IN SIX VOLUMES, CAREFULLY REVISED AND CORRECTED

MATTHEW HENRY'S
COMMENTARY
ON THE WHOLE BIBLE

WHEREIN EACH CHAPTER IS SUMMED UP IN ITS CONTENTS: THE SACRED TEXT
INSERTED AT LARGE IN DISTINCT PARAGRAPHS; EACH PARAGRAPH
REDUCED TO ITS PROPER HEADS: THE SENSE GIVEN,
AND LARGELY ILLUSTRATED

WITH

PRACTICAL REMARKS AND OBSERVATIONS

VOL. III.—JOB TO SONG OF SOLOMON

World Bible Publishers
Iowa Falls, Iowa

PREFACE.

THESE five books of scripture which are contained in this third volume and which I have here endeavoured, according to the measure of the gift given to me, to explain and improve, for the use of those who desire to read them, not only with understanding, but to their edification—though they have the same divine origin, design, and authority, as those that went before, yet, upon some accounts, are of a very different nature from them, and from the rest of the sacred writings, such variety of methods has Infinite Wisdom seen fit to take in conveying the light of divine revelation to the children of men, that this heavenly food might have (as the Jews say of the manna) something in it agreeable to every palate and suited to every constitution. If every eye be not thus opened, every mouth will be stopped, and such as perish in their ignorance will be left without excuse. *We have piped unto you, and you have not danced ; we have mourned unto you, and you have not lamented,* Matt. xi. 17.

I. The books of scripture have hitherto been, for the most part, very plain and easy, narratives of matter of fact, which he that runs may read and understand, and which are milk for babes, such as they can receive and digest, and both entertain and nourish themselves with. The waters of the sanctuary have hitherto been but to the ancles or to the knees, such as a lamb might wade in, to drink of and wash in ; but here we are advanced to a higher form in God's school, and have books put into our hands wherein are *many things dark and hard to be understood*, which we do not apprehend the meaning of so suddenly and so certainly as we could wish, the study of which requires a more close application of mind, a greater intenseness of thought, and the accomplishing of a diligent search, which yet the treasure hid in them, when it is found, will abundantly recompense. The waters of the sanctuary are here *to the loins*, and still as we go forward we shall find the waters still risen in the prophetical books, *waters to swim in* (Ezek. xlvii. 3—5), not fordable, nor otherwise to be passed over—depths in which an elephant will not find footing, *strong meat for strong men.* The same method is observable in the New Testament, where we find the plain history of Christ and his gospel placed first in the Evangelists and the Acts of the Apostles ; then the mystery of both in the Epistles, which are more difficult to be understood ; and, lastly, the prophecies of things to come in the apocalyptic visions. This method, so exactly observed in both the Testaments, directs us in what order to proceed both in studying the things of God ourselves and in teaching them to others ; we must go in the order that the scripture does ; and where can we expect to find a better method of divinity and a better method of preaching ?

1. We must begin with those things that are most plain and easy, as, blessed be God, those things are which are most necessary to salvation and of the greatest use. We must lay our foundation firm, in a sound experimental knowledge of the principles of religion, and then the superstructure will be well reared and will stand firmly. It is not safe to launch out into the deep at first, nor to venture into points difficult and controverted until we have first thoroughly digested the elements of the oracles of God and turned them *in succum et sanguinem—into juice and blood.* Those that begin their Bible at the wrong end commonly use their knowledge of it in the wrong way. And, in training up others, we must be sure to ground them well at first in those truths of God which are plain, and in some measure level to their capacity, which we find they comprehend, and relish, and know how to make use of, and not amuse those that are weak with things above them, things of doubtful disputation, which they cannot apprehend any certainty of nor advantage by. Our Lord Jesus spoke the word to the people *as they were able to hear it* (Mark iv. 33) and had many things to say to his disciples which he did not say because as yet they *could not bear them*, John xvi. 12, 13. And those whom St. Paul *could not speak to as unto spiritual*—though he blamed them for their backwardness, yet he accommodated himself to their weakness, and spoke to them *as unto babes in Christ*, 1 Cor. iii. 1, 2.

2. Yet we must not rest in these things. We must not be always children that have need of milk, but nourished up with that, and gaining strength, we must *go on to perfection* (Heb. vi. 1), that having, *by reason of use, our spiritual senses exercised* (Heb. v. 14), we may come to full age, and put away childish things, and, *forgetting the things which are behind*, that is, so well remembering them (Phil. iii. 13) that we need not be still poring over them as those that are ever

learning the same lesson, we may reach forth to the things which are before. Though we must never think to learn above our Bible, as long as we are here in this world, yet we must still be getting forward in it. *You have dwelt long enough in this mountain;* now turn and take your journey onward in the wilderness towards Canaan. Our motto must be *Plus ultra—Onward.* And then shall we know if thus, by regular steps (Hos. vi. 3), we *follow on to know the Lord* and what the mind of the Lord is.

II. The books of scripture have hitherto been mostly historical, but now the matter is of another nature; it is doctrinal and devotional, preaching and praying; and in this way of writing, as well as in the former, a great deal of excellent knowledge is conveyed, which serves very valuable purposes. It will be of good use to know not only what others did that went before us, and how they fared, but what their notions and sentiments were, what their thoughts and affections were, that we may, with the help of them, form our minds aright. Plutarch's Morals are reputed as useful a treasure in the commonwealth of learning as Plutarch's Lives, and the wise disquisitions and discourses of the philosophers as the records of the historians; nor is this divine philosophy (if I may so call it), which we have in these books, less needful, nor less serviceable, to the church, than the sacred history was. Blessed be God for both.

III. The Jews make these books to be given by a divine inspiration somewhat different from that both of Moses and the prophets. They divided the books of the Old Testament into the Law, the Prophets, and the כתובים—*Writings*, which Epiphanius emphatically translates γραφεῖα—*things written*, and these books are more commonly called among the Greeks Ἁγιόγραφα—*Holy writings:* the Jews attribute them to that distinct kind of inspiration which they call רוח הקדש—*The Holy Spirit.* Moses they supposed to write by the Spirit in a way above all the other prophets, for *with him* God spoke *mouth to mouth, even apparently* (Num. xii. 8) *knew him,* that is, conversed with him *face to face,* Deut. xxxiv. 10. He was made partaker of divine revelation (as Maimonides distinguishes, *De Fund. Legis, c. 7) per vigiliam—while awake,*[*] whereas God manifested himself to all the other prophets in a dream or vision: and he adds that Moses understood the words of prophecy without any perturbation or astonishment of mind, whereas the other prophets commonly fainted and were troubled. But the writers of the Hagiographa they suppose to be inspired in a degree somewhat below that of the other prophets, and to receive divine revelation, not as they did by dreams, and visions, and voices, but (as Maimonides describes it, *More Nevochim—part* 2. *c.* 45) they perceived some power to rise within them, and rest upon them, which urged and enabled them to write or speak far above their own natural ability, in psalms or hymns, or in history, or in rules of good living, still enjoying the ordinary vigour and use of their senses. Let David himself describe it. *The Spirit of the Lord spoke by me, and his word was in my tongue; the God of Israel said, the Rock of Israel spoke to me,* 2 Sam. xxiii. 2, 3. This gives such a magnificent account of the inspiration by which David wrote that I see not why it should be made inferior to that of the other prophets, for David is expressly called *a prophet,* Acts ii. 29, 30. But, since our hand is in with the Jewish masters, let us see what books they account Hagiographa. These five that are now before us come, without dispute, into this rank of sacred writers, and the book of the Lamentations is not unfitly added to them. Indeed the Jews, when they would speak critically, reckon all those songs which we meet with in the Old Testament among the Hagiographa; for though they were penned by prophets, and under the direction of the Holy Ghost, yet, because they were not the proper result of a *visum propheticum—prophetic vision,* they were not strictly prophecy. As to the historical books, they distinguish (but I think it is a distinction without a difference); some of them they assign to the prophets, calling them the *prophetæ priores—the former prophets,* namely, Joshua, Judges, and the two books of the Kings; but others they rank among the Hagiographa, as the book of Ruth (which yet is but an appendix to the book of Judges), the two books of Chronicles, with Ezra, Nehemiah, and the book of Esther, which last the rabbin have a great value for, and think it is to be had in equal esteem with the law of Moses itself, that it shall last as long as that lasts, and shall survive the writings of the Prophets. And, *lastly,* they reckon the book of Daniel among the Hagiographa,[†] for which no reason can be given, since he was not inferior to any of the prophets in the gift of prophecy; and therefore the learned Mr. Smith thinks that their placing him among the Hagiographical writers was fortuitous and by mistake.[‡] Mr. Smith, in his Discourse before quoted, though he supposes this kind of divine inspiration to be more "*pacate* and *serene* than that which was strictly called *prophecy,* not acting so much upon the imagination, but seating itself in the higher and purer faculties of the soul, yet shows that it manifested itself to be of a divine nature, not only as it always elevated pious souls into strains of devotion, or moved them strangely to dictate matters of true piety and goodness, but as it came in abruptly upon the minds of those holy men, and transported them from the temper of mind they were in before, so that

---

[*] See Mr. Smith's Discourses on Prophecy, c. 11.   [†] Hil. Megil. c. 2, § 11.
[‡] Vid. Hottinger. Thesaur. lib. 2, cap. 1, § 3.

they perceived themselves captivated by the power of some higher light than that which their own understanding commonly poured out upon them ; and this, says he, was a kind of vital form to that light of divine and sanctified reason which they were perpetually possessed of and that constant frame of holiness and goodness which dwelt in their hallowed minds." We have reason to *glorify the God of Israel who gave such power unto men* and has here transmitted to us the blessed products of that power.

IV. The style and composition of these books are different from those that go before and those that follow. Our Saviour divides the books of the Old Testament into *the Law, the Prophets,* and *the Psalms* (Luke xxiv. 44), and thereby teaches us to distinguish those books that are poetical, or metrical, from the Law and the Prophets ; and such are all these that are now before us, except Ecclesiastes, which yet, having something restrained in its style, may well enough be reckoned among them. They are books in verse, according to the ancient rules of versifying, though not according to the Greek and Latin *prosodies.* Some of the ancients call these five books *the second Pentateuch of the Old Testament,** five sacred volumes which are as the satellites to the five books of the law of Moses. *Gregory Nazianzen* † *(carm.* 33, *p.* 98) calls these αἱ στιχῆραι πέντε—*the five metrical books* ; first Job (so he reckons them up), then David, then the three of Solomon—Ecclesiastes, the Song, and Proverbs. *Amphilochius,* bishop at Iconium, in his iambic poem to *Seleucus,* reckons them up particularly, and calls them στιχηράς πέντε Βίβλους—*the five verse-books. Epiphanius (lib. de ponder. et mensur. p.* 533) πέντε στιχήρεις—*the five verse-books.* And *Cyril. Hierosol. Collect.* 4, *p.* 30 *(mihi—in my copy),* calls these five books τὰ στιχηρὰ —*books in verse.* Polychronius, in his prologue to Job, says that as *those that are without* call their tragedies and comedies ποιήτικα—*poetics,* so, in sacred writ, those books which are composed in Hebrew metre (of which he reckons Job the first) we call στιχηρὰ βιβλιὰ—*books in verse,* written κατὰ στίχον—*according to order.* What is written in metre, or rhythm, is so called from μέτρος—*a measure,* and ἀρίθμος—*a number,* because regulated by certain measures, or numbers of syllables, which please the ear with their smoothness and cadency, and so insinuate the matter the more movingly and powerfully into the fancy. Sir William Temple,‡ in his essay upon poetry, thinks it is generally agreed to have been the first sort of writing that was used in the world, nay, that, in several nations, poetical compositions preceded the very invention or usage of letters. The Spaniards (he says) found in America many strains of poetry, and such as seemed to flow from a true poetic vein, before any letters were known in those regions. The same (says he) is probable of the Scythians and Grecians : the oracles of Apollo were delivered in verse. Homer and Hesiod wrote their poems (the very Alcoran of the pagan dæmonology) many ages before the appearing of any of the Greek philosophers or historians ; and long before them (if we may give credit to the antiquities of Greece), even before the days of David, Orpheus and Linus were celebrated poets and musicians in Greece ; and at the same time Carmenta, the mother of Evander, who was the first that introduced letters among the natives of Greece, was so called *à carmine—from a song,* because she expressed herself in verse. And in such veneration was this way of writing among the ancients that their poets were called *vates—prophets,* and their muses were deified. But, which is more certain and considerable, the most ancient composition that we meet with in scripture was the song of Moses at the Red Sea (Exod. xv.), which we find before the very first mention of writing, for that occurs not until Exod. xvii. 14, when God bade Moses write a memorial of the war with Amalek. The first, and indeed the true and general end of writing, is the help of memory ; and poetry does in some measure answer that end, and even in the want of writing, much more with writing, helps to preserve the remembrance of ancient things. The book of *the wars of the Lord* (Num. xxi. 14), and the book of Jasher (Josh. x. 13, 2 Sam. i. 18), seem to have been both written in poetic measures. Many sacred songs we meet with in the Old Testament, scattered both in the historical and prophetical books, penned on particular occasions, which, in the opinion of very competent judges, " have in them as true and noble strains of poetry and picture as are met with in any other language whatsoever, in spite of all disadvantages from translations into such different tongues and common prose,‖ nay, are nobler examples of the true sublime style of poetry than any that can be found in the Pagan writers ; the images are so strong, the thoughts so great, the expressions so divine, and the figures so admirably bold and moving, that the wonderful manner of these writers is quite inimitable."§ It is fit that what is employed in the service of the sanctuary should be the best in its kind.

The books here put together are poetical. Job is an heroic poem, the book of Psalms a collection of divine odes or lyrics, Solomon's Song a pastoral and an epithalamium ; they are poetical, and yet sacred and serious, grave and full of majesty. They have a poetic force and flame, without poetic fury and fiction, and strangely command and move the affections, without corrupting the imagination or putting a cheat upon it ; and, while they gratify the ear, they edify the mind and profit the more by pleasing. It is therefore much to be lamented that so powerful an art,

---

* Damascen. Orthod. Fid. 1. 4, cap. 18.   † Vid. Suicer. Thesaur. in στιχηρά.

‡ Miscell. part 2.   ‖ Sir W. Temple, p. 329.   § Sir R. Blackmore's preface to Job.

which was at first consecrated to the honour of God, and has been so often employed in his service, should be debauched, as it has been, and is at this day, into the service of his enemies—that his corn, and wine, and oil, should be prepared for Baal.

V. As the manner of the composition of these books is excellent, and very proper to engage the attention, move the affections, and fix them in the memory, so the matter is highly useful, and such as will be every way serviceable to us. They have in them the very sum and substance of religion, and what they contain is more fitted to our hand, and made ready for use, than any part of the Old Testament, upon which account, if we may be allowed to compare one star with another in the firmament of the scripture, these will be reckoned stars of the first magnitude. *All scripture is profitable* (and this part of it in a special manner) *for instruction* in doctrine, in devotion, and in the right ordering of the conversation. The book of Job directs us what we are to believe concerning God, the book of Psalms how we are to worship him, pay our homage to him, and maintain our communion with him, and then the book of the Proverbs shows very particularly how we are to govern ourselves ἐν πάσῃ ἀναστροφῇ—*in every turn of human life ;* thus shall the *man of God,* by a due attention to these lights, be *perfect, thoroughly furnished for every good work.* And these are placed according to their natural order, as well as according to the order of time ; for very fitly are we first led into the knowledge of God, our judgments rightly formed concerning him, and our mistakes rectified, and then instructed how to worship him and to choose the things that please him. We have here much of natural religion, its principles, its precepts— much of God, his infinite perfections, his relations to man, and his government both of the world and of the church ; here is much of Christ, who is the spring, and soul, and centre, of revealed religion, and whom both Job and David were eminent types of, and had clear and happy prospects of. We have here that which will be of use to enlighten our understandings, and to acquaint us more and more with the things of God, with the deep things of God—speculations to entertain the most contemplative, and discoveries to satisfy the most inquisitive and increase the knowledge of those that are most knowing. Here is that also which, with a divine light, will bring into the soul the heat and influence of a divine fire, will kindle and inflame pious and devout affections, on which wings we may soar upwards until we enter into the holiest. We may here be in the mount with God, to behold his beauty ; and when we come down from that mount, if we retain (as we ought) the impressions of our devotion upon our spirits and make conscience of doing that good which the Lord our God here requires of us, our faces shall shine before all with whom we converse, who shall take occasion thence to *glorify our Father who is in heaven,* Matt. v. 16. Thus great, thus noble, thus truly excellent, is the subject, and thus capable of being improved, which gives me the more reason to be ashamed of the meanness of my performance, that the comment breathes so little of the life and spirit of the text. We often wonder at those that are not at all affected with the great things of God, and have no taste nor relish of them, because they know little of them ; but perhaps we have more reason to wonder at ourselves, that conversing so frequently, so intimately, with them, we are not more affected with them, so as even to be wholly taken up with them, and in a continual transport of delight in the contemplation of them. We hope to be so shortly ; in the mean time, though like the three disciples that were the witnesses of Christ's transfiguration upon the mount we are but dull and sleepy, yet we can say, *Master, it is good to be here ;* here *let us make tabernacles,* Luke ix. 32, 33.

I have nothing here to boast of—nothing at all, but a great deal to be humbled for, that I have not come up to what I have aimed at in respect of fulness and exactness. In the review of the work, I find many defects, and those who are critical, perhaps, will meet with some mistakes in it ; but I have done it with what care I could, and desire to be thankful to God who by his grace has carried me on in his work thus far : let that grace have all the glory (Phil. ii. 13), which *works in us both to will and to do* whatever we will or do that is good or serves any good purpose. What is from God will, I trust, be to him, will be graciously accepted by him, *according to what a man has, and not according to what he has not,* and will be of some use to his church ; and what is from myself (that is, all the defects and errors) will, I trust, be favourably passed by and pardoned. That prayer of *St. Austin* is mine, *Domine Deus, quæcunque dixi in his libris de tuo, agnoscant et tui ; et quæ de meo, et tu ignosce et tui*—*Lord God, whatever I have maintained in these books correspondent with what is contained in thine grant that thy people may approve as well as thyself ; whatever is but the doctrine of my book forgive thou, and grant that thy people may forgive it also.* I must beg likewise to own, to the honour of our great Master, that I have found the work to be its own wages, and that the more we converse with the word of God the more it is to us as *the honey* and the *honeycomb,* Ps. xix. 10. In gathering some gleanings of this harvest for others we may feast ourselves ; and, when we are enabled by the grace of God to do so, we are best qualified to feed others. I was much pleased with a passage I lately met with of Erasmus, that great scholar and celebrated wit, in an epistle dedicatory before his book *De Ratione Concionandi,* where, as one weary of the world and the hurry of it, he expresses an earnest desire to spend the rest of his days in secret communion with Jesus Christ, encouraged by his gracious invitation to those who *labour and are heavy laden* to *come unto him for rest* (Matt. xi. 28), and this alone is that which he thinks will yield him true satisfaction. I think his words worth transcribing, and such as deserve to be inserted among the testimonies of great men to serious godliness. *Neque quisquam facilè credat quàm miserè animus jamdudum affectet ab his laboribus in tranquillam otium secedere, quodque superest vitæ (superest autem vix brevis palmus sive pugillus), solum cum eo solo colloqui, qui clamavit olim (nec hodiè mutat vocem suam), "Venite ad me, omnes qui laboratis et onerati estis, ego reficiam vos ;" quandoquidem in tam turbulento, ne dicam furente, sæculo, in tot molestiis quas vel ipsa tempora publicè invehunt, vel privatim adfert ætas ac valetudo, nihil reperio in quo mens mea libentiùs conquiescat quàm in hoc arcano colloquio—No one will easily believe how anxiously, for a long time past, I have wished to retire from these labours into a scene of tranquillity, and, during the remainder of life (dwindled, it is true, to the shortest span), to converse only with him who once cried (nor does he now retract), " Come unto me, all you that labour and are heavy laden, and I will refresh you," for in this turbulent, not to say furious, age, the many public sources of disquietude, connected with the infirmities of advancing age, leave no solace to my mind to be compared with this secret communion.* In the pleasing contemplation of the divine beauty and benignity we hope to spend a blessed eternity, and therefore in this work it is good to spend as much as may be of our time.

One volume more, containing the prophetical books, will finish the Old Testament, if the Lord continue my life, and leisure, and ability of mind and body for this work. It is begun, and I find it will be larger than any of the other volumes, and longer in the doing ; but, as God by his grace shall furnish me for it and assist me in it (without which grace I am nothing, less than nothing, worse than nothing), it shall be carried on with all convenient speed ; and *sat citò, si sat benè—if with sufficient ability, it will be with sufficient speed.* I desire the prayers of my friends that God would *minister seed to the sower* and *bread to the eaters* (Isa. lv. 10), that he would *multiply the seed sown* and *increase the fruits of our righteousness* (2 Cor. ix. 10), that so he who *sows and those who reap may rejoice together* (John iv. 36) ; and the great Lord of the harvest shall have the glory of all.

M. H.

Chester,
May 13, 1710.

AN

EXPOSITION,

WITH PRACTICAL OBSERVATIONS,

OF THE BOOK OF

J O B.

THIS book of Job stands by itself, is not connected with any other, and is therefore to be considered alone. Many copies of the Hebrew Bible place it after the book of Psalms, and some after the Proverbs, which perhaps has given occasion to some learned men to imagine it to have been written by Isaiah or some of the later prophets. But, as the subject appears to have been much more ancient, so we have no reason to think but that the composition of the book was, and that therefore it is most fitly placed first in this collection of divine morals: also, being doctrinal, it is proper to precede and introduce the book of Psalms, which is devotional, and the book of Proverbs, which is practical; for how shall we worship or obey a God whom we know not? As to this book,

I. We are sure that it is given by inspiration of God, though we are not certain who was the penman of it. The Jews, though no friends to Job, because he was a stranger to the commonwealth of Israel, yet, as faithful conservators of *the oracles of God* committed to them, always retained this book in their sacred canon. The history is referred to by one apostle (James v. 11) and one passage (*ch.* v. 13) is quoted by another apostle, with the usual form of quoting scripture, *It is written,* 1 Cor. iii. 19. It is the opinion of many of the ancients that this history was written by Moses himself in Midian, and delivered to his suffering brethren in Egypt, for their support and comfort under their burdens, and the encouragement of their hope that God would in due time deliver and enrich them, as he did this patient sufferer. Some conjecture that it was written originally in Arabic, and afterwards translated into Hebrew, for the use of the Jewish church, by Solomon (so Monsieur Jurieu) or some other inspired writer. It seems most probable to me that Elihu was the penman of it, at least of the discourses, because (*ch.* xxxii. 15, 16) he mingles the words of a historian with those of a disputant: but Moses perhaps wrote the first two chapters and the last, to give light to the discourses; for in them God is frequently called *Jehovah,* but not once in all the discourses, except *ch.* xii. 9. That name was but little known to the patriarchs before Moses, Exod. vi. 3. If Job wrote it himself, some of the Jewish writers themselves own him a *prophet among the Gentiles;* if Elihu, we find he had a spirit of prophecy which *filled him with matter and constrained him,* *ch.* xxxii. 18.

II. We are sure that it is, for the substance of it, a true history, and not a romance, though the dialogues are poetical. No doubt there was such a man as Job; the prophet Ezekiel names him with Noah and Daniel, Ezek. xiv. 14. The narrative we have here of his prosperity and piety, his strange afflictions and exemplary patience, the substance of his conferences with his friends, and God's discourse with him out of the whirlwind, with his return at length to a very prosperous condition, no doubt is exactly true, though the inspired penman is allowed the usual liberty of putting the matter of which Job and his friends discoursed into his own words.

III. We are sure that it is very ancient, though we cannot fix the precise time either when Job lived or when the book was written. So many, so evident, are its hoary hairs, the marks of its antiquity, that we have reason to think it of equal date with the book of Genesis itself, and that holy Job was contemporary with Isaac and Jacob; though not coheir with them of the promise of the earthly Canaan, yet a joint-expectant with them of the *better country,* that is, *the heavenly.* Probably he was of the posterity of Nahor, Abraham's brother, whose first-born was *Uz* (Gen. xxii. 21), and in whose family religion was for some ages kept up, as appears, Gen. xxxi. 53, where God is called, not only *the God of Abraham,* but *the God of Nahor.* He lived before the age of man was shortened to seventy or eighty, as it was in Moses's time, before sacrifices were confined to one altar, before the general apostasy of the nations from the knowledge and worship of the true God, and while yet there was no other idolatry known than the worship of the sun and moon, and that punished by the Judges, *ch.* xxxi. 26—28. He lived

1

while God was known by the name of *God Almighty* more than by the name of *Jehovah;* for he is called *Shaddai—the Almighty,* above thirty times in this book. He lived while divine knowledge was conveyed, not by writing, but by tradition ; for to that appeals are here made, *ch.* viii. 8 ; xxi. 29 ; xv. 18 ; v. 1. And we have therefore reason to think that he lived before Moses, because here is no mention at all of the deliverance of Israel out of Egypt, or the giving of the law. There is indeed one passage which might be made to allude to the drowning of Pharaoh (*ch.* xxvi. 12) : *He divideth the sea with his power, and by his understanding he smiteth through Rahab,* which name Egypt is frequently called by in scripture, as Ps. lxxxvii. 4 ; lxxxix. 10 ; Isa. li. 9. But that may as well refer to the proud waves of the sea. We conclude therefore that we are here got back to the patriarchal age, and, besides its authority, we receive this book with veneration for its antiquity.

IV. We are sure that it is of great use to the church, and to every good Christian, though there are many passages in it dark and hard to be understood. We cannot perhaps be confident of the true meaning of every Arabic word and phrase we meet with in it. It is a book that finds a great deal of work for the critics ; but enough is plain to make the whole profitable, and it was all written for our learning.

1. This noble poem presents to us, in very clear and lively characters, these five things among others :—(1.) *A monument of primitive theology.* The first and great principles of the light of nature, on which natural religion is founded, are here, in a warm, and long, and learned dispute, not only taken for granted on all sides and not the least doubt made of them, but by common consent plainly laid down as eternal truths, illustrated and urged as affecting commanding truths. Were ever the being of God, his glorious attributes and perfections, his unsearchable wisdom, his irresistible power, his inconceivable glory, his inflexible justice, and his incontestable sovereignty, discoursed of with more clearness, fulness, reverence, and divine eloquence, than in this book ? The creation of the world, and the government of it, are here admirably described, not as matters of nice speculation, but as laying most powerful obligations upon us to fear and serve, to submit to and trust in, our Creator, owner, Lord, and ruler. Moral good and evil, virtue and vice, were never drawn more to the life (the beauty of the one and the deformity of the other) than in this book ; nor the inviolable rule of God's judgment more plainly laid down, That *happy are the righteous, it shall be well with them;* and *woe to the wicked, it shall be ill with them.* These are not questions of the schools to keep the learned world in action, nor engines of state to keep the unlearned world in awe ; no, it appears by this book that they are sacred truths of undoubted certainty, and which all the wise and sober part of mankind have in every age subscribed and submitted to. (2.) It presents us with *a specimen of Gentile piety.* This great saint descended probably not from Abraham, but Nahor ; or, if from Abraham, not from Isaac, but from one of the sons of the concubines that were sent into the east-country (Gen. xxv. 6); or, if from Isaac, yet not from Jacob, but Esau ; so that he was out of the pale of the covenant of peculiarity, no Israelite, no proselyte, and yet none like him for religion, nor such a favourite of heaven upon this earth. It was a truth therefore, before St. Peter perceived it, that *in every nation he that fears God and works righteousness is accepted of him,* Acts x. 35 There were *children of God scattered abroad* (John xi. 52) besides the incorporated *children of the kingdom,* Matt. viii. 11, 12. (3.) It presents us with *an exposition of the book of Providence,* and a clear and satisfactory solution of many of the difficult and obscure passages of it. The prosperity of the wicked and the afflictions of the righteous have always been reckoned two as hard chapters as any in that book ; but they are here expounded, and reconciled with the divine wisdom, purity, and goodness, by the *end of these things.* (4.) It presents us with *a great example of patience* and close adherence to God in the midst of the sorest calamities. Sir Richard Blackmore's most ingenious pen, in his excellent preface to his paraphrase on this book, makes Job a hero proper for an epic poem ; for, says he, " He appears brave in distress and valiant in affliction, maintains his virtue, and with that his character, under the most exasperating provocations that the malice of hell could invent, and thereby gives a most noble example of passive fortitude, a character no way inferior to that of the active hero," &c. (5.) It presents us with *an illustrious type of Christ,* the particulars of which we shall endeavour to take notice of as we go along. In general, Job was a great sufferer, was emptied and humbled, but in order to his greater glory. So Christ abased himself, that we might be exalted. The learned bishop Patrick quotes St. Jerome more than once speaking of Job as a type of Christ, who *for the joy that was set before him endured the cross,* who was persecuted, for a time, by men and devils, and seemed forsaken of God too, but was raised to be an intercessor even for his friends that had added affliction to his misery. When the apostle speaks of the *patience of Job* he immediately takes notice of *the end of the Lord,* that is, of the Lord Jesus (as some understand it), typified by Job, James v. 11.

2. In this book we have, (1.) The history of Job's sufferings, and his patience under them (*ch.* i. ii.), not without a mixture of human frailty, *ch.* iii. (2.) A dispute between him and his friends upon them, in which, [1.] The opponents were Eliphaz, Bildad, and Zophar. [2.] The respondent was Job. [3.] The moderators were, *First,* Elihu, *ch.* xxxii.—xxxvii. *Secondly,* God himself, *ch.* xxxviii.—xli. (3.) The issue of all in Job's honour and prosperity, *ch.* xlii. Upon the whole, we learn that *many are the afflictions of the righteous, but* that when the Lord *delivers them out of them all* the trial of their faith *will be found to praise, and honour, and glory.*

2

CHAP. I.

The history of Job begins here with an account, I. Of his great piety in general (ver. 1), and in a particular instance, ver. 5. II. Of his great prosperity, ver. 2—4. III. Of the malice of Satan against him, and the permission he obtained to try his constancy, ver. 6—12. IV. Of the surprising troubles that befel him, the ruin of his estate (ver. 13—17), and the death of his children, ver. 18, 19. V. Of his exemplary patience and piety under these troubles, ver. 20—22. In all this he is set forth for an example of suffering affliction, from which no prosperity can secure us, but through which integrity and uprightness will preserve us.

THERE was a man in the land of Uz, whose name *was* Job; and that man was perfect and upright, and one that feared God, and eschewed evil. 2 And there were born unto him seven sons and three daughters. 3 His substance also was seven thousand sheep, and three thousand camels, and five hundred yoke of oxen, and five hundred she asses, and a very great household; so that this man was the greatest of all the men of the east.

Concerning Job we are here told,

I. That he was a man; therefore subject to like passions as we are. He was *Ish*, a worthy man, a man of note and eminency, a magistrate, a man in authority. The country he lived in was the land of Uz, in the eastern part of Arabia, which lay towards Chaldea, near Euphrates, probably not far from Ur of the Chaldees, whence Abraham was called. When God called one good man out of that country, yet he *left not himself without witness*, but raised up another in it to be a *preacher of righteousness*. God has his remnant in all places, sealed ones out of every nation, as well as out of every tribe of Israel, Rev. vii. 9. It was the privilege of the land of Uz to have so good a man as Job in it; now it was *Arabia the Happy* indeed: and it was the praise of Job that he was eminently good in so bad a place; the worse others were round about him the better he was. His name *Job*, or *Jjob*, some say, signifies *one hated* and counted as an enemy. Others make it to signify one that grieves or groans; thus the sorrow he carried in his name might be a check to his joy in his prosperity. Dr. Cave derives it from *Jaab—to love*, or *desire*, intimating how welcome his birth was to his parents, and how much he was *the desire of their eyes;* and yet there was a time when he cursed the day of his birth. Who can tell what the day may prove which yet begins with a bright morning?

II. That he was a very good man, eminently pious, and better than his neighbours: *He was perfect and upright.* This is intended to show us, not only what reputation he had among men (that he was generally taken for an honest man), but what was really his character; for it is the judgment of God concerning him, and we are sure that is according to truth. 1. Job was a religious man, *one that feared God*, that is, worshipped him according to his will, and governed himself

by the rules of the divine law in every thing. 2. He was sincere in his religion: He was *perfect;* not sinless, as he himself owns (*ch.* ix. 20): *If I say I am perfect, I shall be proved perverse.* But, having a respect to all God's commandments, aiming at perfection, he was really as good as he seemed to be, and did not dissemble in his profession of piety; his heart was sound and his eye single. Sincerity is gospel perfection. I know no religion without it. 3. He was upright in his dealings both with God and man, was faithful to his promises, steady in his counsels, true to every trust reposed in him, and made conscience of all he said and did. See Isa. xxxiii. 15. Though he was not *of* Israel, he was indeed an *Israelite without guile.* 4. The fear of God reigning in his heart was the principle that governed his whole conversation. This made him perfect and upright, inward and entire for God, universal and uniform in religion; this kept him close and constant to his duty. He *feared God,* had a reverence for his majesty, a regard to his authority, and a dread of his wrath. 5. He dreaded the thought of doing what was wrong; with the utmost abhorrence and detestation, and with a constant care and watchfulness, he *eschewed evil,* avoided all appearances of sin and approaches to it, and this *because of the fear of God,* Neh. v. 15. *The fear of the Lord is to hate evil* (Prov. viii. 13) and then *by the fear of the Lord men depart from evil,* Prov. xvi. 6.

III. That he was a man who prospered greatly in this world, and made a considerable figure in his country. He was prosperous and yet pious. Though it is hard and rare, it is not impossible, for *a rich man to enter into the kingdom of heaven.* With God even this is possible, and by his grace the temptations of worldly wealth are not insuperable. He was pious, and his piety was a friend to his prosperity; for godliness has the promise of the life that now is. He was prosperous, and his prosperity put a lustre upon his piety, and gave him who was so good so much greater opportunity of doing good. The acts of his piety were grateful returns to God for the instances of his prosperity; and, in the abundance of the good things God gave him, he served God the more cheerfully. 1. He had a numerous family. He was eminent for religion, and yet not a hermit, not a recluse, but the father and master of a family. It was an instance of his prosperity that his house was filled with children, which are a *heritage of the Lord,* and his *reward,* Ps. cxxvii. 3. He had *seven sons and three daughters, v.* 2. Some of each sex, and more of the more noble sex, in which the family is built up. Children must be looked upon as blessings, for so they are, especially to good people, that will give them good instructions, and set them good examples, and put up good prayers for them. Job had many children, and yet he was neither oppressive nor uncharitable, but very liberal to the poor, *ch.* xxxi. 17, &c. Those that have great families to provide for ought to consider that what is prudently given in alms is set out to the best interest and put into the best fund for their children's benefit. 2. He had a good estate for the support of his family; his *substance* was considerable, *v.* 3. Riches are called *substance*, in conformity to the common form of speaking; otherwise, to the soul and another world, they are but shadows, *things that are not,* Prov. xxiii. 5. It is only in heavenly wisdom that we *inherit substance,* Prov. viii. 21. In those days, when the earth was not fully peopled, it was as now in some of the plantations, men might have land enough upon easy terms if they had but wherewithal to stock it; and therefore Job's substance is described, not by the acres of land he was lord of, but, (1.) By his cattle—*sheep and camels, oxen and asses.* The numbers of each are here set down, probably not the exact number, but thereabout, a very few under or over. The sheep are put first, because of most use in the family, as Solomon observes (Prov. xxvii. 23, 26, 27): *Lambs for thy clothing, and milk for the food of thy household.* Job, it is likely, had silver and gold as well as Abraham (Gen. xiii. 2); but then men valued their own and their neighbours' estates by that which was for service and present use more than by that which was for show and state, and fit only to be hoarded. As soon as God had made man, and provided for his maintenance by the herbs and fruits, he made him rich and great by giving him *dominion over the creatures,* Gen. i. 28 That therefore being still continued to man, notwithstanding his defection (Gen. ix. 2), is still to be reckoned one of the most considerable instances of men's wealth, honour, and power, Ps. viii. 6. (2.) By his servants. He had a very good household or husbandry, many that were employed for him and maintained by him; and thus he both had honour and did good; yet thus he was involved in a great deal of care and put to a great deal of charge. See the vanity of this world; as goods are increased those must be increased that tend them and occupy them, and *those will be increased that eat them; and what good has the owner thereof save the beholding of them with his eyes?* Eccles. v. 11. In a word, *Job was the greatest of all the men of the east;* and they were the richest in the world: those were rich indeed who were *replenished more than the east,* Isa. ii. 6. Margin. Job's wealth, with his wisdom, entitled him to the honour and power he had in his country, which he describes (*ch.* xxix.), and made him sit chief. Job was upright and honest, and yet grew rich, nay, *therefore* grew rich; for honesty is the best policy, and piety and charity are ordinarily the surest ways of thriving. He had a great household and much business, and yet kept up the fear and worship of God; and he and his house

served the Lord. The account of Job's piety and prosperity comes before the history of his great afflictions, to show that neither will secure us from the common, no, nor from the uncommon calamities of human life. Piety will not secure us, as Job's mistaken friends thought, for *all things come alike to all;* prosperity will not, as a careless world thinks, Isa. xlvii. 8. I sit *as a queen* and therefore shall *see no sorrow.*

4 And his sons went and feasted *in their* houses, every one his day; and sent and called for their three sisters to eat and to drink with them. 5 And it was so, when the days of *their* feasting were gone about, that Job sent and sanctified them, and rose up early in the morning, and offered burnt offerings *according* to the number of them all: for Job said, It may be that my sons have sinned, and cursed God in their hearts. Thus did Job continually.

We have here a further account of Job's prosperity and his piety.

I. His great comfort in his children is taken notice of as an instance of his prosperity; for our temporal comforts are borrowed, depend upon others, and are as those about us are. Job himself mentions it as one of the greatest joys of his prosperous estate that his *children were about him, ch.* xxix. 5. They kept a circular feast at some certain times (*v.* 4); they *went and feasted in their houses.* It was a comfort to this good man, 1. To see his children grown up and settled in the world. All his sons were in houses of their own, probably married, and to each of them he had given a competent portion to set up with. Those that had been olive-plants round his table were removed to tables of their own. 2. To see them thrive in their affairs, and able to feast one another, as well as to feed themselves. Good parents desire, promote, and rejoice in, their children' wealth and prosperity as their own. 3. To see them in health, no sickness in their houses, for that would have spoiled their feasting and turned it into mourning. 4. Especially to see them live in love, and unity, and mutual good affection, no jars or quarrels among them, no strangeness, no shyness one of another, no strait-handedness, but, though every one knew his own, they lived with as much freedom as if they had had all in common. It is comfortable to the hearts of parents, and comely in the eyes of all, to see brethren thus knit together. *Behold, how good and how pleasant it is!* Ps. cxxxiii. 1. 5. It added to his comfort to see the brothers so kind to their sisters, that they sent for them to feast with them; for they were so modest that they would not have gone if they had not been sent for. Those brothers that slight their sisters, care not for their company, and have no concern for their comfort, are ill-bred, ill-natured, and very unlike Job's sons. It seems their feast was so sober and decent that their sisters were good company for them at it. 6. They feasted in their own houses, not in public houses, where they would be more exposed to temptations, and which were not so creditable. We do not find that Job himself feasted with them. Doubtless they invited him, and he would have been the most welcome guest at any of their tables; nor was it from any sourness or moroseness of temper, or for want of natural affection, that he kept away, but he was old and dead to these things, like Barzillai (2 Sam. xix. 35), and considered that the young people would be more free and pleasant if there were none but themselves. Yet he would not restrain his children from that diversion which he denied himself. Young people may be allowed a youthful liberty, provided they flee youthful lusts.

II. His great care about his children is taken notice of as an instance of his piety: for that we are really which we are relatively. Those that are good will be good to their children, and especially do what they can for the good of their souls. Observe (*v.* 5) Job's pious concern for the spiritual welfare of his children.

1. He was jealous over them with a godly jealousy; and so we ought to be over ourselves and those that are dearest to us, as far as is necessary to our care and endeavour for their good. Job had given his children a good education, had comfort in them and good hope concerning them; and yet he said, "*It may be, my sons have sinned* in the days of their feasting more than at other times, have been too merry, have taken too great a liberty in eating and drinking, and have *cursed God in their hearts*," that is, "have entertained atheistical or profane thoughts in their minds, unworthy notions of God and his providence, and the exercises of religion." When they were *full* they were ready to *deny God, and to say, Who is the Lord?* (Prov. xxx. 9), ready to *forget* God and to say, The *power of our hand* has *gotten us this wealth,* Deut. viii. 12, &c. Nothing alienates the mind more from God than the indulgence of the flesh.

2. As soon as the days of their feasting were over he called them to the solemn exercises of religion. Not while their feasting lasted (let them take their time for that; there is a time for all things), but when it was over, their good father reminded them that they must know when to desist, and not think to fare sumptuously every day; though they had their days of feasting the *week* round, they must not think to have them the *year* round; they had something else to do. Note, Those that are merry must find a time to be serious.

3. He sent to them to prepare for solemn ordinances, *sent and sanctified them,* ordered them to examine their own consciences and repent of what they had done amiss in their feasting, to lay aside their vanity and compose themselves for religious exercises. Thus he kept his authority over them for their good, and they submitted to it, though they had got into houses of their own. Still he was the priest of the family, and at his altar they all attended, valuing their share in his prayers more than their share in his estate. Parents cannot give grace to their children (it is God that sanctifies), but they ought by seasonable admonitions and counsels to further their sanctification. In their baptism they were sanctified to God; let it be our desire and endeavour that they may be sanctified for him.

4. He offered sacrifice for them, both to atone for the sins he feared they had been guilty of in the days of their feasting and to implore for them mercy to pardon and grace to prevent the debauching of their minds and corrupting of their manners by the liberty they had taken, and to preserve their piety and purity.

For he with mournful eyes had often spied,
Scattered on Pleasure's smooth but treacherous tide,
The spoils of virtue overpowered by sense,
And floating wrecks of ruined innocence.—Sir R. BLACKMORE.

Job, like Abraham, had an altar for his family, on which, it is likely, he offered sacrifice daily; but, on this extraordinary occasion, he offered more sacrifices than usual, and with more solemnity, *according to the number of them all,* one for each child. Parents should be particular in their addresses to God for the several branches of their family. "For this child I prayed, according to its particular temper, genius, and condition," to which the prayers, as well as the endeavours, must be accommodated. When these sacrifices were to be offered, (1.) He rose early, as one in care that his children might not lie long under guilt and as one whose heart was upon his work and his desire towards it. (2.), He required his children to attend the sacrifice, that they might join with him in the prayers he offered with the sacrifice, that the sight of the killing of the sacrifice might humble them much for their sins, for which they deserved to die, and the sight of the offering of it up might lead them to a Mediator. This serious work would help to make them serious again after the days of their gaiety.

5. Thus he did *continually,* and not merely whenever an occasion of this kind recurred; for *he that is washed needs to wash his feet,* John xiii. 10. The acts of repentance and faith must be often renewed, because we often repeat our transgressions. All days, every day, he offered up his sacrifices, was constant to his devotions, and did not omit them any day. The occasional exercises of religion will not excuse us from those that are stated. He that serves God uprightly will serve him continually.

5

6 Now there was a day when the sons of God came to present themselves before the LORD, and Satan came also among them. 7 And the LORD said unto Satan, Whence comest thou? Then Satan answered the LORD, and said, From going to and fro in the earth, and from walking up and down in it. 8 And the LORD said unto Satan, Hast thou considered my servant Job, that *there is* none like him in the earth, a perfect and an upright man, one that feareth God, and escheweth evil? 9 Then Satan answered the LORD, and said, Doth Job fear God for nought? 10 Hast not thou made a hedge about him, and about his house, and about all that he hath on every side? thou hast blessed the work of his hands, and his substance is increased in the land. 11 But put forth thine hand now, and touch all that he hath, and he will curse thee to thy face. 12 And the LORD said unto Satan, Behold, all that he hath *is* in thy power; only upon himself put not forth thine hand. So Satan went forth from the presence of the LORD.

Job was not only so rich and great, but withal so wise and good, and had such an interest both in heaven and earth, that one would think the mountain of his prosperity stood so strong that it could not be moved; but here we have a thick cloud gathering over his head, pregnant with a horrible tempest. We must never think ourselves secure from storms while we are in this lower region. Before we are told how his troubles surprised and seized him here in this visible world, we are here told how they were concerted in the world of spirits, that the devil, having a great enmity to Job for his eminent piety, begged and obtained leave to torment him. It does not at all derogate from the credibility of Job's story in general to allow that this discourse between God and Satan, in these verses, is parabolical, like that of Micaiah (1 Kings xxii. 19, &c.), and an allegory designed to represent the malice of the devil against good men and the divine check and restraint which that malice is under; only thus much further is intimated, that the affairs of this earth are very much the subject of the counsels of the unseen world. That world is dark to us, but we lie very open to it. Now here we have,

I. Satan among the sons of God (*v.* 6), an *adversary* (so *Satan* signifies) to God, to men, to all good: he thrust himself into an assembly of the *sons of God* that came to pre-sent themselves before the Lord. This means either, 1. A meeting of the saints on earth. Professors of religion, in the patriarchal age, were called *sons of God* (Gen. vi. 2); they had then religious assemblies and stated times for them. The King came in to see his guests; the eye of God was on all present. But there was a serpent in paradise, a Satan among the sons of God; when they come together he is among them, to distract and disturb them, stands at their right hand to resist them. *The Lord rebuke thee, Satan!* Or, 2. A meeting of the angels in heaven. They are the sons of God, ch. xxxviii. 7. They came to give an account of their negociations on earth and to receive new instructions. Satan was one of them originally; but *how hast thou fallen, O Lucifer!* He shall no more stand in that congregation, yet he is here represented as coming among them, either summoned to appear as a criminal or connived at, for the present, though an intruder.

II. His examination, how he came thither (*v.* 7): *The Lord said unto Satan, Whence comest thou?* He knew very well whence he came, and with what design he came thither, that as the good angels came to do good he came for a permission to do hurt; but he would, by calling him to an account, show him that he was under check and control. *Whence comest thou?* He asks this, 1. As wondering what brought him thither. *Is Saul among the prophets?* Satan among the sons of God? Yes, for he *transforms himself into an angel of light* (2 Cor. xi. 13, 14), and would seem one of them. Note, It is possible that a man may be a child of the devil and yet be found in the assemblies of the sons of God in this world, and *there* may pass undiscovered by men, and yet be challenged by the all-seeing God. *Friend, how camest thou in hither?* Or, 2. As enquiring what he had been doing before he came thither. The same question was perhaps put to the rest of those that presented themselves before the Lord, "Whence came you?" We are accountable to God for all our haunts and all the ways we traverse.

III. The account he gives of himself and of the tour he had made. I come (says he) *from going to and fro on the earth.* 1. He could not pretend he had been doing any good, could give no such account of himself as the sons of God could, who *presented themselves before the Lord,* who came from executing his orders, serving the interest of his kingdom, and ministering to the heirs of salvation. 2. He would not own he had been doing any hurt, that he had been drawing men from their allegiance to God, deceiving and destroying souls; no. *I have done no wickedness,* Prov. xxx. 20. *Thy servant went nowhere.* In saying that he had *walked to and fro through the earth,* he intimates that he had kept himself within the bounds allotted him, and had not transgressed his bounds; for *the dragon is cast out into the earth* (Rev. xii. 9) and not yet confined to his place of torment. While we are on this earth we are within his reach, and with so much subtlety, swiftness, and industry, does he penetrate into all the corners of it, that we cannot be in any place secure from his temptations. 3. He yet seems to give some representation of his own character. (1.) Perhaps it is spoken proudly, and with an air of haughtiness, as if he were indeed the *prince of this world*, as if *the kingdoms of the world and the glory of them* were his (Luke iv. 6), and he had now been walking in circuit through his own territories. (2.) Perhaps it is spoken fretfully, and with discontent. He had been walking to and fro, and could find no rest, but was as much a fugitive and a vagabond as Cain in the land of Nod. (3.) Perhaps it is spoken carefully: "I have been hard at work, going to and fro," or (as some read it) "searching about in the earth," really in quest of an opportunity to do mischief. He walks about seeking whom he may devour. It concerns us therefore to be sober and vigilant.

IV. The question God puts to him concerning Job (*v.* 8): *Hast thou considered my servant Job?* As when we meet with one that has been in a distant place, where we have a friend we dearly love, we are ready to ask, "You have been in such a place; pray did you see my friend there?" Observe, 1. How honourably God speaks of Job: He is *my servant*. Good men are God's servants, and he is pleased to reckon himself honoured in their services, and they are to him for *a name and a praise* (Jer. xiii. 11) *and a crown of glory*, Isa. lxii. 3. "Yonder is *my servant Job;* there is none like him, none I value like him, of all the princes and potentates of the earth; one such saint as he is worth them all: *none like him* for uprightness and serious piety; many do well, but *he excelleth them all;* there is not to be found *such great faith, no, not in Israel.*" Thus Christ, long after, commended the centurion and the woman of Canaan, who were both of them, like Job, strangers to that commonwealth. The saints glory in God—*Who is like thee among the gods?* and he is pleased to glory in them—*Who is like Israel among the people?* So here, *none like Job*, none in earth, that state of imperfection. Those in heaven do indeed far outshine him; those who are least in that kingdom are greater than he; but *on earth there is not his like.* There is none like him in that land; so some good men are the glory of their country. 2. How closely he gives to Satan this good character of Job: *Hast thou set thy heart to my servant Job?* designing hereby, (1.) To aggravate the apostasy and misery of that wicked spirit: "How unlike him art thou!" Note, The holiness and happiness of the saints are the shame and torment of the devil and the devil's children. (2.) To

answer the devil's seeming boast of the interest he had in this earth. "I have been walking to and fro in it," says he, "and it is all my own; all flesh have corrupted their way; they all sit still, and are at rest in their sins," Zech. i. 10, 11. "Nay, hold," saith God, "Job, is my faithful servant." Satan may boast, but he shall not triumph. (3.) To anticipate his accusations, as if he had said, "Satan, I know thy errand; thou hast come to inform against Job; but *hast thou considered him?* Does not his unquestionable character give thee the lie?" Note, God knows all the malice of the devil and his instruments against his servants; and we have an advocate ready to appear for us, even before we are accused.

V. The devil's base insinuation against Job, in answer to God's encomium of him. He could not deny but that Job feared God, but suggested that he was mercenary in his religion, and therefore a hypocrite (*v.* 9): *Doth Job fear God for nought?* Observe, 1. How impatient the devil was of hearing Job praised, though it was God himself that praised him. Those are like the devil who cannot endure that any body should be praised but themselves, but grudge the just share of reputation others have, as Saul (1 Sam. xviii. 5, &c.) and the Pharisees, Matt. xxi. 15. 2. How much at a loss he was for something to object against him; he could not accuse him of any thing that was bad, and therefore charged him with by-ends in doing good. Had the one half of that been true which his angry friends, in the heat of dispute, charged him with (*ch.* xv. 4, xxii. 5), Satan would no doubt have brought it against him now; but no such thing could be alleged, and therefore, 3. See how slily he censured him as a hypocrite, not asserting that he was so, but only asking, "Is he not so?" This is the common way of slanderers, whisperers, backbiters, to suggest that by way of query which yet they have no reason to think is true. Note, It is not strange if those that are approved and accepted of God be unjustly censured by the devil and his instruments; if they are otherwise unexceptionable, it is easy to charge them with hypocrisy, as Satan charged Job, and they have no way to clear themselves, but patiently to wait for the judgment of God. As there is nothing we should dread more than being hypocrites, so there is nothing we need dread less than being called and counted so without cause. 4. How unjustly he accused him as mercenary, to prove him a hypocrite. It was a great truth that Job did not fear God for nought; he got much by it, for godliness is great gain: but it was a falsehood that he would not have feared God if he had not got this by it, as the event proved. Job's friends charged him with hypocrisy because he was greatly afflicted, Satan because he greatly prospered. It is no hard matter for those to calumniate that seek an occasion. It is not mercenary to look at the eternal recompence in our obedience; but to aim at temporal advantages in our religion, and to make it subservient to them, is spiritual idolatry, worshipping the creature more than the Creator, and is likely to end in a fatal apostasy. Men cannot long *serve God and mammon.*

VI. The complaint Satan made of Job's prosperity, *v.* 10. Observe, 1. What God had done for Job. He had protected him, made a hedge about him, for the defence of his person, his family, and all his possessions. Note, God's peculiar people are taken under his special protection, they and all that belong to them; divine grace makes a hedge about their spiritual life, and divine providence about their natural life, so they are safe and easy. He had prospered him, not in idleness or injustice (the devil could not accuse him of them), but in the way of honest diligence: *Thou hast blessed the work of his hands.* Without that blessing, be the hands ever so strong, ever so skilful, the work will not prosper; but, with that, *his substance has wonderfully increased in the land.* The blessing of the Lord makes rich: Satan himself owns it. 2. What notice the devil took of it, and how he improved it against him. The devil speaks of it with vexation. "I see thou hast *made a hedge about him, round about;*" as if he had walked it round, to see if he could spy a single gap in it, for him to enter in at, to do him a mischief; but he was disappointed: it was a complete hedge. *The wicked* one *saw it and was grieved,* and argued against Job that the only reason why he served God was because God prospered him. "No thanks to him to be true to the government that prefers him, and to serve a Master that pays him so well."

VII. The proof Satan undertakes to give of the hypocrisy and mercenariness of Job's religion, if he might but have leave to strip him of his wealth. "Let it be put to this issue," says he (*v.* 11); "make him poor, frown upon him, turn thy hand against him, and then see where his religion will be; touch what he has and it will appear what he is. *If he curse thee not to thy face,* let me never be believed, but posted for a liar and false accuser. Let me perish if he curse thee not;" so some supply the imprecation, which the devil himself modestly concealed, but the profane swearers of our age impudently and daringly speak out. Observe, 1. How slightly he speaks of the affliction he desired that Job might be tried with: "Do but touch all that he has, do but begin with him, do but threaten to make him poor; a little cross will change his tone." 2. How spitefully he speaks of the impression it would make upon Job: "He will not only let fall his devotion, but turn it into an open defiance—not only think hardly of thee, but

even curse thee to thy face." The word translated curse is *barac,* the same that ordinarily, and originally, signifies to *bless;* but cursing God is so impious a thing that the holy language would not admit the name: but that where the sense requires it it must be so understood is plain from 1 Kings xxi. 10—13, where the word is used concerning the crime charged on Naboth, that he did blaspheme God and the king. Now, (1.) It is likely that Satan did think that Job, if impoverished, would renounce his religion and so disprove his profession, and if so (as a learned gentleman has observed in his *Mount of Spirits*) Satan would have made out his own universal empire among the children of men. God declared Job the best man then living: now, if Satan can prove him a hypocrite, it will follow that God had not one faithful servant among men and that there was no such thing as true and sincere piety in the world, but religion was all a sham, and Satan was king *de facto—in fact,* over all mankind. But it appeared that *the Lord knows those that are his* and is not deceived in any. (2.) However, if Job should retain his religion, Satan would have the satisfaction to see him sorely afflicted. He hates good men, and delights in their griefs, as God has *pleasure in their prosperity.*

VIII. The permission God gave to Satan to afflict Job for the trial of his sincerity. Satan desired God to do it: *Put forth thy hand now.* God allowed him to do it (*v.* 12): "*All that he has is in thy hand;* make the trial as sharp as thou canst; do thy worst at him." Now, 1. It is matter of wonder that God should give Satan such a permission as this, should *deliver the soul of his turtle-dove* into the hand of the adversary, such a lamb to such a lion; but he did it for his own glory, the honour of Job, the explanation of Providence, and the encouragement of his afflicted people in all ages, to make a case which, being adjudged, might be a useful precedent. He suffered Job to be tried, as he suffered Peter to be sifted, but took care that *his faith should not fail* (Luke xxii. 32) and then the trial of it was *found unto praise, and honour, and glory,* 1 Pet. i. 7. But, 2. It is matter of comfort that God has the devil *in a chain,* in a great chain, Rev. xx. 1. He could not afflict Job without leave from God first asked and obtained, and then no further than he had leave: "*Only upon himself put not forth thy hand;* meddle not with his body, but only with his estate." It is a limited power that the devil has; he has no power to debauch men but what they give him themselves, nor power to afflict men but what is *given him from above.*

IX. Satan's departure from this meeting of the sons of God. Before they broke up, Satan went forth (as Cain, Gen. iv. 16) *from the presence of the Lord;* no longer detained before him (as Doeg was, 1 Sam. xxi. 7) than till he had accomplished his malicious purpose. He went forth, 1. Glad that he had gained his point, proud of the permission he had to do mischief to a good man; and, 2. Resolved to lose no time, but speedily to put his project in execution. He went forth now, not to go to and fro, rambling through the earth, but with a direct course, to fall upon poor Job, who is carefully going on in the way of his duty, and knows nothing of the matter. What passes between good and bad spirits concerning us we are not aware of.

13 And there was a day when his sons and his daughters *were* eating and drinking wine in their eldest brother's house: 14 And there came a messenger unto Job, and said, The oxen were plowing, and the asses feeding beside them: 15 And the Sabeans fell *upon them*, and took them away; yea, they have slain the servants with the edge of the sword; and I only am escaped alone to tell thee. 16 While he *was* yet speaking, there came also another, and said, The fire of God is fallen from heaven, and hath burned up the sheep, and the servants, and consumed them; and I only am escaped alone to tell thee. 17 While he *was* yet speaking, there came also another, and said, The Chaldeans made out three bands, and fell upon the camels, and have carried them away, yea, and slain the servants with the edge of the sword; and I only am escaped alone to tell thee. 18 While he *was* yet speaking, there came also another, and said, Thy sons and thy daughters *were* eating and drinking wine in their eldest brother's house: 19 And, behold, there came a great wind from the wilderness, and smote the four corners of the house, and it fell upon the young men, and they are dead; and I only am escaped alone to tell thee.

We have here a particular account of Job's troubles.

I. Satan brought them upon him on the very day that his children began their course of feasting, at their *eldest brother's house* (v. 13), where, he having (we may suppose) the double portion, the entertainment was the richest and most plentiful. The whole family, no doubt, was in perfect repose, and all were easy and under no apprehension of trouble, now when they revived this custom; and this time Satan chose, that the trouble, coming now, might be the more grievous. *The night of my pleasure has he turned into fear,* Isa. xxi. 4.

II. They all come upon him at once; while one messenger of evil tidings was speaking another came, and, before he had told his story, a third, and a fourth, followed immediately. Thus Satan, by the divine permission, ordered it, 1. That there might appear a more than ordinary displeasure of God against him in his troubles, and by that he might be exasperated against divine Providence, as if it were resolved, right or wrong, to ruin him, and not give him time to speak for himself. 2. That he might not have leisure to consider and recollect himself, and reason himself into a gracious submission, but might be overwhelmed and overpowered by a complication of calamities. If he have not room to pause a little, he will be apt to speak in haste, and then, if ever, he will curse his God. Note, The children of God are often in heaviness through manifold temptations; deep calls to deep; waves and billows come one upon the neck of another. Let one affliction therefore quicken and help us to prepare for another; for, how deep soever we have drunk of the bitter cup, as long as we are in this world we cannot be sure that we have drunk our share and that it will finally pass from us.

III. They took from him all that he had, and made a full end of his enjoyments. The detail of his losses answers to the foregoing inventory of his possessions.

1. He had 500 *yoke of oxen*, and 500 *she-asses*, and a competent number of servants to attend them; and all these he lost at once, *v.* 14, 15. The account he has of this lets him know, (1.) That it was not through any carelessness of his servants; for then his resentment might have spent itself upon them: *The oxen were ploughing*, not playing, and the asses not suffered to stray and so taken up as waifs, but *feeding beside them*, under the servant's eye, each in their place; and those that passed by, we may suppose, blessed them, and said, *God speed the plough*. Note, All our prudence, care, and diligence, cannot secure us from affliction, no, not from those afflictions which are commonly owing to imprudence and negligence. *Except the Lord keep the city, the watchman*, though ever so wakeful, *wakes but in vain.* Yet it is some comfort under a trouble if it found us in the way of our duty, and not in any by-path. (2.) That it was through the wickedness of his neighbours the Sabeans, probably a sort of robbers that lived by spoil and plunder. They carried off the oxen and asses, and slew the servants that faithfully and bravely did their best to defend them, and *one only escaped*, not in kindness to him or his master, but that Job might have the certain intelligence of it by an eye-witness before he heard it by a flying report, which would have brought it upon him gradually.

We have no reason to suspect that either Job or his servants had given any provocation to the Sabeans to make this inroad, but Satan put it into their hearts to do it, to do it now, and so gained a double point, for he made both Job to suffer and them to sin. Note, When Satan has God's permission to do mischief he will not want mischievous men to be his instruments in doing it, for he is a *spirit that works in the children of disobedience.*

2. He had 7000 *sheep,* and shepherds that kept them; and all those he lost at the same time by lightning, *v.* 16. Job was perhaps, in his own mind, ready to reproach the Sabeans, and fly out against them for their injustice and cruelty, when the next news immediately directs him to look upwards : *The fire of God has fallen from heaven.* As thunder is his voice, so lightning is his fire : but this was such an extraordinary lightning, and levelled so directly against Job, that all his sheep and shepherds were not only killed, but consumed by it at once, and one shepherd only was left alive to carry the news to poor Job. The devil, aiming to make him curse God and renounce his religion, managed this part of the trial very artfully, in order thereto. (1.) His sheep, with which especially he used to honour God in sacrifice, were all taken from him, as if God were angry at his offerings and would punish him in those very things which he had employed in his service. Having misrepresented Job to God as a false servant, in pursuance of his old design to set Heaven and earth at variance, he here misrepresented God to Jacob as a hard Master, who would not protect those flocks out of which he had so many burnt-offerings. This would tempt Job to say, *It is in vain to serve God.* (2.) The messenger called the lightning the *fire of God* (and innocently enough), but perhaps Satan thereby designed to strike into his mind this thought, that God had *turned to be his enemy and fought against him,* which was much more grievous to him than all the insults of the Sabeans. He owned (*ch.* xxxi. 23) that *destruction from God was a terror to him.* How terrible then were the tidings of this destruction, which came immediately from the hand of God! Had the fire from heaven consumed the sheep upon the altar, he might have construed it into a token of God's favour; but, the fire consuming them in the pasture, he could not but look upon it as a token of God's displeasure. There had not been the like since Sodom was burned.

3. He had 3000 *camels,* and servants tending them; and he lost them all at the same time by the Chaldeans, who came in three bands, and drove them away, and slew the servants, *v.* 17. If the fire of God, which fell upon Job's honest servants, who were in the way of their duty, had fallen upon the Sabean and Chaldean robbers who were doing mischief, God's judgments therein would

have been like the great mountains, evident and conspicuous; but when the way of the wicked prospers, and they carry off their booty, while just and good men are suddenly cut off, God's righteousness is like the great deep, the bottom of which we cannot find, Ps. xxxvi. 6.

4. His dearest and most valuable possessions were his ten children; and, to conclude the tragedy, news is brought him, at the same time, that they were killed and buried in the ruins of the house in which they were feasting, and all the servants that waited on them, except one that came express with the tidings of it, *v.* 18, 19. This was the greatest of Job's losses, and which could not but go nearest him; and therefore the devil reserved it for the last, that, if the other provocations failed, this might make him curse God. Our children are pieces of ourselves; it is very hard to part with them, and touches a good man in as tender a part as any. But to part with them all at once, and for them to be all cut off in a moment, who had been so many years his cares and hopes, went to the quick indeed. (1.) They all died together, and not one of them was left alive. David, though a wise and good man, was very much discomposed by the death of one son. How hard then did it bear upon poor Job who lost them all, and, in one moment, was written childless! (2.) They died suddenly. Had they been taken away by some lingering disease, he would have had notice to expect their death, and prepare for the breach; but this came upon him without giving him any warning. (3.) They died when they were feasting and making merry. Had they died suddenly when they were praying, he might the better have borne it. He would have hoped that death had found them in a good frame if their blood had been mingled with their *sacrifices;* but to have it mingled with their feast, where he himself used to be jealous of them that they had *sinned, and cursed God in their hearts*—to have that day come upon them unawares, like a thief in the night, when perhaps their heads were overcharged with surfeiting and drunkenness—this could not but add much to his grief, considering what a tender concern he always had for his children's souls, and that they were now out of the reach of the sacrifices he used to offer *according to the number of them all.* See how all things come alike to all. Job's children were constantly prayed for by their father, and lived in love one with another, and yet came to this untimely end. (4.) They died by a wind of the devil's raising, who is *the prince of the power of the air* (Eph. ii. 2), but it was looked upon to be an immediate hand of God, and a token of his wrath. So Bildad construed it (*ch.* viii. 4): *Thy children have sinned against him, and he has cast them away in their transgression.* (5.) They were taken away when he had most need of them to comfort him under all his other losses. Such

10

miserable comforters are all creatures. In God only we have a present help at all times.

20 Then Job arose, and rent his mantle, and shaved his head, and fell down upon the ground, and worshipped, 21 And said, Naked came I out of my mother's womb, and naked shall I return thither : the LORD gave, and the LORD hath taken away ; blessed be the name of the LORD. 22 In all this Job sinned not, nor charged God foolishly.

The devil had done all he desired leave to do against Job, to provoke him to curse God. He had touched all he had, touched it with a witness; he whom the rising sun saw the richest of all the men in the east was before night poor to a proverb. If his riches had been, as Satan insinuated, the only principle of his religion, now that he had lost his riches he would certainly have lost his religion ; but the account we have, in these verses, of his pious deportment under his affliction, sufficiently proved the devil a liar and Job an honest man.

I. He conducted himself like a man under his afflictions, not stupid and senseless, like a stock or stone, not unnatural and unaffected at the death of his children and servants ; no (v. 20), he *arose, and rent his mantle, and shaved his head,* which were the usual expressions of great sorrow, to show that he was sensible of the hand of the Lord that had gone out against him ; yet he did not break out into any indecencies, nor discover any extravagant passion. He did not faint away, but arose, as a champion to the combat; he did not, in a heat, throw off his clothes, but very gravely, in conformity to the custom of the country, rent his mantle, his cloak, or outer garment ; he did not passionately tear his hair, but deliberately shaved his head. By all this it appeared that he kept his temper, and bravely maintained the possession and repose of his own soul, in the midst of all these provocations. The time when he began to show his feelings is observable ; it was not till he heard of the death of his children, and then he arose, then he rent his mantle. A worldly unbelieving heart would have said, " Now that the meat is gone it is well that the mouths are gone too ; now that there are no portions it is well that there are no children :" but Job knew better, and would have been thankful if Providence had spared his children, though he had had little or nothing for them, for *Jehovah-jireh—the Lord will provide.* Some expositors, remembering that it was usual with the Jews to rend their clothes when they heard blasphemy, conjecture that Job rent his clothes in a holy indignation at the blasphemous thoughts which Satan now cast into his mind, tempting him to curse God.

II. He conducted himself like a wise and good man under his affliction, like a *perfect and upright man,* and *one that feared God* and *eschewed the evil* of sin more than that of outward trouble.

1. He humbled himself under the hand of God, and accommodated himself to the providences he was under, as one that knew how to want as well as how to abound. When God called to weeping and mourning he wept and mourned, *rent his mantle and shaved his head ;* and, as one that abased himself even to the dust before God, he *fell down upon the ground,* in a penitent sense of sin and a patient submission to the will of God, *accepting the punishment of his iniquity.* Hereby he showed his sincerity; for *hypocrites cry not when God binds them,* ch. xxxvi. 13. Hereby he prepared himself to get good by the affliction ; for how can we improve the grief which we will not feel ?

2. He composed himself with quieting considerations, that he might not be disturbed and put out of the possession of his own soul by these events. He reasons from the common state of human life, which he describes with application to himself : *Naked came I* (as others do) *out of my mother's womb, and naked shall I return thither,* into the lap of our common mother—the earth, as the child, when it is sick or weary, lays its head in its mother's bosom. *Dust we were* in our original, and *to dust we return* in our exit (Gen. iii. 19), *to the earth as we were* (Eccl. xii. 7), *naked shall we return thither,* whence we were taken, namely, to the clay, *ch.* xxxiii. 6. St. Paul refers to this of Job, 1 Tim. vi. 7. *We brought nothing* of this world's goods *into the world,* but have them from others ; and *it is certain that we can carry nothing out,* but must leave them to others. We come into the world naked, not only unarmed, but unclothed, helpless, shiftless, not so well covered and fenced as other creatures. The sin we are born in makes us naked, to our shame, in the eyes of the holy God. We go out of the world naked ; the body does, though the sanctified soul goes clothed, 2 Cor. v. 3. Death strips us of all our enjoyments ; clothing can neither warm nor adorn a dead body. This consideration silenced Job under all his losses. (1.) He is but where he was at first. He looks upon himself only as naked, not maimed, not wounded ; he was himself still his own man, when nothing else was his own, and therefore but reduced to his first condition. *Nemo tam pauper potest esse quam natus est—no one can be so poor as he was when born.—Min. Felix.* If we are impoverished, we are not wronged, nor much hurt, for we are but as we were born. (2.) He is but where he must have been at last, and is only unclothed, or unloaded rather, a little sooner than he expected. If we put off our clothes before we go to bed, it is some inconvenience, but it may be the better borne when it is near bed-time.

3. He gave glory to God, and expressed himself upon this occasion with a great veneration for the divine Providence, and a meek submission to its disposals. We may well rejoice to find Job in this good frame, because this was the very thing upon which the trial of his integrity was put, though he did not know it. The devil said that he would, under his affliction, curse God; but he blessed him, and so proved himself an honest man.

(1.) He acknowledged the hand of God both in the mercies he had formerly enjoyed and in the afflictions he was now exercised with: *The Lord gave, and the Lord has taken away.* We must own the divine Providence, [1.] In all our comforts. God gave us our being, *made us, and not we ourselves,* gave us our wealth; it was not our own ingenuity or industry that enriched us, but God's blessing on our cares and endeavours. He gave us power to get wealth, not only made the creatures for us, but bestowed upon us our share. [2.] In all our crosses. The same that gave hath taken away; and may he not do what he will with his own? See how Job looks above instruments, and keeps his eye upon the first Cause. He does not say, "The Lord gave, and the Sabeans and Chaldeans have taken away; God made me rich, and the devil has made me poor;" but, "He that gave has taken;" and for that reason he is dumb, and has nothing to say, because God did it. He that gave all may take what, and when, and how much he pleases. Seneca could argue thus, *Abstulit, sed et dedit—he took away, but he also gave;* and Epictetus excellently (cap. 15), "When thou art deprived of any comfort, suppose a child taken away by death, or a part of thy estate lost, say not ἀπώλεσα ἀυτὸ—*I have lost it;* but, ἀπέδωκα—*I have restored it to the right owner;* but thou wilt object (says he), κακὸς ὁ ἀφελόμενος—*he is a bad man that has robbed me;* to which he answers, τί δέ σοι μέλει—*What is it to thee by what hand he that gives remands what he gave?*

(2.) He adored God in both. When all was gone he fell down and worshipped. Note, Afflictions must not divert us from, but quicken us to, the exercises of religion. Weeping must not hinder sowing, nor hinder worshipping. He eyed not only the hand of God, but the name of God, in his afflictions, and gave glory to that: *Blessed be the name of the Lord.* He has still the same great and good thoughts of God that ever he had, and is as forward as ever to speak them forth to his praise; he can find in his heart to bless God even when he takes away as well as when he gives. Thus must we *sing both of mercy and judgment,* Ps. ci. 1. [1.] He blesses God for what was given, though now it was taken away. When our comforts are removed from us we must thank God that ever we had them and had them so much longer than we deserved. Nay, [2.] He

adores God even in taking away, and gives him honour by a willing submission; nay, he gives him thanks for good designed him by his afflictions, for gracious supports under his afflictions, and the believing hopes he had of a happy issue at last.

Lastly, Here is the honourable testimony which the Holy Ghost gives to Job's constancy and good conduct under his afflictions. He passed his trials with applause, v. 22. In all this Job did not act amiss, for he did not attribute folly to God, nor in the least reflect upon his wisdom in what he had done. Discontent and impatience do in effect charge God with folly. Against the workings of these therefore Job carefully watched; and so must we, acknowledging that as God has done right, but we have done wickedly, so God has done wisely, but we have done foolishly, **very** foolishly. Those who not only keep their temper under crosses and provocations, but keep up good thoughts of God and sweet communion with him, whether their praise be of men or no, it will be of God, as Job's here was.

CHAP. II.

We left Job honourably acquitted upon a fair trial between God and Satan concerning him. Satan had leave to touch, to touch and take, all he had, and was confident that he would then curse God to his face; but, on the contrary, he blessed him, and so he was proved an honest man and Satan a false accuser. Now, one would have thought, this would be conclusive, and that Job would never have his reputation called in question again; but Job is known to be armour of proof, and therefore is here set up for a mark, and brought upon his trial, a second time. I. Satan moves for another trial, which should touch his bone and his flesh, ver. 1–6. II. God, for holy ends, permits it, ver. 6. III. Satan smites him with a very painful and loathsome disease, ver. 7, 8. IV. His wife tempts him to curse God, but he resists the temptation, ver. 9, 10. V. His friends come to condole with him and to comfort him, ver. 11–13. And in this that good man is set forth for an example of suffering affliction and of patience.

AGAIN there was a day when the sons of God came to present themselves before the LORD, and Satan came also among them to present himself before the LORD. 2 And the LORD said unto Satan, From whence comest thou? And Satan answered the LORD, and said, From going to and fro in the earth, and from walking up and down in it. 3 And the LORD said unto Satan, Hast thou considered my servant Job, that *there is* none like him in the earth, a perfect and an upright man, one that feareth God, and escheweth evil? and still he holdeth fast his integrity, although thou movedst me against him, to destroy him without cause. 4 And Satan answered the LORD, and said, Skin for skin, yea, all that a man hath will he give for his life. 5 But put forth thine hand now, and touch his bone and his flesh, and he will curse thee to thy face. 6 And the LORD said unto Satan, Behold, he *is* in thine hand; but save his life.

Satan, that sworn enemy to God and all good men, is here pushing forward his malicious prosecution of Job, whom he hated because God loved him, and did all he could to separate between him and his God, to sow discord and make mischief between them, urging God to afflict him and then urging him to blaspheme God. One would have thought that he had enough of his former attempt upon Job, in which he was so shamefully baffled and disappointed; but malice is restless: the devil and his instruments are so. Those that calumniate good people, and accuse them falsely, will have their saying, though the evidence to the contrary be ever so plain and full and they have been cast in the issue which they themselves have put it upon. Satan will have Job's cause called over again. The malicious, unreasonable, importunity of that great persecutor of the saints is represented (Rev. xii. 10) by his accusing them before our God day and night, still repeating and urging that against them which has been many a time answered: so did Satan here accuse Job day after day. Here is,

I. The court set, and the prosecutor, or accuser, making his appearance (*v.* 1, 2), as before, *ch.* i. 6, 7. The angels attended God's throne and Satan among them. One would have expected him to come and confess his malice against Job and his mistake concerning him, to cry, *Peccavi—I have done wrong,* for belying one whom God spoke well of, and to beg pardon; but, instead of that, he comes with a further design against Job. He is asked the same question as before, *Whence comest thou?* and answers as before, *From going to and fro in the earth:* as if he had been doing no harm, though he had been abusing that good man.

II. The judge himself of counsel for the accused, and pleading for him (*v.* 3): " *Hast thou considered my servant Job* better than thou didst, and art thou now at length convinced that he is a faithful servant of mine, *a perfect and an upright man;* for thou seest he *still holds fast his integrity?* This is now added to his character, as a further achievement; instead of letting go his religion, and cursing God, he holds it faster than ever, as that which he has now more than ordinary occasion for. He is the same in adversity that he was in prosperity, and rather better, and more hearty and lively in blessing God than ever he was, and takes root the faster for being thus shaken. See, 1. How Satan is condemned for his allegations against Job: " *Thou movedst me against him,* as an accuser, *to destroy him without cause.*" Or, " Thou in vain movedst me to destroy him, for I will never do that." Good men, when they are *cast down,* are *not destroyed,* 2 Cor. iv. 9. How well is it for us that

neither men nor devils are to be our judges, for perhaps they would destroy us, right or wrong; but our judgment proceeds from the Lord, whose judgment never errs nor is biassed. 2. How Job is commended for his constancy notwithstanding the attacks made upon him: " Still he holds fast his integrity, as his weapon, and thou canst not disarm him—as his treasure, and thou canst not rob him of that; nay, thy endeavours to do it make him hold it the faster; instead of losing ground by the temptation, he gets ground." God speaks of it with wonder, and pleasure, and something of triumph in the power of his own grace: *Still he holds fast his integrity.* Thus the trial of Job's faith was found to his *praise and honour,* 1 Pet i. 7. Constancy crowns integrity.

III. The accusation further prosecuted, *v.* 4. What excuse can Satan make for the failure of his former attempt? What can he say to palliate it, when he had been so very confident that he should gain his point? Why, truly, he has this to say, *Skin for skin, and all that a man has, will he give for his life.* Something of truth there is in this, that self-love and self-preservation are very powerful commanding principles in the hearts of men. Men love themselves better than their nearest relations, even their children, that are parts of themselves, will not only venture, but give, their estates to save their lives. All account life sweet and precious, and, while they are themselves in health and at ease, they can keep trouble from their hearts, whatever they lose. We ought to make a good use of this consideration, and, while God continues to us our life and health and the use of our limbs and senses, we should the more patiently bear the loss of other comforts. See Matt. vi. 25. But Satan grounds upon this an accusation of Job, slily representing him, 1. As unnatural to those about him, and one that laid not to heart the death of his children and servants, nor cared how many of them had their skins (as I may say) stripped over their ears, so long as he slept in a whole skin himself; as if he that was so tender of his children's souls could be careless of their bodies, and, like the ostrich, hardened against his young ones, as though they were not his. 2. As wholly selfish, and minding nothing but his own ease and safety; as if his religion made him sour, and morose, and ill-natured. Thus are the ways and people of God often misrepresented by the devil and his agents.

IV. A challenge given to make a further trial of Job's integrity (*v.* 5): " *Put forth thy hand now* (for I find my hand too short to reach him, and too weak to hurt him) *and touch his bone and his flesh* (that is with him the only tender part, *make him sick with smiting him,* Mic. vi. 13), and then, I dare say, *he will curse thee to thy face,* and let go his integrity." Satan knew it, and we find it by experience, that nothing is more likely

13

to ruffle the thoughts and put the mind into disorder than acute pain and distemper of body. There is no disputing against sense. St. Paul himself had much ado to bear a thorn in the flesh, nor could he have borne it without special grace from Christ, 2 Cor. xii. 7, 9.

V. A permission granted to Satan to make this trial, *v.* 6. Satan would have had God put forth his hand and do it; but he *afflicts not willingly*, nor takes any pleasure in *grieving the children of men*, much less his own children (Lam. iii. 33), and therefore, if it must be done, let Satan do it, who delights in such work: "*He is in thy hand,* do thy worst with him; but with a proviso and limitation, *only save his life,* or his soul. Afflict him, but not to death." Satan hunted for the precious life, would have taken that if he might, in hopes that dying agonies would force Job to curse his God; but God had mercy in store for Job after this trial, and therefore he must survive it, and, however he is afflicted, must have his life given him for a prey. If God did not chain up the roaring lion, how soon would he devour us! As far as he permits the wrath of Satan and wicked men to proceed against his people he will make it turn to his praise and theirs, and *the remainder thereof he will restrain,* Ps. lxxvi. 10. "Save his soul," that is, "his reason" (so some), "preserve to him the use of that, for otherwise it will be no fair trial; if, in his delirium, he should curse God, that will be no disproof of his integrity. It would be the language not of his heart, but of his distemper." Job, in being thus maligned by Satan, was a type of Christ, the first prophecy of whom was that Satan should *bruise his heel* (Gen. iii. 15), and so he was foiled, as in Job's case. Satan tempted him to let go his integrity, his adoption (Matt. iv. 6): *If thou be the Son of God.* He entered into the heart of Judas who betrayed Christ, and (some think) with his terrors put Christ into his agony in the garden. He had permission to touch his bone and his flesh without exception of his life, because by dying he was to do that which Job could not do— *destroy him that had the power of death, that is, the devil.*

7 So went Satan forth from the presence of the LORD, and smote Job with sore boils from the sole of his foot unto his crown. 8 And he took him a potsherd to scrape himself withal; and he sat down among the ashes. 9 Then said his wife unto him, Dost thou still retain thine integrity? curse God, and die. 10 But he said unto her, Thou speakest as one of the foolish women speaketh. What? shall we receive good at the hand of God, and

shall we not receive evil? In all this did not Job sin with his lips.

The devil, having got leave to tear and worry poor Job, presently fell to work with him, as a tormentor first and then as a tempter. His own children he tempts first, and draws them to sin, and afterwards torments, when thereby he has brought them to ruin; but this child of God he tormented with affliction, and then tempted to make a bad use of his affliction. That which he aimed at was to make Job curse God; now here we are told what course he took both to move him to it and move it to him, both to give him the provocation, else it would be to no purpose to urge him to it, and to give him the information, else he would not have thought of it: thus artfully is the temptation managed with all the subtlety of the old serpent, who is here playing the same game against Job that he played against our first parents (Gen. iii.), aiming to seduce him from his allegiance to his God and to rob him of his integrity.

I. He provokes him to curse God by smiting him with sore boils, and so making him a burden to himself, *v.* 7, 8. The former attack was extremely violent, but Job kept his ground, bravely made good the pass and carried the day. Yet he is still but girding on the harness; there is worse behind. The clouds return after the rain. Satan, by the divine permission, follows his blow, and now *deep calls unto deep.*

1. The disease with which Job was seized was very grievous: Satan *smote him with boils, sore boils,* all over him, from head to foot, with *an evil inflammation* (so some render it), an erysipelas, perhaps, in a higher degree. One boil, when it is gathering, is torment enough, and gives a man abundance of pain and uneasiness. What a condition was Job then in, that had boils all over him, and no part free, and those of as raging a heat as the devil could make them, and, as it were, *set on fire of hell!* The small-pox is a very grievous and painful disease, and would be much more terrible than it is but that we know the extremity of it ordinarily lasts but a few days; how grievous then was the disease of Job, who was smitten all over with sore boils or grievous ulcers, which made him sick at heart, put him to exquisite torture, and so spread themselves over him that he could lie down no way for any ease. If at any time we be exercised with sore and grievous distempers, let us not think ourselves dealt with any otherwise than as God has sometimes dealt with the best of his saints and servants. We know not how much Satan may have a hand (by divine permission) in the diseases with which the children of men, and especially the children of God, are afflicted, what infections that prince of the air may spread, what inflammations may come from that fiery serpent. We read of

one whom Satan had bound many years, Luke xiii. 16. Should God suffer that roaring lion to have his will against any of us, how miserable would he soon make us!

2. His management of himself, in this distemper, was very strange, v. 8.

(1.) Instead of healing salves, *he took a potsherd*, a piece of a broken pitcher, *to scrape himself withal*. A very sad pass this poor man had come to. When a man is sick and sore he may bear it the better if he be well tended and carefully looked after. Many rich people have with a soft and tender hand charitably ministered to the poor in such a condition as this; even Lazarus had some ease from the tongues of the dogs that came and *licked his sores;* but poor Job has no help afforded him. [1.] Nothing is done to his sores but what he does himself, with his own hands. His children and servants are all dead, his wife unkind, ch. xix. 17. He has not wherewithal to fee a physician or surgeon; and, which is most sad of all, none of those he had formerly been kind to had so much sense of honour and gratitude as to minister to him in his distress, and lend him a hand to dress or wipe his running sores, either because the disease was loathsome and noisome or because they apprehended it to be infectious. Thus it was in the former days, as it will be in the last days, men were *lovers of their own selves, unthankful, and without natural affection.* [2.] All that he does to his sores is to *scrape them;* they are not bound up with soft rags, not mollified with ointment, not washed or kept clean, no healing plasters laid on them, no opiates, no anodynes, ministered to the poor patient, to alleviate the pain and compose him to rest, nor any cordials to support his spirits; all the operation is the scraping of the ulcers, which, when they had come to a head and began to die, made his body all over like a scurf, as is usual in the end of the small-pox. It would have been an endless thing to dress his boils one by one; he therefore resolves thus to do it by wholesale—a remedy which one would think as bad as the disease. [3.] He has nothing to do this with but a *potsherd*, no surgeon's instrument proper for the purpose, but that which would rather rake into his wounds, and add to his pain, than give him any ease. People that are sick and sore have need to be under the discipline and direction of others, for they are often but bad managers of themselves.

(2.) Instead of reposing in a soft and warm bed, he *sat down among the ashes*. Probably he had a bed left him (for, though his fields were stripped, we do not find that his house was burnt or plundered), but he chose to sit in the ashes, either because he was weary of his bed or because he would put himself into the place and posture of a penitent, who, in token of his self-abhorrence, lay in dust and ashes, ch. xlii. 6; Isa. lviii. 5; Jon. iii. 6. Thus did he humble himself under the mighty hand of God, and bring his mind to the meanness and poverty of his condition. He complains (ch. vii. 5) that his flesh was *clothed with worms* and *clods of dust;* and therefore *dust to dust, ashes to ashes.* If God lay him among the ashes, there he will contentedly sit down. A low spirit becomes low circumstances, and will help to reconcile us to them. The Septuagint reads it, He sat *down upon a dunghill without the city* (which is commonly said, in mentioning this story); but the original says no more than that he sat *in the midst of the ashes,* which he might do in his own house.

II. He urges him, by the persuasions of his own wife, to curse God, v. 9. The Jews (who covet much to be wise above what is written) say that Job's wife was Dinah, Jacob's daughter: so the Chaldee paraphrase. It is not likely that she was; but, whoever it was, she was to him like Michal to David, a scoffer at his piety. She was spared to him, when the rest of his comforts were taken away, for this purpose, to be a troubler and tempter to him. If Satan leaves any thing that he has permission to take away, it is with a design of mischief. It is his policy to send his temptations by the hand of those that are dear to us, as he tempted Adam by Eve and Christ by Peter. We must therefore carefully watch that we be not drawn to say or do a wrong thing by the influence, interest, or entreaty, of any, no, not those for whose opinion and favour we have ever so great a value. Observe how strong this temptation was. 1. She banters Job for his constancy in his religion: *"Dost thou still retain thy integrity?* Art thou so very obstinate in thy religion that nothing will cure thee of it? so tame and sheepish as thus to truckle to a God who is so far from rewarding thy services with marks of his favour that he seems to take a pleasure in making thee miserable, strips thee, and scourges thee, without any provocation given? Is this a God to be still loved, and blessed, and served?"

Dost thou not see that thy devotion's vain?
What have thy prayers procured but woe and pain?
Hast thou not yet thy int'rest understood?
Perversely righteous, and absurdly good?
Those painful sores, and all thy losses, show
How Heaven regards the foolish saint below.
Incorrigibly pious! Can't thy God
Reform thy stupid virtue with his rod?—Sir R. BLACKMORE.

Thus Satan still endeavours to draw men from God, as he did our first parents, by suggesting hard thoughts of him, as one that envies the happiness and delights in the misery of his creatures, than which nothing is more false. Another artifice he uses is to drive men from their religion by loading them with scoffs and reproaches for their adherence to it. We have reason to expect it, but we are fools if we heed it. Our Master himself has undergone it, we shall be abundantly recompensed for it, and with much more reason may we retort it upon the scoffers, "Are you such fools as still to retain

15

your impiety, when you might *bless God and live?*" 2. She urges him to renounce his religion, to blaspheme God, set him at defiance, and dare him to do his worst : " *Curse God and die ;* live no longer in dependence upon God, wait not for relief from him, but be thy own deliverer by being thy own executioner; end thy troubles by ending thy life; better die once than be always dying thus; thou mayest now despair of having any help from thy God, even curse him, and hang thyself." These are two of the blackest and most horrid of all Satan's temptations, and yet such as good men have sometimes been violently assaulted with. Nothing is more contrary to natural conscience than blaspheming God, nor to natural sense than self-murder; therefore the suggestion of either of these may well be suspected to come immediately from Satan. Lord, *lead us not into temptation*, not into such, not into any temptation, but *deliver us from the evil one.*

III. He bravely resists and overcomes the temptation, *v.* 10. He soon gave her an answer (for Satan spared him the use of his tongue, in hopes he would curse God with it), which showed his constant resolution to cleave to God, to keep his good thoughts of him, and not to let go his integrity. See,

1. How he resented the temptation. He was very indignant at having such a thing mentioned to him : "What! Curse God? I abhor the thought of it. *Get thee behind me, Satan."* In other cases Job reasoned with his wife with a great deal of mildness, even when she was unkind to him (*ch.* xix. 17) : *I entreated her for the children's sake of my own body.* But, when she persuaded him to curse God, he was much displeased : *Thou speakest as one of the foolish women speaketh.* He does not call her *a fool* and *an atheist*, nor does he break out into any indecent expressions of his displeasure, as those who are sick and sore are apt to do, and think they may be excused; but he shows her the evil of what she said, that she spoke the language of the infidels and idolaters, who, when they are *hardly bestead, fret themselves, and curse their king and their God*, Isa. viii. 21. We have reason to suppose that in such a pious household as Job had his wife was one that had been well affected to religion, but that now, when all their estate and comfort were gone, she could not bear the loss with that temper of mind that Job had; but that she should go about to infect his mind with her wretched distemper was a great provocation to him, and he could not forbear thus showing his resentment. Note, (1.) Those are angry and sin not who are angry only at sin and take a temptation as the greatest affront, who *cannot bear those that are evil*, Rev. ii. 2. When Peter was a Satan to Christ he told him plainly, *Thou art an offence to me.* (2.) If those whom we think wise and good at any time speak·that which is foolish and bad, we ought to reprove them faithfully for it and

show them the evil of what they say, that we suffer them not sin upon them. (3.) Temptations to curse God ought to be rejected with the greatest abhorrence, and not so much as to be parleyed with. Whoever persuades us to that must be looked upon as our enemy, to whom if we yield it is at our peril. Job did not curse God and then think to come off with Adam's excuse: " *The woman whom thou gavest to be with me* persuaded me to do it" (Gen. iii. 12), which had in it a tacit reflection on God, his ordinance and providence. No; if thou scornest, if thou cursest, thou alone shalt bear it.

2. How he reasoned against the temptation : *Shall we receive good at the hand of God, and shall we not receive evil also?* Those whom we reprove we must endeavour to convince ; and it is no hard matter to give a reason why we should still hold fast our integrity even when we are stripped of every thing else. He considers that, though good and evil are contraries, yet they do not come from contrary causes, but both from the hand of God (Isa. xlv. 7, Lam. iii. 38), and therefore that in both we must have our eye up unto him, with thankfulness for the good he sends and without fretfulness at the evil. Observe the force of his argument.

(1.) What he argues for, not only the bearing, but the receiving of evil: *Shall we not receive evil*, that is, [1.] " Shall we not expect to receive it ? If God give us so many good things, shall we be surprised, or think it strange, if he sometimes afflict us, when he has told us that prosperity and adversity are set the one over against the other ?" 1 Pet. iv. 12. [2.] " Shall we not set ourselves to receive it aright?" The word signifies to receive as a gift, and denotes a pious affection and disposition of soul under our afflictions, neither despising them nor fainting under them, accounting them gifts (Phil. i. 29), accepting them as punishments of our iniquity (Lev. xxvi. 41), acquiescing in the will of God in them (" Let him do with me as seemeth him good"), and accommodating ourselves to them, as those that know how to want as well as how to abound, Phil. iv. 12. When the heart is humbled and weaned, by humbling weaning providences, then we *receive correction* (Zeph. iii. 2) and take up our cross.

(2.) What he argues from: " Shall we receive so much good as has come to us from the hand of God during all those years of peace and prosperity that we have lived, and shall we not now receive evil, when God thinks fit to lay it on us ?" Note, The consideration of the mercies we receive from God, both past and present, should make us receive our afflictions with a suitable disposition of spirit. If we receive our share of the common good in the seven years of plenty, shall we not receive our share of the common evil in the years of famine? *Qui sentit commodum, sentire debet et onus—he who feels the privilege, should prepare for the privation.* If we have so much that pleases us, why should we not be content with that which pleases God ? If we receive so many comforts, shall we not receive some afflictions, which will serve as foils to our comforts, to make them the more valuable (we are taught the worth of mercies by being made to want them sometimes), and as allays to our comforts, to make them the less dangerous, to keep the balance even, and to prevent our being *lifted up above measure?* 2 Cor. xii. 7. If we receive so much good for the body, shall we not receive some good for the soul; that is, some afflictions, by which we partake of God's holiness (Heb. xii. 10), something which, by saddening the countenance, makes the heart better? Let murmuring therefore, as well as boasting, be for ever excluded.

IV. Thus, in a good measure, Job still held fast his integrity, and Satan's design against him was defeated : *In all this did not Job sin with his lips ;* he not only said this well, but all he said at this time was under the government of religion and right reason. In the midst of all these grievances he did not speak a word amiss ; and we have no reason to think but that he also preserved a good temper of mind, so that, though there might be some stirrings and risings of corruption in his heart, yet grace got the upper hand and he took care that the root of bitterness might not spring up to trouble him, Heb. xii. 15. The *abundance of his heart* was for God, produced good things, and suppressed the evil that was there, which was out-voted by the better side. If he did think any evil, yet he *laid his hand upon his mouth* (Prov. xxx. 32), stifled the evil thought and let it go no further, by which it appeared, not only that he had true grace, but that it was strong and victorious: in short, that he had not forfeited the character of a *perfect and upright man ;* for so *he* appears to be who, in the midst of such temptations, *offends not in word,* Jam. iii. 2 ; Ps. xvii. 3.

11 Now when Job's three friends heard of all this evil that was come upon him, they came every one from his own place ; Eliphaz the Temanite, and Bildad the Shuhite, and Zophar the Naamathite : for they had made an appointment together to come to mourn with him and to comfort him. 12 And when they lifted up their eyes afar off, and knew him not, they lifted up their voice, and wept; and they rent every one his mantle, and sprinkled dust upon their heads toward heaven. 13 So they sat down with him upon the ground seven days and seven nights, and none spake a word

unto him : for they saw that *his* grief was very great.

We have here an account of the kind visit which Job's three friends paid him in his affliction. The news of his extraordinary troubles spread into all parts, he being an eminent man both for greatness and goodness, and the circumstances of his troubles being very uncommon. Some, who were his enemies, triumphed in his calamities, *ch.* xvi. 10; xix. 18 ; xxx. 1, &c. Perhaps they made ballads on him. But his friends concerned themselves for him, and endeavoured to comfort him. *A friend loveth at all times, and a brother is born for adversity.* Three of them are here named (*v.* 11), Eliphaz, Bildad, and Zophar. We shall afterwards meet with a fourth, who it should seem was present at the whole conference, namely, Elihu. Whether he came as a friend of Job or only as an auditor does not appear. These three are said to be his *friends,* his intimate acquaintance, as David and Solomon had each of them one in their court that was called *the king's friend.* These three were eminently wise and good men, as appears by their discourses. They were old men, very old, had a great reputation for knowledge, and much deference was paid to their judgment, *ch.* xxxii. 6. It is probable that they were men of figure in their country—princes, or heads of houses. Now observe,

I. That Job, in his prosperity, had contracted a friendship with them. If they were his equals, yet he had not that jealousy of them—if his inferiors, yet he had not that disdain of them, which was any hindrance to an intimate converse and correspondence with them. To have such friends added more to his happiness in the day of his prosperity than all the head of cattle he was master of. Much of the comfort of this life lies in acquaintance and friendship with those that are prudent and virtuous ; and he that has a few such friends ought to value them highly. Job's three friends are supposed to have been all of them of the posterity of Abraham, which, for some descents, even in the families that were shut out from the covenant of peculiarity, retained some good fruits of that pious education which the father of the faithful gave to those under his charge. Eliphaz descended from Teman, the grandson of Esau (Gen. xxxvi. 11), Bildad (it is probable) from Shuah, Abraham's son by Keturah, Gen. xxv. 2. Zophar is thought by some to be the same with Zepho, a descendant from Esau, Gen. xxxvi. 11. The preserving of so much wisdom and piety among those that were strangers to the covenants of promise was a happy presage of God's grace to the Gentiles, when the partition-wall should in the latter days be taken down. Esau was rejected ; yet many that came from him inherited some of the best blessings.

II. That they continued their friendship

with Job in his adversity, when most of his friends had forsaken him, *ch.* xix. 14. In two ways they showed their friendship:—

1. By the kind visit they paid him in his affliction, to mourn with him and to comfort him, *v.* 11. Probably they had been wont to visit him in his prosperity, not to hunt or hawk with him, not to dance or play at cards with him, but to entertain and edify themselves with his learned and pious converse; and now that he was in adversity they come to share with him in his griefs, as formerly they had come to share with him in his comforts. These were wise men, whose *heart was in the house of mourning,* Eccl. vii. 4. Visiting the afflicted, sick or sore, fatherless or childless, in their sorrow, is made a branch of *pure religion and undefiled* (Jam. i. 27), and, if done from a good principle, will be abundantly recompensed shortly, Matt. xxv. 36.

(1.) By visiting the sons and daughters of affliction we may contribute to the improvement, [1.] Of our own graces; for many a good lesson is to be learned from the troubles of others; we may look upon them and receive instruction, and be made wise and serious. [2.] Of their comforts. By putting a respect upon them we encourage them, and some good word may be spoken to them which may help to make them easy. Job's friends came, not to satisfy their curiosity with an account of his troubles and the strangeness of the circumstances of them, much less, as David's false friends, to make invidious remarks upon him (Ps. xli. 6—8), but to mourn with him, to mingle their tears with his, and so to comfort him. It is much more pleasant to visit those in affliction to whom comfort belongs than those to whom we must first speak conviction.

(2.) Concerning these visitants observe, [1.] That they were not sent for, but came of their own accord (*ch.* vi. 22), whence Mr. Caryl observes that *it is good manners to be an unbidden guest at the house of mourning,* and, in comforting our friends, to anticipate their invitations. [2.] That they made an appointment to come. Note, Good people should make appointments among themselves for doing good, so exciting and binding one another to it, and assisting and encouraging one another in it. For the carrying on of any pious design let hand join in hand. [3.] That they came with a design (and we have reason to think it was a sincere design) to comfort him, and yet proved miserable comforters, through their unskilful management of his case. Many that aim well do, by mistake, come short of their aim.

2. By their tender sympathy with him and concern for him in his affliction. When they saw him at some distance he was so disfigured and deformed with his sores that *they knew him not,* v. 12. His face was *foul with weeping* (*ch.* xvi. 16), like Jerusalem's Nazarites, which had been *ruddy as the rubies,* but were now *blacker than a coal,* Lam.

iv. 7, 8. What a change will a sore disease, or, without that, oppressing care and grief, make in the countenance, in a little time! *Is this Naomi?* Ruth i. 19. So, *Is this Job?* How hast thou fallen! How is thy glory stained and sullied, and all thy honour laid in the dust! God fit us for such changes! Observing him thus miserably altered, they did not leave him, in a fright or loathing, but expressed so much the more tenderness towards him. (1.) Coming to mourn with him, they vented their undissembled grief in all the then usual expressions of that passion. *They wept* aloud; the sight of them (as is usual) revived Job's grief, and set him a weeping afresh, which fetched floods of tears from their eyes. *They rent their clothes, and sprinkled dust upon their heads,* as men that would strip themselves, and abase themselves, with their friend that was stripped and abased. (2.) Coming to comfort him, *they sat down with him upon the ground,* for so he received visits; and they, not in compliment to him, but in true compassion, put themselves into the same humble and uneasy place and posture. They had many a time, it is likely, sat with him on his couches and at his table, in his prosperity, and were therefore willing to share with him in his grief and poverty because they had shared with him in his joy and plenty. It was not a modish short visit that they made him, just to look upon him and be gone; but, as those that could have had no enjoyment of themselves if they had returned to their place while their friend was in so much misery, they resolved to stay with him till they saw him mend or end, and therefore took lodgings near him, though he was not now able to entertain them as he had done, and they must therefore bear their own charges. Every day, for seven days together, at the hours in which he admitted company, they came and sat with him, as his companions in tribulation, and exceptions from that rule, *Nullus ad amissas ibit amicus opes —Those who have lost their wealth are not to expect the visits of their friends.* They sat with him, but *none spoke a word* to him, only they all attended to the particular narratives he gave of his troubles. They were silent, as men astonished and amazed. *Curæ leves loquuntur, ingentes stupent—Our lighter griefs have a voice; those which are more oppressive are mute.*

So long a time they held their peace, to show
A reverence due to such prodigious woe.—Sir R. BLACKMORE.

They spoke not a word to him, whatever they said one to another, by way of instruction, for the improvement of the present providence. They said nothing to that purport to which afterwards they said much—nothing to grieve him (*ch.* iv. 2), because they saw his grief was very great already, and they were loth at first to add affliction to the afflicted. There is a *time to keep silence,* when either *the wicked is before us,* and by speaking we may harden them (Ps. xxxix. 1), or when by speaking we may *offend the generation of God's children*, Ps. lxxiii. 15. Their not entering upon the following solemn discourses till the seventh day may perhaps intimate that it was the sabbath day, which doubtless was observed in the patriarchal age, and to that day they adjourned the intended conference, because probably then company resorted, as usual, to Job's house, to join with him in his devotions, who might be edified by the discourse. Or, rather, by their silence so long they would intimate that what they afterwards said was well considered and digested and the result of many thoughts. *The heart of the wise studies to answer.* We should think twice before we speak once, especially in such a case as this, think long, and we shall be the better able to speak short and to the purpose.

CHAP. III.

"You have heard of the patience of Job," says the apostle, Jam. v. 11. So we have, and of his impatience too. We wondered that a man should be so patient as he was (ch. i. and ii.), but we wonder also that a good man should be so impatient as he is in this chapter, where we find him cursing his day, and, in passion, I. Complaining that he was born, ver. 1—10. II. Complaining that he did not die as soon as he was born, ver. 11—19. III. Complaining that his life was now continued when he was in misery, ver. 20—26. In this it must be owned that Job sinned with his lips, and it is written, not for our imitation, but our admonition, that he who thinks he stands may take heed lest he fall.

AFTER this opened Job his mouth, and cursed his day. 2 And Job spake, and said, 3 Let the day perish wherein I was born, and the night *in which* it was said, There is a man child conceived. 4 Let that day be darkness; let not God regard it from above, neither let the light shine upon it. 5 Let darkness and the shadow of death stain it; let a cloud dwell upon it; let the blackness of the day terrify it. 6 *As for* that night, let darkness seize upon it; let it not be joined unto the days of the year, let it not come into the number of the months. 7 Lo, let that night be solitary, let no joyful voice come therein. 8 Let them curse it that curse the day, who are ready to raise up their mourning. 9 Let the stars of the twilight thereof be dark; let it look for light, but *have* none; neither let it see the dawning of the day: 10 Because it shut not up the doors of my *mother's* womb, nor hid sorrow from mine eyes.

Long was Job's heart hot within him; and, while he was musing, the fire burned, and the more for being stifled and suppressed. At length he spoke with his tongue, but not such a good word as David spoke after a long pause: *Lord, make me to know my end*, Ps. xxxix. 3, 4. Seven days the prophet Ezekiel sat down astonished with the captives, and then (probably on the sabbath day) *the word of the Lord came to him*, Ezek. iii. 15, 16. So long Job and his friends sat thinking, but said nothing; *they* were afraid of speaking what they thought, lest they should grieve him, and *he* durst not give vent to his thoughts, lest he should offend them. They came to comfort him, but, finding his afflictions very extraordinary, they began to think comfort did not belong to him, suspecting him to be a hypocrite, and therefore they said nothing. But losers think they may have leave to speak, and therefore Job first gives vent to his thoughts. Unless they had been better, it would however have been well if he had kept them to himself. In short, he cursed his day, the day of his birth, wished he had never been born, could not think or speak of his own birth without regret and vexation. Whereas men usually observe the annual return of their birth-day with rejoicing, he looked upon it as the unhappiest day of the year, because the unhappiest of his life, being the inlet into all his woe. Now,

I. This was bad enough. The extremity of his trouble and the discomposure of his spirits may excuse it in part, but he can by no means be justified in it. Now he has forgotten the good he was born to, the lean kine have eaten up the fat ones, and he is filled with thoughts of the evil only, and wishes he had never been born. The prophet Jeremiah himself expressed his painful sense of his calamities in language not much unlike this: *Woe is me, my mother, that thou hast borne me!* Jer. xv. 10. *Cursed be the day wherein I was born*, Jer. xx. 14, &c. We may suppose that Job in his prosperity had many a time blessed God for the day of his birth, and reckoned it a happy day; yet now he brands it with all possible marks of infamy. When we consider the iniquity in which we were conceived and born we have reason enough to reflect with sorrow and shame upon the day of our birth, and to say that the *day of our death*, by which we are *freed from sin* (Rom. vi. 7), is far *better.* Eccl. vii. 1. But to curse the day of our birth because then we entered upon the calamitous scene of life is to quarrel with the God of nature, to despise the dignity of our being, and to indulge a passion which our own calm and sober thoughts will make us ashamed of. Certainly there is no condition of life a man can be in in this world but he may in it (if it be not his own fault) so honour God, and work out his own salvation, and make sure a happiness for himself in a better world, that he will have no reason at all to wish he had never been born, but a great deal of reason to say that he had his being to good purpose. Yet it must be owned, if there were not another life after this, and divine consolations to support us in the prospect of it, so many are the sorrows and troubles of this that we might sometimes be tempted to say that we were *made in vain*

(Ps. lxxxix. 47), and to wish we had never been. There are those in hell who with good reason wish they had never been born, as Judas, Matt. xxvi. 24. But, on this side hell, there can be no reason for so vain and ungrateful a wish. It was Job's folly and weakness to curse his day. We must say of it, This was his infirmity; but good men have sometimes failed in the exercise of those graces which they have been most eminent for, that we may understand that when they are said to be *perfect* it is meant that they were upright, not that they were sinless. *Lastly,* Let us observe it, to the honour of the spiritual life above the natural, that though many have cursed the day of their first birth, never any cursed the day of their new-birth, nor wished they never had had grace, and the Spirit of grace, given them. Those are the most excellent gifts, above life and being itself, and which will never be a burden.

II. Yet it was not so bad as Satan promised himself. Job cursed his day, but he did not curse his God—was weary of his life, and would gladly have parted with that, but not weary of his religion; he resolutely cleaves to that, and will never let it go. The dispute between God and Satan concerning Job was not whether Job had his infirmities, and whether he was subject to like passions as we are (that was granted), but whether he was a hypocrite, who secretly hated God, and, if he were provoked, would show his hatred; and, upon trial, it proved that he was no such man. Nay, all this may consist with his being a pattern of patience; for, though he did thus speak unadvisedly with his lips, yet both before and after he expressed great submission and resignation to the holy will of God and repented of his impatience; he condemned himself for it, and therefore God did not condemn him, nor must we, but watch the more carefully over ourselves, lest we sin after the similitude of this transgression.

1. The particular expressions which Job used in cursing his day are full of poetical fancy, flame, and rapture, and create as much difficulty to the critics as the thing itself does to the divines: we need not be particular in our observations upon them. When he would express his passionate wish that he had never been, he falls foul upon the day, and wishes,

(1.) That earth might forget it : *Let it perish (v. 3); let it not be joined to the days of the year, v. 6.* "Let it be not only not inserted in the calendar in red letters, as the day of the king's nativity useth to be" (and Job was a king, *ch. xxix. 25*), "but let it be erased and blotted out, and buried in oblivion. Let not the world know that ever such a man as I was born into it, and lived in it, who am made such a spectacle of misery."

(2.) That Heaven might frown upon it : *Let not God regard it from above, v. 4.* "Every thing is indeed as it is with God;

that day is honourable on which he puts honour, and which he distinguishes and crowns with his favour and blessing, as he did the seventh day of the week; but let my birth-day never be so honoured ; let it be *nigro carbone notandus—marked as with a black coal* for an evil day by him that determines the times before appointed. The father and fountain of light appointed the greater light to rule the day and the less lights to rule the night ; but let that want the benefit of both." [1.] *Let that day be darkness (v. 4) ;* and, if the light of the day be darkness, *how great is that darkness!* how terrible! because then we look for light.' Let the gloominess of the day represent Job's condition, whose sun went down at noon. [2.] As for that night too, let it want the benefit of moon and stars, and *let darkness seize upon it,* thick darkness, darkness that may be felt, which will not befriend the repose of the night by its silence, but rather disturb it with its terrors.

(3.) That all joy might forsake it : "Let it be a melancholy night, solitary, and not a merry night of music or dancing. *Let no joyful voice come therein (v. 7);* let it be a long night, and not *see the eye-lids of the morning (v. 9),* which bring joy with them."

(4.) That all curses might follow it (v. 8) : "Let none ever desire to see it, or bid it welcome when it comes, but, on the contrary, *let those curse it that curse the day.* Whatever day any are tempted to curse, let them at the same time bestow one curse upon my birth-day, particularly those that make it their trade to raise up mourning at funerals with their ditties of lamentation. Let those that curse the day of the death of others in the same breath curse the day of my birth." Or those who are so fierce and daring as to be ready to raise up the *Leviathan* (for that is the word here), who, being about to strike the whale or crocodile, curse it with the bitterest curse they can invent, hoping by their incantations to weaken it, and so to make themselves master of it. Probably some such custom might there be used, to which our divine poet alludes. "Let it be as odious as *the day wherein men bewail the greatest misfortune,* or the time *wherein they see the most dreadful apparition ;*" so bishop Patrick, I suppose taking the Leviathan here to signify the devil, as others do, who understand it of the curses used by conjurors and magicians in raising the devil, or when they have raised a devil that they cannot lay.

2. But what is the ground of Job's quarrel with the day and night of his birth? It is *because it shut not up the doors of his mother's womb, v. 10.* See the folly and madness of a passionate discontent, and how absurdly and extravagantly it talks when the reins are laid on the neck of it. Is this Job, who was so much admired for his wisdom that *unto him men gave ear, and kept silence at his counsel,* and *after his words they spoke not again? ch. xxix. 21, 22.* Surely his wis-

20

dom failed him, (1.) When he took so much pains to express his desire that he had never been born, which, at the best, was a vain wish, for it is impossible to make that which has been not to have been. (2.) When he was so liberal of his curses upon a day and a night that could not be hurt, or made any the worse for his curses. (3.) When he wished a thing so very barbarous to his own mother as that she had not brought him forth when her full time had come, which must inevitably have been her death, and a miserable death. (4.) When he despised the goodness of God to him in giving him a being (such a being, so noble and excellent a life, such a life, so far above that of any other creature in this lower world), and undervalued the gift, as not worth the acceptance, only because *transit cum onere---it was clogged with a proviso of trouble*, which now at length came upon him, after many years' enjoyment of its pleasures. What a foolish thing it was to wish that his eyes had never seen the light, that so they might not have seen sorrow, which yet he might hope to see through, and beyond which he might see joy! Did Job believe and hope that he should *in his flesh see God at the latter day* (*ch.* xix. 26), and yet would he wish he had never had a being capable of such a bliss, only because, for the present, he had sorrow in the flesh? God by his grace arm us against this foolish and hurtful lust of impatience.

11 Why died I not from the womb? *why* did I *not* give up the ghost when I came out of the belly? 12 Why did the knees prevent me? or why the breasts that I should suck? 13 For now should I have lain still and been quiet, I should have slept: then had I been at rest, 14 With kings and counsellors of the earth, which built desolate places for themselves; 15 Or with princes that had gold, who filled their houses with silver: 16 Or as a hidden untimely birth I had not been; as infants *which* never saw light. 17 There the wicked cease *from* troubling; and there the weary be at rest. 18 *There* the prisoners rest together; they hear not the voice of the oppressor. 19 The small and great are there; and the servant *is* free from his master.

Job, perhaps reflecting upon himself for his folly in wishing he had never been born, follows it, and thinks to mend it, with another, little better, that he had died as soon as he was born, which he enlarges upon in these verses. When our Saviour would set forth a very calamitous state of things he seems to allow such a saying as this, *Blessed are the barren, and the wombs that never bore,*

and the paps which never gave suck (Luke xxiii. 29); but blessing the barren womb is one thing and cursing the fruitful womb is another! It is good to make the best of afflictions, but it is not good to make the worst of mercies. Our rule is, *Bless, and curse not.* Life is often put for all good, and death for all evil; yet Job here very absurdly complains of life and its supports as a curse and plague to him, and covets death and the grave as the greatest and most desirable bliss. Surely Satan was deceived in Job when he applied that maxim to him, *All that a man hath will he give for his life;* for never any man valued life at a lower rate than he did.

I. He ungratefully quarrels with life, and is angry that it was not taken from him as soon as it was given him (*v.* 11, 12): *Why died not I from the womb?* See here, 1. What a weak and helpless creature man is when he comes into the world, and how slender the thread of life is when it is first drawn. We are ready to die from the womb, and to breathe our last as soon as we begin to breathe at all. We can do nothing for ourselves, as other creatures can, but should drop into the grave if the knees did not prevent us; and the lamp of life, when first lighted, would go out of itself if the breasts given us, that we should suck, did not supply it with fresh oil. 2. What a merciful and tender care divine Providence took of us at our entrance into the world. It was owing to this that we *died not from the womb* and did not *give up the ghost when we came out of the belly.* Why were we not cut off as soon as we were born? Not because we did not deserve it. Justly might such weeds have been plucked up as soon as they appeared; justly might such cockatrices have been crushed in the egg. Nor was it because we did, or could, take any care of ourselves and our own safety: no creature comes into the world so shiftless as man. It was not our might, or the power of our hand, that preserved us these beings, but God's power and providence upheld our frail lives, and his pity and patience spared our forfeited lives. It was owing to this that the knees prevented us. Natural affection is put into parents' hearts by the hand of the God of nature: and hence it was that the blessings of the breast attended those of the womb. 3. What a great deal of vanity and vexation of spirit attends human life. If we had not a God to serve in this world, and better things to hope for in another world, considering the faculties we are endued with and the troubles we are surrounded with, we should be strongly tempted to wish that we had *died from the womb,* which would have prevented a great deal both of sin and misery.

He that is born to-day, and dies to-morrow,
Loses some hours of joy, but months of sorrow.

4. The evil of impatience, fretfulness, and

discontent. When they thus prevail they are unreasonable and absurd, impious and ungrateful. To indulge them is a slighting and undervaluing of God's favour. How much soever life is embittered, we must say, "It was of the Lord's mercies that we died not from the womb, that we were not consumed." Hatred of life is a contradiction to the common sense and sentiments of mankind, and to our own at any other time. Let discontented people declaim ever so much against life, they will be loth to part with it when it comes to the point. When the old man in the fable, being tired with his burden, threw it down with discontent and called for Death, and Death came to him and asked him what he would have with him, he then answered, "Nothing, but to help me up with my burden."

II. He passionately applauds death and the grave, and seems quite in love with them. To desire to die that we may be with Christ, that we may be free from sin, and that we may be *clothed upon with our house which is from heaven,* is the effect and evidence of grace; but to desire to die only that we may be quiet in the grave, and delivered from the troubles of this life, savours of corruption. Job's considerations here may be of good use to reconcile us to death when it comes, and to make us easy under the arrest of it; but they ought not to be made use of as a pretence to quarrel with life while it is continued, or to make us uneasy under the burdens of it. It is our wisdom and duty to make the best of that which is, be it living or dying, and so to *live to the Lord* and *die to the Lord,* and to be his in both, Rom. xiv. 8. Job here frets himself with thinking that if he had but died as soon as he was born, and been carried from the womb to the grave, 1. His condition would have been as good as that of the best: I should have been (says he, *v.* 14) *with kings and counsellors of the earth,* whose pomp, power, and policy, cannot set them out of the reach of death, nor secure them from the grave, nor distinguish theirs from common dust in the grave. Even princes, who had gold in abundance, could not with it bribe Death to overlook them when he came with commission; and, though they filled their houses with silver, yet they were forced to leave it all behind them, no more to return to it. Some, by the *desolate places* which the kings and counsellors are here said *to build for themselves,* understand the sepulchres or monuments they prepared for themselves in their life-time; as Shebna (Isa. xxii. 16) *hewed himself out a sepulchre;* and by the gold which the princes had, and the silver with which they filled their houses, they understand the treasures which, they say, it was usual to deposit in the graves of great men. Such arts have been used to preserve their dignity, if possible, on the other side death, and to keep themselves from lying

even with those of inferior rank; but it will not do: death is, and will be, an irresistible leveller. *Mors sceptra ligonibus æquat—Death mingles sceptres with spades. Rich and poor meet together* in the grave; and there a *hidden untimely birth* (*v.* 16), a child that either never saw light or but just opened its eyes and peeped into the world, and, not liking it, closed them again and hastened out of it, lies as soft and easy, lies as high and safe, as kings, and counsellors, and princes, that had gold. "And therefore," says Job, "would I had lain there in the dust, rather than live to lie here in the ashes!" 2. His condition would have been much better than now it was (*v.* 13): "*Then should I have lain still, and been quiet,* which now I cannot do, I cannot be, but am still tossing and unquiet; then *I should have slept,* whereas now sleep departeth from my eyes; *then had I been at rest,* whereas now I am restless." Now that life and immortality are brought to a much clearer light by the gospel than before they were placed in good Christians can give a better account than this of the gain of death: "Then should I have been present with the Lord; then should I have seen his glory face to face, and no longer through a glass darkly." But all that poor Job dreamed of was rest and quietness in the grave out of the fear of evil tidings and out of the feeling of sore boils. *Then should I have been quiet;* and had he kept his temper, his even easy temper still, which he was in as recorded in the two foregoing chapters, entirely resigned to the holy will of God and acquiescing in it, he might have been quiet now; his soul, at least, might have dwelt at ease, even when his body lay in pain, Ps. xxv. 13. Observe how finely he describes the repose of the grave, which (provided the soul also be at rest in God) may much assist our triumphs over it. (1.) Those that now are troubled will there be out of the reach of trouble (*v.* 17): *There the wicked cease from troubling.* When persecutors die they can no longer persecute; their *hatred and envy* will then *perish.* Herod had vexed the church, but, when he became a prey for worms, he ceased from troubling. When the persecuted die they are out of the danger of being any further troubled. Had Job been at rest in his grave, he would have had no disturbance from the Sabeans and Chaldeans, none of all his enemies would have created him any trouble. (2.) Those that are now toiled will there see the period of their toils. *There the weary are at rest.* Heaven is more than a rest to the souls of the saints, but the grave is a rest to their bodies. Their pilgrimage is a weary pilgrimage; sin and the world they are weary of; their services, sufferings, and expectations, they are wearied with; but in the grave they *rest from all their labours,* Rev. xiv. 13; Isa. lvii. 2. They are easy there, and make no complaints; there believers sleep in Jesus.

22

(3.) Those that were here enslaved are there at liberty. Death is the prisoner's discharge, the relief of the oppressed, and the servant's manumission (v. 18): *There the prisoners,* though they walk not at large, yet they *rest together,* and are not put to work, to grind in that prison-house. They are no more insulted and trampled upon, menaced and terrified, by their cruel task-masters: *They hear not the voice of the oppressor.* Those that were here doomed to perpetual servitude, that could call nothing their own, no, not their own bodies, are there no longer under command or control: *There the servant is free from his master,* which is a good reason why those that have power should use it moderately, and those that are in subjection should bear it patiently, yet a little while. (4.) Those that were at a vast distance from others are there upon a level (v. 19): *The small and great are there,* there the same, there all one, all alike free among the dead. The tedious pomp and state which attend the great are at an end there. All the inconveniencies of a poor and low condition are likewise over; death and the grave know no difference.

> Levelled by death, the conqueror and the slave,
> The wise and foolish, cowards and the brave,
> Lie mixed and undistinguished in the grave.
> Sir R. Blackmore.

20 Wherefore is light given to him that is in misery, and life unto the bitter *in* soul; 21 Which long for death, but it *cometh* not; and dig for it more than for hid treasures; 22 Which rejoice exceedingly, *and* are glad, when they can find the grave? 23 *Why is light given* to a man whose way is hid, and whom God hath hedged in? 24 For my sighing cometh before I eat, and my roarings are poured out like the waters. 25 For the thing which I greatly feared is come upon me, and that which I was afraid of is come unto me. 26 I was not in safety, neither had I rest, neither was I quiet; yet trouble came.

Job, finding it to no purpose to wish either that he had not been born or had died as soon as he was born, here complains that his life was now continued and not cut off. When men are set on quarrelling there is no end of it; the corrupt heart will carry on the humour. Having cursed the day of his birth, here he courts the day of his death. The beginning of this strife and impatience is as the letting forth of water.

I. He thinks it hard, in general, that miserable lives should be prolonged (v. 20—22): *Wherefore is light in life given to those that are bitter in soul?* Bitterness of soul, through spiritual grievances, makes life itself bitter. *Why doth he give light?* (so it is in the original): he means *God,* yet does not

name him, though the devil had said, " He will curse thee to thy face;" but he tacitly reflects on the divine Providence as unjust and unkind in continuing life when the comforts of life are removed. Life is called *light,* because pleasant and serviceable for walking and working. It is candle-light; the longer it burns the shorter it is, and the nearer to the socket. This light is said to be given us; for, if it were not daily renewed to us by a fresh gift, it would be lost. But Job reckons that to those who are in misery it is δῶρον ἄδωρον—*gift and no gift,* a gift that they had better be without, while the light only serves them to see their own misery by. Such is the vanity of human life that it sometimes becomes a vexation of spirit; and so alterable is the property of death that, though dreadful to nature, it may become desirable even to nature itself. He here speaks of those, 1. Who long for death, when they have out-lived their comforts and usefulness, are burdened with age and infirmities, with pain or sickness, poverty or disgrace, and yet it comes not; while, at the same time, it comes to many who dread it and would put it far from them. The continuance and period of life must be according to God's will, not according to ours. It is not fit that we should be consulted how long we would live and when we would die; our times are in a better hand than our own. 2. Who *dig for it as for hidden treasures,* that is, would give any thing for a fair dismission out of this world, which supposes that *then* the thought of men's being their own executioners was not so much as entertained or suggested, else those who longed for it needed not take much pains for it, they might soon come at it (as Seneca tells them) if they pleased. 3. Who bid it welcome, and *are glad* when they can find the grave and see themselves stepping into it. If the miseries of this life can prevail, contrary to nature, to make death itself desirable, shall not much more the hopes and prospects of a better life, to which death is our passage, make it so, and set us quite above the fear of it? It may be a sin to long for death, but I am sure it is no sin to long for heaven.

II. He thinks himself, in particular, hardly dealt with, that he might not be eased of his pain and misery by death when he could not get ease in any other way. To be thus impatient of life for the sake of the troubles we meet with is not only unnatural in itself, but ungrateful to the giver of life, and argues a sinful indulgence of our own passion and a sinful inconsideration of our future state. Let it be our great and constant care to get ready for another world, and then let us leave it to God to order the circumstances of our removal thither as he thinks fit: " Lord, when and how thou pleasest;" and this with such an indifference that, if he should refer it to us, we would refer it to him again. Grace teaches us, in the midst of life's greatest comforts, to be willing to die, and, in the midst of its greatest crosses, to be willing to live. Job, to excuse himself in this earnest desire which he had to die, pleads the little comfort and satisfaction he had in life.

1. In his present afflicted state troubles were continually felt, and were likely to be so. He thought he had cause enough to be weary of living, for, (1.) He had no comfort of his life: *My sighing comes before I eat,* v. 24. The sorrows of life prevented and anticipated the supports of life; nay, they took away his appetite for his necessary food. His griefs returned as duly as his meals, and affliction was his daily bread. Nay, so great was the extremity of his pain and anguish that he did not only sigh, but roar, and his *roarings were poured out like the waters* in a full and constant stream. Our Master was acquainted with grief, and we must expect to be so too. (2.) He had no prospect of bettering his condition: *His way was hidden,* and God had *hedged him in, v.* 23. He saw no way open of deliverance, nor knew he what course to take; his way was *hedged up with thorns,* that he could not find his path. See *ch.* xxiii. 8; Lam. iii. 7.

2. Even in his former prosperous state troubles were continually feared; so that *then* he was never easy, *v.* 25, 26. He knew so much of the vanity of the world, and the troubles to which, of course, he was born, that he was *not in safety, neither had he rest* then. That which made his grief now the more grievous was that he was not conscious to himself of any great degree either of negligence or security in the day of his prosperity, which might provoke God thus to chastise him. (1.) He had not been negligent and unmindful of his affairs, but kept up such a fear of trouble as was necessary to the maintaining of his guard. He was afraid for his children when they were feasting, lest they should offend God (*ch.* i. 5), afraid for his servants lest they should offend his neighbours; he took all the care he could of his own health, and managed himself and his affairs with all possible precaution; yet all would not do. (2.) He had not been secure, nor indulged himself in ease and softness, had not trusted in his wealth, nor flattered himself with the hopes of the perpetuity of his mirth; yet trouble came, to convince and remind him of the vanity of the world, which yet he had not forgotten when he lived at ease. Thus his way was hidden, for he knew not wherefore God contended with him. Now this consideration, instead of aggravating his grief, might rather serve to alleviate it. Nothing will make trouble easy so much as the testimony of our consciences for us, that, in some measure, we did our duty in a day of prosperity; and an expectation of trouble will make it sit the lighter when it comes. The less it is a surprise the less it is a terror.

24

CHAP. IV.

Job having warmly given vent to his passion, and so broken the ice, his friends here come gravely to give vent to their judgment upon his case, which perhaps they had communicated to one another apart, compared notes upon it and talked it over among themselves, and found they were all agreed in their verdict, that Job's afflictions certainly proved him to be a hypocrite; but they did not attack Job with this high charge till by the expressions of his discontent and impatience, in which they thought he reflected on God himself, he had confirmed them in the bad opinion they had before conceived of him and his character. Now they set upon him with great fear. The dispute begins, and it soon becomes fierce. The opponents are Job's three friends. Job himself is respondent. Elihu appears, first, as moderator, and at length God himself gives judgment upon the controversy and the management of it. The question in dispute is whether Job was an honest man or no, the same question that was in dispute between God and Satan in the first two chapters. Satan had yielded it, and durst not pretend that his cursing his day was a constructive cursing of his God; no, he cannot deny but that Job still holds fast his integrity; but Job's friends will needs have it that, if Job were an honest man, he would not have been thus sorely and thus tediously afflicted, and therefore urge him to confess himself a hypocrite in the profession he had made of religion: "No," says Job, "that I will never do; I have offended God, but my heart, notwithstanding, has been upright with him;" and still he holds fast the comfort of his integrity. Eliphaz, who, it is likely, was the senior, or of the best quality, begins with him in this chapter, in which, I. He begins, in which, I. He compliments Job with an acknowledgment of the eminence and usefulness of the profession he had made of religion, ver. 3, 4. III. He charges him with hypocrisy in his profession, grounding his charge upon his present troubles and his conduct under them, ver. 5, 6. IV. To make good the inference, he maintains that man's wickedness is that which always brings God's judgments, ver. 7—11. V. He corroborates his assertion by a vision which he had, in which he was reminded of the incontestable purity and justice of God, and the meanness, weakness, and sinfulness of man, ver. 12—21. By all this he aims to bring down Job's spirit and to make him both penitent and patient under his afflictions.

THEN Eliphaz the Temanite answered and said, 2 *If* we assay to commune with thee, wilt thou be grieved? but who can withhold himself from speaking? 3 Behold, thou hast instructed many, and thou hast strengthened the weak hands. 4 Thy words have upholden him that was falling, and thou hast strengthened the feeble knees. 5 But now it is come upon thee, and thou faintest; it toucheth thee, and thou art troubled. 6 *Is* not *this* thy fear, thy confidence, thy hope, and the uprightness of thy ways?

In these verses,

I. Eliphaz excuses the trouble he is now about to give to Job by his discourse (*v.* 2): "*If we assay a word with thee*, offer a word of reproof and counsel, wilt thou be grieved and take it ill? We have reason to fear thou wilt; but there is no remedy: *"Who can refrain from words?"* Observe, 1. With what modesty he speaks of himself and his own attempt. He will not undertake the management of the cause alone, but very humbly joins his friends with him: "We will commune with thee." Those that plead God's cause must be glad of help, lest it suffer through their weakness. He will not promise much, but begs leave to assay or attempt, and try if he could propose any thing that might be pertinent, and suit Job's case. In difficult matters it becomes us to pretend no further, but only to try what may be said or done. Many excellent discourses have gone under the modest title of *Essays.* 2. With what tenderness he speaks of Job, and his present afflicted condition: "If we tell thee our mind, *wilt thou be grieved?* Wilt thou take it ill? Wilt thou lay it to thy own heart as thy affliction or to our charge as our fault? Shall we be reckoned unkind and cruel if we deal plainly and faithfully with thee? We desire we may not; we hope we shall not, and should be sorry if that should be ill resented which is well intended." Note, We ought to be afraid of grieving any, especially those that are already in grief, lest we add affliction to the afflicted, as David's enemies, Ps. lxix. 26. We should show ourselves backward to say that which we foresee will be grievous, though ever so necessary. God himself, though he afflicts justly, does not afflict willingly, Lam. iii. 33. 3. With what assurance he speaks of the truth and pertinency of what he was about to say: *Who can withhold himself from speaking?* Surely it was a pious zeal for God's honour, and the spiritual welfare of Job, that laid him under this necessity of speaking. "Who can forbear speaking in vindication of God's honour, which we hear reproved, in love to thy soul, which we see endangered?" Note, It is foolish pity not to reprove our friends, even our friends in affliction, for what they say or do amiss, only for fear of offending them. Whether men take it well or ill, we must with wisdom and meekness do our duty and discharge a good conscience.

II. He exhibits a twofold charge against Job.

1. As to his particular conduct under this affliction. He charges him with weakness and faint-heartedness, and this article of his charge there was too much ground for, *v.* 3—5. And here,

(1.) He takes notice of Job's former serviceableness to the comfort of others. He owns that Job had instructed many, not only his own children and servants, but many others, his neighbours and friends, as many as fell within the sphere of his activity. He did not only encourage those who were teachers by office, and countenance them, and pay for the teaching of those who were poor, but he did himself instruct many. Though a great man, he did not think it below him (king Solomon was a preacher); though a man of business, he found time to do it, went among his neighbours, talked to them about their souls, and gave them good counsel. O that this example of Job were imitated by our great men! If he met with those who were ready to fall into sin, or sink under their troubles, his words upheld them: a wonderful dexterity he had in offering that which was proper to fortify persons against temptations, to support them under their burdens, and to comfort afflicted consciences. He had, and used, the tongue of the learned, knew how to speak a word in season to those that were weary, and employed himself much in that good work. With suitable counsels and comforts he *strengthened the weak hands* for work and service and the spiritual warfare, and the feeble knees for bearing up the

man in his journey and under his load. It is not only our duty to *lift up our own hands that hang down*, by quickening and encouraging ourselves in the way of duty (Heb. xii. 12), but we must also strengthen the weak hands of others, as there is occasion, and do what we can to confirm their feeble knees, by saying *to those that are of a fearful heart, Be strong*, Isa. xxxv. 3, 4. The expressions seem to be borrowed thence. Note, Those who have abundance of spiritual riches should abound in spiritual charity. A good word, well and wisely spoken, may do more good than perhaps we think of. But why does Eliphaz mention this here? [1.] Perhaps he praises him thus for the good he had done that he might make the intended reproof the more passable with him. Just commendation is a good preface to a just reprehension, will help to remove prejudices, and will show that the reproof comes not from ill will. Paul praised the Corinthians before he chided them, 1 Cor. xi. 2. [2.] He remembers how Job had comforted others as a reason why he might justly expect to be himself comforted; and yet, if conviction was necessary in order to comfort, they must be excused if they applied themselves to that first. The *Comforter shall reprove*, John xvi. 8. [3.] He speaks this, perhaps, in a way of pity, lamenting that through the extremity of his affliction he could not apply those comforts to himself which he had formerly administered to others. It is easier to give good counsel than to take it, to preach meekness and patience than to practise them. *Facile omnes, cùm valemus, rectum consilium ægrotis damus—We all find it easy, when in health, to give good advice to the sick.—Terent.* [4.] Most think that he mentions it as an aggravation of his present discontent, upbraiding him with his knowledge, and the good offices he had done for others, as if he had said, "Thou that hast taught others, why dost thou not teach thyself? Is not this an evidence of thy hypocrisy, that thou hast prescribed that medicine to others which thou wilt not now take thyself, and so contradictest thyself, and actest against thy own known principles? Thou that teachest another to faint, dost thou faint? Rom. ii. 21. Physician, heal thyself." Those who have rebuked others must expect to hear of it if they themselves become obnoxious to rebuke.

(2.) He upbraids him with his present low-spiritedness, *v.* 5. "*Now that it has come upon thee*, now that it is thy turn to be afflicted, and the bitter cup that goes round is put into thy hand, now that *it touches thee, thou faintest, thou art troubled.*" Here, [1.] He makes too light of Job's afflictions: "It *touches* thee." The very word that Satan himself had used, *ch.* i. 11; ii. 5. Had Eliphaz felt but the one-half of Job's affliction, he would have said, "It smites me, it wounds me;" but, speaking of Job's afflictions, he makes a mere trifle of it: "It touches thee and thou canst not bear to be touched. *Noli me tangere—Touch me not.* [2.] He makes too much of Job's resentments, and aggravates them: "Thou faintest, or thou art beside thyself; thou ravest, and knowest not what thou sayest." Men in deep distress must have grains of allowance, and a favourable construction put upon what they say; when we make the worst of every word we do not as we would be done by.

2. As to his general character before this affliction. He charges him with wickedness and false-heartedness, and this article of his charge was utterly groundless and unjust. How unkindly does he banter him, and upbraid him with the great profession of religion he had made, as if it had all now come to nothing and proved a sham (*v.* 6): " *Is not this thy fear, thy confidence, thy hope, and the uprightness of thy ways?* Does it not all appear now to be a mere pretence? For, hadst thou been sincere in it, God would not thus have afflicted thee, nor wouldst thou have behaved thus under the affliction." This was the very thing Satan aimed at, to prove Job a hypocrite, and disprove the character God had given of him. When he could not himself do this to God, but he still saw and said, *Job is perfect and upright,* then he endeavoured, by his friends, to do it to Job himself, and to persuade him to confess himself a hypocrite. Could he have gained that point he would have triumphed. *Habes confitentem reum—Out of thy own mouth will I condemn thee.* But, by the grace of God, Job was enabled to hold fast his integrity, and would not bear false witness against himself. Note, Those that pass rash and uncharitable censures upon their brethren, and condemn them as hypocrites, do Satan's work, and serve his interest, more than they are aware of. I know not how it comes to pass that this verse is differently read in several editions of our common English Bibles; the original, and all the ancient versions, put *thy hope* before *the uprightness of thy ways.* So does the Geneva, and most of the editions of the last translation; but I find one of the first, in 1612, has it, *Is not this thy fear, thy confidence, the uprightness of thy ways, and thy hope?* Both the Assembly's Annotations and Mr. Pool's have that reading: and an edition in 1660 reads it, " *Is not thy fear thy confidence, and the uprightness of thy ways thy hope?* Does it not appear now that all the religion both of thy devotion and of thy conversation was only in hope and confidence that thou shouldst grow rich by it? Was it not all mercenary?" The very thing that Satan suggested. *Is not thy religion thy hope, and are not thy ways thy confidence?* so Mr. Broughton. Or, "Was it not? Didst thou not think that that would be thy protection? But thou art deceived." Or, "Would it not have been so? If it had been sincere, would it not have kept thee from this despair? It is true, *if thou*

26

faint in the day of adversity, thy strength, thy grace, *is small* (Prov. xxiv. 10); but it does not therefore follow that thou hast no grace, no strength at all. A man's character is not to be taken from a single act.

7 Remember, I pray thee, who *ever* perished, being innocent? or where were the righteous cut off? 8 Even as I have seen, they that plough iniquity, and sow wickedness, reap the same. 9 By the blast of God they perish, and by the breath of his nostrils are they consumed. 10 The roaring of the lion, and the voice of the fierce lion, and the teeth of the young lions, are broken. 11 The old lion perisheth for lack of prey, and the stout lion's whelps are scattered abroad.

Eliphaz here advances another argument to prove Job a hypocrite, and will have not only his impatience under his afflictions to be evidence against him, but even his afflictions themselves, being so very great and extraordinary, and there being no prospect at all of his deliverance out of them. To strengthen his argument he here lays down these two principles, which seem plausible enough:—

I. That good men were never thus ruined. For the proof of this he appeals to Job's own observation (*v.* 7): " *Remember, I pray thee;* recollect all that thou hast seen, heard, or read, and give me an instance of any one that was innocent and righteous, and yet perished as thou dost, and was cut off as thou art." If we understand it of a final and eternal destruction, his principle is true. None that are innocent and righteous perish for ever: it is only a *man of sin* that is a *son of perdition,* 2 Thess. ii. 3. But then it is ill applied to Job; he did not thus perish, nor was he cut off: a man is never undone till he is in hell. But, if we understand it of any temporal calamity, his principle is not true. *The righteous perish* (Isa. lvii. 1); *there is one event both to the righteous and to the wicked* (Eccl. ix. 2), both in life and death; the great and certain difference is after death. Even before Job's time (as early as it was) there were instances sufficient to contradict this principle. Did not righteous Abel *perish being innocent?* and was he not cut off in the beginning of his days? Was not righteous Lot burnt out of house and harbour, and forced to retire to a melancholy cave? Was not righteous Jacob *a Syrian ready to perish?* Deut. xxvi. 5. Other such instances, no doubt, there were, which are not on record.

II. That wicked men were often thus ruined. For the proof of this he vouches his own observation (*v.* 8): " *Even as I have seen,* many a time, *those that plough iniquity, and sow wickedness, reap accordingly; by the blast of God they perish, v.* 9. We have daily instances of that; and therefore, since thou dost thus perish and art consumed, we have reason to think that, whatever profession of religion thou hast made, thou hast but ploughed iniquity and sown wickedness. Even as I have seen in others, so do I see in thee."

1. He speaks of sinners in general, politic busy sinners, that take pains in sin, for they plough iniquity; and expect gain by sin, for they sow wickedness. Those that plough plough in hope; but what is the issue? *They reap the same.* They shall of the *flesh reap corruption* and ruin, Gal. vi. 7, 8. The harvest will be *a heap in the day of grief and desperate sorrow,* Isa. xvii. 11. He shall reap *the same,* that is, the proper product of that seedness. That which the sinner sows, he *sows not that body that shall be,* but God will give it a body, a body of death, *the end of those things,* Rom. vi. 21. Some, by iniquity and wickedness, understand wrong and injury done to others. Those who plough and sow them shall reap the same, that is, they shall be paid in their own coin. Those who are troublesome shall be troubled, 2 Thess. i. 6; Josh. vii. 25. The *spoilers shall be spoiled* (Isa. xxxiii. 1), and those that led captive shall *go captive,* Rev. xiii. 10. He further describes their destruction (*v.* 9): *By the blast of God they perish.* The projects they take so much pains in are defeated; God cuts asunder the cords of those ploughers, Ps. cxxix. 3, 4. They themselves are destroyed, which is the just punishment of their iniquity. *They perish,* that is, they are destroyed utterly; *they are consumed,* that is, they are destroyed gradually; and this by the blast and breath of God, that is, (1.) By his wrath. His anger is the ruin of sinners, who are therefore called *vessels of wrath,* and his breath is said to kindle Tophet, Isa. xxx. 33. *Who knows the power of his anger?* Ps. xc. 11. (2.) By his word. He speaks and it is done, easily and effectually. The Spirit of God, in the word, consumes sinners; with that he slays them, Hos. vi. 5. Saying and doing are not two things with God. The man of sin is said to be consumed with the *breath of Christ's mouth,* 2 Thess. ii. 8. Compare Isa. xi. 4; Rev. xix. 21. Some think that in attributing the destruction of sinners to the blast of God, and the *breath of his nostrils,* he refers to the wind which blew the house down upon Job's children, as if they were therefore *sinners above all men because they suffered such things.* Luke xiii. 2.

2. He speaks particularly of tyrants and cruel oppressors, under the similitude of lions, *v.* 10, 11. Observe, (1.) How he describes their cruelty and oppression. The Hebrew tongue has five several names for lions, and they are all here used to set forth the terrible tearing power, fierceness, and cruelty, of proud oppressors. They roar, and rend, and prey upon all about them, and bring up their young ones to do so too, Ezek. xix. 3.

The devil is a roaring lion; and they partake of his nature, and do his lusts. They are strong as lions, and subtle (Ps. x. 9; xvii. 12); and, as far as they prevail, they lay all desolate about them. (2.) How he describes their destruction, the destruction both of their power and of their persons. They shall be restrained from doing further hurt and reckoned with for the hurt they have done. An effectual course shall be taken, [1.] That they shall not terrify. The voice of their roaring shall be stopped. [2.] That they shall not tear. God will disarm them, will take away their power to do hurt: *The teeth of the young lions are broken.* See Ps. iii. 7. Thus shall the remainder of wrath be restrained. [3.] That they shall not enrich themselves with the spoil of their neighbours. Even *the old lion* is famished, and *perishes for lack of prey.* Those that have surfeited on spoil and rapine are perhaps reduced to such straits as to die of hunger at last. [4.] That they shall not, as they promise themselves, leave a succession: *The stout lion's whelps are scattered abroad,* to seek for food themselves, which the old ones used to bring in for them, Nah. ii. 12. *The lion did tear in pieces for his whelps,* but now they must shift for themselves. Perhaps Eliphaz intended, in this, to reflect upon Job, as if he, being the *greatest of all the men of the east,* had got his estate by spoil and used his power in oppressing his neighbours, but now his power and estate were gone, and his family was scattered: if so, it was a pity that a man whom God praised should be thus abused.

12 Now a thing was secretly brought to me, and mine ear received a little thereof. 13 In thoughts from the visions of the night, when deep sleep falleth on men, 14 Fear came upon me, and trembling, which made all my bones to shake. 15 Then a spirit passed before my face; the hair of my flesh stood up: 16 It stood still, but I could not discern the form thereof: an image *was* before mine eyes, *there was* silence, and I heard a voice, *saying,* 17 Shall mortal man be more just than God? shall a man be more pure than his maker? 18 Behold, he put no trust in his servants; and his angels he charged with folly: 19 How much less *in* them that dwell in houses of clay, whose foundation *is* in the dust, *which* are crushed before the moth? 20 They are destroyed from morning to evening: they perish for ever without any regarding *it.* 21 Doth not their excellency *which is* in

them go away? they die, even without wisdom.

Eliphaz, having undertaken to convince Job of the sin and folly of his discontent and impatience, here vouches a vision he had been favoured with, which he relates to Job for his conviction. What comes immediately from God all men will pay a particular deference to, and Job, no doubt, as much as any. Some think Eliphaz had this vision now *lately,* since he came to Job, putting words into his mouth wherewith to reason with him; and it would have been well if he had kept to the purport of this vision, which would serve for a ground on which to reprove Job for his murmuring, but not to condemn him as a hypocrite. Others think he had it *formerly;* for God did, in this way, often communicate his mind to the children of men in those first ages of the world, *ch.* xxxiii. 15. Probably God had sent Eliphaz this messenger and message some time or other, when he was himself in an unquiet discontented frame, to calm and pacify him. Note, As we should comfort others with that wherewith we have been comforted (2 Cor. i. 4), so we should endeavour to convince others with that which has been powerful to convince us. The people of God had not then any written word to quote, and therefore God sometimes notified to them even common truths by the extraordinary ways of revelation. We that have Bibles have there (thanks be to God) a more sure word to depend upon than even visions and voices, 2 Pet. i. 19. Observe,

I. The manner in which this message was sent to Eliphaz, and the circumstances of the conveyance of it to him. 1. It was *brought to him secretly,* or by stealth. Some of the sweetest communion gracious souls have with God is in secret, where no eye sees but that of him who is all eye. God has ways of bringing conviction, counsel, and comfort, to his people, unobserved by the world, by private whispers, as powerfully and effectually as by the public ministry. *His secret is with them,* Ps. xxv. 14. As the evil spirit often steals good words out of the heart (Matt. xiii. 19), so the good Spirit sometimes steals good words into the heart, or ever we are aware. 2. *He received a little thereof, v.* 12. And it is but a little of divine knowledge that the best receive in this world. We know little in comparison with what is to be known, and with what we shall know when we come to heaven. *How little a portion is heard of God! ch.* xxvi. 14. *We know but in part,* 1 Cor. xiii. 12. See his humility and modesty. He pretends not to have understood it fully, but something of it he perceived. 3. It was brought to him in the *visions of the night* (*v.* 13), when he had retired from the world and the hurry of it, and all about him was composed and quiet. Note, The more we are withdrawn from the

world and the things of it the fitter we are for communion with God. When we are *communing with our own hearts, and are still* (Ps. iv. 4), then is a proper time for the Holy Spirit to commune with us. When others were asleep Eliphaz was ready to receive this visit from Heaven, and probably, like David, was *meditating upon God in the night-watches;* in the midst of those good thoughts this thing was brought to him. We should hear more from God if we thought more of him; yet some are surprised with convictions in the night, *ch.* xxxiii. 14, 15. 4. It was prefaced with terrors: *Fear came upon him, and trembling, v.* 14. It should seem, before he either heard or saw any thing, he was seized with this trembling, which shook his bones, and perhaps the bed under him. A holy awe and reverence of God and his majesty being struck upon his spirit, he was thereby prepared for a divine visit. Whom God intends to honour he first humbles and lays low, and will have us all to serve him with holy fear, and to rejoice with trembling.

II. The messenger by whom it was sent—*a spirit,* one of the good angels, who are employed not only as the ministers of God's providence, but sometimes as the ministers of his word. Concerning this apparition which Eliphaz saw we are here told (*v.* 15, 16), 1. That it was real, and not a dream, not a fancy. *An image* was before his eyes; he plainly saw it; at first it passed and re-passed before his face, moved up and down, but at length it *stood still* to speak to him. If some have been so knavish as to impose false visions on others, and some so foolish as to be themselves imposed upon, it does not therefore follow but that there may have been apparitions of spirits, both good and bad. 2. That it was indistinct, and somewhat confused. He *could not discern the form thereof,* so as to frame any exact idea of it in his own mind, much less to give a description of it. His conscience was to be awakened and informed, not his curiosity gratified. We know little of spirits; we are not capable of knowing much of them, nor is it fit that we should: all in good time; we must shortly remove to the world of spirits, and shall then be better acquainted with them. 3. That it put him into a great consternation, so that his hair stood on end. Ever since man sinned it has been terrible to him to receive an express from heaven, as conscious to himself that he can expect no good tidings thence; apparitions therefore, even of good spirits, have always made deep impressions of fear, even upon good men. How well is it for us that God sends us his messages, not by spirits, but by men like ourselves, *whose terror shall not make us afraid!* See Dan. vii. 28; x. 8, 9.

III. The message itself. Before it was delivered *there was silence,* profound silence, *v.* 16. When we are to speak either from God or to him it becomes us to address ourselves to it with a solemn pause, and so to set bounds about the mount on which God is to come down, and not be hasty to utter any thing. It was in a still small voice that the message was delivered, and this was it (*v.* 17): "*Shall mortal man be more just than God*, the immortal God? *Shall a man be* thought to be, or pretend to be, *more pure than his Maker?* Away with such a thought!" 1. Some think that Eliphaz aims hereby to prove that Job's great afflictions were a certain evidence of his being a wicked man. A mortal man would be thought unjust and very impure if he should thus correct and punish a servant or subject, unless he had been guilty of some very great crime: "If therefore there were not some great crimes for which God thus punishes thee, man would be more just than God, which is not to be imagined." 2. I rather think it is only a reproof of Job's murmuring and discontent: "Shall a man pretend to be more just and pure than God? more truly to understand, and more strictly to observe, the rules and laws of equity than God?" Shall *Enosh*, mortal miserable man, be so insolent; nay, shall *Geber*, the strongest and most eminent man, man at his best estate, pretend to compare with God, or stand in competition with him?" Note, It is most impious and absurd to think either others or ourselves more just and pure than God. Those that quarrel and find fault with the directions of the divine law, the dispensations of the divine grace, or the disposals of the divine providence, make themselves more just and pure than God; and those who thus *reprove God, let them answer it.* What! sinful man! (for he would not have been mortal if he had not been sinful) short-sighted man! Shall he pretend to be more just, more pure, than God, who, being his Maker, is his Lord and owner? Shall the clay contend with the potter? What justice and purity there is in man, God is the author of it, and therefore is himself more just and pure. See Ps. xciv. 9, 10.

IV. The comment which Eliphaz makes upon this, for so it seems to be; yet some take all the following verses to be spoken in vision. It comes all to one.

1. He shows how little the angels themselves are in comparison with God, *v.* 18. Angels are God's servants, waiting servants, working servants; they are his ministers (Ps. civ. 4); bright and blessed beings they are, but God neither needs them nor is benefited by them and is himself infinitely above them, and therefore, (1.) He put no trust in them, did not repose a confidence in them, as we do in those we cannot live without. There is no service in which he employs them but, if he pleased, he could have it done as well without them. He never made them his confidants, or of his cabinet-council, Matt. xxiv. 36. He does not leave his business wholly to them, but *his own eyes run to*

and fro through the earth, 2 Chron. xvi. 9. See this phrase, *ch.* xxxix. 11. Some give this sense of it: "So mutable is even the angelical nature that God would not trust angels with their own integrity; if he had, they would all have done as some did, left their first estate; but he saw it necessary to give them supernatural grace to confirm them." (2.) He charges them with folly, vanity, weakness, infirmity, and imperfection, in comparison with himself. If the world were left to the government of the angels, and they were trusted with the sole management of affairs, they would take false steps, and every thing would not be done for the best, as now it is. Angels are intelligences, but finite ones. Though not chargeable with iniquity, yet with imprudence. This last clause is variously rendered by the critics. I think it would bear this reading, repeating the negation, which is very common: *He will put no trust in his saints; nor will he glory in his angels (in angelis suis non ponet gloriationem) or make his boast* of them, as if their praises, or services, added any thing to him: it is his glory that he is infinitely happy without them.

2. Thence he infers how much less man is, how much less to be trusted in or gloried in. If there is such a distance between God and angels, what is there between God and man! See how man is represented here in his meanness.

(1.) Look upon man in his life, and he is very mean, *v.* 19. Take man in his best estate, and he is a very despicable creature in comparison with the holy angels, though honourable if compared with the brutes. It is true, angels are spirits, and the souls of men are spirits; but, [1.] Angels are pure spirits; the souls of men *dwell in houses of clay:* such the bodies of men are. Angels are free; human souls are housed, and the body is a cloud, a clog, to it; it is its cage; it is its prison. It is a house of clay, mean and mouldering; an earthen vessel, soon broken, as it was first formed, according to the good pleasure of the potter. It is a cottage, not a house of cedar or a house of ivory, but of clay, which would soon be in ruins if not kept in constant repair. [2.] Angels are fixed, but the very *foundation* of that house of clay in which man dwells *is in the dust.* A house of clay, if built upon a rock, might stand long; but, if founded in the dust, the uncertainty of the foundation will hasten its fall, and it will sink with its own weight. As man was made out of the earth, so he is maintained and supported by that which cometh out of the earth. Take away that, and his body returns to its earth. We stand but upon the dust; some have a higher heap of dust to stand upon than others, but still it is the earth that stays us to and will shortly swallow us up. [3.] Angels are immortal, but man is soon crushed; the *earthly house of his tabernacle is dissolved;* he *dies and wastes away, is crushed like a moth* between one's fingers, as easily, as quickly ; one may almost as soon kill a man as kill a moth. A little thing will destroy his life. He is *crushed before the face of the moth*, so the word is. If some lingering distemper, which consumes like a moth, be commissioned to destroy him, he can no more resist it than he can resist an acute distemper, which comes roaring upon him like a lion. See Hos. v. 12—14. Is such a creature as this to be trusted in, or can any service be expected from him by that God who puts no trust in angels themselves ?

(2.) Look upon him in his death, and he appears yet more despicable, and unfit to be trusted. Men are mortal and dying, *v.* 20, 21. [1.] In death *they are destroyed*, and *perish for ever*, as to this world; it is the final period of their lives, and all their employments and enjoyments here ; their place will know them no more. [2.] They are dying daily, and continually wasting : *Destroyed from morning to evening*. Death is still working in us, like a mole digging our grave at each remove, and we so continually lie exposed that we are killed all the day long. [3.] Their life is short, and in a little time they are cut off. It lasts perhaps but from morning to evening. It is but a day (so some understand it); their birth and death are but the sun-rise and sun-set of the same day. [4.] In death all their excellency passes away ; beauty, strength, learning, not only cannot secure them from death, but must die with them, nor shall their pomp, their wealth, or power, descend after them. [5.] Their wisdom cannot save them from death: *They die without wisdom*, die for want of wisdom, by their own foolish management of themselves, digging their graves with their own teeth. [6.] It is so common a thing that nobody heeds it, nor takes any notice of it : *They perish without any regarding it*, or laying it to heart. The deaths of others are much the subject of common talk, but little the subject of serious thought. Some think the eternal damnation of sinners is here spoken of, as well as their temporal death : *They are destroyed, or broken to pieces, by death, from morning to evening ; and, if they repent not, they perish for ever* (so some read it), *v.* 20. They perish for ever because they regard not God and their duty ; they *consider not their latter end*, Lam. i. 9. They have no excellency but that which death takes away, and they die, they die the second death, for want of wisdom to lay hold on eternal life. Shall such a mean, weak, foolish, sinful, dying creature as this pretend to be *more just than God and more pure than his Maker?* No, instead of quarrelling with his afflictions, let him wonder that he is out of hell.

CHAP. V.

Eliphaz, in the foregoing chapter, for the making good of his charge against Job, had vouched a word from heaven, sent him in a vision. In this chapter he appeals to those that bear record on earth, to the saints, the faithful witnesses of God's truth in all ages, ver. 1. They will testify, 1. That the sin of sinners is their ruin, ver. 2—5. II. That yet affliction is the common lot of

30

mankind, ver. 6, 7. III. That when we are in affliction it is our wisdom and duty to apply to God, for he is able and ready to help us, ver. 8—16. IV. That the afflictions which are borne well will end well ; and Job particularly, if he would come to a better temper, might assure himself that God had great mercy in store for him, ver. 17—27. So that he concludes his discourse in somewhat a better humour than he began it.

CALL now, if there be any that will answer thee ; and to which of the saints wilt thou turn ? 2 For wrath killeth the foolish man, and envy slayeth the silly one. 3 I have seen the foolish taking root : but suddenly I cursed his habitation. 4 His children are far from safety, and they are crushed in the gate, neither *is there* any to deliver *them*. 5 Whose harvest the hungry eateth up, and taketh it even out of the thorns, and the robber swalloweth up their substance.

A very warm dispute being begun between Job and his friends, Eliphaz here makes a fair motion to put the matter to a reference. In all debates perhaps the sooner this is done the better if the contenders cannot end it between themselves. So well assured is Eliphaz of the goodness of his own cause that he moves Job himself to choose the arbitrators (*v.* 1): *Call now, if there be any that will answer thee ;* that is, 1. " If there be any that suffer as thou sufferest. Canst thou produce an instance of any one that was really a saint that was reduced to such an extremity as thou art now reduced to? God never dealt with any that love his name as he deals with thee, and therefore surely thou art none of them." 2. " If there be any that say as thou sayest. Did ever any good man curse his day as thou dost ? Or will any of the saints justify thee in these heats or passions, or say that these are the spots of God's children? Thou wilt find none of the saints that will be either thy advocates or my antagonists. *To which of the saints wilt thou turn?* Turn to which thou wilt, and thou wilt find they are all of my mind. I have the *communis sensus fidelium—the unanimous vote of the faithful* on my side ; they will all subscribe to what I am going to say. Observe, (1.) Good people are called *saints* even in the Old Testament; and therefore I know not why we should, in common speaking (unless because we must *loqui cum vulgo—speak as our neighbours*), appropriate the title to those of the New Testament, and not say St. Abraham, St. Moses, and St. Isaiah, as well as St. Matthew and St. Mark; and St. David the psalmist, as well as St. David the British bishop. Aaron is expressly called *the saint of the Lord*. (2.) All that are themselves saints will turn to those that are so, will choose them for their friends and converse with them, will choose them for their judges and consult them. See Ps. cxix. 79. The saints shall *judge the world*, 1 Cor. vi. 1, 2. *Walk in the way of good men*

(Prov. ii. 20), *the old way, the footsteps of the flock.* Every one chooses some sort of people or other to whom he studies to recommend himself, and whose sentiments are to him the test of honour and dishonour. Now all true saints endeavour to recommend themselves to those that are such, and to stand right in their opinion. (3.) There are some truths so plain, and so universally known and believed, that one may venture to appeal to any of the saints concerning them. However there are some things about which they unhappily differ, there are many more, and more considerable, in which they are agreed; as the evil of sin, the vanity of the world, the worth of the soul, the necessity of a holy life, and the like. Though they do not all live up, as they should, to their belief of these truths, yet they are all ready to bear their testimony to them.

Now there are two things which Eliphaz here maintains, and in which he doubts not but all the saints concur with him:—

I. That the sin of sinners directly tends to their own ruin (*v.* 2): *Wrath kills the foolish man,* his own wrath, and therefore he is foolish for indulging it; it is a fire in his bones, in his blood, enough to put him into a fever. *Envy* is the rottenness of the bones, and so *slays the silly one* that frets himself with it. " So it is with thee," says Eliphaz, " while thou quarrellest with God thou doest thyself the greatest mischief; thy anger at thy own troubles, and thy envy at our prosperity, do but add to thy pain and misery: turn to the saints, and thou wilt find they understand their interest better." Job had told his wife she spoke as the foolish women; now Eliphaz tells him he acted as the foolish men, the silly ones. Or it may be meant thus: " If men are ruined and undone, it is always their own folly that ruins and undoes them. They kill themselves by some lust or other; therefore, no doubt, Job, thou hast done some foolish thing, by which thou hast brought thyself into this calamitous condition." Many understand it of God's wrath and jealousy. Job needed not be uneasy at the prosperity of the wicked, for the world's smiles can never shelter them from God's frowns; they are foolish and silly if they think they will. God's anger will be the death, the eternal death, of those on whom it fastens. What is hell but God's anger without mixture or period?

II. That their prosperity is short and their destruction certain, *v.* 3—5. He seems here to parallel Job's case with that which is commonly the case of wicked people 1. Job had prospered for a time, seemed confirmed, and was secure in his prosperity; and it is common for foolish wicked men to do so : *I have seen them taking root*—planted, and, in their own and others' apprehension, fixed, and likely to continue. See Jer. xii. 2; Ps. xxxvii. 35, 36. We see worldly men taking root in the earth; on earthly things they fix the standing of their hopes, and from them they draw the sap of their comforts. The outward estate may be flourishing, but the soul cannot prosper that takes root in the earth. 2. Job's prosperity was now at an end, and so has the prosperity of other wicked people quickly been. (1.) Eliphaz foresaw their ruin with an eye of faith. Those who looked only at present things blessed their habitation, and thought them happy, blessed it long, and wished themselves in their condition. But Eliphaz cursed it, suddenly cursed it, as soon as he saw them begin to take root, that is, he plainly foresaw and foretold their ruin; not that he prayed for it *(I have not desired the woeful day),* but he prognosticated it. *He went into the sanctuary,* and there *understood their end* and heard their doom read (Ps. lxxiii. 17, 18), that the *prosperity of fools will destroy them,* Prov. i. 32. Those who believe the word of God can see a *curse in the house of the wicked* (Prov. iii. 33), though it be ever so finely and firmly built, and ever so full of all good things; and they can foresee that the curse will, in time, infallibly consume it with the timber thereof, and the stones thereof, Zech. v. 4. (2.) He saw, at length, what he had foreseen. He was not disappointed in his expectation concerning him; the event answered it; his family was undone, and his estate ruined. In these particulars he plainly and very inviously reflects on Job's calamities. [1.] His children were crushed, *v.* 4. They thought themselves safe in their eldest brother's house, but were *far from safety,* for they were *crushed in the gate.* Perhaps the door or gate of the house was highest built, and fell heaviest upon them, *and there was none to deliver them* from perishing in the ruins. This is commonly understood of the destruction of the families of wicked men, by the execution of justice upon them, to oblige them to restore what they have ill-gotten. They leave it to their children; but the descent shall not bar the entry of the rightful owners, who will crush their children, and cast them by due course of law (and there shall be none to help them), or perhaps by oppression, Ps. cix. 9, &c. [2.] His estate was plundered, *v.* 5. Job's was so. The hungry robbers, the Sabeans and Chaldeans, ran away with it, and swallowed it; and this, says he, I have often observed in others. What has been got by spoil and rapine has been lost in the same way. The careful owner hedged it about with thorns, and then thought it safe; but the fence proved insignificant against the greediness of the spoilers (if hunger will break through stone walls, much more through thorn hedges), and against the divine curse, which will go through the thorns and briers, and *burn them together,* Isa. xxvii. 4.

6 Although affliction cometh not forth of the dust, neither doth trouble spring out of the ground; 7 Yet man

is born unto trouble, as the sparks fly upward. 8 I would seek unto God, and unto God would I commit my cause : 9 Which doeth great things and unsearchable ; marvellous things without number : 10 Who giveth rain upon the earth, and sendeth waters upon the fields : 11 To set up on high those that be low ; that those which mourn may be exalted to safety. 12 He disappointeth the devices of the crafty, so that their hands cannot perform *their* enterprise. 13 He taketh the wise in their own craftiness : and the counsel of the froward is carried headlong. 14 They meet with darkness in the daytime, and grope in the noonday as in the night. 15 But he saveth the poor from the sword, from their mouth, and from the hand of the mighty. 16 So the poor hath hope, and iniquity stoppeth her mouth.

Eliphaz, having touched Job in a very tender part, in mentioning both the loss of his estate and the death of his children as the just punishment of his sin, that he might not drive him to despair, here begins to encourage him, and puts him in a way to make himself easy. Now he very much changes his voice (Gal. iv. 20), and speaks in the accents of kindness, as if he would atone for the hard words he had given him.

I. He reminds him that no affliction comes by chance, nor is to be attributed to second causes: It *doth not come forth of the dust,* nor *spring out of the ground,* as the grass doth, *v.* 6. It doth not come of course, at certain seasons of the year, as natural productions do, by a chain of second causes. The proportion between prosperity and adversity is not so exactly observed by Providence as that between day and night, summer and winter, but according to the will and counsel of God, when and as he thinks fit. Some read it, *Sin comes not forth out of the dust, nor iniquity out of the ground.* If men be bad, they must not lay the blame upon the soil, the climate, or the stars, but on themselves. *If thou scornest, thou alone shalt bear it.* We must not attribute our afflictions to fortune, for they are from God, nor our sins to fate, for they are from ourselves; so that, whatever trouble we are in, we must own that God sends it upon us and we procure it to ourselves: the former is a reason why we should be very patient, the latter why we should be very penitent, when we are afflicted.

II. He reminds him that trouble and affliction are what we have all reason to expect in this world: *Man is brought to trouble* (*v.* 7), not as man (had he kept his innocency he would have been born to pleasure), but as

sinful man, as *born of a woman* (*ch.* xiv. 1), who was in the transgression. Man is born in sin, and therefore born to trouble. Even those that are born to honour and estate are yet born to trouble in the flesh. In our fallen state it has become natural to us to sin, and the natural consequence of that is affliction, Rom. v. 12. There is nothing in this world we are born to, and can truly call our own, but sin and trouble; both are as the sparks that fly upwards. Actual transgressions are the sparks that fly out of the furnace of original corruption; and, being called *transgressors from the womb,* no wonder that we *deal very treacherously,* Isa. xlviii. 8. Such too is the frailty of our bodies, and the vanity of all our enjoyments, that our troubles also thence arise as naturally *as the sparks fly upwards*—so many are they, so thick and so fast does one follow another. Why then should we be surprised at our afflictions as strange, or quarrel with them as hard, when they are but what we are born to? Man is born to *labour* (so it is in the margin), is sentenced to eat his bread in the sweat of his face, which should inure him to hardness, and make him bear his afflictions the better.

III. He directs him how to behave himself under his affliction (*v.* 8): *I would seek unto God; surely I would:* so it is in the original. Here is, 1 A tacit reproof to Job for not seeking to God, but quarrelling with him: "Job, if I had been in thy case, I would not have been so peevish and passionate as thou art. I would have acquiesced in the will of God." It is easy to say what we would do if we were in such a one's case; but, when it comes to the trial, perhaps it will be found not so easy to do as we say. 2. Very good and seasonable advice to him, which Eliphaz transfers to himself in a figure: "For my part, the best way I should think I could take, if I were in thy condition, would be to apply to God." Note, We should give our friends no other counsel than what we would take ourselves if we were in their case, that we may be easy under our afflictions, may get good by them, and may see a good issue of them. (1.) We must by prayer fetch in mercy and grace from God, seek to him as a Father and friend, though he contend with us, as one who is alone able to support and succour us. His favour we must seek when we have lost all we have in the world; to him we must address ourselves as the fountain and Father of all good, all consolation. *Is any afflicted? let him pray.* It is heart's-ease, a salve for every sore. (2.) We must by patience refer ourselves and our cause to him : *To God would I commit my cause;* having spread it before him, I would leave it with him; having laid it at his feet, I would lodge it in his hand. *Here I am, let the Lord do with me as seemeth him good.*" If our cause be indeed a good cause, we need not fear committing it to God, for he is both just and kind. Those that would seek so as to speed must refer themselves to God.

IV. He encourages him thus to seek to God, and commit his cause to him. It will not be in vain to do so, for he is one in whom we shall find effectual help.

1. He recommends to his consideration God's almighty power and sovereign dominion. In general, he *doeth great things* (v. 9), great indeed, for he can do any thing, he doth do every thing, and all according to the counsel of his own will—great indeed, for the operations of his power are, (1.) *Unsearchable*, and such as can never be fathomed, can never be found out *from the beginning to the end*, Eccl. iii. 11. The works of nature are mysterious; the most curious searches come far short of full discoveries and the wisest philosophers have owned themselves at a loss. The designs of Providence are much more deep and unaccountable, Rom. xi. 33. (2.) *Numerous*, and such as can never be reckoned up. He doeth great *things without number;* his power is never exhausted, nor will all his purposes ever be fulfilled till the end of time. (3). They are *marvellous*, and such as never can be sufficiently admired; eternity itself will be short enough to be spent in the admiration of them. Now, by the consideration of this, Eliphaz intends, [1.] To convince Job of his fault and folly in quarrelling with God. We must not pretend to pass a judgment upon his works, for they are unsearchable and above our enquiries; nor must we strive with our Maker, for he will certainly be too hard for us, and is able to crush us in a moment. [2.] To encourage Job to seek unto God, and to refer his cause to him. What more encouraging than to see that he is one to whom power belongs? He can do great things and marvellous for our relief, when we are brought ever so low.

2. He gives some instances of God's dominion and power.

(1.) God doeth great things in the kingdom of nature : *He gives rain upon the earth* (v. 10), put here for all the gifts of common providence, all the *fruitful seasons* by which he *filleth our hearts with food and gladness,* Acts xiv. 17. Observe, When he would show what great things God does he speaks of his giving rain, which, because it is a common thing, we are apt to look upon as a little thing, but, if we duly consider both how it is produced and what is produced by it, we shall see it to be a great work both of power and goodness.

(2.) He doeth great things in the affairs of the children of men, not only enriches the poor and comforts the needy, by the rain he sends (v. 10), but, in order to the advancing of those that are low, he *disappoints the devices of the crafty ;* for v. 11 is to be joined to v. 12. Compare with Luke i. 51—53. He hath *scattered the proud in the imagination of their hearts,* and so hath *exalted those of low*

degree, and *filled the heart with good things.* See,

[1.] How he frustrates the counsels of the proud and politic, v. 12—14. There is a supreme power that manages and overrules men who think themselves free and absolute, and fulfils its own purposes in spite of their projects. Observe, *First,* The froward, that walk contrary to God and the interests of his kingdom, are often very crafty ; for they are the seed of the old serpent that was noted for his subtlety. They think themselves wise, but, at the end, will be fools. *Secondly,* The froward enemies of God's kingdom have their devices, their enterprises, and their counsels, against it, and against the loyal faithful subjects of it. They are restless and unwearied in their designs, close in their consultations, high in their hopes, deep in their politics, and fast-linked in their confederacies, Ps. ii. 1, 2. *Thirdly,* God easily can, and (as far as is for his glory) certainly will, blast and defeat all the designs of his and his people's enemies. How were the plots of Ahithophel, Sanballat, and Haman baffled ! How were the confederacies of Syria and Ephraim against Judah, of Gebal, and Ammon, and Amalek, against God's Israel, the kings of the earth and the princes against the Lord and against his anointed, broken ! The hands that have been stretched out against God and his church have not performed their enterprise, nor have the weapons formed against Sion prospered. *Fourthly,* That which enemies have designed for the ruin of the church has often turned to their own ruin (v. 13): *He takes the wise in their own craftiness,* and *snares them in the work of their own hands,* Ps. vii. 15, 16 ; ix. 15, 16. This is quoted by the apostle (1 Cor. iii. 19) to show how the learned men of the heathen were befooled by their own vain philosophy. *Fifthly,* When God infatuates men they are perplexed, and at a loss, even in those things that seem most plain and easy (v. 14) : *They meet with darkness* even *in the day-time :* nay (as in the margin), *They run themselves into darkness* by the violence and precipitation of their own counsels. See *ch.* xii. 20, 24, 25.

[2.] How he favours the cause of the poor and humble, and espouses that. *First,* He exalts the humble, v. 11. Those whom proud men contrive to crush he raises from under their feet, and sets them in safety, Ps. xii. 5. The lowly in heart, and those that mourn, he advances, comforts, and makes to *dwell on high,* in the *munitions of rocks,* Isa. xxxiii. 16. Sion's mourners are the sealed ones, marked for safety, Ezek. ix. 4. *Secondly,* He delivers the oppressed, v. 15. The designs of the crafty are to ruin the poor. Tongue, and hand, and sword, and all, are at work in order to this ; but God takes under his special protection those who, being poor and unable to help themselves, being his poor and devoted to his praise, have committed themselves to him. He saves them from the mouth that speaks hard things against them and the hand that does hard things against them; for he can, when he pleases, tie the tongue and wither the hand. The effect of this is (*v.* 16), 1. That weak and timorous saints are comforted: *So the poor,* who began to despair, *has hope.* The experiences of some are encouragements to others to hope the best in the worst of times; for it is the glory of God to send help to the helpless and hope to the hopeless. 2. That daring threatening sinners are confounded: *Iniquity stops her mouth,* being surprised at the strangeness of the deliverance, ashamed of its enmity against those who appear to be the favourites of Heaven, mortified at the disappointment, and compelled to acknowledge the justice of God's proceedings, having nothing to object against them. Those that domineered over God's poor, that frightened them, menaced them, and falsely accused them, will not have a word to say against them when God appears for them. See Ps. lxxvi. 8, 9; Isa. xxvi. 11; Mic. vii. 16.

17 Behold, happy *is* the man whom God correcteth : therefore despise not thou the chastening of the Almighty : 18 For he maketh sore, and bindeth up: he woundeth, and his hands make whole. 19 He shall deliver thee in six troubles : yea, in seven there shall no evil touch thee. 20 In famine he shall redeem thee from death : and in war from the power of the sword. 21 Thou shalt be hid from the scourge of the tongue : neither shalt thou be afraid of destruction when it cometh. 22 At destruction and famine thou shalt laugh : neither shalt thou be afraid of the beasts of the earth. 23 For thou shalt be in league with the stones of the field : and the beasts of the field shall be at peace with thee. 24 And thou shalt know that thy tabernacle *shall be* in peace ; and thou shalt visit thy habitation, and shalt not sin. 25 Thou shalt know also that thy seed *shall be* great, and thine offspring as the grass of the earth. 26 Thou shalt come to *thy* grave in a full age, like as a shock of corn cometh in in his season. 27 Lo this, we have searched it, so it *is ;* hear it, and know thou *it* for thy good.

Eliphaz, in this concluding paragraph of his discourse, gives Job (what he himself knew not how to take) a comfortable prospect of the issue of his afflictions, if he did but recover his temper and accommodate himself to them. Observe,

I. The seasonable word of caution and exhortation that he gives him (*v.* 17): "*Despise not thou the chastening of the Almighty.* Call it a chastening, which comes from the father's love and is designed for the child's good. Call it the chastening of the Almighty, with whom it is madness to contend, to whom it is wisdom and duty to submit, and who will be a God all-sufficient (for so the word signifies) to all those that trust in him. Do not *despise* it ;" it is a copious word in the original. 1. "Be not averse to it. Let grace conquer the antipathy which nature has to suffering, and reconcile thyself to the will of God in it." We need the rod and we deserve it; and therefore we ought not to think it either strange or hard if we feel the smart of it. Let not the heart rise against a bitter pill or potion, when it is prescribed for our good. 2. "Do not think ill of it; do not put it from thee (as that which is either hurtful or at least not useful, which there is no occasion for nor advantage by) only because for the present it is not joyous, but grievous." We must never scorn to stoop to God, nor think it a thing below us to come under his discipline, but reckon, on the contrary, that God really magnifies man when he thus *visits and tries him, ch.* vii. 17, 18. 3. "Do not overlook and disregard it, as if it were only a chance, and the production of second causes, but take great notice of it as the voice of God and a messenger from heaven." More is implied than is expressed : "*Reverence the chastening of the Lord ;* have a humble awful regard to his correcting hand, and tremble when the lion roars, Amos iii. 8. Submit to the chastening, and study to answer the call, to answer the end of it, and then you reverence it." When God by an affliction draws upon us for some of the effects he has entrusted us with we must honour his bill by accepting it, and subscribing it, resigning him his own when he calls for it."

II. The comfortable words of encouragement which he gives him thus to accommodate himself to his condition, and (as he himself had expressed it) to receive evil at the hand of God, and not despise it as a gift not worth the accepting.

1. If his affliction was thus borne, (1.) The nature and property of it would be altered. Though it looked like a man's misery, it would really be his bliss : *Happy is the man whom God correcteth* if he make but a due improvement of the correction. A good man is happy though he be afflicted, for, whatever he has lost, he has not lost his enjoyment of God nor his title to heaven. Nay, he is happy because he is afflicted ; correction is an evidence of his sonship and a means of his sanctification ; it mortifies his corruptions, weans his heart from the world, draws him nearer to God, brings him to his Bible, brings him to his knees, works him for, and so is working for him, a far more exceeding and eternal weight of glory. *Happy* there-

fore *is the man whom God correcteth*, Jam. i. 12. (2.) The issue and consequence of it would be very good, *v.* 18. [1.] Though *he makes sore* the body with sore boils, the mind with sad thoughts, yet he *binds up* at the same time, as the skilful tender surgeon binds up the wounds he had occasion to make with his incision-knife. When God makes sores by the rebukes of his providence he binds up by the consolations of his Spirit, which oftentimes abound most as afflictions do abound, and counterbalance them, to the unspeakable satisfaction of the patient sufferers. [2.] Though *he wounds*, yet *his hands make whole* in due time; as he supports his people, and makes them easy under their afflictions, so in due time he delivers them, and makes a way for them to escape. All is well again; and he comforts them *according to the time wherein he afflicted them.* God's usual method is first to wound and then to heal, first to convince and then to comfort, first to humble and then to exalt; and (as Mr. Caryl observes) he never makes a wound too great, too deep, for his own cure. *Una eademque manus vulnus opemque tulit—The hand that inflicts the wound applies the cure.* God tears the wicked and goes away; let those heal that will, if they can (Hos. v. 14); but the humble and penitent may say, *He has torn and he will heal us*, Hos. vi. 1. This is general, but,

2. In the following verses Eliphaz addresses himself directly to Job, and gives him many precious promises of great and kind things which God would do for him if he did but humble himself under his hand. Though then they had no Bibles that we know of, yet Eliphaz had sufficient warrant to give Job these assurances, from the general discoveries God had made of his good will to his people. And, though in every thing which Job's friends said they were not directed by the Spirit of God (for they spoke both of God and Job some things that were not right), yet the general doctrines they laid down expressed the pious sense of the patriarchal age, and as St. Paul quoted *v.* 13 for canonical scripture, and as the command *v.* 17 is no doubt binding on us, so these promises here may be, and must be, received and applied as divine promises, and we may *through patience and comfort of this* part of *scripture have hope.* Let us therefore give diligence to make sure our interest in these promises, and then view the particulars of them and take the comfort of them.

(1.) It is here promised that as afflictions and troubles recur supports and deliverances shall be graciously repeated, be it ever so often: *In six troubles he shall* be ready to *deliver thee; yea, and in seven, v.* 19. This intimates that, as long as we are here in this world, we must expect a succession of troubles, that the clouds will return after the rain. After six troubles may come a seventh; after many, look for more; but out of them all will God deliver those that are his, 2 Tim.

iii. 11; Ps. xxxiv. 19. Former deliverances are not, as among men, excuses from further deliverances, but earnests of them, Prov. xix. 19.

(2.) That, whatever troubles good men may be in, *there shall no evil touch them;* they shall do them no real harm; the malignity of them, the sting, shall be taken out; they may hiss, but they cannot hurt, Ps. xci. 10. The *evil one toucheth not* God's children, 1 John v. 18. Being kept from sin, they are kept from the evil of every trouble.

(3.) That, when desolating judgments are abroad, they shall be taken under special protection, *v.* 20. Do many perish about them for want of the necessary supports of life? They shall be supplied. " *In famine he shall redeem thee from death;* whatever becomes of others, thou shalt be *kept alive*, Ps. xxxiii. 19. Verily, *thou shalt be fed*, nay, even *in the days of famine thou shalt be satisfied*, Ps. xxxvii. 3, 19. *In* time of *war*, when thousands fall on the right and left hand, he shall redeem thee *from the power of the sword.* If God please, it shall not touch thee; or if it wound thee, if it kill thee, it shall not hurt thee; it can but kill the body, nor has it power to do that unless it be given from above."

(4.) That, whatever is maliciously said against them, it shall not affect them to do them any hurt, *v.* 21. " *Thou shalt* not only be protected from the killing sword of war, but shalt *be hidden from the scourge of the tongue*, which, like a scourge, is vexing and painful, though not mortal." The best men, and the most inoffensive, cannot, even in their innocency, secure themselves from calumny, reproach, and false accusation. From these a man cannot hide himself, but God can hide him, so that the most malicious slanders shall be so little heeded by him as not to disturb his peace, and so little heeded by others as not to blemish his reputation: and the remainder of wrath God can and does restrain, for it is owing to the hold he has of the consciences of bad men that the scourge of the tongue is not the ruin of all the comforts of good men in this world.

(5.) That they shall have a holy security and serenity of mind, arising from their hope and confidence in God, even in the worst of times. When dangers are most threatening they shall be easy, believing themselves safe; and they *shall not be afraid of destruction*, no, not when they see it coming (*v.* 21), nor *of the beasts of the field* when they set upon them, nor of men as cruel as beasts; nay, *at destruction and famine thou shalt laugh* (*v.* 22), not so as to despise any of God's chastenings or make a jest of his judgments, but so as to triumph in God, in his power and goodness, and therein to triumph over the world and all its grievances, to be not only easy, but cheerful and joyful, in tribulation. Blessed Paul laughed at destruction when he said, *O death! where is thy sting?*

when, in the name of all the saints, he defied all the calamities of this present time to *separate us from the love of God*, concluding that *in all these things we are more than conquerors*, Rom. viii. 35, &c. See Isa. xxxvii. 22.

(6.) That, being at peace with God, there shall be a covenant of friendship between them and the whole creation, *v.* 23. "When thou walkest over thy grounds thou shalt not need to fear stumbling, for *thou shalt be at league with the stones of the field*, not to dash thy foot against any of them, nor shalt thou be in danger from *the beasts of the field*, for they shall all be at peace with thee;" compare Hos. ii. 18, *I will make a covenant for them with the beasts of the field*. This implies that while man is at enmity with his Maker the inferior creatures are at war with him; but *tranquillus Deus tranquillat omnia— a reconciled God reconciles all things*. Our covenant with God is a covenant with all the creatures that they shall do us no hurt, but be ready to serve us and do us good.

(7.) That their houses and families shall be comfortable to them, *v.* 24. Peace and piety in the family will make it so. "*Thou shalt know* and be assured *that thy tabernacle* is and *shall be in peace ;* thou mayest be confident both of its present and its future prosperity." *That peace is thy tabernacle* (so the word is); peace is the house in which those dwell who dwell in God, and are at home in him. "*Thou shalt visit*" (that is, enquire into the affairs of) *thy habitation, and take a review of them, and shalt not sin.*" [1.] God will provide a settlement for his people, mean perhaps and movable, a cottage, a tabernacle, but a fixed and quiet habitation. "Thou shalt not sin," or *wander ;* that is, as some understand it, "thou shalt not be a fugitive and a vagabond" (Cain's curse), "but shalt dwell in the land, and verily, not uncertainly as vagrants, shalt thou be fed." [2.] Their families shall be taken under the special protection of the divine Providence, and shall prosper as far as is for their good. [3.] They shall be assured of peace, and of the continuance and entail of it. "Thou shalt know, to thy unspeakable satisfaction, that peace is sure to thee and thine, having the word of God for it." Providence may change, but the promise cannot. [4.] They shall have wisdom to govern their families aright, to order their affairs with discretion, and to look well to the ways of their household, which is here called *visiting their habitation*. Masters of families must not be strangers at home, but must have a watchful eye over what they have and what their servants do. [5.] They shall have grace to manage the concerns of their families after a godly sort, and not to sin in the management of them. They shall call their servants to account without passion, pride, covetousness, worldliness, or the like ; they shall look into their affairs without discontent at what is or distrust of what shall be. Family piety

crowns family peace and prosperity. The greatest blessing, both in our employments and in our enjoyments, is to be kept from sin in them. When we are abroad it is comfortable to hear that our tabernacle is in peace ; and when we return home it is comfortable to visit our habitation with satisfaction in our success, that we have not failed in our business, and with a good conscience, that we have not offended God.

(8.) That their posterity shall be numerous and prosperous. Job had lost all his children ; "but," says Eliphaz, "if thou return to God, he will again build up thy family, and thy seed shall be many and as great as ever, and thy offspring increasing and flourishing *as the grass of the earth* (*v.* 25), and thou shalt know it." God has blessings in store for the seed of the faithful, which they shall have if they do not stand in their own light and forfeit them by their folly. It is a comfort to parents to see the prosperity, especially the spiritual prosperity, of their children ; if they are truly good, they are truly great, how small a figure soever they may make in the world.

(9.) That their death shall be seasonable, and they shall finish their course, at length, with joy and honour, *v.* 26. It is a great mercy, [1.] To live to a full age, and not to have the number of our months cut off in the midst. If the providence of God do not give us long life, yet, if the grace of God give us to be satisfied with the time allotted us, we may be said to come to a full age. That man lives long enough that has done his work and is fit for another world. [2.] To be willing to die, to come cheerfully to the grave, and not to be forced thither, as he whose soul was required of him. [3.] To die seasonably, as the corn is cut and housed when it is fully ripe ; not till then, but then not suffered to stand a day longer, lest it shed. Our times are in God's hand ; it is well they are so, for he will take care that those who are his shall die in the best time : however their death may seem to us untimely, it will be found not unseasonable.

3. In the last verse he recommends these promises to Job, (1.) As faithful sayings, which he might be confident of the truth of : "*Lo, this we have searched, and so it is.* We have indeed received these things by tradition from our fathers, but we have not taken them upon trust ; we have carefully searched them, have compared spiritual things with spiritual, have diligently studied them, and been confirmed in our belief of them from our own observation and experience ; and we are all of a mind that so it is." Truth is a treasure that is well worth digging for, diving for ; and then we shall know both how to value it ourselves and how to communicate it to others when we have taken pains in searching for it. (2.) As well worthy of all acceptation, which he might improve to his great advantage : *Hear it, and know*

thou it for thy good. It is not enough to hear and know the truth, but we must improve it, and be made wiser and better by it, receive the impressions of it, and submit to the commanding power of it. *Know it for thyself* (so the word is), with application to thyself, and thy own case; not only " This is true," but " this is true concerning me." That which we thus hear and know for ourselves we hear and know for our good, as we are nourished by the meat which we digest. That is indeed a good sermon to us which does us good.

CHAP. VI.

Eliphaz concluded his discourse with an air of assurance; very confident he was that what he had said was so plain and so pertinent that nothing could be objected in answer to it. But, though he that is first in his own cause seems just, yet his neighbour comes and searches him. Job is not convinced by all he had said, but still justifies himself in his complaints and condemns him for the weakness of his arguing. I. He shows that he had just cause to complain as he did of his troubles, and so it would appear to any impartial judge, ver. 2—7. II. He continues his passionate wish that he might speedily be cut off by the stroke of death, and so be eased of all his miseries, ver. 8—13. III. He reproves his friends for their uncharitable censures of him and their unkind treatment, ver. 14—30. It must be owned that Job, in all this, spoke much that was reasonable, but with a mixture of passion and human infirmity. And in this contest, as indeed in most contests, there was fault on both sides.

BUT Job answered and said, 2 Oh that my grief were thoroughly weighed, and my calamity laid in the balances together! 3 For now it would be heavier than the sand of the sea: therefore my words are swallowed up. 4 For the arrows of the Almighty *are* within me, the poison whereof drinketh up my spirit: the terrors of God do set themselves in array against me. 5 Doth the wild ass bray when he hath grass? or loweth the ox over his fodder? 6 Can that which is unsavoury be eaten without salt? or is there *any* taste in the white of an egg? 7 The things *that* my soul refused to touch *are* as my sorrowful meat.

Eliphaz, in the beginning of his discourse, had been very sharp upon Job, and yet it does not appear that Job gave him any interruption, but heard him patiently till he had said all he had to say. Those that would make an impartial judgment of a discourse must hear it out, and take it entire. But, when he had concluded, he makes his reply, in which he speaks very feelingly.

I. He represents his calamity, in general, as much heavier than either he had expressed it or they had apprehended it, *v.* 2, 3. He could not fully describe it; they would not fully apprehend it, or at least would not own that they did; and therefore he would gladly appeal to a third person, who had just weights and just balances with which to weigh his grief and calamity, and would do it with an impartial hand. He wished that they would set his grief and all the expressions of it in one scale, his calamity and all the particulars

of it in the other, and (though he would not altogether justify himself in his grief) they would find (as he says, *ch.* xxiii. 2) that *his stroke was heavier than his groaning;* for, whatever his grief was, his calamity was *heavier than the sand of the sea:* it was complicated, it was aggravated, every grievance weighty, and all together numerous as the sand. "Therefore (says he) *my words are swallowed up;*" that is, "Therefore you must excuse both the brokenness and the bitterness of my expressions. Do not think it strange if my speech be not so fine and polite as that of an eloquent orator, or so grave and regular as that of a morose philosopher: no, in these circumstances I can pretend neither to the one nor to the other; my words are, as I am, quite swallowed up." Now, 1. He hereby complains of it as his unhappiness that his friends undertook to administer spiritual physic to him before they thoroughly understood his case and knew the worst of it. It is seldom that those who are at ease themselves rightly weigh the afflictions of the afflicted. Every one feels most from his own burden; few feel from other people's. 2. He excuses the passionate expressions he had used when he cursed his day. Though he could not himself justify all he had said, yet he thought his friends should not thus violently condemn it, for really the case was extraordinary, and that might be connived at in such a man of sorrows as he now was which in any common grief would by no means be allowed. 3. He bespeaks the charitable and compassionate sympathy of his friends with him, and hopes, by representing the greatness of his calamity, to bring them to a better temper towards him. To those that are pained it is some ease to be pitied.

II. He complains of the trouble and terror of mind he was in as the sorest part of his calamity, *v.* 4. Herein he was a type of Christ, who, in his sufferings, complained most of the sufferings of his soul. *Now is my soul troubled,* John xii. 27. *My soul is exceedingly sorrowful,* Matt. xxvi. 38. *My God, my God, why hast thou forsaken me?* Matt. xxvii. 46. Poor Job sadly complains here, 1. Of what he felt▸ *The arrows of the Almighty are within me.* It was not so much the troubles themselves he was under that put him into this confusion, his poverty, disgrace, and bodily pain; but that which cut him to the heart, and put him into this agitation, was to think that the God he loved and served had brought all this upon him and laid him under these marks of his displeasure. Note, Trouble of mind is the sorest trouble. *A wounded spirit who can bear!* Whatever burden of affliction, in body or estate, God is pleased to lay upon us, we may well afford to submit to it as long as he continues to us the use of our reason and the peace of our consciences; but, if in either of these we be disturbed, our case is sad indeed and very pitiable. The way to prevent God's fiery darts of trouble is with the shield of faith to quench Satan's fiery darts of temptation. Observe, He calls them the *arrows of the Almighty;* for it is an instance of the power of God above that of any man that he can with his arrows reach the soul. He that made the soul can make his sword to approach to it. The poison or heat of these arrows is said to drink up his spirit, because it disturbed his reason, shook his resolution, exhausted his vigour, and threatened his life; and therefore his passionate expressions, though they could not be justified, might be excused. 2. Of what he feared. He saw himself charged by *the terrors of God,* as by an army set in battle-array, and surrounded by them. God, by his terrors, fought against him. As he had no comfort when he retired inward into his own bosom, so he had none when he looked upward towards Heaven. He that used to be encouraged with the consolations of God not only wanted those, but was amazed with the terrors of God.

HI. He reflects upon his friends for their severe censures of his complaints and their unskilful management of his case. 1. Their reproofs were causeless. He complained, it is true, now that he was in this affliction, but he never used to complain, as those do who are of a fretful unquiet spirit, when he was in prosperity: he did not *bray when he had grass,* nor *low over his fodder, v.* 5. But, now that he was utterly deprived of all his comforts, he must be a stock or a stone, and not have the sense of an ox or a wild ass, if he did not give some vent to his grief. He was forced to eat unsavoury meats, and was so poor that he had not a grain of salt wherewith to season them, nor to give a little taste to the white of an egg, which was now the choicest dish he had at his table, *v.* 6. Even that food which once he would have scorned to touch he was now glad of, and it was his *sorrowful meat, v.* 7. Note, It is wisdom not to use ourselves or our children to be nice and dainty about meat and drink, because we know not how we or they may be reduced, nor how that which we now disdain may be made acceptable by necessity. 2. Their comforts were sapless and insipid; so some understand *v.* 6, 7. He complains he had nothing now offered to him for his relief that was proper for him, no cordial, nothing to revive and cheer his spirits; what they had afforded was in itself as tasteless as the white of an egg, and, when applied to him, as loathsome and burdensome as the most sorrowful meat. I am sorry he should say thus of what Eliphaz had excellently well said, *ch.* v. 8, &c. But peevish spirits are too apt thus to abuse their comforters.

8 Oh that I might have my request; and that God would grant *me* the thing that I long for! 9 Even that it would please God to destroy me;
38

that he would let loose his hand, and cut me off! 10 Then should I yet have comfort; yea, I would harden myself in sorrow: let him not spare; for I have not concealed the words of the Holy One. 11 What *is* my strength, that I should hope? and what *is* mine end, that I should prolong my life? 12 *Is* my strength the strength of stones? or *is* my flesh of brass? 13 *Is* not my help in me? and is wisdom driven quite from me?

Ungoverned passion often grows more violent when it meets with some rebuke and check. The troubled sea rages most when it dashes against a rock. Job had been courting death, as that which would be the happy period of his miseries, *ch.* iii. For this Eliphaz had gravely reproved him, but he, instead of unsaying what he had said, says it here again with more vehemence than before; and it is as ill said as almost any thing we meet with in all his discourses, and is recorded for our admonition, not our imitation.

I. He is still most passionately desirous to die, as if it were not possible that he should ever see good days again in this world, or that, by the exercise of grace and devotion, he might make even these days of affliction good days. He could see no end of his trouble but death, and had not patience to wait the time appointed for that. He has a request to make; there is a thing he longs for (*v.* 8); and what is that? One would think it should be, "That it would please God to deliver me, and restore me to my prosperity again;" no, *That it would please God to destroy me, v.* 9. "As once he let loose his hand to make me poor, and then to make me sick, let him loose it once more to put an end to my life. Let him give the fatal stroke; it shall be to me the *coup de grace—the stroke of favour,*" as, in France, they call the last blow which dispatches those that are broken on the wheel. There was a time when *destruction from the Almighty was a terror* to Job (*ch.* xxxi. 23), yet now he courts the destruction of the flesh, but in hopes that the spirit should be saved in the day of the Lord Jesus. Observe, Though Job was extremely desirous of death, and very angry at its delays, yet he did not offer to destroy himself, nor to take away his own life, only he begged *that it would please God to destroy him.* Seneca's morals, which recommend self-murder as the lawful redress of insupportable grievances, were not then known, nor will ever be entertained by any that have the least regard to the law of God and nature. How uneasy soever the soul's confinement in the body may be, it must by no means break prison, but wait for a fair discharge.

II. He puts this desire into a prayer, that God would grant him this request, that it would please God to do this for him. It was his sin so passionately to desire the hastening of his own death, and offering up that desire to God made it no better ; nay, what looked ill in his wish looked worse in his prayer, for we ought not to ask any thing of God but what we can ask in faith, and we cannot ask any thing in faith but what is agreeable to the will of God. Passionate prayers are the worst of passionate expressions, for we should *lift up pure hands without wrath.*

III. He promises himself effectual relief, and the redress of all his grievances, by the stroke of death (*v.* 10): " *Then should I yet have comfort,* which now I have not, nor ever expect till then." See, 1. The vanity of human life ; so uncertain a good is it that it often proves men's greatest burden and nothing is so desirable as to get clear of it. Let grace make us willing to part with it whenever God calls ; for it may so happen that even sense may make us desirous to part with it before he calls. 2. The hope which the righteous have in their death. If Job had not had a good conscience, he could not have spoken with this assurance of comfort on the other side death, which turns the tables between the rich man and Lazarus. *Now he is comforted, and thou art tormented.*

IV. He challenges death to do its worst. If he could not die without the dreadful prefaces of bitter pains and agonies, and strong convulsions, if he must be racked before he be executed, yet, in prospect of dying at last, he would make nothing of dying pangs : " *I would harden myself in sorrow,* would open my breast to receive death's darts, and not shrink from them. *Let him not spare;* I desire no mitigation of that pain which will put a happy period to all my pains. Rather than not die, let me die so as to feel myself die." These are passionate words, which might better have been spared. We should soften ourselves in sorrow, that we may receive the good impressions of it, and by the sadness of the countenance our hearts, being made tender, may be made better ; but, if we harden ourselves, we provoke God to proceed in his controversy ; *for when he judgeth he will overcome.* It is great presumption to dare the Almighty, and to say, *Let him not spare;* for *are we stronger than he?* 1 Cor. x. 22. We are much indebted to sparing mercy ; it is bad indeed with us when we are weary of that. Let us rather say with David, *O spare me a little.*

V. He grounds his comfort upon the testimony of his conscience for him that he had been faithful and firm to his profession of religion, and in some degree useful and serviceable to the glory of God in his generation : *I have not concealed the words of the Holy One.* Observe, 1. Job had the words of the Holy One committed to him. The people of God were at that time blessed with divine revelation. 2. It was his comfort that

he had not concealed them, had not received the grace of God therein in vain. (1.) He had not kept them from himself, but had given them full scope to operate upon him, and in every thing to guide and govern him. He had not stifled his convictions, *imprisoned the truth in unrighteousness,* nor done any thing to hinder the digestion of this spiritual food and the operation of this spiritual physic. Let us never conceal God's word from ourselves, but always receive it in the light of it. (2.) He had not kept them to himself, but had been ready, on all occasions, to communicate his knowledge for the good of others, was never ashamed nor afraid to own the word of God to be his rule, nor remiss in his endeavours to bring others into an acquaintance with it. Note, Those, and those only, may promise themselves comfort in death who are good, and do good, while they live.

VI. He justifies himself, in this extreme desire of death, from the deplorable condition he was now in, *v.* 11, 12. Eliphaz, in the close of his discourse, had put him in hopes that he should yet see a good issue of his troubles ; but poor Job puts these cordials away from him, refuses to be comforted, abandons himself to despair, and very ingeniously, yet perversely, argues against the encouragements that were given him. Disconsolate spirits will reason strangely against themselves. In answer to the pleasing prospects Eliphaz had flattered him with, he here intimates, 1. That he had no reason to expect any such thing : " *What is my strength, that I should hope?* You see how I am weakened and brought low, how unable I am to grapple with my distempers, and therefore what reason have I to hope that I should out-live them, and see better days? *Is my strength the strength of stones?* Are my muscles brass and my sinews steel? No, they are not, and therefore I cannot hold out always in this pain and misery, but must needs sink under the load. Had I strength to grapple with my distemper, I might hope to look through it; but, alas! I have not. The *weakening of my strength in the way* will certainly be the *shortening of my days,*" Ps. cii. 23. Note, All things considered, we have no reason to reckon upon the long continuance of life in this world. *What is our strength?* It is depending strength. We have no more strength than God gives us ; for in him we live and move. It is decaying strength ; we are daily spending the stock, and by degrees it will be exhausted. It is disproportionable to the encounters we may meet with ; what is our strength to be depended upon, when two or three days' sickness will make us weak as water? Instead of expecting a long life, we have reason to wonder that we have lived hitherto and to feel that we are hastening off apace. 2. That he had no reason to desire any such thing : " *What is my end, that I should desire to prolong my life?* What comfort can I promise myself in life, comparable to the comfort I promise myself in death?" Note, Those who, through grace, are ready for another world, cannot see much to invite their stay in this world, or to make them fond of it. That, if it be God's will, we may do him more service and may get to be fitter and riper for heaven, is an end for which we may wish the prolonging of life, in subserviency to our chief end; but, otherwise, what can we propose to ourselves in desiring to tarry here? The longer life is the more grievous will its burdens be (Eccl. xii. 1), and the longer life is the less pleasant will be its delights, 2 Sam. xix. 34, 35. We have already seen the best of this world, but we are not sure that we have seen the worst of it.

VII. He obviates the suspicion of his being delirious (v. 13): *Is not my help in me?* that is, "Have I not the use of my reason, with which, I thank God, I can help myself, though you do not help me? Do you think wisdom is driven quite from me, and that I am gone distracted? No, I am not mad, most noble Eliphaz, but *speak the words of truth and soberness.*" Note, Those who have grace in them, who have the evidence of it and have it in exercise, have wisdom in them, which will be their help in the worst of times. *Sat lucis intus—They have light within.*

14 To him that is afflicted pity *should be showed* from his friend; but he forsaketh the fear of the Almighty. 15 My brethren have dealt deceitfully as a brook, *and* as the stream of brooks they pass away; 16 Which are blackish by reason of the ice, *and* wherein the snow is hid: 17 What time they wax warm, they vanish: when it is hot, they are consumed out of their place. 18 The paths of their way are turned aside; they go to nothing, and perish. 19 The troops of Tema looked, the companies of Sheba waited for them. 20 They were confounded because they had hoped; they came thither, and were ashamed. 21 For now ye are nothing; ye see *my* casting down, and are afraid.

Eliphaz had been very severe in his censures of Job; and his companions, though as yet they had said little, yet had intimated their concurrence with him. Their unkindness therein poor Job here complains of, as an aggravation of his calamity and a further excuse of his desire to die; for what satisfaction could he ever expect in this world when those that should have been his comforters thus proved his tormentors?

I. He shows what reason he had to expect kindness from them. His expectation was grounded upon the common principles of humanity (v. 14): " *To him that is afflicted,* and that is wasting and melting under his affliction, *pity should be shown from his friend;* and he that does not show that pity *forsakes the fear of the Almighty.*" Note, 1. Compassion is a debt owing to those that are in affliction. The least which those that are at ease can do for those that are pained and in anguish is to pity them,—to manifest the sincerity of a tender concern for them, and to sympathize with them,—to take cognizance of their case, enquire into their grievances, hear their complaints, and mingle their tears with theirs,—to comfort them, and to do all they can to help and relieve them: this well becomes the members of the same body, who should feel for the grievances of their fellow-members, not knowing how soon the same may be their own. 2. Inhumanity is impiety and irreligion. *He that withholds compassion from his friend forsakes the fear of the Almighty.* So the Chaldee. *How dwells the love of God in that man?* 1 John iii. 17. Surely those have no fear of the rod of God upon themselves who have no compassion for those that feel the smart of it. See Jam. i. 27. 3. Troubles are the trials of friendship. When a man is afflicted he will see who are his friends indeed and who are but pretenders; for *a brother is born for adversity,* Prov. xvii. 17; xviii. 24.

II. He shows how wretchedly he was disappointed in his expectations from them (v. 15): " *My brethren,* who should have helped me, *have dealt deceitfully as a brook.*" They came by appointment, with a great deal of ceremony, to mourn with him and to comfort him (ch. ii. 11); and some extraordinary things were expected from such great men, such good men, such wise, learned, knowing men, and Job's particular friends. None questioned but that the drift of their discourses would be to comfort Job with the remembrance of his former piety, the assurance of God's favour to him, and the prospect of a glorious issue; but, instead of this, they most barbarously fall upon him with their reproaches and censures, condemn him as a hypocrite, insult over his calamities, and pour vinegar, instead of oil, into his wounds, and thus they deal deceitfully with him. Note, It is fraud and deceit not only to violate our engagements to our friends, but to frustrate their just expectations from us, especially the expectations we have raised. Note, further, It is our wisdom to cease from man. We cannot expect too little from the creature nor too much from the Creator. It is no new thing even for brethren to *deal deceitfully* (Jer. ix. 4, 5; Mic. vii. 5); let us therefore put our confidence in the rock of ages, not in broken reeds—in the fountain of life, not in broken cisterns. God will out-do our hopes as much as men come short of them. This disappointment which Job met with he here illustrates by the failing of brooks in summer.

1. The similitude is very elegant, *v.* 15—20. (1.) Their pretensions are fitly compared to the great show which the brooks make when they are swoln with the waters of a land flood, by the melting of the ice and snow, which make them blackish or muddy, *v.* 16. (2.) His expectations from them, which their coming so solemnly to comfort him had raised, he compares to the expectation which the weary thirsty travellers have of finding water in the summer where they have often seen it in great abundance in the winter, *v.* 19. *The troops of Tema and Sheba,* the caravans of the merchants of those countries, whose road lay through the deserts of Arabia, looked and waited for supply of water from those brooks. " Hard by here," says one, " A little further," says another, " when I last travelled this way, there was water enough; we shall have that to refresh us." Where we have met with relief or comfort we are apt to expect it again ; and yet it does not follow ; for, (3.) The disappointment of his expectation is here compared to the confusion which seizes the poor travellers when they find heaps of sand where they expected floods of water. In the winter, when they were not thirsty, there was water enough. Every one will applaud and admire those that are full and in prosperity. But in the heat of summer, when they needed water, then it failed them ; it was consumed (*v.* 17) ; it was turned aside, *v.* 18. When those who are rich and high are sunk and impoverished, and stand in need of comfort, then those who before gathered about them stand aloof from them, those who before commended them are forward to run them down. Thus those who raise their expectations high from the creature will find it fail them when it should help them ; whereas those who make God their confidence have help *in the time of need,* Heb. iv. 16. Those who make gold their hope will sooner or later be ashamed of it, and of their confidence in it (Ezek. vii. 19) ; and the greater their confidence was the greater their shame will be: *They were confounded because they had hoped, v.* 20. We prepare confusion for ourselves by our vain hopes : the reeds break under us because we lean upon them. If we build a house upon the sand, we shall certainly be confounded, for it will fall in the storm, and we must thank ourselves for being such fools as to expect it would stand. We are not deceived unless we deceive ourselves.

2. The application is very close (*v.* 21): *For now you are nothing.* They seemed to be somewhat, but in conference they added nothing to him. Allude to Gal. ii. 6. He was never the wiser, never the better, for the visit they made him. Note, Whatever complacency we may take, or whatever confidence we may put, in creatures, how great soever they may seem and how dear soever they may be to us, one time or other we shall say of them, *Now you are nothing.* When Job was in prosperity his friends were something to him, he took complacency in them and their society ; but " *Now you are nothing,* now I can find no comfort but in God." It were well for us if we had always such convictions of the vanity of the creature, and its insufficiency to make us happy, as we have sometimes had, or shall have on a sick-bed, a death-bed, or in trouble of conscience : " *Now you are nothing.* You are not what you have been, what you should be, what you pretend to be, what I thought you would have been ; *for you see my casting down and are afraid.* When you saw me in my elevation you caressed me ; but now that you see me in my dejection you are shy of me, are afraid of showing yourselves kind, lest I should thereby be emboldened to beg something of you, or to borrow" (compare *v.* 22); " you are afraid lest, if you own me, you should be obliged to keep me." Perhaps they were afraid of catching his distemper or of coming within smell of the noisomeness of it. It is not good, either out of pride or niceness, for love of our purses or of our bodies, to be shy of those who are in distress and afraid of coming near them. Their case may soon be our own.

22 Did I say, Bring unto me ? or, Give a reward for me of your substance ? 23 Or, Deliver me from the enemy's hand ? or, Redeem me from the hand of the mighty ? 24 Teach me, and I will hold my tongue : and cause me to understand wherein I have erred. 25 How forcible are right words ! but what doth your arguing reprove ? 26 Do ye imagine to reprove words, and the speeches of one that is desperate, *which are* as wind ? 27 Yea, ye overwhelm the fatherless, and ye dig *a pit* for your friend. 28 Now therefore be content, look upon me ; for *it is* evident unto you if I lie. 29 Return, I pray you, let it not be iniquity ; yea, return again, my righteousness *is* in it. 30 Is there iniquity in my tongue ? cannot my taste discern perverse things ?

Poor Job goes on here to upbraid his friends with their unkindness and the hard usage they gave him. He here appeals to themselves concerning several things which tended both to justify him and to condemn them. If they would but think impartially, and speak as they thought, they could not but own,

I. That, though he was necessitous, yet he was not craving, nor burdensome to his friends. Those that are so, whose troubles serve them to beg by, are commonly less pitied than the silent poor. Job would be glad to see his friends, but he did not say, *Bring unto me* (v. 22), or, *Deliver me, v.* 23. He did not desire to put them to any expense, did not urge his friends either, 1. To make a collection for him, to set him up again in the world. Though he could plead that his losses came upon him by the hand of God and not by any fault or folly of his own,—that he was utterly ruined and impoverished, —that he had lived in good condition, and that when he had wherewithal he was charitable and ready to help those that were in distress,—that his friends were rich, and able to help him, yet he did not say, *Give me of your substance.* Note, A good man, when troubled himself, is afraid of being troublesome to his friends. Or, 2. To raise the country for him, to help him to recover his cattle out of the hands of the Sabeans and Chaldeans, or to make reprisals upon them : " Did I send for you to *deliver me out of the hand of the mighty ?* No, I never expected you should either expose yourselves to any danger or put yourselves to any charge upon my account. I will rather sit down content under my affliction, and make the best of it, than sponge upon my friends." St. Paul worked with his hands, that he might not be burdensome to any. Job's not asking their help did not excuse them from offering it when he needed it and it was in the power of their hands to give it; but it much aggravated their unkindness when he desired no more from them than a good look, and a good word, and yet could not obtain them. It often happens that from man, even when we expect little, we have less, but from God, even when we expect much, we have more, Eph. iii. 20.

II. That, though he differed in opinion from them, yet he was not obstinate, but ready to yield to conviction, and to strike sail to truth as soon as ever it was made to appear to him that he was in an error (v. 24, 25) : " If, instead of invidious reflections and uncharitable insinuations, you will give me plain instructions and solid arguments, which shall carry their own evidence along with them, I am ready to acknowledge my error and own myself in a fault : *Teach me, and I will hold my tongue ;* for I have often found, with pleasure and wonder, *how forcible right words are.* But the method you take will never make proselytes : *What doth your arguing reprove ?* Your hypothesis is false, your surmises are groundless, your management is weak, and your application peevish and uncharitable." Note, 1. Fair reasoning has a commanding power, and it is a wonder if men are not conquered by it; but railing and foul language are impotent and foolish, and it is no wonder if men are exasperated and hardened by them. 2. It is the undoubted character of every honest man that he is truly desirous to have his mistakes rectified, and to be made to understand wherein he has erred ; and he will

acknowledge that right words, when they appear to him to be so, though contrary to his former sentiments, are both forcible and acceptable.

III. That, though he had been indeed in a fault, yet they ought not to have given him such hard usage (v. 26, 27) : " *Do you imagine,* or contrive with a great deal of art" (for so the word signifies), " *to reprove words,* some passionate expressions of mine in this desperate condition, as if they were certain indications of reigning impiety and atheism? A little candour and charity would have served to excuse them, and to put a better construction upon them. Shall a man's spiritual state be judged of by some rash and hasty words, which a surprising trouble extorts from him ? Is it fair, is it kind, is it just, to criticise in such a case ? Would you yourselves be served thus ?" Two things aggravated their unkind treatment of him :— 1. That they took advantage of his weakness and the helpless condition he was in : *You overwhelm the fatherless,* a proverbial expression, denoting that which is most barbarous and inhuman. "The fatherless cannot secure themselves from insults, which emboldens men of base and sordid spirits to insult them and trample upon them; and you do so by me." Job, being a childless father, thought himself as much exposed to injury as a fatherless child (Ps. cxxvii. 5) and had reason to be offended with those who therefore triumphed over him. Let those who overwhelm and overpower such as upon any account may be looked upon as fatherless know that therein they not only put off the compassions of man, but fight against the compassions of God, who is, and will be, a Father of the fatherless and a helper of the helpless. 2. That they made pretence of kindness : " *You dig a pit for your friend ;* not only you are unkind to me, who am your friend, but, under colour of friendship, you ensnare me." When they came to see and sit with him he thought he might speak his mind freely to them, and that the more bitter his complaints to them were the more they would endeavour to comfort him. This made him take a greater liberty than otherwise he would have done. David, though he smothered his resentments when the wicked were before him, would probably have given vent to them if none had been by but friends, Ps. xxxix. 1. But this freedom of speech, which their professions of concern for him made him use, had exposed him to their censures, and so they might be said to dig a pit for him. Thus, when our hearts are hot within us, what is ill done we are apt to misrepresent as if done designedly.

IV. That, though he had let fall some passionate expressions, yet in the main he was in the right, and that his afflictions, though very extraordinary, did not prove him to be a hypocrite or a wicked man. His righteousness he holds fast, and will not let it go. For the evincing of it he here appeals, 1. To what they saw in him (*v.* 28): "*Be content, and look upon me ;* what do you see in me that bespeaks me either a madman or a wicked man ? Nay, look in my face, and you may discern there the indications of a patient and submissive spirit, for all this. Let the show of my countenance witness for me that, though I have cursed my day, I do not curse my God." Or rather, "Look upon my ulcers and sore boils, and by them it will be evident to you that I do not lie," that is, "that I do not complain without cause. Let your own eyes convince you that my condition is very sad, and that I do not quarrel with God by making it worse than it is." 2. To what they heard from him, *v.* 30. "You hear what I have to say : *Is there iniquity in my tongue?* that iniquity that you charge me with ? Have I blasphemed God or renounced him ? Are not my present arguings right ? Do not you perceive, by what I say, that I can discern perverse things ? I can discover your fallacies and mistakes, and, if I were myself in an error, I could perceive it. Whatever you think of me, I know what I say." 3. To their own second and sober thoughts (*v.* 29): "*Return, I pray you,* consider the thing over again without prejudice and partiality, and let not the result be iniquity, let it not be an unrighteous sentence ; and you will find *my righteousness is in it,*" that is, "I am in the right in this matter ; and, though I cannot keep my temper as I should, I keep my integrity, and have not said, nor done, nor suffered, any thing which will prove me other than an honest man." A just cause desires nothing more than a just hearing, and if need be a re-hearing.

CHAP. VII.

Job, in this chapter, goes on to express the bitter sense he had of his calamities and to justify himself in his desire of death. I. He complains to himself and his friends of his troubles, and the constant agitation he was in, ver. 1—6. II. He turns to God, and expostulates with him (ver. 7, to the end), in which, 1. He pleads the final period which death puts to our present state, ver. 7—10. 2. He passionately complains of the miserable condition he was now in, ver. 11—16. 3. He wonders that God will thus contend with him, and begs for the pardon of his sins and a speedy release out of his miseries, ver. 17—21. It is hard to methodise the speeches of one who owned himself almost desperate, ch. vi. 26.

*I*S *there* not an appointed time to man upon earth ? *are not* his days also like the days of a hireling ? 2 As a servant earnestly desireth the shadow, and as a hireling looketh for *the reward of* his work : 3 So am I made to possess months of vanity, and wearisome nights are appointed to me. 4 When I lie down, I say, When shall I arise, and the night be gone ? and I am full of tossings to and fro unto the dawning of the day. 5 My flesh is clothed with worms and clods of dust ; my skin is broken, and become loathsome. 6 My days are swifter than a weaver's shuttle, and are spent without hope.

Job is here excusing what he could not justify, even his inordinate desire of death. Why should he not wish for the termination of life, which would be the termination of his miseries ? To enforce this reason he argues,

I. From the general condition of man upon earth (*v.* 1): "He *is of few days, and full of trouble.* Every man must die shortly, and every man has some reason (more or less) to desire to die shortly; and therefore why should you impute it to me as so heinous a crime that I wish to die shortly ?" Or thus : "Pray mistake not my desires of death, as if I thought the time appointed of God could be anticipated : no, I know very well that that is fixed ; only in such language as this I take the liberty to express my present uneasiness : *Is there not an appointed time (a warfare,* so the word is) to *man upon earth ?* and *are not his days* here *like the days of a hireling ?*" Observe, 1. Man's present place. He is upon earth, which God *has given to the children of men,* Ps. cxv. 16. This bespeaks man's meanness and inferiority. How much below the inhabitants of yonder elevated and refined regions is he situated ! It also bespeaks God's mercy to him. He is yet upon the earth, not under it ; on earth, not in hell. Our time on earth is limited and short, according to the narrow bounds of this earth ; but heaven cannot be measured, nor the days of heaven numbered. 2. His continuance in that place. Is there not a time appointed for his abode here ? Yes, certainly there is, and it is easy to say by whom the appointment is made, even by him that made us and set us here. We are not to be on this earth always, nor long, but for a certain time, which is determined by him in whose hand our times are. We are not to think that we are governed by the blind fate of the Stoics, nor by the blind fortune of the Epicureans, but by the wise, holy, and sovereign counsel of God. 3. His condition during that continuance. Man's life is *a warfare,* and *as the days of a hireling.* We are every one of us to look upon ourselves in this world, (1.) As soldiers, exposed to hardship and in the midst of enemies ; we must serve and be under command ; and, when our warfare is accomplished, we must be disbanded, dismissed with either shame or honour, according to what we have done in the body. (2.) As day-labourers, that have the work of the day to do in its day and must make up their account at night.

II. From his own condition at this time. He had as much reason, he thought, to wish for death, as a poor servant or hireling that is tired with his work has to wish for the shadows of the evening, when he shall receive his penny and go to rest, *v.* 2. The darkness of the night is as welcome to the labourer as the light of the morning is to the watchman, Ps. cxxx. 6. The God of nature has provided for the repose of labourers, and no wonder that they desire it. *The sleep of the labouring man is sweet,* Eccl. v. 12. No pleasure more grateful, more relishing, to the luxurious than rest to the laborious; nor can any rich man take so much satisfaction in the return of his rent-days as the hireling in his day's wages. The comparison is plain, the application is concise and somewhat obscure, but we must supply a word or two, and then it is easy: exactness of language is not to be expected from one in Job's condition. "*As a servant earnestly desires the shadow, so* and for the same reason I earnestly desire death; for *I am made to possess,* &c. Hear his complaint.

1. His days were useless, and had been so a great while. He was wholly taken off from business, and utterly unfit for it. Every day was a burden to him, because he was in no capacity of doing good, or of spending it to any purpose. *Et vitæ partem non attigit ullam—He could not fill up his time with any thing that would turn to account.* This he calls *possessing months of vanity, v.* 3. It very much increases the affliction of sickness and age, to a good man, that he is thereby forced from his usefulness. He insists not so much upon it that they are days in which he has no pleasure as that they are days in which he does no good; on that account they are months of vanity. But when we are disabled to work for God, if we will but sit still quietly for him, it is all one; we shall be accepted.

2. His nights were restless, *v.* 3, 4. The night relieves the toil and fatigue of the day, not only to the labourers, but to the sufferers: if a sick man can but get a little sleep in the night, it helps nature, and it is hoped that he will do well, John xi. 12. However, be the trouble what it will, sleep gives some intermission to the cares, and pains, and griefs, that afflict us; it is the parenthesis of our sorrows. But poor Job could not gain this relief. (1.) His nights were wearisome, and, instead of taking any rest, he did but tire himself more with tossing to and fro until morning. Those that are in great uneasiness, through pain of body or anguish of mind, think by changing sides, changing places, changing postures, to get some ease; but, while the cause is the same within, it is all to no purpose; it is but a resemblance of a fretful discontented spirit, that is ever shifting, but never easy. This made him dread the night as much as the servant desires it, and, when he lay down, to say, *When will the night be gone?* (2.) These *wearisome nights* were *appointed* to him. God, who determines the times before appointed, had allotted him such nights as these. Whatever is at any time grievous to us, it is good to see it appointed for us, that we may acquiesce in the event, not only as unavoidable

because appointed, but as therefore designed for some holy end. When we have comfortable nights we must see them also appointed to us and be thankful for them; many better than we have wearisome nights.

3. His body was noisome, *v.* 5. His sores bred worms, the scabs were like clods of dust, and his skin was broken; so evil was the disease which cleaved fast to him. See what vile bodies we have, and what little reason we have to pamper them or be proud of them; they have in themselves the principles of their own corruption: as fond as we are of them now, the time may come when we may loathe them and long to get rid of them.

4. His life was hastening apace towards a period, *v.* 6. He thought he had no reason to expect a long life, for he found himself declining fast (*v.* 6): *My days are swifter than a weaver's shuttle,* that is, "My time is now but short, and there are but a few sands more in my glass, which will speedily run out." Natural motions are more swift near the centre. Job thought his days ran swiftly because he thought he should soon be at his journey's end; he looked upon them as good as spent already, and he was therefore without hope of being restored to his former prosperity. It is applicable to man's life in general. Our days are like a weaver's shuttle, thrown from one side of the web to the other in the twinkling of an eye, and then back again, to and fro, until at length it is quite exhausted of the thread it carried, and then we *cut off, like a weaver, our life,* Isa. xxxviii. 12. Time hastens on apace; the motion of it cannot be stopped, and, when it is past, it cannot be recalled. While we are living, as we are sowing (Gal. vi. 8), so we are weaving. Every day, like the shuttle, leaves a thread behind it. Many weave the spider's web, which will fail them, *ch.* viii. 14. If we are weaving to ourselves holy garments and robes of righteousness, we shall have the benefit of them when our work comes to be reviewed and every man shall reap as he sowed and wear as he wove.

7 O remember that my life *is* wind: mine eye shall no more see good. 8 The eye of him that hath seen me shall see me no *more:* thine eyes *are* upon me, and I *am* not. 9 *As* the cloud is consumed and vanisheth away: so he that goeth down to the grave shall come up no *more.* 10 He shall return no more to his house, neither shall his place know him any more. 11 Therefore I will not refrain my mouth; I will speak in the anguish of my spirit; I will complain in the bitterness of my soul. 12 *Am* I a sea, or a whale, that thou settest a watch over me? 13 When I say, My bed shall comfort

me, my couch shall ease my complaint; 14 Then thou scarest me with dreams, and terrifiest me through visions: 15 So that my soul chooseth strangling, *and* death rather than my life. 16 I loathe *it;* I would not live alway: let me alone; for my days *are* vanity.

Job, observing perhaps that his friends, though they would not interrupt him in his discourse, yet began to grow weary, and not to heed much what he said, here turns to God, and speaks to him. If men will not hear us, God will; if men cannot help us, he can; for his arm is not shortened, neither is his ear heavy. Yet we must not go to school to Job here to learn how to speak to God; for, it must be confessed, there is a great mixture of passion and corruption in what he here says. But, if God be not extreme to mark what his people say amiss, let us also make the best of it. Job is here begging of God either to ease him or to end him. He here represents himself to God,

I. As a dying man, surely and speedily dying. It is good for us, when we are sick, to think and speak of death, for sickness is sent on purpose to put us in mind of it; and, if we be duly mindful of it ourselves, we may in faith put God in mind of it, as Job does here (*v.* 7): *O remember that my life is wind.* He recommends himself to God as an object of his pity and compassion, with this consideration, that he was a very weak frail creature, his abode in this world short and uncertain, his removal out of it sure and speedy, and his return to it again impossible and never to be expected—that his life was wind, as the lives of all men are, noisy perhaps and blustering, like the wind, but vain and empty, soon gone, and, when gone, past recal. God had compassion on Israel, *remembering that they were but flesh, a wind that passeth away and cometh not again,* Ps. lxxviii. 38, 39. Observe,

1. The pious reflections Job makes upon his own life and death. Such plain truths as these concerning the shortness and vanity of life, the unavoidableness and irrecoverableness of death, *then* do us good when we think and speak of them with application to ourselves. Let us consider then, (1.) That we must shortly take our leave of all the things that are seen, that are temporal. The eye of the body must be closed, and shall no more see good, the good which most men set their hearts upon; for their cry is, *Who will make us to see good?* Ps. iv. 6. If we be such fools as to place our happiness in visible good things, what will become of us when they shall be for ever hidden from our eyes, and we shall no more see good? Let us therefore live by that faith which is the substance and evidence of things not seen. (2.) That we must then remove to an invisi-

ble world: *The eye of him that hath* here *seen me shall see me no more* there. It is ᾅδης— *an unseen state, v.* 8. Death removes our lovers and friends into darkness (Ps. lxxxviii. 18), and will shortly remove us out of their sight; when we *go hence we shall be seen no more* (Ps. xxxix. 13), but go to converse with the things that are not seen, that are eternal. (3.) That God can easily, and in a moment, put an end to our lives, and send us to another world (*v.* 8): " *Thy eyes are upon me and I am not;* thou canst look me into eternity, frown me into the grave, when thou pleasest."

Shouldst thou, displeased, give me a frowning look,
I sink, I die, as if with lightning struck.—Sir R. BLACKMORE.

He takes away our breath, and we die; nay, he but *looks on the earth* and it *trembles,* Ps. civ. 29, 30. (4.) That, when we are once removed to another world, we must never return to this. There is constant passing from this world to the other, but *vestigia nulla retrorsum—there is no repassing.* "Therefore, Lord, show me kindness while I am here, for I shall return no more to receive kindness in this world." Or, "Therefore, Lord, kindly ease me by death, for that will be a perpetual ease. I shall return no more to the calamities of this life." When we are dead we are gone, to return no more, [1.] From our house under ground (*v.* 9): *He that goeth down to the grave shall come up no more* until the general resurrection, shall come up no more to his place in this world. Dying is work that is to be done but once, and therefore it had need be well done: an error there is past retrieve. This is illustrated by the blotting out and scattering of a cloud. It is consumed and vanisheth away, is resolved into air and never knits again. Other clouds arise, but the same cloud never returns: so a new generation of the children of men is raised up, but the former generation is quite consumed and vanishes away. When we see a cloud which looks great, as if it would eclipse the sun and drown the earth, of a sudden dispersed and disappearing, let us say, "Just such a thing is the life of man; it is *a vapour that appears for a little while and then vanishes away.*" [2.] To return no more to our house above ground (*v.* 10): *He shall return no more to his house,* to the possession and enjoyment of it, to the business and delights of it. Others will take possession, and keep it till they also resign to another generation. The rich man in hell desired that Lazarus might be sent to his house, knowing it was to no purpose to ask that he might have leave to go himself. Glorified saints shall return no more to the cares, and burdens, and sorrows of their house; nor damned sinners to the gaieties and pleasures of their house. Their place shall no more know them, no more own them, have no more acquaintance with them, nor be any more under their influence. It concerns us to secure a better place when we die, for this will no more own us.

2. The passionate inference he draws from it. From these premises he might have drawn a better conclusion than this (*v.* 11): *Therefore I will not refrain my mouth; I will speak; I will complain.* Holy David, when he had been meditating on the frailty of human life, made a contrary use of it (Ps. xxxix. 9, *I was dumb, and opened not my mouth);* but Job, finding himself near expiring, hastens as much to make his complaint as if he had been to make his last will and testament or as if he could not die in peace until he had given vent to his passion. When we have but a few breaths to draw we should spend them in the holy gracious breathings of faith and prayer, not in the noisome noxious breathings of sin and corruption. Better die praying and praising than die complaining and quarrelling.

II. As a distempered man, sorely and grievously distempered both in body and mind. In this part of his representation he is very peevish, as if God dealt hardly with him and laid upon him more than was meet: "*Am I a sea, or a whale* (*v.* 12), a raging sea, that must be kept within bounds, to check its proud waves, or an unruly whale, that must be restrained by force from devouring all the fishes of the sea? Am I so strong that there needs so much ado to hold me? so boisterous that no less than all these mighty bonds of affliction will serve to tame me and keep me within compass?" We are very apt, when we are in affliction, to complain of God and his providence, as if he laid more restraints upon us than there is occasion for; whereas we are never in heaviness but when there is need, nor more than the necessity demands. 1. He complains that he could not rest in his bed, *v.* 13, 14. There we promise ourselves some repose, when we are fatigued with labour, pain, or travelling: "*My bed shall comfort me, and my couch shall ease my complaint.* Sleep will for a time give me some relief;" it usually does so; it is appointed for that end; many a time it has eased us, and we have awaked refreshed, and with new vigour. When it is so we have great reason to be thankful; but it was not so with poor Job: his bed, instead of comforting him, terrified him; and his couch, instead of easing his complaint, added to it; for, if he dropped asleep, he was disturbed with frightful dreams, and when those awaked him still he was haunted with dreadful apparitions. This was it that made the night so unwelcome and wearisome to him as it was (*v.* 4): When *shall I arise?* Note, God can, when he pleases, meet us with terror even where we promise ourselves ease and repose; nay, he can make us a terror to ourselves, and, as we have often contracted guilt by the rovings of an unsanctified fancy, he can likewise, by the power of our own imagination, create us much grief, and so make that our punishment which has often been our sin. In Job's

dreams, though they might partly arise from his distemper (in fevers, or small pox, when the body is all over sore, it is common for the sleep to be unquiet), yet we have reason to think Satan had a hand, for he delights to terrify those whom it is out of his reach to destroy; but Job looked up to God, who permitted Satan to do this (*thou scarest me*), and mistook Satan's representations for the *terrors of God setting themselves in array against him.* We have reason to pray to God that our dreams may neither defile nor disquiet us, neither tempt us to sin nor torment us with fear, that he who keeps Israel, and neither slumbers nor sleeps, may keep us when we slumber and sleep, that the devil may not then do us a mischief, either as an insinuating serpent or as a roaring lion, and to bless God if we lie down and our sleep is sweet and we are not thus scared. 2. He covets to rest in his grave, that bed where there are no tossings to and fro, nor any frightful dreams, *v.* 15, 16. (1.) He was sick of life, and hated the thoughts of it: "*I loathe it;* I have had enough of it. *I would not live always,* not only not live always in this condition, in pain and misery, but not live always in the most easy and prosperous condition, to be continually in danger of being thus reduced. *My days are vanity* at the best, empty of solid comfort, exposed to real griefs; and I would not be for ever tied to such uncertainty." Note, A good man would not (if he might) live always in this world, no, not though it smile upon him, because it is a world of sin and temptation and he has a better world in prospect. (2.) He was fond of death, and pleased himself with the thoughts of it: his *soul* (his judgment, he thought, but really it was his passion) *chose strangling and death rather than life;* any death rather than such a life as this. Doubtless this was Job's infirmity; for though a good man would not wish to live always in this world, and would choose strangling and death rather than sin, as the martyrs did, yet he will be content to live as long as pleases God, not choose death rather than life, because life is our opportunity of glorifying God and getting ready for heaven.

17 What *is* man, that thou shouldest magnify him? and that thou shouldest set thine heart upon him? 18 And *that* thou shouldest visit him every morning, *and* try him every moment? 19 How long wilt thou not depart from me, nor let me alone till I swallow down my spittle? 20 I have sinned; what shall I do unto thee, O thou preserver of men? why hast thou set me as a mark against thee, so that I am a burden to myself? 21 And why dost thou not pardon my transgression, and take away mine iniquity?

for now shall I sleep in the dust; and thou shalt seek me in the morning, but I *shall* not *be*.

Job here reasons with God,

I. Concerning his dealings with man in general (*v.* 17, 18): *What is man, that thou shouldst magnify him?* This may be looked upon either, 1. As a passionate reflection upon the proceedings of divine justice; as if the great God did diminish and disparage himself in contending with man. "Great men think it below them to take cognizance of those who are much their inferiors so far as to reprove and correct their follies and indecencies; why then does God magnify man, by visiting him, and trying him, and making so much ado about him? Why will he thus pour all his forces upon one that is such an unequal match for him? Why will he visit him with afflictions, which, like a quotidian ague, return as duly and constantly as the morning light, and try, every moment, what he can bear?" We mistake God, and the nature of his providence, if we think it any lessening to him to take notice of the meanest of his creatures. Or, 2. As a pious admiration of the condescensions of divine grace, like that, Ps. viii. 4; cxliv. 3. He owns God's favour to man in general, even when he complains of his own particular troubles. "*What is man*, miserable man, a poor, mean, weak creature, *that thou*, the great and glorious God, shouldst deal with him as thou dost? What is man," (1.) "That thou shouldst put such honour upon him, *shouldst magnify him*, by taking him into covenant and communion with thyself?" (2.) "That thou shouldst concern thyself so much about him, *shouldst set thy heart upon him*, as dear to thee, and one that thou hast a kindness for?" (3.) "*That thou shouldst visit him* with thy compassions *every morning*, as we daily visit a particular friend, or as the physician visits his patients every morning to help them?" (4.) "That thou shouldst *try him*, shouldst feel his pulse and observe his looks, *every moment*, as in care about him and jealous over him?" That such a worm of the earth as man is should be the darling and favourite of heaven is what we have reason for ever to admire.

II. Concerning his dealings with him in particular. Observe,

1. The complaint he makes of his afflictions, which he here aggravates, and (as we are all too apt to do) makes the worst of, in three expressions:—(1.) That he was the butt to God's arrows: "*Thou hast set me as a mark against thee*," *v.* 20. "My case is singular, and none is shot at as I am." (2.) That he was a *burden to himself*, ready to sink under the load of his own life. How much delight soever we take in ourselves God can, when he pleases, make us burdens to ourselves. • What comfort can we take in ourselves if God appear against us as an

enemy and we have not comfort in him. (3.) That he had no intermission of his griefs (*v.* 19): "*How long* will it be ere thou cause thy rod to *depart from me*, or abate the rigour of the correction, at least for so long as that I may *swallow down my spittle?*" It should seem, Job's distemper lay much in his throat, and almost choked him, so that he could not swallow his spittle. He complains (*ch.* xxx. 18) that it *bound him about like the collar of his coat*. "Lord," says he, "wilt not thou give me some respite, some breathing time?" *ch.* ix. 18.

2. The concern he is in about his sins. The best men have sin to complain of, and the better they are the more they will complain of it. (1.) He ingenuously owns himself guilty before God: *I have sinned*. God had said of him that he was a *perfect and an upright man;* yet he says of himself, *I have sinned*. Those may be upright who yet are not sinless; and those who are sincerely penitent are accepted, through a Mediator, as evangelically perfect. Job maintained, against his friends, that he was not a hypocrite, not a wicked man; and yet he owned to his God that he had sinned. If we have been kept from gross acts of sin, it does not therefore follow that we are innocent. The best must acknowledge, before God, that they have sinned. His calling God the *observer*, or *preserver*, of men, may be looked upon as designed for an aggravation of his sin: "Though God has had his eye upon me, his eye upon me for good, yet I have sinned against him." When we are in affliction it is seasonable to confess sin, as the procuring cause of our affliction. Penitent confessions would drown and silence passionate complaints. (2.) He seriously enquires how he may make his peace with God: "*What shall I do unto thee*, having done so much against thee?" Are we convinced that we have sinned, and are we brought to own it? We cannot but conclude that something must be done to prevent the fatal consequences of it. The matter must not rest as it is, but some course must be taken to undo what has been ill done. And, if we are truly sensible of the danger we have run ourselves into, we shall be willing to do any thing, to take a pardon upon any terms; and therefore shall be *inquisitive as to what we shall do* (Mic. vi. 6, 7), what we shall do to God, not to satisfy the demands of his justice (that is done only by the Mediator), but to qualify ourselves for the tokens of his favour, according to the tenour of the gospel-covenant. In making this enquiry it is good to eye God as the preserver or Saviour of men, not their destroyer. In our repentance we must keep up good thoughts of God, as one that delights not in the ruin of his creatures, but would rather they should return and live. "Thou art the Saviour of men; be my Saviour, for I cast myself upon thy mercy."

(3.) He earnestly begs for the forgiveness of his sins, *v.* 21. The heat of his spirit, as, on the one hand, it made his complaints the more bitter, so, on the other hand, it made his prayers the more lively and importunate; as here: "*Why dost thou not pardon my transgression?* Art thou not a God of infinite mercy, that art ready to forgive? Hast not thou wrought repentance in me? Why then dost thou not give me the pardon of my sin, and make me to hear the voice of that joy and gladness?" Surely he means more than barely the removing of his outward trouble, and is herein earnest for the return of God's favour, which he complained of the want of, *ch.* vi. 4. "Lord, pardon my sins, and give me the comfort of that pardon, and then I can easily bear my afflictions," Matt. ix. 2; Isa. xxxiii. 24. When the mercy of God pardons the transgression that is committed by us the grace of God takes away the iniquity that reigns in us. Wherever God removes the guilt of sin he breaks the power of sin. (4.) To enforce his prayer for pardon he pleads the prospect he had of dying quickly: *For now shall I sleep in the dust.* Death will lay us in the dust, will lay us to sleep there, and perhaps presently, now in a little time. Job had been complaining of restless nights, and that sleep departed from his eyes (*v.* 3, 4, 13, 14); but those who cannot sleep on a bed of down will shortly sleep in a bed of dust, and not be scared with dreams nor tossed to and fro: "*Thou shalt seek me in the morning,* to show me favour, but *I shall not be;* it will be too late then. If my sins be not pardoned while I live, I am lost and undone for ever." Note, The consideration of this, that we must shortly die, and perhaps may die suddenly, should make us all very solicitous to get our sins pardoned and our iniquity taken away.

CHAP. VIII.

Job's friends are like Job's messengers; the latter followed one another close with evil tidings, the former followed him with harsh censures: both, unawares, served Satan's design; these to drive him from his integrity, those to drive him from the comfort of it. Eliphaz did not reply to what Job had said in answer to him, but left it to Bildad, whom he knew to be of the same mind with himself in this affair. Those are not the wisest of the company, but the weakest rather, who covet to have all the talk. Let others speak in their turn, and let the first keep silence, 1 Cor. xiv. 30, 31. Bildad had undertaken to show that because Job was sorely afflicted he was certainly a wicked man. Bildad is much of the same mind, and will conclude Job a wicked man unless God do speedily appear for his relief. In this chapter he endeavours to convince Job, I. That he had spoken too passionately, ver. 2. II. That he and his children had suffered justly, ver. 3, 4. III. That, if he were a true penitent, God would soon turn his captivity, ver. 5—7. IV. That it was a usual thing for Providence to extinguish the joys and hopes of wicked men as his were extinguished; and therefore that they had reason to suspect him for a hypocrite, ver. 8—19. V. That they would be abundantly confirmed in their suspicion unless God did speedily appear for his relief, ver. 20—22.

THEN answered Bildad the Shuhite, and said, 2 How long wilt thou speak these *things?* and how long shall the words of thy mouth be like a strong wind? 3 Doth God pervert judgment? or doth the Almighty pervert justice? 4 If thy children have sinned against him, and he have cast

them away for their transgression; 5 If thou wouldest seek unto God betimes, and make thy supplication to the Almighty; 6 If thou *wert* pure and upright; surely now he would awake for thee, and make the habitation of thy righteousness prosperous. 7 Though thy beginning was small, yet thy latter end should greatly increase.

Here, I. Bildad reproves Job for what he had said (*v.* 2), checks his passion, but perhaps (as is too common) with greater passion. We thought Job spoke a great deal of good sense and much to the purpose, and that he had reason and right on his side; but Bildad, like an eager angry disputant, turns it all off with this, *How long wilt thou speak these things?* taking it for granted that Eliphaz had said enough to silence him, and that therefore all he said was impertinent. Thus (as Caryl observes) reproofs are often grounded upon mistakes. Men's meaning is not taken aright, and then they are gravely rebuked as if they were evil-doers. Bildad compares Job's discourse to a *strong wind.* Job had excused himself with this, that his speeches were but *as wind* (ch. vi. 26), and therefore they should not make such ado about them: "Yea, but" (says Bildad) "they are as strong wind, blustering and threatening, boisterous and dangerous, and therefore we are concerned to fence against them."

II. He justifies God in what he had done. This he had no occasion to do at this time (for Job did not condemn God, as he would have it thought he did), or he might at least have done it without reflecting upon Job's children, as he does here. Could he not be an advocate for God but he must be an accuser of the brethren? 1. He is right in general, that *God doth not pervert judgment,* nor ever go contrary to any settled rule of justice, *v.* 3. Far be it from him that he should and from us that we should suspect him. He never oppresses the innocent, nor lays a greater load on the guilty than they deserve. He is God, the Judge; and shall not the Judge of all the earth do right? Gen. xviii. 25. If there should be unrighteousness with God, *how should he judge the world?* Rom. iii. 5, 6. He is *Almighty, Shaddai—all-sufficient.* Men pervert justice sometimes for fear of the power of others (but God is Almighty, and stands in awe of none), sometimes to obtain the favour of others; but God is all-sufficient, and cannot be benefited by the favour of any. It is man's weakness and impotency that he often is unjust; it is God's omnipotence that he cannot be so. 2. Yet he is not fair and candid in the application. He takes it for granted that Job's children (the death of whom was one of the greatest of his afflictions) had been guilty of some notorious wickedness, and that the unhappy circumstances of their death were sufficient evidence that they were sinners above all the children of the east, *v.* 4. Job readily owned that God did not pervert judgment; and yet it did not therefore follow either that his children were cast-aways or that they died for some great transgression. It is true that we and our children have sinned against God, and we ought to justify him in all he brings upon us and ours; but extraordinary afflictions are not always the punishment of extraordinary sins, but sometimes the trial of extraordinary graces; and, in our judgment of another's case (unless the contrary appears), we ought to take the more favourable side, as our Saviour directs, Luke xiii. 2—4. Here Bildad missed it.

III. He put Job in hope that, if he were indeed upright, as he said he was, he should yet see a good issue of his present troubles: *"Although thy children have sinned against him, and are cast away in their transgression* (they have died in their own sin), yet if thou be pure and upright thyself, and as an evidence of that wilt now seek unto God and submit to him, all shall be well yet," *v.* 5—7. This may be taken two ways, either, 1. As designed to prove Job a hypocrite and a wicked man, though not by the greatness, yet by the continuance, of his afflictions. "When thou wast impoverished, and thy children were killed, if thou hadst been pure and upright, and approved thyself so in the trial, God would before now have returned in mercy to thee and comforted thee according to the time of thy affliction; but, because he does not so, we have reason to conclude thou art not so *pure and upright* as thou pretendest to be. If thou hadst conducted thyself well under the former affliction, thou wouldst not have been struck with the latter." Herein Bildad was not in the right; for a good man may be afflicted for his trial, not only very sorely, but very long, and yet, if for life, it is in comparison with eternity but for a moment. But, since Bildad put it to this issue, God was pleased to join issue with him, and proved his servant Job an honest man by Bildad's own argument; for, soon after, he blessed his latter end more than his beginning. Or, 2. As designed to direct and encourage Job, that he might not thus run himself into despair, and give up all for gone; there might yet be hope if he would take the right course. I am apt to think Bildad here intended to condemn Job, yet would be thought to counsel and comfort him. (1.) He gives him good counsel, yet perhaps not expecting he would take it, the same that Eliphaz had given him (*ch.* v. 8), to *seek unto God*, and that *betimes* (that is, speedily and seriously), and not to be dilatory and trifling in his return and repentance. He advises him not to complain, but to petition, to *make* his *supplication to the Almighty* with humility and faith, and to see that there

was (what he feared had hitherto been wanting) sincerity in his heart ("thou must be *pure and upright*") and honesty in his house —"that must be *the habitation of thy righteousness,* and not filled with ill-gotten goods, else God will not hear thy prayers," Ps. lxvi. 18. It is only the prayer of the upright that is the acceptable and prevailing prayer, Prov. xv. 8. (2.) He gives him good hopes that he shall yet again see good days, secretly suspecting, however, that he was not qualified to see them. He assures him that, if he would be early in seeking God, God would awake for his relief, would remember him and return to him, though now he seemed to forget him and forsake him—that if his habitation were righteous it should be prosperous; for honesty is the best policy, and inward piety a sure friend to outward prosperity. When we return to God in a way of duty we have reason to hope that he will return to us in a way of mercy. Let not Job object that he had so little left to begin the world with again that it was impossible he should ever prosper as he had done; no, "Though thy beginning should be ever so small, a little meal in the barrel and a little oil in the cruse, God's blessing shall multiply that to a great increase." This is God's way of enriching the souls of his people with graces and comforts, not *per saltum—as by a bound,* but *per gradum—step by step.* The beginning is small, but the progress is to perfection. Dawning light grows to noonday, a grain of mustard seed to a great tree. Let us not therefore despise the day of small things, but hope for the day of great things

8 For enquire, I pray thee, of the former age, and prepare thyself to the search of their fathers: 9 (For we *are but of* yesterday, and know nothing, because our days upon earth *are* a shadow:) 10 Shall not they teach thee, *and* tell thee, and utter words out of their heart? 11 Can the rush grow up without mire? can the flag grow without water? 12 Whilst it *is* yet in his greenness, *and* not cut down, it withereth before any *other* herb. 13 So *are* the paths of all that forget God; and the hypocrite's hope shall perish: 14 Whose hope shall be cut off, and whose trust *shall be* a spider's web. 15 He shall lean upon his house, but it shall not stand: he shall hold it fast, but it shall not endure. 16 He *is* green before the sun, and his branch shooteth forth in his garden. 17 His roots are wrapped about the heap, *and* seeth the place

of stones. 18 If he destroy him from his place, then *it* shall deny him, *saying*, I have not seen thee. 19 Behold, this *is* the joy of his way, and out of the earth shall others grow

Bildad here discourses very well of the sad catastrophe of hypocrites and evil-doers and the fatal period of all their hopes and joys. He will not be so bold as to say with Eliphaz that none that were righteous were ever cut off thus (*ch.* iv. 7); yet he takes it for granted that God, in the course of his providence, does ordinarily bring wicked men, who seemed pious and were prosperous, to shame and ruin in this world, and that, by making their prosperity short, he discovers their piety to be counterfeit. Whether this will certainly prove that all who are thus ruined must be concluded to have been hypocrites he will not say, but rather suspect, and thinks the application is easy.

I. He proves this truth, of the certain destruction of all the hopes and joys of hypocrites, by an appeal to antiquity and the concurring sentiment and observation of all wise and good men; and an undoubted truth it is, if we take in the other world, that, if not in this life, yet in the life to come, hypocrites will be deprived of all their trusts and all their triumphs: whether Bildad so meant or no, we must so take it. Let us observe the method of his proof, *v.* 8—10.

1. He insists not on his own judgment and that of his companions: *We are but of yesterday, and know nothing, v.* 9. He perceived that Job had no opinion of their abilities, but thought they knew little. "We will own," says Bildad, "that we know nothing, are as ready to confess our ignorance as thou art to condemn it; for we are but of yesterday in comparison, *and our days upon earth are* short and transient, and hastening away as *a shadow.* And hence," (1.) "We are not so near the fountain-head of divine revelation" (which then, for aught that appears, was conveyed by tradition) "as the former age was; and therefore we must enquire what they said and recount what we have been told of their sentiments." Blessed be God, now that we have the word of God in writing, and are directed to search that, we need not *enquire of the former age*, nor *prepare ourselves to the search of their fathers;* for, though we ourselves are but of yesterday, the word of God in the scripture is as nigh to us as it was to them (Rom. x. 8), and it is the *more sure word of prophecy, to which we must take heed.* If we study and keep God's precepts, we may by them *understand more than the ancients*, Ps. cxix. 99, 100. (2.) "We do not live so long as those of the former age did, to make observations upon the methods of divine providence, and therefore cannot be such competent judges as they in a cause of this nature." Note, The

50

shortness of our lives is a great hindrance to the improvement of our knowledge, and so are the frailty and weakness of our bodies. *Vita brevis, ars longa—life is short, the progress of art boundless.*

2. He refers to the testimony of the ancients and to the knowledge which Job himself had of their sentiments. "Do thou *enquire of the former age*, and let them tell thee, not only their own judgment in this matter, but the judgment also of *their fathers, v.* 8. *They will teach thee*, and inform thee (*v.* 10), that all along, in their time, the judgments of God followed wicked men This they will *utter out of their hearts*, that is, as that which they firmly believe themselves, which they are greatly affected with and desirous to acquaint and affect others with." Note, (1.) For the right understanding of divine Providence, and the unfolding of the difficulties of it, it will be of use to compare the observations and experiences of former ages with the events of our own day; and, in order thereto, to consult history, especially the sacred history, which is the most ancient, infallibly true, and written designedly for our learning. (2.) Those that would fetch knowledge from the former ages must search diligently, *prepare for the search*, and take pains for the search. (3.) Those words are most likely to reach to the hearts of the learners that come from the hearts of the teachers. *Those shall teach thee* best that *utter words out of their heart*, that speak by experience, and not by rote, of spiritual and divine things. The learned bishop Patrick suggests that Bildad being a Shuhite, descended from Shuah one of Abraham's sons by Keturah (Gen. xxv. 2), in this appeal which he makes to history he has a particular respect to the rewards which the blessing of God secured to the posterity of faithful Abraham (who hitherto, and long after, continued in his religion) and to the extirpation of those eastern people, neighbours to Job (in whose country they were settled), for their wickedness, whence he infers that it is God's usual way to prosper the just and root out the wicked, though for a while they may flourish.

II. He illustrates this truth by some similitudes.

1. The hopes and joys of the hypocrite are here compared to a rush or flag, *v.* 11—13. (1.) It grows up out of the mire and water. The hypocrite cannot gain his hope without some false rotten ground or other out of which to raise it, and with which to support it and keep it alive, any more than the rush can grow without mire. He grounds it on his worldly prosperity, the plausible profession he makes of religion, the good opinion of his neighbours, and his own good conceit of himself, which are no solid foundation on which to build his confidence. It is all but mire and water; and the hope that grows out of it is but rush and flag. (2.) It

may look green and gay for a while (the rush outgrows the grass), but it is light, and hollow, and empty, and good for nothing. It is green for show, but of no use. (3.) It withers presently, *before any other herb, v.* 12. Even *while it is in its greenness* it is dried away and gone in a little time. Note, The best state of hypocrites and evil-doers borders upon withering; even when it is green it is going. The grass is *cut down and withers* (Ps. xc. 6); but the rush is *not cut down* and yet *withers, withers before it grows up* (Ps. cxxix. 6): as it has no use, so it has no continuance. *So are the paths of all that forget God* (*v.* 13); they take the same way that the rush does, *for the hypocrite's hope shall perish*. Note, [1.] Forgetfulness of God is at the bottom of men's hypocrisy, and of the vain hopes with which they flatter and deceive themselves in their hypocrisy. Men would not be hypocrites if they did not forget that the God with whom they have to do searches the heart and requires truth there, that he is a Spirit and has his eye on our spirits; and hypocrites would have no hope if they did not forget that God is righteous, and will not be mocked with the torn and the lame. [2.] The hope of hypocrites is a great cheat upon themselves, and, though it may flourish for a while, it will certainly perish at last, and they with it.

2. They are here compared to *a spider's web*, or *a spider's house* (as it is in the margin), a cobweb, *v.* 14, 15. The hope of the hypocrite, (1) Is woven out of his own bowels; it is the creature of his own fancy, and arises merely from a conceit of his own merit and sufficiency. There is a great deal of difference between the work of the bee and that of the spider. A diligent Christian, like the laborious bee, fetches in all his comfort from the heavenly dews of God's word; but the hypocrite, like the subtle spider, weaves his out of a false hypothesis of his own concerning God, as if he were altogether such a one as himself. (2.) He is very fond of it, as the spider of her web; pleases himself with it, wraps himself in it, calls it his house, *leans upon it*, and *holds it fast*. It is said of the spider that *she takes hold with her hands, and is in kings' palaces*, Prov. xxx. 28. So does a carnal worldling hug himself in the fulness and firmness of his outward prosperity; he prides himself in that house as his palace, fortifies himself in it as his castle, and makes use of it as the spider of her web, to ensnare those he has a mind to prey upon. So does a formal professor; he flatters himself in his own eyes, doubts not of his salvation, is secure of heaven, and cheats the world with his vain confidences. (3.) It will easily and certainly be swept away, as the cobweb with the besom, when God shall come to purge his house. The prosperity of worldly people will fail them when they expect to find safety and happiness in it. They seek to hold fast their estates, but God is plucking them

out of their hands; and whose shall all those things be, which they have provided? or what the better will they be for them? The confidences of hypocrites will fail them. *I tell you, I know you not.* The house built on the sand will fall in the storm, when the builder most needs it and promised himself the benefit of it. *When a wicked man dies his expectation perishes.* The ground of his hopes will prove false; he will be disappointed of the thing he hoped for, and his foolish hope with which he buoyed himself up will be turned into endless despair; and thus his hope will be cut off, his web, that refuge of lies, swept away, and he crushed in it.

3. The hypocrite is here compared to a flourishing and well-rooted tree, which, though it do not wither of itself, yet will easily be cut down and its place know it no more. The secure and prosperous sinner may think himself wronged when he is compared to a rush and a flag; he thinks he has a better root. "We will allow him his conceit," says Bildad, "and give him all the advantage he can desire, and yet bring him in suddenly cut off." He is here represented as Nebuchadnezzar was in his own dream (Dan. iv. 10) by a great tree. (1.) See this tree fair and flourishing (*v.* 16) like a *green bay-tree* (Ps. xxxvii. 35), *green before the sun*, that keeps its greenness in defiance of the scorching sun-beams, and *his branch shoots forth* under the protection of his garden-wall and with the benefit of his garden-soil. See it fixed, and taking deep root, never likely to be overthrown by stormy winds, *for his roots are interwoven with the stones* (*v.* 17); it grows in firm ground, not, as the rush, in mire and water. Thus does a wicked man, when he prospers in the world, think himself secure; his wealth is a *high wall in his own conceit*. (2.) See this tree felled and forgotten notwithstanding, *destroyed from his place* (*v.* 18), and so entirely extirpated that there shall remain no sign or token where it grew. The very place shall say, *I have not seen thee;* and the standers by shall say the same. *I sought him, but he could not be found*, Ps. xxxvii. 36. He made a great show and a great noise for a time, but he has gone of a sudden, and *neither root nor branch* is *left him*, Mal. iv. 1. *This is the joy* (that is, this is the end and conclusion) *of the wicked man's way* (*v.* 19); this is that which all his joy comes to. *The way of the ungodly shall perish*, Ps. i. 6. His hope, he thought, would in the issue be turned into joy; but this is the issue, this is the joy. *The harvest shall be a heap in the day of grief and of desperate sorrow*, Isa. xvii. 11. This is the best of it; and what then is the worst of it? But shall he not leave a family behind him to enjoy what he has? No, *out of the earth* (not out of his roots) *shall others grow*, that are nothing akin to him, and shall fill up his place, and rule over that for which he laboured. Others (that is, others of the same spirit and disposition) shall grow up in his place, and be as

secure as ever he was, not warned by his fall. The way of worldlings is their folly, and yet there is a race of those that *approve their sayings*, Ps. xlix. 13.

20 Behold, God will not cast away a perfect *man*, neither will he help the evildoers: 21 Till he fill thy mouth with laughing, and thy lips with rejoicing. 22 They that hate thee shall be clothed with shame ; and the dwelling place of the wicked shall come to nought.

Bildad here, in the close of his discourse, sums up what he has to say in a few words, setting before Job life and death, the blessing and the curse, assuring him that as he was so he should fare, and therefore they might conclude that as he fared so he was. 1. On the one hand, if he were a perfect upright man, God would not *cast him away*, *v.* 20. Though now he seemed forsaken of God, he would yet return to him, and by degrees would *turn his mourning into dancing* (Ps. xxx. 11), and comforts should flow in upon him so plentifully that his *mouth* should be *filled with laughing*, *v.* 21. So affecting should the happy change be, Ps. cxxvi. 2. Those that loved him would rejoice with him; but those that hated him, and had triumphed in his fall, would be ashamed of their insolence, when they should see him restored to his former prosperity. Now it is true that *God will not cast away an upright man ;* he may be cast down for a time, but he shall not be cast away for ever. It is true that, if not in this world, yet in another, the mouth of the righteous shall be *filled with rejoicing*. Though their sun should set under a cloud, yet it shall rise again clear, never more to be clouded ; though they go mourning to the grave, that shall not hinder their entrance into the joy of their Lord. It is true that the enemies of 'the saints will be *clothed with shame* when they see them crowned with honour. But it does not therefore follow that, if Job were not perfectly restored to his former prosperity, he would forfeit the character of a perfect man. 2. On the other hand, if he were a wicked man and an evil-doer, God would not help him, but leave him to perish in his present distresses (*v.* 20), and his *dwelling-place* should *come to nought*, 22. And here also it is true that God *will not help the evil-doers ;* they throw themselves out of his protection, and forfeit his favour. He *will not take the ungodly by the hand* (so it is in the margin), will not have fellowship and communion with them ; for *what communion* can there be *between light and darkness?* He will not lend them his hand to pull them out of the miseries, the eternal miseries, into which they have plunged themselves ; they will then stretch out their hand to him for help, but it will be too late : he will not take them by the hand. *Between us and you there is a*

great gulf fixed. It is true that *the dwelling-place of the wicked*, sooner or later, *will come to nought*. Those only *who make God their dwelling-place* are safe for ever, Ps. xc. 1 ; xci. 1. Those who make other things their refuge will be disappointed. Sin brings ruin on persons and families. Yet to argue (as Bildad, I doubt, slily does) that because Job's family was sunk, and he himself at present seemed helpless, therefore he certainly was an ungodly wicked man, was neither just nor charitable, as long as there appeared no other evidence of his wickedness and ungodliness. Let us *judge nothing before the time*, but wait till the secrets of all hearts shall be made manifest, and the present difficulties of Providence be solved to universal and everlasting satisfaction, when the *mystery of God shall be finished*.

CHAP. IX.

In this and the following chapter we have Job's answer to Bildad's discourse, wherein he speaks honourably of God, humbly of himself, and feelingly of his troubles ; but not one word by way of reflection upon his friends, or their unkindness to him, nor in direct reply to what Bildad had said. He wisely keeps to the merits of the cause, and makes no remarks upon the person that managed it, nor seeks occasion against him. In this chapter we have, I. The doctrine of God's justice laid down, ver. 2. II. The proof of it, from his wisdom, and power, and sovereign dominion, ver. 3–13. III. The application of it, in which, 1. He condemns himself, as not able to contend with God either in law or battle, ver. 14–21. 2. He maintains his point, that we cannot judge of men's character by their outward condition, ver. 22–24. 3. He complains of the greatness of his troubles, the confusion he was in, and the loss he was at what to say or do, ver. 25–35.

THEN Job answered and said, 2 I know *it is* so of a truth : but how should man be just with God ? 3 If he will contend with him, he cannot answer him one of a thousand. 4 *He is* wise in heart, and mighty in strength : who hath hardened *himself* against him, and hath prospered ? 5 Which removeth the mountains, and they know not : which overturneth them in his anger. 6 Which shaketh the earth out of her place, and the pillars thereof tremble. 7 Which commandeth the sun, and it riseth not ; and sealeth up the stars. 8 Which alone spreadeth out the heavens, and treadeth upon the waves of the sea. 9 Which maketh Arcturus, Orion, and Pleiades, and the chambers of the south. 10 Which doeth great things past finding out ; yea, and wonders without number. 11 Lo, he goeth by me, and I see *him* not : he passeth on also, but I perceive him not. 12 Behold, he taketh away, who can hinder him ? who will say unto him, What doest thou ? 13 *If* God will not withdraw his anger, the proud helpers do stoop under him.

Bildad began with a rebuke to Job for talking so much, *ch.* viii. 2. Job makes no answer to that, though it would have been easy enough to retort it upon himself; but in what he next lays down as his principle, that God never perverts judgment, Job agrees with him: *I know it is so of a truth, v.* 2. Note, We should be ready to own how far we agree with those with whom we dispute, and should not slight, much less resist, a truth, though produced by an adversary and urged against us, but receive it in the light and love of it, though it may have been misapplied. "*It is so of a truth,* that wickedness brings men to ruin and the godly are taken under God's special protection. These are truths which I subscribe to; but how can any man make good his part with God?" *In his sight shall no flesh living be justified,* Ps. cxliii. 2. *How should man be just with God?* Some understand this as a passionate complaint of God's strictness and severity, that he is a God whom there is no dealing with; and it cannot be denied that there are, in this chapter, some peevish expressions, which seem to speak such language as this. But I take this rather as a pious confession of man's sinfulness, and his own in particular, that, if God should deal with any of us according to the desert of our iniquities, we should certainly be undone.

I. He lays this down for a truth, that man is an unequal match for his Maker, either in dispute or combat.

1. In dispute (*v.* 3): *If he will contend with him,* either at law or at an argument, *he cannot answer him one of a thousand.* (1.) God can ask a thousand puzzling questions which those that quarrel with him, and arraign his proceedings, cannot give an answer to. When God spoke to Job out of the whirlwind he asked him a great many questions (*Dost thou know* this? *Canst thou do* that?) to none of which Job could give an answer, *ch.* xxxviii., xxxix. God can easily manifest the folly of the greatest pretenders to wisdom. (2.) God can lay to our charge a thousand offences, can draw up against us a thousand articles of impeachment, and we cannot answer him so as to acquit ourselves from the imputation of any of them, but must, by silence, give consent that they are all true. We cannot set aside one as foreign, another as frivolous, and another as false. We cannot, as to one, deny the fact, and plead not guilty, and, as to another, deny the fault, confess and justify. No, we are not able to answer him, but must *lay our hand upon our mouth,* as Job did (*ch.* xl. 4, 5), and cry, *Guilty, guilty.*

2. In combat (*v.* 4): "*Who hath hardened himself against him and hath prospered?*" The answer is very easy. You cannot produce any instance, from the beginning of the world to this day, of any daring sinner who has *hardened himself against God,* has obstinately persisted in rebellion against him, who did not find God too hard for him and pay dearly for his folly. Such transgressors

have not prospered or had peace; they have had no comfort in their way nor any success. What did ever man get by trials of skill, or trials of titles, with his Maker? All the opposition given to God is but setting briers and thorns before a consuming fire; so foolish, so fruitless, so destructive, is the attempt, Isa. xxvii. 4; Ezek. xxviii. 24; 1 Cor. x. 22. Apostate angels hardened themselves against God, but did not prosper, 2 Pet. ii. 4. The dragon fights, but is cast out, Rev. xii. 9. Wicked men harden themselves against God, dispute his wisdom, disobey his laws, are impenitent for their sins and incorrigible under their afflictions; they reject the offers of his grace, and resist the strivings of his Spirit; they make nothing of his threatenings, and make head against his interest in the world. But have they prospered? Can they prosper? No; they are but *treasuring up for themselves wrath against the day of wrath.* Those that roll this stone will find it return upon them.

II. He proves it by showing what a God he is with whom we have to do: *He is wise in heart,* and therefore we cannot answer him at law; he is *mighty in strength,* and therefore we cannot fight it out with him. It is the greatest madness that can be to think to contend with a God of infinite wisdom and power, who knows every thing and can do every thing, who can be neither outwitted nor overpowered. The devil promised himself that Job, in the day of his affliction, would curse God and speak ill of him, but, instead of that, he sets himself to honour God and to speak highly of him. As much pained as he is, and as much taken up with his own miseries, when he has occasion to mention the wisdom and power of God he forgets his complaints, dwells with delight, and expatiates with a flood of eloquence, upon that noble useful subject. Evidences of the wisdom and power of God he fetches,.

1. From the kingdom of nature, in which the God of nature acts with an uncontrollable power and does what he pleases; for all the orders and all the powers of nature are derived from him and depend upon him.

(1.) When he pleases he alters the course of nature, and turns back its streams, *v.* 5— 7. By the common law of nature the mountains are settled and are therefore called *everlasting mountains,* the earth is established and cannot be removed (Ps. xciii. 1) and the pillars thereof are immovably fixed, the sun rises in its season, and the stars shed their influences on this lower world; but when God pleases he can not only drive out of the common track, but invert the order and change the law of nature. [1.] Nothing more firm than the mountains. When we speak of removing mountains we mean that which is impossible; yet the divine power can make them change their seat: *He removes them and they know not,* removes them whether they will or no; he can make them lower their heads; he can level them, and overturn them in his anger; he can spread the mountains as easily as the husbandman spreads the mole-hills, be they ever so high, and large, and rocky. Men have much ado to pass over them, but God, when he pleases, can make them pass away. He made Sinai shake, Ps. lxviii. 8. *The hills skipped*, Ps. cxiv. 4. *The everlasting mountains were scattered*, Hab. iii. 6. [2.] Nothing more fixed than the earth on its axletree; yet God can, when he pleases, *shake the earth out of its place*, heave it off its centre, and make even *its pillars to tremble;* what seemed to support it will itself need support when God gives it a shock. See how much we are indebted to God's patience. God has power enough to shake the earth from under that guilty race of mankind which makes it groan under the burden of sin, and so to *shake the wicked out of it* (Job xxxviii. 13); yet he continues the earth, and man upon it, and does not make it, as once, to swallow up the rebels. [3.] Nothing more constant than the rising sun, it never misses its appointed time; yet God, when he pleases, can suspend it. He that at first commanded it to rise can countermand it. Once the sun was told to stand, and another time to retreat, to show that it is still under the check of its great Creator. Thus great is God's power; and how great then is his goodness, which causes his sun to shine even upon the evil and unthankful, though he could withhold it! He that made the stars also, can, if he pleases, seal them up, and hide them from our eyes. By earthquakes and subterraneous fires mountains have sometimes been removed and the earth shaken: in very dark and cloudy days and nights it seems to us as if the sun were forbidden to rise and the stars were sealed up, Acts xxvii. 20. It is sufficient to say that Job here speaks of what God can do; but, if we must understand it of what he has done in fact, all these verses may perhaps be applied to Noah's flood, when the mountains of the earth were shaken, and the sun and stars were darkened; and the world that now is we believe to be reserved for that fire which will consume the mountains, and melt the earth, with its fervent heat, and which will turn the sun into darkness.

(2.) As long as he pleases he preserves the settled course and order of nature; and this is a continued creation. He himself alone, by his own power, and without the assistance of any other, [1.] *Spreads out the heaven* (v. 8), not only did spread them out at first, but still spreads them out (that is, keeps them spread out), for otherwise they would of themselves roll together like a scroll of parchment. [2.] *He treads upon the waves of the sea;* that is, he suppresses them and keeps them under, that they return not to deluge the earth (Ps. civ. 9), which is given as a reason why we should all fear God and stand in awe of him, Jer. v. 22. He is mightier than the proud waves, Ps. xciii. 4; lxv. 7. [3.] He

makes the constellations; three are named for all the rest (v. 9), *Arcturus, Orion,* and *Pleiades,* and in general *the chambers of the south.* The stars of which these are composed he made at first, and put into that order, and he still makes them, preserves them in being, and guides their motions; he makes them to be what they are to man, and inclines the hearts of men to observe them, which the beasts are not capable of doing. Not only those stars which we see and give names to, but those also in the other hemisphere, about the antarctic pole, which never come in our sight, called here *the chambers of the south,* are under the divine direction and dominion. How wise is he then, and how mighty!

2. From the kingdom of Providence, that special Providence which is conversant about the affairs of the children of men. Consider what God does in the government of the world, and you will say, He is *wise in heart* and *mighty in strength.* (1.) He does many things and great, many and great to admiration, v. 10. Job here says the same that Eliphaz had said (ch. v. 9), and in the original in the very same words, not declining to speak after him, though now his antagonist. God is a great God, and *doeth great things,* a wonder-working God; his works of wonder are so many that we cannot number them and so mysterious that we cannot find them out. O the depth of his counsels! (2.) He acts invisibly and undiscerned, v. 11. "*He goes by me* in his operations, *and I see him not, I perceive him not. His way is in the sea,*" Ps. lxxvii. 19. The operations of second causes are commonly obvious to sense, but God does all about us and yet *we see him not,* Acts xvii. 23. Our finite understandings cannot fathom his counsels, apprehend his motions, or comprehend the measures he takes; we are therefore incompetent judges of God's proceedings, because we know not what he does nor what he designs. The *arcana imperii—secrets of government,* are things above us, which therefore we must not pretend to expound or comment upon. (3.) He acts with an incontestable sovereignty, v. 12. He takes away our creature-comforts and confidences when and as he pleases, takes away health, estate, relations, friends, takes away life itself; whatever goes, it is he that takes it; by what hand soever it is removed, his hand must be acknowledged in its removal. The Lord *takes away,* and *who can hinder him? Who can turn him away?* (Margin, *Who shall make him restore?*) Who can dissuade him or alter his counsels? Who can resist him or oppose his operations? Who can control him or call him to an account? What action can be brought against him? Or *who will say unto him, What doest thou?* Or, Why doest thou so? Dan. iv. 35. God is not obliged to give us a reason of what he does. The meaning of his proceedings we know not now; it will be time enough to know hereafter, when it will

appear that what seemed now to be done by prerogative was done in infinite wisdom and for the best. (4.) He acts with an irresistible power, which no creature can resist, *v.* 13. *If God will not withdraw his anger* (which he can do when he pleases, for he is *Lord of his anger*, lets it out or calls it in according to his will), *the proud helpers do stoop under him*; that is, He certainly breaks and crushes those that proudly help one another against him. Proud men set themselves against God and his proceedings. In this opposition they join hand in hand. *The kings of the earth set themselves, and the rulers take counsel together,* to throw off his yoke, to run down his truths, and to persecute his people. *Men of Israel, help,* Acts xxi. 28 ; Ps. lxxxiii. 8. If one enemy of God's kingdom fall under his judgment, the rest come proudly to help that, and think to deliver that out of his hand : but in vain ; unless he pleases to withdraw his anger (which he often does, for it is the day of his patience) the proud helpers stoop under him, and fall with those whom they designed to help. *Who knows the power of God's anger ?* Those who think they have strength enough to help others will not be able to help themselves against it.

14 How much less shall I answer him, *and* choose out my words *to reason* with him ? 15 Whom, though I were righteous, *yet* would I not answer, *but* I would make supplication to my judge. 16 If I had called, and he had answered me ; *yet* would I not believe that he had hearkened unto my voice. 17 For he breaketh me with a tempest, and multiplieth my wounds without cause. 18 He will not suffer me to take my breath, but filleth me with bitterness. 19 If *I speak* of strength, lo, *he is* strong : and if of judgment, who shall set me a time *to plead ?* 20 If I justify myself, mine own mouth shall condemn me : *if I say,* I *am* perfect, it shall also prove me perverse. 21 *Though* I *were* perfect, *yet* would I not know my soul : I would despise my life.

What Job had said of man's utter inability to contend with God he here applies to himself, and in effect despairs of gaining his favour, which (some think) arises from the hard thoughts he had of God, as one who, having set himself against him, right or wrong, would be too hard for him. I rather think it arises from the sense he had of the imperfection of his own righteousness, and the dark and cloudy apprehensions which at present he had of God's displeasure against him.

I. He durst not dispute with God (*v.* 14) :

" *If the proud helpers do stoop under him, how much less shall I* (a poor weak creature, so far from being a helper that I am very helpless) *answer him ?* What can I say against that which God does ? If I go about to reason with him, he will certainly be too hard for me." If the potter make the clay into a vessel of dishonour, or break in pieces the vessel he has made, shall the clay or the broken vessel reason with him ? So absurd is the man who replies against God, or thinks to talk the matter out with him. No, let all flesh be silent before him.

II. He durst not insist upon his own justification before God. Though he vindicated his own integrity to his friends, and would not yield that he was a hypocrite and a wicked man, as they suggested, yet he would never plead it as his righteousness before God. " I will never venture upon the covenant of innocency, nor think to come off by virtue of that." Job knew so much of God, and knew so much of himself, that he durst not insist upon his own justification before God.

1. He knew so much of God that he durst not stand a trial with him, *v.* 15—19. He knew how to make his part good with his friends, and thought himself able to deal with them ; but, though his cause had been better than it was, he knew it was to no purpose to debate it with God. (1.) God knew him better than he knew himself and therefore (*v.* 15), " *Though I were righteous* in my own apprehension, and my own heart did not condemn me, *yet God is greater than my heart,* and knows those secret faults and errors of mine which I do not and cannot understand, and is able to charge me with them, and therefore *I would not answer.*" St. Paul speaks to the same purport : *I know nothing by myself,* am not conscious to myself of any reigning wickedness, and *yet I am not hereby justified,* 1 Cor. iv. 4. " I dare not put myself upon that issue, lest God should charge that upon me which I did not discover in myself." Job will therefore waive that plea, and *make supplication to his Judge,* that is, will cast himself upon God's mercy, and not think to come off by his own merit. (2.) He had no reason to think that there was any thing in his prayers to recommend them to the divine acceptance, or to fetch in an answer of peace, no worth or worthiness at all to which to ascribe their success, but it must be attributed purely to the grace and compassion of God, who answers before we call and not because we call, and gives gracious answers to our prayers, but not for our prayers (*v.* 16): " *If I had called, and he had answered,* had given the thing I called to him for, yet, so weak and defective are my best prayers, that *I would not believe he had* therein *hearkened to my voice ;* I could not say that he had *saved with his right hand and answered me*" (Ps. lx. 5), " but that he did it purely for his own name's sake." Bishop Patrick expounds it thus : " If I had made suppli-

cation, and he had granted my desire, I would not think my prayer had done the business.' *Not for your sakes, be it known to you.* (3.) His present miseries, which God had brought him into notwithstanding his integrity, gave him too sensible a conviction that, in the ordering and disposing of men's outward condition in this world, God acts by sovereignty, and, though he never does wrong to any, yet he does not ever give full right to all (that is, the best do not always fare best, nor the worst fare worst) in this life, because he reserves the full and exact distribution of rewards and punishments for the future state. Job was not conscious to himself of any extraordinary guilt, and yet fell under extraordinary afflictions, *v.* 17, 18. Every man must expect the wind to blow upon him and ruffle him, but Job was *broken with a tempest.* Every man, in the midst of these thorns and briers, must expect to be scratched; but Job was wounded, and his wounds were multiplied. Every man must expect a cross daily, and to taste sometimes of the bitter cup; but poor Job's troubles came so thickly upon him that he had no breathing time, and he was filled with bitterness. And he presumes to say that all this was *without cause,* without any great provocation given. We have made the best of what Job said hitherto, though contrary to the judgment of many good interpreters; but here, no doubt, *he spoke unadvisedly with his lips;* he reflected on God's goodness in saying that he was not suffered *to take his breath* (while yet he had such good use of his reason and speech as to be able to talk thus) and on his justice in saying that it was without cause. Yet it is true that as, on the one hand, there are many who are chargeable with more sin than the common infirmities of human nature, and yet feel no more sorrow than that of the common calamities of human life, so, on the other hand, there are many who feel more than the common calamities of human life and yet are conscious to themselves of no more than the common infirmities of human nature. (4.) He was in no capacity at all to make his part good with God, *v.* 19. [1.] Not by force of arms. "I dare not enter the lists with the Almighty; for *if I speak of strength,* and think to come off by that, *lo, he is strong,* stronger than I, and will certainly overpower me." There is no disputing (said one once to Cæsar) with him that commands legions. Much less is there any with him that has legions of angels at command. *Can thy heart endure* (thy courage and presence of mind) *or can thy hands be strong* to defend thyself, *in the days that I shall deal with thee?* Ezek. xxii. 14. [2.] Not by force of arguments. "I dare not try the merits of the cause. *If I speak of judgment,* and insist upon my right, *who will set me a time to plead?* There is no higher power to which I may appeal, no superior court to appoint a hearing of the cause; for he is supreme and from him proceeds every man's judgment, which he must abide by."

2. He knew so much of himself that he durst not stand a trial, *v.* 20, 21. "*If I go about to justify myself,* and to plead a righteousness of my own, my defence will be my offence, and *my own mouth shall condemn me* even when it goes about to acquit me." A good man, who knows the deceitfulness of his own heart, and is jealous over it with a godly jealousy, and has often discovered that amiss there which had long lain undiscovered, is suspicious of more evil in himself than he is really conscious of, and therefore will by no means think of justifying himself before God. *If we say we have no sin, we* not only *deceive ourselves,* but we affront God; for we sin in saying so, and give the lie to the scripture, which has *concluded all under sin.* "*If I say, I am perfect,* I am sinless, God has nothing to lay to my charge, my very saying so shall *prove me perverse,* proud, ignorant, and presumptuous. Nay, *though I were perfect,* though God should pronounce me just, *yet would I not know my soul,* I would not be in care about the prolonging of my life while it is loaded with all these miseries." Or, "Though I were free from gross sin, though my conscience should not charge me with any enormous crime, yet would I not believe my own heart so far as to insist upon my innocency nor think my life worth striving for with God." In short, it is folly to contend with God, and our wisdom, as well as duty, to submit to him and throw ourselves at his feet.

22 This *is* one *thing,* therefore I said *it,* He destroyeth the perfect and the wicked. 23 If the scourge slay suddenly, he will laugh at the trial of the innocent. 24 The earth is given into the hand of the wicked: he covereth the faces of the judges thereof; if not, where, *and* who *is* he?

Here Job touches briefly upon the main point now in dispute between him and his friends. They maintained that those who are righteous and good always prosper in this world, and none but the wicked are in misery and distress; he asserted, on the contrary, that it is a common thing for the wicked to prosper and the righteous to be greatly afflicted. This is the one thing, the chief thing, wherein he and his friends differed; and they had not proved their assertion, therefore he abides by his: "I said it, and say it again, that all things come alike to all." Now, 1. It must be owned that there is very much truth in what Job here means, that temporal judgments, when they are sent abroad, fall both upon good and bad, and the destroying angel seldom distinguishes (though once he did) between the houses of Israelites and the houses of Egyptians. In the judgment of Sodom indeed, which is called *the vengeance of eternal fire* (Jude 7), *far be it from* God *to slay the righteous with the wicked, and that the righteous should be as the wicked* (Gen. xviii. 25); but, in judgments merely temporal, the righteous have their share, and sometimes the greatest share. *The sword devours one as well as another,* Josiah as well as Ahab. Thus God *destroys the perfect and the wicked,* involves them both in the same common ruin; good and bad were sent together into Babylon, Jer. xxiv. 5, 9. *If the scourge slay suddenly,* and sweep down all before it, God will be well pleased to see how the same scourge which is the perdition of the wicked is the trial of the innocent and of their faith, which *will be found unto praise, and honour, and glory,* 1 Pet. i. 7; Ps. lxvi. 10.

> Against the just th' Almighty's arrows fly,
> For he delights the innocent to try,
> To show their constant and their Godlike mind,
> Not by afflictions broken, but refined.—Sir R. BLACKMORE.

Let this reconcile God's children to their troubles; they are but trials, designed for their honour and benefit, and, if God be pleased with them, let not them be displeased; if he *laugh at the trial of the innocent,* knowing how glorious the issue of it will be, at destruction and famine let them also laugh (*ch.* v. 22), and triumph over them, saying, *O death! where is thy sting?* On the other hand, the wicked are so far from being made the marks of God's judgments that *the earth is given into their hand,* v. 24 (they enjoy large possessions and great power, have what they will and do what they will), *into the hand of the wicked one* (in the original, the word is singular); the devil, that wicked one, is called *the god of this world,* and boasts that into his hands it is delivered, Luke iv. 6. Or *into the hand of a wicked man,* meaning (as bishop Patrick and the Assembly's Annotations conjecture) some noted tyrant then living in those parts, whose great wickedness and great prosperity were well known both to Job and his friends. The wicked have the earth given them, but the righteous have heaven given them, and which is better—heaven without earth or earth without heaven? God, in his providence, advances wicked men, while he *covers the faces of* those who are fit to be *judges,* who are wise and good, and qualified for government, and buries them alive in obscurity, perhaps suffers them to be run down and condemned, and to have their faces covered as criminals by those wicked ones into whose hand the earth is given. We daily see that this is done; *if* it be *not* God that does it, *where and who is he* that does it? To whom can it be ascribed but to him that rules in the kingdoms of men, and gives them to whom he will? Dan. iv. 32. Yet, 2. It must be owned that there is too much passion in what Job here says. The manner of expression is peevish. When he meant that God afflicts he ought not to have said, *He destroys both the perfect and the wicked;* when he

meant that God pleases himself with the trial of the innocent he ought not to have said, *He laughs at it,* for he doth not afflict willingly. When the spirit is heated, either with dispute or with discontent, we have need to set a watch before the door of our lips, that we may observe a due decorum in speaking of divine things.

25 Now my days are swifter than a post: they flee away, they see no good. 26 They are passed away as the swift ships: as the eagle *that* hasteth to the prey. 27 If I say, I will forget my complaint, I will leave off my heaviness, and comfort *myself:* 28 I am afraid of all my sorrows, I know that thou wilt not hold me innocent. 29 *If* I be wicked, why then labour I in vain? 30 If I wash myself with snow water, and make my hands never so clean; 31 Yet shalt thou plunge me in the ditch, and mine own clothes shall abhor me. 32 For *he is* not a man, as I *am, that* I should answer him, *and* we should come together in judgment. 33 Neither is there any daysman betwixt us, *that* might lay his hand upon us both. 34 Let him take his rod away from me, and let not his fear terrify me: 35 *Then* would I speak, and not fear him; but *it is* not so with me.

Job here grows more and more querulous, and does not conclude this chapter with such reverent expressions of God's wisdom and justice as he began with. Those that indulge a complaining humour know not to what indecencies, nay, to what impieties, it will hurry them. *The beginning of* that *strife* with God *is as the letting forth of water; therefore leave it off before it be meddled with.* When we are in trouble we are allowed to complain to God, as the Psalmist often, but must by no means complain of God, as Job here.

I. His complaint here of the passing away of the days of his prosperity is proper enough (*v.* 25, 26): " *My days* (that is, all my good days) are gone, never to return, gone of a sudden, gone ere I was aware. Never did any courier that went express" (like Cushi and Ahimaaz) " with good tidings make such haste as all my comforts did from me. Never did ship sail to its port, never did eagle fly upon its prey, with such incredible swiftness; nor does there remain any trace of my prosperity, any more than there does of an eagle in the air or a ship in the sea," Prov. xxx. 19. See here, 1. How swift the motion of time is. It is always upon the wing, hastening to its period; it stays for no man. What little need have we of pastimes, and what great need to redeem time, when time runs out, runs on so fast towards eternity, which comes as time goes! 2. How vain the enjoyments of time are, which we may be quite deprived of while yet time continues. Our day may be longer than the sun-shine of our prosperity; and, when that is gone, it is as if it had not been. The remembrance of having done our duty will be pleasing afterwards; so will not the remembrance of our having got a great deal of worldly wealth when it is all lost and gone. "*They flee away*, past recal; *they see no good,* and leave none behind them."

II. His complaint of his present uneasiness is excusable, v. 27, 28. 1. It should seem, he did his endeavour to quiet and compose himself as his friends advised him. That was the good he would do: he would fain *forget his complaints* and praise God, would *leave off his heaviness and comfort himself*, that he might be fit for converse both with God and man; but, 2. He found he could not do it: " *I am afraid of all my sorrows.* When I strive most against my trouble it prevails most over me and proves too hard for me!" It is easier, in such a case, to know what we should do than to do it, to know what temper we should be in than to get into that temper and keep in it. It is easy to preach patience to those that are in trouble, and to tell them they must forget their complaints and comfort themselves; but it is not so soon done as said. Fear and sorrow are tyrannizing things, not easily brought into the subjection they ought to be kept in to religion and right reason. But,

III. His complaint of God as implacable and inexorable was by no means to be excused. It was the language of his corruption. He knew better, and, at another time, would have been far from harbouring any such hard thoughts of God as now broke in upon his spirit and broke out in these passionate complaints. Good men do not always speak like themselves; but God, who considers their frame and the strength of their temptations, gives them leave afterwards to unsay what was amiss by repentance and will not lay it to their charge.

1. Job seems to speak here, (1.) As if he despaired of obtaining from God any relief or redress of his grievances, though he should produce ever so good proofs of his integrity: " *I know that thou wilt not hold me innocent.* My afflictions have continued so long upon me, and increased so fast, that I do not expect thou wilt ever clear up my innocency by delivering me out of them and restoring me to a prosperous condition. Right or wrong, I must be treated as a wicked man; my friends will continue to think so of me, and God will continue upon me the afflictions which give them occasion to think so. *Why then do I labour in vain to* clear myself and maintain my own integrity?"

v. 29. It is to no purpose to speak in a cause that is already prejudged. With men it is often labour in vain for the most innocent to go about to clear themselves; they must be adjudged guilty, though the evidence be ever so plain for them. But it is not so in our dealings with God, who is the patron of oppressed innocency and to whom it was never in vain to commit a righteous cause. Nay, he not only despairs of relief, but expects that his endeavour to clear himself will render him yet more obnoxious (*v.* 30, 31): " *If I wash myself with snow water,* and make my integrity ever so evident, it will be all to no purpose; judgment must go against me. *Thou shalt plunge me in the ditch*" (the pit of destruction, so some, or rather the filthy kennel, or sewer), which will make me so offensive in the nostrils of all about me that *my own clothes shall abhor me* and I shall even loathe to touch myself." He saw his afflictions coming from God. Those were the things that blackened him in the eye of his friends; and, upon that score, he complained of them, and of the continuance of them, as the ruin, not only of his comfort, but of his reputation. Yet these words are capable of a good construction. If we be ever so industrious to justify ourselves before men, and to preserve our credit with them,—if we keep our hands ever so clean from the pollutions of gross sin, which fall under the eye of the world,—yet God, who knows our hearts, can charge us with so much secret sin as will for ever take off all our pretensions to purity and innocency, and make us see ourselves odious in the sight of the holy God. Paul, while a Pharisee, made his hands very clean; but when the commandment came and discovered to him his heart-sins, made him know lust, that *plunged him in the ditch.* (2.) As if he despaired to have a fair hearing with God, and that were hard indeed. [1.] He complains that he was not upon even terms with God (*v.* 32): " *He is not a man, as I am.* I could venture to dispute with a man like myself (the potsherds may strive with the potsherds of the earth), but he is infinitely above me, and therefore I dare not enter the lists with him; I shall certainly be cast if I contend with him." Note, *First,* God is not a man as we are. Of the greatest princes we may say, "They are men as we are," but not of the great God. His thoughts and ways are infinitely above ours, and we must not measure him by ourselves. Man is foolish and weak, frail and fickle, but God is not. We are depending dying creatures; he is the independent and immortal Creator. *Secondly,* The consideration of this should keep us very humble and very silent before God. Let us not make ourselves equal with God, but always eye him as infinitely above us. [2.] That there was no arbitrator or umpire to adjust the differences between him and God and to determine the controversy (*v.* 33):

Neither is there any days-man between us. This complaint that there was not is in effect a wish that there were, and so the LXX. read it: *O that there were a mediator between us!* Job would gladly refer the matter, but no creature was capable of being a referee, and therefore he must even refer it still to God himself and resolve to acquiesce in his judgment. Our Lord Jesus is the blessed days-man, who has mediated between heaven and earth, has laid his hand upon us both; to him the Father has committed all judgment, and we must. But this matter was not then brought to so clear a light as it is now by the gospel, which leaves no room for such a complaint as this. [3.] That the terrors of God, which set themselves in array against him, put him into such confusion that he knew not how to address God with the confidence with which he was formerly wont to approach him, *v.* 34, 35. "Besides the distance which I am kept at by his infinite transcendency, his present dealings with me are very discouraging: *Let him take his rod away from me.*" He means not so much his outward afflictions as the load which lay upon his spirit from the apprehensions of God's wrath; that was *his fear* which *terrified him.* "Let that be removed; let me recover the sight of his mercy, and not be amazed with the sight of nothing but his terrors, and *then I would speak* and order my cause before him. *But it is not so with me;* the cloud is not at all dissipated; the wrath of God still fastens upon me, and preys on my spirits, as much as ever; and what to do I know not."

2. From all this let us take occasion, (1.) To stand in awe of God, and to fear the power of his wrath. If good men have been put into such consternation by it, *where shall the ungodly and the sinner appear?* (2.) To pity those that are wounded in spirit, and pray earnestly for them, because in that condition they know not how to pray for themselves. (3.) Carefully to keep up good thoughts of God in our minds, for hard thoughts of him are the inlets of much mischief. (4.) To bless God that we are not in such a disconsolate condition as poor Job was here in, but that we walk in the light of the Lord; let us rejoice therein, but *rejoice with trembling.*

CHAP. X

Job owns here that he was full of confusion (ver. 15), and as he was so was his discourse: he knew not what to say, and perhaps sometimes scarcely knew what he said. In this chapter, I. He complains of the hardships he was under (ver. 1—7), and then comforts himself with this, that he was in the hand of the God that made him, and pleads that, ver. 8—13. II. He complains again of the severity of God's dealings with him (ver. 14—17), and then comforts himself with this, that death would put an end to his troubles, ver. 18—22.

M Y soul is weary of my life; I will leave my complaint upon myself; I will speak in the bitterness of my soul. 2 I will say unto God, Do not condemn me; show me wherefore thou contendest with me. 3 *Is it* good unto thee that thou shouldest oppress, that thou shouldest despise the work of thine hands, and shine upon the counsel of the wicked? 4 Hast thou eyes of flesh? or seest thou as man seeth? 5 *Are* thy days as the days of man? *are* thy years as man's days, 6 That thou enquirest after mine iniquity, and searchest after my sin? 7 Thou knowest that I am not wicked; and *there is* none that can deliver out of thine hand.

Here is, I. A passionate resolution to persist in his complaint, *v.* 1. Being daunted with the dread of God's majesty, so that he could not plead his cause with him, he resolves to give himself some ease by giving vent to his resentments. He begins with vehement language: "*My soul is weary of my life,* weary of this body, and impatient to get clear of it, fallen out with life, and displeased at it, sick of it, and longing for death." Through the weakness of grace he went contrary to the dictates even of nature itself. We should act more like men did we act more like saints. Faith and patience would keep us from being weary of our lives (and *cruel to them,* as some read it), even when Providence has made them most wearisome to us; for that is to be weary of God's correction. Job, being weary of his life and having ease no other way, resolves to complain, resolves to speak. He will not give vent to his soul by violent hands, but he will give vent to the bitterness of his soul by violent words. Losers think they may have leave to speak; and unbridled passions, as well as unbridled appetites, are apt to think it an excuse for their excursions that they cannot help them: but what have we wisdom and grace for, but to keep the mouth as with a bridle? Job's corruption speaks here, yet grace puts in a word. 1. He will complain, but he will *leave his complaint upon himself.* He would not impeach God, nor charge him with unrighteousness or unkindness; but, though he knew not particularly the ground of God's controversy with him and the cause of action, yet, in the general, he would suppose it to be in himself and willingly bear all the blame. 2. He will speak, but it shall be the *bitterness of his soul* that he will express, not his settled judgment. If I speak amiss, it is *not I, but sin that dwells in me,* not my soul, but its bitterness.

II. A humble petition to God. He will speak, but the first word shall be a prayer, and, as I am willing to understand it, it is a good prayer, *v.* 2. 1. That he might be delivered from the sting of his afflictions, which is sin: "*Do not condemn me;* do not separate me for ever from thee. Though I lie under the cross, let me not lie under the curse; though I smart by the rod of a Father,

59

let me not be cut off by the sword of a Judge. Thou dost correct me; I will bear that as well as I can; but O do not condemn me!" It is the comfort of those who are in Christ Jesus that, though they are in affliction, there is *no condemnation to them*, Rom. viii. 1. Nay, they are *chastened of the Lord that they may not be condemned with the world*, 1 Cor. xi. 32. This therefore we should deprecate above any thing else, when we are in affliction. "However thou art pleased to deal with me, Lord, do not condemn me; my friends condemn me, but do not thou." 2. That he might be made acquainted with the true cause of his afflictions, and that is sin too : Lord, *show me wherefore thou contendest with me.* When God afflicts us he contends with us, and when he contends with us there is always a reason. He is never angry without a cause, though we are; and it is desirable to know what the reason is, that we may repent of, mortify, and forsake the sin for which God has a controversy with us. In enquiring it out, let conscience have leave to do its office and to deal faithfully with us, as Gen. xlii. 21.

III. A peevish expostulation with God concerning his dealings with him. Now he speaks in the bitterness of his soul indeed, not without some ill-natured reflections upon the righteousness of his God.

1. He thinks it unbecoming the goodness of God, and the mercifulness of his nature, to deal so hardly with his creature as to lay upon him more than he can bear (v. 3): *Is it good unto thee that thou shouldst oppress?* No, certainly it is not; what he approves not in men (Lam. iii. 34—36) he will not do himself. Lord, in dealing with me, thou seemest to oppress thy subject, to despise thy workmanship, and to countenance thy enemies. Now, Lord, what is the meaning of this? Such is thy nature that this cannot be a pleasure to thee; and such is thy name that it cannot be an honour to thee. Why then dealest thou thus with me? *What profit is there in my blood?*" Far be it from Job to think that God did him wrong, but he is quite at a loss how to reconcile his providences with his justice, as good men have often been, and must wait until the day shall declare it. Let us therefore now harbour no hard thoughts of God, because we shall then see there was no cause for them.

2. He thinks it unbecoming the infinite knowledge of God to put his prisoner thus upon the rack, as it were, by torture, to extort a confession from him, v. 4—6. (1.) He is sure that God does not discover things, nor judge of them, as men do: He has not *eyes of flesh* (v. 4), for he is a Spirit. Eyes of flesh cannot see in the dark, but darkness hides not from God. Eyes of flesh are but in one place at a time, and can see but a little way; but the *eyes of the Lord are in every place*, and *run to and fro through the whole earth.* Many things are hidden from eyes of flesh, the most curious and piercing; there

is a path which even *the vulture's eye has not seen:* but nothing is, or can be, hidden from the eye of God, to which all things are naked and open. Eyes of flesh see the outward appearance only, and may be imposed upon by a *deceptio visûs—an illusion of the senses;* but God sees every thing truly. His sight cannot be deceived, for he tries the heart, and is a witness to the thoughts and intents of that. Eyes of flesh discover things gradually, and, when we gain the sight of one thing, we lose the sight of another; but God sees every thing at one view. Eyes of flesh are soon tired, must be closed every night that they may be refreshed, and will shortly be darkened by age and shut up by death; but the keeper of Israel neither slumbers nor sleeps, nor does his sight ever decay. *God sees not as man sees,* that is, he does not judge as man judges, at the best *secundum allegata et probata—according to what is alleged and proved,* as the thing appears rather than as it is, and too often according to the bias of the affections, passions, prejudices, and interest; *but we are sure that the judgment of God is according to truth,* and that he knows truth, not by information, but by his own inspection. Men discover secret things by search, and examination of witnesses, comparing evidence and giving conjectures upon it, wheedling or forcing the parties concerned to confess; but God needs not any of these ways of discovery : *he sees not as man sees.* (2.) He is sure that as God is not short-sighted, like man, so he is not short-lived (v. 5): " *Are thy days as the days of man,* few and evil? Do they roll on in succession, or are they subject to change, like the days of man? No, by no means." Men grow wiser by experience and more knowing by daily observation; with them truth is the daughter of time, and therefore they must take time for their searches, and, if one experiment fail, must try another. But it is not so with God; to him nothing is past, nothing future, but every thing present. The days of time, by which the life of man is measured, are nothing to the years of eternity, in which the life of God is wrapped up. (3.) He therefore thinks it strange that God should thus prolong his torture, and continue him under the confinement of this affliction, and neither bring him to a trial nor grant him a release, as if he must take time to *enquire after his iniquity* and use means to *search after his sin,* v. 6. Not as if Job thought that God did thus torment him that he might find occasion against him; but his dealings with him had such an aspect, which was dishonourable to God, and would tempt men to think him a hard master. " Now, Lord, if thou wilt not consult my comfort, consult thy own honour; do something *for thy great name,* and *do not disgrace the throne of thy glory,*" Jer. xiv. 21.

3. He thinks it looked like an abuse of his omnipotence to keep a poor prisoner in custody, whom he knew to be innocent, only

because there was none that could deliver him out of his hand (*v.* 7): *Thou knowest that I am not wicked.* He had already owned himself a sinner, and guilty before God; but he here stands to it that he was not wicked, not devoted to sin, not an enemy to God, not a dissembler in his religion, that *he had not wickedly departed from his God,* Ps. xviii. 21. "*But there is none that can deliver out of thy hand,* and therefore there is no remedy; I must be content to lie there, waiting thy time, and throwing myself on thy mercy, in submission to thy sovereign will." Here see, (1.) What ought to quiet us under our troubles—that it is to no purpose to contend with Omnipotence. (2.) What will abundantly comfort us—if we are able to appeal to God, as Job here, " Lord, *thou knowest that I am not wicked.* I cannot say that I am not wanting, or I am not weak; but, through grace, I can say, *I am not wicked:* thou knowest I am not, for *thou knowest I love thee.*"

8 Thine hands have made me and fashioned me together round about; yet thou dost destroy me. 9 Remember, I beseech thee, that thou hast made me as the clay; and wilt thou bring me into dust again? 10 Hast thou not poured me out as milk, and curdled me like cheese? 11 Thou hast clothed me with skin and flesh, and hast fenced me with bones and sinews. 12 Thou hast granted me life and favour, and thy visitation hath preserved my spirit. 13 And these *things* hast thou hid in thine heart: I know that this *is* with thee.

In these verses we may observe,

I. How Job eyes God as his Creator and preserver, and describes his dependence upon him as the author and upholder of his being. This is one of the first things we are all concerned to know and consider.

1. That God made us, he, and not our parents, who were only the instruments of his power and providence in our production. *He made us, and not we ourselves. His hands have made and fashioned* these bodies of ours and every part of them (*v.* 8), and they are *fearfully and wonderfully made.* The soul also, which animates the body, is his gift. Job takes notice of both here. (1.) The body is *made as the clay* (*v.* 9), cast into shape, into this shape, as the clay is formed into a vessel, according to the skill and will of the potter. We are earthen vessels, mean in our original, and soon broken in pieces, made *as the clay.* Let not therefore *the thing formed say unto him that formed it, Why hast thou made me thus?* We must not be proud of our bodies, because the matter is from the earth, yet not dishonour our bodies, because the mould and shape are from the divine

wisdom. The formation of human bodies in the womb is described by an elegant similitude (*v.* 10, *Thou hast poured me out like milk, which is coagulated into cheese*), and by an induction of some particulars, *v.* 11. Though we come into the world naked, yet the body is itself both clothed and armed. The skin and flesh are its clothing; the bones and sinews are its armour, not offensive, but defensive. The vital parts, the heart and lungs, are thus clothed, not to be seen—thus fenced, not to be hurt. The admirable structure of human bodies is an illustrious instance of the wisdom, power, and goodness of the Creator. What a pity is it that these bodies should be instruments of unrighteousness which are capable of being temples of the Holy Ghost! (2.) The soul is the life, the soul is the man, and this is the gift of God: *Thou hast granted me life,* breathed into me the breath of life, without which the body would be but a worthless carcase. God is the Father of spirits: he made us living souls, and endued us with the powers of reason; he gave us *life and favour,* and life is a favour —a great favour, more than meat, more than raiment—a distinguishing favour, a favour that puts us into a capacity of receiving other favours. Now Job was in a better mind than he was when he quarrelled with life as a burden, and asked, *Why died I not from the womb?* Or by life and favour may be meant life and all the comforts of life, referring to his former prosperity. Time was when he walked in the light of the divine favour, and thought, as David, that through that favour his mountain stood strong.

2. That God maintains us. Having lighted the lamp of life, he does not leave it to burn upon its own stock, but continually supplies it with fresh oil: " *Thy visitation has preserved my spirit,* kept me alive, protected me from the adversaries of life, the death we are in the midst of and the dangers we are continually exposed to, and blessed me with all the necessary supports of life and the daily supplies it needs and craves."

II. How he pleads this with God, and what use he makes of it. He reminds God of it (*v.* 9): *Remember, I beseech thee, that thou hast made me.* What then? Why, 1. "Thou hast made me, and therefore thou hast a perfect knowledge of me (Ps cxxxix. 1 —13), and needest not to examine me by scourging, nor to put me upon the rack for the discovery of what is within me." 2. "Thou hast made me, as the clay, by an act of sovereignty; and wilt thou by a like act of sovereignty unmake me again? If so, I must submit." 3. "Wilt thou destroy the work of thy own hands?" It is a plea the saints have often used in prayer, *We are the clay and thou our potter,* Isa. lxiv. 8. *Thy hands have made me and fashioned me,* Ps. cxix. 73. So here, *Thou madest me;* and wilt thou destroy me (*v.* 8), *wilt thou bring me into dust again? v.* 9. " Wilt thou not pity me? Wilt thou not spare and help me, and stand by *the work of thy own hands?* Ps. cxxxviii. 8. Thou madest me, and knowest my strength; wilt thou then suffer me to be pressed above measure? Was I made to be made miserable? Was I preserved only to be reserved for these calamities?" If we plead this with ourselves as an inducement to duty, "God made me and maintains me, and therefore I will serve him and submit to him," we may plead it with God as an argument for mercy: *Thou hast made me,* new-make me; *I am thine, save me.* Job knew not how to reconcile God's former favours and his present frowns, but concludes (*v.* 13), " *These things hast thou hidden in thy heart.* Both are according to the counsel of thy own will, and therefore undoubtedly consistent, however they seem." When God thus strangely changes his way, though we cannot account for it, we are bound to believe there are good reasons for it hidden in his heart, which will be manifested shortly. It is not with us, or in our reach, to assign the cause, but I *know that this is with thee.* Known unto God are all his works.

14 If I sin, then thou markest me, and thou wilt not acquit me from mine iniquity. 15 If I be wicked, woe unto me; and *if* I be righteous, *yet* will I not lift up my head. *I am* full of confusion; therefore see thou mine affliction; 16 For it increaseth. Thou huntest me as a fierce lion: and again thou showest thyself marvellous upon me. 17 Thou renewest thy witnesses against me, and increasest thine indignation upon me; changes and war *are* against me. 18 Wherefore then hast thou brought me forth out of the womb? Oh that I had given up the ghost, and no eye had seen me! 19 I should have been as though I had not been; I should have been carried from the womb to the grave. 20 *Are* not my days few? cease *then, and* let me alone, that I may take comfort a little, 21 Before I go *whence* I shall not return, *even* to the land of darkness and the shadow of death; 22 A land of darkness, as darkness *itself; and* of the shadow of death, without any order, and *where* the light *is* as darkness.

Here we have,

I. Job's passionate complaints. On this harsh and unpleasant string he harps much, in which, though he cannot be justified, he may be excused. He complained not for nothing, as the murmuring Israelites, but

had cause to complain. If we think it looks ill in him, let it be a warning to us to keep our temper better.

1. He complains of the strictness of God's judgment and the rigour of his proceedings against him, and is ready to call it *summum jus—justice bordering on severity.* (1.) That he took all advantages against him: " *If I sin, then thou markest me, v.* 14. If I do but take one false step, misplace a word, or cast a look awry, I shall be sure to hear of it. Conscience, thy deputy, will be sure to upbraid me with it, and to tell me that this gripe, this twitch of pain, is to punish me for that." If God should thus mark iniquities, we should be undone; but we must acknowledge the contrary, that, though we sin, God does not deal in extremity with us. (2.) That he prosecuted those advantages to the utmost: *Thou wilt not acquit me from my iniquity.* While his troubles continued he could not take the comfort of his pardon, nor hear that voice of joy and gladness; so hard is it to see love in God's heart when we see frowns in his face and a rod in his hand. (3.) That, whatever was his character, his case at present was very uncomfortable, *v.* 15. [1.] If he be wicked, he is certainly undone in the other world: *If I be wicked, woe to me.* Note, A sinful state is a woeful state. This we should each of us believe, as Job here, with application to ourselves: " *If I be wicked,* though prosperous and living in pleasure, yet woe to me." Some especially have reason to dread double woes if they be wicked. "I that have knowledge, that have made a great profession of religion, that have been so often under strong convictions, and have made so many fair promises—I that was born of such good parents, blessed with a good education, that have lived in good families, and long enjoyed the means of grace —*if I be wicked,* woe, and a thousand woes, to me." [2.] If he be *righteous,* yet he dares not *lift up his head,* dares not answer as before, *ch.* ix. 15. He is so oppressed and overwhelmed with his troubles that he cannot look up with any comfort or confidence. Without were fightings, within were fears; so that, between both, he was full of confusion, not only confusion of face for the disgrace he was brought down to and the censures of his friends, but confusion of spirit; his mind was in a constant hurry, and he was almost distracted, Ps. lxxxviii. 15.

2. He complains of the severity of the execution. God (he thought) did not only punish him for every failure, but punish him in a high degree, *v.* 16, 17. His affliction was, (1.) Grievous, very grievous, marvellous, exceedingly marvellous. God *hunted him* as a lion, *as a fierce lion* hunts and runs down his prey. God was not only strange to him, but *showed himself marvellous upon him,* by bringing him into uncommon troubles and so making him a prodigy, a wonder unto many. All wondered that God would inflict

and that Job could bear so much. That which made his afflictions most grievous was that he felt God's *indignation* in them; it was this that made them taste so bitter and lie so heavy. They were God's *witnesses* against him, tokens of his displeasure; this made the sores of his body wounds in his spirit. (2.) It was growing, still growing worse and worse. This he insists much upon; when he hoped the tide would turn, and begin to ebb, still it flowed higher and higher. His affliction increased, and God's indignation in the affliction. He found himself no better, no way better. These witnesses were renewed against him, that, if one did not reach to convict him, another might. *Changes and war* were against him. If there was any change with him, it was not for the better; still he was kept in a state of war. As long as we are here in this world we must expect that the clouds will return after the rain, and perhaps the sorest and sharpest trials may be reserved for the last. God was at war with him, and it was a great change. He did not use to be so, which aggravated the trouble and made it truly marvellous. God usually shows himself kind to his people; if at any time he shows himself otherwise, it is *his strange work, his strange act,* and he does in it show himself marvellous.

3. He complains of his life, and that ever he was born to all this trouble and misery (*v.* 18, 19): " If this was designed for my lot, *why was I brought out of the womb,* and not smothered there, or stifled in the birth ?" This was the language of his passion, and it was a relapse into the same sin he fell into before. He had just now called life a *favour* (*v.* 12), yet now he calls it a *burden,* and quarrels with God for giving it, or rather laying it upon him. Mr. Caryl gives this a good turn in favour of Job. " We may charitably suppose," says he, " that that which troubled Job was that he was in a condition of life which (as he conceived) hindered the main end of his life, which was the glorifying of God. His harp was hung on the willow-trees, and he was quite out of tune for praising God. Nay, he feared lest his troubles should reflect dishonour upon God and give occasion to his enemies to blaspheme; and therefore he wishes, *O that I had given up the ghost !* A godly man reckons that he lives to no purpose if he do not live to the praise and glory of God." If that was his meaning, it was grounded on a mistake; for we may *glorify the Lord in the fires.* But this use we may make of it, not to be over-fond of life, since the case has been such sometimes, even with wise and good men, that they have complained of it. Why should we dread giving up the ghost, or covet to be seen of men, since the time may come when we may be ready to wish we had given up the ghost and no eye had seen us ? Why should we inordinately lament the death of our children in their infancy, that *are as if they had not been,*

and are *carried from the womb to the grave,* when perhaps we ourselves may sometimes wish it had been our own lot ?

II. Job's humble requests. ·He prays, 1. That God would *see his affliction* (*v* 15), take cognizance of his case, and take it into his compassionate consideration. Thus David prays (Ps. xxv. 18), *Look upon my affliction and my pain.* Thus we should, in our troubles, refer ourselves to God, and may comfort ourselves with this, that he knows our souls in adversity. 2. That God would grant him some ease. If he could not prevail for the removal of his trouble, yet might he not have some intermission? " Lord, let me not be always upon the rack, always in extremity: *O let me alone, that I may take comfort a little !* *v.* 20. Grant me some respite, some breathing-time, some little enjoyment of myself." This he would reckon a great favour. Those that are not duly thankful for constant ease should think how welcome one hour's ease would be if they were in constant pain. Two things he pleads :—(1.) That life and its light were very short: " *Are not my days few ? v.* 20. Yes, certainly they are, very few. Lord, let them not be all miserable, all in the extremity of misery. I have but a little time to live; let me have some comfort of life while it does last." This plea fastens on the goodness of God's nature, the consideration of which is very comfortable to an afflicted spirit. And, if we would use this as a plea with God for mercy (" *Are not my days few?* Lord, pity me "), we should use it as a plea with ourselves, to quicken us to duty : "*Are not my days few ?* Then it concerns me to redeem time, to improve opportunities, what my hand finds to do to do it with all my might, that I may be ready for the days of eternity, which shall be many." (2.) That death and its darkness were very near and would be very long (*v.* 21, 22): " Lord, give me some ease before I die," that is, " lest I die of my pain." Thus David pleads (Ps. xiii. 3), " *Lest I sleep the sleep of death,* and then it will be too late to expect relief; for *wilt thou show wonders to the dead ?*" Ps. lxxxviii. 10. " Let me have a little comfort before I die, that I may take leave of this world calmly, and not in such confusion as I am now in." Thus earnest should we be for grace, and thus should we plead, " Lord, renew me in the inward man; Lord, sanctify me before I die, for otherwise it will never be done." See how he speaks here of the state of the dead. [1.] It is a fixed state, whence we shall not return ever again to live such a life as we now live, *ch.* vii. 10. At death we must bid a final farewell to this world. The body must then be laid where it will lie long, and the soul adjudged to that state in which it must be for ever. That had need be well done which is to be done but once, and done for eternity. [2.] It is a very melancholy state ; so it appears to us. Holy souls, at death, remove to a land of light, where there is no death; but their bodies they leave to a *land of darkness and the shadow of death.* He heaps up expressions here of the same import to show that he has as dreadful apprehensions of death and the grave as other men naturally have, so that it was only the extreme misery he was in that made him wish for it. Come and let us look a little into the grave, and we shall find, *First,* That there is no order there: it is *without any order,* perpetual night, and no succession of day. All there lie on the same level, and there is no distinction between prince and peasant, but *the servant is there free from his master, ch.* iii. 19. No order is observed in bringing people to the grave, not the eldest first, not the richest, not the poorest, and yet every one in his own order, the order appointed by the God of life. *Secondly,* That there is no light there. In the grave there is thick darkness, darkness that cannot be felt indeed, yet cannot but be feared by those that enjoy the light of life. In the grave there is no knowledge, no comfort, no joy, no praising God, no working out our salvation, and therefore no light. Job was so much ashamed that others should see his sores, and so much afraid to see them himself, that the darkness of the grave, which would hide them and huddle them up, would upon that account be welcome to him. Darkness comes upon us; and therefore let us walk and work while we have the light with us. The grave being a land of darkness, it is well we are carried thither with our eyes closed, and then it is all one. The grave is a land of darkness to man; our friends that have gone thither we reckon removed into darkness, Ps. lxxxviii. 18. But that it is not so to God will appear by this, that the dust of the bodies of the saints, though scattered, though mingled with other dust, will none of it be lost, for God's eye is upon every grain of it and it shall be forth-coming in the great day.

CHAP. XI.

Poor Job's wounds were yet bleeding, his sore still runs and ceases not, but none of his friends bring him any oil, any balm; Zophar, the third, pours into them as much vinegar as the two former had done. I. He exhibits a very high charge against Job, as proud and false in justifying himself, ver. 1—4. II. He appeals to God for his conviction, and begs that God would take him to task (ver. 5) and that Job might be made sensible, 1. Of God's unerring wisdom and his inviolable justice, ver. 6. 2. Of his unsearchable perfections, ver. 7—9. 3. Of his incontestable sovereignty and uncontrollable power, ver. 10. 4. Of the cognizance he takes of the children of men, ver. 11, 12. III. He assures him that, upon his repentance and reformation (ver. 13, 14), God would restore him to his former prosperity and safety (ver. 15—19); but that, if he were wicked it was in vain to expect it, ver. 20.

THEN answered Zophar the Naamathite, and said, 2 Should not the multitude of words be answered? and should a man full of talk be justified? 3 Should thy lies make men hold their peace? and when thou mockest, shall no man make thee ashamed? 4 For thou hast said, My doctrine *is.* pure, and I am clean in thine eyes. 5 But oh that God would

speak, and open his lips against thee; 6 And that he would show thee the secrets of wisdom, that *they are* double to that which is! Know therefore that God exacteth of thee *less* than thine iniquity *deserveth.*

It is sad to see what intemperate passions even wise and good men are sometimes betrayed into by the heat of disputation, of which Zophar here is an instance. Eliphaz began with a very modest preface, *ch.* iv. 2. Bildad was a little more rough upon Job, *ch.* viii. 2. But Zophar falls upon him without mercy, and gives him very bad language: *Should a man full of talk be justified? And should thy lies make men hold their peace?* Is this the way to comfort Job? No, nor to convince him neither. Does this become one that appears as an advocate for God and his justice? *Tantæne animis cœlestibus iræ?—In heavenly breasts can such resentment dwell?* Those that engage in controversy will find it very hard to keep their temper. All the wisdom, caution, and resolution they have will be little enough to prevent their breaking out into such indecencies as we here find Zophar guilty of.

I. He represents Job otherwise than what he was, *v.* 2, 3. He would have him thought idle and impertinent in his discourse, and one that loved to hear himself talk; he gives him the lie, and calls him *a mocker;* and all this that it might be looked upon as a piece of justice to chastise him. Those that have a mind to fall out with their brethren, and to fall foul upon them, find it necessary to put the worst colours they can upon them and their performances, and, right or wrong, to make them odious. We have read and considered Job's discourses in the foregoing chapters, and have found them full of good sense and much to the purpose, that his principles are right, his reasonings strong, many of his expressions weighty and very considerable, and that what there is in them of heat and passion a little candour and charity will excuse and overlook; and yet Zophar here invidiously represents him, 1. As a man that never considered what he said, but uttered what came uppermost, only to make a noise with the multitude of words, hoping by that means to carry his cause and run down his reprovers: *Should not the multitude of words be answered?* Truly, sometimes it is no great matter whether it be or no; silence perhaps is the best confutation of impertinence and puts the greatest contempt upon it. *Answer not a fool according to his folly.* But, if it be answered, let reason and grace have the answering of it, not pride and passion. *Should a man full of talk* (margin, *a man of lips,* that is all tongue, *vox et præterea nihil—mere voice) be justified?* Should he be justified in his loquacity, as in effect he is if he be not reproved for it? No, for *in the mul-*

titude of words there wanteth not sin. Should he be justified by it? Shall many words pass for valid pleas? Shall he carry the day with the flourishes of language? No, he shall not be accepted with God, or any wise men, *for his much speaking,* Matt. vi. 7. 2. As a man that made no conscience of what he said—a liar, and one that hoped by the impudence of lies to silence his adversaries *(should thy lies make men hold their peace?)*—a mocker, one that bantered all mankind, and knew how to put false colours upon any thing, and was not ashamed to impose upon every one that talked with him : *When thou mockest shall no man make thee ashamed?* Is it not time to speak, to stem such a violent tide as this? Job was not mad, but spoke the words of truth and soberness, and yet was thus misrepresented. Eliphaz and Bildad had answered him, and said what they could to make him ashamed; it was therefore no instance of Zophar's generosity to set upon a man so violently who was already thus harassed. Here were three matched against one.

II. He charges Job with saying that which he had not said (*v.* 4): *Thou hast said, My doctrine is pure.* And what if he had said so? It was true that Job was sound in the faith, and orthodox in his judgment, and spoke better of God than his friends did. If he had expressed himself unwarily, yet it did not therefore follow but that his doctrine was true. But he charges him with saying, *I am clean in thy eyes.* Job had not said so : he had indeed said, *Thou knowest that I am not wicked* (*ch.* x. 7); but he had also said, *I have sinned,* and never pretended to a spotless perfection. He had indeed maintained that he was not a hypocrite as they charged him; but to infer thence that he would not own himself a sinner was an unfair insinuation. We ought to put the best construction on the words and actions of our brethren that they will bear; but contenders are tempted to put the worst.

III. He appeals to God, and wishes him to appear against Job. So very confident is he that Job is in the wrong that nothing will serve him but that God must immediately appear to silence and condemn him. We are commonly ready with too much assurance to interest God in our quarrels, and to conclude that, if he would but speak, he would take our part and speak for us, as Zophar here : *O that God would speak!* for he would certainly *open his lips against thee;* whereas, when God did speak, he opened his lips for Job against his three friends. We ought indeed to leave all controversies to be determined by the judgment of God, which we are sure *is according to truth;* but those are not always in the right who are most forward to appeal to that judgment and prejudge it against their antagonists. Zophar despairs to convince Job himself, and therefore desires God would convince him of two things which it is good for every one of us duly to

consider, and under all our afflictions cheerfully to confess :—

1. The unsearchable depth of God's counsels. Zophar cannot pretend to do it, but he desires that God himself would show Job so much of the secrets of the divine wisdom as might convince him *that they are* at least *double to that which is, v.* 6. Note, (1.) There are secrets in the divine wisdom, *arcana imperii—state-secrets.* God's way is in the sea. Clouds and darkness are round about him. He has reasons of state which we cannot fathom and must not pry into. (2.) What we know of God is nothing to what we cannot know. What is hidden is more than double to what appears, Eph. iii. 9. (3.) By employing ourselves in adoring the depth of those divine counsels of which we cannot find the bottom we shall very much tranquilize our minds under the afflicting hand of God. (4.) God knows a great deal more evil of us than we do of ourselves; so some understand it. When God gave David a sight and sense of sin he said that he had *in the hidden part made him to know wisdom,* Ps. li. 6.

2. The unexceptionable justice of his proceedings. "Know therefore that, how sore soever the correction is that thou art under, *God exacteth of thee less than thy iniquity deserves,*" or (as some read it), "he *remits thee part of thy iniquity,* and does not deal with thee according to the full demerit of it." Note, (1.) When the debt of duty is not paid it is justice to insist upon the debt of punishment. (2.) Whatever punishment is inflicted upon us in this world we must own that it is less than our iniquities deserve, and therefore, instead of complaining of our troubles, we must be thankful that we are out of hell, Lam. iii. 39 ; Ps. ciii. 10.

7 Canst thou by searching find out God? canst thou find out the Almighty unto perfection? 8 *It is* as high as heaven; what canst thou do? deeper than hell; what canst thou know? 9 The measure thereof *is* longer than the earth, and broader than the sea. 10 If he cut off, and shut up, or gather together, then who can hinder him? 11 For he knoweth vain men : he seeth wickedness also; will he not then consider *it?* 12 For vain man would be wise, though man be born *like* a wild ass's colt.

Zophar here speaks very good things concerning God and his greatness and glory, concerning man and his vanity and folly : these two compared together, and duly considered, will have a powerful influence upon our submission to all the dispensations of the divine Providence.

I. See here what God is, and let him be adored.

1. He is an incomprehensible Being, infi-

nite and immense, whose nature and perfections our finite understandings cannot possibly form any adequate conceptions of, and whose counsels and actings we cannot therefore, without the greatest presumption, pass a judgment upon. We that are so little acquainted with the divine nature are incompetent judges of the divine providence; and, when we censure the dispensations of it, we talk of things that we do not understand. We cannot find out God; how dare we then find fault with him? Zophar here shows, (1.) That God's nature infinitely exceeds the capacities of our understandings: " *Canst thou find out God, find him out to perfection?* No, *What canst thou do? What canst thou know? v.* 7, 8. Thou, a poor, weak, shortsighted creature, a worm of the earth, that art but of yesterday? Thou, though ever so inquisitive after him, ever so desirous and industrious to find him out, yet darest thou attempt the search, or canst thou hope to speed in it? We may, by searching find God (Acts xvii. 27), but we cannot find him out in any thing he is pleased to conceal; we may apprehend him, but we cannot comprehend him; we may know that he is, but cannot know what he is. The eye can see the ocean but not see over it. We may, by a humble, diligent, and believing search, find out something of God, but cannôt find him out to perfection; we may know, but cannot know fully, what God is, nor find out his work *from the beginning to the end,* Eccl. iii. 11. Note, God is unsearchable. The ages of his eternity cannot be numbered, nor the spaces of his immensity measured; the depths of his wisdom cannot be fathomed, nor the reaches of his power bounded; the brightness of his glory can never be described, nor the treasures of his goodness reckoned up. This is a good reason why we should always speak of God with humility and caution and never prescribe to him nor quarrel with him, why we should be thankful for what he has revealed of himself and long to be where we shall see him as he is, 1 Cor. xiii. 9, 10. (2.) That it infinitely exceeds the limits of the whole creation: *It is higher than heaven* (so some read it), *deeper than hell,* the great abyss, *longer than the earth, and broader than the sea,* many parts of which are to this day undiscovered, and more were then. It is quite out of our reach to comprehend God's nature. *Such knowledge is too wonderful for us,* Ps. cxxxix. 6. We cannot fathom God's designs, nor find out the reasons of his proceedings. His judgments are a great deep. Paul attributes such immeasurable dimensions to the divine love as Zophar here attributes to the divine wisdom, and yet recommends it to our acquaintance. Eph. iii. 18, 19, *That you may know the breadth, and length, and depth, and height, of the love of Christ.*

2. God is a sovereign Lord (*v.* 10): *If he cut off* by death (margin, *If he make a change,* for death is a change; if he make a change in nations, in families, in the posture of our affairs),—if he *shut up* in prison, or in the net of affliction (Ps. lxvi. 11),—if he seize any creature as a hunter his prey, he will gather it (so bishop Patrick) and who shall force him to restore? or if he *gather together,* as tares for the fire, or *if he gather to himself man's spirit and breath* (ch. xxxiv. 14), *then who can hinder him?* Who can either arrest the sentence or oppose the execution? Who can control his power or arraign his wisdom and justice? If he that made all out of nothing think fit to reduce all to nothing, or to their first chaos again,—if he that separated between light and darkness, dry land and sea, at first, please to gather them together again,—if he that made unmakes, *who can turn him away,* alter his mind or stay his hand, impede or impeach his proceedings?

3. God is a strict and just observer of the children of men (*v.* 11): *He knows vain men.* We know little of him, but he knows us perfectly: *He sees wickedness also,* not to approve it (Hab. i. 13), but to animadvert upon it. (1.) He observes vain men. Such all are *(every man, at his best estate, is altogether vanity),* and he considers it in his dealings with them. He knows what the projects and hopes of vain men are, and can blast and defeat them, the workings of their foolish fancies; he sits in heaven, and laughs at them. He takes knowledge of the vanity of men (that is, their little sins; so some) their vain thoughts and vain words, and unsteadiness in that which is good. (2.) He observes bad men: *He sees* gross *wickedness also,* though committed ever so secretly and ever so artfully palliated and disguised. All the wickedness of the wicked is naked and open before the all-seeing eye of God: *Will he not then consider it?* Yes, certainly he will, and will reckon for it, though for a time he seem to keep silence.

II. See here what man is, and let him be humbled, *v.* 12. God sees this concerning vain man that he *would be wise,* would be thought so, *though he is born like a wild ass's colt,* so sottish and foolish, unteachable and untameable. See what man is. 1. He is a vain creature—*empty ;* so the word is. God made him full, but he emptied himself, impoverished himself, and now he is *raca,* a creature that has nothing in him. 2. He is a foolish creature, has become *like the beasts that perish* (Ps. xlix. 20, lxxiii. 22), an idiot, born like an ass, the most stupid animal, an ass's colt, not yet brought to any service. If ever he come to be good for any thing, it is owing to the grace of Christ, who once, in the day of his triumph, served himself by an ass's colt. 3. He is a wilful ungovernable creature. An ass's colt may be made good for something, but the wild ass's colt will never be reclaimed, nor regards the crying of the driver. See Job xxxix. 5—7.

Man thinks himself as much at liberty, and his own master, as the wild ass's colt does, that is *used to the wilderness* (Jer. ii. 24), eager to gratify his own appetites and passions. 4. Yet he is a proud creature and self-conceited. He *would be wise,* would be thought so, values himself upon the honour of wisdom, though he will not submit to the laws of wisdom. He would be wise, that is, he reaches after forbidden wisdom, and, like his first parents, aiming to be wise above what is written, loses the tree of life for the tree of knowledge. Now is such a creature as this fit to contend with God or call him to an account? Did we but better know God and ourselves, we should better know how to conduct ourselves towards God

13 If thou prepare thine heart, and stretch out thine hands toward him; 14 If iniquity *be* in thine hand, put it far away, and let not wickedness dwell in thy tabernacles. 15 For then shalt thou lift up thy face without spot; yea, thou shalt be stedfast, and shalt not fear: 16 Because thou shalt forget *thy* misery, *and* remember *it* as waters *that* pass away: 17 And *thine* age shall be clearer than the noonday; thou shalt shine forth, thou shalt be as the morning. 18 And thou shalt be secure, because there is hope; yea, thou shalt dig *about thee, and* thou shalt take thy rest in safety. 19 Also thou shalt lie down, and none shall make *thee* afraid; yea, many shall make suit unto thee. 20 But the eyes of the wicked shall fail, and they shall not escape, and their hope *shall be as* the giving up of the ghost.

Zophar, as the other two, here encourages Job to hope for better times if he would but come to a better temper.

I. He gives him good counsel (*v.* 13, 14), as Eliphaz did (*ch.* v. 8), and Bildad, *ch.* viii. 5. He would have him repent and return to God. Observe the steps of that return. 1. He must look within, and get his mind changed and the tree made good. He must *prepare his heart;* there the work of conversion and reformation must begin. The heart that wandered from God must be reduced—that was defiled with sin and put into disorder must be cleansed and put in order again—that was wavering and unfixed must be settled and established; so the word here signifies. The heart is then prepared to seek God when it is determined and fully resolved to make a business of it and to go through with it. 2. He must look up, and *stretch out his hands towards God,* that is, must stir up himself to take hold on God, must pray to him with earnestness and im-

portunity, striving in prayer, and with expectation to receive mercy and grace from him. To *give the hand to the Lord* signifies to yield ourselves to him and to covenant with him, 2 Chron. xxx. 8. This Job must do, and, for the doing of it, must prepare his heart. Job had prayed, but Zophar would have him to pray in a better manner, not as an appellant, but as a petitioner and humble suppliant. 3. He must amend what was amiss in his own conversation, else his prayers would be ineffectual (*v.* 14): "*If iniquity be in thy hand* (that is, if there be any sin which thou dost yet live in the practice of) *put it far away,* forsake it with detestation and a holy indignation, stedfastly resolving not to return to it, nor ever to have any thing more to do with it. Ezek. xviii. 31; Hos. xiv. 9; Isa. xxx. 22. If any of the gains of iniquity, any goods gotten by fraud or oppression, be in thy hand, make restitution thereof" (as Zaccheus, Luke xix. 8), "and *shake thy hands from holding* them," Isa. xxxiii. 15. The guilt of sin is not removed if the gain of sin be not restored. 4. He must do his utmost to reform his family too: "*Let not wickedness dwell in thy tabernacles;* let not thy house harbour or shelter any wicked persons, any wicked practices, or any wealth gotten by wickedness." He suspected that Job's great household had been ill-governed, and that, where there were many, there were many wicked, and the ruin of his family was the punishment of the wickedness of it; and therefore, if he expected God should return to him, he must reform what was amiss there, and, though wickedness might come into his tabernacles, he must not suffer it to dwell there, Ps. ci. 3, &c.

II. He assures him of comfort if he took this counsel, *v.* 15, &c. If he would repent and reform, he should, without doubt, be easy and happy, and all would be well. Perhaps Zophar might insinuate that, unless God did speedily make such a change as this in his condition, he and his friends would be confirmed in their opinion of him as a hypocrite and a dissembler with God. A great truth, however, is conveyed, That *the work of righteousness will be peace, and the effect of righteousness quietness and assurance for ever,* Isa. xxxii. 17. Those that sincerely turn to God may expect,

1. A holy confidence towards God: "*Then shalt thou lift up thy face towards heaven* without spot; thou mayest come boldly to the throne of grace, and not with that terror and amazement expressed," *ch.* ix. 34. If our hearts condemn us not for hypocrisy and impenitency, then have we confidence in our approaches to God and expectations from him, 1 John iii. 21. If we are looked upon in the face of the anointed, our faces, that were dejected, may be lifted up—that were polluted, being washed with the blood of Christ, may be lifted up without spot. We may *draw near in full assurance of faith* when

we are *sprinkled from an evil conscience,* Heb. x. 22. Some understand this of the clearing up of his credit before men, Ps. xxxvii. 6. If we make our peace with God, we may with cheerfulness look our friends in the face.

2. A holy composedness in themselves: *Thou shalt be stedfast, and shalt not fear, not be afraid of evil tidings,* thy heart being fixed, Ps. cxii. 7. Job was now full of confusion (*ch.* x. 15), while he looked upon God as his enemy and quarrelled with him; but Zophar assures him that, if he would submit and humble himself, his mind would be composed, and he would be freed from those frightful apprehensions he had of God, which put him into such an agitation. The less we are frightened the more we are fixed, and consequently the more fit we are for our services and for our sufferings.

3. A comfortable reflection upon their past troubles (*v.* 16): "*Thou shalt forget thy misery,* as the mother forgets her travailing pains, for joy that the child is born; thou shalt be perfectly freed from the impressions it makes upon thee, and *thou shalt remember it as waters that pass away,* or are poured out of a vessel, which leave no taste or tincture behind them, as other liquors do. The wounds of thy present affliction shall be perfectly healed, not only without a remaining scar, but without a remaining pain." Job had endeavoured to forget his complaint (*ch.* ix. 27), but found he could not; his soul *had still in remembrance the wormwood and the gall:* but here Zophar puts him in a way to forget it; let him by faith and prayer bring his griefs and cares to God, and leave them with him, and then he shall forget them. Where sin sits heavily affliction sits lightly. If we duly remember our sins, we shall, in comparison with them, forget our misery, much more if we obtain the comfort of a sealed pardon and a settled peace. He whose iniquity is forgiven shall *not say, I am sick,* but shall forget his sickness, Isa. xxxiii. 24.

4. A comfortable prospect of their future peace. This Zophar here thinks to please Job with, in answer to the many despairing expressions he had used, as if it were to no purpose for him to hope ever to see good days again in this world: "Yea, but thou mayest" (says Zophar) "and good nights too." A blessed change he here puts him in hopes of.

(1.) That though now his light was eclipsed it should shine out again, and more brightly than ever (*v.* 17),—that even his setting sun should out-shine his noon-day sun, and his evening be fair and clear as the morning, in respect both of honour and pleasure,—that his light should shine *out of obscurity* (Isa. lviii. 10), and the thick and dark cloud, from behind which his sun should break forth, would serve as a foil to its lustre,—that it should shine even in old age, and those evil days should be good days to him. Note, Those that truly turn to God then begin to

shine forth; their path is as the shining light which increases, the period of their day will be the perfection of it, and their evening to this world will be their morning to a better.

(2.) That, though now he was in a continual fear and terror, he should live in a holy rest and security, and find himself continually safe and easy (*v.* 18): *Thou shalt be secure, because there is hope.* Note, Those who have a good hope, through grace, in God, and of heaven, are certainly safe, and have reason to be secure, how difficult soever the times are through which they pass in this world. He that walks uprightly may thus walk surely, because, though there are trouble and danger, yet there is hope that all will be well at last. Hope is *an anchor of the soul,* Heb. vi. 19. "*Thou shalt dig about thee,*" that is, "Thou shalt be as safe as an army in its intrenchments." Those that submit to God's government shall be taken under his protection, and then they are safe both day and night. [1.] By day, when they employ themselves abroad: "*Thou shalt dig in safety,* thou and thy servants for thee, and not be again set upon by the plunderers, who fell upon thy servants at plough," *ch.* i. 14, 15. It is no part of the promised prosperity that he should live in idleness, but that he should have a calling and follow it, and, when he was about the business of it, should be under the divine protection. Thou shalt dig and be safe, not rob and be safe, revel and be safe. The way of duty is the way of safety. [2.] By night, when they repose themselves at home: *Thou shalt take thy rest* (and *the sleep of the labouring man is sweet*) *in safety,* notwithstanding the dangers of the darkness. The pillar of cloud by day shall be a pillar of fire by night: "*Thou shalt lie down* (*v.* 19), not forced to wander where there is no place to lay thy head on, nor forced to watch and sit up in expectation of assaults; but thou shalt go to bed at bedtime, and not only shall none hurt thee, but none shall make thee afraid nor so much as give thee an alarm." Note, It is a great mercy to have quiet nights and undisturbed sleeps; those say so that are within the hearing of the noise of war. And the way to be quiet is to seek unto God and keep ourselves in his love. Nothing needs make those afraid who *return to God as their rest* and take him for their habitation.

(3.) That, though now he was slighted, yet he should be courted: "*Many shall make suit to thee,* and think it their interest to secure thy friendship." Suit is made to those that are eminently wise or reputed to be so, that are very rich or in power. Zophar knew Job so well that he foresaw that, how low soever this present ebb was, if once the tide turned, it would flow as high as ever; and he would be again the darling of his country. Those that rightly make suit to God will probably see the day when others will make suit to them, as the foolish virgins to the wise, *Give us of your oil.*

III. Zophar concludes with a brief account of the doom of wicked people (*v.* 20): *But the eyes of the wicked shall fail.* It should seem, he suspected that Job would not take his counsel, and here tells him what would then come of it, setting death as well as life before him. See what will become of those who persist in their wickedness, and will not be reformed. 1. They shall not reach the good they flatter themselves with the hopes of in this world and in the other. Disappointments will be their doom, their shame, their endless torment. Their eyes shall fail with expecting that which will never come. *When a wicked man dies his expectation perishes,* Prov. xi. 7. *Their hope shall be as a puff of breath* (margin), vanished and gone past recal. Or their hope will perish and expire as a man does when he gives up the ghost; it will fail them when they have most need of it and when they expected the accomplishment of it; it will die away, and leave them in utter confusion. 2. They shall not avoid the evil which sometimes they frighten themselves with the apprehensions of. They shall not escape the execution of the sentence passed upon them, can neither out-brave it nor outrun it. Those that will not fly to God will find it in vain to think of flying from him.

CHAP. XII.

In this and the two following chapters we have Job's answer to Zophar's discourse, in which, as before, he first reasons with his friends (see ch. xiii. 19) and then turns to his God, and directs his expostulations to him, from thence to the end of his discourse. In this chapter he addresses himself to his friends, and, I. He condemns what they had said of him, and the judgment they had given of his character, ver. 1—5. II. He contradicts and confronts what they had said of the destruction of wicked people in this world, showing that they often prosper, ver. 6—11. III. He consents to what they had said of the wisdom, power, and sovereignty of God, and the dominion of his providence over the children of men and all their affairs; he confirms this, and enlarges upon it, ver. 12—25.

AND Job answered and said, 2 No doubt but ye *are* the people, and wisdom shall die with you. 3 But I have understanding as well as you; I *am* not inferior to you: yea, who knoweth not such things as these? 4 I am *as* one mocked of his neighbour, who calleth upon God, and he answereth him: the just upright *man is* laughed to scorn. 5 He that is ready to slip with *his* feet *is as* a lamp despised in the thought of him that is at ease.

The reproofs Job here gives to his friends, whether they were just or no, were very sharp, and may serve for a rebuke to all that are proud and scornful, and an exposure of their folly.

I. He upbraids them with their conceitedness of themselves, and the good opinion they seemed to have of their own wisdom in comparison with him, than which nothing is more weak and unbecoming, nor better deserves to be ridiculed, as it is here. 1. He represents them as claiming the monopoly of wisdom, *v.* 2. He speaks ironically: " *No doubt you are the people;* you think yourselves fit to dictate and give law to all mankind, and your own judgment to be the standard by which every man's opinion must be measured and tried, as if nobody could discern between truth and falsehood, good and evil, but you only; and therefore every top-sail must lower to you, and, right or wrong, we must all say as you say, and you three must be the people, the majority, to have the casting vote." Note, It is a very foolish and sinful thing for any to think themselves wiser than all mankind besides, or to speak and act confidently and imperiously, as if they thought so. Nay, he goes further : " You not only think there are none, but that there will be none, as wise as you, and therefore that *wisdom must die with you,* that all the world must be fools when you are gone, and in the dark when your sun has set." Note, It is folly for us to think that there will be any great irreparable loss of us when we are gone, or that we can be ill spared, since God has the residue of the Spirit, and can raise up others, more fit than we are, to do his work. When wise men and good men die it is a comfort to think that wisdom and goodness shall not die with them. Some think Job here reflects upon Zophar's comparing him (as he thought) and others to the wild ass's colt, *ch.* xi. 12. "Yes," says he, " we must be asses; you are the only men." 2. He does himself the justice to put in his claim as a sharer in the gifts of wisdom (*v.* 3): " *But I have understanding (a heart) as well as you;* nay, *I fall not lower than you ;*" as it is in the margin. "I am as well able to judge of the methods and meanings of the divine providence, and to construe the hard chapters of it, as you are." He says not this to magnify himself. It was no great applause of himself to say, *I have understanding as well as you ;* no, nor to say, " I understand this matter as well as you ;" for what reason had either he or they to be proud of understanding that which was obvious and level to the capacity of the meanest? " *Yea, who knows not such things as these ?* What things you have said that are true are plain truths, and common themes, which there are many that can talk as excellently of as either you or I" But he says it to humble them, and check the value they had for themselves as doctors of the chair. Note, (1.) It may justly keep us from being proud of our knowledge to consider how many there are that know as much as we do, and perhaps much more and to better purpose. (2.) When we are tempted to be harsh in our censures of those we differ from and dispute with we ought to consider that they also have understanding as well as we, a capacity of judging, and a right of judging for themselves; nay, perhaps they are not inferior to us, but superior, and it is possible that they may be in the right and we in the wrong; and therefore we ought not to judge or despise them (Rom. xiv. 3), nor pretend to be masters (Jam. iii. 1), while *all we are brethren*, Matt. xxiii. 8. It is a very reasonable allowance to be made to all we converse with, all we contend with, that they are rational creatures as well as we.

II. He complains of the great contempt with which they had treated him. Those that are haughty and think too well of themselves are commonly scornful and ready to trample upon all about them. Job found it so, at least he thought he did (*v.* 4): *I am as one mocked.* I cannot say there was cause for this charge; we will not think Job's friends designed him any abuse, nor aimed at any thing but to convince him, and so, in the right method, to comfort him; yet he cries out, *I am as one mocked.* Note, We are apt to call reproofs reproaches, and to think ourselves mocked when we are but advised and admonished; this peevishness is our folly, and a great wrong to ourselves and to our friends. Yet we cannot but say there was colour for this charge; they came to comfort him, but they vexed him, gave him counsels and encouragements, but with no great opinion that either the one or the other would take effect; and therefore he thought they mocked him, and this added much to his grief. Nothing is more grievous to those that have fallen from the height of prosperity into the depth of adversity than to be trodden on, and insulted over, when they are down; and on this head they are too apt to be suspicious. Observe,

1. What aggravated this grievance to him. Two things:—(1.) That they were his *neighbours*, his friends, his companions (so the word signifies), and the scoffs of such are often most spitefully given, and always most indignantly received. Ps. lv. 12, 13, *It was not an enemy that reproached me; then I would have* slighted it, and so *borne it; but it was thou, a man, my equal.* (2.) That they were professors of religion, such as *called upon God*, and said that he *answered them:* for some understand that of the persons mocking. "They are such as have a regard to heaven, and an interest in heaven, whose prayers I would therefore be glad of and thankful for, whose good opinion I cannot but covet, and therefore whose censures are the more grievous." Note, It is sad that any who call upon God should mock their brethren (Jam. iii. 9, 10), and it cannot but lie heavily on a good man to be thought ill of by those whom he thinks well of, yet this is no new thing.

2. What supported him under it. (1.) That he had a God to go to, with whom he could lodge his appeal; for some understand those words of the person mocked, that he *calls upon God and he answers him;* and so it agrees with *ch.* xvi. 20. *My friends scorn me, but my eye poureth out tears to God.* If

our friends be deaf to our complaints, God is not; if they condemn us, God knows our integrity; if they make the worst of us, he will make the best of us; if they give us cross answers, he will give us kind ones. (2.) That his case was not singular, but very common: *The just upright man is laughed to scorn.* By many he is laughed at even for his justice and his uprightness, his honesty towards men and his piety towards God; these are derided as foolish things, which silly people needlessly hamper themselves with, as if religion were a jest and therefore to be made a jest of. By most he is laughed at for any little infirmity or weakness, notwithstanding his justice and uprightness, without any consideration had of that which is so much his honour. Note, It was of old the lot of honest good people to be despised and derided; we are not therefore to think it strange (1 Pet. iv. 12), no, nor to think it hard, if it be our lot; *so persecuted they* not only *the prophets*, but even the saints of the patriarchal age (Matt. v. 12), and can we expect to fare better than they?

3. What he suspected to be the true cause of it, and that was, in short, this: they were themselves rich and at ease, and therefore they despised him who had fallen into poverty. It is the way of the world; we see instances of it daily. Those that prosper are praised, but of those that are going down it is said, " Down with them." *He that is ready to slip with his feet* and fall into trouble, though he has formerly shone as a lamp, is then looked upon as a lamp going out, like the snuff of a candle, which we throw to the ground and tread upon, and is accordingly *despised in the thought of him that is at ease, v.* 5. Even the just upright man, that is in his generation as a burning and shining light, if he enter into temptation (Ps. lxxiii. 2) or come under a cloud, is looked upon with contempt. See here, (1.) What is the common fault of those that live in prosperity. Being full, and easy, and merry themselves, they look scornfully upon those that are in want, pain, and sorrow; they overlook them, take no notice of them, and study to forget them. See Ps. cxxiii. 4. The chief butler drinks wine in bowls, but makes nothing of the afflictions of Joseph. Wealth without grace often makes men thus haughty, thus careless of their poor neighbours. (2.) What is the common fate of those that fall into adversity. Poverty serves to eclipse all their lustre; though they are lamps, yet, if taken out of golden candlesticks, and put, like Gideon's, into earthen pitchers, nobody values them as formerly, but those that live at ease despise them.

6 The tabernacles of robbers prosper, and they that provoke God are secure; into whose hand God bringeth *abundantly.* 7 But ask now the beasts, and they shall teach thee; and

the fowls of the air, and they shall tell thee: 8 Or speak to the earth, and it shall teach thee: and the fishes of the sea shall declare unto thee. 9 Who knoweth not in all these that the hand of the LORD hath wrought this? 10 In whose hand *is* the soul of every living thing, and the breath of all mankind. 11 Doth not the ear try words? and the mouth taste his meat?

Job's friends all of them went upon this principle, that wicked people cannot prosper long in this world, but some remarkable judgment or other will suddenly light on them: Zophar had concluded with it, that *the eyes of the wicked shall fail, ch.* xi. 20. This principle Job here opposes, and maintains that God, in disposing men's outward affairs, acts as a sovereign, reserving the exact distribution of rewards and punishments for the future state.

I. He asserts it as an undoubted truth that wicked people may, and often do, prosper long in this world, *v.* 6. Even great sinners may enjoy great prosperity. Observe, 1. How he describes the sinners. They are *robbers*, and such as provoke God, the worst kind of sinners, blasphemers and persecutors. Perhaps he refers to the Sabeans and Chaldeans, who had robbed him, and had always lived by spoil and rapine, and yet they prospered; all the world saw they did, and there is no disputing against sense; one observation built upon matter of fact is worth twenty notions framed by an hypothesis. Or more generally, All proud oppressors are robbers and pirates. It is supposed that what is injurious to men is provoking to God, the patron of right and the protector of mankind. It is not strange if those that violate the bonds of justice break through the obligations of all religion, bid defiance even to God himself, and make nothing of provoking him. 2. How he describes their prosperity. It is very great; for, (1.) Even *their tabernacles prosper*, those that live with them and those that come after them and descend from them. It seems as if a blessing were entailed upon their families; and that is sometimes preserved to succeeding generations which was got by fraud. (2.) They *are secure*, and not only feel no hurt, but fear none, are under no apprehensions of danger either from threatening providences or an awakened conscience. But those *that provoke God* are never the more safe for their being secure. (3.) *Into their hand God brings abundantly.* They have *more than heart could wish* (Ps. lxxiii. 7), not for necessity only, but for delight—not for themselves only, but for others—not for the present only, but for hereafter; and this from the hand of Providence too. God brings plentifully to them. We cannot therefore

judge of men's piety by their plenty, nor of what they have in their heart by what they have in their hand.

II. He appeals even to the inferior creatures for the proof of this—the beasts, and fowls, and trees, and even the earth itself; consult these, and they shall tell thee, *v.* 7, 8. Many a good lesson we may learn from them, but what are they here to teach us?

1. We may from them learn that *the tabernacles of robbers prosper* (so some); for, (1.) Even among the brute creatures the greater devour the less and the stronger prey upon the weaker, and men are as the fishes of the sea, Hab. i. 14. If sin had not entered, we may suppose there would have been no such disorder among the creatures, but the wolf and the lamb would have lain down together. (2.) These creatures are serviceable to wicked men, and so they declare their prosperity. Ask the herds and the flocks to whom they belong, and they will tell you that such a robber, such an oppressor, is their owner: the fishes and fowls will tell you that they are served up to the tables, and feed the luxury, of proud sinners. The earth brings forth her fruits to them (*ch.* ix. 24), and the whole creation groans under the burden of their tyranny, Rom. viii. 20, 22. Note, All the creatures which wicked men abuse, by making them the food and fuel of their lusts, will witness against them another day, Jam. v. 3, 4.

2. We may from them learn the wisdom, power, and goodness of God, and that sovereign dominion of his into which plain and self-evident truth all these difficult dispensations must be resolved. Zophar had made a vast mystery of it, *ch.* xi. 7. "So far from that," says Job, "that what we are concerned to know we may learn even from the inferior creatures; for *who knows not from all these? v.* 9. Any one may easily gather from the book of the creatures that *the hand of the Lord has wrought this,*" that is, "that there is a wise Providence which guides and' governs all these things by rules which we are neither acquainted with nor are competent judges of." Note, From God's sovereign dominion over the inferior creatures we should learn to acquiesce in all his disposals of the affairs of the children of men, though contrary to our measures.

III. He resolves all into the absolute propriety which God has in all the creatures (*v.* 10): *In whose hand is the soul of every living thing.* All the creatures, and mankind particularly, derive their being from him, owe their being to him, depend upon him for the support of it, lie at his mercy, are under his direction and dominion and entirely at his disposal, and at his summons must resign their lives. All souls are his; and may he not do what he will with his own? The name *Jehovah* is used here (*v.* 9), and it is the only time that we meet with it in all the discourses between Job and his friends; for

God was, in that age, more known by the name of *Shaddai—the Almighty.*

IV. Those words—(v. 11), *Doth not the ear try words, as the mouth tastes meat?* may be taken either as the conclusion to the foregoing discourse or the preface to what follows. The mind of man has as good a faculty of discerning between truth and error, when duly stated, as the palate has of discerning between what is sweet and what is bitter. Job therefore demands from his friends a liberty to judge for himself of what they had said, and desires them to use the same liberty in judging of what he had said; nay, he seems to appeal to any man's impartial judgment in this controversy; let the ear try the words on both sides, and it would be found that he was in the right. Note, The ear must try words before it receives them so as to subscribe to them. As by the taste we judge what food is wholesome to the body and what not, so by the spirit of discerning we must judge what doctrine is sound, and savoury, and wholesome, and what not, 1 Cor. x. 15; xi. 13.

12 With the ancient *is* wisdom ; and in length of days understanding. 13 With him *is* wisdom and strength, he hath counsel and understanding. 14 Behold, he breaketh down, and it cannot be built again : he shutteth up a man, and there can be no opening. 15 Behold, he withholdeth the waters, and they dry up : also he sendeth them out, and they overturn the earth. 16 With him *is* strength and wisdom: the deceived and the deceiver *are* his. 17 He leadeth counsellors away spoiled, and maketh the judges fools. 18 He looseth the bond of kings, and girdeth their loins with a girdle. 19 He leadeth princes away spoiled, and overthroweth the mighty. 20 He removeth away the speech of the trusty, and taketh away the understanding of the aged. 21 He poureth contempt upon princes, and weakeneth the strength of the mighty. 22 He discovereth deep things out of darkness, and bringeth out to light the shadow of death. 23 He increaseth the nations, and destroyeth them : he enlargeth the nations, and straiteneth them *again.* 24 He taketh away the heart of the chief of the people of the earth, and causeth them to wander in a wilderness *where there is* no way. 25 They grope in the dark without light, and he maketh them to stagger like *a* drunken *man.*

This is a noble discourse of Job's concerning the wisdom, power, and sovereignty of God, in ordering and disposing of all the affairs of the children of men, according to the counsel of his own will, which none dares gainsay or can resist. Take both him and them out of the controversy in which they were so warmly engaged, and they all spoke admirably well; but, in *that,* we sometimes scarcely know what to make of them. It were well if wise and good men, that differ in their apprehensions about minor things, would see it to be for their honour and comfort, and the edification of others, to dwell most upon those great things in which they are agreed. On this subject Job speaks like himself. Here are no passionate complaints, no peevish reflections, but every thing masculine and great.

I. He asserts the unsearchable wisdom and irresistible power of God. It is allowed that among men there is *wisdom and understanding, v.* 12. But it is to be found only with some few, *with the ancient,* and those who are blessed with length of days, who get it by long experience and constant experience ; and, when they have got the wisdom, they have lost their strength and are unable to execute the results of their wisdom. But now *with God there are* both *wisdom and strength,* wisdom to design the best and strength to accomplish what is designed. He does not get counsel or understanding, as we do, by observation, but he has it essentially and eternally in himself, *v.* 13. What is the wisdom of ancient men compared with the wisdom of the ancient of days! It is but little that we know, and less that we can do; but God can do every thing, and *no thought can be withheld from him.* Happy are those who have this God for their God, for they have infinite wisdom and strength engaged for them. Foolish and fruitless are all the attempts of men against him (*v.* 14): *He breaketh down, and it cannot be built again.* Note, There is no contending with the divine providence, nor breaking the measures of it. As he had said before (*ch.* ix. 12), *He takes away, and who can hinder him?* so he says again. What God says cannot be gainsaid, nor what he does undone. There is no rebuilding what God will have to lie in ruins; witness the tower of Babel, which the undertakers could not go on with, and the desolations of Sodom and Gomorrah, which could never be repaired. See Isa. xxv. 2 ; Ezek. xxvi. 14; Rev. xviii. 21. There is no releasing those whom God has condemned to a perpetual imprisonment; if *he shut up* a man by sickness, reduce him to straits, and embarrass him in his affairs, *there can be no opening.* He shuts up in the grave, and none can break open those sealed doors—shuts up in hell, in chains of darkness, and none can pass that great gulf fixed.

II. He gives an instance, for the proof of this doctrine in nature, *v.* 15. God has the command of *the waters, binds them as in a gar-*

ment (Prov. xxx. 4), holds them *in the hollow of his hand* (Isa. xl. 12); and he can punish the children of men either by the defect or by the excess of them. As men break the laws of virtue by extremes on each hand, both defects and excesses, while virtue is in the mean, so God corrects them by extremes, and denies them the mercy which is in the mean. 1. Great droughts are sometimes great judgments: *He withholds the waters, and they dry up;* if the heaven be as brass, the earth is as iron; if the rain be denied, fountains dry up and their streams are wanted, fields are parched and their fruits are wanted, Amos iv. 7. 2. Great wet is sometimes a great judgment. He raises the waters, and *overturns the earth,* the productions of it, the buildings upon it. A sweeping rain is said to *leave no food,* Prov. xxviii. 3. See how many ways God has of contending with a sinful people and taking from them abused, forfeited, mercies; and how utterly unable we are to contend with him. If we might invert the order, this verse would fitly refer to Noah's flood, that ever memorable instance of the divine power. God then, in wrath, sent the waters out, and they overturned the earth; but in mercy he withheld them, shut the windows of heaven and the fountains of the great deep, and then, in a little time, they dried up.

III. He gives many instances of it in God's powerful management of the children of men, crossing their purposes and serving his own by them and upon them, overruling all their counsels, overpowering all their attempts, and overcoming all their oppositions. What changes does God make with men! what turns does he give them! how easily, how surprisingly!

1. In general (v. 16): *With him are strength and reason* (so some translate it), strength and consistency with himself: it is an elegant word in the original. With him are the very quintessence and extract of wisdom. *With him are power and all that is;* so some read it. He is what he is of himself, and by him and in him all things subsist. Having this strength and wisdom, he knows how to make use, not only of those who are wise and good, who willingly and designedly serve him, but even of those who are foolish and bad, who, one would think, could be made no way serviceable to the designs of his providence: *The deceived and the deceiver are his;* the simplest men that are deceived are not below his notice; the subtlest men that deceive cannot with all their subtlety escape his cognizance. The world is full of deceit; the one half of mankind cheats the other, and God suffers it to be so, and from both will at last bring glory to himself. The deceivers make tools of the deceived, but the great God makes tools of them both, wherewith he works, and none can hinder him. He has wisdom and might enough to manage all the fools and knaves in the world, and knows how to serve his own purposes by them, notwithstanding the weakness of the one and the wickedness of the other. When Jacob by a fraud got the blessing the design of God's grace was served; when Ahab was drawn by a false prophecy into an expedition that was his ruin the design of God's justice was served; and in both *the deceived and the deceiver* were at his disposal. See Ezek. xiv. 9. God would not suffer the sin of the deceiver, nor the misery of the deceived, if he knew not how to set bounds to both and bring glory to himself out of both. *Hallelujah, the Lord God omnipotent* thus reigns; and it is well he does, for otherwise there is so little wisdom and so little honesty in the world that it would all have been in confusion and ruin long ago.

2. He next descends to the particular instances of the wisdom and power of God in the revolutions of states and kingdoms; for thence he fetches his proofs, rather than from the like operations of Providence concerning private persons and families, because the more high and public the station is in which men are placed the more changes that befal them are taken notice of, and consequently the more illustriously does Providence shine forth in them. And it is easy to argue, If God can thus turn and toss the great ones of the earth, like a ball in a large place (as the prophet speaks, Isa. xxii. 18), much more the little ones; and with him to whom states and kingdoms must submit it is surely the greatest madness for us to contend. Some think that Job here refers to the extirpation of those powerful nations, the Rephaim, the Zuzim, the Emim, and the Horites (mentioned Gen. xiv. 5, 6, Deut. ii. 10, 20), in which perhaps it was particularly noticed how strangely they were infatuated and enfeebled: if so, it is designed to show that whenever the like is done in the affairs of nations it is God that does it, and we must therein observe his sovereign dominion, even over those that think themselves most powerful, politic, and absolute. Compare this with that of Eliphaz, ch. v. 12, &c. Let us gather up the particular changes here specified, which God makes upon persons, either for the destruction of nations and the planting of others in their room or for the turning out of a particular government and ministry and the elevation of another in its room, which may be a blessing to the kingdom; witness the glorious Revolution in our own land twenty years ago, in which we saw as happy an exposition as ever was given of this discourse of Job's. (1.) Those that were wise are sometimes strangely infatuated, and in this the hand of God must be acknowledged (v. 17): *He leadeth counsellors away spoiled,* as trophies of his victory over them, spoiled of all the honour and wealth they have got by their policy, nay, spoiled of the wisdom itself for which they have been celebrated and the success they promised themselves in their pro-

jects. His counsel stands, while all their devices are brought to nought and their designs baffled, and so they are spoiled both of the satisfaction and of the reputation of their wisdom. *He maketh the judges fools.* By a work on their minds he deprives them of their qualifications for business, and so they become really fools; and by his disposal of their affairs he makes the issue and event of their projects to be quite contrary to what they themselves intended, and so he makes them look like fools. The counsel of Ahithophel, one in whom this scripture was remarkably fulfilled, became foolishness, and he, according to his name, *the brother of a fool.* See Isa. xix. 13, *The princes of Zoan have become fools; they have seduced Egypt, even those that are the stay of the tribes thereof.* Let not the wise man therefore glory in his wisdom, nor the ablest counsellors and judges be proud of their station, but humbly depend upon God for the continuance of their abilities. Even the aged, who seem to hold their wisdom by prescription, and think they have got it by their own industry and therefore have an indefeasible title to it, may yet be deprived of it, and often are, by the infirmities of age, which make them twice children: He *taketh away the understanding of the aged, v.* 20. The aged, who were most depended on for advice, fail those that depended on them. We read of an old and yet foolish king, Eccl. iv. 13. (2.) Those that were high and in authority are strangely brought down, impoverished, and enslaved, and it is God that humbles them (*v.* 18): *He looseth the bond of kings,* and taketh from them the power wherewith they ruled their subjects, perhaps enslaved them and ruled them with rigour; he strips them of all the ensigns of their honour and authority, and all the supports of their tyranny, unbuckles their belts, so that the sword drops from their side, and then no marvel if the crown quickly drops from their head, on which immediately follows the *girding of their loins with a girdle,* a badge of servitude, for servants went with their loins girt. Thus *he leads* great *princes away spoiled* of all their power and wealth, and that in which they pleased and prided themselves, *v.* 19. Note, Kings are not exempt from God's jurisdiction. To us they are gods, but men to him, and subject to more than the common changes of human life. (3.) Those that were strong are strangely weakened, and it is God that weakens them (*v.* 21) and *overthrows the mighty, v.* 19. Strong bodies are weakened by age and sickness; powerful armies moulder and come to nothing, and their strength will not secure them from a fatal overthrow. No force can stand before Omnipotence, no, not that of Goliath. (4.) Those that were famed for eloquence, and entrusted with public business, are strangely silenced, and have nothing to say (*v.* 20): *He removeth away the speech of the trusty,* so that they cannot speak

as they intended and as they used to do, with freedom and clearness, but blunder, and falter, and make nothing of it. Or they cannot speak what they intended, but the contrary, as Balaam, who blessed those whom he was called to curse. Let not the orator therefore be proud of his rhetoric, nor use it to any bad purposes, lest God take it away, who made man's mouth. (5.) Those that were honoured and admired strangely fall into disgrace (*v.* 21): He *poureth contempt upon princes.* He leaves them to themselves to do mean things, or alters the opinions of men concerning them. If princes themselves dishonour God and despise him, if they offer indignities to the people of God and trample upon them, they shall be lightly esteemed, and God will pour contempt upon them. See Ps. cvii. 40. Commonly none more abject in themselves, nor more abused by others when they are down, than those who were haughty and insolent when they were in power. (6.) That which was secret, and lay hidden, is strangely brought to light and laid open (*v.* 22): *He discovers deep things out of darkness.* Plots closely laid are discovered and defeated; wickedness closely committed and artfully concealed is discovered, and the guilty are brought to condign punishment—secret treasons (Eccl. x. 20), secret murders, secret whoredoms. The cabinet-councils of princes are before God's eye, 2 Kings vi. 11. (7.) Kingdoms have their ebbings and flowings, their waxings and wanings; and both are from God (*v.* 23): *He* sometimes *increases their numbers,* and enlarges their bounds, so that they make a figure among the nations and become formidable; but after a while, by some undiscerned cause perhaps, they are destroyed and straitened, made few and poor, cut short and many of them cut off, and so they are rendered despicable among their neighbours, and those that were the head become the tail of the nations. See Ps. cvii. 38, 39. (8.) Those that were bold and courageous, and made nothing of dangers, are strangely cowed and dispirited; and this also is the Lord's doing (*v.* 24): *He taketh away the heart of the chief of the people,* that were their leaders and commanders, and were most famed for their martial fire and great achievements; when any thing is to be done they are heartless, and ready to flee at the shaking of a leaf. Ps. lxxvi. 5. (9.) Those that were driving on their projects with full speed are strangely bewildered and at a loss; they know not where they are nor what they do, are unsteady in their counsels and uncertain in their motions, off and on, this way and that way, wandering like men in a desert (*v.* 24), groping like men in the dark, and staggering like men in drink, *v.* 25. Isa. lix. 10. Note, God can soon nonplus the deepest politicians and bring the greatest wits to their wits' end, to show that wherein they deal proudly he is above them.

Thus are the revolutions of kingdoms wonderfully brought about by an overruling Providence. Heaven and earth are shaken, but the Lord sits King for ever, and with him we look for *a kingdom that cannot be shaken.*

CHAP. XIII.

Job here comes to make application of what he had said in the foregoing chapter; and now we have him not in so good a temper as he was in then: for, I. He is very bold with his friends, comparing himself with them, notwithstanding the mortifications he was under, ver. 1, 2. Condemning them for their falsehood, their forwardness to judge, their partiality and deceitfulness under colour of pleading God's cause (ver. 4—8), and threatening them with the judgments of God for their so doing (ver. 9—12), desiring them to be silent (ver. 5, 13, 17), and turning from them to God, ver. 3. II. He is very bold with his God. 1. In some expressions his faith is very bold, yet that is not more bold than welcome, ver. 15, 16, 18. But, 2. In other expressions his passion is rather too bold in expostulations with God concerning the deplorable condition he was in (ver. 14, 19, &c.), complaining of the confusion he was in (ver. 20 - 22), and the loss he was at to find out the sin that provoked God thus to afflict him, and in short of the rigour of God's proceedings against him, ver. 23—28.

LO, mine eye hath seen all *this,* mine ear hath heard and understood it. 2 What ye know, *the same* do I know also : I *am* not inferior unto you. 3 Surely I would speak to the Almighty, and I desire to reason with God. 4 But ye *are* forgers of lies, ye *are* all physicians of no value. 5 O that ye would altogether hold your peace! and it should be your wisdom. 6 Hear now my reasoning, and hearken to the pleadings of my lips. 7 Will ye speak wickedly for God? and talk deceitfully for him? 8 Will ye accept his person? will ye contend for God? 9 Is it good that he should search you out? or as one man mocketh another, do ye *so* mock him? 10 He will surely reprove you, if ye do secretly accept persons. 11 Shall not his excellency make you afraid? and his dread fall upon you? 12 Your remembrances *are* like unto ashes, your bodies to bodies of clay.

Job here warmly expresses his resentment of the unkindness of his friends.

I. He comes up with them as one that understood the matter in dispute as well as they, and did not need to be taught by them, *v.* 1, 2. They compelled him, as the Corinthians did Paul, to commend himself and his own knowledge, yet not in a way of self-applause, but of self-justification. All he had before said his eye had seen confirmed by many instances, and his ear had heard seconded by many authorities, and he well understood it and what use to make of it. Happy are those who not only see and hear, but understand, the greatness, glory, and sovereignty of God. This, he thought, would justify what he had said before (*ch.* xii. 3), which he repeats here (*v.* 2): " *What you know, the same do I know also,* so that I need not come to you to be taught; *I am not inferior unto you* in wisdom." Note, Those who enter into disputation enter into

temptation to magnify themselves and vilify their brethren more than is fit, and therefore ought to watch and pray against the workings of pride.

II. He turns from them to God (*v.* 3): *Surely I would speak to the Almighty;* as if he had said, " I can promise myself no satisfaction in talking to you. O that I might have liberty *to reason with God!* He would not be so hard upon me as you are." The prince himself will perhaps give audience to a poor petitioner with more mildness, patience, and condescension, than the servants will. Job would rather argue with God himself than with his friends. See here, 1. What confidence those have towards God whose hearts condemn them not of reigning hypocrisy: they can, with humble boldness, appear before him and appeal to him. 2. What comfort those have in God whose neighbours unjustly condemn them: if they may not speak to them with any hopes of a fair hearing, yet they may speak to the Almighty; they have easy access to him and shall find acceptance with him.

III. He condemns them for their unjust and uncharitable treatment of him, *v.* 4. 1. They falsely accused him, and that was unjust: *You are forgers of lies.* They framed a wrong hypothesis concerning the divine Providence, and misrepresented it, as if it did never remarkably afflict any but wicked men in this world, and thence they drew a false judgment concerning Job, that he was certainly a hypocrite. For this gross mistake, both in doctrine and application, he thinks an indictment of forgery lies against them. To speak lies is bad enough, though but at second hand, but to forge them with contrivance and deliberation is much worse; yet against this wrong neither innocency nor excellency will be a fence. 2. They basely deceived him, and that was unkind. They undertook his cure, and pretended to be his physicians; but they were all *physicians of no value,* " idol-physicians, who can do me no more good than an idol can." They were worthless physicians, who neither understood his case nor knew how to prescribe to him— mere empirics, who pretended to great things, but in conference added nothing to him : he was never the wiser for all they said. Thus to broken hearts and wounded consciences all creatures, without Christ, are physicians of no value, on which one may spend all and be never the better, but rather grow worse, Mark v. 26.

IV. He begs they would be silent and give him a patient hearing, *v.* 5, 6. 1. He thinks it would be a credit to them if they would say no more, having said too much already : " *Hold your peace, and it shall be your wisdom,* for thereby you will conceal your ignorance and ill-nature, which now appear in all you say." They pleaded that they could not forbear speaking (*ch.* iv. 2, xi. 2, 3); but he tells them that they would better have consulted

75

their own reputation if they had enjoined themselves silence. Better say nothing than nothing to the purpose or that which tends to the dishonour of God and the grief of our brethren. *Even a fool, when he holds his peace, is accounted wise,* because nothing appears to the contrary, Prov. xvii. 28. And, as silence is an evidence of wisdom, so it is a means of it, as it gives time to think and hear. 2. He thinks it would be a piece of justice to him to hear what he had to say *Hear now my reasoning.* Perhaps, though they did not interrupt him in his discourse, yet they seemed careless, and did not much heed what he said. He therefore begged that they would not only hear, but hearken. Note, We should be very willing and glad to hear what those have to say for themselves whom, upon any account, we are tempted to have hard thoughts of. Many a man, if he could but be fairly heard, would be fairly acquitted, even in the consciences of those that run him down.

V. He endeavours to convince them of the wrong they did to God's honour, while they pretended to plead for him, v. 7, 8. They valued themselves upon it that they spoke for God, were advocates for him, and had undertaken to justify him and his proceedings against Job; and, being (as they thought) of counsel for the sovereign, they expected not only the ear of the court and the last word, but judgment on their side. But Job tells them plainly, 1. That God and his cause did not need such advocates: "*Will you think to contend for God,* as if his justice were clouded and wanted to be cleared up, or as if he were at a loss what to say and wanted you to speak for him? Will you, who are so weak and passionate, put in for the honour of pleading God's cause?" Good work ought not to be put into bad hands. *Will you accept his person?* If those who have not right on their side carry their cause, it is by the partiality of the judge in favour of their persons; but God's cause is so just that it needs no such methods for the support of it. He is a God, and can plead for himself (Judg. vi. 31); and, if you were for ever silent, the heavens would declare his righteousness. 2. That God's cause suffered by such management. Under pretence of justifying God in afflicting Job they magisterially condemned him as a hypocrite and a bad man. "This" (says he) "is *speaking wickedly*" (for uncharitableness and censoriousness are wickedness, great wickedness; it is an offence to God to wrong our brethren); "it is talking *deceitfully,* for you condemn one whom yet perhaps your own consciences, at the same time, cannot but acquit. Your principles are false and your arguings fallacious, and will it excuse you to say, *It is for God?*" No, for a good intention will not justify, much less will it sanctify, a bad word or action. God's truth needs not our lie, nor God's cause either our sinful policies or our sinful passions. The wrath of man works

not the righteousness of God, nor may we *do evil that good may come,* Rom. iii. 7, 8. Pious frauds (as they call them) are impious cheats; and devout persecutions are horrid profanations of the name of God, as theirs who *hated their brethren,* and *cast them out, saying, Let the Lord be glorified,* Isa. lxvi. 5; John xvi. 2.

VI. He endeavours to possess them with a fear of God's judgment, and so to bring them to a better temper. Let them not think to impose upon God as they might upon a man like themselves, nor expect to gain his countenance in their bad practices by pretending a zeal for him and his honour. "As one man mocks another by flattering him, do you think so to mock him and deceive him?" Assuredly those who think to put a cheat upon God will prove to have put a cheat upon themselves. *Be not deceived, God is not mocked.* That they might not think thus to jest with God, and affront him, Job would have them to consider both God and themselves, and then they would find themselves unable to enter into judgment with him.

1. Let them consider what a God he is into whose service they had thus thrust themselves, and to whom they really did so much disservice, and enquire whether they could give him a good account of what they did. Consider, (1.) The strictness of his scrutiny and enquiries concerning them (v. 9): "*Is it good that he should search you out?* Can you bear to have the principles looked into which you go upon in your censures, and to have the bottom of the matter found out?" Note, It concerns us all seriously to consider whether it will be to our advantage or no that God searches the heart. It is good to an upright man who means honestly that God should search him; therefore he prays for it: *Search me, O God! and know my heart.* God's omniscience is a witness of his sincerity. But it is bad to him who looks one way and rows another that God should search him out, and lay him open to his confusion. (2.) The severity of his rebukes and displeasure against them (v. 10): "*If you do accept persons,* though but secretly and in heart, *he will surely reprove you;* he will be so far from being pleased with your censures of me, though under colour of vindicating him, that he will resent them as a great provocation, as any prince or great man would if a base action were done under the sanction of his name and under the colour of advancing his interest." Note, What we do amiss we shall certainly be reproved for, one way or other, one time or other, though it be done ever so secretly. (3.) The terror of his majesty, which if they would duly stand in awe of they would not do that which would make them obnoxious to his wrath (v. 11): "*Shall not his excellency make you afraid?* You that have great knowledge of God, and profess religion and a fear of him, how dare you talk at this rate and give yourselves so great a liberty

of speech? *Ought you not to walk and talk in the fear of God?* Neh. v. 9. *Should not his dread fall upon you*, and give a check to your passions?" Methinks Job speaks this as one that did himself know the terror of the Lord, and lived in a holy fear of him, whatever his friends suggested to the contrary. Note, [1.] There is in God a dreadful excellency. He is the most excellent Being, has all excellencies in himself and in each infinitely excels any creature. His excellencies in themselves are amiable and lovely. He is the most beautiful Being; but considering man's distance from God by nature, and his defection and degeneracy by sin, his excellencies are dreadful. His power, holiness, justice, yea, and his goodness too, are dreadful excellencies. They shall fear the Lord and his goodness. [2.] A holy awe of this dreadful excellency should fall upon us and make us afraid. This would awaken impenitent sinners and bring them to repentance, and would influence all to be careful to please him and afraid of offending him.

2. Let them consider themselves, and what an unequal match they were for this great God (v. 12): " *Your remembrances* (all that is in you for which you hope to be remembered when you are gone) *are like unto ashes*, worthless and weak, and easily trampled on and blown away. *Your bodies are like bodies of clay*, mouldering and coming to nothing. Your memories, you think, will survive your bodies, but, alas! they are like ashes which will be shovelled up with your dust." Note, the consideration of our own meanness and mortality should make us afraid of offending God, and furnishes a good reason why we should not despise and trample upon our brethren. Bishop Patrick gives another sense of this verse: " Your remonstrances on God's behalf are no better than dust, and the arguments you accumulate but like so many heaps of dirt."

13 Hold your peace, let me alone, that I may speak, and let come on me what *will.* 14 Wherefore do I take my flesh in my teeth, and put my life in mine hand? 15 Though he slay me, yet will I trust in him: but I will maintain mine own ways before him. 16 He also *shall be* my salvation: for a hypocrite shall not come before him. 17 Hear diligently my speech, and my declaration with your ears. 18 Behold now, I have ordered *my* cause; I know that I shall be justified. 19 Who *is* he *that* will plead with me? for now, if I hold my tongue, I shall give up the ghost. 20 Only do not two *things* unto me: then will I not hide myself from thee. 21 Withdraw thine hand far from me: and

let not thy dread make me afraid. 22 Then call thou, and I will answer: or let me speak, and answer thou me.

Job here takes fresh hold, fast hold, of his integrity, as one that was resolved not to let it go, nor suffer it to be wrested from him. His firmness in this matter is commendable and his warmth excusable.

I. He entreats his friends and all the company to let him alone, and not interrupt him in what he was about to say (v. 13), but diligently to hearken to it, v. 17. He would have his own protestation to be decisive, for none but God and himself knew his heart. " Be silent therefore, and let me hear no more of you, but hearken diligently to what I say, and let my own oath for confirmation be an end of the strife."

II. He resolves to adhere to the testimony his own conscience gave of his integrity; and though his friends called it obstinacy that should not shake his constancy: " I will speak in my own defence, and *let come on me what will*, v. 13. Let my friends put what construction they please upon it, and think the worse of me for it; I hope God will not make my necessary defence to be my offence, as you do. He will justify me (v. 18) and then nothing can come amiss to me." Note, Those that are upright, and have the assurance of their uprightness, may cheerfully welcome every event. Come what will, *bene præparatum pectus—they are ready for it.* He resolves (v. 15) that he will *maintain his own ways.* He would never part with the satisfaction he had in having walked uprightly with God; for, though he could not justify every word he had spoken, yet, in the general, his ways were good, and he would maintain his uprightness; and why should he not, since that was his great support under his present exercises, as it was Hezekiah's, *Now, Lord, remember how I have walked before thee?* Nay, he would not only not betray his own cause, or give it up, but he would openly avow his sincerity; for (v. 19) " *If I hold my tongue*, and do not speak for myself, my silence now will for ever silence me, for *I shall* certainly *give up the ghost*," v. 19. " If I cannot be cleared, yet let me be eased, by what I say," as Elihu, ch. xxxii. 17, 20.

III. He complains of the extremity of pain and misery he was in (v. 14): *Wherefore do I take my flesh in my teeth?* That is, 1. " Why do I suffer such agonies? I cannot but wonder that God should lay so much upon me when he knows I am not a wicked man." He was ready, not only to rend his clothes, but even to tear his flesh, through the greatness of his affliction, and saw himself at the brink of death, and his life in his hand, yet his friends could not charge him with any enormous crime, nor could he himself discover any; no marvel then that he was in such confusion. 2. " Why do I stifle and smother the protestations of my innocency?" When a man with great difficulty keeps in what he would say, he bites his lips. "Now," says he, "why may not I take liberty to speak, since I do but vex myself, add to my torment, and endanger my life, by refraining?" Note, It would vex the most patient man, when he has lost every thing else, to be denied the comfort (if he deserves it) of a good conscience and a good name.

IV. He comforts himself in God, and still keeps hold of his confidence in him. Observe here,

1. What he depends upon God for—justification and salvation, the two great things we hope for through Christ. (1.) Justification (*v.* 18): *I have ordered my cause, and, upon the whole matter, I know that I shall be justified.* This he knew because he knew that his Redeemer lived, *ch.* xix. 25. Those whose hearts are upright with God, in walking not after the flesh but after the Spirit, may be sure that through Christ there shall be no condemnation to them, but that, whoever lays any thing to their charge, they shall be justified: they may know that they shall. (2.) Salvation (*v.* 16): *He also shall be my salvation.* He means it not of temporal salvation (he had little expectation of that); but concerning his eternal salvation he was very confident that God would not only be his Saviour to make him happy, but his salvation, in the vision and fruition of whom he should be happy. And the reason why he depended on God for salvation was because *a hypocrite shall not come before him.* He knew himself not to be a hypocrite, and that none but hypocrites are rejected of God, and therefore concluded he should not be rejected. Sincerity is our evangelical perfection; nothing will ruin us but the want of that.

2. With what constancy he depends upon him: *Though he slay me, yet will I trust in him, v.* 15. This is a high expression of faith, and what we should all labour to come up to —to trust in God, though he slay us, that is, we must be well pleased with God as a friend even when he seems to come forth against us as an enemy, *ch.* xxiii. 8—10. We must believe that all shall work for good to us even when all seems to make against us, Jer. xxiv. 5. We must proceed and persevere in the way of our duty, though it cost us all that is dear to us in this world, even life itself, Heb. xi. 35. We must depend upon the performance of the promise when all the ways leading to it are shut up, Rom. iv. 18. We must rejoice in God when we have nothing else to rejoice in, and cleave to him, yea, though we cannot for the present find comfort in him. In a dying hour we must derive from him living comforts; and this is to trust in him though he slay us.

V. He wishes to argue the case even with God himself, if he might but have leave to settle the preliminaries of the treaty, *v.* 20

—22. He had desired (*v.* 3) to *reason with God,* and is still of the same mind. He *will not hide himself,* that is, he will not decline the trial, nor dread the issue of it, but under two provisos :—1. That his body might not be tortured with this exquisite pain: "*Withdraw thy hand far from me ;* for, while I am in this extremity, I am fit for nothing. I can make a shift to talk with my friends, but I know not how to address myself to thee." When we are to converse with God we have need to be composed, and as free as possible from every thing that may make us uneasy. 2. That his mind might not be terrified with the tremendous majesty of God: "*Let not thy dread make me afraid ;* either let the manifestations of thy presence be familiar or let me be enabled to bear them without disorder and disturbance." Moses himself trembled before God, so did Isaiah and Habakkuk. *O God! thou art terrible even in thy holy places.* "Lord," says Job, "let me not be put into such a consternation of spirit, together with this bodily affliction; for then I must certainly drop the cause, and shall make nothing of it." See what a folly it is for men to put off their repentance and conversion to a sick-bed and a death-bed. How can even a good man, much less a bad man, reason with God, so as to be justified before him, when he is upon the rack of pain and under the terror of the arrests of death? At such a time it is very bad to have the great work to do, but very comfortable to have it done, as it was to Job, who, if he might but have a little breathing-time, was ready either, (1.) To hear God speaking to him by his word, and return an answer: *Call thou, and I will answer ;* or, (2.) To speak to him by prayer, and expect an answer: *Let me speak, and answer thou me, v.* 22. Compare this with *ch.* ix. 34, 35, where he speaks to the same purport. In short, the badness of his case was at present such a damp upon him as he could not get over; otherwise he was well assured of the goodness of his cause, and doubted not but to have the comfort of it at last, when the present cloud was over. With such holy boldness may the upright come to the throne of grace, not doubting but to find mercy there.

23 How many *are* mine iniquities and sins? make me to know my transgression and my sin. 24 Wherefore hidest thou thy face, and holdest me for thine enemy? 25 Wilt thou break a leaf driven to and fro? and wilt thou pursue the dry stubble? 26 For thou writest bitter things against me, and makest me to possess the iniquities of my youth. 27 Thou puttest my feet also in the stocks, and lookest narrowly unto all my paths; thou settest a print upon the heels of my

feet. 28 And he, as a rotten thing, consumeth, as a garment that is moth eaten.

Here, I. Job enquires after his sins, and begs to have them discovered to him. He looks up to God, and asks him what was the number of them *(How many are my iniquities?)* and what were the particulars of them: *Make me to know my transgressions, v.* 23. His friends were ready enough to tell him how numerous and how heinous they were, *ch.* xxii. 5. "But, Lord," says he, "let me know them from thee; *for thy judgment is according to truth,* theirs is not." This may be taken either, 1. As a passionate complaint of hard usage, that he was punished for his faults and yet was not told what his faults were. Or, 2. As a prudent appeal to God from the censures of his friends. He desired that all his sins might be brought to light, as knowing they would then appear not so many, nor so mighty, as his friends suspected him to be guilty of. Or, 3. As a pious request, to the same purport with that which Elihu directed him to, *ch.* xxxiv. 32. *That which I see not, teach thou me.* Note, A true penitent is willing to know the worst of himself; and we should all desire to know what our transgressions are, that we may be particular in the confession of them and on our guard against them for the future.

II. He bitterly complains of God's withdrawings from him *(v.* 24): *Wherefore hidest thou thy face?* This must be meant of something more than his outward afflictions; for the loss of estate, children, health, might well consist with God's love; when that was all, he blessed the name of the Lord; but *his soul was also sorely vexed,* and that is it which he here laments. 1. That the favours of the Almighty were suspended. God hid his face as one strange to him, displeased with him, shy and regardless of him. 2. That the terrors of the Almighty were inflicted and impressed upon him. God held him for his enemy, shot his arrows at him *(ch.* vi. 4), and set him as a mark, *ch.* vii. 20. Note, The Holy Ghost sometimes denies his favours and discovers his terrors to the best and dearest of his saints and servants in this world. This case occurs, not only in the production, but sometimes in the progress of the divine life. Evidences for heaven are eclipsed, sensible communications interrupted, dread of divine wrath impressed, and the returns of comfort, for the present, despaired of, Ps. lxxvii. 7—9; lxxxviii. 7, 15, 16. These are grievous burdens to a gracious soul, that values God's loving-kindness as better than life, Prov. xviii. 14. *A wounded spirit who can bear?* Job, by asking here, *Why hidest thou thy face?* teaches us that, when at any time we are under the sense of God's withdrawings, we are concerned to enquire into the reason of them—what is the sin for which he corrects us and what the

good he designs us. Job's sufferings were typical of the sufferings of Christ, from whom not only men hid their faces (Isa. liii. 3), but God hid his, witness the darkness which surrounded him on the cross when he cried out, *My God, my God, why hast thou forsaken me?* If this were done to these green trees, what shall be done to the dry? They will for ever be forsaken.

III. He humbly pleads with God his own utter inability to stand before him *(v.* 25): "*Wilt thou break a leaf, pursue the dry stubble?* Lord, is it for thy honour to trample upon one that is down already, or to crush one that neither has nor pretends to any power to resist thee?" Note, We ought to have such an apprehension of the goodness and compassion of God as to believe that he will not *break the bruised reed,* Matt. xii. 20.

IV. He sadly complains of God's severe dealings with him. He owns it was for his sins that God thus contended with him, but thinks it hard,

1. That his former sins, long since committed, should now be remembered against him, and he should be reckoned with for the old scores *(v.* 26): *Thou writest bitter things against me.* Afflictions are bitter things. Writing them denotes deliberation and determination, written as a warrant for execution; it denotes also the continuance of his affliction, for that which is written remains, and, "Herein *thou makest me to possess the iniquities of my youth,*" that is, "thou punishest me for them, and thereby puttest me in mind of them, and obligest me to renew my repentance for them." Note, (1.) God sometimes writes very bitter things against the best and dearest of his saints and servants, both in outward afflictions and inward disquiet, trouble in body and trouble in mind, that he may humble them, and prove them, and do them good in their latter end. (2.) That the sins of youth are often the smart of age both in respect of sorrow within (Jer. xxxi. 18, 19) and suffering without, *ch.* xx. 11. Time does not wear out the guilt of sin. (3.) That when God writes bitter things against us his design therein is to make us possess our iniquities, to bring forgotten sins to mind, and so to bring us to remorse for them as to break us off from them. *This is all the fruit, to take away our sin.*

2. That his present mistakes and miscarriages should be so strictly taken notice of, and so severely animadverted upon *(v.* 27): "*Thou puttest my feet also in the stocks,* not only to afflict me and expose me to shame, not only to keep me from escaping the strokes of thy wrath, but that thou mayest critically remark all my motions and look narrowly to all my paths, to correct me for every false step, nay, for but a look awry or a word misapplied; nay, thou *settest a print upon the heels of my feet,* scorest down every thing I do amiss, to reckon for it; or no sooner have I trodden wrong, though ever so little, than

immediately I smart for it ; the punishment treads upon the very heels of the sin. Guilt, both of the oldest and of the freshest date, is put together to make up the cause of my calamity." Now, (1.) It was not true that God did thus seek advantages against him. He is not thus extreme to mark what we do amiss ; if he were, there were no abiding for us, Ps. cxxx. 3. But he is so far from this that he deals not with us according to the desert, no, not of our manifest sins, which are not *found by secret search,* Jer. ii. 34. This therefore was the language of Job's melancholy ; his sober thoughts never represented God thus as a hard Master. (2.) But we should keep such a strict and jealous eye as this upon ourselves and our own steps, both for the discovery of sin past and the prevention of it for the future. It is good for us all to *ponder the path of our feet.*

V. He finds himself wasting away apace under the heavy hand of God, *v.* 28. *He* (that is, man) *as a rotten thing,* the principle of whose putrefaction is in itself, *consumes, even like a moth-eaten garment,* which becomes continually worse and worse. Or, *He* (that is, God) *like rottenness, and like a moth, consumes me.* Compare this with Hos. v. 12, *I will be unto Ephraim as a moth, and to the house of Judah as rottenness ;* and see Ps. xxxix. 11. Note, Man, at the best, wears fast ; but, under God's rebukes especially, he is soon gone. While there is so little soundness in the soul, no marvel there is so little soundness in the flesh, Ps. xxxviii. 3.

CHAP. XIV.

Job had turned from speaking to his friends, finding it to no purpose to reason with them, and here he goes on to speak to God and himself. He had reminded his friends of their frailty and mortality (ch. xiii. 12) ; here he reminds himself of his own, and pleads it with God for some mitigation of his miseries. We have here an account, I. Of man's life, that it is, 1. Short, ver. 1. 2. Sorrowful, ver. 1. 3. Sinful, ver. 4. 4. Stinted, ver. 5, 14. II. Of man's death, that it puts a final period to our present life, to which we shall not again return (ver. 7—12), that it hides us from the calamities of life (ver. 13), destroys the hopes of life (ver. 18, 19), sends us away from the business of life (ver. 20), and keeps us in the dark concerning our relations in this life, how much soever we have formerly been in care about them, ver. 21, 22. III. The use Job makes of all this. 1. He pleads it with God, who, he thought, was too strict and severe with him (ver. 16, 17), begging that, in consideration of his frailty, he would not contend with him (ver. 3), but grant him some respite, ver. 6. 2. He engages himself to prepare for death (ver. 14), and encourages himself to hope that it will help us both to get good by the death of others and to get ready for our own.

MAN *that is* born of a woman *is* of few days, and full of trouble. 2 He cometh forth like a flower, and is cut down : he fleeth also as a shadow, and continueth not. 3 And dost thou open thine eyes upon such a one, and bringest me into judgment with thee ? 4 Who can bring a clean *thing* out of an unclean ? not one. 5 Seeing his days *are* determined, the number of his months *are* with thee, thou hast appointed his bounds that he cannot pass ; 6 Turn from him,

that he may rest, till he shall accomplish, as a hireling, his day.

We are here led to think,

I. Of the original of human life. God is indeed its great original, for he *breathed into man the breath of life* and in him we live ; but we date it from our birth, and thence we must date both its frailty and its pollution. 1. Its frailty : *Man, that is born of a woman, is* therefore *of few days, v.* 1. This may refer to the first woman, who was called *Eve,* because she was the mother of all living. Of her, who being deceived by the tempter was first in the transgression, we are all born, and consequently derive from her that sin and corruption which both shorten our days and sadden them. Or it may refer to every man's immediate mother. The woman is the weaker vessel, and we know that *partus sequitur ventrem—the child takes after the mother.* Let not the strong man therefore glory in his strength, or in the strength of his father, but remember that he is born of a woman, and that, when God pleases, the *mighty men become as women,* Jer. li. 30. 2. Its pollution (*v.* 4) : *Who can bring a clean thing out of an unclean ?* If man be born of a woman that is a sinner, how can it be otherwise than that he should be a sinner? See *ch.* xxv. 4. *How can he be clean that is born of a woman ?* Clean children cannot come from unclean parents any more than pure streams from an impure spring or grapes from thorns. Our habitual corruption is derived with our nature from our parents, and is therefore bred in the bone. Our blood is not only attainted by a legal conviction, but tainted with an hereditary disease. Our Lord Jesus, being made sin for us, is said to be *made of a woman,* Gal. iv. 4.

II. Of the nature of human life : it is *a flower,* it is a *shadow, v.* 2. The flower is fading, and all its beauty soon withers and is gone. The shadow is fleeting, and its very being will soon be lost and drowned in the shadows of the night. Of neither do we make any account; in neither do we put any confidence

III. Of the shortness and uncertainty of human life : Man is *of few days.* Life is here computed, not by months or years, but by days, for we cannot be sure of any day but that it may be our last. These days are few, fewer than we think of, few at the most, in comparison with the days of the first patriarchs, much more in comparison with the days of eternity, but much fewer to most, who come short of what we call *the age of man.* Man sometimes no sooner comes forth than he *is cut down*—comes forth out of the womb than he dies in the cradle—comes forth into the world and enters into the business of it than he is hurried away as soon as he has laid his hand to the plough. If not cut down immediately, yet *he flees as a shadow,* and never continues in one stay, in one shape, but the fashion of it passes away; so does this world, and our life in it, 1 Cor. vii. 31.

IV. Of the calamitous state of human life. Man, as he is short-lived, so he is sad-lived. Though he had but a few days to spend here, yet, if he might rejoice in those few, it were well (a short life and a merry one is the boast of some); but it is not so. During these few days he is *full of trouble,* not only troubled, but full of trouble, either toiling or fretting, grieving or fearing. No day passes without some vexation, some hurry, some disorder or other. Those that are fond of the world shall have enough of it. He is *satur tremore—full of commotion.* The fewness of his days creates him a continual trouble and uneasiness in expectation of the period of them, and he always hangs in doubt of his life. Yet, since man's days are so full of trouble, it is well that they are few, that the soul's imprisonment in the body, and banishment from the Lord, are not perpetual, are not long. When we come to heaven our days will be many, and perfectly free from trouble, and in the mean time faith, hope, and love, balance the present grievances.

V. Of the sinfulness of human life, arising from the sinfulness of the human nature. So some understand that question (*v.* 4), *Who can bring a clean thing out of an unclean?*—a clean performance from an unclean principle? Note, Actual transgressions are the natural product of habitual corruption, which is *therefore* called *original* sin, because it is the original of all our sins. This holy Job here laments, as all that are sanctified do, running up the streams to the fountain (Ps. li. 5); and some think he intends it as a plea with God for compassion: "Lord, be not extreme to mark my sins of human frailty and infirmity, for thou knowest my weakness. *O remember that I am flesh!*" The Chaldee paraphrase has an observable reading of this verse: *Who can make a man clean that is polluted with sin? Cannot one? that is, God. Or who but God, who is one, and will spare him?* God, by his almighty grace, can change the skin of the Ethiopian, the skin of Job, though clothed with worms.

VI. Of the settled period of human life, *v.* 5.

1. Three things we are here assured of :— (1.) That our life will come to an end; our days upon earth are not numberless, are not endless, no, they are numbered, and will soon be finished, Dan. v. 26. (2.) That it is determined, in the counsel and decree of God, how long we shall live and when we shall die. The number of our months is with God, at the disposal of his power, which cannot be controlled, and under the view of his omniscience, which cannot be deceived. It is certain that God's providence has the ordering of the period of our lives: our times are in his hand. The powers of nature depend upon him, and act under him. In him we live and move. Diseases are his servants; he kills and makes alive. Nothing

comes to pass by chance, no, not the execution done by a bow drawn at a venture. It is therefore certain that God's prescience has determined it before; for *known unto God are all his works.* Whatever he does he determined, yet with a regard partly to the settled course of nature (the end and the means are determined together) and to the settled rules of moral government, punishing evil and rewarding good in this life. We are no more governed by the Stoic's blind fate than by the Epicurean's blind fortune. (3.) That the bounds God has fixed we cannot pass; for his counsels are unalterable, his foresight being infallible.

2. These considerations Job here urges as reasons, (1.) Why God should not be so strict in taking cognizance of him and of his slips and failings (*v.* 3): "Since I have such a corrupt nature within, and am liable to so much trouble, which is a constant temptation from without, *dost thou open thy eyes* and fasten them *upon such a one,* extremely to mark what I do amiss? ch. xiii. 27. And dost thou *bring me,* such a worthless worm as I am, *into judgment with thee* who art so quick sighted to discover the least failing, so holy to hate it, so just to condemn it, and so mighty to punish it?" The consideration of our own inability to contend with God, of our own sinfulness and weakness, should engage us to pray, *Lord, enter not into judgment with thy servant.* (2.) Why he should not be so severe in his dealings with him: "Lord, I have but a little time to live. I must certainly and shortly go hence, and the few days I have to spend here are, at the best, full of trouble. O let me have a little respite! *v.* 6. Turn from afflicting a poor creature thus, and let him rest awhile; allow him some breathing time, *until he shall accomplish as a hireling his day.* It is appointed to me once to die; let that one day suffice me, and let me not thus be continually dying, dying a thousand deaths. Let it suffice that my life, at best, is *as the day of a hireling,* a day of toil and labour. I am content to accomplish that, and will make the best of the common hardships of human life, the burden and heat of the day; but let me not feel those uncommon tortures, let not my life be as the day of a malefactor, all execution-day." Thus may we find some relief under great troubles by recommending ourselves to the compassion of that God who knows our frame and will consider it, and our being out of frame too.

7 For there is hope of a tree, if it be cut down, that it will sprout again, and that the tender branch thereof will not cease. 8 Though the root thereof wax old in the earth, and the stock thereof die in the ground; 9 *Yet* through the scent of water it will bud, and bring forth boughs like a plant.

10 But man dieth, and wasteth away: yea, man giveth up the ghost, and where *is* he ? 11 *As* the waters fail from the sea, and the flood decayeth and drieth up : 12 So man lieth down, and riseth not : till the heavens *be* no more, they shall not awake, nor be raised out of their sleep. 13 O that thou wouldest hide me in the grave, that thou wouldest keep me secret, until thy wrath be past, that thou wouldest appoint me a set time, and remember me ! 14 If a man die, shall he live *again* ? all the days of my appointed time will I wait, till my change come. 15 Thou shalt call, and I will answer thee : thou wilt have a desire to the work of thine hands.

We have seen what Job has to say concerning life; let us now see what he has to say concerning death, which his thoughts were very much conversant with, now that he was sick and sore. It is not unseasonable, when we are in health, to think of dying ; but it is an inexcusable incogitancy if, when we are already taken into the custody of death's messengers, we look upon it as a thing at a distance. Job had already shown that death will come, and that its hour is already fixed. Now here he shows,

I. That death is a removal for ever out of this world. This he had spoken of before (*ch.* vii. 9, 10), and now he mentions it again ; for, though it be a truth that needs not be proved, yet it needs to be much considered, that it may be duly improved.

1. A man cut down by death will not revive again, as a tree cut down will. What hope there is of a tree he shows very elegantly, *v.* 7—9. If the body of the tree be cut down, and only the stem or stump left in the ground, though it seem dead and dry, yet it will shoot out young boughs again, as if it were but newly planted. The moisture of the earth and the rain of heaven are, as it were, scented and perceived by the stump of a tree, and they have an influence upon it to revive it; but the dead body of a man would not perceive them, nor be in the least affected by them. In Nebuchadnezzar's dream, when his being deprived of the use of his reason was signified by the cutting down of a tree, his return to it again was signified by the leaving of the stump in the earth with a band of iron and brass to be *wet with the dew of heaven,* Dan. iv. 15. But man has no such prospect of a return to life. The vegetable life is a cheap and easy thing : the scent of water will recover it. The animal life, in some insects and fowls, is so : the heat of the sun retrieves it. But the rational soul, when once retired, is too great, too noble, a thing to be

recalled by any of the powers of nature ; it is out of the reach of sun or rain, and cannot be restored but by the immediate operations of Omnipotence itself ; for (*v.* 10) *man dieth and wasteth away, yea, man giveth up the ghost, and where is he ?* Two words are here used for man :—*Geber, a mighty man,* though mighty, dies ; *Adam, a man of the earth,* because earthy, gives up the ghost. Note, Man is a dying creature. He is here described by what occurs, (1.) Before death : he *wastes away ;* he is continually wasting, dying daily, spending upon the quick stock of life. Sickness and old age are wasting things to the flesh, the strength, the beauty. (2.) In death : *he gives up the ghost ;* the soul leaves the body, and returns to God who gave it, the Father of spirits. (3.) After death : *Where is he ?* He is not where he was ; his place knows him no more ; but *is he nowhere?* So some read it. Yes, he is somewhere ; and it is a very awful consideration to think where those are that have given up the ghost, and where we shall be when we give it up. It has gone to the world of spirits, gone into eternity, gone to return no more to this world.

2. A man laid down in the grave will not rise up again, *v.* 11, 12. Every night we lie down to sleep, and in the morning we awake and rise again ; but at death we must lie down in the grave, not to awake or rise again to such a world, such a state, as we are now in, never to awake or arise *until the heavens,* the faithful measures of time, shall *be no more,* and consequently time itself shall come to an end and be swallowed up in eternity ; so that the life of man may fitly be compared to the waters of a land-flood, which spread far and make a great show, but they are shallow, and when they are cut off from the sea or river, the swelling and overflowing of which was the cause of them, they soon decay and dry up, and their place knows them no more. The waters of life are soon exhaled and disappear. The body, like some of those waters, sinks and soaks into the earth, and is buried there ; the soul, like others of them, is drawn upwards, to mingle with the waters above the firmament. The learned Sir Richard Blackmore makes this also to be a dissimilitude. If the waters decay and be dried up in the summer, yet they will return again in the winter; but it is not so with the life of man. Take part of his paraphrase in his own words :—

A flowing river, or a standing lake,
May their dry banks and naked shores forsake;
Their waters may exhale and upward move,
Their channel leave to roll in clouds above ;
But the returning winter will restore
What in the summer they had lost before:
But if, O man ! thy vital streams desert
Their purple channels and defraud the heart,
With fresh recruits they ne'er will be supplied,
Nor feel their leaping life's returning tide.

II. That yet there will be a return of man to life again in another world, at the end of time, when *the heavens* are *no more.* Then *they shall awake and be raised out of their sleep.* The resurrection of the dead was doubtless an article of Job's creed, as appears, *ch.* xix

26, and to that, it should seem, he has an eye here, where, in the belief of that, we have three things :—

1. A humble petition for a hiding-place in the grave, *v.* 13. It was not only in a passionate weariness of this life that he wished to die, but in a pious assurance of a better life, to which at length he should arise. *O that thou wouldst hide me in the grave!* The grave is not only a resting-place, but a hiding-place, to the people of God. God has the key of the grave, to let in now and to let out at the resurrection. He *hides men in the grave,* as we hide our treasure in a place of secresy and safety; and he who hides will find, and nothing shall be lost. "O that thou wouldst hide me, not only from the storms and troubles of this life, but for the bliss and glory of a better life! Let me lie in the grave, reserved for immortality, in secret from all the world, but not from thee, not from those eyes which saw my substance when first curiously wrought in *the lowest parts of the earth,*" Ps. cxxxix. 15, 16. There let me lie, (1.) *Until thy wrath be past.* As long as the bodies of the saints lie in the grave, so long there are some remains of that wrath which they were by nature children of, so long they are under some of the effects of sin; but, when the body is raised, it is wholly past—death, the last enemy, will then be totally destroyed. (2.) Until the *set time* comes for my being remembered, as Noah was remembered in the ark (Gen. viii. 1), where God not only hid him from the destruction of the old world, but reserved him for the reparation of a new world. The bodies of the saints shall not be forgotten in the grave. There is a time appointed, a time set, for their being enquired after. We cannot be sure that we shall look through the darkness of our present troubles and see good days after them in this world; but, if we can but get well to the grave, we may with an eye of faith look through the darkness of that, as Job here, and see better days on the other side of it, in a better world.

2. A holy resolution patiently to attend the will of God both in his death and in his resurrection (*v.* 14): *If a man die, shall he live again? All the days of my appointed time will I wait until my change come.* Job's friends proving miserable comforters, he set himself to be the more his own comforter. His case was now bad, but he pleases himself with the expectation of a change. I think it cannot be meant of his return to a prosperous condition in this world. His friends indeed flattered him with the hopes of that, but he himself all along despaired of it. Comforts founded upon uncertainties at best must needs be uncertain comforts; and therefore, no doubt, it is something more sure than that which he here bears up himself with the expectation of. The change he waits for must therefore be understood either, (1.) Of the change of the resurrection, when the vile body shall be changed (Phil. iii. 21), and a great and glorious change it will be; and then that question, *If a man die, shall he live again?* must be taken by way of admiration. "Strange! Shall these dry bones live! If so, all the time appointed for the continuance of the separation between soul and body my separate soul shall wait until that change comes, when it shall be united again to the body, *and my flesh also shall rest in hope.*" Ps. xvi. 9. Or, (2.) Of the change at death. "*If a man die, shall he live again?* No, not such a life as he now lives; and therefore I will patiently wait until that change comes which will put a period to my calamities, and not impatiently wish for the anticipation of it, as I have done." Observe here, [1.] That it is a serious thing to die; it is a work by itself. It is a change; there is a visible change in the body, its appearance altered, its actions brought to an end, but a greater change with the soul, which quits the body, and removes to the world of spirits, finishes its state of probation and enters upon that of retribution. This change will come, and it will be a final change, not like the transmutations of the elements, which return to their former state. No, we must die, not thus to live again. It is but once to die, and that had need be well done that is to be done but once. An error here is fatal, conclusive, and not again to be rectified. [2.] That therefore it is the duty of every one of us to wait for that change, and to continue waiting all the days of our appointed time. The time of life is an appointed time; that time is to be reckoned by days; and those days are to be spent in waiting for our change. That is, *First,* We must expect that it will come, and think much of it. *Secondly,* We must desire that it would come, as those that long to be with Christ. *Thirdly,* We must be willing to tarry until it does come, as those that believe God's time to be the best. *Fourthly,* We must give diligence to get ready against it comes, that it may be a blessed change to us.

3. A joyful expectation of bliss and satisfaction in this (*v.* 15): Then *thou shalt call, and I will answer thee.* Now, he was under such a cloud that he could not, he durst not, answer (*ch.* ix. 15, 35; xiii. 22); but he comforted himself with this, that there would come a time when God would call and he should answer. Then, that is, (1.) At the resurrection, "Thou shalt call me out of the grave, by the voice of the archangel, and I will answer and come at the call." The body is the *work of God's hands,* and he will have a desire to that, having prepared a glory for it. Or, (2.) At death: "Thou shalt call my body to the grave, and my soul to thyself, and I will answer, Ready, Lord, ready—Coming, coming; here I am." Gracious souls can cheerfully answer death's summons, and appear to his writ. Their spirits are not forcibly required from them (as Luke xii. 20), but willingly resigned by them, and the earthly tabernacle not violently pulled down,

but voluntarily laid down, with this assurance, "Thou *wilt have a desire to the work of thy hands.* Thou hast mercy in store for me, not only as made by thy providence, but new-made by thy grace; otherwise *he that made them will not save them.* Note, Grace in the soul is the work of God's own hands, and therefore he will not forsake it in this world (Ps. cxxxviii. 8), but will have a desire to it, to perfect it in the other, and to crown it with endless glory.

16 For now thou numberest my steps : dost thou not watch over my sin ? 17 My transgression *is* sealed up in a bag, and thou sewest up mine iniquity. 18 And surely the mountain falling cometh to nought, and the rock is removed out of his place. 19 The waters wear the stones : thou washest away the things which grow *out* of the dust of the earth; and thou destroyest the hope of man. 20 Thou prevailest for ever against him, and he passeth : thou changest his countenance, and sendest him away. 21 His sons come to honour, and he knoweth *it* not; and they are brought low, but he perceiveth *it* not of them. 22 But his flesh upon him shall have pain, and his soul within him shall mourn.

Job here returns to his complaints; and, though he is not without hope of future bliss, he finds it very hard to get over his present grievances.

I. He complains of the particular hardships he apprehended himself under from the strictness of God's justice, *v.* 16, 17. *Therefore* he longed to go hence to that world where God's wrath will be past, because now he was under the continual tokens of it, as a child, under the severe discipline of the rod, longs to be of age. "When shall my change come ? *For now thou* seemest to me to *number my steps,* and *watch over my sin,* and *seal it up in a bag,* as bills of indictment are kept safely, to be produced against the prisoner." See Deut. xxxii. 34. "Thou takest all advantages against me; old scores are called over, every infirmity is animadverted upon, and no sooner is a false step taken than I am beaten for it." Now, 1. Job does right to the divine justice in owning that he smarted for his sins and transgressions, that he had done enough to deserve all that was laid upon him; for there was sin in all his steps, and he was guilty of transgression enough to bring all this ruin upon him, if it were strictly enquired into: he is far from saying that he perishes being innocent. But, 2. He does wrong to the divine goodness in suggesting that God was extreme to mark what he did amiss, and made the worst of

84

every thing. He spoke to this purport, ch. xiii. 27. It was unadvisedly said, and therefore we will not dwell too much upon it. God does indeed see all our sins ; he sees sin in his own people ; but he is not severe in reckoning with us, nor is the law ever stretched against us, but we are punished less than our iniquities deserve. God does indeed seal and sew up, against the day of wrath, the transgression of the impenitent, but the sins of his people he blots out as a cloud.

II. He complains of the wasting condition of mankind in general. We live in a dying world. *Who knows the power of God's anger, by which we are consumed and troubled, and in which all our days are passed away ?* See Ps. xc. 7—9, 11. And who can bear up against his rebukes ? Ps. xxxix. 11.

1. We see the decays of the earth itself. (1.) Of the strongest parts of it, *v.* 18. Nothing will last always, for we see even mountains moulder and come to nought; they wither and fall as a leaf; rocks wax old and pass away by the continual beating of the sea against them. *The waters wear the stones* with constant dropping, *non vi, sed sæpe cadendo*—not by the violence, but by the constancy with which they fall. On this earth every thing is the worse for the wearing. *Tempus edax rerum*—*Time devours all things.* It is not so with the heavenly bodies. (2.) Of the natural products of it. The things which grow out of the earth, and seem to be firmly rooted in it, are sometimes by an excess of rain washed away, *v.* 19. Some think he pleads this for relief : "Lord, my patience will not hold out always ; even rocks and mountains will fail at last; therefore cease the controversy."

2. No marvel then if we see the decays of man upon the earth, for he is of the earth, earthy. Job begins to think his case is not singular, and therefore he ought to reconcile himself to the common lot. We perceive by many instances, (1.) How vain it is to expect much from the enjoyments of life : "*Thou destroyest the hope of man,*" that is, "puttest an end to all the projects he had framed and all the prospects of satisfaction he had flattered himself with." Death will be the destruction of all those hopes which are built upon worldly confidences and confined to worldly comforts. Hope in Christ, and hope in heaven, death will consummate and not destroy. (2.) How vain it is to struggle against the assaults of death (*v.* 20): *Thou prevailest for ever against him.* Note, Man is an unequal match for God. Whom God contends with he will certainly prevail against, prevail for ever against, so that they shall never be able to make head again. Note further, The stroke of death is irresistible ; it is to no purpose to dispute its summons. God prevails against man and he passes away, and lo he is not. Look upon a dying man, and see, [1.] How his looks are altered : *Thou changest his countenance,* and this in

two ways:—*First*, By the disease of his body. When a man has been a few days sick what a change is there in his countenance! How much more when he has been a few minutes dead! The countenance which was majestic and awful becomes mean and despicable—that was lovely and amiable becomes ghastly and frightful. *Bury my dead out of my sight.* Where then is the admired beauty? Death changes the countenance, and then sends us away out of this world, gives us one dismission hence, never to return. *Secondly*, By the discomposure of his mind. Note, The approach of death will make the strongest and stoutest to change countenance; it will make the most merry smiling countenance to look grave and serious, and the most bold daring countenance to look pale and timorous. [2.] How little he is concerned in the affairs of his family, which once lay so near his heart. When he is in the hands of the harbingers of death, suppose struck with a palsy or apoplexy, or delirious in a fever, or in conflict with death, tell him then the most agreeable news, or the most painful, concerning his children, it is all alike, he knows it not, he perceives it not, *v.* 21. He is going to that world where he will be a perfect stranger to all those things which here filled and affected him. The consideration of this should moderate our cares concerning our children and families. God will know what comes of them when we are gone. To him therefore let us commit them, with him let us leave them, and not burden ourselves with needless fruitless cares concerning them. [3.] How dreadful the agonies of death are (*v.* 22): *While his flesh is upon him* (so it may be read), that is, the body he is so loth to lay down, *it shall have pain; and while his soul is within him*, that is, the spirit he is so loth to resign, it shall mourn. Note, Dying work is hard work; dying pangs are, commonly, sore pangs. It is folly therefore for men to defer their repentance to a death-bed, and to have that to do which is the one thing needful when they are really unfit to do any thing: but it is true wisdom, by making our peace with God in Christ and keeping a good conscience, to treasure up comforts which will support and relieve us against the pains and sorrows of a dying hour.

CHAP. XV.

Perhaps Job was so clear, and so well satisfied, in the goodness of his own cause, that he thought, if he had not convinced, yet he had at least silenced all his three friends; but, it seems, he had not: in this chapter they begin a second attack upon him, each of them charging him afresh with as much vehemence as before. It is natural to us to be fond of our own sentiments, and therefore to be firm to them, and with difficulty to be brought to recede from them. Eliphaz here keeps close to the principles upon which he had condemned Job, and, I. He reproves him for justifying himself, and fathers on him many evil things which are unfairly inferred thence, ver. 2—13. II. He persuades him to humble himself before God and to take shame to himself, ver. 14—16. III. He reads him a long lecture concerning the woeful estate of wicked people, who harden their hearts against God and the judgments which are prepared for them, ver. 17—35. A good use may be made both of his reproofs (for they are plain) and of his doctrine (for it is sound), though both the one and the other are misapplied to Job.

THEN answered Eliphaz the Temanite, and said, 2 Should a wise man utter vain knowledge, and fill his belly with the east wind? 3 Should he reason with unprofitable talk? or with speeches wherewith he can do no good? 4 Yea, thou castest off fear, and restrainest prayer before God. 5 For thy mouth uttereth thine iniquity, and thou choosest the tongue of the crafty. 6 Thine own mouth condemneth thee, and not I: yea, thine own lips testify against thee. 7 *Art* thou the first man *that* was born? or wast thou made before the hills? 8 Hast thou heard the secret of God? and dost thou restrain wisdom to thyself? 9 What knowest thou, that we know not? *what* understandest thou, which *is* not in us? 10 With us *are* both the grayheaded and very aged men, much elder than thy father. 11 *Are* the consolations of God small with thee? is there any secret thing with thee? 12 Why doth thine heart carry thee away? and what do thy eyes wink at, 13 That thou turnest thy spirit against God, and lettest *such* words go out of thy mouth? 14 What *is* man, that he should be clean? and *he which is* born of a woman, that he should be righteous? 15 Behold, he putteth no trust in his saints; yea, the heavens are not clean in his sight. 16 How much more abominable and filthy *is* man, which drinketh iniquity like water?

Eliphaz here falls very foul upon Job, because he contradicted what he and his colleagues had said, and did not acquiesce in it and applaud it, as they expected. Proud people are apt thus to take it very much amiss if they may not have leave to dictate and give law to all about them, and to censure those as ignorant and obstinate, and all that is naught, who cannot in every thing say as they say. Several great crimes Eliphaz here charges Job with, only because he would not own himself a hypocrite.

I. He charges him with folly and absurdity (*v.* 2, 3), that, whereas he had been reputed a wise man, he had now quite forfeited his reputation; any one would say that his wisdom had departed from him, he talked so extravagantly and so little to the purpose. Bildad began thus (*ch.* viii. 2), and Zophar, *ch.* xi. 2, 3. It is common for angry disputants thus to represent one another's reasonings as impertinent and ridiculous more than there is cause, forgetting the doom of him that calls his brother *Raca*, and *Thou fool*. It is true, 1. That there is in the world a great deal of vain knowledge, science falsely so called, that is useless, and therefore worthless. 2. That this is the knowledge that puffs up, with which men swell in a fond conceit of their own accomplishments. 3. That, whatever vain knowledge a man may have in his head, if he would be thought a wise man he must not utter it, but let it die with himself as it deserves. 4. Unprofitable talk is evil talk. We must give an account in the great day not only for wicked words, but for idle words. Speeches therefore which do no good, which do no service either to God or our neighbour, or no justice to ourselves, which are no way to the use of edifying, were better unspoken. Those words which are as wind, light and empty, especially which are as the east wind, hurtful and pernicious, it will be pernicious to fill either ourselves or others with, for they will pass very ill in the account. 5. Vain knowledge or unprofitable talk ought to be reproved and checked, especially in a wise man, whom it worst becomes and who does most hurt by the bad example of it.

II. He charges him with impiety and irreligion (*v.* 4): " *Thou castest off fear,*" that is, "the fear of God, and that regard to him which thou shouldst have; and then *thou restrainest prayer.*" See what religion is summed up in, fearing God and praying to him, the former the most needful principle, the latter the most needful practice. Where no fear of God is no good is to be expected; and those who live without prayer certainly live without God in the world. Those who restrain prayer do thereby give evidence that they cast off fear. Surely those have no reverence of God's majesty, no dread of his wrath, and are in no care about their souls and eternity, who make no applications to God for his grace. Those who are prayerless are fearless and graceless. When the fear of God is cast off all sin is let in and a door opened to all manner of profaneness. It is especially bad with those who have had some fear of God, but have now cast it off—have been frequent in prayer, but now restrain it. How have they fallen! How is their first love lost! It denotes a kind of force put upon themselves. The fear of God would cleave to them, but they throw it off; prayer would be uttered, but they restrain it; and, in both, they baffle their convictions. Those who either omit prayer or straiten and abridge themselves in it, quenching the spirit of adoption and denying themselves the liberty they might take in the duty, restrain prayer. This is bad enough, but it is worse to restrain others from prayer, to prohibit and discourage prayer, as Darius, Dan. vi. 7. Now,

1. Eliphaz charges this upon Job, either, (1.) As that which was his own practice. He thought that Job talked of God with such liberty as if he had been his equal, and that he charged him so vehemently with hard usage of him, and challenged him so often to a fair

trial, that he had quite thrown off all religious regard to him. This charge was utterly false, and yet wanted not some colour. We ought not only to take care that we keep up prayer and the fear of God, but that we never drop any unwary expressions which may give occasion to those who seek occasion to question our sincerity and constancy in religion. Or, (2.) As that which others would infer from the doctrine he maintained. " If this be true" (thinks Eliphaz) "which Job says, that a man may be thus sorely afflicted and yet be a good man, then farewell all religion, farewell prayer and the fear of God. If all things come alike to all, and the best men may have the worst treatment in this world, every one will be ready to say, *It is vain to serve God; and what profit is it to keep his ordinances?* Mal. iii. 14. *Verily I have cleansed my hands in vain,* Ps. lxxiii. 13, 14. Who will be honest if the tabernacles of robbers prosper? *ch.* xii. 6. If there be no forgiveness with God (*ch.* vii. 21), who will fear him? Ps. cxxx. 4. If he *laugh at the trial of the innocent* (*ch.* ix. 23), if he be so difficult of access (*ch.* ix. 32), who will pray to him?" Note, It is a piece of injustice which even wise and good men are too often guilty of, in the heat of disputation, to charge upon their adversaries those consequences of their opinions which are not fairly drawn from them and which really they abhor. This is not doing as we would be done by.

2. Upon this strained innuendo Eliphaz grounds that high charge of impiety (*v.* 5): *Thy mouth utters thy iniquity—teaches it,* so the word is. "Thou teachest others to have the same hard thoughts of God and religion that thou thyself hast." It is bad to *break even the least of the commandments,* but worse to *teach men so,* Matt. v. 19. If we ever thought evil, let us lay our hand upon our mouth to suppress the evil thought (Prov. xxx. 32), and let us by no means utter it; that is putting an *imprimatur* to it, publishing it with allowance, to the dishonour of God and the damage of others. Observe, When men have cast off fear and prayer their mouths utter iniquity. Those that cease to do good soon learn to do evil. What can we expect but all manner of iniquity from those that arm not themselves with the grace of God against it? But *thou choosest the tongue of the crafty,* that is, "Thou utterest thy iniquity with some show and pretence of piety, mixing some good words with the bad, as tradesmen do with their wares to help them off." The mouth of iniquity could not do so much mischief as it does without the tongue of the crafty. The serpent beguiled Eve through his subtlety. See Rom. xvi. 18. The tongue of the crafty speaks with design and deliberation; and therefore those that use it may be said to *choose* it, as that which will serve their purpose better than the tongue of the upright: but it will be found, at last, that honesty is the best policy. Eli-

phaz, in his first discourse, had proceeded against Job upon mere surmise (*ch.* iv. 6, 7), but now he has got proof against him from his own discourses (*v.* 6): *Thy own mouth condemns thee, and not I.* But he should have considered that he and his fellows had provoked him to say that which now they took advantage of ; and that was not fair. Those are most effectually condemned that are condemned by themselves, Tit. iii. 11 ; Luke xix. 22. Many a man needs no more to sink him than for his own tongue to fall upon him.

III. He charges him with intolerable arrogancy and self-conceitedness. It was a just, and reasonable, and modest demand that Job had made (*ch.* xii. 3), Allow that *I have understanding as well as you ;* but see how they seek occasion against him : that is misconstrued, as if he pretended to be wiser than any man. Because he will not grant to them the monopoly of wisdom, they will have it thought that he claims it to himself, *v.* 7—9. As if he thought he had the advantage of all mankind, 1. In length of acquaintance with the world, which furnishes men with so much the more experience : " *Art thou the first man that was born ;* and, consequently, senior to us, and better able to give the sense of antiquity and the judgment of the first and earliest, the wisest and purest, ages ? Art thou prior to Adam ?" So it may be read. " Did not he suffer for sin; and yet wilt not thou, who art so great a sufferer, own thyself a sinner ? *Wast thou made before the hills,* as Wisdom herself was ? Prov. viii. 23, &c. Must God's counsels, which are as the great mountains (Ps. xxxvi. 6), and immovable as the everlasting hills, be subject to thy notions and bow to them ? Dost thou know more of the world than any of us do ? No, thou art but of yesterday even as we are," *ch.* viii. 9. Or, 2. In intimacy of acquaintance with God (*v.* 8): " *Hast thou heard the secret of God ?* Dost thou pretend to be of the cabinet-council of heaven, that thou canst give better reasons than others can for God's proceedings?" There are secret things of God, which belong not to us, and which therefore we must not pretend to account for. Those are daringly presumptuous who do. He also represents him, (1.) As assuming to himself such knowledge as none else had : " *Dost thou restrain wisdom to thyself,* as if none were wise besides ?" Job had said (*ch.* xiii. 2), *What you know, the same do I know also ;* and now they return upon him, according to the usage of eager disputants, who think they have a privilege to commend themselves : *What knowest thou that we know not ?* How natural are such replies as these in the heat of argument ! But how simple do they look afterwards, upon the review ! (2.) As opposing the stream of antiquity, a venerable name, under the shade of which all contending parties strive to shelter themselves : " *With us are the gray-headed and very aged men, v.* 10. We have the fathers on our side ; all the ancient doc-

tors of the church are of our opinion." A thing soon said, but not so soon proved; and, when proved, truth is not so soon discovered and proved by it as most people imagine. David preferred right scripture-knowledge before that of antiquity (Ps. cxix. 100 : *I understand more than the ancients, because I keep thy precepts.* Or perhaps one or more, if not all three, of these friends of Job, were older than he (*ch.* xxxii. 6), and therefore they thought he was bound to acknowledge them to be in the right. This also serves contenders to make a noise with to very little purpose. If they are older than their adversaries, and can say they knew such a thing before their opponents were born, this will not serve to justify them in being arrogant and overbearing; for the oldest are not always the wisest, *ch.* xxxii. 9.

IV. He charges him with a contempt of the counsels and comforts that were given him by his friends (*v.* 11): *Are the consolations of God small with thee ?* 1. Eliphaz takes it ill that Job did not value the comforts which he and his friends administered to him more than it seems he did, and did not welcome every word they said as true and important. It is true they had said some very good things, but, in their application to Job, they were miserable comforters. Note, We are apt to think that great and considerable which we ourselves say, when others perhaps with good reason think it small and trifling. Paul found that those who *seemed to be somewhat, yet, in conference, added nothing to him,* Gal. ii. 6. 2. He represents this as a slight put upon divine consolations in general, as if they were of small account with him, whereas really they were not. If he had not highly valued them, he could not have borne up as he did under his sufferings. Note, (1.) The consolations of God are not in themselves small. Divine comforts are great things, that is, the comfort which is from God, especially the comfort which is in God. (2.) The consolations of God not being small in themselves, it is very lamentable if they be small with us. It is a great affront to God, and an evidence of a degenerate depraved mind, to disesteem and undervalue spiritual delights and despise the pleasant land. " What !" (says Eliphaz) " *is there any secret thing with thee ?* Hast thou some cordial to support thyself with, that is a *proprium,* an *arcanum,* that nobody else can pretend to, or knows any thing of ?" Or, " Is there some secret sin harboured and indulged in thy bosom, which hinders the operation of divine comforts ?" None disesteem divine comforts but those that secretly affect the world and the flesh.

V. He charges him with opposition to God himself and to religion (*v.* 12, 13): " *Why doth thy heart carry thee away* into such indecent irreligious expressions?" Note, *Every man is tempted when he is drawn away of his own lust,* Jam. i. 14. If we fly off from God and our duty, or fly out into any thing amiss, it is our own heart that carries us away. *If thou scornest, thou alone shalt bear it.* There is a violence, an ungovernable impetus, in the turnings of the soul; the corrupt heart carries men away, as it were, by force, against their convictions. "What is it that thy eyes wink at? Why so careless and mindless of what is said to thee, hearing it as if thou wert half asleep? Why so scornful, disdaining what we say, as if it were below thee to take notice of it? What have we said that deserves to be thus slighted—nay, *that thou turnest thy spirit against God?*" It was bad that his heart was carried away from God, but much worse that it was turned against God. But those that forsake God will soon break out in open enmity to him. But how did this appear? Why, "Thou lettest such words go out of thy mouth, reflecting on God, and his justice and goodness." It is the character of the wicked that they *set their mouth against the heavens* (Ps. lxxiii. 9), which is a certain indication that the spirit is turned against God. He thought Job's spirit was soured against God, and so turned from what it had been, and exasperated at his dealings with him. Eliphaz wanted candour and charity, else he would not have put such a harsh construction upon the speeches of one that had such a settled reputation for piety and was now in temptation. This was, in effect, to give the cause on Satan's side, and to own that Job had done as Satan said he would, had *cursed God to his face.*

VI. He charges him with justifying himself to such a degree as even to deny his share in the common corruption and pollution of the human nature (*v.* 14): *What is man, that he should be clean?* that is, that he should pretend to be so, or that any should expect to find him so. What is *he that is born of a woman,* a sinful creature, *that he should be righteous?* Note, 1. Righteousness is cleanness; it makes us acceptable to God and easy to ourselves, Ps. xviii. 24. 2. Man, in his fallen state, cannot pretend to be clean and righteous before God, either to acquit himself to God's justice or recommend himself to his favour. 3. He is to be adjudged unclean and unrighteous because born of a woman, from whom he derives a corrupt nature, which is both his guilt and his pollution. With these plain truths Eliphaz thinks to convince Job, whereas he had just now said the same (*ch.* xiv. 4): *Who can bring a clean thing out of an unclean?* But does it therefore follow that Job is a hypocrite, and a wicked man, which is all that he denied? By no means. Though man, as born of a woman, is not clean, yet, as born again of the Spirit, he is clean. 4. Further to evince this he here shows, (1.) That the brightest creatures are imperfect and impure before God, *v.* 15. God places no confidence in saints and angels; he employs both, but trusts neither with his service, without giving them

fresh supplies of strength and wisdom for it, as knowing they are not sufficient of themselves, neither more nor better than his grace makes them. He takes no complacency in the heavens themselves. How pure soever they seem to us, in his eye they have many a speck and many a flaw: *The heavens are not clean in his sight.* If the stars (says Mr. Caryl) have no light in the sight of the sun, what light has the sun in the sight of God! See Isa. xxiv. 23. (2.) That man is much more so (*v.* 16): *How much more abominable and filthy is man!* If saints are not to be trusted, much less sinners. If the heavens are not pure, which are as God made them, much less man, who is degenerated. Nay, he is abominable and filthy in the sight of God, and if ever he repent he is so in his own sight, and therefore he abhors himself. Sin is an odious thing, it makes men hateful. The body of sin is so, and is therefore called *a dead body,* a loathsome thing. Is it not a filthy thing, and enough to make any one sick, to see a man eating swine's food or drinking some nauseous and offensive stuff? Such is the filthiness of man that he *drinks iniquity* (that abominable thing which the Lord hates) as greedily, and with as much pleasure, as a man drinks water when he is thirsty. It is his constant drink; it is natural to sinners to commit iniquity. It gratifies, but does not satisfy, the appetites of the old man. It is like water to a man in a dropsy. The more men sin the more they would sin.

17 I will show thee, hear me; and that *which* I have seen I will declare; 18 Which wise men have told from their fathers, and have not hid *it:* 19 Unto whom alone the earth was given, and no stranger passed among them. 20 The wicked man travaileth with pain all *his* days, and the number of years is hidden to the oppressor. 21 A dreadful sound *is* in his ears: in prosperity the destroyer shall come upon him. 22 He believeth not that he shall return out of darkness, and he is waited for of the sword. 23 He wandereth abroad for bread, *saying,* Where *is it?* he knoweth that the day of darkness is ready at his hand. 24 Trouble and anguish shall make him afraid; they shall prevail against him, as a king ready to the battle. 25 For he stretcheth out his hand against God, and strengtheneth himself against the Almighty. 26 He runneth upon him, *even* on *his* neck, upon the thick bosses of his bucklers: 27 Because he covereth his face with his fatness

and maketh collops of fat on *his* flanks. 28 And he dwelleth in desolate cities, *and* in houses which no man inhabiteth, which are ready to become heaps. 29 He shall not be rich, neither shall his substance continue, neither shall he prolong the perfection thereof upon the earth. 30 He shall not depart out of darkness; the flame shall dry up his branches, and by the breath of his mouth shall he go away. 31 Let not him that is deceived trust in vanity: for vanity shall be his recompence. 32 It shall be accomplished before his time, and his branch shall not be green. 33 He shall shake off his unripe grape as the vine, and shall cast off his flower as the olive. 34 For the congregation of hypocrites *shall be* desolate, and fire shall consume the tabernacles of bribery. 35 They conceive mischief, and bring forth vanity, and their belly prepareth deceit.

Eliphaz, having reproved Job for his answers, here comes to maintain his own thesis, upon which he built his censure of Job. His opinion is that those who are wicked are certainly miserable, whence he would infer that those who are miserable are certainly wicked, and that therefore Job was so.   Observe,

I. His solemn preface to this discourse, in which he bespeaks Job's attention, which he had little reason to expect, he having given so little heed to and put so little value upon what Job had said (*v* 17): "*I will show thee that which is worth hearing, and not reason, as thou dost, with unprofitable talk.*" Thus apt are men, when they condemn the reasonings of others, to commend their own.   He promises to teach him, 1. From his own experience and observation: "*That which I have* myself *seen*, in divers instances, *I will declare.*" It is of good use to take notice of the providences of God concerning the children of men, from which many a good lesson may be learned.   What good observations we have made, and have found benefit by ourselves, we should be ready to communicate for the benefit of others; and we may speak boldly when we declare what we have seen.   2. From the wisdom of the ancients (*v.* 18): *Which wise men have told from their fathers.*   Note, The wisdom and learning of the moderns are very much derived from those of the ancients.   Good children will learn a good deal from their good parents; and what we have learned from our ancestors we must transmit to our posterity and not hide from the generations to come   See Ps. lxxviii. 3—6. If the thread of the knowledge of many ages be cut off by the carelessness of one, and nothing be done to preserve it pure

and entire, all that succeed fare the worse. The authorities Eliphaz vouched were authorities indeed, men of rank and figure (*v.* 19), *unto whom alone the earth was given,* and therefore you may suppose them favourites of Heaven and best capable of making observations concerning the affairs of this earth. The dictates of wisdom come with advantage from those who are in places of dignity and power, as Solomon; yet there is a wisdom *which none of the princes of this world knew,* 1 Cor. ii. 7, 8.

II. The discourse itself.   He here aims to show,

1. That those who are wise and good do ordinarily prosper in this world.   This he only hints at (*v.* 19), that those of whose mind he was were such as had the earth given to them, and to them only; they enjoyed it entirely and peaceably, and no stranger passed among them, either to share with them or give disturbance to them.   Job had said, *The earth is given into the hand of the wicked,* ch. ix. 24.   "No," says Eliphaz, "it is given into the hands of the saints, and runs along with the faith committed unto them; and they are not robbed and plundered by strangers and enemies making inroads upon them, as thou art by the Sabeans and Chaldeans."   But because many of God's people have remarkably prospered in this world, as Abraham, Isaac, and Jacob, it does not therefore follow that those who are crossed and impoverished, as Job, are not God's people.

2. That wicked people, and particularly oppressors and tyrannizing rulers, are subject to continual terrors, live very uncomfortably, and perish very miserably.   On this head he enlarges, showing that even those who impiously dare God's judgments yet cannot but dread them and will feel them at last.   He speaks in the singular number— *the wicked man,* meaning (as some think) Nimrod, or perhaps Chedorlaomer, or some such mighty hunter before the Lord.   I fear he meant Job himself, whom he expressly charges both with the tyranny and with the timorousness here described, *ch.* xxii. 9, 10. Here he thinks the application easy, and that Job might, in this description, as in a glass, see his own face.   Now,

(1.) Let us see how he describes the sinner who lives thus miserably.   He does not begin with that, but brings it in as a reason of his doom, *v.* 25—28.   It is no ordinary sinner, but one of the first rate, an *oppressor* (*v.* 20), a *blasphemer, and a persecutor,* one that *neither fears God nor regards man.* [1.] He bids defiance to God, and to his authority and power, *v.* 25.   Tell him of the divine law, and its obligations; he breaks those bonds asunder, and will not have, no, not him that made him, to restrain him or rule over him.   Tell him of the divine wrath, and its terrors; he bids the Almighty do his worst, he will have his will, he will have his

way, in spite of him, and will not be controlled by law, or conscience, or the notices
of a judgment to come. *He stretches out his
hand against God*, in defiance of him and of
the power of his wrath. God is indeed out
of his reach, but he stretches out his hand
against him, to show that, if it were in his
power, he would ungod him. This applies
to the audacious impiety of some sinners who
are really *haters of God* (Rom. i. 30), and
whose carnal mind is not only an enemy to
him, but enmity itself, Rom. viii. 7. But,
alas! the sinner's malice is as impotent as
it is impudent; what can he do? *He
strengthens himself (he would be valiant*, so
some read it) *against the Almighty.* He
thinks with his exorbitant despotic power to
change times and laws (Dan. vii. 25), and, in
spite of Providence, to carry the day for rapine and wrong, clear of the check of conscience. Note, It is the prodigious madness
of presumptuous sinners that they enter the
lists with Omnipotence. *Woe unto him that
strives with his Maker.* That is generally
taken for a further description of the sinner's
daring presumption (*v.* 26): *He runs upon
him*, upon God himself, in a direct opposition to him, to his precepts and providences,
even upon his neck, as a desperate combatant,
when he finds himself an unequal match for
his adversary, flies in his face, though, at
the same time, he falls on his sword's point,
or the sharp spike of his buckler. Sinners,
in general, run from God; but the presumptuous sinner, who sins with a high hand,
runs upon him, fights against him, and bids
defiance to him; and it is easy to foretel
what will be the issue. [2.] He wraps himself up in security and sensuality (*v.* 27):
He covers his face with his fatness. This
signifies both the pampering of his flesh
with daily delicious fare and the hardening
of his heart thereby against the judgments of
God. Note, The gratifying of the appetites
of the body, feeding and feasting that to the
full, often turns to the damage of the soul
and its interests. Why is God forgotten and
slighted, but because the belly is made a god
of and happiness placed in the delights of
sense? Those that fill themselves with wine
and strong drink abandon all that is serious
and flatter themselves with hopes that *to-
morrow shall be as this day*, Isa. lvi. 12.
Woe to those that are thus at ease in Zion,
Amos vi. 1, 3, 4; Luke xii. 19. The fat
that covers his face makes him look bold and
haughty, and that which covers his flanks
makes him lie easy and soft, and feel little;
but this will prove poor shelter against the
darts of God's wrath. [3.] He enriches himself with the spoils of all about him, *v.* 28.
He dwells in cities which he himself has
made desolate by expelling the inhabitants
out of them, that he might be placed alone
in them, Isa. v. 8 Proud and cruel men
take a strange pleasure in ruins, when they
are of their own making, in *destroying cities*

(Ps. ix. 6) and triumphing in the destruction,
since they cannot make them their own but
by making them *ready to become heaps*, and
frightening the inhabitants out of them.
Note, Those that aim to engross the world
to themselves, and grasp at all, lose the comfort of all, and make themselves miserable
in the midst of all. How does this tyrant
gain his point, and make himself master of
cities that have all the marks of antiquity
upon them? We are told (*v.* 35) that he
does it by malice and falsehood, the two
chief ingredients of *his* wickedness who was
a liar and a murderer from the beginning,
They conceive mischief, and then they effect
it by *preparing deceit*, pretending to protect
those whom they design to subdue, and
making leagues of peace the more effectually
to carry on the operations of war. From
such wicked men God deliver all good men.
(2.) Let us see now what is the miserable
condition of this wicked man, both in spiritual and temporal judgments.
[1.] His inward peace is continually disturbed. He seems to those about him to be
easy, and they therefore envy him and wish
themselves in his condition; but he who
knows what is in men tells us that a wicked
man has so little comfort and satisfaction in
his own breast that he is rather to be pitied
than envied. *First*, His own conscience accuses him, and with the pangs and throes of
that *he travaileth in pain all his days*, *v.* 20.
He is continually uneasy at the thought of
the cruelties he has been guilty of and the
blood in which he has imbrued his hands.
His sins stare him in the face at every turn.
*Diri conscia facti mens habet attonitos—Con-
scious guilt astonishes and confounds.* Secondly, He is vexed at the uncertainty of the
continuance of his wealth and power: *The
number of years is hidden to the oppressor.* He
knows, whatever he pretends, that they will
not last always, and has reason to fear that
they will not last long, and this he frets at.
Thirdly, He is under a *certain fearful expectation of judgment and fiery indignation* (Heb.
x. 27), which puts him into, and keeps him
in, a continual terror and consternation, so
that he dwells with Cain in the land of Nod,
or *commotion* (Gen. iv. 16), and is made like
*Pashur, Magor-missabib—a terror round
about*, Jer. xx. 3, 4. *A dreadful sound is in
his ears*, *v.* 21. He knows that both heaven
and earth are incensed against him, that God
is angry with him and that all the world
hates him; he has done nothing to make his
peace with either, and therefore he thinks
that every one who *meets him will slay him*,
Gen. iv. 14. Or he is like a man absconding
for debt, who thinks every man a bailiff. Fear
came in, at first, with sin (Gen. iii. 10) and
still attends it. Even in prosperity he is apprehensive that the destroyer will come upon
him, either some destroying angel sent of
God to avenge his quarrel or some of his
injured subjects who will be their own

avengers. Those who are the *terror of the mighty in the land of the living* usually *go down slain to the pit* (Ezek. xxxii. 25), the expectation of which makes them a terror to themselves. This is further set forth (*v.* 22): *He is*, in his own apprehension, *waited for of the sword*; for he knows that *he who killeth with the sword must be killed with the sword*, Rev. xiii. 10. A guilty conscience represents to the sinner a *flaming sword turning every way* (Gen. iii. 24) and himself inevitably running on it. Again (*v.* 23): *He knows that the day of darkness* (or the *night* of darkness rather) *is ready at his hand*, that it is appointed to him and cannot be put by, that it is hastening on apace and cannot be put off. This day of darkness is something beyond death; it is that *day of the Lord* which to all wicked people will be darkness and not light and in which they will be doomed to utter, endless, darkness. Note, Some wicked people, though they seem secure, have already received the sentence of death, eternal death, within themselves, and plainly see hell gaping for them. No marvel that it follows (*v.* 24), *Trouble and anguish* (that inward tribulation and anguish of soul spoken of Rom. ii. 8, 9, which are the effect of God's *indignation and wrath* fastening upon the conscience) *shall make him afraid* of worse to come. What is the hell before him if this be the hell within him? And though he would fain shake off his fears, drink them away, and jest them away, it will not do; *they shall prevail against him*, and overpower him, *as a king ready to the battle*, with forces too strong to be resisted. He that would keep his peace, let him keep a good conscience. *Fourthly*, If at any time he be in trouble, he despairs of getting out (*v.* 22): *He believeth not that he shall return out of darkness*, but he gives himself up for gone and lost in an endless night. Good men expect *light at evening time, light out of darkness;* but what reason have those to expect that they shall return out of the darkness of trouble who would not return from the darkness of sin, but *went on in it?* Ps. lxxxii. 5. It is the misery of damned sinners that they know they shall never return out of that utter darkness, nor pass the gulf there fixed. *Fifthly*, He perplexes himself with continual care, especially if Providence ever so little frown upon him, *v.* 23. Such a dread he has of poverty, and such a waste does he discern upon his estate, that he is already, in his own imagination, *wandering abroad for bread*, going a begging for a meal's meat, and saying, *Where is it?* The rich man, in his abundance, cried out, *What shall I do?* Luke xii. 17. Perhaps he pretends fear of wanting, as an excuse of his covetous practices; and justly may he be brought to this extremity at last. We read of those who *were full*, but have *hired out themselves for bread* (1 Sam. ii. 5), which this sinner will not do. He cannot dig; he is too fat (*v.* 27): but to

beg he may well be ashamed. See Ps. cix. 10. David never saw the righteous so far forsaken as to beg their bread; for, verily, they shall be fed by the charitable unasked, Ps. xxxvii. 3, 25. But the wicked want it, and cannot expect it should be readily given them. How should those find mercy who never showed mercy?

[2.] His outward prosperity will soon come to an end, and all his confidence and all his comfort will come to an end with it. How can he prosper when God runs upon him? so some understand that, *v.* 26. Whom God runs *upon* he will certainly run *down;* for when he judges he will overcome. See how the judgments of God cross this worldly wicked man in all his cares, desires, and projects, and so complete his misery. *First*, He is in care to get, but *he shall not be rich, v.* 29. His own covetous mind keeps him from being truly rich. He is not rich that has not enough, and he has not enough that does not think he has. It is contentment only that is great gain. Providence remarkably keeps some from being rich, defeating their enterprises, breaking their measures, and keeping them always behind-hand. Many that get much by fraud and injustice, yet do not grow rich : it goes as it comes; it is got by one sin and spent upon another. *Secondly*, He is in care to keep what he has got, but in vain : *His substance shall not continue ;* it will dwindle and come to nothing. God blasts it, and what came up in a night perishes in a night. *Wealth gotten by vanity will certainly be diminished.* Some have themselves lived to see the ruin of those estates which have been raised by oppression; but, where this is not the case, that which is left goes with a curse to those who succeed. *De male quæsitis vix gaudet tertius hæres*—Ill-gotten property will scarcely be enjoyed by the third generation. He purchases estates *to him and his heirs for ever;* but to what purpose? *He shall not prolong the perfection thereof upon the earth;* neither the credit nor the comfort of his riches shall be prolonged; and, when those are gone, where is the perfection of them? How indeed can we expect the perfection of any thing to be prolonged upon the earth, where every thing is transitory, and we soon see the end of all perfection? *Thirdly*, He is in care to leave what he has got and kept to his children after him. But in this he is crossed; the branches of his family shall perish, in whom he hoped to live and flourish and to have the reputation of making them all great men. *They shall not be green, v.* 32. *The flame shall dry them up, v.* 30. He shall shake them off as blossoms that never knit, or as the *unripe grape, v.* 33. They shall die in the beginning of their days and never come to maturity. Many a man's family is ruined by his iniquity. *Fourthly*, He is in care to enjoy it a great while himself; but in that also he is crossed. 1. He may perhaps be taken from it (v. 30): *By the breath of God's mouth shall he go away,* and leave his wealth to others; that is, by God's wrath, which, *like a stream of brimstone, kindles* the fire that devours him (Isa. xxx. 33), or by his word; he speaks, and it is done immediately. *This night thy soul shall be required of thee;* and so *the wicked is driven away in his wickedness,* the worldling in his worldliness. 2. It may perhaps be taken from him, and fly away like an eagle towards heaven: *It shall be accomplished* (or cut off) *before his time* (v. 32); that is, he shall survive his prosperity, and see himself stripped of it. *Fifthly,* He is in care, when he is in trouble, how to get out of it (not how to get good by it); but in this also he is crossed (v. 30): *He shall not depart out of darkness.* When he begins to fall, like Haman, all men say, "Down with him." It was said of him (v. 22), *He believeth not that he shall return out of darkness.* He frightened himself with the perpetuity of his calamity, and God also shall *choose his delusions* and *bring his fears upon him* (Isa. lxvi. 4), as he did upon Israel, Num. xiv. 28. God says *Amen* to his distrust and despair. *Sixthly,* He is in care to secure his partners, and hopes to secure himself by his partnership with them; but that is in vain too, v. 34, 35. *The congregation* of them, the whole confederacy, they and all their tabernacles, *shall be desolate* and consumed with fire. Hypocrisy and bribery are here charged upon them; that is, deceitful dealing both with God and man—God affronted under colour of religion, man wronged under colour of justice. It is impossible that these should end well. *Though hand join in hand* for the support of these perfidious practices, *yet shall not the wicked go unpunished.*

(3.) The use and application of all this. Will the prosperity of presumptuous sinners end thus miserably? Then (v. 31) *let not him that is deceived trust in vanity.* Let the mischiefs which befal others be our warnings, and let not us rest on that broken reed which always failed those who leaned on it. [1.] Those who trust to their sinful ways of getting wealth *trust in vanity,* and *vanity will be their recompence,* for they shall not get what they expected. Their arts will deceive them and perhaps ruin them in this world. [2.] Those who trust to their wealth when they have gotten it, especially to the wealth they have gotten dishonestly, trust in vanity; for it will yield them no satisfaction. The guilt that cleaves to it will ruin the joy of it. They sow the wind, and will reap the whirlwind, and will own at length, with the utmost confusion, that *a deceived heart turned them aside,* and that they cheated themselves with *a lie in their right hand.*

CHAP. XVI.

This chapter begins Job's reply to that discourse of Eliphaz which we had in the foregoing chapter; it is but the second part of the same song of lamentation with which he had before bemoaned himself, and is set to the same melancholy tune. I. He upbraids his friends with their unkind usage of him, ver. 1—5. II.

He represents his own case as very deplorable upon all accounts, ver. 6—16. III. He still holds fast his integrity, concerning which he appeals to God's righteous judgment from the unrighteous censures of his friends, ver. 17—22.

THEN Job answered and said, 2 I have heard many such things: miserable comforters *are* ye all. 3 Shall vain words have an end? or what emboldeneth thee that thou answerest? 4 I also could speak as ye *do:* if your soul were in my soul's stead, I could heap up words against you, and shake mine head at you. 5 *But* I would strengthen you with my mouth, and the moving of my lips should assuage *your grief.*

Both Job and his friends took the same way that disputants commonly take, which is to undervalue one another's sense, and wisdom, and management. The longer the saw of contention is drawn the hotter it grows; and the *beginning of* this sort of *strife is as the letting forth of water; therefore leave it off before it be meddled with.* Eliphaz had represented Job's discourses as idle, and unprofitable, and nothing to the purpose; and Job here gives his the same character. Those who are free in passing such censures must expect to have them retorted; it is easy, it is endless: but *cui bono?—what good does it do?* It will stir up men's passions, but will never convince their judgments, nor set truth in a clear light. Job here reproves Eliphaz, 1. For needless repetitions (v. 2): " *I have heard many such things.* You tell me nothing but what I knew before, nothing but what you yourselves have before said; you offer nothing new; it is the same thing over and over again." This Job thinks as great a trial of his patience as almost any of his troubles. The inculcating of the same things thus by an adversary is indeed provoking and nauseous, but by a teacher it is often necessary, and must not be grievous to the learner, to whom *precept must be upon precept, and line upon line.* Many things we have heard which it is good for us to hear again, that we may understand and remember them better, and be more affected with them and influenced by them. 2. For unskilful applications. They came with a design to comfort him, but they went about it very awkwardly, and when they touched Job's case, quite mistook it: " *Miserable comforters are you all,* who, instead of offering any thing to alleviate the affliction, add affliction to it, and make it yet more grievous." The patient's case is sad indeed when his medicines are poisons and his physicians his worst disease. What Job says here of his friends is true of all creatures, in comparison with God, and, one time or other, we shall be made to see it and own it, that miserable comforters are they all. When we are under convictions of sin, terrors of conscience, and the arrests of death, it is only the blessed Spirit that can comfort effectually; all others, without him, do it miserably, and sing songs to a heavy heart, to no purpose. 3. For endless impertinence. Job wishes that *vain words might have an end, v.* 3. If vain, it were well that they were never begun, and the sooner they are ended the better. Those who are so wise as to speak to the purpose will be so wise as to know when they have said enough of a thing and when it is time to break off. 4. For causeless obstinacy. *What emboldeneth thee, that thou answerest?* It is a great piece of confidence, and unaccountable, to charge men with those crimes which we cannot prove upon them, to pass a judgment on men's spiritual state upon the view of their outward condition, and to re-advance those objections which have been again and again answered, as Eliphaz did. 5. For the violation of the sacred laws of friendship, doing by his brother as he would not have been done by and as his brother would not have done by him. This is a cutting reproof, and very affecting, *v.* 4, 5. (1.) He desires his friends, in imagination, for a little while, to change conditions with him, to put their souls in his soul's stead, to suppose themselves in misery like him and him at ease like them. This was no absurd or foreign supposition, but what might quickly become true in fact. So strange, so sudden, frequently, are the vicissitudes of human affairs, and such the turns of the wheel, that the spokes soon change places. Whatever our brethren's sorrows are, we ought by sympathy to make them our own, because we know not how soon they may be so. (2.) He represents the unkindness of their conduct towards him, by showing what he could do to them if they were in his condition: *I could speak as you do.* It is an easy thing to trample upon those that are down, and to find fault with what those say that are in extremity of pain and affliction: " *I could heap up words against you,* as you do against me; and how would you like it? how would you bear it?" (3.) He shows them what they should do, by telling them what in that case he would do (*v.* 5): "*I would strengthen you,* and say all I could to assuage your grief, but nothing to aggravate it." It is natural to sufferers to think what they would do if the tables were turned. But perhaps our hearts may deceive us; we know not what we should do. We find it easier to discern the reasonableness and importance of a command when we have occasion to claim the benefit of it than when we have occasion to do the duty of it. See what is the duty we owe to our brethren in their affliction. [1.] We should say and do all we can to strengthen them, suggesting to them such considerations as are proper to encourage their confidence in God and to support their sinking spirits. Faith and patience are the strength of the afflicted; whatever helps these graces con-

firms the feeble knees. [2.] To assuage their grief—the causes of their grief, if possible, or at least their resentment of those causes. Good words cost nothing; but they may be of good service to those that are in sorrow, not only as it is some comfort to them to see their friends concerned for them, but as they may be so reminded of that which, through the prevalency of grief, was forgotten. Though hard words (we say) break no bones, yet kind words may help to make broken bones rejoice; and those have the *tongue of the learned* that know how to *speak a word in season to the weary.*

6 Though I speak, my grief is not assuaged: and *though* I forbear, what am I eased? 7 But now he hath made me weary: thou hast made desolate all my company. 8 And thou hast filled me with wrinkles, *which* is a witness *against me:* and my leanness rising up in me beareth witness to my face. 9 He teareth *me* in his wrath, who hateth me: he gnasheth upon me with his teeth; mine enemy sharpeneth his eyes upon me. 10 They have gaped upon me with their mouth; they have smitten me upon the cheek reproachfully; they have gathered themselves together against me. 11 God hath delivered me to the ungodly, and turned me over into the hands of the wicked. 12 I was at ease, but he hath broken me asunder: he hath also taken *me* by my neck, and shaken me to pieces, and set me up for his mark. 13 His archers compass me round about, he cleaveth my reins asunder, and doth not spare; he poureth out my gall upon the ground. 14 He breaketh me with breach upon breach, he runneth upon me like a giant. 15 I have sewed sackcloth upon my skin, and defiled my horn in the dust. 16 My face is foul with weeping, and on my eyelids *is* the shadow of death.

Job's complaint is here as bitter as any where in all his discourses, and he is at a stand whether to smother it or to give it vent. Sometimes the one and sometimes the other is a relief to the afflicted, according as the temper or the circumstances are; but Job found help by neither, *v.* 6. 1. Sometimes giving vent to grief gives ease; but, " *Though I speak*" (says Job), " *my grief is not assuaged,* my spirit is never the lighter for the pouring out of my complaint; nay, what I speak is so misconstrued as to be turned to the aggravation of my grief." 2. At other times keeping silence makes the trouble the easier and the sooner forgotten; but (says Job) *though I forbear* I am never the nearer; *what am I eased?* If he complained he was censured as passionate; if not, as sullen. If he maintained his integrity, that was his crime; if he made no answer to their accusations, his silence was taken for a confession of his guilt.

Here is a doleful representation of Job's grievances. O what reason have we to bless God that we are not making such complaints! He complains,

I. That his family was scattered (*v.* 7): " *He hath made me weary*, weary of speaking, weary of forbearing, weary of my friends, weary of life itself; my journey through the world proves so very uncomfortable that I am quite tired with it." This made it as tiresome as any thing, that all his company was made desolate, his children and servants being killed and the poor remains of his great household dispersed. The company of good people, that used to meet at his house for religious worship, was now scattered, and he spent his sabbaths in silence and solitude. He had company indeed, but such as he would rather have been without, for they seemed to triumph in his desolation. If lovers and friends are put far from us, we must see and own God's hand in it, making our company desolate.

II. That his body was worn away with diseases and pains, so that he had become a perfect skeleton, nothing but skin and bones, *v.* 8. His face was furrowed, not with age, but sickness: *Thou hast filled me with wrinkles.* His flesh was wasted with the running of his sore boils, so that *his leanness rose up in him*, that is, his bones, that before were not seen, stuck out, *ch.* xxxiii. 21. These are called *witnesses against him*, witnesses of God's displeasure against him, and such witnesses as his friends produced against him to prove him a wicked man. Or, "They are witnesses *for* me, that my complaint is not causeless," or "witnesses *to* me, that I am a dying man, and must be gone shortly."

III. That his enemy was a terror to him, threatened him, frightened him, looked sternly upon him, and gave all the indications of rage against him (*v.* 9): *He tears me in his wrath.* But who is this enemy? 1. Eliphaz, who showed himself very much exasperated against him, and perhaps had expressed himself with such marks of indignation as are here mentioned: at least, what he said tore Job's good name and thundered nothing but terror to him; his eyes were sharpened to spy out matter of reproach against Job, and very barbarously both he and the rest of them used him. Or, 2. Satan. He was his enemy that hated him, and perhaps, by the divine permission, terrified him with apparitions, as (some think) he terrified our Saviour, which put him into

his agonies in the garden; and thus he aimed to make him curse God. It is not improbable that this is the enemy he means. Or, (3.) God himself. If we understand it of him, the expressions are indeed as rash as any he used. God hates none of his creatures; but Job's melancholy did thus represent to him the terrors of the Almighty: and nothing can be more grievous to a good man than to apprehend God to be his enemy. If the wrath of a king be as messengers of death, what is the wrath of the King of kings!

IV. That all about him were abusive to him, *v.* 10. They came upon him with open mouth to devour him, as if they would swallow him alive, so terrible were their threats and so scornful was their conduct to him. They offered him all the indignities they could invent, and even smote him *on the cheek;* and herein many were confederate. *They gathered themselves together against him*, even the abjects, Ps. xxxv. 15. Herein Job was a type of Christ, as many of the ancients make him : these very expressions are used in the predictions of his sufferings, Ps. xxii. 13, *They gaped upon me with their mouths;* and (Mic. v. 1), *They shall smite the Judge of Israel with a rod upon the cheek*, which was literally fulfilled, Matt. xxvi. 67. How were those increased that troubled him!

V. That God, instead of delivering him out of their hands, as he hoped, delivered him into their hands (*v.* 11): *He hath turned me over into the hands of the wicked.* They could have had no power against him if it had not been given them from above. He therefore looks beyond them to God who gave them their commission, as David did when Shimei cursed him; but he thinks it strange, and almost thinks it hard, that those should have power against him who were God's enemies as much as his. God sometimes makes use of wicked men as his sword to one another (Ps. xvii. 13) and his rod to his own children, Isa. x. 5. Herein also Job was a type of Christ, who was delivered into wicked hands, to be crucified and slain, by the *determinate counsel and fore-knowledge of God*, Acts ii. 23.

VI. That God not only delivered him into the hands of the wicked, but took him into his own hands too, into which it is a fearful thing to fall (*v.* 12): " *I was at ease* in the comfortable enjoyment of the gifts of God's bounty, not fretting and uneasy, as some are in the midst of their prosperity, who thereby provoke God to strip them; yet *he has broken me asunder*, put me upon the rack of pain, and torn me limb from limb." God, in afflicting him, had seemed, 1. As if he were furious. Though fury is not in God, he thought it was, when he took him *by the neck* (as a strong man in a passion would take a child) and shook him to pieces, triumphing in the irresistible power he had to do what he would with him. 2. As if he were partial. "He has distinguished me from the rest of mankind by this hard usage of me : *He has set me up for his mark*, the butt at which he is pleased to let fly all his arrows : at me they are directed, and they come not by chance ; against me they are levelled, as if I were the greatest sinner of all the men of the east or were singled out to be made an example." When God set him up for a mark *his archers* presently *compassed him round.* God has archers at command, who will be sure to hit the mark that he sets up. Whoever are our enemies, we must look upon them as God's archers, and see him directing the arrow. *It is the Lord ; let him do what seemeth him good.* 3. As if he were cruel, and his wrath as relentless as his power was resistless. As if he contrived to touch him in the tenderest part, *cleaving his reins asunder* with acute pains ; perhaps they were nephritic pains, those of the stone, which lie in the region of the kidneys. As if he had no mercy in reserve for him, he does not spare nor abate any thing of the extremity. And as if he aimed at nothing but his death, and his death in the midst of the most grievous tortures : *He pours out my gall upon the ground*, as when men have taken a wild beast, and killed it, they open it, and pour out the gall with a loathing of it. He thought his blood was poured out, as if it were not only not precious, but nauseous. 4. As if he were unreasonable and insatiable in his executions (*v.* 14) : "*He breaketh me with breach upon breach*, follows me with one wound after another." So his troubles came at first ; while one messenger of evil tidings was speaking another came : and so it was still ; new boils were rising every day, so that he had no prospect of the end of his troubles. Thus he thought that God ran upon him *like a giant*, whom he could not possibly stand before or confront ; as the giants of old ran down all their poor neighbours, and were too hard for them. Note, Even good men, when they are in great and extraordinary troubles, have much ado not to entertain hard thoughts of God.

VII. That he had divested himself of all his honour, and all his comfort, in compliance with the afflicting providences that surrounded him. Some can lessen their own troubles by concealing them, holding their heads as high and putting on as good a face as ever ; but Job could not do so : he received the impressions of them, and, as one truly penitent and truly patient, he humbled himself under the mighty hand of God, *v.* 15, 16. 1. He now laid aside all his ornaments and soft clothing, consulted not either his ease or finery in his dress, but sewed sackcloth upon his skin ; that clothing he thought good enough for such a defiled distempered body as he had. Silks upon sores, such sores, he thought, would be unsuitable ; sackcloth would be more becoming. Those are fond indeed of gay clothing that

will not be weaned from it by sickness and old age, and, as Job was (*v.* 8), by *wrinkles and leanness.* He not only put on sackcloth, but sewed it on, as one that resolved to continue his humiliation as long as the affliction continued. 2. He insisted not upon any points of honour, but humbled himself under humbling providences : *He defiled his horn in the dust*, and refused the respect that used to be paid to his dignity, power, and eminency. Note, When God brings down our condition, that should bring down our spirits. Better lay the horn in the dust than lift it up in contradiction to the designs of Providence and have it broken at last. Eliphaz had represented Job as high and haughty, and unhumbled under his affliction. "No," says Job, "I know better things ; the dust is now the fittest place for me." 3. He banished mirth as utterly unseasonable, and set himself to sow in tears (*v.* 16) : "*My face is foul with weeping* so constantly for my sins, for God's displeasure against me, and for my friends' unkindness : this has brought a *shadow of death upon my eyelids.*" He had not only wept away all his beauty, but almost wept his eyes out. In this also he was a type of Christ, who was a man of sorrows, and much in tears, and pronounced those blessed that mourn, *for they shall be comforted.*

17 Not for *any* injustice in mine hands : also my prayer *is* pure. 18 O earth, cover not thou my blood, and let my cry have no place. 19 Also now, behold, my witness *is* in heaven, and my record *is* on high. 20 My friends scorn me : *but* mine eye poureth out *tears* unto God. 21 O that one might plead for a man with God, as a man *pleadeth* for his neighbour ! 22 When a few years are come, then I shall go the way *whence* I shall not return.

Job's condition was very deplorable ; but had he nothing to support him, nothing to comfort him ? Yes, and he here tells us what it was.

I. He had the testimony of his conscience for him that he had walked uprightly, and had never allowed himself in any gross sin. None was ever more ready than he to acknowledge his sins of infirmity ; but, upon search, he could not charge himself with any enormous crime, for which he should be made more miserable than other men, *v.* 17.

1. He had kept a conscience void of offence, (1.) Towards men : "*Not for any injustice in my hands*, any wealth that I have unjustly got or kept." Eliphaz had represented him as a tyrant and an oppressor. "No," says he, "I never did any wrong to any man, but always despised the gain of oppression." (2.) Towards God : *Also my*

prayer is pure; but prayer cannot be pure as long as there is *injustice in our hands,* Isa. i. 15. Eliphaz had charged him with hypocrisy in religion, but he specifies prayer, the great act of religion, and professes that in that he was pure, though not from all infirmity, yet from reigning and allowed guile: it was not like the prayers of the Pharisees, who looked no further than to be seen of men, and to serve a turn.

2. This assertion of his own integrity he backs with a solemn imprecation of shame and confusion to himself if it were not true, *v.* 18. (1.) If there were any injustice in his hands, he wished it might not be concealed: *O earth! cover thou not my blood,* that is, "the innocent blood of others, which I am suspected to have shed." Murder will out; and "let it," says Job, "if I have ever been guilty of it," Gen. iv. 10, 11. The day is coming when *the earth shall disclose her blood* (Isa. xxvi. 21), and a good man is far from dreading that day. (2.) If there were any impurity in his prayers, he wished they might not be accepted: *Let my cry have no place.* He was willing to be judged by that rule, *If I regard iniquity in my heart, the Lord will not hear me,* Ps. lxvi. 18. There is another probable sense of these words, that he does hereby, as it were, lay his death upon his friends, who broke his heart with their harsh censures, and charges the guilt of his blood upon them, begging of God to avenge it and that the cry of his blood might have no place in which to lie hid, but might come up to heaven and be heard by him that makes inquisition for blood.

II. He could appeal to God's omniscience concerning his integrity, *v.* 19. The witness in our own bosoms for us will stand us in little stead if we have not a witness in heaven for us too; for God *is greater than our hearts,* and we are not to be our own judges. This therefore is Job's triumph, *My witness is in heaven.* Note, It is an unspeakable comfort to a good man, when he lies under the censure of his brethren, that there is a God in heaven who knows his integrity and will clear it up sooner or later. See John v. 31, 37. This one witness is instead of a thousand.

III. He had a God to go to before whom he might unbosom himself, *v.* 20, 21. See here, 1. How the case stood between him and his friends. He knew not how to be free with them, nor could he expect either a fair hearing with them or fair dealing from them. "My friends (so they call themselves) scorn me; they set themselves not only to resist me, but to expose me; they are of counsel against me, and use all their art and eloquence" (so the word signifies) "to run me down." The scorns of friends are more cutting than those of enemies; but we must expect them, and provide accordingly. 2. How it stood between him and God. He doubted not but that, (1.) God did now take

cognizance of his sorrows: *My eye pours out tears to God.* He had said (*v.* 16) that he wept much; here he tells us in what channel his tears ran, and which way they were directed. His sorrow was not that of the world, but he sorrowed after a godly sort, wept before the Lord, and offered to him the sacrifice of a broken heart. Note, Even tears, when sanctified to God, give ease to troubled spirits; and, if men slight our grief, this may comfort us, that God regards them. (2.) That he would in due time clear up his innocency (*v.* 21): *O that one might plead for a man with God!* If he could but now have the same freedom at God's bar that men commonly have at the bar of the civil magistrate, he doubted not but to carry his cause, for the Judge himself was a witness to his integrity. The language of this wish is like that in Isa. l. 7, 8, *I know that I shall not be ashamed, for he is near that justifies me.* Some give a gospel sense of this verse, and the original will very well bear it; *and he will plead* (that is, there is one that will plead) *for man with God, even the Son of man for his friend, or neighbour.* Those who pour out tears before God, though they cannot plead for themselves, by reason of their distance and defects, have a friend to plead for them, even the Son of man, and on this we must bottom all our hopes of acceptance with God.

IV. He. had a prospect of death which would put a period to all his troubles. Such confidence had he towards God that he could take pleasure in thinking of the approach of death, when he should be determined to his everlasting state, as one that doubted not but it would be well with him then: *When a few years have come (the years of number* which are determined and appointed to me) *then I shall go the way whence I shall not return.* Note, 1. To die is to *go the way whence we shall not return.* It is to go a journey, a long journey, a journey for good and all, to remove from this to another country, from the world of sense to the world of spirits. It is a journey to our long home; there will be no coming back to our state in this world nor any change of our state in the other world. 2. We must all of us very certainly, and very shortly, go this journey; and it is comfortable to those who keep a good conscience to think of it, for it is the crown of their integrity.

CHAP. XVII.

In this chapter, I. Job reflects upon the harsh censures which his friends had passed upon him, and, looking upon himself as a dying man (ver. 1), he appeals to God, and begs of him speedily to appear for him, and right him, because they had wronged him, and he knew not how to right himself, ver. 2—7. But he hopes that, though it should be a surprise, it will be no stumbling-block, to good people, to see him thus abused, ver. 8, 9. II. He reflects upon the vain hopes they had fed him with, that he should yet see good days, showing that his days were just at an end, and with his body all his hopes would be buried in the dust, ver. 10—16. His friends becoming strange to him, which greatly grieved him, he makes death and the grave familiar to him, which yielded him some comfort.

M Y breath is corrupt, my days are extinct, the graves *are ready* for me. 2 *Are there* not mockers with me? and doth not mine eye continue in their provocation? 3 Lay down now, put me in a surety with thee; who *is* he *that* will strike hands with me? 4 For thou hast hid their heart from understanding : therefore shalt thou not exalt *them.* 5 He that speaketh flattery to *his* friends, even the eyes of his children shall fail. 6 He hath made me also a byword of the people; and aforetime I was as a tabret. 7 Mine eye also is dim by reason of sorrow, and all my members *are* as a shadow. 8 Upright *men* shall be astonied at this, and the innocent shall stir up himself against the hypocrite. 9 The righteous also shall hold on his way, and he that hath clean hands shall be stronger and stronger.

Job's discourse is here somewhat broken and interrupted, and he passes suddenly from one thing to another, as is usual with men in trouble; but we may reduce what is here said to three heads :—

I. The deplorable condition which poor Job was now in, which he describes, to aggravate the great unkindness of his friends to him and to justify his own complaints. Let us see what his case was.

1. He was a dying man, *v.* 1. He had said (*ch.* xvi. 22), "*When a few years have come,* I shall go that long journey." But here he corrects himself. "Why do I talk of years to come? Alas! I am just setting out on that journey, am now ready to be offered, and the time of my departure is at hand. *My breath is* already *corrupt,* or broken off; my spirits are spent; I am a gone man." It is good for every one of us thus to look upon ourselves as dying, and especially to think of it when we are sick. We are dying, that is, (1.) Our life is going; for the breath of life is going. It is continually *going forth; it is in our nostrils* (Isa. ii. 22), the door at which it entered (Gen. ii. 7); there it is upon the threshold, ready to depart. Perhaps Job's distemper obstructed his breathing, and short breath will, after a while, be no breath. Let *the Anointed of the Lord be the breath of our nostrils,* and let us get spiritual life breathed into us, and that breath will never be corrupted. (2.) Our time is ending : *My days are extinct, are put out,* as a candle which, from the first lighting, is continually wasting and burning down, and will by degrees burn out of itself, but may by a thousand accidents be extinguished. Such is life. It concerns us therefore carefully to redeem the days of time, and to spend them in getting ready for

the days of eternity, which will never be extinct. (3.) We are expected in our long home: *The graves are ready for me.* But would not one grave serve? Yes, but he speaks of the *sepulchres of his fathers,* to which he must be gathered : "The graves where they are laid are ready for me also," graves in consort, the congregation of the dead. Wherever we go there is but a step between us and the grave. Whatever is unready, that is ready; it is a bed soon made. If the graves be ready for us, it concerns us to be ready for the graves. *The graves for me* (so it runs), denoting not only his expectation of death, but his desire of it · " I have done with the world, and have nothing now to wish for but a grave."

2. He was a despised man (*v.* 6) : "*He*" (that is, Eliphaz, so some, or rather God, whom he all along acknowledges to be the author of his calamities) "*has made me a byword of the people,* the talk of the country, a laughing-stock to many, a gazing-stock to all; *and aforetime* (or to men's faces, publicly) *I was as a tabret,* that whoever chose might play upon." They made ballads of him; his name became a proverb; it is so still, *As poor as Job.* "He has now *made me a by-word,*" a reproach of men, whereas, aforetime, in my prosperity, I was as a tabret, *deliciæ humani generis—the darling of the human race,* whom they were all pleased with. It is common for those who were honoured in their wealth to be despised in their poverty.

3. He was a man of sorrows, *v.* 7. He wept so much that he had almost lost his sight : *My eye is dim by reason of sorrow, ch.* xvi. 16. The sorrow of the world thus works darkness and death. He grieved so much that he had fretted all the flesh away and become a perfect skeleton, nothing but skin and bones : "*All my members are as a shadow.* I have become so poor and thin that I am not to be called a man, but the *shadow of a man.*"

II. The ill use which his friends made of his miseries. They trampled upon him, and insulted over him, and condemned him as a hypocrite, because he was thus grievously afflicted. Hard usage! Now observe,

1. How Job describes it, and what construction he puts upon their discourses with him. He looks upon himself as basely abused by them. (1.) They abused him with their foul censures, condemning him as a bad man, justly reduced thus and exposed to contempt, *v.* 2. "They are *mockers,* who deride my calamities, and insult over me, because I am thus brought low. They are so *with me,* abusing me to my face, pretending friendship in their visit, but intending mischief. I cannot get clear of them; they are continually tearing me, and they will not be wrought upon, either by reason or pity, to let fall the prosecution." (2.) They abused him too with their fair promises, for in them

they did but banter him. He reckons them (v. 5) among those that speak flattery to their friends. They all came to mourn with him. Eliphaz began with a commendation of him, *ch.* iv. 3. They had all promised him that he would be happy if he would take their advice. Now all this he looked upon as flattery, and as designed to vex him so much the more. All this he calls their *provocation, v.* 2. They did what they could to provoke him and then condemned him for his resentment of it; but he thinks himself excusable when his eye *continued* thus *in their provocation:* it never ceased, and he never could look off it. Note, The unkindness of those that trample upon their friends in affliction, that banter and abuse them then, is enough to try, if not to tire, the patience even of Job himself.

2. How he condemns it. (1.) It was a sign that *God had hidden their heart from understanding* (v. 4), and that in this matter they were infatuated, and their wonted wisdom had departed from them. Wisdom is a gift of God, which he grants to some and withholds from others, grants at some times and withholds at other times. Those that are void of compassion are so far void of understanding. Where there is not the tenderness of a man one may question whether there be the understanding of a man. (2.) It would be a lasting reproach and diminution to them: *Therefore shalt thou not exalt them.* Those are certainly kept back from honour whose hearts are hidden from understanding. When God infatuates men he will abase them. Surely those who discover so little acquaintance with the methods of Providence shall not have the honour of deciding this controversy! That is reserved for a man of better sense and better temper, such a one as Elihu afterwards appeared to be. (3.) It would entail a curse upon their families. He that thus violates the sacred laws of friendship forfeits the benefit of it, not only for himself, but for his posterity: "*Even the eyes of his children shall fail,* and, when they look for succour and comfort from their own and their father's friends, they shall look in vain as I have done, and be as much disappointed as I am in you." Note, Those that wrong their neighbours may thereby, in the end, wrong their own children more than they are aware of.

3. How he appeals from them to God (v. 3): *Lay down now, put me in a surety with thee,* that is, "Let me be assured that God will take the hearing and determining of the cause into his own hands, and I desire no more. Let some one engage for God to bring on this matter." Thus those whose hearts condemn them not have confidence towards God, and can with humble and believing boldness beg of him to search and try them. Some make Job here to glance at the mediation of Christ, for he speaks of a surety with God, without whom he durst

not appear before God, nor try his cause at his bar; for, though his friends' accusations of him were utterly false, yet he could not justify himself before God but in a mediator. Our English annotations give this reading of the verse: "*Appoint, I pray thee, my surety with thee,* namely, Christ who is with thee in heaven, and has undertaken to be my surety: let him plead my cause, and stand up for me; and *who is he then that will strike upon my hand?*" that is, "Who dares then contend with me? Who shall lay any thing to my charge if Christ be an advocate for me?" Rom. viii. 32, 33. Christ is the surety of the better testament (Heb. vii. 22), a surety of God's appointing; and, if he undertake for us, we need not fear what can be done against us.

III. The good use which the righteous should make of Job's afflictions from God, from his enemies, and from his friends, v. 8, 9. Observe here,

1. How the saints are described. (1.) They are *upright men,* honest and sincere, and that act from a steady principle, with a single eye. This was Job's own character (*ch.* i. 1), and probably he speaks of such upright men especially as had been his intimates and associates. (2.) They are *the innocent,* not perfectly so, but innocence is what they aim at and press towards. Sincerity is evangelical innocency, and those that are upright are said to be *innocent from the great transgression,* Ps. xix. 13. (3.) They are *the righteous,* who walk in the way of righteousness. (4.) They have *clean hands,* kept clean from the gross pollutions of sin, and, when spotted with infirmities, *washed with innocency,* Ps. xxvi. 6.

2. How they should be affected with the account of Job's troubles. Great enquiry, no doubt, would be made concerning him, and every one would speak of him and his case; and what use will good people make of it? (1.) It will amaze them: *Upright men shall be astonished at this;* they will wonder to hear that so good a man as Job should be so grievously afflicted in body, name, and estate, that God should lay his hand so heavily upon him, and that his friends, who ought to have comforted him, should add to his grief, that such a remarkable saint should be such a remarkable sufferer, and so useful a man laid aside in the midst of his usefulness; what shall we say to these things? Upright men, though satisfied in general that God is wise and holy in all he does, yet cannot but be astonished at such dispensations of Providence, paradoxes which will not be unfolded till the mystery of God shall be finished. (2.) It will animate them. Instead of being deterred from and discouraged in the service of God, by the hard usage which this faithful servant of God met with, they shall be so much the more emboldened to proceed and persevere in it. That which was St. Paul's care (1 Thess. iii. 3) was Job's, that no good

man should be moved, either from his holiness or his comfort, by these afflictions, that none should, for the sake hereof, think the worse of the ways or work of God. And that which was St. Paul's comfort was his too, that *the brethren in the Lord would wax confident by his bonds,* Phil. i. 14. They would hereby be animated, [1.] To oppose sin and to confront the corrupt and pernicious inferences which evil men would draw from Job's sufferings, as that God has forsaken the earth, that it is in vain to serve him, and the like: *The innocent shall stir up himself against the hypocrite,* will not bear to hear this (Rev. ii. 2), but will withstand him to his face, will stir up himself to search into the meaning of such providences and study these hard chapters, that he may read them readily, will stir up himself to maintain religion's just but injured cause against all its opposers. Note, The boldness of the attacks which profane people make upon religion should sharpen the courage and resolution of its friends and advocates. It is time to stir when proclamation is made in the gate of the camp, *Who is on the Lord's side?* When vice is daring it is no time for virtue, through fear, to hide itself. [2.] To persevere in religion. *The righteous,* instead of drawing back, or so much as starting back, at this frightful spectacle, or standing still to deliberate whether he should proceed or no (allude to 2 Sam. ii. 23), *shall* with so much the more constancy and resolution *hold on his way* and press forward. "Though in me he foresees that bonds and afflictions abide him, yet *none of these things shall move him,*" Acts xx. 24. Those who keep their eye upon heaven as their end will keep their feet in the paths of religion as their way, whatever difficulties and discouragements they meet with in it. [3.] In order thereunto to grow in grace. He will not only hold on his way notwithstanding, but will grow *stronger and stronger.* By the sight of other good men's trials, and the experience of his own, he will be made more vigorous and lively in his duty, more warm and affectionate, more resolute and undaunted; the worse others are the better he will be; that which dismays others emboldens him. The blustering wind makes the traveller gather his cloak the closer about him and gird it the faster. Those that are truly wise and good will be continually growing wiser and better. Proficiency in religion is a good sign of sincerity in it.

10 But as for you all, do ye return, and come now : for I cannot find *one wise man* among you. 11 My days are past, my purposes are broken off, *even* the thoughts of my heart. 12 They change the night into day : the light *is* short because of darkness. 13 If I wait, the grave *is* mine house : I have made my bed in the darkness.

14 I have said to corruption, Thou *art* my father: to the worm, *Thou art* my mother, and my sister. 15 And where *is* now my hope ? as for my hope, who shall see it ? 16 They shall go down to the bars of the pit, when *our* rest together *is* in the dust.

Job's friends had pretended to comfort him with the hopes of his return to a prosperous estate again; now he here shows,

I. That it was their folly to talk so (v. 10): "*Return, and come now,* be convinced that you are in an error, and let me persuade you to be of my mind; *for I cannot find one wise man among you,* that knows how to explain the difficulties of God's providence or how to apply the consolations of his promises." Those do not go wisely about the work of comforting the afflicted who fetch their comforts from the possibility of their recovery and enlargement in this world; though that is not to be despaired of, it is at the best uncertain; and if it should fail, as perhaps it may, the comfort built upon it will fail too. It is therefore our wisdom to comfort ourselves, and others, in distress, with that which will not fail, the promise of God, his love and grace, and a well-grounded hope of eternal life.

II. That it would be much more his folly to heed them; for,

1. All his measures were already broken and he was full of confusion, v. 11, 12. He owns he had, in his prosperity, often pleased himself both with projects of what he should do and prospects of what he should enjoy; but now he looked upon his days as past, or drawing towards a period; all those purposes were broken off and those expectations dashed. He had had thoughts about enlarging his border, increasing his stock, and settling his children, and many pious thoughts, it is likely, of promoting religion in his country, redressing grievances, reforming the profane, relieving the poor, and raising funds perhaps for charitable uses; but he concluded that all these thoughts of his heart were now at an end, and that he should never have the satisfaction of seeing his designs effected. Note, The period of our days will be the period of all our contrivances and hopes for this world; but, if with full purpose of heart we cleave to the Lord, death will not break off that purpose. Job, being thus put upon new counsels, was under a constant uneasiness (v. 12): *The thoughts of his heart* being broken, they *changed the night into day and shortened the light.* Some, in their vanity and riot, turn night into day and day into night; but Job did so through trouble and anguish of spirit, which were a hindrance, (1.) To the repose of the night, keeping his eyes waking, so that the night was as wearisome to him as the day, and the tossings of the night tired him as much as the toils of the day. (2.)

To the entertainments of the day. "The light of the morning is welcome, but, by reason of this inward darkness, the comfort of it is soon gone, and the day is to me as dismal as the black and dark night," Deut. xxviii. 67. See what reason we have to be thankful for the health and ease which enable us to welcome both the shadows of the evening and the light of the morning.

2. All his expectations from this world would very shortly be buried in the grave with him; so that it was a jest for him to think of such mighty things as they had flattered him with the hopes of, *ch.* v. 19; viii. 21; xi. 17. "Alas! you do but make a fool of me."

(1.) He saw himself just dropping into the grave. A convenient house, an easy bed, and agreeable relations, are some of those things in which we take satisfaction in this world: Job expected not any of these above ground; all he felt, and all he had in view, was unpleasing and disagreeable, but under ground he expected them. [1.] He counted upon no house but the grave (*v.* 13): "If I wait, if there be any place where I shall ever be easy again, it must be in the grave. I should deceive myself if I should count upon any out-let from my trouble but what death will give me. Nothing is so sure as that." Note, In all our prosperity it is good to keep death in prospect. Whatever we expect, let us be sure to expect that; for that may prevent other things which we expect, but nothing will prevent that. But see how he endeavours not only to reconcile himself to the grave, but to recommend it to himself: " It is my house." The grave is a house; to the wicked it is a prison-house (*ch.* xxiv. 19, 20); to the godly it is *Bethabara, a passage-house* in their way home. "It is my house, mine by descent, I am born to it; it is my father's house. It is mine by purchase. I have made myself obnoxious to it." We must every one of us shortly remove to this house, and it is our wisdom to provide accordingly; let us think of removing, and send before to our long home. [2.] He counted upon no quiet bed but in the darkness: "There," says he, "*I have made my bed.* It is made, for it is ready, and I am just going to it." The grave is a bed, for we shall rest in it in the evening of our day on earth, and rise from it in the morning of our everlasting day, Isa. lvii. 2. Let this make good people willing to die; it is but going to bed; they are weary and sleepy, and it is time that they were in their beds. Why should they not go willingly, when their father calls? "Nay, *I have made my bed*, by preparation for it, have endeavoured to make it easy, by keeping conscience pure, by seeing Christ lying in this bed, and so turning it into a bed of spices, and by looking beyond it to the resurrection. [3.] He counted upon no agreeable relations but what he had in the grave (*v.* 14): *I have cried to corruption* (that is, to the grave, where the body will corrupt), *Thou art*

my father (for our bodies were formed out of the earth), and *to the worms* there, *You are my mother and my sister,* to whom I am allied (for *man is a worm*) and with whom I must be conversant, for the *worms shall cover us, ch.* xxi. 26. Job complained that his kindred were estranged from him (*ch.* xix. 13, 14); therefore here he claims acquaintance with other relations that would cleave to him when those disowned him. Note, *First,* We are all of us near akin to corruption and the worms. *Secondly,* It is therefore good to make ourselves familiar with them, by conversing much with them in our thoughts and meditations, which would very much help us above the inordinate love of life and fear of death.

(2.) He saw all his hopes from this world dropping into the grave with him (*v.* 15, 16): "Seeing I must shortly leave the world, *where is now my hope?* How can I expect to prosper who do not expect to live?" He is not hopeless, but his hope is not where they would have it be. *If in this life only* he had *hope*, he was *of all men most miserable.* "No, as for my hope, that hope which I comfort and support myself with, who shall see it? It is something out of sight that I hope for, not things that are seen, that are temporal, but things not seen, that are eternal." What is his hope he will tell us (*ch.* xix. 25), *Non est mortale quod opto, immortale peto—I seek not for that which perishes, but for that which abides for ever.* "But, as for the hopes you would buoy me up with, they shall go down with me to the bars of the pit. You are dying men, and cannot make good your promises. I am a dying man, and cannot enjoy the good you promise. Since, therefore, our rest will be together in the dust, let us all lay aside the thoughts of this world and set our hearts upon another." We must shortly be in the dust, for dust we are, dust and ashes in the pit, under *the bars of the pit*, held fast there, never to loose the bands of death till the general resurrection. But we shall rest there; we shall rest together there. Job and his friends could not agree now, but they will both be quiet in the grave; the dust of that will shortly stop their mouths and put an end to the controversy. Let the foresight of this cool the heat of all contenders and moderate the disputers of this world.

CHAP. XVIII.

In this chapter Bildad makes a second assault upon Job. In his first discourse (ch. viii.) he had given him encouragement to hope that all should yet be well with him. But here there is not a word of that; he has grown more peevish, and is so far from being convinced by Job's reasonings that he is but more exasperated. I. He sharply reproves Job as haughty and passionate, and obstinate in his opinion, ver. 1—4. II. He enlarges upon the doctrine he had before maintained, concerning the misery of wicked people and the ruin that attends them, ver. 5—21. In this he seems, all along, to have an eye to Job's complaints of the miserable condition he was in, that he was in the dark, bewildered, ensnared, terrified, and hastening out of the world. "This," says Bildad, "is the condition of a wicked man; and therefore thou art one."

THEN answered Bildad the Shuhite, and said, 2 How long *will*

it be ere ye make an end of words?
mark, and afterwards we will speak.
3 Wherefore are we counted as beasts,
and reputed vile in your sight? 4 He
teareth himself in his anger: shall the
earth be forsaken for thee? and shall
the rock be removed out of his place?

Bildad here shoots his arrows, even bitter
words, against poor Job, little thinking that,
though he was a wise and good man, in this
instance he was serving Satan's design in
adding to Job's affliction.

I. He charges him with idle endless talk,
as Eliphaz had done (*ch.* xv. 2, 3): *How long
will it be ere you make an end of words? v.
2.* Here he reflects, not only upon Job himself, but either upon all the managers of the
conference (thinking perhaps that Eliphaz
and Zophar did not speak so closely to the
purpose as they might have done) or upon
some that were present, who possibly took
part with Job, and put in a word now and
then in his favour, though it be not recorded.
Bildad was weary of hearing others speak,
and impatient till it came to his turn, which
cannot be observed to any man's praise, for
we ought to be swift to hear and slow to
speak. It is common for contenders to monopolize the reputation of wisdom, and then
to insist upon it as their privilege to be dictators. How unbecoming this conduct is in
others every one can see; but few that are
guilty of it can see it in themselves. Time
was when Job had the last word in all debates (*ch.* xxix. 22): *After my words they spoke
not again.* Then he was in power and prosperity; but now that he was impoverished
and brought low he could scarcely be allowed
to speak at all, and every thing he said was
as much vilified as formerly it had been
magnified. *Wisdom* therefore (as the world
goes) *is good with an inheritance* (Eccl. vii.
11); for *the poor man's wisdom is despised,*
and, because he is poor, *his words are not
heard,* Eccl. ix. 16.

II. With a regardlessness of what was said
to him, intimated in that, *Mark, and afterwards we will speak.* And it is to no purpose to speak, though what is said be ever
so much to the purpose, if those to whom it
is addressed will not mark and observe it.
Let the *ear be opened to hear as the learned,*
and then the tongues of the learned will do
good service (Isa. l. 4) and not otherwise.
It is an encouragement to those that speak
of the things of God to see the hearers attentive.

III. With a haughty contempt and disdain
of his friends and of that which they offered
(*v.* 3): *Wherefore are we counted as beasts?*
This was invidious. Job had indeed called
them *mockers,* had represented them both as
unwise and as unkind, wanting both in the
reason and tenderness of men, but he did
not count them beasts; yet Bildad so repre-

sents the matter, 1. Because his high spirit
resented what Job had said as if it had been
the greatest affront imaginable. Proud men
are apt to think themselves slighted more
than really they are. 2. Because his hot
spirit was willing to find a pretence to be
hard upon Job. Those that incline to be
severe upon others will have it thought that
others have first been so upon them.

IV. With outrageous passion: *He teareth
himself in his anger, v.* 4. Herein he seems
to reflect upon what Job had said (*ch.* xiii.
14): *Wherefore do I take my flesh in my teeth?*
"It is thy own fault," says Bildad. Or he
reflected upon what he said *ch.* xvi. 9, where
he seemed to charge it upon God, or, as
some think, upon Eliphaz: *He teareth me in
his wrath.* "No," says Bildad; "thou alone
shalt bear it." *He teareth himself in his
anger.* Note, Anger is a sin that is its own
punishment. Fretful passionate people tear
and torment themselves. *He teareth his soul*
(so the word is); every sin wounds the soul,
tears that, wrongs that (Prov. viii. 36), unbridled passion particularly.

V. With a proud and arrogant expectation
to give law even to Providence itself: "*Shall
the earth be forsaken for thee?* Surely not;
there is no reason for that, that the course of
nature should be changed and the settled rules
of government violated to gratify the humour
of one man. Job, dost thou think the world
cannot stand without thee; but that, if thou
art ruined, all the world is ruined and forsaken with thee?" Some make it a reproof
of Job's justification of himself, falsely insinuating that either Job was a wicked man
or we must deny a Providence and suppose
that God has forsaken the earth and the rock
of ages is removed. It is rather a just reproof of his passionate complaints. When
we quarrel with the events of Providence we
forget that, whatever befals us, it is, 1. According to the eternal purpose and counsel
of God. 2. According to the written word.
Thus it is written that in the world we must
have tribulation, that, since we sin daily, we
must expect to smart for it; and, 3. According to the usual way and custom, the track
of Providence, nothing but what is common
to men; and to expect that God's counsels
should change, his method alter, and his
word fail, to please us, is as absurd and unreasonable as to think that *the earth should
be forsaken for us and the rock removed out
of its place.*

5 Yea, the light of the wicked shall
be put out, and the spark of his fire
shall not shine. 6 The light shall be
dark in his tabernacle, and his candle
shall be put out with him. 7 The steps
of his strength shall be straitened, and
his own counsel shall cast him down.
8 For he is cast into a net by his own
feet, and he walketh upon a snare.

9 The gin shall take *him* by the heel, *and* the robber shall prevail against him. 10 The snare *is* laid for him in the ground, and a trap for him in the way.

The rest of Bildad's discourse is entirely taken up in an elegant description of the miserable condition of a wicked man, in which there is a great deal of certain truth, and which will be of excellent use if duly considered—that a sinful condition is a sad condition, and that iniquity will be men's ruin if they do not repent of it. But it is not true that all wicked people are visibly and openly made thus miserable in this world; nor is it true that all who are brought into great distress and trouble in this world are *therefore* to be deemed and adjudged wicked men, when no other proof appears against them; and therefore, though Bildad thought the application of it to Job was easy, yet it was not safe nor just. In these verses we have,

I. The destruction of the wicked foreseen and foretold, under the similitude of darkness (*v.* 5, 6): *Yea, the light of the wicked shall be put out.* Even his *light*, the best and brightest part of him, shall be put out; even that which he rejoiced in shall fail him. Or the *yea* may refer to Job's complaints of the great distress he was in and the darkness he should shortly make his bed in. "Yea," says Bildad, "so it is; thou art clouded, and straitened, and made miserable, and no better could be expected; for *the light of the wicked shall be put out*, and therefore thine shall." Observe here, 1. The wicked may have some light for a while, some pleasure, some joy, some hope within, as well as wealth, and honour, and power without. But his light is but a spark (*v.* 5), a little thing and soon extinguished. It is but a candle (*v.* 6), wasting, and burning down, and easily blown out. It is not the light of the Lord (that is sun-light), but the *light of his own fire* and *sparks of his own kindling*, Isa. l. 11. 2. His light will certainly be put out at length, quite put out, so that not the least spark of it shall remain with which to kindle another fire. Even while he is in his tabernacle, while he is in the body, which is the tabernacle of the soul (2 Cor. v. 1), the light shall be dark; he shall have no true solid comfort, no joy that is satisfying, no hope that is supporting. Even *the light that is in him is darkness; and how great is that darkness!* But, when he is put out of this tabernacle by death, *his candle shall be put out with him.* The period of his life will be the final period of all his days and will turn all his hopes into endless despair. *When a wicked man dies his expectation shall perish*, Prov. xi. 7. *He shall lie down in sorrow.*

II. The preparatives for that destruction represented under the similitude of a beast or bird caught in a snare, or a malefactor arrested and taken into custody in order to his punishment, *v.* 7—10. 1. Satan is preparing for his destruction. He is *the robber that shall prevail against him* (*v.* 9); for, as he was a murderer, so he was a robber, from the beginning. He, as the tempter, lays snares for sinners in the way, wherever they go, and he shall prevail. If he make them sinful like himself, he will make them miserable like himself. He *hunts for the precious life.* 2. He is himself preparing for his own destruction by going on in sin, and so *treasuring up wrath against the day of wrath.* God gives him up, as he deserves and desires, to his own counsels, and then *his own counsels cast him down, v.* 7. His sinful projects and pursuits bring him into mischief. He is *cast into a net by his own feet* (*v.* 8), runs upon his own destruction, is *snared in the work of his own hands* (Ps. ix. 16); his *own tongue falls upon him*, Ps. lxiv. 8. *In the transgression of an evil man there is a snare.* 3. God is preparing for his destruction. The sinner by his sin is preparing the fuel and then God by his wrath is preparing the fire. See here, (1.) How the sinner is infatuated, to run himself into the snare; and whom God will destroy he infatuates. (2.) How he is embarrassed: *The steps of his strength, his mighty designs and efforts, shall be straitened, so that he shall not compass what he intended*; and the more he strives to extricate himself the more will he be entangled. Evil men wax worse and worse. (3.) How he is secured and kept from escaping the judgments of God that are in pursuit of him. *The gin shall take him by the heel.* He can no more escape the divine wrath that is in pursuit of him than a man, so held, can flee from the pursuer. God *knows how to reserve the wicked for the day of judgment*, 2 Pet. ii. 9.

11 Terrors shall make him afraid on every side, and shall drive him to his feet. 12 His strength shall be hungerbitten, and destruction *shall be* ready at his side. 13 It shall devour the strength of his skin: *even* the firstborn of death shall devour his strength. 14 His confidence shall be rooted out of his tabernacle, and it shall bring him to the king of terrors. 15 It shall dwell in his tabernacle, because *it is* none of his: brimstone shall be scattered upon his habitation. 16 His roots shall be dried up beneath, and above shall his branch be cut off. 17 His remembrance shall perish from the earth, and he shall have no name in the street. 18 He shall be driven from light into darkness, and chased out of the world. 19 He shall neither have son nor nephew

among his people, nor any remaining in his dwellings. 20 They that come after *him* shall be astonied at his day, as they that went before were affrighted. 21 Surely such *are* the dwellings of the wicked, and this *is* the place *of him that* knoweth not God.

Bildad here describes the destruction itself which wicked people are reserved for in the other world, and which, in some degree, often seizes them in this world. Come, and see what a miserable condition the sinner is in when his day comes to fall.

I. See him disheartened and weakened by continual terrors arising from the sense of his own guilt and the dread of God's wrath (*v.* 11, 12): *Terror shall make him afraid on every side.* The terrors of his own conscience shall haunt him, so that he shall never be easy. Wherever he goes, these shall follow him; which way soever he looks, these shall stare him in the face. It will make him tremble to see himself fought against by the whole creation, to see Heaven frowning on him, hell gaping for him, and earth sick of him. He that carries his own accuser, and his own tormentor, always in his bosom, cannot but be afraid on every side. This will drive him to his feet, like the malefactor, who, being conscious of his guilt, takes to his heels and *flees when none pursues*, Prov. xxviii. 1. But his feet will do him no service; they are fast in the snare, *v.* 9. The sinner may as soon overpower the divine omnipotence as flee from the divine omniscience, Amos ix. 2, 3. No marvel that the sinner is dispirited and distracted with fear, for, 1. He sees his ruin approaching: *Destruction shall be ready at his side*, to seize him whenever justice gives the word, so that he is *brought into desolation in a moment*, Ps. lxxiii. 19. 2. He feels himself utterly unable to grapple with it, either to escape it or to bear up under it. That which he relied upon as *his strength* (his wealth, power, pomp, friends, and the hardiness of his own spirit) *shall* fail him in the time of need, and *be hunger-bitten*, that is, it shall do him no more service than a famished man, pining away for hunger, would do in work or war. The case being thus with him, no marvel that he is a terror to himself. Note, The way of sin is a way of fear, and leads to everlasting confusion, of which the present terrors of an impure and unpacified conscience are earnests, as they were to Cain and Judas.

II. See him devoured and swallowed up by a miserable death; and miserable indeed a wicked man's death is, how secure and jovial soever his life was. 1. See him dying, arrested by *the first-born of death* (some disease, or some stroke that has in it a more than ordinary resemblance of death itself; *so great a death*, as it is called, 2 Cor. i. 10,

a messenger of death that has in it an uncommon strength and terror), weakened by the harbingers of death, which *devour the strength of his skin*, that is, it shall bring rottenness into his bones and consume them. *His confidence shall then be rooted out of his tabernacle* (*v.* 14), that is, all that he trusted to for his support shall be taken from him, and he shall have nothing to rely upon, no, not his own tabernacle. His own soul was his confidence, but that shall be rooted out of the tabernacle of the body, as a tree that cumbered the ground. "Thy soul shall be required of thee." 2. See him dead, and see his case then with an eye of faith. (1.) He is then brought to *the king of terrors*. He was surrounded with terrors while he lived (*v.* 11), and death was the king of all those terrors; they fought against the sinner in death's name, for it is by reason of death that sinners are *all their lifetime subject to bondage* (Heb. ii. 15), and at length they will be brought to that which they so long feared, as a captive to the conqueror. Death is terrible to nature; our Saviour himself prayed, *Father, save me from this hour.* But to the wicked it is in a special manner *the king of terrors*, both as it is a period to that life in which they placed their happiness and a passage to that life where they will find their endless misery. How happy then are the saints, and how much indebted to the Lord Jesus, by whom death is so far abolished, and the property of it altered, that this king of terrors becomes a friend and servant! (2.) He is then *driven from light into darkness* (*v.* 18), from the light of this world, and his prosperous condition in it, into darkness, the darkness of the grave, the darkness of hell, into utter darkness, never to see light (Ps. xlix. 19), not the least gleam, nor any hopes of it. (3.) He is then *chased out of the world*, hurried and dragged away by the messengers of death, sorely against his will, chased as Adam out of paradise, for the world is his paradise. It intimates that he would fain stay here; he is loth to depart, but go he must; all the world is weary of him, and therefore chases him out, as glad to get rid of him. This is death to a wicked man.

III. See his family sunk and cut off, *v.* 15. The wrath and curse of God light and lie, not only upon his head and heart, but upon his house too, to consume it with the *timber and stones thereof*, Zech. v. 4. Death itself shall dwell in his tabernacle, and, having expelled him, shall take possession of his house, to the terror and destruction of all that he leaves behind. Even the dwelling shall be ruined for the sake of its owner: *Brimstone shall be scattered upon his habitation*, rained upon it as upon Sodom, to the destruction of which this seems to have reference. Some think he here upbraids Job with the burning of his sheep and servants with fire from heaven. The reason is here given why his tabernacle is thus marked for ruin: *Because it is none of his;* that is, it was unjustly got, and kept, from the rightful owner, and therefore let him not expect either the comfort or the continuance of it. His children shall perish, either with him or after him, *v.* 16. So that, *his roots being* in his own person *dried up beneath, above his branch* (every child of his family) *shall be cut off.* Thus the houses of Jeroboam, Baasha, and Ahab, were cut off; none that descended from them were left alive. Those who take root in the earth may expect it will thus be dried up; but, if we be rooted in Christ, even our leaf shall not wither, much less shall our branch be cut off. Those who consult the true honour of their family, and the welfare of its branches, will be afraid of withering it by sin. The extirpation of the sinner's family is mentioned again (*v.* 19): *He shall neither have son nor nephew,* child nor grandchild, to enjoy his estate and bear up his name, *nor shall there be any remaining in his dwelling* akin to him. Sin entails a curse upon posterity, and the iniquity of the fathers is often visited upon the children. Herein, also, it is probable that Bildad reflects upon the death of Job's children and servants, as a further proof of his being a wicked man; whereas all that are written childless are not thereby written graceless; there is a name *better than that of sons and daughters.*

IV. See his memory buried with him, or made odious; he shall either be forgotten or spoken of with dishonour (*v.* 17): *His remembrance shall perish from the earth;* and, if it perish thence, it perishes wholly, for it was never written in heaven, as the names of the saints are, Luke x. 20. All his honour shall be laid and lost in the dust, or stained with perpetual infamy, so that *he shall have no name in the street,* departing without being desired. Thus the judgments of God follow him, after death, in this world, as an indication of the misery his soul is in after death, and an earnest of that everlasting shame and contempt to which he shall rise in the great day. *The memory of the just is blessed, but the name of the wicked shall rot,* Prov. x. 7.

V. See a universal amazement at his fall, *v.* 20. Those that see it are affrighted, so sudden is the change, so dreadful the execution, so threatening to all about him: and those that come after, and hear the report of it, are astonished at it; their ears are made to tingle, and their hearts to tremble, and they cry out, *Lord, how terrible art thou in thy judgments!* A place or person utterly ruined is said to be *made an astonishment,* Deut. xxviii. 37; 2 Chron. vii. 21; Jer. xxv. 9, 18. Horrible sins bring strange punishments.

VI. See all this averred as the unanimous sense of the patriarchal age, grounded upon their knowledge of God and their many observations of his providence (*v.* 21): *Surely such are the dwellings of the wicked, and this*

is the place (this the condition) *of him that knows not God!* See here what is the beginning, and what is the end, of the wickedness of this wicked world. 1. The beginning of it is ignorance of God, and it is a wilful ignorance, for there is that to be known of him which is sufficient to leave them for ever inexcusable. They know not God, and then they commit all iniquity. Pharaoh knows not the Lord, and therefore will not obey his voice. 2. The end of it, and that is utter destruction. *Such,* so miserable, *are the dwellings of the wicked.* Vengeance will be taken of those that *know not God,* 2 Thess. i. 8. For those whom he has not honour from he will get himself honour upon. Let us therefore stand in awe and not sin, for it will certainly be bitterness in the latter end.

CHAP. XIX.

This chapter is Job's answer to Bildad's discourse in the foregoing chapter. Though his spirit was grieved and much heated, and Bildad was very peevish, yet he gave him leave to say all he designed to say, and did not break in upon him in the midst of his argument; but, when he had done, he gave him a fair answer, in which, I. He complains of unkind usage. And very unkindly he takes it, 1. That his comforters added to his affliction, ver. 2—7. 2. That his God was the author of his affliction, ver. 8—12. 3. That his relations and friends were strange to him, and shy of him, in his affliction, ver. 13—19. 4. That he had no compassion shown him in his affliction, ver. 20—22. II. He comforts himself with the believing hopes of happiness in the other world, though he had so little comfort in this, making a very solemn confession of his faith, with a desire that it might be recorded as an evidence of his sincerity, ver. 23—27. III. He concludes with a caution to his friends not to persist in their hard censures of him, ver. 28, 29. If the remonstrance Job here makes of his grievances may serve sometimes to justify our complaints, yet his cheerful views of the future state, at the same time, may shame us Christians, and may serve to silence our complaints, or at least to balance them.

THEN Job answered and said, 2 How long will ye vex my soul, and break me in pieces with words? 3 These ten times have ye reproached me: ye are not ashamed *that* ye make yourselves strange to me. 4 And be it indeed *that* I have erred, mine error remaineth with myself. 5 If indeed ye will magnify *yourselves* against me, and plead against me my reproach: 6 Know now that God hath overthrown me, and hath compassed me with his net. 7 Behold, I cry out of wrong, but I am not heard: I cry aloud, but *there is* no judgment.

Job's friends had passed a very severe censure upon him as a wicked man because he was so grievously afflicted; now here he tells them how ill he took it to be so censured. Bildad had twice begun with a *How long* (ch. viii. 2, xviii. 2), and therefore Job, being now to answer him particularly, begins with a *How long* too, *v.* 2. What is not liked is commonly thought long; but Job had more reason to think those long who assaulted him than they had to think him long who only vindicated himself. Better cause may be shown for defending ourselves, if we have right on our side, than for offending our brethren, though we have right on our side. Now observe here,

I. How he describes their unkindness to him and what account he gives of it. 1. They *vexed his soul,* and that is more grievous than the vexation of the bones, Ps. vi. 2, 3. They were his friends; they came to comfort him, pretended to counsel him for the best; but with a great deal of gravity, and affectation of wisdom and piety, they set themselves to rob him of the only comfort he had now left him in a good God, a good conscience, and a good name; and this vexed him to the heart. 2. They *broke him in pieces with words,* and those were surely hard and very cruel words that would break a man to pieces: they grieved him, and so broke him; and therefore there will be a reckoning hereafter for all the hard speeches spoken against Christ and his people, Jude 15. 3. They *reproached him* (v. 3), gave him a bad character and laid to his charge things that he knew not. To an ingenuous mind reproach is a cutting thing. 4. They *made themselves strange to him,* were shy of him now that he was in his troubles, and seemed as if they did not know him (*ch.* ii. 12), were not free with him as they used to be when he was in his prosperity. Those are governed by the spirit of the world, and not by any principles of true honour or love, who make themselves strange to their friends, or God's friends, when they are in trouble. *A friend loves at all times.* 5. They not only estranged themselves from him, but *magnified themselves against him* (v. 5), not only looked shy of him, but looked big upon him, and insulted over him, magnifying themselves to depress him. It is a mean thing, it is a base thing, thus to trample upon those that are down. 6. *They pleaded against him his reproach,* that is, they made use of his affliction as an argument against him to prove him a wicked man. They should have pleaded for him his integrity, and helped him to take the comfort of that under his affliction, and so have pleaded that against his reproach (as St. Paul, 2 Cor. i. 12); but, instead of that, they pleaded his reproach against his integrity, which was not only unkind, but very unjust; for where shall we find an honest man if reproach may be admitted for a plea against him?

II. How he aggravates their unkindness. 1. They had thus abused him often (v. 3): *These ten times you have reproached me,* that is, very often, as Gen. xxxi. 7; Num. xiv. 22. Five times they had spoken, and every speech was a double reproach. He spoke as if he had kept a particular account of their reproaches, and could tell just how many they were. It is but a peevish and unfriendly thing to do so, and looks like a design of retaliation and revenge. We better befriend our own peace by forgetting injuries and unkindnesses than by remembering them and scoring them up. 2. They continued still to abuse him, and seemed resolved to persist in it: "How long will you do it?" v. 2, 5. "I

see you will magnify yourselves against me, notwithstanding all I have said in my own justification." Those that speak too much seldom think they have said enough; and, when the mouth is opened in passion, the ear is shut to reason. 3. They were not ashamed of what they did, v. 3. They had reason to be ashamed of their hard-heartedness, so ill becoming men, of their uncharitableness, so ill becoming good men, and of their deceitfulness, so ill becoming friends: but were they ashamed? No, though they were told of it again and again, yet they could not blush.

III. How he answers their harsh censures, by showing them that what they condemned was capable of excuse, which they ought to have considered. 1. The errors of his judgment were excusable (v. 4): "*Be it indeed that I have erred,* that I am in the wrong through ignorance or mistake," which may well be supposed concerning men, concerning good men. *Humanum est errare—Error cleaves to humanity;* and we must be willing to suppose it concerning ourselves. It is folly to think ourselves infallible. "But be it so," said Job, "*my error remaineth with myself,*" that is, "I speak according to the best of my judgment, with all sincerity, and not from a spirit of contradiction." Or, "If I be in an error, I keep it to myself, and do not impose it upon others as you do. I only prove myself and my own work by it. I meddle not with other people, either to teach them or to judge them." Men's errors are the more excusable if they keep them to themselves, and do not disturb others with them. *Hast thou faith? Have it to thyself.* Some give this sense of these words: "If I be in an error, it is I that must smart for it; and therefore you need not concern yourselves: nay, it is I that do smart, and smart severely, for it; and therefore you need not add to my misery by your reproaches." 2. The breakings out of his passion, though not justifiable, yet were excusable, considering the vastness of his grief and the extremity of his misery. "If you will go on to cavil at every complaining word I speak, will make the worst of it and improve it against me, yet take the cause of the complaint along with you, and weigh that, before you pass a judgment upon the complaint, and turn it to my reproach: *Know then that God has overthrown me,*" v. 6. Three things he would have them consider:—(1.) That his trouble was very great. He was overthrown, and could not help himself, enclosed as in a net, and could not get out. (2.) That God was the author of it, and that, in it, he fought against him: "It was his hand that overthrew me; it is in his net that I am enclosed; and therefore you need not appear against me thus. I have enough to do to grapple with God's displeasure; let me not have yours also. Let God's controversy with me be ended before you begin yours." It is barbarous to *persecute him whom God hath smitten and to talk to the grief of one whom he hath wounded,* Ps. lxix. 26. (3.) That he could not obtain any hope of the redress of his grievances, *v.* 7. He complained of his pain, but got no ease—begged to know the cause of his affliction, but could not discover it—appealed to God's tribunal for the clearing of his innocency, but could not obtain a hearing, much less a judgment, upon his appeal: *I cry out of wrong, but I am not heard.* God, for a time, may seem to turn away his ear from his people, to be angry at their prayers and overlook their appeals to him, and they must be excused if, in that case, they complain bitterly. Woe unto us if God be against us !

8 He hath fenced up my way that I cannot pass, and he hath set darkness in my paths. 9 He hath stripped me of my glory, and taken the crown *from* my head. 10 He hath destroyed me on every side, and I am gone : and mine hope hath he removed like a tree. 11 He hath also kindled his wrath against me, and he counteth me unto him as *one of* his enemies. 12 His troops come together, and raise up their way against me, and encamp round about my tabernacle. 13 He hath put my brethren far from me, and mine acquaintance are verily estranged from me. 14 My kinsfolk have failed, and my familiar friends have forgotten me. 15 They that dwell in mine house, and my maids, count me for a stranger : I am an alien in their sight. 16 I called my servant, and he gave *me* no answer; I intreated him with my mouth. 17 My breath is strange to my wife, though I intreated for the children's *sake* of mine own body. 18 Yea, young children despised me ; I arose, and they spake against me 19 All my inward friends abhorred me : and they whom I loved are turned against me. 20 My bone cleaveth to my skin and to my flesh, and I am escaped with the skin of my teeth. 21 Have pity upon me, have pity upon me, O ye my friends ; for the hand of God hath touched me. 22 Why do ye persecute me as God, and are not satisfied with my flesh ?

Bildad had very disingenuously perverted Job's complaints by making them the description of the miserable condition of a wicked man; and yet he repeats them here,

to move their pity, and to work upon their good nature, if they had any left in them.

I. He complains of the tokens of God's displeasure which he was under, and which infused the wormwood and gall into the affliction and misery. How doleful are the accents of his complaints ! "*He hath kindled his wrath against me,* which flames and terrifies me, which burns and pains me," *v.* 11. What is the fire of hell but the wrath of God ? Seared consciences will feel it hereafter, but do not fear it now. Enlightened consciences fear it now, but shall not feel it hereafter. Job's present apprehension was that *God counted him as one of his enemies ;* and yet, at the same time, God loved him, and gloried in him, as his faithful friend. It is a gross mistake, but a very common one, to think that whom God afflicts he treats as his enemies ; whereas, on the contrary, *as many as he loves he rebukes and chastens ;* it is the discipline of his sons. Which way soever Job looked he thought he saw the tokens of God's displeasure against him. 1. Did he look back upon his former prosperity ? He saw God's hand putting an end to that (*v.* 9) : "*He has stripped me of my glory,* my wealth, honour, power, and all the opportunity I had of doing good. My children were my glory, but I have lost them ; and whatever was a crown to my head he has taken it from me, and has laid all my honour in the dust." See the vanity of worldly glory : it is what we may be soon stripped of ; and, whatever strips us, we must see and own God's hand in it and comply with his design. 2. Did he look down upon his present troubles ? He saw God giving them their commission, and their orders to attack him. They are *his troops,* that act by his direction, which *encamp against me, v.* 12. It did not so much trouble him that his miseries came upon him in troops as that they were *God's* troops, in whom it seemed as if God fought against him and intended his destruction. God's troops *encamped around his tabernacle,* as soldiers lay siege to a strong city, cutting off all provisions from being brought into it and battering it continually ; thus was Job's tabernacle besieged. Time was when God's hosts encamped round him for safety : *Hast thou not made a hedge about him ?* Now, on the contrary, they surrounded him, to his terror, and *destroyed him on every side, v.* 10. 3. Did he look forward for deliverance ? He saw the hand of God cutting off all hopes of that (*v.* 8) : "*He hath fenced up my way, that I cannot pass.* I have now no way left to help myself, either to extricate myself out of my troubles or to ease myself under them. Would I make any motion, take any steps towards deliverance ? I find *my way hedged up;* I cannot do what I would ; nay, if I would please myself with the prospect of a deliverance hereafter, I cannot do it ; it is not only out of my reach, but out of my sight : God *hath set darkness in my paths,* and there is none to tell me how long," Ps. lxxiv. 9. He concludes (*v.* 10), " I am gone, quite lost and undone for this world; *my hope hath he removed like a tree* cut down, or plucked up by the roots, which will never grow again." Hope in this life is a perishing thing, but the hope of good men, when it is cut off from this world, is but removed like a tree, transplanted from this nursery to the garden of the Lord. We shall have no reason to complain if God thus remove our hopes from the sand to the rock, from things temporal to things eternal.

II. He complains of the unkindness of his relations and of all his old acquaintance. In this also he owns the hand of God (*v.* 13): *He has put my brethren far from me,* that is, " He has laid those afflictions upon me which frighten them from me, and make them stand aloof from my sores." As it was their sin God was not the author of it; it is Satan that alienates men's minds from their brethren in affliction. But, as it was Job's trouble, God ordered it for the completing of his trial. As we must eye the hand of God in all the injuries we receive from our enemies (" the Lord has bidden Shimei curse David"), so also in all the slights and unkindnesses we receive from our friends, which will help us to bear them the more patiently. Every creature is that to us (kind or unkind, comfortable or uncomfortable) which God makes it to be. Yet this does not excuse Job's relations and friends from the guilt of horrid ingratitude and injustice to him, which he had reason to complain of; few could have borne it so well as he did. He takes notice of the unkindness, 1. Of his kindred and acquaintance, his neighbours, and such as he had formerly been familiar with, who were bound by all the laws of friendship and civility, to concern themselves for him, to visit him, to enquire after him, and to be ready to do him all the good offices that lay in their power; yet these were *estranged from him, v.* 13. They took no more care about him than if he had been a stranger whom they never knew. His kinsfolk, who claimed relation to him when he was in prosperity, now failed him; they came short of their former professions of friendship to him and his present expectations of kindness from them. Even his familiar friends, whom he was mindful of, had now forgotten him, had forgotten both his former friendliness to them and his present miseries : they had heard of his troubles, and designed him a visit; but truly they forgot it, so little affected were they with it. Nay, his inward friends, the men of his secret, whom he was most intimate with and laid in his bosom, not only forgot him, but abhorred him, kept as far off him as they could, because he was poor and could not entertain them as he used to do, and because he was sore and a loathsome spectacle. Those whom he loved, and who therefore were worse than publicans if they did not

love him now that he was in distress, not only turned from him, but were turned against him, and did all they could to make him odious, so to justify themselves in being so strange to him, *v.* 19. So uncertain is the friendship of men ; but, if God be our friend, he will not fail us in a time of need. But let none that pretend either to humanity or Christianity ever use their friends as Job's friends used him : adversity is the proof of friendship. 2. Of his domestics and family relations. Sometimes indeed we find that, beyond our expectation, there is a friend that sticks closer than a brother ; but the master of a family ordinarily expects to be attended on and taken care of by those of his family, even when, through weakness of body or mind, he has become despicable to others. But poor Job was misused by his own family, and some of his worst foes were those of his own house. He mentions not his children ; they were all dead, and we may suppose that the unkindness of his surviving relations made him lament the death of his children so much the more : " If they had been alive," would he think, "I should have had comfort in them." As for those that were now about him, (1.) His own servants slighted him. His maids did not attend him in his illness, but *counted him for a stranger and an alien, v.* 15. His other servants never heeded him ; if he called to them they would not come at his call, but pretended that they did not hear him. If he asked them a question, they would not vouchsafe to *give him an answer, v.* 16. Job had been a good master to them, and did not *despise their cause when they pleaded with him* (*ch.* xxxi. 13), and yet they were rude to him now, and despised his cause when he pleaded with them. We must not think it strange if we receive evil at the hand of those from whom we have deserved well. Though he was now sickly, yet he was not cross with his servants, and imperious, as is too common, but he entreated his servants with his mouth, when he had authority to command ; and yet they would not be civil to him, neither kind nor just. Note, Those that are sick and in sorrow are apt to take things ill, and be jealous of a slight, and to lay to heart the least unkindness done to them : when Job was in affliction even his servants' neglect of him troubled him. (2.) But, one would think, when all forsook him, the wife of his bosom should have been tender of him : no, because he would not curse God and die, as she persuaded him, his breath was strange to her too ; she did not care for coming near him, nor took any notice of what he said, *v.* 17. Though he spoke to her, not with the authority, but with the tenderness of a husband, did not command, but entreated her by that conjugal love which their children were the pledges of, yet she regarded him not. Some read it, " Though I lamented, or bemoaned myself, for the children," that is, " for the death of the children of my own body," an affliction in which she was equally concerned with him. Now, it appeared, the devil spared her to him, not only to be his tempter, but to be his tormentor. By what she said to him at first, *Curse God and die,* it appeared that she had little religion in her; and what can one expect that is kind and good from those that have not the fear of God before their eyes and are not governed by conscience? (3.) Even the little children who were born in his house, the children of his own servants, who were his servants by birth, despised him, and spoke against him (*v.* 18); though he arose in civility to speak friendly to them, or with authority to check them, they let him know that they neither feared him nor loved him.

III. He complains of the decay of his body; all the beauty and strength of that were gone. When those about him slighted him, if he had been in health, and at ease, he might have enjoyed himself. But he could take as little pleasure in himself as others took in him (*v.* 20): *My bone cleaves now to my skin,* as formerly it did to my flesh; it was this that filled *him with wrinkles* (*ch.* xvi. 8); he was a perfect skeleton, nothing but skin and bones. Nay, his skin too was almost gone, little remained unbroken but the *skin of his teeth,* his gums and perhaps his lips; all the rest was fetched off by his sore boils. See what little reason we have to indulge the body, which, after all our care, may be thus consumed by the diseases which it has in itself the seeds of.

IV. Upon all these accounts he recommends himself to the compassion of his friends, and justly blames their harshness with him. From this representation of his deplorable case, it was easy to infer, 1. That they ought to pity him, *v.* 21. This he begs in the most moving melting language that could be, enough (one would think) to break a heart of stone: "*Have pity upon me, have pity upon me, O you my friends!* if you will do nothing else for me, be sorry for me, and show some concern for me; *have pity upon me, for the hand of God hath touched me.* My case is sad indeed, for I have fallen into the hands of the living God, my spirit is touched with the sense of his wrath, a calamity of all other the most piteous." Note, It becomes friends to pity one another when they are in any trouble, and not to shut up the bowels of compassion. 2. That, however, they ought not to persecute him; if they would not ease his affliction by their pity, yet they must not be so barbarous as to add to it by their censures and reproaches (*v.* 22): "*Why do you persecute me as God?* Surely his rebukes are enough for one man to bear; you need not add your wormwood and gall to the cup of affliction he puts into my hand, it is bitter enough without that: God has a sovereign power over me, and may do what he pleases with me; but do you think that you may do

so too?" No, we must aim to be like the Most Holy and the Most Merciful, but not like the Most High and Most Mighty. God gives not account of any of his matters, but we must give account of ours. If they did delight in his calamity, let them be satisfied with his flesh, which was wasted and gone, but let them not, as if that were too little, wound his spirit, and ruin his good name. Great tenderness is due to those that are in affliction, especially to those that are troubled in mind.

23 Oh that my words were now written! oh that they were printed in a book! 24 That they were graven with an iron pen and lead in the rock for ever! 25 For I know *that* my redeemer liveth, and *that* he shall stand at the latter *day* upon the earth: 26 And *though* after my skin *worms* destroy this *body,* yet in my flesh shall I see God: 27 Whom I shall see for myself, and mine eyes shall behold, and not another; *though* my reins be consumed within me. 28 But ye should say, Why persecute we him, seeing the root of the matter is found in me? 29 Be ye afraid of the sword: for wrath *bringeth* the punishments of the sword, that ye may know *there is* a judgment.

In all the conferences between Job and his friends we do not find any more weighty and considerable lines than these; would one have expected it? Here is much both of Christ and heaven in these verses: and he that said such things as these *declared plainly that he sought the better country, that is, the heavenly;* as the patriarchs of that age did, Heb. xi. 14. We have here Job's creed, or confession of faith. His belief in God the Father Almighty, the Maker of heaven and earth, and the principles of natural religion, he had often professed: but here we find him no stranger to revealed religion; though the revelation of the promised Seed, and the promised inheritance, was then discerned only like the dawning of the day, yet Job was taught of God to believe in a living Redeemer, and to *look for the resurrection of the dead and the life of the world to come,* for of these, doubtless, he must be understood to speak. These were the things he comforted himself with the expectation of, and not a deliverance from his trouble or a revival of his happiness in this world, as some would understand him; for besides that the expressions he here uses, of the Redeemer's *standing at the latter day upon the earth,* of his seeing God, and *seeing him for himself,* are wretchedly forced if they be understood of any temporal deliverance, it is very plain that he had no expectation at all of his return to a prosperous condition in this world. He had just now said that *his way was fenced up*, (*v.* 8) and his *hope removed like a tree, v.* 10. Nay, and after this he expressed his despair of any comfort in this life, *ch.* xxiii. 8, 9 ; xxx. 23. So that we must necessarily understand him of the redemption of his soul from the power of the grave, and his reception to glory, which is spoken of, Ps. xlix. 15. We have reason to think that Job was just now under an extraordinary impulse of the blessed Spirit, which raised him above himself, gave him light, and gave him utterance, even to his own surprise. And some observe that, after this, we do not find in Job's discourses such passionate, peevish, unbecoming, complaints of God and his providence as we have before met with: this hope quieted his spirit, stilled the storm, and, having here cast anchor within the veil, his mind was kept steady from this time forward. Let us observe,

I. To what intent Job makes this confession of his faith here. Never did any thing come in more pertinently, or to better purpose. 1. Job was now accused, and this was his appeal. His friends reproached him as a hypocrite and contemned him as a wicked man ; but he appeals to his creed, to his faith, to his hope, and to his own conscience, which not only acquitted him from reigning sin, but comforted him with the expectation of a blessed resurrection. *These are not the words of him that has a devil.* He appeals to the coming of the Redeemer, from this wrangle at the bar to the judgment of the bench, even to him to whom all judgment is committed, who he knew would right him. The consideration of God's day coming will make it a *very small thing with us to be judged of man's judgment,* 1 Cor. iv. 3, 4. How easily may we bear the unjust calumnies and reproaches of men while we expect the glorious appearance of our Redeemer, and his redeemed, at the last day, and that there will then be a resurrection of names, as well as bodies ! 2. Job was now afflicted, and this was his cordial ; when he was pressed above measure this kept him from fainting—he believed that he should *see the goodness of the Lord in the land of the living ;* not in this world, for that is the land of the dying.

II. With what a solemn preface he introduces it, *v.* 23, 24. He breaks off his complaints abruptly, to triumph in his comforts, which he does, not only for his own satisfaction, but for the edification of others. Those now about him, he feared, would little regard what he said, and so it proved. He therefore wished it might be recorded for the generations to come. *O that my words were now written,* the words I am now about to say ! As if he had said, "I own I have spoken many unadvised words, which I could wish might be forgotten, for they will neither do me credit nor do others good. But I am now going to speak deliberately, and that which

I desire may be published to all the world and preserved for the generations to come, *in perpetuam rei memoriam—for an abiding memorial,* and therefore that it may be written plainly and *printed,* or drawn out in large and legible characters, so that he that runs may read it ; and that it may not be left in loose papers, but put into *a book ;* or, if that should perish, that it may be *engraven* like an inscription upon a monument, *with an iron pen in lead, or in the stone;* let the engraver use all his art to make it a durable appeal to posterity." That which Job here somewhat passionately wished for God graciously granted him. His words are written ; they are printed in God's book ; so that, wherever that book is read, there shall this be told for a memorial concerning Job. He believed, therefore he spoke.

III. What his confession itself is ; what are the words which he would have to be written ; we here have them written, *v.* 25—27. Let us observe them.

1. He believes the glory of the Redeemer and his own interest in him (*v.* 25) : *I know that my Redeemer liveth,* that he is in being and is my life, *and that he shall stand at last,* or stand the last, or at the latter day, *upon* (or above) *the earth.* He shall be raised up, or, He shall be, at the latter day, (that is, in the fulness of time : the gospel day is called *the last time* because that is the last dispensation) upon the earth : so it points at his incarnation ; or, He shall be lifted up from the earth (so it points at his crucifixion), or raised up out of the earth (so it is applicable to his resurrection), or, as we commonly understand it, At the end of time he shall appear over the earth, for *he shall come in the clouds, and every eye shall see him,* so close shall he come to this earth. He shall stand *upon the dust* (so the word is), upon all his enemies, which shall be put as dust under his feet ; and he shall tread upon them and triumph over them. Observe here, (1.) That there is a Redeemer provided for fallen man, and Jesus Christ is that Redeemer. The word is *Goël* which is used for the next of kin, to whom, by the law of Moses, the right of redeeming a mortgaged estate did belong, Lev. xxv. 25. Our heavenly inheritance was mortgaged by sin ; we are ourselves utterly unable to redeem it ; Christ is near of kin to us, the next kinsman that is able to redeem ; he has paid our debt, satisfied God's justice for sin, and so has taken off the mortgage and made a new settlement of the inheritance Our persons also want a Redeemer ; we are sold for sin, and sold under sin ; our Lord Jesus has wrought out a redemption for us, and proclaims redemption to us, and so he is truly the Redeemer. (2.) He is a living Redeemer. As we are made by a living God, so we are saved by a living Redeemer, who is both almighty and eternal, and is therefore able to save to the uttermost. *Of him it is witnessed that he liveth,* Heb. vii. 8 ; Rev. i. 18.

We are dying, but he liveth, and hath assured us that *because he lives we shall live also,* John xiv. 19. (3.) There are those that through grace have an interest in this Redeemer, and can, upon good grounds, call him theirs. When Job had lost all his wealth and all his friends, yet he was not separated from Christ, nor cut off from his relation to him : "Still he is my Redeemer." That next kinsman adhered to him when all his other kindred forsook him, and he had the comfort of it. (4.) Our interest in the Redeemer is a thing that may be known ; and, where it is known, it may be triumphed in, as sufficient to balance all our griefs: *I know* (observe with what an air of assurance he speaks it, as one confident of this very thing), *I know that my Redeemer lives.* His friends had often charged him with ignorance or vain knowledge ; but he knows enough, and knows to good purpose, who knows Christ to be his Redeemer. (5.) There will be a latter day, a last day, a day when *time shall be no more,* Rev. x. 6. That is a day we are concerned to think of every day. (6.) Our Redeemer will at that day stand upon the earth, or over the earth, to summon the dead out of their graves, and determine them to an unchangeable state; for to him all judgment is committed. He shall stand, at the last, on the dust to which this earth will be reduced by the conflagration.

2. He believes the happiness of the redeemed, and his own title to that happiness, that, at Christ's second coming, believers shall be raised up in glory and so made perfectly blessed in the vision and fruition of God ; and this he believes with application to himself. (1.) He counts upon the corrupting of his body in the grave, and speaks of it with a holy carelessness and unconcernedness : *Though, after my skin* (which is already wasted and gone, none of it remaining but *the skin of my teeth, v.* 20) *they destroy* (those that are appointed to destroy it, the grave and the worms in it of which he had spoken, *ch.* xvii. 14) *this body.* The word *body* is added : "Though they destroy this, this skeleton, this shadow (*ch.* xvii. 7), this that I lay my hand upon," or (pointing perhaps to his weak and withered limbs) "this that you see, call it what you will ; I expect that shortly it will be a feast for the worms." Christ's body saw not corruption, but ours must. And Job mentions this, that the glory of the resurrection he believed and hoped for might shine the more brightly. Note, It is good for us often to think, not only of the approaching death of our bodies, but of their destruction and dissolution in the grave ; yet let not that discourage our hope of their resurrection, for the same power that made man's body at first, out of common dust, can raise it out of its own dust. This body which we now take such care about, and make such provision for, will in a little time be destroyed. Even *my reins* (says Job) *shall be consumed within me (v.* 27) ; the innermost part of the body, 110

which perhaps putrefies first. (2.) He comforts himself with the hopes of happiness on the other side death and the grave : *After I shall awake* (so the margin reads it), *though this body be destroyed, yet out of my flesh shall I see God.* [1.] Soul and body shall come together again. That body which must be destroyed in the grave shall be raised again, a glorious body : *Yet in my flesh I shall see God.* The separate soul has eyes wherewith to see God, eyes of the mind ; but Job speaks of seeing him with eyes of flesh, *in my flesh, with my eyes ;* the same body that died shall rise again, a true body, but a glorified body, fit for the employments and entertainments of that world, and therefore a *spiritual body,* 1 Cor. xv. 44. Let us *therefore* glorify God with our bodies because there is such a glory designed for them. [2.] Job and God shall come together again : *In my flesh shall I see God,* that is, the glorified Redeemer, who is God. *I shall see God in my flesh* (so some read it), the Son of God clothed with a body which will be visible even to eyes of flesh. Though the body, in the grave, seem despicable and miserable, yet it shall be dignified and made happy in the vision of God. Job now complained that he could not get a sight of God (*ch.* xxiii. 8, 9), but hoped to see him shortly, never more to lose the sight of him, and that sight of him will be the more welcome after the present darkness and distance. Note, It is the blessedness of the blessed that they shall see God, shall see him as he is, see him face to face, and no longer through a glass darkly. See with what pleasure holy Job enlarges upon this (*v.* 27): "*Whom I shall see for myself,*" that is, "see and enjoy, see to my own unspeakable comfort and satisfaction. I shall see him as mine, as mine with an appropriating sight," Rev. xxi. 3. *God himself shall be with them and be their God ;* they shall be *like him, for they shall see him as he is,* that is seeing for themselves, 1 John iii. 2. *My eyes shall behold him, and not another.* First, "He, and not another for him, shall be seen, not a type or figure of him, but he himself." Glorified saints are perfectly sure that they are not imposed upon ; it is no *deceptio visús —illusion of the senses. Secondly,* "I, and not another for me, shall see him. Though my flesh and body be consumed, yet I shall not need a proxy ; I shall see him with my own eyes." This was what Job hoped for, and what he earnestly desired, which, some think, is the meaning of the last clause: *My reins are spent in my bosom,* that is, "all my desires are summed up and concluded in this; this will crown and complete them all; let me have this, and I shall have nothing more to desire; it is enough; it is all. With this the prayers of David, the son of Jesse, are ended.

IV. The application of this to his friends. His creed spoke comfort to himself, but warning and terror to those that set themselves against him.

1. It was a word of caution to them not to proceed and persist in their unkind usage of him, *v.* 28. He had reproved them for what they had said, and now tells them what they should say for the reducing of themselves and one another to a better temper. " *Why persecute we him* thus? Why do we grieve him and vex him, by censuring and condemning him, *seeing the root of the matter,* or the root of the word, *is found in him?*" Let this direct us, (1.) In our care concerning ourselves. We are all concerned to see to it that the root of the matter be found in us. A living, quickening, commanding, principle of grace in the heart, is the root of the matter, as necessary to our religion as the root to the tree, to which it owes both its fixedness and its fruitfulness. Love to God and our brethren, faith in Christ, hatred of sin—these are the root of the matter; other things are but leaves in comparison with these. Serious godliness is the one thing needful. (2.) In our conduct towards our brethren. We are to believe that many have the root of the matter in them who are not in every thing of our mind—who have their follies, and weaknesses, and mistakes—and to conclude that it is at our peril if we persecute any such. Woe be to him that offends one of these little ones! God will resent and revenge it. Job and his friends differed in some notions concerning the methods of Providence, but they agreed in the root of the matter, the belief of another world, and therefore should not persecute one another for these differences.

2. It was a word of terror to them. Christ's second coming will be very dreadful to those that are found *smiting their fellow servants* (Matt. xxiv. 49), and therefore (*v.* 29), " *Be you afraid of the sword,* the flaming sword of God's justice, which turns every way; fear, lest you make yourselves obnoxious to it. Good men need to be frightened from sin by the terrors of the Almighty, particularly from the sin of rashly judging their brethren, Matt. vii. 1; Jam. iii. 1. Those that are peevish and passionate with their brethren, censorious of them and malicious towards them, should know, not only that their wrath, whatever it pretends, works not the righteousness of God, but that, (1.) They may expect to smart for it in this world: *It brings the punishments of the sword.* Wrath leads to such crimes as expose men to the sword of the magistrate. God himself often takes vengeance for it, and those that showed no mercy shall find no mercy. (2.) If they repent not, that will be an earnest of worse. By these you may know there is a judgment, not only a present government, but a future judgment, in which hard speeches must be accounted for.

CHAP. XX.

One would have thought that such an excellent confession of faith as Job made, in the close of the foregoing chapter, would satisfy his friends, or at least mollify them; but they do not seem to have taken any notice of it, and therefore Zophar here takes his turn, enters the lists with Job, and attacks him with as much vehemence as before. I. His preface is short, but hot, ver. 2, 3. II. His discourse is long, and all upon one subject, the very same that Bildad was large upon (ch. xviii.), the certain misery of wicked people and the ruin that awaits them. 1. He asserts, in general, that the prosperity of a wicked person is short, and his ruin sure, ver. 4—9. 2. He proves the misery of his condition by many instances—that he should have a diseased body, a troubled conscience, a ruined estate, a beggared family, an infamous name,—and that he himself should perish under the weight of divine wrath: all this is most curiously described here in lofty expressions and lively similitudes; and it often proves true in this world, and always in another, without repentance, ver. 10—29. But the great mistake was, and (as bishop Patrick expresses it) all the flaw in his discourse (which was common to him with the rest), that he imagined God never varied from this method, and therefore Job was, without doubt, a very bad man, though it did not appear that he was, any other way than by his infelicity.

THEN answered Zophar the Naamathite, and said, 2 Therefore do my thoughts cause me to answer, and for *this* I make haste. 3 I have heard the check of my reproach, and the spirit of my understanding causeth me to answer. 4 Knowest thou *not* this of old, since man was placed upon earth, 5 That the triumphing of the wicked *is* short, and the joy of the hypocrite *but* for a moment? 6 Though his excellency mount up to the heavens, and his head reach unto the clouds; 7 *Yet* he shall perish for ever like his own dung: they which have seen him shall say, Where *is* he? 8 He shall fly away as a dream, and shall not be found: yea, he shall be chased away as a vision of the night. 9 The eye also *which* saw him shall *see him* no more; neither shall his place any more behold him.

Here, I. Zophar begins very passionately, and seems to be in a great heat at what Job had said. Being resolved to condemn Job for a bad man, he was much displeased that he talked so like a good man, and, as it should seem, broke in upon him, and began abruptly (*v.* 2): *Therefore do my thoughts cause me to answer.* He takes no notice of what Job had said to move their pity, or to evidence his own integrity, but fastens upon the reproof he gave them in the close of his discourse, counts that a reproach, and thinks himself *therefore* obliged to answer, because Job had bidden them be afraid of the sword, that he might not seem to be frightened by his menaces. The best counsel is too often ill taken from an antagonist, and therefore usually may be well spared. Zophar seemed more in haste to speak than became a wise man; but he excuses his haste with two things:—1. That Job had given him a strong provocation (*v.* 3): " *I have heard the check of my reproach,* and cannot bear to hear it any longer." Job's friends, I doubt, had spirits too high to deal with a man in his low condition; and high spirits are impatient of contradiction, and think themselves

111

affronted if all about them do not say as they say · they cannot bear a check but they call it *the check of their reproach*, and then they are bound in honour to return it, if not to draw upon him that gave it. 2. That his own heart gave him a strong instigation. His thoughts caused him to answer (*v.* 2), for *out of the abundance of the heart the mouth speaks;* but he fathers the instigation (*v.* 3) upon *the spirit of his understanding:* that indeed should cause us to answer; we should rightly apprehend a thing and duly consider it before we speak of it; but whether it did so here or no is a question. Men often mistake the dictates of their passion for the dictates of their reason, and therefore think they do well to be angry.

II. Zophar proceeds very plainly to show the ruin and destruction of wicked people, insinuating that because Job was destroyed and ruined he was certainly a wicked man and a hypocrite. Observe,

1. How this doctrine is introduced, *v.* 4, where he appeals, (1.) To Job's own knowledge and conviction: "*Knowest thou not this?* Canst thou be ignorant of a truth so plain? Or canst thou doubt of a truth which has been confirmed by the suffrages of all mankind?" Those know little who do not know that the wages of sin is death. (2.) To the experience of all ages. It was known of old, since man was placed upon the earth; that is, ever since man was made he has had this truth written in his heart, that the sin of sinners will be their ruin; and ever since there were instances of wickedness (which there were soon after man was placed on the earth) there were instances of the punishments of it, witness the exclusions of Adam and Cain. When sin entered into the world death entered with it: all the world knows that evil pursues sinners, whom *vengeance suffers not to live* (Acts xxviii. 4), and subscribes to that (Isa. iii. 11), *Woe to the wicked; it shall be ill with him*, sooner or later.

2. How it is laid down (*v.* 5): *The triumphing of the wicked is short, and the joy of the hypocrite but for a moment.* Observe, (1.) He asserts the misery, not only of those who are openly wicked and profane, but of hypocrites, who secretly practise wickedness under a show and profession of religion, because such a wicked man he looked upon Job to be; and it is true that a form of godliness, if it be made use of for a cloak of maliciousness, does but make bad worse. Dissembled piety is double iniquity, and the ruin that attends it will be accordingly. The hottest place in hell will be the portion of hypocrites, as our Saviour intimates, Matt. xxiv. 51. (2.) He grants that wicked men may for a time prosper, may be secure and easy, and very merry. You may see them in triumph and joy, triumphing and rejoicing in their wealth and power, their grandeur and success, triumphing and rejoicing over their poor honest neighbours whom they vex

and oppress: they feel no evil, they fear none. Job's friends were loth to own, at first, that wicked people might prosper at all (*ch.* iv. 9), until Job proved it plainly (*ch.* ix. 24, xii. 6), and now Zophar yields it; but, (3.) He lays it down for a certain truth that they will not prosper long. Their joy is but for a moment, and will quickly end in endless sorrow. Though he be ever so great, and rich, and jovial, the hypocrite will be humbled, and mortified, and made miserable.

3. How it is illustrated, *v.* 6—9. (1.) He supposes his prosperity to be very high, as high as you can imagine, *v.* 6. It is not his wisdom and virtue, but his worldly wealth or greatness, that he accounts *his excellency*, and values himself upon. We will suppose that *to mount up to the heavens*, and, since his spirit always rises with his condition, you may suppose that with it *his head reaches to the clouds.* He is every way advanced; the world has done the utmost it can for him. He looks down upon all about him with disdain, while they look up to him with admiration, envy, or fear. We will suppose him to bid fair for a universal monarchy. And, though he cannot but have made himself many enemies before he arrived to this pitch of prosperity, yet he thinks himself as much out of the reach of their darts as if he were in the clouds. (2.) He is confident that his ruin will accordingly be very great, and his fall the more dreadful for his having risen so high: *He shall perish for ever, v.* 7. His pride and security were the certain presages of his misery. This will certainly be true of all impenitent sinners in the other world; they shall be undone, for ever undone. But Zophar means his ruin in this world; and indeed sometimes notorious sinners are remarkably cut off by present judgments; they have reason enough to fear what Zophar here threatens even the triumphant sinner with. [1.] A shameful destruction: *He shall perish like his own dung* or dunghill, so loathsome is he to God and all good men, and so willing will the world be to part with him, Ps. cxix. 119; Isa. lxvi. 24. [2.] A surprising destruction. He will be brought into desolation in a moment (Ps. lxxiii. 19), so that those about him, that saw him but just now, will ask, "*Where is he?* Could he that made so great a figure vanish and expire so suddenly?" [3.] A swift destruction, *v.* 8. *He shall fly away* upon the wings of his own terrors, and be *chased away* by the just imprecations of all about him, who would gladly get rid of him. [4.] An utter destruction. It will be total; he shall go away *like a dream*, or *vision of the night*, which was a mere phantasm, and, whatever in it pleased the fancy, it is quite gone, and nothing of it remains but what serves us to laugh at the folly of. It will be final (*v.* 9): *The eye that saw him*, and was ready to adore him, *shall see him no more*, and the place he filled shall no more behold him, having

given him an eternal farewell when he went to his own place, as Judas, Acts i. 25.

10 His children shall seek to please the poor, and his hands shall restore their goods. 11 His bones are full of *the sin* of his youth, which shall lie down with him in the dust. 12 Though wickedness be sweet in his mouth, *though* he hide it under his tongue ; 13 *Though* he spare it, and forsake it not; but keep it still within his mouth: 14 *Yet* his meat in his bowels is turned, *it is* the gall of asps within him. 15 He hath swallowed down riches, and he shall vomit them up again : God shall cast them out of his belly. 16 He shall suck the poison of asps : the viper's tongue shall slay him. 17 He shall not see the rivers, the floods, the brooks of honey and butter. 18 That which he laboured for shall he restore, and shall not swallow *it* down: according to *his* substance *shall* the restitution *be,* and he shall not rejoice *therein.* 19 Because he hath oppressed *and* hath forsaken the poor ; *because* he hath violently taken away a house which he builded not ; 20 Surely he shall not feel quietness in his belly, he shall not save of that which he desired. 21 There shall none of his meat be left; therefore shall no man look for his goods. 22 In the fulness of his sufficiency he shall be in straits: every hand of the wicked shall come upon him.

The instances here given of the miserable condition of the wicked man in this world are expressed with great fulness and fluency of language, and the same thing returned to again and repeated in other words. Let us therefore reduce the particulars to their proper heads, and observe,

I. What his wickedness is for which he is punished.

1. The lusts of the flesh, here called the *sins of his youth* (v. 11); for those are the sins which, at that age, people are most tempted to. The forbidden pleasures of sense are said to be *sweet in his mouth* (v. 12); he indulges himself in all the gratifications of the carnal appetite, and takes an inordinate complacency in them, as yielding the most agreeable delights. That is the satisfaction which *he hides under his tongue,* and rolls there, as the most dainty delicate thing that can be. *He keeps it still within his mouth* (v. 13); let him have that, and he desires no more ; he will never part with that for the spiritual and divine pleasures of religion, which he has no

relish of nor affection for. His keeping it still in his mouth denotes his obstinately persisting in his sin (*he spares it* when he should kill and mortify it, *and forsakes it not,* but holds it fast, and goes on frowardly in it), and also his re-acting of his sin by revolving it and remembering it with pleasure, as that adulterous woman (Ezek. xxiii. 19) who *multiplied her whoredoms by calling to remembrance the days of her youth;* so does this wicked man here. Or his hiding it and keeping it under his tongue denotes his industrious concealment of his beloved lust. Being a hypocrite, his haunts of sin are secret, that he may save the credit of his profession ; but he who knows what is in the heart knows what is under the tongue too, and will discover it shortly.

2. The love of the world and the wealth of it. It is in worldly wealth that he places his happiness, and therefore he sets his heart upon it. See here, (1.) How greedy he is of it (*v.* 15): *He has swallowed down riches* as eagerly as ever a hungry man swallowed down meat; and is still crying, "Give, give." It is that which he desired (*v.* 20); it was, in his eye, the best gift, and that which he coveted earnestly. (2.) What pains he takes for it : It is *that which he laboured for* (*v.* 18), not by honest diligence in a lawful calling, but by an unwearied prosecution of all ways and methods, *per fas, per nefas—right or wrong,* to be rich. We must *labour,* not *to be rich* (Prov. xxiii. 4), but to be charitable, *that we may have to give* (Eph. iv. 28), not to spend. (3.) What great things he promises himself from it, intimated in *the rivers, the floods, the brooks of honey and butter* (*v.* 17); his being disappointed of them supposes that he had flattered himself with the hopes of them : he expected rivers of sensual delights.

3. Violence and oppression, and injustice in his poor neighbours, *v.* 19. This was the sin of the giants of the old world, and a sin that, as much as any, brings God's judgments upon nations and families. It is charged upon this wicked man, (1.) That *he has forsaken the poor,* taken no care of them, shown no kindness to them, nor made any provision for them. At first perhaps, for a pretence, he gave alms like the Pharisees, to gain a reputation ; but, when he had served his turn by this practice, he left it off, and forsook the poor, whom before he seemed to be concerned for. Those who do good, but not from a good principle, though they may abound in it, will not abide in it. (2.) That he has *oppressed* them, crushed them, taken all advantages against them to do them a mischief. To enrich himself, he has robbed the spital, and made the poor poorer. (3.) That he has *violently taken away their houses,* which he had no right to, as Ahab took Naboth's vineyard, not by secret fraud, by forgery, perjury, or some trick in law, but avowedly, and by open violence.

II. What his punishment is for this wickedness.

1. He shall be disappointed in his expectations, and shall not find that satisfaction in his worldly wealth which he vainly promised himself (v. 17): *He shall never see the rivers, the floods, the brooks of honey and butter,* with which he hoped to glut himself. The world is not that to those who love it, and court it, and admire it, which they fancy it will be. The enjoyment sinks far below the raised expectation.

2. He shall be diseased and distempered in his body; and how little comfort a man has in riches if he has not health! Sickness and pain, especially if they be in extremity, embitter all his enjoyments. This wicked man has all the delights of sense wound up to the height of pleasurableness; but what real happiness can he enjoy when *his bones are full of the sins of his youth* (v. 11), that is, of the effects of those sins? By his drunkenness and gluttony, his uncleanness and wantonness, when he was young, he contracted those diseases which are painful to him long after, and perhaps make his life very miserable, and, as Solomon speaks, consume his flesh and his body, Prov. v. 11. Perhaps he was given to fight when he was young, and then made nothing of a cut or a bruise in a fray; but he feels it in his bones long after. But can he get no ease, no relief? No, he is likely to carry his pains and diseases with him to the grave, or rather they are likely to carry him thither, and so the sins of his youth shall *lie down with him in the dust;* the very putrefying of his body in the grave is to him the effect of sin (*ch.* xxiv. 19), so that his iniquity is upon his bones there, Ezek. xxxii. 27. The sin of sinners follows them to the other side death.

3. He shall be disquieted and troubled in his mind: *Surely he shall not feel quietness in his belly,* v. 20. He has not that ease in his own mind that people think he has, but is in continual agitation. The ill-gotten wealth which he has swallowed down makes him sick, and, like undigested meat, is always upbraiding him. Let none expect to enjoy that comfortably which they have gotten unjustly. The unquietness of his mind arises, (1.) From his conscience looking back, and filling him with the fear of the wrath of God against him for his wickedness. Even that wickedness which was sweet in the commission, and was rolled under the tongue as a delicate morsel, becomes bitter in the reflection, and, when it is reviewed, fills him with horror and vexation. *In his bowels it is turned* (v. 14) like John's book, *in his mouth as sweet as honey,* but, *when he had eaten it, his belly was bitter,* Rev. x. 10. Such a thing is sin; it is turned into *the gall of asps,* than which nothing is more bitter, *the poison of asps* (v. 16), than which nothing more fatal, and so it will be to him; what he sucked so sweetly, and with so much pleasure, will prove to him the poison of asps; so will all unlawful gains be. The fawning tongue will

prove the viper's tongue. All the charming graces that are thought to be in sin will, when conscience is awakened, turn into so many raging furies. (2.) From his cares, looking forward, v. 22. *In the fulness of his sufficiency,* when he thinks himself most happy, and most sure of the continuance of his happiness, *he shall be in straits,* that is, he shall think himself so, through the anxieties and perplexities of his own mind, as that rich man who, when his ground brought forth plentifully, cried out, *What shall I do?* Luke xii. 17.

4. He shall be dispossessed of his estate; that shall sink and dwindle away to nothing, so that *he shall not rejoice therein, v.* 18. He shall not only never rejoice truly, but not long rejoice at all. (1.) What he has unjustly swallowed he shall be compelled to disgorge (v. 15): *He swallowed down riches,* and then thought himself sure of them, and that they were as much his own as the meat he had eaten; but he was deceived: *he shall vomit them up again;* his own conscience perhaps may make him so uneasy in the keeping of what he has gotten that, for the quiet of his own mind, he shall make restitution, and that not with the pleasure of a virtue, but the pain of a vomit, and with the utmost reluctancy. Or, if he do not himself refund what he has violently taken away, God will, by his providence, force him to it, and bring it about, one way or other, that ill-gotten goods shall return to the right owners: *God shall cast them out of his belly,* while yet the love of the sin is not cast out of his heart. So loud shall the clamours of the poor, whom he has impoverished, be against him, that he shall be forced to send his children to them to soothe them and beg their pardon (v. 10): *His children shall seek to please the poor,* while his own hands shall restore them their goods with shame (v. 18): *That which he laboured for,* by all the arts of oppression, *shall he restore,* and shall not so swallow it down as to digest it; it shall not stay with him, but *according to his shame shall the restitution be;* having gotten a great deal unjustly, he shall restore a great deal, so that when every one has his own he will have but little left for himself. To be made to restore what was unjustly gotten, by the sanctifying grace of God, as Zaccheus was, is a great mercy; he voluntarily and cheerfully restored four-fold, and yet had a great deal left to *give to the poor,* Luke xix. 8. But to be forced to restore, as Judas was, merely by the horrors of a despairing conscience, has none of that benefit and comfort attending it, for he *threw down the pieces of silver and went and hanged himself.* (2.) He shall be stripped of all he has and become a beggar. He that spoiled others shall himself be spoiled (Isa. xxxiii. 1); for *every hand of the wicked shall be upon him.* The innocent, whom he has wronged, sit down by their loss, saying, as David, *Wickedness proceedeth*

from the wicked, but my hand shall not be upon him, 1 Sam. xxiv. 13. But though they have forgiven him, though they will make no reprisals, divine justice will, and often makes the wicked to avenge the quarrel of the righteous, and squeezes and crushes one bad man by the hand of another upon him. Thus, when he is plucked on all sides, *he shall not save of that which he desired* (v. 20), not only he shall not save it all, but he shall save nothing of it. *There shall none of his meat* (which he coveted so much, and fed upon with so much pleasure) *be left*, v. 21. All his neighbours and relations shall look upon him to be in such bad circumstances that, when he is dead, no man shall look for his goods, none of his kindred shall expect to be a penny the better for him, nor be willing to take out letters of administration for what he leaves behind him. In all this Zophar reflects upon Job, who had lost all and was reduced to the last extremity.

23 *When* he is about to fill his belly, *God* shall cast the fury of his wrath upon him, and shall rain *it* upon him while he is eating. 24 He shall flee from the iron weapon, *and* the bow of steel shall strike him through. 25 It is drawn, and cometh out of the body; yea, the glittering sword cometh out of his gall : terrors *are* upon him. 26 All darkness *shall be* hid in his secret places : a fire not blown shall consume him; it shall go ill with him that is left in his tabernacle. 27 The heaven shall reveal his iniquity; and the earth shall rise up against him. 28 The increase of his house shall depart, *and his goods* shall flow away in the day of his wrath. 29 This *is* the portion of a wicked man from God, and the heritage appointed unto him by God.

Zophar, having described the many embarrassments and vexations which commonly attend the wicked practices of oppressors and cruel men, here comes to show their utter ruin at last.

I. Their ruin will take its rise from God's wrath and vengeance, v. 23. The hand of the wicked was upon him (v. 22), *every hand of the wicked*. His hand was against every one, and therefore every man's hand will be against him. Yet, in grappling with these, he might go near to make his part good; but his heart cannot endure, nor his hands be strong, when *God shall deal with him* (Ezek. xxii. 14), *when God shall cast the fury of his wrath upon him and rain it upon him*. Every word here speaks terror. It is not only the justice of God that is engaged against him, but his wrath, the deep resentment of

provocations given to himself; it is *the fury of his wrath,* incensed to the highest degree; it is cast upon him with force and fierceness; it is rained upon him in abundance; it comes on his head like the fire and brimstone upon Sodom, to which the psalmist also refers, Ps. xi. 6. *On the wicked God shall rain fire and brimstone.* There is no fence against this, but in Christ, who is the only covert from the storm and tempest, Isa. xxxii. 2. This wrath shall be cast upon him *when he is about to fill his belly,* just going to glut himself with what he has gotten and promising himself abundant satisfaction in it. Then, when he is eating, shall this tempest surprise him, when he is secure and easy, and in apprehension of no danger; as the ruin of the old world and Sodom came when they were in the depth of their security and the height of their sensuality, as Christ observes, Luke xvii. 26, &c. Perhaps Zophar here reflects on the death of Job's children when they were eating and drinking.

II. Their ruin will be inevitable, and there will be no possibility of escaping it (v. 24): *He shall flee from the iron weapon.* Flight argues guilt. He will not humble himself under the judgments of God, nor seek means to make his peace with him. All his care is to escape the vengeance that pursues him, but in vain : if he escape the sword, yet *the bow of steel shall strike him through.* God has weapons of all sorts; he has both *whet his sword and bent his bow* (Ps. vii. 12, 13); he can deal with his enemies *cominus vel eminus—at hand or afar off.* He has a sword for those that think to fight it out with him by their strength, and a bow for those that think to avoid him by their craft. See Isa. xxiv. 17, 18; Jer. xlviii. 43, 44. He that is marked for ruin, though he may escape one judgment, will find another ready for him.

III. It will be a total terrible ruin. When the dart that has struck him through (for when God shoots he is sure to hit his mark, when he strikes he strikes home) comes to be *drawn out of his body,* when *the glittering sword* (the *lightning,* so the word is), the flaming sword, the sword that is bathed in heaven (Isa. xxxiv. 5), *comes out of his gall,* O what *terrors are upon him!* How strong are the convulsions, how violent are the dying agonies! How terrible are the arrests of death to a wicked man!

IV. Sometimes it is a ruin that comes upon him insensibly, v. 26. 1. The darkness he is wrapped up in is a hidden darkness : it is *all darkness,* utter darkness, without the least mixture of light, and it is *hid in his secret place,* whither he has retreated and where he hopes to shelter himself; he never retires into his own conscience but he finds himself in the dark and utterly at a loss. 2. The fire he is consumed by is *a fire not blown,* kindled without noise, a consumption which every body sees the effect of, but nobody sees the cause of. It is plain that the gourd is withered, but the worm at the root, that causes it to wither, is out of sight. He is wasted by a soft gentle fire—surely, but very slowly. When the fuel is very combustible, the fire needs no blowing, and that is his case; he is ripe for ruin. *The proud, and those that do wickedly, shall be stubble,* Mal. iv. 1. *An unquenchable fire shall consume him* (so some read it), and that is certainly true of hell-fire.

V. It is a ruin, not only to himself, but to his family: *It shall go ill with him that is left in his tabernacle,* for the curse shall reach him, and he shall be cut off perhaps by the same grievous disease. There is an entail of wrath upon the family, which will destroy both his heirs and his inheritance, *v.* 28. 1. His posterity will be rooted out: *The increase of his house shall depart,* shall either be cut off by untimely deaths or forced to run their country. Numerous and growing families, if wicked and vile, are soon reduced, dispersed, and extirpated, by the judgments of God. 2. His estate will be sunk. *His goods shall flow away* from his family as fast as ever they flowed into it, when *the day of God's wrath* comes, for which, all the while his estate was in the getting by fraud and oppression, he was treasuring up wrath.

VI. It is a ruin which will manifestly appear to be just and righteous, and what he has brought upon himself by his own wickedness; for (*v.* 27) *the heaven shall reveal his iniquity,* that is, the God of heaven, who sees all the secret wickedness of the wicked, will, by some means or other, let all the world know what a base man he has been, that they may own the justice of God in all that is brought upon him. *The earth also shall rise up against him,* both to discover his wickedness and to avenge it. *The earth shall disclose her blood,* Isa. xxvi. 21. *The earth will rise up against him* (as the stomach rises against that which is loathsome), and will no longer keep him. *The heaven reveals his iniquity,* and therefore will not receive him. Whither then must he go but to hell? If the God of heaven and earth be his enemy, neither heaven nor earth will show him any kindness, but all the hosts of both are and will be at war with him.

VII. Zophar concludes like an orator (*v.* 29): *This is the portion of a wicked man from God;* it is allotted him, it is designed him, as his portion. He will have it at last, as a child has his portion, and he will have it for a perpetuity; it is what he must abide by: *This is the heritage of his decree from God;* it is the settled rule of his judgment, and fair warning is given of it. *O wicked man! thou shalt surely die,* Ezek. xxxiii. 8. Though impenitent sinners do not always fall under such temporal judgments as are here described (therein Zophar was mistaken), yet the wrath of God abides upon them, and they are made miserable by spiritual judg-

116

ments, which are much worse, their consciences being either, on the one hand, a terror to them, and then they are in continual amazement, or, on the other hand, seared and silenced, and then they are given up to a reprobate sense and bound over to eternal ruin. Never was any doctrine better explained, or worse applied, than this by Zophar, who intended by all this to prove Job a hypocrite. Let us receive the good explication, and make a better application, for warning to ourselves to stand in awe and not to sin.

CHAP. XXI.

This is Job's reply to Zophar's discourse, in which he complains less of his own miseries than he had done in his former discourses (finding that his friends were not moved by his complaints to pity him in the least), and comes closer to the general question that was in dispute between him and them, Whether outward prosperity, and the continuance of it, were a mark of the true church and the true members of it, so that the ruin of a man's prosperity is sufficient to prove him a hypocrite, though no other evidence appear against him: this they asserted, but Job denied. I. His preface here is designed for the moving of their affections, that he might gain their attention, ver. 1—6. II. His discourse is designed for the convincing of their judgments and the rectifying of their mistakes. He owns that God does sometimes hang up a wicked man as it were in chains, in terrorem—as a terror to others, by some visible remarkable judgment in this life, but denies that he always does so; nay, he maintains that commonly he does otherwise, suffering even the worst of sinners to live all their days in prosperity and to go out of the world without any visible mark of his wrath upon them. 1. He describes the great prosperity of wicked people, ver. 7—13. 2. He shows their great impiety, in which they are hardened by their prosperity, ver. 14—16. 3. He foretels their ruin at length, but after a long reprieve, ver. 17—21. 4. He observes a very great variety in the ways of God's providence towards men, even towards bad men, ver. 22—26. 5. He overthrows the ground of their severe censures of him, by showing that the destruction of the wicked is reserved for the other world, and that they often escape to the last in this world (ver. 27, to the end), and in this Job was clearly in the right.

BUT Job answered and said, 2 Hear diligently my speech, and let this be your consolations. 3 Suffer me that I may speak; and after that I have spoken, mock on. 4 As for me, *is* my complaint to man? and if *it were* so, why should not my spirit be troubled? 5 Mark me, and be astonished, and lay *your* hand upon *your* mouth. 6 Even when I remember I am afraid, and trembling taketh hold on my flesh.

Job here recommends himself, both his case and his discourse, both what he suffered and what he said, to the compassionate consideration of his friends. 1. That which he entreats of them is very fair, that they would suffer him to speak (*v.* 3) and not break in upon him, as Zophar had done, in the midst of his discourse. Losers, of all men, may have leave to speak; and, if those that are accused and censured are not allowed to speak for themselves, they are wronged without remedy, and have no way to come at their right. He entreats that they would hear diligently his speech (*v.* 2) as those that were willing to understand him, and, if they were under a mistake, to have it rectified; and that they would *mark him* (*v.* 5), for we may as well not hear as not heed and observe what we hear. 2. That which he urges for this is very reasonable. (1.) They came to comfort him. "Now," says he, " *let this be your consolations* (*v.* 2); if you have no other comforts ·to administer to me, yet deny me not this; be so kind, so just, as to give me a patient hearing, and that shall pass for your consolations of me." Nay, they could not know how to comfort him if they would not give him leave to open his case and tell his own story. Or, "It will be a consolation to yourselves, in the reflection, to have dealt tenderly with your afflicted friend, and not harshly." (2.) He would hear them speak when it came to their turn. "After I have spoken you may go on with what you have to say, and I will not hinder you, no, though you go on to mock me." Those that engage in controversy must reckon upon having hard words given them, and resolve to bear reproach patiently; for, generally, those that mock will mock on, whatever is said to them. (3.) He hoped to convince them. "If you will but give me a fair hearing, mock on if you can, but I believe I shall say that which will change your note and make you pity me rather than mock me." (4.) They were not his judges (v. 4): "*Is my complaint to man?* No, if it were I see it would be to little purpose to complain. But my complaint is to God, and to him do I appeal. Let him be Judge between you and me. Before him we stand upon even terms, and therefore I have the privilege of being heard as well as you. If my complaint were to men, my spirit would be troubled, for they would not regard me, nor rightly understand me; but my complaint is to God, who will suffer me to speak, though you will not." It would be sad if God should deal as unkindly with us as our friends sometimes do. (5.) There was that in his case which was very surprising and astonishing, and therefore both needed and deserved their most serious consideration. It was not a common case, but a very extraordinary one. [1.] He himself was amazed at it, at the troubles God had laid upon him and the censures of his friends concerning him (v. 6): "*When I remember* that terrible day in which I was on a sudden stripped of all my comforts, that day in which I was stricken with sore boils,— when I remember all the hard speeches with which you have grieved me,—I confess *I am afraid, and trembling takes hold of my flesh,* especially when I compare this with the prosperous condition of many wicked people, and the applauses of their neighbours, with which they pass through the world." Note, The providences of God, in the government of the world, are sometimes very astonishing even to wise and good men, and bring them to their wits' end. [2.] He would have them wonder at it (v. 5): "*Mark me, and be astonished.* Instead of expounding my troubles, you should awfully adore the unsearchable mysteries of Providence in afflicting one thus of whom you know no evil; you should therefore *lay your hand upon your mouth,* silently wait the issue, and judge nothing before the time. *God's way is in the sea, and his path in the great waters.* When we can-

not account for what he does, in suffering the wicked to prosper and the godly to be afflicted, nor fathom the depth of those proceedings, it becomes us to sit down and admire them. *Upright men shall be astonished at this, ch.* xvii. 8. Be you so."

7 Wherefore do the wicked live, become old, yea, are mighty in power? 8 Their seed is established in their sight with them, and their offspring before their eyes. 9 Their houses *are* safe from fear, neither *is* the rod of God upon them. 10 Their bull gendereth, and faileth not; their cow calveth, and castest not her calf. 11 They send forth their little ones like a flock, and their children dance. 12 They take the timbrel and harp, and rejoice at the sound of the organ. 13 They spend their days in wealth, and in a moment go down to the grave. 14 Therefore they say unto God, Depart from us; for we desire not the knowledge of thy ways. 15 What *is* the Almighty, that we should serve him? and what profit should we have, if we pray unto him? 16 Lo, their good *is* not in their hand: the counsel of the wicked is far from me.

All Job's three friends, in their last discourses, had been very copious in describing the miserable condition of a wicked man in this world. "It is true," says Job, "remarkable judgments are sometimes brought upon notorious sinners, but not always; for we have many instances of the great and long prosperity of those that are openly and avowedly wicked; though they are hardened in their wickedness by their prosperity, yet they are still suffered to prosper."

I. He here describes their prosperity in the height, and breadth, and length of it. "If this be true, as you say, pray tell me *wherefore do the wicked live?*" v. 7.

1. The matter of fact is taken for granted, for we see instances of it every day. (1.) They live, and are not suddenly cut off by the strokes of divine vengeance. Those yet speak who have set their mouths against the heavens. Those yet act who have stretched out their hands against God. Not only they live (that is, they are reprieved), but they *live in prosperity,* 1 Sam. xxv. 6. Nay, (2.) They *become old;* they have the honour, satisfaction, and advantage of living long, long enough to raise their families and estates. We read of a *sinner a hundred years old,* Isa. lxv. 20. But this is not all. (3.) They are *mighty in power,* are preferred to places of authority and trust, and not only make a great figure, but bear a great sway. *Vivit imo, et in senatum venit—*

He not only lives, but appears in the senate.
Now wherefore is it so? Note, It is worth
while to enquire into the reasons of the outward prosperity of wicked people. It is not
because God has forsaken the earth, because
he does not see, or does not hate, or cannot
punish their wickedness; but it is because
the measure of their iniquities is not full.
This is the day of God's patience, and, in
some way or other, he makes use of them and
their prosperity to serve his own counsels,
while it ripens them for ruin; but the chief
reason is because he will make it to appear
there is another world which is the world of
retribution, and not this.

2. The prosperity of the wicked is here
described to be,

(1.) Complete and consummate. [1.] They
are multiplied, and their family is built up,
and they have the satisfaction of seeing it
(*v.* 8): *Their seed is established in their sight.*
This is put first, as that which gives both a
pleasant enjoyment and a pleasing prospect.
[2.] They are easy and quiet, *v.* 9. Whereas
Zophar had spoken of their continual frights
and terrors, Job says, *Their houses are safe*
both from danger and from the fear of it (*v.* 9),
and so far are they from the killing wounds of
God's sword or arrows that they do not feel the
smart of so much as *the rod of God upon them.*
[3.] They are rich and thrive in their estates.
Of this he gives only one instance, *v.* 10.
Their cattle increase, and they meet with no
disappointment in them; not so much as a
cow casts her calf, and then their much
must needs grow more. This is promised,
Exod. xxiii. 26; Deut. vii. 14. [4.] They are
merry and live a jovial life (*v.* 11, 12): *They
send forth their little ones* abroad among their
neighbours, *like a flock,* in great numbers, to
sport themselves. They have their balls and
music-meetings, at which *their children dance;*
and dancing is fittest for children, who know
not better how to spend their time and whose
innocency guards them against the mischiefs
that commonly attend it. Though the parents are not so very youthful and frolicsome
as to dance themselves, yet *they take the timbrel and harp;* they pipe, and their children
dance after their pipe, and they know no grief
to put their instruments out of tune or to
withhold their hearts from any joy. Some
observe that this is an instance of their vanity, as well as of their prosperity. Here is
none of that care taken of their children
which Abraham took of his, to *teach them the
way of the Lord,* Gen. xviii. 19. Their children do not pray, or say their catechism, but
dance, and sing, and *rejoice at the sound of
the organ.* Sensual pleasures are all the delights of carnal people, and as men are themselves so they breed their children.

(2.) Continuing and constant (*v.* 13): *They
spend their days,* all their days, *in wealth,* and
never know what it is to want—in mirth, and
never know what sadness means; and at last,
without any previous alarms to frighten them,

118

without any anguish or agony, *in a moment they
go down to the grave,* and there are no bands
in their death. If there were not another life
after this, it were most desirable to die by the
quickest shortest strokes of death. Since we
must *go down to the grave,* if that were the
furthest of our journey, we should wish to *go
down in a moment,* to swallow the bitter pill,
and not chew it.

II. He shows how they abuse their prosperity and are confirmed and hardened by it
in their impiety, *v.* 14, 15.

1. Their gold and silver serve to steel them,
to make them more insolent, and more impudent, in their wickedness. Now he mentions
this either, (1.) To increase the difficulty. It
is strange that any wicked people should prosper thus, but especially that those should prosper who have arrived at such a pitch of wickedness as openly to bid defiance to God himself, and tell him to his face that they care not
for him; nay, and that their prosperity should
be continued, though they bear up themselves
upon that, in their opposition to God; with
that weapon they fight against him, and yet
are not disarmed. Or, (2.) To lessen the difficulty. God suffers them to prosper; but let
us not wonder at it, for *the prosperity of fools
destroys them,* by hardening them in sin,
Prov. i. 32; Ps. lxxiii. 7—9.

2. See how light these prospering sinners
make of God and religion, as if because they
have so much of this world they had no need
to look after another.

(1.) See how ill affected they are to God
and religion; they abandon them, and cast
off the thoughts of them. [1.] They dread
the presence of God; they *say unto him,
"Depart from us;* let us never be troubled
with the apprehension of our being under
God's eye nor be restrained by the fear of
him." Or they bid him depart as one they
do not need, nor have any occasion to make
use of. The world is the portion they have
chosen, and take up with, and think themselves happy in; while they have that they
can live without God. Justly will God say
Depart (Matt. xxv. 41) to those who have
bidden him depart; and justly does he now
take them at their word. [2.] They dread the
knowledge of God, and of his will, and of their
duty to him: *We desire not the knowledge of
thy ways.* Those that are resolved not to walk
in God's ways desire not to know them, because their knowledge will be a continual reproach to their disobedience, John iii. 19.

(2.) See how they argue against God and
religion (*v.* 15): *What is the Almighty?*
Strange that ever creatures should speak
so insolently, that ever reasonable creatures
should speak so absurdly and unreasonably.
The two great bonds by which we are drawn
and held to religion are those of duty and
interest; now they here endeavour to break
both these bonds asunder. [1.] They will
not believe it is their duty to be religious:
What is the Almighty, that we should serve

him? Like Pharaoh (Exod. v. 2), *Who is the Lord, that I should obey his voice?* Observe, *First,* How slightly they speak of God: *What is the Almighty?* As if he were a mere name, a mere cipher, or one they have nothing to do with and that has nothing to do with them. *Secondly,* How hardly they speak of religion. They call it a *service,* and mean a hard service. Is it not enough, they think, to keep up a fair correspondence with the Almighty, but they must serve him, which they look upon as a task and drudgery. *Thirdly,* How highly they speak of themselves: " *That we should serve him;* we who are rich and mighty in power, shall we be subject and accountable to him? No, we are lords," Jer. ii. 31. [2.] They will not believe it is their interest to be religious: *What profit shall we have if we pray unto him?* All the world are for what they can get, and *therefore* wisdom's merchandise is neglected, because they think there is nothing to be got by it. *It is vain to serve God,* Mal. iii. 13, 14. Praying will not pay debts nor portion children; nay, perhaps serious godliness may hinder a man's preferment and expose him to losses; and what then? Is nothing to be called gain but the wealth and honour of this world? If we obtain the favour of God, and spiritual and eternal blessings, we have no reason to complain of losing by our religion. But, if we have not profit by prayer, it is our own fault (Isa. lviii. 3, 4), it is because we ask amiss, Jam. iv. 3. Religion itself is not a vain thing; if it be so to us, we may thank ourselves for resting in the outside of it, Jam. i. 26.

III. He shows their folly herein, and utterly disclaims all concurrence with them (v. 19): *Lo, their good is not in their hand,* that is, they did not get it without God, and therefore they are very ungrateful to slight him thus. It was *not their might, nor the power of their hand,* that got them this wealth, and therefore they ought to remember God who gave it them. Nor can they keep it without God, and therefore they are very unwise to lose their interest in him and bid him to depart from them. Some give this sense of it: " Their good is in their barns and their bags, hoarded up there; it is not in their hand, to do good to others with it; and then what good does it do them?" " Therefore," says Job, " *the counsel of the wicked is far from me.* Far be it from me that I should be of their mind, say as they say, do as they do, and take my measures from them. Their *posterity approve their sayings,* though *their way be their folly* (Ps. xlix. 13); but I know better things than to walk in their counsel.

17 How oft is the candle of the wicked put out? and *how oft* cometh their destruction upon them? *God* distributeth sorrows in his anger. 18

They are as stubble before the wind, and as chaff that the storm carrieth away. 19 God layeth up his iniquity for his children : he rewardeth him, and he shall know *it.* 20 His eyes shall see his destruction, and he shall drink of the wrath of the Almighty. 21 For what pleasure *hath* he in his house after him, when the number of his months is cut off in the midst? 22 Shall *any* teach God knowledge? seeing he judgeth those that are high. 23 One dieth in his full strength, being wholly at ease and quiet. 24 His breasts are full of milk, and his bones are moistened with marrow. 25 And another dieth in the bitterness of his soul, and never eateth with pleasure. 26 They shall lie down alike in the dust, and the worms shall cover them.

Job had largely described the prosperity of wicked people; now, in these verses,

I. He opposes this to what his friends had maintained concerning their certain ruin in this life. "Tell me *how often* do you see *the candle of the wicked put out?* Do you not as often see it burnt down to the socket, until it goes out of itself? *v.* 17. How often do you see *their destruction come upon them,* or *God distributing sorrows in his anger* among them? Do you not as often see their mirth and prosperity continuing to the last?" Perhaps there are as many instances of notorious sinners ending their days in pomp as ending them in misery, which observation is sufficient to invalidate their arguments against Job and to show that no certain judgment can be made of men's character by their outward condition.

II. He reconciles this to the holiness and justice of God. Though wicked people prosper thus all their days, yet we are not therefore to think that God will let their wickedness always go unpunished. No, 1. Even while they prosper thus they are *as stubble and chaff before the stormy wind,* v. 18. They are light and worthless, and of no account either with God or with wise and good men. They are fitted to destruction, and continually lie exposed to it, and in the height of their pomp and power there is but a step between them and ruin. 2. Though they spend all their days in wealth God is *laying up their iniquity for their children* (v. 19), and he will visit it upon their posterity when they are gone. The oppressor lays up his goods for his children, to make them gentlemen, but God lays up his iniquity for them, to make them beggars. He keeps an exact account of the fathers' sins, *seals them up among his treasures* (Deut. xxxii. 34), and will justly punish the children, while the riches, to which the curse cleaves, are found as assets in their hands. 3. Though they prosper in this world, yet they shall be reckoned with in another world. God *rewards him* according to his deeds at last (v. 19), though the sentence passed against his evil works be not executed speedily. Perhaps he may not now be made to fear the wrath to come, but he may flatter himself with hopes that he shall have peace though he go on; but he shall be made to feel it in the day of the revelation of the righteous judgment of God. He shall know it (v. 20): *His eyes shall see his destruction* which he would not be persuaded to believe. They *will not see, but they shall see,* Isa. xxvi. 11. The eyes that have been wilfully shut against the grace of God shall be opened to see his destruction. *He shall drink of the wrath of the Almighty;* that shall be the portion of his cup. Compare Ps. xi. 6 with Rev. xiv. 10. The misery of damned sinners is here set forth in a few words, but very terrible ones. They lie under the wrath of an Almighty God, who, in their destruction, both shows his wrath and makes known his power; and, if this will be his condition in the other world, what good will his prosperity in this world do him? *What pleasure has he in his house after him?* v. 21. Our Saviour has let us know how little pleasure the rich man in hell had in his house after him, when the remembrance of the good things he had received in his life-time would not cool his tongue, but added much to his misery, as did also the sorrow he was in lest his five brethren, whom he left in his house after him, should follow him to that place of torment, Luke xvi. 25—28. So little will the gain of the world profit him that has lost his soul.

III. He resolves this difference which Providence makes between one wicked man and another into the wisdom and sovereignty of God (v. 22): *Shall any pretend to teach God knowledge?* Dare we arraign God's proceedings or blame his conduct? Shall we take upon us to tell God how he should govern the world, what sinner he should spare and whom he should punish? He has both authority and ability to judge those that are high. Angels in heaven, princes and magistrates on earth, are accountable to God, and must receive their doom from him. He manages them, and makes what use he pleases of them. Shall he then be accountable to us, or receive advice from us? He is the Judge of all the earth, and therefore no doubt he will do right (Gen. xviii. 25, Rom. iii. 6), and those proceedings of his providence which seem to contradict one another he can make, not only mutually to agree, but jointly to serve his own purposes. The little difference there is between one wicked man's dying impenitent in peace and pomp and another wicked man's dying so in pain and misery, when both will at last meet

in hell, he illustrates by the little difference there is between one man's dying suddenly and another's dying slowly, when they will both meet shortly in the grave. So vast is the disproportion between time and eternity that, if hell be the lot of every sinner at last, it makes little difference if one goes singing thither and another sighing. See,

1. How various the circumstances of people's dying are. There is one way into the world, we say, but many out; yet, as some are born by quick and easy labour, others by that which is hard and lingering, so dying is to some much more terrible than to others; and, since the death of the body is the birth of the soul into another world, death-bed agonies may not unfitly be compared to child-bed throes. Observe the difference. (1.) One dies suddenly, *in his full strength,* not weakened by age or sickness (v. 23), *being wholly at ease and quiet,* under no apprehension at all of the approach of death, nor in any fear of it; but, on the contrary, because *his breasts are full of milk and his bones moistened with marrow* (v. 24), that is, he is healthful and vigorous, and of a good constitution (like a milch cow that is fat and in good liking), he counts upon nothing but to live many years in mirth and pleasure. Thus fair does he bid for life, and yet he is cut off in a moment by the stroke of death. Note, It is a common thing for persons to be taken away by death when they are in their full strength, in the highest degree of health, when they least expect death, and think themselves best armed against it, and are ready not only to set death at a distance, but to set it at defiance. Let us therefore never be secure; for we have known many well and dead in the same week, the same day, the same hour, nay, perhaps, the same minute. Let us therefore be always ready. (2.) Another dies slowly, and with a great deal of previous pain and misery (v. 25), *in the bitterness of his soul,* such as poor Job was himself now in, *and never eats with pleasure,* has no appetite to his food nor any relish of it, through sickness, or age, or sorrow of mind. What great reason have those to be thankful that are in health and always eat with pleasure! And what little reason have those to complain who sometimes do not eat thus, when they hear of many that never do!

2. How undiscernible this difference is in the grave. As rich and poor, so healthful and unhealthful, meet there (v. 26): *They shall lie down alike in the dust, and the worms shall cover them,* and feed sweetly on them. Thus, if one wicked man die in a palace and another in a dungeon, they will meet in the congregation of the dead and damned, and the worm that dies not, and the fire that is not quenched, will be the same to them, which makes those differences inconsiderable and not worth perplexing ourselves about.

27 Behold, I know your thoughts,

and the devices *which* ye wrongfully imagine against me. 28 For ye say, Where *is* the house of the prince? and where *are* the dwelling places of the wicked? 29 Have ye not asked them that go by the way? and do ye not know their tokens, 30 That the wicked is reserved to the day of destruction? they shall be brought forth to the day of wrath. 31 Who shall declare his way to his face? and who shall repay him *what* he hath done? 32 Yet shall he be brought to the grave, and shall remain in the tomb. 33 The clods of the valley shall be sweet unto him, and every man shall draw after him, as *there are* innumerable before him. 34 How then comfort ye me in vain, seeing in your answers there remaineth falsehood?

In these verses,

I. Job opposes the opinion of his friends, which he saw they still adhered to, that the wicked are sure to fall into such visible and remarkable ruin as Job had now fallen into, and none but the wicked, upon which principle they condemned Job as a wicked man. "*I know your thoughts,*" says Job (*v.* 27); "I know you will not agree with me; for your judgments are tinctured and biassed by your piques and prejudices against me, *and the devices which you wrongfully imagine against* my comfort and honour: and how can such men be convinced?" Job's friends were ready to say, in answer to his discourse concerning the prosperity of the wicked, "*Where is the house of the prince? v.* 28. Where is Job's house, or the house of his eldest son, in which his children were feasting? Enquire into the circumstances of Job's house and family, and then ask, *Where are the dwelling-places of the wicked?* and compare them together, and you will soon see that Job's house is in the same predicament with the houses of tyrants and oppressors, and may therefore conclude that doubtless he was such a one."

II. He lays down his own judgment to the contrary, and, for proof of it, appeals to the sentiments and observations of all mankind. So confident is he that he is in the right that he is willing to refer the cause to the next man that comes by (*v.* 29): "*Have you not asked those that go by the way*—any indifferent person, any that will answer you? I say not, as Eliphaz (*ch.* v. 1), to which of the *saints,* but to which of the *children of men* will you turn? Turn to which you will, and you will find them all of my mind, that the punishment of sinners is designed more for the other world than for this, according to the prophecy of Enoch, the seventh from

Adam, Jude 14. *Do you not know the tokens* of this truth, which all that have made any observations upon the providences of God concerning mankind in this world can furnish you with?" Now,

1. What is it that Job here asserts? Two things:—(1.) That impenitent sinners will certainly be punished in the other world, and, usually, their punishment is put off until then. (2.) That therefore we are not to think it strange if they prosper greatly in this world and fall under no visible token of God's wrath. *Therefore* they are spared now, because they are to be punished then; *therefore* the *workers of iniquity flourish, that they may be destroyed for ever,* Ps. xcii. 7. The sinner is here supposed, [1.] To live in a great deal of power, so as to be not only the *terror of the mighty in the land of the living* (Ezek. xxxii. 27), but the terror of the wise and good too, whom he keeps in such awe that none dares *declare his way to his face, v.* 31. None will take the liberty to reprove him, to tell him of the wickedness of his way, and what will be in the end thereof; so that he sins securely, and is not made to know either shame or fear. *The prosperity of fools destroys them,* by setting them (in their own conceit) above reproofs, by which they might be brought to that repentance which alone will prevent their ruin. Those are marked for destruction that are let alone in sin, Hos. iv. 17. And, if none dares declare his way to his face, much less dare any repay him what he has done and make him refund what he has obtained by injustice. He is one of those great flies which break through the cobwebs of the law, that hold only the little ones. This emboldens sinners in their sinful ways that they can brow-beat justice and make it afraid to meddle with them. But there is a day coming when those shall be told of their faults who now would not bear to hear of them, those shall have their sins set in order before them, and their way declared to their face, to their everlasting confusion, who would not have it done here, to their conviction, and those who would not repay the wrongs they had done shall have them repaid to them. [2.] To die, and be buried in a great deal of pomp and magnificence, *v.* 32, 33. There is no remedy; he must die; that is the lot of all men; but every thing you can think of shall be done to take off the reproach of death. *First,* He shall have a splendid funeral—a poor thing for any man to be proud of the prospect of; yet with some it passes for a mighty thing. Well, *he shall be brought to the grave* in state, surrounded with all the honours of the heralds' office and all the respect his friends can then pay to his remains. *The rich man died, and was buried,* but no mention is made of the poor man's burial, Luke xvi. 22. *Secondly,* He shall have a stately monument erected over him *He shall remain in the tomb* with a *Hic jacet* —Here lies, over him, and a large encomium.

121

Perhaps it is meant of the embalming of his body to preserve it, which was a piece of honour anciently done by the Egyptians to their great men. He *shall watch in the tomb* (so the word is), shall abide solitary and quiet there, as a watchman in his tower. *Thirdly, The clods of the valley shall be sweet to him;* there shall be as much done as can be with rich odours to take off the noisomeness of the grave, as by lamps to set aside the darkness of it, which perhaps was referred to in the foregoing phrase of *watching in the tomb.* But it is all a jest; what is the light, or what the perfume, to a man that is dead? *Fourthly,* It shall be alleged, for the lessening of the disgrace of death, that it is the common lot : He has only yielded to fate, *and every man shall draw after him, as there are innumerable before him.* Note, Death is the way of all the earth: when we are to cross that darksome valley we must consider, 1. That there are innumerable before us; it is a tracked road, which may help to take off the terror of it. To die is *ire ad plures—to go to the great majority.* 2. That every man shall draw after us. As there is a plain track before, so there is a long train behind; we are neither the first nor the last that pass through that dark entry. Every one must go in his own order, the order appointed of God.

2. From all this Job infers the impertinency of their discourses, *v. 34.* (1.) Their foundation is rotten, and they went upon a wrong hypothesis: *"In your answers there remains falsehood;* what you have said stands not only unproved but disproved, and lies under such an imputation of falsehood as you cannot clear it from." (2.) Their building was therefore weak and tottering : *" You comfort me in vain.* All you have said gives me no relief; you tell me that I shall prosper again if I turn to God, but you go upon this presumption, that piety shall certainly be crowned with prosperity, which is false; and therefore how can your inference from it yield me any comfort?" Note, Where there is not truth there is little comfort to be expected

CHAP. XXII.

Eliphaz here leads on a third attack upon poor Job, in which Bildad followed him, but Zophar drew back, and quitted the field. It was one of the unhappinesses of Job, as it is of many an honest man, to be misunderstood by his friends. He had spoken of the prosperity of wicked men in this world as a mystery of Providence, but they took it for a reflection upon Providence, as countenancing their wickedness; and they reproached him accordingly. In this chapter, I. Eliphaz checks him for his complaints of God, and of his dealings with him, as if he thought God had done him wrong, ver. 2—4. II. He charges him with many high crimes and misdemeanours, for which he supposes God was now punishing him. 1. Oppression and injustice, ver. 5—11. 2. Atheism and infidelity, ver. 12—14. III. He compares his case to that of the old world, ver. 15—20. IV. He gives him very good counsel, assuring him that, if he would take it, God would return in mercy to him and he should return to his former prosperity, ver. 21—30.

THEN Eliphaz the Temanite answered and said, 2 Can a man be profitable unto God, as he that is wise may be profitable unto himself?

3 *Is it* any pleasure to the Almighty, that thou art righteous? or *is it* gain *to him,* that thou makest thy ways perfect? 4 Will he reprove thee for fear of thee? will he enter with thee into judgment?

Eliphaz here insinuates that, because Job complained so much of his afflictions, he thought God was unjust in afflicting him; but it was a strained *innuendo.* Job was far from thinking so. What Eliphaz says here is therefore unjustly applied to Job, but in itself it is very true and good,

I. That when God does us good it is not because he is indebted to us; if he were, there might be some colour to say, when he afflicts us, " He does not deal fairly with us." But whoever pretends that he has by any meritorious action made God his debtor, let him prove this debt, and he shall be sure not to lose it, Rom. xi. 35. *Who has given to him, and it shall be recompensed to him again?* But Eliphaz here shows that the righteousness and perfection of the best man in the world are no real benefit or advantage to God, and therefore cannot be thought to merit any thing from him. 1. Man's piety is no profit to God, no gain, *v. 1, 2.* If we could by any thing merit from God, it would be by our piety, our being righteous, and making our way perfect. If that will not merit, surely nothing else will. If a man cannot make God his debtor by his godliness, and honesty, and obedience to his laws, much less can he by his wit, and learning, and worldly policy. Now Eliphaz here asks whether any man can possibly be *profitable to God.* It is certain that he cannot. By no means. *He that is wise may be profitable to himself.* Note, Our wisdom and piety are that by which we ourselves are, and are likely to be, great gainers. *Wisdom is profitable to direct,* Eccl. x. 10. *Godliness is profitable to all things,* 1 Tim. iv. 8. *If thou be wise, thou shalt be wise for thyself,* Prov. ix. 12. The gains of religion are infinitely greater than the losses of it, and so it will appear when they are balanced. But can a man be thus profitable to God? No, for such is the perfection of God that he cannot receive any benefit or advantage by men; what can be added to that which is infinite? And such is the weakness and imperfection of man that he cannot offer any benefit or advantage to God. Can the light of a candle be profitable to the sun or the drop of the bucket to the ocean? He that is wise is profitable to himself, for his own direction and defence, his own credit and comfort; he can with his wisdom entertain himself and enrich himself; but can he so be profitable to God? No; God needs not us nor our services. We are undone, for ever undone, without him; but he is happy, for ever happy, without us. *Is it any gain to him,* any real addition to his glory or wealth, *if we make our way perfect?* Suppose it were absolutely perfect, yet what is God the better? Much less when it is so far short of being perfect. 2. It is no pleasure to him. God has indeed expressed himself in his word well pleased with the righteous; his countenance beholds them and his delight is in them and their prayers; but all that adds nothing to the infinite satisfaction and complacency which the Eternal Mind has in itself. God can enjoy himself without us, though we could have but little enjoyment of ourselves without our friends. This magnifies his condescension, in that, though our services be no real profit or pleasure to him, yet he invites, encourages, and accepts them.

II. That when God restrains or rebukes us it is not because he is in danger from us, or jealous of us (*v.* 4): " *Will he reprove thee for fear of thee*, and take thee down from thy prosperity lest thou shouldst grow too great for him, as princes sometimes have thought it a piece of policy to curb the growing greatness of a subject, lest he should become formidable?" Satan indeed suggested to our first parents that God forbade them the tree of knowledge for fear of them, lest they should be as gods, and so become rivals with him; but it was a base insinuation. God rebukes the good because he loves them, but he never rebukes the great because he fears them. He does not *enter into judgment* with men, that is, pick a quarrel with them and seek occasion against them, through fear lest they should eclipse his honour or endanger his interest. Magistrates punish offenders for fear of them. Pharaoh oppressed Israel because he feared them. It was for fear that Herod slew the children of Bethlehem and that the Jews persecuted Christ and his apostles. But God does not, as they did, pervert justice for fear of any. See *ch.* xxxv. 5—8.

5 *Is* not thy wickedness great? and thine iniquities infinite? 6 For thou hast taken a pledge from thy brother for nought, and stripped the naked of their clothing. 7 Thou hast not given water to the weary to drink, and thou hast withholden bread from the hungry. 8 But *as for* the mighty man, he had the earth; and the honourable man dwelt in it. 9 Thou hast sent widows away empty, and the arms of the fatherless have been broken. 10 Therefore snares *are* round about thee, and sudden fear troubleth thee; 11 Or darkness, *that* thou canst not see; and abundance of waters cover thee. 12 *Is* not God in the height of heaven? and behold the height of the stars, how high they are! 13 And thou sayest, How doth God know? can he judge through the dark cloud? 14

Thick clouds *are* a covering to him, that he seeth not; and he walketh in the circuit of heaven.

Eliphaz and his companions had condemned Job, in general, as a wicked man and a hypocrite; but none of them had descended to particulars, nor drawn up any articles of impeachment against him, until Eliphaz did so here, where he positively and expressly charges him with many high crimes and misdemeanours, which, if he had really been guilty of them, might well have justified them in their harsh censures of him. "Come," says Eliphaz, "we have been too long beating about the bush, too tender of Job and afraid of grieving him, which has but confirmed him in his self-justification. It is high time to deal plainly with him. We have condemned him by parables, but that does not answer the end; he is not prevailed with to condemn himself. We must therefore plainly tell him, *Thou art the man*, the tyrant, the oppressor, the atheist, we have been speaking of all this while. *Is not thy wickedness great?* Certainly it is, or else thy troubles would not be so great. I appeal to thyself, and thy own conscience; are not *thy iniquities infinite*, both in number and heinousness?" Strictly taken, nothing is infinite but God; but he means this, that his sins were more than could be counted and more heinous than could be conceived. Sin, being committed against Infinite Majesty, has in it a kind of infinite malignity. But when Eliphaz charges Job thus highly, and ventures to descend to particulars too, laying to his charge that which he knew not, we may take occasion hence, 1. To be angry at those who unjustly censure and condemn their brethren. For aught I know, Eliphaz, in accusing Job falsely, as he does here, was guilty of as great a sin and as great a wrong to Job as the Sabeans and Chaldeans that robbed him; for a man's good name is more precious and valuable than his wealth. It is against all the laws of justice, charity, and friendship, either to raise or receive calumnies, jealousies, and evil surmises, concerning others; and it is the more base and disingenuous if we thus vex those that are in distress and add to their affliction. Eliphaz could produce no instances of Job's guilt in any of the particulars that follow here, but seems resolved to calumniate boldly, and throw all the reproach he could on Job, not doubting but that some would cleave to him. 2. To pity those who are thus censured and condemned. Innocency itself will be no security against a false and foul tongue. Job, whom God himself praised as the best man in the world, is here represented by one of his friends, and he a wise and good man too, as one of the greatest villains in nature. Let us not think it strange if at any time we be thus blackened, but learn how to pass by evil report as well as good, and commit our cause, as Job did his, to him that judgeth righteously.

Let us see the particular articles of this charge

I. He charged him with oppression and injustice, that, when he was in prosperity, he not only did no good with his wealth and power, but did a great deal of hurt with them. This was utterly false, as appears by the account Job gives of himself (*ch.* xxix. 12, &c.) and the character God gave of him, *ch.* i. And yet,

1. Eliphaz branches out this charge into divers particulars, with as much assurance as if he could call witnesses to prove upon oath every article of it. He tells him, (1.) That he had been cruel and unmerciful to the poor. As a magistrate he ought to have protected them and seen them provided for; but Eliphaz suspects that he never did them any kindness, but all the mischief his power enabled him to do,—that, for an inconsiderable debt, he demanded, and carried away by violence, a pawn of great value, even from his brother, whose honesty and sufficiency he could not but know (*v.* 6), *Thou hast taken a pledge from thy brother for nought*, or, as the LXX. read it, *Thou hast taken thy brethren for pledges*, and that for nought, imprisoned them, enslaved them, because they had nothing to pay,—that he had taken the very clothes of his insolvent tenants and debtors, so that he had *stripped them naked*, and left them so (the law of Moses forbade this, Exod. xxii. 26, Deut. xxiv. 13),—that he had not been charitable to the poor, no, not to poor travellers, and poor widows: "*Thou hast not given* so much as a cup of cold *water* (which would have cost thee nothing) *to the weary to drink*, when he begged for it (*v.* 7) and was ready to perish for want of it, nay, *thou hast withholden bread from the hungry* in their extremity, hast not only not given it, but hast forbidden the giving of it, which is *withholding good from those to whom it is really due*, Prov. iii. 27. Poor widows, who while their husbands were living troubled nobody, but now were forced to seek relief, thou hast sent away empty from thy doors with a sad heart, *v.* 9. Those who came to thee for justice, thou didst send away unheard, unhelped; nay, though they came to thee full, thou didst squeeze them, and send them away empty; and, worst of all, *the arms of the fatherless have been broken;* those that could help themselves but little thou hast quite disabled to help themselves." This, which is the blackest part of the charge, is but insinuated: *The arms of the fatherless have been broken.* He does not say, "Thou hast broken them," but he would have it understood so. and if they be broken, and those who have power do not relieve them, they are chargeable with it. "They have been broken by those under thee, and thou hast connived at it, which brings thee under the guilt." (2.) That he had been partial to the

rich and great (*v.* 8): "*As for the mighty man*, if he was guilty of any crime, he was never questioned for it : *he had the earth ;* he *dwelt in it.* If he brought an action ever so unjustly, or if an action were ever so justly brought against him, yet he was sure to carry his cause in thy courts. The poor were not fed at thy door, while the rich were feasted at thy table." Contrary to this is Christ's rule for hospitality (Luke xiv. 12—14); and Solomon says, *He that gives to the rich shall come to poverty.*

2. He attributes all his present troubles to these supposed sins (*v.* 10, 11): "Those that are guilty of such practices as these commonly bring themselves into just such a condition as thou art now in; and therefore we conclude thou hast been thus guilty." (1.) "The providence of God usually crosses and embarrasses such; and *snares are*, accordingly, *round about thee*, so that, which way soever thou steppest or lookest, thou findest thyself in distress; and others are as hard upon thee as thou hast been upon the poor." (2.) "Their own consciences may be expected to terrify and accuse them. No sin makes a louder cry there than unmercifulness; and, accordingly, *sudden fear troubles thee;* and, though thou wilt not own it, it is guilt of this kind that creates thee all this terror." Zophar had insinuated this, *ch.* xx 19, 20. (3.) "They are brought to their wits' end, so amazed and bewildered that they know not what to do, and that also is thy case; for thou art *in darkness that thou canst not see* wherefore God contends with thee nor what is the best course for thee to take *for abundance of waters cover thee*," that is, "thou art in a mist, in the midst of dark waters, in the thick clouds of the sky." Note, Those that have not shown mercy may justly be denied the comfortable hope that they shall find mercy; and then what can they expect but snares, and darkness, and continual fear?

II. He charged him with atheism, infidelity, and gross impiety, and thought this was at the bottom of his injustice and oppressiveness: he that did not fear God did not regard man. He would have it thought that Job was an Epicurean, who did indeed own the being of God, but denied his providence, and fancied that he confined himself to the entertainments of the upper world and never concerned himself in the inhabitants and affairs of this.

1. Eliphaz referred to an important truth, which he thought, if Job had duly considered it, would have prevented him from being so passionate in his complaints and bold in justifying himself (*v.* 12): *Is not God in the height of heaven?* Yes, no doubt he is. No heaven so high but God is there; and in the highest heavens, the heavens of the blessed, the residence of his glory, he is present in a special manner. There he is pleased to manifest himself in a way peculiar to the upper world, and thence

he is pleased to manifest himself in a way suited to this lower world. There is his throne; there is his court: he is called *the Heavens,* Dan. iv. 26. Thus Eliphaz proves that a man cannot be profitable to God (*v.* 2), that he ought not to contend with God (it is his folly if he does), and that we ought always to address ourselves to God with very great reverence; for when we *behold the height of the stars, how high they are,* we should, at the same time, also consider the transcendent majesty of God, who is above the stars, and how high he is.

2. He charged it upon Job that he made a bad use of this doctrine, which he might have made so good a use of, *v.* 13. "This is *holding the truth in unrighteousness,* fighting against religion with its own weapons, and turning its own artillery upon itself: thou art willing to own that *God is in the height of heaven* but thence thou inferrest, *How doth God know?*" Bad men expel the fear of God out of their hearts by banishing the eye of God out of the world (Ezek. viii. 12), and care not what they do if they can but persuade themselves that God does not know. Eliphaz suspected that Job had such a notion of God as this, that, because he is in the height of heaven, (1.) It is therefore impossible for him to see and hear what is done at so great a distance as this earth, especially since there is a *dark cloud* (*v.* 13), many *thick clouds* (*v.* 14), that come between him and us, and *are a covering to him,* so that he cannot see, much less can he judge of, the affairs of this lower world; as if God had *eyes of flesh, ch.* x. 4. The interposing firmament is to him as transparent crystal, Ezek. i. 22. Distance of place creates no difficulty to him who fills immensity, any more than distance of time to him who is eternal. Or, (2.) That it is therefore below him, and a diminution to his glory, to take cognizance of this inferior part of the creation: *He walks in the circuit of heaven,* and has enough to do to enjoy himself and his own perfections and glory in that bright and quiet world; why should he trouble himself about us? This is gross absurdity, as well as gross impiety, which Eliphaz here fathers upon Job; for it supposes that the administration of government is a burden and disparagement to the supreme governor and that the acts of justice and mercy are a toil to a mind infinitely wise, holy, and good. If the sun, a creature, and inanimate, can with his light and influence reach this earth, and every part of it (Ps. xix. 6), even from that vast height of the visible heavens in which he is, and in the circuit of which he walks, and that through many a thick and dark cloud, shall we question it concerning the Creator?

15 Hast thou marked the old way which wicked men have trodden? 16 Which were cut down out of time,

whose foundation was overflown with a flood: 17 Which said unto God, Depart from us: and what can the Almighty do for them? 18 Yet he filled their houses with good *things:* but the counsel of the wicked is far from me. 19 The righteous see *it,* and are glad: and the innocent laugh them to scorn. 20 Whereas our substance is not cut down, but the remnant of them the fire consumeth.

Eliphaz, having endeavoured to convict Job, by setting his sins (as he thought) in order before him, here endeavours to awaken him to a sight and sense of his misery and danger by reason of sin; and this he does by comparing his case with that of the sinners of the old world; as if he had said, "Thy condition is bad now, but, unless thou repent, it will be worse, as theirs was—theirs *who were overflown with a flood,* as the old world (*v.* 16), and theirs the *remnant of whom the fire consumed* " (*v.* 20), namely, the Sodomites, who, in comparison of the old world, were but a remnant. And these two instances of the wrath of God against sin and sinners are more than once put together, for warning to a careless world, as by our Saviour (Luke xvii. 26, &c.) and the apostle, 2 Pet. ii. 5, 6. Eliphaz would have Job to *mark the old way which wicked men have trodden* (*v.* 15) and see what came of it, what the end of their way was. Note, There is an old way which wicked men have trodden. Religion had but newly entered when sin immediately followed it. But though it is an old way, a broad way, a tracked way, it is a dangerous way and it leads to destruction; and it is good for us to mark it, that we may not dare to walk in it. Eliphaz here puts Job in mind of it, perhaps in opposition to what he had said of the prosperity of the wicked; as if he had said, "Thou canst find out here and there a single instance, it may be, of a wicked man ending his days in peace; but what is that to those two great instances of the final perdition of ungodly men—the drowning of the whole world and the burning of Sodom?" destructions by wholesale, in which he thinks Job may, as in a glass, see his own face. Observe, 1. The ruin of those sinners (*v.* 16): *They were cut down out of time;* that is, they were cut off in the midst of their days, when, as man's time then went, many of them might, in the course of nature, have lived some hundreds of years longer, which made their immature extirpation the more grievous. They were *cut down out of time,* to be hurried into eternity. And their foundation, the earth on which they built themselves and all their hopes, was *overflown with a flood,* the flood which was *brought in upon the world of the ungodly,* 2 Pet. ii. 5. Note, Those who build upon the sand choose a foundation which will be *over-flown* when *the rains descend and the floods come* (Matt. vii. 27), and then their building must needs fall and they perish in the ruins of it, and repent of their folly when it is too late. 2. The sin of those sinners, which brought that ruin (*v.* 17): *They said unto God, Depart from us.* Job had spoken of some who said so and yet prospered, ch. xxi. 14. " But these did not (says Eliphaz); they found to their cost what it was to set God at defiance. Those who were resolved to lay the reins on the neck of their appetites and passions began with this; they said unto God, *Depart;* they abandoned all religion, hated the thoughts of it, and desired to live *without God in the world;* they shunned his word, and silenced conscience, his deputy. *And what can the Almighty do for them?"* Some make this to denote the justness of their punishment. They said to God, *Depart from us;* and then *what could the Almighty do with them but cut them off?* Those who will not submit to God's golden sceptre must expect to be broken to pieces with his iron rod. Others make it to denote the injustice of their sin: But *what hath the Almighty done against them?* What iniquity have they found in him, or wherein has he wearied them? Mic. vi. 3; Jer. ii. 5. Others make it to denote the reason of their sin: They say unto God, *Depart,* asking *what the Almighty can do to them.* " What has he done to oblige us? What can he do in a way of wrath to make us miserable, or in a way of favour to make us happy ?" As they argue, Zeph. i. 12. *The Lord will not do good, neither will he do evil.* Eliphaz shows the absurdity of this in one word, and that is, calling God *the Almighty;* for, if he be so, what cannot he do? But it is not strange if those cast off all religion who neither dread God's wrath nor desire his favour. 3. The aggravation of this sin: *Yet he had filled their houses with good things, v.* 18. Both those of the old world and those of Sodom had great plenty of all the delights of sense; for *they ate, they drank, they bought, they sold,* &c. (Luke xvii. 27), so that they had no reason to ask *what the Almighty could do for them,* for they lived upon his bounty, no reason to bid him depart from them who had been so kind to them. Many have their houses full of goods but their hearts empty of grace, and thereby are marked for ruin. 4. The protestation which Eliphaz makes against the principles and practices of those wicked people : *But the counsel of the wicked is far from me.* Job had said so (*ch.* xxi. 16) and Eliphaz will not be behind with him. If they cannot agree in their own principles concerning God, yet they agree in renouncing the principles of those that live without God in the world. Note, Those that differ from each other in some matters of religion, and are engaged in disputes about them, yet ought unanimously

and vigorously to appear against atheism and irreligion, and to take care that their disputes do not hinder either their vigour or unanimity in that common cause of God, that righteous cause. 5. The pleasure and satisfaction which the righteous shall have in this. (1.) In seeing the wicked destroyed, *v.* 19. They shall *see it,* that is, observe it, and take notice of it (Hos. xiv. 9); and they shall be *glad,* not to see their fellow-creatures miserable, or any secular turn of their own served, or point gained, but to see God glorified, the word of God fulfilled, the power of oppressors broken, and thereby the oppressed relieved—to see sin shamed, atheists and infidels confounded, and fair warning given to all others to shun such wicked courses. Nay, they shall *laugh them to scorn,* that is, they justly might do it, they shall do it, as God does it, in a holy manner, Ps. ii. 4; Prov. i. 26. They shall take occasion thence to expose the folly of sinners and show how ridiculous their principles are, though they call themselves wits. *Lo, this is the man that made not God his strength;* and see what comes of it, Ps. lii. 7. Some understand this of righteous Noah and his family, who beheld the destruction of the old world and rejoiced in it, as he had grieved for their impiety. Lot, who saw the ruin of Sodom, had the same reason to rejoice, 2 Pet. ii. 7, 8. (2.) In seeing themselves distinguished (*v.* 20): " *Whereas our substance is not cut down,* as theirs was, and as thine is; we continue to prosper, which is a sign that we are the favourites of Heaven, and in the right." The same rule that served him to condemn Job served him to magnify himself and his companions by. *His* substance is cut down; therefore he is a wicked man; *ours* is not; therefore we are righteous. But it is a deceitful rule to judge by; for none knows love or hatred by all that is before him. If others be consumed, if the very remnant of them be consumed, and we be not, instead of censuring them and lifting up ourselves, as Eliphaz does here, we ought to be thankful to God and take it for a warning to ourselves to prepare for similar calamities.

21 Acquaint now thyself with him, and be at peace : thereby good shall come unto thee. 22 Receive, I pray thee, the law from his mouth, and lay up his words in thine heart. 23 If thou return to the Almighty, thou shalt be built up, thou shalt put away iniquity far from thy tabernacles. 24 Then shalt thou lay up gold as dust, and the *gold* of Ophir as the stones of the brooks. 25 Yea, the Almighty shall be thy defence, and thou shalt have plenty of silver. 26 For then shalt thou have thy delight in the Almighty,

and shalt lift up thy face unto God. 27 Thou shalt make thy prayer unto him, and he shall hear thee, and thou shalt pay thy vows. 28 Thou shalt also decree a thing, and it shall be established unto thee : and the light shall shine upon thy ways. 29 When *men* are cast down, then thou shalt say, *There is* lifting up ; and he shall save the humble person. 30 He shall deliver the island of the innocent : and it is delivered by the pureness of thine hands.

Methinks I can almost forgive Eliphaz his hard censures of Job, which we had in the beginning of the chapter, though they were very unjust and unkind, for this good counsel and encouragement which he gives him in these verses with which he closes his discourse, and than which nothing could be better said, nor more to the purpose. Though he thought him a bad man, yet he saw reason to have hopes concerning him, that, for all this, he would be both pious and prosperous. But it is strange that out of the same mouth, and almost in the same breath, both sweet waters and bitter should proceed. Good men, though they may perhaps be put into a heat, yet sometimes will talk themselves into a better temper, and, it may be, sooner than another could talk them into it. Eliphaz had laid before Job the miserable condition of a wicked man, that he might frighten him into repentance. Here, on the other hand, he shows him the happiness which those may be sure of that do repent, that he might allure and encourage him to it. Ministers must try both ways in dealing with people, must speak to them from Mount Sinai by the terrors of the law, and from Mount Sion by the comforts of the gospel, must set before them both life and death, good and evil, the blessing and the curse. Now here observe,

I. The good counsel which Eliphaz gives to Job; and good counsel it is to us all, though, as to Job, it was built upon a false supposition that he was a wicked man and now a stranger and enemy to God. 1. *Acquaint now thyself with God. Acquiesce in God;* so some. It is our duty at all times, especially when we are in affliction, to accommodate ourselves to, and quiet ourselves in, all the disposals of the divine Providence. *Join thyself to him* (so some); fall in with his interests, and act no longer in opposition to him. Our translators render it well, "*Acquaint thyself with him;* be not such a stranger to him as thou hast made thyself by casting off the fear of him and restraining prayer before him." It is the duty and interest of every one of us to acquaint himself with God. We must get the knowledge of him, fix our affections on him, join ourselves

to him in a covenant of friendship, and then set up, and keep up, a constant correspondence with him in the ways he has appointed. It is our honour that we are made capable of this acquaintance, our misery that by sin we have lost it, our privilege that through Christ we are invited to return to it ; and it will be our unspeakable happiness to contract and cultivate this acquaintance. 2. "*Be at peace,* at peace with thyself, not fretful, uneasy, and in confusion ; let not thy heart be troubled, but be quiet and calm, and well composed. Be at peace with thy God; be reconciled to him. Do not carry on this unholy war. Thou complainest that God is thy enemy ; be thou his friend." It is the great concern of every one of us to make our peace with God, and it is necessary in order to our comfortable acquaintance with him ; for *how can two walk together except they be agreed?* Amos iii. 3. This we must do quickly, now, before it be too late. *Agree with thy adversary while thou art in the way.* This we are earnestly urged to do. Some read it, "Acquaint thyself, *I pray thee,* with him, and be at peace." God himself beseeches us ; ministers, in Christ's stead, pray us to be reconciled. Can we gainsay such entreaties ? 3. *Receive the law from his mouth, v.* 22. "Having made thy peace with God, submit to his government, and resolve to be ruled by him, that thou mayest keep thyself in his love." We receive our being and maintenance from God. From him we hope to receive our bliss, and from him we must receive law. *Lord, what wilt thou have me to do?* Acts ix. 6. Which way soever we receive the intimations of his will we must have our eye to him ; whether he speaks by scripture, ministers, conscience, or Providence, we must take the word as from his mouth and bow our souls to it. Though, in Job's time, we do not know that there was any written word, yet there was a revelation of God's will to be received. Eliphaz looked upon Job as a wicked man, and was pressing him to repent and reform. Herein consists the conversion of a sinner—his receiving the law from God's mouth and no longer from the world and the flesh. Eliphaz, being now in contest with Job, appeals to the word of God for the ending of the controversy. "Receive that, and be determined by it." *To the law and to the testimony.* 4. *Lay up his word in thy heart.* It is not enough to receive it, but we must retain it, Prov. iii. 18. We must lay it up as a thing of great value, that it may be safe ; and we must lay it up in our hearts, as a thing of great use, that it may be ready to us when there is occasion and we may neither lose it wholly nor be at a loss for it in a time of need. 5. *Return to the Almighty, v.* 23. "Do not only turn from sin, but turn to God and thy duty. Do not only turn towards the Almighty in some good inclinations and good beginnings, but *return to him;* return home to him, quite to him, so as to reach to the Almighty, by a universal reformation, an effectual thorough change of thy heart and life, and a firm resolution to cleave to him;" so Mr. Poole. 6. *Put away iniquity far from thy tabernacle.* This was the advice Zophar gave him, *ch.* xi. 14. *"Let not wickedness dwell in thy tabernacle.* Put iniquity far off, the further the better, not only from thy heart and hand, but from thy house. Thou must not only not be wicked thyself, but must reprove and restrain sin in those that are under thy charge." Note, Family reformation is needful reformation; we and our house must serve the Lord.

II. The good encouragement which Eliphaz gives Job, that he shall be very happy, if he will but take this good counsel. In general, *"Thereby good shall come unto thee (v.* 21); the good that has now departed from thee, all the good thy heart can desire, temporal, spiritual, eternal good, shall come to thee. God shall come to thee, into covenant and communion with thee; and he brings all good with him, all good in him. Thou art now ruined and brought down, but, if thou return to God, *thou shalt be built up* again, and thy present ruins shall be repaired. Thy family shall be built up in children, thy estate in wealth, and thy soul in holiness and comfort." The promises which Eliphaz here encourages Job with are reducible to three heads:—

1. That his estate should prosper, and temporal blessings should be bestowed abundantly on him; for godliness has the promise of the life that now is. It is promised,

(1.) That he shall be very rich (*v.* 24): *"Thou shalt lay up gold as dust,* in such great abundance, and *shalt have plenty of silver* (*v.* 25), whereas now thou art poor and stripped of all." Job had been rich. Eliphaz suspected he got his riches by fraud and oppression, and therefore they were taken from him: but if he would return to God and his duty, [1.] He should have more wealth than ever he had, not only thousands of sheep and oxen, the wealth of farmers, but thousands of gold and silver, the wealth of princes, *ch.* iii. 15. Abundantly more riches, true riches, are to be got by the service of God than by the service of the world. [2.] He should have it more sure to him: *"Thou shalt lay it up* in good hands, and hold that which is got by thy piety by a surer tenure than that which thou didst get by thy iniquity." *Thou shalt have silver of strength* (for so the word is), which, being honestly got, will wear well —silver like steel. [3.] He should, by the grace of God, be kept from setting his heart so much upon it as Eliphaz thought he had done; and then wealth is a blessing indeed when we are not ensnared with the love of it. Thou shalt *lay up gold;* but how? Not as thy treasure and portion, but *as dust,* and *as the stones of the brooks.* So little shalt thou value it or expect from it that thou shalt lay it at thy feet (Acts iv. 35), not in thy bosom.

(2.) That yet he shall be very safe. Whereas men's riches usually expose them to danger, and he had owned that in his prosperity he *was not in safety* (*ch.* iii. 26), now he might be secure; for *the Almighty shall be thy defender;* nay, he shall be *thy defence, v.* 25. He *shall be thy gold;* so it is in the margin, and it is the same word that is used (*v.* 24) for gold, but it signifies also a strong-hold, because *money is a defence,* Eccl. vii. 12. Worldlings make gold their god, saints make God their gold; and those that are enriched with his favour and grace may truly be said *to have abundance of the best gold,* and best laid up. We read it, *"He shall be thy defence* against the incursions of neighbouring spoilers: thy wealth shall not then lie exposed as it did to Sabeans and Chaldeans," which, some think, is the meaning of that, *Thou shalt put away iniquity far from thy tabernacle,* taking it as a promise. "The iniquity or wrong designed against thee shall be put off and shall not reach thee." Note, Those must needs be safe that have Omnipotence itself for their defence, Ps. xci. 1—3.

2. That his soul should prosper, and he should be enriched with spiritual blessings, which are the best blessings.

(1.) That he should live a life of complacency in God (*v.* 26): *"For then shalt thou have thy delight in the Almighty;* and *thus* the Almighty comes to be thy gold by thy delighting in him, as worldly people delight in their money. He shall be thy wealth, thy defence, thy dignity; for he shall be thy delight." The way to have our heart's desire is to make God our heart's delight, Ps. xxxvii. 4. If God give us himself to be our joy, he will deny us nothing that is good for us. "Now, God is a terror to thee; he is so by thy own confession (*ch.* vi. 4; xvi. 9; xix. 11); but, if thou wilt return to him, then, and not till then, *he will be thy delight;* and it shall be as much a pleasure to thee to think of him as ever it was a pain." No delight is comparable to the delight which gracious souls have in the Almighty; and those that acquaint themselves with him, and submit themselves entirely to him, shall find his favour to be, not only their strength, but their song.

(2.) That he should have a humble holy confidence towards God, such as those are said to have *whose hearts condemn them not,* 1 John iii. 21. "Then *shalt* thou *lift up thy face to God* with boldness, and not be afraid, as thou now art, to draw near to him. Thy countenance is now fallen, and thou lookest dejected; but, when thou hast made thy peace with God, thou shalt blush no more, tremble no more, and hang thy head no more, as thou dost now, but shalt cheerfully, and with a gracious assurance, show thyself to him, pray before him, and expect blessings from him.

(3.) That he should maintain a constant communion with God "The correspondence, once settled, shall be kept up to thy unspeakable satisfaction. Letters shall be both statedly and occasionally interchanged between thee and heaven," *v.* 27. [1.] "Thou shalt by prayer send letters to God : *Thou shalt make thy prayer*" (the word is, *Thou shalt multiply* thy prayers) "unto him, and he will not think thy letters troublesome, though many and long. The oftener we come to the throne of grace the more welcome. Under all thy burdens, in all thy wants, cares, and fears, thou shalt send to heaven for guidance and strength, wisdom, comfort, and good success." [2.] "He shall, by his providence and grace, answer those letters, and give thee what thou askest of him, either in kind or kindness : *He shall hear thee*, and make it to appear he does so by what he does for thee and in thee." [3.] "Then thou shalt by thy praises reply to the gracious answers which he sent thee : *Thou shalt pay thy vows*, and that shall be acceptable to him and fetch in further mercy." Note, When God performs that which in our distress we prayed for we must make conscience of performing that which we then promised, else we do not deal honestly. If we promised nothing else we promised to be thankful, and that is enough, for it includes all, Ps. cxvi. 14.

(4.) That he should have inward satisfaction in the management of all his outward affairs (*v.* 28): "*Thou shalt decree a thing and it shall be established unto thee,*" that is, "Thou shalt frame all thy projects and purposes with so much wisdom, and grace, and resignation to the will of God, that the issue of them shall be to thy heart's content, just as thou wouldst have it to be. Thou shalt *commit thy works unto the Lord* by faith and prayer, and then *thy thoughts shall be established;* thou shalt be easy and pleased, whatever occurs, Prov. xvi. 3. This the grace of God shall work in thee; nay, sometimes the providence of God shall give thee the very thing thou didst desire and pray for, and give it thee in thy own way, and manner, and time. *Be it unto thee even as thou wilt.*" When at any time an affair succeeds just according to the scheme we laid, and our measures are in nothing broken, nor are we put upon new counsels, then we must own the performance of this promise, *Thou shalt decree a thing and it shall be established unto thee.* "Whereas now thou complainest of darkness round about thee, then *the light shall shine on thy ways;*" that is, "God shall guide and direct thee, and then it will follow, of course, that he shall prosper and succeed thee in all thy undertakings. God's wisdom shall be thy guide, his favour thy comfort, and thy ways shall be so under both those lights that thou shalt have a comfortable enjoyment of what is present and a comfortable prospect of what is future," Ps. xc. 17.

(5.) That even in times of common calamity and danger he should have abundance of joy and hope (*v.* 29): "*When men are cast down* round about thee, cast down in their affairs,

cast down in their spirits, sinking, desponding, and ready to despair, *then shalt thou say, There is lifting up.* Thou shalt find that in thyself which will not only bear thee up under thy troubles, and keep thee from fainting, but lift thee up above thy troubles and enable thee to rejoice evermore. When men's *hearts fail them for fear*, then shall Christ's disciples *lift up their heads for joy*, Luke xxi. 26—28. Thus are they made to *ride upon the high places of the earth* (Isa. lviii. 14), and that which will lift them up is the belief of this, that God will save the humble person. Those that humble themselves shall be exalted, not only in honour, but in comfort.

3. That he should be a blessing to his country and an instrument of good to many (*v.* 30): *God shall*, in answer to thy prayers, *deliver the island of the innocent*, and have a regard therein to *the pureness of thy hands*, which is necessary to the acceptableness of our prayers, 1 Tim. ii. 8. But, because we may suppose the innocent not to need deliverance (it was guilty Sodom that wanted the benefit of Abraham's intercession), I incline to the marginal reading, *The innocent shall deliver the island,* by their advice (Eccl. ix. 14, 15) and by their prayers and their interest in heaven, Acts xxvii. 24. Or, *He shall deliver those that are not innocent, and they are delivered by the pureness of thy hands;* so it may be read, and most probably. Note, A good man is a public good. Sinners fare the better for saints, whether they are aware of it or no. If Eliphaz intended hereby (as some think he did) to insinuate that Job's prayers were not prevailing, nor his hands pure (for then he would have relieved others, much more himself), he was afterwards made to see his error, when it appeared that Job had a better interest in heaven than he had; for he and his three friends, who in this matter were not innocent, were delivered by *the pureness of Job's hands*, ch. xlii. 8.

CHAP. XXIII.

This chapter begins Job's reply to Eliphaz. In this reply he takes no notice of his friends, either because he saw it was to no purpose or because he liked the good counsel Eliphaz gave him in the close of his discourse so well that he would make no answer to the peevish reflections he began with; but he appeals to God, begs to have his cause heard, and doubts not but to make it good, having the testimony of his own conscience concerning his integrity. Here seems to be a struggle between flesh and spirit, fear and faith, throughout this chapter. I. He complains of his calamitous condition, and especially of God's withdrawings from him, so that he could not get his appeal heard (ver. 2—5), nor discern the meaning of God's dealings with him (ver. 8, 9), nor gain any hope of relief, ver. 13, 14. This made deep impressions of trouble and terror upon him, ver. 15—17. But, II. In the midst of these complaints he comforts himself with the assurance of God's clemency (ver. 6, 7) and his own integrity, which God himself was a witness to, ver. 10—12. Thus was the light of his day like that spoken of, Zech. xiv. 6, 7, neither perfectly clear nor perfectly dark, but "at evening time it was light."

THEN Job answered and said, 2 Even to day *is* my complaint bitter : my stroke is heavier than my groaning. 3 Oh that I knew where I might find him! *that* I might come *even* to his seat ! 4 I would order *my* cause before him, and fill my mouth with arguments. 5 I would know the words *which* he would answer me, and understand what he would say unto me. 6 Will he plead against me with *his* great power? No; but he would put *strength* in me. 7 There the righteous might dispute with him; so should I be delivered for ever from my judge

Job is confident that he has wrong done him by his friends, and therefore, ill as he is, he will not give up the cause, nor let them have the last word. Here,

I. He justifies his own resentments and representations of his trouble (*v.* 2): *Even to day*, I own, *my complaint is bitter;* for the affliction, the cause of the complaint, is so. There are *wormwood and gall in the affliction and misery; my soul has them still in remembrance* and is embittered by them, Lam. iii. 19, 20. *Even to day is my complaint* counted *rebellion* (so some read it); his friends construed the innocent expressions of his grief into reflections upon God and his providence, and called them *rebellion*. "But," says he, "I do not complain more than there is cause; *for my stroke is heavier than my groaning*. Even to-day, after all you have said to convince and comfort me, still the pains of my body and the wounds of my spirit are such that I have reason enough for my complaints, if they were more bitter than they are." We wrong God if our groaning be heavier than our stroke, like froward children, who, when they cry for nothing, have justly something given them to cry for; but we do not wrong ourselves though our stroke be heavier than our groaning, for little said is soon amended.

II. He appeals from the censures of his friends to the just judgment of God; and this he thought was an evidence for him that he was not a hypocrite, for then he durst not have made such an appeal as this. St. Paul comforted himself in this, that *he that judged him was the Lord*, and therefore he valued not man's judgment (1 Cor. iv. 3, 4), but he was willing to wait till the appointed day of decision came; whereas Job is impatient, and passionately wishes to have the judgment-day anticipated, and to have his cause tried quickly, as it were, by a special commission. The apostle found it necessary to press it much upon suffering Christians patiently to expect the Judge's coming, James v. 7—9.

1. He is so sure of the equity of God's tribunal that he longs to appear before it (*v.* 3): *O that I knew where I might find him !* This may properly express the pious breathings of a soul convinced that it has by sin lost God and is undone for ever if it recover not its interest in his favour. "O that I knew how I might recover his favour! How I might come into covenant and communion with him !" Mic vi. 6, 7. It is the cry of a poor deserted soul. " *Saw you him whom my soul loveth ? O that I knew where I might find him !* O that

he who has laid open the way to himself would direct me into it and lead me in it !" But Job here seems to complain too boldly that his friends wronged him and he knew not which way to apply himself to God to have justice done him, else he would go even to his seat, to demand it. A patient waiting for death and judgment is our wisdom and duty, and, if we duly consider things, that cannot be without a holy fear and trembling; but a passionate wishing for death or judgment, without any such fear and trembling, is our sin and folly, and ill becomes us. Do we know what death and judgment are, and are we so very ready for them, that we need not time to get readier ? *Woe to those that* thus, in a heat, *desire the day of the Lord*, Amos v. 18.

2. He is so sure of the goodness of his own cause that he longs to be opening it at God's bar (*v.* 4): "*I would order my cause before him*, and set it in a true light. I would produce the evidences of my sincerity in a proper method, and would *fill my mouth with arguments* to prove it." We may apply this to the duty of prayer, in which we have *boldness to enter into the holiest* and to come even to the footstool of the throne of grace. We have not only liberty of access, but liberty of speech. We have leave, (1.) To be particular in our requests, *to order our cause before God*, to speak the whole matter, to lay before him all our grievances, in what method we think most proper; we durst not be so free with earthly princes as a humble holy soul may be with God. (2.) To be importunate in our requests. We are allowed, not only to pray, but to plead, not only to ask, but to argue; nay, to *fill our mouths with arguments*, not to move God (he is perfectly apprized of the merits of the cause without our showing), but to move ourselves, to excite our fervency and encourage our faith in prayer.

3. He is so sure of a sentence in favour of him that he even longed to hear it (*v.* 5): "*I would know the words which he would answer me*," that is, "I would gladly hear what God will say to this matter in dispute between you and me, and will entirely acquiesce in his judgment." This becomes us, in all controversies; let the word of God determine them; let us know what he answers, and understand what he says. Job knew well enough what his friends would answer him; they would condemn him, and run him down. "But" (says he) "*I would fain know what God would answer me;* for I am sure his judgment is according to truth, which theirs is not. I cannot understand them; they talk so little to the purpose. But what he says I should understand and therefore be fully satisfied in."

III. He comforts himself with the hope that God would deal favourably with him in this matter, *v.* 6, 7. Note, It is of great use to us, in every thing wherein we have to do with God, to keep up good thoughts of him. He believes, 1. That God would not overpower him, that he would not deal with him either by absolute sovereignty or in strict justice, not with a high hand, nor with a strong hand: *Will he plead against me with his great power?* No. Job's friends pleaded against him with all the power they had; but will God do so? No; his power is all just and holy, whatever men's is. Against those that are obstinate in their unbelief and impenitency God will *plead with his great power;* their destruction will come *from the glory of his power.* But with his own people, that love him and trust in him, he will deal in tender compassion. 2. That, on the contrary, he would empower him to plead his own cause before God: "*He would put strength in me,* to support me and bear me up, in maintaining my integrity." Note, The same power that is engaged against proud sinners is engaged for humble saints, who prevail with God by strength derived from him, as Jacob did, Hos. xii. 3. See Ps. lxviii. 35. 3. That the issue would certainly be comfortable, *v.* 7. There, in the court of heaven, when the final sentence is to be given, *the righteous might dispute with him* and come off in his righteousness. Now, even the upright are often *chastened of the Lord,* and they cannot dispute against it; integrity itself is no fence either against calamity or calumny; but in that day *they shall not be condemned with the world,* though God may afflict by prerogative. *Then you shall discern between the righteous and the wicked* (Mal. iii. 18), so vast will be the difference between them in their everlasting state; whereas now we can scarcely distinguish them, so little is the difference between them as to their outward condition, for all things come alike to all. Then, when the final doom is given, "*I shall be delivered for ever from my Judge,*" that is, "I shall be saved from the unjust censures of my friends and from that divine sentence which is now so much a terror to me. Those that are delivered up to God as their owner and ruler shall be for ever delivered from him as their judge and avenger; and there is no flying from his justice but by flying to his mercy.

8 Behold, I go forward, but he *is* not *there;* and backward, but I cannot perceive him: 9 On the left hand, where he doth work, but I cannot behold *him:* he hideth himself on the right hand, that I cannot see *him:* 10 But he knoweth the way that I take: *when* he hath tried me, I shall come forth as gold. 11 My foot hath held his steps, his way have I kept, and not declined. 12 Neither have I gone back from the commandment of his lips; I have esteemed the words of his mouth more than my necessary *food.*

Here, I. Job complains that he cannot understand the meaning of God's providences concerning him, but is quite at a loss about them (*v.* 8, 9): *I go forward, but he is not there,* &c. Eliphaz had bid him acquaint himself with God. "So I would, with all my heart," says Job, "if I knew how to get acquainted with him." He had himself a great desire to appear before God, and get a hearing of his case, but the Judge was not to be found. Look which way he would, he could see no sign of God's appearing for him to clear up his innocency. Job, no doubt, believed that God is every where present; but three things he seems to complain of here:—1. That he could not fix his thoughts, nor form any clear judgment of things in his own mind. His mind was so hurried and discomposed with his troubles that he was like a man in a fright, or at his wits' end, who runs this way and that way, but, being in confusion, brings nothing to a head. By reason of the disorder and tumult his spirit was in he could not fasten upon that which he knew to be in God, and which, if he could but have mixed faith with it and dwelt upon it in his thoughts, would have been a support to him. It is the common complaint of those who are sick or melancholy that, when they would think of that which is good, they can make nothing of it. 2. That he could not find out the cause of his troubles, nor the sin which provoked God to contend with him. He took a view of his whole conversation, turned to every side of it, and could not perceive wherein he had sinned more than others, for which he should thus be punished more than others; nor could he discern what other end God should aim at in afflicting him thus. 3. That he could not foresee what would be in the end hereof, whether God would deliver him at all, nor, if he did, when or which way. He saw not his signs, nor was there any to tell him how long; as the church complains, Ps. lxxiv. 9. He was quite at a loss to know what God designed to do with him; and, whatever conjecture he advanced, still something or other appeared against it.

II. He satisfies himself with this, that God himself was a witness to his integrity, and therefore did not doubt but the issue would be good.

1. After Job had almost lost himself in the labyrinth of the divine counsels, how contentedly does he sit down, at length, with this thought: "Though I know not the way that he takes (for *his way is in the sea and his path in the great waters,* his thoughts and ways are infinitely above ours and it would be presumption in us to pretend to judge of them), yet *he knows the way that I take,*" *v.* 10. That is, (1.) He is acquainted with it. His friends judged of that which they did not know, and therefore charged him with that which he was never guilty of; but God, who knew every step he had taken, would not do so, Ps. cxxxix. 3. Note, It is a great

comfort to those who mean honestly that God understands their meaning, though men do not, cannot, or will not. (2.) He approves of it: "He knows that, however I may sometimes have *taken a false step*, yet I have still *taken a good way*, have *chosen the way of truth*, and therefore he knows it," that is, he accepts it, and is well pleased with it, as he is said to *know the way of the righteous*, Ps. i. 6. This comforted the prophet, Jer. xii. 3. *Thou hast tried my heart towards thee.* From this Job infers, *When he hath tried me I shall come forth as gold.* Those that *keep the way of the Lord* may comfort themselves, when they are in affliction, with these three things: —[1.] That they are but tried. It is not intended for their hurt, but for their honour and benefit; *it is the trial of their faith*, 1 Pet. i. 7. [2.] That, when they are sufficiently tried, they shall come forth out of the furnace, and not be left to consume in it as dross or reprobate silver. The trial will have an end. *God will not contend for ever.* [3.] That they shall come forth as gold, pure in itself and precious to the refiner. They shall come forth as gold approved and improved, found to be good and made to be better. Afflictions are to us as we are; those that go gold into the furnace will come out no worse.

2. Now that which encouraged Job to hope that his present troubles would thus end well was the testimony of his conscience for him, that he had lived a good life in the fear of God.

(1.) That God's way was the way he walked in (v. 11): "*My foot hath held his steps*," that is, "held to them, adhered closely to them; the steps he takes. I have endeavoured to conform myself to his example." Good people are followers of God. Or, "I have accommodated myself to his providence, and endeavoured to answer all the intentions of that, to follow Providence step by step." Or, "His steps are the steps he has appointed me to take; the way of religion and serious godliness—that way I have kept, and have not declined from it, not only not turned back from it by a total apostasy, but not turned aside out of it by any wilful transgression." His holding God's steps, and keeping his way, intimate that the tempter had used all his arts by fraud and force to draw him aside; but, with care and resolution, he had by the grace of God hitherto persevered, and those that will do so must hold and keep, hold with resolution and keep with watchfulness.

(2.) That God's word was the rule he walked by, v. 12. He governed himself by *the commandment of God's lips*, and would not go back from that, but go forward according to it. Whatever difficulties we may meet with in the way of God's commandments, though they lead us through a wilderness, yet we must never think of going back, but must press on towards the mark. Job kept closely to the law of God in his

132

conversation, for both his judgment and his affection led him to it: *I have esteemed the words of his mouth more than my necessary food;* that is, he looked upon it as his necessary food; he could as well have lived without his daily bread as without the word of God. *I have laid it up* (so the word is), as those that lay up provision for a siege, or as Joseph laid up corn before the famine. Eliphaz had told him to *lay up God's words in his heart*, ch. xxii. 22. "I do," says he, "and always did, *that I might not sin against him*, and that, like the good householder, I might bring forth for the good of others." Note, The word of God is to our souls what our necessary food is to our bodies; it sustains the spiritual life and strengthens us for the actions of life; it is that which we cannot subsist without, and which nothing else can make up the want of: and we ought therefore so to esteem it, to take pains for it, hunger after it, feed upon it with delight, and nourish our souls with it; and this will be our rejoicing in the day of evil, as it was Job's here.

13 But he *is* in one *mind*, and who can turn him? and *what* his soul desireth, even *that* he doeth. 14 For he performeth *the thing that is* appointed for me: and many such *things are* with him. 15 Therefore am I troubled at his presence: when I consider, I am afraid of him. 16 For God maketh my heart soft, and the Almighty troubleth me: 17 Because I was not cut off before the darkness, *neither* hath he covered the darkness from my face.

Some make Job to complain here that God dealt unjustly and unfairly with him in proceeding to punish him without the least relenting or relaxation, though he had such incontestable evidences to produce of his innocency. I am loth to think holy Job would charge the holy God with iniquity; but his complaint is indeed bitter and peevish, and he reasons himself into a sort of *patience per force*, which he cannot do without reflecting upon God as dealing hardly with him, but he must bear it because he cannot help it; the worst he says is that God deals unaccountably with him.

I. He lays down good truths, and truths which were capable of a good improvement, v. 13, 14. 1. That God's counsels are immutable: *He is in one mind, and who can turn him?* *He is one* (so some read it) or *in one;* he has no counsellors by whose interest he might be prevailed with to alter his purpose: he is one with himself, and never alters his mind, never alters his measures. Prayer has prevailed to change God's way and his providence, but never was his will or purpose changed; for *known unto God are all his works.* 2. That his power is irresistible:

What his soul desires or designs *even that he does,* and nothing can stand in his way or put him upon new counsels. Men desire many things which they may not do, or cannot do, or dare not do. But God has an incontestable sovereignty; his will is so perfectly pure and right that it is highly fit he should pursue all its determinations. And he has an uncontrollable power. *None can stay his hand. Whatever the Lord pleased that did he* (Ps. cxxxv. 6), and always will, for it is always best. 3. That all he does is according to the counsel of his will (*v.* 14): *He performs the thing that is appointed for me.* Whatever happens to us, it is God that performs it (Ps. lvii. 2), and an admirable performance the whole will appear to be when the mystery of God shall be finished. He performs all that, and that only, which was appointed, and in the appointed time and method. This may silence us, for what is appointed cannot be altered. But to consider that, when God was appointing us to eternal life and glory as our end, he was appointing to this condition, this affliction, whatever it is, in our way, this may do more than silence us, it may satisfy us that it is all for the best; though what he does we know not now, yet we shall know hereafter. 4. That all he does is according to the custom of his providence: *Many such things are with him,* that is, He does many things in the course of his providence which we can give no account of, but must resolve into his absolute sovereignty. Whatever trouble we are in others have been in the like. Our case is not singular; the same *afflictions are accomplished in our brethren,* 1 Pet. v. 9. Are we sick or sore, impoverished and stripped? Are our children removed by death or our friends unkind? This is what *God has appointed for us, and many such things are with him. Shall the earth be forsaken for us?*

II. He makes but a bad use of these good truths. Had he duly considered them, he might have said, "Therefore am I easy and pleased, and well reconciled to the way of my God concerning me; therefore will I rejoice in hope that my troubles will issue well at last." But he said, *Therefore am I troubled at his presence, v.* 15. Those are indeed of troubled spirits who are troubled at the presence of God, as the psalmist, who *remembered God and was troubled,* Ps. lxxvii. 3. See what confusion poor Job was now in, for he contradicted himself: just now he was troubled for God's absence (*v.* 8, 9); now he is troubled at his presence. *When I consider, I am afraid of him.* What he now felt made him fear worse. There is indeed that which, if we consider it, will show that we have cause to be afraid of God—his infinite justice and purity, compared with our own sinfulness and vileness; but if, withal, we consider his grace in a Redeemer, and our compliance with that grace, our fears will vanish and we shall see cause to hope in him. See what

impressions were made upon him by the wounds of his spirit. 1. He was very fearful (*v.* 16): *The Almighty troubled him,* and so *made his heart soft,* that is, utterly unable to bear any thing, and afraid of every thing that stirred. There is a gracious softness, like that of Josiah, whose heart was tender, and trembled at the word of God; but this is meant of a grievous softness, which apprehends every thing that is present to be pressing and every thing future to be threatening. 2. He was very fretful, peevish indeed, for he quarrels with God, (1.) Because he did not die before his troubles, that he might never have seen them *(Because I was not cut off before the darkness, v.* 17), and yet if, in the height of his prosperity, he had received a summons to the grave, he would have thought it hard. This may help to reconcile us to death, whenever it comes, that we do not know what evil we may be taken away from. But when trouble comes it is folly to wish we had not lived to see it and it is better to make the best of it. (2.) Because he was left to live so long in his troubles, and the darkness was not covered from his face by his being hidden in the grave. We should bear the darkness better than thus if we would but remember that to the upright there sometimes arises a marvellous light in the darkness; however, there is reserved for them a more marvellous light after it.

CHAP. XXIV.

Job having by his complaints in the foregoing chapter given vent to his passion, and thereby gained some ease, breaks them off abruptly, and now applies himself to a further discussion of the doctrinal controversy between him and his friends concerning the prosperity of wicked people. That many live at ease who yet are ungodly and profane, and despise all the exercises of devotion, he had shown, ch. xxi. Now here he goes further, and shows that many who are mischievous to mankind, and live in open defiance to all the laws of justice and common honesty, yet thrive and succeed in their unrighteous practices; and we do not see them reckoned with in this world. What he had said before (ch. xii. 6), "The tabernacles of robbers prosper," he here enlarges upon. He lays down his general proposition (ver. 1), that the punishment of wicked people is not so visible and apparent as his friends supposed, and then proves it by an induction of particulars. 1. Those that openly do wrong to their poor neighbours are not reckoned with, nor the injured righted (ver. 2—12), though the former are very barbarous, ver. 21, 22. II. Those that secretly practise mischief often go undiscovered and unpunished, ver. 13—17. III. That God punishes such by secret judgments and reserves them for future judgments (ver. 18—20, and ver. 23—25), so that, upon the whole matter, we cannot say that all who are in trouble are wicked; for it is certain that all who are in prosperity are not righteous.

W HY, seeing times are not hidden from the Almighty, do they that know him not see his days? 2 *Some* remove the landmarks; they violently take away flocks, and feed *thereof.* 3 They drive away the ass of the fatherless, they take the widow's ox for a pledge. 4 They turn the needy out of the way: the poor of the earth hide themselves together. 5 Behold, *as* wild asses in the desert, go they forth to their work; rising betimes for a prey: the wilderness *yieldeth* food for them *and* for *their* children. 6 They reap *every one* his corn in the field : and they gather the vintage of the wicked. 7 They cause the naked to lodge without clothing, that *they have* no covering in the cold. 8 They are wet with the showers of the mountains, and embrace the rock for want of a shelter. 9 They pluck the fatherless from the breast, and take a pledge of the poor. 10 They cause *him* to go naked without clothing, and they take away the sheaf *from* the hungry ; 11 *Which* make oil within their walls, *and* tread *their* winepresses, and suffer thirst. 12 Men groan from out of the city, and the soul of the wounded crieth out : yet God layeth not folly *to them.*

Job's friends had been very positive in it that they should soon see the fall of wicked people, how much soever they might prosper for a while. By no means, says Job ; *though times are not hidden from the Almighty,* yet *those that know him do not presently see his day, v.* 1. 1. He takes it for granted that times are not hidden from the Almighty ; past times are not hidden from his judgment (Eccl. iii. 15), present times are not hidden from his providence (Matt. x. 29), future times are not hidden from his prescience, Acts xv. 18. God governs the world, and therefore we may be sure he takes cognizance of it. Bad times are not hidden from him, though the bad men that make the times bad say one to another, He has *forsaken the earth,* Ps. xciv. 6, 7. Every man's times are in his hand, and under his eye, and therefore it is in his power to make the times of wicked men in this world miserable. He foresees the time of every man's death, and therefore, if wicked men die before they are punished for their wickedness, we cannot say, " They escaped him by surprise ;" he foresaw it, nay, he ordered it. Before Job will enquire into the reasons of the prosperity of wicked men he asserts God's omniscience, as one prophet, in a similar case, asserts his righteousness (Jer. xii. 1), another his holiness (Hab. i. 13), another his goodness to his own people, Ps. lxxiii. 1. General truths must be held fast, though we may find it difficult to reconcile them to particular events. 2. He yet asserts that those who know him (that is, wise and good people who are acquainted with him, and with whom his secret is) *do not see his day,*—the day of his judging for them ; this was the thing he complained of in his own case (*ch.* xxiii. 8), that he could not see God appearing on his behalf to plead his cause,—the day of his judging against open and notorious sinners, that is called *his day,* Ps. xxxvii. 13. We believe that day will come, but we do not see it, because it is future, and its presages are secret. 3. Though this is a

mystery of Providence, yet there is a reason for it, and we shall shortly know why the judgment is deferred ; even the wisest, and those who know God best, do not yet see it. God will exercise their faith and patience, and excite their prayers for the coming of his kingdom, for which they are to *cry day and night to him,* Luke xviii. 7.

For the proof of this, that wicked people prosper, Job specifies two sorts of unrighteous ones, whom all the world saw thriving in their iniquity :—

I. Tyrants, and those that do wrong under pretence of law and authority. It is a melancholy sight which has often been *seen under the sun, wickedness in the place of judgment* (Eccl. iii. 16), the unregarded *tears of the oppressed,* while *on the side of the oppressors there was power* (Eccl. iv. 1), the *violent perverting of justice and judgment,* Eccl. v. 8. 1. They disseize their neighbours of their real estates, which came to them by descent from their ancestors. They *remove the land-marks,* under pretence that they were misplaced (*v.* 2), and so they encroach upon their neighbours' rights and think they effectually secure that to their posterity which they have got wrongfully, by making that to be an evidence for them which should have been an evidence for the rightful owner. This was forbidden by the law of Moses (Deut. xix. 14), under a curse, Deut. xxvii. 17. Forging or destroying deeds is now a crime equivalent to this. 2. They dispossess them of their personal estates, under colour of justice . *They violently take away flocks,* pretending they are forfeited, *and feed thereof;* as the rich man took the poor man's ewe lamb, 2 Sam. xii. 4. If a poor fatherless child has but an ass of his own to get a little money with, they find some colour or other to take it away, because the owner is not able to contest with them. It is all one if a widow has but an ox for what little husbandry she has ; under pretence of distraining for some small debt, or arrears of rent, this ox shall be taken for a pledge, though perhaps it is the widow's all. God has taken it among the titles of his honour to be a *Father of the fatherless and a judge of the widows ;* and therefore those will not be reckoned his friends that do not to their utmost protect and help them ; but those he will certainly reckon with as his enemies that vex and oppress them. 3. They take all occasions to offer personal abuses to them, *v.* 4. They will mislead them if they can when they meet them on the high-way, so that the poor and needy are forced to hide themselves from them, having no other way to secure themselves from them. They love in their hearts to banter people, and to make fools of them, and do them a mischief if they can, especially to triumph over poor people, whom they turn out of the way of getting relief, threaten to punish them as vagabonds, and so force them to abscond, and laugh at them when they have done. Some understand those barbarous actions (*v.* 9, 10) to be done by those oppressors that pretend law for what they do : *They pluck the fatherless from the breast ;* that is, having made poor infants fatherless, they make them motherless too ; having taken away the father's life, they break the mother's heart, and so starve the children and leave them to perish. Pharaoh and Herod plucked the children from the breast to the sword ; and we read of *children brought forth to the murderers,* Hos. ix. 13. Those are inhuman murderers indeed that can with so much pleasure suck innocent blood. *They take a pledge of the poor,* and so they rob the spital ; nay, they take the poor themselves for a pledge (as some read it), and probably it was under this pretence that they *plucked the fatherless from the breast,* distraining them for slaves, as Neh. v. 5. Cruelty to the poor is great wickedness and cries aloud for vengeance. Those who show no mercy to such as lie at their mercy shall themselves have judgment without mercy. Another instance of their barbarous treatment of those they have advantage against is that they take from them even their necessary food and raiment ; they squeeze them so with their extortion that they *cause them to go naked without clothing* (*v.* 10) and so catch their death. And if a poor hungry family has gleaned a sheaf of corn, to make a little cake of, that they may eat it and die, even that they take away from them, being well pleased to see them perish for want, while they themselves are fed to the full. 4. They are very oppressive to the labourers they employ in their service. They not only give them no wages, though the labourer is worthy of his hire (and this is a crying sin, Jam. v. 4), but they will not so much as give them meat and drink : *Those that carry their sheaves are hungry ;* so some read it (*v.* 10), and it agrees with *v.* 11, that those who *make oil within their walls,* and with a great deal of toil labour at the wine-presses, yet suffer thirst, which was worse than muzzling the mouth of the ox that treads out the corn. Those masters forget that they have a Master in heaven who will not allow the necessary supports of life to their servants and labourers, not caring whether they can live by their labour or no. 5. It is not only among the poor country people, but in the cities also, that we see the tears of the oppressed (*v.* 12): *Men groan from out of the city,* where the rich merchants and traders are as cruel with their poor debtors as the landlords in the country are with their poor tenants. In cities such cruel actions as these are more observed than in obscure corners of the country and the wronged have easier access to justice to right themselves ; and yet the oppressors there fear neither the restraints of the law nor the just censures of their neighbours, but the oppressed groan and cry out

like wounded men, and can no more ease and help themselves, for the oppressors are inexorable and deaf to their groans.

II. He speaks of robbers, and those that do wrong by downright force, as the bands of the Sabeans and Chaldeans, which had lately plundered him. He does not mention them particularly, lest he should seem partial to his own cause, and to judge of men (as we are apt to do) by what they are to us ; but among the Arabians, the children of the east (Job's country), there were those that lived by spoil and rapine, making incursions upon their neighbours, and robbing travellers. See how they are described here, and what mischief they do, *v.* 5—8. 1. Their character is that they are *as wild asses in the desert,* untamed, untractable, unreasonable, Ishmael's character (Gen. xvi. 12), fierce and furious, and under no restraint of law or government, Jer. ii. 23, 24. They choose the deserts for their dwelling, that they may be lawless and unsociable, and that they may have opportunity of doing the more mischief. The desert is indeed the fittest place for such wild people, *ch.* xxxix. 6. But no desert can set men out of the reach of God's eye and hand. 2. Their trade is to steal, and to make a prey of all about them. They have chosen it as their trade ; it is their work, because there is more to be got by it, and it is got more easily, than by an honest calling. They follow it as their trade ; they follow it closely ; they *go forth to* it as *their work,* as man goes forth to his labour, Ps. civ. 23. They are diligent and take pains at it : They *rise betimes for a prey.* If a traveller be out early, they will be out as soon to rob him. They live by it as a man lives by his trade : *The wilderness* (not the grounds there but the roads there) *yieldeth food for them and for their children ;* they maintain themselves and their families by robbing on the high-way, and bless themselves in it without any remorse of compassion or conscience, and with as much security as if it were honestly got ; as Ephraim, Hos. xii. 7, 8. 3. See the mischief they do to the country. They not only rob travellers, but they make incursions upon their neighbours, and *reap every one his corn in the field* (*v.* 6), that is, they enter upon other people's ground, cut their corn, and carry it away as freely as if it were their own. Even *the wicked gather the vintage,* and it is their wickedness ; or, as we read it, They gather the vintage of the wicked, and so one wicked man is made a scourge to another. What the wicked got by extortion (which is their way of stealing) these robbers get from them in their way of stealing ; thus oftentimes are the spoilers spoiled, Isa. xxxiii. 1. 4. The misery of those that fall into their hands (*v.* 7, 8): *They cause the naked,* whom they have stripped, not leaving them the clothes to their backs, *to lodge,* in the cold nights, *without clothing,* so that *they are wet with the showers of the mountains, and, for want of a* better *shelter, embrace the rock,* and are glad of a cave or den in it to preserve them from the injuries of the weather. Eliphaz had charged Job with such inhumanity as this, concluding that Providence would not thus have stripped him if he had not first *stripped the naked of their clothing,* ch. xxii. 6. Job here tells him there were those that were really guilty of those crimes with which he was unjustly charged and yet prospered and had success in their villanies, the curse they laid themselves under working invisibly; and Job thinks it more just to argue as he did, from an open notorious course of wickedness inferring a secret and future punishment, than to argue as Eliphaz did, who from nothing but present trouble inferred a course of past secret iniquity. The impunity of these oppressors and spoilers is expressed in one word (*v.* 12): *Yet God layeth not folly to them,* that is, he does not immediately prosecute them with his judgments for these crimes, nor make them examples, and so evince their folly to all the world. He that *gets riches, and not by right, at his end shall be a fool,* Jer. xvii. 11. But while he prospers he passes for a wise man, and God lays not folly to him until he saith, *Thou fool, this night thy soul shall be required of thee,* Luke xii. 20.

13 They are of those that rebel against the light; they know not the ways thereof, nor abide in the paths thereof. 14 The murderer rising with the light killeth the poor and needy, and in the night is as a thief. 15 The eye also of the adulterer waiteth for the twilight, saying, No eye shall see me: and disguiseth *his* face. 16 In the dark they dig through houses, *which* they had marked for themselves in the daytime: they know not the light. 17 For the morning *is* to them even as the shadow of death: if *one* know *them, they are in* the terrors of the shadow of death.

These verses describe another sort of sinners who *therefore* go unpunished, because they go undiscovered. *They rebel against the light, v.* 13. Some understand it figuratively: they sin against the light of nature, the light of God's law, and that of their own consciences; they profess to know God, but they rebel against the knowledge they have of him, and will not be guided and governed, commanded and controlled, by it. Others understand it literally: they have the day-light, and choose the night as the most advantageous season for their wickedness. Sinful works are *therefore* called *works of darkness,* because he *that does evil hates the light* (John iii. 20), *knows not the ways thereof,* that is, keeps out of the way of it, or, if he happen 136

to be seen, abides not where he thinks he is known. So that he here describes the worst of sinners,—those that sin wilfully, and against the convictions of their own consciences, whereby they add rebellion to their sin,—those that sin deliberately, and with a great deal of plot and contrivance, using a thousand arts to conceal their villanies, fondly imagining that, if they can but hide them from the eye of men, they are safe, but forgetting that *there is no darkness or shadow of death* in which *the workers of iniquity can hide themselves* from God's eye, ch. xxxiv. 22. In this paragraph Job specifies three sorts of sinners that shun the light:—1. Murderers, *v.* 14. They *rise with the light,* as soon as ever the day breaks, to kill the poor travellers that are up early and abroad about their business, going to market with a little money or goods; and though it is so little that they are really to be called poor and needy, who with much ado get a sorry livelihood by their marketings, yet, to get it, the murderer will both take his neighbour's life and venture his own, will rather play at such small game than not play at all; nay, he kills for killing sake, thirsting more for blood than booty. See what care and pains wicked men take to compass their wicked designs, and let the sight shame us out of our negligence and slothfulness in doing good.

Ut jugulent homines, surgunt de nocte latrones,
Tuque ut te ser es non expergisceris?———

Rogues nightly rise to murder men for pelf;
Will you not rouse you to preserve yourself?

2. Adulterers. *The eyes* that are *full of adultery* (2 Pet. ii. 14), the unclean and wanton eyes, *wait for the twilight, v.* 15. The eye of the adulteress did so, Prov. vii. 9. Adultery hides its head for shame. The sinners themselves, even the most impudent, do what they can to hide their sin: *si non caste, tamen caute—if not chastely, yet cautiously;* and, after all the wretched endeavours of the factors for hell to take away the reproach of it, it is and ever will be a *shame even to speak of those things which are done of them in secret,* Eph. v. 12. It hides its head also for fear, knowing that *jealousy is the rage of a husband,* who *will not spare in the day of vengeance,* Prov. vi. 34, 35. See what pains those take that make provision for the flesh to fulfil the lusts of it, pains to compass, and then to conceal, that provision which, after all, will be death and hell at last. Less pains would serve to mortify and crucify the flesh, which would be life and heaven at last. Let the sinner change his heart, and then he needs not disguise his face, but may lift it up without spot. 3. Housebreakers, *v.* 16. These *mark houses in the day-time,* mark the avenues of a house, and on which side they can most easily force their entrance, and then, in the night, dig through them, either to kill, or steal, or commit adultery. The night favours the assault,

and makes the defence the more difficult; for the *good man of the house knows not what hour the thief will come* and therefore is asleep (Luke xii. 39) and he and his lie exposed. For this reason our law makes burglary, which is the breaking and entering of a dwelling-house in the night time with a felonious intent, to be felony without benefit of clergy.

And, *lastly,* Job observes (and perhaps observes it as part of the present, though secret, punishment of such sinners as these) that they are in a continual terror for fear of being discovered (*v.* 17): *The morning is to them even as the shadow of death.* The light of the day, which is welcome to honest people, is a terror to bad people. They curse the sun, not as the Moors, because it scorches them, but because it discovers them. *If one know them,* their consciences fly in their faces, and they are ready to become their own accusers; for *they are in the terrors of the shadow of death.* Shame came in with sin, and everlasting shame is at the end of it. See the misery of sinners—they are exposed to continual frights; and yet see their folly—they are afraid of coming under the eye of men, but have no dread of God's eye, which is always upon them: they are not afraid of doing that which yet they are so terribly afraid of being known to do.

18 He *is* swift as the waters; their portion is cursed in the earth: he beholdeth not the way of the vineyards. 19 Drought and heat consume the snow waters: *so doth* the grave *those which* have sinned. 20 The womb shall forget him; the worm shall feed sweetly on him; he shall be no more remembered; and wickedness shall be broken as a tree. 21 He evil entreateth the barren *that* beareth not: and doeth not good to the widow. 22 He draweth also the mighty with his power: he riseth up, and no *man* is sure of life. 23 *Though* it be given him *to be* in safety, whereon he resteth; yet his eyes *are* upon their ways. 24 They are exalted for a little while, but are gone and brought low; they are taken out of the way as all *other*, and cut off as the tops of the ears of corn. 25 And if *it be* not *so* now, who will make me a liar, and make my speech nothing worth?

Job here, in the conclusion of his discourse,

I. Gives some further instances of the wickedness of these cruel bloody men. 1. Some are pirates and robbers at sea. To this many learned interpreters apply those

difficult expressions (*v.* 18), He is swift upon the waters. Privateers choose those ships that are the best sailers. In these swift ships they cruise from one channel to another, to pick up prizes; and this brings them in so much wealth that their *portion is cursed in the earth*, and they *behold not the way of the vineyards*, that is (as bishop Patrick explains it), they despise the employment of those who till the ground and plant vineyards as poor and unprofitable. But others make this a further description of the conduct of those sinners that are afraid of the light: if they be discovered, they get away as fast as they can, and choose to lurk, not in the vineyards, for fear of being discovered, but in some cursed portion, a lonely and desolate place, which nobody looks after. 2. Some are abusive to those that are in trouble, and add affliction to the afflicted. Barrenness was looked upon as a great reproach, and those that fall under that affliction they upbraid with it, as Peninnah did Hannah, on purpose to vex them and make them to fret, which is a barbarous thing. This is *evil entreating the barren that beareth not* (*v.* 21), or those that are childless, and so want the arrows others have in their quiver, which enable them to deal with their enemy in the gate, Ps. cxxvii. 5. They take that advantage against and are oppressive to them. As the fatherless, so the childless, are in some degree helpless. For the same reason it is a cruel thing to hurt the widow, to whom we ought to do good; and not doing good, when it is in our power, is doing hurt. 3. There are those who, by inuring themselves to cruelty, come at last to be so exceedingly boisterous that they are *the terror of the mighty in the land of the living* (*v.* 22): "*He draws the mighty* into a snare with his power; even the greatest are not able to stand before him when he is in his mad fits: *he rises up* in his passion, and lays about him with so much fury that *no man is sure of his life;* nor can he at the same time be sure of his own, for *his hand is against every man* and *every man's hand against him*," Gen. xvi. 12. One would wonder how any man can take pleasure in making all about him afraid of him, yet there are those that do.

II. He shows that these daring sinners prosper, and are at ease for a while, nay, and often end their days in peace, as Ishmael, who, though he was a man of such a character as is here given, yet both *lived and died in the presence of all his brethren*, as we are told, Gen. xvi. 12; xxv. 18: Of these sinners here it is said, 1. That it is *given them to be in safety, v.* 23　They seem to be under the special protection of the divine Providence; and one would wonder how they escape with life through so many dangers as they run themselves into. 2. That they rest upon this, that is, they rely upon this as sufficient to warrant all their violences. *Because sentence against their evil works is not executed speedily* they think that there is no great evil in them, and that God is not displeased with them, nor will ever call them to an account. Their prosperity is their security. 3. That *they are exalted for a while.* They seem to be the favourites of heaven, and value themselves as making the best figure on earth. They are set up in honour, set up (as they think) out of the reach of danger, and lifted up in the pride of their own spirits. 4. That, at length, they are carried out of the world very silently and gently, and without any remarkable disgrace or terror. "They go down to the grave as easily as snow-water sinks into the dry ground when it is melted by the sun;" so bishop Patrick explains *v.* 19. To the same purport he paraphrases *v.* 20, *The womb shall forget him,* &c. "God sets no such mark of his displeasure upon him but that his mother may soon forget him. The hand of justice does not hang him on a gibbet for the birds to feed on; but he is carried to his grave like other men, to be the sweet food of worms. There he lies quietly, and neither he nor his wickedness is any more remembered than a tree which is broken to shivers." And *v.* 24, *They are taken out of the way as all others,* that is, "they are shut up in their graves like all other men; nay, they die as easily (without those tedious pains which some endure) as an ear of corn is cropped with your hand." Compare this with Solomon's observation (Eccl. viii. 10), *I saw the wicked buried, who had come and gone from the place of the holy, and they were forgotten.*

III. He foresees their fall however, and that their death, though they die in ease and honour, will be their ruin. God's *eyes are upon their ways, v.* 23. Though he keep silence, and seem to connive at them, yet he takes notice, and keeps account of all their wickedness, and will make it to appear shortly that their most secret sins, which they thought *no eye should see* (*v.* 15), were under his eye and will be called over again. Here is no mention of the punishment of these sinners in the other world, but it is intimated in the particular notice taken of the consequences of their death. 1. The consumption of the body in the grave, though common to all, yet to them is in the nature of a punishment for their sin. The *grave shall consume those that have sinned;* that land of darkness will be the lot of those that *love darkness rather than light.* The bodies they pampered shall be a feast for worms, which shall feed as sweetly on them as ever they fed on the pleasures and gains of their sins. 2. Though they thought to make themselves a great name by their wealth, and power, and mighty achievements, yet *their memorial perished with them,* Ps. ix. 6. He that made himself so much talked of *shall,* when he is dead, *be no more remembered* with honour; his *name shall rot,* Prov. x. 7. Those that durst not

give him his due character while he lived shall not spare him when he is dead; so that the womb that bore him, his own mother, shall forget him, that is, shall avoid making mention of him, and shall think *that* the greatest kindness she can do him, since no good can be said of him. That honour which is got by sin will soon turn into shame. 3. The wickedness they thought to establish in their families shall be broken as a tree; all their wicked projects shall be blasted, and all their wicked hopes dashed and buried with them. 4. Their pride shall be brought down and laid in the dust (*v.* 24); and, in mercy to the world, they shall be taken out of the way, and all their power and prosperity shall be cut off. You may seek them, and they shall not be found. Job owns that wicked people will be miserable at last, miserable on the other side death, but utterly denies what his friends asserted, that ordinarily they are miserable in this life.

IV. He concludes with a bold challenge to all that were present to disprove what he had said if they could (*v.* 25): " *If it be not so now,* as I have declared, and if it do not thence follow that I am unjustly condemned and censured, let those that can undertake to prove that my discourse is either, 1. False in itself, and then they prove me a liar; or, 2. Foreign, and nothing to the purpose, and then they prove my speech frivolous and nothing worth." That indeed which is false is nothing worth; where there is not truth, how can there be goodness? But those that speak the words of truth and soberness need not fear having what they say brought to the test, but can cheerfully submit it to a fair examination, as Job does here.

CHAP. XXV.

Bildad here makes a very short reply to Job's last discourse, as one that began to be tired of the cause. He drops the main question concerning the prosperity of wicked men, as being unable to answer the proofs Job had produced in the foregoing chapter: but, because he thought Job had made too bold with the divine majesty in his appeals to the divine tribunal (ch. xxiii.), he in a few words shows the infinite distance there is between God and man, teaching us, I. To think highly and honourably of God, ver. 2, 3, 5. II. To think meanly of ourselves, ver. 4, 6. These, however misapplied to Job, are two good lessons for us all to learn.

THEN answered Bildad the Shuhite, and said, 2 Dominion and fear *are* with him, he maketh peace in his high places. 3 Is there any number of his armies? and upon whom doth not his light arise? 4 How then can man be justified with God? or how can he be clean *that is* born of a woman? 5 Behold even to the moon, and it shineth not; yea, the stars are not pure in his sight. 6 How much less man, *that is* a worm? and the son of man, *which is* a worm?

Bildad is to be commended here for two things:—1. For speaking no more on the subject about which Job and he differed. Perhaps he began to think Job was in the right, and then it was justice to say no more concerning it, as one that contended for truth, not for victory, and therefore, for the finding of truth, would be content to lose the victory · or, if he still thought himself in the right, yet he knew when he had said enough, and would not wrangle endlessly for the last word. Perhaps indeed one reason why he and the rest of them let fall this debate was because they perceived that Job and they did not differ so much in opinion as they thought: they owned that wicked people might prosper a while, and Job owned they would be destroyed at last; how little then was the difference! If disputants would understand one another better, perhaps they would find themselves nearer one another than they imagined. 2. For speaking so well on the matter about which Job and he were agreed. If we would all get our hearts filled with awful thoughts of God and humble thoughts of ourselves, we should not be so apt as we are to fall out about matters of doubtful disputation, which are trifling or intricate.

Two ways Bildad takes here to exalt God and abase man:—

I. He shows how glorious God is, and thence infers how guilty and impure man is before him, *v.* 2—4. Let us see then,

1. What great things are here said of God, designed to possess Job with a reverence of him, and to check his reflections upon him and upon his dealings with him: (1.) God is the sovereign Lord of all, and *with him is terrible majesty. Dominion and fear are with him, v.* 2. He that gave being has an incontestable authority to give laws, and can enforce the laws he gives. He that made all has a right to dispose of all according to his own will, with an absolute sovereignty. Whatever he will do he does, and may do; and none can say unto him, *What doest thou?* or *Why doest thou so?* Dan. iv. 35. His having dominion (or being *Dominus—Lord)* bespeaks him both owner and ruler of all the creatures. They are all his, and they are all under his direction and at his disposal. Hence it follows that he is to be feared (that is, reverenced and obeyed), that he is feared by all that know him (the seraphim cover their faces before him), and that, first or last, all will be made to fear him. Men's dominion is often despicable, often despised, but God is always terrible. (2.) The glorious inhabitants of the upper world are all perfectly observant of him and entirely acquiesce in his will: *He maketh peace in his high places.* He enjoys himself in a perfect tranquillity. The holy angels never quarrel with him, nor with one another, but entirely acquiesce in his will, and unanimously execute it without murmuring or disputing. Thus the will of God is done in heaven; and thus we pray that it may be done by us and others on earth. The sun, moon, and stars, keep their courses, and never clash with one another: nay, even in this lower region,

which is often disturbed with storms and tempests, yet when God pleases he commands peace, by *making the storm a calm,* Ps. cvii. 29; lxv. 7. Observe, The high places are *his* high places; for *the heaven, even the heavens, are the Lord's* (Ps. cxv. 16) in a peculiar manner. Peace is God's work; where it is made it is he that makes it, Isa. lvii. 19. In heaven there is perfect peace; for there is perfect holiness, and there is God, who is love. (3.) He is a God of irresistible power: *Is there any number of his armies? v.* 3. The greatness and power of princes are judged of by their armies. God is not only himself almighty, but he has numberless numbers of armies at his beck and disposal,—standing armies that are never disbanded,—regular troops, and well disciplined, that are never to seek, never at a loss, that never mutiny,—veteran troops, that have been long in his service,—victorious troops, that never failed of success nor were ever foiled. All the creatures are his hosts, angels especially. He is Lord of all, Lord of hosts. He has numberless armies, and yet makes peace. He could make war upon us, but is willing to be at peace with us; and even the heavenly hosts were sent to proclaim *peace on earth* and *good will towards men,* Luke ii. 14. (4.) His providence extends itself to all: *Upon whom does not his light arise?* The light of the sun is communicated to all parts of the world, and, take the year round, to all equally. See Ps. xix. 6. That is a faint resemblance of the universal cognizance and care God takes of the whole creation, Matt. v 45. All are under the light of his knowledge and are naked and open before him. All partake of the light of his goodness: it seems especially to be meant of *that.* He is good to all; the earth is full of his goodness. He is *Deus optimus—God, the best of beings,* as well as *maximus—the greatest:* he has power to destroy; but his pleasure is to show mercy. All the creatures live upon his bounty.

2. What low things are here said of man, and very truly and justly (*v.* 4): *How then can man be justified with God? Or how can he be clean?* Man is not only mean, but vile, not only earthy, but filthy; he cannot be justified, he cannot be clean, (1.) In comparison with God. Man's righteousness and holiness, at the best, are nothing to God's, Ps. lxxxix. 6. (2.) In debate with God. He that will quarrel with the word and providence of God must unavoidably go by the worst. God will be justified, and then man will be condemned, Ps. li. 4; Rom. iii. 4. There is no error in God's judgment, and therefore there lies no exception against it, nor appeal from it. (3.) In the sight of God. If God is so great and glorious, how can man, who is guilty and impure, appear before him? Note, [1.] Man, by reason of his actual transgressions, is obnoxious to God's justice and cannot in himself be justi-

fied before him: he can neither plead *Not guilty,* nor plead any merit of his own to balance or extenuate his guilt. The scripture has concluded all under sin. [2.] Man, by reason of his original corruption, as he is born of a woman, is odious to God's holiness, and cannot be clean in his sight. God sees his impurity, and it is certain that by it he is rendered utterly unfit for communion and fellowship with God in grace here and for the vision and fruition of him in glory hereafter. We have need therefore to be born again of water and of the Holy Ghost, and to be bathed again and again in the blood of Christ, that fountain opened.

II. He shows how dark and defective even the heavenly bodies are in the sight of God, and in comparison with him, and thence infers how little, and mean, and worthless, man is. 1. The lights of heaven, though beauteous creatures, are before God as clods of earth (*v.* 5): *Behold even to the moon,* walking in brightness, and the stars, those glorious lamps of heaven, which the heathen were so charmed with the lustre of that they worshipped them---yet, in God's sight, in comparison with him, they shine not, they are not pure; they have no glory, by reason of the glory which excelleth, as a candle, though it burn, yet does not shine when it is set in the clear light of the sun. The glory of God, shining in his providences, eclipses the glory of the brightest creatures, Isa. xxiv. 23. *The moon shall be confounded, and the sun ashamed, when the Lord of hosts shall reign in Mount Sion.* The heavenly bodies are often clouded; we plainly see spots in the moon, and, with the help of glasses, may sometimes discern spots upon the sun too: but God sees spots in them that we do not see. How durst Job then so confidently appeal to God, who would discover that amiss in him which he was not aware of in himself? 2. The children of men, though noble creatures, are before God but as worms of the earth (*v.* 6): *How much less* does *man* shine in honour, how much less is he pure in righteousness *that is a worm, and the son of man,* whoever he be, *that is a worm!—a vermin* (so some), not only mean and despicable, but noxious and detestable; *a mite* (so others), the smallest animal, which cannot be discerned with the naked eye, but through a magnifying glass. Such a thing is man. (1.) So mean, and little, and inconsiderable, in comparison with God and with the holy angels: so worthless and despicable, having his original in corruption, and hastening to corruption. What little reason has man to be proud, and what great reason to be humble! (2.) So weak and impotent, and so easily crushed, and therefore a very unequal match for Almighty God. Shall man be such a fool as to contend with his Maker, who can tread him to pieces more easily than we can a worm? (3.) So sordid and filthy. Man is not pure for he is a worm, hatched in putrefaction, and therefore odious to God. Let us therefore wonder at God's condescension in taking such worms as we are into covenant and communion with himself, especially at the condescension of the Son of God, in emptying himself so far as to say, *I am a worm, and no man,* Ps. xxii. 6.

CHAP. XXVI.

This is Job's short reply to Bildad's short discourse, in which he is so far from contradicting him that he confirms what he had said, and out-does him in magnifying God and setting forth his power, to show what reason he had still to say, as he did (ch. xiii. 2), "What you know, the same do I know also." I. He shows that Bildad's discourse was foreign to the matter he was discoursing of—though very true and good, yet not to the purpose, ver. 2—4. II. That it was needless to the person he was discoursing with; for he knew it, and believed it, and could speak of it as well as he, and better, and could add to the proofs which he had produced of God's power and greatness, which he does in the rest of his discourse (ver. 5—13), concluding that, when they had both said what they could, all came short of the merit of the subject and it was still far from being exhausted, ver. 14.

BUT Job answered and said, 2 How hast thou helped *him that is* without power? *how* savest thou the arm *that hath* no strength? 3 How hast thou counselled *him that hath* no wisdom? and *how* hast thou plentifully declared the thing as it is? 4 To whom hast thou uttered words? and whose spirit came from thee?

One would not have thought that Job, when he was in so much pain and misery, could banter his friend as he does here and make himself merry with the impertinency of his discourse. Bildad thought that he had made a fine speech, that the matter was so weighty, and the language so fine, that he had gained the reputation both of an oracle and of an orator; but Job peevishly enough shows that his performance was not so valuable as he thought it and ridicules him for it. He shows,

I. That there was no great matter to be found in it (*v.* 3): *How hast thou plentifully declared the thing as it is?* This is spoken ironically, upbraiding Bildad with the good conceit he himself had of what he had said. 1. He thought he had spoken very clearly, had *declared the thing as it is.* He was very fond (as we are all apt to be) of his own notions, and thought they only were right, and true, and intelligible, and all other notions of the thing were false, mistaken, and confused; whereas, when we speak of the glory of God, we cannot declare the thing as it is, for we see it through a glass darkly, or but by reflection, and shall not see him as he is till we come to heaven. Here *we cannot order our speech concerning him,* ch. xxxvii. 19. 2. He thought he had spoken very fully, though in few words, that he had plentifully declared it, and, alas! it was but poorly and scantily that he declared it, in comparison with the vast compass and copiousness of the subject.

II. That there was no great use to be made of it. *Cui bono—What good hast thou done* by all that thou hast said? *How hast thou,* with all this mighty flourish, *helped him that is with-*

out power? v. 2. How hast thou, with thy grave dictates, *counselled* him *that has no wisdom? v. 3.* Job would convince him, 1. That he had done God no service by it, nor made him in the least beholden to him. It is indeed our duty, and will be our honour, to speak on God's behalf; but we must not think that he needs our service, or is indebted to us for it, nor will he accept it if it come from a spirit of contention and contradiction, and not from a sincere regard to God's glory. 2. That he had done his cause no service by it. He thought his friends were mightily beholden to him for helping them, at a dead lift, *to* make their part good against Job, when they were quite at a loss, and had no strength, no wisdom. Even weak disputants, when warm, are apt to think truth more beholden to them than it really is. 3. That he had done him no service by it. He pretended to convince, instruct, and comfort, Job; but, alas! what he had said was so little to the purpose that it would not avail to rectify any mistakes, nor to assist him either in bearing his afflictions or in getting good by them: *" To whom hast thou uttered words? v.* 4. Was it to me that thou didst direct thy discourse? And dost thou take me for such a child as to need these instructions? Or dost thou think them proper for one in my condition?" Every thing that is true and good is not suitable and seasonable. To one that was humbled, and broken, and grieved in spirit, as Job was, he ought to have preached of the grace and mercy of God, rather than of his greatness and majesty, to have laid before him the consolations rather than the terrors of the Almighty. Christ knows how to speak what is proper for the weary (Isa. l. 4), and his ministers should learn rightly to divide the word of truth, and not make those sad whom God would not have made sad, as Bildad did; and therefore Job asks him, *Whose spirit came from thee?* that is, "What troubled soul would ever be revived, and relieved, and brought to itself, by such discourses as these?" Thus are we often disappointed in our expectations from our friends who should comfort us, but the Comforter, who is the Holy Ghost, never mistakes in his operations nor misses of his end.

5 Dead *things* are formed from under the waters, and the inhabitants thereof. 6 Hell *is* naked before him, and destruction hath no covering. 7 He stretcheth out the north over the empty place, *and* hangeth the earth upon nothing. 8 He bindeth up the waters in his thick clouds; and the cloud is not rent under them. 9 He holdeth back the face of his throne, *and* spreadeth his cloud upon it. 10 He hath compassed the waters with bounds, until the day and night come

to an end. 11 The pillars of heaven tremble and are astonished at his reproof. 12 He divideth the sea with his power, and by his understanding he smiteth through the proud. 13 By his spirit he hath garnished the heavens; his hand hath formed the crooked serpent. 14 Lo, these *are* parts of his ways: but how little a portion is heard of him? but the thunder of his power who can understand?

The truth received a great deal of light from the dispute between Job and his friends concerning those points about which they differed; but now they are upon a subject in which they were all agreed, the infinite glory and power of God. How does truth triumph, and how brightly does it shine, when there appears no other strife between the contenders than which shall speak most highly and honourably of God and be most copious in showing forth his praise! It were well if all disputes about matters of religion might end thus, in *glorifying God* as Lord of all, and our Lord, *with one mind and one mouth* (Rom. xv. 6); for to that we have all attained, in that we are all agreed.

I. Many illustrious instances are here given of the wisdom and power of God in the creation and preservation of the world.

1. If we look about us, to the earth and waters here below, we shall see striking instances of omnipotence, which we may gather out of these verses. (1.) *He hangs the earth upon nothing, v.* 7. The vast terraqueous globe neither rests upon any pillars nor hangs upon any axle-tree, and yet, by the almighty power of God, is firmly fixed in its place, poised with its own weight. The art of man could not hang a feather upon nothing, yet the divine wisdom hangs the whole earth so. It is *ponderibus librata suis—poised by its own weight,* so says the poet; it is *upheld by the word of God's power,* so says the apostle. What is hung upon nothing may serve us to set our feet on, and bear the weight of our bodies, but it will never serve us to set our hearts on, nor bear the weight of our souls. (2.) *He sets bounds to the waters of the sea,* and compasses them in (*v.* 10), that they may not *return to cover the earth;* and these bounds shall continue unmoved, unshaken, unworn, *till the day and night come to an end,* when time shall be no more. Herein appears the dominion which Providence has over the raging waters of the sea, and so it is an instance of his power, Jer. v. 22. We see too the care which Providence takes of the poor sinful inhabitants of the earth, who, though obnoxious to his justice and lying at his mercy, are thus preserved from being overwhelmed, as they were once by the waters of a flood, and will continue to be so, because they are reserved

unto fire. (3.) He *forms dead things under the waters. Rephaim—giants, are formed under the waters,* that is, vast creatures, of prodigious bulk, as whales, giant-like creatures, among the innumerable inhabitants of the water. So bishop Patrick. (4.) By mighty storms and tempests he shakes the mountains, which are here called *the pillars of heaven* (v. 11), and even *divides the sea, and smites through its proud waves, v.* 12. At the presence of the Lord the *sea flies* and the *mountains skip,* Ps. cxiv. 3, 4. See Hab. iii. 6, &c. A storm furrows the waters, and does, as it were, divide them; and then a calm smites through the waves, and lays them flat again. See Ps. lxxxix. 9, 10. Those who think Job lived at, or after, the time of Moses, apply this to the dividing of the Red Sea before the children of Israel, and the drowning of the Egyptians in it. *By his understanding he smiteth through Rahab;* so the word is, and Rahab is often put for Egypt; as Ps. lxxxvii. 4; Isa. li. 9.

2. If we consider hell beneath, though it is out of our sight, yet we may conceive the instances of God's power there. By *hell and destruction* (v. 6) we may understand the grave, and those who are buried in it, that they are under the eye of God, though laid out of our sight, which may strengthen our belief of the resurrection of the dead. God knows where to find, and whence to fetch, all the scattered atoms of the consumed body. We may also consider them as referring to the place of the damned, where the separate souls of the wicked are in misery and torment. That is hell and destruction, which are said to be *before the Lord* (Prov. xv. 11), and here to be *naked before him,* to which it is probable there is an allusion, Rev. xiv. 10, where sinners are to be tormented *in the presence of the holy angels* (who attended the Shechinah) and *in the presence of the Lamb.* And this may give light to v. 5, which some ancient versions read thus (and I think more agreeably to the signification of the word *Rephaim) : Behold, the giants groan under the waters, and those that dwell with them;* and then follows, *Hell is naked before him,* typified by the drowning of the giants of the old world; so the learned Mr. Joseph Mede understands it, and with it illustrates Prov. xxi. 16, where hell is called *the congregation of the dead;* and it is the same word which is here used, and which he would there have rendered *the congregation of the giants,* in allusion to the drowning of the sinners of the old world. And is there any thing in which the majesty of God appears more dreadful than in the eternal ruin of the ungodly and the groans of the inhabitants of the land of darkness? Those that will not with angels fear and worship shall for ever with devils fear and tremble; and God therein will be glorified.

3. If we look up to heaven above, we shall see instances of God's sovereignty and power.

(1.) *He stretches out the north over the empty place, v.* 7. So he did at first, when *he stretched out the heavens like a curtain* (Ps. civ. 2); and he still continues to keep them stretched out, and will do so till the general conflagration, when they shall be *rolled together as a scroll,* Rev. vi. 14. He mentions the north because his country (as ours) lay in the northern hemisphere; and the air is the empty place over which it is stretched out. See Ps. lxxxix. 12. What an empty place is this world in comparison with the other! (2.) He keeps the waters that are said to be *above the firmament* from pouring down upon the earth, as once they did (v. 8): *He binds up the waters in his thick clouds,* as if they were tied closely in a bag, till there is occasion to use them; and, notwithstanding the vast weight of water so raised and laid up, yet *the cloud is not rent under them,* for then they would burst and pour out as a spout; but they do, as it were, distil through the cloud, and so come drop by drop, in mercy to the earth, in small rain, or great rain, as he pleases. (3.) He conceals the glory of the upper world, the dazzling lustre of which we poor mortals could not bear (v. 9): *He holds back the face of his throne,* that light in which he dwells, *and spreads a cloud upon it,* through which *he judges,* ch. xxii. 13. God will have us to live by faith, not by sense; for this is agreeable to a state of probation. It were not a fair trial if the face of God's throne were as visible now as it will be in the great day.

> Lest his high throne, above expression bright,
> With deadly glory should oppress our sight,
> To break the dazzling force he draws a screen
> Of sable shades, and spreads his clouds between.
>   Sir R. BLACKMORE.

(4.) The bright ornaments of heaven are the work of his hands (v. 13): *By his Spirit,* the eternal Spirit that moved upon the face of the waters, *the breath of his mouth* (Ps. xxxiii. 6), *he has garnished the heavens,* not only made them, but beautified them, has curiously bespangled them with stars by night and painted them with the light of the sun by day. God, having made man to look upward *(Os homini sublime dedit—To man he gave an erect countenance),* has *therefore* garnished the heavens, to invite him to look upward, that, by pleasing his eye with the dazzling light of the sun and the sparkling light of the stars, their number, order, and various magnitudes, which, as so many golden studs, beautify the canopy drawn over our heads, he may be led to admire the great Creator, the Father and fountain of lights, and to say, " If the pavement be so richly inlaid, what must the palace be! If the visible heavens be so glorious, what are those that are out of sight!" From the beauteous garniture of the ante-chamber we may infer the precious furniture of the presence-chamber. If stars be so bright, what are angels! What is meant here by *the crooked serpent* which his hands have formed is not certain. Some make it part of the garnishing of the heavens, the milky-way, say some; some particular constellation, so called, say others. It is the same word that is used for leviathan (Isa. xxvii. 1), and probably may be meant of the whale or crocodile, in which appears much of the power of the Creator; and why may not Job conclude with that inference, when God himself does so? *ch.* xli.

II. He concludes, at last, with an awful *et cætera* (v. 14): *Lo, these are parts of his ways,* the out-goings of his wisdom and power, the ways in which he walks and by which he makes himself known to the children of men. Here, 1. He acknowledges, with adoration, the discoveries that were made of God. These things which he himself had said, and which Bildad had said, are his ways, and this is heard of him; this is something of God. But, 2. He admires the depth of that which is undiscovered. This that we have said is but part of his ways, a small part. What we know of God is nothing in comparison with what is in God and what God is. After all the discoveries which God has made to us, and all the enquiries we have made after God, still we are much in the dark concerning him, and must conclude, *Lo, these are but parts of his ways.* Something we hear of him by his works and by his word; but, alas! *how little a portion is heard of him!* heard by us, heard from us! We know but in part; we prophesy but in part. When we have said all we can, concerning God, we must even do as St. Paul does (Rom. xi. 33); despairing to find the bottom, we must sit down at the brink, and adore the depth : *O the depth of the wisdom and knowledge of God!* It is but a little portion that we hear and know of God in our present state. He is infinite and incomprehensible; our understandings and capacities are weak and shallow, and the full discoveries of the divine glory are reserved for the future state. Even *the thunder of his power* (that is, his powerful thunder), one of the lowest of his ways here in our own region, we cannot understand. See *ch.* xxxvii. 4, 5. Much less can we understand the utmost force and extent of his power, the terrible efforts and operations of it, and particularly *the power of his anger,* Ps. xc. 11. God is great, and we know him not.

CHAP. XXVII

MOREOVER Job continued his parable, and said, 2 *As* God liveth, *who* hath taken away my judgment; and the Almighty, *who* hath vexed my soul; 3 All the while my breath *is* in me, and the spirit of God *is* in my nostrils; 4 My lips shall not speak wickedness, nor my tongue utter deceit. 5 God forbid that I should justify you: till I die I will not remove mine integrity from me. 6 My righteousness I hold fast, and will not let it go: my heart shall not reproach *me* so long as I live.

Job's discourse here is called a *parable (mashal),* the title of Solomon's proverbs, because it was grave and weighty, and very instructive, and he spoke as one having authority. It comes from a word that signifies *to rule,* or *have dominion;* and some think it intimates that Job now triumphed over his opponents, and spoke as one that had baffled them. We say of an excellent preacher that he knows how *dominari in concionibus—to command his hearers.* Job did so here. A long strife there had been between Job and his friends; they seemed disposed to have the matter compromised; and therefore, since an *oath for confirmation is an end of strife* (Heb. vi. 16), Job here backs all he had said in maintenance of his own integrity with a solemn oath, to silence contradiction, and take the blame entirely upon himself if he prevaricated. Observe,

I. The form of his oath (v. 2): *As God liveth, who hath taken away my judgment.* Here, 1. He speaks highly of God, in calling him *the living God* (which means *everliving,* the eternal God, that has life in himself) and in appealing to him as the sole and sovereign Judge. We can swear by no greater, and it is an affront to him to swear by any other. 2. Yet he speaks hardly of him, and unbecomingly, in saying that he had taken away his judgment (that is, refused to do him justice in this controversy and to appear in defence of him), and that by continuing his troubles, on which his friends grounded their censures of him, he had taken from him the opportunity he hoped ere now to have of clearing himself. Elihu reproved him for this word (*ch.* xxxiv. 5); for God is righteous in all his ways, and takes away no man's judgment. But see how apt we are to despair of favour if it be not shown us immediately, so poor-spirited are we and so soon weary of waiting God's time. He also charges it upon God that he had *vexed his soul,* had not only not appeared for him, but had appeared against him, and, by laying such grievous afflictions upon him had quite embittered his life to him and all the comforts of it. We, by our impatience, vex our own souls and then complain of God that he has vexed them. Yet see Job's confidence in the goodness both of his cause and of his God, that though God seemed to be angry with him, and to act against him for the present, yet he could cheerfully commit his cause to him.

II. The matter of his oath, *v.* 3, 4. 1. That he would not *speak wickedness, nor utter deceit*—that, in general, he would never allow himself in the way of lying, that, as in this debate he had all along spoken as he thought, so he would never wrong his conscience by speaking otherwise; he would never maintain any doctrine, nor assert any matter of fact, but what he believed to be true; nor would he deny the truth, how much soever it might make against him: and, whereas his friends charged him with being a hypocrite, he was ready to answer, upon oath, to all their interrogatories, if called to do so. On the one hand he would not, for all the world, deny the charge if he knew himself guilty, but would declare the truth, the whole truth, and nothing but the truth, and take to himself the shame of his hypocrisy. On the other hand, since he was conscious to himself of his integrity, and that he was not such a man as his friends represented him, he would never betray his integrity, nor charge himself with that which he was innocent of. He would not be brought, no, not by the rack of their unjust censures, falsely to accuse himself. If we must not bear false witness against our neighbour, then not against ourselves. 2. That he would adhere to this resolution as long as he lived (*v.* 3): *All the while my breath is in me.* Our resolutions against sin should be thus constant, resolutions for life. In things doubtful and indifferent, it is not safe to be thus peremptory. We know not what reason we may see to change our mind: God may reveal to us that which we now are not aware of. But in so plain a thing as this we cannot be too positive that we will never speak wickedness. Something of a reason for his resolution is here implied—that our breath will not be always in us. We must shortly breathe our last, and therefore, while our breath is in us, we must never breathe wickedness and deceit, nor allow ourselves to say or do any thing which will make against us when our breath shall depart. The breath in us is called *the spirit of God,* because he breathed it into us; and this is another reason why we must not speak wickedness. It is God that gives us life and breath, and therefore, while we have breath, we must praise him.

III. The explication of his oath (*v.* 5, 6): "*God forbid that I should justify you* in your uncharitable censures of me, by owning myself a hypocrite: no, *until I die I will not remove my integrity from me; my righteousness I hold fast, and will not let it go.*" 1. He would always be an honest man, would hold fast his integrity, and not curse God, as Sa-

tan, by his wife, urged him to do, *ch.* ii. 9. Job here thinks of dying, and of getting ready for death, and therefore resolves never to part with his religion, though he had lost all he had in the world. Note, The best preparative for death is perseverance to death in our integrity. "*Until I die,*" that is, "though I die by this affliction, I will not thereby be put out of conceit with my God and my religion. *Though he slay me, yet will I trust in him.*" 2. He would always stand to it that he was an honest man; he would not remove, he would not part with, the conscience, and comfort, and credit of his integrity; he was resolved to defend it to the last. "God knows, and my own heart knows, that I always meant well, and did not allow myself in the omission of any known duty or the commission of any known sin. This is my rejoicing, and no man shall rob me of it; I will never lie against my right." It has often been the lot of upright men to be censured and condemned as hypocrites; but it well becomes them to bear up boldly against such censures, and not to be discouraged by them nor think the worse of themselves for them; as the apostle (Heb. xiii. 18): *We have a good conscience in all things, willing to live honestly.*

> Hic murus aheneus esto, nil conscire sibi.
> Be this thy brazen bulwark of defence,
> Still to preserve thy conscious innocence.

Job complained much of the reproaches of his friends; but (says he) *my heart shall not reproach me,* that is, "I will never give my heart cause to reproach me, but will keep a conscience void of offence; and, while I do so, I will not give my heart leave to reproach me." *Who shall lay any thing to the charge of God's elect? It is God that justifies.* To resolve that our hearts shall not reproach us when we give them cause to do so is to affront God, whose deputy conscience is, and to wrong ourselves; for it is a good thing, when a man has sinned, to have a heart within him to smite him for it, 2 Sam. xxiv. 10. But to resolve that our hearts shall not reproach us while we still hold fast our integrity is to baffle the designs of the evil spirit (who tempts good Christians to question their adoption, *If thou be the Son of God*) and to concur with the operations of the good Spirit, who witnesses to their adoption.

7 Let mine enemy be as the wicked, and he that riseth up against me as the unrighteous. 8 For what *is* the hope of the hypocrite, though he hath gained, when God taketh away his soul? 9 Will God hear his cry when trouble cometh upon him? 10 Will he delight himself in the Almighty? will he always call upon God?

Job having solemnly protested the satisfaction he had in his integrity, for the further clearing of himself, here expresses the dread he had of being found a hypocrite.

I. He tells us how he startled at the thought of it, for he looked upon the condition of a hypocrite and a wicked man to be certainly the most miserable condition that any man could be in (*v.* 7): *Let my enemy be as the wicked,* a proverbial expression, like that (Dan. iv. 19), *The dream be to those that hate thee.* Job was so far from indulging himself in any wicked way, and flattering himself in it, that, if he might have leave to wish the greatest evil he could think of to the worst enemy he had in the world, he would wish him the portion of a wicked man, knowing that worse he could not wish him. Not that we may lawfully wish any man to be wicked, or that any man who is not wicked should be treated as wicked; but we should all choose to be in the condition of a beggar, an out-law, a galley-slave, any thing, rather than in the condition of the wicked, though in ever so much pomp and outward prosperity.

II. He gives us the reasons of it.

1. Because the hypocrite's hopes will not be crowned (*v.* 8): *For what is the hope of the hypocrite?* Bildad had condemned it (*ch.* viii. 13, 14), and Zophar (*ch.* xi. 20), and Job here concurs with them, and reads the death of the hypocrite's hope with as much assurance as they had done; and this fitly comes in as a reason why he would not remove his integrity, but still hold it fast. Note, The consideration of the miserable condition of wicked people, and especially hypocrites, should engage us to be upright (for we are undone, for ever undone, if we be not) and also to get the comfortable evidence of our uprightness; for how can we be easy if the great concern lie at uncertainties? Job's friends would persuade him that all his hope was but the hope of the hypocrite, *ch.* iv. 6. "Nay," says he, "I would not, for all the world, be so foolish as to build upon such a rotten foundation; for *what is the hope of the hypocrite?*" See here, (1.) The hypocrite deceived. *He has gained,* and he has hope; this is his bright side. It is allowed that he has gained by his hypocrisy, has gained the praise and applause of men and the wealth of this world. Jehu gained a kingdom by his hypocrisy and the Pharisees many a widow's house. Upon this gain he builds his hope, such as it is. He hopes he is in good circumstances for another world, because he finds he is so for this, and he blesses himself in his own way. (2.) The hypocrite undeceived. He will at last see himself wretchedly cheated; for, [1.] God shall *take away his soul,* sorely against his will. Luke xii. 20, *Thy soul shall be required of thee.* God, as the Judge, takes it away to be tried and determined to its everlasting state. He shall then fall into the hands of the living God, to be dealt with immediately. [2.] What will his hope be then? It will be vanity and a lie; it will stand him in no

stead. The wealth of this world, which he hoped in, he must leave behind him, Ps. xlix. 17. The happiness of the other world, which he hoped for, he will certainly miss of. He hoped to go to heaven, but he will be shamefully disappointed; he will plead his external profession, privileges, and performances, but all his pleas will be overruled as frivolous: *Depart from me, I know you not.* So that, upon the whole, it is certain that a formal hypocrite, with all his gains and all his hopes, will be miserable in a dying hour.

2. Because the hypocrite's prayer will not be heard (*v.* 9): *Will God hear his cry when trouble comes upon him?* No, he will not; it cannot be expected he should. If true repentance come upon him, God will hear his cry and accept him (Isa. i. 18); but, if he continue impenitent and unchanged, let him not think to find favour with God. Observe, (1.) Trouble will come upon him, certainly it will. Troubles in the world often surprise those that are most secure of an uninterrupted prosperity. However, death will come, and trouble with it, when he must leave the world and all his delights in it. The judgment of the great day will come; fearfulness will surprise the hypocrites, Isa. xxxiii. 14. (2.) Then he will cry to God, will pray, and pray earnestly. Those who in prosperity slighted God, either prayed not at all or were cold and careless in prayer, when trouble comes will make their application to him and cry as men in earnest. But, (3.) Will God hear him then? In the troubles of this life, God has told us that he will not hear the prayers of those who regard iniquity in their hearts (Ps. lxvi. 19) and set up their idols there (Ezek. xiv. 4), nor of those who turn away their ear from hearing the law, Prov. xxviii. 9. *Get you to the gods whom you have served,* Judg. x. 14. In the judgment to come, it is certain, God will not hear the cry of those who lived and died in their hypocrisy. Their doleful lamentations will all be unpitied. *I will laugh at your calamity.* Their importunate petitions will all be thrown out and their pleas rejected. Inflexible justice cannot be biassed, nor the irreversible sentence revoked. See Matt. vii. 22, 23, Luke xiii. 26, and the case of the foolish virgins, Matt. xxv. 11.

3. Because the hypocrite's religion is neither comfortable nor constant (*v.* 10): *Will he delight himself in the Almighty?* No, not at any time (for his delight is in the profits of the world and the pleasures of the flesh, more than in God), especially not in the time of trouble. *Will he always call upon God?* No, in prosperity he will not call upon God, but slight him; in adversity he will not call upon God but curse him; he is weary of his religion when he gets nothing by it, or is in danger of losing. Note, (1.) Those are hypocrites who, though they profess religion, neither take pleasure in it nor persevere in it, **who**

reckon their religion a task and a drudgery, a weariness, and snuff at it, who make use of it only to serve a turn, and lay it aside when the turn is served, who will call upon God while it is in fashion, or while the pang of devotion lasts, but leave it off when they fall into other company, or when the hot fit is over. (2.) The reason why hypocrites do not persevere in religion is because they have no pleasure in it. Those that do not delight in the Almighty will not always call upon him. The more comfort we find in our religion the more closely we shall cleave to it. Those who have no delight in God are easily inveigled by the pleasures of sense, and so drawn away from their religion; and they are easily run down by the crosses of this life, and so driven away from their religion, and will not always call upon God.

11 I will teach you by the hand of God: *that* which *is* with the Almighty will I not conceal. 12 Behold, all ye yourselves have seen *it;* why then are ye thus altogether vain? 13 This *is* the portion of a wicked man with God, and the heritage of oppressors, *which* they shall receive of the Almighty. 14 If his children be multiplied, *it is* for the sword: and his offspring shall not be satisfied with bread. 15 Those that remain of him shall be buried in death: and his widows shall not weep. 16 Though he heap up silver as the dust, and prepare raiment as the clay; 17 He may prepare *it,* but the just shall put *it* on, and the innocent shall divide the silver. 18 He buildeth his house as a moth, and as a booth *that* the keeper maketh. 19 The rich man shall lie down, but he shall not be gathered: he openeth his eyes, and he *is* not. 20 Terrors take hold on him as waters, a tempest stealeth him away in the night. 21 The east wind carrieth him away, and he departeth: and as a storm hurleth him out of his place. 22 For *God* shall cast upon him, and not spare: he would fain flee out of his hand. 23 *Men* shall clap their hands at him, and shall hiss him out of his place.

Job's friends had seen a great deal of the misery and destruction that attend wicked people, especially oppressors; and Job, while the heat of disputation lasted, had said as much, and with as much assurance, of their prosperity; but now that the heat of the battle was nearly over he was willing to own how far he agreed with them, and where the

difference between his opinion and theirs lay. 1. He agreed with them that wicked people are miserable people, that God will surely reckon with cruel oppressors, and one time or other, one way or other, his justice will make reprisals upon them for all the affronts they have put upon God and all the wrongs they have done to their neighbours. This truth is abundantly confirmed by the entire concurrence even of these angry disputants in it. But, 2. In *this* they differed—they held that these deserved judgments are presently and visibly brought upon wicked oppressors, that *they travail with pain all their days,* that in prosperity *the destroyer comes upon them,* that they *shall not be rich,* nor their *branch green,* and that *their destruction shall be accomplished before their time* (so Eliphaz, ch. xv. 20, 21, 29, 32), that the *steps of their strength shall be straitened,* that *terrors shall make them afraid on every side* (so Bildad, ch. xviii. 7, 11), that he himself *shall vomit up his riches,* and that *in the fulness of his sufficiency he shall be in straits,* so Zophar, ch. xx. 15, 22. Now Job held that, in many cases, judgments do not fall upon them quickly, but are deferred for some time. That vengeance strikes slowly he had already shown (*ch.* xxi. and xxiv.); now he comes to show that it strikes surely and severely, and that reprieves are no pardons.

I. Job here undertakes to set this matter in a true light (*v.* 11, 12): *I will teach you.* We must not disdain to learn even from those who are sick and poor, yea, and peevish too, if they deliver what is true and good. Observe, 1. What he would teach them: "*That which is with the Almighty,*" that is, "the counsels and purposes of God concerning wicked people, which are hidden with him, and which you cannot hastily judge of; and the usual methods of his providence concerning them." This, says Job, *will I not conceal.* What God has not concealed from us we must not conceal from those we are concerned to teach. *Things revealed belong to us and our children.* 2. How he would teach them: *By the hand of God,* that is, by his strength and assistance. Those who undertake to teach others must look to the hand of God to direct them, to open their ear (Isa. l. 4), and to open their lips. Those whom God teaches with a strong hand are best able to teach others, Isa. viii. 11. 3. What reason they had to learn those things which he was about to teach them (*v.* 12), that it was confirmed by their own observation—*You yourselves have seen it* (but what we have heard, and seen, and known, we have need to be taught, that we may be perfect in our lesson), and that it would set them to rights in their judgment concerning him—"*Why then are you thus altogether vain,* to condemn me for a wicked man because I am afflicted?" Truth, rightly understood and applied, would cure us of that vanity of mind which arises from our mistakes. That particularly which he offers now to lay before them is *the portion of a wicked man with God*, particularly of oppressors, *v.* 13. Compare *ch.* xx. 29. Their portion in the world may be wealth and preferment, but their portion with God is ruin and misery. They are above the control of any earthly power, it may be, but the Almighty can deal with them.

II. He does it, by showing that wicked people may, in some instances, prosper, but that ruin follows them in those very instances; and that is their portion, that is their heritage, that is it which they must abide by.

1. They may prosper in their children, but ruin attends them. *His children* perhaps *are multiplied* (*v.* 14) or *magnified* (so some); they are very numerous and are raised to honour and great estates. Worldly people are said to be *full of children* (Ps. xvii. 14), and, as it is in the margin there, *their children are full.* In them the parents hope to live and in their preferment to be honoured. But the more children they leave, and the greater prosperity they leave them in, the more and the fairer marks do they leave for the arrows of God's judgments to be levelled at, his three sore judgments, *sword, famine, and pestilence*, 2 Sam. xxiv. 13. (1.) Some of them shall die by the sword, the sword of war perhaps (they brought them up to live by their sword, as Esau, Gen. xxvii. 40, and those that do so commonly die by the sword, first or last), or by the sword of justice for their crimes, or the sword of the murderer for their estates. (2.) Others of them shall die by famine (*v.* 14): *His offspring shall not be satisfied with bread.* He thought he had secured to them large estates, but it may happen that they may be reduced to poverty, so as not to have the necessary supports of life, at least not to live comfortably. They shall be so needy that they shall not have a competency of necessary food, and so greedy, or so discontented, that what they have they shall not be satisfied with, because not so much, or not so dainty, as what they have been used to. *You eat, but you have not enough*, Hag. i. 6. (3.) Those that *remain shall be buried in death*, that is, shall die of the plague, which is called *death* (Rev. vi. 8), and be buried privately and in haste, as soon as they are dead, without any solemnity, *buried with the burial of an ass;* and even their *widows shall not weep;* they shall not have wherewithal to put them in mourning. Or it denotes that these wicked men, as they live undesired, so they die unlamented, and even their widows will think themselves happy that they have got rid of them.

2. They may prosper in their estates, but ruin attends *them* too, *v.* 16—18. (1.) We will suppose them to be rich in money and plate, in clothing and furniture. *They heap up silver* in abundance *as the dust*, and *prepare raiment as the clay;* they have heaps of clothes about them, as plentiful as heaps of clay. Or it intimates that they have such abundance of clothes that they are even a burden to them. *They lade themselves with thick clay*, Hab. ii. 6. See what is the care and business of worldly people—to heap up worldly wealth. Much would have more, until the silver is cankered and the garments are moth-eaten, Jam. v. 2, 3. But what comes of it? He shall never be the better for it himself; death will strip him, death will rob him, if he be not robbed and stripped sooner, Luke xii. 20. Nay, God will so order it that *the just shall wear his raiment and the innocent shall divide his silver.* [1.] They shall have it, and divide it among themselves. In some way or other Providence shall so order it that good men shall come honestly by that wealth which the wicked man came dishonestly by. *The wealth of the sinner is laid up for the just*, Prov. xiii. 22. God disposes of men's estates as he pleases, and often makes their wills against their wills. The just, whom he hated and persecuted, shall have rule over all his labour, and, in due time, recover with interest what was violently taken from him. The Egyptians' jewels were the Israelites' pay. Solomon observes (Eccl. ii. 26) that God makes the sinners drudges to the righteous; for to *the sinner he gives travail to gather and heap up, that he may give to him that is good before God.* [2.] They shall do good with it. The innocent shall not hoard the silver, as he did that gathered it, but shall divide it to the poor, shall *give a portion to seven and also to eight*, which is laying up the best securities. Money is like manure, good for nothing if it be not spread. When God enriches good men they must remember they are but stewards and must give an account. What bad men bring a curse upon their families with the ill-getting of good men bring a blessing upon their families with the well-using of. *He that by unjust gain increaseth his substance shall gather it for him that will pity the poor*, Prov. xxviii. 8. (2.) We will suppose them to have built themselves strong and stately houses; but they are like the house which the moth makes for herself in an old garment, out of which she will soon be shaken, *v.* 18. He is very secure in it, as a moth, and has no apprehension of danger; but it will prove of as short continuance as *a booth which the keeper makes*, which will quickly be taken down and gone, and his place shall know him no more.

3. Destruction attends their persons, though they lived long in health and at ease (*v.* 19): *The rich man shall lie down* to sleep, to repose himself in the abundance of his wealth (*Soul, take thy ease*), shall lie down in it as his strong city, and seem to others to be very happy and very easy; *but he shall not be gathered*, that is, he shall not have his mind composed, and settled, and gathered in, to enjoy his wealth. He does not sleep so contentedly as people think he does. He *lies down*, but *his abundance will not suffer him to sleep*, at least not so sweetly as the *labouring*

man, Eccl. v. 12. He lies down, but he is full of tossings to and fro till the dawning of the day, and then *he opens his eyes and he is not ;* he sees himself, and all he has, hastening away, as it were, in the twinkling of an eye. His cares increase his fears, and both together make him uneasy, so that, when we attend him to his bed, we do not find him happy there. But, in the close, we are called to attend his exit, and see how miserable he is in death and after death.

(1.) He is miserable in death. It is to him the king of terrors, v. 20, 21. When some mortal disease seizes him what a fright is he in! *Terrors take hold of him as waters,* as if he were surrounded by the flowing tides. He trembles to think of leaving this world, and much more of removing to another. This mingles *sorrow and wrath with his sickness,* as Solomon observes, Eccl. v. 17. These terrors put him either [1.] Into a silent and sullen despair; and then the tempest of God's wrath, the tempest of death, may be said *to steal him away in the night,* when no one is aware or takes any notice of it. Or, [2.] Into an open and clamorous despair; and then he is said *to be carried away,* and hurled out of his place as with a storm, and with an east wind, violent, and noisy, and very dreadful. Death, to a godly man, is like a fair gale of wind to convey him to the heavenly country, but, to a wicked man, it is like an east wind, a storm, a tempest, that hurries him away in confusion and amazement, to destruction.

(2.) He is miserable after death. [1.] His soul falls under the just indignation of God, and it is the terror of that indignation which puts him into such amazement at the approach of death (v. 22): *For God shall cast upon him and not spare.* While he lived he had the benefit of sparing mercy; but now the day of God's patience is over, and he will not spare, but pour out upon him the full vials of his wrath. What God casts down upon a man there is no flying from nor bearing up under. We read of his *casting down great stones from heaven* upon the Canaanites (Josh. x. 11), which made terrible execution among them; but what was that to his casting down his anger in its full weight upon the sinner's conscience, like the *talent of lead?* Zech. v. 7, 8. The damned sinner, seeing the wrath of God break in upon him, would fain flee out of his hand; but he cannot: the gates of hell are locked and barred, and the great gulf fixed, and it will be in vain to call for the shelter of rocks and mountains. Those who will not be persuaded now to fly to the arms of divine grace, which are stretched out to receive them, will not be able to flee from the arms of divine wrath, which will shortly be stretched out to destroy them. [2.] His memory falls under the just indignation of all mankind (v. 23): *Men shall clap their hands at him,* that is, they shall rejoice in the judgments of God, by which he is cut off, and be well pleased in his fall. *When the wicked pe-*

rish there is shouting, Prov. xi. 10. When God buries him men shall hiss him out of his place, and leave on his name perpetual marks of infamy. In the same place where he has been caressed and cried up he shall be laughed at (Ps. lii. 7) and his ashes shall be trampled on.

CHAP. XXVIII.

The strain of this chapter is very unlike the rest of this book. Job forgets his sores, and all his sorrows, and talks like a philosopher or a virtuoso. Here is a great deal both of natural and moral philosophy in this discourse; but the question is, How does it come in here? Doubtless it was not merely for an amusement, or diversion from the controversy; though, if it had been only so, perhaps it would not have been much amiss. When disputes grow hot, better lose the question than lose our temper. But this is pertinent and to the business in hand. Job and his friends had been discoursing about the dispensations of Providence towards the wicked and the righteous. Job had shown that some wicked men live and die in prosperity, while others are presently and openly arrested by the judgments of God. But, if any ask the reason why some are punished in this world and not others, they must be told it is a question that cannot be answered. The knowledge of the reasons of state in God's government of the world is kept from us, and we must neither pretend to it nor reach after it. Zophar had wished that Job would show Job the "secrets of wisdom," ch. xi. 6. No, says Job, "secret things belong not to us, but things revealed," Deut. xxix. 29. And here he shows, I. Concerning worldly wealth, how industriously that is sought for and pursued by the children of men, what pains they take, what contrivances they have, and what hazards they run to get it, ver. 1—11. II. Concerning wisdom, ver. 12. In general, the price of it is very great; it is of inestimable value, ver. 15—19. The place of it is very secret, ver. 14, 20, 22. In particular, there is a wisdom which is hidden in God (ver. 23—27) and there is a wisdom which is revealed to the children of men, ver. 28. Our enquiries into the former must be checked, into the latter quickened, for that is it which is our concern.

SURELY there is a vein for the silver, and a place for gold *where* they fine *it.* 2 Iron is taken out of the earth, and brass *is* molten *out of* the stone. 3 He setteth an end to darkness, and searcheth out all perfection: the stones of darkness, and the shadow of death. 4 The flood breaketh out from the inhabitant; *even the waters* forgotten of the foot: they are dried up, they are gone away from men. 5 *As for* the earth, out of it cometh bread: and under it is turned up as it were fire. 6 The stones of it *are* the place of sapphires: and it hath dust of gold. 7 *There is* a path which no fowl knoweth, and which the vulture's eye hath not seen: 8 The lion's whelps have not trodden it, nor the fierce lion passed by it. 9 He putteth forth his hand upon the rock; he overturneth the mountains by the roots. 10 He cutteth out rivers among the rocks; and his eye seeth every precious thing. 11 He bindeth the floods from overflowing; and *the thing that is* hid bringeth he forth to light.

Here Job shows, 1. What a great way the wit of man may go in diving into the depths of nature and seizing the riches of it, what a great deal of knowledge and wealth men may, by their ingenious and industrious searches, make themselves masters of. But does it therefore follow that men may, by their wit, comprehend the reasons why some wicked people prosper and others are punished, why some good people prosper and others are afflicted? No, by no means. The caverns of the earth may be discovered, but not the counsels of heaven. 2. What a great deal of care and pains worldly men take to get riches. He had observed concerning the wicked man (*ch.* xxvii. 16) that he *heaped up silver as the dust;* now here he shows whence that silver came which he was so fond of and how it was obtained, to show what little reason wicked rich men have to be proud of their wealth and pomp. Observe here,

I. The wealth of this world is hidden in the earth. Thence the silver and the gold, which afterwards they refine, are fetched, *v.* 1. There they lay mixed with a great deal of dirt and dross, like a worthless thing, of no more account than common earth; and abundance of them will so lie neglected, till the earth and all the works therein shall be burnt up. Holy Mr. Herbert, in his poem called *Avarice,* takes notice of this, to shame men out of the love of money:—

> Money, thou bane of bliss, thou source of woe,
>   Whence com'st thou, that thou art so fresh and fine?
> I know thy parentage is base and low;
>   Man found thee poor and dirty in a mine.
>
> Surely thou didst so little contribute
>   To this great kingdom which thou now hast got
> That he was fain, when thou wast destitute,
>   To dig thee out of thy dark cave and grot.
>
> Man calleth thee his wealth, who made thee rich,
> And while he digs out thee falls in the ditch.

Iron and brass, less costly but more serviceable metals, are *taken out of the earth* (*v.* 2), and are there found in great abundance, which abates their price indeed, but is a great kindness to man, who could much better be without gold than without iron. Nay, *out of the earth comes bread,* that is, bread-corn, the necessary support of life, *v.* 5. Thence man's maintenance is fetched, to remind him of his own original; he is of the earth, and is hastening to the earth. *Under it is turned up as it were fire,* precious stones, that sparkle as fire—brimstone, that is apt to take fire—coal, that is proper to feed fire. As we have our food, so we have our fuel, out of the earth. There the sapphires and other gems are, and thence gold-dust is digged up, *v.* 6. The wisdom of the Creator has placed these things, 1. Out of our sight, to teach us not to set our eyes upon them, Prov. xxiii. 5. 2. Under our feet, to teach us not to lay them in our bosoms, nor to set our hearts upon them, but to trample upon them with a holy contempt. See how full the *earth is of God's riches* (Ps. civ. 24) and infer thence, not only how great a God he is *whose the earth is* and *the fulness thereof* (Ps. xxiv. 1), but how full heaven must needs be of God's riches, which is the city of the great King, in comparison with which this earth is a poor country.

II. The wealth that is hidden in the earth cannot be obtained but with a great deal of difficulty. 1. It is hard to be found out: there is but here and there *a vein for the silver, v.* 1. The precious stones, though bright themselves, yet, because buried in obscurity and out of sight, are called *stones of darkness and the shadow of death.* Men may search long before they light on them. 2. When found out it is hard to be fetched out. Men's wits must be set on work to contrive ways and means to get this hidden treasure into their hands. They must with their lamps *set an end to darkness;* and if one expedient miscarry, one method fail, they must try another, till they have *searched out all perfection,* and turned every stone to effect it, *v.* 3. They must grapple with subterraneous waters (*v.* 4, 10, 11), and force their way through rocks which are, as it were, the roots of the mountains, *v.* 9. Now God has made the getting of gold, and silver, and precious stones, so difficult, (1.) For the exciting and engaging of industry. *Dii laboribus omnia vendunt—Labour is the price which the gods affix to all things.* If valuable things were too easily obtained men would never learn to take pains. But the difficulty of gaining the riches of this earth may suggest to us what violence the kingdom of heaven suffers. (2.) For the checking and restraining of pomp and luxury. What is for necessity is had with a little labour from the surface of the earth; but what is for ornament must be dug with a great deal of pains out of the bowels of it. To be fed is cheap, but to be fine is chargeable.

III. Though the subterraneous wealth is thus hard to obtain, yet men will have it. He that loves silver is not satisfied with silver, and yet is not satisfied without it; but those that have much must needs have more. See here, 1. What inventions men have to get this wealth. They *search out all perfection, v.* 3. They have arts and engines to dry up the waters, and carry them off, when they break in upon them in their mines and threaten to drown the work, *v.* 4. They have pumps, and pipes, and canals, to clear their way, and, obstacles being removed, they tread *the path which no fowl knoweth* (*v.* 7, 8), unseen by the vulture's eye, which is piercing and quick-sighted, and untrodden by the lion's whelps, which traverse all the paths of the wilderness. 2. What pains men take, and what vast charge they are at, to get this wealth. They work their way through the rocks and undermine the mountains, *v.* 10. 3. What hazards they run. Those that dig in the mines have their lives in their hands; for they are obliged to *bind the floods from overflowing* (*v.* 11), and are continually in danger of being suffocated by damps or crushed or buried alive by the fall of the earth upon them. See how foolish man adds to his own burden. He is sentenced to eat bread in the sweat of his face; but, as if that were not enough, he will get gold and silver at the peril of his life, though the more is gotten the less valuable it is. In Solomon's time silver was as stones. But,

4. Observe what it is that carries men through all this toil and peril: *Their eye sees every precious thing, v.* 10. Silver and gold are precious things with them, and they have them in their eye in all these pursuits. They fancy they see them glittering before their faces, and, in the prospect of laying hold of them, they make nothing of all these difficulties; for they make something of their toil at last: *That which is hidden bringeth he forth to light, v.* 11. What was hidden under ground is laid upon the bank; the metal that was hidden in the ore is refined from its dross and brought forth pure out of the furnace; and then he thinks his pains well bestowed. Go to the miners then, thou sluggard in religion; consider their ways, and be wise. Let their courage, diligence, and constancy in seeking the wealth that perisheth shame us out of slothfulness and faint-heartedness in labouring for the true riches. *How much better is it to get wisdom than gold!* How much easier and safer! Yet gold is sought for, but grace neglected. Will the hopes of *precious things* out of the earth (so they call them, though really they are paltry and perishing) be such a spur to industry, and shall not the certain prospect of truly precious things in heaven be much more so?

12 But where shall wisdom be found? and where *is* the place of understanding? 13 Man knoweth not the price thereof; neither is it found in the land of the living. 14 The depth saith, It *is* not in me: and the sea saith, *It is* not with me. 15 It cannot be gotten for gold, neither shall silver be weighed *for* the price thereof. 16 It cannot be valued with the gold of Ophir, with the precious onyx, or the sapphire. 17 The gold and the crystal cannot equal it: and the exchange of it *shall not be for* jewels of fine gold. 18 No mention shall be made of coral, or of pearls: for the price of wisdom *is* above rubies. 19 The topaz of Ethiopia shall not equal it, neither shall it be valued with pure gold.

Job, having spoken of the wealth of the world, which men put such a value upon and take so much pains for, here comes to speak of another more valuable jewel, and that is, *wisdom and understanding*, the knowing and enjoying of God and ourselves. Those that found out all those ways and means to enrich themselves thought themselves very wise; but Job will not own theirs to be wisdom. He supposes them to gain their point, and to bring to light what they sought for (*v.* 11), and yet asks, " *Where is wisdom?* for it is not here." This their way is their folly. We must therefore seek

150

it somewhere else, and it will be found nowhere but in the principles and practices of religion. There is more true knowledge, satisfaction, and happiness, in sound divinity, which shows us the way to the joys of heaven, than in natural philosophy or mathematics, which help us to find a way into the bowels of the earth. Two things cannot be found out concerning this wisdom:—

I. The price of it, for that is inestimable; its worth is infinitely more than all the riches in this world: *Man knows not the price thereof* (*v.* 13), that is, 1. Few put a due value upon it. Men know not the worth of it, its innate excellency, their need of it, and of what unspeakable advantage it will be to them; and therefore, though they have many a price in their hand to get this wisdom, yet they *have no heart to it,* Prov. xvii. 16. The cock in the fable knew not the value of the precious stone he found in the dunghill, and therefore would rather have lighted on a barleycorn. Men know not the worth of grace, and therefore will take no pains to get it. 2. None can possibly give a valuable consideration for it, with all the wealth this world can furnish them with. This Job enlarges upon *v.* 15, &c., where he makes an inventory of the *bona notabilia—the most valuable treasures* of this world. Gold is five times mentioned; silver comes in also; and then several precious stones, the onyx and sapphire, pearls and rubies, and the topaz of Ethiopia. These are the things that are highest prized in the world's markets: but if a man would give, not only these, heaps of these, but all the substance of his house, all he is worth in the world, for wisdom, it would utterly be contemned. These may give a man some advantage in seeking wisdom, as they did to Solomon, but there is no purchasing wisdom with these. It is a gift of *the Holy Ghost,* which *cannot be bought with money,* Acts viii. 20. As it does not run in the blood, and so come to us by descent, so it cannot be got for money, nor does it come to us by purchase. Spiritual gifts are conferred without money and without price, because no money can be a price for them. Wisdom is likewise a more valuable gift to him that has it, makes him richer and happier, than gold or precious stones. It is *better to get wisdom than gold.* Gold is another's, wisdom our own; gold is for the body and time, wisdom for the soul and eternity. Let that which is most precious in God's account be so in ours. See Prov. iii. 14, &c.

II. The place of it, for that is undiscoverable. *Where shall wisdom be found? v.* 12. He asks this, 1. As one that truly desired to find it. This is a question we should all put. While the most of men are asking, " Where shall money be found?" we should ask, *Where may wisdom be found?* that we may seek it and find it, not vain philosophy, or carnal policy, but true religion; for that is the only true wisdom, that is it which best improves our faculties and best secures our spiritual and eternal welfare. This is that which we should cry after and dig for, Prov. ii. 3, 4. 2. As one that utterly despaired of finding it any where but in God, and any way but by divine revelation : *It is not found in* this *land of the living, v.* 13. We cannot attain to a right understanding of God and his will, of ourselves and our duty and interest, by reading any books or men, but by reading God's book° and the men of God. Such is the degeneracy of human nature that there is no true wisdom to be found with any but those who are born again, and who, through grace, partake of the divine nature. As for others, even the most ingenious and industrious, they can tell us no tidings of this lost wisdom. (1.) Ask the miners, and by them *the depth will say,* It *is not in me, v.* 14. Those who dig into the bowels of the earth, to rifle the treasures there, cannot in these dark recesses find this rare jewel, nor with all their art make themselves masters of it. (2.) Ask the mariners, and by them *the sea will say,* It *is not in me.* It can never be got either by trading on the waters or diving into them, can never be *sucked from the abundance of the seas or the treasures hidden in the sand.* Where there is a vein for the silver there is no vein for wisdom, none for grace. Men can more easily break through the difficulties they meet with in getting worldly wealth than through those they meet with in getting heavenly wisdom, and they will take more pains to learn how to live in this world than how to live for ever in a better world. So blind and foolish has man become that it is in vain to ask him, *Where is the place of wisdom,* and which is the road that leads to it?

20 Whence then cometh wisdom ? and where *is* the place of understanding ? 21 Seeing it is hid from the eyes of all living, and kept close from the fowls of the air. 22 Destruction and death say, We have heard the fame thereof with our ears. 23 God understandeth the way thereof, and he knoweth the place thereof. 24 For he looketh to the ends of the earth, *and* seeth under the whole heaven ; 25 To make the weight for the winds ; and he weigheth the waters by measure. 26 When he made a decree for the rain, and a way for the lightning of the thunder : 27 Then did he see it, and declare it ; he prepared it, yea, and searched it out. 28 And unto man he said, Behold, the fear of the Lord, that *is* wisdom ; and to depart from evil *is* understanding.

The question which Job had asked (*v.* 12)

he asks again here; for it is too worthy, too weighty, to be let fall, until we speed in the enquiry. Concerning this we must seek till we find, till we get some satisfactory account of it. By a diligent prosecution of this enquiry he brings it, at length, to this issue, that there is a twofold wisdom, one *hidden in God,* which is secret and *belongs not to us,* the other made known by him and revealed to man, which *belongs to us and to our children.*

I. The knowledge of God's secret will, the will of his providence, is out of our reach, and what God has reserved to himself. It *belongs to the Lord our God.* To know the particulars of what God will do hereafter, and the reasons of what he is doing now, is the knowledge Job first speaks of.

1. This knowledge is hidden from us. It is high, we cannot attain unto it (*v.* 21, 22) : *It is hid from the eyes of all living,* even of philosophers, politicians, and saints ; it is *kept close from the fowls of the air ;* though they fly high and in the open firmament of heaven, though they seem somewhat nearer that upper world where the source of this wisdom is, though their eyes behold afar off (*ch.* xxxix. 29), yet they cannot penetrate into the counsels of God. No, man is *wiser than the fowls of heaven,* and yet comes short of this wisdom. Even those who, in their speculations, soar highest, and think themselves, like the fowls of the air, above the heads of other people, yet cannot pretend to this knowledge. Job and his friends had been arguing about the methods and reasons of the dispensations of Providence in the government of the world. " What fools are we" (says Job) " to fight in the dark thus, to dispute about that which we do not understand !" The line and plummet of human reason can never fathom the abyss of the divine counsels. Who can undertake to give the rationale of Providence, or account for the maxims, measure, and methods of God's government, those *arcana imperii—cabinet counsels* of divine wisdom ? Let us then be content not to know the future events of Providence until time discover them (Acts i. 7) and not to know the secret reasons of Providence until eternity discover them. God is now a God that hideth himself (Isa. xlv. 15); *clouds and darkness are round about him.* Though this wisdom be hidden from all living, yet *destruction and death say, We have heard the fame of it.* Though they cannot give an account of themselves (for there is *no wisdom, nor device, nor knowledge at all in the grave,* much less this), yet there is a world on the other side death and the grave, on which those dark regions border, and to which we must pass through them, and there we shall see clearly what we are now in the dark about. " Have a little patience," says Death to the inquisitive soul : " I will fetch thee shortly to a place where even this wisdom will be found." When *the mystery of God shall be finished* it will be laid open, and we shall know as we are

known; when the veil of flesh is rent, and the interposing clouds are scattered, we shall know what God does, though we know not now, John xiii. 7.

2. This knowledge is hidden in God, as the apostle speaks, Eph. iii. 9. *Known unto God are all his works,* though they are not known to us, Acts xv. 18. There are good reasons for what he does, though we cannot assign them (*v.* 23): *God understands the way thereof.* Men sometimes do they know not what, but God never does. Men do what they did not design to do; new occurrences put them upon new counsels, and oblige them to take new measures. But God does all according to the purpose which he purposed in himself, and which he never alters. Men sometimes do that which they cannot give a good reason for, but in every will of God there is a counsel: he knows both what he does and why he does it, the whole series of events and the order and place of every occurrence. This knowledge he has in perfection, but keeps to himself. Two reasons are here given why God must needs understand his own way, and he only:—

(1.) Because all events are now directed by an all-seeing and almighty Providence, *v.* 24, 25. He that governs the world is, [1.] Omniscient; *for he looks to the ends of the earth,* both in place and time; distant ages, distant regions, are under his view. We do not understand our own way, much less can we understand God's way, because we are short-sighted. How little do we know of what is doing in the world, much less of what will be done! But *the eyes of the Lord are in every place;* nay, they *run to and fro through the earth.* Nothing is, or can be, hidden from him; and therefore the reasons why some wicked people prosper remarkably and others are remarkably punished in this world, which are secret to us, are known to him. One day's events, and one man's affairs, have such a reference to, and such a dependence upon, another's, that he only to whom all events and all affairs are naked and open, and who sees the whole at one entire and certain view, is a competent Judge of every part. [2.] He is omnipotent. He can do every thing, and is very exact in all he does. For proof of this Job mentions the winds and waters, *v.* 25. What is lighter than the wind? Yet God hath ways of poising it. He knows how *to make the weight for the winds,* which he *brings out of his treasuries* (Ps. cxxxv. 7), keeping a very particular account of what he draws out, as men do of what they pay out of their treasuries, not at random, as men bring out their trash. Nothing sensible is to us more unaccountable than the wind. We *hear the sound of it, yet cannot tell whence it comes, nor whither it goes;* but God gives it out by weight, wisely ordering both from what point it shall blow and with what strength. The waters of the sea, and the rain-waters, he both weighs and measures, allot-

152

ting the proportion of every tide and every shower. A great and constant communication there is between clouds and seas, the waters above the firmament and those under it. Vapours go up, rains come down, air is condensed into water, water rarefied into air; but the great God keeps an exact account of all the stock with which this trade is carried on for the public benefit and sees that none of it be lost. Now if, in these things, Providence be so exact, much more in dispensing frowns and favours, rewards and punishments, to the children of men, according to the rules of equity.

(2.) Because all events were from eternity designed and determined by an infallible prescience and immutable decree, *v.* 26, 27. When he settled the course of nature he fore-ordained all the operations of his government. [1.] He settled the course of nature. Job mentions particularly *a decree for the rain* and *a way for the thunder and lightning.* The general manner and method, and the particular uses and tendencies, of these strange performances, both their causes and their effects, were appointed by the divine purpose; hence God is said to *prepare lightnings for the rain,* Ps. cxxxv. 7; Jer. x. 13. [2.] When he did that he laid all the measures of his providence, and drew an exact scheme of the whole work from first to last. Then, from eternity, did he see in himself, and declare to himself, the plan of his proceedings. Then he prepared it, fixed it, and established it, set every thing in readiness for all his works, so that, when any thing was to be done, nothing was to seek, nor could any thing unforeseen occur, to put it either out of its method or out of its time; for all was ordered as exactly as if he had studied it and searched it out, so that, whatever he does, *nothing can be put to it nor taken from it,* and therefore *it shall be for ever,* Eccl. iii. 14. Some make Job to speak of wisdom here as a person, and translate it, *Then he saw her and showed her,* &c., and then it is parallel with that of Solomon concerning the essential wisdom of the Father, the eternal Word, Prov. viii. 22, &c. *Before the earth was, then was I by him,* John i. 1, 2.

II. The knowledge of God's revealed will, the will of his precept, and this is within our reach; it is level to our capacity, and will do us good (*v.* 28): *Unto man he said, Behold, the fear of the Lord that is wisdom.* Let it not be said that when God concealed his counsels from man, and forbade him that tree of knowledge, it was because he grudged him any thing that would contribute to his real bliss and satisfaction; no, he let him know as much as he was concerned to know in order to his duty and happiness; he shall be entrusted with as much of his sovereign mind as is needful and fit for a subject, but he must not think himself fit to be a privy-counsellor. He said to *Adam* (so some), to the first man, in the day in which he was created; he told him plainly it was not for him to amuse himself with over-curious searches into the mysteries of creation, nor to pretend to solve all the phenomena of nature; he would find it neither possible nor profitable to do so. No less wisdom (says archbishop Tillotson) than that which made the world can thoroughly understand the philosophy of it. But let him look upon this as his wisdom, to fear the Lord and to depart from evil; let him learn that, and he is learned enough; let this knowledge serve his turn. When God forbade man the tree of knowledge he allowed him the tree of life, and this is that tree, Prov. iii. 18. We cannot attain true wisdom but by divine revelation. *The Lord giveth wisdom,* Prov. ii. 6. Now the matter of that is not found in the secrets of nature or providence, but in the rules for our own practice. Unto man he said, not, " Go up to heaven, to fetch happiness thence;" or, " Go down to the deep, to draw it up thence." No, *the word is nigh thee,* Deut. xxx. 14. *He hath shown thee, O man!* not what is great, but *what is good,* not what the Lord thy God designs to do with thee, but what he *requires of thee,* Mic. vi. 8. *Unto you, O men! I call,* Prov. viii. 4. Lord, what is man that he should be thus minded, thus visited! Behold, mark, take notice of this; he that has ears let him hear what the God of heaven says to the children of men: *The fear of the Lord, that is the wisdom.* Here is, 1. The description of true religion, pure religion, and undefiled; it is to *fear the Lord and depart from evil,* which agrees with God's character of Job, *ch.* i. 1. The *fear of the Lord* is the spring and summary of all religion. There is a slavish fear of God, springing from hard thoughts of him, which is contrary to religion, Matt. xxv. 24. There is a selfish fear of God springing from dreadful thoughts of him, which may be a good step towards religion, Acts ix. 5. But there is a filial fear of God, springing from great and high thoughts of him, which is the life and soul of all religion. And, wherever this reigns in the heart, it will appear by a constant care to *depart from evil,* Prov. xvi. 6. This is essential to religion. We must first cease to do evil, or we shall never learn to do well. *Virtus est vitium fugere—Even in our flight from vice some virtue lies.* 2. The commendation of religion: it is *wisdom* and *understanding.* To be truly religious is to be truly wise. As the wisdom of God appears in the institution of religion, so the wisdom of man appears in the practice and observance of it. It is understanding, for it is the best knowledge of truth; it is wisdom, for it is the best management of our affairs. Nothing more surely guides our way and gains our end than being religious.

CHAP. XXIX.

After that excellent discourse concerning wisdom in the foregoing chapter Job sat down and paused awhile, not because he had talked himself out of breath, but because he would not, without the leave of the company, engross the talk to himself, but would give room for his friends, if they pleased, to make their remarks on what he had said; but they had nothing to say, and there-fore, after he had recollected himself a little, he went on with his discourse concerning his own affairs, as recorded in this and the two following chapters, in which, I. He describes the height of the prosperity from which he had fallen. And, II. The depth of the adversity into which he had fallen; and then he does to move the pity of his friends, and to justify, or at least excuse, his own complaints. But then, III. To obviate his friends' censures of him, he makes a very ample and particular protestation of his own integrity notwithstanding. In this chapter he looks back to the days of his prosperity, and shows, 1. What comfort and satisfaction he had in his house and family, ver. 1—6. 2. What a great deal of honour and power he had in his country, and what respect was paid him by all sorts of people, ver. 7—10. 3. What abundance of good he did in his place, as a magistrate, ver. 11—17. 4. What a just prospect he had of the continuance of his comfort at home (ver. 18—20) and of his interest abroad, ver. 21—25. All this he enlarges upon, to aggravate his present calamities; like Naomi, " I went out full," but am brought " home again empty."

MOREOVER Job continued his parable, and said, 2 O that I were as *in* months past, as *in* the days *when* God preserved me; 3 When his candle shined upon my head, *and when* by his light I walked *through* darkness; 4 As I was in the days of my youth, when the secret of God *was* upon my tabernacle; 5 When the Almighty *was* yet with me, *when* my children *were* about me; 6 When I washed my steps with butter, and the rock poured me out rivers of oil.

Losers may have leave to speak, and there is nothing they speak of more feelingly than of the comforts they are stripped of. Their former prosperity is one of the most pleasing subjects of their thoughts and talk. It was so to Job, who begins here with a wish (*v.* 2): *O that I were as in months past!* so he brings in this account of his prosperity. His wish is, 1. " O that I were in as good a state as I was in then, that I had as much wealth, honour, and pleasure, as I had then!" This he wishes, from a concern he had, not so much for his ease, as for his reputation and the glory of his God, which he thought were eclipsed by his present sufferings. " O that I might be restored to my prosperity, and then the censures and reproaches of my friends would be effectually silenced, even upon their own principles, and for ever rolled away!" If this be our end in desiring life, health, and prosperity, that God may be glorified, and the credit of our holy profession rescued, preserved, and advanced, the desire is not only natural, but spiritual. 2. " O that I were in as good a frame of spirit as I was in then!" That which Job complained most of now was a load upon his spirits, through God's withdrawing from him; and therefore he wishes he now had his spirit as much enlarged and encouraged in the service of God as he had then, and that he had as much freedom and fellowship with him as he then thought himself happy in. This was *in the days of his youth* (v. 4), when he was in the prime of his time for the enjoyment of those things and could relish them with the highest gust. Note, Those that prosper in the days of their youth know not what black and cloudy days they are yet reserved for.

Two things made the months past pleasant to Job:—

1. That he had comfort in his God. This was the chief thing he rejoiced in, in his prosperity, as the spring of it and the sweetness of it, that he had the favour of God and the tokens of that favour. He did not attribute his prosperity to a happy turn of fortune, nor to his own might, nor to the power of his own hand, but makes the same acknowledgment that David does. Ps. xxx. 7, *Thou, by thy favour, hast made my mountain stand strong.* A gracious soul delights in God's smiles, not in the smiles of this world. Four things were then very pleasant to holy Job:—1. The confidence he had in the divine protection. They were *the days when God preserved me, v.* 2. Even then he saw himself exposed, and did not make *his wealth his strong city* nor *trust in the abundance of his riches,* but *the name of the Lord was his strong tower;* in that only he thought himself safe, and to that he ascribed it that he was then safe and that his comforts were preserved to him. The devil saw a hedge about him of God's making (*ch.* i. 10), and Job saw it himself, and owned it was *God's visitation that preserved his spirit, ch.* x. 12. Those only whom God protects are safe and may be easy; and therefore those who have ever so much of this world must not think themselves safe unless God preserve them. 2. The complacency he had in the divine favour (*v.* 3): *God's candle shone upon his head,* that is, God lifted up the light of his countenance upon him, gave him the assurances and sweet relishes of his love. The best of the communications of the divine favour to the saints in this world is but the candle-light, compared with what is reserved for them in the future state. But such abundant satisfaction did Job take in the divine favour that, by the light of that, he walked through darkness; that guided him in his doubts, comforted him in his griefs, bore him up under his burdens, and helped him through all his difficulties. Those that have the brightest sun-shine of outward prosperity must yet expect some moments of darkness. They are sometimes crossed, sometimes at a loss, sometimes melancholy. But those that are interested in the favour of God, and know how to value it, can, by the light of that, walk cheerfully and comfortably through all the darkness of this vale of tears. That puts gladness into the heart enough to counterbalance all the grievances of this present time. 3. The communion he had with the divine word (*v.* 4): *The secret of God was upon my tabernacle,* that is, God conversed freely with him, as one bosom-friend with another. He knew God's mind, and was not in the dark about it, as, of late, he had been. *The secret of the Lord is* said to be *with those that fear him,* for he *shows them* that in *his covenant* which others see not, Ps. xxv. 14. God communicates his favour and grace to his people, and receives

the returns of their devotion in a way secret to the world. Some read it, *When the society of God was in my tabernacle,* which Rabbi Solomon understands of an assembly of God's people that used to meet at Job's house for religious worship, in which he presided; this he took a great deal of pleasure in, and the scattering of it was a trouble to him. Or it may be understood of the angels of God pitching their tents about his habitation. 4. The assurance he had of the divine presence (*v.* 5): *The Almighty was yet with me.* Now he thought God had departed from him, but in those days he was *with him,* and that was all in all to him. God's presence with a man in his house, though it be but a cottage, makes it both a castle and a palace.

II. That he had comfort in his family. Every thing was agreeable there: he had both mouths for his meat and meat for his mouths; the want of either is a great affliction. 1. He had a numerous offspring to enjoy his estate: *My children were about me.* He had many children, enough to compass him round, and they were observant of him and obsequious to him; they were about him, to know what he would have and wherein they might serve him. It is a comfort to tender parents to see their children about them. Job speaks very feelingly of this comfort now that he was deprived of it. He thought it an instance of God's being with him that his children were about him; and yet we reckon amiss if, when we have lost our children, we cannot comfort ourselves with this, that we have not lost our God. 2. He had a plentiful estate for the support of this numerous family, *v.* 6. His dairy abounded to such a degree that he might, if he pleased, *wash his steps with butter;* and his olive-yards were so fruitful, beyond expectation, that it seemed as if the *rock poured him out rivers of oil.* He reckons his wealth, not by his silver and gold, which were for hoarding, but by his butter and oil, which were for use; for what is an estate good for unless we take the good of it ourselves and do good with it to others?

7 When I went out to the gate through the city, *when* I prepared my seat in the street! 8 The young men saw me, and hid themselves: and the aged arose, *and* stood up. 9 The princes refrained talking, and laid *their* hand on their mouth. 10 The nobles held their peace, and their tongue cleaved to the roof of their mouth. 11 When the ear heard *me,* then it blessed me; and when the eye saw *me,* it gave witness to me: 12 Because I delivered the poor that cried, and the fatherless, and *him that had* none to help him. 13 The blessing of him that was ready

to perish came upon me: and I caused the widow's heart to sing for joy. 14 I put on righteousness, and it clothed me: my judgment *was* as a robe and a diadem. 15 I was eyes to the blind, and feet *was* I to the lame. 16 I *was* a father to the poor: and the cause *which* I knew not I searched out. 17 And I brake the jaws of the wicked, and plucked the spoil out of his teeth.

We have here Job in a post of honour and power. Though he had comfort enough in his own house, yet he did not confine himself to that. We are not born for ourselves, but for the public. When any business was to be done in the gate, the place of judgment, Job *went out to* it *through the city* (v. 7), not in an affectation of pomp, but in an affection to justice. Observe, Judgment was administered in the gate, in the street, in the places of concourse, to which every man might have a free access, that every one who would might be a witness to all that was said and done, and that when judgment was given against the guilty others might hear and fear. Job being a prince, a judge, a magistrate, a man in authority, among the children of the east, we are here told,

I. What a profound respect was paid to him by all sorts of people, not only for the dignity of his place, but for his personal merit, his eminent prudence, integrity, and good management. 1. The people honoured him and stood in awe of him, *v.* 8. The gravity and majesty of his looks and mien, and his known strictness in animadverting upon every thing that was evil and indecent, commanded all about him into due decorum. *The young men,* who could not keep their countenances, or, it may be, were conscious to themselves of something amiss, *hid themselves,* and got out of his way; *and the aged,* though they kept their ground, yet would not keep their seats: they *arose and stood up* to do homage to him; those who expected honour from others gave honour to him. Virtue and piety challenge respect from all, and usually have it; but those that not only *are* good, but *do* good, are worthy of double honour. Modesty becomes those that are young and in subjection as much as majesty becomes those that are aged and in power. Honour and fear are due to magistrates, and must be rendered to them, Rom. xiii. 7. But, if a great and good man was thus reverenced, how is the great and good God to be feared! 2. The princes and nobles paid great deference to him, *v.* 9, 10. Some think that these were inferior magistrates under him, and that the respect they paid him was due to his place, as their sovereign and supreme. It should rather seem that they were his equals in place, and joined in commission with him, **and** that the peculiar honour they gave him

was gained by his extraordinary abilities and services. It was agreed that he excelled them all in quickness of apprehension, soundness of judgment, closeness of application, clearness and copiousness of expression; and therefore he was among his fellows an oracle of law, and counsel, and justice, and what he said all attended to and acquiesced in. When he came into court, especially when he stood up to speak to any business, *the princes refrained talking, the nobles held their peace,* that they might the more diligently hearken to what he said and might be sure to understand his meaning. Those that had been forward to speak their own thoughts, loved to hear themselves talk, and cared not much what any body else said, yet, when it came to Job's turn to speak, were as desirous to know his thoughts as ever they had been to vent their own. Those that suspected their own judgment were satisfied in his, and admired with what dexterity he split the hair and untied the knots which puzzled them and which they knew not what to make of. When the princes and nobles wrangled among themselves all agreed to refer the matters in dispute to Job and to abide by his judgment. Happy the men that are blessed with such eminent gifts as these; they have great opportunities of honouring God and doing good, but have great need to watch against pride. Happy the people that are blessed with such eminent men; it is a token for good to them.

II. What a great deal of good he did in his place. He was very serviceable to his country with the power he had; and here we shall see what it was which Job valued himself by in the day of his prosperity. It is natural to men to have some value for themselves, and we may judge something of our own character by observing what that is upon which we value ourselves. Job valued himself, not by the honour of his family, the great estate he had, his large income, his full table, the many servants he had at his command, the ensigns of his dignity, his equipage and retinue, the splendid entertainments he gave, and the court that was made to him, but by his usefulness. Goodness is God's glory, and it will be ours; if we are merciful as God is, we are perfect as he is.

1. He valued himself by the interest he had in the esteem, affections, and prayers, of sober people; not by the studied panegyrics of the wits and poets, but the unconstrained praises of all about him. All that heard what he said, and saw what he did, how he laid out himself for the public good with all the authority and tender affection of a father to his country, blessed him, and gave witness to him, *v.* 11. Many a good word they said of him, and many a good prayer they put up for him. He did not think it an honour to make every body fear him (*Oderint dum metuant—Let them hate, provided they also fear*) nor to be arbitrary, and to have his own will and way, not caring

what people said of him; but, like Mordecai, to be *accepted of the multitude of his brethren,* Esth. x. 3. He did not so much value the applauses of those at a distance as the attestations of those that were the witnesses of his conduct, that constantly attended him, saw him, and heard him, and could speak of their own knowledge, especially theirs who had themselves been the better for him and could speak by their own experience: such was the blessing of him who was ready to perish (v. 13) and who by Job's means was rescued from perishing. Let great men, and men of estates, thus do good, and they shall have praise of the same; and let those who have good done to them look upon it as a just debt they owe to their protectors and benefactors to bless them and give witness to them, to use their interest on earth for their honour and in heaven for their comfort, to praise them and pray for them. Those are ungrateful indeed who grudge these small returns.

2. He valued himself by the care he took of those that were least able to help themselves, the poor and the needy, the widows and fatherless, the blind and the lame, who could not be supposed either to merit his favour or ever to be in a capacity to recompense it. (1.) If the poor were injured or oppressed, they might cry to Job, and, if he found the allegations of their petitions true, they had not only his ear and his bowels, but his hand too: He *delivered the poor that cried* (v. 12) and would not suffer them to be trampled upon and run down. Nay (v. 16), he was *a father to the poor,* not only a judge to protect them and to see that they were not wronged, but a father to provide for them and to see that they did not want, to counsel and direct them, and to appear and act for them upon all occasions. It is no disparagement to the son of a prince to be a father to the poor. (2.) The fatherless that had none to help them found Job ready to help them, and, if they were in straits, to deliver them. He helped them to make the best of what little they had, helped them to pay what they owed and to get in what was owing to them, helped them out into the world, helped them into business, helped them to it, and helped them in it; thus should the fatherless be helped. (3.) Those that were ready to perish he saved from perishing, relieving those that were hungry and ready to perish for want, taking care of those that were sick, that were outcasts, that were falsely accused, or in danger of being turned out of their estates unjustly, or, upon any other account, were ready to perish. The extremity of the peril, as it quickened Job to appear the more vigorously for them, so it made his seasonable kindness the more affecting and the more obliging, and brought their blessings the more abundantly upon him. (4.) The widows that were sighing for grief, and trembling for fear, he made to sing for joy, so carefully

did he protect them and provide for them, and so heartily did he espouse their interest. It is a pleasure to a good man, and should be so to a great man, to give those occasion to rejoice that are most acquainted with grief. (5.) Those that were upon any account at a loss Job gave suitable and seasonable relief to (v. 15): *I was eyes to the blind,* counselling and advising those for the best that knew not what to do, and *feet to the lame,* assisting those with money and friends that knew what they should do, but knew not how to compass it. Those we best help whom we help out in that very thing wherein they are defective and most need help. We may come to be blind or lame ourselves, and therefore should pity and succour those that are so, Isa. xxxv. 3, 4; Heb. xii. 13.

3. He valued himself by the conscience he made of justice and equity in all his proceedings. His friends had unjustly censured him as an oppressor. "So far from that," says he, "I always made it my business to maintain and support right." (1.) He devoted himself to the administration of justice (v. 14): *I put on righteousness and it clothed me,* that is, he had an habitual disposition to execute justice and put on a fixed resolution to do it. It was *the girdle of his lions,* Isa. xi. 5. It kept him tight and steady in all his motions. He always appeared in it, as in his clothing, and never without it. Righteousness will clothe those that put it on; it will keep them warm, and be comfortable to them; it will keep them safe, and fence them against the injuries of the season; it will adorn them, and recommend them to the favour both of God and man. (2.) He took pleasure in it, and, as I may say, a holy delight. He looked upon it as his greatest glory to do justice to all and injury to none: *My judgment was as a robe and a diadem.* Perhaps he did not himself wear a robe and a diadem; he was very indifferent to those ensigns of honour; those were most fond of them who had least intrinsic worth to recommend them. But the settled principles of justice, by which he was governed and did govern, were to him instead of all those ornaments. If a magistrate do the duty of his place, that is an honour to him far beyond his gold or purple, and should be, accordingly, his delight; and truly if he do not make conscience of his duty, and in some measure answer the end of his elevation, his robe and diadem, his gown and cap, his sword and mace, are but a reproach, like the purple robe and crown of thorns with which the Jews studied to ridicule our Saviour; for, as clothes on a dead man will never make him warm, so robes on a base man will never make him honourable. (3.) He took pains in the business of his place (v. 16): *The cause which I knew not I searched out.* He diligently enquired into the matters of fact, patiently and impartially heard both sides, set every thing in its true light, and

cleared it from false colours; he laid all circumstances together, that he might find out the truth and the merits of every cause, and then, and not till then, gave judgment upon it. He never answered a matter before he heard it, nor did he judge a man to be righteous, however he seemed, for his being *first in his own cause,* Prov. xviii. 17.

4. He valued himself by the check he gave to the violence of proud and evil men (*v.* 17): *I broke the jaws of the wicked.* He does not say that he broke their necks. He did not take away their lives, but he broke their jaws, he took away their power of doing mischief; he humbled them, mortified them, and curbed their insolence, and so plucked the spoil out of their teeth, delivered the persons and estates of honest men from being made a prey of by them. When they had got the spoil between their teeth, and were greedily swallowing it down, he bravely rescued it, as David did the lamb out of the mouth of the lion, not fearing, though they roared and raged like a lion disappointed of his prey. Good magistrates must thus be a terror and restraint to evil-doers and a protection to the innocent, and, in order to this, they have need to arm themselves with zeal, and resolution, and an undaunted courage. A judge upon the bench has as much need to be bold and brave as a commander in the field.

18 Then I said, I shall die in my nest, and I shall multiply *my* days as the sand. 19 My root *was* spread out by the waters, and the dew lay all night upon my branch. 20 My glory *was* fresh in me, and my bow was renewed in my hand. 21 Unto me *men* gave ear, and waited, and kept silence at my counsel. 22 After my words they spake not again; and my speech dropped upon them. 23 And they waited for me as for the rain; and they opened their mouth wide *as* for the latter rain. 24 *If* I laughed on them, they believed *it* not; and the light of my countenance they cast not down. 25 I chose out their way, and sat chief, and dwelt as a king in the army, as one *that* comforteth the mourners.

That which crowned Job's prosperity was the pleasing prospect he had of the continuance of it. Though he knew, in general, that he was liable to trouble, and therefore was not secure (*ch.* iii. 26, *I was not in safety, neither had I rest*), yet he had no particular occasion for fear, but as much reason as ever any man had to count upon the lengthening out of his tranquillity.

I. See here what his thoughts were in his prosperity (*v.* 18): *Then I said, I shall die in my nest.* Having made himself a warm and easy nest, he hoped nothing would disturb him in it, nor remove him out of it, till death removed him. He knew he had never stolen any coal from the altar which might fire his nest; he saw no storm arising to shake down his nest; and therefore concluded, *To morrow shall be as this day;* as David (Ps. xxx. 6), *My mountain stands strong, and shall not be moved.* Observe, 1. In the midst of his prosperity he thought of dying, and the thought was not uneasy to him. He knew that, though his nest was high, it did not set him out of the reach of the darts of death. 2. Yet he flattered himself with vain hopes, (1.) That he should live long, should *multiply his days as the sand.* He means as the sand on the sea-shore; whereas we should rather reckon our days by the sand in the hour-glass, which will have run out in a little time. See how apt even good people are to think of death as a thing at a distance, and to put far from them that evil day, which will really be to them a good day. (2.) That he should die in the same prosperous state in which he had lived. If such an expectation as this arise from a lively faith in the providence and promise of God, it is well, but if from a conceit of our own wisdom, and the stability of these earthly things, it is ill-grounded and turns into sin. We hope Job's confidence was like David's (Ps. xxvii. 1, *Whom shall I fear?*), not like the rich fool's (Luke xii. 19), *Soul, take thy ease.*

II. See what was the ground of these thoughts.

1. If he looked at home, he found he had a good foundation. His stock was all his own, and none of all his neighbours had any demand upon him. He found no bodily distemper growing upon him; his estate did not lie under any incumbrance; nor was he sensible of any worm at the root of it. He was getting forward in his affairs, and not going behind-hand; he lost no reputation, but gained rather; he knew no rival that threatened either to eclipse his honour or abridge his power. See how he describes this, *v.* 19, 20. He was like a tree whose root is not only spread out, which fixes it and keeps it firm, so that it is in no danger of being overturned, but *spread out by the waters,* which feed it, and make it fruitful and flourishing, so that it is in no danger of withering. And, as he thought himself blessed with the fatness of the earth, so also with the kind influences of heaven too; for the *dew lay all night upon his branch.* Providence favoured him, and made all his enjoyments comfortable and all his enterprises successful. Let none think to support their prosperity with what they draw from this earth without that blessing which is derived from above. God's favour being continued to Job, in the virtue of that his glory was still fresh in him. Those about him had still something new to say in his praise, and needed not to repeat the old sto-

ries: and it is only by constant goodness that men's glory is thus preserved fresh and kept from withering and growing stale. His *bow* also *was renewed in his hand*, that is, his power to protect himself and annoy those that assailed him still increased, so that he thought he had as little reason as any man to fear the insults of the Sabeans and Chaldeans.

2. If he looked abroad, he found he had a good interest and well confirmed. As he had no reason to dread the power of his enemies, so neither had he any reason to distrust the fidelity of his friends. To the last moment of his prosperity they continued their respect to him and their dependence on him. What had he to fear who so gave counsel as in effect to give law to all his neighbours? Nothing surely could be done against him when really nothing was done without him.

(1.) He was the oracle of his country. He was consulted as an oracle, and his dictates were acquiesced in as oracles, *v.* 21. When others could not be heard all men *gave ear* to him, *and kept silence at his counsel*, knowing that, as nothing could be said against it, so nothing needed to be added to it. And therefore, *after his words, they spoke not again, v.* 22. Why should men meddle with a subject that has already been exhausted?

(2.) He was the darling of his country. All about him were well pleased with every thing he said and did, as David's people were with him, 2 Sam. iii. 36. He had the hearts and affections of all his neighbours, all his servants, tenants, subjects; never was man so much admired nor so well beloved. [1.] Those were thought happy to whom he spoke, and they thought themselves so. Never were the dews of heaven so acceptable to the parched ground as his wise discourses were to those that attended on them, especially to those to whom they were particularly accommodated and directed. His speech dropped upon them, and they waited for it as for the rain (*v.* 22, 23), wondering at the gracious words which proceeded out of his mouth, catching at them, laying hold on them, and treasuring them up as apophthegms. His servants that stood continually before him to hear his wisdom would not have envied Solomon's. Those are wise, or are likely to be so, that know how to value wise discourse, that wish for it, and wait for it, and drink it in as the earth does *the rain that comes often upon it*, Heb. vi. 7. And those who have such an interest as Job had in the esteem of others, whose *ipse dixit—bare assertion* goes so far, as they have a great opportunity of doing good, so they must take great care lest they do hurt, for a bad word out of their mouths is very infectious. [2.] Much more happy were those thought on whom he smiled, and they thought themselves so, *v.* 24. "*If I laughed on them*, designing thereby to show myself pleased in them, or pleasant with them, it was such a favour that

they believed it not for joy," or because it was so rare a thing to see this grave man smile. *Many seek the ruler's favour.* Job was a ruler whose favour was courted and valued at a high rate. He to whom a great prince gave a kiss was envied by another to whom he only gave a golden cup. Familiarity often breeds contempt; but if Job at any time saw fit, for his own diversion, to make himself free with those about him, yet it did not in the least diminish the veneration they had for him: *The light of his countenance they cast not down.* So wisely did he dispense his favours as not to make them cheap, and so wisely did they receive them as not to make themselves unworthy of them another time.

(3.) He was the sovereign of his country, *v.* 25. He *chose out their way*, sat at the helm, and steered for them, all referring themselves to his conduct and submitting themselves to his command. To this perhaps, in many countries, monarchy owed its rise: such a man as Job, that so far excelled all his neighbours in wisdom and integrity, could not but sit chief, and the fool will, of course, be servant to the wise in heart: and, if the wisdom did but for a while run in the blood, the honour and power would certainly attend it and so by degrees become hereditary. Two things recommended Job to the sovereignty:—[1.] That he had the authority of a commander or general. He *dwelt as a king in the army*, giving orders which were not to be disputed. Every one that has the spirit of wisdom has not the spirit of government, but Job had both, and, when there was occasion, could assume state, as the king in the army does, and say, "Go," "Come," and "Do this," Matt. viii. 9. [2.] That yet he had the tenderness of a comforter. He was as ready to succour those in distress as if it had been his office to comfort the mourners. Eliphaz himself owned he had been very good in that respect (*ch.* iv. 3): *Thou hast strengthened the weak hands.* And this he now reflected upon with pleasure, when he was himself a mourner. But we find it easier to comfort others with the comforts wherewith we ourselves have been formerly comforted than to comfort ourselves with those comforts wherewith we have formerly comforted others.

I know not but we may look upon Job as a type and figure of Christ in his power and prosperity. Our Lord Jesus is such a King as Job was, the poor man's King, who loves righteousness and hates iniquity, and upon whom the blessing of a world ready to perish comes; see Ps. lxxii. 2, &c. To him therefore let us give ear, and let him sit chief in our hearts.

CHAP. XXX.

It is a melancholy "But now" which this chapter begins with. Adversity is here described as much to the life as prosperity was in the foregoing chapter, and the height of that did but increase the depth of this. God sets the one over-against the other, and so did Job, that his afflictions might appear the more grievous, and consequently his case the more pitiable. I. He had lived in great honour, but now he had fallen into disgrace, and was as much vilified, even by the meanest, as ever he had been magnified by the greatest; this he insists much on, ver 1–14. II.

He had had much inward comfort and delight, but now he was a terror and burden to himself (ver. 15, 16) and overwhelmed with sorrow, ver. 28—31. III. He had long enjoyed a good state of health, but now he was sick and in pain, ver. 17—19, 29, 30. IV. Time was when the secret of God was with him, but now his communication with heaven was cut off, ver. 20—22. V. He had promised himself a long life, but now he saw death at the door, ver. 23. One thing he mentions, which aggravated his affliction, that it surprised him when he looked for peace. But two things gave him some relief:—1. That his troubles would not follow him to the grave, ver. 24. 2. That his conscience witnessed for him that, in his prosperity, he had sympathized with those that were in misery, ver. 25.

BUT now *they that are* younger than I have me in derision, whose fathers I would have disdained to have set with the dogs of my flock. 2 Yea, whereto *might* the strength of their hands *profit* me, in whom old age was perished? 3 For want and famine *they were* solitary; fleeing into the wilderness in former time desolate and waste. 4 Who cut up mallows by the bushes, and juniper roots *for* their meat. 5 They were driven forth from among *men*, (they cried after them as *after* a thief;) 6 To dwell in the cliffs of the valleys, *in* caves of the earth, and *in* the rocks. 7 Among the bushes they brayed; under the nettles they were gathered together. 8 *They were* children of fools, yea, children of base men: they were viler than the earth. 9 And now am I their song, yea, I am their byword. 10 They abhor me, they flee far from me, and spare not to spit in my face. 11 Because he hath loosed my cord, and afflicted me, they have also let loose the bridle before me. 12 Upon *my* right *hand* rise the youth; they push away my feet, and they raise up against me the ways of their destruction. 13 They mar my path, they set forward my calamity, they have no helper. 14 They came *upon me* as a wide breaking in *of waters:* in the desolation they rolled themselves *upon me.*

Here Job makes a very large and sad complaint of the great disgrace he had fallen into, from the height of honour and reputation, which was exceedingly grievous and cutting to such an ingenuous spirit as Job's was. Two things he insists upon as greatly aggravating his affliction :—

I. The meanness of the persons that affronted him. As it added much to his honour, in the day of his prosperity, that princes and nobles showed him respect and paid a deference to him, so it added no less to his disgrace in his adversity that he was spurned by the footmen, and trampled upon by those that were not only every way his inferiors, but were the meanest and most contemptible of all mankind. None can be represented as more base than those are here represented who insulted Job, upon all accounts. 1. They were young, younger than he (*v.* 1), *the youth* (*v.* 12), who ought to have behaved themselves respectfully towards him for his age and gravity. Even the children, in their play, played upon him, as the children of Bethel upon the prophet, *Go up, thou baldhead.* Children soon learn to be scornful when they see their parents so. 2. They were of a mean extraction. Their fathers were so very despicable that such a man as Job would have disdained to take them into the lowest service about his house, as that of tending the sheep and attending the shepherds with the dogs of his flock, *v.* 1. They were so shabby that they were not fit to be seen among his servants, so silly that they were not fit to be employed, and so false that they were not fit to be trusted in the meanest post. Job here speaks of what he might have done, not of what he did : he was not of such a spirit as to set any of the children of men with the dogs of his flock ; he knew the dignity of human nature better than to do so. 3. They and their families were the unprofitable burdens of the earth, and good for nothing. Job himself, with all his prudence and patience, could make nothing of them, *v.* 2. The young were not fit for labour, they were so lazy, and went about their work so awkwardly : *Whereto might the strength of their hands profit me?* The old were not to be advised with in the smallest matters, for in them was old age indeed, but their *old age was perished,* they were twice children. 4. They were extremely poor, *v.* 3. They were ready to starve, for they would not dig, and to beg they were ashamed. Had they been brought to necessity by the providence of God, their neighbours would have sought them out as proper objects of charity and would have relieved them ; but, being brought into straits by their own slothfulness and wastefulness, nobody was forward to relieve them. Hence they were forced to flee into the deserts both for shelter and sustenance, and were put to sorry shifts indeed, when they *cut up mallows by the bushes,* and were glad to eat them, for want of food that was fit for them, *v.* 4. See what hunger will bring men to : one half of the world does not know how the other half lives ; yet those that have abundance ought to think sometimes of those whose fare is very coarse and who are brought to a short allowance of that too. But we must own the righteousness of God, and not think it strange, if slothfulness clothe men with rags and the idle soul be made to suffer hunger. This beggarly world is full of the devil's poor. 5. They were very scandalous wicked people, not only the burdens, but the plagues, of the places where they lived, arrant scoundrels, the scum of the country : *They were driven forth from among men, v.* 5. They were such lying, thieving, lurking, mischievous people, that the best service the magistrates could do was to rid the country of them, while the very mob cried after them as after a thief. *Away with such fellows from the earth; it is not fit they should live.* They were lazy and would not work, and therefore they were exclaimed against as thieves, and justly; for those that do not earn their own bread by honest labour do, in effect, steal the bread out of other people's mouths. An idle fellow is a public nuisance; but it is better to drive such into a workhouse than, as here, into a wilderness, which will punish them indeed, but never reform them. They were forced to dwell in *caves of the earth,* and *they brayed* like asses *among the bushes, v.* 6, 7. See what is the lot of those that have the cry of the country, the cry of their own conscience, against them; they cannot but be in a continual terror and confusion. *They groan among the trees* (so Broughton) *and smart among the nettles;* they are stung and scratched there, where they hoped to be sheltered and protected. See what miseries wicked people bring themselves to in this world; yet this is nothing to what is in reserve for them in the other world. 6. They were all that is base, *v.* 8. They had nothing at all in them to recommend them to any man's esteem. They were a vile kind; yea, a kind without fame, people that nobody could give a good word to nor had a good wish for; they were banished from the earth as being *viler than the earth.* One would not think it possible that ever the human nature should sink so low, and degenerate so far, as it did in these people. When we thank God that we are men we have reason to thank him that we are not such men. But such as these were abusive to Job, (1.) In revenge, because when he was in prosperity and power, like a good magistrate, he put in execution the laws which were in force against vagabonds, and rogues, and sturdy beggars, which these base people now remembered against him. (2.) In triumph over him, because they thought he had now become like one of them. Isa. xiv. 10, 11. The abjects, men of mean spirits, insult over the miserable, Ps. xxxv. 15.

II. The greatness of the affronts that were given him. It cannot be imagined how abusive they were.

1. They made ballads on him, with which they made themselves and their companions merry (*v.* 9): *I am their song and their by-word.* Those have a very base spirit that turn the calamities of their honest neighbours into a jest, and can sport themselves with their griefs.

2. They shunned him as a loathsome spectacle, abhorred him, fled far from him, (*v.* 10), as an ugly monster or as one infected. Those that were themselves driven out from among men would have had him driven out. For,

3. They expressed the greatest scorn and indignation against him. They spat

160

in his face, or were ready to do so; they tripped up his heels, pushed away his feet (*v.* 12), kicked him, either in wrath, because they hated him, or in sport, to make themselves merry with him, as they did with their companions at foot-ball. The best of saints have sometimes received the worst of injuries and indignities from a spiteful, scornful, wicked world, and must not think it strange; our Master himself was thus abused.

4. They were very malicious against him, and not only made a jest of him, but made a prey of him—not only affronted him, but set themselves to do him all the real mischief they could devise: *They raise up against me the ways of their destruction;* or (as some read it), *They cast upon me the cause of their woe;* that is, "They lay the blame of their being driven out upon me;" and it is common for criminals to hate the judges and laws by which they are punished. But under this pretence, (1.) They accused him falsely, and misrepresented his former conversation, which is here called *marring his path.* They reflected upon him as a tyrant and an oppressor because he had done justice upon them; and perhaps Job's friends grounded their uncharitable censures of him (*ch.* xxii. 6, &c.) upon the unjust and unreasonable clamours of these sorry people; and it was an instance of their great weakness and inconsideration, for who can be innocent if the accusations of such persons may be heeded? (2.) They not only triumphed in his calamity, but set it forward, and did all they could to add to his miseries and make them more grievous to him. It is a great sin to forward the calamity of any, especially of good people. In this *they have no helper,* nobody to set them on or to countenance them in it, nobody to bear them out or to protect them, but they do it of their own accord; they are fools in other things, but wise enough to do mischief, and need no help in inventing that. Some read it thus, *They hold my heaviness a profit, though they be never the better.* Wicked people, though they get nothing by the calamities of others, yet rejoice in them.

5. Those that did him all this mischief were numerous, unanimous, and violent (*v.* 14): *They came upon me as a wide breaking in of waters,* when the dam is broken; or, "They came as soldiers into a broad breach which they have made in the wall of a besieged city, pouring in upon me with the utmost fury;" and in this they took a pride and a pleasure: *They rolled themselves in the desolation* as a man rolls himself in a soft and easy bed, and they rolled themselves upon him with all the weight of their malice.

III. All this contempt put upon him was caused by the troubles he was in (*v.* 11): *" Because he has loosed my cord,* has taken away the honour and power with which I was girded (*ch.* xii. 18), has scattered what I had got together and untwisted all my affairs—because he has afflicted me, therefore *they have let loose the bridle before me,"* that is, "have given themselves a liberty to say and do what they please against me." Those that by Providence are stripped of their honour may expect to be loaded with contempt by inconsiderate ill-natured people. "Because he hath loosed *his* cord" (the original has that reading also), that is, "because he has taken off his bridle of restraint from off their malice, they cast away the bridle from me," that is, "they make no account of my authority, nor stand in any awe of me." It is owing to the hold God has of the consciences even of bad men, and the restraints he lays upon them, that we are not continually thus insulted and abused; and, if at any time we meet with such ill treatment, we must acknowledge the hand of God in taking off those restraints, as David did when Shimei cursed him: *So let him curse, for the Lord hath bidden him.* Now in all this, 1. We may see the uncertainty of worldly honour, and particularly of popular applause, how suddenly a man may fall from the height of dignity into the depth of disgrace. What little cause therefore have men to be ambitious or proud of that which may be so easily lost, and what little confidence is to be put in it! Those that to-day cry *Hosannah* may to-morrow cry *Crucify.* But there is an honour which comes from God, which if we secure, we shall find it not thus changeable and loseable. 2. We may see that it has often been the lot of very wise and good men to be trampled upon and abused. And, 3. That those who look only at the things that are seen despise those whom the world frowns upon, though they are ever so much the favourites of Heaven. Nothing is more grievous in poverty than that it renders men contemptible. *Turba Remi sequitur fortunam, ut semper odit damnatos—The Roman populace, faithful to the turns of fortune, still persecute the fallen.* 4. We may see in Job a type of Christ, who was thus made a *reproach of men* and *despised of the people* (Ps. xxii. 6; Isa. liii. 3), and who hid not his face from shame and spitting, but bore the indignity better than Job did.

15 Terrors are turned upon me : they pursue my soul as the wind : and my welfare passeth away as a cloud. 16 And now my soul is poured out upon me ; the days of affliction have taken hold upon me. 17 My bones are pierced in me in the night season : and my sinews take no rest. 18 By the great force *of my disease* is my garment changed : it bindeth me about as the collar of my coat. 19 He hath cast me into the mire, and I am become like dust and ashes. 20 I cry unto thee, and thou dost not hear me :

I stand up, and thou regardest me *not.* 21 Thou art become cruel to me : with thy strong hand thou opposest thyself against me. 22 Thou liftest me up to the wind ; thou causest me to ride *upon it,* and dissolvest my substance. 23 For I know *that* thou wilt bring me *to* death, and *to* the house appointed for all living. 24 Howbeit he will not stretch out *his* hand to the grave, though they cry in his destruction. 25 Did not I weep for him that was in trouble? was *not* my soul grieved for the poor? 26 When I looked for good, then evil came *unto me :* and when I waited for light, there came darkness. 27 My bowels boiled, and rested not : the days of affliction prevented me. 28 I went mourning without the sun : I stood up, *and* I cried in the congregation. 29 I am a brother to dragons, and a companion to owls. 30 My skin is black upon me, and my bones are burned with heat. 31 My harp also is *turned* to mourning, and my organ into the voice of them that weep.

In this second part of Job's complaint, which is very bitter, and has a great many sorrowful accents in it, we may observe a great deal that he complains of and some little that he comforts himself with.

I. Here is much that he complains of.

1. In general, it was a day of great affliction and sorrow. (1.) Affliction seized him, and surprised him. It seized him (*v.* 16): *The days of affliction have taken hold upon me, have caught me* (so some); *they have arrested me,* as the bailiff arrests the debtor, claps him on the back, and secures him. When trouble comes with commission it will take fast hold, and not lose its hold. It surprised him (*v.* 27): "*The days of affliction prevented me,*" that is, "they came upon me without giving me any previous warning. I did not expect them, nor make any provision for such an evil day." Observe, He reckons his affliction by days, which will soon be numbered and finished, and are nothing to the ages of eternity, 2 Cor. iv. 17. (2.) He was in great sorrow by reason of it. His *bowels boiled* with grief, *and rested not, v.* 27. The sense of his calamities was continually preying upon his spirits without any intermission. He *went mourning* from day to day, always sighing, always weeping ; and such a cloud was constantly upon his mind that he went, in effect, *without the sun, v.* 28. He had nothing that he could take any comfort in. He abandoned himself to perpetual sorrow, as one that, like Jacob, resolved to go to the

grave mourning. He walked out of the sun (so some) in dark shady places, as melancholy people use to do. If he went into the congregation, to join with them in solemn worship, instead of standing up calmly to desire their prayers, he *stood up and cried* aloud, through pain of body, or anguish of mind, like one half distracted. If he appeared in public, to receive visits, when the fit came upon him he could not contain himself, nor preserve due decorum, but stood up and shrieked aloud. Thus he was *a brother to dragons and owls* (v. 29), both in choosing solitude and retirement, as they do (Isa. xxxiv. 13), and in making a fearful hideous noise as they do; his inconsiderate complaints were fitly compared to their inarticulate ones.

2. The terror and trouble that seized his soul were the sorest part of his calamity, *v.* 15, 16. (1.) If he looked forward, he saw every thing frightful before him: if he endeavoured to shake off his terrors, they turned furiously upon him: if he endeavoured to escape from them, they pursued his soul as swiftly and violently as the wind. He complained, at first, of the *terrors of God setting themselves in array against him*, ch. vi. 4. And still, which way soever he looked, they turned upon him; which way soever he fled, they pursued him. *My soul* (Heb., *my principal one, my princess);* the soul is the principal part of the man; it is our glory; it is every way more excellent than the body, and therefore that which pursues the soul, and threatens that, should be most dreaded. (2.) If he looked back, he saw all the good he had formerly enjoyed removed from him, and nothing left him but the bitter remembrance of it: *My welfare* and prosperity *pass away*, as suddenly, swiftly, and irrecoverably, *as a cloud.* (3.) If he looked within, he found his spirit quite sunk and unable to bear his infirmity, not only wounded, but *poured out upon him, v.* 16. He was not only weak as water, but, in his own apprehension, lost as water spilt upon the ground. Compare Ps. xxii. 14, *My heart is melted like wax.*

3. His bodily diseases were very grievous; for, (1.) He was full of pain, piercing pain, pain that went to the bone, to all his bones, *v.* 17. It was a *sword in his bones*, which *pierced him in the night season*, when he should have been refreshed with sleep. His nerves were affected with strong convulsions; his *sinews took no rest* By reason of his pain, he could take no rest, but sleep departed from his eyes. *His bones were burnt with heat, v.* 30. He was in a constant fever, which dried up the radical moisture, and even consumed the marrow in his bones. See how frail our bodies are, which carry in themselves the seeds of our own disease and death. (2.) He was full of sores. Some that are pained in their bones, yet sleep in a whole skin, but, Satan's commission against Job extending both to his bone and to his flesh,

he spared neither. His *skin was black upon him, v.* 30. The blood settled, and the sores suppurated and by degrees scabbed over, which made his skin look black. Even his garment had its colour changed with the continual running of his boils, and the soft clothing he used to wear had now grown so stiff that all his garments were *like his collar, v.* 18. It would be noisome to describe what a condition poor Job was in for want of clean linen and good attendance, and what filthy rags all his clothes were. Some think that, among other diseases, Job was ill of a quinsy or swelling in his throat, and that it was this which bound him about like a stiff collar. Thus was he *cast into the mire* (v. 19), *compared to mire* (so some); his body looked more like a heap of dirt than any thing else. Let none be proud of their clothing nor proud of their cleanness; they know not but some disease or other may *change their garments*, and even *throw them into the mire*, and make them noisome both to themselves and others. *Instead of sweet smell, there shall be a stench*, Isa. iii. 24. We are but dust and ashes at the best, and our bodies are vile bodies; but we are apt to forget it, till God, by some sore disease, makes us sensibly to feel and own what we are. "*I have become already like* that *dust and ashes* into which I must shortly be resolved: wherever I go I carry my grave about with me."

4. That which afflicted him most of all was that God seemed to be his enemy and to fight against him. It was *he* that *cast him into the mire* (v. 19), and seemed to trample on him when he had him there. This cut him to the heart more than any thing else, (1.) That God did not appear for him. He addressed himself to him, but gained no grant—appealed to him, but gained no sentence; he was very importunate in his applications, but in vain (v. 20): " *I cry unto thee*, as one in earnest, *I stand up*, and cry, as one waiting for an answer, but thou hearest not, *thou regardest not*, for any thing I can perceive." If our most fervent prayers bring not in speedy and sensible returns, we must not think it strange. Though the seed of Jacob did never seek in vain, yet they have often thought that they did and that God has not only been deaf, but angry, at the prayers of his people, Ps. lxxx. 4. (2.) That God did appear against him. That which he here says of God is one of the worst words that ever Job spoke (v. 21): *Thou hast become cruel to me.* Far be it from the God of mercy and grace that he should be cruel to any (his compassions fail not), but especially that he should be so to his own children. Job was unjust and ungrateful when he said so of him: but harbouring hard thoughts of God was the sin which did, at this time, most easily beset him. Here, [1.] He thought God fought against him and stirred up his whole strength to ruin him: *With thy strong hand thou opposest thyself*, or art an adversary against me.

He had better thoughts of God (*ch.* xxiii. 6) when he concluded he would *not plead against him with his great power.* God has an absolute sovereignty and an irresistible strength, but he never uses either the one or the other for the crushing or oppressing of any. [2.] He thought he insulted over him (*v.* 22): *Thou liftest me up to the wind,* as a feather or the chaff which the wind plays with ; so unequal a match did Job think himself for Omnipotence, and so unable was he to help himself when he was made to ride, not in triumph, but in terror, upon the wings of the wind, and the judgments of God did even *dissolve his substance,* as a cloud is dissolved and dispersed by the wind. Man's substance, take him in his best estate, is nothing before the power of God ; it is soon dissolved.

5. He expected no other now than that God, by these troubles, would shortly make an end of him : " If I be made to ride upon the wind, I can count upon no other than to break my neck shortly ;" and he speaks as if God had no other design upon him than that in all his dealings with him: " *I know that thou wilt bring me,* with so much the more terror, *to death,* though I might have been brought thither without all this ado, for it is *the house appointed for all living,*" *v.* 23. The grave is a house, a narrow, dark, cold, ill-furnished house, but it will be our residence, where we shall rest and be safe. It is our long home, our own home; for it is our mother's lap, and in it we are gathered to our fathers. It is a house appointed for us by him that has appointed us the bounds of all our habitations. It is appointed for all living. It is the common receptacle, where rich and poor meet; it is appointed for the general rendezvous. We must all be brought thither shortly. It is God that brings us to it, for the keys of death and the grave are in his hand, and we may all know that, sooner or later, he will bring us thither. It would be well for us if we would duly consider it. *The living know that they shall die ;* let us, each of us, know it with application.

6. There were two things that aggravated his trouble, and made it the less tolerable :— (1.) That it was a very great disappointment to his expectation (*v.* 26): " *When I looked for good,* for more good, or at least for the continuance of what I had, *then evil came*"— such uncertain things are all our worldly enjoyments, and such a folly is it to feed ourselves with great expectations from them. Those that wait for light from the sparks of their creature comforts will be wretchedly disappointed and will *make their bed in the darkness.* (2.) That it was a very great change in his condition (*v.* 31): " *My harp is* not only laid by, and hung upon the willow-trees, but it is *turned to mourning, and my organ into the voice of those that weep.*" Job, in his prosperity, had taken *the timbrel and harp,*

and *rejoiced at the sound of the organ, ch.* xxi. 12. Notwithstanding his gravity and grace, he had found time to be cheerful ; but now his tune was altered. Let those therefore that rejoice be *as though they rejoiced not,* for they know not how soon their *laughter* will be *turned into mourning and their joy into heaviness.* Thus we see how much Job complains of; but,

II. Here is something in the midst of all with which he comforts himself, and it is but a little. 1. He foresees, with comfort, that death will be the period of all his calamities (*v.* 24): Though God now, with a strong hand, opposed himself against him, " yet," says he, " *he will not stretch out his hand to the grave.*" The hand of God's wrath would bring him to death, but would not follow him beyond death; his soul would be safe and happy in the world of spirits, his body safe and easy in the dust. Though men *cry in his destruction* (though, when they are dying, there is a great deal of agony and out-cry, many a sigh, and groan, and complaint), yet in the grave they feel nothing, they fear nothing, but all is quiet there. "Though in hell, which is called *destruction,* they cry, yet not in the grave; and, being delivered from the second death, the first to me will be an effectual relief." Therefore he wished he might be *hidden in the grave, ch.* xiv. 13. 2. He reflects with comfort upon the concern he always had for the calamities of others when he was himself at ease (*v.* 25): *Did not I weep for him that was in trouble ?* Some think he herein complains of God, thinking it very hard that he who had shown mercy to others should not himself find mercy. I would rather take it as a quieting consideration to himself; his conscience witnessed for him that he had always sympathized with persons in misery and done what he could to help them, and therefore he had reason to expect that, at length, both God and his friends would pity him. Those who mourn with them that mourn will bear their own sorrows the better when it comes to their turn to drink of the bitter cup. *Did not my soul burn for the poor ?* so some read it, comparing it with that of St. Paul, 2 Cor. xi. 29, *Who is offended, and I burn not ?* As those who have been unmerciful and hard-hearted to others may expect to hear of it from their own consciences, when they are themselves in trouble, so those who have considered the poor and succoured them shall have the remembrance thereof to make their bed easy in their sickness, Ps. xli. 1, 3.

CHAP. XXXI.

Job had often protested his integrity in general ; here he does it in particular instances, not in a way of commendation (for he does not here proclaim his good deeds), but in his own just and necessary vindication, to clear himself from those crimes with which his friends had falsely charged him, which is a debt every man owes to his own reputation. Job's friends had been particular in their articles of impeachment against him, and therefore he is so in his protestation, which seems to refer especially to what Eliphaz had accused him of, ch. xxii. 6, &c. They had produced no witnesses against him, neither could they prove the things whereof they now accused him, and therefore he may well be admittted to purge himself upon oath, which he does very solemnly, and with many awful imprecations of God's wrath if he were guilty of those crimes. This protestation con firms God's character of him, that there was none like him in the earth. Perhaps some of his accusers durst not have joined with him; for he not only acquits himself from those gross sins which lie open to the eye of the world, but from many secret sins which, if he had been guilty of them, nobody could have charged him with, because he will prove himself no hypocrite. Nor does he only maintain the cleanness of his practices, but shows also that in them he went upon good principles, that the reason of his eschewing evil was because he feared God, and his piety was at the bottom of his justice and charity; and this crowns the proof of his sincerity. I. The sins from which he here acquits himself are, 1. Wantonness and uncleanness of heart, ver. 1—4. 2. Fraud and injustice in commerce, ver. 4—8. 3. Adultery, ver. 9—12. 4. Haughtiness and severity towards his servants, ver. 13—15. 5. Unmercifulness to the poor, the widows, and the fatherless, ver. 16—23. 6. Confidence in his worldly wealth, ver. 24, 25. 7. Idolatry, ver. 26—28. 8. Revenge, ver. 29—31. 9. Neglect of poor strangers, ver. 32. 10. Hypocrisy in concealing his own sins and cowardice in conniving at the sins of others, ver. 33, 34. 11. Oppression, and the violent invasion of other people's rights, ver. 38—40. And, towards the close, he appeals to God's judgment concerning his integrity, ver. 35—37. Now, II. In all this we may see, 1. The sense of the patriarchal age concerning good and evil and what was so long ago condemned as sinful, that is, both hateful and hurtful. 2. A noble pattern of piety and virtue proposed to us for our imitation, which, if our consciences can witness for us that we conform to it, will be our rejoicing, as it was Job's, in the day of evil.

I MADE a covenant with mine eyes; why then should I think upon a maid? 2 For what portion of God *is there* from above? and *what* inheritance of the Almighty from on high? 3 *Is* not destruction to the wicked? and a strange *punishment* to the workers of iniquity? 4 Doth not he see my ways, and count all my steps? 5 If I have walked with vanity, or if my foot hath hasted to deceit; 6 Let me be weighed in an even balance, that God may know mine integrity. 7 If my step hath turned out of the way, and mine heart walked after mine eyes, and if any blot hath cleaved to mine hands; 8 *Then* let me sow, and let another eat; yea, let my offspring be rooted out.

The lusts of the flesh, and the love of the world, are the two fatal rocks on which multitudes split; against these Job protests he was always careful to stand upon his guard.

I. Against the lusts of the flesh. He not only kept himself clear from adultery, from defiling his neighbours' wives (*v.* 9), but from all lewdness with any women whatsoever. He kept no concubine, no mistress, but was inviolably faithful to the marriage bed, though his wife was none of the wisest, best, or kindest. From the beginning it was so, that a man should have but one wife and cleave to her only; and Job kept closely to that institution and abhorred the thought of transgressing it; for, though his greatness might tempt him to it, his goodness kept him from it. Job was now in pain and sickness of body, and under that affliction it is in a particular manner comfortable if our consciences can witness for us that we have been careful to preserve our bodies in chastity and to possess those vessels in sanctification and honour, pure from the lusts of uncleanness. Now observe here,

1. What the resolutions were which, in this matter, he kept to (*v.* 1): *I made a covenant with my eyes,* that is, "I watched against the occasions of the sin; *why then should I think upon a maid?*" that is, "by that means, through the grace of God, I kept myself from the very first step towards it." So far was he from wanton dalliances, or any act of lasciviousness, that, (1.) He would not so much as admit a wanton look. *He made a covenant with his eyes,* made this bargain with them, that he would allow them the pleasure of beholding the light of the sun and the glory of God shining in the visible creation, provided they would never fasten upon any object that might occasion any impure imaginations, much less any impure desires, in his mind; and under this penalty, that, if they did, they must smart for it in penitential tears. Note, Those that would keep their hearts pure must guard their eyes, which are both the outlets and inlets of uncleanness. Hence we read of *wanton* eyes (Isa. iii. 16) and *eyes full of adultery*, 2 Pet. ii. 14. The first sin began in the eye, Gen. iii. 6. What we must not meddle with we must not lust after; and what we must not lust after we must not look at; not the forbidden wealth (Prov. xxiii. 5), not the forbidden wine (Prov. xxiii. 31), not the forbidden woman, Matt. v. 28. (2.) He would not so much as allow a wanton thought: "*Why then should I think upon a maid* with any unchaste fancy or desire towards her?" Shame and sense of honour might restrain him from soliciting the chastity of a beautiful virgin, but only grace and the fear of God would restrain him from so much as thinking of it. Those are not chaste that are not so in spirit as well as body, 1 Cor. vii. 34. See how Christ's exposition of the seventh commandment agrees with the ancient sense of it, and how much better Job understood it than the Pharisees, though they sat in Moses's chair.

2. What the reasons were which, in this matter, he was governed by. It was not for fear of reproach among men, though that is to be considered (Prov. vi. 33), but for fear of the wrath and curse of God. He knew very well, (1.) That uncleanness is a sin that forfeits all good, and shuts us out from the hope of it (*v.* 2): *What portion of God is there from above?* What blessing can such impure sinners expect from the pure and holy God, or what token of his favour? What inheritance of the Almighty can they look for from on high? There is no portion, no inheritance, no true happiness, for a soul, but what is in God, in the Almighty, and what comes from above, from on high. Those that wallow in uncleanness render themselves utterly unfit for communion with God, either in grace here or in glory hereafter, and become allied to unclean spirits, which are for ever separated from him; and then what portion, what inheritance, can they have with God?

No unclean thing shall enter into the New Jerusalem, that holy city. (2.) It is a sin that incurs divine vengeance, *v.* 3. It will certainly be the sinner's ruin if it be not repented of in time. *Is not destruction,* a swift and sure destruction, *to* those *wicked* people, *and a strange punishment to the workers of* this *iniquity?* Fools make a mock at this sin, make a jest of it; it is with them a peccadillo, a trick of youth. But they deceive themselves with vain words, for because of these things, how light soever they make of them, the wrath of God, the insupportable wrath of the eternal God, *comes upon the children of disobedience,* Eph. v. 6. There are some sinners whom God sometimes goes out of the common road of Providence to meet with; such are these. The destruction of Sodom is a strange punishment. *Is there not alienation* (so some read it) *to the workers of iniquity?* This is the sinfulness of the sin that it alienates the mind from God (Eph. iv. 18, 19), and this is the punishment of the sinners that they shall be eternally set at a distance from him, Rev. xxii. 15. (3.) It cannot be hidden from the all-seeing God. A wanton thought cannot be so close, nor a wanton look so quick, as to escape his cognizance, much less any act of uncleanness so secretly done as to be out of his sight. If Job was at any time tempted to this sin, he restrained himself from it, and all approaches to it, with this pertinent thought (*v.* 4), *Doth not he see my ways;* as Joseph did (Gen. xxxix. 9), *How can I do it, and sin against God?* Two things Job had an eye to:—[1.] God's omniscience. It is a great truth that God's eyes are *upon all the ways of men* (Prov. v. 20, 21); but Job here mentions it with application to himself and his own actions: *Doth not he see my ways? O God! thou hast searched me and known me.* God sees what rule we walk by, what company we walk with, what end we walk towards, and therefore what ways we walk in. [2.] His observance. "He not only sees, but takes notice; he *counts all my steps,* all my false steps in the way of duty, all my by-steps into the way of sin." He not only sees our ways in general, but takes cognizance of our particular steps in these ways, every action, every motion. He keeps account of all, because he will call us to account, will bring every work into judgment. God takes a more exact notice of us than we do of ourselves; for who ever counted his own steps? yet God counts them. Let us therefore walk circumspectly.

II. He stood upon his guard against the love of the world, and carefully avoided all sinful indirect means of getting wealth. He dreaded all forbidden profit as much as all forbidden pleasure. Let us see,

1. What his protestation is. In general, he had been honest and just in all his dealings, and never, to his knowledge, did any body any wrong. (1.) He never *walked with vanity* (*v.* 5), that is, he never durst tell a lie

to get a good bargain. It was never his way to banter, or equivocate, or make many words in his dealings. Some men's constant walk is a constant cheat. They either make what they have more than it is, that they may be trusted, or less than it is, that nothing may be expected from them. But Job was a different man. His wealth was not acquired by vanity, though now diminished, Prov. xiii. 11. (2.) He never *hasted to deceit.* Those that deceive must be quick and sharp, but Job's quickness and sharpness were never turned that way. He never made haste to be rich by deceit, but always acted cautiously, lest, through inconsideration, he should do an unjust thing. Note, What we have in the world may be either used with comfort or lost with comfort if it was honestly obtained. (3.) His *steps never turned out of the way,* the way of justice and fair dealing; from that he never deviated, *v.* 7. He not only took care not to walk in a constant course and way of deceit, but he did not so much as take one step out of the way of honesty. In every particular action and affair we must closely tie ourselves up to the rules of righteousness. (4.) His heart did not *walk after his eyes,* that is, he did not covet what he saw that was another's, nor wish it his own. Covetousness is called the *lust of the eye,* 1 John ii. 16. Achan saw, and then took, the accursed thing. That heart must needs wander that walks after the eyes; for then it looks no further than the things that are seen, whereas it ought to be in heaven, whither the eyes cannot reach: it should follow the dictates of religion and right reason: if it follow the eye, it will be misled to that for which *God will bring men into judgment,* Eccl. xi. 9. (5.) That no *blot had cleaved to his hands,* that is, he was not chargeable with getting any thing dishonestly, or keeping that which was another's, whenever it appeared to be so. Injustice is a blot, a blot to the estate, a blot to the owner; it spoils the beauty of both, and therefore is to be dreaded. Those that deal much in the world may perhaps have a blot come upon their hands, but they must wash it off again by repentance and restitution, and not let it *cleave to their hands.* See Isa. xxxiii. 15.

2. How he ratifies his protestation. So confident is he of his own honesty that, (1.) He is willing to have his goods searched (*v.* 6): *Let me be weighed in an even balance,* that is, "Let what I have got be enquired into and it will be found to weigh well"—a sign that it was not obtained by vanity, for then *Tekel* would have been written on it—*weighed in the balance and found too light.* An honest man is so far from dreading a trial that he desires it rather, being well assured that God knows his integrity and will approve it, and that the trial of it will be to his praise and honour. (2.) He is willing to forfeit the whole cargo if there be found any prohibited or contraband goods, any thing but what he

came honestly by (*v.* 8): "*Let me sow, and let another eat,*" which was already agreed to be the doom of oppressors (*ch.* v. 5), "*and let my offspring, all the trees that I have planted, be rooted out.*" This intimates that he believed the sin did deserve this punishment, that usually it is thus punished, but that though now his estate was ruined (and at such a time, if ever, his conscience would have brought his sin to his mind), yet he knew himself innocent and would venture all the poor remains of his estate upon the issue of the trial.

9 If mine heart have been deceived by a woman, or *if* I have laid wait at my neighbour's door; 10 *Then* let my wife grind unto another, and let others bow down upon her. 11 For this *is* a heinous crime; yea, it *is* an iniquity *to be punished by* the judges. 12 For it *is* a fire *that* consumeth to destruction, and would root out all mine increase. 13 If I did despise the cause of my manservant or of my maidservant, when they contended with me; 14 What then shall I do when God riseth up? and when he visiteth, what shall I answer him? 15 Did not he that made me in the womb make him? and did not one fashion us in the womb?

Two more instances we have here of Job's integrity:—

I. That he had a very great abhorrence of the sin of adultery. As he did not wrong his own marriage bed by keeping a concubine (he did not so much as think upon a maid, *v.* 1), so he was careful not to offer any injury to his neighbour's marriage bed. Let us see here, 1. How clear he was from this sin, *v.* 9. (1.) He did not so much as covet his neighbour's wife; for even *his heart was not deceived by a woman.* The beauty of another man's wife did not kindle in him any unchaste desires, nor was he ever moved by the allurements of an adulterous woman, such as is described, Prov. vii. 6, &c. See the original of all the defilements of the life; they come from a deceived heart. Every sin is deceitful, and none more so than the sin of uncleanness. (2.) He never compassed or imagined any unchaste design. He never *laid wait at his neighbour's door,* to get an opportunity to debauch his wife in his absence, when the good man was not at home, Prov. vii. 19. See *ch.* xxiv. 15. 2. What a dread he had of this sin, and what frightful apprehensions he had concerning the malignity of it—that it was a *heinous crime* (*v.* 11), one of the greatest vilest sins a man can be guilty of, highly provoking to God, and destructive to the prosperity of the soul. With respect to the mischievousness of it, and the punish-

ment it deserved, he owns that, if he were guilty of that heinous crime, (1.) His family might justly be made infamous in the highest degree (*v.* 10): *Let my wife grind to another.* Let her be a *slave* (so some), a *harlot,* so others. God often punishes the sins of one with the sin of another, the adultery of the husband with the adultery of the wife, as in David's case (2 Sam. xii. 11), which does not in the least excuse the treachery of the adulterous wife; but, how unrighteous soever she is, God is righteous. See Hos. iv. 13, *Your spouses shall commit adultery.* Note, Those who are not just and faithful to their relations must not think it strange if their relations be unjust and unfaithful to them. (2.) He himself might justly be made a public example: *For it is an iniquity to be punished by the judges;* yea, though those who are guilty of it are themselves judges, as Job was. Note, Adultery is a crime which the civil magistrate ought to take cognizance of and punish: so it was adjudged even in the patriarchal age, before the law of Moses made it capital. It is an evil work, to which the sword of justice ought to be a terror. (3.) It might justly become the ruin of his estate; nay, he knew it would be so (*v.* 12): *It is a fire.* Lust is a fire in the soul: those that indulge it are said to burn. It consumes all that is good there (the convictions, the comforts), and lays the conscience waste. It kindles the fire of God's wrath, which, if not extinguished by the blood of Christ, will burn to the lowest hell. It will *consume* even *to* that eternal *destruction.* It consumes the body, Prov. v. 11. It consumes the substance; it *roots out all the increase.* Burning lusts bring burning judgments. Perhaps it alludes to the burning of Sodom, which was intended for an example to those who should afterwards, in like manner, live ungodly.

II. That he had a very great tenderness for his servants and ruled them with a gentle hand. He had a great household and he managed it well. By this he evidenced his sincerity that he had grace to govern his passion as well as his appetite; and he that in these two things has the rule of his own spirit is *better than the mighty,* Prov. xvi. 32. Here observe, 1. What were Job's condescensions to his servants (*v.* 13): He did not *despise the cause of his man-servant,* no, nor of his *maid-servant, when they contended with him.* If they contradicted him in any thing, he was willing to hear their reasons. If they had offended him, or were accused to him, he would patiently hear what they had to say for themselves, in their own vindication or excuse. Nay, if they complained of any hardship he put upon them, he did not browbeat them, and bid them hold their tongues, but gave them leave to tell their story, and redressed their grievances as far as it appeared they had right on their side. He was tender of them, not only when they served and pleased him, but even when they contended with him. Herein he was a great example to masters, to *give to their servants that which is just and equal;* nay, to do the same things to them that they expect from them (Col. iv. 1, Eph. vi. 9), and not to rule them with rigour, and carry it with a high hand. Many of Job's servants were slain in his service (*ch.* i. 15—17); the rest were unkind and undutiful to him, and despised his cause, though he never despised theirs (*ch.* xix. 15, 16); but he had this comfort that in his prosperity he had behaved well towards them. Note, When relations are either removed from us or embittered to us the testimony of our consciences that we have done our duty to them will be a great support and comfort to us. 2. What were the considerations that moved him to treat his servants thus kindly. He had, herein, an eye to God, both as his Judge and their Maker. (1.) As his Judge. He considered, " If I should be imperious and severe with my servants, *what then shall I do when God riseth up?* He considered that he had a Master in heaven, to whom he was accountable, who will rise up and will visit; and *we* are concerned to consider *what we shall do in the day of his visitation* (Isa. x. 3), and, considering that we should be undone if God should then be strict and severe with us, we ought to be very mild and gentle towards all with whom we have to do. Consider what would become of us if God should be extreme to mark what we do amiss, should take all advantages against us and insist upon all his just demands from us—if he should visit every offence, and take every forfeiture—if he should always chide, and keep his anger for ever. And let not us be rigorous with our inferiors. Consider what will become of us if we be cruel and unmerciful to our brethren. The cries of the injured will be heard; the sins of the injurious will be punished. Those that showed no mercy shall find none; and what shall we do then? (2.) As his and his servants' Creator, *v.* 15. When he was tempted to be harsh with his servants, to deny them their right and turn a deaf ear to their reasonings, this thought came very seasonably into his mind, " *Did not he that made me in the womb make him?* I am a creature as well as he, and my being is derived and depending as well as his. He partakes of the same nature that I do and is the work of the same hand : *Have we not all one Father ?*" Note, Whatever difference there is among men in their outward condition, in their capacity of mind, or strength of body, or place in the world, he that made the one made the other also, which is a good reason why we should not mock at men's natural infirmities, nor trample upon those that are in any way our inferiors, but, in every thing, do as we would be done by. It is a rule of justice, *Parium par sit ratio—Let equals be equally estimated and treated;* and therefore since there is so great a parity

among men, they being all made of the same mould, by the same power, for the same end, notwithstanding the disparity of our outward condition, we are bound so far to set ourselves upon the level with those we deal with as to do to them, in all respects, as we would they should do to us.

16 If I have withheld the poor from *their* desire, or have caused the eyes of the widow to fail; 17 Or have eaten my morsel myself alone, and the fatherless hath not eaten thereof; 18 (For from my youth he was brought up with me, as *with* a father, and I have guided her from my mother's womb;) 19 If I have seen any perish for want of clothing, or any poor without covering ; 20 If his loins have not blessed me, and *if* he were *not* warmed with the fleece of my sheep ; 21 If I have lifted up my hand against the fatherless, when I saw my help in the gate : 22 *Then* let mine arm fall from my shoulder blade, and mine arm be broken from the bone. 23 For destruction *from* God *was* a terror to me, and by reason of his highness I could not endure.

Eliphaz had particularly charged Job with unmercifulness to the poor (*ch.* xxii. 6, &c.): Thou hast *withholden bread from the hungry, stripped the naked of their clothing,* and sent *widows away empty.* One would think he could not have been so very positive and express in his charge unless there had been some truth in it, some ground, for it; and yet it appears, by Job's protestation, that it was utterly false and groundless; he was never guilty of any such thing. See here,

I. The testimony which Job's conscience gave in concerning his constant behaviour towards the poor. He enlarges most upon this head because in this matter he was most particularly accused. He solemnly protests,

1. That he had never been wanting to do good to them, as there was occasion, to the utmost of his ability. He was always compassionate to the poor, and careful of them, especially the widows and fatherless, that were destitute of help. (1.) He was always ready to grant their desires and answer their expectations, *v.* 16. If a poor person begged a kindness of him, he was ready to gratify him ; if he could but perceive by the widow's mournful craving look that she expected an alms from him, though she had not confidence enough to ask it, he had compassion enough to give it, and *never caused the eyes of the widow to fail.* (2.) He put a respect upon the poor, and did them honour ; for he took the fatherless children to eat with him at his own table: they should fare as he fared,

and be familiar with him, and he would show himself pleased with their company as if they had been his own, v. 17. As it is one of the greatest grievances of poverty that it exposes to contempt, so it is none of the least supports to the poor to be respected. (3.) He was very tender of them, and had a fatherly concern for them, v. 18. He was a father to the fatherless, took care of orphans, brought them up with him under his own eye, and gave them, not only maintenance, but education. He was a guide to the widow, who had lost the guide of her youth; he advised her in her affairs, took cognizance of them, and undertook the management of them. Those that need not our alms may yet have occasion for our counsel, and it may be a real kindness to them. This Job says he did *from his youth, from his mother's womb.* He had something of tenderness and compassion woven in his nature; he began betimes to do good, ever since he could remember; he had always some poor widow or fatherless child under his care. His parents taught him betimes to pity and relieve the poor, and brought up orphans with him. (4.) He provided food convenient for them; they ate of the same morsels that he did (v. 17), did not eat after him, of the crumbs that fell from his table, but with him, of the best dish upon his table. Those that have abundance must not eat their morsels alone, as if they had none but themselves to take care of, nor indulge their appetite with a dainty bit by themselves, but take others to share with them, as David took Mephibosheth. (5.) He took particular care to clothe those that were without covering, which would be more expensive to him than feeding them, v. 19. Poor people may perish for want of clothing as well as for want of food—for want of clothing to lie in by night or to go abroad in by day. If Job knew of any that were in this distress, he was forward to relieve them, and instead of giving rich and gaudy liveries to his servants, while the poor were turned off with rags that were ready to be thrown to the dunghill, he had good warm strong clothes made on purpose for them of *the fleece of his sheep* (v. 20), so that their *loins*, whenever they girt those garments about them, *blessed him;* they commended his charity, blessed God for him, and prayed God to bless him. Job's sheep were burned with fire from heaven, but this was his comfort that, when he had them, he came honestly by them, and used them charitably, fed the poor with their flesh and clothed them with their wool.

2. That he had never been accessory to the wronging of any that were poor. It might be said, perhaps, that he was kind here and there to a poor orphan that was a favourite, but to others he was oppressive. No, he was tender to all and injurious to none. He never so much as *lifted up his hand against the fatherless* (v. 21), never

threatened or frightened them, or offered to strike them; never used his power to crush those that stood in his way or squeeze what he could out of them, though he *saw his help in the gate,* that is, though he had interest enough, both in the people and in the judges, both to enable him to do it and to bear him out when he had done it. Those that have it in their power to do a wrong thing and go through with it, and a prospect of getting by it, and yet do justly, and love mercy, and are firm to both, may afterwards reflect upon their conduct with much comfort, as Job does here.

II. The imprecation with which he confirms this protestation (v. 22): "If I have been oppressive to the poor, *let my arm fall from my shoulder-blade and my arm be broken from the bone,*" that is, "let the flesh rot off from the bone and one bone be disjointed and broken off from another." Had he not been perfectly clear in this matter, he durst not thus have challenged the divine vengeance. And he intimates that it is a righteous thing with God to break the arm that is lifted up against the fatherless, as he withered Jeroboam's arm that was stretched out against a prophet.

III. The principles by which Job was restrained from all uncharitableness and unmercifulness. He durst not abuse the poor; for though, with his help in the gate, he could overpower them, yet he could not make his part good against that God who is the patron of oppressed poverty and will not let oppressors go unpunished (v. 23): "*Destruction from God was a terror to me,* whenever I was tempted to this sin, and *by reason of his highness I could not endure the thought* of making him my enemy." He stood in awe, 1. Of the majesty of God, as a God above him. He thought of his highness, the infinite distance between him and God, which possessed him with such a reverence of him as made him very circumspect in his whole conversation. Those who oppress the poor, and pervert judgment and justice, forget that *he who is higher than the highest regards,* and *there is a higher than they,* who is able to deal with them (Eccl. v. 8); but Job considered this. 2. Of the wrath of God, as a God that would certainly be against him if he should wrong the poor. *Destruction from God,* because it would be a certain and an utter ruin to him if he were guilty of this sin, was a constant terror to him, to restrain him from it. Note, Good men, even the best, have need to restrain themselves from sin with the fear of destruction from God, and all little enough. This should especially restrain us from all acts of injustice and oppression that God himself is the avenger thereof. Even when salvation from God is a comfort to us, yet destruction from God should be a terror to us. Adam, in innocency, was awed with a threatening.

24 If I have made gold my hope,

or have said to the fine gold, *Thou art* my confidence ; 25 If I rejoiced because my wealth *was* great, and because mine hand had gotten much ; 26 If I beheld the sun when it shined, or the moon walking *in* brightness ; 27 And my heart hath been secretly enticed, or my mouth hath kissed my hand : 28 This also *were* an iniquity *to be punished by* the judge : for I should have denied the God *that is* above. 29 If I rejoiced at the destruction of him that hated me, or lifted up myself when evil found him : 30 Neither have I suffered my mouth to sin by wishing a curse to his soul. 31 If the men of my tabernacle said not, Oh that we had of his flesh ! we cannot be satisfied. 32 The stranger did not lodge in the street : *but* I opened my doors to the traveller.

Four articles more of Job's protestation we have in these verses, which, as all the rest, not only assure us what he was and did, but teach us what we should be and do :—

I. He protests that he never set his heart upon the wealth of this world, nor took the things of it for his portion and happiness. He had gold ; he had fine gold. His *wealth was great,* and he *had gotten much.* Our wealth is either advantageous or pernicious to us according as we stand affected to it. If we make it our rest and our ruler, it will be our ruin ; if we make it our servant, and an instrument of righteousness, it will be a blessing to us. Job here tells us how he stood affected to his worldly wealth. 1. He put no great confidence in it : he did not *make gold his hope, v.* 24. Those are very unwise that do, and enemies to themselves, who depend upon it as sufficient to make them happy, who think themselves safe and honourable, and sure of comfort, in having abundance of this world's goods. Some make it their hope and confidence for another world, as if it were a certain token of God's favour ; and those who have so much sense as not to think so yet promise themselves that it will be a portion for them in this life, whereas the things themselves are uncertain and our satisfaction in them is much more so. It is hard to have riches and not to trust in riches ; and it is this which makes it so difficult for *a rich man to enter into the kingdom of God,* Matt. xix. 23 ; Mark x. 24. 2. He took no great complacency in it (*v.* 25) : *If I rejoiced because my wealth was great* and boasted that *my hand had gotten much.* He took no pride in his wealth, as if it added any thing to his real excellency, nor did he think that his might

and the power of his hand obtained it for him, Deut. viii. 17. He took no pleasure in it in comparison with the spiritual things which were the delight of his soul. His joy did not terminate in the gift, but passed through it to the giver. When he was in the midst of his abundance he never said, *Soul, take thy ease* in these things, *eat, drink, and be merry,* nor blessed himself in his riches. He did not inordinately rejoice in his wealth, which helped him to bear the loss of it so patiently as he did. The way to *weep as though we wept not* is to *rejoice as though we rejoiced not.* The less pleasure the enjoyment is the less pain the disappointment will be.

II. He protests that he never gave the worship and glory to the creature which are due to God only ; he was never guilty of idolatry, *v.* 26—28. We do not find that Job's friends charged him with this. But there were those, it seems, at that time, who were so sottish as to worship the sun and moon, else Job would not have mentioned it. Idolatry is one of the old ways which wicked men have trodden, and the most ancient idolatry was the worshipping of the sun and moon, to which the temptation was most strong, as appears Deut. iv. 19, where Moses speaks of the danger which the people were in of being driven to worship them. But as yet it was practised secretly, and durst not appear in open view, as afterwards the most abominable idolatries did. Observe,

1. How far Job kept from this sin. He not only never bowed the knee to Baal (which, some think, was designed to represent the sun), never fell down and worshipped the sun, but he kept his eye, his heart, and his lips, clean from this sin. (1,) He never so much as beheld the sun or the moon in their pomp and lustre with any other admiration of them than what led him to give all the glory of their brightness and usefulness to their Creator. Against spiritual as well as corporal adultery he made a covenant with his eyes ; and this was his covenant, that, whenever he looked at the lights of heaven, he should by faith look through them, and beyond them, to the Father of lights. (2.) He kept his heart with all diligence, that it should not be secretly enticed to think that there is a divine glory in their brightness, or a divine power in their influence, and that therefore divine honours are to be paid to them. Here is the source of idolatry ; it begins in the heart. Every man is tempted to that, as to other sins, when he is *drawn away by his own lust and enticed.* (3.) He did not so much as put a compliment upon these pretended deities, did not perform the least and lowest act of adoration : *His mouth did not kiss his hand,* which, it is likely, was a ceremony then commonly used even by some that yet would not be thought idolaters. It is an old-fashioned piece of civil respect among ourselves, in making a bow, to kiss

the hand, a form which, it seems, was anciently used in giving divine honours to the sun and moon. They could not reach to kiss them, as *the men that sacrificed kissed the calves* (Hos. xiii. 2, 1 Kings xix. 18); but, to show their good will, they kissed their hand, reverencing those as their masters which God has made servants to this lower world, to hold the candle for us. Job never did it.

2. How ill Job thought of this sin, *v.* 28. (1.) He looked upon it as an affront to the civil magistrate: It *were an iniquity to be punished by the judge,* as a public nuisance, and hurtful to kings and provinces. Idolatry debauches men's minds, corrupts their manners, takes off the true sense of religion which is the great bond of societies, and provokes God to give men up to a reprobate sense, and to send judgments upon a nation; and therefore the conservators of the public peace are concerned to restrain it by punishing it. (2.) He looked upon it as a much greater affront to the God of heaven, and no less than high treason against his crown and dignity: For *I should have denied the God that is above,* denied his being as God and his sovereignty as God above. Idolatry is, in effect, atheism; hence the Gentiles are said to be *without God (atheists) in the world.* Note, We should be afraid of every thing that does but tacitly deny the God above, his providence, or any of his perfections.

III. He protests that he was so far from doing or designing mischief to any that he neither desired nor delighted in the hurt of the worst enemy he had. The forgiving of those that do us evil, it seems, was Old-Testament duty, though the Pharisees made the law concerning it of no effect, by teaching, *Thou shalt love thy neighbour and hate thy enemy,* Matt. v. 43. Observe here;

1. Job was far from revenge. He did not only not return the injuries that were done him, not only not destroy those who hated him; but, (1.) He did not so much as rejoice when any mischief befel them, *v.* 29. Many who would not wilfully hurt those who stand in their light, or have done them a diskindness, yet are secretly pleased and laugh in their sleeve (as we say) when hurt is done them. But Job was not of that spirit. Though Job was a very good man, yet, it seems, there were those that hated him; but evil found them. He saw their destruction, and was far from rejoicing in it; for that would justly have brought the destruction upon him, as it is intimated, Prov. xxiv. 17, 18. (2.) He did not so much as wish in his own mind that evil might befal them, *v.* 30. He never *wished a curse to his soul* (curses to the soul are the worst of curses), never desired his death; he knew that, if he did, it would turn into sin to him. He was careful *not to offend with his tongue* (Ps. xxxix. 1), would not *suffer his mouth to sin,* and therefore durst not imprecate any evil, no, not to his worst enemy.

170

If others bear malice to us, that will not justify us in bearing malice to them.

2. He was violently urged to revenge, and yet he kept himself thus clear from it (*v.* 31): *The men of his tabernacle,* his domestics, his servants, and those about him, were so enraged at Job's enemy who hated him, that they could have eaten him, if Job would but have set them on or given them leave. *"O that we had of his flesh!* Our master is satisfied to forgive him, but *we cannot be so satisfied."* See how much beloved Job was by his family, how heartily they espoused his cause, and what enemies they were to his enemies; but see what a strict hand Job kept upon his passions, that he would not avenge himself, though he had those about him that blew the coals of his resentment. Note, (1.) A good man commonly does not himself lay to heart the affronts that are done him so much as his friends do for him. (2.) Great men have commonly those about them that stir them up to revenge. David had so, 1 Sam. xxiv. 4; xxvi. 8; 2 Sam. xvi. 9. But if they keep their temper, notwithstanding the spiteful insinuations of those about them, afterwards it shall be no grief of heart to them, but shall turn very much to their praise.

IV. He protests that he had never been unkind or inhospitable to strangers (*v.* 32) · *The stranger lodged not in the street,* as angels might lately have done in the streets of Sodom if Lot alone had not entertained them. Perhaps by that instance Job was taught (as we are, Heb. xiii. 2) not to be forgetful to entertain strangers. He that is at home must consider those that are from home, and put his soul into their soul's stead, and then do as he would be done by. Hospitality is a Christian duty, 1 Pet. iv. 9. Job, in his prosperity, was noted for good house-keeping: *He opened his door to the road* (so it may be read); he kept the street-door open, that he might see who passed by and invite them in, as Abraham, Gen. xviii. 1.

33 If I covered my transgressions as Adam, by hiding mine iniquity in my bosom: 34 Did I fear a great multitude, or did the contempt of families terrify me, that I kept silence, *and* went not out of the door? 35 Oh that one would hear me! behold, my desire *is, that* the Almighty would answer me, and *that* mine adversary had written a book. 36 Surely I would take it upon my shoulder, *and* bind it *as* a crown to me. 37 I would declare unto him the number of my steps; as a prince would I go near unto him. 38 If my land cry against me, or that the furrows likewise thereof complain; 39 If I have eaten the fruits thereof

without money, or have caused the owners thereof to lose their life : 40 Let thistles grow instead of wheat, and cockle instead of barley. The words of Job are ended.

We have here Job's protestation against three more sins, together with his general appeal to God's bar and his petition for a hearing there, which, it is likely, was intended to conclude his discourse (and therefore we will consider it last), but that another particular sin occurred, from which he thought it requisite to acquit himself. He clears himself from the charge,

I. Of dissimulation and hypocrisy. The general crime of which his friends accused him was that, under the cloak of a profession of religion, he had kept up secret haunts of sin, and that really he was as bad as other people, but had the art of concealing it. Zophar insinuated (*ch.* xx. 12) that he *hid his iniquity under his tongue.* "No," says Job, "I never did (*v.* 33), *I never covered my transgression as Adam,* never palliated a sin with frivolous excuses, nor made fig-leaves the shelter of my shame, nor ever *hid my iniquity in my bosom,* as a fondling, a darling, that I could by no means part with, or as stolen goods which I dreaded the discovery of." It is natural to us to cover our sins ; we have it from our first parents. We are loth to confess our faults, willing to extenuate them and make the best of ourselves, to devolve the blame upon others, as Adam on his wife, not without a tacit reflection upon God himself. But *he that* thus *covers his sins shall not prosper,* Prov. xxviii. 13. Job, in this protestation, intimates two things, which were certain evidences of his integrity :—1. That he was not guilty of any great transgression or iniquity, inconsistent with sincerity, which he had now industriously concealed. In this protestation he had dealt fairly, and, while he denies some sins, was not conscious to himself that he allowed himself in any. 2. That what transgression and iniquity he had been guilty of (*Who is there that lives and sins not ?*) he had always been ready to own it, and, as soon as ever he perceived he had said or done amiss, he was ready to unsay it and undo it, as far as he could, by repentance, confessing it both to God and man, and forsaking it : this is doing honestly.

II. From the charge of cowardice and base fear. His courage in that which is good he produces as an evidence of his sincerity in it (*v.* 34) : *Did I fear a great multitude, that I kept silence?* No, all that knew Job knew him to be a man of undaunted resolution in a good cause, that boldly appeared, spoke, and acted, in defence of religion and justice, and did not fear the face of man nor was ever threatened or brow-beaten out of his duty, but set his face as a flint. Observe, 1. What great conscience Job had made of his duty

as a magistrate, or a man of reputation, in the place where he lived. He did not, he durst not, keep silence when he had a call to speak in an honest cause, or keep within doors when he had a call to go abroad to do good. The case may be such that it may be our sin to be silent and retired, as when we are called to reprove sin and bear our testimony against it, to vindicate the truths and ways of God, to do justice to those who are injured or oppressed, or in any way to serve the public or to do honour to our religion. 2. What little account Job made of the discouragements he met with in the way of his duty. He valued not the clamours of the mob, feared not a great multitude, nor did he value the menaces of the mighty : *The contempt of families never terrified him.* He was not deterred by the number or quality, the scorns or insults, of the injurious from doing justice to the injured ; no, he scorned to be swayed and biassed by any such considerations, nor ever suffered a righteous cause to be run down by a high hand. He feared the great God, not the great multitude, and his curse, not the contempt of families.

III. From the charge of oppression and violence, and doing wrong to his poor neighbours. And here observe,

1. What his protestation is—that the estate he had he both got and used honestly, so that his *land* could not *cry out against him nor the furrows thereof complain* (*v.* 38), as they do against those who get the possession of them by fraud and extortion, Hab. ii. 9—11. The whole creation is said to groan under the sin of man ; but that which is unjustly gained and held cries out against a man, and accuses him, condemns him, and demands justice against him for the injury. Rather than his oppression shall go unpunished the very ground and the furrows of it shall witness against him, and be his prosecutors. Two things he could say safely concerning his estate :—(1.) That he *never ate the fruits of it without money,* v. 39. What he purchased he paid for, as Abraham for the land he bought (Gen. xxiii. 16), and David, 2 Sam. xxiv. 24. The labourers that he employed had their wages duly paid them, and, if he made use of the fruits of those lands that he let out, he paid his tenants for them, or allowed it in their rent. (2.) That he never caused the owners thereof to lose their life, never got an estate, as Ahab got Naboth's vineyard, by killing the heir and seizing the inheritance, never starved those that held lands of him nor killed them with hard bargains and hard usage. No tenant, no workman, no servant, he had, could complain of him.

2. How he confirms his protestation. He does it, as often before, with a suitable imprecation (*v.* 40) : "If I have got my estate unjustly, *let thistles grow instead of wheat,* the worst of weeds instead of the best of

grains." When men get estates unjustly they are justly deprived of the comfort of them, and disappointed in their expectations from them. They sow their land, but they sow not that body that shall be. God will give it a body. It was sown wheat, but shall come up thistles. What men do not come honestly by will never do them any good. Job, towards the close of his protestation, appeals to the judgment-seat of God concerning the truth of it (*v.* 35—37): *O that he would hear me,* even *that the Almighty would answer me!* This was what he often desired and often complained that he could not obtain; and, now that he had drawn up his own defence so particularly, he leaves it upon record, in expectation of a hearing, files it, as it were, till his cause be called.

(1.) A trial is moved for, and the motion earnestly pressed: "*O that one,* any one, *would hear me;* my cause is so good, and my evidence so clear, that I am willing to refer it to any indifferent person whatsoever; but my desire is that the Almighty himself would determine it." An upright heart does not dread a scrutiny. He that means honestly wishes he had a window in his breast, that all men might see the intents of his heart. But an upright heart does particularly desire to be determined in every thing by the judgment of God, which we are sure is according to truth. It was holy David's prayer, *Search me, O God! and know my heart;* and it was blessed Paul's comfort, *He that judgeth me is the Lord.*

(2.) The prosecutor is called, the plaintiff summoned, and ordered to bring in his information, to say what he has to say against the prisoner, for he stands upon his deliverance: "*O that my adversary had written a book*—that my friends, who charge me with hypocrisy, would draw up their charge in writing, that it might be reduced to a certainty, and that we might the better join issue upon it." Job would be very glad to see the libel, to have a copy of his indictment. He would not hide it under his arm, but *take it upon his shoulder,* to be seen and read of all men, nay, he would *bind it as a crown* to him, would be pleased with it, and look upon it as his ornament; for, [1.] If it discovered to him any sin he had been guilty of, which he did not yet see, he should be glad to know it, that he might repent of it and get it pardoned. A good man is willing to know the worst of himself and will be thankful to those that will faithfully tell him of his faults. [2.] If it charged him with what was false, he doubted not but to disprove the allegations, that his innocency would be cleared up as the light, and he should come off with so much the more honour. But, [3.] He believed that, when his adversaries came to consider the matter so closely as they must do if they put the charge in writing, the accusations would be trivial and minute, and every one that saw them would say, "If this

172

was all they had to say against him, it was a shame they gave him so much trouble."

(3.) The defendant is ready to make his appearance and to give his accusers all the fair play they can desire. He will *declare unto them the number of his steps, v.* 37. He will let them into the history of his own life, will show them all the stages and scenes of it. He will give them a narrative of his conversation, what would make against him as well as what would make for him, and let them make what use they pleased of it; and so confident he is of his integrity that as a prince to be crowned, rather than as a prisoner to be tried, he would *go near to him,* both to his accuser to hear his charge and to his judge to hear his doom. Thus the testimony of his conscience was his rejoicing.

Hic murus aheneus esto, nil conscire sibi—

Be this thy brazen bulwark of defence,
Still to preserve thy conscious innocence.

Those that have kept their hands without spot from the world, as Job did, may lift up their faces without spot unto God, and may comfort themselves with the prospect of his judgment when they lie under the unjust censures of men. *If our hearts condemn us not, then have we confidence towards God.*

Thus *the words of Job are ended;* that is, he has now said all he would say in answer to his friends: he afterwards said something in a way of self-reproach and condemnation (*ch.* xl. 4, 5, xlii. 2, &c.), but here ends what he had to say in a way of self-defence and vindication. If this suffice not he will say no more; he knows when he has said enough and will submit to the judgment of the bench. Some think the manner of expression intimates that he concluded with an air of assurance and triumph. He now keeps the field and doubts not but to win the field. *Who shall lay any thing to the charge of God's elect? It is God that justifies.*

CHAP. XXXII.

The stage is clear, for Job and his three friends have sat down, and neither he nor they have any thing more to say; it is therefore very seasonable for a moderator to interpose, and Elihu is the man. In this chapter we have, I. Some account of him, his parentage, his presence at this dispute, and his sentiments concerning it, ver. 1—5. II. The apology he made for his bold undertaking to speak to a question which had been so largely and learnedly argued by his seniors. He pleads, 1. That, though he had not the experience of an old man, yet he had the understanding of a man, ver. 6—10. 2. That he had patiently heard all they had to say, ver. 11—13. 3. That he had something new to offer, ver. 14—17. 4. That his mind was full of this matter, and it would be a refreshment to him to give it vent, ver. 18—20. 5. That he was resolved to speak impartially, ver. 21, 22. And he did speak so well to this matter that Job made no reply to him, and God gave him no rebuke when he checked both Job himself and his other three friends.

SO these three men ceased to answer Job, because he *was* righteous in his own eyes. 2 Then was kindled the wrath of Elihu the son of Barachel the Buzite, of the kindred of Ram: against Job was his wrath kindled, because he justified himself rather than God. 3 Also against his three friends was his wrath kindled, because they had found no answer, and *yet* had condemned Job. 4 Now Elihu had waited till Job had spoken, because they *were* elder than he. 5 When Elihu saw that *there was* no answer in the mouth of *these* three men, then his wrath was kindled.

Usually young men are the disputants and old men the moderators; but here, when old men were the disputants, as a rebuke to them for their unbecoming heat, a young man is raised up to be the moderator. Divers of Job's friends were present, that came to visit him and to receive instruction. Now here we have,

I. The reason why his three friends were now silent. They *ceased to answer him,* and let him have his saying, *because he was righteous in his own eyes.* This was the reason they gave why they said no more, because it was to no purpose to argue with a man that was so opinionative, *v.* 1. Those that are self-conceited are indeed hard to be wrought upon; there is more hope of a fool (a fool of God's making) than of those who are fools of their own making, Prov. xxvi. 12. But they did not judge fairly concerning Job: he was really righteous before God, and not righteous in his own eyes only; so that it was only to save their own credit that they made this the reason of their silence, as peevish disputants commonly do when they find themselves run a-ground and are not willing to own themselves unable to make their part good.

II. The reasons why Elihu, the fourth, now spoke. His name *Elihu* signifies *My God is he.* They had all tried in vain to convince Job, but *my God is he* that can and will do it, and did it at last: he only can open the understanding. He is said to be a *Buzite,* from Buz, Nahor's second son (Gen. xxii. 21), and *of the kindred of Ram,* that is, *Aram* (so some), whence the Syrians or Aramites descended and were denominated, Gen. xxii. 21. *Of the kindred of Abram;* so the Chaldee-paraphrase, supposing him to be first called *Ram—high,* then *Abram—a high father,* and lastly *Abraham—the high father of a multitude.* Elihu was not so well known as the rest, and therefore is more particularly described thus.

1. Elihu spoke because he was angry and thought he had good cause to be so. When he had made his observations upon the dispute he did not go away and calumniate the disputants, striking them secretly with a malicious censorious tongue, but what he had to say he would say before their faces, that they might vindicate themselves if they could. (1.) He was angry at Job, because he thought he did not speak so reverently of God as he ought to have done; and that was too true (*v.* 2): *He justified himself more than God,* that is, took more care and pains to clear himself from the imputation of unrighteousness

in being thus afflicted than to clear God from the imputation of unrighteousness in afflicting him, as if he were more concerned for his own honour than for God's; whereas he should, in the first place, have justified God and cleared his glory, and then he might well enough have left his own reputation to shift for itself. Note, A gracious heart is jealous for the honour of God, and cannot but be angry when that is neglected or postponed, or when any injury is done it. Nor is it any breach of the law of meekness to be angry at our friends when they are offensive to God. *Get thee behind me, Satan,* says Christ to Simon. Elihu owned Job to be a good man, and yet would not say as he said when he thought he said amiss: it is too great a compliment to our friends not to tell them of their faults. (2.) He was angry at his friends because he thought they had not conducted themselves so charitably towards Job as they ought to have done (*v.* 3): *They had found no answer, and yet had condemned Job.* They had adjudged him to be a hypocrite, a wicked man, and would not recede from that sentence concerning him; and yet they could not prove it so, nor disprove the evidences he produced of his integrity. They could not make good the premises, and yet held fast the conclusion. They had no reply to make to his arguments, and yet they would not yield, but, right or wrong, would run him down; and this was not fair. Seldom is a quarrel begun, and more seldom is a quarrel carried on to the length that this was, in which there is not a fault on both sides. Elihu, as became a moderator, took part with neither, but was equally displeased with the mistakes and mismanagement of both. Those that in good earnest seek for truth must thus be impartial in their judgments concerning the contenders, and not reject what is true and good on either side for the sake of what is amiss, nor approve or defend what is amiss for the sake of what is true and good, but must learn to separate between the precious and the vile.

2. Elihu spoke because he thought that it was time to speak, and that now, at length, it had come to his turn, *v.* 4, 5. (1.) He had waited on Job's speeches, had patiently heard him out, until the words of Job were ended. (2.) He had waited on his friends' silence, so that, as he would not interrupt him, so he would not prevent them, not because they were wiser than he, but because they were older than he, and therefore it was expected by the company that they should speak first; and Elihu was very modest, and would by no means offer to abridge them of their privilege. Some certain rules of precedency must be observed, for the keeping of order. Though inward real honour will attend true wisdom and worth, yet, since every man will think himself or his friend the wisest and worthiest, this can afford no certain rule for the outward ceremonial honour, which there-

fore must attend seniority either of age or office; and this respect the seniors may the better require because they paid it when they were juniors, and the juniors may the better pay because they shall have it when they come to be seniors.

6 And Elihu the son of Barachel the Buzite answered and said, I *am* young, and ye *are* very old; wherefore I was afraid, and durst not show you mine opinion. 7 I said, Days should speak, and multitude of years should teach wisdom. 8 But *there is* a spirit in man: and the inspiration of the Almighty giveth them understanding. 9 Great men are not *always* wise: neither do the aged understand judgment. 10 Therefore I said, Hearken to me; I also will show mine opinion, 11 Behold, I waited for your words; I gave ear to your reasons, whilst ye searched out what to say. 12 Yea, I attended unto you, and, behold, *there was* none of you that convinced Job, *or* that answered his words: 13 Lest ye should say, We have found out wisdom: God thrusteth him down, not man. 14 Now he hath not directed *his* words against me: neither will I answer him with your speeches.

Elihu here appears to have been,

I. A man of great modesty and humility. Though a young man, and a man of abilities, yet not pert, and confident, and assuming: his face shone, and, like Moses, he did not know it, which made it shine so much the brighter. Let it be observed by all, especially by young people, as worthy their imitation, 1. What a diffidence he had of himself and of his own judgment (*v.* 6): "*I am young, and therefore I was afraid, and durst not show you my opinion,* for fear I should either prove mistaken or do that which was unbecoming me." He was so observant of all that passed, and applied his mind so closely to what he heard, that he had formed in himself a judgment of it. He neither neglected it as foreign, nor declined it as intricate; but, how clear soever the matter was to himself, he was afraid to deliver his mind upon it, because he differed in his sentiments from those that were older than he. Note, It becomes us to be suspicious of our own judgment in matters of doubtful disputation, to be swift to hear the sentiments of others and slow to speak our own, especially when we go contrary to the judgment of those for whom, upon the score of their learning and piety, we justly have a veneration. 2. What a deference he paid to his

seniors, and what great expectations he had from them, (*v.* 7): *I said, Days should speak.* Note, Age and experience give a man great advantage in judging of things, both as they furnish a man with so much the more matter for his thoughts to work upon and as they ripen and improve the faculties he is to work with, which is a good reason why old people should take pains both to learn themselves and to teach others (else the advantages of their age are a reproach to them), and why young people should attend on their instructions. It is good *lodging with an old disciple,* Acts xxi. 16; Tit. ii. 4. Elihu's modesty appeared in the patient attention he gave to what his seniors said, *v.* 11, 12. He waited for their words as one that expected much from them, agreeably to the opinion he had of these grave men. He gave ear to their reasons, that he might take their meaning, and fully understand what was the drift of their discourse and what the force of their arguments. He attended to them with diligence and care, and this, (1.) Though they were slow, and took up a great deal of time in searching out what to say. Though they had often to seek for matter and words, paused and hesitated, and were unready at their work, yet he overlooked that, and *gave ear to their reasons,* which, if really convincing, he would not think the less so for the disadvantages of the delivery of them. (2.) Though they trifled and made nothing of it, though none of them answered Job's words nor said what was proper to convince him, yet he attended to them, in hopes they would bring it to some head at last. We must often be willing to hear what we do not like, else we cannot prove all things. His patient attendance on their discourses he pleads, [1.] As that which entitled him to a liberty of speech in his turn and empowered him to require their attention. *Hanc veniam petimusque damusque vicissim—This liberty we mutually allow and ask.* Those that have heard may speak, and those that have learned may teach. [2.] As that which enabled him to pass a judgment upon what they had said. He had observed what they aimed at, and therefore knew what to say to it. Let us thoroughly apprized of the sentiments of our brethren before we censure them; for *he that answers a matter before he hears it,* or when he has heard it only by halves, *it is folly and shame to him,* and bespeaks him both impertinent and imperious.

II. A man of great sense and courage, and one that knew as well when and how to speak as when and how to keep silence. Though he had so much respect to his friends as not to interrupt them with his speaking, yet he had so much regard to truth and justice (his better friends) as not to betray them by his silence. He boldly pleads,

1. That man is a rational creature, and therefore that every man has for himself a judgment of discretion and ought to be al-

lowed a liberty of speech in his turn. He means the same that Job did *(ch.* xii. 3, *But I have understanding as well as you)* when he says *(v.* 8), *But there is a spirit in man;* only he expresses it a little more modestly, that one man has understanding as well as another, and no man can pretend to have the monopoly of reason or to engross all the trade of it. Had he meant *I have revelation as well as you* (as some understand it), he must have proved it; but, if he meant only *I have reason as well as you,* they cannot deny it, for it is every man's honour, and it is no presumption to claim it, nor could they gainsay his inference from it *(v.* 10): *Therefore hearken to me.* Learn here, (1.) That the soul is a spirit, neither material itself nor dependent upon matter, but capable of conversing with things spiritual, which are not the objects of sense. (2.) It is an understanding spirit. It is able to discover and receive truth, to discourse and reason upon it, and to direct and rule accordingly. (3.) This understanding spirit is in every man; it is the light *that lighteth every man,* John i. 9. (4.) It is the inspiration of the Almighty that gives us this understanding spirit; for he is the Father of spirits and fountain of understanding. See Gen. ii. 7; Eccl. xii. 7; Zech. xii. 1.

2. That those who are advanced above others in grandeur and gravity do not always proportionably go beyond them in knowledge and wisdom *(v.* 9): *Great men are not always wise;* it is a pity but they were, for then they would never do hurt with their greatness and would do so much the more good with their wisdom. Men should be preferred for their wisdom, and those that are in honour and power have most need of wisdom and have the greatest opportunity of improving in it; and yet it does not follow that great men are always wise, and therefore it is folly to subscribe to the dictates of any with an implicit faith. The aged do not always understand judgment; even *they* may be mistaken, and therefore must not expect to bring every thought into obedience to them: nay, *therefore* they must not take it as an affront to be contradicted, but rather take it as a kindness to be instructed, by their juniors: *Therefore I said, hearken to me, v.* 10. We must be willing to hear reason from those that are every way inferior to us, and to yield to it. He that has a good eye can see further upon level ground than he that is purblind can from the top of the highest mountain. *Better is a poor and wise child than an old and foolish king,* Eccl. iv. 13.

3. That it was requisite for something to be said, for the setting of this controversy in a true light, which, by all that had hitherto been said, was but rendered more intricate and perplexed *(v.* 13): "I must speak, *lest you should say, We have found out wisdom,* lest you should think your argument against Job conclusive and irrefragable, and that Job cannot be convinced and humbled by

any other argument than this of yours, *that God casteth him down and not man,* that it appears by his extraordinary afflictions that God is his enemy, and therefore he is certainly a wicked man. I must show you that this is a false hypothesis and that Job may be convinced without maintaining it." Or, "Lest you should think you have found out the wisest way, to reason no more with him, but leave it to God to thrust him down." It is time to speak when we hear errors advanced and disputed for, especially under pretence of supporting the cause of God with them. It is time to speak when God's judgments are vouched for the patronising of men's pride and passion and their unjust uncharitable censures of their brethren; then we must speak on God's behalf.

4. That he had something new to offer, and would endeavour to manage the dispute in a better manner than it had hitherto been managed, *v.* 14. He thinks he may expect a favourable hearing; for, (1.) He will not reply to Job's protestations of his integrity, but allows the truth of them, and therefore does not interpose as his enemy : *" He hath not directed his words against me.* I have nothing to say against the main scope of his discourse, nor do I differ from his principles. I have only a gentle reproof to give him for his passionate expressions." (2.) He will not repeat their arguments, nor go upon their principles: *" Neither will I answer him with your speeches*—not with the same matter, for should I only say what has been said I might justly be silenced as impertinent,—nor in the same manner; I will not be guilty of that peevishness towards him myself which I dislike in you." The controversy that has already been fully handled a wise man will let alone, unless he can amend and improve what has been done; why should he *actum agere*—do that which has been done already ?

15 They were amazed, they answered no more : they left off speaking. 16 When I had waited, (for they spake not, but stood still, *and* answered no more;) 17 *I said,* I will answer also my part, I also will show mine opinion. 18 For I am full of matter, the spirit within me constraineth me. 19 Behold, my belly *is* as wine *which* hath no vent ; it is ready to burst like new bottles. 20 I will speak, that I may be refreshed : I will open my lips and answer. 21 Let me not, I pray you, accept any man's person, neither let me give flattering titles unto man. 22 For I know not to give flattering titles ; *in so doing* my maker would soon take me away.

Three things here apologize for Elihu's interposing as he does in this controversy which had already been canvassed by such acute and learned disputants :—

1. That the stage was clear, and he did not break in upon any of the managers on either side : *They were amazed* (v. 15); *they stood still, and answered no more,* v. 16. They not only left off speaking themselves, but they stood still, to hear if any of the company would speak their minds, so that (as we say) he had room and fair play given him. They seemed not fully satisfied themselves with what they had said, else they would have adjourned the court, and not have stood still, expecting what might further be offered. And therefore *I said* (v. 17), " *I will answer also my part.* I cannot pretend to give a definitive sentence ; no, the judgment is the Lord's, and by him it must be determined who is in the right and who is in the wrong; but, since you have each of you shown your opinion, I also will show mine, and let it take its fate with the rest." When what is offered, even by the meanest, is offered thus modestly, it is a pity but it should be fairly heard and considered. I see no inconvenience in supposing that Elihu here discovers himself to be the penman of this book, and that he here writes as an historian, relating the matter of fact, that, after he had bespoken their attention in the foregoing verses, they were amazed, they left off whispering among themselves, did not gainsay the liberty of speech he desired, but stood still to hear what he would say, being much surprised at the admirable mixture of boldness and modesty that appeared in his preface.

2. That he was uneasy, and even in pain, to be delivered of his thoughts upon this matter. They must give him leave to speak, for he cannot forbear ; while he is *musing the fire burns* (Ps. xxxix. 3), *shut up in his bones,* as the prophet speaks, Jer. xx. 9. Never did nurse, when her breasts were gorged, so long to have them drawn as Elihu did to deliver his mind concerning Job's case, v. 18—20. If any of the disputants had hit that which he thought was the right joint, he would contentedly have been silent; but, when he thought they all missed it, he was eager to be trying his hand at it. He pleads, (1.) That he had a great deal to say : " *I am full of matter,* having carefully attended to all that has hitherto been said, and made my own reflections upon it. When aged men are drawn dry, and have spent their stock, in discoursing of the divine Providence, God can raise up others, even young men, and fill them with matter for the edifying of his church ; for it is a subject that can never be exhausted, though those that speak upon it may. (2.) That he was under a necessity of saying it : " *The spirit within me* not only instructs me what to say, but puts me on to say it ; so that if I have not vent (such a ferment are my thoughts in) I shall *burst like bottles of new wine* when it is working," v. 19. See what a great grief it is to a good

176

minister to be silenced and thrust into a corner; he is full of matter, full of Christ, full of heaven, and would speak of these things for the good of others, but he may not. (3.) That it would be an ease and satisfaction to himself to deliver his mind (v. 20): *I will speak, that I may be refreshed,* not only that I may be eased of the pain of stifling my thoughts, but that I may have the pleasure of endeavouring, according to my place and capacity, to do good. It is a great refreshment to a good man to have liberty to speak for the glory of God and the edification of others.

3. That he was resolved to speak, with all possible freedom and sincerity, what he thought was true, not what he thought would please (v. 21, 22) : " *Let me not accept any man's person,* as partial judges do, that aim to enrich themselves, not to do justice. I am resolved to flatter no man." He would not speak otherwise than he thought, either, (1.) In compassion to Job, because he was poor and in affliction, would not make his case better than he really took it to be, for fear of increasing his grief ; " but, let him bear it as he can, he shall be told the truth." Those that are in affliction must not be flattered, but dealt faithfully with. When trouble is upon any it is foolish pity to suffer sin upon them too (Lev. xix. 17), for that is the worst addition that can be to their trouble. Thou shalt not countenance, any more than discountenance, *a poor man in his cause* (Exod. xxiii. 3), nor regard a sad look any more than a big look, so as, for the sake of it, to pervert justice, for that is accepting persons. Or, (2.) In compliment to Job's friends, because they were in prosperity and reputation. Let them not expect that he should say as they said, any further than he was convinced that they say right, nor applaud their dictates for the sake of their dignities. No, though Elihu is a young man, and upon his preferment, he will not dissemble truth to court the favour of great men. It is a good resolution he has taken up—*I know not to give flattering titles to men ; I never used myself to flattering language ;*" and it is a good reason he gives for that resolution—*In so doing my Maker would soon take me away.* It is good to keep ourselves in awe with a holy fear of God's judgments. He that made us will take us away in his wrath if we do not conduct ourselves as we should. He hates all dissimulation and flattery, and will soon *put lying lips to silence* and *cut off flattering lips,* Ps. xii. 3. The more closely we eye the majesty of God as our Maker, the more we dread his wrath and justice, and less danger shall we be in of a sinful fearing or flattering of men.

CHAP. XXXIII.

Pompous prefaces, like the teeming mountain, often introduce poor performances ; but Elihu's discourse here does not disappoint the expectations which his preface had raised. It is substantial, and lively, and very much to the purpose. He had, in the foregoing chapter, said what he had to say to Job's three friends ; and now he comes up close to Job himself and directs his speech to him. I. He bespeaks Job's favourable acceptance of what he should say, and desires he would take him for that person whom he had so often wished for, that would plead with him, and receive his plea on God's behalf, ver. 1—7. II. He does, in God's name, bring an action against him, for words which he had spoken, in the heat of disputation, reflecting upon God as dealing hardly with him, ver. 8—11. III. He endeavours to convince him of his fault and folly herein, by showing him, 1. God's sovereign dominion over man, ver. 12, 13. 2. The care God takes of man, and the various ways and means he uses to do his soul good, which we have reason to think he designs when he lays bodily afflictions upon him, ver. 14. (1.) Job had sometimes complained of unquiet dreams, ch. vii. 14. "Why," says Elihu, "God sometimes speaks conviction and instruction to men by such dreams," ver. 15—18. (2.) Job had especially complained of his sicknesses and pains; and, as to these, he shows largely that they were so far from being tokens of God's wrath, as Job took them, or evidences of Job's hypocrisy, as his friends took them, that they were really wise and gracious methods, which divine grace took for the increase of his acquaintance with God, to work patience, experience, and hope, ver. 19—30. And, lastly, he concludes with a request to Job, either to answer him or give him leave to go on, ver. 31—33.

WHEREFORE, Job, I pray thee, hear my speeches, and hearken to all my words. 2 Behold, now I have opened my mouth, my tongue hath spoken in my mouth. 3 My words *shall be of* the uprightness of my heart : and my lips shall utter knowledge clearly. 4 The Spirit of God hath made me, and the breath of the Almighty hath given me life. 5 If thou canst answer me, set *thy words* in order before me, stand up. 6 Behold, I *am* according to thy wish in God's stead : I also am formed out of the clay. 7 Behold, my terror shall not make thee afraid, neither shall my hand be heavy upon thee.

Several arguments Elihu here uses to persuade Job not only to give him a patient hearing, but to believe that he designed him a good office, and to take it kindly, and be willing to receive the instructions he was now about to give him. Let Job consider, 1. That Elihu does not join with his three friends against him. He has, in the foregoing chapter, declared his dislike of their proceedings, disclaimed their hypothesis, and quite set aside the method they took of healing Job. "*Wherefore, Job, I pray thee, hear my speech, v.* 1. They were all in the same song, all spoke in the same strain; but I am trying a new way, *therefore hearken to all my words,* and not to some of them only ;" for we cannot judge of a discourse unless we take it entire and hearken to it all. 2. That he intended to make a solemn business of it, not to put in a word by the by, or give a short repartee, to show his wit: after long silence he *opened his mouth* (v. 2), with deliberation and design. Upon mature consideration he had already begun to speak, and was prepared to go on if Job would encourage him by his attention. 3. That he was resolved to speak as he thought and not otherwise (v. 3) : *My words shall be of the uprightness of my heart,* the genuine product of my convictions and sentiments." There was reason to suspect that Job's three friends did not think, in their consciences, that Job was so bad a man as they had in

their discourses, merely for the support of their hypothesis, represented him to be ; and that was not fair. It is a base thing to condemn those with our tongues, to serve a turn, whom at the same time we cannot but in our consciences think well of. Elihu is an honest man, and scorns to do so. 4. That what he said should be easy, and not dark and hard to be understood : *My lips shall utter knowledge clearly.* Job shall readily comprehend his meaning, and perceive what he aims at. Those that speak of the things of God should carefully avoid all obscurity and perplexedness both of notion and expression, and speak as plainly and clearly as they can ; for by that it will appear that they do themselves understand what they speak of, that they mean honestly, and design the edification of those they speak to. 5. That he would, in his discourse, make the best use he could of the reason and understanding God had given him, that life, that rational soul which he received from *the Spirit of God* and *the breath of the Almighty, v.* 4. He owns himself unfit to enter into the lists with his seniors, yet he desires they will not despise his youth, for that he is God's workmanship as well as they, made by the same hand, endued with the same noble powers and faculties, and designed for the same great end ; and therefore why may not the God that made him make use of him as an instrument of good to Job ? With this consideration also we should quicken ourselves (and perhaps Elihu made that use of it) to do good in our places according to our capacity. God has made us, and given us life, and therefore we should study to use our life to some good purpose, to spend it in glorifying God and serving our generation according to his will, that we may answer the end of our creation and it may not be said that we were made in vain. 6. That he would be very willing to hear what Job could object against what he had to say (v. 5): " *If thou canst, answer me.* If thou hast so much strength and spirit left thee, and art not quite spent with the distemper and the dispute, *set thy words in order,* and they shall have their due consideration." Those that can speak reason will hear reason. 7. That he had often wished for one that would appear for God, with whom he might freely expostulate, and to whom, as arbitrator, he might refer the matter, and such a one Elihu would be (v. 6) : *I am, according to thy wish, in God's stead.* How pathetically had Job wished (*ch.* xvi. 21), *O that one might plead for a man with God !* and (*ch.* xxiii. 3), *O that I knew where I might find him !* Only he would make it his bargain that *his dread should not make him afraid, ch.* xiii. 21. "Now," says Elihu, "look upon me, for this once, as in God's stead. I will undertake to plead his cause with thee and to show thee wherein thou hast affronted him and what he has against thee ; and what appeals or complaints thou hast to make to God make them to me." 8.

That he was not an unequal match for him: "*I also am formed out of the clay.* I also, as well as the first man (Gen. ii. 7), I also as well as thou." Job had urged this with God as a reason why he should not bear hard upon him (*ch.* x. 9), *Remember that thou hast made me as the clay.* "I," says Elihu, " am *formed out of the clay* as well as thou," *formed of the same clay,* so some read it. It is good for us all to consider that we are formed out of the clay; and well for us it is that those who are to us in God's stead are so, that he speaks to us by men like ourselves, according to Israel's wish upon a full trial, Deut. v. 24. God has wisely deposited the treasure in earthen vessels like ourselves, 2 Cor. iv. 7. 9. That he would have no reason to be frightened at the assault he made upon him (*v.* 7): "*My terror shall not make thee afraid,*" (1.) " As thy friends have done with their arguings. I will not reproach thee as they have done, nor draw up such a heavy charge against thee, Nor," (2.) "As God would do if he should appear to reason with thee. I stand upon the same level with thee, and am made of the same mould, and therefore cannot impose that terror upon thee which thou mayest justly dread from the appearance of the divine Majesty." If we would rightly convince men, it must be by reason, not by terror, by fair arguing, not by a heavy hand.

8 Surely thou hast spoken in mine hearing, and I have heard the voice of *thy* words, *saying,* 9 I am clean without transgression, I *am* innocent; neither *is there* iniquity in me. 10 Behold, he findeth occasions against me, he counteth me for his enemy, 11 He putteth my feet in the stocks, he marketh all my paths. 12 Behold, *in* this thou art not just: I will answer thee, that God is greater than man. 13 Why dost thou strive against him? for he giveth not account of any of his matters.

In these verses,

I. Elihu particularly charges Job with some indecent expressions that had dropped from him, reflecting upon the justice and goodness of God in his dealings with him. He does not ground the charge upon report, but was himself an ear-witness of what he here reproves him for (*v.* 8): "*Thou hast spoken it in my hearing,* and in the hearing of all this company." He had it not at second hand; if so, he would have hoped it was not so bad as it was represented. He did not hear it from Job in private conversation, for then he would not have been so ill-bred as to repeat it thus publicly; but Job had said it openly, and therefore it was fit he should be openly reproved for it. *Those that sin before all rebuke before all.* When we hear any thing said that tends to God's dis-

honour we ought publicly to bear our testimony against it. What is said amiss in our hearing we are concerned to reprove; for *you are my witnesses, saith the Lord,* to confront the accuser. 1. Job had represented himself as innocent (*v.* 9): Thou hast said, *I am clean without transgression.* Job had not said this *totidem verbis—in so many words;* nay, he had owned himself to have sinned and to be impure before God; but he had indeed said, *Thou knowest that I am not wicked, my righteousness I hold fast,* and the like, on which Elihu might ground this charge. It was true that Job was a perfect and an upright man and not such à one as his friends had represented him; but he ought not to have insisted so much upon it, as if God had therefore done him wrong in afflicting him. Yet, it should seem, Elihu did not deal fairly in charging Job with saying that he was clean and innocent from all transgression, when he only pleaded that he was upright and innocent from the great transgression. But those that speak passionately and unwarily must thank themselves if they be misunderstood; they should have taken more care. 2. He had represented God as severe in marking what he did amiss and taking all advantages against him (*v.* 10, 11), as if he sought opportunity to pick quarrels with him. *He findeth occasions against me,* which supposes seeking them. To this purport Job had spoken, *ch.* xiv. 16, 17, *Dost thou not watch over my sin? He counteth me for his enemy;* so he had expressly said, *ch.* xiii. 24 ; xix. 11. "*He putteth my feet in the stocks,* that, as I cannot contend with him, so I may not be able to flee from him;" this he had said, *ch.* xiii. 27. *He marketh all my paths;* so he had said, *ch.* xiii. 27.

II. He endeavours to convince him that he had spoken amiss in speaking thus, and that he ought to humble himself before God for it, and by repentance to unsay it (*v.* 12): *Behold, in this thou art not just. Here thou art not in the right,* so some read it. See the difference between the charge which Elihu exhibited against Job and that which was preferred against him by his other friends; they would not own that he was just at all, but Elihu only says, " In this, in saying this, thou art not just." 1. "Thou dost not deal justly with God." To be just is to render to all their due; now we do not render to God his due, nor are we just to him, if we do not acknowledge his equity and kindness in all the dispensations of his providence towards us, that he is righteous in all his ways, and that, however it be, yet he is good. 2. "Thou dost not speak the language of a righteous man. I do not deny but thou art such a one, but in this thou dost not make it to appear." Many that are just yet, in some particular instances, do not speak and act like themselves; and as, on the one hand, we must not fail to tell even a good man wherein he mistakes and does amiss, nor flatter him in his errors and passions, for in that we are not kind, so on the other hand we must not draw men's characters, nor pass a judgment on them, from one instance, or some few misplaced words, for in that we are not just. *In many things we all offend,* and therefore must be candid in our censures. Two things Elihu proposes to Job's consideration, to convince him that he had said amiss:—(1.) That God is infinitely above us, and therefore it is madness to contend with him; for if he plead against us with his great power we cannot stand before him. *I will answer thee,* says Elihu, in one word, which carries its own evidence along with it, *That God is greater than man*; no doubt he is, infinitely greater. Between God and man there is no proportion. Job had himself said a great deal, and admirably well, concerning the greatness of God, his irresistible power and incontestable sovereignty, his terrible majesty and unsearchable immensity. "Now," said Elihu, "do but consider what thou thyself hast said concerning the greatness of God, and apply it to thyself; if he is greater than man, he is greater than thou, and thou wilt see reason enough to repent of these ill-natured, ill-favoured, reflections upon him, and to blush at thy folly, and tremble to think of thy own presumption." Note, There is enough in this one plain unquestionable truth, *That God is greater than man,* if duly improved, for ever to put to silence and to shame all our complaints of his providence and our exceptions against his dealings with us. He is not only more wise and powerful than we are, and therefore it is to no purpose to contend with him who will be too hard for us, but more holy, just, and good, for these are the transcendent glories and excellencies of the divine nature; in these God is greater than man, and therefore it is absurd and unreasonable to find fault with him, for he is certainly in the right. (2.) That God is not accountable to us (*v.* 13): *Why dost thou strive against him?* Those that complain of God strive against him, implead him, impeach him, bring an action against him. And why do they do so? For what cause? To what purpose? Note, It is an unreasonable thing for us, weak, foolish, sinful, creatures, to strive with a God of infinite wisdom, power, and goodness. Woe to the clay that strives with the potter; *for he gives no account of any of his matters.* He is under no obligation to show us a reason for what he does, neither to tell us what he designs to do (in what method, at what time, by what instruments) nor to tell us why he deals thus with us. He is not bound either to justify his own proceedings or to satisfy our demands and enquiries; his judgments will certainly justify themselves; if we do not satisfy ourselves in them, it is our own fault. It is therefore daring impiety for us to arraign God at our bar, or challenge him to show cause for what he doeth,

to say unto him, *What doest thou?* or, *Why doest thou so?* He gives not account of all his matters (so some read it); he reveals as much as it is fit for us to know, as follows here (*v.* 14), but still there are secret things, which belong not to us, which it is not for us to pry into.

14 For God speaketh once, yea twice, *yet man* perceiveth it not. 15 In a dream, in a vision of the night, when deep sleep falleth upon men, in slumberings upon the bed; 16 Then he openeth the ears of men, and sealeth their instruction, 17 That he may withdraw man *from his* purpose, and hide pride from man. 18 He keepeth back his soul from the pit, and his life from perishing by the sword.

Job had complained that God kept him wholly in the dark concerning the meaning of his dealings with him, and therefore concluded he dealt with him as his enemy. "No," says Elihu, "he speaks to you, but you do not perceive him; so that the fault is yours, not his; and he is designing your real good even in those dispensations which you put this harsh construction upon." Observe in general, 1. What a friend God is to our welfare: *He speaketh to us once, yea, twice, v.* 14. It is a token of his favour that, notwithstanding the distance and quarrel between us and him, yet he is pleased to speak to us. It is an evidence of his gracious design that he is pleased to speak to us of our own concerns, to show us what is our duty and what our interest, what he requires of us and what we may expect from him, to tell us of our faults and warn us of our danger, to show us the way and to lead us in it. This he does once, yea, twice, that is, again and again; when one warning is neglected he gives another, not willing that any should perish. *Precept must be upon precept, and line upon line;* it is so, that sinners may be left inexcusable. 2. What enemies we are to our own welfare: *Man perceives it not,* that is, he does not heed it or regard it, does not discern or understand it, is not aware that it is the voice of God, nor does he receive the things revealed, for they are foolishness to him; he stops his ear, stands in his own light, rejects the counsel of God against himself, and so is never the wiser, no not for the dictates of wisdom itself. God speaks to us by conscience, by providences, and by ministers, of all which Elihu here discourses at large, to show Job that God was both telling him his mind and doing him a kindness, even now that he seemed to keep him in the dark and so treat him as a stranger, and to keep him in distress and so treat him as an enemy. There was not then, that we know of, any divine revelation in writing, and therefore that is not here mentioned among the ways by which God speaks to men, though now it is the principal way.

In these verses he shows how God teaches and admonishes the children of men by their own consciences. Observe,

I. The proper season and opportunity for these admonitions (*v.* 15): *In a dream, in slumberings upon the bed,* when men are retired from the world and the business and conversation of it. It is a good time for them to retire into their own hearts, and commune with them, when they are upon their beds, solitary and still, Ps. iv. 4. It is the time God takes for dealing personally with men. 1. When he sent angels, extraordinary messengers, on his errands, he commonly chose that time for the delivery of their messages, when by deep sleep falling on men the bodily senses were all locked up and the mind more free to receive the immediate communications of divine light. Thus he made his mind known to the prophets by visions and dreams (Num. xii. 6); thus he warned Abimelech (Gen. xx. 3), Laban (Gen. xxxi. 24), Joseph (Matt. i. 20); thus he made known to Pharaoh and Nebuchadnezzar things that should come to pass hereafter. 2. When he stirred up conscience, that ordinary deputy of his, in the soul, to do its office, he took that opportunity, either when deep sleep fell on men (for, though dreams mostly come from fancy, some may come from conscience) or in slumberings, when men are between sleeping and waking, reflecting at night upon the business of the foregoing day or projecting in the morning the business of the ensuing day; then is a proper time for their hearts to reproach them for what they have done ill and to admonish them what they should do. See Isa. xxx. 21.

II. The power and force with which those admonitions come, *v.* 16. When God designs men's good by the convictions and dictates of their own consciences, 1. He gives them admission, and makes them to be heeded: *Then he opens the ears of men,* which were before shut against the voice of this charmer, Ps. lviii. 5. He opens the heart, as he opened Lydia's, and so opens the ears. He takes away that which stopped the ear, so that the conviction finds or forces its way; nay, he works in the soul a submission to the regimen of conscience and a compliance with its rules, for that follows upon God's opening the ear, Isa. l. 5. *God has opened my ear, and I was not rebellious.* 2. He gives them a lodgment in the heart and makes them to abide: *He sealeth their instruction,* that is, the instruction that is designed for them and is suited to them; this he makes their souls to receive the deep and lasting impression of, as the wax of the seal. When the heart is delivered into divine instructions, as into a mould, then the work is done.

III. The end and design of these admoni-

tions that are sent. 1. To keep men from sin, and particularly the sin of pride (*v.* 17). *That he may withdraw man from his purpose,* that is, from his evil purposes, may change the temper of his mind and the course of his life, his disposition and inclination, or prevent some particular sin he is in danger of falling into, that he may withdraw man from his work, may make him leave off man's work, which is working for the world and the flesh, and may set him to work the work of God. Many a man has been stopped in the full career of a sinful pursuit by the seasonable checks of his own conscience, saying, *Do not this abominable thing which the Lord hates.* Particularly, God does, by this means, *hide pride from man,* that is, hide those things from him which are the matter of his pride, and take his mind off from dwelling upon them, by setting before him what reason he has to be humble. That he may *take away pride from man* (so some read it), that he may pluck up that root of bitterness which is the cause of so much sin. All those whom God has mercy in store for he will humble and hide pride from. Pride makes people eager and resolute in the prosecution of their purposes; they will have their way, therefore God withdraws them from their purposes, by mortifying their pride. 2. To keep men from ruin, *v.* 18. While sinners are pursuing their evil purposes, and indulging their pride, their souls are hastening apace to the pit, to the sword, to destruction, both in this world and that to come; but when God, by the admonitions of conscience, withdraws them from sin, he thereby *keeps back* their souls *from the pit,* from the bottomless pit, and saves them from perishing by *the sword* of divine vengeance, so iniquity shall not be their ruin. That which turns men from sin saves them from hell, *saves a soul from death,* James v. 20. See what a mercy it is to be under the restraints of an awakened conscience. Faithful are the wounds, and kind are the bonds, of that friend, for by them the soul is kept from perishing eternally.

19 He is chastened also with pain upon his bed, and the multitude of his bones with strong *pain:* 20 So that his life abhorreth bread, and his soul dainty meat. 21 His flesh is consumed away, that it cannot be seen; and his bones *that* were not seen stick out. 22 Yea, his soul draweth near unto the grave, and his life to the destroyers. 23 If there be a messenger with him, an interpreter, one among a thousand, to show unto man his uprightness: 24 Then he is gracious unto him, and saith, Deliver him from going down to the pit: I have found

a ransom. 25 His flesh shall be fresher than a child's : he shall return to the days of his youth : 26 He shall pray unto God, and he will be favourable unto him : and he shall see his face with joy : for he will render unto man his righteousness. 27 He looketh upon men, and *if any* say, I have sinned, and perverted *that which was* right, and it profited me not ; 28 He will deliver his soul from going into the pit, and his life shall see the light.

God has spoken once to sinners by their own consciences, to keep them from the paths of the destroyer, but they perceive it not; they are not aware that the checks their own hearts give them in a sinful way are from God, but they are imputed to melancholy or the preciseness of their education; and therefore God speaks twice ; he speaks a second time, and tries another way to convince and reclaim sinners, and that is by providences, afflictive and merciful (in which he speaks twice), and by the seasonable instructions of good ministers setting in with them. Job complained much of his diseases and judged by them that God was angry with him ; his friends did so too : but Elihu shows that they were all mistaken, for God often afflicts the body in love, and with gracious designs of good to the soul, as appears in the issue. This part of Elihu's discourse will be of great use to us for the due improvement of sickness, in and by which God speaks to men. Here is,

I. The patient described in his extremity. See what work sickness makes (*v.* 19, &c.) when God sends it with commission. *Do this, and it doeth it.* 1. The sick man is full of pain all over him (*v.* 19): *He is chastened with pain upon his bed,* such pain as confines him to his bed, or so extreme the pain is that he can get no ease, no, not on his bed, where he would repose himself. Pain and sickness will turn a bed of down into a bed of thorns, on which he that used to sleep now tosses to and fro till the dawning of the day. The ·case, as here put, is very bad. Pain is borne with more difficulty than sickness, and with that the patient here is chastened, not a dull heavy pain, but strong and acute ; and frequently the stronger the patient the stronger the pain, for the more sanguine the complexion is the more violent, commonly, the disease is. It is not the smarting of the flesh that is complained of, but the aching of the bones. It is an inward rooted pain ; and not only the bones of one limb, but *the multitude of the bones,* are thus chastened. See what frail, what vile bodies we have, which, though receiving no external hurt, may be thus pained from causes within themselves. See what work sin makes, what mischief it does. Pain is the fruit of sin ;

yet, by the grace of God, the pain of the body is often made a means of good to the soul. 2. He has quite lost his appetite, the common effect of sickness (*v.* 20): *His life abhorreth bread,* the most necessary food, *and dainty meat,* which he most delighted in, and formerly relished with a great deal of pleasure. This is a good reason why we should *not* be *desirous of dainties, because they are deceitful meat,* Prov. xxiii. 3. We may be soon made as sick of them as we are now fond of them ; and those who live in luxury when they are well, if ever they come, by reason of sickness, to loathe dainty meat, may, with grief and shame, read their sin in their punishment. Let us not inordinately love the taste of meat, for the time may come when we may even loathe the sight of meat, Ps. cvii. 18. 3. He has become a perfect skeleton, nothing but skin and bones, *v.* 21. By sickness, perhaps a few days' sickness, *his flesh,* which was fat, and fair, *is consumed away,* that it cannot be seen ; it is strangely wasted and gone : *and his bones,* which were buried in flesh, now *stick out;* you may count his ribs, may tell all his bones. The soul that is well nourished with the bread of life sickness will not make lean, but it soon makes a change in the body.

'He who, before, had such a beauteous air,
And, pampered with his ease, seemed plump and fair
Doth all his friends (amazing change!) surprise
With pale lean cheeks and ghastly hollow eyes ;
His bones (a horrid sight) start through his skin,
Which lay before, in flesh and fat, unseen.''

Sir R. BLACKMORE

4. He is given up for gone, and his life despaired of (*v.* 22): *His soul draws near to the grave,* that is, he has all the symptoms of death upon him, and in the apprehension of all about him, as well as in his own, he is a dying man. The pangs of death, here called *the destroyers,* are just ready to seize him ; they compass him about, Ps. cxvi. 3. Perhaps it intimates the very dreadful apprehensions which those have of death as a destroying thing, when it stares them in the face, who, when it was at a distance, made light of it. All agree when it comes to the point, whatever they thought of it before, that it is a serious thing to die.

II. The provision made for his instruction, in order to a sanctified use of his affliction, that, when God in that way speaks to man, he may be heard and understood, and not speak in vain, *v.* 23. He is happy *if there be a messenger with him* to attend him in his sickness, to convince, counsel, and comfort him, *an interpreter* to expound the providence and give him to understand the meaning of it, *a man of wisdom* that knows the voice of the rod and its interpretation ; for, when God speaks by afflictions, we are frequently so unversed in the language, that we have need of an interpreter, and it is well if we have such a one. The advice and help of a good minister are as needful and seasonable, and should be as acceptable, in sickness, as of a good physician, especially if he be well skilled in the art of explaining and improving providences; he is then *one of a thousand,* and to be valued accordingly. His business at such a time is *to show unto man his uprightness,* that is, God's uprightness, that in faithfulness he afflicts him and does him no wrong, which it is necessary to be convinced of in order to our making a due improvement of the affliction: or, rather, it may mean man's uprightness, or rectitude. 1. The uprightness that *is.* If it appear that the sick person is truly pious, the interpreter will not do as Job's friends had done, make it his business to prove him a hypocrite because he is afflicted, but on the contrary will show him his uprightness, notwithstanding his afflictions, that he may take the comfort of it, and be easy, whatever the event is. 2. The uprightness, the reformation, that *should be,* in order to life and peace. When men are made to see the way of uprightness to be the only way, and a sure way to salvation, and to choose it, and walk in it accordingly, the work is done.

III. God's gracious acceptance of him, upon his repentance, *v.* 24. When he sees that the sick person is indeed convinced that sincere repentance, and that uprightness which is gospel perfection, are his interest as well as duty, then he that waits to be gracious, and shows mercy upon the first indication of true repentance, *is gracious unto him,* and takes him into his favour and thoughts for good. Wherever God finds a gracious heart he will be found a gracious God; and, 1. He will give a gracious order for his discharge. He says, *Deliver him* (that is, let him be delivered) *from going down to the pit,* from that death which is the wages of sin. When afflictions have done their work they shall be removed. When we return to God in a way of duty he will return to us in a way of mercy. Those shall be delivered from going down to the pit who receive God's messengers, and rightly understand his interpreters, so as to subscribe to his uprightness. 2. He will give a gracious reason for this order: *I have found a ransom,* or propitiation; Jesus Christ is that ransom, so Elihu calls him, as Job had called him his Redeemer, for he is both the purchaser and the price, the priest and the sacrifice; so high was the value put upon souls that nothing less would redeem them, and so great the injury done by sin that nothing less would atone for it than the blood of the Son of God, who *gave his life a ransom for many.* This is a ransom of God's finding, a contrivance of Infinite Wisdom; we could never have found it ourselves, and the angels themselves could never have found it. It is *the wisdom of God in a mystery, the hidden wisdom,* and such an invention as is and will be the everlasting wonder of those principalities and powers that desire to look into it. Observe how God glories in the invention here, εὕρηκα, εὕρηκα—"*I have found, I*

have found, the ransom: I, even I, am he that has done it.*"

IV. The recovery of the sick man hereupon. Take away the cause and the effect will cease. When the patient becomes a penitent see what a blessed change follows. 1. His body recovers its health, *v.* 25. This is not always the consequence of a sick man's repentance and return to God, but sometimes it is; and recovery from sickness is a mercy indeed when it arises from the remission of sin; then it is in love to the soul that the body is *delivered from the pit of corruption* when God *casts our sins behind his back,* Isa. xxxviii. 17. That is the method of a blessed recovery. *Son, be of good cheer, thy sins be forgiven thee:* and then, *Rise, take up thy bed, and walk,* Matt. ix. 2, 6. So here, interest him in the ransom, and then *his flesh shall be fresher than a child's* and there shall be no remains of his distemper, but *he shall return to the days of his youth,* to the beauty and strength which he had then. When the distemper that oppressed nature is removed how strangely does nature help itself, in which the power and goodness of the God of nature must be thankfully acknowledged! By such merciful providences as these, which afflictions give occasion for, God speaketh once, yea, twice, to the children of men, letting them know (if they would but perceive it) their dependence upon him and his tender compassion of them. 2. His soul recovers its peace, *v.* 26. (1.) The patient, being a penitent, is a supplicant, and has learned to pray. He knows God will be sought unto for his favours, and therefore *he shall pray unto God,* pray for pardon, pray for health. *Is any afflicted, any sick? Let him pray.* When he finds himself recovering he shall not then think that prayer is no longer necessary, for we need the grace of God as much for the sanctifying of a mercy as for the sanctifying of an affliction. (2.) His prayers are accepted. God *will be favourable to him,* and be well pleased with him; his anger shall be turned away from him, and the light of God's countenance shall shine upon his soul; and then it follows, (3.) That he has the comfort of communion with God. He shall now see the face of God, which before was hid from him, and he shall see it with joy, for what sight can be more reviving? See Gen. xxxiii. 10, *As though I had seen the face of God.* All true penitents rejoice more in the returns of God's favour than in any instance whatsoever of prosperity or pleasure, Ps. iv. 6, 7. (4.) He has a blessed tranquillity of mind, arising from the sense of his justification before God, who *will render unto* this *man his righteousness.* He shall receive the atonement, that is, the comfort of it, Rom. v. 11. Righteousness shall be imputed to him, and peace thereupon spoken, the joy and gladness of which he shall then be made to hear though he could not hear them in the day of his affliction. God will now deal with him as a righteous man, with whom it shall be well. He shall *receive the blessing from the Lord, even righteousness,* Ps. xxiv. 5. God shall give him grace to go and sin no more. Perhaps this may denote the reformation of his life after his recovery. As he shall pray unto God, whom before he had slighted, so he shall render to man his righteousness, whom before he had wronged, shall make restitution, and for the future do justly.

V. The general rule which God will go by in dealing with the children of men inferred from this instance, v. 27, 28. As sick people, upon their submission, are restored, so all others that truly repent of their sins shall find mercy with God. See here, 1. What sin is, and what reason we have not to sin. Would we know the nature of sin and the malignity of it? It is the perverting of that which is right; it is a most unjust unreasonable thing; it is the rebellion of the creature against the Creator, the usurped dominion of the flesh over the spirit, and a contradiction to the eternal rules and reasons of good and evil. It is *perverting the right ways of the Lord* (Acts xiii. 10), and therefore the ways of sin are called *crooked ways,* Ps. cxxv. 5. Would we know what is to be got by sin? *It profiteth us not.* The works of darkness are unfruitful works. When profit and loss come to be balanced all the gains of sin, put them all together, will come far short of countervailing the damage. All true penitents are ready to own this, and it is a mortifying consideration. Rom. vi. 21, *What fruit had you then in those things whereof you are now ashamed?* 2. See what repentance is, and what reason we have to repent. Would we approve ourselves true penitents? We must then, with a broken and contrite heart, confess our sins to God, 1 John i. 9. We must confess the fact of sin *(I have sinned)* and not deny the charge, or stand upon our own justification; we must confess the fault of sin, the iniquity, the dishonesty of it *(I have perverted that which was right);* we must confess the folly of sin—" so foolish have I been and ignorant, for *it profited me not;* and therefore what have I to do any more with it?" Is there not good reason why we should make such a penitent confession as this? For, (1.) God expects it. *He looks upon men,* when they have sinned, to see what they will do next, whether they will go on in it or whether they will bethink themselves and return. He hearkens and hears whether any say, *What have I done?* Jer. viii. 6. He looks upon sinners with an eye of compassion, desiring to hear this from them; for he has no pleasure in their ruin. He looks upon them, and, as soon as he perceives these workings of repentance in them, he encourages them and is ready to accept them (Ps. xxxii. 5, 6), as the father went forth to meet the returning prodigal. (2.) It will turn to our unspeakable advantage.

The promise is general. If any humble himself thus, whoever he be, [1.] ·He shall not come into condemnation, but be saved from the wrath to come: *He shall deliver his soul from going into the pit,* the pit of hell; iniquity shall not be his ruin. [2.] He shall be happy in everlasting life and joy: *His life shall see the light,* that is, all good, in the vision and fruition of God. To obtain this bliss, if the prophet had bidden us do some great thing, would we not have done it? How much more when he only says unto us, *Wash and be clean,* confess and be pardoned, repent and be saved?

29 Lo, all these *things* worketh God oftentimes with man, 30 To bring back his soul from the pit, to be enlightened with the light of the living. 31 Mark well, O Job, hearken unto me: hold thy peace, and I will speak. 32 If thou hast any thing to say, answer me: speak, for I desire to justify thee. 33 If not, hearken unto me: hold thy peace, and I shall teach thee wisdom.

We have here the conclusion of this first part of Elihu's discourse, in which, 1. He briefly sums up what he had said, showing that God's great and gracious design, in all the dispensations of his providence towards the children of men, is to save them from being for ever miserable and bring them to be for ever happy, v. 29, 30. *All these things God is working with the children of men.* He deals with them by conscience, by providences, by ministers, by mercies, by afflictions. He makes them sick, and makes them well again. All these are his operations; he has *set the one over against the other* (Eccl. vii. 14), but his hand is in all; it is he that performs all things for us. All providences are to be looked upon as God's workings with man, his strivings with him. He uses a variety of methods to do men good; if one affliction do not do the work, he will try another; if neither do, he will try a mercy; and he will send a messenger to interpret both. He often works such things as these twice, thrice; so it is in the original, referring to v. 14. He *speaks once, yea, twice:* if that prevail not, he works twice, yea, thrice; he changes his method *(we have piped, we have mourned),* returns again to the same method, repeats the same applications. Why does he take all this pains with man? It is *to bring back his soul from the pit,* v. 30. If God did not take more care of us than we do of ourselves, we should be miserable; we would destroy ourselves, but he would have us saved, and devises means, by his grace, to undo that by which we were undoing ourselves. The former method, by dream and vision, was to *keep back the soul from the pit* (v. 18), that is, to prevent sin, that we might not fall into it. This, by sickness and the word, is to bring back the soul, to recover those that have fallen into sin, that they may not lie still and perish in it. With respect to all that by repentance are brought back from the pit, it is that they may be *enlightened with the light of the living*, that they may have present comfort and everlasting happiness. Whom God saves from sin and hell, which are darkness, he will bring to heaven, the inheritance of the saints in light; and this he aims at in all his institutions and all his dispensations. *Lord, what is man, that thou shouldst thus visit him!* This should engage us to comply with God's designs, to work with him for our own good, and not to counter-work him. This will render those that perish for ever inexcusable, that so much was done to save them and they would not be healed. 2. He bespeaks Job's acceptance of what he had offered and begs of him to *mark it well, v.* 31. What is intended for our good challenges our regard. If Job will observe what is said, (1.) He is welcome to make what objections he can against it (*v.* 32): "*If thou hast any thing to say* for thyself, in thy own vindication, *answer me;* though I am fresh, and thou art spent, I will not run thee down with words: *Speak, for I desire to justify thee*, and am not as thy other friends that desired to condemn thee." Elihu contends for truth, not, as they did, for victory. Note, Those we reprove we should desire to justify, and be glad to see them clear themselves from the imputations they lie under, and therefore give them all possible advantage and encouragement to do so. (2.) If he has nothing to say against what is said, Elihu lets him know that he has something more to say, which he desires him patiently to attend to (*v.* 33): *Hold thy peace, and I will teach thee wisdom.* Those that would both show wisdom and learn wisdom must hearken and keep silence, be swift to hear and slow to speak. Job was wise and good; but those that are so may yet be wiser and better, and must therefore set themselves to improve by the means of wisdom and grace.

CHAP. XXXIV.

Elihu, it is likely, paused awhile, to see if Job had any thing to say against his discourse in the foregoing chapter; but he sitting silent, and it is likely intimating his desire that he would go on, he here proceeds. And, I. He bespeaks not only the audience, but the assistance of the company, ver. 2—4. II. He charges Job with some more indecent expressions that had dropped from him, ver. 5—9. III. He undertakes to convince him that he had spoken amiss, by showing very fully, 1. God's incontestable justice, ver. 10—12, 17, 19, 23. 2. His sovereign dominion, ver. 13—15. 3. His almighty power, ver. 20, 24. 4. His omniscience, ver. 21, 22, 25. 5. His severity against sinners, ver. 26—28. 6. His overruling providence, ver. 29, 30. IV. He teaches him what he should say, ver. 31, 32. And then, lastly, he leaves the matter to Job's own conscience, and concludes with a sharp reproof of him for his peevishness and discontent, ver. 33—37. All this Job not only bore patiently, but took kindly, because he saw that Elihu meant well; and, whereas his other friends had accused him of that from which his own conscience acquitted him, Elihu charged him with that only for which, it is probable, his own heart, now upon the reflection, began to smite him.

FURTHERMORE Elihu answered and said, 2 Hear my words, O ye wise *men;* and give ear unto me,

ye that have knowledge. 3 For the ear trieth words, as the mouth tasteth meat. 4 Let us choose to us judgment: let us know among ourselves what *is* good. 5 For Job hath said, I am righteous: and God hath taken away my judgment. 6 Should I lie against my right? my wound *is* incurable without transgression. 7 What man *is* like Job, *who* drinketh up scorning like water? 8 Which goeth in company with the workers of iniquity, and walketh with wicked men. 9 For he hath said, It profiteth a man nothing that he should delight himself with God.

Here, I. Elihu humbly addresses himself to the auditors, and endeavours, like an orator, to gain their good-will and their favourable attention. 1. He calls them *wise men*, and men that *had knowledge, v.* 2. It is comfortable dealing with such as understand sense. *I speak as to wise men*, who can *judge what I say*, 1 Cor. x. 15. Elihu differed in opinion from them, and yet he calls them wise and knowing men. Peevish disputants think all fools that are not of their mind; but it is a piece of justice which we owe to those who are wise to acknowledge it, though our sentiments do not agree with theirs. 2. He appeals to their judgment, and therefore submits to their trial, *v.* 3. *The ear* of the judicious *tries words*, whether what is said be true or false, right or wrong, and he that speaks must stand the test of the intelligent. As we must prove all things we hear, so we must be willing that what we speak should be proved. 3. He takes them into partnership with him in the examination and discussion of this matter, *v.* 4. He does not pretend to be sole dictator, nor undertake to say what is just and good and what is not, but he is willing to join with them in searching it out, and desires a consultation: "Let us agree to lay aside all animosities and feuds, all prejudices and affectation of contradiction, and all stiffness in adhering to the opinion we have once espoused, and *let us choose to ourselves judgment;* let us fix right principles on which to proceed, and then take right methods for finding out truth; and *let us know among ourselves*, by comparing notes and communicating our reasons, *what is good* and what is otherwise." Note, We are then likely to discern what is right when we agree to assist one another in searching it out.

II. He warmly accuses Job for some passionate words which he had spoken, that reflected on the divine government, appealing to the house whether he ought not to be called to the bar and checked for them.

1. He recites the words which Job had

spoken, as nearly as he can remember. (1.) He had insisted upon his own innocency Job hath said, *I am righteous, v.* 5), and, when urged to confess his guilt, had stiffly maintained his plea of, *Not guilty: Should I lie against my right? v.* 6. Job had spoken to this purport, *My righteousness I hold fast, ch.* xxvii. 6. (2.) He had charged God with injustice in his dealings with him, that he had wronged him in afflicting him and had not righted him: *God has taken away my judgment;* so Job had said, *ch.* xxvii. 2. (3.) he had despaired of relief and concluded that God could not, or would not, help him: *My wound is incurable,* and likely to be mortal, and yet *without transgression; not for any injustice in my hand, ch.* xvi. 16, 17. (4.) He had, in effect, said that there is nothing to be got in the service of God and that no man will be the better at last for his religion (*v.* 9): *He hath said* that which gives occasion to suspect that he thinks *it profiteth a man nothing that he should delight himself with God.* It is granted that there is a present pleasure in religion; for what is it but so delight ourselves with God, in communion with him, in concurrence with him, in walking with him as Enoch did? this is a true notion of religion, and bespeaks its ways to be pleasantness. Yet the advantage of it is denied, as if it were *vain to serve God,* Mal. iii. 14. This Elihu gathers as Job's opinion, by an innuendo from what he said (*ch.* ix. 22), *He destroys the perfect and the wicked,* which has a truth in it (for all things come alike to all), but it was ill expressed, and gave too much occasion for this imputation, and therefore Job sat down silently under it and attempted not his own vindication, whence Mr. Caryl well observes that good men sometimes speak worse than they mean, and that a good man will rather bear more blame than he deserves than stand to excuse himself when he has deserved any blame.

2. He charges Job very high upon it. In general, *What man is like Job? v.* 7. "Did you ever know such a man as Job, or ever hear a man talk at such an extravagant rate?" He represents him, (1.) As sitting in the seat of the scornful: "He *drinketh up scorning like water,*" that is, "he takes a great deal of liberty to reproach both God and his friends, takes a pleasure in so doing, and is very liberal in his reflections." Or, "He is very greedy in receiving and hearkening to the scorns and contempts which others cast upon their brethren, is well pleased with them and extols them." Or, as some explain it, "By these foolish expressions of his he makes himself the object of scorn, lays himself very open to reproach, and gives occasion to others to laugh at him; while his religion suffers by them, and the reputation of that is wounded through his side." We have need to pray that God will never leave us to ourselves to say or do any thing which may *make us a reproach to the foolish,* Ps.

xxxix. 8. (2.) As walking in the course of the ungodly, and standing in the way of sinners: He *goes in company with the workers of iniquity* (*v.* 8), not that in his conversation he did associate with them, but in his opinion he did favour and countenance them, and strengthen their hands. If (as it follows, *v.* 9, for the proof of this) *it profits a man nothing to delight himself in God,* why should he not lay the reins on the neck of his lusts and herd with the workers of iniquity? He that says, I have *cleansed my hands in vain,* does not only *offend against the generation of God's children* (Ps. lxxiii. 13, 14), but gratifies his enemies, and says as they say.

10 Therefore hearken unto me, ye men of understanding: far be it from God, *that he should do* wickedness; and *from* the Almighty, *that he should commit* iniquity. 11 For the work of a man shall he render unto him, and cause every man to find according to *his* ways. 12 Yea, surely God will not do wickedly, neither will the Almighty pervert judgment. 13 Who hath given him a charge over the earth? or who hath disposed the whole world? 14 If he set his heart upon man, *if* he gather unto himself his spirit and his breath; 15 All flesh shall perish together, and man shall turn again unto dust.

The scope of Elihu's discourse is to reconcile Job to his afflictions and to pacify his spirit under them. In order to this he had shown, in the foregoing chapter, that God meant him no hurt in afflicting him, but intended it for his spiritual benefit. In this chapter he shows that he did him no wrong in afflicting him, nor punished him more than he deserved. If the former could not prevail to satisfy him, yet this ought to silence him. In these verses he directs his discourse to all the company: "*Hearken to me, you men of understanding* (*v.* 10), and show yourselves to be intelligent by assenting to this which I say." And this is that which he says, That the righteous God never did, nor ever will do, any wrong to any of his creatures, but his ways are equal, ours are unequal. The truth here maintained respects the justice and equity of all God's proceedings. Now observe in these verses,

I. How plainly this truth is laid down, both negatively and positively. 1. He does wrong to none: *God cannot do wickedness,* nor *the Almighty commit iniquity, v.* 10. It is inconsistent with the perfection of his nature, and so it is also with the purity of his will (*v.* 12): *God will not do wickedly, neither will the Almighty pervert judgment.* He neither can nor will do a wrong thing, nor deal hardly with any man. He will never inflict the evil of punishment but where he finds the evil of sin, nor in any undue proportion, for that would be to commit iniquity and do wickedly. If appeals be made to him, or he be to give a definitive sentence, he will have an eye to the merits of the cause and not respect the person, for that were to pervert judgment. He will never either do any man wrong or deny any man right, but *the heavens will shortly declare his righteousness.* Because he is God, and therefore is infinitely perfect and holy, he can neither do wrong himself nor countenance it in others, any more than he can die, or lie, or deny himself. Though he be Almighty, yet he never uses his power, as mighty men often do, for the support of injustice. He is *Shaddai*—God *all-sufficient,* and therefore he cannot be *tempted with evil* (James i. 13), to do an unrighteous thing. 2. He ministers justice to all (*v.* 11): *The work of a man shall he render unto him.* Good works shall be rewarded and evil works either punished or satisfied for; so that sooner or later, in this world or in that to come, he will cause every man to find according to his ways. This is the standing rule of distributive justice, to give to every man according to his work. *Say to the righteous, it shall be well with them; woe to the wicked, it shall be ill with them.* If services persevered in now go unrewarded, and sins persisted in now go unpunished, yet there is a day coming when God will fully render to every man according to his works, with interest for the delay.

II. How warmly it is asserted, 1. With an assurance of the truth of it: *Yea, surely, v.* 12. It is a truth which none can deny or call in question; it is what we may take for granted and are all agreed in, That God will not do wickedly. 2. With an abhorrence of the very thought of the contrary (*v.* 10): *Far be it from God that he should do wickedness,* and from us that we should imagine such a thing, that we should entertain the least suspicion of it or say any thing that looks like charging him with it.

III. How evidently It is proved by two arguments :—

1. His independent absolute sovereignty and dominion (*v.* 13): *Who has given him a charge over the earth* and deputed him to manage the affairs of men upon the earth? Or, Who besides has disposed the whole world of mankind? He has the sole administration of the kingdoms of men, and has it of himself, nor is he entrusted with it by or for any other. (1.) It is certain that the government is his, and he does according to his will in all the hosts both of heaven and earth; and therefore he is not to be charged with injustice; for *shall not the Judge of all the earth do right?* Gen. xviii. 25. How shall God either rule or judge the world if there be, or could be, any *unrighteousness with him?* Rom. iii. 5, 6. He that is entitled to such unlimited power must certainly have in himself unspotted purity. This is also a good reason why we should acquiesce in all God's dealings with us. Shall not he that disposes of the whole world dispose of us and our concerns? (2.) It is as certain that he does not derive his power from any, nor is it a dispensation that is committed to him, but his power is original, and, like his being, of himself; and therefore, if he were not perfectly just, all the world and the affairs of it would soon be in the utmost confusion. The highest powers on earth have a God above them, to whom they are accountable, because it is not far from them to do iniquity. But *therefore* God has none above him, because it is not possible that he should do any thing (such is the perfection of his nature) that should need to be controlled. And, if he be an absolute sovereign, we are bound to submit to him, for there is no higher power to which we may appeal, so that there virtue is a necessity.

2. His irresistible power (*v.* 14): *If he set his heart upon man,* to contend with him, much more *if* (as some read it) *he set his heart against man,* to ruin him, if he should deal with man either by *summa potestas—mere sovereignty,* or by *summum jus—strict justice,* there were no standing before him; man's spirit and breath would soon be gone and *all flesh would perish together, v.* 15. Many men's honesty is owing purely to their impotency; they do not do wrong because they cannot support it when it is done, or it is not in their power to do it. But God is able to crush any man easily and suddenly, and yet does not by arbitrary power crush any man, which therefore must be attributed to the infinite perfection of his nature, and that is immutable. See here, (1.) What God can do with us. He can soon bring us to dust; there needs not any positive act of his omnipotence to do it; if he do but withdraw that concurrence of his providence by which we live, *if he gather unto himself that spirit and breath* which was from his hand at first and is still in his hand, we expire immediately, like an animal in an air-pump when the air is exhausted. (2.) What he may do with us without doing us any wrong. He may recal the being he gave, of which we are but tenants at will, and which also we have forfeited; and therefore, as long as that is continued of his mere favour, we have no reason to cry out of wrong, whatever other comforts are removed.

16 If now *thou hast* understanding, hear this : hearken to the voice of my words. 17 Shall even he that hateth right govern? and wilt thou condemn him that is most just? 18 *Is it fit* to say to a king, *Thou art* wicked? *and* to princes, *Ye are* ungodly? 19 *How much less to him* that accepteth not the persons of princes, nor regardeth

the rich more than the poor? for they all *are* the work of his hands. 20 In a moment shall they die, and the people shall be troubled at midnight, and pass away: and the mighty shall be taken away without hand. 21 For his eyes *are* upon the ways of man, and he seeth all his goings. 22 *There is* no darkness, nor shadow of death, where the workers of iniquity may hide themselves. 23 For he will not lay upon man more *than right*; that he should enter into judgment with God. 24 He shall break in pieces mighty men without number, and set others in their stead. 25 Therefore he knoweth their works, and he overturneth *them* in the night, so that they are destroyed. 26 He striketh them as wicked men in the open sight of others; 27 Because they turned back from him, and would not consider any of his ways: 28 So that they cause the cry of the poor to come unto him, and he heareth the cry of the afflicted. 29 When he giveth quietness, who then can make trouble? and when he hideth *his* face, who then can behold him? whether *it be done* against a nation, or against a man only: 30 That the hypocrite reign not, lest the people be ensnared.

Elihu here addresses himself more directly to Job. He had spoken to the rest (*v.* 10) as *men of understanding;* now, speaking to Job, he puts an *if* upon his understanding: *If thou hast understanding,* hear this and observe it, *v.* 16.

I. Hear this, That God is not to be quarrelled with for any thing that he does. It is daring presumption to arraign and condemn God's proceedings, as Job had done by his discontents. It was, 1. As absurd as it would be to advance one to power that is a professed enemy to justice: *Shall even he that hates right govern? v.* 17. The righteous Lord so loves righteousness that, in comparison with him, even Job himself, though a perfect and upright man, might be said to hate right; and shall he govern? Shall he pretend to direct God or correct what he does? Shall such unrighteous creatures as we are give law to the righteous God? or must he take his measures from us? When we consider the corruption of our nature, and the contrariety there is in us to the eternal rule of equity, we cannot but see it to be an impudent impious thing for us to prescribe to God. 2. It was as absurd as it would be to call a most righteous innocent person to the bar, and to give judgment against him, though it ap-

peared ever so plainly, upon the trial, that he was most just: *Wilt thou condemn him that is righteous in all his ways,* and cannot but be so? 3. It is more absurd and unbecoming than it would be to say to a sovereign prince, *Thou art wicked,* and to judges upon the bench, *You are ungodly, v.* 18. This would be looked upon as an insufferable affront to majesty and to magistracy; no king, no prince, would bear it. In favour of government, we presume it is a right sentence that is passed, unless the contrary be very evident; but, whatever we think, it is not fit to tell a king to his face that he is wicked. Nathan reproved David by a parable. But, whatever a high priest or a prophet might do, it is not for an ordinary subject to make so bold with the powers that are. How absurd is it then to say so to God—to impute iniquity to him, who, having no respect of persons, is in no temptation to do an unjust thing! *He regardeth not the rich more than the poor,* and therefore it is fit he should rule, and it is not fit we should find fault with him, *v.* 19. Note, Rich and poor stand upon the same level before God. A great man shall fare never the better, nor find any favour, for his wealth and greatness; nor shall a poor man fare ever the worse for his poverty, nor an honest cause be starved. Job, now that he was poor, should have as much favour with God, and be as much regarded by him, as when he was rich; *for they are all the work of his hands.* Their persons are so: the poor are made by the same hand, and of the same mould, as the rich. Their conditions are so: the poor were made poor by the divine providence, as well as the rich made rich; and therefore the poor shall fare never the worse for that which is their lot, not their fault.

II. Hear this, That God is to be acknowledged and submitted to in all that he does. Divers considerations Elihu here suggests to Job, to beget in him great and high thoughts of God, and so to persuade him to submit and proceed no further in his quarrel with him.

1. God is almighty, and able to deal with the strongest of men when he enters into judgment with them (*v.* 20); even *the people,* the body of a nation, though ever so numerous, *shall be troubled,* unhinged, and put into disorder, when God pleases; even *the mighty* man, the prince, though ever so honourable, ever so formidable among men, *shall,* if God speak the word, *be taken away* out of his throne, nay, out of the land of the living; they shall die; they shall pass away. What cannot he do that has all the powers of death at his command? Observe the suddenness of this destruction: *In a moment shall they die.* It is not a work of time, with God, to bring down his proud enemies, but, when he pleases, it is soon done; nor is he bound to give them warning, no, not an hour's warning. *This night thy soul shall be required.* Observe the season of it: *They shall be trou-*

bled at midnight, when they are secure and careless, and unable to help themselves; as the Egyptians when their first-born were slain. This is the immediate work of God: they are taken away, *without hand,* insensibly, by secret judgments. God can himself humble the greatest tyrant, without the assistance or agency of any man. Whatever hand he sometimes uses in the accomplishing of his purposes, he needs none, but can do it without hand. Nor is it one single mighty man only that he can thus overpower, but even hosts of them (*v.* 24): *He shall break in pieces mighty men without number;* for no combined power can stand it out against Omnipotence. Yet, when God destroys tyranny, he does not design anarchy; if those are brought down that ruled ill, it does not therefore follow that people must have no rulers; for, when he breaks mighty men, he *sets others in their stead,* that will rule better, or, if they do not, *he overturns them* also *in the night,* or in a night, *so that they are destroyed, v.* 25. Witness Belshazzar. Or, if he designs them space to repent, he does not presently destroy them, but *he strikes them as wicked men, v.* 26. Some humbling mortifying judgments are brought upon them; these wicked rulers are stricken as other wicked men, as surely, as sorely, stricken in their bodies, estates, or families, and this for warning to their neighbours; the stroke is given *in terrorem—as an alarm to others,* and therefore is given *in the open sight of others,* that they also may see and fear, and tremble before the justice of God. If kings stand not before him, how shall we stand!

2. God is omniscient, and can discover that which is most secret. As the strongest cannot oppose his arm, so the most subtle cannot escape his eye; and therefore, if some are punished either more or less than we think they should be, instead of quarrelling with God, it becomes us to ascribe it to some secret cause known to God only. For, (1.) Every thing is open before him (*v.* 21): *His eyes are upon the ways of man;* not only they are within reach of his eye, so that he can see them, but his eye is upon them, so that he actually observes and inspects them. He sees us all, and sees all our goings; go where we will, we are under his eye; all our actions, good and evil, are regarded and recorded. and reserved to be brought into judgment when the books shall be opened. (2.) Nothing is or can be concealed from him (*v.* 22): *There is no darkness nor shadow of death* so close, so thick, so solitary, so remote from light or sight as that in it *the workers of iniquity may hide themselves* from the discovering eye and avenging hand of the righteous God. Observe here, [1.] The workers of iniquity would hide themselves if they could from the eye of the world for shame (and that perhaps they may do), and from the eye of God for fear, as Adam among the trees of the garden. The day is coming when mighty men, and

chief captains, will call to the rocks and mountains to hide them. [2.] They would gladly be hid even by the shadow of death, be hid in the grave, and lie for ever there, rather than appear before the judgment-seat of Christ. (3.) It is in vain to think of flying from God's justice, or absconding when his wrath is in pursuit of us. The workers of iniquity may find ways and means to hide themselves from men, but not from God: *He knows their works (v.* 25), both what they do and what they design.

3. God is righteous, and, in all his proceedings, goes according to the rules of equity. Even when he is overturning mighty men, and breaking them in pieces, yet *he will not lay upon man more than right, v.* 23. As he will not punish the innocent, so he will not exact of those that are guilty more than their iniquities deserve; and of the proportion between the sin and the punishment Infinite Wisdom shall be the judge. He will not give any man cause to complain that he deals hardly with him, nor shall any man *enter into judgment with God,* or bring an action against him. If he do, God will be justified when he speaks and clear when he judges. Therefore Job was very much to be blamed for his complaints of God, and is here well-advised to let fall his action, for he would certainly be cast or non-suited. *It is not for man ever to purpose to enter into judgment with the Omnipotent;* so some read the whole verse. Job had often wished to plead his cause before God. Elihu asks, "To what purpose? The judgment already given concerning thee will certainly be affirmed; no errors can be found in it, nor any exceptions taken to it, but, after all, it must rest as it is." All is well that God does, and will be found so. To prove that when God destroys the mighty men, and *strikes them as wicked men,* he does not *lay upon them more than right,* he shows what their wickedness was (*v.* 27, 28); and let any compare that with their punishment, and then judge whether they did not deserve it. In short, these unjust judges, whom God will justly judge, neither *feared God nor regarded man,* Luke xviii. 2. (1.) They were rebels to God: They *turned back from him,* cast off the fear of him, and abandoned the very thoughts of him; for *they would not consider any of his ways,* took no heed either to his precepts or to his providences, but lived without God in the world. This is at the bottom of all the wickedness of the wicked, they turn back from God; and it is because they do not consider, not because they cannot, but because they will not. From inconsideration comes impiety, and thence all immorality. (2.) They were tyrants to all mankind, *v.* 28. They will not call upon God for themselves; but they *cause the cry of the poor to come to him,* and that cry is against them. They are injurious and oppressive to the poor, wrong them, crush them, impoverish them yet more, and add affliction to the afflicted, who *cry*

unto God, make their complaint to him, and he hears them and pleads their cause. Their case is bad who have the prayers and tears of the poor against them; for the cry of the oppressed will, sooner or later, draw down vengeance on the heads of the oppressors, and no one can say that this is *more than right*, Exod. xxii. 23.

4. God has an uncontrollable dominion in all the affairs of the children of men, and so guides and governs whatever concerns both communities and particular persons, that, as what he designs cannot be defeated, so what he does cannot be changed, *v.* 29. Observe, (1.) The frowns of all the world cannot trouble those whom God quiets with his smiles. *When he gives quietness* who then *can make trouble? v.* 29. This is a challenge to all the powers of hell and earth to disquiet those to whom God speaks peace, and for whom he creates it. If God give outward peace to a nation, he can secure what he gives, and disable the enemies of it to give it any disturbance. If God give inward peace to a man only, the quietness and everlasting assurance which are the effect of righteousness, neither the accusations of Satan nor the afflictions of this present time, no, nor the arrests of death itself, can give trouble. What can make those uneasy whose *souls dwell at ease in God?* See Phil. iv. 7. (2.) The smiles of all the world cannot quiet those whom God troubles with his frowns; for if he, in displeasure, *hide his face,* and withhold the comfort of his favour, *who then can behold him?* that is, Who can behold a displeased God, so as to bear up under his wrath or turn it away? Who can make him show his face when he resolves to hide it, or see through the clouds and darkness which are round about him? Or, Who can behold a disquieted sinner, so as to give him effectual relief? Who can stand a friend to him to whom God is an enemy? None can relieve the distresses of the outward condition without God. *If the Lord do not help thee, whence shall I?* 2 Kings vi. 27. Nor can any relieve the distresses of the mind against God and his terrors. If he impress the sense of his wrath upon a guilty conscience, all the comforts the creature can administer are ineffectual. *As vinegar upon nitre, so are songs to a heavy heart.* The irresistibleness of God's operations must be acknowledged in his dealings both with communities and with particular persons: what he does cannot be controlled, *whether it be done against a nation* in its public capacity *or against a man only* in his private affairs. The same Providence that governs mighty kingdoms presides in the concerns of the meanest individual; and neither the strength of a whole nation can resist his power nor the smallness of a single person evade his cognizance; but what he does shall be done effectually and victoriously.

5. God is wise, and careful of the public welfare, and therefore provides *that the hy-* pocrite *reign not, lest the people be ensnared, v.* 30. See here, (1.) The pride of hypocrites. They aim to reign; the praise of men, and power in the world, are their reward, what they aim at. (2.) The policy of tyrants. When they aim to set up themselves they sometimes make use of religion as a cloak and cover for their ambition and by their hypocrisy come to the throne. (3.) The danger the people are in when hypocrites reign. They are likely to be ensnared in sin, or trouble, or both. Power, in the hands of dissemblers, is often destructive to the rights and liberties of a people, which they are more easily wheedled out of than forced out of. Much mischief has been done likewise to the power of godliness under the pretence of a form of godliness. (4.) The care which divine Providence takes of the people, to prevent this danger, *that the hypocrite reign not,* either that he do not reign at all or that he do not reign long. If God has mercy in store for a people, he will either prevent the rise or hasten the ruin of hypocritical rulers.

31 Surely it is meet to be said unto God, I have borne *chastisement*, I will not offend *any more:* 32 *That which* I see not teach thou me: if I have done iniquity, I will do no more. 33 *Should it be* according to thy mind? he will recompense it, whether thou refuse, or whether thou choose; and not I: therefore speak what thou knowest. 34 Let men of understanding tell me, and let a wise man hearken unto me. 35 Job hath spoken without knowledge, and his words *were* without wisdom. 36 My desire *is that* Job may be tried unto the end because of *his* answers for wicked men. 37 For he addeth rebellion unto his sin, he clappeth *his hands* among us, and multiplieth his words against God.

In these verses,

I. Elihu instructs Job what'he should say under his affliction, *v.* 31, 32. Having reproved him for his peevish passionate words, he here puts better words into his mouth. When we reprove for what is amiss we must direct to what is good, that our reproofs may be the *reproofs of instruction,* Prov. vi. 23. He does not impose it upon Job to use these words, but recommends it to him, as that which was *meet to be said.* In general, he would have him repent of his misconduct, and indecent expressions, under his affliction. Job's other friends would have had him own himself a wicked man, and by overdoing they undid. Elihu will oblige him only to own that he had, in the management of this controversy, *spoken unadvisedly with his lips.* Let us remember this, in giving reproofs, and not make the matter worse than it is; for the stretching of the crime may defeat the prosecution. Elihu drives the right nail, and speeds accordingly. He directs Job, 1. To humble himself before God for his sins, and to accept the punishment of them: *" I have borne chastisement.* What I suffer comes justly upon me, and therefore I will bear it, and not only justify God in it, but acknowledge his goodness." Many are chastised that do not bear chastisement, do not bear it well, and so, in effect, do not bear it at all. Penitents, if sincere, will take all well that God does, and will bear chastisement as a medicinal operation intended for good. 2. To pray to God to discover his sins to him (*v.* 32): *" That which I see not teach thou me.* Lord, upon the review, I find much amiss in me and much done amiss by me, but I have reason to fear there is much more that I am not aware of, greater abominations, which through ignorance, mistake, and partiality to myself, I do not yet see; Lord, give me to see it, awaken my conscience to do its office faithfully:" A good man is willing to know the worst of himself, and particularly, under affliction, desires to be told wherefore God contends with him and what God designs in correcting him. 3. To promise reformation (*v.* 31): *I will not offend any more.* " If I have done iniquity (or *seeing I have), I will do so no more;* whatever thou shalt discover to me to have been amiss, by thy grace I will amend it for the future." This implies a confession that we have offended, true remorse and godly sorrow for the offence, and a humble compliance with God's design in afflicting us, which is to separate between us and our sins. The penitent here completes his repentance; for it is not enough to be sorry for our sins, but we must go and sin no more, and, as here, bind ourselves with the bond of a fixed resolution never more to return to folly. This is meet to be said in a stedfast purpose, and meet to be said to God in a solemn promise and vow.

II. He reasons with him concerning his discontent and uneasiness under his affliction, *v.* 33. We are ready to think every thing that concerns us should be just as we would have it; but Elihu here shows, 1. That it is absurd and unreasonable to expect this: *" Should it be according to thy mind?"* No, what reason for that?" Elihu here speaks with a great deference to the divine will and wisdom, and a satisfaction therein: it is highly fit that every thing should be according to God's mind. He speaks also with a just disdain of the pretensions of those that are proud, and would be their own carvers: *Should it be according to thy mind?* Should we always have the good we have a mind to enjoy? We should then wrongfully encroach upon others and foolishly ensnare ourselves. Must we never be afflicted, because we have no mind to it? Is it fit that sinners should feel no smart, that scholars

190

should be under no discipline? Or, if we must be afflicted, is it fit that we should choose what rod we will be beaten with? No; it is fit that every thing should be according to God's mind, and not ours; for he is the Creator, and we are creatures. He is infinitely wise and knowing; we are foolish and short-sighted. He is in one mind; we are in many. 2. That it is in vain, and to no purpose, to expect it: *" He will recompense it whether thou refuse or whether thou choose.* God will take his own way, fulfil his own counsel, and recompense according to the sentence of his own justice, whether thou art pleased or displeased; he will neither ask thy leave nor ask thy advice, but, what he pleases, that will he do. It is therefore thy wisdom to be easy, and make a virtue of necessity; *make the best of that which is,* because it is out of thy power to make it otherwise. If thou pretend to choose and refuse," that is, " to prescribe to God and except against what he does, so will not I—I will acquiesce in all he does; and *therefore speak what thou knowest;* say what thou wilt do, whether thou wilt oppose or submit. The matter lies plainly before thee; be at a point; thou art in God's hand, not in mine."

III. He appeals to all intelligent indifferent persons whether there was not a great deal of sin and folly in that which Job said. 1. He would have the matter thoroughly examined, and brought to an issue (*v.* 36)· *" My desire is that Job may be tried unto the end.* If any will undertake to justify what he has said, let them do it; if not, let us all agree to bear our testimony against it." Many understand it of his trial by afflictions: " Let his troubles be continued till he be thoroughly humbled, and his proud spirit brought down, till he be made to see his error and to retract what he has so presumptuously said against God and his providence. Let the trial be continued till the end be obtained." 2. He appeals both to God and man, and desires the judgment of both upon it. (1.) Some read *v.* 36 as an appeal to God: *O, my Father! let Job be tried.* So the margin of our Bibles, for the same word signifies *my desire* and *my father;* and some suppose that he lifted up his eyes when he said this, meaning, " O my Father who art in heaven! let Job be tried till he be subdued." When we are praying for the benefit of afflictions either to ourselves or others we must eye God as a Father, because they are fatherly corrections and a part of our filial education, Heb. xii. 7. (2.) He appeals to the by-standers (*v.* 34): *" Let men of understanding tell me* whether they can put any more favourable construction upon Job's words than I have put, and whether he has not spoken very ill and ought not to cry, *Peccavi—I have done wrong."* In what Job had said he thought it appeared, [1.] That he did not rightly understand himself, but had talked foolishly, *v.* 35. He cannot say that Job is without knowledge and wisdom; but, in this matter, *he has spoken without knowledge,* and, whatever his heart is, *his words were without prudence.* What he said to his wife may be retorted upon himself *(He speaks as one of the foolish men speak)* and for the same reason, *Shall we not receive evil as well as good* at God's hand? *ch.* ii. 10. Sometimes we need and deserve those reproofs ourselves which we have given to others. Those that reproach God's wisdom really reproach their own. [2.] That he had not a due regard to God, but had talked wickedly. If what he had said *be tried to the end,* that is, if one put it to the utmost stretch and make the worst of it, it will be found, *First,* That he has taken part with God's enemies: *His answers have been for wicked men;* that is, what he had said tended to strengthen the hands and harden the hearts of wicked people in their wickedness, he having carried the matter of their prosperity much further than he needed. Let wicked men, like Baal, plead for themselves if they will, but far be it from us that we should answer for them, or say any thing in favour of them. *Secondly,* That he has insulted God's friends, and hectored over them: "*He clappeth his hands among us;* and, if he be not thoroughly tried and humbled, will grow yet more insolent and imperious, as if he had gotten the day and silenced us all." To speak ill is bad enough, but to clap our hands and triumph in it when we have done, as if error and passion had won the victory, is much worse. *Thirdly,* That he has spoken against God himself, and, by standing to what he had said, *added rebellion to his sin.* To speak, though but one word, against God, by whom we speak and for whom we ought to speak, is a great sin; what is it then to multiply words against him, as if we would out-talk him? What is it to repeat them, instead of unsaying them? Those that have sinned, and, when they are called to repent, thus go on frowardly, add rebellion to their sin and make it exceedingly sinful. *Errare possum, Hæreticus esse nolo—I may fall into error, but I will not plunge into heresy.*

CHAP. XXXV

Job being still silent, Elihu follows his blow, and here, a third time, undertakes to show him that he had spoken amiss, and ought to recant. Three improper sayings he here charges him with, and returns answer to them distinctly:—I. He had represented religion as an indifferent unprofitable thing, which God enjoins for his own sake, not for ours; Elihu evinces the contrary, ver. 1—8. II. He had complained of God as deaf to the cries of the oppressed, against which imputation Elihu here justifies God, ver. 9—13. III. He had despaired of the return of God's favour to him, because it was so long deferred, but Elihu hows him the true cause of the delay, ver. 14—16.

ELIHU spake moreover, and said, 2 Thinkest thou this to be right, *that* thou saidst, My righteousness *is* more than God's? 3 For thou saidst, What advantage will it be unto thee? *and,* What profit shall I have, *if I be cleansed* from my sin? 4 I will answer thee, and thy companions with

thee. 5 Look unto the heavens, and see; and behold the clouds *which* are higher than thou. 6 If thou sinnest, what doest thou against him? or *if* thy transgressions be multiplied, what doest thou unto him? 7 If thou be righteous, what givest thou him? or what receiveth he of thine hand? 8 Thy wickedness *may hurt* a man as thou *art;* and thy righteousness *may profit* the son of man.

We have here,

I. The bad words which Elihu charges upon Job, v. 2, 3. To evince the badness of them he appeals to Job himself, and his own sober thoughts, in the reflection: *Thinkest thou this to be right?* This intimates Elihu's confidence that the reproof he now gave was just, for he could refer the judgment of it even to Job himself. Those that have truth and equity on their side sooner or later will have every man's conscience on their side. It also intimates his good opinion of Job, that he thought better than he spoke, and that, though he had spoken amiss, yet, when he perceived his mistake, he would not stand to it. When we have said, in our haste, that which was not right, it becomes us to own that our second thoughts convince us that it was wrong. Two things Elihu here reproves Job for:—1. For justifying himself more than God, which was the thing that first provoked him, *ch.* xxxii. 2. "Thou hast, in effect, said, *My righteousness is more than God's,*" that is, "I have done more for God than ever he did for me; so that, when the accounts are balanced, he will be brought in debtor to me. As if Job thought his services had been paid less than they deserved and his sins punished more than they deserved, which is a most unjust and wicked thought for any man to harbour and especially to utter. When Job insisted so much upon his own integrity, and the severity of God's dealings with him, he did in effect say, *My righteousness is more than God's;* whereas, though we be ever so good and our afflictions ever so great, we are chargeable with unrighteousness and God is not. 2. For disowning the benefits and advantages of religion because he suffered these things: *What profit shall I have if I be cleansed from my sin? v.* 3. This is gathered from *ch.* ix. 30, 31, *Though I make my hands ever so clean,* what the nearer am I? *Thou shalt plunge me in the ditch.* And *ch.* x. 15, *If I be wicked, woe to me;* but, if I be righteous, it is all the same. The psalmist, when he compared his own afflictions with the prosperity of the wicked, was tempted to say, *Verily I have cleansed my heart in vain,* Ps. lxxiii. 13. And, if Job said so, he did in effect say, *My righteousness is more than God's (v.* 2); for, if he got nothing by his religion, God was more beholden to him than he was to God. But, though there might be some colour for it, yet it was not fair to charge these words upon Job, when he himself had made them the wicked words of prospering sinners (*ch.* xxi. 15, *What profit shall we have if we pray to him?*) and had immediately disclaimed them. *The counsel of the wicked is far from me, ch.* xxi. 16. It is not a fair way of disputing to charge men with those consequences of their opinions which they expressly renounce.

II. The good answer which Elihu gives to this (*v.* 4): "*I will* undertake to *answer thee, and thy companions with thee,*" that is, all those that approve thy sayings and are ready to justify thee in them, and all others that say as thou sayest: I have that to offer which will silence them all." To do this he has recourse to his old maxim (*ch.* xxxiii. 12), *that God is greater than man.* This is a truth which, if duly improved, will serve many good purposes, and particularly this to prove that God is debtor to no man. The greatest of men may be a debtor to the meanest; but such is the infinite disproportion between God and man that the great God cannot possibly receive any benefit by man, and therefore cannot be supposed to lie under any obligation to man; for, if he be obliged by his purpose and promise, it is only to himself. That is a challenge which no man can take up (Rom. xi. 35), *Who hath first given to God,* let him prove it, *and it shall be recompensed to him again.* Why should we demand it, as a just debt, to gain by our religion (as Job seemed to do), when the God we serve does not gain by it? 1. Elihu needs not prove that God is above man; it is agreed by all; but he endeavours to affect Job and us with it, by an ocular demonstration of the height of the heavens and the clouds, *v.* 5. They are far above us, and God is far above them; how much then is he set out of the reach either of our sins or of our services! *Look unto the heavens, and behold the clouds.* God made man erect, *cœlumque tueri jussit—and bade him look up to heaven.* Idolaters looked up, and worshipped the hosts of heaven, the sun, moon, and stars; but we must look up to heaven, and worship the Lord of those hosts. They are higher than we, but God is infinitely above them. His *glory is above the heavens* (Ps. viii. 1) and the knowledge of him higher than heaven, *ch.* xi. 8. 2. But hence he infers that God is not affected, either one way or other, by any thing that we do. (1.) He owns that men may be either bettered or damaged by what we do (*v.* 8): *Thy wickedness,* perhaps, may *hurt a man as thou art,* may occasion him trouble in his outward concerns. A wicked man may wound, or rob, or slander his neighbour, or may draw him into sin and so prejudice his soul. Thy righteousness, thy justice, thy charity, thy wisdom, thy piety, may perhaps *profit the*

son of man. Our goodness *extends to the saints that are in the earth,* Ps. xvi. 3. To men like ourselves we are in a capacity either of doing injury or of showing kindness; and in both these the sovereign Lord and Judge of all will interest himself, will reward those that do good and punish those that do hurt to their fellow-creatures and fellow-subjects. But, (2.) He utterly denies that God can really be either prejudiced or advantaged by what any, even the greatest men of the earth, do, or can do. [1.] The sins of the worst sinners are no damage to him (*v.* 6): "*If thou sinnest* wilfully, and of malice prepense, against him, with a high hand, nay, *if thy transgressions be multiplied,* and the acts of sin be ever so often repeated, yet *what doest thou against him?*" This is a challenge to the carnal mind, and defies the most daring sinner to do his worst. It speaks much for the greatness and glory of God that it is not in the power of his worst enemies to do him any real prejudice. Sin is said to *be against God* because so the sinner intends it and so God takes it, and it is an injury to his honour; yet it cannot *do any thing against him.* The malice of sinners is impotent malice: it cannot destroy his being or perfections, cannot dethrone him from his power and dominion, cannot diminish his wealth and possessions, cannot disturb his peace and repose, cannot defeat his counsels and designs, nor can it derogate from his essential glory. Job therefore spoke amiss in saying *What profit is it that I am cleansed from my sin?* God was no gainer by his reformation; and who then would gain if he himself did not? [2.] The services of the best saints are no profit to him (*v.* 7): *If thou be righteous, what givest thou to him?* He needs not our service; or, if he did want to have the work done, he has better hands than ours at command. Our religion brings no accession at all to his felicity. He is so far from being beholden to us that we are beholden to him for making us righteous and accepting our righteousness; and therefore we can demand nothing from him, nor have any reason to complain if we have not what we expect, but to be thankful that we have better than we deserve.

9 By reason of the multitude of oppressions they make *the oppressed* to cry: they cry out by reason of the arm of the mighty. 10 But none saith, Where *is* God my maker, who giveth songs in the night; 11 Who teacheth us more than the beasts of the earth, and maketh us wiser than the fowls of heaven? 12 There they cry, but none giveth answer, because of the pride of evil men. 13 Surely God will not hear vanity, neither will the Almighty regard it.

Elihu here returns an answer to another word that Job had said, which, he thought, reflected much upon the justice and goodness of God, and therefore ought not to pass without a remark. Observe,

I. What it was that Job complained of; it was this, That God did not regard the cries of the oppressed against their oppressors (v. 9): "*By reason of the multitude of oppressions,* the many hardships which proud tyrants put upon poor people and the barbarous usage they give them, *they make the oppressed to cry;* but it is to no purpose : God does not appear to right them. They cry out, they cry on still, *by reason of the arm of the mighty,* which lies heavily upon them." This seems to refer to those words of Job (*ch.* xxiv. 12), *Men groan from out of the city, and the soul of the wounded cries out* against the oppressors, *yet God lays not folly to them,* does not reckon with them for it. This is a thing that Job knows not what to make of, nor how to reconcile to the justice of God and his government. *Is there a righteous God, and can it be that he should so slowly hear, so slowly see?*

II. How Elihu solves the difficulty. If the cries of the oppressed be not heard, the fault is not in God; he is ready to hear and help them. But the fault is in themselves; they *ask and have not,* but it is *because they ask amiss,* James iv. 3. *They cry out by reason of the arm of the mighty,* but it is a complaining cry, a wailing cry, not a penitent praying cry, the cry of nature and passion, not of grace. See Hos. vii. 14, *They have not cried unto me with their heart when they howled upon their beds.* How then can we expect that they should be answered and relieved?

1. They do not enquire after God, nor seek to acquaint themselves with him, under their affliction (v. 10): *But none saith, Where is God my Maker?* Afflictions are sent to direct and quicken us to *enquire early after God,* Ps. lxxviii. 34. But many that groan under great oppressions never mind God, nor take notice of his hand in their troubles; if they did, they would bear their troubles more patiently and be more benefited by them. Of the many that are afflicted and oppressed, few get the good they might get by their affliction. It should drive them to God, but how seldom is this the case! It is lamentable to see so little religion among the poor and miserable part of mankind. Every one complains of his troubles; *but none saith, Where is God my Maker?* that is, none repent of their sins, none return to him that smites them, none seek the face and favour of God, and that comfort in him which would balance their outward afflictions. They are wholly taken up with the wretchedness of their condition, as if that would excuse them in living without God in the world which should engage them to cleave the more closely to him. Observe, (1.) God is our Maker,

the author of our being, and, under that notion, it concerns us to regard and remember him, Eccl. xii. 1. *God my Makers,* in the plural number, which some think is, if not an indication, yet an intimation, of the Trinity of persons in the unity of the Godhead. *Let us make man.* (2.) It is our duty therefore to enquire after him. Where is he, that we may pay our homage to him, may own our dependence upon him and obligations to him? Where is he, that we may apply to him for maintenance and protection, may receive law from him, and may seek our happiness in his favour, from whose power we received our being? (3.) It is to be lamented that he is so little enquired after by the children of men. All are asking, Where is mirth? Where is wealth? Where is a good bargain? But none ask, *Where is God my Maker?*

2. They do not take notice of the mercies they enjoy in and under their afflictions, nor are thankful for them, and therefore cannot expect that God should deliver them out of their afflictions. (1.) He provides for our inward comfort and joy under our outward troubles, and we ought to make use of that, and wait his time for the removal of our troubles: He *gives songs in the night,* that is, when our condition is ever so dark, and sad, and melancholy, there is that in God, in his providence and promise, which is sufficient, not only to support us, but to fill us with joy and consolation, and enable us in every thing to give thanks, and even to rejoice in tribulation. When we only pore upon the afflictions we are under, and neglect the consolations of God which are treasured up for us, it is just with God to reject our prayers. (2.) He preserves to us the use of our reason and understanding (v. 11): *Who teaches us more than the beasts of the earth,* that is, who has endued us with more noble powers and faculties than they are endued with and has made us capable of more excellent pleasures and employments here and for ever. Now this comes in here, [1.] As that which furnishes us with matter for thanksgiving, even under the heaviest burden of affliction. Whatever we are deprived of, we have our immortal souls, those jewels of more worth than all the world, continued to us; even those that kill the body cannot hurt *them.* And if our affliction prevail not to disturb the exercise of their faculties, but we enjoy the use of our reason and the peace of our consciences, we have much reason to be thankful, how pressing soever our calamities otherwise are. [2.] As a reason why we should, under our afflictions, enquire after God our Maker, and seek unto him. This is the greatest excellency of reason, that it makes us capable of religion, and it is in that especially that we are *taught more than the beasts and the fowls.* They have wonderful instincts and sagacities in seeking out their food, their physic, their shelter; but none of them are capable of enquiring, *Where is God my Maker?* Some-

thing like logic, and philosophy, and politics, has been observed among the brute-creatures, but never any thing of divinity or religion; these are peculiar to man. If therefore the oppressed only *cry by reason of the arm of the mighty*, and do not look up to God, they do no more than the brutes (who complain when they are hurt), and they forget that instruction and wisdom by which they are advanced so far above them. God relieves the brute-creatures because they cry to him according to the best of their capacity, *ch.* xxxviii. 41; Ps. civ. 21. But what reason have men to expect relief, who are capable of enquiring after God as their Maker and yet cry to him no otherwise than as brutes do?

3. They are proud and unhumbled under their afflictions, which were sent to mortify them and to hide pride from them (*v.* 12): *There they cry*—there they lie exclaiming against their oppressors, and filling the ears of all about them with their complaints, not sparing to reflect upon God himself and his providence—*but none gives answer*. God does not work deliverance for them, and perhaps men do not much regard them; and why so? It is *because of the pride of evil men;* they are evil men; they *regard iniquity in their hearts,* and therefore God will not hear their prayers, Ps. lxvi. 18; Isa. i. 15. *God hears not* such *sinners*. They have, it may be, brought themselves into trouble by their own wickedness; they are the devil's poor; and then who can pity them? Yet this is not all: they are proud still, and *therefore* they do not seek unto God (Ps. x. 4), or, if they do cry unto him, *therefore* he does not give answer, for he hears only the *desire of the humble* (Ps. x. 17) and delivers those by his providence whom he has first by his grace prepared and made fit for deliverance, which we are not if, under humbling afflictions, our hearts remain unhumbled and our pride unmortified. The case is plain then, If we cry to God for the removal of the oppression and affliction we are under, and it is not removed, the reason is not because the Lord's hand is shortened or his ear heavy, but because the affliction has not done its work; we are not sufficiently humbled, and therefore must thank ourselves that it is continued.

4. They are not sincere, and upright, and inward with God, in their supplications to him, and therefore he does not hear and answer them (*v.* 13): *God will not hear vanity*, that is, the hypocritical prayer, which is a vain prayer, coming out of feigned lips. It is a vanity to think that God should hear it, who searches the heart and requires *truth in the inward part*

14 Although thou sayest thou shalt not see him, *yet* judgment *is* before him; therefore trust thou in him. 15 But now, because *it is* not *so*, he hath visited in his anger; yet he knoweth

it not in great extremity: 16 Therefore doth Job open his mouth in vain; he multiplieth words without knowledge.

Here is, I. Another improper word for which Elihu reproves Job (*v.* 14): *Thou sayest thou shalt not see him;* that is, 1. "Thou complainest that thou dost not understand the meaning of his severe dealings with thee, nor discern the drift and design of them," *ch.* xxiii. 8, 9. And, 2. "Thou despairest of seeing his gracious returns to thee, of seeing better days again, and art ready to give up all for gone;" as Hezekiah (Isa. xxxviii. 11), *I shall not see the Lord.* As, when we are in prosperity, we are ready to think our mountain will never be brought low, so when we are in adversity we are ready to think our valley will never be filled, but, in both, to conclude that *to morrow must be as this day*, which is as absurd as to think, when the weather is either fair or foul, that it will be always so, that the flowing tide will always flow, or the ebbing tide will always ebb.

II. The answer which Elihu gives to this despairing word that Job had said, which is this, 1. That, when he looked up to God, he had no just reason to speak thus despairingly: *Judgment is before him*, that is, "He knows what he has to do, and will do all in infinite wisdom and justice; he has the entire plan and model of providence before him, and knows what he will do, which we do not, and therefore we understand not what he does. There is a day of judgment before him, when all the seeming disorders of providence will be set to rights and the dark chapters of it will be expounded. Then thou shalt see the full meaning of these dark events, and the final period of these dismal events; then thou shalt see his face with joy; *therefore trust in him*, depend upon him, wait for him, and believe that the issue will be good at last." When we consider that God is infinitely wise, and righteous, and faithful, and that he is a God of judgment (Isa. xxx. 18), we shall see no reason to despair of relief from him, but all the reason in the world to hope in him, that it will come in due time, in the best time. 2. That, if he had not yet seen an end of his troubles, the reason was because he did not thus trust in God and wait for him (*v.* 15)· "*Because it is not so,* because thou dost not thus trust in him, therefore the affliction which came at first from love has now displeasure mixed with it. Now God *has visited* thee *in his anger*, taking it very ill that thou canst not find in thy heart to trust him, but harbourest such hard misgiving thoughts of him." If there be any mixtures of divine wrath in our afflictions, we may thank ourselves; it is because we do not behave aright under them; we quarrel with God, are fretful and impatient, and distrustful of the divine Providence.

This was Job's case. *The foolishness of man perverts his way, and then his heart frets against the Lord,* Prov. xix. 3. Yet Elihu thinks that Job, being in great extremity, did not know and consider this as he should, that it was his own fault that he was not yet delivered. He concludes therefore that *Job opens his mouth in vain* (v. 16) in complaining of his grievances and crying for redress, or in justifying himself and clearing up his own innocency; it is all in vain, because he does not trust in God and wait for him, and has not a due regard to him in his afflictions. He had said a great deal, had *multiplied words,* but all *without knowledge,* all to no purpose, because he did not encourage himself in God and humble himself before him. It is in vain for us either to appeal to God or to acquit ourselves if we do not study to answer the end for which affliction is sent, and in vain to pray for relief if we do not trust in God; for let not that man who distrusts God *think that he shall receive any thing from him,* James i. 7. Or this may refer to all that Job had said. Having shown the absurdity of some passages in his discourse, he concludes that there were many other passages which were in like manner the fruits of his ignorance and mistake. He did not, as his other friends, condemn him for a hypocrite, but charged him only with Moses's sin, *speaking unadvisedly with his lips* when his spirit was provoked. When at any time we do so (and who is there that offends not in word?) it is a mercy to be told of it, and we must take it patiently and kindly as Job did, not repeating, but recanting, what we have said amiss.

CHAP. XXXVI.

Elihu, having largely reproved Job for some of his unadvised speeches, which Job had nothing to say in the vindication of, here comes more generally to set him to rights in his notions of God's dealings with him. His other friends had stood to it that, because he was a wicked man, therefore his afflictions were so great and so long. But Elihu only maintained that the affliction was sent for his trial, and that therefore it was lengthened out because Job was not, as yet, thoroughly humbled under it, nor had duly accommodated himself to it. He urges many reasons, taken from the wisdom and righteousness of God, his care of his people, and especially his greatness and almighty power, with which, in this and the following chapter, he persuades him to submit to the hand of God. Here we have, I. His preface, ver. 2—4. II. The account he gives of the methods of God's providence towards the children of men, according as they conduct themselves, ver. 5—15. III. The fair warning and good counsel he gives to Job thereupon, ver. 16—21. IV. His demonstration of God's sovereignty and omnipotence, which he gives instances of in the operations of common providence, and which is a reason why we should all submit to him in his dealings with us, ver. 22—33. This he prosecutes and enlarges upon in the following chapter.

ELIHU also proceeded, and said, 2 Suffer me a little, and I will show thee that *I have* yet to speak on God's behalf. 3 I will fetch my knowledge from afar, and will ascribe righteousness to my Maker. 4 For truly my words *shall* not *be* false : he that is perfect in knowledge *is* with thee.

Once more Elihu begs the patience of the auditory, and Job's particularly, for he has not said all that he has to say, but he will not detain them long. *Stand about me a little* (so some read it), v. 2. "Let me have your attendance, your attention, awhile longer, and I will speak but this once, as plainly and as much to the purpose as I can." To gain this he pleads, 1. That he had a good cause, and a noble and very fruitful subject : *I have yet to speak on God's behalf.* He spoke as an advocate for God, and therefore might justly expect the ear of the court. Some indeed pretend to speak on God's behalf who really speak for themselves; but those who sincerely appear in the cause of God, and speak in behalf of his honour, his truths, his ways, his people, shall be sure neither to want instructions *(it shall be given them in that same hour what they shall speak)* nor to lose their cause or their fee. Nor need they fear lest they should exhaust their subject. Those that have spoken ever so much may yet find more to be spoken on God's behalf. 2. That he had something to offer that was uncommon, and out of the road of vulgar observation : *I will fetch my knowledge from afar* (v. 3), that is, "we will have recourse to our first principles and the highest notions we can make use of to serve any purpose." It is worth while to go far for this knowledge of God, to dig for it, to travel for it; it will recompense our pains, and, though far-fetched, is not dear-bought. 3. That his design was undeniably honest; for all he aimed at was to ascribe righteousness to his Maker, to maintain and clear this truth, that God is righteous in all his ways. In speaking of God, and speaking for him, it is good to remember that he is our Maker, to call him so, and therefore to be ready to do him and the interests of his kingdom the best service we can. If he be our Maker, we have our all from him, must use our all for him, and be very jealous for his honour. 4. That his management should be very just and fair (v. 4): "*My words shall not be false,* neither disagreeable to the thing itself nor to my own thoughts and apprehensions. It is truth that I am contending for, and that for truth's sake, with all possible sincerity and plainness." He will make use of plain and solid arguments and not the subtleties and niceties of the schools. "He who is perfect or upright in knowledge is now reasoning with thee; and therefore let him not only have a fair hearing, but let what he says be taken in good part, as meant well." The perfection of our knowledge in this world is to be honest and sincere in searching out truth, in applying it to ourselves, and in making use of what we know for the good of others.

5 Behold, God *is* mighty, and despiseth not *any* : he *is* mighty in strength *and* wisdom. 6 He preserveth not the life of the wicked : but giveth right to the poor. 7 He withdraweth not his eyes from the righteous : but with kings *are they* on the throne;

yea, he doth establish them for ever, and they are exalted. 8 And if *they be* bound in fetters, *and* be holden in cords of affliction; 9 Then he showeth them their work, and their transgressions that they have exceeded. 10 He openeth also their ear to discipline, and commandeth that they return from iniquity. 11 If they obey and serve *him,* they shall spend their days in prosperity, and their years in pleasures. 12 But if they obey not, they shall perish by the sword, and they shall die without knowledge. 13 But the hypocrites in heart heap up wrath: they cry not when he bindeth them. 14 They die in youth, and their life *is* among the unclean.

Elihu, being to speak on God's behalf, and particularly to ascribe righteousness to his Maker, here shows that the disposals of divine Providence are all, not only according to the eternal counsels of his will, but according to the eternal rules of equity. God acts as a righteous governor, for,

I. He does not think it below him to take notice of the meanest of his subjects, nor does poverty or obscurity set any at a distance from his favour. If men are mighty, they are apt to look with a haughty disdain upon those that are not of distinction and make no figure; but *God is mighty,* infinitely so, and yet he *despises not any, v.* 5. He humbles himself to take cognizance of the affairs of the meanest, to do them justice and to show them kindness. Job thought himself and his cause slighted because God did not immediately appear for him. "No," says Elihu, *God despises not any,* which is a good reason why we should honour all men. *He is mighty in strength and wisdom,* and yet does not look with contempt upon those that have but a little strength and wisdom, if they but mean honestly. Nay, for this reason he despises not any, because his wisdom and strength are incontestably infinite and therefore the condescensions of his grace can be no diminution to him. Those that are wise and good will not look upon any with scorn and disdain.

II. He gives no countenance to the greatest, if they be bad (*v.* 6): *He preserves not the life of the wicked.* Though their life may be prolonged, yet not under any special care of the divine Providence, but only its common protection. Job had said that *the wicked live, become old, and are mighty in power, ch.* xxi. 7. "No," says Elihu: "he seldom suffers wicked men to become old. He preserves not their life so long as they expected, nor with that comfort and satisfaction which are indeed our life; and their preservation is but a reservation for the day of wrath," Rom. ii. 5.

196

III. He is always ready to right those that are any way injured, and to plead their cause (*v.* 6): He *gives right to the poor,* avenges their quarrel upon their persecutors and forces them to make restitution of what they have robbed them of. If men will not right the injured poor, God will.

IV. He takes a particular care for the protection of his good subjects, *v.* 7. He not only looks on them, but he never looks off them: *He withdraws not his eyes from the righteous.* Though they may seem sometimes neglected and forgotten, and that befals them which looks like an oversight of Providence, yet the tender careful eye of their heavenly Father never withdraws from them. If our eye be ever towards God in duty, his eye will be ever upon us in mercy, and, when we are at the lowest, will not overlook us.

1. Sometimes he prefers good people to places of trust and honour (*v.* 7): *With kings are they on the throne,* and every sheaf is made to bow to theirs. When righteous persons are advanced to places of honour and power, it is in mercy to them; for God's grace in them will both arm them against the temptations that attend preferment and enable them to improve the opportunity it gives them of doing good. It is also in mercy to those over whom they are set: *When the righteous bear rule the city rejoices.* If the righteous be advanced, they are established. Those that in honour keep a good conscience stand upon sure ground, and high places are not such slippery ground to them as they are to others. But, because it is not often that we see good men made great men in this world, this may be supposed to refer to the honour to which the righteous shall rise when their Redeemer shall *stand at the latter day upon the earth;* for then only they shall be exalted for ever, and established for ever; then shall they all shine forth as the sun, and be made kings and priests to our God.

2. If at any time he bring them into affliction, it is for the good of their souls, *v.* 8—10. Some good people are preferred to honour and power, but others are in trouble. Now observe, (1.) The distress supposed (*v.* 8): *If they be bound in fetters,* laid in prison as Joseph was, or *holden in the cords of* any other *affliction,* confined by pain and sickness, hampered by poverty, bound in their counsels, and, notwithstanding all their struggles, held long in this distress. This was Job's case; he was caught, and kept fast, *in the cords of anguish* (as some read it) ; but observe, (2.) The design God has, in bringing his people into such distresses as these; it is for the benefit of their souls, the consideration of which should reconcile us to affliction and make us think well of it. Three things God intends when he afflicts us :—[1.] To discover past sins to us, and to bring them to our remembrance. Then he shows them that amiss in them which before they did not see. He discovers to them the fact of sin: *He shows*

them their work. Sin is our own work. If there be any good in us, it is God's work; and we are concerned to see what work we have made by sin. He discovers the fault of sin, shows them *their transgressions* of the law of God, and withal the sinfulness of sin, *that they have exceeded,* and have been beyond measure sinful. True penitents lay a load upon themselves, do not extenuate, but aggravate, their sins, and own that they have exceeded in them. Affliction sometimes answers to the sin; it serves, however, to awaken the conscience and puts men upon considering. [2.] To dispose our hearts to receive present instructions: Then *he opens their ear to discipline, v.* 10. Whom God chastens *he teaches* (Ps. xciv. 12), and the affliction makes people willing to learn, softens the wax, that it may receive the impression of the seal; yet it does not do this of itself, but the grace of God working with and by it; it is he that opens the ear, that opens the heart, who has the key of David. [3.] To deter and draw us off from iniquity for the future. This is the errand on which the affliction is sent; it is a command to *return from iniquity,* to have no more to do with sin, to turn from it with an aversion to it and a resolution never to return to it any more, Hos. xiv. 8.

3. If the affliction do its work, and accomplish that for which it is sent, he will comfort them again, according to the time that he has afflicted them (*v.* 11): *If they obey and serve him,*—if they comply with his design and serve his purpose in these dispensations, —if, when the affliction is removed, they continue in the same good mind that they were in when they were under the smart of it and perform the vows they made then,—if they live in obedience to God's commands, particularly those which relate to his service and worship, and in all instances make conscience of their duty to him,—then *they shall spend their days in prosperity* again *and their years in true pleasures.* Piety is the only sure way to prosperity and pleasure; this is a certain truth, and yet few will believe it. If we faithfully serve God, (1.) We have the promise of outward prosperity, the promise of the life that now is, and the comforts of it, as far as is for God's glory and our good; and who would desire them any further? (2.) We have the possession of inward pleasures, the comfort of communion with God and a good conscience, and that great peace which those have that love God's law. If we rejoice not in the Lord always, and in hope of eternal life, it is our own fault; and what better pleasures can we spend our years in?

4. If the affliction do not do its work, let them expect the furnace to be heated seven times hotter till they are consumed (*v.* 12): *If they obey not,* if they are not bettered by their afflictions, are not reclaimed and reformed, they shall perish by the sword of God's wrath. Those whom his rod does not

cure his sword will kill; and the consuming fire will prevail if the refining fire do not; for when God judges he will overcome. If *Ahaz, in his distress, trespass yet more against the Lord, this is that king Ahaz* that is marked for ruin, 2 Chron. xxviii. 22; Jer. vi. 29, 30. God would have instructed them by their afflictions, but they received not instruction, would not take the hints that were given them; and therefore *they shall die without knowledge,* ere they are aware, without any further previous notices given them; or *they shall die because they were without knowledge* notwithstanding the means of knowledge which they were blessed with. Those that *die without knowledge* die without grace and are undone for ever.

V. He brings ruin upon hypocrites, the secret enemies of his kingdom (such as Elihu described, *v.* 12), who, though they were numbered among the righteous whom Elihu had spoken of before, yet did not obey God, but, being children of disobedience and darkness, become children of wrath and perdition; these are the *hypocrites in heart, who heap up wrath, v.* 13. See the nature of hypocrisy: it lies in the heart, which is for the world and the flesh when the outside seems to be for God and religion. Many that are saints in show and saints in word are hypocrites in heart. That spring is corrupt, and there is an evil treasure there. See the mischievousness of hypocrisy: hypocrites *heap up wrath.* They are doing that every day which is provoking to God, and will be reckoned with for it all together in the great day. *They treasure up wrath against the day of wrath,* Rom. ii. 5. Their sins are *laid up in store with God among his treasures,* Deut. xxxii. 34. Compare Jam. v. 3. As what goes up a vapour comes down a shower, so what goes up sin, if not repented of, will come down wrath. They think they are heaping up wealth, heaping up merits, but, when the treasures are opened, it will prove they were heaping up wrath. Observe, 1. What they do to heap up wrath. What is it that is so provoking? It is this, *They cry not when he binds them,* that is, when they are in affliction, bound with the cords of trouble, their hearts are hardened, they are stubborn and unhumbled, and will not cry to God nor make their application to him. They are stupid and senseless as stocks and stones, despising the chastening of the Lord. 2. What are the effects of that wrath? *They die in youth, and their life is among the unclean, v.* 14. This is the portion of hypocrites, whom Christ denounced many woes against. If they continue impenitent, (1.) They shall die a sudden death, *die in youth,* when death is most a surprise, and death (that is, the consequence of it) is always such to hypocrites; as those that die in youth die when they hoped to live, so hypocrites, at death, go to hell, when they hoped to go to heaven. *When a wicked man dies his expectations shall perish.* (2.) They shall die the second death. *Their life,* after death (for so it comes in here), *is among the unclean,* among the *fornicators* (so some), among the worst and vilest of sinners, notwithstanding their specious and plausible profession. It is among the *Sodomites* (so the margin), those filthy wretches, who, *going after strange flesh, are set forth for an example, suffering the vengeance of eternal fire,* Jude 7. The souls of the wicked live after death, but they live among the unclean, the unclean spirits, the devil and his angels, for ever separated from the new Jerusalem, into which *no unclean thing shall enter.*

15 He delivereth the poor in his affliction, and openeth their ears in oppression. 16 Even so would he have removed thee out of the strait *into* a broad place, where *there is* no straitness; and that which should be set on thy table *should be* full of fatness. 17 But thou hast fulfilled the judgment of the wicked: judgment and justice take hold *on thee.* 18 Because *there is* wrath, *beware* lest he take thee away with *his* stroke: then a great ransom cannot deliver thee. 19 Will he esteem thy riches? *no,* not gold, nor all the forces of strength. 20 Desire not the night, when people are cut off in their place. 21 Take heed, regard not iniquity: for this hast thou chosen rather than affliction. 22 Behold, God exalteth by his power: who teacheth like him? 23 Who hath enjoined him his way? or who can say, Thou hast wrought iniquity?

Elihu here comes more closely to Job; and,

I. He tells him what God would have done for him before this if he had been duly humbled under his affliction. "We all know how ready God is to *deliver the poor in his affliction* (v. 15); he always was so. The poor in spirit, those that are of a broken and contrite heart, he looks upon with tenderness, and, when they are in affliction, is ready to help them. He *opens their ears,* and makes them to hear joy and gladness, even *in* their *oppressions;* while he does not yet deliver them he speaks to them good words and comfortable words, for the encouragement of their faith and patience, the silencing of their fears, and the balancing of their griefs; and *even so* (v. 16) would he have done to thee if thou hadst submitted to his providence and conducted thyself well; he would have delivered and comforted thee, and we should have had none of these complaints. If thou hadst accommodated thyself to the will of God, thy liberty and plenty would have been restored to thee with advantage" 1. "Thou wouldst

have been enlarged, and not confined thus by thy sickness and disgrace: *He would have removed thee into a broad place where is no straitness,* and thou wouldst no longer have been cramped thus and have had all thy measures broken." 2. "Thou wouldst have been enriched, and wouldst not have been left in this poor condition; thou wouldst have had thy table richly spread, not only with food convenient, but with the finest of the wheat" (see Deut. xxxii. 14) "and the fattest of the flesh." Note, It ought to silence us under our afflictions to consider that, if we were better, it would be every way better with us: if we had answered the ends of an affliction, the affliction would be removed; and deliverance would come if we were ready for it. God would have done well for us if we had conducted ourselves well; Ps. lxxxi. 13, 14; Isa. xlviii. 18.

II. He charges him with standing in his own light, and makes him the cause of the continuance of his own trouble (v. 17): "*But thou hast fulfilled the judgment of the wicked,*" that is, "Whatever thou art really, in this thing thou hast conducted thyself like a wicked man, hast spoken and done like the wicked, hast gratified them and served their cause; and *therefore* judgment and justice take hold on thee as a wicked man, because thou goest in company with them, actest as if thou wert in their interest, aiding and abetting. *Thou hast maintained the cause of the wicked;* and such as a man's cause is such will the judgment of God be upon him;" so bishop Patrick. It is dangerous being on the wrong side: accessaries to treason will be dealt with as principals.

III. He cautions him not to persist in his frowardness. Several good cautions he gives him to this purport.

1. Let him not make light of divine vengeance, nor be secure, as if he were in no danger of it (v. 18): "*Because there is wrath*" (that is, "because God is a righteous governor, who resents all the affronts given to his government, because he has revealed his wrath from heaven against all ungodliness and unrighteousness of men, and because thou hast reason to fear that thou art under God's displeasure) therefore *beware lest he take thee away* suddenly *with his stroke,* and be so wise as to make thy peace with him quickly and get his anger turned away from thee." A warning to this purport Job had given his friends (ch. xix. 29): *Be you afraid of the sword, for wrath brings the punishment of the sword.* Thus contenders are apt, with too much boldness, to bind one another over to the judgment of God and threaten one another with his wrath; but he that keeps a good conscience needs not fear the impotent menaces of proud men. But this was a friendly caution to Job, and necessary. Even good men have need to be kept to their duty by the fear of God's wrath. "Thou art a wise and good man, but beware lest he take

thee away, for the wisest and best have enough in them to deserve his stroke."

2. Let him not promise himself that, if God's wrath should kindle against him, he could find out ways to escape the strokes of it. (1.) There is no escaping by money, no purchasing a pardon with silver, or gold, and such corruptible things : " Even *a great ransom cannot deliver thee* when God enters into judgment with thee. His justice cannot be bribed, nor any of the ministers of his justice. *Will he esteem thy riches,* and take from them a commutation of the punishment? *No, not gold, v.* 19. If thou hadst as much wealth as ever thou hadst, that would not ease thee, would not secure thee from the strokes of God's wrath, in the day of the revelation of which *riches profit not,*" Prov. xi. 4. See Ps. xlix. 7, 8. (2.) There is no escaping by rescue : " If *all the forces of strength* were at thy command, if thou couldst muster ever so many servants and vassals to appear for thee to force thee out of the hands of divine vengeance, it were all in vain ; God would not regard it. There is *none that can deliver out of his hand.*" (3.) There is no escaping by absconding (*v.* 20) : " *Desire not the night,* which often favours the retreat of a conquered army and covers it ; think not that thou canst so escape the righteous judgment of God, for the *darkness hideth not from him,*" Ps. cxxxix. 11, 12. See *ch.* xxxiv. 22. " Think not, because in the night people retire to their place, go up to their beds, and it is then easy to escape being discovered by them, that God also ascends to his place, and cannot see thee. No ; he *neither slumbers nor sleeps.* His eyes are open upon the children of men, not only in all places, but at all times. No rocks nor mountains can shelter us from his eye. Some understand it of the night of death ; that is the night by which men are *cut off from their place,* and Job had earnestly breathed for that night, as the hireling desires the evening, *ch.* vii. 2. " But do not do so," says Elihu ; " for thou knowest not what the night of death is." Those that passionately wish for death, in hopes to make that their shelter from God's wrath, may perhaps be mistaken. There are those whom wrath pursues into that night.

3. Let him not continue his unjust quarrel with God and his providence, which hitherto he had persisted in when he should have submitted to the affliction (*v.* 21) : " *Take heed,* look well to thy own spirit, and *regard not iniquity,* return not to it (so some), for it is at thy peril if thou do." Let us never dare to think a favourable thought of sin, never indulge it, nor allow ourselves in it. Elihu thinks Job had need of this caution, he having *chosen iniquity rather than affliction,* that is, having chosen rather to gratify his own pride and humour in contending with God than to mortify it by a submission to him and accepting the punishment. We may take it more generally, and observe that those who choose iniquity rather than affliction make a very foolish choice. Those that ease their cares by sinful pleasures, increase their wealth by sinful pursuits, escape their troubles by sinful projects, and evade sufferings for righteousness' sake by sinful compliances against their consciences, make a choice they will repent of; for there is more evil in the least sin than in the greatest affliction. It is an evil, and only evil.

4. Let him not dare to prescribe to God, nor give him his measures (*v.* 22, 23) : " *Behold, God exalteth by his power,*" that is, " He does, may, and can set up and pull down whom he pleases, and therefore it is not for thee nor me to contend with him." The more we magnify God the more do we humble and abase ourselves. Now consider, (1.) That God is an absolute sovereign: *He exalts by his* own *power,* and not by strength derived from any other. He exalts whom he pleases, exalts those that were afflicted and cast down, by the strength and power which he gives his people; and therefore *who has enjoined him his way?* Who presides above him in his way? Is there any superior from whom he has his commission and to whom he is accountable? No ; he himself is supreme and independent. *Who puts him in mind of his way?* so some. Does the eternal Mind need a remembrancer? No ; his own way, as well as ours, is ever before him. He has not received orders or instructions from any (Isa. xl. 13, 14), nor is he accountable to any. He enjoins to all the creatures their way; let not us then enjoin him his, but leave it to him to govern the world, who is fit to do it. (2.) That he is an incomparable teacher: *Who teaches like him?* It is absurd for us to teach him who is himself the fountain of light, truth, knowledge, and instruction. *He that teaches man knowledge,* and so as none else can, *shall not he know?* Ps. xciv. 9. 10. Shall we light a candle to the sun? Observe, When Elihu would give glory to God as a ruler he praises him as a teacher, for rulers must teach. God does so. He binds with the cords of a man. In this, as in other things, he is unequalled. None so fit to direct his own actions as he himself is. He knows what he has to do, and how to do it for the best, and needs no information nor advice. Solomon himself had a privy-council to advise him, but the King of kings has none. Nor is any so fit to direct our actions as he is. None teaches with such authority and convincing evidence, with such condescension and compassion, nor with such power and efficacy, as God does. He teaches by the Bible, and that is the best book, teaches by his Son, and he is the best Master. (3.) That he is unexceptionably just in all his proceedings: *Who can say, Thou hast wrought iniquity?* Not, Who *dares* say it? (many do iniquity, and those who tell them of it do so at their peril), but Who *can* say it? Who has any cause to say it? Who can say it

and prove it? It is a maxim undoubtedly true, without limitation, that *the King of kings can do no wrong.*

24 Remember that thou magnify his work, which men behold. 25 Every man may see it; man may behold *it* afar off. 26 Behold, God *is* great, and we know *him* not, neither can the number of his years be searched out. 27 For he maketh small the drops of water: they pour down rain according to the vapour thereof: 28 Which the clouds do drop *and* distil upon man abundantly. 29 Also can *any* understand the spreadings of the clouds, *or* the noise of his tabernacle? 30 Behold, he spreadeth his light upon it, and covereth the bottom of the sea. 31 For by them judgeth he the people; he giveth meat in abundance. 32 With clouds he covereth the light; and commandeth it *not to shine* by *the cloud* that cometh betwixt. 33 The noise thereof showeth concerning it, the cattle also concerning the vapour.

Elihu is here endeavouring to possess Job with great and high thoughts of God, and so to persuade him into a cheerful submission to his providence.

I. He represents the work of God, in general, as illustrious and conspicuous, *v.* 24. His whole work is so. God does nothing mean. This is a good reason why we should acquiesce in all the operations of his providence concerning us in particular. His visible works, those of nature, and which concern the world in general, are such as we admire and commend, and in which we observe the Creator's wisdom, power, and goodness; shall we then find fault with his dispensations concerning us, and the counsels of his will concerning our affairs? We are here called to *consider the work of God,* Eccl. vii. 13. 1. It is plain before our eyes, nothing more obvious: it is what *men behold.* Every man that has but half an eye may see it, may behold it afar off. Look which way we will, we see the productions of God's wisdom and power; we see that done, and that doing, concerning which we cannot but say, This is *the work of God,* the finger of God; it is the Lord's doing. Every man may see, afar off, the heaven and all its lights, the earth and all its fruits, to be the work of Omnipotence; much more when we behold them nigh at hand. Look at the minutest works of nature through a microscope; do they not appear curious? The eternal power and godhead of the Creator are *clearly seen and understood* by the *things that are made,* Rom. i. 20. Every man, even those that have not the be-

200

nefit of divine revelation, may see this; for *there is no speech or language where the voice* of these natural constant preachers *is not heard,* Ps. xix. 3. 2. It ought to be marvellous in our eyes. The beauty and excellency of the work of God, and the agreement of all the parts of it, are what we must remember to magnify and highly to extol, not only justify it as right and good, and what cannot be blamed, but magnify it as wise and glorious, and such as no creature could contrive or produce. Man may see his works, and is capable of discerning his hand in them (which the beasts are not), and therefore ought to praise them and give him the glory of them.

II. He represents God, the author of them, as infinite and unsearchable, *v.* 26. The streams of being, power, and perfection should lead us to the fountain. *God is great,* infinitely so,—great in power, for he is omnipotent and independent,—great in wealth, for he is self-sufficient and all-sufficient,—great in himself,—great in all his works,—great, and therefore greatly to be praised,—great, and therefore *we know him not.* We know that he is, but not what he is. We know what he is not, but not what he is. We know in part, but not in perfection. This comes in here as a reason why we must not arraign his proceedings, nor find fault with what he does, because it is speaking evil of the things that we understand not and answering a matter before we hear it. We know not the duration of his existence, for it is infinite. *The number of his years cannot* possibly *be searched out,* for he is eternal; there is no number of them. He is a Being without beginning, succession, or period, who ever was, and ever will be, and ever the same, the great *I AM.* This is a good reason why we should not prescribe to him, nor quarrel with him, because, as he is, such are his operations, quite out of our reach.

III. He gives some instances of God's wisdom, power, and sovereign dominion, in the works of nature and the dispensations of common providence, beginning in this chapter with the clouds and the rain that descends from them. We need not be critical in examining either the phrase or the philosophy of this noble discourse. The general scope of it is to show that God is infinitely great, and the Lord of all, the first cause and supreme director of all the creatures, and *has all power in heaven and earth* (whom therefore we ought, with all humility and reverence, to adore, to speak well of, and to give honour to), and that it is presumption for us to prescribe to him the rules and methods of his special providence towards the children of men, or to expect from him an account of them, when the operations even of common providences about the meteors are so various and so mysterious and unaccountable. Elihu, to affect Job with God's sublimity and sovereignty, had directed him (*ch.* xxxv. 5) to look unto the clouds. In these verses he shows us what we may observe in the clouds we see which will lead us to consider the glorious perfections of their Creator. Consider the clouds,

1. As springs to this lower world, the source and treasure of its moisture, and the great bank through which it circulates—a very necessary provision, for its stagnation would be as hurtful to this lower world as that of the blood to the body of man. It is worth while to observe in this common occurrence, (1.) That the clouds above distil upon the earth below. If the heavens become brass, the earth becomes iron; therefore thus the promise of plenty runs, *I will hear the heavens and they shall hear the earth.* This intimates to us that every good gift is from above, from him who is both Father of lights and Father of the rain, and it instructs us to direct our prayers to him and to look up. (2.) That they are here said to *distil upon man (v. 28)*; for, though indeed God *causes it to rain in the wilderness where no man is (ch. xxxviii. 26, Ps. civ. 11)*, yet special respect is had to man herein, to whom the inferior creatures are all made serviceable and from whom the actual return of the tribute of praise is required. Among men, he *causes his rain to fall upon the just and upon the unjust,* Matt. v. 45. (3.) They are said to distil the water in *small drops,* not in spouts, as when the *windows of heaven were opened,* Gen. vii. 11. God waters the earth with that with which he once drowned it, only dispensing it in another manner, to let us know how much we lie at his mercy, and how kind he is, in giving rain by drops, that the benefit of it may be the further and the more equally diffused, as by an artificial water-pot. (4.) Though sometimes the rain comes in very small drops, yet, at other times, it pours down in great rain, and this difference between one shower and another must be resolved into the divine Providence which orders it so. (5.) Though it comes down in drops, yet it distils upon man *abundantly (v. 28)*, and therefore is called *the river of God which is full of water,* Ps. lxv. 9. (6.) The clouds *pour down according to the vapour* that they draw up, *v. 27.* So just the heavens are to the earth, but the earth is not so in the return it makes. (7.) The produce of the clouds is sometimes a great terror, and at other times a great favour, to the earth, *v. 31.* When he pleases *by them he judges the people* he is angry with. Storms, and tempests, and excessive rains, destroying the fruits of the earth and causing inundations, come from the clouds; but, on the other hand, from them, usually, he gives meat in abundance; they drop fatness upon the pastures that are clothed with flocks, and the valleys that are *covered with corn,* Ps. lxv. 11—13. (8.) Notice is sometimes given of the approach of rain, *v. 33. The noise thereof,* among other things, *shows concerning it.* Hence we read (1 Kings xviii. 41) of *the sound*

of abundance of rain, or (as it is in the margin) *a sound of a noise of rain,* before it came; and a welcome harbinger it was then. As the noise, so the face of the sky, shows concerning it, Luke xii. 56. The cattle also, by a strange instinct, are apprehensive of a change in the weather nigh at hand, and seek for shelter, shaming man, who will not foresee the evil and hide himself.

2. As shadows to the upper world (*v. 29*): *Can any understand the spreading of the clouds?* They are spread over the earth as a curtain or canopy; how they come to be so, how stretched out, and how poised, as they are, we cannot understand, though we daily see they are so. Shall we then pretend to understand the reasons and methods of God's judicial proceedings with the children of men, whose characters and cases are so various, when we cannot account for the spreadings of the clouds, which *cover the light? v. 32.* It is a cloud coming *betwixt, v. 32; ch.* xxvi. 9. And this we are sensible of, that, by the interposition of the clouds ,between us and the sun, we are, (1.) Sometimes favoured; for they serve as an umbrella to shelter us from the violent heat of the sun, which otherwise would beat upon us. A *cloud of dew in the heat of harvest* is spoken of as a very great refreshment, Isa. xviii. 4. (2.) Sometimes we are by them frowned upon; for they darken the earth at noon-day and eclipse the light of the sun. Sin is compared to a cloud (Isa. xliv. 22), because it comes between us and the light of God's countenance and obstructs the shining of it. But though the clouds darken the sun for a time, and pour down rain, yet *(post nubila Phœbus—the sun shines forth after the rain),* after he has wearied the cloud, *he spreads his light upon it, v. 30.* There is a *clear shining after rain,* 2 Sam. xxiii. 4. The sunbeams are darted forth, and reach to *cover* even *the bottom of the sea,* thence to exhale a fresh supply of vapours, and so raise recruits for the clouds, *v. 30.* In all this, we must remember to magnify the work of God.

CHAP. XXXVII.

Elihu here goes on to extol the wonderful power of God in the meteors and all the changes of the weather: if, in those changes, we submit to the will of God, take the weather as it is and make the best of it, why should we not do so in other changes of our condition? Here he observes the hand of God, I. In the thunder and lightning, ver. 1—5. II. In the frost and snow, the rains and wind, ver. 6—13. III. He applies it to Job, and challenges him to solve the phenomena of these works of nature, that, confessing his ignorance in them, he might own himself an incompetent judge in the proceedings of divine Providence, ver. 14—22. And then, IV. Concludes with his principle, which he undertook to make out, That God is great and greatly to be feared, ver. 23, 24.

A T this also my heart trembleth, and is moved out of his place. 2 Hear attentively the noise of his voice, and the sound *that* goeth out of his mouth. 3 He directeth it under the whole heaven, and his lightning unto the ends of the earth. 4 After it a voice roareth: he thundereth with the voice of his excellency; and he will not stay them when his voice is heard.

5 God thundereth marvellously with his voice; great things doeth he, which we cannot comprehend.

Thunder and lightning, which usually go together, are sensible indications of the glory and majesty, the power and terror, of Almighty God, one to the ear and the other to the eye; in these God leaves not himself without witness of his greatness, as, in the rain from heaven and fruitful seasons, he leaves not himself without witness of his goodness (Acts xiv. 17), even to the most stupid and unthinking. Though there are natural causes and useful effects of them, which the philosophers undertake to account for, yet they seem chiefly designed by the Creator to startle and awaken the slumbering world of mankind to the consideration of a God above them. The eye and the ear are the two learning senses; and therefore, though such a circumstance is possible, they say it was never known in fact that any one was born both blind and deaf. By the word of God divine instructions are conveyed to the mind through the ear, by his works through the eye; but, because those ordinary sights and sounds do not duly affect men, God is pleased sometimes to astonish men by the eye with his lightnings and by the ear with his thunder. It is very probable that at this time, when Elihu was speaking, it thundered and lightened, for he speaks of the phenomena as present; and, God being about to speak (*ch.* xxxviii. 1), these were, as afterwards on Mount Sinai, the proper prefaces to command attention and awe. Observe here, 1. How Elihu was himself affected, and desired to affect Job, with the appearance of God's glory in the thunder and lightning (*v.* 1, 2): "For my part," says Elihu, "*my heart trembles* at it; though I have often heard it, often seen it, yet it is still terrible to me, and makes every joint of me tremble, and my heart beat as if it would move *out of its place.*" Thunder and lightning have been dreadful to the wicked: the emperor Caligula would run into a corner, or under a bed, for fear of them. Those who are very much astonished, we say, are *thunder-struck.* Even good people think thunder and lightning very awful; and that which makes them the more terrible is the hurt often done by lightning, many having been killed by it. Sodom and Gomorrah were laid in ruins by it. It is a sensible indication of what God could do to this sinful world, and what he *will do,* at last, by the fire to which it is reserved. Our hearts, like Elihu's, should tremble at it for fear of God's judgments, Ps. cxix. 120. He also calls upon Job to attend to it (*v.* 2): *Hear attentively the noise of his voice.* Perhaps as yet it thundered at a distance, and could not be heard without listening: or rather,

Though the thunder itself will be heard, and whatever we are doing we cannot help attending to it, yet, to apprehend and understand the instructions God thereby gives us, we have need to hear with great attention and application of mind. Thunder is called *the voice of the Lord* (Ps. xxix. 3, &c.), because by it God speaks to the children of men to fear before him, and it should put us in mind of that mighty word by which the world was at first made, which is called thunder. Ps. civ. 7, *At the voice of thy thunder they hasted away,* namely, the waters, when God said, *Let them be gathered into one place.* Those that are themselves affected with God's greatness should labour to affect others. 2. How he describes them. (1.) Their original, not their second causes, but the first. God directs the thunder, and the lightning is his, *v.* 3. Their production and motion are not from chance, but from the counsel of God and under the direction and dominion of his providence, though to us they seem accidental and ungovernable. (2.) Their extent. The claps of thunder roll *under the whole heaven,* and are heard far and near; so are the lightnings darted to *the ends of the earth;* they come out of the one part under heaven and shine to the other, Luke xvii. 24. Though the same lightning and thunder do not reach to all places, yet they reach to very distant places in a moment, and there is no place but, some time or other, has these alarms from heaven. (3.) Their order. The lightning is first directed, and *after it a voice roars, v.* 4. The flash of fire, and the noise it makes in a watery cloud, are really at the same time; but, because the motion of light is much quicker than that of sound, we see the lightning some time before we hear the thunder, as we see the firing of a great gun at a distance before we hear the report of it. The thunder is here called *the voice of God's excellency,* because by it he proclaims his transcendent power and greatness. *He sends forth his voice and that a mighty voice,* Ps. lxviii. 33. (4.) Their violence. *He will not stay them,* that is, he does not need to check them, or hold them back, lest they should grow unruly and out of his power to restrain them, but lets them take their course, says to them, Go, and they go—Come, and they come—Do this, and they do it. He will not stay the rains and showers that usually follow upon the thunder (which he had spoken of, *ch.* xxxvi. 27, 29), so some, but will pour them out upon the earth *when his voice is heard.* Thunder-showers are sweeping rains, and for them he *makes the lightnings,* Ps. cxxxv. 7. (5.) The inference he draws from all this, *v.* 5. Does God thunder thus marvellously with his voice? We must then conclude that his other works are great, and such as we cannot comprehend. From this one instance we may argue to all, that, in the dispensations of his providence, there is that which is too great, too strong, for us to oppose or strive against, and too high, too deep, for us to arraign or quarrel with.

6 For he saith to the snow, Be thou *on* the earth; likewise to the small rain, and to the great rain of his strength. 7 He sealeth up the hand of every man; that all men may know his work. 8 Then the beasts go into dens, and remain in their places. 9 Out of the south cometh the whirlwind: and cold out of the north. 10 By the breath of God frost is given: and the breadth of the waters is straitened. 11 Also by watering he wearieth the thick cloud: he scattereth his bright cloud: 12 And it is turned round about by his counsels: that they may do whatsoever he commandeth them upon the face of the world in the earth. 13 He causeth it to come, whether for correction, or for his land, or for mercy.

The changes and extremities of the weather, wet or dry, hot or cold, are the subject of a great deal of our common talk and observation; but how seldom do we think and speak of these things, as Elihu does here, with an awful regard to God the director of them, who shows his power and serves the purposes of his providence by them! We must take notice of the glory of God, not only in the thunder and lightning, but in the more common revolutions of the weather, which are not so terrible and which make less noise. As,

I. In the snow and rain, *v.* 6. Thunder and lightning happen usually in the summer, but here he takes notice of the winter-weather. Then *he saith to the snow, Be thou on the earth;* he commissions it, he commands it, he appoints it, where it shall light and how long it shall lie. He speaks, and it is done: as in the creation of the world, *Let there be light,* so in the works of common providence, *Snow, be thou on the earth.* Saying and doing are not two things with God, though they are with us. When he speaks the word *the small rain* distils and *the great rain* pours down as he pleases—*the winter-rain* (so the LXX.), for in those countries, when the winter was past, the rain was over and gone, Cant. ii. 11. The distinction in the Hebrew between the small rain and the great rain is this, that the former is called a shower of *rain,* the latter of *rains,* many showers in one; but all are the showers *of his strength:* the power of God is to be observed as much in the small rain that soaks into the earth as in the great rain that batters on the house-top and washes away all before it. Note, The providence of God is to be

acknowledged, both by husbandmen in the fields and travellers upon the road, in every shower of rain, whether it does them a kindness or a diskindness. It is sin and folly to contend with God's providence in the weather; if he send the snow or rain, can we hinder them? Or shall we be angry at them? It is as absurd to quarrel with any other disposal of Providence concerning ourselves or ours. The effect of the extremity of the winter-weather is that it obliges both men and beasts to retire, making it uncomfortable and unsafe for them to go abroad. 1. Men retire to their houses from their labours in the field, and keep within doors (*v.* 7): *He seals up the hand of every man.* In frost and snow, husbandmen cannot follow their business, nor some tradesmen, nor travellers, when the weather is extreme. The plough is laid by, the shipping laid up, nothing is to be done, nothing to be got, that men, being taken off from their own work, *may know his work,* and contemplate that, and give him the glory of that, and, by the consideration of that work of his in the weather which seals up their hands, be led to celebrate his other great and marvellous works. Note, When we are, upon any account, disabled from following our worldly business, and taken off from it, we should spend our time rather in the exercises of piety and devotion (in acquainting ourselves with the works of God and praising him in them) than in foolish idle sports and recreations. When our hands are sealed up our hearts should be thus opened, and the less we have at any time to do in the world the more we should do for God and our souls. When we are confined to our houses we should thereby be driven to our Bibles and our knees. 2. *The beasts* also *retire to* their *dens and remain in their close places, v.* 8. It is meant of the wild beasts, which, being wild, must seek a shelter for themselves, to which by instinct they are directed, while the tame beasts, which are serviceable to man, are housed and protected by his care, as Exod. ix. 20. The ass has no den but his master's crib, and thither he goes, not only to be safe and warm, but to be fed. Nature directs all creatures to shelter themselves from a storm; and shall man alone be unprovided with an ark?

II. In the winds, which blow from different quarters and produce different effects (*v.* 9): *Out of the hidden place* (so it may be read) *comes the whirlwind;* it turns round, and so it is hard to say from which point it comes, but it comes from *the secret chamber,* as the word signifies, which I am not so willing to understand of the *south,* because he says here (*v.* 17) that the wind out of the south is so far from being a whirlwind that it is a warming, quieting, wind. But at this time, perhaps, Elihu saw a whirlwind-cloud coming out of the south and making towards them, out of which the Lord spoke soon after, *ch.* xxxviii. 1. Or, if turbulent winds which bring showers come out of the south, cold and drying blasts come out of the north to scatter the vapours and clear the air of them.

III. In the frost, *v.* 10. See the cause of it: *It is given by the breath of God*, that is, by the word of his power and the command of his will; or, as some understand it, by the wind, which is the breath of God, as the thunder is his voice; it is caused by the cold freezing wind out of the north. See the effect of it: *The breadth of the waters is straitened*, that is, the waters that had spread themselves, and flowed with liberty, are congealed, benumbed, arrested, bound up in crystal fetters. This is such an instance of the power of God as, if it were not common, would be next to a miracle.

IV. In the clouds, the womb where all these watery meteors are conceived, of which he had spoken, *ch.* xxxvi. 28. Three sorts of clouds he here speaks of:—1. Close, black, thick clouds, pregnant with showers; and these with watering *he wearies* (*v.* 11), that is, they spend themselves, and are exhausted by the rain into which they melt and are dissolved, pouring out water till they are weary and can pour out no more. See what pains, as I may say, the creatures, even those above us, take to serve man: the clouds water the earth till they are weary; they spend and are spent for our benefit, which shames and condemns us for the little good we do in our places, though it would be to our own advantage, for *he that watereth shall be watered also himself.* 2. Bright thin clouds, clouds without water; and these *he scattereth;* they are dispersed of themselves, and not dissolved into rain, but what becomes of them we know not. The bright cloud, in the evening, when the sky is red, is scattered, and proves an earnest of a fair day, Matt. xvi. 2. 3. Flying clouds, which do not dissolve, as the thick cloud, into a close rain, but are carried upon the wings of the wind from place to place, dropping showers as they go; and these are said to be *turned round about by his counsels, v.* 12. The common people say that the rain is determined by the planets, which is as bad divinity as it is philosophy, for it is guided and governed by the counsel of God, which extends even to those things that seem most casual and minute, *that they may do whatsoever he commands them;* for the stormy winds, and the clouds that are driven by them, fulfil his word; and by this means he *causes it to rain upon one city and not upon another,* Amos iv. 7, 8. Thus his will is done *upon the face of the world in the earth,* that is, among the children of men, to whom God has an eye in all these things, or whom it is said that he *made them to dwell on the face of all the earth,* Acts xvii. 26. The inferior creatures, being incapable of doing moral actions, are incapable of receiving rewards and punishments: but, among the children of men, God causes the rain to come, either for the correction of his land

or for a mercy to it, *v.* 13. (1.) Rain sometimes turns into a judgment. It is a scourge to a sinful land; as once it was for the destruction of the whole world, so it is now often for the correction or discipline of some parts of it, by hindering seedness and harvest, raising the waters, and damaging the fruits. Some have said that our nation has received much more prejudice by the excess of rain than by the want of it. (2.) At other times it is a blessing. It is *for his land,* that this may be made fruitful; and, besides that which is just necessary, he gives *for mercy,* to fatten it and make it more fruitful. See what a necessary dependence we have upon God, when the very same thing, according to the proportion in which it is given, may be either a great judgment or a great mercy, and without God we cannot have either a shower or a fair gleam.

14 Hearken unto this, O Job: stand still, and consider the wondrous works of God. 15 Dost thou know when God disposed them, and caused the light of his cloud to shine? 16 Dost thou know the balancings of the clouds, the wondrous works of him which is perfect in knowledge? 17 How thy garments *are* warm, when he quieteth the earth by the south *wind?* 18 Hast thou with him spread out the sky, *which is* strong, *and* as a molten looking glass? 19 Teach us what we shall say unto him; *for* we cannot order *our speech* by reason of darkness. 20 Shall it be told him that I speak? if a man speak, surely he shall be swallowed up.

Elihu here addresses himself closely to Job, desiring him to apply what he had hitherto said to himself. He begs that he would hearken to this discourse (*v.* 14), that he would pause awhile: *Stand still, and consider the wondrous works of God.* What we hear is not likely to profit us unless we consider it, and we are not likely to consider things fully unless we stand still and compose ourselves to the consideration of them. The works of God, being wondrous, both deserve and need our consideration, and the due consideration of them will help to reconcile us to all his providences. Elihu, for the humbling of Job, shows him,

I. That he had no insight into natural causes, could neither see the springs of them nor foresee the effects of them (*v.* 15—17): *Dost thou know* this and know that which are *the wondrous works of him who is perfect in knowledge?* We are here taught, 1. The perfection of God's knowledge. It is one of the most glorious perfections of God that he is perfect in knowledge; he is omniscient. His knowledge is intuitive: he *sees,* and does not know by report. It is intimate and entire: he knows things truly, and not by their colours—thoroughly, and not by piecemeal. To his knowledge there is nothing distant, but all near—nothing future, but all present —nothing hid, but all open. We ought to acknowledge this in all his wondrous works, and it is sufficient to satisfy us in those wondrous works which we know not the meaning of that they are the works of one that knows what he does.   2. The imperfection of our knowledge. The greatest philosophers are much in the dark concerning the powers and works of nature. We are a paradox to ourselves, and every thing about us is a mystery. The gravitation of bodies, and the cohesion of the parts of matter, are most certain, and yet unaccountable. It is good for us to be made sensible of our own ignorance. Some have confessed their ignorance, and those that would not do this have betrayed it. But we must all infer from it what incompetent judges we are of the divine politics, when we understand so little even of the divine mechanics. (1.) We know not what orders God has given concerning the clouds, nor what orders he will give, *v.* 15. That all is done by determination and with design we are sure ; but what is determined, and what designed, and when the plan was laid, we know not. God often *causes the light of his cloud to shine,* in the rainbow (so some), in the lightning (so others); but did we foresee, or could we foretel, when he would do it? If we foresee the change of weather a few hours before, by vulgar observation, or when second causes have begun to work by the weather-glass, yet how little do these show us of the purposes of God by these changes! (2.) We know not how the clouds are poised in the air, the *balancing* of them, which is one of the wondrous works of God. They are so balanced, so spread, that they never rob us of the benefit of the sun (even the cloudy day is day), so balanced that they do not fall at once, nor burst into cataracts or water-spouts. The rainbow is an intimation of God's favour in balancing the clouds so as to keep them from drowning the world. Nay, so are they balanced that they impartially distribute their showers on the earth, so that, one time or other, every place has its share. (3.) We know not how the comfortable change comes when the winter is past, *v.* 17. [1.] How the weather becomes warm after it has been cold. We know how our garment came to be warm upon us, that is, how we come to be warm in our clothes, by reason of the warmth of the air we breathe in. Without God's blessing we should clothe ourselves, yet not be warm, Hag. i. 6. But, when he so orders it, the clothes are warm upon us, which, in the extremity of cold weather, would not serve to keep us warm. [2.] How it becomes calm after it has been stormy : *He quiets the earth by the south wind,* when the

spring comes. As he has a blustering freezing north wind, so he has a thawing, composing, south wind; the Spirit is compared to both, because he both convinces and comforts, Cant. iv. 16.

II. That he had no share at all in the first making of the world (*v.* 18): "*Hast thou with him spread out the sky ?* Thou canst not pretend to have stretched it out without him, no, nor to have stretched it out in conjunction with him ; for he was far from needing any help either in contriving or in working." The creation of the vast expanse of the visible heavens (Gen. i. 6—8), which we see in being to this day, is a glorious instance of the divine power, considering, 1. That, though it is fluid, yet it is firm. It *is strong,* and has its name from its stability. It still is what it was, and suffers no decay, nor shall the ordinances of heaven be altered till the lease expires with time. 2. That, though it is large, it is bright and most curiously fine : It is a *molten looking-glass,* smooth and polished, and without the least flaw or crack. In this, as in a looking-glass, we may *behold the glory of God* and the wisdom of *his handy work,* Ps. xix. 1. When we look up to heaven above we should remember it is a mirror or looking-glass, not to show us our own faces, but to be a faint representation of the purity, dignity, and brightness of the upper world and its glorious inhabitants.

III. That neither he nor they were able to speak of the glory of God in any proportion to the merit of the subject, *v.* 19, 20. 1. He challenges Job to be their director, if he durst undertake the task. He speaks it ironically : "*Teach us,* if thou canst, *what we shall say unto him, v.* 19. Thou hast a mind to reason with God, and wouldst have us to contend with him on thy behalf ; teach us then what we shall say. Canst thou see further into this abyss than we can? If thou canst, favour us with thy discoveries, furnish us with instructions." 2. He owns his own insufficiency both in speaking to God and in speaking of him : *We cannot order our speech by reason of darkness.* Note, The best of men are much in the dark concerning the glorious perfections of the divine nature and the administrations of the divine government. Those that through grace know much of God, yet know little, yea, nothing, in comparison with what is to be known, and what will be known, when that which is perfect shall come and the veil shall be rent. When we would speak of God we speak confusedly and with great uncertainty, and are soon at a loss and run aground, not for want of matter, but for want of words. As we must always begin with fear and trembling, lest we speak amiss *(De Deo etiam vera dicere periculosum est— Even while affirming what is true concerning God we incur risk),* so we must conclude with shame and blushing, for having spoken no better. Elihu himself had, for his part, spoken well on God's behalf, and yet is so far from expecting a fee, or thinking that God was beholden to him for it, or that he was fit to be standing counsel for him, that (1.) He is even ashamed of what he has said, not of the cause, but of his own management of it : *"Shall it be told him that I speak ? v.* 20. Shall it be reported to him as a meritorious piece of service, worthy his notice ? By no means ; let it never be spoken of," for he fears that the subject has suffered by his undertaking it, as a fine face is wronged by a bad painter, and his performance is so far from meriting thanks that it needs pardon. When we have done all we can for God we must acknowledge that we are unprofitable servants and have nothing at all to boast of. He is afraid of saying any more : *If a man speak,* if he undertake to plead for God, much more if he offer to plead against him, *surely he shall be swallowed up.* If he speak presumptuously, God's wrath shall soon consume him ; but, if ever so well, he will soon lose himself in the mystery and be overpowered by the divine lustre. Astonishment will strike him blind and dumb.

21 And now *men* see not the bright light which *is* in the clouds : but the wind passeth, and cleanseth them. 22 Fair weather cometh out of the north: with God *is* terrible majesty. 23 *Touching* the Almighty, we cannot find him out: *he is* excellent in power, and in judgment, and in plenty of justice : he will not afflict. 24 Men do therefore fear him : he respecteth not any *that are* wise of heart.

Elihu here concludes his discourse with some short but great sayings concerning the glory of God, as that which he was himself impressed, and desired to impress others, with a holy awe of. He speaks concisely, and in haste, because, it should seem, he perceived that God was about to take the work into his own hands. 1. He observes that God who has said that he will *dwell in the thick darkness* and *make that his pavilion* (2 Chron. vi. 1, Ps. xviii. 11) is in that awful chariot advancing towards them, as if he were preparing his throne for judgment, surrounded with *clouds and darkness,* Ps. xcvii. 2, 9. He saw the cloud, with a whirlwind in the bosom of it, coming out of the south ; but now it hung so thick, so black, over their heads, that they could none of them *see the bright light which* just before *was in the clouds.* The light of the sun was now eclipsed. This reminded him of the darkness by reason of which he could not speak (*v.* 19), and made him afraid to go on, *v.* 20. Thus the disciples *feared when they entered into a cloud,* Luke ix. 34. Yet he looks to the north, and sees it clear that way, which gives him hope that the clouds are not gathering for

a deluge ; they are covered, but not surrounded, with them. He expects that *the wind will pass* (so it may be read) *and cleanse them,* such a wind as passed over the earth to clear it from the waters of Noah's flood (Gen. viii. 1), in token of the return of God's favour ; and then *fair weather will come out of the north* (*v.* 22) and all will be well. God will not always frown, nor contend for ever. 2. He hastens to conclude, now that God is about to speak ; and therefore delivers much in a few words, as the sum of all that he had been discoursing of, which, if duly considered, would not only clench the nail he had been driving, but make way for what God would say. He observes, (1.) That *with God is terrible majesty.* He is a God of glory and such transcendent perfection as cannot but strike an awe upon all his attendants and a terror upon all his adversaries. *With God is terrible praise* (so some), for he is *fearful in praises,* Exod. 15. 11. (2.) That when we speak *touching the Almighty* we must own that *we cannot find him out;* our finite understandings cannot comprehend his infinite perfections, *v.* 23. Can we put the sea into an egg-shell? We cannot trace the steps he takes in his providence. *His way is in the sea.* (3.) That *he is excellent in power.* It is the excellency of his power that he can do whatever he pleases in heaven and earth. The universal extent and irresistible force of his power are the excellency of it ; no creature has an arm like him, so long, so strong. (4.) That he is no less excellent in wisdom and righteousness, *in judgment and plenty of justice,* else there would be little excellency in his power. We may be sure that he who can do every thing will do every thing for the best, for he is infinitely wise, and will not in any thing do wrong, for he is infinitely just. When he executes judgment upon sinners, yet there is plenty of justice in the execution, and he inflicts not more than they deserve. (5.) That *he will not afflict,* that is, that he will not afflict willingly ; it is no pleasure to him to grieve the children of men, much less his own children. He never afflicts but when there is cause and when there is need, and ne does not overburden us with affliction, but considers our frame. Some read it thus : *" The Almighty, whom we cannot find out, is great in power, but he will not afflict in judgment, and with him is plenty of justice,* nor is he extreme to mark what we do amiss. (6.) He values not the censures of those who are wise in their own conceit : *He respecteth them not, v.* 24. He will not alter his counsels to oblige them, nor can those that prescribe to him prevail with him to do as they would have him do. He regards the prayer of the humble, but not the policies of the crafty. No, the foolishness of God is wise than men, 1 Cor. 1. 25. (7.) From all this it is easy to infer that, since God is great, he is greatly to be feared ; nay, because he is gracious and will not afflict, *men do therefore fear him,* for *there is forgiveness with him, that he may be feared,* Ps. 130. 4. It is the duty and interest of all men to fear God. *Men shall fear him* (so some); sooner or later they shall fear him. Those that will not fear the Lord and his goodness shall for ever tremble under the pourings out of the vials of his wrath.

CHAP. XXXVIII.

In most disputes the strife is who shall have the last word. Job's friends had, in this controversy, tamely yielded it to Job, and then he to Elihu. But, after all the wranglings of the counsel at bar, the judge upon the bench must have the last word; so God had here, and so he will have in every controversy, for every man's judgment proceeds from him and by his definitive sentence every man must stand or fall and every cause be won or lost. Job had often appealed to God, and had talked boldly how he would order his cause before him, and as a prince would he go near unto him; but, when God took the throne, Job had nothing to say in his own defence, but was silent before him. It is not so easy a matter as some think it to contest with the Almighty. Job's friends had sometimes appealed to God too: "O that God would speak!" ch. xi. 5. And now, at length, God does speak, when Job, by Elihu's clear and close arguings, was mollified a little, and mortified, and so prepared to hear what God had to say. It is the office of ministers to prepare the way of the Lord. That which the great God designs in this discourse is to humble Job, and bring him to repent of, and to recant, his passionate indecent expressions concerning God's providential dealings with him; and this he does by calling upon Job to compare God's eternity with his own time, God's omniscience with his own ignorance, and God's omnipotence with his own impotency. I. He begins with an awakening challenge and demand in general, ver. 2, 3. II. He proceeds in divers particular instances and proofs of Job's utter inability to contend with God, because of his ignorance and weakness; for, 1. He knew nothing of the founding of the earth, ver. 4—7. 2. Nothing of the limiting of the sea, ver. 8—11. 3. Nothing of the morning light, ver. 12—15. 4. Nothing of the dark recesses of the sea and earth, ver. 16—21. 5. Nothing of the springs in the clouds (ver. 22—27), nor the secret counsels by which they are directed. 6. He could do nothing towards the production of the rain, or frost, or lightning (ver. 28—30, 34, 35, 37, 38), nothing towards the directing of the stars and their influences (ver. 31—33), nothing towards the making of his own soul, ver. 36. And, lastly, he could not provide for the lions and the ravens, ver. 39—41. If, in these ordinary works of nature, Job was puzzled, how durst he pretend to dive into the counsels of God's government and to judge of them? In this (as bishop Patrick observes) God takes up the argument begun by Elihu (who came nearest to the truth) and prosecutes it in inimitable words, excelling his, and all other men's, in the loftiness of the style, as much as thunder does a whisper.

THEN the Lord answered Job out of the whirlwind, and said, 2 Who *is* this that darkeneth counsel by words without knowledge? 3 Gird up now thy loins like a man; for I will demand of thee, and answer thou me.

Let us observe here, 1. Who speaks—*The Lord,* Jehovah, not a created angel, but the eternal Word himself, the second person in the blessed Trinity, for it is he by whom the worlds were made, and that was no other than the Son of God. The same speaks here that afterwards spoke from Mount Sinai. Here he begins with the creation of the world, there with the redemption of Israel out of Egypt, and from both is inferred the necessity of our subjection to him. Elihu had said, *God speaks to men and they do not perceive it* (ch. xxxiii. 14); but this they could not but perceive, and yet we have *a more sure word of prophecy,* 2 Pet. i. 19. 2. When he spoke—*Then.* When they had all had their saying, and yet had not gained their point, then it was time for God to interpose, whose judgment is according to truth. When

we know not who is in the right, and perhaps are doubtful whether we ourselves are, this may satisfy us, That God will determine shortly *in the valley of decision,* Joel iii. 14. Job had silenced his three friends, and yet could not convince them of his integrity in the main. Elihu had silenced Job, and yet could not bring him to acknowledge his mismanagement of this dispute. But now God comes, and does both, convinces Job first of his unadvised speaking and makes him cry, *Peccavi—I have done wrong;* and, having humbled him, he puts honour upon him, by convincing his three friends that they had done him wrong. These two things God will, sooner or later, do for his people: he will show them their faults, that they may be themselves ashamed of them, and he will show others their righteousness, and bring it forth as the light, that they may be ashamed of their unjust censures of them. 3. How he spoke—*Out of the whirlwind,* the rolling and involving cloud, which Elihu took notice of, *ch.* xxxvii. 1, 2, 9. A whirlwind prefaced Ezekiel's vision (Ezek. i. 4), and Elijah's, 1 Kings xix. 11. God is said to have *his way in the whirlwind* (Nah. i. 3), and, to show that even the stormy wind fulfils his word, here it was made the vehicle of it. This shows what a mighty voice God's is, that it was not lost, but perfectly audible, even in the noise of a whirlwind. Thus God designed to startle Job, and to command his attention. Sometimes God answers his own people in terrible corrections, as out of the whirlwind, but always in righteousness. 4. To whom he spoke: He *answered Job,* directed his speech to him, to convince him of what was amiss, before he cleared him from the unjust aspersions cast upon him. It is God only that can effectually convince of sin, and those shall be humbled whom he designs to exalt. Those that desire to hear from God, as Job did, shall certainly hear from him at length. 5. What he said. We may conjecture that Elihu, or some other of the auditory, wrote down *verbatim* what was delivered out of the whirlwind, for we find (Rev. x. 4) that, when the thunders uttered their voices, John was prepared to write. Or, if it was not written then, yet, the penman of the book being inspired by the Holy Ghost, we are sure that we have here a very true and exact report of what was said. *The Spirit* (says Christ) *shall bring to your remembrance,* as he did here, *what I have said to you.* The preface is very searching. (1.) God charges him with ignorance and presumption in what he had said (*v.* 2): "*Who is this* that talks at this rate? Is it Job? What! a man? That weak, foolish, despicable, creature—shall he pretend to prescribe to me what I must do or to quarrel with me for what I have done? Is it Job? What! my servant Job, a perfect and an upright man? Can he so far forget himself, and act unlike himself? Who, where, is he *that darkens*

207

counsel thus by words without knowledge? Let him show his face if he dare, and stand to what he has said." Note, Darkening the counsels of God's wisdom with our folly is a great affront and provocation to God. Concerning God's counsels we must own that we are without knowledge. They are a deep which we cannot fathom; we are quite out of our element, out of our aim, when we pretend to account for them. Yet we are too apt to talk of them as if we understood them, with a great deal of niceness and boldness; but, alas! we do but darken them, instead of explaining them. We confound and perplex ourselves and one another when we dispute of the order of God's decrees, and the designs, and reasons, and methods, of his operations of providence and grace. A humble faith and sincere obedience shall see further and better into the secret of the Lord than all the philosophy of the schools, and the searches of science, so called. This first word which God spoke is the more observable because Job, in his repentance, fastens upon it as that which silenced and humbled him, *ch.* xlii. 3. This he repeated and echoed as the arrow that stuck fast in him: "I am the fool that has darkened counsel." There was some colour to have turned it upon *Elihu,* as if God meant *him,* for he spoke last, and was speaking when the whirlwind began; but Job applied it to himself, as it becomes us to do when faithful reproofs are given, and not (as most do) to billet them upon other people. (2.) He challenges him to give such proofs of his knowledge as would serve to justify his enquiries into the divine counsels (*v.* 3): "*Gird up now thy loins like a stout man;* prepare thyself for the encounter; *I will demand of thee,* will put some questions to thee, *and answer me* if thou canst, before I answer thine." Those that go about to call God to an account must expect to be catechised and called to an account themselves, that they may be made sensible of their ignorance and arrogance. God here puts Job in mind of what he had said, *ch.* xiii. 22. *Call thou, and I will answer.* "Now make thy words good."

4 Where wast thou when I laid the foundations of the earth? declare, if thou hast understanding. 5 Who hath laid the measures thereof, if thou knowest? or who hath stretched the line upon it? 6 Whereupon are the foundations thereof fastened? or who laid the corner stone thereof; 7 When the morning stars sang together, and all the sons of God shouted for joy? 8 Or *who* shut up the sea with doors, when it brake forth, *as if* it had issued out of the womb? 9 When I made the cloud the garment thereof, and

208

thick darkness a swaddlingband for it, 10 And brake up for it my decreed *place,* and set bars and doors, 11 And said, Hitherto shalt thou come, but no further: and here shall thy proud waves be stayed?

For the humbling of Job, God here shows him his ignorance even concerning the earth and the sea. Though so near, though so bulky, yet he could give no account of their origination, much less of heaven above or hell beneath, which are at such a distance, or of the several parts of matter which are so minute, and then, least of all, of the divine counsels.

I. Concerning the founding of the earth. "If he have such a mighty insight, as he pretends to have, into the counsels of God, let him give some account of the earth he goes upon, which is given to the children of men."

1. Let him tell where he was when this lower world was made, and whether he was advising or assisting in that wonderful work (*v.* 4): "*Where wast thou when I laid the foundations of the earth?* Thy pretensions are high; canst thou pretend to this? Wast thou present when the world was made?" See here, (1.) The greatness and glory of God: *I laid the foundations of the earth.* This proves him to be the only living and true God, and a God of power (Isa. xl. 21, Jer. x. 11, 12), and encourages us to trust in him at all times, Isa. li. 13, 16. (2.) The meanness and contemptibleness of man: *Where wast thou* then? Thou that hast made such a figure among the children of the east, and settest up for an oracle, and a judge of the divine counsels, where wast thou when the foundations of the earth were laid?" So far were we from having any hand in the creation of the world, which might entitle us to a dominion in it, or so much as being witnesses of it, by which we might have gained an insight into it, that we were not then in being. The first man was not, much less were we. It is the honour of Christ that he was present when this was done (Prov. viii. 22, &c., John i. 1, 2); but *we are of yesterday and know nothing.* Let us not therefore find fault with the works of God, nor prescribe to him. He did not consult us in making the world, and yet it is well made; why should we expect then that he should take his measures from us in governing it?

2. Let him describe how this world was made, and give a particular account of the manner in which this strong and stately edifice was formed and erected: "*Declare, if thou hast* so much *understanding* as thou fanciest thyself to have, what were the advances of that work." Those that pretend to have understanding above others ought to give proof of it. Show me thy faith by thy works, thy knowledge by thy words. Let Job declare,

if he can, (1.) How the world came to be so finely framed, with so much exactness, and such an admirable symmetry and proportion of all the parts of it (v. 5): "Stand forth, and *tell who laid the measures thereof* and *stretched out the line upon it.* Wast thou the architect that formed the model and then drew the dimensions by rule according to it? The vast bulk of the earth is moulded as regularly as if it had been done by line and measure; but who can describe how it was cast into this figure? Who can determine its circumference and diameter, and all the lines that are drawn on the terrestrial globe? It is to this day a dispute whether the earth stands still or turns round; how then can we determine by what measures it was first formed? (2.) How it came to be so firmly fixed. Though it is hung upon nothing, yet it is established, that it cannot be moved; but who can tell *upon what the foundations of it are fastened,* that it may not sink with its own weight, or *who laid the corner-stone thereof,* that the parts of it may not fall asunder? *v.* 6. *What God does, it shall be for ever* (Eccl. iii. 14); and therefore, as we cannot find fault with God's work, so we need not be in fear concerning it; it will last, and answer the end, the works of his providence as well as the work of creation; the measures of neither can never be broken; and the work of redemption is no less firm, of which Christ himself is both the foundation and the corner-stone. The church stands as fast as the earth.

3. Let him repeat, if he can, the songs of praise which were sung at that solemnity (v. 7), *when the morning-stars sang together,* the blessed angels (the first-born of the Father of light), who, in the morning of time, shone as brightly as the morning star, going immediately before the light which God commanded to shine out of darkness upon the seeds of this lower world, the earth, which was without form and void. They were *the sons of God,* who *shouted for joy* when they saw the foundations of the earth laid, because, though it was not made for them, but for the children of men, and though it would increase their work and service, yet they knew that the eternal Wisdom and Word, whom they were to worship (Heb. i. 6), would *rejoice in the habitable parts of the earth,* and that much of his *delight would be in the sons of men,* Prov. viii. 31. The angels are called *the sons of God* because they bear much of his image, are with him in his house above, and serve him as a son does his father. Now observe here, (1.) The glory of God, as the Creator of the world, is to be celebrated with joy and triumph by all his reasonable creatures; for they are qualified and appointed to be the collectors of his praises from the inferior creatures, who can praise him merely as objects that exemplify his workmanship. (2.) The work of angels is to praise God. The more we abound in holy, humble, thank-

ful, joyful praise, the more we do the will of God as they do it; and, whereas we are so barren and defective in praising God, it is a comfort to think that they are doing it in a better manner. (3.) They were unanimous in singing God's praises; they sang together with one accord, and there was no jar in their harmony. The sweetest concerts are in praising God. (4.) They all did it, even those who afterwards fell and left their first estate. Even those who have praised God may, by the deceitful power of sin, be brought to blaspheme him, and yet God will be eternally praised.

II. Concerning the limiting of the sea to the place appointed for it, *v.* 8, &c. This refers to the third day's work, when God said (Gen. i. 9), *Let the waters under the heaven be gathered together unto one place, and it was so.* 1. Out of the great deep or chaos, in which earth and water were intermixed, in obedience to the divine command the waters *broke forth like a child out of the* teeming *womb,* v. 8. Then the waters that had covered the deep, and stood above the mountains, retired with precipitation. At *God's rebuke they fled,* Ps. civ. 6, 7. 2. This newborn babe is clothed and swaddled, *v.* 9. *The cloud* is made *the garment thereof,* with which it is covered, and *thick darkness* (that is, shores vastly remote and distant from one another and quite in the dark one to another) *is a swaddling-band for it.* See with what ease the great God manages the raging sea; notwithstanding the ·violence of its tides, and the strength of its billows, he manages it as the nurse does the child in swaddling clothes. It is not said, He made *rocks and mountains* its swaddling bands, but *clouds and darkness,* something that we are not aware of and should think least likely for such a purpose. 3. There is a cradle too provided for this babe: *I broke up for it my decreed place,* v. 10. Valleys were sunk for it in the earth, capacious enough to receive it, and there it is laid to sleep; and, if it be sometimes tossed with winds, that (as bishop Patrick observes) is but the rocking of the cradle, which makes it sleep the faster. As for the sea, so for every one of us, there is a decreed place; for he that determined the times before appointed determined also the bounds of our habitation. 4. This babe being made unruly and dangerous by the sin of man, which was the original of all unquietness and danger in this lower world, there is also a prison provided for it; *bars and doors are set,* v. 10. And it is said to it, by way of check to its insolence, *Hitherto shalt thou come, but no further.* The sea is God's, for he made it, he restrains it; he says to it, *Here shall thy proud waves be stayed,* v. 11. This may be considered as an act of God's power over the sea. Though it is so vast a body, and though its motion is sometimes extremely violent, yet God has it under check. Its waves rise no higher, its tides roll no further, than God permits; and this is mentioned as a reason why we should stand in awe of God (Jer. v. 22), and yet why we should encourage ourselves in him, for he that stops the noise of the sea, even the noise of her waves, can, when he pleases, still the tumult of the people, Ps. lxv. 7. It is also to be looked upon as an act of God's mercy to the world of mankind and an instance of his patience towards that provoking race. Though he could easily cover the earth again with the waters of the sea (and, methinks, every flowing tide twice a day threatens us, and shows what the sea could do, and would do, if God would give it leave), yet he restrains them, being not willing that any should perish, and having *reserved the world that now is unto fire,* 2 Pet. iii. 7.

12 Hast thou commanded the morning since thy days; *and* caused the dayspring to know his place; 13 That it might take hold of the ends of the earth, that the wicked might be shaken out of it? 14 It is turned as clay *to* the seal; and they stand as a garment. 15 And from the wicked their light is withholden, and the high arm shall be broken. 16 Hast thou entered into the springs of the sea? or hast thou walked in the search of the depth? 17 Have the gates of death been opened unto thee? or hast thou seen the doors of the shadow of death? 18 Hast thou perceived the breadth of the earth? declare if thou knowest it all. 19 Where *is* the way *where* light dwelleth? and *as for* darkness, where *is* the place thereof, 20 That thou shouldest take it to the bound thereof, and that thou shouldest know the paths *to* the house thereof? 21 Knowest thou *it,* because thou wast then born? or *because* the number of thy days *is* great? 22 Hast thou entered into the treasures of the snow? or hast thou seen the treasures of the hail, 23 Which I have reserved against the time of trouble, against the day of battle and war? 24 By what way is the light parted, *which* scattereth the east wind upon the earth?

The Lord here proceeds to ask Job many puzzling questions, to convince him of his ignorance, and so to shame him for his folly in prescribing to God. If we will but try ourselves with such interrogatories as these, we shall soon be brought to own that what we know is nothing in comparison with what

210

we know not. Job is here challenged to give an account of six things :—

I. Of the springs of the morning, the dayspring from on high, *v.* 12—15. As there is no visible being of which we may be more firmly assured that it is, so there is none which we are more puzzled in describing, nor more doubtful in determining what it is, than the light. We welcome the morning, and are glad of the day-spring; but, 1. It is not commanded since our days, but what it is it was long before we were born, so that it was neither made by us nor designed primarily for us, but we take it as we find it and as the many generations had it that went before us. The day-spring knew its place before we knew ours, for we are but of yesterday. 2. It was not we, it was not any man that commanded the morning-light at first, or appointed the place of its springing up and shining forth, or the time of it. The constant and regular succession of day and night was no contrivance of ours; it is the glory of God that it shows, and his handy work, not ours, Ps. xix. 1, 2. 3. It is quite out of our power to alter this course : " *Hast thou countermanded the morning since thy days?* Hast thou at any time raised the morning light sooner than its appointed time, to serve thy purpose when thou hast waited for the morning, or ordered the day-spring for thy convenience to any other place than its own? No, never. Why then wilt thou pretend to direct the divine counsels, or expect to have the methods of Providence altered in favour of thee?" We may as soon break the covenant of the day and of the night as any part of God's covenant with his people, and particularly this, *I will chasten them with the rod of men.* 4. It is God that has appointed the day-spring to visit the earth, and diffuses the morning light through the air, which receives it as readily as the clay does the seal (*v.* 14), immediately admitting the impressions of it, so as of a sudden to be all over enlightened by it, as the seal stamps its image on the wax; *and they stand as a garment,* or as if they were clothed with a garment. The earth puts on a new face every morning, and dresses itself as we do, puts on light as a garment, and is then to be seen. 5. This is made a terror to evil-doers. Nothing is more comfortable to mankind than the light of the morning; it is pleasant to the eyes, it is serviceable to life and the business of it, and the favour of it is universally extended, for *it takes hold of the ends of the earth* (*v.* 13), and we should dwell, in our hymns to the light, on its advantages to the earth. But God here observes how unwelcome it is to those that do evil, and therefore hate the light. God makes the light a minister of his justice as well as of his mercy. It is designed *to shake the wicked out of the earth,* and for that purpose *it takes hold of the ends of it,* as we take hold of the ends of a garment to shake the dust and moths out of it. Job had observed what a terror the morning light is to criminals, because it discovers them (*ch.* xxiv. 13, &c.), and God here seconds the observation, and asks him whether the world was indebted to him for that kindness? No, the great Judge of the world sends forth the beams of the morning light as his messengers to detect criminals, that they may not only be defeated in their purposes and put to shame, but that they may be brought to condign punishment (*v.* 15), that their light may be *withholden* from them (that is, that they may lose their comfort, their confidence, their liberties, their lives) and that their *high arm*, which they have lifted up against God and man, may be *broken*, and they deprived of their power to do mischief. Whether what is here said of the morning light was designed to represent, as in a figure, the light of the gospel of Christ, and to give a type of it, I will not say; but I am sure it may serve to put us in mind of the encomiums given to the gospel just at the rising of its morning-star by Zecharias in his *Benedictus* (Luke i. 78, By the *tender mercy of our God the day-spring from on high has visited us, to give light to those that sit in darkness,* whose hearts are turned to it *as clay to the seal,* 2 Cor. iv. 6), and by the virgin Mary in her *Magnificat* (Luke i. 51), showing that God, in his gospel, has *shown strength with his arm, scattered the proud, and put down the mighty,* by that light by which he designed to shake the wicked, to shake wickedness itself out of the earth, and break its high arm.

II. Of the springs of the sea (*v.* 16): *"Hast thou entered into* them, or *hast thou walked in the search of the depth?* Knowest thou what lies in the bottom of the sea, the treasures there hidden in the sands? Or canst thou give an account of the rise and original of the waters of the sea? Vapours are continually exhaled out of the sea. Dost thou know how the recruits are raised by which it is continually supplied? Rivers are constantly poured into the sea. Dost thou know how they are continually discharged, so as not to overflow the earth? Art thou acquainted with the secret subterraneous passages by which the waters circulate?" God's way in the government of the world is said to be *in the sea,* and *in the great waters* (Ps. lxxvii. 19), intimating that it is hidden from us and not to be pried into by us.

III. Of the gates of death: *Have* these *been open to thee? v.* 16. Death is a grand secret. 1. We know not beforehand when, and how, and by what means, we or others shall be brought to death, by what road we must go the way whence we shall not return, what disease or what disaster will be the door to let us into the house appointed for all living. *Man knows not his time.* 2. We cannot describe what death is, how the knot is untied between body and soul, nor how the *spirit of a man goes upward* (Eccl. iii. 21), to

be we know not what and live we know not how, as Mr. Norris expresses it; with what dreadful curiosity (says he) does the soul launch out into the vast ocean of eternity and resign to an untried abyss! Let us make it sure that the gates of heaven shall be opened to us on the other side death, and then we need not fear the opening of the gates of death, though it is a way we are to go but once. 3. We have no correspondence at all with separate souls, nor any acquaintance with their state. It is an unknown undiscovered region to which they are removed; we can neither hear from them nor send to them. While we are here, in a world of sense, we speak of the world of spirits as blind men do of colours, and when we remove thither we shall be amazed to find how much we are mistaken.

IV. Of the breadth of the earth (*v.* 18): *Hast thou perceived* that? The knowledge of this might seem most level to him and within his reach; yet he is challenged to declare this if he can. We have our residence on the earth, God has given it to the children of men. But who ever surveyed it, or could give an account of the number of its acres? It is but a point to the universe? yet, small as it is, we cannot be exact in declaring the dimensions of it. Job had never sailed round the world, nor any before him; so little did men know the breadth of the earth that it was but a few ages ago that the vast continent of America was discovered, which had, time out of mind, lain hidden. The divine perfection is longer than the earth and broader than the sea; it is therefore presumption for us, who perceive not the breadth of the earth, to dive into the depth of God's counsels.

V. Of the place and way of light and darkness. Of the day-spring he had spoken before (*v.* 12) and he returns to speak of it again (*v.* 19): *Where is the way where light dwells?* And again (*v.* 24): *By what way is the light parted?* He challenges him to describe, 1. How the light and darkness were at first made. When God, in the beginning, first spread darkness upon the face of the deep, and afterwards commanded the light to shine out of darkness, by that mighty word, *Let there be light,* was Job a witness to the order, to the operation? can he tell where the fountains of light and darkness are, and where those mighty princes keep their courts distinct, while in one world they rule alternately? Though we long ever so much either for the shining forth of the morning or the shadows of the evening, we know not whither to send, or go, to fetch them, nor can tell *the paths to the house thereof, v.* 20. We were not then born, nor is the number of our days so great that we can describe the birth of that first-born of the visible creation, *v.* 21. Shall we then undertake to discourse of God's counsels, which were from eternity, or to find out the paths to the house thereof, to solicit for the alteration of them? God glories in it that he forms the light and creates the darkness; and if we must take those as we find them, take those as they come, and quarrel with neither, but make the best of both, then we must, in like manner, accommodate ourselves to the peace and the evil which God likewise created. Isa. xlv. 7. 2. How they still keep their turns interchangeably. It is God that *makes the outgoings of the morning and of the evening to rejoice* (Ps. lxv. 8); for it is his order, and no order of ours, that is executed by the outgoings of the morning light and the darkness of the night. We cannot so much as tell whence they come nor whither they go (*v.* 24): *By what way is the light parted* in the morning, when, in an instant, it shoots itself into all the parts of the air above the horizon, as if the morning light flew upon the wings of an east wind, so swiftly, so strongly, is it carried, scattering the darkness of the night, as the east wind does the clouds? Hence we read of the *wings of the morning* (Ps. cxxxix. 9), on which the light is conveyed *to the uttermost parts of the sea*, and *scattered like an east wind upon the earth*. It is a marvellous change that passes over us every morning by the return of the light and every evening by the return of the darkness; but we expect them, and so they are no surprise nor uneasiness to us. If we would, in like manner, reckon upon changes in our outward condition, we should neither in the brightest noon expect perpetual day nor in the darkest midnight despair of the return of the morning. God has set the one over against the other, like the day and night; and so must we, Eccl. vii. 14.

VI. Of the *treasures of the snow and hail* (*v.* 22, 23): "*Hast thou entered* into these and taken a view of them?" In the clouds the snow and hail are generated, and thence they come in such abundance that one would think there were treasures of them laid up in store there, whereas indeed they are produced *extempore—suddenly*, as I may say, and *pro re nata—for the occasion*. Sometimes they come so opportunely, to serve the purposes of Providence, in God's fighting for his people and against his and their enemies, that one would think they were laid up as magazines, or stores of arms, ammunition, and provisions, against the time of trouble, *the day of battle and war*, when God will either contend with the world in general (as in the deluge, when the windows of heaven were opened, and the waters fetched out of these treasures to drown a wicked world, that waged war with Heaven) or with some particular persons or parties, as when God out of these treasures fetched great hail-stones wherewith to fight against the Canaanites, Josh. x. 11. See what folly it is to strive against God, who is thus prepared for battle and war, and how much it is our interest to make our peace with him and to keep ourselves in his love. God can fight as effectually with snow and hail, if he please, as with thunder and lightning or the sword of an angel!

212

25 Who hath divided a watercourse for the overflowing of waters, or a way for the lightning of thunder; 26 To cause it to rain on the earth, *where* no man *is; on* the wilderness, wherein *there is* no man; 27 To satisfy the desolate and waste *ground;* and to cause the bud of the tender herb to spring forth? 28 Hath the rain a father? or who hath begotten the drops of dew? 29 Out of whose womb came the ice? and the hoary frost of heaven, who hath gendered it? 30 The waters are hid as *with* a stone, and the face of the deep is frozen. 31 Canst thou bind the sweet influences of Pleiades, or loose the bands of Orion? 32 Canst thou bring forth Mazzaroth in his season? or canst thou guide Arcturus with his sons? 33 Knowest thou the ordinances of heaven? canst thou set the dominion thereof in the earth? 34 Canst thou lift up thy voice to the clouds, that abundance of waters may cover thee? 35 Canst thou send lightnings, that they may go, and say unto thee, Here we *are?* 36 Who hath put wisdom in the inward parts? or who hath given understanding to the heart? 37 Who can number the clouds in wisdom? or who can stay the bottles of heaven, 38 When the dust groweth into hardness, and the clods cleave fast together? 39 Wilt thou hunt the prey for the lion? or fill the appetite of the young lions, 40 When they couch in *their* dens, *and* abide in the covert to lie in wait? 41 Who provideth for the raven his food? when his young ones cry unto God, they wander for lack of meat.

Hitherto God had put such questions to Job as were proper to convince him of his ignorance and short-sightedness. Now he comes, in the same manner, to show his impotency and weakness. As it is but little that he knows, and therefore he ought not to arraign the divine counsels, so it is but little that he can do, and therefore he ought not to oppose the proceedings of Providence. Let him consider what great things God does, and try whether he can do the like, or whether he thinks himself an equal match for him.

I. God has thunder, and lightning, and rain, and frost, at command, but Job has not, and therefore let him not dare to compare himself with God, or to contend with him. Nothing is more uncertain than what weather it shall be, nor more out of our reach to appoint; it shall be what weather pleases God, not what pleases us, unless, as becomes us, whatever pleases God pleases us. Concerning this observe here,

1. How great God is.

(1.) He has a sovereign dominion over the waters, has appointed them their course, even then when they seem to overflow and to be from under his check, v. 25. He has *divided a water-course,* directs the rain where to fall, even when the shower is most violent, with as much certainty as if it were conveyed by canals or conduit-pipes. Thus the hearts of kings are said to be *in God's hand;* and as the rains, those rivers of God, he turns them whithersoever he will. Every drop goes as it is directed. God has *sworn that the waters of Noah shall no more return to cover the earth;* and we see that he is able to make good what he has promised, for he has the rain in a water-course.

(2.) He has dominion over the lightning and the thunder, which go not at random, but in the way that he directs them. They are mentioned here because he *prepares the lightnings for the rain,* Ps. cxxxv. 7. Let not those that fear God be afraid of the lightning or the thunder, for they are not blind bullets, but go the way that God himself, who means no hurt to them, directs.

(3.) In directing the course of the rain he does not neglect the wilderness, the desert land (v. 26, 27), *where no man is.* [1.] Where there is no man to be employed in taking care of the productions. God's providence reaches further than man's industry. If he had not more kindness for many of the inferior creatures than man has, it would go ill with them. God can make the earth fruitful without any art or pains of ours, Gen. ii. 5, 6. When *there was not a man to till the ground,* yet there went up a mist and watered it. But we cannot make it fruitful without God; it is he that gives the increase. [2.] Where there is no man to be provided for nor to take the benefit of the fruits that are produced. Though God does with very peculiar favour visit and regard man, yet he does not overlook the inferior creatures, but causes *the bud of the tender herb to spring forth for food for all flesh,* as well as *for the service of man.* Even the wild asses shall have their thirst quenched, Ps. civ. 11. God has enough for all, and wonderfully provides even for those creatures that man neither has service from nor makes provision for.

(4.) He is, in a sense, *the Father of the rain, v.* 28. It has no other father. He produces it by his power; he governs and directs it, and makes what use he pleases of it. Even the small drops of the dew he distils upon the earth, as the God of nature; and, as the God of grace, he rains righteousness upon us and is himself as the dew unto Israel. See Hos. xiv. 5, 6; Mic. v. 7.

(5.) The ice and the frost, by which the waters are congealed and the earth incrus-

tated, are produced by his providence, v. 29, 30. These are very common things, which lessens the strangeness of them. But, considering what a vast change is made by them in a very little time, how the waters are hid as with a stone, as with a grave-stone, laid upon them (so thick, so strong, is the ice that covers them), and the face even of the deep is sometimes frozen, we may well ask, " *Out of whose womb came the ice?* What created power could produce such a wonderful work?" No power but that of the Creator himself. Frost and snow come from him, and therefore should lead our thoughts and meditations to him who does such great things, past finding out. And we shall the more easily bear the inconveniencies of winter-weather if we learn to make this good use of it.

2. How weak man is. Can he do such things as these? Could Job? No, v. 34, 35. (1.) He cannot command one shower of rain for the relief of himself or his friends: " *Canst thou lift up thy voice to the clouds,* that bottles of heaven, *that abundance of waters may cover thee,* to water thy fields when they are dry and parched?" If we lift up our voice to God, to pray for rain, we may have it (Zech. x. 1); but if we lift up our voice to the clouds, to demand it, they will soon tell us they are not at our beck, and we shall go without it, Jer. xiv. 22. The heavens will not hear the earth unless God hear them, Hos. ii. 21. See what poor, indigent, depending creatures we are; we cannot do without rain, nor can we have it when we will. (2.) He cannot commission one flash of lightning, if he had a mind to make use of it for the terror of his enemies (v. 35): " *Canst thou send lightnings, that they may go* on thy errand, and do the execution thou desirest? Will they come at thy call, and say unto thee, *Here we are?*" No, the ministers of God's wrath will not be ministers of ours. Why should they, since the *wrath of man works not the righteousness of God?* See Luke ix. 55.

II. God has the stars of heaven under his command and cognizance, but we have them not under ours. Our meditations are now to rise higher, far above the clouds, to the glorious lights above. God mentions particularly, not the planets, which move in lower orbs, but the fixed stars, which are much higher. It is supposed that they have an influence upon this earth, notwithstanding their vast distance, not upon the minds of men or the events of providence (men's fate is not determined by their stars), but upon the ordinary course of nature; they are set for signs and seasons, for days and years, Gen. i. 14. And if the stars have such a dominion over this earth (v. 33), though they have their place in the heavens and are but mere matter, much more has he who is their Maker and ours, and who is an Eternal Mind. Now see how weak we are. 1. We cannot alter the influences of the stars (v. 31), not theirs that are instrumental to produce the pleasures of the spring : *Canst thou bind the sweet influ-ences of Pleiades ?*—the seven stars, that con-stellation which lies in so small a compass (none in less), and yet sheds very benign in-fluences upon the earth. Nor can we alter theirs that introduce the rigour of the winter: *Canst thou loose the bands of Orion?*—that magnificent constellation which makes so great a figure (none greater), and dispenses rough and unpleasing influences, which we cannot control nor repel. Both summer and winter will have their course. God can change them when he pleases, can make the spring cold, and so bind the sweet influences of Pleiades, and the winter warm, and so loose the bands of Orion ; but we cannot. 2. It is not in our power to order the motions of the stars, nor are we entrusted with the guidance of them. God, who *calls the stars by their names* (Ps. cxlvii. 4), calls them forth in their respective seasons, appointing them the time of their rising and setting. But this is not our province; we cannot *bring forth Mazzaroth*—the stars in the southern signs, nor *guide Arcturus*—those in the northern, *v.* 32. God can bring forth the stars to battle (as he did when in their courses they fought against Sisera) and guide them in the attacks they are ordered to make; but man cannot do so. 3. We are not only un-concerned in the government of the stars (the government they are under, and the go-vernment they are entrusted with, for they both rule and are ruled), but utterly unac-quainted with it ; we *know not the ordinances of heaven, v.* 33. So far are we from being able to change them that we can give no ac-count of them ; they are a secret to us. Shall we then pretend to know God's counsels, and the reasons of them ? If it were left to us to set the dominion of the stars upon the earth, we should soon be at a loss. Shall we then teach God how to govern the world ?

III. God is the author and giver, the father and fountain, of all wisdom and understand-ing, *v.* 36. The souls of men are nobler and more excellent beings than the stars of hea-ven themselves, and shine more brightly. The powers and faculties of reason with which man is endued, and the wonderful per-formances of thought, bring him into some alliance to the blessed angels ; and whence comes this light, but from the Father of lights ? *Who* else *has put wisdom into the inner parts* of man, and *given understanding to the heart?* 1. The rational soul itself, and its capacities, come from him as the God of nature ; for he forms the spirit of man within him. We did not make our own souls, nor can we describe how they act, nor how they are united to our bodies. He only that made them knows them, and knows how to ma-nage them. He fashioneth men's hearts alike in some things, and yet unlike in others. 2. True wisdom, with its furniture and im-provement, comes from him as the God of grace and the Father of every good and per-

214

fect gift. Shall we pretend to be wiser than God, when we have all our wisdom from him ? Nay, shall we pretend to be wise above our sphere, and beyond the limits which he that gave us our understanding sets to it ? He designed we should with it serve God and do our duty, but never intended we should with it set up for directors of the stars or the lightning.

IV. God has the clouds under his cogni-zance and government, but so have not we, *v.* 37. Can any man, with all his wisdom, undertake to *number the clouds*, or (as it may be read) to *declare and describe the nature of them?* Though they are near us, in our own atmosphere, yet we know little more of them than of the stars which are at so great a dis-tance. And when the clouds have poured down rain in abundance, so that *the dust grows into* solid mire and *the clods cleave fast to-gether* (*v.* 38), *who can stay the bottles of hea-ven?* Who can stop them, that it may not always rain? The power and goodness of God are herein to be acknowledged, that he gives the earth rain enough, but does not surfeit it, softens it, but does not drown it, makes it fit for the plough, but not unfit for the seed. As we cannot command a shower of rain, so we cannot command a fair day, without God; so neces-sary, so constant, is our dependence upon him.

V. God provides food for the inferior crea-tures, and it is by his providence, not by any care or pains of ours, that they are fed. The following chapter is wholly taken up with the instances of God's power and goodness about animals, and therefore some transfer to it the last three verses of this chapter, which speak of the provision made, 1. For the lions, *v.* 39, 40. "Thou dost not pretend that the clouds and stars have any dependence upon thee, for they are above thee ; but on the earth thou thinkest thyself paramount ; let us try that then : *Wilt thou hunt the prey for the lion ?* Thou valuest thyself upon thy posses-sions of cattle which thou wast once owner of, the oxen, and asses, and camels, that were fed at thy crib ; but wilt thou undertake the main-tenance of the lions, and *the young lions, when they couch in their dens*, waiting for a prey? No, thou needest not do it, they can shift for them-selves without thee : thou canst not do it, for thou hast not wherewithal to satisfy them : thou darest not do it ; shouldst thou come to feed them, they would seize upon thee. But I do it." See the all-sufficiency of the divine providence: it has wherewithal to satisfy the desire of every living thing, even the most ra-venous. See the bounty of the divine Provi-dence, that, wherever it has given life, it will give livelihood, even to those creatures that are not only not serviceable, but dangerous, to man. And see its sovereignty, that it suffers some creatures to be killed for the support of other creatures. The harmless sheep are torn to pieces, to *fill the appetite of the young lions*, who yet sometimes are made to lack and suffer hunger, **to** punish them for their cruelty, while those that fear God want no good thing. 2. For the young ravens, *v.* 41. As ravenous beasts, so ravenous birds, are fed by the divine Providence. *Who* but God *provides for the raven his food?* Man does not; he takes care only of those creatures that are, or may be, useful to him. But God has a regard to all the works of his hands, even the meanest and least valuable. The ravens' *young ones* are in a special manner necessitous, and God supplies them, Ps. cxlvii. 9. God's feeding the fowls, especially these fowls (Matt. vi. 26), is an encouragement to us to trust him for our daily bread. See here, (1.) What distress the young ravens are often in : *They wander for lack of meat.* The old ones, they say, neglect them, and do not provide for them as other birds do for their young : and indeed those that are ravenous to others are commonly barbarous to their own, and unnatural. (2.) What they are supposed to do in that distress : They *cry,* for they are noisy clamorous creatures, and this is interpreted a crying to God. It being the cry of nature, it is looked upon as directed to the God of nature. The putting of so favourable a construction as this upon the cries of the young ravens may encourage us in our prayers, though we can but cry, *Abba, Father.* (3.) What God does for them. Some way or other he provides for them, so that they grow up, and come to maturity. And he that takes this care of the young ravens certainly will not be wanting to his people or theirs. This, being but one instance of many of the divine compassion, may give us occasion to think how much good our God does, every day, beyond what we are aware of.

CHAP. XXXIX.

God proceeds here to show Job what little reason he had to charge him with unkindness who was so compassionate to the inferior creatures and took such a tender care of them, or to boast of himself, and his own good deeds before God, which were nothing to the divine mercies. He shows him also what great reason he had to be humble who knew so little of the nature of the creatures about him and had so little influence upon them, and to submit to that God on whom they all depend. He discourses particularly, I. Concerning the wild goats and the hinds, ver. 1—4. II. Concerning the wild ass, ver. 5—8. III. Concerning the unicorn, ver. 9—12. IV. Concerning the peacock, ver. 13. V. Concerning the ostrich, ver. 13—18. VI. Concerning the horse, ver. 19—25. VII. Concerning the hawk and the eagle, ver. 26—30.

K NOWEST thou the time when the wild goats of the rock bring forth? *or* canst thou mark when the hinds do calve? 2 Canst thou number the months *that* they fulfil? or knowest thou the time when they bring forth? 3 They bow themselves, they bring forth their young ones, they cast out their sorrows. 4 Their young ones are in good liking, they grow up with corn ; they go forth, and return not unto them. 5 Who hath sent out the wild ass free? or who hath loosed the bands of the wild ass? 6 Whose house I have made the wilderness, and the barren land his dwellings. 7 He scorneth the multitude of the city, neither regardeth he the crying of the driver. 8 The range of the mountains *is* his pasture, and he searcheth after every green thing. 9 Will the unicorn be willing to serve thee, or abide by thy crib? 10 Canst thou bind the unicorn with his band in the furrow? or will he harrow the vallies after thee? 11 Wilt thou trust him, because his strength *is* great? or wilt thou leave thy labour to him? 12 Wilt thou believe him, that he will bring home thy seed, and gather *it into* thy barn?

God here shows Job what little acquaintance he had with the untamed creatures that run wild in the deserts and live at large, but are the care of the divine Providence. As,

I. The *wild goats* and the *hinds.* That which is taken notice of concerning them is the bringing forth and bringing up of their young ones. For, as every individual is fed, so every species of animals is preserved, by the care of the divine Providence, and, for aught we know, none extinct to this day. Observe here, 1. Concerning the production of their young, (1.) Man is wholly ignorant of the time when they bring forth, *v.* 1, 2. Shall we pretend to tell what is in the womb of Providence, or what a day will bring forth, who know not the time of the pregnancy of a hind or a wild goat? (2.) Though they bring forth their young with a great deal of difficulty and sorrow, and have no assistance from man, yet, by the good providence of God, their young ones are safely produced, and their sorrows cast out and forgotten, *v.* 3. Some think it is intimated (Ps. xxix. 9) that God by thunder helps the hinds in calving. Let it be observed, for the comfort of women in labour, that God helps even the hinds to bring forth their young; and shall he not much more succour them, and save them in child-bearing, who are his children in covenant with him? 2. Concerning the growth of their young (*v.* 4): *They are in good liking;* though they are brought forth in sorrow, after their dams have suckled them awhile they shift for themselves in the corn-fields, and are no more burdensome to them, which is an example to children, when they have grown up, not to be always hanging upon their parents and craving from them, but to put forth themselves to get their own livelihood and to requite their parents.

II. The *wild ass,* a creature we frequently read of in Scripture, some say untameable. Man is said to be born as the wild ass's colt, so hard to be governed. Two things Providence has allotted to the wild ass —1. An unbounded liberty (*v.* 5): *Who* but God *has sent out the wild ass free?* He has given a disposition to it, and therefore a dispensation for it. The tame ass is bound to labour; the wild ass has no bonds on him. Note, Freedom from service, and liberty to range at pleasure, are but the privileges of a wild ass. It is a pity that any of the children of men should covet such a liberty, or value themselves on it. It is better to labour and be good for something than ramble and be good for nothing. But if, among men, Providence sets some at liberty and suffers them to live at ease, while others are doomed to servitude, we must not marvel at the matter: it is so among the brute-creatures. 2. An uninclosed lodging (*v.* 6): *Whose house I have made the wilderness,* where he has room enough to traverse his ways, and snuff up the wind at his pleasure, as the wild ass is said to do (Jer. ii. 24), as if he had to live upon the air, for it is *the barren land* that is *his dwelling.* Observe, The tame ass, that labours, and is serviceable to man, has his master's crib to go to both for shelter and food, and lives in a fruitful land: but the wild ass, that will have his liberty, must have it in a barren land. He that will not labour, let him not eat. He that will shall eat the labour of his hands, and have also to give to him that needs. Jacob, the shepherd, has good red pottage to spare, when Esau, a sportsman, is ready to perish for hunger. A further description of the liberty and livelihood of the wild ass we have, *v.* 7, 8. (1.) He has no owner, nor will he be in subjection: *He scorns the multitude of the city.* If they attempt to take him, and in order to that surround him with a multitude, he will soon get clear of them, and *the crying of the driver* is nothing to him. He laughs at those that live in the tumult and bustle of cities (so bishop Patrick), thinking himself happier in the wilderness; and opinion is the rate of things. (2.) Having no owner, he has no feeder, nor is any provision made for him, but he must shift for himself: *The range of the mountains is his pasture,* and a bare pasture it is; there he *searches after here and there a green thing,* as he can find it and pick it up; whereas the labouring asses have green things in plenty, without their searching for them. From the untameableness of this and other creatures we may infer how unfit we are to give law to Providence, who cannot give law even to a wild ass's colt.

III. The unicorn—*rhem,* a strong creature (Num. xxiii. 22), a stately proud creature, Ps. xcii. 10. He is able to serve, but not willing; and God here challenges Job to force him to it. Job expected every thing should be just as he would have it. " Since thou dost pretend" (says God) " to bring every thing beneath thy sway, begin with the unicorn, and try thy skill upon him. Now that thy oxen and asses are all gone, try whether he will be willing to serve thee in their stead (*v.* 9) and whether he will be content with the provision thou usedst to make

216

for them: *Will he abide by thy crib?* No;" 1. " Thou canst not tame him, nor *bind him with his band,* nor set him to *draw the harrow,*" *v.* 10. There are creatures that are willing to serve man, that seem to take a pleasure in serving him, and to have a love for their masters; but there are such as will never be brought to serve him, which is the effect of sin. Man has revolted from his subjection to his Maker, and is therefore justly punished with the revolt of the inferior creatures from their subjection to him; and yet, as an instance of God's good-will to man, there are some that are still serviceable to him. Though the wild bull (which some think is meant here by the unicorn) will not serve him, nor submit to his band in the furrows, yet there are tame bullocks that will, and other animals that are not *feræ naturæ*—*of a wild nature,* in whom man may have a property, for whom he provides, and to whose service he is entitled. *Lord, what is man, that thou art thus mindful of him?* 2. " Thou darest not trust him; though *his strength is great,* yet thou wilt not *leave thy labour to him,* as thou dost with thy asses or oxen, which a little child may lead or drive, leaving to them all the pains. Thou wilt never depend upon the wild bull, as likely to come to thy harvest-work, much less to go through it, to *bring home thy seed and gather it into thy barn,*" *v.* 11, 12. And, because he will not serve about the corn, he is not so well fed as the tame ox, whose mouth was not to be muzzled in treading out the corn; but *therefore* he will not draw the plough, because he that made him never designed him for it. A disposition to labour is as much the gift of God as an ability for it; and it is a great mercy if, where God gives strength for service, he gives a heart; it is what we should pray for, and reason ourselves into, which the brutes cannot do; for, as among beasts, so among men, those may justly be reckoned wild and abandoned to the deserts who have no mind either to take pains or to do good.

13 *Gavest thou* the goodly wings unto the peacocks? or wings and feathers unto the ostrich? 14 Which leaveth her eggs in the earth, and warmeth them in dust, 15 And forgetteth that the foot may crush them, or that the wild beast may break them. 16 She is hardened against her young ones, as though *they were* not her's; her labour is in vain without fear; 17 Because God hath deprived her of wisdom, neither hath he imparted to her understanding. 18 What time she lifteth up herself on high, she scorneth the horse and his rider.

The ostrich is a wonderful animal, a very large bird, but it never flies. Some have called it *a winged camel.* God here gives an account of it, and observes,

I. Something that it has in common with the peacock, that is, beautiful feathers (*v.* 13): *Gavest thou proud wings unto the peacocks?* so some read it. Fine feathers make proud birds. The peacock is an emblem of pride; when he struts, and shows his fine feathers, Solomon in all his glory is not arrayed like him. The ostrich too has goodly feathers, and yet is a foolish bird; for wisdom does not always go along with beauty and gaiety. Other birds do not envy the peacock or the ostrich their gaudy colours, nor complain for want of them; why then should we repine if we see others wear better clothes than we can afford to wear? God gives his gifts variously, and those gifts are not always the most valuable that make the finest show. Who would not rather have the voice of the nightingale than the tail of the peacock, the eye of the eagle and her soaring wing, and the natural affection of the stork, than the beautiful wings and feathers of the ostrich, which can never rise above the earth, and is without natural affection?

II. Something that is peculiar to itself,

1. Carelessness of her young. It is well that this is peculiar to herself, for it is a very bad character. Observe, (1.) How she exposes her eggs; she does not retire to some private place, and make a nest there, as the sparrows and swallows do (Ps. lxxxiv. 3), and there lay eggs and hatch her young. Most birds, as well as other animals, are strangely guided by natural instinct in providing for the preservation of their young. But the ostrich is a monster in nature, for she drops her eggs any where upon the ground and takes no care to hatch them. If the sand and the sun will hatch them, well and good; they may for her, for she will not warm them, *v.* 14. Nay, she takes no care to preserve them: *The foot of the traveller may crush them,* and *the wild beast break them, v.* 15. But how then are any young ones brought forth, and whence is it that the species has not perished? We must suppose either that God, by a special providence, with the heat of the sun and the sand (so some think), hatches the neglected eggs of the ostrich, as he feeds the neglected young ones of the raven, or that, though the ostrich *often* leaves her eggs thus, yet not *always.* (2.) The reason why she does thus expose her eggs. It is, [1.] For want of natural affection (*v.* 16): *She is hardened against her young ones.* To be hardened against any is unamiable, even in a brute-creature, much more in a rational creature that boasts of humanity, especially to be hardened against young ones, that cannot help themselves and therefore merit compassion, that give no provocation and therefore merit no hard usage: but it is worst of all for her to be hardened against her own young ones, as though they were not hers, whereas really they are parts of her-

self. Her labour in laying her eggs is in vain and all lost, because she has not that fear and tender concern for them that she should have. Those are most likely to lose their labour that are least in fear of losing it. [2.] For want of wisdom (*v.* 17): *God has deprived her of wisdom.* This intimates that the art which other animals have to nourish and preserve their young is God's gift, and that, where it exists not, God denies it, that by the folly of the ostrich, as well as by the wisdom of the ant, we may learn to be wise; for, *First,* As careless as the ostrich is of her eggs so careless many people are of their own souls; they make no provision for them, no proper nest in which they may be safe, leave them exposed to Satan and his temptations, which is a certain evidence that they are deprived of wisdom. *Secondly,* So careless are many parents of their children; some of their bodies, not providing for their own house, their own bowels, and therefore worse than infidels, and as bad as the ostrich; but many more are thus careless of their children's souls, take no care of their education, send them abroad into the world untaught, unarmed, forgetting what corruption there is in the world through lust, which will certainly crush them. Thus their labour in rearing them comes to be in vain; it were better for their country that they had never been born. *Thirdly,* So careless are too many ministers of their people, with whom they should reside; but they leave them in the earth, and forget how busy Satan is to sow tares while men sleep. They overlook those whom they should oversee, and are really hardened against them.

2. Care of herself. She leaves her eggs in danger, but, if she herself be in danger, no creature shall strive more to get out of the way of it than the ostrich, *v.* 18. Then she lifts up her wings on high (the strength or which then stands her in better stead than their beauty), and, with the help of them, runs so fast that a horseman at full speed cannot overtake her: *She scorneth the horse and his rider.* Those that are least under the law of natural affection often contend most for the law of self-preservation. Let not the rider be proud of the swiftness of his horse when such an animal as the ostrich shall out-run him.

19 Hast thou given the horse strength? hast thou clothed his neck with thunder? 20 Canst thou make him afraid as a grasshopper? the glory of his nostrils *is* terrible. 21 He paweth in the valley, and rejoiceth in *his* strength: he goeth on to meet the armed men. 22 He mocketh at fear, and is not affrighted; neither turneth he back from the sword. 23 The quiver rattleth against him, the glittering

spear and the shield. 24 He swallow-eth the ground with fierceness and rage : neither believeth he that *it is* the sound of the trumpet. 25 He saith among the trumpets, Ha, ha ; and he smelleth the battle afar off, the thunder of the captains, and the shouting.

God, having displayed his own power in those creatures that are strong and despise man, here shows it in one scarcely inferior to any of them in strength, and yet very tame and serviceable to man, and that is the horse, especially *the horse that is prepared against the day of battle* and is serviceable to man at a time when he has more than ordinary occasion for his service. It seems, there was, in Job's country, a noble generous breed of horses. Job, it is probable, kept many, though they are not mentioned among his possessions, cattle for use in husbandry being there valued more than those for state and war, which alone horses were then reserved for, and they were not then put to such mean services as with us they are commonly put to. Concerning the great horse, that stately beast, it is here observed, 1. That he has a great deal of strength and spirit (*v.* 19): *Hast thou given the horse strength?* He uses his strength for man, but has it not from him : God gave it to him, who is the fountain of all the powers of nature, and yet he himself *delights not in the strength of the horse* (Ps. cxlvii. 10), but has told us that *a horse is a vain thing for safety,* Ps. xxxiii. 17. For running, drawing, and carrying, no creature that is ordinarily in the service of man has so much strength as the horse has, nor is of so stout and bold a spirit, not to be made afraid as a grasshopper, but daring and forward to face danger. It is a mercy to man to have such a servant, which, though very strong, submits to the management of a child, and rebels not against his owner. But let not the strength of a horse be trusted to, Hos. xiv. 3; Ps. xx. 7; Isa. xxxi. 1, 3. 2. That his neck and nostrils look great. His neck is *clothed with thunder,* with a large and flowing mane, which makes him formidable and is an ornament to him. *The glory of his nostrils,* when he snorts, flings up his head, and throws foam about, *is terrible, v.* 20. Perhaps there might be at that time, and in that country, a more stately breed of horses than any we have now. 3. That he is very fierce and furious in battle, and charges with an undaunted courage, though he pushes on in imminent danger of his life. (1.) See how frolicsome he is (*v.* 21): *He paws in the valley,* scarcely knowing what ground he stands upon. He is proud of his strength, and he has much more reason to be so as using his strength in the service of man, and under his direction, than the wild ass that uses it in contempt of man, and in a revolt from him *v.* 8. (2.) See how

218

forward he is to engage : *He goes on to meet the armed men,* animated, not by the goodness of the cause, or the prospect of honour, but only by *the sound of the trumpet, the thunder of the captains, and the shouting* of the soldiers, which are as bellows to the fire of his innate courage, and make him spring forward with the utmost eagerness, as if he cried, *Ha ! ha ! v.* 25. How wonderfully are the brute-creatures fitted for and inclined to the services for which they were designed. (3.) See how fearless he is, how he despises death and the most threatening dangers. (*v.* 22): *He mocks at fear,* and makes a jest of it; slash at him with a sword, rattle the quiver, brandish the spear, to drive him back, he will not retreat, but press forward, and even inspires courage into his rider. (4.) See how furious he is. He curvets and prances, and runs on with so much violence and heat against the enemy that one would think he even *swallowed the ground with fierceness and rage, v.* 24. High mettle is the praise of a horse rather than of a man, whom fierceness and rage ill become. This description of the war-horse will help to explain that character which is given of presumptuous sinners, Jer. viii. 6. *Every one turneth to his course, as the horse rusheth into the battle.* When a man's heart is fully set in him to do evil, and he is carried on in a wicked way by the violence of inordinate appetites and passions, there is no making him afraid of the wrath of God and the fatal consequences of sin. Let his own conscience set before him the curse of the law, the death that is the wages of sin, and all the terrors of the Almighty in battle-array; he mocks at this fear, and is not affrighted, neither turns he back from the flaming sword of the cherubim. Let ministers lift up their voice like a trumpet, to proclaim the wrath of God against him, *he believes not that it is the sound of the trumpet,* nor that God and his heralds are in earnest with him; but what will be in the end hereof it is easy to foresee.

26 Doth the hawk fly by thy wisdom, *and* stretch her wings toward the south? 27 Doth the eagle mount up at thy command, and make her nest on high? 28 She dwelleth and abideth on the rock, upon the crag of the rock, and the strong place. 29 From thence she seeketh the prey, *and* her eyes behold afar off. 30 Her young ones also suck up blood : and where the slain *are,* there *is* she.

The birds of the air are proofs of the wonderful power and providence of God, as well as the beasts of the earth; God here refers particularly to two stately ones:—1. The *hawk,* a noble bird of great strength and sagacity, and yet a bird of prey, *v.* 26. This bird is here taken notice of for her flight, which is swift and strong, and especially for the course she steers *towards the south*, whither she follows the sun in winter, out of the colder countries in the north, especially when she is to cast her plumes and renew them. This is her wisdom, and it was God that gave her this wisdom, not man. Perhaps the extraordinary wisdom of the hawk's flight after her prey was not used then for men's diversion and recreation, as it has been since. It is a pity that the reclaimed hawk, which is taught to fly at man's command and to make him sport, should at any time be abused to the dishonour of God, since it is from God that she receives that wisdom which makes her flight entertaining and serviceable. 2. The *eagle*, a royal bird, and yet a bird of prey too, the permission of which, nay, the giving of power to which, may help to reconcile us to the prosperity of oppressors among men. The eagle is here taken notice of, (1.) For the height of her flight. No bird soars so high, has so strong a wing, nor can so well bear the light of the sun. Now, *"Doth she mount at thy command? v.* 27. Is it by any strength she has from thee? or dost thou direct her flight? No; it is by the natural power and instinct God has given her that she will soar out of thy sight, much more out of thy call." (2.) For the strength of her nest. Her house is her castle and strong-hold; she makes it *on high* and *on the rock, the crag of the rock* (*v.* 28), which sets her and her young out of the reach of danger. Secure sinners think themselves as safe in their sins as the eagle in her nest on high, in the *clefts of the rock; but I will bring thee down thence, saith the Lord,* Jer. xlix. 16. The higher bad men sit above the resentments of the earth the nearer they ought to think themselves to the vengeance of Heaven. (3.) For her quicksightedness (*v.* 29): *Her eyes behold afar off*, not upwards, but downwards, in quest of her prey. In this she is an emblem of a hypocrite, who, while, in the profession of religion, he seems to rise towards heaven, keeps his eye and heart upon the prey on earth, some temporal advantage, some widow's house or other that he hopes to devour, under pretence of devotion. (4.) For the way she has of maintaining herself and her young. She preys upon living animals, which she seizes and tears to pieces, and then carries to her young ones, which are taught to *suck up blood;* they do it by instinct, and know no better; but for men that have reason and conscience to thirst after blood is what could scarcely be believed if there had not been in every age wretched instances of it. She also preys upon the dead bodies of men : *Where the slain are, there is she.* These birds of prey (in another sense than the horse, *v.* 25) *smell the battle afar off.* Therefore, when a great slaughter is to be made among the enemies of the church, the fowls are invited to *the supper of the great God, to eat the flesh of kings and cap-*

tains, Rev. xix. 17, 18. Our Saviour refers to this instinct of the eagle, Matt. xxiv. 28. *Wheresoever the carcase is, there will the eagles be gathered together.* Every creature will make towards that which is its proper food; for he that provides the creatures their food has implanted in them that inclination. These and many such instances of natural power and sagacity in the inferior creatures, which we cannot account for, oblige us to confess our own weakness and ignorance and to give glory to God as the fountain of all being, power, wisdom, and perfection.

CHAP. XL.

Many humbling confounding questions God had put to Job, in the foregoing chapter; now, in this chapter, I. He demands an answer to them, ver. 1, 2. II. Job submits in a humble silence, ver. 3—5. III. God proceeds to reason with him, for his conviction, concerning the infinite distance and disproportion between him and God, showing that he was by no means an equal match for God. He challenges him (ver. 6, 7) to vie with him, if he durst, for justice (ver. 8), power (ver. 9), majesty (ver. 10), and dominion over the.proud (ver. 11—14), and he gives an instance of his power in one particular animal, here called "Behemoth," ver. 15—24.

MOREOVER the Lord answered Job, and said, 2 Shall he that contendeth with the Almighty instruct *him?* he that reproveth God, let him answer it. 3 Then Job answered the Lord, and said, 4 Behold, I am vile; what shall I answer thee? I will lay mine hand upon my mouth. 5 Once have I spoken; but I will not answer: yea, twice; but I will proceed no further.

Here is, I. A humbling challenge which God gave to Job. After he had heaped up many hard questions upon him, to show him, by his manifest ignorance in the works of nature, what an incompetent judge he was of the methods and designs of Providence, he clenches the nail with one demand more, which stands by itself here as the application of the whole. It should seem, God paused awhile, as Elihu had done, to give Job time to say what he had to say, or to think of what God had said; but Job was in such confusion that he remained silent, and therefore God here put him upon replying, *v.* 1, 2. This is not said to be spoken *out of the whirlwind,* as before; and therefore some think God said it in a still small voice, which wrought more upon Job than the whirlwind did, as upon Elijah, 1 Kings xix. 12, 13. *My doctrine shall drop as the rain,* and then it does wonders. Though Job had not spoken any thing, yet God is said to answer him; for he knows men's thoughts, and can return a suitable answer to their silence. Here, 1. God puts a convincing question to him: " *Shall he that contendeth with the Almighty instruct him?* Shall he pretend to dictate to God's wisdom or prescribe to his will? Shall God receive instruction from every peevish complainer, and change the measures he has taken to please him?' It is a question with disdain. *Shall any teach God knowledge? ch.* xxi. 22.

It is intimated that those who quarrel with God do, in effect, go about to teach him how to mend his work. For if we contend with men like ourselves, as not having done well, we ought to instruct them how to do better; but is it a thing to be suffered that any man should teach his Maker? He that contends with God is justly looked upon as his enemy; and shall he pretend so far to have prevailed in the contest as to prescribe to him? We are ignorant and short-sighted, but before him all things are naked and open; we are depending creatures, but he is the sovereign Creator; and shall we pretend to instruct him? Some read it, *Is it any wisdom to contend with the Almighty?* The answer is easy. No; it is the greatest folly in the world. Is it wisdom to contend with him whom it will certainly be our ruin to oppose and unspeakably our interest to submit to? 2. He demands a speedy reply to it: *"He that reproaches God let him answer* this question to his own conscience, and answer it thus, *Far be it from me to contend with the Almighty* or to *instruct him.* Let him answer all those questions which I have put, if he can. Let him answer for his presumption and insolence, answer it at God's bar, to his confusion." Those have high thoughts of themselves, and mean thoughts of God, who reprove any thing he says or does.

II. Job's humble submission thereupon. Now Job came to himself, and began to melt into godly sorrow. When his friends reasoned with him he did not yield; but the voice of the Lord is powerful. *When the Spirit of truth shall come, he shall convince.* They had condemned him for a wicked man; Elihu himself had been very sharp upon him (*ch.* xxxiv. 7, 8, 37); but God had not given him such hard words. We may sometimes have reason to expect better treatment from God, and a more candid construction of what we do, than we meet with from our friends. This the good man is here overcome by, and yields himself a conquered captive to the grace of God. 1. He owns himself an offender, and has nothing to say in his own justification (*v.* 4): *"Behold, I am vile,* not only mean and contemptible, but vile and abominable, in my own eyes." He is now sensible that he has sinned, and therefore calls himself *vile.* Sin debases us, and penitents abase themselves, reproach themselves, are ashamed, yea, even confounded. "I have acted undutifully to my Father, ungratefully to my benefactor, unwisely for myself; and therefore I am vile." Job now vilifies himself as much as ever he had justified and magnified himself. Repentance changes men's opinion of themselves. Job had been too bold in demanding a conference with God, and thought he could make his part good with him: but now he is convinced of his error, and owns himself utterly unable to stand before God or to produce any thing worth his notice, the veriest dunghill-worm

that ever crawled upon God's ground. While his friends talked with him, he answered them, for he thought himself as good as they; but, when God talked with him, he had nothing to say, for, in comparison with him, he sees himself nothing, less than nothing, worse than nothing, vanity and vileness itself; and therefore, *What shall I answer thee?* God demanded an answer, *v.* 2. Here he gives the reason of his silence; it was not because he was sullen, but because he was convinced he had been in the wrong. Those that are truly sensible of their own sinfulness and vileness dare not justify themselves before God, but are ashamed that ever they entertained such a thought, and, in token of their shame, lay their hand upon their mouth. 2. He promises not to offend any more as he had done; for Elihu had told him that this was meet to be said unto God. When we have spoken amiss we must repent of it and not repeat it nor stand to it. He enjoins himself silence (*v.* 4): *"I will lay my hand upon my mouth,* will keep that as with a bridle, to suppress all passionate thoughts which may arise in my mind, and keep them from breaking out in intemperate speeches." It is bad to think amiss, but it is much worse to speak amiss, for that is an allowance of the evil thought and gives it an *imprimatur—a sanction;* it is publishing the seditious libel; and therefore, *if thou hast thought evil, lay thy hand upon thy mouth* and let it go no further (Prov. xxx. 32) and that will be an evidence for thee that tnat which thou thoughtest thou allowest not. Job had suffered his evil thoughts to vent themselves: *"Once have I spoken* amiss, *yea, twice,"* that is, "divers times, in one discourse and in another; but I have done: *I will not answer;* I will not stand to what I have said, nor say it again; *I will proceed no further."* Observe here what true repentance is. (1.) It is to rectify our errors, and the false principles we went upon in doing as we did. What we have long, and often, and vigorously maintained, once, yea, twice, we must retract as soon as we are convinced that it is a mistake, not adhere to it any longer, but take shame to ourselves for holding it so long. (2.) It is to return from every by-path and to proceed not one step further in it: *"I will not add"* (so the word is); "I will never indulge my passion so much again, nor give myself such a liberty of speech, will never say as I have said nor do as I have done." Till it comes to this, we come short of repentance. Further observe, Those who dispute with God will be silenced at last. Job had been very bold and forward in demanding a conference with God, and talked very boldly, how plain he would make his case, and how sure he was that he should be justified. *As a prince he would go near unto him* (*ch.* xxxi. 37); he would *come even to his seat* (*ch.* xxiii. 3); but he has soon enough of it; he lets fall his plea and will not answer. "Lord, the wisdom and right are all on thy side, and I have done foolishly and wickedly in questioning them."

6 Then answered the LORD unto Job out of the whirlwind, and said, 7 Gird up thy loins now like a man : I will demand of thee, and declare thou unto me. 8 Wilt thou also disannul my judgment? wilt thou condemn me, that thou mayest be righteous? 9 Hast thou an arm like God? or canst thou thunder with a voice like him? 10 Deck thyself now *with* majesty and excellency; and array thyself with glory and beauty. 11 Cast abroad the rage of thy wrath : and behold every one *that is* proud, and abase him. 12 Look on every one *that is* proud, *and* bring him low; and tread down the wicked in their place. 13 Hide them in the dust together; *and* bind their faces in secret. 14 Then will I also confess unto thee that thine own right hand can save thee.

Job was greatly humbled for what God had already said, but not sufficiently; he was brought low, but not low enough; and therefore God here proceeds to reason with him in the same manner and to the same purport as before, *v.* 6. Observe, 1. Those who duly receive what they have heard from God, and profit by it, shall hear more from him. 2. Those who are truly convinced of sin, and penitent for it, yet have need to be more thoroughly convinced and to be made more deeply penitent. Those who are under convictions, who have their sins set in order before their eyes and their hearts broken for them, must learn from this instance not to catch at comfort too soon; it will be everlasting when it comes, and therefore it is necessary that we be prepared for it by deep humiliation, that the wound be searched to the bottom and not skinned over, and that we do not make more haste out of our convictions than good speed. When our hearts begin to melt and relent within us, let those considerations be dwelt upon and pursued which will help to make a thorough effectual thaw of it.

God begins with a challenge (*v.* 7), as before (*ch.* xxxviii. 3): "*Gird up thy loins now like a man;* if thou hast the courage and confidence thou hast pretended to, show them now; but thou wilt soon be made to see and own thyself no match for me." This is that which every proud heart must be brought to at last, either by its repentance or by its ruin; and thus low must every mountain and hill be, sooner or later, brought. We must acknowledge,

I. That we cannot vie with God for justice, that the Lord is righteous and holy in his dealings with us, but that we are unrighteous and unholy in our conduct towards him; we have a great deal to blame ourselves for, but nothing to blame him for (*v.* 8): "*Wilt thou disannul my judgment?* Wilt thou take exceptions to what I say and do, and bring a writ of error, to reverse the judgment I have given as erroneous and unjust?" Many of Job's complaints had too much of a tendency this way : *I cry out of wrong,* says he, *but I am not heard;* but such language as this is by no means to be suffered. God's judgment cannot, must not, be disannulled, for we are sure it is according to truth, and therefore it is a great piece of impudence and iniquity in us to call it in question. "*Wilt thou,*" says God, "*condemn me, that thou mayest be righteous?* Must my honour suffer for the support of thy reputation? Must I be charged as dealing unjustly with thee because thou canst not otherwise clear thyself from the censures thou liest under?" Our duty is to condemn ourselves, that God may be righteous. David is *therefore* ready to own the evil he has done in God's sight, that *God may be justified when he speaks and clear when he judges,* Ps. li. 4. See Neh. ix. 33; Dan. ix. 7. But those are very proud, and very ignorant both of God and themselves, who, to clear themselves, will condemn God; and the day is coming when, if the mistake be not rectified in time by repentance, the eternal judgment will be both the confutation of the plea and the confusion of the prisoner, for the heavens shall declare God's righteousness and all the world shall become guilty before him.

II. That we cannot vie with God for power; and therefore, as it is great impiety, so it is great impudence to contest with him, and is as much against our interest as it is against reason and justice (*v.* 9): "*Hast thou an arm like God,* equal to his in length and strength? *Or canst thou thunder with a voice like him,* as he did (*ch.* xxxvii. 1, 2), or does now out of the whirlwind?" To convince Job that he was not so able as he thought himself to contest with God, he shows him, 1. That he could never fight it out with him, nor carry his cause by force of arms. Sometimes, among men, controversies have been decided by battle, and the victorious champion is adjudged to have justice on his side; but, if the controversy were put upon that issue between God and man, man would certainly go by the worse, for all the forces he could raise against the Almighty would be but like briers and thorns before a consuming fire, Isa. xxvii. 4. "*Hast thou, a poor weak worm of the earth,* an arm comparable to his who upholds all things?" The power of creatures, even of angels themselves, is derived from God, limited by him, and dependent on him; but the power of God is original, independent, and unlimited. He can do every thing without us; we can do nothing without him; and therefore we have not an arm like God.

2. That he could never talk it out with him, nor carry his cause by noise and big words, which sometimes among men go a great way towards the gaining of a point: " *Canst thou thunder with a voice like him ?* No ; his voice will soon drown thine and one of his thunders will overpower and overrule all thy whispers." Man cannot speak so convincingly, so powerfully, nor with such a commanding conquering force as God can, who *speaks, and it is done.* His creating voice is called his *thunder* (Ps. civ. 7), so is that voice of his with which he terrifies and discomfits his enemies, 1 Sam. ii. 10. *Out of heaven shall he thunder upon them.* The wrath of a king may sometimes be like the roaring of a lion, but can never pretend to imitate God's thunder.

III. That we cannot vie with God for beauty and majesty, *v.* 10. " If thou wilt enter into a comparison with him, and appear more amiable, put on thy best attire : *Deck thyself now with majesty and excellency.* Appear in all the martial pomp, in all the royal pageantry that thou hast ; make the best of every thing that will set thee off : *Array thyself with glory and beauty,* such as may awe thy enemies and charm thy friends ; but what is it all to the divine majesty and beauty ? No more than the light of a glow-worm to that of the sun when he goes forth in his strength." God decks himself with such majesty and glory as are the terror of devils and all the powers of darkness and make them tremble ; he arrays himself with such glory and beauty as are the wonder of angels and all the saints in light and make them rejoice. David could dwell all his days in God's house, to behold the beauty of the Lord. But, in comparison with this, what is all the majesty and excellency by which princes think to make themselves feared, and all the glory and beauty by which lovers think to make themselves beloved ? If Job think, in contending with God, to carry the day by looking great and making a figure, he is quite mistaken. *The sun shall be ashamed, and the moon confounded, when God shines forth.*

IV. That we cannot vie with God for dominion over the proud, *v.* 11—14. Here the cause is put upon this short issue : if Job can humble and abase proud tyrants and oppressors as easily and effectually as God can, it shall be acknowledged that he has some colour to compete with God. Observe here,

1. The justice Job is here challenged to do, and that is to bring the proud low with a look. If Job will pretend to be a rival with God, especially if he pretend to be a judge of his actions, he must be able to do this.

(1.) It is here supposed that God can do it and will do it himself, else he would not have put it thus upon Job. By this God proves himself to be God, that he resists the proud, sits Judge upon them, and is able to bring them to ruin. Observe here, [1.] That

proud people are wicked people, and pride is at the bottom of a great deal of the wickedness that is in this world both towards God and man. [2.] Proud people will certainly be abased and brought low ; for *pride goes before destruction.* If they bend not, they will break ; if they humble not themselves by true repentance, God will humble them, to their everlasting confusion. The wicked will be *trodden down in their place,* that is, Wherever they are found, though they pretend to have a place of their own, and to have taken root in it, yet even there they shall be trodden down, and all the wealth, and power, and interest, to which their place entitles them, will not be their security. [3.] The wrath of God, scattered among the proud, will humble them, and break them, and bring them down. If he casts abroad the rage of his wrath, as he will do at the great day and sometimes does in this life, the stoutest heart cannot hold out against him. *Who knows the power of his anger ?* [4.] God can and does easily abase proud tyrants ; he can *look upon them, and bring them low,* can overwhelm them with shame, and fear, and utter ruin, by one angry look, as he can, by a gracious look, revive the hearts of the contrite ones. [5.] He can and will at last do it effectually (*v.* 13), not only bring them to the dust, from which they might hope to arise, but *hide them in the dust,* like the proud Egyptian whom Moses slew and *hid in the sand* (Exod. ii. 12), that is, they shall be brought not only to death, but to the grave, that pit out of which there is no return. They were proud of the figure they made, but they shall be buried in oblivion and be no more remembered than those that are hidden in the dust, out of sight and out of mind. They were linked in leagues and confederacies to do mischief, and are now bound in bundles. They are hidden *together;* not their rest, but their shame together *is in the dust, ch.* xvii. 16. Nay, they are treated as malefactors (who, when condemned, had their faces covered, as Haman's was : He *binds their faces in secret)* or as dead men : Lazarus, in the grave, had his face bound about. Thus complete will be the victory that God will gain, at last, over proud sinners that set themselves in opposition to him. Now by this he proves himself to be God. Does he thus hate proud men ? Then he is holy. Will he thus punish them ? Then he is the just Judge of the world. Can he thus humble them ? Then he is the Lord Almighty. When he had abased proud Pharaoh, and hidden him in the sand of the Red Sea, Jethro thence inferred that doubtless *the Lord is greater than all gods, for wherein the proud* enemies of his *Israel dealt proudly he was above them,* he was too hard for them, Exod. xviii. 11. See Rev. xix. 1, 2.

(2.) It is here proposed to Job to do it. He had been passionately quarrelling with God and his providence, casting abroad the rage of his wrath towards heaven, as if he thought thereby to bring God himself to his mind. "Come," says God, "try thy hand first upon proud men, and thou wilt soon see how little they value the rage of thy wrath; and shall I then regard it, or be moved by it?" Job had complained of the prosperity and power of tyrants and oppressors, and was ready to charge God with mal-administration for suffering it; but he ought not to find fault, except he could mend. If God, and he only, has power enough to humble and bring down proud men, no doubt he has wisdom enough to know when and how to do it, and it is not for us to prescribe to him or to teach him how to govern the world. Unless we had an arm like God we must not think to take his work out of his hands.

2. The justice which is here promised to be done him if he can perform such mighty works as these (*v.* 14): "*Then will I also confess unto thee that thy right hand* is sufficient to save thee, though, after all, it would be too weak to contend with me." It is the innate pride and ambition of man that he would be his own saviour (would have his own hands sufficient for him and be independent), but it is presumption to pretend that he is. Our own hands cannot save us by recommending us to God's grace, much less by rescuing us from his justice. Unless we could by our own power humble our enemies, we cannot pretend by our own power to save ourselves; but, if we could, God himself would confess it. He never did nor ever will defraud any man of his just praise, nor deny him the honour he has merited. But, since we cannot do this, we must confess unto him that our own hands cannot save us, and therefore into his hand we must commit ourselves.

15 Behold now behemoth, which I made with thee; he eateth grass as an ox. 16 Lo now, his strength *is* in his loins, and his force *is* in the navel of his belly. 17 He moveth his tail like a cedar: the sinews of his stones are wrapped together. 18 His bones *are* as strong pieces of brass; his bones *are* like bars of iron. 19 He *is* the chief of the ways of God: he that made him can make his sword to approach *unto him.* 20 Surely the mountains bring him forth food, where all the beasts of the field play, 21 He lieth under the shady trees, in the covert of the reed, and fens. 22 The shady trees cover him *with* their shadow; the willows of the brook compass him about. 23 Behold, he drinketh up a river, *and* hasteth not: he trusteth that he can draw up Jordan

into his mouth. 24 He taketh it with his eyes: *his* nose pierceth through snares.

God, for the further proving of his own power and disproving of Job's pretensions, concludes his discourse with the description of two vast and mighty animals, far exceeding man in bulk and strength, one he calls *behemoth,* the other *leviathan.* In these verses we have the former described. "*Behold now behemoth,* and consider whether thou art able to contend with him who made that beast and gave him all the power he has, and whether it is not my wisdom rather to submit to him and make thy peace with him." *Behemoth* signifies *beasts* in general, but must here be meant of some one particular species. Some understand it of the *bull;* others of an amphibious animal, well known (they say) in Egypt, called the *river-horse (hippopotamus),* living among the fish in the river Nile, but coming out to feed upon the earth. But I confess I see no reason to depart from the ancient and most generally received opinion, that it is the elephant that is here described, which is a very strong stately creature, of very large stature above any other, of wonderful sagacity, and of so great a reputation in the animal kingdom that among so many four-footed beasts as we have had the natural history of (*ch.* xxxviii. and xxxix.) we can scarcely suppose this should be omitted. Observe,

I. The description here given of the behemoth.

1. His body is very strong and well built. *His strength is in his loins, v.* 16. *His bones,* compared with those of other creatures, *are like bars of iron, v.* 18. His back-bone is so strong that, though his tail be not large, yet he moves it like a cedar, with a commanding force, *v.* 17. Some understand it of the trunk of the elephant, for the word signifies any extreme part, and in that there is indeed a wonderful strength. So strong is the elephant in his back and loins, and the sinews of his thighs, that he will carry a large wooden tower, and a great number of fighting men in it. No animal whatsoever comes near the elephant for strength of body, which is the main thing insisted on in this description.

2. He feeds on the productions of the earth and does not prey upon other animals: He *eats grass as an ox* (*v.* 15), the *mountains bring him forth food* (*v.* 20), and the beasts of the field do not tremble before him nor flee from him, as from a lion, but they play about him, knowing they are in no danger from him. This may give us occasion, (1.) To acknowledge the goodness of God in ordering it so that a creature of such bulk, which requires so much food, should not feed upon flesh (for then multitudes must die to keep him alive), but should be content with the grass of the field, to prevent such destruction of lives as otherwise must have ensued. (2.)

To commend living upon herbs and fruits without flesh, according to the original appointment of man's food, Gen. i. 29. Even the strength of an elephant, as of a horse and an ox, may be supported without flesh; and why not that of a man? Though therefore we use the liberty God has allowed us, yet *be not among riotous eaters of flesh,* Prov. xxiii. 20. (3.) To commend a quiet and peaceable life. Who would not rather, like the elephant, have his neighbours easy and pleasant about him, than, like the 'lion, have them all afraid of him?

3. He *lodges under the shady trees* (v. 21), which *cover him with their shadow* (v. 22), where he has a free and open air to breathe in, while lions, which live by prey, when they would repose themselves, are obliged to retire into a close and dark den, to live therein, and to abide in the covert of that, *ch.* xxxviii. 40. Those who are a terror to others cannot but be sometimes a terror to themselves too; but those will be easy who will let others be easy about them; and the reed and fens, and the willows of the brook, though a very weak and slender fortification, yet are sufficient for the defence and security of those who *therefore* dread no harm, because they design none.

4. That he is a very great and greedy drinker, not of wine or strong drink (to be greedy of that is peculiar to man, who by his drunkenness makes a beast of himself), but of fair water. (1.) His size is prodigious, and therefore he must have supply accordingly, v. 23. He drinks so much that one would think he could drink up a river, if you would give him time, and not hasten him. Or, when he drinks, *he hasteth not,* as those do that drink in fear; he is confident of his own strength and safety, and therefore makes no haste when he drinks, no more haste than good speed. (2.) His eye anticipates more than he can take; for, when he is very thirsty, having been long kept without water, *he trusts that he can drink up Jordan in his mouth,* and even *takes it with his eyes,* v. 24. As a covetous man causes his eyes to fly upon the wealth of this world, which he is greedy of, so this great beast is said to snatch, or draw up, even a river with his eyes. (3.) His nose has in it strength enough for both; for, when he goes greedily to drink with it, he *pierces through snares* or nets, which perhaps are laid in the waters to catch fish. He makes nothing of the difficulties that lie in his way, so great is his strength and so eager his appetite.

II. The use that is to be made of this description. We have taken a view of this mountain of a beast, this over-grown animal, which is here set before us, not merely as a show (as sometimes it is in our country) to satisfy our curiosity and to amuse us, but as an argument with us to humble ourselves before the great God; for, 1. He made this vast animal, which is so fearfully and wonderfully made; it is the work of his hands,

224

the contrivance of his wisdom, the production of his power; it is *behemoth which I made, v.* 15. Whatever strength this, or any other creature, has, it is derived from God, who therefore must be acknowledged to have all power originally and infinitely in himself, and such an arm as it is not for us to contest with. This beast is here called *the chief,* in its kind, *of the ways of God* (v. 19), an eminent instance of the Creator's power and wisdom. Those that will peruse the accounts given by historians of the elephant will find that his capacities approach nearer to those of reason than the capacities of any other brute-creature whatsoever, and therefore he is fitly called *the chief of the ways of God,* in the inferior part of the creation, no creature below man being preferable to him. 2. He made him with man, as he made other four-footed beasts, on the same day with man (Gen. i. 25, 26), whereas the fish and fowl were made the day before; he made him to live and move on the same earth, in the same element, and therefore man and beast are said to be jointly preserved by divine Providence as fellow-commoners, Ps. xxxvi. 6. "It is *behemoth, which I made with thee;* I made that beast as well as thee, and he does not quarrel with me; why then dost thou? Why shouldst thou demand peculiar favours because I made thee (*ch.* x. 9), when I made the *behemoth* likewise with thee? I made thee as well as that beast, and therefore can as easily manage thee at pleasure as that beast, and will do it whether thou refuse or whether thou choose. I made him with thee, that thou mayest look upon him and receive instruction." We need not go far for proofs and instances of God's almighty power and sovereign dominion; they are near us, they are with us, they are under our eye wherever we are. 3. *He that made him can make his sword to approach to him* (v. 19), that is, the same hand that made him, notwithstanding his great bulk and strength, can unmake him again at pleasure and kill an elephant as easily as a worm or a fly, without any difficulty, and without the imputation either of waste or wrong. God that gave to all the creatures their being may take away the being he gave; for may he not do what he will with his own? And he *can* do it; he that has power to create with a word no doubt has power to destroy with a word, and can as easily speak the creature into nothing as at first he spoke it out of nothing. The *behemoth* perhaps is here intended (as well as the *leviathan* afterwards) to represent those proud tyrants and oppressors whom God had just now challenged Job to abase and bring down. They think themselves as well fortified against the judgments of God as the elephant with his bones of brass and iron; but he that made the soul of man knows all the avenues to it, and can make the sword of justice, his wrath, to approach to it, and touch it in the most tender and sensible part. He that framed the engine, and put the parts of it together, knows how to take it in pieces. Woe to him therefore that strives with his Maker, for he that made him has therefore power to make him miserable, and will not make him happy unless he will be ruled by him.

CHAP. XLI.

The description here given of the leviathan, a very large, strong, formidable fish, or water-animal, is designed yet further to convince Job of his own impotency, and of God's omnipotence, that he might be humbled for his folly in making so bold with him as he had done. I. To convince Job of his own weakness he is here challenged to subdue and tame this leviathan if he can, and make himself master of him (ver. 1–9), and, since he cannot do this, he must own himself utterly unable to stand before the great God, ver. 10. II. To convince Job of God's power and terrible majesty several particular instances are here given of the strength and terror of the leviathan, which is no more than what God has given him, nor more than he has under his check, ver. 11, 12. The face of the leviathan is here described to be terrible (ver. 13, 14), his scales close (ver. 15—17), his breath and neesings sparkling (ver. 18—21), his flesh firm (ver. 22—24), his strength and spirit, when he is attacked, insuperable (ver. 25—30), his motions turbulent, and disturbing to the waters (ver. 31, 32), so that, upon the whole, he is a very terrible creature, and man is no match for him, ver. 33, 34.

CANST thou draw out leviathan with a hook? or his tongue with a cord *which* thou lettest down? 2 Canst thou put a hook into his nose? or bore his jaw through with a thorn? 3 Will he make many supplications unto thee? will he speak soft *words* unto thee? 4 Will he make a covenant with thee? wilt thou take him for a servant for ever? 5 Wilt thou play with him as *with* a bird? or wilt thou bind him for thy maidens? 6 Shall thy companions make a banquet of him? shall they part him among the merchants? 7 Canst thou fill his skin with barbed irons? or his head with fish spears? 8 Lay thine hand upon him, remember the battle, do no more. 9 Behold, the hope of him is in vain: shall not *one* be cast down even at the sight of him? 10 None *is so* fierce that dare stir him up: who then is able to stand before me?

Whether this leviathan be a whale or a crocodile is a great dispute among the learned, which I will not undertake to determine; some of the particulars agree more easily to the one, others to the other; both are very strong and fierce, and the power of the Creator appears in them. The ingenious Sir Richard Blackmore, though he admits the more received opinion concerning the *behemoth*, that it must be meant of the *elephant*, yet agrees with the learned Bochart's notion of the *leviathan*, that it is the *crocodile*, which was so well known in the river of Egypt. I confess that that which inclines me rather to understand it of the whale is not only because it is much larger and a nobler animal, but because, in the history of the Creation, there is such an express notice taken of it as

is not of any other species of animals whatsoever (Gen. i. 21, *God created great whales*), by which it appears, not only that whales were well known in those parts in the time of Moses, who lived a little after Job, but that the creation of whales was generally looked upon as a most illustrious proof of the eternal power and godhead of the Creator; and we may conjecture that this was the reason (for otherwise it seems unaccountable) why Moses there so particularly mentions the creation of the whales, because God had so lately, in this discourse with Job, more largely insisted upon the bulk and strength of that creature than of any other, as the proof of his power; and the *leviathan* is here spoken of as an inhabitant of the sea (*v.* 31), which the crocodile is not; and Ps. civ. 25, 26, *there*, in *the great and wide sea, is that leviathan.* Here in these verses,

I. He shows how unable Job was to master the leviathan. 1. That he could not catch him, as a little fish, with angling, *v.* 1, 2. He had no bait wherewith to deceive him, no hook wherewith to catch him, no fish-line wherewith to draw him out of the water, nor a thorn to run through his gills, on which to carry him home. 2. That he could not make him his prisoner, nor force him to cry for quarter, or surrender himself at discretion, *v.* 3, 4. "He knows his own strength too well to *make many supplications to thee,* and to *make a covenant with thee* to be thy servant on condition thou wilt save his life." 3. That he could not entice him into a cage, and keep him there as a bird for the children to play with, *v.* 5. There are creatures so little, so weak, as to be easily restrained thus, and triumphed over; but the leviathan is not one of these: he is made to be the terror, not the sport and diversion, of mankind. 4. That he could not have him served up to his table; he and his companions could not make a banquet of him; his flesh is too strong to be fit for food, and, if it were not, he is not easily caught. 5. That they could not enrich themselves with the spoil of him: *Shall they part him among the merchants,* the bones to one, the oil to another? If they can catch him, they will; but it is probable that the art of fishing for whales was not brought to perfection then, as it has been since. 6. That they could not destroy him, could not *fill his head with fish-spears, v.* 7. He kept out of the reach of their instruments of slaughter, or, if they touched him, they could not touch him to the quick. 7. That it was to no purpose to attempt it: *The hope of* taking *him is in vain, v.* 9. If men go about to seize him, so formidable is he that the very sight of him will appal them, and make a stout man ready to faint away: *Shall not one be cast down even at the sight of him?* and will not that deter the pursuers from their attempt? Job is told, at his peril, to *lay his hand upon him, v.* 8. "Touch him if thou dare; *remember the battle,* how unable thou art to encounter such a force, and what is therefore likely to be the issue of the battle, *and do no more,* but desist from the attempt." It is good to remember the battle before we engage in a war, and put off the harness in time if we foresee it will be to no purpose to gird it on. Job is hereby admonished not to proceed in his controversy with God, but to make his peace with him, remembering what the battle will certainly end in if he come to an engagement. See Isa. xxvii. 4, 5.

II. Thence he infers how unable he was to contend with the Almighty. *None is so fierce,* none so fool-hardy, *that he dares to stir up* the leviathan (*v.* 10), it being known that he will certainly be too hard for them; and *who then is able to stand before God,* either to impeach and arraign his proceedings or to out-face the power of his wrath? If the inferior creatures that are put under the feet of man, and over whom he has dominion, keep us in awe thus, how terrible must the majesty of our great Lord be, who has a sovereign dominion over us and against whom man has been so long in rebellion! *Who can stand before him when once he is angry?*

11 Who hath prevented me, that I should repay *him? whatsoever is* under the whole heaven is mine. 12 I will not conceal his parts, nor his power, nor his comely proportion. 13 Who can discover the face of his garment? *or* who can come *to him* with his double bridle? 14 Who can open the doors of his face? his teeth *are* terrible round about. 15 **His** scales *are his* pride, shut up together *as with* a close seal. 16 One is so near to another, that no air can come between them. 17 They are joined one to another, they stick together, that they cannot be sundered. 18 By his neesings a light doth shine, and his eyes *are* like the eyelids of the morning. 19 Out of his mouth go burning lamps, *and* sparks of fire leap out. 20 Out of his nostrils goeth smoke, as *out* of a seething pot or caldron. 21 His breath kindleth coals, and a flame goeth out of his mouth. 22 In his neck remaineth strength, and sorrow is turned into joy before him. 23 The flakes of his flesh are joined together: they are firm in themselves; they cannot be moved. 24 His heart is as firm as a stone; yea, as hard as a piece of the nether *millstone.* 25 When he raiseth up himself, the mighty are afraid:

by reason of breakings they purify themselves. 26 The sword of him that layeth at him cannot hold: the spear, the dart, nor the habergeon. 27 He esteemeth iron as straw, *and* brass as rotten wood. 28 The arrow cannot make him flee: slingstones are turned with him into stubble. 29 Darts are counted as stubble: he laugheth at the shaking of a spear. 30 Sharp stones *are* under him: he spreadeth sharp pointed things upon the mire. 31 He maketh the deep to boil like a pot: he maketh the sea like a pot of ointment. 32 He maketh a path to shine after him; *one* would think the deep *to be* hoary. 33 Upon earth there is not his like, who is made without fear. 34 He beholdeth all high *things:* he *is* a king over all the children of pride.

God, having in the foregoing verses shown Job how unable he was to deal with the leviathan, here sets forth his own power in that massy mighty creature. Here is,

I. God's sovereign dominion and independency laid down, *v.* 11. 1. That he is indebted to none of his creatures. If any pretend he is indebted to them, let them make their demand and prove their debt, and they shall receive it in full and not by composition: "*Who has prevented me?*" that is, "who has laid any obligations upon me by any services he has done me? Who can pretend to be before-hand with me? If any were, I would not long be behind-hand with them; I would soon repay them." The apostle quotes this for the silencing of all flesh in God's presence, Rom. xi. 35. *Who hath first given to him, and it shall be recompensed to him again?* As God does not inflict upon us the evils we have deserved, so he does bestow upon us the favours we have not deserved. 2. That he is the rightful Lord and owner of all the creatures: "*Whatsoever is under the whole heaven,* animate or inanimate, *is mine* (and particularly this leviathan), at my command and disposal, what I have an incontestable property in and dominion over." All is his; we are his, all we have and do; and therefore we cannot make God our debtor; but *of thy own, Lord, have we given thee.* All is his, and therefore, if he were indebted to any, he has wherewithal to repay them; the debt is in good hands. All is his, and therefore he needs not our services, nor can he be benefited by them. *If I were hungry I would not tell thee, for the world is mine and the fulness thereof,* Ps. l. 12.

II. The proof and illustration of it, from the wonderful structure of the leviathan, *v.* 12. 1. The parts of his body, the power he exerts, especially when he is set upon, and the comely proportion of the whole of him, are what God will not conceal, and therefore what we must observe and acknowledge the power of God in. Though he is a creature of monstrous bulk, yet there is in him a *comely proportion.* In our eye beauty lies in that which is small *(inest sua gratia parvis— little things have a gracefulness all their own)* because we ourselves are so; but in God's eye even the leviathan is comely; and, if he pronounce even the whale, even the crocodile, so, it is not for us to say of any of the works of his hands that they are ugly or ill-favoured; it is enough to say so, as we have cause, of our own works. God here goes about to give us an anatomical view (as it were) of the leviathan; for his works appear most beautiful and excellent, and his wisdom and power appear most in them, when they are taken in pieces and viewed in their several parts and proportions. (1.) The leviathan, even *prima facie—at first sight*, appears formidable and inaccessible, *v.* 13, 14. Who dares come so near him while he is alive as to discover or take a distinct view of *the face of the garment*, the skin with which he is clothed as with a garment, so near him as to bridle him like a horse and so lead him away, so near him as to be within reach of his jaws, which are like *a double bridle?* Who will venture to look into his mouth, as we do into a horse's mouth? He that *opens the doors of his face* will see *his teeth terrible round about*, strong and sharp, and fitted to devour; it would make a man tremble to think of having a leg or an arm between them. (2.) *His scales are* his beauty and strength, and therefore *his pride, v.* 15—17. The crocodile is indeed remarkable for his scales; if we understand it of the whale, we must understand by these *shields* (for so the word is) the several coats of his skin; or there might be whales in that country with scales. That which is remarkable concerning the scales is that *they stick* so close *together*, by which he is not only kept warm, for no air can pierce him, but kept safe, for no sword can pierce him through those scales. Fishes, that live in the water, are fortified accordingly by the wisdom of Providence, which gives clothes as it gives cold. (3.) He scatters terror with his very breath and looks; if he sneeze or spout up water, it is like a light shining, either with the froth or the light of the sun shining through it, *v.* 18. The eyes of the whale are reported to shine in the night-time like a flame, or, as here, *like the eye-lids of the morning:* the same they say of the crocodile. The breath of this creature is so hot and fiery, from the great natural heat within, that *burning lamps and sparks of fire*, smoke and a flame, are said to *go out of his mouth*, even such as one would think sufficient to set coals on fire, *v.* 19—21. Probably these hyperbolical expressions are used concerning the leviathan

to intimate the terror of the wrath of God, for that is it which all this is designed to convince us of. *Fire out of his mouth devours*, Ps. xviii. 7, 8. *The breath of the Almighty*, like a *stream of brimstone, kindles Tophet*, and will for ever keep it burning, Isa. xxx. 33. The wicked one shall be *consumed with the breath of his mouth*, 2 Thess. ii. 8. (4.) He is of invincible strength and most terrible fierceness, so that he frightens all that come in his way, but is not himself frightened by any. Take a view of his neck, and there remains strength, *v.* 22. His head and his body are well set together. *Sorrow rejoices* (or *rides in triumph) before him*, for he makes terrible work wherever he comes. Or, Those storms which are the sorrow of others are his joy; what is tossing to others is dancing to him. His flesh is well knit, *v.* 23. *The flakes* of it *are joined* so closely *together*, and *are so firm*, that it is hard to pierce it; he is as if he were all bone. *His flesh is of brass*, which Job had complained his was not, *ch.* vi. 12. *His heart is as firm as a stone, v.* 24. He has spirit equal to his bodily strength, and, though he is bulky, he is sprightly, and not unwieldy. As his flesh and skin cannot be pierced, so his courage cannot be daunted; but, on the contrary, he daunts all he meets and puts them into a consternation (*v.* 25): *When he raises up himself* like a moving mountain in the great waters even *the mighty are afraid* lest he should overturn their ships or do them some other mischief. *By reason of the breakings* he makes in the water, which threaten death, *they purify themselves*, confess their sins, betake themselves to their prayers, and get ready for death. We read (*ch.* iii. 8) of those who, when they raise up a leviathan, are in such a fright that they curse the day. It was a fear which, it seems, used to drive some to their curses and others to their prayers; for, as now, so then there were seafaring men of different characters and on whom the terrors of the sea have contrary effects; but all agree there is a great fright among them when the leviathan raises up himself. (5.) All the instruments of slaughter that are used against him do him no hurt and therefore are no terror to him, *v.* 26—29. *The sword* and *the spear*, which wound nigh at hand, are nothing to him; the *darts, arrows*, and *sling-stones*, which wound at a distance, do him no damage; nature has so well armed him *cap-a-pie—at all points*, against them all. The defensive weapons which men use when they engage with the leviathan, as *the habergeon*, or breast-plate, often serve men no more than their offensive weapons; *iron and brass* are to him *as straw and rotten wood*, and he laughs at them. It is the picture of a hard-hearted sinner, that despises the terrors of the Almighty and laughs at all the threatenings of his word. The leviathan so little dreads the weapons that are used against him that, to show how hardy he is, he chooses to lie on

the *sharp stones, the sharp-pointed things* (v
30), and lies as easy there as if he lay on the
soft mire. Those that would endure hardness must inure themselves to it. (6.) His
very motion in the water troubles it and puts
it into a ferment, v. 31, 32. When he rolls,
and tosses, and makes a stir in the water, or
is in pursuit of his prey, *he makes the deep to
boil like a pot*, he raises a great froth and
foam upon the water, such as is upon a boiling pot, especially *a pot of* boiling *ointment;*
and *he makes a path to shine after him*, which
even *a ship in the midst of the sea* does not,
Prov. xxx. 19. One may trace the leviathan
under water by the bubbles on the surface;
and yet who can take that advantage against
him in pursuing him? Men track hares in
the snow and kill them, but he that tracks
the leviathan dares not come near him.

2. Having given this particular account of
*his parts, and his power, and his comely pro-
portion*, he concludes with four things in
general concerning this animal:—(1.) That
he is a non-such among the inferior creatures: *Upon earth there is not his like*, v. 33.
No creature in this world is comparable to
him for strength and terror. Or the earth
is here distinguished from the sea: *His dominion is not upon the earth* (so some), but
in the waters. None of all the savage creatures upon earth come near him for bulk and
strength, and it is well for man that he is
confined to the waters and there has *a watch
set upon him* (*ch.* vii. 12) by the divine Providence, for, if such a terrible creature were
allowed to roam and ravage upon this earth,
it would be an unsafe and uncomfortable
habitation for the children of men, for whom
it is intended. (2.) That he is more bold
and daring than any other creature whatsoever: He *is made without fear.* The creatures are as they are made; the leviathan
has courage in his constitution, nothing can
frighten him; other creatures, quite contrary,
seem as much designed for flying as this for
fighting. So, among men, some are in their
natural temper bold, others are timorous.
(3.) That he is himself very proud; though
lodged in the deep, yet *he beholds all high
things*, v. 34. The rolling waves, the impending
rocks, the hovering clouds, and the ships under
sail with top and top-gallant, this mighty animal beholds with contempt, for he does not
think they either lessen him or threaten him.
Those that are great are apt to be scornful.
(4.) *That he is a king over all the children of
pride*, that is, he is the proudest of all proud
ones. He has more to be proud of (so Mr.
Caryl expounds it) than the proudest people
in the world have; and so it is a mortification to the haughtiness and lofty looks of
men. Whatever bodily accomplishments men
are proud of, and puffed up with, the leviathan
excels them and is a *king over them.* Some
read it so as to understand it of God: *He
that beholds all high things, even he, is King
over all the children of pride;* he can tame

the behemoth (*ch.* xl. 19) and the leviathan, big as they are, and stout-hearted as
they are. This discourse concerning those
two animals was brought in to prove that it
is God only who can *look upon proud men
and abase them, bring them low* and *tread
them down*, and *hide them in the dust* (*ch.* xl.
11—13), and so it concludes with a *quod
erat demonstrandum—which was to be demonstrated;* there is one that *beholds all high
things*, and, wherein men deal proudly, is
above them; he is *King over all the children
of pride*, whether brutal or rational, and can
make them all either bend or break before
him, Isa. ii. 11. *The lofty looks of man shall
be humbled, and the haughtiness of men shall
be bowed down, and* thus *the Lord alone shall
be exalted.*

CHAP. XLII.

Solomon says, " Better is the end of a thing than the beginning
thereof," Eccl. vii. 8. It was so here in the story of Job: at
evening-time it was light. Three things we have met with in
this book which, I confess, have troubled me very much; but
we find all the three grievances redressed, thoroughly redressed,
in this chapter, every thing set to-rights. I. It has been a great
trouble to us to see such a holy man as Job was so fretful, and
peevish, and uneasy to himself, and especially to hear him
quarrel with God and speak indecently to him; but, though he
thus fall, he is not utterly cast down, for here he recovers his
temper, comes to himself and to his right mind again by repentance, is sorry for what he has said amiss, unsays it, and
humbles himself before God, ver. 1—6. II. It has been likewise
a great trouble to us to see Job and his friends so much at variance, not only differing in their opinions, but giving one another a great many hard words, and passing severe censures one
upon another, though they were all very wise and good men;
but here we have this grievance redressed likewise, the differences
between them happily adjusted, the quarrel taken up, all the
peevish reflections they had cast upon one another forgiven and
forgotten, and all joining in sacrifices and prayers, mutually
accepted of God, ver. 7—9. III. It has troubled us to see a man
of such eminent piety and usefulness as Job was so grievously
afflicted, so pained, so sick, so poor, so reproached, so slighted,
and made the very centre of all the calamities of human life;
but here we have this grievance redressed too, Job healed of all
his ailments, more honoured and beloved than ever, enriched
with an estate double to what he had before, surrounded with
all the comforts of life, and as great an instance of prosperity as
ever he had been of affliction and patience, ver. 10—17. All this
is written for our learning, that we, under these and the like discouragements that we meet with, through patience and comfort
of this scripture may have hope.

THEN Job answered the LORD,
and said, 2 I know that thou
canst do every *thing*, and *that* no
thought can be withholden from thee.
3 Who *is* he that hideth counsel without knowledge? therefore have I uttered that I understood not; things
too wonderful for me, which I knew
not. 4 Hear, I beseech thee, and I
will speak: I will demand of thee, and
declare thou unto me. 5 I have heard
of thee by the hearing of the ear: but
now mine eye seeth thee. 6 Wherefore I abhor *myself*, and repent in dust
and ashes.

The words of Job justifying himself were
ended, *ch.* xxxi. 40. After that he said no
more to that purport. The words of Job
judging and condemning himself began, *ch.*
xl. 4, 5. Here he goes on with words to the
same purport. Though his patience had not
its perfect work, his repentance for his impatience had. He is here thoroughly hum-

bled for his folly and unadvised speaking, and it was forgiven him. Good men will see and own their faults at last, though it may be some difficulty to bring them to do this. *Then*, when God had said all that to him concerning his own greatness and power appearing in the creatures, *then Job answered the Lord* (*v.* 1), not by way of contradiction (he had promised not so to answer again, *ch.* xl. 5), but by way of submission; and thus we must all answer the calls of God.

I. He subscribes to the truth of God's unlimited power, knowledge, and dominion, to prove which was the scope of God's discourse out of the whirlwind, *v.* 2. Corrupt passions and practices arise either from some corrupt principles or from the neglect and disbelief of the principles of truth; and therefore true repentance begins in *the acknowledgment of the truth*, 2 Tim. ii. 25. Job here owns his judgment convinced of the greatness, glory, and perfection of God, from which would follow the conviction of his conscience concerning his own folly in speaking irreverently to him. 1. He owns that God can do every thing. What can be too hard for him that made behemoth and leviathan, and manages both as he pleases? He knew this before, and had himself discoursed very well upon the subject, but now he knew it with application. *God had spoken* it once, and then he heard it twice, that *power belongs to God;* and therefore it is the greatest madness and presumption imaginable to contend with him. "*Thou canst do every thing*, and therefore canst raise me out of this low condition, which I have so often foolishly despaired of as impossible: I now believe thou art able to do this." 2. That *no thought can be withholden from him*, that is, (1.) There is no thought of ours that he can be hindered from the knowledge of. Not a fretful, discontented, unbelieving thought is in our minds at any time but God is a witness to it. It is in vain to contest with him; for we cannot hide our counsels and projects from him, and, if he discover them, he can defeat them. (2.) There is no thought of his that he can be hindered from the execution of. *Whatever the Lord pleased, that did he.* Job had said this passionately, complaining of it (*ch.* xxiii. 13), *What his soul desireth even that he doeth;* now he says, with pleasure and satisfaction, that *God's counsels shall stand.* If God's thoughts concerning us be *thoughts of good, to give us an unexpected end*, he cannot be withheld from accomplishing his gracious purposes, whatever difficulties may seem to lie in the way.

II. He owns himself to be guilty of that which God had charged him with in the beginning of his discourse, *v.* 3. "Lord, the first word thou saidst was, *Who is this that darkens counsel by words without knowledge?* There needed no more; that word convinced me. I own *I am the man* that has been so foolish. That word reached my conscience,

and set my sin in order before me. It is too plain to be denied, too bad to be excused. I have hidden *counsel without knowledge.* I have ignorantly overlooked the counsels and designs of God in afflicting me, and therefore have quarrelled with God, and insisted too much upon my own justification: *Therefore I uttered that which I understood not,*' that is, "I have passed a judgment upon the dispensations of Providence, though I was utterly a stranger to the reasons of them." Here, 1. He owns himself ignorant of the divine counsels; and so we are all. God's judgments are a great deep, which we cannot fathom, much less find out the springs of. We see what God does, but we neither know why he does it, what he is aiming at, nor what he will bring it to. These are things too wonderful for us, out of our sight to discover, out of our reach to alter, and out of our jurisdiction to judge of. They are things which we know not; it is quite above our capacity to pass a verdict upon them. The reason why we quarrel with Providence is because we do not understand it; and we must be content to be in the dark about it, until the mystery of God shall be finished. 2. He owns himself imprudent and presumptuous in undertaking to discourse of that which he did not understand and to arraign that which he could not judge of. *He that answereth a matter before he heareth it, it is folly and shame to him.* We wrong ourselves, as well as the cause which we undertake to determine, while we are no competent judges of it.

III. He will not answer, but he will *make supplication to his Judge*, as he had said, *ch.* ix. 15. "*Hear, I beseech thee, and I will speak* (*v.* 4), not speak either as plaintiff or defendent (*ch.* xiii. 22), but as a humble petitioner, not as one that will undertake to teach and prescribe, but as one that desires to learn and is willing to be prescribed to. Lord, put no more hard questions to me, for I am not able to answer thee one of a thousand of those which thou hast put; but give me leave to ask instruction from thee, and do not deny it me, do not upbraid me with my folly and self-sufficiency," Jam. i. 5. Now he is brought to the prayer Elihu taught him, *That which I see not teach thou me.*

IV. He puts himself into the posture of a penitent, and therein goes upon a right principle. In true repentance there must be not only conviction of sin, but contrition and godly sorrow for it, sorrow *according to God*, 2 Cor. vii. 9. Such was Job's sorrow for his sins.

1. Job had an eye to God in his repentance, thought highly of him, and went upon that as the principle of it (*v.* 5): "*I have heard of thee by the hearing of the ear* many a time from my teachers when I was young, from my friends now of late. I have known something of thy greatness, and power, and sovereign dominion; and yet was not brought,

by what I heard, to submit myself to thee as I ought. The notions I had of these things served me only to talk of, and had not a due influence upon my mind. *But now* thou hast by immediate revelation discovered thyself to me in thy glorious majesty; *now my eyes see thee;* now I feel the power of those truths which before I had only the notion of, and therefore now I repent, and unsay what I have foolishly said." Note, (1.) It is a great mercy to have a good education, and to know the things of God by the instructions of his word and ministers. *Faith comes by hearing,* and then it is most likely to come when we hear attentively and with the *hearing of the ear*, (2.) When the understanding is enlightened by the Spirit of grace our knowledge of divine things as far exceeds what we had before as that by ocular demonstration exceeds that by report and common fame. By the teachings of men God reveals his Son to us; but by the teachings of his Spirit he reveals his Son in us (Gal. i. 16), and so *changes us into the same image,* 2 Cor. iii. 18. (3.) God is pleased sometimes to manifest himself most fully to his people by the rebukes of his word and providence. "Now that I have been afflicted, now that I have been told of my faults, now my eye sees thee. *The rod and reproof give wisdom. Blessed is the man whom thou chastenest and teachest.*

2, Job had an eye to himself in his repentance, thought hardly of himself, and thereby expressed his sorrow for his sins (*v.* 6): *Wherefore I abhor myself, and repent in dust and ashes.* Observe, (1.) It concerns us to be deeply humbled for the sins we are convinced of, and not to rest in a slight superficial displeasure against ourselves for them. Even good people, that have no gross enormities to repent of, must be greatly afflicted in soul for the workings and breakings out of pride, passion, peevishness, and discontent, and all their hasty unadvised speeches; for these we must be pricked to the heart and be in bitterness. Till the enemy be effectually humbled, the peace will be insecure. (2.) Outward expressions of godly sorrow well become penitents; Job repented in dust and ashes. These, without an inward change, do but mock God; but, where they come from sincere contrition of soul, the sinner by them gives glory to God, takes shame to himself, and may be instrumental to bring others to repentance. Job's afflictions had brought him to the ashes *(ch.* ii. 8, he *sat down among the ashes),* but now his sins brought him thither. True penitents mourn for their sins as heartily as ever they did for any outward afflictions, and are in bitterness as for an only son or a first-born, for they are brought to see more evils in their sins than in their troubles. (3.) Self-loathing is evermore the companion of true repentance. Ezek. vi. 9, *They shall loathe themselves for the evils which they have committed.* We must not only be angry at ourselves for the wrong and da-

mage we have by sin done to our own souls, but must abhor ourselves, as having by sin made ourselves odious to the pure and holy God, who cannot endure to look upon iniquity. If sin be truly an abomination to us, sin in ourselves will especially be so; the nearer it is to us the more loathsome it will be. (4.) The more we see of the glory and majesty of God, and the more we see of the vileness and odiousness of sin and of ourselves because of sin, the more we shall abase and abhor ourselves for it. "Now my eye sees what a God he is whom I have offended, the brightness of that majesty which by wilful sin I have spit in the face of, the tenderness of that mercy which I have spurned at the bowels of; now I see what a just and holy God he is whose wrath I have incurred; wherefore I abhor myself. *Woe is me, for I am undone,"* Isa. vi. 5. God had challenged Job to *look upon proud men and abase them.* "I cannot," says Job, "pretend to do it; I have enough to do to get my own proud heart humbled, to abase that and bring that low." Let us leave it to God to govern the world, and make it our care, in the strength of his grace, to govern ourselves and our own hearts well.

7 And it was *so*, that after the LORD had spoken these words unto Job, the LORD said to Eliphaz the Temanite, My wrath is kindled against thee, and against thy two friends: for ye have not spoken of me *the thing that is* right, as my servant Job *hath.* 8 Therefore take unto you now seven bullocks and seven rams, and go to my servant Job, and offer up for yourselves a burnt offering; and my servant Job shall pray for you: for him will I accept: lest I deal with you *after your* folly, in that ye have not spoken of me *the thing which is* right, like my servant Job. 9 So Eliphaz the Temanite and Bildad the Shuhite *and* Zophar the Naamathite went, and did according as the LORD commanded them: the LORD also accepted Job.

Job, in his discourses, had complained very much of the censures of his friends and their hard usage of him, and had appealed to God as Judge between him and them, and thought it hard that judgment was not immediately given upon the appeal. While God was catechising Job out of the whirlwind one would have thought that he only was in the wrong, and that the cause would certainly go against him; but here, to our great surprise, we find it quite otherwise, and the definitive sentence given in Job's favour. Wherefore judge nothing before the time. Those who are truly righteous before God may have their righteousness clouded and eclipsed by great and uncommon afflictions, by the severe censures of men, by their own frailties and foolish passions, by the sharp reproofs of the word and conscience, and the deep humiliation of their own spirits under the sense of God's terrors; and yet, in due time, these clouds shall all blow over, and God will *bring forth their righteousness as the light and their judgment as the noon-day*, Ps. xxxvii. 6. He cleared Job's righteousness here, because he, like an honest man, held it fast and would not let it go. We have here,

I. Judgment given against Job's three friends, upon the controversy between them and Job. Elihu is not censured here, for he distinguished himself from the rest in the management of the dispute, and acted, not as a party, but as a moderator; and moderation will have its praise with God, whether it have with men or no. In the judgment here given Job is magnified and his three friends are mortified. While we were examining the discourses on both sides we could not discern, and therefore durst not determine, who was in the right; something of truth we thought they both had on their side, but we could not cleave the hair between them; nor would we, for all the world, have had to give the decisive sentence upon the case, lest we should have determined wrong. But it is well that the judgment is the Lord's, and we are sure that his judgment is according to truth; to it we will refer ourselves, and by it we will abide. Now, in the judgment here given,

1. Job is greatly magnified and comes off with honour. He was but one against three, a beggar now against three princes, and yet, having God on his side, he needed not fear the result, though thousands set themselves against him. Observe here, (1.) When God appeared for him: *After the Lord had spoken these words unto Job, v.* 7. After he had convinced and humbled him, and brought him to repentance for what he had said amiss, then he owned him in what he had said well, comforted him, and put honour upon him; not till then: for we are not ready for God's approbation till we judge and condemn ourselves; but then he thus pleaded his cause, for he that *has torn will heal* us, he that *has smitten will bind us.* The Comforter shall convince, John xvi. 8. See in what method we are to expect divine acceptance; we must first be humbled under divine rebukes. After God, by speaking these words, had caused grief, he returned and had compassion, according to the multitude of his mercies; for he will not contend for ever, but will debate in measure, and stay his rough wind in the day of his east wind. Now that Job had humbled himself God exalted him. True penitents shall find favour with God, and what they have said and done amiss shall no more be mentioned against them. Then God is well

pleased with us when we are brought to abhor ourselves. (2.) How he appeared for him. It is taken for granted that all his offences are forgiven; for if he be dignified, as we find he is here, no doubt he is justified. Job had sometimes intimated, with great assurance, that God would clear him at last, and he was not made ashamed of the hope. [1.] God calls him again and again *his servant Job*, four times in two verses, and he seems to take a pleasure in calling him so, as before his troubles (*ch.* i. 8), *"Hast thou considered my servant Job?"* Though he is poor and despised, he is my servant notwithstanding, and as dear to me as when he was in prosperity. Though he has his faults, and has appeared to be a man subject to like passions as others, though he has contended with me, has gone about to disannul my judgment, and has darkened counsel by words without knowledge, yet he sees his error and retracts it, and therefore he is my servant Job still." If we still hold fast the integrity and fidelity of servants to God, as Job did, though we may for a time be deprived of the credit and comfort of the relation, we shall be restored to it at last, as he was. The devil had undertaken to prove Job a hypocrite, and his three friends had condemned him as a wicked man; but God will acknowledge those whom he accepts, and will not suffer them to be run down by the malice of hell or earth. If God says, *Well done, good and faithful servant*, it is of little consequence who says otherwise. [2.] He owns that he had *spoken of him the thing that was right*, beyond what his antagonists had done. He had given a much better and truer account of the divine Providence than they had done They had wronged God by making prosperity a mark of the true church and affliction a certain indication of God's wrath; but Job had done him right by maintaining that God's love and hatred are to be judged of by what is in men, not by what is before them, Eccl. ix. 1. Observe, *First*, Those do the most justice to God and his providence who have an eye to the rewards and punishments of another world more than to those of this, and with the prospect of those solve the difficulties of the present administration. Job had referred things to the future judgment, and the future state, more than his friends had done, and therefore he spoke of God that which was right, better than his friends had done. *Secondly*, Though Job had spoken some things amiss, even concerning God, whom he made too bold with, yet he is commended for what he spoke that was right. We must not only not reject that which is true and good, but must not deny it its due praise, though there appear in it a mixture of human frailty and infirmity. *Thirdly*, Job was in the right, and his friends were in the wrong, and yet he was in pain and they were at ease—a plain evidence that we cannot judge of men and their sentiments by looking in their faces or purses. He only can do it infallibly who sees men's hearts. [3.] He will pass his word for Job that, notwithstanding all the wrong his friends had done him, he is so good a man, and of such a humble, tender, forgiving spirit, that he will very readily pray for them, and use his interest in heaven on their behalf: *"My servant Job will pray for you.* I know he will. I have pardoned him, and he has the comfort of pardon, and therefore he will pardon you." [4.] He appoints him to be the priest of this congregation, and promises to accept him and his mediation for his friends. "Take your sacrifices to my servant Job, *for him will I accept."* Those whom God washes from their sins he makes to himself kings and priests. True penitents shall not only find favour as petitioners for themselves, but be accepted as intercessors for others also. It was a great honour that God hereby put upon Job, in appointing him to offer sacrifice for his friends, as formerly he used to do for his own children, *ch.* i. 5. And a happy presage it was of his restoration to his prosperity again, and indeed a good step towards it, that he was thus restored to the priesthood. Thus he became a type of Christ, through whom alone we and our spiritual sacrifices are *acceptable to God;* see 1 Pet. ii. 5. " Go *to my servant Job,* to my servant Jesus" (from whom for a time he hid his face), "put your sacrifices into his hand, make use of him as your Advocate, for him will I accept, but, out of him, you must expect to be dealt with according to your folly." And, as Job prayed and offered sacrifice for those that had grieved and wounded his spirit, so Christ prayed and died for his persecutors, and ever lives *making intercession for the transgressors.*

2. Job's friends are greatly mortified, and come off with disgrace. They were good men and belonged to God, and therefore he would not let them lie still in their mistake any more than Job, but, having humbled him by a discourse out of the whirlwind, he takes another course to humble them. Job, who was dearest to him, was first chidden, but the rest in their turn. When they heard Job talked to, it is probable, they flattered themselves with a conceit that they were in the right and Job was in all the fault, but God soon took them to task, and made them know the contrary. In most disputes and controversies there is something amiss on both sides, either in the merits of the cause or in the management, if not in both; and it is fit that both sides should be told of it, and made to see their errors. God addresses this to Eliphaz, not only as the senior, but as the ringleader in the attack made upon Job. Now, (1.) God tells them plainly that they had *not spoken of him the thing that was right, like Job,* that is, they had censured and condemned Job upon a false hypothesis, had represented God fighting against Job as an

enemy when really he was only trying him as a friend, and this was not right. Those do not say well of God who represent his fatherly chastisements of his own children as judicial punishments and who cut them off from his favour upon the account of them. Note, It is a dangerous thing to judge uncharitably of the spiritual and eternal state of others, for in so doing we may perhaps condemn those whom God has accepted, which is a great provocation to him; it is offending his little ones, and he takes himself to be wronged in all the wrongs that are done to them. (2.) He assures them he was angry with them : *My wrath is kindled against thee and thy two friends.* God is very angry with those who despise and reproach their brethren, who triumph over them, and judge hardly of them, either for their calamities or for their infirmities. Though they were wise and good men, yet, when they spoke amiss, God was angry with them and let them know that he was. (3.) He requires from them a sacrifice, to make atonement for what they had said amiss. They must bring each of them *seven bullocks,* and each of them *seven rams,* to be offered up to God for a *burnt-offering;* for it should seem that, before the law of Moses, all sacrifices, even those of atonement, were wholly burnt, and therefore were so called. They thought they had spoken wonderfully well, and that God was beholden to them for pleading his cause and owed them a good reward for it; but they are told that, on the contrary, he is displeased with them, requires from them a sacrifice, and threatens that, otherwise, he will deal with them after their folly. God is often angry at that in us which we are ourselves proud of and sees much amiss in that which we think was done well. (4.) He orders them to go to Job, and beg of him to offer their sacrifices, and pray for them, otherwise they should not be accepted. By this God designed, [1.] To humble them and lay them low. They thought that they only were the favourites of Heaven, and that Job had no interest there; but God gives them to understand that he had a better interest there than they had, and stood fairer for God's acceptance than they did. The day may come when those who despise and censure God's people will court their favour, and be *made to know that God has loved them,* Rev. iii. 9. The foolish virgins will beg oil of the wise. [2.] To oblige them to make their peace with Job, as the condition of their making their peace with God. *If thy brother has aught against thee* (as Job had a great deal against them), *first be reconciled to thy brother and then come and offer thy gift.* Satisfaction must first be made for wrong done, according as the nature of the thing requires, before we can hope to obtain from God the forgiveness of sin. See how thoroughly God espoused the cause of his servant Job and engaged in it. God will not be reconciled to those that have offended

Job till they have first begged his pardon and he be reconciled to them. Job and his friends had differed in their opinion about many things, and had been too keen in their reflections one upon another, but now they were to be made friends; in order to that, they are not to argue the matter over again and try to give it a new turn (that might be endless), but they must agree in a sacrifice and a prayer, and that must reconcile them: they must unite in affection and devotion when they could not concur in the same sentiments. Those who differ in judgment about minor things are yet one in Christ the great sacrifice, and meet at the same throne of grace, and therefore ought to love and bear with one another. Once more, observe, When God was angry with Job's friends, he did himself put them in a way to make their peace with him. Our quarrels with God always begin on our part, but the reconciliation begins on his.

II. The acquiescence of Job's friends in this judgment given, *v.* 9. They were good men, and, as soon as they understood what the mind of the Lord was, they did as he commanded them, and that speedily and without gainsaying, though it was against the grain to flesh and blood to court him thus whom they had condemned. Note, Those who would be reconciled to God must carefully use the prescribed means and methods of reconciliation. Peace with God is to be had only in his own way and upon his own terms, and they will never seem hard to those who know how to value the privilege, but they will be glad of it upon any terms, though ever so humbling. Job's friends had all joined in accusing Job, and now they join in begging his pardon. Those that have sinned together should repent together. Those that appeal to God, as both Job and his friends had often done, must resolve to stand by his award, whether pleasing or unpleasing to their own mind. And those that conscientiously observe God's commands need not doubt of his favour : *The Lord also accepted Job,* and his friends in answer to his prayer. It is not said, He accepted *them* (though that is implied), but, He accepted *Job* for them ; so he has *made us accepted in the beloved,* Eph. i. 6 ; Matt. iii. 17. Job did not insult over his friends upon the testimony God had given concerning him, and the submission they were obliged to make to him ; but, God being graciously reconciled to him, he was easily reconciled to them, and then God accepted him. This is that which we should aim at in all our prayers and services, to be accepted of the Lord ; this must be the summit of our ambition, not to have praise of men, but to please God.

10 And the LORD turned the captivity of Job, when he prayed for his friends: also the LORD gave Job twice as much as he had before. 11 Then came there unto him all his brethren, and all his sisters, and all they that had been of his acquaintance before, and did eat bread with him in his house : and they bemoaned him, and comforted him over all the evil that the LORD had brought upon him : every man also gave him a piece of money, and every one an earring of gold. 12 So the LORD blessed the latter end of Job more than his beginning: for he had fourteen thousand sheep, and six thousand camels, and a thousand yoke of oxen, and a thousand she asses. 13 He had also seven sons and three daughters. 14 And he called the name of the first, Jemima; and the name of the second, Kezia ; and the name of the third, Keren-happuch. 15 And in all the land were no women found *so* fair as the daughters of Job : and their father gave them inheritance among their brethren. 16 After this lived Job a hundred and forty years, and saw his sons, and his sons' sons, *even* four generations. 17 So Job died, *being* old and full of days.

You have heard of the patience of Job (says the apostle, Jam. v. 11) *and have seen the end of the Lord,* that is, what end the Lord, at length, put to his troubles. In the beginning of this book we had Job's patience under his troubles, for an example ; here, in the close, for our encouragement to follow that example, we have the happy issue of his troubles and the prosperous condition to which he was restored after them, which confirms us in counting those happy which endure. Perhaps, too, the extraordinary prosperity which Job was crowned with after his afflictions was intended to be to us Christians a type and figure of the glory and happiness of heaven, which the afflictions of this present time are working for us, and in which they will issue at last ; this will be more than double to all the delights and satisfactions we now enjoy, as Job's after-prosperity was to his former, though then he was the greatest of all the men of the east. He that rightly endures temptation, when he is tried, shall receive a *crown of life* (Jam. i. 12), as Job, when he was tried, received all the wealth, and honour, and comfort, which here we have an account of.

I. God returned in ways of mercy to him; and his thoughts concerning him *were thoughts of good and not of evil, to give the expected* (nay, the *unexpected) end,* Jer. xxix. 11. His troubles began in Satan's malice, which God restrained ; his restoration began in God's mercy, which Satan could not oppose. Job's sorest complaint, and indeed the sorrowful accent of all his complaints, on which he laid the greatest emphasis, was that God appeared against him. But now God plainly appeared for him, and *watched over him to build and to plant, like as he had* (at least in his apprehension) *watched over him to pluck up and to throw down,* Jer. xxxi. 28. This put a new face upon his affairs immediately, and every thing now looked as pleasing and promising as before it had looked gloomy and frightful. 1. God *turned his captivity,* that is, he redressed his grievances and took away all the causes of his complaints; he loosed him from the bond with which Satan had now, for a great while, bound him, and delivered him out of those cruel hands into which he had delivered him. We may suppose that now all his bodily pains and distempers were healed so suddenly and so thoroughly that the cure was next to miraculous: *His flesh became fresher than a child's, and he returned to the days of his youth;* and, what was more, he felt a very great alteration in his mind; it was calm and easy, and the tumult was all over, his disquieting thoughts had all vanished, his fears were silenced, and the consolations of God were now as much the delight of his soul as his terrors had been its burden. The tide thus turned, his troubles began to ebb as fast as they had flowed, just then *when he was praying for his friends,* praying over his sacrifice which he offered for them. Mercy did not return when he was disputing with his friends, no, not though he had right on his side, but when he was praying for them; for God is better served and pleased with our warm devotions than with our warm disputations. When Job completed his repentance by this instance of his *forgiving men their trespasses,* then God completed his remission by turning his captivity. Note, We are really doing our business when we are praying for our friends, if we pray in a right manner, for in those prayers there is not only faith, but love. Christ has taught us to pray with and for others in teaching us to say, *Our Father;* and, in seeking mercy for others, we may find mercy ourselves. Our Lord Jesus has his exaltation and dominion there, where he *ever lives making intercession.* Some, by the turning of Job's captivity, understand the restitution which the Sabeans and Chaldeans made of the cattle which they had taken from him, God wonderfully inclining them to do it; and with these he began the world again. Probably it was so; those spoilers had *swallowed down his riches,* but they were forced to *vomit them up again,* ch. xx. 15. But I rather understand this more generally of the turn now given. 2. God doubled his possessions: *Also the Lord gave Job twice as much as he had before.* It is probable that he did at first, in some way or other, intimate to him that it was his gracious purpose, by degrees, in due time to bring him to such a height of prosperity that he should have twice as much as

234

ever he had, for the encouraging of his hope and the quickening of his industry, and that it might appear that this wonderful increase was a special token of God's favour. And it may be considered as intended, (1.) To balance his losses. He suffered for the glory of God, and therefore God made it up to him with advantage, and allowed him more than interest upon interest. God will take care that none shall lose by him. (2.) To recompense his patience and his confidence in God, which (notwithstanding the workings of corruption) he did not cast away, but still held fast, and that is it which has *a great recompence of reward,* Heb. x. 35. Job's friends had often put their severe censure of Job upon this issue, *If thou wert pure and upright, surely now he would awake for thee,* ch. viii. 6. But he does not awake for thee; therefore thou art not upright. " Well," says God, " though your argument be not conclusive, I will even by that demonstrate the integrity of my servant Job; his latter end shall greatly increase, and by that it shall appear, since you will have it so, that it was not for any injustice in his hands that he suffered the loss of all things." Now it appeared that Job had reason to bless God for taking away (as he did, ch. i. 21), since it made so good a return.

II. His old acquaintance, neighbours, and relations, were very kind to him, *v.* 11. They had been estranged from him, and this was not the least of the grievances of his afflicted state; he bitterly complained of their unkindness, ch. xix. 13, &c. But now they visited him with all possible expressions of affection and respect. 1. They put honour upon him, in coming to dine with him as formerly, but (we may suppose) privately bringing their entertainment along with them, so that he had the reputation of feasting them without the expense. 2. They sympathized with him, and showed a tender concern for him, such as becomes brethren. They bemoaned him when they talked over all the calamities of his afflicted state, and comforted him when they took notice of God's gracious returns to him. They wept for his griefs, and rejoiced in his joys, and proved not such miserable comforters as his three friends, that, at first, were so forward and officious to attend him. These were not such great men nor such learned and eloquent men as those, but they proved much more skilful and kind in comforting Job. God sometimes chooses the foolish and weak things of the world, as for conviction, so for comfort. 3. They made a collection among them for the repair of his losses and the setting of him up again. They did not think it enough to say, *Be warmed, Be filled,* but gave him such things as would be of use to him, Jam. ii. 16. *Every one gave him a piece of money* (some more, it is likely, and some less, according to their ability) *and every one an ear-ring of gold* (an ornament much used by the children of the east), which would be as good as money to him   this was a superfluity which they could well spare, and the rule is, That our abundance must be a supply to our brethren's necessity. But why did Job's relations now, at length, show this kindness to him? (1.) God put it in their hearts to do so; and every creature is that to us which he makes it to be. Job had acknowledged God in their estrangement from him, for which he now rewarded him in turning them to him again. (2.) Perhaps some of them withdrew from him because they thought him a hypocrite, but, now that his integrity was made manifest, they returned to him and to communion with him again. When God was friendly to him they were all willing to be friendly too, Ps. cxix. 74, 79. Others of them, it may be, withdrew because he was poor, and sore, and a rueful spectacle, but now that he began to recover they were willing to renew their acquaintance with him. Swallow-friends, that are gone in winter, will return in the spring, though their friendship is of little value. (3.) Perhaps the rebuke which God had given to Eliphaz and the other two for their unkindness to Job awakened the rest of his friends to return to their duty. Reproofs to others we should thus take as admonitions and instructions to us. 4. Job *prayed for his friends,* and then they flocked about him, overcome by his kindness, and every one desiring an interest in his prayers. The more we pray for our friends and relations the more comfort we may expect in them.

III. His estate strangely increased, by the blessing of God upon the little that his friends gave him. He thankfully received their courtesy, and did not think it below him to have his estate repaired by contributions. He did not, on the one hand, urge his friends to raise money for him; he acquits himself from that (*ch.* vi. 22), *Did I say, Bring unto me or give me a reward of your substance?* Yet what they brought he thankfully accepted, and did not upbraid them with their former unkindnesses, nor ask them why they did not do this sooner. He was neither so covetous and griping as to ask their charity, nor so proud and ill-natured as to refuse it when they offered it; and, being in so good a temper, God gave him that which was far better than their money and ear-rings, and that was his blessing, *v.* 12. The Lord comforted him now according to the days wherein he had afflicted him, and *blessed his latter end more than his beginning.* Observe, 1. *The blessing of the Lord makes rich;* it is he that gives us power to get wealth and gives success in honest endeavours. Those therefore that would thrive must have an eye to God's blessing, and never go out of it, no, not into the warm sun; and those that have thriven must not sacrifice to their own net, but acknowledge their obligations to God for his blessing. 2. That blessing can make very rich and sometimes makes good people so. Those that become rich by getting think

they can easily make themselves very rich by saving; but, as those that have little must depend upon God to make it much, so those that have much must depend upon God to make it more and to double it; else *you have sown much and bring in little,* Hag. i. 6. 3. The last days of a good man sometimes prove his best days, his last works his best works, his last comforts his best comforts; for his path, like that of the morning-light, shines more and more to the perfect day. Of a wicked man it is said, *His last state is worse than his first* (Luke xi. 26), but of the upright man, *His end is peace;* and sometimes the nearer it is the clearer are the views of it. In respect of outward prosperity God is pleased sometimes to make the latter end of a good man's life more comfortable than the former part of it has been, and strangely to outdo the expectations of his afflicted people, who thought they should never live to see better days, that we may not despair even in the depths of adversity. We know not what good times we may yet be reserved for in our latter end. *Non, si malè nunc, et olim sic erit—It may yet be well with us, though now it is otherwise.* Job, in his affliction, had wished to be as in months past, as rich as he had been before, and quite despaired of that; but God is often better to us than our own fears, nay, than our own wishes, for Job's possessions were doubled to him; the number of his cattle, his sheep and camels, his oxen and she-asses, is just double here to what it was, *ch.* i. 3. This is a remarkable instance of the extent of the divine providence to things that seem minute, as this of the exact number of a man's cattle, as also of the harmony of providence, and the reference of one event to another; for *known unto God are all his works, from the beginning to the end.* Job's other possessions, no doubt, were increased in proportion to his cattle, lands, money, servants, &c. So that if, before, he was the greatest of all the men of the east, what was he now?

IV. His family was built up again, and he had great comfort in his children, *v.* 13—15. The last of his afflictions that are recorded (*ch.* i.), and the most grievous, was the death of all his children at once. His friends upbraided him with it (*ch.* viii. 4), but God repaired even that breach in process of time, either by the same wife, or, she being dead, by another. 1. The number of his children was the same as before, *seven sons and three daughters.* Some give this reason why they were not doubled as his cattle were, because his children that were dead were not lost, but gone before to a better world; and therefore, if he have but the same number of them, they may be reckoned doubled, for he has two fleeces of children (as I may say) *mahanaim* —*two hosts,* one in heaven, the other on earth, and in both he is rich. 2. The names of his daughters are here registered (*v.* 14), because, in the significations of them, they seemed designed to perpetuate the remembrance of

235

God's great goodness to him in the surprising change of his condition. He called the first *Jemima—The day* (whence perhaps *Diana* had her name), because of the shining forth of his prosperity after a dark night of affliction. The next *Kezia*, a spice of a very fragrant smell, because (says bishop Patrick) God had healed his ulcers, the smell of which was offensive. The third *Keren-happuch* (that is, *Plenty restored*, or *A horn of paint*), because (says he) God had wiped away the tears which fouled his face, *ch.* xvi. 16. Concerning these daughters we are here told, (1.) That God adorned them with great beauty, *no women so fair as the daughters of Job, v.* 15. In the Old Testament we often find women praised for their beauty, as Sarah, Rebekah, and many others; but we never find any women in the New Testament whose beauty is in the least taken notice of, no, not the virgin Mary herself, because the beauty of holiness is that which is brought to a much clearer light by the gospel. (2.) That their father (God enabling him to do it) supplied them with great fortunes: *He gave them inheritance among their brethren,* and did not turn them off with small portions, as most did. It is probable that they had some extraordinary personal merit, which Job had an eye to in the extraordinary favour he showed them. Perhaps

they excelled their brethren in wisdom and piety; and therefore, that they might continue in his family, to be a stay and blessing to it, he made them co-heirs with their brethren.

V. His life was long. What age he was when his troubles came we are nowhere told, but here we are told he lived 140 years, whence some conjecture that he was 70 when he was in his troubles, and that so his age was doubled, as his other possessions. 1. He lived to have much of the comfort of this life, for he saw his posterity to the fourth generation, *v.* 16. Though his children were not doubled to him, yet in his children's children (and those are the crown of old men) they were more than doubled. As God appointed to Adam another seed instead of that which was slain (Gen. iv. 25), so he did to Job with advantage. God has ways to repair the losses and balance the griefs of those who are written childless, as Job was when he had buried all his children. 2. He lived till he was satisfied, for he died full of days, satisfied with living in this world, and willing to leave it; not peevishly so, as in the days of his affliction, but piously so, and thus, as Eliphaz had encouraged him to hope, he *came to his grave like a shock of corn in his season.*

AN

EXPOSITION,

WITH PRACTICAL OBSERVATIONS,

OF THE BOOK OF

PSALMS.

WE have now before us one of the choicest and most excellent parts of all the Old Testament; nay, so much is there in it of CHRIST and his gospel, as well as of God and his law, that it has been called *the abstract*, or *summary, of both Testaments.* The History of Israel, which we were long upon, led us to camps and council-boards, and there entertained and instructed us in the knowledge of God. The book of Job brought us into the schools, and treated us with profitable disputations concerning God and his providence. But this book brings us into the sanctuary, draws us off from converse with men, with the politicians, philosophers, or disputers of this world, and directs us into communion with God, by solacing and reposing our souls in him, lifting up and letting out our hearts towards him. Thus may we be in the mount with God; and we understand not our interests if we say not, *It is good to be here.* Let us consider,

I. The title of this book. It is called, 1. The *Psalms;* under that title it is referred to, Luke xxiv. 44. The Hebrew calls it *Tehillim*, which properly signifies *Psalms of praise*, because many of them are such; but *Psalms* is a more general word, meaning all metrical compositions fitted to be sung, which may as well be historical, doctrinal, or supplicatory, as laudatory. Though singing be properly the voice of joy, yet the intention of songs is of a much greater latitude, to assist the memory, and both to express and to excite all the other affections as well as this of joy. The priests had a mournful muse as well as joyful ones; and the divine institution of singing psalms is thus largely intended; for we are directed not only to praise God, but to teach and admonish ourselves and one another *in psalms, and hymns, and spiritual songs,* Col. iii. 16. 2. It is called the *Book of Psalms;* so it is quoted by St. Peter, Acts i. 20. It is a collection of psalms, of all the psalms that were divinely inspired, which, though composed at several times and upon several occasions, are here put together without any reference to or dependence upon one another ; thus they were preserved from being scattered and lost, and were in so much greater readiness for the service of the church. See what a good Master we serve, and what pleasantness there is in wisdom's ways, when we are not only commanded to sing at our work, and have cause enough given us to do so, but have words also put in our mouths and songs prepared to our hands.

II. The author of this book. It is, no doubt, derived originally from the blessed Spirit. They are spiritual songs, words which the Holy Ghost taught. The penman of most of them was David the son of Jesse, who is therefore called the *sweet psalmist of Israel*, 2 Sam. xxiii. 1. Some that have not his name in their titles yet are expressly ascribed to him elsewhere, as Ps. ii. (Acts iv. 25) and Ps. xcvi. and cv. (1 Chron. xvi.). One psalm is expressly said to be *the prayer of Moses* (Ps. xc.) ; and that some of the psalms were penned by Asaph is intimated, 2 Chron. xxix. 30, where they are said to *praise the Lord in the words of David and Asaph*, who is there called a *seer* or *prophet*. Some of the psalms seem to have been penned long after, as Ps. cxxxvii., at the time of the captivity in Babylon ; but the far greater part of them were certainly penned by David himself, whose genius lay towards poetry and music, and who was raised up, qualified, and animated, for the establishing of the ordinance of singing psalms in the church of God, as Moses and Aaron were, in their day, for the settling of the ordinances of sacrifice ; theirs is superseded, but his remains, and will to the end of time, when it shall be swallowed up in the songs of eternity. Herein David was a type of Christ, who descended from him, not from Moses, because he came to take away sacrifice (the family of Moses was soon lost and extinct), but to establish and perpetuate joy and praise ; for of the family of David in Christ there shall be no end.

III. The scope of it. It is manifestly intended, 1. To assist the exercises of natural religion, and to kindle in the souls of men those devout affections which we owe to God as our Creator, owner, ruler, and benefactor. The book of Job helps to prove our first principles of the divine perfections and providence ; but this helps to improve them in prayers and praises, and professions of desire towards him, dependence on him, and an entire devotedness and resignation to him. Other parts of scripture show that God is infinitely above man, and his sovereign Lord ; but this shows us that he may, notwithstanding, be conversed with by us sinful worms of the earth ; and there are ways in which, if it be not our own fault, we may keep up communion with him in all the various conditions of human life. 2. To advance the excellencies of revealed religion, and in the most pleasing powerful manner to recommend it to the world. There is indeed little or nothing of the ceremonial law in all the book of *Psalms*. Though sacrifice and offering were yet to continue many ages, yet they are here represented as things which God did not desire (Ps. xl. 6, li. 16), as things comparatively little, and which in time were to vanish away. But the word and law of God, those parts of it which are moral and of perpetual obligation, are here all along magnified and made honourable, nowhere more. And Christ, the crown and centre of revealed religion, the foundation, corner, and top-stone, of that blessed building, is here clearly spoken of in type and prophecy, his sufferings and the glory that should follow, and the kingdom that he should set up in the world, in which God's covenant with David, concerning his kingdom, was to have its accomplishment. What a high value does this book put upon the word of God, his statutes and judgments, his covenant and the great and precious promises of it ; and how does it recommend them to us as our guide and stay, and our heritage for ever !

IV. The use of it. All scripture, being given by inspiration of God, is profitable to convey divine light into our understandings ; but this book is of singular use with that to convey divine life and power, and a holy warmth, into our affections. There is no one book of scripture that is more helpful to the devotions of the saints than this, and it has been so in all ages of the church, ever since it was written and the several parts of it were delivered to the chief musician for the service of the church. 1. It is of use to be sung. Further than David's psalms we *may* go, but we *need* not, for hymns and spiritual songs. What the rules of the Hebrew metre were even the learned are not certain. But these psalms ought to be rendered according to the metre of every language, at least so as that they may be sung for the edification of the church. And methinks it is a great comfort to us, when we are singing David's psalms, that we are offering the very same praises to God that were offered to him in the days of David and the other godly kings of Judah. So rich, so well made, are these divine poems, that they can never be exhausted, can never be worn thread-bare. 2. It is of use to be read and opened by the ministers of Christ, as containing great and excellent truths, and rules concerning good and evil. Our Lord Jesus expounded the psalms to his disciples, the gospel psalms, and opened their understandings (for he had the key of David) to understand them, Luke xxiv. 44. 3. It is of use to be read and meditated upon by all good people. It is a full fountain, out of which we may all be drawing water with joy. (1.) The Psalmist's experiences are of great use for our direction, caution, and encouragement. In telling us, as he often does, what passed between God and his soul, he lets us know what we may expect from God, and what he will expect, and require, and graciously accept, from us. David was a man after God's own heart, and therefore those who find themselves in some measure according to his heart have reason to hope that they are renewed by the grace of God, after the image of God, and may have much comfort in the testimony of their consciences for them that they can heartily say *Amen* to David's prayers and praises. (2.) Even the Psalmist's expressions too are of great use ; and by them the Spirit helps our praying infirmities, because we know not what to pray for as we ought. In all our approaches to God, as well as in our first returns to God, we are directed to *take with us words*

(Hos. xiv. 2), these words, words which the Holy Ghost teaches. If we make David's psalms familiar to us, as we ought to do, whatever errand we have at the throne of grace, by way of confession, petition, or thanksgiving, we may thence be assisted in the delivery of it; whatever devout affection is working in us, holy desire or hope, sorrow or joy, we may there find apt words wherewith to clothe it, sound speech which cannot be condemned. It will be good to collect the most proper and lively expressions of devotion which we find here, and to methodize them, and reduce them to the several heads of prayer, that they may be the more ready to us. Or we may take sometimes one choice psalm and sometimes another, and pray it over, that is, enlarge upon each verse in our own thoughts, and offer up our meditations to God as they arise from the expressions we find there. The learned Dr. Hammond, in his preface to his paraphrase on the Psalms (sect. 29), says, " That going over a few psalms with these interpunctions of mental devotion, suggested, animated, and maintained, by the native life and vigour which is in the psalms, is much to be preferred before the saying over of the whole Psalter, since nothing is more fit to be averted in religious offices than their degenerating into heartless dispirited recitations." If, as St. Austin advises, we form our spirit by the affection of the psalm, we may then be sure of acceptance with God in using the language of it. Nor is it only our devotion, and the affections of our mind, that the book of Psalms assists, teaching us how to offer praise so as to glorify God, but it is also a directory to the actions of our lives, and teaches us how to *order our conversation aright, so as that,* in the end, *we may see the salvation of God,* Ps. l. 23. The Psalms were thus serviceable to the Old-Testament church, but to us Christians they may be of more use than they could be to those who lived before the coming of Christ; for, as Moses's sacrifices, so David's songs, are expounded and made more intelligible by the gospel of Christ, which lets us within the veil; so that if to David's prayers and praises we add St. Paul's prayers in his epistles, and the new songs in the Revelation, we shall be thoroughly furnished for this good work; for the scripture, perfected, makes the man of God perfect.

As to the division of this book, we need not be solicitous; there is no connexion (or very seldom) between one psalm and another, nor any reason discernible for the placing of them in the order wherein we here find them; but it seems to be ancient, for that which is now the second psalm was so in the apostles' time, Acts xiii. 33. The vulgar Latin joins the 9th and 10th together; all popish authors quote by that, so that, thenceforward, throughout the book, their number is one short of ours; our xi. is their x. our cxix. their cxviii. But then they divide the 147th into two, and so make up the number of 150. Some have endeavoured to reduce the psalms to proper heads, according to the matter of them, but there is often such a variety of matter in one and the same psalm that this cannot be done with any certainty. But the seven penitential Psalms have been in a particular manner singled out by the devotions of many. They are reckoned to be Ps. vi., xxxii., xxxviii., li., cii., cxxx., and cxliii. The Psalms were divided into five books, each concluding with *Amen, Amen,* or *Hallelujah;* the first ending with Ps. xli., the second with Ps. lxxii., the third with Ps. lxxxix., the fourth with Ps. cvi., the fifth with Ps. cl. Others divide them into three fifties; others into sixty parts, two for every day of the month, one for the morning, the other for the evening. Let good Christians divide them for themselves, so as may best increase their acquaintance with them, that they may have them at hand upon all occasions and may sing them in the spirit and with the understanding.

PSALM I.

This is a psalm of instruction concerning good and evil, setting before us life and death, the blessing and the curse, that we may take the right way which leads to happiness and avoid that which will certainly end in our misery and ruin. The different character and condition of godly people and wicked people, those that serve God and those that serve him not, is here plainly stated in a few words; so that every man, if he will be faithful to himself, may here see his own face and then read his own doom. That division of the children of men into saints and sinners, righteous and unrighteous, the children of God and the children of the wicked one, as it is ancient, ever since the struggle began between sin and grace, the seed of the woman and the seed of the serpent, so it is lasting, and will survive all other divisions and subdivisions of men into high and low, rich and poor, bond and free; for by this men's everlasting state will be determined, and the distinction will last as long as heaven and hell. This psalm shows us, I. The holiness and happiness of a godly man, ver. 1—3. II. The sinfulness and misery of a wicked man, ver. 4, 5. III. The ground and reason of both, ver. 6. Whoever collected the psalms of David (probably it was Ezra) with good reason put this psalm first, as a preface to the rest, because it is absolutely necessary to the acceptance of our devotions that we be righteous before God (for it is only the prayer of the upright that is his delight), and therefore that we be right in our notions of blessedness and in our choice of the way that leads to it. Those are not fit to put up good prayers who do not walk in good ways.

BLESSED *is* the man that walketh not in the counsel of the ungodly, nor standeth in the way of sinners, nor sitteth in the seat of the scornful. 2 But his delight *is* in the law of the LORD; and in his law doth he meditate day and night. 3 And he shall be like a tree planted by the rivers of water, that bringeth forth his fruit in his season; his leaf also shall not wither; and whatsoever he doeth shall prosper.

The psalmist begins with the character and condition of a godly man, that those may first take the comfort of that to whom it belongs. Here is,

I. A description given of the godly man's spirit and way, by which we are to try ourselves. The Lord knows those that are his by name, but we must know them by their character; for that is agreeable to a state of probation, that we may study to answer to the character, which is indeed both the command of the law which we are bound in duty to obey and the condition of the promise which we are bound in interest to fulfil. The character of a good man is here given by the rules he chooses to walk by and to take his measures from. What we take at our setting out, and at every turn, for the guide of our conversation, whether the course of this world or the word of God, is of material consequence. An error in the choice of our standard and leader is original and fatal; but, if we be right here, we are in a fair way to do well.

1. A godly man, that he may avoid the evil, utterly renounces the companionship of evil-doers, and will not be led by them (*v.* 1): *He walks not in the council of the ungodly,* &c. This part of his character is put first, because those that will keep the commandments of their God must say to evil-doers, *Depart from us* (cxix. 115), and departing from evil is that in which wisdom begins. (1.) He sees evil-doers round about him; the world is full of them; they walk on every side. They are here described by three characters, *ungodly, sinners,* and *scornful.* See by what steps men arrive at the height of impiety. *Nemo repente fit turpissimus—None reach the height of vice at once.* They are *ungodly* first, casting off the fear of God and living in the neglect of their duty to him: but they rest not there. When the services of religion are laid aside, they come to be *sinners,* that is, they break out into open rebellion against God and engage in the service of sin and Satan. Omissions make way for commissions, and by these the heart is so hardened that at length they come to be *scorners,* that is, they openly defy all that is sacred, scoff at religion, and make a jest of sin. Thus is the way of iniquity down-hill; the bad grow worse, sinners themselves become tempters to others and advocates for Baal. The word which we translate *ungodly* signifies such as are unsettled, aim at no certain end and walk by no certain rule, but are at the command of every lust and at the beck of every temptation. The word for *sinners* signifies such as are determined for the practice of sin and set it up as their trade. The *scornful* are those that set *their mouths against the heavens.* These the good man sees with a sad heart; they are a constant vexation to his righteous soul. But, (2.) He shuns them wherever he sees them. He does not do as they do; and, that he may not, he does not converse familiarly with them. [1.] He does *not walk in the counsel of the ungodly.* He is not present at their councils, nor does he advise with them; though they are ever so witty, and subtle, and learned, if they are ungodly, they shall not be the men of his counsel. He does not consent to them, nor *say as they say,* Luke xxiii. 51. He does not take his measures from their principles, nor act according to the advice which they give and take. The ungodly are forward to give their advice against religion, and it is managed so artfully that we have reason to think ourselves happy if we escape being tainted and ensnared by it. [2.] He *stands not in the way of sinners;*

he avoids doing as they do; their way shall not be his way; he will not come into it, much less will he continue in it, as the sinner does, who *sets himself in a way that is not good,* xxxvi. 4. He avoids (as much as may be) being where they are. That he may not imitate them, he will not associate with them, nor choose them for his companions. He does not stand in their way, to be picked up by them (Prov. vii. 8), but keeps as far from them as from a place or person infected with the plague, for fear of the contagion, Prov. iv. 14, 15. He that would be kept from harm must keep out of harm's way. [3.] He *sits not in the seat of the scornful;* he does not repose himself with those that sit down secure in their wickedness and please themselves with the searedness of their own consciences. He does not associate with those that sit in close cabal to find out ways and means for the support and advancement of the devil's kingdom, or that sit in open judgment, magisterially to condemn the generation of the righteous. The seat of the drunkards is the *seat of the scornful,* lxix. 12. Happy is the man that never sits in it, Hos. vii. 5.

2. A godly man, that he may do that which is good and cleave to it, submits to the guidance of the word of God and makes that familiar to him, *v.* 2. This is that which keeps him out of the way of the ungodly and fortifies him against their temptations. *By the words of thy lips I have kept me from the path of the deceiver,* xvii. 4. We need not court the fellowship of sinners, either for pleasure or for improvement, while we have fellowship with the word of God and with God himself in and by his word. *When thou awakest it shall talk with thee,* Prov. vi. 22. We may judge of our spiritual state by asking, " What is the law of God to us? What account do we make of it? What place has it in us?" See here, (1.) The entire affection which a good man has for the law of God: *His delight is in it.* He delights in it, though it be a law, a yoke, because it is the law of God, which is holy, just, and good, and which he freely consents to, and so delights in, *after the inner man,* Rom. vii. 16, 22. All who are well pleased that there is a God must be well pleased that there is a Bible, a revelation of God, of his will, and of the only way to happiness in him. (2.) The intimate acquaintance which a good man keeps up with the word of God: *In that law doth he meditate day and night;* and by this it appears that his delight is in it, for what we love we love to think of, cxix. 97. To meditate in God's word is to discourse with ourselves concerning the great things contained in it, with a close application of mind, a fixedness of thought, till we be suitably affected with those things and experience the savour and power of them in our hearts. This we must do *day and night;* we must have a constant habitual regard to the word of God as the rule of our actions and the

spring of our comforts, and we must have it in our thoughts, accordingly, upon every occasion that occurs, whether night or day. No time is amiss for meditating on the word of God, nor is any time unseasonable for those visits. We must not only set ourselves to meditate on God's word morning and evening, at the entrance of the day and of the night, but these thoughts should be interwoven with the business and converse of every day and with the repose and slumbers of every night. *When I awake I am still with thee.*

II. An assurance given of the godly man's happiness, with which we should encourage ourselves to answer the character of such. 1. In general, he is *blessed, v.* 1. God blesses him, and that blessing will make him happy. Blessednesses are to him, blessings of all kinds, of the upper and nether springs, enough to make him completely happy; none of the ingredients of happiness shall be wanting to him. When the psalmist undertakes to describe a blessed man, he describes a good man; for, after all, those only are happy, truly happy, that are holy, truly holy; and we are more concerned to know the way to blessedness than to know wherein that blessedness will consist. Nay, goodness and holiness are not only the way to happiness (Rev. xxii. 14) but happiness itself; supposing there were not another life after this, yet that man is a happy man that keeps in the way of his duty. 2. His blessedness is here illustrated by a similitude (*v.* 3): *He shall be like a tree,* fruitful and flourishing. This is the effect, (1.) Of his pious practice; he meditates in the law of God, turns that *in succum et sanguinem—into juice and blood,* and that makes him like a tree. The more we converse with the word of God the better furnished we are for every good word and work. Or, (2.) Of the promised blessing; he is blessed of the Lord, and therefore *he shall be like a tree.* The divine blessing produces real effects. It is the happiness of a godly man, [1.] That he is planted by the grace of God. These trees were by nature wild olives, and will continue so till they are grafted anew, and so planted by a power from above. Never any good tree grew of itself; it is *the planting of the Lord,* and therefore he must in it be glorified. Isa. lxi. 3, *The trees of the Lord are full of sap.* [2.] That he is placed by the means of grace, here called *the rivers of water,* those rivers which *make glad the city of our God* (xlvi. 4); from these a good man receives supplies of strength and vigour, but in secret undiscerned ways. [3.] That his practices shall be fruit, abounding to a good account, Phil. iv. 17. To those whom God first blessed he said, *Be fruitful* (Gen. i. 22), and still the comfort and honour of fruitfulness are a recompence for the labour of it. It is expected from those who enjoy the mercies of grace that, both in the temper of their minds and in the tenour of their lives, they comply with the intentions of that grace, and then they bring forth fruit. And, be it observed to the praise of the great dresser of the vineyard, they bring forth their fruit (that which is required of them) *in due season,* when it is most beautiful and most useful, improving every opportunity of doing good and doing it in its proper time. [4.] That his profession shall be preserved from blemish and decay: *His leaf also shall not wither.* As to those who bring forth only the leaves of profession, without any good fruit, even their leaf will wither and they shall be as much ashamed of their profession as ever they were proud of it; but, if the word of God rule in the heart, that will keep the profession green, both to our comfort and to our credit; and the laurels thus won shall never wither. [5.] That prosperity shall attend him wherever he goes, soul-prosperity. *Whatever he does,* in conformity to the law, *it shall prosper* and succeed to his mind, or above his hope.

In singing these verses, being duly affected with the malignant and dangerous nature of sin, the transcendent excellencies of the divine law, and the power and efficacy of God's grace, from which our fruit is found, we must teach and admonish ourselves, and one another, to watch against sin and all approaches towards it, to converse much with the word of God, and to abound in the fruit of righteousness; and, in praying over them, we must seek to God for his grace both to fortify us against every evil word and work and to furnish us for every good word and work.

4 The ungodly *are* not so : but *are* like the chaff which the wind driveth away. 5 Therefore the ungodly shall not stand in the judgment, nor sinners in the congregation of the righteous. 6 For the LORD knoweth the way of the righteous : but the way of the ungodly shall perish.

Here is, I. The description of the ungodly given, *v.* 4. 1. In general, they are the reverse of the righteous, both in character and condition: *They are not so.* The LXX. emphatically repeat this: *Not so the ungodly; they are not so;* they are led by the counsel of the wicked, in the way of sinners, to the seat of the scornful; they have no delight in the law of God, nor ever think of it; they bring forth no fruit but grapes of Sodom; they cumber the ground. 2. In particular, whereas the righteous are like valuable, useful, fruitful trees, *they are like the chaff which the wind drives away,* the very lightest of the chaff, the dust which the owner of the floor desires to have driven away, as not capable of being put to any use. Would you value them? Would you weigh them? They are like chaff, of no worth at all in God's account, how highly soever they may value themselves. Would you know the temper of their minds? They are light and vain; they have no substance in them, no solidity; they are easily driven to and fro by every wind and temptation, and have no stedfastness. Would you know their end? The wrath of God will drive them away in their wickedness, as the wind does the chaff, which is never gathered nor looked after more. The chaff may be, for a while, among the wheat; but he is coming *whose fan is in his hand* and who will *thoroughly purge his floor.* Those that by their own sin and folly make themselves as chaff will be found so before the whirlwind and fire of divine wrath (xxxv. 5), so unable to stand before it or to escape it, Isa. xvii. 13.

II. The doom of the ungodly read, *v.* 5. 1. They will be cast, upon their trial, as traitors convicted: *They shall not stand in the judgment,* that is, they shall be found guilty, shall hang down the head with shame and confusion, and all their pleas and excuses will be overruled as frivolous. There is a judgment to come, in which every man's present character and work, though ever so artfully concealed and disguised, shall be truly and perfectly discovered, and appear in their own colours, and accordingly every man's future state will be, by an irreversible sentence, determined for eternity. The ungodly must appear in that judgment, to receive according to the things done in the body. They may hope to come off, nay, to come off with honour, but their hope will deceive them: *They shall not stand in the judgment,* so plain will the evidence be against them and so just and impartial will the judgment be upon it. 2. They will be for ever shut out from the society of the blessed. They shall not stand *in the congregation of the righteous,* that is, in the *judgment* (so some), that court wherein the saints, as assessors with Christ, shall judge the world, those holy myriads with which he shall come to execute *judgment upon all,* Jude 14; 1 Cor. vi. 2. Or in *heaven.* There will be seen, shortly, a *general assembly of the church of the first-born, a congregation of the righteous,* of all the saints, and none but saints, and saints made perfect, such a congregation as never was in this world, 2 Thess. ii. 1. The wicked shall not have a place in that congregation. Into the new Jerusalem none unclean nor unsanctified shall enter; they shall see the righteous enter into the kingdom, and themselves, to their everlasting vexation, thrust out, Luke xiii. 27. The wicked and profane, in this world, ridiculed the righteous and their congregation, despised them, and cared not for their company; justly therefore will they be for ever separated from them. Hypocrites in this world, under the disguise of a plausible profession, may thrust themselves into the congregation of the righteous and remain undisturbed and undiscovered there; but Christ cannot be imposed upon, though his ministers may; the day is coming when he will separate *between the sheep and the goats, the tares and the wheat;* see Matt. xiii. 41, 49. That *great day* (so the Chaldee here calls it) will be a day of discovery, a day of distinction, and a day of final division. Then you shall return and discern between the righteous and the wicked, which here it is sometimes hard to do, Mal. iii. 18.

III. The reason rendered of this different state of the godly and wicked, *v.* 6. 1. God must have all the glory of the prosperity and happiness of the righteous. They are blessed because *the Lord knows their way;* he chose them into it, inclined them to choose it, leads and guides them in it, and orders all their steps. 2. Sinners must bear all the blame of their own destruction. *Therefore* the ungodly perish, because the very way in which they have chosen and resolved to walk leads directly to destruction; it naturally tends towards ruin and therefore must necessarily end in it. Or we may take it thus, The Lord approves and is well pleased with the way of the righteous, and therefore, under the influence of his gracious smiles, it shall prosper and end well; but he is angry at the way of the wicked, all they do is offensive to him, and therefore it shall perish, and they in it. It is certain that every man's judgment proceeds from the Lord, and it is well or ill with us, and is likely to be so to all eternity, accordingly as we are or are not accepted of God. Let this support the drooping spirits of the righteous, that the Lord knows their way, knows their hearts (Jer. xii. 3), knows their secret devotions (Matt. vi. 6), knows their character, how much soever it is blackened and blemished by the reproaches of men, and will shortly make them and their way manifest before the world, to their immortal joy and honour. Let this cast a damp upon the security and jollity of sinners, that their way, though pleasant now, will perish at last.

In singing these verses, and praying over them, let us possess ourselves with a holy dread of the wicked man's portion, and deprecate it with a firm and lively expectation of the judgment to come, and stir up ourselves to prepare for it, and with a holy care to approve ourselves to God in every thing, entreating his favour with our whole hearts.

PSALM II.

As the foregoing psalm was moral, and showed us our duty, so this is evangelical, and shows us our Saviour. Under the type of David's kingdom (which was of divine appointment, met with much opposition, but prevailed at last) the kingdom of the Messiah, the Son of David, is prophesied of, which is the primary intention and scope of the psalm; and I think there is less in it of the type, and more of the anti-type, than in any of the gospel psalms, for there is nothing in it but what is applicable to Christ, but some things that are not at all applicable to David (ver. 6, 7): "Thou art my Son" (ver. 8), "I will give thee the uttermost parts of the earth," and (ver. 12), "Kiss the Son." It is interpreted of Christ, Acts iv. 27; xiii. 33; Heb. i. 5. The Holy Ghost here foretels, I. The opposition that should be given to the kingdom of the Messiah, ver. 1—3. II. The baffling and chastising of that opposition, ver. 4, 5. III. The setting up of the kingdom of Christ, notwithstanding that opposition, ver. 6. IV. The confirmation and establishment of it, ver. 7. V. A promise of the enlargement and success of it, ver. 8, 9. VI. A call and exhortation to kings and princes to yield themselves the willing subjects of this kingdom, ver. 10—12. Or thus: We have here, I. Threatenings denounced against the adversaries of Christ's kingdom, ver. 1—6. II. Promises made to Christ himself, the head of this kingdom, ver. 7—9. III. Counsel given to all to espouse the interests of this kingdom, ver. 10—12. This psalm, as the former, is very fitly prefixed to this book of devotions, because, as it is necessary to our acceptance with God that we should be subject to the precepts of his law, so it is likewise that we should be subject to the grace of his gospel, and come to him in the name of a Mediator.

WHY do the heathen rage, and the people imagine a vain thing? 2 The kings of the earth set themselves, and the rulers take counsel together, against the LORD, and against his anointed, *saying*, 3 Let us break their bands asunder, and cast away their cords from us. 4 He that sitteth in the heavens shall laugh : the LORD shall have them in derision. 5 Then shall he speak unto them in his wrath, and vex them in his sore displeasure. 6 Yet have I set my king upon my holy hill of Zion.

We have here a very great struggle about the kingdom of Christ, hell and heaven contesting it ; the seat of the war is this earth, where Satan has long had a usurped kingdom and exercised dominion to such a degree that he has been called *the prince of the power of the* very *air* we breathe in and *the god of the world* we live in. He knows very well that, as the Messiah's kingdom rises and gets ground, his falls and loses ground ; and therefore, though it will be set up certainly, it shall not be set up tamely. Observe here,

I. The mighty opposition that would be given to the Messiah and his kingdom, to his holy religion and all the interests of it, *v.* 1 —3. One would have expected that so great a blessing to this world would be universally welcomed and embraced, and that every sheaf would immediately bow to that of the Messiah and all the crowns and sceptres on earth would be laid at his feet ; but it proves quite contrary. Never were the notions of any sect of philosophers, though ever so absurd, nor the powers of any prince or state, though ever so tyrannical, opposed with so much violence as the doctrine and government of Christ—a sign that it was from heaven originally, for the opposition was plainly from hell originally.

1. We are here told who would appear as adversaries to Christ and the devil's instruments in this opposition to his kingdom. Princes and people, court and country, have sometimes separate interests, but here they are united against Christ ; not the mighty only, but the mob, the *heathen*, the *people*, numbers of them, communities of them ; though usually fond of liberty, yet they were averse to the liberty Christ came to procure and proclaim. Not the mob only, but the mighty (among whom one might have expected more sense and consideration) appear violent against Christ. Though his kingdom is not of this world, nor in the least calcu-

lated to weaken their interests, but very likely, if they pleased, to strengthen them, yet the kings of the earth and rulers are up in arms immediately. See the effects of the old enmity in the seed of the serpent against the seed of the woman, and how general and malignant the corruption of mankind is. See how formidable the enemies of he church are ; they are numerous ; they are potent The unbelieving Jews are here called *heathen*, so wretchedly had they degenerated from the faith and holiness of their ancestors ; they stirred up the heathen, the Gentiles, to persecute the Christians. As the Philistines and their lords, Saul and his courtiers, the disaffected party and their ringleaders, opposed David's coming to the crown, so Herod and Pilate, the Gentiles and the Jews, did their utmost against Christ and his interest in men, Acts iv. 27.

2. Who it is that they quarrel with, and muster up all their forces against ; it is *against the Lord and against his anointed*, that is, against all religion in general and the Christian religion in particular. It is certain that all who are enemies to Christ, whatever they pretend, are enemies to God himself ; they *have hated both me and my Father*, John xv. 24. The great author of our holy religion is here called *the Lord's anointed*, or *Messiah*, or *Christ*, in allusion to the anointing of David to be king. He is both authorized and qualified to be the church's head and king, is duly invested in the office and every way fitted for it ; yet there are those that are against him ; nay, *therefore* they are against him, because they are impatient of God's authority, envious at Christ's advancement, and have a rooted enmity to the Spirit of holiness.

3. The opposition they give is here described. (1.) It is a most spiteful and malicious opposition. They *rage* and fret ; they gnash their teeth for vexation at the setting up of Christ's kingdom ; it creates them the utmost uneasiness, and fills them with indignation, so that they have no enjoyment of themselves ; see Luke xiii. 14 ; John xi. 47 ; Acts v. 17, 33 ; xix. 28. Idolaters raged at the discovery of their folly, the chief priests and Pharisees at the eclipsing of their glory and the shaking of their usurped dominion. Those that did evil raged at the light. (2.) It is a deliberate and politic opposition. They *imagine* or meditate, that is, they contrive means to suppress the rising interests of Christ's kingdom and are very confident of the success of their contrivances ; they promise themselves that they shall run down religion and carry the day. (3.) It is a resolute and obstinate opposition. They *set themselves*, set their faces as a flint and their hearts as an adamant, in defiance of reason, and conscience, and all the terrors of the Lord ; they are proud and daring, like the Babel-builders, and will persist in their resolution, come what will. (4.) It is a combined and confederate opposition. They *take coun-*

sel *together*, to assist and animate one another in this opposition; they carry their resolutions *nemine contradicente — unanimously*, that they will push on the unholy war against the Messiah with the utmost vigour: and thereupon councils are called, cabals are formed, and all their wits are at work to find out ways and means for the preventing of the establishment of Christ's kingdom, lxxxiii. 5.

4. We are here told what it is they are exasperated at and what they aim at in this opposition (*v.* 3): *Let us break their bands asunder.* They will not be under any government; they are children of Belial, that cannot endure the yoke, at least the yoke of the Lord and his anointed. They will be content to entertain such notions of the kingdom of God and the Messiah as will serve them to dispute of and to support their own dominion with: if the Lord and his anointed will make them rich and great in the world, they will bid them welcome; but if they will restrain their corrupt appetites and passions, regulate and reform their hearts and lives, and bring them under the government of a pure and heavenly religion, truly then *they will not have this man to reign over them*, Luke xix. 14. Christ has *bands and cords* for us; those that will be saved by him must be ruled by him; but they are *cords of a man*, agreeable to right reason, and *bands of love*, conducive to our true interest: and yet against those the quarrel is. Why do men oppose religion but because they are impatient of its restraints and obligations? They would break asunder the bands of conscience they are under and the cords of God's commandments by which they are called to tie themselves out from all sin and to tie themselves up to all duty; they will not receive them, but cast them away as far from them as they can.

5. They are here reasoned with concerning it, *v.* 1. Why do they do this? (1.) They can show no good cause for opposing so just, holy, and gracious a government, which will not interfere with the secular powers, nor introduce any dangerous principles hurtful to kings or provinces; but, on the contrary, if universally received, would bring a heaven upon earth. (2.) They can hope for no good success in opposing so powerful a kingdom, with which they are utterly unable to contend. It is *a vain thing;* when they have done their worst Christ will have a church in the world and that church shall be glorious and triumphant. It is *built upon a rock, and the gates of hell shall not prevail against it.* The moon walks in brightness, though the dogs bark at it.

II. The mighty conquest gained over all this threatening opposition. If heaven and earth be the combatants, it is easy to foretel which will be the conqueror. Those that make this mighty struggle are the people of the earth, and the kings of the earth, who, being of the earth, are earthy; but he whom they contest with is one that *sits in the heavens, v.* 4. He is in the heaven, a place of such a vast prospect that he can oversee them all and all their projects; and such is his power that he can overcome them all and all their attempts. He sits there, as one easy and at rest, out of the reach of all their impotent menaces and attempts. There he sits as Judge in all the affairs of the children of men, perfectly secure of the full accomplishment of all his own purposes and designs, in spite of all opposition, xxix. 10. The perfect repose of the Eternal Mind may be our comfort under all the disquietments of our mind. We are tossed on earth, and in the sea, but he sits in the heavens, where he has prepared his throne for judgment; and therefore,

1. The attempts of Christ's enemies are easily ridiculed. God *laughs* at them as a company of fools. He *has them*, and all their attempts, *in derision*, and therefore *the virgin, the daughter of Zion, has despised them*, Isa. xxxvii. 22. Sinners' follies are the just sport of God's infinite wisdom and power; and those attempts of the kingdom of Satan which in our eyes are formidable in his are despicable. Sometimes God is said to *awake*, and *arise*, and *stir up himself*, for the vanquishing of his enemies; here he is said to *sit still* and vanquish them; for the utmost operations of God's omnipotence create no difficulty at all, nor the least disturbance to his eternal rest.

2. They are justly punished, *v.* 5. Though God despises them as impotent, yet he does not therefore wink at them, but is justly displeased with them as impudent and impious, and will make the most daring sinners to know that he is so and to tremble before him. (1.) Their sin is a provocation to him. He is wroth; he is sorely displeased. We cannot expect that God should be reconciled to us, or well pleased in us, but in and through the anointed; and therefore, if we affront and reject him, we sin against the remedy and forfeit the benefit of his interposition between us and God. (2.) His anger will be a vexation to them; if he but speak to them in his wrath, even the breath of his mouth will be their confusion, slaughter, and consumption, Isa. xi. 4; 2 Thess. ii. 8. He speaks, and it is done; he speaks in wrath, and sinners are undone. As a word made us, so a word can unmake us again. *Who knows the power of his anger?* The enemies rage, but cannot vex God. God sits still, and yet vexes them, puts them into a consternation (as the word is), and brings them to their wits' end: his setting up this kingdom of his Son, in spite of them, is the greatest vexation to them that can be. They were vexatious to Christ's good subjects; but the day is coming when vexation shall be recompensed to them.

3. They are certainly defeated, and all their counsels turned headlong (*v.* 6): *Yet have I set my king upon my holy hill of Zion.* David was advanced to the throne, and became

master of the strong-hold of Zion, notwith-standing the disturbance given him by the malcontents in his kingdom, and particularly the affronts he received from the garrison of Zion, who taunted him with their blind and their lame, their maimed soldiers, 2 Sam. v. 6. The Lord Jesus is exalted to the right hand of the Father, has all power both in heaven and in earth, and is head over all things to the church, notwithstanding the restless endeavours of his enemies to hinder his advancement. (1.) Jesus Christ is a King, and is invested by him who is the fountain of power with the dignity and authority of a sovereign prince in the kingdom both of providence and grace. (2.) God is pleased to call him *his* King, because he is appointed by him, and entrusted for him with the sole administration of government and judgment. He is his King, for he is dear to the Father, and one in whom he is well pleased. (3.) Christ took not this honour to himself, but was called to it, and he that called him owns him : *I have set him;* his commandment, his commission, he received from the Father. (4.) Being called to this honour, he was confirmed in it; high places (we say) are slippery places, but Christ, being raised, is fixed : "*I have set him,* I have settled him." (5.) He is set upon *Zion,* the hill of God's holiness, a type of the gospel church, for on that the temple was built, for the sake of which the whole mount was called *holy.* Christ's throne is set up in his church, that is, in the hearts of all believers and in the societies they form. The evangelical law of Christ is said to *go forth from Zion* (Isa. ii. 3, Mic. iv. 2), and therefore that is spoken of as the head-quarters of this general, the royal seat of this prince, in whom the children of men shall be joyful.

We are to sing these verses with a holy exultation, triumphing over all the enemies of Christ's kingdom (not doubting but they will all of them be quickly made his footstool), and triumphing in Jesus Christ as the great trustee of power ; and we are to pray, in firm belief of the assurance here given, "Father in heaven, *Thy kingdom come;* let thy Son's kingdom come."

7 I will declare the decree : the LORD hath said unto me, Thou *art* my Son ; this day have I begotten thee. 8 Ask of me, and I shall give *thee* the heathen *for* thine inheritance, and the uttermost parts of the earth *for* thy possession. 9 Thou shalt break them with a rod of iron ; thou shalt dash them in pieces like a potter's vessel.

We have heard what the kings of the earth have to say against Christ's kingdom, and have heard it gainsaid by him that sits in heaven ; let us now hear what the Messiah

himself has to say for his kingdom, to make good his claims, and it is what all the powers on earth cannot gainsay

I. The kingdom of the Messiah is founded upon a decree, an eternal decree, of God the Father. It was not a sudden resolve, it was not the trial of an experiment, but the result of the counsels of the divine wisdom and the determinations of the divine will, before all worlds, neither of which can be altered—the *precept* or *statute* (so some read it), the *covenant* or *compact* (so others,) the federal transactions between the Father and the Son concerning man's redemption, represented by the covenant of royalty made with David and his seed, lxxxix. 3. This our Lord Jesus often referred to as that which, all along in his undertaking, he governed himself by ; *This is the will of him that sent me,* John vi. 40. *This commandment have I received of my Father,* John x. 18 ; xiv. 31.

II. There is a declaration of that decree as far as is necessary for the satisfaction of all those who are called and commanded to yield themselves subjects to this king, and to leave those inexcusable who will not have him to reign over them. The decree was secret ; it was what the Father said to the Son, when he possessed him in the beginning of his way, before his works of old ; but it is declared by a faithful witness, who had lain in the bosom of the Father from eternity, and came into the world as the prophet of the church, to declare him, John i. 18. The fountain of all being is, without doubt, the fountain of all power ; and it is by, from, and under him, that the Messiah claims. He has his right to rule from what Jehovah said to him, by whose word all things were made and are governed. Christ here makes a two-fold title to his kingdom :—1. A title by inheritance (*v.* 7): *Thou art my Son, this day have I begotten thee.* This scripture the apostle quotes (Heb. i. 5) to prove that Christ has a more excellent name than the angels, but that he *obtained it by inheritance, v.* 4. He is the Son of God, not by adoption, but his begotten Son, the only begotten of the Father, John i. 14. And the Father owns him, and will have this declared to the world as the reason why he is constituted King upon the holy hill of Zion ; he is therefore unquestionably entitled to, and perfectly qualified for, that great trust. He is the Son of God, and therefore of the same nature with the Father, has in him all the fulness of the godhead, infinite wisdom, power, and holiness. The supreme government of the church is too high an honour and too hard an undertaking for any mere creature ; none can be fit for it but he who is *one with the Father* and was *from eternity by him as one brought up with him,* thoroughly apprized of all his counsels, Prov. viii. 30. He is the Son of God, and therefore dear to him, his beloved Son, in whom he is well pleased ; and upon this account we are to receive him as a

King; for because *the Father loveth the Son he hath given all things into his hand,* John iii. 35; v. 20. Being a Son, he is heir of all things, and, the Father having made the worlds by him, it is easy to infer thence that by him also he governs them; for he is the eternal Wisdom and the eternal Word. If God hath said unto him, "*Thou art my Son,*" it becomes each of us to say to him, "Thou art my Lord, my sovereign." Further, to satisfy us that his kingdom is well-grounded upon his sonship, we are here told what his sonship is grounded on: *This day have I begotten thee,* which refers both to his eternal generation itself, for it is quoted (Heb. i. 5) to prove that he is the *brightness of his Father's glory and the express image of his person* (v. 3), and to the evidence and demonstration given of it by his resurrection from the dead, for to that also it is expressly applied by the apostle, Acts xiii. 33. *He hath raised up Jesus again, as it is written, Thou art my Son, this day have I begotten thee.* It was by the resurrection from the dead, that sign of the prophet Jonas, which was to be the most convincing of all, that he was *declared to be the Son of God with power,* Rom. i. 4. Christ is said to be the *first-begotten* and *first-born from the dead,* Rev. i. 5; Col. i. 18. Immediately after his resurrection he entered upon the administration of his mediatorial kingdom; it was then that he said, *All power is given unto me,* and to that especially he had an eye when he taught his disciples to pray, *Thy kingdom come.* 2. A title by agreement, v. 8, 9. The agreement is, in short, this: the Son must undertake the office of an intercessor, and, upon that condition, he shall have the honour and power of a universal monarch; see Isa. liii. 12, *Therefore will I divide him a portion with the great, because he made intercession for the transgressors. He shall be a priest upon his throne, and the counsel of peace shall be between them both,* Zech. vi. 13. (1.) The Son must ask. This supposes his putting himself voluntarily into a state of inferiority to the Father, by taking upon him the human nature; for, as God, he was equal in power and glory with the Father and had nothing to ask. It supposes the making of a satisfaction by the virtue of which the intercession must be made, and the paying of a price, on which this large demand was to be grounded; see John xvii. 4, 5. The Son, in asking the heathen for his inheritance, aims, not only at his own honour, but at their happiness in him; so that he intercedes for them, ever lives to do so, and is therefore able to save to the uttermost. (2.) The Father will grant more than to the half of the kingdom, even to the kingdom itself. It is here promised him, [1.] That his government shall be universal: he shall have *the heathen* for his inheritance, not the Jews only, to whose nation the church had been long confined, but the Gentiles also. Those in *the uttermost parts of*

the earth (as this nation of ours) shall be his *possession,* and he shall have multitudes of willing loyal subjects among them. Baptized Christians are the possession of the Lord Jesus; they are to him for a name and a praise. God the Father gives them to him when by his Spirit and grace he works upon them to submit their necks to the yoke of the Lord Jesus. This is in part fulfilled; a great part of the Gentile world received the gospel when it was first preached, and Christ's throne was set up there where Satan's seat had long been. But it is to be yet further accomplished when *the kingdoms of this world shall become the kingdoms of the Lord and of his Christ,* Rev. xi. 15. *Who shall live when God doeth this?* [2.] That it shall be victorious: *Thou shalt break them* (those of them that oppose thy kingdom) *with a rod of iron,* v. 9. This was in part fulfilled when the nation of the Jews, those that persisted in unbelief and enmity to Christ's gospel, were destroyed by the Roman power, which was represented (Dan. ii. 40) by feet of iron, as here by a rod of iron. It had a further accomplishment in the destruction of the Pagan powers, when the Christian religion came to be established; but it will not be completely fulfilled till all opposing rule, principality, and power, shall be finally put down, 1 Cor. xv. 24. See cx. 5, 6. Observe, How powerful Christ is and how weak the enemies of his kingdom are before him; he has a rod of iron wherewith to crush those that will not submit to his golden sceptre; they are but like a potter's vessel before him, suddenly, easily, and irreparably dashed in pieces by him; see Rev. ii. 27. "Thou shalt do it, that is, thou shalt have *leave* to do it." Nations shall be ruined, rather than the gospel church shall not be built and established *I have loved thee, therefore will I give men for thee,* Isa. xliii. 4. "Thou shalt have power to do it; none shall be able to stand before thee; and thou shalt do it effectually." Those that will not bow shall break.

In singing this, and praying it over, we must give glory to Christ as the eternal Son of God and our rightful Lord, and must take comfort from this promise, and plead it with God, that the kingdom of Christ shall be enlarged and established and shall triumph over all opposition.

10 Be wise now therefore, O ye kings : be instructed, ye judges of the earth. 11 Serve the LORD with fear, and rejoice with trembling. 12 Kiss the Son, lest he be angry, and ye perish *from* the way, when his wrath is kindled but a little. Blessed *are* all they that put their trust in him.

We have here the practical application of this gospel doctrine concerning the kingdom of the Messiah, by way of exhortation to the kings and judges of the earth. They hear that it is in vain to oppose Christ's government; let them therefore be so wise for themselves as to submit to it. He that has power to destroy them shows that he has no pleasure in their destruction, for he puts them into a way to make themselves happy, *v.* 10. Those that would be wise must be instructed; and those are truly wise that receive instruction from the word of God. Kings and judges stand upon a level with common persons before God; and it is as necessary for them to be religious as for any others. Those that give law and judgment to others must receive law from Christ, and it will be their wisdom to do so. What is said to them is said to all, and is required of every one of us, only it is directed to kings and judges because of the influence which their example will have upon their inferiors, and because they were men of rank and power that opposed the setting up of Christ's kingdom, *v.* 2. We are exhorted,

I. To reverence God and to stand in awe of him, *v.* 11. This is the great duty of natural religion. God is great, and infinitely above us, just and holy, and provoked against us, and therefore we ought to fear him and tremble before him; yet he is our Lord and Master, and we are bound to serve him, our friend and benefactor, and we have reason to rejoice in him; and these are very well consistent with each other, for, 1. We must serve God in all ordinances of worship, and all instances of a godly conversation, but with a holy fear, a jealousy over ourselves, and a reverence of him. Even kings themselves, whom others serve and fear, must serve and fear God; there is the same infinite distance between them and God that there is between the meanest of their subjects and him. 2. We must rejoice in God, and, in subordination to him, we may rejoice in other things, but still with a holy trembling, as those that know what a glorious and jealous God he is, whose eye is always upon us. Our salvation must be wrought out *with fear and trembling*, Phil. ii. 12. We ought to rejoice in the setting up of the kingdom of Christ, but to *rejoice with trembling*, with a holy awe of him, a holy fear for ourselves, lest we come short, and a tender concern for the many precious souls to whom his gospel and kingdom are a savour of death unto death. Whatever we rejoice in, in this world, it must always be with trembling, lest we grow vain in our joy and be puffed up with the things we rejoice in, and because of the uncertainty of them and the damp which by a thousand accidents may soon be cast upon our joy. To *rejoice with trembling is to rejoice as though we rejoiced not*, 1 Cor. vii. 30.

II. To welcome Jesus Christ and to submit to him, *v.* 12. This is the great duty of the Christian religion; it is that which is required of all, even kings and judges, and it is our wisdom and interest to do it. Observe here,

1. The command given to this purport: *Kiss the Son.* Christ is called the *Son* because so he was declared (*v.* 7), *Thou art my Son.* He is the Son of God by eternal generation, and, upon that account, he is to be adored by us. He is the *Son of man* (that is, the Mediator, John v. 27), and, upon that account, to be received and submitted to. He is called the *Son*, to include both, as God is often called emphatically the *Father*, because he is the Father of our Lord Jesus Christ, and in him our Father, and we must have an eye to him under both considerations. Our duty to Christ is here expressed figuratively: *Kiss the Son*, not with a betraying kiss, as Judas kissed him, and as all hypocrites, who pretend to honour him, but really affront him; but with a believing kiss. (1.) With a kiss of agreement and reconciliation. Kiss, and be friends, as Jacob and Esau; let the quarrel between us and God terminate; let the acts of hostility cease, and let us be at peace with God in Christ, who is our peace. (2.) With a kiss of adoration and religious worship. Those that worshipped idols kissed them, 1 Kings xix. 18; Hos. xiii. 2. Let us study how to do honour to the Lord Jesus, and to give unto him the glory due unto his name. *He is thy Lord, and worship thou him*, xlv. 11. We must *worship the Lamb*, as well as him that sits on the throne, Rev. v. 9—13. (3.) With a kiss of affection and sincere love: "*Kiss the Son;* enter into a covenant of friendship with him, and let him be very dear and precious to you; love him above all, love him in sincerity, love him much, as she did to whom much was forgiven, and, in token of it, kissed his feet," Luke vii. 38. (4.) With a kiss of allegiance and loyalty, as Samuel kissed Saul, 1 Sam. x. 1. Swear fealty and homage to him, submit to his government, take his yoke upon you, and give up yourselves to be governed by his laws, disposed of by his providence, and entirely devoted to his interest.

2. The reasons to enforce this command; and they are taken from our own interest, which God, in his gospel, shows a concern for. Consider,

(1.) The certain ruin we run upon if we refuse and reject Christ: "*Kiss the Son;* for it is at your peril if you do not." [1.] "It will be a great provocation to him. Do it, *lest he be angry.*" The Father is angry already; the Son is the Mediator that undertakes to make peace; if we slight him, the *Father's wrath abides upon us* (John iii. 36), and not only so, but there is an addition of the Son's wrath too, to whom nothing is more displeasing than to have the offers of his grace slighted and the designs of it frustrated. The Son can be angry, though a Lamb; he is the lion of the tribe of Judah, and the wrath of this king, this King of kings, will be as the roaring of a lion, and will drive even mighty men and chief captains to seek in vain for shelter in rocks and mountains,

Rev. vi. 16. If the Son be angry, who shall intercede for us? There remains no more sacrifice, no other name by which we can be saved. Unbelief is a sin against the remedy. [2.] It will be utter destruction to yourselves: *Lest you perish from the way*, or *in* the way so some, *in* the way of your sins, and *from* the way of your vain hopes; *lest your way perish* (as i. 6), lest you prove to have missed the way to happiness. Christ is the way; take heed lest you be cut off from him as your way to God. It intimates that they were, or at least thought themselves, in the way; but, by neglecting Christ, they perished from it, which aggravates their ruin, that they go to hell from the way to heaven, are not far from the kingdom of God and yet never arrive there.

(2.) The happiness we are sure of if we yield ourselves to Christ. When his wrath is kindled, though *but a little*, the least spark of that fire is enough to make the proudest sinner miserable if it fasten upon his conscience; for it will burn to the lowest hell: one would think it should therefore follow, "When his wrath is kindled, woe be to those that despise him;" but the Psalmist startles at the thought, deprecates that dreadful doom and pronounces those blessed that escape it. Those that trust in him, and so kiss him, are truly happy; but they will especially appear to be so when the wrath of Christ is kindled against others. Blessed will those be in the day of wrath, who, by trusting in Christ, have made him their refuge and patron; when the hearts of others fail them for fear they shall lift up their heads with joy; and then those who now despise Christ and his followers will be forced to say, to their own greater confusion, "Now we see that *blessed are all those*, and those only, *that trust in him.*"

In singing this, and praying it over, we should have our hearts filled with a holy awe of God, but at the same time borne up with a cheerful confidence in Christ, in whose mediation we may comfort and encourage ourselves and one another. *We are the circumcision, that rejoice in Christ Jesus*

PSALM III.

As the foregoing psalm, in the type of David in preferment, showed us the royal dignity of the Redeemer, so this, by the example of David in distress, shows us the peace and holy security of the redeemed, how safe they really are, and think themselves to be, under the divine protection. David, being now driven out from his palace, from the royal city, from the holy city, by his rebellious son Absalom, I. Complains to God of his enemies, ver. 1, 2. II. Confides in God, and encourages himself in him as his God, notwithstanding, ver. 3. III. Recollects the satisfaction he had in the gracious answers God gave to his prayers, and his experience of his goodness to him, ver. 4, 5. IV. Triumphs over his fears (ver. 6) and over his enemies, whom he prays against, ver. 7. V. Gives God the glory and takes to himself the comfort of the divine blessing and salvation which are sure to all the people of God, ver. 8. Those speak best of the truths of God who speak experimentally; so David here speaks of the power and goodness of God, and of the safety and tranquillity of the godly.

A Psalm of David, when he fled from Absalom his son.

L ORD, how are they increased that trouble me? many *are* they that

rise up against me. 2 Many *there be* which say of my soul, *There is* no help for him in God. Selah. 3 But thou, O Lord, *art* a shield for me; my glory, and the lifter up of mine head.

The title of this psalm and many others is as a key hung ready at the door, to open it, and let us into the entertainments of it; when we know upon what occasion a psalm was penned we know the better how to expound it. This was composed, or at least the substance of it was meditated and digested in David's thoughts, and offered up to God, when he fled from Absalom his son, who formed a conspiracy against him, to take away, not his crown only, but his life; we have the story, 2 Sam. xv., &c. 1. David was now in great grief; when, in his flight, he went up the Mount of Olives, he wept greatly, with his head covered, and marching bare-foot; yet *then* he composed this comfortable psalm. He wept and prayed, wept and sung, wept and believed; this was sowing in tears. Is any afflicted? Let him pray; nay, let him sing psalms, let him sing this psalm. Is any afflicted with undutiful disobedient children? David was; and yet that did not hinder his joy in God, nor put him out of tune for holy songs. 2. He was now in great danger; the plot against him was laid deep, the party that sought his ruin was very formidable, and his own son at the head of them, so that his affairs seemed to be at the last extremity; yet *then* he kept hold of his interest in God and improved that. Perils and frights should drive us to God, not drive us from him. 3. He had now a great deal of provocation given him by those from whom he had reason to expect better things, from his son, whom he had been indulgent of, from his subjects, whom he had been so great a blessing to; this he could not but resent, and it was enough to break in upon any man's temper; yet he was so far from any indecent expressions of passion and indignation that he had calmness enough for those acts of devotion which require the greatest fixedness and freedom of thought. The sedateness of his mind was evinced by the Spirit's coming upon him; for the Spirit chooses to move upon the still waters. Let no unkindness, no, not of a child or a friend, ever be laid so much to heart as to disfit us for communion with God. 4. He was now suffering for his sin in the matter of Uriah; this was the evil which, for that sin, God threatened to *raise up against him out of his own house* (2 Sam. xii. 11), which, no doubt, he observed, and took occasion thence to renew his repentance for it. Yet he did not *therefore* cast away his confidence in the divine power and goodness, nor despair of succour. Even our sorrow for sin must not hinder either our joy in God or our hope in God. 5. He seemed cowardly in fleeing from Absalom, and quitting his royal city, before he had had one struggle for it; and yet, by this psalm, it appears he was full of true courage arising from his faith in God. True Christian fortitude consists more in a gracious security and serenity of mind, in patiently bearing and patiently waiting, than in daring enterprises with sword in hand.

In these three verses he applies to God. Whither else should we go but to him when any thing grieves us or frightens us? David was now at a distance from his own closet, and from the courts of God's house, where he used to pray; and yet he could find a way open heaven-ward. Wherever we are we may have access to God, and may draw nigh to him whithersoever we are driven. David, in his flight, attends his God,

I. With a representation of his distress, v. 1, 2. He looks round, and as it were takes a view of his enemies' camp, or receives information of their designs against him, which he brings to God, not to his own council-board. Two things he complains of, concerning his enemies:—1. That they were very many: *Lord, how are they increased!* beyond what they were at first, and beyond whatever he thought they would have been. Absalom's faction, like a snow-ball, strangely gathered in its motion. He speaks of it as one amazed, and well he might, that a people he had so many ways obliged should almost generally revolt from him, rebel against him, and choose for their head such a foolish and giddy young man as Absalom was. How slippery and deceitful are the many! And how little fidelity and constancy are to be found among men! David had had the hearts of his subjects as much as ever any king had, and yet now, of a sudden, he had lost them. As people must not trust too much to princes (cxlvi. 3), so princes must not build too much upon their interest in the people. Christ, the Son of David, had many enemies. When a great multitude came to seize him, when the crowd cried, *Crucify him, Crucify him,* how were those then increased that troubled him! Even good people must not think it strange if the stream be against them and the powers that threaten them grow more and more formidable. 2. That they were very malicious. They rose up against him; they aimed to trouble him; but that was not all: they said of his soul, *There is no help for him in God.* That is, (1.) They put a spiteful and invidious construction upon his troubles, as Job's friends did upon his, concluding that, because his servants and subjects forsook him thus and did not help him, God had deserted him and abandoned his cause, and he was therefore to be looked *on,* or rather to be looked *off,* as a hypocrite and a wicked man. (2.) They blasphemously reflected upon God as unable to relieve him: "His danger is so great that God himself cannot help him." It is strange that so great unbelief should be found in any,

especially in many, in Israel, as to think any party of men too strong for Omnipotence to deal with. (3.) They endeavoured to shake his confidence in God and drive him to despair of relief from him: "They have said it *to* my soul;" so it may be read; compare xi. 1; xlii. 10. This grieved him worst of all, that they had so bad an opinion of him as to think it possible to take him off from that foundation. The mere temptation was a buffeting to him, *a thorn in his flesh,* nay, a *sword in his bones.* Note, A child of God startles at the very thought of despairing of help in God; you cannot vex him with any thing so much as if you offer to persuade him that *there is no help for him in God.* David comes to God, and tells him what his enemies said of him, as Hezekiah spread Rabshakeh's blasphemous letter before the Lord. "They say, *There is no help for me in thee;* but, Lord, if it be so, I am undone. They say to my soul, *There is no salvation*" (for so the word is) "*for him in God;* but, Lord, do thou say unto my soul, *I am thy salvation* (xxxv. 3) and that shall satisfy me, and in due time silence them." To this complaint he adds *Selah,* which occurs about seventy times in the book of psalms. Some refer it to the music with which, in David's time, the psalms were sung; others to the sense, and that it is a note commanding a solemn pause. *Selah—Mark that,* or, "*Stop there,* and consider a little." As here, they say, There is no help for him in God, *Selah.* "Take time for such a thought as this. *Get thee behind me, Satan. The Lord rebuke thee!* Away with such a vile suggestion!"

II. With a profession of his dependence upon God, v. 3. An active believer, the more he is beaten off from God, either by the rebukes of Providence or the reproaches of enemies, the faster hold he will take of him and the closer will he cleave to him; so David here, when his enemies said, *There is no help for him in God,* cries out with so much the more assurance, "*But thou, O Lord! art a shield for me;* let them say what they will, I am sure thou wilt never desert me, and I am resolved I will never distrust thee." See what God is to his people, what he will be, what they have found him, what David found in him. 1. Safety: "*Thou art a shield for me,* a shield *about* me" (so some), "to secure me on all sides, since my enemies surrounded me." Not only *my shield* (Gen. xv. 1), which denotes an interest in the divine protection, but a shield *for* me, which denotes the present benefit and advantage of that protection. 2. Honour: *Thou art my glory.* Those whom God owns for his are not only safe and easy, but really look great, and have true honour put upon them, far above that which the great ones of the earth are proud of. David was now in disgrace; the crown had fallen from his head; but he will not think the worse of himself while he has God for his glory, Isa lx. 19. *"Thou art my glory*; thy glory I reckon mine" (so some); "this is what I aim at, and am ambitious of, whatever my lot is, and whatever becomes of my honour—that I may be to my God for a name and a praise." 3. Joy and deliverance: *Thou art the lifter up of my head;* thou wilt lift up my head *out of* my troubles, and restore me to my dignity again, in due time; or, at least, thou wilt lift up my head *under* my troubles, so that I shall not droop nor be discouraged, nor shall my spirits fail." If, in the worst of times, God's people can lift up their heads with joy, knowing that all shall work for good to them, they will own it is God that is the lifter up of their head, that gives them both cause to rejoice and hearts to rejoice.

In singing this, and praying it over, we should possess ourselves with an apprehension of the danger we are in from the multitude and malice of our spiritual enemies, who seek the ruin of our souls by driving us from our God, and we should concern ourselves in the distresses and dangers of the church of God, which is every where spoken against, every where fought against; but, in reference to both, we should encourage ourselves in our God, who owns and protects and will in due time crown his own interest both in the world and in the hearts of his people.

4 I cried unto the LORD with my voice, and he heard me out of his holy hill. Selah. 5 I laid me down and slept; I awaked; for the LORD sustained me. 6 I will not be afraid of ten thousands of people, that have set *themselves* against me round about. 7 Arise, O LORD; save me, O my God : for thou hast smitten all mine enemies *upon* the cheek bone ; thou hast broken the teeth of the ungodly. 8 Salvation *belongeth* unto the LORD : thy blessing *is* upon thy people. Selah.

David, having stirred up himself by the irritations of his enemies to take hold on God as his God, and so gained comfort in looking upward when, if he looked round about him, nothing appeared but what was discouraging, here looks back with pleasing reflections upon the benefit he had derived from trusting in God and looks forward with pleasing expectations of a very bright and happy issue to which the dark dispensation he was now under would shortly be brought.

I. See with what comfort he looks back upon the communion he had had with God, and the communications of his favour to him, either in some former troubles he had been in, and through God's goodness got through, or in this hitherto. David had been exercised with many difficulties, often oppressed and brought very low; but still he had found

God all-sufficient. He now remembered with pleasure,

1. That his troubles had always brought him to his knees, and that, in all his difficulties and dangers, he had been enabled to acknowledge God and to lift up his heart to him, and his voice too (this will be a comfortable reflection when we are in trouble): *I cried unto God with my voice.* Care and grief do us good and no hurt when they set us a praying, and engage us, not only to speak to God, but to cry to him, as those that are in earnest. And though God understands the language of the heart, when the *voice is not heard* (1 Sam. i. 13), and values not the hypocritical prayers of those who *cause their voice to be heard on high* (Isa. lviii. 4), *vox et præterea nihil—mere sound,* yet, when the earnestness of the voice comes from the fervency of the heart, it shall be taken notice of, in the account, that we cried unto God with our *voice.*

2. That he had always found God ready to answer his prayers: *He heard me out of his holy hill,* from heaven, the high and holy place, from the ark on Mount Sion, whence he used to give answers to those that sought to him. David had ordered Zadok to *carry back the ark into the city* when he was flying from Absalom (2 Sam. xv. 25), knowing that God was not tied, no, not to the ark of his presence, and that, notwithstanding the distance of place, he could by faith receive answers of peace from the holy hill. No such things can fix a gulf between the communications of God's grace towards us and the operations of his grace in us, between his favour and our faith. The ark of the covenant was in Mount Zion, and all the answers to our prayers come from the promises of that covenant. Christ was *set King upon the holy hill of Zion* (ii 6), and it is through him, whom the Father hears always, that our prayers are heard.

3. That he had always been very safe and very easy under the divine protection (*v.* 5): " *I laid myself down and slept,* composed and quiet ; *and awaked* refreshed, *for the Lord sustained me."* (1.) This is applicable to the common mercies of every night, which we ought to give thanks for alone, and with our families, every morning. Many have not where to lay their head (but wander in deserts), or, if they have, dare not lie down for fear of the enemy ; but we have laid ourselves down in peace. Many lie down and cannot sleep, but are full of tossings to and fro till the dawning of the day, through pain of body, or anguish of mind, or the continual alarms of fear in the night; but we lie down and sleep in safety, though incapable of doing any thing then for our own preservation. Many lie down and sleep, and never awake again, they sleep the sleep of death, as the first-born of the Egyptians; but we lie down and sleep, and awake again to the light and comfort of another day; and whence is it,

but because the Lord has sustained us with sleep as with food? We have been safe under his protection and easy in the arms of his good providence. (2.) It seems here to be meant of the wonderful quietness and calmness of David's spirit, in the midst of his dangers. Having by prayer committed himself and his cause to God, and being sure of his protection, his heart was fixed, and he was easy. The undutifulness of his son, the disloyalty of his subjects, the treachery of many of his friends, the hazard of his person, the fatigues of his march, and the uncertainty of the event, never deprived him of an hour's sleep, nor gave any disturbance to his repose; for the Lord, by his grace and the consolations of his Spirit, powerfully sustained him and made him easy. It is a great mercy when we are in trouble to have our minds stayed upon God, so as never either to eat or sleep with trembling and astonishment. (3.) Some of the ancients apply i to the resurrection of Christ. In his sufferings he offered up strong cries, and was heard; and therefore, though he laid down and slept the sleep of death, yet he awaked the third day, for the Lord sustained him, that he should not see corruption.

4. That God had often broken the power and restrained the malice of his enemies, had *smitten them upon the cheek-bone* (v. 7), had silenced them and spoiled their speaking, blemished them and put them to shame, smitten them on the cheek reproachfully, had disabled them to do the mischief they intended; for he had broken their teeth. Saul and the Philistines, who were sometimes ready to swallow him up, could not effect what they designed. The teeth that are gnashed or sharpened against God's people shall be broken. When, at any time, the power of the church's enemies seems threatening, it is good to remember how often God has broken it; and we are sure that his arm is not shortened. He can stop their mouths and tie their hands.

II. See with what confidence he looks forward to the dangers he had yet in prospect. Having put himself under God's protection and often found the benefit of it, 1. His *fears were all stilled and silenced, v.* 6. With what a holy bravery does he bid defiance to the impotent menaces and attempts of his enemies! "*I will not be afraid of ten thousands of people,* that either in a foreign invasion or an intestine rebellion *set themselves,* or encamp, *against me round about.*" No man seemed less safe (his enemies are numerous, *ten thousands;* they are spiteful and resolute, "They have set themselves against me; nay, they have prevailed far, and seem to have gained their point; for they are against me round about on every side, thousands against one"), and yet no man was more secure: "I will not be afraid, for all this; they cannot hurt me, and therefore they shall not frighten me; whatever prudent methods I take for my

250

own preservation, I will not disquiet myself, distrust my God, nor doubt of a good issue at last." When David, in his flight from Absalom, bade Zadok carry back the ark, he spoke doubtfully of the issue of his present troubles, and concluded, like a humble penitent, *Here I am; let him do to me what seemeth to him good,* 2 Sam. xv. 26. But now, like a strong believer, he speaks confidently, and has no fear concerning the event. Note, A cheerful resignation to God is the way to obtain a cheerful satisfaction and confidence in God. 2. His prayers were quickened and encouraged, v. 7. He believed God was his Saviour, and yet prays; nay, he *therefore* prays, *Arise, O Lord! save me, O my God!* Promises of salvation do not supersede, but engage, our petitions for it. He will for this be enquired of. 3. His faith became triumphant. He began the psalm with complaints of the strength and malice of his enemies, but concludes it with exultation in the power and grace of his God, and now sees more with him than against him, *v.* 8. Two great truths he here builds his confidence upon and fetches comfort from. (1.) That *salvation belongeth unto the Lord;* he has power to save, be the danger ever so great; it is his prerogative to save, when all other helps and succours fail; it is his pleasure, it is his property, it is his promise to those that are his, whose salvation is not of themselves, but of the Lord. Therefore all that have the Lord for their God, according to the tenour of the new covenant, are sure of salvation; for he that is their God is the God of salvation. (2.) That his blessing is upon his people; he not only has power to save them, but he has assured them of his kind and gracious intentions towards them. He has, in his word, pronounced a blessing upon his people; and we are bound to believe that that blessing does accordingly rest upon them, though there be not the visible effects of it. Hence we may conclude that God's people, though they may lie under the reproaches and censures of men, are surely blessed of him, who blesses indeed, and therefore can command a blessing.

In singing this, and praying it over, we must own the satisfaction we have had in depending upon God and committing ourselves to him, and encourage ourselves, and one another to continue still hoping and quietly waiting for the salvation of the Lord.

PSALM IV

David was a preacher, a royal preacher, as well as Solomon; many of his psalms are doctrinal and practical as well as devotional; the greatest part of this psalm is so, in which Wisdom cries to men, to the sons of men (as Prov. viii. 4, 5), to receive instruction. The title does not tell us, as that of the former did, that it was penned on any particular occasion, nor are we to think that all the psalms were occasional, though some were, but that many of them were designed in general for the instruction of the people of God, who attended in the courts of his house, the assisting of their devotions, and the directing of their conversations: such a one I take this psalm to be. Let us not make the prophecy of scripture to be of more private interpretation than needs must, 2 Pet. i. 20. Here, I. David begins with a short prayer (ver. 1) and that prayer preaches. II. He directs his speech to the children of men, and, 1. In God's name reproves them for the dishonour they do to God and the damage they do to their own souls, ver. 2. 2. He sets before them the happiness of godly people, for their encouragement to be religious, ver. 3. 3. He calls upon them to consider their ways, ver. 4. III. He exhorts them to serve God and trust in him, ver. 5. IV. He gives an account of his own experiences of the grace of God working in him, 1. Enabling him to choose God's favour for his felicity, ver. 6. 2. Filling his heart with joy therein, ver. 7. 3. Quieting his spirit in the assurance of the divine protection he was under, night and day, ver. 8.

To the chief musician on Neginoth. A psalm of David.

HEAR me when I call, O God of my righteousness : thou hast enlarged me *when I was* in distress ; have mercy upon me, and hear my prayer. 2 O ye sons of men, how long *will ye turn* my glory into shame ? *how long* will ye love vanity, *and* seek after leasing ? Selah. 3 But know that the LORD hath set apart him that is godly for himself : the LORD will hear when I call unto him. 4 Stand in awe, and sin not : commune with your own heart upon your bed, and be still. Selah. 5 Offer the sacrifices of righteousness, and put your trust in the LORD.

The title of the psalm acquaints us that David, having penned it by divine inspiration for the use of the church, delivered it to the chief musician, or master of the song, who (according to the divine appointment of psalmody made in his time, which he was chiefly instrumental in the establishment of) presided in that service. We have a particular account of the constitution, the modelling of the several classes of singers, each with a chief, and the share each bore in the work, 1 Chron. xxv. Some *prophesied according to the order of the king, v.* 2. Others *prophesied with a harp, to give thanks, and to praise the Lord, v.* 3. Of others it is said that they were to *lift up the horn, v.* 5. But of them all, that they were *for song in the house of the Lord* (*v.* 6) and were *instructed in the songs of the Lord, v.* 7. This psalm was committed to one of the chiefs, to be sung on *neginoth* —*stringed instruments* (Hab. iii. 19), which were played on with the hand ; with music of that kind the choristers were to sing this psalm : and it should seem that then *they* only sung, not the people ; but the New-Testament appoints all Christians to sing (Eph. v. 19, Col. iii. 16), from whom it is expected that they do it decently, not artfully ; and therefore there is not now so much occasion for musical instruments as there was then : the melody is to be made in the heart. In these verses,

I. David addresses himself to God, *v.* 1. Whether the *sons of men,* to whom he is about to speak, will hear, or whether they will forbear, he hopes and prays that God will give him a gracious audience, and an answer of peace : "*Hear me when I call,* and accept my adorations, grant my petitions, and judge upon my appeals ; *have mercy upon me, and hear me.*" All the notice God is pleased to take of our prayers, and all the returns he is pleased to make to them, must be ascribed, not to our merit, but purely to his mercy. "Hear me for thy mercy-sake" is our best plea. Two things David here pleads further : —1. "Thou art *the God of my righteousness ;* not only a righteous God thyself, but the author of my righteous dispositions, who hast by thy grace wrought that good that is in me, hast made me a righteous man ; therefore *hear me,* and so attest thy own work in me ; thou art also the patron of my righteous cause, the protector of my wronged innocency, to whom I commit my way, and whom I trust to *bring forth my righteousness as the light.*" When men condemn us unjustly, this is our comfort, *It is God that justifies ;* he is the God of a believer's righteousness. 2. "*Thou hast* formerly *enlarged me when I was in distress,* enlarged my heart in holy joy and comfort under my distresses, enlarged my condition by bringing me out of my distresses ; therefore *now,* Lord, *have mercy upon me, and hear me.*" The experience we have had of God's goodness to us in enlarging us when we have been in distress is not only a great encouragement to our faith and hope for the future, but a good plea with God in prayer. "*Thou hast ; wilt thou not ?* For thou art God, and changest not ; thy work is perfect."

II. He addresses himself to the children of men, for the conviction and conversion of those that are yet strangers to God, and that will not have the Messiah, the Son of David, to reign over them.

1. He endeavours to convince them of the folly of their impiety (*v.* 2) "*O you sons of men*" (of *great* men, so some, men of high degree, understanding it of the partisans of Saul or Absalom), "*how long will you* oppose me and my government, and continue disaffected to it, under the influence of the false and groundless suggestions of those that wish evil to me ?" Or it may be taken more generally. God, by the psalmist, here reasons with sinners to bring them to repentance. "You that go on in the neglect of God and his worship, and in contempt of the kingdom of Christ and his government, consider what you do." (1.) "You debase yourselves, for you are *sons of men*" (the word signifies man as a noble creature) ; "consider the dignity of your nature, and the excellency of those powers of reason with which you are endued, and do not act thus irrationally and unbecoming yourselves." Let the *sons of men* consider and show themselves men. (2.) "You dishonour your Maker, and *turn his glory into shame.*" **They** may well be taken as God's own words, charging sinners with the wrong they do him in his honour : or, if

David's words, the term glory may be understood of God, whom he called *his glory*, iii. 3. Idolaters are charged with *changing the glory of God* into shame, Rom. i. 23. All wilful sinners do so by disobeying the commands of his law, despising the offers of his grace, and giving the affection and service to the creature which are due to God only. Those that profane God's holy name, that ridicule his word and ordinances, and, while they profess to know him, in works deny him, do what in them lies to *turn his glory into shame.* (3.) "You put a cheat upon yourselves: *You love vanity*, and *seek after leasing*, or *lying*, or that which is *a lie.* You are yourselves vain and lying, and you love to be so." Or, "You set your hearts upon that which will prove, at last, but vanity and a lie." Those that love the world, and seek the things that are beneath, love vanity, and seek lies; as those also do that please themselves with the delights of sense, and portion themselves with the wealth of this world; for these will deceive them, and so ruin them. "How long will you do this? Will you never be wise for yourselves, never consider your duty and interest? *When shall it once be?*" Jer. xiii. 27. The God of heaven thinks the time long that sinners persist in dishonouring him and in deceiving and ruining themselves.

2. He shows them the peculiar favour which God has for good people, the special protection they are under, and the singular privileges to which they are entitled, *v.* 3. This comes in here, (1.) As a reason why they should not oppose or persecute him that is godly, nor think to run him down. It is at their peril if they *offend one of these little ones*, whom God has *set apart for himself*, Matt. xviii. 6. God reckons that those who touch them touch the apple of his eye; and he will make their persecutors to know it, sooner or later. They have an interest in heaven, God will hear them, and therefore let none dare to do them any injury, for God will hear their cry and plead their cause, Exod. xxii. 23. It is generally supposed that David speaks of his own designation to the throne; he is the *godly* man whom *the Lord has set apart* for that honour, and who does not usurp it or assume it to himself: "The opposition therefore which you give to him and to his advancement is very criminal, for therein you fight against God, and it will be vain and ineffectual." God has, in like manner, set apart the Lord Jesus for himself, that merciful One; and those that attempt to hinder his advancement will certainly be baffled, for the Father hears him always. Or, (2.) As a reason why they should themselves be good, and walk no longer in the counsel of the ungodly: "You have hitherto sought vanity; be truly religious, and you will be truly happy here and for ever; for," [1.] "God will secure to himself his interest in you." *The Lord has set apart him that is godly*, every particular godly man, *for himself*, in his eternal choice, in his

effectual calling, in the special disposals of his providence and operations of his grace; his people are *purified unto him a peculiar people.* Godly men are God's separated, sealed, ones; he knows those that are his, and has set his image and superscription upon them; he distinguishes them with uncommon favours: *They shall be mine, saith the Lord, in that day when I make up my jewels. Know this;* let godly people know it, and let them never alienate themselves from him to whom they are thus appropriated; let wicked people know it, and take heed how they hurt those whom God protects. [2.] "God will secure to you an interest in himself." This David speaks with application: *The Lord will hear when I call unto him.* We should think ourselves happy if we had the ear of an earthly prince; and is it not worth while upon any terms, especially such easy ones, to gain the ear of the King of kings? Let us know this, and forsake lying vanities for our own mercies.

3. He warns them against sin, and exhorts them both to frighten and to reason themselves out of it (*v.* 4): "*Stand in awe and sin not*" (*be angry and sin not*, so the LXX., and some think the apostle takes that exhortation from him, Eph. iv. 26); "*commune with your own hearts;* be converted, and, in order thereunto, consider and fear." Note, (1.) We must not sin, must not miss our way and so miss our aim. (2.) One good remedy against sin is to stand in awe. *Be moved* (so some), in opposition to carelessness and carnal security. "Always keep up a holy reverence of the glory and majesty of God, and a holy dread of his wrath and curse, and dare not to provoke him." (3.) One good means of preventing sin, and preserving a holy awe, is to be frequent and serious in *communing with our own hearts:* "*Talk with your hearts;* you have a great deal to say to them; they may be spoken with at any time; let it not be unsaid." A thinking man is in a fair way to be a wise and a good man. "*Commune with your hearts;* examine them by serious self-reflection, that you may acquaint yourselves with them and amend what is amiss in them; employ them in solemn pious meditations; let your thoughts fasten upon that which is good and keep closely to it. Consider your ways, and observe the directions here given in order to the doing of this work well and to good purpose." [1.] "Choose a solitary time; do it when you lie awake *upon your beds.* Before you turn yourself to go to sleep at night" (as some of the heathen moralists have directed) "examine your consciences with respect to what you have done that day, particularly what you have done amiss, that you may repent of it. When you awake in the night meditate upon God, and the things that belong to your peace." David himself practised what he here counsels others to do (lxiii. 6), *I remember thee on my bed.* Upon a sick-bed, particularly, we should consider our ways and

commune with our own hearts about them. [2.] "Compose yourselves into a serious frame : *Be still.* When you have asked conscience a question be silent, and wait for an answer ; even in unquiet times keep your spirits calm and quiet.

4. He counsels them to make conscience of their duty (*v.* 5): *Offer to God the sacrifice of righteousness.* We must not only cease to do evil, but learn to do well. Those that were disaffected to David and his government would soon come to a better temper, and return to their allegiance, if they would but worship God aright ; and those that know the concerns that lie between them and God will be glad of the Mediator, the Son of David. It is required here from every one of us, (1.) That we serve him : " *Offer sacrifices to him,* your own selves first, and your best sacrifices." But they must be *sacrifices of righteousness,* that is, good works, all the fruits of the reigning love of God and our neighbour, and all the instances of a religious conversation, which are better than all burnt-offerings and sacrifices. " Let all your devotions come from an upright heart ; let all your alms be sacrifices of righteousness." The sacrifices of the unrighteous God will not accept ; they are an abomination, Isa. i. 11, &c. (2.) That we confide in him. " First make conscience of offering the sacrifices of righteousness and then you are welcome to put your trust in the Lord. Serve God without any diffidence of him, or any fear of losing by him. Honour him, by trusting in him only, and not in your wealth nor in an arm of flesh ; trust in his providence, and lean not to your own understanding ; trust in his grace, and go not about to establish your own righteousness or sufficiency.

In singing these verses we must preach to ourselves the doctrine of the provoking nature of sin, the lying vanity of the world, and the unspeakable happiness of God's people ; and we must press upon ourselves the duties of fearing God, conversing with our own hearts, and offering spiritual sacrifices ; and in praying over these verses we must beg of God grace thus to think and thus to do.

6 *There be* many that say, Who will show us *any* good ? LORD, lift thou up the light of thy countenance upon us. 7 Thou hast put gladness in my heart, more than in the time *that* their corn and their wine increased. 8 I will both lay me down in peace, and sleep : for thou, LORD, only makest me dwell in safety.

We have here,

I. The foolish wish of worldly people: *There be many that say, Who will show us any good ? Who will make us to see good ?* What good they meant is intimated, *v.* 7. It was the increase of their corn and wine ; all they desired was plenty of the wealth of this world,

that they might enjoy abundance of the delights of sense. Thus far they are right, that they are desirous of good and solicitous about it ; but there are these things amiss in this wish :—1. They enquire, in general, " Who will make us happy ?" but do not apply themselves to God who alone can ; and so they expose themselves to be ill-advised, and show they would rather be beholden to any than to God, for they would willingly live without him. 2. They enquire for good that may be seen, seeming good, sensible good ; and they show no concern for the good things that are out of sight and are the objects of faith only. The source of idolatry was a desire of gods that they might see, therefore they worshipped the sun ; but, as we must be taught to worship an unseen God, so to seek an unseen good, 2 Cor. iv. 18. We look with an eye of faith further than we can see with an eye of sense. 3. They enquire for *any* good, not for the chief good ; all they want is outward good, present good, partial good, good meat, good drink, a good trade, and a good estate ; and what are all these worth without a good God and a good heart ? Any good will serve the turn of most men, but a gracious soul will not be put off so. This way, this wish, of carnal worldlings is their folly, yet *many there be* that join in it ; and their doom will be accordingly. " *Son, remember that thou in thy life-time receivedst thy good things,* the penny thou didst agree for."

II. The wise choice which godly people make. David, and the pious few that adhered to him, dissented from that wish, and joined in this prayer, *Lord, lift thou up the light of thy countenance upon us.* 1. He disagrees from the vote of the many. God had set him apart for himself by distinguishing favours, and therefore he sets himself apart by a distinguishing character. " They are for any good, for worldly good, but so am not I ; I will not say as they say ; any good will not serve my turn ; the wealth of the world will never make a portion for my soul, and therefore I cannot take up with it." 2. He and his friends agree in their choice of God's favour as their felicity ; it is this which in their account is better than life and all the comforts of life. (1.) This is what they most earnestly desire and seek after ; this is the breathing of their souls, "*Lord, lift thou up the light of thy countenance upon us.* Most are for other things, but we are for this." Good people, as they are distinguished by their practices, so they are by their prayers, not the length and language of them, but the faith and fervency of them ; those whom God has set apart have a prayer by themselves, which, though others may speak the words of it, they only offer up in sincerity ; and this is a prayer which they all say *Amen* to ; " Lord, let us have thy favour, and let us know that we have it, and we desire no more ; that is enough to make us happy. Lord, be at peace with us, accept of us, manifest thyself to us, let us be satisfied *of* thy loving-kindness and we will be satisfied *with* it." Observe, Though David speaks of himself only in the 7th and 8th verses, he speaks, in this prayer, for others also,—"*upon us*," as Christ taught us to pray, "*Our Father.*" All the saints come to the throne of grace on the same errand, and in this they are one, they all desire God's favour as their chief good. We should beg it for others as well as for ourselves, for in God's favour there is enough for us all and we shall have never the less for others sharing in what we have! (2.) This is what, above any thing, they rejoice in (*v.* 7): "*Thou hast* hereby often *put gladness into my heart;* not only supported and refreshed me, but filled me with joy unspeakable; and therefore this is what I will still pursue, what I will seek after all the days of my life." When God puts grace in the heart he *puts gladness in the heart;* nor is any joy comparable to that which gracious souls have in the communications of the divine favour, no, not the joy of harvest, of a plentiful harvest, when the corn and wine increase. This is gladness in the heart, inward, solid, substantial joy. The mirth of worldly people is but a flash, a shadow; *even in laughter their heart is sorrowful,* Prov. xiv. 13. "Thou hast *given* gladness in my heart; so the word is. True joy is God's gift, *not as the world giveth,* John xiv. 27. The saints have no reason to envy carnal worldlings their mirth and joy, but should pity them rather, for they may know better and will not. (3.) This is what they entirely confide in, and in this confidence they are always easy, *v.* 8. He had laid himself down and slept (iii. 5), and so he will still: "*I will lay myself down* (having the assurance of thy favour) *in peace,* and with as much pleasure as those whose corn and wine increase, and who lie down as Boaz did in his threshing-floor, at the end of the heap of corn, to sleep there when *his heart was merry* (Ruth iii. 7), *for thou only makest me to dwell in safety.* Though I am alone, yet I am not alone, for God is with me; though I have no guards to attend me, the Lord alone is sufficient to protect me; he can do it himself when all other defences fail." If he have the light of God's countenance, [1.] He can enjoy himself. His soul returns to God, and reposes itself in him as its rest, and so he lays himself down and sleeps in peace. He has what he would have and is sure that nothing can come amiss to him. [2.] He fears no disturbance from his enemies, sleeps quietly, and is very secure, because God himself has undertaken to keep him safe. When he comes to sleep the sleep of death, and to lie down in the grave, to make his bed in the darkness, he will then, with good old Simeon, *depart in peace* (Luke ii. 29), being assured that God will receive his soul, to be safe with himself, and that his body also shall be made to dwell in safety in the grave. [3.] He commits all his affairs to God, and contentedly leaves the

issue of them with him. It is said of the husbandman that, having *cast his seed into the ground, he sleeps and rises night and day, and the seed springs and grows up, he knows not how,* Mark iv. 26, 27. So a good man, having by faith and prayer cast his care upon God, sleeps and rests night and day, and is very easy, leaving it to his God to perform all things for him and prepared to welcome his holy will.

In singing these verses, and praying over them, let us, with a holy contempt of the wealth and pleasure of this world, as insufficient to make us happy, earnestly seek the favour of God and pleasingly solace ourselves in that favour; and, with a holy indifferency about the issue of all our worldly concerns, let us commit ourselves and all our affairs to the guidance and custody of the divine Providence, and be satisfied that all shall be made to work for good to us if we keep ourselves in the love of God.

PSALM V.

This psalm is a prayer, a solemn address to God, at a time when the psalmist was brought into distress by the malice of his enemies. Many such times passed over David, nay, there was scarcely any time of his life to which this psalm may not be accommodated, for in this he was a type of Christ, that he was continually beset with enemies, and his powerful and prevalent appeals to God, when he was so beset, pointed at Christ's dependence on his Father and triumphs over the powers of darkness in the midst of his sufferings. In this psalm, I. David settles a correspondence between his soul and God, promising to pray, and promising himself that God would certainly hear him, ver. 1—3. II. He gives to God the glory, and takes to himself the comfort, of God's holiness, ver. 4—6. III. He declares his resolution to keep close to the public worship of God, ver. 7. IV. He prayed, 1. For himself, that God would judge him, ver. 8. 2. Against his enemies, that God would destroy them, ver. 9, 10. 3. For all the people of God, that God would give them joy, and keep them safe, ver. 11, 12. And this is all of great use to direct us in prayer.

To the chief musician upon Nehiloth. A psalm of David.

G IVE ear to my words, O LORD, consider my meditation. 2 Hearken unto the voice of my cry, my King, and my God: for unto thee will I pray. 3 My voice shalt thou hear in the morning, O LORD; in the morning will I direct *my prayer* unto thee, and will look up. 4 For thou *art* not a God that hath pleasure in wickedness: neither shall evil dwell with thee. 5 The foolish shall not stand in thy sight: thou hatest all workers of iniquity. 6 Thou shalt destroy them that speak leasing: the LORD will abhor the bloody and deceitful man.

The title of this psalm has nothing in it peculiar but that it is said to be upon *Nehiloth,* a word nowhere else used. It is conjectured (and it is but a conjecture) that it signifies *wind*-instruments, with which this psalm was sung, as *Neginoth* was supposed to signify the *stringed*-instruments. In these verses David had an eye to God,

I. As a prayer-hearing God; such he has always been ever since men began to call upon the name of the Lord, and yet is still as ready to hear prayer as ever. Observe how David here styles him: *O Lord* (*v.* 1, 3), *Jehovah*, a self-existent, self-sufficient, Being, whom we are bound to adore, and, "*my King and my God* (*v.* 2), whom I have avouched for my God, to whom I have sworn allegiance, and under whose protection I have put myself as my King." We believe that the God we pray to is a King and a God, King of kings and God of gods; but that is not enough: the most commanding encouraging principle of prayer, and the most powerful or prevailing plea in prayer, is to look upon him as *our* King and *our* God, to whom we lie under peculiar obligations and from whom we have peculiar expectations. Now observe,

1. What David here prays for, which may encourage our faith and hopes in all our addresses to God. If we pray fervently, and in faith, we have reason to hope, (1.) That God will take cognizance of our case, the representation we make of it and the requests we make upon it; for so he prays here: *Give ear to my words, O Lord!* Though God is in heaven, he has an ear open to his people's prayers, and it is not heavy, that he cannot hear. Men perhaps will not or cannot hear us; our enemies are so haughty that they will not, our friends at such a distance that they cannot; but God, though high, though in heaven, can, and will. (2.) That he will take it into his wise and compassionate consideration, and will not slight it, or turn it off with a cursory answer; for so he prays: *Consider my meditation.* David's prayers were not his words only, but his meditations; as meditation is the best preparative for prayer, so prayer is the best issue of meditation. Meditation and prayer should go together, xix. 14. It is when we thus consider our prayers, and then only, that we may expect that God will consider them, and take that to his heart which comes from ours. (3.) That he will, in due time, return a gracious answer of peace; for so he prays (*v.* 2): *Hearken to the voice of my cry.* His prayer was a *cry;* it was *the voice of his cry,* which denotes fervency of affection and importunity of expression; and such effectual fervent prayers of a righteous man avail much and do wonders.

2. What David here promises, as the condition on his part to be performed, fulfilled, and kept, that he might obtain this gracious acceptance; this may guide and govern us in our addresses to God, that we may present them aright, for we ask, and have not, if we ask amiss. Four things David here promises, and so must we:—(1.) That he will pray, that he will make conscience of praying, and make a business of it: *Unto thee will I pray.* "Others live without prayer, but I will pray." Kings on their own thrones (so David was) must be beggars at God's throne. "Others pray to strange gods, and expect relief from them, but to thee, to thee

only, will I pray." The assurances God has given us of his readiness to hear prayer should confirm our resolution to live and die praying. (2.) That he will pray *in the morning.* His praying voice shall be heard then, and then shall his prayer be directed; that shall be the date of his letters to heaven, not that only ("Morning, and evening, and at noon, will I pray, nay, seven times a day, will I praise thee"), but that certainly. Morning prayer is our duty; we are the fittest for prayer when we are in the most fresh, and lively, and composed frame, got clear of the slumbers of the night, revived by them, and not yet filled with the business of the day We have then most need of prayer, considering the dangers and temptations of the day to which we are exposed, and against which we are concerned, by faith and prayer, to fetch in fresh supplies of grace. (3.) That he will have his eye single and his heart intent in the duty: *I will direct my prayer,* as a marksman directs his arrow to the white; with such a fixedness and steadiness of mind should we address ourselves to God. Or as we direct a letter to a friend at such a place so must we direct our prayers to God as our Father in heaven; and let us always send them by the Lord Jesus, the great Mediator, and then they will be sure not to miscarry. All our prayers must be directed to God; his honour and glory must be aimed at as our highest end in all our prayers. Let our first petition be, *Hallowed,* glorified, *be thy name,* and then we may be sure of the same gracious answer to it that was given to Christ himself: *I have glorified it, and I will glorify it yet again.* (4.) That he will patiently wait for an answer of peace: " I *will look up,* will look after my prayers, and *hear what God the Lord will speak* (lxxxv. 8; Hab. ii. 1), that, if he grant what I asked, I may be thankful —if he deny, I may be patient—if he defer, I may continue to pray and wait and may not faint." We must look *up,* or look *out,* as he that has shot an arrow looks to see how near it has come to the mark. We lose much of the comfort of our prayers for want of observing the returns of them. Thus praying, thus waiting, as the lame man looked stedfastly on Peter and John (Acts iii. 4), we may expect that God will give ear to our words and consider them, and to him we may refer ourselves, as David here, who does not pray, " Lord, do this, or the other, for me;" but, " Hearken to me, consider my case, and do in it as seemeth good unto thee."

II. As a sin-hating God, *v.* 4—6. David takes notice of this, 1. As a warning to himself, and all other praying people, to remember that, as the God with whom we have to do is gracious and merciful, so he is pure and holy; though he is ready to hear prayer, yet, if we regard iniquity in our heart, he will not hear our prayers, lxvi. 18. 2. As an encouragement to his prayers against his enemies; they were wicked men, and therefore enemies to God, and such as he had no pleasure in. See here, (1.) The holiness of God's nature. When he says, *Thou art not a God that has pleasure in wickedness,* he means, "Thou art a God that hates it, as directly contrary to thy infinite purity and rectitude, and holy will." Though the workers of iniquity prosper, let none thence infer that God has pleasure in wickedness, no, not in that by which men pretend to honour him, as those do that hate their brethren, and cast them out, and say, *Let the Lord be glorified.* God has no pleasure in wickedness, though covered with a cloak of religion. Let those therefore who delight in sin know that God has no delight in them; nor let any say, when he is tempted, *I am tempted of God,* for God is not the author of sin, neither *shall evil dwell with him,* that is, it shall not always be countenanced and suffered to prosper. Dr. Hammond thinks this *refers* to that law of Moses which would not permit strangers, who persisted in their idolatry, to dwell in the land of Israel. (2.) The justice of his government. The foolish *shall not stand in his sight,* that is, shall not be smiled upon by him, nor admitted to attend upon him, nor shall they be acquitted in the judgment of the great day. The workers of iniquity are very foolish. Sin is folly, and sinners are the greatest of all fools; not fools of God's making (those are to be pitied), for he hates nothing that he has made, but fools of their own making, and those he hates. Wicked people hate God; justly therefore are they hated of him, and it will be their endless misery and ruin. "Those whom thou hatest thou shalt destroy; particularly two sorts of sinners, who are here marked for destruction:—[1.] Those that are fools, that speak leasing or lying, and that are deceitful. There is a particular emphasis laid on these sinners (Rev. xxi. 8), *All liars,* and (*ch.* xxii. 15), *Whosoever loves and makes a lie;* nothing is more contrary than this, and therefore nothing more hateful to the God of truth. [2.] Those that are cruel: *Thou wilt abhor the bloody man;* for inhumanity is no less contrary, no less hateful, to the God of mercy, whom mercy pleases. Liars and murderers are in a particular manner said to resemble the devil and to be his children, and therefore it may well be expected that God should abhor them. These were the characters of David's enemies; and such as these are still the enemies of Christ and his church, men perfectly lost to all virtue and honour; and the worse they are the surer we may be of their ruin in due time.

In singing these verses, and praying them over, we must engage and stir up ourselves to the duty of prayer, and encourage ourselves in it, because we shall not seek the Lord in vain; and must express our detestation of sin, and our awful expectation of that day of Christ's appearing which will be the day of the perdition of ungodly men.

7 But as for me, I will come *into*

thy house in the multitude of thy mercy; *and* in thy fear will I worship toward thy holy temple. 8 Lead me, O LORD, in thy righteousness because of mine enemies; make thy way straight before my face. 9 For *there is* no faithfulness in their mouth; their inward part *is* very wickedness; their throat *is* an open sepulchre; they flatter with their tongue. 10 Destroy thou them, O God; let them fall by their own counsels; cast them out in the multitude of their transgressions; for they have rebelled against thee. 11 But let all those that put their trust in thee rejoice: let them ever shout for joy, because thou defendest them: let them also that love thy name be joyful in thee. 12 For thou, LORD, wilt bless the righteous; with favour wilt thou compass him as *with* a shield.

In these verses David gives three characters—of himself, of his enemies, and of all the people of God, and subjoins a prayer to each of them.

I. He gives an account of himself and prays for himself, *v.* 7, 8

1. He is stedfastly resolved to keep closely to God and to his worship. Sinners go away from God, and so make themselves odious to his holiness and obnoxious to his justice: "*But, as for me,* that shall not keep me from thee." God's holiness and justice are so far from being a terror to the upright in heart, to drive them from God, that they are rather by them invited to cleave to him. David resolves, (1.) To worship God, to pay his homage to him, and give unto God the glory due unto his name. (2.) To worship him publicly: "*I will come into thy house,* the courts of thy house, to worship there with other faithful worshippers." David was much in secret worship, prayed often alone (*v.* 2, 3), and yet was very constant and devout in his attendance on the sanctuary. The duties of the closet are designed to prepare us for, not to excuse us from, public ordinances. (3.) To worship him reverently and with a due sense of the infinite distance there is between God and man: "*In thy fear will I worship,* with a holy awe of God upon my spirit," Heb. xii. 28. God is greatly to be feared by all his worshippers. (4.) To take his encouragement, in worship, from God himself only. [1.] From his infinite mercy. It is in the multitude of God's mercy (the inexhaustible treasures of mercy that are in God and the innumerable proofs and instances of it which we receive from him) that David confides, and not in any merit or righteousness of his own, in his approaches to God. The mercy

of God should ever be both the foundation of our hopes and the fountain of our joy in every thing wherein we have to do with him. [2.] From the instituted medium of worship, which was then the temple, here called *the temple of his holiness*, as a type of Christ, the great and only Mediator, who sanctifies the service as the temple sanctified the gold, and to whom we must have an eye in all our devotions as the worshippers then had to the temple.

2. He earnestly prays that God, by his grace, would guide and preserve him always in the way of his duty (*v.* 8): *Lead me in thy righteousness, because of my enemies*—Heb. "*Because of those who observe me*, who watch for my halting and seek occasion against me." See here, (1.) The good use which David made of the malice of his enemies against him. The more curious they were in spying faults in him, that they might have whereof to accuse him, the more cautious he was to avoid sin and all appearances of it, and the more solicitous to be always found in the good way of God and duty. Thus, by wisdom and grace, good may come out of evil. (2.) The right course which David took for the baffling of those who sought occasion against him. He committed himself to a divine guidance, begged of God both by his providence and by his grace to direct him in the right way, and keep him from turning aside out of it, at any time, in any instance whatsoever, that the most critical and captious of his enemies, like Daniel's, might find no occasion against him. The way of our duty is here called *God's way*, and *his righteousness*, because he prescribes to us by his just and holy laws, which if we sincerely set before us as our rule, we may in faith beg of God to direct us in all particular cases. How this prayer of David's was answered to him see 1 Sam. xviii. 14, 15.

II. He gives an account of his enemies, and prays against them, *v.* 9, 10. 1. If his account of them is true, as no doubt it is, they have a very bad character; and, if they had not been bad men indeed, they could not have been enemies to a man after God's own heart. He had spoken (*v.* 6) of God's hating the bloody and deceitful men. "Now, Lord," says he, "that is the character of my enemies: they are deceitful; there is no trusting them, for there is no faithfulness in their mouth." They thought it was no sin to tell a deliberate lie if it might but blemish David, and render him odious. "*Lord, lead me*," says he (*v.* 8), "for such as these are the men I have to do with, against whose slanders innocency itself is no security. Do they speak fair? Do they talk of peace and friendship? *They flatter with their tongues;* it is designed to cover their malice, and to gain their point the more securely. Whatever they pretend of religion or friendship, two sacred things, they are true to neither: *Their inward part is wickedness* itself; it is *very*

wickedness. They are likewise bloody; for *their throat is an open sepulchre,* cruel as the grave, gaping to devour and to swallow up, insatiable as the grave, which never says, It is enough," Prov. xxx. 15, 16. This is quoted (Rom. iii. 13) to show the general corruption of mankind; for they are all naturally prone to malice, Tit. iii. 3. The grave is opened for them all, and yet they are as open graves to one another. 2. If his prayer against them is heard, as no doubt it is, they are in a bad condition. As men are, and do, so they must expect to fare. He prays to God to destroy them (according to what he had said (*v.* 6), "Thou shalt destroy men of this character," so *let them fall;* and sinners would soon throw themselves into ruin if they were let alone), to *cast them out* of his protection and favour, out of the heritage of the Lord, out of the land of the living; and woe to those whom God casts out. "They have by their sins deserved destruction; there is enough to justify God in their utter rejection: *Cast them out in the multitude of their transgressions,* by which they have filled up the measure of their iniquity and have become ripe for ruin." Persecuting God's servants fills the measure as soon as any thing, 1 Thess. ii. 15, 16. Nay, they may be easily made to *fall by their own counsels;* that which they do to secure themselves, and do mischief to others, by the over-ruling providence of God may be made a means of their destruction, vii. 15; ix. 15. He pleads, "*They have rebelled against thee.* Had they been only my enemies, I could safely have forgiven them; but they are rebels against God, his crown and dignity; they oppose his government, and will not repent, to give him glory, and therefore I plainly foresee their ruin." His prayer for their destruction comes not from a spirit of revenge, but from a spirit of prophecy, by which he foretold that all who rebel against God will certainly be destroyed by their own counsels. If it is a righteous thing with God to recompense tribulation to those that trouble his people, as we are told it is (2 Thess. i. 6), we pray that it may be done whenever we pray, *Father, thy will be done.*

III. He gives an account of the people of God, and prays for them, concluding with an assurance of their bliss, which he doubted not of his own interest in. Observe, 1. The description he gives of God's people. They are the righteous (*v.* 12); for they *put their trust in God,* are well assured of his power and all-sufficiency, venture their all upon his promise, and are confident of his protection in the way of their duty; and they *love his name,* are well pleased with all that by which God has made himself known, and take delight in their acquaintance with him. This is true and pure religion, to live a life of complacency in God and dependence on him. 2. His prayer for them: "*Let them rejoice;* let them have cause to rejoice and hearts to rejoice; fill them with joy, with great joy and unspeakable; let them shout for joy, with constant joy and perpetual; *let them ever shout for joy,* with holy joy, and that which terminates in God; *let them be joyful in thee,* in thy favour, in thy salvation, not in any creature. Let them rejoice *because thou defendest them,* coverest them, or overshadowest them, dwellest among them." Perhaps here is an allusion to the pillar of cloud and fire, which was to Israel a visible token of God's special presence with them and the special protection they were under. Let us learn of David to pray, not for ourselves only, but for others, for all good people, for all that trust in God and love his name, though not in every thing of our mind nor in our interest. Let all that are entitled to God's promises have a share in our prayers; grace be with all that love Christ in sincerity. This is to concur with God. 3. His comfort concerning them, *v.* 12. He takes them into his prayers because they are God's peculiar people; therefore he doubts not but his prayers shall be heard, and they shall always rejoice; for, (1.) They are happy in the assurance of God's blessing: " *Thou, Lord, wilt bless the righteous,* wilt command a blessing upon them. Thou hast in thy word pronounced them blessed, and therefore wilt make them truly so. *Those whom thou blessest are blessed indeed.*" (2.) "They are safe under the protection of thy favour; with that thou wilt *crown* him" (so some read it); "it is his honour, will be to him a diadem of beauty, and make him truly great: with that thou *wilt compass him,* wilt surround him, on every side, *as with a shield.*" A shield, in war, guards only one side, but the favour of God is to the saints a defence on every side; like the hedge about Job, round about, so that, while they keep themselves under the divine protection, they are entirely safe and ought to be entirely satisfied.

In singing these verses, and praying them over, we must by faith put ourselves under God's guidance and care, and then please ourselves with his mercy and grace and with the prospect of God's triumphs at last over all his enemies and his people's triumphs in him and in his salvation.

PSALM VI.

David was a weeping prophet as well as Jeremiah, and this psalm is one of his lamentations: either it was penned in a time, or at least calculated for a time, of great trouble, both outward and inward. Is any afflicted? Is any sick? Let him sing this psalm. The method of this psalm is very observable, and what we shall often meet with. He begins with doleful complaints, but ends with joyful praises; like Hannah, who went to prayer with a sorrowful spirit, but, when she had prayed, went her way, and her countenance was no more sad. Three things the psalmist is here complaining of:—1. Sickness of body. 2. Trouble of mind, arising from the sense of sin, the meritorious cause of pain and sickness. 3. The insults of his enemies upon occasion of both. Now here, I. He pours out his complaints before God, deprecates his wrath, and begs earnestly for the return of his favour, ver. 1—7. II. He assures himself of an answer of peace, shortly, to his full satisfaction, ver. 8—10. This psalm is like the book of Job.

To the chief musician on Neginoth upon Sheminith. A psalm of David.

O LORD, rebuke me not in thine anger, neither chasten me in thy

258

hot displeasure. 2 Have mercy upon me, O LORD; for I *am* weak: O LORD, heal me; for my bones are vexed. 3 My soul is also sore vexed: but thou, O LORD, how long? 4 Return, O LORD, deliver my soul: oh save me for thy mercies' sake. 5 For in death *there is* no remembrance of thee: in the grave who shall give thee thanks? 6 I am weary with my groaning; all the night make I my bed to swim; I water my couch with my tears. 7 Mine eye is consumed because of grief; it waxeth old because of all mine enemies.

These verses speak the language of a heart truly humbled under humbling providences, of a broken and contrite spirit under great afflictions, sent on purpose to awaken conscience and mortify corruption. Those heap up wrath who cry not when God binds them; but those are getting ready for mercy who, under God's rebukes, sow in tears, as David does here. Let us observe here,

I. The representation he makes to God of his grievances. He pours out his complaint before him. Whither else should a child go with his complaints, but to his father? 1. He complains of bodily pain and sickness (*v.* 2): *My bones are vexed.* His bones and his flesh, like Job's, were touched. Though David was a king, yet he was sick and pained; his imperial crown could not keep his head from aching. Great men are men, and subject to the common calamities of human life. Though David was a stout man, a man of war from his youth, yet this could not secure him from distempers, which will soon make even the strong men to bow themselves. Though David was a good man, yet neither could his goodness keep him in health. *Lord, behold, he whom thou lovest is sick.* Let this help to reconcile us to pain and sickness, that it has been the lot of some of the best saints, and that we are directed and encouraged by their example to show before God our trouble in that case, who *is for the body,* and takes cognizance of its ailments. 2. He complains of inward trouble: *My soul is also sorely vexed;* and that is much more grievous than the vexation of the bones. *The spirit of a man will sustain his infirmity,* if that be in good plight; but, if that be wounded, the grievance is intolerable. David's sickness brought his sin to his remembrance, and he looked upon it as a token of God's displeasure against him; that was the vexation of his soul; that made him cry, *I am weak, heal me.* It is a sad thing for a man to have his bones and his soul vexed at the same time; but this has been sometimes the lot of God's own people: nay, and this completed his complicated trouble, that it was continued upon him a great while, which is here intimated in that expostulation (*v.* 3), *Thou, O Lord! how long?* To the living God we must, at such a time, address ourselves, who is the only physician both of body and mind, and not to the Assyrians, not to the god of Ekron.

II. The impression which his troubles made upon him. They lay very heavily; he *groaned till he was weary*, wept till he *made his bed to swim*, and *watered his couch* (*v.* 6), wept till he had almost wept his eyes out (*v.* 7): *My eye is consumed because of grief.* David had more courage and consideration than to mourn thus for any outward affliction; but, when sin sat heavily upon his conscience and he was made to possess his iniquities, when his soul was wounded with the sense of God's wrath and his withdrawings from him, then he thus grieves and mourns in secret, and even his soul refuses to be comforted. This not only kept his eyes waking, but kept his eyes weeping. Note, 1. It has often been the lot of the best of men to be men of sorrows; our Lord Jesus himself was so. Our way lies through a vale of tears, and we must accommodate ourselves to the temper of the climate. 2. It well becomes the greatest spirits to be tender, and to relent, under the tokens of God's displeasure. David, who could face Goliath himself and many another threatening enemy with an undaunted bravery, yet melts into tears at the remembrance of sin and under the apprehensions of divine wrath; and it was no diminution at all to his character to do so. 3. True penitents weep in their retirements. The Pharisees disguised their faces, that they might *appear unto men to mourn;* but David mourned in the night upon the bed where he lay communing with his own heart, and no eye was a witness to his grief, but the eye of him who is all eye. Peter went out, covered his face, and wept. 4. Sorrow for sin ought to be great sorrow; so David's was; he wept so bitterly, so abundantly, that he watered his couch. 5. The triumphs of wicked men in the sorrows of the saints add very much to their grief. David's eye waxed old because of his enemies, who rejoiced in his afflictions and put bad constructions upon his tears. In this great sorrow David was a type of Christ, who often wept, and who cried out, *My soul is exceedingly sorrowful,* Heb. v. 7.

III. The petitions which he offers up to God in this sorrowful and distressed state. 1. That which he dreads as the greatest evil is the anger of God. This was the wormwood and the gall in the affliction and the misery; it was the infusion of this that made it indeed a bitter cup; and therefore he prays (*v.* 1), *O Lord! rebuke me not in thy anger,* though I have deserved it, *neither chasten me in thy hot displeasure.* He does not pray, "Lord, rebuke me not; Lord, chasten me not; for, *as many as God loves he rebukes and chastens, as a father the son in whom he delights.* He can bear the rebuke and chastening well enough if God, at the same time,

lift up the light of his countenance upon him and by his Spirit make him to hear the joy and gladness of his loving-kindness; the affliction of his body will be tolerable if he have but comfort in his soul. No matter though sickness make his bones ache, if God's wrath do not make his heart ache; therefore his prayer is, " *Lord, rebuke me not in thy wrath;* let me not lie under the impressions of that, for that will sink me." Herein David was a type of Christ, whose sorest complaint, in his sufferings, was of the trouble of his soul and of the suspension of his Father's smiles. He never so much as whispered a complaint of the rage of his enemies—"Why do they crucify me?" or the unkindness of his friends—"Why do they desert me?" But he *cried with a loud voice, My God, my God, why hast thou forsaken me?* Let us thus deprecate the wrath of God more than any outward trouble whatsoever and always beware of treasuring up wrath against a day of affliction. 2. That which he desires as the greatest good, and which would be to him the restoration of all good, is the favour and friendship of God. He prays, (1.) That God would pity him and look upon him with compassion. He thinks himself very miserable, and misery is the proper object of mercy. Hence he prays, " *Have mercy upon me, O Lord!* in wrath remember mercy, and deal not with me in strict justice." (2.) That God would pardon his sins; for that is the proper act of mercy, and is often chiefly intended in that petition, *Have mercy upon me.* (3.) That God would put forth his power for his relief: " *Lord, heal me* (v. 2), *save me* (v. 4), speak the word, and I shall be whole, and all will be well." (4.) That he would be at peace with him: " *Return, O Lord!* receive me into thy favour again, and be reconciled to me. Thou hast seemed to depart from me and neglect me, nay, to set thyself at a distance, as one angry; but now, Lord, return and show thyself nigh to me." (5.) That he would especially preserve the inward man and the interests of that, whatever might become of the body: " *O Lord! deliver my soul* from sinning, from sinking, from perishing for ever." It is an unspeakable privilege that we have a God to go to in our afflictions, and it is our duty to go to him, and thus to wrestle with him, and we shall not seek in vain.

IV. The pleas with which he enforces his petitions, not to move God (he knows our cause and the true merits of it better than we can state them), but to move himself. 1. He pleads his own misery, and that his misery had continued long: " *I am weak, I am* troubled, *sorely troubled; O Lord! how long* shall I be so?" 2. He pleads God's mercy; and thence we take some of our best encouragements in prayer: *Save me, for thy mercies' sake.* 3. He pleads God's glory (v. 5): " *For in death there is no remembrance of thee.* Lord, if thou deliver me and comfort me, I will not only give thee thanks for my deliverance, and stir up others to join with me in these thanksgivings, but I will spend the new life thou shalt entrust me with in thy service and to thy glory, and all the remainder of my days I will preserve a grateful remembrance of thy favours to me, and be quickened thereby in all instances of service to thee; but, if I die, I shall be cut short of that opportunity of honouring thee and doing good to others, for *in the grave who will give the thanks ?*" Not but that separate souls live and act, and the souls of the faithful joyfully remember God and give thanks to him. But, (1.) In the second death (which perhaps David, being now troubled in soul under the wrath of God, had some dreadful apprehensions of) there is no pleasing remembrance of God; devils and damned spirits blaspheme him and do not praise him. " Lord, let me not lie always under this wrath, for that is *sheol,* it is *hell* itself, and lays me under an everlasting disability to praise thee." Those that sincerely seek God's glory, and desire and delight to praise him, may pray in faith, " Lord, send me not to that dreadful place, where there is no devout remembrance of thee, nor are any thanks given to thee." (2.) Even the death of the body puts an end to our opportunity and capacity of glorifying God in this world, and serving the interests of his kingdom among men by opposing the powers of darkness and bringing many on this earth to know God and devote themselves to him. Some have maintained that the joys of the saints in heaven are more desirable, infinitely more so, than the comforts of saints on earth; yet the services of saints on earth, especially such eminent ones as David was, are more laudable, and redound more to the glory of the divine grace, than the services of the saints in heaven, who are not employed in maintaining the war against sin and Satan, nor in edifying the body of Christ. Courtiers in the royal presence are most happy, but soldiers in the field are more useful; and therefore we may, with good reason, pray that if it be the will of God, and he has any further work for us or our friends to do in this world, he will yet spare us, or them, to serve him. To depart and be with Christ is most happy for the saints themselves; but for them to abide in the flesh is more profitable for the church. This David had an eye to when he pleaded this, *In the grave who shall give thee thanks ?* xxx. 9; lxxxviii. 10; cxv. 17; Isa. xxxviii. 18. And this Christ had an eye to when he said, *I pray not that thou shouldst take them out of the world.*

We should sing these verses with a deep sense of the terrors of God's wrath, which we should therefore dread and deprecate above any thing; and with thankfulness if this be not our condition, and compassion to those who are thus afflicted: if we be thus troubled, let it comfort us that our case is not

without precedent, nor, if we humble ourselves and pray, as David did, shall it be long without redress.

8 Depart from me, all ye workers of iniquity; for the Lᴏʀᴅ hath heard the voice of my weeping. 9 The Lᴏʀᴅ hath heard my supplication; the Lᴏʀᴅ will receive my prayer. 10 Let all mine enemies be ashamed and sore vexed: let them return *and* be ashamed suddenly.

What a sudden change is here for the better! He that was groaning, and weeping, and giving up all for gone (*v.* 6, 7), here looks and speaks very pleasantly. Having made his requests known to God, and lodged his case with him, he is very confident the issue will be good and his sorrow is turned into joy.

I. He distinguishes himself from the wicked and ungodly, and fortifies himself against their insults (*v.* 8): *Depart from me, all you workers of iniquity.* When he was in the depth of his distress, 1. He was afraid that God's wrath against him would give him his portion with the workers of iniquity; but now that this cloud of melancholy had blown over he was assured that his soul would not be gathered with sinners, for they are not his people. He began to suspect himself to be one of them because of the heavy pressures of God's wrath upon him; but now that all his fears were silenced he bade them depart, knowing that his lot was among the chosen. 2. The workers of iniquity had teased him, and taunted him, and asked him, " Where is thy God ?" triumphing in his despondency and despair; but now he had wherewith to answer those that reproached him, for God, who was about to return in mercy to him, had now comforted his spirit and would shortly complete his deliverance. 3. Perhaps they had tempted him to do as they did, to quit his religion and betake himself for ease to the pleasures of sin. But now, " *depart from me;* I will never lend an ear to your counsel; you would have had me to curse God and die, but I will bless him and live." This good use we should make of God's mercies to us, we should thereby have our resolution strengthened never to have any thing more to do with sin and sinners. David was a king, and he takes this occasion to renew his purpose of using his power for the suppression of sin and the reformation of manners, lxxv. 4; ci. 3. When God has done great things for us, this should put us upon studying what we shall do for him. Our Lord Jesus seems to borrow these words from the mouth of his father David, when, having all judgment committed to him, he shall say, *Depart from me, all you workers of iniquity* (Luke xiii. 27), and so teaches us to say so now, cxix. 115.

II. He assures himself that God was, and would be, propitious to him, notwithstanding the present intimations of wrath which he was under. 1. He is confident of a gracious answer to this prayer which he is now making. While he is yet speaking, he is aware that God hears (as Isa. lxv. 24, Dan. ix. 20), and therefore speaks of it as a thing done, and repeats it with an air of triumph, " *The Lord hath heard*" (*v.* 8), and again (*v.* 9), " *The Lord hath heard.*" By the workings of God's grace upon his heart he knew his prayer was graciously accepted, and therefore did not doubt but it would in due time be effectually answered. His tears had a voice, a loud voice, in the ears of the God of mercy: *The Lord has heard the voice of my weeping.* Silent tears are not speechless ones. His prayers were cries to God: " *The Lord has heard the voice of my supplication,* has put his *Fiat—Let it be done,* to my petitions, and so it will appear shortly." 2. Thence he infers the like favourable audience of all his other prayers : " He *has heard the voice of my supplication,* and therefore he *will receive my prayer;* for he gives, and does not upbraid with former grants."

III. He either prays for the conversion or predicts the destruction of his enemies and persecutors, *v.* 10. 1. It may very well be taken as a prayer for their conversion : " Let them all be ashamed of the opposition they have given me and the censures they have passed upon me. Let them be (as all true penitents are) vexed at themselves for their own folly; let them return to a better temper and disposition of mind, and let them be ashamed of what they have done against me and take shame to themselves." 2. If they be not converted, it is a prediction of their confusion and ruin. *They shall be ashamed and sorely vexed* (so it may be read), and that justly. They rejoiced that David was vexed (*v.* 2, 3), and therefore, as usually happens, the evil returns upon themselves; they also shall be sorely vexed. Those that will not give glory to God shall have their faces filled with everlasting shame.

In singing this, and praying over it, we must give glory to God, as a God ready to hear prayer, must own his goodness to us in hearing our prayers, and must encourage ourselves to wait upon him and to trust in him in the greatest straits and difficulties.

PSALM VII.

It appears by the title that this psalm was penned with a particular reference to the malicious imputations that David was unjustly laid under by some of his enemies. Being thus wronged, I. He applies to God for favour, ver. 1, 2. II. He appeals to God concerning his innocency as to those things whereof he was accused, ver. 3—5. III. He prays to God to plead his cause and judge for him against his persecutors, ver. 6-9. IV. He expresses his confidence in God that he would do so, and would return the mischief upon the head of those that designed it against him, ver. 10—16. V. He promises to give God the glory of his deliverance, ver. 17. In this David was a type of Christ, who was himself, and still is in his members, thus injured, but will certainly be righted at last.

Shiggaion of David, which he sang unto the Lord concerning the words of Cush the Benjamite.

O LORD my God, in thee do I put my trust : save me from all them that persecute me, and deliver me : 2 Lest he tear my soul like a lion, rending *it* in pieces, while *there is* none to deliver. 3 O LORD my God, if I have done this ; if there be iniquity in my hands ; 4 If I have rewarded evil unto him that was at peace with me ; (yea, I have delivered him that without cause is mine enemy :) 5 Let the enemy persecute my soul, and take *it;* yea, let him tread down my life upon the earth, and lay mine honour in the dust. Selah. 6 Arise, O LORD, in thine anger, lift up thyself because of the rage of mine enemies : and awake for me *to* the judgment *that* thou hast commanded. 7 So shall the congregation of the people compass thee about: for their sakes therefore return thou on high. 8 The LORD shall judge the people : judge me, O LORD, according to my righteousness, and according to mine integrity *that is* in me. 9 Oh let the wickedness of the wicked come to an end ; but establish the just : for the righteous God trieth the hearts and reins.

Shiggaion is a *song* or *psalm* (the word is used so only here and Hab. iii. 1)—a *wandering* song (so some), the matter and composition of the several parts being different, but artificially put together — a *charming* song (so others), very delightful. David not only penned it, but sang it himself in a devout religious manner unto the Lord, *concerning the words* or affairs *of Cush the Benjamite,* that is, of Saul himself, whose barbarous usage of David bespoke him rather a Cushite, or Ethiopian, than a true-born Israelite. Or, more likely, it was some kinsman of Saul named *Cush,* who was an inveterate enemy to David, misrepresented him to Saul as a traitor, and (which was very needless) exasperated Saul against him, one of those children of men, children of Belial indeed, whom David complains of (1 Sam. xxvi. 19), that made mischief between him and Saul. David, thus abused, has recourse to the Lord. The injuries men do us should drive us to God, for to him we may commit our cause. Nay, he sings to the Lord; his spirit was not ruffled by it, nor cast down, but so composed and cheerful that he was still in tune for sacred songs and it did not occasion one jarring string in his harp. Thus let the injuries we receive from men, instead of provoking our passions, kindle and excite our devotions. In these verses,

I. He puts himself under God's protection and flies to him for succour and shelter (*v.* 1): " *Lord, save me, and deliver me* from the power and malice of *all those that perse-cute me*, that they may not have their will against me." He pleads, 1. His relation to God. "Thou art *my God*, and therefore whither else should I go but to thee? Thou art my God, and therefore my shield (Gen. xv. 1), my God, and therefore I am one of thy servants, who may expect to be protected." 2. His confidence in God : "Lord, save me, for I depend upon thee : *In thee do I put my trust*, and not in any arm of flesh." Men of honour will not fail those that repose a trust in them, especially if they themselves have encouraged them to do so, which is our case. 3. The rage and malice of his enemies, and the imminent danger he was in of being swallowed up by them : "Lord, save me, or I am gone ; he will *tear my soul like a lion* tearing his prey," with so much pride, and pleasure, and power, so easily, so cruelly. St. Paul compares Nero to a lion (2 Tim. iv. 17), as David here compares Saul. 4. The failure of all other helpers : "Lord, be thou pleased to deliver me, for otherwise *there is none to deliver*," v. 2. It is the glory of God to help the helpless.

II. He makes a solemn protestation of his innocency as to those things whereof he was accused, and by a dreadful imprecation appeals to God, the searcher of hearts, concerning it, v. 3—5. Observe, in general, 1. When we are falsely accused by men it is a great comfort if our own consciences acquit us—

——————— Hic murus aheneus esto,
Nil conscire sibi.—————————
Be this thy brazen bulwark of defence,
Still to preserve thy conscious innocence.—

and not only they cannot prove their calumnies (Acts xxiv. 13), but our hearts can disprove them, to our own satisfaction. 2. God is the patron of wronged innocency. David had no court on earth to appeal to. His prince, who should have righted him, was his sworn enemy But he had the court of heaven to fly to, and a righteous Judge there, whom he could call *his God*. And here see, (1.) What the indictment is which he pleads not guilty to. He was charged with a traitorous design against Saul's crown and life, that he compassed and imagined to depose and murder him, and, in order to that, levied war against him. This he utterly denies. He never did this ; there was no iniquity of this kind in his hand (v. 3) ; he abhorred the thought of it. He never *rewarded evil* to Saul when he was *at peace with him*, nor to any other, v. 4. Nay, as some think it should be rendered, he never rendered evil for evil, never did those mischief that had injured him. (2.) What evidence he produces of his innocency. It is hard to prove a negative, and yet this was a negative which David could produce very good proof of : *I have delivered him that without cause is my enemy*, v. 4. By *this* it appeared, beyond contradiction, that David had no design against Saul's life—that, once and again, Providence so ordered

262

it that Saul lay at his mercy, and there were those about him that would soon have dispatched him, but David generously and conscientiously prevented it, when he cut off his skirt (1 Sam. xxiv. 4) and afterwards when he took away his spear (1 Sam. xxvi. 12), to attest for him what he could have done. Saul himself owned both these to be undeniable proofs of David's integrity and good affection to him. If we render good for evil, and deny ourselves the gratifications of our passion, our so doing may turn to us for a testimony, more than we think of, another day. (3.) What doom he would submit to if he were guilty (v. 5) : *Let the enemy persecute my soul* to the death, and my good name when I am gone : let him *lay my honour in the dust*. This intimates, [1.] That, if he had been indeed injurious to others, he had reason to expect that they would repay him in the same coin. He that has his hand against every man must reckon upon it that every man's hand will be against him. [2.] That, in that case, he could not with any confidence go to God and beg of him to deliver him or plead his cause. It is a presumptuous dangerous thing for any that are guilty, and suffer justly, to appeal to God, as if they were innocent and suffered wrongfully ; such must humble themselves and accept the punishment of their iniquity, and not expect that the righteous God will patronise their unrighteousness. [3.] That he was abundantly satisfied in himself concerning his innocency. It is natural to us to wish well to ourselves ; and therefore a curse to ourselves, if we swear falsely, has been thought as awful a form of swearing as any. With such an oath, or imprecation, David here ratifies the protestation of his innocency, which yet will not justify us in doing the like for every light and trivial cause ; for the occasion here was important.

III. Having this testimony of his conscience concerning his innocency, he humbly prays to God to appear for him against his persecutors, and backs every petition with a proper plea, as one that knew how to order his cause before God.

1. He prays that God would manifest his wrath against his enemies, and pleads their wrath against him : "Lord, they are unjustly angry at me, be thou justly angry with them and let them know that thou art so, v. 6. *In thy anger lift up thyself* to the seat of judgment, and make thy power and justice conspicuous, *because of the rage*, the furies, the outrages (the word is plural) *of my enemies*." Those need not fear men's wrath against them who have God's wrath for them. *Who knows the power of his anger?*

2. He prays that God would plead his cause.

(1.) He prays, *Awake for me to judgment* (that is, let my cause have a hearing), to *the judgment which thou hast commanded ;* this speaks, [1.] The divine power ; as he blesses effectually, and is therefore said to *command the blessing*, so he judges effectually, and is therefore said to *command the judgment*, which is such as none can countermand; for it certainly carries execution along with it. [2.] The divine purpose and promise: "It is the judgment which thou hast determined to pass upon all the enemies of thy people. Thou hast commanded the princes and judges of the earth to give redress to the injured and vindicate the oppressed; Lord, awaken thyself to that judgment." He that loves righteousness, and requires it in others, will no doubt execute it himself. Though he seem to connive at wrong, as one asleep, he will awake in due time (lxxviii. 65) and will make it to appear that the delays were no neglects.

(2.) He prays (v. 7), "*Return thou on high*, maintain thy own authority, resume thy royal throne of which they have despised the sovereignty, and the judgment-seat of which they have despised the sentence. Return on high, that is, visibly and in the sight of all, that it may be universally acknowledged that heaven itself owns and pleads David's cause." Some make this to point at the resurrection and ascension of Jesus Christ, who, when he returned to heaven (returned on high in his exalted state), had all judgment committed to him. Or it may refer to his second coming, when he shall return on high to this world, to execute judgment upon all. This return his injured people wait for, and pray for, and to it they appeal from the unjust censures of men.

(3.) He prays again (v. 8), "*Judge me*, judge for me, give sentence on my side." To enforce this suit, [1.] He pleads that his cause was now brought into the proper court: *The Lord shall judge the people*, v. 8. It is his place; it is his promise. *God is the Judge;* "Therefore, Lord, judge me." He is the Judge of all the earth, and therefore no doubt he will do right and all will be obliged to acquiesce in his judgment. [2.] He insists upon his integrity as to all the matters in variance between him and Saul, and desires only to be judged, in this matter, according to his righteousness, and the sincerity of his heart in all the steps he had taken towards his preferment. [3.] He foretels that it would be much for the glory of God and the edification and comfort of his people if God would appear for him: "*So shall the congregation of the people compass thee about*; therefore do it for their sakes, that they may attend thee with their praises and services in the courts of thy house." *First*, They will do it of their own accord. God's appearing on David's behalf, and fulfilling his promise to him, would be such an instance of his righteousness, goodness, and faithfulness, as would greatly enlarge the hearts of all his faithful worshippers and fill their mouths with praise. David was the darling of his country, especially of all the good people in it; and therefore, when they saw him in a fair way to the throne, they

would greatly rejoice and give thanks to God; crowds of them would attend his footstool with their praises for such a blessing to their land. *Secondly*, If David come into power, as God has promised him, he will take care to bring people to church by his influence upon them, and the ark shall not be neglected, as it was *in the days of Saul*, 1 Chron. xiii 3.

3. He prays, in general, for the conversion of sinners and the establishment of saints (v. 9): "*O let the wickedness*, not only of my wicked enemies, but *of all the wicked, come to an end! but establish the just.*" Here are two things which every one of us must desire and may hope for:—(1.) The destruction of sin, that it may be brought to an end in ourselves and others. When corruption is mortified, when every wicked way and thought are forsaken, and the stream which ran violently towards the world and the flesh is driven back and runs towards God and heaven, then the wickedness of the wicked comes to an end. When there is a general reformation of manners, when atheists and profane are convinced and converted, when a stop is put to the spreading of the infection of sin, so that evil men proceed no further, their folly being made manifest, when the wicked designs of the church's enemies are baffled, and their power is broken, and the man of sin is destroyed, then the *wickedness of the wicked comes to an end*. And this is that which all that love God, and for his sake hate evil, desire and pray for. (2.) The perpetuity of righteousness: *But establish the just*. As we pray that the bad may be made good, so we pray that the good may be made better, that they may not be seduced by the wiles of the wicked nor shocked by their malice, that they may be confirmed in their choice of the ways of God and in their resolution to persevere therein, may be firm to the interests of God and religion and zealous in their endeavours to bring *the wickedness of the wicked to an end*. His plea to enforce this petition is, *For the righteous God trieth the hearts and the reins;* and therefore he knows the secret wickedness of the wicked and knows how to bring it to an end, and the secret sincerity of the just he is witness to and has secret ways of establishing.

As far as we have the testimony of an unbiassed conscience for us that in any instance we are wronged and injuriously reflected on, we may, in singing these verses, lodge our appeal with the righteous God, and be assured that he will own our righteous cause, and will one day, in the last day at furthest, bring forth our integrity as the light.

10 My defence *is* of God, which saveth the upright in heart. 11 God judgeth the righteous, and God is angry *with the wicked* every day. 12 If he turn not, he will whet his sword; he hath bent his bow, and made it

ready. 13 He hath also prepared for him the instruments of death; he ordaineth his arrows against the persecutors. 14 Behold, he travaileth with iniquity, and hath conceived mischief, and brought forth falsehood. 15 He made a pit, and digged it, and is fallen into the ditch *which* he made. 16 His mischief shall return upon his own head, and his violent dealing shall come down upon his own pate. 17 I will praise the LORD according to his righteousness: and will sing praise to the name of the LORD most high.

David having lodged his appeal with God by prayer and a solemn profession of his integrity, in the former part of the psalm, in this latter part does, as it were, take out judgment upon the appeal, by faith in the word of God, and the assurance it gives of the happiness and safety of the righteous and the certain destruction of wicked people that continue impenitent.

I. David is confident that he shall find God his powerful protector and Saviour, and the patron of his oppressed innocency (*v.* 10): "*My defence is of God.* Not only, God is my defender, and I shall find him so; but I look for defence and safety in no other; my hope for shelter in a time of danger is placed in God alone; if I have defence, it must be of God." *My shield is upon God* (so some read it); there is that in God which gives an assurance of protection to all that are his. His name is a strong tower, Prov xviii. 10. Two things David builds this confidence upon:—1. The particular favour God has for all that are sincere: *He saves the upright in heart,* saves them with an everlasting salvation, and therefore will *preserve them to his heavenly kingdom;* he saves them out of their present troubles, as far as is good for them; their integrity and uprightness will preserve them. The upright in heart are safe, and ought to think themselves so, under the divine protection. 2. The general respect he has for justice and equity: *God judgeth the righteous;* he owns every righteous cause, and will maintain it in every righteous man, and will protect him. *God is a righteous Judge* (so some read it), who not only doeth righteousness himself, but will take care that righteousness be done by the children of men and will avenge and punish all unrighteousness.

II. He is no less confident of the destruction of all his persecutors, even as many of them as would not *repent, to give glory to God.* He reads their doom here, for their good, if possible, that they might cease from their enmity, or, however, for his own comfort, that he might not be afraid of them nor aggrieved at their prosperity and success for a time. He goes into the sanctuary of God, and there understands,

1. That they are children of wrath. They are not to be envied, for God is angry with them, is *angry with the wicked every day.* They are every day doing that which is provoking to him, and he resents it, and treasures it up *against the day of wrath.* As his mercies are new every morning towards his people, so his anger is new every morning against the wicked, upon the fresh occasions given for it by their renewed transgressions. God is angry with the wicked even in the merriest and most prosperous of their days, even in the days of their devotion; for, if they be suffered to prosper, it is in wrath; if they pray, their very prayers are an abomination. The wrath of God abides upon them (John iii. 36) and continual additions are made to it.

2. That they are children of death, as all the children of wrath are, sons of perdition, marked out for ruin. See their destruction.

(1.) God will destroy them. The destruction they are reserved for is *destruction from the Almighty,* which ought to be a terror to every one of us, for it comes from the *wrath of God, v.* 13, 14. It is here intimated, [1.] That the destruction of sinners may be prevented by their conversion, for it is threatened with that proviso: *If he turn not* from his evil way, if he do not let fall his enmity against the people of God, then let him expect it will be his ruin; but, if he turn, it is implied that his sin shall be pardoned and all shall be well. Thus even the threatenings of wrath are introduced with a gracious implication of mercy, enough to justify God for ever in the destruction of those that perish; they might have turned and lived, but they chose rather to go on and die and their blood is therefore upon their own heads. [2.] That, if it be not thus prevented by the conversion of the sinner, it will be prepared for him by the justice of God. In general (*v.* 13), *He has prepared for him the instruments of death,* of all that death which is the wages of sin. If God will slay, he will not want instruments of death for any creature; even the least and weakest may be made so when he pleases. *First,* Here is variety of instruments, all which breathe threatenings and slaughter. Here is a sword, which wounds and kills at hand, a bow and arrows, which wound and kill at a distance those who think to get out of the reach of God's vindictive justice. If the sinner *flees from the iron weapon,* yet the *bow of steel shall strike him through,* Job xx. 24. *Secondly,* These instruments of death are all said to be made ready. God has them not to seek, but always at hand. *Judgments are prepared for scorners. Tophet is prepared of old. Thirdly,* While God is preparing his instruments of death, he gives the sinners timely warning of their danger, and space to repent and prevent it. He is slow to punish, and *long-suffering to us-ward, not willing that any should perish. Fourthly,* The longer the destruction is delayed, to give time for repentance, the sorer will it be and the heavier will it fall and lie for ever if that time be not so improved; while God is waiting the sword is in the whetting and the bow in the drawing. *Fifthly,* The destruction of impenitent sinners, though it come slowly, yet comes surely; for it is *ordained,* they are of old ordained to it. *Sixthly,* Of all sinners persecutors are set up as the fairest marks of divine wrath; against them, more than any other, God has ordained his arrows. They set God at defiance, but cannot set themselves out of the reach of his judgments.

(2.) They will destroy themselves, *v.* 14—16. The sinner is here described as taking a great deal of pains to ruin himself, more pains to damn his soul than, if directed aright, would save it. His conduct is described, [1.] By the pains of a labouring woman that brings forth a false conception, *v.* 14. The sinner's head with its politics *conceives mischief*, contrives it with a great deal of art, lays the plot deep, and keeps it close; the sinner's heart with its passions *travails with iniquity*, and is in pain to be delivered of the malicious projects it is hatching against the people of God. But what does it come to when it comes to the birth? It is falsehood; it is a cheat upon himself; it is a lie in his right hand. He cannot compass what he intended, nor, if he gain his point, will he gain the satisfaction he promised himself. He brings forth *wind* (Isa. xxvi. 18), *stubble* (Isa. xxxiii. 11), *death* (James i. 15), that is, *falsehood.* [2.] By the pains of a labouring man that works hard to dig a pit, and then falls into it and perishes in it. *First,* This is true, in a sense, of all sinners. They prepare destruction for themselves by preparing themselves for destruction, loading themselves with guilt and submitting themselves to their corruptions. *Secondly,* It is often remarkably true of those who contrive mischief against the people of God or against their neighbours; by the righteous hand of God it is made to *return upon their own heads.* What they designed for the shame and destruction of others proves to be their own confusion.

———Nec lex est justior ulla
Quàm necis artifices arte perire suâ———

There is not a juster law than that the author of a murderous contrivance shall perish by it.

Some apply it to Saul, who fell upon his sword.

In singing this psalm we must do as David here does (*v.* 17), *praise the Lord according to his righteousness*, that is, give him the glory of that gracious protection under which he takes his afflicted people and of that just vengeance with which he will pursue those that afflict them. Thus we must sing to the praise of the Lord most high, who, when his enemies deal proudly, shows that he is above them.

PSALM VIII. (S)

This psalm is a solemn meditation on, and admiration of, the glory and greatness of God, of which we are all concerned to think highly and honourably. It begins and ends with the same acknowledgment of the transcendent excellency of God's name. It is proposed for proof (ver. 1) that God's name is excellent in all the earth, and then it is repeated as proved (with a " quod erat demonstrandum"—which was to be demonstrated) in the last verse. For the proof of God's glory the psalmist gives instances of his goodness to man; for God's goodness is his glory. God is to be glorified, I. For making known himself and his great name to us, ver. 1. II. For making use of the weakest of the children of men, by them to serve his own purposes, ver. 2. III. For making even the heavenly bodies useful to man, ver. 3, 4. IV. For making him to have dominion over the creatures in this lower world, and thereby placing him but little lower than the angels, ver. 5—8. This psalm is, in the New Testament, applied to Christ and the work of our redemption which he wrought out; the honour given by the children of men to him (ver. 2, compared with Matt. xxi. 16) and the honour put upon the children of men by him, both in his humiliation, when he was made a little lower than the angels, and in his exaltation, when he was crowned with glory and honour. Compare ver. 5, 6, with Heb. ii. 6—8, 1 Cor. xv. 27. When we are observing the glory of God in the kingdom of nature and Providence we should be led by that, and through that, to the contemplation of his glory in the kingdom of grace.

To the chief musician upon Gittith, A psalm of David.

O LORD our Lord, how excellent *is* thy name in all the earth! who hast set thy glory above the heavens. 2 Out of the mouth of babes and sucklings hast thou ordained strength because of thine enemies, that thou mightest still the enemy and the avenger.

The psalmist here sets himself to give to God the glory due to his name. Dr. Hammond grounds a conjecture upon the title of this psalm concerning the occasion of penning it. It is said to be upon *Gittith*, which is generally taken for the tune, or musical instrument, with which this psalm was to be sung; but he renders it upon the *Gittite*, that is, *Goliath the Gittite*, whom he vanquished and slew (1 Sam. xvii.); that enemy was stilled by him who was, in comparison, but a babe and a suckling. The conjecture would be probable enough but that we find two other psalms with the same title, lxxxi. and lxxxiv. Two things David here admires:—

I. How plainly God displays his glory himself, *v.* 1. He addresses himself to God with all humility and reverence, as the Lord and his people's Lord: *O Lord our Lord!* If we believe that God is the Lord, we must avouch and acknowledge him to be ours. He is ours, for he made us, protects us, and takes special care of us. He must be ours, for we are bound to obey him and submit to him; we must own the relation, not only when we come to pray to God, as a plea with him to show us mercy, but when we come to praise him, as an argument with ourselves to give him glory: and we shall never think we can do that with affection enough if we consider, 1. How brightly God's glory shines even in this lower world : *How excellent is his name in all the earth !* The works of creation and Providence evince and proclaim to all the world that there is an infinite Being, the fountain of all being, power, and perfection, the sovereign ruler, powerful protector, and bountiful benefactor of all the creatures. How great, how illustrious, how magnificent, is his name in all the earth ! The light of it shines in men's faces every where (Rom. i. 20); if they shut their eyes against it, that is their fault. There is no speech or language but the voice of God's name either is heard in it or may be. But this looks further, to the gospel of Christ, by which the name of God, as it is notified by divine revelation, which before was great in Israel only, came to be so in all the earth, the utmost ends of which have thus been made to *see God's great salvation,* Mark xvi. 15, 16. 2. How much more brightly it shines in the upper world: *Thou hast set thy glory above the heavens.* (1.) God is infinitely more glorious and excellent than the noblest of creatures and those that shine most brightly. (2.) Whereas we, on this earth, only hear God's excellent name, and praise that, the angels and blessed spirits above see his glory, and praise that, and yet he is exalted far above even their blessing and praise. (3.) In the exaltation of the Lord Jesus to the right hand of God, who is the brightness of his Father's glory and the express image of his person, God set his glory above the heavens, far above all principalities and powers.

II. How powerfully he proclaims it by the weakest of his creatures (*v.* 2): *Out of the mouth of babes and sucklings hast thou ordained strength,* or perfected praise, the praise of thy strength, Matt. xxi. 16. This intimates the glory of God, 1. In the kingdom of nature. The care God takes of little children (when they first come into the world the most helpless of all animals), the special protection they are under, and the provision nature has made for them, ought to be acknowledged by every one of us, to the glory of God, as a great instance of his power and goodness, and the more sensibly because we have all had the benefit of it, for to this we owe it that we *died not from the womb,* that the knees then prevented us, *and the breasts, that we should suck.* "This is such an instance of thy goodness, as may for ever put to silence the enemies of thy glory, who say, There is no God." 2. In the kingdom of Providence. In the government of this lower world he makes use of the children of men, some that know him and others that do not (Isa. xlv. 4), and these such as have been babes and sucklings; nay, sometimes he is pleased to serve his own purposes by the ministry of such as are still, in wisdom and strength, little better than babes and sucklings. 3. In the kingdom of grace, the kingdom of the Messiah. It is here foretold that by the apostles, who were looked upon but as babes, *unlearned and ignorant men* (Acts iv. 13), mean and despicable, and *by the foolishness of their preaching,* the devil's kingdom should be thrown down, as Jericho's walls were by the sound of rams' horns. The gospel is called *the arm of the Lord* and *the rod of his strength ;* this was ordained to work wonders, not out of the mouth of philosophers or orators, politicians or statesmen, but of a company of poor fishermen, who lay under the greatest external

disadvantages; yea, we hear children crying, *Hosanna to the Son of David,* when the chief priests and Pharisees owned him not, but despised and rejected him; to that therefore our Saviour applied this (Matt. xxi. 16) and by it stilled the enemy. Sometimes the grace of God appears wonderfully in young children, and he *teaches* those *knowledge, and makes* those *to understand doctrine, who are* but *newly weaned from the milk and drawn from the breasts,* Isa. xxviii. 9. Sometimes the power of God brings to pass great things in his church by very weak and unlikely instruments, and confounds the noble, wise, and mighty, by the base, and weak, and foolish things of the world, that no flesh may glory in his presence, but the excellency of the power may the more evidently appear to be of God, and not of man, 1 Cor. i. 27, 28. This he does *because of his enemies,* because they are insolent and haughty, that he may still them, may put them to silence, and put them to shame, and so be justly avenged on the avengers; see Acts iv. 14; vi. 10. The devil is the great enemy and avenger, and by the preaching of the gospel he was in a great measure stilled, his oracles were silenced, the advocates of his cause were confounded, and unclean spirits themselves were not suffered to speak.

In singing this let us give God the glory of his great name, and of the great things he has done by the power of his gospel, in the chariot of which the exalted Redeemer rides forth conquering and to conquer, and ought to be attended, not only with our praises, but with our best wishes. Praise is perfected (that is, God is in the highest degree glorified) when strength is ordained out of the mouth of babes and sucklings.

3 When I consider thy heavens, the work of thy fingers, the moon and the stars, which thou hast ordained; 4 What is man, that thou art mindful of him? and the son of man, that thou visitest him? 5 For thou hast made him a little lower than the angels, and hast crowned him with glory and honour. 6 Thou madest him to have dominion over the works of thy hands; thou hast put all *things* under his feet: 7 All sheep and oxen, yea, and the beasts of the field; 8 The fowl of the air, and the fish of the sea, *and whatsoever* passeth through the paths of the seas. 9 O LORD our Lord, how excellent *is* thy name in all the earth!

David here goes on to magnify the honour of God by recounting the honours he has put upon man, especially the man Christ Jesus. The condescensions of the divine grace call for our praises as much as the elevations of the divine glory. How God has condescended in favour to man the psalmist here observes with wonder and thankfulness, and recommends it to our thoughts. See here,

I. What it is that leads him to admire the condescending favour of God to man; it is his consideration of the lustre and influence of the heavenly bodies, which are within the view of sense (*v.* 3): *I consider thy heavens,* and there, particularly, *the moon and the stars.* But why does he not take notice of the sun, which much excels them all? Probably because it was in a night-walk, by moon-light, that he entertained and instructed himself with this meditation, when the sun was not within view, but only the moon and the stars, which, though they are not altogether so serviceable to man as the sun is, yet are no less demonstrations of the wisdom, power, and goodness of the Creator. Observe, 1. It is our duty to consider the heavens. We see them, we cannot but see them. By this, among other things, man is distinguished from the beasts, that, while *they* are so framed as to look downwards to the earth, man is made erect to look upwards towards heaven. *Os homini sublime dedit, cœlumque tueri jussit—To man he gave an erect countenance, and bade him gaze on the heavens,* that thus he may be directed to set his affections on things above; for what we see has not its due influence upon us unless we consider it. 2. We must always consider the heavens as God's heavens, not only as all the world is, even the earth and the fulness thereof, but in a more peculiar manner. *The heavens, even the heavens, are the Lord's* (cxv. 16); they are the place of the residence of his glory and we are taught to call him *Our Father in heaven.* 3. They are *therefore* his, because they are the work of his fingers. He made them; he made them easily. The stretching out of the heavens needed not any outstretched arm; it was done with a word; it was but *the work of his fingers.* He made them with very great curiosity and fineness, like a nice piece of work which the artist makes with his fingers. 4. Even the inferior lights, the moon and stars, show the glory and power of the Father of lights, and furnish us with matter for praise. 5. The heavenly bodies are not only the creatures of the divine power, but subject to the divine government. God not only made them, but *ordained* them, and the ordinances of heaven can never be altered. But how does this come in here to magnify God's favour to man? (1.) When we consider how the glory of God shines in the upper world we may well wonder that he should take cognizance of such a mean creature as man, that he who resides in that bright and blessed part of the creation, and governs it, should humble himself to behold the things done upon this earth; see cxiii. 5, 6. (2.) When we consider of what great use the heavens are to men on earth, and how the lights of heavens are *divided unto all nations* (Deut. iv. 19, Gen. i. 15), we may well say, "*Lord, what is man* that thou shouldst settle the ordinances of heaven with an eye

to him and to his benefit, and that his comfort and convenience should be so consulted in the making of the lights of heaven and directing their motions!"

II. How he expresses this admiration (*v.* 4): "*Lord, what is man* (*enosh,* sinful, weak, miserable man, a creature so forgetful of thee and his duty to thee) *that thou art* thus *mindful of him,* that thou takest cognizance of him and of his actions and affairs, that in the making of the world thou hadst a respect to him! What is the *son of man, that thou visitest him,* that thou not only feedest him and clothest him, protectest him and providest for him, in common with other creatures, but visitest him as one friend visits another, art pleased to converse with him and concern thyself for him! What is man—(so mean a creature), that he should be thus honoured—(so sinful a creature), that he should be thus countenanced and favoured!" Now this refers,

1. To mankind in general. Though man is a worm, and the son of man is a worm (Job xxv. 6), yet God puts a respect upon him, and shows him abundance of kindness; man is, above all the creatures in this lower world, the favourite and darling of Providence. For, (1.) He is of a very honourable rank of beings. We may be sure he takes precedence of all the inhabitants of this lower world, for he is made but a *little lower than the angels* (*v.* 5), lower indeed, because by his body he is allied to the earth and to the beasts that perish, and yet by his soul, which is spiritual and immortal, he is so near akin to the holy angels that he may be truly said to be but *a little lower than they,* and is, in order, next to them. He is but for a little while lower than the angels, while his great soul is cooped up in a house of clay, but the children of the resurrection shall be ἰσάγγελοι—*angels' peers* (Luke xx. 36) and no longer lower than they. (2.) He is endued with noble faculties and capacities: *Thou hast crowned him with glory and honour.* He that gave him his being has distinguished him, and qualified him for a dominion over the inferior creatures; for, having *made him wiser than the beasts of the earth and the fowls of heaven* (Job xxxv. 11), he has made him fit to rule them and it is fit that they should be ruled by him. Man's reason is his crown of glory; let him not profane that crown by disturbing the use of it nor forfeit that crown by acting contrary to its dictates. (3.) He is invested with a sovereign dominion over the inferior creatures, under God, and is constituted their lord. He that made them, and knows them, and whose own they are, has *made man to have dominion over them, v.* 6. His charter, by which he holds this royalty, bears equal date with his creation (Gen. i. 28) and was renewed after the flood, Gen. ix. 2. God has put all things under man's feet, that he might serve himself, not only of the labour, but of the productions and lives of the inferior creatures; they are all delivered into his hand, nay, they are all *put*

under his feet. He specifies some of the inferior animals (v. 7, 8), not only *sheep and oxen,* which man takes care of and provides for, but *the beasts of the field,* as well as those of the flood, yea, and those creatures which are most at a distance from man, as *the fowl of the air,* yea, *and the fish of the sea,* which live in another element and pass unseen through the paths of the seas. Man has arts to take these; though many of them are much stronger and many of them much swifter than he, yet, one way or other, he is too hard for them, Jam. iii. 7. *Every kind of beasts, and birds, and things in the sea, is tamed, and has been tamed.* He has likewise liberty to use them as he has occasion. *Rise, Peter, kill and eat,* Acts x. 13. Every time we partake of fish or of fowl we realize this dominion which man has over the works of God's hands; and this is a reason for our subjection to God, our chief Lord, and to his dominion over us.

2. But this refers, in a particular manner, to Jesus Christ. Of him we are taught to expound it, Heb. ii. 6—8, where the apostle, to prove the sovereign dominion of Christ both in heaven and in earth, shows that he is that man, that son of man, here spoken of, whom God *has crowned with glory and honour* and made to *have dominion over the works of his hands.* And it is certain that the greatest favour that ever was shown to the human race, and the greatest honour that ever was put upon the human nature, were exemplified in the incarnation and exaltation of the Lord Jesus; these far exceed the favours and honours done us by creation and providence, though they also are great and far more than we deserve. We have reason humbly to value ourselves by it and thankfully to admire the grace of God in it, (1.) That Jesus Christ assumed the nature of man, and, in that nature, humbled himself. He became the *Son of man,* a partaker of flesh and blood; being so, God visited him, which some apply to his sufferings for us, for it is said (Heb. ii. 9), *For the suffering of death,* a visitation in wrath, *he was crowned with glory and honour.* God visited him; having laid upon him the iniquity of us all, he reckoned with him for it, visited him with a rod and with stripes, that we by them might be healed. He was, *for a little while* (so the apostle interprets it), made lower than the angels, when he took upon him the form of a servant and made himself of no reputation. (2.) That, in that nature, he is exalted to be Lord of all. God the Father exalted him, because he had humbled himself, *crowned him with glory and hon ur,* the glory which he had with him before the worlds were, set him at his own right hand, constituted him not only the *head of the church,* but *head over all things to the church,* and gave all things into his hand, entrusted him with the administration of the kingdom of providence in conjunction with and subserviency to the kingdom of grace. All the creatures are put under his feet; and, even in the days of his

flesh, he gave some specimens of his power over them, as when he commanded the winds and the seas, and appointed a fish to pay his tribute. With good reason therefore does the psalmist conclude as he began, *Lord, how excellent is thy name in all the earth,* which has been honoured with the presence of the Redeemer, and is still enlightened by his gospel and governed by his wisdom and power!

In singing this and praying it over, though we must not forget to acknowledge, with suitable affections, God's common favours to mankind, particularly in the serviceableness of the inferior creatures to us, yet we must especially set ourselves to give glory to our Lord Jesus, by confessing that he is Lord, submitting to him as our Lord, and waiting till we see all things put under him and all his enemies made his footstool.

PSALM IX.

In this psalm, I. David praises God for pleading his cause, and giving him victory over his enemies and the enemies of his country (ver. 1—6), and calls upon others to join with him in his songs of praise, ver. 11, 12. II. He prays to God that he might have still further occasion to praise him, for his own deliverances and the confusion of his enemies, ver. 13, 14, 19, 20. III. He triumphs in the assurance he had of God's judging the world (ver. 7, 8), protecting his oppressed people (ver. 9, 10, 18), and bringing his and their implacable enemies to ruin, ver. 15—17. This is very applicable to the kingdom of the Messiah, the enemies of which have been in part destroyed already, and shall be yet more and more, till they all be made his footstool, which we are to assure ourselves of, that God may have the glory and we may take the comfort.

To the chief musician upon Muth-labben.

A psalm of David.

I WILL praise *thee,* O Lord, with my whole heart; I will show forth all thy marvellous works. 2 I will be glad and rejoice in thee: I will sing praise to thy name, O thou most High. 3 When mine enemies are turned back, they shall fall and perish at thy presence. 4 For thou hast maintained my right and my cause; thou satest in the throne judging right. 5 Thou hast rebuked the heathen, thou hast destroyed the wicked, thou hast put out their name for ever and ever. 6 O thou enemy, destructions are come to a perpetual end: and thou hast destroyed cities; their memorial is perished with them. 7 But the Lord shall endure for ever: he hath prepared his throne for judgment. 8 And he shall judge the world in righteousness, he shall minister judgment to the people in uprightness. 9 The Lord also will be a refuge for the oppressed, a refuge in times of trouble. 10 And they that know thy name will put their trust in thee: for thou, Lord, hast not forsaken them that seek thee.

The title of this psalm gives a very uncertain sound concerning the occasion of penning it. It is upon *Muth-labben,* which some make to refer to the death of Goliath, others of Nabal, others of Absalom; but I incline to think it signifies only some tune, or some musical instrument, to which this psalm was intended to be sung; and that the enemies David is here triumphing in the defeat of are the Philistines, and the other neighbouring nations that opposed his settlement in the throne, whom he contested with and subdued in the beginning of his reign, 2 Sam. v. 8. In these verses, °

I. David excites and engages himself to praise God for his mercies and the great things he had of late done for him and his government, *v.* 1, 2. Note, 1. God expects suitable returns of praise from those for whom he has done marvellous works. 2. If we would praise God acceptably, we must praise him in sincerity, with our hearts, and not only with our lips, and be lively and fervent in the duty, with our *whole heart.* 3. When we give thanks for some one particular mercy we should take occasion thence to remember former mercies and so to *show forth all his marvellous works.* 4. Holy joy is the life of thankful praise, as thankful praise is the language of holy joy: *I will be glad and rejoice in thee.* 5. Whatever occurs to make us glad, our joy must pass through it, and terminate in God only: *I will be glad and rejoice in thee,* not in the gift so much as in the giver. 6. Joy and praise are properly expressed by singing psalms. 7. When God has shown himself to be above the proud enemies of the church we must take occasion thence to give glory to him as the *Most High.* 8. The triumphs of the Redeemer ought to be the triumphs of the redeemed; see Rev. xii. 10; xix. 5; xv. 3, 4.

II. He acknowledges the almighty power of God as that which the strongest and stoutest of his enemies were no way able to contest with or stand before, *v.* 3. But, 1. They are forced to turn back. Their policy and their courage fail them, so that they cannot, they dare not, push forward in their enterprises, but retire with precipitation. 2. When once they turn back, they fall and perish; even their retreat will be their ruin, and they will save themselves no more by flying than by fighting. If Haman begin to fall before Mordecai, he is a lost man, and shall prevail no more; see Esther vi. 13. 3. The presence of the Lord, and the glory of his power, are sufficient for the destruction of his and his people's enemies. That is easily done which a man does with his very presence; with *that* God confounds his enemies, such a presence has he. This was fulfilled when our Lord Jesus, with one word, *I am he,* made his enemies to *fall back at his presence* (John xviii. 6) and he could, at the same time, have made them perish. 4. When the enemies of God's church are put to confusion we must ascribe their discomfiture to the power, not of instruments, but of his presence, and give him all the glory.

III. He gives to God the glory of his righteousness, in his appearing on his behalf (*v.* 4): "*Thou hast maintained my right and my cause,* that is, my righteous cause; when that came on, *thou satest in the throne, judging right.* Observe, 1. God sits in the throne of judgment. To him it belongs to decide controversies, to determine appeals, to avenge the injured, and to punish the injurious; for he has said, *Vengeance is mine.* 2. We are sure that the judgment of God is according to truth and that with him there is no unrighteousness. Far be it from God that he should pervert justice. If there seem to us to be some irregularity in the present decisions of Providence, yet these, instead of shaking our belief of God's justice, may serve to strengthen our belief of the judgment to come, which will set all to-rights. 3. Whoever disown and desert a just and injured cause, we may be sure that the righteous God will maintain it and plead it with jealousy, and will never suffer it to be run down.

IV. He records, with joy, the triumphs of the God of heaven over all the powers of hell and attends those triumphs with his praises, *v.* 5. By three steps the power and justice of God had proceeded against the heathen, and wicked people, who were enemies to the king God had lately set up upon his holy hill of Zion. 1. He had checked them: "*Thou hast rebuked the heathen,* hast given them real proofs of thy displeasure against them." This he did before he destroyed them, that they might take warning by the rebukes of Providence and so prevent their own destruction. (2.) He had cut them off: *Thou hast destroyed the wicked.* The wicked are marked for destruction, and some are made monuments of God's vindictive justice and destructive power in this world. (3.) He had buried them in oblivion and perpetual infamy, had put out their name for ever, that they should never be remembered with any respect.

V. He exults over the enemy whom God thus appears against (*v.* 6): *Thou hast destroyed cities.* Either, "Thou, O enemy! hast destroyed our cities, at least in intention and imagination," or "Thou, O God! hast destroyed their cities by the desolation brought upon their country." It may be taken either way; for the psalmist will have the enemy to know, 1. That their destruction is just and that God was but reckoning with them for all the mischief which they had done and designed against his people. The malicious and vexatious neighbours of Israel, as the Philistines, Moabites, Ammonites, Edomites, and Syrians, had made incursions upon them (when there was no king in Israel to fight their battles), had destroyed their cities and done what they could to make their memorial perish with them. But now the wheel was turned upon them; their destructions of Israel had come to a perpetual end; they shall now cease to spoil and must themselves be spoiled, Isa. xxxiii. 1. 2. That it is total and final, such a destruction as should make a perpetual end of them, so that the very memorial of their cities should perish with them. So devouring a thing is time, and much more such desolations do the righteous judgments of God make upon sinners, that great and populous cities have been reduced to such ruins that their very memorial has perished, and those who have sought them could not find where they stood; but we look for a city that has stronger foundations.

VI. He comforts himself and others in God, and pleases himself with the thoughts of him. 1. With the thoughts of his eternity. On this earth we see nothing durable, even strong cities are buried in rubbish and forgotten; *but the Lord shall endure for ever, v.* 7. There is no change of his being; his felicity, power, and perfection, are out of the reach of all the combined forces of hell and earth; they may put an end to our liberties, our privileges, our lives, but our God is still the same, and sits even upon the floods, unshaken, undisturbed, xxix. 10; xciii. 2. 2. With the thoughts of his sovereignty both in government and judgment: *He has prepared his throne,* has fixed it by his infinite wisdom, has fixed it by his immutable counsel. It is the great support and comfort of good people, when the power of the church's enemies is threatening and the posture of its affairs melancholy and perplexed, that God now rules the world and will shortly judge the world. 3. With the thoughts of his justice and righteousness in all the administrations of his government. He does all every day, he will do all at the last day, according to the eternal unalterable rules of equity (*v.* 8): *He shall judge the world,* all persons and all controversies, *shall minister judgment to the people* (shall determine their lot both in this and in the future state) in righteousness and *in uprightness,* so that there shall not be the least colour of exception against it. 4. With the thoughts of that peculiar favour which God bears to his own people and the special protection which he takes them under. The Lord, who endures for ever, is their everlasting strength and protection; he that judges the world will be sure to judge for them, when at any time they are injured or distressed (*v.* 9): *He will be a refuge for the oppressed,* a high place, a strong place, for the oppressed, *in times of trouble.* It is the lot of God's people to be oppressed in this world and to have troublous times appointed to them. Perhaps God may not immediately appear for them as their deliverer and avenger; but, in the midst of their distresses, they may by faith flee to him as their refuge and may depend upon his power and promise for their safety, so that no real hurt shall be done them. 5. With the thoughts of that sweet satisfaction and repose of mind which those have that

make God their refuge (*v.* 10): "*Those that know thy name will put their trust in thee,* as I have done" (for the grace of God is the same in all the saints, "and then they will find, as I have found, that thou dost not forsake those that seek thee;" for the favour of God is the same towards all the saints. Note, (1.) The better God is known the more he is trusted. Those who know him to be a God of infinite wisdom will trust him *further than they can see him* (Job xxxv. 14); those who know him to be a God of almighty power will trust him when creature-confidences fail and they have nothing else to trust to (2 Chron. xx. 12); and those who know him to be a God of infinite grace and goodness will trust him *though he slay them,* Job xiii. 15. Those who know him to be a God of inviolable truth and faithfulness will rejoice in his word of promise, and rest upon that, though the performance be deferred and intermediate providences seem to contradict it. Those who know him to be the Father of spirits, and an everlasting Father, will trust him with their souls as their main care and trust in him at all times, even to the end. (2.) The more God is trusted the more he is sought unto. If we trust God we shall seek him by faithful and fervent prayer, and by a constant care to approve ourselves to him in the whole course of our conversation. (3.) God never did, nor ever will, disown or desert any that duly seek to him and trust in him. Though he afflict them, he will not leave them comfortless; though he seem to forsake them for a while, yet he will gather them with everlasting mercies.

11 Sing praises to the Lord, which dwelleth in Zion: declare among the people his doings. 12 When he maketh inquisition for blood, he remembereth them: he forgetteth not the cry of the humble. 13 Have mercy upon me, O Lord; consider my trouble *which I suffer* of them that hate me, thou that liftest me up from the gates of death: 14 That I may show forth all thy praise in the gates of the daughter of Zion: I will rejoice in thy salvation. 15 The heathen are sunk down in the pit *that* they made: in the net which they hid is their own foot taken. 16 The Lord is known *by* the judgment *which* he executeth: the wicked is snared in the work of his own hands. Higgaion. Selah. 17 The wicked shall be turned into hell, *and* all the nations that forget God. 18 For the needy shall not alway be forgotten: the expectation of the poor shall *not* perish for ever. 19 Arise, O

LORD; let not man prevail, let the heathen be judged in thy sight. 20 Put them in fear, O LORD: *that* the nations may know themselves *to be but* men. Selah.

In these verses,

I. David, having praised God himself, calls upon and invites others to praise him likewise, *v.* 11. Those who believe God is greatly to be praised not only desire to do that work better themselves, but desire that others also may join with them in it and would gladly be instrumental to bring them to it: *Sing praises to the Lord who dwelleth in Zion.* As the special residence of his glory is in heaven, so the special residence of his grace is in his church, of which Zion was a type. There he meets his people with his promises and graces, and there he expects they should meet him with their praises and services. In all our praises we should have an eye to God as dwelling in Zion, in a special manner present in the assemblies of his people, as their protector and patron. He resolved himself to show forth God's marvellous works (*v.* 1), and here he calls upon others to *declare among the people his doings.* He commands his own subjects to do it, for the hohour of God, of their country, and of their holy religion; he courts his neighbours to do it, to sing praises, not, as hitherto, to their false gods, but to Jehovah who dwelleth in Zion, to the God of Israel, and to own among the heathen that *the Lord has done great things for his people Israel,* cxxvi. 3, 4. Let them particularly take notice of the justice of God in avenging the blood of his people Israel on the Philistines and their other wicked neighbours, who had, in making war upon them, used them barbarously and given them no quarter, *v.* 12. When God comes to *make inquisition for blood* by his judgments on earth, before he comes to do it by the judgment of the great day, *he remembers them,* remembers every drop of the innocent blood which they have shed, and will return it sevenfold upon the head of the bloodthirsty; he will give them blood to drink, for they are worthy. This assurance he might well build upon that word (Deut. xxxii. 43), *He will avenge the blood of his servants.* Note, There is a day coming when God will make inquisition for blood, when he will discover what has been shed secretly, and avenge what has been shed unjustly; see Isa. xxvi. 21; Jer. li. 35. In that day it will appear how precious the blood of God's people is to him (lxxii. 14), when it must all be accounted for. It will then appear that he has not forgotten *the cry of the humble,* neither the cry of their blood nor the cry of their prayers, but that both are sealed up among his treasures.

II. David, having praised God for former mercies and deliverances, earnestly prays that God would still appear for him; for he sees not yet all things put under him.

1. He prays, (1.) That God would be compassionate to him (*v.* 13): " *Have mercy upon me,* who, having misery only, and no merit, to speak for me, must depend upon mere mercy for relief." (2.) That he would be concerned for him. He is not particular in his request, lest he should seem to prescribe to God; but submits himself to the wisdom and will of God in this modest request, " *Lord, consider my trouble,* and do for me as thou thinkest fit."

2. He pleads, (1.) The malice of his enemies, the trouble which he suffered from those that hated him, and hatred is a cruel passion. (2.) The experience he had had of divine succours and the expectation he now had of the continuance of them, as the necessity of his case required: " *O thou that liftest me up,* that canst do it, that hast done it, that wilt do it, whose prerogative it is to lift up thy people *from the gates of death !*" We are never brought so low, so near to death, but God can raise us up. If he has saved us from spiritual and eternal death, we may thence take encouragement to hope that in all our distresses he will be a very present help to us. (3.) His sincere purpose to praise God when his victories should be completed (*v.* 14): " *Lord, save me,* not that I may have the comfort and credit of the deliverance, but that thou mayest have the glory, *that I may show forth all thy praise,* and that publicly, *in the gates of the daughter of Zion:*" there God was said to dwell (*v.* 11) and there David would attend him, with joy in God's salvation, typical of the great salvation which was to be wrought out by the Son of David.

III. David by faith foresees and foretels the certain ruin of all wicked people, both in this world and in that to come.

1. In this world, *v.* 15, 16. God executes judgment upon them when the measure of their iniquities is full, and does it, (1.) So as to put shame upon them and make their fall inglorious; for they sink into the pit which they themselves digged (vii. 15), they are taken in the net which they themselves laid for the ensnaring of God's people, and they are snared in the work of their own hands. In all the struggles David had with the Philistines they were the aggressors, 2 Sam. v. 17, 22. And other nations were subdued by those wars in which they embroiled themselves. The overruling providence of God frequently so orders it that persecutors and oppressors are brought to ruin by those very projects which they intended to be destructive to the people of God. Drunkards kill themselves; prodigals beggar themselves; the contentious bring mischief upon themselves. Thus men's sins may be read in their punishment, and it becomes visible to all that the destruction of sinners is not only meritoriously, but efficiently, of themselves, which will fill them with the utmost confu-

sion. (2.) So as to get honour to himself: *The Lord is known,* that is, he makes himself known, by these judgments which he executes. It is known that there is a God who judges in the earth, that he is a righteous God, and one that hates sin and will punish it. In these judgments the wrath of God is revealed from heaven against all ungodliness and unrighteousness of men. The psalmist therefore adds here a note extraordinary, commanding special regard, *Higgaion;* it is a thing to be carefully observed and meditated upon. What we see of present judgments, and what we believe of the judgment to come, ought to be the subject of our frequent and serious meditations.

. 2. In the other world (*v.* 17): *The wicked shall be turned into hell,* as captives into the prison-house, even *all the nations that forget God.* Note, (1.) Forgetfulness of God is the cause of all the wickedness of the wicked. (2.) There are nations of those that forget God, multitudes that live without God in the world, many great and many mighty nations, that never regard him nor desire the knowledge of his ways. (3.) Hell will, at last, be the portion of such, a state of everlasting misery and torment—*Sheol,* a pit of destruction, in which they and all their comforts will be for ever lost and buried. Though there be nations of them, yet they shall be turned into hell, like sheep into the slaughter-house (xlix. 14), and their being so numerous will not be any security or ease to them, nor any loss to God or the least impeachment of his goodness.

IV. David encourages the people of God to wait for his salvation, though it should be long deferred, *v.* 18. The needy may think themselves, and others may think them, forgotten for a while, and their expectation of help from God may seem to have perished and to have been for ever frustrated. But he that believes does not make haste; the vision is for an appointed time, and at the end it shall speak. We may build upon it as undoubtedly true that God's people, God's elect, shall not always be forgotten, nor shall they be disappointed of their hopes from the promise. God will not only remember them, at last, but will make it to appear that he never did forget them; it is impossible he should, though a woman may forget her sucking child.

V. He concludes with prayer that God would humble the pride, break the power, and blast the projects, of all the wicked enemies of his church: "*Arise, O Lord!* (*v.* 19), stir up thyself, exert thy power, take thy seat, and deal with all these proud and daring enemies of thy name, and cause, and people." 1. "Lord, restrain them, and set bounds to their malice: *Let not man prevail;* consult thy own honour, and let not weak and mortal man prevail against the kingdom and interest of the almighty and immortal God. *Shall mortal man be too hard for God, too*

272

strong *for his Maker?*" 2. "Lord, reckon with them: *Let the heathen be judged in thy sight,* that is, let them be plainly called to an account for all the dishonour done to thee and the mischief done to thy people." Impenitent sinners will be punished in God's sight; and, when their day of grace is over, the bowels even of infinite mercy will not relent towards them, Rev. xiv. 10. 3. "Lord, frighten them: *Put them in fear, O Lord!* (*v.* 20), strike a terror upon them, make them afraid with thy judgments." God knows how to make the strongest and stoutest of men to tremble and to flee when none pursues, and thereby he makes them know and own that they are but men; they are but weak men, unable to stand before the holy God—sinful men, the guilt of whose consciences makes them subject to alarms. Note, It is a very desirable thing, much for the glory of God and the peace and welfare of the universe, that men should know and consider themselves to be but men, depending creatures, mutable, mortal, and accountable.

In singing this psalm we must give to God the glory of his justice in pleading his people's cause against his and their enemies, and encourage ourselves to wait for the year of the redeemed and the year of recompences for the controversy of Zion, even the final destruction of all anti-christian powers and factions, to which many of the ancients apply this psalm.

PSALM X. ⑩

The Septuagint translation joins this psalm with the ninth, and makes them but one; but the Hebrew makes it a distinct psalm, and the scope and style are certainly different. In this psalm, I. David complains of the wickedness of the wicked, describes the dreadful pitch of impiety at which they had arrived (to the great dishonour of God and the prejudice of his church and people), and notices the delay of God's appearing against them, ver. 1—11. He prays to God to appear against them for the relief of his people and comforts himself with hopes that he would do so in due time, ver. 12—18.

WHY standest thou afar off, O Lord? *why* hidest thou *thyself* in times of trouble ? 2 The wicked in *his* pride doth persecute the poor : let them be taken in the devices that they have imagined. 3 For the wicked boasteth of his heart's desire, and blesseth the covetous, *whom* the Lord abhorreth. 4 The wicked, through the pride of his countenance, will not seek *after God:* God *is* not in all his thoughts. 5 His ways are always grievous; thy judgments *are* far above out of his sight : *as for* all his enemies, he puffeth at them. 6 He hath said in his heart, I shall not be moved : for *I shall* never *be* in adversity. 7 His mouth is full of cursing and deceit and fraud : under his tongue *is* mischief and vanity. 8 He sitteth in the lurking places of the villages : in the secret places doth he murder the innocent: his eyes are privily set against the poor. 9 He lieth in wait secretly as a lion in his den: he lieth in wait to catch the poor: he doth catch the poor, when he draweth him into his net. 10 He croucheth, *and* humbleth himself, that the poor may fall by his strong ones. 11 He hath said in his heart, God hath forgotten: he hideth his face; he will never see *it.*

David, in these verses, discovers,

I. A very great affection to God and his favour; for, in the time of trouble, that which he complains of most feelingly is God's withdrawing his gracious presence (*v.* 1): *Why standest thou afar off,* as one unconcerned in the indignities done to thy name and the injuries done to the people?" Note, God's withdrawings are very grievous to his people at any time, but especially in times of trouble. Outward deliverance is afar off and is hidden from us, and then we think God is afar off and we therefore want inward comfort; but that is our own fault; it is because we judge by outward appearance; we stand afar off from God by our unbelief, and then we complain that God stands afar off from us.

II. A very great indignation against sin, the sins that made the times perilous, 2 Tim. iii. 1. He beholds the transgressors and is grieved, is amazed, and brings to his heavenly Father their evil report, not in a way of vain-glory, boasting before God that he was not as *these publicans* (Luke xviii. 11), much less venting any personal resentments, piques, or passions, of his own; but as one that laid to heart that which is offensive to God and all good men, and earnestly desired a reformation of manners. Passionate and satirical invectives against bad men do more hurt than good; if we will speak of their badness, let it be to God in prayer, for he alone can make them better. This long representation of the wickedness of the wicked is here summed up in the first words of it (*v.* 2), *The wicked in his pride doth persecute the poor,* where two things are laid to their charge, pride and persecution, the former the cause of the latter. Proud men will have all about them to be of their mind, of their religion, to say as they say, to submit to their dominion, and acquiesce in their dictates; and those that either eclipse them or will not yield to them they malign and hate with an inveterate hatred. Tyranny, both in state and church, owes its origin to pride. The psalmist, having begun this description, presently inserts a short prayer, a prayer in a parenthesis, which is an advantage and no prejudice to the sense: *Let them be taken,* as proud people often are, *in the devices that they have imagined, v.* 2. Let their counsels be turned headlong, and let them fall headlong by them. These two heads of the charge are here enlarged upon.

1. They are proud, very proud, and extremely conceited of themselves; justly therefore did he wonder that God did not speedily appear against them, for he hates pride, and resists the proud. (1.) The sinner proudly glories in his power and success. He *boasts of his heart's desire,* boasts that he can do what he pleases (as if God himself could not control him) and that he has all he wished for and has carried his point. Ephraim said, *I have become rich, I have found me out substance,* Hos. xii. 8. "Now, Lord, is it for thy glory to suffer a sinful man thus to pretend to the sovereignty and felicity of a God?" (2.) He proudly contradicts the judgment of God, which, we are sure, is according to truth; for he *blesses the covetous, whom the Lord abhors.* See how God and men differ in their sentiments of persons: God abhors covetous worldlings, who make money their God and idolize it; he looks upon them as his enemies, and will have no communion with them. *The friendship of the world is enmity to God.* But proud persecutors bless them, and approve their sayings, xlix. 13. They applaud those as wise whom God pronounces foolish (Luke xii. 20); they justify those as innocent whom God condemns as deeply guilty before him; and they admire those as happy, in having their portion in this life, whom God declares, upon that account, truly miserable. *Thou, in thy lifetime, receivedst thy good things.* (3.) He proudly casts off the thoughts of God, and all dependence upon him and devotion to him (*v.* 4): *The wicked, through the pride of his countenance,* that pride of his heart which appears in his very countenance (Prov. vi. 17), *will not seek after God,* nor entertain the thoughts of him. *God is not in all his thoughts,* not in any of them. *All his thoughts are that there is no God.* See here, [1.] The nature of impiety and irreligion; it is *not seeking after God* and *not having him in our thoughts.* There is no enquiry made after him (Job xxxv. 10, Jer. ii. 6), no desire towards him, no communion with him, but a secret wish to have no dependence upon him and not to be beholden to him. Wicked people will not seek after God (that is, will not call upon him); they live without prayer, and that is living without God. They have many thoughts, many projects and devices, but no eye to God in any of them, no submission to his will nor aim at his glory. [2.] The cause of this impiety and irreligion; and that is pride. Men will not seek after God because they think they have no need of him, their own hands are sufficient for them; they think it a thing below them to be religious, because religious people are few, and mean, and despised, and the restraints of religion will be a disparagement to them. (4.) He proudly makes light of God's commandments and judgments (*v.* 5): *His ways*

are always grievous; he is very daring and resolute in his sinful courses; he will have his way, though ever so tiresome to himself and vexatious to others; he travails with pain in his wicked courses, and yet his pride makes him wilful and obstinate in them. God's judgments (what he commands and what he threatens for the breach of his commands) are *far above out of his sight;* he is not sensible of his duty by the law of God nor of his danger by the wrath and curse of God. Tell him of God's authority over him, he turns it off with this, that he never saw God and therefore does not know that there is a God, he is *in the height of heaven,* and *quæ supra nos nihil ad nos—we have nothing to do with things above us.* Tell him of God's judgments which will be executed upon those that go on still in their trespasses, and he will not be convinced that there is any reality in them; they are *far above out of his sight,* and therefore he thinks they are mere bugbears. (5.) He proudly despises all his enemies, and looks upon them with the utmost disdain; he puffs at those whom God is preparing to be a scourge and ruin to him, as if he could baffle them all, and was able to make his part good with them. But, as it is impolitic to despise an enemy, so it is impious to despise any instrument of God's wrath. (6.) He proudly sets trouble at defiance and is confident of the continuance of his own prosperity (*v.* 6): *He hath said in his heart,* and pleased himself with the thought, *I shall not be moved,* my goods are laid up for many years, and *I shall never be in adversity:* like Babylon, that said, *I shall be a lady for ever,* Isa. xlvii. 7; Rev. xviii. 7. Those are nearest ruin who thus set it furthest from them.

2. They are persecutors, cruel persecutors. For the gratifying of their pride and covetousness, and in opposition to God and religion, they are very oppressive to all within their reach. Observe, concerning these persecutors, (1.) That they are very bitter and malicious (*v.* 7): *His mouth is full of cursing.* Those he cannot do a real mischief to, yet he will spit his venom at, and breathe out the slaughter which he cannot execute. Thus have God's faithful worshippers been anathematized and cursed, with bell, book, and candle. Where there is a heart full of malice there is commonly a mouth full of curses. (2.) They are very false and treacherous. There is mischief designed, but it is hidden under the tongue, not to be discerned, for *his mouth is full of deceit* and vanity. He has learned of the devil to deceive, and so to destroy; with this his hatred is covered, Prov. xxvi. 26. He cares not what lies he tells, nor what oaths he breaks, nor what arts of dissimulation he uses, to compass his ends. (3.) That they are very cunning and crafty in carrying on their designs. They have ways and means to concert what they intend, that they may the more effectually

accomplish it. Like Esau, that cunning hunter, *he sits in the lurking places, in the secret places,* and *his eyes are privily set* to do mischief (*v.* 8), not because he is ashamed of what he does (if he blushed, there were some hopes he would repent), nor because he is afraid of the wrath of God, for he imagines God will never call him to an account (*v.* 11), but because he is afraid lest the discovery of his designs should be the breaking of them. Perhaps it refers particularly to robbers and highwaymen, who lie in wait for honest travellers, to make a prey of them and what they have. (4.) That they are very cruel and barbarous. Their malice is against *the innocent,* who never provoked them—against *the poor,* who cannot resist them and over whom it will be no glory to triumph. Those are perfectly lost to all honesty and honour against whose mischievous designs neither innocence nor poverty will be any man's security. Those that have power ought to protect the innocent and provide for the poor; yet these will be the destroyers of those whose guardians they ought to be. And what do they aim at? It is to *catch the poor,* and *draw them into their net,* that is, get them into their power, not to strip them only, but to *murder them.* They hunt for the precious life. It is God's poor people that they are persecuting, against whom they bear a mortal hatred for his sake whose they are and whose image they bear, and therefore they lie in wait to murder them: *He lies in wait as a lion* that thirsts after blood, and feeds with pleasure upon the prey. The devil, whose agent he is, is compared to a roaring lion that seeks not what, but whom, he may devour. (5.) That they are base and hypocritical (*v.* 10): *He crouches and humbles himself,* as beasts of prey do, that they may get their prey within their reach. This intimates that the sordid spirits of persecutors and oppressors will stoop to any thing, though ever so mean, for the compassing of their wicked designs; witness the scandalous practices of Saul when he hunted David. It intimates, likewise, that they cover their malicious designs with the pretence of meekness and humility, and kindness to those they design the greatest mischief to; they seem to humble themselves to take cognizance of the poor, and concern themselves in their concernments, when it is in order to make them fall, to make a prey of them. (6.) That they are very impious and atheistical, *v.* 11. They could not thus break through all the laws of justice and goodness towards man if they had not first shaken off all sense of religion, and risen up in rebellion against the light of its most sacred and self-evident principles: *He hath said in his heart, God has forgotten.* When his own conscience rebuked him for his wickedness, and threatened him with the consequences of it, and asked how he would answer it to the righteous Judge of heaven and earth, he turned it off with this, *God has forsaken the earth*, Ezek. viii. 12; ix. 9. This is a blasphemous reproach, [1.] Upon God's omniscience and providence, as if he could not, or did not, see what men do in this lower world. [2.] Upon his holiness and the rectitude of his nature, as if, though he did see, yet he did not dislike, but was willing to connive at, the most unnatural and inhuman villanies. [3.] Upon his justice and the equity of his government, as if, though he did see and dislike the wickedness of the wicked, yet he would never reckon with them, nor punish them for it, either because he could not or durst not, or because he was not inclined to do so. Let those that suffer by proud oppressors hope that God will, in due time, appear for them; for those that are abusive to them are abusive to God Almighty too.

In singing this psalm and praying it over, we should have our hearts much affected with a holy indignation at the wickedness of the oppressors, a tender compassion of the miseries of the oppressed, and a pious zeal for the glory and honour of God, with a firm belief that he will, in due time, give redress to the injured and reckon with the injurious.

12 Arise, O LORD; O God, lift up thine hand: forget not the humble. 13 Wherefore doth the wicked contemn God? he hath said in his heart, Thou wilt not require *it.* 14 Thou hast seen *it*; for thou beholdest mischief and spite, to requite *it* with thy hand: the poor committeth himself unto thee; thou art the helper of the fatherless. 15 Break thou the arm of the wicked and the evil *man*: seek out his wickedness *till* thou find none. 16 The LORD *is* King for ever and ever: the heathen are perished out of his land. 17 LORD, thou hast heard the desire of the humble: thou wilt prepare their heart, thou wilt cause thine ear to hear: 18 To judge the fatherless and the oppressed, that the man of the earth may no more oppress.

David here, upon the foregoing representation of the inhumanity and impiety of the oppressors, grounds an address to God, wherein observe,

I. What he prays for. 1. That God would himself appear (*v.* 12): *"Arise, O Lord! O God! lift up thy hand,* manifest thy presence and providence in the affairs of this lower world. *Arise, O Lord!* to the confusion of those who say that thou hidest thy face. Manifest thy power, exert it for the maintaining of thy own cause, lift up thy hand to give a fatal blow to these oppressors; let thy everlasting arm be made bare."* 2. That he would

appear for his people: *"Forget not the humble, the afflicted,* that are poor, that are made poorer, and are poor in spirit. Their oppressors, in their presumption, say that thou hast forgotten them; and they, in their despair, are ready to say the same. Lord, make it to appear that they are both mistaken."* 3. That he would appear against their persecutors, *v.* 15. (1.) That he would disable them from doing any mischief: *Break thou the arm of the wicked,* take away his power, *that the hypocrite reign not, lest the people be ensnared,* Job xxxiv. 30. We read of oppressors whose dominion was taken away, but their lives were prolonged (Dan. vii. 12), that they might have time to repent. (2.) That he would deal with them for the mischief they had done: *"Seek out his wickedness;* let that be all brought to light which he thought should for ever lie undiscovered; let that be all brought to account which he thought should for ever go unpunished; bring it out *till thou find none,* that is, till none of his evil deeds remain unreckoned for, none of his evil designs undefeated, and none of his partisans undestroyed.

II. What he pleads for the encouraging of his own faith in these petitions.

1. He pleads the great affronts which these proud oppressors put upon God himself: "Lord, it is thy own cause that we beg thou wouldst appear in; the enemies have made it so, and therefore it is not for thy glory to let them go unpunished" (*v.* 13): *Wherefore do the wicked contemn God?* He does so; for he says, *"Thou wilt not require it;* thou wilt never call us to an account for what we do," than which they could not put a greater indignity upon the righteous God. The psalmist here speaks with astonishment, (1.) At the wickedness of the wicked: "Why do they speak so impiously, why so absurdly?" It is a great trouble to good men to think what contempt is cast upon the holy God by the sin of sinners, upon his precepts, his promises, his threatenings, his favours, his judgments; all are despised and made light of. *Wherefore do the wicked thus contemn God?* It is because they do not know him. (2.) At the patience and forbearance of God towards them: "Why are they suffered thus to contemn God? Why does he not immediately vindicate himself and take vengeance on them?" It is because the day of reckoning is yet to come, when the measure of their iniquity is full.

2. He pleads the notice God took of the impiety and iniquity of these oppressors (*v.* 14): "Do the persecutors encourage themselves with a groundless fancy that thou wilt never see it? Let the persecuted encourage themselves with a well-grounded faith, not only that thou hast seen it, but that thou dost behold it, even all the mischief that is done by the hands, and all the spite and malice that lurk in the hearts, of these oppressors; it is all known to thee, and observed by thee; nay, not only thou hast seen it and dost behold it, but thou wilt requite it, wilt recompense it

into their bosoms, by thy just and avenging hand."

3. He pleads the dependence which the oppressed had upon him: " *The poor commits himself unto thee,* each of them does so, I among the rest. They rely on thee as their patron and protector, they refer themselves to thee as their Judge, in whose determination they acquiesce and at whose disposal they are willing to be. *They leave themselves with thee"* (so some read it), " not prescribing, but subscribing, to thy wisdom and will. They thus give thee honour as much as their oppressors dishonour thee. They are thy willing subjects, and put themselves under thy protection ; therefore protect them."

4. He pleads the relation in which God is pleased to stand to us, (1.) As a great God. He *is King for ever and ever, v.* 16. And it is the office of a king to administer justice for the restraint and terror of evil-doers and the protection and praise of those that do well. To whom should the injured subjects appeal but to the sovereign? *Help, my Lord, O King! Avenge me of my adversary.* "Lord, let all that pay homage and tribute to thee as their King have the benefit of thy government and find thee their refuge. Thou art an everlasting King, which no earthly prince is, and therefore canst and wilt, by an eternal judgment, dispense rewards and punishments in an everlasting state, when time shall be no more ; and to that judgment the poor refer themselves." (2.) As a good God. He is the helper of the fatherless (*v.* 14), of those who have no one else to help them and have many to injure them. He has appointed kings to *defend the poor and fatherless* (lxxxii. 3), and therefore much more will he do so himself ; for he has taken it among the titles of his honour to be a Father to the fatherless (lxviii. 5), a helper of the helpless.

5. He pleads the experience which God's church and people had had of God's readiness to appear for them. (1.) He had dispersed and extirpated their enemies (*v.* 16): " *The heathen have perished out of his land ;* the remainders of the Canaanites, the seven devoted nations, which have long been as thorns in the eyes and goads in the sides of Israel, are now, at length, utterly rooted out; and this is an encouragement to us to hope that God will, in like manner, break the arm of the oppressive Israelites, who were, in some respects, worse than heathens." (2.) He had heard and answered their prayers (*v.* 17): " *Lord, thou hast* many a time *heard the desire of the humble,* and never saidst to a distressed suppliant, *Seek in vain.* Why may not we hope for the continuance and repetition of the wonders, the favours, which our father told us of ?"

6. He pleads their expectations from God pursuant to their experience of him : " *Thou hast heard, therefore thou will cause thy ear to hear,* as, vi. 9. Thou art the same, and thy power, and promise, and relation to thy

people are the same, and the work and work · ings of grace are the same in them ; why therefore may we not hope that he who has been will still be, will ever be, a God hearing prayer ?" But observe, (1.) In what method God hears prayer. He first prepares the heart of his people and then gives them an answer of peace ; nor may we expect his gracious answer, but in this way ; so that God's working upon us is the best earnest of his working for us. He prepares the heart for prayer by kindling holy desires, and strengthening our most holy faith, fixing the thoughts and raising the affections, and then he graciously accepts the prayer ; he prepares the heart for the mercy itself that is wanting and prayed for, makes us fit to receive it and use it well, and then gives it in to us. The preparation of the heart is from the Lord, and we must seek unto him for it (Prov. xvi. 1) and take that as a leading favour. (2.) What he will do in answer to prayer, *v.* 18. [1.] He will plead the cause of the persecuted, will judge the fatherless and oppressed, will judge for them, clear up their innocency, restore their comforts, and recompense them for all the loss and damage they have sustained. [2.] He will put an end to the fury of the persecutors. Hitherto they shall come, but no further ; here shall the proud waves of their malice be stayed ; an effectual course shall be taken *that the man of the earth may no more oppress.* See how light the psalmist now makes of the power of that proud persecutor whom he had been describing in this psalm, and how slightly he speaks of him now that he had been considering God's sovereignty. *First,* He is but *a man of the earth,* a man *out of* the earth (so the word is), sprung out of the earth, and therefore mean, and weak, and hastening to the earth again. Why then should we be afraid of the fury of the oppressor when he is but *man that shall die, a son of man that shall be as grass?* Isa. li. 12. He that protects us is the Lord of heaven ; he that persecutes us is but a man of the earth. *Secondly,* God has him in a chain, and can easily restrain the remainder of his wrath, so that he cannot do what he would. When God speaks the word Satan shall by his instruments no more deceive (Rev. xx. 3), no more oppress.

In singing these verses we must commit religion's just but injured cause to God, as those that are heartily concerned for its honour and interests, believing that he will, in due time, plead it with jealousy.

PSALM XI.

In this psalm we have David's struggle with and triumph over a strong temptation to distrust God and betake himself to indirect means for his own safety in a time of danger. It is supposed to have been penned when he began to feel the resentments of Saul's envy, and had had the javelin thrown at him once and again. He was then advised to run his country. " No," says he, " I trust in God, and therefore will keep my ground." Observe, I. How he represents the temptation, and perhaps parleys with it, ver. 1—3. II. How he answers it, and puts it to silence with the consideration of God's dominion and providence (ver. 4), his favour to the righteous, and the wrath which the wicked are reserved for, ver. 5—7. In times of public fear, when the insults of the church's enemies are daring and threatening, it will be profitable to meditate on this psalm.

To the chief musician. A psalm of David.

IN the LORD put I my trust: how say ye to my soul, Flee *as* a bird to your mountain? 2 For, lo, the wicked bend *their* bow, they make ready their arrow upon the string, that they may privily shoot at the upright in heart. 3 If the foundations be destroyed, what can the righteous do?

Here is, I. David's fixed resolution to make God his confidence: *In the Lord put I my trust, v.* 1. Those that truly fear God and serve him are welcome to put their trust in him, and shall not be made ashamed of their doing so. And it is the character of the saints, who have taken God for their God, that they make him their hope. Even when they have other things to stay themselves upon, yet they do not, they dare not, stay upon them, but on God only. Gold is not their hope, nor are horses and chariots their confidence, but God only; and therefore, when second causes frown, yet their hopes do not fail them, because the first cause is still the same, is ever so. The psalmist, before he gives an account of the temptation he was in to distrust God, records his resolution to trust in him, as that which he was resolved to live and die by.

II. His resentment of a temptation to the contrary: "*How say you to my soul,* which has thus returned to God as its rest and reposes in him, *Flee as a bird to your mountain,* to be safe there out of the reach of the fowler?" This may be taken either,

1. As the serious advice of his timorous friends; so many understand it, and with great probability. Some that were hearty well-wishers to David, when they saw how much Saul was exasperated against him and how maliciously he sought his life, pressed him by all means to flee for the same to some place of shelter, and not to depend too much upon the anointing he had received, which, they thought, was more likely to occasion the loss of his head than to save it. That which grieved him in this motion was not that to flee now would savour of cowardice, and ill become a soldier, but that it would savour of unbelief and would ill become a saint who had so often said, *In the Lord put I my trust.* Taking it thus, the two following verses contain the reason with which these faint-hearted friends of David backed this advice. They would have him flee, (1.) Because he could not be safe where he was, *v.* 2. "Observe," say they, "how *the wicked bend their bow;* Saul and his instruments aim at thy life, and the uprightness of thy heart will not be thy security." See what an enmity there is in the wicked against the upright, in the seed of the serpent against the seed of the woman; what pains they take, what preparations they make, to do them a mischief: *They privily shoot* at them, or, *in darkness,* that they may not see the evil designed, to avoid it, nor others, to prevent it, no, nor God himself, to punish

it. (2.) Because he could be no longer useful where he was. "For," say they, "*if the foundations be destroyed*" (as they were by Saul's mal-administration), "if the civil state and government be unhinged and all out of course" (lxxv. 3, lxxxii. 5), "what canst thou do with thy righteousness to redress the grievances? Alas! it is to no purpose to attempt the saving of a kingdom so wretchedly shattered; whatever the righteous can do signifies nothing." *Abi in cellam, et dic, Miserere mei, Domine—Away to thy cell, and there cry, Pity me, O Lord!* Many are hindered from doing the service they might do to the public, in difficult times, by a despair of success.

2. It may be taken as a taunt wherewith his enemies bantered him, upbraiding him with the professions he used to make of confidence in God, and scornfully bidding him try what stead that would stand him in now. "You say, God is your mountain; flee to him now, and see what the better you will be." Thus they endeavoured to shame the counsel of the poor, saying, There is *no help for them in God,* xiv. 6; iii. 2. The confidence and comfort which the saints have in God, when all the hopes and joys in the creature fail them, are a riddle to a carnal world and are ridiculed accordingly. Taking it thus, the two following verses are David's answer to this sarcasm, in which, (1.) He complains of the malice of those who did thus abuse him (*v.* 2): *They bend their bow and make ready their arrows;* and we are told (lxiv. 3) what their arrows are, even bitter words, such words as these, by which they endeavour to discourage hope in God, which David felt as a sword in his bones. (2.) He resists the temptation with a gracious abhorrence, *v.* 3. He looks upon this suggestion as striking at the foundations which every Israelite builds upon: "If you destroy the foundations, if you take good people off from their hope in God, if you can persuade them that their religion is a cheat and a jest and can banter them out of that, you ruin them, and break their hearts indeed, and make them of all men the most miserable." The principles of religion are the foundations on which the faith and hope of the righteous are built. These we are concerned, in interest as well as duty, to hold fast against all temptations to infidelity; for, if these be destroyed, if we let these go, *What can the righteous do?* Good people would be undone if they had not a God to go to, a God to trust to, and a future bliss to hope for.

4 The LORD *is* in his holy temple, the LORD's throne *is* in heaven: his eyes behold, his eyelids try, the children of men. 5 The LORD trieth the righteous: but the wicked and him that loveth violence his soul hateth. 6 Upon the wicked he shall rain snares, fire and brimstone, and a hor-

rible tempest: *this shall be* the portion of their cup. 7 For the righteous LORD loveth righteousness; his countenance doth behold the upright.

The shaking of a tree (they say) makes it take the deeper and faster root. The attempt of David's enemies to discourage his confidence in God engages him to cleave so much the more closely to his first principles, and to review them, which he here does, abundantly to his own satisfaction and the silencing of all temptations to infidelity. That which was shocking to his faith, and has been so to the faith of many, was the prosperity of wicked people in their wicked ways, and the straits and distresses which the best men are sometimes reduced to: hence such an evil thought as this was apt to arise, *Surely it is vain to serve God,* and we may call the proud happy. But, in order to stifle and shame all such thoughts, we are here called to consider,

I. That there is a God in heaven: *The Lord is in his holy temple* above, where, though he is out of our sight, we are not out of his. Let not the enemies of the saints insult over them, as if they were at a loss and at their wits' end: no, they have a God, and they know where to find him and how to direct their prayer unto him, as their Father in heaven. Or, He is in his holy temple, that is, in his church; he is a God in covenant and communion with his people, through a Mediator, of whom the temple was a type. We need not say, "Who shall go up to heaven, to fetch us thence a God to trust to?" No, the word is nigh us, and God in the word; his Spirit is in his saints, those living temples, and the Lord is that Spirit.

II. That this God governs the world. The Lord has not only his residence, but his throne, in heaven, and he has *set the dominion thereof in the earth* (Job xxxviii. 33); for, having *prepared his throne in the heavens, his kingdom ruleth over all,* ciii. 19. Hence the heavens are said *to rule,* Dan. iv. 26. Let us by faith see God on his throne, on his throne of glory, infinitely transcending the splendour and majesty of earthly princes—on his throne of government, giving law, giving motion, and giving aim, to all the creatures—on his throne of judgment, rendering to every man according to his works—and on his throne of grace, to which his people may come boldly for mercy and grace; we shall then see no reason to be discouraged by the pride and power of oppressors, or any of the afflictions that attend the righteous.

III. That this God perfectly knows every man's true character: *His eyes behold, his eye-lids try, the children of men;* he not only sees them, but he sees through them, not only knows all they say and do, but knows what they think, what they design, and how they really stand affected, whatever they pretend. We may know what men seem to be, but he knows what they are, as the refiner knows

what the value of the gold is when he has tried it. God is said to try *with his eyes,* and *his eye-lids,* because he knows men, not as earthly princes know men, by report and representation, but by his own strict inspection, which cannot err nor be imposed upon. This may comfort us when we are deceived in men, even in men that we think we have tried, that God's judgment of men, we are sure, is according to truth.

IV. That, if he afflict good people, it is for their trial and therefore for their good, *v.* 5. The Lord tries all the children of men that he may *do them good in their latter end,* Deut. viii. 16. Let not that therefore shake our foundations nor discourage our hope and trust in God.

V. That, however persecutors and oppressors may prosper and prevail awhile, they now lie under, and will for ever perish under, the wrath of God. 1. He is a holy God, and therefore hates them, and cannot endure to look upon them: *The wicked, and him that loveth violence, his soul hateth;* for nothing is more contrary to the rectitude and goodness of his nature. Their prosperity is so far from being an evidence of God's love that their abuse of it does certainly make them the objects of his hatred. He that hates nothing that he has made, yet hates those who have thus ill-made themselves. Dr. Hammond offers another reading of this verse: *The Lord trieth the righteous and the wicked* (distinguishes infallibly between them, which is more than we can do), and *he that loveth violence hateth his own soul,* that is, persecutors bring certain ruin upon themselves (Prov. viii. 36), as follows here. 2. He is a righteous Judge, and therefore he will punish them, *v.* 6. Their punishment will be, (1.) Inevitable: *Upon the wicked he shall rain snares.* Here is a double metaphor, to denote the unavoidableness of the punishment of wicked men. It shall be rained upon them from heaven (Job xx. 23), against which there is no fence and from which there is no escape; see Josh x. 11; 1 Sam. ii. 10. It shall surprise them as a sudden shower sometimes surprises the traveller in a summer's day. It shall be as snares upon them, to hold them fast, and keep them prisoners, till the day of reckoning comes. (2.) Very terrible. It is *fire, and brimstone, and a horrible tempest,* which plainly alludes to the destruction of Sodom and Gomorrah, and very fitly, for that destruction was intended for a figure of *the vengeance of eternal fire,* Jude 7. The fire of God's wrath, fastening upon the brimstone of their own guilt, will burn certainly and furiously, will burn to the lowest hell and the utmost line of eternity. What a horrible tempest are the wicked hurried away in at death! What a lake of fire and brimstone must they make their bed in for ever, in the congregation of the dead and damned! It is this that is here meant; it is this that shall be the portion of their cup, the heritage appointed them by the Almighty and allotted to them, Job xx. 29. This is the cup of trembling which shall be put into their hands, which they must *drink the dregs* of, lxxv. 8. Every man has the portion of his cup assigned him. Those who choose the Lord for the portion of their cup shall have what they choose, and be for ever happy in their choice (xvi. 5); but those who reject his grace shall be made to drink the cup of his fury, Jer. xxv. 15; Isa. li. 17; Hab. ii. 16.

VI. That, though honest good people may be run down and trampled upon, yet God does and will own them, and favour them, and smile upon them, and that is the reason why God will severely reckon with persecutors and oppressors, because those whom they oppress and persecute are dear to him; so that *whosoever toucheth them toucheth the apple of his eye, v.* 7. 1. He loves them and the work of his own grace in them. He is himself a righteous God, and therefore loves righteousness wherever he finds it and pleads the cause of the righteous that are injured and oppressed; he delights to execute judgment for them, ciii. 6. We must herein be followers of God, must love righteousness as he does, that we may keep ourselves always in his love. He looks graciously upon them: *His countenance doth behold the upright;* he is not only at peace with them, but well pleased in them, and he comforts them, and puts gladness into their hearts, by letting them know that he is so. He, like a tender father, looks upon them with pleasure, and they, like dutiful children, are pleased and abundantly satisfied with his smiles. They walk in the light of the Lord.

In singing this psalm we must encourage and engage ourselves to trust in God at all times, must depend upon him to protect our innocence and make us happy, must dread his frowns as worse than death and desire his favour as better than life.

PSALM XII. (12)

It is supposed that David penned this psalm in Saul's reign, when there was a general decay of honesty and piety both in court and country, which he here complains of to God, and very feelingly, for he himself suffered by the treachery of his false friends and the insolence of his sworn enemies. I. He begs help of God, because there were none among men whom he durst trust, ver. 1, 2. II. He foretels the destruction of his proud and threatening enemies, ver. 3, 4. III. He assures himself and others that, how ill soever things went now (ver. 8), God would preserve and secure to himself his own people (ver. 5, 7), and would certainly make good his promises to them, ver. 6. Whether this psalm was penned in Saul's reign or no, it is certainly calculated for a bad reign ; and perhaps David, in spirit, foresaw that some of his successors would bring things to as bad a pass as is here described, and treasured up this psalm for the use of the church then. "O tempora, O mores!—Oh the times! Oh the manners!"

To the chief musician upon Sheminith. A psalm of David.

HELP, Lord; for the godly man ceaseth; for the faithful fail from among the children of men. 2 They speak vanity every one with his neighbour: *with* flattering lips *and* with a double heart do they speak. 3

The Lord shall cut off all flattering lips, *and* the tongue that speaketh proud things : 4 Who have said,With our tongue will we prevail ; our lips *are* our own : who *is* lord over us ? 5 For the oppression of the poor, for the sighing of the needy, now will I arise, saith the Lord ; I will set *him* in safety *from him that* puffeth at him. 6 The words of the Lord *are* pure words : *as* silver tried in a furnace of earth, purified seven times. 7 Thou shalt keep them, O Lord, thou shalt preserve them from this generation for ever. 8 The wicked walk on every side, when the vilest men are exalted.

This psalm furnishes us with good thoughts for bad times, in which, though the prudent will keep silent (Amos v. 13) because a man may then be made an offender for a word, yet we may comfort ourselves with such suitable meditations and prayers as are here got ready to our hand.

I. Let us see here what it is that makes the times bad, and when they may be said to be so. Ask the children of this world what it is in their account that makes the times bad, and they will tell you, Scarcity of money, decay of trade, and the desolations of war, make the times bad. But the scripture lays the badness of the times upon causes of another nature. 2 Tim. iii. 1, *Perilous times shall come,* for iniquity shall abound; and that is the thing David here complains of.

1. When there is a general decay of piety and honesty among men the times are then truly bad (*v.* 1): *When the godly man ceases and the faithful fail.* Observe how these two characters are here put together, the godly and the faithful. As there is no true policy, so there is no true piety, without honesty. Godly men are faithful men, *fast* men, so they have sometimes been called ; their word is as confirming as their oath, as binding as their bond; they make conscience of being true both to God and man. They are here said to cease and fail, either by death or by desertion, or by both. Those that were godly and faithful were taken away, and those that were left had sadly degenerated and were not what they had been ; so that there were few or no good people that were Israelites indeed to be met with. Perhaps he meant that there were no godly faithful men among Saul's courtiers; if he meant there were few or none in Israel, we hope he was under the same mistake that Elijah was, who thought he only was left alone, when God had 7000 who kept their integrity (Rom. xi. 3); or he meant that there were few in comparison; there was a general decay of religion and virtue (and the times are bad, very bad, when

it is so), not a man to be found that executes judgment, Jer. v. 1.

2. When dissimulation and flattery have corrupted and debauched all conversation, then the times are very bad (*v.* 2), when men are generally so profligate that they make no conscience of a lie, are so spiteful as to design against their neighbours the worst of mischiefs, and yet so base as to cover the design with the most specious and plausible pretences and professions of friendship. Thus *they speak vanity* (that is, falsehood and a lie) *every one to his neighbour, with flattering lips and a double heart.* They will kiss and kill (as Joab did Abner and Amasa in David's own time), will smile in your face and cut your throat. This is the devil's image complete, a complication of malice and falsehood. The times are bad indeed when there is no such thing as sincerity to be met with, when an honest man knows not whom to believe nor whom to trust, nor dares put confidence in a friend, in a guide, Mic. vii. 5, 6; Jer. ix. 4, 5. Woe to those who help to make the times thus perilous.

3. When the enemies of God, and religion, and religious people, are impudent and daring, and threaten to run down all that is just and sacred, then the times are very bad, when proud sinners have arrived at such a pitch of impiety as to say, "*With our tongue will we prevail* against the cause of virtue; *our lips are our own* and we may say what we will; *who is lord over us,* either to restrain us or to call us to an account?" *v.* 4. This bespeaks, (1.) A proud conceit of themselves and confidence in themselves, as if the point were indeed gained by eating forbidden fruit, and they were as gods, independent and self-sufficient, infallible in their knowledge of good and evil and therefore fit to be oracles, irresistible in their power and therefore fit to be lawgivers, that could prevail with their tongues, and, like God himself, speak and it is done. (2.) An insolent contempt of God's dominion as if he had no propriety in them— *Our lips are our own* (an unjust pretension, for who made man's mouth, in whose hand is his breath, and whose is the air he breathes in?) and as if he had no authority either to command them or to judge them: *Who is Lord over us?* Like Pharaoh, Exod. v. 2. This is as absurd and unreasonable as the former; for he in whom we live, and move, and have our being, must needs be, by an indisputable title, Lord over us.

4. When the poor and needy are oppressed, and abused, and puffed at, then the times are very bad. This is implied (*v.* 5) where God himself takes notice of *the oppression of the poor* and *the sighing of the needy;* they are oppressed because they are poor, have all manner of wrong done them merely because they are not in a capacity to right themselves. Being thus oppressed, they dare not speak for themselves, lest their defence should be made their offence; but they sigh, secretly

bemoaning their calamities, and pouring out their souls in sighs before God. If their oppressors be spoken to on their behalf, they puff at them, make light of their own sin and the misery of the poor, and lay neither to heart; see x. 5.

5. When wickedness abounds, and goes barefaced, under the protection and countenance of those in authority, then the times are very bad, v. 8. *When the vilest men are exalted* to places of trust and power (who, instead of putting the laws in execution against vice and injustice and punishing the wicked according to their merits, patronise and protect them, give them countenance, and support their reputation by their own example), then *the wicked walk on every side;* they swarm in all places, and go up and down seeking to deceive, debauch, and destroy others; they are neither afraid nor ashamed to discover themselves; they declare their sin as Sodom and there is none to check or control them. Bad men are base men, the vilest of men, and they are so though they are ever so highly exalted in this world. Antiochus the illustrious the scripture calls *a vile person,* Dan. xi. 21. But it is bad with a kingdom when such are preferred; no marvel if wickedness then grows impudent and insolent. *When the wicked bear rule the people mourn.*

II. Let us now see what good thoughts we are here furnished with for such bad times; and what times we may yet be reserved for we cannot tell. When times are thus bad it is comfortable to think,

1. That we have a God to go to, from whom we may ask and expect the redress of all our grievances. This he begins with (v. 1): "*Help, Lord, for the godly man ceaseth.* All other helps and helpers fail; even the godly and faithful, who should lend a helping hand to support the dying cause of religion, are gone, and therefore whither shall we seek but to thee?" Note, When godly faithful people cease and fail it is time to cry, *Help, Lord!* The abounding of iniquity threatens a deluge. "Help, Lord, help the virtuous; few seek to hold fast their integrity, and to stand in the gap; help to save thy own interest in the world from sinking. *It is time for thee, Lord, to work.*"

2. That God will certainly reckon with false and proud men, and will punish and restrain their insolence. They are above the control of men and set them at defiance. Men cannot discover the falsehood of flatterers, nor humble the haughtiness of those that speak proud things; but the righteous God will *cut off all flattering lips,* that give the traitor's kiss and speak words softer than oil when war is in the heart; he will pluck out *the tongue that speaks proud things* against God and religion, v. 3. Some translate it as a prayer, "May God cut off those false and spiteful lips." *Let lying lips be put to silence.*

3. That God will, in due time, work de-

liverance for his oppressed people, and shelter them from the malicious designs of their persecutors (v. 5): *Now, will I arise, saith the Lord.* This promise of God, which David here delivered by the spirit of prophecy, is an answer to that petition which he put up to God by the spirit of prayer. "Help, Lord," says he; "I will," says God; "here I am, with seasonable and effectual help." (1.) It is seasonable, in the fittest time. [1.] When the oppressors are in the height of their pride and insolence—when they say, *Who is lord over us?*—then is God's time to let them know, to their cost, that he is above them. [2.] When the oppressed are in the depth of their distress and despondency, when they are sighing like Israel in Egypt by reason of the cruel bondage, then is God's time to appear for them, as for Israel when they were most dejected and Pharaoh was most elevated. *Now will I arise.* Note, There is a time fixed for the rescue of oppressed innocency; that time will come, and we may be sure it is the fittest time, cii. 13. (2.) It is effectual: *I will set him in safety,* or in salvation, not only protect him, but restore him to his former prosperity, will *bring him out into a wealthy place* (lxvi. 12), so that, upon the whole, he shall lose nothing by his sufferings.

4. That, though men are false, God is faithful; though they are not to be trusted, God is. They speak vanity and flattery, but *the words of the Lord are pure words* (v. 6), not only all true, but all pure, like silver tried in a furnace of earth or a crucible. It denotes, (1.) The sincerity of God's word, every thing is really as it is there represented and not otherwise; it does not jest with us, nor impose upon us, nor has it any other design towards us than our own good. (2.) The preciousness of God's word; it is of great and intrinsic value, like silver refined to the highest degree; it has nothing in it to depreciate it. (3.) The many proofs that have been given of its power and truth; it has been often tried, all the saints in all ages have trusted it and so tried it, and it never deceived them nor frustrated their expectation, but they have all set to their seal that God's word is true, with an *Experto crede* —*Trust one that has made trial;* they have found it so. Probably this refers especially to these promises of succouring and relieving the poor and oppressed. Their friends put them in hopes that they will do something for them, and yet prove a broken reed; but the words of God are what we may rely upon; and the less confidence is to be put in men's words let us with the more assurance trust in God's word.

5. That God will secure his chosen remnant to himself, how bad soever the times are (v. 7): *Thou shalt preserve them from this generation for ever.* This intimates that, as long as the world stands, there will be a generation of proud and wicked men in it, more or less, who will threaten by their wretched arts to ruin religion, by *wearing out the saints of the Most High,* Dan. vii. 25. But let God alone to maintain his own interest and to preserve his own people. He will keep them from this generation, (1.) From being debauched by them and drawn away from God, from mingling with them and learning their works. In times of general apostasy the Lord knows those that are his, and they shall be enabled to keep their integrity. (2.) From being destroyed and rooted out by them. The church is built upon a rock, and so well fortified that the gates of hell shall not prevail against it. In the worst of times God has his remnant, and in every age will reserve to himself a holy seed and preserve that to his heavenly kingdom.

In singing this psalm, and praying it over, we must bewail the general corruption of manners, thank God that things are not worse than they are, but pray and hope that they will be better in God's due time.

PSALM XIII. (13)

This psalm is the deserted soul's case and cure. Whether it was penned upon any particular occasion does not appear, but in general, I. David sadly complains that God had long withdrawn from him and delayed to relieve him, ver. 1, 2. II. He earnestly prays to God to consider his case and comfort him, ver. 3, 4. III. He assures himself of an answer of peace, and therefore concludes the psalm with joy and triumph, because he concludes his deliverance to be as good as wrought, ver. 5, 6.

To the chief musician. A psalm of David.

HOW long wilt thou forget me, O Lord? for ever? how long wilt thou hide thy face from me? 2 How long shall I take counsel in my soul, *having* sorrow in my heart daily? how long shall mine enemy be exalted over me? 3 Consider *and* hear me, O Lord my God: lighten mine eyes, lest I sleep the *sleep of* death; 4 Lest mine enemy say, I have prevailed against him; *and* those that trouble me rejoice when I am moved. 5 But I have trusted in thy mercy; my heart shall rejoice in thy salvation. 6 I will sing unto the Lord, because he hath dealt bountifully with me.

David, in affliction, is here pouring out his soul before God; his address is short, but the method is very observable, and of use for direction and encouragement.

I. His troubles extort complaints (v. 1, 2); and the afflicted have liberty to *pour out their complaint before the Lord,* cii. title. It is some ease to a troubled spirit to give vent to its griefs, especially to give vent to them at the throne of grace, where we are sure to find one who is afflicted in the afflictions of his people and is troubled with the feeling of their infirmities; thither we have boldness of access by faith, and there we have παῤῥησία —*freedom of speech.* Observe here,

1. What David complains of. (1.) God's unkindness; so he construed it, and it was his infirmity. He thought God had forgot-

281

ten him, had forgotten his promises to him, his covenant with him, his former loving-kindness which he had shown him and which he took to be an earnest of further mercy, had forgotten that there was such a man in the world, who needed and expected relief and succour from him.· Thus Zion said, *My God has forgotten me* (Isa xlx. 14), Israel said, *My way is hidden from the Lord*, Isa. xl. 27. Not that any good man can doubt the omniscience, goodness, and faithfulness of God; but it is a peevish expression of prevailing fear, which yet, when it arises from a high esteem and earnest desire of God's favour, though it be indecent and culpable, shall be passed by and pardoned, for the second thought will retract it and repent of it. God hid his face from him, so that he wanted that inward comfort in God which he used to have, and herein was a type of Christ upon the cross, crying out, *My God, why hast thou forsaken me?* God sometimes hides his face from his own children, and leaves them in the dark concerning their interest in him; and this they lay to heart more than any outward trouble whatsoever. (2.) His own uneasiness. [1.] He was racked with care, which filled his head: *I take counsel in my soul:* "I am at a loss, and am *inops consilii*—*without a friend to advise with* that I can put any confidence in, and therefore am myself continually projecting what to do to help myself; but none of my projects are likely to take effect, so that I am at my wits' end, and in a continual agitation." Anxious cares are heavy burdens with which good people often load themselves more than they need. [2.] He was overwhelmed with sorrow, which filled his heart: *I have sorrow in my heart daily.* He had a constant disposition to sorrow and it preyed upon his spirits, not only in the night, when he was silent and solitary, but by day too, when lighter griefs are diverted and dissipated by conversation and business; nay, every day brought with it fresh occasions of grief; *the clouds returned after the rain.* The bread of sorrow is sometimes the saint's daily bread. Our Master himself was a man of sorrows. (3.) His enemies' insolence, which added to his grief. Saul his great enemy, and others under him, were exalted over him, triumphed in his distress, pleased themselves with his grief, and promised themselves a complete victory over him. This he complained of as reflecting dishonour upon God, and his power and promise. 2. How he expostulates with God hereupon: "*How long* shall it be thus?" And, "Shall it be thus *for ever?*" Long afflictions try our patience and often tire it. It is a common temptation, when trouble lasts long, to think it will last always; despondency then turns into despair, and those that have long been without joy begin, at last, to be without hope. "Lord, tell me how long thou wilt hide thy face, and assure me that it shall not be for ever, but

that thou wilt return at length in mercy to me, and then I shall the more easily bear my present troubles."

II. His complaints stir up his prayers, *v.* 3, 4. We should never allow ourselves to make any complaints but what are fit to be offered up to God and what drive us to our knees. Observe here,

1. What his petitions are: *Consider* my case, *hear* my complaints, and *enlighten my eyes*, that is, (1.) "Strengthen my faith;" for faith is the eye of the soul, with which it sees above, and sees through, the things of sense. "Lord, enable me to look beyond my present troubles and to foresee a happy issue of them." (2.) "Guide my way; enable me to look about me, that I may avoid the snares which are laid for me." (3.) "Refresh my soul with the joy of thy salvation." That which revives the drooping spirits is said to *enlighten the eyes*, 1 Sam. xiv. 27; Ezra ix. 8. "Lord, scatter the cloud of melancholy which darkens my eyes, and let my countenance be made pleasant."

2. What his pleas are. He mentions his relation to God and interest in him *(O Lord my God!)* and insists upon the greatness of the peril, which called for speedy relief and succour. If his eyes were not enlightened quickly, (1.) He concludes that he must perish: "I shall *sleep the sleep of death;* I cannot live under the weight of all this care and grief." Nothing is more killing to a soul than the want of God's favour, nothing more reviving than the return of it. (2.) That then his enemies would triumph: "*Lest my enemy say*, So would I have it; lest Saul, lest Satan, be gratified in my fall." It would gratify the pride of his enemy: He will say, "*I have prevailed*, I have gotten the day, and been too hard for him and his God." It would gratify the malice of his enemies: They will *rejoice when I am moved*. And will it be for God's honour to suffer them thus to trample upon all that is sacred both in heaven and earth?

III. His prayers are soon turned into praises *(v.* 5, 6): But *my heart shall rejoice and I will sing to the Lord.* What a surprising change is here in a few lines! In the beginning of the psalm we have him drooping, trembling, and ready to sink into melancholy and despair; but, in the close of it, rejoicing in God, and elevated and enlarged in his praises. See the power of faith, the power of prayer, and how good it is to draw near to God. If we bring our cares and griefs to the throne of grace, and leave them there, we may go away like Hannah, and our *countenance will be no more sad*, 1 Sam. i. 18. And here observe the method of his comfort. 1. God's mercy is the support of his faith. "My case is bad enough, and I am ready to think it deplorable, till I consider the infinite goodness of God; but, finding I have that to trust to, I am comforted, though I have no merit of my own.

In former distresses *I have trusted in the mercy of God,* and I never found that it failed me; his mercy has in due time relieved me and my confidence in it has in the mean time supported me. Even in the depth of this distress, when God hid his face from me, when without were fightings and within were fears, yet *I trusted in the mercy of God* and that was as an anchor in a storm, by the help of which, though I was tossed, I was not overset." And still *I do trust in thy mercy;* so some read it. " I refer myself to that, with an assurance that it will do well for me at last." This he pleads with God, knowing what pleasure he takes *in those that hope in his mercy,* cxlvii. 11. 2. His faith in God's mercy filled his heart with *joy in his salvation;* for joy and peace come by *believing,* Rom. xv. 13. *Believing, you rejoice,* 1 Pet. i. 8. Having put his trust in the mercy of God, he is fully assured of salvation, and that his heart, which was now daily grieving, should *rejoice in that salvation.* Though weeping endure long, joy will return. 3. His joy in God's salvation would fill his mouth with songs of praise *(v.* 6): " *I will sing unto the Lord,* sing in remembrance of what he has done formerly; though I should never recover the peace I have had, I will die blessing God that ever I had it. He has dealt bountifully with me formerly, and he shall have the glory of that, however he is pleased to deal with me now. I will sing in hope of what he will do for me at last, being confident that all will end well, will end everlastingly well. But he speaks of it as a thing past *(He has dealt bountifully with me),* because by faith he had received the earnest of the salvation and he was as confident of it as if it had been done already.

In singing this psalm and praying it over, if we have not the same complaints to make that David had, we must thank God that we have not, dread and deprecate his withdrawings, sympathise with those that are troubled in mind, and encourage ourselves in our most holy faith and joy.

PSALM XIV. (14)

It does not appear upon what occasion this psalm was penned nor whether upon any particular occasion. Some say David penned it when Saul persecuted him; others, when Absalom rebelled against him. But they are mere conjectures, which have not certainty enough to warrant us to expound the psalm by them. The apostle, in quoting part of this psalm (Rom. iii. 10, &c.) to prove that Jews and Gentiles are all under sin (ver. 9) and that all the world is guilty before God (ver. 19), leads us to understand it, in general, as a description of the depravity of human nature, the sinfulness of the sin we are conceived and born in, and the deplorable corruption of a great part of mankind, even of the world that lies in wickedness, 1 John v. 19. But as in those psalms which are designed to discover our remedy in Christ there is commonly an allusion to David himself, yea, and some passages that are to be understood primarily of him (as in psalm ii., xvi., xxii., and others), so in this psalm, which is designed to discover our wound by sin, there is an allusion to David's enemies and persecutors, and other oppressors of good men at that time, to whom some passages have an immediate reference. In all the psalms from the 3d to this (except the 8th) David had been complaining of those that hated and persecuted him, insulted him and abused him; now here he traces all those bitter streams to the fountain, the general corruption of nature, and sees that not his enemies only, but all the children of men, were thus corrupted. Here is, I. A charge exhibited against a wicked world, ver. 1. II. The proof of the charge, ver. 2, 3. III. A serious expostulation with sinners, especially with persecutors, upon it, ver. 4—6. IV. A believing prayer for the salvation of Israel and a joyful expectation of it, ver. 7.

To the chief musician. A psalm of David.

THE fool hath said in his heart, *There is* no God. They are corrupt, they have done abominable works, *there is* none that doeth good. 2 The LORD looked down from heaven upon the children of men, to see if there were any that did understand, *and* seek God. 3 They are all gone aside, they are *all* together become filthy : *there is* none that doeth good, no, not one.

If we apply our hearts as Solomon did (Eccl. vii. 25) *to search out the wickedness of folly, even of foolishness and madness,* these verses will assist us in the search and will show us that sin is exceedingly sinful. Sin is the disease of mankind, and it appears here to be malignant and epidemic.

1. See how malignant it is *(v.* 1) in two things :—

(1.) The contempt it puts upon the honour of God : for there is something of practical atheism at the bottom of all sin. *The fool hath said in his heart, There is no God.* We are sometimes tempted to think, " Surely there never was so much atheism and profaneness as there is in our days ;" but we see the former days were no better ; even in David's time there were those who had arrived at such a height of impiety as to deny the very being of a God and the first and self-evident principles of religion. Observe, [1.] The sinner here described. He is one that *saith in his heart, There is no God;* he is an atheist. "There is no *Elohim,* no Judge or governor of the world, no providence presiding over the affairs of men." They cannot doubt of the being of God, but will question his dominion. He says this *in his heart ;* it is not his judgment, but his imagination. He cannot satisfy himself that there is none, but he wishes there were none, and pleases himself with the fancy that it is possible there may be none. He cannot be sure there is one, and therefore he is willing to think there is none. He dares not speak it out, lest he be confuted, and so undeceived, but he whispers it secretly *in his heart,* for the silencing of the clamours of his conscience and the emboldening of himself in his evil ways. [2.] The character of this sinner. He is a fool; he is simple and unwise, and this is an evidence of it; he is wicked and profane, and this is the cause of it. Note, Atheistical thoughts are very foolish wicked thoughts, and they are at the bottom of a great deal of the wickedness that is in this world. The word of God is a *discerner of these thoughts,* and puts a just brand on him that harbours them. *Nabal is his name, and folly is with him ;* for he thinks against the clearest light, against his own knowledge and convictions, and the common sentiments of all the wise and sober part of mankind. No man will say, *There is no God* till he is so hardened in sin that it has become his interest that there should be none to call him to an account.

(2.) The disgrace and debasement it puts upon the nature of man. Sinners are corrupt, quite degenerated from what man was in his innocent estate : *They have become filthy* (*v.* 3), putrid. All their faculties are so disordered that they have become odious to their Maker and utterly incapable of answering the ends of their creation. *They are corrupt* indeed ; for, [1.] They do no good, but are the unprofitable burdens of the earth; they do God no service, bring him no honour, nor do themselves any real kindness. [2.] They do a great deal of hurt. *They have done abominable works,* for such all sinful works are. Sin is an abomination to God ; it is that *abominable thing which he hates* (Jer. xliv. 4), and, sooner or later, it will be so to the sinner ; it will be *found to be hateful* (xxxvi. 2), an *abomination of desolation,* that is, making desolate, Matt. xxiv. 15. This follows upon their saying, *There is no God ;* for those that *profess they know God, but in works deny him, are abominable, and to every good work reprobate,* Tit. i. 16.

2. See how epidemic this disease is ; it has infected the whole race of mankind. To prove this, God himself is here brought in for a witness, and he is an eye-witness, *v.* 2, 3. Observe, (1.) His enquiry: *The Lord looked down from heaven,* a place of prospect, which commands this lower world ; thence, with an all-seeing eye, he took a view of all *the children of men,* and the question was, *Whether there were any* among them *that did understand* themselves aright, their duty and interests, and did seek God and set him before them. He that made this search was not only one that could find out a good man if he was to be found, though ever so obscure, but one that would be glad to find out one, and would be sure to take notice of him, as of Noah in the old world. (2.) The result of this enquiry, *v.* 3. Upon search, upon his search, it appeared, *They have all gone aside,* the apostasy is universal, *there is none that doeth good, no, not one,* till the free and mighty grace of God has wrought a change. Whatever good is in any of the children of men, or is done by them, it is not of themselves ; it is God's work in them. When God had made the world he looked upon his own work, and *all was very good* (Gen. i. 31) ; but, some time after, he looked upon man's work, and, behold, all was very bad (Gen. vi. 5), every operation of the thought of man's heart was evil, only evil, and that continually. They have gone aside from the right way of their duty, the way that leads to happiness, and have turned into the paths of the destroyer.

In singing this let us lament the corruption of our own nature, and see what need we have of the grace of God ; and, since that which is born of the flesh is flesh, let us not marvel that we are told we must be born again.

284

4 Have all the workers of iniquity no knowledge ? who eat up my people *as* they eat bread, and call not upon the Lord. 5 There were they in great fear : for God *is* in the generation of the righteous. 6 Ye have shamed the counsel of the poor, because the Lord *is* his refuge. 7 Oh that the salvation of Israel *were come* out of Zion ! when the Lord bringeth back the captivity of his people, Jacob shall rejoice, *and* Israel shall be glad.

In these verses the psalmist endeavours,

I. To convince sinners of the evil and danger of the way they are in, how secure soever they are in that way. Three things he shows them, which, it may be, they are not very willing to see—their wickedness, their folly, and their danger, while they are apt to believe themselves very wise, and good, and safe. See here,

1. Their wickedness. This is described in four instances :—(1.) They are themselves *workers of iniquity ;* they design it, they practise it, and take as much pleasure in it as ever any man did in his business. (2) They *eat up God's people* with as much greediness *as they eat bread,* such an innate and inveterate enmity they have to them, and so heartily do they desire their ruin, because they really hate God, whose people they are. It is meat and drink to persecutors to be doing mischief ; it is as agreeable to them as their necessary food. They eat up God's people easily, daily, securely, without either check of conscience when they do it or remorse of conscience when they have done it; as Joseph's brethren *cast him into a pit* and then *sat down to eat bread,* Gen. xxxvii. 24, 25. See Mic. iii. 2, 3. (3.) They *call not upon the Lord.* Note, Those that care not for God's people, for God's poor, care not for God himself, but live in contempt of him. The reason why people run into all manner of wickedness, even the worst, is because they do not call upon God for his grace. What good can be expected from those that live without prayer ? (4) They *shame the counsel of the poor,* and upbraid them with making God their refuge, as David's enemies upbraided him, xi. 1. Note, Those are very wicked indeed, and have a great deal to answer for, who not only shake off religion and live without it themselves, but say and do what they can to put others out of conceit with it that are well-inclined—with the duties of it, as if they were mean, melancholy, and unprofitable, and with the privileges of it, as if they were insufficient to make a man safe and happy. Those that banter religion and religious people will find, to their cost, it is ill jesting with edged-tools and dangerous persecuting those that make God their refuge. *Be you not mockers, lest your bands be made strong.* He shows them,

2. Their folly: *They have no knowledge;* this is obvious, for if they had any knowledge of God, if they did rightly understand themselves, and would but consider things as men, they would not be so abusive and barbarous as they are to the people of God.

3. Their danger (*v.* 5): *There were they in great fear.* There, where they ate up God's people, their own consciences condemned what they did, and filled them with secret terrors; they sweetly sucked the blood of the saints, but in their bowels it is turned, and become the gall of asps. Many instances there have been of proud and cruel persecutors who have been made like Pashur, *Magormissabibs*—*terrors to themselves* and all about them. Those that will not fear God perhaps may be made to fear at the shaking of a leaf.

II. He endeavours to comfort the people of God, 1. With what they have. They have God's presence (*v.* 5): He *is in the generation of the righteous.* They have his protection (*v.* 6): *The Lord is their refuge.* This is as much their security as it is the terror of their enemies, who may jeer them for their confidence in God, but cannot jeer them out of it. In the judgment-day it will add to the terror and confusion of sinners to see God own the generation of the righteous, which they have hated and bantered. 2. With what they hope for; and that is the *salvation of Israel, v.* 7. When David was driven out by Absalom and his rebellious accomplices, he comforted himself with an assurance that God would in due time *turn again his captivity*, to the joy of all his good subjects. But surely this pleasing prospect looks further. He had, in the beginning of the psalm, lamented the general corruption of mankind; and, in the melancholy view of that, wishes for the salvation which in the fulness of time was to come out of Zion—salvation from sin, that great salvation which should be wrought out by the Redeemer, who was expected *to come to Zion, to turn away ungodliness from Jacob*, Rom. xi. 26. The world is bad; O that the Messiah would come and change its character! There is a universal corruption; O for the times of reformation! Those will be as joyful times as these are melancholy ones. Then shall God *turn again the captivity of his people;* for the Redeemer shall *ascend on high, and lead captivity captive*, and Jacob shall then rejoice. The triumphs of Zion's King will be the joys of Zion's children. The second coming of Christ, finally to extinguish the dominion of sin and Satan, will be the completing of this salvation, which is the hope, and will be the joy, of every Israelite indeed. With the assurance of that we should, in singing this, comfort ourselves and one another, with reference to the present sins of sinners and sufferings of saints.

PSALM XV.

The scope of this short but excellent psalm is to show us the way to heaven, and to convince us that, if we would be happy, we must be holy and honest. Christ, who is himself the way, and in whom we must walk as our way, has also shown us the same way that is here prescribed, Matt. xix. 17. "If thou wilt enter into life, keep the commandments." In this psalm, I. By the question (ver. 1) we are directed and excited to enquire for the way. II. By the answer to that question, in the rest of the psalm, we are directed to walk in that way, ver. 2—5. III. By the assurance given in the close of the psalm of the safety and happiness of those who answer these characters **we are** encouraged to walk in that way, ver. 5.

A psalm of David. (15)

LORD, who shall abide in thy tabernacle? who shall dwell in thy holy hill? 2 He that walketh uprightly, and worketh righteousness, and speaketh the truth in his heart. 3 *He that* backbiteth not with his tongue, nor doeth evil to his neighbour, nor taketh up a reproach against his neighbour. 4 In whose eyes a vile person is contemned; but he honoureth them that fear the LORD. *He that* sweareth to *his own* hurt, and changeth not. 5 *He that* putteth not out his money to usury, nor taketh reward against the innocent. He that doeth these *things* shall never be moved.

Here is, I. A very serious and weighty question concerning the characters of a citizen of Zion (*v.* 1): "*Lord, who shall abide in thy tabernacle?* Let me know who shall go to heaven." Not, who by name (in this way the *Lord* only knows those that are his), but who by description: "What kind of people are those whom thou wilt own and crown with distinguishing and everlasting favours?" This supposes that it is a great privilege to be a citizen of Zion, an unspeakable honour and advantage,—that all are not thus privileged, but a remnant only,—and that men are not entitled to this privilege by their birth and blood: all shall not *abide in God's tabernacle* that have Abraham to their father, but, according as men's hearts and lives are, so will their lot be. It concerns us all to put this question to ourselves, *Lord, what shall I be, and do, that I may abide in thy tabernacle?* Luke xviii. 18; Acts xvi. 30. 1. Observe to whom this enquiry is addressed—to God himself. Note, Those that would find the way to heaven must look up to God, must take direction from his word and beg direction from his Spirit. It is fit he himself should give laws to his servants, and appoint the conditions of his favours, and tell who are his and who not. 2. How it is expressed in Old-Testament language. (1.) By the *tabernacle* we may understand the church militant, typified by Moses's tabernacle, fitted to a wilderness-state, mean and movable. There God manifests himself, and there he meets his people, as of old in the tabernacle of the testimony, the tabernacle of meeting. Who shall dwell in this tabernacle? Who shall be accounted a true living member of God's church, admitted among the spiritual priests to lodge in the courts of this tabernacle? We are concerned to enquire this, because many pretend to a place in this tabernacle who really have no part nor lot in the matter. (2.) By the *holy hill* we may understand the church triumphant, alluding to Mount Zion, on which the temple was to be built by Solomon. It is the happiness of glorified saints that they dwell in that holy hill; they are at home there: they shall be for ever there. It concerns us to know who shall dwell there, that we may make it sure to ourselves that we shall have a place among them, and may then take the comfort of it, and rejoice in prospect of that holy hill.

II. A very plain and particular answer to this question. Those that desire to know their duty, with a resolution to do it, will find the scripture a very faithful director and conscience a faithful monitor. Let us see then the particular characters of a citizen of Zion.

1. He is one that is sincere and entire in his religion: He *walketh uprightly*, according to the condition of the covenant (Gen. xvii. 1), " *Walk before me, and be thou perfect*" (it is the same word that is here used) " and then thou shalt find me a God all-sufficient." He is really what he professes to be, is sound at heart, and can approve himself to God, in his integrity, in all he does; his conversation is uniform, and he is of a piece with himself, and endeavours to stand complete in all the will of God. His eye perhaps is weak, but it is single; he has his spots indeed, but he does not paint; he is an *Israelite indeed in whom is no guile*, John i. 47; 2 Cor. i. 12. I know no religion but sincerity.

2. He is one that is conscientiously honest and just in all his dealings, faithful and fair to all with whom he has to do: He *worketh righteousness;* he walks in all the ordinances and commandments of the Lord, and takes care to give all their due, is just both to God and man; and, in speaking to both, he speaks that which is *the truth in his heart;* his prayers, professions, and promises, to God, come not out of feigned lips, nor dares he tell a lie, or so much as equivocate, in his converse or commerce with men. He walks by the rules of righteousness and truth, and scorns and abhors the gains of injustice and fraud. He reckons that that cannot be a good bargain, nor a saving one, which is made with a lie, and that he who wrongs his neighbour, though ever so plausibly, will prove, in the end, to have done the greatest injury to himself.

3. He is one that contrives to do all the good he can to his neighbours, but is very careful to do hurt to no man, and is, in a particular manner, tender of his neighbour's reputation, *v.* 3. He *does no evil* at all *to his neighbour* willingly or designedly, nothing to offend or grieve his spirit, nothing to prejudice the health or ease of his body, nothing to injure him in his estate or secular interests, in his family or relations; but walks by that

286

golden rule of equity, To do as he would be done by. He is especially careful not to injure his neighbour in his good name, though many, who would not otherwise wrong their neighbours, make nothing of that. If any man, in this matter, bridles not his tongue, his religion is vain. He knows the worth of a good name, and therefore *he backbites not*, defames no man, speaks evil of no man, makes not others' faults the subject of his common talk, much less of his sport and ridicule, nor speaks of them with pleasure, nor at all but for edification. He makes the best of every body, and the worst of nobody. He does not *take up a reproach*, that is, he neither raises it nor receives it; he gives no credit nor countenance to a calumny, but frowns upon a backbiting tongue, and so silences it, Prov. xxv. 23. If an ill-natured character of his neighbour be given him, or an ill-natured story be told him, he will disprove it if he can; if not, it shall die with him and go no further. His *charity will cover a multitude of sins.*

4. He is one that values men by their virtue and piety, and not by the figure they make in the world, *v.* 5. (1.) He thinks the better of no man's wickedness for his pomp and grandeur: *In his eyes a vile person is contemned.* Wicked people are vile people, worthless and good for nothing (so the word signifies), as dross, as chaff, and as salt that has lost its savour. They are vile in their choices (Jer. ii. 13), in their practices, Isa. xxxii. 6. For this wise and good men contemn them, not denying them civil honour and respect as men, as men in authority and power perhaps (1 Pet. ii. 17, Rom. xiii. 7), but, in their judgment of them, agreeing with the word of God. They are so far from envying them that they pity them, despising their gains (Isa. xxxiii. 15), as turning to no account, their dainties (cxli. 4), their pleasures (Heb. xi. 24, 25) as sapless and insipid. They despise their society (cxix. 115; 2 Kings iii. 14); they despise their taunts and threats, and are not moved by them, nor disturbed at them; they despise the feeble efforts of their impotent malice (ii. 1, 4), and will shortly triumph in their fall, lii. 6, 7. God despises them, and they are of his mind. (2.) He thinks the worse of no man's piety for his poverty and meanness, *but he knows those that fear the Lord.* He reckons that serious piety, wherever it is found, puts an honour upon a man, and makes his face to shine, more than wealth, or wit, or a great name among men, does or can. He honours such, esteems them very highly in love, desires their friendship and conversation and an interest in their prayers, is glad of an opportunity to show them respect or do them a good office, pleads their cause and speaks of them with veneration, rejoices when they prosper, grieves when they are removed, and their memory, when they are gone, is precious with him. By this we may judge of

ourselves in some measure. What rules do we go by in judging of others?

5. He is one that always prefers a good conscience before any secular interest or advantage whatsoever; for, if he has promised upon oath to do any thing, though afterwards it appear much to his damage and prejudice in his worldly estate, yet he adheres to it and *changes not, v.* 4. See how weak-sighted and short-sighted even wise and good men may be; they may *swear to their own hurt,* which they were not aware of when they took the oath. But see how strong the obligation of an oath is, that a man must rather suffer loss to himself and his family than wrong his neighbour by breaking his oath. An oath is a sacred thing, which we must not think to play fast and loose with.

6. He is one that will not increase his estate by any unjust practices, *v.* 5. (1.) Not by extortion : *He putteth not out his money to usury,* that he may live at ease upon the labours of others, while he is in a capacity for improving it by his own industry. Not that it is any breach of the law of justice or charity for the lender to share in the profit which the borrower makes of his money, any more than for the owner of the land to demand rent from the occupant, money being, by art and labour, as improvable as land. But a citizen of Zion will freely lend to the poor, according to his ability, and not be rigorous and severe in recovering his right from those that are reduced by Providence. (2.) Not by bribery : He will not *take a reward against the innocent ;* if he be any way employed in the administration of public justice, he will not, for any gain, or hope of it, to himself, do any thing to the prejudice of a righteous cause.

III. The psalm concludes with a ratification of this character of the citizen of Zion. He is like Zion-hill itself, which cannot be moved, but abides for ever, cxxv. 1. Every true living member of the church, like the church itself, is built upon a rock, which the gates of hell cannot prevail against : *He that doeth these things shall never be moved ;* shall not be moved *for ever,* so the word is. The grace of God shall always be sufficient for him, to preserve him safe and blameless to the heavenly kingdom. Temptations shall not overcome him, troubles shall not overwhelm him, nothing shall rob him of his present peace nor his future bliss.

In singing this psalm we must teach and admonish ourselves, and one another, to answer the characters here given of the citizen of Zion, that we may never be moved from God's tabernacle on earth, and may arrive, at last, at that holy hill where we shall be for ever out of the reach of temptation and danger.

PSALM XVI. ⑯

This psalm has something of David in it, but much more of Christ. It begins with such expressions of devotion as may be applied to Christ ; but concludes with such confidence of a resurrection (and so timely a one as to prevent corruption) as must be applied

to Christ, to him only, and cannot be understood of David, as both St. Peter and St. Paul have observed, Acts ii. 24; xiii. 36. For David died, and was buried, and saw corruption. I. David speaks of himself as a member of Christ, and so he speaks the language of all good Christians, professing his confidence in God (ver. 1), his consent to him (ver. 2), his affection to the people of God (ver. 3), his adherence to the true worship of God (ver. 4), and his entire complacency and satisfaction in God and the interest he had in him, ver. 5—7. II. He speaks of himself as a type of Christ, and so he speaks the language of Christ himself, to whom all the rest of the psalm is expressly and at large applied, Acts ii. 25, &c. David speaks concerning him (not concerning himself), "I foresaw the Lord always before my face," &c. And this he spoke, being a prophet, ver. 30, 31. He spoke, 1. Of the special presence of God with the Redeemer in his services and sufferings, ver. 8. 2. Of the prospect which the Redeemer had of his own resurrection and the glory that should follow, which carried him cheerfully through his undertaking, ver. 9—11.

Michtam of David.

PRESERVE me, O God: for in thee do I put my trust. 2 *O my soul,* thou hast said unto the LORD, Thou *art* my Lord : my goodness *extendeth* not to thee ; 3 *But* to the saints that *are* in the earth, and *to* the excellent, in whom *is* all my delight. 4 Their sorrows shall be multiplied *that* hasten *after* another *god :* their drink offerings of blood will I not offer, nor take up their names into my lips. 5 The LORD *is* the portion of mine inheritance and of my cup : thou maintainest my lot. 6 The lines are fallen unto me in pleasant *places ;* yea, I have a goodly heritage. 7 I will bless the LORD, who hath given me counsel : my reins also instruct me in the night seasons.

This psalm is entitled *Michtam,* which some translate *a golden* psalm, a very precious one, more to be valued by us than gold, yea, than much fine gold, because it speaks so plainly of Christ and his resurrection, who is the true treasure hidden in the field of the Old Testament.

I. David here flies to God's protection with a cheerful believing confidence in it (*v.* 1): " *Preserve me, O God!* from the deaths, and especially from the sins, to which I am continually exposed ; *for in thee,* and in thee only, *do I put my trust.*" Those that by faith commit themselves to the divine care, and submit themselves to the divine guidance, have reason to hope for the benefit of both. This is applicable to Christ, who prayed, *Father, save me from this hour,* and trusted in God that he would deliver him.

II. He recognises his solemn dedication of himself to God as his God (*v.* 2): " *O my soul! ! thou hast said unto the Lord, Thou art my Lord,* and therefore thou mayest venture to trust him." Note, 1. It is the duty and interest of every one of us to acknowledge the Lord for our Lord, to subject ourselves to him, and then to stay ourselves upon him. *Adonai* signifies *My stayer,* the strength of my heart. 2. This must be done with our souls. " *O my soul!* thou hast said it." Covenanting with God must be heart-work; all that is within us must be employed therein and engaged thereby. 3. Those who have avouched the Lord for their Lord should be often putting themselves in mind of what they have done. "Hast thou said unto the Lord, *Thou art my Lord?* Say it again then, stand to it, abide by it, and never unsay it. Hast thou said it? Take the comfort of it, and live up to it. He is thy Lord, and worship thou him, and let thy eye be ever towards him."

III. He devotes himself to the honour of God in the service of the saints (v. 2, 3): *My goodness extends not to thee, but to the saints.* Observe, 1. Those that have taken the Lord for their Lord must, like him, be good and do good; we do not expect happiness without goodness. 2. Whatever good there is in us, or is done by us, we must humbly acknowledge that it extends not to God; so that we cannot pretend to merit any thing by it. God has no need of our services; he is not benefited by them, nor can they add any thing to his infinite perfection and blessedness. The wisest, and best, and most useful, men in the world cannot be profitable to God, Job xxii. 2; xxxv. 7. God is infinitely above us, and happy without us, and whatever good we do it is all from him; so that we are indebted to him, not he to us: David owns it (1 Chron. xxix. 14), *Of thy own have we given thee.* 3. If God be ours, we must, for his sake, extend our goodness to those that are his, to the saints in the earth; for what is done to them he is pleased to take as done to himself, having constituted them his receivers. Note, (1.) There are saints in the earth; and saints on earth we must all be, or we shall never be saints in heaven. Those that are renewed by the grace of God, and devoted to the glory of God, are saints on earth. (2.) The saints in the earth are excellent ones, great, mighty, magnificent ones, and yet some of them so poor in the world that they need to have David's goodness extended to them. God makes them excellent by the grace he gives them. *The righteous is more excellent than his neighbour,* and then he accounts them excellent. They are precious in his sight and honourable; they are his jewels, his peculiar treasure. Their God is their glory, and a diadem of beauty to them. (3.) All that have taken the Lord for their God delight in his saints as excellent ones, because they bear his image, and because he loves them. David, though a king, was a *companion of all that feared God* (cxix. 63), even the meanest, which was a sign that his delight was in them. (4.) It is not enough for us to delight in the saints, but, as there is occasion, our goodness must extend to them; we must be ready to show them the kindness they need, distribute to their necessities, and abound in the labour of love to them. This is applicable to Christ. The salvation he wrought out for us was no gain to God, for our ruin would have been no loss to him; but the goodness and benefit of it extend to us men, in whom he delighteth, Prov. viii. 31. *For their sakes,* says he, *I sanctify myself,* John xvii. 19. Christ delights even in the saints on earth, notwithstanding their weaknesses and manifold infirmities, which is a good reason why we should.

IV. He disclaims the worship of all false gods and all communion with their worshippers, v. 4. Here, 1. He reads the doom of idolaters, who hasten after another God, being mad upon their idols, and pursuing them as eagerly as if they were afraid they would escape from them: *Their sorrows shall be multiplied,* both by the judgments they bring upon themselves from the true God whom they forsake and by the disappointment they will meet with in the false gods they embrace. Those that multiply gods multiply griefs to themselves; for, whoever thinks one God too little, will find two too many, and yet hundreds not enough. 2. He declares his resolution to have no fellowship with them nor with their unfruitful works of darkness: "*Their drink-offerings of blood will I not offer,* not only because the gods they are offered to are a lie, but because the offerings themselves are barbarous." At God's altar, because the blood made atonement, the drinking of it was most strictly prohibited, and the drink-offerings were of wine; but the devil prescribed to his worshippers to drink of the blood of the sacrifices, to teach them cruelty. "I will have nothing to do" (says David) "with those bloody deities, nor so much as take their names into my lips with any delight in them or respect to them." Thus must we hate idols and idolatry with a perfect hatred. Some make this also applicable to Christ and his undertaking, showing the nature of the sacrifice he offered (it was not the blood of bulls and goats, which was offered according to the law; that was never named, nor did he ever make any mention of it, but his own blood), showing also the multiplied sorrows of the unbelieving Jews, who hastened after another king, Cæsar, and are still hastening after another Messiah, whom they in vain look for.

V. He repeats the solemn choice he had made of God for his portion and happiness (v. 5), takes to himself the comfort of the choice (v. 6), and gives God the glory of it, v. 7. This is very much the language of a devout and pious soul in its gracious exercises. 1. Choosing the Lord for its portion and happiness. "Most men take the world for their chief good, and place their felicity in the enjoyments of it; but this I say, *The Lord is the portion of my inheritance and of my cup,* the portion I make choice of, and will gladly take up with, how poor soever my condition is in this world. Let me have the love and favour of God, and be accepted of him; let me have the comfort of communion with God, and satisfaction in the communications of his graces and comforts; let me have an interest in his promises, and a title by promise to everlasting life and happiness in the future state; and I have enough, I need no more, I desire no more, to complete my felicity." Would we do well and wisely for ourselves, we must take God, in Christ, to be, (1.) The portion of our inheritance in the other world. Heaven is an inheritance. God himself is the inheritance of the saints there, whose everlasting bliss is to enjoy him. We must take that for our inheritance, our home, our rest, our lasting, everlasting, good, and look upon this world to be no more ours than the country through which our road lies when we are on a journey. (2.) The portion of our cup in this world, with which we are nourished, and refreshed, and kept from fainting. Those have not God for theirs who do not reckon his comforts the most reviving cordials, acquaint themselves with them, and make use of them as sufficient to counterbalance all the grievances of this present time and to sweeten the most bitter cup of affliction.

2. Confiding in him for the securing of this portion : " *Thou maintainest my lot.* Thou that hast by promise made over thyself to me, to be mine, wilt graciously make good what thou hast promised, and never leave me to myself to forfeit this happiness, nor leave it in the power of my enemies to rob me of it. Nothing shall pluck me out of thy hands, nor separate me from thy love, and the sure mercies of David." The saints and their bliss are kept by the power of God.

3. Rejoicing in this portion, and taking a complacency in it (*v.* 6): *The lines have fallen to me in pleasant places.* Those have reason to say so that have God for their portion; they have a worthy portion, a goodly heritage. What can they have better? What can they desire more? *Return unto thy rest, O my soul !* and look no further. Note, Gracious persons, though they still covet more of God, never covet more than God; but, being satisfied of his loving-kindness, they are abundantly satisfied with it, and envy not any their carnal mirth and sensual pleasures and delights, but account themselves truly happy in what they have, and doubt not but to be completely happy in what they hope for. Those whose lot is cast, as David's was, in a land of light, in a valley of vision, where God is known and worshipped, have, upon that account, reason to say, *The lines have fallen to me in pleasant places ;* much more those who have not only the means, but the end, not only Immanuel's land, but Immanuel's love.

4. Giving thanks to God for it, and for grace to make this wise and happy choice (*v.* 7): " *I will bless the Lord who has given me counsel,* this counsel, to take him for my portion and happiness." So ignorant and foolish are we that, if we be left to ourselves, our hearts will follow our eyes, and we shall choose our own delusions, and forsake our own mercies for lying vanities; and therefore,

if we have indeed taken God for our portion and preferred spiritual and eternal blessings before those that are sensible and temporal, we must thankfully acknowledge the power and goodness of divine grace directing and enabling us to make that choice. If we have the pleasure of it, let God have the praise of it.

5. Making a good use of it. God having given him counsel by his word and Spirit, his own *reins* also (his own thoughts) instructed him in the night-season ; when he was silent and solitary, and retired from the world, then his own conscience (which is called the *reins,* Jer. xvii. 10) not only reflected with comfort upon the choice he had made, but instructed or admonished him concerning the duties arising out of this choice, catechized him, and engaged and quickened him to live as one that had God for his portion, by faith to live upon him and to live to him. Those who have God for their portion, and who will be faithful to him, must give their own consciences leave to deal thus faithfully and plainly with them.

All this may be applied to Christ, who made the Lord his portion and was pleased with that portion, made his Father's glory his highest end and made it his meat and drink to seek that and to do his will, and delighted to prosecute his undertaking, pursuant to his Father's counsel, depending upon him to maintain his lot and to carry him through his undertaking. We may also apply it to ourselves, in singing it, renewing our choice of God as ours, with a holy complacency and satisfaction.

8 I have set the LORD always before me : because *he is* at my right hand, I shall not be moved. 9 Therefore my heart is glad, and my glory rejoiceth : my flesh also shall rest in hope. 10 For thou wilt not leave my soul in hell ; neither wilt thou suffer thine Holy One to see corruption. 11 Thou wilt show me the path of life : in thy presence *is* fulness of joy ; at thy right hand *there are* pleasures for evermore.

All these verses are quoted by St. Peter in his first sermon, after the pouring out of the Spirit on the day of pentecost (Acts ii. 25–28); and he tells us expressly that David in them speaks concerning Christ and particularly of his resurrection. Something we may allow here of the workings of David's own pious and devout affections towards God, depending upon his grace to perfect every thing that concerned him, and looking for the blessed hope, and a happy state on the other side death, in the enjoyment of God ; but in these holy elevations towards God and heaven he was carried by the spirit of prophecy quite beyond the consideration of himself and his own case, to foretel the glory of the Messiah, in such expressions as were peculiar to that, and could not be understood of himself. The New Testament furnishes us with a key to let us into the mystery of these lines.

I. These verses must certainly be applied to Christ; of him speaks the prophet this, as did many of the Old-Testament prophets, who *testified beforehand the sufferings of Christ and the glory that should follow* (1 Pet. i. 11), and that is the subject of this prophecy here. It is foretold (as he himself showed concerning this, no doubt, among other prophecies in this psalm, Luke xxiv. 44, 46) that *Christ should suffer, and rise from the dead,* 1 Cor. xv. 3, 4.

1. That he should suffer and die. This is implied here when he says (*v.* 8), *I shall not be moved;* he supposed that he should be struck at, and have a dreadful shock given him, as he had in his agony, when his soul was exceedingly sorrowful, and he prayed that the cup might pass from him. When he says, " *My flesh shall rest,*" it is implied that he must put off the body, and therefore must go through the pains of death. It is likewise plainly intimated that his soul must go into a state of separation from the body, and that his body, so deserted, would be in imminent danger of seeing corruption—that he should not only die, but be buried, and abide for some time under the power of death.

2. That he should be wonderfully borne up by the divine power in suffering and dying. (1.) That he should not be moved, should not be driven off from his undertaking nor sink under the weight of it, that he should not fail nor be discouraged (Isa xlii. 4), but should proceed and persevere in it, till he could say, *It is finished.* Though the service was hard and the encounter hot, and he trod the wine-press alone, yet he was not moved, did not give up the cause, but set his face as a flint, Isa. l. 7—9. *Here am I, let these go their way.* Nay, (2.) That his heart should rejoice and his glory be glad, that he should go on with his undertaking, not only resolutely, but cheerfully, and with unspeakable pleasure and satisfaction, witness that saying (John xvii. 11), *Now I am no more in the world, but I come to thee,* and that (John xviii. 11), *The cup that my Father has given me, shall I not drink it?* and many the like. By his glory is meant his *tongue,* as appears, Acts ii. 26. For our tongue is our glory, and never more so than when it is employed in glorifying God. Now there were three things which bore him up and carried him on thus cheerfully:—[1.] The respect he had to his Father's will and glory in what he did : *I have set the Lord always before me.* He still had an eye to his Father's commandment (John x. 18, xiv. 31), the will of him that sent him. He aimed at his Father's honour and the re-storing of the interests of his kingdom among men, and this kept him from being moved by the difficulties he met with; for he always did those things that pleased his Father. [2.] The

290

assurance he had of his Father's presence with him in his sufferings : *He is at my right hand,* a present help to me, nigh at hand in the time of need. *He is near that justifieth me* (Isa. l. 8); he is at my right hand, to direct and strengthen it, and hold it up, lxxxix. 21. When he was in his agony an angel was sent from heaven to strengthen him, Luke xxii. 43. To this the victories and triumphs of the cross were all owing ; it was the Lord at his right hand that *struck through kings,* cx. 5 ; Isa. xlii. 1, 2. [3.] The prospect he had of a glorious issue of his sufferings. It was *for the joy set before him* that *he endured the cross,* Heb. xii. 2. He rested in hope, and that made his rest glorious, Isa. xi. 10. He knew he should be justified in the Spirit by his resurrection, and straightway glorified. See John xiii. 31, 32.

3. That he should be brought through his sufferings, and brought from under the power of death by a glorious resurrection. (1.) That his soul should not be left in hell, that is, his human spirit should not be long left, as other men's spirits are, in a state of separation from the body, but should, in a little time, return and be re-united to it, never to part again. (2.) That being God's holy One in a peculiar manner, sanctified to the work of redemption and perfectly free from sin, he should not see corruption nor feel it. This implies that he should not only be raised from the grave, but raised so soon that his dead body should not so much as begin to corrupt, which, in the course of nature, it would have done if it had not been raised the third day. We, who have so much corruption in our souls, must expect that our bodies also will corrupt (Job xxiv. 19); but that holy One of God who knew no sin saw no corruption. Under the law it was strictly ordered that those parts of the sacri-fices which were not burnt upon the altar should by no means be kept till the third day, lest they should putrefy (Lev. vii. 15, 18), which perhaps pointed at Christ's rising the third day, that he might not see corruption —neither was a bone of him broken.

4. That he should be abundantly recom-pensed for his sufferings, with the joy set be-fore him, *v.* 11. He was well assured, (1.) That he should not miss of his glory: " *Thou wilt show me the path of life,* and lead me to that life through this darksome valley.*" In confidence of this, when he gave up the ghost, he said, *Father, into thy hands I commit my spirit;* and, a little before, *Father, glorify me with thy own self.* (2.) That he should be received into the presence of God, to sit at his right hand. His being admitted into God's presence would be the acceptance of his ser-vice and his being set at his right hand the recompence of it. (3.) Thus, as a reward for the sorrows he underwent for our redemp-tion, he should have a *fulness of joy, and plea-sures for evermore ;* not only the glory he had with God, as God, before all worlds, but the joy and pleasure of a Mediator, in seeing his

seed, and the success and prosperity of his undertaking, Isa. liii. 10, 11.

II. Christ being the Head of the body, the church, these verses may, for the most part, be applied to all good Christians, who are guided and animated by the Spirit of Christ; and, in singing them, when we have first given glory to Christ, in whom, to our everlasting comfort, they have had their accomplishment, we may then encourage and edify ourselves and one another with them, and may hence learn, 1. That it is our wisdom and duty to set the Lord always before us, and to see him continually at our right hand, wherever we are, to eye him as our chief good and highest end, our owner, ruler, and judge, our gracious benefactor, our sure guide and strict observer; and, while we do thus, we shall not be moved either from our duty or from our comfort. Blessed Paul set the Lord before him, when, though bonds and afflictions did await him, he could bravely say, *None of these things move me,* Acts xx. 24. 2. That, if our eyes be ever towards God, our hearts and tongues may ever rejoice in him; it is our own fault if they do not. If the heart rejoice in God, out of the abundance of that let the mouth speak, to his glory, and the edification of others. 3. That dying Christians, as well as a dying Christ, may cheerfully put off the body, in a believing expectation of a joyful resurrection: *My flesh also shall rest in hope.* Our bodies have little rest in this world, but in the grave they shall rest as in their beds, Isa. lvii. 2. We have little to hope for from this life, but we shall rest in hope of a better life; we may put off the body in that hope. Death *destroys the hope of man* (Job xiv. 19), but not the hope of a good Christian, Prov. xiv. 32. He has hope in his death, living hopes in dying moments, hopes that the body shall not be left for ever in the grave, but, though it see corruption for a time, it shall, at the end of the time, be raised to immortality; Christ's resurrection is an earnest of ours if we be his. 4. That those who live piously with God in their eye may die comfortably with heaven in their eye. In this world sorrow is our lot, but in heaven there is joy. All our joys here are empty and defective, but in heaven there is a fulness of joy. Our pleasures here are transient and momentary, and such is the nature of them that it is not fit they should last long; but those at God's right hand are pleasures for evermore; for they are the pleasures of immortal souls in the immediate vision and fruition of an eternal God.

PSALM XVII.

A prayer of David.

HEAR the right, O LORD, attend unto my cry, give ear unto my prayer, *that goeth* not out of feigned lips. 2 Let my sentence come forth from thy presence; let thine eyes behold the things that are equal. 3 Thou hast proved mine heart; thou hast visited *me* in the night; thou hast tried me, *and* shalt find nothing; I am purposed *that* my mouth shall not transgress. 4 Concerning the works of men, by the word of thy lips I have kept *me from* the paths of the destroyer. 5 Hold up my goings in thy paths, *that* my footsteps slip not. 6 I have called upon thee, for thou wilt hear me, O God: incline thine ear unto me, *and hear* my speech. 7 Show thy marvellous lovingkindness, O thou that savest by thy right hand them which put their trust *in thee* from those that rise up *against them.*

This psalm is a prayer. As there is a time to weep and a time to rejoice, so there is a time for praise and a time for prayer. David was now persecuted, probably by Saul, who hunted him like a partridge on the mountains; without were fightings, within were fears, and both urged him as a suppliant to the throne of mercy. He addresses himself to God in these verses both by way of appeal *(Hear the right, O Lord!* let my righteous cause have a hearing before thy tribunal, and give judgment upon it) and by way of petition *(Give ear unto my prayer v.* 1, and again *v.* 6, *Incline thy ear unto me and hear my speech)*; not that God needs to be thus pressed with our importunity, but he gives us leave thus to express our earnest desire of his gracious answers to our prayers. These things he pleads with God for audience, 1. That he was sincere, and did not dissemble with God in his prayer: *It goeth not out of feigned lips.* He meant as he spoke, and the feelings of his mind agreed with the expressions of his mouth. Feigned prayers are fruitless; but, if our hearts lead our prayers, God will meet them with his favour. 2. That he had been used to pray at other times, and it was not his distress and danger that now first brought him to his duty: "*I have called upon thee* formerly *(v.* 6); therefore, Lord, hear me now." It will be a great comfort to us if trouble, when it comes, find the wheels of prayer a-going, for then we may come with the more boldness to the throne of grace. Tradesmen are willing to oblige those that have been long their customers. 3. That he was encouraged by his faith to expect God would take notice of his prayers: "*I know thou wilt hear me,* and therefore, O God, *incline thy ear to*

291

me." Our believing dependence upon God is a good plea to enforce our desires towards him. Let us now see,

I. What his appeal is; and here observe,

1. What the court is to the cognizance and determination of which he makes his appeal; it is the court of heaven. "Lord, do thou hear the right, for Saul is so passionate, so prejudiced, that he will not hear it. Lord, *let my sentence come forth from thy presence, v.* 2. Men sentence me to be pursued and cut off as an evil-doer. Lord, I appeal from them to thee." This he did in a public remonstrance before Saul's face (1 Sam. xxiv. 12, *The Lord judge between me and thee)*, and he repeats it here in his private devotions. Note, (1.) The equity and extent of God's government and judgment are a very great support to injured innocency. If we are blackened, and abused, and misrepresented, by unrighteous men, it is a comfort that we have a righteous God to go to, who will take our part, who is the patron of the oppressed, whose judgment is according to truth, by the discoveries of which every person and every cause will appear in a true light, stripped of all false colours, and by the decisions of which all unrighteous dooms will be reversed, and to every man will be rendered according to his work. (2.) Sincerity dreads no scrutiny, no, not that of God himself, according to the tenour of the covenant of grace: *Let thy eyes behold the things that are equal.* God's omniscience is as much the joy of the upright as it is the terror of hypocrites, and is particularly comfortable to those who are falsely accused and in any wise have wrong done them.

2. What the evidence is by which he hopes to make good his appeal; it is the trial God had made of him (*v.* 3): *Thou hast proved my heart.* God's sentence is *therefore* right, because he always proceeds upon his knowledge, which is more certain and infallible than that which men attain to by the closest views and the strictest investigations.

(1.) He knew God had tried him, [1.] By his own conscience, which is God's deputy in the soul. *The spirit of a man is the candle of the Lord,* with this God had searched him, and *visited him in the night,* when he *communed with his own heart upon his bed.* He had submitted to the search, and had seriously reviewed the actions of his life, to discover what was amiss, but could find nothing of that which his enemies charged him with. [2.] By providence. God had tried him by the fair opportunity he had, once and again, to kill Saul; he had tried him by the malice of Saul, the treachery of his friends, and the many provocations that were given him; so that, if he had been the man he was represented to be, it would have appeared; but, upon all these trials, there was nothing found against him, no proof at all of the things whereof they accused him.

(2.) God tried his heart, and could witness to the integrity of that; but, for the further proof

292

of his integrity, he himself takes notice of two things concerning which his conscience bore him record:—[1.] That he had a fixed resolution against all sins of the tongue: "*I have purposed* and fully determined, in the strength of God's grace, *that my mouth shall not transgress.*" He does not say, "I hope that it will not," or, "I wish that it may not," but, "I have fully purposed that it shall not:" with this bridle he kept his mouth, xxxix. 1. Note, Constant resolution and watchfulness against sins of the tongue will be a good evidence of our integrity. *If any offend not in word, the same is a perfect man,* Jam. iii. 2. He does not say, "My mouth never shall transgress" (for in many things we all offend), but, "I have purposed that it shall not;" and he that searches the heart knows whether the purpose be sincere. [2.] That he had been as careful to refrain from sinful actions as from sinful words (*v.* 4): "*Concerning the* common *works of men,* the actions and affairs of human life, *I have,* by the direction of thy word, *kept myself from the paths of the destroyer.*" Some understand it particularly, that he had not been himself a destroyer of Saul, when it lay in his power, nor had he permitted others to be so, but said to Abishai, *Destroy him not,* 1 Sam. xxvi. 9. But it may be taken more generally; he kept himself from all evil works, and endeavoured, according to the duty of his place, to keep others from them too. Note, *First,* The ways of sin are paths of the destroyer, of the devil, whose name is *Abaddon* and *Apollyon,* a destroyer, who ruins souls by decoying them into the paths of sin. *Secondly,* It concerns us all to keep out of the paths of the destroyer; for, if we walk in those ways that lead to destruction, we must thank ourselves if destruction and misery be our portion at last. *Thirdly,* It is by the word of God, as our guide and rule, that we must keep out of the paths of the destroyer, by observing its directions and admonitions, cxix 9. *Fourthly,* If we carefully avoid all the paths of sin, it will be very comfortable in the reflection, when we are in trouble. If we *keep ourselves, that the wicked one touch us not* with his temptations (1 John v. 18), we may hope he will not be able to touch us with his terrors.

II. What his petition is; it is, in short, this. That he might experience the good work of God in him, as an evidence of and qualification for the good will of God towards him: this is grace and peace from God the Father. 1. He prays for the work of God's grace in him (*v.* 5): "*Hold up my goings in thy paths.* Lord, I have, by thy grace, kept myself from the paths of the destroyer; by the same grace let me be kept in thy paths; let me not only be restrained from doing that which is evil, but quickened to abound always in that which is good. Let my goings be held in thy paths, that I may not turn back from them nor turn aside out of them; let them be held up in thy paths, that I may not stumble and fall into sin, that I may not trifle and neglect my duty. Lord, as thou hast kept me hitherto, so keep me still." Those that are, through grace, going in God's paths, have need to pray, and do pray, that their goings may be held up in those paths; for we stand no longer than he is pleased to hold us, we go no further than he is pleased to lead us, bear us up, and carry us. David had been kept in the way of his duty hitherto, and yet he does not think that this would be his security for the future, and therefore prays, "Lord, still hold me up." Those that would proceed and persevere in the way of God must, by faith and prayer, fetch in daily fresh supplies of grace and strength from him. David was sensible that his way was slippery, that he himself was weak, and not so well fixed and furnished as he should be, that there were those who watched for his halting and would improve the least slip against him, and therefore he prays, "Lord, hold me up, that my foot slip not, that I may never say nor do any thing that looks either dishonest or distrustful of thee and thy providence and promise." 2. He prays for the tokens of God's favour to him, *v.* 7. Observe here, (1.) How he eyes God as the protector and Saviour of his people, so he calls him, and thence he takes his encouragement in prayer: *O thou that .savest by thy right hand* (by thy own power, and needest not the agency of any other) *those who put their trust in thee from those that rise up against them.* It is the character of God's people that they trust in him; he is pleased to make them confidants, for his secret is with the righteous; and they make him their trust, for to him they commit themselves. Those that trust in God have many enemies, many that rise up against them and seek their ruin; but they have one friend that is able to deal with them all, and, if he be for them, no matter who is against them. He reckons it his honour to be their Saviour. His almighty power is engaged for them, and they have all found him ready to save them. The margin reads it, *O thou that savest those who trust in thee from those that rise up against thy right hand.* Those that are enemies to the saints are rebels against God and his right hand, and therefore, no doubt, he will, in due time, appear against them. (2.) What he expects and desires from God: *Show thy marvellous loving-kindness.* The word signifies, [1.] Distinguishing favours. "Set apart thy loving-kindnesses for me; put me not off with common mercies, but be gracious to me, *as thou usest to do to those who love thy name.*" [2.] Wonderful favours. "O make thy loving-kindness admirable! Lord, testify thy favour to me in such a way that I and others may wonder at it." God's loving-kindness is marvellous for the freeness and the fulness of it; in some instances it appears, in a special manner, marvellous (cxviii. 23), and it will certainly appear so in the salvation of the saints, when Christ shall come to be *glorified in the saints and to be admired in all those that believe.*

8 Keep me as the apple of the eye, hide me under the shadow of thy wings, 9 From the wicked that oppress me, *from* my deadly enemies, *who* compass me about. 10 They are inclosed in their own fat: with their mouth they speak proudly. 11 They have now compassed us in our steps: they have set their eyes bowing down to the earth; 12 Like as a lion *that* is greedy of his prey, and as it were a young lion lurking in secret places. 13 Arise, O LORD, disappoint him, cast him down: deliver my soul from the wicked, *which is* thy sword: 14 From men *which are* thy hand, O LORD, from men of the world, *which have* their portion in *this* life, and whose belly thou fillest with thy hid *treasure:* they are full of children, and leave the rest of their *substance* to their babes. 15 As for me, I will behold thy face in righteousness: I shall be satisfied, when I awake, with thy likeness.

We may observe, in these verses,

I. What David prays for. Being compassed about with enemies that sought his life, he prays to God to preserve him safely through all their attempts against him, to the crown to which he was anointed. This prayer is both a prediction of the preservation of Christ through all the hardships and difficulties of his humiliation, to the glories and joys of his exalted state, and a pattern to Christians to commit the keeping of their souls to God, trusting him to *preserve them to his heavenly kingdom.* He prays,

1. That he himself might be protected (*v.* 8): "Keep me safe, hide me close, where I may not be found, where I may not be come at. Deliver my soul, not only my mortal life from death, but my immortal spirit from sin." Those who put themselves under God's protection may in faith implore the benefit of it.

(1.) He prays that God would keep him, [1]. With as much care as a man keeps the apple of his eye with, which nature has wonderfully fenced and teaches us to guard. If we keep God's law as the *apple of our eye* (Prov. vii. 2), we may expect that God will so keep us; for it is said concerning his people that whoso *touches them touches the apple of his eye,* Zech. ii. 8. [2.] With as much tenderness as the hen gathers her young ones under her wings with; Christ uses the similitude, Matt. xxiii. 37. "*Hide me under the shadow of thy wings,* where I may be both safe and warm." Or, perhaps, it rather alludes to the wings of the cherubim shadowing the mercy-seat: "Let me be taken under the protection of that glorious grace which is peculiar to God's Israel." What David here prays for was performed to the Son of David, our Lord Jesus, of whom it is said (Isa. xlix. 2) that God hid *him in the shadow of his hand,* hid him *as a polished shaft in his quiver.*

(2.) David further prays, " Lord, keep me from the wicked, from men of the world," [1.] " From being, and doing, like them, from walking in their counsel, and standing in their way, and eating of their dainties." [2.] " From being destroyed and run down by them. Let them not have their will against me; let them not triumph over me."

2. That all the designs of his enemies to bring him either into sin or into trouble might be defeated (*v.* 13): "*Arise, O Lord !* appear for me, disappoint him, and cast him down in his own eyes by the disappointment." While Saul persecuted David, how often did he miss his prey, when he thought he had him sure ! And how were Christ's enemies disappointed by his resurrection, who thought they had gained their point when they had put him to death !

¶II. What he pleads for the encouraging of his own faith in these petitions, and his hope of speeding. He pleads,

1. The malice and wickedness of his enemies: " They are such as are not fit to be countenanced, such as, if I be not delivered from them by the special care of God himself, will be my ruin. Lord, see what wicked men those are that oppress me, and waste me, and run me down." (1.) " They are very spiteful and malicious; they are *my deadly enemies,* that thirst after my blood, my heart's blood— *enemies against the soul,* so the word is. David's enemies did what they could to drive him to sin and drive him away from God; they bade him *go serve other gods* (1 Sam. xxvi. 19), and therefore he had reason to pray against them. Note, Those are our worst enemies, and we ought so to account them, that are enemies to our souls. (2.) " They are very secure and sensual, insolent and haughty (*v.* 10): *They are enclosed in their own fat,* wrap themselves, hug themselves, in their own honour, and power, and plenty, and then make light of God, and set his judgments at defiance, lxxiii. 7 ; Job xv. 27. They wallow in pleasure, and promise themselves that to-morrow shall be as this day. And therefore with their mouth they speak proudly, glorying in themselves, blaspheming God, trampling upon his people, and insulting them." See Rev. xiii. 5, 6. " Lord, are not such men as these fit to be mortified and humbled, and made to know themselves? Will it not be for thy glory *to look upon these proud men and abase them ?*" (3.) " They are restless and unwearied in their attempts against me : They *compass me about, v.* 9. They have now in a manner gained their point; they have surrounded us, they have compassed us in our steps, they track us wherever we go, follow us as close as the

hound does the hare, and take all advantages against us, being both too many and too quick for us. And yet they pretend to look another way, and set their eyes bowing down to the earth, as if they were meditating, retired into themselves, and thinking of something else ;" or (as some think), "They are watchful and intent upon it, to do us a mischief; they are down-looked, and never let slip any opportunity of compassing their design." (4.) "The ringleader of them (that was Saul) is in a special manner bloody and barbarous, politic and projecting (*v.* 12), *like a lion* that lives by prey and is therefore greedy of it." It is as much the meat and drink of a wicked man to do mischief as it is of a good man to do good. He is like *a young lion lurking in secret places,* disguising his cruel designs. This is fitly applied to Saul, who sought David *on the rocks of the wild goats* (1 Sam. xxiv. 2) and in *the wilderness of Ziph* (*ch.* xxvi. 2), where lions used to lurk for their prey.

2. The power God have over them, to control and restrain them. He pleads, (1.) " Lord, they are *thy sword ;* and will any father suffer his sword to be drawn against his own children ?" As this is a reason why we should patiently bear the injuries of men, that they are but the instruments of the trouble (it comes originally from God, to whose will we are bound to submit), so it is an encouragement to us to hope both that their wrath shall praise him and that the remainder thereof he will restrain, that they are God's sword, which he can manage as he pleases, which cannot move without him, and which he will sheathe when he has done his work with it. (2.) "They are *thy hand,* by which thou dost chastise thy people and make them feel thy displeasure." He therefore expects deliverance from God's hand because from God's hand the trouble came. *Una eademque manus vulnus opemque tulit — The same hand wounds and heals.* There is no flying from God's hand but by flying to it. It is very comfortable, when we are in fear of the power of man, to see it dependent upon and in subjection to the power of God; see Isa. x. 6, 7, 15.

3. Their outward prosperity (*v.* 14): " Lord, appear against them, for, (1.) " They are entirely devoted to the world, and care not for thee and thy favour. They are *men of the world,* actuated by the spirit of the world, walking according to the course of this world, in love with the wealth and pleasure of this world, eager in the pursuits of it (making them their business) and at ease in the enjoyments of it—making them their bliss. They *have their portion in this life;* they look upon the good things of this world as the best things, and sufficient to make them happy, and they choose them accordingly, place their felicity in them, and aim at them as their chief good; they rest satisfied with them, their souls take their ease in them, and they look no further, nor are in any care to pro-

vide for another life. These things are their consolation (Luke vi. 24), *their good things* (Luke xvi. 25), *their reward* (Matt. vi. 5), the penny they agreed for, Matt. xx. 13. Now, Lord, shall men of this character be supported and countenanced against those who honour thee by preferring thy favour before all the wealth in this world, and taking thee for their portion?" xvi. 5. (2.) They have abundance of the world. [1.] They have enlarged appetites, and a great deal wherewith to satisfy them: *Their bellies thou fillest with thy hidden treasures.* The things of this world are called *treasures*, because they are so accounted; otherwise, to a soul, and in comparison with eternal blessings, they are but trash. They are hidden in the several parts of the creation, and hidden in the sovereign disposals of Providence. They are God's hidden treasures, for the earth is his and the fulness thereof, though the men of the world think it is their own and forget God's property in it. Those that fare deliciously every day have their *bellies filled with these hidden treasures ;* and they will but *fill the belly* (1 Cor. vi. 13); they will not fill the soul; they are not bread for that, nor can they satisfy, Isa. lv. 2. They are husks, and ashes, and wind ; and yet most men, having no care for their souls, but all for their bellies, take up with them. [2.] They have numerous families, and a great deal to leave to them : *They are full of children*, and yet their pasture is not overstocked ; they have enough for them all, and *leave the rest of their substance to their babes*, to their grand-children; and this is their heaven, it is their bliss, it is their all. "Lord," said David, "*deliver me from them ;* let me not have my portion with them. Deliver me from their designs against me; for, they having so much wealth and power, I am not able to deal with them unless the Lord be on my side."

4. He pleads his own dependence upon God as his portion and happiness. "They have their portion in this life, but as for me (*v.* 15) I am none of them, I have but little of the world. *Nec habeo, nec careo, nec curo*—*I neither have, nor need, nor care for it.* It is the vision and fruition of God that I place my happiness in; that is it I hope for, and comfort myself with the hopes of, and thereby distinguish myself from those who have their portion in this life." Beholding God's face with satisfaction may be considered, (1.) As our duty and comfort in this world. We must in righteousness (clothed with Christ's righteousness, having a good heart and a good life) by faith behold God's face and set him always before us, must entertain ourselves from day to day with the contemplation of the beauty of the Lord; and, when we awake every morning, we must be satisfied with his likeness set before us in his word, and with his likeness stamped upon us by his renewing grace. Our experience of God's favour to us, and our con-

formity to him, should yield us more satisfaction than those have whose belly is filled with the delights of sense. 2. As our recompence and happiness in the other world. With the prospect of that he concluded the foregoing psalm, and so this. That happiness is prepared and designed only for the righteous that are justified and sanctified. They shall be put in possession of it when they awake, when the soul awakes, at death, out of its slumber in the body, and when the body awakes, at the resurrection, out of its slumber in the grave. That blessedness will consist in three things:—[1.] The immediate vision of God and his glory: *I shall behold thy face*, not, as in this world, through a glass darkly. The knowledge of God will there be perfected and the enlarged intellect filled with it. [2.] The participation of his likeness. Our holiness will there be perfect. This results from the former (1 John iii. 2): *When he shall appear we shall be like him, for we shall see him as he is.* [3.] A complete and full satisfaction resulting from all this: *I shall be satisfied*, abundantly satisfied with it. There is no satisfaction for a soul but in God, and in his face and likeness, his good-will towards us and his good work in us; and even that satisfaction will not be perfect till we come to heaven.

PSALM XVIII. (18)

This psalm we met with before, in the history of David's life, 2 Sam. xxii. That was the first edition of it ; here we have it revived, altered a little, and fitted for the service of the church. It is David's thanksgiving for the many deliverances God had wrought for him ; these he desired always to preserve fresh in his own memory and to diffuse and entail the knowledge of them. It is an admirable composition. The poetry is very fine, the images are bold, the expressions lofty, and every word is proper and significant ; but the piety far exceeds the poetry. Holy faith, and love, and joy, and praise, and hope, are here lively, active, and upon the wing. I. He triumphs in God, ver. 1—3. II. He magnifies the deliverances God had wrought for him, ver. 4—19. III. He takes the comfort of his integrity, which God had thereby cleared up, ver. 20—28. IV. He gives to God the glory of all his achievements, ver. 29—42. V. He encourages himself with the expectation of what God would further do for him and his, ver. 43—50.

To the chief musician, *A psalm* of David, the servant of the Lord, who spoke unto the Lord the words of this song, in the day *that* the Lord delivered him from the hand of all his enemies, and from the hand of Saul: and he said,

I WILL love thee, O Lord, my strength. 2 The Lord *is* my rock, and my fortress, and my deliverer ; my God, my strength, in whom I will trust; my buckler, and the horn of my salvation, *and* my high tower. 3 I will call upon the Lord, *who is worthy* to be praised : so shall I be saved from mine enemies. 4 The sorrows of death compassed me, and the floods of ungodly men made me afraid. 5 The sorrows of hell compassed me about : the snares of death prevented me. 6 In my distress I called upon the LORD, and cried unto my God: he heard my voice out of his temple, and my cry came before him, *even* into his ears. 7 Then the earth shook and trembled; the foundations also of the hills moved and were shaken, because he was wroth. 8 There went up a smoke out of his nostrils, and fire out of his mouth devoured: coals were kindled by it. 9 He bowed the heavens also, and came down: and darkness *was* under his feet. 10 And he rode upon a cherub, and did fly: yea, he did fly upon the wings of the wind. 11 He made darkness his secret place; his pavilion round about him *were* dark waters *and* thick clouds of the skies. 12 At the brightness *that was* before him his thick clouds passed, hail *stones* and coals of fire. 13 The LORD also thundered in the heavens, and the Highest gave his voice; hail *stones* and coals of fire. 14 Yea, he sent out his arrows, and scattered them; and he shot out lightnings, and discomfited them. 15 Then the channels of waters were seen, and the foundations of the world were discovered at thy rebuke, O LORD, at the blast of the breath of thy nostrils. 16 He sent from above, he took me, he drew me out of many waters. 17 He delivered me from my strong enemy, and from them which hated me: for they were too strong for me. 18 They prevented me in the day of my calamity: but the LORD was my stay. 19 He brought me forth also into a large place; he delivered me, because he delighted in me.

The title gives us the occasion of penning this psalm; we had it before (2 Sam. xxii. 1), only here we are told that the psalm was delivered *to the chief musician,* or precentor, in the temple-songs. Note, The private compositions of good men, designed by them for their own use, may be serviceable to the public, that others may not only borrow light from their candle, but heat from their fire. Examples sometimes teach better than rules. And David is here called *the servant of the Lord,* as Moses was, not only as every good man is God's servant, but because, with his sceptre, with his sword, and with his pen, he greatly promoted the interests of God's kingdom in Israel. It was more his honour that he was a servant of the Lord than that he was king of a great kingdom; and so he

296

himself accounted it (cxvi. 16): *O Lord! truly I am thy servant.* In these verses,

I. He triumphs in God and his relation to him. The first words of the psalm, *I will love thee, O Lord! my strength,* are here prefixed as the scope and contents of the whole. Love to God is the first and great commandment of the law, because it is the principle of all our acceptable praise and obedience; and this use we should make of all the mercies God bestows upon us, our hearts should thereby be enlarged in love to him. This he requires and will accept; and we are very ungrateful if we grudge him so poor a return. An interest in the person loved is the lover's delight; this string therefore he touches, and on this he harps with much pleasure (v. 2): "*The Lord* Jehovah *is my* God; and then he is my *rock, my fortress,* all that I need and can desire in my present distress." For there is that in God which is suited to all the exigencies and occasions of his people that trust in him. "He is my rock, and strength, and fortress;" that is, 1. "I have found him so in the greatest dangers and difficulties." 2. "I have chosen him to be so, disclaiming all others, and depending upon him alone to protect me." Those that truly love God may thus triumph in him as theirs, and may with confidence call upon him, v. 3. This further use we should make of our deliverances, we must not only love God the better, but love prayer the better— *call upon him as long as we live,* especially in time of trouble, with an assurance that so we shall be saved; for thus it is written, *Whosoever shall call upon the name of the Lord shall be saved,* Acts ii. 21.

II. He sets himself to magnify the deliverances God had wrought for him, that he might be the more affected in his returns of praise. It is good for us to observe all the circumstances of a mercy, which magnify the power of God and his goodness to us in it.

1. The more imminent and threatening the danger was out of which we were delivered the greater is the mercy of the deliverance. David now remembered how the forces of his enemies poured in upon him, which he calls *the floods of Belial,* shoals of the children of Belial, likely to overpower him with numbers. They surrounded him, *compassed him about;* they surprised him, and by that means were very near seizing him; their snares prevented him, and, when without were fightings, within were fears and sorrows, v. 4, 5. His spirit was overwhelmed, and he looked upon himself as a lost man; see cxvi. 3.

2. The more earnest we have been with God for deliverance, and the more direct answer it is to our prayers, the more we are obliged to be thankful. David's deliverances were so, v. 6. David was found a praying man, and God was found a prayer-hearing God. If we pray as he did, we shall speed as

he did. Though distress drive us to prayer, God will not therefore be deaf to us; nay, being a God of pity, he will be the more ready to succour us.

3. The more wonderful God's appearances are in any deliverance the greater it is : such were the deliverances wrought for David, in which God's manifestation of his presence and glorious attributes is most magnificently described, *v.* 7, &c. Little appeared of man, but much of God, in these deliverances. (1.) He appeared a God of almighty power; for he made the earth shake and tremble, and moved even the *foundations of the hills (v.* 7), as of old at Mount Sinai. When the men of the earth were struck with fear, then the earth might be said to *tremble ;* when the great men of the earth were put into confusion, then the hills moved. (2.) He showed his anger and displeasure against the enemies and persecutors of his people : *He was wroth, v.* 7. His wrath smoked, it burned, it was fire, it was devouring fire (*v.* 8), and *coals were kindled by it.* Those that by their own sins make themselves as coals (that is, fuel) to this fire will be consumed by it. He that ordains his arrows against the persecutors sends them forth when he pleases, and they are sure to hit the mark and do execution ; for those arrows are lightnings, *v.* 14.· (3.) He showed his readiness to plead his people's cause and work deliverance for them; for he rode upon a cherub and did fly, for the maintaining of right and the relieving of his distressed servants, *v.* 10. No opposition, no obstruction, can be given to him *who rides upon the wings of the wind, who rides on the heavens, for the help of his people, and, in his excellency, on the skies.* (4.) He showed his condescension, in taking cognizance of David's case : *He bowed the heavens and came down* (*v.* 9), did not send an angel, but came himself, as one afflicted in the afflictions of his people. (5.) He wrapped himself in darkness, and yet commanded light to shine out of darkness for his people, Isa. xlv. 15. He is a God that hideth himself; for he *made darkness his pavilion, v.* 11. His glory is invisible, his counsels are unsearchable, and his proceedings unaccountable, and so, as to us, clouds and darkness are round about him; we know not the way that he takes, even when he is coming towards us in ways of mercy ; but, when his designs are secret, they are kind ; for, though he hide himself, he is the God of Israel, the Saviour. And, *at his brightness, the thick clouds pass* (*v.* 12), comfort returns, the face of affairs is changed, and that which was gloomy and threatening becomes serene and pleasant.

4. The greater the difficulties are that lie in the way of deliverance the more glorious the deliverance is. For the rescuing of David, the waters were to be divided till the very channels were seen; the earth was to be cloven till the very foundations of it were discovered, *v.* 15. There were waters deep and many, waters out of which he was to be drawn (*v.* 16), as Moses, who had his name from being drawn out of the water literally, as David was figuratively. His enemies were strong, and they hated him ; had he been left to himself, they would have been too strong for him, *v.* 17. And they were too quick for him; for they *prevented him in the day of his calamity, v.* 18. But, in the midst of his troubles, the Lord was his stay, so that he did not sink. Note, God will not only deliver his people out of their troubles in due time, but he will sustain them and bear them up under their troubles in the mean time.

5. That which especially magnified the deliverance was that his comfort was the fruit of it and God's favour was the root and fountain of it. (1.) It was an introduction to his preferment, *v.* 19. " He brought me forth also out of my straits into a large place, where I had room, not only to turn, but to thrive in." (2.) It was a token of God's favour to him, and that made it doubly sweet : " *He delivered me because he delighted in me,* not for my merit, but for his own grace ,and good-will." Compare this with 2 Sam. xv. 26, *If he thus say, I have no delight in thee, here I am.* We owe our salvation, that great deliverance, to the delight God had in the Son of David, in whom he has declared himself to be well pleased.

In singing this we must triumph in God, and trust in him : and we may apply it to Christ the Son of David. The sorrows of death surrounded him ; in his distress he prayed (Heb. v. 7); God made the earth to shake and tremble, and the rocks to cleave, and brought him out, in his resurrection, into a large place, because he delighted in him and in his undertaking.

20 The LORD rewarded me according to my righteousness ; according to the cleanness of my hands hath he recompensed me. 21 For I have kept the ways of the LORD, and have not wickedly departed from my God. 22 For all his judgments *were* before me, and I did not put away his statutes from me. 23 I was also upright before him, and I kept myself from mine iniquity. 24 Therefore hath the LORD recompensed me according to my righteousness, according to the cleanness of my hands in his eyesight. 25 With the merciful thou wilt show thyself merciful ; with an upright man thou wilt show thyself upright ; 26 With the pure thou wilt show thyself pure ; and with the froward thou wilt show thyself froward. 27 For thou wilt save the afflicted people ; but wilt

bring down high looks. 28 For thou wilt light my candle: the LORD my God will enlighten my darkness.

Here, I. David reflects with comfort upon his own integrity, and rejoices in the testimony of his conscience that he had had his conversation in godly sincerity and not with fleshly wisdom, 2 Cor. i. 12. His deliverances were an evidence of this, and this was the great comfort of his deliverances. His enemies had misrepresented him, and perhaps, when his troubles continued long, he began to suspect himself; but, when God visibly took his part, he had both the credit and the comfort of his righteousness. 1. His deliverances cleared his innocency before men, and acquitted him from those crimes which he was falsely accused of. This he calls *rewarding him according to his righteousness* (v. 20, 24), that is, determining the controversy between him and his enemies, according to the justice of his cause and the cleanness of his hands, from that sedition, treason, and rebellion, with which he was charged. He had often appealed to God concerning his innocency; and now God had given judgment upon the appeal (as he always will) according to equity. 2. They confirmed the testimony of his own conscience for him, which he here reviews with a great deal of pleasure, v. 21—23. His own heart knows, and is ready to attest it, (1.) That he had kept firmly to his duty, and had not departed, not wickedly, not wilfully departed, from his God. Those that forsake the ways of the Lord do, in effect, depart from their God, and it is a wicked thing to do so. But though we are conscious to ourselves of many a stumble, and many a false step taken, yet if we recover ourselves by repentance, and go on in the way of our duty, it shall not be construed into a departure, for it is not a wicked departure, from our God. (2.) That he had kept his eye upon the rule of God's commands (v. 22): "*All his judgments were before me;* and I had a respect to them all, despised none as little, disliked none as hard, but made it my care and business to conform to them all. His statutes I did not put away from me, out of my sight, out of my mind, but kept my eye always upon them, and did not as those who, because they would quit the ways of the Lord, desire not the knowledge of those ways." (3.) That he had kept himself from his iniquity, and thereby had approved himself upright before God. Constant care to abstain from that sin, whatever it be, which most easily besets us, and to mortify the habit of it, will be a good evidence for us that we are upright before God. As David's deliverances cleared his integrity, so did the exaltation of Christ clear his, and for ever roll away the reproach that was cast upon him; and therefore he is said to be *justified in the Spirit,* 1 Tim. iii. 16.

II. He takes occasion thence to lay down the rules of God's government and judgment, that we may know not only what God expects from us, but what we may expect from him, v. 25, 26. 1. Those that show mercy to others (even they need mercy, and cannot depend upon the merit, no, not of their works of mercy) shall find mercy with God, Matt. v. 7. 2. Those that are faithful to their covenants with God, and the relations wherein they stand to him, shall find him all that to them which he has promised to be. Wherever God finds an upright man, he will be found an upright God. 3. Those that serve God with a pure conscience shall find that the words of the Lord are pure words, very sure to be depended on and very sweet to be delighted in. 4. Those that resist God, and walk contrary to him, shall find that he will resist them, and walk contrary to them, Lev. xxvi. 21, 24.

III. Hence he speaks comfort to the humble ("*Thou wilt save the afflicted people,* that are wronged and bear it patiently"), terror to the proud ("*Thou wilt bring down high looks,* that aim high, and expect great things for themselves, and look with scorn and disdain upon the poor and pious"), and encouragement to himself—"*Thou wilt light my candle,* that is, thou wilt revive and comfort my sorrowful spirit, and not leave me melancholy; thou wilt recover me out of my troubles and restore me to peace and prosperity; thou wilt make my honour bright, which is now eclipsed; thou wilt guide my way, and make it plain before me, that I may avoid the snares laid for me; thou wilt light my candle to work by, and give me an opportunity of serving thee and the interests of thy kingdom among men."

Let those that walk in darkness, and labour under many discouragements in singing these verses, encourage themselves that God himself will be a light to them.

29 For by thee I have run through a troop; and by my God have I leaped over a wall. 30 *As for* God, his way *is* perfect: the word of the LORD is tried: he *is* a buckler to all those that trust in him. 31 For who *is* God save the LORD? or who *is* a rock save our God? 32 *It is* God that girdeth me with strength, and maketh my way perfect. 33 He maketh my feet like hinds' *feet,* and setteth me upon my high places. 34 He teacheth my hands to war, so that a bow of steel is broken by mine arms. 35 Thou hast also given me the shield of thy salvation: and thy right hand hath holden me up, and thy gentleness hath made me great. 36 Thou hast enlarged my steps under me, that my feet did not slip.

37 I have pursued mine enemies, and overtaken them : neither did I turn again till they were consumed. 38 I have wounded them that they were not able to rise : they are fallen under my feet. 39 For thou hast girded me with strength unto the battle : thou hast subdued under me those that rose up against me. 40 Thou hast also given me the necks of mine enemies ; that I might destroy them that hate me. 41 They cried, but *there was* none to save *them : even* unto the LORD, but he answered them not. 42 Then did I beat them small as the dust before the wind : I did cast them out as the dirt in the streets. 43 Thou hast delivered me from the strivings of the people ; *and* thou hast made me the head of the heathen : a people *whom* I have not known shall serve me. 44 As soon as they hear of me, they shall obey me: the strangers shall submit themselves unto me. 45 The strangers shall fade away, and be afraid out of their close places. 46 The LORD liveth ; and blessed *be* my rock ; and let the God of my salvation be exalted. 47 *It is* God that avengeth me, and subdueth the people unto me. 48 He delivereth me from mine enemies : yea, thou liftest me up above those that rise up against me : thou hast delivered me from the violent man. 49 Therefore will I give thanks unto thee, O LORD, among the heathen, and sing praises unto thy name. 50 Great deliverance giveth he to his king ; and showeth mercy to his anointed, to David, and to his seed for evermore.

In these verses,

I. David looks back, with thankfulness, upon the great things which God had done for him. He had not only wrought deliverance for him, but had given him victory and success, and made him triumph over those who thought to triumph over him. When we set ourselves to praise God for one mercy we must be led by that to observe the many more with which we have been compassed about, and followed, all our days. Many things had contributed to David's advancement, and he owns the hand of God in them all, to teach us to do likewise, in reviewing the several steps by which we have risen to our prosperity. 1. God had given him all his skill and understanding in military af-fairs, which he was not bred up to nor designed for, his genius leading him more to music, and poetry, and a contemplative life: *He teaches my hands to war, v.* 34 2. God had given him bodily strength to go through the business and fatigue of war : God *girded him with strength (v.* 32, 39) to such a degree that he could break even a bow of steel, *v.* 34. What service God designs men for he will be sure to fit them for. 3. God had likewise given him great swiftness, not to flee from the enemies but to fly upon them (*v.* 33): *He makes my feet like hinds' feet, v.* 36. " *Thou hast enlarged my steps under me ;* but" (whereas those that take large steps are apt to tread awry) "my feet did not slip." He was so swift that he pursued his enemies and overtook them, *v.* 37. 4. God had made him very bold and daring in his enterprises, and given him spirit proportionable to his strength. If a troop stood in his way, he made nothing of running through them ; if a wall, he made nothing of leaping over it (*v.* 29) ; if ramparts and bulwarks, he soon mounted them, and by divine assistance set his feet upon the high places of the enemy, *v.* 33. 5. God had protected him, and kept him safe, in the midst of the greatest perils. Many a time he put his life in his hand, and yet it was wonderfully preserved : " *Thou hast given me the shield of thy salvation (v.* 35), and that has compassed me on every side. By that I have been delivered from the strivings of the people who aimed at my destruction (*v.* 43), particularly from the violent man" (*v.* 48), that is, Saul, who more than once threw a javelin at him. 6. God had prospered him in his designs ; he it was that made his way perfect (*v.* 32) and it was his right hand that held him up, *v.* 35. 7. God had given him victory over his enemies, the Philistines, Moabites, Ammonites, and all that fought against Israel : those especially he means, yet not excluding the house of Saul, which opposed his coming to the crown, and the partisans of Absalom and Sheba, who would have deposed him. He enlarges much upon the goodness of God to him in defeating his enemies, attributing his victories, not to his own sword or bow, nor to the valour of his mighty men, but to the favour of God : *I pursued* them (*v.* 37), *I wounded them* (*v.* 38); *for thou hast girded me with strength (v.* 39), else I could not have done it. All the praise is ascribed to God: *Thou hast subdued them under me, v.* 39. Thou hast *given me their necks* (*v.* 40), not only to trample upon them (as Josh. x. 24), but to cut them off. Even those who hated David whom God loved, and were enemies to the Israel of God, in their distress cried unto the Lord : but in vain ; he answered them not. How could they expect he should when it was he whom they fought against ? And, when he disowned them (as he will all those that act against his people), no other succours could stand them in stead : *There was none to save them, v.* 41.

Those whom God has abandoned are easily vanquished: *Then did I beat them small as the dust, v.* 42. But those whose cause is just he avenges (*v.* 47), and those whom he favours will certainly be *lifted up above those that rise up against them, v.* 48. 8. God had raised him to the throne, and not only delivered him and kept him alive, but dignified him and made him great (*v.* 35): *Thy gentleness has increased me*—thy *discipline* and *instruction ;* so some. The good lessons David learned in his affliction prepared him for the dignity and power that were intended him; and the lessening of him helped very much to increase his greatness. God made him not only a great conqueror, but a great ruler: *Thou hast made me the head of the heathen* (*v.* 43); all the neighbouring nations were tributaries to him. See 2 Sam. viii. 6, 11. In all this David was a type of Christ, whom the Father brought safely through his conflicts with the powers of darkness, and made victorious over them, and gave to be head over all things to his church, which is his body.

II. David looks up with humble and reverent adorations of the divine glory and perfection. When God had, by his providence, magnified him, he endeavours, with his praises, to magnify God, to bless him and exalt him, *v.* 46. He gives honour to him, 1. As a living God: *The Lord liveth, v.* 46. We had our lives at first from, and we owe the continuance of them to, that God who has life in himself and is therefore fitly called *the living God.* The gods of the heathen were dead gods. The best friends we have among men are dying friends. But God lives, lives for ever, and will not fail those that trust in him, but, because he lives, they shall live also ; for he is their life. 2. As a finishing God: *As for God,* he is not only perfect himself, but *his way his perfect, v.* 30. He is known by his name *Jehovah* (Exod. vi. 3), a God performing and perfecting what he begins in providence as well as creation, Gen. ii. 1. If it was God that made David's way perfect (*v.* 32), much more is his own way so. There is no flaw in God's works, nor any fault to be found with what he does, Eccl. iii. 14. And what he undertakes he will go through with, whatever difficulties lie in the way; what God begins to build he is able to finish. 3. As a faithful God: *The word of the Lord is tried.* "I have tried it" (says David), "and it has not failed me." All the saints, in all ages, have tried it, and it never failed any that trusted in it. It is tried as silver is tried, refined from all such mixture and alloy as lessen the value of men's words. David, in God's providences concerning him, takes notice of the performance of his promises to him, which, as it puts sweetness into the providence, so it puts honour upon the promise. 4. As the protector and defender of his people. David found him so to him : " *He is the God of my salva-*

tion (*v.* 46), by whose power and grace I am and hope to be saved ; but not of mine only: he is *a buckler to all those that trust in him* (*v.* 30); he shelters and protects them all, is both able and ready to do so." 5. As a non-such in all this, *v.* 31. There is a God, and *who is God save Jehovah ?* That God is a rock, for the support and shelter of his faithful worshippers ; and *who is a rock save our God ?* Thus he not only gives glory to God, but encourages his own faith in him. Note, (1.) Whoever pretend to be deities, it is certain that there is no God, save the Lord; all others are counterfeits, Isa. xliv. 8 ; Jer. x. 10. (2.) Whoever pretend to be our felicities, there is no rock, save our God ; none that we can depend upon to make us happy.

III. David looks forward, with a believing hope that God would still do him good. He promises himself, 1. That his enemies should be completely subdued, and that those of them that yet remained should be made his footstool,—that his government should be extensive, so that even a people whom he had not known should serve him (*v.* 43),—that his conquests, and, consequently, his acquests, should be easy (*As soon as they hear of me they shall obey me, v.* 44),—and that his enemies should be convinced that it was to no purpose to oppose him ; even those that had retired to their fastnesses should not trust to them, but be afraid out of their close places, having seen so much of David's wisdom, courage, and success. Thus the Son of David, though he sees not yet all things put under him, yet knows he shall reign till all opposing rule, principality, and power shall be quite put down. 2. That his seed should be for ever continued in the Messiah, who, he foresaw, should come from his loins, *v.* 50. He *shows mercy to his anointed,* his Messiah, *to David* himself, the anointed of the God of Jacob in the type, *and to his seed for evermore. He saith not unto seeds, as of many, but to his seed, as of one, that is Christ,* Gal. iii. 16. It is he only that shall reign for ever, and of the increase of whose government and peace there shall be no end. Christ is called *David,* Hos. iii. 5. God has called him *his king,* ii. 6. Great deliverance God does give, and will give, to him, and to his church and people, here called *his seed, for evermore.*

In singing these verses we must give God the glory of the victories of Christ and his church hitherto and of all the deliverances and advancements of the gospel kingdom, and encourage ourselves and one another with an assurance that the church militant will be shortly triumphant, will be eternally so.

PSALM XIX.

There are two excellent books which the great God has published for the instruction and edification of the children of men ; this psalm treats of them both, and recommends them both to our diligent study. I. The book of the creatures, in which we may easily read the power and godhead of the Creator, ver. 1—6. II. The book of the scriptures, which makes known to us the will of God concerning our duty. He shows the excellency and usefulness of that book (ver. 7—11) and then teaches us how to improve it, ver. 12—14.

To the chief musician. A psalm of David.

THE heavens declare the glory of God; and the firmament showeth his handywork. 2 Day unto day uttereth speech, and night unto night showeth knowledge. 3 *There is* no speech nor language, *where* their voice is not heard. 4 Their line is gone out through all the earth, and their words to the end of the world. In them hath he set a tabernacle for the sun, 5 Which *is* as a bridegroom coming out of his chamber, *and* rejoiceth as a strong man to run a race. 6 His going forth *is* from the end of the heaven, and his circuit unto the ends of it: and there is nothing hid from the heat thereof.

From the things that are seen every day by all the world the psalmist, in these verses, leads us to the consideration of the invisible things of God, whose being appears incontestably evident and whose glory shines transcendently bright in the visible heavens, the structure and beauty of them, and the order and influence of the heavenly bodies. This instance of the divine power serves not only to show the folly of atheists, who see there is a heaven and yet say, "There is no God," who see the effect and yet say, "There is no cause," but to show the folly of idolaters also, and the vanity of their imagination, who, though the heavens declare the glory of God, yet gave that glory to the lights of heaven which those very lights directed them to give to God only, the Father of lights. Now observe here,

I. What that is which the creatures notify to us. They are in many ways useful and serviceable to us, but in nothing so much as in this, that they declare the glory of God, by showing his handy-works, *v.* 1. They plainly speak themselves to be God's handy-works; for they could not exist from eternity; all succession and motion must have had a beginning; they could not make themselves, that is a contradiction; they could not be produced by a casual hit of atoms, that is an absurdity, fit rather to be bantered than reasoned with: therefore they must have a Creator, who can be no other than an eternal mind, infinitely wise, powerful, and good. Thus it appears they are God's works, the *work of his fingers* (viii. 3), and therefore they declare his glory. From the excellency of the work we may easily infer the infinite perfection of its great author. From the brightness of the heavens we may collect that the Creator is light; their vastness of extent bespeaks his immensity, their height his transcendency and sovereignty, their influence upon this earth his dominion, and providence, and universal beneficence: and all declare his

almighty power, by which they were at first made, and continue to this day according to the ordinances that were then settled.

II. What are some of those things which notify this?. 1. The heavens and the firmament—the vast expanse of air and ether, and the spheres of the planets and fixed stars. Man has this advantage above the beasts, in the structure of his body, that whereas they are made to look downwards, as their spirits must go, he is made erect, to look upwards, because upwards his spirit must shortly go and his thoughts should now rise. 2. The constant and regular succession of day and night (*v.* 2): *Day unto day, and night unto night,* speak the glory of that God who first divided between the light and the darkness, and has, from the beginning to this day, preserved that established order without variation, according to God's covenant with Noah (Gen. viii. 22), that, *while the earth remains, day and night shall not cease,* to which covenant of providence the covenant of grace is compared for its stability, Jer. xxxiii. 20; xxxi. 35. The counterchanging of day and night, in so exact a method, is a great instance of the power of God, and calls us to observe that, as in the kingdom of nature, so in that of providence, *he forms the light and creates the darkness* (Isa. xlv. 7), and sets the one over-against the other. It is likewise an instance of his goodness to man; for he *makes the outgoings of the morning and evening to rejoice,* lxv. 8. He not only glorifies himself, but gratifies us, by this constant revolution; for, as the light of the morning befriends the business of the day, so the shadows of the evening befriend the repose of the night; every day and every night speak the goodness of God, and, when they have finished their testimony, leave it to the next day, to the next night, to say the same. 3. The light and influence of the sun do, in a special manner, declare the glory of God; for of all the heavenly bodies that is the most conspicuous in itself and most useful to this lower world, which would be all dungeon, and all desert, without it. It is not an improbable conjecture that David penned this psalm when he had the rising sun in view, and from the brightness of it took occasion to declare the glory of God. Concerning the sun observe here, (1.) The place appointed him. In the heavens God has *set a tabernacle for the sun.* The heavenly bodies are called *hosts of heaven,* and therefore are fitly said to *dwell in tents,* as soldiers in their encampments. The sun is said to have a tabernacle set him, not only because he is in continual motion and never has a fixed residence, but because the mansion he has will, at the end of time, be taken down like a tent, when the heavens shall be rolled together like a scroll and the sun shall be turned into darkness. (2.) The course assigned him. That glorious creature was not made to be idle, but *his going forth* (at least as it appears to our eye) *is from one* point of the heavens, *and his circuit* thence to the opposite point, and thence (to complete his diurnal revolution) to the same point again; and this with such steadiness and constancy that we can certainly foretel the hour and the minute at which the sun will rise at such a place, any day to come. (3.) The brightness wherein he appears. He is *as a bridegroom coming out of his chamber,* richly dressed and adorned, as fine as hands can make him, looking pleasantly himself and making all about him pleasant; for *the friend of the bridegroom rejoices greatly to hear the bridegroom's voice,* John iii. 29. (4.) The cheerfulness wherewith he makes his tour. Though it seems a vast round which he has to walk, and he has not a moment's rest, yet in obedience to the law of his creation, and for the service of man, he not only does it, but does it with a great deal of pleasure and *rejoices as a strong man to run a race.* With such satisfaction did Christ, the Sun of righteousness, finish the work that was given him to do. (5.) His universal influence on this earth: *There is nothing hidden from the heat thereof,* no, not metals in the bowels of the earth, which the sun has an influence upon.

III. To whom this declaration is made of the glory of God. It is made to all parts of the world (*v.* 3, 4): *There is no speech nor language* (no nation, for the nations were divided *after their tongues,* Gen. x. 31,32) *where their voice is not heard. Their line has gone through all the earth* (the equinoctial line, suppose) *and* with it *their words to the end of the world,* proclaiming the eternal power of the God of nature, *v.* 4. The apostle uses this as a reason why the Jews should not be angry with him and others for preaching the gospel to the Gentiles, because God had already made himself known to the Gentile world by the works of creation, and left not himself without witness among them (Rom. x. 18), so that they were without excuse if they were idolaters, Rom. i. 20, 21. And those were without blame who, by preaching the gospel to them, endeavoured to turn them from their idolatry. If God used these means to prevent their apostasy, and they proved ineffectual, the apostles did well to use other means to recover them from it. *They have no speech or language* (so some read it) *and yet their voice is heard.* All people may hear these natural immortal preachers speak to them in their own tongue the wonderful works of God.

In singing these verses we must give God the glory of all the comfort and benefit we have by the lights of heaven, still looking above and beyond them to the Sun of righteousness.

7 The law of the LORD *is* perfect, converting the soul: the testimony of the LORD *is* sure, making wise the simple. 8 The statutes of the LORD *are* right, rejoicing the heart: the commandment of the LORD *is* pure, enlightening the eyes. 9 The fear of the LORD *is* clean, enduring for ever: the judgments of the LORD *are* true *and* righteous altogether. 10 More to be desired *are they* than gold, yea, than much fine gold: sweeter also than honey and the honeycomb. 11 Moreover by them is thy servant warned: *and* in keeping of them *there is* great reward. 12 Who can understand *his* errors? cleanse thou me from secret *faults.* 13 Keep back thy servant also from presumptuous *sins;* let them not have dominion over me: then shall I be upright, and I shall be innocent from the great transgression. 14 Let the words of my mouth, and the meditation of my heart, be acceptable in thy sight, O LORD, my strength, and my redeemer.

God's glory (that is, his goodness to man) appears much in the works of creation, but much more in and by divine revelation. The holy scripture, as it is a rule both of our duty to God and of our expectation from him, is of much greater use and benefit to us than day or night, than the air we breathe in, or the light of the sun. The discoveries made of God by his works might have served if man had retained his integrity; but, to recover him out of his fallen state, another course must be taken; that must be done by the word of God. And here,

I. The psalmist gives an account of the excellent properties and uses of the word of God, in six sentences (*v.* 7—9), in each of which the name *Jehovah* is repeated, and no vain repetition, for the law has its authority and all its excellency from the law-maker. Here are six several titles of the word of God, to take in the whole of divine revelation, precepts and promises, and especially the gospel. Here are several good properties of it, which prove its divine original, which recommend it to our affection, and which extol it above all other laws whatsoever. Here are several good effects of the law upon the minds of men, which show what it is designed for, what use we are to make of it, and how wonderful the efficacy of divine grace is, going along with it, and working by it. 1. *The law of the Lord is perfect.* It is perfectly free from all corruption, perfectly filled with all good, and perfectly fitted for the end for which it is designed; and it will make the man of God perfect, 2 Tim. iii. 17. Nothing is to be added to it nor taken from it. It is of use to *convert the soul,* to bring us back to ourselves, to our God, to our duty; for it shows us our sinfulness and misery in our departures from God and the indispensable necessity of our return to him. (2.) *The testimony of the Lord* (which witnesses for him to us) *is sure*, incontestably and inviolably sure, what we may give credit to, may rely upon, and may be confident it will not deceive us. It is a sure discovery of divine truth, a sure direction in the way of duty. It is a sure fountain of living comforts and a sure foundation of lasting hopes. It is of use to make us wise, wise to salvation, 2 Tim. iii. 15. It will give us an insight into things divine and a foresight of things to come. It will employ us in the best work and secure to us our true interests. It will make even *the simple* (poor contrivers as they may be for the present world) wise for their souls and eternity. Those that are humbly simple, sensible of their own folly and willing to be taught, shall be made wise by the word of God, xxv. 9. 3. *The statutes of the Lord* (enacted by his authority, and binding on all wherever they come) *are right*, exactly agreeing with the eternal rules and principles of good and evil, that is, with the right reason of man and the right counsels of God. All God's precepts, concerning all things, are right (cxix. 128), just as they should be; and they will set us to rights if we receive them and submit to them; and, because they are right, they *rejoice the heart*. The law, as we see it in the hands of Christ, gives cause for joy; and, when it is written in our hearts, it lays a foundation for lasting joy, by restoring us to our right mind. 4. *The commandment of the Lord is pure;* it is clear, without darkness; it is clean, without dross and defilement. It is itself purified from all alloy, and is purifying to those that receive and embrace it. It is the ordinary means which the Spirit uses in *enlightening the eyes;* it brings us to a sight and sense of our sin and misery, and directs us in the way of duty. 5. *The fear of the Lord* (true religion and godliness prescribed in the word, reigning in the heart, and practised in the life) *is clean*, clean itself, and will make us clean (John xv. 3); it will cleanse our way, cxix. 9. And it *endureth for. ever;* it is of perpetual obligation and can never be repealed. The ceremonial law is long since done away, but the law concerning the fear of God is ever the same. Time will not alter the nature of moral good and evil. 6. *The judgments of the Lord* (all his precepts, which are framed in infinite wisdom) *are true;* they are grounded upon the most sacred and unquestionable truths; they are *righteous*, all consonant to natural equity; and they are so *altogether:* there is no unrighteousness in any of them, but they are all of a piece.

II. He expresses the great value he had for the word of God, and the great advantage he had, and hoped to have, from it, *v.* 10, 11.

1. See how highly he prized the commandments of God. It is the character of all good people that they prefer their religion and the word of God, (1.) Far before all the wealth of the world. It is *more desirable than gold*, than

fine gold, *than much fine gold.* Gold is of the earth, earthly; but grace is the image of the heavenly. Gold is only for the body and the concerns of time; but grace is for the soul and the concerns of eternity. (2.) Far before all the pleasures and delights of sense. The word of God, received by faith, is sweet to the soul, *sweeter than honey and the honeycomb.* The pleasures of sense are the delight of brutes, and therefore debase the great soul of man; the pleasures of religion are the delight of angels, and exalt the soul. The pleasures of sense are deceitful, will soon surfeit, and yet never satisfy; but those of religion are substantial and satisfying, and there is no danger of exceeding in them.

2. See what use he made of the precepts of God's word: *By them is thy servant warned.* The word of God is a word of warning to the children of men; it warns us of the duty we are to do, the dangers we are to avoid, and the deluge we are to prepare for, Ezek. iii. 17; xxxiii. 7. It warns the wicked not to go on in his wicked way, and warns the righteous not to turn from his good way. All that are indeed God's servants take this warning.

3. See what advantage he promised himself by his obedience to God's precepts: *In keeping them there is great reward.* Those who make conscience of their duty will not only be no losers by it, but unspeakable gainers. There is a reward, not only after keeping, but in keeping, God's commandments, a present great reward of obedience in obedience. Religion is health and honour; it is peace and pleasure; it will make our comforts sweet and our crosses easy, life truly valuable and death itself truly desirable.

III. He draws some good inferences from this pious meditation upon the excellency of the word of God. Such thoughts as these should excite in us devout affections, and then they are to good purpose.

1. He takes occasion hence to make a penitent reflection upon his sins; for *by the law is the knowledge of sin.* " Is the commandment thus holy, just, and good? Then *who can understand his errors?* I cannot, whoever can." From the rectitude of the divine law he learns to call his sins his *errors.* If the commandment be true and righteous, every transgression of the commandment is an error, as grounded upon a mistake; every wicked practice takes rise from some corrupt principle; it is a deviation from the rule we are to work by, the way we are to walk in. From the extent, and strictness, and spiritual nature, of the divine law, he learns that his sins are so many that he cannot understand the number of them, and so exceedingly sinful that he cannot understand the heinousness and malignity of them. We are guilty of many sins which, through our carelessness and partiality to ourselves, we are not aware of; many we have been guilty of which we have forgotten; so that, when we have been ever so particular in the confession of sin, we

must conclude with an *et cætera—and such like;* for God knows a great deal more evil of us than we do of ourselves. In many things we all offend, and who can tell how often he offends? It is well that we are under grace, and not under the law, else we were undone.

2. He takes occasion hence to pray against sin. All the discoveries of sin made to us by the law should drive us to the throne of grace, there to pray, as David does here, (1.) For mercy to pardon. Finding himself unable to specify all the particulars of his transgressions, he cries out, *Lord, cleanse me from my secret faults;* not secret to God, so none are, nor only such as were secret to the world, but such as were hidden from his own observation of himself. The best of men have reason to suspect themselves guilty of many secret faults, and to pray to God to cleanse them from that guilt and not to lay it to their charge; for even our sins of infirmity and inadvertency, and our secret sins, would be our ruin, if God should deal with us according to the desert of them. Even secret faults are defiling, and render us unfit for communion with God; but, when they are pardoned, we are cleansed from them, 1 John i. 7. (2.) For grace to help in time of need. Having prayed that his sins of infirmity might be pardoned, he prays that presumptuous sins might be prevented, *v.* 13. All that truly repent of their sins, and have them pardoned, are in care not to relapse into sin, nor to return again to folly, as appears by their prayers, which concur with David's here, where observe, [1.] His petition: " Keep me from ever being guilty of a wilful presumptuous sin." We ought to pray that we may be kept from sins of infirmity, but especially from presumptuous sins, which most offend God and wound conscience, which wither our comforts and shock our hopes. " However, let none such *have dominion over me,* let me not be at the command of any such sin, nor be enslaved by it." [2.] His plea: " *So shall I be upright;* I shall appear upright; I shall preserve the evidence and comfort of my uprightness; and I *shall be innocent from the great transgression;*" so he calls a presumptuous sin, because no sacrifice was accepted for it, Num. xv. 28—30. Note, *First,* Presumptuous sins are very heinous and dangerous. Those that sin against the habitual convictions and actual admonitions of their own consciences, in contempt and defiance of the law and its sanctions, that sin with a high hand, sin presumptuously, and it is a great transgression. *Secondly,* Even good men ought to be jealous of themselves, and afraid of sinning presumptuously, yea, though through the grace of God they have hitherto been kept from them. Let none be high-minded, but fear. *Thirdly,* Being so much exposed, we have great need to pray to God, when we are pushing forward towards a presumptuous sin, to keep us back from it, either by his providence preventing

304

the temptation or by his grace giving us victory over it.

3. He takes occasion humbly to beg the divine acceptance of those his pious thoughts and affections, *v.* 14. Observe the connexion of this with what goes before. He prays to God to keep him from sin, and then begs he would accept his performances; for, if we favour our sins, we cannot expect God should favour us or our services, lxvi. 18. Observe, (1.) What his services were—the *words of his mouth and the meditations of his heart,* his holy affections offered up to God. The pious meditations of the heart must not be smothered, but expressed in the words of our mouth, for God's glory and the edification of others; and the words of our mouth in prayer and praise must not be formal, but arising from the meditation of the heart, xlv. 1. (2.) What was his care concerning these services—that they might be acceptable with God; for, if our services be not acceptable to God, what do they avail us? Gracious souls must have all they aim at if they be accepted of God, for that is their bliss. (3.) What encouragement he had to hope for this, because God was his strength and his redeemer. If we seek assistance from God as our strength in our religious duties, we may hope to find acceptance with God in the discharge of our duties; for by his strength we have power with him.

In singing this we should get our hearts much affected with the excellency of the word of God and delivered into it, we should be much affected with the evil of sin, the danger we are in of it and the danger we are in by it, and we should fetch in help from heaven against it.

PSALM XX. (20)

It is the will of God that prayers, intercessions, and thanksgivings, should be made, in a special manner, for kings and all in authority. This psalm is a prayer, and the next a thanksgiving, for the king. David was a martial prince, much in war. Either this psalm was penned upon occasion of some particular expedition of his, or, in general, as a form to be used in the daily service of the church for him. In this psalm we may observe, I. What it is they beg of God for the king, ver. 1—4. II. With what assurance they beg it. The people triumph (ver. 5), the prince (ver. 6), both together (ver. 7, 8), and so he concludes with a prayer to God for audience, ver. 9. In this, David may well be looked upon as a type of Christ, to whose kingdom and its interests among men the church was, in every age, a hearty well-wisher.

To the chief musician. A psalm of David.

THE LORD hear thee in the day of trouble; the name of the God of Jacob defend thee. 2 Send thee help from the sanctuary, and strengthen thee out of Zion. 3 Remember all thy offerings, and accept thy burnt sacrifice. Selah. 4 Grant thee according to thine own heart, and fulfil all thy counsel. 5 We will rejoice in thy salvation, and in the name of our God we will set up *our* banners: the LORD fulfil all thy petitions.

This prayer for David is entitled *a psalm of David;* nor was it any absurdity at all for him who was divinely inspired to draw up a directory, or form of prayer, to be used in the congregation for himself and those in authority under him; nay, it is very proper for those who desire the prayers of their friends to tell them particularly what they would have to be asked of God for them. Note, Even great and good men, and those that know ever so well how to pray for themselves, must not despise, but earnestly desire, the prayers of others for them, even those that are their inferiors in all respects. Paul often begged of his friends to pray for him. Magistrates and those in power ought to esteem and encourage praying people, to reckon them their strength (Zech. xii. 5. 10), and to do what they can for them, that they may have an interest in their prayers and may do nothing to forfeit it. Now observe here,

I. What it is that they are taught to ask of God for the king.

1. That God would answer his prayers: *The Lord hear thee in the day of trouble* (v. 1), and *the Lord fulfil all thy petitions, v.* 5. Note, (1.) Even the greatest of men may be much in trouble. It was often a day of trouble with David himself, of disappointment and distress, of treading down and of perplexity. Neither the crown on his head nor the grace in his heart would exempt him from trouble. (2.) Even the greatest of men must be much in prayer. David, though a man of business, a man of war, was constant to his devotions; though he had prophets, and priests, and many good people among his subjects, to pray for him, he did not think that excused him from praying for himself. Let none expect benefit by the prayers of the church, or of their ministers or friends for them, who are capable of praying for themselves, and yet neglect it. The prayers of others for us must be desired, not to supersede, but to second, our own for ourselves. Happy the people that have praying princes, to whose prayers they may thus say, *Amen.*

2. That God would protect his person, and preserve his life, in the perils of war: " *The name of the God of Jacob defend thee,* and set thee out of the reach of thy enemies." (1.) " Let God by his providence keep thee safe, even the God who preserved Jacob in the days of his trouble." David had mighty men for his guards, but he commits himself, and his people commit him, to the care of the almighty God. (2.) " Let God by his grace keep thee easy from the fear of evil.—Prov. xviii. 10, *The name of the Lord is a strong tower, into which the righteous run* by faith, *and are safe;* let David be enabled to shelter himself in that strong tower, as he has done many a time."

3. That God would enable him to go on in his undertakings for the public good—that, in the day of battle, he would *send him help out of the sanctuary, and strength out of Zion,* not from common providence, but from the ark of the covenant and the peculiar fa-

vour God bears to his chosen people Israel. That he would help him, in performance of the promises and in answer to the prayers made in the sanctuary. Mercies out of the sanctuary are the sweetest mercies, such as are the tokens of God's peculiar love, the blessing of God, even our own God. Strength out of Zion is spiritual strength, strength in the soul, in the inward man, and that is what we should most desire both for ourselves and others in services and sufferings.

4. That God would testify his gracious acceptance of the sacrifices he offered with his prayers, according to the law of that time, before he went out on this dangerous expedition: *The Lord remember all thy offerings and accept thy burnt-sacrifices* (v. 3) or *turn them to ashes;* that is, "The Lord give thee the victory and success which thou didst by prayer with sacrifices ask of him, and thereby give as full proof of his acceptance of the sacrifice as ever he did by kindling it with fire from heaven." By this we may now know that God accepts our spiritual sacrifices, if by his Spirit he kindles in our souls a holy fire of pious and divine affection and with that makes our hearts burn within us.

5. That God would crown all his enterprises and noble designs for the public welfare with the desired success (v. 4): *The Lord grant thee according to thy own heart.* This they might in faith pray for, because they knew David was a man after God's own heart, and would design nothing but what was pleasing to him. Those who make it their business to glorify God may expect that God will, in one way or other, gratify them; and those who walk in his counsel may promise themselves that he will fulfil theirs. *Thou shalt devise a thing and it shall be established unto thee.*

II. What confidence they had of an answer of peace to these petitions for themselves and their good king (v. 5): " *We will rejoice in thy salvation.* We that are subjects will rejoice in the preservation and prosperity of our prince;" or, rather, "In thy salvation, O God! in thy power and promise to save, will we rejoice; that is it which we depend upon now, and which, in the issue, we shall have occasion greatly to rejoice in." Those that have their eye still upon the salvation of the Lord shall have their hearts filled with the joy of that salvation: *In the name of our God will we set up our banners.* 1. "We will wage war in his name; we will see that our cause be good and make his glory our end in every expedition; we will ask counsel at his mouth, and take him along with us; we will follow his direction, implore his aid and depend upon it, and refer the issue to him." David went against Goliath in the name of the Lord of hosts, 1 Sam. xvii. 45. (2.) " We will celebrate our victories in his name. When we lift up our banners in triumph, and set up our trophies, it shall be in the name of our God; he shall have all the glory of our success, and no instrument shall have any part of the honour that is due to him."

In singing this we ought to offer up to God our hearty good wishes to the good government we are under and to the prosperity of it. But we may look further; these prayers for David are prophecies concerning Christ the Son of David, and in them they were abundantly answered; he undertook the work of our redemption, and made war upon the powers of darkness. In the day of trouble, when his soul was exceedingly sorrowful, the Lord heard him, heard him in that he feared (Heb. v. 7), *sent him help out of the sanctuary,* sent an angel from heaven to strengthen him, took cognizance of his offering when he made his soul an offering for sin, and accepted his burnt-sacrifice, turned it to ashes, the fire that should have fastened upon the sinner fastening upon the sacrifice, with which God was well pleased. And he granted him according to his own heart, made him to see of the travail of his soul, to his satisfaction, prospered his good pleasure in his hand, fulfilled all his petitions for himself and us; for him the Father heareth always and his intercession is ever prevailing.

6 Now know I that the LORD saveth his anointed; he will hear him from his holy heaven with the saving strength of his right hand. 7 Some *trust* in chariots, and some in horses: but we will remember the name of the LORD our God. 8 They are brought down and fallen: but we are risen, and stand upright. 9 Save, LORD: let the king hear us when we call.

Here is, I. Holy David himself triumphing in the interest he had in the prayers of good people (*v.* 6): "*Now know I* (I that pen the psalm know it) *that the Lord saveth his anointed,* because he hath stirred up the hearts of the seed of Jacob to pray for him." Note, It bodes well to any prince and people, and may justly be taken as a happy presage, when God pours upon them a spirit of prayer. If he see us seeking him, he will be found of us; if he cause us to hope in his word, he will establish his word to us. Now that so many who have an interest in heaven are praying for him he doubts not but that God will hear him, and grant him an answer of peace, which will, 1. Take its rise from above: *He will hear him from his holy heaven,* of which the sanctuary was a type (Heb. ix. 23), from the throne he hath prepared in heaven, of which the mercy-seat was a type. 2. It shall take its effect here below: He will hear him *with the saving strength of his right hand;* he will give a real answer to his prayers, and the prayers of his friends for him, not by letter, nor by word of mouth, but, which is much better, by his right hand, by the saving strength of his right hand. He

306

will make it to appear that he hears him by what he does for him

II. His people triumphing in God and their relation to him, and his revelation of himself to them, by which they distinguish themselves from those that live without God in the world. 1. See the difference between worldly people and godly people, in their confidences, *v.* 7. The children of this world trust in second causes, and think all is well if those do but smile upon them; they trust *in chariots and in horses,* and the more of them they can bring into the field the more sure they are of success in their wars; probably David has here an eye to the Syrians, whose forces consisted much of chariots and horsemen, as we find in the history of David's victories over them, 2 Sam. viii. 4; x. 18. "But," say the Israelites, "we neither have chariots and horses to trust to nor do we want them, nor, if we had them, would we build our hopes of success upon that; *but we will remember,* and rely upon, *the name of the Lord our God,* upon the relation we stand in to him as the Lord our God and the knowledge we have of him by his name," that is, all that whereby he makes himself known; this we will remember and upon every remembrance of it will be encouraged. Note, Those who make God and his name their praise may make God and his name their trust. 2. See the difference in the issue of their confidences and by that we are to judge of the wisdom of the choice; things are as they prove; see who will be ashamed of their confidence and who not, *v.* 8. "Those that trusted in their chariots and horses are brought down and fallen, and their chariots and horses were so far from saving them that they helped to sink them, and made them the easier and the richer prey to the conqueror, 2 Sam. viii. 4. But we that trust in the name of the Lord our God not only stand upright, and keep our ground, but have risen, and have got ground against the enemy, and have triumphed over them." Note, A believing obedient trust in God and his name is the surest way both to preferment and to establishment, to rise and to stand upright, and this will stand us in stead when creature-confidences fail those that depend upon them.

III. They conclude their prayer for the king with a *Hosanna,* "*Save now, we beseech thee,* O Lord!" *v.* 9. As we read this verse, it may be taken as a prayer that God would not only bless the king, "Save, Lord, give him success," but that he would make him a blessing to them, "*Let the king hear us* when we call to him for justice and mercy." Those that would have good of their magistrates must thus pray for them, for they, as all other creatures, are that to us (and no more) which God makes them to be. Or it may refer to the Messiah, that King, that King of kings; let him hear us when we call; let him come to us according to the promise, in the time appointed; let him, as the great Master of requests, receive all our petitions and present them to his Father. But many interpreters give another reading of this verse, by altering the pause, *Lord, save the king, and hear us when we call;* and so it is a summary of the whole psalm and is taken into our English Liturgy: *O Lord! save the king, and mercifully hear us when we call upon thee.*

In singing these verses we should encourage ourselves to trust in God, and stir up ourselves to pray earnestly, as we are in duty bound, for those in authority over us, that under them we may lead quiet and peaceable lives in all godliness and honesty.

PSALM XXI.

As the foregoing psalm was a prayer for the king that God would protect and prosper him, so this is a thanksgiving for the success God had blessed him with. Those whom we have prayed for we ought to give thanks for, and particularly for kings, in whose prosperity we share. They are here taught, I. To congratulate him on his victories, and the honour he had achieved, ver. 1-6. II. To confide in the power of God for the completing of the ruin of the enemies of his kingdom, ver. 7—13. In this there is an eye to Messiah the Prince, and the glory of his kingdom; for to him divers passages in this psalm are more applicable than to David himself.

To the chief musician. A psalm of David.

THE king shall joy in thy strength, O Lord; and in thy salvation how greatly shall he rejoice! 2 Thou hast given him his heart's desire, and hast not withholden the request of his lips. Selah. 3 For thou preventest him with the blessings of goodness: thou settest a crown of pure gold on his head. 4 He asked life of thee, *and* thou gavest *it* him, *even* length of days for ever and ever. 5 His glory *is* great in thy salvation: honour and majesty hast thou laid upon him. 6 For thou hast made him most blessed for ever: thou hast made him exceeding glad with thy countenance.

David here speaks for himself in the first place, professing that his joy was in God's strength and in his salvation, and not in the strength or success of his armies. He also directs his subjects herein to rejoice with him, and to give God all the glory of the victories he had obtained; and all with an eye to Christ, of whose triumphs over the powers of darkness David's victories were but shadows. 1. They here congratulate the king on his joys and concur with him in them (*v.* 1): "*The king rejoices,* he uses to rejoice *in thy strength,* and so do we; what pleases the king pleases us," 2 Sam. iii. 36. Happy the people the character of whose king it is that he makes God's strength his confidence and God's salvation his joy, that is pleased with all the advancements of God's kingdom and trusts God to bear him out in all he does for the service of it. Our Lord Jesus, in his great undertaking, relied upon help from heaven, and pleased himself with the prospect of that great salvation which he

was thereby to work out. 2. They give God all the praise of those things which were the matter of their king's rejoicing. (1.) That God had heard his prayers (*v.* 2): *Thou hast given him his heart's desire* (and there is no prayer accepted but what is the heart's desire), the very thing they begged of God for him, xx. 4. Note, God's gracious returns of prayer do, in a special manner, require our humble returns of praise. When God gives to Christ the heathen for his inheritance, gives him to see his seed, and accepts his intercession for all believers, he gives him his heart's desire. (2.) That God had surprised him with favours, and much outdone his expectations (*v.* 3): *Thou preventest him with the blessings of goodness.* All our blessings are blessings of goodness, and are owing, not at all to any merit of ours, but purely and only to God's goodness. But the psalmist here reckons it in a special manner obliging that these blessings were given in a preventing way; this fixed his eye, enlarged his soul, and endeared his God, as one expresses it. When God's blessings come sooner and prove richer than we imagine, when they are given before we prayed for them, before we were ready for them, nay, when we feared the contrary, then it may be truly said that he prevented us with them. Nothing indeed prevented Christ, but to mankind never was any favour more preventing than our redemption by Christ and all the blessed fruits of his mediation. (3.) That God had advanced him to the highest honour and the most extensive power: "*Thou hast set a crown of pure gold upon his head* and kept it there, when his enemies attempted to throw it off." Note, Crowns are at God's disposal; no head wears them but God sets them there, whether in judgment to his land or for mercy the event will show. On the head of Christ God never set a crown of gold, but of thorns first, and then of glory. (4.) That God had assured him of the perpetuity of his kingdom, and therein had done more for him than he was able either to ask or think (*v.* 4): "When he went forth upon a perilous expedition *he asked his life of thee,* which he then put into his hand, *and thou* not only *gavest him that,* but withal gavest him *length of days for ever and ever,* didst not only prolong his life far beyond his expectation, but didst assure him of a blessed immortality in a future state and of the continuance of his kingdom in the Messiah that should come of his loins." See how God's grants often exceed our petitions and hopes, and infer thence how rich he is in mercy to those that call upon him. See also and rejoice in the length of the days of Christ's kingdom. He was dead, indeed, that we might live through him; but he is alive, and lives for evermore, and *of the increase of his government and peace there shall be no end;* and because he thus lives we shall thus live also. (5.) That God had advanced him to the highest honour and dignity (*v.* 5):

" *His glory is great,* far transcending that of all the neighbouring princes, in the salvation thou hast wrought for him and by him." The glory which every good man is ambitious of is to see the salvation of the Lord. *Honour and majesty hast thou laid upon him,* as a burden which he must bear, as a charge which he must account for. Jesus Christ *received from God the Father honour and glory* (2 Pet. i. 17), the glory which he had with him before the worlds were, John xvii. 5. And on him is laid the charge of universal government and to him all power in heaven and earth is committed. (6.) That God had given him the satisfaction of being the channel of all bliss to mankind (*v.* 6): " *Thou hast set him to be blessings for ever*" (so the margin reads it), " thou has made him to be a universal everlasting blessing to the world, in whom the families of the earth are, and shall be, blessed; and so thou hast made him exceedingly glad with the countenance thou hast given to his undertaking and to him in the prosecution of it." See how the spirit of prophecy gradually rises here to that which is peculiar to Christ, for none besides is blessed for ever, much less a blessing for ever to that eminency that the expression denotes: and of him it is said that God made him full of joy with his countenance.

In singing this we should rejoice in his joy and triumph in his exaltation.

7 For the king trusteth in the LORD, and through the mercy of the most High he shall not be moved. 8 Thine hand shall find out all thine enemies: thy right hand shall find out those that hate thee. 9 Thou shalt make them as a fiery oven in the time of thine anger : the LORD shall swallow them up in his wrath, and the fire shall devour them. 10 Their fruit shalt thou destroy from the earth, and their seed from among the children of men. 11 For they intended evil against thee: they imagined a mischievous device, *which* they are not able *to perform.* 12 Therefore shalt thou make them turn their back, *when* thou shalt make ready *thine arrows* upon thy strings against the face of them. 13 Be thou exalted, LORD, in thine own strength: *so* will we sing and praise thy power.

The psalmist, having taught his people to look back with joy and praise on what God had done for him and them, here teaches them to look forward with faith, and hope, and prayer, upon what God would further do for them: *The king rejoices in God* (*v.* 1), and therefore we will be thankful; *the king trusteth in God* (*v.* 7), therefore will we be encouraged. The joy and confidence of Christ

our King is the ground of all our joy and confidence.

I. They are confident of the stability of David's kingdom. *Through the mercy of the Most High,* and not through his own merit or strength, *he shall not be moved.* His prosperous state shall not be disturbed; his faith and hope in God, which are the stay of his spirit, shall not be shaken. The mercy of the Most High (the divine goodness, power, and dominion) is enough to secure our happiness, and therefore our trust in that mercy should be enough to silence all our fears. God being at Christ's right hand in his sufferings (xvi. 8) and he being at God's right hand in his glory, we may be sure he shall not, he cannot, be moved, but continues ever.

II. They are confident of the destruction of all the impenitent implacable enemies of David's kingdom. The success with which God had blessed David's arms hitherto was an earnest of the rest which God would give him from all his enemies round about, and a type of the total overthrow of all Christ's enemies who would not have him to reign over them. Observe, 1. The description of his enemies. They are such as hate him, *v.* 8. They hated David because God had set him apart for himself, hated Christ because they hated the light ; but both were hated without any just cause, and in both God was hated, John xv. 23, 25. 2. The designs of his enemies (*v.* 11): *They intended evil against thee, and imagined a mischievous device ;* they pretended to fight against David only, but their enmity was against God himself. Those that aimed to un-king David aimed, in effect, to un-God Jehovah. What is devised and designed against religion, and against the instruments God raises up to support and advance it, is very evil and mischievous, and God takes it as devised and designed against himself and will so reckon for it. (3.) The disappointment of them : "They devise what they are *not able to perform,*" *v.* 11. Their malice is impotent, and they *imagine a vain thing,* ii. 1. (4.) The discovery of them (*v.* 8): " *Thy hand shall find them out.* Though ever so artfully disguised by the pretences and professions of friendship, though mingled with the faithful subjects of this kingdom and hardly to be distinguished from them, though flying from justice and absconding in their close places, yet thy hand shall find them out wherever they are." There is no escaping God's avenging eye, no going out of the reach of his hand ; rocks and mountains will be no better shelter at last than fig-leaves were at first. (5.) The destruction of them ; it will be an utter destruction (Luke xix. 27); they shall be swallowed up and devoured, *v.* 9. Hell, the portion of all Christ's enemies, is the complete misery both of body and soul. *Their fruit and their seed shall be destroyed, v.* 10. The enemies of God's kingdom, in every age, shall fall under the same doom, and the whole generation of them will at last be rooted out, and all opposing rule, principality, and power, shall be put down. The arrows of God's wrath shall confound them and put them to flight, being levelled at the face of them, v. 12. That will be the lot of daring enemies that face God. The fire of God's wrath will consume them (v. 9); they shall not only be cast into a furnace of fire (Matt. xlii. 42), but he shall make them themselves as a fiery oven or furnace; they shall be their own tormentors; the reflections and terrors of their own consciences will be their hell. Those that might have had Christ to rule and save them, but rejected him and fought against him, shall find that even the remembrance of that will be enough to make them, to eternity, a fiery oven to themselves: it is the worm that dies not.

III. In this confidence they beg of God that he would still appear for his anointed (v. 13), that he would act for him in his own strength, by the immediate operations of his power as Lord of hosts and Father of spirits, making little use of means and instruments. And, 1. Hereby he would exalt himself and glorify his own name. "We have but little strength, and are not so active for thee as we should be, which is our shame; Lord, take the work into thy own hands, do it without us, and it will be thy glory." 2. Hereupon they would exalt him: *So will we sing, and praise thy power*, the more triumphantly." The less God has of our service when a deliverance is in the working the more he must have of our praises when it is wrought without us.

PSALM XXII.

The Spirit of Christ, which was in the prophets, testifies in this psalm, as clearly and fully as any where in all the Old Testament, "the sufferings of Christ and the glory that should follow" (1 Pet. i. 11); of him, no doubt, David here speaks, and not of himself, or any other man. Much of it is expressly applied to Christ in the New Testament, all of it may be applied to him, and some of it must be understood of him only. The providences of God concerning David were so very extraordinary that we may suppose there were some wise and good men who then could not but look upon him as a figure of him that was to come. But the composition of his psalms especially, in which he found himself wonderfully carried out by the spirit of prophecy far beyond his own thought and intention, was (we may suppose) an abundant satisfaction to himself that he was not only a father of the Messiah, but a figure of him. In this psalm he speaks, I. Of the humiliation of Christ (ver. 1—21), where David, as a type of Christ, complains of the very calamitous condition he was in upon many accounts. 1. He complains, and mixes comforts with his complaints; he complains (ver. 1, 2), but comforts himself (ver. 3—5), complains again (ver. 6—8), but comforts himself again, ver. 9, 10. 2. He complains, and mixes prayers with his complaints; he complains of the power and rage of his enemies (ver. 12, 13, 16, 18), of his own bodily weakness and decay (ver. 14, 15, 17); but prays that God would not be far from him (ver. 11, 19), that he would save and deliver him, ver. 19—21. II. Of the exaltation of Christ, that his undertaking should be for the glory of God (ver. 22—25), for the salvation and joy of his people (ver. 26—29), and for the perpetuating of his own kingdom, ver. 30, 31. In singing this psalm we must keep our thoughts fixed upon Christ, and be so affected with his sufferings as to experience the fellowship of them, and so affected with his grace as to experience the power and influence of it.

To the chief musician upon Aijeleth Shahar. A psalm of David.

MY God, my God, why hast thou forsaken me? *why art thou so* far from helping me, *and from* the words of my roaring? 2 O my God, I cry in the daytime, but thou hearest

not; and in the night season, and am not silent. 3 But thou *art* holy, O *thou* that inhabitest the praises of Israel. 4 Our fathers trusted in thee : they trusted, and thou didst deliver them. 5 They cried unto thee, and were delivered : they trusted in thee, and were not confounded. 6 But I *am* a worm, and no man ; a reproach of men, and despised of the people. 7 All they that see me laugh me to scorn : they shoot out the lip, they shake the head, *saying*, 8 He trusted on the LORD *that* he would deliver him : let him deliver him, seeing he delighted in him. 9 But thou *art* he that took me out of the womb : thou didst make me hope *when I was* upon my mother's breasts. 10 I was cast upon thee from the womb : thou *art* my God from my mother's belly.

Some think they find Christ in the title of this psalm, upon *Aijeleth Shahar—The hind of the morning*. Christ is as the swift hind upon the mountains of spices (Cant. viii. 14), as the loving hind and the pleasant roe, to all believers (Prov. v. 19); he giveth goodly words like Naphtali, who is compared to a *hind let loose*, Gen. xlix. 21. He is the hind of the morning, marked out by the counsels of God from eternity, to be run down by those dogs that compassed him, v. 16. But others think it denotes only the tune to which the psalm was set. In these verses we have,

I. A sad complaint of God's withdrawings, v. 1, 2.

1. This may be applied to David, or any other child of God, in the want of the tokens of his favour, pressed with the burden of his displeasure, roaring under it, as one overwhelmed with grief and terror, crying earnestly for relief, and, in this case, apprehending himself forsaken of God, unhelped, unheard, yet calling him, again and again, "*My God*," and continuing to cry day and night to him and earnestly desiring his gracious returns. Note, (1.) Spiritual desertions are the saints' sorest afflictions; when their evidences are clouded, divine consolations suspended, their communion with God interrupted, and the terrors of God set in array against them, how sad are their spirits, and how sapless all their comforts! (2.) Even their complaint of these burdens is a good sign of spiritual life and spiritual senses exercised. To cry out, "My God, why am I sick? Why am I poor?" would give cause to suspect discontent and worldliness. But, *Why hast thou forsaken-me?* is the language of a heart binding up its happiness in God's favour. (3.) When we are lamenting God's withdrawings, yet still we must call him our

God, and continue to call upon him as ours. When we want the faith of assurance we must live by a faith of adherence. " However it be, yet God is good, and he is mine; *though he slay me, yet will I trust in him;* though he do not answer me immediately, I will continue praying and waiting; though he be silent, I will not be silent."

2. But it must be applied to Christ; for, in the first words of this complaint, he poured out his soul before God when he was upon the cross (Matt. xxvii. 46); probably he proceeded to the following words, and, some think, repeated the whole psalm, if not aloud (because they cavilled at the first words), yet to himself. Note, (1.) Christ, in his sufferings, cried earnestly to his Father for his favour and presence with him. He cried *in the day-time,* upon the cross, *and in the night-season,* when he was in his agony in the garden. *He offered up strong crying and tears to him that was able to save him,* and with some fear too, Heb. v. 7. (2.) Yet God forsook him, was far from helping him, and did not hear him, and it was this that he complained of more than all his sufferings. God delivered him into the hands of his enemies; it was by his determinate counsel that he was crucified and slain, and he did not give in sensible comforts. But, Christ having made himself sin for us, in conformity thereunto the Father laid him under the present impressions of his wrath and displeasure against sin. *It pleased the Lord to bruise him and put him to grief,* Isa. liii. 10. But even then he kept fast hold of his relation to his Father as his God, by whom he was now employed, whom he was now serving, and with whom he should shortly be glorified.

II. Encouragement taken, in reference hereunto, v. 3—5. Though God did not hear him, did not help him, yet, 1. He will think well of God: " *But thou art holy,* not unjust, untrue, nor unkind, in any of thy dispensations. Though thou dost not immediately come in to the relief of thy afflicted people, yet thou lovest them, art true to thy covenant with them, and dost not countenance the iniquity of their persecutors, Hab. i. 13. And, as thou art infinitely pure and upright thyself, so thou delightest in the services of thy upright people: *Thou inhabitest the praises of Israel;* thou art pleased to manifest thy glory, and grace, and special presence with thy people, in the sanctuary, where they attend thee with their praises. There thou art always ready to receive their homage, and of the tabernacle of meeting thou hast said, *This is my rest for ever.*" This bespeaks God's wonderful condescension to his faithful worshippers—(that, though he is attended with the praises of angels, yet he is pleased to inhabit the praises of Israel), and it may comfort us in all our complaints—that, though God seem, for a while, to turn a deaf ear to them, yet he is so well pleased with his people's praises that he will, in due

time, give them cause to change their note: *Hope in God, for I shall yet praise him.* Our Lord Jesus, in his sufferings, had an eye to the holiness of God, to preserve and advance the honour of that, and of his grace in inhabiting the praises of Israel notwithstanding the iniquities of their holy things. 2. He will take comfort from the experiences which the saints in former ages had of the benefit of faith and prayer (v. 4, 5): " *Our fathers trusted in thee, cried unto thee, and thou didst deliver them;* therefore thou wilt, in due time, deliver me, for never any that hoped in thee were made ashamed of their hope, never any that sought thee sought thee in vain. And thou art still the same in thyself and the same to thy people that ever thou wast. They were our fathers, and thy people are *beloved for the fathers' sake,*" Rom. xi. 28. The entail of the covenant is designed for the support of the seed of the faithful. He that was our fathers' God must be ours and will therefore be ours. Our Lord Jesus, in his sufferings, supported himself with this—that all the fathers who were types of him in his sufferings, Noah, Joseph, David, Jonah, and others, were in due time delivered and were types of his exaltation too; therefore he knew that *he also should not be confounded,* Isa. l. 7.

III. The complaint renewed of another grievance, and that is the contempt and reproach of men. This complaint is by no means so bitter as that before of God's withdrawings; but, as that touches a gracious soul, so this a generous soul, in a very tender part, v. 6—8. Our fathers were honoured, the patriarchs in their day, first or last, appeared great in the eye of the world, Abraham, Moses, David; but Christ is *a worm, and no man.* It was great condescension that he became man, a step downwards, which is, and will be, the wonder of angels; yet, as if it were too much, too great, to be a man, he becomes a worm, and no man. He was *Adam—a mean man,* and *Enosh—a man of sorrows,* but *lo Ish—not a considerable man;* for he took upon him the form of a servant, and *his visage was marred more than any man's,* Isa. lii. 14. Man, at the best, is a worm; but he became *a worm, and no man.* If he had not made himself a worm, he could not have been trampled upon as he was. The word signifies such a worm as was used in dyeing scarlet or purple, whence some make it an allusion to his bloody sufferings. See what abuses were put upon him. 1. He was reproached as a bad man, as a blasphemer, a sabbath-breaker, a wine-bibber, a false prophet, an enemy to Cæsar, a confederate with the prince of the devils. 2. He was despised of the people as a mean contemptible man, not worth taking notice of, his country in no repute, his relations poor mechanics, his followers none of the rulers, or the Pharisees, but the mob. 3. He was ridiculed as a foolish man, and one that not only deceived others, but himself too. Those that saw him hanging on the cross laughed him to scorn. So far were they from pitying him, or concerning themselves for him, that they added to his afflictions, with all the gestures and expressions of insolence upbraiding him with his fall. They make mouths at him, make merry over him, and make a jest of his sufferings: *They shoot out the lip, they shake their head*, saying, This was he that said *he trusted God would deliver him; now let him deliver him.* David was sometimes taunted for his confidence in God; but in the sufferings of Christ this was literally and exactly fulfilled. Those very gestures were used by those that reviled him (Matt. xxvii. 39); they wagged their heads, nay, and so far did their malice make them forget themselves that they used the very words (*v.* 43), *He trusted in God; let him deliver him.* Our Lord Jesus, having undertaken to satisfy for the dishonour we had done to God by our sins, did it by submitting to the lowest possible instance of ignominy and disgrace.

IV. Encouragement taken as to this also (*v.* 9, 10): Men despise me, *but thou art he that took me out of the womb.* David and other good men have often, for direction to us, encouraged themselves with this, that God was not only the *God of their fathers,* as before (*v.* 4), but the God of their infancy, who began by times to take care of them, as soon as they had a being, and therefore, they hope, will never cast them off. He that did so well for us in that helpless useless state will not leave us when he has reared us and nursed us up into some capacity of serving him. See the early instances of God's providential care for us, 1. In the birth: *He took us also out of the womb,* else we had died there, or been stifled in the birth. Every man's particular time begins with this pregnant proof of God's providence, as time, in general, began with the creation, that pregnant proof of his being. 2. At the breast: "*Then didst thou make me hope;*" that is, "thou didst that for me, in providing sustenance for me and protecting me from the dangers to which I was exposed, which encourages me to hope in thee all my days." The blessings of the breasts, as they crown the blessings of the womb, so they are earnests of the blessings of our whole lives; surely he that fed us then will never starve us, Job iii. 12. 3. In our early dedication to him: *I was cast upon thee from the womb,* which perhaps refers to his circumcision on the eighth day; he was then by his parents committed and given up to God as his God in covenant; for circumcision was a seal of the covenant; and this encouraged him to trust in God. Those have reason to think themselves safe who were so soon, so solemnly, *gathered under the wings of the divine majesty.* 4. In the experience we have had of God's goodness to us all along ever since, drawn out in a constant uninterrupted series

of preservations and supplies: *Thou art my God,* providing for me and watching over me for good, *from my mother's belly,* that is; from my coming into the world unto this day. And if, as soon as we became capable of exercising reason, we put our confidence in God and committed ourselves and our way to him, we need not doubt but he will always remember the *kindness of our youth and the love of our espousals,* Jer. ii. 2. This is applicable to our Lord Jesus, over whose incarnation and birth the divine Providence watched with a peculiar care, when he was born in a stable, laid in a manger, and immediately exposed to the malice of Herod, and forced to flee into Egypt. *When he was a child God loved him and called him thence* (Hos. xi. 1), and the remembrance of this comforted him in his sufferings. Men reproached him, and discouraged his confidence in God; but God had honoured him and encouraged his confidence in him.

11 Be not far from me; for trouble *is* near; for *there is* none to help. 12 Many bulls have compassed me: strong *bulls* of Bashan have beset me round. 13 They gaped upon me *with* their mouths, *as* a ravening and a roaring lion. 14 I am poured out like water, and all my bones are out of joint: my heart is like wax; it is melted in the midst of my bowels. 15 My strength is dried up like a potsherd; and my tongue cleaveth to my jaws; and thou hast brought me into the dust of death. 16 For dogs have compassed me: the assembly of the wicked have inclosed me: they pierced my hands and my feet. 17 I may tell all my bones: they look *and* stare upon me. 18 They part my garments among them, and cast lots upon my vesture. 19 But be not thou far from me, O Lord: O my strength, haste thee to help me. 20 Deliver my soul from the sword; my darling from the power of the dog. 21 Save me from the lion's mouth: for thou hast heard me from the horns of the unicorns.

In these verses we have Christ suffering and Christ praying, by which we are directed to look for crosses and to look up to God under them.

I. Here is Christ suffering. David indeed was often in trouble, and beset with enemies; but many of the particulars here specified are such as were never true of David, and therefore must be appropriated to Christ in the depth of his humiliation.

1. He is here deserted by his friends: *Trouble* and distress are *near,* and *there is*

none to help, none to uphold, *v.* 11. He trod the wine-press alone; for all his disciples forsook him and fled. It is God's honour to help when all other helps and succours fail.

2. He is here insulted and surrounded by his enemies, such as were of a higher rank, who, for their strength and fury, are compared to bulls, *strong bulls of Bashan* (*v.* 12), fat and fed to the full, haughty and sour; such were the chief priests and elders that persecuted Christ; and others of a lower rank, who are compared to *dogs* (*v.* 16), filthy and greedy, and unwearied in running him down. There was an assembly of the wicked plotting against him (*v.* 16); for the chief priests sat in council, to consult of ways and means to take Christ. These enemies were numerous and unanimous: " Many, and those of different and clashing interests among themselves, as Herod and Pilate, have agreed to compass me. They have carried their plot far, and seem to have gained their point, for they have *beset me round, v.* 12. They have enclosed me, *v.* 16. They are formidable and threatening (*v.* 13): *They gaped upon me with their mouths,* to show me that they would swallow me up; and this with as much strength and fierceness as a roaring ravening lion leaps upon his prey."

3. He is here crucified. The very manner of his death is described, though never in use among the Jews: *They pierced my hands and my feet* (*v.* 16), which were nailed to the accursed tree, and the whole body left so to hang, the effect of which must needs be the most exquisite pain and torture. There is no one passage in all the Old Testament which the Jews have so industriously corrupted as this, because it is such an eminent prediction of the death of Christ and was so exactly fulfilled.

4. He is here dying (*v.* 14, 15), dying in pain and anguish, because he was to satisfy for sin, which brought in pain, and for which we must otherwise have lain in everlasting anguish. Here is, (1.) The dissolution of the whole frame of his body: *I am poured out like water,* weak as water, and yielding to the power of death, emptying himself of all the supports of his human nature. (2.) The dislocation of his bones. Care was taken that not one of them should be broken (John xix. 36), but they were all out of joint by the violent stretching of his body upon the cross as upon a rack. Or it may denote the fear that seized him in his agony in the garden, when he began to be sore amazed, the effect of which perhaps was (as sometimes it has been of great fear, Dan. v. 6), that the *joints of his loins were loosed and his knees smote one against another.* His bones were put out of joint that he might put the whole creation into joint again, which sin had put out of joint, and might make our broken bones to rejoice. (3.) The colliquation of his spirits: *My heart is like wax,* melted to receive the impressions of God's wrath against the sins

he undertook to satisfy for, melting away like the vitals of a dying man; and, as this satisfied for the hardness of our hearts, so the consideration of it should help to soften them. When Job speaks of his inward trouble he says, *The Almighty makes my heart soft,* Job xxiii. 16, and see Ps. lviii. 2. (4.) The failing of his natural force: *My strength is dried up;* so that he became parched and brittle like a potsherd, the radical moisture being wasted by the fire of divine wrath preying upon his spirits. Who then can stand before God's anger? Or who knows the power of it? *If this was done in the green tree, what shall be done in the dry?* (5.) The clamminess of his mouth, a usual symptom of approaching death: *My tongue cleaveth to my jaws;* this was fulfilled both in his thirst upon the cross (John xix. 28) and in his silence under his sufferings; for, *as a sheep before the shearers is dumb, so he opened not his mouth,* nor objected against any thing done to him. (6.) His giving up the ghost: " *Thou hast brought me to the dust of death;* I am just ready to drop into the grave;" for nothing less would satisfy divine justice. The life of the sinner was forfeited, and therefore the life of the sacrifice must be the ransom for it. The sentence of death passed upon Adam was thus expressed: *Unto dust thou shalt return.* And therefore Christ, having an eye to that sentence in his obedience to death, here uses a similar expression: *Thou hast brought me to the dust of death.*

5. He was stripped. The shame of nakedness was the immediate consequence of sin; and therefore our Lord Jesus was stripped of his clothes, when he was crucified, that he might clothe us with the robe of his righteousness, and that the shame of our nakedness might not appear. Now here we are told, (1.) How his body looked when it was thus stripped: *I may tell all my bones, v.* 17. His blessed body was lean and emaciated with labour, grief, and fasting, during the whole course of his ministry, which made him look as if he was nearly 50 years old when he was yet but 33, as we find, John viii. 57. His wrinkles now witnessed for him that he was far from being what he was called, *a gluttonous man and a wine-bibber.* Or his bones might be numbered, because his body was distended upon the cross, which made it easy to count his ribs. *They look and stare upon me,* that is, my bones do, being distorted, and having no flesh to cover them, as Job says (ch. xvi. 8), *My leanness, rising up in me, beareth witness to my face.* Or " the standers by, the passers by, are amazed to see my bones start out thus; and, instead of pitying me, are pleased even with such a rueful spectacle." (2.) What they did with his clothes, which they took from him (*v.* 18): *They part my garments among them,* to every soldier a part, and *upon my vesture,* the seamless coat, *do they cast lots.* This very circumstance was exactly fulfilled, John xix. 23, 24. And though

it was no great instance of Christ's suffering, yet it is a great instance of the fulfilling of the scripture in him. *Thus it was written, and* therefore *thus it behoved Christ to suffer.* Let this therefore confirm our faith in him as the true Messiah, and inflame our love to him as the best of friends, who loved us and suffered all this for us.

II. Here is Christ praying, and with that supporting himself under the burden of his sufferings. Christ, in his agony, prayed, prayed earnestly, prayed that the cup might pass from him. When the prince of this world with his terrors set upon him, *gaped upon him as a roaring lion,* he fell upon the ground and prayed. And of that David's praying here was a type. He calls God his *strength, v.* 19. When we cannot rejoice in God as our song, yet let us stay ourselves upon him as our strength, and take the comfort of spiritual supports when we cannot come at spiritual delights. He prays, 1. That God would be with him, and not set himself at a distance from him : *Be not thou far from me* (*v.* 11), and again, *v.* 19. "Whoever stands aloof from my sore, Lord, do not thou." The nearness of trouble should quicken us to draw near to God and then we may hope that he will draw near to us. 2. That he would help him and make haste to help him, help him to bear up under his troubles, that he might not fail nor be discouraged, that he might neither shrink from his undertaking nor sink under it. And the Father *heard him in that he feared* (Heb. v. 7) and enabled him to go through with his work. 3. That he would deliver him and save him, *v.* 20, 21. (1.) Observe what the jewel is which he is in care for, " The safety of my soul, my darling ; let that be redeemed from the power of the grave, xlix. 15. Father, into thy hands I commit that, to be conveyed safely to paradise." The psalmist here calls his soul his *darling,* his *only one* (so the word is): " *My soul is my only one.* I have but one soul to take care of, and therefore the greater is my shame if I neglect it and the greater will the loss be if I let it perish. Being my only one, it ought to be my darling, for the eternal welfare of which I ought to be deeply concerned. I do not use my soul as my darling, unless I take care to preserve it from every thing that would hurt it and to provide all necessaries for it, and be entirely tender of its welfare. 2.) Observe what the danger is from which he prays to be delivered, *from the sword,* the flaming sword of divine wrath, which turns every way. This he dreaded more than any thing, Gen. iii. 24. God's anger was the wormwood and the gall in the bitter cup that was put into his hands. " O deliver my soul from that. Lord, though I lose my life, let me not lose thy love. Save me from *the power of the dog,* and *from the lion's mouth.*" This seems to be meant of Satan, that old enemy who bruised the heel of the seed of the woman, the prince of this world, with whom

he was to engage in close combat and whom he saw coming, John xiv. 30. " Lord, save me from being overpowered by his terrors." He pleads, " Thou hast formerly *heard me from the horns of the unicorn,*" that is," saved me from him in answer to my prayer." This may refer to the victory Christ had obtained over Satan and his temptations (Matt. iv.), when the devil left him for a season (Luke iv. 13), but now returned in another manner to attack him with his terrors. " Lord, thou gavest me the victory then, give it me now, that I may spoil principalities and powers, and *cast out the prince of this world.*" Has God delivered us *from the horns of the unicorn,* that we be not tossed ? Let that encourage us to hope that we shall be delivered from the lion's mouth, that we be not torn. He that has delivered doth and will deliver This prayer of Christ, no doubt, was answered, for the Father heard him always. And, though he did not deliver him from death, yet he suffered him not to see corruption, but, the third day, raised him out of the dust of death, which was a greater instance of God's favour to him than if he had helped him down from the cross ; for that would have hindered his undertaking, whereas his resurrection crowned it.

In singing this we should meditate on the sufferings and resurrection of Christ till we experience in our own souls the power of his resurrection and the fellowship of his sufferings.

22 I will declare thy name unto my brethren : in the midst of the congregation will I praise thee. 23 Ye that fear the LORD, praise him ; all ye the seed of Jacob, glorify him ; and fear him, all ye the seed of Israel. 24 For he hath not despised nor abhorred the affliction of the afflicted ; neither hath he hid his face from him ; but when he cried unto him, he heard. 25 My praise *shall be* of thee in the great congregation : I will pay my vows before them that fear him. 26 The meek shall eat and be satisfied : they shall praise the LORD that seek him : your heart shall live for ever. 27 All the ends of the world shall remember and turn unto the LORD : and all the kindreds of the nations shall worship before thee. 28 For the kingdom *is* the LORD's : and he *is* the governor among the nations. 29 All *they that be* fat upon earth shall eat and worship : all they that go down to the dust shall bow before him : and none can keep alive his own soul. 30 A seed shall serve him ; it shall be accounted to

the Lord for a generation. 31 They shall come, and shall declare his righteousness unto a people that shall be born, that he hath done *this.*

The same that began the psalm complaining, who was no other than Christ in his humiliation, ends it here triumphing, and it can be no other than Christ in his exaltation. And, as the first words of the complaint were used by Christ himself upon the cross, so the first words of the triumph are expressly applied to him (Heb. ii. 12) and are made his own words : *I will declare thy name unto my brethren, in the midst of the church will I sing praise unto thee.* The certain prospect which Christ had of the joy set before him not only gave him a satisfactory answer to his prayers, but turned his complaints into praises; he saw of the travail of his soul, and was well satisfied, witness that triumphant word wherewith he breathed his last : *It is finished.*

Five things are here spoken of, the view of which were the satisfaction and triumph of Christ in his sufferings :—

I. That he should have a church in the world, and that those that were given him from eternity should, in the fulness of time, be gathered in to him. This is implied here; that he should *see his seed*, Isa. liii. 10. It pleased him to think, 1. That by the declaring of God's name, by the preaching of the everlasting gospel in its plainness and purity, many should be effectually called to him and to God by him. And for this end ministers should be employed to publish this doctrine to the world, and that they should be so much his messengers and his voice that their doing it should be accounted his doing it; their word is his, and by them he declares God's name. 2. That those who are thus called in should be brought into a very near and dear relation to him as his brethren ; for he is not only not ashamed, but greatly well pleased, to call them so; not the believing Jews only, his countrymen, but those of the Gentiles also who became fellow-heirs and of the same body, Heb. ii. 11. Christ is our elder brother, who takes care of us, and makes provision for us, and expects that our desire should be towards him and that we should be willing he should rule over us. 3. That these his brethren should be incorporated into a congregation, a great congregation ; such is the universal church, the whole family that is named from him, into which all the *children of God that were scattered abroad are collected*, and in which they are united (John xi. 52, Eph. i. 10), and that they should also be incorporated into smaller societies, members of that great body, many religious assemblies for divine worship, on which the face of Christianity should appear and in which the interests of it should be supported and advanced. 4. That these should be accounted the seed of Jacob and Israel (*v.* 23), that on them, though Gentiles, the blessing of Abraham

might come (Gal. iii. 14), and to them might pertain the adoption, the glory, the covenant, and the service of God, as much as ever they did to *Israel according to the flesh*, Rom. ix. 4, Heb. viii. 10. The gospel church is called *the Israel of God*, Gal. vi. 16.

II. That God should be greatly honoured and glorified in him by that church. His Father's glory was that which he had in his eye throughout his whole undertaking (John xvii. 4), particularly in his sufferings, which he entered upon with this solemn request, *Father, glorify thy name*, John xii. 27, 28. He foresees with pleasure, 1. That God would be glorified by the church that should be gathered to him, and that for this end they should be called and gathered in that they might be unto God *for a name and a praise*. Christ by his ministers will declare God's name to his brethren, as God's mouth to them, and then by them, as the mouth of the congregation to God, will God's name be praised. All that fear the Lord will praise him (*v.* 23), even every Israelite indeed. See cxviii. 2—4; cxxxv. 19, 20. The business of Christians, particularly in their solemn religious assemblies, is to praise and glorify God with a holy awe and reverence of his majesty, and therefore those that are here called upon to praise God are called upon to fear him. 2. That God would be glorified in the Redeemer and in his undertaking. *Therefore* Christ is said to *praise God in the church*, not only because he is the Master of the assemblies in which God is praised, and the Mediator of all the praises that are offered up to God, but because he is the matter of the church's praise. See Eph. iii. 21. All our praises must centre in the work of redemption and a great deal of reason we have to be thankful, (1.) That Jesus Christ was owned by his Father in his undertaking, notwithstanding the apprehension he was sometimes under that his Father had forsaken him (*v.* 24): *For he hath not despised nor abhorred the affliction of the afflicted* one (that is, of the suffering Redeemer), but has graciously accepted it as a full satisfaction for sin, and a valuable consideration on which to ground the grant of eternal life to all believers. Though it was offered for us poor sinners, he did not despise nor abhor it for our sakes ; nor did he turn his face from him that offered it, as Saul was angry with his own son because he interceded for David, whom he looked upon as his enemy. But when he cried unto him, when his blood cried for peace and pardon for us, he heard him. This, as it is the matter of our rejoicing, ought to be the matter of our thanksgiving. Those who have thought their prayers slighted and unheard, if they continue to pray and wait, will find they have not sought in vain. (2.) That he himself will go on with his undertaking and complete it. Christ says, *I will pay my vows, v.* 25. Having engaged to bring many sons to glory, he will perform his engagement to the utmost, and will lose none.

III. That all humble gracious souls should have a full satisfaction and happiness in him, *v.* 26. It comforted the Lord Jesus in his sufferings that in and through him all true believers should have everlasting consolation. 1. The poor in spirit shall be rich in blessings, spiritual blessings; the hungry shall be filled with good things. Christ's sacrifice being accepted, the saints shall feast upon the sacrifice, as, under the law, upon the peace-offerings, and so partake of the altar: *The meek shall eat and be satisfied,* eat of the bread of life, feed with an appetite upon the doctrine of Christ's mediation, which is meat and drink to the soul that knows its own nature and case. Those that hunger and thirst after righteousness in Christ shall have all they can desire to satisfy them and make them easy, and shall not labour, as they have done, for that which satisfies not. 2. Those that are much in praying shall be much in thanksgiving: *Those shall praise the Lord that seek him,* because through Christ they are sure of finding him, in the hopes of which they have reason to praise him even while they are seeking him; and the more earnest they are in seeking him the more will their hearts be enlarged in his praises when they have found him. 3. The souls that are devoted to him shall be for ever happy with him: " *Your heart shall live for ever.* Yours that are meek, that are satisfied in Christ, that continue to seek God; whatever becomes of your bodies, *your hearts shall live for ever;* the graces and comforts you have shall be perfected in everlasting life. Christ has said, *Because I live, you shall live also* (John xiv. 19); and therefore that life shall be as sure and as long as his."

IV. That the church of Christ, and with it the kingdom of God among men, should extend itself to all corners of the earth and should take in all sorts of people.

1. That it should reach far (*v.* 27, 28), that, whereas the Jews had long been the only professing people of God, now all the ends of the world should come into the church, and, the partition-wall being taken down, the Gentiles should be taken in. It is here prophesied, (1.) That they should be converted: They *shall remember, and turn to the Lord.* Note, Serious reflection is the first step, and a good step it is, towards true conversion. We must consider and turn. The prodigal came first to himself, and then to his father. (2.) That then they should be admitted into communion with God and with the assemblies that serve him: *They shall worship before thee,* for *in every place incense shall be offered to God,* Mal. i. 11; Isa. lxvi. 23. Those that turn to God will make conscience of worshipping before him. And good reason there is why all the kindreds of the nations should do homage to God, for (*v.* 28) *the kingdom is the Lord's;* his, and his only, is the universal monarchy. [1.] The kingdom of nature is the Lord Jehovah's, and his providence rules among the nations, and upon that account we are bound

to worship him; so that the design of the Christian religion is to revive natural religion and its principles and laws. Christ died to bring us to God, the God that made us, from whom we had revolted, and to reduce us to our native allegiance. [2.] The kingdom of grace is the Lord Christ's, and he, as Mediator, is appointed governor among the nations, head over all things to his church. Let every tongue therefore confess that he is Lord.

2. That it should include many of different ranks, *v.* 29. High and low, rich and poor, bond and free, meet in Christ. (1.) Christ shall have the homage of many of the great ones. *Those that are fat upon the earth,* that live in pomp and power, *shall eat and worship;* even those that fare deliciously, when they have eaten and are full, shall bless the Lord their God for their plenty and prosperity. (2.) The poor also shall receive his gospel: *Those that go down to the dust,* that sit in the dust (cxiii. 7), that can scarcely keep life and soul together, *shall bow before him,* before the Lord Jesus, who reckons it his honour to be the poor man's King (lxxii. 12) and whose protection does, in a special manner, draw their allegiance. Or this may be understood in general of dying men, whether poor or rich. See then what is our condition —we are going down to the dust to which we are sentenced and where shortly we must make our bed. Nor can we keep alive our own souls; we cannot secure our own natural life long, nor can we be the authors of our own spiritual and eternal life. It is therefore our great interest, as well as duty, to bow before the Lord Jesus, to give up ourselves to him to be his subjects and worshippers; for this is the only way, and it is a sure way, to secure our happiness when we go down to the dust. Seeing we cannot keep alive our own souls, it is our wisdom, by an obedient faith, to commit our souls to Jesus Christ, who is able to save them and keep them alive for ever.

V. That the church of Christ, and with it the kingdom of God among men, should continue to the end, through all the ages of time. Mankind is kept up in a succession of generations; so that there is always a generation passing away and a generation coming up. Now, as Christ shall have honour from that which is passing away and leaving the world (*v.* 29, *those that go down to the dust shall bow before him,* and it is good to die bowing before Christ; *blessed are the dead who thus die in the Lord),* so he shall have honour from that which is rising up, and setting out, in the world, *v.* 30. Observe, 1. Their application to Christ: *A seed shall serve him,* shall keep up the solemn worship of him and profess and practise obedience to him as their Master and Lord. Note, God will have a church in the world to the end of time; and, in order to that, there shall be a succession of professing Christians and gospel ministers from generation to generation. *A seed shall* serve him; there shall be a remnant, more or less, to whom shall pertain the service of God and to whom God will give grace to serve him,—perhaps not the seed of the same persons, for grace does not run in a blood (he does not say *their* seed, but *a* seed),—perhaps but few, yet enough to preserve the entail. 2. Christ's acknowledgement of them : *They shall be accounted to him for a generation;* he will be the same to them that he was to those who went before them; his kindness to his friends shall not die with them, but shall be drawn out to their heirs and successors, and instead of the fathers shall be the children, whom all shall acknowledge to be a *seed that the Lord hath blessed,* Isa. lxi. 9; lxv. 23. The generation of the righteous God will graciously own as his treasure, his children. 3. Their agency for him (*v.* 31): *They shall come,* shall rise up in their day, not only to keep up the virtue of the generation that is past, and to do the work of their own generation, but to serve the honour of Christ and the welfare of souls in the generations to come; they shall transmit to them the gospel of Christ (that sacred deposit) pure and entire, even to a people that shall be born hereafter; to them they shall declare two things:—(1.) That there is an everlasting righteousness, which Jesus Christ has brought in. This righteousness of his, and not any of our own, they shall declare to be the foundation of all our hopes and the fountain of all our joys. See Rom. i. 16, 17. (2.) That the work of our redemption by Christ is the Lord's own doing (cxviii. 23) and no contrivance of ours. We must declare to our children that God has done this; it is his wisdom in a mystery; it is his arm revealed.

In singing this we must triumph in the name of Christ as above every name, must give him honour ourselves, rejoice in the honours others do him, and in the assurance we have that there shall be a people praising him on earth when we are praising him in heaven.

PSALM XXIII.

Many of David's psalms are full of complaints, but this is full of comforts, and the expressions of delight in God's great goodness and dependence upon him. It is a psalm which has been sung by good Christians, and will be while the world stands, with a great deal of pleasure and satisfaction. I. The psalmist here claims relation to God, as his shepherd, ver. 1. II. He recounts his experience of the kind things God had done for him as his shepherd, ver. 2, 3, 5. III. Hence he infers that he should want no good (ver. 1), that he needed to fear no evil (ver. 4), that God would never leave nor forsake him in a way of mercy; and therefore he resolves never to leave nor forsake God in a way of duty, ver. 6. In this he has certainly an eye, not only to the blessings of God's providence, which made his outward condition prosperous, but to the communications of God's grace, received by a lively faith, and returned in a warm devotion, which filled his soul with joy unspeakable. And, as in the foregoing psalm he represented Christ dying for his sheep, so here he represents Christians receiving the benefit of all the care and tenderness of that great and good shepherd.

A psalm of David.

THE LORD *is* my shepherd; I shall not want. 2 He maketh me to lie down in green pastures : he leadeth me beside the still waters. 3

He restoreth my soul : he leadeth me in the paths of righteousness for his name's sake. 4 Yea, though I walk through the valley of the shadow of death, I will fear no evil : for thou *art* with me; thy rod and thy staff they comfort me. 5 Thou preparest a table before me in the presence of mine enemies: thou anointest my head with oil; my cup runneth over. 6 Surely goodness and mercy shall follow me all the days of my life : and I will dwell in the house of the LORD for ever.

From three very comfortable premises David, in this psalm, draws three very comfortable conclusions, and teaches us to do so too. We are saved by hope, and that hope will not make us ashamed, because it is well grounded. It is the duty of Christians to encourage themselves in the Lord their God; and we are here directed to take that encouragement both from the relation wherein he stands to us and from the experience we have had of his goodness according to that relation.

I. From God's being his shepherd he infers that he shall not want any thing that is good for him, *v.* 1. See here, 1. The great care that God takes of believers. He is their shepherd, and they may call him so. Time was when David was himself a shepherd; he was taken from following the ewes great with young (lxxviii. 70, 71), and so he knew by experience the cares and tender affections of a good shepherd towards his flock. He remembered what need they had of a shepherd, and what a kindness it was to them to have one that was skilful and faithful; he once ventured his life to rescue a lamb. By this therefore he illustrates God's care of his people; and to this our Saviour seems to refer when he says, *I am the shepherd of the sheep; the good shepherd,* John x. 11. He that is the shepherd of the whole church in general (lxxx. 1), is the shepherd of every particular believer; the meanest is not below his cognizance, Isa. xl. 11. He takes them into his fold, and then takes care of them, protects them, and provides for them, with more care and constancy than a shepherd can, that makes it his business to keep the flock. If God be as a shepherd to us, we must be as sheep, inoffensive, meek, and quiet, silent before the shearers, nay, and before the butcher too, useful and sociable; we must know the shepherd's voice, and follow him. 2. The great confidence which believers have in God: "If the Lord is my shepherd, my feeder, I may conclude I shall not want any thing that is really necessary and good for me." If David penned this psalm before his coming to the crown, though destined to it, he had as much reason to fear wanting as any man. Once he sent his men a begging for him to Nabal, and another time went himself a begging to Ahimelech; and yet, when he considers that God is his shepherd, he can boldly say, *I shall not want.* Let not those fear starving that are at God's finding and have him for their feeder. More is implied than is expressed, not only, *I shall not want,* but, " I shall be supplied with whatever I need ; and, if I have not every thing I desire, I may conclude it is either not fit for me or not good for me, or I shall have it in due time."

II. From his performing the office of a good shepherd to him he infers that he needs not fear any evil in the greatest dangers and difficulties he could be in, *v.* 2—4. He experiences the benefit of God's presence with him and care of him now, and therefore expects the benefit of them when he most needs it. See here,

1. The comforts of a living saint. God is his shepherd and his God—a God all-sufficient to all intents and purposes. David found him so, and so have we. See the happiness of the saints as the sheep of God's pasture. (1.) They are well placed, well laid . *He maketh me to lie down in green pastures.* We have the supports and comforts of this life from God's good hand, our daily bread from him as our Father. The greatest abundance is but a dry pasture to a wicked man, who relishes that only in it which pleases the senses ; but to a godly man, who tastes the goodness of God in all his enjoyments, and by faith relishes that, though he has but little of the world, it is a green pasture, xxxvii. 16 ; Prov. xv. 16, 17. God's ordinances are the green pastures in which food is provided for all believers ; the word of life is the nourishment of the new man. It is milk for babes, pasture for the sheep, never barren, never eaten bare, never parched, but always a green pasture for faith to feed in. God makes his saints to lie down ; he gives them quiet and contentment in their own minds, whatever their lot is ; their souls dwell at ease in him, and that makes every pasture green. Are we blessed with the green pastures of the ordinances ? Let us not think it enough to pass through them, but let us lie down in them, abide in them ; this is my rest for ever. It is by a constancy of the means of grace that the soul is fed. (2.) They are well guided, well led. The shepherd of Israel guides Joseph like a flock ; and every believer is under the same guidance : *He leadeth me beside the still waters.* Those that feed on God's goodness must follow his direction ; he leads them by his providence, by his word, by his Spirit, disposes their affairs for the best, according to his counsel, disposes their affections and actions according to his command, directs their eye, their way, and their heart, into his love. The still waters by which he leads them yield them, not only a pleasant prospect, but many a cooling draught, many a reviving cordial, when they are thirsty and weary. God pro-

vides for his people not only food and rest, but refreshment also and pleasure. The consolations of God, the joys of the Holy Ghost, are these still waters, by which the saints are led, streams which flow from the fountain of living waters and make glad the city of our God. God leads his people, not to the standing waters which corrupt and gather filth, nor to the troubled sea, nor to the rapid rolling floods, but to the silent purling waters ; for the still but running waters agree best with those spirits that flow out towards God and yet do it silently. The divine guidance they are under is stripped of its metaphor (*v.* 3) : *He leadeth me in the paths of righteousness,* in the way of my duty ; in that he instructs me by his word and directs me by conscience and providence. These are the paths in which all the saints desire to be led and kept, and never to turn aside out of them. And those only are led by the still waters of comfort that walk in the paths of righteousness. The way of duty is the truly pleasant way. It is the work of righteousness that is peace. In these paths we cannot walk unless God both lead us into them and lead us in them. (3.) They are well helped when any thing ails them : *He restoreth my soul.* [1.] " He restores me when I wander." No creature will lose itself sooner than a sheep, so apt it is to go astray, and then so unapt to find the way back. The best saints are sensible of their proneness to *go astray like lost sheep* (cxix. 176) ; they miss their way, and turn aside into by-paths ; but when God shows them their error, gives them repentance, and brings them back to their duty again, he restores the soul ; and, if he did not do so, they would wander endlessly, and be undone. When, after one sin, David's heart smote him, and, after another, Nathan was sent to tell him, *Thou art the man,* God restored his soul. Though God may suffer his people to fall into sin, he will not suffer them to lie still in it. [2.] " He recovers me when I am sick, and revives me when I am faint, and so restores the soul which was ready to depart." He is the Lord our God that heals us, Exod. xv. 26. Many a time we should have fainted unless we had believed ; and it was the good shepherd that kept us from fainting.

2. See here the courage of a dying saint (*v.* 4): " Having had such experience of God's goodness to me all my days, in six troubles and in seven, I will never distrust him, no, not in the last extremity ; the rather because all he has done for me hitherto was not for any merit or desert of mine, but purely for his name's sake, in pursuance of his word, in performance of his promise, and for the glory of his own attributes and relations to his people. That name therefore shall still be my strong tower, and shall assure me that he who has led me, and fed me, all my life long, will not leave me at last." Here is,

(1.) Imminent danger supposed : " *Though*

I walk through the valley of the shadow of death, that is, though I am in peril of death, though in the midst of dangers, deep as a valley, dark as a shadow, and dreadful as death itself," or, rather, " though I am under the arrests of death, have received the sentence of death within myself, and have all the reason in the world to look upon myself as a dying man, yet I am easy." Those that are sick, those that are old, have reason to look upon themselves as in the valley of the shadow of death. Here is one word indeed which sounds terrible; it is *death,* which we must all count upon; *there is no discharge in that war.* But, even in the supposition of the distress, there are four words which lessen the terror :—It is death indeed that is before us; but, [1.] It is but the *shadow* of death ; there is no substantial evil in it ; the shadow of a serpent will not sting nor the shadow of a sword kill. [2.] It is the *valley* of the shadow, deep indeed, and dark, and dirty; but the valleys are fruitful, and so is death itself fruitful of comforts to God's people. [3.] It is but a *walk* in this valley, a gentle pleasant walk. The wicked are chased out of the world, and their souls are required ; but the saints take a walk to another world as cheerfully as they take their leave of this. [4.] It is a walk *through* it ; they shall not be lost in this valley, but get safely to the mountain of spices on the other side of it.

(2.) This danger made light of, and triumphed over, upon good grounds. Death is a king of terrors, but not to the sheep of Christ ; they tremble at it no more than sheep do that are appointed for the slaughter. "Even in *the valley of the shadow of death I will fear no evil. None of these things move me.*" Note, A child of God may meet the messengers of death and receive its summons with a holy security and serenity of mind. The sucking child may play upon the hole of this asp ; and the weaned child, that, through grace, is weaned from this world, may put his hand upon this cockatrice's den, bidding a holy defiance to death, as Paul, *O death ! where is thy sting ?* And there is ground enough for this confidence, [1.] Because there is no evil in it to a child of God ; death cannot separate us from the love of God, and therefore it can do us no real arm ; it kills the body, but cannot touch the soul. Why should it be dreadful when there is nothing in it hurtful? [2.] Because the saints have God's gracious presence with them in their dying moments ; he is then at their right hand, and therefore why should they be moved ? The good shepherd will not only conduct, but convoy, his sheep through this valley, where they are in danger of being set upon by the beasts of prey, the ravening wolves : he will not only convoy them, but comfort them when they most need comfort. His presence shall comfort them : *Thou art with me.* His word and Spirit shall comfort them—*his rod and staff,* alluding to the shepherd's crook, or the rod under which

the sheep passed when they were counted (Lev. xxvii. 32), or the staff with which the shepherds drove away the dogs that would scatter or worry the sheep. It is a comfort to the saints, when they come to die, that God takes cognizance of them *(he knows those that are his),* that he will rebuke the enemy, that he will guide them with his rod and sustain them with his staff. The gospel is called *the rod of Christ's strength* (cx. 2), and there is enough in that to comfort the saints when they come to die, and *underneath* them are *the everlasting arms.*

III. From the good gifts of God's bounty to him now he infers the constancy and perpetuity of his mercy, *v.* 5, 6. Here we may observe,

1. How highly he magnifies God's gracious vouchsafements to him (*v.* 5): " *Thou preparest a table before me ;* thou hast provided for me all things pertaining both to life and godliness, all things requisite both for body and soul, for time and eternity:" such a bountiful benefactor is God to all his people ; and it becomes them abundantly to utter his great goodness, as David here, who acknowledges, (1.) That he had food convenient, a table spread, a cup filled, meat for his hunger, drink for his thirst. (2.) That he had it carefully and readily provided for him. His table was not spread with any thing that came next to hand, but prepared, and prepared *before him.* (3.) That he was not stinted, was not straitened, but had abundance : " *My cup runs over,* enough for myself and my friends too." (4.) That he had not only for necessity, but for ornament and delight : *Thou anointest my head with oil.* Samuel anointed him king, which was a certain pledge of further favour ; but this is rather an instance of the plenty with which God had blessed him, or an allusion to the extraordinary entertainment of special friends, whose heads they anointed with oil, Luke vii. 46. Nay, some think he still looks upon himself as a sheep, but such a one as the *poor man's ewe-lamb* (2 Sam. xii. 3), that did eat of his own meat, and drank of his own cup, and lay in his bosom ; not only thus nobly, but thus tenderly, are the children of God looked after. Plentiful provision is made for their bodies, for their souls, for the life that now is and for that which is to come. If Providence do not bestow upon us thus plentifully for our natural life, it is our own fault if it be not made up to us in spiritual blessings.

2. How confidently he counts upon the continuance of God's favours, *v.* 6. He had said (*v.* 1), *I shall not want ;* but now he speaks more positively, more comprehensively : *Surely goodness and mercy shall follow me all the days of my life.* His hope rises, and his faith is strengthened, by being exercised. Observe, (1.) What he promises himself—goodness and mercy, all the streams of mercy flowing from the fountain, pardoning mercy, protecting mercy, sustaining mercy,

supplying mercy. (2.) The manner of the conveyance of it: It shall *follow* me, as the water out of the rock followed the camp of Israel through the wilderness; it shall follow into all places and all conditions, shall be always ready. (3.) The continuance of it: It shall follow me *all my life long*, even to the last; for whom God loves he loves to the ĕnd. (4.) The constancy of it: *All the days of my life*, as duly as the day comes; it shall be *new every morning* (Lam. iii. 22, 23) like the manna that was given to the Israelites daily. (5.) The certainty of it: *Surely* it shall. It is as sure as the promise of the God of truth can make it; and we know whom we have believed. (6.) Here is a prospect of the perfection of bliss in the future state. So some take the latter clause: "Goodness and mercy having followed me all the days of my life on this earth, when that is ended I shall remove to a better world, to *dwell in the house of the Lord for ever*, in our Father's house above, where there are many mansions. *With what I have I am pleased much; with what I hope for I am pleased more.*" All this, and heaven too! Then we serve a good Master.

3. How resolutely he determineš to cleave to God and to his duty. We read the last clause as David's covenant with God: *I will dwell in the house of the Lord for ever* (as long as I live), and I will praise him while I have any being." We must dwell in his house as servants, that desired to have their ears bored to the door-post, to serve him for ever. If God's goodness to us be like the morning light, which shines more and more to the perfect day, let not ours to him be like the morning cloud and the early dew that passeth away. Those that would be satisfied with the fatness of God's house must keep close to the duties of it.

PSALM XXIV.

This psalm is concerning the kingdom of Jesus Christ, I. His providential kingdom, by which he rules the world, ver. 1, 2.   II. The kingdom of his grace, by which he rules in his church.   1. Concerning the subjects of that kingdom; their character (ver. 4, 6), their charter, ver. 5.   2. Concerning the King of that kingdom; and a summons to all to give him admission, ver. 7—10. It is supposed that the psalm was penned upon occasion of David's bringing up the ark to the place prepared for it, and that the intention of it was to lead the people above the pomp of external ceremonies to a holy life and faith in Christ, of whom the ark was a type.

A psalm of David.

THE earth *is* the LORD's, and the fulness thereof; the world, and they that dwell therein. 2 For he hath founded it upon the seas, and established it upon the floods.

Here is, I. God's absolute propriety in this part of the creation where our lot is cast, *v.* 1. We are not to think that the heavens, even the heavens only, are the Lord's, and the numerous and bright inhabitants of the upper world, and that this earth, being so small and inconsiderable a part of the creation, and at such a distance from the royal palace above, is neglected, and that he claims no interest in it. No, even the earth is his, and this lower world; and, though he has prepared the throne of his glory in the heavens, yet his kingdom rules over all, and even the worms of this earth are not below his cognizance, nor from under his dominion. 1. When God gave the earth to the children of men he still reserved to himself the property, and only let it out to them as tenants, or usufructuaries: *The earth is the Lord's and the fulness thereof.* The mines that are lodged in the bowels of it, even the richest, the fruits it produces, all the beasts of the forest and the cattle upon a thousand hills, our lands and houses, and all the improvements that are made of this earth by the skill and industry of man, are all his. These indeed, in the kingdom of grace, are justly looked upon as emptiness; for they are vanity of vanities, nothing to a soul; but, in the kingdom of providence, they are fulness. *The earth is full of God's riches, so is the great and wide sea also.* All the parts and regions of the earth are the Lord's, all under his eye, all in his hand: so that, wherever a child of God goes, he may comfort himself with this, that he does not go off his Father's ground. That which falls to our share of the earth and its productions is but lent to us; it is the Lord's; what is our own against all the world is not so against his claims. That which is most remote from us, as that which passes through the paths of the sea, or is hidden in the bottom of it, is the Lord's, and he knows where to find it. 2. The habitable part of this earth (Prov. viii. 31) is his in a special manner—*the world and those that dwell therein.* We ourselves are not our own, our bodies, our souls, are not. *All souls are mine*, says God; for he is the former of our bodies and the Father of our spirits. Our tongues are not our own; they are to be at his service. Even those of the children of men that know him not, nor own their relation to him, are his. Now this comes in here to show that, though God is graciously pleased to accept the devotions and services of his peculiar chosen people (*v.* 3—5), it is not because he needs them, or can be benefited by them, for the earth is his and all in it, Exod. xix.⋅5; Ps. l. 12. It is likewise to be applied to the dominion Christ has, as Mediator, over the utmost parts of the earth, which are given him for his possession: the Father loveth the Son and hath given all things into his hand, power over all flesh. The apostle quotes this scripture twice together in his discourse about things offered to idols, 1 Cor. x. 26, 28. "If it be sold in the shambles, eat it, and ask no questions; *for the earth is the Lord's;* it is God's good creature, and you have a right to it. But, if one tell you it was offered to an idol, forbear, *for the earth is the Lord's,* and there is enough besides." This is a good reason why we should be content with our allotment in this world, and not envy others theirs; *the earth is the Lord's,* and may he not do what he will with his own, and give to some more of it, to others less, as it pleases him?

II. The ground of this propriety. The earth is his by an indisputable title, *for he hath founded it upon the seas* and *established it upon the floods, v.* 2. It is his; for, 1. He made it, formed it, founded it, and fitted it for the use of man. The matter is his, for he made it out of nothing; the form is his, for he made it according to the eternal counsels and ideas of his own mind. He made it himself, he made it for himself; so that he is sole, entire, and absolute owner, and none can let us a title to any part, but by, from, and under him; see lxxxix. 11, 12. 2. He made it so as no one else could. It is the creature of omnipotence, for it is founded upon the seas, upon the floods, a weak and unstable foundation (one would think) to build the earth upon, and yet, if almighty power please, it shall serve to bear the weight of this earth. The waters which at first covered the earth, and rendered it unfit to be a habitation for man, were ordered under it, that the dry land might appear, and so they are as a foundation to it; see civ. 8, 9. 3. He continues it, he has *established* it, fixed it, so that, though one generation passes and another comes, the earth abides, Eccl. i. 4. And his providence is a continued creation, cxix. 90. The founding of the earth upon the floods should remind us how slippery and uncertain all earthly things are; their foundation is not only sand, but water; it is therefore our folly to build upon them.

3 Who shall ascend into the hill of the LORD? or who shall stand in his holy place? 4 He that hath clean hands, and a pure heart; who hath not lifted up his soul unto vanity, nor sworn deceitfully. 5 He shall receive the blessing from the LORD, and righteousness from the God of his salvation. 6 This *is* the generation of them that seek him, that seek thy face, O Jacob. Selah.

From this world, and the fulness thereof, the psalmist's meditations rise, of a sudden, to the great things of another world, the foundation of which is not on the seas, nor on the floods. The things of this world God has given to the children of men and we are much indebted to his providence for them; but they will not make a portion for us. And therefore,

I. Here is an enquiry after better things, *v.* 3. This earth is God's footstool; but, if we had ever so much of it, we must be here but a while, must shortly go hence, and *Who then shall ascend into the hill of the Lord?* Who shall go to heaven hereafter, and, as an earnest of that, shall have communion

with God in holy ordinances now? A soul that knows and considers its own nature, origin, and immortality, when it has viewed the earth and the fulness thereof, will sit down unsatisfied; there is not found among all the creatures a help meet for man, and therefore it will think of ascending towards God, towards heaven, will ask, " What shall I do to rise to that high place, that hill, where the Lord dwells and manifests himself, that I may be acquainted with him, and to abide in that happy holy place where he meets his people and makes them holy and happy? What shall I do that I may be of those whom God owns for his peculiar people and who are his in another manner than the earth is his and its fulness?" This question is much the same with that, xv. 1. The hill of Zion on which the temple was built typified the church, both visible and invisible. When the people attended the ark to its holy place David puts them in mind that these were but patterns of heavenly things, and therefore that by them they should be led to consider the heavenly things themselves.

II. An answer to this enquiry, in which we have,

1. The properties of God's peculiar people, who shall have communion with him in grace and glory. (1.) They are such as keep themselves from all the gross acts of sin. They have *clean hands;* not spotted with the pollutions of the world and the flesh. None that were ceremonially unclean might enter into the mountain of the temple, which signified that cleanness of conversation which is required in all those that have fellowship with God. The hands lifted up in prayer must be pure hands, no blot of unjust gain cleaving to them, nor any thing else that defiles the man and is offensive to the holy God. (2.) They are such as make conscience of being really (that is, of being inwardly) as good as they seem to be outwardly. They have *pure hearts.* We make nothing of our religion if we do not make heart-work of it. It is not enough that our hands be clean before men, but we must also wash our hearts from wickedness, and not allow ourselves in any secret heart-impurities, which are open before the eye of God. Yet in vain do those pretend to have pure and good hearts whose hands are defiled with the acts of sin. That is a pure heart which is sincere and without guile in covenanting with God, which is carefully guarded, that the wicked one, the unclean spirit, touch it not, which is purified by faith, and conformed to the image and will of God; see Matt. v. 8. (3.) They are such as do not set their affections upon the things of this world, do not *lift up their souls unto vanity,* whose hearts are not carried out inordinately towards the wealth of the world, the praise of men, or the delights of sense, who do not choose these things for their portion, nor reach forth after them, because they believe them to be vanity, uncertain and un-

satisfying. (4.) They are such as deal honestly both with God and man. In their covenant with God, and their contracts with men, they have not sworn deceitfully, nor broken their promises, violated their engagements, nor taken any false oath. Those that have no regard to the obligations of truth or the honour of God's name are unfit for a place in God's holy hill. (5.) They are a praying people (v. 6): *This is the generation of those that seek him.* In every age there is a remnant of such as these, men of this character, who are *accounted to the Lord for a generation,* xxii. 30. And they are such as seek God, *that seek thy face, O Jacob!* [1.] They join themselves to God, to seek him, not only in earnest prayer, but in serious endeavours to obtain his favour and keep themselves in his love. Having made it the summit of their happiness, they make it the summit of their ambition to be accepted of him, and therefore take care and pains to approve themselves to him. It is to the hill of the Lord that we must ascend, and, the way being up-hill, we have need to put forth ourselves to the utmost, as those that seek diligently. [2.] They join themselves to the people of God, to seek God with them. Being brought into communion with God, they come into the communion of saints; conforming to the patterns of the saints that have gone before (so some understand this), they seek God's face, as Jacob (so some), who was *therefore* surnamed *Israel,* because he wrestled with God and prevailed, sought him and found him; and, associating with the saints of their own day, they shall court the favour of God's church (Rev. iii. 9), shall be glad of an acquaintance with God's people (Zech. viii. 23), shall incorporate themselves with them, and, when they *subscribe with their hands to the Lord,* shall *call themselves by the name of Jacob,* Isa. xliv. 5. As soon as ever Paul was converted he *joined himself to the disciples,* Acts ix. 26. They shall seek God's face *in Jacob* (so some), that is, in the assemblies of his people. *Thy face, O God of Jacob!* so our margin supplies it, and makes it easy. As all believers are the spiritual seed of Abraham, so all that strive in prayer are the spiritual seed of Jacob, to whom God never said, *Seek you me in vain.*

2. The privileges of God's peculiar people, *v.* 5. They shall be made truly and for ever happy. (1.) They shall be blessed : they shall receive the blessing from the Lord, all the fruits and gifts of God's favour, according to his promise ; and those whom God blesses are blessed indeed, for it is his prerogative to command the blessing. (2.) They shall be justified and sanctified. These are the spiritual blessings in heavenly things which they shall receive, even righteousness, the very thing they hunger and thirst after, Matt. v. 6. Righteousness is blessedness, and it is from God only that we must expect it, for we have no righteousness of our own. They shall re-

ceive the reward of their righteousness (so some), the *crown of righteousness which the righteous Judge shall give,* 2 Tim. iv. 8. (3.) They shall be saved ; for God himself will be the God of their salvation. Note, Where God gives righteousness he certainly designs salvation. Those that are made meet for heaven shall be brought safely to heaven, and then they will find what they have been seeking, to their endless satisfaction.

7 Lift up your heads, O ye gates ; and be ye lift up, ye everlasting doors; and the King of glory shall come in. 8 Who *is* this King of glory ? The LORD strong and mighty, the LORD mighty in battle. 9 Lift up your heads, O ye gates; even lift *them* up, ye everlasting doors ; and the King of glory shall come in. 10 Who is this King of glory ? The LORD of hosts, he *is* the King of glory. Selah.

What is spoken once is spoken a second time in these verses; such repetitions are usual in songs, and have much beauty in them. Here is, 1. Entrance once and again demanded for the King of glory ; the doors and gates are to be thrown open, thrown wide open, to give him admission, for behold he stands at the door and knocks, ready to come in. 2. Enquiry once and again made concerning this mighty prince, in whose name entrance is demanded : *Who is this King of glory ?* As, when any knock at our door, it is common to ask, *Who is there ?* 3. Satisfaction once and again given concerning the royal person that makes the demand: *It is the Lord, strong and mighty, the Lord, mighty in battle, the Lord of hosts, v.* 8, 10. Now,

I. This splendid entry here described it is probable refers to the solemn bringing in of the ark into the tent David pitched for it or the temple Solomon built for it; for, when David prepared materials for the building of it, it was proper for him to prepare a psalm for the dedication of it. The porters are called upon to open the doors, and they are called *everlasting doors,* because much more durable than the door of the tabernacle, which was but a curtain. They are taught to ask, *Who is this King of glory ?* And those that bore the ark are taught to answer in the language before us, and very fitly, because the ark was a symbol or token of God's presence, Josh. iii. 11. Or it may be taken as a poetical figure designed to represent the subject more affectingly. God, in his word and ordinances, is thus to be welcomed by us, 1. With great readiness; the doors and gates must be thrown open to him. Let the word of the Lord come into the innermost and uppermost place in our souls ; and, if we had 600 necks, we should bow them all to the authority of it. 2. With all reverence, remembering how great a God he is with whom we have to do, in all our approaches to him.

II. Doubtless it points at Christ, of whom the ark, with the mercy-seat, was a type. 1. We may apply it to the ascension of Christ into heaven and the welcome given to him there. When he had finished his work on earth he ascended *in the clouds of heaven*, Dan. vii. 13, 14. The gates of heaven must then be opened to him, those doors that may be truly called *everlasting*, which had been shut against us, to keep the way of the tree of life, Gen. iii. 24. Our Redeemer found them shut, but, having by his blood made atonement for sin and gained a title to *enter into the holy place* (Heb. ix. 12), as one having authority, he demanded entrance, not for himself only, but for us ; for, as the forerunner, he has for us entered and *opened the kingdom of heaven to all believers.* The keys not only of hell and death, but of heaven and life, must be put into his hand. His approach being very magnificent, the angels are brought in asking, *Who is this King of glory ?* For angels keep the gates of the New Jerusalem, Rev. xxi. 12. When the first-begotten was brought into the upper world the angels were to worship him (Heb. i. 6) ; and, accordingly, they here ask with wonder, " Who is he?—this that cometh *with dyed garments from Bozrah* (Isa. lxiii. 1—3), for he appears in that world *as a Lamb that had been slain.* It is answered that he is *strong and mighty, mighty in battle,* to save his people and subdue his and their enemies. 2. We may apply it to Christ's entrance into the souls of men by his word and Spirit, that they may be his temples. Christ's presence in them is like that of the ark in the temple ; it sanctifies them. *Behold, he stands at the door and knocks,* Rev. iii. 20. It is required that the gates and doors of the heart be opened to him, not only as admission is given to a guest, but as possession is delivered to the rightful owner, after the title has been contested. This is the gospel call and demand, that we let Jesus Christ, the King of glory, come into our souls, and welcome him with hosannas, *Blessed is he that cometh.* That we may do this aright we are concerned to ask, *Who is this King of glory?*—to acquaint ourselves with him, whom we are to believe in, and to love above all. And the answer is ready : He is *Jehovah,* and will be *Jehovah our righteousness,* an all-sufficient Saviour to us, if we give him entrance and entertainment. He is *strong and mighty,* and *the Lord of hosts ;* and therefore it is at our peril if we deny him entrance : for he is able to avenge the affront ; he can force his way, and can break those in pieces with his iron rod that will not submit to his golden sceptre.

In singing this let our hearts cheerfully answer to this call, as it is in the first words of the next psalm, *Unto thee, O Lord ! do I lift up my soul.*

PSALM XXV.

This psalm is full of devout affection to God, the out-goings of holy desires towards his favour and grace and the lively actings of faith in his promises. We may learn out of it, I. What it is to pray, ver. 1, 15. II. What we must pray for, the pardon of sin (ver. 6, 7, 18), direction in the way of duty (ver. 4, 5), the favour

322

of God (ver. 16), deliverance out of our troubles (ver. 17, 18), preservation from our enemies (ver. 20, 21), and the salvation of the church of God, ver. 22. III. What we may plead in prayer, our confidence in God (ver. 2, 3, 5, 20, 21), our distress and the malice of our enemies (ver. 17, 19), our sincerity, ver. 21. IV. What precious promises we have to encourage us in prayer, of guidance and instruction (ver. 8, 9, 12), the benefit of the covenant (ver. 10), and the pleasure of communion with God, ver. 13, 14. It is easy to apply the several passages of this psalm to ourselves in the singing of it ; for we have often troubles, and always sins, to complain of at the throne of grace.

A psalm of David.

UNTO thee, O Lord, do I lift up my soul. 2 O my God, I trust in thee: let me not be ashamed, let not mine enemies triumph over me. 3 Yea, let none that wait on thee be ashamed: let them be ashamed which transgress without cause. 4 Show me thy ways, O Lord; teach me thy paths. 5 Lead me in thy truth, and teach me: for thou *art* the God of my salvation; on thee do I wait all the day. 6 Remember, O Lord, thy tender mercies and thy lovingkindnesses; for they *have been* ever of old. 7 Remember not the sins of my youth, nor my transgressions: according to thy mercy remember thou me for thy goodness' sake, O Lord.

Here we have David's professions of desire towards God and dependence on him. He often begins his psalms with such professions, not to move God, but to move himself, and to engage himself to answer those professions.

I. He professes his desire towards God: *Unto thee, O Lord ! do I lift up my soul, v.* 1. In the foregoing psalm (*v.* 4) it was made the character of a good man that he *has not lifted up his soul to vanity ;* and a call was given to the everlasting gates to lift up their heads for the *King of glory to come in, v.* 1. To this character, to this call, David here answers, " Lord, I lift up my soul, not to vanity, but to thee." Note, In worshipping God we must lift up our souls to him. Prayer is the ascent of the soul to God; God must be eyed and the soul employed. *Sursum corda—Up with your hearts,* was anciently used as a call to devotion. With a holy contempt of the world and the things of it, by a fixed thought and active faith, we must set God before us, and let out our desires towards him as the fountain of our happiness.

II. He professes his dependence upon God and begs for the benefit and comfort of that dependence (*v.* 2): *O my God ! I trust in thee.* His conscience witnessed for him that he had no confidence in himself nor in any creature, and that he had no diffidence of God or of his power or promise. He pleases himself with this profession of faith in God. Having put his trust in God, he is easy, is well satisfied, and quiet from the fear of evil; and he pleads it with God whose honour it is to help those that honour him by trusting in him. What men put a confidence in is either their joy or their shame, according as it proves. Now David here, under the direction of faith, prays earnestly, 1. That shame might not be his lot: " *Let me not be ashamed* of my confidence in thee; let me not be shaken from it by any prevailing fears, and let me not be, in the issue, disappointed of what I depend upon thee for; but, Lord, *keep what I have committed unto thee.*" Note, If we make our confidence in God our stay, it shall not be our shame; and, if we triumph in him, our enemies shall not triumph over us, as they would if we should now sink under our fears, or should, in the issue, come short of our hopes. 2. That it might not be the lot of any that trusted in God. All the saints have obtained a like precious faith; and therefore, doubtless, it will be alike successful in the issue. Thus the communion of saints is kept up, even by their praying one for another. True saints will make supplication for all saints. It is certain that none who, by a believing attendance, wait on God, and, by a believing hope, wait for him, shall be made ashamed of it. 3. That it might be the lot of the transgressors: *Let those be ashamed that transgress without cause,* or *vainly,* as the word is. (1.) Upon no provocation. They revolt from God and their duty, from David and his government (so some), without any occasion given them, not being able to pretend any iniquity they have found in God, or that in any thing he has wearied them. The weaker the temptation is by which men are drawn to sin the stronger the corruption is by which they are driven to it. Those are the worst transgressors that sin for sinning-sake. (2.) To no purpose. They know their attempts against God are fruitless; they imagine a vain thing, and therefore they will soon be ashamed of it.

III. He begs direction from God in the way of his duty, *v.* 4, 5. Once and again he here prays to God to teach him. He was a knowing man himself, but the most intelligent, the most observant, both need and desire to be taught of God; from him we must be ever learning. Observe,

1. What he desired to learn: " *Teach me,* not fine words or fine notions, but *thy ways, thy paths, thy truth,* the ways in which thou walkest towards me, which are *all mercy and truth* (*v.* 10), and the ways in which thou wouldst have me to walk towards thee." Those are best taught who understand their duty, and know *the good things they should do,* Eccl. ii. 3. God's *paths* and his *truth* are the same; divine laws are all founded upon divine truths. The way of God's precepts is the way of truth, cxix. 30. Christ is both the way and the truth, and therefore we must learn Christ.

2. What he desired of God, in order to this. (1.) That he would enlighten his understanding concerning his duty: " *Show me thy way,* and so *teach me.*" In doubtful cases we should pray earnestly that God would make it plain to us what he would have us to do. (2.) That he would incline his will to it, and strengthen him in it: " *Lead me,* and so teach

me." Not only as we lead one that is dimsighted, to keep him from missing his way, but as we lead one that is sick, and feeble, and faint, to help him forward in the way and to keep him from fainting and falling. We go no further in the way to heaven than God is pleased to lead us and to hold us up.

3. What he pleads, (1.) His great expectation from God: *Thou art the God of my salvation.* Note, Those that choose the salvation of God as their end, and make him the God of their salvation, may come boldly to him for direction in the way that leads to that end. If God save us, he will teach us and lead us. He that gives salvation will give instruction. (2.) His constant attendance on God: *On thee do I wait all the day.* Whence should a servant expect direction what to do but from his own master, on whom he waits all the day? If we sincerely desire to know our duty, with a resolution to do it, we need not question but that God will direct us in it.

IV. He appeals to God's infinite mercy, and casts himself upon that, not pretending to any merit of his own (*v.* 6): " *Remember, O Lord! thy tender mercies,* and, for the sake of those mercies, lead me, and teach me; for they *have been ever of old.*" 1. "Thou always wast a merciful God; it is thy name, it is thy nature and property, to show mercy." 2. "Thy counsels and designs of mercy were from everlasting; the vessels of mercy were, before all worlds, ordained to glory." 3. "The instances of thy mercy to the church in general, and to me in particular, were early and ancient, and constant hitherto; they began of old, and never ceased. Thou hast taught me from my youth up, teach me now."

V. He is in a special manner earnest for the pardon of his sins (*v.* 7): " *O remember not the sins of my youth.* Lord, remember thy mercies (*v.* 6), which speak for me, and not my sins, which speak against me." Here is, 1. An implicit confession of sin; he specifies particularly the sins of his youth. Note, Our youthful faults and follies should be matter of our repentance and humiliation long after, because time does not wear out the guilt of sin. Old people should mourn for the sinful mirth and be in pain for the sinful pleasures of their youth. He aggravates his sins, calling them his *transgressions;* and the more holy, just, and good the law is, which sin is the transgression of, the more exceedingly sinful it ought to appear to us. 2. An express petition for mercy, (1.) That he might be acquitted from guilt: " *Remember not the sins of my youth;* that is, remember them not against me, lay them not to my charge, enter not into judgment with me for them." When God pardons sin he is said to *remember it no more,* which denotes a plenary remission; he forgives and forgets. (2.) That he might be accepted in God's sight: "Remember thou me; think on me for good, and come in seasonably for my succour." We need desire no more to make us happy than for God to remember us with favour. His plea is, "according to thy mercy, and for thy goodness-sake." Note, It is God's goodness and not ours, his mercy and not our own merit, that must be our plea for the pardon of sin and all the good we stand in need of. This plea we must always rely upon, as those that are sensible of our poverty and unworthiness and as those that are satisfied of the riches of God's mercy and grace.

8 Good and upright *is* the LORD : therefore will he teach sinners in the way. 9 The meek will he guide in judgment: and the meek will he teach his way. 10 All the paths of the LORD *are* mercy and truth unto such as keep his covenant and his testimonies. 11 For thy name's sake, O LORD, pardon mine iniquity ; for it *is* great. 12 What man *is* he that feareth the LORD ? him shall he teach in the way *that* he shall choose. 13 His soul shall dwell at ease ; and his seed shall inherit the earth. 14 The secret of the LORD *is* with them that fear him ; and he will show them his covenant.

God's promises are here mixed with David's prayers. Many petitions there were in the former part of the psalm, and many we shall find in the latter; and here, in the middle of the psalm, he meditates upon the promises, and by a lively faith sucks and is satisfied from these breasts of consolation; for the promises of God are not only the best foundation of prayer, telling us what to pray for and encouraging our faith and hope in prayer, but they are a present answer to prayer. Let the prayer be made according to the promise, and then the promise may be read as a return to the prayer; and we are to believe the prayer is heard because the promise will be performed. But, in the midst of the promises, we find one petition which seems to come in somewhat abruptly, and should have followed upon *v.* 7. It is that (*v.* 11), *Pardon my iniquity.* But prayers for the pardon of sin are never impertinent; we mingle sin with all our actions, and therefore should mingle such prayers with all our devotions. He enforces this petition with a double plea. The former is very natural: " *For thy name's sake pardon my iniquity,* because thou hast proclaimed thy name gracious and merciful, pardoning iniquity, for thy glory-sake, for thy promise-sake, for thy own sake," Isa. xliii. 25. But the latter is very surprising: " *Pardon my iniquity, for it is great,* and the greater it is the more will divine mercy be magnified in the forgiveness of it." It is the glory of a great God to forgive great sins, to forgive iniquity, transgression, and sin, Exod. xxxiv. 7. " It is great, and therefore I am undone,

324

for ever undone, if infinite mercy do not interpose for the pardon of it. It is great; I see it to be so." The more we see of the heinousness of our sins the better qualified we are to find mercy with God. When we confess sin we must aggravate it.

Let us now take a view of the great and precious promises which we have in these verses, and observe,

I. To whom these promises belong and who may expect the benefit of them. We are all sinners; and can we hope for any advantage by them? Yes (*v.* 8), He will teach sinners, though they be sinners; for Christ came into the world to save sinners, and, in order to that, to teach sinners, to call sinners to repentance. These promises are sure to those who though they have been sinners, have gone astray, yet now keep God's word, 1. To such as keep his covenant and his testimonies (*v.* 10), such as take his precepts for their rule and his promises for their portion, such as, having taken God to be to them a God, live upon that, and, having given up themselves to be to him a people, live up to that. Though, through the infirmity of the flesh, they sometimes break the command, yet by a sincere repentance when at any time they do amiss, and a constant adherence by faith to God as their God, they keep the covenant and do not break that. 2. To such as fear him (*v.* 12 and again *v.* 14), such as stand in awe of his majesty and worship him with reverence, submit to his authority and obey him with cheerfulness, dread his wrath and are afraid of offending him.

II. Upon what these promises are grounded, and what encouragement we have to build upon them. Here are two things which ratify and confirm all the promises:—1. The perfections of God's nature. We value the promise by the character of him that makes it. We may therefore depend upon God's promises; for *good and upright is the Lord,* and therefore he will be as good as his word. He is so kind that he cannot deceive us, so true that he cannot break his promise. *Faithful is he who hath promised,* who also will do it. He was good in making the promise, and therefore will be upright in performing it. 2. The agreeableness of all he says and does with the perfections of his nature (*v.* 10) : *All the paths of the Lord* (that is, all his promises and all his providences) *are mercy and truth ;* they are, like himself, good and upright. All God's dealings with his people are according to the mercy of his purposes and the truth of his promises; all he does comes from love, covenant-love; and they may see in it his mercy displayed and his word fulfilled. What a rich satisfaction may this be to good people, that, whatever afflictions they are exercised with, *All the paths of the Lord are mercy and truth,* and so it will appear when they come to their journey's end.

III. What these promises are.
1. That God will instruct and direct them

in the way of their duty. This is most insisted upon, because it is an answer to David's prayers (*v.* 4, 5), *Show me thy ways and lead me.* We should fix our thoughts, and act our faith, most on those promises which suit our present case. (1.) He will *teach sinners in the way*, because they are sinners, and therefore need teaching. When they see themselves sinners, and desire teaching, then he will teach them the way of reconciliation to God, the way to a well-grounded peace of conscience, and the way to eternal life. He does, by his gospel, make this way known to all, and, by his Spirit, open the understanding and guide penitent sinners that enquire after it. The devil leads men blindfold to hell, but God enlightens men's eyes, sets things before them in a true light, and so leads them to heaven. (2.) *The meek will he guide*, the meek will he teach, that is, those that are humble and low in their own eyes, that are distrustful of themselves, desirous to be taught, and honestly resolved to follow the divine guidance. *Speak, Lord, for thy servant hears.* These he will guide *in judgment*, that is, by the rule of the written word; he will guide them in that which is practical, which relates to sin and duty, so that they may keep conscience void of offence; and he will do it judiciously (so some), that is, he will suit his conduct to their case; he will teach sinners with wisdom, tenderness, and compassion, and as they are able to bear. He will teach them his way. All good people make God's way their way, and desire to be taught that; and those that do so shall be taught and led in that way. (3.) *Him that feareth the Lord he will teach in the way that he shall choose*, either in the way that God shall choose or that the good man shall choose. It comes all to one, for he that fears the Lord chooses the things that please him. If we choose the right way, he that directed our choice will direct our steps, and will lead us in it. If we choose wisely, God will give us grace to walk wisely.

2. That God will make them easy. (*v.* 13): *His soul shall dwell at ease, shall lodge in goodness,* marg. Those that devote themselves to the fear of God, and give up themselves to be taught of God, will be easy, if it be not their own fault. The soul that is sanctified by the grace of God, and, much more, that is comforted by the peace of God, dwells at ease. Even when the body is sick and lies in pain, yet the soul may dwell at ease in God, may return to him, and repose in him as its rest. Many things occur to make us uneasy, but there is enough in the covenant of grace to counterbalance them all and to make us easy.

3. That he will give to them and theirs as much of this world as is good for them: *His seed shall inherit the earth.* Next to our care concerning our souls is our care concerning our seed, and God has a blessing in store for the generation of the upright. Those that fear God shall inherit the earth, shall have a competency in it and the comfort of it, and

their children shall fare the better for their prayers when they are gone.

4. That God will admit them into the secret of communion with himself (*v.* 14): *The secret of the Lord is with those that fear him.* They understand his word; for, *if any man do his will, he shall know of the doctrine whether it be of God,* John vii. 17. Those that receive the truth in the love of it, and experience the power of it, best understand the mystery of it. They know the meaning of his providence, and what God is doing with them, better than others. *Shall I hide from Abraham the things that I do?* Gen. xviii. 17. He calls them not *servants,* but *friends,* as he called Abraham. They know by experience the blessings of the covenant and the pleasure of that fellowship which gracious souls have with the Father and with his Son Jesus Christ. This honour have all his saints.

15 Mine eyes *are* ever toward the LORD; for he shall pluck my feet out of the net. 16 Turn thee unto me, and have mercy upon me; for I *am* desolate and afflicted. 17 The troubles of my heart are enlarged: *O* bring thou me out of my distresses. 18 Look upon mine affliction and my pain; and forgive all my sins. 19 Consider mine enemies; for they are many; and they hate me with cruel hatred. 20 O keep my soul, and deliver me: let me not be ashamed; for I put my trust in thee. 21 Let integrity and uprightness preserve me; for I wait on thee. 22 Redeem Israel, O God, out of all his troubles.

David, encouraged by the promises he had been meditating upon, here renews his addresses to God, and concludes the psalm, as he began, with professions of dependence upon God and desire towards him.

I. He lays open before God the calamitous condition he was in. His feet were in the net, held fast and entangled, so that he could not extricate himself out of his difficulties, *v.* 15. He was *desolate and afflicted, v.* 16. It is common for those that are afflicted to be desolate; their friends desert them then, and they are themselves disposed to sit alone and keep silence, Lam. iii. 28. David calls himself *desolate and solitary* because he depended not upon his servants and soldiers, but relied as entirely upon God as if he had no prospect at all of help and succour from any creature. Being in distress, in many distresses, *the troubles of his heart were enlarged* (*v.* 17), he grew more and more melancholy and troubled in mind. Sense of sin afflicted him more than any thing else: this it was that broke and wounded his spirit, and made his outward troubles lie heavily upon him. He was in *affliction and pain, v.* 18. His enemies that persecuted him were many and malicious (they hated him), and very barbarous; it was *with a cruel hatred* that they hated him, *v.* 19. Such were Christ's enemies and the persecutors of his church.

II. He expresses the dependence he had upon God in these distresses (*v.* 15): *My eyes are ever towards the Lord.* Idolaters were for gods that they could see with their bodily eyes, and they had their eyes ever towards their idols, Isa. xvii. 7, 8. But it is an eye of faith that we must have towards God, who is a Spirit, Zech. ix. 1. Our meditation of him must be sweet, and we must always set him before us: in all our ways we must acknowledge him and do all to his glory. Thus we must live a life of communion with God, not only in ordinances, but in providences, not only in the acts of devotion, but in the whole course of our conversation. David had the comfort of this in his affliction; for, because his eyes were ever towards the Lord, he doubted not but he would pluck his feet out of the net, that he would deliver him from the corruptions of his own heart (so some), from the designs of his enemies against him, so others. Those that have their eye ever towards God shall not have their feet long in the net. He repeats his profession of dependence upon God (*v.* 20)—*Let me not be ashamed; for I put my trust in thee;* and of expectation from him—*I wait on thee, v.* 21. It is good thus to hope and quietly to wait for the salvation of the Lord.

III. He prays earnestly to God for relief and succour,

1. For himself.

(1.) See how he begs, [1.] For the remission of sin (*v.* 18): *Forgive all my sins.* Those were his heaviest burdens, and which brought upon him all other burdens. He had begged (*v.* 7) for the pardon of the sins of his youth, and (*v.* 11) for the pardon of some one particular iniquity that was remarkably great, which, some think, was his sin in the matter of Uriah. But here he prays, Lord, *forgive all, take away all iniquity.* It is observable that, as to his affliction, he asks for no more than God's regard to it: " *Look upon my affliction and my pain, and do with it as thou pleasest.*" But, as to his sin, he asks for no less than a full pardon: *Forgive all my sins.* When at any time we are in trouble we should be more concerned about our sins, to get them pardoned, than about our afflictions, to get them removed. Yet he prays, [2.] For the redress of his grievances. His mind was troubled for God's withdrawings from him and under the sense he had of his displeasure against him for his sin; and therefore he prays (*v.* 16), *Turn thou unto me.* And, if God turn to us, no matter who turns from us. His condition was troubled, and, in reference to that, he prays, " *O bring thou me out of my distresses.* I see no way of deliverance open; but thou canst either find one or make one." His enemies were spiteful; and, in reference to that, he prays, " *O keep my soul* from falling into their hands, or else *deliver me* out of their hands."

(2.) Four things he mentions by way of plea to enforce these petitions, and refers himself and them to God's consideration:—
[1.] He pleads God's mercy: *Have mercy upon me.* Men of the greatest merits would be undone if they had not to do with a God of infinite mercies. [2.] He pleads his own misery, the distress he was in, his affliction and pain, especially the troubles of his heart, all which made him the proper object of divine mercy. [3.] He pleads the iniquity of his enemies: " Lord, consider them, how cruel they are, and deliver me out of their hands." [4.] He pleads his own integrity, *v.* 21. Though he had owned himself guilty before God, and had confessed his sins against him, yet, as to his enemies, he had the testimony of his conscience that he had done them no wrong, which was his comfort when they hated him with cruel hatred; and he prays that this might *preserve him.* This intimates that he did not expect to be safe any longer than he continued in his *integrity and uprightness,* and that, while he did continue in it, he did not doubt of being safe. Sincerity will be our best security in the worst of times. Integrity and uprightness will be a man's preservation more than the wealth and honour of the world can be. These will preserve us to the heavenly kingdom. We should therefore pray to God to preserve us in our integrity and then be assured that that will preserve us.

2. For the church of God (*v.* 22): *Redeem Israel, O God! out of all his troubles.* David was now in trouble himself, but he thinks it not strange, since trouble is the lot of all God's Israel. Why should any one member fare better than the whole body? David's troubles were enlarged, and very earnest he was with God to deliver him, yet he forgets not the distresses of God's church; for, when we have ever so much business of our own at the throne of grace, we must still remember to pray for the public. Good men have little comfort in their own safety while the church is in distress and danger. This prayer is a prophecy that God would, at length, give David rest, and therewith give Israel rest from all their enemies round about. It is a prophecy of the sending of the Messiah in due time to *redeem Israel from his iniquities* (cxxx. 8) and so to redeem them from their troubles. It refers also to the happiness of the future state. In heaven, and in heaven only, will God's Israel be perfectly redeemed from all troubles.

PSALM XXVI.

Holy David is in this psalm putting himself upon a solemn trial, not by God and his country, but by God and his own conscience, to both which he appeals touching his integrity (ver. 1, 2), the proof of which he alleges, I. His constant regard to God and his grace, ver. 3. II. His rooted antipathy to sin and sinners, ver. 4, 5. III. His sincere affection to the ordinances of God, and his care about them, ver. 6—8. Having thus proved his integrity, I. He deprecates the doom of the wicked, ver. 9, 10. 2. He casts himself upon the mercy and grace of God, with a resolution to hold fast his integrity, and his hope in God, ver. 11, 12. In singing this psalm we must teach and admonish ourselves, and one another, what we must be and do that we may have the favour of God, and comfort in our own consciences, and comfort ourselves with it, as David does, if we can say that in any measure we have, through grace, answered to these characters. The learned Amyraldus, in his argument of this psalm, suggests that David is here, by the spirit of prophecy, carried out to speak of himself as a type of Christ, of whom what he here says of his spotless innocence, was fully and eminently true, and of him only, and to him we may apply it in singing this psalm. "We are complete in him."

A psalm of David.

JUDGE me, O LORD ; for I have walked in mine integrity: I have trusted also in the LORD ; *therefore* I shall not slide. 2 Examine me, O LORD, and prove me ; try my reins and my heart. 3 For thy lovingkindness *is* before mine eyes : and I have walked in thy truth. 4 I have not sat with vain persons, neither will I go in with dissemblers. 5 I have hated the congregation of evil doers ; and will not sit with the wicked.

It is probable that David penned this psalm when he was persecuted by Saul and his party, who, to give some colour to their unjust rage, represented him as a very bad man, and falsely accused him of many high crimes and misdemeanours, dressed him up in the skins of wild beasts that they might bait him. Innocency itself is no fence to the name, though it is to the bosom, against the darts of calumny. Herein he was a type of Christ, who was made a reproach of men, and foretold to his followers that they also must have all manner of evil said against them falsely. Now see what David does in this case.

I. He appeals to God's righteous sentence (*v.* 1): "*Judge me, O God !* be thou Judge between me and my accusers, between the persecutor and the poor prisoner; bring me off with honour, and put those to shame that falsely accuse me." Saul, who was himself supreme judge in Israel, was his adversary, so that in a controversy with him he could appeal to no other than to God himself. As to his offences against God, he prays, *Lord, enter not into judgment with me* (cxliii. 2), *remember not my transgressions* (xxv. 7), in which he appeals to God's mercy; but, as to his offences against Saul, he appeals to God's justice and begs of him to judge for him, as xliii. 1. Or thus: he cannot justify himself against the charge of sin ; he owns his iniquity is great and he is undone if God, in his infinite mercy, do not forgive him; but he can justify himself against the charge of hypocrisy, and has reason to hope that, according to the tenour of the covenant of grace, he is one of those that may expect to find favour with God. Thus holy Job often owns he has sinned and yet he holds fast his integrity. Note, It is a comfort to those who are falsely accused that there is a righteous God, who, sooner or later, will clear up their innocency, and a comfort

to all who are sincere in religion that God himself is a witness to their sincerity.

II. He submits to his unerring search (*v.* 2) : *Examine me, O Lord ! and prove me,* as gold is proved, whether it be standard. God knows every man's true character, for he knows the thoughts and intents of the heart, and sees through every disguise. David prays, *Lord, examine me,* which intimates that he was well pleased that God did know him and truly desirous that he would discover him to himself and discover him to all the world. So sincere was he in his devotion to his God and his loyalty to his prince (in both which he was suspected to be a pretender) that he wished he had a window in his bosom, that whoever would might look into his heart.

III. He solemnly protests his sincerity (*v.* 1): "*I have walked in my integrity ;* my conversation has agreed with my profession, and one part of it has been of a piece with another." It is vain to boast of our integrity unless we can make it out that by the grace of God we have walked in our integrity, and that our conversation in the world has been in simplicity and godly sincerity. He produces here several proofs of his integrity, which encouraged him to trust in the Lord as his righteous Judge, who would patronise and plead his righteous cause, with an assurance that he should come off with reputation *(therefore I shall not slide),* and that those should not prevail who consulted to cast him down from his excellency, to shake his faith, blemish his name, and prevent his coming to the crown, lxii. 4. Those that are sincere in religion may trust in God that they shall not slide, that is, that they shall not apostatize from their religion.

1. He had a constant regard to God and to his grace, *v.* 3. (1.) He aimed at God's favour as his end and chief good : *Thy lovingkindness is before my eyes.* This will be a good evidence of our sincerity, if what we do in religion we do from a principle of love to God, and good thoughts of him as the best of beings and the best of friends and benefactors, and from a grateful sense of God's goodness to us in particular, which we have had the experience of all our days. If we set God's loving-kindness before us as our pattern, to which we endeavour to conform ourselves, being *followers of him that is good* in his goodness (1 Pet. iii. 13),—if we set it before us as our great engagement and encouragement to our duty, and are afraid of doing any thing to forfeit God's favour and in care by all means to keep ourselves in his love,—this will not only be a good evidence of our integrity, but will have a great influence upon our perseverance in it. (2.) He governed himself by the word of God as his rule : "*I have walked in thy truth,* that is, according to thy law, for thy law is truth." Note, Those only may expect the benefit of God's loving-kindness that live up to his truths, and his laws that are grounded upon

them. Some understand it of his conforming himself to God's example in truth and faithfulness, as well as in goodness and loving-kindness. Those certainly walk well that are followers of God as dear children.

2. He had no fellowship with the unfruitful works of darkness, nor with the workers of those works, *v.* 4, 5. By this it appeared he was truly loyal to his prince that he never associated with those that were disaffected to his government, with any of those *sons of Belial that despised him*, 1 Sam. x. 27. He was in none of their cabals, nor joined with them in any of their intrigues ; he cursed not the king, no, not in his heart. And this also was an evidence of his faithfulness to his God, that he never associated with those who he had any reason to think were disaffected to religion, or were open enemies, or false friends, to its interests. Note, Great care to avoid bad company is both a good evidence of our integrity and a good means to preserve us in it. Now observe here, (1.) That this part of his protestation looks both backward upon the care he had hitherto taken in this matter, and forward upon the care he would still take : *" I have not sat with them*, and I *will not go in with them."* Note, Our good practices hitherto are then evidences of our integrity when they are accompanied with resolutions, in God's strength, to persevere in them to the end, and not to draw back ; and our good resolutions for the future we may then take the comfort of when they are the continuation of our good practices hitherto. (2.) That David shunned the company, not only of wicked persons, but of vain persons, that were wholly addicted to mirth and gaiety and had nothing solid or serious in them. The company of such may perhaps be the more pernicious of the two to a good man because he will not be so ready to stand upon his guard against the contagion of vanity as against that of downright wickedness. (3.) That the company of dissemblers is as dangerous company as any, and as much to be shunned, in prudence as well as piety. Evil-doers pretend friendship to those whom they would decoy into their snares, but they dissemble. *When they speak fair, believe them not.* (4.) Though sometimes he could not avoid being in the company of bad people, yet he would not *go in with them*, he would not choose such for his companions nor seek an opportunity of acquaintance and converse with them. He might fall in with them, but he would not, by appointment and assignation, go in with them. Or, if he happened to be with them, he would not sit with them ; he would not continue with them; he would be in their company no longer than his business made it necessary : he would not concur with them, not say as they said, nor do as they did, as those that *sit in the seat of the scornful*, i. 1. He would not sit in counsel with them upon ways and means to do mischief, nor sit in judgment with them to con-

328

demn the generation of the righteous. (5.) We must not only in our practice avoid bad company, but in our principles and affections we must have an aversion to it. David here says, not only " I have shunned it," but, " *I have hated* it," cxxxix. 21. (6.) The congregation of evil-doers, the club, the confederacy of them, is in a special manner hateful to good people. I have hated *ecclesiam malignantium—the church of the malignant ;* so the vulgar Latin reads it. As good men, in concert, make one another better, and are enabled to do so much the more good, so bad men, in combination, make one another worse, and do so much the more mischief. In all this David was a type of Christ, who, though he received sinners and ate with them, to instruct them and do them good, yet, otherwise, was holy, harmless, undefiled, and separate from sinners, particularly from the Pharisees, those dissemblers. He was also an example to Christians, when they join themselves to Christ, to *save themselves from this untoward generation*, Acts ii. 40.

6 I will wash mine hands in innocency : so will I compass thine altar, O LORD : 7 That I may publish with the voice of thanksgiving, and tell of all thy wondrous works. 8 LORD, I have loved the habitation of thy house, and the place where thine honour dwelleth. 9 Gather not my soul with sinners, nor my life with bloody men : 10 In whose hands *is* mischief, and their right hand is full of bribes. 11 But as for me, I will walk in mine integrity : redeem me, and be merciful unto me. 12 My foot standeth in an even place : in the congregations will I bless the LORD.

In these verses,

I. David mentions, as a further evidence of his integrity, the sincere affection he had to the ordinances of God, the constant care he took about them, and the pleasure he took in them. Hypocrites and dissemblers may indeed be found attending on God's ordinances, as the proud Pharisee went up to the temple to pray with the penitent publican ; but it is a good sign of sincerity if we attend upon them as David here tells us he did, *v.* 6—8.

1. He was very careful and conscientious in his preparation for holy ordinances : *I will wash my hands in innocency.* He not only refrained from the society of sinners, but kept himself clean from the pollutions of sin, and this with an eye to the place he had among those that compassed God's altar. " I will wash, and so will I compass the altar, knowing that otherwise I shall not be welcome." This is like that (1 Cor. xi. 28), *Let a man examine himself, and so let him eat, so pre-*

pared. This denotes, (1.) Habitual preparation: "*I will wash my hands in innocency;* I will carefully watch against all sin, and keep my conscience pure from those dead works which defile it and forbid my drawing nigh to God." See xxiv. 3, 4. (2.) Actual preparation. It alludes to the ceremony of the priests' washing when they went in to minister, Exod. xxx. 20, 21. Though David was no priest, yet, as every worshipper ought, he would look to the substance of that which the priests were enjoined the shadow of. In our preparations for solemn ordinances we must not only be able to clear ourselves from the charge of reigning infidelity or hypocrisy, and to protest our innocency of that (which was signified by *washing the hands,* Deut. xxi. 6), but we must take pains to cleanse ourselves from the spots of remaining iniquity by renewing our repentance, and making a fresh application of the blood of Christ to our consciences for the purifying and pacifying of them. He that is washed (that is, is in a justified state) has need thus to *wash his feet* (John xiii. 10), to wash his hands, to wash them in innocency; he that is penitent is *pene innocens—almost innocent;* and he that is pardoned is so far innocent that his sins shall not be mentioned against him.

2. He was very diligent and serious in his attendance upon them: *I will compass thy altar,* alluding to the custom of the priests, who, while the sacrifice was in offering, walked round the altar, and probably the offerers likewise did so at some distance, denoting a diligent regard to what was done and a dutiful attendance in the service. " *I will compass it;* I will be among the crowds that do compass it, among the thickest of them." David, a man of honour, a man of business, a man of war, thought it not below him to attend with the multitude on God's altars and could find time for that attendance. Note, (1.) All God's people will be sure to wait on God's altar, in obedience to his commands and in pursuance of his favour. Christ is our altar, not as the altar in the Jewish church, which was fed by them, but an altar that we eat of and *live upon,* Heb. xiii. 10. (2.) It is a pleasant sight to see God's altar compassed and to see ourselves among those that compass it.

3. In all his attendance on God's ordinances he aimed at the glory of God and was much in the thankful praise and adoration of him. He had an eye to the place of worship as the place where God's honour dwelt (*v.* 8), and therefore made it his business there to honour God and to give him the glory due to his name, to publish with the voice of thanksgiving all God's wondrous works. God's gracious works, which call for our thanksgiving, are all wondrous works, which call for our admiration. We ought to publish them, and tell of them, for his glory, and the excitement of others to praise him; and we ought to do it with the voice of thanksgiving,

as those that are sensible of our obligations, by all ways possible, to acknowledge with gratitude the favours we have received from God.

4. He did this with delight and from a principle of true affection to God and his institutions. Touching this he appeals to God: " *Lord,* thou knowest how dearly *I have loved the habitation of thy house* (*v.* 8), the tabernacle where thou art pleased to manifest thy residence among thy people and receive their homage, *the place where thy honour dwells.*" David was sometimes forced by persecution into the countries of idolaters and was hindered from attending God's altars, which perhaps his persecutors, that laid him under that restraint, did themselves upbraid him with as his crime. See 1 Sam. xx. 27. "But, Lord," says he, "though I cannot come to the habitation of thy house, I love it; my heart is there, and it is my greatest trouble that I am not there." Note, All that truly love God truly love the ordinances of God, and *therefore* love them because in them he manifests his honour and they have an opportunity of honouring him. Our Lord Jesus loved his Father's honour, and made it his business to glorify him; he loved the habitation of his house, his church among men, loved it and gave himself for it, that he might build and consecrate it. Those who love communion with God, and delight in approaching to him, find it to be a constant pleasure, a comfortable evidence of their integrity, and a comfortable earnest of their endless felicity.

II. David, having given proofs of his integrity, earnestly prays, with a humble confidence towards God (such as those have whose hearts condemn them not), that he might not fall under the doom of the wicked (*v.* 9, 10). *Gather not my soul with sinners.* Here, 1. David describes these sinners, whom he looked upon to be in a miserable condition, so miserable that he could not wish the worst enemy he had in the world to be in a worse. " They are *bloody men,* that thirst after blood and lie under a great deal of the guilt of blood. They do mischief, and mischief is always in their hands. Though they get by their wickedness (for *their right hand is full of bribes* which they have taken to pervert justice), yet that will make their case never the better; for *what is a man profited if he gain the world and lose his soul?*" 2. He dreads having his lot with them. He never loved them, nor associated with them, in this world, and therefore could in faith pray that he might not have his lot with them in the other world. Our souls must shortly be gathered, to return to God that gave them and will call for them again. See Job xxxiv. 14. It concerns us to consider whether our souls will then be gathered with saints or with sinners, whether bound in the bundle of life with the Lord for ever, as the souls of the faithful are (1 Sam. xxv. 29), or bound in the bundle of tares for the fire, Matt. xiii. 30. Death gathers us to our people, to those that are our people while we live, whom we choose to associate with, and with whom we cast in our lot, to those death will gather us, and with them we must take our lot, to eternity. Balaam desired to die the death of the righteous; David dreaded dying the death of the wicked; so that both sides were of that mind, which if we be of, and will live up to it, we are happy for ever. Those that will not be companions with sinners in their mirth, nor eat of their dainties, may in faith pray not to be companions with them in their misery, nor to drink of their cup, their cup of trembling.

III. David, with a holy humble confidence, commits himself to the grace of God, *v.* 11, 12. 1. He promises that by the grace of God he would persevere in his duty: " *As for me, whatever others do, I will walk in my integrity.*" Note, When the testimony of our consciences for us that we have walked in our integrity is comfortable to us this should confirm our resolutions to continue therein. 2. He prays for the divine grace both to enable him to do so and to give him the comfort of it: " *Redeem me* out of the hands of my enemies, *and be merciful to me,* living and dying." Be we ever so confident of our integrity, yet still we must rely upon God's mercy and the great redemption Christ has wrought out, and pray for the benefit of them. 3. He pleases himself with his steadiness: " *My foot stands in an even place,* where I shall not stumble and whence I shall not fall." This he speaks as one that found his resolutions fixed for God and godliness, not to be shaken by the temptations of the world, and his comforts firm in God and his grace, not to be disturbed by the crosses and troubles of the world. 4. He promises himself that he should yet have occasion to praise the Lord, that he should be furnished with matter for praise, that he should have a heart for praises, and that, though he was now perhaps banished from public ordinances, yet he should again have an opportunity of blessing God in the congregation of his people. Those that hate the congregation of evil-doers shall be joined to the congregation of the righteous and join with them in praising God; and it is pleasant doing that in good company; the more the better: it is the more like heaven.

PSALM XXVII.

Some think David penned this psalm before his coming to the throne, when he was in the midst of his troubles, and perhaps upon occasion of the death of his parents; but the Jews think he penned it when he was old, upon occasion of the wonderful deliverance he had from the sword of the giant, when Abishai succoured him (2 Sam. xxi. 16, 17) and his people thereupon resolved he should never venture his life again in battle, lest he should quench the light of Israel. Perhaps it was not penned upon any particular occasion; but it is very expressive of the pious and devout affections with which gracious souls are carried out towards God at all times, especially in times of trouble. Here is, I. The courage and holy bravery of his faith, ver. 1–3. II. The complacency he took in communion with God and the benefit he experienced by it, ver. 4–6. III. His desire towards God, and his favour and grace, ver. 7–9, 11, 12. IV. His expectations from God, and the encouragement he gives to others to hope in him, ver. 10, 13, 14. And let our hearts be thus affected in singing this psalm.

A psalm of David.

THE Lord *is* my light and my salvation; whom shall I fear? the Lord *is* the strength of my life; of whom shall I be afraid? 2 When the wicked, *even* mine enemies and my foes, came upon me to eat up my flesh, they stumbled and fell. 3 Though a host should encamp against me, my heart shall not fear: though war should rise against me, in this *will* I *be* confident. 4 One *thing* have I desired of the Lord, that will I seek after; that I may dwell in the house of the Lord all the days of my life, to behold the beauty of the Lord, and to enquire in his temple. 5 For in the time of trouble he shall hide me in his pavilion: in the secret of his tabernacle shall he hide me; he shall set me up upon a rock. 6 And now shall mine head be lifted up above mine enemies round about me: therefore will I offer in his tabernacle sacrifices of joy; I will sing, yea, I will sing praises unto the Lord.

We may observe here,

I. With what a lively faith David triumphs in God, glories in his holy name, and in the interest he had in him. 1. *The Lord is my light.* David's subjects called him *the light of Israel,* 2 Sam. xxi. 17. And he was indeed a burning and a shining light: but he owns that he shone, as the moon does, with a borrowed light; what light God darted upon him reflected upon them: *The Lord is my light.* God is a light to his people, to show them the way when they are in doubt, to comfort and rejoice their hearts when they are in sorrow. It is in his light that they now walk on in their way, and in his light they hope to see light for ever. 2. " He is *my salvation,* in whom I am safe and by whom I shall be saved." 3. " He is *the strength of my life,* not only the protector of my exposed life, who keeps me from being slain, but the strength of my frail weak life, who keeps me from fainting, sinking, and dying away." God, who is a believer's light, is the strength of his life, not only by whom, but in whom, he lives and moves. In God therefore let us strengthen ourselves.

II. With what an undaunted courage he triumphs over his enemies; no fortitude like that of faith. If God be for him, who can be against him? *Whom shall I fear? Of whom shall I be afraid?* If Omnipotence be his guard, he has no cause to fear; if he knows it to be so, he has no disposition to fear. If God be his light, he fears no shades; if God be his salvation, he fears no colours. He triumphs over his enemies that were already routed, *v.* 2. His enemies came upon him, *to eat up his flesh,* aiming at no less and assured of that, but they fell; not, "He smote them and they fell," but, "*They stumbled and fell;*" they were so confounded and weakened that they could not go on with their enterprise. Thus those that came to take Christ with a word's speaking were made to stagger and fall to the ground, John xviii. 6. The ruin of some of the enemies of God's people is an earnest of the complete conquest of them all. And therefore, these having fallen, he is fearless of the rest: "Though they be numerous, *a host* of them,—though they be daring and their attempts threatening, — though they *encamp against me,* an army against one man,—though they wage war upon me, yet *my heart shall not fear.*" Hosts cannot hurt us if the Lord of hosts protect us. Nay, in this assurance that God is for me *I will be confident.*" Two things he will be confident of:—1. That he shall be safe. "If God is my salvation, *in the time of trouble he shall hide me;* he shall set me out of danger and above the fear of it." God will not only find out a shelter for his people in distress (as he did Jer. xxxvi. 26), but he will himself be their hiding-place, Ps. xxxii. 7. His providence will, it may be, keep them safe; at least his grace will make them easy. His name is the strong tower into which by faith they run, Prov. xviii. 10. "*He shall hide me,*" not in the strongholds of En-gedi (1 Sam. xxiii. 29), but *in the secret of his tabernacle.*" The gracious presence of God, his power, his promise, his readiness to hear prayer, the witness of his Spirit in the hearts of his people—these are the secret of his tabernacle, and in these the saints find cause for that holy security and serenity of mind in which they dwell at ease. This sets them upon a rock which will not sink under them, but on which they find firm footing for their hopes; nay, it sets them *up upon a rock* on high, where the raging threatening billows of a stormy sea cannot touch them; it is a rock that is *higher than we,* lxi. 2. 2. That he shall be victorious (*v.* 6): "*Now shall my head be lifted up above my enemies,* not only so as that they cannot reach it with their darts, but so as that I shall be exalted to bear rule over them." David here, by faith in the promise of God, triumphs before the victory, and is as sure, not only of the laurel, but of the crown, as if it were already upon his head.

III. With what a gracious earnestness he prays for a constant communion with God in holy ordinances, *v.* 4. It greatly encouraged his confidence in God that he was conscious to himself of an entire affection to God and to his ordinances, and that he was in his element when in the way of his duty and in the way of increasing his acquaintance with him. If our hearts can witness for us that we delight in God above any creature, that may encourage us to depend upon him; for it is

a sign we are of those whom he protects as his own. Or it may be taken thus: He desired to dwell in the house of the Lord that there he might be safe from the enemies that surrounded him. Finding himself surrounded by threatening hosts, he does not say, "*One thing have I desired,*" in order to my safety, that I may have my army augmented to such a number," or that I may be master of such a city or such a castle, but "*that I may dwell in the house of the Lord,* and then I am well." Observe,

1. What it is he desires—*to dwell in the house of the Lord.* In the courts of God's house the priests had their lodgings, and David wished he had been one of them. Disdainfully as some look upon God's ministers, one of the greatest and best of kings that ever was would gladly have taken his lot, have taken his lodging, among them. Or, rather, he desires that he might duly and constantly attend on the public service of God, with other faithful Israelites, according as the duty of every day required. He longed to see an end of the wars in which he was now engaged, not that he might live at ease in his own palace, but that he might have leisure and liberty for a constant attendance in God's courts. Thus Hezekiah, a genuine son of David, wished for the recovery of his health, not that he might go up to the thrones of judgment, but that he might *go up to the house of the Lord,* Isa. xxxviii. 22. Note, All God's children desire to dwell in God's house; where should they dwell else? Not to sojourn there as a wayfaring man, that turns aside to tarry but for a night, nor to dwell there for a time only, as the servant that abides not in the house for ever, but to dwell there all the days of their life; for there the Son abides ever. Do we hope that praising God will be the blessedness of our eternity? Surely then we ought to make it the business of our time.

2. How earnestly he covets this: "This is the *one thing I have desired of the Lord* and which I will seek after." If he were to ask but one thing of God, this should be it; for this he had at heart more than any thing. He desired it as a good thing; he desired it of the Lord as his gift and a token of his favour. And, having fixed his desire upon this as the one thing needful, he sought after it; he continued to pray for it, and contrived his affairs so as that he might have this liberty and opportunity. Note, Those that truly desire communion with God will set themselves with all diligence to seek after it, Prov. xviii. 1.

3. What he had in his eye in it. He would dwell in God's house, not for the plenty of good entertainment that was there, in the feasts upon the sacrifices, nor for the music and good singing that were there, but *to behold the beauty of the Lord and to enquire in his temple.* He desired to attend in God's courts, (1.) That he might have the pleasure

of meditating upon God. He knew something of the beauty of the Lord, the infinite and transcendent amiableness of the divine being and perfections; his holiness is his beauty (cx. 3); his goodness is his beauty, Zech. ix. 17. The harmony of all his attributes is the beauty of his nature. With an eye of faith and holy love we with pleasure behold this beauty, and observe more and more in it that is amiable, that is admirable. When with fixedness of thought, and a holy flame of devout affections, we contemplate God's glorious excellencies, and entertain ourselves with the tokens of his peculiar favour to us, this is that view of the beauty of the Lord which David here covets, and it is to be had in his ordinances, for there he manifests himself. (2.) That he might have the satisfaction of being instructed in his duty; for concerning this he would *enquire in God's temple.* Lord, *what wilt thou have me to do?* For the sake of these two things he desired that one thing, to *dwell in the house of the Lord all the days of his life;* for blessed are those that do so; they will be still praising him (lxxxiv. 4), both in speaking to him and in hearing from him. Mary's sitting at Christ's feet to hear his word Christ calls the *one thing needful,* and *the good part.*

4. What advantage he promised himself by it. Could he but have a place in God's house, (1.) There he should be quiet and easy: there troubles would not find him, for he should be hid in secret; there troubles would not reach him, for he should be set on high, *v.* 5. Joash, one of David's seed, was hidden in the house of the Lord six years, and there not only preserved from the sword, but reserved to the crown, 2 Kings xi. 3. The temple was thought a safe place for Nehemiah to abscond in, Neh. vi. 10. The safety of believers however is not in the walls of the temple, but in the God of the temple and their comfort in communion with him. (2.) There he should be pleasant and cheerful: there he would offer sacrifices of joy, *v.* 6. For God's work is its own wages. There *he would sing, yea, he would sing praises to the Lord.* Note, Whatever is the matter of our joy ought to be the matter of our praise; and, when we attend upon God in holy ordinances, we ought to be much in joy and praise. It is for the glory of our God that we should sing in his ways; and, whenever God lifts us up above our enemies, we ought to exalt him in our praises. *Thanks be to God, who always causeth us to triumph,* 2 Cor. ii. 14.

7 Hear, O LORD, *when* I cry with my voice : have mercy also upon me, and answer me. 8 *When thou saidst,* Seek ye my face; my heart said unto thee, Thy face, LORD, will I seek. 9 Hide not thy face *far* from me; put not thy servant away in anger : thou hast been my help ; leave me not, nei-

ther forsake me, O God of my salvation. 10 When my father and my mother forsake me, then the LORD will take me up. 11 Teach me thy way, O LORD, and lead me in a plain path, because of mine enemies. 12 Deliver me not over unto the will of mine enemies : for false witnesses are risen up against me, and such as breathe out cruelty. 13 *I had fainted,* unless I had believed to see the goodness of the LORD in the land of the living. 14 Wait on the LORD : be of good courage, and he shall strengthen thine heart : wait, I say, on the LORD.

David in these verses expresses,

I. His desire towards God, in many petitions. If he cannot now go up to the house of the Lord, yet, wherever he is, he can find a way to the throne of grace by prayer.

1. He humbly bespeaks, because he firmly believes he shall have, a gracious audience : " *Hear, O Lord, when I cry,* not only with my heart, but, as one in earnest, *with my voice* too." He bespeaks also an answer of peace, which he expects, not from his own merit, but God's goodness : *Have mercy upon me, and answer me, v.* 7. If we pray and believe, God will graciously hear and answer.

2. He takes hold of the kind invitation God had given him to this duty, *v.* 8. It is presumption for us to come into the presence of the King of kings uncalled, nor can we draw near with any assurance unless he *hold forth to us the golden sceptre.* David therefore going to pray fastens, in his thoughts, upon the call God had given him to the throne of his grace, and reverently touches, as it were, the top of the golden sceptre which was thereby held out to him. *My heart said unto thee* (so it begins in the original) or *of thee, Seek you my face;* he first revolved that, and preached that over again to himself (and that is the best preaching; it is hearing twice what God speaks once)—*Thou saidst* (so it may be supplied), *Seek you my face;* and then he returns what he had so meditated upon, in this pious resolution, *Thy face, Lord, will I seek.* Observe here, (1.) The true nature of religious worship; it is seeking the face of God. This it is in God's precept: *Seek you my face;* he would have us seek him for himself, and make his favour our chief good; and this it is in the saint's purpose and desire : " *Thy face, Lord, will I seek,* and nothing less will I take up with." The opening of his hand will satisfy the desire of other living things (cxlv 16), but it is only the shining of his face that will satisfy the desire of a living soul, iv. 6, 7. (2.) The kind invitation of a gracious God to this duty : *Thou saidst, Seek you my face;* it is not only a permission, but a precept; and his commanding us to seek implies a promise

of finding ; for he is too kind to say, *Seek you me in vain.* God calls us to seek his face in our conversion to him and in our converse with him. He calls us, by the whispers of his Spirit to and with our spirits, to seek his face ; he calls us by his word, by the stated returns of opportunities for his worship, and by special providences, merciful and afflictive. When we are foolishly making our court to lying vanities God is, in love to us, calling us in him to seek our own mercies. (3.) The ready compliance of a gracious soul with this invitation. The call is immediately returned: *My heart answered, Thy face, Lord, will I seek.* The call was general : *" Seek you my face ;"* but, like David, we must apply it to ourselves, *" I will seek it."* The word does us no good when we transfer it to others, and do not ourselves accept the exhortation. The call was, *Seek you my face ;* the answer is express, *Thy face, Lord, will I seek ;* like that (Jer. iii. 22), *Behold, we come unto thee.* A gracious heart readily echoes to the call of a gracious God, being made willing in the day of his power.

3. He is very particular in his requests. (1.) For the favour of God, that he might not be shut out from that (*v.* 9): *" Thy face, Lord, will I seek,* in obedience to thy command ; therefore *hide not thy face from me ;* let me never want the reviving sense of thy favour ; love me, and let me know that thou lovest me; *put not thy servant away in anger."* He owns he had deserved God's displeasure, but begs that, however God might correct him, he would not cast him away from his presence; for what is hell but that? (2.) For the continuance of his presence with him: *" Thou hast been my help* formerly, and *thou art the God of my salvation ;* and therefore whither shall I go but to thee? *O leave me not, neither forsake me ;* withdraw not the operations of thy power from me, for then I am helpless ; withdraw not the tokens of thy good-will to me, for then I am comfortless."* (3.) For the benefit of a divine guidance (*v.* 11): *" Teach me thy way, O Lord !* give me to understand the meaning of thy providences towards me and make them plain to me; and give me to know my duty in every doubtful case, that I may not mistake it, but may walk rightly, and that I may not do it with hesitation, but may walk surely."* It is not policy, but plainness (that is, downright honesty) that will direct us into and keep us in the way of our duty. He begs to be guided *in a plain path, because of his enemies,* or (as the margin reads it) his *observers.* His enemies watched for his halting, that they might find occasion against him. Saul eyed David, 1 Sam. xviii. 9. This quickened him to pray, " Lord, *lead me in a plain path,* that they may have nothing ill, or nothing that looks ill, to lay to my charge." (4.) For the benefit of a divine protection (*v.* 12): *" Deliver me not over to the will of my enemies.* Lord, let them not gain their point, for it aims at my life, and no less, and in such

a way as that I have no fence against them, but thy power over their consciences ; for *false witnesses have risen up against me,* that aim further than to take away my reputation or estate, for they *breathe out cruelty ;* it is the blood, the precious blood, they thirst after." Herein David was a type of Christ ; for false witnesses rose up against him, and such as breathed out cruelty ; but, though he was delivered into their wicked hands, he was not delivered over to their will, for they could not prevent his exaltation.

II. He expresses his dependence upon God,

1. That he would help and succour him when all other helps and succours failed him (*v.* 10): *" When my father and my mother forsake me,* the nearest and dearest friends I have in the world, from whom I may expect most relief and with most reason, when they die, or are at a distance from me, or are disabled to help me in the time of need, or are unkind to me or unmindful of me, and will not help me, when I am as helpless as ever poor orphan was that was left fatherless and motherless, then I know *the Lord will take me up,* as a poor wandering sheep is taken up, and saved from perishing."* His time to help those that trust in him is when all other helpers fail, when it is most for his honour and their comfort. With him *the fatherless find mercy.* This promise has often been fulfilled in the letter of it. Forsaken orphans have been taken under the special care of the divine Providence, which has raised up relief and friends for them in a way that one would not have expected. God is a surer and better friend than our earthly parents are or can be.

2. That in due time he should see the displays of his goodness, *v.* 13. He believed he should *see the goodness of the Lord in the land of the living ;* and, if he had not done so, he would *have fainted* under his afflictions. Even the best saints are subject to faint when their troubles become grievous and tedious, their spirits are overwhelmed, and their flesh and heart fail. But then faith is a sovereign cordial ; it keeps them from desponding under their burden and from despairing of relief, keeps them hoping, and praying, and waiting, and keeps up in them good thoughts of God, and the comfortable enjoyment of themselves. But what was it the belief of which kept David from fainting ?—*that he should see the goodness of the Lord,* which now seemed at a distance. Those that walk by faith in the goodness of the Lord shall in due time walk in the sight of that goodness. This he hopes to see in the land of the living, that is, (1.) In this world, that he should outlive his troubles and not perish under them. It is his comfort, not so much that he shall see the land of the living as that he shall see the goodness of God in it ; for that is the comfort of all creature-comforts to a gracious soul. (2.) In the land of Canaan, and in Jerusalem where the lively oracles were. In comparison with the heathen, that were dead in sin, the land

of Israel might fitly be called *the land of the living;* there God was known, and there David hoped to see his goodness; see 2 Sam. xv. 25, 26. Or, (3.) In heaven. It is that land alone that may truly be called *the land of the living,* where there is no more death. This earth is the land of the dying. There is nothing like the believing hope of eternal life, the foresights of that glory, and foretastes of those pleasures, to keep us from fainting under all the calamities of this present time.

3. That in the mean time he should be strengthened to bear up under his burdens (*v.* 14); whether he says it to himself, or to his friends, it comes all to one; this is that which encourages him : *He shall strengthen thy heart,* shall sustain the spirit, and then the spirit shall sustain the infirmity. In that strength, (1.) Keep close to God and to your duty. *Wait on the Lord* by faith, and prayer, and a humble resignation to his will; *wait, I say, on the Lord;* whatever you do, grow not remiss in your attendance upon God. (2.) Keep up your spirits in the midst of the greatest dangers and difficulties : *Be of good courage;* let your hearts be fixed, trusting in God, and your minds stayed upon him, and then let none of these things move you. Those that wait upon the Lord have reason to be of good courage.

PSALM XXVIII.

The former part of this psalm is the prayer of a saint militan and now in distress (ver. 1—3), to which is added the doom of God's implacable enemies, ver. 4, 5. The latter part of the psalm is the thanksgiving of a saint triumphant, and delivered out of his distresses (ver. 6—8), to which is added a prophetical prayer for all God's faithful loyal subjects, ver. 9. So that it is hard to say which of these two conditions David was in when he penned it. Some think he was now in trouble seeking God, but at the same time preparing to praise him for his deliverance, and by faith giving him thanks for it, before it was wrought. Others think he was now in triumph, but remembered, and recorded for his own and others' benefit, the prayers he made when he was in affliction, that the mercy might relish the better, when it appeared to be an answer to them.

A psalm of David.

UNTO thee will I cry, O LORD my rock; be not silent to me : lest, *if* thou be silent to me, I become like them that go down into the pit. 2 Hear the voice of my supplications, when I cry unto thee, when I lift up my hands toward thy holy oracle. 3 Draw me not away with the wicked, and with the workers of iniquity, which speak peace to their neighbours, but mischief *is* in their hearts. 4 Give them according to their deeds, and according to the wickedness of their endeavours : give them after the work of their hands; render to them their desert. 5 Because they regard not the works of the LORD, nor the operation of his hands, he shall destroy them, and not build them up.

In these verses David is very earnest in prayer.

I. He prays that God would graciously hear and answer him, now that, in his distress, he called upon him, *v.* 1, 2. Observe his faith in prayer: *O Lord, my rock,* denoting his belief of God's power (he is a rock) and his dependence upon that power—" He is *my rock,* on whom I build my hope." Observe his fervency in prayer : " *To thee will I cry,* as one in earnest, being ready to sink, unless thou come in with seasonable succour." And observe how solicitous he is to obtain an answer: " *Be not silent to me,* as one angry at my prayers, lxxx. 4. Lord, speak to me, answer me *with· good words and comfortable words* (Zech. i. 13); though the thing I pray for be not given me, yet let God speak to me joy and gladness, and make me to hear them. Lord, speak for me, in answer to my prayers, plead my cause, command deliverances for me, and thus hear and answer the voice of my supplications." Two things he pleads :— 1. The sad despair he should be in if God slighted him : " *If thou be silent to me,* and I have not the tokens of thy favour, I am *like those that go down into the pit* (that is, I am a dead man, lost and undone); if God be not my friend, appear not to me and appear not for me, my hope and my help will have perished." Nothing can be so cutting, so killing, to a gracious soul, as the want of God's favour and the sense of his displeasure. *I shall be like those that go down to hell* (so some understand it) ; for what is the misery of the damned but this, that God is for ever silent to them and deaf to their cry? Those are in some measure qualified for God's favour, and may expect it, who are thus possessed with a dread of his wrath, and to whom his frowns are worse than death. 2. The good hopes he had that God would favour him : *I lift up my hands towards thy holy oracle,* which denotes, not only an earnest desire, but an earnest expectation, thence to receive an answer of peace. The most holy place within the veil is here, as elsewhere, called the *oracle;* there the ark and the mercy-seat were, there God was said to *dwell between the cherubim,* and thence he spoke to his people, Num. vii. 89. That was a type of Christ, and it is to him that we must lift up our eyes and hands, for through him all good comes from God to us. It was also a figure of heaven (Heb. ix. 24); and from God as our Father in heaven we are taught to expect an answer to our prayers. The scriptures are called *the oracles of God,* and to them we must have an eye in our prayers and expectations. There is the word on which God hath caused and encouraged us to hope.

II. He deprecates the doom of wicked people, as before (xxvi. 9, " *Gather not my soul with sinners):* Lord, I attend thy holy oracle, *draw me not away* from that *with the wicked, and with the workers of iniquity,*" *v.* 3. 1. " Save me from being entangled in the snares they have laid for me. They flatter and cajole me, and speak peace to me; but they have a design upon me, for *mischief is in their heart;* they aim to disturb me, nay, to destroy me. Lord, suffer me not to be drawn away and ruined by their cursed plots ; for they have, can have, no power, no success, against me, except it be given them from above." 2. " Save me from being infected with their sins and from doing as they do. Let me not be drawn away by their fallacious arguments, or their allurements, from thy holy oracle (where I desire to dwell all the days of my life), to practise any wicked works ;" see cxli. 4. " Lord, never leave me to myself, to use such arts of deceit and treachery for my safety as they use for my ruin. Let no event of Providence be an invincible temptation to me, to draw me either into the imitation or into the interest of wicked people." Good men dread the way of sinners ; the best are sensible of the danger they are in of being drawn aside into it ; and therefore we should all pray earnestly to God for his grace to keep us in our integrity. 3. " Save me from being involved in their doom ; let me not be led forth with the workers of iniquity, for I am not one of those that speak peace while war is in their hearts." Note, Those that are careful not to partake with sinners in their sins have reason to hope that they shall not partake with them in their plagues, Rev. xviii. 4.

III. He imprecates the just judgments of God upon the workers of iniquity (*v.* 4) : *Give them according to their deeds.* This is not the language of passion or revenge, nor is it inconsistent with the duty of praying for our enemies. But, 1. Thus he would show how far he was from complying with the workers of iniquity, and with what good reason he had begged not to be drawn away with them, because he was convinced that they could not be made more miserable than to be dealt with according to their deeds. 2. Thus he would express his zeal for the honour of God's justice in governing the world. " Lord, they think all well that they do, and justify themselves in their wicked practices. Lord, *give them after the work of their hands,* and so undeceive those about them, who think there is no harm in what they do because it goes unpunished," xciv. 1, 2. 3. This prayer is a prophecy that God will, sooner or later, render to all impenitent sinners according to their deserts. If what has been done amiss be not undone by repentance, there will certainly come a reckoning day, when God will render to every man who persists in his evil deeds according to them. It is a prophecy particularly of the destruction of destroyers : *"They speak peace to their neighbours, but mischief is in their hearts;* Lord, *give them according to their deeds,* let the spoilers be spoiled, and let those be treacherously dealt with who have thus dealt treacherously ;" see Isa. xxxiii. 1 ; Rev. xviii. 6 ; xiii. 10. Observe, He foretels that God will reward them, not only according to their deeds, but *according to the wickedness of their endeavours;* for sinners shall be

reckoned with, not only for the mischief they have done, but for the mischief they would have done, which they designed, and did what they could to effect. And, if God go by this rule in dealing with the wicked, surely he will do so in dealing with the righteous, and will reward them, not only for the good they have done, but for the good they have endeavoured to do, though they could not accomplish it.

IV. He foretels their destruction for their contempt of God and his hand (*v.* 5) : " *Because they regard not the works of the Lord and the operations of his hands,* by which he manifests himself and speaks to the children of men, *he will destroy them* in this world and in the other, *and not build them up.*" Note, A stupid regardlessness of the works of God is the cause of the sin of sinners, and so becomes the cause of their ruin. Why do men question the being or attributes of God, but because they do not duly regard his handyworks, which declare his glory, and in which the invisible things of him are clearly seen ? Why do men forget God, and live without him, nay, affront God, and live in rebellion against him, but because they consider not the instances of that wrath of his which is revealed *from heaven against all ungodliness and unrighteousness of men?* Why do the enemies of God's people hate and persecute them, and devise mischief against them, but because they regard not the works God has wrought for his church, by which he has made it appear how dear it is to him ? See Isa. v. 12.

In singing this we must arm ourselves against all temptations to join with the workers of iniquity, and animate ourselves against all the troubles we may be threatened with by the workers of iniquity.

6 Blessed *be* the Lord, because he hath heard the voice of my supplications. 7 The Lord *is* my strength and my shield ; my heart trusted in him, and I am helped : therefore my heart greatly rejoiceth ; and with my song will I praise him. 8 The Lord *is* their strength, and he *is* the saving strength of his anointed. 9 Save thy people, and bless thine inheritance: feed them also, and lift them up for ever.

In these verses,

I. David gives God thanks for the audience of his prayers as affectionately as a few verses before he had begged it : *Blessed be the Lord, v.* 6. How soon are the saints' sorrows turned into songs and their prayers into praises ! It was in faith that David prayed (*v.* 2), *Hear the voice of my supplications ;* and by the same faith he gives thanks (*v.* 6) that *God has heard the voice of his supplications.* Note, 1. Those that pray in faith may rejoice in hope. " He hath heard me (graciously accepted me) and I am as sure of a real answer as if I had it already." 2. What we win by prayer we must wear with praise. Has God heard our supplications? Let us then bless his name.

II. He encourages himself to hope in God for the perfecting of every thing that concerned him. Having given to God the glory of his grace (*v.* 6), he is humbly bold to take the comfort of it, *v.* 7. This is the method of attaining peace: let us begin with praise that it is attainable. Let us first bless God and then bless ourselves. Observe, 1. His dependence upon God: "*The Lord is my strength,* to support me, and carry me on, through all my services and sufferings. He is *my shield,* to protect me from all the malicious designs of my enemies against me. I have chosen him to be so, I have always found him so, and I expect he will still be so." 2. His experience of the benefit of that dependence: "*My heart trusted in him,* and in his power and promise; and it has not been in vain to do so, for *I am helped,* I have been often helped; not only God has given to me, in his due time, the help I trusted to him for, but my very trusting in him has helped me, in the mean time, and kept me from fainting," xxvii. 13. The very actings of faith are present aids to a drooping spirit, and often help it at a dead lift. 3. His improvement of this experience. (1.) He had the pleasure of it: *Therefore my heart greatly rejoices.* The joy of a believer is seated in the heart, while, in the laughter of the fool, the heart is sorrowful. It is great joy, *joy unspeakable and full of glory.* The heart that truly believes shall in due time greatly rejoice; it is *joy and peace in believing* that we are to expect. (2.) God shall have the praise of it: *when my heart greatly rejoices, with my song will I praise him.* Thus must we express our gratitude; it is the least we can do; and others will hereby be invited and encouraged to trust in him too.

III. He pleases himself with the interest which all good people, through Christ, have in God (*v.* 8): "*The Lord is their strength;* not mine only, but the strength of every believer." Note, The saints rejoice in their friends' comforts as well as their own; for, as we have not the less benefit from the light of the sun, so neither from the light of God's countenance, for others' sharing therein; for we are sure there is enough for all and enough for each. This is our communion with all saints, that God is their strength and ours, Christ their Lord and ours, 1 Cor. i. 2. He is their strength, the strength of all Israel, because he is *the saving strength of his anointed,* that is, 1. Of David in the type. God, in strengthening him that was their king and fought their battles, strengthened the whole kingdom. He calls himself God's *anointed* because it was the unction he had received that exposed him to the envy of his enemies, and therefore entitled him to the divine protection. 2. Of Christ, his anointed, his Messiah, in the anti-type. God was his saving strength, qualified him for his undertaking

and carried him through it; see lxxxix. 21; Isa. xlix. 5; l. 7, 9. And so he becomes their strength, the strength of all the saints; he strengthened him that is the church's head, and from him diffuses strength to all the members, has commanded his strength, and so *strengthens what he has wrought for us,* lxviii. 28; lxxx. 17, 18.

IV. He concludes with a short but comprehensive prayer for the church of God, *v.* 9. He prays for Israel, not as his people ("save my people, and bless my inheritance"), though they were so, but, "*thine.*" God's interest in them lay nearer his heart than his own. *We are thy people* is a good plea, Isa. lxiv. 9; lxiii. 19. *I am thine, save me.* God's people are his inheritance, dear to him, and precious in his eyes; what little glory he has from this world he has from them. *The Lord's portion is his people.* That which he begs of God for them is, 1. That he would save them from their enemies and the dangers they were exposed to. 2. That he would bless them with all good, flowing from his favour, in performance of his promise, and amounting to a happiness for them. 3. That he would *feed them,* bless them with plenty, and especially the plenty of his ordinances, which are food to the soul. *Rule them;* so the margin. "Direct their counsels and actions aright, and overrule their affairs for good. Feed them, and rule them; set pastors, set rulers, over them, that shall do their office with wisdom and understanding." 4. That he would *lift them up for ever,* lift them up out of their troubles and distresses, and do this, not only for those of that age, but for his people in every age to come, even to the end. "Lift them up into thy glorious kingdom, lift them up as high as heaven." There, and there only, will the saints be lifted up for ever, never more to sink or be depressed. Observe, Those, and those only, whom God feeds and rules, who are willing to be taught, and guided, and governed, by him, shall be saved, and blessed, and lifted up for ever.

PSALM XXIX.

It is the probable conjecture of some very good interpreters that David penned this psalm upon occasion, and just at the time, of a great storm of thunder, lightning, and rain, as the eighth psalm was his meditation in a moon-light night and the nineteenth in a sunny morning. It is good to take occasion from the sensible operations of God's power in the kingdom of nature to give glory to him. So composed was David, and so cheerful, even in a dreadful tempest, when others trembled, that then he penned this psalm; for, "though the earth be removed, yet will we not fear." I. He calls upon the dead ones of the world to give glory to God, ver. 1, 2. II. To convince them of the goodness of that God whom they were to adore, he takes notice of his power and terror in the thunder, and lightning, and thunder-showers (ver. 3—9), his sovereign dominion over the world (ver. 10), and his special favour to his church, ver. 11. Great and high thoughts of God should fill us in singing this psalm.

A psalm of David.

GIVE unto the LORD, O ye mighty, give unto the LORD glory and strength. 2 Give unto the LORD the glory due unto his name; worship the LORD in the beauty of holiness. 3 The voice of the LORD *is* upon the waters: the God of glory thundereth:

the Lord *is* upon many waters. 4 The voice of the Lord *is* powerful ; the voice of the Lord *is* full of majesty. 5 The voice of the Lord breaketh the cedars ; yea, the Lord breaketh the cedars of Lebanon. 6 He maketh them also to skip like a calf ; Lebanon and Sirion like a young unicorn. 7 The voice of the Lord divideth the flames of fire. 8 The voice of the Lord shaketh the wilderness ; the Lord shaketh the wilderness of Kadesh. 9 The voice of the Lord maketh the hinds to calve, and discovereth the forests : and in his temple doth every one speak of *his* glory. 10 The Lord sitteth upon the flood ; yea, the Lord sitteth King for ever. 11 The Lord will give strength unto his people ; the Lord will bless his people with peace.

In this psalm we have,

I. A demand of the homage of the great men of the earth to be paid to the great God. Every clap of thunder David interpreted as a call to himself and other princes to give glory to the great God. Observe, 1. Who they are that are called to this duty : " *O you mighty* (*v.* 1), you sons of the mighty, who have power, and on whom that power is devolved by succession and inheritance, who have royal blood running in your veins !" It is much for the honour of the great God that the great men of this world should pay their homage to him ; and they are bound to do it, not only because, high as they are, he is infinitely above them, and therefore they must bow to him, but because they have their power from him, and are to use it for him, and this tribute of acknowledgment they owe to him for it. 2. How often this call is repeated : *Give unto the Lord*, and again, and a third time, *Give unto the Lord*. This intimates that the mighty men are backward to this duty and are with difficulty persuaded to it, but that it is of great consequence to the interests of God's kingdom among men that princes should heartily espouse them. Jerusalem flourishes when the *kings of the earth bring their glory and honour into it*, Rev. xxi. 24. 3. What they are called to—to *give unto the Lord*, not as if he needed any thing, or could be benefited by any gifts of ours, nor as if we had any thing to give him that is not his own already *(Who hath first given to him ?)*, but the recognition of his glory, and of his dominion over us, he is pleased to interpret as a gift to him : " *Give unto the Lord* your ownselves, in the first place, and then your services. *Give unto the Lord glory and strength ;* acknowledge his glory and strength, and give praise to him as a God of infinite majesty and irre-

sistible power; and whatever glory or strength he has by his providence entrusted you with offer it to him, to be used for his honour, in his service. Give him your crowns ; let them be laid at his feet ; give him your sceptres, your swords, your keys ; put all into his hand, that you, in the use of them, may be to him for a name and a praise." Princes value themselves by their glory and strength ; these they must ascribe to God, owning him to be infinitely more glorious and powerful than they. This demand of homage from the mighty may be looked upon as directed either to the grandees of David's own kingdom, the peers of the realm, the princes of the tribes (and it is to excite them to a more diligent and constant attendance at God's altars, in which he had observed them very remiss), or to the neighbouring kings whom he by his sword had made tributaries to Israel and now would persuade to become tributaries to the God of Israel. Crowned heads must bow before the King of kings. What is here said to the mighty is said to all: *Worship God ;* it is the sum and substance of the everlasting gospel, Rev. xiv. 6, 7. Now we have here, (1.) The nature of religious worship ; it is *giving to the Lord the glory due to his name, v.* 2. God's name is that whereby he has made himself known. There is a glory due to his name. It is impossible that we should give him all the glory due to his name ; when we have said and done our best for the honour of God's name, still we come infinitely short of the merit of the subject ; but when we answer that revelation which he has made of himself, with suitable affections and adorations, then we give him some of that glory which is due to his name. If we would, in hearing and praying, and other acts of devotion, receive grace from God, we must make it our business to give glory to God. (2.) The rule of the performance of religious exercises : *Worship the Lord in the beauty of holiness,* which denotes, [1.] The object of our worship ; the glorious majesty of God is called *the beauty of holiness,* 2 Chron. xx. 21. In the worship of God we must have an eye to his beauty, and adore him, not only as infinitely awful and therefore to be feared above all, but as infinitely amiable and therefore to be loved and delighted in above all ; especially we must have an eye to the beauty of his holiness ; this the angels fasten upon in their praises, Rev. iv. 8. Or, [2.] The place of worship. The sanctuary then was the *beauty of holiness,* xlviii. 1, 2 ; Jer. xvii. 12. The beauty of the sanctuary was the exact agreement of the worship there performed with the divine appointment—the pattern in the mount. Now, under the gospel, solemn assemblies of Christians (which purity is the beauty of) are the places where God is to be worshipped. Or, [3.] The manner of worship. We must be holy in all our religious performances, devoted to God, and to his will and glory. There is a beauty in holiness, and it is that which puts an acceptable beauty upon all the acts of worship.

II. Good reason given for this demand. We shall see ourselves bound to give glory to God if we consider,

1. His sufficiency in himself, intimated in his name *Jehovah—I am that I am,* which is repeated here no fewer than eighteen times in this short psalm, twice in every verse but three, and once in two of those three; I do not recollect that there is the like in all the book of psalms. Let the mighty ones of the earth know him by this name and give him the glory due to it.

2. His sovereignty over all things. Let those that rule over men know there is a God that rules over them, that rules over all. The psalmist here sets forth God's dominion,

(1.) In the kingdom of nature. In the wonderful effects of natural causes, and the operations of the powers of nature, we ought to take notice of God's glory and strength, which we are called upon to ascribe to him; in the thunder, and lightning, and rain, we may see, [1.] His glory. It is the God of glory that thunders, v. 3. It is God that thunders (thunder is the *noise of his voice,* Job. xxxvii. 2), and it declares him a God of glory, so awful is the sound of the thunder, and so bright the flash of its companion, the lightning; to the hearing and to the sight nothing is more affecting than these, as if by those two learning senses God would give such proofs of his glory to the minds of men as should leave the most stupid inexcusable. Some observe that there were then some particular reasons why thunder should be called *the voice of the Lord,* not only because it comes from above, is not under the direction or foresight of any man, speaks aloud, and reaches far, but because God often spoke in thunder, particularly at Mount Sinai, and by thunder discomfited the enemies of Israel. To speak it the voice of the God of glory, it is here said to be *upon thewaters,* upon *many waters* (v. 3); it reaches over the vast ocean, the waters under the firmament; it rattles among the thick clouds, the waters above the firmament. Every one that hears the thunder (his ears being made to tingle with it) will own that *the voice of the Lord is full of majesty* (xxix.4), enough to make the highest humble (for none can *thunder with a voice like him)* and the proudest tremble—for, if his voice be so terrible, what is his arm? Every time we hear it thunder, let our hearts be thereby filled with great, and high, and honourable thoughts of God, in the holy adorings and admirings of whom the power of godliness does so much consist. *O Lord our God! thou art very great.* [2.] His power (v. 4): *The voice of the Lord is powerful,* as appears by the effects of it; for it works wonders. Those that write natural histories relate the prodigious effects of thunder and lightning, even out of the ordinary course of natural causes, which must be resolved into the omnipotence of the God of nature.

First, Trees have been rent and split by thunderbolts, v. 5, 6. *The voice of the Lord,* in the thunder, often *broke the cedars,* even those of Lebanon, the strongest, the stateliest. Some understand it of the violent winds which shook the cedars, and sometimes tore off their aspiring tops. Earthquakes also shook the ground itself on which the trees grew, and made *Lebanon and Sirion* to dance; *the wilderness of Kadesh* also was in like manner shaken (v. 8), the trees by winds, the ground by earthquakes, and both by thunders, of which I incline rather to understand it. The learned Dr. Hammond understands it of the consternation and conquest of the neighbouring kingdoms that warred with Israel and opposed David, as the Syrians, whose country lay near the forest of Lebanon, the Amorites that bordered on Mount Hermon, and the Moabites and Ammonites that lay about the wilderness of Kadesh. *Secondly,* Fires have been kindled by lightnings and houses and churches thereby consumed; hence we read of hot thunderbolts (lxxviii. 48); accordingly the voice of the Lord, in the thunder, is here said to *divide the flames of fire* (v. 7), that is, to scatter them upon the earth, as God sees fit to direct them and do execution by them. *Thirdly,* The terror of thunder makes the hinds to calve sooner, and some think more easily, than otherwise they would. The hind is a timorous creature, and much affected with the noise of thunder; and no marvel, when sometimes proud and stout men have been made to tremble at it. The emperor Caligula would hide himself under his bed when it thundered. Horace, the poet, owns that he was reclaimed from atheism by the terror of thunder and lightning, which he describes somewhat like this of David, *lib.* 1, *ode* 34. The thunder is said here to *discover the forest,* that is, it so terrifies the wild beasts of the forest that they quit the dens and thickets in which they hid themselves and so are discovered. Or it throws down the trees, and so discovers the ground that was shaded by them. Whenever it thunders let us think of this psalm; and, whenever we sing this psalm, let us think of the dreadful thunder-claps we have sometimes heard, and thus bring God's word and his works together, that by both we may be directed and quickened to give unto him the glory due unto his name; and let us bless him that there is another voice of his besides this dreadful one, by which God now speaks to us, even the still small voice of his gospel, the terror of which shall not make us afraid.

(2.) In the kingdom of providence, v. 10. God is to be praised as the governor of the world of mankind. He *sits upon the flood;* he sits King for ever. He not only sits at rest in the enjoyment of himself, but he sits as King in the throne which he has *prepared in the heavens* (ciii. 19), where he takes cognizance of, and gives orders about, all the affairs of the children of men, and does all according to his will, according to the counsel of his will. Observe, [1.] The power of his kingdom: He *sits upon the flood*. As he has founded the earth, so he has founded his own throne, upon the floods, xxiv. 2. The ebbings and flowings of this lower world, and the agitations and revolutions of the affairs in it, give not the least shake to the repose nor to the counsels of the Eternal Mind. The opposition of his enemies is compared to the floods (xciii. 3, 4); but the Lord sits upon it; he crushes it, conquers it, and completes his own purposes in despite of all the devices that are in men's hearts. The word here translated *the flood* is never used but concerning Noah's flood; and therefore some think it is that which is here spoken of. God did sit upon that flood as a Judge executing the sentence of his justice upon the world of the ungodly that was swept away by it. And he still sits upon the flood, restraining the waters of Noah, that they turn not again to cover the earth, according to his promise never to *destroy the earth any more by a flood*, Gen. ix. 11; Isa. liv. 9. [2.] The perpetuity of his kingdom: He *sits King for ever ;* no period can, or shall, be put to his government. The administration of his kingdom is consonant to his counsels from eternity and pursuant to his designs for eternity.

(3.) In the kingdom of grace. Here his glory shines most brightly, [1.] In the adorations he receives from the subjects of that kingdom, *v.* 9. *In his temple*, where his people attend his discoveries of himself and his mind and attend him with their praises, *every one speaks of his glory.* In the world every man sees it, or at least *may behold it afar off* (Job xxxvi. 25); but it is only in the temple, in the church, that it is spoken of to his honour. *All his works do praise him* (that is, they minister matter for praise), but his saints only do bless him, and speak of his glory in his works, cxlv. 10. [2.] In the favours he bestows upon the subjects of that kingdom, *v.* 11. *First,* He will qualify them for his service: *He will give strength to his people*, to fortify them against every evil work and to furnish them for every good work; out of weakness they shall be made strong; nay, he will perfect strength in weakness. *Secondly,* He will encourage them in his service: *He will bless his people with peace.* Peace is a blessing of inestimable value, which God designs for all his people. The *work of righteousness is peace (great peace have those that love thy law) ;* but much more the crown of righteousness: the end of the righteous is peace; it is endless peace. When the thunder of God's wrath shall make sinners tremble the saints shall lift up their heads with joy.

PSALM XXX.

This is a psalm of thanksgiving for the great deliverances which God had wrought for David, penned upon occasion of the dedicating of his house of cedar, and sung in that pious solemnity, though there is not any thing in it that has particular reference to that occasion. Some collect from divers passages in the psalm itself that it was penned upon his recovery from a dangerous fit of sickness, which might happen to be about the time of the dedication of his house. I. He here praises God for the deliverances

he had wrought for him, ver. 1.–3. II. He calls upon others to praise him too, and encourages them to trust in him, ver. 4, 5. III. He blames himself for his former security, ver. 6, 7. IV. He recollects the prayers and complaints he had made in his distress, ver. 8.–10. With them he stirs up himself to be very thankful to God for the present comfortable change, ver. 11, 12. In singing this psalm we ought to remember with thankfulness any like deliverances wrought for us, for which we must stir up ourselves to praise him and by which we must be engaged to depend upon him.

A psalm *and* song *at* the dedication of the house of David.

I WILL extol thee, O LORD; for thou hast lifted me up, and hast not made my foes to rejoice over me. 2 O LORD my God, I cried unto thee, and thou hast healed me. 3 O LORD, thou hast brought up my soul from the grave : thou hast kept me alive, that I should not go down to the pit. 4 Sing unto the LORD, O ye saints of his, and give thanks at the remembrance of his holiness. 5 For his anger *endureth but* a moment; in his favour *is* life: weeping may endure for a night, but joy *cometh* in the morning.

It was the laudable practice of the pious Jews, and, though not expressly appointed, yet allowed and accepted, when they had built a new house, to *dedicate it to God*, Deut. xx. 5. David did so when his house was built, and he took possession of it (2 Sam. v. 11); for royal palaces do as much need God's protection, and are as much bound to be at his service, as ordinary houses. Note, The houses we dwell in should, at our first entrance upon them, be dedicated to God, as little sanctuaries. We must solemnly commit ourselves, our families, and all our family affairs, to God's guidance and care, must pray for his presence and blessing, must devote ourselves and all ours to his glory, and must resolve both that we will put away iniquity far from our tabernacles and that we and our houses will serve the Lord both in the duties of family worship and in all instances of gospel obedience. Some conjecture that this psalm was sung at the re-dedication of David's house, after he had been driven out of it by Absalom, who had defiled it with his incest, and that it is a thanksgiving for the crushing of that dangerous rebellion. In these verses,

I. David does himself give God thanks for the great deliverances he had wrought for him (*v.* 1): " *I will extol thee, O Lord !* I will exalt thy name, will praise thee as one high and lifted up. I will do what I can to advance the interests of thy kingdom among men. I will extol thee, for thou hast lifted me up, not only up out of the pit in which I was sinking, but up to the throne of Israel." **He** *raiseth up the poor out of the dust.* In consideration of the great things God has done to exalt us, both by his providence and by his grace, we are bound, in gratitude, to do all we can to extol his name, though the most we can do is but little. Three things magnify David's deliverance:—1. That it was the defeat of his enemies. They were not suffered to triumph over him, as they would have done (though it is a barbarous thing) if he had died of this sickness or perished in this distress: see xli. 11. 2. That it was an answer to his prayers (*v.* 2): *I cried unto thee.* All the expressions of the sense we have of our troubles should be directed to God, and every cry be a cry to him; and giving way, in this manner, to our grief, will ease a burdened spirit. " *I cried to thee, and thou hast* not only neard me, but *healed me,* healed the distempered body, healed the disturbed and disquieted mind, healed the disordered distracted affairs of the kingdom." This is what God glories in, *I am the Lord that healeth thee* (Exod. xv. 26), and we must give him the glory of it. 3. That it was the saving of his life; for he was brought to the last extremity, dropping into the grave, and ready *to go down into the pit,* and yet rescued and kept alive, *v.* 3. The more imminent our dangers have been, the more eminent our deliverances have been, the more comfortable are they to ourselves and the more illustrious proofs of the power and goodness of God. A life from the dead ought to be spent in extolling the God of our life.

II. He calls upon others to join with him in praise, not only for the particular favours God had bestowed upon him, but for the general tokens of his good-will to all his saints (*v.* 4): *Sing unto the Lord, O you saints of his!* All that are truly saints he owns for his. There is a remnant of such in this world, and from them it is expected that they sing unto him; for they are created and sanctified, made and made saints, that they may be to him for a name and a praise. His saints in heaven sing to him; why should not those on earth be doing the same work, as well as they can, in concert with them? 1. They believe him to be a God of unspotted purity; and therefore let them sing to him: " Let them *give thanks at the remembrance of his holiness;* let them praise his holy name, for holiness is his memorial throughout all generations." God is a holy God; his holiness is his glory; that is the attribute which the holy angels, in their praises, fasten most upon, Isa. vi. 3; Rev. iv. 8. We ought to be much in the mention and remembrance of God's holiness; and holy souls can give thanks at the mention of God's holiness. It is matter of joy to the saints that God is a holy God; for then they hope he will make them holy, more holy. None of all God's perfections carries in it more terror to the wicked, nor more comfort to the godly, than his holiness. It is a good sign that we are in some measure partakers of his holiness if we can heartily rejoice and give thanks at the remembrance of it. 2. They have experienced him to be a God gracious and merciful; and therefore let them sing to him. (1.) We have found his frowns very short. Though we have deserved that they

should be everlasting, and that he should be angry with us till he had consumed us, and should never be reconciled, yet *his anger endureth but for a moment, v.* 5. When we offend him he is angry; but, as he is slow to anger and not soon provoked, so, when he is angry, upon our repentance and humiliation his anger is soon turned away and he is willing to be at peace with us. If he hide his face from his own children, and suspend the wonted tokens of his favour, it is but *in a little wrath* and *for a small moment;* but he will *gather them with everlasting kindness,* Isa. liv. 7, 8. If *weeping endureth for a night,* and it be a wearisome night, yet, as sure as the light of the morning returns after the darkness of the night, so sure will joy and comfort return in a short time, in due time, to the people of God; for the covenant of grace is as firm as the covenant of the day. This word has often been fulfilled to us in the letter Weeping has endured for a night, but the grief has been soon over and the grievance gone. Observe, As long as God's anger continues so long the saints' weeping continues; but, if that be but for a moment, the affliction is but for a moment, and when the light of God's countenance is restored the affliction is easily pronounced light and momentary. (2.) We have found his smiles very sweet: *In his favour is life,* that is, all good. The return of his favour to an afflicted soul is as life from the dead; nothing can be more reviving. Our happiness is bound up in God's favour; if we have that, we have enough, whatever else we want. It is the life of the soul, it is spiritual life, the earnest of life eternal.

6 And in my prosperity I said, I shall never be moved. 7 Lᴏʀᴅ, by thy favour thou hast made my mountain to stand strong : thou didst hide thy face, *and* I was troubled. 8 I cried to thee, O Lᴏʀᴅ; and unto the Lᴏʀᴅ I made supplication. 9 What profit *is there* in my blood, when I go down to the pit ? Shall the dust praise thee ? shall it declare thy truth ? 10 Hear, O Lᴏʀᴅ, and have mercy upon me : Lᴏʀᴅ, be thou my helper. 11 Thou hast turned for me my mourning into dancing : thou hast put off my sackcloth, and girded me with gladness ; 12 To the end that *my* glory may sing praise to thee, and not be silent. O Lᴏʀᴅ my God, I will give thanks unto thee for ever.

We have, in these verses, an account of three several states that David was in successively, and of the workings of his heart towards God in each of those states—what he said and did, and how his heart stood affected; in the first of these we may see what we are too apt to be, and in the other two what we should be.

1. He had long enjoyed prosperity, and then he grew secure and over-confident of the continuance of it (*v.* 6, 7): "*In my prosperity, when I was in health of body and God had given me rest from all my enemies, I said I shall never be moved;* I never thought either of having my body distempered or my government disturbed, nor had any apprehensions of danger upon any account." Such complete victories had he obtained over those that opposed him, and such a confirmed interest had he in the hearts of his people, such a firmness of mind and such a strong constitution of body, that he thought his prosperity fixed like a mountain; yet this he ascribes, not to his own wisdom or fortitude, but to the divine goodness. *Thou, through thy favour, hast made my mountain to stand strong, v.* 7. He does not look upon it as his *heaven* (as worldly people do, who make their prosperity their felicity), only his *mountain;* it is earth still, only raised a little higher than the common level. This he thought, by the favour of God, would be perpetuated to him, imagining perhaps that, having had so many troubles in the beginning of his days, he had had his whole share and should have none in his latter end, or that God, who had given him such tokens of his favour, would never frown upon him. Note, 1. We are very apt to dream, when things are well with us, that they will always be so, and never otherwise. *To-morrow shall be as this day.* As if we should think, when the weather is once fair, that it will be ever fair; whereas nothing is more certain than that it will change. 2. When we see ourselves deceived in our expectations, it becomes us to reflect, with shame, upon our security, as our folly, as David does here, that we may be wiser another time and may rejoice in our prosperity as though we rejoiced not, because the fashion of it passes away.

II. On a sudden he fell into trouble, and then he prayed to God, and pleaded earnestly for relief and succour.

1. His mountain was shaken and he with it; it proved, when he grew secure, that he was least safe: " *Thou didst hide thy face and I was troubled,* in mind, body, or estate." In every change of his condition he still kept his eye upon God, and, as he ascribed his prosperity to God's favour, so in his adversity he observed the hiding of God's face to be the cause of it. If God hide his face, a good man is certainly troubled, though no other calamity befal him; when the sun sets night certainly follows, and the moon and all the stars cannot make day.

2. When his mountain was shaken he lifted up his eyes above the hills. Prayer is a salve for every sore; he made use of it accordingly. *Is any afflicted?* Is any troubled? *Let him pray.* Though God hid his face from him, yet he prayed. If God, in wisdom

and justice, turn from us, yet it will be in us the greatest folly and injustice imaginable is we turn from him. No; let us learn to pray in the dark (*v.* 8): *I cried to thee, O Lord!* It seems God's withdrawings made his prayers the more vehement. We are here told, for it seems he kept account of it,

(1.) What he pleaded, *v.* 9. [1.] That God would be no gainer by his death: *What profit is there in my blood?* implying that he would willingly die if he could thereby do any real service to God or his country (Phil. ii. 17), but he saw not what good could be done by his dying in the bed of sickness, as might be if he had died in the bed of honour. "Lord," says he, "wilt thou sell one of thy own *people for nought and not increase thy wealth by the price?*" xliv. 12. Nay, [2.] That, in his honour, God would seem to be a loser by his death: *Shall the dust praise thee?* The sanctified spirit, which returns to God, shall praise him, shall be still praising him; but the dust, which returns to the earth, shall not praise him, nor declare his truth. The services of God's house cannot be performed by the dust; it cannot praise him; there is none of that device or working in the grave, for it is the land of silence. The promises of God's covenant cannot be performed to the dust. "Lord," says David, "if I die now, what will become of the promise made to me? Who shall declare the truth of that?" The best pleas in prayer are those that are taken from God's honour; and then we ask aright for life when we have that in view, that we may live and praise him.

(2.) What he prayed for, *v.* 10. He prayed for mercy to pardon *(Have mercy upon me),* and for grace to help in time of need—*Lord, be thou my helper.* On these two errands we also may come boldly to the throne of grace, Heb. iv. 16.

III. In due time God delivered him out of his troubles and restored him to his former prosperity. His prayers were answered and his *mourning was turned into dancing, v.* 11. God's anger now endured but for a moment, and David's weeping but for a night. The sackcloth with which, in a humble compliance with the divine Providence, he had clad himself, was loosed; his griefs were balanced; his fears were silenced; his comforts returned; and he was girded with gladness: joy was made his ornament, was made his strength, and seemed to cleave to him, as the girdle cleaves to the loins of a man. As David's plunge into trouble from the height of prosperity, and then when he least expected it, teaches us to rejoice as though we rejoiced not, because we know not how near trouble may be, so his sudden return to a prosperous condition teaches us to weep as though we wept not, because we know not how soon the storm may become a calm and the formidable blast may become a favourable gale. But what temper of mind was he in upon this happy change of the face of his affairs? What does he say now? He tells us, *v.* 12. 1. His complaints were turned into praises. He looked upon it that God girded him with gladness to the end that he might be the *sweet psalmist of Israel* (2 Sam. xxiii. 1), that his *glory might sing praise to God,* that is, his tongue (for our tongue is our glory, and never more so than when it is employed in praising God) or his soul, for that is our glory above the beasts, that must be employed in blessing the Lord, and with that we must make melody to him in singing psalms. Those that are kept from being silent in the pit must not be silent in the land of the living, but fervent, and constant, and public, in praising God. 2. These praises were likely to be everlasting: *I will give thanks unto thee for ever.* This bespeaks a gracious resolution that he would persevere to the end in praising God and a gracious hope that he should never want fresh matter for praise and that he should shortly be where this would be the everlasting work. *Blessed are those that dwell in God's house; they will be still praising him.* Thus must we learn to accommodate ourselves to the various providences of God that concern us, to want and to abound, to sing of mercy and judgment, and to sing unto God for both.

PSALM XXXI.

It is probable that David penned this psalm when he was persecuted by Saul; some passages in it agree particularly to the narrow escapes he had, at Keilah (1 Sam. xxiii. 13), then in the wilderness of Maon, when Saul marched on one side of the hill and he on the other, and, soon after, in the cave in the wilderness of En-gedi; but that it was penned upon any of those occasions we are not told. It is a mixture of prayers, and praises, and professions of confidence in God, all which do well together and are helpful to one another. I. David professes his cheerful confidence in God, and, in that confidence, prays for deliverance out of his present troubles, ver. 1—8. II. He complains of the very deplorable condition he was in, and, in the sense of his calamities, still prays that God would graciously appear for him against his persecutors, ver. 9—18. III. He concludes the psalm with praise and triumph, giving glory to God, and encouraging himself and others to trust in him, ver. 19—24.

To the chief musician. A psalm of David.

IN thee, O LORD, do I put my trust; let me never be ashamed : deliver me in thy righteousness. 2 Bow down thine ear to me ; deliver me speedily : be thou my strong rock, for a house of defence to save me. 3 For thou *art* my rock and my fortress ; therefore for thy name's sake lead me, and guide me. 4 Pull me out of the net that they have laid privily for me : for thou *art* my strength. 5 Into thine hand I commit my spirit : thou hast redeemed me, O LORD God of truth. 6 I have hated them that regard lying vanities : but I trust in the LORD. 7 I will be glad and rejoice in thy mercy : for thou hast considered my trouble ; thou hast known my soul in adversities ; 8 And hast not shut me up into

342

the hand of the enemy : thou hast set my feet in a large room.

Faith and prayer must go together. He that believes, let him pray—*I believe, therefore have I spoken:* and he that prays, let him believe, for the prayer of faith is the prevailing prayer. We have both here.

I. David, in distress, is very earnest with God in prayer for succour and relief. This eases a burdened spirit, fetches in promised mercies, and wonderfully supports and comforts the soul in the expectation of them. He prays, 1. That God would deliver him (*v.* 1), that his life might be preserved from the malice of his enemies, and that an end might be put to their persecutions of him, that God, not only in mercy, but in righteousness, would deliver him, as a righteous Judge betwixt him and his unrighteous persecutors, that he would bow down his ear to his petitions, to his appeals, and deliver him, *v.* 2. It is condescension in God to take cognizance of the case of the greatest and best of men; he humbles himself to do it. The psalmist prays also that he would deliver him speedily, lest, if the deliverance were long deferred, his faith should fail. 2. That, if he did not immediately deliver him out of his troubles, yet he would protect and shelter him in his troubles : "*Be thou my strong rock,* immovable, impregnable, as a fastness framed by nature, and my *house of defence,* a fortress framed by art, and all *to save me.*" Thus may we pray that God's providence would secure to us our lives and comforts, and that by his grace we may be enabled to think ourselves safe in him, Prov. xviii. 10. 3. That his case having much in it of difficulty, both in respect of duty and in respect of prudence, he might be under the divine guidance : "*Lord, lead me and guide me* (*v.* 3), so order my steps, so order my spirit, that I may never do any thing unlawful and unjustifiable—against my conscience, nor unwise and indiscreet—against my interest." Those that resolve to follow God's direction may in faith pray for it. 4. That his enemies being very crafty, as well as very spiteful, God would frustrate and baffle their designs against him (*v.* 4): "*Pull me out of the net that they have laid privily for me,* and keep me from the sin, the trouble, the death, they aim to entrap me in."

II. In this prayer he gives glory to God by a repeated profession of his confidence in him and dependence on him. This encouraged his prayers and qualified him for the mercies he prayed for (*v.* 1): "*In thee, O Lord! do I put my trust,* and not in myself, or any sufficiency of my own, or in any creature; *let me never be ashamed,* let me not be disappointed of any of that good which thou hast promised me and which therefore I have promised myself in thee." 1. He had chosen God for his protector, and God had, by his promise, undertaken to be so (*v.* 3): "*Thou* art my rock and my fortress, *by thy covenant with me and my believing consent to that covenant; therefore* be my strong rock," *v. 2.* Those that have in sincerity avouched the Lord for theirs may expect the benefit of his being so; for God's relations to us carry with them both name and thing. *Thou art my strength, v. 4.* If God be our strength, we may hope that he will both put his strength in us and put forth his strength for us. 2. He gave up his soul in a special manner to him (*v. 5*): *Into thy hands I commit my spirit.* (1.) If David here looks upon himself as a dying man, by these words he resigns his departing soul to God who gave it, and to whom, at death, the spirit returns. "Men can but kill the body, but I trust in God to *redeem my soul from the power of the grave,*" xlix. 15. He is willing to die if God will have it so; but let my soul *fall into the hands of the Lord, for his mercies are great.* With these words our Lord Jesus yielded up the ghost upon the cross, and made his soul an offering, a free-will offering, for sin, voluntarily laying down his life a ransom. By Stephen's example we are taught, in our dying moments, to eye Christ at God's right hand, and to commit our spirits to him: *Lord Jesus, receive my spirit.* But, (2.) David is here to be looked upon as a man in distress and trouble. And, [1.] His great care is about his soul, his spirit, his better part. Note, Our outward afflictions should increase our concern for our souls. Many think that while they are perplexed about their worldly affairs, and Providence multiplies their cares about them, they may be excused if they neglect their souls; whereas the greater hazard our lives and secular interests lie at the more we are concerned to look to our souls, that, though the outward man perish, the inward man may suffer no damage (2 Cor. iv. 16), and that we may keep possession of our souls when we can keep possession of nothing else, Luke xxi. 19. [2.] He thinks the best he can do for his soul is to commit it into the hand of God, and lodge that great trust with him. He had prayed (*v. 4*) to be plucked out of the net of outward trouble, but, as not insisting upon that (God's will be done), he immediately lets fall that petition, and commits the spirit, the inward man, into God's hand. "Lord, however it goes with me, as to my body, let it go well with my soul." Note, It is the wisdom and duty of every one of us solemnly to commit our spirits into the hands of God, to be sanctified by his grace, devoted to his honour, employed in his service, and fitted for his kingdom. That which encourages us to commit our spirits into the hand of God is that he has not only created, but redeemed, them; the particular redemptions of the Old-Testament church and the Old-Testament saints were typical of our redemption by Jesus Christ, Gen. xlviii. 16. The redemption of the soul is so precious that it must have ceased for

ever if Christ had not undertaken it; but, by redeeming our souls, he has not only acquired an additional right and title to them, which obliges us to commit them to him as his own, but has shown the extraordinary kindness and concern he has for them, which encourages us to commit them to him, to be preserved to his heavenly kingdom (2 Tim. i. 12): "*Thou hast redeemed me, O Lord God of truth!* redeemed me according to a promise which thou wilt be true to."

III. He disclaimed all confederacy with those that made an arm of flesh their confidence (*v. 6*): *I have hated those that regard lying vanities*—idolaters (so some), who expect aid from false gods, which are vanity and a lie—astrologers, and those that give heed to them, so others. David abhorred the use of enchantments and divinations; he consulted not, nor ever took notice of, the flight of birds or entrails of beasts, good omens or bad omens; they are lying vanities, and he not only did not regard them himself, but hated the wickedness of those that did. He trusted in God only, and not in any creature. His interest in the court or country, his retreats or strongholds, even Goliath's sword itself—these were lying vanities, which he could not depend upon, but trusted in the Lord only. See xl. 4; Jer. xvii. 5.

IV. He comforted himself with his hope in God, and made himself, not only easy, but cheerful, with it, *v. 7.* Having relied on God's mercy, he will be glad and rejoice in it; and those know not how to value their hope in God who cannot find joy enough in that hope to counterbalance their grievances and silence their griefs.

V. He encouraged himself in this hope with the experiences he had had of late, and formerly, of God's goodness to him, which he mentions to the glory of God; he that has delivered doth and will. 1. God had taken notice of his afflictions and all the circumstances of them: "*Thou hast considered my trouble,* with wisdom to suit relief to it, with condescension and compassion regarding the low estate of thy servant." 2. He had observed the temper of his spirit and the workings of his heart under his afflictions: "*Thou hast known my soul in adversities,* with a tender concern and care for it." God's eye is upon our souls when we are in trouble, to see whether they be humbled for sin, submissive to the will of God, and bettered by the affliction. If the soul, when cast down under affliction, has been lifted up to him in true devotion, he knows it. 3. He had rescued him out of the hands of Saul when he had him safe enough in Keilah (1 Sam. xxiii. 7): "*Thou hast not shut me up into the hand of the enemy,* but set me at liberty, in *a large room,* where I may shift for my own safety," *v. 8.* Christ's using those words (*v. 5*) upon the cross may warrant us to apply all this to Christ, who trusted in his Father and was supported and delivered by him, and (because he humbled himself) highly exalted, which it is proper to think of when we sing these verses, as also therein to acknowledge the experience we have had of God's gracious presence with us in our troubles and to encourage ourselves to trust in him for the future.

9 Have mercy upon me, O LORD, for I am in trouble : mine eye is consumed with grief, *yea*, my soul and my belly. 10 For my life is spent with grief, and my years with sighing : my strength faileth because of mine iniquity, and my bones are consumed. 11 I was a reproach among all mine enemies, but especially among my neighbours, and a fear to mine acquaintance : they that did see me without fled from me. 12 I am forgotten as a dead man out of mind : I am like a broken vessel. 13 For I have heard the slander of many : fear *was* on every side : while they took counsel together against me, they devised to take away my life. 14 But I trusted in thee, O LORD : I said, Thou *art* my God. 15 My times *are* in thy hand : deliver me from the hand of mine enemies, and from them that persecute me. 16 Make thy face to shine upon thy servant : save me for thy mercies' sake. 17 Let me not be ashamed, O LORD ; for I have called upon thee : let the wicked be ashamed, *and* let them be silent in the grave. 18 Let the lying lips be put to silence ; which speak grievous things proudly and contemptuously against the righteous.

In the foregoing verses David had appealed to God's righteousness, and pleaded his relation to him and dependence on him; here he appeals to his mercy, and pleads the greatness of his own misery, which made his case the proper object of that mercy. Observe,

I. The complaint he makes of his trouble and distress (*v.* 9): "*Have mercy upon me, O Lord! for I am in trouble,* and need thy mercy." The remembrance he makes of his condition is not much unlike some even of Job's complaints. 1. His troubles had fixed a very deep impression upon his mind and made him a man of sorrows. So great was his grief that his very soul was consumed with it, and his life spent with it, and he was continually sighing, *v.* 9, 10. Herein he was a type of Christ, who was intimately acquainted with grief and often in tears. We may guess by David's complexion, which was ruddy and sanguine, by his genius for music,

and by his daring enterprises in his early days, that his natural disposition was both cheerful and firm, that he was apt to be cheerful, and not to lay trouble to his heart; yet here we see what he is brought to : he has almost wept out his eyes, and sighed away his breath. Let those that are airy and gay take heed of running into extremes, and never set sorrow at defiance; God can find out ways to make them melancholy if they will not otherwise learn to be serious. 2. His body was affected with the sorrows of his mind (*v.* 10): *My strength fails, my bones are consumed,* and all *because of my iniquity.* As to Saul, and the quarrel he had with him, he could confidently insist upon his righteousness; but, as it was an affliction God laid upon him, he owns he had deserved it, and freely confesses his iniquity to have been the procuring cause of all his trouble; and the sense of sin touched him to the quick and wasted him more than all his calamities. 3. His friends were unkind and became shy of him. He was *a fear to his acquaintance,* when they saw him they *fled from him, v.* 11. They durst not harbour him nor give him any assistance, durst not show him any countenance, nor so much as be seen in his company, for fear of being brought into trouble by it, now that Saul had proclaimed him a traitor and outlawed him. They saw how dearly Ahimelech the priest had paid for aiding and abetting him, though ignorantly; and therefore, though they could not but own he had a great deal of wrong done him, yet they had not the courage to appear for him. He was forgotten by them, *as a dead man out of mind* (*v.* 12), and looked upon with contempt *as a broken vessel.* Those that showed him all possible respect when he was in honour at court, now that he had fallen into disgrace, though unjustly, were strange to him. Such swallow-friends the world is full of, that are gone in winter. Let those that fall on the losing side not think it strange if they be thus deserted, but make sure a friend in heaven, that will not fail them, and make use of him. 4. His enemies were unjust in their censures of him. They would not have persecuted him as they did if they had not first represented him as a bad man ; he was a *reproach among all his enemies, but especially among his neighbours, v.* 11. Those that had been the witnesses of his integrity, and could not but be convinced in their consciences that he was an honest man, were the most forward to represent him quite otherwise, that they might curry favour with Saul. Thus he *heard the slander of many ;* every one had a stone to throw at him, because *fear was on every side ;* that is, they durst not do otherwise, for he that would not join with his neighbours to abuse David was looked upon as disaffected to Saul. Thus the best of men have been represented under the worst characters by those that resolved to give them the worst treatment. 5. His life was aimed at and he went in continual peril of it. Fear was on every side, and he knew that, whatever counsel his enemies took against him, the design was not to take away his liberty, but to take away his life (*v.* 13), a life so valuable, so useful, to the good services of which all Israel owed so much, and which was never forfeited. Thus, in all the plots of the Pharisees and Herodians against Christ, still the design was to take away his life; such are the enmity and cruelty of the serpent's seed.

II. His confidence in God in the midst of these troubles. Every thing looked black and dismal round about him, and threatened to drive him to despair: "*But I trusted in thee, O Lord!* (*v.* 14) and was thereby kept from sinking." His enemies robbed him of his reputation among men, but they could not rob him of his comfort in God, because they could not drive him from his confidence in God. Two things he comforted himself with in his straits, and he went to God and pleaded them with him:—1. "*Thou art my God;* I have chosen thee for mine, and thou hast promised to be mine;" and, if he be ours and we can by faith call him so, it is enough, when we can call nothing else ours. "Thou art my God; and therefore to whom shall I go for relief but to thee?" Those need not be straitened in their prayers who can plead this; for, if God undertake to be our God, he will do that for us which will answer the compass and vast extent of that engagement. 2. *My times are in thy hand.* Join this with the former and it makes the comfort complete. If God have our times in his hand, he can help us; and, if he be our God, he will help us; and then what can discourage us? It is a great support to those who have God for their God that their times are in his hand and he will be sure to order and dispose of them for the best, to all those who commit their spirits also into his hand, to suit them to their times, as David here, *v.* 5. The time of life is in God's hands, to lengthen or shorten, embitter or sweeten, as he pleases, according to the counsel of his will. Our times (all events that concern us, and the timing of them) are at God's disposal; they are not in our own hands, for the way of man is not in himself, not in our friends' hands, nor in our enemies' hands, but in God's; *every man's judgment proceedeth from him.* David does not, in his prayers, prescribe to God, but subscribe to him. "Lord, my times are in thy hand, and I am well pleased that they are so: they could not be in a better hand. Thy will be done."

III. His petitions to God, in his faith and confidence, 1. He prays that God would deliver him out of the hand of his enemies (*v.* 15), and save him (*v.* 16), and this for his mercies' sake, and not for any merit of his own. Our opportunities are in God's hand (so some read it), and therefore he knows how to choose the best and fittest time for

our deliverance, and we must be willing to wait that time. When David had Saul at his mercy in the cave those about him said, "*This is the time* in which God will deliver thee," 1 Sam. xxiv. 4. "No," says David, "the time has not come for my deliverance till it can be wrought without sin; and I will wait for that time; for it is God's time, and that is the best time." 2. That God would give him the comfort of his favour in the mean time (*v.* 16): "*Make thy face to shine upon thy servant;* let me have the comfortable tokens and evidences of thy favour to me, and that shall put gladness in my heart in the midst of all my griefs." 3. That his prayers to God might be answered and his hopes in God accomplished (*v.* 17): "*Let me not be ashamed* of my hopes and prayers, *for I have called upon thee,* who never saidst to thy people, Seek in vain, and hope in vain." 4. That shame and silence might be the portion of wicked people, and particularly of his enemies. They were confident of their success against David, and that they should run him down and ruin him. "Lord," says he, "let them be made ashamed of that confidence by the disappointment of their expectations," as those that opposed the building of the wall about Jerusalem, when it was finished, were *much cast down in their own eyes,* Neh. vi. 16. *Let them be silent in the grave.* Note, Death will silence the rage and clamour of cruel persecutors, whom reason would not silence. In the grave the wicked cease from troubling. Particularly, he prays for (that is, he prophesies) the silencing of those that reproach and calumniate the people of God (*v.* 18): *Let lying lips be put to silence, that speak grievous things proudly and contemptuously against the righteous.* This is a very good prayer which, (1.) We have often occasion to put up to God; for those that set their mouth against the heavens commonly revile the heirs of heaven. Religion, and the strict and serious professors of it, are every where spoken against, [1.] With a great deal of malice: They speak *grievous things,* on purpose to vex them, and hoping, with what they say, to do them a real mischief. They speak *hard things* (so the word is), which bear hard upon them, and by which they hope to fasten indelible characters of infamy upon them. [2.] With a great deal of falsehood: They are *lying lips,* taught by the father of lies and serving his interest. [3.] With a great deal of scorn and disdain: They speak *proudly and contemptuously,* as if the righteous, whom God has honoured, were the most despicable people in the world, and not worthy to be set with the dogs of their flock. One would think they thought it no sin to tell a deliberate lie if it might but serve to expose a good man either to hatred or contempt. *Hear, O our God! for we are despised.* (2.) We may pray in faith; for these lying lips shall be put to silence. God has many ways of doing it. Sometimes he convinces the consciences of those that reproach his people, and turns their hearts. Sometimes by his providence he visibly confutes their calumnies, and brings forth the righteousness of his people as the light. However, there is a day coming when God will convince ungodly sinners of the falsehood of all the hard speeches they have spoken against his people and will execute judgment upon them, Jude 14, 15. Then shall this prayer be fully answered, and to that day we should have an eye in the singing of it, engaging ourselves likewise by well-doing, if possible, to *silence the ignorance of foolish men*, 1 Pet. ii. 15.

19 *Oh* how great *is* thy goodness, which thou hast laid up for them that fear thee; *which* thou hast wrought for them that trust in thee before the sons of men! 20 Thou shalt hide them in the secret of thy presence from the pride of man: thou shalt keep them secretly in a pavilion from the strife of tongues. 21 Blessed *be* the LORD: for he hath showed me his marvellous kindness in a strong city. 22 For I said in my haste, I am cut off from before thine eyes: nevertheless thou heardest the voice of my supplications when I cried unto thee. 23 O love the LORD, all ye his saints: *for* the LORD preserveth the faithful, and plentifully rewardeth the proud doer. 24 Be of good courage, and he shall strengthen your heart, all ye that hope in the LORD.

We have three things in these verses :—

I. The believing acknowledgment which David makes of God's goodness to his people in general, *v.* 19, 20.

1. God is good to all, but he is, in a special manner, good to Israel. His goodness to them is wonderful, and will be, to eternity, matter of admiration: *O how great is thy goodness!* How profound are the counsels of it! how rich are the treasures of it! how free and extensive are the communications of it! Those very persons whom men load with slanders God loads with benefits and honours. Those who are interested in this goodness are described to be such as fear God and trust in him, as stand in awe of his greatness and rely on his grace. This goodness is said to be *laid up for them* and *wrought for them*. (1.) There is a goodness laid up for them in the other world, an inheritance *reserved in heaven* (1 Pet. i. 4), and there is a goodness wrought for them in this world, goodness wrought in them. There is enough in God's goodness both for the portion and inheritance of all his children when they come to their full age, and for their maintenance and education during their minority. There is enough in bank and enough in hand. (2.) This goodness is laid up in his promise for all that fear God, to whom assurance is given that they shall want no good thing. But it is wrought, in the actual performance of the promise, for those that trust in him—that by faith take hold of the promise, put it in suit, and draw out to themselves the benefit and comfort of it. If what is laid up for us in the treasures of the everlasting covenant be not wrought for us, it is our own fault, because we do not believe. But those that trust in God, as they have the comfort of his goodness in their own bosoms, so they have the credit of it (and the credit of an estate goes far with some); it is wrought for them *before the sons of men.* God's goodness to them puts an honour upon them and rolls away their reproach; *for all that see them shall acknowledge them, that they are the seed which the Lord hath blessed,* Isa. lxi. 9.

2. God preserves man and beast; but he is, in a special manner, the protector of his own people (*v.* 20): *Thou shalt hide them.* As his goodness is hid and reserved for them, so they are hid and preserved for it. The saints are God's hidden ones. See here, (1.) The danger they are in, which arises from the pride of man and from the strife of tongues; proud men insult over them and would trample on them and tread them down; contentious men pick quarrels with them; and, when tongues are at strife, good people often go by the worst. The pride of men endangers their liberty; the strife of tongues in perverse disputings endangers truth. But, (2.) See the defence they are under: *Thou shalt hide them in the secret of thy presence, in a pavilion.* God's providence shall keep them safe from the malice of their enemies. He has many ways of sheltering them. When Baruch and Jeremiah were sought for *the Lord hid them,* Jer. xxxvi. 26. God's grace shall keep them safe from the evil of the judgments that are abroad; to them they have no sting; and they shall be hidden in the day of the Lord's anger, for there is no anger at them. His comforts shall keep them easy and cheerful; his sanctuary, where they have communion with him, shelters them from the fiery darts of terror and temptation; and the mansions in his house above shall be shortly, shall be eternally, their hiding-place from all danger and fear.

II. The thankful returns which David makes for God's goodness to him in particular, *v.* 21, 22. Having admired God's goodness to all the saints, he here owns how good he had found him. 1. Without were fightings; but God had wonderfully preserved his life: " *He has shown me his marvellous lovingkindness,* he has given me an instance of his care of me and favour to me, beyond what I could have expected." God's loving-kindness to his people, all things considered, is wonderful: but some instances of it, even in this world, are in a special manner marvellous in their eyes; as this here, when God preserved David from the sword of Saul, in caves and woods, as safe as if he had been in a strong city. In Keilah, that strong city, God showed him great mercy, both in making him an instrument to rescue the inhabitants out of the hands of the Philistines and then in rescuing him from the same men who would have ungratefully delivered him up into the hand of Saul, 1 Sam. xxiii. 5, 12. This was marvellous loving-kindness indeed, upon which he writes, with wonder and thankfulness, *Blessed be the Lord.* Special preservations call for particular thanksgivings. 2. Within were fears; but God was better to him than his fears, *v.* 22. He here keeps an account, (1.) Of his own folly, in distrusting God, which he acknowledges, to his shame. Though he had express promises to build upon, and great experience of God's care concerning him in many straits, yet he had entertained this hard and jealous thought of God, and could not forbear telling it him to his face. *" I am cut off from before thy eyes; thou hast quite forsaken me, and I must not expect to be looked upon or regarded by thee any more. I shall one day perish by the hand of Saul,* and so be cut off before thy eyes, be ruined while thou lookest on," 1 Sam. xxvii. 1. This he said in his *flight* (so some read it), which denotes the distress of his affairs. Saul was just at his back, and ready to seize him, which made the temptation strong. *In my haste* (so we read it), which denotes the disturbance and discomposure of his mind, which made the temptation surprising, so that it found him off his guard. Note, It is a common thing to speak amiss when we speak in haste and without consideration; but what we speak amiss in haste we must repent of at leisure, particularly that which we have spoken distrustfully of God. (2.) Of God's wonderful goodness to him notwithstanding. Though his faith failed, God's promise did not: *Thou heardest the voice of my supplication,* for all this. He mentions his own unbelief as a foil to God's fidelity, serving to make his loving-kindness the more marvellous, the more illustrious. When we have thus distrusted God he might justly take us at our word, and bring our fears upon us, as he did on Israel, Num. xiv. 28; Isa. lxvi. 4. But he has pitied and pardoned us, and our unbelief has not made his promise and grace of no effect; for he knows our frame.

III. The exhortation and encouragement which he hereupon gives to all the saints, *v.* 23, 24. 1. He would have them set their love on God (*v.* 23): *O love the Lord! all you his saints.* Those that have their own hearts full of love to God cannot but desire that others also may be in love with him; for in his favour there is no need to fear a rival. It is the character of the saints that they do love God; and yet they must be still called

upon to love him, to love him more and love him better, and give proofs of their love. We must love him, not only for his goodness, because *he preserves the faithful*, but for his justice, because he *plentifully rewards the proud doer* (who would ruin those whom he preserves), according to their pride. Some take it in a good sense; he plentifully rewards the magnificent (or excellent) doer, that is daringly good, whose heart, like Jehoshaphat's, is lifted up in the ways of the Lord. He rewards him that does well, but plentifully rewards him that does excellently well. 2. He would have them set their hope in God (*v.* 24): *" Be of good courage;* have a good heart on it; whatever difficulties or dangers you may meet with, the God you trust in shall by that trust strengthen your heart."* Those that hope in God have reason to be of good courage, and let their hearts be strong, for, as nothing truly evil can befal them, so nothing truly good for them shall be wanting to them.

In singing this we should animate ourselves and one another to proceed and persevere in our Christian course, whatever threatens us, and whoever frowns upon us.

PSALM XXXII.

This psalm, though it speaks not of Christ, as many of the psalms we have hitherto met with have done, has yet a great deal of gospel in it. The apostle tells us that David, in this psalm, describes "the blessedness of the man unto whom God imputes righteousness without works," Rom. iv. 6. We have here a summary, I. Of gospel grace in the pardon of sin (ver. 1, 2), in divine protection (ver. 7), and divine guidance, ver. 8. II. Of gospel duty. To confess sin (ver. 3–5), to pray (ver. 6), to govern ourselves well (ver. 9, 10), and to rejoice in God, ver. 11. The way to obtain these privileges is to make conscience of these duties, which we ought to think of—of the former for our comfort, of the latter for our quickening, when we sing this psalm. Grotius thinks it was designed to be sung on the day of atonement.

A psalm of David, Maschil.

BLESSED *is he whose* transgression *is* forgiven, *whose* sin *is* covered. 2 Blessed *is* the man unto whom the LORD imputeth not iniquity, and in whose spirit *there is* no guile. 3 When I kept silence, my bones waxed old through my roaring all the day long. 4 For day and night thy hand was heavy upon me: my moisture is turned into the drought of summer. Selah. 5 I acknowledged my sin unto thee, and mine iniquity have I not hid. I said, I will confess my transgressions unto the LORD; and thou forgavest the iniquity of my sin. Selah. 6 For this shall every one that is godly pray unto thee in a time when thou mayest be found: surely in the floods of great waters they shall not come nigh unto him.

This psalm is entitled *Maschil*, which some take to be only the name of the tune to which it was set and was to be sung. But others think it is significant; our margin reads it,

A psalm of David giving instruction, and there is nothing in which we have more need of instruction than in the nature of true blessedness, wherein it consists and the way that leads to it—what we must do that we may be happy. There are several things in which these verses instruct us. In general, we are here taught that our happiness consists in the favour of God, and not in the wealth of this world—in spiritual blessings, and not the good things of this world. When David says (i. 1), *Blessed is the man that walks not in the counsel of the ungodly,* and (cxix. 1), *Blessed are the undefiled in the way,* the meaning is, " This is the character of the blessed man ; and he that has not this character cannot expect to be happy :" but when it is here said, *Blessed is the man whose iniquity is forgiven,* the meaning is, " This is the ground of his blessedness : this is that fundamental privilege from which all the other ingredients of his blessedness flow." In particular, we are here instructed,

I. Concerning the nature of the pardon of sin. This is that which we all need and are undone without ; we are therefore concerned to be very solicitous and inquisitive about it. 1. It is the forgiving of transgression. *Sin is the transgression of the law.* Upon our repentance, the transgression is forgiven ; that is, the obligation to punishment which we lay under, by virtue of the sentence of the law, is vacated and cancelled ; it is *lifted off* (so some read it), that by the pardon of it we may be eased of a burden, a heavy burden, like a load on the back, that makes us stoop, or a load on the stomach, that makes us sick, or a load on the spirits, that makes us sink. The remission of sins gives rest and relief to those that were *weary and heavily laden,* Matt. xi. 28. 2. It is the covering of sin, as nakedness is covered, that it may not appear to our shame, Rev. iii. 18. One of the first symptoms of guilt in our first parents was blushing at their own nakedness. Sin makes us loathsome in the sight of God and utterly unfit for communion with him, and, when conscience is awakened, it makes us loathsome to ourselves too ; but, when sin is pardoned, it is covered with the robe of Christ's righteousness, like the coats of skins wherewith God clothed Adam and Eve (an emblem of the remission of sins), so that God is no longer displeased with us, but perfectly reconciled. They are not covered from us (no ; *My sin is ever before me)* nor covered from God's omniscience, but from his vindictive justice. When he pardons sin he *remembers it no more,* he *casts it behind his back,* it *shall be sought for and not found,* and the sinner, being thus reconciled to God, begins to be reconciled to himself. 3. It is the not imputing of iniquity, not laying it to the sinner's charge, not proceeding against him for it according to the strictness of the law, not dealing with him as he deserves. The righteousness of Christ being imputed to us, and we

being made *the righteousness of God in him,* our iniquity is not imputed, God having *laid upon him the iniquity of us all* and made him *sin for us.* Observe, Not to impute iniquity is God's act, for he is the Judge. *It is God that justifies.*

II. Concerning the character of those whose sins are pardoned : *in whose spirit there is no guile.* He does not say, " There is no *guilt"* (for who is there that lives and sins not ?), but no *guile ;* the pardoned sinner is one that does not dissemble with God in his professions of repentance and faith,nor in his prayers for peace or pardon, but in all these is sincere and means as he says—that does not repent with a purpose to sin again, and then sin with a purpose to repent again, as a learned interpreter glosses upon it. Those that design honestly, that are really what they profess to be, are the Israelites indeed, in whom is no guile.

III. Concerning the happiness of a justified state : *Blessednesses are to the man whose iniquity is forgiven,* all manner of blessings, sufficient to make him completely blessed. That is taken away which incurred the curse and obstructed the blessing ; and then God will pour out blessings till there be no room to receive them. The forgiveness of sin is that article of the covenant which is the reason and ground of all the rest. *For I will be merciful to their unrighteousness,* Heb. viii. 12.

IV. Concerning the uncomfortable condition of an unhumbled sinner, that sees his guilt, but is not yet brought to make a penitent confession of it. This David describes very pathetically, from his own sad experience (v. 3, 4) : *While I kept silence my bones waxed old.* Those may be said to keep silence who stifle their convictions, who, when they cannot but see the evil of sin and their danger by reason of it, ease themselves by not thinking of it and diverting their minds to something else, as Cain to the building of a city,—who *cry not when God binds them,—* who will not unburden their consciences by a penitent confession, nor seek for peace, as they ought, by faithful and fervent prayer,— and who choose rather to pine away in their iniquities than to take the method which God has appointed of finding rest for their souls. Let such expect that their smothered convictions will be a fire in their bones, and the wounds of sin, not opened, will fester, and grow intolerably painful. If conscience be seared, the case is so much the more dangerous ; but, if it be startled and awake, it will be heard. The hand of divine wrath will be felt lying heavily upon the soul, and the anguish of the spirit will affect the body ; to that degree David experienced it, so that when he was young his bones waxed old ; and even his silence made him *roar all the day long,* as if he had been under some grievous pain and distemper of body, when really the cause of all his uneasiness was the struggle he felt in his own bosom between his convictions and his corruptions. Note, *He that covers his sin shall not prosper ;* some inward trouble is required in repentance, but there is much worse in impenitency.

V. Concerning the true and only way to peace of conscience. We are here taught to confess our sins, that they may be forgiven, to declare them, that we may be justified. This course David took: *I acknowledged my sin unto thee,* and no longer *hid my iniquity, v.* 5. Note, Those that would have the comfort of the pardon of their sins must take shame to themselves by a penitent confession of them. We must confess the fact of sin, and be particular in it *(Thus and thus have I done),* confess the fault of sin, aggravate it, and lay a load upon ourselves for it *(I have done very wickedly),* confess the justice of the punishment we have been under for it *(The Lord is just in all that is brought upon us),* and that we deserve much worse—*I am no more worthy to be called thy son.* We must confess sin with shame and holy blushing, with fear and holy trembling.

VI. Concerning God's readiness to pardon sin to those who truly repent of it: " *I said, I will confess* (I sincerely resolved upon it, hesitated no longer, but came to a point, that I would make a free and ingenuous confession of my sins) *and* immediately *thou forgavest the iniquity of my sin,* and gavest me the comfort of the pardon in my own conscience; immediately I found rest to my soul." Note, God is more ready to pardon sin, upon our repentance, than we are to repent in order to the obtaining of pardon. It was with much ado that David was here brought to confess his sins ; he was put to the rack before he was brought to do it (*v.* 3, 4), he held out long, and would not surrender till it came to the last extremity ; but, when he did offer to surrender, see how quickly, how easily, he obtained good terms : " I did but say, *I will confess, and thou forgavest.*" Thus the father of the prodigal saw his returning son *when he was yet afar off,* and ran to meet him with the kiss that sealed his pardon. What an encouragement is this to poor penitents, and what an assurance does it give us that, *if we confess our sins,* we shall find God, not only *faithful and just,* but gracious and kind, *to forgive us our sins !*

VII. Concerning the good use that we are to make of the experience David had had of God's readiness to forgive his sins (*v.* 6): *For this shall every one that is godly pray unto thee.* Note, 1. All godly people are praying people. As soon as ever Paul was converted, *Behold, he prays,* Acts ix. 11. You may as soon find a living man without breath as a living Christian without prayer. 2. The instructions given us concerning the happiness of those whose sins are pardoned, and the easiness of obtaining the pardon, should engage and encourage us to pray, and particularly to pray, *God be merciful to us sinners.* For this shall every one that is well inclined

be earnest with God in prayer, and *come boldly to the throne of grace,* with hopes to *obtain mercy,* Heb. iv. 16. 3. Those that would speed in prayer must seek the Lord in *a time when he will be found.* When, by his providence, he calls them to seek him, and by his Spirit stirs them up to seek him, they must *go speedily to seek the Lord* (Zech. viii. 21) and lose no time, lest death cut them off, and then it will be too late to seek him, Isa. lv. 6. *Behold, now is the accepted time,* 2 Cor. vi. 2. 4. Those that are sincere and abundant in prayer will find the benefit of it when they are in trouble : *Surely in the floods of great waters,* which are very threatening, *they shall not come nigh them,* to terrify them, or create them any uneasiness, much less shall they overwhelm them. Those that have God *nigh unto them in all that which they call upon him for,* as all upright, penitent, praying people have, are so guarded, so advanced, that no waters—no, not great waters—no, not floods of them, can come nigh them, to hurt them. As the temptations of the *wicked one touch them not* (1 John v. 18), so neither do the troubles of this evil world ; these fiery darts, of both kinds, drop short of them.

7 Thou *art* my hiding place ; thou shalt preserve me from trouble ; thou shalt compass me about with songs of deliverance. Selah. 8 I will instruct thee and teach thee in the way which thou shalt go : I will guide thee with mine eye. 9 Be ye not as the horse, *or* as the mule, *which* have no understanding : whose mouth must be held in with bit and bridle, lest they come near unto thee. 10 Many sorrows *shall be* to the wicked : but he that trusteth in the LORD, mercy shall compass him about. 11 Be glad in the LORD, and rejoice, ye righteous : and shout for joy, all *ye that are* upright in heart.

David is here improving the experience he had had of the comfort of pardoning mercy.

I. He speaks to God, and professes his confidence in him and expectation from him, *v.* 7. Having tasted the sweetness of divine grace to a penitent sinner, he cannot doubt of the continuance of that grace to a praying saint, and that in that grace he should find both safety and joy. 1. Safety : " *Thou art my hiding-place ;* when by faith I have recourse to thee I see all the reason in the world to be easy, and to think myself out of the reach of any real evil. *Thou shalt preserve me from trouble,* from the sting of it, and from the strokes of it as far as is good for me. *Thou shalt preserve me from* such trouble as I was in *while I kept silence,*" *v.* 3. When God has pardoned our sins, if he leave us to ourselves, we shall soon run as far in debt again as ever and plunge ourselves again into the same gulf; and therefore, when we have received the comfort of our remission, we must fly to the grace of God to be preserved from returning to folly again, and having our hearts again hardened through the deceitfulness of sin. God keeps his people from trouble by keeping them from sin. 2. Joy: " Thou shalt not only deliver me, but *compass me about with songs of deliverance;* which way soever I look I shall see occasion to rejoice and to praise God; and my friends also shall compass me about in the great congregation, to join with me in songs of praise: they shall join their songs of deliverance with mine. As *every one that is godly shall pray with me,* so they shall give thanks with me."

II. He turns his speech to the children of men. Being himself converted, he does what he can to *strengthen his brethren* (Luke xxii. 32): *I will instruct thee,* whoever thou art that desirest instruction, *and teach thee in the way which thou shalt go, v.* 8. Thus, in another of his penitential psalms, he resolves that when God should have restored to him the joy of his salvation he would teach transgressors his ways, and do what he could to convert sinners to God, as well as to comfort those that were converted, li. 12, 13. When Solomon became a penitent he immediately became a preacher, Eccl. i. 1. Those are best able to teach others the grace of God who have themselves had the experience of it: and those who are themselves taught of God ought to *tell others what he has done for their souls* (lxvi. 16) and so teach them. *I will guide thee with my eye.* Some apply this to God's conduct and direction. He teaches us by his word and guides us with his eye, by the secret intimations of his will in the hints and turns of Providence, which he enables his people to understand and take direction from, as a master makes a servant know his mind by a wink of his eye. When Christ turned and looked upon Peter he guided him with his eye. But it is rather to be taken as David's promise to those who sat under his instruction, his own children and family especially: " *I will counsel thee; my eye shall be upon thee*" (so the margin reads it); "I will give thee the best counsel I can and then observe whether thou takest it or no." Those that are taught in the word should be under the constant inspection of those that teach them; spiritual guides must be overseers. In this application of the foregoing doctrine concerning the blessedness of those whose sins are pardoned we have a word to sinners and a word to saints; and this is rightly dividing the word of truth and giving to each their portion.

1. Here is a word of caution to sinners, and a good reason is given for it. (1.) The caution is, not to be unruly and ungovernable: *Be you not as the horse and the mule, which have no understanding, v.* 9. When the psalmist would reproach himself for the sins he repented of he compared himself to a *beast before God (so foolish have I been and*

350

ignorant, lxxiii. 22) and therefore warns others not to be so. It is our honour and happiness that we have understanding, that we are capable of being governed by reason and of reasoning with ourselves. Let us therefore use the faculties we have, and act rationally. The horse and mule must be managed *with bit and bridle, lest they come near* us, to do us a mischief, or (as some read it) that they may come near to us, to do us service, that they *may obey us,* Jam. iii. 3. Let us not be like them; let us not be hurried by appetite and passion, at any time, to go contrary to the dictates of right reason and to our true interest. If sinners would be governed and determined by these, they would soon become saints and would not go a step further in their sinful courses; where there is renewing grace there is no need of the bit and bridle of restraining grace. (2.) The reason for this caution is because the way of sin which we would persuade you to forsake will certainly end in sorrow (*v.* 10): *Many sorrows shall be to the wicked,* which will not only spoil their vain and carnal mirth, and put an end to it, but will make them pay dearly for it. Sin will have sorrow, if not repented of, everlasting sorrow. It was part of the sentence, *I will greatly multiply thy sorrows.* "Be wise for yourselves therefore, and turn from your wickedness, that you may prevent those sorrows, those many sorrows."

2. Here is a word of comfort to saints, and a good reason is given for that too. (1.) They are assured that if they will but trust in the Lord, and keep closely to him, *mercy shall compass them about* on every side (*v.* 10), so that they shall not depart from God, for that mercy shall keep them in, nor shall any real evil break in upon them, for that mercy shall keep it out. (2.) They are therefore commanded to *be glad in the Lord, and* to *rejoice* in him, to such a degree as even to *shout for joy, v.* 11. Let them be so transported with this holy joy as not to be able to contain themselves; and let them affect others with it, that they also may see that a life of communion with God is the most pleasant and comfortable life we can live in this world. This is that present bliss which the upright in heart, and they only, are entitled to and qualified for.

PSALM XXXIII.

This is a psalm of praise; it is probable that David was the penman of it, but we are not told so, because God would have us look above the penmen of sacred writ, to that blessed Spirit that moved and guided them. The psalmist, in this psalm, I. Calls upon the righteous to praise God, ver. 1—3. II. Furnishes us with matter for praise. We must praise God, 1. For his justice, goodness, and truth, appearing in his word, and in all his works, ver. 4, 5. 2. For his power appearing in the work of creation, ver. 6—9. 3. For the sovereignty of his providence in the government of the world, ver. 10, 11, and again ver. 13—17. 4. For the peculiar favour which he bears to his own chosen people, which encourages them to trust in him, ver. 12 and again ver. 18—22. We need not be at a loss for proper thoughts in singing this psalm, which so naturally expresses the pious affections of a devout soul towards God.

R EJOICE in the LORD, O ye righteous : *for* praise is comely for the upright. 2 Praise the LORD with harp : sing unto him with the psaltery *and* an instrument of ten strings. 3 Sing unto him a new song ; play skilfully with a loud noise. 4 For the word of the LORD *is* right ; and all his works *are done* in truth. 5 He loveth righteousness and judgment: the earth is full of the goodness of the LORD. 6 By the word of the LORD were the heavens made ; and all the host of them by the breath of his mouth. 7 He gathereth the waters of the sea together as a heap : he layeth up the depth in storehouses. 8 Let all the earth fear the LORD : let all the inhabitants of the world stand in awe of him. 9 For he spake, and it was *done;* he commanded, and it stood fast. 10 The LORD bringeth the counsel of the heathen to nought : he maketh the devices of the people of none effect. 11 The counsel of the LORD standeth for ever, the thoughts of his heart to all generations.

Four things the psalmist expresses in these verses :—

I. The great desire he had that God might be praised. He did not think he did it so well himself, but that he wished others also might be employed in this work ; the more the better, in this concert : it is the more like heaven. 1. Holy joy is the heart and soul of praise, and that is here pressed upon all good people (*v.* 1): *Rejoice in the Lord, you righteous ;* so the foregoing psalm concluded and so this begins ; for all our religious exercises should both begin and end with a holy complacency and triumph in God as the best of beings and best of friends. 2. Thankful praise is the breath and language of holy joy ; and that also is here required of us (*v.* 2): "*Praise the Lord ;* speak well of him, and give him the glory due to his name." 3. Religious songs are the proper expressions of thankful praise ; those are here required (*v.* 3) : "*Sing unto him a new song,* the best you have, not that which by frequent use is worn thread-bare, but that which, being new, is most likely to move the affections, a new song for new mercies and upon every new occasion, for those compassions which are new every morning." Music was·then used, by the appointment of David, with the temple-songs, that they might be the better sung ; and this also is here called for (*v.* 2): *Sing unto him with the psaltery.* Here is, (1.) A good rule for this duty : "Do it *skilfully,* and *with a loud noise ;* let it have the best both of head and heart ; let it be done intelligently and with a clear head, affectionately and with a warm heart." (2.) A good reason

for this duty : *For praise is .comely for the upright.* It is well pleasing to God (the garments of praise add much to the comeliness which God puts upon his people) and it is an excellent ornament to our profession. *It becomes the upright,* whom God has put so much honour upon, to give honour to him. The upright praise God in a comely manner, for they praise him with their hearts, that is praising him with their glory ; whereas the praises of hypocrites are awkward and uncomely, like *a parable in the mouth of fools,* Prov. xxvi. 7.

II. The high thoughts he had of God, and of his infinite perfections, *v.* 4, 5. God makes himself known to us, 1. In his *word,* here put for all divine revelation, all that which God at sundry times and in divers manners spoke to the children of men, and that is all *right,* there is nothing amiss in it ; his commands exactly agree with the rules of equity and the eternal reasons of good and evil. His promises are all wise and good and inviolably sure, and there is no iniquity in his threatenings, but even those are designed for our good, by deterring us from evil. God's word is right, and therefore all our deviations from it are wrong, and we are then in the right when we agree with it. 2. In his *works,* and those are all *done in truth,* all according to his counsels, which are called the *scriptures of truth,* Dan. x. 21. The copy in all God's works agrees exactly with the great original, the plan laid in the Eternal Mind, and varies not in the least jot. God has made it to appear in his works, (1.) That he is a God of inflexible justice : *He loveth righteousness and judgment.* There is nothing but righteousness in the sentence he passes and judgment in the execution of it. He never did nor can do wrong to any of his creatures, but is always ready to give redress to those that are wronged, and does it with delight. He takes pleasure in those that are righteous. He is himself the righteous Lord, and therefore loveth righteousness. (2.) That he is a God of inexhaustible bounty : *The earth is full of his goodness,* that is, of the proofs and instances of it. The benign influences which the earth receives from above, and the fruits it is thereby enabled to produce, the provision that is made both for man and beast, and the common blessings with which all the nations of the earth are blessed, plainly declare that *the earth is full of his goodness*—the darkest, the coldest, the hottest, and the most dry and desert part of it not excepted. What a pity is it that this earth, which is so full of God's goodness, should be so empty of his praises, and that of the multitudes that live upon his bounty there are so few that live to his glory !

III. The conviction he was under of the almighty power of God, evidenced in the creation of the world. We "believe in God," and therefore we praise him as "the Father Almighty, maker of heaven and earth," so we are here taught to praise him. Observe,

1. How God made the world, and brought all things into being. (1.) How easily: All things were made, *by the word of the Lord and by the breath of his mouth.* Christ is the Word, the Spirit is the breath, so that God the Father made the world, as he rules it and redeems it, by his Son and Spirit. *He spoke, and he commanded* (v. 9), and that was enough; there needed no more. With men saying and doing are two things, but it is not so with God. By the Word and Spirit of God as the world was made, so was man, that little world. God said, *Let us make man,* and he *breathed into him the breath of life.* By the Word and Spirit the church is built, that new world, and grace wrought in the soul, that new man, that new creation. What cannot that power do which with a word made a world! (2.) How effectually it was done: *And it stood fast.* What God does he does to purpose; he does it and it stands fast. *Whatsoever God doeth, it shall be for ever,* Eccl. iii. 14. It is by virtue of that command to stand fast that things *continue to this day according to God's ordinance,* cxix. 91.

2. What he made. He made all things, but notice is here taken, (1.) Of *the heavens, and the host of them, v.* 6. The visible heavens, and the sun, moon, and stars, their hosts—the highest heavens, and the angels, their hosts. (2.) Of the waters, and the treasures of them, *v.* 7. The earth was at first covered with the water, and, being heavier, must of course subside and sink under it; but, to show from the very first that the God of nature is not tied to the ordinary method of nature and the usual operations of his powers, with a word's speaking *he gathered the waters together on a heap,* that the dry land might appear, yet left them not to continue on a heap, but *laid up the depth in store-houses,* not only in the flats where the seas make their beds, and in which they are locked up by the sand on the shore as in store-houses, but in secret subterraneous caverns, where they are hidden from the eyes of all living, but were reserved as in a store-house for that day when those fountains of the great deep were to be broken up; and they are still laid up there in store, for what use the great Master of the house knows best.

3. What use is to be made of this (v. 8): *Let all the earth fear the Lord,* and *stand in awe of him;* that is, let all the children of men worship him and give glory to him, xcv. 5, 6. The everlasting gospel gives this as the reason why we must worship God, because he made the heaven, and the earth, and the sea, Rev. xiv. 6. 7. Let us all fear him, that is, dread his wrath and displeasure, and be afraid of having him our enemy and of standing it out against him. Let us not dare to offend him who having this power no doubt has all power in his hand. It is dangerous being at war with him who has the host of

heaven for his armies and the depths of the sea for his magazines, and therefore it is wisdom to desire conditions of peace, see Jer. v. 22.

IV. The satisfaction he had of God's sovereignty and dominion, *v.* 10, 11. He overrules all the counsels of men, and makes them, contrary to their intention, serviceable to his counsels. Come and see with an eye of faith God in the throne, 1. Frustrating the devices of his enemies: *He bringeth the counsel of the heathen to nought,* so that what they imagine against him and his kingdom proves *a vain thing* (ii. 1); the counsel of Ahithophel is turned into foolishness; Haman's plot is baffled. Though the design be laid ever so deep, and the hopes raised upon it ever so high, yet, if God says *it shall not stand, neither shall it come to pass;* it is all to no purpose. 2. Fulfilling his own decrees: *The counsel of the Lord standeth for ever.* It is immutable in itself, *for he is in one mind, and who can turn him?* The execution of it may be opposed, but cannot in the least be obstructed by any created power. Through all the revolutions of time God never changed his measures, but in every event, even that which to us is most surprising, the eternal counsel of God is fulfilled, nor can any thing prevent its being accomplished in its time. With what pleasure to ourselves may we in singing this give praise to God! How easy may this thought make us at all times, that God governs the world, that he did it in infinite wisdom before we were born, and will do it when we are silent in the dust!

12 Blessed *is* the nation whose God *is* the LORD; *and* the people *whom* he hath chosen for his own inheritance. 13 The LORD looketh from heaven; he beholdeth all the sons of men. 14 From the place of his habitation he looketh upon all the inhabitants of the earth. 15 He fashioneth their hearts alike; he considereth all their works. 16 There is no king saved by the multitude of a host: a mighty man is not delivered by much strength. 17 A horse *is* a vain thing for safety: neither shall he deliver *any* by his great strength. 18 Behold, the eye of the LORD *is* upon them that fear him, upon them that hope in his mercy; 19 To deliver their soul from death, and to keep them alive in famine. 20 Our soul waiteth for the LORD: he *is* our help and our shield. 21 For our heart shall rejoice in him, because we have trusted in his holy name. 22 Let thy mercy, O LORD, be upon us, according as we hope in thee.

We are here taught to give to God the glory, I. Of his common providence towards all the children of men. Though he has endued man with understanding and freedom of will, yet he reserves to himself the government of him, and even of those very faculties by which he is qualified to govern himself. 1. The children of men are all under his eye, even their hearts are so; and all the motions and operations of their souls, which none know but they themselves, he knows better than they themselves, *v.* 13, 14. Though the residence of God's glory is in the highest heavens, yet thence he not only has a prospect of all the earth, but a particular inspection of all the inhabitants of the earth. He not only beholds them, but he *looks upon them;* he looks narrowly upon them (so the word here used is sometimes rendered), so narrowly that not the least thought can escape his observation. Atheists think that, because he dwells above in heaven, he cannot, or will not, take notice of what is done here in this lower world; but thence, high as it is, he sees us all, and all persons and things are naked and open before him. 2. Their hearts, as well as their times, are all in his hand: *He fashions their hearts.* He made them at first, formed the spirit of each man within him, then when he brought him into being. Hence he is called *the Father of spirits:* and this is a good argument to prove that he perfectly knows them. The artist that made the clock, can account for the motions of every wheel. David uses this argument with application to himself, cxxxix. 1, 14. He still moulds the hearts of men, turns them as the rivers of water, which way soever he pleases, to serve his own purposes, darkens or enlightens men's understandings, stiffens or bows their wills, according as he is pleased to make use of them. He that fashions men's hearts fashions them alike. It is in hearts as in faces, though there is a great difference, and such a variety as that no two faces are exactly of the same features, nor any two hearts exactly of the same temper, yet there is such a similitude that, in some things, all faces and all hearts agree, *as in water face answers to face,* Prov. xxvii. 19. *He fashions them together* (so some read it); as the wheels of a watch, though of different shapes, sizes, and motions, are yet all put together, to serve one and the same purpose, so the hearts of men and their dispositions, however varying from each other and seeming to contradict one another, are yet all overruled to serve the divine purpose, which is one. 3. They, and all they do, are obnoxious to his judgment; *for he considers all their works,* not only knows them, but weighs them, that he may render to every man according to his works, in the day, in the world, of retribution, in the judgment, and to eternity. 4. All the powers of the creature have a dependence upon him, and are of no account, of no avail at all, without him, *v.* 16, 17. It is much

for the honour of God that not only no force can prevail in opposition to him, but that no force can act but in dependence on him and by a power derived from him. (1.) The strength of a king is nothing without God. No king is sacred by his royal prerogatives, or the authority with which he is invested; for the powers that are, of that kind, are ordained of God, and are what he makes them, and no more. David was a king, and a man of war from his youth, and yet acknowledged God to be his only protector and Saviour. (2.) The strength of an army is nothing without God. *The multitude of a host* cannot secure those under whose command they act, unless God make them a security to them. A great army cannot be sure of victory; for, when God pleases, one shall chase a thousand. (3.) The strength of a giant is nothing without God. *A mighty man,* such as Goliath was, *is not delivered by* his *much strength,* when his day comes to fall. Neither the firmness and activity of his body nor the stoutness and resolution of his mind will stand him in any stead, any further than God is pleased to give him success. *Let not the strong man* then *glory in his strength,* but let us all strengthen ourselves in the Lord our God, go forth, and go on, in his strength. (4.) The strength of a horse is nothing without God (*v.* 17): *A horse is a vain thing for safety.* In war horses were then so highly accounted of, and so much depended on, that God forbade the kings of Israel to *multiply horses* (Deut. xvii. 16), lest they should be tempted to trust to them and their confidence should thereby be taken off from God. David houghed the horses of the Syrians (2 Sam. viii. 4); here he houghs all the horses in the world, by pronouncing a horse a vain thing for safety in the day of battle. If the war-horse be unruly and ill-managed, he may hurry his rider into danger instead of carrying him out of danger. If he be killed under him, he may be his death, instead of saving his life. It is therefore our interest to make sure God's favour towards us, and then we may be sure of his power engaged for us, and need not fear whatever is against us.

II. We are to give God the glory of his special grace. In the midst of his acknowledgments of God's providence he pronounces those blessed that have Jehovah for their God, who governs the world, and has wherewithal to help them in every time of need, while those were miserable who had this and the other Baal for their god, which was so far from being able to hear and help them that it was itself senseless and helpless (*v.* 12): *Blessed is the nation whose God is the Lord,* even Israel, who had the knowledge of the true God and were taken into covenant with him, and all others who own God for theirs and are owned by him; for they also, whatever nation they are of, are of the spiritual seed of Abraham. 1. It is their wisdom that they take the Lord for their God, that they direct their homage and adoration there where it is due and where the payment of it will not be in vain. 2. It is their happiness that they are the people whom God has chosen for his own inheritance, whom he is pleased with, and honoured in, and whom he protects and takes care of, whom he cultivates and improves as a man does his inheritance, Deut. xxxii. 9. Now let us observe here, to the honour of divine grace, (1.) The regard which God has to his people, *v.* 18, 19. God beholds all the sons of men with an eye of observation, but his eye of favour and complacency is upon those that fear him. He looks upon them with delight, as the father on his children, as the bridegroom on his spouse, Isa. lxii. 5. While those that depend on arms and armies, on chariots and horses, perish in the disappointment of their expectations, God's people, under his protection, are safe, for he shall deliver their soul from death when there seems to be but a step between them and it. If he do not deliver the body from temporal death, yet he will deliver the soul from spiritual and eternal death. Their souls, whatever happens, shall live and praise him, either in this world or in a better. From his bounty they shall be supplied with all necessaries. He shall *keep them alive in famine;* when others die for want, they shall live, which shall make it a distinguishing mercy. When visible means fail, God will find out some way or other to supply them. He does not say that he will give them abundance (they have no reason either to desire it or to expect it), but he will keep them alive; they shall not starve; and, when destroying judgments are abroad, it ought to be reckoned a great favour, for it is a very striking one, and lays us under peculiar obligations, to have our lives given us for a prey. Those that have the Lord for their God shall find him their help and their shield, *v.* 20. In their difficulties he will assist them; they shall be helped over them, helped through them. In their dangers he will secure them, so that they shall not receive any real damage. (2.) The regard which God's people have to him and which we ought to have in consideration of this. [1.] We must wait for God. We must attend the motions of his providence, and accommodate ourselves to them, and patiently expect the issue of them. Our souls must wait for him, *v.* 20. We must not only in word and tongue profess a believing regard to God, but it must be inward and sincere, a secret and silent attendance on him. [2.] We must rely on God, *hope in his mercy,* in the goodness of his nature, though we have not an express promise to depend upon. Those that fear God and his wrath must hope in God and his mercy; for there is no flying from God, but by flying to him. These pious dispositions will not only consist together, but befriend each other, a holy fear of God and yet at the same time a hope in his mercy. This is *trusting in his holy name* (*v.* 21), in all

that whereby he has made known himself to us, for our encouragement to serve him. [3.] We must rejoice in God, *v.* 21. Those do not truly rest in God, or do not know the unspeakable advantage they have by so doing, who do not rejoice in him at all times; because those that hope in God hope for an eternal fulness of joy in his presence. [4.] We must seek to him for that mercy which we hope in, *v.* 22. Our expectations from God are not to supersede, but to quicken and encourage, our applications to him; he will be sought unto for that which he has promised, and therefore the psalm concludes with a short but comprehensive prayer, "*Let thy mercy, O Lord! be upon us;* let us always have the comfort and benefit of it, not according as we merit from thee, but *according as we hope in thee,* that is, according to the promise which thou hast in thy word given to us and according to the faith which thou hast by thy Spirit and grace wrought in us." If, in singing these verses, we put forth a dependence upon God, and let out our desires towards him, we make melody with our hearts to the Lord.

PSALM XXXIV.

This psalm was penned upon a particular occasion, as appears by the title, and yet there is little in it peculiar to that occasion, but that which is general, both by way of thanksgiving to God and instruction to us. I. He praises God for the experience which he and others had had of his goodness, ver. 1—6. II. He encourages all good people to trust in God and to seek to him, ver. 7—10. III. He gives good counsel to us all, as unto children, to take heed of sin, and to make conscience of our duty both to God and man, ver. 11—14. IV. To enforce this good counsel he shows God's favour to the righteous and his displeasure against the wicked, in which he sets before us good and evil, the blessing and the curse, ver. 15—22. So that, in singing this psalm, we are both to give glory to God and to teach and admonish ourselves and one another.

A psalm of David when he changed his behaviour before Abimelech, who drove him away, and he departed.

I WILL bless the Lord at all times: his praise *shall* continually *be* in my mouth. 2 My soul shall make her boast in the LORD: the humble shall hear *thereof,* and be glad. 3 O magnify the LORD with me, and let us exalt his name together. 4 I sought the LORD, and he heard me, and delivered me from all my fears. 5 They looked unto him, and were lightened: and their faces were not ashamed. 6 This poor man cried, and the LORD heard *him,* and saved him out of all his troubles. 7 The angel of the LORD encampeth round about them that fear him, and delivereth them. 8 O taste and see that the LORD *is* good: blessed *is* the man *that* trusteth in him. 9 O fear the LORD, ye his saints: for *there is* no want to them that fear him. 10 The young lions do lack, and suffer hunger: but they that seek the LORD shall not want any good *thing.*

The title of this psalm tells us both who penned it and upon what occasion it was penned. David, being forced to flee from his country, which was made too hot for him by the rage of Saul, sought shelter as near it as he could, in the land of the Philistines. There it was soon discovered who he was, and he was brought before the king, who, in the narrative, is called *Achish* (his proper name), here *Abimelech* (his title); and lest he should be treated as a spy, or one that came thither upon design, he feigned himself to be a mad-man (such there have been in every age, that even by idiots men might be taught to give God thanks for the use of their reason), that Achish might dismiss him as a contemptible man, rather than take cognizance of him as a dangerous man. And it had the effect he desired; by this stratagem he escaped the hand that otherwise would have handled him roughly. Now, 1. We cannot justify David in this dissimulation. It ill became an honest man to feign himself to be what he was not, and a man of honour to feign himself to be a fool and a mad-man. If, in sport, we mimic those who have not so good an understanding as we think we have, we forget that God might have made their case ours. 2. Yet we cannot but wonder at the composure of his spirit, and how far he was from any change of that, when he changed his behaviour. Even when he was in that fright, or rather in that danger only, his heart was so fixed, trusting in God, that even then he penned this excellent psalm, which has as much in it of the marks of a calm sedate spirit as any psalm in all the book; and there is something curious too in the composition, for it is what is called an alphabetical psalm, that is, a psalm in which every verse begins with each letter in its order as it stands in the Hebrew alphabet. Happy are those who can thus keep their temper, and keep their graces in exercise, even when they are tempted to change their behaviour. In this former part of the psalm,

I. David engages and excites himself to praise God. Though it was his fault that he changed his behaviour, yet it was God's mercy that he escaped, and the mercy was so much the greater in that God did not deal with him according to the desert of his dissimulation, and we must in every thing give thanks. He resolves, 1. That he will praise God constantly: *I will bless the Lord at all times,* upon all occasions. He resolves to keep up stated times for this duty, to lay hold of all opportunities for it, and to renew his praises upon every fresh occurrence that furnished him with matter. If we hope to spend our eternity in praising God, it is fit that we should spend as much as may be of our time in this work. 2. That he will praise him openly: *His praise shall continually be in my mouth.* Thus he would show how forward he was to own his obligations to the mercy of God and how desirous to make others also sensible of theirs. 3. That he will praise him

heartily: "*My soul shall make her boast in the Lord,* in my relation to him, my interest in him, and expectations from him." It is not vainglory to glory in the Lord.

II. He calls upon others to join with him herein. He expects they will (v. 2): "*The humble shall hear thereof,* both of my deliverance and of my thankfulness, *and be glad* that a good man has so much favour shown him and a good God so much honour done him." Those have most comfort in God's mercies, both to others and to themselves, that are humble, and have the least confidence in their own merit and sufficiency. It pleased David to think that God's favours to him would rejoice the heart of every Israelite. Three things he would have us all to concur with him in :—

1. In great and high thoughts of God, which we should express in magnifying him and exalting his name, v. 3. We cannot make God greater or higher than he is; but if we adore him as infinitely great, and higher than the highest, he is pleased to reckon this magnifying and exalting him. This we must do together. God's praises sound best in concert, for so we praise him as the angels do in heaven. Those that share in God's favour, as all the saints do, should concur in his praises; and we should be as desirous of the assistance of our friends in returning thanks for mercies as in praying for them. We have reason to join in thanksgiving to God,

(1.) For his readiness to hear prayer, which all the saints have had the comfort of; for he never said to any of them, *Seek you me in vain.* [1.] David, for his part, will give it under his hand that he has found him a prayer-hearing God (v. 4): "*I sought the Lord,* in my distress, entreated his favour, begged his help, *and he heard me,* answered my request immediately, *and delivered me from all my fears,* both from the death I feared and from the disquietude and disturbance produced by my fear of it." The former he does by his providence working for us, the latter by his grace working in us, to silence our fears and still the tumult of the spirits; this latter is the greater mercy of the two, because the thing we fear is our trouble only, but our unbelieving distrustful fear of it is our sin; nay, it is often more our torment too than the thing itself would be, which perhaps would only touch the bone and the flesh, while the fear would prey upon the spirits and put us out of the possession of our own soul. David's prayers helped to silence his fears; having sought the Lord, and left his case with him, he could wait the event with great composure. "But David was a great and eminent man, we may not expect to be favoured as he was; have any others ever experienced the like benefit by prayer?" Yes, [2.] Many besides him have *looked unto God* by faith and prayer, *and have been lightened by it,* v. 5. It has wonderfully revived and comforted them; witness Hannah, who, when she had prayed, *went her way, and did eat, and her countenance was no more sad.* When we look to the world we are darkened, we are perplexed, and at a loss; but, when we look to God, from him we have the light both of direction and joy, and our way is made both plain and pleasant. These here spoken of, that looked unto God, had their expectations raised, and the event did not frustrate them: *Their faces were not ashamed* of their confidence. "But perhaps these also were persons of great eminence, like David himself, and upon that account were highly favoured, or their numbers made them considerable;" nay, [3.] *This poor man cried,* a single person, mean and inconsiderable, whom no man looked upon with any respect or looked after with any concern; yet he was as welcome to the throne of grace as David or any of his worthies: *The Lord heard him,* took cognizance of his case and of his prayers, *and saved him out of all his troubles,* v. 6. God will *regard the prayer of the destitute,* cii. 17. See Isa. lvii. 15.

(2.) For the ministration of the good angels about us (v. 7): *The angel of the Lord,* a guard of angels (so some), but as unanimous in their service as if they were but one, or a guardian angel, *encamps round about those that fear God,* as the life-guard about the prince, *and delivers them.* God makes use of the attendance of the good spirits for the protection of his people from the malice and power of evil spirits; and the holy angels do us more good offices every day than we are aware of. Though in dignity and in capacity of nature they are very much superior to us,—though they retain their primitive rectitude, which we have lost,—though they have constant employment in the upper world, the employment of praising God, and are entitled to a constant rest and bliss there,—yet in obedience to their Maker, and in love to those that bear his image, they condescend to minister to the saints, and stand up for them against the powers of darkness; they not only visit them, but encamp round about them, acting for their good as really, though not as sensibly, as for Jacob's (Gen. xxxii. 1), and Elisha's, 2 Kings vi. 17. All the glory be to the God of the angels.

2. He would have us to join with him in kind and good thoughts of God (v. 8): *O taste and see that the Lord is good!* The goodness of God includes both the beauty and amiableness of his being and the bounty and beneficence of his providence and grace; and accordingly, (1.) We must taste that he is a bountiful benefactor, relish the goodness of God in all his gifts to us, and reckon that the savour and sweetness of them. Let God's goodness be rolled under the tongue as a sweet morsel. (2.) We must see that he is a beautiful being, and delight in the contemplation of his infinite perfections. By taste and sight we both make discoveries and take complacency. Taste and see God's goodness, that is, take notice of it and take the comfort of it, 1 Pet. ii. 3. He is good, for he makes all those that trust in him truly blessed; let

us therefore be so convinced of his goodness as thereby to be encouraged in the worst of times to trust in him.

3. He would have us join with him in a resolution to seek God and serve him, and continue in his fear (v. 9): *O fear the Lord! you his saints.* When we taste and see that he is good we must not forget that he is great and greatly to be feared; nay, even his goodness is the proper object of a filial reverence and awe. *They shall fear the Lord and his goodness,* Hos. iii. 5. *Fear the Lord;* that is, worship him, and make conscience of your duty to him in every thing, not fear him and shun him, but fear him and seek him (v. 10) as a people seek unto their God; address yourselves to him and portion yourselves in him. To encourage us to fear God and seek him, it is here promised that those that do so, even in this wanting world, *shall want no good thing* (Heb. *They shall not want all good things);* they shall so have all good things that they shall have no reason to complain of the want of any. As to the things of the other world, they shall have grace sufficient for the support of the spiritual life (2 Cor. xii. 9; Ps. lxxxiv. 11); and, as to this life, they shall have what is necessary to the support of it from the hand of God: as a Father, he will feed them with food convenient. What further comforts they desire they shall have, as far as Infinite Wisdom sees good, and what they want in one thing shall be made up in another. What God denies them he will give them grace to be content without and then they do not want it, Deut. iii. 26. Paul had all and abounded, because he was content, Phil. iv. 11, 18. Those that live by faith in God's all-sufficiency want nothing; for in him they have enough. *The young lions often lack and suffer hunger*—those that live upon common providence, as the lions do, shall want that satisfaction which those have that live by faith in the promise; those that trust to themselves, and think their own hands sufficient for them, shall want (for *bread is not always to the wise)*—but verily those shall be fed that trust in God and desire to be at his finding. Those that are ravenous, and prey upon all about them, shall want; but *the meek shall inherit the earth.* Those shall not want who with quietness work and mind their own business; plain-hearted Jacob has pottage enough, when Esau, the cunning hunter, is ready to perish for hunger.

11 Come, ye children, hearken unto me: I will teach you the fear of the LORD. 12 What man *is he that* desireth life, *and* loveth *many* days, that he may see good? 13 Keep thy tongue from evil, and thy lips from speaking guile. 14 Depart from evil, and do good; seek peace, and pursue it. 15 The eyes of the LORD *are* upon the righteous, and his ears *are open* unto

their cry. 16 The face of the LORD *is* against them that do evil, to cut off the remembrance of them from the earth. 17 *The righteous* cry, and the LORD heareth, and delivereth them out of all their troubles. 18 The LORD *is* nigh unto them that are of a broken heart ; and saveth such as be of a contrite spirit. 19 Many *are* the afflictions of the righteous : but the LORD delivereth him out of them all. 20 He keepeth all his bones: not one of them is broken. 21 Evil shall slay the wicked : and they that hate the righteous shall be desolate. 22 The LORD redeemeth the soul of his servants : and none of them that trust in him shall be desolate.

David, in this latter part of the psalm, undertakes to teach children. Though a man of war, and anointed to be king, he did not think it below him; though now he had his head so full of cares and his hands of business, yet he could find heart and time to give good counsel to young people, from his own experience. It does not appear that he had now any children of his own, at least any that were grown up to a capacity of being taught; but, by divine inspiration, he instructs the children of his people. Those that were in years would not be taught by him, though he had offered them his service (xxxii. 8) ; but he has hopes that the tender branches will be more easily bent and that children and young people will be more tractable, and therefore he calls together a congregation of them (*v.* 11): "*Come, you children,* that are now in your learning age, and are now to lay up a stock of knowledge which you must live upon all your days, you children that are foolish and ignorant, and need to be taught." Perhaps he intends especially those children whose parents neglected to instruct and catechise them ; and it is as great a piece of charity to put those children to school whose parents are not in a capacity to teach them as to feed those children whose parents have not bread for them. Observe, 1. What he expects from them : "*Hearken unto me,* leave your play, lay by your toys, and hear what I have to say to you ; not only give me the hearing, but observe and obey me." 2. What he undertakes to teach them—*the fear of the Lord,* inclusive of all the duties of religion. David was a famous musician, a statesman, a soldier ; but he does not say to the children, "I will teach you to play on the harp, or to handle the sword or spear, or to draw the bow, or I will teach you the maxims of state-policy;" but I will teach you *the fear of the Lord,* which is better than all arts and sciences, better than all burnt-offerings and sacrifices. That is it which we should be so-

licitous both to learn ourselves and to teach our children.

I. He supposes that we all aim to be happy (*v.* 12): *What man is he that desireth life?* that is, as it follows, not only to see many days, but to see good comfortable days. *Non est vivere, sed valere, vita*—*It is not being, but well being, that constitutes life.* It is asked, "Who wishes to live a long and pleasant life?" and it is easily answered, *Who does not?* Surely this must look further than time and this present world ; for man's life on earth at best consists but of few days and those full of trouble. What man is he that would be eternally happy, that would see many days, as many as the days of heaven, that would see good in that world where all bliss is in perfection, without the least alloy? Who would see the good before him now, by faith and hope, and enjoy it shortly? Who would? Alas! very few have that in their thoughts. Most ask, *Who will show us any good?* But few ask, *What shall we do to inherit eternal life?* This question implies that there are some such.

II. He prescribes the true and only way to happiness both in this world and that to come, *v.* 13, 14. Would we pass comfortably through the world, and out of the world, our constant care must be to keep a good conscience ; and, in order to that, 1. We must learn to bridle our tongues, and be careful what we say, that we never speak amiss, to God's dishonour or our neighbour's prejudice : *Keep thy tongue from evil speaking, lying, and slandering.* So great a way does this go in religion that, *if any offend not in word, the same is a perfect man;* and so little a way does religion go without this that of him who *bridles not his tongue* it is declared, *His religion is vain.* 2. We must be upright and sincere in every thing we say, and not double-tongued. Our words must be the indications of our minds ; our lips must be kept from speaking guile either to God or man. 3. We must leave all our sins, and resolve we will have no more to do with them. We must *depart from evil,* from evil works and evil workers ; from the sins others commit and which we have formerly allowed ourselves in. 4. It is not enough not to do hurt in the world, but we must study to be useful, and live to some purpose. We must not only depart from evil, but we must *do good,* good for ourselves, especially for our own souls, employing them well, furnishing them with a good treasure, and fitting them for another world; and, as we have ability and opportunity, we must do good to others also. 5. Since nothing is more contrary to that love which never fails (which is the summary both of law and gospel, both of grace and glory) than strife and contention, which bring confusion and every evil work, we must *seek peace and pursue it;* we must show a peaceable disposition, study the things that make for peace, do nothing to break the peace and to make mischief. If peace seem to flee from us, we must pursue it; *follow peace with*

357

all men, spare no pains, no expense, to preserve and recover peace; be willing to deny ourselves a great deal, both in honour and interest, for peace' sake. These excellent directions in the way to life and good are transcribed into the New Testament and made part of our gospel duty, 1 Pet. iii. 10, 11. And perhaps David, in warning us that we speak no guile, reflects upon his own sin in changing his behaviour. Those that truly repent of what they have done amiss will warn others to take heed of doing likewise.

III. He enforces these directions by setting before us the happiness of the godly in the love and favour of God and the miserable state of the wicked under his displeasure. Here are life and death, good and evil, the blessing and the curse, plainly stated before us, that we may choose life and live. See Isa. iii. 10, 11.

1. *Woe to the wicked, it shall be ill with them,* however they may bless themselves in their own way. (1.) God is against them, and then they cannot but be miserable. Sad is the case of that man who by his sin has made his Maker his enemy, his destroyer. *The face of the Lord is against those that do evil, v.* 16. Sometimes God is said to *turn his face from them* (Jer. xviii. 17), because they have forsaken him; here he is said to *set his face against them,* because they have fought against him; and most certainly God is able to out-face the most proud and daring sinners and can frown them into hell. (2.) Ruin is before them; this will follow of course if God be against them, for he is able both to kill and to cast into hell. [1.] The land of the living shall be no place for them nor theirs. When God sets his face against them he will not only cut them off, but *cut off the remembrance of them;* when they are alive he will bury them in obscurity, when they are dead he will bury them in oblivion. He will root out their posterity, by whom they would be remembered. He will pour disgrace upon their achievements, which they gloried in and for which they thought they should be remembered. It is certain that there is no lasting honour but that which comes from God. [2.] There shall be a sting in their death: *Evil shall slay the wicked, v.* 21. Their death shall be miserable; and so it will certainly be, though they die on a bed of down or on the bed of honour. Death, to them, has a curse in it, and is the king of terrors; to them it is evil, only evil. It is very well observed by Dr. Hammond that the *evil* here, which slays the wicked, is the same word, in the singular number, that is used (*v.* 19) for the afflictions of the righteous, to intimate that godly people have many troubles, and yet they do them no hurt, but are made to work for good to them, for God will deliver them out of them all; whereas wicked people have fewer troubles, fewer evils befal them, perhaps but one, and yet that one may prove their utter ruin. One trouble with a curse in it kills

and slays, and does execution; but many, with a blessing in them, are harmless, nay, gainful. [3.] Desolation will be their everlasting portion. Those that are wicked themselves often hate the righteous, name and thing, have an implacable enmity to them and their righteousness; but they *shall be desolate,* shall be condemned as guilty, and laid waste for ever, shall be for ever forsaken and abandoned of God and all good angels and men; and those that are so are desolate indeed.

2. Yet *say to the righteous, It shall be well with them.* All good people are under God's special favour and protection. We are here assured of this under a great variety of instances and expressions.

(1.) God takes special notice of good people, and takes notice who have their eyes ever to him and who make conscience of their duty to him: *The eyes of the Lord are upon the righteous* (*v.* 15), to direct and guide them, to protect and keep them. Parents that are very fond of a child will not let it be out of their sight; none of God's children are ever from under his eye, but on them he looks with a singular complacency, as well as with a watchful and tender concern.

(2.) They are sure of an answer of peace to their prayers. All God's people are a praying people, and they cry in prayer, which denotes great importunity; but is it to any purpose? Yes, [1.] God takes notice of what we say (*v.* 17): They *cry, and the Lord hears them,* and hears them so as to make it appear he has a regard to them. *His ears are open to their prayers,* to receive them all, and to receive them readily and with delight. Though he has been a God hearing prayer ever since men began to call upon the name of the Lord, yet his ear is not heavy. There is no rhetoric, nothing charming, in a cry, yet God's ears are open to it, as the tender mother's to the cry of her sucking child, which another would take no notice of: *The righteous cry, and the Lord heareth, v.* 17. This intimates that it is the constant practice of good people, when they are in distress, to cry unto God, and it is their constant comfort that God hears them. [2.] He not only takes notice of what we say, but is ready to us for our relief (*v.* 18): *He is nigh to those that are of a broken heart, and saves them.* Note, *First,* It is the character of the righteous, whose prayers God will hear, that they are of a broken heart and a contrite spirit (that is, humbled for sin and emptied of self); they are low in their own eyes, and have no confidence in their own merit and sufficiency, but in God only. *Secondly,* Those who are so have God nigh unto them, to comfort and support them, that the spirit may not be broken more than is meet, lest it should fail before him. See Isa. lvii. 15. Though God is high, and dwells on high, yet he is near to those who, being of a contrite spirit, know how to value his favour, and will save them from sinking under their burdens; he is near them to good purpose.

(3.) They are taken under the special protection of the divine government (*v.* 20): *He keepeth all his bones ;* not only his soul, but his body; not only his body in general, but every bone in it: *Not one of them is broken.* He that has a broken heart shall not have a broken bone; for David himself had found that, when he had a contrite heart, the *broken bones* were *made to rejoice,* li. 8, 17. One would not expect to meet with any thing of Christ here, and yet this scripture is said to be fulfilled in him (John xix. 36) when the soldiers broke the legs of the two thieves that were crucified with him, but did not break his, they being under the protection of this promise as well as of the type, even the paschal-lamb *(a bone of him shall not be broken) ;* the promises, being made good to Christ, through him are sure to all the seed. It does not follow but that a good man may have a broken bone; but, by the watchful providence of God concerning him, such a calamity is often wonderfully prevented, and the preservation of his bones is the effect of this promise; and, if he have a broken bone, sooner or later it shall be made whole, at furthest at the resurrection, when that which is sown in weakness shall be raised in power.

(4.) They are, and shall be, delivered out of their troubles. [1.] It is supposed that they have their share of crosses in this world, perhaps a greater share than others. In the world they must have tribulation, that they may be conformed both to the will of God and to the example of Christ (*v.* 19): *Many are the afflictions of the righteous,* witness David and his afflictions, cxxxii. 1. There are those that hate them (*v.* 21) and they are continually aiming to do them a mischief; their God loves them, and therefore corrects them; so that, between the mercy of heaven and the malice of hell, the afflictions of the righteous must needs be many. [2.] God has engaged for their deliverance and salvation: *He delivers them out of all their troubles* (*v.* 17, 19); he saves them (*v.* 18), so that, though they may fall into trouble, it shall not be their ruin. This promise of their deliverance is explained, *v.* 22. Whatever troubles befal them, *First,* They shall not hurt their better part. *The Lord redeemeth the soul of his servants* from the power of the grave (xlix. 15) and from the sting of every affliction. He keeps them from sinning in their troubles, which is the only thing that would do them a mischief, and keeps them from despair, and from being put out of the possession of their own souls. *Secondly,* They shall not hinder their everlasting bliss. *None of those that trust in him shall be desolate ;* that is, they shall not be comfortless, for they shall not be cut off from their communion with God. No man is desolate but he whom God has forsaken, nor is any man undone till he is in hell. Those that are God's faithful servants, that make it their care to please him and their business to honour him,

and in doing so trust him to protect and reward them, and, with good thoughts of him, refer themselves to him, have reason to be easy whatever befals them, for they are safe and shall be happy.

In singing these verses let us be confirmed in the choice we have made of the ways of God; let us be quickened in his service, and greatly encouraged by the assurances he has given of the particular care he takes of all those that faithfully adhere to him.

PSALM XXXV.

David, in this psalm, appeals to the righteous Judge of heaven and earth against his enemies that hated and persecuted him. It is supposed that Saul and his party are the persons he means, for with them he had the greatest struggles. I. He complains to God of the injuries they did him ; they strove with him, fought against him (ver. 1), persecuted him (ver. 3), sought his ruin (ver. 4, 7), accused him falsely (ver. 11), abused him basely (ver. 15, 16), and all his friends (ver. 20), and triumphed over him, ver. 21, 25, 26. II. He pleads his own innocency, that he never gave them any provocation (ver. 7, 19), but, on the contrary, had studied to oblige them, ver. 12—14. III. He prays to God to protect and defend him, and appear for him (ver. 1, 2), to comfort him (ver. 3), to be nigh to him and rescue him (ver. 17, 22), to plead his cause (ver. 23, 24), to defeat all the designs of his enemies against him (ver. 3, 4), to disappoint their expectations of his fall (ver. 19, 25, 26), and, lastly, to countenance all his friends, and encourage them, ver. 27. IV. He prophesies the destruction of his persecutors, ver. 4—6, 8 V. He promises himself that he shall yet see better days (ver. 9, 10), and promises God that he will then attend him with his praises, ver 18, 28. In singing this psalm, and praying over it, we must take heed of applying it to any little peevish quarrels and enmities of our own, and of expressing by it any uncharitable revengeful resentments of injuries done to us ; for Christ has taught us to forgive our enemies and not to pray against them, but to pray for them, as he did ; but, 1. We may comfort ourselves with the testimony of our consciences concerning our innocency, with reference to those that are any way injurious to us, and with hopes that God will, in his own way and time, right us, and, in the mean time, support us. 2. We ought to apply it to the public enemies of Christ and his kingdom, typified by David and his kingdom, to resent the indignities done to Christ's honour, to pray to God to plead the just and injured cause of Christianity and serious godliness, and to believe that God will, in due time, glorify his own name in the ruin of all the irreconcilable enemies of his church, that will not repent to give him glory.

A psalm of David.

PLEAD *my cause,* O LORD, with them that strive with me : fight against them that fight against me. 2 Take hold of shield and buckler, and stand up for mine help. 3 Draw out also the spear, and stop *the way* against them that persecute me : say unto my soul, I *am* thy salvation. 4 Let them be confounded and put to shame that seek after my soul : let them be turned back and brought to confusion that devise my hurt. 5 Let them be as chaff before the wind : and let the angel of the LORD chase *them.* 6 Let their way be dark and slippery : and let the angel of the LORD persecute them. 7 For without cause have they hid for me their net *in* a pit, *which* without cause they have digged for my soul. 8 Let destruction come upon him at unawares ; and let his net that he hath hid catch himself : into that very destruction let him fall. 9 And my soul shall be joyful in the LORD : it shall rejoice in his salvation. 10

All my bones shall say, Lord, who *is* like unto thee, which deliverest the poor from him that is too strong for him, yea, the poor and the needy from him that spoileth him ?

In these verses we have,

I. David's representation of his case to God, setting forth the restless rage and malice of his persecutors. He was God's servant, expressly appointed by him to be what he was, followed his guidance, and aimed at his glory in the way of duty, had lived (as St. Paul speaks) *in all good conscience before God unto this day ;* and yet there were those that strove with him, that did their utmost to oppose his advancement, and made all the interest they could against him ; they fought against him (*v.* 1), not only undermined him closely and secretly, but openly avowed their opposition to him and set themselves to do him all the mischief they could. They persecuted him with an unwearied enmity, *sought after his soul* (*v.* 4), that is, his life, no less would satisfy their bloody minds ; they aimed to disquiet his spirit and put that into disorder. Nor was it a sudden passion against him that they harboured, but inveterate malice : They *devised his hurt*, laid their heads together, and set their wits on work, not only to do him a mischief, but to find out ways and means to ruin him. They treated him, who was the greatest blessing of his country, as if he had been the curse and plague of it ; they hunted him as a dangerous beast of prey ; they digged a pit for him and laid a net in it, that they might have him at their mercy, *v.* 7. They took a great deal of pains in persecuting him, for they digged a pit (vii. 15); and very close and crafty they were in carrying on their designs ; the old serpent taught them subtlety : they hid their net from David and his friends ; but in vain, for they could not hide it from God. And, *lastly,* he found himself an unequal match for them. His enemy, especially Saul, was *too strong for him* (*v.* 10), for he had the army at his command, and assumed to himself the sole power of making laws and giving judgment, attainted and condemned whom he pleased, carried not a sceptre, but a javelin, in his hand, to cast at any man that stood in his way ; such was the manner of the king, and all about him were compelled to do as he bade them, right or wrong. The king's word is a law, and every thing must be carried with a high hand ; he has fields, and vineyards, and preferments, at his disposal, 1 Sam. xxii. 7. But David is poor and needy, has nothing to make friends with, and therefore has none to take his part but men (as we say) of broken fortunes (1 Sam. xxii. 2) ; and therefore no marvel that Saul spoiled him of what little he had got and the interest he had made. If the kings of the earth set themselves against the Lord and his anointed, who can contend with them ? Note, It is no new thing for the most righteous men, and the most righteous cause, to meet with many mighty and malicious enemies : Christ himself is striven with and fought against, and war is made upon the holy seed ; and we are not to marvel at the matter : it is a fruit of the old enmity in the seed of the serpent against the seed of the woman.

II. His appeal to God concerning his integrity and the justice of his cause. If a fellow-subject had wronged him, he might have appealed to his prince, as St. Paul did to Cæsar ; but, when his prince wronged him, he appealed to his God, who is prince and Judge of the kings of the earth : *Plead my cause, O Lord! v.* 1. Note, A righteous cause may, with the greatest satisfaction imaginable, be laid before a righteous God, and referred to him to give judgment upon it; for he perfectly knows the merits of it, holds the balance exactly even, and with him there is no respect of persons. God knew that they were, without cause, his enemies, and that they had, without cause, digged pits for him, *v.* 7. Note, It will be a comfort to us, when men do us wrong, if our consciences can witness for us that we have never done them any. It was so to St. Paul. Acts xxv. 10, *To the Jews have I done no wrong.* We are apt to justify our uneasiness at the injuries men do us by this, That we never gave them any cause to use us so ; whereas this should, more than any thing, make us easy, for then we may the more confidently expect that God will plead our cause.

III. His prayer to God to manifest himself both for him and to him, in this trial. 1. For him. He prays that God would *fight against* his enemies, so as to disable them to hurt him, and defeat their designs against him (*v.* 1), that he would *take hold of shield and buckler*, for the Lord is a man of war (Exod. xv. 3), *and* that he would *stand up for his help* (*v.* 2), for he had few that would stand up for him, and, if he had ever so many, they would stand him in no stead without God. He prays that God would *stop their way* (*v.* 3), that they might not overtake him when he fled from them. This prayer we may put up against our persecutors, that God would restrain them and stop their way. 2. To him : *" Say unto my soul, I am thy salvation;* let me have inward comfort under all these outward troubles, to support my soul which they strike at. Let God be my salvation, not only my Saviour out of my present troubles, but my everlasting bliss. Let me have that salvation not only which he is the author of, but which consists in his favour ; and let me know my interest in it ; let me have the comfortable assurance of it in my own breast."

If God, by his Spirit, witness to our spirits that he is our salvation, we have enough, need desire no more to make us happy ; and this is a powerful support when men persecute us. If God be our friend, no matter who is our enemy.

IV. His prospect of the destruction of his enemies, which he prays for, not in malice or revenge. We find how patiently he bore Shimei's curses *(so let him curse, for the Lord has bidden him)* ; and we cannot suppose that he who was so meek in his conversation would give vent to any intemperate heat or passion in his devotion; but, by the spirit of prophecy, he foretells the just judgments of God that would come upon them for their great wickedness, their malice, cruelty, and perfidiousness, and especially their enmity to the counsels of God, the interests of religion, and that reformation which they knew David, if ever he had power in his hand, would be an instrument of. They seemed to be hardened in their sins, and to be of the number of those who have sinned unto death and are not to be prayed for, Jer. vii. 16; xi. 14; xiv. 11; 1 John v. 16. As for Saul himself, David, it is probable, knew that God had rejected him and had forbidden Samuel to mourn for him, 1 Sam. xvi. 1. And these predictions look further, and read the doom of the enemies of Christ and his kingdom, as appears by comparing Rom. xi. 9, 10. David here prays, 1. Against his many enemies (*v.* 4—6): *Let them be confounded,* &c. Or, as Dr. Hammond reads it, *They shall be confounded, they shall be turned back.* This may be taken as a prayer for their repentance, for all penitents are put to shame for their sins and turned back from them. Or, if they were not brought to repentance, David prays that they might be defeated and disappointed in their designs against him and so put to shame. Though they should in some degree prevail, yet he foresees that it would be to their own ruin at last: *They shall be as chaff before the wind,* so unable will wicked men be to stand before the judgments of God and so certainly will they be driven away by them, i. 4. Their way shall be *dark and slippery, darkness and slipperiness* (so the margin reads it); the way of sinners is so, for they walk in darkness and in continual danger of falling into sin, into hell; and it will prove so at last, for *their foot shall slide in due time,* Deut. xxxii. 35. But this is not the worst of it. Even chaff before the wind may perhaps be stopped, and find a place of rest, and, though the way be dark and slippery, it is possible that a man may keep his footing; but it is here foretold that the *angel of the Lord shall chase them* (*v.* 5) so that they shall find no rest, *shall persecute them* (*v.* 6) so that they cannot possibly escape the pit of destruction. As God's angels encamp about those that fear him, so they encamp against those that fight against him. They are the ministers of his justice, as well as of his mercy. Those that make God their enemy make all the holy angels their enemies. 2. Against his one mighty enemy (*v.* 8): *Let destruction come upon him.* It is probable that he means Saul, who laid snares for him and aimed at his destruction. David vowed

that his hand should not be upon him; he would not be judge in his own cause. But, at the same time, he foretold that *the Lord would smite him* (1 Sam. xxvi. 10), and here that the net he had hidden should catch himself, and into *that very destruction he should fall.* This was remarkably fulfilled in the ruin of Saul; for he had laid a plot to make David *fall by the hand of the Philistines* (1 Sam. xviii. 25), that was the net which he hid for him under pretence of doing him honour, and in that very net was he himself taken, for he fell by the hand of the Philistines when his day came to fall.

V. His prospect of his own deliverance, which, having committed his cause to God, he did not doubt of, *v.* 9, 10. 1. He hoped that he should have the comfort of it: " *My soul shall be joyful,* not in my own ease and safety, but *in the Lord* and in his favour, in his promise and *in his salvation* according to the promise." Joy in God and in his salvation is the only true, solid, satisfying joy. Those whose souls are sorrowful in the Lord, who sow in tears and sorrow after a godly sort, need not question but that in due time their souls shall be joyful in the Lord; for gladness is sown for them, and they shall at last *enter into the joy of their Lord.* 2. He promised that then God should have the glory of it (*v.* 10): *All my bones shall say, Lord, who is like unto thee?* (1.) He will praise God with the whole man, with all that is within him, and with all the strength and vigour of his soul, intimated by his bones, which are within the body and are the strength of it. (2.) He will praise him as one of peerless and unparalleled perfection. We cannot express how great and good God is, and therefore must praise him by acknowledging him to be a non-such. *Lord, who is like unto thee?* No such patron of oppressed innocency, no such punisher of triumphant tyranny. The formation of our bones so wonderfully, so curiously (Eccl. xi. 5, Ps. cxxxix. 16), the serviceableness of our bones, and the preservation of them, and especially the life which, at the resurrection, shall be breathed upon the dry bones and make them flourish as a herb, oblige every bone in our bodies, if it could speak, to say, Lord, *who is like unto thee?* and willingly to undergo any services or sufferings for him.

11 False witnesses did rise up; they laid to my charge *things* that I knew not. 12 They rewarded me evil for good *to* the spoiling of my soul. 13 But as for me, when they were sick, my clothing *was* sackcloth: I humbled my soul with fasting; and my prayer returned into mine own bosom. 14 I behaved myself as though *he had been* my friend *or* brother: I bowed down heavily, as one that mourneth

for his mother. 15 But in mine adversity they rejoiced, and gathered themselves together : *yea,* the abjects gathered themselves together against me, and I knew *it* not; they did tear *me,* and ceased not : 16 With hypocritical mockers in feasts, they gnashed upon me with their teeth.

Two very wicked things David here lays to the charge of his enemies, to make good his appeal to God against them—perjury and ingratitude.

I. Perjury, *v.* 11. When Saul would have David attainted of treason, in order to his being outlawed, perhaps he did it with the formalities of a legal prosecution, produced witnesses who swore some treasonable words or overt acts against him, and he being not present to clear himself (or, if he was, it was all the same), Saul adjudged him a traitor. This he complains of here as the highest piece of injustice imaginable : *False witnesses did rise up*, who would swear any thing; *they laid to my charge things that I knew not,* nor ever thought of. See how much the honours, estates, liberties, and lives, even of the best men, lie at the mercy of the worst, against whose false oaths innocency itself is no fence; and what reason we have to acknowledge with thankfulness the hold God has of the consciences even of bad men, to which it is owing that there is not more mischief done in that way than is. This instance of the wrong done to David was typical, and had its accomplishment in the Son of David, against whom false witnesses did arise, Matt. xxvi. 60. If we be at any time charged with what we are innocent of let us not think it strange, as though some new thing happened to us; so persecuted they the prophets, even the great prophet.

II. Ingratitude. Call a man ungrateful and you can call him no worse. This was the character of David's enemies (*v.* 12): *They rewarded me evil for good.* A great deal of good service he had done to his king, witness his harp, witness Goliath's sword, witness the foreskins of the Philistines; and yet his king vowed his death, and his country was made too hot for him. This is *to the spoiling of his soul ;* this base unkind usage robs him of his comfort, and cuts him to the heart, more than any thing else. Nay, he had deserved well not only of the public in general, but of those particular persons that were now most bitter against him. Probably it was then well known whom he meant; it may be Saul himself for one, whom he was sent for to attend upon when he was melancholy and ill, and to whom he was serviceable to drive away the evil spirit, not with his harp, but with his prayers; to others of the courtiers, it is likely, he had shown this respect, while he lived at court, who now were, of all others, most abusive to him. Herein he was a type

of Christ, to whom this wicked world was very ungrateful. John x. 32, *Many good works have I shown you from my Father; for which of those do you stone me ?* David here shows,

1. How tenderly, and with what a cordial affection, he had behaved towards them in their afflictions (*v.* 13, 14): *They were sick.* Note, Even the palaces and courts of princes are not exempt from the jurisdiction of death and the visitation of sickness. Now when these people were sick, (1.) David mourned for them and sympathized with them in their grief. They were not related to him; he was under no obligations to them; he would lose nothing by their death, but perhaps be a gainer by it; and yet he behaved himself as though they had been his nearest relations, purely from a principle of compassion and humanity. David was a man of war, and of a bold stout spirit, and yet was thus susceptible of the impressions of sympathy, forgot the bravery of the hero, and seemed wholly made up of love and pity ; it was a rare composition of hardiness and tenderness, courage and compassion, in the same breast. Observe, He mourned as for a brother or mother, which intimates that it is our duty, and well becomes us, to lay to heart the sickness, and sorrow, and death of our near relations. Those that do not are justly stigmatized as without natural affection. (2.) He prayed for them. He discovered not only the tender affection of a man, but the pious affection of a saint. He was concerned for their precious souls, and, since he could not otherwise be helpful to them, he helped them with his prayers to God for mercy and grace; and the prayers of one who had so great an interest in heaven were of more value than perhaps they knew and considered. With his prayers he joined humiliation and self-affliction, both in his diet (he fasted, at least from pleasant bread) and in his dress; he clothed himself with sackcloth, thus expressing his grief, not only for / their affliction, but for their sin; for this was the guise and practice of a penitent. We ought to mourn for the sins of those that do not mourn for them themselves. His fasting also put an edge upon his praying, and was an expression of the fervour of it; he was so intent in his devotions that he had no appetite to meat, nor would allow himself time for eating : " *My prayer returned into my own bosom ;* I had the comfort of having done my duty, and of having approved myself a loving neighbour, though I could not thereby win upon them nor make them my friends." We shall not lose by the good offices we have done to any, how ungrateful soever they are; for our rejoicing will be this, *the testimony of our conscience.*

2. How basely and insolently and with what a brutish enmity, and worse than brutish, they had behaved towards him (*v.* 15, 16): *In my adversity they rejoiced.* When he fell under the frowns of Saul, was banished the court, and persecuted as a criminal, they were

pleased, were glad at his calamities, and got together in their drunken clubs to make themselves and one another merry with the disgrace of this great favourite. Well might he call them *abjects*, for nothing could be more vile and sordid than to triumph in the fall of a man of such unstained honour and consummate virtue. But this was not all. (1.) They tore him, rent his good name without mercy, said all the ill they could of him and fastened upon him all the reproach their cursed wit and malice could reach to. (2.) *They gnashed upon him with their teeth ;* they never spoke of him but with the greatest indignation imaginable, as those that would have eaten him up if they could. David was the fool in the play, and his disappointment all the table-talk of the hypocritical mockers at feasts; it was the song of the drunkards. The comedians, who may fitly be called *hypocritical mockers* (for what does a hypocrite signify but a stage-player?) and whose comedies, it is likely, were acted at feasts and balls, chose David for their subject, bantered and abused him, while the auditory, in token of their agreement with the plot, hummed, and *gnashed upon him with their teeth.* Such has often been the hard fate of the best of men. The apostles were made a spectacle to the world. David was looked upon with illwill for no other reason than because he was caressed by the people. It is a vexation of spirit which attends even a right work that *for this a man is envied of his neighbour,* Eccl. iv. 4. And *who can stand before envy?* Prov. xxvii. 4.

17 Lord, how long wilt thou look on? rescue my soul from their destructions, my darling from the lions. 18 I will give thee thanks in the great congregation: I will praise thee among much people. 19 Let not them that are mine enemies wrongfully rejoice over me: *neither* let them wink with the eye that hate me without a cause. 20 For they speak not peace: but they devise deceitful matters against *them that are* quiet in the land. 21 Yea, they opened their mouth wide against me, *and* said, Aha, aha, our eye hath seen *it.* 22 *This* thou hast seen, O Lord: keep not silence: O Lord, be not far from me. 23 Stir up thyself, and awake to my judgment, *even* unto my cause, my God and my Lord. 24 Judge me, O Lord my God, according to thy righteousness; and let them not rejoice over me. 25 Let them not say in their hearts, Ah, so would we have it: let them not say, We have swallowed him up. 26 Let

them be ashamed and brought to confusion together that rejoice at mine hurt: let them be clothed with shame and dishonour that magnify *themselves* against me. 27 Let them shout for joy, and be glad, that favour my righteous cause: yea, let them say continually, Let the Lord be magnified, which hath pleasure in the prosperity of his servant. 28 And my tongue shall speak of thy righteousness *and* of thy praise all the day long.

In these verses, as before,

I. David describes the great injustice, malice, and insolence, of his persecutors, pleading this with God as a reason why he should protect him from them and appear against them. 1. They were very unrighteous; they were his enemies wrongfully, for he never gave them any provocation: *They hated him without a cause ;* nay, for that for which they ought rather to have loved and honoured him. This is quoted, with application to Christ, and is said to be fulfilled in him. John xv. 25, *They hated me without cause.* 2. They were very rude; they could not find in their hearts to show him common civility: *They speak not peace ;* if they met him, they had not the good manners to give him the time of the day; like Joseph's brethren, that could not *speak peaceably to him,* Gen xxxvii. 4. 3. They were very proud and scornful (*v.* 21): *They opened their mouth wide against me ;* they shouted and huzzaed when they saw his fall; they bawled after him when he was forced to quit the court, "Aha! aha! this is the day we longed to see." 4. They were very barbarous and base, for they trampled upon him when he was down, rejoiced at his hurt, and *magnified themselves against him, v.* 26. *Turba Remi sequitur fortunam, ut semper, et odit damnatos—The Roman crowd, varying their opinions with every turn of fortune, are sure to execrate the fallen.* Thus, when the Son of David was run upon by the rulers, the people cried, *Crucify him, crucify him.* 5. They set themselves against all the sober good people that adhered to David (*v.* 20): *They devised deceitful matters,* to trepan and ruin *those that were quiet in the land.* Note, (1.) It is the character of the godly in the land that they are the quiet in the land, that they live in all dutiful subjection to government and governors, in the Lord, and endeavour, as much as in them lies, to live peaceably with all men, however they may have been misrepresented as enemies to Cæsar and hurtful to kings and provinces. *I am for peace,* cxx. 7. (2.) Though the people of God are, and study to be, a quiet people, yet it has been the common practice of their enemies to devise deceitful matters against them. All the hellish arts of malice and falsehood are made use of to render them odious or despicable; their words and actions are misconstrued, even that which they abhor is fathered upon them, laws are made to ensnare them (Dan. vi. 4, &c.), and all to ruin them and root them out. Those that hated David thought scorn, like Haman, to lay hands on him alone, but contrived to involve all the religious people of the land in the same ruin with him.

2. He appeals to God against them, the *God to whom vengeance belongs*, appeals to his knowledge (v. 22): *This thou hast seen.* They had falsely accused him, but God, who knows all things, knew that he did not falsely accuse them, nor make them worse than really they were. They had carried on their plots against him with a great degree of secresy (v. 15): "I knew it not, till long after, when they themselves gloried in it; but thy eye was upon them in their close cabals and thou art a witness of all they have said and done against me and thy people." He appeals to God's justice: *Awake to my judgment, even to my cause*, and let it have a hearing at thy bar, v. 23. "*Judge me, O Lord my God!* pass sentence upon this appeal, *according to the righteousness* of thy nature and government," v. 24. See this explained by Solomon, 1 Kings viii. 31, 32. When thou art appealed to, *hear in heaven, and judge, by condemning the wicked and justifying the righteous.*

III. He prays earnestly to God to appear graciously for him and his friends, against his and their enemies, that by his providence the struggle might issue to the honour and comfort of David and to the conviction and confusion of his persecutors. 1. He prays that God would act for him, and not stand by as a spectator (v. 17): "*Lord, how long wilt thou look on?* How long wilt thou connive at the wickedness of the wicked? *Rescue my soul from the destructions* they are plotting against it; rescue *my darling*, my only one, *from the lions.* My soul is my only one, and therefore the greater is the shame if I neglect it and the greater the loss if I lose it: it is my only one, and therefore ought to be my darling, ought to be carefully protected and provided for. It is my soul that is in danger; Lord, rescue it. It does, in a peculiar manner, belong to the Father of spirits, therefore claim thy own; it is thine, save it. *Lord, keep not silence*, as if thou didst consent to what is done against me! *Lord, be not far from me* (v. 22), as if I were a stranger that thou wert not concerned for; let not me be beheld afar off, as the proud are." 2. He prays that his enemies might not have cause to rejoice (v. 19): *Let them not rejoice over me* (and again, v. 24); not so much because it would be a mortification to him to be trampled upon by the abjects, as because it would turn to the dishonour of God and the reproach of his confidence in God. It would harden the hearts of his enemies in their wickedness and confirm them

in their enmity to him, and would be a great discouragement to all the pious Jews that were friends to his righteous cause. He prays that he might never be in such imminent danger as that they should *say in their hearts, Ah! so would we have it* (v. 25), much more that he might not be reduced to such extremity that they should say, *We have swallowed him up;* for then they will reflect upon God himself. But, on the contrary, that they might be *ashamed and brought to confusion together* (v. 26, as before, v. 4); he desires that his innocency might be so cleared that they might be ashamed of the calumnies with which they had loaded him, that his interest might be so confirmed that they might be ashamed of their designs against him and their expectations of his ruin, that they might either be brought to that shame which would be a step towards their reformation or that that might be their portion which would be their everlasting misery. 3. He prays that his friends might have cause to rejoice and give glory to God, v. 27. Notwithstanding the arts that were used to blacken David, and make him odious, and to frighten people from owning him, there were some that favoured his righteous cause, that knew he was wronged and bore a good affection to him; and he prays for them, (1.) That they might rejoice with him in his joys. It is a great pleasure to all that are good to see an honest man, and an honest cause, prevail and prosper; and those that heartily espouse the interests of God's people, and are willing to take their lot with them even when they are run down and trampled upon, shall in due time shout for joy and be glad, for the righteous cause will at length be a victorious cause. (2.) That they might join with him in his praises: *Let them say continually, The Lord be magnified*, by us and others, *who hath pleasure in the prosperity of his servant.* Note, [1.] The great God has pleasure in the prosperity of good people, not only of his family, the church in general, but of every particular servant in his family. He has pleasure in the prosperity both of their temporal and of their spiritual affairs, and delights not in their griefs; for he does not afflict willingly; and we ought therefore to have pleasure in their prosperity, and not to envy it. [2.] When God in his providence shows his goodwill to the prosperity of his servants, and the pleasure he takes in it, we ought to acknowledge it with thankfulness, to his praise, and to say, *The Lord be magnified.*

IV. The mercy he hoped to win by prayer he promises to wear with praise: "*I will give thee thanks*, as the author of my deliverance (v. 18), *and my tongue shall speak of thy righteousness*, the justice of thy judgments and the equity of all thy dispensations;" and this, 1. Publicly, as one that took a pleasure in owning his obligations to his God, so far was he from being ashamed of them. He will do it in the great congregation, and among much people, that God might be honoured and many edified. 2. Constantly. He will speak God's praise *every day* (so it may be read) and *all the day long ;* for it is a subject that will never be exhausted, no, not by the endless praises of saints and angels.

PSALM XXXVI.

It is uncertain when, and upon what occasion, David penned this psalm, probably when he was struck at either by Saul or by Absalom ; for in it he complains of the malice of his enemies against him, but triumphs in the goodness of God to him. We are here led to consider, and it will do us good to consider seriously, I. The sinfulness of sin, and how mischievous it is, ver. 1—4. II. The goodness of God, and how gracious he is, 1. To all his creatures in general, ver. 5, 6. 2. To his own people in a special manner, ver. 7—9. By this the psalmist is encouraged to pray for all the saints (ver. 10), for himself in particular and his own preservation (ver. 11), and to triumph in the certain fall of his enemies, ver. 12. If, in singing this psalm, our hearts be duly affected with the hatred of sin and satisfaction in God's lovingkindness, we sing it with grace and understanding.

To the chief musician. A psalm of David the servant of the Lord.

THE transgression of the wicked saith within my heart, *that there is* no fear of God before his eyes. 2 For he flattereth himself in his own eyes, until his iniquity be found to be hateful. 3 The words of his mouth *are* iniquity and deceit : he hath left off to be wise, *and* to do good. 4 He deviseth mischief upon his bed ; he setteth himself in a way *that is* not good ; he abhorreth not evil.

David, in the title of this psalm, is styled *the servant of the Lord ;* why in this, and not in any other, except in xviii. *(title),* no reason can be given ; but so he was, not only as every good man is God's servant, but as a king, as a prophet, as one employed in serving the interests of God's kingdom among men more immediately and more eminently than any other in his day. He glories in it, cxvi. 16. It is no disparagement, but an honour, to the greatest of men, to be the servants of the great God ; it is the highest preferment a man is capable of in this world.

David, in these verses, describes the wickedness of the wicked ; whether he means his persecutors in particular, or all notorious gross sinners in general, is not certain. But we have here sin in its causes and sin in its colours, in its root and in its branches.

I. Here is the root of bitterness, from which all the wickedness of the wicked comes. It takes rise, 1. From their contempt of God and the want of a due regard to him (*v.* 1) : " *The transgression of the wicked* (as it is described afterwards, *v.* 3, 4) *saith within my heart* (makes me to conclude within myself) *that there is no fear of God before his eyes ;* for, if there were, he would not talk and act so extravagantly as he does ; he would not, he durst not, break the laws of God, and violate his covenants with him, if he had any awe of his majesty or dread of his wrath." Fitly therefore is it brought into the form of indictments by our law that the criminal, *not having the fear of God before his eyes,* did so

and so. The wicked did not openly renounce the fear of God, but their transgression whispered it secretly into the minds of all those that knew any thing of the nature of piety and impiety. David concluded concerning those who lived at large that they lived without God in the world. 2. From their conceit of themselves and a cheat they wilfully put upon their own souls (*v.* 2) : *He flattereth himself in his own eyes ;* that is, while he goes on in sin he thinks he does wisely and well for himself, and either does not see or will not own the evil and danger of his wicked practices ; he calls evil good and good evil ; his licentiousness he pretends to be but his just liberty, his fraud passes for his prudence and policy, and his persecuting the people of God, he suggests to himself, is a piece of necessary justice. If his own conscience threaten him for what he does, he says, *God will not require it ; I shall have peace though I go on.* Note, Sinners are self-destroyers, by being self-flatterers. Satan could not deceive them if they did not deceive themselves. But will the cheat last always ? No ; the day is coming when the sinner will be undeceived, when *his iniquity shall be found to be hateful.* Iniquity is a hateful thing ; it is that *abominable thing which the Lord hates,* and which his pure and jealous eye cannot endure to look upon. It is hurtful to the sinner himself, and therefore ought to be hateful to him ; but it is not so ; he rolls it under his tongue as a sweet morsel, because of the secular profit and sensual pleasure which may attend it ; yet *the meat in his bowels will be turned, it will be the gall of asps,* Job xx. 13, 14. When their consciences are convinced, and sin appears in its true colours and makes them a terror to themselves —when the cup of trembling is put into their hands and they are made to drink the dregs of it—then their iniquity will be found hateful, and their self-flattery their unspeakable folly, and an aggravation of their condemnation.

II. Here are the cursed branches which spring from this root of bitterness. The sinner defies God, and even deifies himself, and then what can be expected but that he should go all to naught ? These two were the first inlets of sin. Men do not fear God, and therefore they flatter themselves, and then, 1. They make no conscience of what they say, true or false, right or wrong (*v.* 3) : *The words of his mouth are iniquity and deceit,* contrived to do wrong, and yet to cover it with specious and plausible pretences. It is no marvel if those that deceive themselves contrive how to deceive all mankind ; for to whom will those be true who are false to their own souls ? 2. What little good there has been in them is gone ; the sparks of virtue are extinguished, their convictions baffled, their good beginnings come to nothing : They have *left off to be wise and to do good.* They seemed to be under the direction of wisdom and the government of religion, but they have broken these bonds asunder ; they have shaken off their religion, and therewith their wisdom. Note, Those that leave off to do good leave off to be wise. 3. Having left off to do good, they contrive to do hurt and to be vexatious to those about them that are good and do good (*v.* 4): *He devises mischief upon his bed.* Note,(1.) Omissions make way for commissions. When men leave off doing good, leave off praying, leave off their attendance on God's ordinances and their duty to him, the devil easily makes them his agents, his instruments to draw those that will be drawn into sin, and, with respect to those that will not, to draw them into trouble. Those that leave off to do good begin to do evil; the devil, being an apostate from his innocency, soon became a tempter to Eve and a persecutor of righteous Abel. (2.) It is bad to do mischief, but it is worse to devise it, to do it deliberately and with resolution, to set the wits on work to contrive to do it most effectually, to do it with plot and management, with the subtlety, as well as the malice, of the old serpent, to devise it upon the bed, where we should be meditating upon God and his word, Mic. ii. 1. This argues the sinner's heart fully set in him to do evil. 4. Having entered into the way of sin, that way that is not good, that has good neither in it nor at the end of it, they persist and resolve to persevere in that way. *He sets himself* to execute the mischief he has devised, and nothing shall be withholden from him which he has purposed to do, though it be ever so contrary both to his duty and to his true interest. If sinners did not steel their hearts and brazen their faces with obstinacy and impudence, they could not go on in their evil ways, in such a direct opposition to all that is just and good. 5. Doing evil themselves, they have no dislike at all of it in others: *He abhors not evil*, but, on the contrary, takes pleasure in it, and is glad to see others as bad as himself. Or this may denote his impenitency in sin. Those that have done evil, if God give them repentance, abhor the evil they have done and themselves because of it; it is bitter in the reflection, however sweet it was in the commission. But these hardened sinners have such seared stupified consciences that they never reflect upon their sins afterwards with any regret or remorse, but stand to what they have done, as if they could justify it before God himself.

Some think that David, in all this, particularly means Saul, who had cast off the fear of God and left off all goodness, who pretended kindness to him when he gave him his daughter to wife, but at the same time was devising mischief against him. But we are under no necessity of limiting ourselves so in the exposition of it; there are too many among us to whom the description agrees, which is to be greatly lamented.

5 Thy mercy, O LORD, *is* in the heavens; *and* thy faithfulness *reacheth* unto the clouds. 6 Thy righteous-

366

ness *is* like the great mountains; thy judgments *are* a great deep: O LORD, thou preservest man and beast. 7 How excellent *is* thy lovingkindness, O God! therefore the children of men put their trust under the shadow of thy wings. 8 They shall be abundantly satisfied with the fatness of thy house; and thou shalt make them drink of the river of thy pleasures. 9 For with thee *is* the fountain of life: in thy light shall we see light. 10 O continue thy lovingkindness unto them that know thee; and thy righteousness to the upright in heart. 11 Let not the foot of pride come against me, and let not the hand of the wicked remove me. 12 There are the workers of iniquity fallen: they are cast down, and shall not be able to rise.

David, having looked round with grief upon the wickedness of the wicked, here looks up with comfort upon the goodness of God, a subject as delightful as the former was distateful and very proper to be set in the balance against it. Observe,

I. His meditations upon the grace of God. He sees the world polluted, himself endangered, and God dishonoured, by the transgressions of the wicked; but, of a sudden, he turns his eye, and heart, and speech, to God "However it be, yet thou art good." He here acknowledges,

1. The transcendent perfections of the divine nature. Among men we have often reason to complain, There is *no truth nor mercy*, (Hos. iv. 1), *no judgment nor justice*, Isa. v. 7. But all these may be found in God without the least alloy. Whatever is missing, or amiss, in the world, we are sure there is nothing missing, nothing amiss, in him that governs it. (1.) He is a God of inexhaustible goodness: *Thy mercy, O Lord! is in the heavens.* If men shut up the bowels of their compassion, yet with God, at the throne of his grace, we shall find mercy. When men are devising mischief against us God's thoughts concerning us, if we cleave closely to him, are thoughts of good. On earth we meet with little content and a great deal of disquiet and disappointment; but in the heavens, where the mercy of God reigns in perfection and to eternity, there is all satisfaction; there therefore, if we would be easy, let us have our conversation, and there let us long to be. How bad soever the world is, let us never think the worse of God nor of his government; but, from the abundance of wickedness that is among men, let us take occasion, instead of reflecting upon God's purity, as if he countenanced sin, to admire his patience, that he bears so much with those that so impudently

provoke him, nay, and causes his sun to shine and his rain to fall upon them. If God's mercy were not in the heavens (that is, infinitely above the mercies of any creature), he would, long ere this, have drowned the world again. See Isa. lv. 8, 9; Hos. xi. 9. (2.) He is a God of inviolable truth: *Thy faithfulness reaches unto the clouds.* Though God suffers wicked people to do a great deal of mischief, yet he is and will be faithful to his threatenings against sin, and there will come a day when he will reckon with them; he is faithful also to his covenant with his people, which cannot be broken, nor one jot or tittle of the promises of it defeated by all the malice of earth and hell. This is matter of great comfort to all good people, that, though men are false, God is faithful; men speak vanity, but the words of the Lord are pure words. God's faithfulness reaches so high that it does not change with the weather, as men's does, for it reaches to the *skies* (so it should be read, as some think), above the clouds, and all the changes of the lower region. (3.) He is a God of incontestable justice and equity : *Thy righteousness is like the great mountains,* so immovable and inflexible itself and so conspicuous and evident to all the world; for no truth is more certain nor more plain than this, That the Lord is righteous in all his ways, and that he never did, nor ever will do, any wrong to any of his creatures. Even *when clouds and darkness are round about him,* yet *judgment and justice are the habitation of his throne,* xcvii. 2. (4.) He is a God of unsearchable wisdom and design : " *Thy judgments are a great deep,* not to be fathomed with the line and plummet of any finite understanding." As his power is sovereign, which he owes not any account of to us, so his method is singular and mysterious, which cannot be accounted for by us: *His way is in the sea and his path in the great waters.* We know that he does all wisely and well; but what he does we know not now; it will be time enough to know hereafter.

2. The extensive care and beneficence of the divine Providence: " *Thou preservest man and beast,* not only protectest them from mischief, but suppliest them with that which is needful for the support of life." The beasts, though not capable of knowing and praising God, are yet graciously provided for; their eyes wait on him, and he gives them their meat in due season. Let us not wonder that God gives food to bad men, for he feeds the brute-creatures; and let us not fear but that he will provide well for good men; he that feeds the young lions will not starve his own children.

3. The peculiar favour of God to the saints. Observe,

(1.) Their character, *v.* 7. They are such as are allured by the *excellency of God's loving-kindness to put their trust under the shadow of his wings.* [1.] God's loving-kindness is precious to them. They relish it; they taste a

transcendent sweetness in it; they admire God's beauty and benignity above any thing in this world, nothing so amiable, so desirable. Those know not God that do not admire his loving-kindness; and those know not themselves that do not earnestly covet it. [2.] They therefore repose an entire confidence in him. They have recourse to him, put themselves under his protection, and then think themselves safe and find themselves easy, as the chickens under the wings of the hen, Matt. xxiii. 37. It was the character of proselytes that they came to *trust under the wings of the God of Israel* (Ruth ii. 12); and what more proper to gather proselytes than the excellency of his loving-kindness ? What more powerful to engage our complacency to him and on him ? Those that are thus drawn by love will cleave to him.

(2.) Their privilege. Happy, thrice happy, the people whose God is the Lord, for in him they have, or may have, or shall have, a complete happiness. [1.] Their desires shall be answered (*v.* 8): *They shall be abundantly satisfied with the fatness of thy house,* their wants supplied, their cravings gratified, and their capacities filled. In God all-sufficient they shall have enough, all that which an enlightened enlarged soul can desire or receive. The gains of the world and the delights of sense will surfeit, but never satisfy, Isa. lv. 2. But the communications of divine favour and grace will satisfy, but never surfeit. A gracious soul, though still desiring more of God, never desires more than God. The gifts of Providence so far satisfy them that they are content with such things as they have. *I have all, and abound,* Phil. iv. 18. The benefit of holy ordinances is the fatness of God's house, sweet to a sanctified soul and strengthening to the spiritual and divine life. With this they are abundantly satisfied; they desire nothing more in this world than to live a life of communion with God and to have the comfort of the promises. But the full, the abundant satisfaction is reserved for the future state, the house not made with hands, eternal in the heavens. Every vessel will be full there. [2.] Their joys shall be constant: *Thou shalt make them drink of the river of thy pleasures.* *First,* There are pleasures that are truly divine. " They are *thy pleasures,* not only which come from thee as the giver of them, but which terminate in thee as the matter and centre of them." Being purely spiritual, they are of the same nature with those of the glorious inhabitants of the upper world, and bear some analogy even to the delights of the Eternal Mind. *Secondly,* There is a river of these pleasures, always full, always fresh, always flowing. There is enough for all, enough for each; see xlvi. 4. The pleasures of sense are putrid puddle-water; those of faith are pure and pleasant, *clear as crystal,* Rev. xxii. 1. *Thirdly,* God has not only provided this river of pleasures for his people, but he makes them to drink of it, works in them a gracious appetite to these pleasures, and by his Spirit fills their souls with joy and peace in believing. In heaven they shall be for ever drinking of those *pleasures that are at God's right hand,* satiated with a *fulness of joy,* xvi. 11. [3.] Life and light shall be their everlasting bliss and portion, *v.* 9. Having God himself for their felicity, *First,* In him they have a fountain of life, from which those rivers of pleasure flow, *v.* 8. The God of nature is the fountain of natural life. In him we live, and move, and have our being. The God of grace is the fountain of spiritual life. All the strength and comfort of a sanctified soul, all its gracious principles, powers, and performances, are from God. He is the spring and author of all its sensations of divine things, and all its motions towards them : he quickens whom he will; and whosoever will may come, and take from him of the waters of life freely. He is the fountain of eternal life. The happiness of glorified saints consists in the vision and fruition of him, and in the immediate communications of his love, without interruption or fear of cessation. *Secondly,* In him they have light in perfection, wisdom, knowledge, and joy, all included in this light : *In thy light we shall see light,* that is, 1. " In the knowledge of thee in grace, and the vision of thee in glory, we shall have that which will abundantly suit and satisfy our understandings." That divine light which shines in the scripture, and especially in the face of Christ, the light of the world, has all truth in it. When we come to see God face to face, within the veil, we shall see light in perfection, we shall know enough then, 1 Cor. xiii. 12 ; 1 John iii. 2. 2. " In communion with thee now; by the communications of thy grace to us and the return of our devout affections to thee, and in the fruition of thee shortly in heaven, we shall have a complete felicity and satisfaction. In thy favour we have all the good we can desire." This is a dark world ; we see little comfort in it ; but in the heavenly light there is true light, and no false light, light that is lasting and never wastes. In this world we see God, and enjoy him by creatures and means ; but in heaven *God himself shall be with us* (Rev. xxi. 3) and we shall see and enjoy him immediately.

II. We have here David's prayers, intercessions, and holy triumphs, grounded upon these meditations.

1. He intercedes for all saints, begging that they may always experience the benefit and comfort of God's favour and grace, *v.* 10. (1.) The persons he prays for are those that know God, that are acquainted with him, acknowledge him, and avouch him for theirs —the upright in heart, that are sincere in their profession of religion, and faithful both to God and man. Those that are not upright with God do not know him as they should. (2.) The blessing he begs for them is God's loving-kindness (that is, the tokens of his favour towards them) and his righteousness

(that is, the workings of his grace in them); or his loving-kindness and righteousness are his goodness according to promise ; they are mercy and truth. (3.) The manner in which he desires this blessing may be conveyed : *O continue it, draw it out,* as the mother draws out her breasts to the child, and then the child draws out the milk from the breasts. Let it be drawn out to a length equal to the line of eternity itself. The happiness of the saints in heaven will be in perfection, and yet in continual progression (as some think); for the fountain there will be always full and the streams always flowing. *In these is continuance,* Isa. lxiv. 5.

2. He prays for himself, that he might be preserved in his integrity and comfort (*v.* 11): " *Let not the foot of pride come against me,* to trip up my heels, or trample upon me ; *and let not the hand of the wicked,* which is stretched out against me, prevail to *remove me,* either from my purity and integrity, by any temptation, or from my peace and comfort, by any trouble." Let not those who fight against God triumph over those who desire to cleave to him. Those that have experienced the pleasure of communion with God cannot but desire that nothing may ever remove them from him

3. He rejoices in hope of the downfal of all his enemies in due time (*v.* 12): " *There,* where they thought to gain the point against me, *they have themselves fallen,* been taken in that snare which they laid for me." *There,* in the other world (so some), where the saints stand in the judgment, and have a place in God's house, the workers of iniquity are cast in the judgment, *are cast down* into hell, into the bottomless pit, out of which they shall assuredly never be able to rise from under the insupportable weight of God's wrath and curse. It is true we are not to rejoice when any particular enemy of ours falls; but the final overthrow of all the workers of iniquity will be the everlasting triumph of glorified saints.

PSALM XXXVII.

This psalm is a sermon, and an excellent useful sermon it is, calculated not (as most of the psalms) for our devotion, but for our conversation ; there is nothing in it of prayer or praise, but it is all instruction ; it is " Maschil—a teaching psalm ;" it is an exposition of some of the hardest chapters in the book of Providence, the advancement of the wicked and the disgrace of the righteous, a solution of the difficulties that arise thereupon, and an exhortation to conduct ourselves as becomes us under such dark dispensations. The work of the prophets (and David was one) was to explain the law. Now the law of Moses had promised temporal blessings to the obedient, and denounced temporal miseries against the disobedient, which principally referred to the body of the people, the nation as a nation ; for, when they came to be applied to particular persons, many instances occurred of sinners in prosperity and saints in adversity ; to reconcile those instances with the word that God had spoken is the scope of the prophet in this psalm, in which, I. He forbids us to fret at the prosperity of the wicked in their wicked ways, ver. 1, 7, 8. II. He gives very good reasons why we should not fret at it. 1. Because of the scandalous character of the wicked (ver. 12, 14, 21, 32) notwithstanding their prosperity, and the honourable character of the righteous, ver. 21, 26, 30, 31. 2. Because of the destruction and ruin which the wicked are nigh to (ver. 2, 9, 10, 20, 35, 36, 38) and the salvation and protection which the righteous are sure of from all the malicious designs of the wicked, ver. 13, 15, 17, 28, 33, 39, 40. 3. Because of the particular mercy God has in store for all good people and the favour he shows them, ver. 11, 16, 18, 19, 22—25, 28, 29, 37. III. He prescribes very good remedies against this sin of envying the prosperity of the wicked, and great encouragement to use those remedies, ver. 3—6, 27, 34. In singing this psalm we must teach and admonish one another rightly to understand the providence of God and to accommodate ourselves to it, at all times carefully to do our duty and then patiently to leave the event with God and to believe that, how black soever things may look for the present, it shall be "well with those that fear God, that fear before him."

A psalm of David.

FRET not thyself because of evil-doers, neither be thou envious against the workers of iniquity. 2 For they shall soon be cut down like the grass, and wither as the green herb. 3 Trust in the LORD, and do good ; *so* shalt thou dwell in the land, and verily thou shalt be fed. 4 Delight thyself also in the LORD ; and he shall give thee the desires of thine heart. 5 Commit thy way unto the LORD ; trust also in him ; and he shall bring *it* to pass. 6 And he shall bring forth thy righteousness as the light, and thy judgment as the noonday.

The instructions here given are very plain; much need not be said for the exposition of them, but there is a great deal to be done for the reducing of them to practice, and there they will look best.

I. We are here cautioned against discontent at the prosperity and success of evil-doers (v. 1, 2): *Fret not thyself, neither be thou envious.* We may suppose that David speaks this to himself first, and preaches it to his own heart (in his communing with that upon his bed), for the suppressing of those corrupt passions which he found working there, and then leaves it in writing for instruction to others that might be in similar temptation. That is preached best, and with most probability of success, to others, which is first preached to ourselves. Now, 1. When we look abroad we see the world full of evil-doers and workers of iniquity, that flourish and prosper, that have what they will and do what they will, that live in ease and pomp themselves and have power in their hands to do mischief to those about them. So it was in David's time ; and therefore, if it is so still, let us not marvel at the matter, as though it were some new or strange thing. 2. When we look within we find ourselves tempted to fret at this, and to be envious against these scandals and burdens, these blemishes and common nuisances, of this earth. We are apt to fret at God, as if he were unkind to the world and unkind to his church in permitting such men to live, and prosper, and prevail, as they do. We are apt to fret ourselves with vexation at their success in their evil projects. We are apt to envy them the liberty they take in getting wealth, and perhaps by unlawful means, and in the indulgence of their lusts, and to wish that we could shake off the restraints of conscience and do so too. We are tempted to think them the only happy people, and to incline to imitate them, and to join ourselves with them, that

we may share in their gains and eat of their dainties ; and this is that which we are warned against : *Fret not thyself, neither be thou envious.* Fretfulness and envy are sins that are their own punishments ; they are the uneasiness of the spirit and the rottenness of the bones ; it is therefore in kindness to ourselves that we are warned against them. Yet that is not all ; for, 3. When we look forward with an eye of faith we shall see no reason to envy wicked people their prosperity, for their ruin is at the door and they are ripening apace for it, v. 2. They flourish, but as the grass, and as the green herb, which nobody envies nor frets at. The flourishing of a godly man is like that of a fruitful tree (i. 3), but that of the wicked man is like grass and herbs, which are very short-lived. (1.) They will soon wither of themselves. Outward prosperity is a fading thing, and so is the life itself to which it is confined. (2.) They will sooner be cut down by the judgments of God. Their triumphing is short, but their weeping and wailing will be everlasting.

II. We are here counselled to live a life of confidence and complacency in God, and that will keep us from fretting at the prosperity of evil-doers ; if we do well for our own souls, we shall see little reason to envy those that do so ill for theirs. Here are three excellent precepts, which we are to be ruled by, and, to enforce them, three precious promises, which we may rely upon.

1. We must make God our hope in the way of duty and then we shall have a comfortable subsistence in this world, v. 3. (1.) It is required that we *trust in the Lord and do good,* that we confide in God and conform to him. The life of religion lies much in a believing reliance on God, his favour, his providence, his promise, his grace, and a diligent care to serve him and our generation, according to his will. We must not think to trust in God and then live as we list. No; it is not trusting God, but tempting him, if we do not make conscience of our duty to him. Nor must we think to do good, and then to trust to ourselves, and our own righteousness and strength. No ; we must both trust in the Lord and do good. And then, (2.) It is promised that we shall be well provided for in this world : *So shalt thou dwell in the land, and verily thou shalt be fed.* He does not say, "So shalt thou get preferment, dwell in a palace, and be feasted." This is not necessary; a man's life consists not in the abundance of these things; but, "Thou shalt have a place to live in, and that in the land, in Canaan, the valley of vision, and thou shalt have food convenient for thee." This is more than we deserve ; it is as much as a good man will stipulate for (Gen. xxviii. 20) and it is enough for one that is going to heaven. "Thou shalt have a settlement, a quiet settlement, and a maintenance, a comfortable maintenance : *Verily thou shalt be fed.*" Some read it, *Thou shalt be fed by faith,*

as the just are said to live by faith, and it is good living, good feeding, upon the promises. *"Verily thou shalt be fed,* as Elijah in the famine, with what is needful for thee." God himself is a shepherd, a feeder, to all those that trust in him, xxiii. 1.

2. We must make God our heart's delight and then we shall have our heart's desire, *v.* 4. We must not only depend upon God, but solace ourselves in him. We must be well pleased that there is a God, that he is such a one as he has revealed himself to be, and that he is our God in covenant. We must delight ourselves in his beauty, bounty, and benignity; our souls must return to him, and repose in him, as their rest, and their portion for ever. Being satisfied of his loving-kindness, we must be satisfied with it, and make that our exceeding joy, xliii. 4. We were commanded (*v.* 3) to do good, and then follows this command to delight in God, which is as much a privilege as a duty. If we make conscience of obedience to God, we may then take the comfort of a complacency in him. And even this pleasant duty of delighting in God has a promise annexed to it, which is very full and precious, enough to recompense the hardest services: *He shall give thee the desires of thy heart.* He has not promised to gratify all the appetites of the body and the humours of the fancy, but to grant all the desires of the heart, all the cravings of the renewed sanctified soul. What is the desire of the heart of a good man? It is this, to know, and love, and live to God, to please him and to be pleased in him.

3. We must make God our guide, and submit in every thing to his guidance and disposal; and then all our affairs, even those that seem most intricate and perplexed, shall be made to issue well and to our satisfaction, *v.* 5, 6. (1.) The duty is very easy; and, if we do it aright, it will make us easy: *Commit thy way unto the Lord; roll thy way upon the Lord* (so the margin reads it), Prov. xvi. 3; Ps. lv. 22. *Cast thy burden upon the Lord,* the burden of thy care, 1 Pet. v. 7. We must roll it off ourselves, so as not to afflict and perplex ourselves with thoughts about future events (Matt. vi. 25), not to cumber and trouble ourselves either with the contrivance of the means or with expectation of the end, but refer it to God, leave it to him by his wise and good providence to order and dispose of all our concerns as he pleases. *Reveal thy way unto the Lord* (so the LXX.), that is, "By prayer spread thy case, and all thy cares about it, before the Lord" (as Jephthah *uttered all his words before the Lord in Mizpeh,* Judg. xi. 11), "and then trust in him to bring it to a good issue, with a full satisfaction that all is well that God does." We must do our duty (that must be our care) and then leave the event with God. *Sit still, and see how the matter will fall,* Ruth iii. 18. We must follow Providence, and not force it, subscribe to Infinite Wisdom and not pre-

scribe. (2.) The promise is very sweet. [1.] In general, *"He shall bring that to pass,* whatever it is, which thou hast committed to him, if not to thy contrivance, yet to thy content. He will find means to extricate thee out of thy straits, to prevent thy fears, and bring about thy purposes, to thy satisfaction." [2.] In particular, "He will take care of thy reputation, and bring thee out of thy difficulties, not only with comfort, but with credit and honour: *He shall bring forth thy righteousness as the light and thy judgment as the noon-day"* (*v.* 6), that is, "he shall make it to appear that thou art an honest man, and that is honour enough." *First,* It is implied that the righteousness and judgment of good people may, for a time, be clouded and eclipsed, either by remarkable rebukes of Providence (Job's great afflictions darkened his righteousness) or by the malicious censures and reproaches of men, who give them bad names which they no way deserve, and lay to their charge things which they know not. *Secondly,* It is promised that God will, in due time, roll away the reproach they are under, clear up their innocency, and bring forth their righteousness, to their honour, perhaps in this world, at furthest in the great day, Matt. xiii. 43. Note, If we take care to keep a good conscience, we may leave it to God to take care of our good name.

7 Rest in the Lᴏʀᴅ, and wait patiently for him: fret not thyself because of him who prospereth in his way, because of the man who bringeth wicked devices to pass. 8 Cease from anger, and forsake wrath: fret not thyself in any wise to do evil. 9 For evildoers shall be cut off: but those that wait upon the Lᴏʀᴅ, they shall inherit the earth. 10 For yet a little while, and the wicked *shall* not *be :* yea, thou shalt diligently consider his place, and it *shall* not *be.* 11 But the meek shall inherit the earth ; and shall delight themselves in the abundance of peace. 12 The wicked plotteth against the just, and gnasheth upon him with his teeth. 13 The Lᴏʀᴅ shall laugh at him : for he seeth that his day is coming. 14 The wicked have drawn out the sword, and have bent their bow, to cast down the poor and needy, *and* to slay such as be of upright conversation. 15 Their sword shall enter into their own heart, and their bows shall be broken. 16 A little that a righteous man hath *is* better than the riches of many wicked. 17 For the arms of the wicked shall be

broken : but the LORD upholdeth the righteous. 18 The LORD knoweth the days of the upright : and their inheritance shall be for ever. 19 They shall not be ashamed in the evil time : and in the days of famine they shall be satisfied. 20 But the wicked shall perish, and the enemies of the LORD *shall be* as the fat of lambs : they shall consume ; into smoke shall they consume away.

In these verses we have,

I. The foregoing precepts inculcated; for we are so apt to disquiet ourselves with needless fruitless discontents and distrusts that it is necessary there should be precept upon precept, and line upon line, to suppress them and arm us against them. 1. Let us compose ourselves by believing in God : *"Rest in the Lord, and wait patiently for him (v. 7),* that is, be well reconciled to all he does and acquiesce in it, for that is best that is, because it is what God has appointed; and be well satisfied that he will still make all to work for good to us, though we know not how or which way." *Be silent to the Lord* (so the word is), not with a sullen, but a submissive silence. A patient bearing of what is laid upon us, with a patient expectation of what is further appointed for us, is as much our interest as it is our duty, for it will make us always easy; and there is a great deal of reason for it, for it is making a virtue of necessity. 2. Let us not discompose ourselves at what we see in this world: *" Fret not thyself because of him who prospers in his wicked way,* who, though he is a bad man, yet thrives and grows rich and great in the world; no, nor because of him who does mischief with his power and wealth, and brings wicked devices to pass against those that are virtuous and good, who seems to have gained his point and to have run them down. If thy heart begins to rise at it, stroke down thy folly, and *cease from anger (v. 8),* check the first stirrings of discontent and envy, and do not harbour any hard thoughts of God and his providence upon this account. Be not angry at any thing that God does, but forsake that wrath ; it is the worst kind of wrath that can be. *Fret not thyself in any wise to do evil;* do not envy them their prosperity, lest thou be tempted to fall in with them and to take the same evil course that they take to enrich and advance themselves or some desperate course to avoid them and their power." Note, A fretful discontented spirit lies open to many temptations; and those that indulge it are in danger of doing evil.

II. The foregoing reasons, taken from the approaching ruin of the wicked notwithstanding their prosperity, and the real happiness of the righteous notwithstanding their troubles, are here much enlarged upon and the same things repeated in a pleasing variety of expression. We were cautioned (*v.* 7) not to envy the wicked either worldly prosperity or the success of their plots against the righteous, and the reasons here given respect these two temptations severally:—

1. Good people have no reason to envy the worldly prosperity of wicked people, nor to grieve or be uneasy at it, (1.) Because the prosperity of the wicked will soon be at an end (*v.* 9): *Evil-doers shall be cut off* by some sudden stroke of divine justice in the midst of their prosperity; what they have got by sin will not only flow away from them (Job xx. 28), but they shall be carried away with it. See the end of these men (lxxiii. 17), how dear their ill-got gain will cost them, and you will be far from envying them or from being willing to espouse their lot, for better, for worse. Their ruin is sure, and it is very near (*v.* 10): *Yet a little while, and the wicked shall not be* what they now are; *they are brought into desolation in a moment,* lxxiii. 19. Have a little patience, for the *Judge stands before the door,* Jam. v. 8, 9. Moderate your passion, *for the Lord is at hand,* Phil. iv. 5. And when their ruin comes it will be an utter ruin; he and his shall be extirpated; the day that comes shall *leave him neither root nor branch* (Mal. iv. 1): *Thou shalt diligently consider his place,* where but the other day he made a mighty figure, but *it shall not be,* you will not find it; he shall leave nothing valuable, nothing honourable, behind him. To the same purport (*v.* 20), *The wicked shall perish;* their death is their perdition, because it is the termination of all their joy and a passage to endless misery. *Blessed are the dead that die in the Lord;* but undone, for ever undone, are the dead that die in their sins. The wicked are the enemies of the Lord ; such those make themselves who will not have him to reign over them, and as such he will reckon with them: *They shall consume as the fat of lambs, they shall consume into smoke.* Their prosperity, which gratifies their sensuality, is like the fat of lambs, not solid or substantial, but loose and washy; and, when their ruin comes, they shall fall as sacrifices to the justice of God and be consumed as the fat of the sacrifices was upon the altar, whence it ascended in smoke. The day of God's vengeance on the wicked is represented as a *sacrifice of the fat of the kidneys of rams* (Isa. xxxiv. 6); for he will be honoured by the ruin of his enemies, as he was by the sacrifices. Damned sinners are sacrifices, Mark ix. 49. This is a good reason why we should not envy them their prosperity; while they are fed to the full, they are but in the fattening for the day of sacrifice, *like a lamb in a large place* (Hos. iv. 16), and the more they prosper the more will God be glorified in their ruin. (2.) Because the condition of the righteous, even in this life, is every way better and more desirable than that of the wicked, *v.* 16. In general,

a little that a righteous man has of the honour, wealth, and pleasure of this world, *is better than the riches of many wicked*. Observe, [1.] The wealth of the world is so dispensed by the divine Providence that it is often the lot of good people to have but a little of it, and of wicked people to have abundance of it; for thus God would show us that the things of this world are not the best things, for, if they were, those would have most that are best and dearest to God. [2.] That a godly man's little is really better than a wicked man's much; see Prov. xv. 16, 17; xvi. 8; xxviii. 6. A godly man's estate, though ever so little, is better than a wicked man's estate, though ever so much; for it comes from a better hand, from a hand of special love and not merely from a hand of common providence,—it is enjoyed by a better title (God gives it to them by promise, Gal. iii. 18),—it is theirs by virtue of their relation to Christ, who is the heir of all things,—and it is put to a better use: it is sanctified to them by the blessing of God. *Unto the pure all things are pure*, Tit. i. 15. A little wherewith God is served and honoured is better than a great deal prepared for Baal or for a base lust. The promises here made to the righteous secure them such a happiness that they need not envy the prosperity of evil-doers. Let them know to their comfort, *First*, That *they shall inherit the earth*, as much of it as Infinite Wisdom sees good for them; they have the promise of the *life that now is*, 1 Tim. iv. 8. If all the earth were necessary to make them happy, they should have it. All is theirs, even *the world*, and *things present*, as well as *things to come*, 1 Cor. iii. 21, 22. They have it by inheritance, a safe and honourable title, not by permission only and connivance. When evil-doers are cut off the righteous sometimes inherit what they gathered. *The wealth of the sinner is laid up for the just*, Job xxvii. 17; Prov. xiii. 22. This promise is here made, 1. To those that live a life of faith (*v*. 9): *Those that wait upon the Lord*, as dependents on him, expectants from him, and suppliants to him, *shall inherit the earth*, as a token of his present favour to them and an earnest of better things intended for them in the other world. God is a good Master, that provides plentifully and well, not only for his working servants, but for his waiting servants. 2. To those that live a quiet and peaceable life (*v*. 11): *The meek shall inherit the earth*. They are in least danger of being injured and disturbed in the possession of what they have and they have most satisfaction in themselves and consequently the sweetest relish of their creature-comforts. Our Saviour has made this a gospel-promise, and a confirmation of the blessing he pronounced on the meek, Matt. v. 5. *Secondly*, That they *shall delight themselves in the abundance of peace*, *v*. 11. Perhaps they have not abundance of wealth to delight in;

but they have that which is better, abundance of peace, inward peace and tranquillity of mind, peace with God, and then peace in God, that great peace which those have that love God's law, whom *nothing shall offend* (cxix. 165), that abundance of peace which is in the kingdom of Christ (lxxii. 7), that peace which the world cannot give (John xiv. 27), and which the wicked cannot have, Isa. lvii. 21. This they shall delight themselves in, and in it they shall have a continual feast; while those that have abundance of wealth do but cumber and perplex themselves with it and have little delight in it. *Thirdly*, That God *knows their days*, *v*. 18. He takes particular notice of them, of all they do and of all that happens to them. He keeps account of the days of their service, and not one day's work shall go unrewarded, and of the days of their suffering, that for those also they may receive a recompence. He knows their bright days, and has pleasure in their prosperity; he knows their cloudy and dark days, the days of their affliction, and as the day is so shall the strength be. *Fourthly*, That *their inheritance shall be for ever*. Their time on earth is reckoned by days, which will soon be numbered. God takes cognizance of them, and gives them the blessings of every day in its day; but it was never intended that their inheritance should be confined within the limits of those days. No, that must be the portion of an immortal soul, and therefore must last as long as that lasts, and will run parallel with the longest line of eternity itself: *Their inheritance shall be for ever;* not their inheritance in the earth, but that incorruptible indefeasible one which is laid up for them in heaven. Those that are sure of an everlasting inheritance in the other world have no reason to envy the wicked their transitory possessions and pleasures in this world. *Fifthly*, That in the worst of times it shall go well with them (*v*. 19): *They shall not be ashamed* of their hope and confidence in God, nor of the profession they have made of religion; for the comfort of that will stand them in stead, and be a real support to them, in evil times. When others droop they shall lift up their heads with joy and confidence: Even *in the days of famine*, when others are dying for hunger round about them, *they shall be satisfied*, as Elijah was; in some way or other God will provide food convenient for them, or give them hearts to be satisfied and content without it, so that, if they should be hardly bestead and hungry, they shall not (as the wicked do) *fret themselves and curse their king and their God* (Isa. viii. 21), but rejoice in God as the God of their salvation even when *the fig-tree does not blossom*, Hab. iii. 17, 18.

2. Good people have no reason to fret at the occasional success of the designs of the wicked against the just. Though they do bring some of their wicked devices to pass, which makes us fear they will gain

their point and bring them all to pass, yet let us cease from anger, and not fret ourselves so as to think of giving up the cause. For,

(1.) Their plots will be their shame, *v.* 12, 13. It is true *the wicked plotteth against the just;* there is a rooted enmity in the seed of the wicked one against the righteous seed; their aim is, if they can, to destroy their righteousness, or, if that fail, then to destroy them. With this end in view they have acted with a great deal both of cursed policy and contrivance (they plot, they practise, against the just), and of cursed zeal and fury—*they gnash upon them with their teeth,* so desirous are they, if they could get it into their power, to eat them up, and so full of rage and indignation are they because it is not in their power; but by all this they do but make themselves ridiculous. *The Lord shall laugh at them,* ii. 4, 5. They are proud and insolent, but God shall pour contempt upon them. He is not only displeased with them, but he despises them and all their attempts as vain and ineffectual, and their malice as impotent and in a chain; *for he sees that his day is coming,* that is, [1.] The day of God's reckoning, the day of the revelation of his righteousness, which now seems clouded and eclipsed. Men have their day now. *This is your hour,* Luke xxii. 53. But God will have his day shortly, a day of recompences, a day which will set all to rights, and render that ridiculous which now passes for glorious. *It is a small thing to be judged of man's judgment,* 1 Cor. iv. 3. God's day will give a decisive judgment. [2.] The day of their ruin. The wicked man's day, the day set for his fall, that day *is coming,* which denotes delay; it has not yet come, but certainly it will come. The believing prospect of that day will enable the virgin, the daughter of Zion, to despise the rage of her enemies and *laugh them to scorn,* Isa. xxxvii. 22.

(2.) Their attempts will be their destruction, *v.* 14, 15. See here, [1.] How cruel they are in their designs against good people. They prepare instruments of death, *the sword* and *the bow,* no less will serve; they hunt for the precious life. That which they design is *to cast down and slay;* it is the blood of the saints they thirst after. They carry on the design very far, and it is near to be put in execution: They *have drawn the sword, and bent the bow;* and all these military preparations are made against the helpless, *the poor and needy* (which proves them to be very cowardly), and against the guiltless, *such as are of upright conversation,* that never gave them any provocation, nor offered injury to them or any other person, which proves them to be very wicked. Uprightness itself will be no fence against their malice. But, [2.] How justly their malice recoils upon themselves: *Their sword shall turn into their own heart,* which implies the preservation of the righteous from their malice and the filling up of the measure of

their own iniquity by it. Sometimes that very thing proves to be their own destruction which they projected against their harmless neighbours; however, God's sword, which their provocations have drawn against them, will give them their death's wound.

(3.) Those that are not suddenly cut off shall yet be so disabled for doing any further mischief that the interests of the church shall be effectually secured: *Their bows shall be broken* (*v.* 15); the instruments of their cruelty shall fail them and they shall lose those whom they had made tools of to serve their bloody purposes with; nay, *their arms shall be broken,* so that they shall not be able to go on with their enterprises, *v.* 17. *But the Lord upholds the righteous,* so that they neither sink under the weight of their afflictions nor are crushed by the violence of their enemies. He upholds them both in their integrity and in their prosperity; and those that are so upheld by the rock of ages have no reason to envy the wicked the support of their broken reeds.

21 The wicked borroweth, and payeth not again: but the righteous showeth mercy, and giveth. 22 For *such as be* blessed of him shall inherit the earth ; and *they that be* cursed of him shall be cut off. 23 The steps of a *good* man are ordered by the LORD : and he delighteth in his way. 24 Though he fall, he shall not be utterly cast down : for the LORD upholdeth *him with* his hand. 25 I have been young, and *now* am old ; yet have I not seen the righteous forsaken, nor his seed begging bread. 26 *He is* ever merciful, and lendeth ; and his seed *is* blessed. 27 Depart from evil, and do good ; and dwell for evermore. 28 For the LORD loveth judgment, and forsaketh not his saints ; they are preserved for ever : but the seed of the wicked shall be cut off. 29 The righteous shall inherit the land, and dwell therein for ever. 30 The mouth of the righteous speaketh wisdom, and his tongue talketh of judgment. 31 The law of his God *is* in his heart ; none of his steps shall slide. 32 The wicked watcheth the righteous, and seeketh to slay him. 33 The LORD will not leave him in his hand, nor condemn him when he is judged.

These verses are much to the same purport with the foregoing verses of this psalm, for it is a subject worthy to be dwelt upon. Observe here,

I. What is required of us as the way to our

happiness, which we may learn both from the characters here laid down and from the directions here given. If we would be blessed of God, 1. We must make conscience of giving every body his own ; for *the wicked borrows and pays not again, v.* 21. It is the first thing which the Lord our God requires of us, that we do justly, and render to all their due. It is not only a shameful paltry thing, but a sinful wicked thing, not to repay what we have borrowed. Some make this an instance, not so much of the wickedness of the wicked as of the misery and poverty to which they are reduced by the just judgment of God, that they shall be necessitated to borrow for their supply and then be in no capacity to repay again, and so lie at the mercy of their creditors. Whatever some men seem to think of it, as it is a great sin for those that are able to deny the payment of their just debts, so it is a great misery not to be able to pay them. 2. We must be ready to all acts of charity and beneficence ; for, as it is an instance of God's goodness to the righteous that he puts it into the power of his hand to be kind and to do good (and so some understand it, God's blessing increases his little to such a degree that he has abundance to spare for the relief of others), so it is an instance of the goodness of the righteous man that he has a heart proportionable to his estate : *He shows mercy, and gives, v.* 21. *He is ever merciful,* or every day, or all the day, merciful, *and lends,* and sometimes there is as true charity in lending as in giving ; and giving and lending are acceptable to God when they proceed from a merciful disposition in the heart, which, if it be sincere, will be constant, and will keep us from being weary of well-doing. He that is truly merciful will be ever merciful. 3. We must leave our sins, and engage in the practice of serious godliness (*v.* 27) : *Depart from evil and do good.* Cease to do evil and abhor it ; learn to do well and cleave to it ; this is true religion. 4. We must abound in good discourse, and with our tongues must glorify God and edify others. It is part of the character of a righteous man (*v.* 30) that his *mouth speaketh wisdom ;* not only he speaks wisely, but he speaks wisdom, like Solomon himself, for the instruction of those about him. *His tongue talks* not of things idle and impertinent, but *of judgment,* that is, of the word and providence of God and the rules of wisdom for the right ordering of the conversation. Out of the abundance of a good heart will the mouth speak that which is good and to the use of edifying. 5. We must have our wills brought into an entire subjection to the will and word of God (*v.* 31) : *The law of God, of his God, is in his heart ;* and in vain do we pretend that God is our God if we do not receive his law into our hearts and resign ourselves to the government of it. It is but a jest and a mockery to speak wisdom, and to talk of judgment (*v.* 30), unless we have the law in our hearts, and we

think as we speak. The law of God must be a commanding ruling principle in the heart ; it must be a light there, a spring there, and then the conversation will be regular and uniform : *None of his steps will slide ;* it will effectually prevent backsliding into sin, and the uneasiness that follows from it.

II. What is assured to us, as instances of our happiness and comfort, upon these conditions.

1. That we shall have the blessing of God, and that blessing shall be the spring, and sweetness, and security of all our temporal comforts and enjoyments (*v.* 22) : *Such as are blessed of God,* as all the righteous are, with a Father's blessing, by virtue of that *shall inherit the earth,* or *the land* (for so the same word is translated, *v.* 29), the land of Canaan, that glory of all lands. Our creature-comforts are comforts indeed to us when we see them flowing from the blessing of God, from his favour, his promise, and his covenant with us ; and, if we are sure of the blessing of God, we are sure not to want any thing that is good for us in this world. *The earth shall yield us her increase* if God, as *our own God, give us his blessing,* lxvii. 6. And as *those whom God blesses are* thus *blessed indeed (for they shall inherit the land),* so *those whom he curses are cursed indeed ;* they *shall be cut off* and rooted out, and their extirpation by the divine curse will set off the establishment of the righteous by the divine blessing and be a foil to it.

2. That God will direct and dispose of our actions and affairs so as may be most for his glory (*v.* 23) : *The steps of a good man are ordered by the Lord.* By his grace and Holy Spirit he directs the thoughts, affections, and designs of good men. He has all hearts in his hand, but theirs by their own consent. By his providence he overrules the events that concern them, so as to make their way plain before them, both what they should do and what they may expect. Observe, God orders the steps of a good man ; not only his way in general, by his written word, but his particular steps, by the whispers of conscience, saying, *This is the way, walk in it.* He does not always show him his way at a distance, but leads him step by step, as children are led, and so keeps him in a continual dependence upon his guidance ; and this, (1.) Because *he delights in his way,* and is well pleased with the paths of righteousness wherein he walks. *The Lord knows the way of the righteous* (i. 6), knows it with favour, and therefore directs it. (2.) That he may delight in his way. Because God orders his way according to his own will, therefore he delights in it ; for, as he loves his own image upon us, so he is well pleased with what we do under his guidance.

3. That God will keep us from being ruined by our falls either into sin or into trouble (*v.* 24) : *Though he fall, he shall not be utterly cast down.* (1.) A good man may be overtaken in a fault, but the grace of God shall recover

him to repentance, so that he shall not be utterly cast down. Though he may, for a time, lose the joys of God's salvation, yet they shall be restored to him; for God shall uphold him with his hand, uphold him with his free Spirit. The root shall be kept alive, though the leaf wither; and there will come a spring after the winter. (2.) A good man may be in distress, his affairs embarrassed, his spirits sunk, but he shall not be utterly cast down; God will be the strength of his heart when his flesh and heart fail, and will uphold him with his comforts, so that the spirit he has made shall not fail before him.

4. That we shall not want the necessary supports of this life (*v.* 25): "*I have been young and now am old*, and, among all the changes I have seen in men's outward condition and the observations I have made upon them, *I never saw the righteous forsaken* of God and man, as I have sometimes seen wicked people abandoned both by heaven and earth; nor do I ever remember to have seen the seed of the righteous reduced to such an extremity as to beg their bread." David had himself begged his bread of Ahimelech the priest, but it was when Saul hunted him; and our Saviour has taught us to except the case of persecution for righteousness' sake out of all the temporal promises (Mark x. 30), because that has such peculiar honours and comforts attending it as make it rather a gift (as the apostle reckons it, Phil. i. 29) than a loss or grievance. But there are very few instances of good men, or their families, that are reduced to such extreme poverty as many wicked people bring themselves to by their wickedness. He had not *seen the righteous forsaken, nor his seed begging their bread. Forsaken* (so some expound it); if they do want God will raise them up friends to supply them, without a scandalous exposing of themselves to the reproach of common beggars; or, if they go from door to door for meat, it shall not be with despair, as the wicked man *that wanders abroad for bread, saying, Where is it?* Job xv. 23. Nor shall he be denied, as the prodigal, that *would fain have filled his belly, but no man gave unto him*, Luke xv. 16. Nor shall he grudge if he be not satisfied, as David's enemies, when they *wandered up and down for meat*, lix. 15. Some make this promise relate especially to those that are charitable and liberal to the poor, and to intimate that David never observed any that brought themselves to poverty by their charity. It is *withholding more than is meet that tends to poverty*, Prov. xi. 24.

5. That God will not desert us, but graciously protect us in our difficulties and straits (*v.* 28): *The Lord loves judgment;* he delights in doing justice himself and he delights in those that do justice; and therefore he forsakes not his saints in affliction when others make themselves strange to them and become shy of them, but he takes care that they be *preserved for ever*, that is, that the saints in

every age be taken under his protection, that the succession be preserved to the end of time, and that particular saints be preserved from all the temptations and through all the trials of this present time, to that happiness which shall be for ever. He will *preserve them to his heavenly kingdom;* that is a preservation for ever, 2 Tim. iv. 18; Ps. xii. 7.

6. That we shall have a comfortable settlement in this world, and in a better when we leave this. That we shall *dwell for evermore* (*v.* 27), and not be *cut off* as the *seed of the wicked, v.* 28. That we *shall inherit the land* which the Lord our God gives us *and dwell therein for ever, v.* 29. Those shall not be tossed that make God their rest and are at home in him. But on this earth there is no dwelling for ever, no continuing city; it is in heaven only, that city which has foundations, that the righteous shall dwell for ever; that will be their everlasting habitation.

7. That we shall not become a prey to our adversaries, who seek our ruin, *v.* 32, 33. There is an adversary that takes all opportunities to do us a mischief, a wicked one that watches the righteous (as a roaring lion watches his prey) and seeks to slay him. There are wicked men that do so, that are very subtle (they watch the righteous, that they may have an opportunity to do them a mischief effectually and may have a pretence wherewith to justify themselves in the doing of it), and very spiteful, for they seek to slay him. But it may very well be applied to the wicked one, the devil, that old serpent, who has his wiles to entrap the righteous, his devices which we should not be ignorant of,—that great red dragon, who seeks to slay them,—that roaring lion, who goes about continually, restless and raging, and seeking whom he may devour. But it is here promised that he shall not prevail, neither Satan nor his instruments. (1.) He shall not prevail as a field-adversary: *The Lord will not leave him in his hand;* he will not permit Satan to do what he would, nor will he withdraw his strength and grace from his people, but will enable them to resist and overcome him, and *their faith shall not fail*, Luke xxii. 31, 32. A good man may fall into the hands of a messenger of Satan, and be sorely buffeted, but God will not leave him in his hands, 1 Cor. x. 13. (2.) He shall not prevail as a law-adversary: *God will not condemn him when he is judged*, though urged to do it by the accuser of the brethren, who *accuses them before our God day and night.* His false accusations will be thrown out, as those exhibited against Joshua (Zech. iii, 1, 2), *The Lord rebuke thee, O Satan! It is God that justifies*, and then *who shall lay any thing to the charge of God's elect?*

34 Wait on the LORD, and keep his way, and he shall exalt thee to inherit the land: when the wicked are cut off, thou shalt see *it*. 35 I have

seen the wicked in great power, and spreading himself like a green bay tree. 36 Yet he passed away, and, lo, he *was* not : yea, I sought him, but he could not be found. 37 Mark the perfect *man,* and behold the upright : for the end of *that* man *is* peace. 38 But the transgressors shall be destroyed together : the end of the wicked shall be cut off. 39 But the salvation of the righteous *is* of the LORD : *he is* their strength in the time of trouble. 40 And the LORD shall help them, and deliver them : he shall deliver them from the wicked, and save them, because they trust in him.

The psalmist's conclusion of this sermon (for that is the nature of this poem) is of the same purport with the whole, and inculcates the same things.

I. The duty here pressed upon us is still the same (*v.* 34): *Wait on the Lord and keep his way.* Duty is ours, and we must mind it and make conscience of it, keep God's way and never turn out of it nor loiter in it, keep close, keep going ; but events are God's, and we must refer ourselves to him for the disposal of them ; we must wait on the Lord, attend the motions of his providence, carefully observe them, and conscientiously accommodate ourselves to them. If we make conscience of *keeping God's way,* we may with cheerfulness wait on him and commit to him our way ; and we shall find him a good Master both to his working servants and to his waiting servants.

II. The reasons to enforce this duty are much the same too, taken from the certain destruction of the wicked and the certain salvation of the righteous. This good man, being tempted to envy the prosperity of the wicked, that he might fortify himself against the temptation, *goes into the sanctuary of God* and leads us thither (lxxiii. 17); there he understands their end, and thence gives us to understand it, and, by comparing that with the end of the righteous, baffles the temptation and puts it to silence. Observe,

1. The misery of the wicked at last, however they may prosper awhile: *The end of the wicked shall be cut off* (*v.* 38) ; and that cannot be well that will undoubtedly end so ill. The wicked, in their end, will be cut off from all good and all hopes of it ; a final period will be put to all their joys, and they will be for ever separated from the fountain of life to all evil. (1.) Some instances of the remarkable ruin of wicked people David had himself observed in this world—that the pomp and prosperity of sinners would not secure them from the judgments of God when their day should come to fall (*v.* 36, 35): *I have seen a wicked man* (the word is singular),

suppose Saul or Ahithophel (for David was an old man when he penned this psalm), *in great power, formidable* (so some render it), *the terror of the mighty in the land of the living,* carrying all before him with a high hand, and seeming to be firmly fixed and finely flourishing, *spreading himself like a green bay-tree,* which produces all leaves and no fruit ; like a native home-born Israelite (so Dr. Hammond), likely to take root. But what became of him ? Eliphaz, long before, had learned, when he saw the foolish taking root, to curse his habitation, Job v. 3. And David saw cause for it ; for this bay-tree withered away as soon as the fig-tree Christ cursed: *He passed away as a dream,* as a shadow, such was he and all the pomp and power he was so proud of. He was gone in an instant : *He was not ; I sought him* with wonder, *but he could not be found.* He had acted his part and then quitted the stage, and there was no miss of him. (2.) The total and final ruin of sinners, of all sinners, will shortly be made as much a spectacle to the saints as they are now sometimes made a spectacle to the world (*v.* 34): *When the wicked are cut off* (and cut off they certainly will be) *thou shalt see it,* with awful adorations of the divine justice. *The transgressors shall be destroyed together, v.* 38. In this world God singles out here one sinner and there another, out of many, to be made an example *in terrorem—as a warning;* but in the day of judgment there will be a general destruction of all the transgressors, and not one shall escape. Those that have sinned together shall be damned together. *Bind them in bundles, to burn them.*

2. The blessedness of the righteous, at last. Let us see what will be the end of God's poor despised people. (1.) Preferment. There have been times the iniquity of which has been such that men's piety has hindered their preferment in this world, and put them quite out of the way of raising estates ; but those that keep God's way may be assured that in due time he will *exalt them to inherit the land* (*v.* 34) ; he will advance them to a place in the heavenly mansions, to dignity, and honour, and true wealth, in the New Jerusalem, to inherit that good land, that land of promise, of which Canaan was a type ; he will exalt them above all contempt and danger. (2.) Peace, *v.* 37. Let all people *mark the perfect man, and behold the upright ;* take notice of him to admire him and imitate him, keep your eye upon him to observe what comes of him, and you will find that *the end of that man is peace.* Sometimes the latter end of his days proves more comfortable to him than the beginning was ; the storms blow over, and he is comforted again, after the time that he was afflicted. However, if all his days continue dark and cloudy, perhaps his dying day may prove comfortable to him and his sun may set in brightness ; or, if it should set under a cloud, yet his future state will be peace, everlasting peace. Those that walk in their up-

rightness while they live shall enter into peace when they die, Isa. lvii. 2. A peaceful death has concluded the troublesome life of many a good man; and all is well that thus ends everlastingly well. Balaam himself wished that his death and his last end might be like that of the righteous Num. xxiii. 10. (3.) Salvation, *v.* 39, 40. *The salvation of the righteous* (which may be applied to the great salvation of which *the prophets enquired and searched diligently,* 1 Pet. i. 10) *is of the Lord;* it will be the Lord's doing. The eternal salvation, that salvation of God which those shall see that *order their conversation aright* (1. 23), is likewise of the Lord. And he that intends Christ and heaven for them will be a God all-sufficient to them: *He is their strength in time of trouble,* to support them under it and carry them through it. *He shall help them and deliver them,* help them to do their duties, to bear their burdens, and to maintain their spiritual conflicts, help them to bear their troubles well and *get good by them,* and, in due time, shall deliver them out of their troubles. He shall deliver them from the wicked that would overwhelm them and swallow them up, shall secure them there, where the wicked cease from troubling. He shall *save them,* not only keep them safe, but make them happy, *because they trust in him,* not because they have merited it from him, but because they have committed themselves to him and reposed a confidence in him, and have thereby honoured him.

PSALM XXXVIII.

This is one of the penitential psalms; it is full of grief and complaint from the beginning to the end. David's sins and his afflictions are the cause of his grief and the matter of his complaints. It should seem he was now sick and in pain, which reminded him of his sins and helped to humble him for them; he was, at the same time, deserted by his friends and persecuted by his enemies; so that the psalm is calculated for the depth of distress and a complication of calamities. He complains, I. Of God's displeasure, and of his own sin which provoked God against him, ver. 1—5. II. Of his bodily sickness, ver. 6—10. III. Of the unkindness of his friends, ver. 11. IV. Of the injuries which his enemies did him, pleading his good conduct towards them, yet confessing his sins against God, ver. 12—20. Lastly, he concludes the psalm with earnest prayers to God for his gracious presence and help, ver. 21, 22. In singing this psalm we ought to be much affected with the malignity of sin; and, if we have not such troubles as are here described, we know not how soon we may have, and therefore must sing of them by way of preparation, and we know that others have them, and therefore we must sing of them by way of sympathy.

A psalm of David to bring to remembrance.

O LORD, rebuke me not in thy wrath: neither chasten me in thy hot displeasure. 2 For thine arrows stick fast in me, and thy hand presseth me sore. 3 *There is* no soundness in my flesh because of thine anger; neither *is there any* rest in my bones because of my sin. 4 For mine iniquities are gone over mine head: as a heavy burden they are too heavy for me. 5 My wounds stink *and* are corrupt because of my foolishness. 6 I am troubled; I am bowed down greatly; I go mourning all the day

long. 7 For my loins are filled with a loathsome *disease:* and *there is* no soundness in my flesh. 8 I am feeble and sore broken: I have roared by reason of the disquietness of my heart. 9 Lord, all my desire *is* before thee; and my groaning is not hid from thee. 10 My heart panteth, my strength faileth me: as for the light of mine eyes, it also is gone from me. 11 My lovers and my friends stand aloof from my sore; and my kinsmen stand afar off.

The title of this psalm is very observable; it is a psalm *to bring to remembrance;* the 70th psalm, which was likewise penned in a day of affliction, is so entitled. It is designed, 1. To bring to his own remembrance. We will suppose it penned when he was sick and in pain, and then it teaches us that times of sickness are times to bring to remembrance, to bring the sin to remembrance, for which God contended with us, to awaken our consciences to deal faithfully and plainly with us, and set our sins in order before us, for our humiliation. *In a day of adversity consider.* Or we may suppose it penned after his recovery, but designed as a record of the convictions he was under and the workings of his heart when he was in affliction, that upon every review of this psalm he might call to mind the good impressions then made upon him and make a fresh improvement of them. To the same purport was the writing of Hezekiah when he had been sick. 2. To put others in mind of the same things which he was himself mindful of, and to teach them what to think and what to say when they are sick and in affliction; let them think as he did, and speak as he did.

I. He deprecates the wrath of God and his displeasure in his affliction (*v.* 1): *O Lord! rebuke me not in thy wrath.* With this same petition he began another prayer for the visitation of the sick, vi. 1. This was most upon his heart, and should be most upon ours when we are in affliction, that, however God rebukes and chastens us, it may not be in wrath and displeasure, for that will be wormwood and gall in the affliction and misery. Those that would escape the wrath of God must pray against that more than any outward affliction, and be content to bear any outward affliction while it comes from, and consists with, the love of God.

II. He bitterly laments the impressions of God's displeasure upon his soul (*v.* 2): *Thy arrows stick fast in me.* Let Job's complaint (ch. vii. 4) expound this of David. By the arrows of the Almighty he means the terrors of God, which did set themselves in array against him. He was under a very melancholy frightful apprehension of the wrath of God against him for his sins, and thought he could look for nothing but judgment and fiery indignation to devour him. God's arrows, as they are sure to hit the mark, so they are sure to stick where they hit, to stick fast, till he is pleased to draw them out and to bind up with his comforts the wound he has made with his terrors. This will be the everlasting misery of the damned—the arrows of God's wrath will stick fast in them and the wound will be incurable. " *Thy hand,* thy heavy hand, *presses me sore,* and I am ready to sink under it; it not only lies hard upon me, but it lies long; and who knows the power of God's anger, the weight of his hand?" Sometimes God shot his arrows, and stretched forth his hand, for David (xviii. 14), but now against him; so uncertain is the continuance of divine comforts, where yet the continuance of divine grace is assured. He complains of God's wrath as that which inflicted the bodily distemper he was under (*v.* 3): *There is no soundness in my flesh because of thy anger.* The bitterness of it, infused in his mind, affected his body; but that was not the worst: it caused the disquietude of his heart, by reason of which he forgot the courage of a soldier, the dignity of a prince, and all the cheerfulness of the sweet psalmist of Israel, and roared terribly, *v.* 8. Nothing will disquiet the heart of a good man so much as the sense of God's anger, which shows what a fearful thing it is to fall into his hands. The way to keep the heart quiet is to keep ourselves in the love of God and to do nothing to offend him.

III. He acknowledges his sin to be the procuring provoking cause of all his troubles, and groans more under the load of guilt than any other load, *v.* 3. He complains that his flesh had no soundness, his bones had no rest, so great an agitation he was in. "It is *because of thy anger;* that kindles the fire which burns so fiercely;" but, in the next words, he justifies God herein, and takes all the blame upon himself: " It is *because of my sin.* I have deserved it, and so have brought it upon myself. My own iniquities do correct me." If our trouble be the fruit of God's anger, we may thank ourselves; it is our sin that is the cause of it. Are we restless? It is sin that makes us so. If there were not sin in our souls, there would be no pain in our bones, no illness in our bodies. It is sin therefore that this good man complains most of, 1. As a burden, a heavy burden (*v.* 4): " *My iniquities have gone over my head,* as proud waters over a man that is sinking and drowning, or as a heavy burden upon my head, pressing me down more than I am able to bear or to bear up under." Note, Sin is a burden. The power of sin dwelling in us is a weight, Heb. xii. 1. All are clogged with it; it keeps men from soaring upward and pressing forward. All the saints are complaining of it as a body of death they are loaded with, Rom. vii. 24. The guilt of sin committed by us is a burden, a heavy burden; it is a burden to God (he is pressed under it,

Amos ii. 13), a burden to the whole creation, which groans under it, Rom. viii. 21, 22. It will, first or last, be a burden to the sinner himself, either a burden of repentance when he is pricked to the heart for it, labours, and is heavy-laden, under it, or a burden of ruin when it sinks him to the lowest hell and will for ever detain him there; it will be a talent of lead upon him, Zech. v. 8. Sinners are said to bear their iniquity. Threatenings are burdens. 2. As wounds, dangerous wounds (*v.* 5): " *My wounds stink and are corrupt* (as wounds in the body rankle, and fester, and grow foul, for want of being dressed and looked after), and it is through my own *foolishness.*" Sins are wounds (Gen. iv. 23), painful mortal wounds. Our wounds by sin are often in a bad condition, no care taken of them, no application made to them, and it is owing to the sinner's foolishness in not confessing sin, xxxii. 3, 4. A slight sore, neglected, may prove of fatal consequence, and so may a slight sin slighted and left unrepented of.

IV. He bemoans himself because of his afflictions, and gives ease to his grief by giving vent to it and pouring out his complaint before the Lord.

1. He was troubled in mind, his conscience was pained, and he had no rest in his own spirit; and a wounded spirit who can bear? He was *troubled,* or distorted, *bowed down greatly,* and went *mourning all the day long, v.* 6. He was always pensive and melancholy, which made him a burden and terror to himself. His spirit was feeble and sorely broken, and his heart disquieted, *v.* 8. Herein David, in his sufferings, was a type of Christ, who, being in his agony, cried out, *My soul is exceedingly sorrowful.* This is a sorer affliction than any other in this world; whatever God is pleased to lay upon us, we have no reason to complain as long as he preserves to us the use of our reason and the peace of our consciences.

2. He was sick and weak in body; his loins were filled with a loathsome disease, some swelling, or ulcer, or inflammation (some think a plague-sore, such as Hezekiah's boil), and there was *no soundness in his flesh,* but, like Job, he was all over distempered. See, (1.) What vile bodies these are which we carry about with us, what grievous diseases they are liable to, and what an offence and grievance they may soon be made by some diseases to the souls that animate them, as they always are a cloud and clog. (2.) That the bodies both of the greatest and of the best of men have in them the same seeds of diseases that the bodies of others have, and are liable to the same disasters. David himself, though so great a prince and so great a saint, was not exempt from the most grievous diseases: there was no soundness even in his flesh. Probably this was after his sin in the matter of Uriah, and thus did he smart in his flesh for his fleshly lusts. When, at any

time, we are distempered in our bodies, we ought to remember how God has been dishonoured in and by our bodies. He was *feeble and sorely broken, v. 8.* His *heart panted,* and was in a continual palpitation, *v.* 10. His *strength* and limbs *failed* him. As for *the light of his eyes,* that *had gone from him,* either with much weeping or by a defluxion of rheum upon them, or perhaps through the lowness of his spirits and the frequent returns of fainting. Note, Sickness will tame the strongest body and the stoutest spirit. David was famed for his courage and great exploits; and yet, when God contended with him by bodily sickness and the impressions of his wrath upon his mind, his hair is cut, his heart fails him, and he becomes weak as water. Therefore let not the strong man glory in his strength, nor any man set grief at defiance, however it may be thought at a distance.

3. His friends were unkind to him (*v.* 11): *My lovers* (such as had been merry with him in the day of his mirth) now *stand aloof from my sore;* they would not sympathize with him in his griefs, nor so much as come within hearing of his complaints, but, like the priest and Levite (Luke x. 31), *passed by on the other side.* Even *his kinsmen,* that were bound to him by blood and alliance, *stood afar off.* See what little reason we have to trust in man or to wonder if we be disappointed in our expectations of kindness from men. Adversity tries friendship, and separates between the precious and the vile. It is our wisdom to make sure a friend in heaven, who will not stand aloof from our sore and from whose love no tribulation nor distress shall be able to separate us. David, in his troubles, was a type of Christ in his agony, Christ on his cross, feeble and sorely broken, and then deserted by his friends and kinsmen, who beheld afar off.

V. In the midst of his complaints, he comforts himself with the cognizance God graciously took both of his griefs and of his prayers (*v.* 9): "*Lord, all my desire is before thee.* Thou knowest what I want and what I would have: *My groaning is not hidden from thee.* Thou knowest the burdens I groan under and the blessings I groan after." The *groanings which cannot be uttered* are not hidden from him that *searches the heart and knows what is the mind of the Spirit,* Rom. viii. 26, 27.

In singing this, and praying it over, whatever burden lies upon our spirits, we should by faith cast it upon God, and all our care concerning it, and then be easy.

12 They also that seek after my life lay snares *for me :* and they that seek my hurt speak mischievous things, and imagine deceits all the day long. 13 But I, as a deaf *man,* heard not ; and *I was* as a dumb man *that* openeth not his mouth. 14 Thus I was as a man that heareth not, and in whose mouth *are* no reproofs. 15 For in thee, O LORD, do I hope : thou wilt hear, O Lord my God. 16 For I said, *Hear me,* lest *otherwise* they should rejoice over me : when my foot slippeth, they magnify *themselves* against me. 17 For I *am* ready to halt, and my sorrow *is* continually before me. 18 For I will declare mine iniquity ; I will be sorry for my sin. 19 But mine enemies *are* lively, *and* they are strong : and they that hate me wrongfully are multiplied. 20 They also that render evil for good are mine adversaries; because I follow *the thing that* good *is.* 21 Forsake me not, O LORD : O my God, be not far from me. 22 Make haste to help me, O Lord my salvation.

In these verses,

I. David complains of the power and malice of his enemies, who, it should seem, not only took occasion from the weakness of his body and the trouble of his mind to insult over him, but took advantage thence to do him a mischief. He has a great deal to say against them, which he humbly offers as a reason why God should appear for him, as xxv. 19, *Consider my enemies.* 1. "They are very spiteful and cruel : *They seek my hurt;* nay, they *seek after my life,*" *v.* 12. That life which was so precious in the sight of the Lord and all good men was aimed at, as if it had been forfeited, or a public nuisance. Such is the enmity of the serpent's seed against the seed of the woman ; it would wound the head, though it can but reach the heel. It is the blood of the saints that is thirsted after. 2. "They are very subtle and politic. They *lay snares,* they *imagine deceits,* and herein they are restless and unwearied : they do it *all the day long.* They speak mischievous things one to another; every one has something or other to propose that may be a mischief to me." Mischief, covered and carried on by deceit, may well be called a *snare.* 3. "They are very insolent and abusive : *When my foot slips,* when I fall into any trouble, or when I make any mistake, misplace a word, or take a false step, they magnify themselves against me ; they are pleased with it, and promise themselves that it will ruin my interest, and that if I slip I shall certainly fall and be undone." 4. "They are not only unjust, but very ungrateful : They *hate me wrongfully, v.* 19. I never did them any ill turn, nor so much as bore them any ill-will, nor ever gave them any provocation ; nay, *they render evil for good, v.* 20. Many a kindness I have done them, for which I might have expected a return of kindness ; but *for my love they are my adversaries,*" cix. 4. Such a rooted enmity there is in the hearts of wicked men to goodness for its own sake that they hate it, even when they themselves have the benefit of it; they hate prayer even in those that pray for them, and hate peace even in those that would be at peace with them. Very ill-natured indeed those are whom no courtesy will oblige, but who are rather exasperated by it. 5. "They are very impious and devilish: *They are my adversaries* merely *because I follow the thing that good is."* They hated him, not only for his kindness to them, but for his devotion and obedience to God; they hated him because they hated God and all that bear his image. If we suffer ill for doing well, we must not think it strange; from the beginning it was so (Cain slew Abel, because his works were righteous); nor must we think it hard, because it will not be always so; for so much the greater will our reward be. 6. "They are many and mighty: They *are lively; they are strong; they are multiplied, v.* 19. *Lord, how are those increased that trouble me?"* iii. 1. Holy David was weak and faint; his heart panted, and his strength failed; he was melancholy and of a sorrowful spirit, and persecuted by his friends; but at the same time his wicked enemies were strong and lively, and their number increased. Let us not therefore pretend to judge of men's characters by their outward condition; none knows love or hatred by all that is before him. It should seem that David in this, as in other complaints he makes of his enemies, has an eye to Christ, whose persecutors were such as are here described, perfectly lost to all honour and virtue. None hate Christianity but such as have first divested themselves of the first principles of humanity and broken through its most sacred bonds.

II. He reflects, with comfort, upon his own peaceable and pious behaviour under all the injuries and indignities that were done him. It is then only that our enemies do us a real mischief when they provoke us to sin (Neh. vi. 13), when they prevail to put us out of the possession of our own souls, and drive us from God and our duty. If by divine grace we are enabled to prevent this mischief, we quench their fiery darts, and are saved from harm. If still we hold fast our integrity and our peace, who can hurt us? This David did here. 1. He kept his temper, and was not ruffled nor discomposed by any of the slights that were put upon him or the mischievous things that were said or done against him (*v.* 13, 14): "*I, as a deaf man, heard not;* I took no notice of the affronts put upon me, did not resent them, nor was put into disorder by them, much less did I meditate revenge, or study to return the injury." Note, The less notice we take of the unkindness and injuries that are done us the more we consult the quiet of our own minds. Being deaf, he was dumb, as a man *in whose mouth there are no reproofs;* he was as silent as if he had nothing to say for himself, for fear of putting himself into a heat and incensing his enemies yet more against him; he would not only not recriminate upon them, but not so much as vindicate himself, lest his necessary defence should be construed his offence. Though they sought after his life, and his silence might be taken for a confession of his guilt, yet he was as a dumb man that opens not his mouth. Note, When our enemies are most clamorous it is generally our prudence to be silent, or to say little, lest we make bad worse. David could not hope by his mildness to win upon his enemies, nor by his soft answers to turn away their wrath; for they were men of such base spirits that they rendered him evil for good; and yet he conducted himself thus meekly towards them, that he might prevent his own sin and might have the comfort of it in the reflection. Herein David was a type of Christ, who was as a sheep dumb before the shearer, and, when he was reviled, reviled not again; and both are examples to us not to render railing for railing. 2. He kept close to his God by faith and prayer, and so both supported himself under these injuries and silenced his own resentments of them. (1.) He trusted in God (*v.* 15): "*I was as a man that opens not his mouth,* for *in thee, O Lord! do I hope.* I depend upon thee to plead my cause and clear my innocency, and, some way or other, to put my enemies to silence and shame." His lovers and friends, that should have owned him, and stood by him, and appeared as witnesses for him, withdrew from him, *v.* 10. But God is a friend that will never fail us if we hope in him. "*I was as a man that heareth not, for thou wilt hear.* Why need I hear, and God hear too?" He *careth for you* (1 Pet. v. 7), and why need you care and God care too? "*Thou wilt answer"* (so some) "and therefore I will say nothing." Note, It is a good reason why we should bear reproach and calumny with silence and patience, because God is a witness to all the wrong that is done us, and, in due time, will be a witness for us and against those that do us wrong; therefore let us be silent, because, if we be, then we may expect that God will appear for us, for this is an evidence that we trust in him; but, if we undertake to manage for ourselves, we take God's work out of his hands and forfeit the benefit of his appearing for us. Our Lord Jesus, when he suffered, threatened not, because he *committed himself to him that judges righteously* (1 Pet. ii. 23); and we shall lose nothing, at last, by doing so. *Thou shalt answer, Lord, for me.* (2.) He called upon God (*v.* 16): *For I said,* Hear me (that is supplied); "*I said so"* (as *v.* 15); "in thee do I hope, for thou wilt hear, lest they should rejoice over me. I comforted myself with that when I was apprehensive that they would overwhelm me." It is a great support to us, when men are false and unkind, that we have a God to go to whom we may be free with and who will be faithful to us.

III. He here bewails his own follies and infirmities. 1. He was very sensible of the present workings of corruption in him, and that he was now ready to repine at the providence of God and to be put into a passion by the injuries men did him : *I am ready to halt, v.* 17. This will best be explained by a reflection like this which the psalmist made upon himself in a similar case (lxxiii. 2): *My feet were almost gone, when I saw the prosperity of the wicked.* So here : *I was ready to halt,* ready to say, *I have cleansed my hands in vain.* His sorrow was continual : *All the day long have I been plagued* (lxxiii. 13, 14), and it was continually before him ; he could not forbear poring upon it, and that made him almost ready to halt between religion and irreligion. The fear of this drove him to his God : " In thee do I hope, not only that thou wilt plead my cause, but that thou wilt prevent my falling into sin." Good men, by setting their sorrow continually before them, have been ready to halt, who, by setting God always before them, have kept their standing. 2. He remembered against himself his former transgressions, acknowledging that by them he had brought these troubles upon himself and forfeited the divine protection. Though before men he could justify himself, before God he will judge and condemn himself (*v.* 18): " *I will declare my iniquity,* and not cover it ; *I will be sorry for my sin,* and not make a light matter of it ;" and this helped to make him silent under the rebukes of Providence and the reproaches of men. Note, If we be truly penitent for sin, that will make us patient under affliction, and particularly under unjust censures. Two things are required in repentance :—(1.) Confession of sin : " *I will declare my iniquity ;* I will not only in general own myself a sinner, but I will make a particular acknowledgment of what I have done amiss." We must declare our sins before God freely and fully, and with their aggravating circumstances, that we may give glory to God and take shame to ourselves. (2.) Contrition for sin : *I will be sorry for it.* Sin will have sorrow ; every true penitent grieves for the dishonour he has done to God and the wrong he has done to himself. " I will be in care or fear about my sin" (so some), " in fear lest it ruin me and in care to get it pardoned."

IV. He concludes with very earnest prayers to God for his gracious presence with him and seasonable powerful succour in his distress (*v.* 21, 22): " *Forsake me not, O Lord!* though my friends forsake me, and though I deserve to be forsaken by thee. Be not far from me, as my unbelieving heart is ready to fear thou art." Nothing goes nearer to the heart of a good man in affliction than to be under the apprehension of God's deserting him in wrath ; nor does any thing therefore

come more feelingly from his heart than this prayer : " *Lord, be not thou far from me ; make haste for my help ;* for I am ready to perish, and in danger of being lost if relief do not come quickly." God gives us leave, not only to call upon him when we are in trouble, but to hasten him. He pleads, "Thou art *my God,* whom I serve, and on whom I depend to bear me out ; and *my salvation,* who alone art able to save me, who hast engaged thyself by promise to save me, and from whom alone I expect salvation." Is any afflicted ? let him thus pray, let him thus plead, let him thus hope, in singing this psalm.

PSALM XXXIX.

David seems to have been in a great strait when he penned this psalm, and, upon some account or other, very uneasy ; for it is with some difficulty that he conquers his passion, and composes his spirit himself to take that good counsel which he had given to others (xxxvii.) to rest in the Lord, and wait patiently for him, without fretting ; for it is easier to give the good advice than to give the good example of quietness under affliction. What was the particular trouble which gave occasion for the conflict David was now in does not appear. Perhaps it was the death of some dear friend or relation that was the trial of his patience, and that suggested to him these meditations of mortality ; and at the same time, it should seem too, he himself was weak and ill, and under some prevailing distemper. His enemies likewise were seeking advantages against him, and watched for his halting, that they might have something to reproach him for. Thus aggrieved, I. He relates the struggle that was in his breast between grace and corruption, between passion and patience, ver. 1—3. II. He meditates upon the doctrine of man's frailty and mortality, and prays to God to instruct him in it, ver. 4—6. III. He applies to God for the pardon of his sins, the removal of his afflictions, and the lengthening out of his life till he was ready for death, ver. 7—13. This is a funeral psalm, and very proper for the occasion ; in singing it we should get our hearts duly affected with the brevity, uncertainty, and calamitous state of human life ; and those on whose comforts God has, by death, made breaches, will find this psalm of great use to them, in order to their obtaining what we ought much to aim at under such an affliction, which is to get it sanctified to us for our spiritual benefit and to get our hearts reconciled to the holy will of God in it.

To the chief musician, *even* to Jeduthun. A psalm of David.

I SAID, I will take heed to my ways, that I sin not with my tongue : I will keep my mouth with a bridle, while the wicked is before me. 2 I was dumb with silence, I held my peace, *even* from good ; and my sorrow was stirred. 3 My heart was hot within me, while I was musing the fire burned : *then* spake I with my tongue, 4 LORD, make me to know mine end, and the measure of my days, what it *is ; that* I may know how frail I *am.* 5 Behold, thou hast made my days *as* a handbreadth ; and mine age *is* as nothing before thee : verily every man at his best state *is* altogether vanity. Selah. 6 Surely every man walketh in a vain show : surely they are disquieted in vain : he heapeth up *riches,* and knoweth not who shall gather them.

David here recollects, and leaves upon record, the workings of his heart under his afflictions ; and it is good for us to do so, that what was thought amiss may be amended, and what was well thought of may be improved the next time.

I. He remembered the covenants he had made with God to walk circumspectly, and to be very cautious both of what he did and what he said. When at any time we are tempted to sin, and are in danger of falling into it, we must call to mind the solemn vows we have made against sin, against the particular sin we are upon the brink of. God can, and will, remind us of them (Jer. ii. 20, *Thou saidst, I will not transgress*), and therefore we ought to remind ourselves of them. So David did here.

1. He remembers that he had resolved, in general, to be very cautious and circumspect in his walking (*v.* 1): *I said, I will take heed to my ways;* and it was well said, and what he would never unsay and therefore must never gainsay. Note, (1.) It is the great concern of every one of us to take heed to our ways, that is, to walk circumspectly, while others walk at all adventures. (2.) We ought stedfastly to resolve that we will take heed to our ways, and frequently to renew that resolution. Fast bind, fast find. (3.) Having resolved to take heed to our ways, we must, upon all occasions, remind ourselves of that resolution, for it is a covenant never to be forgotten, but which we must be always mindful of.

2. He remembers that he had in particular covenanted against tongue-sins—that he would not sin with his tongue, that he would not speak amiss, either to offend God or *offend the generation of the righteous*, lxxiii. 15. It is not so easy as we could wish not to sin in thought; but, if an evil thought should arise in his mind, he would lay his hand upon his mouth, and suppress it, that it should go no further: and this is so great an attainment that, *if any offend not in word, the same is a perfect man;* and so needful a one that of him who *seems to be religious, but bridles not his tongue*, it is declared *His religion is vain.* David had resolved, (1.) That he would at all times watch against tongue-sins: "*I will keep a bridle*, or muzzle, *upon my mouth.*" He would keep a bridle upon it, as upon an unruly horse, to guide and direct it, to check and curb it, to keep it in the right way and on a good pace; see Jam. iii. 3. Watchfulness in the habit is the bridle upon the head; watchfulness in the act and exercise is the hand upon the bridle. He would keep a muzzle upon it, as upon an unruly dog that is fierce and does mischief; by particular stedfast resolution corruption is restrained from breaking out at the lips, and so is muzzled. (2.) That he would double his guard against them when there was most danger of scandal—*when the wicked is before me.* When he was in company with the wicked he would take heed of saying any thing that might harden them or give occasion to them to blaspheme. If good men fall into bad company, they must take heed

382

what they say. Or, *when the wicked is before me*, in my thoughts. When he was contemplating the pride and power, the prosperity and flourishing estate, of evil-doers, he was tempted to speak amiss; and therefore then he would take special care what he said. Note, The stronger the temptation to a sin is the stronger the resolution must be against it.

II. Pursuant to these covenants he made a shift with much ado to bridle his tongue (*v.* 2): *I was dumb with silence; I held my peace even from good.* His silence was commendable; and the greater the provocation was the more praiseworthy was his silence. Watchfulness and resolution, in the strength of God's grace, will do more towards the bridling of the tongue than we can imagine, though it be an unruly evil. But what shall we say of his keeping silence *even from good?* Was it his wisdom that he refrained from good discourse when the wicked were before him, because he would not cast pearls before swine? I rather think it was his weakness; because he might not say any thing, he would say nothing, but ran into an extreme, which was a reproach to the law, for that prescribes a mean between extremes. The same law which forbids all corrupt communication requires *that which is good and to the use of edifying*, Eph. iv. 29.

III. The less he spoke the more he thought and the more warmly. Binding the distempered part did but draw the humour to it: *My sorrow was stirred, my heart was hot within me, v.* 3. He could bridle his tongue, but he could not keep his passion under; though he suppressed the smoke, that was as a fire in his bones, and, while he was musing upon his afflictions and upon the prosperity of the wicked, the fire burned. Note, Those that are of a fretful discontented spirit ought not to pore much, for, while they suffer their thoughts to dwell upon the causes of the calamity, the fire of their discontent is fed with fuel and burns the more furiously. Impatience is a sin that has its ill cause within ourselves, and that is musing, and its ill effects upon ourselves, and that is no less than burning. If therefore we would prevent the mischief of ungoverned passions, we must redress the grievance of ungoverned thoughts.

IV. When he did speak, at last, it was to the purpose: *At the last I spoke with my tongue.* Some make what he said to be the breach of his good purpose, and conclude that, in what he said, he sinned with his tongue; and so they make what follows to be a passionate wish *that he might die*, like Elijah (1 Kings xix. 4) and Job, *ch.* vi. 8, 9. But I rather take it to be, not the breach of his good purpose, but the reformation of his mistake in carrying it too far; he had kept silence from good, but now he would so keep silence no longer. He had nothing to say to the wicked that were before him, for to them he knew not how to place his words, but, after long musing, the first word he said was a prayer, and a devout meditation upon a subject which it will be good for us all to think much of.

1. He prays to God to make him sensible of the shortness and uncertainty of life and the near approach of death (*v.* 4): *Lord, make me to know my end and the measure of my days.* He does not mean, " Lord, let me know how long I shall live and when I shall die." We could not, in faith, pray such a prayer; for God has nowhere promised to let us know, but has, in wisdom, locked up that knowledge among the secret things which belong not to us, nor would it be good for us to know it. But, *Lord, make me to know my end,* means, " Lord, give me wisdom and grace to consider it (Deut. xxxii. 29) and to improve what I know concerning it." *The living know that they shall die* (Eccl. ix. 5), but few care for thinking of death; we have therefore need to pray that God by his grace would conquer that aversion which is in our corrupt hearts to the thoughts of death. " Lord, make me to consider," (1.) " What death is. It is my end, the end of my life, and all the employments and enjoyments of life. It is the end of all men," Eccl. vii. 2. It is a final period to our state of probation and preparation, and an awful entrance upon a state of recompence and retribution. To the wicked man it is the end of all joys; to a godly man it is the end of all griefs. " Lord, give me to know my end, to be better acquainted with death, to make it more familiar to me (Job xvii. 14), and to be more affected with the greatness of the change. Lord, give me to consider what a serious thing it is to die." (2.) " How near it is. Lord, give me to consider the measure of my days, that they are measured in the counsel of God" (the end is a fixed end, so the word signifies; *my days are determined,* Job xiv. 5) "and that the measure is but short: My days will soon be numbered and finished." When we look upon death as a thing at a distance we are tempted to adjourn the necessary preparations for it; but, when we consider how short life is, we shall see ourselves concerned to do what our hand finds to do, not only with all our might, but with all possible expedition. (3.) That it is continually working in us: " Lord, give me to consider how frail I am, how scanty the stock of life is, and how faint the spirits which are as the oil to keep that lamp burning." We find by daily experience that the earthly house of this tabernacle is mouldering and going to decay: " Lord, make us to consider this, that we may secure mansions in the house not made with hands."

2. He meditates upon the brevity and vanity of life, pleading them with God for relief under the burdens of life, as Job often, and pleading them with himself for his quickening to the business of life.

(1.) Man's life on earth is short and of no continuance, and that is a reason why we should sit loose to it and prepare for the end

of it (*v.* 5): *Behold, thou hast made my days as a hand-breadth,* the breadth of four fingers, a certain dimension, a small one, and· the measure whereof we have always about us, always before our eyes. We need no rod, no pole, no measuring line, wherewith to take the dimension of our days, nor any skill in arithmetic wherewith to compute the number of them. No; we have the standard of them at our fingers' end, and there is no multiplication of it; it is but one hand-breadth in all. Our time is short, and God has made it so; for *the number of our months is with him.* It is short, and he knows it to be so: It *is as nothing before thee.* He remembers *how short our time is,* lxxxix. 47. *It is nothing in comparison with thee;* so some. All time is nothing to God's eternity, much less our share of time.

(2.) Man's life on earth is vain and of no value, and therefore it is folly to be fond of it and wisdom to make sure of a better life. Adam is Abel—*man is vanity,* in his present state. He is not what he seems to be, has not what he promised himself. He and all his comforts lie at a continual uncertainty; and if there were not another life after this, all things considered, he were made in vain. He is vanity; he is mortal, he is mutable. Observe, [1.] How emphatically this truth is expressed here. *First, Every man is vanity,* without exception; high and low, rich and poor, all meet in this. *Secondly,* He is so *at his best estate,* when he is young, and strong, and healthful, in wealth and honour, and the height of prosperity; when he is most easy, and merry, and secure, and thinks his mountain stands strong. *Thirdly,* He is *altogether vanity,* as vain as you can imagine. *All man is all vanity* (so it may be read); every thing about him is uncertain; nothing is substantial and durable but what relates to the new man. *Fourthly, Verily* he is so. This is a truth of undoubted certainty, but which we are very unwilling to believe and need to have solemnly attested to us, as indeed it is by frequent instances. *Fifthly, Selah* is annexed, as a note commanding observation. " Stop here, and pause awhile, that you may take time to consider and apply this truth, that every man is vanity." We ourselves are so. [2.] For the proof of the vanity of man, as mortal, he here mentions three things, and shows the vanity of each of them, *v.* 6. *First,* The vanity of our joys and honours: *Surely every man walks* (even when he walks in state, when he walks in pleasure) in a shadow, in an image, *in a vain show.* When he makes a figure his fashion passes away, and his great pomp is but great fancy, Acts xxv. 23. It is but a show, and therefore a vain show, like the rainbow, the gaudy colours of which must needs vanish and disappear quickly when the substratum is but a cloud, a vapour; such is life (Jam. iv. 14), and therefore such are all the gaieties of it. *Secondly,* The vanity of our griefs and fears *Surely they are disquieted in vain.* Our disquietudes are often groundless (we vex ourselves without any just cause, and the occasions of our trouble are often the creatures of our own fancy and imagination), and they are always fruitless; we disquiet ourselves in vain, for we cannot, with all our disquietment, alter the nature of things nor the counsel of God; things will be as they are when we have disquieted ourselves ever so much about them. *Thirdly*, The vanity of our cares and toils. Man takes a great deal of pains to *heap up riches*, and they are but like heaps of manure in the furrows of the field, good for nothing unless they be spread. But, when he has filled his treasures with his trash, he *knows not who shall gather them*, nor to whom they shall descend when he is gone; for he shall not take them away with him. He asks not, *For whom do I labour?* and that is his folly, Eccl. iv. 8. But, if he did ask, he could not tell whether he should be a wise man or a fool, a friend or a foe, Eccl. ii. 19. *This is vanity.*

7 And now, Lord, what wait I for? my hope *is* in thee. 8 Deliver me from all my transgressions: make me not the reproach of the foolish. 9 I was dumb, I opened not my mouth; because thou didst *it*. 10 Remove thy stroke away from me: I am consumed by the blow of thine hand. 11 When thou with rebukes dost correct man for iniquity, thou makest his beauty to consume away like a moth : surely every man *is* vanity. Selah. 12 Hear my prayer, O LORD, and give ear unto my cry; hold not thy peace at my tears : for I *am* a stranger with thee, *and* a sojourner, as all my fathers *were.* 13 O spare me, that I may recover strength, before I go hence, and be no more.

The psalmist, having meditated on the shortness and uncertainty of life, and the vanity and vexation of spirit that attend all the comforts of life, here, in these verses, turns his eyes and heart heaven-ward. When there is no solid satisfaction to be had in the creature it is to be found in God, and in communion with him; and to him we should be driven by our disappointments in the world. David here expresses,

I. His dependence on God, *v.* 7. Seeing all is vanity, and man himself is so, 1. He despairs of a happiness in the things of the world, and disclaims all expectations from it: " *Now, Lord, what wait I for?* Even nothing from the things of sense and time; I have nothing to wish for, nothing to hope for, from this earth." Note, The consideration of the vanity and frailty of human life should deaden our desires to the things of

this world and lower our expectations from it. " If the world be such a thing as this, God deliver me from having, or seeking, my portion in it." We cannot reckon upon constant health and prosperity, nor upon comfort in any relation; for it is all as uncertain as our continuance here. " Though I have sometimes foolishly promised myself this and the other from the world, I am now of another mind." 2. He takes hold of happiness and satisfaction in God: *My hope is in thee.* Note, When creature-confidences fail, it is our comfort that we have a God to go to, a God to trust to, and we should thereby be quickened to take so much the faster hold of him by faith.

II. His submission to God, and his cheerful acquiescence in his holy will, *v.* 9. If our hope be in God for a happiness in the other world, we may well afford to reconcile ourselves to all the dispensations of his providence concerning us in this world: *" I was dumb; I opened not my mouth* in a way of complaint and murmuring." He now again recovered that serenity and sedateness of mind which were disturbed, *v.* 2. Whatever comforts he is deprived of, whatever crosses he is burdened with, he will be easy. *" Because thou didst it;* it did not come to pass by chance, but according to thy appointment." We may here see, 1. A good God doing all, and ordering all events concerning us. Of every event we may say, " This is the finger of God; it is the Lord's doing," whoever were the instruments. 2. A good man, for that reason, saying nothing against it. He is dumb, he has nothing to object, no question to ask, no dispute to raise upon it. All that God does is well done.

III. His desire towards God, and the prayers he puts up to him. *Is any afflicted? let him pray*, as David here,

1. For the pardoning of his sin and the preventing of his shame, *v.* 8. Before he prays (*v.* 10), *Remove thy stroke from me*, he prays (*v.* 8), " *Deliver me from all my offences*, from the guilt I have contracted, the punishment I have deserved, and the power of corruption by which I have been enslaved." When God forgives our sins he delivers us from them, he delivers us from them all. He pleads, *Make me not a reproach to the foolish.* Wicked people are foolish people; and they then show their folly most when they think to show their wit, by scoffing at God's people. When David prays that God would pardon his sins, and not make him a reproach, it is to be taken as a prayer for peace of conscience (" Lord, leave me not to the power of melancholy, which the foolish will laugh at me for "), and as a prayer for grace, that God would never leave him to himself, so far as to do any thing that might make him a reproach to bad men. Note, This is a good reason why we should both watch and pray against sin, because the credit of our profession is nearly concerned in the preservation of our integrity.

2. For the removal of his affliction, that he might speedily be eased of his present burdens (*v.* 10): *Remove thy stroke away from me.* Note, When we are under the correcting hand of God our eye must be to God himself, and not to any other, for relief. He only that inflicts the stroke can remove it; and we may then in faith, and with satisfaction, pray that our afflictions may be removed, when our sins are pardoned (Isa. xxxviii. 17), and when, as here, the affliction is sanctified and has done its work, and we are humbled under the hand of God.

(1.) He pleads the great extremity he was reduced to by his affliction, which made him the proper object of God's compassion: *I am consumed by the blow of thy hand.* His sickness prevailed to such a degree that his spirits failed, his strength was wasted, and his body emaciated. "The blow, or conflict, of thy hand has brought me even to the gates of death." Note, The strongest, and boldest, and best of men cannot bear up under, much less make head against, the power of God's wrath. It was not his case only, but any man will find himself an unequal match for the Almighty, *v.* 11. When God, at any time, contends with us, when with rebukes he corrects us, [1.] We cannot impeach the equity of his controversy, but must acknowledge that he is righteous in it; for, whenever he corrects man, it is for iniquity. Our ways and our doings procure the trouble to ourselves, and we are beaten with a rod of our own making. It is the yoke of our transgressions, though it be *bound with his hand,* Lam. i. 14. [2.] We cannot oppose the effects of his controversy, but he will be too hard for us. As we have nothing to move in arrest of his judgment, so we have no way of escaping the execution. God's rebukes make man's *beauty to consume away like a moth;* we often see, we sometimes feel, how much the body is weakened and decayed by sickness in a little time; the countenance is changed; where are the ruddy cheek and lip, the sprightly eye, the lively look, the smiling face? It is the reverse of all this that presents itself to view. What a poor thing is beauty; and what fools are those that are proud of it, or in love with it, when it will certainly, and may quickly, be consumed thus! Some make the moth to represent man, who is as easily crushed as a moth with the touch of a finger, Job. iv. 19. Others make it to represent the divine rebukes, which silently and insensibly waste and consume us, as the moth does the garment. All this abundantly proves what he had said before, that surely every man is vanity, weak and helpless; so he will be found when God comes to contend with him.

(2.) He pleads the good impressions made upon him by his affliction. He hoped that the end was accomplished for which it was sent, and that therefore it would be removed in mercy; and unless an affliction has done its work, though it may be removed, it is not

removed in mercy. [1.] It had set him a weeping, and he hoped God would take notice of that. When the Lord God called to mourning, he answered the call and accommodated himself to the dispensation, and therefore could, in faith, pray, *Lord, hold not thy peace at my tears, v.* 12. He that does not willingly afflict and grieve the children of men, much less his own children, will not hold his peace at their tears, but will either speak deliverance for them (and, if he speak, it is done) or in the mean time speak comfort to them and make them to hear joy and gladness. [2.] It had set him a praying; and afflictions are sent to stir up prayer. If they have that effect, and when we are afflicted we pray more, and pray better, than before, we may hope that God will hear our prayer and give ear to our cry; for the prayer which by his providence he gives occasion for, and which by his Spirit of grace he indites, shall not return void. [3.] It had helped to wean him from the world and to take his affections off from it. Now he began, more than ever, to look upon himself as *a stranger and sojourner* here, like all his fathers, not at home in this world, but travelling through it to another, to a better, and would never reckon himself at home till he came to heaven. He pleads it with God: "Lord, take cognizance of me, and of my wants and burdens, for I am a stranger here, and therefore meet with strange usage; I am slighted and oppressed as a stranger; and whence should I expect relief but from thee, from that other country to which I belong?"

3. He prays for a reprieve yet a little longer (*v.* 13): "*O spare me,* ease me, raise me up from this illness, that I may recover strength both in body and mind, that I may get into a more calm and composed frame of spirit, and may be better prepared for another world, *before I go hence* by death, *and* shall *be no more* in this world." Some make this to be a passionate wish that God would send him help quickly or it would be too late, like that, Job x. 20, 21. But I rather take it as a pious prayer that God would continue him here till by his grace he had made him fit to go hence, and that he might finish the work of life before his life was finished. *Let my soul live, and it shall praise thee.*

PSALM XL.

It should seem David penned this psalm upon occasion of his deliverance, by the power and goodness of God, from some great and pressing trouble, by which he was in danger of being overwhelmed; probably it was some trouble of mind arising from a sense of sin and of God's displeasure against him for it; whatever it was, the same Spirit that indited his praises for that deliverance was in him, at the same time, a Spirit of prophecy, testifying of the sufferings of Christ and the glory that should follow; or, ere he was aware, he was led to speak of his undertaking, and the discharge of his undertaking, in words that must be applied to Christ only; and therefore how far the praises that here go before that illustrious prophecy, and the prayers that follow, may safely and profitably be applied to him it will be worth while to consider. In this psalm, I. David records God's favour to him in delivering him out of his deep distress, with thankfulness to his praise, ver. 1—5. II. Thence he takes occasion to speak of the work of our redemption by Christ, ver. 6—10. III. That gives him encouragement to pray to God for mercy and grace both for himself and for his friends, ver. 11—17. If, in singing this psalm, we mix faith with the prophecy of Christ, and join in sincerity with the praises and prayers here offered up, we make melody with our hearts to the Lord.

To the chief musician. A psalm of David.

I WAITED patiently for the LORD; and he inclined unto me, and heard my cry. 2 He brought me up also out of a horrible pit, out of the miry clay, and set my feet upon a rock, *and* established my goings. 3 And he hath put a new song in my mouth, *even* praise unto our God: many shall see *it*, and fear, and shall trust in the LORD. 4 Blessed *is* that man that maketh the LORD his trust, and respecteth not the proud, nor such as turn aside to lies. 5 Many, O LORD my God, *are* thy wonderful works *which* thou hast done, and thy thoughts *which are* to us-ward: they cannot be reckoned up in order unto thee: if I would declare and speak *of them*, they are more than can be numbered.

In these verses we have,

I. The great distress and trouble that the psalmist had been in. He had been plunged into a horrible pit and into miry clay (*v.* 2), out of which he could not work himself, and in which he found himself sinking yet further. He says nothing here either of the sickness of his body or the insults of his enemies, and therefore we have reason to think it was some inward disquiet and perplexity of spirit that was now his greatest grievance. Despondency of spirit under the sense of God's withdrawings, and prevailing doubts and fears about the eternal state, are indeed a horrible pit and miry clay, and have been so to many a dear child of God.

II. His humble attendance upon God and his believing expectations from him in those depths: *I waited patiently for the Lord, v.* 1. *Waiting, I waited.* He expected relief from no other than from God; the same hand that tears must heal, that smites must bind up (Hos. vi. 1), or it will never be done. From God he expected relief, and he was big with expectation, not doubting but it would come in due time. There is power enough in God to help the weakest, and grace enough in God to help the unworthiest, of all his people that trust in him. But he waited patiently, which intimates that the relief did not come quickly; yet he doubted not but it would come, and resolved to continue believing, and hoping, and praying, till it did come. Those whose expectation is from God may wait with assurance, but must wait with patience. Now this is very applicable to Christ. His agony, both in the garden and on the cross, was the same continued, and it was a horrible pit and miry clay. Then was his soul troubled and exceedingly sorrowful; but then he prayed, *Father, glorify thy name; Father, save me;* then he kept hold of his relation to his Father, "My

God, my God," and thus waited patiently for him.

III. His comfortable experience of God's goodness to him in his distress, which he records for the honour of God and his own and others' encouragement.

1. God answered his prayers: *He inclined unto me and heard my cry.* Those that wait patiently for God, though they may wait long, do not wait in vain. Our Lord Jesus was *heard in that he feared*, Heb. v. 7. Nay, he was sure that the Father heard him always.

2. He silenced his fears, and stilled the tumult of his spirits, and gave him a settled peace of conscience (*v.* 2): "*He brought me up out of that horrible pit* of despondency and despair, scattered the clouds, and shone brightly upon my soul, with the assurances of his favour; and not only so, but *set my feet upon a rock and established my goings.*" Those that have been under the prevalency of a religious melancholy, and by the grace of God have been relieved, may apply this very feelingly to themselves; they are brought up out of a horrible pit. (1.) The mercy is completed by the setting of their feet upon a rock, where they find firm footing, are as much elevated with the hopes of heaven as they were before cast down with the fears of hell. Christ is the rock on which a poor soul may stand fast, and on whose mediation alone between us and God we can build any solid hopes or satisfaction. (2.) It is continued in the establishment of their goings. Where God has given a stedfast hope he expects there should be a steady regular conversation; and, if that be the blessed fruit of it, we have reason to acknowledge, with abundance of thankfulness, the riches and power of his grace.

3. He filled him with joy, as well as peace, in believing: "*He has put a new song in my mouth;* he has given me cause to rejoice and a heart to rejoice." He was brought, as it were, into a new world, and that filled his mouth with a new song, *even praise to our God;* for to his praise and glory must all our songs be sung. Fresh mercies, especially such as we never before received, call for new songs. This is applicable to our Lord Jesus in his reception to paradise, his resurrection from the grave, and his exaltation to the joy and glory set before him; he was brought out of the horrible pit, set upon a rock, and had a new song put into his mouth.

IV. The good improvement that should be made of this instance of God's goodness to David.

1. David's experience would be an encouragement to many to hope in God, and, for that end, he leaves it here upon record: *Many shall see, and fear, and trust in the Lord.* They shall fear the Lord and his justice, which brought David, and the Son of David, into that horrible pit, and shall say, *If this be done to the green tree, what shall be done to the dry?* They shall fear the Lord and his goodness, in filling the mouth of David, and the Son of

David, with new songs of joy and praise. There is a holy reverent fear of God, which is not only consistent with, but the foundation of, our hope in him. They shall not fear him and shun him, but fear him and trust in him in their greatest straits, not doubting but to find him as able and ready to help as David did in his distress. God's dealings with our Lord Jesus are our great encouragement to trust in God ; when it pleased the Lord to bruise him, and put him to grief for our sins, he demanded our debt from him ; and when he raised him from the dead, and set him at his own right hand, he made it to appear that he had accepted the payment he made and was satisfied with it ; and what greater encouragement can we have to fear and worship God and to *trust in him?* See Rom. iv. 25 ; v. 1, 2. The psalmist invites others to make God their hope, as he did, by pronouncing those happy that do so (*v.* 4) : " *Blessed is the man that makes the Lord his trust,* and him only (that has great and good thoughts of him, and is entirely devoted to him), *and respects not the proud,* does not do as those do that trust in themselves, nor depends upon those who proudly encourage others to trust in them; for both the one and the other turn aside to lies, as indeed all those do that turn aside from God." This is applicable, particularly, to our faith in Christ. Blessed are those that trust in him, and in his righteousness alone, and respect not the proud Pharisees, that set up their own righteousness in competition with that, that will not be governed by their dictates, nor turn aside to lies, with the unbelieving Jews, who *submit not to the righteousness of God,* Rom. x. 3. Blessed are those that escape this temptation.

2. The joyful sense he had of this mercy led him to observe, with thankfulness, the many other favours he had received from God, *v.* 5. When God puts new songs into our mouth we must not forget our former songs, but repeat them : " *Many, O Lord my God ! are thy wonderful works which thou hast done,* both for me and others ; this is but one of many." Many are the benefits with which we are daily loaded both by the providence and by the grace of God. (1.) They are his works, not only the gifts of his bounty, but the operations of his power. He works for us, he works in us, and thus he favours us with matter, not only for thanks, but for praise. (2.) They are his wonderful works, the contrivance of them admirable, his condescension to us in bestowing them upon us admirable; eternity itself will be short enough to be spent in the admiration of them. (3.) All his wonderful works are the product of his thoughts to us-ward. He does all *according to the counsel of his own will* (Eph. i. 11), the purposes of his grace *which he purposed in himself,* Eph. iii. 11. They are the projects of infinite wisdom, the designs of everlasting love (1 Cor. ii. 7, Jer. xxxi. 3), *thoughts of good and not of evil,* Jer. xxix. 11. His

gifts and callings will *therefore* be without repentance, because they are not sudden resolves, but the result of his thoughts, his many thoughts, to us-ward. (4.) They are innumerable ; they cannot be methodised or *reckoned up in order.* There is an order in all God's works, but there are so many that present themselves to our view at once that we know not where to begin nor which to name next ; the order of them, and their natural references and dependencies, and how the links of the golden chain are joined, are a mystery to us, and what we shall not be able to account for till the veil be rent and the mystery of God finished. Nor can they be counted, not the very heads of them. When we have said the most we can of the wonders of divine love to us we must conclude with an *et cætera—and such like,* and adore the depth, despairing to find the bottom.

6 Sacrifice and offering thou didst not desire ; mine ears hast thou opened : burnt offering and sin offering hast thou not required. 7 Then said I, Lo, I come : in the volume of the book *it is* written of me, 8 I delight to do thy will, O my God : yea, thy law *is* within my heart. 9 I have preached righteousness in the great congregation : lo, I have not refrained my lips, O Lord, thou knowest. 10 I have not hid thy righteousness within my heart ; I have declared thy faithfulness and thy salvation : I have not concealed thy lovingkindness and thy truth from the great congregation.

The psalmist, being struck with amazement at the wonderful works that God had done for his people, is strangely carried out here to foretel that work of wonder which excels all the rest and is the foundation and fountain of all, that of our redemption by our Lord Jesus Christ. God's thoughts, which were to us-ward concerning that work, were the most curious, the most copious, the most gracious, and therefore to be most admired. This paragraph is quoted by the apostle (Heb. x. 5, &c.) and applied to Christ and his undertaking for us. As in the institutions, so in the devotions, of the Old Testament, there is more of Christ than perhaps the Old-Testament saints were aware of ; and, when the apostle would show us the Redeemer's voluntary undertaking of his work, he does not fetch his account out of the book of God's secret counsels, which belong not to us, but from the things revealed. Observe,

I. The utter insufficiency of the legal sacrifices to atone for sin in order to our peace with God and our happiness in him : *Sacrifice and offering thou didst not desire;* thou wouldst not have the Redeemer to offer them. Something he must have to offer, but not these (Heb. viii. 3); therefore he must not be of the house of Aaron, Heb. vii. 14. Or, In the days of the Messiah burnt-offering and sin-offering will be no longer required, but all those ceremonial institutions will be abolished. But that is not all: even while the law concerning them was in full force it might be said, God did not desire them, nor accept them, for their own sake. They could not take away the guilt of sin by satisfying God's justice. The life of a sheep, which is so much inferior in value to that of a man (Matt. xii. 12), could not pretend to be an equivalent, much less an expedient to preserve the honour of God's government and laws and repair the injury done to that honour by the sin of man. They could not take away the terror of sin by pacifying the conscience, nor the power of sin by sanctifying the nature; it was impossible, Heb. ix. 9; x. 1—4. What there was in them that was valuable resulted from their reference to Jesus Christ, of whom they were types—shadows indeed, but shadows of good things to come, and trials of the faith and obedience of God's people, of their obedience to the law and their faith in the gospel. But the substance must come, which is Christ, who must bring that glory to God and that grace to man which it was impossible those sacrifices should ever do.

II. The designation of our Lord Jesus to the work and office of Mediator: *My ears hast thou opened.* God the Father disposed him to the undertaking (Isa. l. 5, 6) and then obliged him to go through with it. *My ear hast thou digged.* It is supposed to allude to the law and custom of binding servants to serve for ever by boring their ear to the door-post; see Exod. xxi. 6. Our Lord Jesus was so in love with his undertaking that he would not go out free from it, and therefore engaged to persevere for ever in it; and for this reason *he is able to save us to the uttermost,* because he has engaged to serve his Father to the uttermost, who upholds him in it, Isa. xlii. 1.

III. His own voluntary consent to this undertaking: " *Then said I, Lo, I come;* then, when sacrifice and offering would not do, rather than the work should be undone, I said, Lo, I come, to enter the lists with the powers of darkness, and to advance the interests of God's glory and kingdom." This intimates three things:—1. That he freely offered himself to this service, to which he was under no obligation at all prior to his own voluntary engagement. It was no sooner proposed to him than, with the greatest cheerfulness, he consented to it, and was wonderfully well pleased with the undertaking. Had he not been perfectly voluntary in it, he could not have been a surety, he could not have been a sacrifice; for it is by this will (this *animus offerentis—mind of the offerer*) that we are sanctified, Heb. x. 10. 2. That he firmly obliged himself to it: " I come; I promise to come in the fulness of

time." And therefore the apostle says, " It was when he came into the world that he had an actual regard to this promise, by which he had *engaged his heart to approach unto God.*" He thus entered into bonds, not only to show the greatness of his love, but because he was to have the honour of his undertaking before he had fully performed it. Though the price was not paid, it was secured to be paid, so that he was the Lamb slain from the foundation of the world. 3. That he frankly owned himself engaged: He said, Lo, I come, said it all along to the Old-Testament saints, who therefore knew him by the title of ὁ ἐρχόμενος —*He that should come.* This word was the foundation on which they built their faith and hope, and which they looked and longed for the accomplishment of.

IV. The reason why he came, in pursuance of his undertaking—because *in the volume of the book it was written of him,* 1. In the close rolls of the divine decree and counsel; there it was written that his ear was opened, and he said, Lo, I come; there the covenant of redemption was recorded, the counsel of peace between the Father and the Son; and to that he had an eye in all he did, the commandment he received of his Father. 2. In the letters patent of the Old Testament. Moses and all the prophets testified of him; in all the volumes of that book something or other was written of him, which he had an eye to, that all might be accomplished, John xix. 28.

V. The pleasure he took in his undertaking. Having freely offered himself to it, he did not fail, nor was discouraged, but proceeded with all possible satisfaction to himself (v. 8, 9): *I delight to do thy will, O my God!* It was to Christ his meat and drink to go on with the work appointed to him (John iv. 34); and the reason here given is, *Thy law is within my heart;* it is written there, it rules there, it is an active commanding principle there. It is meant of the law concerning the work and office of the Mediator, what he was to do and suffer; this law was dear to him and had an influence upon him in his whole undertaking. Note, When the law of God is written in our hearts our duty will be our delight.

VI. The publication of the gospel to the children of men, even *in the great congregation,* v. 9, 10. The same that as a priest wrought out redemption for us, as a prophet, by his own preaching first, then by his apostles, and still by his word and Spirit, makes it known to us. The *great salvation began to be spoken by the Lord,* Heb. ii. 3. It is the gospel of Christ that is preached to all nations. Observe, 1. What it is that is preached: It is *righteousness* (v. 9), God's righteousness (v. 10), the everlasting righteousness which Christ has brought in (Dan. ix. 24); compare Rom. i. 16, 17. It is God's *faithfulness* to his promise, and the salvation which had long been looked for. It is God's *lovingkindness* and his *truth*, his mercy according to his word. Note, In the work of our redemption we ought to take notice how brightly all the divine attributes shine, and give to God the praise of each of them. 2. To whom it is preached—*to the great congregation, v.* 9 and again *v.* 10. When Christ was here on earth he preached to multitudes, thousands at a time. The gospel was preached both to Jews and Gentiles, to great congregations of both. Solemn religious assemblies are a divine institution, and in them the glory of God, in the face of Christ, ought to be both praised to the glory of God and preached for the edification of men. 3. How it is preached—freely and openly: *I have not refrained my lips; I have not hid it; I have not concealed it.* This intimates that whoever undertook to preach the gospel of Christ would be in great temptation to hide it and conceal it, because it must be preached with great contention and in the face of great opposition; but Christ himself, and those whom he called to that work, set their faces *as a flint* (Isa. l. 7) and were wonderfully carried on in it. It is well for us that they were so, for by this means our eyes come to see this joyful light and our ears to hear this joyful sound, which otherwise we might for ever have perished in ignorance of.

11 Withhold not thou thy tender mercies from me, O Lord : let thy lovingkindness and thy truth continually preserve me. 12 For innumerable evils have compassed me about : mine iniquities have taken hold upon me, so that I am not able to look up; they are more than the hairs of mine head : therefore my heart faileth me. 13 Be pleased, O Lord, to deliver me : O Lord, make haste to help me. 14 Let them be ashamed and confounded together that seek after my soul to destroy it ; let them be driven backward and put to shame that wish me evil. 15 Let them be desolate for a reward of their shame that say unto me, Aha, aha. 16 Let all those that seek thee rejoice and be glad in thee : let such as love thy salvation say continually, The Lord be magnified. 17 But I *am* poor and needy; *yet* the Lord thinketh upon me : thou *art* my help and my deliverer ; make no tarrying, O my God.

The psalmist, having meditated upon the work of redemption, and spoken of it in the person of the Messiah, now comes to make improvement of the doctrine of his mediation between us and God, and therefore speaks in his own person. Christ having done his

Father's will, and finished his work, and given orders for the preaching of the gospel to every creature, we are encouraged to come boldly to the throne of grace, for mercy and grace.

I. This may encourage us to pray for the mercy of God, and to put ourselves under the protection of that mercy, *v.* 11. "Lord, thou hast not spared thy Son, nor withheld him; *withhold not thou thy tender mercies* then, which thou hast laid up for us in him; for wilt thou not *with him also freely give us all things?* Rom. viii. 32. *Let thy lovingkindness and thy truth continually preserve me.*" The best saints are in continual danger, and see themselves undone if they be not continually preserved by the grace of God ; and the everlasting lovingkindness and truth of God are what we have to depend upon for our preservation to the heavenly kingdom, lxi. 7.

II. This may encourage us in reference to the guilt of sin, that Jesus Christ has done that towards our discharge from it which sacrifice and offering could not do. See here, 1. The frightful sight he had of sin, *v.* 12. This was it that made the discovery he was now favoured with of a Redeemer very welcome to him. He saw his iniquities to be evils, the worst of evils ; he saw that they *compassed him about ;* in all the reviews of his life, and his reflections upon each step of it, still he discovered something amiss. The threatening consequences of his sin surrounded him. Look which way he would, he saw some mischief or other waiting for him, which he was conscious to himself his sins had deserved. He saw them taking hold of him, arresting him, as the bailiff does the poor debtor ; he saw them to be innumerable, and *more than the hairs of his head.* Convinced awakened consciences are apprehensive of danger from the numberless number of the sins of infirmity which seem small as hairs, but, being numerous, are very dangerous. *Who can understand his errors?* God numbers our hairs (Matt. x. 30), which yet we cannot number; so he keeps an account of our sins, which we keep no account of. The sight of sin so oppressed him that he could not hold up his head—*I am not able to look up ;* much less could he keep up his heart—*therefore my heart fails me.* Note, The sight of our sins in their own colours would drive us to distraction, if we had not at the same time some sight of a Saviour. 2. The careful recourse he had to God under the sense of sin (*v.* 13); seeing himself brought by his sins to the very brink of ruin, eternal ruin, with what a holy passion does he cry out, "*Be pleased, O Lord ! to deliver me* (*v.* 13); O save me from the wrath to come, and the present terrors I am in through the apprehensions of that wrath! I am undone. I die, I perish, without speedy relief. In a case of this nature, where the bliss of an immortal soul is concerned, delays are dangerous ; therefore, *O Lord! make haste to help me.*"

III. This may encourage us to hope for

victory over our spiritual enemies that seek after our souls to destroy them (*v.* 14), the roaring lion that goes about continually seeking to devour. If Christ has triumphed over them, we, through him, shall be more than conquerors. In the belief of this we may pray, with humble boldness, *Let them be ashamed and confounded together,* and *driven backward, v.* 14. *Let them be desolate, v.* 15. Both the conversion of a sinner and the glorification of a saint are great disappointments to Satan, who does his utmost, with all his power and subtlety, to hinder both. Now, our Lord Jesus having undertaken to bring about the salvation of all his chosen, we may in faith pray that, in both these ways, that great adversary may be confounded. When a child of God is brought into that horrible pit, and the miry clay, Satan cries *Aha! aha!* thinking he has gained his point; but he shall rage when he sees the brand plucked out of the fire, and shall be *desolate, for a reward of his shame. The Lord rebuke thee, O Satan ! The accuser of the brethren is cast out.*

IV. This may encourage all that seek God, and love his salvation, to rejoice in him and to praise him, *v.* 16. See here, 1. The character of good people. Conformably to the laws of natural religion, they seek God, desire his favour, and in all their exigencies apply to him, as a people should seek unto their God ; and conformably to the laws of revealed religion they *love his salvation,* that great salvation of which the prophets enquired and searched diligently, which the Redeemer undertook to work out when he said, *Lo, I come.* All that shall be saved love the salvation, not only as a salvation from hell, but a salvation from sin. 2. The happiness secured to good people by this prophetic prayer. Those that seek God shall *rejoice and be glad in him,* and with good reason, for he will not only be found of them but will be their bountiful rewarder. Those that love his salvation shall be filled with the joy of his salvation, and shall *say continually, The Lord be magnified;* and thus they shall have a heaven upon earth. Blessed are those that are thus still praising God.

V. This may encourage the saints, in distress and affliction, to trust in God and comfort themselves in him, *v.* 17. David himself was one of these : *I am poor and needy* (a king, perhaps now on the throne, and yet, being troubled in spirit, he calls himself *poor and needy,* in want and distress, lost and undone without a Saviour), *yet the Lord thinketh upon me* in and through the Mediator, by whom we are made accepted. Men forget the poor and needy, and seldom think of them ; but God's thoughts towards them (which he had spoken of *v.* 5) are their support and comfort. They may assure themselves that God is their help under their troubles, and will be, in due time, their deliverer out of their troubles, and will make no long tarrying; for *the vision is for an appointed*

390

time, and therefore, *though it tarry,* we may *wait for it,* for it shall come; *it will come, it will not tarry.*

PSALM XLI.

God's kindness and truth have often been the support and comfort of the saints when they have had most experience of men's unkindness and treachery. David here found them so, upon a sick-bed; he found his enemies very barbarous, but his God very gracious. I. He here comforts himself in his communion with God under his sickness, by faith receiving and laying hold of God's promises to him (ver. 1—3) and lifting up his heart in prayer to God, ver. 4. II. He here represents the malice of his enemies against him, their malicious censures of him, their spiteful reflections upon him, and their insolent conduct towards him, ver. 5—9. III. He leaves his case with God, not doubting but that he would own and favour him (ver. 10—12), and so the psalm concludes with a doxology, ver. 13. Is any afflicted with sickness? let him sing the beginning of this psalm. Is any persecuted by enemies? let him sing the latter end of it; and we may any of us, in singing it, meditate upon both the calamities and comforts of good people in this world.

To the chief musician. A psalm of David.

BLESSED *is* he that considereth the poor : the LORD will deliver him in time of trouble. 2 The LORD will preserve him, and keep him alive; *and* he shall be blessed upon the earth : and thou wilt not deliver him unto the will of his enemies. 3 The LORD will strengthen him upon the bed of languishing : thou wilt make all his bed in his sickness. 4 I said, LORD, be merciful unto me : heal my soul; for I have sinned against thee.

In these verses we have,

I. God's promises of succour and comfort to those that consider the poor ; and,

1. We may suppose that David makes mention of these with application either, (1.) To his friends, who were kind to him, and very considerate of his case, now that he was in affliction : *Blessed is he that considers* poor David. Here and there he met with one that sympathized with him, and was concerned for him, and kept up his good opinion of him and respect for him, notwithstanding his afflictions, while his enemies were so insolent and abusive to him ; on these he pronounced this blessing, not doubting but that God would recompense to them all the kindness they had done him, particularly when they also came to be in affliction. The provocations which his enemies gave him did but endear his friends so much the more to him. Or, (2.) To himself. He had the testimony of his conscience for him that he had considered the poor, that when he was in honour and power at court he had taken cognizance of the wants and miseries of the poor and had provided for their relief, and therefore was sure God would, according to his promise, strengthen and comfort him in his sickness.

2. We must regard them more generally with application to ourselves. Here is a comment upon that promise, *Blessed are the merciful, for they shall obtain mercy.* Observe, (1.) What the mercy is which is required of us. It is to consider the poor or afflicted, whether in mind, body, or estate. These we are to consider with prudence and tender-

ness; we must take notice of their affliction and enquire into their state, must sympathize with them and judge charitably concerning them. We must wisely consider the poor; that is, we must ourselves be instructed by the poverty and affliction of others; it must be *Maschil* to us, that is the word here used. (2.) What the mercy is that is promised to us if we thus show mercy. He that considers the poor (if he cannot relieve them, yet he considers them, and has a compassionate concern for them, and in relieving them acts considerately and with discretion) shall be considered by his God: he shall not only be recompensed in the resurrection of the just, but he *shall be blessed upon the earth.* This branch of godliness, as much as any, has the promise of the life that now is and is usually recompensed with temporal blessings. Liberality to the poor is the surest and safest way of thriving; such as practise it may be sure of seasonable and effectual relief from God, [1.] In all troubles: He *will deliver them in the day of evil,* so that when the times are at the worst it shall go well with them, and they shall not fall into the calamities in which others are involved; if any be hidden in the day of the Lord's anger, *they* shall. Those who thus distinguish themselves from those that have hard hearts God will distinguish from those that have hard usage. Are they in danger? he will preserve and keep them alive; and those who have a thousand times forfeited their lives, as the best have, must acknowledge it as a great favour if they have their *lives given them for a prey.* He does not say, "They shall be preferred," but, "*They shall be preserved and kept alive,*" when the arrows of death fly thickly round about them? Do their enemies threaten them? God will not *deliver them into the will of their enemies;* and the most potent enemy we have can have no power against us but what is given him from above. The good-will of a God that loves us is sufficient to secure us from the ill-will of all that hate us, men and devils; and that good-will we may promise ourselves an interest in if we have considered the poor and helped to relieve and rescue them. [2.] Particularly in sickness (*v.* 3): *The Lord will strengthen him,* both in body and mind, *upon the bed of languishing,* on which he had long lain sick, and *he will make all his bed*—a very condescending expression, alluding to the care of those that nurse and tend sick people, especially of mothers for their children when they are sick, which is to make their beds easy for them; and that bed must needs be well made which God himself has the making of. He will make all his bed from head to foot, so that no part shall be uneasy; he will *turn* his bed (so the word is), to shake it up and make it very easy; or he will turn it into a bed of health. Note, God has promised his people that he will strengthen them, and make them easy, under their bodily pains and sicknesses. He

has not promised that they shall never be sick, nor that they shall not lie long languishing, nor that their sickness shall not be unto death; but he has promised to enable them to bear their affliction with patience, and cheerfully to wait the issue. The soul shall by his grace be made to dwell at ease when the body lies in pain.

II. David's prayer, directed and encouraged by these promises (*v.* 4): *I said, Heal my soul.* It is good for us to keep some account of our prayers, that we may not unsay, in our practices, any thing that we said in our prayers. Here is, 1. His humble petition: *Lord, be merciful to me.* He appeals to mercy, as one that knew he could not stand the test of strict justice. The best saints, even those that have been merciful to the poor, have not made God their debtor, but must throw themselves on his mercy. When we are under the rod we must thus recommend ourselves to the tender mercy of our God: *Lord, heal my soul.* Sin is the sickness of the soul; pardoning mercy heals it; renewing grace heals it; and this spiritual healing we should be more earnest for than for bodily health. 2. His penitent confession: "*I have sinned against thee,* and therefore my soul needs healing. I am a sinner, a miserable sinner; therefore, *God, be merciful to me,*" Luke xviii. 13. It does not appear that this has reference to any particular gross act of sin, but, in general, to his many sins of infirmity, which his sickness set in order before him, and the dread of the consequences of which made him pray, *Heal my soul.*

5 Mine enemies speak evil of me, When shall he die, and his name perish? 6 And if he come to see *me,* he speaketh vanity: his heart gathereth iniquity to itself; *when* he goeth abroad, he telleth *it.* 7 All that hate me whisper together against me: against me do they devise my hurt. 8 An evil disease, *say they,* cleaveth fast unto him: and *now* that he lieth he shall rise up no more. 9 Yea, mine own familiar friend, in whom I trusted, which did eat of my bread, hath lifted up *his* heel against me. 10 But thou, O Lord, be merciful unto me, and raise me up, that I may requite them. 11 By this I know that thou favourest me, because mine enemy doth not triumph over me. 12 And as for me, thou upholdest me in mine integrity, and settest me before thy face for ever. 13 Blessed *be* the Lord God of Israel from everlasting, and to everlasting. Amen, and Amen.

David often complains of the insolent conduct of his enemies towards him when he was sick, which, as it was very barbarous in them, so it could not but be very grievous to him. They had not indeed arrived at that modern pitch of wickedness of poisoning his meat and drink, or giving him something to make him sick; but, when he was sick, they insulted over him (*v.* 5): *My enemies speak evil of me,* designing thereby to grieve his spirit, to ruin his reputation, and so to sink his interest. Let us enquire,

I. What was the conduct of his enemies towards him. 1. They longed for his death: *When shall he die, and his name perish* with him? He had but an uncomfortable life, and yet they grudged him that. But it was a useful life; he was, upon all accounts, the greatest ornament and blessing of his country; and yet, it seems, there were some who were sick of him, as the Jews were of Paul, crying out, *Away with such a fellow from the earth.* We ought not to desire the death of any; but to desire the death of useful men, for their usefulness, has much in it of the venom of the old serpent. They envied him his name, and the honour he had won, and doubted not but, if he were dead, that would be laid in the dust with him; yet see how they were mistaken: when he had served his generation he did die (Acts xiii. 36), but did his name perish? No; it lives and flourishes to this day in the sacred writings, and will to the end of time; for *the memory of the just is,* and shall be, *blessed.* 2 They picked up every thing they could to reproach him with (*v.* 6): " *If he come to see me* " (as it has always been reckoned a piece of neighbourly kindness to visit the sick) " *he speaks vanity;* that is, he pretends friendship, and that his errand is to mourn with me and to comfort me; he tells me he is very sorry to see me so much indisposed, and wishes me my health; but it is all flattery and falsehood." We complain, and justly, of the want of sincerity in our days, and that there is scarcely any true friendship to be found among men; but it seems, by this, that the former days were no better than these. David's friends were all compliment, and had nothing of that affection for him in their hearts which they made profession of. Nor was that the worst of it; it was upon a mischievous design that they came to see him, that they might make invidious remarks upon every thing he said or did, and might represent it as they pleased to others, with their own comments upon it, so as to render him odious or ridiculous: *His heart gathereth iniquity to itself,* puts ill constructions upon every thing; and then, when he goes among his companions, he tells it to them, that they may tell it to others. *Report, say they, and we will report it,* Jer. xx. 10. If he complained much of his illness, they would reproach him for his pusillanimity; if he scarcely complained at all, they would reproach him for his stupidity. If he prayed, or gave them good counsel, they would ban-

ter it, and call it *canting;* if he kept silence from good, when the wicked were before him, they would say that he had forgotten his religion now that he was sick. There is no fence against those whose malice thus gathers iniquity. 3. They promised themselves that he would never recover from this sickness, nor ever wipe off the odium with which they had loaded him. They *whispered together against him* (*v.* 7), speaking that secretly in one another's ears which they could not for shame speak out, and which, if they did, they knew would be confuted. Whisperers and backbiters are put together among the worst of sinners, Rom. i. 29, 30. They whispered, that their plot against him might not be discovered and so defeated; there is seldom whispering (we say) but there is lying, or some mischief on foot. Those whisperers devised evil to David. Concluding he would die quickly, they contrived how to break all the measures he had concerted for the public good, to prevent the prosecution of them, and to undo all that he had hitherto been doing. This he calls *devising hurt against him;* and they doubted not but to gain their point: *An evil disease (a thing of Belial),* say they, *cleaves fast to him.* The reproach with which they had loaded his name, they hoped, would cleave so fast to it that it would perish with him, and then they should gain their point. They went by a modern maxim, *Fortiter calumniari, aliquid adhærebit*—Fling an abundance of calumny, and some will be sure to stick. " The disease he is now under will certainly make an end of him; for it is the punishment of some great enormous crime, which he will not be brought to repent of, and proves him, however he has appeared, a son of Belial." Or, " It is inflicted by Satan, who is called *Belial,*" *the wicked one,* 2 Cor. vi. 15. " It is " (according to a loose way of speaking some have) " a devilish disease, and therefore it will *cleave fast to him;* and *now that he lieth,* now that his distemper prevails so far as to oblige him to keep his bed, *he shall rise up no more;* we shall get rid of him, and divide the spoil of his preferments." We are not to think it strange if, when good men are sick, there be those that hope for their death, as well as those that fear it, which makes the world not worthy of them, Rev. xi. 10. 4. There was one particularly, in whom he had reposed a great deal of confidence, that took part with his enemies and was as abusive to him as any of them (*v.* 9): *My own familiar friend;* probably he means Ahithophel, who had been his bosom-friend and prime-minister of state, in whom he trusted as one inviolably firm to him, whose advice he relied much upon in dealing with his enemies, and who *did eat of his bread,* that is, with whom he had been very intimate and whom he had taken to sit at the table with him, nay, whom he had maintained and given a livelihood to, and so obliged, both in gratitude and interest, to adhere to him. Those that had their maintenance *from the king's palace* did not think it *meet for them to see the king's dishonour* (Ezra iv. 14), much less to do him dishonour. Yet this base and treacherous confidant of David's forgot all the eaten bread, and *lifted up his heel against him* that had lifted up his head; not only deserted him, but insulted him, kicked at him, endeavoured to supplant him. Those are wicked indeed whom no courtesy done them, nor confidence reposed in them, will oblige; and let us not think it strange if we receive abuses from such: David did, and the Son of David; for of Judas the traitor David here, in the Spirit, spoke; our Saviour himself so expounds this, and *therefore* gave Judas the sop, that the scripture might be fulfilled, *He that eats bread with me has lifted up his heel against me,* John xiii. 18, 26. Nay, have not we ourselves behaved thus perfidiously and disingenuously towards God? We *eat of his bread* daily, and yet *lift up the heel against him,* as Jeshurun, that *waxed fat and kicked,* Deut. xxxii. 15.

II. How did David bear this insolent ill-natured conduct of his enemies towards him?

1. He prayed to God that they might be disappointed. He said nothing to them, but turned himself to God: *O Lord! be thou merciful to me,* for they are unmerciful, *v.* 10. He had prayed in reference to the guilt of his sins (*v.* 4), *Lord, be merciful to me;* and now again, in reference to the insults of his enemies, *Lord, be merciful to me,* for this is a prayer which will suit every case. God's mercy has in it a redress for every grievance. "They endeavour to run me down, but, Lord, do thou raise me up from this bed of languishing, from which they think I shall never arise. Raise me up *that I may requite them,* that I may render them good for evil" (so some), for that was David's practice, vii. 4; xxxv. 13. A good man will even wish for an opportunity of making it to appear that he bears no malice to those that have been injurious to him, but, on the contrary, that he is ready to do them any good office. Or, "That, as a king, I may put them under the marks of my just displeasure, banish them the court, and forbid them my table for the future," which would be a necessary piece of justice, for warning to others. Perhaps in this prayer is couched a prophecy of the exaltation of Christ, whom God raised up, that he might be a just avenger of all the wrongs done to him and to his people, particularly by the Jews, whose utter destruction followed not long after.

2. He assured himself that they would be disappointed (*v.* 11): "*By this I know that thou favourest me* and my interest, *because my enemy doth not triumph over me.*" They hoped for his death, but he found himself, through mercy, recovering, and this would add to the comfort of his recovery, (1.) That it would be a disappointment to his adversaries; they would be crest-fallen and

wretchedly ashamed, and there would be no occasion to upbraid them with their disappointment; they would fret at it themselves. Note, Though we may not take a pleasure in the fall of our enemies, we may take a pleasure in the frustrating of their designs against us. (2.) That it would be a token of God's favour to him, and a certain evidence that he did favour him, and would continue to do so. Note, When we can discern the favour of God to us in any mercy, personal or public, that doubles it and sweetens it.

3. He depended upon God, who had thus delivered him from many an evil work, to *preserve him to his heavenly kingdom,* as blessed Paul, 2 Tim. iv. 18. "As for me, forasmuch as thou favourest me, as a fruit of that favour, and to qualify me for the continuance of it, *thou upholdest me in my integrity, and,* in order to that, *settest me before thy face,* hast thy eye always upon me for good;" or, "Because thou dost, by thy grace, uphold me in my integrity, I know that thou wilt, in thy glory, set me for ever before thy face." Note, (1.) When at any time we suffer in our reputation our chief concern should be about our integrity, and then we may cheerfully leave it to God to secure our reputation. David knows that, if he can but persevere in his integrity, he needs not fear his enemies' triumphs over him. (2.) The best man in the world holds his integrity no longer than God upholds him in it; for by his grace we are what we are; if we be left to ourselves, we shall not only fall, but fall away. (3.) It is a great comfort to us that, however weak we are, God is able to uphold us in our integrity, and will do it if we commit the keeping of it to him. (4.) If the grace of God did not take a constant care of us, we should not be upheld in our integrity; his eye is always upon us, else we should soon start aside from him. (5.) Those whom God now upholds in their integrity he will set before his face for ever, and make happy in the vision and fruition of himself. *He that endures to the end shall be saved.*

4. The psalm concludes with a solemn doxology, or adoration of God as *the Lord God of Israel, v.* 13. It is not certain whether this verse pertains to this particular psalm (if so, it teaches us this, That a believing hope of our preservation through grace to glory is enough to fill our hearts with joy and our mouths with everlasting praise, even in our greatest straits) or whether it was added as the conclusion of the first book of *Psalms,* which is reckoned to end here (the like being subjoined to lxxii., lxxxix., cvi.), and then it teaches us to make God the Omega who is the Alpha, to make him the end who is the beginning of every good work. We are taught, (1.) To give glory to God as the *Lord God of Israel,* a God in covenant with his people, who has done great and kind things for them and has more and better in reserve. (2.) To give him glory as an eternal God, that has both his being and his blessedness *from*

everlasting and to everlasting. (3.) To do this with great affection and fervour of spirit, intimated in the double seal set to it—*Amen, and Amen.* Be it so now, be it so to all eternity. We say *Amen* to it, and let all others say *Amen* too.

PSALM XLII.

If the book of Psalms be, as some have styled it, a mirror or looking-glass of pious and devout affections, this psalm in particular deserves, as much as any one psalm, to be so entitled, and is as proper as any to kindle and excite such in us: gracious desires are here strong and fervent; gracious hopes and fears, joys and sorrows, are here struggling, but the pleasing passion comes off a conqueror. Or we may take it for a conflict between sense and faith, sense objecting and faith answering. I. Faith begins with holy desires towards God and communion with him, ver. 1, 2. II. Sense complains of the darkness and cloudiness of the present condition, aggravated by the remembrance of the former enjoyments, ver. 3, 4. III. Faith silences the complaint with the assurance of a good issue at last, ver. 5. IV. Sense renews its complaints of the present dark and melancholy state, ver. 6, 7. V. Faith holds up the heart, notwithstanding, with hope that the day will dawn, ver. 8. VI. Sense repeats its lamentations (ver. 9, 10) and sighs out the same remonstrance it had before made of its grievances. VII. Faith gets the last word (ver. 11), for the silencing of the complaints of sense, and, though it be almost the same with that ver. 5, yet now it prevails and carries the day. The title does not tell us who was the penman of this psalm, but most probably it was David, and we may conjecture that it was penned by him at a time when, either by Saul's persecution or Absalom's rebellion, he was driven from the sanctuary and cut off from the privilege of waiting upon God in public ordinances. The strain of it is much the same with lxiii., and therefore we may presume it was penned by the same hand and upon the same or a similar occasion. In singing it, if we be either in outward affliction or inward distress, we may accommodate to ourselves the melancholy expressions we find here; if not, we must, in singing them, sympathize with those whose case they speak too plainly, and thank God it is not our own case; but those passages in it which express and excite holy desires towards God, and dependence on him, we must earnestly endeavour to bring our minds up to.

To the chief musician, Maschil, for the sons of Korah.

AS the hart panteth after the water brooks, so panteth my soul after thee, O God. 2 My soul thirsteth for God, for the living God : when shall I come and appear before God ? 3 My tears have been my meat day and night, while they continually say unto me, Where *is* thy God ? 4 When I remember these *things*, I pour out my soul in me : for I had gone with the multitude, I went with them to the house of God, with the voice of joy and praise, with a multitude that kept holyday. 5 Why art thou cast down,. O my soul ? and *why* art thou disquieted in me ? hope thou in God : for I shall yet praise him *for* the help of his countenance.

Holy love to God as the chief good and our felicity is the power of godliness, the very life and soul of religion, without which all external professions and performances are but a shell and carcase : now here we have some of the expressions of that love. Here is,

I. Holy love thirsting, love upon the wing, soaring upwards in holy desires towards the Lord and towards the remembrance of his name (v. 1, 2) : "*My soul panteth, thirsteth, for God,* for nothing more than God, but still for more and more of him." Now observe,

1. When it was that David thus expressed his vehement desire towards God. It was,

(1.) When he was debarred from his outward opportunities of waiting on God, when he was banished to the land of Jordan, a great way off from the courts of God's house. Note, Sometimes God teaches us effectually to know the worth of mercies by the want of them, and whets our appetite for the means of grace by cutting us short in those means. We are apt to loathe that manna, when we have plenty of it, which will be very precious to us if ever we come to know the scarcity of it. (2.) When he was deprived, in a great measure, of the inward comfort he used to have in God. He now went mourning, but he went on panting. Note, If God, by his grace, has wrought in us sincere and earnest desires towards him, we may take comfort from these when we want those ravishing delights we have sometimes had in God, because lamenting after God is as sure an evidence that we love him as rejoicing in God. Before the psalmist records his doubts, and fears, and griefs, which had sorely shaken him, he premises this, That he looked upon the living God as his chief good, and had set his heart upon him accordingly, and was resolved to live and die by him; and, casting anchor thus at first, he rides out the storm.

2. What is the object of his desire and what it is he thus thirsts after. (1.) He pants after God, he thirsts for God, not the ordinances themselves, but the God of the ordinances. A gracious soul can take little satisfaction in God's courts if it do not meet with God himself there : " *O that I knew where I might find him!* that I might have more of the tokens of his favour, the graces and comforts of his Spirit, and the earnests of his glory." (2.) He has, herein, an eye to God as the living God, that has life in himself, and is the fountain of life and all happiness to those that are his, the living God, not only in opposition to dead idols, the works of men's hands, but to all the dying comforts of this world, which perish in the using. Living souls can never take up their rest any where short of a living God. (3.) He longs to *come and appear before God,*—to make himself known to him, as being conscious to himself of his own sincerity,—to attend on him, as a servant appears before his master, to pay his respects to him and receive his commands,—to give an account to him, as one from whom our judgment proceeds. To appear before God is as much the desire of the upright as it is the dread of the hypocrite. The psalmist knew he could not come into God's courts without incurring expense, for so was the law, that *none should appear before God empty ;* yet he longs to come, and will not grudge the charges.

3. What is the degree of this desire. It is very importunate ; it is his soul that pants, his soul that thirsts, which denotes not only the sincerity, but the strength, of his desire. His longing for the water of the well of Bethlehem was nothing to this. He compares it

to the *panting of a hart,* or deer, which is naturally hot and dry, especially of a hunted buck, *after the water-brooks.* Thus earnestly does a gracious soul desire communion with God, thus impatient is it in the want of that communion, so impossible does it find it to be satisfied with any thing short of that communion, and so insatiable is it in taking the pleasures of that communion when the opportunity of it returns, still thirsting after the full enjoyment of him in the heavenly kingdom.

II. Holy love mourning for God's present withdrawings and the want of the benefit of solemn ordinances (*v.* 3): "*My tears have been my meat day and night* during this forced absence from God's house." His circumstances were sorrowful, and he accommodated himself to them, received the impressions and returned the signs of sorrow. Even the royal prophet was a weeping prophet when he wanted the comforts of God's house. His tears were mingled with his meat; nay, they were *his meat day and night;* he fed, he feasted, upon his own tears, when there was such just cause for them; and it was a satisfaction to him that he found his heart so much affected with a grievance of this nature. Observe, He did not think it enough to shed a tear or two at parting from the sanctuary, to weep a farewell-prayer when he took his leave, but, as long as he continued under a forced absence from that place of his delight, he never looked up, but wept day and night. Note, Those that are deprived of the benefit of public ordinances constantly miss them, and therefore should constantly mourn for the want of them, till they are restored to them again. Two things aggravated his grief:—

1. The reproaches with which his enemies teased him: *They continually say unto me, Where is thy God?* (1.) Because he was absent from the ark, the token of God's presence. Judging of the God of Israel by the gods of the heathen, they concluded he had lost his God. Note, Those are mistaken who think that when they have robbed us of our Bibles, and our ministers, and our solemn assemblies, they have robbed us of our God; for, though God has tied us to them when they are to be had, he has not tied himself to them. We know where our God is, and where to find him, when we know not where his ark is, nor where to find that. Wherever we are there is a way open heaven-ward. (2.) Because God did not immediately appear for his deliverance they concluded that he had abandoned him; but herein also they were deceived: it does not follow that the saints have lost their God because they have lost all their other friends. However, by this base reflection on God and his people, they added affliction to the afflicted, and that was what they aimed at. Nothing is more grievous to a gracious soul than that which is intended to shake its hope and confidence in God.

2. The remembrance of his former liberties and enjoyments, *v.* 4. *Son, remember thy good things,* is a great aggravation of evil things, so much do our powers of reflection and anticipation add to the grievance of this present time. David remembered the *days of old,* and then *his soul was poured out in him;* he melted away, and the thought almost broke his heart. He poured out his soul within him in sorrow, and then poured out his soul before God in prayer. But what was it that occasioned this painful melting of spirit? It was not the remembrance of the pleasures at court, or the entertainments of his own house, from which he was now banished, that afflicted him, but the remembrance of the free access he had formerly had to God's house and the pleasure he had in attending the sacred solemnities there. (1.) He *went to the house of God,* though in his time it was but a tent; nay, if this psalm was penned, as many think it was, at the time of his being persecuted by Saul, the ark was then in a private house, 2 Sam. vi. 3. But the meanness, obscurity, and inconveniency of the place did not lessen his esteem of that sacred symbol of the divine presence. David was a courtier, a prince, a man of honour, a man of business, and yet very diligent in attending God's house and joining in public ordinances, even in the days of Saul, when he and his great men *enquired not at it,* 1 Chron. xiii. 3. Whatever others did, David and his house would serve the Lord. (2.) He *went with the multitude,* and thought it no disparagement to his dignity to be at the head of a crowd in attending upon God. Nay, this added to the pleasure of it, that he was accompanied with a multitude, and therefore it is twice mentioned, as that which he greatly lamented the want of now. The more the better in the service of God; it is the more like heaven, and a sensible help to our comfort in the communion of saints. (3.) He went *with the voice of joy and praise,* not only with joy and praise in his heart, but with the outward expressions of it, proclaiming his joy and speaking forth the high praises of his God. Note, When we wait upon God in public ordinances we have reason to do it both with cheerfulness and thankfulness, to take to ourselves the comfort and give to God the glory of our liberty of access to him. (4.) He went to keep holydays, not to keep them in vain mirth and recreation, but in religious exercises. Solemn days are spent most comfortably in solemn assemblies.

III. Holy love hoping (*v.* 5): *Why art thou cast down, O my soul?* His sorrow was upon a very good account, and yet it must not exceed its due limits, nor prevail to depress his spirits; he therefore communes with his own heart, for his relief. "Come, my soul, I have something to say to thee in thy heaviness." Let us consider, 1. The cause of it. "Thou art cast down, as one stooping and sinking under a burden, Prov. xii. 25. Thou art disquieted, in confusion and disorder; now why art thou so?" This may be taken as an enquiring question : "Let the cause of this uneasiness be duly weighed, and see whether it be a just cause." Our disquietudes would in many cases vanish before a strict scrutiny into the grounds and reasons of them. "*Why am I cast down?* Is there a cause, a real cause? Have not others more cause, that do not make so much ado? Have not we, at the same time, cause to be encouraged?" Or it may be taken as an expostulating question ; those that commune much with their own hearts will often have occasion to chide them, as David here. "Why do I thus dishonour God by my melancholy dejections? Why do I discourage others and do so much injury to myself? Can I give a good account of this tumult?" 2. The cure of it : *Hope thou in God, for I shall yet praise him.* A believing confidence in God is a sovereign antidote against prevailing despondency and disquietude of spirit. And therefore, when we chide ourselves for our dejections, we must charge ourselves to hope in God ; when the soul embraces itself it sinks ; if it catch hold on the power and promise of God, it keeps the head above water. *Hope in God,* (1.) That he shall have glory from us : "*I shall yet praise him ;* I shall experience such a change in my state that I shall not want matter for praise, and such a change in my spirit that I shall not want a heart for praise." It is the greatest honour and happiness of a man, and the greatest desire and hope of every good man, to be unto God for a name and a praise. What is the crown of heaven's bliss but this, that there we shall be for ever praising God? And what is our support under our present woes but this, that we shall yet praise God, that they shall not prevent nor abate our endless hallelujahs? (2.) That we shall have comfort in him. We shall praise him *for the help of his countenance,* for his favour, the support we have by it and the satisfaction we have in it. Those that know how to value and improve the light of God's countenance will find in that a suitable, seasonable, and sufficient help, in the worst of times, and that which will furnish them with constant matter for praise. David's believing expectation of this kept him from sinking, nay, it kept him from drooping ; his harp was a palliative cure of Saul's melancholy, but his hope was an effectual cure of his own.

6 O my God, my soul is cast down within me : therefore will I remember thee from the land of Jordan, and of the Hermonites, from the hill Mizar. 7 Deep calleth unto deep at the noise of thy waterspouts : all thy waves and thy billows are gone over me. 8 *Yet* the LORD will command his lovingkindness in the daytime, and in the

night his song *shall be* with me, *and* my prayer unto the God of my life. 9 I will say unto God my rock, Why hast thou forgotten me? why go I mourning because of the oppression of the enemy? 10 *As* with a sword in my bones, mine enemies reproach me; while they say daily unto me, Where *is* thy God? 11 Why art thou cast down, O my soul? and why art thou disquieted within me? hope thou in God : for I shall yet praise him, *who is* the health of my countenance, and my God.

Complaints and comforts here, as before, take their turn, like day and night in the course of nature.

I. He complains of the dejections of his spirit, but comforts himself with the thoughts of God, v. 6. 1. In his troubles. His soul was dejected, and he goes to God and tells him so : *O my God! my soul is cast down within me.* It is a great support to us, when upon any account we are distressed, that we have liberty of access to God, and liberty of speech before him, and may open to him the causes of our dejection. David had communed with his own heart about its own bitterness, and had not as yet found relief ; and therefore he turns to God, and opens before him the trouble. Note, When we cannot get relief for our burdened spirits by pleading with ourselves, we should try what we can do by praying to God and leaving our case with him. We cannot still these winds and waves ; but we know who can. 2. In his devotions. His soul was elevated, and, finding the disease very painful, he had recourse to that as a sovereign remedy. "My soul is plunged ; therefore, to prevent its sinking, I will remember thee, meditate upon thee, and call upon thee, and try what that will do to keep up my spirit." Note, The way to forget the sense of our miseries is to remember the God of our mercies. It was an uncommon case when the psalmist *remembered God and was troubled,* lxxvii. 3. He had often remembered God and was comforted, and therefore had recourse to that expedient now. He was now driven to the utmost borders of the land of Canaan, to shelter himself there from the rage of his persecutors—sometimes to *the country about Jordan,* and, when discovered there, to *the land of the Hermonites,* or to a hill called *Mizar,* or *the little hill ;* but, (1.) Wherever he went he took his religion along with him. In all these places, he remembered God, and lifted up his heart to him, and kept his secret communion with him. This is the comfort of the banished, the wanderers, the travellers, of those that are strangers in a strange land, that *undique ad cœlos tantundem est viæ— wherever they are there is a way open heaven-*

ward. (2.) Wherever he was he retained his affection for the courts of God's house; from the land of Jordan, or from the top of the hills, he used to look a long look, a longing look, towards the place of the sanctuary, and wish himself there. Distance and time could not make him forget that which his heart was so much upon and which lay so near it.

II. He complains of the tokens of God's displeasure against him, but comforts himself with the hopes of the return of his favour in due time.

1. He saw his troubles coming from God's wrath, and that discouraged him (*v.* 7): "*Deep calls unto deep*, one affliction comes upon the neck of another, as if it were called to hasten after it; and thy water-spouts give the signal and sound the alarm of war." It may be meant of the terror and disquietude of his mind under the apprehensions of God's anger. One frightful thought summoned another, and made way for it, as is usual in melancholy people. He was overpowered and overwhelmed with a deluge of grief, like that of the old world, when the windows of heaven were opened and the fountains of the great deep were broken up. Or it is an allusion to a ship at sea in a great storm, tossed by the roaring waves, which go over it, cvii. 25. Whatever waves and billows of affliction go over us at any time we must call them God's waves and his billows, that we may humble ourselves under his mighty hand, and may encourage ourselves to hope that though we be threatened we shall not be ruined; for the waves and billows are under a divine check. *The Lord on high is mightier than the noise of these many waters.* Let not good men think it strange if they be exercised with many and various trials, and if they come thickly upon them; God knows what he does, and so shall they shortly. Jonah, in the whale's belly, made use of these words of David, Jon. ii. 3 (they are exactly the same in the original), and of him they were literally true, *All thy waves and thy billows have gone over me;* for the book of psalms is contrived so as to reach every one's case.

2. He expected his deliverance to come from God's favour (*v.* 8): *Yet the Lord will command his lovingkindness.* Things are bad, but they shall not always be so. *Non si male nunc et olim sic erit—Though affairs are now in an evil plight, they may not always be so.* After the storm there will come a calm, and the prospect of this supported him when deep called unto deep. Observe, (1.) What he promised himself from God: *The Lord will command his lovingkindness.* He eyes the favour of God as the fountain of all the good he looked for. That is life; that is better than life; and with that God will gather those from whom he has, *in a little wrath, hid his face*, Isa. liv. 7, 8. God's conferring his favour is called his *commanding* it. This intimates the freeness of it; we cannot pretend to merit it, but it is bestowed in a way

of sovereignty, he gives like a king. It intimates also the efficacy of it; he speaks his lovingkindness, and makes us to hear it; speaks, and it is done. He *commands deliverance* (xliv. 4), *commands the blessing* (cxxxiii. 3), as one having authority. By commanding his lovingkindness, he commands down the waves and the billows, and they shall obey him. This he will do *in the daytime*, for God's lovingkindness will make day in the soul at any time. Though *weeping* has *endured for a night*, a long night, yet *joy will come in the morning*. (2.) What he promised for himself to God. If God command his lovingkindness for him, he will meet it, and bid it welcome, with his best affections and devotions. [1.] He will rejoice in God: *In the night his song shall be with me.* The mercies we receive in the day we ought to return thanks for at night; when others are sleeping we should be praising God. See cxix. 62, *At midnight will I rise to give thanks.* In silence and solitude, when we are retired from the hurries of the world, we must be pleasing ourselves with the thoughts of God's goodness. Or in the night of affliction: "Before the day dawns, in which God commands his lovingkindness, I will sing songs of praise in the prospect of it." Even in tribulation the saints can *rejoice in hope of the glory of God*, sing in hope, and praise in hope, Rom. v. 2, 3. It is God's prerogative to *give songs in the night*, Job xxxv. 10. [2.] He will seek to God in a constant dependence upon him: *My prayer shall be to the God of my life.* Our believing expectation of mercy must not supersede, but quicken, our prayers for it. God is the God of our life, in whom we live and move, the author and giver of all our comforts; and therefore to whom should we apply by prayer, but to him? And from him what good may not we expect? It would put life into our prayers in them to eye God as the God of our life; for then it is for our lives, and the lives of our souls, that we stand up to make request.

III. He complains of the insolence of his enemies, and yet comforts himself in God as his friend, *v.* 9—11.

1. His complaint is that his enemies oppressed and reproached him, and this made a great impression upon him. (1.) They oppressed him to such a degree that he went mourning from day to day, from place to place, *v.* 9. He did not break out into indecent passions, though abused as never man was, but he silently wept out his grief, and went mourning; and for this we cannot blame him: it must needs grieve a man that truly loves his country, and seeks the good of it, to see himself persecuted and hardly used, as if he were an enemy to it. Yet David ought not hence to have concluded that God had forgotten him and cast him off, nor thus to have expostulated with him, as if he did him as much wrong in suffering him to be trampled upon as those did that trampled upon

him : *Why go I mourniny ?* and *why hast thou forgotten me ?* We may complain to God, but we are not allowed thus to complain of him. (2.) They reproached him so cuttingly that it was a *sword in his bones, v.* 10. He had mentioned before what the reproach was that touched him thus to the quick, and here he repeats it : *They say daily unto me, Where is thy God?*—a reproach which was very grievous to him, both because it reflected dishonour upon God and was intended to discourage his hope in God, which he had enough to do to keep up in any measure, and which was but too apt to fail of itself.

2. His comfort is that God is his *rock* (*v.* 9)—a rock to build upon, a rock to take shelter in. The rock of ages, in whom is everlasting strength, would be his rock, his strength in the inner man, both for doing and suffering. To him he had access with confidence. To God his rock he might say what he had to say, and be sure of a gracious audience. He therefore repeats what he had before said (*v.* 5), and concludes with it (*v.* 11) : *Why art thou cast down, O my soul?* His griefs and fears were clamorous and troublesome ; they were not silenced though they were again and again answered. But here, at length, his faith came off a conqueror and forced the enemies to quit the field. And he gains this victory, (1.) By repeating what he had before said, chiding himself, as before, for his dejections and disquietudes, and encouraging himself to trust in the name of the Lord and to stay himself upon his God. Note, It may be of great use to us to think our good thoughts over again, and, if we do not gain our point with them at first, perhaps we may the second time ; however, where the heart goes along with the words, it is no vain repetition. We have need to press the same thing over and over again upon our hearts, and all little enough. (2.) By adding one word to it ; *there* he hoped to praise God for the salvation that was in his countenance ; *here,* " I will praise him," says he, " as the salvation of my countenance from the present cloud that is upon it ; if God smile upon me, that will make me look pleasant, look up, look forward, look round, with pleasure." He adds, *and my God,* " related to me, in covenant with me ; all that he is, all that he has, is mine, according to the true intent and meaning of the promise." This thought enabled him to triumph over all his griefs and fears. God's being with the saints in heaven, and being their God, is that which will *wipe away all tears from their eyes,* Rev. xxi. 3, 4.

PSALM XLIII.

This psalm, it is likely, was penned upon the same occasion with the former, and, having no title, may be looked upon as an appendix to it ; the malady presently returning, he had immediate recourse to the same remedy, because he had entered it in his book, with a "probatum est—it has been proved," upon it. The second verse of this psalm is almost the very same with the ninth verse of the foregoing psalm, as the fifth of this is exactly the same with the eleventh of that. Christ himself, who had the Spirit without measure, when there was occasion prayed a second and third time " saying the same words," Matt. xxvi. 44. In this psalm, I. David appeals to God concerning the injuries that were done him by his enemies, ver. 1, 2. II. He prays to God

to restore to him the free enjoyment of public ordinances again, and promises to make a good improvement of them, ver. 3, 4. III. He endeavours to still the tumult of his own spirit with a lively hope and confidence in God (ver. 5), and if, in singing this psalm, we labour after these, we sing with grace in our hearts.

JUDGE me, O God, and plead my cause against an ungodly nation: O deliver me from the deceitful and unjust man. 2 For thou *art* the God of my strength : why dost thou cast me off? why go I mourning because of the oppression of the enemy ? 3 **O** send out thy light and thy truth : let them lead me ; let them bring me unto thy holy hill, and to thy tabernacles. 4 Then will I go unto the altar of God, unto God my exceeding joy: yea, upon the harp will I praise thee, O God my God. 5 Why art thou cast down, O my soul? and why art thou disquieted within me ? hope in God: for I shall yet praise him, *who is* the health of my countenance, and my God.

David here makes application to God, by faith and prayer, as his judge, his strength, his guide, his joy, his hope, with suitable affections and expressions.

I. As his Judge, his righteous Judge, who he knew would judge him, and who (being conscious of his own integrity) he knew would judge for him (*v.* 1) : *Judge me, O God! and plead my cause.* There were those that impeached him ; against them he is defendant, and from their courts, where he stood unjustly convicted and condemned, he appeals to the court of heaven, the supreme judicature, praying to have their judgment given against him reversed and his innocency cleared. There were those that had injured him ; against them he is plaintiff, and exhibits his complaint to him who is the avenger of wrong, praying for justice for himself and upon them. Observe, 1. Who his enemies were with whom he had this struggle. Here was a sinful body of men, whom he calls an *ungodly* or *unmerciful nation.* Those that are unmerciful make it appear that they are ungodly ; for, those that have any fear or love of their master will have compassion on their fellow-servants. And here was one bad man the head of them, a deceitful and unjust man, most probably Saul, who not only showed no kindness to David, but dealt most perfidiously and dishonestly with him. If Absalom was the man he meant, his character was no better. As long as there are such bad men out of hell, and nations of them, it is not strange that good men, who are yet out of heaven, meet with hard and base treatment. Some think that David, by the spirit of prophecy, calculated this psalm for the use of the Jews in their captivity in Babylon, and that the Chaldeans are the ungodly nation here meant ; to them it was very applicable, but only as other similar scriptures, none of which are of private interpretation. God might design it for their use, whether David did or no. 2. What is his prayer with reference to them : *Judge me.* As to the quarrel God had with him for sin, he prays, " *Enter not into judgment with me,* for then I shall be condemned;" but, as to the quarrel his enemies had with him he prays, " Lord, *judge me,* for I know that I shall be justified; *plead my cause against them,* take my part, and in thy providence appear on my behalf." He that has an honest cause may expect that God will plead it. " Plead my cause so as to deliver me from them, that they may not have their will against me." We must reckon our cause sufficiently pleaded if we be delivered, though our enemies be not destroyed.

II. As his strength, his all-sufficient strength; so he eyes God (*v.* 2): " *Thou art the God of my strength, my God, my strength,* from whom all my strength is derived, in whom I strengthen myself, who hast often strengthened me, and without whom I am weak as water and utterly unable either to do or suffer any thing for thee." David now went mourning, destitute of spiritual joys, yet he found God to be the God of his strength. If we cannot comfort ourselves in God, we may stay ourselves upon him, and may have spiritual supports when we want spiritual delights. David here pleads this with God : " Thou art the God on whom I depend as my strength ; why then dost thou cast me off ?" This was a mistake; for God never cast off any that trusted in him, whatever melancholy apprehensions they may have had of their own state. "Thou art the God of my strength ; why then is my enemy too strong for me, and why go I mourning because of his oppressive power ?" It is hard to reconcile the mighty force of the church's enemies with the almighty power of the church's God ; but the day will reconcile them when all his enemies shall become his footstool.

III. As his guide, his faithful guide (*v.* 3): *Lead me, bring me to thy holy hill.* He prays, 1. That God by his providence would bring him back from his banishment, and open a way for him again to the free enjoyment of the privileges of God's sanctuary. His heart is upon *the holy hill and the tabernacles,* not upon his family-comforts, his court-preferments, or his diversions; he could bear the want of these, but he is impatient to see God's tabernacles again ; nothing so amiable in his eyes as those ; thither he would gladly be brought back. In order to this he prays, " *Send out thy light and thy truth;* let me have this as a fruit of thy favour, which is light, and the performance of thy promise, which is truth." We need desire no more to make us happy than the good that flows from God's favour and is included in his promise. That mercy, that truth, is enough, is all; and, when we see these in God's providences, we see ourselves under a very safe conduct. Note, Those whom God leads he leads to his holy hill, and

to his tabernacles ; those therefore who pretend to be led by the Spirit, and yet turn their backs upon instituted ordinances, certainly deceive themselves. 2. That God by his grace would bring him into communion with himself, and prepare him for the vision and fruition of himself in the other world. Some of the Jewish writers by the *light* and *truth* here understand Messiah the Prince and Elias his forerunner : these have come, in answer to the prayers of the Old Testament ; but we are still to pray for God's light and truth, the Spirit of light and truth, who supplies the want of Christ's bodily presence, to lead us into the mystery of godliness and to guide us in the way to heaven. When God sends his light and truth into our hearts, these will guide us to the upper world in all our devotions as well as in all our aims and expectations ; and, if we conscientiously follow that light and that truth, they will certainly bring us to the holy hill above.

IV. As his joy, his exceeding joy. If God guide him to his tabernacles, if he restore him to his former liberties, he knows very well what he has to do : *Then will I go unto the altar of God, v.* 4. He will get as near as he can unto God, his exceeding joy. Note, 1. Those that come to the tabernacles should come to the altar; those that come to ordinances should qualify themselves to come, and then come to special ordinances, to those that are most affecting and most binding. The nearer we come, the closer we cleave, to God, the better. 2. Those that come to the altar of God must see to it that therein they come unto God, and draw near to him with the heart, with a true heart : we come in vain to holy ordinances if we do not in them come to the holy God. 3. Those that come unto God must come to him as their exceeding joy, not only as their future bliss, but as their present joy, and that not a common, but an exceeding joy, far exceeding all the joys of sense and time. The phrase, in the original, is very emphatic —*unto God the gladness of my joy,* or of my triumph. Whatever we rejoice or triumph in God must be the joy of it ; all our joy in it must terminate in him, and must pass through the gift to the giver. 4. When we come to God as our exceeding joy our comforts in him must be the matter of our praises to him as God, and our God : *Upon the harp will I praise thee, O God! my God.* David excelled at the harp (1 Sam. xvi. 16, 18), and with that in which he excelled he would praise God; for God is to be praised with the best we have ; it is fit he should be, for he is the best.

V. As his hope, his never-failing hope, *v* 5. Here, as before, David quarrels with himself for his dejections and despondencies, and owns he did ill to yield to them, and that he had no reason to do so : *Why art thou cast down, O my soul?* He then quiets himself in the believing expectation he had of giving glory to God (*Hope in God, for I shall yet praise him*) and of enjoying glory with God : *He is the health of my countenance and my God.* That is what we cannot too much insist upon, for it is what we must live and die by.

PSALM XLIV.

We are not told either who was the penman of this psalm or when and upon what occasion it was penned, upon a melancholy occasion, we are sure, not so much to the penman himself (then we could have found occasions enough for it in the history of David and his afflictions), but to the church of God in general; and therefore, if we suppose it penned by David, yet we must attribute it purely to the Spirit of prophecy, and must conclude that that Spirit (whatever he himself had) had in view the captivity of Babylon, or the sufferings of the Jewish church under Antiochus, or rather the afflicted state of the Christian church in its early days (to which ver. 22 is applied by the apostle, Rom. viii. 36), and indeed in all its days on earth, for it is its determined lot that it must enter into the kingdom of heaven through many tribulations. And, if we have any gospel-psalms pointing at the privileges and comforts of Christians, why should we not have one pointing at their trials and exercises? It is a psalm calculated for a day of fasting and humiliation upon occasion of some public calamity, either pressing or threatening. In it the church is taught, I. To own with thankfulness, to the glory of God, the great things God has done for their fathers, ver. 1—8. II. To exhibit a memorial of their present calamitous estate, ver. 9—16. III. To file a protestation of their integrity and adherence to God notwithstanding, ver. 17—22. IV. To lodge a petition at the throne of grace for succour and relief, ver. 22—26. In singing this psalm we ought to give God the praise of what he has formerly done for his people, to represent our own grievances, or sympathize with those parts of the church that are in distress, to engage ourselves, whatever happens, to cleave to God and duty, and then cheerfully to wait the event.

To the chief musician for the sons of Korah, Maschil.

W E have heard with our ears, O God, our fathers have told us, *what* work thou didst in their days, in the times of old. 2 *How* thou didst drive out the heathen with thy hand, and plantedst them; *how* thou didst afflict the people, and cast them out. 3 For they got not the land in possession by their own sword, neither did their own arm save them: but thy right hand, and thine arm, and the light of thy countenance, because thou hadst a favour unto them. 4 Thou art my King, O God: command deliverances for Jacob. 5 Through thee will we push down our enemies: through thy name will we tread them under that rise up against us. 6 For I will not trust in my bow, neither shall my sword save me. 7 But thou hast saved us from our enemies, and hast put them to shame that hated us. 8 In God we boast all the day long, and praise thy name for ever. Selah.

Some observe that most of the psalms that are entitled *Maschil—psalms of instruction,* are sorrowful psalms; for afflictions give instructions, and sorrow of spirit opens the ear to them. *Blessed is the man whom thou chastenest and teachest.*

In these verses the church, though now trampled upon, calls to remembrance the days of her triumph, of her triumph in God and over her enemies. This is very largely mentioned here, 1. As an aggravation of the present distress. The yoke of servitude cannot but lie very heavily on the necks of those

that used to wear the crown of victory; and the tokens of God's displeasure must needs be most grievous to those that have been long accustomed to the tokens of his favour. 2. As an encouragement to hope that God would yet turn again their captivity and return in mercy to them; accordingly he mixes prayers and comfortable expectations with his record of former mercies. Observe,

I. Their commemoration of the great things God had formerly done for them.

1. In general (*v.* 1): *Our fathers have told us what work thou didst in their days.* Observe, (1.) The many operations of providence are here spoken of as one work—"They have told us the *work* which thou didst;" for there is a wonderful harmony and uniformity in all that God does, and the many wheels make but one wheel (Ezek. x. 13), many works make but one work. (2.) It is a debt which every age owes to posterity to keep an account of God's works of wonder, and to transmit the knowledge of them to the next generation. Those that went before us told us what God did in their days, we are bound to tell those that come after us what he has done in our days, and let them do the like justice to those that shall succeed them; thus shall *one generation praise his works to another* (cxlv. 4), the *fathers to the children shall make known his truth,* Isa. xxxviii. 19. (3.) We must not only make mention of the work God has done in our own days, but must also acquaint ourselves and our children with what he did in the times of old, long before our own days; and of this we have in the scripture a sure word of history, as sure as the word of prophecy. (4.) Children must diligently attend to what their parents tell them of the wonderful works of God, and keep it in remembrance, as that which will be of great use to them. (5.) Former experiences of God's power and goodness are strong supports to faith and powerful pleas in prayer under present calamities. See how Gideon insists upon it (Judg. vi. 13): *Where are all his miracles which our fathers told us of?*

2. In particular, their fathers had told them, (1.) How wonderfully God planted Israel in Canaan at first, *v.* 2, 3. He drove out the natives, to make room for Israel, afflicted them, and cast them out, gave them as dust to Israel's sword and as driven stubble to their bow. The many complete victories which Israel obtained over the Canaanites, under the command of Joshua, were not to be attributed to themselves, nor could they challenge the glory of them. [1.] They were not owing to their own merit, but to God's favour and free grace: It was *through the light of thy countenance, because thou hadst a favour to them. Not for thy righteousness, or the uprightness of thy heart, doth God drive them out from before thee* (Deut. ix. 5, 6), but because God would *perform the oath which he swore unto their fathers,* Deut. vii. 8. The less praise this allows us the more comfort it

administers to us, that we may see all our successes and enlargements coming to us from the favour of God and the light of his countenance. [2.] They were not owing to their own might, but to God's power engaged for them, without which all their own efforts and endeavours would have been fruitless. It was not by their own sword that they got the land in possession, though they had great numbers of mighty men; nor did their own arm save them from being driven back by the Canaanites and put to shame; but it was God's *right hand* and his *arm.* He fought for Israel, else they would have fought in vain; it was through him that they did valiantly and victoriously. It was God that planted Israel in that good land, as the careful husbandman plants a tree, from which he promises him-self fruit, See lxxx. 8. This is applicable to the planting of the Christian church in the world, by the preaching of the gospel. Paganism was wonderfully driven out, as the Canaanites, not all at once, but by little and little, not by any human policy or power (for God chose to do it by the weak and foolish things of the world), but by the wisdom and power of God—Christ by his Spirit went forth conquering and to conquer; and the remembrance of that is a great support and comfort to those that groan under the yoke of antichristian tyranny, for to the state of the church under the power of the New-Testament Babylon, some think (and particularly the learned Amyraldus), the complaints in the latter part of this psalm may very fitly be accommodated. He that by his power and goodness planted a church for himself in the world will certainly support it by the same power and goodness; and the *gates of hell shall not prevail against it.*

(2.) How frequently he had given them success against their enemies that attempted to disturb them in the possession of that good land (*v.* 7): *Thou hast,* many a time, *saved us from our enemies,* and hast put to flight, and so put to shame, *those that hated us,* witness the successes of the judges against the nations that oppressed Israel. Many a time have the persecutors of the Christian church, and those that hate it, been put to shame by the power of truth, Acts vi. 10.

II. The good use they make of this record, and had formerly made of it, in consideration of the great things God had done for their fathers of old.

1. They had taken God for their sovereign Lord, had sworn allegiance to him, and put themselves under his protection (*v.* 4): *Thou art my King, O God!* He speaks in the name of the church, as (lxxiv. 12), *Thou art my King of old.* God, as a king, has made laws for his church, provided for the peace and good order of it, judged for it, pleaded its cause, fought its battles, and protected it; it is his kingdom in the world, and ought to be subject to him, and to pay him tribute. Or the psalmist speaks for himself here:

" Lord, *Thou art my King;* whither shall I go with my petitions, but to thee? The favour I ask is not for myself, but for thy church." Note, It is every one's duty to improve his personal interest at the throne of grace for the public welfare and prosperity of the people of God; as Moses, " *If I have found grace in thy sight,* guide thy people," Exod. xxxiii. 13.

2. They had always applied to him by prayer for deliverance when at any time they were in distress: *Command deliverances for Jacob.* Observe, (1.) The enlargedness of their desire. They pray for deliverances, not one, but many, as many as they had need of, how many soever they were, a series of deliverances, a deliverance from every danger. (2.) The strength of their faith in the power of God. They do not say, *Work deliverances,* but, *Command them,* which denotes his doing it easily and instantly—*Speak and it is done* (such was the faith of the centurion, Matt. viii. 8, *Speak the word only, and my servant shall be healed*): it denotes also his doing it effectually: " Command it, as one having authority, whose command will be obeyed." *Where the word of a king is there is power,* much more the word of the King of kings.

3. They had trusted and triumphed in him. As they owned it was not their own sword and bow that had saved them (*v.* 3), so neither did they trust to their own sword or bow to save them for the future (*v.* 6): " *I will not trust in my bow,* nor in any of my military preparations, as if those would stand me in stead without God. No; *through thee will we push down our enemies* (*v.* 5); we will attempt it in thy strength, relying only upon that, and not upon the number or valour of our forces; and, having thee on our side, we will not doubt of success in the attempt. *Through thy name* (by virtue of thy wisdom directing us, thy power strengthening us and working for us, and thy promise securing success to us) we shall, we *will, tread those under that rise up against us.*"

4. They had made him their joy and praise (*v.* 8): " *In God we have boasted;* in him we do and will boast, every day, and all the day long." When their enemies boasted of their strength and successes, as Sennacherib and Rabshakeh hectored Hezekiah, they owned they had nothing to boast of, in answer thereunto, but their relation to God and their interest in him; and, if he were for them, they could set all the world at defiance. *Let him that glories glory in the Lord,* and let that for ever exclude all other boasting. Let those that trust in God make their boast in him, for they know whom they have trusted; let them *boast in him all the day long,* for it is a subject that can never be exhausted. But let them withal *praise his name for ever;* if they have the comfort of his name, let them give unto him the glory due to it.

9 But thou hast cast off, and put us

to shame; and goest not forth with our armies. 10 Thou makest us to turn back from the enemy: and they which hate us spoil for themselves. 11 Thou hast given us like sheep *appointed* for meat; and hast scattered us among the heathen. 12 Thou sellest thy people for nought, and dost not increase *thy wealth* by their price. 13 Thou makest us a reproach to our neighbours, a scorn and a derision to them that are round about us. 14 Thou makest us a byword among the heathen, a shaking of the head among the people. 15 My confusion *is* continually before me, and the shame of my face hath covered me, 16 For the voice of him that reproacheth and blasphemeth; by reason of the enemy and avenger.

The people of God here complain to him of the low and afflicted condition that they were now in, under the prevailing power of their enemies and oppressors, which was the more grievous to them because *they* were now trampled upon, who had always been used, in their struggles with their neighbours, to win the day and get the upper hand, and because those were now their oppressors whom they had many a time triumphed over and made tributaries, and especially because they had boasted in their God with great assurance that he would still protect and prosper them, which made the distress they were in, and the disgrace they were under, the more shameful. Let us see what the complaint is.

I. That they wanted the usual tokens of God's favour to them and presence with them (*v.* 9): " *Thou hast cast off;* thou seemest to have cast us off and our cause, and to have cast off thy wonted care of us and concern for us, and so hast put us to shame, for we boasted of the constancy and perpetuity of thy favour. Our armies go forth as usual, but they are put to flight; we gain no ground, but lose what we have gained, for thou goest not forth with them, for, if thou didst, which way soever they turned they would prosper; but it is quite contrary." Note, God's people, when they are cast down, are tempted to think themselves cast off and forsaken of God; but it is a mistake. *Hath God cast away his people? God forbid,* Rom. xi. 1.

II. That they were put to the worst before their enemies in the field of battle (*v.* 10): *Thou makest us to turn back from the enemy,* as Joshua complained when they met with a repulse at Ai (Josh. vii. 8): "We are dispirited, and have lost the ancient valour of Israelites; we flee, we fall, before those that used to flee and fall before us; and then those

that hate us have the plunder of our camp and of our country; they spoil for themselves, and reckon all their own that they can lay their hands on. Attempts to shake off the Babylonish yoke have been ineffectual, and we have rather lost ground by them."

III. That they were doomed to the sword and to captivity (*v.* 11): " *Thou hast given us like sheep appointed for meat.* They make no more scruple of killing an Israelite than of killing a sheep; nay, like the butcher, they make a trade of it, they take a pleasure in it as a hungry man in his meat; and we are led with as much ease, and as little resistance, as a lamb to the slaughter; many are slain, and the rest scattered among the heathen, continually insulted by their malice or in danger of being infected by their iniquities." They looked upon themselves as bought and sold, and charged it upon God, *Thou sellest thy people,* when they should have charged it upon their own sin. *For your iniquities have you sold yourselves,* Isa. l. 1. However, thus far was right that they looked above the instruments of their trouble and kept their eye upon God, as well knowing that their worst enemies had no power against them *but what was given them from above;* they own it was God that *delivered them into the hands of the ungodly,* as that which is sold is delivered to the buyer. *Thou sellest them for nought, and dost not increase in their price* (so it may be read); "thou dost not sell them by auction, to those that will bid most for them, but in haste, to those that will bid first for them; any one shall have them that will." Or, as we read it, *Thou dost not increase thy wealth by their price,* intimating that they could have suffered this contentedly if they had been sure that it would redound to the glory of God and that his interest might be some way served by their sufferings; but it was quite contrary: Israel's disgrace turned to God's dishonour, so that he was so far from being a gainer in his glory by the sale of them that it should seem he was greatly a loser by it; see Isa. lii. 5; Ezek. xxxvi. 20.

IV. That they were loaded with contempt, and all possible ignominy was put upon them. In this also they acknowledge God: " *Thou makest us a reproach;* thou bringest those calamities upon us which occasion the reproach, and thou permittest their virulent tongues to smite us." They complain, 1. That they were ridiculed and bantered, and were looked upon as the most contemptible people under the sun; their troubles were turned to their reproach, and upon the account of them they were derided. 2. That their neighbours, those about them, from whom they could not withdraw, were most abusive to them, *v.* 13. 3. That the heathen, the people that were strangers to the commonwealth of Israel and aliens to the covenants of promise, made them a by-word, and shook the head at them, as triumphing in their fall, *v.* 14. 4. That the reproach was constant and incessant (*v.* 15): *My confusion is continually before me.* The church in general, the psalmist in particular, were continually teased and vexed with the insults of the enemy. Concerning those that are going down every one cries, "Down with them." 5. That it was very grievous, and in a manner overwhelmed him: *The shame of my face has covered me.* He blushed for sin, or rather for the dishonour done to God, and then it was a holy blushing. 6. That it reflected upon God himself; the reproach which the enemy and the avenger cast upon them was downright blasphemy against God, *v.* 16, and 2 Kings xix. 3. There was therefore strong reason to believe that God would appear for them. As there is no trouble more grievous to a generous and ingenuous mind than reproach and calumny, so there is none more grievous to a holy gracious soul than blasphemy and dishonour done to God.

17 All this is come upon us; yet have we not forgotten thee, neither have we dealt falsely in thy covenant. 18 Our heart is not turned back, neither have our steps declined from thy way; 19 Though thou hast sore broken us in the place of dragons, and covered us with the shadow of death. 20 If we have forgotten the name of our God, or stretched out our hands to a strange god; 21 Shall not God search this out? for he knoweth the secrets of the heart. 22 Yea, for thy sake are we killed all the day long; we are counted as sheep for the slaughter. 23 Awake, why sleepest thou, O Lord? arise, cast *us* not off for ever. 24 Wherefore hidest thou thy face, *and* forgettest our affliction and our oppression? 25 For our soul is bowed down to the dust: our belly cleaveth unto the earth. 26 Arise for our help, and redeem us for thy mercies' sake.

The people of God, being greatly afflicted and oppressed, here apply to him; whither else should they go?

I. By way of appeal, concerning their integrity, which he only is an infallible judge of, and which he will certainly be the rewarder of. Two things they call God to witness to :—

1. That, though they suffered these hard things, yet they kept close to God and to their duty (*v.* 17): "*All this has come upon us,* and it is as bad perhaps as bad can be, *yet have we not forgotten thee,* neither cast off the thoughts of thee nor deserted the worship of thee; for, though we cannot deny but that we have dealt foolishly, yet we have not *dealt falsely in thy covenant,* so as to cast thee off and take to

other gods. Though idolaters were our conquerors, we did not therefore entertain any more favourable thoughts of their idols and idolatries; though thou hast seemed to forsake us and withdraw from us, yet we have not therefore forsaken thee." The trouble they had been long in was very great: "We have been *sorely broken in the place of dragons,* among men as fierce, and furious, and cruel, as dragons. We have been *covered with the shadow of death,* that is, we have been under deep melancholy and apprehensive of nothing short of death. We have been wrapped up in obscurity, and buried alive; and thou hast thus broken us, thou hast thus covered us (*v.* 19), yet we have not harboured any hard thoughts of thee, nor meditated a retreat from thy service. Though thou hast slain us, we have continued to trust in thee: *Our heart has not turned back;* we have not secretly withdrawn our affections from thee, neither have our steps, either in our religious worship or in our conversation, *declined from thy way* (*v.* 18), the way which thou hast appointed us to walk in." When the heart turns back the steps will soon decline; for it is the evil heart of unbelief that inclines to depart from God. Note, We may the better bear our troubles, how pressing soever, if in them we still hold fast our integrity. While our troubles do not drive us from our duty to God we should not suffer them to drive us from our comfort in God; for he will not leave us if we do not leave him. For the proof of their integrity they take God's omniscience to witness, which is as much the comfort of the upright in heart as it is the terror of hypocrites (*v.* 20, 21): "*If we have forgotten the name of our God,* under pretence that he had forgotten us, or in our distress have *stretched out our hands to a strange god,* as more likely to help us, *shall not God search this out?* Shall he not know it more fully and distinctly than we know that which we have with the greatest care and diligence searched out? Shall he not judge it, and call us to an account for it?" Forgetting God was a heart-sin, and stretching out the hand to a strange god was often a secret sin, Ezek. viii. 12. But heart-sins and secret sins are known to God, and must be reckoned for; for *he knows the secrets of the heart,* and therefore is an infallible judge of the words and actions.

2. That they suffered these hard things because they kept close to God and to their duty (*v.* 22): "It is *for thy sake that we are killed all the day long,* because we stand related to thee, are called by thy name, call upon thy name, and will not worship other gods." In this the Spirit of prophecy had reference to those who suffered even unto death for the testimony of Christ, to whom it is applied, Rom. viii. 36. So many were killed, and put to such lingering deaths, that they were in the killing all the day long; so universally was this practised that when a man became a

Christian he reckoned himself as a *sheep appointed for the slaughter.*

II. By way of petition, with reference to their present distress, that God would, in his own due time, work deliverance for them. 1. Their request is very importunate: *Awake, arise, v.* 23. *Arise for our help; redeem us* (*v.* 26); come speedily and powerfully to our relief, lxxx. 2. *Stir up thy strength, and come and save us.* They had complained (*v.* 12) that God had sold them; here they pray (*v.* 26) that God would redeem them; for there is no appealing from God, but by appealing to him. If he sell us, it is not any one else that can redeem us; the same hand that tears must heal, that smites must bind up, Hos. vi. 1. They had complained (*v.* 9), *Thou hast cast us off;* but here they pray (*v.* 23), " *Cast us not off for ever;* let us not be finally forsaken of God." 2. The expostulations are very moving: *Why sleepest thou? v.* 23. He that keeps Israel neither slumbers nor sleeps; but, when he does not immediately appear for the deliverance of his people, they are tempted to think he sleeps. The expression is figurative (as lxxviii. 65, *Then the Lord awaked as one out of sleep);* but it was applicable to Christ in the letter (Matt. viii. 24); he was asleep when his disciples were in a storm, and they awoke him, saying, *Lord, save us, we perish.* " *Wherefore hidest thou thy face,* that we may not see thee and the light of thy countenance ?" Or, "that thou mayest not see us and our distresses? Thou forgettest our affliction and our oppression, for it still continues, and we see no way open for our deliverance." And, 3. The pleas are very proper, not their own merit and righteousness, though they had the testimony of their consciences concerning their integrity, but they plead the poor sinner's pleas. (1.) Their own misery, which made them the proper objects of the divine compassion (*v.* 25): " *Our soul is bowed down to the dust* under prevailing grief and fear. We have become as creeping things, the most despicable animals: *Our belly cleaves unto the earth;* we cannot lift up ourselves, neither revive our own drooping spirits nor recover ourselves out of our low and sad condition, and we lie exposed to be trodden on by every insulting foe." 2. God's mercy: "*O redeem us for thy mercies' sake;* we depend upon the goodness of thy nature, which is the glory of thy name (Exod. xxxiv. 6), and upon those sure mercies of David which are conveyed by the covenant to all his spiritual seed."

PSALM XLV.

This psalm is an illustrious prophecy of Messiah the Prince: it is all over gospel, and points at him only, as a bridegroom espousing the church to himself and as a king ruling in it and ruling for it. It is probable that our Saviour has reference to this psalm when he compares the kingdom of heaven, more than once, to a nuptial solemnity, the solemnity of a royal nuptial, Matt. xxii. 2; xxv. 1. We have no reason to think it has any reference to Solomon's marriage with Pharaoh's daughter; if I thought that it had reference to any other than the mystical marriage between Christ and his church, I would rather apply it to some of David's marriages, because he was a man of war, such a one as the bridegroom here is described to be, which Solomon was not. But I take it to be purely and only meant of

404

Jesus Christ; of him speaks the prophet this, of him and of no other man ; and to him (ver. 6, 7) it is applied in the New Testament (Heb. i. 8), nor can it be understood of any other. The preface speaks the excellency of the song, ver. 1. The psalm speaks, I. Of the royal bridegroom, who is Christ. 1. The transcendent excellency of his person, ver. 2. 2. The glory of his victories, ver. 3—5. 3. The righteousness of his government, ver. 6, 7. 4. The splendour of his court, ver. 8, 9. II. Of the royal bride, which is the church. 1. Her consent gained, ver. 10, 11. 2. The nuptials solemnized, ver. 12—15. 3. The issue of this marriage, ver. 16, 17. In singing this psalm our hearts must be filled with high thoughts of Christ, with an entire submission and satisfaction in his government, and with an earnest desire of the enlarging and perpetuating of his church in the world.

To the chief musician upon Shoshannim, for the sons of Korah, Maschil. A song of loves.

MY heart is inditing a good matter: I speak of the things which I have made touching the king : my tongue *is* the pen of a ready writer. 2 Thou art fairer than the children of men : grace is poured into thy lips : therefore God hath blessed thee for ever. 3 Gird thy sword upon *thy* thigh, O *most* mighty, with thy glory and thy majesty. 4 And in thy majesty ride prosperously because of truth and meekness *and* righteousness ; and thy right hand shall teach thee terrible things. 5 Thine arrows *are* sharp in the heart of the king's enemies ; *whereby* the people fall under thee.

Some make *Shoshannim,* in the title, to signify an instrument of six strings ; others take it in its primitive signification for lilies or roses, which probably were strewed, with other flowers, at nuptial solemnities ; and then it is easily applicable to Christ, who calls himself the *rose of Sharon and the lily of the valleys,* Cant. ii. 1. It is *a song of loves,* concerning the holy love that is between Christ and his church. It is a *song of the well-beloved,* the virgins, the companions of the bride (*v.* 14), prepared to be sung by them. The virgin-company that attend the Lamb on Mount Zion are said to *sing a new song,* Rev. xiv. 3, 4.

I. The preface (*v.* 1) speaks, 1. The dignity of the subject. It is *a good matter,* and it is a pity that such a moving art as poetry should ever be employed about a bad matter. It is *touching the King,* King Jesus, and his kingdom and government. Note, Those that speak of Christ speak of a good matter, no subject so noble, so copious, so fruitful, so profitable, and so well-becoming us ; it is a shame that this good matter is not more the matter of our discourse. 2. The excellency of the management. This song was a confession with the mouth of faith in the heart concerning Christ and his church. (1.) The matter was well digested, as it well deserved : *My heart is inditing it,* which perhaps is meant of that Spirit of prophecy that dictated the psalm to David, that Spirit of Christ which was in the prophets, 1 Pet. i. 11. But it is applicable to his devout meditations and affections in his heart, out of the abundance of which his mouth spoke. Things concerning Christ ought to be thought of by us with all possible seriousness, with fixedness of thought and a fire of holy love, especially when we are to speak of those things. We then speak best of Christ and divine things when we speak from the heart that which has warmed and affected us; and we should never be rash in speaking of the things of Christ, but weigh well beforehand what we have to say, lest we speak amiss. See Eccl. v. 2. (2.) It was well expressed: *I will speak of the things which I have made.* He would express himself, [1.] With all possible clearness, as one that did himself understand and was affected with the things he spoke of. Not, " I will speak the things I have heard from others," that is speaking by rote; but, " the things which I have myself studied." Note, What God has wrought in our souls, as well as what he has wrought for them, we must declare to others, lxvi. 16. [2.] With all possible cheerfulness, freedom, and fluency : " *My tongue is as the pen of a ready writer,* guided by my heart in every word as the pen is by the hand." We call the prophets the *penmen* of scripture, whereas really they were but the pen. The tongue of the most subtle disputant, and the most eloquent orator, is but the pen with which God writes what he pleases. Why should we quarrel with the pen if bitter things be written against us, or idolize the pen if it write in our favour? David not only spoke what he thought of Christ, but wrote it, that it might spread the further and last the longer. His tongue was as the pen of a ready writer, that lets nothing slip. When the heart is inditing a good matter it is a pity but the tongue should be as *the pen of a ready writer,* to leave it upon record.

II. In these verses the Lord Jesus is represented,

1. As most beautiful and amiable in himself. It is a marriage-song; and therefore the transcendent excellencies of Christ are represented by the beauty of the royal bridegroom (*v.* 2): *Thou art fairer than the children of men,* than any of them. He proposed (*v.* 1) to speak of the King, but immediately directs his speech to him. Those that have an admiration and affection for Christ love to go to him and tell him so. Thus we must profess our faith, that we see his beauty, and our love, that we are pleased with it: *Thou are fair, thou art fairer than the children of men.* Note, Jesus Christ is in himself, and in the eyes of all believers, more amiable and lovely than the children of men. The beauties of the Lord Jesus, as God, as Mediator, far surpass those of human nature in general and those which the most amiable and excellent of the children of men are endowed with; there is more in Christ to engage our love than there is or can be in any creature. Our beloved is more than another beloved. The beauties of this lower

world, and its charms, are in danger of drawing away our hearts from Christ, and therefore we are concerned to understand how much he excels them all, and how much more worthy he is of our love.

2. As the great favourite of heaven. He is *fairer than the children of men,* for God has done more for him than for any of the children of men, and all his kindness to the children of men is for his sake, and passes through his hands, through his mouth. (1.) He has grace, and he has it for us : *Grace is poured into thy lips.* By his word, his promise, his gospel, the good-will of God is made known to us and the good work of God is begun and carried on in us. He received all grace from God, all the endowments that were requisite to qualify him for his work and office as Mediator, that from his fulness we might receive, John i. 16. It was not only poured into his heart, for his own strength and encouragement, but poured into his lips, that by the words of his mouth in general, and the kisses of his mouth to particular believers, he might communicate both holiness and comfort. From this grace poured into his lips proceeded those gracious words which all admired, Luke iv. 22. The gospel of grace is poured into his lips; for it *began to be spoken by the Lord,* and from him we receive it. He has the words of eternal life. *The spirit of prophecy is put into thy lips;* so the Chaldee. (2.) He has the blessing, and he has it for us. " Therefore, because thou art the great trustee of divine grace for the use and benefit of the children of men, *therefore God has blessed thee for ever,* has made thee an everlasting blessing, so as that in thee all the nations of the earth shall be blessed." Where God gives his grace he will give his blessing. We are blessed with spiritual blessings in Christ Jesus, Eph. i. 3.

3. As victorious over all his enemies. The royal bridegroom is a man of war, and his nuptials do not excuse him from the field of battle (as was allowed by the law, Deut. xxiv. 5); nay, they bring him to the field of battle, for he is to rescue his spouse by dint of sword out of her captivity, to conquer her, and to conquer for her, and then to marry her. Now we have here,

(1.) His preparations for war (*v.* 3): *Gird thy sword upon thy thigh, O Most Mighty!* The word of God is the sword of the Spirit. By the promises of that word, and the grace contained in those promises, souls are made willing to submit to Jesus Christ and become his loyal subjects; by the threatenings of that word, and the judgments executed according to them, those that stand it out against Christ will, in due time, be brought down and ruined. By the gospel of Christ many Jews and Gentiles were converted, and, at length, the Jewish nation was destroyed, according to the predictions of it, for their implacable enmity to it; and paganism was quite abolished. The sword here girt on Christ's thigh is the same which is said to *proceed out of his mouth,* Rev.

xix. 15. When the gospel was sent forth to be preached to all nations, then our Redeemer girded his sword upon his thigh.

(2.) His expedition to this holy war: He goes forth *with his glory and his majesty*, as a great king takes the field with abundance of pomp and magnificence—his sword, his glory, and majesty. In his gospel he appears transcendently great and excellent, bright and blessed, in the honour and majesty which the Father has laid upon him. Christ, both in his person and in his gospel, had nothing of external glory or majesty, nothing to charm men (for he had no form nor comeliness), nothing to awe men, for he *took upon him the form of a servant;* it was all spiritual glory, spiritual majesty. There is so much grace, and therefore glory, in that word, *He that believes shall be saved,* so much terror, and therefore majesty, in that word, *He that believes not shall be damned,* that we may well say, in the chariot of that gospel, which these words are the sum of, the Redeemer rides forth in glory and majesty. *In thy majesty ride prosperously, v. 4. Prosper thou; ride thou.* This speaks the promise of his Father, that he should prosper according to *the good pleasure of the Lord,* that he should *divide the spoil with the strong,* in recompence of his sufferings. Those cannot but prosper to whom God says, Prosper, Isa. lii. 10—12. And it denotes the good wishes of his friends, praying that he may prosper in the conversion of souls to him, and the destruction of all the powers of darkness that rebel against him." " *Thy kingdom come;* Go on and prosper."

(3.) The glorious cause in which he is engaged—*because of truth, and meekness, and righteousness,* which were, in a manner, sunk and lost among men, and which Christ came to retrieve and rescue. [1.] The gospel itself is *truth, meekness, and righteousness;* it commands by the power of truth and righteousness; for Christianity has these, incontestably, on its side, and yet it is to be promoted by meekness and gentleness, 1 Cor. iv. 12, 13; 2 Tim. ii. 25. [2.] Christ appears in it in his *truth, meekness,* and *righteousness,* and these are his glory and majesty, and because of these he shall prosper. Men are brought to believe on him because he is true, to learn of him because he is meek, Matt. xi. 29 (the gentleness of Christ is of mighty force, 2 Cor. x. 1), and to submit to him because he is righteous and rules with equity. [3.] The gospel, as far as it prevails with men, sets up in their hearts *truth, meekness, and righteousness,* rectifies their mistakes by the light of truth, controls their passions by the power of meekness, and governs their hearts and lives by the laws of righteousness. Christ came, by setting up his kingdom among men, to restore those glories to a degenerate world, and to maintain the cause of those just and rightful rulers under him that by error, malice, and iniquity, had been deposed.

406

(4.) The success of his expedition: " *Thy right hand shall teach thee terrible things;* thou shalt experience a wonderful divine power going along with thy gospel, to make it victorious, and the effects of it will be terrible things." [1.] In order to the conversion and reduction of souls to him, there are terrible things to be done; the heart must be pricked, conscience must be startled, and the terrors of the Lord must make way for his consolations. This is done by the right hand of Christ. The Comforter shall continue, John xvi. 8. [2.] In the conquest of the gates of hell and its supporters, in the destruction of Judaism and Paganism, terrible things will be done, which will make *men's hearts fail them for fear* (Luke xxi. 26) and great men and chief captains call to the *rocks and mountains to fall on them,* Rev. vi. 15 The next verse describes these terrible things (*v.* 5): *Thy arrows are sharp in the heart of the king's enemies. First,* Those that were by nature enemies are thus wounded, in order to their being subdued and reconciled. Convictions are like the arrows of the bow, which are sharp in the heart on which they fasten, and bring people to fall under Christ, in subjection to his laws and government. Those that thus fall on this stone shall be broken, Matt. xxi. 44. *Secondly,* Those that persist in their enmity are thus wounded, in order to their being ruined. The arrows of God's terrors are sharp in their hearts, whereby they shall fall under him, so as to be made his footstool, cx. 1. Those that would not have him to reign over them shall be brought forth and slain before him (Luke xix. 27); those that would not submit to his golden sceptre shall be broken to pieces by his iron rod.

6 Thy throne, O God, *is* for ever and ever: the sceptre of thy kingdom *is* a right sceptre. 7 Thou lovest righteousness, and hatest wickedness: therefore God, thy God, hath anointed thee with the oil of gladness above thy fellows. 8 All thy garments *smell* of myrrh, and aloes, *and* cassia, out of the ivory palaces, whereby they have made thee glad. 9 Kings' daughters *were* among thy honourable women: upon thy right hand did stand the queen in gold of Ophir.

We have here the royal bridegroom filling his throne with judgment and keeping his court with splendour.

I. He here fills his throne with judgment. It is God the Father that says to the Son here, *Thy throne, O God! is for ever and ever,* as appears Heb. i. 8, 9, where this is quoted to prove that he is God and has a *more excellent name than the angels.* The Mediator is God, else he neither would have been able to do the Mediator's work nor fit to wear the

Mediator's crown. Concerning his government observe, 1. The eternity of it; it is *for ever and ever.* It shall continue on earth throughout all the ages of time, in despite of all the opposition of the gates of hell; and in the blessed fruits and consequences of it it shall last as long as the days of heaven, and run parallel with the line of eternity itself. Perhaps even then the glory of the Redeemer, and the blessedness of the redeemed, shall be in a continual infinite progression; for it is promised that not only of his government, but of *the increase of his government and peace, there shall be no end* (Isa. ix. 7); even when the kingdom shall be *delivered up to God even the Father* (1 Cor. xv. 24) the throne of the Redeemer will continue. 2. The equity of it: *The sceptre of thy kingdom,* the administration of thy government, *is right,* exactly according to the eternal counsel and will of God, which is the eternal rule and reason of good and evil. Whatever Christ does he does none of his subjects any wrong, but gives redress to those that do suffer wrong: *He loves righteousness, and hates wickedness, v.* 7. He himself loves to do righteousness, and hates to do wickedness; and he loves those that do righteousness, and hates those that do wickedness. By the holiness of his life, the merit of his death, and the great design of his gospel, he has made it to appear that he loves righteousness (for by his example, his satisfaction, and his precepts, he has brought in an everlasting righteousness), and that he hates wickedness, for never did God's hatred of sin appear so conspicuously as it did in the sufferings of Christ. 3. The establishment and elevation of it: *Therefore God, even thy God* (Christ, as Mediator, called God *his God,* John xx. 17, as commissioned by him, and the head of those that are taken into covenant with him), *has anointed thee with the oil of gladness. Therefore,* that is, (1.) "In order to this righteous government of thine, God has given thee his Spirit, that divine unction, to qualify thee for thy undertaking," Isa. lxi. 1. *The Spirit of the Lord God is upon me, because he has anointed me.* What God called him to he fitted him for, Isa. xi. 2. The Spirit is called *the oil of gladness* because of the delight wherewith Christ was filled in carrying on his undertaking. He was anointed with the Spirit *above all his fellows,* above all those that were anointed, whether priests or kings. (2.) "In recompence of what thou hast done and suffered for the advancement of righteousness and the destruction of sin God has anointed thee with the oil of gladness, has brought thee to all the honours and all the joys of thy exalted state." *Because he humbled himself,* God has *highly exalted him,* Phil. ii. 8, 9. His anointing him denotes the power and glory to which he is exalted; he is invested in all the dignities and authorities of the Messiah. And his anointing him with the oil of gladness denotes *the*

joy that was set before him (so his exaltation is expressed, Heb. xii. 2) both in the light of his *Father's countenance* (Acts ii. 28) and in the success of his undertaking, which he shall *see, and be satisfied,* Isa. liii. 11. This he is anointed with *above all his fellows,* above all believers, who are his brethren, and who partake of the anointing—they by measure, he without measure. But the apostle brings it to prove his pre-eminence above the angels, Heb. i. 4, 9. The salvation of sinners is the joy of angels (Luke xv. 10), but much more of the Son.

II. He keeps his court with splendour and magnificence. 1. His robes of state, wherein he appears, are taken notice of, not for their pomp, which might strike an awe upon the spectator, but their pleasantness and the gratefulness of the odours with which they were perfumed (*v.* 8): *They smell of myrrh, aloes, and cassia* (the *oil of gladness* with which he and his garments were anointed); these were some of the ingredients of the holy anointing oil which God appointed, the like to which was not to be made up for any common use (Exod. xxx. 23, 24), which was typical of the unction of the Spirit which Christ, the great high priest of our profession, received, and to which therefore there seems here to be a reference. It is the savour of these good ointments, his graces and comforts, that draws souls to him (Cant. i. 3, 4) and makes him *precious to believers,* 1 Pet. ii. 7. 2. His royal palaces are said to be *ivory* ones, such as were then reckoned most magnificent. We read of an ivory house that Ahab made, 1 Kings xxii. 39. The mansions of light above are the *ivory palaces,* whence all the joys both of Christ and believers come, and where they will be for ever in perfection; for by them he is made glad, and all that are his with him; for they shall enter into the joy of their Lord. 3. The beauties of his court shine very brightly. In public appearances at court, when the pomp of it is shown, nothing is supposed to contribute so much to it as the splendour of the ladies, which is alluded to here, *v.* 9. (1.) Particular believers are here compared to the ladies at court, richly dressed in honour of the sovereign: *Kings' daughters are among thy honourable women,* whose looks, and mien, and ornaments, we may suppose, from the height of their extraction, to excel all others. All true believers are born from above; they are the children of the King of kings. These attend the throne of the Lord Jesus daily with their prayers and praises, which is really their honour, and he is pleased to reckon it his. The numbering of kings' daughters among his honourable women, or maids of honour, intimates that the kings whose daughters they were should be tributaries to him and dependents on him, and would therefore think it a preferment to their daughters to attend him. (2.) The church in general, constituted of these particular believers, is here compared to the queen herself—the queen-consort, whom, by an everlasting covenant, he hath betrothed to himself. She stands *at his right hand*, near to him, and receives honour from him, in the richest array, *in gold of Ophir*, in robes woven with golden thread or with a gold chain and other ornaments of gold. This is *the bride, the Lamb's wife*, whose graces, which are her ornaments, are compared to *fine linen, clean and white* (Rev. xix. 8), for their purity, here to *gold of Ophir*, for their costliness; for, as we owe our redemption, so we owe our adorning, not to corruptible things, but to *the precious blood of the Son of God*.

10 Hearken, O daughter, and consider, and incline thine ear; forget also thine own people, and thy father's house; 11 So shall the king greatly desire thy beauty: for he *is* thy Lord; and worship thou him. 12 And the daughter of Tyre *shall be there* with a gift; *even* the rich among the people shall intreat thy favour. 13 The king's daughter *is* all glorious within; her clothing *is* of wrought gold. 14 She shall be brought unto the king in raiment of needle-work: the virgins her companions that follow her shall be brought unto thee. 15 With gladness and rejoicing shall they be brought: they shall enter into the king's palace. 16 Instead of thy fathers shall be thy children, whom thou mayest make princes in all the earth. 17 I will make thy name to be remembered in all generations: therefore shall the people praise thee for ever and ever.

This latter part of the psalm is addressed to the royal bride, standing on the right hand of the royal bridegroom. God, who said to the Son, *Thy throne is for ever and ever*, says this to the church, which, upon the account of her espousals to the Son, he here calls his *daughter*.

I. He tells her of the duties expected from her, which ought to be considered by all those that come into relation to the Lord Jesus: "*Hearken*, therefore, *and consider* this, *and incline thy ear*, that is, submit to those conditions of thy espousals, and bring thy will to comply with them." This is the method of profiting by the word of God. *He that has ears, let him hear*, let him hearken diligently; he that hearkens, let him consider and weigh it duly; he that considers, let him incline and yield to the force of what is laid before him. And what is it that is here required?

1. She must renounce all others. (1.) Here is the law of her espousals

408

"*Forget thy own people and thy father's house*," according to the law of marriage. Retain not the affection thou hast had for them, nor covet to return to them again; banish all such remembrance (not only of thy people that were dear to thee, but of thy father's house that were dearer) as may incline thee to look back, as Lot's wife to Sodom." When Abraham, in obedience to God's call, had quitted his native soil, he was not so much *mindful of the country whence he came out*. This shows, [1.] How necessary it was for those who were converted from Judaism or paganism to the faith of Christ wholly to cast out the old leaven, and not to bring into their Christian profession either the Jewish ceremonies or the heathen idolatries, for these would make such a mongrel religion in Christianity as the Samaritans had. [2.] How necessary it is for us all, when we give up our names to Jesus Christ, to hate father and mother, and all that is dear to us in this world, in comparison, that is, to love them less than Christ and his honour, and our interest in him, Luke xiv. 26.

(2.) Here is good encouragement given to the royal bride thus entirely to break off from her former alliances: *So shall the king greatly desire thy beauty*, which intimates that the mixing of her old rites and customs, whether Jewish or Gentile, with her religion, would blemish her beauty and would hazard her interest in the affections of the royal bridegroom, but that, if she entirely conformed to his will, he would delight in her. The beauty of holiness, both on the church and on particular believers, is in the sight of Christ of great price and very amiable. Where that is he says, *This is my rest for ever; here will I dwell, for I have desired it*. Among the golden candlesticks he walks with pleasure, Rev. ii. 1.

2. She must reverence him, must love, honour, and obey him: *He is thy Lord, and worship thou him*. The church is to be subject to Christ as the wife to the husband (Eph. v. 24), to call him Lord, as Sarah called Abraham, and to obey him (1 Pet. iii. 6), and so not only to submit to his government, but to give him divine honours. We must worship him as God, and our Lord; for this is the will of God, that *all men should honour the Son even as they honour the Father;* nay, in so doing it is reckoned that they honour the Father. If we confess that Christ is Lord, and pay our homage to him accordingly, it is *to the glory of God the Father*, Phil. ii. 11.

II. He tells her of the honours designed for her.

1. Great court should be made to her, and rich presents brought her (v. 12): "The *daughter of Tyre*," a rich and splendid city, "the *daughter of the King of Tyre* shall be *there with a gift;* every royal family round about shall send a branch, as a representative of the whole, to seek thy favour and to make

an interest in thee; *even the rich among the people*, whose wealth might be thought to exempt them from dependence at court, even they shall entreat thy favour, for his sake to whom thou art espoused, that by thee they may make him their friend." The Jews, the pretending Jews, who are rich to a proverb (as rich as a Jew), shall come and worship before the church's feet in the Philadelphian period, and shall *know that Christ has loved her*, Rev. iii. 9. When the Gentiles, being converted to the faith of Christ, join themselves to the church, they then *come with a gift*, 2 Cor. viii. 5; Rom. xv. 16. When with themselves they devote all they have to the honour of Christ, and the service of his kingdom, they then *come with a gift*.

2. She shall be very splendid, and highly esteemed in the eyes of all, (1.) For her personal qualifications, the endowments of her mind, which every one shall admire (*v.* 13): *The king's daughter is all glorious within.* Note, The glory of the church is spiritual glory, and that is indeed all glory; it is the glory of the soul, and that is the man; it is glory in God's sight, and it is an earnest of eternal glory. The glory of the saints falls not within the view of a carnal eye. As their life, so their glory, is hidden with Christ in God, neither can the natural man know it, for it is spiritually discerned; but those who do so discern it highly value it. Let us see here what is that true glory which we should be ambitious of, not that which *makes a fair show in the flesh*, but which is in *the hidden man of the heart, in that which is not corruptible* (1 Pet. iii. 4), *whose praise is not of men, but of God*, Rom. ii. 29. (2.) For her rich apparel. Though all her glory is within, that for which she is truly valuable, yet *her clothing* also *is of wrought gold;* the conversation of Christians, in which they appear in the world, must be enriched with good works, not gay and gaudy ones, like paint and flourish, but substantially good, like gold; and it must be accurate and exact, like wrought gold, which is worked with a great deal of care and caution.

3. Her nuptials shall be celebrated with a great deal of honour and joy (*v.* 14, 15): *She shall be brought to the king*, as the Lord God brought the woman to the man (Gen. ii. 22), which was a type of this mystical marriage between Christ and his church. None are brought to Christ but whom the Father brings, and he has undertaken to do it; none besides are so brought *to the king* (*v.* 14) as to *enter into the king's palace, v.* 15.

(1.) This intimates a two-fold bringing of the spouse to Christ. [1]. In the conversion of souls to Christ; then they are espoused to him, privately contracted, as chaste virgins, 2 Cor. xi. 2; Rom. vii. 4. [2.] In the completing of the mystical body, and the glorification of all the saints, at the end of time; then the *bride, the Lamb's wife*, shall be made completely ready, when all that belong to the election of grace shall be called in and called home, and all gathered together to Christ, 2 Thess. ii. 1. Then is the marriage of the Lamb come (Rev. xix 7; xxi. 2), and the virgins *go forth to meet the bridegroom*, Matt. xxv. 1. Then they shall *enter into the king's palaces*, into the heavenly mansions, to be ever with the Lord.

(2.) In both these espousals, observe, to the honour of the royal bride, [1.] Her wedding clothes—*raiment of needle-work*, the righteousness of Christ, the graces of the Spirit; both curiously wrought by divine wisdom. [2.] Her bride-maids—*the virgins her companions*, the wise virgins who have oil in their vessels as well as in their lamps, those who, being joined to the church, cleave to it and follow it, these shall go in to the marriage. [3.] The mirth with which the nuptials will be celebrated: *With gladness and rejoicing shall she be brought.* When the prodigal is brought home to his father *it is meet that we should make merry and be glad* (Luke xv. 32); and when the marriage of the Lamb has come *let us be glad and rejoice* (Rev. xix. 7); for the *day of his espousals is the day of the gladness of his heart*, Cant. iii. 11.

4. The progeny of this marriage shall be illustrious (*v.* 16): *Instead of thy fathers shall be thy children.* Instead of the Old-Testament church, the economy of which had waxed old, and ready to *vanish away* (Heb. viii. 13), as the fathers that are going off, there shall be a New-Testament church, a Gentile-church, that shall be grafted into the same olive and partake of its *root and fatness* (Rom. xi. 17); more and more eminent shall be *the children of the desolate* than the *children of the married wife*, Isa. liv. 1. This promise to Christ is of the same import with that Isa. liii. 10, *He shall see his seed;* and these shall be made *princes in all the earth;* there shall be some of all nations brought into subjection to Christ, and so made princes, *made to our God kings and priests*, Rev. i. 6. Or it may intimate that there should be a much greater number of Christian kings than ever there was of Jewish kings (those in Canaan only, these in all the earth), nursing fathers and nursing mothers to the church, which shall *suck the breasts of kings.* They are princes of Christ's making; for *by him kings reign and princes decree justice.*

5. The praise of this marriage shall be perpetual in the praises of the royal bridegroom (*v.* 18): *I will make thy name to be remembered.* His Father has given him *a name above every name*, and here promises to make it perpetual, by keeping up a succession of ministers and Christians in every age, that shall bear up his name, which shall thus *endure for ever* (lxxii. 17), by being remembered in all the generations of time; for the entail of Christianity shall not be cut off. "Therefore, because they shall remember thee in all generations, they shall praise thee for ever

409

and ever." Those that help to support the honour of Christ on earth shall in heaven see his glory, and share in it, and be for ever praising him. In the believing hope of our everlasting happiness in the other world let us always keep up the remembrance of Christ, as our only way thither, in our generation; and, in assurance of the perpetuating of the kingdom of the Redeemer in the world, let us transmit the remembrance of him to succeeding generations, that his name *may endure for ever and be as the days of heaven.*

PSALM XLVI.

This psalm encourages us to hope and trust in God, and his power, and providence, and gracious presence with his church in the worst of times, and directs us to give him the glory of what he has done for us and what he will do: probably it was penned upon occasion of David's victories over the neighbouring nations (2 Sam. viii.), and the rest which God gave him from all his enemies round about. We are here taught, I. To take comfort in God when things look very black and threatening, ver. 1—5. II. To mention, to his praise, the great things he has wrought for his church against its enemies, ver. 6—9. III. To assure ourselves that God who has glorified his own name will glorify it yet again, and to comfort ourselves with that, ver. 10, 11. We may, in singing it, apply it either to our spiritual enemies, and the encouragement we have to hope that through Christ we shall be more than conquerors over them, or to the public enemies of Christ's kingdom in the world and their threatening insults, endeavouring to preserve a holy security and serenity of mind when they seem most formidable. It is said of Luther that, when he heard any discouraging news, he would say, Come let us sing the forty-sixth psalm.

To the chief musician for the sons of Korah. A song upon Alamoth.

GOD *is* our refuge and strength, a very present help in trouble. 2 Therefore will not we fear, though the earth be removed, and though the mountains be carried into the midst of the sea; 3 *Though* the waters thereof roar *and* be troubled, *though* the mountains shake with the swelling thereof. Selah. 4 *There is* a river, the streams whereof shall make glad the city of God, the holy *place* of the tabernacles of the most high. 5 God *is* in the midst of her; she shall not be moved: God shall help her, *and that* right early.

The psalmist here teaches us by his own example.

I. To triumph in God, and his relation to us and presence with us, especially when we have had some fresh experiences of his appearing in our behalf (*v.* 1): *God is our refuge and strength;* we have found him so, he has engaged to be so, and he ever will be so. Are we pursued? God is our refuge to whom we may flee, and in whom we may be safe and think ourselves so; secure upon good grounds, Prov. xviii. 10. Are we oppressed by troubles? Have we work to do and enemies to grapple with? God is our strength, to bear us up under our burdens, to fit us for all our services and sufferings; he will by his grace put strength into us, and on him we may stay ourselves. Are we in distress? He is a help, to do all that for us which we need, *a present help, a help found* (so the word

is), one whom we have found to be so, a help on which we may write *Probatum est—It is tried,* as Christ is called a *tried stone,* Isa. xxviii. 16. Or, *a help at hand,* one that never is to seek for, but that is always near. Or, a *help sufficient,* a help accommodated to every case and exigence; whatever it is, he is a very present help; we cannot desire a better help, nor shall ever find the like in any creature.

II. To triumph over the greatest dangers: *God is our strength and our help,* a God all-sufficient to us; *therefore will not we fear.* Those that with a holy reverence fear God need not with any amazement to be afraid of the power of hell or earth. If God be for us who can be against us; to do us any harm? It is our duty, it is our privilege, to be thus fearless; it is an evidence of a clear conscience, of an honest heart, and of a lively faith in God and his providence and promise: "*We will not fear, though the earth be removed,* though all our creature-confidences fail us and sink us; nay, though that which should support us threaten to swallow us up, as the earth did Korah," for whose sons this psalm was penned, and, some think, by them; yet while we keep close to God, and have him for us, we will not fear, for we have no cause to fear;

——Si fractus illabatur orbis,
Impavidum ferient ruinæ.——Hor.

—Let Jove's dread arm with thunder rend the spheres,
Beneath the crush of worlds undaunted he appears.

Observe here, 1. How threatening the danger is. We will suppose the earth to be removed, and thrown into the sea, even the mountains, the strongest and firmest parts of the earth, to lie buried in the unfathomed ocean; we will suppose the sea to roar and rage, and make a dreadful noise, and its foaming billows to insult the shore with so much violence as even to *shake the mountains, v.* 3. Though kingdoms and states be in confusion, embroiled in wars, tossed with tumults, and their governments in continual revolution—though their powers combine against the church and people of God, aim at no less than their ruin, and go very near to gain their point—yet will not we fear, knowing that all these troubles will end well for the church. See xciii. 4. If the earth be removed, those have reason to fear who have laid up their treasures on earth, and set their hearts upon it; but not those who have laid up for themselves treasures in heaven, and who expect to be most happy when *the earth and all the works that are therein shall be burnt up.* Let those be troubled at the troubling of the waters who build their confidence on such a floating foundation, but not those who are led to *the rock that is higher than they,* and find firm footing upon that rock. 2. How well-grounded the defiance of this danger is, considering how well guarded the church is, and that interest which we are concerned for. It is not any private particular concern of our own that we are in pain about; no, it is the city of God, *the holy place of the tabernacles of the Most High;* it is the ark of God for which our hearts tremble. But, when we consider what God has provided for the comfort and safety of his church, we shall see reason to have our hearts fixed, and set above the fear of evil tidings. Here is, (1.) Joy to the church, even in the most melancholy and sorrowful times (*v.* 4): *There is a river the streams whereof shall make* it *glad,* even then when the waters of the sea roar and threaten it. It alludes to the waters of Siloam, which *went softly by Jerusalem* (Isa. viii. 6, 7); though of no great depth or breadth, yet the waters of it were made serviceable to the defence of Jerusalem in Hezekiah's time, Isa. xxii. 10, 11. But this must be understood spiritually; the covenant of grace is the river, the promises of which are the streams; or the Spirit of grace is the river (John vii. 38, 39), the comforts of which are *the streams, that make glad the city of our God.* God's word and ordinances are rivers and streams with which God makes his saints glad in cloudy and dark days. God himself is to his church a place of *broad rivers and streams,* Isa. xxxiii. 21. The streams that make glad the city of God are not rapid, but gentle, like those of Siloam. Note, The spiritual comforts which are conveyed to the saints by soft and silent whispers, and which come not with observation, are sufficient to counterbalance the most loud and noisy threatenings of an angry and malicious world. (2.) Establishment to the church. Though heaven and earth are shaken, yet *God is in the midst of her, she shall not be moved, v.* 5. God has assured his church of his special presence with her and concern for her; his honour is embarked in her, he has set up his tabernacle in her and has undertaken the protection of it, and therefore she shall not be moved, that is, [1.] Not destroyed, not removed, as the earth may be, *v.* 2. The church shall survive the world, and be in bliss when that is in ruins. It is *built upon a rock,* and the *gates of hell shall not prevail against it.* [2.] Not disturbed, not much moved, with fears of the issue. If God be for us, if God be with us, we need not be moved at the most violent attempts made against us. (3.) Deliverance to the church, though her dangers be very great: *God shall help her;* and who then can hurt her? He shall help her under her troubles, that she shall not sink; nay, that the more she is afflicted the more she shall multiply. God shall help her out of her troubles, *and that right early*—when the morning appears; that is, very speedily, for he is *a present help* (*v.* 1), and very seasonably, when things are brought to the last extremity and when the relief will be most welcome. This may be applied by particular believers to themselves; if God be in our hearts, in the midst of us, by his word dwelling richly in us, we shall be established, we shall be helped; let us therefore trust and not be afraid; all is well, and will end well.

6 The heathen raged, the kingdoms were moved: he uttered his voice, the earth melted. 7 The LORD of hosts *is* with us; the God of Jacob *is* our refuge. Selah. 8 Come, behold the works of the LORD, what desolations he hath made in the earth. 9 He maketh wars to cease unto the end of the earth; he breaketh the bow, and cutteth the spear in sunder; he burneth the chariot in the fire. 10 Be still, and know that I *am* God: I will be exalted among the heathen, I will be exalted in the earth. 11 The LORD of hosts *is* with us; the God of Jacob *is* our refuge. Selah.

These verses give glory to God both as King of nations and as King of saints.

I. As King of nations, ruling the world by his power and providence, and overruling all the affairs of the children of men to his own glory; he does according to his will among the inhabitants of the earth, and none may say, *What doest thou?* 1. He checks the rage and breaks the power of the nations that oppose him and his interests in the world (*v.* 6): *The heathen raged* at David's coming to the throne, and at the setting up of the kingdom of the Son of David; compare ii. 1, 2. *The kingdoms were moved* with indignation, and rose in a tumultuous furious manner to oppose it; but God *uttered his voice, spoke to them in his wrath,* and they were moved in another sense, they were struck into confusion and consternation, put into disorder, and all their measures broken; the earth itself melted under them, so that they found no firm footing; their earthly hearts failed them for fear, and dissolved like snow before the sun. Such a melting of the spirits of the enemies is described, Judg. v. 4, 5; and see Luke xxi. 25, 26. 2. When he pleases to draw his sword, and give it commission, he can make great havoc among the nations and lay all waste (*v.* 8): *Come, behold the works of the Lord;* they are to be observed (lxvi. 5), and to be sought out, cxi. 2. All the operations of Providence must be considered as the works of the Lord, and his attributes and purposes must be taken notice of in them. Particularly take notice of the *desolations he has made in the earth,* among the enemies of his church, who thought to lay the land of Israel desolate. The destruction they designed to bring upon the church has been turned upon themselves. War is a tragedy which commonly destroys the stage it is acted on; David carried the war into the enemies' country; and O what desolations did it make there! Cities were burnt, countries laid waste, and armies of men cut off and laid in heaps upon heaps. Come and see the effects of desolating judgments, and stand in awe of God; say, *How terrible art thou in thy works!* lxvi. 3. Let all that oppose him see this with terror, and expect the same cup of trembling to be put into their hands; let all that fear him and trust in him see it with pleasure, and not be afraid of the most formidable powers armed against the church. Let them gird themselves, but *they shall be broken to pieces.* 3. When he pleases to sheathe his sword, he puts an end to the wars of the nations and crowns them with peace, *v.* 9. War and peace depend on his word and will, as much as storms and calms at sea do, cvii. 25, 29. *He makes wars to cease unto the end of the earth,* sometimes in pity to the nations, that they may have a breathing-time, when, by long wars with each other, they have run themselves out of breadth. Both sides perhaps are weary of the war, and willing to let it fall; expedients are found out for accommodation; martial princes are removed, and peace-makers set in their room; and then the bow is broken by consent, the spear cut asunder and turned into a pruning-hook, and the sword beaten into a ploughshare, and the chariots of war are burned, there being no more occasion for them; or, rather, it may be meant of what he does, at other times, in favour of his own people. He makes those wars to cease that were waged against them and designed for their ruin. He breaks the enemies' bow that was drawn against them. *No weapon formed against Zion shall prosper,* Isa. liv. 17. The total destruction of Gog and Magog is prophetically described by the burning of their weapons of war (Ezek. xxxix. 9, 10), which intimates likewise the church's perfect security and assurance of lasting peace, which made it needless to lay up those weapons of war for their own service. The bringing of a long war to a good issue is a work of the Lord, which we ought to behold with wonder and thankfulness.

II. As King of saints, and as such we must own that *great and marvellous are his works,* Rev. xv. 3. He does and will do great things,

1. For his own glory (*v.* 10): *Be still, and know that I am God.* (1.) Let his enemies be still, and threaten no more, but know it, to their terror, that he is God, one infinitely above them, and that will certainly be too hard for them; let them rage no more, for it is all in vain: *he that sits in heaven, laughs at them;* and, in spite of all their impotent malice against his name and honour, he will be exalted among the heathen and not merely among his own people, he will be exalted in the earth and not merely in the church. Men will set up themselves, will have their own way and do their own will; but let them know that God will be exalted, he will have his way will do his own will, will glorify his own name, and *wherein they deal proudly he will be above them,* and make them know that he is so. (2.) Let his own people be still; let them be calm and sedate, and tremble no more, but know, to their comfort, that the Lord is God, he is

God alone, and will be exalted above the heathen; let him alone to maintain his honour, to fulfil his own counsels and to support his own interest in the world. Though we be depressed, yet let us not be dejected, for we are sure that God will be exalted, and that may satisfy us; he will work for his great name, and then no matter what becomes of our little names. When we pray, *Father, glorify thy name,* we ought to exercise faith upon the answer given to that prayer when Christ himself prayed it, *I have both glorified it and I will glorify it yet again.* Amen, Lord, so be it.

2. For his people's safety and protection. He triumphs in the former: *I will be exalted;* they triumph in this, *v.* 7 and again *v.* 11. It is the burden of the song, " *The Lord of hosts is with us;* he is on our side, he takes our part, is present with us and president over us; *the God of Jacob is our refuge,* to whom we may flee, and in whom we may confide and be sure of safety." Let all believers triumph in this. (1.) They have the presence of a God of power, of all power: *The Lord of hosts is with us.* God is the Lord of hosts, for he has all the creatures which are called *the hosts of heaven and earth* at his beck and command, and he makes what use he pleases of them, as the instruments either of his justice or of his mercy. This sovereign Lord is with us, sides with us, acts with us, and has promised he will never leave us. Hosts may be against us, but we need not fear them if the Lord of hosts be with us. (2.) They are under the protection of a God in covenant, who not only is able to help them, but is engaged in honour and faithfulness to help them. He is the God of Jacob, not only Jacob the person, but Jacob the people; nay, and of all praying people, the spiritual seed of wrestling Jacob; and he is our refuge, by whom we are sheltered and in whom we are satisfied, who by his providence secures our welfare when without are fightings, and who by his grace quiets our minds, and establishes them, when within are fears. The Lord of hosts, the God of Jacob, has been, is, and will be with us—has been, is, and will be our refuge: the original includes all; and well may *Selah* be added to it. Mark this, and take the comfort of it, and say, *If God be for us, who can be against us?*

PSALM XLVII.

The scope of this psalm is to stir us up to praise God, to stir up all people to do so; and, I. We are directed in what manner to do it, publicly, cheerfully, and intelligently, ver. 1, 6, 7. II. We are furnished with matter for praise. 1. God's majesty, ver. 2. 2. His sovereign and universal dominion, ver. 2, 7—9. 3. The great things he had done, and will do, for his people, ver. 3—5. Many suppose that this psalm was penned upon occasion of the bringing up of the ark to Mount Zion, which ver. 5 seems to refer to (" God has gone up with a shout");—but it looks further, to the ascension of Christ into the heavenly Zion, after he had finished his undertaking on earth, and to the setting up of his kingdom in the world, to which the heathen should become willing subjects. In singing this psalm we are to give honour to the exalted Redeemer, to rejoice in his exaltation, and to celebrate his praises, confessing that he is Lord, to the glory of God the Father.

To the chief musician. A psalm for the sons of Korah.

O CLAP your hands, all ye people; shout unto God with the voice of triumph. 2 For the LORD most high *is* terrible; *he is* a great King over all the earth. 3 He shall subdue the people under us, and the nations under our feet. 4 He shall choose our inheritance for us, the excellency of Jacob whom he loved. Selah.

The psalmist, having his own heart filled with great and good thoughts of God, endeavours to engage all about him in the blessed work of praise, as one convinced that God is worthy of all blessing and praise, and as one grieved at his own and others' backwardness to and barrenness in this work. Observe, in these verses,

I. Who are called upon to praise God: *"All you people,* all you people of Israel;" those were his own subjects, and under his charge, and therefore he will engage them to praise God, for on them he has an influence. Whatever others do, he and his house, he and his people, shall praise the Lord. Or, "All you people and nations of the earth;" and so it may be taken as a prophecy of the conversion of the Gentiles and the bringing of them into the church; see Rom. xv. 11.

II. What they are called upon to do: *"O clap your hands,* in token of your own joy and satisfaction in what God has done for you, of your approbation, nay, your admiration, of what God has done in general, and of your indignation against all the enemies of God's glory, Job xxvii. 23. *Clap your hands,* as men transported with pleasure, that cannot contain themselves; *shout unto God,* not to make him hear (his ear is not heavy), but to make all about you hear, and take notice how much you are affected and filled with the works of God. Shout *with the voice of triumph* in him, and in his power and goodness, that others may join with you in the triumph." Note, Such expressions of pious and devout affections as to some may seem indecent and imprudent ought not to be hastily censured and condemned, much less ridiculed, because, if they come from an upright heart, God will accept the strength of the affection and excuse the weakness of the expressions of it.

III. What is suggested to us as matter for our praise. 1. That the God with whom we have to do is a God of awful majesty (*v.* 2): *The Lord most high is terrible.* He is infinitely above the noblest creatures, higher than the highest; there are those perfections in him that are to be reverenced by all, and particularly that power, holiness, and justice, that are to be dreaded by all those that contend with him. 2. That he is a God of sovereign and universal dominion. He is a King that reigns alone, and with an absolute power, *a King over all the earth;* all the creatures, being made by him, are subject to him,

and therefore he is *a great King,* the King of kings. 3. That he takes a particular care of his people and their concerns, has done so and ever will; (1.) In giving them victory and success (*v.* 3), subduing the people and nations under them, both those that stood in their way (xliv. 2) and those that made attempts upon them. This God had done for them, witness the planting of them in Canaan, and their continuance there unto this day. This they doubted not but he would still do for them by his servant David, who prospered which way soever he turned his victorious arms. But this looks forward to the kingdom of the Messiah, which was to be set over all the earth, and not confined to the Jewish nation. Jesus Christ shall subdue the Gentiles; he shall bring *them in as sheep into the fold* (so the word signifies), not for slaughter, but for preservation. He shall subdue their affections, and make them a *willing people in the day of his power,* shall bring their thoughts into obedience to him, and reduce those who had gone astray, under the guidance of the *great shepherd and bishop of souls,* 1 Pet. ii. 25. (2.) In giving them rest and settlement (*v.* 4): *He shall choose our inheritance for us.* He had chosen the land of Canaan to be an inheritance for Israel; it was the land which the Lord their God spied out for them; see Deut. xxxii. 8. This justified their possession of that land, and gave them a good title; and this sweetened their enjoyment of it, and made it comfortable; they had reason to think it a happy lot, and to be satisfied in it, when it was that which Infinite Wisdom chose for them. And the setting up of God's sanctuary in it made it *the excellency,* the honour, *of Jacob* (Amos vi. 8); and he chose so good an inheritance for Jacob because he loved him, Deut. vii. 8. Apply this spiritually, and it bespeaks, [1.] The happiness of the saints, that God himself has chosen their inheritance for them, and it is a goodly heritage: *he* has chosen it who knows the soul, and what will serve to make it happy; and he has chosen so well that he himself has undertaken to be the *inheritance of his people* (xvi. 5), and he has laid up for them in the other world an inheritance incorruptible, 1 Pet. i. 4. This will be indeed the excellency of Jacob, for whom, because he loved them, he prepared such a happiness as eye has not seen. [2.] The faith and submission of the saints to God. This is the language of every gracious soul, "God shall choose my inheritance for me; let him appoint me my lot, and I will acquiesce in the appointment. He knows what is good for me better than I do for myself, and therefore I will have no will of my own but what is resolved into his."

5 God is gone up with a shout, the LORD with the sound of a trumpet. 6 Sing praises to God, sing praises: sing praises unto our King, sing praises.

413

7 For God *is* the King of all the earth: sing ye praises with understanding. 8 God reigneth over the heathen : God sitteth upon the throne of his holiness. 9 The princes of the people are gathered together, *even* the people of the God of Abraham : for the shields of the earth *belong* unto God : he is greatly exalted.

We are here most earnestly pressed to praise God, and to sing his praises ; so backward are we to this duty that we have need to be urged to it by precept upon precept, and line upon line ; so we are here (*v.* 6) : *Sing praises to God*, and again, *Sing praises, Sing praises to our King*, and again, *Sing praises.* This intimates that it is a very necessary and excellent duty, that it is a duty we ought to be frequent and abundant in ; we may sing praises again and again in the same words, and it is no vain repetition if it be done with new affections. Should not a people praise their God? Dan. v. 4. Should not subjects praise their king? God is our God, our King, and therefore we must praise him ; we must sing his praises, as those that are pleased with them and that are not ashamed of them. But here is a needful rule subjoined (*v.* 7) : *Sing you praises with understanding*, with *Maschil.* 1. "Intelligently ; as those that do yourselves understand why and for what reasons you praise God and what is the meaning of the service." This is the gospel-rule (1 Cor. xiv. 15), *to sing with the spirit and with the understanding also ;* it is only with the heart that we make melody to the Lord, Eph. v. 19. It is not an acceptable service if it be not a reasonable service. 2. "Instructively, as those that desire to make others understand God's glorious perfections, and to teach them to praise him." Three things are mentioned in these verses as just matter for our praises, and each of them will admit of a double sense :—

I. We must praise God going up (*v.* 5) : *God has gone up with a shout*, which may refer, 1. To the carrying up of the ark to the hill of Zion, which was done with great solemnity, David himself dancing before it, the priests, it is likely, blowing the trumpets, and the people following with their loud huzzas. The ark being the instituted token of God's special presence with them, when that was brought up by warrant from him he might be said to *go up.* The emerging of God's ordinances out of obscurity, in order to the more public and solemn administration of them, is a great favour to any people, which they have reason to rejoice in and give thanks for. 2. To the ascension of our Lord Jesus into heaven, when he had finished his work on earth, Acts i. 9. Then *God went up with a shout*, the shout of a King, of a conqueror, as one who, having *spoiled principalities and powers*, then *led captivity captive*, lxviii. 18.

414

He went up as a Mediator, typified by the ark and the mercy-seat over it, and was brought up as the ark was into the most holy place, *into heaven itself ;* see Heb. ix. 24. We read not of a shout, or of the sound of a trumpet, at the ascension of Christ, but they were the inhabitants of the upper world, those sons of God, that then shouted for joy, Job xxxviii. 7. He shall come again in the same manner as he went (Acts i. 11) and we are sure that he shall come again with a shout and the sound of a trumpet.

II. We must praise God reigning, *v.* 7. 8. God is not only our King, and therefore we owe our homage to him, but he is *King of all the earth* (*v.* 7), over all the kings of the earth, and therefore in every place the incense of praise is to be offered up to him. Now this may be understood, 1. Of the kingdom of providence. God, as Creator, and the God of nature, *reigns over the heathen*, disposes of them and all their affairs, as he pleases, though they know him not, nor have any regard to him : *He sits upon the throne of his holiness*, which he has prepared in the heavens, and there he rules over all, even over the heathen, serving his own purposes by them and upon them. See here the extent of God's government ; all are born within his allegiance ; even the heathen that serve other gods are ruled by the true God, our God, whether they will or no. See the equity of his government ; it is a throne of holiness, on which he sits, whence he gives warrants, orders, and judgment, in which we are sure there is no iniquity. 2. Of the kingdom of the Messiah. Jesus Christ, who is God, and whose *throne is for ever and ever, reigns over the heathen ;* not only he is entrusted with the administration of the providential kingdom, but he shall set up the kingdom of his grace in the Gentile world, and rule in the hearts of multitudes that were bred up in heathenism, Eph. ii. 12, 13. This the apostle speaks of as a great mystery that the *Gentiles should be fellow-heirs*, Eph. iii. 6. Christ *sits upon the throne of his holiness*, his throne in the heavens, where all the administrations of his government are intended to show forth God's holiness and to advance holiness among the children of men.

III. We must praise God as attended and honoured by *the princes of the people, v.* 9. This may be understood, 1. Of the congress or convention of the states of Israel, the heads and rulers of the several tribes, at the solemn feasts, or to despatch the public business of the nation. It was the honour of Israel that they were *the people of the God of Abraham*, as they were Abraham's seed and taken into his covenant ; and, thanks be to God, this blessing of Abraham has come upon the isles of the Gentiles, Gal. iii. 14 It was their happiness that they had a settled government, *princes of their people*, who were the *shields of their land.* Magistracy is the shield of a nation, and it is a great mercy to any people to have this shield, especially when their princes, *their shields, belong unto the Lord*, are devoted to his honour, and their power is employed in his service, for then he is greatly exalted. It is likewise the honour of God that, in another sense, the *shields of the earth do belong to him ;* magistracy is his institution, and he serves his own purposes by it in the government of the world, turning the hearts of kings as the rivers of water, which way soever he pleases. It was well with Israel when the princes of their people were gathered together to consult for the public welfare. The unanimous agreement of the great ones of a nation in the things that belong to its peace is a very happy omen, which promises abundance of blessings. 2. It may be applied to the calling of the Gentiles into the church of Christ, and taken as a prophecy that in the days of the Messiah the kings of the earth and their people should join themselves to the church, and bring their glory and power into the New Jerusalem, that they should all become *the people of the God of Abraham*, to whom it was promised that he should be *the father of many nations*. The *volunteers* of the people (so it may be read); it is the same word that is used in cx. 3, *Thy people shall be willing ;* for those that are gathered to Christ are not forced, but made freely willing, to be his. When the *shields of the earth*, the ensigns of royal dignity (1 Kings xiv. 27, 28,), are surrendered to the Lord Jesus, as the keys of a city are presented to the conqueror or sovereign, when princes use their power for the advancement of the interests of religion, then Christ is greatly exalted.

PSALM XLVIII.

This psalm, as the two former, is a triumphant song ; some think it was penned on occasion of Jehoshaphat's victory (2 Chron. xx.), others of Sennacherib's defeat, when his army laid siege to Jerusalem in Hezekiah's time ; but, for aught I know, it might be penned by David upon occasion of some eminent victory obtained in his time ; yet not so calculated for that but that it might serve any other similar occasion in aftertimes, and be applicable also to the glories of the gospel church, of which Jerusalem was a type, especially when it shall come to be a church triumphant, the "heavenly Jerusalem" (Heb. xii. 22), "the Jerusalem which is above," Gal. iv. 26. Jerusalem is here praised, I. For its relation to God, ver. 1, 2. II. For God's care of it, ver. 3. III. For the terror it strikes upon its enemies, ver. 4—7. IV. For the pleasure it gives to its friends, who delight to think, 1. Of what God has done, does, and will do for it, ver. 8. 2. Of the gracious discoveries he makes of himself in and for that holy city, ver. 9, 10. 3. Of the effectual provision which is made for its safety, ver. 11—13. 4. Of the assurance we have of the perpetuity of God's covenant with the children of Zion, ver. 14. In singing this psalm we must be affected with the privilege we have as members of the gospel church, and must express and excite our sincere good-will to all its interests.

A song *and* psalm for the sons of Korah.

GREAT *is* the LORD, and greatly to be praised in the city of our God, *in* the mountain of his holiness. 2 Beautiful for situation, the joy of the whole earth, *is* mount Zion, *on* the sides of the north, the city of the great King. 3 God is known in her palaces for a refuge. 4 For, lo, the kings were assembled, they passed by together. 5 They saw *it, and* so they marvelled ;

they were troubled, *and* hasted away. 6 Fear took hold upon them there, *and* pain, as of a woman in travail. 7 Thou breakest the ships of Tarshish with an east wind.

The psalmist is designing to praise Jerusalem and to set forth the grandeur of that city ; but he begins with the praises of God and his greatness (*v.* 1), and ends with the praises of God and his goodness, *v.* 14. For, whatever is the subject of our praises, God must be both the Alpha and Omega of them. And, particularly, whatever is said to the honour of the church must redound to the honour of the church's God.

What is here said to the honour of Jerusalem is,

I. That the King of heaven owns it : it is *the city of our God* (*v.* 1), which he chose out of all the cities of Israel to put his name there. Of Zion he said kinder things than ever he said of any place upon earth. *This is my rest for ever ; here will I dwell, for I have desired it*, cxxxii. 13, 14. It is *the city of the great King* (*v.* 2), the King of all the earth, who is pleased to declare himself in a special manner present there. This our Saviour quotes to prove that to swear by Jerusalem is profanely to swear by God himself (Matt. v. 35), *for it is the city of the great King*, who has chosen it for the special residence of his grace, as heaven is of his glory. 1. It is enlightened with the knowledge of God. *In Judah God is known, and his name is great*, but especially in Jerusalem, the head-quarters of the priests, whose lips were to keep this knowledge. In Jerusalem *God is great* (*v.* 1) who in other places was made little of, was made nothing of. Happy the kingdom, the city, the family, the heart, in which God is great, in which he is uppermost, in which he is all. There *God is known* (*v.* 3) and where he is known he will be great ; none contemn God but those that are ignorant of him. 2. It is devoted to the honour of God. It is therefore called *the mountain of his holiness*, for *holiness to the Lord* is written upon it and all the furniture of it, Zech. xiv. 20, 21. This is the privilege of the church of Christ, that it is *a holy nation, a peculiar people ;* Jerusalem, the type of it, is called *the holy city*, bad as it was (Matt. xxvii. 53), till that was set up, but never after. 3. It is the place appointed for the solemn service and worship of God ; there he is greatly praised, and *greatly to be praised, v.* 1. Note, The clearer discoveries are made to us of God and his greatness the more it is expected that we should abound in his praises. Those that from all parts of the country brought their offerings to Jerusalem had reason to be thankful that God would not only permit them thus to attend him, but promise to accept them, and meet them with a blessing, and reckon himself praised and honoured by their services. Herein Jerusalem typified the gospel church; for what little tribute of praise God has from this earth arises from that church upon earth, which is therefore his tabernacle among men. 4. It is taken under his special protection (*v.* 3): He is *known for a refuge*; that is, he has approved himself such a one, and as such a one he is there applied to by his worshippers. Those that know him will *trust in him, and seek to him,* ix. 10. God was known, not only in the streets, but even in the palaces of Jerusalem, for a refuge; the great men had recourse to God and acquaintance with him. And then religion was likely to flourish in the city when it reigned in the palaces. 5. Upon all these accounts, Jerusalem, and especially Mount Zion, on which the temple was built, were universally beloved and admired—*beautiful for situation,* and *the joy of the whole earth, v.* 2. The situation must needs be every way agreeable, when Infinite Wisdom chose it for the place of the sanctuary; and that which made it beautiful was that it was the mountain of holiness, for there is a beauty in holiness. This earth is, by sin, covered with deformity, and therefore justly might that spot of ground which was thus beautified with holiness he called *the joy of the whole earth,* that is, what the whole earth had reason to rejoice in, that God would thus in very deed dwell with man upon the earth. Mount Zion was on the north side of Jerusalem, and so was a shelter to the city from the cold and bleak winds that blew from that quarter; or, if fair weather was expected out of the north, they were thus directed to look Zion-ward for it.

II. That the kings of the earth were afraid of it. That God was known in their palaces for a refuge they had had a late instance, and a very remarkable one. Whatever it was, 1. They had had but too much occasion to fear their enemies; for *the kings were assembled, v.* 4. The neighbouring princes were confederate against Jerusalem; their heads and horns, their policies and powers, were combined for its ruin; they were assembled with all their forces; they passed, advanced, and marched on together, not doubting but they should soon make themselves masters of that city which should have been the joy, but was the envy of the whole earth. 2. God made their enemies to fear them. The very sight of Jerusalem struck them into a consternation and gave check to their fury, as the sight of the tents of Jacob frightened Balaam from his purpose to curse Israel (Num. xxiv. 2): *They saw it and marvelled, and hasted away, v.* 5. Not *Veni, vidi, vici—I came, I saw, I conquered;* but, on the contrary, *Veni, vidi, victus sum— I came, I saw, I was defeated.* Not that there was any thing to be seen in Jerusalem that was so very formidable; but the sight of it brought to mind what they had heard concerning the special presence of God in that city and the divine protection it was under, and God impressed such terrors on their minds thereby as made them retire with precipita-

tion. Though they were kings, though they were many in confederacy, yet they knew themselves an unequal match for Omnipotence, and therefore *fear came upon them, and pain, v.* 6. Note, God can dispirit the stoutest of his church's enemies, and soon put those in pain that live at ease. The fright they were in upon the sight of Jerusalem is here compared to the throes of a woman in travail, which are sharp and grievous, which sometimes come suddenly (1 Thess. v. 3), which cannot be avoided, and which are effects of sin and the curse. The defeat hereby given to their designs upon Jerusalem is compared to the dreadful work made with a fleet of ships by a violent storm, when some are split, others shattered, all dispersed (*v.* 7): *Thou breakest the ships of Tarshish with an east wind;* effects at sea lie thus exposed. The terrors of God are compared to an east wind (Job xxvii. 20, 21); these shall put them into confusion, and break all their measures. *Who knows the power of God's anger?*

8 As we have heard, so have we seen in the city of the LORD of hosts, in the city of our God: God will establish it for ever. Selah. 9 We have thought of thy lovingkindness, O God, in the midst of thy temple. 10 According to thy name, O God, so *is* thy praise unto the ends of the earth: thy right hand is full of righteousness. 11 Let mount Zion rejoice, let the daughters of Judah be glad, because of thy judgments. 12 Walk about Zion, and go round about her: tell the towers thereof. 13 Mark ye well her bulwarks, consider her palaces; that ye may tell *it* to the generation following. 14 For this God *is* our God for ever and ever: he will be our guide *even* unto death.

We have here the good use and improvement which the people of God are taught to make of his late glorious and gracious appearances for them against their enemies, that they might work for their good.

I. Let our faith in the word of God be hereby confirmed. If we compare what God has done with what he has spoken, we shall find that, as *we have heard, so have we seen* (*v.* 8), and what we have seen obliges us to believe what we have heard. 1. "As we have heard done in former providences, in the days of old, so have we seen done in our own days." Note, God's latter appearances for his people against his and their enemies are consonant to his former appearances, and should put us in mind of them. 2. "As we have heard in the promise and prediction, so have we seen in the performance and accomplishment. We have heard that God is the Lord of hosts, and that Jerusalem is the city of our God, is dear to him, is his particular care; and now we have seen it; we have seen the power of our God; we have seen his goodness; we have seen his care and concern for us, that he is a *wall of fire round about Jerusalem and the glory in the midst of her."* Note, In the great things that God has done, and is doing, for his church, it is good to take notice of the fulfilling of the scriptures; and this would help us the better to understand both the providence itself and the scripture that is fulfilled in it.

II. Let our hope of the stability and perpetuity of the church be hereby encouraged. "From what we have seen, compared with what we have heard, in the city of our God, we may conclude that God will establish it for ever." This was not fulfilled in Jerusalem (that city was long since destroyed, and all its glory laid in the dust), but has its accomplishment in the gospel church. We are sure that that shall be established for ever; it is built upon a rock, and the gates of hell cannot prevail against it, Matt. xvi. 18. God himself has undertaken the establishment of it; it is the Lord that has founded Zion, Isa. xiv. 32. And what we have seen, compared with what we have heard, may encourage us to hope in that promise of God upon which the church is built.

III. Let our minds be hereby filled with good thoughts of God. "From what we have heard, and seen, and hope for, we may take occasion to think much of God's loving-kindness, whenever we meet *in the midst of his temple,"* v. 9. All the streams of mercy that flow down to us must be traced up to the fountain of God's lovingkindness. It is not owing to any merit of ours, but purely to his mercy, and the peculiar favour he bears to his people. This therefore we must think of with delight, think of frequently and fixedly. What subject can we dwell upon more noble, more pleasant, more profitable? We must have God's lovingkindness always before our eyes (xxvi. 3), especially when we attend upon him in his temple. When we enjoy the benefit of public ordinances undisturbed, when we meet in his temple and there is none to make us afraid, we should take occasion thence to think of his lovingkindness.

IV. Let us give to God the glory of the great things which he has done for us, and mention them to his honour (v. 10): "*According to thy name, O God! so is thy praise,* not only in Jerusalem, but to the ends of the earth." By the late signal deliverance of Jerusalem God had made himself a name; that is, he had gloriously discovered his wisdom, power, and goodness, and made all the nations about sensible of it; and *so was his praise;* that is, some in all parts would be found giving glory to him accordingly. As far as his name goes his praise will go, at least it should go, and, at length, it shall go, when all the ends of the world shall praise him, xxii. 27; Rev. xi. 15. Some, by his *name,* understand especially that glorious name of his, *the Lord of hosts;* according to that name, so

is his praise; for all the creatures, even to the ends of the earth, are under his command. But his people must, in a special manner, acknowledge his justice in all he does for them. "*Righteousness fills thy right hand;"* that is, all the operations of thy power are consonant to the eternal rules of equity.

V. Let all the members of the church in particular take to themselves the comfort of what God does for his church in general (v. 11): "*Let Mount Zion rejoice,* the priests and Levites that attend the sanctuary, and then *let* all *the daughters of Judah,* the country towns, and the inhabitants of them, be glad: let the women in their songs and dances, as usual on occasion of public joys, celebrate with thankfulness the great salvation which God has wrought for us." Note, When we have given God the praise we may then take the pleasure of the extraordinary deliverances of the church, and *be glad because of God's judgments* (that is, the operations of his providence), all which we may see wrought in wisdom (therefore called *judgments)* and working for the good of his church.

VI. Let us diligently observe the instances and evidences of the church's beauty, strength, and safety, and faithfully transmit our observations to those that shall come after us (v. 12, 13): *Walk about Zion.* Some think this refers to the ceremony of the triumph; let those who are employed in that solemnity walk round the walls (as they did, Neh. xii. 31), singing and praising God. In doing this let *them tell the towers and mark well the bulwarks,* 1. That they might magnify the late wonderful deliverance God had wrought for them. Let them observe, with wonder, that the towers and bulwarks are all in their full strength and none of them damaged, the palaces in their beauty and none of them blemished; there is not the least damage done to the city by the kings that were assembled against it (v. 4): *Tell this to the generation following,* as a wonderful instance of God's care of his holy city, that the enemies should not only not ruin or destroy it, but not so much as hurt or deface it. 2. That they might fortify themselves against the fear of the like threatening danger another time. And so, (1.) We may understand it literally of Jerusalem, and the strong-hold of Zion. Let the daughters of Judah see the towers and bulwarks of Zion, with a pleasure equal to the terror with which the kings their enemies saw them, v. 5. Jerusalem was generally looked upon as an impregnable place, as appears, Lam. iv. 12. *All the inhabitants of the world would not have believed that an enemy should enter the gates of Jerusalem;* nor could they have entered if the inhabitants had not sinned away their defence. *Set your heart to her bulwarks.* This intimates that the principal bulwarks of Zion were not the objects of sense, which they might set their eye upon, but the objects of faith, which they must set their hearts upon. It was well enough fortified indeed both by nature and art; but its bulwarks that were mostly to be relied upon were the special presence of God in it, the beauty of holiness he had put upon it, and the promises he had made concerning it. " Consider Jerusalem's strength, and tell it to the generations to come, that they may do nothing to weaken it, and that, if at any time it be in distress, they may not basely surrender it to the enemy as not tenable." Calvin observes here that when they are directed to transmit to posterity a particular account of the towers, and bulwarks, and palaces of Jerusalem, it is intimated that in process of time they would all be destroyed and remain no longer to be seen; for, otherwise, what need was there to preserve the description and history of them? When the disciples were admiring the buildings of the temple their Master told them that in a little time one stone of it should not be *left upon another*, Matt. xxiv. 1, 2. Therefore, (2.) This must certainly be applied to the gospel church, that Mount Zion, Heb. xii. 22. " Consider the towers, and bulwarks, and palaces of that, that you may be invited and encouraged to join yourselves to it and embark in it. See it founded on Christ, the rock fortified by the divine power, guarded by him that neither slumbers nor sleeps. See what precious ordinances are its palaces, what precious promises are its bulwarks; tell this to the generation following, that they may with purpose of heart espouse its interests and cleave to it."

VII. Let us triumph in God, and in the assurances we have of his everlasting loving-kindness, *v.* 14. Tell this to the generation following; transmit this truth as a sacred deposit to your posterity, That *this God*, who has now done such great things for us, *is our God for ever and ever;* he is constant and unchangeable in his love to us and care for us. 1. If God be our God, he is ours for ever, not only through all the ages of time, but to eternity; for it is the everlasting blessedness of glorified saints that *God himself will be with them and will be their God*, Rev. xxi. 3. 2. If he be our God, *he will be our guide*, our faithful constant guide, to show us our way and to lead us in it; he will be so, *even unto death*, which will be the period of our way, and will bring us to our rest. He will lead and keep us even to the last. He will be our guide *above* death (so some); he will so guide us as to set us above the reach of death, so that it shall not be able to do us any real hurt. He will be our guide *beyond* death (so others); he will conduct us safely to a happiness on the other side death, to a life in which there shall be no more death. If we take the Lord for our God, he will conduct and convey us safely to death, through death, and beyond death—down to death and up again to glory.

PSALM XLIX.

This psalm is a sermon, and so is the next. In most of the psalms we have the penman praying or praising; in these we have him preaching; and it is our duty, in singing psalms, to teach and admonish ourselves and one another. The scope and design of this discourse is to convince the men of this world of their sin and folly in setting their hearts upon the things of this world, and so to persuade them to seek the things of a better world; as also to comfort the people of God, in reference to their own troubles and the grief that arises from the prosperity of the wicked. 1. In the preface he proposes to awaken worldly people out of their security (ver. 1—3) and to comfort himself and other godly people in a day of distress, ver. 4, 5. II. In the rest of the psalm, 1. He endeavours to convince sinners of their folly in doting upon the wealth of this world, by showing them, (1.) That they cannot, with all their wealth, save their friends from death, ver. 6—9. (2.) They cannot save themselves from death, ver. 10. (3.) They cannot secure to themselves a happiness in this world, ver. 11, 12. Much less, (4.) Can they secure to themselves a happiness in the other world, ver. 14. 2. He endeavours to comfort himself and other good people, (1.) Against the fear of death, ver. 15. (2.) Against the fear of the prospering power of wicked people, ver. 16—20. In singing this psalm let us receive these instructions, and be wise.

To the chief musician.   A psalm for the sons of Korah.

HEAR this, all *ye* people; give ear, all *ye* inhabitants of the world : 2 Both low and high, rich and poor, together. 3 My mouth shall speak of wisdom; and the meditation of my heart *shall be* of understanding. 4 I will incline mine ear to a parable : I will open my dark saying upon the harp. 5 Wherefore should I fear in the days of evil, *when* the iniquity of my heels shall compass me about ?

This is the psalmist's preface to his discourse concerning the vanity of the world and its insufficiency to make us happy; and we seldom meet with an introduction more solemn than this is ; for there is no truth of more undoubted certainty, nor of greater weight and importance, and the consideration of which will be of more advantage to us.

I. He demands the attention of others to that which he was about to say (*v.* 1, 2): *Hear this, all you people;* hear it and heed it, hear it and consider it; what is spoken once, hear twice. *Hear and give ear*, lxii. 9, 11. Not only, " Hear, all you Israelites, and give ear all the inhabitants of Canaan," but, *Hear, all you people, and give ear, all you inhabitants of the world :* for this doctrine is not peculiar to those that are blessed with divine revelation, but even the light of nature witnesses to it. All men may know, and therefore let all men consider, that their riches will not profit them in the day of death. *Both low and high, both rich and poor,* must come together, to hear the word of God; let both therefore hear this with application. Let those that are high and rich in the world hear of the vanity of their worldly possessions and not be proud of them, nor secure in the enjoyment of them, but lay them out in doing good, that with them they may make to themselves friends; let those that are poor and low hear this and be content with their little, and not envy those that have abundance. Poor people are as much in danger from an inordinate desire towards the wealth of the world as rich people from an inordinate delight in it. He gives a good reason why his discourse should be regarded (*v.* 3): *My mouth shall speak of wisdom ;* what he had to say, 1. Was true and good. It is wisdom and understanding; it will make those wise and intelligent that receive it and submit to it. It is not doubtful but certain, not trivial but weighty, not a matter of nice speculation but of admirable use to guide us in the right way to our great end. 2. It was what he had himself well digested. What his mouth spoke was the *meditation of his heart* (as xix. 14; xlv. 1); it was what God put into his mind, what he had himself seriously considered, and was fully apprized of the meaning of and convinced of the truth of. That which ministers speak from their own hearts is most likely to reach the hearts of their hearers.

II. He engages his own attention (*v.* 4): *I will incline my ear to a parable.* It is called a *parable*, not because it is figurative and obscure, but because it is a wise discourse and very instructive. It is the same word that is used concerning Solomon's proverbs. The psalmist will himself incline his ear to it. This intimates, 1. That he was taught it by the Spirit of God and did not speak of himself. Those that undertake to teach others must first learn themselves. 2. That he thought himself nearly concerned in it, and was resolved not to venture his own soul upon that bottom which he dissuaded others from venturing theirs upon. 3. That he would not expect others should attend to that which he himself did not attend to as a matter of the greatest importance. Where God *gives the tongue of the learned* he first *wakens the ear to hear as the learned,* Isa. l. 4.

III. He promises to make the matter as plain and as affecting as he could: *I will open my dark saying upon the harp.* What he learned for himself he would not conceal or confine to himself, but would communicate, for the benefit of others. 1. Some understood it not, it was a riddle to them ; tell them of the vanity of the things that are seen, and of the reality and weight of invisible things, and they say, *Ah Lord God! doth he not speak parables?* For the sake of such, he would open this dark saying, and make it so plain that he that runs might read it. 2. Others understood it well enough, but they were not moved by it, it never affected them, and for their sake he would open it upon the harp, and try that expedient to work upon them, to win upon them. *A verse may find him who a sermon flies.* Herbert.

IV. He begins with the application of it to himself, and that is the right method in which to treat of divine things. We must first preach to ourselves before we undertake to admonish or instruct others. Before he comes to set down the folly of carnal security (*v.* 6), he here lays down, from his own experience, the benefit and comfort of a holy gracious security, which those enjoy who trust in God, and not in their worldly wealth: *Wherefore should I fear?* he means, *Where-*

fore should *I fear their fear* (Isa. viii. 12), the fears of worldly people. 1. "Wherefore should I be afraid of them? Wherefore should I fear in the days of trouble and persecution, *when the iniquity of my heels,* or of my supplanters that endeavour to trip up my heels, *shall compass me about,* and they shall surround me with their mischievous attempts? Why should I be afraid of those all whose power lies in their wealth, which will not enable them to redeem their friends? I will not fear their power, for it cannot enable them to ruin me." The great men of the world will not appear at all formidable when we consider what little stead their wealth will stand them in. We need not fear their casting us down from our excellency who cannot support themselves in their own excellency. 2. "Wherefore should I be afraid like them?" The days of old age and death are the *days of evil,* Eccl. xii. 1. In the day of judgment *the iniquity of our heels* (or of our steps, our past sins) will compass us about, will be set in order before us. *Every work will be brought into judgment, with every secret thing;* and *every one of us must give account of himself.* In these days worldly wicked people will be afraid ; nothing more dreadful to those that have set their hearts upon the world than to think of leaving it ; death to them is the king of terrors, because, after death, comes the judgment, when their sins will surround them as so many furies ; but wherefore should a good man fear death, who has God with him? xxiii. 4. When his iniquities compass him about, he sees them all pardoned, his conscience is purified and pacified, and then even in the judgment-day, when the hearts of others fail them for fear, he can lift up his head with joy, Luke xxi. 26, 28. Note, The children of God, though ever so poor, are in this truly happy, above the most prosperous of the children of this world, that they are well guarded against the terrors of death and the judgment to come.

6 They that trust in their wealth, and boast themselves in the multitude of their riches ; 7 None *of them* can by any means redeem his brother, nor give to God a ransom for him : 8 (For the redemption of their soul *is* precious, and it ceaseth for ever :) 9 That he should still live for ever, *and* not see corruption. 10 For he seeth *that* wise men die, likewise the fool and the brutish person perish, and leave their wealth to others. 11 Their inward thought *is, that* their houses *shall* continue for ever, *and* their dwelling places to all generations ; they call *their* lands after their own names. 12 Nevertheless man *being* in honour abideth not : he is like the beasts *that*

perish. 13 This their way *is* their folly: yet their posterity approve their sayings. Selah. 14 Like sheep they are laid in the grave; death shall feed on them; and the upright shall have dominion over them in the morning; and their beauty shall consume in the grave from their dwelling.

In these verses we have,

I. A description of the spirit and way of worldly people, whose portion is in this life, xvii. 14. It is taken for granted that they have wealth, and a multitude of riches (*v.* 6), houses and lands of inheritance, which they call their own, *v.* 11. God often gives abundance of the good things of this world to bad men who live in contempt of him and rebellion against him, by which it appears that they are not the best things in themselves (for then God would give most of them to his best friends), and that they are not the best things for us, for then those would not have so much of them who, being marked for ruin, are to be ripened for it by their prosperity, Prov. i. 32. A man may have abundance of the wealth of this world and be made better by it, may thereby have his heart enlarged in love, and thankfulness, and obedience, and may do that good with it which will be fruit abounding to his account; and therefore it is not men's having riches that denominates them worldly, but their setting their hearts upon them as the best things; and so these worldly people are here described. 1. They repose a confidence in their riches: *They trust in their wealth* (*v.* 6); they depend upon it as their portion and happiness, and expect that it will secure them from all evil and supply them with all good, and that they need nothing else, no, not God himself. Their gold is their hope (Job xxxi. 24), and so it becomes their God. Thus our Saviour explains the difficulty of the salvation of rich people (Mark x. 24): *How hard is it for those that trust in riches to enter into the kingdom of God!* See 1 Tim. vi. 17. 2. They take a pride in their riches: *They boast themselves in the multitude of them,* as if they were sure tokens of God's favour and certain proofs of their own ingenuity and industry *(my might, and the power of my hand, have gotten me this wealth),* as if they made them truly great and happy, and more really excellent than their neighbours. They boast that they have all they would have (x. 3) and can set all the world at defiance *(I sit as a queen, and shall be a lady for ever)*; therefore *they call their lands after their own names,* hoping thereby to perpetuate their memory; and, if their lands do retain the names by which they called them, it is but a poor honour; but they often change their names when they change their owners. 3. They flatter themselves with an expectation of the perpetuity of their worldly possessions (*v.* 11):

Their inward thought is that their houses shall continue for ever, and with this thought they please themselves. Are not all thoughts inward? Yes; but it intimates, (1.) That this thought is deeply rooted in their minds, is rolled and revolved there, and carefully lodged in the innermost recesses of their hearts. A godly man has thoughts of the world, but they are his outward thoughts; his inward thought is reserved for God and heavenly things: but a worldly man has only some floating foreign thoughts of the things of God, while his fixed thought, his inward thought, is about the world; that lies nearest his heart, and is upon the throne there. (2.) There it is industriously concealed. They cannot, for shame, say that they expect their houses to continue for ever, but inwardly they think so. If they cannot persuade themselves that they shall continue for ever, yet they are so foolish as to think *their houses* shall, and their dwelling-places; and suppose they should, what good will that do them when they shall be no longer theirs? But they will not; for the world passes away, and the fashion of it. All things are devoured by the teeth of time.

II. A demonstration of their folly herein. In general (*v.* 13), *This their way is their folly.* Note, The way of worldliness is a very foolish way: those that lay up their treasure on earth, and set their affections on things below, act contrary both to right reason and to their true interest. God himself pronounced him *a fool* who thought his goods were laid up for many years, and that they would be a portion for his soul, Luke xii. 19, 20. And yet their posterity approve their sayings, agree with them in the same sentiments, say as they say and do as they do, and tread in the steps of their worldliness. Note, The love of the world is a disease that runs in the blood; men have it by kind, till the grace of God cures it. To prove the folly of carnal worldlings he shows,

1. That with all their wealth they cannot save the life of the dearest friend they have in the world, nor purchase a reprieve for him when he is under the arrest of death (*v.* 7—9): *None of them can by any means redeem his brother,* his brother worldling, who would give him counter-security out of his own estate, if he would but be bail for him: and gladly he would, in hopes that he might do the same kindness for him another time. But their words will not be taken one for another, nor will one man's estate be the ransom of another man's life. God does not value it; it is of no account with him; and the true value of things is as they stand in his books. His justice will not accept it by way of commutation or equivalent. The Lord of our brother's life is the Lord of our estate, and may take both if he please, without either difficulty to himself or wrong to us; and therefore one cannot be ransom for another. We cannot bribe death, that our

brother should still live, much less that he should live for ever, in this world, nor bribe the grave, that he should not see corruption; for we must needs die, and return to the dust, and there is no discharge from that war. What folly is it to trust to that, and boast of that, which will not enable us so much as for one hour to respite the execution of the sentence of death upon a parent, a child, or a friend that is to us as our own soul! It is certainly true that *the redemption of the soul is precious and ceaseth for ever;* that is, life, when it is going, cannot be arrested, and when it is gone it cannot be recalled, by any human art, or worldly price. But this looks further, to the eternal redemption which was to be wrought out by the Messiah, whom the Old-Testament saints had an eye to as the Redeemer. Everlasting life is a jewel of too great a value to be purchased by the wealth of this world. We are *not redeemed with corruptible things, such as silver and gold,* 1 Pet. i. 18, 19. The learned Dr. Hammond applies the 8th and 9th verses expressly to Christ: " *The redemption of the soul shall be precious,* shall be high-prized, it shall cost very dear; but, being once wrought, it shall cease for ever, it shall never need to be repeated, Heb. ix. 25, 26; x. 12. And he (that is, the Redeemer) *shall yet live for ever, and shall not see corruption;* he shall rise again before he sees corruption, and then shall live for evermore," Rev. i. 18. Christ did that for us which all the riches of the world could not do; well therefore may he be dearer to us than any worldly things. Christ did that for us which a brother, a friend, could not do for us, no, not one of the best estate or interest; and therefore those that *love father or brother more than him are not worthy of him.* This likewise shows the folly of worldly people, who sell their souls for that which would never buy them.

2. That with all their wealth they cannot secure themselves from the stroke of death. The worldling sees, and it vexes him to see it, that *wise men die, likewise the fool and the brutish person perish, v.* 10. Therefore he cannot but expect that it will, at length, come to his own turn; he cannot find any encouragement to hope that he himself shall continue for ever, and therefore foolishly comforts himself with this, that, though he shall not, his house shall. Some rich people are wise, they are politicians, but they cannot out-wit death, nor evade his stroke, with all their art and management; others are fools and brutish *(Fortuna favet fatuis—Fools are Fortune's favourites);* these, though they do no good, yet perhaps do no great hurt in the world: but that shall not excuse them; they shall perish, and be taken away by death, as well as the wise that did mischief with their craft. Or by the wise and the foolish we may understand the godly and the wicked; the godly die, and their death is their deliverance; the wicked perish, and their death is

their destruction; but, however, they leave their wealth to others. (1.) They cannot continue with it, nor will it serve to procure them a reprieve. That is a frivolous plea, though once it served a turn (Jer. xli. 8), *Slay us not, for we have treasures in the field.* (2.) They cannot carry it away with them, but must leave it behind them. (3.) They cannot foresee who will enjoy it when they have left it; they must leave it to others, but to whom they know not, perhaps to a fool (Eccl. ii. 19), perhaps to an enemy.

3. That, as their wealth will stand them in no stead in a dying hour, so neither will their honour (*v.* 12): *Man, being in honour, abides not.* We will suppose a-man advanced to the highest pinnacle of preferment, as great and happy as the world can make him, man in splendour, man at his best estate, surrounded and supported with all the advantages he can desire; yet then he abides not. His honour does not continue; that is a fleeting shadow. He himself does not, he tarries not all night; this world is an inn, in which his stay is so short that he can scarcely be said to get a night's lodging in it; so little rest is there in these things; he has but a baiting time. *He is like the beasts that perish;* that is, he must as certainly die as the beasts, and his death will be as final a period to his state in this world as theirs is; his dead body likewise will putrefy as theirs does; and (as Dr. Hammond observes) frequently the greatest honours and wealth, unjustly gotten by the parent, descend not to any one of his posterity (as the beasts, when they die, leave nothing behind them to their young ones, but the wide world to feed in), but fall into other hands immediately, for which he never designed to gather them.

4. That their condition on the other side death will be very miserable. The world they dote upon will not only not save them from death, but will sink them so much the lower into hell (*v.* 14): *Like sheep they are laid in the grave.* Their prosperity did but feed them like sheep for the slaughter (Hos. iv. 16), and then death comes, and shuts them up in the grave like fat sheep in a fold, *to be brought forth to the day of wrath,* Job xxi. 30. Multitudes of them, like flocks of sheep dead of some disease, are thrown into the grave, and there death shall feed on them, the second death, *the worm that dies not,* Job xxiv. 20. Their own guilty consciences, like so many vultures, shall be continually preying upon them, with, *Son, remember,* Luke xvi. 25. Death insults and triumphs over them, as it is represented in the fall of the king of Babylon, at which *hell from beneath is moved,* Isa. xiv. 9, &c. While a saint can ask proud Death, *Where is thy sting?* Death will ask the proud sinner, *Where is thy wealth, thy pomp?* and the more he was fattened with prosperity the more sweetly will death feed on him. And in the morning of the resurrection, when all that sleep in the dust

shall awake (Dan. xii. 2), *the upright shall have dominion over them,* shall not only be advanced to the highest dignity and honour when they are filled with everlasting shame and contempt, elevated to the highest heavens when they are sunk to the lowest hell, but they shall be assessors with Christ in passing judgment upon them, and shall applaud the justice of God in their ruin. When the rich man in hell begged that Lazarus might bring him a drop of water to cool his tongue he owned that that upright man had dominion over him, as the foolish virgins also owned the dominion of the wise, and that they lay much at their mercy, when they begged, *Give us of your oil.* Let this comfort us in reference to the oppressions which the upright are now often groaning under, and the dominion which the wicked have over them. The day is coming when the tables will be turned (Esther ix. 1) and the upright will have the dominion. Let us now judge of things as they will appear at that day. But what will become of all the beauty of the wicked? Alas! that shall all be *consumed in the grave from their dwelling ;* all that upon which they valued themselves, and for which others caressed and admired them, was adventitious and borrowed ; it was paint and varnish, and they will rise in their own native deformity. The beauty of holiness is that which the grave, that consumes all other beauty, cannot touch, or do any damage to. Their beauty shall consume, the grave (or hell) being a habitation to every one of them; and what beauty can be there where there is nothing but the blackness of darkness for ever?

15 But God will redeem my soul from the power of the grave : for he shall receive me. Selah. 16 Be not thou afraid when one is made rich, when the glory of his house is increased ; 17 For when he dieth he shall carry nothing away : his glory shall not descend after him. 18 Though while he lived he blessed his soul: and *men* will praise thee, when thou doest well to thyself. 19 He shall go to the generation of his fathers ; they shall never see light. 20 Man *that is* in honour, and understandeth not, is like the beasts *that* perish.

Good reason is here given to good people,

I. Why they should not be afraid of death. There is no cause for that fear if they have such a comfortable prospect as David here has of a happy state on the other side death, *v.* 15. He had shown (*v.* 14) how miserable the dead are that die in their sins, where he shows how blessed the dead are that die in the Lord. The distinction of men's outward condition, how great a difference soever it makes in life, makes none at death; rich and poor meet in the grave. But the distinction of men's spiritual state, though, in this life, it makes a small difference, where all things come alike to all, yet, at and after death, it makes a very great one. *Now he is comforted, and thou art tormented.* The righteous has hope in his death, so has David here hope in God concerning his soul. Note, The believing hopes of the soul's redemption from the grave, and reception to glory, are the great support and joy of the children of God in a dying hour. They hope,

1. That God will redeem their souls from the power of the grave, which includes, (1.) The preserving of the soul from going to the grave with the body. The grave has a power over the body, by virtue of the sentence (Gen. iii. 19), and it is cruel enough in executing that power (Cant. viii. 6); but it has no such power over the soul. It has power to silence, and imprison, and consume the body; but the soul then moves, and acts, and converses, more freely than ever (Rev. vi. 9, 10); it is immaterial and immortal. When death breaks the dark lantern, yet it does not extinguish the candle that was pent up in it. (2.) The reuniting of the soul and body at the resurrection. The soul is often put for the life; that indeed falls under the power of the grave for a time, but it shall, at length, be redeemed from it, when *mortality shall be swallowed up of life.* The God of life, that was its Creator at first, can and will be its Redeemer at last. (3.) The salvation of the soul from eternal ruin: "*God shall redeem my soul from the sheol of hell* (*v.* 15), the wrath to come, that pit of destruction into which the wicked shall be cast," *v.* 14. It is a great comfort to dying saints that they shall not be hurt of the second death (Rev. ii. 11), and therefore the first death has no sting and the grave no victory.

2. That he will receive them to himself. He redeems their souls, that he may receive them. Ps. xxxi. 5, *Into thy hands I commit my spirit, for thou hast redeemed it.* He will receive them into his favour, will admit them into his kingdom, into the mansions that are prepared for them (John xiv. 2, 3), those everlasting habitations, Luke xvi. 9.

II. Why they should not be afraid of the prosperity and power of wicked people in this world, which, as it is their pride and joy, has often been the envy, and grief, and terror of the righteous, which yet, all things considered, there is no reason for.

1. He supposes the temptation very strong to envy the prosperity of sinners, and to be afraid that they will carry all before them with a high hand, that with their wealth and interest they will run down religion and religious people, and that they will be found the truly happy people; for he supposes, (1.) That they are made rich, and so are enabled to give law to all about them and have every thing at command. *Pecuniæ*

obediunt omnes et omnia—Every person and every thing obey the commanding influence of money. (2.) That the glory of their house, from very small beginnings, is increased greatly, which naturally makes men haughty, insolent, and imperious, *v.* 16. Thus they seem to be the favourites of heaven, and therefore formidable. (3.) That they are very easy and secure in themselves and in their own minds (*v.* 18): *In his life-time he blessed his soul;* that is, he thought himself a very happy man, such a one as he would be, and a very good man, such a one as he should be, because he prospered in the world. He blessed his soul, as that rich fool who said to his soul, "*Soul, take thy ease,* and be not disturbed either with cares and fears about the world or with the rebukes and ad-monitions of conscience. All is well, and will be well for ever." Note, [1.] It is of great consequence to consider what that is in which we bless our souls, upon the score of which we think well of ourselves. Be-lievers *bless themselves in the God of truth* (Isa. lxv. 16) and think themselves happy if he be theirs; carnal people bless themselves in the wealth of the world, and think them-selves happy if they have abundance of that. [2.] There are many whose precious souls lie under God's curse, and yet they do them-selves bless them; they applaud that in them-selves which God condemns, and speak peace to themselves when God denounces war against them. Yet this is not all. (4.) They are in good reputation among their neigh-bours: "*Men will praise thee,* and cry thee up, as having done well for thyself in raising such an estate and family." This is the sen-timent of all the children of this world, that those do best for themselves that do most for their bodies, by heaping up riches, though, at the same time, nothing is done for the soul, nothing for eternity; and accordingly they *bless the covetous, whom the Lord abhors,* x. 3. If men were to be our judges, it were our wisdom thus to recommend ourselves to their good opinion: but what will it avail us to be approved of men if God condemn us? Dr. Hammond understands this of the good man here spoken to, for it is the second per-son, not of the wicked man spoken of: "*He, in his life-time, blessed his soul, but thou shalt be praised for doing well unto thyself.* The worldling magnified himself; but thou that dost not, like him, speak well of thyself, but do well for thyself, in securing thy eternal welfare, thou shalt be praised, if not of men, yet of God, which will be thy everlasting honour."

2. He suggests that which is sufficient to take off the strength of the temptation, by directing us to look forward to the end of prosperous sinners (lxxiii. 17): "Think what they will be in the other world, and you will see no cause to envy them what they are and have in this world."

(1.) In the other world they will be never

the better for all the wealth and prosperity they are now so fond of. It is a miserable portion, which will not last so long as they must (*v.* 17): *When he dies* it is taken for granted that he goes into another world him-self, but *he shall carry nothing away with him* of all that which he has been so long heaping up. The greatest and wealthiest cannot therefore be the happiest, because they are never the better for their living in this world; as they came naked into it, they shall go naked out of it. But those have something to show in the other world for their living in this world who can say, through grace, that though they came corrupt, and sin-ful, and spiritually naked, into it, they go re-newed, and sanctified, and well clothed with the righteousness of Christ, out of it. Those that are rich in the graces and comforts of the Spirit have something which, when they die, they shall carry away with them, something which death cannot strip them of, nay, which death will be the improvement of; but, as for worldly possessions, as we *brought nothing into the world* (what we have we had from others), so it is certain that we shall carry nothing out, but leave it to others, 1 Tim. vi. 7. They shall descend, but *their glory,* that which they called and counted their glory, and gloried in, *shall not descend after them* to lessen the disgrace of death and the grave, to bring them off in the judgment, or abate the torments of hell. Grace is glory that will ascend with us, but no earthly glory will descend after us.

(2.) In the other world they will be in-finitely the worse for all their abuses of the wealth and prosperity they enjoyed in this world (*v.* 19): *The soul shall go to the genera-tion of his fathers,* his worldly wicked fathers, whose sayings he approved and whose steps he trod in, his fathers who would not hearken to the word of God, Zech. i. 4. He shall go to be there where they are that shall never see light, shall never have the least glimpse of comfort and joy, being condemned to utter darkness. Be not afraid then of the pomp and power of wicked people; for the end of the man that is in honour, if he be not wise and good, will be miserable; if he under-stand not, he is to be pitied rather than envied. A fool, a wicked man, in honour, is really as despicable an animal as any under the sun; he is *like the beasts that perish* (*v.* 20); nay, it is better to be a beast than to be a man that makes himself like a beast. Men in honour that understand, that know and do their duty and make conscience of it, are as gods, and children of the Most High. But men in honour that understand not, that are proud, and sensual, and oppressive, are as beasts, and they shall perish, like the beasts, ingloriously as to this world, though not, like the beasts, indemnified as to another world. Let prosperous sinners therefore be afraid for themselves, but let not even suffering saints be afraid of them.

PSALM L.

This psalm, as the former, is a psalm of instruction, not of prayer or praise; it is a psalm of reproof and admonition, in singing which we are to teach and admonish one another. In the foregoing psalm, after a general demand of attention, God by his prophet deals (ver. 3) with the children of this world, to convince them of their sin and folly in setting their hearts upon the wealth of this world; in this psalm, after a like preface, he deals with those that were, in profession, the church's children, to convince them of their sin and folly in placing their religion in ritual services, while they neglected practical godliness; and this is as sure a way to ruin as the other. This psalm is intended, 1. As a proof to the carnal Jews, both those that rested in the external performances of their religion, and were remiss in the more excellent duties of prayer and praise, and those that expounded the law to others, but lived wicked lives themselves. 2. As a prediction of the abolishing of the ceremonial law, and of the introducing of a spiritual way of worship, in and by the kingdom of the Messiah, John iv. 23, 24. 3. As a representation of the day of judgment, in which God will call men to an account concerning their observance of those things which they have thus been taught; men shall be judged "according to what is written in the books;" and therefore Christ is fitly represented speaking as a Judge, then when he speaks as a Lawgiver. Here is, I. The glorious appearance of the Prince that gives law and judgment, ver. 1—6. II. Instruction given to his worshippers, to turn their sacrifices into prayers, ver. 7—15. III. A rebuke to those that pretend to worship God, but live in disobedience to his commands (ver. 16—20), their doom read (ver. 21, 22), and warning given to all to look to their conversation as well as to their devotions, ver. 23. These instructions and admonitions we must take to ourselves, and give to one another, in singing this psalm.

A psalm of Asaph.

THE mighty God, *even* the LORD, hath spoken, and called the earth from the rising of the sun unto the going down thereof. 2 Out of Zion, the perfection of beauty, God hath shined. 3 Our God shall come, and shall not keep silence: a fire shall devour before him, and it shall be very tempestuous round about him. 4 He shall call to the heavens from above, and to the earth, that he may judge his people. 5 Gather my saints together unto me; those that have made a covenant with me by sacrifice. 6 And the heavens shall declare his righteousness: for God *is* judge himself. Selah.

It is probable that Asaph was not only the chief musician, who was to put a tune to this psalm, but that he was himself the penman of it; for we read that in Hezekiah's time they praised God *in the words of David and of Asaph the seer,* 2 Chron. xxix. 30. Here is, I. The court called, in the name of the King of kings (*v.* 1): *The mighty God, even the Lord, hath spoken—*El, Elohim, Jehovah, the God of infinite power, justice, and mercy, Father, Son, and Holy Ghost. God is the Judge, the Son of God came for judgment into the world, and the Holy Ghost is the Spirit of judgment. All the earth is called to attend, not only because the controversy God had with his people Israel for their hypocrisy and ingratitude might safely be referred to any man of reason (nay, let the house of Israel itself *judge between God and his vineyard,* Isa. v. 3), but because all the children of men are concerned to know the right way of worshipping God, in spirit and in truth, because when the kingdom of the

424

Messiah should be set up all should be instructed in the evangelical worship, and invited to join in it (see Mal. 1. 11, Acts x. 34), and because in the day of final judgment all nations shall be gathered together to receive their doom, and every man shall give an account of himself unto God.

II. The judgment set, and the Judge taking his seat. As, when God gave the law to Israel in the wilderness, it is said, *He came from Sinai, and rose up from Seir, and shone forth from Mount Paran, and came with ten thousands of his saints, and then from his right hand went a fiery law* (Deut. xxxiii. 2), so, with allusion to that, when God comes to reprove them for their hypocrisy, and to send forth his gospel to supersede the legal institutions, it is said here, 1. That *he shall shine out of Zion,* as then from the top of Sinai, *v.* 2. Because in Zion his oracle was now fixed, thence his judgments upon that provoking people were denounced, and thence the orders issued for the execution of them (Joel ii. 1): *Blow you the trumpet in Zion.* Sometimes there are more than ordinary appearances of God's presence and power working with and by his word and ordinances, for the convincing of men's consciences and the reforming and refining of his church; and then God, who always dwells in Zion, may be said to *shine out of Zion.* Moreover, he may be said to *shine out of Zion* because the gospel, which set up spiritual worship, was to *go forth from Mount Zion* (Isa. ii. 3, Mic. iv. 2), and the preachers of it were to *begin at Jerusalem* (Luke xxiv. 47), and Christians are said to come unto Mount Zion, to receive their instructions, Heb. xii. 22, 28. Zion is here called *the perfection of beauty,* because it was the holy hill; and holiness is indeed the perfection of beauty. 2. That he *shall come, and not keep silence,* shall no longer seem to wink at the sins of men, as he had done (*v.* 21), but shall show his displeasure at them, and shall also cause that mystery to be published to the world by his holy apostles which had long *lain hid, that the Gentiles should be fellow-heirs* (Eph. iii. 5, 6) and that the partition-wall of the ceremonial law should be taken down; this shall now no longer be concealed. In the great day *our God shall come and shall not keep silence,* but shall make those to hear his judgment that would not hearken to his law. 3. That his appearance should be very majestic and terrible: *A fire shall devour before him.* The fire of his judgments shall make way for the rebukes of his word, in order to the awakening of the hypocritical nation of the Jews, that the sinners in Zion, being afraid of that devouring fire (Isa. xxxiii. 14), might be startled out of their sins. When his gospel kingdom was to be set up Christ *came to send fire on the earth,* Luke xii. 49. The Spirit was given in cloven tongues as of fire, introduced by a rushing mighty wind, which was very tempestuous, Acts ii. 2, 3. And in the last judgment Christ shall come in flaming fire, 2 Thess. i. 8. See Dan. vii. 9; Heb. x. 27. 4. That as on Mount Sinai he came with *ten thousands of his saints*, so he shall now *call to the heavens from above*, to take notice of this solemn process (*v.* 4), as Moses often *called heaven and earth to witness* against Israel (Deut. iv. 26, xxxi. 28, xxxii. 1), and God by his prophets, Isa. i. 2; Mic. vi. 2. The equity of the judgment of the great day will be attested and applauded by heaven and earth, by saints and angels, even all the holy myriads.

III. The parties summoned (*v.* 5): *Gather my saints together unto me.* This may be understood either, 1. Of saints indeed: " Let them be gathered to God through Christ; let the few pious Israelites be set by themselves;" for to them the following denunciations of wrath do not belong; rebukes to hypocrites ought not to be terrors to the upright. When God will reject the services of those that only offered sacrifice, resting in the outside of the performance, he will graciously accept those who, in sacrificing, *make a covenant with him*, and so attend to and answer the end of the institution of sacrifices. The design of the preaching of the gospel, and the setting up of Christ's kingdom, was to gather together in one the children of God, John xi. 52. And at the second coming of Jesus Christ all his saints shall be *gathered together unto him* (2 Thess. ii. 1) to be assessors with him in the judgment; for *the saints shall judge the world*, 1 Cor. vi. 2. Now it is here given as a character of the saints that they have made a covenant with God by sacrifice. Note, (1.) Those only shall be gathered to God as his saints who have, in sincerity, covenanted with him, who have taken him to be their God and given up themselves to him to be his people, and thus have joined themselves unto the Lord. (2.) It is only by sacrifice, by Christ the great sacrifice (from whom all the legal sacrifices derived what value they had), that we poor sinners can covenant with God so as to be accepted of him. There must be an atonement made for the breach of the first covenant before we can be admitted again into covenant. Or, 2. It may be understood of saints in profession, such as the people of Israel were, who are called *a kingdom of priests* and *a holy nation*, Exod. xix. 6. They were, as a body politic, taken into covenant with God, the covenant of peculiarity; and it was done with great solemnity, *by sacrifice*, Exod. xxiv. 8. " Let them come and hear what God has to say to them; let them receive the reproofs God sends them now by his prophets, and the gospel he will, in due time, send them by his Son, which shall supersede the ceremonial law. If these be slighted, let them expect to hear from God another way, and to be judged by that word which they will not be ruled by."

IV. The issue of this solemn trial foretold (*v.* 6): *The heavens shall declare his righteousness*, those heavens that were called to be witnesses to the trial (*v.* 4); the *people in heaven shall say, Hallelujah. True and righteous are his judgments*, Rev. xix. 1, 2. The righteousness of God in all the rebukes of his word and providence, in the establishment of his gospel (which *brings in an everlasting righteousness*, and in which *the righteousness of God is revealed*), and especially in the judgment of the great day, is what the heavens will declare; that is, 1. It will be universally known, and proclaimed to all the world. *As the heavens declare the glory*, the wisdom and power, of God the *Creator* (xix. 1), so they shall no less openly declare the glory, the justice and righteousness, of God the *Judge;* and so loudly do they proclaim both that *there is no speech nor language where their voice is not heard*, as it follows there, *v.* 3. 2. It will be incontestably owned and proved; who can deny what the heavens declare? Even sinners' own consciences will subscribe to it, and hell as well as heaven will be forced to acknowledge the righteousness of God. The reason given is, *for God is Judge himself*, and therefore, (1.) He will be just; for it is impossible he should do any wrong to any of his creatures, he never did, nor ever will. When men are employed to judge for him they may do unjustly; but, when he is Judge himself, there can be no injustice done. *Is God unrighteous, who takes vengeance?* The apostle, for this reason, startles at the thought of it; *God forbid! for then how shall God judge the world?* Rom. iii. 5, 6. These decisions will be perfectly just, for against them there will lie no exception, and from them there will lie no appeal. (2.) He will be justified; *God is Judge*, and therefore he will not only execute justice, but he will oblige all to own it; for he *will be clear when he judges*, li. 4.

7 Hear, O my people, and I will speak; O Israel, and I will testify against thee: I *am* God, *even* thy God. 8 I will not reprove thee for thy sacrifices or thy burnt offerings, *to have been* continually before me. 9 I will take no bullock out of thy house, *nor* he goats out of thy folds. 10 For every beast of the forest *is* mine, *and* the cattle upon a thousand hills. 11 I know all the fowls of the mountains : and the wild beasts of the field *are* mine. 12 If I were hungry, I would not tell thee : for the world *is* mine, and the fulness thereof. 13 Will I eat the flesh of bulls, or drink the blood of goats ? 14 Offer unto God thanksgiving ; and pay thy vows unto the most high : 15 And call upon me in the day of trouble : I will deliver thee, and thou shalt glorify me.

God is here dealing with those that placed all their religion in the observances of the ceremonial law, and thought those sufficient.

I. He lays down the original contract between him and Israel, in which they had avouched him to be their God, and he them to be his people, and so both parties were agreed (*v.* 7): *Hear, O my people! and I will speak.* Note, It is justly expected that whatever others do, when he speaks, his people should give ear; who will, if they do not? And then we may comfortably expect that God will speak to us when we are ready to hear what he says; even when he testifies against us in the rebukes and threatenings of his word and providences we must be forward to hear what he says, to hear even *the rod and him that has appointed it.*

II. He puts a slight upon the legal sacrifices, *v.* 8, &c. Now,

1. This may be considered as looking back to the use of these under the law. God had a controversy with the Jews; but what was the ground of the controversy? Not their neglect of the ceremonial institutions; no, they had not been wanting in the observance of them, their burnt-offerings had been continually before God, they took a pride in them, and hoped by their offerings to procure a dispensation for their lusts, as the adulterous woman, Prov. vii. 14. Their constant sacrifices, they thought, would both expiate and excuse their neglect of the weightier matters of the law. Nay, if they had, in some degree, neglected these institutions, yet that should not have been the cause of God's quarrel with them, for it was but a small offence in comparison with the immoralities of their conversation. They thought God was mightily beholden to them for the many sacrifices they had brought to his altar, and that they had made him very much their debtor by them, as if he could not have maintained his numerous family of priests without their contributions; but God here shows them the contrary, (1.) That he did not need their sacrifices. What occasion had he for their bullocks and goats who has the command of all *the beasts of the forest,* and the *cattle upon a thousand hills* (*v.* 9, 10), has an incontestable propriety in them and dominion over them, has them all always under his eye and within his reach, and can make what use he pleases of them; they all wait on him, and are all at his disposal? civ. 27—29. Can we add any thing to his store whose all the wild fowl and wild beasts are, the world itself and the fulness thereof? *v.* 11, 12. God's infinite self-sufficiency proves our utter insufficiency to add any thing to him. (2.) That he could not be benefited by their sacrifices. Their goodness, of this kind, could not possibly extend to him, nor, if they were in this matter righteous, was he the better (*v.* 13): *Will I eat the flesh of bulls?* It is as absurd to think that their sacrifices could, of themselves, and by virtue of any innate

excellency in them, add any pleasure or praise to God, as it would be to imagine that an infinite Spirit could be supported by meat and drink, as our bodies are. It is said indeed of the demons whom the Gentiles worshipped that they did *eat the fat of their sacrifices, and drink the wine of their drink-offerings* (Deut. xxxii. 38): they regaled themselves in the homage they robbed the true God of; but will the great Jehovah be thus entertained? No; *to obey is better than sacrifice,* and to love God and our neighbour *better than all burnt-offerings,* so much better that God by his prophets often told them that their sacrifices were not only not acceptable, but abominable, to him, while they lived in sin; instead of pleasing him, he looked upon them as a mockery, and therefore an affront and provocation to him; see Prov. xv. 8; Isa. i. 11, &c.; lxvi. 3; Jer. vi. 20; Amos v. 21. They are therefore here warned not to rest in these performances; but to conduct themselves, in all other instances, towards God as their God.

2. This may be considered as looking forward to the abolishing of these by the gospel of Christ. Thus Dr. Hammond understands it. When God shall set up the kingdom of the Messiah he shall abolish the old way of worship by sacrifice and offerings; he will no more have those to be *continually before him* (*v.* 8); he will no more require of his worshippers to bring him their bullocks and their goats, to be burnt upon his altar, *v.* 9. For indeed he never appointed this as that which he had any need of, or took any pleasure in, for, besides that all we have is his already, he has far more beasts in the forest and upon the mountains, which we know nothing of nor have any property in, than we have in our folds; but he instituted it to prefigure the great sacrifice which his own Son should in the fulness of time offer upon the cross, to make atonement for sin, and all the other spiritual sacrifices of acknowledgment with which God, through Christ, will be well pleased.

III. He directs to the best sacrifices of prayer and praise as those which, under the law, were preferred before all burnt-offerings and sacrifices, and on which then the greatest stress was laid, and which now, under the gospel, come in the room of those carnal ordinances which were imposed until the times of reformation. He shows us here (*v.* 14, 15) what is good, and what the Lord our God requires of us, and will accept, when sacrifices are slighted and superseded. 1. We must make a penitent acknowledgment of our sins: *Offer to God confession,* so some read it, and understand it of the confession of sin, in order to our giving glory to God and taking shame to ourselves, that we may never return to it. *A broken and contrite heart* is the sacrifice which *God will not despise,* li. 17. If the sin was not abandoned the sin-offering was not accepted. 2. We must give God thanks for his mercies to us: *Offer to God thanksgiving*, every day, often every day *(seven times a day will I praise thee)*, and upon special occasions; and *this shall please the Lord*, if it come from a humble thankful heart, full of love to him and joy in him, *better than an ox or bullock that has horns and hoofs*, lxix. 30, 31. 3. We must make conscience of performing our covenants with him: *Pay thy vows to the Most High*, forsake thy sins, and do thy duty better, pursuant to the solemn promises thou hast made him to that purport. When we give God thanks for any mercy we have received we must be sure to pay the vows we made to him when we were in the pursuit of the mercy, else our thanksgivings will not be accepted. Dr. Hammond applies this to the great gospel ordinance of the eucharist, in which we are to give thanks to God for his great love in sending his Son to save us, and to pay our vows of love and duty to him, and to give alms. Instead of all the Old Testament types of a Christ to come, we have that blessed memorial of a Christ already come. 4. In the day of distress we must address ourselves to God by faithful and fervent prayer (*v.* 15): *Call upon me in the day of trouble*, and not upon any other god. Our troubles, though we see them coming from God's hand, must drive us to him, and not drive us from him. We must thus acknowledge him in all our ways, depend upon his wisdom, power, and goodness, and refer ourselves entirely to him, and so give him glory. This is a cheaper, easier, readier way of seeking his favour than by a peace-offering, and yet more acceptable. 5. When he, in answer to our prayers, delivers us, as he has promised to do in such way and time as he shall think fit, we must glorify him, not only by a grateful mention of his favour, but by living to his praise. Thus must we keep up our communion with God, meeting him with our prayers when he afflicts us and with our praises when he delivers us.

16 But unto the wicked God saith, What hast thou to do to declare my statutes, or *that* thou shouldest take my covenant in thy mouth? 17 Seeing thou hatest instruction, and castest my words behind thee. 18 When thou sawest a thief, then thou consentedst with him, and hast been partaker with adulterers. 19 Thou givest thy mouth to evil, and thy tongue frameth deceit. 20 Thou sittest *and* speakest against thy brother; thou slanderest thine own mother's son. 21 These *things* hast thou done, and I kept silence; thou thoughtest that I was altogether *such a one* as thyself: *but* I will reprove thee, and set *them* in order before thine eyes. 22 Now

consider this, ye that forget God, lest I tear *you* in pieces, and *there be* none to deliver. 23 Whoso offereth praise glorifieth me: and to him that ordereth *his* conversation *aright* will I show the salvation of God.

God, by the psalmist, having instructed his people in the right way of worshipping him and keeping up their communion with him, here directs his speech to the wicked, to hypocrites, whether they were such as professed the Jewish or the Christian religion: hypocrisy is wickedness for which God will judge. Observe here,

I. The charge drawn up against them. 1 They are charged with invading and usurping the honours and privileges of religion (*v.* 16): *What hast thou to do*, O wicked man! *to declare my statutes?* This is a challenge to those that are really profane, but seemingly godly, to show what title they have to the cloak of religion, and by what authority they wear it, when they use it only to cover and conceal the abominable impieties of their hearts and lives. Let them make out their claim to it if they can. Some think it points prophetically at the scribes and Pharisees that were the teachers and leaders of the Jewish church at the time when the kingdom of the Messiah, and that evangelical way of worship spoken of in the foregoing verses, were to be set up. They violently opposed that great revolution, and used all the power and interest which they had by sitting in Moses's seat to hinder it; but the account which our blessed Saviour gives of them (Matt. xxiii.), and St. Paul (Rom. ii. 21, 22), makes this expostulation here agree very well to them. They took on them to declare God's statutes, but they hated Christ's instruction; and therefore what had they to do to expound the law, when they rejected the gospel? But it is applicable to all those that are practisers of iniquity, and yet professors of piety, especially if withal they be preachers of it. Note, It is very absurd in itself, and a great affront to the God of heaven, for those that are wicked and ungodly to declare his statutes and to take his covenant in their mouths. It is very possible, and too common, for those that declare God's statutes to others to live in disobedience to them themselves, and for those that take God's covenant in their mouths yet in their hearts to continue their covenant with sin and death; but they are guilty of a usurpation, they take to themselves an honour which they have no title to, and there is a day coming when they will be thrust out as intruders. *Friend, how camest thou in hither?* 2. They are charged with transgressing and violating the laws and precepts of religion. (1.) They are charged with a daring contempt of the word of God (*v.* 17): *Thou hatest instruction.* They loved to give instruction, and to tell others what they should do, for this fed their pride and made them look great, and by this craft they got their living; but they hated to receive instruction from God himself, for that would be a check upon them and a mortification to them. "Thou hatest discipline, the reproofs of the word and the rebukes of Providence." No wonder that those who hate to be reformed hate the means of reformation. *Thou castest my words behind thee.* They seemed to set God's words before them, when they sat in Moses's seat, and undertook to teach others out of the law (Rom. ii. 19); but in their conversations they cast God's word behind them, and did not care for seeing that rule which they were resolved not to be ruled by. This is despising the commandment of the Lord. (2.) A close confederacy with the worst of sinners (*v.* 18): "*When thou sawest a thief*, instead of reproving him and witnessing against him, as those should do that declare God's statutes, *thou consentedst with him*, didst approve of his practices, and desire to be a partner with him and to share in the profits of his cursed trade; *and thou hast been partaker with adulterers*, hast done as they did, and encouraged them to go on in their wicked courses, hast done these things and hast *had pleasure in those that do them*," Rom. i. 32. (3.) A constant persisting in the worst of tongue-sins (*v.* 19): "*Thou givest thy mouth to evil*, not only allowest thyself in, but addictest thyself wholly to, all manner of evil-speaking." [1.] Lying: *Thy tongue frames deceit*, which denotes contrivance and deliberation in lying. It *knits* or *links* deceit, so some. One lie begets another, and one fraud requires another to cover it. [2.] Slandering (*v.* 20): "*Thou sittest, and speakest against thy brother*, dost basely abuse and misrepresent him, magisterially judge and censure him, and pass sentence upon him, as if thou wert his master to whom he must stand or fall, whereas he is thy brother, as good as thou art, and upon the level with thee, for he is *thy own mother's son*. He is thy near relation, whom thou oughtest to love, to vindicate, and stand up for, if others abused him; yet thou dost thyself abuse him, whose faults thou oughtest to cover and make the best of; if really he had done amiss, yet thou dost most falsely and unjustly charge him with that which he is innocent of; *thou sittest* and doest this, as a judge upon the bench, with authority; thou sittest in the seat of the scornful, to deride and backbite those whom thou oughtest to respect and be kind to." Those that do ill themselves commonly delight in speaking ill of others.

II. The proof of this charge (*v.* 21): "*These things thou hast done;* the fact is too plain to be denied, the fault too bad to be excused; these things God knows, and thy own heart knows, thou hast done." The sins of sinners will be proved upon them, beyond contradiction, in the judgment of the great day: "*I*

will reprove thee, or convince thee, so that thou shalt have not one word to say for thyself." The day is coming when impenitent sinners will have their mouths for ever stopped and be struck speechless. What confusion will they be filled with when God shall set their sins in order before their eyes! They would not see their sins to their humiliation, but cast them behind their backs, covered them, and endeavoured to forget them, nor would they suffer their own consciences to put them in mind of them; but the day is coming when God will make them see their sins to their everlasting shame and terror; he will set them in order, original sin, actual sins, sins against the law, sins against the gospel, against the first table, against the second table, sins of childhood and youth, of riper age, and old age. He will set them in order, as the witnesses are set in order, and called in order, against the criminal, and asked what they have to say against him.

III. The Judge's patience, and the sinner's abuse of that patience: *I kept silence*, did not give thee any disturbance in thy sinful way, but let thee alone to take thy course; sentence against thy evil works was respited, and not executed speedily." Note, The patience of God is very great towards provoking sinners. He sees their sins and hates them; it would be neither difficulty nor damage to him to punish them, and yet he waits to be gracious and gives them space to repent, that he may render them inexcusable if they repent not. His patience is the more wonderful because the sinner makes such an ill use of it: "*Thou thoughtest that I was altogether such a one as thyself*, as weak and forgetful as thyself, as false to my word as thyself, nay, as much a friend to sin as thyself." Sinners take God's silence for consent and his patience for connivance; and therefore the longer they are reprieved the more are their hearts hardened; but, if they turn not, they shall be made to see their error when it is too late, and that the God they provoke is just, and holy, and terrible, and not such a one as themselves.

IV. The fair warning given of the dreadful doom of hypocrites (*v.* 22): "*Now consider this, you that forget God*, consider that God knows and keeps account of all your sins, that he will call you to an account for them, that patience abused will turn into the greater wrath, that though you forget God and your duty to him he will not forget you and your rebellions against him: consider this in time, before it be too late; for if these things be not considered, and the consideration of them improved, he will *tear you in pieces, and there will be none to deliver*." It is the doom of hypocrites to be *cut asunder*, Matt. xxiv. 51. Note, 1. Forgetfulness of God is at the bottom of all the wickedness of the wicked. Those that know God, and yet do not obey him, do certainly forget him. 2. Those that forget God forget themselves; and it will never be right with them till they consider, and so recover themselves. Consideration is the first step towards conversion. 3. Those that will not consider the warnings of God's word will certainly be torn in pieces by the executions of his wrath. 4. When God comes to tear sinners in pieces, there is no delivering them out of his hand. They cannot deliver themselves, nor can any friend they have in the world deliver them.

V. Full instructions given to us all how to prevent this fearful doom. Let us hear the conclusion of the whole matter; we have it, *v.* 23, which directs us what to do that we may attain our chief end. 1. Man's chief end is to glorify God, and we are here told that *whoso offers praise glorifies him;* whether he be Jew or Gentile, those spiritual sacrifices shall be accepted from him. We must praise God, and we must sacrifice praise, direct it to God, as every sacrifice was directed; put it into the hands of the priest, our Lord Jesus, who is also the altar; see that it be made by fire, sacred fire, that it be kindled with the flame of holy and devout affection; we must be fervent in spirit, praising the Lord. This he is pleased, in infinite condescension, to interpret as glorifying him. Hereby we give him the glory due to his name and do what we can to advance the interests of his kingdom among men. 2. Man's chief end, in conjunction with this, is to enjoy God; and we are here told that those who *order their conversation aright shall see his salvation.* (1.) It is not enough for us to offer praise, but we must withal order our conversation aright. Thanksgiving is good, but thanks-living is better. (2.) Those that would have their conversation right must take care and pains to order it, to dispose it according to rule, to understand their way and to direct it. (3.) Those that take care of their conversation make sure their salvation; them God will make to see his salvation, for it is a salvation ready to be revealed; he will make them to see it and enjoy it, to see it, and to see themselves happy for ever in it. Note, The right ordering of the conversation is the only way, and it is a sure way, to obtain the great salvation.

PSALM LI.

Though David penned this psalm upon a very particular occasion, yet it is of as general use as any of David's psalms; it is the most eminent of the penitential psalms, and most expressive of the cares and desires of a repenting sinner. It is a pity indeed that in our devout addresses to God we should have any thing else to do than to praise God, for that is the work of heaven; but we make other work for ourselves by our own sins and follies: we must come to the throne of grace in the posture of penitents, to confess our sins and sue for the grace of God; and, if therein we would take with us words, we can nowhere find any more apposite than in this psalm, which is the record of David's repentance for his sin in the matter of Uriah, which was the greatest blemish upon his character: all the rest of his faults were nothing to this; it is said of him (1 Kings xv. 5), That "he turned not aside from the commandment of the Lord all the days of his life, save only in the matter of Uriah the Hittite." In this psalm, I. He confesses his sin, ver. 3—6. II. He prays earnestly for the pardon of his sin, ver. 1, 2, 7, 9. III. For peace of conscience, ver. 8, 12. IV. For grace to go and sin no more, ver. 10, 11, 14. V. For liberty of access to God, ver. 15. VI. He promises to do what he could for the good of the souls of others (ver. 13) and for the glory of God, ver. 16, 17, 19. And, lastly, concludes with a prayer for Zion and Jerusalem, ver. 18. Those whose consciences charge them with any gross sin should, with a believing regard to Jesus Christ, the Mediator, again and

again pray over this psalm; nay, though we have not been guilty of adultery and murder, or any the like enormous crime, yet in singing it, and praying over it, we may very sensibly apply it all to ourselves, which if we do with suitable affections we shall, through Christ, find mercy to pardon and grace for seasonable help.

To the chief musician. A psalm of David, when Nathan the prophet came unto him, after he had gone in to Bathsheba.

HAVE mercy upon me, O God, according to thy lovingkindness : according unto the multitude of thy tender mercies blot out my transgressions. 2 Wash me throughly from mine iniquity, and cleanse me from my sin. 3 For I acknowledge my transgressions : and my sin *is* ever before me. 4 Against thee, thee only, have I sinned, and done *this* evil in thy sight : that thou mightest be justified when thou speakest, *and* be clear when thou judgest. 5 Behold, I was shapen in iniquity; and in sin did my mother conceive me. 6 Behold, thou desirest truth in the inward parts : and in the hidden *part* thou shalt make me to know wisdom.

The title has reference to a very sad story, that of David's fall. But, though he fell, he was not utterly cast down, for God graciously upheld him and raised him up. 1. The sin which, in this psalm, he laments, was the folly and wickedness he committed with his neighbour's wife, a sin not to be spoken of, nor thought of, without detestation. His debauching of Bathsheba was the inlet to all the other sins that followed; it was as the letting forth of water. This sin of David's is recorded for warning to all, that he who thinks he stands may take heed lest he fall. 2. The repentance which, in this psalm, he expresses, he was brought to by the ministry of Nathan, who was sent of God to convince him of his sin, after he had continued above nine months (for aught that appears) without any particular expressions of remorse and sorrow for it. But though God may suffer his people to fall into sin, and to lie a great while in it, yet he will, by some means or other, recover them to repentance, bring them to himself and to their right mind again. Herein, generally, he uses the ministry of the word, which yet he is not tied to. But those that have been overtaken in any fault ought to reckon a faithful reproof the greatest kindness that can be done them and a wise reprover their best friend. *Let the righteous smite me, and it shall be excellent oil.* 3. David, being convinced of his sin, poured out his soul to God in prayer for mercy and grace. Whither should backsliding children return, but to the Lord their God, from whom they have backslidden, and who alone can heal their backslidings? 4. He drew up, by divine inspiration, the workings of his heart towards God, upon this occasion,

429

into a psalm, that it might be often repeated, and long after reviewed; and this he committed to the chief musician, to be sung in the public service of the church. (1.) As a profession of his own repentance, which he would have to be generally taken notice of, his sin having been notorious, that the plaster might be as wide as the wound. Those that truly repent of their sins will not be ashamed to own their repentance; but, having lost the honour of innocents, they will rather covet the honour of penitents. (2.) As a pattern to others, both to bring them to repentance by his example and to instruct them in their repentance what to do and what to say. Being converted himself, he thus *strengthens his brethren* (Luke xxii. 32), and *for this cause he obtained mercy*, 1 Tim. i. 16.

In these words we have,

I. David's humble petition, *v.* 1, 2. His prayer is much the same with that which our Saviour puts into the mouth of his penitent publican in the parable: *God be merciful to me a sinner!* Luke xviii. 13. David was, upon many accounts, a man of great merit; he had not only done much, but suffered much, in the cause of God; and yet, when he is convinced of sin, he does not offer to balance his evil deeds with his good deeds, nor can he think that his services will atone for his offences; but he flies to God's infinite mercy, and depends upon that only for pardon and peace: *Have mercy upon me, O God!* He owns himself obnoxious to God's justice, and therefore casts himself upon his mercy; and it is certain that the best man in the world will be undone if God be not merciful to him. Observe,

1. What his plea is for this mercy: "*Have mercy upon me, O God!* not according to the dignity of my birth, as descended from the prince of the tribe of Judah, not according to my public services as Israel's champion, or my public honours as Israel's king;" his plea is not, *Lord, remember David and all his afflictions, how he vowed to build a place for the ark* (cxxxii. 1, 2); a true penitent will make no mention of any such thing; but "Have mercy upon me for mercy's sake. I have nothing to plead with thee but," (1.) "The freeness of thy mercy, according to thy lovingkindness, thy clemency, the goodness of thy nature, which inclines thee to pity the miserable." (2.) "The fulness of thy mercy. There are in thee not only lovingkindness and tender mercies, but abundance of them, a multitude of tender mercies for the forgiveness of many sinners, of many sins, to multiply pardons as we multiply transgressions."

2. What is the particular mercy that he begs—the pardon of sin. *Blot out my transgressions*, as a debt is blotted or crossed out of the book, when either the debtor has paid it or the creditor has remitted it. "Wipe out my transgressions, that they may not appear to demand judgment against me, nor stare

me in the face to my confusion and terror." The blood of Christ, sprinkled upon the conscience, to purify and pacify that, blots out the transgression, and, having reconciled us to God, reconciles us to ourselves, *v.* 2. "*Wash me thoroughly from my iniquity;* wash my soul from the guilt and stain of my sin by thy mercy and grace, for it is only from a ceremonial pollution that the water of separation will avail to cleanse me. Multiply to wash me; the stain is deep, for I have lain long soaking in the guilt, so that it will not easily be got out. O wash me much, wash me thoroughly. *Cleanse me from my sin.*" Sin defiles us, renders us odious in the sight of the holy God, and uneasy to ourselves; it unfits us for communion with God in grace or glory. When God pardons sin he cleanses us from it, so that we become acceptable to him, easy to ourselves, and have liberty of access to him. Nathan had assured David, upon his first profession of repentance, that his sin was pardoned. *The Lord has taken away thy sin; thou shalt not die*, 2 Sam. xii. 13. Yet he prays, *Wash me, cleanse me, blot out my transgressions;* for God will be sought unto even for that which he has promised; and those whose sins are pardoned must pray that the pardon may be more and more cleared up to them. God had forgiven him, but he could not forgive himself; and therefore he is thus importunate for pardon, as one that thought himself unworthy of it and knew how to value it.

II. David's penitential confessions, *v.* 3—5. 1. He was very free to own his guilt before God: *I acknowledge my transgressions;* this he had formerly found the only way of easing his conscience, xxxii. 4, 5. Nathan said, *Thou art the man. I am*, says David; *I have sinned.*

2. He had such a deep sense of it that he was continually thinking of it with sorrow and shame. His contrition for his sin was not a slight sudden passion, but an abiding grief: "*My sin is ever before me*, to humble me and mortify me, and make me continually blush and tremble. It is *ever against me*" (so some); "I see it before me as an enemy, accusing and threatening me." David was, upon all occasions, put in mind of his sin, and was willing to be so, for his further abasement. He never walked on the roof of his house without a penitent reflection on his unhappy walk there when thence he saw Bathsheba; he never lay down to sleep without a sorrowful thought of the bed of his uncleanness, never sat down to meat, never sent his servant on an errand, or took his pen in hand, but it put him in mind of his making Uriah drunk, the treacherous message he sent by him, and the fatal warrant he wrote and signed for his execution. Note, The acts of repentance, even for the same sin, must be often repeated. It will be of good use for us to have our sins ever before us, that by the remembrance of our past sins we may be kept humble, may be armed against temptation,

quickened to duty, and made patient under the cross.

(1.) He confesses his actual transgressions (*v.* 4): *Against thee, thee only, have I sinned.* David was a very great man, and yet, having done amiss, submits to the discipline of a penitent, and thinks not his royal dignity will excuse him from it. Rich and poor must here meet together; there is one law of repentance for both; the greatest must be judged shortly, and therefore must judge themselves now. David was a very good man, and yet, having sinned, he willingly accommodates himself to the place and posture of a penitent. The best men, if they sin, should give the best example of repentance. [1.] His confession is particular: "*I have done this evil,* this that I am now reproved for, this that my own conscience now upbraids me with." Note, It is good to be particular in the confession of sin, that we may be the more express in praying for pardon, and so may have the more comfort in it. We ought to reflect upon the particular heads of our sins of infirmity and the particular circumstances of our gross sins. [2.] He aggravates the sin which he confesses and lays a load upon himself for it: *Against thee, and in thy sight.* Hence our Saviour seems to borrow the confession which he puts into the mouth of the returning prodigal: *I have sinned against heaven, and before thee,* Luke xv. 18. Two things David laments in his sin:—*First,* That it was committed against God. To him the affront is given, and he is the party wronged. It is his truth that by wilful sin we deny, his conduct that we despise, his command that we disobey, his promise that we distrust, his name that we dishonour, and it is with him that we deal deceitfully and disingenuously From this topic Joseph fetched the great argument against sin (Gen. xxxix. 9), and David here the great aggravation of it: *Against thee only.* Some make this to intimate the prerogative of his crown, that, as a king, he was not accountable to any but God; but it is more agreeable to his present temper to suppose that it expresses the deep contrition of his soul for his sin, and that it was upon right grounds. He here sinned against Bathsheba and Uriah, against his own soul, and body, and family, against his kingdom, and against the church of God, and all this helped to humble him; but none of these were sinned against so as God was, and therefore this he lays the most sorrowful accent upon: *Against thee only have I sinned. Secondly,* That it was committed in God's sight. "This not only proves it upon me, but renders it exceedingly sinful." This should greatly humble us for all our sins, that they have been committed under the eye of God, which argues either a disbelief of his omniscience or a contempt of his justice. [3.] He justifies God in the sentence passed upon him—that *the sword should never depart from his house,* 2 Sam. xii. 10,

11. He is very forward to own his sin, and aggravate it, not only that he might obtain the pardon of it himself, but that by his confession he might give honour to God. *First,* That God might be justified in the threatenings he had spoken by Nathan. "Lord, I have nothing to say against the justice of them; I deserve what is threatened, and a thousand times worse." Thus Eli acquiesced in the like threatenings (1 Sam. iii. 18), *It is the Lord.* And Hezekiah (2 Kings xx. 19), *Good is the word of the Lord, which thou hast spoken. Secondly,* That God might be clear when he judged, that is, when he executed those threatenings. David published his confession of sin that when hereafter he should come into trouble none might say God had done him any wrong; for he owns the Lord is righteous: this will all true penitents justify God by condemning themselves. *Thou art just in all that is brought upon us.*

(2.) He confesses his original corruption (*v.* 5): *Behold, I was shapen in iniquity.* He does not call upon God to behold it, but upon himself. "Come, my soul, look unto the rock out of which I was hewn, and thou wilt find I was shapen in iniquity. Had I duly considered this before, I find I should not have made so bold with the temptation, nor have ventured among the sparks with such tinder in my heart; and so the sin might have been prevented. Let me consider it now, not to excuse or extenuate the sin— *Lord, I did so; but indeed I could not help it, my inclination led me to it*" (for as that plea is false, with due care and watchfulness, and improvement of the grace of God, he might have helped it, so it is what a true penitent never offers to put in), "but let me consider it rather as an aggravation of the sin: Lord, I have not only been guilty of adultery and murder, but I have an adulterous murderous nature; therefore I abhor myself." David elsewhere speaks of the admirable structure of his body (cxxxix. 14, 15); it was *curiously wrought;* and yet here he says it was shapen in iniquity, sin was twisted in with it; not as it came out of God's hands, but as it comes through our parents' loins. He elsewhere speaks of the piety of his mother, that she was God's handmaid, and he pleads his relation to her (cxvi. 16, lxxxvi. 16), and yet here he says *she conceived him in sin;* for though she was, by grace, a child of God, she was, by nature, a daughter of Eve, and not excepted from the common character. Note, It is to be sadly lamented by every one of us that we brought into the world with us a corrupt nature, wretchedly degenerated from its primitive purity aud rectitude; we have from our birth the snares of sin in our bodies, the seeds of sin in our souls, and a stain of sin upon both. This is what we call *original sin,* because it is as ancient as our original, and because it is the original of all our actual transgressions. This is that foolishness which is bound in the heart of a child, that proneness to evil and backwardness to good which is the burden of the regenerate and the ruin of the unregenerate; it is a bent to backslide from God.

III. David's acknowledgment of the grace of God (*v.* 6), both his good-will towards us *(thou desirest truth in the inward parts,* thou wouldst have us all honest and sincere, and true to our profession") and his good work in us—" *In the hidden part thou hast made,"* or shalt make, *" me to know wisdom."* Note, 1. Truth and wisdom will go very far towards making a man a good man. A clear head and a sound heart (prudence and sincerity) bespeak the man of God perfect. 2. What God requires of us he himself works in us, and he works it in the regular way, enlightening the mind, and so gaining the will. But how does this come in here? (1.) God is hereby justified and cleared: " Lord, thou wast not the author of my sin; there is no blame to be laid upon thee; but I alone must bear it; for thou hast many a time admonished me to be sincere, and hast made me to know that which, if I had duly considered it, would have prevented my falling into this sin; had I improved the grace thou hast given me, I should have kept my integrity." (2.) The sin is hereby aggravated: " Lord, thou desirest truth; but where was it when I dissembled with Uriah? *Thou hast made me to know wisdom;* but I have not lived up to what I have known." (3.) He is hereby encouraged, in his repentance, to hope that God would graciously accept him; for, [1.] God had made him sincere in his resolutions never to return to folly again: *Thou desirest truth in the inward part;* this is that which God has an eye to in a returning sinner, that *in his spirit there be no guile,* xxxii. 2. David was conscious to himself of the uprightness of his heart towards God in his repentance, and therefore doubted not but God would accept him. [2.] He hoped that God would enable him to make good his resolutions, that in the hidden part, in the new man, which is called the *hidden man of the heart* (1 Pet. iii. 4), he would make him to know wisdom, so as to discern and avoid the designs of the tempter another time. Some read it as a prayer: " Lord, in this instance, I have done foolishly; for the future make me to know wisdom." Where there is truth God will give wisdom; those that sincerely endeavour to do their duty shall be taught their duty.

7 Purge me with hyssop, and I shall be clean : wash me, and I shall be whiter than snow. 8 Make me to hear joy and gladness ; *that* the bones *which* thou hast broken may rejoice. 9 Hide thy face from my sins, and blot out all mine iniquities. 10 Create in me a clean heart, O God; and renew a right spirit within me. 11 Cast me not away from thy presence and

take not thy holy spirit from me. 12 Restore unto me the joy of thy salvation ; and uphold me *with thy* free spirit. 13 *Then* will I teach transgressors thy ways ; and sinners shall be converted unto thee.

I. See here what David prays for. Many excellent petitions he here puts up, to which if we do but add, " for Christ's sake," they are as evangelical as any other.

1. He prays that God would cleanse him from his sins and the defilement he had contracted by them (*v.* 7): *Purge me with hyssop;* that is, pardon my sins, and let me know that they are pardoned, that I may be restored to those privileges which by sin I have forfeited and lost." The expression here alludes to a ceremonial distinction, that of cleansing the leper, or those that were unclean by the touch of a body by sprinkling water, or blood, or both upon them with a bunch of hyssop, by which they were, at length, discharged from the restraints they were laid under by their pollution. " Lord, let me be as well assured of my restoration to thy favour, and to the privilege of communion with thee, as they were thereby assured of their re-admission to their former privileges." But it is founded upon gospel-grace : *Purge me with hyssop,* that is, with the blood of Christ applied to my soul by a lively faith, as water of purification was sprinkled with a bunch of hyssop. It is the blood of Christ (which is therefore called *the blood of sprinkling,* Heb. xii. 24), that purges the conscience from dead works, from that guilt of sin and dread of God which shut us out of communion with him, as the touch of a dead body, under the law, shut a man out from the courts of God's house. If this blood of Christ, which cleanses from all sin, cleanse us from our sin, then we shall be clean indeed, Heb. x. 2. If we be washed in this fountain opened, we shall be whiter than snow, not only acquitted but accepted; so those are that are justified. Isa. i. 18, *Though your sins have been as scarlet, they shall be white as snow.*

2. He prays that, his sins being pardoned, he might have the comfort of that pardon. He asks not to be comforted till first he is cleansed; but if sin, the bitter root of sorrow, be taken away, he can pray in faith, " *Make me to hear joy and gladness* (*v.* 8), that is, let me have a well-grounded peace, of thy creating, thy speaking, so that the bones which thou hast broken by convictions and threatenings may rejoice, may not only be set again, and eased from the pain, but may be sensibly comforted, and, as the prophet speaks, may flourish as a herb." Note, (1.) The pain of a heart truly broken for sin may well be compared to that of a broken bone ; and it is the same Spirit who as a Spirit of bondage smites and wounds and **as a**

Spirit of adoption heals and binds up. (2.) The comfort and joy that arise from a sealed pardon to a penitent sinner are as refreshing as perfect ease from the most exquisite pain. (3.) It is God's work, not only to speak this joy and gladness, but to make us hear it and take the comfort of it. He earnestly desires that God would lift up the light of his countenance upon him, and so put gladness into his heart, that he would not only be reconciled to him, but, which is a further act of grace, let him know that he was so.

3. He prays for a complete and effectual pardon. This is that which he is most earnest for as the foundation of his comfort (*v.* 9): "*Hide thy face from my sins*, that is, be not provoked by them to deal with me as I deserve; they are ever before me, let them be cast behind thy back. *Blot out all my iniquities* out of the book of thy account; blot them out, as a cloud is blotted out and dispelled by the beams of the sun," Isa. xliv. 22.

4. He prays for sanctifying grace; and this every true penitent is as earnest for as for pardon and peace, *v.* 10. He does not pray, "Lord, preserve me my reputation," as Saul, *I have sinned, yet honour me before this people.* No; his great concern is to get his corrupt nature changed: the sin he had been guilty of was, (1.) An evidence of its impurity, and therefore he prays, *Create in me a clean heart, O God!* He now saw, more than ever, what an unclean heart he had, and sadly laments it, but sees it is not in his own power to amend it, and therefore begs of God (whose prerogative it is to create) that he would create in him a clean heart. He only that made the heart can new-make it; and to his power nothing is impossible. He created the world by the word of his power as the God of nature, and it is by the word of his power as the God of grace that *we are clean* (John xv. 3), that we *are sanctified*, John xvii. 17. (2.) It was the cause of its disorder, and undid much of the good work that had been wrought in him; and therefore he prays, "*Lord, renew a right spirit within me;* repair the decays of spiritual strength which this sin has been the cause of, and set me to rights again. Renew a *constant* spirit within me, so some. He had, in this matter, discovered much inconstancy and inconsistency with himself, and therefore he prays, "Lord, fix me for the time to come, that I may never in like manner depart from thee."

5. He prays for the continuance of God's good-will towards him and the progress of his good work in him, *v.* 11. (1.) That he might never be shut out from God's favour: "*Cast me not away from thy presence,* as one whom thou abhorrest and canst not endure to look upon." He prays that he might not be thrown out of God's protection, but that, wherever he went, he might have the divine presence with him, might be under the guidance of his wisdom and in the custody of his power, and that he might not be forbid-

den communion with God: "Let me not be banished thy courts, but always have liberty of access to thee by prayer." He does not deprecate the temporal judgments which God by Nathan had threatened to bring upon him. "God's will be done; but, Lord, rebuke me not in thy wrath. If the sword come into my house never to depart from it, yet let me have a God to go to in my distresses, and all shall be well." (2.) That he might never be deprived of God's grace: *Take not thy Holy Spirit from me.* He knew he had by his sin grieved the Spirit and provoked him to withdraw, and that because he also was flesh God might justly have said that his Spirit should no more strive with him nor work upon him, Gen. vi. 3. This he dreads more than any thing. We are undone if God take his Holy Spirit from us. Saul was a sad instance of this. How exceedingly sinful, how exceedingly miserable, was he, when the Spirit of the Lord had departed from him! David knew it, and therefore begs thus earnestly: "Lord, whatever thou take from me, my children, my crown, my life, yet *take not thy Holy Spirit from me*" (see 2 Sam. vii. 15), "but continue thy Holy Spirit with me, to perfect the work of my repentance, to prevent my relapse into sin, and to enable me to discharge my duty both as a prince and as a psalmist."

6. He prays for the restoration of divine comforts and the perpetual communications of divine grace, *v.* 12. David finds two ill effects of his sin:—(1.) It had made him sad, and therefore he prays, *Restore unto me the joy of thy salvation.* A child of God knows no true nor solid joy but the joy of God's salvation, joy in God his Saviour and in the hope of eternal life. By wilful sin we forfeit this joy and deprive ourselves of it; our evidences cannot but be clouded and our hopes shaken. When we give ourselves so much cause to doubt of our interest in the salvation, how can we expect the joy of it? But, when we truly repent, we may pray and hope that God will restore to us those joys. Those that sow in penitential tears shall reap in the joys of God's salvation when the times of refreshing shall come. (2.) It had made him weak, and therefore he prays, "*Uphold me with thy free Spirit:* I am ready to fall, either into sin or into despair; Lord, sustain me; my own spirit" (though the spirit of a man will go far towards the sustaining of his infirmity) "is not sufficient; if I be left to myself, I shall certainly sink; therefore uphold me with thy Spirit, let him counterwork the evil spirit that would cast me down from my excellency. Thy Spirit is a free spirit, a free agent himself, working freely" (and that makes those free whom he works upon, for where the Spirit of the Lord is there is liberty)—"thy ingenuous princely Spirit." He was conscious to himself of having acted, in the matter of Uriah, very disingenuously and unlike a prince; his be-

433

haviour was base and paltry; "Lord," says he, "let thy Spirit inspire my soul with noble and generous principles, that I may always act as becomes me." A free spirit will be a firm and fixed spirit, and will uphold us. The more cheerful we are in our duty the more constant we shall be to it.

II. See what David here promises, *v.* 13. Observe,

1. What good work he promises to do: *I will teach transgressors thy ways.* David had been himself a transgressor, and therefore could speak experimentally to transgressors, and resolves, having himself found mercy with God in the way of repentance, to teach others God's ways, that is, (1.) Our way to God by repentance; he would teach others that had sinned to take the same course that he had taken, to humble themselves, to confess their sins, and seek God's face; and, (2.) God's way towards us in pardoning mercy; how ready he is to receive those that return to him. He taught the former by his own example, for the direction of sinners in repenting; he taught the latter by his own experience, for their encouragement. By this psalm he is, and will be to the world's end, teaching transgressors, telling them what God had done for his soul. Note, Penitents should be preachers. Solomon was so, and blessed Paul.

2. What good effect he promises himself from his doing this: "*Sinners shall be converted unto thee,* and shall neither persist in their wanderings from thee, nor despair of finding mercy in their returns to thee." The great thing to be aimed at in teaching transgressors is their conversion to God; that is a happy point gained, and happy are those that are instrumental to contribute towards it, Jam. v. 20.

14 Deliver me from bloodguiltiness, O God, thou God of my salvation: *and* my tongue shall sing aloud of thy righteousness. 15 O Lord, open thou my lips; and my mouth shall show forth thy praise. 16 For thou desirest not sacrifice; else would I give *it :* thou delightest not in burnt offering. 17 The sacrifices of God *are* a broken spirit: a broken and a contrite heart, O God, thou wilt not despise. 18 Do good in thy good pleasure unto Zion : build thou the walls of Jerusalem. 19 Then shalt thou be pleased with the sacrifices of righteousness, with burnt offering and whole burnt offering : then shall they offer bullocks upon thine altar.

I. David prays against the guilt of sin, and prays for the grace of God, enforcing both petitions from a plea taken from the glory of God, which he promises with thankfulness to show forth. 1. He prays against the guilt of sin, that he might be delivered from that, and promises that then he would praise God, *v.* 14. The particular sin he prays against is blood-guiltiness, the sin he had now been guilty of, having slain Uriah with the sword of the children of Ammon. Hitherto perhaps he had stopped the mouth of conscience with that frivolous excuse, that he did not kill him himself; but now he was convinced that he was the murderer, and, hearing the blood cry to God for vengeance, he cries to God for mercy: "*Deliver me from blood-guiltiness;* let me not lie under the guilt of this kind which I have contracted, but let it be pardoned to me, and let me never be left to myself to contract the like guilt again." Note, It concerns us all to pray earnestly against the guilt of blood. In this prayer he eyes God as the God of salvation. Note, Those to whom God is the God of salvation he will deliver from guilt; for the salvation he is the God of is salvation from sin. We may therefore plead this with him, "Lord, thou art the God of my salvation, therefore deliver me from the dominion of sin." He promises that, if God would deliver him, *his tongue should sing aloud of his righteousness;* God should have the glory both of pardoning mercy and of preventing grace. God's righteousness is often put for his grace, especially in the great business of justification and sanctification. This he would comfort himself in and therefore sing of; and this he would endeavour both to acquaint and to affect others with; he would *sing aloud* of it. This all those should do that have had the benefit of it, and owe their all to it. 2. He prays for the grace of God and promises to improve that grace to his glory (*v.* 15): "*O Lord ! open thou my lips,* not only that I may teach and instruct sinners" (which the best preacher cannot do to any purpose unless God give him the opening of the mouth, and the tongue of the learned), "but *that my mouth may show forth thy praise,* not only that I may have abundant matter for praise, but a heart enlarged in praise." Guilt had closed his lips, had gone near to stop the mouth of prayer; he could not for shame, he could not for fear, come into the presence of that God whom he knew he had offended, much less speak to him; his heart condemned him, and therefore he had little confidence towards God. It cast a damp particularly upon his praises; when he had lost the joys of his salvation his harp was hung upon the willow-trees; therefore he prays, "*Lord, open my lips,* put my heart in tune for praise again." To those that are tongue-tied by reason of guilt the assurance of the forgiveness of their sins says effectually, *Ephphatha—Be opened;* and, when the lips are opened, what should they speak but the praises of God, as Zacharias did ? Luke i. 64.

II. David offers the sacrifice of a penitent contrite heart, as that which he knew God would be pleased with. 1. He knew well that the sacrificing of beasts was in itself of no account with God (*v.* 16): *Thou desirest not sacrifice (else would I give it* with all my heart to obtain pardon and peace); *thou delightest not in burnt-offering.* Here see how glad David would have been to give thousands of rams to make atonement for sin. Those that are thoroughly convinced of their misery and danger by reason of sin would spare no cost to obtain the remission of it, Mic. vi. 6, 7. But see how little God valued this. As trials of obedience, and types of Christ, he did indeed require sacrifices to be offered; but he had no delight in them for any intrinsic worth or value they had. *Sacrifice and offering thou wouldst not.* As they cannot make satisfaction for sin, so God cannot take any satisfaction in them, any otherwise than as the offering of them is expressive of love and duty to him. 2. He knew also how acceptable true repentance is to God (*v.* 17): *The sacrifices of God are a broken spirit.* See here, (1.) What the good work is that is wrought in every true penitent—a broken spirit, a broken and a contrite heart. It is a work wrought upon the heart; that is it that God looks at, and requires, in all religious exercises, particularly in the exercises of repentance. It is a sharp work wrought there, no less than the breaking of the heart; not in despair (as we say, when a man is undone, His heart is broken), but in necessary humiliation and sorrow for sin. It is a heart breaking with itself, and breaking from its sin; it is a heart pliable to the word of God, and patient under the rod of God, a heart subdued and brought into obedience; it is a heart that is tender, like Josiah's, and trembles at God's word. Oh that there were such a heart in us! (2.) How graciously God is pleased to accept of this. It is *the sacrifices of God*, not one, but many; it is instead of all burnt-offering and sacrifice. The breaking of Christ's body for sin is the only sacrifice of atonement, for no sacrifice but that could take away sin; but the breaking of our hearts for sin is a sacrifice of acknowledgment, a sacrifice of God, for to him it is offered up; he requires it, he prepares it (he provides this lamb for a burnt-offering), and he will accept of it. That which pleased God was not the feeding of a beast, and making much of it, but killing it; so it is not the pampering of our flesh, but the mortifying of it, that God will accept. The sacrifice was bound, was bled, was burnt; so the penitent heart is bound by convictions, bleeds in contrition, and then burns in holy zeal against sin and for God. The sacrifice was offered upon the altar that sanctified the gift; so the broken heart is acceptable to God only through Jesus Christ; there is no true repentance without faith in him; and this is the sacrifice which he will not despise. Men despise that which is broken, but God will not. He despised the sacrifice of torn and broken beasts, but he will not despise

that of a torn and broken heart. He will not overlook it; he will not refuse or reject it; though it make God no satisfaction for the wrong done him by sin, yet he does not despise it. The proud Pharisee despised the broken-hearted publican, and he thought very meanly of himself; but God did not despise him. More is implied than is expressed; the great God overlooks heaven and earth, to look with favour upon a *broken and contrite heart*, Isa. lxvi. 1, 2; lvii. 15.

III. David intercedes for Zion and Jerusalem, with an eye to the honour of God. See what a concern he had,

1. For the good of the church of God (*v.* 18): *Do good in thy good pleasure unto Zion*, that is, (1.) "To all the particular worshippers in Zion, to all that love and fear thy name; keep them from falling into such wounding wasting sins as these of mine; defend and succour all that fear thy name." Those that have been in spiritual troubles themselves know how to pity and pray for those that are in like manner afflicted. Or, (2.) To the public interests of Israel. David was sensible of the wrong he had done to Judah and Jerusalem by his sin, how it had weakened the hands and saddened the hearts of good people, and opened the mouths of their adversaries; he was likewise afraid lest, he being a public person, his sin might bring judgments upon the city and kingdom, and therefore he prays to God to secure and advance those public interests which he had damaged and endangered. He prays that God would prevent those national judgments which his sin had deserved, that he would continue those blessings, and carry on that good work, which it had threatened to retard and put a stop to. He prays, not only that God would do good to Zion, as he did to other places, by his providence, but that he would do it in his *good pleasure*, with the peculiar favour he bore to that place which he had chosen to put his name there, that the walls of Jerusalem, which perhaps were now in the building, might be built up, and that good work finished. Note, [1.] When we have most business of our own, and of greatest importance at the throne of grace, yet then we must not forget to pray for the church of God; nay, our Master has taught us in our daily prayers to begin with that, *Hallowed be thy name, Thy kingdom come.* [2.] The consideration of the prejudice we have done to the public interests by our sins should engage us to do them all the service we can, particularly by our prayers.

2. For the honour of the churches of God, *v.* 19. If God would show himself reconciled to him and his people, as he had prayed, then they should go on with the public services of his house, (1.) Cheerfully to themselves. The sense of God's goodness to them would enlarge their hearts in all the instances and expressions of thankfulness and obedience. They will then come to his tabernacle with

burnt-offerings, with whole burnt-offerings, which were intended purely for the glory of God, and they shall offer, not lambs and rams only, but bullocks, the costliest sacrifices, upon his altar. (2.) Acceptably to God: *"Thou shalt be pleased with them,* that is, we shall have reason to hope so when we perceive the sin taken away which threatened to hinder thy acceptance."* Note, It is a great comfort to a good man to think of the communion that is between God and his people in their public assemblies, how he is honoured by their humble attendance on him and they are happy in his gracious acceptance of it.

PSALM LII.

David, no doubt, was in very great grief when he said to Abiathar (1 Sam. xxii. 22), "I have occasioned the death of all the persons of thy father's house," who were put to death upon Doeg's malicious information; to give some vent to that grief, and to gain some relief to his mind under it, he penned this psalm, wherein, as a prophet, and therefore with as good an authority as if he had been now a prince upon the throne, I. He arraigns Doeg for what he had done, ver. 1. II. He accuses him, convicts him, and aggravates his crimes, ver. 2—4. III. He passes sentence upon him, ver. 5. IV. He foretels the triumphs of the righteous in the execution of the sentence, ver. 6, 7. V. He comforts himself in the mercy of God and the assurance he had that he should yet praise him, ver. 8, 9. In singing this psalm we should conceive a detestation of the sin of lying, foresee the ruin of those that persist in it, and please ourselves with the assurance of the preservation of God's church and people, in spite of all the malicious designs of the children of Satan, that father of lies.

To the chief musician, Maschil. *A psalm of* David, when Doeg the Edomite came and told Saul, and said unto him, David has come to the house of Ahimelech.

WHY boastest thou thyself in mischief, O mighty man ? the goodness of God *endureth* continually. 2 Thy tongue deviseth mischiefs; like a sharp razor, working deceitfully. 3 Thou lovest evil more than good; *and* lying rather than to speak righteousness. Selah. 4 Thou lovest all devouring words, O *thou* deceitful tongue. 5 God shall likewise destroy thee for ever, he shall take thee away, and pluck thee out of *thy* dwelling place, and root thee out of the land of the living. Selah.

The title is a brief account of the story which the psalm refers to. David now, at length, saw it necessary to quit the court, and shift for his own safety, for fear of Saul, who had once and again attempted to murder him. Being unprovided with arms and victuals, he, by a wile, got Ahimelech the priest to furnish him with both. Doeg an Edomite happened to be there, and he went and informed Saul against Ahimelech, representing him as confederate with a traitor, upon which accusation Saul grounded a very bloody warrant, to kill all the priests; and Doeg, the prosecutor, was the executioner, 1 Sam. xxii. 9, &c. In these verses,

I David argues the case fairly with this proud and mighty man, *v.* 1. Doeg, it is probable, was mighty in respect of bodily strength; but, if he was, he gained no reputation to it by his easy victory over the unarmed priests of the Lord; it is no honour for those that wear a sword to hector those that wear an ephod. However, he was, by his office, a *mighty man,* for he was set over the servants of Saul, chamberlain of the household. This was he that boasted himself, not only in the power he had to do mischief, but in the mischief he did. Note, It is bad to do ill, but it is worse to boast of it and glory in it when we have done, not only not to be ashamed of a wicked action, but to justify it, not only to justify it, but to magnify it and value ourselves upon it. Those that glory in their sin glory in their shame, and then it becomes yet more shameful ; mighty men are often mischievous men, and *boast of their heart's desire,* x. 3. It is uncertain how the following words come in: *The goodness of God endures continually.* Some make it the wicked man's answer to this question. The patience and forbearance of God (those great proofs of his goodness) are abused by sinners to the hardening of their hearts in their wicked ways; because sentence against their evil works is not executed speedily, nay, because God is continually doing them good, therefore they boast in mischief; as if their prosperity in their wickedness were an evidence that there is no harm in it. But it is rather to be taken as an argument against him, to show, 1. The sinfulness of his sin : " God is continually doing good, and those that therein are like him have reason to glory in their being so ; but thou art continually doing mischief, and therein art utterly unlike him, and contrary to him, and yet gloriest in being so." 2. The folly of it: "Thou thinkest, with the mischief which thou boastest of (so artfully contrived and so successfully carried on), to run down and ruin the people of God ; but thou wilt find thyself mistaken : *the goodness of God endures continually* for their preservation, and then they need *not fear what man can do unto them."* The enemies in vain boast in their mischief while we have God's mercy to boast in.

II. He draws up a high charge against him in the court of heaven, as he had drawn up a high charge against Ahimelech in Saul's court, *v.* 2—4. He accuses him of the wickedness of his tongue (that unruly evil, full of deadly poison) and the wickedness of his heart, which that was an evidence of. Four things he charges him with:—1. Malice. His tongue does *mischief,* not only pricking like a needle, but cutting *like a sharp razor.* Scornful bantering words would not content him ; he loved devouring words, words that would ruin the priests of the Lord, whom he hated. 2. Falsehood. It was a *deceitful tongue* that he did this mischief with (*v.* 4); he loved lying (*v.* 3), and this sharp razor did *work deceitfully* (*v.* 2), that is, before he had this occasion given him to discover his malice against the priests, he had acted very plausibly towards them ; though he was an Edomite, he attended the altars, and brought his offerings, and paid his respects to the priests, as decently as any Israelite ; therein he put a force upon himself (for he was *detained before the Lord*), but thus he gained an opportunity of doing them so much the greater mischief. Or it may refer to the information itself which he gave in against Ahimelech ; for the matter of fact was, in substance, true, yet it was misrepresented, and false colours were put upon it, and therefore he might well be said to love lying, and to have a deceitful tongue. He told the truth, but not all the truth, as a witness ought to do; had he told that David made Ahimelech believe he was then going upon Saul's errand, the kindness he showed him would have appeared to be not only not traitorous against Saul, but respectful to him. It will not save us from the guilt of lying to be able to say, "There was some truth in what we said," if we pervert it, and make it to appear otherwise than it was. 3. Subtlety in sin : "*Thy tongue devises mischiefs;* that is, it speaks the mischief which thy heart devises." The more there is of craft and contrivance in any wickedness the more there is of the devil in it. 4. Affection to sin : "*Thou lovest evil more than good;* that is, thou lovest evil, and hast no love at all to that which is good; thou takest delight in lying, and makest no conscience of doing right. Thou wouldst rather please Saul by telling a lie than please God by speaking truth." Those are of Doeg's spirit who, instead of being pleased (as we ought all to be) with an opportunity of doing a man a kindness in his body, estate, or good name, are glad when they have a fair occasion to do a man a mischief, and readily close with an opportunity of that kind ; that is loving evil more than good. It is bad to speak devouring words, but it is worse to love them either in others or in ourselves.

III. He reads his doom and denounces the judgments of God against him for his wickedness (*v.* 5): "Thou hast destroyed the priests of the Lord and cut them off, and therefore *God shall likewise destroy thee for ever.*" Sons of perdition actively shall be sons of perdition passively, as Judas and the man of sin. Destroyers shall be destroyed; those especially that hate, and persecute, and destroy the priests of the Lord, his ministers and people, who are made to our God priests, a royal priesthood, shall be taken away with a swift and everlasting destruction. Doeg is here condemned, 1. To be driven out of the church: *He shall pluck thee out of the tabernacle*, not thy dwelling-place, but God's (so it is most probably understood) ; " thou shalt be cut off from the favour of God, and his presence, and all communion with him, and shalt have no benefit either by oracle or offering." Justly was he deprived of all the privileges of God's house who had been so mischievous to his servants ; he had come sometimes to God's tabernacle, and attended in his courts, but he was detained there ; he was weary of his service, and sought an opportunity to defame his family ; it was very fit therefore that he should be taken away, and plucked out thence ; we should forbid any one our house that should serve us so. Note, We forfeit the benefit of ordinances if we make an ill use of them. 2. To be driven out of the world : "*He shall root thee out of the land of the living*, in which thou thoughtest thyself so deeply rooted." When good men die they are transplanted from the land of the living on earth, the nursery of the plants of righteousness, to that in heaven, the garden of the Lord, where they shall take root for ever ; but, when wicked men die, they are rooted out of the land of the living, to perish for ever, as fuel to the fire of divine wrath. This will be the portion of those that contend with God.

6 The righteous also shall see, and fear, and shall laugh at him : 7 Lo, *this is* the man *that* made not God his strength ; but trusted in the abundance of his riches, *and* strengthened himself in his wickedness. 8 But I *am* like a green olive tree in the house of God : I trust in the mercy of God for ever and ever. 9 I will praise thee for ever, because thou hast done *it :* and I will wait on thy name ; for *it is* good before thy saints.

David was at this time in great distress ; the mischief Doeg had done him was but the beginning of his sorrows ; and yet here we have him triumphing, and that is more than rejoicing, in tribulation. Blessed Paul, in the midst of his troubles, is in the midst of his triumphs, 2 Cor. ii. 14. David here triumphs,

I. In the fall of Doeg. Yet, lest this should look like personal revenge, he does not speak of it as his own act, but the language of other righteous persons. They shall observe God's judgments on Doeg, and speak of them, 1. To the glory of God : *They shall see and fear* (*v.* 6) ; that is, they shall reverence the justice of God, and stand in awe of him, as a God of almighty power, before whom the proudest sinner cannot stand and before whom therefore we ought every one of us to humble ourselves. Note, God's judgments on the wicked should strike an awe upon the righteous and make them afraid of offending God and incurring his displeasure, cxix. 120 ; Rev. xv. 3, 4. 2. To the shame of Doeg. They shall laugh at him, not with a ludicrous, but a rational serious laughter, as *he that sits in heaven shall laugh at him*, ii. 4. He shall appear ridiculous, and worthy to be laughed at. We are told how they shall triumph in God's just judgments on him (*v.* 7): *Lo, this is the man that made not God his strength.* The fall and ruin of a wealthy mighty man cannot but be generally taken notice of, and every one is apt to make his remarks upon it ; now this is the remark which the righteous should make upon Doeg's fall, that no better could come of it, since he took the wrong method of establishing himself in his wealth and power.

If a newly-erected fabric tumbles down, every one immediately enquires where was the fault in the building of it. Now that which ruined Doeg's prosperity was, (1.) That he did not build it upon a rock : *He made not God his strength,* that is, he did not think that the continuance of his prosperity depended upon the favour of God, and therefore took no care to make sure that favour nor to keep himself in God's love, made no conscience of his duty to him nor sought him in the least. Those wretchedly deceive themselves that think to support themselves in their power and wealth without God and religion. (2.) That he did build it upon the sand. He thought his wealth would support itself : *He trusted in the abundance of his riches,* which, he imagined, were *laid up for many years ;* nay, he thought his wickedness would help to support it. He was resolved to stick at nothing for the securing and advancing of his honour and power. Right or wrong, he would get what he could and keep what he had, and be the ruin of any one that stood in his way ; and this, he thought, would strengthen him. Those may have any thing that will make conscience of nothing. But now see what it comes to ; see what untempered mortar he built his house with, now that it has fallen and he is himself buried in the ruins of it.

II. In his own stability, *v.* 8, 9. "This mighty man is plucked up by the roots ; *but I am like a green olive-tree,* planted and rooted, fixed and flourishing ; he is turned out of God's dwelling-place, but I am established in it, not detained, as Doeg, by any thing but the abundant satisfaction I meet with there." Note, Those that by faith and love dwell in the house of God shall be like green olive-trees there ; the wicked are said to flourish like a green bay-tree (xxxvii. 35), which bears no useful fruit, though it has abundance of large leaves ; but the righteous flourish like a green olive-tree, which is fat as well as flourishing (xcii. 14) and with *its fatness honours God and man* (Judg. ix. 9), deriving its root and fatness from the good olive, Rom. xi. 17. Now what must we do that we may be as green olive-trees ? 1. We must live a life of faith and holy confidence in God and his grace : " I see what comes of men's trusting in the abundance of their riches, and therefore *I trust in the mercy of God for ever and ever*—not in the world, but in God, not in my own merit, but in God's mercy, which dispenses its gifts freely, even to the unworthy, and has in it an all-sufficiency to be our portion and happiness." This mercy is for ever ; it is constant and unchangeable, and its gifts will continue to all eternity. We must therefore for ever trust in it, and never come off from that foundation. 2. We must live a life of thankfulness and holy joy in God (*v.* 9): "*I will praise thee for ever, because thou hast done it,* hast avenged the blood of thy priests upon their bloody enemy, and given him blood to drink,

and hast performed thy promise to me," which he was as sure would be done in due time as if it were done already. It contributes very much to the beauty of our profession, and to our fruitfulness in every grace, to be much in praising God ; and it is certain that we never want matter for praise. 3. We must live a life of expectation and humble dependence upon God : "*I will wait on thy name ;* I will attend upon thee in all those ways wherein thou hast made thyself known, hoping for the discoveries of thy favour to me and willing to tarry till the time appointed for them ; *for it is good before thy saints,*" or *in the opinion and judgment of thy saints,* with whom David heartily concurs. *Communis sensus fidelium*—*All the saints are of this mind,* (1.) That God's name is good in itself, that God's manifestations of himself to his people are gracious and very kind ; there is no other name given than his that can be our refuge and strong tower. (2.) That it is very good for us to wait on that name, that there is nothing better to calm and quiet our spirits when they are ruffled and disturbed, and to keep us in the way of duty when we are tempted to use any indirect courses for our own relief, than to *hope and quietly wait for the salvation of the Lord,* Lam. iii. 26. All the saints have experienced the benefit of it, who never attended him in vain, never followed his guidance but it ended well, nor were ever made ashamed of their believing expectations from him. What is good before all the saints let us therefore abide and abound in, and in this particularly : *Turn thou to thy God ; keep mercy and judgment, and wait on thy God continually,* Hos. xii. 6.

PSALM LIII.

God speaks once, yea, twice, and it were well if man would even then perceive it ; God, in this psalm, speaks twice, for this is the same almost verbatim with the fourteenth psalm. The scope of it is to convince us of our sins, to set us a blushing and trembling because of them ; and this is what we are with so much difficulty brought to that there is need of line upon line to this purport. The word, as a convincing word, is compared to a hammer, the strokes whereof must be frequently repeated. God, by the psalmist here, I. Shows us how bad we are, ver. 1. II. Proves it upon us by his own certain knowledge, ver. 2, 3. III. He speaks terror to persecutors, the worst of sinners, ver. 4, 5. IV. He speaks encouragement to God's persecuted people, ver. 6. Some little variation there is between Ps. xiv. and this, but none considerable, only between ver. 5, 6, there, and ver. 5 here ; some expressions there used are here left out, concerning the shame which the wicked put upon God's people, and, instead of that, is here foretold the shame which God would put upon the wicked, which alteration, with some others, he made by divine direction when he delivered it the second time to the chief musician. In singing it we ought to lament the corruption of the human nature, and the wretched degeneracy of the world we live in, yet rejoicing in hope of the great salvation.

To the chief musician upon Mahalath, Maschil. *A psalm* of David.

THE fool hath said in his heart, *There is* no God. Corrupt are they, and have done abominable iniquity : *there is* none that doeth good. 2 God looked down from heaven upon the children of men, to see if there were *any* that did understand, that did seek God. 3 Every one of them is gone back : they are altogether become filthy; *there is* none that doeth good, no, not one. 4 Have the workers of iniquity no knowledge? who eat up my people *as* they eat bread : they have not called upon God. 5 There were they in great fear, *where* no fear was: for God hath scattered the bones of him that encampeth *against* thee : thou hast put *them* to shame, because God hath despised them. 6 Oh that the salvation of Israel *were come* out of Zion! When God bringeth back the captivity of his people, Jacob shall rejoice, *and* Israel shall be glad.

This psalm was opened before, and therefore we shall here only observe, in short, some things concerning sin, in order to the increasing of our sorrow for it and hatred of it. 1. The fact of sin. Is that proved? Can the charge be made out? Yes, God is a witness to it, an unexceptionable witness: from the place of his holiness he looks on the children of men, and sees how little good there is among them, *v.* 2. All the sinfulness of their hearts and lives is naked and open before him. 2. The fault of sin. Is there any harm in it? Yes, it is iniquity (*v.* 1, 4); it is an unrighteous thing; it is that which there is no good in (*v.* 1, 3); it is an evil thing; it is the worst of evils; it is that which makes this world such an evil world as it is; it is going back from God, *v.* 3. 3. The fountain of sin. How comes it that men are so bad? Surely it is because *there is no fear of God before their eyes: they say in their hearts,* " *There is no God* at all to call us to an account, none that we need to stand in awe of." Men's bad practices flow from their bad principles; if they profess to know God, yet in works, because in thoughts, they deny him. 4. The folly of sin. He is a fool (in the account of God, whose judgment we are sure is right) that harbours such corrupt thoughts. Atheists, whether in opinion or practice, are the greatest fools in the world. Those that do not seek God do not understand; they are like brute-beasts that have no understanding; for man is distinguished from the brutes, not so much by the powers of reason as by a capacity for religion. *The workers of iniquity,* whatever they pretend to, *have no knowledge;* those may truly be said to know nothing that do not know God, *v.* 4. 5. The filthiness of sin. Sinners are corrupt (*v.* 1); their nature is vitiated and spoiled, and the more noble the nature is the more vile it is when it is depraved, as that of the angels. *Corruptio optimi est pessima—The best things, when corrupted, become the worst.* Their iniquity is abominable; it is odious to the holy God, and it renders them so; whereas otherwise he *hates nothing that he has made.* It makes men filthy, altogether filthy. Wilful sinners are offensive in the nostrils of the God of

heaven and of the holy angels. What decency soever proud sinners pretend to, it is certain that wickedness is the greatest defilement in the world. 6. The fruit of sin. See to what a degree of barbarity it brings men at last; when men's hearts are hardened through the deceitfulness of sin see their cruelty to their brethren, that are bone of their bone—because they will not *run with them to the same excess of riot,* they *eat them up as they eat bread;* as if they had not only become beasts, but beasts of prey. And see their contempt of God at the same time. *They have not called upon* him, but scorn to be beholden to him. 7. The fear and shame that attend sin (*v.* 5): *There were those in great fear* who had made God their enemy; their own guilty consciences frightened them, and filled them with horror, though otherwise there was no apparent cause of fear. *The wicked flees when none pursues.* See the ground of this fear; it is because God has formerly *scattered the bones of those that encamped against* his people, not only broken their power and dispersed their forces, but slain them, and reduced their bodies to dry bones, like those *scattered at the grave's mouth,* cxli. 7. Such will be the fate of those that lay siege to the *camp of the saints and the beloved city,* Rev. xx. 9. The apprehensions of this cannot but put those into frights that eat up God's people. This enables the virgin, the daughter of Zion, to put them to shame, and expose them, *because God has despised them,* to laugh at them, because he that sits in heaven laughs at them. We need not look upon those enemies with fear whom God looks upon with contempt. If he despises them, we may. 8. The faith of the saints, and their hope and power touching the cure of this great evil, *v.* 6. There will come a Saviour, a great salvation, a salvation from sin. Oh that it might be hastened! for it will bring in glorious and joyful times. There were those in the Old-Testament times that looked and hoped, that prayed and waited, for this redemption. (1.) God will, in due time, save his church from the sinful malice of its enemies, which will bring joy to Jacob and Israel, that have long been in a mournful melancholy state. Such salvations were often wrought, and all typical of the everlasting triumphs of the glorious church. (2.) He will save all believers from their own iniquities, that they may not be led captive by them, which will be everlasting matter of joy to them. From this work the Redeemer had his name—*Jesus,* for *he shall save his people from their sins,* Matt. i. 21.

PSALM LIV.

The key of this psalm hangs at the door, for the title tells us upon what occasion it was penned—when the inhabitants of Ziph, men of Judah (types of Judas the traitor), betrayed David to Saul, by informing him where he was and putting him in a way how to seize him. This they did twice (1 Sam. xxiii. 19; xxvi. 1), and it is upon record to their everlasting infamy. The psalm is sweet; the former part of it, perhaps, was meditated when he was in his distress and put into writing when the danger was over, with the addition of the last two verses, which express his thankfulness for the deliverance, which yet might be written in faith, even when he was in the midst of his fright. Here, 1. He complains to God of the malice of his enemies, and prays for help against them, ver. 1—3. II. He comforts himself with an assurance of the divine favour and protection, and that, in due time, his enemies should be confounded and he delivered, ver. 4—7. What time we are in distress we may comfortably sing this psalm.

To the chief musician on Neginoth, Maschil. A psalm of David, when the Ziphim came and said to Saul, Doth not David hide himself with us?

SAVE me, O God, by thy name, and judge me by thy strength. 2 Hear my prayer, O God; give ear to the words of my mouth. 3 For strangers are risen up against me, and oppressors seek after my soul: they have not set God before them. Selah.

We may observe here, 1. The great distress that David was now in, which the title gives an account of. The Ziphim came of their own accord, and informed Saul where David was, with a promise to deliver him into his hand. One would have thought that when David had retired into the country he would not be pursued, into a desert country he would not be discovered, and into his own country he would not be betrayed; and yet it seems he was. Never let a good man expect to be safe and easy till he comes to heaven. How treacherous, how officious, were these Ziphim! It is well that God is faithful, for men are not to be trusted, Mic. vii. 5. 2. His prayer to God for succour and deliverance, *v.* 1, 2. He appeals to God's strength, by which he was able to help him, and to his name, by which he was engaged to help him, and begs he would save him from his enemies and judge him, that is, plead his cause and judge for him. David has no other plea to depend upon than God's name, no other power to depend upon than God's strength, and those he makes his refuge and confidence. This would be the effectual answer of his prayers (*v.* 2), which even in his flight, when he had not opportunity for solemn address to God, he was ever and anon lifting up to heaven: *Hear my prayer,* which comes from my heart, *give ear to the words of my mouth.* 3. His plea, which is taken from the character of his enemies, *v.* 3. (1.) They are *strangers;* such were the Ziphites, unworthy the name of Israelites. "They have used me more basely and barbarously than the Philistines themselves would have done." The worst treatment may be expected from those who, having broken through the bonds of relation and alliance, make themselves strangers. (2.) They are *oppressors;* such was Saul, who, as a king, should have used his power for the protection of all his good subjects, but abused it for their destruction. Nothing is so grievous as oppression in *the seat of judgment,* Eccl. iii. 16. Paul's greatest perils were by his *own countrymen* and by *false brethren* (2 Cor. xi. 26), and so were David's. (3.) They were very formidable and threatening; they not only hated him and wished him ill, but they

rose up against him in a body, joining their power to do him a mischief. (4.) They were very spiteful and malicious: *They seek after my soul;* they hunt for the precious life; no less will satisfy them. We may, in faith, pray that God would not by his providence give success, lest it should look like giving countenance, to such cruel bloody men. (5.) They were very profane and atheistical, and, for this reason, he thought God was concerned in honour to appear against them: *They have not set God before them,* that is, they have quite cast off the thoughts of God; they do not consider that his eye is upon them, that, in fighting against his people, they fight against him, nor have they any dread of the certain fatal consequences of such an unequal engagement. Note, From those who do not set God before them no good is to be expected; nay, what wickedness will not such men be guilty of? What bonds of nature, or friendship, or gratitude, or covenant, will hold those that have broken through the fear of God? *Selah—Mark this.* Let us all be sure to set God before us at all times; for, if we do not we are in danger of becoming desperate.

4 Behold, God *is* mine helper: the Lord *is* with them that uphold my soul. 5 He shall reward evil unto mine enemies: cut them off in thy truth. 6 I will freely sacrifice unto thee: I will praise thy name, O LORD; for *it is* good. 7 For he hath delivered me out of all trouble: and mine eye hath seen *his desire* upon mine enemies.

We have here the lively actings of David's faith in his prayer, by which he was assured that the issue would be comfortable, though the attempt upon him was formidable.

I. He was sure that he had God on his side, that God took his part (*v.* 4); he speaks it with an air of triumph and exultation, *Behold, God is my helper.* If we be for him, he is for us; and, if he be for us, we shall have such help in him that we need not fear any power engaged against us. Though men and devils aim to be our destroyers, they shall not prevail while God is our helper: *The Lord is with those that uphold my soul.* Compare cxviii. 7, "*The Lord taketh my part with those that help me.* There are some that uphold me, and God is one of them; he is the principal one; none of them could help me if he did not help them." Every creature is that to us (and no more) that God makes it to be. He means, "The Lord is he that upholds my soul, and keeps me from tiring in my work and sinking under my burdens." He that by his providence upholds all things by his grace upholds the souls of his people. God, who will in due time save his people, does, in the mean time, sustain them and bear them up, so that the spirit he has made shall not fail before him.

II. God taking part with him, he doubted not but his enemies should both flee and fall before him (*v.* 5): "*He shall reward evil unto my enemies that observe me*, seeking an opportunity to do me a mischief. The evil they designed against me the righteous God will return upon their own heads." David would not render evil to them, but he knew God would: *I as a deaf man heard not, for thou wilt hear.* The enemies we forgive, if they repent not, God will judge; and for this reason we must not avenge ourselves, because God has said, *Vengeance is mine.* But he prays, *Cut them off in thy truth.* This is not a prayer of malice, but a prayer of faith; for it has an eye to the word of God, and only desires the performance of that. There is truth in God's threatenings as well as in his promises, and sinners that repent not will find it so to their cost.

III. He promises to give thanks to God for all the experiences he had had of his goodness to him (*v.* 6): *I will sacrifice unto thee.* Though sacrifices were expensive, yet, when God required that his worshippers should in that way praise him, David would not only offer them, but offer them freely and without grudging. All our spiritual sacrifices must, in this sense, be free-will-offerings; for God loves a cheerful giver. Yet he will not only bring his sacrifice, which was but the shadow, the ceremony; he will mind the substance: *I will praise thy name.* A thankful heart, and the calves of our lips giving thanks to his name, are the sacrifices God will accept: "*I will praise thy name, for it is good.* Thy name is not only great but good, and therefore to be praised. To praise thy name is not only what we are bound to, but it is good, it is pleasant, it is profitable; it is good for us (xcii. 1); therefore *I will praise thy name.*"

IV. He speaks of his deliverance as a thing done (*v.* 7): I will praise thy name, and say, "*He has delivered me;* this shall be my song then." That which he rejoices in is a complete deliverance—*He has delivered me from all trouble;* and a deliverance to his heart's content—*My eye has seen its desire upon my enemies*, not seen them cut off and ruined, but forced to retreat, tidings being brought to Saul that the Philistines were upon him, 1 Sam. xxiii. 27, 28. All David desired was to be himself safe; when he saw Saul draw off his forces he saw his desire. *He has delivered me from all trouble.* Either, 1. With this thought David comforted himself when he was in distress: *He has delivered me from all trouble* hitherto, and many a time I have gained my point, and seen my desire on my enemies; therefore he will deliver me out of this trouble." We should thus, in our greatest straits, encourage ourselves with our past experiences. Or, 2. With this thought he magnified his present deliverance when the

fright was over, that it was an earnest of further deliverance. He speaks of the completing of his deliverance as a thing done, though he had as yet many troubles before him, because, having God's promise for it, he was as sure of it as if it had been done already. "He that has begun to deliver me from this trouble will deliver me from all troubles, and will at length give me to see my desire upon my enemies." This may perhaps point at Christ, of whom David was a type; God would deliver him out of all the troubles of his state of humiliation, and he was perfectly sure of it; and all things are said to be put under his feet; for, though we see not yet all things put under him, yet we are sure he shall reign till all his enemies be made his footstool, and he shall see his desire upon them. However, it is an encouragement to all believers to make that use of their particular deliverances which St. Paul does (like David here), 2 Tim. iv. 17, 18, *He that delivered me from the mouth of the lion shall deliver me from every evil work, and will preserve me to his heavenly kingdom.*

PSALM LV.

It is the conjecture of many expositors that David penned this psalm upon occasion of Absalom's rebellion, and that the particular enemy he here speaks of, that dealt treacherously with him, was Ahithophel; and some will therefore make David's troubles here typical of Christ's sufferings, and Ahithophel's treachery a figure of Judas's, because they both hanged themselves. But there is nothing in it that is particularly applied to Christ in the New Testament. David was in great distress when he penned this psalm. I. He prays that God would manifest his favour to him, and pleads his own sorrow and fear, ver. 1—8. II. He prays that God would manifest his displeasure against his enemies, and pleads their great wickedness and treachery, ver. 9—15 and again ver. 20, 21. III. He assures himself that God would, in due time, appear for him against his enemies, comforts himself with the hopes of it, and encourages others to trust in God, ver. 16—19 and again ver. 22, 23. In singing this psalm we may, if there be occasion, apply it to our own troubles; if not, we may sympathize with those to whose case it comes nearer, foreseeing that there will be, at last, indignation and wrath to the persecutors, salvation and joy to the persecuted.

To the chief musician on Neginoth, Maschil. *A psalm* of David.

GIVE ear to my prayer, O God; and hide not thyself from my supplication. 2 Attend unto me, and hear me: I mourn in my complaint, and make a noise; 3 Because of the voice of the enemy, because of the oppression of the wicked: for they cast iniquity upon me, and in wrath they hate me. 4 My heart is sore pained within me: and the terrors of death are fallen upon me. 5 Fearfulness and trembling are come upon me, and horror hath overwhelmed me. 6 And I said, Oh that I had wings like a dove! *for then* would I fly away, and be at rest. 7 Lo, *then* would I wander far off, *and* remain in the wilderness. Selah. 8 I would hasten my escape from the windy storm *and* tempest.

In these verses we have,

I. David praying. Prayer is a salve for every sore and a relief to the spirit under every burden: *Give ear to my prayer, O God!* *v.* 1, 2. He does not set down the petitions he offered up to God in his distress, but begs that God would hear the prayers which, at every period, his heart lifted up to God, and grant an answer of peace to them: *Attend to me, hear me.* Saul would not hear his petitions; his other enemies regarded not his pleas; but, " Lord, be thou pleased to hearken to me. *Hide not thyself from my supplication,* either as one unconcerned and not regarding it, nor seeming to take any notice of it, or as one displeased, angry at me, and therefore at my prayer." If we, in our prayers, sincerely lay open ourselves, our case, our hearts, to God, we have reason to hope that he will not hide himself, his favours, his comforts, from us.

II. David weeping; for in this he was a type of Christ that he was a man of sorrows and often in tears (*v.* 2): " *I mourn in my complaint*" (or in my *meditation,* my *melancholy musings*), " and I make a noise; I cannot forbear such sighs and groans, and other expressions of grief, as discover it to those about me." Great griefs are sometimes noisy and clamorous, and thus are, in some measure, lessened, while those increase that are stifled, and have no vent given them. But what was the matter? *v.* 3. It is *because of the voice of the enemy,* the menaces and insults of Absalom's party, that swelled, and hectored, and stirred up the people to cry out against David, and shout him out of his palace and capital city, as afterwards the chief priests stirred up the mob to cry out against the Son of David, *Away with him— Crucify him.* Yet it was not the voice of the enemy only that fetched tears from David's eyes, but their oppression, and the hardship he was thereby reduced to: *They cast iniquity upon me.* They could not justly charge David with any mal-administration in his government, could not prove any act of oppression or injustice upon him, but they loaded him with calumnies. Though they found no iniquity in him relating to his trust as a king, yet they cast all manner of iniquity upon him, and represented him to the people as a tyrant fit to be expelled. Innocency itself is no security against violent and lying tongues. They hated him themselves, nay, in wrath they hated him; there was in their enmity both the heat and violence of anger, or sudden passion, and the implacableness of hatred and rooted malice; and therefore they studied to make him odious, that others also might hate him. This made him mourn, and the more because he could remember the time when he was the darling of the people, and answered to his name, *David—a beloved one.*

III. David trembling, and in great consternation. We may well suppose him to be so upon the breaking out of Absalom's conspiracy and the general defection of the people, even those that he had little reason to

suspect. 1. See what fear seized him. David was a man of great boldness, and in some very eminent instances had signalized his courage, and yet, when the danger was surprising and imminent, his heart failed him. Let not the stout man therefore glory in his courage any more than the strong man in his strength. Now David's *heart is sorely pained within him; the terrors of death have fallen upon him, v.* 4. Fearfulness of mind and trembling of body came upon him, and horror covered and overwhelmed him, *v.* 5. When without are fightings no marvel that within are fears; and, if it was upon the occasion of Absalom's rebellion, we may suppose that the remembrance of his sin in the matter of Uriah, which God was now reckoning with him for, added as much more to the fright. Sometimes David's faith made him, in a manner, fearless, and he could boldly say, when surrounded with enemies, *I will not be afraid what man can do unto me.* But at other times his fears prevail and tyrannise; for the best men are not always alike strong in faith. 2. See how desirous he was, in this fright, to retire into a desert, any where to be far enough from hearing the voice of the enemy and seeing their oppressions. He said (*v.* 6), said it to God in prayer, said it to himself in meditation, said it to his friends in complaint, *O that I had wings like a dove!* Much as he had been sometimes in love with Jerusalem, now that it had become a rebellious city he longed to get clear of it, and, like the prophet, wished he had *in the wilderness a lodging place of way-faring men, that he might leave his people and go from them; for they were an assembly of treacherous men,* Jer. ix. 2. This agrees very well with David's resolution upon the breaking out of that plot, *Arise, let us flee, and make speed to depart,* 2 Sam. xv. 14. Observe, (1.) How he would make his escape. He was so surrounded with enemies that he saw not how he could escape but upon the wing, and therefore he wishes, *O that I had wings!* not like a hawk that flies strongly, but *like a dove* that flies swiftly; he wishes for wings, not to fly upon the prey, but to fly from the birds of prey, for such his enemies were. The wings of a dove were most agreeable to him who was of a dove-like spirit, and therefore the wings of an eagle would not become him. The dove flies low, and takes shelter as soon as she can, and thus would David fly. (2.) What he would make his escape from—*from the wind, storm, and tempest,* the tumult and ferment that the city was now in, and the danger to which he was exposed. Herein he was like a dove, that cannot endure noise. (3.) What he aimed at in making this escape, not victory but rest: " *I would fly away and be at rest, v.* 6. I would fly any where, if it were to a barren frightful wilderness, ever so far off, so I might be quiet," *v.* 7. Note, Peace and quietness in silence and solitude are what the wisest and best of men have most earnestly coveted, and the more when they have been vexed and wearied with the noise and clamour of those about them. Gracious souls wish to retire from the hurry and bustle of this world, that they may sweetly enjoy God and themselves; and, if there be any true peace on this side heaven, it is they that enjoy it in those retirements. This makes death desirable to a child of God, that it is a final escape from all the storms and tempests of this world to perfect and everlasting rest.

9 Destroy, O Lord, *and* divide their tongues: for I have seen violence and strife in the city. 10 Day and night they go about it upon the walls thereof: mischief also and sorrow *are* in the midst of it. 11 Wickedness *is* in the midst thereof: deceit and guile depart not from her streets. 12 For *it was* not an enemy *that* reproached me; then I could have borne *it :* neither *was it* he that hated me *that* did magnify *himself* against me; then I would have hid myself from him : 13 But *it was* thou, a man mine equal, my guide, and mine acquaintance. 14 We took sweet counsel together, *and* walked unto the house of God in company. 15 Let death seize upon them, *and* let them go down quick into hell : for wickedness *is* in their dwellings, *and* among them.

David here complains of his enemies, whose wicked plots had brought him, though not to his faith's end, yet to his wits' end, and prays against them by the spirit of prophecy. Observe here,

I. The character he gives of the enemies he feared. They were of the worst sort of men, and his description of them agrees very well with Absalom and his accomplices. 1. He complains of the city of Jerusalem, which strangely fell in with Absalom and fell off from David, so that he had none there but his own guards and servants that he could repose any confidence in : *How has that faithful city become a harlot !* David did not take the representation of it from others; but with his own eyes, and with a sad heart, did himself see nothing but *violence and strife in the city* (v. 9); for, when they grew disaffected and disloyal to David, they grew mischievous one to another. If he walked the rounds upon the walls of the city, he saw that violence and strife went about it day and night, and mounted its guards, *v.* 10. All the arts and methods which the rebels used for the fortifying of the city were made up of violence and strife, and there were no remains of honesty or love among them. If he looked into the heart of the city, mischief and injury, mutual wrong and vexation, were

in the midst of it : *Wickedness,* all manner of wickedness, *is in the midst thereof. Jusque datum sceleri—Wickedness was legalized.* Deceit and guile, and all manner of treacherous dealing, *departed not from her streets, v.* 11. It may be meant of their base and barbarous usage of David's friends and such as they knew were firm and faithful to him; they did them all the mischief they could, by fraud or force. Is this the character of Jerusalem, the royal city, and, which is more, the holy city, and in David's time too, so soon after the thrones of judgment and the testimony of Israel were both placed there? *Is this the city that men call the perfection of beauty?* Lam. ii. 15. Is Jerusalem, the head-quarters of God's priests, so ill taught? Can Jerusalem be ungrateful to David himself, its own illustrious founder, and be made too hot for him, so that he cannot reside in it? Let us not be surprised at the corruptions and disorders of this church on earth, but long to see the New Jerusalem, where there is no violence nor strife, no mischief nor guile, and into which no unclean thing shall enter, nor any thing that disquiets. 2. He complains of one of the ringleaders of the conspiracy, that had been very industrious to foment jealousies, to misrepresent him and his government, and to incense the city against him. It was one that reproached him, as if he either abused his power or neglected the use of it, for that was Absalom's malicious suggestion : *There is no man deputed of the king to hear thee,* 2 Sam. xv. 3. That and similar accusations were industriously spread among the people; and who was most active in it? "Not a sworn enemy, not Shimei, nor any of the nonjurors; then I could have borne it, for I should not have expected better from them" (and we find how patiently he did bear Shimei's curses); "not one that professed to hate me, then I would have stood upon my guard against him, would have hidden myself and counsels from him, so that it would not have been in his power to betray me. *But it was thou, a man, my equal,"* v. 13. The Chaldee-paraphrase names Ahithophel as the person here meant, and nothing in that plot seems to have discouraged David so much as to hear that Ahithophel was *among the conspirators with Absalom* (2 Sam. xv. 31), for he was *the king's counsellor,* 1 Chron. xxvii. 33. "*It was thou, a man, my equal,* one whom I esteemed as myself, a friend as my own soul, whom I had laid in my bosom and made equal with myself, to whom I had communicated all my secrets and who knew my mind as well as I myself did,—my guide, with whom I advised and by whom I was directed in all my affairs, whom I made president of the council and prime-minister of state,—my intimate acquaintance and familiar friend; this is the man that now abuses me. I have been kind to him, but I find him thus basely ungrateful. I have put a trust in him, but I find him thus basely treacherous; nay, and he could not have done me the one-half of the mischief he does if I had not shown him so much respect." All this must needs be very grievous to an ingenuous mind, and yet this was not all; this traitor had seemed a saint, else he had never been David's bosom-friend (v. 14): "*We took counsel together,* spent many an hour together, with a great deal of pleasure, in religious discourse," or, as Dr. Hammond reads it, "*We joined ourselves together to the assembly;* I gave him the right hand of fellowship in holy ordinances, and then *we walked to the house of God in company,* to attend the public service." Note, (1.) There always has been, and always will be, a mixture of good and bad, sound and unsound, in the visible church, between whom, perhaps for a long time, we can discern no difference; but the searcher of hearts does. David, who went to the house of God in his sincerity, had Ahithophel in company with him, who went in his hypocrisy. The Pharisee and the publican went together to the temple to pray; but, sooner or later, those that are perfect and those that are not will be made manifest. (2.) Carnal policy may carry men on very far and very long in a profession of religion while it is in fashion, and will serve a turn. In the court of pious David none was more devout than Ahithophel, and yet his heart was not right in the sight of God. (3.) We must not wonder if we be sadly deceived in some that have made great pretensions to those two sacred things, religion and friendship; David himself, though a very wise man, was thus imposed upon, which may make similar disappointments the more tolerable to us.

II. His prayers against them, which we are both to stand in awe of and to comfort ourselves in, as prophecies, but not to copy into our prayers against any particular enemies of our own. He prays, 1. That God would disperse them, as he did the Babel-builders (v. 9): "*Destroy, O Lord! and divide their tongues;* that is, blast their counsels, by making them to disagree among themselves, and clash with one another. Send an evil spirit among them, that they may not understand one another, but be envious and jealous one of another." This prayer was answered in the turning of Ahithophel's counsel into foolishness, by setting up the counsel of Hushai against it. God often destroys the church's enemies by dividing them;·nor is there a surer way to the destruction of any people than their division. A kingdom, an interest, divided against itself, cannot long stand. 2. That God would destroy them, as he did Dathan and Abiram, and their associates, who were confederate against Moses, whose throat being an open sepulchre, the earth therefore opened and swallowed them up. This was then a new thing which God executed, Num. xvi. 30. But David prays that it might now be repeated, or something equi-

valent (v. 15): "*Let death seize upon them* by divine warrant, and *let them go down quickly into hell;* let them be dead, and buried, and so utterly destroyed, in a moment; for wickedness is wherever they are; it is in the midst of them." The souls of impenitent sinners go down quick, or alive, into hell, for they have a perfect sense of their miseries, and shall *therefore* live still, that they may be still miserable. This prayer is a prophecy of the utter, the final, the everlasting ruin of all those who, whether secretly or openly, oppose and rebel against the Lord's Messiah.

16 As for me, I will call upon God; and the LORD shall save me. 17 Evening, and morning, and at noon, will I pray, and cry aloud: and he shall hear my voice. 18 He hath delivered my soul in peace from the battle *that was* against me: for there were many with me. 19 God shall hear, and afflict them, even he that abideth of old. Selah. Because they have no changes, therefore they fear not God. 20 He hath put forth his hands against such as be at peace with him: he hath broken his covenant. 21 *The words* of his mouth were smoother than butter, but war *was* in his heart: his words were softer than oil, yet *were* they drawn swords. 22 Cast thy burden upon the LORD, and he shall sustain thee: he shall never suffer the righteous to be moved. 23 But thou, O God, shalt bring them down into the pit of destruction: bloody and deceitful men shall not live out half their days; but I will trust in thee.

In these verses,

I. David perseveres in his resolution to call upon God, being well assured that he should not seek him in vain (v. 16): "*As for me,* let them take what course they please to secure themselves, let violence and strife be their guards, prayer shall be mine; this I have found comfort in, and therefore this will I abide by: *I will call upon God,* and commit myself to him, and *the Lord shall save me;*" for whosoever shall call on the name of the Lord, in a right manner, shall be saved, Rom. x. 13. He resolves to be both fervent and frequent in this duty. 1. He will pray fervently: "*I will pray and cry aloud. I will meditate*" (so the former word signifies); "I will speak with my own heart, and the prayer shall come thence." Then we pray aright when we pray with all that is within us, think first and then pray over our thoughts; for the true nature of prayer is lifting up the heart to God. Having meditated, he will cry, he will cry aloud; the fervour of his spirit in prayer shall be expressed and yet more excited by the intenseness and earnestness of his voice. 2. He will pray frequently, every day, and three times a day—*evening, and morning, and at noon.* It is probable that this had been his constant practice, and he resolves to continue it now that he is in his distress. Then we may come the more boldly to the throne of grace in trouble when we do not then first begin to seek acquaintance with God, but it is what we have constantly practised, and the trouble finds the wheels of prayer going. Those that think three meals a day little enough for the body ought much more to think three solemn prayers a day little enough for the soul, and to count it a pleasure, not a task. As it is fit that in the morning we should begin the day with God, and in the evening close it with him, so it is fit that in the midst of the day we should retire awhile to converse with him. It was Daniel's practice to pray three times a day (Dan. vi. 10), and noon was one of Peter's hours of prayer, Acts x. 9. Let not us be weary of praying often, for God is not weary of hearing. "He shall hear my voice, and not blame me for coming too often, but the oftener the better, the more welcome."

II. He assures himself that God would in due time give an answer of peace to his prayers.

1. That he himself should be delivered and his fears prevented; those fears with which he was much disordered (*v.* 4, 5) by the exercise of faith were now silenced, and he begins to rejoice in hope (*v.* 18): *God has delivered my soul in peace,* that is, he will deliver it; David is as sure of the deliverance as if it were already wrought. His enemies were at war with him, and the battle was against him, but God delivered him in peace, that is, brought him off with as much comfort as if he had never been in danger. If he did not deliver him in victory, yet he delivered him in peace, inward peace. He delivered his soul in peace; by patience and holy joy in God he kept possession of that. Those are safe and easy whose hearts and minds are kept by that peace of God which *passes all understanding,* Phil. iv. 7. David, in his fright, thought all were against him; but now he sees there were many with him, more than he imagined; his interest proved better than he expected, and this he gives to God the glory of: for it is he that raises us up friends when we need them, and makes them faithful to us. There were many with him; for though his subjects deserted him, and went over to Absalom, yet God was with him and the good angels. With an eye of faith he now sees himself surrounded, as Elisha was, with chariots of fire and horses of fire, and therefore triumphs thus, *There are many with me,* more *with me than against me,* 2 Kings vi. 16, 17.

2. That his enemies should be reckoned with, and brought down. They had frightened him with their menaces (*v.* 3), but here he says enough to frighten them and make them tremble with more reason, and no remedy; for they could not ease themselves of their fears as David could, by faith in God.

(1.) David here gives their character as the reason why he expected God would bring them down. [1.] They are impious and profane, and stand in no awe of God, of his authority or wrath (*v.* 19): "*Because they have no changes* (no afflictions, no interruption to the constant course of their prosperity, no crosses to empty them from vessel to vessel) *therefore they fear not God;* they live in a constant neglect and contempt of God and religion, which is the cause of all their other wickedness, and by which they are certainly marked for destruction." [2.] They are treacherous and false, and will not be held by the most sacred and solemn engagements (*v.* 20): "*He has put forth his hand against such as are at peace with him,* that never provoked him, nor gave him any cause to quarrel with them; nay, to whom he had given all possible encouragement to expect kindness from him. He has put forth his hand against those whom he had given his hand to, and has broken his covenant both with God and man, has perfidiously violated his engagement to both," than which nothing makes men riper for ruin. [3.] They are base and hypocritical, pretending friendship while they design mischief (*v.* 21): "*The words of his mouth*" (probably, he means Ahithophel particularly) "*were smoother than butter and softer than oil,* so courteous was he and obliging, so free in his professions of respect and kindness and the proffers of his service; yet, at the same time, *war was in his heart,* and all this courtesy was but a stratagem of war, and those very words had such a mischievous design in them that they were as *drawn swords* designed to stab." They smile in a man's face, and cut his throat at the same time, as Joab, that kissed and killed. Satan is such an enemy; he flatters men into their ruin. *When he speaks fair, believe him not.*

(2.) David here foretels their ruin. [1.] God shall afflict them, and bring them into straits and frights, and recompense tribulation to those that have troubled his people, and this in answer to the prayers of his people: *God shall hear and afflict them,* hear the cries of the oppressed and speak terror to their oppressors, *even he that abides of old,* who is God from everlasting, and world without end, and who sits Judge from the beginning of time, and has always presided in the affairs of the children of men. Mortal men, though ever so high and strong, will easily be crushed by an eternal God and are a very unequal match for him. This the saints have comforted themselves with in reference to the threatening power of the church's enemies (Hab. i. 12): *Art thou not from everlasting, O Lord?* [2.] God shall *bring them down,* not only to the dust, but *to the pit of destruction* (*v.* 23), to the bottomless pit, which is called *destruction*, Job xxvi. 6. He afflicted them (*v.* 19) to see if that would humble and re-form them; but, they not being wrought upon by that, he shall at last bring them to ruin. Those that are not reclaimed by the rod of affliction will certainly be brought down into the pit of destruction. They are *bloody and deceitful men* (that is, the worst of men) and therefore *shall not live out half their days*, not half so long as men ordinarily live, and as they might have lived in a course of nature, and as they themselves expected to live. They shall live as long as the Lord of life, the righteous Judge, has appointed, with whom the number of our months is; but he has determined to cut them off by an untimely death in the midst of their days. They were bloody men, and cut others off, and therefore God will justly cut them off: they were deceitful men, and defrauded others of the one-half perhaps of what was their due, and now God will cut them short, though not of that which was their due, yet of that which they counted upon.

III. He encourages himself and all good people to commit themselves to God, with confidence in him. He himself resolves to do so (*v.* 23): "*I will trust in thee*, in thy providence, and power, and mercy, and not in my own prudence, strength, or merit; when bloody and deceitful men are cut off in the midst of their days I shall still live by faith in thee." And this he will have others to do (*v.* 22): "*Cast thy burden upon the Lord,* whoever thou art that art burdened, and whatever the burden is. "*Cast thy gift upon the Lord*" (so some read it); "whatever blessings God has bestowed upon thee to enjoy commit them all to his custody, and particularly commit the keeping of thy soul to him." Or, "Whatever it is that thou desirest God should give thee, leave it to him to give it to thee in his own way and time. *Cast thy care upon the Lord*, so the LXX., to which the apostle refers, 1 Pet. v. 7. Care is a burden; it makes the heart stoop (Prov. xii. 25); we must cast it upon God by faith and prayer, commit our·way and works to him; let him do as seemeth him good, and we will be satisfied. To cast our burden upon God is to stay ourselves on his providence and promise, and to be very easy in the assurance that all shall work for good. If we do so, it is promised, 1. That he will sustain us, both support and supply us, will himself carry us in the arms of his power, as the nurse carries the sucking-child, will strengthen our spirits so by his Spirit as that they shall sustain the infirmity. He has not promised to free us immediately from that trouble which gives rise to our cares and fears; but he will provide that we be not tempted above what we are able, and that we shall be able according as we are tempted. 2. That he will never suffer the righteous to be moved, to be so shaken by any troubles as to quit either their duty to God or their comfort in him. However, he will not suffer them to be moved for ever (as some read it); though they fall, they shall not be utterly cast down.

PSALM LVI.

It seems by this, and many other psalms, that even in times of the greatest trouble and distress David never hung his harp upon the willow-trees, never unstrung it or laid it by; but that when his dangers and fears were greatest he was still in tune for singing God's praises. He was in imminent peril when he penned this psalm, at least when he meditated it; yet even then his meditation of God was sweet. I. He complains of the malice of his enemies, and begs mercy for himself and justice against them, ver. 1, 2, 5—7. II. He confides in God, being assured that he took his part, comforting himself with this, that therefore he was safe and should be victorious, and that while he lived he should praise God, ver. 3, 4, 8—13. How pleasantly may a good Christian, in singing this psalm, rejoice in God, and praise him for what he will do, as well as for what he has done.

To the chief musician, upon Jonath-elem-rechokim, Michtam of David, when the Philistines took him in Gath.

BE merciful unto me, O God : for man would swallow me up; he fighting daily oppresseth me. 2 Mine enemies would daily swallow *me* up : for *they be* many that fight against me, O thou most high. 3 What time I am afraid, I will trust in thee. 4 In God I will praise his word, in God I have put my trust; I will not fear what flesh can do unto me. 5 Every day they wrest my words : all their thoughts *are* against me for evil. 6 They gather themselves together, they hide themselves, they mark my steps, when they wait for my soul. 7 Shall they escape by iniquity ? in *thine* anger cast down the people, O God.

David, in this psalm, by his faith throws himself into the hands of God, even when he had by his fear and folly thrown himself into the hands of the Philistines; it was when they took him in Gath, whither he fled for fear of Saul, forgetting the quarrel they had with him for killing Goliath; but they soon put him in mind of it, 1 Sam. xxi. 10, 11. Upon that occasion he changed his behaviour, but with so little ruffle to his temper that then he penned both this psalm and the 34th. This is called *Michtam—a golden psalm*. So some other psalms are entitled, but this has something peculiar in the title; it is upon *Jonath-elem-rechokim*, which signifies *the silent dove afar off*. Some apply this to David himself, who wished for the wings of a dove on which to fly away. He was innocent and inoffensive, mild and patient, as a dove, was at this time driven from his nest, from the sanctuary (lxxxiv. 3), was forced to wander afar off, to seek for shelter in distant countries; there he was like the doves of the valleys, mourning and melancholy; but silent, neither murmuring against God nor railing at the instruments of his trouble; herein a type of Christ, who was as a sheep, dumb before the shearers, and a pattern to Christians, who, wherever they are and whatever injuries are done them, ought to be as silent doves. In this former part of the psalm,

I. He complains to God of the malice and wickedness of his enemies, to show what reason he had to fear them, and what cause, what need, there was that God should appear against them (*v.* 1): *Be merciful unto me, O God!* That petition includes all the good we come to the throne of grace for; if we obtain mercy there, we obtain all we can desire, and need no more to make us happy. It implies likewise our best plea, not our merit, but God's mercy, his free rich mercy. He prays that he might find mercy with God, for with men he could find no mercy. When he fled from the cruel hands of Saul he fell into the cruel hands of the Philistines. "Lord" (says he), "be thou merciful to me now, or I am undone." The mercy of God is what we may flee to and trust to, and in faith pray for, when we are surrounded on all sides with difficulties and dangers. He complains, 1. That his enemies were very numerous (*v.* 2): "*They are many that fight against me,* and think to overpower me with numbers; take notice of this, *O thou Most High!* and make it to appear that wherein they deal proudly thou art above them." It is a point of honour to come in to the help of one against many. And, if God be on our side, how many soever they are that fight against us, we may, upon good grounds, boast that there are more with us; for (as that great general said) "How many do we reckon him for?" 2. That they were very barbarous: they would *swallow him up, v.* 1 and again *v.* 2. They sought to devour him; no less would serve; they came upon him with the utmost fury, like beasts of prey, to eat up his flesh, xxvii. 2. *Man* would swallow him up, those of his own kind, from whom he might have expected humanity. The ravenous beasts prey not upon those of their own species; yet a bad man would devour a good man if he could. "They are men, weak and frail; make them to know that they are so," ix. 20. 3. That they were very unanimous (*v.* 6): *They gather themselves together;* though they were many, and of different interests among themselves, yet they united and combined against David, as Herod and Pilate against the Son of David. 4. That they were very powerful, quite too hard for him if God did not help him: "*They fight against me* (*v.* 2); *they oppress me, v.* 1. I am almost overcome and borne down by them, and reduced to the last extremity." 5. That they were very subtle and crafty (*v.* 6): "*They hide themselves;* they industriously cover their designs, that they may the more effectually prosecute and pursue them. They hide themselves as a lion in his den, that they may mark my steps;" that is, "they observe every thing I say and do with a critical eye, that they may have something to accuse me of" (thus Christ's enemies watched him, Luke xx. 20), or "they have an eye upon all my motions, that they may gain an opportunity to do me a mischief, and may lay their snares for me. 6. That they were very spiteful and malicious. They put invidious constructions upon every thing he said, though ever so honestly meant and prudently expressed (*v.* 5): "*They wrest my words,* put them upon the rack, to extort that out of them which was never in them;" and so they made him an offender for a word (Isa. xxix. 21), misrepresenting it to Saul, and aggravating it, to incense him yet more against him. They made it their whole business to ruin David; all their thoughts were against him for evil, which put evil interpretations upon all his words. 7. That they were very restless and unwearied. They continually waited for his soul; it was the life, the precious life, they hunted for; it was his death they longed for, *v.* 6. They fought daily against him (*v.* 1), and would daily swallow him up (*v.* 2), and every day they wrested his words, *v.* 5. Their malice would not admit the least cessation of arms, or the acts of hostility, but they were continually pushing at him. Such as this is the enmity of Satan and his agents against the kingdom of Christ and the interests of his holy religion, which if we cordially espouse, we must not think it strange to meet with such treatment as this, as though some strange thing happened to us. Our betters have been thus used. So persecuted they the prophets.

II. He encourages himself in God, and in his promises, power, and providence, *v.* 3, 4. In the midst of his complaints, and before he has said what he has to say of his enemies, he triumphs in the divine protection. 1. He resolves to make God his confidence, then when dangers were most threatening and all other confidences failed: "*What time I am afraid,* in the day of my fear, when I am most terrified from without and most timorous within, then *I will trust in thee,* and thereby my fears shall be silenced." Note, There are some times which are, in a special manner, times of fear with God's people; in these times it is their duty and interest to trust in God as their God, and to know whom they have trusted. This will fix the heart and keep it in peace. 2. He resolves to make God's promises the matter of his praises, and so we have reason to make them (*v.* 4): "*In God I will praise,* not only his work which he has done, but *his word* which he has spoken; I will give him thanks for a promise, though not yet performed. *In God* (in his strength and by his assistance) I will both glory in his word and give him the glory of it. Some understand by *his word* his providences, every event that he orders and appoints: "When I speak well of God I will with him speak well of every thing that he does." 3. Thus supported, he will bid defiance to all adverse powers: "*When in God I have put my trust,* I am safe, I am easy, and *I will not fear what flesh can do unto me;* it is but flesh, and cannot do much; nay, it can do nothing but by divine permission." As we must not trust to an arm of flesh when it is engaged for us, so we must not be afraid of an arm of flesh when it is stretched out against us.

III. He foresees and foretels the fall of those that fought against him, and of all others that think to establish themselves in and by any wicked practices (v. 7): *Shall they escape by iniquity?* They hope to escape God's judgments, as they escape men's, by violence and fraud, and the arts of injustice and treachery; but shall they escape? No, certainly they shall not. The sin of sinners will never be their security, nor will either their impudence or their hypocrisy bring them off at God's bar; God will in his anger cast down and cast out such people, Rom. ii. 3. None are raised so high, or settled so firmly, but that the justice of God can bring them down, both from their dignities and from their confidences. *Who knows the power of God's anger,* how high it can reach, and how forcibly it can strike?

8 Thou tellest my wanderings: put thou my tears into thy bottle: *are they* not in thy book? 9 When I cry *unto thee,* then shall mine enemies turn back: this I know; for God *is* for me. 10 In God will I praise *his* word: in the LORD will I praise *his* word. 11 In God have I put my trust: I will not be afraid what man can do unto me. 12 Thy vows *are* upon me, O God: I will render praises unto thee. 13 For thou hast delivered my soul from death: *wilt* not *thou deliver* my feet from falling, that I may walk before God in the light of the living?

Several things David here comforts himself with in the day of his distress and fear.

I. That God took particular notice of all his grievances and all his griefs, v. 8. 1. Of all the inconveniences of his state: *Thou tellest my wanderings,* my *flittings,* so the old translation. David was now but a young man (under thirty) and yet he had had many removes, from his father's house to the court, thence to the camp, and now driven out to sojourn where he could find a place, but not allowed to rest any where; he was hunted like a partridge upon the mountains; continual terrors and toils attended him; but this comforted him, that God kept a particular account of all his motions, and numbered all the weary steps he took, by night or by day. Note, God takes cognizance of all the afflictions of his people; and he does not cast out from his care and love those whom men have cast out from their acquaintance

448

and converse. 2. Of all the impressions thus made upon his spirit. When he was wandering he was often weeping, and therefore prays, "*Put thou my tears into thy bottle,* to be preserved and looked upon; nay, I know they are *in thy book,* the book of thy remembrance." God has a bottle and a book for his people's tears, both those for their sins and those for their afflictions. This intimates, (1.) That he observes them with compassion and tender concern; he is afflicted in their afflictions, and knows their souls in adversity. As the blood of his saints, and their deaths, are precious in the sight of the Lord, so are their tears, not one of them shall fall to the ground. *I have seen thy tears,* 2 Kings xx. 5. *I have heard Ephraim bemoaning himself,* Jer. xxxi. 18. (2.) That he will remember them and review them, as we do the accounts we have booked. Paul was mindful of Timothy's tears (2 Tim. i. 4), and God will not forget the sorrows of his people. The tears of God's persecuted people are bottled up and sealed among God's treasures; and, when these books come to be opened, they will be found vials of wrath, which will be poured out upon their persecutors, whom God will surely reckon with for all the tears they have forced from his people's eyes; and they will be breasts of consolation to God's mourners, whose sackcloth will be turned into garments of praise. God will comfort his people according to the time wherein he has afflicted them, and give to those to reap in joy who sowed in tears. What was sown a tear will come up a pearl.

II. That his prayers would be powerful for the defeat and discomfiture of his enemies, as well as for his own support and encouragement (v. 9): "*When I cry unto thee, then shall my enemies turn back;* I need no other weapons than prayers and tears; *this I know,* for *God is for me,* to plead my cause, to protect and deliver me; and, if God be for me, who can be against me so as to prevail?" The saints have God for them; they may know it; and to him they must cry when they are surrounded with enemies; and, if they do this in faith, they shall find a divine power exerted and engaged for them; their enemies shall be made to turn back, their spiritual enemies, against whom we fight best upon our knees, Eph. vi. 18.

III. That his faith in God would set him above the fear of man, v. 10, 11. Here he repeats, with a strong pathos, what he had said (v. 4), "*In God will I praise his word;* that is, I will firmly depend upon the promise for the sake of him that made it, who is true and faithful, and has wisdom, power, and goodness enough to make it good." When we give credit to a man's bill we honour him that drew it; so when we do, and suffer, for God, in a dependence upon his promise, not staggering at it, we give glory to God, we praise his word, and so give praise to him. Having thus put his trust in

God, he looks with a holy contempt upon the threatening power of man : " *In God have I put my trust,* and in him only, and therefore *I will not be afraid what man can do unto me* (v. 11), though I know very well what he would do if he could," v. 1, 2. This triumphant word, so expressive of a holy magnanimity, the apostle puts into the mouth of every true believer, whom he makes a Christian hero, Heb. xiii. 6. We may each of us boldly say, *The Lord is my helper,* and then *I will not fear what man shall do unto me ;* for he has no power but what he has given him from above.

IV. That he was in bonds to God (v 12) : " *Thy vows are upon me, O God!*—not upon me as a burden which I am loaded with, but as a badge which I glory in, as that by which I am known to be thy menial servant—not upon me as fetters that hamper me (such are superstitious vows), but upon me as a bridle that restrains me from what would be hurtful to me, and directs me in the way of my duty. Thy vows are upon me, the vows I have made to thee, to which thou art not only a witness, but a party, and which thou hast commanded and encouraged me to make." It is probable that he means especially those vows which he had made to God in the day of his trouble and distress, which he would retain the remembrance of, and acknowledge the obligations of, when his fright was over. Note, It ought to be the matter of our consideration and joy that *the vows of God are upon us*—our baptismal vows renewed at the Lord's table, our occasional vows under convictions, under corrections, by these we are bound to live to God.

V. That he should still have more and more occasion to praise him : *I will render praises unto thee.* This is part of the performance of his vows ; for vows of thankfulness properly accompany prayers for mercy, and when the mercy is received must be made good. When we study what we shall render this is the least we can resolve upon, to render praises to God—poor returns for rich receivings ! Two things he will praise God for :—1. For what he had done for him (v. 13) : " *Thou hast delivered my soul,* my life, *from death,* which was just ready to seize me." If God have delivered us from sin, either from the commission of it by preventing grace or from the punishment of it by pardoning mercy, we have reason to own that he has thereby delivered our souls from death, which is the wages of sin. If we, who were by nature dead in sin, are quickened together with Christ, and are made spiritually alive, we have reason to own that God has delivered our souls from death. 2. For what he would do for him : " *Thou hast delivered my soul from death,* and so hast given me a new life, and thereby hast given me an earnest of further mercy, that thou wilt *deliver my feet from falling ;* thou hast done the greater, and therefore thou wilt do the less ; thou

hast begun a good work, and therefore thou wilt carry it on and perfect it." This may be taken either as the matter of his prayer, pleading his experience, or as the matter of his praise, raising his expectations ; and those that know how to praise in faith will give God thanks for mercies in promise and prospect, as well as in possession. See here, (1.) What David hopes for, that God would deliver his feet from falling either into sin, which would wound his conscience, or into the appearance of sin, from which his enemies would take occasion to wound his good name. Those that think they stand must take heed lest they fall, because the best stand no longer than God is pleased to uphold them. We are weak, our way is slippery, many stumbling-blocks are in it, our spiritual enemies are industrious to thrust us down, and therefore we are concerned by faith and prayer to commit ourselves to his care who *keeps the feet of his saints.* (2.) What he builds this hope upon : " *Thou hast delivered my soul from death,* and therein hast magnified thy power and goodness, and put me into a capacity of receiving further mercy from thee ; and now wilt thou not secure and crown thy own work ?" God never brought his people out of Egypt to slay them in the wilderness. He that in conversion delivers the soul from so great a death as sin is will not fail *to preserve it to his heavenly kingdom.* (3.) What he designs in these hopes : *That I may walk before God in the light of the living,* that is, [1.] "That I may get to heaven, the only land of light and life ; for in this world darkness and death reign." [2.] "That I may do my duty while this life lasts." Note, This we should aim at, in all our desires and expectations of deliverance both from sin and trouble, that we may do God so much the better service—*that, being delivered out of the hands of our enemies, we may serve him without fear.*

PSALM LVII.

This psalm is very much like that which goes next before it ; it was penned upon a like occasion, when David was both in danger of trouble and in temptation to sin ; it begins as that did, " Be merciful to me ;" the method also is the same. I. He begins with prayer and complaint, yet not without some assurance of speeding in his request, ver. 1—6. II. He concludes with joy and praise, ver. 7—11. So that hence we may take direction and encouragement, both in our supplications and in our thanksgivings, and may offer both to God, in singing this psalm.

To the chief musician, Al-taschith, Michtam of David, when he fled from Saul in the cave.

BE merciful unto me, O God, be merciful unto me : for my soul trusteth in thee : yea, in the shadow of thy wings will I make my refuge, until *these* calamities be overpast. 2 I will cry unto God most high ; unto God that performeth *all things* for me. 3 He shall send from heaven, and save me *from* the reproach of him that would swallow me up. Selah. God shall send forth his mercy and his truth. 4 **My** soul *is* among lions : *and* I lie *even among* them that are set on fire, *even* the sons of men, whose teeth *are* spears and arrows, and their tongue a sharp sword. 5 Be thou exalted, O God, above the heavens; *let* thy glory *be* above all the earth. 6 They have prepared a net for my steps; my soul is bowed down : they have digged a pit before me, into the midst whereof they are fallen *themselves.* Selah.

The title of this psalm has one word new in it, *Al-taschith*—*Destroy not.* Some make it to be only some known tune to which this psalm was set; others apply it to the occasion and matter of the psalm. *Destroy not;* that is, David would not let Saul be destroyed, when now in the cave there was a fair opportunity of killing him, and his servants would fain have done so. No, says David, *destroy him not,* 1 Sam. xxiv. 4, 6. Or, rather, God would not let David be destroyed by Saul; he suffered him to persecute David, but still under this limitation, *Destroy him not;* as he permitted Satan to afflict Job, *Only save his life.* David must not be destroyed, for *a blessing is in him* (Isa. lxv. 8), even Christ, the best of blessings. When David was in the cave, in imminent peril, he here tells us what were the workings of his heart towards God; and happy are those that have such good thoughts as these in their minds when they are in danger !

I. He supports himself with faith and hope in God, and prayer to him, *v.* 1, 2. Seeing himself surrounded with enemies, he looks up to God with that suitable prayer : *Be merciful to me, O Lord !* which he again repeats, and it is no vain repetition : *Be merciful unto me.* It was the publican's prayer, Luke xviii. 13. It is a pity that any should use it slightly and profanely, should cry, *God be merciful to us,* or, *Lord, have mercy upon us,* when they mean only to express their wonder, or surprise, or vexation, but God and his mercy are not in all their thoughts. It is with much devout affection that David here prays, "*Be merciful unto me, O Lord !* look with compassion upon me, and in thy love and pity redeem me." To recommend himself to God's mercy, he here professes,

1. That all his dependence is upon God : *My soul trusteth in thee, v.* 1. He did not only profess to trust in God, but his soul did indeed rely on God only, with a sincere devotion and self-dedication, and an entire complacency and satisfaction. He goes to God, and, at the footstool of the throne of his grace, humbly professes his confidence in him : *In the shadow of thy wings will I make my refuge,* as the chickens take shelter under the wings of the hen when the birds

450

of prey are ready to strike at them, *until these calamities be over-past.* (1.) He was confident his troubles would end well, in due time; *these calamities will be over-past;* the storm will blow over. *Non si male nunc et olim sic erit*—*Though now distressed, I shall not always be so.* Our Lord Jesus comforted himself with this in his sufferings, Luke xxii. 37. *The things concerning me have an end.* (2.) He was very easy under the divine protection in the mean time. [1.] He comforted himself in the goodness of God's nature, by which he is inclined to succour and protect his people, as the hen is by instinct to shelter her young ones. God comes upon the wing to the help of his people, which denotes a speedy deliverance (xviii. 10); and he takes them under his wing, which denotes warmth and refreshment, even when the calamities are upon them; see Matt. xxiii. 37. [2.] In the promise of his word and the covenant of his grace; for it may refer to the out-stretched *wings of the cherubim,* between which God is said to dwell (lxxx. 1) and whence he gave his oracles. "To God, as the God of grace, will I fly, and his promise shall be my refuge, and a sure passport it will be through all these dangers." God, by his promise, offers himself to us, to be trusted ; we by our faith must accept of him, and put our trust in him.

2. That all his desire is towards God (*v.* 2): "*I will cry unto God most high,* for succour and relief; to him that is most high will I lift up my soul, and pray earnestly, *unto God that performs all things for me.*" Note, (1.) In every thing that befalls us we ought to see and own the hand of God ; whatever is done is of his performing ; in it his counsel is accomplished and the scripture is fulfilled. (2.) Whatever God performs concerning his people, it will appear, in the issue, to have been performed for them and for their benefit. Though God be high, *most high,* yet he condescends so low as to take care that all things be made to work for good to them. (3.) This is a good reason why we should, in all our straits and difficulties, cry unto him, not only pray, but pray earnestly.

3. That all his expectation is from God (*v.* 3) : *He shall send from heaven, and save me.* Those that make God their only refuge, and fly to him by faith and prayer, may be sure of salvation, in his way and time. Observe here, (1.) Whence he expects the salvation—from heaven. Look which way he will, on this earth, refuge fails, no help appears ; but he looks for it from heaven. Those that lift up their hearts to things above may thence expect all good. (2.) What the salvation is that he expects. He trusts that God will save him *from the reproach of those that would swallow him up,* that aimed to ruin him, and, in the mean time, did all they could to vex him. Some read it, *He shall send from heaven and save me, for he has put to shame him that would swallow me up;* he has disap-

pointed their designs against me hitherto, and therefore he will perfect my deliverance. (3.) What he will ascribe his salvation to: *God shall send forth his mercy and truth.* God is good in himself and faithful to every word that he has spoken, and so he makes it appear when he works deliverance for his people. We need no more to make us happy than to have the benefit of the mercy and truth of God, xxv. 10.

II. He represents the power and malice of his enemies (*v.* 4): *My soul is among lions.* So fierce and furious was Saul, and those about him, against David, that he might have been as safe in a den of lions as among such men, who were continually roaring against him and ready to make a prey of him. They are set on fire, and breathe nothing but flame ; they set on fire the course of nature, inflaming one another against David, and *they were themselves set on fire of hell,* Jam. iii. 6. They were sons of men, from whom one might have expected something of the reason and compassion of a man ; but they were beasts of prey in the shape of men ; their *teeth,* which they gnashed upon him, and with which they hoped to tear him to pieces and to eat him up, *were spears and arrows* fitted for mischiefs and murders ; and their *tongue,* with which they cursed him and wounded his reputation, was *as a sharp sword* to cut and kill; see xlii. 10. A spiteful tongue is a dangerous weapon, wherewith Satan's instruments fight against God's people. He describes their malicious projects against him (*v.* 6) and shows the issue of them: " *They have prepared a net for my steps,* in which to take me, that I might not again escape out of their hands ; *they have digged a pit before me,* that I might, ere I was aware, run headlong into it." See the policies of the church's enemies; see the pains they take to do mischief. But let us see what comes of it. 1. It is indeed some disturbance to David: *My soul is bowed down.* It made him droop, and hang the head, to think that there should be those that bore him so much ill-will. But, 2. It was destruction to themselves ; they dug a pit for David, *into the midst whereof they have fallen.* The mischief they designed against David returned upon themselves, and they were embarrassed in their counsels ; then when Saul was pursuing David the Philistines were invading *him ;* nay, in the cave, when Saul thought David should fall into his hands, he fell into the hands of David, and lay at his mercy.

III. He prays to God to glorify himself and his own great name (*v.* 5): " Whatever becomes of me and my interest, *be thou exalted, O God ! above the heavens,* be thou praised by the holy angels, those glorious inhabitants of the upper world ; *and let thy glory be above* or over *all the earth ;* let all the inhabitants of this earth be brought to know and praise thee." Thus God's glory should lie nearer our hearts, and we should be more concerned

for it, than for any particular interests of our own. When David was in the greatest distress and disgrace he did not pray, *Lord, exalt me,* but, *Lord, exalt thy own name.* Thus the Son of David, when his soul was troubled, and he prayed, *Father, save me from this hour,* immediately withdrew that petition, and presented this in the room of it, *For this cause came I to this hour ; Father, glorify thy name,* John xii. 27, 28. Or it may be taken as a plea to enforce his petition for deliverance : " Lord, *send from heaven to save me,* and thereby thou wilt glorify thyself as the God both of heaven and earth." Our best encouragement in prayer is taken from the glory of God, and to that therefore, more than our own comfort, we should have an eye in all our petitions for particular mercies ; for this is made the first petition in the Lord's prayer, as that which regulates and directs all the rest, *Father in heaven, hallowed be thy name.*

7 My heart is fixed, O God, my heart is fixed : I will sing and give praise. 8 Awake up, my glory ; awake, psaltery and harp: I *myself* will awake early. 9 I will praise thee, O Lord, among the people : I will sing unto thee among the nations. 10 For thy mercy *is* great unto the heavens, and thy truth unto the clouds. 11 Be thou exalted, O God, above the heavens : *let* thy glory *be* above all the earth.

How strangely is the tune altered here ! David's prayers and complaints, by the lively actings of faith, are here, all of a sudden, turned into praises and thanksgivings ; his sackcloth is loosed, he is girded with gladness, and his hallelujahs are as fervent as his hosannas. This should make us in love with prayer, that, sooner or later, it will be swallowed up in praise. Observe,

I. How he prepares himself for the duty of praise (*v.* 7): *My heart is fixed, O God !* *my heart is fixed.* My heart is *erect,* or *lifted up* (so some), which was bowed down, *v.* 6. *My heart is fixed,* 1. With reference to God's providences ; it is prepared for every event, being *stayed upon God,* cxii. 7 ; Isa. xxvi. 3. *My heart is fixed,* and then *none of these things move me,* Acts xx. 24. If by the grace of God we be brought into this even composed frame of spirit, we have great reason to be thankful. 2. With reference to the worship of God : *My heart is fixed* to *sing and give praise.* It is implied that the heart is the main thing required in all acts of devotion ; nothing is done to purpose, in religion, further than it is done with the heart. The heart must be fixed, fixed for the duty, fitted and put in frame for it, fixed in the duty by a close application, *attending on the Lord without distraction.*

II. How he excites himself to the duty of

praise (*v.* 8): *Awake up my glory*, that is, my tongue (our tongue is our glory, and never more so than when it is employed in praising God), or my soul, that must be first awakened; dull and sleepy devotions will never be acceptable to God. We must stir up ourselves, and all that is within us, to praise God; with a holy fire must that sacrifice be kindled, and ascend in a holy flame. David's tongue will lead, and his psaltery and harp will follow, in these hymns of praise. *I myself will awake*, not only. " I will not be dead, and drowsy, and careless, in this work," but, " I will be in the most lively frame, as one newly awakened out of a refreshing sleep." He will awake *early* to this work, early in the morning, to begin the day with God, early in the beginnings of a mercy. When God is coming towards us with his favours we must go forth to meet him with our praises.

III. How he pleases himself, and (as I may say) even prides himself, in the work of praise; so far is he from being ashamed to own his obligations to God, and dependence upon him, that he resolves to *praise him among the people* and to *sing unto him among the nations, v.* 9. This intimates, 1. That his own heart was much affected and enlarged in praising God; he would even make the earth ring with his sacred songs, that all might take notice how much he thought himself indebted to the goodness of God. 2. That he desired to bring others in to join with him in praising God. He will publish God's praises *among the people*, that the knowledge, and fear, and love of God might be propagated, and the ends of the earth might see his salvation. When David was driven out into heathen lands he would not only not worship their gods, but he would openly avow his veneration for the God of Israel, would take his religion along with him wherever he went, would endeavour to bring others in love with it, and leave the sweet savour of it behind him. David, in his psalms, which fill the universal church, and will to the end of time, may be said to be still *praising God among the people* and *singing to him among the nations ;* for all good people make use of his words in praising God. Thus St. John, in his writings, is said to *prophesy again before many peoples and nations*, Rev. x. 11.

IV. How he furnishes himself with matter for praise, *v.* 10. That which was the matter of his hope and comfort *(God shall send forth his mercy and his truth, v.* 3) is here the matter of his thanksgiving: *Thy mercy is great unto the heavens*, great beyond conception and expression; and *thy truth unto the clouds*, great beyond discovery, for what eye can reach that which is wrapped up in the clouds? God's mercy and truth reach to the heavens, for they will bring all such to heaven as lay up their treasure in them and build their hopes upon them. God's mercy and truth are praised even to the heavens, that is, by all the bright and blessed inhabitants of

the upper world, who are continually exalting God's praises to the highest, while David, on earth, is endeavouring to spread his praises to the furthest, *v.* 9.

V. How he leaves it at last to God to glorify his own name (*v.* 11): *Be thou exalted, O God !* The same words which he had used (*v.* 5) to sum up his prayers in he here uses again (and no vain repetition) to sum up his praises in: " Lord, I desire to exalt thy name, and that all the creatures may exalt it; but what can the best of us do towards it ? Lord, take the work into thy own hands; do it thyself : *Be thou exalted, O God !* In the praises of the church triumphant thou art exalted to the heavens, and in the praises of the church militant thy glory is throughout all the earth; but thou art above all the blessing and praise of both (Neh. ix. 5), and therefore, Lord, exalt thyself *above the heavens* and *above all the earth. Father, glorify thy own name. Thou hast glorified it, glorify it yet again."*

PSALM LVIII.

It is the probable conjecture of some (Amyraldus particularly) that before Saul began to persecute David by force of arms, and raised the militia to seize him, he formed a process against him by course of law, upon which he was condemned unheard, and attainted as a traitor, by the great council, or supreme court of judicature, and then proclaimed " qui caput gerit lupinum—an outlawed wolf," whom any man might kill and no man might protect. The elders, in order to curry favour with Saul, having passed this bill of attainder, it is supposed that David penned this psalm on the occasion. I. He describes their sin, and aggravates that, ver. 1—5. II. He imprecates and foretels their ruin, and the judgments which the righteous God would bring upon them for their injustice (ver. 6—9), which would redound, 1. To the comfort of the saints, ver. 10. 2. To the glory of God, ver. 11. Sin appears here both exceedingly sinful and exceedingly dangerous, and God a just avenger of wrong, with which we should be affected in singing this psalm.

To the chief musician, Al-taschith, Michtam of David.

DO ye indeed speak righteousness, O congregation ? do ye judge uprightly, O ye sons of men ? 2 Yea, in heart ye work wickedness; ye weigh the violence of your hands in the earth. 3 The wicked are estranged from the womb : they go astray as soon as they be born, speaking lies. 4 Their poison *is* like the poison of a serpent : *they are* like the deaf adder *that* stoppeth her ear ; 5 Which will not hearken to the voice of charmers, charming never so wisely.

We have reason to think that this psalm refers to the malice of Saul and his janizaries against David, because it bears the same inscription *(Al-taschith*, and *Michtam of David)* with that which goes before and that which follows, both which appear, by the title, to have been penned with reference to that persecution through which God preserved him *(Al-taschith—Destroy not)*, and therefore the psalms he then penned were precious to him, *Michtams—David's jewels*, as Dr. Hammond translates it.

In these verses David, not as a king, for

he had not yet come to the throne, but as a prophet, in God's name arraigns and convicts his judges, with more authority and justice than they showed in prosecuting him. Two things he charges them with :—

I. The corruption of their government. They were a congregation, a bench of justices, nay, perhaps, a congress or convention of the states, from whom one might have expected fair dealing, for they were men learned in the laws, had been brought up in the study of these statutes and judgments, which were so righteous that those of other nations were not to be compared with them. One would not have thought a congregation of such could be bribed and biassed with pensions, and yet, it seems, they were, because the son of Kish could do that for them which the son of Jesse could not, 1 Sam. xxii. 7. He had vineyards, and fields, and preferments, to give them, and therefore, to please him, they would do any thing, right or wrong. Of all the melancholy views which Solomon took of this earth and its grievances, nothing vexed him so much as to see that in the *place of judgment wickedness was there,* Eccl. iii. 16. So it was in Saul's time. 1. The judges would not do right, would not protect or vindicate oppressed innocency (v. 1): "*Do you indeed speak righteousness, or judge uprightly?* No; you are far from it; your own consciences cannot but tell you that you do not discharge the trust reposed in you as magistrates, by which you are bound to be *a terror to evildoers and a praise to those that do well.* Is this the justice you pretend to administer? Is this the patronage, this the countenance, which an honest man and an honest cause may expect from you? Remember you are sons of men; mortal and dying, and that you stand upon the same level before God with the meanest of those you trample upon, and must yourselves be called to an account and judged. You are *sons of men,* and therefore we may appeal to yourselves, and to that law of nature which is written in every man's heart: *Do you indeed speak righteousness?* And will not your second thoughts correct what you have done?" Note, It is good for us often to reflect upon what we say with this serious question, *Do we indeed speak righteousness?* that we may unsay what we have spoken amiss and may proceed no further in it. 2. They did a great deal of wrong; they used their power for the support of injury and oppression (v. 2): *In heart you work wickedness* (all the wickedness of the life is wrought in the heart). It intimates that they wrought with a great deal of plot and management, not by surprise, but with premeditation and design, and with a strong inclination to it and resolution in it. The more there is of the heart in any act of wickedness the worse it is, Eccl. viii. 11. And what was their wickedness? It follows, "*You weigh the violence of your hands in the earth*" (or *in the land),* "the peace of which you are appointed

to be the conservators of." They did all the violence and injury they could, either to enrich or avenge themselves, and they weighed it; that is, 1. They did it with a great deal of craft and caution : "*You frame it by rule and lines*" (so the word signifies), "that it may effectually answer your mischievous intentions; such masters are you of the art of oppression." 2. They did it under colour of justice. They held the balances (the emblem of justice) in their hands, as if they designed to do right, and right is expected from them, but the result is violence and oppression, which are practised the more effectually for being practised under the pretext of law and right.

II. The corruption of their nature. This was the root of bitterness from which that gall and wormwood sprang (v. 3): *The wicked, who in heart work wickedness, are estranged from the womb,* estranged from God and all good, *alienated from the divine life,* and its principles, powers, and pleasures, Eph. iv. 18. A sinful state is a state of estrangement from that acquaintance with God and service of him which we were made for. Let none wonder that these wicked men dare do such things, for wickedness is bred in the bone with them; they brought it into the world with them; they have in their natures a strong inclination to it; they learned it from their wicked parents, and have been trained up in it by a bad education. They are called, and not miscalled, *transgressors from the womb;* one can therefore expect no other than that they will *deal very treacherously;* see Isa. xlviii. 8. They go astray from God and their duty as soon as they are born, (that is, as soon as possibly they can); the foolishness that is bound up in their hearts appears with the first operations of reason; as the wheat springs up, the tares spring up with it. Three instances are here given of the corruption of nature : — 1. Falsehood. They soon learn to speak lies, and *bend their tongues, like their* bows, for that purpose, Jer. ix. 3. How soon will little children tell a lie to excuse a fault, or in their own commendation! No sooner can they speak than they speak to God's dishonour; tongue-sins are some of the first of our actual transgressions. 2. Malice. *Their poison* (that is, their ill-will, and the spite they bore to goodness and all good men, particularly to David) was *like the poison of a serpent,* innate, venomous, and very mischievous, and that which they can never be cured of. We pity a dog that is poisoned by accident, but hate a serpent that is poisonous by nature. Such was the cursed enmity in this serpent's brood against the Lord and his anointed. 3. Untractableness. They are malicious, and nothing will work upon them, no reason, no kindness, to mollify them, and bring them to a better temper. *They are like the deaf adder that stops her ear,* v. 4, 5. The psalmist, having compared these wicked men, whom he here complains of, to serpents, for their poisonous malice, takes occasion thence, upon another account, to compare them to the deaf adder or viper, concerning which there was then this vulgar tradition, that whereas, by music or some other art, they had a way of charming serpents, so as either to destroy them or at least disable them to do mischief, this deaf adder would lay one ear to the ground and stop the other with her tail, so that she could not hear the voice of the enchantment, and so defeated the intention of it and secured herself. The using of this comparison neither verifies the story, nor, if it were true, justifies the use of this enchantment; for it is only an allusion to the report of such a thing, to illustrate the obstinacy of sinners in a sinful way. God's design, in his word and providence, is to cure serpents of their malignity; to this end how wise, how powerful, how well-chosen are the charms! How forcible the right words! But all in vain with most men; and what is the reason? It is because they will not hearken. None so deaf as those that will not hear. We *have piped unto men, and they have not danced; how* should they, when they have stopped their ears?

6 Break their teeth, O God, in their mouth: break out the great teeth of the young lions, O Lord. 7 Let them melt away as waters *which* run continually: *when* he bendeth *his bow to shoot* his arrows, let them be as cut in pieces. 8 As a snail *which* melteth, let *every one of them* pass away: *like* the untimely birth of a woman, *that* they may not see the sun. 9 Before your pots can feel the thorns, he shall take them away as with a whirlwind, both living, and in *his* wrath. 10 The righteous shall rejoice when he seeth the vengeance: he shall wash his feet in the blood of the wicked. 11 So that a man shall say, Verily *there is* a reward for the righteous: verily he is a God that judgeth in the earth.

In these verses we have,

I. David's prayers against his enemies, and all the enemies of God's church and people; for it is as such that he looks upon them, so that he was actuated by a public spirit in praying against them, and not by any private revenge. 1. He prays that they might be disabled to do any further mischief (*v.* 6): *Break their teeth, O God!* Not so much that they might not feed themselves as that they might not be able to make prey of others, iii. 7. He does not say, "Break their necks" (no; let them live to repent, *slay them not, lest my people forget*), but, "Break their teeth,

for they are lions, they are young lions, that live by rapine." 2. That they might be disappointed in the plots they had already laid, and might not gain their point: "*When he bends his bow,* and takes aim *to shoot his arrows* at the upright in heart, *let them be as cut in pieces, v.* 7. Let them fall at his feet, and never come near the mark." 3. That they and their interest might waste and come to nothing, that they might *melt away as waters that run continually;* that is, as the waters of a land-flood, which, though they seem formidable for a while, soon soak into the ground or return to their channels, or, in general, as *water spilt upon the ground, which cannot be gathered up again,* but gradually dries away and disappears. Such shall the *floods of ungodly men* be, which sometimes *make us afraid* (xviii. 4); so shall the proud waters be reduced, which threaten to go over our soul, cxxiv. 4, 5. Let us by faith then see what they shall be and then we shall not fear what they are. He prays (*v.* 8) that they might *melt as a snail,* which wastes by its own motion, in every stretch it makes leaving some of its moisture behind, which, by degrees, must needs consume it, though it makes a path to shine after it. He that like a snail in her house is *plenus sui—full of himself,* that pleases himself and trusts to himself, does but consume himself, and will quickly bring himself to nothing. And he prays that they might be *like the untimely birth of a woman,* which dies as soon as it begins to live and never *sees the sun.* Job, in his passion, wished he himself had been such a one (Job iii. 16), but he knew not what he said. We may, in faith, pray against the designs of the church's enemies, as the prophet does (Hos. ix. 14, *Give them, O Lord! what wilt thou give them? Give them a miscarrying womb and dry breasts),* which explains this prayer of the psalmist.

II. His prediction of their ruin (*v.* 9): "*Before your pots can feel the* heat of a fire of *thorns* made under them (which they will presently do, for it is a quick fire and violent while it lasts), so speedily, with such a hasty and violent flame, God shall hurry them away, as terribly and as irresistibly as with a whirlwind, as it were alive, as it were in fury."

1. The proverbial expressions are somewhat difficult, but the sense is plain, (1.) That the judgments of God often surprise wicked people in the midst of their jollity, and hurry them away of a sudden. When they are beginning to walk in the light of their own fire, and the sparks of their own kindling, they are made to *lie down in sorrow* (Isa. l. 11), and their laughter proves like the crackling of thorns under a pot, the comfort of which is soon gone, ere they can say, *Alas! I am warm,* Eccl. vii. 6. (2.) That there is no standing before the destruction that comes from the Almighty; for *who knows the power of God's anger?* When God will take sin-

ners away, dead or alive, they cannot contest with him. *The wicked are driven away in their wickedness.* Now,

2. There are two things which the psalmist promises himself as the good effects of sinners' destruction :—(1.) That saints would be encouraged and comforted by it (*v.* 10): *The righteous shall rejoice when he sees the vengeance.* The pomp and power, the prosperity and success, of the wicked, are a discouragement to the righteous ; they sadden their hearts, and weaken their hands, and are sometimes a strong temptation to them to question their foundations, lxxiii. 2, 13. But when they see the judgments of God hurrying them away, and just vengeance taken on them for all the mischief they have done to the people of God, they rejoice in the satisfaction thereby given to their doubts and the confirmation thereby given to their faith in the providence of God and his justice and righteousness in governing the world; they shall rejoice in the victory thus gained over that temptation by seeing *their end,* lxxiii. 17. *He shall wash his feet in the blood of the wicked ;* that is, there shall be abundance of bloodshed (lxviii. 23), and it shall be as great a refreshment to the saints to see God glorified in the ruin of sinners as it is to a weary traveller to have his feet washed. It shall likewise contribute to their sanctification; the sight of the vengeance shall make them tremble before God (cxix. 120) and shall convince them of the evil of sin, and the obligations they lie under to that God who pleads their cause and will suffer no man to do them wrong and go unpunished for it. The joy of the saints in the destruction of the wicked is then a holy joy, and justifiable, when it helps to make them holy and to purify them from sin. (2.) That sinners would be convinced and converted by it, *v.* 11. The vengeance God sometimes takes on the wicked in this world will bring men to say, *Verily, there is a reward for the righteous.* Any man may draw this inference from such providences, and many a man shall, who before denied even these plain truths or doubted of them. Some shall have this confession extorted from them, others shall have their minds so changed that they shall willingly own it, and thank God who has given them to see it and see it with satisfaction, That God is, and, [1.] That he is the bountiful rewarder of his saints and servants: *Verily (however it be,* so it may be read) *there is a fruit to the righteous ;* whatever damage a man may sustain, whatever hazard he may run, and whatever hardship he may undergo for his religion, he shall not only be no loser by it, but an unspeakable gainer in the issue. Even in this world there is a reward for the righteous; they shall be recompensed in the earth. Those shall be taken notice of, honoured, and protected, that seemed slighted, despised, and abandoned. [2.] That he is the righteous governor of the world, and will

surely reckon with the enemies of his kingdom : *Verily,* however it be, though wicked people prosper, and bid defiance to divine justice, yet it shall be made to appear, to their confusion, that the world is not governed by chance, but by a Being of infinite wisdom and justice ; *there is a God that judges in the earth,* though he has prepared his throne in the heavens. He presides in all the affairs of the children of men, and directs and disposes them according to the counsel of his will, to his own glory; and he will punish the wicked, not only in the world to come, but *in the earth,* where they have laid up their treasure and promised themselves a happiness—*in the earth,* that the Lord may be known by the judgments which he executes, and that they may be taken as earnests of a judgment to come. *He is a God* (so we read it), not a weak man, not an angel, not a mere name, not (as the atheists suggest) a creature of men's fear and fancy, not a deified hero, not the sun and moon, as idolaters imagined, but a God, a self-existent perfect Being; he it is that judges the earth; his favour therefore let us seek, from whom every man's judgment proceeds, and to him let all judgment be referred.

PSALM LIX.

This psalm is of the same nature and scope with six or seven foregoing psalms ; they are all filled with David's complaints of the malice of his enemies and of their cursed and cruel designs against him, his prayers and prophecies against them, and his comfort and confidence in God as his God. The first is the language of nature, and may be allowed ; the second of a prophetical spirit, looking forward to Christ and the enemies of his kingdom, and therefore not to be drawn into a precedent; the third of grace and a most holy faith, which ought to be imitated by every one of us. In this psalm, I. He prays to God to defend and deliver him from his enemies, representing them as very bad men, barbarous, malicious, and atheistical, ver. 1—7. II. He foresees and foretels the destruction of his enemies, which he would give to God the glory of, ver. 8—17. As far as it appears that any of the particular enemies of God's people fall under these characters, we may, in singing this psalm, read their doom and foresee their ruin.

To the chief musician, Al-taschith, Michtam of David, when Saul sent and they watched the house to kill him.

DELIVER me from mine enemies, O my God : defend me from them that rise up against me. 2 Deliver me from the workers of iniquity, and save me from bloody men. 3 For, lo, they lie in wait for my soul : the mighty are gathered against me ; not *for* my transgression, nor *for* my sin, O LORD. 4 They run and prepare themselves without *my* fault: awake to help me, and behold. 5 Thou therefore, O LORD God of hosts, the God of Israel, awake to visit all the heathen : be not merciful to any wicked transgressors. Selah. 6 They return at evening : they make a noise like a dog, and go round about the city. 7 Behold, they belch out with their mouth : swords *are* in their lips : for who, *say they*, doth hear ?

The title of this psalm acquaints us particularly with the occasion on which it was penned; it was when Saul sent a party of his guards to beset David's house in the night, that they might seize him and kill him; we have the story 1 Sam. xix. 11. It was when his hostilities against David were newly begun, and he had but just before narrowly escaped Saul's javelin. These first eruptions of Saul's malice could not but put David into disorder and be both grievous and terrifying, and yet he kept up his communion with God, and such a composure of mind as that he was never out of frame for prayer and praises; happy are those whose intercourse with heaven is not intercepted nor broken in upon by their cares, or griefs, or fears, or any of the hurries (whether outward or inward) of an afflicted state. In these verses,

I. David prays to be delivered out of the hands of his enemies, and that their cruel designs against him might be defeated (*v.* 1, 2): "*Deliver me from my enemies, O my God!* thou art *God*, and canst deliver me, *my* God, under whose protection I have put myself; and thou hast promised me to be a God all-sufficient, and therefore, in honour and faithfulness, thou wilt deliver me. Set me on high out of the reach of the power and malice of those that rise up against me, and above the fear of it. Let me be safe, and see myself so, safe and easy, safe and satisfied. O deliver me! and save me." He cries out as one ready to perish, and that had his eye to God only for salvation and deliverance. He prays (*v.* 4), "*Awake to help me*, take cognizance of my case, behold that with an eye of pity, and exert thy power for my relief." Thus the disciples, in the storm, awoke Christ, saying, *Master, save us, we perish.* And thus earnestly should we pray daily to be defended and delivered from our spiritual enemies, the temptations of Satan, and the corruptions of our own hearts, which war against our spiritual life.

II. He pleads for deliverance. Our God gives us leave not only to pray, but to plead with him, to order our cause before him and to fill our mouth with arguments, not to move him, but to move ourselves. David does so here.

1. He pleads the bad character of his enemies. They are *workers of iniquity*, and therefore not only his enemies, but God's enemies; they are *bloody men*, and therefore not only his enemies, but enemies to all mankind. " Lord, let not the workers of iniquity prevail against one that is a worker of righteousness, nor bloody men against a merciful man."

2. He pleads their malice against him, and the imminent danger he was in from them, *v.* 3. "Their spite is great; they aim at my soul, my life, my better part. They are subtle and very politic : *They lie in wait*, taking an

opportunity to do me a mischief. They are all mighty, men of honour and estates, and interest in court and country. They are in a confederacy; they are united by league, and actually *gathered* together *against me*, combined both in consultation and action. They are very ingenious in their contrivances, and very industrious in the prosecution of them (*v.* 4): *They run and prepare themselves*, with the utmost speed and fury, to do me a mischief." He takes particular notice of the brutish conduct of the messengers that Saul sent to take him (*v.* 6): " *They return at evening* from the posts assigned them in the day, to apply themselves to their works of darkness (their night-work, which may well be their day-shame), and then *they make a noise like a hound* in pursuit of the hare." Thus did David's enemies, when they came to take him, raise an out cry against him as a rebel, a traitor, a man not fit to live; with this clamour they went *round about the city*, to bring a bad reputation upon David, if possible to set the mob against him, at least to prevent their being incensed against them, which otherwise they had reason to fear they would be, so much was David their darling. Thus the persecutors of our Lord Jesus, who are compared to dogs (xxii. 16), ran him down with noise; for else they could not have taken him, at least *not on the feast-day, for there would have been an uproar among the people.* They belch out with their mouth the malice that boils in their hearts, *v.* 7. *Swords are in their lips;* that is, reproaches that wound my heart with grief (xlii. 10), and slanders that stab and wound my reputation. They were continually suggesting that which drew and whetted Saul's sword against him, and the fault is laid upon the false accusers. The sword perhaps would not have been in Saul's hand if it had not been first in their lips.

3. He pleads his own innocency, not as to God (he was never backward to own himself guilty before him), but as to his persecutors; what they charged him with was utterly false, nor had he ever said or done any thing to deserve such treatment from them (*v.* 3): " *Not for my transgression, nor for my sin, O Lord!* thou knowest, who knowest all things." And again (*v.* 4), *without my fault.* Note, (1.) The innocency of the godly will not secure them from the malignity of the wicked. Those that are harmless like doves, yet, for Christ's sake, are hated of all men, as if they were noxious like serpents, and obnoxious accordingly. (2.) Though our innocency will not secure us from troubles, yet it will greatly support and comfort us under our troubles. The testimony of our conscience for us that we have behaved ourselves well towards those that behave themselves ill towards us will be very much our rejoicing in the day of evil. (3.) If we are conscious to ourselves of our innocency, we may with humble confidence appeal to God and beg of

him to plead our injured cause, which he will do in due time.

4. He pleads that his enemies were profane and atheistical, and bolstered themselves up in their enmity to David, with the contempt of God: *For who*, say they, *doth hear? v.* 7. Not God himself, **x.** 11; xciv. 7. Note, It is not strange if those regard not what they say who have made themselves believe that God regards not what they say.

III. He refers himself and his cause to the just judgment of God, *v.* 5. "The Lord, the Judge, be Judge between me and my persecutors." In this appeal to God he has an eye to him as *the Lord of hosts*, that has power to execute judgment, having all creatures, even hosts of angels, at his command; he views him also as *the God of Israel*, to whom he was, in a peculiar manner, King and Judge, not doubting that he would appear on the behalf of those that were upright, that were Israelites indeed. When Saul's hosts persecuted him, he had recourse to God as *the Lord of all hosts;* when those maligned him who in spirit were strangers to the commonwealth of Israel he had recourse to God as *the God of Israel.* He desires (that is, he is very sure) that God will *awake to visit all the nations*, will make an early and exact enquiry into the controversies and quarrels that are among the children of men; there will be a day of visitation (Isa. **x.** 3), and to that day David refers himself, with this solemn appeal, *Be not merciful to any wicked transgressors. Selah—Mark that.* 1. If David had been conscious to himself that he was a wicked transgressor, he would not have expected to find mercy; but, as to his enemies, he could say he was no transgressor at all (*v.* 3, 4): "*Not for my transgression*, and therefore thou wilt appear for me." As to God, he could say he was no *wicked* transgressor; for, though he had transgressed, he was a penitent transgressor, and did not obstinately persist in what he had done amiss. 2. He knew his enemies were wicked transgressors, wilful, malicious, and hardened in their transgressions both against God and man, and therefore he sues for justice against them, judgment without mercy. Let not those expect to find mercy who never showed mercy, for such are wicked transgressors.

8 But thou, O LORD, shalt laugh at them; thou shalt have all the heathen in derision. 9 *Because of* his strength will I wait upon thee: for God *is* my defence. 10 The God of my mercy shall prevent me: God shall let me see *my desire* upon mine enemies. 11 Slay them not, lest my people forget: scatter them by thy power; and bring them down, O Lord our shield. 12 *For* the sin of their mouth *and* the words of their lips let them

even be taken in their pride ; and for cursing and lying *which* they speak. 13 Consume *them* in wrath, consume *them*, that they *may* not *be:* and let them know that God ruleth in Jacob unto the ends of the earth. Selah. 14 And at evening let them return ; *and* let them make a noise like a dog, and go round about the city. 15 Let them wander up and down for meat, and grudge if they be not satisfied. 16 But I will sing of thy power ; yea, I will sing aloud of thy mercy in the morning: for thou hast been my defence and refuge in the day of my trouble. 17 Unto thee, O my strength, will I sing : for God *is* my defence, *and* the God of my mercy.

David here encourages himself, in reference to the threatening power of his enemies, with a pious resolution to wait upon God and a believing expectation that he should yet praise him.

I. He resolves to wait upon God (*v.* 9): "*Because of his strength*" (either the strength of his enemies, the fear of which drove him to God, or because of God's strength, the hope of which drew him to God) "*will I wait upon thee*, with a believing dependence upon thee and confidence in thee." It is our wisdom and duty, in times of danger and difficulty, to wait upon God; for he is our defence, our high place, in whom we shall be safe. He hopes, 1. That God will be to him a God of mercy (*v.* 10): "*The God of my mercy shall prevent me* with the blessings of his goodness and the gifts of his mercy, prevent my fears, prevent my prayers, and be better to me than my own expectations." It is very comfortable to us, in prayer, to eye God, not only as the God of mercy, but as the God of our mercy, the author of all good in us and the giver of all good to us. Whatever mercy there is in God, it is laid up for us, and is ready to be laid out upon us. Justly does the psalmist call God's mercy *his mercy*, for all the blessings of the new covenant are called *the sure mercies of David* (Isa. lv. 3); and they are *sure to all the seed.* 2. That he will be to his persecutors a God of vengeance. His expectation of this he expresses partly by way of prediction and partly by way of petition, which come all to one; for his prayer that it might be so amounts to a prophecy that it shall be so. Here are several things which he foretels concerning his enemies, or observers, that sought occasions against him and opportunity to do him a mischief, in all which he should see his desire, not a passionate or revengeful desire, but a believing desire upon them, *v.* 10. (1.) He foresees that God would expose them to scorn, as they had indeed made themselves ridiculous, *v.* 8.

" They think **God** *does not hear them,* does not heed them; *but thou, O Lord! shalt laugh at them* for their folly, to think that he who planted the ear shall not hear, and *thou shalt have* not them only, but all such other heathenish people that live without God in the world, *in derision."* Note, Atheists and persecutors are worthy to be laughed at and had in derision. See Ps. ii. 4 ; Prov. i. 26 ; Isa. xxxvii. 22. (2.) That God would make them standing monuments of his justice (*v.* 11): *Slay them not ;* let them not be killed outright, *lest my people forget.* If the execution be soon done, the impressions of it will not be deep, and therefore will not be durable, but will quickly wear off. Swift destructions startle men for the present, but they are soon forgotten, for which reason he prays that this might be gradual: "*Scatter them by thy power,* and let them carry about with them, in their wanderings, such tokens of God's displeasure as may spread the notice of their punishment to all parts of the country." Thus Cain himself, though a murderer, was not slain, lest the vengeance should be forgotten, but was sentenced to be *a fugitive and a vagabond.* Note, When we think God's judgments come slowly upon sinners we must conclude that God has wise and holy ends in the gradual proceedings of his wrath. " So scatter them as that they may never again unite to do mischief, *bring them down, O Lord, our shield !"* If God has undertaken the protection of his people as their shield, he will doubtless humble and abase all those that fight against them. (3.) That they might be dealt with according to their deserts (*v.* 12): *For the sin of their mouth, even for the words of their lips* (for every word they speak has sin in it), *let them* for this *be taken in their pride,* even for their cursing others and themselves (a sin Saul was subject to, 1 Sam. xiv. 28, 44), and lying. Note, There is a great deal of malignity in tongue-sins, more than is commonly thought of. Note, further, Cursing, and lying, and speaking proudly, are some of the worst of the sins of the tongue; and that man is truly miserable whom God deals with according to the deserts of these, *making his own tongue to fall on him.* (4.) That God would glorify himself, as Israel's God and King, in their destruction (*v.* 13): " *Consume them in wrath, consume them ;* that is, follow them with one judgment after another, till they be utterly ruined ; let them be sensibly, but gradually wasted, that they themselves, while they are in the consuming, may know, and that the standers-by may likewise draw this inference from it, *That God ruleth in Jacob unto the ends of the earth."* Saul and his party think to rule and carry all before them, but they shall be made to know that there is a higher than they, that there is one who does and will overrule them. The design of God's judgments is to convince men that the Lord reigns, that he fulfils his own counsels, gives law to all the creatures, and

458

disposes all things to his own glory, so that the greatest of men are under his check, and he makes what use he pleases of them. He *rules in Jacob ;* for there he keeps his court; there he is known, and his name is great. But he *rules to the end of the earth ;* for all nations are within the territories of his kingdom. He *rules to the ends of the earth,* even over those that know him not, but he *rules for Jacob* (so it may be read); he has an eye to the good of his church in the government of the world; the administrations of that government, even to the ends of the earth, are *for Jacob his servant's sake and for Israel's his elect,* Isa. xlv. 4. (5.) That he would make their sin their punishment, *v.* 14, compare *v.* 6. Their sin was their hunting for David to make a prey of him ; their punishment should be that they should be reduced to such extreme poverty that they should hunt about for meat to satisfy their hunger, and should miss of it as they missed of David. Thus they should be, not cut off at once, but scattered (*v.* 11), and gradually consumed (*v.* 13); those that die by famine die by inches, and feel themselves die, Lam. iv. 9. He foretels that they should be forced to beg their bread from door to door. [1.] That they should do it with the greatest regret and reluctancy imaginable. *To beg they are ashamed* (which makes it the greater punishment to them), and therefore they do it at evening, when it begins to be dark, that they may not be seen, at the time when other beasts of prey creep forth, civ. 20. [2.] That yet they should be very clamorous and loud in their complaints, which would proceed from a great indignation at their condition, which they cannot in the least degree reconcile themselves to : *They shall make a noise like a dog.* When they were in quest of David they made a noise like an angry dog snarling and barking; now, when they are in quest of meat, they shall make a noise like a hungry dog howling and wailing. Those that repent of their sins *mourn,* when in trouble, *like doves ;* those whose hearts are hardened make a noise, when in trouble, like dogs, *like a wild bull in a net, full of the fury of the Lord.* See Hos. vii. 14, *They have not cried unto me with their heart when they howled on their beds for corn and wine.* [3.] That they should meet with little relief, but the hearts of people should be very much hardened towards them, so that they should *go round about the city,* and *wander up and down for meat* (*v.* 15), and should get nothing but by dint of importunity (according to our marginal reading, *If they be not satisfied, they will tarry all night),* so that what people do give them is not with good-will, but only to get rid of them, lest by their continual coming they weary them. [4.] That they should be insatiable, which is the greatest misery of all in a poor condition. *They are greedy dogs which can never have enough* (Isa. lvi. 11), and *they grudge if they be not satisfied.* A contented man, if he has not what he would have, yet does not grudge, does not quarrel with Providence, nor fret within himself; but those whose God is their belly, if that be not filled and its appetites gratified, fall out both with God and themselves. It is not poverty, but discontent, that makes a man unhappy.

II. He expects to praise God, that God's providence would find him matter for praise and that God's grace would work in him a heart for praise, *v.* 16, 17. Observe,

1. What he would praise God for. (1.) He would praise his power and his mercy; both should be the subject-matter of his song. Power, without mercy, is to be dreaded; mercy, without power, is not what a man can expect much benefit from; but God's power by which he is able to help us, and his mercy by which he is inclined to help us, will justly be the everlasting praise of all the saints. (2.) He would praise him because he had, many a time, and all along, found him his defence and his refuge in the day of trouble. God brings his people into trouble, that they may experience his power and mercy in protecting and sheltering them, and may have occasion to praise him. (3.) He would praise him because he had still a dependence upon him and a confidence in him, as his strength to support him and carry him on in his duty, his defence to keep him safe from evil, and the God of his mercy to make him happy and easy. He that is all this to us is certainly worthy of our best affections, praises, and services.

2. How he would praise God. (1.) He would *sing.* As that is a natural expression of joy, so it is an instituted ordinance for the exerting and exciting of holy joy and thankfulness. (2.) He would *sing aloud,* as one much affected with the glory of God, that was not ashamed to own it, and that desired to affect others with it. He will sing of God's power, but he will sing aloud of his mercy; the consideration of that raises his affections more than any thing else. (3.) He would sing aloud *in the morning,* when his spirits were most fresh and lively. God's compassions are new every morning, and therefore it is fit to begin the day with his praises. (4.) He would *sing unto God* (*v.* 17), to his honour and glory, and with him in his eye. As we must direct our prayers to God, so to him we must direct our praises, and must look up, making melody to the Lord.

PSALM LX.

After many psalms which David penned in a day of distress this comes which was calculated for a day of triumph; it was penned after he was settled in the throne, upon occasion of an illustrious victory which God blessed his forces with over the Syrians and Edomites; it was when David was in the zenith of his prosperity, and the affairs of his kingdom seem to have been in a better posture than ever they were either before or after. See 2 Sam. viii. 3, 13; 1 Chron. xviii. 3, 12. David, in prosperity, was as devout as David in adversity. In this psalm, I. He reflects upon the bad state of the public interests, for many years, in which God had been contending with them, ver. 1—3. II. He takes notice of the happy turn lately given to their affairs, ver. 4. III. He prays for the deliverance of God's Israel from their enemies, ver. 5. IV. He triumphs in hope of their victories over their enemies, and begs of God to carry them on and complete them, ver. 6—12. In singing this psalm we may have an

eye both to the acts of the church and to the state of our own souls, both which have their struggles.

To the chief musician, upon Shushan-eduth, Michtam of David, to teach, when he strove with Aram-naharaim, and with Aramzobah, when Joab returned and smote of Edom in the valley of salt 12,000.

O GOD, thou hast cast us off, thou hast scattered us, thou hast been displeased; O turn thyself to us again. 2 Thou hast made the earth to tremble; thou hast broken it: heal the breaches thereof; for it shaketh. 3 Thou hast showed thy people hard things: thou hast made us to drink the wine of astonishment. 4 Thou hast given a banner to them that feared thee, that it may be displayed because of the truth. Selah. 5 That thy beloved may be delivered; save *with* thy right hand, and hear me.

The title gives us an account, 1. Of the general design of the psalm. It is *Michtam—David's jewel,* and it is *to teach.* The Levites must teach it to the people, and by it teach them both to trust in God and to triumph in him; we must, in it, teach ourselves and one another. In a day of public rejoicing we have need to be taught to direct our joy to God and to terminate it in him, to give none of that praise to the instruments of our deliverance which is due to him only, and to encourage our hopes with our joys. 2. Of the particular occasion of it. It was at a time, (1.) When he was at war with the Syrians, and still had a conflict with them, both those of Mesopotamia and those of Zobah. (2.) When he had gained a great victory over the Edomites, by his forces, under the command of Joab, who had left 12,000 of the enemy dead upon the spot. David has an eye to both these concerns in this psalm: he is in care about his strife with the Assyrians, and in reference to that he prays; he is rejoicing in his success against the Edomites, and in reference to that he triumphs with a holy confidence in God that he would complete the victory. We have our cares at the same time that we have our joys, and they may serve for a balance to each other, that neither may exceed. They may likewise furnish us with matter both for prayer and praise, for both must be laid before God with suitable affections and devotions. If one point be gained, yet in another we are still striving: the Edomites are vanquished, but the Syrians are not; therefore *let not him that girds on the harness boast as if he had put it off.*

In these verses, which begin the psalm, we have,

I. A melancholy memorial of the many disgraces and disappointments which God had, for some years past, put the people under. During the reign of Saul, especially in the latter end of it, and during David's struggle with the house of Saul, while he reigned over Judah only, the affairs of the kingdom were much perplexed, and the neighbouring nations were vexatious to them. 1. He complains of *hard things* which they had seen (that is, which they had suffered), while the Philistines and other ill-disposed neighbours took all advantages against them, *v.* 3. God sometimes shows even his own people hard things in this world, that they may not take up their rest in it, but may dwell at ease in him only. 2. He owns God's displeasure to be the cause of all the hardships they had undergone: " *Thou hast been displeased* by us, displeased against us (*v.* 1), and in thy displeasure hast cast us off and scattered us, hast put us out of thy protection, else our enemies could not have prevailed thus against us. They would never have picked us up and made a prey of us if thou hadst not broken *the staff of bands* (Zech. xi. 14) by which we were united, and so scattered us." Whatever our trouble is, and whoever are the instruments of it, we must own the hand of God, his righteous hand, in it. 3. He laments the ill effects and consequences of the miscarriages of the late years. The whole nation was in a convulsion: *Thou hast made the earth* (or *the land) to tremble, v.* 2. The generality of the people had dreadful apprehensions of the issue of these things. The good people themselves were in a consternation: " *Thou hast made us to drink the wine of astonishment* (*v.*3); we were like men intoxicated, and at our wits' end, not knowing how to reconcile these dispensations with God's promises and his relation to his people; we are amazed, can do nothing, nor know we what to do." Now this is mentioned here to teach, that is, for the instruction of the people. When God is turning his hand in our favour, it is good to remember our former calamities, (1.) That we may retain the good impressions they made upon us, and may have them revived. Our souls must still have the affliction and the misery in remembrance, that they may be *humbled within us,* Lam. iii. 19, 20. (2.) That God's goodness to us, in relieving us and raising us up, may be more magnified; for it is as life from the dead, so strange, so refreshing. Our calamities serve as foils to our joys. (3.) That we may not be secure, but may always rejoice with trembling, as those that know not how soon we may be returned into the furnace again, which we were lately taken out of as the silver is when it is not thoroughly refined.

II. A thankful notice of the encouragement God had given them to hope that, though things had been long bad, they would now begin to mend (*v.* 4): " *Thou hast given a banner to those that fear thee* (for, as bad as the times are, there is a remnant among us that desire to fear thy name, for whom thou

hast a tender concern), *that it may be displayed* by thee, *because of the truth* of thy promise which thou wilt perform, and to be displayed by them, in defence of truth and equity," xlv. 4. This banner was David's government, the establishment and enlargement of it over all Israel. The pious Israelites, who feared God and had a regard to the divine designation of David to the throne, took his elevation as a token for good, and like the lifting up of a banner to them, 1. It united them, as soldiers are gathered together to their colours. Those that were *scattered* (*v.* 1), divided among themselves, and so weakened and exposed, coalesced in him when he was fixed upon the throne. 2. It animated them, and put life and courage into them, as the soldiers are animated by the sight of their banner. 3. It struck a terror upon their enemies, to whom they could now hang out a flag of defiance. Christ, the Son of David, is given *for an ensign of the people* (Isa. xi. 10), for a banner to those that fear God; in him, as the centre of their unity, they are gathered together in one; to him they seek, in him they glory and take courage. His love is the banner over them; in his name and strength they wage war with the powers of darkness, and under him the church becomes terrible as an army with banners.

III. A humble petition for seasonable mercy. 1. That God would be reconciled to them, though he had been displeased with them. In his displeasure their calamities began, and therefore in his favour their prosperity must begin: *O turn thyself to us again!* (*v.* 1) smile upon us, and take part with us; be at peace with us, and in that peace we shall have peace. *Tranquillus Deus tranquillat omnia—A God at peace with us spreads peace over all the scene.* 2. That they might be reconciled to one another, though they had been broken and wretchedly divided among themselves: " *Heal the breaches of our land* (*v.* 2), not only the breaches made upon us by our enemies, but the breaches made among ourselves by our unhappy divisions." Those are breaches which the folly and corruption of man makes, and which nothing but the wisdom and grace of God can make up and repair, by pouring out a spirit of love and peace, by which only a shaken shattered kingdom is set to rights and saved from ruin. 3. That thus they might be preserved out of the hands of their enemies (*v.* 5): " *That thy beloved may be delivered,* and not made a prey of, *save with thy right hand,* with thy own power and by such instruments as thou art pleased to make the men of thy right hand, *and hear me.*" Those that fear God are his beloved; they are dear to him as the apple of his eye. They are often in distress, but they shall be delivered. God's own right hand shall save them; for those that have his heart have his hand. *Save them, and hear me.* Note, God's praying people may take the general deliverances of the church as answers to their prayers in particular. If we improve what interest we have at the throne of grace for blessings for the public, and those blessings be bestowed, besides the share we have with others in the benefit of them we may each of us say, with peculiar satisfaction, "God has therein heard me, and answered me."

6 God hath spoken in his holiness; I will rejoice, I will divide Shechem, and mete out the valley of Succoth. 7 Gilead *is* mine, and Manasseh *is* mine; Ephraim also *is* the strength of mine head; Judah *is* my lawgiver; 8 Moab *is* my washpot; over Edom will I cast out my shoe: Philistia, triumph thou because of me. 9 Who will bring me *into* the strong city? who will lead me into Edom? 10 *Wilt* not thou, O God, *which* hadst cast us off? and *thou*, O God, *which* didst not go out with our armies? 11 Give us help from trouble: for vain *is* the help of man. 12 Through God we shall do valiantly: for he *it is that* shall tread down our enemies.

David is here rejoicing in hope and praying in hope; such are the triumphs of the saints, not so much upon the account of what they have in possession as of what they have in prospect (*v.* 6): "*God has spoken in his holiness* (that is, he has given me his word of promise, has *sworn by his holiness, and he will not lie unto David*, lxxxix. 35), therefore *I will rejoice*, and please myself with the hopes of the performance of the promise, which was intended for more than a pleasing promise." Note, God's word of promise, being a firm foundation of hope, is a full fountain of joy to all believers.

I. David here rejoices; and it is in prospect of two things:—

1. The perfecting of this revolution in his own kingdom. God having *spoken in his holiness* that David shall be king, he doubts not but the kingdom is all his own, as sure as if it were already in his hand: *I will divide Shechem* (a pleasant city in Mount Ephraim) *and mete out the valley of Succoth*, as my own. *Gilead is mine, and Manasseh is mine*, and both are entirely reduced, *v.* 7. Ephraim would furnish him with soldiers for his life-guards and his standing forces; Judah would furnish him with able judges for his courts of justice; and thus Ephraim would be *the strength of his head* and Judah *his lawgiver.* Thus may an active believer triumph in the promises, and take the comfort of all the good contained in them; for they are all yea and amen in Christ. "*God has spoken in his holiness*, and then pardon is mine, peace mine, grace mine, Christ mine, heaven mine, God

himself mine." *All is yours, for you are Christ's*, 1 Cor. iii. 22, 23.

2. The conquering of the neighbouring nations, which had been vexatious to Israel, were still dangerous, and opposed the throne of David, *v.* 8. Moab shall be enslaved, and put to the meanest drudgery. *The Moabites became David's servants*, 2 Sam. viii. 2. Edom shall be made a dunghill to throw old shoes upon; at least David shall take possession of it as his own, which was signified by *drawing off his shoe* over it, Ruth iv. 7. As for the Philistines, let them, if they dare, triumph over him as they had done; he will soon force them to change their note. Rather let those that know their own interest triumph because of him; for it would be the greatest kindness imaginable to them to be brought into subjection to David and communion with Israel. But the war is not yet brought to an end; there is a *strong city*, Rabbah (perhaps) of the children of Ammon, which yet holds out; Edom is not yet subdued. Now, (1.) David is here enquiring for help to carry on the war: "*Who will bring me into the strong city?* What allies, what auxiliaries, can I depend upon, to make me master of the enemies' country and their strongholds?" Those that have begun a good work cannot but desire to make a thorough work of it, and to bring it to perfection. (2.) He is expecting it from God only: "*Wilt not thou, O God?* For thou hast *spoken in thy holiness;* and wilt not thou be as good as thy word?" He takes notice of the frowns of Providence they had been under: *Thou hadst*, in appearance, *cast us off; thou didst not go forth with our armies.* When they were defeated and met with disappointments, they owned it was because they wanted (that is, because they had forfeited) the gracious presence of God with them; yet they do not therefore fly off from him, but rather take so much the faster hold of him; and the less he has done for them of late the more they hoped he would do. At the same time that they own God's justice in what was past they hope in his mercy for what was to come: "*Though thou hadst cast us off*, yet thou wilt not contend for ever, thou wilt not always chide; though *thou hadst cast us off*, yet thou hast begun to show mercy; and wilt thou not perfect what thou hast begun?" The Son of David, in his sufferings, seemed to be cast off by his Father when he cried out, *Why hast thou forsaken me?* and yet even then he obtained a glorious victory over the powers of darkness and their strong city, a victory which will undoubtedly be completed at last; for he has gone forth conquering and to conquer. The Israel of God, his spiritual Israel, are likewise, through him, more than conquerors. Though sometimes they may be tempted to think that God has cast them off, and may be foiled in particular conflicts, yet God will bring them into the strong city at last *Vincimur in prælio, sed non in bello*

—*We are foiled in a battle, but not in the whole war.* A lively faith in the promise will assure us, not only that *the God of peace shall tread Satan under our feet shortly,* but that *it is our Father's good pleasure to give us the kingdom.*

II. He prays in hope. His prayer is, *Give us help from trouble, v.* 11. Even in the day of their triumph they see themselves in trouble, because still in war, which is troublesome even to the prevailing side. None therefore can delight in war but those that love to fish in troubled waters. The *help from trouble* they pray for is preservation from those they were at war with. Though now they were conquerors, yet (so uncertain are the issues of war), unless God gave them help in the next engagement, they might be defeated; therefore, *Lord, send us help from the sanctuary. Help from trouble* is rest from war, which they prayed for, as those that contended for equity, not for victory. *Sic quærimus pacem—Thus we seek for peace.* The hope with which they support themselves in this prayer has two things in it:—1. A diffidence of themselves and all their creature-confidences: *Vain is the help of man.* Then only we are qualified to receive help from God when we are brought to own the insufficiency of all creatures to do that for us which we expect him to do. 2. A confidence in God, and in his power and promise (*v.* 12): "*Through God we shall do valiantly,* and so we shall do victoriously; for *he it is,* and he only, *that shall tread down our enemies,* and shall have the praise of doing it." Note, (1.) Our confidence in God must be so far from superseding that it must encourage and quicken our endeavours in the way of our duty. Though *it is God that performs all things for us,* yet there is something to be done by us. (2.) Hope in God is the best principle of true courage. Those that do their duty under his conduct may afford to do it valiantly; for what need those fear who have God on their side? (3.) It is only through God, and by the influence of his grace, that we do valiantly; it is he that puts strength into us, and inspires us, who of ourselves are weak and timorous, with courage and resolution. (4.) Though we do ever so valiantly, the success must be attributed entirely to him; for *he it is that shall tread down our enemies,* and not we ourselves. All our victories, as well as our valour, are from him, and therefore at his feet all our crowns must be cast.

PSALM LXI.

462

of our hope, of our prayers and of our praises; and some passages in this psalm are very peculiar.

To the chief musician upon Neginah. *A psalm of David.*

HEAR my cry, O God; attend unto my prayer. 2 From the end of the earth will I cry unto thee, when my heart is overwhelmed: lead me to the rock *that* is higher than I. 3 For thou hast been a shelter for me, *and* a strong tower from the enemy. 4 I will abide in thy tabernacle for ever: I will trust in the covert of thy wings. Selah.

In these verses we may observe,

I. David's close adherence and application to God by prayer in the day of his distress and trouble: "Whatever comes, *I will cry unto thee* (*v.* 2),—not cry unto other gods, but to thee only,—not fall out with thee because thou afflictest me, but still look unto thee, and wait upon thee,—not speak to thee in a cold and careless manner, but cry to thee with the greatest importunity and fervency of spirit, as one that will not let thee go except thou bless me." This he will do, 1. Notwithstanding his distance from the sanctuary, the house of prayer, where he used to attend as in the court of requests: "*From the end of the earth,* or of *the land,* from the most remote and obscure corner of the country, *will I cry unto thee.*" Note, Wherever we are we may have liberty of access to God, and may find a way open to the throne of grace. *Undique ad cœlos tantundem est viæ—Heaven is equally accessible from all places.* "Nay, because I am here in the end of the earth, in sorrow and solitude, therefore *I will cry unto thee.*" Note, That which separates us from our other comforts should drive us so much the nearer to God, the fountain of all comfort. 2. Notwithstanding the dejection and despondency of his spirit: "Though *my heart is overwhelmed,* it is not so sunk, so burdened, but that it may be lifted up to God in prayer; if it is not capable of being thus raised up, it is certainly too much cast down. Nay, because my heart is ready to be overwhelmed, therefore *I will cry unto thee,* for by that means it will be supported and relieved." Note, Weeping must quicken praying, and not deaden it. *Is any afflicted? Let him pray,* Jam. v. 13; Ps. cii., title.

II. The particular petition he put up to God when his heart was overwhelmed and he was ready to sink: *Lead me to the rock that is higher than I;* that is, 1. "To the rock which is too high for me to get up to unless thou help me to it. Lord, give me such an assurance and satisfaction of my own safety as I can never attain to but by thy special grace working such a faith in me." 2. "To the rock on the top of which I shall be set further out of the reach of my troubles, and nearer the serene and quiet region, than I can be by any power or wisdom of my own." God's power and promise are a rock that is higher than we. This rock is Christ; those are safe that are in him. We cannot get upon this rock unless God by his power lead us. *I will put thee in the cleft of the rock,* Exod. xxxiii. 22. We should therefore by faith and prayer put ourselves under the divine management, that we may be taken under the divine protection.

III. His desire .and expectation of an answer of peace. He begs in faith (*v.* 1): "*Hear my cry, O God! attend unto my prayer;* that is, let me have the present comfort of knowing that I am heard (xx. 6), and in due time let me have that which I pray for."

IV. The ground of this expectation, and the plea he uses to enforce his petition (*v.* 3): "*Thou hast been a shelter for me;* I have found in thee a rock higher than I: therefore I trust thou wilt still lead me to that rock." Note, Past experiences of the benefit of trusting in God, as they should engage us still to keep close to him, so they should encourage us to hope that it will not be in vain. "Thou hast been my *strong tower from the enemy,* and thou art as strong as ever, and thy name is as much a refuge to the righteous as ever it was," Prov. xviii. 10.

V. His resolution to continue in the way of duty to God and dependence on him, *v.* 4. 1. The service of God shall be his constant work and business. All those must make it so who expect to find God their shelter and strong tower: none but his menial servants have the benefit of his protection. *I will abide in thy tabernacle for ever.* David was now banished from the tabernacle, which was his greatest grievance, but he is assured that God by his providence would bring him back to his tabernacle, because he had by his grace wrought in him such a kindness for the tabernacle as that he was resolved to make it his perpetual residence, xxvii. 4. He speaks of abiding in it *for ever* because that tabernacle was a type and figure of heaven, Heb. ix. 8, 9, 24. Those that dwell in God's tabernacle, as it is a house of duty, during their short *ever* on earth, shall dwell in that tabernacle which is the house of glory during an endless *ever.* 2. The grace of God and the covenant of grace shall be his constant comfort: *I will make my refuge in the covert of his wings,* as the chickens seek both warmth and safety under the wings of the hen. Those that have found God a shelter to them ought still to have recourse to him in all their straits. This advantage those have that abide in God's tabernacle, that in the time of trouble he shall there hide them.

5 For thou, O God, hast heard my vows: thou hast given *me* the heritage of those that fear thy name. 6 Thou wilt prolong the king's life: *and* his years as many generations. 7 He shall abide before God for ever: O prepare mercy and truth, *which* may preserve him. 8 So will I sing praise unto thy name for ever, that I may daily perform my vows.

In these verses we may observe,

I. With what pleasure David looks back upon what God had done for him formerly (*v.* 5): *Thou, O God! hast heard my vows,* that is, 1. "The vows themselves which I made, and with which I bound my soul: thou hast taken notice of them; thou hast accepted them, because made in sincerity, and been well pleased with them; thou hast been mindful of them, and put me in mind of them." God put Jacob in mind of his vows, Gen. xxxi. 13; xxxv. 1. Note, God is a witness to all our vows, all our good purposes, and all our solemn promises of new obedience. He keeps an account of them, which should be a good reason with us, as it was with David here, why we should perform our vows, *v.* 8. For he that hears the vows we made will make us hear respecting them if they be not made good. 2. "The prayers that went along with those vows; those thou hast graciously heard and answered," which encouraged him now to pray, *O God! hear my cry.* He that never did say to the seed of Jacob, Seek you me in vain, will not now begin to say so. "Thou hast heard my vows, and given a real answer to them; for *thou hast given me a heritage of those that fear thy name.*" Note, (1.) There is a peculiar people in the world that fear God's name, that with a holy awe and reverence accept of and accommodate themselves to all the discoveries he is pleased to make of himself to the children of men. (2.) There is a heritage peculiar to that peculiar people; present comforts, earnests of their future bliss. God himself is their inheritance, their portion for ever. The Levites that had God for their inheritance must take up with him, and not expect a lot like their brethren; so those that fear God have enough in him, and therefore must not complain if they have but little of the world. (3.) We need desire no better heritage than that of those who fear God. If God deal with us as he uses to deal with those that love his name we need not desire to be any better dealt with.

II. With what assurance he looks forward to the continuance of his life (*v.* 6): *Thou shalt prolong the king's life.* This may be understood either, 1. Of himself. If it was penned before he came to the crown, yet, being anointed by Samuel, and knowing what God had spoken in his holiness, he could in faith call himself *the king,* though now persecuted as an out-law; or perhaps it was penned when Absalom sought to dethrone him, and force him into exile. There were those that aimed to shorten his life, but he trusted to God to prolong his life, which he did to the age of man set by Moses (namely, seventy years), which, being spent in serving his generation according to the will of God (Acts. xiii. 36), might be reckoned *as many generations*, because many generations would be the better for him. His resolution was to abide in God's tabernacle for ever (*v.* 4), in a way of duty; and now his hope is that he shall abide before God for ever, in a way of comfort. Those abide to good purpose in this world that abide before God, that serve him and walk in his fear; and those that do so shall abide before him for ever. He speaks of himself in the third person, because the psalm was delivered to the chief musician for the use of the church, and he would have the people, in singing it, to be encouraged with an assurance that, notwithstanding the malice of his enemies, their king, as they wished, should live for ever. Or, 2. Of the Messiah, the King of whom he was a type. It was a comfort to David to think, whatever became of him, that the years of the Lord's Anointed would be as many generations, and that *of the increase of his government and peace there should be no end.* The Mediator shall abide before God for ever, for he always appears in the presence of God for us, and ever lives, making intercession; and, because he lives, we shall live also.

III. With what importunity he begs of God to take him and keep him always under his protection: *O prepare mercy and truth which may preserve him!* God's promises and our faith in them are not to supersede, but to quicken and encourage prayer. David is sure that God will prolong his life, and therefore prays that he would preserve it, not that he would prepare him a strong lifeguard, or a well-fortified castle, but that he would prepare mercy and truth for his preservation; that is, that God's goodness would provide for his safety according to the promise. We need not desire to be better secured than under the protection of God's mercy and truth. This may be applied to the Messiah: " Let him be sent in the fulness of time, in *performance of the truth to Jacob and the mercy to Abraham.*" Micah. vii. 20; Luke i. 72, 73.

IV. With what cheerfulness he vows the grateful returns of duty to God (*v.* 8): *So will I sing praise unto thy name for ever.* Note, God's preservation of us calls upon us to praise him; and *therefore* we should desire to live, that we may praise him: *Let my soul live, and it shall praise thee.* We must make praising God the work of our time, even to the last (as long as our lives are prolonged we must continue praising God), and then it shall be made the work of our eternity, and we shall be praising him for ever. *That I may daily perform my vows.* His praising God was itself the performance of his vows, and it disposed his heart to the performance of his vows in other instances. Note, 1. The vows we have made we must conscientiously

perform. 2. Praising God and paying our vows to him must be our constant daily work; every day we must be doing something towards it, because it is all but little in comparison with what is due, because we daily receive fresh mercies, and because, if we think much to do it daily, we cannot expect to be doing it eternally.

PSALM LXII.

This psalm has nothing in it directly either of prayer or praise, nor does it appear upon what occasion it was penned, nor whether upon any particular occasion, whether mournful or joyful. But in it, I. David with a great deal of pleasure professes his own confidence in God and dependence upon him, and encourages himself to continue waiting on him, ver. 1—7. II. With a great deal of earnestness he excites and encourages others to trust in God likewise, and not in any creature, ver. 8—12. In singing it we should stir up ourselves to wait on God.

To the chief musician, to Jeduthun. A psalm of David.

TRULY my soul waiteth upon God: from him *cometh* my salvation. 2 He only *is* my rock and my salvation; *he is* my defence; I shall not be greatly moved. 3 How long will ye imagine mischief against a man? ye shall be slain all of you: as a bowing wall *shall ye be, and as* a tottering fence. 4 They only consult to cast *him* down from his excellency: they delight in lies: they bless with their mouth, but they curse inwardly. Selah. 5 My soul, wait thou only upon God; for my expectation *is* from him. 6 He only *is* my rock and my salvation: *he is* my defence; I shall not be moved. 7 In God *is* my salvation and my glory: the rock of my strength, *and* my refuge, *is* in God.

In these verses we have,

I. David's profession of dependence upon God, and upon him only, for all good (*v.* 1): *Truly my soul waiteth upon God.* *Nevertheless* (so some) or " *However it be,* whatever difficulties or dangers I may meet with, though God frown upon me and I meet with discouragements in my attendance on him, yet still my soul waits upon God" (or *is silent to God,* as the word is), " says nothing against what he does, but quietly expects what he will do." We are in the way both of duty and comfort when our souls wait upon God, when we cheerfully refer ourselves, and the disposal of all our affairs, to his will and wisdom, when we acquiesce in and accommodate ourselves to all the dispensations of his providence, and patiently expect a doubtful event, with an entire satisfaction in his righteousness and goodness, *however it be. Is not my soul subject to God?* So the LXX. So it is, certainly so it ought to be; our wills must be melted into his will. *My soul has respect to God, for from him cometh my salvation.* He doubts not but his salvation will come, though now he was threatened and in danger, and he expects it to come from God, and from him only; for *in vain is it hoped for from hills and mountains*, Jer. iii. 23; Ps. cxxi. 1, 2. "From him I know it will come, and therefore on him will I patiently wait till it does come, for his time is the best time." We may apply it to our eternal salvation, which is called *the salvation of God* (l. 23); from him it comes; he prepared it for us, he prepares us for it, and preserves us to it, and therefore let our souls wait on him, to be conducted through this world to that eternal salvation, in such way as he thinks fit.

II. The ground and reason of this dependence (*v.* 2): *He only is my rock and my salvation; he is my defence.* 1. He has been so many a time; in him I have found shelter, and strength, and succour. He has by his grace supported me and borne me up under my troubles, and by his providence defended me from the insults of my enemies and delivered me out of the troubles into which I was plunged; and therefore *I trust he will deliver me*," 2 Cor. i. 10. 2. "He only can be my rock and my salvation. Creatures are insufficient; they are nothing without him, and therefore I will look above them to him." 3. "He has by covenant undertaken to be so. Even he that is the rock of ages is my rock; he that is the God of salvation is my salvation; he that is the Most High is my high place; and therefore I have all the reason in the world to confide in him."

III. The improvement he makes of his confidence in God.

1. Trusting in God, his heart is fixed. "If God is my strength and mighty deliverer, *I shall not be greatly moved* (that is, I shall not be undone and ruined), but I shall not be sunk." Or, "I shall not be much disturbed and disquieted in my own breast. I may be put into some fright, but I shall not be afraid with any amazement, nor so as to be put out of the possession of my own soul. I may be perplexed, but not in despair," 2 Cor. iv. 8. This hope in God will be an anchor of the soul, sure and stedfast.

2. His enemies are slighted, and all their attempts against him looked upon by him with contempt, *v.* 3, 4. If God be for us, we need not fear what man can do against us, though ever so mighty and malicious. He here, (1.) Gives a character of his enemies: *They imagine mischief*, design it with a great deal of the serpent's venom and contrive it with a great deal of the serpent's subtlety, and this *against a man*, one of their own kind, against one single man, that is not an equal match for them, for they are many; they continued their malicious persecution though Providence had often defeated their mischievous designs. "*How long will you do it?* Will you never be convinced of your error? Will your malice never have spent itself?" They are unanimous in their consultations to cast an excellent man *down from his excellency*, to

draw an honest man from his integrity, to entangle him in sin, which is the only thing that can effectually cast us down from our excellency, to thrust a man, whom God has exalted, down from his dignity, and so to fight against God. Envy was at the bottom of their malice; they were grieved at David's advancement, and therefore plotted, by diminishing his character and blackening that (which was casting him down from his excellency) to hinder his preferment. In order to this they calumniate him, and love to hear such bad characters given of him and such bad reports raised and spread concerning him as they themselves know to be false: *They delight in lies.* And as they make no conscience of lying concerning him, to do him a mischief, so they make no conscience of lying to him, to conceal the mischief they design, and accomplish it the more effectually: *They bless with their mouth* (they compliment David to his face), *but they curse inwardly;* in their hearts they wish him all mischief, and privately they are plotting against him and in their cabals carrying on some evil design or other, by which they hope to ruin him. It is dangerous putting our trust in men who are thus false; but God is faithful. (2.) He reads their doom, pronounces a sentence of death upon them, not as a king, but as a prophet: *You shall be slain all of you*, by the righteous judgments of God. Saul and his servants were slain by the Philistines on Mount Gilboa, according to this prediction. Those who seek the ruin of God's chosen are but preparing ruin for themselves. God's church is built upon a rock which will stand, but those that fight against it, and its patrons and protectors, shall be as *a bowing wall and a tottering fence*, which, having a rotten foundation, sinks with its own weight, falls of a sudden, and buries those in the ruins of it that put themselves under the shadow and shelter of it. David, having put his confidence in God, thus foresees the overthrow of his enemies, and, in effect, sets them at defiance and bids them do their worst.

3. He is himself encouraged to continue waiting upon God (*v.* 5—7): *My soul, wait thou only upon God.* Note, The good we do we should stir up ourselves to continue doing, and to do yet more and more, as those that have, through grace, experienced the comfort and benefit of it. We have found it good to wait upon God, and therefore should charge our souls, and even charm them, into such a constant dependence upon him as may make us always easy. He had said (*v.* 1), *From him cometh my salvation;* he says (*v.* 5), *My expectation is from him.* His salvation was the principal matter of his expectation; let him have that from God, and he expects no more. His salvation being from God, all his other expectations are from him. "If God will save my soul, as to every thing else let him do what he pleases with me,

and I will acquiesce in his disposals, knowing they shall *all turn to my salvation*," Phil. i. 19. He repeats (*v.* 6) what he had said concerning God (*v.* 2), as one that was not only assured of it, but greatly pleased with it, and that dwelt much upon it in his thoughts: *He only is my rock and my salvation; he is my defence,* I know he is; but there he adds, *I shall not be greatly moved,* here, *I shall not be moved at all.* Note, The more faith is acted the more active it is. *Crescit eundo—It grows by being exercised.* The more we meditate upon God's attributes and promises, and our own experience, the more ground we get of our fears, which, like Haman, when they begin to fall, shall fall before us, and we shall be *kept in perfect peace,* Isa. xxvi. 3. And, as David's faith in God advances to an unshaken stayedness, so his joy in God improves itself into a holy triumph (*v.* 7): *In God is my salvation and my glory.* Where our salvation is there our glory is; for what is our salvation but the glory to be revealed, the eternal weight of glory? And there our glorying must be. In God let us boast all the day long. "The *rock of my strength* (that is, my strong rock, on which I build my hopes and stay myself) *and my refuge,* to which I flee for shelter when I am pursued, *is in God,* and in him only. I have no other to flee to, no other to trust to; the more I think of it the better satisfied I am in the choice I have made." Thus does he *delight himself in the Lord, and then ride upon the high places of the earth,* Isa. lviii. 14.

8 Trust in him at all times; ye people, pour out your heart before him : God *is* a refuge for us. Selah. 9 Surely men of low degree *are* vanity, *and* men of high degree *are* a lie : to be laid in the balance, they *are* altogether *lighter* than vanity. 10 Trust not in oppression, and become not vain in robbery : if riches increase, set not your heart *upon them.* 11 God hath spoken once ; twice have I heard this ; that power *belongeth* unto God. 12 Also unto thee, O Lord, *belongeth* mercy : for thou renderest to every man according to his work.

Here we have David's exhortation to others to trust in God and wait upon him, as he had done. Those that have found the comfort of the ways of God themselves will invite others into those ways ; there is enough in God for all the saints to draw from, and we shall have never the less for others sharing with us.

I. He counsels all to wait upon God, as he did, *v.* 8. Observe,

1. To whom he gives this good counsel : *You people* (that is, all people); all shall be welcome to trust in God, for he is the *confi-*

466

dence of all the ends of the earth, lxv. 5. *You people of the house of Israel* (so the Chaldee); they are especially engaged and invited to trust in God, for he is the God of Israel; and should not a people seek unto their God?

2. What the good counsel is which he gives. (1.) To confide in God : "*Trust in him ;* deal with him, and be willing to deal upon trust; depend upon him to perform all things for you, upon his wisdom and goodness, his power and promise, his providence and grace. Do this *at all times.*" We must have an habitual confidence in God always, must live a life of dependence upon him, must so trust in him at all times as not at any time to put that confidence in ourselves, or in any creature, which is to be put in him only; and we must have an actual confidence in God upon all occasions, trust in him upon every emergency, to guide us when we are in doubt, to protect us when we are in danger, to supply us when we are in want, to strengthen us for every good word and work. (2.) To converse with God : *Pour out your heart before him.* The expression seems to allude to the pouring out of the drink-offerings before the Lord. When we make a penitent confession of sin our hearts are therein *poured out before God,* 1 Sam. vii. 6. But here it is meant of prayer, which, if it be as it should be, is the pouring out of the heart before God. We must lay our grievances before him, offer up our desires to him with all humble freedom, and then entirely refer ourselves to his disposal, patiently submitting our wills to his : this is pouring out our hearts.

3. What encouragement he gives us to take this good counsel : *God is a refuge for us,* not only my refuge (*v.* 7), but a refuge for us all, even as many as will flee to him and take shelter in him.

II. He cautions us to take heed of misplacing our confidence, in which, as much as in any thing, *the heart is deceitful,* Jer. xvii. 5—9. Those that trust in God truly (*v.* 1) will trust in him only, *v.* 5. 1. Let us not trust in the men of this world, for they are broken reeds (*v.* 9): *Surely men of low degree are vanity,* utterly unable to help us, and *men of high degree are a lie,* that will deceive us if we trust to them. Men of low degree, one would think, might be relied on for their multitude and number, their bodily strength and service, and men of high degree for their wisdom, power, and influence; but neither the one nor the other are to be depended on. Of the two, men of high degree are mentioned as the more deceiving; for they are *a lie,* which denotes not only vanity, but iniquity. We are not so apt to depend upon men of low degree as upon the king and the captain of the host, who, by the figure they make, tempt us to trust in them, and so, when they fail us, prove a lie. But lay them *in the balance,* the balance of the scripture, or rather make trial of them, see how they will prove, whether they will answer your expectations from them or no, and you will write *Tekel* upon them; they are alike *lighter than vanity;* there is no depending upon their wisdom to advise us, their power to act for us, their good-will to us, no, nor upon their promises, in comparison with God, nor otherwise than in subordination to him. 2. Let us not trust in the wealth of this world, let not that be made our strong city (*v.* 10): *Trust not in oppression;* that is, in riches got by fraud and violence, because where there is a great deal it is commonly got by indirect scraping or saving (our Saviour calls it the *mammon of unrighteousness,* Luke xvi. 9), or in the arts of getting riches. "Think not, either because you have got abundance or are in the way of getting, that therefore you are safe enough; for this is becoming *vain in robbery,* that is, cheating yourselves while you think to cheat others." He that *trusted in the abundance of his riches strengthened himself in his wickedness* (lii. 7); but at his end he will be a fool, Jer. xvii. 11. Let none be so stupid as to think of supporting themselves in their sin, much less of supporting themselves in this sin. Nay, because it is hard to have riches and not to trust in them, if they increase, though by lawful and honest means, we must take heed lest we let out our affections inordinately towards them: "*Set not your heart upon them;* be not eager for them, do not take a complacency in them as the rest of your souls, nor put a confidence in them as your portion; be not over-solicitous about them; do not value yourselves and others by them; make not the wealth of the world your chief good and highest end: in short, do not make an idol of it." This we are most in danger of doing when riches increase. When the grounds of the rich man brought forth plentifully, then he said to his soul, *Take thy ease* in these things, Luke xii. 19. It is a smiling world that is most likely to draw the heart away from God, on whom only it should be set.

III. He gives a very good reason why we should make God our confidence, because he is a God of infinite power, mercy, and righteousness, *v.* 11, 12. This he himself was well assured of and would have us be assured of it: *God has spoken once; twice have I heard this;* that is, 1. "God has spoken it, and I have heard it, once, yea, twice. He has spoken it, and I have heard it by the light of reason, which easily infers it from the nature of the infinitely perfect Being and from his works both of creation and providence. He has spoken it, and I have heard once, yea, twice (that is, many a time), by the events that have concerned me in particular. He has spoken it and I have heard it by the light of revelation, by dreams and visions (Job iv. 15), by the glorious manifestation of himself upon Mount Sinai" (to which, some think, it does especially refer), "and by the written word." God has often told us

what a great and good God he is, and we ought as often to take notice of what he has told us. Or, 2. "Though God spoke it but once, I heard it twice, heard it diligently, not only with my outward ears, but with my soul and mind." To some God speaks twice and they will not hear once; but to others he speaks but once, and they hear twice. Compare Job xxxiii. 14. Now what is it which is thus spoken and thus heard? (1.) That the God with whom we have to do is infinite in power. *Power belongs to God;* he is almighty, and can do every thing; with him nothing is impossible. All the powers of all the creatures are derived from him, depend upon him, and are used by him as he pleases. His is the power, and to him we must ascribe it. This is a good reason why we should trust in him at all times and live in a constant dependence upon him; for he is able to do all that for us which we trust in him for. (2.) That he is a God of infinite goodness. Here the psalmist turns his speech to God himself, as being desirous to give him the glory of his goodness, which is his glory: *Also unto thee, O Lord! belongeth mercy.* God is not only the greatest, but the best, of beings. Mercy is with him, cxxx. 4, 7. He is merciful in a way peculiar to himself; he is the *Father of mercies,* 2 Cor. i. 3. This is a further reason why we should trust in him, and answers the objections of our sinfulness and unworthiness; though we deserve nothing but his wrath, yet we may hope for all good from his mercy, which is over all his works. (3.) That he never did, nor ever will do, any wrong to any of his creatures: *For thou renderest to every man according to his work.* Though he does not always do this visibly in this world, yet he will do it in the day of recompence. No service done him shall go unrewarded, nor any affront given him unpunished, unless it be repented of. By this it appears that power and mercy belong to him. If he were not a God of power, there are sinners that would be too great to be punished. And if he were not a God of mercy there are services that would be too worthless to be rewarded. This seems especially to bespeak the justice of God in judging upon appeals made to him by wronged innocency; he will be sure to judge according to truth, in giving redress to the injured and avenging them on those that have been injurious to them, 1 Kings viii. 32. Let those therefore that are wronged commit their cause to him and trust to him to plead it.

PSALM LXIII.

This psalm has in it as much of warmth and lively devotion as any of David's psalms in so little a compass. As the sweetest of Paul's epistles were those that bore date out of a prison, so some of the sweetest of David's psalms were those that were penned, as this was, in a wilderness. That which grieved him most in his banishment was the want of public ordinances; these he here longs to be restored to the enjoyment of; and the present want did but whet his appetite. Yet it is not the ordinances, but the God of the ordinances, that his heart is upon. And here we have, I. His desire towards God, ver. 1, 2. II. His esteem of God, ver. 3, 4. III. His satisfaction in God, ver. 5. IV. His secret communion with God, ver. 6. V. His joyful dependence upon God, ver. 7, 8. VI. His holy triumph in God over his enemies and in the assurance of his own safety, ver. 9–11. A devout and pious soul has little need of direction how to sing this psalm, so naturally does it speak its own genuine language; and an unsanctified soul, that is unacquainted and unaffected with divine things, is scarcely capable of singing it with understanding.

A psalm of David, when he was in the wilderness of Judah.

O GOD, thou *art* my God; early will I seek thee: my soul thirsteth for thee, my flesh longeth for thee in a dry and thirsty land, where no water is; 2 To see thy power and thy glory, so *as* I have seen thee in the sanctuary.

The title tells us when the psalm was penned, when David was *in the wilderness of Judah;* that is, *in the forest of Hareth* (1 Sam. xxii. 5) or in *the wilderness of Ziph*, 1 Sam. xxiii. 15. 1. Even in Canaan, though a fruitful land and the people numerous, yet there were wildernesses, places less fruitful and less inhabited than other places. It will be so in the world, in the church, but not in heaven; there it is all city, all paradise, and no desert ground; *the wilderness* there *shall blossom as the rose*. 2. The best and dearest of God's saints and servants may sometimes have their lot cast in a wilderness, which speaks them lonely and solitary, desolate and afflicted, wanting, wandering, and unsettled, and quite at a loss what to do with themselves. 3. All the straits and difficulties of a wilderness must not put us out of tune for sacred songs; but even then it is our duty and interest to keep up a cheerful communion with God. There are psalms proper for a wilderness, and we have reason to thank God that it is the wilderness of Judah we are in, not the wilderness of Sin.

David, in these verses, *stirs up himself to take hold on God,*

I. By a lively active faith: *O God! thou art my God*. Note, In all our addresses to God we must eye him as God, and our God, and this will be our comfort in a wilderness-state. We must acknowledge that God is, that we speak to one that really exists and is present with us, when we say, *O God!* which is a serious word; pity it should ever be used as a by-word. And we must own his authority over us and propriety in us, and our relation to him: "*Thou art my God*, mine by creation and therefore my rightful owner and ruler, mine by covenant and my own consent." We must speak it with the greatest pleasure to ourselves, and thankfulness to God, as those that are resolved to abide by it: *O God! thou art my God*.

II. By pious and devout affections, pursuant to the choice he had made of God and the covenant he had made with him.

1. He resolves to seek God, and his favour and grace: *Thou art my God*, and therefore *I will seek thee;* for *should not a people seek unto their God?* Isa. viii. 19. We must seek him; we must covet his favour as our chief good and consult his glory as our

468

highest end; we must seek acquaintance with him by his word and seek mercy from him by prayer. We must seek him, (1.) Early, with the utmost care, as those that are afraid of missing him; we must begin our days with him, begin every day with him: *Early will I seek thee*. (2.) Earnestly: "*My soul thirsteth for thee* and *my flesh longeth for thee* (that is, my whole man is affected with this pursuit) here *in a dry and thirsty land*." Observe, [1.] His complaint in the want of God's favourable presence. He was in a dry and thirsty land; so he reckoned it, not so much because it was a wilderness as because it was at a distance from the ark, from the word and sacraments. This world is a *weary land* (so the word is); it is so to the worldly that have their portion in it—it will yield them no true satisfaction; it is so to the godly that have their passage through it—it is a valley of Baca; they can promise themselves little from it. [2.] His importunity for that presence of God: *My soul thirsteth, longeth, for thee*. His want quickened his desires, which were very intense; he thirsted as the hunted hart for the water-brooks; he would take up with nothing short of it. His desires were almost impatient; he longed, he languished, till he should be restored to the liberty of God's ordinances. Note, Gracious souls look down upon the world with a holy disdain and look up to God with a holy desire.

2. He longs to enjoy God. What is it that he does so passionately wish for? What is his petition and what is his request? It is this (*v.* 2), *To see thy power and thy glory, so as I have seen thee in the sanctuary*. That is, (1.) "To see it here in this wilderness as I have seen it in the tabernacle, to see it in secret as I have seen it in the solemn assembly." Note, When we are deprived of the benefit of public ordinances we should desire and endeavour to keep up the same communion with God in our retirements that we have had in the great congregation. A closet may be turned into a little sanctuary. Ezekiel had the visions of the Almighty in Babylon, and John in the isle of Patmos. When we are alone we may have the Father with us, and that is enough. (2.) "To see it again in the sanctuary as I have formerly seen it there." He longs to be brought out of the wilderness, not that he might see his friends again and be restored to the pleasures and gaieties of the court, but that he might have access to the sanctuary, not to see the priests there, and the ceremony of the worship, but *to see thy power and glory* (that is, thy glorious power, or thy powerful glory, which is put for all God's attributes and perfections), "that I may increase in my acquaintance with them and have the agreeable impressions of them made upon my heart"—so to *behold the glory of the Lord* as to *be changed into the same image*, 2 Cor. iii. 18. "That I may see thy power and glory," he does not say, as I have seen them,

but "as I have seen *thee.*" We cannot see the essence of God, but we see him in seeing by faith his attributes and perfections. These sights David here pleases himself with the remembrance of. Those were precious minutes which he spent in communion with God; he loved to think them over again; these he lamented the loss of, and longed to be restored to. Note, That which has been the delight and is the desire of gracious souls, in their attendance on solemn ordinances, is to see God and his power and glory in them.

3 Because thy lovingkindness *is* better than life, my lips shall praise thee. 4 Thus will I bless thee while I live : I will lift up my hands in thy name. 5 My soul shall be satisfied as *with* marrow and fatness; and my mouth shall praise *thee* with joyful lips : 6 When I remember thee upon my bed, *and* meditate on thee in the *night* watches.

How soon are David's complaints and prayers turned into praises and thansgivings! After two verses that express his desire in seeking God, here are some that express his joy and satisfaction in having found him. Faithful prayers may quickly be turned into joyful praises, if it be not our own fault. *Let the hearts of those rejoice that seek the Lord* (cv. 3), and let them praise him for working those desires in them, and giving them assurance that he will satisfy them. David was now in a wilderness, and yet had his heart much enlarged in blessing God. Even in affliction we need not want matter for praise, if we have but a heart to it. Observe,

I. What David will praise God for (*v.*' 3) : *Because thy lovingkindness is better than life,* than *lives,* life and all the comforts of life, life in its best estate, long life and prosperity. God's lovingkindness is in itself, and in the account of all the saints, better than life. It is our spiritual life, and that is better than temporal life, xxx. 5. It is better, a thousand times, to die in God's favour than to live under his wrath. David in the wilderness finds, by comfortable experience, that God's lovingkindness is better than life; and *therefore* (says he) *my lips shall praise thee.* Note, Those that have their hearts refreshed with the tokens of God's favour ought to have them enlarged in his praises. A great deal of reason we have to bless God that we have better provisions and better possessions than the wealth of this world can afford us, and that in the service of God, and in communion with him, we have better employments and better enjoyments than we can have in the business and converse of this world.

II. How he will praise God, and how long, *v.* 4. He resolves to live a life of thankful-

ness to God and dependence on him. Observe, 1. His manner of blessing God: "*Thus will I bless thee,* thus as I have now begun; the present devout affections shall not pass away, like the morning cloud, but shine more and more, like the morning sun." Or, " I will bless thee with the same earnestness and fervency with which I have prayed to thee." 2. His continuance and perseverance therein : *I will bless thee while I live.* Note, Praising God must be the work of our whole lives; we must always retain a grateful sense of his former favours and repeat our thanksgivings for them. We must every day give thanks to him for the benefits with which we are daily loaded. We must in every thing give thanks, and not be put out of frame for this duty by any of the afflictions of this present time. Whatever days we live to see, how dark and cloudy soever, though the days come of which we say, *We have no pleasure in them,* yet still every day must be a thanksgiving-day, even to our dying-day. In this work we must spend our time because in this work we hope to spend a blessed eternity. 3. His constant regard to God upon all occasions, which should accompany his praises of him : *I will lift up my hands in thy name.* We must have an eye to God's name (to all that by which he has made himself known) in all our prayers and praises, which we are taught to begin with,—*Hallowed be thy name,* and to conclude with,—*Thine is the glory.* This we must have an eye to in our work and warfare ; we must lift up our hands to our duty and against our special enemies in God's name, that is, in the strength of his Spirit and grace, lxxi. 16; Zech. x. 12. We must make all our vows in God's name; to him we must engage ourselves and in a dependence upon his grace. And when we lift up the hands that hang down, in comfort and joy, it must be in God's name; from him our comforts must be fetched, and to him they must be devoted. *In thee do we boast all the day long.*

III. With what pleasure and delight he would praise God, *v.* 5. 1. With inward complacency: *My soul shall be satisfied as with marrow and fatness,* not only as with bread, which is nourishing, but as with marrow, which is pleasant and delicious, Isa. xxv. 6. David hopes he shall return again to the enjoyment of God's ordinances, and then he shall thus be satisfied, and the more for his having been for a time under restraint. Or, if not, yet in God's loving kindness, and in conversing with him in solitude, he shall be thus satisfied. Note, There is that in a gracious God, and in communion with him, which gives abundant satisfaction to a gracious soul, xxxvi. 8; lxv. 4. And there is that in a gracious soul which takes abundant satisfaction in God and communion with him. The saints have a contentment with God ; they desire no more than his favour to make them happy: and they have a transcendent complacency in God, in comparison with which all the delights of sense are sapless and without relish, as puddle-water in comparison with the wine of this consolation. 2. With outward expressions of this satisfaction; he will praise God *with joyful lips.* He will praise him, (1.) Openly. His mouth and lips shall praise God. When with the heart man believes and is thankful, with the mouth confession must be made of both, to the glory of God; not that the performances of the mouth are accepted without the heart (Matt. xv. 8), but out of the abundance of the heart the mouth must speak (xlv. 1), both for the exciting of our own devout affections and for the edification of others. (2.) Cheerfully. We must praise God with joyful lips; we must address ourselves to that and other duties of religion with great cheerfulness, and speak forth the praises of God from a principle of holy joy. Praising lips must be joyful lips.

IV. How he would entertain himself with thoughts of God when he was most retired (v. 6): I will praise thee *when I remember thee upon my bed.* We must praise God upon every remembrance of him. Now that David was shut out from public ordinances he abounded the more in secret communion with God, and so did something towards making up his loss. Observe here, 1. How David employed himself in thinking of God. God was in all his thoughts, which is the reverse of the wicked man's character, x. 4. The thoughts of God were ready to him: "*I remember thee;* that is, when I go to think, I find thee at my right hand, present to my mind." This subject should first offer itself, as that which we cannot forget or overlook. And they were fixed in him: *I meditate on thee.*" Thoughts of God must not be transient thoughts, passing through the mind, but abiding thoughts, dwelling in the mind. 2. When David employed himself thus—*upon his bed* and in the night-watches. David was now wandering and unsettled, but, wherever he came, he brought his religion along with him. Upon my *beds* (so some); being hunted by Saul, he seldom lay two nights together in the same bed; but wherever he lay, if, as Jacob, upon the cold ground and with a stone for his pillow, good thoughts of God lay down with him. David was so full of business all day, shifting for his own safety, that he had scarcely leisure to apply himself solemnly to religious exercises, and therefore, rather than want time for them, he denied himself his necessary sleep. He was now in continual peril of his life, so that we may suppose care and fear many a time held his eyes waking and gave him wearisome nights; but then he entertained and comforted himself with thoughts of God. Sometimes we find David in tears upon his bed (vi. 6), but thus he wiped away his tears. When sleep departs from our eyes (through pain, or sickness of body, or any disturbance

470

in the mind) our souls, by remembering God, may be at ease, and repose themselves. Perhaps an hour's pious meditation will do us more good than an hour's sleep would have done. See xvi. 7; xvii. 3; iv. 4; cxix. 62. There were night-watches kept in the tabernacle for praising God (cxxxiv. 1), in which, probably, David, when he had liberty, joined with the Levites; and now that he could not keep place with them he kept time with them, and wished himself among them.

7 Because thou hast been my help, therefore in the shadow of thy wings will I rejoice. 8 My soul followeth hard after thee: thy right hand upholdeth me. 9 But those *that* seek my soul, to destroy *it,* shall go into the lower parts of the earth. 10 They shall fall by the sword: they shall be a portion for foxes. 11 But the king shall rejoice in God; every one that sweareth by him shall glory: but the mouth of them that speak lies shall be stopped.

David, having expressed his desires towards God and his praises of him, here expresses his confidence in him and his joyful expectations from him (v. 7): *In the shadow of thy wings I will rejoice,* alluding either to the wings of the cherubim stretched out over the ark of the covenant, between which God is said to dwell ("I will rejoice in thy oracles, and in covenant and communion with thee"), or to the wings of a fowl, under which the helpless young ones have shelter, as the eagle's young ones (Exod. xix. 4, Deut. xxxii. 11), which speaks the divine power, and the young ones of the common hen (Matt. xxiii. 37), which speaks more of divine tenderness. It is a phrase often used in the psalms (xvii. 8; xxxvi. 7; lvii. 1; lxi. 4; xci. 4), and no where else in this sense, except Ruth ii. 12, where Ruth, when she became a proselyte, is said to *trust under the wings of the God of Israel.* It is our duty to *rejoice in the shadow of God's wings,* which denotes our recourse to him by faith and prayer, as naturally as the chickens, when they are cold or frightened, run by instinct under the wings of the hen. It intimates also our reliance upon him as able and ready to help us and our refreshment and satisfaction in his care and protection. Having committed ourselves to God, we must be easy and pleased, and quiet from the fear of evil. Now let us see further,

I. What were the supports and encouragements of David's confidence in God. Two things were as props to that hope which the word of God was the only foundation of:—

1. His former experiences of God's power in relieving him: "*Because thou hast been my help* when other helps and helpers failed me, therefore I will still rejoice in thy salva-

tion, will trust in thee for the future, and will do it with delight and holy joy. Thou hast been not only my helper, but my help;" for we could never have helped ourselves, nor could any creature have been helpful to us, but by him. Here we may set up our Ebenezer, saying, *Hitherto the Lord has helped us,* and must therefore resolve that we will never desert him, never distrust him, nor ever droop in our walking with him.

2. The present sense he had of God's grace carrying him on in these pursuits (*v.* 8): *My soul follows hard after thee,* which speaks a very earnest desire and a serious vigorous endeavour to keep up communion with God; if we cannot always have God in our embraces, yet we must always have him in our eye, reaching forth towards him as our prize, Phil. iii. 14. To press hard after God is to follow him closely, as those that are afraid of losing the sight of him, and to follow him swiftly, as those that long to be with him. This David did, and he owns, to the glory of God, *Thy right hand upholds me.* God upheld him, (1.) Under his afflictions, that he might not sink under them. *Underneath are the everlasting arms.* (2.) In his devotions. God upheld him in his holy desires and pursuits, that he might not grow weary in well-doing. Those that follow hard after God would soon fail and faint if God's right hand did not uphold them. It is he that strengthens us in the pursuit of him, quickens our good affections, and comforts us while we have not yet attained what we are in the pursuit of. It is by the power of God (that is his right hand) that we are kept from falling. Now this was a great encouragement to the psalmist to hope that he would, in due time, give him that which he so earnestly desired, because he had by his grace wrought in him those desires and kept them up.

II. What it was that David triumphed in the hopes of.

1. That his enemies should be ruined, *v.* 9, 10. There were those that *sought his soul to destroy it,* not only his life (which they struck at, both to prevent his coming to the crown and because they envied and hated him for his wisdom, piety, and usefulness), but his soul, which they sought to destroy by banishing him from God's ordinances, which are the nourishment and support of the soul (so doing what they could to starve it), and by sending him to serve other gods, so doing what they could to poison it, 1 Sam. xxvi. 19. But he foresees and foretels, (1.) That they shall *go into the lower parts of the earth,* to the grave, to hell; their enmity to David would be their death and their damnation, their ruin, their eternal ruin. (2.) That they shall fall by the sword, by the sword of God's wrath and his justice, by the sword of man, Job xix. 28, 29. They shall die a violent death, Rev. xiii. 10. This was fulfilled in Saul, who fell by the sword, his own sword; David foretold this, yet he would not execute

it when it was in the power of his hand, once and again; for precepts, not prophecies, are our rule. (3.) That *they shall be a portion for foxes;* either their dead bodies shall be a prey to ravenous beasts (Saul lay a good while unburied) or their houses and estates shall be a habitation for wild beasts, Isa. xxxiv. 14. Such as this will be the doom of Christ's enemies, that oppose his kingdom and interest in the world: *Bring them forth and slay them before me,* Luke xix. 27.

2. That he himself should gain his point at last (*v.* 11), that he should be advanced to the throne to which he had been anointed: *The king shall rejoice in God.* (1.) He calls himself *the king,* because he knew himself to be so in the divine purpose and designation; thus Paul, while yet in the conflict, writes himself *more than a conqueror,* Rom. viii. 37. Believers are made kings, though they are not to have the dominion till the morning of the resurrection. (2.) He doubts not but that though he was now sowing in tears he should reap in joy· *The king shall rejoice.* (3.) He resolves to make God the Alpha and Omega of all his joys. He shall *rejoice in God.* Now this is applicable to the glories and joys of the exalted Redeemer. Messiah the Prince shall rejoice in God; he has already entered into the joy set before him, and his glory will be completed at his second coming. Two things would be the good effect of David's advancement:—[1.] It would be the consolation of his friends. *Every one that swears to him* (that is, to David), that comes into his interest and takes an oath of allegiance to him, *shall glory* in his success; or *every one that swears by him* (that is, by the blessed name of God, and not by any idol, Deut. vi. 13), and then it means all good people, that make a sincere and open profession of God's name; they shall glory in God; they shall glory in David's advancement. *Those that fear thee will be glad when they see me.* Those that heartily espouse the cause of Christ shall glory in its victory at last. *If we suffer with him, we shall reign with him.* [2.] It would be the confutation of his enemies: *The mouth of those that speak lies,* of Saul, and Doeg, and others that misrepresented David and insulted over him, as if his cause was desperate, *shall be* quite *stopped;* they shall not have one word more to say against him, but will be for ever silenced and shamed. Apply this to Christ's enemies, to those that speak lies to him, as all hypocrites do, that tell him they love him while their hearts are not with him; their mouth shall be stopped with that word, *I know you not whence you are;* they shall be for ever speechless, Matt. xxii. 12. The mouths of those also that speak lies against him, that *pervert the right ways of the Lord* and speak ill of his holy religion, will be stopped in that day when the Lord shall come to reckon for all the hard speeches which ungodly sinners have spoken against him. Christ's second

coming will be the everlasting triumph of all his faithful friends and followers, who may therefore now triumph in the believing hopes of it.

PSALM LXIV.

This whole psalm has reference to David's enemies, persecutors, and slanderers ; many such there were, and a great deal of trouble they gave him, almost all his days, so that we need not guess at any particular occasion of penning this psalm. I. He prays to God to preserve him from their malicious designs against him, ver. 1, 2. II. He gives a very bad character of them, as men marked for ruin by their own wickedness, ver. 3—6. III. By the spirit of prophecy he foretels their destruction, which would redound to the glory of God and the encouragement of his people, ver. 7—10. In singing this psalm we must observe the effect of the old enmity that is in the seed of the woman against the seed of the serpent, and assure ourselves that the serpent's head will be broken, at last, to the honour and joy of the holy seed.

To the chief musician. A psalm of David.

HEAR my voice, O God, in my prayer : preserve my life from fear of the enemy. 2 Hide me from the secret counsel of the wicked; from the insurrection of the workers of iniquity : 3 Who whet their tongue like a sword, *and* bend *their bows to shoot* their arrows, *even* bitter words : 4 That they may shoot in secret at the perfect : suddenly do they shoot at him, and fear not. 5 They encourage themselves *in* an evil matter : they commune of laying snares privily ; they say,Who shall see them? 6 They search out iniquities ; they accomplish a diligent search : both the inward *thought* of every one *of them,* and the heart, *is* deep.

David, in these verses, puts in before God a representation of his own danger and of his enemies' character, to enforce his petition that God would protect him and punish them.

I. He earnestly begs of God to preserve him (*v.* 1, 2): *Hear my voice, O God! in my prayer;* that is, grant me the thing I pray for, and this is it, *Lord, preserve my life from fear of the enemy,* that is, from the enemy that I am in fear of. He makes request for his life, which is, in a particular manner, dear to him, because he knows it is designed to be very serviceable to God and his generation. When his life is struck at it cannot be thought he should altogether hold his peace, Esth. vii. 2, 4. And, if he plead his fear of the enemy, it is no disparagement to his courage ; his father Jacob, that prince with God, did so before him. Gen. xxxii. 11, *Deliver me from the hand of Esau, for I fear him.* Preserve *my life from fear,* not only from the thing itself which I fear, but from the disquieting fear of it ; this is, in effect, the preservation of the life, for fear has torment, particularly the fear of death, by reason of which some are all their life-time subject to bondage. He prays, " *Hide me from the secret counsel of the wicked,* from the mischief which they secretly consult among themselves to do

against me, and *from the insurrection of the workers of iniquity,* who join forces, as they join counsels, to do me a mischief." Observe, The secret counsel ends in an insurrection ; treasonable practices begin in treasonable confederacies and conspiracies. "Hide me from them, that they may not find me, that they may not reach me. Let me be safe under thy protection."

II. He complains of the great malice and wickedness of his enemies : " Lord, hide me from them, for they are the worst of men, not fit to be connived at ; they are dangerous men, that will stick at nothing ; so that I am undone if thou do not take my part."

1. They are very spiteful in their calumnies and reproaches, *v.* 3, 4. They are described as military men, with their sword and bow, archers that take aim exactly, secretly, and suddenly, and shoot at the harmless bird that apprehends not herself in any danger. But, (1.) Their tongues are their swords, flaming swords, two-edged swords, drawn swords, drawn in anger, with which they cut, and wound, and kill, the good name of their neighbours. The tongue is a little member, but, like the sword, it *boasts great things,* Jam. iii. 5. It is a dangerous weapon. (2.) *Bitter words* are *their arrows*—scurrilous reflections, opprobrious nicknames, false representations, slanders, and calumnies, the fiery darts of the wicked one, set on fire of hell. For these their malice *bends their bows,* to send out these arrows with so much the more force. (3.) The upright man is their mark ; against him their spleen is, and they cannot speak peaceably either of him or to him. The better any man is the more he is envied by those that are themselves bad, and the more ill is said of him. (4.) They manage it with a great deal of art and subtlety. They *shoot in secret,* that those they shoot at may not discover them and avoid the danger, for *in vain is the net spread in the sight of any bird.* And *suddenly do they shoot,* without giving a man lawful warning or any opportunity to defend himself. *Cursed be he that thus smites his neighbour secretly* in his reputation, Deut. xxvii. 24. There is no guard against a pass made by a false tongue. (5.) Herein *they fear not,* that is, they are confident of their success, and doubt not but by these methods they shall gain the point which their malice aims at. Or, rather, they fear not the wrath of God, which will be the portion of a false tongue. They are impudent and daring in the mischief they do to good people, as if they must never be called to an account for it.

2. They are very close and very resolute in their malicious projects, *v.* 5. (1.) They strengthen and corroborate themselves and one another in this evil matter, and, by joining together in it they make one another the more bitter and the more bold. *Fortiter calumniari, aliquid adhærebit*—Lay on an abundance of reproach; part will be sure to stick.

It is bad to do a wrong thing, but worse to encourage ourselves and one another in doing it; this is doing the devil's work for him. It is a sign that the heart is hardened to the highest degree when it is thus fully set to do evil and fears no colours. It is the office of conscience to discourage men in an evil matter, but, when that is baffled, the case is desperate. (2.) They consult with themselves and one another how to do the most mischief and most effectually: *They commune of laying snares privily.* All their communion is in sin and all their communication is how to sin securely. They hold councils of war for finding out the most effectual expedients to do mischief; every snare they lay was talked of before, and was laid with all the contrivance of their wicked wits combined. (3.) They please themselves with an atheistical conceit that God himself takes no notice of their wicked practices: *They say, Who shall see them?* A practical disbelief of God's omniscience is at the bottom of all the wickedness of the wicked.

3. They are very industrious in putting their projects in execution (*v.* 6): "*They search out iniquity;* they take a great deal of pains to find out some iniquity or other to lay to my charge; they dig deep, and look far back, and put things to the utmost stretch, that they may have something to accuse me of;" or, "They are industrious to find out new arts of doing mischief to me; in this they accomplish a diligent search; they go through with it, and spare neither cost nor labour. *Evil men dig up mischief.* Half the pains that many take to damn their souls would serve to save them. They are masters of all the arts of mischief and destruction, for *the inward thought of every one of them, and the heart, are deep,* deep as hell, desperately wicked, who can know it? By the unaccountable wickedness of their wit and of their will, they show themselves to be, both in subtlety and malignity, the genuine offspring of the old serpent.

7 But God shall shoot at them *with* an arrow; suddenly shall they be wounded. 8 So they shall make their own tongue to fall upon themselves: all that see them shall flee away. 9 And all men shall fear, and shall declare the work of God; for they shall wisely consider of his doing. 10 The righteous shall be glad in the LORD, and shall trust in him; and all the upright in heart shall glory.

We may observe here,

I. The judgments of God which should certainly come upon these malicious persecutors of David. Though they encouraged themselves in their wickedness, here is that which, if they would believe and consider it, was enough to discourage them. And it is observable how the punishment answers the sin. 1. They shot at David secretly and suddenly, to wound him; but God shall shoot at them, for he *ordains his arrows against the persecutors* (vii. 13), *against the face of them,* xxi. 12. And God's arrows will hit surer, and fly swifter, and pierce deeper, than theirs do or can. They have many arrows, but they are only bitter words, and words are but wind: the curse causeless shall not come. But God has one arrow that will be their death, his curse which is never causeless, and therefore shall come; with it they shall be suddenly wounded, that is, their wound by it will be a surprise upon them, because they were secure and not apprehensive of any danger. 2. Their tongues fell upon him, but God shall *make their tongues to fall upon themselves.* They do it by the desert of their sin; God does it by the justice of his wrath, *v.* 8. When God deals with men according to the desert of their tongue-sins, and brings those mischiefs upon them which they have passionately and maliciously imprecated upon others, then he makes their own tongues to fall upon them; and it is weight enough to sink a man to the lowest hell, like a talent of lead. Many have cut their own throats, and many more have damned their own souls, with their tongues, and it will be an aggravation of their condemnation. *O Israel! thou hast destroyed thyself,* art *snared in the words of thy mouth. If thou scornest, thou alone shalt bear it.* Those that love cursing, it shall come unto them. Sometimes men's secret wickedness is brought to light by their own confession, and then their own tongue falls upon them.

II. The influence which these judgments should have upon others; for it is done *in the open sight of all,* Job xxxiv. 26.

1. Their neighbours shall shun them and shift for their own safety. They *shall flee away,* for fear of partaking in their plagues and being involved in their ruin, so dreadful will it be and such a noise will it make in the country. They shall flee away, as the men of Israel did from the tents of Korah, Dathan, and Abiram, Num. xvi. 27. Some think this was fulfilled in the death of Saul, when not only his army was dispersed, but the inhabitants of the neighbouring country were so terrified with the fall, not only of their king but of his three sons, that they quitted their cities and fled, 1 Sam. xxxi. 7.

2. Spectators shall reverence the providence of God therein, *v.* 9. (1.) They shall understand and observe God's hand in all (and, unless we do so, we are not likely to profit by the dispensations of Providence, Hos. xiv. 9): *They shall wisely consider his doing.* There is need of consideration and serious thought rightly to apprehend the matter of fact, and need of wisdom to put a true interpretation upon it. God's doing is well worth our considering (Eccl. vii. 13), but it must be considered wisely, that we put not

473

a corrupt gloss upon a pure text. (2.) They shall be affected with a holy awe of God upon the consideration of it. All men (all that have any thing of the reason of a man in them) shall fear and tremble because of God's judgments, cxix. 120. They shall fear to do the like, fear being found persecutors of God's people. *Smite the scorner and the simple shall beware.* (3.) They shall declare the work of God. They shall speak to one another and to all about them of the justice of God in punishing persecutors. What we wisely consider ourselves we should wisely declare to others, for their edification and the glory of God. *This is the finger of God.*

3. Good people shall in a special manner take notice of it, and it shall affect them with a holy pleasure, *v.* 10. (1.) It shall increase their joy: *The righteous shall be glad in the Lord,* not glad of the misery and ruin of their fellow-creatures, but glad that God is glorified, and his word fulfilled, and the cause of injured innocency pleaded effectually. (2.) It shall encourage their faith. They shall commit themselves to him in the way of duty and be willing to venture for him with an entire confidence in him. (3.) Their joy and faith shall both express themselves in a holy boasting: *All the upright in heart,* that keep a good conscience and approve themselves to God, *shall glory,* not in themselves, but in the favour of God, in his righteousness and goodness, their relation to him and interest in him. *Let him that glories glory in the Lord.*

PSALM LXV.

In this psalm we are directed to give to God the glory of his power and goodness, which appear, I. In the kingdom of grace (ver. 1), hearing prayer (ver. 2), pardoning sin (ver. 3), satisfying the souls of the people (ver. 4), protecting and supporting them, ver. 5. II. In the kingdom of Providence, fixing the mountains (ver. 6), calming the sea (ver. 7), preserving the regular succession of day and night (ver. 8), and making the earth fruitful, ver. 9—13. These are blessings we are all indebted to God for, and therefore we may easily accommodate this psalm to ourselves in singing it.

To the chief musician. A psalm *and* song of David.

PRAISE waiteth for thee, O God, in Sion : and unto thee shall the vow be performed. 2 O thou that hearest prayer, unto thee shall all flesh come. 3 Iniquities prevail against me: *as for* our transgressions, thou shalt purge them away. 4 Blessed *is the man whom* thou choosest, and causest to approach *unto thee, that* he may dwell in thy courts : we shall be satisfied with the goodness of thy house, *even* of thy holy temple. 5 *By* terrible things in righteousness wilt thou answer us, O God of our salvation ; *who art* the confidence of all the ends of the earth, and of them that are afar off *upon* the sea.

The psalmist here has no particular concern of his own at the throne of grace, but

begins with an address to God, as the master of an assembly and the mouth of a congregation ; and observe,

I. How he gives glory to God, *v.* 1. 1. By humble thankfulness: *Praise waiteth for thee, O God! in Zion,* waits in expectation of the mercy desired, waits till it arrives, that it may be received with thankfulness at its first approach. When God is coming towards us with his favours we must go forth to meet him with our praises, and wait till the day dawn. " Praise waits, with an entire satisfaction in thy holy will and dependence on thy mercy." When we stand ready in every thing to give thanks, then praise waits for God. " Praise waits thy acceptance " The *Levites* by night *stood in the house of the Lord,* ready to sing their songs of praise at the hour appointed (cxxxiv. 1, 2), and thus their praise waited for him. *Praise is silent unto thee* (so the word is), as wanting words to express the great goodness of God, and being struck with a silent admiration at it. As there are holy *groanings which cannot be uttered,* so there are holy adorings which cannot be uttered, and yet shall be accepted by him that *searches the heart and knows what is the mind of the spirit.* Our praise is silent, that the praises of the blessed angels, who excel in strength, may be heard. Let it not be told him that I speak, for if a man offer to *speak forth all God's praise surely he shall be swallowed up,* Job xxxvii. 20. *Before thee praise is reputed as silence* (so the Chaldee), so far exalted is God above all our blessing and praise. Praise is due to God from all the world, but it waits for him in Zion only, in his church, among his people. All his works praise him (they minister matter for praise), but only his saints bless him by actual adorations. The redeemed church sing their new song upon Mount Zion, Rev. xiv. 1, 3. In Zion was God's dwelling-place, lxxvi. 2. Happy are those who dwell with him there, for they will be still praising him. 2. By sincere faithfulness: *Unto thee shall the vow be performed,* that is, the sacrifice shall be offered up which was vowed. We shall not be accepted in our thanksgivings to God for the mercies we have received unless we make conscience of paying the vows which we made when we were in pursuit of the mercy; for better it is not to vow than to vow and not to pay.

II. What he gives him glory for.

1. For hearing prayer (*v.* 2): *Praise waits for thee;* and why is it so ready? (1.) " Because thou art ready to grant our petitions. *O thou that hearest prayer!* thou canst answer every prayer, for thou art able to do for us more than we are able to ask or think (Eph. iii. 20), and thou wilt answer every prayer of faith, either in kind or kindness." It is much for the glory of God's goodness, and the encouragement of ours, that he is a God hearing prayer, and has taken it among the titles of his honour to be so ; and we are

much wanting to ourselves if we do not take all occasions to give him his title. (2.) Because, for that reason, we are ready to run to him when we are in our straits. "*Therefore,* because thou art a God hearing prayer, *unto thee shall all flesh come;* justly does every man's praise wait for thee, because every man's prayer waits on thee when he is in want or distress, whatever he does at other times. Now only the seed of Israel come to thee, and the proselytes to their religion; but, when thy *house shall be called a house of prayer to all people,* then unto thee shall all flesh come, and be welcome," Rom. x. 12, 13. To him let us come, and come boldly, because he is a God that hears prayer.

2. For pardoning sin. In this *who is a God like unto him?* Micah vii. 18. By this he proclaims his name (Exod. xxxiv. 7), and therefore, upon this account, praise waits for him, *v.* 3. "Our sins reach to the heavens, *iniquities prevail against* us, and appear so numerous, so heinous, that when they are set in order before us we are full of confusion and ready to fall into despair. They prevail so against us that we cannot pretend to balance them with any righteousness of our own, so that when we appear before God our own consciences accuse us and we have no reply to make; and yet, *as for our transgressions, thou shalt,* of thy own free mercy and for the sake of a righteousness of thy own providing, *purge them away,* so that we shall not come into condemnation for them." Note, The greater our danger is by reason of sin the more cause we have to admire the power and riches of God's pardoning mercy, which can invalidate the threatening force of our manifold transgressions and our mighty sins.

3. For the kind entertainment he gives to those that attend upon him and the comfort they have in communion with him. Iniquity must first be purged away (*v.* 3) and then we are welcome to compass God's altars, *v.* 4. Those that come into communion with God shall certainly find true happiness and full satisfaction in that communion.

(1.) They are blessed. Not only blessed is the nation (xxxiii. 12), but *blessed is the man,* the particular person, how mean soever, *whom thou choosest, and causest to approach unto thee, that he may dwell in thy courts;* he is a happy man, for he has the surest token of the divine favour and the surest pledge and earnest of everlasting bliss. Observe here, [1.] What it is to come into communion with God, in order to this blessedness. *First,* It is to approach to him by laying hold on his covenant, setting our best affections upon him, and letting out our desires towards him; it is to converse with him as one we love and value. *Secondly,* It is to dwell in his courts, as the priests and Levites did, that were at home in God's house; it is to be constant in the exercises of religion, and apply ourselves closely to them as we do

to that which is the business of our dwelling-place. [2.] How we come into communion with God, not recommended by any merit of our own, nor brought in by any management of our own, but by God's free choice: "*Blessed is the man whom thou choosest,* and so distinguishest from others who are left to themselves;" and it is by his effectual special grace pursuant to that choice; whom he chooses he causes to approach, not only invites them, but inclines and enables them, to draw nigh to him. He draws them, John vi. 44.

(2.) They shall be satisfied. Here the psalmist changes the person, not, *He* shall be satisfied (the man whom thou choosest), but, *We* shall, which teaches us to apply the promises to ourselves and by an active faith to put our own names into them: *We shall be satisfied with the goodness of thy house, even of thy holy temple.* Note, [1.] God's holy temple is his house; there he dwells, where his ordinances are administered. [2.] God keeps a good house. There is abundance of goodness in his house, righteousness, grace, and all the comforts of the everlasting covenant; there is enough for all, enough for each; it is ready, always ready; and all on free cost, without money and without price. [3.] In those things there is that which is satisfying to a soul, and with which all gracious souls will be satisfied. Let them have the pleasure of communion with God, and that suffices them; they have enough, they desire no more.

4. For the glorious operations of his power on their behalf (*v.* 5): *By terrible things in righteousness wilt thou answer us, O God of our salvation!* This may be understood of the rebukes which God in his providence sometimes gives to his own people; he often answers them by terrible things, for the awakening and quickening of them, but always in righteousness; he neither does them any wrong nor means them any hurt, for even then he is the God of their salvation. See Isa. xlv. 15. But it is rather to be understood of his judgments upon their enemies; God answers his people's prayers by the destructions made, for their sakes, among the heathen, and the recompence he renders to their proud oppressors, as a righteous God, the God to whom vengeance belongs, and as the God that protects and saves his people. By *wonderful* things (so some read it), things which are very surprising, and which we looked not for, Isa. lxiv. 3. Or, "By things which strike an awe upon us thou wilt answer us." The holy freedom that we are admitted to in God's courts, and the nearness of our approach to him, must not at all abate our reverence and godly fear of him; for he is *terrible in his holy places.*

5. For the care he takes of all his people, however distressed, and whithersoever dispersed. He is *the confidence of all the ends of the earth* that is, of all the saints all the world over and not theirs only that were of

the seed of Israel; for he is the God of the Gentiles as well as of the Jews, the confidence *of those that are afar off* from his holy temple and its courts, that dwell in the islands of the Gentiles, or that are in distress *upon the sea.* They trust in thee, and cry to thee, when they are at their wits' end, cvii. 27, 28. By faith and prayer we may keep up our communion with God, and fetch in comfort from him, wherever we are, not only in the solemn assemblies of his people, but also afar off upon the sea.

6 Which by his strength setteth fast the mountains; *being* girded with power : 7 Which stilleth the noise of the seas, the noise of their waves, and the tumult of the people. 8 They also that dwell in the uttermost parts are afraid at thy tokens : thou makest the outgoings of the morning and evening to rejoice. 9 Thou visitest the earth, and waterest it : thou greatly enrichest it with the river of God, *which* is full of water : thou preparest them corn, when thou hast so provided for it. 10 Thou waterest the ridges thereof abundantly : thou settlest the furrows thereof : thou makest it soft with showers : thou blessest the springing thereof. 11 Thou crownest the year with thy goodness ; and thy paths drop fatness. 12 They drop *upon* the pastures of the wilderness : and the little hills rejoice on every side. 13 The pastures are clothed with flocks ; the valleys also are covered over with corn; they shout for joy, they also sing.

That we may be the more affected with the wonderful condescensions of the God of grace, it is of use to observe his power and sovereignty as the God of nature, the riches and bounty of his providential kingdom.

I. He establishes the earth and it abides, cxix. 90. *By his* own *strength* he *setteth fast the mountains* (*v.* 6), did set them fast at first and still keeps them firm, though they are sometimes shaken by earthquakes.

——— Feriuntque summos
Fulmina montes.

The lightning blasts the loftiest hills.

Hence they are called *everlasting mountains,* Hab. iii. 6. Yet God's covenant with his people is said to stand more firmly than they, Isa. liv. 10.

II. He stills the sea, and it is quiet, *v.* 7. The sea in a storm makes a great noise, which adds to its threatening terror; but, when God pleases, he commands silence among the waves and billows, and lays them to sleep, turns the storm into a calm quickly, cvii. 29. And by this change in the sea, as well as by the former instance of the unchangeableness

476

of the earth, it appears that he whose the sea and the dry land are is girded with power. And by this our Lord Jesus gave a proof of his divine power, that he *commanded the winds and waves, and they obeyed him.* To this instance of the quieting of the sea he adds, as a thing much of the same nature, that he stills *the tumult of the people,* the common people. Nothing is more unruly and disagreeable than the insurrections of the mob, the insults of the rabble; yet even these God can pacify, in secret ways, which they themselves are not aware of. Or it may be meant of the outrage of the people that were enemies to Israel, ii. 1. God has many ways to still them and will for ever silence their tumults.

III. He renews the morning and evening, and their revolution is constant, *v.* 8. This regular succession of day and night may be considered, 1. As an instance of God's great power, and so it strikes an awe upon all : *Those that dwell in the uttermost parts of the earth are afraid at thy* signs or *tokens ;* they are by them convinced that there is a supreme deity, a sovereign monarch, before whom they ought to fear and tremble; for in these things the invisible things of God are clearly seen; and therefore they are said to be *set for signs,* Gen. i. 14. Many of those that dwell in the remote and dark corners of the earth were so afraid at these tokens that they were driven to worship them (Deut. iv. 19), not considering that they were God's tokens, undeniable proofs of his power and godhead, and therefore they should have been led by them to worship him. 2. As an instance of God's great goodness, and so it brings comfort to all : *Thou makest the outgoings of the morning,* before the sun rises, *and of the evening,* before the sun sets, *to rejoice.* As it is God that scatters the light of the morning and draws the curtains of the evening, so he does both in favour to man, and makes both to rejoice, gives occasion to us to rejoice in both; so that how contrary soever light and darkness are to each other, and how inviolable soever the partition between them (Gen. i. 4), both are equally welcome to the world in their season. It is hard to say which is more welcome to us, the light of the morning, which befriends the business of the day, or the shadows of the evening, which befriend the repose of the night. Does the watchman wait for the morning? So does the hireling earnestly desire the shadow. Some understand it of the morning and evening sacrifice, which good people greatly rejoiced in and in which God was constantly honoured. Thou makest them to *sing* (so the word is); for every morning and every evening songs of praise were sung by the Levites; it was that which the duty of every day required. We are to look upon our daily worship, alone and with our families, to be both the most needful of our daily occupations and the most delightful of our daily comforts; and, if therein we keep up our communion with God, the outgoings both of the morning and of the evening are thereby made truly to rejoice.

IV. He waters the earth and makes it fruitful. On this instance of God's power and goodness he enlarges very much, the psalm being probably penned upon occasion either of a more than ordinarily plentiful harvest or of a seasonable rain after long drought. How much the fruitfulness of this lower part of the creation depends upon the influence of the upper is easy to observe; if the heavens be as brass, the earth is as iron, which is a sensible intimation to a stupid world that every good and perfect gift is from above, *omnia desuper—all from above;* we must lift up our eyes above the hills, lift them up to the heavens, where the original springs of all blessings are, out of sight, and thither must our praises return, as the first-fruits of the earth were in the heave-offerings lifted up towards heaven by way of acknowledgment that thence they were derived. All God's blessings, even spiritual ones, are expressed by his raining righteousness upon us. Now observe how the common blessing of rain from heaven and fruitful seasons is here described.

1. How much there is in it of the power and goodness of God, which is here set forth by a great variety of lively expressions. (1.) God that made the earth hereby visits it, sends to it, gives proof of his care of it, *v.* 9. It is a visit in mercy, which the inhabitants of the earth ought to return in praises. (2.) God, that made it dry land, hereby waters it, in order to its fruitfulness. Though the productions of the earth flourished before God had caused it to rain, yet even then there was a mist which answered the intention, and *watered the whole face of the ground*, Gen. ii. 5, 6. Our hearts are dry and barren unless God himself be as the dew to us and water us; and the plants of his own planting he will water and make them to increase. (3.) Rain is *the river of God, which is full of water;* the clouds are the springs of this river, which do not flow at random, but in the channel which God cuts out for it. The showers of rain, as the rivers of water, he turns which way soever he pleases. (4.) This river of God enriches the earth, which without it would quickly be a poor thing. The riches of the earth, which are produced out of its surface, are abundantly more useful and serviceable to man than those which are hidden in its bowels; we might live well enough without silver and gold, but not without corn and grass.

2. How much benefit is derived from it to the earth and to man upon it. (1.) To the earth itself. The rain in season gives it a new face; nothing is more reviving, more refreshing, than the *rain upon the new-mown grass*, lxxii. 6. Even *the ridges* of the earth, off which the rain seems to slide, are watered *abundantly*, for they drink in the rain which comes often upon them; *the furrows* of it, which are turned up by the plough, in order to the seedness, are settled by the rain and made fit to receive the seed (*v.* 10); they are settled by being made soft. That which makes the soil of the heart tender settles it; for the heart is established with that grace. Thus the springing of the year is blessed; and if the spring, that first quarter of the year, be blessed, that is an earnest of a blessing upon the whole year, which God is therefore said to *crown with his goodness* (*v.* 11), to compass it on every side as the head is compassed with a crown, and to complete the comforts of it as the end of a thing is said to crown it. And his paths are said to *drop fatness;* for whatever fatness there is in the earth, which impregnates its productions, it comes from the out-goings of the divine goodness. Wherever God goes he leaves the tokens of his mercy behind him (Joel ii. 13, 14) and makes his path thus to shine after him. These communications of God's goodness to this lower world are very extensive and diffusive (*v.* 12): *They drop upon the pastures of the wilderness*, and not merely upon the pastures of the inhabited land. The deserts, which man takes no care of and receives no profit from, are under the care of the divine Providence, and the profits of them redound to the glory of God, as the great benefactor of the whole creation, though not immediately to the benefit of man; and we ought to be thankful not only for that which serves us, but for that which serves any part of the creation, because thereby it turns to the honour of the Creator. The wilderness, which makes not such returns as the cultivated grounds do, receives as much of the rain of heaven as the most fruitful soil; for God does good to the evil and unthankful. So extensive are the gifts of God's bounty that in them the hills, *the little hills, rejoice on every side*, even the north side, that lies most from the sun. Hills are not above the need of God's providence; little hills are not below the cognizance of it. But as, when he pleases, he can make them tremble (cxiv. 6), so when he pleases he can make them rejoice. (2.) To man upon the earth. God, by providing rain for the earth, prepares corn for man, *v.* 9. *As for the earth, out of it comes bread* (Job xxviii. 5), for out of it comes corn; but every grain of corn that comes out of it God himself prepared; and therefore he provides rain for the earth, that thereby he may prepare corn for man, under whose feet he has put the rest of the creatures and for whose use he has fitted them. When we consider that the yearly produce of the corn is not only an operation of the same power that raises the dead, but an instance of that power not much unlike to that (as appears by that of our Saviour, John xii. 24), and that the constant benefit we have from it is an instance of that goodness which endures for ever, we shall have reason to think that it is

477

no less than a God that prepares corn for us. Corn and cattle are the two staple commodities with which the husbandman, who deals immediately in the fruits of the earth, is enriched ; and both are owing to the divine goodness in watering the earth, *v.* 13. To this it is owing that the pastures are clothed with flocks, *v.* 13. So well stocked are the pastures that they seem to be covered over with the cattle that are laid in them, and yet the pasture not overcharged; so well fed are the cattle that they are the ornament and the glory of the pastures in which they are fed. The valleys are so fruitful that they seem to be *covered over with corn,* in the time of harvest. The lowest parts of the earth are commonly the most fruitful, and one acre of the humble valleys is worth five of the lofty mountains. But both corn-ground and pasture-ground, answering the end of their creation, are said to *shout for joy and sing,* because they are serviceable to the honour of God and the comfort of man, and because they furnish us with matter for joy and praise : as there is no earthly joy above the joy of harvest, so there was none of the feasts of the Lord, among the Jews, solemnized with greater expressions of thankfulness than the *feast of in-gathering at the end of the year,* Exod. xxiii. 16. Let all these common gifts of the divine bounty, which we yearly and daily partake of, increase our love to God as the best of beings, and engage us to glorify him with our bodies, which he thus provides so well for.

PSALM LXVI.

This is a thanksgiving-psalm, and it is of such a general use and application that we need not suppose it penned upon any particular occasion. All people are here called upon to praise God, I. For the general instances of his sovereign dominion and power in the whole creation, ver. 1—7. II. For the special tokens of his favour to the church, his peculiar people, ver. 8—12. And then, III. The psalmist praises God for his own experiences of his goodness to him in particular, especially in answering his prayers, ver. 13—20. If we have learned in every thing to give thanks for ancient and modern mercies, public and personal mercies, we shall know how to sing this psalm with grace and understanding.

To the chief musician. A song *or* psalm.

MAKE a joyful noise unto God, all ye lands : 2 Sing forth the honour of his name : make his praise glorious. 3 Say unto God, How terrible *art thou in* thy works ! through the greatness of thy power shall thine enemies submit themselves unto thee. 4 All the earth shall worship thee, and shall sing unto thee ; they shall sing *to* thy name. Selah. 5 Come and see the works of God : *he is* terrible *in his* doing toward the children of men. 6 He turned the sea into dry *land :* they went through the flood on foot : there did we rejoice in him. 7 He ruleth by his power for ever ; his eyes behold the nations : let not the rebellious exalt themselves. Selah.

478

I. In these verses the psalmist calls upon all people to praise God, *all lands, all the earth,* all the inhabitants of the world that are capable of praising God, *v.* 1. 1. This speaks the glory of God, that he is worthy to be praised by all, for he is good to all and furnishes every nation with matter for praise. 2. The duty of man, that all are obliged to praise God ; it is part of the law of creation, and therefore is required of every creature. 3. A prediction of the conversion of the Gentiles to the faith of Christ ; the time should come when all lands should praise God, and this incense should in every place be offered to him. 4. A hearty good-will which the psalmist had to this good work of praising God. He will abound in it himself, and wishes that God might have his tribute paid him by all the nations of the earth and not by the land of Israel only. He excites all lands, (1.) To *make a joyful noise to God.* Holy joy is that devout affection which should animate all our praises ; and, though it is not making a noise in religion that God will accept of (hypocrites are said to *cause their voice to be heard on high,* Isa. lviii. 4), yet, in praising God, [1.] We must be hearty and zealous, and must do what we do with all our might, with all that is within us. [2.] We must be open and public, as those that are not ashamed of our Master. And both these are implied in making a noise, a joyful noise. (2.) To sing with pleasure, and to *sing forth,* for the edification of others, *the honour of his name,* that is, of all that whereby he has made himself known, *v.* 2. That which is the honour of God's name ought to be the matter of our praise. (3.) To *make his praise glorious* as far as we can. In praising God we must do it so as to glorify him, and that must be the scope and drift of all our praises. *Reckon it your greatest glory to praise God,* so some. It is the highest honour the creature is capable of to be to the Creator for a name and a praise.

II. He had called upon all lands to praise God (*v.* 1), and he foretels (*v.* 4) that they shall do so : *All the earth shall worship thee ;* some in all parts of the earth, even the remotest regions, for *the everlasting gospel shall be preached to every nation and kindred;* and this is the purport of it, *Worship him that made heaven and earth,* Rev. xiv. 6, 7. Being thus sent forth, it shall not return void, but shall bring all the earth, more or less, to worship God, and sing unto him. In gospel times God shall be worshipped by the singing of psalms. They shall *sing to God,* that is, *sing to his name,* for it is only to his declarative glory, that by which he has made himself known, not to his essential glory, that we can contribute any thing by our praises.

III. That we may be furnished with matter for praise, we are here called upon *to come and see the works of God;* for *his own works praise him,* whether we do or no ; and the reason why we do not praise him more and better is because we do not duly and attentively observe them. Let us therefore see God's works and observe the instances of his wisdom, power, and faithfulness in them (*v.* 5), and then speak of them, and speak of them to him (*v.* 3): *Say unto God, How terrible art thou in thy works, terrible in thy doings!* 1. God's works are wonderful in themselves, and such as, when duly considered, may justly fill us with amazement. God *is terrible* (that is, admirable) in his works, through the greatness of his power, which is such, and shines so brightly, so strongly, in all he does, that it may be truly said there are *not any works like unto his works.* Hence he is said to be *fearful in praises,* Exod. xv. 11. In all his doings towards the children of men he is terrible, and to be eyed with a holy awe. Much of religion lies in a reverence for the divine Providence. 2. They are formidable to his enemies, and have many a time forced and frightened them into a feigned submission (*v.* 3): *Through the greatness of thy power,* before which none can stand, *shall thy enemies submit themselves unto thee; they shall lie unto thee* (so the word is), that is, they shall be compelled, sorely against their wills, to make their peace with thee upon any terms. Subjection extorted by fear is seldom sincere, and therefore force is no proper means of propagating religion, nor can there be much joy of such proselytes to the church as will in the end be found liars unto it, Deut. xxxiii. 29. 3. They are comfortable and beneficial to his people, *v.* 6. When Israel came out of Egypt, *he turned the sea into dry land* before them, which encouraged them to follow God's guidance through the wilderness; and, when they were to enter Canaan, for their encouragement in their wars Jordan was divided before them, and *they went through that flood on foot;* and such foot, so signally owned by heaven, might well pass for cavalry, rather than infantry, in the wars of the Lord. There did the enemies tremble before them (Exod. xv. 14, 15, Josh. v. 1), but *there did we rejoice in him,* both trust his power (for relying on God is often expressed by rejoicing in him) and sing his praise, cvi. 12. There did we rejoice; that is, our ancestors did, and we in their loins. The joys of our fathers were our joys, and we ought to look upon ourselves as sharers in them. 4. They are commanding to all. God by his works keeps up his dominion in the world (*v.* 7): *He rules by his power for ever; his eyes behold the nations.* (1.) God has a commanding eye; from the height of heaven his eye commands all the inhabitants of the world, and he has a clear and full view of them all. *His eyes run to and fro through the earth;* the most remote and obscure nations are under his inspection. (2.) He has a commanding arm; his power rules, rules for ever, and is never weakened, never obstructed. *Strong is his hand, and high is his right hand.* Hence he infers, *Let not the rebellious exalt*

themselves; let not those that have revolting and rebellious hearts dare to rise up in any overt acts of rebellion against God, as Adonijah exalted himself, saying, *I will be king.* Let not those that are in rebellion against God exalt themselves as if there were any probability that they should gain their point. No; let them be still, for God hath said, *I will be exalted,* and man cannot gainsay it.

8 O bless our God, ye people, and make the voice of his praise to be heard : 9 Which holdeth our soul in life, and suffereth not our feet to be moved. 10 For thou, O God, hast proved us : thou hast tried us, as silver is tried. 11 Thou broughtest us into the net ; thou laidst affliction upon our loins. 12 Thou hast caused men to ride over our heads ; we went through fire and through water : but thou broughtest us out into a wealthy place.

In these verses the psalmist calls upon God's people in a special manner to praise him. Let all lands do it, but Israel's land particularly. Bless our God ; bless him as ours, a God in covenant with us, and that takes care of us as his own. Let them *make the voice of his praise to be heard* (*v.* 8) ; for from whom should it be heard but from those who are his peculiar favourites and select attendants ? Two things we have reason to bless God for :—

I. Common protection (*v.* 9) : *He holdeth our soul in life,* that it may not drop away of itself ; for, being continually in our hands, it is apt to slip through our fingers. We must own that it is the good providence of God that keeps life and soul together and his visitation that preserves our spirit. *He puts our soul in life,* so the word is. He that gave us our being, by a constant renewed act upholds us in our being, and his providence is a continued creation. When we are ready to faint and perish he restores our soul, and so puts it, as it were, into a new life, giving new comforts. *Non est vivere, sed valere, vita* —*It is not existence, but happiness, that deserves the name of life.* But we are apt to stumble and fall, and are exposed to many destructive accidents, killing disasters as well as killing diseases, and therefore as to these also we are guarded by the divine power. He *suffers not our feet to be moved,* preventing many unforeseen evils, which we ourselves were not aware of our danger from. To him we owe it that we have not, long ere this, fallen into endless ruin. *He will keep the feet of his saints.*

II. Special deliverance from great distress Observe,

1. How grievous the distress and danger were, *v.* 11, 12. What particular trouble of the church this refers to does not appear ; it

might be the trouble of some private persons or families only. But, whatever it was, they were surprised with it as a bird with a snare, enclosed and entangled in it as a fish in a net; they were pressed down with it, and kept under as with a load *upon their loins, v.* 11. But they owned the hand of God in it. We are never in the net but God brings us into it, never under affliction but God lays it upon us. Is any thing more dangerous than fire and water? *We went through both,* that is, afflictions of different kinds; the end of one trouble was the beginning of another; when we had got clear of one sort of dangers we found ourselves involved in dangers of another sort. Such may be the troubles of the best of God's saints, but he has promised, *When thou passest through the waters, through the fire, I will be with thee,* Isa. xliii. 2. Yet proud and cruel men may be as dangerous as fire and water, and more so. *Beware of men,* Matt. x. 17 When men rose up against us, that was fire and water, and all that is threatening (cxxiv. 2, 3, 4), and that was the case here: " *Thou hast caused men to ride over our heads,* to trample upon us and insult over us, to hector and abuse us, nay, and to make perfect slaves of us; they have said to our souls, *Bow down, that we may go over,*" Isa. li. 23. While it is the pleasure of good princes to rule in the hearts of their subjects it is the pride of tyrants to ride over their heads; yet the afflicted church in this also owns the hand of God: "Thou hast caused them thus to abuse us;" for the most furious oppressor has no power but what is given him from above.

2. How gracious God's design was in bringing them into this distress and danger. See what the meaning of it is (*v.* 10): *Thou, O God! hast proved us, and tried us.* Then we are likely to get good by our afflictions, when we look upon them under this notion, for then we may see God's grace and love at the bottom of them and our own honour and benefit in the end of them. By afflictions we are proved as silver in the fire. (1.) That our graces, by being tried, may be made more evident and so we may be approved, as silver, when it is touched and marked sterling, and this will be *to our praise at the appearing of Jesus Christ* (1 Pet. i. 7) and perhaps in this world. Job's integrity and constancy were manifested by his afflictions. (2.) That our graces, by being exercised, may be made more strong and active, and so we may be improved, as silver when it is refined by the fire and made more clear from its dross; and this will be to our unspeakable advantage, for thus we are made partakers of God's holiness, Heb. xii. 10. Public troubles are for the purifying of the church, Dan. xi. 35; Rev. ii. 10; Deut. viii. 2.

3. How glorious the issue was at last. The troubles of the church will certainly end well; these do so, for (1.) The outlet of the trouble is happy. They are in fire and water, but

480

they get through them: " *We went through fire and water,* and did not perish in the flames or floods." Whatever the troubles of the saints are, blessed be God, there is a way through them. (2.) The inlet to a better state is much more happy: *Thou broughtest us out into a wealthy place,* into a *well-watered* place (so the word is), *like the gardens of the Lord,* and therefore fruitful. God brings his people into trouble that their comforts afterwards may be the sweeter and that their affliction may thus yield the peaceable fruit of righteousness, which will make the poorest place in the world a wealthy place.

13 I will go into thy house with burnt offerings: I will pay thee my vows, 14 Which my lips have uttered, and my mouth hath spoken, when I was in trouble. 15 I will offer unto thee burnt sacrifices of fatlings, with the incense of rams; I will offer bullocks with goats. Selah. 16 Come *and* hear, all ye that fear God, and I will declare what he hath done for my soul. 17 I cried unto him with my mouth, and he was extolled with my tongue. 18 If I regard iniquity in my heart, the Lord will not hear *me:* 19 *But* verily God hath heard *me;* he hath attended to the voice of my prayer. 20 Blessed *be* God, which hath not turned away my prayer, nor his mercy from me.

The psalmist, having before stirred up all people, and all God's people in particular, to bless the Lord, here stirs up himself and engages himself to do it.

I. In his devotions to his God, *v.* 13—15. He had called upon others to sing God's praises and to make a joyful noise with them; but, for himself, his resolutions go further, and he will praise God, 1. By costly sacrifices, which, under the law, were offered to the honour of God. All people had not wherewithal to offer these sacrifices, or wanted zeal to be at such an expense in praising God; but David, for his part, being able, is as willing, in this chargeable way to pay his homage to God (*v.* 13): *I will go into thy house with burnt-offerings.* His sacrifices should be public, in the place which God had chosen: " I will go into thy house with them." Christ is our temple, to whom we must bring our spiritual gifts, and by whom they are sanctified. They should be the best of the kind— *burnt-sacrifices,* which were wholly consumed upon the altar, to the honour of God, and of which the offerer had no share; and burnt-sacrifices *of fatlings,* not the lame or the lean, but the best fed, and such as would be most acceptable at his own table. God, who is the best, must be served with the best we have.

The feast God makes for us is a *feast of fat things, full of marrow* (Isa. xxv. 6), and such sacrifices should we bring to him. He will *offer bullocks with goats*, so liberal will he be in his return of praise, and not strait-handed: he would not offer that which cost him nothing, but that which cost him a great deal. And this *with the incense of rams*, that is, with the fat of rams, which being burnt upon the altar, the smoke of it would ascend like the smoke of incense. Or *rams with incense*. The incense typifies Christ's intercession, without which the fattest of our sacrifices will not be accepted. 2. By a conscientious performance of his vows. We do not acceptably praise God for our deliverance out of trouble unless we make conscience of paying the vows we made when we were in trouble. This was the psalmist's resolution (*v.* 13, 14), *I will pay thee my vows, which my lips have uttered when I was in trouble.* Note, (1.) It is very common, and very commendable, when we are under the pressure of any affliction, or in the pursuit of any mercy, to make vows, and solemnly to speak them before the Lord, to bind ourselves out from sin and bind ourselves more closely to our duty; not as if this were an equivalent, or valuable consideration, for the favour of God, but a qualification for receiving the tokens of that favour. (2.) The vows which we made when we were in trouble must not be forgotten when the trouble is over, but be carefully performed, for better it is not to vow than to vow and not pay.

II. In his declarations to his friends, *v.* 16. He calls together a congregation of good people to hear his thankful narrative of God's favours to him: "*Come and hear, all you that fear God*, for, 1. You will join with me in my praises and help me in giving thanks." And we should be as desirous of the assistance of those that fear God in returning thanks for the mercies we have received as in praying for those we want. 2. "You will be edified and encouraged by that which I have to say. *The humble shall hear of it and be glad*, xxxiv. 2. *Those that fear thee will be glad when they see me* (cxix. 74), and therefore let me have their company, and I will declare to them, not to vain carnal people that will banter it and make a jest of it" (pearls are not to be cast before swine); "but to those that fear God, and will make a good use of it, I will declare what God has done for my soul," not in pride and vain-glory, that he might be thought more a favourite of heaven than other people, but for the honour of God, to which we owe this as a just debt, and for the edification of others. Note, God's people should communicate their experiences to each other. We should take all occasions to tell one another of the great and kind things which God has done for us, especially which he has done for our souls, the spiritual blessings with which he has blessed us in heavenly things; these we should be most af-

fected with ourselves, and therefore with these we should be desirous to affect others. Now what was it that God had done for his soul? (1.) He had wrought in him a love to the duty of prayer, and had by his grace enlarged his heart in that duty (*v.* 17): *I cried unto him with my mouth.* But if God, among other things done for our souls, had not given us the Spirit of adoption, teaching and enabling us to cry, *Abba, Father*, we should never have done it. That God has given us leave to pray, a command to pray, encouragements to pray, and (to crown all) a heart to pray, is what we have reason to mention with thankfulness to his praise; and the more if, when we cried to him with our mouth, *he was extolled with our tongue*, that is, if we were enabled by faith and hope to give glory to him when we were seeking for mercy and grace from him, and to praise him for mercy in prospect though not yet in possession. By crying to him we do indeed extol him. He is pleased to reckon himself honoured by the humble believing prayers of the upright, and this is a great thing which he has done for our souls, that he has been pleased so far to unite interests with us that, in seeking our own welfare, we seek his glory. *His exaltation was under my tongue* (so it may be read); that is, I was considering in my mind how I might exalt and magnify his name. When prayers are in our mouths praises must be in our hearts. (2.) He had wrought in him a dread of sin as an enemy to prayer (*v.* 18): *If I regard iniquity in my heart, I know very well the Lord will not hear me.* The Jewish writers, some of them that have the leaven of the Pharisees, which is hypocrisy, put a very corrupt gloss upon these words: *If I regard iniquity in my heart*, that is (say they), If I allow myself only in heart-sins, and iniquity does not break out in my words and actions, *God will not hear me*, that is, he will not be offended with me, will take no notice of it, so as to lay it to my charge; as if heart-sins were no sins in God's account. The falsehood of this our Saviour has shown in his spiritual exposition of the law, Matt. v. But the sense of this place is plain: *If I regard iniquity in my heart*, that is, "If I have favourable thoughts of it, if I love it, indulge it, and allow myself in it, if I treat it as a friend and bid it welcome, make provision for it and am loth to part with it, if I roll it under my tongue as a sweet morsel, though it be but a heart sin that is thus countenanced and made much of, if I delight in it after the inward man, God will not hear my prayer, will not accept it, nor be pleased with it, nor can I expect an answer of peace to it." Note, Iniquity, regarded in the heart, will certainly spoil the comfort and success of prayer; for *the sacrifice of the wicked is an abomination to the Lord.* Those that continue in love and league with sin have no interest either in the promise or in the Mediator, and therefore cannot expect to speed in prayer. (3.) He had graciously granted him an answer of peace to his prayers (*v.* 19): "*But verily God has heard me;* though, being conscious to myself of much amiss in me, I began to fear that my prayers would be rejected, yet, to my comfort, I found that God was pleased to regard them." This God did for his soul, by answering his prayer, he gave him a token of his favour and an evidence that he had wrought a good work in him. And therefore he concludes (*v.* 20), *Blessed be God.* The two foregoing verses are the major and minor propositions of a syllogism: *If I regard iniquity in my heart, God will not hear my prayer;* that is the proposition: *but verily God has heard me;* that is the assumption, from which he might have rationally inferred, "Therefore I do not regard iniquity in my heart;" but, instead of taking the comfort to himself, he gives the praise to God: *Blessed be God.* Whatever are the premises, God's glory must always be the conclusion. *God has heard me*, and therefore *blessed be God.* Note, What we win by prayer we must wear with praise. Mercies in answer to prayer do, in a special manner, oblige us to be thankful. He has *not turned away my prayer, nor his mercy.* Lest it should be thought that the deliverance was granted for the sake of some worthiness in his prayer, he ascribes it to God's mercy. This he adds by way of correction: "It was not my prayer that fetched the deliverance, but his mercy that sent it." *Therefore* God does not turn away our prayer, because he does not turn away his own mercy, for that is the foundation of our hopes and the fountain of our comforts, and therefore ought to be the matter of our praises.

PSALM LXVII.

This psalm relates to the church and is calculated for the public. Here is, I. A prayer for the prosperity of the church of Israel, ver. 1. II. A prayer for the conversion of the Gentiles and the bringing of them into the church, ver. 2—5. III. A prospect of happy and glorious times when God shall do this, ver. 6, 7. Thus was the psalmist carried out by the spirit of prophecy to foretel the glorious estate of the Christian church, in which Jews and Gentiles should unite in one flock, the beginning of which blessed work ought to be the matter of our joy and praise, and the completing of it of our prayer and hope, in singing this psalm.

To the chief musician on Neginoth. A psalm or song.

G OD be merciful unto us, and bless us; *and* cause his face to shine upon us. Selah. 2 That thy way may be known upon earth, thy saving health among all nations. 3 Let the people praise thee, O God; let all the people praise thee. 4 O let the nations be glad and sing for joy: for thou shalt judge the people righteously, and govern the nations upon earth. Selah. 5 Let the people praise thee, O God; let all the people praise thee. 6 *Then* shall the earth yield her increase; *and* God, *even* our own God, shall bless us. 7 God shall bless us; and all the ends of the earth shall fear him.

The composition of this psalm is such as denotes the penman's affections to have been very warm and lively, by which spirit of devotion he was elevated to receive the spirit of prophecy concerning the enlargement of God's kingdom.

I. He begins with a prayer for the welfare and prosperity of the church then in being, in the happiness of which he should share, and think himself happy, *v.* 1. Our Saviour, in teaching us to say, *Our Father*, has intimated that we ought to pray with and for others; so the psalmist here prays not, *God be merciful to me, and bless me*, but to us, and bless *us;* for we must make supplication for all saints, and be willing and glad to take our lot with them. We are here taught, 1. That all our happiness comes from God's mercy and takes rise in that; and therefore the first thing prayed for is, *God be merciful to us,* to us sinners, and pardon our sins (Luke xviii. 13), to us miserable sinners, and help us out of our miseries. 2. That it is conveyed by God's blessing, and secured in that: *God bless us;* that is, give us an interest in his promises, and confer upon us all the good contained in them. God's speaking well to us amounts to his doing well for us. *God bless us* is a comprehensive prayer; it is a pity such excellent words should ever be used slightly and carelessly, and as a byword. 3. That it is completed in the light of his countenance: *God cause his face to shine upon us;* that is, God by his grace qualify us for his favour and then give us the tokens of his favour. We need desire no more to make us happy than to have God's face shine upon us, to have God love us, and let us know that he loves us: *To shine with us* (so the margin reads it); *with us* doing our endeavour, and let it crown that endeavour with success. If we by faith walk with God, we may hope that his face will shine with us.

II. He passes from this to a prayer for the conversion of the Gentiles (*v.* 2): *That thy way may be known upon earth.* "Lord, I pray not only that thou wilt be merciful to us and bless us, but that thou wilt be merciful to all mankind, *that thy way may be known upon earth.*" Thus public-spirited must we be in our prayers. *Father in heaven, hallowed be thy name, thy kingdom come.* We shall have never the less of God's mercy, and blessing, and favour, for others coming in to share with us. Or it may be taken thus: *God be merciful to us Jews, and bless us, that* thereby thy way may be known upon earth, that by the peculiar distinguishing tokens of thy favour to us others may be allured to come and join themselves to us, saying, *We will go with you, for we have heard that God is with you,*" Zech. viii. 23.

1. These verses, which point at the conversion of the Gentiles, may be taken, (1.) As a prayer; and so it speaks the desire of the Old-Testament saints; so far were they from wishing to monopolize the privileges of the

church that they desired nothing more than the throwing down of the enclosure and the laying open of the advantages. See then how the spirit of the Jews, in the days of Christ and his apostles, differed from the spirit of their fathers. The Israelites indeed that were of old desired that God's name might be known among the Gentiles; those counterfeit Jews were enraged at the preaching of the gospel to the Gentiles; nothing in Christianity exasperated them so much as that did. (2.) As a prophecy that it shall be as he here prays. Many scripture-prophecies and promises are wrapped up in prayers, to intimate that the answer of the church's prayer is as sure as the performance of God's promises.

2. Three things are here prayed for, with reference to the Gentiles :—

(1.) That divine revelation might be sent among them, *v.* 2. Two things he desires might be known upon earth, even among all nations, and not to the nation of the Jews only:—[1.] God's way, the rule of duty: "Let them all know, as well as we do, *what is good and what the Lord our God requires of them;* let them be blessed and honoured with the same righteous statutes and judgments which are so much the praise of our nation and the envy of all its neighbours," Deut. iv. 8. [2.] His saving health, or his salvation. The former is wrapped up in his law, this in his gospel. If God make known his way to us, and we walk in it, he will show us his saving health, l. 23. Those that have themselves experimentally known the pleasantness of God's ways, and the comforts of his salvation, cannot but desire and pray that they may be known to others, even among all nations. All upon earth are bound to walk in God's way, all need his salvation, and there is in it enough for all; and therefore we should pray that both the one and the other may be made known to all.

(2.) That divine worship may be set up among them, as it will be where divine revelation is received and embraced (*v.* 3): "*Let the people praise thee, O God!* let them have matter for praise, let them have hearts for praise; yea, let not only some, but *all the people, praise thee,*" all nations in their national capacity, some of all nations. It is again repeated (*v.* 5) as that which the psalmist's heart was very much upon. Those that delight in praising God themselves cannot but desire that others also may be brought to praise him, that he may have the honour of it and they may have the benefit of it. It is a prayer, [1.] That the gospel might be preached to them, and then they would have cause enough to praise God, as for the dayspring after a long and dark night. *Ortus est sol—The sun has risen.* Acts viii. 8. [2.] That they might be converted and brought into the church, and then they would have a disposition to praise God, the living and true God, and not the dumb and dunghill deities

they had worshipped, Dan. v. 4. Then their hard thoughts of God would be silenced, and they would see him, in the gospel glass, to be love itself, and the proper object of praise. [3.] That they might be incorporated into solemn assemblies, and might praise God in a body, that they might all together praise him with one mind and one mouth. Thus a face of religion appears upon a land when God is publicly owned and the ordinances of religious worship are duly celebrated in religious assemblies

(3.) That the divine government may be acknowledged and cheerfully submitted to (*v.* 4): *O let the nations be glad, and sing for joy!* Holy joy, joy in God and in his name, is the heart and soul of thankful praise. That *all the people* may *praise thee, let the nations be glad.* Those that *rejoice in the Lord always will in every thing give thanks.* The joy he wishes to the nations is holy joy; for it is joy in God's dominion, joy that *God has taken to himself his great power and has reigned,* which the unconverted *nations are angry at,* Rev. xi. 17, 18. Let them be glad, [1.] That *the kingdom is the Lord's* (xxii. 28.), that he, as an absolute sovereign, shall govern the nations upon earth, that by the kingdom of his providence he shall overrule the affairs of kingdoms according to the counsel of his will, though they neither know him nor own him, and that in due time he shall disciple all nations by the preaching of his gospel (Matt. xxviii. 19) and set up the kingdom of his grace among them upon the ruin of the devil's kingdom—that he shall make them a willing people in the day of his power, and even *the kingdoms of this world shall become the kingdoms of the Lord and of his Christ.* [2.] That *every man's judgment proceeds from the Lord.* "Let them be glad that *thou shalt judge the people righteously,* that thou shalt give a law and gospel which shall be a righteous rule of judgment, and shalt pass an unerring sentence, according to that rule, upon all the children of men, against which there will lie no exception." Let us all be glad that we are not to be one another's judges, but that he that judges us is the Lord, whose judgment we are sure is according to truth.

III. He concludes with a joyful prospect of all good when God shall do this, when the nations shall be converted and brought to praise God.

1. The lower world shall smile upon them, and they shall have the fruits of that (*v.* 6): *Then shall the earth yield her increase.* Not but that God gave rain from heaven and fruitful seasons to the nations when they *sat in darkness* (Acts xiv. 17); but when they were converted the earth yielded its increase to God; the meat and the drink then became a *meat-offering and a drink-offering to the Lord our God* (Joel ii. 14); and then it was fruitful to some good purpose. Then it yielded its increase more than before to

the comfort of men, who through Christ acquired a covenant-title to the fruits of it and had a sanctified use of it. Note, The success of the gospel sometimes brings outward mercies along with it; righteousness exalts a nation. See Isa. iv. 2; lxii. 9.

2. The upper world shall smile upon them, and they shall have the favours of that, which is much better: *God, even our own God, shall bless us, v.* 6. And again (*v.* 7), *God shall bless us.* Note, (1.) There are a people in the world that can, upon good grounds, call God their God. (2.) Believers have reason to glory in their relation to God and the interest they have in him. It is here spoken with an air of triumph· *God, even our own God.* (3.) Those who through grace call God their own may with a humble confidence expect a blessing from him. If he be our God, he will bless us with special blessings. (4.) The blessing of God, as ours in covenant, is that which sweetens all our creature-comforts to us, and makes them comforts indeed; then we receive the increase of the earth as a mercy indeed when with it God, even our own God, gives us his blessing.

3. All the world shall hereby be brought to do like them: *The ends of the earth shall fear him,* that is, worship him, which is to be done with a godly fear. The blessings God bestows upon us call upon us not only to love him, but to fear him, to keep up high thoughts of him and to be afraid of offending him. When the gospel begins to spread it shall get ground more and more, till it reach to the ends of the earth. The leaven hidden in the meal shall diffuse itself, till the whole be leavened. And the many blessings which those will own themselves to have received that are brought into the church invite others to join themselves to them. It is good to cast in our lot with those that are the blessed of the Lord.

PSALM LXVIII.

This is a most excellent psalm, but in many places the genuine sense is not easy to come at; for in this, as in some other scriptures, there are things dark and hard to be understood. It does not appear when, or upon what occasion, David penned this psalm; but probably it was when, God having given him rest from all his enemies round about, he brought the ark (which was both the token of God's presence and a type of Christ's mediation) from the house of Obed-edom to the tent he had pitched for it in Zion; for the first words are the prayer which Moses used at the removing of the ark, Num. x. 35. From this he is led, by the Spirit of prophecy, to speak glorious things concerning the Messiah, his ascension into heaven, and the setting up of his kingdom in the world. I He begins with prayer, both against God's enemies (ver. 1, 2) and for his people, ver. 3. II. He proceeds to praise, which takes up the rest of the psalm, calling upon all to praise God (ver. 4, 26, 32) and suggesting many things as matter for praise. 1. The greatness and goodness of God, ver. 4—6. 2. The wonderful works God had wrought for his people formerly, bringing them through the wilderness (ver. 7, 8), settling them in Canaan (ver. 9, 10), giving them victory over their enemies (ver. 11, 12), and delivering them out of the hands of their oppressors, ver. 13, 14. 3. The special presence of God in his church, ver. 15—17. 4. The ascension of Christ (ver. 18) and the salvation of his people by him, ver. 19, 20. 5. The victories which Christ would obtain over his enemies, and the favours he would bestow upon his church, ver. 21—28. 6. The enlargement of the church by the accession of the Gentiles to it, ver. 29—31. And so he concludes the psalm with an awful acknowledgment of the glory and grace of God, ver. 32—35. With all these great things we should endeavour to be duly affected in singing this psalm.

To the chief musician. A psalm *or* song of David.

L ET God arise, let his enemies be scattered: let them also that hate him flee before him. 2 As smoke is driven away, *so* drive *them* away: as wax melteth before the fire, *so* let the wicked perish at the presence of God. 3 But let the righteous be glad; let them rejoice before God: yea, let them exceedingly rejoice. 4 Sing unto God, sing praises to his name: extol him that rideth upon the heavens by his name JAH, and rejoice before him. 5 A father of the fatherless, and a judge of the widows, *is* God in his holy habitation. 6 God setteth the solitary in families: he bringeth out those which are bound with chains: but the rebellious dwell in a dry *land.*

In these verses,

I. David prays that God would appear in his glory,

1. For the confusion of his enemies (*v.* 1, 2): " *Let God arise,* as a judge to pass sentence upon them, as a general to take the field and do execution upon them; *and let them be scattered,* and flee before him, as unable to keep their ground, much less to make head against him. Let God arise, as the sun when he goes forth in his strength; and the children of darkness shall be scattered, as the shadows of the evening flee before the rising sun. Let them be driven away as smoke by the wind, which ascends as if it would eclipse the sun, but is presently dispelled, and there appears no remainder of it. Let them melt *as wax before the fire,* which is quickly dissolved." Thus does David comment upon Moses's prayer, and not only repeat it with application to himself and his own times, but enlarge upon it, to direct us how to make use of scripture-prayers. Nay, it looks further, to the Redeemer's victory over the enemies of his kingdom, for he was the angel of the covenant, that guided Israel through the wilderness. Note, (1.) There are, and have been, and ever will be, such as are enemies to God and hate him, that join in with the old serpent against the kingdom of God among men and against the seed of the woman. (2.) They are the wicked, and none but the wicked, that are enemies to God, the children of the wicked one. (3.) Though we are to pray for our enemies as such, yet we are to pray against God's enemies as such, against their enmity to him and their attempts upon his kingdom. (4.) If God but arise, all his impenitent and implacable enemies, that will not repent to give him glory, will certainly and speedily be scattered, and driven away, and made to perish at his presence; for none ever hardened his heart against God and prospered. The day of judgment will be the day of the complete and final *per-*

dition of ungodly men (2 Pet. iii. 7), who shall melt like wax before that flaming fire in which the Lord shall then appear, 2 Thess. i. 8.

2. For the comfort and joy of his own people (v. 3): " Let the righteous be glad, that are now in sorrow; let them rejoice before God in his favourable presence. God is the joy of his people; let them rejoice whenever they come before God, yea, let them exceedingly rejoice, let them rejoice with gladness." Note, Those who rejoice in God have reason to rejoice with exceeding joy; and this joy we ought to wish to all the saints, for it belongs to them. Light is sown for the righteous.

II. He praises God for his glorious appearances, and calls upon us to praise him, to sing to his name, and extol him,

1. As a great God, infinitely great (v. 4): He rides upon the heavens, by his name JAH. He is the spring of all the motions of the heavenly bodies, directs and manages them, as he that rides in the chariot sets it a-going, has a supreme command of the influences of heaven; he rides upon the heavens for the help of his people (Deut. xxxiii. 26), so swiftly, so strongly, and so much above the reach of opposition. He rules these by his name Jah, or Jehovah, a self-existent self-sufficient being, the fountain of all being, power, motion, and perfection; this is his name for ever. When we thus extol God we must rejoice before him. Holy joy in God will very well consist with that reverence and godly fear wherewith we ought to worship him.

2. As a gracious God, a God of mercy and tender compassion. He is great, but he despises not any, no, not the meanest; nay, being a God of great power, he uses his power for the relief of those that are distressed, v. 5, 6. The fatherless, the widows, the solitary, find him a God all-sufficient to them. Observe how much God's goodness is his glory. He that rides on the heavens by his name Jah, one would think, should immediately have been adored as King of kings and Lord of lords, and the sovereign director of all the affairs of states and nations; he is so, but this he rather glories in, that he is a Father of the fatherless. Though God be high, yet has he respect unto the lowly. Happy are those that have an interest in such a God as this. He that rides upon the heavens is a Father worth having; thrice happy are the people whose God is the Lord. (1.) When families are bereaved of their head God takes care of them, and is himself their head; and the widows and the fatherless children shall find that in him which they have lost in the relation that is removed, and infinitely more and better. He is a Father of the fatherless, to pity them, to bless them, to teach them, to provide for them, to portion them. He will preserve them alive (Jer. xlix. 11), and with him they shall find mercy, Hos. xiv. 3. They have liberty to call him Father, and to plead their relation to him as their guardian,

cxlvi. 9; x. 14, 18. He is a judge or patron of the widows, to give them counsel and to redress their grievances, to own them and plead their cause, Prov. xxii. 23. He has an ear open to all their complaints and a hand open to all their wants. He is so in his holy habitation, which may be understood either of the habitation of his glory in heaven (there he has prepared his throne of judgment, which the fatherless and widow have free recourse to, and are taken under the protection of, ix. 4, 7), or of the habitation of his grace on earth; and so it is a direction to the widows and fatherless how to apply to God; let them go to his holy habitation, to his word and ordinances; there they may find him and find comfort in him. (2.) When families are to be built up he is the founder of them: God sets the solitary in families, brings those into comfortable relations that were lonely, gives those a convenient settlement that were unsettled (cxiii. 9); he makes those dwell at home that were forced to seek for relief abroad (so Dr. Hammond), putting those that were destitute into a way of getting their livelihood, which is a very good way for man's charity, as it is of God's bounty.

3. As a righteous God, (1.) In relieving the oppressed. He brings out those that are bound with chains, and sets those at liberty who were unjustly imprisoned and brought into servitude. No chains can detain those whom God will make free. (2.) In reckoning with the oppressors: The rebellious dwell in a dry land and have no comfort in that which they have got by fraud and injury. The best land will be a dry land to those that by their rebellion have forfeited the blessing of God, which is the juice and fatness of all our enjoyments. The Israelites were brought out of Egypt into the wilderness, but were there better provided for than the Egyptians themselves, whose land, if Nilus failed them, as it sometimes did, was a dry land.

7 O God, when thou wentest forth before thy people, when thou didst march through the wilderness; Selah: 8 The earth shook, the heavens also dropped at the presence of God: even Sinai itself was moved at the presence of God, the God of Israel. 9 Thou, O God, didst send a plentiful rain, whereby thou didst confirm thine inheritance, when it was weary. 10 Thy congregation hath dwelt therein: thou, O God, hast prepared of thy goodness for the poor. 11 The Lord gave the word: great was the company of those that published it. 12 Kings of armies did flee apace: and she that tarried at home divided the spoil. 13 Though ye have lien among the pots, yet shall

ye be as the wings of a dove covered with silver, and her feathers with yellow gold. 14 When the Almighty scattered kings in it, it was *white* as snow in Salmon.

The psalmist here, having occasion to give God thanks for the great things he had done for him and his people of late, takes occasion thence to praise him for what he had done for their fathers in the days of old. Fresh mercies should put us in mind of former mercies and revive our grateful sense of them. Let it never be forgotten,

I. That God himself was the guide of Israel through the wilderness; when he had brought them out of their chains he did not leave them in the dry land, but he himself went before them in a *march through the wilderness, v. 7.* It was not a journey, but a march, for they went as soldiers, as an army with banners. The Egyptians promised themselves that the wilderness had shut them in, but they were deceived; God's Israel, having him for their leader, marched through the wilderness and were not lost in it. Note, If God bring his people into a wilderness, he will be sure to go before them in it and bring them out of it. Cant. viii. 5.

II. That he manifested his glorious presence with them at Mount Sinai, *v.* 8. Never did any people see the glory of God, nor hear his voice, as Israel did, Deut. iv. 32, 33. Never had any people such an excellent law given them, so expounded, so enforced. Then the *earth shook*, and the neighbouring countries, it is likely, felt the shock; terrible thunders there were, accompanied no doubt with thunder-showers, in which the heavens seemed to drop; while the divine doctrine *dropped as the rain*, Deut. xxxii. 2. *Sinai itself*, that vast mountain, that long ridge of mountains, *was moved at the presence of God;* see Judg. v. 4, 5; Deut. xxxiii. 2; Hab. iii. 3. This terrible appearance of the Divine Majesty, as it would possess them with a fear and dread of him, so it would encourage their faith in him and dependence upon him. Whatever mountains of difficulty lay in the way of their happy settlement, he that could move Sinai itself could remove them, could get over them.

III. That he provided very comfortably for them both in the wilderness and in Canaan (*v.* 9, 10): *Thou didst send a plentiful rain and hast prepared of thy goodness for the poor.* This may refer, 1. To the victualling of their camp with manna in the wilderness, which was rained upon them, as were also the quails (lxxviii. 24, 27), and it might be fitly called a rain of liberality or munificence, for it was a memorable instance of the divine bounty. This confirmed the camp of Israel (here called *God's inheritance*, because he had chosen them to be a peculiar treasure to himself) *when it was weary* and ready to perish: this confirmed their faith, and was a standing proof of God's

power and goodness. Even in the wilderness God found a comfortable dwelling for Israel, which was his congregation. Or, 2. To the seasonable supplies granted them in Canaan, that land *flowing with milk and honey*, which is said to *drink water of the rain of heaven*, Deut. xi. 11. When sometimes that fruitful land was ready to be turned into barrenness, for the iniquity of those that dwelt therein, God, in judgment, remembered mercy, and sent them a plentiful rain, which refreshed it again, so that the congregation of Israel dwelt therein, and there was provision enough, even to satisfy their poor with bread. This looks further to the spiritual provision made for God's Israel; the Spirit of grace and the gospel of grace are the plentiful rain with which God confirms his inheritance, and from which their fruit is found, Isa. xlv. 8. Christ himself is this rain, lxxii. 6. *He shall come as showers that water the earth.*

IV. That he often gave them victory over their enemies; armies, and kings of armies, appeared against them, from their first coming into Canaan, and all along in the times of the judges, till David's days, but, first or last, they gained their point against them, *v.* 11, 12, 14. Observe here, 1. That God was their commander-in-chief: *The Lord gave the word*, as general of their armies. He raised up judges for them, gave them their commissions and instructions, and assured them of success. *God spoke in his holiness*, and then *Gilead is mine.* 2. That they had prophets, as God's messengers, to make known his mind to them. God gave them his word (*the word of the Lord* came unto them) and then *great was the company of the preachers*—prophets and *prophetesses*, for the word is feminine. When God has messages to send he will not want messengers. Or perhaps it may allude to the women's joining in the triumph when the victory was obtained, as was usual (Exod. xv. 20, 1 Sam. xviii. 7), in which they took notice of the word of God, triumphing in that as much as in his works. 3. That their enemies were defeated, and put to confusion: *Kings of armies did flee*, did flee with the greatest terror and precipitation imaginable, did not fight and flee, but flee and flee, retired without striking a stroke; they fled apace, fled and never rallied again. 4. That they were enriched with the plunder of the field: *She that tarried at home divided the spoil.* Not only the men, the soldiers that abode by the stuff, who were, by a statute of distributions, to share the prey (1 Sam. xxx. 24), but even the women that tarried at home had a share, which intimates the abundance of spoil that should be taken. 5. That these great things which God did for them were sanctified to them and contributed to their reformation (*v.* 14): *When the Almighty scattered kings for her* (for the church) *she was white as snow in Salmon*, purified and refined by the mercies of God; *when the host went forth against the enemy they kept them-*

selves from every wicked thing, and so the host returned victorious, and Israel by the victory were confirmed in their purity and piety. This account of Israel's victories is applicable to the victories obtained by the exalted Redeemer for those that are his, over death and hell. By the resurrection of Christ our spiritual enemies were made to flee, their power was broken, and they were for ever disabled to hurt any of God's people. This victory was first notified by the women (the she-publishers) to the disciples (Matt. xxviii. 7) and by them it was preached to all the world, while believers that tarry at home, that did not themselves contribute any thing towards it, enjoy the benefit of it, and divide the spoil.

V. That from a low and despised condition they had been advanced to splendour and prosperity. When they were bond-slaves in Egypt, and afterwards when they were oppressed sometimes by one potent neighbour and sometimes by another, they did, as it were, *lie among the pots* or rubbish, as despised broken vessels, or as vessels in which there was no pleasure—they were black, and dirty, and discoloured. But God, at length, *delivered them from the pots* (lxxxi. 6), and in David's time they were in a fair way to be one of the most prosperous kingdoms in the world, amiable in the eyes of all about them, *like the wings of a dove covered with silver, v.* 13. "And so," says Dr. Hammond, "under Christ's kingdom, the heathen idolaters that were brought to the basest and most despicable condition of any creatures, worshipping wood and stone, and given up to the vilest lusts, should from that detestable condition be advanced to the service of Christ, and the practice of all Christian virtues, the greatest inward beauties in the world." It may be applied also to the deliverance of the church out of a suffering state and the comforts of particular believers after their despondencies.

15 The hill of God *is as* the hill of Bashan; a high hill *as* the hill of Bashan. 16 Why leap ye, ye high hills? *this is* the hill *which* God desireth to dwell in; yea, the Lord will dwell *in it* for ever. 17 The chariots of God *are* twenty thousand, *even* thousands of angels: the Lord *is* among them, *as in* Sinai, in the holy *place.* 18 Thou hast ascended on high, thou hast led captivity captive: thou hast received gifts for men; yea, *for* the rebellious also, that the Lord God might dwell *among them.* 19 Blessed *be* the Lord, *who* daily loadeth us *with benefits,* *even* the God of our salvation. Selah. 20 *He that is* our God *is* the God of salvation: and unto God the Lord

belong the issues from death. 21 But God shall wound the head of his enemies, *and* the hairy scalp of such a one as goeth on still in his trespasses.

David, having given God praise for what he had done for Israel in general, as the God of Israel (*v.* 8), here comes to give him praise as Zion's God in a special manner; compare ix. 11. *Sing praises to the Lord who dwelleth in Zion,* for which reason Zion is called *the hill of God.*

I. He compares it with the hill of Bashan and other high and fruitful hills, and prefers it before them, *v.* 15, 16. It is true, Zion was but little and low in comparison with them, and was not covered over with flocks and herds as they were, yet, upon this account, it has the pre-eminence above them all, that it is *the hill of God,* the hill *which he desires to dwell in,* and where he chooses to manifest the tokens of his peculiar presence, cxxxii. 13, 14. Note, It is much more honourable to be holy to God than to be high and great in the world. "*Why leap you, you high hills?* Why do you insult over poor Zion, and boast of your own height? This is the hill which God has chosen, and therefore though you exceed it in bulk, and be first-rates, yet, because on this the royal flag is hoisted, you must all strike sail to it." Zion was especially honourable because it was a type of the gospel church, which is therefore called Mount Zion (Heb. xii. 22), and this is intimated here, when he said, *The Lord will dwell in it for ever,* which must have its accomplishment in the gospel Zion. There is no kingdom in the world comparable to the kingdom of the Redeemer, no city comparable to that which is incorporated by the gospel charter, for there God dwells and will dwell for ever.

II. He compares it with Mount Sinai, of which he had spoken (*v.* 8), and shows that it has the Shechinah or divine presence in it as really, though not as sensibly, as Sinai itself had, *v.* 17. Angels are *the chariots of God,* his chariots of war, which he makes use of against his enemies, his chariots of conveyance, which he sends for his friends, as he did for Elijah (and Lazarus is said to be carried by the angels), his chariots of state, in the midst of which he shows his glory and power. They are vastly numerous: *Twenty thousands,* even thousands multiplied. There is an *innumerable company of angels* in the heavenly Jerusalem, Heb. xii. 22. The enemies David fought with had chariots (2 Sam. viii. 4), but what were they, for number or strength, to the chariots of God? While David had these on his side he needed not to fear those that trusted in *chariots and horses,* xx. 7. God appeared on Mount Sinai, attended with myriads of angels, by whose dispensation the law was given, Acts vii. 53 *He comes with ten thousands of saints,* Deut. xxxiii. 2. And still in Zion God manifests his glory, and is really present, with a numerous retinue of his heavenly hosts, signified by the cherubim between which God is said *to dwell.* So that, as some read the last words of the verse, *Sinai is in the sanctuary;* that is, the sanctuary was to Israel instead of Mount Sinai, whence they received divine oracles. Our Lord Jesus has these chariots at command. When the first-begotten was brought into the world it was with this charge, *Let all the angels of God worship him* (Heb. i. 6); they attended him upon all occasions, and he is now among them, *angels, principalities, and powers, being made subject to him,* 1 Pet. iii. 22. And it is intimated in the New Testament that the angels are present in the solemn religious assemblies of Christians, 1 Cor. xi. 10. Let the woman have a veil on her head *because of the angels;* and see Eph. iii. 10.

III. The glory of Mount Zion was the King whom God *set on that holy hill* (ii. 6), who *came to the daughter of Zion,* Matt. xxi. 5. Of his ascension the psalmist here speaks, and to it his language is expressly applied (Eph. iv. 8): *Thou hast ascended on high* (*b* 18); compare xlvii. 5, 6. Christ's ascending on high is here spoken of as a thing past, so sure was it; and spoken of to his honour, so great was it. It may include his whole exalted state, but points especially at his ascension into heaven to the right hand of the Father, which was as much our advantage as his advancement. For, 1. He then triumphed over the gates of hell. He led *captivity captive;* that is, he led his captives in triumph, as great conquerors used to do, *making a show of them openly,* Col. ii. 15. He led those captive who had led us captive, and who, if he had not interposed, would have held us captive for ever. Nay, he *led captivity itself captive,* having quite broken the power of sin and Satan. As he was the death of death, so he was the captivity of captivity, Hos. xiii. 14. This intimates the complete victory which Jesus Christ obtained over our spiritual enemies; it was such that through him *we also are more than conquerors,* that is, triumphers, Rom. viii. 37. 2. He then opened the gates of heaven to all believers: *Thou hast received gifts for men.* He *gave gifts to men,* so the apostle reads it, Eph. iv. 8. For he received that he might give; on his head the anointing of the Spirit was poured, that from him it might descend to the skirts of his garments. And he gave what he had received; having received power to give eternal life, he bestows it upon *as many as were given him,* John xvii. 2. *Thou hast received gifts for men,* not for angels; fallen angels not to be made saints, nor standing angels made gospel ministers, Heb. ii. 5. Not for Jews only, but for all men; whoever will may reap the benefit of these gifts. The apostle tells us what these gifts were (Eph. iv. 11), *prophets, apostles, evangelists, pastors and teachers,* the institution of a gospel ministry and the quali-

fication of men for it, both which are to be valued as the gifts of heaven and the fruits of Christ's ascension. *Thou hast received gifts in man* (so the margin), that is, in the human nature which Christ was pleased to clothe himself with, that he might be a *merciful and faithful high priest in things pertaining to God.* In him, as Mediator, *all fulness dwells,* that *from his fulness we might receive.* To magnify the kindness and love of Christ to us in receiving these gifts for us, the psalmist observes, (1.) The forfeiture we had made of them. He received them for the *rebellious also,* for those that had been rebellious; so all the children of men had been in their fallen state. Perhaps it is especially meant of the Gentiles, that had been *enemies in their minds by wicked works,* Col. i. 21. For them these gifts are received, to them they are given, that they might lay down their arms, that their enmity might be slain, and that they might return to their allegiance. This magnifies the grace of Christ exceedingly that through him rebels are, upon their submission, not only pardoned, but preferred. They have commissions given them under Christ, which some say, in our law, amounts to the reversing of an attainder. Christ came to a rebellious world, not to condemn it, but that through him it might be saved. (2.) The favour designed us in them: He *received gifts for the rebellious,* that *the Lord God might dwell among them,* that he might set up a church in a rebellious world, in which he would dwell by his word and ordinances, as of old in the sanctuary, that he might set up his throne, and Christ might dwell in the hearts of particular persons that had been rebellious. The gracious intention of Christ's undertaking was to rear up the *tabernacle of God among men,* that he might dwell with them and they might themselves be living temples to his praise, Ezek. xxxvii. 27.

IV. The glory of Zion's King is that he is a Saviour and benefactor to all his willing people and a consuming fire to all those that persist in rebellion against him, *v.* 19—21. We have here good and evil, life and death, the blessing and the curse, set before us, like that (Mark xvi. 16), *He that believes shall be saved; he that believes not shall be damned.*

1. Those that take God for their God, and so give up themselves to him to be his people, shall be loaded with his benefits, and to them he will be a God of salvation. If in sincerity we avouch God to be our God, and seek to him as such, (1.) He will continually do us good and furnish us with occasion for praise. Having mentioned the gifts Christ received for us (*v.* 18), fitly does he subjoin, in the next words, *Blessed be the Lord;* for it is owing to the mediation of Christ that we live, and live comfortably, and are daily loaded with benefits. So many, so weighty, are the gifts of God's bounty to us that he may be truly said to *load us* with them; he *pours out*

blessings till there is no room to receive them, Mal. iii. 10. So constant are they, and so unwearied is he in doing us good, that he *daily* loads us with them, according as the necessity of every day requires. (2.) He will at length be unto us the God of salvation, of everlasting salvation, the *salvation of God*, which he will *show to those that order their conversation aright* (l. 23), the salvation of the soul. He that *daily loads us with benefits* will not put us off with present things for a portion, but will be the God of our salvation; and what he gives us now he gives as the God of salvation, pursuant to the great design of our salvation. *He is our God*, and therefore he will be the God of eternal salvation to us; for that only will answer the vast extent of his covenant-relation to us as our God. But has he power to complete this salvation? Yes, certainly; *for unto God the Lord belong the issues from death*. The keys of hell and death are put into the hand of the Lord Jesus, Rev. i. 18. He, having made an escape from death himself in his resurrection, has both authority and power to rescue those that are his from the dominion of death, by altering the property of it to them when they die and giving them a complete victory over it when they shall rise again; for *the last enemy that shall be destroyed is death*. And to those that shall thus for ever escape death, and shall find such an outlet from it as not to be hurt of the second death, to them surely deliverances from temporal death are mercies indeed and come from God as the God of their salvation. 2 Cor. i. 10.

2. Those that persist in their enmity to him will certainly be ruined (*v.* 21): *God shall wound the head of his enemies*,—of Satan the old serpent (of whom it was by the first promise foretold that *the seed of the woman* should *break his head*, Gen. iii. 15), —of all the powers of the nations, whether Jews or Gentiles, that oppose him and his kingdom among men (cx. 6, *He shall wound the heads over many countries*),—of all those, whoever they are, that will *not have him to reign over them*, for those he accounts his enemies, and they shall be *brought forth and slain before him*, Luke xix. 27. He will *wound the hairy scalp of such a one as goeth on still in his trespasses*. Note, Those who go on still in their trespasses, and hate to be reformed, God looks upon as his enemies and will treat them accordingly. In calling the head *the hairy scalp* perhaps there is an allusion to Absalom, whose bushy hair was his halter. Or it denotes either the most fierce and barbarous of his enemies, who let their hair grow, to make themselves look the more frightful, or the most fine and delicate of his enemies, who are nice about their hair: neither the one nor the other can secure themselves from the fatal wounds which divine justice will give to the heads of those that go on in their sins.

22 The Lord said, I will bring again

from Bashan, I will bring *my people* again from the depths of the sea: 23 That thy foot may be dipped in the blood of *thine* enemies, *and* the tongue of thy dogs in the same. 21 They have seen thy goings, O God ; *even* the goings of my God, my King, in the sanctuary. 25 The singers went before, the players on instruments *followed* after; among *them were* the damsels playing with timbrels. 26 Bless ye God in the congregations, *even* the Lord, from the fountain of Israel. 27 There *is* little Benjamin *with* their ruler, the princes of Judah *and* their council, the princes of Zebulun, *and* the princes of Naphtali. 28 Thy God hath commanded thy strength : strengthen, O God, that which thou hast wrought for us. 29 Because of thy temple at Jerusalem shall kings bring presents unto thee. 30 Rebuke the company of spearmen, the multitude of the bulls, with the calves of the people, *till every one* submit himself with pieces of silver: scatter thou the people *that* delight in war. 31 Princes shall come out of Egypt; Ethiopia shall soon stretch out her hands unto God.

In these verses we have three things :—

I. The gracious promise which God makes of the redemption of his people, and their victory over his and their enemies (*v.* 22, 23): *The Lord said*, in his own gracious purpose and promise, "I will do great things for my people, as the God of their salvation," *v.* 20. God will not fail the expectations of those who by faith take him for their God. It is promised, 1. That he will set them in safety from their danger, as he had done formerly: " I will *again bring them from the depths of the sea*," as he did Israel when he brought them out of the slavery of Egypt into the ease and liberty of the wilderness; "and *I will again bring them from Bashan*," as he did Israel when he brought them from their wants and wanderings in the wilderness into the fulness and settlement of the land of Canaan; for the land of Bashan was on the other side Jordan, where they had wars with Sihon and Og, and whence their next removal was into Canaan. Note, The former appearances of God's power and goodness for his people should encourage their faith and hope in him for the future, that what he has done he will do again. He will *set his hand again the second time to recover the remnant of his people* (Isa. xi. 11); and we may perhaps see repeated *all the wonders which our fathers told us of.* But this is not all: 2. That he will make them victorious over their enemies (*v.* 23): *That thy feet may be dipped, as thou passest along, in the blood of thy enemies,* shed like water in great abundance, and the *tongue of thy dogs* may lap *in the same.* Dogs licked the blood of Ahab ; and, in the destruction of the anti-christian generation, we read of blood up *to the horses' bridles,* Rev. xiv. 20. The victories with which God blessed David's forces over the enemies of Israel are here prophesied of, but as types of Christ's victory over death and the grave for himself and for all believers, in his resurrection (and theirs by virtue of his) out of the earth, and of the destruction of the enemies of Christ and his church, who shall have blood given them to drink, for they are worthy.

II. The welcome entertainment which God's own people shall give to these glorious discoveries of his grace, both in his word and in his works. Has he spoken in his holiness ? Has he said he will *bring again from Bashan?* What then is required of us in return to this ?

1. That we observe his motions (*v.* 24): " *They have seen,* thy people have seen, *thy goings, O God!* While others regard not the work of the Lord, nor the operation of his hands, they have seen *the goings of my God, my King, in the sanctuary.*" See here, (1.) How an active faith appropriates God ; he is God and King ; but that is not all, he is *my* God and *my* King. Those who thus take him for theirs may see him, in all his outgoings, acting as their God, as their King, for their good, and in answer to their prayers. (2.) Where God's most remarkable outgoings are, even in the sanctuary, in and by his word and ordinances, and among his people in the gospel church especially, in and by which is made known the manifold wisdom of God. These outgoings of his *in the sanctuary* far outshine the outgoings of the morning and the evening, and more loudly proclaim his eternal power and godhead. (3.) What is our duty in reference to these outgoings, which is to observe them. *This is the finger of God. Surely God is with us of a truth.*

2. That we give him glory in the most devout and solemn manner. When we see *his goings in his sanctuary,* (1.) Let those that are immediately employed in the service of the temple praise him, *v.* 25. It was expected that the Levites, some of whom were singers and others players on instruments, who had the nearest views of his *outgoings in his sanctuary,* should lead in his praises. And, it being a day of extraordinary triumph, *among them were damsels playing with timbrels,* to complete the concert. " Thus (says Dr. Hammond) when Christ has gone up to heaven the apostles shall celebrate and publish it to all the world, and even the women that were witnesses of it shall affectionately join

490

with them in divulging it." (2.) Let all the people of Israel in their solemn religious assembly give glory to God : *Bless God,* not only in temples, but in the synagogues, or schools of the prophets, or wherever there is a congregation of those that *come forth from the fountain of Israel,* that are of the seed of Jacob, let them concur in blessing God. Public mercies, which we jointly share in, call for public thanksgivings, which all should join in. " Thus (says Dr. Hammond) all Christians shall be obliged solemnly to magnify the name of the Messiah, and, to that end, frequently to assemble together in congregations." And, (3.) Let those among them who, upon any account, are the most eminent, and make a figure, go before the rest in praising God, *v.* 27. There was *little Benjamin* (that was the royal tribe in Saul's time) *with their rulers, the princes of Judah* (that was the royal tribe in David's time), and *their council,* their captains or leaders. In the beginning of David's reign there had been long war between Judah and Benjamin, but now they both join in praises for success against the common enemy. But why are the tribes of Zebulun and Naphtali particularly mentioned ? Perhaps because those tribes, lying towards the north, lay most exposed to the incursions of the Syrians, and other neighbours that molested them, and therefore should be in a particular manner thankful for these victories over them. Dr. Hammond gives another reason, That these were the two learned tribes. *Naphtali giveth goodly words* (Gen. xlix. 21) and Zebulun had those that *handle the pen of the writer,* Judg. v. 14. These shall join in praising God, their princes especially. It is much for the honour of God when those that are above others in dignity, power, and reputation, go before them in the worship of God and are forward in using their influence and interest for the advancing of any service that is to be done to him. Dr. Hammond notes hence that the kingdom of the Messiah should, at length, be submitted to by all the potentates and learned men in the world

3. That we seek unto him, and depend upon him, for the perfecting of what he has begun, *v.* 28. In the former part of the verse the psalmist speaks to Israel : " *Thy God has commanded thy strength;* that is, whatever is done for thee, or whatever strength thou hast to help thyself, it comes from God, his power and grace, and the word which he has commanded ; thou hast no reason to fear while thou hast strength of God's commanding, and no reason to boast while thou hast no strength but what is of his commanding." In the latter part he speaks to God, encouraged by his experiences : " *Strengthen, O God! that which thou hast wrought for us.* Lord, confirm what thou hast commanded, perform what thou hast promised, and bring to a happy end that good work which thou hast so gloriously begun." What God has

wrought he will strengthen; where he has given true grace he will give more grace. Some make this whole verse to be a believer's address to the Messiah, whom David calls *God*, as he had done, xlv. 6, 8. *" Thy God"* (God the Father) *" has commanded thy strength,* has made thee strong for himself, as the *man of his right hand* (lxxx. 17), has treasured up strength in thee for us; therefore we pray that thou, O God the Son! wilt *strengthen what thou hast wrought for us,* wilt accomplish thy undertaking for us by finishing thy good work in us."

III. The powerful invitation and inducement which would hereby be given to those that are without to come in and join themselves to the church, *v.* 29—31. This was in part fulfilled by the accession of many proselytes to the Jewish religion in the days of David and Solomon; but it was to have its full accomplishment in the conversion of the Gentile nations to the faith of Christ, and the making of them fellow-heirs, and of the same body, with the seed of Israel, Eph. iii. 6. 1. Some shall submit for fear (*v.* 30): *" The company of spearmen,* that stand it out against Christ and his gospel, that are not willing to be ruled by him, that persecute the preachers and professors of his name, that are furious and outrageous as a multitude of bulls, fat and wanton as the calves of the people" (which is a description of those Jews and Gentiles that opposed the gospel of Christ and did what they could to prevent the setting up of his kingdom in the world), *"* Lord, rebuke them, abate their pride, assuage their malice, and confound their devices, till, conquered by the convictions of their consciences and the many checks of providence, they be every one of them brought, at length, to *submit themselves with pieces of silver,* as being glad to make their peace with the church upon any terms." Even Judas submitted himself with pieces of silver when he returned them with this confession, *I have betrayed innocent blood.* And see Rev. iii. 9. Many, by being rebuked, have been happily saved from being ruined. But as for those that will not submit, notwithstanding these rebukes, he prays for their dispersion, which amounts to a prophecy of it: *Scatter thou the people that delight in war,* who take such a pleasure in opposing Christ that they will never be reconciled to him. This may refer to the unbelieving Jews, who delighted in making war upon the holy seed, and would not submit themselves, and were therefore scattered over the face of the earth. David had himself been a man of war, but could appeal to God that he never delighted in war and bloodshed for its own sake; as for those that did, and therefore would not submit to the fairest terms of peace, he does not doubt but God would scatter them. Those are lost to all the sacred principles of humanity, as well as Christianity, that can delight in war and take a pleasure in contention let them

expect that, sooner or later, they shall have enough of it, Isa. xxxiii. 1; Rev. xiii. 10. 2. Others shall submit willingly (*v.* 29, 31): *Because of thy temple at Jerusalem* (this David speaks of in faith, for the temple of Jerusalem was not built in his time, only the materials and model were prepared) *kings shall bring presents unto thee;* rich presents shall be brought, such as are fit for kings to bring; even kings themselves, that stand much upon the punctilios of honour and prerogative, shall court the favour of Christ at a great expense. There is that in God's temple, that beauty and benefit in the service of God and in communion with him, and in the gospel of Christ which went forth from Jerusalem, that is enough to invite kings themselves to bring presents to God, to present themselves to him as living sacrifices, and with themselves the best performances. He mentions *Egypt* and *Ethiopia,* two countries out of which subjects and suppliants were least to be expected (*v.* 31): *Princes shall come out of Egypt* as ambassadors to seek God's favour and submit to him; and they shall be accepted, for *the Lord of hosts shall* thereupon *bless them, saying, Blessed be Egypt my people,* Isa. xix. 25. Even Ethiopia, that had stretched out her hands against God's Israel (2 Chron. xiv. 9), should now *stretch out her hands unto God,* in prayer, in presents, and to take hold on him, and that soon. *Agree with thy adversary quickly.* Out of all nations some shall be gathered in to Christ and be owned by him.

32 Sing unto God, ye kingdoms of the earth; O sing praises unto the Lord; Selah: 33 To him that rideth upon the heavens of heavens, *which were* of old; lo, he doth send out his voice, *and that* a mighty voice. 34 Ascribe ye strength unto God: his excellency *is* over Israel, and his strength *is* in the clouds. 35 O God, *thou art* terrible out of thy holy places: the God of Israel *is* he that giveth strength and power unto *his* people. Blessed *be* God.

The psalmist, having prayed for and prophesied of the conversion of the Gentiles, here invites them to come in and join with the devout Israelites in praising God, intimating that their accession to the church would be the matter of their joy and praise (*v.* 32): Let the *kingdoms of the earth sing praises to the Lord;* they all ought to do it, and, when they become the kingdoms of the Lord and of his Christ, they will do it. God is here proposed to them as the proper object of praise upon several accounts:—

I. Because of his supreme and sovereign dominion: *He rides upon the heavens of heavens which were of old* (*v.* 33); compare *v.* 4. He has from the beginning, nay from before all time, prepared his throne; he sits on the circuit of heaven, guides all the motions of the heavenly bodies; and from the highest heavens, which are the residence of his glory, he dispenses the influences of his power and goodness to this lower world.

II. Because of his awful and terrible majesty: *He sends out his voice, and that a mighty voice.* This may refer either generally to the thunder, which is called *the voice of the Lord* and is said to be *powerful and full of majesty* (xxix. 3, 4), or in particular to that thunder in which God spoke to Israel at Mount Sinai.

III. Because of his mighty power: *Ascribe you strength unto God* (v. 34); acknowledge him to be a God of such irresistible power that it is folly to contend with him and wisdom to submit to him; acknowledge that he has power sufficient both to protect his faithful subjects and to destroy his stubborn adversaries; and give him the glory of all the instances of his omnipotence. *Thine is the kingdom and power*, and therefore *thine is the glory.* We must acknowledge his power, 1. In the kingdom of grace: *His excellency is over Israel;* he shows his sovereign care in protecting and governing his church; that is the excellency of his power, which is employed for the good of his people. 2. In the kingdom of providence: *His strength is in the clouds*, whence comes the thunder of his power, the *small rain, and the great rain of his strength.* Though God has his strength in the clouds, yet he condescends to gather his Israel under the shadow of his wings, Deut. xxxiii. 26.

IV. Because of the glory of his sanctuary and the wonders wrought there (v. 35): *O God! thou art terrible out of thy holy places.* God is to be admired and adored with reverence and godly fear by all those that attend him in his holy places, that receive his oracles, that observe his operations according to them, and that pay their homage to him. He displays that out of his holy places which declares aloud that he will be sanctified in those that come nigh unto him. Out of heaven, his holy place above, he does, and will, show himself a terrible God. Nor is any attribute of God more dreadful to sinners than his holiness.

V. Because of the grace bestowed upon his people: *The God of Israel is he that gives strength and power unto his people*, which the gods of the nations, that were vanity and a lie, could not give to their worshippers; how should they help them, when they could not help themselves? All Israel's strength against their enemies came from God; they owned they had *no might of their own*, 2 Chron. xx. 12. And all our sufficiency for our spiritual work and warfare is from the grace of God. It is through Christ strengthening us that we can do all things, and not otherwise; and therefore he must have the glory of all we do (cxv. 1) and our humble thanks for en-

492

abling us to do it and accepting the work of his own hands in us. If it be the God of Israel that gives strength and power unto his people, they ought to say, *Blessed be God.* If all be from him, let all be to him.

PSALM LXIX.

David penned this psalm when he was in affliction; and in it, I. He complains of the great distress and trouble he was in and earnestly begs of God to relieve and succour him, ver. 1—21. II. He imprecates the judgments of God upon his persecutors, ver. 22—29. III. He concludes with the voice of joy and praise, in an assurance that God would help and succour him, and would do well for the church, ver. 30—36. Now, in this, David was a type of Christ, and divers passages in this psalm are applied to Christ in the New Testament and are said to have their accomplishment in him (ver. 4, 9, 21), and ver. 22 refers to the enemies of Christ. So that (like the twenty-second psalm) it begins with the humiliation and ends with the exaltation of Christ, one branch of which was the destruction of the Jewish nation for persecuting him, which the imprecations here are predictions of. In singing this psalm we must have an eye to the sufferings of Christ, and the glory that followed, not forgetting the sufferings of Christians too, and the glory that shall follow them; for it may lead us to think of the ruin reserved for the persecutors and the rest reserved for the persecuted

To the chief musician upon Shoshannim. *A psalm* of David.

SAVE me, O God; for the waters are come in unto *my* soul. 2 I sink in deep mire, where *there is* no standing: I am come into deep waters, where the floods overflow me. 3 I am weary of my crying: my throat is dried: mine eyes fail while I wait for my God. 4 They that hate me without a cause are more than the hairs of mine head: they that would destroy me, *being* mine enemies wrongfully, are mighty: then I restored *that* which I took not away. 5 O God, thou knowest my foolishness; and my sins are not hid from thee. 6 Let not them that wait on thee, O Lord GOD of hosts, be ashamed for my sake: let not those that seek thee be confounded for my sake, O God of Israel. 7 Because for thy sake I have borne reproach; shame hath covered my face. 8 I am become a stranger unto my brethren, and an alien unto my mother's children. 9 For the zeal of thine house hath eaten me up; and the reproaches of them that reproached thee are fallen upon me. 10 When I wept, *and* chastened my soul with fasting, that was to my reproach. 11 I made sackcloth also my garment; and I became a proverb to them. 12 They that sit in the gate speak against me; and I *was* the song of the drunkards.

In these verses David complains of his troubles, intermixing with those complaints some requests for relief.

I. His complaints are very sad, and he pours them out before the Lord, as one that hoped thus to ease himself of a burden that lay very heavy upon him.

1. He complains of the deep impressions that his troubles made upon his spirit (*v.* 1, 2): "The *waters of affliction*, those bitter waters, *have come unto my soul*, not only threaten my life, but disquiet my mind; they fill my head with perplexing cares and my heart with oppressive grief, so that I cannot enjoy God and myself as I used to do." We shall bear up under our troubles if we can but keep them from our hearts; but, when they put us out of the possession of our own souls, our case is bad. *The spirit of a man will sustain his infirmity;* but what shall we do when the spirit is wounded? That was David's case here. His thoughts sought for something to confide in, and with which to support his hope, but he found nothing: He sunk *in deep mire, where there was no standing*, no firm footing; the considerations that used to support and encourage him now failed him, or were out of the way, and he was ready to give himself up for gone. He sought for something to comfort himself with, but found himself *in deep waters that overflowed* him, overwhelmed him; he was like a sinking drowning man, in such confusion and consternation. This points at Christ's sufferings in his soul, and the inward agony he was in when he said, *Now is my soul troubled;* and, *My soul is exceedingly sorrowful;* for it was his soul that he made an offering for sin. And it instructs us, when we are in affliction, to commit the keeping of our souls to God, that we may be neither soured with discontent nor sink into despair.

2. He complains of the long continuance of his troubles (*v.* 3): *I am weary of my crying.* Though he could not keep his head above water, yet he cried to his God, and the more death was in his view the more life was in his prayers; yet he had not immediately an answer of peace given in, no, nor so much of that support and comfort in praying which God's people used to have; so that he was almost weary of crying, grew hoarse, and his *throat* so *dried* that he could cry no more. Nor had he his wonted satisfaction in believing, hoping, and expecting relief: *My eyes fail while I wait for my God;* he had almost looked his eyes out, in expectation of deliverance. Yet his pleading this with God is an indication that he is resolved not to give up believing and praying. His throat is dried, but his heart is not; his eyes fail, but his faith does not. Thus our Lord Jesus, on the cross, cried out, *Why hast thou forsaken me?* yet, at the same time, he kept hold of his relation to him: *My God, my God.*

3. He complains of the malice and multitude of his enemies, their injustice and cruelty, and the hardships they put upon him, *v.* 4. They hated him, they would destroy him, for hatred aims at the destruction of the person hated; but what was his iniquity, what was his sin, what provocation had he

given them, that they were so spiteful towards him? None at all : "*They hate me without a cause;* I never did them the least injury, that they should bear me such ill-will." Our Saviour applies this to himself (John xv. 25): *They hated me without a cause.* We are apt to use this in justification of our passion against those that hate us, that we never gave them cause to hate us. But it is rather an argument why we should bear it patiently, because then we suffer as Christ did, and may then expect that God will give us redress. "*They are my enemies wrongfully*, for I have been no enemy to them." In a world where unrighteousness reigns so much we must not wonder if we meet with those that are our enemies wrongfully. Let us take care that we never do wrong and then we may the better bear it if we receive wrong. These enemies were not to be despised, but were very formidable both for their number —*They are more than the hairs of my head* (Christ's enemies were numerous; those that came to seize him were a great multitude; how were those increased that troubled him!) and for their strength—They *are mighty* in authority and power. We are weak, but our enemies are strong; for *we wrestle against principalities and powers. Then I restored that which I took not away.* Applying this to David, it was what his enemies compelled him to (they made him suffer for that offence which he had never been guilty of); and it was what he consented to, that, if possible, he might pacify them and make them to be at peace with him. He might have insisted upon the laws of justice and honour, the former not requiring and the latter commonly thought to forbid the restoring of that which we took not away, for that is to wrong ourselves both in our wealth and in our reputation. Yet the case may be such sometimes that it may become our duty. Blessed Paul, though free from all men, yet, for the honour of Christ and the edification of the church, made himself a servant to all. But, applying it to Christ, it is an observable description of the satisfaction which he made to God for our sin by his blood: *Then he restored that which he took not away ;* he underwent the punishment that was due to us, paid our debt, suffered for our offence. God's glory, in some instances of it, was taken away by the sin of man; man's honour, and peace, and happiness, were taken away; it was not he that took them away, and yet by the merit of his death he restored them.

4. He complains of the unkindness of his friends and relations, and this is a grievance which with an ingenuous mind cuts as deeply as any (*v.* 8): "*I have become a stranger to my brethren ;* they made themselves strange to me and use me as a stranger, are shy of conversing with me and ashamed to own me." This was fulfilled in Christ, whose *brethren did not believe on him* (John vii. 5), who *came to his own and his own received him not* (John

i. 11), and who was forsaken by his disciples, whom he had been free with as his brethren.

5. He complains of the contempt that was put upon him and the reproach with which he was continually loaded. And in this especially his complaint points at Christ, who for our sakes submitted to the greatest disgrace and made himself of no reputation. We having by sin injured God in his honour, Christ made him satisfaction, not only by divesting himself of the honours due to an incarnate deity, but by submitting to the greatest dishonours that could be done to any man. Two things David here takes notice of as aggravations of the indignities done him :—(1.) The ground and matter of the reproach, *v.* 10, 11. They ridiculed him for that by which he both humbled himself and honoured God. When men lift up themselves in pride and vain glory they are justly laughed at for their folly ; but David chastened his soul, and clothed himself with sackcloth, and from his abasing himself they took occasion to trample upon him. When men dishonour God it is just that their so doing should turn to their dishonour ; but when David, purely in devotion to God and to testify his respect to him, *wept, and chastened his soul with fasting,* and *made sackcloth his garment,* as humble penitents used to do, instead of commending his devotion and recommending it as a great example of piety, they did all they could both to discourage him in it and to prevent others from following his good example ; for *that was to his reproach.* They laughed at him as a fool for mortifying himself thus ; and even for this he *became a proverb to them ;* they made him the common subject of their banter. We must not think it strange if we be ill spoken of for that which is well done, and in which we have reason to hope that we are accepted of God. Our Lord Jesus was stoned for his good works (John x. 32), and when he cried, *Eli, Eli—My God, my God,* was bantered, as if he called for Elias. (2.) The persons that reproached him, *v.* 12. [1.] Even the gravest and the most honourable, from whom better was expected : *Those that sit in the gate speak against me,* and their reproaches pass for the dictates of senators and the decrees of judges, and are credited accordingly. [2.] The meanest, and the most despicable, the abjects (xxxv. 15), the scum of the country, the *children of fools,* yea, the *children of base men,* Job xxx. 8. Such drunkards as these make themselves vile, and he was the song of the drunkards ; they made themselves and their companions merry with him. See the bad consequences of the sin of drunkenness ; it makes men *despisers of those that are good,* 2 Tim. iii. 3. When *the king was made sick with bottles of wine he stretched out his hand with scorners,* Hos. vii. 5. The bench of the drunkards is the seat of the scornful. See what is commonly the lot of the best of men : those that are the praise of the wise are the song of fools. But it is easy to those that rightly judge of things to despise being thus despised.

II. His confessions of sin are very serious (*v.* 5) : " *O God ! thou knowest my foolishness,* both what is and what is not ; my sins that I am guilty of are not hidden from thee, and therefore thou knowest how innocent I am of those crimes which they charge upon me." Note, Even when, as to men's unjust accusations, we plead *Not guilty,* yet, before God, we must acknowledge ourselves to have deserved all that is brought upon us, and much worse. This is the genuine confession of a penitent, who knows that he cannot prosper in covering his sin, and that *therefore* it is his wisdom to acknowledge it, because it is naked and open before God. 1. He knows the corruption of our nature : *Thou knowest the foolishness* that is bound up in my heart. All our sins take rise from our foolishness. 2. He knows the transgressions of our lives ; they are not hidden from him, no, not our heart-sins, no, not those that are committed most secretly. They are all done in his sight, and are never cast behind his back till they are repented of and pardoned. This may aptly be applied to Christ, for he knew no sin, yet he was made sin for us ; and God knew it, nor was it hidden from him, when it pleased the Lord to bruise him and put him to grief.

III. His supplications are very earnest. 1. For himself (*v.* 1) : " *Save me, O God !* save me from sinking, from despairing." Thus Christ was heard in that he feared, for he was saved from letting fall his undertaking, Heb. v. 7. 2. For his friends (*v.* 6) : *Let not those that wait on thee, O Lord God of hosts ! and that seek thee, O God of Israel !* (under these two characters we ought to seek God, and in seeking him to wait on him, as the *God of hosts,* who has all power to help, and as the *God of Israel* in covenant with his people, whom therefore he is engaged in honour and truth to help) *be ashamed and confounded for my sake.* This intimates his fear that if God did not appear for him it would be a discouragement to all other good people and would give their enemies occasion to triumph over them, and his earnest desire that whatever became of him all that seek God, and wait upon him, might be kept in heart and kept in countenance, and might neither be discouraged in themselves nor exposed to contempt from others. If Jesus Christ had not been owned and accepted of his Father in his sufferings, all that seek God, and wait for him, would have been ashamed and confounded ; but they have confidence towards God, and in his name come boldly to the throne of grace.

IV. His plea is very powerful, *v.* 7, 9. Reproach was one of the greatest of his burdens : " Lord, roll away the reproach, and plead my cause, for, 1. It is for thee that I am reproached, for serving thee and trusting in thee : *For thy sake I have borne reproach.*" Those that are evil spoken of for well-doing may with a humble confidence leave it to God to *bring forth their righteousness as the light.* 2. "It is with thee that I am reproached: *The zeal of thy house has eaten me up,* that is, has made me forget myself, and do that which they wickedly turn to my reproach. Those that hate thee and thy house for that reason hate me, because they know how zealously affected I am to it. It is this that has made them ready to eat me up and has eaten up all the love and respect I had among them." Those that blasphemed God, and spoke ill of his word and ways, did therefore reproach David for believing in his word and walking in his ways. Or it may be construed as an instance of David's zeal for God's house, that he resented all the indignities done to God's name as if they had been done to his own name. He laid to heart all the dishonour done to God and the contempt cast upon religion; these he laid nearer to his heart than any outward troubles of his own. And *therefore* he had reason to hope God would interest himself in the reproaches cast upon him, because he had always interested himself in the reproaches cast upon God. Both the parts of this verse are applied to Christ. (1.) It was an instance of his love to his Father that *the zeal of his house did even eat him up* when he whipped the buyers and sellers out of the temple, which reminded his disciples of this text, John ii. 17. (2.) It was an instance of his self-denial, and that he pleased not himself, that the *reproaches of those that reproached God fell upon him* (Rom. xv. 3), and therein he set us an example.

13 But as for me, my prayer *is* unto thee, O LORD, *in* an acceptable time: O God, in the multitude of thy mercy hear me, in the truth of thy salvation. 14 Deliver me out of the mire, and let me not sink: let me be delivered from them that hate me, and out of the deep waters. 15 Let not the water-flood overflow me, neither let the deep swallow me up, and let not the pit shut her mouth upon me. 16 Hear me, O LORD; for thy lovingkindness *is* good: turn unto me according to the multitude of thy tender mercies. 17 And hide not thy face from thy servant; for I am in trouble: hear me speedily. 18 Draw nigh unto my soul, *and* redeem it: deliver me because of mine enemies. 19 Thou hast known my reproach, and my shame, and my dishonour: mine adversaries *are* all before thee. 20 Reproach hath broken my heart; and I am full of heaviness: and I looked *for some* to take pity, but *there was* none; and for comfort-

ers, but I found none. 21 They gave me also gall for my meat; and in my thirst they gave me vinegar to drink.

David had been speaking before of the spiteful reproaches which his enemies cast upon him; here he adds, *But, as for me, my prayer is unto thee.* They spoke ill of him for his fasting and praying, and for that he was made the song of the drunkards; but, notwithstanding that, he resolves to continue praying. Note, Though we may be jeered for well-doing, we never be jeered out of it. Those can bear but little for God, and their confessing his name before men, that cannot bear a scoff and a hard word rather than quit their duty. David's enemies were very abusive to him, but this was his comfort, that he had a God to go to, with whom he would lodge his cause. "They think to carry their cause by insolence and calumny; but I use other methods. Whatever they do, *As for me, my prayer is unto thee, O Lord!*" And it was in an acceptable time, not the less acceptable for being a time of affliction. God will not drive us from him, though it is need that drives us to him; nay, it is the more acceptable, because the misery and distress of God's people make them so much the more the objects of his pity: it is seasonable for him to help them when all other helps fail, and they are undone, and feel that they are undone, if he do not help them. We find this expression used concerning Christ. Isa. xlix. 8, *In an acceptable time have I heard thee.* Now observe,

I. What his requests are. 1. That he might have a gracious audience given to his complaints, the cry of his affliction, and the desire of his heart. *Hear me* (v. 13), and again, *Hear me, O Lord!* (v. 16), *Hear me speedily* (v. 17), not only hear what I say, but grant what I ask. Christ knew that *the Father heard him always,* John xi. 42. 2. That he might be rescued out of his troubles, might be saved from sinking under the load of grief *(Deliver me out of the mire;* let me not stick in it, so some, but help me out, and *set my feet on a rock,* xl. 2), might be saved from his enemies, that they might not swallow him up, nor have their will against him: "*Let me be delivered from those that hate me,* as a lamb from the paw of a lion, v. 14. Though I have come into deep waters (v. 2), where I am ready to conclude that the floods will overflow me, yet let my fears be prevented and silenced; let not the waterflood, though it flow upon me, overflow me, v. 15. Let me not fall into the gulf of despair; let not that deep swallow me up; let not that pit shut her mouth upon me, for then I am undone." He gave himself up for lost in the beginning of the psalm; yet now he has his head above water, and is not so weary of crying as he thought himself. 3. That God would turn to him (v. 16), that he would smile upon him, and not hide his face from him, v. 17. The tokens of God's favour to us, and the light of his countenance shining upon us, are enough to keep our spirits from sinking in the deepest mire of outward troubles, nor need we desire any more to make us safe and easy, *v.* 18. "Draw nigh to my soul, to manifest thyself to it, and that shall redeem it."

II. What his pleas are to enforce these petitions. 1. He pleads God's mercy and truth (*v.* 13): *In the multitude of thy mercy hear me.* There is mercy in God, a multitude of mercies, all kinds of mercy, inexhaustible mercy, mercy enough for all, enough for each; and hence we must take our encouragement in praying. The truth also of his salvation (the truth of all those promises of salvation which he has made to those that trust in him) is a further encouragement. He repeats his argument taken from the mercy of God: "*Hear me, for thy lovingkindness is good.* It is so in itself; it is rich and plentiful and abundant. It is so in the account of all the saints; it is very precious to them, it is their life, their joy, their all. O let me have the benefit of it! Turn to me, *according to the multitude of thy tender mercies,*" *v.* 16. See how highly he speaks of the goodness of God: in him there are mercies, tender mercies, and a multitude of them. If we think well of God, and continue to do so under the greatest hardships, we need not fear but God will do well for us; for *he takes pleasure in those that hope in his mercy,* cxlvii. 11. 2. He pleads his own distress and affliction: "*Hide not thy face* from me, *for I am in trouble* (*v.* 17), and therefore need thy favour; therefore it will come seasonably, and therefore I shall know how to value it." He pleads particularly the reproach he was under and the indignities that were done him (*v.* 19): *Thou hast known my reproach, my shame, and my dishonour.* See what a stress is laid upon this; for, in the sufferings of Christ for us, perhaps nothing contributed more to the satisfaction he made for sin, which had been so injurious to God in his honour, than the reproach, and shame, and dishonour he underwent, which God took notice of, and accepted as more than an equivalent for the everlasting shame and contempt which our sins had deserved, and therefore we must by repentance take shame to ourselves and bear the reproach of our youth. And if at any time we be called out to suffer reproach, and shame, and dishonour, for his sake, this may be our comfort, that he knows it, and, as he is before-hand with us, so he will not be behind-hand with us. The psalmist speaks the language of an ingenuous nature when he says (*v.* 20): *Reproach has broken my heart; I am full of heaviness;* for it bears hard upon one that knows the worth of a good name to be put under a bad character; but when we consider what an honour it is to be dishonoured for God, and what a favour it is to be counted worthy to suffer shame for his name (as they deemed it, Acts v. 41),

we shall see there is no reason at all why it should sit so heavily or be any heart-breaking to us. 3. He pleads the insolence and cruelty of his enemies (*v.* 18): *Deliver me because of my enemies,* because they were such as he had before described them, *v.* 4. "*My adversaries are all before thee* (*v.* 19); thou knowest what sort of men they are, what danger I am in from them, what enemies they are to thee, and how much thou art reflected upon in what they do and design against me." One instance of their barbarity is given (*v.* 21): *They gave me gall for my meat* (the word signifies a bitter herb, and is often joined with wormwood) *and in my thirst they gave me vinegar to drink.* This was literally fulfilled in Christ, and did so directly point to him that he would not say *It is finished* till this was fulfilled; and, in order that his enemies might have occasion to fulfil it, he said, *I thirst,* John xix. 28, 29. Some think that the hyssop which they put to his mouth with the vinegar was the bitter herb which they gave him with the vinegar for his meat. See how particularly the sufferings of Christ were foretold, which proves the scripture to be the word of God, and how exactly the predictions were fulfilled in Jesus Christ, which proves him to be the true Messiah. This is he that should come, and we are to look for no other. 4. He pleads the unkindness of his friends and his disappointment in them (*v.* 20): *I looked for some to take pity, but there was none;* they all failed him like the brooks in summer. This was fulfilled in Christ, for in his sufferings all his disciples forsook him and fled. We cannot expect too little from men (miserable comforters are they all); nor can we expect too much from God, for he is the Father of mercy and the God of all comfort and consolation.

22 Let their table become a snare before them : and *that which should have been* for *their* welfare, *let it become* a trap. 23 Let their eyes be darkened, that they see not; and make their loins continually to shake. 24 Pour out thine indignation upon them, and let thy wrathful anger take hold of them. 25 Let their habitation be desolate; *and* let none dwell in their tents. 26 For they persecute *him* whom thou hast smitten; and they talk to the grief of those whom thou hast wounded. 27 Add iniquity unto their iniquity : and let them not come into thy righteousness. 28 Let them be blotted out of the book of the living, and not be written with the righteous. 29 But I *am* poor and sorrowful: let thy salvation, O God, set me up on high.

These imprecations are not David's prayers against his enemies, but prophecies of the destruction of Christ's persecutors, especially the Jewish nation, which our Lord himself foretold with tears, and which was accomplished about forty years after the death of Christ. The first two verses of this paragraph are expressly applied to the judgments of God upon the unbelieving Jews by the apostle (Rom. xi. 9, 10), and therefore the whole must look that way. The rejection of the Jews for rejecting Christ, as it was a signal instance of God's justice and an earnest of the vengeance which God will at last take on all that are obstinate in their infidelity, so it was, and continues to be, a convincing proof of the truth of the Christian religion. One great objection against it, at first, was, that it set aside the ceremonial law; but its doing so was effectually justified, and that objection removed, when God so remarkably set it aside by the utter destruction of the temple, and the sinking of those, with the Mosaic economy, that obstinately adhered to it in opposition to the gospel of Christ. Let us observe here,

I. What the judgments are which should come upon the crucifiers of Christ; not upon all of them, for there were those who had a hand in his death and yet repented and found mercy (Acts ii. 23; iii. 14, 15), but upon those of them and their successors who justified it by an obstinate infidelity and rejection of his gospel, and by an inveterate enmity to his disciples and followers. See 1 Thess. ii. 15, 16. It is here foretold,

1. That their sacrifices and offerings should be a mischief and prejudice to them (*v.* 22): *Let their table become a snare.* This may be understood of the altar of the Lord, which is called *his table and theirs* because in feasting upon the sacrifices they were partakers of the altar. This should have been for their welfare or peace (for they were peace-offerings), but it became a snare and a trap to them; for by their affection and adherence to the altar they were held fast in their infidelity and hardened in their prejudices against Christ, that altar which those had no right to eat of who continued to serve the tabernacle, Heb. xiii. 10. Or it may be understood of their common creature-comforts, even their necessary food; they had given Christ gall and vinegar, and therefore justly shall their meat and drink be made gall and vinegar to them. When the supports of life and delights of sense, through the corruption of our nature, become an occasion of sin to us, and are made the food and fuel of our sensuality, then our table is a snare, which is a good reason why we should never feed ourselves without fear, Jude 12.

2. That they should never have the comfort either of that knowledge or of that peace which believers are blessed with in the gospel of Christ (*v.* 23), that they should be given up, (1.) To a judicial blindness: *Let their eyes be darkened,* that they see not the glory of God in the face of Christ. Their sin was that they would not see, but shut their eyes against the light, loving darkness rather; their punishment was that they should not see, but be given up to their own hearts' lusts, which were hardening, and the god of this world should be permitted to blind their minds, 2 Cor. iv. 4. This was foretold concerning them (Isa. vi. 10), and Christ ratified it, Matt. xiii. 14, 15; John xii. 40. (2.) To a judicial terror. There is a gracious terror, which opens the way to comfort, such as that of Paul (Acts ix. 6); he trembled and was astonished. But this is a terror that shall never end in peace, but shall make their loins continually to shake, through horror of conscience, as Belshazzar, when the joints of his loins were loosed. "Let them be driven to despair, and filled with constant confusion." This was fulfilled in the desperate counsels of the Jews when the Romans came upon them.

3. That they should fall and lie under God's anger and fiery indignation (*v.* 24): *Pour out thy indignation upon them.* Note, Those who reject God's great salvation proffered to them may justly fear that his indignation will be poured out upon them; for those that submit not to the Son of his love will certainly be made the generation of his wrath. It is the doom passed on those who believe not in Christ that the *wrath of God abideth on them* (John iii. 36); it takes hold of them, and will never let them go. Salvation itself will not save those that are not willing to be ruled by it. Behold the goodness and severity of God!

4. That their place and nation should be utterly taken away, the very thing they were afraid of, and to prevent which, as they pretended, they persecuted Christ (John xi. 48): *Let their habitation be desolate* (*v.* 25), which was fulfilled when their country was laid waste by the Romans, and *Zion, for their sakes, was ploughed as a field,* Mic. iii. 12. The temple was the house which they were in a particular manner proud of, but this was *left unto them desolate,* Matt. xxiii. 38. Yet that is not all; it ought to be some satisfaction to us, if we be cut off from the enjoyment of our possessions, that others will have the benefit of them when we are dislodged: but it is here added, *Let none dwell in their tents,* which was remarkably fulfilled in Judah and Jerusalem, for after the destruction of the Jews it was long ere the country was inhabited to any purpose. But this is applied particularly to Judas, by St. Peter, Acts i. 20. For, he being *felo de se*—a suicide, we may suppose his estate was confiscated, so that *his habitation was desolate and no man* of his own kindred *dwelt therein.*

5. That their way to ruin should be downhill, and nothing should stop them, nor interpose to prevent it (*v.* 27): " Lord, leave them to themselves, to *add iniquity to ini-*

quity." Those that are bad, if they be given up to their own hearts' lusts, will certainly be worse; they will add sin to sin, nay, they will *add rebellion to their sin,* Job xxxiv. 37. It is said of the Jews that they *filled up their sin always,* 1 Thess. ii. 16. *Add the punishment of iniquity to their iniquity* (so some read it), for the same word signifies both sin and punishment, so close is their connexion. If men will sin, God will reckon for it. But those that have multiplied to sin may yet find mercy, for God multiplies to pardon, through the righteousness of the Mediator; and therefore, that they might be precluded from all hopes of mercy, he adds, *Let them not come into thy righteousness,* to receive the benefit of the righteousness of God, which is by faith in a Mediator, Phil. iii. 9. Not that God shuts out any from that righteousness, for the gospel excludes none that do not by their unbelief exclude themselves; but let them be left to take their own course and they will never come into this government; for being ignorant of the demands of God's righteousness, and going about to establish the merit of their own, they *have not submitted themselves to the righteousness of God,* Rom. x. 3. And those that are so proud and self-willed that they will not come into God's righteousness shall have their doom accordingly; they themselves have decided it: they *shall not come into his righteousness.* Let not those expect any benefit by it that are not willing and glad to be beholden to it.

6. That they should be cut off from all hopes of happiness (*v.* 28): *Let them be blotted out of the book of the living;* let them not be suffered to live any longer, since, the longer they live, the more mischief they do. Multitudes of the unbelieving Jews fell by sword and famine, and none of those who had embraced the Christian faith perished among them; the nation, as a nation, was blotted out, and became not a people. Many understand it of their rejection from God's covenant and all the privileges of it; that is *the book of the living:* "Let the commonwealth of Israel itself, Israel according to the flesh, now become alienated from that covenant of promise which hitherto it has had the monopoly of. Let it appear that they were never written in the Lamb's book of life, but reprobate silver let *men call them, because the Lord has rejected them.* Let them *not be written with the righteous ;* that is, let them not have a place in the congregation of the saints when they shall all be gathered in the general assembly of those whose names are written in heaven," i. 5.

II. What the sin is for which these dreadful judgments should be brought upon them (*v.* 26): *They persecute him whom thou hast smitten, and talk to the grief of thy wounded.* 1. Christ was he whom God had smitten, for *it pleased the Lord to bruise him,* and he was esteemed *stricken, smitten of God, and afflicted,* and therefore men *hid their faces from*

him, Isa. liii. 3, 4, 10. They persecuted him with a rage reaching up to heaven; they cried, *Crucify him, crucify him.* Compare that of St. Peter with this, Acts ii. 23. Though he was *delivered by the counsel and foreknowledge of God,* it was *with wicked hands that they crucified and slew him.* They talked to the grief of the Lord Jesus when he was upon the cross, saying, *He trusted in God, let him deliver him,* than which nothing could be said more grieving. 2. The suffering saints were God's wounded, wounded in his cause and for his sake, and them they persecuted, and *talked to their grief.* For these things *wrath came upon them to the uttermost,* 1 Thess. ii. 16 ; and see Matt. xxiii. 34, &c. This may be understood more generally, and it teaches us that nothing is more provoking to God than to insult over those whom he has smitten, and to add affliction to the afflicted, upon which it justly follows here, *Add iniquity to iniquity ;* see Zech. i. 15. Those that are of a wounded spirit, under trouble and fear about their spiritual state, ought to be very tenderly dealt with, and care must be taken not to *talk to their grief and not to make the heart of the righteous sad.*

III. What the psalmist thinks of himself in the midst of all (*v.* 29): "*But I am poor and sorrowful ;* that is the worst of my case, under outward afflictions, yet *written among the righteous,* and not under God's indignation as they are." It is better to be poor and sorrowful, with the blessing of God, than rich and jovial and under his curse. For those who come into God's righteousness shall soon see an end of their poverty and sorrow, and his salvation shall set them up on high, which is the thing that David here prays for, Isa. lxi. 10. This may be applied to Christ. He was, in his humiliation, poor and sorrowful, a man of sorrows, and that had not where to lay his head. But God highly exalted him; the salvation wrought for him, the salvation wrought by him, *set him up on high, far above all principalities and powers.*

30 I will praise the name of God with a song, and will magnify him with thanksgiving. 31 *This* also shall please the LORD better than an ox *or* bullock that hath horns and hoofs. 32 The humble shall see *this, and* be glad : and your heart shall live that seek God. 33 For the LORD heareth the poor, and despiseth not his prisoners. 34 Let the heaven and earth praise him, the seas, and every thing that moveth therein. 35 For God will save Zion, and will build the cities of Judah : that they may dwell there, and have it in possession. 36 The seed also of his servants shall inherit it : and

they that love his name shall dwell therein.

The psalmist here, both as a type of Christ and as an example to Christians, concludes a psalm with holy joy and praise which he began with complaints and remonstrances of his griefs.

I. He resolves to praise God himself, not doubting but that therein he should be accepted of him (v. 30, 31): "*I will praise the name of God,* not only with my heart, but with my song, and *magnify him with thanksgiving;*" for he is pleased to reckon himself magnified by the thankful praises of his people. It is intimated that all Christians ought to glorify God with their praises, *in psalms, and hymns, and spiritual songs.* And *this shall please the Lord,* through Christ the Mediator of our praises as well as of our prayers, better than the most valuable of the legal sacrifices (*v.* 31), *an ox or bullock.* This is a plain intimation that in the days of the Messiah an end should be put, not only to the sacrifices of atonement, but to those of praise and acknowledgment which were instituted by the ceremonial law; and, instead of them, spiritual sacrifices of praise and thanksgiving are accepted—the calves of our lips, not the calves of the stall, Heb. xiii. 15. It is a great comfort to us that humble and thankful praises are more pleasing to God than the most costly pompous sacrifices are or ever were.

II. He encourages other good people to rejoice in God and continue seeking him (*v.* 32, 33): *The humble shall see this and be glad.* They shall observe, to their comfort, 1. The experiences of the saints. They shall see how ready God is to hear the poor when they cry to him, and to give them that which they call upon him for, how far he is from despising his prisoners; though men despise them, he favours them with his gracious visits and will find a time to enlarge them. *The humble shall see this and be glad,* not only because when one member is honoured all the members rejoice with it, but because it is an encouragement to them in their straits and difficulties to trust in God. It shall revive the hearts of those who seek God to see more seals and subscriptions to this truth, that Jacob's God never said to Jacob's seed, *Seek you me in vain.* 2. The exaltation of the Saviour, for of him the psalmist had been speaking, and of himself as a type of him. When his sorrows are over, and he enters into the joy that was set before him, when he is heard and discharged from his imprisonment in the grave, the humble shall look upon it and be glad, and those that seek God through Christ shall live and be comforted, concluding that, if they suffer with him, they shall also reign with him.

III. He calls upon all the creatures to praise God, the heaven, and earth, and sea, and the inhabitants of each, *v.* 34. Heaven

and earth, and the hosts of both, were made by him, and therefore *let heaven and earth praise him.* Angels in heaven, and saints on earth, may each of them in their respective habitations furnish themselves with matter enough for constant praise. Let the fishes of the sea, though mute to a proverb, praise the Lord, for the sea is his, and he made it. The praises of the world must be offered for God's favours to his church, *v.* 35, 36. For God will save Zion, the holy mountain, where his service was kept up. He will save all that are sanctified and set apart to him, all that employ themselves in his worship, and all those over whom Christ reigns; for he was King upon the holy hill of Zion. He has mercy in store for the cities of Judah, of which tribe Christ was. God will do great things for the gospel church, in which let all that wish well to it rejoice. For, 1. It shall be peopled and inhabited. There shall be added to it such as shall be saved. *The cities of Judah shall be built,* particular churches shall be formed and incorporated according to the gospel model, that there may be a remnant to *dwell there* and to *have it in possession,* to enjoy the privileges conferred upon it and to pay the tributes and services required from it. Those that love his name, that have a kindness for religion in general, shall embrace the Christian religion, and take their place in the Christian church; they shall dwell therein, as citizens, and of the household of God. 2. It shall be perpetuated and inherited. Christianity was not to be *res unius ætatis*—a transitory thing. No: *The seed of his servants shall inherit it.* God will secure and raise up for himself a seed to serve him, and they shall inherit the privileges of their fathers; for the promise is to you and your children, as it was of old. *I will be a God to thee, and thy seed after thee.* The land of promise shall never be lost for want of heirs, for God *can out of stones raise up children unto Abraham* and will do so rather than the entail shall be cut off. David shall never want a man to stand before him. The Redeemer shall see his seed, and prolong his days in them, till the mystery of God shall be finished and the mystical body completed. And since the holy seed is the substance of the world, and if that were all gathered in the world would be at an end quickly, it is just that for this assurance of the preservation of it heaven and earth should praise him.

PSALM LXX.

This psalm is adapted to a state of affliction; it is copied almost word for word from the fortieth, and, some think for that reason, is entitled, "a psalm to bring to remembrance;" for it may be of use sometimes to pray over the prayers we have formerly made to God upon similar occasions, which may be done with new affections. David here prays that God would send, I. Help to himself, ver. 1, 5. II. Shame to his enemies, ver. 2, 3. III. Joy to his friends, ver. 4. These five verses were the last five verses of Ps. xl. He seems to have intended this short prayer to be both for himself and us a salve for every sore, and therefore to be always in mind; and in singing we may apply it to our particular troubles, whatever they are.

To the chief musician. *A psalm* of David, to bring to remembrance.

*M*AKE *haste*, O God, to deliver me; make haste to help me, O Lord. 2 Let them be ashamed and confounded that seek after my soul: let them be turned backward, and put to confusion, that desire my hurt. 3 Let them be turned back for a reward of their shame that say, Aha, aha. 4 Let all those that seek thee rejoice and be glad in thee: and let such as love thy salvation say continually, Let God be magnified. 5 But I *am* poor and needy: make haste unto me, O God: thou *art* my help and my deliverer; O Lord, make no tarrying.

The title tells us that this psalm was designed to bring to remembrance; that is, to put God in remembrance of his mercy and promises (for so we are said to do when we pray to him and plead with him. Isa. xliii. 26, *Put me in remembrance*)—not that the Eternal Mind needs a remembrancer, but this honour he is pleased to put upon the prayer of faith. Or, rather, to put himself and others in remembrance of former afflictions, that we may never be secure, but always in expectation of troubles, and of former devotions, that when the clouds return after the rain we may have recourse to the same means which we have formerly found effectual for fetching in comfort and relief. We may in prayer use the words we have often used before: our Saviour in his agony prayed thrice, saying the same words; so David here uses the words he had used before, yet not without some alterations, to show that he did not design to tie himself or others to them as a form. God looks at the heart, not at the words.

I. David here prays that God would make haste to relieve and succour him (*v.* 1, 5): *I am poor and needy*, in want and distress, and much at a loss within myself. Poverty and necessity are very good pleas in prayer to a God of infinite mercy, who despises not the sighing of a contrite heart, who has pronounced a blessing upon the poor in spirit, and who fills the hungry with good things. He prays, 1. That God would appear for him to deliver him from his troubles in due time. 2. That in the mean time he would come in to his aid, to help him under his troubles, that he might not sink and faint. 3. That he would do this quickly: *Make haste* (*v.* 1), and again (*v.* 5), *Make haste, make no tarrying.* Sometimes God seems to delay helping his own people, that he may excite such earnest desires as these. *He that believes does not make haste*, so as to anticipate or outrun the divine counsels, so as to force a way of escape or to take any unlawful methods of relief; but he may make haste by going forth to meet God in humble prayer that he would

500

hasten the desired succour. "*Make haste unto me*, for the longing desire of my soul is towards thee; I shall perish if I be not speedily helped. I have no other to expect relief from: *Thou art my help and my deliverer.* Thou hast engaged to be so to all that seek thee; I depend upon thee to be so to me; I have often found thee so; and thou art sufficient, all-sufficient, to be so; therefore make haste to me."

II. He prays that God would fill the faces of his enemies with shame, *v.* 2, 3. Observe, 1. How he describes them; they sought after his soul—his life, to destroy that—his mind, to disturb that, to draw him from God to sin and to despair. They desired his hurt, his ruin; when any calamity befel him or threatened him they said, "*Aha, aha! so would we have it;* we shall gain our point now, and see him ruined." Thus spiteful, thus insolent, were they. 2. What his prayer is against them: "*Let them be ashamed;* let them be brought to repentance, so filled with shame as that they may seek thy name (lxxxiii. 16); let them see their fault and folly in fighting against those whom thou dost protect, and be *ashamed of their envy*, Isa. xxvi. 11. However, let their designs against me be frustrated and their measures broken; let them be turned back from their malicious pursuits, and then they will be ashamed and confounded, and, like the enemies of the Jews, *much cast down in their own eyes*," Neh. vi. 16.

III. He prays that God would fill the hearts of his friends with joy (*v.* 4), that all those who seek God and love his salvation, who desire it, delight in it, and depend upon it, may have continual matter for joy and praise and hearts for both; and then he doubts not but that he should put in for a share of the blessing he prays for; and so may we if we answer the character. 1. Let us make the service of God our great business and the favour of God our great delight and pleasure, for that is seeking him and loving his salvation. Let the pursuit of a happiness in God be our great care and the enjoyment of it our great satisfaction. A heart to love the salvation of the Lord, and to prefer it before any secular advantages whatsoever, so as cheerfully to quit all rather than hazard our salvation, is a good evidence of our interest in it and title to it. 2. Let us then be assured that, if it be not our own fault, the joy of the Lord shall fill our minds and the high praises of the Lord shall fill our mouths. Those that seek God, if they seek him early and seek him diligently, shall rejoice and be glad in him, for their seeking him is an evidence of his good-will to them and an earnest of their finding him, cv. 3. There is pleasure and joy even in seeking God, for it is one of the fundamental principles of religion that God is the *rewarder of all those that diligently seek him.* Those that love God's salvation shall say with pleasure, with constant pleasure (for praising God, if we make it our continual work, will be our continual feast), *Let God be magnified*, as he will be, to eternity, in the salvation of his people. All who wish well to the comfort of the saints, and to the glory of God, cannot but say a hearty *amen* to this prayer, that those who love God's salvation may say continually, *Let God be magnified.*

PSALM LXXI.

David penned this psalm in his old age, as appears by several passages in it, which makes many think that it was penned at the time of Absalom's rebellion; for that was the great trouble of his latter days. It might be occasioned by Sheba's insurrection, or some trouble that happened to him in that part of his life of which it was foretold that the sword should not depart from his house. But he is not over-particular in representing his case, because he intended it for the general use of God's people in their afflictions, especially those they meet with in their declining years; for this psalm, above any other, is fitted for the use of the old disciples of Jesus Christ. I. He begins the psalm with believing prayers, with prayers that God would deliver him and save him (ver. 2, 4) and not cast him off (ver. 9) or be far from him (ver. 12), and that his enemies might be put to shame, ver. 13. He pleads his confidence in God (ver. 1, 3, 5, 7), the experience he had had of help from God (ver. 6), and the malice of his enemies against him, ver. 10, 11. II. He concludes the psalm with believing praises, ver. 14, &c. Never was his hope more established, ver. 16, 18, 20, 21. Never were his joys and thanksgivings more enlarged, ver. 15, 19, 22—24. He is in an ecstasy of joyful praise; and, in the singing of it, we too should have our faith in God encouraged and our hearts raised in blessing his holy name.

IN thee, O LORD, do I put my trust: let me never be put to confusion. 2 Deliver me in thy righteousness, and cause me to escape: incline thine ear unto me, and save me. 3 Be thou my strong habitation, whereunto I may continually resort: thou hast given commandment to save me; for thou *art* my rock and my fortress. 4 Deliver me, O my God, out of the hand of the wicked, out of the hand of the unrighteous and cruel man. 5 For thou *art* my hope, O Lord GOD: *thou art* my trust from my youth. 6 By thee have I been holden up from the womb: thou art he that took me out of my mother's bowels: my praise *shall be* continually of thee. 7 I am as a wonder unto many; but thou *art* my strong refuge. 8 Let my mouth be filled *with* thy praise *and with* thy honour all the day. 9 Cast me not off in the time of old age; forsake me not when my strength faileth. 10 For mine enemies speak against me; and they that lay wait for my soul take counsel together, 11 Saying, God hath forsaken him: persecute and take him; for *there is* none to deliver *him*. 12 O God, be not far from me: O my God, make haste for my help. 13 Let them be confounded *and* consumed that are adversaries to my soul; let them be covered *with* reproach and dishonour that seek my hurt.

Two things in general David here prays for—that he might not be confounded and that his enemies and persecutors might be confounded.

I. He prays that he might never be made ashamed of his dependence upon God nor disappointed in his believing expectations from him. With this petition every true believer may come boldly to the throne of grace; for God will never disappoint the hope that is of his own raising. Now observe here,

1. How David professes his confidence in God, and with what pleasure and grateful variety of expression he repeats his profession of that confidence, still presenting the profession of it to God and pleading it with him. We praise God, and so please him, by telling him (if it be indeed true) what an entire confidence we have in him (v. 1): "*In thee, O Lord!* and in thee only, *do I put my trust.* Whatever others do, I choose the God of Jacob for my help." Those that are entirely satisfied with God's all-sufficiency and the truth of his promise, and in dependence upon that, as sufficient to make them amends, are freely willing to do and suffer, to lose and venture, for him, may truly say, *In thee, O Lord! do I put my trust.* Those that will deal with God must deal upon trust; if we are shy of dealing with him, it is a sign we do not trust him. *Thou art my rock and my fortress* (v. 3); and again, "*Thou art my refuge, my strong refuge*" (v. 7); that is, "I fly to thee, and am sure to be safe in thee, and under thy protection. If thou secure me, none can hurt me. *Thou art my hope and my trust*" (v. 5); that is, "thou hast proposed thyself to me in thy word as the proper object of my hope and trust; I have hoped in thee, and never found it in vain to do so."

2. How his confidence in God is supported and encouraged by his experiences (v. 5, 6): "*Thou hast been my trust from my youth;* ever since I was capable of discerning between my right hand and my left, I stayed myself upon thee, and saw a great deal of reason to do so; for *by thee have I been holden up from the womb.*" Ever since he had the use of his reason he had been a dependent upon God's goodness, because ever since he had had a being he had been a monument of it. Note, The consideration of the gracious care which the divine Providence took of us in our birth and infancy should engage us to an early piety and constant devotedness to his honour. He that was our help from our birth ought to be our hope from our youth. If we received so much mercy from God before we were capable of doing him any service, we should lose no time when we are capable. This comes in here as a support to the psalmist in his present distress; not only that God had given him his life and being, bringing him out of his mother's bowels into the world, and providing that he should not die from the womb, nor give up the ghost when he came out of the belly, but that he

had betimes made him one of his family: "Thou art he that took me out of my mother's bowels into the arms of thy grace, under the shadow of thy wings, into the bond of thy covenant; thou tookest me into thy church, as a son of thy handmaid, and born in thy house, cxvi. 16. And therefore," (1.) "I have reason to hope that thou wilt protect me; thou that hast held me up hitherto wilt not let me fall now; thou that madest me wilt not forsake the work of thy own hands; thou that helpedst me when I could not help myself wilt not abandon me now that I am as helpless as I was then." (2.) "Therefore I have reason to resolve that I will devote myself unto thee: *My praise shall therefore be continually of thee;*" that is, "I will make it my business every day to praise thee and will take all occasions to do it."

3. What his requests to God are, in this confidence.

(1.) That he might *never be put to confusion* (v. 1), that he might not be disappointed of the mercy he expected and so made ashamed of his expectation. Thus we may all pray in faith that our confidence in God may not be our confusion. Hope of the glory of God is hope that makes not ashamed.

(2.) That he might be delivered out of the hand of his enemies (v. 2): "*Deliver me in thy righteousness.* As thou art the righteous Judge of the world, pleading the cause of the injured and punishing the injurious, cause me in some way or other to escape" (God will, with the temptation, make a way to escape, 1 Cor. x. 13): "*Incline thy ear unto my prayers,* and, in answer to them, save me out of my troubles, v. 4. Deliver me, O my God! out of the hands of those that are ready to pull me in pieces." Three things he pleads for deliverance:—[1.] The encouragement God had given him to expect it: *Thou hast given commandment to save me* (v. 3); that is, thou hast promised to do it, and such efficacy is there in God's promises that they are often spoken of as commands, like that, *Let there be light, and there was light.* He speaks, and it is done. [2.] The character of his enemies; they are *wicked, unrighteous, cruel men,* and it will be for the honour of God to appear against them (v. 4), for he is a holy, just, and good God. [3.] The many eyes that were upon him (v. 7): "*I am as a wonder unto many;* every one waits to see what will be the issue of such extraordinary troubles as I have fallen into and such extraordinary confidence as I profess to have in God." Or, "I am looked upon as a monster, am one whom every body shuns, and therefore am undone if the Lord be not my refuge. Men abandon me, but God will not."

(3.) That he might always find rest and safety in God (v. 3): *Be thou my strong habitation;* be thou to me *a rock of repose, whereto I may continually resort.* Those that are at home in God, that live a life of communion with him and confidence in him, that continually resort unto him by faith and prayer, having their eyes ever towards him, may promise themselves a strong habitation in him, such as will never fall of itself nor can ever be broken through by any invading power; and they shall be welcome to resort to him continually upon all occasions, and not be upbraided as coming too often.

(4.) That he might have continual matter for thanksgiving to God, and might be continually employed in that pleasant work (v. 8): "*Let my mouth be filled with thy praise,* as now it is with my complaints, and then I shall not be ashamed of my hope, but my enemies will be ashamed of their insolence." Those that love God love to be praising him, and desire to be doing it all the day, not only in their morning and evening devotions, not only *seven times a day* (cxix. 164), but *all the day,* to intermix with all they say something or other that may redound to the honour and praise of God. They resolve to do it while they live; they hope to be doing it eternally in a better world.

(5.) That he might not be neglected now in his declining years (v. 9): *Cast me not off now in the time of* my *old age; forsake me not when my strength fails.* Observe here, [1.] The natural sense he had of the infirmities of age: *My strength fails.* Where there was strength of body and vigour of mind, strong sight, a strong voice, strong limbs, alas! in old age they fail; the life is continued, but the strength is gone, or that which is is *labour and sorrow,* xc. 10. [2.] The gracious desire he had of the continuance of God's presence with him under these infirmities: *Lord, cast me not off; do not then forsake me.* This intimates that he should look upon himself as undone if God should abandon him. To be cast off and forsaken of God is a thing to be dreaded at any time, especially in the time of old age and when our strength fails us; for it is God that is the strength of our heart. But it intimates that he had reason to hope God would not desert him; the faithful servants of God may be comfortably assured that he will not cast them off in old age, nor forsake them when their strength fails them. He is a Master that is not wont to cast off old servants. In this confidence David here prays again (v. 12): "*O God! be not far from me;* let me not be under the apprehension of thy withdrawings, for then I am miserable. *O my God!* a God in covenant with me, *make haste for my help,* lest I perish before help come."

II. He prays that his enemies might be made ashamed of their designs against him. Observe, 1. What it was which they unjustly said against him, v. 10, 11. Their plot was deep and desperate; it was against his life: *They lay wait for my soul* (v. 10), and are adversaries to that, v. 13. Their powers and policies were combined: *They take counsel together.* And very insolent they were in their deportment: They say, *God has forsaken him; persecute and take him.* Here their premises are utterly false, that because a good man was in great trouble and had continued long in it, and was not so soon delivered as perhaps he expected, therefore God had forsaken him and would have no more to do with him. All are not forsaken of God who think themselves so or whom others think to be so. And, as their premises were false, so their inference was barbarous. If God has forsaken him, then persecute and take him, and doubt not but to make a prey of him. This is *talking to the grief of one whom God has smitten,* lxix. 26. But thus they endeavour to discourage David, as Sennacherib endeavoured to intimidate Hezekiah by suggesting that God was his enemy and fought against him. *Have I now come up without the Lord against this city, to destroy it?* Isa. xxxvi. 10. It is true, if God has forsaken a man, there is none to deliver him; but *therefore* to insult over him ill becomes those who are conscious to themselves that they deserve to be for ever forsaken of God. But *rejoice not against me, O my enemy! though I fall, I shall rise.* He that seems to forsake for a small moment will gather with everlasting kindness. 2. What it was which he justly prayed for, from a spirit of prophecy, not a spirit of passion (*v.* 13): "*Let them be confounded and consumed that are adversaries to my soul.*" If they will not be confounded by repentance, and so saved, let them be confounded with everlasting dishonour, and so ruined." God will turn into shame the glory of those who turn into shame the glory of God and his people.

14 But I will hope continually, and will yet praise thee more and more. 15 My mouth shall show forth thy righteousness *and* thy salvation all the day; for I know not the numbers *thereof.* 16 I will go in the strength of the Lord God: I will make mention of thy righteousness, *even* of thine only. 17 O God, thou hast taught me from my youth: and hitherto have I declared thy wondrous works. 18 Now also when I am old and greyheaded, O God, forsake me not; until I have showed thy strength unto *this* generation, *and* thy power to every one *that* is to come. 19 Thy righteousness also, O God, *is* very high, who hast done great things: O God, who *is* like unto thee! 20 *Thou,* which hast showed me great and sore troubles, shalt quicken me again, and shalt bring me up again from the depths of the earth. 21 Thou shalt increase my greatness, and comfort me on every side. 22 I

will also praise thee with the psaltery, *even* thy truth, O my God: unto thee will I sing with the harp, O thou Holy One of Israel. 23 My lips shall greatly rejoice when I sing unto thee; and my soul, which thou hast redeemed. 24 My tongue also shall talk of thy righteousness all the day long: for they are confounded, for they are brought unto shame, that seek my hurt.

David is here in a holy transport of joy and praise, arising from his faith and hope in God; we have both together *v.* 14, where there is a sudden and remarkable change of his voice; his fears are all silenced, his hopes raised, and his prayers turned into thanksgivings. "Let my enemies say what they will, to drive me to despair, *I will hope continually,* hope in all conditions, in the most cloudy and dark day; I will live upon hope and will hope to the end." Since we hope in one that will never fail us, let not our hope in him fail us, and then we shall praise him yet more and more. "The more they reproach me the more closely will I cleave to thee; I *will praise thee more* and better than ever I have done yet." The longer we live the more expert we should grow in praising God and the more we should abound in it. *I will add over and above all thy praise,* all the praise I have hitherto offered, for it is all too little. When we have said all we can, to the glory of God's grace, there is still more to be said; it is a subject that can never be exhausted, and therefore we should never grow weary of it. Now observe, in these verses,

I. How his heart is established in faith and hope; and it is a good thing that the heart be so established. Observe,

1. What he hopes in, *v.* 16. (1.) In the power of God: "*I will go in the strength of the Lord God,* not sit down in despair, but stir up myself to and exert myself in my work and warfare, will go forth and go on, not in any strength of my own, but in God's strength —disclaiming my own sufficiency and depending on him only as all-sufficient—in the strength of his providence and in the strength of his grace." We must always go about God's work in his strength, having our eyes up unto him to work in us both to will and to do. (2.) In the promise of God: "*I will make mention of thy righteousness,* that is, thy faithfulness to every word which thou hast spoken, the equity of thy disposals, and thy kindness to thy people that trust in thee. This I will make mention of as my plea in prayer for thy mercy." We may very fitly apply it to the righteousness of Christ, which is called the *righteousness of God by faith,* and which is *witnessed by the law and the prophets;* we must depend upon God's strength

for assistance and upon Christ's righteousness for acceptance. *In the Lord have I righteousness and strength,* Isa. xlv. 24.

2. What he hopes for.

(1.) He hopes that God will not leave him in his old age, but will be the same to him to the end that he had been all along, v. 17, 18. Observe here, [1.] What God had done for him when he was young: *Thou hast taught me from my youth.* The good education and good instructions which his parents gave him when he was young he owns himself obliged to give God thanks for as a great favour. It is a blessed thing to be taught of God from our youth, from our childhood to know the holy scriptures, and it is what we have reason to bless God for. [2.] What he had done for God when he was middle-aged: He had *declared all God's wondrous works.* Those that have got good when they are young must be doing good when they are grown up, and must continue to communicate what they have received. We must own that all the works of God's goodness to us are wondrous works, admiring he should do so much for us who are so undeserving, and we must make it our business to declare them, to the glory of God and the good of others. [3.] What he desired of God now that he was old: *Now that I am old and gray-headed,* dying to this world and hastening to another, *O God! forsake me not.* This is what he earnestly desires and confidently hopes for. Those that have been taught of God from their youth, and have made it the business of their lives to honour him, may be sure that he will not leave them when they are old and gray-headed, will not leave them helpless and comfortless, but will make the evil days of old age their best days, and such as they shall have occasion to say they have pleasure in. [4.] What he designed to do for God in his old age: " I will not only *show thy strength,* by my own experience of it, *to this generation,* but I will leave my observations upon record for the benefit of posterity, and so show it *to every one that is to come.*" As long as we live we should be endeavouring to glorify God and edify one another; and those that have had the largest and longest experience of the goodness of God to them should improve their experiences for the good of their friends. It is a debt which the old disciples of Christ owe to the succeeding generations to leave behind them a solemn testimony to the power, pleasure, and advantage of religion, and the truth of God's promises.

(2.) He hopes that God would revive him and raise him up out of his present low and disconsolate condition (v. 20): *Thou who hast made me to see and feel great and sore troubles,* above most men, *shalt quicken me again.* Note, [1.] The best of God's saints and servants are sometimes exercised with great and sore troubles in this world. [2.] God's hand is to be eyed in all the troubles of the saints, and that will help to extenuate them and

make them seem light. He does not say, " Thou hast burdened me with those troubles," but " shown them to me," as the tender father shows the child the rod to keep him in awe. [3.] Though God's people be brought ever so low he can revive them and raise them up. Are they dead? he can quicken them again. See 2 Cor. i. 9. Are they buried, as dead men out of mind? he can bring *them up again from the depths of the earth,* can cheer the most drooping spirit and raise the most sinking interest. [4.] If we have a due regard to the hand of God in our troubles, we may promise ourselves, in due time, a deliverance out of them. Our present troubles, though great and sore, shall be no hindrance to our joyful resurrection from the depths of the earth, witness our great Master, to whom this may have some reference; his Father showed him great and sore troubles, but quickened him and brought him up from the grave.

(3.) He hopes that God would not only deliver him out of his troubles, but would advance his honour and joy more than ever (v. 21): " Thou shalt not only restore me to *my greatness* again, but shalt *increase* it, and give me a better interest, after this shock, than before; thou shalt not only comfort me, but *comfort me on every side,* so that I shall see nothing black or threatening on any side." Note, Sometimes God makes his people's troubles contribute to the increase of their greatness, and their sun shines the brighter for having been under a cloud. If he make them contribute to the increase of their goodness, that will prove in the end the increase of their greatness, their glory; and if he comfort them on every side, according to the time and degree wherein he has afflicted them on every side, they will have no reason to complain. When our Lord Jesus was quickened again, and brought back from the depths of the earth, his greatness was increased, and he entered on the joy set before him.

(4.) He hopes that all his enemies would be put to confusion, v. 24. He speaks of it with the greatest assurance as a thing done, and triumphs in it accordingly: *They are confounded, they are brought to shame, that seek my hurt.* His honour would be their disgrace and his comfort their vexation.

II. Let us now see how his heart is enlarged in joy and praises, how he rejoices in hope, and sings in hope; for we are saved by hope.

1. He will speak of God's righteousness and his salvation, as great things, things which he was well acquainted with, and much affected with, which he desired God might have the glory of and others might have the comfortable knowledge of (v. 15): *My mouth shall show forth thy righteousness and thy salvation ;* and again (v. 24), *My tongue shall talk of thy righteousness,* and this *all the day.* God's righteousness, which David seems here to be in a particular manner affected with, includes a great deal: the rectitude of his

nature, the equity of his providential dis-posals, the righteous laws he has given us to be ruled by, the righteous promises he has given us to depend upon, and the everlasting righteousness which his Son has brought in for our justification. God's righteousness and his salvation are here joined together; let no man think to put them asunder, nor expect salvation without righteousness, l. 23. If these two are made the objects of our de-sire, let them be made the subjects of our discourse all the day, for they are subjects that can never be exhausted.

2. He will speak of them with wonder and admiration, as one astonished at the dimen-sions of divine love and grace, the height and depth, the length and breadth, of it: "*I know not the numbers thereof, v.* 15. Though I cannot give a particular account of thy favours to me, they are so many, so great (if *I would count them, they are more in number than the sand,* xl. 5), yet, knowing them to be numberless, I will be still speaking of them, for in them I shall find new matter," *v.* 19. The righteousness that is in God is very high; that which is done by him for his people is very great: put both together, and we shall say, *O God! who is like unto thee?* This is praising God, acknowledging his per-fections and performances to be, (1.) Above our conception; they are very high and great, so high that we cannot apprehend them, so great that we cannot comprehend them. (2.) Without any parallel; no being like him, no works like his: *O God! who is like unto thee?* None in heaven, none on earth, no angel, no king. God is a non-such; we do not rightly praise him if we do not own him to be so.

3. He will speak of them with all the ex-pressions of joy and exultation, *v.* 22, 23. Observe,

(1.) How he would eye God in praising him. [1.] As a faithful God: *I will praise thee, even thy truth.* God is made known by his word; if we praise that, and the truth of that, we praise him. By faith we set to our seal that God is true; and so we praise his truth. [2.] As a God in covenant with him: " *O my God!* whom I have consented to and avouched for mine." As in our prayers, so in our praises, we must look up to God as our God, and give him the glory of our in-terest in him and relation to him. [3.] As the *Holy One of Israel,* Israel's God in a peculiar manner, glorious in his holiness among that people and faithful to his cove-nant with them. . It is God's honour that he is a Holy One; it is his people's honour that he is the Holy One of Israel.

(2.) How he will express his joy and exulta-tion. [1.] With his hand, in sacred music— *with the psaltery, with the harp;* at these David excelled, and the best of his skill shall be employed in setting forth God's praises to such advantage as might affect others. [2.] With his lips, in sacred songs: " *Unto thee will I sing,* to thy honour, and with a desire

to be accepted of thee. *My lips shall greatly rejoice when I sing unto thee,* knowing they cannot be better employed." [3.] In both with his heart: " *My soul* shall rejoice *which thou hast redeemed.*" Note, *First,* Holy joy is the very heart and life of thankful praise. *Secondly,* We do not make melody to the Lord, in singing his praises, if we do not do it with our hearts. My lips shall rejoice, but that is nothing; lip-labour, though ever so well laboured, if that be all, is but lost labour in serving God; the soul must be at work, and with all that is within us we must bless his holy name, else all about us is worth little. *Thirdly,* Redeemed souls ought to be joyful thankful souls. The work of redemption ought, above all God's works, to be celebrated by us in our praises. The Lamb that was slain, and has redeemed us to God, must therefore be counted worthy of all blessing and praise.

PSALM LXXII.

The foregoing psalm was penned by David when he was old, and, it should seem, so was this too; for Solomon was now standing fair for the crown; that was his prayer for himself, this for his son and successor, and with these two the prayers of David the son of Jesse are ended, as we find in the close of this psalm. If we have but God's presence with us while we live, and good hopes concerning those that shall come after us that they shall be praising God on earth when we are praising him in heaven, it is enough. This is entitled "a psalm for Solomon:" it is probable that David dictated it, or, rather, that it was by the blessed Spirit dictated to him, when, a little before he died, by divine direction he settled the succession, and gave orders to proclaim Solomon king, 1 Kings i. 30, &c. But, though Solo-mon's name is here made use of, Christ's kingdom is here pro-phesied of under the type and figure of Solomon's. David knew what the divine oracle was, That "of the fruit of his loins, ac-cording to the flesh, he would raise up Christ to sit on his throne," Acts ii. 30. To him he here bears witness, and had the prospect of the glories of his kingdom he comforted himself in his dying moments when he foresaw that his house would not be so with God, not so great, not so good, as he wished. David, in spirit, I. Begins with a short prayer for his successor, ver. l. II. He passes immediately into a long prediction of the glories of his reign, ver. 2—17. And, III. He concludes with praise to the God of Israel, ver. 18—20. In singing this psalm we must have an eye to Christ, praising him as a King, and pleasing our-selves with our happiness as his subjects.

A psalm for Solomon.

GIVE the king thy judgments, O God, and thy righteousness un-to the king's son.

This verse is a prayer for the king, even the king's son.

I. We may apply it to Solomon: *Give him thy judgments, O God! and thy righteous-ness;* make him a man, a king; make him a good man, a good king. 1. It is the prayer of a father for his child, a dying blessing, such as the patriarchs bequeathed to their children. The best thing we can ask of God for our children is that God will give them wisdom and grace to know and do their duty; that is better than gold. Solomon learned to pray for himself as his father had prayed for him, not that God would give him riches and honour, but a wise and understanding heart. It was a comfort to David that his own son was to be his successor, but more so that he was likely to be both judicious and righteous. David had given him a good edu-cation (Prov. iv. 3), had taught him *good judgment and righteousness,* yet that would not do unless God gave him his judgments. Parents cannot give grace to their children, but may by prayer bring them to the God of grace, and shall not seek him in vain, for their prayer shall either be answered or it shall return with comfort into their own bosom. 2. It is the prayer of a king for his successor. David had executed judgment and justice during his reign, and now he prays that his son might do so too. Such a concern as this we should have for posterity, desiring and endeavouring that those who come after us may do God more and better service in their day than we have done in ours. Those have little love either to God or man, and are of a very narrow selfish spirit, who care not what becomes of the world and the church when they are gone. 3. It is the prayer of subjects for their king. It should seem, David penned this psalm for the use of the people, that they, in singing, might pray for Solomon. Those who would live quiet and peaceable lives must pray for kings and all in authority, that God would give them his judgments and righteousness. II. We may apply it to Christ; not that he who intercedes for us needs us to intercede for him; but, 1. It is a prayer of the Old-Testament church for sending the Messiah, as the church's King, King *on the holy hill of Zion*, of whom the King of kings had said, *Thou art my Son*, ii. 6, 7. " Hasten his coming to whom all judgment is committed;" and we must thus hasten the second coming of Christ, when he shall *judge the world in righteousness.* 2. It is an expression of the satisfaction which all true believers take in the authority which the Lord Jesus has received from the Father: " Let him have all power both in heaven and earth, and be the Lord our righteousness; let him be the great trustee of divine grace for all that are his; give it to him, that he may give it to us."

2 He shall judge thy people with righteousness, and thy poor with judgment. 3 The mountains shall bring peace to the people, and the little hills, by righteousness. 4 He shall judge the poor of the people, he shall save the children of the needy, and shall break in pieces the oppressor. 5 They shall fear thee as long as the sun and moon endure, throughout all generations. 6 He shall come down like rain upon the mown grass : as showers *that* water the earth. 7 In his days shall the righteous flourish ; and abundance of peace so long as the moon endureth. 8 He shall have dominion also from sea to sea, and from the river unto the ends of the earth. 9 They that dwell in the wilderness shall bow before him; and his ene-

mies shall lick the dust. 10 The kings of Tarshish and of the isles shall bring presents: the kings of Sheba and Seba shall offer gifts. 11 Yea, all kings shall fall down before him : all nations shall serve him. 12 For he shall deliver the needy when he crieth ; the poor also, and *him* that hath no helper. 13 He shall spare the poor and needy, and shall save the souls of the needy. 14 He shall redeem their soul from deceit and violence : and precious shall their blood be in his sight. 15 And he shall live, and to him shall be given of the gold of Sheba : prayer also shall be made for him continually ; *and* daily shall he be praised. 16 There shall be a handful of corn in the earth upon the top of the mountains ; the fruit thereof shall shake like Lebanon : and *they* of the city shall flourish like grass of the earth. 17 His name shall endure for ever : his name shall be continued as long as the sun : and *men* shall be blessed in him : all nations shall call him blessed.

This is a prophecy of the prosperity and perpetuity of the kingdom of Christ under the shadow of the reign of Solomon. It comes in, 1. As a plea to enforce the prayer: " Lord, *give him thy judgments and thy righteousness,* and then *he shall judge thy people with righteousness,* and so shall answer the end of his elevation, *v.* 2. Give him thy grace, and then thy people, committed to his charge, will have the benefit of it." *Because God loved Israel, he made him king over them to do judgment and justice,* 2 Chron. ix. 8. We may in faith wrestle with God for that grace which we have reason to think will be of common advantage to his church. 2. As an answer of peace to the prayer. As by the prayer of faith we return answers to God's promises of mercy, so by the promises of mercy God returns answers to our prayers of faith. That this prophecy must refer to the kingdom of the Messiah is plain, because there are many passages in it which cannot be applied to the reign of Solomon. There was indeed a great deal of righteousness and peace, at first, in the administration of his government; but, before the end of his reign, there were both trouble and unrighteousness. The kingdom here spoken of is to last as long as the sun, but Solomon's was soon extinct. Therefore even the Jewish expositors understand it of the kingdom of the Messiah.

Let us observe the many great and precious promises here made, which were to have their full accomplishment only in the

506

kingdom of Christ; and yet some of them were in part fulfilled in Solomon's reign.

I. That it should be a *righteous government* (v. 2): *He shall judge thy people with righteousness.* Compare Isa. xi. 4. All the laws of Christ's kingdom are consonant to the eternal rules of equity; the chancery it erects to relieve against the rigours of the broken law is indeed a court of equity; and against the sentence of his last judgment there will lie no exception. The peace of his kingdom shall be supported by righteousness (v. 3); for then only is the peace like a river, when the *righteousness is as the waves of the sea.* The world will be judged in righteousness, Acts xvii. 31.

II. That it should be a peaceable government: *The mountains shall bring peace, and the little hills (v. 3)*; that is (says Dr. Hammond), both the superior and the inferior courts of judicature in Solomon's kingdom. There shall be *abundance of peace, v. 7.* Solomon's name signifies *peaceable*, and such was his reign; for in it Israel enjoyed the victories of the foregoing reign and preserved the tranquillity and repose of that reign. But peace is, in a special manner, the glory of Christ's kingdom; for, as far as it prevails, it reconciles men to God, to themselves, and to one another, and slays all enmities; for he is our peace.

III. That the poor and needy should be, in a particular manner, taken under the protection of this government: *He shall judge thy poor, v. 2.* Those are God's poor that are impoverished by keeping a good conscience, and those shall be provided for with a distinguishing care, shall be judged for with judgment, with a particular cognizance taken of their case and a particular vengeance taken for their wrongs. *The poor of the people,* and *the children of the needy,* he will be sure so to judge as to save, *v. 4.* This is insisted upon again (v. 12, 13), intimating that Christ will be sure to carry his cause on behalf of his injured poor. *He will deliver the needy* that lie at the mercy of their oppressors, *the poor also,* both because they have *no helper* and it is for his honour to help them and because they cry unto him and he has promised, in answer to their prayers, to help them; they by prayer *commit themselves unto him,* x. 14. *He will spare the needy* that throw themselves on his mercy, and will not be rigorous and severe with them; he *will save their souls,* and that is all they desire. *Blessed are the poor in spirit, for theirs is the kingdom of heaven.* Christ is the poor man's King.

IV. That proud oppressors shall be reckoned with: *He shall break them in pieces (v. 4),* shall take away their power to hurt, and punish them for all the mischief they have done. This is the office of a good king, *Parcere subjectis, et debellare superbos—To spare the vanquished and debase the proud.* The devil is the great oppressor, whom Christ will break in pieces and of whose kingdom he will be the destruction. *With the breath of his mouth shall he slay that wicked one* (Isa. xi. 4), and shall deliver the souls of his people *from deceit and violence, v. 14.* He shall save from the power of Satan, both as an old serpent working by deceit to ensnare them and as a roaring lion working by violence to terrify and devour them. So *precious shall their blood be unto him* that not a drop of it shall be shed, by the deceit or violence of Satan or his instruments, without being reckoned for. Christ is a King, who, though he calls his subjects sometimes to resist unto blood for him, yet is not prodigal of their blood, nor will ever have it parted with but upon a valuable consideration to his glory and theirs, and the filling up of the measure of their enemies' iniquity.

V. That religion shall flourish under Christ's government (v. 5): *They shall fear thee as long as the sun and moon endure.* Solomon indeed built the temple, and the fear and worship of God were well kept up, for some time, under his government, but it did not last long; this therefore must point at Christ's kingdom, all the subjects of which are brought to and kept in the fear of God; for the Christian religion has a direct tendency to, and a powerful influence upon, the support and advancement of natural religion. Faith in Christ will set up, and keep up, the fear of God; and therefore this is the everlasting gospel that is preached, *Fear God, and give honour to him,* Rev. xiv. 7. And, as Christ's government promotes devotion towards God, so it promotes both justice and charity among men (v. 7): *In his days shall the righteous flourish ;* righteousness shall be practised, and those that practise righteousness shall be preferred. Righteousness shall abound and be in reputation, shall command and be in power. The law of Christ, written in the heart, disposes men to be honest and just, and to render to all their due; it likewise disposes men to live in love, and so it produces abundance of peace and beats swords into ploughshares. Both holiness and love shall be perpetual in Christ's kingdom, and shall never go to decay, for the subjects of it shall *fear God as long as the sun and moon endure ;* Christianity, in the profession of it, having got footing in the world, shall keep its ground till the end of time, and having, in the power of it, got footing in the heart, it will continue there till, by death, the sun, and the moon, and the stars (that is, the bodily senses) are darkened. Through all the changes of the world, and all the changes of life, Christ's kingdom will support itself; and, if the fear of God continue as long as the sun and moon, abundance of peace will. The peace of the church, the peace of the soul, shall run parallel with its purity and piety, and last as long as these last.

VI. That Christ's government shall be very comfortable to all his faithful loving subjects (*v.* 6): *He shall,* by the graces and comforts of his Spirit, *come down like rain upon the mown grass ;* not on that which is cut down, but that which is left growing, that it may spring again, though it was beheaded. The gospel of Christ distils as the rain, which softens the ground that was hard, moistens that which was dry, and so makes it green and fruitful, Isa. lv. 10. Let our hearts *drink in the rain,* Heb. vi. 7.

VII. That Christ's kingdom shall be extended very far, and greatly enlarged; considering,

1. The extent of his territories (*v.* 8): *He shall have dominion from sea to sea* (from the South Sea to the North, or from the Red Sea to the Mediterranean) *and from the river* Euphrates, or Nile, *to the ends of the earth.* Solomon's dominion was very large (1 Kings iv. 21), according to the promise, Gen. xv. 18. But no sea, no river, is named, that it might, by these proverbial expressions, intimate the universal monarchy of the Lord Jesus. His gospel has been, or shall be, preached *to all nations* (Matt. xxiv. 14), and the *kingdoms of the world* shall *become his kingdoms* (Rev. xi. 15) when the fulness of the Gentiles shall be brought in. His territories shall be extended to those countries, (1.) That were strangers to him : *Those that dwell in the wilderness,* out of all high roads, that seldom hear news, shall hear the glad tidings of the Redeemer and redemption by him, *shall bow before him,* shall believe in him, accept of him, worship him, and take his yoke upon them. Before the Lord Jesus we must all either bow or break ; if we break, we are ruined—if we bow, we are certainly made for ever. (2.) That were enemies to him, and had fought against him : *They shall lick the dust;* they shall be brought down and laid in the dust, shall bite the ground for vexation, and be so hunger-bitten that they shall be glad of dust, the serpent's meat (Gen. iii. 15), for of his seed they are ; and over whom shall not he rule, when his enemies themselves are thus humbled and brought low ?

2. The dignity of his tributaries. He shall not only reign over those that dwell in the wilderness, the peasants and cottagers, but over those that dwell in the palaces (*v.* 10): *The kings of Tarshish, and of the isles,* that lie most remote from Israel and are *the isles of the Gentiles* (Gen. x. 5), *shall bring presents* to him as their sovereign Lord, by and under whom they hold their crowns and all their crown-lands. They shall court his favour, and make an interest in him, that they may hear his wisdom. This was literally fulfilled in Solomon (for *all the kings of the earth sought the wisdom of Solomon, and brought every man his present,* 2 Chron. ix. 23, 24), and in Christ too, when the wise men of the east, who probably were men of the first rank in their own country, came to worship him and *brought him presents,* Matt. ii. 11. They shall present themselves to him ; that is the best present we can bring to Christ, and without that no other present is acceptable, Rom. xii. 1. They *shall offer gifts,* spiritual sacrifices of prayer and praise, offer them to Christ as their God, on Christ as their altar, which sanctifies every gift. Their conversion to God is called the *offering up,* or *sacrificing, of the Gentiles,* Rom. xv. 16. And so is their devotion to God, Heb. xiii. 15, 16. Yea, all kings shall, sooner or later, *fall down before him,* either to do their duty to him or to receive their doom from him, *v.* 11. They shall fall before him, either as his willing subjects or as his conquered captives, as suppliants for his mercy or expectants of his judgment. And, when the kings submit, the people come in of course : *All nations shall serve him;* all shall be invited into his service ; some of all nations shall come into it, and in every nation *incense shall be offered to him and a pure offering,* Mal. i. 11 ; Rev. vii. 9.

VIII. That he shall be honoured and beloved by all his subjects (*v.* 15): *He shall live;* his subjects shall desire his life *(O king! live for ever)* and with good reason ; for he has said, *Because I live, you shall live also; and of him it is witnessed that he liveth, ever liveth, making intercession,* Heb. vii. 8, 25. He shall live, and live prosperously ; and, 1. Presents shall be made to him. Though he shall be able to live without them, for he needs neither the gifts nor the services of any, yet to him *shall be given of the gold of Sheba*—gold, the best of metals, gold of Sheba, which probably was the finest gold ; for he that is best must be served with the best. Those that have abundance of the wealth of this world, that have gold at command, must give it to Christ, must serve him with it, do good with it. *Honour the Lord with thy substance.* 2. Prayers shall be made for him, and that continually. The people prayed for Solomon, and that helped to make him and his reign so great a blessing to them. It is the duty of subjects to make prayers, intercessions, and giving of thanks, for kings and all in authority, not in compliment to them, as is too often done, but in concern for the public welfare. But how is this applied to Christ ? He needs not our prayers, nor can have any benefit by them. But the Old-Testament saints prayed for his coming, prayed continually for it ; for they called him, *He that should come.* And now that he has come we must pray for the success of his gospel and the advancement of his kingdom, which he calls praying for him (Hosanna to the Son of David, prosperity to his reign), and we must pray for his second coming. It may be read, *Prayer shall be made through him,* or for his sake ; whatsoever we ask of the Father shall be in his name and in dependence upon his intercession. 3. Praises shall be made of him, and high encomiums given or his wisdom, justice, and goodness: *Daily shall he be praised.* By praying daily in his name we give him honour. Subjects ought to speak well of the government that is a blessing to them; and much more ought all Christians to praise Jesus Christ, daily to praise him; for they owe their all to him, and to him they lie under the highest obligations.

IX. That under his government there shall be a wonderful increase both of meat and mouths, both of the fruits of the earth in the country and of the people inhabiting the cities, *v.* 16. 1. The country shall grow rich. Sow but a *handful of corn on the top of the mountains,* whence one would expect but little, and yet *the fruit of it shall shake like Lebanon;* it shall come up like a wood, so thick, and tall, and strong, like the cedars of Lebanon. Even upon the tops of the mountains the earth shall bring forth by handfuls; that is an expression of great plenty (Gen. xli. 47), as the grass upon the house-top is said to be that wherewith the mower fills not his hand. This is applicable to the wonderful productions of the seed of the gospel in the days of the Messiah. A handful of that seed, sown in the mountainous and barren soil of the Gentile world, produced a wonderful harvest gathered in to Christ, fruit that shook like Lebanon. The fields were *white to the harvest,* John iv. 35; Matt. ix. 37. The grain of mustard-seed grew up to a great tree. 2. The towns shall grow populous: *Those of the city shall flourish like grass,* for number, for verdure. The gospel church, the city of God among men, shall have all the marks of prosperity, many shall be added to it, and those that are shall be happy in it.

X. That his government shall be perpetual, both to his honour and to the happiness of his subjects. The Lord Jesus shall reign for ever, and of him only this must be understood, and not at all of Solomon. It is Christ only that shall *be feared throughout all generations* (*v.* 5) and *as long as the sun and moon endure,* *v.* 7. 1. The honour of the prince is immortal and shall never be sullied (*v.* 17): *His name shall endure for ever,* in spite of all the malicious attempts and endeavours of the powers of darkness to eclipse the lustre of it and to cut off the line of it; it shall be preserved; it shall be perpetuated; it shall be propagated. As the names of earthly princes are continued in their posterity, so Christ's in himself. *Filiabitur nomen ejus—His name shall descend to posterity.* All nations, while the world stands, shall call him blessed, shall bless God for him, continually speak well of him, and think themselves happy in him. To the end of time, and to eternity, his name shall be celebrated, shall be made use of; every tongue shall confess it and every knee shall bow before it. 2. The happiness of the people is universal too; it is complete and everlasting: *Men shall be blessed,* truly and for ever blessed, *in him.* This plainly refers to the promise made unto the fathers that in the Messiah all the nations of the earth should be blessed. Gen. xii. 3.

18 Blessed *be* the LORD God, the God of Israel, who only doeth wondrous things. 19 And blessed *be* his glorious name for ever: and let the whole earth be filled *with* his glory; Amen, and Amen. 20 The prayers of David the son of Jesse are ended.

Such an illustrious prophecy as is in the foregoing verses of the Messiah and his kingdom may fitly be concluded, as it is here, with hearty prayers and praises.

I. The psalmist is here enlarged in thanksgivings for the prophecy and promise, *v.* 18, 19. So sure is every word of God, and with so much satisfaction may we rely upon it, that we have reason enough to give thanks for what he has said, though it be not yet done. We must own that for all the great things he has done for the world, for the church, for the children of men, for his own children, in the kingdom of providence, in the kingdom of grace, for all the power and trust lodged in the hands of the Redeemer, God is worthy to be praised; we must stir up ourselves and all that is within us to praise him after the best manner, and desire that all others may do it. *Blessed be the Lord,* that is, *blessed be his glorious name;* for it is only in his name that we can contribute any thing to his glory and blessedness, and yet that is also *exalted above all blessing and praise.* Let it be blessed for ever, it shall be blessed for ever, it deserves to be blessed for ever, and we hope to be for ever blessing it. We are here taught to bless the name of Christ, and to bless God in Christ, for all that which he has done for us by him. We must bless him, 1. As the Lord God, as a self-existent self-sufficient Being, and our sovereign Lord. 2. As the God of Israel, in covenant with that people and worshipped by them, and who does this in performance of the truth unto Jacob and the mercy to Abraham. 3. As the God *who only does wondrous things,* in creation and providence, and especially this work of redemption, which excels them all. Men's works are little, common, trifling things, and even these they could not do without him. But God does all by his own power, and they are wondrous things which he does, and such as will be the eternal admiration of saints and angels.

II. He is earnest in prayer for the accomplishment of this prophecy and promise: *Let the whole earth be filled with his glory,* as it will be when the *kings of Tarshish, and the isles, shall bring presents to him.* It is sad to think how empty the earth is of the glory of God, how little service and honour he has from a world to which he is such a bountiful benefactor. All those, therefore, that wish well to the honour of God and the welfare of mankind, cannot but desire that the earth may be filled with the discoveries of his glory, suitably returned in thankful acknowledgments of his glory. Let every heart, and every mouth, and every assembly, be filled with the high praises of God. We shall see how earnest David is in this prayer, and how much his heart is in it, if we observe, 1. How he shuts up the prayer with a double seal: "*Amen and amen;* again and again I say, I say it and let all others say the same, so be it. Amen to my prayer; Amen to the prayers of all the saints to this purport—*Hallowed be thy name; thy kingdom come.*" 2. How he even shuts up his life with this prayer, *v.* 20. This was the last psalm that ever he penned, though not placed last in this collection; he penned it when he lay on his death-bed, and with this he breathes his last: "Let God be glorified, let the kingdom of the Messiah be set up, and kept up, in the world, and I have enough, I desire no more. With this let *the prayers of David the son of Jesse be ended.* Even so, come, Lord Jesus, come quickly."

PSALM LXXIII.

This psalm, and the ten that next follow it, carry the name of Asaph in the titles of them. If he was the penman of them (as many think), we rightly call them psalms of Asaph. If he was only the chief musician, to whom they were delivered, our marginal reading is right, which calls them psalms for Asaph. It is probable that he penned them; for we read of the words of David and of Asaph the seer, which were used in praising God in Hezekiah's time, 2 Chron. xxix. 30. Though the Spirit of prophecy by sacred songs descended chiefly on David, who is therefore styled "the sweet psalmist of Israel," yet God put some of that Spirit upon those about him. This is a psalm of great use; it gives us an account of the conflict which the psalmist had with a strong temptation to envy the prosperity of wicked people. He begins his account with a sacred principle, which he held fast, and by the help of which he kept his ground and carried his point, ver. 1. He then tells us, I. How he got into the temptation, ver. 2—14. II. How he got out of the temptation and gained a victory over it, ver. 15—20. III. How he got by the temptation and was the better for it, ver. 21—23. If, in singing this psalm, we fortify ourselves against the like temptation, we do not use it in vain. The experiences of others should be our instructions.

A psalm of Asaph.

TRULY God *is* good to Israel, even to such as are of a clean heart. 2 But as for me, my feet were almost gone; my steps had well nigh slipped. 3 For I was envious at the foolish, *when* I saw the prosperity of the wicked. 4 For *there are* no bands in their death : but their strength *is* firm. 5 They *are* not in trouble *as other* men; neither are they plagued like *other* men. 6 Therefore pride compasseth them about as a chain; violence covereth them *as* a garment. 7 Their eyes stand out with fatness : they have more than heart could wish. 8 They are corrupt, and speak wickedly *concerning* oppression : they speak loftily. 9 They set their mouth against the heavens, and their tongue walketh through the earth. 10 Therefore his people return hither : and waters of a full *cup* are wrung out to them. 11 And they say, How doth God know ? and is there knowledge

in the most high ? 12 Behold, these *are* the ungodly, who prosper in the world; they increase *in* riches. 13 Verily I have cleansed my heart *in* vain, and washed my hands in innocency. 14 For all the day long have I been plagued, and chastened every morning.

This psalm begins somewhat abruptly : *Yet God is good to Israel* (so the margin reads it); he had been thinking of the prosperity of the wicked; while he was thus musing the fire burned, and at last he spoke by way of check to himself for what he had been thinking of. "However it be, yet God is good." Though wicked people receive many of the gifts of his providential bounty, yet we must own that he is, in a peculiar manner, good to Israel; they have favours from him which others have not.

The psalmist designs an account of a temptation he was strongly assaulted with—to envy the prosperity of the wicked, a common temptation, which has tried the graces of many of the saints. Now in this account,

I. He lays down, in the first place, that great principle which he is resolved to abide by and not to quit while he was parleying with this temptation, *v.* 1. Job, when he was entering into such a temptation, fixed for his principle the omniscience of God : *Times are not hidden from the Almighty,* Job xxiv. 1. Jeremiah's principle is the justice of God : *Righteous art thou, O God! when I plead with thee,* Jer. xii. 1. Habakkuk's principle is the holiness of God : *Thou art of purer eyes than to behold iniquity,* Hab. i. 13. The psalmist's, here, is the goodness of God. These are truths which cannot be shaken and which we must resolve to live and die by. Though we may not be able to reconcile all the disposals of Providence with them, we must believe they are reconcilable. Note, Good thoughts of God will fortify us against many of Satan's temptations. *Truly God is good;* he had had many thoughts in his mind concerning the providences of God, but this word, at last, settled him : "For all this, God is good, *good to Israel, even to those that are of a clean heart.*" Note, 1. Those are the Israel of God that are of a clean heart, purified by the blood of Christ, cleansed from the pollutions of sin, and entirely devoted to the glory of God. An upright heart is a clean heart; cleanness is truth in the inward part. 2. God, who is good to all, is in a special manner good to his church and people, as he was to Israel of old. God was good to Israel in redeeming them out of Egypt, taking them into covenant with himself, giving them his laws and ordinances, and in the various providences that related to them; he is, in like manner, good to all those that are of a clean heart, and, whatever happens, we must not think otherwise.

II. He comes now to relate the shock that

was given to his faith in God's distinguishing goodness to Israel, by a strong temptation to envy the prosperity of the wicked, and therefore to think that the Israel of God are no happier than other people and that God is no kinder to them than to others.

1. He speaks of it as a very narrow escape that he had not been quite foiled and overthrown by this temptation (v. 2): "*But as for me*, though I was so well satisfied in the goodness of God to Israel, yet *my feet were almost gone* (the tempter had almost tripped up my heels), *my steps had well-nigh slipped* (I had like to have quitted my religion, and given up all my expectations of benefit by it); *for I was envious at the foolish.*" Note, 1. The faith even of strong believers may sometimes be sorely shaken and ready to fail them. There are storms that will try the firmest anchors. 2. Those that shall never be quite undone are sometimes very near it, and, in their own apprehension, as good as gone. Many a precious soul, that shall live for ever, had once a very narrow turn for its life; almost and well-nigh ruined, but a step between it and fatal apostasy, and yet snatched as a brand out of the burning, which will for ever magnify the riches of divine grace in the nations of those that are saved. Now,

2. Let us take notice of the process of the psalmist's temptation, what he was tempted with and tempted to.

(1.) He observed that foolish wicked people have sometimes a very great share of outward prosperity. He *saw*, with grief, *the prosperity of the wicked, v. 3.* Wicked people are really foolish people, and act against reason and their true interest, and yet every stander-by sees their prosperity. [1.] They seem to have the least share of the troubles and calamities of this life (v. 5): *They are not in the troubles of other men*, even of wise and good men, *neither are they plagued like other men*, but seem as if by some special privilege they were exempted from the common lot of sorrows. If they meet with some little trouble, it is nothing to what others endure that are less sinners and yet greater sufferers. [2.] They seem to have the greatest share of the comforts of this life. They live at ease, and bathe themselves in pleasures, so that *their eyes stand out with fatness, v. 7.* See what the excess of pleasure is; the moderate use of it enlightens the eyes, but those that indulge themselves inordinately in the delights of sense have their eyes ready to start out of their heads. Epicures are really their own tormentors, by putting a force upon nature, while they pretend to gratify it. And well may those feed themselves to the full who have *more than heart could wish*, more than they themselves ever thought of or expected to be masters of. They have, at least, more than a humble, quiet, contented heart could wish, yet not so much as they themselves wish for. There are many who have a great deal of this life in their hands,

but nothing of the other life in their hearts. They are ungodly, live without the fear and worship of God, and yet they prosper and get on in the world, and not only are rich, but *increase in riches, v.* 12. They are looked upon as thriving men ; while others have much ado to keep what they have, they are still adding more, more honour, power, pleasure, by increasing in riches. *They are the prosperous of the age*, so some read it. [3.] Their end seems to be peace. This is mentioned first, as the most strange of all, for peace in death was ever thought to be the peculiar privilege of the godly (xxxvii. 37), yet, to outward appearance, it is often the lot of the ungodly (v. 4): *There are no bands in their death.* They are not taken off by a violent death ; they are foolish, and yet die not as fools die ; for *their hands are not bound nor their feet put into fetters,* 2 Sam. iii. 33, 34. They are not taken off by an untimely death, like the fruit forced from the tree before it is ripe, but are left to hang on, till, through old age, they gently drop of themselves. They do not die of sore and painful diseases : *There are no pangs,* no agonies, *in their death, but their strength is firm* to the last, so that they scarcely feel themselves die. They are of those who *die in their full strength, being wholly at ease and quiet,* not of those that *die in the bitterness of their souls and never eat with pleasure,* Job xxi. 23, 25. Nay, they are not bound by the terrors of conscience in their dying moments ; they are not frightened either with the remembrance of their sins or the prospect of their misery, but die securely. We cannot judge of men's state on the other side death either by the manner of their death or the frame of their spirits in dying. Men may die like lambs, and yet have their place with the goats.

(2.) He observed that they made a very bad use of their outward prosperity and were hardened by it in their wickedness, which very much strengthened the temptation he was in to fret at it. If it had done them any good, if it had made them less provoking to God or less oppressive to man, it would never have vexed him ; but it had quite a contrary effect upon them. [1.] It made them very proud and haughty. Because they live at ease, *pride compasses them as a chain, v.* 6. They show themselves (to all that see them) to be puffed up with their prosperity, as men show their ornaments. *The pride of Israel testifies to his face,* Hos. v. 5 ; Isa. iii. 9. *Pride ties on their chain,* or necklace ; so Dr. Hammond reads it. It is no harm to wear a chain or necklace ; but when pride ties it on, when it is worn to gratify a vain mind, it ceases to be an ornament. It is not so much what the dress or apparel is (though we have rules for that, 1 Tim. ii. 9) as what principle ties it on and with what spirit it is worn. And, as the pride of sinners appears in their dress, so it does in their talk : *They speak loftily* (v. 8) ; they affect *great swelling words of vanity* (2 Pet. ii. 18), bragging of themselves and disdaining all about them. Out of the abundance of the pride that is in their heart they speak big. [2.] It made them oppressive to their poor neighbours (*v.* 6): *Violence covers them as a garment.* What they have got by fraud and oppression they keep and increase by the same wicked methods, and care not what injury they do to others, nor what violence they use, so they may but enrich and aggrandize themselves. *They are corrupt*, like the giants, the sinners of the old world, when *the earth was filled with violence*, Gen. vi. 11, 13. They care not what mischief they do, either for mischief-sake or for their own advantage-sake. *They speak wickedly concerning oppression;* they oppress, and justify themselves in it. Those that speak well of sin speak wickedly of it. *They are corrupt*, that is, dissolved in pleasures and every thing that is luxurious (so some), and then they deride and speak maliciously; they care not whom they wound with the poisoned darts of calumny; from on high they speak oppression. [3.] It made them very insolent in their demeanour towards both God and man (*v.* 9): *They set their mouth against the heavens*, putting contempt upon God himself and his honour, bidding defiance to him and his power and justice. They cannot reach the heavens with their hands, to shake God's throne, else they would; but they show their ill-will by setting their mouth against the heavens. *Their tongue* also *walks through the earth*, and they take liberty to abuse all that come in their way. No man's greatness or goodness can secure him from the scourge of the virulent tongue. They take a pride and pleasure in bantering all mankind; they are pests of the country, for they neither fear God nor regard man. [4.] In all this they were very atheistical and profane. They could not have been thus wicked if they had not learned to say (*v.* 11), *How doth God know? And is there knowledge in the Most High?* So far were they from desiring the knowledge of God, who gave them all the good things they had and would have taught them to use them well, that they were not willing to believe God had any knowledge of them, that he took any notice of their wickedness or would ever call them to an account. As if, because he is *Most High*, he could not or would not see them, Job xxii. 12, 13. Whereas because he is *Most High* therefore he can and will, take cognizance of all the children of men and of all they do, or say, or think. What an affront is it to the God of infinite knowledge, from whom all knowledge is, to ask, *Is there knowledge in him?* Well may he say (*v.* 12), *Behold, these are the ungodly.*

(3.) He observed that while wicked men thus prospered in their impiety, and were made more impious by their prosperity, good people were in great affliction, and he himself in particular, which very much strength-

ened the temptation he was in to quarrel with Providence. [1.] He looked abroad and saw many of God's people greatly at a loss (*v.* 10): "Because the wicked are so very daring *therefore his people return hither;* they are at the same pause, the same plunge, that I am at; they know not what to say to it any more than I do, and the rather because *waters of a full cup are wrung out to them;* they are not only made to drink, and to drink deeply, of the bitter cup of affliction, but to drink all. Care is taken that they lose not a drop of that unpleasant potion; the waters are wrung out unto them, that they may have the dregs of the cup. They pour out abundance of tears when they hear wicked people blaspheme God and speak profanely," as David did, cxix. 136. These are the waters wrung out to them. [2.] He looked at home, and felt himself under the continual frowns of Providence, while the wicked were sunning themselves in its smiles (*v.* 14): "For my part," says he, "*all the day long have I been plagued* with one affliction or another, *and chastened every morning*, as duly as the morning comes." His afflictions were great—he was chastened and plagued; the returns of them were constant, *every morning* with the morning, and they continued, without intermission, *all the day long*. This he thought was very hard, that, when those who blasphemed God were in prosperity, he that worshipped God was under such great affliction. He spoke feelingly when he spoke of his own troubles; there is no disputing against sense, except by faith.

(4.) From all this arose a very strong temptation to cast off his religion. [1.] Some that observed the prosperity of the wicked, especially comparing it with the afflictions of the righteous, were tempted to deny a providence and to think that God had forsaken the earth. In this sense some take *v.* 11. There are those, even among God's professing people, that say, "*How does God know?* Surely all things are left to blind fortune, and not disposed of by an all-seeing God." Some of the heathen, upon such a remark as this, have asked, *Quis putet esse deos?—Who will believe that there are gods?* [2.] Though the psalmist's feet were not so far gone as to question God's omniscience, yet he was tempted to question the benefit of religion, and to say (*v.* 13), *Verily, I have cleansed my heart in vain, and have, to no purpose, washed my hands in innocency.* See here what it is to be religious; it is to cleanse our hearts, in the first place, by repentance and regeneration, and then to wash our hands in innocency by a universal reformation of our lives. It is not in vain to do this, not in vain to serve God and keep his ordinances; but good men have been sometimes tempted to say, "It is in vain," and "Religion is a thing that there is nothing to be got by," because they see wicked people in prosperity. But, however the thing may appear now, when the pure in heart, those blessed ones, shall see God (Matt. v. 8), they will not say that they cleansed their hearts in vain.

15 If I say, I will speak thus ; behold, I should offend *against* the generation of thy children. 16 When I thought to know this, it *was* too painful for me ; 17 Until I went into the sanctuary of God ; *then* understood I their end. 18 Surely thou didst set them in slippery places: thou castedst them down into destruction. 19 How are they *brought* into desolation, as in a moment ! they are utterly consumed with terrors. 20 As a dream when *one* awaketh ; *so*, O Lord, when thou awakest, thou shalt despise their image.

We have seen what a strong temptation the psalmist was in to envy prospering profaneness ; now here we are told how he kept his footing and got the victory.

I. He kept up a respect for God's people, and with that he restrained himself from speaking what he had thought amiss, *v.* 15. He got the victory by degrees, and this was the first point he gained ; he was ready to say, *Verily, I have cleansed my heart in vain*, and thought he had reason to say it, but he kept his mouth with this consideration, " *If I say, I will speak thus, behold, I should* myself revolt and apostatize from, and *so give the greatest offence imaginable to, the generation of thy children.*" Observe here, 1. Though he thought amiss, he took care not to utter that evil thought which he had conceived. Note, It is bad to think ill, but it is worse to speak it, for that is giving the evil thought an *imprimatur—a sanction;* it is allowing it, giving consent to it, and publishing it for the infection of others. But it is a good sign that we repent of the evil imagination of the heart if we suppress it, and the error remains with ourselves. If therefore thou hast been so foolish as to think evil, be so wise as to *lay thy hand upon thy mouth,* and let it go no further, Prov. xxx. 32. *If I say, I will speak thus.* Observe, Though his corrupt heart made this inference from the prosperity of the wicked, yet he did not mention it to those about him till he had debated within himself whether it were fit to be mentioned or no. Note, We must think twice before we speak once, both because some things may be thought which yet may not be spoken and because the second thoughts may correct the mistakes of the first. 2. The reason why he would not speak it was for fear of giving offence to those whom God owned for his children. Note, (1.) There are a people in the world that are the generation of God's children, a set of men that hear and love God as their Father. (2.) We must be

very careful not to say or do any thing which may justly offend *any of these little ones* (Matt. xviii. 6), especially which may offend *the generation of them,* may sadden their hearts, or weaken their hands, or shake their interest. (3.) There is nothing that can give more general offence to the generation of God's children than to say that *we have cleansed our heart in vain* or that it is vain to serve God; for there is nothing more contrary to their universal sentiment and experience nor any thing that grieves them more than to hear God thus reflected on. (4.) Those that wish themselves in the condition of the wicked do in effect quit the tents of God's children.

II. He foresaw the ruin of wicked people. By this he baffled the temptation, as by the former he gave some check to it. Because he durst not speak what he had thought, for fear of giving offence, he began to consider whether he had any good reason for that thought (*v.* 16): " I endeavoured to understand the meaning of this unaccountable dispensation of Providence; but *it was too painful for me.* I could not conquer it by the strength of my own reasoning." It is a problem, not to be solved by the mere light of nature, for, if there were not another life after this, we could not fully reconcile the prosperity of the wicked with the justice of God. But (*v.* 17) *he went into the sanctuary of God;* he applied to his devotions, meditated upon the attributes of God, and the *things revealed, which belong to us and to our children;* he consulted the scriptures, and the lips of the priests who attended the sanctuary; he prayed to God to make this matter plain to him and to help him over this difficulty; and, at length, he understood the wretched end of wicked people, which he plainly foresaw to be such that even in the height of their prosperity they were rather to be pitied than envied, for they were but ripening for ruin. Note, There are many great things, and things needful to be known, which will not be known otherwise than by going into the sanctuary of God, by the word and prayer. The sanctuary must therefore be the resort of a tempted soul. Note, further, We must judge of persons and things as they appear by the light of divine revelation, and then we shall judge righteous judgment ; particularly we must judge by the end. All is well that ends well, everlastingly well; but nothing well that ends ill, everlastingly ill. The righteous man's afflictions end in peace, and therefore he is happy ; the wicked man's enjoyments end in destruction, and therefore he is miserable.

1. The prosperity of the wicked is short and uncertain. The high places in which Providence sets them are *slippery places* (*v.* 18), where they cannot long keep footing ; but, when they offer to climb higher, that very attempt will be the occasion of their sliding and falling. Their prosperity has no firm

ground; it is not built upon God's favour or his promise; and they have not the satisfaction of feeling that it rests on firm ground.

2. Their destruction is sure, and sudden, and very great. This cannot be meant of any temporal destruction; for they were supposed to *spend all their days in wealth* and their death itself had no bands in it: *In a moment they go down to the grave,* so that even that could scarcely be called *their destruction;* it must therefore be meant of eternal destruction on the other side death—hell and destruction. They flourish for a time, but are undone for ever. (1.) Their ruin is sure and inevitable. He speaks of it as a thing done—*They are cast down;* for their destruction is as certain as if it were already accomplished. He speaks of it as God's doing, and therefore it cannot be resisted: *Thou castest them down.* It is *destruction from the Almighty* (Joel i. 15), from *the glory of his power,* 2 Thess. i. 9. Who can support those whom God will cast down, on whom God will lay burdens? (2.) It is swift and sudden; their damnation slumbers not; for *how are they brought into desolation as in a moment! v.* 19. It is easily effected, and will be a great surprise to themselves and all about them. (3.) It is severe and very dreadful. It is a total and final ruin: *They are utterly consumed with terrors.* It is the misery of the damned that the terrors of the Almighty, whom they have made their enemy, fasten upon their guilty consciences, which can neither shelter themselves from them nor strengthen themselves under them; and therefore not their being, but their bliss, must needs be utterly consumed by them; not the least degree of comfort or hope remains to them; the higher they were lifted up in their prosperity the sorer will their fall be when they are cast down into *destructions* (for the word is plural) and suddenly *brought into desolation.*

3. Their prosperity is therefore not to be envied at all, but despised rather, *quod erat demonstrandum—which was the point to be established, v.* 20. *As a dream when one awaketh, so, O Lord ! when thou awakest,* or when they awake (as some read it), *thou shalt despise their image,* their shadow, *and make it to vanish. In the day of the great judgment* (so the Chaldee paraphrase reads it), when they are awaked out of their graves, thou shalt, in wrath, despise their image; for *they shall rise to shame and everlasting contempt.* See here, (1.) What their prosperity now is; it is but an image, a vain show, a fashion of the world that passes away; it is not real, but imaginary, and it is only a corrupt imagination that makes it a happiness; it is not substance, but a mere shadow; it is not what it seems to be, nor will it prove what we promise ourselves from it; it is as a dream, which may please us a little, while we are asleep, yet even then it disturbs our repose; but, how pleasing soever it is, it is all but a

cheat, all false; when we awake we find it so. A hungry man *dreams that he eats, but he awakes and his soul is empty,* Isa. xxix. 8. A man is never the more rich or honourable for dreaming he is so. Who therefore will envy a man the pleasure of a dream? (2.) What will be the issue of it; God will awake to judgment, to plead his own and his people's injured cause; they shall be made to awake out of the sleep of their carnal security, and then God shall despise their image; he shall make it appear to all the world how despicable it is; so that the righteous shall laugh at them, lii. 6, 7. How did God despise that rich man's image when he said, *Thou fool, this night thy soul shall be required of thee!* Luke xii. 19, 20. We ought to be of God's mind, for his judgment is according to truth, and not to admire and envy that which he despises and will despise; for, sooner or later, he will bring all the world to be of his mind.

21 Thus my heart was grieved, and I was pricked in my reins. 22 So foolish *was* I, and ignorant: I was *as* a beast before thee. 23 Nevertheless I *am* continually with thee: thou hast holden *me* by my right hand. 24 Thou shalt guide me with thy counsel, and afterward receive me *to* glory. 25 Whom have I in heaven *but thee?* and *there is* none upon earth *that* I desire beside thee. 26 My flesh and my heart faileth: *but* God *is* the strength of my heart, and my portion for ever. 27 For, lo, they that are far from thee shall perish: thou hast destroyed all them that go a whoring from thee. 28 But *it is* good for me to draw near to God: I have put my trust in the Lord God, that I may declare all thy works.

Behold Samson's riddle again unriddled, *Out of the eater came forth meat, and out of the strong sweetness;* for we have here an account of the good improvement which the psalmist made of that sore temptation with which he had been assaulted and by which he was almost overcome. He that stumbles and does not fall, by recovering himself takes so much the longer steps forward. It was so with the psalmist here; many good lessons he learned from his temptation, his struggles with it, and his victories over it. Nor would God suffer his people to be tempted if his grace were not sufficient for them, not only to save them from harm, but to make them gainers by it; even this shall work for good.

I. He learned to think very humbly of himself and to abase and accuse himself before God (*v.* 21, 22); he reflects with shame upon the disorder and danger he was in, and the vexation he gave himself by entertaining the temptation and parleying with it: *My heart was grieved, and I was pricked in my reins,* as one afflicted with the acute pain of the stone in the region of the kidneys. If evil thoughts at any time enter into the mind of a good man, he does not roll them under his tongue as a sweet morsel, but they are grievous and painful to him; temptation was to Paul as a thorn in the flesh, 2 Cor. xii. 7. This particular temptation, the working of envy and discontent, is as painful as any; where it constantly rests it is the *rottenness of the bones* (Prov. xiv. 30); where it does but occasionally come it is the pricking of the reins. Fretfulness is a corruption that is its own correction. Now in the reflection upon it, 1. He owns it was his folly thus to vex himself " *So foolish was I* to be my own tormentor." Let peevish people thus reproach themselves for, and shame themselves out of, their discontents. " What a fool am I thus to make myself uneasy without a cause?" 2. He owns it was his ignorance to vex himself at this: " So ignorant was I of that which I might have known, and which, if I had known it aright, would have been sufficient to silence my murmurs. *I was as a beast* (Behemoth—*a great beast) before thee.* Beasts mind present things only, and never look before at what is to come; and so did I. If I had not been a great fool, I should never have suffered such a senseless temptation to prevail over me so far. What! to envy wicked men upon account of their prosperity ! To be ready to wish myself one of them, and to think of changing conditions with them! *So foolish was I.*" Note, If good men do at any time, through the surprise and strength of temptation, think, or speak, or act amiss, when they see their error they will reflect upon it with sorrow, and shame, and self-abhorrence, will call themselves *fools* for it. *Surely I am more brutish than any man,* Prov. xxx. 2; Job xlii. 5, 6. Thus David, 2 Sam. xxiv. 10.

II. He took occasion hence to own his dependence on and obligations to the grace of God (*v.* 23): " *Nevertheless,* foolish as I am, *I am continually with thee* and in thy favour; *thou hast holden me by my right hand.*" This may refer either, 1. To the care God had taken of him, and the kindness he had shown him, all along from his beginning hitherto. He had said, in the hour of temptation (*v.* 14), *All the day long have I been plagued ;* but here he corrects himself for that passionate complaint: " Though God has chastened me, he has not cast me off; notwithstanding all the crosses of my life, *I have been continually with thee ;* I have had thy presence with me, and thou hast been nigh unto me in all that which I have called upon thee for; and therefore, though perplexed, yet not in despair. Though God has sometimes written bitter things against me, yet he has still *holden me by my right hand,* both to keep me, that I should not desert him or fly off from him,

and to prevent my sinking and fainting under my burdens, or losing my way in the wildernesses through which I have walked." If we have been kept in the way with God, kept closely in our duty and upheld in our integrity, we must own ourselves indebted to the free grace of God for our preservation: *Having obtained help of God, I continue hitherto.* And, if he has thus maintained spiritual life, the earnest of eternal life, we ought not to complain, whatever calamities of this present time we have met with. Or, 2. To the late experience he had had of the power of divine grace in carrying him through this strong temptation and bringing him off a conqueror: " I was foolish and ignorant, and yet thou hast had compassion on me and taught me (Heb. v. 2), and kept me under thy protection ;" for the unworthiness of man is no bar to the free grace of God. We must ascribe our safety in temptation, and our victory over it, not to our own wisdom, for we are foolish and ignorant, but to the gracious presence of God with us and the prevalency of Christ's intercession for us, that our faith may not fail: " *My feet were almost gone,* and they would have quite gone, past recovery, but that thou hast holden me by my right hand and so kept me from falling."

III. He encouraged himself to hope that the same God who had delivered him from this evil work would *preserve him to his heavenly kingdom,* as St. Paul does (2 Tim. iv. 18): " I am now upheld by thee, therefore *thou shalt guide me with thy counsel,* leading me, as thou hast done hitherto, many a difficult step; and, since I am now continually with thee, thou *shalt afterwards receive me to glory*" v. 24. This completes the happiness of the saints, so that they have no reason to envy the worldly prosperity of sinners. Note, 1. All those who commit themselves to God shall be guided with his counsel, with the counsel both of his word and of his Spirit, the best counsellors. The psalmist had like to have paid dearly for following his own counsels in this temptation and therefore resolves for the future to take God's advice, which shall never be wanting to those that duly seek it with a resolution to follow it. 2. All those who are guided and led by the counsel of God in this world shall be received to his glory in another world. If we make God's glory in us the end we aim at, he will make our glory with him the end we shall for ever be happy in. Upon this consideration, let us never envy sinners, but rather bless ourselves in our own blessedness. If God direct us in the way of our duty, and prevent our turning aside out of it, he will afterwards, when our state of trial and preparation is over, receive us to his kingdom and glory, the believing hopes and prospects of which will reconcile us to all the dark providences that now puzzle and perplex us, and ease us of the pain we have been put into by some threatening temptations.

IV. He was hereby quickened to cleave the

more closely to God, and very much confirmed and comforted in the choice he had made of him, *v.* 25, 26. His thoughts here dwell with delight upon his own happiness in God, as much greater than the happiness of the ungodly that prospered in the world. He saw little reason to envy them what they had in the creature when he found how much more and better, surer and sweeter, comforts he had in the Creator, and what cause he had to congratulate himself on this account. He had complained of his afflictions (*v.* 14); but this makes them very light and easy, *All is well if God be mine.* We have here the breathings of a sanctified soul towards God, and its repose in him, as that to a godly man really which the prosperity of a worldly man is to him in conceit and imagination : *Whom have I in heaven but thee ?* There is scarcely a verse in all the psalms more expressive than this of the pious and devout affections of a soul to God ; here it soars up towards him, follows hard after him, and yet, at the same time, has an entire satisfaction and complacency in him.

1. It is here supposed that God alone is the felicity and chief good of man. He, and he only, that made the soul, can make it happy ; there is none in heaven, none in earth, that can pretend to do it besides.

2. Here are expressed the workings and breathings of a soul towards God accordingly. If God be our felicity,

(1.) Then we must have him *(Whom have I but thee ?)*, we must choose him, and make sure to ourselves an interest in him. What will it avail us that he is the felicity of souls if he be not the felicity of our souls, and if we do not by a lively faith make him ours, by joining ourselves to him in an everlasting covenant ?

(2.) Then our desire must be towards him and our delight in him (the word signifies both) ; we must delight in what we have of God and desire what we yet further hope for. Our desires must not only be offered up to God, but they must all terminate in him, desiring nothing more than God, but still more and more of him. This includes all our prayers, *Lord, give us thyself;* as that includes all the promises, *I will be to them a God. The desire of our souls is to thy name.*

(3.) We must prefer him in our choice and desire before any other. [1.] " *There is none in heaven but thee,* none to seek to or trust in, none to court or covet acquaintance with, but thee." God is in himself more glorious than any celestial being (lxxxix. 6), and must be, in our eyes, infinitely more desirable. Excellent beings there are in heaven, but God alone can make us happy. His favour is infinitely more to us than the refreshment of the dews of heaven or the benign influence of the stars of heaven, more than the friendship of the saints in heaven or the good offices of the angels there. [2.] *I desire none on earth besides thee;* not only none in heaven,

a place at a distance, which we have but little acquaintance with, but none on earth neither, where we have many friends and where much of our present interest and concern lie. " Earth carries away the desires of most men, and yet I have none on earth, no persons, no things, no possessions, no delights, that I desire besides thee or with thee, in comparison or competition with thee." We must desire nothing besides God but what we desire for him *(nil præter te nisi propter te—nothing besides thee except for thy sake)*, nothing but what we desire from him, and can be content without so that it be made up in him. We must desire nothing besides God as needful to be a partner with him in making us happy.

(4.) Then we must repose ourselves in God with an entire satisfaction, *v.* 26. Observe here, [1.] Great distress and trouble supposed : *My flesh and my heart fail.* Note, Others have experienced and we must expect, the failing both of flesh and heart. The body will fail by sickness, age, and death ; and that which touches the bone and the flesh touches us in a tender part, that part of ourselves which we have been but too fond of ; when the flesh fails the heart is ready to fail too ; the conduct, courage, and comfort fail. [2.] Sovereign relief provided in this distress : *But God is the strength of my heart and my portion for ever.* Note, Gracious souls, in their greatest distresses, rest upon God as their spiritual strength and their eternal portion. *First,* " *He is the strength of my heart,* the rock of my heart, a firm foundation, which will bear my weight and not sink under it. *God is the strength of my heart;* I have found him so ; I do so still, and hope ever to find him so." In the distress supposed, he had put the case of a double failure, both *flesh and heart fail;* but, in the relief, he fastens on a single support : he leaves out the flesh and the consideration of that, it is enough that God is *the strength of his heart.* He speaks as one careless of the body (let that fail, there is no remedy), but as one concerned about the soul, to be *strengthened in the inner man. Secondly,* " *He is my portion for ever;* he will not only support me while I am here, but make me happy when I go hence." The saints choose God for their portion, they have him for their portion, and it is their happiness that he will be their portion, a portion that will last as long as the immortal soul lasts.

V. He was fully convinced of the miserable condition of all wicked people. This he learned in the sanctuary upon this occasion, and he would never forget it (*v.* 27) : *"Lo, those that are far from thee,* in a state of distance and estrangement, that desire the Almighty to depart from them, *shall* certainly *perish;* so shall their doom be; they choose to be far from God, and they shall be far from him for ever. *Thou wilt* justly *destroy all those that go a whoring from thee,* that is, all apostates, that in profession have been betrothed to God, but forsake him, their duty to him and their communion with him, to embrace the bosom of a stranger." The doom is severe, no less than perishing and being destroyed. It is universal: "They shall all be destroyed without exception." It is certain: "*Thou hast destroyed ;* it is as sure to be done as if done already; and the destruction of some ungodly men is an earnest of the perdition of all." God himself undertakes to do it, into whose hands it is a fearful thing to fall: "Thou, though infinite in goodness, wilt reckon for thy injured honour and abused patience, and wilt destroy those that go a whoring from thee."

VI. He was greatly encouraged to cleave to God and to confide in him, *v.* 28. *If those that are far from God shall perish,* then, 1. Let this constrain us to live in communion with God; "if it fare so ill with those that live at a distance from him, then it is good, very good, the chief good, that good for a man, in this life, which he should most carefully pursue and secure, it is best for me to draw near to God, and to have God draw near to me;" the original may take in both. *But for my part* (so I would read it) *the approach of God is good for me.* Our drawing near to God takes rise from his drawing near to us, and it is the happy meeting that makes the bliss. Here is a great truth laid down, That it is good to draw near to God; but the life of it lies in the application, " It is good for *me.*" Those are the wise who know what is good for themselves: "*It is good,* says he (and every good man agrees with him in it), *it is good for me to draw near to God ;* it is my duty; it is my interest." 2. Let us therefore live in a continual dependence upon him : "*I have put my trust in the Lord God,* and will never go a whoring from him after any creature confidences." If wicked men, notwithstanding all their prosperity, shall perish and be destroyed, then let us trust in the Lord God, in him, not in them (see cxlvi. 3—5), in him, and not in our worldly prosperity; let us trust in God, and neither fret at them nor be afraid of them ; let us trust in him for a better portion than theirs is. 3. While we do so, let us not doubt but that we shall have occasion to praise his name. Let us trust in the Lord, that we may declare all his works. Note, Those that with an upright heart put their trust in God shall never want matter for thanksgiving to him.

PSALM LXXIV.

This psalm does so particularly describe the destruction of Jerusalem and the temple, by Nebuchadnezzar and the army of the Chaldeans, and can so ill be applied to any other event we meet with in the Jewish history, that interpreters incline to think that either it was penned in a day of affliction (which yet is not so probable), or that it was penned by another Asaph, who lived at the time of the captivity, or Jeremiah (for it is of a piece with his Lamentations,) or some other prophet, and, after the return out of captivity, was delivered to the sons of Asaph, who were called by his name, for the public service of the church. That was the most eminent family of the singers in Ezra's time. See Ezra ii. 41; iii. 10; Neh. xi. 17, 22; xii. 35, 46. The deplorable case of the people of God at that time is here spread before the Lord, and left with him. The prophet, in the name of the church, I. Puts in complaining pleas of the miseries they suffered, for the quickening of their desires in prayer, ver. 1—11. II. He puts in comfortable pleas for the encouraging of their faith in prayer, ver. 12—17. III. He concludes with divers petitions to God for deliverances, ver. 18—23. In singing it we must be affected with the former desolations of the church, for if we are members of the same body, and may apply it to any present distresses or desolations of any part of the Christian church.

Maschil of Asaph.

O GOD, why hast thou cast *us* off for ever? *why* doth thine anger smoke against the sheep of thy pasture? 2 Remember thy congregation, *which* thou hast purchased of old; the rod of thine inheritance, *which* thou hast redeemed; this mount Zion, wherein thou hast dwelt. 3 Lift up thy feet unto the perpetual desolations; *even* all *that* the enemy hath done wickedly in the sanctuary. 4 Thine enemies roar in the midst of thy congregations; they set up their ensigns *for* signs. 5 *A man* was famous according as he had lifted up axes upon the thick trees. 6 But now they break down the carved work thereof at once with axes and hammers. 7 They have cast fire into thy sanctuary, they have defiled *by casting down* the dwelling place of thy name to the ground. 8 They said in their hearts, Let us destroy them together : they have burned up all the synagogues of God in the land. 9 We see not our signs: *there is* no more any prophet: neither *is there* among us any that knoweth how long. 10 O God, how long shall the adversary reproach? shall the enemy blaspheme thy name for ever? 11 Why withdrawest thou thy hand, even thy right hand? pluck *it* out of thy bosom.

This psalm is entitled *Maschil—a psalm to give instruction,* for it was penned in a day of affliction, which is intended for instruction ; and this instruction in general it gives us, That when we are, upon any account, in distress, it is our wisdom and duty to apply to God by faithful and fervent prayer, and we shall not find it in vain to do so. Three things the people of God here complain of :—

I. The displeasure of God against them, as that which was the cause and bitterness of all their calamities. They look above the instruments of their trouble, who, they knew, could have no power against them unless it were given them from above, and keep their eye upon God, by whose determined counsel they were delivered up into the hands of wicked and unreasonable men. Observe the liberty they take to expostulate with God (*v.* 1), we hope not too great a liberty, for Christ himself, upon the cross, cried out, *My God, my God, why hast thou forsaken me ?* So the church here, O God ! why hast thou forsaken us for ever ? Here they speak according to their present dark and melancholy apprehensions; for otherwise, *Has God cast away his people? God forbid,* Rom. xi. 1. The people of God must not think that because they are cast down they are therefore cast off, that because men cast them off therefore God does, and that because he seems to cast them off for a time therefore they are really cast off for ever: yet this expostulation intimates that they dreaded God's casting them off more than any thing, that they desired to be owned of him, whatever they suffered from men, and were desirous to know wherefore he thus contended with them: *Why does thy anger smoke?* that is, why does it rise up to such a degree that all about us take notice of it, and ask, *What means the heat of this great anger?* Deut. xxix. 24. Compare *v.* 20, where the anger of the Lord and his jealousy are said to smoke against sinners. Observe what they plead with God, now that they lay under the tokens and apprehensions of his wrath. 1. They plead their relation to him: "We are *the sheep of thy pasture,* the sheep wherewith thou hast been pleased to stock the pasture, thy peculiar people whom thou art pleased to set apart for thyself and design for thy own glory. That the wolves worry the sheep is not strange; but was ever any shepherd thus displeased at his own sheep? *Remember,* we are *thy congregation* (*v.* 2), incorporated by thee and for thee, and devoted to thy praise; we are *the rod,* or tribe, *of thy inheritance,* whom thou hast been pleased to claim a special property in above other people (Deut. xxxii. 9), and from whom thou hast received the rents and issues of praise and worship more than from the neighbouring nations. Nay, a man's inheritance may lie at a great distance, but we are pleading for *Mount Zion, wherein thou hast dwelt,* which has been the place of thy peculiar delight and residence, thy demesne and mansion." 2. They plead the great things God had done for them and the vast expense he had been at upon them: "It is *thy congregation,* which thou hast not only made with a word's speaking, but *purchased of old* by many miracles of mercy when they were first formed into a people; it is *thy inheritance, which thou hast redeemed* when they were sold into servitude." God *gave Egypt* to ruin *for their ransom, gave men for them* and *people for their life,* Isa. xliii. 3, 4. "Now, Lord, wilt thou now abandon a people that cost thee so dear, and has been so dear to thee?" And, if the redemption of Israel out of Egypt was an encouragement to hope that he would not cast them off, much more reason have we to hope that God will not cast off any whom Christ has redeemed with his own blood; but the people of his purchase shall be for ever the people of his praise. 3. They plead the calamitous state that they were in (*v.* 3): "*Lift up thy feet;* that is, come with speed to repair the desolations that are made in thy sanctuary, which otherwise will be perpetual

and irreparable." It has been sometimes said that the divine vengeance strikes with iron hands, yet it comes with leaden feet; and then those who wait for the day of the Lord, cry, *Lord, lift up thy feet; exalt thy steps;* magnify thyself in the outgoing of thy providence. When the desolations of the sanctuary have continued long we are tempted to think they will be perpetual; but it is a temptation; for God will avenge his own elect, will avenge them speedily, though he bear long with their oppressors and persecutors.

II. They complain of the outrage and cruelty of their enemies, not so much, no, not at all, of what they had done to the prejudice of their secular interests; here are no complaints of the burning of their cities and ravaging of their country, but only what they had done against the sanctuary and the synagogue. The concerns of religion should lie nearer our hearts and affect us more than any worldly concern whatsoever. The desolation of God's house should grieve us more than the desolation of our own houses; for the matter is not great what becomes of us and our families in this world provided God's name may be sanctified, his kingdom may come, and his will be done.

1. The psalmist complains of the desolations of the sanctuary, as Daniel, *ch.* ix. 17. The temple at Jerusalem was the *dwelling-place of God's name,* and therefore the *sanctuary,* or *holy place, v.* 7. In this the enemies did wickedly (*v.* 3), for they destroyed it in downright contempt of God and affront to him. (1.) They *roared in the midst of God's congregations, v.* 4. There where God's faithful people attended on him with a humble reverent silence, or softly speaking, they roared in a riotous revelling manner, being elated with having made themselves masters of that sanctuary of which they had sometimes heard formidable things. (2.) *They set up their ensigns for signs.* The banners of their army they set up in the temple (Israel's strongest castle, as long as they kept closely to God) as trophies of their victory There, where the signs of God's presence used to be, now the enemy had set up their ensigns. This daring defiance of God and his power touched his people in a tender part. (3.) They took a pride in destroying *the carved work* of the temple. As much as formerly men thought it an honour to lend a hand to the building of the temple, and he was thought famous that helped to fell timber for that work, so much now they valued themselves upon their agency in destroying it, *v.* 5, 6. Thus, as formerly those were celebrated for wise men that did service to religion, so now those are applauded as wits that help to run it down. Some read it thus: *They show themselves, as one that lifts up axes on high in a thicket of trees,* for so do they break down the carved work of the temple; they make no more scruple of breaking down the rich wainscot of the temple

than woodcutters do of hewing trees in the forest; such indignation have they at the sanctuary that the most curious carving that ever was seen is beaten down by the common soldiers without any regard had to it, either as a dedicated thing or as a piece of exquisite art. (4.) They set fire to it, and so violated or *destroyed it to the ground, v.* 7. The Chaldeans burnt the house of God, that stately costly fabric, 2 Chron. xxxvi. 19. And the Romans *left not there one stone upon another* (Matt. xxiv. 2), rasing it, rasing it, even to the foundations, till Zion, the holy mountain, was, by Titus Vespasian, ploughed as a field.

2. He complains of the desolations of the synagogues, or schools of the prophets, which, before the captivity, were in use, though much more afterwards. There God's word was read and expounded, and his name praised and called upon, without altars or sacrifices. These also they had a spite to (*v.* 8): *Let us destroy them together;* not only the temple, but all the places of religious worship and the worshippers with them. *Let us destroy them together;* let them be consumed in the same flame. Pursuant to this impious resolve they *burnt up all the synagogues of God in the land* and laid them all waste. So great was their rage against religion that the religious houses, because religious, were all levelled with the ground, that God's worshippers might not glorify God, and edify one another, by meeting in solemn assemblies.

III. The great aggravation of all these calamities was that they had no prospect at all of relief, nor could they foresee an end of them (*v.* 9): " We see our enemy's sign set up in the sanctuary, but *we see not our signs,* none of the tokens of God's presence, no hopeful indications of approaching deliverance. *There is no more any prophet* to tell us how long the trouble will last and when things concerning us shall have an end, that the hope of an issue at last may support us under our troubles." In the captivity in Babylon they had prophets, and had been told how long the captivity should continue, but the day was cloudy and dark (Ezek. xxxiv. 12), and they had not as yet the comfort of these gracious discoveries. God spoke once, yea, twice, good words and comfortable words, but they perceived them not. Observe, They do not complain, " We see not our armies; there are no men of war to command our forces, nor any to go forth with our hosts;" but, " no prophets, none to tell us how long." This puts them upon expostulating with God, as delaying, 1. To assert his honour (*v.* 10): *How long shall the adversary reproach and blaspheme thy name?* In the desolations of the sanctuary our chief concern should be for the glory of God, that that may not be injured by the blasphemies of those who persecute his people for his sake, because they are his; and therefore our

enquiry should be, not " How long shall we be troubled?" but "How long shall God be blasphemed?" 2. To exert his power (*v.* 11): " *Why withdrawest thou thy hand,* and dost not stretch it out, to deliver thy people and destroy thy enemies? *Pluck it out of thy bosom,* and be not *as a man astonished, as a mighty man that cannot save,* or will not," Jer. xiv. 9. When the power of enemies is most threatening it is comfortable to fly to the power of God.

12 For God *is* my King of old, working salvation in the midst of the earth. 13 Thou didst divide the sea by thy strength: thou brakest the heads of the dragons in the waters. 14 Thou brakest the heads of leviathan in pieces, *and* gavest him *to be* meat to the people inhabiting the wilderness. 15 Thou didst cleave the fountain and the flood: thou driedst up mighty rivers. 16 The day *is* thine, the night also *is* thine: thou hast prepared the light and the sun. 17 Thou hast set all the borders of the earth: thou hast made summer and winter.

The lamenting church fastens upon something here which she calls to mind, and *therefore hath she hope* (as Lam. iii. 21), with which she encourages herself and silences her own complaints. Two things quiet the minds of those that are here sorrowing for the solemn assembly :—

I. That God is the God of Israel, a God in covenant with his people (*v.* 12): *God is my King of old.* This comes in both as a plea in prayer to God (xliv. 4, *thou art my King, O God!*) and as a prop to their own faith and hope, to encourage themselves to expect deliverance, considering the *days of old,* lxxvii. 5. The church speaks as a complex body, the same in every age, and therefore calls God, " My King, my King of old," or, " from antiquity;" he of old put himself into that relation to them and appeared and acted for them in that relation. As Israel's King, he wrought salvation in the midst of the nations of the earth; for what he did, in the government of the world, tended towards the salvation of his church. Several things are here mentioned which God had done for his people as their King of old, which encouraged them to commit themselves to him and depend upon him.

1. He had divided the sea before them when they came out of Egypt, not by the strength of Moses or his rod, but by his own strength; and he that could do that could do any thing

2. He had destroyed Pharaoh and the Egyptians. Pharaoh was the *leviathan;* the Egyptians were *the dragons,* fierce and cruel. Observe, (1.) The victory obtained over these

enemies. God broke their heads, baffled their politics, as when Israel, the more they were afflicted by them, multiplied the more. God crushed their powers, though complicated, ruined their country by ten plagues, and at last drowned them all in the Red Sea. *This is Pharaoh and all his multitude*, Ezek. xxxi. 18. It was the Lord's doing; none besides could do it, and he did it with a strong hand and an outstretched arm. This was typical of Christ's victory over Satan and his kingdom, pursuant to the first promise, that the seed of the woman should break the serpent's head. (2.) The improvement of this victory for the encouragement of the church: *Thou gavest him to be meat to the people* of Israel, now going to *inhabit the wilderness*. The spoil of the Egyptians enriched them; they stripped their slain, and so got the Egyptians' arms and weapons, as before they had got their jewels. Or, rather, this providence was meat to their faith and hope, to support and encourage them in reference to the other difficulties they were likely to meet with in the wilderness. It was part of the spiritual meat which they were all made to eat of. Note, The breaking of the heads of the church's enemies is the joy and strength of the hearts of the church's friends. Thus the companions make a banquet even of leviathan, Job xli. 6.

3. God had both ways altered the course of nature, both in fetching streams out of the rock and turning streams into rock, *v.* 15. (1.) He had dissolved the rock into waters: *Thou didst bring out the fountain and the flood* (so some read it); and every one knows whence it was brought, out of the rock, out of the flinty rock. Let this never be forgotten, but let it especially be remembered that the rock was Christ, and the waters out of it were spiritual drink. (2.) He had congealed the waters into rock: *Thou driedst up mighty* rapid *rivers*, Jordan particularly at the time when it overflowed all its banks. He that did these things could now deliver his oppressed people, and break the yoke of the oppressors, as he had done formerly; nay, he would do it, for his justice and goodness, his wisdom and truth, are still the same, as well as his power.

II. That the God of Israel is the God of nature, *v.* 16, 17. It is he that orders the regular successions and revolutions, 1. Of day and night. He is the Lord of all time. The evening and the morning are of his ordaining. It is he that opens the eyelids of the morning light, and draws the curtains of the evening shadow. *He has prepared the moon and the sun* (so some read it), the two great lights, to rule by day and by night alternately. The preparing of them denotes their constant readiness and exact observance of their time, which they never miss a moment. 2. Of summer and winter: "Thou hast *appointed all the bounds of the earth*, and the different climates of its several regions,

for *thou hast made summer and winter*, the frigid and the torrid zones; or, rather, the constant revolutions of the year and its several seasons." Herein we are to acknowledge God, from whom all the laws and powers of nature are derived; but how does this come in here? (1.) He that had power at first to settle, and still to preserve, this course of nature by the diurnal and annual motions of the heavenly bodies, has certainly all power both to save and to destroy, and with him nothing is impossible, nor are any difficulties or oppositions insuperable. (2.) He that is faithful to his covenant with the day and with the night, and preserves the ordinances of heaven inviolable, will certainly make good his promise to his people and never cast off those whom he has chosen, Jer. xxxi. 35, 36; xxxiii. 20, 21. His covenant with Abraham and his seed is as firm as that with Noah and his sons, Gen. viii. 21. (3.) Day and night, summer and winter, being counterchanged in the course of nature, throughout all the borders of the earth, we can expect no other than that trouble and peace, prosperity and adversity, should be, in like manner, counterchanged in all the borders of the church. We have as much reason to expect affliction as to expect night and winter. But we have then no more reason to despair of the return of comfort than we have to despair of day and summer.

18 Remember this, *that* the enemy hath reproached, O LORD, and *that* the foolish people have blasphemed thy name. 19 O deliver not the soul of thy turtledove unto the multitude *of the wicked:* forget not the congregation of thy poor for ever. 20 Have respect unto the covenant: for the dark places of the earth are full of the habitations of cruelty. 21 O let not the oppressed return ashamed: let the poor and needy praise thy name. 22 Arise, O God, plead thine own cause: remember how the foolish man reproacheth thee daily. 23 Forget not the voice of thine enemies: the tumult of those that rise up against thee increaseth continually.

The psalmist here, in the name of the church, most earnestly begs that God would appear for them against their enemies, and put an end to their present troubles. To encourage his own faith, he interests God in this matter (*v.* 22): *Arise, O God! plead thy own cause.* This we may be sure he will do, for he is jealous for his own honour; whatever is his own cause he will plead it with a strong hand, will appear against those that oppose it and with and for those that cordially espouse it. He will arise and plead it, though for a time he seems to neglect it; he will stir up himself, will manifest himself, will do his own work in his own time. Note, The cause of religion is God's own cause and he will certainly plead it. Now, to make it out that the cause is God's, he pleads,

I. That the persecutors are God's sworn enemies: "Lord, they have not only abused us, but they have been, and are, abusive to thee; what is done against us, for thy sake, does, by consequence, reflect upon thee. But that is not all; they have directly and immediately reproached thee, and *blasphemed thy name*," v. 18. This was that which they roared in the sanctuary; they triumphed as if they had now got the mastery of the God of Israel, of whom they had heard such great things. As nothing grieves the saints more than to hear God's name blasphemed, so nothing encourages them more to hope that God will appear against their enemies than when they have arrived at such a pitch of wickedness as to reproach God himself; this fills the measure of their sins apace and hastens their ruin. The psalmist insists much upon this: "We dare not answer their reproaches; Lord, do thou answer them. Remember that the *foolish people have blasphemed thy name* (v. 18) and that still *the foolish man reproaches thee daily.*" Observe the character of those that reproach God; they are foolish. As atheism is folly (xiv. 1), profaneness and blasphemy are no less so. Perhaps those are cried up as the wits of the age that ridicule religion and sacred things; but really they are the greatest fools, and will shortly be made to appear so before all the world. And yet see their malice—They reproach God daily, as constantly as his faithful worshippers pray to him and praise him; see their impudence—They do not hide their blasphemous thoughts in their own bosoms, but proclaim them with a loud voice *(forget not the voice of thy enemies, v. 23)*, and this with a daring defiance of divine justice; they *rise up against thee*, and by their blasphemies even wage war with heaven and take up arms against the Almighty. Their noise and *tumult ascend continually* (so some), as the cry of Sodom came up before God, calling for vengeance, Gen. xviii. 21. *It increases continually* (so we read it); they grow worse and worse, and are hardened in their impieties by their successes. Now, Lord, *remember this; do not forget it.* God needs not to be put in remembrance by us of what he has to do, but thus we must show our concern for his honour and believe that he will vindicate us.

II. That the persecuted are his covenant-people. 1. See what distress they are in. They have fallen into the hands of *the multitude of the wicked, v. 19. How are those increased that trouble them!* There is no standing before an enraged multitude, especially like these, armed with power; and, as they are numerous, so they are barbarous: *The dark places of the earth are full of the habitations of cruelty.* The land of the Chaldeans,

where there was none of the light of the knowledge of the true God (though otherwise it was famed for learning and arts), was indeed a dark place; the inhabitants of it were *alienated from the life of God through the ignorance that was in them,* and therefore they were cruel: where there was no true divinity there was scarcely to be found common humanity. They were especially cruel to the people of God; certainly those have no knowledge who *eat them up,* xiv. 4. They are oppressed (v. 21) because they are poor and unable to help themselves; they are oppressed, and so impoverished and made poor. 2. See what reason they had to hope that God would appear for their relief and not suffer them to be always thus trampled upon. Observe how the psalmist pleads with God for them. (1.) "*It is thy turtle-dove* that is ready to be swallowed up by the multitude of the wicked," v. 19. The church is a dove for harmlessness and mildness, innocency and inoffensiveness, purity and fruitfulness, a dove for mournfulness in a day of distress, a turtle-dove for fidelity and the constancy of love: turtle-doves and pigeons were the only fowls that were offered in sacrifice to God. "Shall thy turtle-dove, that is true to thee and devoted to thy honour, be delivered, its life and soul and all, into the *hand of the multitude of the wicked,* to whom it will soon become an easy and acceptable prey? Lord, it will be thy honour to help the weak, especially to help thy own." (2.) "It is *the congregation of thy poor,* and they are not the less thine for their being poor (for God has *chosen the poor of this world,* Jam. ii. 5), but they have the more reason to expect thou wilt appear for them because they are many: it is *the congregation of thy poor;* let them not be abandoned and forgotten for ever." (3.) "They are in covenant with thee; and wilt thou not *have respect unto the covenant?* v. 20. Wilt thou not perform the promises thou hast, in thy covenant, made to them? Wilt thou not own those whom thou hast brought into the bond of the covenant?" When God delivers his people it is *in remembrance of his covenant,* Lev. xxvi. 42. "Lord, though we are unworthy to be respected, yet have respect to the covenant." (4.) "They trust in thee. and boast of their relation to thee and expectations from thee. O let not them return ashamed of their hope (v. 21), as they will be if they be disappointed." (5.) "If thou deliver them, they will praise thy name and give thee the glory of their deliverance. Appear, Lord, for those that will praise thy name, against those that blaspheme it."

PSALM LXXV.

Though this psalm is attributed to Asaph in the title, yet it does so exactly agree with David's circumstances, at his coming to the crown after the death of Saul, that most interpreters apply it to that juncture, and suppose that either Asaph penned it, in the person of David, as his poet-laureat (probably the substance of the psalm was some speech which David made to a convention of the states, at his accession to the government, and Asaph turned it into verse, and published it in a poem, for the better spreading of it among the people), or that David penned it, and delivered it to Asaph as precentor of the temple. In this psalm, I. David returns God thanks for bringing him to the throne, ver. 1, 9. II. He promises to lay out himself for the public good, in the use of the power God had given him, ver. 2, 3, 10. III. He checks the insolence of those that opposed his coming to the throne, ver. 4, 5. IV. He fetches a reason for all this from God's sovereign dominion in the affairs of the children of men, ver. 6—8. In singing this psalm we must give to God the glory of all the revolutions of states and kingdoms, believing that they are all according to his counsel and that he will make them all to work for the good of his church.

To the chief musician, Al-taschith. A psalm
        or song of Asaph.

UNTO thee, O God, do we give thanks, *unto thee* do we give thanks: for *that* thy name is near thy wondrous works declare. 2 When I shall receive the congregation I will judge uprightly. 3 The earth and all the inhabitants thereof are dissolved: I bear up the pillars of it. Selah. 4 I said unto the fools, Deal not foolishly: and to the wicked, Lift not up the horn: 5 Lift not up your horn on high: speak *not with* a stiff neck.

In these verses,

I. The psalmist gives to God the praise of his advancement to honour and power, and the other great things he had done for him and for his people Israel (*v.* 1): *Unto thee, O God! do we give thanks* for all the favours thou hast bestowed upon us; and again, *unto thee do we give thanks;* for our thanksgivings must be often repeated. Did not we often pray for mercy when we were in pursuit of it; and shall we think it will suffice once or twice to give thanks when we have obtained it? Not only *I* do give thanks, but *we do,* I and all my friends. If we share with others in their mercies, we must join with them in their praises. " *Unto thee, O God!* the author of our mercies (and we will not give that glory to the instruments which is due to thee only), *we give thanks; for that thy name is near* (that the complete accomplishment of thy promise made to David is not far off) *thy wondrous works,* which thou hast already done for him, *declare.*" Note, 1. There are many works which God does for his people that may truly be called *wondrous works,* out of the common course of providence and quite beyond our expectation. 2. These wondrous works declare the nearness of his name; they show that he himself is at hand, nigh to us in what we call upon him for, and that he is about to do some great things for his people, in pursuance of his purpose and promise. 3. When God's wondrous works declare the nearness of his name it is our duty to give him thanks, again and again to give him thanks.

II. He lays himself under an obligation to use his power well, pursuant to the great trust reposed in him (*v.* 2): *When I shall receive the congregation I will judge uprightly.* Here he takes it for granted that God would, in due time, perfect that which concerned him, that though the congregation was very

slow in gathering to him, and great opposition was made to it, yet, at length, he should receive it; for what God has spoken in his holiness he will perform by his wisdom and power. Being thus in expectation of the mercy, he promises to make conscience of his duty: " When I am a judge I will judge, and *judge uprightly;* not as those that went before me, who either neglected judgment or, which was worse, perverted it, either did no good with their power or did hurt." Note, 1. Those that are advanced to posts of honour must remember that they are posts of service, and must set themselves with diligence and application of mind to do the work to which they are called. He does not say, " *When I shall receive the congregation* I will take my ease, and take state upon me, and leave the public business to others;" but, " I will mind it myself." 2. Public trusts are to be managed with great integrity; those that judge must judge uprightly, according to the rules of justice, without respect of persons.

III. He promises himself that his government would be a public blessing to Israel, *v.* 3. The present state of the kingdom was very bad: *The earth and all the inhabitants thereof are dissolved;* and no marvel, when the former reign was so dissolute that all went to wrack and ruin. There was a general corruption of manners, for want of putting the laws in execution against vice and profaneness. They were divided one from another for want of centering, as they ought to have done, in the government God had appointed. They were all to pieces, two against three and three against two, crumbled into factions and parties, which was likely to issue in their ruin; but *I bear up the pillars of it.* Even in Saul's time David did what he could for the public welfare; but he hoped that when he had himself received the congregation he should do much more, and should not only prevent the public ruin, but recover the public strength and beauty. Now, 1. See the mischief of parties; they melt and dissolve a land and the inhabitants of it. 2. See how much one head frequently holds up. The fabric would have sunk if David had not held up the pillars of it. This may well be applied to Christ and his government. The *world and all the inhabitants of it* were dissolved by sin; man's apostasy threatened the destruction of the whole creation. But Christ bore up the pillars of it; he saved the whole world from utter ruin by saving his people from their sins, and into his hand the administration of the kingdom of Providence is committed, for *he upholds all things by the word of his power,* Heb. i. 3.

IV. He checks those that opposed his government, that were against his accession to it and obstructed the administration of it, striving to keep up that vice and profaneness which he had made it his business to suppress (*v.* 4, 5): *I said unto the fools, Deal not foolishly.* He had said so to them in Saul's time. When he had not power to restrain them, yet he had wisdom and grace to reprove them, and to give them good counsel; though they bore themselves high, upon the favour of that unhappy prince, he cautioned them not to be too presumptuous. Or, rather, he does now say so to them. As soon as he came to the crown he issued out a proclamation against vice and profaneness, and here we have the contents of it. 1. To the simple sneaking sinners, the fools in Israel, that corrupted themselves, to them he said, "*Deal not foolishly;* do not act so directly contrary both to your reason and to your interest as you do while you walk contrary to the laws God has given to Israel and the promises he has made to David." Christ, the Son of David, gives us this counsel, issues out this edict, *Deal not foolishly.* He who is made of God to us wisdom bids us be wise for ourselves, and not make fools of ourselves. 2. To the proud daring sinners, the wicked, that set God himself at defiance, he says, "*Lift not up the horn;* boast not of your power and prerogatives; persist not in your contumacy and contempt of the government set over you; *lift not up your horn on high,* as though you could have what you will and do what you will; *speak not with a stiff neck,* in which is an iron sinew, that will never bend to the will of God in the government; for those that will not bend shall break; those whose necks are stiffened are so to their own destruction." This is Christ's word of command in his gospel, that *every mountain will be brought low before him,* Isa. xl. 4. Let not the anti-christian power, with its heads and horns, lift up itself against him, for it shall certainly be broken to pieces; what is said with a stiff neck must be unsaid again with a broken heart, or we are undone. Pharaoh said with a stiff neck, *Who is the Lord?* But God made him know to his cost.

6 For promotion *cometh* neither from the east, nor from the west, nor from the south. 7 But God *is* the judge: he putteth down one, and setteth up another. 8 For in the hand of the LORD *there is* a cup, and the wine is red; it is full of mixture; and he poureth out of the same: but the dregs thereof, all the wicked of the earth shall wring *them* out, *and* drink *them.* 9 But I will declare for ever; I will sing praises to the God of Jacob. 10 All the horns of the wicked also will I cut off; *but* the horns of the righteous shall be exalted.

In these verses we have two great doctrines laid down and two good inferences drawn from them, for the confirmation of what he had before said.

I. Here are two great truths laid down concerning God's government of the world, which we ought to mix faith with, both pertinent to the occasion :—

1. That from God alone kings receive their power (*v.* 6, 7), and therefore to God alone David would give the praise of his advancement; having his power from God he would use it for him, and therefore those were fools that lifted up the horn against him. We see strange revolutions in states and kingdoms, and are surprised at the sudden disgrace of some and elevation of others; we are all full of such changes, when they happen; but here we are directed to look at the author of them, and are taught where the original of power is, and whence promotion comes. Whence comes preferment to kingdoms, to the sovereignty of them? And whence come preferments in kingdoms, to places of power and trust in them? The former depends not upon the will of the people, nor the latter on the will of the prince, but both on the will of God, who has all hearts in his hands; to him therefore those must look who are in pursuit of preferment, and then they begin aright. We are here told, (1.) Negatively, which way we are not to look for the fountain of power: *Promotion comes not from the east, nor from the west, nor from the desert,* that is, neither from the desert on the north of Jerusalem nor from that on the south; so that the fair gale of preferment is not to be expected to blow from any point of the compass, but only from above, directly thence. Men cannot gain promotion either by the wisdom or wealth of the children of the east, nor by the numerous forces of the isles of the Gentiles, that lay westward, nor those of Egypt or Arabia, that lay south; no concurring smiles of second causes will raise men to preferment without the first cause. The learned bishop Lloyd *(Serm. in loc.)* gives this gloss upon it : "All men took the original of power to be from heaven, but from whom there many knew not; the eastern nations, who were generally given to astrology, took it to come from their stars, especially the sun, their god. No, says David, it comes neither from the east nor from the west, neither from the rising nor from the setting of such a planet, or such a constellation, nor from the south, nor from the exaltation of the sun or any star in the mid-heaven." He mentions not the north, because none supposed it to come thence; or because the same word that signifies the north signifies the secret place, and from the secret of God's counsel it does come, or from the oracle in Zion, which lay on the north side of Jerusalem. Note, No wind is so good as to blow promotion, but as he directs who has the winds in his fists. (2.) Positively : *God is the judge,* the governor or umpire. When parties contend for the prize, he *puts down one and sets up another* as he sees fit, so as to serve his own purposes and bring to pass his own counsels. Herein he acts by preroga-

tive, and is not accountable to us for any of these matters; nor is it any damage, danger, or disgrace that he, who is infinitely wise, holy, and good, has an arbitrary and despotic power to set up and put down whom, and when, and how he pleases. This is a good reason why magistrates should rule for God as those that must give account to him, because it is by him that kings reign.

2. That from God alone all must receive their doom (*v.* 8): *In the hand of the Lord there is a cup,* which he puts into the hands of the children of men, a cup of providence, mixed up (as he thinks fit) of many ingredients, a cup of affliction. The sufferings of Christ are called a *cup,* Matt. xx. 22; John xviii. 11. The judgments of God upon sinners are *the cup of the Lord's right hand,* Hab. ii. 16. *The wine is red,* denoting the wrath of God, which is infused into the judgments executed on sinners, and is the wormwood and the gall in the affliction and the misery. It is red as fire, red as blood, for it burns, it kills. It is *full of mixture,* prepared in wisdom, so as to answer the end. There are mixtures of mercy and grace in the cup of affliction when it is put into the hands of God's own people, mixtures of the curse when it is put into the hands of the wicked; it is wine mingled with gall. These vials, (1.) Are poured out upon all; see Rev. xv. 7, xvi. 1, where we read of the angels pouring out the vials of God's wrath upon the earth. Some drops of this wrath may light on good people; when God's judgments are abroad, they have their share in common calamities; but, (2.) The dregs of the cup are reserved for the wicked. The calamity itself is but the vehicle into which the wrath and curse is infused, the top of which has little of the infusion; but the sediment is pure wrath, and that shall fall to the share of sinners; they have the dregs of the cup now in the terrors of conscience, and hereafter in the torments of hell. They shall *wring them out,* that not a drop of the wrath may be left behind, *and they shall drink them,* for the curse shall *enter into their bowels like water and like oil into their bones.* The cup of the Lord's indignation will be to them a cup of trembling, everlasting trembling, Rev. xiv. 10. The wicked man's cup, while he prospers in the world, is full of mixture, but the worst is at the bottom. The wicked are reserved unto the day of judgment.

II. Here are two good practical inferences drawn from these great truths, and they are the same purposes of duty that he began the psalm with. This being so, 1. He will praise God, and give him glory, for the power to which he has advanced him (*v.* 9): *I will declare for ever* that which *thy wondrous works declare, v.* 1. He will praise God for his elevation, not only at first, while the mercy was fresh, but for ever, so long as he lives. The exaltation of the Son of David will be the subject of the saints' everlasting praises. He

524

will give glory to God, not only as his God, but as the God of Jacob, knowing it was for Jacob his servant's sake, and because he loved his people Israel, that he made him king over them. 2. He will use the power with which he is entrusted for the great ends for which it was put into his hands, *v.* 10, as before, *v.* 2, 4. According to the duty of the higher powers, (1.) He resolves to be a terror to evildoers, to humble their pride and break their power: "Though not all the heads, yet *all the horns, of the wicked will I cut off,* with which they push their poor neighbours; I will disable them to do mischief." Thus God promises to raise up carpenters who should *fray the horns of the Gentiles that had scattered Judah and Israel,* Zech. i. 18—21. (2.) He resolves to be a protection and praise to those that do well: *The horns of the righteous shall be exalted ;* they shall be preferred and be put into places of power; and those that are good, and have hearts to do good, shall not want ability and opportunity for it. This agrees with David's resolutions, ci. 3, &c. Herein David was a type of Christ, who with the breath of his mouth shall slay the wicked, but shall *exalt with honour the horn of the righteous,* cxii. 9.

PSALM LXXVI.

This psalm seems to have been penned upon occasion of some great victory obtained by the church over some threatening enemy or other, and designed to grace the triumph. The LXX. call it, " A song upon the Assyrians," whence many good interpreters conjecture that it was penned when Sennacherib's army, then besieging Jerusalem, was entirely cut off by a destroying angel in Hezekiah's time; and several passages in the psalm are very applicable to that work of wonder: but there was a religious triumph upon occasion of another victory, in Jehoshaphat's time, which might as well be the subject of this psalm (2 Chron. xx. 28); and it might be called "a song of Asaph" because always sung by the sons of Asaph. Or it might be penned by Asaph who lived in David's time, upon occasion of the many triumphs with which God delighted to honour that reign. Upon occasion of this glorious victory, whatever it was, I. The psalmist congratulates the happiness of the church in having God so nigh, ver. 1—3. II. He celebrates the glory of God's power, which this was an illustrious instance of, ver. 4—6. III. He infers hence what reason all have to fear before him, ver. 7—9. And, IV. What reason his people have to trust in him and to pay their vows to him, ver. 10—12. It is a psalm proper for a thanksgiving day, upon the account of public successes, and not improper at other times, because it is never out of season to glorify God for the great things he has done for his church formerly, especially for the victories of the Redeemer over the powers of darkness, which all those Old-Testament victories were types of, at least those that are celebrated in the psalms.

To the chief musician on Neginoth. A psalm or song of Asaph.

IN Judah *is* God known: his name *is* great in Israel. 2 In Salem also is his tabernacle, and his dwelling place in Zion. 3 There brake he the arrows of the bow, the shield, and the sword, and the battle. Selah. 4 Thou *art* more glorious *and* excellent than the mountains of prey. 5 The stouthearted are spoiled, they have slept their sleep: and none of the men of might have found their hands. 6 At thy rebuke, O God of Jacob, both the chariot and horse are cast into a dead sleep.

The church is here triumphant even in the

midst of its militant state. The psalmist, in the church's name, triumphs here in God, the centre of all our triumphs.

I. In the revelation God had made of himself to them, *v.* 1. It is the honour and privilege of Judah and Israel that among them *God is known,* and where he is known *his name* will be *great.* God is known as he is pleased to make himself known; and those are happy to whom he discovers himself—happy people that have their land filled with the knowledge of God, happy persons that have their hearts filled with that knowledge. In Judah God was known as he was not known in other nations, which made the favour the greater, inasmuch as it was distinguishing, cxlvii. 19, 20.

II. In the tokens of God's special presence with them in his ordinances, *v.* 2. In the whole land of Judah and Israel God was known and his name was great; but *in Salem, in Zion,* were *his tabernacle* and *his dwelling-place.* There he kept court; there he received the homage of his people by their sacrifices and entertained them by the feasts upon the sacrifices; thither they came to address themselves to him, and thence by his oracles he issued out his orders; there he recorded his name, and of that place he said, *Here will I dwell, for I have desired it.* It is the glory and happiness of a people to have God among them by his ordinances; but his dwelling-place is a tabernacle, a movable dwelling. *Yet a little while is that light with us.*

III. In the victories they had obtained over their enemies (*v.* 3): *There broke he the arrows of the bow.* Observe how threatening the danger was. Though Judah and Israel, Salem and Zion, were thus privileged, yet war is raised against them, and the weapons of war are furbished.

1. Here are bow and arrows, shield and sword, and all for battle; but all are broken and rendered useless. And it was done there, (1.) In Judah and in Israel, in favour of that people near to God. While the weapons of war were used against other nations they answered their end, but, when turned against that holy nation, they were immediately broken. The Chaldee paraphrases it thus: When the house of Israel did his will he placed his majesty among them, and there he broke the arrows of the bow; while they kept closely to his service they were great and safe, and every thing went well with them. Or, (2.) In the tabernacle and dwelling-place in Zion, there he broke the arrows of the bow; it was done in the field of battle, and yet it is said to be done in the sanctuary, because done in answer to the prayers which God's people there made to him and in the performance of the promises which he there made to them, of both which see that instance, 2 Chron. xx. 5, 14. Public successes are owing as much to what is done in the church as to what is done in the camp. Now,

2. This victory redounded very much, (1.)

To the immortal honour of Israel's God (*v.* 4): *Thou art,* and hast manifested thyself to be, *more glorious and excellent than the mountains of prey.* [1.] "Than the great and mighty ones of the earth in general, who are high, and think themselves firmly fixed like mountains, but are really mountains of prey, oppressive to all about them. It is their glory to destroy; it is thine to deliver." [2.] "Than our invaders in particular. When they besieged the cities of Judah, they cast up mounts against them, and raised batteries; but thou art more able to protect us than they are to annoy us." Wherein the enemies of the church deal proudly it will appear that God is above them. (2.) To the perpetual disgrace of the enemies of Israel, *v.* 5, 6. They were *stout-hearted,* men of great courage and resolution, flushed with their former victories, enraged against Israel, confident of success; they were *men of might,* robust and fit for service; they had *chariots and horses,* which were then greatly valued and trusted to in war, xx. 7. But all this force was of no avail when it was levelled against Jerusalem. [1.] *The stout-hearted have despoiled and disarmed themselves* (so some read it); when God pleases he can make his enemies to weaken and destroy themselves. *They have slept,* not the sleep of the righteous, who sleep in Jesus, but *their sleep,* the sleep of sinners, that shall awake to everlasting shame and contempt. [2.] The men of might can no more *find their hands* than the stout-hearted can their spirit. As the bold men are cowed, so the strong men are lamed, and cannot so much as find their hands, to save their own heads, much less to hurt their enemies. [3.] The chariots and horses may be truly said to be *cast into a dead sleep* when their drivers and their riders were so. God did but speak the word, as the God of Jacob that commands deliverances for Jacob, and, at his rebuke, the chariot and horse were both cast into a dead sleep. When the men were laid dead upon the spot by the destroying angel the chariot and horse were not at all formidable. See the power and efficacy of God's rebukes. With what pleasure may we Christians apply all this to the advantages we enjoy by the Redeemer! It is through him that God is known; it is in him that God's name is great; to him it is owing that God has a tabernacle and a dwelling-place in his church. He it was that vanquished the strong man armed, spoiled principalities and powers, and made a show of them openly.

7 Thou, *even* thou, *art* to be feared: and who may stand in thy sight when once thou art angry? 8 Thou didst cause judgment to be heard from heaven; the earth feared, and was still, 9 When God arose to judgment, to save all the meek of the earth. Selah. 10 Surely the wrath of man shall praise

thee: the remainder of wrath shalt thou restrain. 11 Vow, and pay unto the LORD your God: let all that be round about him bring presents unto him that ought to be feared. 12 He shall cut off the spirit of princes : *he is* terrible to the kings of the earth.

This glorious victory with which God had graced and blessed his church is here made to speak three things :—

I. Terror to God's enemies (*v.* 7—9) : " *Thou, even thou, art to be feared ;* thy majesty is to be reverenced, thy sovereignty to be submitted to, and thy justice to be dreaded by those that have offended thee." Let all the world learn by this event to stand in awe of the great God. 1. Let all be afraid of his wrath against the daring impiety of sinners : *Who may stand in thy sight from the minute that thou art angry ?* If God be a consuming fire, how can chaff and stubble stand before him, though his *anger be kindled but a little?* ii. 12. 2. Let all be afraid of his jealousy for oppressed innocency and the injured cause of his own people : " *Thou didst cause judgment to be heard from heaven,* then when thou didst arise to save all the meek of the earth (*v.* 8, 9) ; and then *the earth feared and was still,* waiting what would be the issue of those glorious appearances of thine." Note, (1.) God's people are the *meek of the earth* (Zeph. ii. 3), the *quiet in the land* (xxxv. 20), that can bear any wrong, but do none. (2.) Though the meek of the earth are by their meekness exposed to injury, yet God will, sooner or later, appear for their salvation, and plead their cause. (3.) When God comes to save *all the meek of the earth,* he will *cause judgment to be heard from heaven ;* he will make the world know that he is angry at the oppressors of his people, and takes what is done against them as done against himself. The righteous God long seems to keep silence, yet, sooner or later, he will make judgment to be heard. (4.) When God is speaking judgment from heaven it is time for the earth to compose itself into an awful and reverent silence : *The earth feared and was still,* as silence is made by proclamation when the court sits. *Be still and know that I am God,* xlvi. 10. *Be silent, O all flesh ! before the Lord, for he is raised* up to judgment, Zech. ii. 13. Those that suppose this psalm to have been penned upon the occasion of the routing of Sennacherib's army take it for granted that the descent of the destroying angel, who did the execution, was accompanied with thunder, by which *God caused judgment to be heard from heaven,* and that the earth feared (that is, there was an earthquake), but it was soon over. But this is altogether uncertain.

II. Comfort to God's people, *v.* 10. We live in a very angry provoking world ; we often feel much, and are apt to fear more, from the wrath of man, which seems boundless.

But this is a great comfort to us, 1. That as far as God permits the wrath of man to break forth at any time he will make it turn to his praise, will bring honour to himself and serve his own purposes by it : *Surely the wrath of man shall praise thee,* not only by the checks given to it, when it shall be forced to confess its own impotency, but even by the liberty given to it for a time. The hardships which God's people suffer by the wrath of their enemies are made to redound to the glory of God and his grace ; and the more *the heathen rage* and plot *against the Lord and his anointed* the more will God be praised for setting *his King upon his holy hill of Zion* in spite of them, ii. 1, 6. When the heavenly hosts make this the matter of their thanksgiving-song that God has *taken to himself his great power and has reigned, though the nations were angry* (Rev. xi. 17, 18), then the wrath of man adds lustre to the praises of God. 2. That what will not turn to his praise shall not be suffered to break out : *The remainder of wrath shalt thou restrain.* Men must never permit sin, because they cannot check it when they will ; but God can. He can set bounds to the wrath of man, as he does to the raging sea. *Hitherto it shall come and no further : here shall its proud waves be stayed.* God restrained the remainder of Sennacherib's rage, for he put *a hook in his nose and a bridle in his jaws* (Isa. xxxvii. 29) ; and, though he permitted him to talk big, he restrained him from doing what he designed.

III. Duty to all, *v.* 11, 12. Let all submit themselves to this great God and become his loyal subjects. Observe, 1. The duty required of us all, all that are about him, that have any dependence upon him or any occasion to approach to him ; and who is there that has not ? We are therefore every one of us commanded to do our homage to the King of kings : *Vow and pay ;* that is, take an oath of allegiance to him and make conscience of keeping it. Vow to be his, and pay what you vow. Bind your souls with a bond to him (for that is the nature of a vow), and then live up to the obligations you have laid upon yourselves ; for *better it is not to vow than to vow and not to pay.* And, having taken him for our King, let us bring presents to him, as subjects to their sovereign, 1 Sam. x. 27. *Send you the lamb to the ruler of the land,* Isa. xvi. 1. Not that God needs any present we can bring, or can be benefited by it ; but thus we must give him honour and own that we have our all from him. Our prayers and praises, and especially our hearts, are the presents we should bring to the Lord our God. 2. The reasons to enforce this duty : *Render to all their due, fear to whom fear is due ;* and is it not due to God ? Yes ; (1.) He ought to be feared : *He is the fear* (so the word is) ; his name is glorious and fearful ; and he is the proper object of our fear ; with him is terrible majesty. The God of Abraham is called *the fear of Isaac* (Gen.

xxxi. 42), and we are commanded to *make him our fear*, Isa. viii. 13. When we bring presents to him we must have an eye to him as greatly to be feared; for he is terrible in his holy places. (2.) He will be feared, even by those who think it their own sole prerogative to be feared (*v.* 12): He shall *cut off the spirit of princes;* he shall slip it off as easily as we slip off a flower from the stalk or a bunch of grapes from the vine; so the word signifies. He can dispirit those that are most daring and make them heartless; for he is, or will be, *terrible to the kings of the earth;* and sooner or later, if they be not so wise as to submit themselves to him, he will force them to call in vain to *rocks and mountains to fall on them and hide them from his wrath*, Rev. vi. 16. Since there is no contending with God, it is as much our wisdom as it is our duty to submit to him.

PSALM LXXVII.

This psalm, according to the method of many other psalms, begins with sorrowful complaints but ends with comfortable encouragements. The complaints seem to be of personal grievances, but the encouragements relate to the public concerns of the church, so that it is not certain whether it was penned upon a personal or a public account. If they were private troubles that he was groaning under, it teaches us that what God has wrought for his church in general may be improved for the comfort of particular believers; if it was some public calamity that he is here lamenting, his speaking of it so feelingly, as if it had been some particular trouble of his own, shows how much we should lay to heart the interests of the church of God and make them ours. One of the rabbin says, This psalm is spoken in the dialect of the captives; and therefore some think it was penned in the captivity in Babylon. I. The psalmist complains here of the deep impressions which his troubles made upon his spirits, and the temptation he was in to despair of relief, ver. 1—10. II. He encourages himself to hope that it would be well at last, by the remembrance of God's former appearances for the help of his people, of which he gives several instances, ver. 11—20. In singing this psalm we must take shame to ourselves for all our sinful distrusts of God, and of his providence and promise, and give to him the glory of his power and goodness by a thankful commemoration of what he has done for us formerly and a cheerful dependence on him for the future.

To the chief musician, to Jeduthun. A psalm of Asaph.

I CRIED unto God with my voice, *even* unto God with my voice; and he gave ear unto me. 2 In the day of my trouble I sought the Lord: my sore ran in the night, and ceased not: my soul refused to be comforted. 3 I remembered God, and was troubled: I complained, and my spirit was overwhelmed. Selah. 4 Thou holdest mine eyes waking: I am so troubled that I cannot speak. 5 I have considered the days of old, the years of ancient times. 6 I call to remembrance my song in the night: I commune with mine own heart: and my spirit made diligent search. 7 Will the Lord cast off for ever? and will he be favourable no more? 8 Is his mercy clean gone for ever? doth *his* promise fail for evermore? 9 Hath God forgotten to be gracious? hath he in anger shut up his tender mercies? Selah. 10 And I said, This *is* my infirmity: *but I will*

remember the years of the right hand of the most high.

We have here the lively portraiture of a good man under prevailing melancholy, fallen into and sinking in that horrible pit and that miry clay, but struggling to get out. Drooping saints, that are of a sorrowful spirit, may here as in a glass see their own faces. The conflict which the psalmist had with his griefs and fears seems to have been over when he penned this record of it; for he says (*v.* 1), *I cried unto God, and he gave ear unto me*, which, while the struggle lasted, he had not the comfortable sense of, as he had afterwards; but he inserts it in the beginning of his narrative as an intimation that his trouble did not end in despair; for God heard him, and, at length, he knew that he heard him. Observe,

I. His melancholy prayers. Being afflicted, he prayed (Jam. v. 13), and, being in an agony, he prayed more earnestly (*v.* 1): *My voice was unto God, and I cried, even with my voice unto God*. He was full of complaints, loud complaints, but he directed them to God, and turned them all into prayers, vocal prayers, very earnest and importunate. Thus he gave vent to his grief and gained some ease; and thus he took the right way in order to relief (*v.* 2): *In the day of my trouble I sought the Lord*. Note, Days of trouble must be days of prayer, days of inward trouble especially, when God seems to have withdrawn from us; we must seek him and seek till we find him. In the day of his trouble he did not seek for the diversion of business or recreation, to shake off his trouble that way, but he sought God, and his favour and grace. Those that are under trouble of mind must not think to drink it away, or laugh it away, but must pray it away. *My hand was stretched out in the night and ceased not;* so Dr. Hammond reads the following words, as speaking the incessant importunity of his prayers. Compare cxliii. 5, 6.

II. His melancholy grief. Grief may then be called melancholy indeed, 1. When it admits of no intermission; such was his: *My sore*, or wound, *ran in the night*, and bled inwardly, and it ceased not, no, not in the time appointed for rest and sleep. 2. When it admits of no consolation; and that also was his case: *My soul refused to be comforted;* he had no mind to hearken to those that would be his comforters. *As vinegar upon nitre, so is he that sings songs to a heavy heart*, Prov. xxv. 20. Nor had he any mind to think of those things that would be his comforts; he put them far from him, as one that indulged himself in sorrow. Those that are in sorrow, upon any account, do not only prejudice themselves, but affront God, if they refuse to be comforted.

III. His melancholy musings. He pored so much upon the trouble, whatever it was, personal or public, that, 1. The methods that

527

should have relieved him did but increase his grief, *v.* 3. (1.) One would have thought that the remembrance of God would comfort him, but it did not: *I remembered God and was troubled,* as poor Job (*ch.* xxiii. 15); *I am troubled at his presence; when I consider I am afraid of him.* When he remembered God his thoughts fastened only upon his justice, and wrath, and dreadful majesty, and thus God himself became a terror to him. (2.) One would have thought that pouring out his soul before God would give him ease, but it did not; he *complained, and yet his spirit was overwhelmed,* and sank under the load. 2. The means of his present relief were denied him, *v.* 4. He could not enjoy sleep, which, if it be quiet and refreshing, is a parenthesis to our griefs and cares: " *Thou holdest my eyes waking* with thy terrors, which make me full of *tossings to and fro until the dawning of the day.*" He could not speak, by reason of the disorder of his thoughts, the tumult of his spirits, and the confusion his mind was in: He *kept silence even from good* while *his heart was hot within him;* he was *ready to burst like a new bottle* (Job xxxii. 19), and yet so troubled that he could not speak and refresh himself. Grief never preys so much upon the spirits as when it is thus smothered and pent up.

IV. His melancholy reflections (*v.* 5, 6): " *I have considered the days of old,* and compared them with the present days; and our former prosperity does but aggravate our present calamities: for we see not the wonders that our fathers told us off." Melancholy people are apt to pore altogether upon the days of old and the years of ancient times, and to magnify them, for the justifying of their own uneasiness and discontent at the present posture of affairs. But *say not thou that the former days were better than these,* because it is more than thou knowest whether they were or no, Eccl. vii. 10. Neither let the remembrance of the comforts we have lost make us unthankful for those that are left, or impatient under our crosses. Particularly, he *called to remembrance his song in the night,* the comforts with which he had supported himself in his former sorrows and entertained himself in his former solitude. These songs he remembered, and tried if he could not sing them over again; but he was out of tune for them, and the remembrance of them did but *pour out his soul in him,* xliii. 4. See Job xxxv. 10.

V. His melancholy fears and apprehensions: " *I communed with my own heart, v.* 6. Come, my soul, what will be the issue of these things? What can I think of them and what can I expect they will come to at last? I *made diligent search* into the causes of my trouble, enquiring wherefore God contended with me and what would be the consequences of it. And thus I began to reason, *Will the Lord cast off for ever,* as he does for the present? He is not now favourable;

and *will he be favourable no more? His mercy* is now gone; *and is it clean gone for ever? His promise* now fails; and *does it fail for evermore?* God is not now gracious; but *has he forgotten to be gracious?* His *tender mercies* have been withheld, perhaps in wisdom; but *are they shut up,* shut up *in anger?*" *v.* 7—9. This is the language of a disconsolate deserted soul, walking in darkness and having no light, a case not uncommon even with those that *fear the Lord and obey the voice of his servant,* Isa. l. 10. He may here be looked upon, 1. As groaning under a sore trouble. God hid his face from him, and withdrew the usual tokens of his favour. Note, Spiritual trouble is of all trouble most grievous to a gracious soul; nothing wounds and pierces it like the apprehensions of God's being angry, the suspending of his favour and the superseding of his promise; this wounds the spirit: and who can bear that? 2. As grappling with a strong temptation. Note, God's own people, in a cloudy and dark day, may be tempted to make desperate conclusions about their own spiritual state and the condition of God's church and kingdom in the world, and, as to both, to give up all for gone. We may be tempted to think that God has abandoned us and cast us off, that the covenant of grace fails us, and that the tender mercy of our God shall be for ever withheld from us. But we must not give way to such suggestions as these. If fear and melancholy ask such peevish questions, let faith answer them from the Scripture: *Will the Lord cast off for ever?* God forbid, Rom. xi. 1. No; *the Lord will not cast off his people,* xciv. 14. *Will he be favourable no more?* Yes, he will; *for, though he cause grief, yet will he have compassion,* Lam. iii. 32. *Is his mercy clean gone for ever?* No; his *mercy endures for ever;* as it is *from everlasting,* it is *to everlasting,* ciii. 17. *Doth his promise fail for evermore?* No; *it is impossible for God to lie,* Heb. vi. 18. *Hath God forgotten to be gracious?* No; *he cannot deny himself,* and his own name which he hath proclaimed *gracious and merciful,* Exod. xxxiv. 6. *Has he in anger shut up his tender mercies?* No; they are *new every morning* (Lam. iii. 23); and therefore, *How shall I give thee up, Ephraim?* Hos. xi. 8, 9. Thus was he going on with his dark and dismal apprehensions when, on a sudden, he first checked himself with that word, *Selah,* " Stop there; go no further; let us hear no more of these unbelieving surmises;" and he then chid himself (*v.* 10): *I said, This is my infirmity.* He is soon aware that it is not well said, and therefore, " *Why art thou cast down, O my soul? I said, This is my affliction*" (so some understand it); " this is the calamity that falls to my lot and I must make the best of it; every one has his affliction, his trouble in the flesh; and this is mine, the cross I must take up." Or, rather, "This is my sin; it is my iniquity, the plague of my own heart." These doubts and fears proceed from the want and weakness of faith and the corruption of a distempered mind. Note, (1.) We all know that concerning ourselves of which we must say, " *This is our infirmity*, a sin that most easily besets us." (2.) Despondency of spirit, and distrust of God, under affliction, are too often the infirmities of good people, and, as such, are to be reflected upon by us with sorrow and shame, as by the psalmist here : *This is my infirmity*. When at any time it is working in us we must thus suppress the rising of it, and not suffer the evil spirit to speak. We must argue down the insurrections of unbelief, as the psalmist here : *But I will remember the years of the right hand of the Most High*. He had been considering the *years of ancient times* (*v.* 5), the blessings formerly enjoyed, the remembrance of which did only add to his grief ; but now he considered them as *the years of the right hand of the Most High*, that those blessings of ancient times came from the Ancient of days, from the power and sovereign disposal of his right hand who is *over all, God, blessed for ever*, and this satisfied him ; for may not the Most High with his right hand make wha⁺ changes he pleases ?

11 I will remember the works of the Lord: surely I will remember thy wonders of old. 12 I will meditate also of all thy work, and talk of thy doings. 13 Thy way, O God, *is* in the sanctuary: who *is* so great a God as *our* God! 14 Thou *art* the God that doest wonders: thou hast declared thy strength among the people. 15 Thou hast with *thine* arm redeemed thy people, the sons of Jacob and Joseph. Selah. 16 The waters saw thee, O God, the waters saw thee; they were afraid: the depths also were troubled. 17 The clouds poured out water: the skies sent out a sound: thine arrows also went abroad. 18 The voice of thy thunder *was* in the heaven: the lightnings lightened the world: the earth trembled and shook. 19 Thy way *is* in the sea, and thy path in the great waters, and thy footsteps are not known. 20 Thou leddest thy people like a flock by the hand of Moses and Aaron.

The psalmist here recovers himself out of the great distress and plague he was in, and silences his own fears of God's casting off his people by the remembrance of the great things he had done for them formerly, which tho igh he had in vain tried to quiet himself with (*v.* 5, 6) yet he tried again, and, upon this second trial, found it not in vain It is good to persevere in the proper means for the strengthening of faith, though they do not prove effectual at first : "*I will remember, surely I will*, what God has done for his people of old, till I can thence infer a happy issue of the present dark dispensations," *v.* 11, 12. Note, 1. The works of the Lord, for his people, have been wondrous works. 2. They are recorded for us, that they may be remembered by us. 3. That we may have benefit by the remembrance of them we must meditate upon them, and dwell upon them in our thoughts, and must talk of them, that we may inform ourselves and others further concerning them. 4. The due remembrance of the works of God will be a powerful antidote against distrust of his promise and goodness ; for he is God and changes not. If he begin, he will finish his work and bring forth the top-stone.

Two things, in general, satisfied him very much :—

I. That *God's way is in the sanctuary*, v. 13. It is *in holiness*, so some. When we cannot solve the particular difficulties that may arise in our constructions of the divine providence, this we are sure of, in general, that God is holy in all his works, that they are all worthy of himself and consonant to the eternal purity and rectitude of his nature. He has holy ends in all he does, and will be sanctified in every dispensation of his providence. His way is according to his promise, which he has spoken in his holiness and made known in the sanctuary. What he has done is according to what he has said and may be interpreted by it ; and from what he has said we may easily gather that he will not cast off his people for ever. God's way is for the sanctuary, and for the benefit of it. All he does is intended for the good of his church.

II. That *God's way is in the sea*. Though God is holy, just, and good, in all he does, yet we cannot give an account of the reasons of his proceedings, nor make any certain judgment of his designs : *His path is in the great waters and his footsteps are not known, v.* 19. God's ways are like the deep waters which cannot be fathomed (xxxvi. 6), like the way of a ship in the sea, which cannot be tracked, Prov. xxx. 18, 19. God's proceedings are always to be acquiesced in, but cannot always be accounted for. He specifies some particulars, for which he goes as far back as the infancy of the Jewish church, and from which he gathers, 1. That there is no God to be compared with the God of Israel (*v.* 13): *Who is so great a God as our God?* Let us first give to God the glory of the great things he has done for his people, and acknowledge him, therein, great above all comparison ; and then we may take to ourselves the comfort of what he has done and encourage ourselves with it. 2. That he is a God of almighty power (*v.* 14): " *Thou art the God that* alone *doest wonders,* above the power of any creature; *thou hast* visibly, and beyond any contradiction, *declared thy strength among the people."* What God has done for his church has been a standing declaration of his almighty power, for therein he has made bare his everlasting arm. (1.) God brought Israel out of Egypt, *v.* 15. This was the beginning of mercy to them, and was yearly to be commemorated among them in the passover: *"Thou hast with thy arm,* stretched out in so many miracles, *redeemed thy people* out of the hand of the Egyptians." Though they were delivered by power, yet they are said to be redeemed, as if it had been done by price, because it was typical of the great redemption, which was to be wrought out, in the fulness of time, both by price and power. Those that were redeemed are here called not only *the sons of Jacob,* to whom the promise was made, but *of Joseph* also, who had a most firm and lively belief of the performance of it; for, when he was dying, he made mention of the departing of the children of Israel out of Egypt, and gave commandment concerning his bones. (2.) He divided the Red Sea before them (*v.* 16): *The waters* gave way, and a lane was made through that crowd instantly, as if they had seen God himself at the head of the armies of Israel, and had retired for fear of him. Not only the surface of the waters, but *the depths, were troubled,* and opened to the right and to the left, in obedience to his word of command. (3.) He destroyed the Egyptians (*v.* 17): *The clouds poured out water* upon them, while the pillar of fire, like an umbrella over the camp of Israel, sheltered it from the shower, in which, as in the deluge, the waters that were above the firmament concurred with those that were beneath the firmament to destroy the rebels. Then *the skies sent out a sound; thy arrows also went abroad,* which is explained (*v.* 18): *The voice of thy thunder was heard in the heaven* (that was the sound which the skies sent forth); *the lightnings lightened the world*—those were the arrows which went abroad, by which the host of the Egyptians was discomfited, with so much terror that *the earth of* the adjacent coast *trembled and shook.* Thus God's way was in the sea, for the destruction of his enemies, as well as for the salvation of his people; and yet when the waters returned to their place *his footsteps were not known* (*v.* 19); there was no mark set upon the place, as there was, afterwards, in Jordan, Josh. iv. 9. We do not read in the story of Israel's passing through the Red Sea that there were thunders and lightnings, and an earthquake; yet there might be, and Josephus says there were, such displays of the divine terror upon that occasion. But it may refer to the thunders, lightnings, and earthquakes, that were at Mount Sinai when the law was given. (4.) He took his people Israel under his own guidance and protection

530

(*v.* 20): *Thou leddest thy people like a flock.* They being weak and helpless, and apt to wander like a flock of sheep, and lying exposed to the beasts of prey, God went before them with all the care and tenderness of a shepherd, that they might not fail. The pillar of cloud and fire led them; yet that is not here taken notice of, but the agency of Moses and Aaron, by whose hand God led them; they could not do it without God, but God did it with and by them. Moses was their governor, Aaron their high priest; they were guides, overseers, and rulers to Israel, and by them God led them. The right and happy administration of the two great ordinances of magistracy and ministry is, though not so great a miracle, yet as great a mercy to any people as the pillar of cloud and fire was to Israel in the wilderness.

The psalm concludes abruptly, and does not apply those ancient instances of God's power to the present distresses of the church, as one might have expected. But as soon as the good man began to meditate on these things he found he had gained his point; his very entrance upon this matter *gave him light* and joy (cxix. 130); his fears suddenly and strangely vanished, so that he needed to go no further; he *went his way, and did eat,* and *his countenance was no more sad,* like Hannah, 1 Sam. i. 18

PSALM LXXVIII.

This psalm is historical; it is a narrative of the great mercies God had bestowed upon Israel, the great sins wherewith they had provoked him, and the many tokens of his displeasure they had been under for their sins. The psalmist began, in the foregoing psalm, to relate God's wonders of old, for his own encouragement in a difficult time; there he broke off abruptly, but here resumes the subject, for the edification of the church, and enlarges much upon it, showing not only how good God had been to them, which was an earnest of further finishing mercy, but how basely they had conducted themselves towards God, which justified him in correcting them as he did at this time, and forbade all complaints. Here is, I. The preface to this church history, commanding the attention of the present age to it and recommending it to the study of the generations to come, ver. 1—8. II. The history itself from Moses to David; it is put into a psalm or song that it might be the better remembered and transmitted to posterity, and that the singing of it might affect them with the things here related, more than they would be with a bare narrative of them. The general scope of this psalm we have ver. 9—11, where notice is taken of the present rebukes they were under (ver. 9), the sin which brought them under those rebukes (ver. 10), and the mercies of God to them formerly, which aggravated that sin, ver. 11. As to the particulars, we are here told, 1. What wonderful works God had wrought for them in bringing them out of Egypt (ver. 12—16), providing for them in the wilderness (ver. 23—29), plaguing and ruining their enemies (ver. 43—53), and at length putting them in possession of the land of promise, ver. 54, 55. 2. How ungrateful they were to God for his favours to them and how many and great provocations they were guilty of. How they murmured against God and distrusted him (ver. 17—20), and did but counterfeit repentance and submission when he punished them (ver. 34—37), thus grieving and tempting him, ver. 40—42. How they affronted God with their idolatries after they came to Canaan, ver. 56—58. 3. How God had justly punished them for their sins (ver. 21, 22) in the wilderness, making their sin their punishment (ver. 29—33), and now, of late, when the ark was taken by the Philistines, ver. 59—64. 4. How graciously God had spared them and returned in mercy to them, notwithstanding their provocations. He had forgiven them formerly (ver. 38, 39), and now, of late, had removed the judgments they had brought upon themselves, and brought them under a happy establishment both in church and state, ver. 65—72. As the general scope of this psalm may be of use to us in the singing of it, to put us upon recollecting what God has done for us and for his church formerly, and what we have done against him, so the particulars also may be of use to us, for warning against those sins of unbelief and ingratitude which Israel of old was notoriously guilty of, and the record of which was preserved for our learning. "These things happened unto them for ensamples," 1 Cor. x. 11; Heb. iv. 11

Maschil of Asaph.

GIVE ear, O my people, *to* my law: incline your ears to the words of my mouth. 2 I will open my mouth in a parable: I will utter dark sayings of old: 3 Which we have heard and known, and our fathers have told us. 4 We will not hide *them* from their children, showing to the generation to come the praises of the LORD, and his strength, and his wonderful works that he hath done. 5 For he established a testimony in Jacob, and appointed a law in Israel, which he commanded our fathers, that they should make them known to their children: 6 That the generation to come might know *them, even* the children *which* should be born; *who* should arise and declare *them* to their children: 7 That they might set their hope in God, and not forget the works of God, but keep his commandments: 8 And might not be as their fathers, a stubborn and rebellious generation: a generation *that* set not their heart aright, and whose spirit was not stedfast with God.

These verses, which contain the preface to this history, show that the psalm answers the title; it is indeed *Maschil—a psalm to give instruction ;* if we receive not the instruction it gives, it is our own fault. Here,

I. The psalmist demands attention to what he wrote (*v.* 1): *Give ear, O my people ! to my law.* Some make these the psalmist's words. David, as a king, or Asaph, in his name, as his secretary of state, or scribe to the sweet singer of Israel, here calls upon the people, as his people committed to his charge, to give ear to his law. He calls his instructions his *law* or *edict ;* such was their commanding force in themselves. Every good truth, received in the light and love of it, will have the power of a law upon the conscience; yet that was not all : David was a king, and he would interpose his royal power for the edification of his people. If God, by his grace, make great men good men, they will be capable of doing more good than others, because their word will be a law to all about them, who must therefore give ear and hearken ;. for to what purpose is divine revelation brought to our ears if we will not incline our ears to it, both humble ourselves and engage ourselves to hear it and heed it? Or the psalmist, being a prophet, speaks as God's mouth, and so calls them *his people,* and demands subjection to what was said as to a law. Let him that has an ear thus *hear what the Spirit saith unto the churches,* Rev. ii. 7.

II. Several reasons are given why we should diligently attend to that which is here related.

1. The things here discoursed of are weighty, and deserve consideration, strange, and need it (*v.* 2): *I will open my mouth in a parable,* in that which is sublime and uncommon, but very excellent and well worthy your attention; *I will utter dark sayings,* which challenge your most serious regards as much as the enigmas with which the eastern princes and learned men used to try one another. These are called *dark sayings,* not because they are hard to be understood, but because they are greatly to be admired and carefully to be looked into. This is said to be fulfilled in the parables which our Saviour put forth (Matt. xiii. 35), which were (as this) representations of the state of the kingdom of God among men. 2. They are the monuments of antiquity—*dark sayings of old which our fathers have told us, v.* 3. They are things of undoubted certainty; we have heard them and known them, and there is no room left to question the truth of them. The gospel of Luke is called a *declaration of those things which are most surely believed among us* (Luke i. 1), so were the things here related. The honour we owe to our parents and ancestors obliges us to attend to that which our fathers have told us, and, as far as it appears to be true and good, to receive it with so much the more reverence and regard. 3. They are to be transmitted to posterity, and it lies as a charge upon us carefully to hand them down (*v.* 4); because our fathers told them to us *we will not hide them from our children.* Our children are called *theirs,* for they were in care for their seed's seed, and looked upon them as theirs ; and, in teaching our children the knowledge of God, we repay to our parents some of that debt we owe to them for teaching us. Nay, if we have no children of our own, we must declare the things of God to *their* children, the children of others. Our care must be for posterity in general, and not only for our own posterity ; and for the generation to come hereafter, the children that shall be born, as well as for the generation that is next rising up and the children that are born. That which we are to transmit to our children is not only the knowledge of languages, arts and sciences, liberty and property, but especially the praises of the Lord, and his strength appearing in the wonderful works he has done. Our great care must be to lodge our religion, that great deposit, pure and entire in the hands of those that succeed us. There are two things the full and clear knowledge of which we must preserve the entail of to our heirs :—(1.) The law of God; for this was given with a particular charge to teach it diligently to their children (*v.* 5): *He established a testimony* or covenant, and enacted a law, in Jacob and Israel, gave them precepts and promises, which he *commanded them to make known to their children,* Deut. vi. 7, 20. The church of God, as the historian says of the Roman commonwealth, was

not to be *res unius ætatis—a thing of one age* but was to be kept up from one generation to another; and therefore, as God provided for a succession of ministers in the tribe of Levi and the house of Aaron, so he appointed that parents should train up their children in the knowledge of his law : and, when they had grown up, they must arise *and declare them to their children* (*v.* 6), that, as one generation of God's servants and worshippers passes away, another generation may come, and the church, as the earth, may abide for ever; and thus God's name among men may be as the days of heaven. (2.) The providences of God concerning them, both in mercy and in judgment. The former seem to be mentioned for the sake of this ; since God gave order that his laws should be made known to posterity, it is requisite that with them his works also should be made known, the fulfilling of the promises made to the obedient and the threatenings denounced against the disobedient. Let these be told to our children and our children's children, [1.] That they may take encouragement to conform to the will of God (*v.* 7): *that, not forgetting the works of God* wrought in former days, *they* might *set their hope in God and keep his commandments,* might make his command their rule and his covenant their stay. Those only may with confidence hope for God's salvation that make conscience of doing his commandments. The works of God, duly considered, will very much strengthen our resolution both to set our hope in him and to keep his commandments, for he is able to bear us out in both. [2.] That they may take warning not to conform to the example of their fathers (*v.* 8): *That they might not be as their fathers, a stubborn and rebellious generation.* See here, *First,* What was the character of their fathers. Though they were the seed of Abraham, taken into covenant with God, and, for aught we know, the only professing people he had then in the world, yet they were stubborn and rebellious, and walked contrary to God, in direct opposition to his will. They did indeed profess relation to him, but they did not set their hearts aright; they were not cordial in their engagements to God, nor inward with him in their worship of him, and therefore their *spirit was not stedfast with him,* but upon every occasion they flew off from him. Note, Hypocrisy is the high road to apostasy. Those that do not set their hearts aright will not be stedfast with God, but play fast and loose. *Secondly,* What was a charge to the children : *That they be not as their fathers.* Note, Those that have descended from wicked and ungodly ancestors, if they will but consider the word and works of God, will see reason enough not to tread in their steps. It will be no excuse for a vain conversation that it was received by tradition from our fathers (1 Pet. i. 18); for what we know of them that was evil must be

an admonition to us, that we dread that which was so pernicious to them as we would shun those courses which they took that were ruinous to their health or estates.

9 The children of Ephraim, *being* armed, *and* carrying bows, turned back in the day of battle. 10 They kept not the covenant of God, and refused to walk in his law; 11 And forgat his works, and his wonders that he had showed them. 12 Marvellous things did he in the sight of their fathers, in the land of Egypt, *in* the field of Zoan. 13 He divided the sea, and caused them to pass through ; and he made the waters to stand as a heap. 14 In the daytime also he led them with a cloud, and all the night with a light of fire. 15 He clave the rocks in the wilderness, and gave *them* drink as *out of* the great depths. 16 He brought streams also out of the rock, and caused waters to run down like rivers. 17 And they sinned yet more against him by provoking the most high in the wilderness. 18 And they tempted God in their heart by asking meat for their lust. 19 Yea, they spake against God; they said, Can God furnish a table in the wilderness ? 20 Behold, he smote the rock, that the waters gushed out, and the streams overflowed; can he give bread also ? can he provide flesh for his people ? 21 Therefore the LORD heard *this*, and was wroth: so a fire was kindled against Jacob, and anger also came up against Israel: 22 Because they believed not in God, and trusted not in his salvation : 23 Though he had commanded the clouds from above, and opened the doors of heaven, 24 And had rained down manna upon them to eat, and had given them of the corn of heaven. 25 Man did eat angels' food : he sent them meat to the full 26 He caused an east wind to blow in the heaven : and by his power he brought in the south wind. 27 He rained flesh also upon them as dust, and feathered fowls like as the sand of the sea : 28 And he let *it* fall in the midst of their camp, round about their habitations. 29 So they did eat, and were well filled : for he gave them

their own desire; 30 They were not estranged from their lust. But while their meat *was* yet in their mouths, 31 The wrath of God came upon them, and slew the fattest of them, and smote down the chosen *men* of Israel. 32 For all this they sinned still, and believed not for his wondrous works. 33 Therefore their days did he consume in vanity, and their years in trouble. 34 When he slew them, then they sought him: and they returned and enquired early after God. 35 And they remembered that God *was* their rock, and the high God their redeemer. 36 Nevertheless they did flatter him with their mouth, and they lied unto him with their tongues. 37 For their heart was not right with him, neither were they stedfast in his covenant. 38 But he, *being* full of compassion, forgave *their* iniquity, and destroyed *them* not: yèa, many a time turned he his anger away, and did not stir up all his wrath. 39 For he remembered that they *were but* flesh; a wind that passeth away, and cometh not again.

In these verses,

I. The psalmist observes the late rebukes of Providence that the people of Israel had been under, which they had brought upon themselves by their dealing treacherously with God, v. 9—11. *The children of Ephraim,* in which tribe Shiloh was, though they were well armed and shot with bows, yet *turned back in the day of battle.* This seems to refer to that shameful defeat which the Philistines gave them in Eli's time, when they took the ark prisoner, 1 Sam. iv. 10, 11. Of this the psalmist here begins to speak, and, after a long digression, returns to it again, v. 61. Well might that event be thus fresh in mind in David's time, above forty years after, for the ark, which in that memorable battle was seized by the Philistines, though it was quickly brought out of captivity, was never brought out of obscurity till David fetched it from Kirjath-jearim to his own city. Observe, 1. The shameful cowardice of the children of Ephraim, that warlike tribe, so famed for valiant men, Joshua's tribe; the children of that tribe, though as well armed as ever, turned back when they came to face the enemy. Note, Weapons of war stand men in little stead without a martial spirit, and that is gone if God be gone. Sin dispirits men and takes away the heart. 2. The causes of their cowardice, which were no less shameful; and these were, (1.) A shameful violation of

God's law and their covenant with him (v. 10); they were basely treacherous and perfidious, for *they kept not the covenant of God,* and basely stubborn and rebellious (as they were described, v. 8), for they peremptorily refused to walk in his law, and, in effect, told him to his face they would not be ruled by him. (2.) A shameful ingratitude to God for the favours he had bestowed upon them: They *forgot his works and his wonders,* his works of wonder which they ought to have admired, v. 11. Note, Our forgetfulness of God's works is at the bottom of our disobedience to nis laws

II. He takes occasion hence to consult precedents and to compare this with the case of their fathers, who were in like manner unmindful of God's mercies to them and ungrateful to their founder and great benefactor, and were therefore often brought under his displeasure. The narrative in these verses is very remarkable, for it relates a kind of struggle between God's goodness and man's badness, and mercy, at length, rejoices against judgment.

1. God did great things for his people Israel when he first incorporated them and formed them into a people: *Marvellous things did he in the sight of their fathers,* and not only in their sight, but in their cause, and for their benefit, so strange, so kind, that one would think they should never be forgotten. What he did for them in the land of Egypt is only just mentioned here (v. 12), but afterwards resumed, v. 43. He proceeds here to show, (1.) How he made a lane for them through the Red Sea, and caused them, gave them courage, to pass through, though the waters stood over their heads as a heap, v. 13. See Isa. lxiii. 12, 13, where God is said to *lead them by the hand,* as it were, *through the deep that they should not stumble.* (2.) How he provided a guide for them through the untrodden paths of the wilderness (v. 14); he led them step by step, *in the day time by a cloud,* which also sheltered them from the heat, and *all the night with a light of fire,* which perhaps warmed the air; at least it made the darkness of night less frightful, and perhaps kept off wild beasts, Zech. ii. 5. (3.) How he furnished their camp with fresh water in a dry and thirsty land where no water was, not by opening the bottles of heaven (that would have been a common way), but by broaching a rock (v. 15, 16): He *clave the rocks in the wilderness,* which yielded water, though they were not capable of receiving it either from the clouds above or the springs beneath. Out of the dry and hard rock he gave them drink, not distilled as out of an alembic, drop by drop, but in streams *running down like rivers,* and as out of the great depths. God gives abundantly, and is rich in mercy; he gives seasonably, and sometimes makes us to feel the want of mercies that we may the better know the worth of them. This water which God gave Israel out of the rock was

the more valuable because it was spiritual drink. *Ana that rock was Christ.*

2. When God began thus to bless them they began to affront him (*v.* 17): *They sinned yet more against him,* more than they had done in Egypt, though there they were bad enough, Ezek. xx. 8. They bore the miseries of their servitude better than the difficulties of their deliverance, and never murmured at their taskmasters so much as they did at Moses and Aaron; as if they were *delivered to do all these abominations,* Jer. vii. 10. As sin sometimes takes occasion by the commandment, so at other times it takes occasion by the deliverance, to become more exceedingly sinful. *They provoked the Most High.* Though he is most high, and they knew themselves an unequal match for him, yet they provoked him and even bade defiance to his justice; and this in the wilderness, where he had them at his mercy and therefore they were bound in interest to please him, and where he showed them so much mercy and therefore they were bound in gratitude to please him; yet there they said and did that which they knew would provoke him: *They tempted God in their heart, v.* 18. Their sin began in their heart, and thence it took its malignity. *They do always err in their heart,* Heb. iii. 10. Thus they tempted God, tried his patience to the utmost, whether he would bear with them or no, and, in effect, bade him do his worst. Two ways they provoked him:—(1.) By desiring, or rather demanding, that which he had not thought fit to give them: *They asked meat for their lust.* God had given them meat for their hunger, in the manna, wholesome pleasant food and in abundance; he had given them meat for their faith out of the heads of leviathan which *he broke in pieces,* lxxiv. 14. But all this would not serve; they must have meat for their lust, dainties and varieties to gratify a luxurious appetite. Nothing is more provoking to God than our quarrelling with our allotment and indulging the desires of the flesh. (2.) By distrusting his power to give them what they desired. This was tempting God indeed. They challenged him to give them flesh; and, if he did not, they would say it was because he could not, not because he did not see it fit for them (*v.* 19): *They spoke against God.* Those that set bounds to God's power speak against him. It was as injurious a reflection as could be cast upon God to say, *Can God furnish a table in the wilderness?* They had manna, but they did not think they had a table furnished unless they had boiled and roast, a first, a second, and a third course, as they had in Egypt, where they had both flesh and fish, and sauce too (Exod. xvi. 3, Num. xi. 5), dishes of meat and salvers of fruit. What an unreasonable insatiable thing is luxury! Such a mighty thing did these epicures think a table well furnished to be that they thought it was more than God himself could give them in that wilderness;

534

whereas the *beasts of the forest,* and all the *fowls of the mountains,* are his, l. 10, 11. Their disbelief of God's power was so much the worse in that they did at the same time own that he had done as much as that came to (*v.* 20): *Behold, he smote the rock, that the waters gushed out,* which they and their cattle drank of. And which is easier, to furnish a table in the wilderness, which a rich man can do, or to fetch water out of a rock, which the greatest potentate on the earth cannot do? Never did unbelief, though always unreasonable, ask so absurd a question: "Can he that melted down a rock into streams of water give bread also? Or can he that has given bread provide flesh also?" Is any thing too hard for Omnipotence? When once the ordinary powers of nature are exceeded God has made bare his arm, and we must conclude that nothing is impossible with him. Be it ever so great a thing that we ask, it becomes us to own, *Lord, if thou wilt, thou canst.*

3. God justly resented the provocation and was much displeased with them (*v.* 21): *The Lord heard this, and was wroth.* Note, God is a witness to all our murmurings and distrusts; he hears them and is much displeased with them. *A fire was kindled* for this *against Jacob;* the *fire of the Lord burnt among them,* Num. xi. 1. Or it may be understood of the fire of God's anger which came up against Israel. To unbelievers our God is himself a consuming fire. Those that will not believe the power of God's mercy shall feel the power of his indignation, and be made to confess that *it is a fearful thing to fall into his hands.* Now here we are told, (1.) Why God thus resented the provocation (*v.* 22): *Because* by this it appeared that *they believed not in God;* they did not give credit to the revelation he had made of himself to them, for they durst not commit themselves to him, nor venture themselves with him: *They trusted not in the salvation* he had begun to work for them; for then they would not thus have questioned its progress. Those cannot be said to trust in God's salvation as their felicity at last who cannot find in their hearts to trust in his providence for food convenient in the way to it. That which aggravated their unbelief was the experience they had had of the power and goodness of God, *v.* 23—25. He had given them undeniable proofs of his power, not only on earth beneath, but in heaven above; for *he commanded the clouds from above,* as one that had created them and commanded them into being; he made what use he pleased of them. Usually by their showers they contribute to the earth's producing corn; but now, when God so commanded them, they showered down corn themselves, which is therefore called here *the corn of heaven;* for heaven can do the work without the earth, but not the earth without heaven. God, who has the key of the clouds, *opened the doors of heaven,* and that is more than *opening the windows,* which yet is spoken of as a great

blessing, Mal. iii. 10. To all that by faith and prayer ask, seek, and knock, these doors shall at any time be opened; for the God of heaven is rich in mercy to all that call upon him. He not only keeps a good house, but keeps open house. Justly might God take it ill that they should distrust him when he had been so very kind to them that he *had rained down manna upon them to eat,* substantial food, daily, duly, enough for all, enough for each. *Man did eat angels' food,* such as angels, if they had occasion for food, would eat and be thankful for; or rather such as was given by the ministry of angels, and (as the *Chaldee* reads it) such as descended from the dwelling of angels. Every one, even the least child in Israel, did *eat the bread of the mighty* (so the margin reads it); the weakest stomach could digest it, and yet it was so nourishing that it was strong meat for strong men. And, though the provision was so good, yet they were not stinted, nor ever reduced to short allowance; for *he sent them meat to the full.* If they gathered little, it was their own fault; and yet even then they had no lack, Exod. xvi. 18. The daily provision God makes for us, and has made ever since we came into the world, though it has not so much of miracle as this, has no less of mercy, and is therefore a great aggravation of our distrust of God. (2.) How he expressed his resentment of the provocation, not in denying them what they so inordinately lusted after, but in granting it to them. [1.] Did they question his power? He soon gave them a sensible conviction that he could *furnish a table in the wilderness.* Though the winds seem to blow where they list, yet, when he pleased, he could make them his caterers to fetch in provisions, v. 26. *He caused an east wind to blow and a south wind,* either a south-east wind, or an east wind first to bring in the quails from that quarter and then a south wind to bring in more from that quarter; so that *he rained flesh upon them,* and that of the most delicate sort, not butchers' meat, but wild-fowl, and abundance of it, *as dust, as the sand of the sea* (v. 27), so that the meanest Israelite might have sufficient; and it cost them nothing, no, not the pains of fetching it from the mountains, for *he let it fall in the midst of their camp, round about their habitation,* v. 28. We have the account Num. xi. 31, 32. See how good God is even to the evil and unthankful, and wonder that his goodness does not overcome their badness. See what little reason we have to judge of God's love by such gifts of his bounty as these; dainty bits are no tokens of his peculiar favour. Christ gave dry bread to the disciples that he loved, but a sop dipped in the sauce to Judas that betrayed him. [2.] Did they defy his justice and boast that they had gained their point? He made them pay dearly for their quails; for, though he *gave them their own desire, they were not estranged from their lust* (v. 29, 30); their appetite was insatiable; they

were well filled and yet they were not satisfied; for they knew not what they would have. Such is the nature of lust; it is content with nothing, and the more it is humoured the more humoursome it grows Those that indulge their lust will never be estranged from it. Or it intimates that God's liberality did not make them ashamed of their ungrateful lustings, as it would have done if they had had any sense of honour. But what came of it? *While the meat was yet in their mouth,* rolled under the tongue as a sweet morsel, *the wrath of God came upon them and slew the fattest of them* (v. 31), those that were most luxurious and most daring. See Num. xi. 33, 34. They were fed *as sheep for the slaughter:* the butcher takes the fattest first. We may suppose there were some pious and contented Israelites, that did eat moderately of the quails and were never the worse; for it was not the meat that poisoned them, but their own lust. Let epicures and sensualists here read their doom. The end of those who make a *god of their belly is destruction,* Phil. iii. 19. *The prosperity of fools shall destroy them,* and their ruin will be the greater.

4. The judgments of God upon them did not reform them, nor attain the end, any more than his mercies (v. 32): *For all this, they sinned still;* they murmured and quarrelled with God and Moses as much as ever. Though God *was wroth and smote them, yet they went on frowardly in the way of their heart* (Isa. lvii. 17); *they believed not for his wondrous works.* Though his works of justice were as wondrous and as great proofs of his power as his works of mercy, yet they were not wrought upon by them to fear God, nor convinced how much it was their interest to make him their friend. Those hearts are hard indeed that will neither be melted by the mercies of God nor broken by his judgments.

5. They persisting in their sins, God proceeded in his judgments, but they were judgments of another nature, which wrought not suddenly, but slowly. He punished them not now with such acute diseases as that was which *slew the fattest of them,* but a lingering chronical distemper (v. 33): *Therefore their days did he consume in vanity* in the wilderness *and their years in trouble.* By an irreversible doom they were condemned to wear out thirty-eight tedious years in the wilderness, which indeed were consumed in vanity; for in all those years there was not a step taken nearer Canaan, but they were turned back again, and wandered to and fro as in a labyrinth, not one stroke struck towards the conquest of it: and not only in vanity, but in trouble, for their carcases were condemned to fall in the wilderness and there they all perished but Caleb and Joshua. Note, Those that sin still must expect to be in trouble still. And the reason why we spend our days in so much vanity and trou-

ble, why we live with so little comfort and to so little purpose, is because we do not live by faith.

6. Under these rebukes they professed repentance, but they were not cordial and sincere in this profession. (1.) Their profession was plausible enough (*v.* 34, 35): *When he slew them,* or condemned them to be slain, *then they sought him;* they confessed their fault, and begged his pardon. When some were slain others in a fright cried to God for mercy, and promised they would reform and be very good ; then *they returned to God, and enquired early after him.* So one would have taken them to be such as desired to find him. And they pretended to do this because, however they had forgotten it formerly, now *they remembered that God was their rock* and therefore now that they needed him they would fly to him and take shelter in him, *and that the high God* was *their Redeemer,* who brought them out of Egypt and to whom therefore they might come with boldness. Afflictions are sent to put us in mind of God as our rock and our redeemer; for, in prosperity, we are apt to forget him. (2.) They were not sincere in this profession (*v.* 36, 37): *They did but flatter him with their mouth,* as if they thought by fair speeches to prevail with him to revoke the sentence and remove the judgment, with a secret intention to break their word when the danger was over; they did not *return to God with their whole heart, but feignedly,* Jer. iii. 10. All their professions, prayers, and promises, were extorted by the rack. It was plain that they did not mean as they said, for they did not adhere to it. They thawed in the sun, but froze in the shade. They did but *lie to God with their tongues, for their heart was not with him,* was not right with him, as appeared by the issue, for *they were not stedfast in his covenant.* They were not sincere in their reformation, for they were not constant; and, by thinking thus to impose upon a heart-searching God, they really put as great an affront upon him as by any of their reflections.

7. God hereupon, in pity to them, put a stop to the judgments which were threatened and in part executed (*v.* 38, 39): *But he, being full of compassion, forgave their iniquity.* One would think this counterfeit repentance should have filled up the measure of their iniquity. What could be more provoking than to *lie thus to the holy God,* than thus to *keep back part of the price,* the chief part? Acts v. 3. And *yet he, being full of compassion, forgave their iniquity* thus far, that he did not destroy them and cut them off from being a people, as he justly might have done, but spared their lives till they had reared another generation which should enter into the promised land. *Destroy it not, for a blessing is in it,* Isa. lxv. 8. *Many a time he turned his anger away* (for he is Lord of his anger) *and did not stir up all his wrath,* to deal with them as they de-

served : and why did he not? Not because their ruin would have been any loss to him, but, (1.) Because he was *full of compassion* and, when he was going to destroy them, *his repentings were kindled together,* and he said, *How shall I give thee up, Ephraim? How shall I deliver thee, Israel?* Hos. xi. 8. (2.) Because, though they did not rightly remember that he was their rock, he *remembered that they were but flesh.* He considered the corruption of their nature, which inclined them to evil, and was pleased to make that an excuse for his sparing them, though it was really no excuse for their sin. See Gen. vi. 3. He considered the weakness and frailty of their nature, and what an easy thing it would be to crush them : *They are as a wind that passeth away and cometh not again.* They may soon be taken off, but, when they are gone, they are gone irrecoverably, and then what will become of the covenant with Abraham? They are flesh, they are wind; whence it were easy to argue they may justly, they may immediately, be cut off, and there would be no loss of them : but God argues, on the contrary, therefore he will not destroy them; for the true reason is, *He is full of compassion.*

40 How oft did they provoke him in the wilderness, *and* grieve him in the desert! 41 Yea, they turned back and tempted God, and limited the Holy One of Israel. 42 They remembered not his hand, *nor* the day when he delivered them from the enemy. 43 How he had wrought his signs in Egypt, and his wonders in the field of Zoan : 44 And had turned their rivers into blood; and their floods, that they could not drink. 45 He sent divers sorts of flies among them, which devoured them ; and frogs, which destroyed them. 46 He gave also their increase unto the caterpillar, and their labour unto the locust. 47 He destroyed their vines with hail, and their sycamore trees with frost. 48 He gave up their cattle also to the hail, and their flocks to hot thunderbolts. 49 He cast upon them the fierceness of his anger, wrath, and indignation, and trouble, by sending evil angels *among them.* 50 He made a way to his anger ; he spared not their soul from death, but gave their life over to the pestilence ; 51 And smote all the first-born in Egypt ; the chief of *their* strength in the tabernacles of Ham : 52 But made his own people to go

forth like sheep, and guided them in the wilderness like a flock. 53 And he led them on safely, so that they feared not : but the sea overwhelmed their enemies. 54 And he brought them to the border of his sanctuary, *even to* this mountain, *which* his right hand had purchased. 55 He cast out the heathen also before them, and divided them an inheritance by line, and made the tribes of Israel to dwell in their tents. 56 Yet they tempted and provoked the most high God, and kept not his testimonies ; 57 But turned back, and dealt unfaithfully like their fathers : they were turned aside like a deceitful bow. 58 For they provoked him to anger with their high places, and moved him to jealousy with their graven images. 59 When God heard *this*, he was wroth, and greatly abhorred Israel : 60 So that he forsook the tabernacle of Shiloh, the tent *which* he placed among men; 61 And delivered his strength into captivity, and his glory into the enemy's hand. 62 He gave his people over also unto the sword ; and was wroth with his inheritance. 63 The fire consumed their young men ; and their maidens were not given to marriage. 64 Their priests fell by the sword ; and their widows made no lamentation. 65 Then the Lord awaked as one out of sleep, *and* like a mighty man that shouteth by reason of wine. 66 And he smote his enemies in the hinder part : he put them to a perpetual reproach. 67 Moreover he refused the tabernacle of Joseph, and chose not the tribe of Ephraim : 68 But chose the tribe of Judah, the mount Zion which he loved. 69 And he built his sanctuary like high *palaces*, like the earth which he hath established for ever. 70 He chose David also his servant, and took him from the sheepfolds : 71 From following the ewes great with young he brought him to feed Jacob his people, and Israel his inheritance. 72 So he fed them according to the integrity of his heart; and guided them by the skilfulness of his hands.

The matter and scope of this paragraph are the same with the former, showing what great mercies God had bestowed upon Israel, how provoking they had been, what judgments he had brought upon them for their sins, and yet how, in judgment, he remembered mercy at last. Let not those that receive mercy from God be thereby emboldened to sin, for the mercies they receive will aggravate their sin and hasten the punishment of it; yet let not those that are under divine rebukes for sin be discouraged from repentance, for their punishments are means of repentance, and shall not prevent the mercy God has yet in store for them. Observe,

I. The sins of Israel in the wilderness again reflected on, because written for our admonition (v. 40, 41): *How often did they provoke him in the wilderness!* Not once, nor twice, but many a time ; and the repetition of the provocation was a great aggravation of it, as well as the place, v. 17. God kept an account how often they provoked him, though they did not. Num. xiv. 22, *They have tempted me these ten times.* By provoking him they did not so much anger him as grieve him, for he looked upon them as his children *(Israel is my son, my first-born)*, and the undutiful disrespectful behaviour of children does more grieve than anger the tender parents ; they lay it to heart, and take it unkindly, Isa. i. 2. They grieved him because they put him under a necessity of afflicting them, which he did not willingly. After they had humbled themselves before him they *turned back and tempted God*, as before, and *limited the Holy One of Israel*, prescribing to him what proofs he should give of his power and presence with them and what methods he should take in leading them and providing for them. They limited him to their way and their time, as if he did not observe that they quarrelled with him. It is presumption for us to limit *the Holy One of Israel;* for, being *the Holy One*, he will do what is most for his own glory; and, being *the Holy One of Israel*, he will do what is most for their good ; and we both impeach his wisdom and betray our own pride and folly if we go about to prescribe to him. That which occasioned their limiting God for the future was their forgetting his former favours (v. 42): *They remembered not his hand*, how strong it is and how it had been stretched out for them, nor *the day when he delivered them from the enemy*, Pharaoh, that great enemy who sought their ruin. There are some days made remarkable by signal deliverances, which ought never to be forgotten ; for the remembrance of them would encourage us in our greatest straits.

II. The mercies of God to Israel, which they were unmindful of when they tempted God and limited him ; and this catalogue of the works of wonder which God wrought for them begins higher, and is carried down further, than that before, v. 12, &c.

1. This begins with their deliverance out

of Egypt, and the plagues with which God compelled the Egyptians to let them go: these were the *signs* God *wrought in Egypt* (*v.* 43), the *wonders* he wrought *in the field of Zoan*, that is, in the country of Zoan, as we say, *in Agro N.*, meaning in such a county.

(1.) Several of the plagues of Egypt are here specified, which speak aloud the power of God and his favour to Israel, as well as terror to his and their enemies. As, [1.] The turning of the waters into blood; they had made themselves drunk with the blood of God's people, even the infants, and now God gave them blood to drink, *for they were worthy, v.* 44. [2.] The flies and frogs which infested them, mixtures of insects in swarms, in shoals, *which devoured them, which destroyed them, v.* 45. For God can make the weakest and most despicable animals instruments of his wrath when he pleases; what they want in strength may be made up in number. [3.] The plague of locusts, which devoured their increase, and that which they had laboured for, *v.* 46. They are called *God's great army*, Joel ii. 25. [4.] The *hail*, which *destroyed* their trees, especially *their vines*, the weakest of trees (*v.* 47), and *their cattle*, especially *their flocks* of sheep, the weakest of their cattle, which were killed with *hot thunder-bolts* (*v.* 48), and the *frost*, or congealed rain (as the word signifies), was so violent that it destroyed even the *sycamore-trees*. [5.] The death of the first-born was the last and sorest of the plagues of Egypt, and that which perfected the deliverance of Israel; it was first in intention (Exod. iv. 23), but last in execution; for, if gentler methods would have done the work, this would have been prevented: but it is here largely described, *v.* 49—51. *First,* The anger of God was the cause of it. Wrath had now come upon the Egyptians to the uttermost; Pharaoh's heart having been often hardened after less judgments had softened it, God now *stirred up all his wrath;* for he *cast upon them the fierceness of his anger,* anger in the highest degree, *wrath and indignation* the cause, *and trouble (tribulation and anguish,* Rom. ii. 8, 9) the effect. This from on high he cast upon them and did not spare, and they could not *flee out of his hands,* Job xxvii. 22. *He made a way,* or (as the word is) *he weighed a path, to his anger.* He did not cast it upon them uncertainly, but by weight. His anger was weighed with the greatest exactness in the balances of justice; for, in his greatest displeasure, he never did, nor ever will do, any wrong to any of his creatures: the path of his anger is always weighed. *Secondly,* The angels of God were the instruments employed in this execution: *He sent evil angels among them,* not evil in their own nature, but in respect to the errand upon which they were sent; they were destroying angels, or angels of punishment, which passed through all the land of Egypt, with orders, according to the weighed paths

538

of God's anger, not to kill all, but the first-born only. Good angels become evil angels to sinners. Those that make the holy God their enemy must never expect the holy angels to be their friends. *Thirdly,* The execution itself was very severe: *He spared not their soul from death* but suffered death to ride in triumph among them and *gave their life over to the pestilence,* which cut the thread of life off immediately; for *he smote all the first-born in Egypt* (*v.* 51), *the chief of their strength,* the hopes of their respective families; children are the parents' strength, and the first-born the *chief of their strength.* Thus, because Israel was precious in God's sight, he *gave men for them and people for their life,* Isa. xliii. 4.

(2.) By these plagues on the Egyptians God made a way for *his own people to go forth like sheep,* distinguishing between them and the Egyptians, *as the shepherd divides between the sheep and the goats,* having set his own mark on these sheep by the blood of the lamb sprinkled on their door-posts. *He made them go forth like sheep,* not knowing whither they went, and *guided them in the wilderness,* as a shepherd guides his flock, with all possible care and tenderness, *v.* 52. *He led them on safely,* though in dangerous paths, so that *they feared not,* that is, they needed not to fear; they were indeed frightened at the Red Sea (Exod. xiv. 10), but that was said to them, and done for them, which effectually silenced their fears *But the sea overwhelmed their enemies* that ventured to pursue them into it, *v.* 53. It was a lane to them, but a grave to their persecutors.

2. It is carried down as far as their settlement in Canaan (*v.* 54): *He brought them to the border of his sanctuary,* to that land in the midst of which he set up his sanctuary, which was, as it were, the centre and metropolis, the crown and glory, of it. That is a happy land which is the border of God's sanctuary. It was the happiness of that land that there God was known, and there were his sanctuary and dwelling-place, lxxvi. 1, 2. The whole land in general, and Zion in particular, was *the mountain which his right hand had purchased,* which by his own power he had set apart for himself. See xliv. 3. He *made them to ride on the high places of the earth,* Isa. lviii. 14; Deut. xxxii. 13. They found the Canaanites in the full and quiet possession of that land, but God *cast out the heathen before them,* not only took away their title to it, as the Lord of the whole earth, but himself executed the judgment given against them, and, as Lord of hosts, turned them out of it, and made his people *Israel tread upon their high places,* dividing each tribe *an inheritance by line,* and making them *to dwell* in the houses of those whom they had destroyed. God could have turned the uninhabited uncultivated wilderness (which perhaps was nearly of the same extent as Ca-

naan) into fruitful soil, and have planted them there; but the land he designed for them was to be a type of heaven, and therefore must be *the glory of all lands;* it must likewise be fought for, for *the kingdom of heaven suffers violence.*

III. The sins of Israel after they were settled in Canaan, *v.* 56—58. The children were *like their fathers,* and brought their old corruptions into their new habitations. Though God had done so much for them, yet *they tempted and provoked the most high God* still. He gave them his testimonies, but they did not keep them; they began very promisingly, but 'hey turned back, gave God good words, but dealt unfaithfully, and were *like a deceitful bow,* which seemed likely to send the arrow to the mark, but, when it is drawn, breaks, and drops the arrow at the arche.'s foot, or perhaps makes it recoil in his face. There was no hold of them, nor any confidence to be put in their promises or professions. They seemed sometimes devoted to God, but they presently *turned aside,* and *provoked him to anger with their high places and their graven images.* Idolatry was the sin that did most easily beset them, and which, though they often professed their repentance for, they as often relapsed into. It was spiritual adultery either to worship idols or to worship God by images, as if he had been an idol, and therefore by it they are said to *move him to jealousy,* Deut. xxxii. 16, 21.

IV. The judgments God brought upon them for these sins. Their place in Canaan would no more secure them in a sinful way than their descent from Israel. *You only have I known of all the families of the earth, therefore I will punish you,* Amos iii. 2. Idolatry is winked at among the Gentiles, but not in Israel. 1. God was displeased with them (*v.* 59): *When God heard this,* when he heard the cry of their iniquity, which came up before him, *he was wroth,* he took it very heinously, as well he might, and he greatly abhorred Israel, whom he had greatly loved and delighted in. Those that had been the people of his choice became the generation of his wrath. Presumptuous sins, idolatries especially, render even Israelites odious to God's holiness and obnoxious to his justice. 2. He deserted his tabernacle among them, and removed the defence which was upon that glory, *v.* 60. God never leaves us till we leave him, never withdraws till we have driven him from us. His name is *Jealous,* and he is a jealous God; and therefore no marvel if a people whom he had betrothed to himself be loathed and rejected, and he refuse to cohabit with them any longer, when they have embraced the bosom of a stranger. The *tabernacle at Shiloh* was *the tent God had placed among men,* in which God would *in very deed dwell with men upon the earth;* but, when his people treacherously forsook it, he justly forsook it, and then all its glory departed. Israel has small joy of the tabernacle without the presence of God in it. 3. He gave up all into the hands of the enemy Those whom God forsakes become an easy prey to the destroyer. The Philistines are sworn enemies to the Israel of God, and no less so to the God of Israel, and yet God will make use of them to be a scourge to his people. (1.) God permits them to take the ark prisoner, and carry it off as a trophy of their victory, to show that he had not only forsaken the tabernacle, but even the ark itself, which shall now be no longer a token of his presence (*v.* 61): *He delivered his strength into captivity,* as if it had been weakened and overcome, *and his glory* fell under the disgrace of being abandoned *into the enemy's hand.* We have the story 1 Sam. iv. 11. When the ark has become as a stranger among Israelites, no marvel if it soon be made a prisoner among Philistines. (2.) He suffers the armies of Israel to be routed by the Philistines (*v.* 62, 63): *He gave his people over unto the sword,* to the sword of his own justice and of the enemy's rage, for he *was wroth with his inheritance;* and that wrath of his was the *fire which consumed their young men,* in the prime of their time, by the sword or sickness, and made such a devastation of them that *their maidens were not praised,* that is, *were not given in marriage* (which is honourable in all), because there were no young men for them to be given to, and because the distresses and calamities of Israel were so many and great that the joys of marriage-solemnities were judged unseasonable, and it was said, *Blessed is the womb that beareth not.* General destructions produce a scarcity of men. Isa. xiii. 12, *I will make a man more precious than fine gold,* so that *seven women shall take hold of one man,* Isa. iv. 1; iii. 25. Yet this was not the worst: (3.) Even *their priests,* who attended the ark, *fell by the sword,* Hophni and Phinehas. Justly they fell, for they made themselves vile, and were sinners before the Lord exceedingly; and their priesthood was so far from being their protection that it aggravated their sin and hastened their fall. Justly did they fall by the sword, because they exposed themselves in the field of battle, without call or warrant. We throw ourselves out of God's protection when we go out of our place and out of the way of our duty. When the priests fell *their widows made no lamentation, v.* 64. All the ceremonies of mourning were lost and buried in substantial grief; the widow of Phinehas, instead of lamenting her husband's death, died herself, when she had called her son *Ichabod,* 1 Sam. iv. 19, &c.

V. God's return, in mercy, to them, and his gracious appearances for them after this. We read not of their repentance and return to God, but God was *grieved for the miseries of Israel* (Judg. x. 16) and concerned for his own honour, *fearing the wrath of the enemy, lest they should behave themselves strangely,*

Deut. xxxii. 27. And therefore *then the Lord awaked as one out of sleep* (*v.* 65), *and like a mighty man that shouteth by reason of wine,* not only like one that is raised out of sleep and recovers himself from the slumber which by drinking he was overcome with, who then regards that which before he seemed wholly to neglect, but like one that is refreshed with sleep, and whose heart is made glad by the sober and moderate use of wine, and is therefore the more lively and vigorous, and fit for business. When God had delivered the ark of his strength into captivity, as one jealous of his honour, he soonput forth the arm of his strength to rescue it, stirred up his strength to do great things for his people.

1. He plagued the Philistines who held the ark in captivity, *v.* 66. He smote them with emerods *in the hinder parts,* wounded them behind, as if they were fleeing from him, even when they thought themselves more than conquerors. He put them to reproach, and they themselves helped to make it a perpetual reproach by the golden images of their emerods, which they returned with the ark for a trespass-offering (1 Sam. vi. 5), to remain *in perpetuam rei memoriam—as a perpetual memorial.* Note, Sooner or later God will glorify himself by putting disgrace upon his enemies, even when they are most elevated with their successes.

2. He provided a new settlement for his ark after it had been some months in captivity and some years in obscurity. He did indeed *refuse* the *tabernacle of Joseph;* he never sent it back to Shiloh, in the tribe of Ephraim, *v.* 67. The ruins of that place were standing monuments of divine justice. *Go, see what I did to Shiloh,* Jer. vii. 12. But he did not wholly take away the glory from Israel; the moving of the ark is not the removing of it. Shiloh has lost it, but Israel has not. God will have a church in the world, and a kingdom among men, though this or that place may have its candlestick removed; nay, the rejection of Shiloh is the election of Zion, as, long after, the fall of the Jews was the riches of the Gentiles, Rom. xi. 12. When God *chose not the tribe of Ephraim,* of which tribe Joshua was, he *chose the tribe of Judah* (*v.* 68), because of that tribe Jesus was to be, who is greater than Joshua. Kirjath-jearim, the place to which the ark was brought after its rescue out of the hands of the Philistines, was in the tribe of Judah. There it took possession of that tribe; but thence it was removed to Zion, *that Mount Zion which he loved* (*v.* 68), which was *beautiful for situation, the joy of the whole earth;* there it was that he *built his sanctuary like high palaces* and *like the earth, v.* 69. David indeed erected only a tent for the ark, but a temple was then designed and prepared for, and finished by his son; and that was, (1.) A very stately place. It was built like the palaces of princes, and the great men of the earth, nay, it excelled them all in splendour

540

and magnificence. Solomon built it, and yet here it is said *God built it,* for his father had taught him, perhaps with reference to this undertaking, that *except the Lord build the house those labour in vain* that build it, cxxvii. 1, which is a psalm for Solomon. (2.) A very stable place, like the earth, though not to continue as long as the earth, yet while it was to continue it was as firm as the earth, which God *upholds by the word of his power,* and it was not finally destroyed till the gospel temple was erected, which is to continue *as long as the sun and moon endure* (lxxxix. 36, 37) and against which the *gates of hell shall not prevail.*

3. He set a good government over them, a monarchy, and a monarch after his own heart: *He chose David his servant* out of all the thousands of Israel, and put the sceptre into his hand, out of whose loins Christ was to come, and who was to be a type of him, *v.* 70. Concerning David observe here, (1.) The meanness of his beginning. His extraction indeed was great, for he descended from the prince of the tribe of Judah, but his education was poor. He was bred not a scholar, not a soldier, but a shepherd. He was *taken from the sheep-folds,* as Moses was; for God delights to put honour upon the humble and diligent, to raise the poor out of the dust and to set them among princes; and sometimes he finds those most fit for public action that have spent the beginning of their time in solitude and contemplation. The Son of David was upbraided with the obscurity of his original: *Is not this the carpenter?* David was taken, he does not say from leading the rams, but *from following the ewes,* especially those *great with young,* which intimated that of all the good properties of a shepherd he was most remarkable for his tenderness and compassion to those of his flock that most needed his care. This temper of mind fitted him for government, and made him a type of Christ, who, when he feeds his flock like a shepherd, does with a particular care *gently lead those that are with young,* Isa. xl. 11. (2.) The greatness of his advancement. God preferred him to *feed Jacob his people, v.* 71. It was a great honour that God put upon him, in advancing him to be a king, especially to be king over Jacob and Israel, God's peculiar people, near and dear to him; but withal it was a great trust reposed in him when he was charged with the government of those that were God's own inheritance. God advanced him to the throne that he might feed them, not that he might feed himself, that he might do good, not that he might make his family great. It is the charge given to all the under-shepherds, both magistrates and ministers, that they *feed the flock of God.* (3.) The happiness of his management. David, having so great a trust put into his hands, obtained mercy of the Lord to be found both skilful and faithful in the discharge of it (*v.* 72): *So he fed them;* he ruled them and taught them, guided and

protected them, [1.] Very honestly; he did it *according to the integrity of his heart,* aiming at nothing but the glory of God and the good of the people committed to his charge; the principles of his religion were the maxims of his government, which he administered, not with carnal policy, but with *godly sincerity, by the grace of God.* In every thing he did he meant well and had no by-end in view. [2.] Very discreetly; he did it *by the skilfulness of his hands.* He was not only very sincere in what he designed, but very prudent in what he did, and chose out the most proper means in pursuit of his end, for his God did instruct him to discretion. Happy the people that are under such a government! With good reason does the psalmist make this the finishing crowning instance of God's favour to Israel, for David was a type of Christ the great and good Shepherd, who was humbled first and then exalted, and of whom it was foretold that he should be filled with the *spirit of wisdom and understanding* and should *judge and reprove with equity,* Isa. xi. 3, 4. On the integrity of his heart and the skilfulness of his hands all his subjects may entirely rely, and *of the increase of his government* and people *there shall be no end.*

PSALM LXXIX.

This psalm, if penned with any particular event in view, is with most probability made to refer to the destruction of Jerusalem and the temple, and the woeful havoc made of the Jewish nation by the Chaldeans under Nebuchadnezzar. It is set to the same tune, as I may say, with the Lamentations of Jeremiah, and that weeping prophet borrows two verses out of it (ver. 6, 7) and makes use of them in his prayer, Jer. x. 25. Some think it was penned long before by the spirit of prophecy, prepared for the use of the church in that cloudy and dark day. Others think that it was penned then by the spirit of prayer, either by a prophet named Asaph or by some other prophet for the sons of Asaph. Whatever the particular occasion was, we have here, I. A representation of the very deplorable condition that the people of God were in at this time, ver. 1—5. II. A petition to God for succour and relief, that their enemies might be reckoned with (ver. 6, 7, 10, 12), that their sins might be pardoned (ver. 8, 9), and that they might be delivered, ver. 11. III. A plea taken from the readiness of his people to praise him, ver. 13. In times of the church's peace and prosperity this psalm may, in the singing of it, give us occasion to bless God that we are not thus trampled on and insulted. But it is especially seasonable in a day of treading down and perplexity, for the exciting of our desires towards God and the encouragement of our faith in him as the church's patron.

A psalm of Asaph.

O GOD, the heathen are come into thine inheritance; thy holy temple have they defiled ; they have laid Jerusalem on heaps. 2 The dead bodies of thy servants have they given *to be* meat unto the fowls of the heaven, the flesh of thy saints unto the beasts of the earth. 3 Their blood have they shed like water round about Jerusalem ; and *there was* none to bury *them.* 4 We are become a reproach to our neighbours, a scorn and derision to them that are round about us. 5 How long, LORD ? wilt thou be angry for ever ? shall thy jealousy burn like fire ?

We have here a sad complaint exhibited in the court of heaven. The world is full of complaints, and so is the church too, for it suffers, not only with it, but from it, as *a lily among thorns.* God is complained to; whither should children go with their grievances, but to their father, to such a father as is able and willing to help? The heathen are complained of, who, being themselves aliens from the commonwealth of Israel, were sworn enemies to it. Though they knew not God, nor owned him, yet, God having them in a chain, the church very fitly appeals to him against them; for he is King of nations, to overrule them, to judge among the heathen, and King of saints, to favour and protect them. I. They complain here of the anger of their enemies and the outrageous fury of the oppressor, exerted,

1. Against places, *v.* 1. They did all the mischief they could, (1.) To the holy land; they invaded that, and made inroads into it: " *The heathen have come into thy inheritance,* to plunder that, and lay it waste." Canaan was dearer to the pious Israelites as it was God's inheritance than as it was their own, as it was the land in which God was known and his name was great rather than as it was the land in which they were bred and born and which they and their ancestors had been long in possession of. Note, Injuries done to religion should grieve us more than even those done to common right, nay, to our own right. We should better bear to see our own inheritance wasted than God's inheritance. This psalmist had mentioned it in the foregoing psalm as an instance of God's great favour to Israel that he had *cast out the heathen before them,* lxxviii. 55. But see what a change sin made; now the heathen are suffered to pour in upon them. (2.) To the holy city : *They have laid Jerusalem on heaps,* heaps of rubbish, such heaps as are raised over graves, so some. The inhabitants were buried in the ruins of their own houses, and their dwelling places became their sepulchres, their long homes. (3.) To the holy house. That sanctuary which God had built like high palaces, and which was thought to be established as the earth, was now laid level with the ground : *Thy holy temple have they defiled,* by entering into it and laying it waste. God's own people had defiled it by their sins, and therefore God suffered their enemies to defile it by their insolence.

2. Against persons, against the bodies of God's people; and further their malice could not reach. (1.) They were prodigal of their blood, and killed them without mercy; their eye did not spare, nor did they give any quarter (*v.* 3): *Their blood have they shed like water,* wherever they met with them, *round about Jerusalem,* in all the avenues to the city; whoever *went out or came in* was *waited for of the sword.* Abundance of human blood was shed, so that the channels of water ran with blood. And they shed it with no more reluctancy or regret than if they had spilt so much water, little thinking that every drop

of it will be reckoned for in the day when *God shall make inquisition for blood.* (2.) They were abusive to their dead bodies. When they had killed them they would let none bury them. Nay, those that were buried, even the *dead bodies of God's servants, the flesh of his saints,* whose names and memories they had a particular spite at, they dug up again, and *gave them to be meat to the fowls of the heaven and to the beasts of the earth;* or, at least, they left those so exposed whom they slew; they hung them in chains, which was in a particular manner grievous to the Jews to see, because God had given them an express law against this, as a barbarous thing, Deut. xxi. 23. This inhuman usage of Christ's witnesses is foretold (Rev. xi. 9), and thus even the dead bodies were witnesses against their persecutors. This is mentioned (says Austin, *De Civitate Dei, lib.* i. *cap.* 12) not as an instance of the misery of the persecuted (for the bodies of the saints shall rise in glory, however they became meat to the birds and the fowls), but of the malice of the persecutors.

3. Against their names (*v.* 4): "*We that survive have become a reproach to our neighbours;* they all study to abuse us and load us with contempt, and represent us as ridiculous, or odious, or both, upbraiding us with our sins and with our sufferings, or giving the lie to our relation to God and expectations from him; so that we have become *a scorn and derision to those that are round about us.*" If God's professing people degenerate from what themselves and their fathers were, they must expect to be told of it; and it is well if a just reproach will help to bring us to a true repentance. But it has been the lot of the gospel-Israel to be made unjustly a reproach and derision; the apostles themselves were *counted as the offscouring of all things.*

II. They wonder more at God's anger, *v.* 5. This they discern in the anger of their neighbours, and this they complain most of: *How long, Lord, wilt thou be angry?* Shall it be *for ever?* This intimates that they desired no more than that God would be reconciled to them, that his anger might be turned away, and then the remainder of men's wrath would be restrained. Note, Those who desire God's favour as better than life cannot but dread and deprecate his wrath as worse than death.

6 Pour out thy wrath upon the heathen that have not known thee, and upon the kingdoms that have not called upon thy name. 7 For they have devoured Jacob, and laid waste his dwelling place. 8 O remember not against us former iniquities: let thy tender mercies speedily prevent us: for we are brought very low. 9 Help us, O God of our salvation, for the glory of thy name: and deliver us, and purge away our sins, for thy

542

name's sake. 10 Wherefore should the heathen say, Where *is* their God? let him be known among the heathen in our sight *by* the revenging of the blood of thy servants *which is* shed. 11 Let the sighing of the prisoner come before thee; according to the greatness of thy power preserve thou those that are appointed to die; 12 And render unto our neighbours sevenfold into their bosom their reproach, wherewith they have reproached thee, O Lord. 13 So we thy people and sheep of thy pasture will give thee thanks for ever: we will show forth thy praise to all generations.

The petitions here put up to God are very suitable to the present distresses of the church, and they have pleas to enforce them, interwoven with them, taken mostly from God's honour.

I. They pray that God would so turn away his anger from them as to turn it upon those that persecuted and abused them (*v.* 6): "*Pour out thy wrath,* the full vials of it, *upon the heathen;* let them wring out the dregs of it, and drink them." This prayer is in effect a prophecy, in which the *wrath of God is revealed from heaven against all ungodliness and unrighteousness of men.* Observe here, 1. The character of those he prays against; they are such as have not known God, nor called upon his name. The reason why men do not call upon God is because they do not know him, how able and willing he is to help them. Those that persist in ignorance of God, and neglect of prayer, are the ungodly, who live *without God in the world.* There are kingdoms that know not God and obey not the gospel, but neither their multitude nor their force united will secure them from his just judgments. 2. Their crime: *They have devoured Jacob, v.* 7. That is crime enough in the account of him who reckons that those who touch his people touch the apple of his eye. They have not only disturbed, but devoured, Jacob, not only encroached upon his dwelling place, the land of Canaan, but laid it waste by plundering and depopulating it. (3.) Their condemnation: *Pour out thy wrath* upon them; do not only restrain them from doing further mischief, but reckon with them for the mischief they have done."

II. They pray for the pardon of sin, which they own to be the procuring cause of all their calamities. How unrighteous soever men were, God was righteous in permitting them to do what they did. They pray, 1. That God would not *remember against them their former iniquities* (*v.* 8), either their own former iniquities, that now, when they were old, they might not be made to possess the iniquities of their youth, or the former iniquities of their people, the sins of their ancestors. In the captivity of Babylon former iniquities were brought to account; but God promises not again to do so (Jer. xxxi. 29, 30), and so they pray, " Remember not against us our first sins," which some make to look as far back as the golden calf, because God said, *In the day when I visit I will visit for this sin* of theirs *upon them,* Exod. xxxii. 34. If the children by repentance and reformation cut off the entail of the parents' sin, they may in faith pray that God will not *remember them against them.* When God pardons sin he blots it out and remembers it no more. 2. That he would purge away the sins they had been lately guilty of, by the guilt of which their minds and consciences had been defiled: *Deliver us, and purge away our sins, v.* 9. Then deliverances from trouble are granted in love, and are mercies indeed, when they are grounded upon the pardon of sin and flow from that; we should therefore be more earnest with God in prayer for the removal of our sins than for the removal of our afflictions, and the pardon of them is the foundation and sweetness of our deliverances.

III. They pray that God would work deliverance for them, and bring their troubles to a good end and that speedily: *Let thy tender mercies speedily prevent us, v.* 8. They had no hopes but from God's mercies, his tender mercies; their case was so deplorable that they looked upon themselves as the proper objects of divine compassion, and so near to desperate that, unless divine mercy did speedily interpose to prevent their ruin, they were undone. This whets their importunity: " *Lord, help us; Lord, deliver us;* help us under our troubles, that we may bear them well; help us out of our troubles, that the spirit may not fail. Deliver us from sin, from sinking." Three things they plead.— 1. The great distress they were reduced to: " *We are brought very low,* and, being low, shall be lost if thou help us not." The lower we are brought the more need we have of help from heaven and the more will divine power be magnified in raising us up. 2. Their dependence upon him: "Thou art the *God of our salvation,* who alone canst help. *Salvation belongs to the Lord,* from whom we expect help; for *in the Lord alone is the salvation of his people.*" Those who make God the God of their salvation shall find him so. 3. The interest of his own honour in their case. They plead no merit of theirs; they pretend to none; but, " *Help us for the glory of thy name;* pardon us for thy name's sake." The best encouragements in prayer are those that are taken from God only, and those things whereby he has made himself known. Two things are insinuated in this plea :—(1.) That God's name and honour would be greatly injured if he did not deliver them; for those that derided them blasphemed God, as if he were weak and could not help them, or had withdrawn and would not; therefore they

plead (*v.* 10), " *Wherefore should the heathen say, Where is their God?* He has forsaken them, and forgotten them; and this they get by worshipping a God whom they cannot see." (*Nil præter nubes et cœli numen adorant.* Juv. *—They adore no other divinity than the clouds and the sky.*) That which was their praise (that they served a God that is every where) was now turned to their reproach and his too, as if they served a God that is nowhere. "Lord," say they, "make it to appear that thou art by making it to appear that thou art with us and for us, that when we are asked, *Where is your God?* we may be able to say, He is nigh unto us in all that which we call upon him for, and you see he is so by what he does for us." (2.) That God's name and honour would be greatly advanced if he did deliver them; his mercy would be glorified in delivering those that were so miserable and helpless. By making bare his everlasting arm on their behalf he would make unto himself an everlasting name; and their deliverance would be a type and figure of the great salvation, which in the fulness of time Messiah the Prince would work out, to the glory of God's name.

IV. They pray that God would avenge them on their adversaries, 1. For their cruelty and barbarity (*v.* 10): " Let the avenging of our blood" (according to the ancient law, Gen. ix. 6) " be known among the heathen; let them be made sensible that what judgments are brought upon them are punishments of the wrong they have done to us; let this be in our sight, and by this means *let God be known among the heathen* as *the God to whom vengeance belongs* (xciv. 1) and the God that espouses his people's cause." Those that have intoxicated themselves with the blood of the saints shall have *blood given them to drink,* for they are worthy. 2. For their insolence and scorn (*v.* 12): " *Render to them their reproach.* The indignities which by word and deed they have done to the people of God himself and his name let them be repaid to them with interest." The reproach wherewith men have reproached us only we must leave it to God whether he will render to them or no, and must pray that he would forgive them; but the reproach wherewith they have blasphemed God himself we may in faith pray that God would render seven-fold into their bosoms, so as to strike at their hearts, to humble them, and bring them to repentance. This prayer is a prophecy, of the same import with that of Enoch, that God will convince sinners of all their hard speeches which they have spoken against him (Jude 15) and will return them into their own bosoms by everlasting terrors at the remembrance of them.

V. They pray that God would find out a way for the rescue of his poor prisoners, especially the condemned prisoners, *v.* 11. The case of their brethren who had fallen into the hands of the enemy was very sad; they were kept close prisoners, and, because they durst not be heard to bemoan themselves, they vented their griefs in deep and silent sighs. All their breathing was sighing, and so was their praying. They were appointed to die, as sheep for the slaughter, and had received the sentence of death within themselves. This deplorable case the psalmist recommends, 1. To the divine pity: *"Let their sighs come up before thee,* and be thou pleased to take cognizance of their moans." 2. To the divine power: *"According to the greatness of thy arm,* which no creature can contest with, *preserve thou those that are appointed to die* from the death to which they are appointed." Man's extremity is God's opportunity to appear for his people. See 2 Cor. i. 8—10.

Lastly, They promise the returns of praise for the answers of prayer (*v.* 13): *So we will give thee thanks for ever.* Observe, 1. How they please themselves with their relation to God. "Though we are oppressed and brought low, yet we are the sheep of thy pasture, not disowned and cast off by thee for all this: *We are thine; save us."* 2. How they promise themselves an opportunity of praising God for their deliverance, which they *therefore* desired, and would bid welcome, because it would furnish them with matter for thanksgiving and put their hearts in tune for that excellent work, the work of heaven. 3. How they oblige themselves not only to give God thanks at present, but to *show forth his praise unto all generations,* that is, to do all they could both to perpetuate the remembrance of God's favours to them and to engage their posterity to keep up the work of praise. 4. How they plead this with God: "Lord, appear for us against our enemies; for, if they get the better, they will *blaspheme thee* (*v.* 12); but, if we be delivered, we will praise thee. Lord, we are that people of thine which thou hast *formed for thyself, to show forth thy praise;* if we be cut off, whence shall that rent, that tribute, be raised?" Note, Those lives that are entirely devoted to God's praise are assuredly taken under his protection.

PSALM LXXX.

This psalm is much to the same purport with the foregoing. Some think it was penned upon occasion of the desolation and captivity of the ten tribes, as the foregoing psalm of the two. But many were the distresses of the Israel of God, many perhaps which are not recorded in the sacred history, some whereof might give occasion for the drawing up of this psalm, which is proper to be sung in the day of Jacob's trouble, and if, in singing it, we express a true love to the church and a hearty concern for its interest, with a firm confidence in God's power to help it out of its greatest distresses, we make melody with our hearts to the Lord. The psalmist here, I. Begs for the tokens of God's presence with them and favour to them, ver. 1—3. II. He complains of the present rebukes they were under, ver. 4—7. III. He illustrates the present rebukes of the church, by the comparison of a vine and a vineyard, which had flourished, but was now destroyed, ver. 8—16. IV. He concludes with prayer to God for the preparing of mercy for them and the preparing of them for mercy, ver. 17—19. This, as many psalms before and after, relates to the public interests of God's Israel, which ought to lie nearer to our hearts than any secular interest of our own.

To the chief musician upon Shoshannim, Eduth. A psalm of Asaph.

G IVE ear, O Shepherd of Israel, thou that leadest Joseph like a flock; thou that dwellest *between* the cherubims, shine forth. 2 Before Ephraim and Benjamin and Manasseh stir up thy strength, and come *and* save us. 3 Turn us again, O God, and cause thy face to shine; and we shall be saved. 4 O LORD God of hosts, how long wilt thou be angry against the prayer of thy people? 5 Thou feedest them with the bread of tears; and givest them tears to drink in great measure. 6 Thou makest us a strife unto our neighbours: and our enemies laugh among themselves. 7 Turn us again, O God of hosts, and cause thy face to shine; and we shall be saved.

The psalmist here, in the name of the church, applies to God by prayer, with reference to the present afflicted state of Israel.

I. He entreats God's favour for them (*v.* 1, 2); that is all in all to the sanctuary when it is desolate, and is to be sought in the first place. Observe, 1. How he eyes God in his address as the Shepherd of Israel, whom he had called the *sheep of his pasture* (lxxix. 13), under whose guidance and care Israel was, as the sheep are under the care and conduct of the shepherd. Christ is the great and good Shepherd, to whom we may in faith commit the custody of his sheep that were given to him. He *leads Joseph like a flock,* to the best pastures, and out of the way of danger; if Joseph follow him not as obsequiously as the sheep do the shepherd, it is his own fault. He *dwells between the cherubim,* where he is ready to receive petitions and to give directions. The mercy-seat was between the cherubim; and it is very comfortable in prayer to look up to God as sitting on a throne of grace, and that it is so to us is owing to the great propitiation, for the mercy-seat was the propitiatory. 2. What he expects and desires from God, that he would give ear to the cry of their miseries and of their prayers, that he would shine forth both in his own glory and in favour and kindness to his people, that he would show himself and smile on them, that he would *stir up his strength,* that he would excite it and exert it. It had seemed to slumber: "Lord, awaken it." His cause met with great opposition and the enemies threatened to overpower it: "Lord, put forth thy strength so much the more, and come for salvation to us; be to thy people a powerful help and a present help; Lord, do this *before Ephraim, Benjamin, and Manasseh,"* that is, "in the sight of all the tribes of Israel; let them see it to their satisfaction." Perhaps these three tribes are named because they were the tribes which formed that squadron of the camp of Israel that in their march through the wilderness followed next after the tabernacle; so that before them the ark of God's strength rose to scatter their enemies.

II. He complains of God's displeasure against them. God was angry, and he dreads that more than any thing, *v.* 4. 1. It was great anger. He apprehended that God was *angry against the prayer of his people*, not only that he was angry notwithstanding their prayers, by which they hoped to turn away his wrath from them, but that he was angry with their prayers, though they were his own people that prayed. That God should be angry at the sins of his people and at the prayers of his enemies is not strange; but that he should be angry at the prayers of his people is strange indeed. He not only delayed to answer them (that he often does in love), but he was displeased at them. If he be really angry at the prayers of his people, we may be sure it is because they ask amiss, Jam. iv. 3. They pray, but they do not wrestle in prayer; their ends are not right, or there is some secret sin harboured and indulged in them; they do not lift up pure hands, or they lift them up with wrath and doubting. But perhaps it is only in their own apprehension; he seems angry with their prayers when really he is not; for thus he will try their patience and perseverance in prayer, as Christ tried the woman of Canaan when he said, *It is not meet to take the children's bread and cast it to dogs.* 2. It was anger that had continued a great while: "*How long wilt thou be angry?* We have still continued praying and yet are still under thy frowns." Now the tokens of God's displeasure which they had been long under were both their sorrow and shame. (1.) Their sorrow (*v.* 5): *Thou feedest them with the bread of tears;* they eat their meat from day to day in tears; this is the vinegar in which they *dipped their morsel,* xlii. 3. They had tears given them to drink, not now and then a taste of that bitter cup, but in great measure. Note, There are many that spend their time in sorrow who yet shall spend their eternity in joy. (2.) It was their shame, *v.* 6. God, by frowning upon them, made them a strife unto their neighbours; each strove which should expose them most, and such a cheap and easy prey were they made to them that all the strife was who should have the stripping and plundering of them. Their enemies laughed among themselves to see the frights they were in, the straits they were reduced to, and the disappointments they met with. When God is displeased with his people we must expect to see them in tears and their enemies in triumph.

III. He prays earnestly for converting grace in order to their acceptance with God, and their salvation: *Turn us again, O God! v.* 3. *Turn us again, O God of hosts!* (*v.* 7) and then *cause thy face to shine and we shall be saved.* It is the burden of the song, for we have it again, *v.* 19. They are conscious to themselves that they have gone astray from God and their duty, and have turned aside into sinful ways, and that it was this that provoked God to hide his face from them and to give them up into the hand of their enemies; and therefore they desire to begin their work at the right end : "Lord, turn us to thee in a way of repentance and reformation, and then, no doubt, thou wilt return to us in a way of mercy and deliverance." Observe, 1. No salvation but from God's favour : "*Cause thy face to shine,* let us have thy love and the light of thy countenance, and then we shall be saved." 2. No obtaining favour with God unless we be converted to him. We must turn again to God from the world and the flesh, and then he will cause his face to shine upon us. 3. No conversion to God but by his own grace; we must frame our doings to turn to him (Hos. v. 4) and then pray earnestly for his grace, *Turn thou me, and I shall be turned,* pleading that gracious promise (Prov. i. 23), *Turn you at my reproof; behold, I will pour out my Spirit unto you.* The prayer here is for a national conversion; in this method we must pray for national mercies, that what is amiss may be amended, and then our grievances would be soon redressed. National holiness would secure national happiness.

8 Thou hast brought a vine out of Egypt : thou hast cast out the heathen, and planted it. 9 Thou preparedst *room* before it, and didst cause it to take deep root, and it filled the land. 10 The hills were covered with the shadow of it, and the boughs thereof *were like* the goodly cedars. 11 She sent out her boughs unto the sea, and her branches unto the river. 12 Why hast thou *then* broken down her hedges, so that all they which pass by the way do pluck her ? 13 The boar out of the wood doth waste it, and the wild beast of the field doth devour it. 14 Return, we beseech thee, O God of hosts : look down from heaven, and behold, and visit this vine ; 15 And the vineyard which thy right hand hath planted, and the branch *that* thou madest strong for thyself. 16 *It is* burned with fire, *it is* cut down : they perish at the rebuke of thy countenance. 17 Let thy hand be upon the man of thy right hand, upon the son of man *whom* thou madest strong for thyself. 18 So will not we go back from thee : quicken us, and we will call upon thy name. 19 Turn us again, O LORD God of hosts, cause

thy face to shine; and we shall be saved.

The psalmist is here presenting his suit for the Israel of God, and pressing it home at the throne of grace, pleading with God for mercy and grace for them. The church is here represented as a vine (*v.* 8, 14) and a vineyard, *v.* 15. The root of this vine is Christ, Rom. xi. 18. The branches are believers, John xv. 5. The church is like a vine, weak and needing support, unsightly and having an unpromising outside, but spreading and fruitful, and its fruit most excellent. The church is a choice and noble vine; we have reason to acknowledge the goodness of God that he has planted such a vine in the wilderness of this world, and preserved it to this day. Now observe here,

I. How the vine of the Old-Testament church was planted at first. It was *brought out of Egypt* with a high hand; *the heathen were cast out* of Canaan to make room for it, seven nations to make room for that one. *Thou didst sweep before it* (so some read *v.* 9), to make clear work; the nations were swept away as dirt with the besom of destruction. God, having made room for it, and planted it, caused it to take deep root by a happy establishment of their government both in church and state, which was so firm that, though their neighbours about them often attempted it, they could not prevail to pluck it up.

II. How it spread and flourished. 1. The land of Canaan itself was fully peopled. At first they were not so numerous as to replenish it, Exod. xxiii. 29. But in Solomon's time *Judah and Israel were many as the sand of the sea;* the land was filled with them, and yet such a fruitful land that it was not over-stocked, *v.* 10. The hills of Canaan were covered with their shadow, and the branches, though they extended themselves far, like those of the vine, yet were not weak like them, but as strong as those of the goodly cedars. Israel not only had abundance of men, but those mighty men of valour. 2. They extended their conquests and dominion to the neighbouring countries (*v.* 11): *She sent out her boughs to the sea,* the great sea westward, and *her branches to the river,* to the river of Egypt southward, the river of Damascus northward, or rather the river Euphrates eastward, Gen. xv. 18. Nebuchadnezzar's greatness is represented by a flourishing tree, Dan. iv. 20, 21. But it is observable here concerning this vine that it is praised for its *shadow,* its *boughs,* and its *branches,* but not a word of its fruit, for *Israel was an empty vine,* Hos. x. 1. God came looking for grapes, but, behold, wild grapes, Isa. v. 2. And, if a vine do not bring forth fruit, no tree so useless, so worthless, Ezek. xv. 2, 6.

III. How it was wasted and ruined: "Lord, thou hast done great things for this vine, and why shall it be all undone again? If it were a plant not of God's planting, it were not strange to see it rooted up; but will God desert and abandon that which he himself gave being to?" *v.* 12. *Why hast thou then broken down her hedges?* There was a good reason for this change in God's way towards them. This noble vine had become *the degenerate plant of a strange vine* (Jer. ii. 21), to the reproach of its great owner, and then no marvel if he *took away its hedge* (Isa. v. 5); yet God's former favours to this vine are urged as pleas in prayer to God, and improved as encouragements to faith, that, notwithstanding all this, God would not wholly cast them off. Observe, 1. The malice and enmity of the Gentile nations against Israel. As soon as ever God *broke down their hedges* and left them exposed troops of enemies presently broke in upon them, that waited for an opportunity to destroy them. Those that passed by the way plucked at them; the *boar out of the wood* and the *wild beast of the field* were ready to ravage it, *v.* 13. But, 2. See also the restraint which these cruel enemies were under; for till God had *broken down their hedges* they could not pluck a leaf of this vine. The devil could not hurt Job so long as God continued the *hedge round about him,* Job i. 10. See how much it is the interest of any people to keep themselves in the favour of God and then they need not fear any wild beast of the field, Job v. 23. If we provoke God to withdraw, *our defence has departed from us,* and we are undone. The deplorable state of Israel is described (*v.* 16): *It is burnt with fire; it is cut down:* the people are treated like thorns and briers, that are nigh unto cursing and whose end is to be burned, and no longer like vines that are protected and cherished. They perish not through the rage of the wild beast and the boar, but *at the rebuke of thy countenance;* that was it which they dreaded and to which they attributed all their calamities. It is well or ill with us according as we are under God's smiles or frowns.

IV. What their requests were to God hereupon. 1. That God would help the vine (*v.* 14, 15), that he would graciously take cognizance of its case and do for it as he thought fit: " *Return, we beseech thee, O Lord of hosts!* for thou hast seemed to go away from us. *Look down from heaven,* to which thou hast retired,—from heaven, that place of prospect, whence thou seest all the wrongs that are done us, that place of power, whence thou canst send effectual relief,— from heaven, where thou hast prepared a throne of judgment, to which we appeal, and where thou hast prepared a better country for those that are Israelites indeed,—thence give a gracious look, thence make a gracious visit, to this vine. Take our woeful condition into thy compassionate consideration, and for the particular fruits of thy pity we refer ourselves to thee. Only behold the vineyard, or rather the root, which *thy right hand hath planted*, and which therefore we hope thy right hand will protect, that *branch which thou madest strong for thyself*, to show forth thy praise (Isa. xliii. 21), that with the fruit of it thou mightest be honoured. Lord, it is formed by thyself and for thyself, and therefore it may with a humble confidence be committed to thyself and to thy own care." *As for God, his work is perfect.* What we read the *branch* in the Hebrew is the *son (Ben)*, whom in thy counsel thou hast made strong for thyself. That branch was to come out of the stock of Israel *(my servant the branch,* Zech. iii. 8), and therefore, till he should come, Israel in general, and the house of David in particular, must be preserved, and upheld, and kept in being. *He is the true vine,* John xv. 1; Isa. xi. 1. *Destroy it not for that blessing is in it,* Isa. lxv. 8. 2. That he would help the vine-dresser *(v.* 17, 18): " *Let thy hand be upon the man of thy right hand,"* that king (whoever it was) of the house of David that was now to go in and out before them; " let thy hand be upon him, not only to protect and cover him, but to own him, and strengthen him, and give him success." We have this phrase, Ezra vii. 28, *And I was strengthened as the hand of the Lord my God was upon me.* Their king is called the *man of God's right hand* as he was the representative of their state, which was dear to God, as his Benjamin, the *son of his right hand,* as he was president in their affairs and an instrument in God's right hand of much good to them, defending them from themselves and from their enemies and directing them in the right way, and as he was under-shepherd under him who was the great shepherd of Israel. Princes, who have power, must remember that they are *sons of men,* of *Adam* (so the word is), that, if they are strong, it is God that has made them strong, and he has made them so for himself, for they are his ministers to serve the interests of his kingdom among men, and, if they do this in sincerity, *his hand shall be upon them;* and we should pray in faith that it may be so, adding this promise, that, if God will adhere to our governors, we will adhere to him: *So will not we go back from thee;* we will never desert a cause which we see that God espouses and is the patron of. Let God be our leader and we will follow him. Adding also this prayer, " *Quicken us,* put life into us, revive our dying interests, revive our drooping spirits, and then *we will call upon thy name.* We will continue to do so upon all occasions, having found it not in vain to do so." We cannot call upon God's name in a right manner unless he quicken us; but it is he that puts life into our souls, that puts liveliness into our prayers. But many interpreters, both Jewish and Christian, apply this to the Messiah, the Son of David, the protector and Saviour of the church and the keeper of the vineyard. (1.) He is the man of God's right hand, to whom he has

sworn by his right hand (so the Chaldee), whom he has exalted to his right hand, and who is indeed his right hand, the arm of the Lord, for all power is given to him. (2.) He is that son of man whom he *made strong for himself,* for the glorifying of his name and the advancing of the interests of his kingdom among men. (3.) God's hand is upon him throughout his whole undertaking, to bear him out and carry him on, to protect and animate him, that the *good pleasure of the Lord might prosper in his hand.* (4.) The stability and constancy of believers are entirely owing to the grace and strength which are laid up for us in Jesus Christ, lxviii. 28. In him is our strength found, by which we are enabled to persevere to the end. Let thy hand be upon him; on him let our help be laid who is mighty; let him be made able to save to the uttermost and that will be our security; *so will not we go back from thee.*

Lastly, The psalm concludes with the same petition that had been put up twice before, and yet it is no vain repetition *(v.* 19): *Turn us again.* The title given to God rises, *v.* 3, O God! *v.* 7, O God of hosts! *v.* 19, O Lord *(Jehovah) God of hosts!* When we come to God for his grace, his good-will towards us and his good work in us, we should pray earnestly, continue instant in prayer, and pray more earnestly.

PSALM LXXXI.

This psalm was penned, as is supposed, not upon occasion of any particular providence, but for the solemnity of a particular ordinance, either that of the new-moon in general or that of the feast of trumpets on the new moon of the seventh month, Lev. xxiii. 24; Num. xxix. 1. When David, by the Spirit, introduced the singing of psalms into the temple-service this psalm was intended for that day, to excite and assist the proper devotions of it. All the psalms are profitable; but, if one psalm be more suitable than another to the day and the observances of it, we should choose that. The two great intentions of our religious assemblies, and which we ought to have in our eye in our attendance on them, are answered in this psalm, which are, to give glory to God and to receive instruction from God, to " behold the beauty of the Lord and to enquire in his temple:" accordingly by this psalm we are assisted on our solemn feast-days, I. In praising God for what he is to his people (ver. 1—3), and has done for them, ver. 4—7. II. In teaching and admonishing one another concerning the obligations we lie under to God (ver. 8—10), the danger of revolting from him (ver. 11, 12), and the happiness we should have if we would but keep close to him, ver. 13—16. This, though spoken primarily of Israel of old, is written for our learning, and is therefore to be sung with application.

To the chief musician upon Gittith. *A psalm of Asaph.*

SING aloud unto God our strength: make a joyful noise unto the God of Jacob. 2 Take a psalm, and bring hither the timbrel, the pleasant harp with the psaltery. 3 Blow up the trumpet in the new moon, in the time appointed, on our solemn feast day. 4 For this *was* a statute for Israel, *and* a law of the God of Jacob. 5 This he ordained in Joseph *for* a testimony, when he went out through the land of Egypt: *where* I heard a language *that* I understood not. 6 I removed his shoulder from the burden: his hands were delivered from the pots. 7 Thou calledst in trouble, and I delivered thee; I answered thee in the secret place of thunder : I proved thee at the waters of Meribah. Selah.

When the people of God were gathered together in *the solemn day, the day of the feast of the Lord,* they must be told that they had business to do, for we do not go to church to sleep nor to be idle; no, there is that which the duty of every day requires, work of the day, which is to be done in its day. And here,

I. The worshippers of God are excited to their work, and are taught, by singing this psalm, to stir up both themselves and one another to it, *v.* 1—3. Our errand is, to give unto God the glory due unto his name, and in all our religious assemblies we must mind this as our business. 1. In doing this we must eye God as *our strength,* and as *the God of Jacob, v.* 1. He is the strength of Israel, as a people; for he is a God in covenant with them, who will powerfully protect, support, and deliver them, who fights their battles and makes them do valiantly and victoriously. He is the strength of every Israelite; by his grace we are enabled to go through all our services, sufferings, and conflicts; and to him, as our strength, we must pray, and we must sing praise to him as the God of all the wrestling seed of Jacob, with whom we have a spiritual communion. 2. We must do this by all the expressions of holy joy and triumph. It was then to be done by musical instruments, the *timbrel, harp, and psaltery;* and by blowing *the trumpet,* some think in remembrance of the sound of the trumpet on Mount Sinai, which waxed louder and louder. It was then and is now to be done by singing psalms, singing *aloud,* and making *a joyful noise.* The pleasantness of the harp and the awfulness of the trumpet intimate to us that God is to be worshipped with cheerfulness and holy joy, with reverence and godly fear. Singing aloud and making a noise intimate that we must be warm and affectionate in praising God, that we must with a hearty good-will show forth his praise, as those that are not ashamed to own our dependence on him and obligations to him, and that we should join many together in this work; the more the better; it is the more like heaven. 3. This must be done in the time appointed. No time is amiss for praising God *(Seven times a day will I praise thee;* nay, *at midnight will I rise and give thanks unto thee);* but some are times appointed, not for God to meet us (he is always ready), but for us to meet one another, that we may join together in praising God. The solemn feast-day must be a day of praise; when we are receiving the gifts of God's bounty, and rejoicing in them, then it is proper to sing his praises.

II. They are here directed in their work. 1. They must look up to the divine institu-

548

tion which it is the observation of. In all religious worship we must have an eye to the command (*v.* 4): *This was a statute for Israel,* for the keeping up of a face of religion among them; it was *a law of the God of Jacob,* which all the seed of Jacob are bound by, and must be subject to. Note, Praising God is not only a good thing, which we do well to do, but it is our indispensable duty, which we are obliged to do; it is at our peril if we neglect it; and in all religious exercises we must have an eye to the institution as our warrant and rule : " This I do because God has commanded me; and therefore I hope he will accept me;" then it is done in faith. 2. They must look back upon those operations of divine Providence which it is the memorial of. This solemn service was *ordained for a testimony* (*v.* 5), a standing traditional evidence, for the attesting of the matters of fact. It was a testimony to Israel, that they might know and remember what God had done for their fathers, and would be a testimony against them if they should be ignorant of them and forget them. (1.) The psalmist, in the people's name, puts himself in mind of the general work of God on Israel's behalf, which was kept in remembrance by this and other solemnities, *v.* 5. When God went out against the land of Egypt, to lay it waste, that he might force Pharaoh to let Israel go, then he ordained solemn feast-days to be observed by a statute for ever in their generations, as a memorial of it, particularly the passover, which perhaps is meant by the *solemn feast-day* (*v.* 3); that was appointed just then when God went out through the land of Egypt to destroy the first-born, and passed over the houses of the Israelites, Exod. xii. 23, 24. By it that work of wonder was to be kept in perpetual remembrance, that all ages might in it behold the goodness and severity of God. The psalmist, speaking for his people, takes notice of this aggravating circumstance of their slavery in Egypt that there they heard a language that they understood not; there they were strangers in a strange land. The Egyptians and the Hebrews understood not one another's language; for Joseph spoke to his brethren by an interpreter (Gen. xlii. 23), and the Egyptians are said to be to the house of Jacob *a people of a strange language,* cxiv. 1. To make a deliverance appear the more gracious, the more glorious, it is good to observe every thing that makes the trouble we are delivered from appear the more grievous. (2.) The psalmist, in God's name, puts the people in mind of some of the particulars of their deliverance. Here he changes the person, *v.* 6. God speaks by him, saying, *I removed the shoulder from the burden.* Let him remember this on the feast-day, [1.] That God had brought them out of the house of bondage, had removed their shoulder from the burden of oppression under which they were ready to sink, *had delivered their hands from the pots*, or panniers, or baskets, in which they carried clay or bricks. Deliverance out of slavery is a very sensible mercy and one which ought to be had in everlasting remembrance. But this was not all. [2.] God had delivered them at the Red Sea; then they called in trouble, and he rescued them and disappointed the designs of their enemies against them, Exod. xiv. 10. Then he answered them with a real answer, out of *the secret place of thunder;* that is, out of the pillar of fire, through which God looked upon the host of the Egyptians and troubled it, Exod. xiv. 24, 25. Or it may be meant of the giving of the law at Mount Sinai, which was the secret place, for it was death to gaze (Exod. xix. 21), and it was in thunder that God then spoke. Even the terrors of Sinai were favours to Israel, Deut. iv. 33. [3.] God had borne their manners in the wilderness: "*I proved thee at the waters of Meribah;* thou didst there show thy temper, what an unbelieving murmuring people thou wast, and yet I continued my favour to thee." *Selah—Mark that;* compare God's goodness and man's badness, and they will serve as foils to each other. Now if they, on their solemn feast-days, were thus to call to mind their redemption out of Egypt, much more ought we, on the Christian sabbath, to call to mind a more glorious redemption wrought out for us by Jesus Christ from worse than Egyptian bondage, and the many gracious answers he has given to us, notwithstanding our manifold provocations.

8 Hear, O my people, and I will testify unto thee: O Israel, if thou wilt hearken unto me; 9 There shall no strange god be in thee; neither shalt thou worship any strange god. 10 I *am* the LORD thy God, which brought thee out of the land of Egypt: open thy mouth wide, and I will fill it. 11 But my people would not hearken to my voice; and Israel would none of me. 12 So I gave them up unto their own hearts' lust: *and* they walked in their own counsels. 13 Oh that my people had hearkened unto me, *and* Israel had walked in my ways! 14 I should soon have subdued their enemies, and turned my hand against their adversaries. 15 The haters of the LORD should have submitted themselves unto him: but their time should have endured for ever. 16 He should have fed them also with the finest of the wheat: and with honey out of the rock should I have satisfied thee.

God, by the psalmist, here speaks to Israel,

and in them to us, on whom the ends of the world are come.

I. He demands their diligent and serious attention to what he was about to say (*v.* 8): "*Hear, O my people!* and who should hear me if my people will not? I have heard and answered thee; now wilt thou hear me? Hear what is said with the greatest solemnity and the most unquestionable certainty, for it is what *I will testify unto thee.* Do not only give me the hearing, but *hearken unto me,* that is, be advised by me, be ruled by me." Nothing could be more reasonably nor more justly expected, and yet God puts an *if* upon it: "*If thou wilt hearken unto me.* It is thy interest to do so, and yet it is questionable whether thou wilt or no; for thy neck is an iron sinew."

II. He puts them in mind of their obligation to him as the Lord their God and Redeemer (*v.* 10): *I am the Lord thy God, who brought thee out of the land of Egypt;* this is the preface to the ten commandments, and a powerful reason for the keeping of them, showing that we are bound to it in duty, interest, and gratitude, all which bonds we break asunder if we be disobedient.

III. He gives them an abstract both of the precepts and of the promises which he gave them, as the Lord and their God, upon their coming out of Egypt. 1. The great command was that they should have no other gods before him (*v.* 9): *There shall no strange god be in thee,* none besides thy own God. Other gods might well be called strange gods, for it was very strange that ever any people who had the true and living God for their God should hanker after any other. God is jealous in this matter, for he will not suffer his glory to be given to another; and therefore in this matter they must be circumspect, Exod. xxiii. 13. 2. The great promise was that God himself, as a God all-sufficient, would be nigh unto them in all that which they called upon him for (Deut. iv. 7), that, if they would adhere to him as their powerful protector and ruler, they should always find him their bountiful benefactor : "*Open thy mouth wide and I will fill it,* as the young ravens that cry open their mouths wide and the old ones fill them." See here, (1.) What is our duty—to raise our expectations from God and enlarge our desires towards him. We cannot look for too little from the creature nor too much from the Creator. We are not straitened in him; why therefore should we be straitened in our own bosoms? (2.) What is God's promise. I will fill thy mouth with good things, ciii. 5. There is *enough in God to fill our treasures* (Prov. viii. 21), to *replenish every hungry soul* (Jer. xxxi. 25), to supply all our wants, to answer all our desires, and to make us completely happy. The pleasures of sense will surfeit and never satisfy (Isa. lv. 2); divine pleasures will satisfy and never surfeit. And we may have enough from God if we pray for it in faith. *Ask, and it shall be given you.* He *gives liberally, and upbraids not.* God assured his people Israel that it would be their own fault if he did not do as great and kind things for them as he had done for their fathers. Nothing should be thought too good, too much, to give them, if they would but keep close to God. He *would moreover have given them such and such things,* 2 Sam. xii. 8.

IV. He charges them with a high contempt of his authority as their lawgiver and his grace and favour as their benefactor, *v.* 11. He had done much for them, and designed to do more; but all in vain : *"My people would not hearken to my voice,* but turned a deaf ear to all I said." Two things he complains of :—1. Their disobedience to his commands. They did hear his voice, so as never any people did; but they would not hearken to it, they would not be ruled by it, neither by the law nor by the reason of it. 2. Their dislike of his covenant-relation to them : *They would none of me. They acquiesced not in my word* (so the Chaldee); God was willing to be to them a God, but they were not willing to be to him a people; they did not like his terms. "I would have gathered them, but they would not." They had none of him ; and why had they not ? It was not because they might not; they were fairly invited into covenant with God. It was not because they could not; for the word was nigh them, even in their mouth and in their heart. But it was purely because they would not. God calls them his people, for they were bought by him, bound to him, his by a thousand ties, and yet even they had not hearkened, had not obeyed. "Israel, the seed of Jacob my friend, set me at nought, and *would* have *none of me.*" Note, All the wickedness of the wicked world is owing to the wilfulness of the wicked will. The reason why people are not religious is because they will not be so.

V. He justifies himself with this in the spiritual judgments he had brought upon them (*v.* 12) : *So I gave them up unto their own hearts' lusts,* which would be more dangerous enemies and more mischievous oppressors to them than any of the neighbouring nations ever were. God withdrew his Spirit from them, took off the bridle of restraining grace, left them to themselves, and justly ; they will do as they will, and therefore let them do as they will. *Ephraim is joined to idols; let him alone.* It is a righteous thing with God to give those up to their own hearts' lusts that indulge them, and give up themselves to be led by them; for why should his Spirit always strive ? His grace is his own, and he is debtor to no man, and yet, as he never gave his grace to any that could say they deserved it, so he never took it away from any but such as had first forfeited it : *They would none of me, so I gave them up;* let them take their course. And see what follows : *They walked in their own counsels,* in the way of their heart and in the sight of their eye, both in their worships and in their conversations. "I left them to do as they would,

and then they did all that was ill;" they walked in their own counsels, and not according to the counsels of God and his advice. God therefore was not the author of their sin; he left them to the lusts of their own hearts and the counsels of their own heads ; if they do not well, the blame must lie upon their own hearts and the blood upon their own heads.

VI. He testifies his good-will to them in wishing they had done well for themselves. He saw how sad their case was, and how sure their ruin, when they were delivered up to their own lusts; that is worse than being given up to Satan, which may be in order to reformation (1 Tim. i. 20) and to salvation (1 Cor. v. 5); but to be delivered up to their own hearts' lusts is to be sealed under condemnation. *He that is filthy, let him be filthy still.* What fatal precipices will not these hurry a man to ! Now here God looks upon them with pity, and shows that it was with reluctance that he thus abandoned them to their folly and fate. *How shall I give thee up, Ephraim ?* Hos. xi. 8, 9. So here, *O that my people had hearkened !* See Isa. xlviii. 18. Thus Christ lamented the obstinacy of Jerusalem. *If thou hadst known,* Luke xix. 42. The expressions here are very affecting (*v.* 13 —16), designed to show how unwilling God is that any should perish and desirous that all should come to repentance (he delights not in the ruin of sinful persons or nations), and also what enemies sinners are to themselves and what an aggravation it will be of their misery that they might have been happy upon such easy terms. Observe here,

1. The great mercy God had in store for his people, and which he would have wrought for them if they had been obedient. (1.) He would have given them victory over their enemies and would soon have completed the reduction of them. They should not only have kept their ground, but have gained their point, against the remaining Canaanites, and their encroaching vexatious neighbours (*v.* 14) : *I should have subdued their enemies;* and it is God only that is to be depended on for the subduing of our enemies. Nor would he have put them to the expense and fatigue of a tedious war : he would *soon* have done it ; for he would have *turned his hand against their adversaries,* and then they would not have been able to stand before them. It intimates how easily he would have done it and without any difficulty. With the turn of a hand, nay, *with the breath of his mouth, shall he slay the wicked,* Isa. xi. 4. If he but turn his hand, the *haters of the Lord will submit themselves to him* (*v.* 15); and, though they are not brought to love him, yet they shall be made to fear him and to confess that he is too hard for them and that it is in vain to contend with him. God is honoured, and so is his Israel, by the submission of those that have been in rebellion against them, though it be but a forced and feigned submission. (2.)

He would have confirmed and perpetuated their posterity, and established it upon sure and lasting foundations. In spite of all the attempts of their enemies against them, *their time should have endured for ever,* and they should never have been disturbed in the possession of the good land God had given them, much less evicted and turned out of possession. (3.) He would have given them great plenty of all good things (*v.* 16): *He should have fed them with the finest of the wheat,* with the best grain and the best of the kind. Wheat was the staple commodity of Canaan, and they exported a great deal of it, Ezek. xxvii. 17. He would not only have provided for them the best sort of bread, but *with honey out of the rock would he have satisfied them.* Besides the precious products of the fruitful soil, that there might not be a barren spot in all their land, even the clefts of the rock should serve for bee-hives and in them they should find honey in abundance. See Deut. xxxii. 13, 14. In short, God designed to make them every way easy and happy.

2. The duty God required from them as the condition of all this mercy. He expected no more than that they should *hearken to him,* as a scholar to his teacher, to receive his instructions—as a servant to his master, to receive his commands; and that they should *walk in his ways,* those ways of the Lord which are right and pleasant, that they should observe the institutions of his ordinances and attend the intimations of his providence. There was nothing unreasonable in this.

3. Observe how the reason of the withholding of the mercy is laid in their neglect of the duty: If they had *hearkened to me, I would soon have subdued their enemies.* National sin or disobedience is the great and only thing that retards and obstructs national deliverance. *When I would have healed Israel,* and set every thing to-rights among them, then *the iniquity of Ephraim was discovered,* and so a stop was put to the cure, Hos. vii. 1. We are apt to say, " If such a method had been taken, such an instrument employed, we should soon have subdued our enemies:" but we mistake; if we had hearkened to God, and kept to our duty, the thing would have been done, but it is sin that makes our troubles long and salvation slow. And this is that which God himself complains of, and wishes it had been otherwise. Note, *Therefore* God would have us do our duty to him, that we may be qualified to receive favour from him. He delights in our serving him, not because he is the better for it, but because we shall be.

PSALM LXXXII.

This psalm is calculated for the meridian of princes' courts and courts of justice, not in Israel only, but in other nations; yet it was probably penned primarily for the use of the magistrates of Israel, the great Sanhedrim, and their other elders who were in places of power, and perhaps by David's direction. This psalm is designed to make kings wise, and "to instruct the judges of the earth" (as ii. and x.), to tell them their duty (as 2 Sam. xxiii. 3), and to tell them of their faults, as lviii. 1. We have here, I. The diguity of magistracy and its dependence upon God, ver. 1. II. The duty of magistrates, ver. 3, 4. III. The degeneracy of bad magistrates and the mischief they do, ver. 2,

5. IV. Their doom read, ver. 6, 7. V. The desire and prayer of all good people that the kingdom of God may be set up more and more, ver. 8. Though magistrates may most closely apply this psalm to themselves, yet we may any of us sing it with understanding when we give glory to God, in singing it, as presiding in all public affairs, providing for the protection of injured innocency, and ready to punish the most powerful injustice, and when we comfort ourselves with the belief of his present government and with the hopes of his future judgment.

A psalm of Asaph.

G OD standeth in the congregation of the mighty; he judgeth among the gods. 2 How long will ye judge unjustly, and accept the persons of the wicked? Selah. 3 Defend the poor and fatherless: do justice to the afflicted and needy. 4 Deliver the poor and needy: rid *them* out of the hand of the wicked. 5 They know not, neither will they understand; they walk on in darkness: all the foundations of the earth are out of course.

We have here,

I. God's supreme presidency and power in all councils and courts asserted and laid down, as a great truth necessary to be believed both by princes and subjects (*v.* 1): *God stands,* as chief director, *in the congregation of the mighty,* the mighty One, *in cœtu fortis*—*in the councils of the prince,* the supreme magistrate, and he judges among the gods, the inferior magistrates; both the legislative and the executive power of princes is under his eye and his hand. Observe here,

1. The power and honour of magistrates; they are the *mighty.* They are so in authority, for the public good (it is a great power that they are entrusted with), and they ought to be so in wisdom and courage. They are, in the Hebrew dialect, called *gods;* the same word is used for these subordinate governors that is used for the sovereign ruler of the world. They are *elohim.* Angels are so called both because they are great in power and might and because God is pleased to make use of their service in the government of this lower world; and magistrates in an inferior capacity are likewise the ministers of his providence in general, for the keeping up of order and peace in human societies, and particularly of his justice and goodness in punishing evil-doers and protecting those that do well. Good magistrates, who answer the ends of magistracy, are as God; some of his honour is put upon them; they are his vicegerents, and great blessings to any people. *A divine sentence is in the lips of the king,* Prov. xvi. 10. But, as *roaring lions and ranging bears,* so are *wicked rulers over the poor people,* Prov. xxviii. 15. 2. A good form and constitution of government intimated, and that is a mixed monarchy like ours; here is the mighty one, the sovereign, and here is his congregation, his privy-council, his parliament, his bench of judges, who are called the *gods.* 3. God's incontestable sovereignty maintained in and over all the congregations

of the mighty. *God stands, he judges among them;* they have their power from him and are accountable to him. *By him kings reign.* He is present at all their debates, and inspects all they say and do, and what is said and done amiss will be called over again, and they reckoned with for their mal-administrations. God has their hearts in his hands, and their tongues too, and he directs them *which way soever he will,* Prov. xxi. 1. So that he has a negative voice in all their resolves, and his counsels shall stand, whatever devices are in men's hearts. He makes what use he pleases of them, and serves his own purposes and designs by them; though their hearts little think so, Isa. x. 7. Let magistrates consider this and be awed by it; God is with them in the judgment, 2 Chron. xix. 6; Deut. i. 17. Let subjects consider this and be comforted with it; for good princes and good judges, who mean well, are under a divine direction, and bad ones, who mean ever so ill, are under a divine restraint.

II. A charge given to all magistrates to do good with their power, as they will answer it to him by whom they are entrusted with it, *v.* 3, 4. 1. They are to be the protectors of those who lie exposed to injury and the patrons of those who want advice and assist-ance: *Defend the poor,* who have no money wherewith to make friends or fee counsel, *and the fatherless,* who, while they are young and unable to help themselves, have lost those who would have been the guides of their youth. Magistrates, as they must be fathers to their country in general, so particularly to those in it who are fatherless. Are they called *gods?* Herein they must be followers of him, they must be *fathers of the fatherless.* Job was so, Job xxix. 12. 2. They are to administer justice impartially, and do *right to the afflicted and needy,* who, being weak and helpless, have often wrongs done them; and will be in danger of losing all if magistrates do not, *ex officio—officially,* interpose for their relief. If a poor man has an honest cause, his poverty must be no prejudice to his cause, how great and powerful soever those are that contend with him. 3. They are to rescue those who have already fallen into the hands of oppressors and deliver them (*v.* 4): *Rid them out of the hand of the wicked. Avenge them of their adversary,* Luke xviii. 3. These are clients whom there is nothing to be got by, no pay for serving them, no interest by obliging them; yet these are those whom judges and magistrates must concern themselves for, whose comfort they must consult and whose cause they must espouse.

III. A charge drawn up against bad magistrates, who neglect their duty and abuse their power, forgetting that God standeth among them, *v.* 2, 5. Observe, 1. What the sin is they are here charged with; they *judge unjustly,* contrary to the rules of equity and the dictates of their consciences, giving judgment against those who have right on their

side, out of malice and ill-will, or for those who have an unrighteous cause, out of favour and partial affection. To do unjustly is bad, but to judge unjustly is much worse, because it is doing wrong under colour of right; against such acts of injustice there is least fence for the injured and by them encouragement is given to the injurious. It was as great an evil as any Solomon saw under the sun when he observed *the place of judgment, that iniquity was there,* Eccl. iii. 16; Isa. v. 7. They not only accepted the persons of the rich because they were rich, though that is bad enough, but (which is much worse) they *accepted the persons of the wicked* because they were wicked; they not only countenanced them in their wickedness, but loved them the better for it, and fell in with their interests. Woe unto thee, O land! when thy judges are such as these. 2. What was the cause of this sin. They were told plainly enough that it was their office and duty to protect and deliver the poor; it was many a time given them in charge; yet they judge unjustly, for *they know not, neither will they understand.* They do not care to hear their duty; they will not take pains to study it; they have no desire to take things right, but are governed by interest, not by reason or justice. *A gift in secret blinds their eyes.* They know not because they will not understand. None so blind as those that will not see. They have baffled their own consciences, and so they walk on in darkness, not knowing nor caring what they do nor whither they go. Those that walk on in darkness are walking on to everlasting darkness. 3. What were the consequences of this sin: *All the foundations of the earth* (or *of the land*) *are out of course.* When justice is perverted what good can be expected? *The earth and all the inhabitants thereof are dissolved,* as the psalmist speaks in a like case, lxxv. 3. The miscarriages of public persons are public mischiefs.

6 I have said, Ye *are* gods; and all of you *are* children of the most high. 7 But ye shall die like men, and fall like one of the princes. 8 Arise, O God, judge the earth: for thou shalt inherit all nations.

We have here,

I. Earthly gods abased and brought down, *v.* 6, 7. The dignity of their character is acknowledged (*v.* 6): *I have said, You are gods* They have been honoured with the name and title of gods. God himself called them so in the statute against treasonable words Exod. xxii. 28, *Thou shalt not revile the gods.* And, if they have this style from the fountain of honour, who can dispute it? But what is man, that he should be thus magnified? He called them *gods* because *unto them the word of God came,* so our Saviour expounds it (John x. 35); they had a commission from

God, and were delegated and appointed by him to be the shields of the earth, the conservators of the public peace, and revengers to execute wrath upon those that disturb it, Rom. xiii. 4. All of them are in this sense *children of the Most High.* God has put some of his honour upon them, and employs them in his providential government of the world, as David made his sons chief rulers. Or, "Because *I said, You are gods,* you have carried the honour further than was intended and have imagined yourselves to be *the children of the Most High,*" as the king of Babylon (Isa. xiv. 14), *I will be like the Most High,* and the king of Tyre (Ezek. xxviii. 2), *Thou hast set thy heart as the heart of God.* It is a hard thing for men to have so much honour put upon them by the hand of God, and so much honour paid them, as ought to be by the children of men, and not to be proud of it and puffed up with it, and so to think of themselves above what is meet. But here follows a mortifying consideration: *You shall die like men.* This may be taken either, 1. As the punishment of bad magistrates, such as judged unjustly, and by their misrule put the *foundations of the earth out of course.* God will reckon with them, and will cut them off in the midst of their pomp and prosperity; they shall die like other wicked men, *and fall like one of the* heathen *princes* (and their being Israelites shall not secure them any more than their being judges) or like one of the angels that sinned, or like one of the giants of the old world. Compare this with that which Elihu observed concerning the mighty oppressors in his time. Job xxxiv. 26, *He striketh them as wicked men in the open sight of others.* Let those that abuse their power know that God will take both it and their lives from them; for wherein they deal proudly he will *show himself above them.* Or, 2. As the period of the glory of all magistrates in this world. Let them not be puffed up with their honour nor neglect their work, but let the consideration of their mortality be both mortifying to their pride and quickening to their duty. "You are called gods, but you have no patent for immortality; *you shall die like men,* like common men; and *like one of them, you, O princes! shall fall.*" Note, Kings and princes, all the judges of the earth, though they are gods to us, are men to God, and shall die like men, and all their honour shall be laid in the dust. *Mors sceptra ligonibus æquat—Death mingles sceptres with spades.*

II. The God of heaven exalted and raised high, *v.* 8. The psalmist finds it to little purpose to reason with these proud oppressors; they turned a deaf ear to all he said and walked on in darkness; and therefore he looks up to God, appeals to him, and begs of him *to take unto himself his great power: Arise, O God! judge the earth;* and, when he prays that he would do it, he believes that he will do it: *Thou shalt inherit all nations.*

This has respect, 1. To the kingdom of providence. God governs the world, sets up and puts down whom he pleases; he inherits all nations, has an absolute dominion over them, to dispose of them as a man does of his inheritance. This we are to believe and to comfort ourselves with, that the earth is not given so much *into the hands of the wicked,* the wicked rulers, as we are tempted to think it is, Job ix. 24. But God has reserved the power to himself and overrules them. In this faith we must pray, "*Arise, O God! judge the earth,* appear against those that judge unjustly, and set shepherds over thy people after thy own heart." There is a righteous God to whom we may have recourse, and on whom we may depend for the effectual relief of all that find themselves aggrieved by unjust judges. 2. To the kingdom of the Messiah. It is a prayer for the hastening of that, that Christ would come, who is to judge the earth, and that promise is pleaded, that God shall *give him the heathen for his inheritance.* Thou, O Christ! shalt *inherit all nations,* and be the governor over them, ii. 8; xxii. 28. Let the second coming of Christ set to-rights all these disorders. There are two words with which we may comfort ourselves and one another in reference to the mismanagements of power among men: one is Rev. xix. 6, *Hallelujah, the Lord God omnipotent reigneth;* the other is Rev. xxii. 20, *Surely I come quickly.*

PSALM LXXXIII.

This psalm is the last of those that go under the name of Asaph. It is penned, as most of those, upon a public account, with reference to the insults of the church's enemies, who sought its ruin. Some think it was penned upon occasion of the threatening descent which was made upon the land of Judah in Jehoshaphat's time by the Moabites and Ammonites, those children of Lot here spoken of (ver. 8), who were at the head of the alliance and to whom all the other states here mentioned were auxiliaries. We have the story 2 Chron. xx. 1, where it is said, The children of Moab and Ammon, and others besides them, invaded the land. Others think it was penned with reference to all the confederacies of the neighbouring nations against Israel, from first to last. The psalmist here makes an appeal and application, I. To God's knowledge, by a representation of their designs and endeavours to destroy Israel, ver. 1—8. II. To God's justice and jealousy, both for his church and for his own honour, by an earnest prayer for the defeat of their attempt, that the church might be preserved, the enemies humbled, and God glorified, ver. 9—18. This, in the singing of it, we may apply to the enemies of the gospel-church, all anti-christian powers and factions, representing to God their confederacies against Christ and his kingdom, and rejoicing in the hope that all their projects will be baffled and the gates of hell shall not prevail against the church.

A song *or* psalm of Asaph.

KEEP not thou silence, O God: hold not thy peace, and be not still, O God. 2 For, lo, thine enemies make a tumult: and they that hate thee have lifted up the head. 3 They have taken crafty counsel against thy people, and consulted against thy hidden ones. 4 They have said, Come, and let us cut them off from *being* a nation; that the name of Israel may be no more in remembrance. 5 For they have consulted together with one consent: they are confederate against thee: 6 The tabernacles of Edom, and the Ishmaelites; of Moab, and the Hagarenes; 7 Gebal, and Ammon, and Amalek; the Philistines with the inhabitants of Tyre; 8 Assur also is joined with them: they have holpen the children of Lot. Selah.

The Israel of God were now in danger, and fear, and great distress, and yet their prayer is called, *A song or psalm;* for singing psalms is not unseasonable, no, not when the harps are hung upon the willow-trees.

I. The psalmist here begs of God to appear on the behalf of his injured threatened people (v. 1): "*Keep not thou silence, O God! but give judgment for us against those that do us an apparent wrong.*" Thus Jehoshaphat prayed upon occasion of that invasion (2 Chron. xx. 11), *Behold, how they reward us, to come to cast us out of thy possession.* Sometimes God seems to connive at the unjust treatment which is given to his people; he keeps silence, as one that either did not observe it or did not concern himself in it; he holds his peace, as if he would observe an exact neutrality, and let them fight it out; he is still, and gives not the enemies of his people any disturbance or opposition, but seems to sit by *as a man astonished, or as a mighty man that cannot save.* Then he gives us leave to call upon him, as here, "*Keep not thou silence, O God!* Lord, speak to us by the prophets for our encouragement against our fears" (as he did in reference to that invasion, 2 Chron. xx. 14, &c.); "Lord, speak for us by thy providence and speak against our enemies; speak deliverance to us and disappointment to them." God's speaking is his acting; for with him saying and doing are the same thing.

II. He here gives an account of the grand alliance of the neighbouring nations against Israel, which he begs of God to break, and blast the projects of. Now observe here,

1. Against whom this confederacy is formed; it is against the Israel of God, and so, in effect, against the God of Israel. Thus the psalmist takes care to interest God in their cause, not doubting but that, if it appeared that they were for God, God would make it to appear that he was for them, and then they might set all their enemies at defiance; for who then could be against them? "Lord," says he, "they are thy enemies, and they hate thee." All wicked people are God's enemies (the *carnal mind is enmity against God*), but especially wicked persecutors; they hated the religious worshippers of God, because they hated God's holy religion and the worship of him. This was that which made God's people so zealous against them—that they fought against God: *They are confederate against thee, v. 5.* Were our interest only concerned, we could the better bear it; but, when God himself is struck at, it is time

554

to cry, Help, Lord. *Keep not thou silence, O God!* He proves that they are confederate against God, for they are so against the people of God, who are near and dear to him, his son, his first-born, his portion, and the lot of his inheritance; he may truly be said to fight against me that endeavours to destroy my children, to root out my family, and to ruin my estate. "Lord," says the psalmist, "they are thy enemies, for they consult against thy hidden ones." Note, God's people are his hidden ones, hidden, (1.) In respect of secresy. Their life is *hid with Christ in God; the world knows them not;* if they knew them, they would not hate them as they do. (2.) In respect of safety. God takes them under his special protection, hides them in the hollow of his hand; and yet, in defiance of God and his power and promise to secure his people, they will consult to ruin them and *cast them down from their excellency* (lxii. 4), and to make a prey of those whom the *Lord has set apart for himself,* iv. 3. They resolve to destroy those whom God resolves to preserve.

2. How this confederacy is managed. The devil is at the bottom of it, and therefore it is carried on, (1.) With a great deal of heat and violence: *Thy enemies make a tumult, v. 2. The heathen rage,* ii. 1. *The nations are angry,* Rev. xi. 18. They are noisy in their clamours against the people whom they hope to run down with their loud calumnies. This comes in as a reason why God should not keep silence: "The enemies talk big and talk much; Lord, let them not talk all, but do thou *speak to them in thy wrath,*" ii. 5. (2.) With a great deal of pride and insolence: *They have lifted up the head.* In confidence of their success, they are so elevated as if they could over-top the Most High and over-power the Almighty. (3.) With a great deal of art and policy: They have *taken crafty counsel, v. 3.* The subtlety of the old serpent appears in their management, and they contrive by all possible means, though ever so base, ever so bad, to gain their point. They are *profound to make slaughter* (Hos. v. 2), as if they could outwit Infinite Wisdom. (4.) With a great deal of unanimity. Whatever separate clashing interest they have among themselves, against the people of God they *consult with one consent (v. 5),* nor is *Satan's kingdom divided against itself.* To push on this unholy war, they lay their heads together, and their horns, and their hearts too. *Fas est et ab hoste doceri—Even an enemy may instruct.* Do the enemies of the church act with one consent to destroy it? Are the kings of the earth of one mind to give their power and honour to the beast? And shall not the church's friends be unanimous in serving her interests? If Herod and Pilate are made friends, that they may join in crucifying Christ, surely Paul and Barnabas, Paul and Peter, will soon be made friends, that they may join in preaching Christ.

3. What it is that is aimed at in this confederacy. They consult not like the Gibeonites to make a league with Israel, that they might strengthen themselves by such a desirable alliance, which would have been their wisdom. They consult, not only to clip the wings of Israel, to recover their new conquests, and check the progress of their victorious arms, not only to keep the balance even between them and Israel, and to prevent their power from growing exorbitant; this will not serve. It is no less than the utter ruin and extirpation of Israel that they design (*v.* 4): " *Come, let us cut them off from being a nation*, as they cut off the seven nations of Canaan; let us leave them neither root nor branch, but lay their country so perfectly waste *that the name of Israel may be no more in remembrance*, no, not in history;" for with them they would destroy their Bibles and burn all their records. Such is the enmity of the serpent's seed against the seed of the woman. It is the secret wish of many wicked men that the church of God might not have a being in the world, that there might be no such thing as religion among mankind. Having banished the sense of it out of their own hearts, they would gladly see the whole earth as well rid of it, all its laws and ordinances abolished, all its restraints and obligations shaken off, and all that preach, profess, or practise it cut off. This they would bring it to if it were in their power; but *he that sits in heaven shall laugh at them.*

4. Who they are that are drawn into this confederacy. The nations that entered into this alliance are here mentioned (*v.* 6—8); the Edomites and Ishmaelites, both descendants from Abraham, lead the van; for apostates from the church have been its most bitter and spiteful enemies, witness Julian. These were allied to Israel in blood and yet in alliance against Israel. There are no bonds of nature so strong but the spirit of persecution has broken through them. *The brother shall betray the brother to death.* Moab and Ammon were the children of righteous Lot; but, as an incestuous, so a degenerate race. The Philistines were long a thorn in Israel's side, and very vexatious. How the inhabitants of Tyre, who in David's time were Israel's firm allies, come in among their enemies, I know not; but that *Assur* (that is, the Assyrian) *also is joined with them* is not strange, or that (as the word is) they were *an arm to the children of Lot.* See how numerous the enemies of God's church have always been. *Lord, how are those increased that trouble it!* God's heritage was as a speckled bird; all *the birds round about were against her* (Jer. xii. 9), which highly magnifies the power of God in preserving to himself a church in the world, in spite of the combined force of earth and hell.

9 Do unto them as *unto* the Mi-

dianites ; as *to* Sisera, as *to* Jabin, at the brook of Kison : 10 *Which* perished at En-dor : they became *as* dung for the earth. 11 Make their nobles like Oreb, and like Zeeb : yea, all their princes as Zebah, and as Zalmunna : 12 Who said, Let us take to ourselves the houses of God in possession. 13 O my God, make them like a wheel ; as the stubble before the wind. 14 As the fire burneth a wood, and as the flame setteth the mountains on fire ; 15 So persecute them with thy tempest, and make them afraid with thy storm. 16 Fill their faces with shame ; that they may seek thy name, O LORD. 17 Let them be confounded and troubled for ever ; yea, let them be put to shame, and perish : 18 That *men* may know that thou, whose name alone *is* JEHOVAH, *art* the most high over all the earth.

The psalmist here, in the name of the church, prays for the destruction of those confederate forces, and, in God's name, foretels it ; for this prayer that it might be so amounts to a prophecy that it shall be so, and this prophecy reaches to all the enemies of the gospel-church ; whoever they be that oppose the kingdom of Christ, here they may read their doom. The prayer is, in short, that these enemies, who were confederate against Israel, might be defeated in all their attempts, and that they might prove their own ruin, and so God's Israel might be preserved and perpetuated. Now this is here illustrated,

I. By some precedents. Let that be their punishment which has been the fate of others who have formerly set themselves against God's Israel. The defeat and discomfiture of former combinations may be pleaded in prayer to God and improved for the encouragement of our own faith and hope, because God is the same still that ever he was, the same to his people and the same against his and their enemies ; with him is no variableness. 1. He prays that their armies might be destroyed as the armies of former enemies had been (*v.* 9, 10) : *Do to them as to the Midianites :* let them be routed by their own fears, for so the Midianites were, more than by Gideon's 300 men. Do to them as to the army under the command of Sisera (who was general under Jabin king of Canaan) which God discomfited (Judg. iv. 15) at the brook Kishon, near to which was Endor. *They became as dung on the earth :* their dead bodies were thrown like dung laid in heaps, or spread, to fatten the ground ; they were trodden to dirt by Barak's small but victorious army; and this was fitly made a precedent here, because Deborah made it so to aftertimes when it was fresh. Judg. v. 31, *So let all thy enemies perish, O Lord!* that is, So they shall perish. 2. He prays that their leaders might be destroyed as they had been formerly. The common people would not have been so mischievous if their princes had not set them on, and therefore they are particularly prayed against, *v.* 11, 12. Observe, (1.) What their malice was against the Israel of God. They said, *Let us take to ourselves the houses of God in possession (v.* 12), the *pleasant places* of God (so the word is), by which we may understand the land of Canaan, which was a pleasant land and was Immanuel's land, or the temple, which was indeed God's pleasant place (Isa. lxiv. 11), or (as Dr. Hammond suggests) the pleasant pastures, which these Arabians, who traded in cattle, did in a particular manner seek after. The princes and nobles aimed to enrich themselves by this war; and their armies must be made as dung for the earth, to serve their covetousness and their ambition. (2.) What their lot should be. They shall be made *like Oreb and Zeeb* (two princes of the Midianites, who, when their forces were routed, were taken in their flight by the Ephraimites and slain, Judg. vii. 25), and *like Zeba and Zalmunna,* whom Gideon himself slew, Judg. viii. 21. " Let these enemies of ours be made as easy a prey to us as they ᴡere to the conquerors then." We may not prescribe to God, but we may pray to God that he will deal with the enemies of his church in our days as he did with those in the days of our fathers.

II. He illustrates it by some similitudes, and prays, 1. That God would *make them like a wheel (v.* 13), that they might be in continual motion, unquiet, unsettled, and giddy in all their counsels and resolves, that they might roll down easily and speedily to their own ruin. Or, as some think, that they might be broken by the judgments of God, as the corn is broken, or beaten out, by the wheel which was then used in threshing. Thus, when a *wise king scatters the wicked,* he is said to *bring the wheel over them,* Prov. xx. 26. Those that trust in God have their hearts fixed; those that fight against him are unfixed, like a wheel. 2. That they might be chased as *stubble,* or chaff, *before the* fierce *wind.* " The wheel, though it continually turn round, is fixed on its own axis; but let them have no more fixation than the light stubble has, which the wind hurries away, and nobody desires to save it, but is willing it should go," Ps. i. 4. Thus shall *the wicked be driven away in his wickedness, and chased out of the world.* 3. That they might be consumed, as wood by the fire, or as briers and thorns, as fern or furze, upon the mountains, by the flames, *v.* 14. When the stubble is driven by the wind it will rest, at last, under some hedge, in some ditch or other; but he prays that they might not only be driven away as stubble, but burnt up
556

as stubble. And this will be the end of wicked men (Heb. vi. 8) and particularly of all the enemies of God's church. The application of these comparisons we have *(v.* 15) : *So persecute them with thy tempest,* persecute them to their utter ruin, and make *them afraid with thy storm.* See how sinners are made miserable ; the storm of God's wrath raises terrors in their own hearts, and so they are made completely miserable. God can deal with the proudest and most daring sinner that has bidden defiance to his justice, and can make him afraid as a grasshopper. It is the torment of devils that they tremble.

III. He illustrates it by the good consequences of their confusion, *v.* 16—18. He prays here that God, having filled their hearts with terror, would thereby fill their faces with shame, that they might be ashamed of their enmity to the people of God (Isa. xxvi. 11), ashamed of their folly in acting both against Omnipotence itself and their own true interest. They did what they could to put God's people to shame, but the shame will at length return upon themselves. Now, 1. The beginning of this shame might be a means of their conversion : " Let them be broken and baffled in their attempts, *that they may seek thy name, O Lord!* Let them be put to a stand, that they may have both leisure and reason to pause a little, and consider who it is that they are fighting against and what an unequal match they are for him, and may therefore humble and submit themselves and desire conditions of peace. Let them be made to fear thy name, and perhaps that will bring them to seek thy name." Note, That which we should earnestly desire and beg of God for our enemies and persecutors is that God would bring them to repentance, and we should desire their abasement in order to this, no other confusion to them than what may be a step towards their conversion. 2. If it did not prove a means of their conversion, the perfecting of it would redound greatly to the honour of God. If they will not be ashamed and repent, let them be put to shame and perish ; if they will not be troubled and turned, which would soon put an end to all their trouble, a happy end, *let them be troubled for ever,* and never have peace : this will be for God's glory *(v.* 18), that other men may know and own, if they themselves will not, *that thou, whose name alone is JEHOVAH* (that incommunicable, though not ineffable name) *art the Most High over all the earth.* God's triumphs over his and his church's enemies will be incontestable proofs, (1.) That he is, according to his name Jᴇ-ʜᴏᴠᴀʜ, a self-existent self-sufficient Being, that has all power and perfection in himself. (2.) That he is the most high God, sovereign Lord of all, above all gods, above all kings, above all that exalt themselves and pretend to be high. (3.) That he is so, not only over the land of Israel, but *over all the earth,* even those nations of the earth that do not know him or own him; for his kingdom rules over all. These are great and unquestionable truths, but men will hardly be persuaded to know and believe them; therefore the psalmist prays that the destruction of some might be the conviction of others. The final ruin of all God's enemies, in the great day, will be the effectual proof of this, before angels and men, when the everlasting shame and contempt to which sinners shall rise (Dan. xii. 2) shall redound to the everlasting honour and praise of that God to whom vengeance belongs.

PSALM LXXXIV.

Though David's name be not in the title of this psalm, yet we have reason to think he was the penman of it, because it breathes so much of his excellent spirit and is so much like the sixty-third psalm which was penned by him; it is supposed that David penned this psalm when he was forced by Absalom's rebellion to quit his city, which he lamented his absence from, not so much because it was the royal city as because it was the holy city, witness this psalm, which contains the pious breathings of a gracious soul after God and communion with him. Though it be not entitled, yet it may fitly be looked upon as a psalm or song for the sabbath day, the day of our solemn assemblies. The psalmist here with great devotion expresses his affection, I. To the ordinances of God; his value for them (ver. 1), his desire towards them (ver. 2, 3), his conviction of the happiness of those that did enjoy them (ver. 4—7), and his placing his own happiness so very much in the enjoyment of them, ver. 10. II. To the God of the ordinances; his desire towards him (ver. 8, 9), his faith in him (ver. 11), and his conviction of the happiness of those that put their confidence in him, ver. 12. In singing this psalm we should have the same devout affections working towards God that David had, and then the singing of it will be very pleasant.

To the chief musician upon Gittith. A psalm for the sons of Korah.

HOW amiable *are* thy tabernacles, O Lord of hosts! 2 My soul longeth, yea, even fainteth for the courts of the Lord: my heart and my flesh crieth out for the living God. 3 Yea, the sparrow hath found a house, and the swallow a nest for herself, where she may lay her young, *even* thine altars, O Lord of hosts, my King, and my God. 4 Blessed *are* they that dwell in thy house: they will be still praising thee. Selah. 5 Blessed *is* the man whose strength *is* in thee; in whose heart *are* the ways *of them.* 6 *Who* passing through the valley of Baca make it a well; the rain also filleth the pools. 7 They go from strength to strength, *every one of them* in Zion appeareth before God.

The psalmist here, being by force restrained from waiting upon God in public ordinances, by the want of them is brought under a more sensible conviction than ever of the worth of them. Observe,

I. The wonderful beauty he saw in holy institutions (v. 1): *How amiable are thy tabernacles, O Lord of hosts !* Some think that he here calls God the *Lord of hosts* (that is, in a special manner of the angels, the heavenly hosts) because of the presence of the angels in God's sanctuary; they attended the Shechinah, and were (as some think) signified by

the cherubim. God is the Lord of these hosts, and his tabernacle is: it is spoken of as more than one *(thy tabernacles)* because there were several courts in which the people attended, and because the tabernacle itself consisted of a holy place and a most holy. How amiable are these! How lovely is the sanctuary in the eyes of all that are truly sanctified! Gracious souls see a wonderful, an inexpressible, beauty in holiness, and in holy work. A tabernacle was a mean habitation, but the disadvantage of external circumstances makes holy ordinances not at all the less amiable; for the beauty of holiness is spiritual, and their glory is within.

II. The longing desire he had to return to the enjoyment of public ordinances, or rather of God in them, v. 2. It was an entire desire; body, soul, and spirit concurred in it. He was not conscious to himself of any rising thought to the contrary. It was an intense desire; it was like the desire of the ambitious, or covetous, or voluptuous. He longed, he fainted, he cried out, importunate to be restored to his place in God's courts, and almost impatient of delay. Yet it was not so much the courts of the Lord that he coveted, but he cried out, in prayer, *for the living God* himself. O that I might know him, and be again taken into communion with him! 1 John i. 3. Ordinances are empty things if we meet not with God in the ordinances.

III. His grudging the happiness of the little birds that made their nests in the buildings that were adjoining to God's altars, *v.* 3. This is an elegant and surprising expression of his affection to God's altars: *The sparrow has found a house and the swallow a nest for herself.* These little birds, by the instinct and direction of nature, provide habitations for themselves in houses, as other birds do in the woods, both for their own repose and in which to lay their young; some such David supposes there were in the buildings about the courts of God's house, and wishes himself with them. He would rather live in a bird's nest nigh God's altars than in a palace at a distance from them. He sometimes wished for *the wings of a dove,* on which to *fly into the wilderness* (lv. 6); here for the wings of a sparrow, that he might fly undiscovered into God's courts; and, though to *watch as a sparrow alone upon the house-top* is the description of a very melancholy state and spirit (cii. 7), yet David would be glad to take it for his lot, provided he might be near God's altars. It is better to be serving God in solitude than serving sin with a multitude. The word for a sparrow signifies any little bird, and (if I may offer a conjecture) perhaps when, in David's time, music was introduced so much into the sacred service, both vocal and instrumental, to complete the harmony they had singing-birds in cages hung about the courts of the tabernacle (for we find the singing of birds taken notice of to the glory of God, civ. 12), and David envies the happiness of these, and would gladly change places with them. Observe, David envies the happiness not of those birds that flew over the altars, and had only a transient view of God's courts, but of those that had nests for themselves there. David will not think it enough to sojourn in God's house *as a way-faring man that turns aside to tarry for a night;* but let this be his rest, his home; here he will dwell. And he takes notice that these birds not only have nests for themselves there, but that there they lay their young; for those who have a place in God's courts themselves cannot but desire that their children also may have in God's house, and within his walls, a place and a name, that they may *feed their kids beside the shepherds' tents.* Some give another sense of this verse: " Lord, by thy providence thou hast furnished the birds with nests and resting-places, agreeable to their nature, and to them they have free recourse; but thy altar, which is my nest, my resting-place, which I am as desirous of as ever the wandering bird was of her nest, I cannot have access to. Lord, wilt thou provide better for thy birds than for thy babes? *As a bird that wanders from her nest* so am I, now that I wander from the place of God's altars, for that is my place (Prov. xxvii. 8); I shall never be easy till I return to my place again." Note, Those whose souls are at home, at rest, in God, cannot but desire a settlement near his ordinances. There were two altars, one for sacrifice, the other for incense, and David, in his desire of a place in God's courts, has an eye to both, as we also must, in all our attendance on God, have an eye both to the satisfaction and to the intercession of Christ. And, *lastly,* Observe how he eyes God in this address: Thou art the *Lord of hosts, my King and my God.* Where should a poor distressed suppliant seek for protection but with his king? *And should not a people seek unto their God?* My King, my God, is Lord of hosts; by him and his altars let me live and die.

IV. His acknowledgment of the happiness both of the ministers and of the people that had liberty of attendance on God's altars: *"Blessed are they.* O when shall I return to the enjoyment of that blessedness?" 1. Blessed are the ministers, the priests and Levites, who have their residence about the tabernacle and are in their courses employed in the service of it (*v.* 4): *Blessed are those that dwell in thy house,* that are at home there, and whose business lies there. He is so far from pitying them, as confined to a constant attendance and obliged to perpetual seriousness, that he would sooner envy them than the greatest princes in the world. There are those that bless the covetous, but he blesses the religious. *Blessed are those that dwell in thy house* (not because they have good wages, a part of every sacrifice for themselves, which would enable them to keep a good table, but because they have good work): *They will be still praising thee;* and, if there be a heaven

upon earth, it is in praising God, in continually praising him. Apply this to his house above; blessed are those that dwell there, angels and glorified saints, for they *rest not day nor night from praising God.* Let us therefore spend as much of our time as may be in that blessed work in which we hope to spend a joyful eternity. 2. Blessed are the people, the inhabitants of the country, who, though they do not constantly dwell in God's house as the priests do, yet have liberty of access to it at the times appointed for their solemn feasts, the three great feasts, at which all the males were obliged to give their attendance, Deut. xvi. 16. David was so far from reckoning this an imposition, and a hardship put upon them, that he envies the happiness of those who might thus attend, *v.* 5—7. Those whom he pronounces blessed are here described. (1.) They are such as act in religion from a rooted principle of dependence upon God and devotedness to him: *Blessed is the man whose strength is in thee,* who makes thee his strength and strongly stays himself upon thee, who makes thy name his strong tower into which he runs for safety, Prov. xviii. 10. *Happy is the man whose hope is in the Lord his God,* Ps. xl. 4; cxlvi. 5. Those are truly happy who go forth, and go on, in the exercises of religion, not in their own strength (for then the work is sure to miscarry), but in the strength of the grace of Jesus Christ, from whom all our sufficiency is. David wished to return to God's tabernacles again, that there he might strengthen himself in the Lord his God for service and suffering. (2.) They are such as have a love for holy ordinances: *In whose heart are the ways of them,* that is, who, having placed their happiness in God as their end, rejoice in all the ways that lead to him, all those means by which their graces are strengthened and their communion with him kept up. They not only walk in these ways, but they have them in their hearts, they lay them near their hearts; no care or concern, no pleasure or delight, lies nearer than this. Note, Those who have the new Jerusalem in their eye must have the ways that lead to it in their heart, must mind them, their eyes must look straight forward in them, must ponder the paths of them, must keep close to them, and be afraid of turning aside to the right hand or to the left. If we make God's promise our strength, we must make God's word our rule, and walk by it. (3.) They are such as will break through difficulties and discouragements in waiting upon God in holy ordinances, *v.* 6. When they come up out of the country to worship at the feasts their way lies through many a dry and sandy valley (so some), in which they are ready to perish for thirst; but, to guard against that inconvenience, they dig little pits to receive and keep the rain-water, which is ready to them and others for their refreshment. When they make the pools the rain of heaven fills them. If we be ready to receive the grace of God, that grace shall not be wanting to us, but shall be sufficient for us at all times. Their way lay through many a weeping valley, so Baca signifies, that is (as others understand it), many watery valleys, which in wet weather, when *the rain filled the pools,* either through the rising of the waters or through the dirtiness of the way were impassable; but, by draining and trenching them, they made a road through them for the benefit of those who went up to Jerusalem. Care should be taken to keep those roads in repair that lead to church, as well as those that lead to market. But all this is intended to show, [1.] That they had a good will to the journey. When they were to attend the solemn feasts at Jerusalem they would not be kept back by bad weather, or bad ways, nor make those an excuse for staying at home. Difficulties in the way of duty are designed to try our resolution; and *he that observes the wind shall not sow.* [2.] That they made the best of the way to Zion, contrived and took pains to mend it where it was bad, and bore, as well as they could, the inconveniences that could not be removed. Our way to heaven lies through a valley of Baca, but even that may be made a well if we make a due improvement of the comforts God has provided for the pilgrims to the heavenly city. (4.) They are such as are still pressing forward till they come to their journey's end at length, and do not take up short of it (*v.* 7): *They go from strength to strength;* their company increases by the accession of more out of every town they pass through, till they become very numerous. Those that were near staid till those that were further off called on them, saying, *Come, and let us go to the house of the Lord* (cxxii. 1, 2), that they might go together in a body, in token of their mutual love. Or the particular persons, instead of being fatigued with the tediousness of their journey and the difficulties they met with, the nearer they came to Jerusalem the more lively and cheerful they were, and so went on *stronger and stronger,* Job xvii. 9. Thus it is promised that those that *wait on the Lord shall renew their strength,* Isa. xl. 31. Even where they are weak, there they are strong. They go *from virtue to virtue* (so some); it is the same word that is used for the virtuous woman. Those that press forward in their Christian course shall find God adding grace to their graces, John i. 16. They shall be changed from glory to glory (2 Cor. iii. 18), from one degree of glorious grace to another, till, at length, *every one of them appears before God in Zion,* to give glory to him and receive blessings from him. Note, Those who grow in grace shall, at last, be perfect in glory. The Chaldee reads it, *They go from the house of the sanctuary to the house of doctrine; and the pains which they have taken about the law shall appear before God, whose majesty dwells in Zion.*

We must go from one duty to another, from prayer to the word, from practising what we have learned to learn more; and, if we do this, the benefit of it will appear, to God's glory and our own everlasting comfort.

8 O LORD God of hosts, hear my prayer: give ear, O God of Jacob. Selah. 9 Behold, O God our shield, and look upon the face of thine anointed. 10 For a day in thy courts *is* better than a thousand. I had rather be a doorkeeper in the house of my God, than to dwell in the tents of wickedness. 11 For the LORD God *is* a sun and shield: the LORD will give grace and glory: no good *thing* will he withhold from them that walk uprightly. 12 O LORD of hosts, blessed *is* the man that trusteth in thee.

Here, I. The psalmist prays for audience and acceptance with God, not mentioning particularly what he desired God would do for him. He needed to say no more when he had professed such an affectionate esteem for the ordinances of God, which now he was restrained and banished from. All his desire was, in that profession, plainly before God, and his longing, his groaning, was not hidden from him; therefore he prays (*v.* 8, 9) only that God would hear his prayer and give ear, that he would behold his condition, behold his good affection, and look upon his face, which way it was set, and how his countenance discovered the longing desire he had towards God's courts. He calls himself (as many think) *God's anointed,* for David was anointed by him and anointed for him. In this petition, 1. He has an eye to God under several of his glorious titles—as *the Lord God of hosts,* who has all the creatures at his command, and therefore has all power both in heaven and in earth,—as the *God of Jacob,* a God in covenant with his own people, a God who never said to the praying seed of Jacob, *Seek you me in vain,*—and as *God our shield,* who takes his people under his special protection, pursuant to his covenant with Abraham their father. Gen. xv. 1, *Fear not, Abraham, I am thy shield.* When David could not be hidden in the secret of God's tabernacle (Ps. xxvii. 5), being at a distance from it, yet he hoped to find God his shield ready to him wherever he was. 2. He has an eye to the Mediator; for of him I rather understand those words, *Look upon the face of thy Messiah,* thy anointed one, for of his anointing David spoke, xlv. 7. In all our addresses to God we must desire that he would look upon the face of Christ, accept us for his sake, and be well-pleased with us in him. We must look with an eye of faith, and then God will with an eye of favour look *upon the face of the anointed,* who does show his face when we without him dare not show ours.

II. He pleads his love to God's ordinances and his dependence upon God himself.

1. God's courts were his choice, *v.* 10. A very great regard he had for holy ordinances: he valued them above any thing else, and he expresses his value for them, (1.) By preferring the time of God's worship before all other time: *A day spent in thy courts,* in attending on the services of religion, wholly abstracted from all secular affairs, *is better than a thousand,* not than a thousand in thy courts, but any where else in this world, though in the midst of all the delights of the children of men. Better than a thousand, he does not say *days,* you may supply it with years, with ages, if you will, and yet David will set his hand to it. "A day in thy courts, a sabbath day, a holy day, a feast-day, though but one day, would be very welcome to me; nay" (as some of the rabbin paraphrase it), "though I were to die for it the next day, yet that would be more sweet than years spent in the business and pleasure of this world. One of these days shall with its pleasure *chase a thousand, and two put ten thousand to flight,* to shame, as not worthy to be compared." (2.) By preferring the place of worship before any other place: *I would rather be a door-keeper,* rather be in the meanest place and office, *in the house of my God, than dwell* in state, as master, *in the tents of wickedness.* Observe, He calls even the tabernacle a house, for the presence of God in it made even those curtains more stately than a palace and more strong than a castle. It is the house of my God; the covenant-interest he had in God as his God was the sweet string on which he loved dearly to be harping; those, and those only, who can, upon good ground, call God theirs, delight in the courts of his house. I would rather be a porter in God's house than a prince in those tents where wickedness reigns, rather lie at the threshold (so the word is); that was the beggar's place (Acts iii. 2): "no matter" (says David), "let that be my place rather than none." The Pharisees loved synagogues well enough, provided they might have the uppermost seats there (Matt. xxiii. 6), that they might make a figure. Holy David is not solicitous about that; if he may but be admitted to the threshold, he will say, *Master, it is good to be here.* Some read it, *I would rather be fixed to a post in the house of my God than live at liberty in the tents of wickedness,* alluding to the law concerning servants, who, if they would not go out free, were to have their ear bored to the door-post, Exod. xxi. 5, 6. David loved his master and loved his work so well that he desired to be tied to this service for ever, to be more free to it, but never to go out free from it, preferring bonds to duty far before the greatest liberty to sin. Such a superlative delight have holy hearts in holy duties; no satisfaction in their account comparable to that in communion with God.

2. God himself was his hope, and joy, and all. *Therefore* he loved the house of his God, because his expectation was from his God, and there he used to communicate himself, *v.* 11. See, (1.) What God is, and will be, to his people: *The Lord God is a sun and shield.* We are here in darkness, but, if God be our God, he will be to us a sun, to enlighten and enliven us, to guide and direct us. We are here in danger, but he will be to us a shield to secure us from the fiery darts that fly thickly about us. *With his favour he will compass us as with a shield.* Let us therefore always *walk in the light of the Lord,* and never throw ourselves out of his protection, and we shall find him a sun to supply us with all good and a shield to shelter us from all evil. (2.) What he does, and will, bestow upon them: *The Lord will give grace and glory.* Grace signifies both the good-will of God towards us and the good work of God in us; glory signifies both the honour which he now puts upon us, in giving us the adoption of sons, and that which he has prepared for us in the inheritance of sons. God will give them grace in this world as a preparation for glory, and glory in the other world as the perfection of grace; both are God's gift, his free gift. And as, on the one hand, wherever God gives grace he will give glory (for grace is glory begun, and is an earnest of it), so, on the other hand, he will give glory hereafter to none to whom he does not give grace now, or who receive his grace in vain. And if God will give grace and glory, which are the two great things that concur to make us happy in both worlds, we may be sure that *no good thing will be withheld from those that walk uprightly.* It is the character of all good people that they walk uprightly, that they worship God in spirit and in truth, and have their conversation in the world in simplicity and godly sincerity; and such may be sure that God will withhold *no good thing from them,* that is requisite to their comfortable passage through this world. Make sure grace and glory, and *other things shall be added.* This is a comprehensive promise, and is such an assurance of the present comfort of the saints that, whatever they desire, and think they need, they may be sure that either Infinite Wisdom sees it is not good for them or Infinite Goodness will give it to them in due time. Let it be our care to walk uprightly, and then let us trust God to give us every thing that is good for us.

Lastly, He pronounces those blessed who put their confidence in God, as he did, *v.* 12. Those are blessed who have the liberty of ordinances and the privileges of God's house. But, though we should be debarred from them, yet we are not therefore debarred from blessedness if we trust in God. If we cannot go to the house of the Lord, we may go by faith to the Lord of the house, and in him we shall be happy and may be easy.

PSALM LXXXV.

Interpreters are generally of opinion that this psalm was penned after the return of the Jews out of their captivity in Babylon, when they still remained under some tokens of God's displeasure, which they here pray for the removal of. And nothing appears to the contrary, but that it might be penned then, as well as Ps. cxxxvii. They are the public interests that lie near the psalmist's heart here, and the psalm is penned for the great congregation. The church was here in a deluge; above were clouds, below were waves; every thing was dark and dismal. The church is like Noah in the ark, between life and death, between hope and fear; being so, I. Here is the dove sent forth in prayer. The petitions are against sin and wrath (ver. 4) and for mercy and grace, ver. 7. The pleas are taken from former favours (ver. 1—3) and present distresses, ver. 5, 6. II. Here is the dove returning with an olive branch of peace and good tidings; the psalmist expects her return (ver. 8) and then recounts the favours to God's Israel which by the spirit of prophecy he gave assurance of to others, and by the spirit of faith he took the assurance of to himself, ver. 9—13. In singing this psalm we may be assisted in our prayers to God both for his church in general and for the land of our nativity in particular. The former part will be of use to direct our desires, the latter to encourage our faith and hope in those prayers.

To the chief musician. A psalm for the sons of Korah.

LORD, thou hast been favourable unto thy land: thou hast brought back the captivity of Jacob. 2 Thou hast forgiven the iniquity of thy people, thou hast covered all their sin. Selah. 3 Thou hast taken away all thy wrath : thou hast turned *thyself* from the fierceness of thine anger. 4 Turn us, O God of our salvation, and cause thine anger toward us to cease. 5 Wilt thou be angry with us for ever? wilt thou draw out thine anger to all generations ? 6 Wilt thou not revive us again : that thy people may rejoice in thee? 7 Show us thy mercy, O LORD, and grant us thy salvation.

The church, in affliction and distress, is here, by direction from God, making her application to God. So ready is God to hear and answer the prayers of his people that by his Spirit in the word, and in the heart, he indites their petitions and puts words into their mouths. The people of God, in a very low and weak condition, are here taught how to address themselves to God.

I. They are to acknowledge with thankfulness the great things God had done for them (v. 1—3): "Thou hast done so and so for us and our fathers." Note, The sense of present afflictions should not drown the remembrance of former mercies; but, even when we are brought very low, we must call to remembrance past experiences of God's goodness, which we must take notice of with thankfulness, to his praise. They speak of it here with pleasure, 1. That God had shown himself propitious to their land, and had smiled upon it as his own : "*Thou hast been favourable to thy land,* as thine, with distinguishing favours." Note, The favour of God is the spring-head of all good, and the fountain of happiness, to nations, as well as to particular persons. It was by the favour of God that Israel got and kept possession of Canaan (xliv. 3); and, if he had not con-

tinued very favourable to them, they would have been ruined many a time. 2. That he had rescued them out of the hands of their enemies and restored them to their liberty : "*Thou hast brought back the captivity of Jacob,* and settled those in their own land again that had been driven out and were strangers in a strange land, prisoners in the land of their oppressors." The captivity of Jacob, though it may continue long, will be brought back in due time. 3. That he had not dealt with them according to the desert of their provocations (v. 2): "*Thou hast forgiven the iniquity of thy people,* and not punished them as in justice thou mightest. *Thou hast covered all their sin.*" When God forgives sin he covers it ; and, when he covers the sin of his people, he covers it all. The bringing back of their captivity to them was *then* an instance of God's favour to them, when it was accompanied with the pardon of their iniquity. 4. That he had not continued his anger against them so far, and so long, as they had reason to fear (v. 3): Having co-vered *all their sin,* thou hast *taken away all thy wrath ;*" for when sin is set aside God's anger ceases ; God is pacified if we are purified. See what the pardon of sin is : *Thou hast forgiven the iniquity of thy people,* that is, " *Thou hast turned thy anger from waxing hot,* so as to consume us in the flame of it. In compassion to us thou hast not stirred up all thy wrath, but, when an intercessor has stood before thee in the gap, thou hast turned away thy anger."

II. They are taught to pray to God for grace and mercy, in reference to their present distress ; this is inferred from the former : "Thou hast done well for our fathers; do well for us, for we are the children of the same covenant." 1. They pray for converting grace: "*Turn us, O God of our salvation !* in order to the turning of our captivity ; turn us from iniquity ; turn us to thyself and to our duty ; turn us, and we shall be turned." All those whom God will save sooner or later he will turn. If no conversion, no salvation. 2. They pray for the removal of the tokens of God's displeasure which they were under : "*Cause thine anger towards us to cease,* as thou didst many a time cause it to cease in the days of our fathers, when thou didst take away thy wrath from them." Observe the method, "First turn us to thee, and then cause thy anger to turn from us." When we are reconciled to God, and, not till then, we may expect the comfort of his being reconciled to us. 3. They pray for the manifestation of God's good-will to them (v. 7): "*Show us thy mercy, O Lord!* show thyself merciful to us ; not only have mercy on us, but let us have the comfortable evidences of that mercy; let us know that thou hast mercy on us and mercy in store for us." 4. They pray that God would, graciously to them and gloriously to himself, appear on their behalf: "*Grant us thy salvation ;* grant it by thy promise, and then, no doubt, thou wilt work it by thy providence." Note, The vessels of God's mercy are the heirs of his salvation; he shows mercy to those to whom he grants salvation; for salvation is of mere mercy.

III. They are taught humbly to expostulate with God concerning their present troubles, *v.* 5, 6. Here observe, 1. What they dread and deprecate: "*Wilt thou be angry with us for ever?* We are undone if thou art, but we hope thou wilt not. *Wilt thou draw out thy anger unto all generations?* No; thou art gracious, slow to anger, and swift to show mercy, and wilt not contend for ever. Thou wast not angry with our fathers for ever, but didst soon turn thyself from the fierceness of thy wrath; why then wilt thou be angry with us for ever? Are not thy mercies and compassions as plentiful and powerful as ever they were? Impenitent sinners God will be angry with for ever; for what is hell but the wrath of God drawn out unto endless generations? But shall a hell upon earth be the lot of thy people?" 2. What they desire and hope for: "*Wilt thou not revive us again* (*v.* 6), revive us with comforts spoken to us, revive us with deliverances wrought for us? Thou hast been favourable to thy land formerly, and that revived it; wilt thou not again be favourable, and so revive it again?" God had granted to the children of the captivity *some reviving in their bondage,* Ezra ix. 8. Their return out of Babylon was as *life from the dead,* Ezek. xxxvii. 11, 12. Now, Lord (say they), *wilt thou not revive us again,* and *put thy hand again the second time* to gather us in? Isa. xi. 11; Ps. cxxvi. 1, 4. *Revive thy work in the midst of the years,* Hab. iii. 2. "Revive us again," (1.) "That thy people may rejoice; and so we shall have the comfort of it," Ps. xiv. 7. Give them life, that they may have joy. (2.) "That they may rejoice in thee; and so thou wilt have the glory of it." If God be the fountain of all our mercies, he must be the centre of all our joys.

8 I will hear what God the LORD will speak: for he will speak peace unto his people, and to his saints: but let them not turn again to folly. 9 Surely his salvation *is* nigh them that fear him; that glory may dwell in our land. 10 Mercy and truth are met together; righteousness and peace have kissed *each other.* 11 Truth shall spring out of the earth; and righteousness shall look down from heaven. 12 Yea, the LORD shall give *that which is* good; and our land shall yield her increase. 13 Righteousness shall go before him; and shall set *us* in the way of his steps.

We have here an answer to the prayers and expostulations in the foregoing verses.

I. In general, it is an answer of peace. This the psalmist is soon aware of (*v.* 8), for he *stands upon his watch-tower to hear what God will say unto him,* as the prophet, Hab. ii. 1, 2. *I will hear what God the Lord will speak.* This intimates, 1. The stilling of his passions—his grief, his fear—and the tumult of his spirit which they occasioned: "Compose thyself, O my soul! in a humble silence to attend upon God and wait his motions. I have spoken enough, or too much; now I will hear what God will speak, and welcome his holy will. *What saith my Lord unto his servant?*" If we would have God to hear what we say to him by prayer, we must be ready to hear what he says to us by his word. 2. The raising of his expectation; now that he has been at prayer he looks for something very great, and very kind, from the God that hears prayer. When we have prayed we should look after our prayers, and stay for an answer. Now observe here, (1.) What it is that he promises himself from God, in answer to his prayers: *He will speak peace to his people, and to his saints.* There are a people in the world who are God's people, set apart for him, subject to him, and who shall be saved by him. All his people are his saints, sanctified by his grace and devoted to his glory; these may sometimes want peace, when without are fightings and within are fears; but, sooner or later, God will speak peace to them; if he do not command outward peace, yet he will suggest inward peace, speaking that to their hearts by his Spirit which he has spoken to their ears by his word and ministers and making them to hear joy and gladness. (2.) What use he makes of this expectation. [1.] He takes the comfort of it; and so must we: "*I will hear what God the Lord will speak,* hear the assurances he gives of peace, in answer to prayer." When God speaks peace we must not be deaf to it, but with all humility and thankfulness receive it. [2.] He cautions the saints to do the duty which this calls for: *But let them not turn again to folly;* for it is on these terms, and no other, that peace is to be expected. To those, and those only, peace is spoken, who turn from sin; but, if they return to it again, it is at their peril. All sin is folly, but especially backsliding; it is egregious folly to turn to sin after we have seemed to turn from it, to turn to it after God has spoken peace. God is for peace, but, when he speaks, such are for war.

II. Here are the particulars of this answer of peace. He doubts not but all will be well in a little time, and therefore gives us the pleasing prospect of the flourishing estate of the church in the last five verses of the psalm, which describe the peace and prosperity that God, at length, blessed the children of the captivity with, when, after a great deal of toil and agitation, at length they gained a settlement in their own land. But it may be taken both as a promise also to all who fear God and work righteousness, that they shall be easy and happy, and as a prophecy of the kingdom of the Messiah and the blessings with which that kingdom should be enriched. Here is,

1. Help at hand (v. 9): "*Surely his salvation is nigh,* nigh to us, nigher than we think it is: it will soon be effected, how great soever our difficulties and distresses are, when God's time shall come, and that time is not far off." When the tale of bricks is doubled, then Moses comes. It is nigh to all who fear him; when trouble is nigh salvation is nigh, for God is a very present help in time of trouble to all who are his; whereas *salvation is far from the wicked,* cxix. 155. This may fitly be applied to Christ the author of eternal salvation: it was the comfort of the Old-Testament saints that, though they lived not to see that redemption in Jerusalem which they waited for, yet they were sure it was nigh, and would be welcome, to all that fear God.

2. Honour secured: "*That glory may dwell in our land,* that we may have the worship of God settled and established among us; for that is the glory of a land. When that goes, *Ichabod —the glory has departed;* when that stays glory dwells." This may refer to the Messiah, who was to be *the glory of his people Israel,* and who came and dwelt among them (John i. 4), for which reason their land is called *Immanuel's land,* Isa. viii. 8.

3. Graces meeting, and happily embracing (v. 10, 11): *Mercy and truth, righteousness and peace, kiss each other.* This may be understood, (1.) Of the reformation of the people and of the government, in the administration of which all those graces should be conspicuous and commanding. The rulers and ruled shall all be merciful and true, righteous and peaceable. When there is no truth nor mercy all goes to ruin (Hos. iv. 1; Isa. lix. 14, 15); but when these meet in the management of all affairs, when these give aim, when these give law, when there is such plenty of truth that it sprouts up like the grass of the earth, and of righteousness that it is showered down like rain from heaven, then things go well. When in every congress mercy and truth meet, in every embrace righteousness and peace kiss, and common honesty is indeed common, then glory dwells in a land, as the sin of reigning dishonesty is a reproach to any people. (2.) Of the return of God's favour, and the continuance of it, thereupon. When a people return to God and adhere to him in a way of duty he will return to them and abide with them in a way of mercy. So some understand this, man's truth and God's mercy, man's righteousness and God's peace, meet together. If God find us true to him, to one another, to ourselves, we shall find him merciful. If we make conscience of righteousness, we shall have the comfort of peace. If *truth spring out of the earth,* that is (as Dr.

Hammond expounds it), out of the hearts of men, the proper soil for it to grow in, righteousness (that is, God's mercy) shall look down from heaven, as the sun does upon the world when it sheds its influences on the productions of the earth and cherishes them. (3.) Of the harmony of the divine attributes in the Messiah's undertaking. In him who is both our salvation and our glory *mercy and truth have met together;* God's mercy and truth, and his *righteousness and peace, have kissed each other;* that is, the great affair of our salvation is so well contrived, so well concerted, that God may have mercy upon poor sinners, and be at peace with them, without any wrong to his truth and righteousness. He is true to the threatening, and just in his government, and yet pardons sinners and takes them into covenant with himself. Christ, as Mediator, brings heaven and earth together again, which sin had set at variance; through him *truth springs out of the earth,* that truth which God *desires in the inward part,* and then *righteousness looks down from heaven;* for God is *just, and the justifier of those who believe in Jesus.* Or it may denote that in the kingdom of the Messiah these graces shall flourish and prevail and have a universal command.

4. Great plenty of every thing desirable (v. 12): *The Lord shall give that which is good,* every thing that he sees to be good for us. All good comes from God's goodness; and when mercy, truth, and righteousness, have a sovereign influence on men's hearts and lives, all good may be expected. If we thus *seek the righteousness of God's kingdom, other things shall be added;* Matt. vi. 33. When the glory of the gospel dwells in our land, then it shall yield its increase, for soul-prosperity will either bring outward prosperity along with it or sweeten the want of it. See Ps. lxvii. 6.

5. A sure guidance in the good way (v. 13): *The righteousness* of his promise which he has made to us, assuring us of happiness, and the righteousness of sanctification, that good work which he has wrought in us, these shall go before him to prepare his way, both to raise our expectations of his favour and to qualify us for it; and these shall go before us also, and be our guide to *set us in the way of his steps,* that is, to encourage our hopes and guide our practice, that we may go forth to meet him when he is coming towards us in ways of mercy. Christ, the sun of righteousness, shall bring us to God, and put us into the way that leads to him. John Baptist, a preacher of righteousness, shall go before Christ to prepare his way. Righteousness is a sure guide both in meeting God and in following him.

PSALM LXXXVI.

This psalm is entitled "a prayer of David;" probably it was not penned upon any particular occasion, but was a prayer he often used himself, and recommended to others for their use, especially in a day of affliction. Many think that David penned this prayer as a type of Christ, "who in the days of his flesh offered up strong cries," Heb. v. 7. David, in this prayer (according to the nature of that duty), I. Gives glory to God, ver. 8—10, 12, 13. II. Seeks for grace and favour from God, that God would hear his prayers (ver. 1, 6, 7), preserve and save him, and be merciful to him (ver. 2, 3, 16), that he would give him joy, and grace, and strength, and put honour upon him, ver. 4, 11, 17. He pleads God's goodness (ver. 5, 15) and the malice of his enemies, ver. 14. In singing this we must, as David did, lift up our souls to God with application.

A prayer of David.

BOW down thine ear, O Lord, hear me: for I *am* poor and needy. 2 Preserve my soul; for I *am* holy: O thou my God, save thy servant that trusteth in thee. 3 Be merciful unto me, O Lord: for I cry unto thee daily. 4 Rejoice the soul of thy servant: for unto thee, O Lord, do I lift up my soul. 5 For thou, Lord, *art* good, and ready to forgive; and plenteous in mercy unto all them that call upon thee. 6 Give ear, O Lord, unto my prayer; and attend to the voice of my supplications. 7 In the day of my trouble I will call upon thee: for thou wilt answer me.

This psalm was published under the title of *a prayer of David;* not as if David sung all his prayers, but into some of his songs he inserted prayers; for a psalm will admit the expressions of any pious and devout affections. But it is observable how very plain the language of this psalm is, and how little there is in it of poetic flights or figures, in comparison with some other psalms; for the flourishes of wit are not the proper ornaments of prayer. Now here we may observe,

I. The petitions he puts up to God. It is true, prayer accidentally may preach, but it is most fit that (as it is in this prayer) every passage should be directed to God, for such is the nature of prayer as it is here described (*v.* 4): *Unto thee, O Lord! do I lift up my soul,* as he had said xxv. 1. In all the parts of prayer the soul must ascend upon the wings of faith and holy desire, and be lifted up to God, to meet the communications of his grace, and in an expectation raised very high of great things from him. 1. He begs that God would give a gracious audience to his prayers (*v.* 1): *Bow down thy ear, O Lord! hear me.* When God hears our prayers it is fitly said that he *bows down his ear* to them, for it is admirable condescension in God that he is pleased to take notice of such mean creatures as we are and such defective prayers as ours are. He repeats this again (*v.* 6): "*Give ear, O Lord! unto my prayer,* a favourable ear, though it be whispered, though it be stammered; *attend to the voice of my supplications.*" Not that God needs to have his affection stirred up by any thing that we can say; but thus we must express our desire of his favour. The Son of David spoke it with assurance

and pleasure (John xi. 41, 42), *Father, I thank thee that thou hast heard me; and I know that thou hearest me always.* 2. He begs that God would take him under his special protection, and so be the author of his salvation (*v.* 2): *Preserve my soul; save thy servant.* It was David's soul that was God's servant; for those only serve God acceptably that *serve him with their spirits.* David's concern is about his soul; if we understand it of his natural life, it teaches us that the best self-preservation is to commit ourselves to God's keeping and by faith and prayer to make our Creator our preserver. But it may be understood of his spiritual life, the life of the soul as distinct from the body: "Preserve my soul from that one evil and dangerous thing to souls, even from sin; preserve my soul, and so save me." All those whom God will save he preserves, and will preserve them to his heavenly kingdom. 3. He begs that God would look upon him with an eye of pity and compassion (*v.* 3): *Be merciful to me, O Lord!* It is mercy in God to pardon our sins and to help us out of our distresses; both these are included in this prayer, *God be merciful to me.* "Men show no mercy; we ourselves deserve no mercy; but, Lord, for mercy-sake, be *merciful unto me.*" 4. He begs that God would fill him with inward comfort (*v.* 4): *Rejoice the soul of thy servant.* It is God only that can *put gladness into the heart and make the soul to rejoice,* and then, and not till then, the joy is full; and, as it is the duty of those who are God's servants to *serve him with gladness,* so it is their privilege to be *filled with joy and peace in believing,* and they may in faith pray, not only that God will preserve their souls, but that he will rejoice their souls, and the *joy of the Lord* will be *their strength.* Observe, When he prays, *Rejoice my soul,* he adds, *For unto thee do I lift up my soul.* Then we may expect comfort from God when we take care to keep up our communion with God: prayer is the nurse of spiritual joy.

II. The pleas with which he enforces these petitions. 1. He pleads his relation to God and interest in him: "Thou art my God, to whom I have devoted myself, and on whom I depend, and I am thy servant (*v.* 2), in subjection to thee, and therefore looking for protection from thee." 2. He pleads his distress: "*Hear me, for I am poor and needy,* therefore I want thy help, therefore none else will hear me." God is the poor man's King, whose glory it is to *save the souls of the needy;* those who are poor in spirit, who see themselves empty and necessitous, are most welcome to the God of all grace. 3. He pleads God's good will towards all that seek him (*v.* 5): "To thee do I *lift up my soul* in desire and expectation; *for thou, Lord, art good;*" and whither should beggars go but to the door of the good house-keeper? The goodness of God's nature is a great encouragement to us in all our addresses to him. His goodness appears in two things, giving and forgiving. (1.) He is a sin-pardoning God; not only he can forgive, but he is ready to forgive, more ready to forgive than we are to repent. *I said, I will confess, and thou forgavest,* xxxii. 5. (2.) He is a prayer-hearing God; he is plenteous in mercy, very full, and very free, both rich and liberal unto *all those that call upon him;* he has wherewithal to supply all their needs and is open-handed in granting that supply. 4. He pleads God's good work in himself, by which he had qualified him for the tokens of his favour. Three things were wrought in him by divine grace, which he looked upon as earnests of all good:—(1.) A conformity to God (*v.* 2): *I am holy,* therefore preserve my soul; for those whom the Spirit sanctifies he will preserve. He does not say this in pride and vain glory, but with humble thankfulness to God. *I am one whom thou favourest* (so the margin reads it), whom thou hast *set apart for thyself.* If God has begun a good work of grace in us, we must own that *the time was a time of love. Then was I in his eyes as one that found favour,* and whom God hath taken into his favour he will take under his protection. *All his saints are in thy hand,* Deut. xxxiii. 3. Observe, *I am needy* (*v.* 1), yet *I am holy* (*v.* 2), holy and yet needy, *poor in the world, but rich in faith.* Those who preserve their purity in their greatest poverty may assure themselves that God will preserve their comforts, will preserve their souls. (2.) A confidence in God: *Save thy servant that trusteth in thee.* Those that are holy must nevertheless not trust in themselves, nor in their own righteousness, but only in God and his grace. Those that trust in God may expect salvation from him. (3.) A disposition to communion with God. He hopes God will answer his prayers, because he had inclined him to pray. [1.] To be constant in prayer: *I cry unto thee daily, and all the day, v.* 3. It is thus our duty to pray always, without ceasing, and to continue instant in prayer; and then we may hope to have our prayers heard which we make in the time of trouble, if we have made conscience of the duty at other times, at all times. It is comfortable if an affliction finds the wheels of prayer a-going, and that they are not then to be set a-going. [2.] To be inward with God in prayer, to *lift up his soul* to him, *v.* 4. Then we may hope that God will meet us with his mercies, when we in our prayers send forth our souls as it were to meet him. [3.] To be in a special manner earnest with God in prayer when he was in affliction (*v.* 7): "*In the day of my trouble,* whatever others do, *I will call upon thee,* and commit my case to thee, for thou wilt hear and answer me, and I shall not seek in vain, as those did who cried, *O Baal! hear us; but there was no voice, nor any that regarded,* 1 Kings xviii. 29.

8 Among the gods *there is* none

like unto thee, O Lord; neither *are there any works* like unto thy works. 9 All nations whom thou hast made shall come and worship before thee, O Lord; and shall glorify thy name. 10 For thou *art* great, and doest wondrous things: thou *art* God alone. 11 Teach me thy way, O Lord; I will walk in thy truth: unite my heart to fear thy name. 12 I will praise thee, O Lord my God, with all my heart: and I will glorify thy name for evermore. 13 For great *is* thy mercy toward me: and thou hast delivered my soul from the lowest hell. 14 O God, the proud are risen against me, and the assemblies of violent *men* have sought after my soul; and have not set thee before them. 15 But thou, O Lord, *art* a God full of compassion, and gracious, longsuffering, and plenteous in mercy and truth. 16 O turn unto me, and have mercy upon me; give thy strength unto thy servant, and save the son of thine handmaid. 17 Show me a token for good; that they which hate me may see *it,* and be ashamed: because thou, Lord, hast holpen me, and comforted me.

David is here going on in his prayer.
I. He gives glory to God; for we ought in our prayers to praise him, ascribing kingdom, power, and glory, to him, with the most humble and reverent adorations. 1. As a being of unparalleled perfection, such a one that there is none like him nor any to be compared with him, *v.* 8. *Among the gods,* the false gods, whom the heathens worshipped, the angels, the kings of the earth, among them all, *there is none like unto thee, O Lord!* none so wise, so mighty, so good; *neither are there any works like unto thy works,* which is an undeniable proof that there is none like him; his own works praise him, and the best way we have of praising him is by acknowledging that there is none like him. 2. As the fountain of all being and the centre of all praise (*v.* 9): "*Thou hast made all nations,* made them all of one blood; they all derive their being from thee, and have a constant dependence on thee, and therefore *they shall come and worship before thee and glorify thy name.*" This was in part fulfilled in the multitude of proselytes to the Jewish religion in the days of David and Solomon, but was to have its full accomplishment in the days of the Messiah, when some out of every kingdom and nation should be effectually brought in to praise God, Rev. vii. 9. It was by Christ that God made all nations, for without

him was not any thing made that was made, and therefore through Christ, and by the power of his gospel and grace, all nations shall be brought to *worship before God*, Isa. lxvi. 23. 3. As a being infinitely great (*v.* 10): "Therefore all nations shall worship before thee, because as King of nations *thou art great*, thy sovereignty absolute and incontestable, thy majesty terrible and insupportable, thy power universal and irresistible, thy riches vast and inexhaustible, thy dominion boundless and unquestionable; and, for the proof of this, *thou doest wondrous things*, which all nations admire, and whence they might easily infer that thou art God alone, not only none like thee, but none besides thee." Let us always entertain great thoughts of this great God, and be filled with holy admiration of this God who doeth wonders; and let him alone have our hearts who is God alone. 4. As a being infinitely good. Man is bad, very wicked and vile (*v.* 14); no mercy is to be expected from him; *but thou, O Lord! art a God full of compassion, and gracious, v.* 15. This is that attribute by which he proclaims his name, and by which we are therefore to proclaim it, Exod. xxxiv. 6, 7. It is his goodness that is over all his works, and therefore should fill all our praises; and this is our comfort, in reference to the wickedness of the world we live in, that, however it be, God is good. Men are barbarous, but God is gracious; men are false, but God is faithful. God is not only compassionate, but full of compassion, and in him *mercy rejoiceth against judgment.* He is long-suffering towards us, though we forfeit his favour and provoke him to anger, and he is *plenteous in mercy and truth*, as faithful in performing as he was free in promising. 5. As a kind friend and bountiful benefactor to him. We ought to praise God as good in himself, but we do it most feelingly when we observe how good he has been to us. This therefore the psalmist dwells upon with most pleasure, *v.* 12, 13. He had said (*v.* 9), *All nations shall praise thee, O Lord! and glorify thy name.* It is some satisfaction to a good man to think that others shall praise and glorify God, but it is his greatest care and pleasure to do it himself. "Whatever others do" (says David), " *I will praise thee, O Lord my God!* not only as the Lord, but as my God; and I will do it with all my heart; I will be ready to do it and cordial in it; I will do it with cheerfulness and liveliness, with a sincere regard to thy honour; for *I will glorify thy name*, not for a time, but for evermore. I will do it as long as I live, and hope to be doing it to eternity." With good reason does he resolve to be thus particular in praising God, because God had shown him particular favours: *For great is thy mercy towards me.* The fountain of mercy is inexhaustibly full; the streams of mercy are inestimably rich. When we speak of God's mercy to us, it becomes us thus to

magnify it: *Great is thy mercy towards me.* Of the greatness of God's mercy he gives this instance, *Thou hast delivered my soul from the lowest hell*, from death, from so great a death, as St. Paul (2 Cor. i. 10), from eternal death, so even some of the Jewish writers understand it. David knew he deserved to be cast off for ever into the lowest hell for his sin in the matter of Uriah; but Nathan assured him that the Lord had *taken away his sin*, and by that word he was delivered from the lowest hell, and herein God's mercy was great towards him. Even the best saints owe it, not to their own merit, but to the mercy of God, that they are saved from the lowest hell; and the consideration of that should greatly enlarge their hearts in praising the mercy of God, which they are obliged to glorify for evermore. So glorious, so gracious, a rescue from everlasting misery, justly requires the return of everlasting praise.

II. He prays earnestly for mercy and grace from God. He complains of the restless and implacable malice of his enemies against him (*v.* 14): "Lord, be thou for me; for there are many against me." He then takes notice of their character; they were *proud men* that looked with disdain upon poor David. (Many are made persecutors by their pride.) They were *violent men*, that would carry all before them by force, right or wrong. They were *terrible formidable men* (so some), that did what they could to frighten all about them. He notices their number: There were *assemblies* of them; they were men in authority and met in councils and courts, or men for conversation, and met in clubs; but, being assembled, they were the more capable of doing mischief. He notices their enmity to him: "They *rise up against me* in open rebellion; they not only plot, but they put their plots in execution as far as they can; and the design is not only to depose me, but to destroy me: they seek after my life, to slay me; after my soul, to damn me, if it lay in their power." And, *lastly*, He notices their distance and estrangement from God, which were at the bottom of their enmity to David: "*They have not set thee before them;* and what good can be expected from those that have no fear of God before their eyes? Lord, appear against them, for they are thy enemies as well as mine." His petitions are,

1. For the operations of God's grace in him, *v.* 11. He prays that God would give him, (1.) An understanding heart, that he would inform and instruct him concerning his duty: "*Teach me thy way, O Lord!* the way that thou hast appointed me to walk in; when I am in doubt concerning it, make it plain to me what I should do; let me hear the voice saying, *This is the way*," Isa. xxx. 21. David was well taught in the things of God, and yet was sensible he needed further instruction, and many a time could not trust his own judgment: *Teach me thy way; I will*

walk in thy truth. One would think it should be, *Teach me thy truth, and I will walk in thy way ;* but it comes all to one ; it is the way of truth that God teaches and that we must choose and walk in, Ps. cxix. 30. Christ is the way and the truth, and we must both learn Christ and walk in him. We cannot walk in God's way and truth unless he teach us ; and, if we expect he should teach us, we must resolve to be governed by his teachings, Isa. ii. 3. (2.) An upright heart : *" Unite my heart to fear thy name.* Make me sincere in religion. A hypocrite has a double heart ; let mine be single and entire for God, not divided between him and the world, not straggling from him." Our hearts are apt to wander and hang loose ; their powers and faculties wander after a thousand foreign things ; we have therefore need of God's grace to unite them, that we may serve God with all that is within us, and all little enough to be employed in his service. " Let my heart be fixed for God, and firm and faithful to him, and fervent in serving him ; that is a united heart."

2. For the tokens of God's favour to him, *v.* 16, 17. Three things he here prays for :— (1.) That God would speak peace and comfort to him : *" O turn unto me,* as to one thou lovest and hast a kind and tender concern for. My enemies turn against me, my friends turn from me ; Lord, do thou turn to me and have mercy upon me ; it will be a comfort to me to know that thou pitiest me." (2.) That God would work deliverance for him, and set him in safety : " Give me *thy strength ;* put strength into me, that I may help myself, and put forth thy strength for me, that I may be saved out of the hands of those that seek my ruin." He pleads relation : " I am *thy servant ;* I am so by birth, as *the son of thy handmaid,* born in thy house, and therefore thou art my rightful owner and proprietor, from whom I may expect protection. *I am thine ; save me."* The children of godly parents, who were betimes dedicated to the Lord, may plead it with him ; if they come under the discipline of his family, they are entitled to the privileges of it. (3.) That God would put a reputation on him : " *Show me a token for good ;* make it to appear to others as well as to myself that thou art doing me good, and designing further good for me. Let me have some unquestionable illustrious instances of thy favour to me, *that those who hate me may see it, and be ashamed* of their enmity to me, as they will have reason to be when they perceive that *thou, Lord, hast helped me and comforted me,* and that therefore they have been striving against God, opposing one whom he owns, and that they have been striving in vain to ruin and vex one whom God himself has undertaken to help and comfort." The joy of the saints shall be the shame of their persecutors.

PSALM LXXXVII.

The foregoing psalm was very plain and easy, but in this are things dark and hard to be understood. It is an encomium of Zion, as a type and figure of the gospel-church, to which what is here spoken is very applicable. Zion, for the temple's sake, is here preferred, I. Before the rest of the land of Canaan, as being crowned with special tokens of God's favour, ver. 1—3. II. Before any other place or country whatsoever, as being replenished with more eminent men and with a greater plenty of divine blessings, ver. 4—7. Some think it was penned to express the joy of God's people when Zion was in a flourishing state ; others think it was penned to encourage their faith and hope when Zion was in ruins and was to be rebuilt after the captivity. Though no man cared for her (Jer. xxx. 17, " This is Ziou whom no man seeketh after "), yet God had done great things for her, and spoken glorious things of her, which should all have their perfection and accomplishment in the gospel-church ; to that therefore we must have an eye in singing this psalm.

A psalm or song for the sons of Korah.

HIS foundation *is* in the holy mountains. 2 The LORD loveth the gates of Zion more than all the dwellings of Jacob. 3 Glorious things are spoken of thee, O city of God. Selah.

Some make the first words of the psalm to be part of the title ; it is a psalm or song whose subject is the holy mountains—the temple built in Zion upon Mount Moriah. This is the foundation of the argument, or beginning of the psalm. Or we may suppose the psalmist had now the tabernacle or temple in view and was contemplating the glories of it, and at length he breaks out into this expression, which has reference, though not to what he had written before, yet to what he had thought of ; every one knew what he meant when he said thus abruptly, *Its foundation is in the holy mountains.* Three things are here observed, in praise of the temple :—

1. That it was founded on the holy mountains, *v.* 1. The church has a foundation, so that it cannot sink or totter ; Christ himself is the foundation of it, which God has laid. The Jerusalem above is a city that has foundations. The foundation is upon the mountains. It is built high ; the *mountain of the Lord's house is established upon the top of the mountains,* Isa. ii. 2. It is built firmly ; the mountains are rocky, and on a rock the church is built. The world is founded upon the seas (xxiv. 2), which are continually ebbing and flowing, and are a very weak foundation ; Babel was built in a plain, where the ground was rotten. But the church is built upon the everlasting mountains and the perpetual hills ; for sooner shall the mountains depart, and the hills be removed, than the covenant of God's peace shall be disannulled, and on that the church is built, Isa. liv. 10. The foundation is upon the holy mountains. Holiness is the strength and stability of the church : it is this that will support it and keep it from sinking ; not so much that it *is* built upon mountains as that it is built upon holy mountains—upon the promise of God, for the confirming of which he has sworn by his holiness, upon the sanctification of the Spirit, which will secure the happiness of all the saints. 2. That God had expressed a particular affection for it (*v.* 2) : *The Lord loveth the gates of Zion,* of the temple, of *the houses of doctrine* (so the Chaldee), *more than all the dwellings of Jacob,* whether in Jeru-

salem or any where else in the country. God had said concerning Zion, *This is my rest for ever; here will I dwell.* There he met his people, and conversed with them, received their homage, and showed them the tokens of his favour, and therefore we may conclude how well he loves those gates. Note, (1.) God has a love for the dwellings of Jacob, has a gracious regard to religious families and accepts their family-worship. (2.) Yet he loves the gates of Zion better, not only better than any, but better than all, of the dwellings of Jacob. God was worshipped in the dwellings of Jacob, and family-worship is family-duty, which must by no means be neglected; yet, when they come in competition, public worship *(cæteris paribus—other things being equal)* is to be preferred before private. 3. That there was much said concerning it in the word of God (v. 3): *Glorious things are spoken of thee, O city of God!* We are to judge of things and persons by the figure they make and the estimate put upon them in and by the scripture. Many base things were spoken of the city of God by the enemies of it, to render it mean and odious; but by him whose judgment we are sure is according to truth glorious things are spoken of it. God said of the temple, *My eyes and my heart shall be there perpetually; I have sanctified this house, that my name may be there for ever,* 2 Chron. vii. 16. *Beautiful for situation is Mount Zion,* Ps. xlviii. 2. These are glorious things. Yet more glorious things are spoken of the gospel-church. It is the spouse of Christ, the purchase of his blood; it is a *peculiar people, a holy nation, a royal priesthood,* and the *gates of hell shall not prevail against it.* Let us not be ashamed of the church of Christ in its meanest condition, nor of any that belong to it, nor disown our relation to it, though it be turned ever so much to our reproach, since such glorious things are spoken of it, and not one iota or tittle of what is said shall fall to the ground.

4 I will make mention of Rahab and Babylon to them that know me: behold Philistia, and Tyre, with Ethiopia; this *man* was born there. 5 And of Zion it shall be said, This and that man was born in her: and the highest himself shall establish her. 6 The Lord shall count, when he writeth up the people, *that* this *man* was born there. Selah. 7 As well the singers as the players on instruments *shall be there:* all my springs *are* in thee.

Zion is here compared with other places, and preferred before them; the church of Christ is more glorious and excellent than the nations of the earth. 1. It is owned that other places have their glories (v. 4): " I will make mention of Rahab" (that is, *Egypt)*
568

" *and Babylon, to those that know me* and are about me, and with whom I discourse about public affairs; *behold Philistia and Tyre, with Ethiopia"* (or rather Arabia), " we will observe that *this man was born there;* here and there one famous man, eminent for knowledge and virtue, may be produced, that was, a native of these countries; here and there one that becomes a proselyte and a worshipper of the true God. But some give another sense of it, supposing that it is a prophecy or promise of bringing the Gentiles into the church and of uniting them in one body with the Jews. God says, " *I will reckon Egypt and Babylon with those that know me.* I will reckon them my people as much as Israel when they shall receive the gospel of Christ, and own them as born in Zion, born again there, and admitted to the privileges of Zion as freely as a true-born Israelite." Those that were strangers and foreigners became *fellow-citizens with the saints,* Eph. ii. 19. A Gentile convert shall stand upon a level with a native Jew; compare Isa. xix. 23—25. *The Lord shall say, Blessed be Egypt my people, and Assyria the work of my hands, and Israel my inheritance.* 2. It is proved that the glory of Zion outshines them all, upon many accounts; for, (1.) Zion shall produce many great and good men that shall be famous in their generation, v. 5. Of Zion it shall be said by all her neighbours that *this and that man were born in her,* many men of renown for wisdom and piety, and especially for acquaintance with the words of God and the visions of the Almighty—many prophets and kings, who should be greater favourites of heaven, and greater blessings to the earth, than ever were bred in Egypt or Babylon. The worthies of the church far exceed those of heathen nations, and their names will shine brighter than in perpetual records. *A man, a man was born in her,* by which some understand Christ, that man, that son of man, who is fairer than the children of men; he was born at Bethlehem near Zion, and was the glory of his people Israel. The greatest honour that ever was put upon the Jewish nation was, that of them, *as concerning the flesh, Christ came,* Rom. ix. 5. Or this also may be applied to the conversion of the Gentiles. Of Zion it shall be said that the law which went forth out of Zion, the gospel of Christ, shall be an instrument to beget many souls to God, and the Jerusalem that is from above shall be acknowledged the mother of them all. (2.) Zion's interest shall be strengthened and settled by an almighty power. *The Highest himself shall* undertake to *establish her,* who can do it effectually; the accession of proselytes out of various nations shall be so far from occasioning discord and division that it shall contribute greatly to Zion's strength; for, God himself having founded her upon an everlasting foundation, whatever convulsions and revolutions there are of states and kingdoms, and however heaven and earth may be shaken, these are things which cannot be shaken, but must remain. (3.) Zion's sons shall be registered with honour (v. 6): "*The Lord shall count, when he writes up the people,* and takes a catalogue of his subjects, *that this man was born there,* and so is a subject by birth, by the first birth, being born in his house—by the second birth, being born again of his Spirit." When God comes to reckon with the children of men, that he may render to every man according to his works, he will observe who was born in Zion, and consequently enjoyed the privileges of God's sanctuary, to whom pertained the adoption, and the glory, and the covenants, and the service of God, Rom. ix. 4; iii. 1, 2. For to them much was given, and therefore of them much will be required, and the account will be accordingly; five talents must be improved by those that were entrusted with five. *I know thy works, and where thou dwellest,* and where thou wast born. *Selah.* Let those that dwell in Zion *mark this,* and live up to their profession. (4.) Zion's songs shall be sung with joy and triumph: *As well the singers as the players on instruments shall be there* to praise God, v. 7. It was much to the honour of Zion, and is to the honour of the gospel-church, that there God is served and worshipped with rejoicing: his work is done, and done cheerfully; see lxviii. 25. *All my springs are in thee,* O Zion! So God says; he has deposited treasures of grace in his holy ordinances; there are the springs from which those streams take rise *which make glad the city of our God,* xlvi. 4. So the psalmist says, reckoning the springs from which his dry soul must be watered to lie in the sanctuary, in the word and ordinances, and in the communion of saints. The springs of the joy of a carnal worldling lie in wealth and pleasure; but the springs of the joy of a gracious soul lie in the word of God and prayer. Christ is the true temple; all our springs are in him, and from him all our streams flow. *It pleased the Father,* and all believers are well pleased with it too, *that in him should all fulness dwell.*

PSALM LXXXVIII.

This psalm is a lamentation, one of the most melancholy of all the psalms; and it does not conclude, as usually the melancholy psalms do, with the least intimation of comfort or joy, but, from first to last, it is mourning and woe. It is not upon a public account that the psalmist here complains (here is no mention of the afflictions of the church), but only upon a personal account, especially trouble of mind, and the grief impressed upon his spirits both by his outward afflictions and by the remembrance of his sins and the fear of God's wrath. It is reckoned among the penitential psalms, and it is well when our fears are thus turned into the right channel, and we take occasion from our worldly grievances to sorrow after a godly sort. In this psalm we have, I. The great pressure of spirit that the psalmist was under, ver. 3—6. II. The wrath of God, which was the cause of that pressure, ver. 7, 15—17. III. The wickedness of his friends, ver. 8, 18. IV. The application he made to God by prayer, ver. 1, 2, 9, 13. V. His humble expostulations and pleadings with God, ver. 10, 12, 14. Those who are in trouble of mind may sing this psalm feelingly; those that are not ought to sing it thankfully, blessing God that it is not their case.

A song *or* psalm for the sons of Korah, to the chief musician upon Mahalath Leannoth, Maschil of Heman the Ezrahite.

O LORD God of my salvation, I have cried day *and* night before thee: 2 Let my prayer come before thee: incline thine ear unto my cry; 3 For my soul is full of troubles: and my life draweth nigh unto the grave. 4 I am counted with them that go down into the pit: I am as a man *that hath* no strength: 5 Free among the dead, like the slain that lie in the grave, whom thou rememberest no more: and they are cut off from thy hand. 6 Thou hast laid me in the lowest pit, in darkness, in the deeps. 7 Thy wrath lieth hard upon me, and thou hast afflicted *me* with all thy waves. Selah. 8 Thou hast put away mine acquaintance far from me; thou hast made me an abomination unto them: *I am* shut up, and I cannot come forth. 9 Mine eye mourneth by reason of affliction: LORD, I have called daily upon thee, I have stretched out my hands unto thee.

It should seem, by the titles of this and the following psalm, that Heman was the penman of the one and Ethan of the other. There were two, of these names, who were sons of Zerah the son of Judah, 1 Chron. ii. 4, 6. There were two others famed for wisdom, 1 Kings iv. 31, where, to magnify Solomon's wisdom, he is said to be *wiser than Heman and Ethan.* Whether the Heman and Ethan who were Levites and precentors in the songs of Zion were the same we are not sure, nor which of these, nor whether any of these, were the penmen of these psalms. There was a Heman that was one of the chief singers, who is called *the king's seer, or prophet,* in the words of God (1 Chron. xxv. 5); it is probable that this also was a seer, and yet could see no comfort for himself, an instructor and comforter of others, and yet himself putting comfort away from him. The very first words of the psalm are the only words of comfort and support in all the psalm. There is nothing about him but clouds and darkness; but, before he begins his complaint, he calls God *the God of his salvation,* which intimates both that he looked for salvation, bad as things were, and that he looked up to God for the salvation and depended upon him to be the author of it. Now here we have the psalmist,

I. A man of prayer, one that gave himself to prayer at all times, but especially now that he was in affliction; for *is any afflicted? let him pray.* It is his comfort that he had prayed; it is his complaint that, notwithstanding his prayer, he was still in affliction. He was, 1. Very earnest in prayer: "*I have cried unto thee* (v. 1), and have *stretched out my hands unto thee* (v. 9), as one that would take hold on thee, and even catch at the mercy, with a holy fear of coming short and missing of it." 2. He was very frequent and constant in prayer: *I have called upon thee daily* (v. 9), nay, *day and night*, v. 1. For thus men ought always to pray, and not to faint; God's own elect cry day and night to him, not only morning and evening, beginning every day and every night with prayer, but spending the day and night in prayer. This is indeed praying always; and then we shall speed in prayer, when we continue instant in prayer. 3. He directed his prayer to God, and from him expected and desired an answer (v. 2): "*Let my prayer come before thee*, to be accepted of thee, not before men, to be seen of them, as the Pharisees' prayers." He does not desire that men should hear them, but, "Lord, *incline thy ear unto my cry*, for to that I refer myself; give what answer to it thou pleasest."

II. He was a man of sorrows, and therefore some make him, in this psalm, a type of Christ, whose complaints on the cross, and sometimes before, were much to the same purport with this psalm. He cries out (v. 3): *My soul is full of troubles;* so Christ said, *Now is my soul troubled;* and, in his agony, *My soul is exceedingly sorrowful even unto death,* like the psalmist's here, for he says, *My life draws nigh unto the grave.* Heman was a very wise man, and a very good man, a man of God, and a singer too, and one may therefore suppose him to have been a man of a cheerful spirit, and yet now a man of a sorrowful spirit, troubled in mind, and upon the brink of despair. Inward trouble is the sorest trouble, and that which, sometimes, the best of God's saints and servants have been severely exercised with. *The spirit of man*, of the greatest of men, will not always sustain his infirmity, but will droop and sink under it; *who then can bear a wounded spirit?*

III. He looked upon himself as a dying man, whose heart was ready to break with sorrow (v. 5): *Free among the dead* (one of that ghastly corporation), *like the slain that lie in the grave,* whose rotting and perishing nobody takes notice of or is concerned for, nay, whom thou rememberest no more, to protect or provide for the dead bodies, but they become an easy prey to corruption and the worms; they are *cut off from thy hand,* which used to be employed in supporting them and reaching out to them; but, now there is no more occasion for this, they are cut off from it and cut off by it" (*for God will not stretch out his hand to the grave,* Job xxx. 24); "*thou hast laid me in the lowest pit,* as low as possible, my condition low, my spirits low, *in darkness, in the deep* (v. 6), sinking, and seeing no way open of escape, brought to the last extremity, and ready to give up all for gone." Thus greatly may good men be afflicted, such dismal apprehensions may they have concerning their afflictions, and such dark conclusions may they sometimes be ready to make concerning the issue of them, through the power of melancholy and the weakness of faith.

IV. He complained most of God's displeasure against him, which infused the wormwood and the gall into the affliction and the misery (v. 7): *Thy wrath lies hard upon me.* Could he have discerned the favour and love of God in his affliction, it would have lain light upon him; but it lay hard, very hard, upon him, so that he was ready to sink and faint under it. The impressions of this wrath upon his spirits were God's *waves* with which he afflicted him, which rolled upon him, one on the neck of another, so that he scarcely recovered from one dark thought before he was oppressed with another; these waves beat against him with noise and fury; not some, but all, of God's waves were made use of in afflicting him and bearing him down. Even the children of God's love may sometimes apprehend themselves children of wrath, and no outward trouble can lie so hard upon them as that apprehension.

V. It added to his affliction that his friends deserted him and made themselves strange to him. When we are in trouble it is some comfort to have those about us that love us, and sympathize with us; but this good man had none such, which gives him occasion, not to accuse them, or charge them with treachery, ingratitude, and inhumanity, but to complain to God, with an eye to his hand in this part of the affliction (v. 8): *Thou hast put away my acquaintance far from me.* Providence had removed them, or rendered them incapable of being serviceable to him, or alienated their affections from him; for every creature is that to us (and no more) that God makes it to be. If our old acquaintance be shy of us, and those we expect kindness from prove unkind, we must bear that with the same patient submission to the divine will that we do other afflictions, Job xix. 13. Nay, his friends were not only strange to him, but even hated him, because he was poor and in distress: "*Thou hast made me an abomination to them;* they are not only shy of me, but sick of me, and I am looked upon by them, not only with contempt, but with abhorrence." Let none think it strange concerning such a trial as this, when Heman, who was so famed for wisdom, was yet, when the world frowned upon him, neglected, as a vessel in which is no pleasure.

VI. He looked upon his case as helpless and deplorable: "*I am shut up, and I cannot come forth,* a close prisoner, under the arrests of divine wrath, and no way open of escape." He therefore lies down and sinks under his troubles, because he sees not any probability of getting out of them. For thus he bemoans himself (v. 9): *My eye mourneth by reason of affliction.* Sometimes giving vent to grief by weeping gives some ease to a troubled spirit. Yet weeping must not hinder praying; we must sow in tears : *My eye mourns,* but *I cry unto thee daily.* Let prayers and tears go together, and they shall be accepted together. *I have heard thy prayers, I have seen thy tears.*

10 Wilt thou show wonders to the dead? shall the dead arise *and* praise thee? Selah. 11 Shall thy loving-kindness be declared in the grave? or thy faithfulness in destruction? 12 Shall thy wonders be known in the dark? and thy righteousness in the land of forgetfulness? 13 But unto thee have I cried, O LORD; and in the morning shall my prayer prevent thee. 14 LORD, why castest thou off my soul? *why* hidest thou thy face from me? 15 I *am* afflicted and ready to die from *my* youth up: *while* I suffer thy terrors I am distracted. 16 Thy fierce wrath goeth over me; thy terrors have cut me off. 17 They came round about me daily like water; they compassed me about together. 18 Lover and friend hast thou put far from me, *and* mine acquaintance into darkness.

In these verses,

I. The psalmist expostulates with God concerning the present deplorable condition he was in (*v.* 10—12): " *Wilt thou do a miraculous work to the dead,* and raise them to life again? Shall those that are dead and buried *rise up to praise thee?* No; they leave it to their children to rise up in their room to praise God; none expects that they should do it; and wherefore should they rise, wherefore should they live, but to praise God? The life we are born to at first, and the life we hope to rise to at last, must thus be spent. But *shall thy lovingkindness to thy people be declared in the grave,* either by those or to those that lie buried there? And thy faithfulness to thy promise, shall that be told in destruction? *shall thy wonders be wrought in the dark,* or known there, *and thy righteousness in* the grave, which is *the land of forgetfulness,* where men remember nothing, nor are themselves remembered? Departed souls may indeed know God's wonders and declare his faithfulness, justice, and lovingkindness; but deceased bodies cannot; they can neither receive God's favours in comfort nor return them in praise." Now we will not suppose these expostulations to be the language of despair, as if he thought God could not help him or would not, much less do they imply any disbelief of the resurrection of the dead at the last day; but he thus pleads with God for speedy relief: "Lord, thou art good, thou art faithful, thou art righteous; these attributes of thine will be made known in my

deliverance, but, if it be not hastened, it will come too late; for I shall be dead and past relief, dead and not capable of receiving any comfort, very shortly." Job often pleaded thus, Job vii. 8; x. 21.

II. He resolves to continue instant in prayer, and the more so because the deliverance was deferred (*v.* 13): " *Unto thee have I cried* many a time, and found comfort in so doing, and therefore I will continue to do so; *in the morning shall my prayer prevent thee.*" Note, Though our prayers be not answered immediately, yet we must not therefore give over praying, because *the vision is for an appointed time, and at the end it shall speak and not lie.* God delays the answer in order that he may try our patience and perseverance in prayer. He resolves to seek God early, in the morning, when his spirits were lively, and before the business of the day began to crowd in—in the morning, after he had been tossed with cares, and sorrowful thoughts in the silence and solitude of the night; but how could he say, *My prayer shall prevent thee?* Not as if he could wake sooner to pray than God to hear and answer; for he neither slumbers nor sleeps; but it intimates that he would be up earlier than ordinary to pray, would *prevent* (that is, go before) his usual hour of prayer. The greater our afflictions are the more solicitous and serious we should be in prayer. " My prayer shall present itself before thee, and be betimes with thee, and shall not stay for the encouragement of the beginning of mercy, but reach towards it with faith and expectation even before the day dawns." God often prevents our prayers and expectations with his mercies; let us prevent his mercies with our prayers and expectations.

III. He sets down what he will say to God in prayer. 1. He will humbly reason with God concerning the abject afflicted condition he was now in (*v.* 14): " *Lord, why castest thou off my soul?* What is it that provokes thee to treat me as one abandoned? *Show me wherefore thou contendest with me.*" He speaks it with wonder that God should cast off an old servant, should cast off one that was resolved not to cast him off: " No wonder men cast me off; but, Lord, why dost thou, whose gifts and callings are without repentance? *Why hidest thou thy face,* as one angry at me, that either hast no favour for me or wilt not let me know that thou hast? Nothing grieves a child of God so much as God's hiding his face from him, nor is there any thing he so much dreads as God's casting off his soul. If the sun be clouded, that darkens the earth; but if the sun should abandon the earth, and quite cast it off, what a dungeon would it be! 2. He will humbly repeat the same complaints he had before made, until God have mercy on him. Two things he represents to God as his grievances :—(1.) That God was a terror to him : *I suffer thy terrors, v.* 15. He had continual frightful apprehensions of the wrath of God against him for his sins and the consequences of that wrath. It terrified him to think of God, of falling into his hands and appearing before him to receive his doom from him. He perspired and trembled at the apprehension of God's displeasure against him, and the terror of his majesty. Note, Even those that are designed for God's favours may yet, for a time, suffer his terrors. The spirit of adoption is first a spirit of bondage to fear. Poor Job complained of the terrors of *God setting themselves in array against him*, Job vi. 4. The psalmist here explains himself, and tells us what he means by God's terrors, even his *fierce wrath*. Let us see what dreadful impressions those terrors made upon him, and how deeply they wounded him. [1.] They had almost taken away his life: " *I am so afflicted* with them that I am *ready to die*, and*" (as the word is) "*to give up the ghost. Thy terrors have cut me off*," v. 16. What is hell, that eternal excision, by which damned sinners are for ever cut off from God and all happiness, but God's terrors fastening and preying upon their guilty consciences? [2.] They had almost taken away the use of his reason: *When I suffer thy terrors I am distracted.* This sad effect the terrors of the Lord have had upon many, and upon some good men, who have thereby been put quite out of the possession of their own souls, a most piteous case, and which ought to be looked upon with great compassion. [3.] This had continued long: *From my youth up I suffer thy terrors.* He had been from his childhood afflicted with melancholy, and trained up in sorrow under the discipline of that school. If we begin our days with trouble, and the days of our mourning have been prolonged a great while, let us not think it strange, but let tribulation work patience. It is observable that Heman, who became eminently wise and good, was *afflicted and ready to die*, and suffered God's terrors, *from his youth up.* Thus many have found it was good for them to bear the yoke in their youth, that sorrow has been much better for them than laughter would have been, and that being much afflicted, and often ready to die, when they were young, they have, by the grace of God, got such an habitual seriousness and weanedness from the world as have been of great use to them all their days. Sometimes those whom God designs for eminent services are prepared for them by exercises of this kind. [4.] His affliction was now extreme, and worse than ever. God's terrors now came round about him, so that from all sides he was assaulted with variety of troubles, and he had no comfortable gale from any point of the compass. They broke in upon him together like an inundation of water; and this daily, and all the day; so that he had no rest, no respite, not the least breathing-time, no lucid intervals, nor any gleam of hope. Such was the calamitous state of a

572

very wise and good man; he was so surrounded with terrors that he could find no place of shelter, nor lie any where under the wind. (2.) That no friend he had in the world was a comfort to him (v. 18): *Lover and friend hast thou put far from me;* some are dead, others at a distance, and perhaps many unkind. Next to the comforts of religion are those of friendship and society; therefore to be friendless is (as to this life) almost to be comfortless; and to those who have had friends, but have lost them, the calamity is the more grievous. With this the psalmist here closes his complaint, as if this were that which completed his woe and gave the finishing stroke to this melancholy piece. If our friends are put far from us by scattering providences, nay, if by death our acquaintance are removed into darkness, we have reason to look upon it as a sore affliction, but must acknowledge and submit to the hand of God in it.

PSALM LXXXIX.

Many psalms that begin with complaint and prayer end with joy and praise, but this begins with joy and praise and ends with sad complaints and petitions; for the psalmist first recounts God's former favours, and then with the consideration of them aggravates the present grievances. It is uncertain when it was penned; only, in general, that it was at a time when the house of David was woefully eclipsed; some think it was at the time of the captivity of Babylon, when king Zedekiah was insulted over, and abused, by Nebuchadnezzar, and then they make the title to signify no more than that the psalm was set to the tune of a song of Ethan the son of Zerah, called Maschil; others suppose it to be penned by Ethan, who is mentioned in the story of Solomon, who, outliving that glorious prince, thus lamented the great disgrace done to the house of David in the next reign by the revolt of the ten tribes. I. The psalmist, in the joyful pleasant part of the psalm, gives glory to God, and takes comfort to himself and his friends. This he does more briefly, mentioning God's mercy and truth (ver. 1) and his covenant (ver. 2—4), but more largely in the following verses, wherein, 1. He adores the glory and perfection of God, ver. 5—14. 2. He pleases himself in the happiness of those that are admitted into communion with him, ver. 15—18. 3. He builds all his hope upon God's covenant with David, as a type of Christ, ver. 19—37. II. In the melancholy part of the psalm he laments the present calamitous state of the prince and royal family (ver. 38—45), expostulates with God upon it (ver. 46—49), and then concludes with prayer for redress, ver. 50, 51. In singing this psalm we must have high thoughts of God, a lively faith in his covenant with the Redeemer, and a sympathy with the afflicted parts of the church.

Maschil of Ethan the Ezrahite.

I WILL sing of the mercies of the LORD for ever: with my mouth will I make known thy faithfulness to all generations. 2 For I have said, Mercy shall be built up for ever: thy faithfulness shalt thou establish in the very heavens. 3 I have made a covenant with my chosen, I have sworn unto David my servant, 4 Thy seed will I establish for ever, and build up thy throne to all generations. Selah.

The psalmist has a very sad complaint to make of the deplorable condition of the family of David at this time, and yet he begins the psalm with songs of praise; for we must, in every thing, in every state, give thanks; thus we must glorify the Lord in the fire. We think, when we are in trouble, that we get ease by complaining; but we do more—we get joy, by praising. Let our complaints therefore be turned into thanksgivings; and in these verses we find that which will be matter of praise and thanksgiving for us in the worst of times, whether upon a personal or a public account, 1. However it be, the everlasting God is good and true, *v.* 1. Though we may find it hard to reconcile present dark providences with the goodness and truth of God, yet we must abide by this principle, That God's mercies are inexhaustible and his truth is inviolable; and these must be the matter of our joy and praise: "*I will sing of the mercies of the Lord for ever,* sing a praising song to God's honour, a pleasant song for my own solace, and *Maschil,* an instructive song, for the edification of others." We may be for ever singing God's mercies, and yet the subject will not be drawn dry. We must sing of God's mercies as long as we live, train up others to sing of them when we are gone, and hope to be singing them in heaven world without end; and this is *singing of the mercies of the Lord for ever. With my mouth,* and with my pen (for by that also do we speak), *will I make known thy faithfulness to all generations,* assuring posterity, from my own observation and experience, that God is true to every word that he has spoken, that they may learn to *put their trust in God,* lxxviii. 6. 2. However it be, the everlasting covenant is firm and sure, *v.* 2—4. Here we have, (1.) The psalmist's faith and hope: "Things now look black, and threaten the utter extirpation of the house of David; but *I have said,* and I have warrant from the word of God to say it, that *mercy shall be built up for ever.*" As the goodness of God's nature is to be the matter of our song (*v.* 1), so much more the mercy that is built for us in the covenant; it is still increasing, like a house in the building up, and shall still continue our rest for ever, like a house built up. It shall be built up for ever; for the everlasting habitations we hope for in the new Jerusalem are of this building. If mercy shall be built for ever, then the *tabernacle of David, which has fallen down,* shall *be raised out of its ruins,* and *built up as in the days of old,* Amos ix. 11. *Therefore* mercy shall be built up for ever, because *thy faithfulness shalt thou establish in the very heavens.* Though our expectations are in some particular instances disappointed, yet God's promises are not disannulled; they are *established in the very heavens* (that is, in his eternal counsels); they are above the changes of this lower region and out of the reach of the opposition of hell and earth. The stability of the material heavens is an emblem of the truth of God's word; the heavens may be clouded by vapours arising out of the earth, but they cannot be touched, they cannot be changed. (2.) An abstract of the covenant upon which this faith and hope are built: *I have said it,* says the psalmist, for God *hath sworn it,* that the heirs of promise might be entirely satisfied of the immutability of his counsel. He brings in God speaking (*v.* 3), owning, to the comfort of his people, "*I have made a cove-*

nant, and therefore will make it good." The covenant is made with David; the covenant of royalty is made with him, as the father of his family, and with his seed through him and for his sake, representing the covenant of grace made with Christ as head of the church and with all believers as his spiritual seed. David is here called *God's chosen* and *his servant;* and, as God is not changeable to recede from his own choice, so he is not unrighteous to cast off one that served him. Two things encourage the psalmist to build his faith on this covenant:—[1.] The ratification of it; it was confirmed with an oath: *The Lord has sworn, and he will not repent.* [2.] The perpetuity of it; the blessings of the covenant were not only secured to David himself, but were entailed on his family; it was promised that his family should continue—*Thy seed will I establish for ever,* so that *David shall not want a son to reign* (Jer. xxxiii. 20, 21); and that it should continue a royal family—*I will build up thy throne to all generations,* to all the generations of time. This has its accomplishment only in Christ, of the seed of David, who lives for ever, to whom God has given the throne of his father David, and of the increase of whose government and peace there shall be no end. Of this covenant the psalmist will return to speak more largely, *v.* 19, &c.

5 And the heavens shall praise thy wonders, O LORD: thy faithfulness also in the congregation of the saints. 6 For who in the heaven can be compared unto the LORD? *who* among the sons of the mighty can be likened unto the LORD? 7 God is greatly to be feared in the assembly of the saints, and to be had in reverence of all *them that are* about him. 8 O LORD God of hosts, who *is* a strong LORD like unto thee? or to thy faithfulness round about thee? 9 Thou rulest the raging of the sea: when the waves thereof arise, thou stillest them. 10 Thou hast broken Rahab in pieces, as one that is slain; thou hast scattered thine enemies with thy strong arm. 11 The heavens *are* thine, the earth also *is* thine: *as for* the world and the fulness thereof, thou hast founded them. 12 The north and the south thou hast created them: Tabor and Hermon shall rejoice in thy name. 13 Thou hast a mighty arm: strong is thy hand, *and* high is thy right hand. 14 Justice and judgment *are* the habitation of thy throne: mercy and truth shall go before thy face.

These verses are full of the praises of God. Observe,

I. Where, and by whom, God is to be praised. 1. God is praised by the angels above: *The heavens shall praise thy wonders, O Lord! v.* 5; that is, "the glorious inhabitants of the upper world continually celebrate thy praises." *Bless the Lord, you his angels,* ciii. 20. The works of God are wonders even to those that are best acquainted and most intimately conversant with them; the more God's works are known the more they are admired and praised. This should make us love heaven, and long to be there, that there we shall have nothing else to do but to praise God and his wonders. 2. God is praised by the assemblies of his saints on earth *(praise waits for him in Zion);* and, though their praises fall so far short of the praises of angels, yet God is pleased to take notice of them, and accept of them, and reckon himself honoured by them. "Thy faithfulness and the truth of thy promise, that rock on which the church is built, shall be praised in the congregation of the saints, who owe their all to that faithfulness, and whose constant comfort it is that there is a promise, and that he is faithful who has promised." It is expected from God's saints on earth that they praise him; who should, if they do not? Let every saint praise him, but especially the congregation of saints; when they come together, let them join in praising God. The more the better; it is the more like heaven. Of the honour done to God by the assembly of the saints he speaks again *(v.* 7): *God is greatly to be feared in the assembly of the saints.* Saints should assemble for religious worship, that they may publicly own their relation to God and may stir up one another to give honour to him, and, in keeping up communion with God, may likewise maintain the communion of saints. In religious assemblies God has promised the presence of his grace, but we must also, in them, have an eye to his glorious presence, that the familiarity we are admitted to may not breed the least contempt; for he is terrible in his holy places, and therefore greatly to be feared. A holy awe of God must fall upon us, and fill us, in all our approaches to God, even in secret, to which something may very well be added by the solemnity of public assemblies. God must be had *in reverence of all that are about him,* that attend him continually as his servants or approach him upon any particular errand. See Lev. x. 3. Those only serve God acceptably who serve him with *reverence and godly fear,* Heb. xii. 28.

II. What it is to praise God; it is to acknowledge him to be a being of unparalleled perfection, such a one that there is none like him, nor any to be compared with him, *v.* 6. If there be any beings that can pretend to vie with God, surely they must be found among the angels; but they are all infinitely short of him: *Who in the heaven can*

be compared with the Lord, so as to challenge any share of the reverence and adoration which are due to him only, or to set up in rivalship with him for the homage of the children of men? They are sons of the mighty, but which of them can be likened unto the Lord? Nobles are princes' peers; some parity there is between them. But there is none between God and the angels; they are not his peers. *To whom will you liken me, or shall I be equal? saith the Holy One,* Isa. xl. 25. This is insisted on again (*v.* 8): *Who is a strong Lord like unto thee?* No angel, no earthly potentate, whatsoever, is comparable to God, or *has an arm like him,* or can *thunder with a voice like him.* Thy *faithfulness is round about thee;* that is, "thy angels who are round about thee, attending thee with their praises and ready to go on thy errands, are all faithful." Or, rather, "In every thing thou doest, on all sides, thou approvest thyself faithful to thy word, above whatever prince or potentate was." Among men it is too often found that those who are most able to break their word are least careful to keep it; but God is both strong and faithful; he can do every thing, and yet will never do an unjust thing.

III. What we ought, in our praises, to give God the glory of. Several things are here mentioned. 1. The command God has of the most ungovernable creatures (*v.* 9): *Thou rulest the raging of the sea,* than which nothing is more frightful or threatening, nor more out of the power of man to give check to; it can swell no higher, roll no further, beat no harder, continue no longer, nor do any more hurt, than God suffers it. *" When the waves thereof arise* thou canst immediately hush them asleep, still them, and make them quiet, and turn the storm into a calm." This coming in here as an act of omnipotence, what manner of man then was the Lord Jesus, whom the *winds and seas obeyed?* 2. The victories God has obtained over the enemies of his church. His ruling the raging of the sea and quelling its billows was an emblem of this (*v.* 10): *Thou hast broken Rahab,* many a *proud enemy* (so it signifies), Egypt in particular, which is sometimes called *Rahab,* broken it in pieces, as one that is slain and utterly unable to make head again. "The head being broken, thou hast scattered the remainder with the arm of thy strength." God has more ways than one to deal with his and his church's enemies. We think he should slay them immediately, but sometimes he scatters them, that he may send them abroad to be monuments of his justice, lix. 11. The remembrance of the breaking of Egypt in pieces is a comfort to the church, in reference to the present power of Babylon; for God is still the same. 3. The incontestable property he has in all the creatures of the upper and lower world (*v.* 11, 12): "Men are honoured for their large possessions; but *the heavens are thine, O Lord! the earth also is thine;* therefore we praise thee, therefore we trust in thee, therefore we will not fear what man can do against us. *The world and the fulness thereof,* all the riches contained in it, all the inhabitants of it, both the tenements and the tenants, are all thine; for *thou hast founded them,*" and the founder may justly claim to be the owner. He specifies, (1.) The remotest parts of the world, the north and south, the countries that lie under the two poles, which are uninhabited and little known : " *Thou hast created them,* and therefore knowest them, takest care of them, and hast tributes of praise from them." The north is said to be *hung over the empty place;* yet what fulness there is there God is the owner of it. (2.) The highest parts of the world. He mentions the two highest hills in Canaan—" *Tabor and Hermon*" (one lying to the west, the other to the east); " these shall rejoice in thy name, for they are under the care of thy providence, and they produce offerings for thy altar." The little hills are said to rejoice in their own ꞏfruitfulness, lxv. 12. Tabor is commonly supposed to be that high mountain in Galilee on the top of which Christ was transfigured ; and then indeed it might be said to rejoice in that voice which was there heard, *This is my beloved Son.* 4. The power and justice, the mercy and truth, with which he governs the world and rules in the affairs of the children of men, *v.* 13, 14. (1.) God is able to do every thing; for he is the Lord God Almighty. His arm, his hand, is mighty and strong, both to save his people and to destroy his and their enemies ; none can either resist the force or bear the weight of his mighty hand. *High is his right hand,* to reach the highest, even those that *set their nests among the stars* (Amos ix. 2, 3 ; Obad. 4); his *right hand is exalted* in what he has done, for in thousands of instances he has signalized his power, cxviii. 16. (2.) He never did, nor ever will do, any thing that is either unjust or unwise; for *righteousness and judgment are the habitation of his throne.* None of all his dictates or decrees ever varied from the rules of equity and wisdom, nor could ever any charge God with unrighteousness or folly. Justice and judgment are the *preparing* of his throne (so some), the *establishment* of it, so others. The preparations for his government in his counsels from eternity, and the establishment of it in its consequences to eternity, are all justice and judgment. (3.) He always does that which is kind to his people and consonant to the word which he has spoken : " *Mercy and truth shall go before thy face,* to prepare thy way, as harbingers to make room for thee—mercy in promising, truth in performing—truth in being as good as thy word, mercy in being better." How praiseworthy are these in great men, much more in the great God, in whom they are in perfection !

15 Blessed *is* the people that know

the joyful sound : they shall walk, O Lᴏʀᴅ, in the light of thy countenance. 16 In thy name shall they rejoice all the day : and in thy righteousness shall they be exalted. 17 For thou *art* the glory of their strength : and in thy favour our horn shall be exalted. 18 For the Lᴏʀᴅ *is* our defence ; and the Holy One of Israel *is* our king.

The psalmist, having largely shown the blessedness of the God of Israel, here shows the blessedness of the Israel of God. As *there is none like unto the God of Jeshurun, so, happy art thou, O Israel! there is none like unto thee, O people!* especially as a type of the gospel-Israel, consisting of all true believers, whose happiness is here described.

I. Glorious discoveries are made to them, and glad tidings of good brought to them ; they hear, *they know, the joyful sound, v.* 15. This may allude, 1. To the shout of a victorious army, the shout of a king, Num. xxiii. 21. Israel have the tokens of God's presence with them in their wars; the sound of the *going in the top of the mulberry-trees* was indeed a *joyful sound* (2 Sam. v. 24) ; and they often returned making the earth ring with their songs of triumph; these were joyful sounds. Or, 2. To the sound that was made over the sacrifices and on the solemn feast-day, lxxxi. 1—3. This was the happiness of Israel, that they had among them the free and open profession of God's holy religion, and abundance of joy in their sacrifices. Or, 3. To the sound of the jubilee-trumpet; a joyful sound it was to servants and debtors, to whom it proclaimed release. The gospel is indeed a joyful sound, a sound of victory, of liberty, of communion with God, and the *sound of abundance of rain;* blessed are the people that hear it, and know it, and bid it welcome.

II. Special tokens of God's favour are granted them : " *They shall walk, O Lord!* in the light of thy countenance;* they shall govern themselves by thy directions, shall be guided by thy eye; and they shall delight themselves in thy consolations. They shall have the favour of God; they shall know that they have it, and it shall be continual matter of joy and rejoicing to them. They shall go through all the exercises of a holy life under the powerful influences of God's loving-kindness, which shall make their duty pleasant to them and make ꞏthem sincere in it, aiming at this, as their end, to be accepted of the Lord." We then walk in the light of the Lord when we fetch all our comforts from God's favour and are very careful to keep ourselves in his love.

III. They never want matter for joy Blessed are God's people, for in his name, in all that whereby he has made himself known, if it be not their own fault, *they shall rejoice* all the day. Those that rejoice in Christ Jesus, and make God their exceeding joy, have enough to counterbalance their grievances and silence their griefs; and therefore their joy is full (1 John i. 4) and constant; it is their duty to rejoice evermore.

IV. Their relation to God is their honour and dignity. They are happy, for they are high. *Surely in the Lord,* in the Lord Christ, *they have righteousness and strength,* and so are recommended by him to the divine acceptance; and therefore *in him shall all the seed of Israel glory,* Isa. xlv, 24, 25. So it is here, *v.* 16, 17. 1. "In *thy righteousness shall they be exalted,* and not in any righteousness of their own." We are exalted out of danger, and into honour, purely by the righteousness of Christ, which is a clothing both for dignity and for defence. 2. "Thou art the *glory of their strength,*" that is, "thou art their strength, and it is their glory that thou art so, and what they glory in." Thanks *be to God who always causes us to triumph.* 3. "In thy favour, which through Christ we hope for, *our horn shall be exalted.* The horn denotes beauty, plenty, and power; these those have who are made accepted in the beloved. What greater preferment are men capable of in this world than to be God's favourites?

V. Their relation to God is their protection and safety (*v.* 18): "*For our shield is of the Lord*" (so the margin) "*and our king is from the Holy One of Israel.* If God be our ruler, he will be our defender; and who is he then that can harm us?" It was the happiness of Israel that God himself had the erecting of their bulwarks and the nominating of their king (so some take it); or, rather, that he was himself a *wall of fire round about them,* and, as a Holy One, the author and centre of their holy religion; he was their King, and so their glory in the midst of them. Christ is the Holy One of Israel, that holy thing; and in nothing was that peculiar people more blessed than in this, that *he* was born King of the Jews. Now this account of the blessedness of God's Israel comes in here as that to which it was hard to reconcile their present calamitous state.

19 Then thou spakest in vision to thy holy one, and saidst, I have laid help upon *one that is* mighty; I have exalted *one* chosen out of the people. 20 I have found David my servant; with my holy oil have I anointed him: 21 With whom my hand shall be established: mine arm also shall strengthen him. 22 The enemy shall not exact upon him; nor the son of wickedness afflict him. 23 And I will beat down his foes before his face, and plague them that hate him. 24 But my faithfulness and my mercy

shall be with him: and in my name shall his horn be exalted. 25 I will set his hand also in the sea, and his right hand in the rivers. 26 He shall cry unto me, Thou *art* my father, my God, and the rock of my salvation. 27 Also I will make him *my* firstborn, higher than the kings of the earth. 28 My mercy will I keep for him for evermore, and my covenant shall stand fast with him. 29 His seed also will I make to endure for ever, and his throne as the days of heaven. 30 If his children forsake my law, and walk not in my judgments; 31 If they break my statutes, and keep not my commandments; 32 Then will I visit their transgression with the rod, and their iniquity with stripes. 33 Nevertheless my lovingkindness will I not utterly take from him, nor suffer my faithfulness to fail. 34 My covenant will I not break, nor alter the thing that is gone out of my lips. 35 Once have I sworn by my holiness that I will not lie unto David. 36 His seed shall endure for ever, and his throne as the sun before me. 37 It shall be established for ever as the moon, and *as* a faithful witness in heaven. Selah.

The covenant God made with David and his seed was mentioned before (*v.* 3, 4); but in these verses it is enlarged upon, and pleaded with God, for favour to the royal family, now almost sunk and ruined; yet certainly it looks at Christ, and has its accomplishment in him much more than in David; nay, some passages here are scarcely applicable at all to David, but must be understood of Christ only (who is therefore called *David our king,* Hos. iii. 5), and very great and precious promises they are which are here made to the Redeemer, which are strong foundations for the faith and hope of the redeemed to build upon. The comforts of our redemption flow from the covenant of redemption; all our springs are in that, Isa. lv. 3. *I will make an everlasting covenant with you, even the sure mercies of David,* Acts xiii. 34. Now here we have an account of those sure mercies. Observe,

I. What assurance we have of the truth of the promise, which may encourage us to build upon it. We are here told, 1. How it was spoken (*v.* 19): *Thou didst speak in vision to thy Holy One.* God's promise to David, which is especially referred to here, was spoken in vision to Nathan the prophet, 2 Sam. vii. 12—17. *Then, when the Holy One of Israel was their king (v.* 18), he appointed

David to be his viceroy. But to all the prophets, those holy ones, he *spoke in vision* concerning Christ, and to him himself especially, who had lain in his bosom from eternity, and was made perfectly acquainted with the whole design of redemption, Matt. xi. 27. 2. How it was sworn to and ratified (*v.* 35): *Once have I sworn by my holiness,* that darling attribute. In swearing by his holiness, he swore by himself; for he will as soon cease to be as be otherwise than holy. His swearing once is enough; he needs not swear again, as David did (1 Sam. xx. 17); for his word and oath are two immutable things. As Christ was made a priest, so he was made a king, *by an oath* (Heb. vii. 21); for his kingdom and priesthood are both unchangeable.

II. The choice made of the person to whom the promise is given, *v.* 19, 20. David was a king of God's own choosing, so is Christ, and therefore both are called *God's kings,* Ps. ii. 6. David was mighty, a man of courage and fit for business; he was chosen out of the people, not out of the princes, but the shepherds. God found him out, exalted him, laid help upon him, and ordered Samuel to anoint him. But this is especially to be applied to Christ. 1. He is one that is mighty, every way qualified for the great work he was to undertake, *able to save to the uttermost*—mighty in strength, for he is the Son of God—mighty in love, for he is able experimentally to compassionate those that are tempted. He is *the mighty God,* Isa. ix. 6. 2. He is *chosen out of the people,* one of us, bone of our bone, that takes part with us of flesh and blood. Being ordained for men, he is taken from among men, that his terror might not make us afraid. 3. God has found him. He is a Saviour of God's own providing; for the salvation, from first to last, is purely the Lord's doing. *He has found the ransom,* Job xxxiii. 24. We could never have found a person fit to undertake this great work, Rev. v. 3, 4. 4. God has *laid help upon him,* not only helped him, but treasured up help in him for us, laid it as a charge upon him to help fallen man up again, to help the chosen remnant to heaven. *In me is thy help,* Hos. xiii. 9. 5. He has exalted him, by constituting him the prophet, priest, and king of his church, clothing him with power, raising him from the dead, and setting him at his own right hand. Whom God chooses and uses he will exalt. 6. He has anointed him, has qualified him for his office, and so confirmed him in it, by giving him the Spirit, not by measure, but without measure, infinitely above his fellows. He is called *Messiah,* or *Christ,* the *Anointed.* 7. In all this he designed him to be his own servant, for the accomplishing of his eternal purpose and the advancement of the interests of his kingdom among men.

III. The promises made to this chosen one, to David in the type and the Son of David in the antitype, in which not only gracious, but glorious things are spoken of him.

1. With reference to himself, as king and God's servant: and what makes for him makes for all his loving subjects. It is here promised, (1.) That God would stand by him and strengthen him in his undertaking (*v.* 21): *With him my hand* not only shall be, but *shall be established,* by promise, shall be so established that he shall by it be established and confirmed in all his offices, so that none of them shall be undermined and overthrown, though by the man of sin they shall all be usurped and fought against. Christ had a great deal of hard work to do and hard usage to go through; but he that gave him commission gave him forces sufficient for the execution of his commission: "*My arm also shall strengthen him* to break through and bear up under all his difficulties." No good work can miscarry in the hand of those whom God himself undertakes to strengthen. (2.) That he should be victorious over his enemies, that they should not encroach upon him (*v.* 22): *The son of wickedness shall not exact upon him,* nor afflict him. He that at first broke the peace would set himself against him that undertook to make peace, and do what he could to blast his design: but he could only reach to bruise his heel; further he could not exact upon him nor afflict him. Christ became a surety for our debt, and thereby Satan and death thought to gain advantage against him; but he satisfied the demands of God's justice, and then they could not exact upon him. *The prince of this world cometh, but he has nothing in me,* John xiv. 30. Nay, they not only shall not prevail against him, but they shall fall before him (*v.* 23): *I will beat down his foes before his face;* the prince of this world shall be cast out, principalities and powers spoiled, and he shall be the death of death itself, and the destruction of the grave, Hos. xiii. 14. Some apply this to the ruin which God brought upon the Jewish nation, that persecuted Christ and put him to death. But all Christ's enemies, who hate him and will not have him to reign over them, shall be brought forth and slain before him, Luke xix. 27. (3.) That he should be the great trustee of the covenant between God and men, that God would be gracious and true to us (*v.* 24): *My faithfulness and my mercy shall be with him.* They were with David; God continued merciful to him, and so approved himself faithful. They were with Christ; God made good all his promises to him. But that is not all; God's mercy to us, and his faithfulness to us, are with Christ; he is not only pleased with him, but with us in him; and it is in him that all the promises of God are yea and amen. So that if any poor sinners hope for benefit by the faithfulness and mercy of God, let them know it is with Christ; it is lodged in his hand, and to him they must apply for it (*v.* 28)· *My mercy will I keep for him,* to be disposed of by him,

for evermore; in the channel of Christ's mediation all the streams of divine goodness will for ever run. Therefore it is *the mercy of our Lord Jesus Christ* which we *look for unto eternal life,* Jude 21; John xvii. 2. And, as the mercy of God flows to us through him, so the promise of God is, through him, firm to us: *My covenant shall stand fast with him,* both the covenant of redemption made with him and the covenant of grace made with us in him. The new covenant is *therefore* always new, and firmly established, because it is lodged in the hands of a Mediator, Heb. viii. 6. The covenant stands fast, because it stands upon this basis. And this redounds to the everlasting honour of the Lord Jesus, that to him the great cause between God and man is entirely referred and the Father has committed all judgment to him, that *all men might honour him* (John v. 22, 23); therefore it is here said, *In my name shall his horn be exalted;* this shall be his glory, that God's *name is in him* (Exod. xxiii. 21), and that he acts in God's name. *As the Father gave me commandment, so I do.* (4) That his kingdom should be greatly enlarged (v. 25): *I will set his hand in the sea* (he shall have the dominion of the seas, and the isles of the sea), and *his right hand in the rivers,* the inland countries that are watered with rivers. David's kingdom extended itself to the Great Sea, and the Red Sea, to the river of Egypt and the river Euphrates. But it is in the kingdom of the Messiah that this has its full accomplishment, and shall have more and more, when *the kingdoms of this world shall become the kingdoms of the Lord and of his Christ* (Rev. xi. 15), and *the isles shall wait for his law.* (5.) That he should own God as his Father, and God would own him as his Son, his firstborn, v. 26, 27. This is a comment upon these words in Nathan's message concerning Solomon (for he also was a type of Christ as well as David), *I will be his Father and he shall be my Son* (2 Sam. vii. 14), and the relation shall be owned on both sides. [1.] *He shall cry unto me, Thou art my Father.* It is probable that Solomon did so; but we are sure Christ did so, in the days of his flesh, when he offered up strong cries to God, and called him *holy Father, righteous Father,* and taught us to address ourselves to him as *our Father in heaven.* Christ, in his agony, cried unto God, *Thou art my Father* (Matt. xxvi. 39, 42, *O my Father),* and, upon the cross, *Father, forgive them; Father, into thy hands I commend my spirit.* He looked upon him likewise as his God, and therefore he perfectly obeyed him, and submitted to his will in his whole undertaking (he is *my God and your God,* John xx. 17), and as the rock of his salvation, who would bear him up and bear him out in his undertaking, and make him more than a conqueror, even a complete Saviour; and therefore with an undaunted resolution he *endured the cross, despising the shame,* for he knew he should be both ius-
578

tified and glorified. [2.] *I will make him my firstborn.* I see not how this can be applied to David; it is Christ's prerogative to be *the firstborn of every creature,* and, as such, the *heir of all things,* Col. i. 15; Heb. i. 2, 6. When *all power was given to Christ both in heaven and in earth, and all things were delivered unto him by the Father,* then God made him his firstborn, and far higher, more great and honourable, than the kings of the earth; for he is the King of kings, *angels, authorities, and powers, being made subject to him,* 1 Pet. iii. 22.

2. With reference to his seed. God's covenants always took in the seed of the covenanters; this does so (v. 29, 36): *His seed shall endure for ever,* and with it his throne. Now this will be differently understood according as we apply it to Christ or David.

(1.) If we apply it to David, by his seed we are to understand his successors, Solomon and the following kings of Judah, who descended from the loins of David. It is supposed that they might degenerate, and not walk in the spirit and steps of their father David; in such a case they must expect to come under divine rebukes, such as the house of David was at this time under, v. 38. But let this encourage them, that, though they were corrected, they should not be abandoned or disinherited. This refers to that part of Nathan's message (2 Sam. vii. 14, 15), *If he commit iniquity, I will chasten him,* but *my mercy shall not depart from him.* Thus far David's seed and throne did endure for ever, that, notwithstanding the wickedness of many of his posterity, who were the scandals of his house, yet his family continued, and continued in the imperial dignity, a very long time,—that, as long as Judah continued a kingdom, David's posterity were kings of it, and the royalty of that kingdom was never in any other family, as that of the ten tribes was, in Jeroboam's first, then in Baasha's, &c.,—and that the family of David continued a family of distinction till that Son of David came whose throne should endure for ever; see Luke i. 27, 32; ii. 4, 11. If David's posterity, in after-times, should forsake God and their duty and revolt to the ways of sin, God would bring desolating judgments upon them and ruin the family; and yet he would not take away his lovingkindness from David, nor break his covenant with him; for, in the Messiah, who should come out of his loins, all these promises shall have their accomplishment to the full. Thus, when the Jews were rejected, the apostle shows that God's covenant with Abraham was not broken, because it was fulfilled in his spiritual seed, the heirs of the righteousness of faith, Rom. xi. 7.

(2.) If we apply it to Christ, by his seed we are to understand his subjects, all believers, his spiritual seed, the children which God has given him, Heb. ii. 13. This is that seed which shall be made to endure for ever, and his throne in the midst of them, in the church in the heart, *as the days of heaven.* To the end Christ shall have a people in the world to serve and honour him. *He shall see his seed; he shall prolong his days.* This holy seed shall endure for ever in a glorified state, when time and days shall be no more; and thus Christ's throne and kingdom shall be perpetuated: the kingdom of his grace shall continue through all the ages of time and the kingdom of his glory to the endless ages of eternity.

[1.] The continuance of Christ's kingdom is here made doubtful by the sins and afflictions of his subjects; their iniquities and calamities threaten the ruin of it. This case is here put, that we may not be offended when it comes to be a case in fact, but that we may reconcile it with the stability of the covenant and be assured of that notwithstanding. *First,* It is here supposed that there will be much amiss in the subjects of Christ's kingdom. His children may *forsake God's law* (v. 30) by omissions, and *break his statutes* (v. 31) by commissions. There are spots which are the spots of God's children, Deut. xxxii. 5. Many corruptions there are in the bowels of the church, as well as in the hearts of those who are the members of it, and these corruptions break out. *Secondly,* They are here told that they must smart for it (v. 32): *I will visit their transgression with a rod,* their transgression sooner than that of others. *You only have I known, and therefore I will punish you,* Amos iii. 2. Their being related to Christ shall not excuse them from being called to an account. But observe what affliction is to God's people. 1. It is but a rod, not an axe, not a sword; it is for correction, not for destruction. This denotes gentleness in the affliction; it is the rod of men, such a rod as men use in correcting their children; and it denotes a design of good in and by the affliction, such a rod as yields the peaceable fruit of righteousness. 2. It is a rod in the hand of God *(I will visit them),* he who is wise, and knows what he does, gracious, and will do what is best. 3. It is a rod which they shall never feel the smart of but when there is great need: *If they break my law, then I will visit their transgression with the rod,* but not else. Then it is requisite that God's honour be vindicated, and that they be humbled and reduced.

[2.] The continuance of Christ's kingdom is made certain by the inviolable promise and oath of God, notwithstanding all this (v. 33): *Nevertheless, my kindness will I not* totally and finally *take from him. First,* "Notwithstanding their provocations, yet my covenant shall not be broken." Note, Afflictions are not only consistent with covenant-love, but to the people of God they flow from it. Though David's seed be chastened, it does not follow that they are disinherited; they may be cast down, but they are not cast off. God's favour is continued to his people, 1. For Christ's sake; in him the mercy is laid

up for us, and God says, I *will not take it from him* (v. 33), I *will not lie unto David,* v. 35. We are unworthy, but he is worthy. 2. For the covenant's sake: *My faithfulness shall not fail, my covenant will I not break.* It was supposed that they had broken God's statutes, *profaned and polluted* them (so the word signifies) ; " But," says God, " I will not break, I will not profane and pollute, my covenant;" it is the same word. That which is said and sworn is that God will have a church in the world as long as sun and moon endure, v. 36, 37. The sun and moon are faithful witnesses in heaven of the wisdom, power, and goodness of the Creator, and shall continue while time lasts, which they are the measurers of; but the *seed of Christ shall be established for ever,* as *lights of the world* while the world stands, to shine in it, and, when it is at an end, they shall be established lights shining in the firmament of the Father.

38 But thou hast cast off and abhorred, thou hast been wroth with thine anointed. 39 Thou hast made void the covenant of thy servant: thou hast profaned his crown *by casting it* to the ground. 40 Thou hast broken down all his hedges; thou hast brought his strong holds to ruin. 41 All that pass by the way spoil him: he is a reproach to his neighbours. 42 Thou hast set up the right hand of his adversaries; thou hast made all his enemies to rejoice. 43 Thou hast also turned the edge of his sword, and hast not made him to stand in the battle. 44 Thou hast made his glory to cease, and cast his throne down to the ground. 45 The days of his youth hast thou shortened: thou hast covered him with shame. Selah. 46 How long, LORD? wilt thou hide thyself for ever? shall thy wrath burn like fire? 47 Remember how short my time is: wherefore hast thou made all men in vain? 48 What man *is he that* liveth, and shall not see death? shall he deliver his soul from the hand of the grave? Selah. 49 Lord, where *are* thy former lovingkindnesses, *which* thou swarest unto David in thy truth? 50 Remember, Lord, the reproach of thy servants; *how* I do bear in my bosom *the reproach of* all the mighty people; 51 Wherewith thine enemies have reproached, O LORD; wherewith they have reproached the footsteps of thine anointed. 52 Blessed

be the LORD for evermore. Amen, and Amen.

In these verses we have,

I. A very melancholy complaint of the present deplorable state of David's family, which the psalmist thinks hard to be reconciled to the covenant God made with David. "Thou saidst thou wouldst not *take away thy lovingkindness, but thou hast cast off.*" Sometimes, it is no easy thing to reconcile God's providences with his promises, and yet we are sure they are reconcilable; for God's works fulfil his word and never contradict it. 1. David's house seemed to have lost its interest in God, which was the greatest strength and beauty of it. God had been pleased with his anointed, but now he was *wroth with him* (v. 38), had entered into covenant with the family, but now, for aught he could perceive, he had made void the covenant, not broken some of the articles of it, but cancelled it, *v.* 39. We misconstrue the rebukes of Providence if we think they make void the covenant. When the great anointed one, Christ himself, was upon the cross, God seemed to have cast him off, and was wroth with him, and yet did not make void his covenant with him, for that was established for ever. 2. The honour of the house of David was lost and laid in the dust: *Thou hast profaned his crown* (which was always looked upon as sacred) by *casting it to the ground,* to be trampled on, *v.* 39. *Thou hast made his glory to cease* (so uncertain is all earthly glory, and so soon does it wither) and *thou hast cast his throne down to the ground,* not only dethroned the king, but put a period to the kingdom, *v.* 44. If it was penned in Rehoboam's time, it was true as to the greatest part of the kingdom, five parts of six; if in Zedekiah's time, it was more remarkably true of the poor remainder. Note, Thrones and crowns are tottering things, and are often laid in the dust; but there is a crown of glory reserved for Christ's spiritual seed which fadeth not away. 3. It was exposed and made a prey to all the neighbours, who insulted over that ancient and honourable family (*v.* 40): *Thou hast broken down all his hedges* (all those things that were a defence to them, and particularly that hedge of protection which they thought God's covenant and promise had made about them) and thou *hast made even his strong-holds a ruin,* so that they were rather a reproach to them than any shelter; and then, *All that pass by the way spoil him* (*v.* 41) and make an easy prey of him; see lxxx. 12, 13. The enemies talk insolently: *He is a reproach to his neighbours,* who triumph in his fall from so great a degree of honour. Nay, every one helps forward the calamity (*v.* 42): "*Thou hast set up the right hand of his adversaries,* not only given them power, but inclined them to turn their power this way." If the enemies of the church lift up their hand against it, we must see God setting up their hand; for they could have *no power unless it were given them from above.* But, when God does permit them to do mischief to his church, it pleases them: *Thou hast made all his enemies to rejoice;* and this is for thy glory, that those who hate thee should have the pleasure to see the tears and troubles of those that love thee." 4. It was disabled to help itself (*v.* 43): "*Thou hast turned the edge of his sword,* and made it blunt, that it cannot do execution as it has done; and (which is worse) thou hast turned the edge of his spirit, and taken off his courage, *and hast not made him to stand* as he used to do *in the battle.*" The spirit of men is what the Father and former of spirits makes them; nor can we stand with any strength or resolution further than God is pleased to uphold us. If men's hearts fail them, it is God that dispirits them; but it is sad with the church when those cannot stand who should stand up for it. 5. It was upon the brink of an inglorious exit (*v.* 45): *The days of his youth hast thou shortened;* it is ready to be cut off, like a young man in the flower of his age. This seems to intimate that the psalm was penned in Rehoboam's time, when the house of David was but in the days of its youth, and yet waxed old and began to decay already. Thus it was covered with shame, and it was turned very much to its reproach that a family which, in the first and second reign, looked so great, and made such a figure, should, in the third, dwindle and look so little as the house of David did in Rehoboam's time. But it may be applied to the captivity in Babylon, which, in comparison with what was expected, was but the day of the youth of that kingdom. However, the kings then had remarkably the *days of their youth shortened,* for it was in the days of their youth, when they were about thirty years old, that Jehoiachin and Zedekiah were carried captives to Babylon.

From all this complaint let us learn, 1. What work sin makes with families, noble royal families, with families in which religion has been uppermost; when posterity degenerates, it falls into disgrace, and iniquity stains their glory. 2. How apt we are to place the promised honour and happiness of the church in something external, and to think the promise fails, and the covenant is made void, if we be disappointed of that, a mistake which we now are inexcusable if we fall into, since our Master has so expressly told us that his kingdom is not of this world.

II. A very pathetic expostulation with God upon this. Four things they plead with God for mercy:—

1. The long continuance of the trouble (*v.* 46): *How long, O Lord! wilt thou hide thyself? For ever?* That which grieved them most was that God himself, as one displeased, did not appear to them by his prophets to comfort them, did not appear for them by his providences to deliver them, and

that he had kept them long in the dark; it seemed an eternal night, when God had withdrawn: *Thou hidest thyself for ever.* Nay, God not only hid himself from them, but seemed to set himself against them: "*Shall thy wrath burn like fire?* How long shall it burn? Shall it never be put out? What is hell, but the wrath of God, burning for ever? And is that the lot of thy anointed?"

2. The shortness of life, and the certainty of death: "Lord, let thy anger cease, and return thou, in mercy to us, remembering how short my time is and how sure the period of my time. Lord, since my life is so transitory, and will, ere long, be at an end, let it not be always so miserable that I should rather choose no being at all than such a being." Job pleads thus, *ch.* x. 20, 21. And probably the psalmist here urges it in the name of the house of David, and the present prince of that house, the *days of whose youth were shortened, v* 45.

(1.) He pleads the shortness and vanity of life (*v.* 47): *Remember how short my time is, how transitory I am* (say some), therefore unable to bear the power of thy wrath, and therefore a proper object of thy pity. *Wherefore hast thou made all men in vain?* or, *Unto what vanity hast thou created all the sons of Adam!* Now, this may be understood either, [1.] As declaring a great truth. If the ancient lovingkindnesses spoken of (*v.* 49) be forgotten (those relating to another life), man is indeed made in vain. Considering man as mortal, if there were not a future state on the other side of death, we might be ready to think that man was made in vain, and was in vain endued with the noble powers and faculties of reason and filled with such vast designs and desires; but God would not make man in vain; therefore, Lord, *remember those lovingkindnesses.* Or, [2.] As implying a strong temptation that the psalmist was in. It is certain *God has not made all men,* nor any man, *in vain,* Isa. xlv. 18. For, *First,* If we think that God has made men in vain because so many have short lives, and long afflictions, in this world, it is true that God has made them so, but it is not true that *therefore* they are made in vain. For those whose days are few and full of trouble may yet glorify God and do some good, may keep their communion with God and get to heaven, and then they are not made in vain. *Secondly,* If we think that God has made men in vain because the most of men neither serve him nor enjoy him, it is true that, as to themselves, they were made in vain, better for them had they not been born than not to be born again; but it was not owing to God that they were made in vain; it was owing to themselves; nor are they made in vain as to him, for he has *made all things for himself, even the wicked for the day of evil,* and those whom he is not glorified by he will be glorified upon.

(2.) He pleads the universality and unavoidableness of death (*v.* 48): "*What man*"

(what *strong man,* so the word is) "*is he that liveth and shall not see death?*" The king himself, of the house of David, is not exempted from the sentence, from the stroke. Lord. since he is under a fatal necessity of dying, let not his whole life be made thus miserable. *Shall he deliver his soul from the hand of the grave?* No, he shall not when his time has come. Let him not therefore be delivered into the hand of the grave by the miseries of a dying life, till his time shall come." We must learn here that death is the end of all men; our eyes must shortly be closed to see death; there is no discharge from that war, nor will any bail be taken to save us from the prison of the grave. It concerns us therefore to make sure a happiness on the other side of death and the grave, that, *when we fail, we may be received into everlasting habitations.*

3. The next plea is taken from the kindness God had for and the covenant he made with his servant David (*v.* 49): "*Lord, where are thy former lovingkindnesses,* which thou showedst, nay, *which thou swaredst, to David in thy truth?*" Wilt thou fail of doing what thou hast promised? Wilt thou undo what thou hast done? Art not thou still the same? Why then may not we have the benefit of the former sure mercies of David?" God's unchangeableness and faithfulness assure us that God will not cast off those whom he has chosen and covenanted with.

4. The last plea is taken from the insolence of the enemies and the indignity done to God's anointed (*v.* 50, 51): "*Remember, Lord, the reproach,* and let it be rolled away from us and returned upon our enemies." (1.) They were God's servants that were reproached, and the abuses done to them reflected upon their master, especially since it was for serving him that they were reproached. (2.) The reproach cast upon God's servants was a very grievous burden to all that were concerned for the honour of God: "*I bear in my bosom the reproach of all the mighty people,* and am even overwhelmed with it; it is what I lay much to heart and can scarcely keep up my spirits under the weight of." (3.) "They are thy enemies who do thus reproach us; and wilt thou not appear against them as such? (4.) *They have reproached the footsteps of thy anointed.* They reflected upon all the steps which the king had taken in the course of his administration, tracked him in all his motions, that they might make invidious remarks upon every thing he had said and done. Or, if we may apply it to Christ, the Lord's Messiah, they reproached the Jews with his footsteps, the slowness of his coming. They have reproached the delays of the Messiah; so Dr. Hammond. They called him, *He that should come;* but, because he had not yet come, because he did not now come to deliver them out of the hands of their enemies, when they had none to deliver them, they told him he would never come, they must give over looking for him. The

scoffers of the latter days do, in like manner, reproach the footsteps of the Messiah when they ask, *Where is the promise of his coming?* 2 Pet. iii. 3, 4. The reproaching of the footsteps of the anointed some refer to the serpent's *bruising the heel of the seed of the woman,* or to the sufferings of Christ's followers, who tread in his footsteps, and are reproached for his name's sake.

III. The psalm concludes with praise, even after this sad complaint (*v.* 52): *Blessed be the Lord for evermore, Amen, and amen.* Thus he confronts the reproaches of his enemies. The more others blaspheme God the more we should bless him. Thus he corrects his own complaints, chiding himself for quarrelling with God's providences and questioning his promises; let both these sinful passions be silenced with the praises of God. However it be, yet God is good, and we will never think hardly of him; God is true, and we will never distrust him. Though the glory of David's house be stained and sullied, this shall be our comfort, that God is blessed for ever, and his glory cannot be eclipsed. If we would have the comfort of the stability of God's promise, we must give him the praise of it; in blessing God, we encourage ourselves. Here is a double *Amen*, according to the double signification. *Amen—so it is,* God is blessed for ever. *Amen—be it so,* let God be blessed for ever. He began the psalm with thanksgiving, before he made his complaint (*v.* 1); and now he concludes it with a doxology. Those who give God thanks for what he has done may give him thanks also for what he will do; God will follow those with his mercies who, in a right manner, follow him with their praises.

PSALM XC.

The foregoing psalm is supposed to have been penned as late as the captivity in Babylon; this, it is plain, was penned as early as the deliverance out of Egypt, and yet they are put close together in this collection of divine songs. This psalm was penned by Moses (as appears by the title), the most ancient penman of sacred writ. We have upon record a praising song of his (Exod. xv., which is alluded to Rev. xv. 3), and an instructing song of his, Deut. xxxii. But this is of a different nature from both, for it is called a prayer. It is supposed that this psalm was penned upon occasion of the sentence passed upon Israel in the wilderness for their unbelief, murmuring, and rebellion, that their carcases should fall in the wilderness, that they should be wasted away by a series of miseries for thirty-eight years together, and that none of them that were then of age should enter Canaan. This was calculated for their wanderings in the wilderness, as that other song of Moses (Deut. xxxi. 19, 21) was for their settlement in Canaan. We have the story to which this psalm seems to refer, Num. xiv. Probably Moses penned this prayer to be daily used, either by the people in their tents, or, at least, by the priests in the tabernacle-service, during their tedious fatigue in the wilderness. In it, I. Moses comforts himself and his people with the eternity of God and their interest in him, ver. 1, 2. II. He humbles himself and his people with the consideration of the frailty of man, ver. 3—6. III. He submits himself and his people to the righteous sentence of God passed upon them, ver. 7—11. IV. He commits himself and his people to God by prayer for divine mercy and grace, and the return of God's favour, ver. 12—17. Though it seems to have been penned upon this particular occasion, yet it is very applicable to the frailty of human life in general, and, in singing it, we may easily apply it to the years of our passage through the wilderness of this world, and it furnishes us with meditations and prayers very suitable to the solemnity of a funeral.

A prayer of Moses the man of God.

L ORD, thou hast been our dwelling place in all generations. 2 Before the mountains were brought forth, or ever thou hadst formed the

earth and the world, even from everlasting to everlasting, thou *art* God. 3 Thou turnest man to destruction; and sayest, Return, ye children of men. 4 For a thousand years in thy sight *are but* as yesterday when it is past, and *as* a watch in the night. 5 Thou carriest them away as with a flood; they are *as* a sleep: in the morning *they are* like grass *which* groweth up. 6 In the morning it flourisheth, and groweth up; in the evening it is cut down, and withereth.

This psalm is entitled *a prayer of Moses.* Where, and in what volume, it was preserved from Moses's time till the collection of psalms was begun to be made, is uncertain; but, being divinely inspired, it was under a special protection: perhaps it was written in the book of Jasher, or the book of the wars of the Lord. Moses taught the people of Israel to pray, and put words into their mouths which they might make use of in turning to the Lord. Moses is here called *the man of God,* because he was a prophet, the father of the prophets, and an eminent type of the great prophet. In these verses we are taught,

I. To give God the praise of his care concerning his people at all times, and concerning us in our days (*v.* 1): *Lord, thou hast been to us a habitation,* or *dwelling-place, a refuge* or *help, in all generations.* Now that they had fallen under God's displeasure, and he threatened to abandon them, they plead his former kindnesses to their ancestors. Canaan was a land of pilgrimage to their fathers the patriarchs, who dwelt there in tabernacles; but then God was their habitation, and, wherever they went, they were at home, at rest, in him. Egypt had been a land of bondage to them for many years, but even then God was their refuge; and in him that poor oppressed people lived and were kept in being. Note, True believers are at home in God, and that is their comfort in reference to all the toils and tribulations they meet with in this world. In him we may repose and shelter ourselves as in our dwelling-place.

II. To give God the glory of his eternity (*v.* 2): *Before the mountains were brought forth, before he made the highest part of the dust of the world* (as it is expressed, Prov. viii. 26), *before the earth fell in travail,* or, as we may read it, *before thou hadst formed the earth and the world* (that is, before the beginning of time) thou hadst a being; *even from everlasting to everlasting thou art God,* an eternal God, whose existence has neither its commencement nor its period with time, nor is measured by the successions and revolutions of it, but who art *the same yesterday, to-day, and for ever,* without beginning of days, or end of life, or change of time. Note, Against all the grievances that arise from our own mortality, and the mortality of our friends, we may take comfort from God's immortality. We are dying creatures, and all our comforts in the world are dying comforts, but God is an everliving God, and those shall find him so who have him for theirs.

III. To own God's absolute sovereign dominion over man, and his irresistible incontestable power to dispose of him as he pleases (*v.* 3): *Thou turnest man to destruction,* with a word's speaking, when thou pleasest, to the destruction of the body, of the earthly house; *and* thou *sayest, Return, you children of men.* 1. When God is, by sickness or other afflictions, turning men to destruction, he does thereby call men to return unto him, that is, to repent of their sins and live a new life. This God *speaketh once, yea, twice.* "*Return unto me,* from whom you have revolted," Jer. iv. 1. 2. When God is threatening to *turn men to destruction,* to bring them to death, and they have received a sentence of death within themselves, sometimes he wonderfully restores them, and says, as the old translation reads it, *Again thou sayest, Return* to life and health again. For God kills and makes alive again, brings down to the grave and brings up. 3. When God turns men to destruction, it is according to the general sentence passed upon all, which is this, "*Return, you children of men,* one, as well as another, return to your first principles; let the body return to the earth as it was (*dust to dust,* Gen. iii. 19) and let the soul *return to God who gave it,*" Eccl. xii. 7. 4. Though God turns all men to destruction, yet he will again say, *Return, you children of men,* at the general resurrection, when, though a man dies, yet he shall live again; and "*then shalt thou call and I will answer* (Job xiv. 14, 15); thou shalt bid me return, and I shall return." The body, the soul, shall both return and unite again.

IV. To acknowledge the infinite disproportion there is between God and men, *v.* 4. Some of the patriarchs lived nearly a thousand years; Moses knew this very well, and had recorded it: but what is their long life to God's eternal life? "A thousand years, to us, are a long period, which we cannot expect to survive; or, if we could, it is what we could not retain the remembrance of; but it is, *in thy sight, as yesterday,* as one day, as that which is freshest in mind; nay, it is but as a *watch of the night,*" which was but three hours. 1. A thousand years are nothing to God's eternity; they are less than a day, than an hour, to a thousand years. Betwixt a minute and a million of years there is some proportion, but betwixt time and eternity there is none. The long lives of the patriarchs were nothing to God, not so much as the life of a child (that is born and dies the same day) is to theirs. 2. All the events of a thousand years, whether past or to come, are as present to the Eternal Mind as what was done yesterday, or the last hour, is to

us, and more so. God will say, at the great day, to those whom he has *turned to destruction, Return—Arise you dead.* But it might be objected against the doctrine of the resurrection that it is a long time since it was expected and it has not yet come. Let that be no difficulty, for a thousand years, in God's sight, are but as one day. *Nullum tempus occurrit regi— To the king all periods are alike.* To this purport these words are quoted, 2 Pet. iii. 8.

V. To see the frailty of man, and his vanity even at his best estate (*v.* 5, 6); look upon all the children of men, and we shall see, 1. That their life is a dying life: *Thou carriest them away as with a flood,* that is, they are continually gliding down the stream of time into the ocean of eternity. The flood is continually flowing, and they are carried away with it; as soon as we are born we begin to die, and every day of our life carries us so much nearer death; or we are carried away violently and irresistibly, as with a flood of waters, as with an inundation, which sweeps away all before it; or as the old world was carried away with Noah's flood. Though God promised not so to drown the world again, yet death is a constant deluge. 2. That it is a dreaming life. Men are carried away as with a flood and yet *they are as a sleep;* they consider not their own frailty, nor are aware how near they approach to an awful eternity. Like men asleep, they imagine great things to themselves, till death wakes them, and puts an end to the pleasing dream. Time passes unobserved by us, as it does with men asleep; and, when it is over, it is as nothing. 3. That it is a short and transient life, like that of the grass which grows up and flourishes, in the morning looks green and pleasant, but in the evening the mower cuts it down, and it immediately withers, changes its colour, and loses all its beauty. Death will change us shortly, perhaps suddenly; and it is a great change that death will make with us in a little time. Man, in his prime, does but flourish as the grass, which is weak, and low, and tender, and exposed, and which, when the winter of old age comes, will wither of itself: but he may be mown down by disease or disaster, as the grass is, in the midst of summer. *All flesh is as grass.*

7 For we are consumed by thine anger, and by thy wrath are we troubled. 8 Thou hast set our iniquities before thee, our secret *sins* in the light of thy countenance. 9 For all our days are passed away in thy wrath: we spend our years as a tale *that is told.* 10 The days of our years *are* threescore years and ten; and if by reason of strength *they be* fourscore years, yet *is* their strength labour and sor-

row; for it is soon cut off, and we fly away. 11 Who knoweth the power of thine anger? even according to thy fear, *so is* thy wrath.

Moses had, in the foregoing verses, lamented the frailty of human life in general; the children of men *are as a sleep and as the grass.* But here he teaches the people of Israel to confess before God that righteous sentence of death which they were under in a special manner, and which by their sins they had brought upon themselves. Their share in the common lot of mortality was not enough, but they are, and must live and die, under peculiar tokens of God's displeasure. Here they speak of themselves: *We* Israelites *are consumed and troubled,* and *our days have passed away.*

I. They are here taught to acknowledge the wrath of God to be the cause of all their miseries. *We are consumed, we are troubled,* and it is *by thy anger, by thy wrath (v.* 7); *our days have passed away in thy wrath, v.* 9. The afflictions of the saints often come purely from God's love, as Job's; but the rebukes of sinners, and of good men for their sins, must be seen coming from the anger of God, who takes notice of, and is much displeased with, the sins of Israel. We are too apt to look upon death as no more than a debt owing to nature; whereas it is not so; if the nature of man had continued in its primitive purity and rectitude, there would have been no such debt owing to it. It is a debt to the justice of God, a debt to the law. *Sin entered into the world, and death by sin.* Are we consumed by decays of nature, the infirmities of age, or any chronic disease? We must ascribe it to God's anger. Are we troubled by any sudden or surprising stroke? That also is the fruit of God's wrath, which is thus revealed from heaven against the *ungodliness* and *unrighteousness of men.*

II. They are taught to confess their sins, which had provoked the wrath of God against them (*v.* 8): *Thou hast set our iniquities before thee, even our secret sins.* It was not without cause that God was angry with them. He had said, *Provoke me not, and I will do you no hurt;* but they had provoked him, and will own that, in passing this severe sentence upon them, he justly punished them, 1. For their open contempts of him and the daring affronts they had given him: *Thou hast set our iniquities before thee.* God had herein an eye to their unbelief and murmuring, their distrusting his power and their despising the pleasant land: these he set before them when he passed that sentence on them; these kindled the fire of God's wrath against them and kept good things from them. 2. For their more secret departures from him: "*Thou hast set our secret sins* (those which go no further than the heart, and which are at the bottom of all the overt acts) *in the light of thy countenance;* that is, thou hast discovered these, and brought these also to the account, and made us to see them, who before overlooked them." Secret sins are known to God and shall be reckoned for. Those who in heart return into Egypt, who set up idols in their heart, shall be dealt with as revolters or idolaters. See the folly of those who go about to cover their sins, for they cannot cover them.

III. They are taught to look upon themselves as dying and passing away, and not to think either of a long life or of a pleasant one; for the decree gone forth against them was irreversible (*v.* 9): *All our days are* likely to be *passed away in thy wrath,* under the tokens of thy displeasure; and, though we are not quite deprived of the residue of our years, yet we are likely to *spend* them *as a tale that is told.* The thirty-eight years which, after this, they wore away in the wilderness, were not the subject of the sacred history; for little or nothing is recorded of that which happened to them from the second year to the fortieth. After they came out of Egypt their time was perfectly trifled away, and was not worthy to be the subject of a history, but only of *a tale that is told;* for it was only to pass away time, like telling stories, that they spent those years in the wilderness; all that while they were in the consuming, and another generation was in the raising. When they came out of Egypt *there was not one feeble person among their tribes* (cv. 37); but now they were all feeble. Their joyful prospect of a prosperous glorious life in Canaan was turned into the melancholy prospect of a tedious inglorious death in the wilderness; so that their whole life was now as impertinent a thing as ever any winter-tale was. That is applicable to the state of every one of us in the wilderness of this world: *We spend our years, we bring them to an end,* each year, and all at last, *as a tale that is told—as the breath of our mouth in winter* (so some), which soon disappears—*as a thought* (so some), than which nothing more quick—*as a word,* which is soon spoken, and then vanishes into air—or *as a tale that is told.* The spending of our years is like the telling of a tale. A year, when it is past, is like a tale when it is told. Some of our years are as a pleasant story, others as a tragical one, most mixed, but all short and transient: that which was long in the doing may be told in a short time. Our years, when they are gone, can no more be recalled than the word that we have spoken can. The loss and waste of our time, which are our fault and folly, may be thus complained of: we should spend our years like the despatch of business, with care and industry; but, alas! we do spend them like the telling of a tale, idle, and to little purpose, carelessly, and without regard. Every year passed *as a tale that is told;* but what was the number of them? As they were vain, so they were few (*v.* 10), seventy or eighty at most, which may be understood either, 1. Of the lives of the Israelites in the wilderness; all those that were numbered when they came out of Egypt, above twenty years old, were to die within thirty-eight years; they numbered those only that *were able to go forth to war*, most of whom, we may suppose, were between twenty and forty, who therefore must have all died before eighty years old, and many before sixty, and perhaps much sooner, which was far short of the years of the lives of their fathers. And those that lived to seventy or eighty, yet, being under a sentence of consumption and a melancholy despair of ever seeing through this wilderness-state, their strength, their life, was nothing but *labour and sorrow*, which otherwise would have been made a new life by the joys of Canaan. See what work sin made. Or, 2. Of the lives of men in general, ever since the days of Moses. Before the time of Moses it was usual for men to live about 100 years, or nearly 150; but, since, seventy or eighty is the common stint, which few exceed and multitudes never come near. We reckon those to have lived to the age of man, and to have had as large a share of life as they had reason to expect, who live to be seventy years old; and how short a time is that compared with eternity! Moses was the first that committed divine revelation to writing, which, before, had been transmitted by tradition; now also both the world and the church were pretty well peopled, and therefore there were not now the same reasons for men's living long that there had been. If, by reason of a strong constitution, some reach to eighty years, yet their strength then is what they have little joy of; it does but serve to prolong their misery, and make their death the more tedious; for even *their strength then is labour and sorrow*, much more their weakness; for the years have come which they have no pleasure in. Or it may be taken thus: *Our years are seventy, and the years of some, by reason of strength, are eighty; but the breadth of our years* (for so the latter word signifies, rather than strength), *the whole extent of them, from infancy to old age, is but labour and sorrow.* In the sweat of our face we must eat bread; our whole life is toilsome and troublesome; and perhaps, in the midst of the years we count upon, *it is soon cut off, and we fly away*, and do not live out half our days.

IV. They are taught by all this to stand in awe of the wrath of God (v. 11): *Who knows the power of thy anger?* 1. None can perfectly comprehend it. The psalmist speaks as one afraid of God's anger, and amazed at the greatness of the power of it; who knows how far the power of God's anger can reach and how deeply it can wound? The angels that sinned knew experimentally the power of God's anger; damned sinners in hell know it; but which of us can fully comprehend or describe it? 2. Few do seriously consider it as they ought. *Who knows it,* so as to im-

prove the knowledge of it? Those who make a mock at sin, and make light of Christ, surely do not know the power of God's anger. For, *according to thy fear, so is thy wrath;* God's wrath is equal to the apprehensions which the most thoughtful serious people have of it; let men have ever so great a dread upon them of the wrath of God, it is not greater than there is cause for and than the nature of the thing deserves. God has not in his word represented his wrath as more terrible than really it is; nay, what is felt in the other world is infinitely worse than what is feared in this world. *Who among us can dwell with that devouring fire?*

12 So teach *us* to number our days, that we may apply *our* hearts unto wisdom. 13 Return, O Lord, how long? and let it repent thee concerning thy servants. 14 O satisfy us early with thy mercy; that we may rejoice and be glad all our days. 15 Make us glad according to the days *wherein* thou hast afflicted us, *and* the years *wherein* we have seen evil. 16 Let thy work appear unto thy servants, and thy glory unto their children. 17 And let the beauty of the Lord our God be upon us: and establish thou the work of our hands upon us; yea, the work of our hands establish thou it.

These are the petitions of this prayer, grounded upon the foregoing meditations and acknowledgments. *Is any afflicted? Let him* learn thus to *pray.* Four things they are here directed to pray for:—

I. For a sanctified use of the sad dispensation they were now under. Being condemned to have our days shortened, "*Lord, teach us to number our days* (v. 12); Lord, give us grace duly to consider how few they are, and how little a while we have to live in this world." Note, 1. It is an excellent art rightly *to number our days*, so as not to be out in our calculation, as he was who counted upon many years to come when, that night, his soul was required of him. We must live under a constant apprehension of the shortness and uncertainty of life and the near approach of death and eternity. We must so number our days as to compare our work with them, and mind it accordingly with a double diligence, as those that have no time to trifle. 2. Those that would learn this arithmetic must pray for divine instruction, must go to God, and beg of him to teach them by his Spirit, to put them upon considering and to give them a good understanding. 3. We then number our days to good purpose when thereby our hearts are inclined and engaged to true wisdom, that is, to the practice of serious godliness. To be religious is to be wise; this is a thing to which it is necessary that we apply our hearts, and the matter requires and deserves a close application, to which frequent thoughts of the uncertainty of our continuance here, and the certainty of our removal hence, will very much contribute.

II. For the turning away of God's anger from them, that though the decree had gone forth, and was past revocation, there was no remedy, but they must die in the wilderness: "*Yet return, O Lord!* be thou reconciled to us, and *let it repent thee concerning thy servants* (v. 13); send us tidings of peace to comfort us again after these heavy tidings. How long must we look upon ourselves as under thy wrath, and when shall we have some token given us of our restoration to thy favour? *We are thy servants, thy people* (Isa. lxiv. 9); when wilt thou change thy way towards us?" In answer to this prayer, and upon their profession of repentance (Num. xiv. 39, 40), God, in the next chapter, proceeded with the laws concerning sacrifices (Num. xv. 1, &c.), which was a token that it repented him concerning his servants; for, *if the Lord had been pleased to kill them, he would not have shown them such things as these.*

III. For comfort and joy in the returns of God's favour to them, v. 14, 15. They pray for the mercy of God; for they pretend not to plead any merit of their own. *Have mercy upon us, O God!* is a prayer we are all concerned to say *Amen* to. Let us pray for early mercy, the seasonable communications of divine mercy, that God's *tender mercies may speedily prevent us, early in the morning of* our days, when we are young and flourishing, v. 6. Let us pray for the true satisfaction and happiness which are to be had only in the favour and mercy of God, iv. 6, 7. A gracious soul, if it may but be satisfied of God's lovingkindness, will be satisfied with it, abundantly satisfied, will take up with that, and will take up with nothing short of it. Two things are pleaded to enforce this petition for God's mercy:—1. That it would be a full fountain of future joys: "*O satisfy us with thy mercy,* not only that we may be easy and at rest within ourselves, which we can never be while we lie under thy wrath, but that we *may rejoice and be glad,* not only for a time, upon the first indications of thy favour, but *all our days,* though we are to spend them in the wilderness." With respect to those that make God their chief joy, as their joy may be full (1 John i. 4), so it may be constant, even in this vale of tears; it is their own fault if they are not glad all their days, for his mercy will furnish them with joy in tribulation and nothing can separate them from it. 2. That it would be a sufficient balance to their former griefs: "*Make us glad according to the days wherein thou hast afflicted us;* let the days of our joy in thy favour be as many as the days of our pain for thy displeasure have been and as

pleasant as those have been gloomy. *Lord, thou usest to set the one over-against the other* (Eccl. vii. 14); do so in our case. Let it suffice that we have drunk so long of the cup of trembling; now put into our hands the cup of salvation." God's people reckon the returns of God's lovingkindness a sufficient recompence for all their troubles.

IV. For the progress of the work of God among them notwithstanding, v. 16, 17. 1. That he would manifest himself in carrying it on: "*Let thy work appear upon thy servants;* let it appear that thou hast wrought upon us, to bring us home to thyself and to fit us for thyself." God's servants cannot work for him unless he work upon them, and work in them both to will and to do; and then we may hope the operations of God's providence will be apparent for us when the operations of his grace are apparent upon us. "Let thy work appear, and in it thy glory will appear to us and those that shall come after us." In praying for God's grace God's glory must be our end; and we must therein have an eye to our children as well as to ourselves, that they also may experience God's glory appearing upon them, so as to change them into the same image, from glory to glory. Perhaps, in this prayer, they distinguish between themselves and their children, for so God distinguished in his late message to them (Num. xiv. 31, *Your carcases shall fall in this wilderness, but your little ones will I bring into Canaan*): "Lord," say they, "let *thy work appear upon us,* to reform us, and bring us to a better temper, and then let *thy glory appear to our children,* in performing the promise to them which we have forfeited the benefit of." 2. That he would countenance and strengthen them in carrying it on, in doing their part towards it. (1.) That he would smile upon them in it: *Let the beauty of the Lord our God be upon us;* let it appear that God favours us. Let us have God's ordinances kept up among us and the tokens of God's presence with his ordinances; so some. We may apply this petition both to our sanctification and to our consolation. Holiness is *the beauty of the Lord our God;* let that be upon us in all we say and do; let the grace of God in us, and the light of our good works, make our faces to shine (that is the comeliness God puts upon us, and those are comely indeed who are so beautified), and then let divine consolations put gladness into our hearts, and a lustre upon our countenances, and that also will be the beauty of the Lord upon us, as our God. (2.) That he would prosper them in it: *Establish thou the work of our hands upon us.* God's working upon us (v. 16) does not discharge us from using our utmost endeavours in serving him and working out our salvation. But, when we have done all, we must wait upon God for the success, and beg of him to *prosper our handy works,* to give us to compass what we aim at for his glory. We are so unworthy of divine assistance, and yet so utterly insufficient to bring any thing to pass without it, that we have need to be earnest for it and to repeat the request: *Yea, the work of our hands, establish thou it,* and, in order to that, establish us in it.

PSALM XCI.

Some of the ancients were of opinion that Moses was the penman, not only of the foregoing psalm, which is expressly said to be his, but also of the eight that next follow it ; but that cannot be, for Ps. xcv. is expressly said to be penned by David, and long after Moses, Heb. iv. 7. It is probable that this psalm also was penned by David ; it is a writ of protection for all true believers, not in the name of king David, or under his broad seal ; he needed it himself, especially if the psalm was penned, as some conjecture it was, at the time of the pestilence which was sent for his numbering the people ; but in the name of the King of kings, and under the broad seal of Heaven. Observe, I. The psalmist's own resolution to take God for his keeper (ver. 2), from which he gives both direction and encouragement to others, ver. 9. II. The promises which are here made, in God's name, to all those that do so in sincerity. 1. They shall be taken under the peculiar care of Heaven, ver. 1, 4. 2. They shall be delivered from the malice of the powers of darkness (ver. 3, 5, 6), and that by a distinguishing preservation, ver. 7, 8. 3. They shall be the charge of the holy angels, ver. 10—12. 4. They shall triumph over their enemies, ver. 13. 5. They shall be the special favourites of God himself, ver. 14—16. In singing this we must shelter ourselves under, and then solace ourselves in, the divine protection. Many think that to Christ, as Mediator, these promises do primarily belong (Isa. xlix. 2), not because to him the devil applied one of these promises (Matt. iv. 6), but because to him they are very applicable, and, coming through him, they are more sweet and sure to all believers.

HE that dwelleth in the secret place of the most high shall abide under the shadow of the Almighty. 2 I will say of the LORD, *He is* my refuge and my fortress : my God ; in him will I trust. 3 Surely he shall deliver thee from the snare of the fowler, *and* from the noisome pestilence. 4 He shall cover thee with his feathers, and under his wings shalt thou trust : his truth *shall be thy* shield and buckler. 5 Thou shalt not be afraid for the terror by night ; *nor* for the arrow *that* flieth by day ; 6 *Nor* for the pestilence *that* walketh in darkness ; *nor* for the destruction *that* wasteth at noonday. 7 A thousand shall fall at thy side, and ten thousand at thy right hand ; *but* it shall not come nigh thee. 8 Only with thine eyes shalt thou behold and see the reward of the wicked.

In these verses we have,

I. A great truth laid down in general, That all those who live a life of communion with God are constantly safe under his protection, and may therefore preserve a holy serenity and security of mind at all times (v. 1): *He that dwells,* that sits down, *in the secret place of the Most High, shall abide under the shadow of the Almighty ;* he that by faith chooses God for his guardian shall find all that in him which he needs or can desire. Note, 1. It is the character of a true believer that he *dwells in the secret place of the Most High ;* he is at home in God, returns to God, and reposes in him as his rest ; he acquaints himself with inward religion, and makes heart-

work of the service of God, worships within the veil, and loves to be alone with God, to converse with him in solitude. 2. It is the privilege and comfort of those that do so that they *abide under the shadow of the Almighty ;* he shelters them, and comes between them and every thing that would annoy them, whether storm or sunshine. They shall not only have an admittance, but a residence, under God's protection ; he will be their rest and refuge for ever.

II. The psalmist's comfortable application of this to himself (v. 2): *I will say of the Lord,* whatever others say of him, " *He is my refuge ;* I choose him as such, and confide in him. Others make idols their refuge, but I will say of Jehovah, the true and living God, He is *my refuge :* any other is a *refuge of lies.* He is a refuge that will not fail me ; for he is *my fortress and strong-hold.*" Idolaters called their idols *Mahuzzim,* their *most stronghold* (Dan. xi. 39), but therein they deceived themselves ; those only secure themselves that make the Lord their God, their fortress. There being no reason to question his sufficiency, fitly does it follow, *In him will I trust.* If Jehovah be our God, our refuge, and our fortress, what can we desire which we may not be sure to find in him ? He is neither fickle nor false, neither weak nor mortal ; he is God and not man, and therefore there is no danger of being disappointed in him. We *know whom we have trusted.*

III. The great encouragement he gives to others to do likewise, not only from his own experience of the comfort of it (for in that there might possibly be a fallacy), but from the truth of God's promise, in which there neither is nor can be any deceit (v. 3, 4, &c.) : *Surely he shall deliver thee.* Those who have themselves found the comfort of making God their refuge cannot but desire that others may do so. Now here it is promised,

1. That believers shall be kept from those mischiefs which they are in imminent danger of, and which would be fatal to them (v. 3), *from the snare of the fowler,* which is laid unseen and catches the unwary prey on a sudden, and *from the noisome pestilence,* which seizes men unawares and against which there is no guard. This promise protects, (1.) The natural life, and is often fulfilled in our preservation from those dangers which are very threatening and very near, while yet we ourselves are not apprehensive of them, any more than the bird is of *the snare of the fowler.* We owe it, more than we are sensible, to the care of the divine Providence that we have been kept from infectious diseases and out of the hands of the wicked and unreasonable. (2.) The spiritual life, which is protected by divine grace from the temptations of Satan, which are as the *snares of the fowler,* and from the contagion of sin, which is the *noisome pestilence.* He that has given grace to be the glory of the soul will create a defence upon all that glory.

2. That God himself will be their pro-tector; those must needs be safe who have him for their keeper, and successful for whom he undertakes (*v.* 4): *He shall cover thee,* shall keep thee *secret* (xxxi. 20), and so keep thee safe, xxvii. 5. God protects believers, (1.) With the greatest tenderness and affec-tion, which is intimated in that, *He shall cover thee with his feathers, under his wings,* which alludes to the hen *gathering her chickens under her wings,* Matt. xxiii. 37. By natural in-stinct she not only protects them, but calls them under that protection when she sees them in danger, not only keeps them safe, but cherishes them and keeps them warm. To this the great God is pleased to compare his care of his people, who are helpless as the chickens, and easily made a prey of, but are invited to trust under the shadow of the wings of the divine promise and providence, which is the periphrasis of a proselyte to the true religion, that he has come to *trust under the wings of the God of Israel,* Ruth ii. 12. (2.) With the greatest power and efficacy. Wings and feathers, though spread with the greatest tenderness, are yet weak, and easily broken through, and therefore it is added, *His truth shall be thy shield and buckler,* a strong defence. God is as willing to guard his people as the hen is to guard the chickens, and as able as a man of war in armour.

3. That he will not only keep them from evil, but from the fear of evil, *v.* 5, 6. Here is, (1.) Great danger supposed; the mention of it is enough to frighten us; night and day we lie exposed, and those that are apt to be timorous will in neither period think them-selves safe. When we are retired into our chambers, our beds, and have made all as safe as we can about us, yet there is terror by night, from thieves and robbers, winds and storms, besides those things that are the creatures of fancy and imagination, which are often most frightful of all. We read of *fear in the night,* Cant. iii. 8. There is also a *pestilence that walketh in darkness,* as that was which slew the first-born of the Egyp-tians, and the army of the Assyrians. No locks nor bars can shut out diseases, while we carry about with us in our bodies the seeds of them. But surely in the day-time, when we can look about us, we are not so much in danger; yes, there is an *arrow that flieth by day* too, and yet flies unseen; there is a destruction that wasteth at high-noon, when we are awake and have all our friends about us; even then we cannot secure our-selves, nor can they secure us. It was in the day-time that that pestilence wasted which was sent to chastise David for numbering the people, on occasion of which some think this psalm was penned. But, (2.) Here is great security promised to believers in the midst of this danger: " *Thou shalt not be afraid.* God by his grace will keep thee from disquieting distrustful fear (that fear which hath torment) in the midst of the greatest dangers. Wisdom shall keep thee from being causelessly afraid, and faith shall keep thee from being inordinately afraid. Thou shalt not be afraid of the arrow, as knowing that though it may hit thee it can-not hurt thee; if it take away the natural life, yet it shall be so far from doing any prejudice to the spiritual life that it shall be its perfection." A believer *needs not* fear, and therefore *should not* fear, any arrow, be-cause the point is off, the poison is out. *O death! where is thy sting?* It is also under divine direction, and will hit where God ap-points and not otherwise. Every bullet has its commission. Whatever is done our hea-venly Father's will is done; and we have no reason to be afraid of that.

4. That they shall be preserved in common calamities, in a distinguishing way (*v.* 7): " When death rides in triumph, and diseases rage, so that *thousands and ten thousands* fall, fall by sickness, or fall by the sword in battle, *fall at thy side, at thy right hand,* and the sight of their fall is enough to frighten thee, and if they fall by the pestilence their falling so near thee may be likely to infect thee, *yet it shall not come nigh thee,* the death shall not, the fear of death shall not." Those that pre-serve their purity in times of general corrup-tion may trust God with their safety in times of general desolation. When multitudes die round about us, though thereby we must be awakened to prepare for our own death, yet we must not be *afraid with any amazement,* nor make ourselves subject to bondage, as many do all their life-time, *through fear of death,* Heb. ii. 15. The sprinkling of blood secured the first-born of Israel when thou-sands fell. Nay, it is promised to God's peo-ple that they shall have the satisfaction of seeing, not only God's promises fulfilled to them, but his threatenings fulfilled upon those that hate them (*v.* 8): *Only with thy eyes shalt thou behold and see the just reward of the wicked,* which perhaps refers to the de-struction of the first-born of Egypt by the pestilence, which was both the punishment of the oppressors and the enlargement of the oppressed; this Israel saw when they saw themselves unhurt, untouched. As it will aggravate the damnation of sinners that with their eyes they shall behold and see the re-ward of the righteous (Luke xiii. 28), so it will magnify the salvation of the saints that with their eyes they shall behold and see the destruction of the wicked, Isa. lxvi. 24; Ps. lviii. 10.

9 Because thou hast made the LORD *which is* my refuge, *even* the most high, thy habitation; 10 There shall no evil befall thee, neither shall any plague come nigh thy dwelling. 11 For he shall give his angels charge over thee, to keep thee in all thy ways. 12 They shall bear thee up in *their*

hands, lest thou dash thy foot against a stone. 13 Thou shalt tread upon the lion and adder: the young lion and the dragon shalt thou trample under feet. 14 Because he hath set his love upon me, therefore will I deliver him: I will set him on high, because he hath known my name. 15 He shall call upon me, and I will answer him: I *will be* with him in trouble; I will deliver him, and honour him. 16 With long life will I satisfy him, and show him my salvation.

Here are more promises to the same purport with those in the foregoing verses, and they are exceedingly great and precious, and sure to all the seed.

I. The psalmist assures believers of divine protection, from his own experience; and that which he says is the word of God, and what we may rely upon. Observe, 1. The character of those who shall have the benefit and comfort of these promises; it is much the same with that, *v.* 1. They are such as make *the Most High their habitation* (*v.* 9), as are continually with God and rest in him, as make his name both their temple and their strong tower, as dwell in love and so dwell in God. It is our duty to be at home in God, to make our choice of him, and then to live our life in him as our habitation, to converse with him, and delight in him, and depend upon him; and then it shall be our privilege to be at home in God; we shall be welcome to him as a man to his own habitation, without any let, hindrance, or molestation, from the arrests of the law or the clamours of conscience; then too we shall be safe in him, shall be kept in *perfect peace*, Isa. xxvi. 3. To encourage us to make the Lord our habitation, and to hope for safety and satisfaction in him, the psalmist intimates the comfort he had had in doing so: "He whom thou makest thy *habitation is my refuge;* and I have found him firm and faithful, and in him there is room enough, and shelter enough, both for thee and me." *In my father's house* there *are many mansions*, one needs not crowd another, much less crowd out another. 2. The promises that are sure to all those who have thus made *the Most High* their habitation. (1.) That, whatever happens to them, nothing shall hurt them (*v.* 10): "*There shall no evil befal thee;* though trouble or affliction befal thee, yet there shall be no real evil in it, for it shall come from the love of God and shall be sanctified; it shall come, not for thy hurt, but for thy good; and though, for *the present, it be not joyous but grievous*, yet, in the end, it shall yield so well that thou thyself shalt own *no evil befel thee*. It is not an evil, an only evil, but there is a mixture of good in it and a product of good by it. Nay, not

thy person only, but thy dwelling, shall be taken under the divine protection: *There shall no plague come nigh* that, nothing to do thee or thine any damage." *Nihil accidere bono viro mali potest*—No evil can befal a good man. Seneca *De Providentiâ.* (2.) That the angels of light shall be serviceable to them, *v.* 11, 12. This is a precious promise, and speaks a great deal both of honour and comfort to the saints, nor is it ever the worse for being quoted and abused by the devil in tempting Christ, Matt. iv. 6. Observe, [1.] The charge given to the angels concerning the saints. He who is the Lord of the angels, who gave them their being and gives laws to them, whose they are and whom they were made to serve, *he shall give his angels a charge over thee*, not only over the church in general, but over every particular believer. The angels *keep the charge of the Lord their God;* and this is the charge they receive from him. It denotes the great care God takes of the saints, in that the angels themselves shall be charged with them, and employed for them. The charge is *to keep thee in all thy ways;* here is a limitation of the promise: They *shall keep thee in thy ways*, that is, "as long as thou keepest in the way of thy duty;" those that go out of that way put themselves out of God's protection. This word the devil left out when he quoted the promise to enforce a temptation, knowing how much it made against him. But observe the extent of the promise; it is *to keep thee in all thy ways:* even where there is no apparent danger yet we need it, and where there is the most imminent danger we shall have it. Wherever the saints go the angels are charged with them, as the servants are with the children. [2.] The care which the angels take of the saints, pursuant to this charge: *They shall bear thee up in their hands*, which denotes both their great ability and their great affection. They are able to bear up the saints out of the reach of danger, and they do it with all the tenderness and affection wherewith the nurse carries the little child about in her arms; it speaks us helpless and them helpful. They are condescending in their ministrations; they keep the feet of the saints, lest they *dash them against a stone*, lest they stumble and fall into sin and into trouble. [3.] That the powers of darkness shall be triumphed over by them (*v.* 13): *Thou shalt tread upon the lion and adder.* The devil is called *a roaring lion, the old serpent, the red dragon;* so that to this promise the apostle seems to refer in that (Rom. xvi. 20), The *God of peace shall tread Satan under your feet.* Christ has broken the serpent's head, spoiled our spiritual enemies (Col. ii. 15), and through him *we are more than conquerors:* for Christ calls us, as Joshua called the captains of Israel, to come and set our feet on the necks of vanquished enemies. Some think that this promise had its full accomplishment in Christ, and the miraculous power

589

which he had over the whole creation, healing the sick, casting out devils, and particularly putting it into his disciples' commission that they should *take up serpents,* Mark xvi. 18. It may be applied to that care of the divine Providence by which we are preserved from ravenous noxious creatures *(the wild beasts of the field shall be at peace with thee,* Job v. 23); nay, and have ways and means of taming them, Jam. iii. 7.

II. He brings in God himself speaking words of comfort to the saints, and declaring the mercy he had in store for them, *v.* 14—16. Some make this to be spoken to the angels as the reason of the charge given them concerning the saints, as if he had said, " Take care of them, for they are dear to me, and I have a tender concern for them." And now, as before, we must observe,

1. To whom these promises do belong; they are described by three characters :—(1.) They are such as know God's name. His nature we cannot fully know; but by his name he has made himself known, and with that we must acquaint ourselves. (2.) They are such as have set their love upon him; and those who rightly know him will love him, will place their love upon him as the only adequate object of it, will let out their love towards him with pleasure and enlargement, and will fix their love upon him with a resolution never to remove it to any rival. (3.) They are such as call upon him, as by prayer keep up a constant correspondence with him, and in every difficult case refer themselves to him

2. What the promises are which God makes to the saints. (1.) That he will, in due time, deliver them out of trouble: *I will deliver him* (*v.* 14 and again *v.* 15), denoting a double deliverance, living and dying, a deliverance in trouble and a deliverance out of trouble. If God proportions the degree and continuance of our troubles to our strength, if he keeps us from offending him in our troubles, and makes our death our discharge, at length, from all our troubles, then this promise is fulfilled. See xxxiv. 19; 2 Tim. iii. 11; iv. 18. (2.) That he will, in the mean time, *be with them in trouble, v.* 15. If he does not immediately put a period to their afflictions, yet they shall have his gracious presence with them in their troubles; he will take notice of their sorrows, and *know their souls in adversity,* will visit them graciously by his word and Spirit, and converse with them, will take their part, will support and comfort them, and sanctify their afflictions to them, which will be the surest token of his presence with them in their troubles. (3.) That herein he will answer their prayers : *He shall call upon me;* I will pour upon him the spirit of prayer, *and then I will answer,* answer by promises (lxxxv. 8), answer by providences, bringing in seasonable relief, and answer by graces, *strengthening them with strength in their souls* (cxxxviii. 3); thus he

answered Paul with *grace sufficient,* 2 Cor. xii. 9. (4.) That he will exalt and dignify them : *I will set him on high,* out of the reach of trouble, above the stormy region, on a rock *above the waves,* Isa. xxxiii. 16. They shall be enabled, by the grace of God, to look down upon the things of this world with a holy contempt and indifference, to look up to the things of the other world with a holy ambition and concern ; and then they are set on high. *I will honour him;* those are truly honourable whom God puts honour upon by taking them into covenant and communion with himself and designing them for his kingdom and glory, John xii. 26. (5.) That they shall have a sufficiency of life in this world (*v.* 16): *With length of days will I satisfy him;* that is, [1.] They shall live long enough: they shall be continued in this world till they have done the work they were sent into this world for and are ready for heaven, and that is long enough. Who would wish to live a day longer than God has some work to do, either by him or upon him? [2.] They shall think it long enough; for God by his grace shall wean them from the world and make them willing to leave it. A man may die young, and yet die full of days, *satur dierum—satisfied with living.* A wicked worldly man is not satisfied, no, not with long life ; he still cries, *Give, give.* But he that has his treasure and heart in another world has soon enough of this; he would not live always. (6.) That they shall have an eternal life in the other world. This crowns the blessedness : *I will show him my salvation,* show him *the Messiah* (so some); good old Simeon was then satisfied with long life when he could say, *My eyes have seen thy salvation,* nor was there any greater joy to the Old-Testament saints than to see Christ's day, though at a distance. It is more probable that the word refers to the better country, that is, the heavenly, which the patriarchs desired and sought : he *will show him* that, bring him to that blessed state, the felicity of which consists so much in seeing that face to face which we here see through a glass darkly ; and, in the mean time, he will give him a prospect of it. All these promises, some think, point primarily at Christ, and had their accomplishment in his resurrection and exaltation.

PSALM XCII.

It is a groundless opinion of some of the Jewish writers (who are usually free of their conjectures) that this psalm was penned and sung by Adam in innocency, on the first sabbath. It is inconsistent with the psalm itself, which speaks of the workers of iniquity, when as yet sin had not entered. It is probable that it was penned by David, and, being calculated for the sabbath day, I. Praise, the business of the sabbath, is here recommended, ver. 1—3. II. God's works, which gave occasion for the sabbath, are here celebrated as great and unsearchable in general, ver. 4 —6. In particular, with reference to the works both of providence and redemption, the psalmist sings unto God both of mercy and judgment, the ruin of sinners and the joy of saints, three times counterchanged. 1. The wicked shall perish (ver. 7), but God is eternal, ver. 8. 2. God's enemies shall be cut off, but David shall be exalted, ver 9, 10. 3. David's enemies shall be confounded (ver. 11), but all the righteous shall be fruitful and flourishing, ver. 12—15. In singing this psalm we must take pleasure in giving to God the glory due to his name, and triumph in his works.

A psalm or song for the sabbath day.

*I*T is a good *thing* to give thanks unto the LORD, and to sing praises unto thy name, O most high: 2 To show forth thy lovingkindness in the morning, and thy faithfulness every night, 3 Upon an instrument of ten strings, and upon the psaltery; upon the harp with a solemn sound. 4 For thou, LORD, hast made me glad through thy work: I will triumph in the works of thy hands. 5 O LORD, how great are thy works! *and* thy thoughts are very deep. 6 A brutish man knoweth not; neither doth a fool understand this.

This psalm was appointed to be sung, at least it usually was sung, in the house of the sanctuary on the sabbath day, that day of rest, which was an instituted memorial of the work of creation, of God's rest from that work, and the continuance of it in his providence; for *the Father worketh hitherto.* Note, 1. The sabbath day must be a day, not only of holy rest, but of holy work, and the rest is in order to the work. 2. The proper work of the sabbath is praising God; every sabbath day must be a thanksgiving-day; and the other services of the day must be in order to this, and therefore must by no means thrust this into a corner. One of the Jewish writers refers it to the kingdom of the Messiah, and calls it, *A psalm or song for the age to come,* which shall be all sabbath. Believers, through Christ, enjoy that *sabbatism which remains for the people of God* (Heb. iv. 9), the beginning of the everlasting sabbath. In these verses,

I. We are called upon and encouraged to praise God (*v.* 1—3): *It is a good thing to give thanks unto the Lord.* Praising God is good work: it is good in itself and good for us. It is our duty, the rent, the tribute, we are to pay to our great Lord; we are unjust if we withhold it. It is our privilege that we are admitted to praise God, and have hope to be accepted in it. It is good, for it is pleasant and profitable, work that is its own wages; it is the work of angels, the work of heaven. It is good to give thanks for the mercies we have received, for that is the way of fetching in further mercy: it is fit to sing to his name who is Most High, exalted above all blessing and praise. Now observe here, 1. How we must praise God. We must do it by *showing forth his lovingkindness and his faithfulness.* Being convinced of his glorious attributes and perfections, we must show them forth, as those that are greatly affected with them ourselves and desire to affect others with them likewise. We must show forth, not only his greatness and majesty, his holiness and justice, which magnify him and

strike an awe upon us, but his lovingkindness and his faithfulness; for his goodness is his glory (Exod. xxxiii. 18, 19), and by these he proclaims his name. His mercy and truth are the great supports of our faith and hope, and the great encouragements of our love and obedience; these therefore we must show forth as our pleas in prayer and the matter of our joy. This was then done, not only by singing, but by music joined with it, *upon an instrument of ten strings* (*v.* 3); but then it was to be *with a solemn sound,* not that which was gay, and apt to dissipate the spirits, but that which was grave, and apt to fix them. 2. When we must praise God—*in the morning and every night,* not only on sabbath days, but every day; it is that which the duty of every day requires. We must praise God, not only in public assemblies, but in secret, and in our families, showing forth, to ourselves and those about us, his lovingkindness and faithfulness. We must begin and end every day with praising God, must give him thanks every morning, when we are fresh and before the business of the day comes in upon us, and every night, when we are again composed and retired, and are recollecting ourselves; we must give him thanks every morning for the mercies of the night and every night for the mercies of the day; going out and coming in we must bless God.

II. We have an example set before us in the psalmist himself, both to move us to and to direct us in this work (*v.* 4): *Thou, Lord, hast made me glad through thy work.* Note, 1. Those can best recommend to others the duty of praise who have themselves experienced the pleasantness of it. "God's works are to be praised, for they have many a time rejoiced my heart; and therefore, whatever others may think of them, I must think well and speak well of them." 2. If God has given us the joy of his works, there is all the reason in the world why we should give him the honour of them. Has he made our hearts glad? Let us then make his praises glorious. Has God made us glad through the works of his providence for us, and of his grace in us, and both through the great work of redemption? (1.) Let us thence fetch encouragement for our faith and hope; so the psalmist does: *I will triumph in the works of thy hands.* From a joyful remembrance of what God has done for us we may raise a joyful prospect of what he will do, and triumph in the assurance of it, triumph over all opposition, 2 Thess. ii. 13, 14. (2.) Let us thence fetch matter for holy adorings and admirings of God (*v.* 5): *O Lord! how great are thy works*—great beyond conception, beyond expression, the products of great power and wisdom, of great consequence and importance! men's works are nothing to them. We cannot comprehend the greatness of God's works, and therefore must reverently and awfully wonder at them, and even stand amazed at the magnificence of them. "Men's works are little and trifling, for their thoughts are shallow; but, Lord, *thy works are great and such as cannot be measured ; for thy thoughts are very deep* and such as cannot be fathomed." God's counsels as much exceed the contrivances of our wisdom as his works do the efforts of our power. *His thoughts are above our thoughts,* as his *ways are above our ways,* Isa. lv. 9. *O the depth* of God's designs! Rom. xi. 33. The greatness of God's works should lead us to consider the depth of his thoughts, that counsel of his own will according to which he does all things—what a compass his thoughts fetch and to what a length they reach!

III. We are admonished not to neglect the works of God, by the character of those who do so, *v.* 6. Those are fools, they are brutish, who do not know, who do not understand, how great God's works are, who will not acquaint themselves with them, nor give him the glory of them; they *regard not the work of the Lord* nor *consider the operation of his hands* (xxviii. 5); particularly, they understand not the meaning of their own prosperity (which is spoken of *v.* 7); they take it as a pledge of their happiness, whereas it is a preparative for their ruin. If there are so many who know not the designs of Providence, nor care to know them, those who through grace are acquainted with them, and love to be so, have the more reason to be thankful.

7 When the wicked spring as the grass, and when all the workers of iniquity do flourish ; *it is* that they shall be destroyed for ever: 8 But thou, Lord, *art most* high for evermore. 9 For, lo, thine enemies, O Lord, for, lo, thine enemies shall perish; all the workers of iniquity shall be scattered. 10 But my horn shalt thou exalt like *the horn of* a unicorn: I shall be anointed with fresh oil. 11 Mine eye also shall see *my desire* on mine enemies, *and* mine ears shall hear *my desire* of the wicked that rise up against me. 12 The righteous shall flourish like the palm tree : he shall grow like a cedar in Lebanon. 13 Those that be planted in the house of the Lord shall flourish in the courts of our God. 14 They shall still bring forth fruit in old age; they shall be fat and flourishing; 15 To show that the Lord *is* upright: *he is* my rock, and *there is* no unrighteousness in him.

The psalmist had said (*v.* 4) that from the works of God he would take occasion to triumph ; and here he does so.

I. He triumphs over God's enemies (*v.* 7,

9, 11), triumphs in the foresight of their destruction, not as it would be the misery of his fellow-creatures, but as it would redound to the honour of God's justice and holiness. He is confident of the ruin of sinners, 1. Though they are flourishing (*v.* 7): *When the wicked spring as the grass* in spring (so numerous, so thickly sown, so green, and growing so fast), *and all the workers of iniquity do flourish* in pomp, and power, and all the instances of outward prosperity, are easy and many, and succeed in their enterprises, one would think that all this was in order to their being happy, that it was a certain evidence of God's favour and an earnest of something as good or better in reserve: but it is quite otherwise ; it is *that they shall be destroyed for ever.* The very *prosperity of fools shall slay them,* Prov. i. 32. The sheep that are designed for the slaughter are put into the fattest pasture. 2. Though they are daring, *v.* 9. They are thy enemies, and impudently avow themselves to be so. They are contrary to God, and they fight against God. They are in rebellion against his crown and dignity, and therefore it is easy to foresee that they shall perish; for *who ever hardened his heart against God and prospered?* Note, All the impenitent workers of iniquity shall be deemed and taken as God's enemies, and as such they shall perish and be scattered. Christ reckons those his enemies that will not have him to reign over them ; and they shall be brought forth and slain before him. The workers of iniquity are now associated, and closely linked together, in a combination against God and religion ; but they shall be scattered, and disabled to help one another against the just judgment of God. *In the world to come they shall be separated from the congregation of the righteous ;* so the Chaldee, Ps. i. 5. 3. Though they had a particular malice against the psalmist, and, upon that account, he might be tempted to fear them, yet he triumphs over them (*v.* 11): " *My eye shall see my desire on my enemies that rise up against me ;* I shall see them not only disabled from doing me any further mischief, but reckoned with for the mischief they have done me, and brought either to repentance or ruin :" and this was his desire concerning them. In the Hebrew it is no more than thus, *My eye shall look on my enemies, and my ear shall hear of the wicked.* He does not say what he shall see or what he shall hear, but he shall see and hear that in which God will be glorified and in which he will therefore be satisfied. This perhaps has reference to Christ, to his victory over Satan, death, and hell, the destruction of those that persecuted and crucified him, and opposed his gospel, and to the final ruin of the impenitent at the last day. Those that rise up against Christ will fall before him and be made his footstool.

II. He triumphs in God, and his glory and grace. 1. In the glory of God (*v.* 8): " *But thou, O Lord! art most high for ever-*

more. The workers of iniquity who fight against us may be high for a time, and think to carry all before them with a high hand, but *thou art high, most high, for evermore.* Their height will be humbled and brought down, but thine is everlasting." Let us not therefore fear the pride and power of evil men, nor be discouraged by their impotent menaces, for the moth shall eat them up as a garment, but *God's righteousness shall be for ever*, Isa. li. 7, 8. 2. In the grace of God, his favour and the fruits of it, (1.) To himself (*v.* 10): "Thou, O Lord! that art thyself most high, *shalt exalt my horn.*" The great God is the fountain of honour, and he, being *high for evermore*, himself will exalt his people for ever, for *he is the praise of all his saints*, cxlviii. 14. The wicked are forbidden to *lift up the horn* (lxxv. 4, 5), but those that serve God and the interest of his kingdom with their honour or power, and commit it to him to keep it, to raise it, to use it, and to dispose of it, as he pleases, may hope that he will *exalt their horn as the horn of a unicorn*, to the greatest height, either in this world or the other: *My horn shalt thou exalt*, when *thy enemies perish;* for *then shall the righteous shine forth as the sun*, when the wicked shall be doomed to shame and everlasting contempt. He adds, *I shall be anointed with fresh oil*, which denotes a fresh confirmation in his office to which he had been anointed, or abundance of plenty, so that he should have fresh oil as often as he pleased, or renewed comforts to revive him when his spirits drooped. Grace is the anointing of the Spirit; when this is given to help in the time of need, and is received, as there is occasion, from the fulness that is in Christ Jesus, we are then anointed with fresh oil. Some read it, *When I grow old thou shalt anoint me with fresh oil. My old age shalt thou exalt with rich mercy;* so the LXX. Compare *v.* 14, *They shall bring forth fruit in old age.* The comforts of God's Spirit, and the joys of his salvation, shall be a refreshing oil to the *hoary heads that are found in the way of righteousness.* (2.) To all the saints. They are here represented as *trees of righteousness*, Isa. lxi. 3; Ps. i. 3. Observe, [1.] The good place they are fixed in; they are *planted in the house of the Lord*, *v.* 13. The trees of righteousness do not grow of themselves; they are *planted*, not in common soil, but in paradise, *in the house of the Lord.* Trees are not usually planted in a house; but God's trees are said to be planted in his house because it is from his grace, by his word and Spirit, that they receive all the sap and virtue that keep them alive and make them fruitful. They fix themselves to holy ordinances, take root in them, abide by them, put themselves under the divine protection, and bring forth all their fruits to God's honour and glory. [2.] The good plight they shall be kept in. It is here promised, *First*, That they shall grow, *v.* 12. Where God

gives true grace he will give more grace. God's trees shall grow higher, like the cedars, the tall cedars in Lebanon; they shall grow nearer heaven, and with a holy ambition shall aspire towards the upper world; they shall grow stronger, like the cedars, and fitter for use. *He that has clean hands shall be stronger and stronger. Secondly*, That they shall flourish, both in the credit of their profession and in the comfort and joy of their own souls. They shall be cheerful themselves and respected by all about them. *They shall flourish like the palm-tree*, which has a stately body (Cant. vii. 7), and large boughs, Lev. xxiii. 40; Judg. iv. 5. Dates, the fruit of it, are very pleasant, but it is especially alluded to here as being ever green. The wicked flourish as the grass (*v.* 7), which is soon withered, but the righteous as the palm-tree, which is long-lived and which the winter does not change. It has been said of the palm-tree, *Sub pondere crescit* —*The more it is pressed down the more it grows;* so the righteous flourish under their burdens; the more they are afflicted the more they multiply. Being planted in *the house of the Lord* (there their root is), *they flourish in the courts of our God*—there their branches spread. *Their life is hid with Christ in God.* But their light also shines before men. It is desirable that those who have a place should have a name in God's house, and within his walls, Isa. lvi. 5. Let good Christians aim to excel, that they may be eminent and may flourish, and so may adorn the doctrine of God our Saviour, as flourishing trees adorn the courts of a house. And let those who flourish in God's courts give him the glory of it; it is by virtue of this promise, *They shall be fat and flourishing.* Their flourishing without is from a fatness within, from the *root and fatness of the good olive*, Rom. xi. 17. Without a living principle of grace in the heart the profession will not be long flourishing; but where that is the *leaf also shall not wither*, Ps. i. 3. *The trees of the Lord are full of sap*, civ. 16. See Hos. xiv. 5, 6. *Thirdly*, That they shall be fruitful. Were there nothing but leaves upon them, they would not be trees of any value; but *they shall still bring forth fruit.* The products of sanctification, all the instances of a lively devotion and a useful conversation, good works, by which God is glorified and others are edified, these are the fruits of righteousness, in which it is the privilege, as well as the duty, of the righteous to abound; and their abounding in them is the matter of a promise as well as of a command. It is promised that they shall bring forth fruit in old age. Other trees, when they are old, leave off bearing, but in God's trees the strength of grace does not fail with the strength of nature. The last days of the saints are sometimes their best days, and their last work is their best work. This indeed shows that they are upright; perseverance is the surest evidence of sincerity. But it is here said *to show that the*

Lord is upright (v. 15), that he is true to his promises and faithful to every word that he has spoken, and that he is constant to the work which he has begun. As it is by the promises that believers first partake of a divine nature, so it is by the promises that that divine nature is preserved and kept up; and therefore the power it exerts is an evidence that the *Lord is upright*, and so he will show himself *with an upright man*, xviii. 25. This the psalmist triumphs in: " *He is my rock and there is no unrighteousness in him.* I have chosen him for my rock on which to build, in the clefts of which to take shelter, on the top of which to set my feet. I have found him a rock, strong and stedfast, and his word as firm as a rock. I have found" (and let every one speak as he finds) "that there is no unrighteousness in him." He is as able, and will be as kind, as his word makes him to be. All that ever trusted in God found him faithful and all-sufficient, and none were ever made ashamed of their hope in him.

PSALM XCIII.

This short psalm sets forth the honour of the kingdom of God among men, to his glory, the terror of his enemies, and the comfort of all his loving subjects. It relates both to the kingdom of his providence, by which he upholds and governs the world, and especially to the kingdom of his grace, by which he secures the church, sanctifies and preserves it. The administration of both these kingdoms is put into the hands of the Messiah, and to him, doubtless, the prophet here bears witness, and to his kingdom, speaking of it as present, because sure ; and because, as the eternal Word, even before his incarnation he was Lord of all. Concerning God's kingdom glorious things are here spoken. 1. Have other kings their royal robes? So has he, ver. 1. II. Have they their thrones? So has he, ver. 2. III. Have they their enemies whom they subdue and triumph over? So has he, ver. 3, 4. IV. Is it their honour to be faithful and holy ? So is it his, ver. 5. In singing this psalm we forget ourselves if we forget Christ, to whom the Father has given all power both in heaven and in earth.

THE LORD reigneth, he is clothed with majesty; the LORD is clothed with strength, *wherewith* he hath girded himself: the world also is stablished, that it cannot be moved. 2 Thy throne *is* established of old : thou *art* from everlasting. 3 The floods have lifted up, O LORD, the floods have lifted up their voice ; the floods lift up their waves. 4 The LORD on high *is* mightier than the noise of many waters, *yea, than* the mighty waves of the sea. 5 Thy testimonies are very sure: holiness becometh thine house, O LORD, for ever.

Next to the being of God there is nothing that we are more concerned to believe and consider than God's dominion, that Jehovah is God, and that this God reigns (v. 1), not only that he is King of right, and is the owner and proprietor of all persons and things, but that he is King in fact, and does direct and dispose of all the creatures and all their actions according to the counsel of his own will. This is celebrated here, and in many other psalms : *The Lord reigns.* It is the song of the gospel church, of the glorified church (Rev. xix. 6), *Hallelujah; the Lord*
594

God omnipotent reigns. Here we are told how he reigns.

I. The Lord reigns gloriously: *He is clothed with majesty.* The majesty of earthly princes, compared with God's terrible majesty, is but like the glimmerings of a glow-worm compared with the brightness of the sun when he goes forth in his strength. Are the enemies of God's kingdom great and formidable? Yet let us not fear them, for God's majesty will eclipse theirs.

II. He reigns powerfully. He is not only clothed with majesty, as a prince in his court, but he is *clothed with strength*, as a general in the camp. He has wherewithal to support his greatness and to make it truly formidable. See him not only clad in robes, but clad in armour. Both *strength and honour are his clothing.* He can do every thing, and with him nothing is impossible. With this power *he has girded himself;* it is not derived from any other, nor does the executing of it depend upon any other, but he has it of himself and with it does whatsoever he pleases. Let us not fear the power of man, which is borrowed and bounded, but fear him who has power to kill and cast into hell. 2. To this power it is owing that the world stands to this day. The world also is established; it was so at first, by the creating power of God, when he founded it upon the seas; it is so still, by that providence which upholds all things and is a continued creation; it is so established that though he has *hanged the earth upon nothing* (Job xxvi. 7) yet *it cannot be moved;* all things *continue to this day, according to his ordinance.* Note, The preserving of the powers of nature and the course of nature is what the God of nature must have the glory of; and we who have the benefit thereof daily are very careless and ungrateful if we give him not the glory of it. Though God clothes himself with majesty, yet he condescends to take care of this lower world and to settle its affairs; and, if he established the world, much more will he establish his church, that it cannot be moved.

III. He reigns eternally (v. 2): *Thy throne is established of old.* 1. God's right to rule the world is founded in his making it; he that gave being to it, no doubt, may give law to it, and so his title to the government is incontestable: *Thy throne is established;* it is a title without a flaw in it. And it is ancient: it is *established of old*, from the beginning of time, before any other rule, principality, or power was erected, as it will continue when all other rule, principality, and power shall be put down, 1 Cor. xv. 24. 2. The whole administration of his government was settled in his eternal counsels before all worlds; for he does all according to the purpose which he purposed in himself. The chariots of Providence came down from between the mountains of brass, from those decrees which are fixed as the everlasting mountains (Zech. vi. 1): *Thou art from everlasting,* and therefore *thy throne is established of old;* because God himself was from everlasting, his throne and all the determinations of it were so too; for in an eternal mind there could not but be eternal thoughts.

IV. He reigns triumphantly, *v.* 3, 4. We have here, 1. A threatening storm supposed: *The floods have lifted up, O Lord!* (to God himself the remonstrance is made) *the floods have lifted up their voice,* which speaks terror; nay, they have *lifted up their waves,* which speaks real danger. It alludes to a tempestuous sea, such as the wicked are compared to, Isa. lvii. 20. The *heathen rage* (Ps. ii. 1) and think to ruin the church, to overwhelm it like a deluge, to sink it like a ship at sea. The church is said to *be tossed with tempests* (Isa. liv. 11), and the *floods of ungodly men* make the saints *afraid,* Ps. xviii. 4. We may apply it to the tumults that are sometimes in our own bosoms, through prevailing passions and frights, which put the soul into disorder, and are ready to overthrow its graces and comforts; but, if the Lord reign there, even the winds and seas shall obey him. 2. An immovable anchor cast in this storm (*v.* 4): *The Lord himself is mightier.* Let this keep our minds fixed, (1.) That God is on high, above them, which denotes his safety (they cannot reach him, xxix. 10) and his sovereignty; they are ruled by him, they are overruled, and, wherein they rebel, overcome, Exod. xviii. 11. (2.) That he *is mightier,* does more *wondrous things* than *the noise of many waters;* they cannot disturb his rest or rule; they cannot defeat his designs and purposes. Observe, The power of the church's enemies is but *as the noise of many waters;* there is more of sound than substance in it. *Pharaoh king of Egypt is but a noise,* Jer. xlvi. 17. The church's friends are commonly more frightened than hurt. God is mightier than this noise; he is mighty to preserve his people's interests from being ruined by these many waters and his people's spirits from being terrified by the noise of them. He can, when he pleases, command peace to the church (lxv. 7), peace in the soul, Isa. xxvi. 3. Note, The unlimited sovereignty and irresistible power of the great Jehovah are very encouraging to the people of God, in reference to all the noises and hurries they meet with in this world, Ps. xlvi. 1, 2.

V. He reigns in truth and holiness, *v.* 5. 1. All his promises are inviolably faithful: *Thy testimonies are very sure.* As God is able to protect his church, so he is true to the promises he has made of its safety and victory. His word is passed, and all the saints may rely upon it. Whatever was foretold concerning the kingdom of the Messiah would certainly have its accomplishment in due time. Those testimonies upon which the faith and hope of the Old-Testament saints were built were very sure, and would

not fail tnem. 2. All his people ought to be conscientiously pure: *Holiness becomes thy house, O Lord! for ever.* God's church is his house; it is a holy house, cleansed from sin, consecrated by God, and employed in his service. The holiness of it is its beauty (nothing better becomes the saints than conformity to God's image and an entire devotedness to his honour), and it is its strength and safety; it is the holiness of God's house that secures it against the many waters and their noise. Where there is purity there shall be peace. Fashions change, and that which is becoming at one time is not so at another; but holiness always becomes God's house and family, and those who belong to it; it is perpetually decent; and nothing so ill becomes the worshippers of the holy God as unholiness.

PSALM XCIV.

This psalm was penned when the church of God was under hatches, oppressed and persecuted; and it is an appeal to God, as the Judge of heaven and earth, and an address to him, to appear for his people against his and their enemies. Two things this psalm speaks:—I. Conviction and terror to the persecutors (ver. 1—11), showing them their danger and folly, and arguing with them. II. Comfort and peace to the persecuted (ver. 12—23), assuring them, both from God's promise and from the psalmist's own experience, that their troubles would end well, and God would, in due time, appear to their joy and the confusion of those who set themselves against them. In singing this psalm we must look abroad upon the pride of oppressors with a holy indignation, and the tears of the oppressed with a holy compassion; but, at the same time, look upwards to the righteous Judge with an entire satisfaction, and look forward, to the end of all these things, with a pleasing hope.

O LORD God, to whom vengeance belongeth; O God, to whom vengeance belongeth, show thyself. 2 Lift up thyself, thou judge of the earth: render a reward to the proud. 3 LORD, how long shall the wicked, how long shall the wicked triumph? 4 *How long* shall they utter *and* speak hard things? *and* all the workers of iniquity boast themselves? 5 They break in pieces thy people, O LORD, and afflict thine heritage. 6 They slay the widow and the stranger, and murder the fatherless. 7 Yet they say, The LORD shall not see, neither shall the God of Jacob regard *it.* 8 Understand, ye brutish among the people: and *ye* fools, when will ye be wise? 9 He that planted the ear, shall he not hear? he that formed the eye, shall he not see? 10 He that chastiseth the heathen, shall not he correct? he that teacheth man knowledge, *shall not he know?* 11 The LORD knoweth the thoughts of man, that they *are* vanity.

In these verses we have,

I. A solemn appeal to God against the cruel oppressors of his people, *v.* 1, 2. This speaks terror enough to them, that they have the prayers of God's people against them, who cry day and night to him to avenge them of their adversaries; and shall he not avenge them speedily? Luke xviii. 3, 7. Observe here,

1. The titles they give to God for the encouraging of their faith in this appeal: *O God! to whom vengeance belongeth;* and *thou Judge of the earth.* We may with boldness appeal to him; for, (1.) He is judge, supreme judge, judge alone, from whom every man's judgment proceeds. He that gives law gives sentence upon every man according to his works, by the rule of that law. He has prepared his throne for judgment. He has indeed appointed magistrates to be avengers under him (Rom. xiii. 4), but he is the avenger in chief, to whom even magistrates themselves are accountable; his throne is the last refuge (the *dernier ressort,* as the law speaks) of oppressed innocency. He is universal judge, not of this city or country only, but *judge of the earth,* of the whole earth: none are exempt from his jurisdiction; nor can it be alleged against an appeal to him in any court that it is *coram non judice—before a person not judicially qualified.* (2.) He is just. As he has authority to avenge wrong, so it is his nature, and property, and honour. This also is implied in the title here given to him and repeated with such an emphasis, *O God! to whom vengeance belongs,* who wilt not suffer might always to prevail against right. This is a good reason why we must not avenge ourselves, because God has said, *Vengeance is mine;* and it is daring presumption to usurp his prerogative and step into his throne, Rom. xii. 19. Let this alarm those who do wrong, whether with a close hand, so as not to be discovered, or with a high hand, so as not to be controlled, There is a God to whom vengeance belongs, who will certainly call them to an account; and let it encourage those who suffer wrong to bear it with silence, committing themselves to him who judges righteously.

2. What it is they ask of God. (1.) That he would *glorify himself,* and get honour to his own name. Wicked persecutors thought God had withdrawn and had forsaken the earth. "Lord," say they, "show thyself; make them know that thou art and that thou art ready to *show thyself strong on the behalf of those whose hearts are upright with thee.*" The enemies thought God was conquered because his people were. "Lord," say they, "*lift up thyself, be thou exalted in thy own strength.* Lift up thyself, to be seen, to be feared; and suffer not thy name to be trampled upon and run down." (2.) That he would mortify the oppressors: *Render a reward to the proud;* that is, "Reckon with them for all their insolence, and the injuries they have done to thy people." These prayers are prophecies, which speak terror to all the sons of violence. The righteous God will deal with them according to their merits.

II. A humble complaint to God of the pride and cruelty of the oppressors, and an expostulation with him concerning it, *v.* 3—6. Here observe,

1. The character of the enemies they complain against. They are wicked; they are *workers of iniquity;* they are bad, very bad, themselves, and therefore they hate and persecute those whose goodness shames and condemns them. Those are wicked indeed, and *workers of the worst iniquity,* lost to all honour and virtue, who are cruel to the innocent and hate the righteous.

2. Their haughty barbarous carriage which they complain of. (1.) They are insolent, and take a pleasure in magnifying themselves. They talk high and talk big; they triumph; they speak loud things; they boast themselves, as if their tongues were their own and their hands too, and they were accountable to none for what they say or do, and as if the day were their own, and they doubted not but to carry the cause against God and religion. Those that speak highly of themselves, that triumph and boast, are apt to speak hardly of others; but there will come a day of reckoning for all their hard speeches which ungodly sinners have spoken against God, his truths, and ways, and people, Jude 15. (2.) They are impious, and take a pleasure in running down God's people because they are his (*v.* 5): "*They break in pieces thy people, O Lord!* break their assemblies, their estates, their families, their persons, in pieces, and do all they can to afflict thy heritage, to grieve them, to crush them, to run them down, to root them out." God's people are his heritage; there are those that, for his sake, hate them, and seek their ruin. This is a very good plea with God, in our intercessions for the church: "Lord, it is thine; thou hast a property in it. It is thy heritage; thou hast a pleasure in it, and out of it the rent of thy glory in this world issues. And wilt thou suffer these wicked men to trample upon it thus?" (3.) They are inhuman, and take a pleasure in wronging those that are least able to help themselves (*v.* 6); they not only oppress and impoverish, but *they slay the widow and the stranger;* not only neglect the fatherless, and make a prey of them, but murder them, because they are weak and exposed, and sometimes lie at their mercy. Those whom they should protect from injury they are most injurious to, perhaps because God has taken them into his particular care. Who would think it possible that any of the children of men should be thus barbarous?

3. A modest pleading with God concerning the continuance of the persecution: "Lord, *how long* shall they do thus?" And again, *How long?* When shall this wickedness of the wicked come to an end?

III. A charge of atheism exhibited against the persecutors, and an expostulation with them upon that charge.

1. Their atheistical thoughts are here discovered (*v.* 7): *Yet they say, The Lord shall not see.* Though the cry of their wickedness

is very great and loud, though they rebel against the light of nature and the dictates of their own consciences, yet they have the confidence to say, " *The Lord shall not see ;* he will not only wink at small faults, but shut his eyes at great ones too." Or they think they have managed it so artfully, under colour of justice and religion perhaps, that it will not be adjudged murder. " The God of Jacob, though his people pretend to have such an interest in him, does not regard it either as against justice or as against his own people; he will never call us to an account for it." Thus they deny God's government of the world, banter his covenant with his people, and set the judgment to come at defiance.

2. They are here convicted of folly and absurdity. He that says either that Jehovah the living God shall not see or that the God of Jacob shall not regard the injuries done to his people, *Nabal* is his name and folly is with him ; and yet here he is fairly reasoned with, for his conviction and conversion, to prevent his confusion (*v.* 8): "*Understand, you brutish among the people,* and let reason guide you." Note, The atheistical, though they set up for wits, and philosophers, and politicians, yet are really the *brutish among the people;* if they would but understand, they would believe. God, by the prophet, speaks as if he thought the time long till men would be men, and show themselves so by understanding and considering: "*You fools, when will you be wise,* so wise as to know that God sees and regards all you say and do, and to speak and act accordingly, as those that must give account?" Note, None are so bad but means are to be used for the reclaiming and reforming of them, none so brutish, so foolish, but it should be tried whether they may not yet be made wise ; while there is life there is hope. To prove the folly of those that question God's omniscience and justice the psalmist argues,

(1.) From the works of creation (*v.* 9), the formation of human bodies, which, as it proves that there is a God, proves also that God has infinitely and transcendently in himself all those perfections that are in any creature. *He that planted the ear* (and it is planted in the head, as a tree, in the ground) *shall he not hear ?* No doubt he shall, more and better than we can. *He that formed the eye* (and how curiously it is formed above any part of the body anatomists know and let us know by their dissections) *shall he not see ?* Could he give, would he give, that perfection to a creature which he has not in himself ? Note, [1.] The powers of nature are all derived from the God of nature. See Exod. iv. 11. [2.] By the knowledge of ourselves we may be led a great way towards the knowledge of God—if by the knowledge of our own bodies, and the organs of sense, so as to conclude that if we can see and hear much more can God, then certainly by the knowledge of our own souls and their noble faculties. The gods of the heathen had eyes and saw not, ears and

heard not ; our God has no eyes nor ears, as we have, and yet we must conclude he both sees and hears, because we have our sight and hearing from him, and are accountable to him for our use of them.

(2.) From the works of providence (*v.* 10): *He that chastises the heathen* for their polytheism and idolatry, *shall not he* much more *correct* his own people for their atheism and profaneness ? He that chastises the children of men for oppressing and wronging one another, shall not he correct those that profess to be his own children, and call themselves so, and yet persecute those that are really so ? Shall not we be under his correction, under whose government the whole world is ? Does he regard as King of nations, and shall he not much more regard as the God of Jacob ? Dr. Hammond gives another very probable sense of this : "*He that instructs the nations* (that is, gives them his law), *shall not he correct,* that is, shall not he judge them according to that law, and call them to an account for their violations of it ? In vain was the law given if there will not be a judgment upon it." And it is true that the same word signifies to chastise and to instruct, because chastisement is intended for instruction and instruction should go along with chastisement.

(3.) From the works of grace : *He that teaches man knowledge, shall he not know ?* He not only, as the God of nature, has given the light of reason, but, as the God of grace, has given the light of revelation, has shown man what is true wisdom and understanding ; and he that does this, shall he not know ? Job xxviii. 23, 28. The flowing of the streams is a certain sign of the fulness of the fountain. If all knowledge is from God, no doubt all knowledge is in God. From this general doctrine of God's omniscience, the psalmist not only confutes the atheists, who said, " *The Lord shall not see* (*v.* 7), he will not take cognizance of what we do ;" but awakens us all to consider that God will take cognizance even of what we think (*v.* 11): *The Lord knows the thoughts of man, that they are vanity.* [1.] He knows those thoughts, in particular, concerning God's conniving at the wickedness of the wicked, and knows them to be vain, and laughs at the folly of those who by such fond conceits buoy themselves up in sin. [2.] He knows all the thoughts of the children of men, and knows them to be, for the most part, vain, that the imaginations of the thoughts of men's hearts are evil, only evil, and that continually. Even in good thoughts there is a fickleness and inconstancy which may well be called *vanity.* It concerns us to keep a strict guard upon our thoughts, because God takes particular notice of them. Thoughts are words to God, and vain thoughts are provocations.

12 Blessed *is* the man whom thou chastenest, O Lord, and teachest him out of thy law ; 13 That thou mayest give him rest from the days of adver-

sity, until the pit be digged for the wicked. 14 For the LORD will not cast off his people, neither will he forsake his inheritance. 15 But judgment shall return unto righteousness: and all the upright in heart shall follow it. 16 Who will rise up for me against the evildoers? *or* who will stand up for me against the workers of iniquity? 17 Unless the LORD *had been* my help, my soul had almost dwelt in silence. 18 When I said, My foot slippeth; thy mercy, O LORD, held me up. 19 In the multitude of my thoughts within me thy comforts delight my soul. 20 Shall the throne of iniquity have fellowship with thee, which frameth mischief by a law? 21 They gather themselves together against the soul of the righteous, and condemn the innocent blood. 22 But the LORD is my defence; and my God *is* the rock of my refuge. 23 And he shall bring upon them their own iniquity, and shall cut them off in their own wickedness; *yea,* the LORD our God shall cut them off.

The psalmist, having denounced tribulation to those that trouble God's people, here assures those that are troubled of rest. See 2 Thess. i. 6, 7. He speaks comfort to suffering saints from God's promises and his own experience.

I. From God's promises, which are such as not only save them from being miserable, but secure a happiness to them (*v.* 12): *Blessed is the man whom thou chastenest.* Here he looks above the instruments of trouble, and eyes the hand of God, which gives it another name and puts quite another colour upon it. The enemies break in pieces God's people (*v.* 5); they aim at no less; but the truth of the matter is that God by them chastens his people, as the father the son in whom he delights, and the persecutors are only the rod he makes use of. *Howbeit they mean not so, neither doth their heart think so,* Isa. x. 5—7. Now it is here promised,

1. That God's people shall get good by their sufferings. When he chastens them he will teach them, and blessed is the man who is thus taken under a divine discipline, for *none teaches like God.* Note, (1.) The afflictions of the saints are fatherly chastenings, designed for their instruction, reformation, and improvement. (2.) When the teachings of the word and Spirit go along with the rebukes of Providence they then both manifest men to be blessed and help to make them so; for then they are marks of adoption and means of sanctification. When we are chastened we

598

must pray to be taught, and look into the law as the best expositor of Providence. It is not the chastening itself that does good, but the teaching that goes along with it and is the exposition of it.

2. That they shall see through their sufferings (*v.* 13): *That thou mayest give him rest from the days of adversity.* Note, (1.) There is a rest remaining for the people of God after the days of their adversity, which, though they may be many and long, shall be numbered and finished in due time, and shall not last always. He that sends the trouble will send the rest, that he may comfort them according to the time that he has afflicted them. (2.) God *therefore* teaches his people by their troubles, that he may prepare them for deliverance, and so give them rest from their troubles, that, being reformed, they may be relieved, and that the affliction, having done its work, may be removed.

3. That they shall see the ruin of those that are the instruments of their sufferings, which is the matter of a promise, not as gratifying any passion of theirs, but as redounding to the glory of God: *Until the pit is digged* (or rather while the pit is digging) *for the wicked,* God is ordering peace for them at the same time that he is ordaining his arrows against the persecutors.

4. That, though they may be cast down, yet certainly they shall not be cast off, *v.* 14. Let God's suffering people assure themselves of this, that, whatever their friends do, God will not cast them off, nor throw them out of his covenant or out of his care; he will not forsake them, because they are his inheritance, which he will not quit his title to nor suffer himself to be disseised of. St. Paul comforted himself with this, Rom. xi. 1.

5. That, bad as things are, they shall mend, and, though they are now out of course, yet they shall return to their due and ancient channel (*v.* 15): *Judgment shall return unto righteousness;* the seeming disorders of Providence (for real ones there never were) shall be rectified. God's judgment, that is, his government, looks sometimes as if it were at a distance from righteousness, while the wicked prosper, and the best men meet with the worst usage; but it shall return to righteousness again, either in this world or at the furthest in the judgment of the great day, which will set all to-rights. Then *all the upright in heart shall be after it;* they shall follow it with their praises, and with entire satisfaction; they shall return to a prosperous and flourishing condition, and shine forth out of obscurity; they shall accommodate themselves to the dispensations of divine Providence, and with suitable affections attend all its motions. *They shall walk after the Lord,* Hos. xi. 10. Dr. Hammond thinks this was most eminently fulfilled in the destruction of Jerusalem first, and afterwards of heathen Rome, the crucifiers of Christ and persecutors of Christians, and the rest which the churches

had thereby. *Then judgment returned even to righteousness,* to mercy and goodness, and favour to God's people, who then were as much countenanced as before they had been trampled on.

II. From his own experiences and observations.

1. He and his friends had been oppressed by cruel and imperious men, that had power in their hands and abused it by abusing all good people with it. They were themselves *evil-doers* and *workers of iniquity* (v. 16); they abandoned themselves to all manner of impiety and immorality, and then their throne was a *throne of iniquity, v.* 20. Their dignity served to put a reputation upon sin, and their authority was employed to support it, and to bring about their wicked designs. It is a pity that ever a throne, which should be a terror to evil-doers and a protection and praise to those that do well, should be the seat and shelter of iniquity. That is a throne of iniquity which by the policy of its council *frames mischief,* and by its sovereignty enacts it and turns it into a law. Iniquity is daring enough even when human laws are against it, which often prove too weak to give an effectual check to it; but how insolent, how mischievous, is it when it is backed by a law! Iniquity is not the better, but much the worse, for being enacted by law; nor will it excuse those that practise it to say that they did but do as they were bidden. These workers of iniquity, having *framed mischief by a law, take care to see the law executed;* for *they gather themselves together against the soul of the righteous,* who dare not *keep the statutes of Omri* nor *the law of the house of Ahab;* and they condemn *the innocent blood* for violating their decrees. See an instance in Daniel's enemies; they *framed mischief by a law* when they obtained an impious edict against prayer (Dan. vi. 7), and, when Daniel would not obey it, they *assembled together against* him (v. 11) and *condemned his innocent blood* to the lions. The best benefactors of mankind have often been thus treated, under colour of law and justice, as the worst of malefactors.

2. The oppression they were under bore very hard upon them, and oppressed their spirits too. Let not suffering saints despair, though, when they are persecuted, they find themselves perplexed and cast down; it was so with the psalmist here: His *soul had almost dwelt in silence* (v. 17); he was at his wits' end, and knew not what to say or do; he was, in his own apprehension, at his life's end, ready to drop into the grave, that land of silence. St. Paul, in a like case, *received a sentence of death within himself,* 2 Cor. i. 8, 9. He said, "*My foot slippeth* (v. 18); I am going irretrievably; there is no remedy; I must *fall. I shall one day perish by the hand of Saul.* My hope fails me; I do not find such firm footing for my faith as I have sometimes found." See Ps. lxxiii. 2. He had a multitude of perplexed entangled thoughts

within him concerning the case he was in and the construction to be made of it, and concerning the course he should take and what was likely to be the issue of it.

3. In this distress they sought for help, and succour, and some relief. (1.) They looked about for it and were disappointed (v. 16): "*Who will rise up for me against the evil-doers?* Have I any friend who, in love to me, will appear for me? Has justice any friend who, in a pious indignation at unrighteousness, will plead my injured cause?" He looked, but there was none to save, there was none to uphold. Note, When on the side of the oppressors there is power it is no marvel if the oppressed have no comforter, none that dare own them, or speak a good word for them, Eccl. iv. 1. When St. Paul was brought before Nero's throne of iniquity *no man stood by him,* 2 Tim. iv. 16. (2.) They looked up for it, v. 20. They humbly expostulate with God: "Lord, *shall the throne of iniquity have fellowship with thee?* Wilt thou countenance and support these tyrants in their wickedness? We know thou wilt not." A throne has fellowship with God when it is a throne of justice and answers the end of the erecting of it; for by him kings reign, and when they reign for him their judgments are his, and he owns them as his ministers, and whoever resist them, or rise up against them, shall receive to themselves damnation; but, when it becomes a *throne of iniquity,* it has no longer fellowship with God. Far be it from the just and holy God that he should be the patron of unrighteousness, even in princes and those that sit in thrones, yea, though they be the *thrones of the house of David.*

4. They found succour and relief in God, and in him only. When other friends failed, in him they had a faithful and powerful friend; and it is recommended to all God's suffering saints to trust in him. (1.) God helps at a dead lift (v. 17): "When I had almost *dwelt in silence,* then the Lord was *my help,* kept me alive, kept me in heart; and *unless I had* made him *my help,* by putting my trust in him and expecting relief from him, I could never have kept possession of my own soul; but living by faith in him has kept my head above water, has given me breath, and something to say." (2.) God's goodness is the great support of sinking spirits (v. 18): "*When I said, My foot slips* into sin, into ruin, into despair, then *thy mercy, O Lord! held me up,* kept me from falling, and defeated the design of those who consulted to *cast me down from my excellency,*" lxii. 4. We are beholden not only to God's power, but to his pity, for spiritual supports: *Thy mercy,* the gifts of thy mercy and my hope in thy mercy, *held me up.* God's right hand sustains his people when they look on their right hand and on their left and there is none to uphold; and we are then prepared for his gracious supports when

we are sensible of our own weakness and inability to stand by our own strength, and come to God, to acknowledge it, and to tell him how *our foot slips.* (3.) Divine consolations are the effectual relief of troubled spirits (*v.* 19): " *In the multitude of my thoughts within me,* which are noisy like a multitude, crowding and jostling one another like a multitude, and very unruly and ungovernable, in the multitude of my sorrowful, solicitous, timorous thoughts, *thy comforts delight my soul;* and they are never more delightful than when they come in so seasonably to silence my unquiet thoughts and keep my mind easy." The world's comforts give but little delight to the soul when it is hurried with melancholy thoughts ; they are songs to a heavy heart. But God's comforts will reach the soul, and not the fancy only, and will bring with them that peace and that pleasure which the smiles of the world cannot give and which the frowns of the world cannot take away.

5. God is, and will be, as a righteous Judge, the patron and protector of right and the punisher and avenger of wrong ; this the psalmist had both the assurance of and the experience of. (1.) He will give redress to the injured (*v.* 22): " When none else will, nor can, nor dare, shelter me, *the Lord is my defence,* to preserve me from the evil of my troubles, from sinking under them and being ruined by them ; and he is *the rock of my refuge,* in the clefts of which I may take shelter, and on the top of which I may set my feet, to be out of the reach of danger." God is his people's refuge, to whom they may flee, in whom they are safe and may be secure ; he is the rock of their refuge, so strong, so firm, impregnable, immovable, as a rock : natural fastnesses sometimes exceed artificial fortifications. (2.) He will reckon with the injurious (*v.* 23) *: He shall render to them their own iniquity ;* he shall deal with them according to their deserts, and that very mischief which they did and designed against God's people shall be brought upon themselves : it follows, *He shall cut them off in their wickedness.* A man cannot be more miserable than his own wickedness will make him if God visit it upon him : it will cut him in the remembrance of it ; it will cut him off in the recompence of it. This the psalm concludes with the triumphant assurance of : *Yea, the Lord our God,* who takes our part and owns us for his, *shall cut them off* from any fellowship with him, and so shall make them completely miserable and their pomp and power shall stand them in no stead.

PSALM XCV.

For the expounding of this psalm we may borrow a great deal of light from the apostle's discourse, Heb. iii. and iv., where it appears both to have been penned by David and to have been calculated for the days of the Messiah ; for it is there said expressly (Heb. iv. 7) that the day here spoken of (ver. 7) is to be understood of the gospel day, in which God speaks to us by his Son in a voice which we are concerned to hear, and proposes to us a rest besides that of Canaan. In singing psalms it is intended, I. That we should " make melody unto the Lord ;" this we are here excited to do, and assisted in doing, being lled upon to praise God (ver. 1,

2) as a great God (ver. 3—5) and as our gracious benefactor, ver. 6, 7. II. That we should teach and admonish ourselves and one another ; and we are here taught and warned to hear God's voice (ver. 7), and not to harden our hearts, as the Israelites in the wilderness did (ver. 8, 9), lest we fall under God's wrath and fall short of his rest, as they did, ver. 10, 11. This psalm must be sung with a holy reverence of God's majesty and a dread of his justice, with a desire to please him and a fear to offend him.

O COME, let us sing unto the Lord : let us make a joyful noise to the rock of our salvation. 2 Let us come before his presence with thanksgiving, and make a joyful noise unto him with psalms. 3 For the Lord *is* a great God, and a great King above all gods. 4 In his hand *are* the deep places of the earth : the strength of the hills *is* his also. 5 The sea *is* his, and he made it : and his hands formed the dry *land.* 6 O come, let us worship and bow down : let us kneel before the Lord our maker. 7 For he *is* our God ; and we *are* the people of his pasture, and the sheep of his hand.

The psalmist here, as often elsewhere, stirs up himself and others to praise God ; for it is a duty which ought to be performed with the most lively affections, and which we have great need to be excited to, being very often backward to it and cold in it. Observe,

I. How God is to be praised. 1. With holy joy and delight in him. The praising song must be *a joyful noise, v.* 1 and again *v.* 2. Spiritual joy is the heart and soul of thankful praise. It is the will of God (such is the condescension of his grace) that when we give glory to him as a being infinitely perfect and blessed we should, at the same time, *rejoice in him* as our Father and King, and a God in covenant with us. 2. With humble reverence, and a holy awe of him (*v.* 6): " *Let us worship, and bow down, and kneel before him,* as becomes those who know what an infinite distance there is between us and God, how much we are in danger of his wrath and in need of his mercy." Though *bodily exercise,* alone, *profits little,* yet certainly it is our duty to glorify God with our bodies by the outward expressions of reverence, seriousness, and humility, in the duties of religious worship. 3. We must praise God with our voice ; we must speak forth, sing forth, his praises out of the abundance of a heart filled with love, and joy, and thankfulness—*Sing to the Lord ; make a noise, a joyful noise to him, with psalms*—as those who are ourselves much affected with his greatness and goodness, are forward to own ourselves so, are desirous to be more and more affected therewith, and would willingly be instrumental to kindle and inflame the same pious and devout affection in others also. 4. We must praise God in concert, in the solemn assemblies : " *Come, let us sing ;* let us join in singing to the Lord ; not others without me, nor I alone, but others with me. *Let us come together before his presence*, in the courts of his house, where his people are wont to attend him and to expect his manifestations of himself." Whenever we come into God's presence we must come with thanksgiving that we are admitted to such a favour; and, whenever we have thanks to give, we must *come before God's presence*, set ourselves before him, and present ourselves to him in the ordinances which he has appointed.

II. Why God is to be praised and what must be the matter of our praise. We do not want matter; it were well if we did not want a heart. We must praise God,

1. Because he is *a great God*, and sovereign Lord of all, *v.* 3. He is great, and therefore *greatly to be praised*. He is infinite and immense, and has all perfection in himself. (1.) He has great power: *He is a great King above all gods*, above all deputed deities, all magistrates, to whom he said, *You are gods* (he manages them all, and serves his own purposes by them, and to him they are all accountable), above all counterfeit deities, all pretenders, all usurpers; he can do that which none of them can do; he can, and will, famish and vanquish them all. (2.) He has great possessions. This lower world is here particularly specified. We reckon those great men who have large territories, which they call their own against all the world, which yet are a very inconsiderable part of the universe: how great then is that God whose *the whole earth is, and the fulness thereof*, not only under whose feet it is, as he has an incontestable dominion over all the creatures and a propriety in them, but in whose hand it is, as he has the actual directing and disposing of all (*v.* 4); even *the deep places of the earth*, which are out of our sight, subterraneous springs and mines, *are in his hand;* and *the height of the hills* which are out of our reach, whatever grows or feeds upon them, *is his also*. This may be taken figuratively: the meanest of the children of men, who are as the low places of the earth, are not beneath his cognizance; and the greatest, who are as the strength of the hills, are not above his control. Whatever strength is in any creature it is derived from God and employed for him (*v.* 5): *The sea is his*, and all that is in it (the waves fulfil his word); it is his, for *he made it*, gathered its waters and fixed its shores; *the dry land*, though given to the children of men, is his too, for he still reserved the property to himself; it is his, for *his hands formed* it, when his word made *the dry land* appear. His being the Creator of all makes him, without dispute, the owner of all. This being a gospel psalm, we may very well suppose that it is the Lord Jesus whom we are here taught to praise. He *is a great God;* the mighty God is one of his titles, and *God over all, blessed for evermore*. As Mediator, he is *a great King above all*

gods; by him kings reign; and angels, principalities, and powers, are subject to him; *by him*, as the eternal Word, *all things were made* (John i. 3), and it was fit he should be the restorer and reconciler of all who was the Creator of all, Col. i. 16, 20. To him all power is given both in heaven and in earth, and into his hand all things are delivered. It is he that sets one foot on the sea and the other on the earth, as sovereign Lord of both (Rev. x. 2), and therefore to him we must sing our songs of praise, and before him we must *worship and bow down*.

2. Because he is our God, not only has a dominion over us, as he has over all the creatures, but stands in special relation to us (*v.* 7): *He is our God*, and therefore it is expected we should praise him; who will, if we do not? What else did he make us for but that we should *be to him for a name and a praise?* (1.) He is our Creator, and the author of our being; we must *kneel before the Lord our Maker, v.* 6. Idolaters kneel before gods which they themselves made; we kneel before a God who made us and all the world and who is therefore our rightful proprietor; for his we are, and not our own. (2.) He is our Saviour, and the author of our blessedness. He is here called *the rock of our salvation* (*v.* 1), not only the founder, but the very foundation, of that work of wonder, on whom it is built. *That rock is Christ;* to him therefore we must sing our songs of praises, *to him that sits upon the throne and to the Lamb*. (3.) We are therefore his, under all possible obligations: *We are the people of his pasture and the sheep of his hand*. All the children of men are so; they are fed and led by his Providence, which cares for them, and conducts them, as the shepherd the sheep. We must praise him, not only because he made us, but because he preserves and maintains us, and our breath and ways are in his hand. All the church's children are in a special manner so; Israel *are the people of his pasture and the sheep of his hand;* and therefore he demands their homage in a special manner. The gospel church is his flock. Christ is the great and good Shepherd of it. We, as Christians, are led by his hand into the green pastures, by him we are protected and well provided for, to his honour and service we are entirely devoted as a peculiar people, and therefore to him must be *glory in the churches* (whether it be in the world or no) *throughout all ages*, Eph. iii. 21.

7—To day if ye will hear his voice, 8 Harden not your heart, as in the provocation, *and as in* the day of temptation in the wilderness: 9 When your fathers tempted me, proved me, and saw my work. 10 Forty years long was I grieved with *this* generation, and said, It *is* a people that do err in their heart, and they have not known my ways: 11 Unto whom I sware in my wrath that they should not enter into my rest.

The latter part of this psalm, which begins in the middle of a verse, is an exhortation to those who sing gospel psalms to live gospel lives, and to hear the voice of God's word; otherwise, how can they expect that he should hear the voice of their prayers and praises? Observe,

I. The duty required of all those that *are the people of* Christ's *pasture and the sheep of his hand.* He expects that they *hear his voice,* for he has said, *My sheep hear my voice,* John x. 27. *We are his people,* say they. Are you so? Then *hear his voice.* If you call him *Master,* or *Lord,* then *do the things which he says,* and be his willing obedient people. Hear the voice of his doctrine, of his law, and, in both, of his Spirit; hear and heed; hear and yield. *Hear his voice,* and not the *voice of a stranger. If you will hear his voice;* some take it as a wish, *O that you would hear his voice!* that you would be so wise, and do so well for yourselves; like that, *If thou hadst known* (Luke xix. 42), that is, O that thou hadst known! Christ's voice must be heard *to-day;* this the apostle lays much stress upon, applying it to the gospel day. While he is speaking to you see that you attend to him, for this day of your opportunities will not last always; improve it, therefore, *while it is called to-day,* Heb. iii. 13, 15. Hearing the voice of Christ is the same with believing. *To-day,* if by faith you accept the gospel offer, well and good, but to-morrow it may be too late. In a matter of such vast importance nothing is more dangerous than delay.

II. The sin they are warned against, as inconsistent with the believing obedient ear required, and that is hardness of heart. *If you will hear his voice,* and profit by what you hear, then do *not harden your hearts;* for the seed sown on the rock never brought any fruit to perfection. The Jews *therefore* believed not the gospel of Christ because *their hearts were hardened;* they were not convinced of the evil of sin, and of their danger by reason of sin, and therefore they regarded not the offer of salvation; they would not bend to the yoke of Christ, nor yield to his demands; and, if the sinner's heart be hardened, it is his own act and deed (he hardening it himself) and he alone shall bear the blame for ever.

III. The example they are warned by, which is that of the Israelites in the wilderness.

1. "Take heed of sinning as they did, lest you be shut out of the everlasting rest as they were out of Canaan." *Be not, as your fathers, a stubborn and rebellious generation,* lxxviii. 8. Thus here, *Harden not your heart as you did* (that is, your ancestors) *in the provocation,* or in *Meribah,* the place where they

602

quarrelled with God and Moses (Exod. xvii. 2—7), *and in the day of temptation in the wilderness, v.* 8. So often did they provoke God by their distrusts and murmurings that the whole time of their continuance in the wilderness might be called a *day of temptation,* or *Massah,* the other name given to that place (Exod. xvii. 7), because they tempted the Lord, saying, *Is the Lord among us or is he not?* This was in the wilderness, where they could not help themselves, but lay at God's mercy, and where God wonderfully helped them and gave them such sensible proofs of his power and tokens of his favour as never any people had before or since. Note, (1.) Days of temptation are days of provocation. Nothing is more offensive to God than disbelief of his promise and despair of the performance of it because of some difficulties that seem to lie in the way. (2.) The more experience we have had of the power and goodness of God the greater is our sin if we distrust him. What, to tempt him in the wilderness, where we live upon him! This is as ungrateful as it is absurd and unreasonable. (3.) Hardness of heart is at the bottom of all our distrusts of God and quarrels with him. That is a hard heart which receives not the impressions of divine discoveries and conforms not to the intentions of the divine will, which will not melt, which will not bend. (4.) The sins of others ought to be warnings to us not to tread in their steps. The murmurings of Israel *were written for our admonition,* 1 Cor. x. 11.

2. Now here observe,

(1.) The charge drawn up, in God's name, against the unbelieving Israelites, v. 9, 10. God here, many ages after, complains of their ill conduct towards him, with the expressions of high resentment. [1.] Their sin was unbelief: they *tempted* God and *proved* him; they questioned whether they might take his word, and insisted upon further security before they would go forward to Canaan, by sending spies; and, when those discouraged them, they protested against the sufficiency of the divine power and promise, and would make a captain and return into Egypt, Num. xiv. 3, 4. This is called *rebellion,* Deut. i. 26, 32. [2.] The aggravation of this sin was that they *saw God's work;* they saw what he had done for them in bringing them out of Egypt, nay, what he was now doing for them every day, this day, in the bread he rained from heaven for them and the water out of the rock that followed them, than which they could not have more unquestionable evidences of God's presence with them. With them even seeing was not believing, because they *hardened their hearts,* though they had seen what Pharaoh got by hardening his heart. [3.] The causes of their sin. See what God imputed it to: *It is a people that do err in their hearts, and they have not known my ways.* Men's unbelief and distrust of God, their murmurings and quarrels with him, are the effect of their ignorance and mistake. *First,* Of their ignorance : *They have not known my ways.* They saw his work (v. 9) and he *made known his acts to them* (ciii. 7); and yet they *did not know his ways,* the ways of his providence, in which he walked towards them, or the ways of his commandments, in which he would have them to walk towards him: they did not know, they did not rightly understand and therefore did not approve of these. Note, The reason why people slight and forsake the ways of God is because they do not know them. *Secondly,* Of their mistake : *They do err in their heart;* they wander out of the way; in heart they turn back. Note, Sins are errors, practical errors, errors in heart; such there are, and as fatal as errors in the head. When the corrupt affections pervert the judgment, and so lead the soul out of the ways of duty and obedience, there is an error of the heart. [4.] God's resentment of their sin : *Forty years long was I grieved with this generation.* Note, The sins of God's professing people do not only anger him, but grieve him, especially their distrust of him; and God keeps an account how often (Num. xiv. 22) and how long they grieve him. See the patience of God towards provoking sinners; he was grieved with them forty years, and yet those years ended in a triumphant entrance into Canaan made by the next generation. If our sins have grieved God, surely they should grieve us, and nothing in sin should grieve us so much as that.

(2.) The sentence passed upon them for their sin (v. 11) : " *Unto whom I swore in my wrath, If they shall enter into my rest,* then say I am changeable and untrue:" see the sentence at large, Num. xiv. 21, &c. Observe, [1.] Whence this sentence came—from the wrath of God. He *swore solemnly in his wrath,* his just and holy wrath; but let not men therefore swear profanely in their wrath, their sinful brutish wrath. God is not subject to such passions as we are; but he is said to be angry, very angry, at sin and sinners, to show the malignity of sin and the justice of God's government. That is certainly an evil thing which deserves such a recompence of revenge as may be expected from a provoked Deity. [2.] What it was: *That they should not enter into his rest,* the rest which he had prepared and designed for them, a settlement for them and theirs, that none of those who were enrolled when they came out of Egypt should be found written in the roll of the living at their entering into Canaan, but Caleb and Joshua. [3.] How it was ratified : *I swore it.* It was not only a purpose, but a decree; the oath showed the *immutability of his counsel ; the Lord swore, and will not repent.* It cut off the thought of any reserve of mercy. God's threatenings are as sure as his promises.

Now this case of Israel may be applied to those of their posterity that lived in David's

time, when this psalm was penned; let them hear God's voice, and not harden their hearts as their fathers did, lest, if they were stiff-necked like them, God should be provoked to forbid them the privileges of his temple at Jerusalem, of which he had said, *This is my rest.* But it must be applied to us Christians, because so the apostle applies it. There is a spiritual and eternal rest set before us, and promised to us, of which Canaan was a type ; we are all (in profession, at least) bound for this rest ; yet many that seem to be so come short and shall never enter into it. And what is it that puts a bar in their door? It is sin; it is unbelief, that sin against the remedy, against our appeal. Those that, like Israel, distrust God, and his power and goodness, and prefer the garlick and onions of Egypt before the milk and honey of Canaan, will justly be shut out from his rest : so shall their doom be ; they themselves have decided it. *Let us therefore fear,* Heb. iv. 1.

PSALM XCVI.

This psalm is part of that which was delivered into the hand of Asaph and his brethren (1 Chron. xvi. 7), by which it appears both that David was the penman of it and that it has reference to the bringing up of the ark to the city of David ; whether that long psalm was made first, and this afterwards taken out of it, or this made first and afterwards borrowed to make up that, is not certain. But this is certain, that, though it was sung at the translation of the ark, it looks further, to the kingdom of Christ, and is designed to celebrate the glories of that kingdom, especially the accession of the Gentiles to it. Here is, I. A call given to all people to praise God, to worship him, and give glory to him, as a great and glorious God, ver. 1—9. II. Notice given to all people of God's universal government and judgment, which ought to be the matter of universal joy, ver. 10—13. In singing this psalm we ought to have our hearts filled with great and high thoughts of the glory of God and the grace of the gospel, and with an entire satisfaction in Christ's sovereign dominion and in the expectation of the judgment to come.

O SING unto the LORD a new song : sing unto the LORD, all the earth. 2 Sing unto the LORD, bless his name ; show forth his salvation from day to day. 3 Declare his glory among the heathen, his wonders among all people. 4 For the LORD *is* great, and greatly to be praised : he *is* to be feared above all gods. 5 For all the gods of the nations *are* idols : but the LORD made the heavens. 6 Honour and majesty *are* before him : strength and beauty *are* in his sanctuary. 7 Give unto the LORD, O ye kindreds of the people, give unto the LORD glory and strength. 8 Give unto the LORD the glory *due unto* his name : bring an offering, and come into his courts. 9 O worship the LORD in the beauty of holiness : fear before him, all the earth.

These verses will be best expounded by pious and devout affections working in our souls towards God, with a high veneration for his majesty and transcendent excellency. The call here given us to praise God is very lively, the expressions are raised and repeated, to all which the echo of a thankful heart should make agreeable returns.

I. We are here required to honour God, 1. With songs, *v.* 1, 2. Three times we are here called to *sing unto the Lord;* sing to the Father, to the Son, to the Holy Ghost, as it was *in the beginning,* when *the morning stars sang together, is now,* in the church militant, and *ever shall be,* in the church triumphant. We have reason to do it often, and we have need to be often reminded of it, and stirred up to it. *Sing unto the Lord,* that is, " *Bless his name,* speak well of him, that you may bring others to think well of him." (1.) *Sing a new song,* an excellent song, the product of new affections, clothed with new expressions. We speak of nothing more despicable than " an old song," but the newness of a song recommends it; for there we expect something surprising. A new song is a song for new favours, for those compassions which are new every morning. A new song is a New-Testament song, a song of praise for the new covenant and the precious privileges of that covenant. A new song is a song that shall be ever new, and shall never wax old nor vanish away; it is an everlasting song, that shall never be antiquated or out of date. (2.) Let all the earth sing this song, not the Jews only, to whom hitherto the service of God had been appropriated, who could not *sing the Lord's song in* (would not sing it to) *a strange land;* but let *all the earth,* all that are *redeemed from the earth, learn* and sing *this new song,* Rev. xiv. 3. This is a prophecy of the calling of the Gentiles; all the earth shall have this *new song put into their mouths,* shall have both cause and call to sing it. (3.) Let the subject-matter of this song be *his salvation,* the great salvation which was to be wrought out by the Lord Jesus; that must be shown forth as the cause of this joy and praise. (4.) Let this song be sung constantly, not only in the times appointed for the solemn feasts, but from day to day; it is a subject that can never be exhausted. Let day unto day utter this speech, that, under the influence of gospel devotions, we may daily exemplify a gospel conversation.

2. With sermons (*v.* 3): *Declare his glory among the heathen,* even *his wonders among all people.* (1.) Salvation by Christ is here spoken of as a work of wonder, and that in which the glory of God shines very brightly; in showing forth that salvation we declare God's glory as it shines in the face of Christ. (2.) This salvation was, in the Old-Testament times, as heaven's happiness is now, *a glory to be revealed ;* but in the fulness of time it was declared, and a full discovery made of that, even to babes, which prophets and kings desired and wished to see and might not. (3.) What was then discovered was declared only among the Jews, but it is now declared *among the heathen, among all people ;* the nations which long sat in darkness now see this great light. The apostles' commission to preach the gospel to every creature is copied from this : *Declare his glory among the heathen.*

3. With religious services, *v.* 7—9. Hitherto, though in every nation those that feared God and wrought righteousness were accepted of him, yet instituted ordinances were the peculiarities of the Jewish religion; but, in gospel-times, the kindreds of the people shall be invited and admitted into the service of God and be as welcome as ever the Jews were. The court of the Gentiles shall no longer be an outward court, but shall be laid in common with the court of Israel. All the earth is here summoned to fear before the Lord, to worship him according to his appointment. *In every place incense shall be offered to his name,* Mal. i. 11 ; Zech. xiv. 17; Isa. lxvi. 23. This indeed spoke mortification to the Jews, but, withal, it gave a prospect of that which would redound very much to the glory of God and to the happiness of mankind. Now observe how the acts of devotion to God are here described. (1.) We must *give unto the Lord;* not as if God needed any thing, or could receive any thing, from us or any creature, which was not his own before, much less be benefited by it; but we must in our best affections, adorations, and services, return to him what we have received from him, and do it freely, as what we give; for *God loves a cheerful giver.* It is debt, it is rent, it is tribute, it is what must be paid, and, if not, will be recovered, and yet, if it come from holy love, God is pleased to accept it as a gift. (2.) We must acknowledge God to be the sovereign Lord and pay homage to him accordingly (*v.* 7): *Give unto the Lord glory and strength, glory and empire,* or *dominion,* so some. As a king, he is clothed with robes of glory and girt with the girdle of power, and we must subscribe to both. *Thine is the kingdom,* and therefore *thine is the power and the glory.* "Give the glory to God; do not take it to yourselves, nor give it to any creature." (3.) We must *give unto the Lord the glory due unto his name,* that is, to the discovery he has been pleased to make of himself to the children of men. In all the acts of religious worship this is that which we must aim at, to honour God, to pay him some of that reverence which we owe him as the best of beings and the fountain of our being. (4.) We must *bring an offering into his courts.* We must bring ourselves, in the first place, the *offering up of the Gentiles,* Rom. xv. 16. We must offer up the *sacrifices of praise continually* (Heb. xiii. 15), must often appear before God in public worship and never appear before him empty. (5.) We must *worship him in the beauty of holiness,* in the solemn assembly where divine institutions are religiously observed, the beauty of which is their holiness, that is, their conformity to the rule. We must worship him with holy hearts, sanctified by the grace of God, devoted to the glory of God,

and purified from the pollutions of sin. (6.) We must *fear before him;* all the acts of worship must be performed from a principle of the fear of God and with a holy awe and reverence.

II. In the midst of these calls to praise God and give glory to him glorious things are here said of him, both as motives to praise and matter of praise: *The Lord is great, and* therefore *greatly to be praised* (*v.* 4) and *to be feared,* great and honourable to his attendants, great and terrible to his adversaries. Even the new song proclaims God great as well as good; for his goodness is his glory; and, when the everlasting gospel is preached, it is this, *Fear God, and give glory to him,* Rev. xiv. 6, 7. 1. He is great in his sovereignty over all that pretend to be deities; none dare vie with him: *He is to be feared above all gods*—all princes, who were often deified after their deaths, and even while they lived were adored as petty gods —or rather all idols, *the gods of the nations, v.* 5. All the earth being called to sing the new song, they must be convinced that the Lord Jehovah, to whose honour they must sing it, is the one only living and true God, infinitely above all rivals and pretenders; he is great, and they are little; he is all, and they are *nothing;* so the word used for idols signifies, for we know that *an idol is nothing in the world,* 1 Cor. viii. 4. 2. He is great in his right, even to the noblest part of the creation; for it is his own work and derives its being from him: *The Lord made the heavens* and all their hosts; they *are the work of his fingers* (viii. 3), so nicely, so curiously, are they made. The gods of the nations were all made-gods, the creatures of men's fancies; but our God is the Creator of the sun, moon, and stars, those lights of heaven, which they imagined to be gods and worshipped as such. 3. He is great in the manifestation of his glory both in the upper and lower world, among his angels in heaven and his saints on earth (*v.* 6): *Splendour and majesty are before him,* in his immediate presence above, where the angels cover their faces, as unable to bear the dazzling lustre of his glory. *Strength and beauty are in his sanctuary,* both that above and this below. In God there is every thing that is awful and yet every thing that is amiable. If we attend him in his sanctuary, we shall behold his beauty, for *God is love,* and experience his strength, for *he is our rock.* Let us therefore go forth in his strength, enamoured with his beauty.

10 Say among the heathen *that* the LORD reigneth: the world also shall be established that it shall not be moved: he shall judge the people righteously. 11 Let the heavens rejoice, and let the earth be glad; let the sea roar, and the fulness thereof. 12 Let the field be joyful, and all that *is* there-

in: then shall all the trees of the wood rejoice 13 Before the LORD: for he cometh, for he cometh to judge the earth: he shall judge the world with righteousness, and the people with his truth.

We have here instructions given to those who were to preach the gospel to the nations what to preach, or to those who had themselves received the gospel what account to give of it to their neighbours, what to *say among the heathen;* and it is an illustrious prophecy of the setting up of the kingdom of Christ upon the ruins of the devil's kingdom, which began immediately after his ascension and will continue in the doing till the mystery of God be finished.

I. Let it be told *that the Lord reigns,* the Lord Christ reigns, that King whom God determined to set upon his holy hill of Zion. See how this was first said *among the heathen* by Peter, Acts x. 42. Some of the ancients added a gloss to this, which by degrees crept into the text, *The Lord reigneth from the tree* (so Justin Martyr, Austin, and others, quote it), meaning the cross, when he had this title written over him, *The King of the Jews.* It was because he became obedient to death, even the death of the cross, that God exalted him, and gave him a name above every name, a throne above every throne. Some of the heathen came betimes to enquire after him that was *born King of the Jews,* Matt. ii. 2. Now let them know that he has come and his kingdom is set up.

II. Let it be told that Christ's government will be the world's happy settlement. *The world also shall be established, that it shall not be moved.* The natural world shall be established. The standing of the world, and its stability, are owing to the mediation of Christ. Sin had given it a shock, and still threatens it; but Christ, as Redeemer, upholds all things, and preserves the course of nature. The world of mankind shall be established, shall be preserved, till all that belong to the election of grace are called in, though a guilty provoking world. The Christian religion, as far as it is embraced, shall establish states and kingdoms, and preserve good order among men. The church in the world shall be established (so some), that it *cannot be moved; for it is built upon a rock, and the gates of hell shall never prevail against it;* it is a *kingdom that cannot be shaken.*

III. Let them be told that Christ's government will be incontestably just and righteous: *He shall judge the people righteously* (*v.* 10), *judge the world with righteousness, and with his truth, v.* 13. Judging is here put for ruling; and though this may be extended to the general judgment of the world at the last day, which will be *in righteousness* (Acts xvii. 31), yet it refers more immediately to Christ's first coming, and the setting up of his kingdom in the world by the gospel. He says himself, *For judgment have I come into this world* (John ix. 39, xii. 31), and declares that *all judgment was committed to him,* John v. 22, 27. His ruling and judging with righteousness and truth signify, 1. That all the laws and ordinances of his kingdom shall be consonant to the rules and principles of eternal truth and equity, that is, to the rectitude and purity of the divine nature and will. 2. That all his administrations of government shall be just and faithful, and according to what he has said. 3. That he shall rule in the hearts and consciences of men by the commanding power of truth and the Spirit of righteousness and sanctification. When Pilate asked our Saviour, *Art thou a king?* he answered, *For this cause came I into the world, that I should bear witness unto the truth* (John xviii. 37); for he rules by truth, commands men's wills by informing their judgments aright.

IV. Let them be told that his coming draws nigh, that this King, this Judge, *standeth before the door ; for he cometh, for he cometh.* Enoch, the seventh from Adam, said so. *Behold, the Lord cometh,* Jude 14. Between this and his first coming the revolutions of many ages intervened, and yet he came at the set time, and so sure will his second coming be ; though it is now long since it was said, *Behold, he comes in the clouds* (Rev. i. 7) and he has not yet come. See 2 Pet. iii. 4, &c.

V. Let them be called upon to rejoice in this honour that is put upon the Messiah, and this great trust that is to be lodged in his hand (*v.* 11, 12): *Let heaven and earth rejoice, the sea, the field,* and *all the trees of the wood.* The dialect here is poetical ; the meaning is, 1. That the days of the Messiah will be joyful days, and, as far as his grace and government are submitted to, will bring joy along with them. We have reason to give that place, that soul, joy into which Christ is admitted. See an instance of both, Acts viii. When Samaria received the gospel *there was great joy in that city* (*v.* 8), and, when the eunuch was baptized, *he went on his way rejoicing, v.* 39. 2. That it is the duty of every one of us to bid Christ and his kingdom welcome ; for, though he comes conquering and to conquer, yet he comes peaceably. *Hosanna, Blessed is he that cometh ;* and again, *Hosanna, Blessed be the kingdom of our father David* (Mark xi. 9, 10); not only *let the daughter of Zion rejoice that her King comes* (Zech. ix. 9), but let all rejoice. 3. That the whole creation will have reason to rejoice in the setting up of Christ's kingdom, even *the sea* and *the field ;* for, as by the sin of the first Adam the whole creation was made *subject to vanity,* so by the grace of the second Adam it shall, some way or other, first or last, be *delivered from the bondage of corruption into the glorious liberty of the children of God,* Rom. viii. 20, 21. 4.

That there will, in the first place, be *joy in heaven, joy in the presence of the angels of God ;* for, when the First-begotten was brought into the world, they sang their anthems to his praise, Luke ii. 14. 5. That God will graciously accept the holy joy and praises of all the hearty well-wishers to the kingdom of Christ, be their capacity ever so mean. *The sea* can but *roar,* and how *the trees of the wood* can show that they *rejoice* I know not ; but *he that searches the heart knows what is the mind of the Spirit,* and understands the language, the broken language, of the weakest.

PSALM XCVII.

This psalm dwells upon the same subject, and is set to the same tune, with the foregoing psalm. Christ is the Alpha and the Omega of both ; they are both penned, and are both to be sung to his honour ; and we make nothing of them if we do not, in them, make melody with our hearts to the Lord Jesus. He it is that reigns, to the joy of all mankind (ver. 1) ; and his government speaks, I. Terror to his enemies ; for he is a prince of inflexible justice and irresistible power, ver. 2—7. II. Comfort to his friends and loyal subjects, arising from his sovereign dominion, the care he takes of his people, and the provision he makes for them, ver. 8—12. In singing this psalm we must be affected with the glory of the exalted Redeemer, must dread the lot of his enemies, and think ourselves happy if we are of those that "kiss the son."

THE LORD reigneth ; let the earth rejoice ; let the multitude of isles be glad *thereof.* 2 Clouds and darkness *are* round about him : righteousness and judgment *are* the habitation of his throne. 3 A fire goeth before him, and burneth up his enemies round about. 4 His lightnings enlightened the world : the earth saw, and trembled. 5 The hills melted like wax at the presence of the LORD, at the presence of the Lord of the whole earth. 6 The heavens declare his righteousness, and all the people see his glory. 7 Confounded be all they that serve graven images, that boast themselves of idols : worship him, all *ye* gods.

What was to be said among the heathen in the foregoing psalm (*v.* 10) is here said again (*v.* 1) and is made the subject of this psalm, and of psalm xcix. *The Lord reigns ;* that is the great truth here laid down. The Lord Jehovah reigns ; he that made the world governs it ; he that gave being gives motion and power, gives law and commission, gives success and event. Every man's judgment proceeds from the Lord, from his counsel and providence, and in all affairs, both public and private, he performs the thing which he himself has appointed. The Lord Jesus reigns ; the providential kingdom is twisted in with the mediatorial and the administration of both is in the hand of Christ, who therefore is both the *head of the church* and *head over all things to the church.* The kingdom of Christ is so constituted that,

I. It may be matter of joy to all ; and it will be so if it be not their own fault. *Let the earth rejoice,* for hereby it is *established* (xcvi. 10); it is honoured and enriched, and, in part, rescued from the vanity which by sin it is made subject to. Not only let the people of Israel rejoice in him as King of the Jews, and the daughter of Zion as her King, but let all the earth rejoice in his elevation; for the kingdoms of the world shall, more or less, sooner or later, become his kingdoms: *Let the multitude of isles*, the many or great isles, *be glad thereof*. This is applicable to our country, which is a great isle, and has many belonging to it; at least, it speaks comfort in general to the Gentiles, whose countries are called *the isles of the Gentiles*, Gen. x. 5. There is enough in Christ for the multitude of the isles to rejoice in; for, though many have been made happy in him, yet still there is room. All have reason to rejoice in Christ's government. 1. In the equity of it. There is an incontestable justice in all the acts of his government, both legislative and judicial. Sometimes indeed *clouds and darkness are round about him;* his dispensations are altogether unaccountable; *his way is in the sea and his path in the great waters.* We are not aware of what he designs, what he drives at; nor is it fit that we should be let into the secrets of his government. There is a depth in his counsels, which we must not pretend to fathom. But still *righteousness and judgment are the habitation of his throne;* a golden thread of justice runs through the whole web of his administration. In this he resides, for it is his habitation. In this he rules, for it is *the habitation of his throne. His commandments are*, and will be, *all righteous. Righteousness and judgment are the basis of his throne* (so Dr. Hammond); for *therefore* his *throne is for ever and ever*, because his *sceptre is a right sceptre*, xlv. 6. *The throne is established in righteousness.* Even *the heavens declare his righteousness* (v. 6); it is as conspicuous and as illustrious as the heavens themselves. The angels of heaven will declare it, who are employed as messengers in the administration of his government and therefore know more of it than any of his creatures. His righteousness is incontestable; for who can contradict or dispute what the *heavens declare?* l. 6. 2. In the extent of it in the upper and lower world. (1.) All the men on earth are under his government; either he is served by them or he serves himself by them. *All the people see his glory,* or may see it. The glory of God, in the face of Christ, was made to shine in distant countries, among many people, more or less among all people; the gospel was preached, for aught we know, in all languages, Acts ii. 5, 11. Miracles were wrought in all nations, and so *all the people saw his glory. Have they not heard?* Rom. x. 18. (2.) All the angels in heaven are so. Perhaps we should not have found this truth in those words (v. 7), *Worship him, all you gods,* if we had not been directed to it by the inspired apostle, who, from the Septuagint ver-

sion of those words, makes the Messiah to be introduced into the upper world at the ascension with this charge (Heb. i. 6), *Let all the angels of God worship him,* which helps us to a key to this whole psalm, and shows us that it must be applied to the exalted Redeemer, who has gone into heaven, *and is on the right hand of God,* which intimates that all power is given him both in heaven and earth, *angels, authorities, and powers, being made subject unto him,* 1 Pet. iii. 22. This speaks the honour of Christ, that he has such worshippers, and the honour of all good Christians, that they have such fellow-worshippers.

II. Christ's government, though it may be matter of joy to all, will yet be matter of terror to some, and it is their own fault that it is so, *v.* 3—5, 7. Observe,

1. When the kingdom of Christ was to be set up in the world, after his ascension, it would meet with many enemies, and much opposition would be given to it. He that reigns, to the *joy of the whole earth,* yet, as he has his subjects, so he has *his enemies* (v. 3), that not only will not have him to reign over them, but would not have him to reign at all, that not only will not *enter into the kingdom of heaven themselves,* but do all they can to *hinder those that are entering,* Matt. xxiii. 13. This was fulfilled in the enmity of the unbelieving Jews to the gospel of Christ, and the violent persecution which in all places they stirred up against the preachers and professors of it. These enemies are here called *hills* (v. 5), for their height, and strength, and immovable obstinacy. It was the *princes of this world* that *crucified the Lord of glory,* 1 Cor. ii. 8; Ps. ii 2.

2. The opposition which the Jews gave to the setting up of Christ's kingdom turned to their own ruin. Their persecuting the apostles, and *forbidding them to speak to the Gentiles,* filled up their sin, and brought *wrath upon them to the uttermost,* 1 Thess. ii. 15, 16. That wrath is here compared, (1.) To consuming fire, which *goes before him, and burns up his enemies,* that have made themselves like chaff and stubble, and have *set the briers and thorns before him in battle,* Isa. xxvii. 4. This fire of divine wrath will not only burn the rubbish upon the hills, but will even *melt the hills* themselves *like wax, v.* 5. When our God appears as a consuming fire even rocks will be wax before him. The most resolute and daring opposition will be baffled *at the presence of the Lord.* His very presence is enough to shame and sink it, for he is *the Lord of the whole earth,* by whom all the children of men are manageable and to whom they are accountable. Men hate and persecute God's people, because they think him absent, that the Lord has *forsaken the earth;* but, when he manifests his presence, they melt. (2.) To amazing *lightnings* (v. 4), which strike a terror upon many. The judgments God brought upon the enemies of Christ's kingdom were such

as all the world took notice of with terror: *The earth saw and trembled,* and the ears of all that heard were made to tingle. This was fulfilled in the destruction of Jerusalem and the Jewish nation by the Romans, about forty years after Christ's resurrection, which, like fire, wholly destroyed that people, and, like lightning, astonished all their neighbours (Deut. xxix. 24); but the heavens declare God's righteousness in it, and all the people, to this day, see his glory, in those lasting monuments of his justice, the scattered Jews.

3. Idolaters also would be put to confusion by the setting up of Christ's kingdom (*v.* 7): *Confounded be all those who serve graven images,* the Gentile world, who *did service to those that by nature are no gods* (Gal. iv. 8), who boasted themselves of idols as their protectors and benefactors. Did those that served idols boast of them, and shall the servants of the living God distrust him, or be ashamed of him? *Let those be ashamed that serve graven images.* (1.) This is a prayer for the conversion of the Gentiles, that those who have been so long serving dumb idols may be convinced of their error, ashamed of their folly, and may, by the power of Christ's gospel, be brought to serve the only living and true God, and may be as much ashamed of their idols as ever they were proud of them. See Isa. ii. 20, 21. (2.) This is a prophecy of the ruin of those that would not be reformed and reclaimed from their idolatry; they shall be confounded by the destruction of Paganism in the Roman empire, which was fulfilled about 300 years after Christ, so much to the terror of idolaters that some think it was the revolution under Constantine that made even the mighty men say to the rocks, *Fall on us and hide us,* Rev. vi. 15, 16. This prayer and prophecy are still in force against antichristian idolaters, who may here read their doom: *Confounded be all those that worship graven images, v.* 7. See Jer. xlviii. 13.

8 Zion heard, and was glad; and the daughters of Judah rejoiced because of thy judgments, O LORD. 9 For thou, LORD, *art* high above all the earth : thou art exalted far above all gods. 10 Ye that love the LORD, hate evil : he preserveth the souls of his saints; he delivereth them out of the hand of the wicked. 11 Light is sown for the righteous, and gladness for the upright in heart. 12 Rejoice in the LORD, ye righteous ; and give thanks at the remembrance of his holiness.

The kingdom of the Messiah, like the pillar of cloud and fire, as it has a dark side towards the Egyptians, so it has a bright side towards the Israel of God. It is set up in spite of opposition; and then *the earth saw and trembled* (v. 4), but *Zion heard and was glad,* very glad, to hear of the conversion of some and of the confusion of others, that is, the conquest of all that stood it out against Christ. *Rejoice greatly, O daughter of Zion! for behold thy king comes unto thee,* Zech. ix. 9. And not Zion only, where the temple was, but even *the daughters of Judah, rejoiced;* the common people, the inhabitants of the villages, they shall triumph in Christ's victories. The command (*v.* 1) is, *Let the earth rejoice;* but it is only the sons of Zion and the daughters of Judah that do rejoice. All should bid the kingdom of the Messiah welcome, but few do. Now here observe,

I. The reasons that are given for Zion's joy in the government of the Redeemer. The faithful servants of God may well *rejoice* and be *glad,* 1. Because God is glorified, and whatever redounds to his hônour is very much his people's pleasure. They rejoice *because of thy judgments, O Lord!* which may take in both the judgments of his mouth and the judgments of his hand, the word of his gospel and his works wrought for the propagating of it, miracles and marvellous providences; for in these we must own, "*Thou, Lord, art high above all the earth* (v. 9); thou hast manifested thy sovereignty in the kingdom of nature, and thy command of all its powers, and thy dominion over all nations, over all hearts; thou art *exalted far above all gods*"—all deputed gods, that is, princes— all counterfeit gods, that is, idols. The exaltation of Christ, and the advancement of God's glory among men thereby, are the rejoicing of all the saints. 2. Because care is taken for their safety. Those that pay allegiance to Christ as a King shall be sure of his protection. Princes are the shields of the earth ; Christ is so to his subjects; they may put their trust under his shadow and rejoice in it, for (v. 10) *He preserves the souls of the saints;* he preserves their lives as long as he has any work for them to do, and wonderfully *delivers them* many a time *out of the hand of the wicked,* their persecutors that thirst after their blood; for *precious in the sight of the Lord is the death of his saints.* But something more is meant than their lives; for those that will be his disciples must be willing to lay down their lives, and not indent for the securing of them. It is the *immortal soul* that Christ preserves, the *inward man,* which may be renewed more and more when the *outward man decays.* He will *preserve the souls of his saints* from sin, from apostasy, and despair, under their greatest trials; he will *deliver them out oᶠ the hands of the wicked one* that *seeks to devour them; he will preserve them* safely *to his heavenly kingdom,* 2 Tim. iv. 18. They have therefore reason to be glad, being thus safe. 3. Because provision is made for their comfort. Those that rejoice in Christ Jesus, and in his exaltation, have fountains of joy treasured up for them, which will be opened sooner or later (*v.* 11): *Light is sown for the righteous,* that is, *gladness for the upright in heart.* The subjects of Christ's kingdom are told to expect tribulation in the world. They must suffer by its malice, and must not share in its mirth; yet let them know, to their comfort, that *light is sown* for them; it is designed and prepared for them. What is sown will come up again in due time; though, like a winter seedness, it may lie long under the clods, and seem to be lost and buried, yet it will return in a rich and plentiful increase. God's goodness shall be sure of a *harvest* in the *appointed weeks. Those that sow in tears shall,* without fail, *reap in joy,* cxxvi. 5, 6. Christ told his disciples, at parting (John xvi. 20), *You shall be sorrowful, but your sorrow shall be turned into joy.* Gladness is sure to the *upright in heart,* to those only that are sincere in religion. *The joy of the hypocrite is but for a moment.* There is no serenity without a lasting sincerity,

II. The rules that are given for Zion's joy. 1. Let it be a pure and holy joy. "You that love the Lord Jesus, that *love his appearing* and kingdom, that love his word and his exaltation, see that you hate evil, the evil of sin, every thing that is offensive to him and will throw you out of his favour." Note, A true love to God will show itself in a real hatred of all sin, as that abominable thing which he hates. The joy of the saints should likewise confirm their antipathy to sin and divine comforts should put their mouths out of taste for sensual pleasures. 2. Let the joy terminate in God (*v.* 12): *Rejoice in the Lord, you righteous.* Let all the streams of comfort, which flow to us in the channel of Christ's kingdom, lead us to the fountain, and oblige us to *rejoice in the Lord.* All the lines of joy must meet in him as in the centre. See Phil. iii. 3; iv. 4. 3. Let it express itself in praise and thanksgiving: *Give thanks at the remembrance of his holiness.* Whatever is the matter of our rejoicing ought to be the matter of our thanksgiving, and particularly the holiness of God. Those that hate sin themselves are glad that God does so, in hopes that therefore he will not suffer it to have dominion over them. Note, (1.) We ought to be much in the remembrance of God's holiness, the infinite purity, rectitude, and perfection of the divine nature. We must be ever mindful of his holy covenant, which he has confirmed with an oath *by his holiness.* (2.) We ought to give thanks at the remembrance of his holiness, not only give him the glory of it as it is an honour to him, but give him thanks for it as it is a favour to us; and an unspeakable favour it will be if, through grace, we are *partakers of his holiness.* It is God's holiness which, above all his attributes, the angels celebrate. Isa. vi. 3, *Holy, holy, holy.* Sinners tremble, but saints rejoice, *at the remembrance of God's holiness,* Ps. xxx. 4.

PSALM XCVIII.

This psalm is to the same purport with the two foregoing psalms; it is a prophecy of the kingdom of the Messiah, the setting of it up in the world, and the bringing of the Gentiles into it. The Chaldee entitles it a prophetic psalm. It sets forth, I. The glory of the Redeemer, ver. 1–3. II. The joy of the redeemed, ver. 4–9. If we in a right manner give to Christ this glory, and upon right grounds take to ourselves this joy, in singing this psalm, we sing it with understanding. If those who saw Christ's day at a distance, and in the promise only, must rejoice and triumph thus, much more reason have we to do so who see these things accomplished and share in the better things provided for us, Heb. xi. 40.

A psalm.

O SING unto the LORD a new song; for he hath done marvellous things: his right hand, and his holy arm, hath gotten him the victory. 2 The LORD hath made known his salvation: his righteousness hath he openly showed in the sight of the heathen. 3 He hath remembered his mercy and his truth toward the house of Israel: all the ends of the earth have seen the salvation of our God.

We are here called upon again to *sing unto the Lord a new song,* as before, xcvi. 1. "Sing a most excellent song, the best song you have." Let the song of Christ's love be like Solomon's on that subject, a *song of songs.* A song of praise for redeeming love is a *new song,* such a song as had not been sung before; for this is a mystery which was hidden from ages and generations. Converts sing a *new song,* very different from what they had sung; they change their wonder and change their joy, and therefore change their note. If the grace of God put a new heart into our breasts, it will therewith put a new song into our mouths. In the new Jerusalem there will be new songs sung, that will be new to eternity, and never wax old. Let this new song be sung to the praise of God, in consideration of these four things:—

I. The wonders he has wrought: *He has done marvellous things, v.* 1. Note, The work of our salvation by Christ is a work of wonder. If we take a view of all the steps of it from the contrivance of it, and the counsels of God concerning it before all time, to the consummation of it, and its everlasting consequences when time shall be no more, we shall say, God has in it *done marvellous things:* it is all his doing and it is *marvellous in our eyes.* The more it is known the more it will be admired.

II. The conquests he has won: *His right hand and his holy arm have gotten him the victory.* Our Redeemer has surmounted all the difficulties that lay in the way of our redemption, has broken through them all, and was not discouraged by the services or sufferings appointed him. He has subdued all the enemies that opposed it, has gotten the victory over Satan, disarmed him, and cast him out of his strong-holds, has *spoiled principalities and powers* (Col. ii. 15), has *taken the prey from the mighty* (Isa. xlix. 24), and given death his death's wound. He has gotten a clear and complete victory, not only for himself, but for us also, for we through him are more than conquerors. He got this victory by his own power; there was *none to help, none to uphold,* none that durst venture into the service; but his *right hand and his holy arm,* which are always stretched out with good success, because they are never stretched out but in a good cause, these have *gotten him the victory,* have *brought him relief or deliverance.* God's power and faithfulness, called here *his right hand and his holy arm,* brought relief to the Lord Jesus, in raising him from the dead, and exalting him personally to the right hand of God; so Dr. Hammond.

III. The discoveries he has made to the world of the work of redemption. What he has wrought for us he has revealed to us, and both by his Son; the gospel-revelation is that on which the gospel-kingdom is founded —*the word which God sent,* Acts x. 36. The *opening of the sealed book* is that which is to be celebrated with songs of praise (Rev. v. 8), because by it was brought to light the mystery which had long been hid in God. Observe, 1. The subject of this discovery—his salvation and his righteousness, *v.* 3. Righteousness and salvation are often put together; as Isa. lxi. 10; xlvi. 13; li. 5, 6, 8. Salvation denotes the redemption itself, and righteousness the way in which it was wrought, by the righteousness of Christ. Or the salvation includes all our gospel-privileges and the righteousness all our gospel-duties; both are made known, for God has joined them together, and we must not separate them. Or righteousness is here put for the way of our justification by Christ, which is revealed in the gospel to be by faith, Rom. i. 17. 2. The plainness of this discovery. He has openly shown it, not in types and figures as under the law, but it is written as with a sunbeam, that he that runs may read it. Ministers are appointed to preach it with all plainness of speech. 3. The extent of this discovery. It is made in the sight of the heathen, and not of the Jews only: *All the ends of the earth have seen the salvation of our God;* for to the Gentiles was the word of salvation sent.

IV. The accomplishment of the prophecies and promises of the Old Testament, in this (*v.* 3): *He has remembered his mercy and his truth towards the house of Israel.* God had mercy in store for the seed of Abraham, and had given them many and great assurances of the kindness he designed them in the latter days; and it was in pursuance of all those that he raised up his Son Jesus to be not only a *light to lighten the Gentiles,* but *the glory of his people Israel;* for he sent him, in the first place, to bless *them.* God is said, in sending Christ, to *perform the mercy promised to our fathers, and to remember the holy covenant,* Luke i. 72. It was in consideration of that, and not of their merit.

4 Make a joyful noise unto the

Lord, all the earth: make a loud noise, and rejoice, and sing praise. 5 Sing unto the Lord with the harp; with the harp, and the voice of a psalm. 6 With trumpets and sound of cornet make a joyful noise before the Lord, the King. 7 Let the sea roar, and the fulness thereof; the world, and they that dwell therein. 8 Let the floods clap *their* hands: let the hills be joyful together 9 Before the Lord; for he cometh to judge the earth: with righteousness shall he judge the world, and the people with equity.

The setting up of the kingdom of Christ is here represented as a matter of joy and praise. I. Let all the children of men rejoice in it, for they all have, or may have, benefit by it. Again and again we are here called upon by all ways and means possible to express our joy in it and give God praise for it: *Make a joyful noise,* as before, xcv. 1, 2. *Make a loud noise,* as those that are affected with those glad tidings and are desirous to affect others with them. *Rejoice and sing praise,* sing *Hosannas* (Matt. xxi. 9), sing *Hallelujahs,* Rev. xix. 6. Let him be welcomed to the throne, as new kings are, with acclamations of joy and loud shouts, till the earth ring again, as when Solomon was proclaimed, 1 Kings i. 40. And let the shouts of the crowd be accompanied with the *singers and players on instruments* (Ps. lxxxvii. 7, lxviii. 25), as is usual in such solemnities. 1. Let sacred songs attend the new King: "*Sing praise, sing with the voice of a psalm.* Express your joy; thus proclaim it, thus excite it yet more, and thus propagate it among others." 2. Let these be assisted with sacred music, not only with the soft and gentle melody of *the harp,* but since it is a victorious King whose glory is to be celebrated, who goes forth conquering and to conquer, let him be proclaimed with the martial sound of the *trumpet* and *cornet, v.* 6. Let all this joy be directed to God, and expressed in a solemn religious manner: *Make a joyful noise to the Lord, v.* 4. *Sing to the Lord* (*v.* 5); do it *before the Lord, the King, v.* 6. Carnal mirth is an enemy to this holy joy. When David danced before the ark he pleaded that *it was before the Lord;* and the piety and devotion of the intention not only vindicated what he did, but commended it. We must rejoice *before the Lord* whenever we draw near to him (Deut. xii. 12), before *the Lord Jesus,* and before him, not only as the Saviour, but as the King, the King of kings, the church's King, and our King.

II. Let the inferior creatures rejoice in it, *v.* 7—9. This is to the same purport with what we had before (xcvi. 11—13): *Let the sea roar,* and let that be called, not as it used to be, a *dreadful noise*, but a *joyful noise;* for the coming of Christ, and the salvation wrought out by him, have quite altered the property of the troubles and terrors of this world, so that when the floods *lift up their voice, lift up their waves*, we must not construe that to be the sea roaring against us, but rather rejoicing with us. Let the *floods* express their joy, as men do when they *clap their hands;* and let the hills, that trembled for fear before God when he came down to give the law at Mount Sinai, dance for joy before him when his gospel is preached and that word of the Lord goes forth from Zion in a still small voice: *Let the hills be joyful together before the Lord.* This intimates that the kingdom of Christ would be a blessing to the whole creation; but that, as the inferior creatures declare the glory of the Creator (xix. 1), so they declare the glory of the Redeemer, for by him all things not only subsist in their being, but consist in their order. It intimates likewise that the children of men would be wanting in paying their due respects to the Redeemer, and therefore that he must look for his honour from the sea and the floods, which would shame the stupidity and ingratitude of mankind. And perhaps respect is here had to the *new heavens* and the *new earth*, which we yet, according to his promise, look for (2 Pet. iii. 13), and this second mention of his coming (after the like, Ps. xcvi.) may principally refer to his second coming, when all these things shall be so dissolved as to be refined; then shall he come to *judge the world with righteousness.* In the prospect of that day all that are sanctified do rejoice, and even the sea, and the floods, and the hills, would rejoice if they could. One would think that Virgil had these psalms in his eye, as well as the oracles of the Cumean Sibyl, in his fourth eclogue, where he either ignorantly or basely applies to Asinius Pollio the ancient prophecies, which at that time were expected to be fulfilled; for he lived in the reign of Augustus Cæsar, a little before our Saviour's birth. He owns they looked for the birth of a child from heaven that should be a great blessing to the world, and restore the golden age:—

 Jam nova progenies cœlo demittitur alto—
 A new race descends from the lofty sky;

and that should take away sin:—

 Te duce, si qua manent sceleris vestigia nostri,
 Irrita perpetuâ solvent formidine terras—
 Thy influence shall efface every stain of corruption,
 And free the world from alarm.

Many other things he says of this long-looked-for child, which Ludovicus Vives, in his notes on that eclogue, thinks applicable to Christ; and he concludes, as the psalmist here, with a prospect of the rejoicing of the whole creation herein:—

 Aspice, venturo lætentur ut omnia sæclo—
 See how this promis'd age makes all rejoice.

And, if all rejoice, why should not we?

PSALM XCIX.

Still we are celebrating the glories of the kingdom of God among men, and are called upon to praise him, as in the foregoing psalms; but those psalms looked forward to the times of the gospel, and prophesied of the graces and comforts of those times; this psalm seems to dwell more upon the Old-Testament dispensation and the manifestation of God's glory and grace in that. The Jews were not, in expectation of the Messiah's kingdom and the evangelical worship, to neglect the divine regimen they were then under, and the ordinances that were then given them, but in them to see God reigning, and to worship before him according to the law of Moses. Prophecies of good things to come must not lessen our esteem of good things present. To Israel indeed pertained the promises, which they were bound to believe; but to them pertained also the giving of the law, and the service of God, which they were also bound dutifully and conscientiously to attend to, Rom. ix. 4. And this they are called to do in this psalm, where yet there is much of Christ, for the government of the church was in the hands of the eternal Word before he was incarnate; and, besides, the ceremonial services were types and figures of evangelical worship. The people of Israel are here required to praise and exalt God, and to worship before him, in consideration of these two things:— I. The happy constitution of the government they were under, both in sacred and civil things, ver. 1—5. II. Some instances of the happy administration of it, ver. 6—9. In singing this psalm we must set ourselves to exalt the name of God, as it is made known to us in the gospel, which we have much more reason to do than those had who lived under the law.

T**HE L**ORD reigneth; let the people tremble: he sitteth *between* the cherubims; let the earth be moved. 2 The LORD *is* great in Zion; and he *is* high above all the people. 3 Let them praise thy great and terrible name; *for* it *is* holy. 4 The king's strength also loveth judgment; thou dost establish equity, thou executest judgment and righteousness in Jacob. 5 Exalt ye the LORD our God, and worship at his footstool; *for* he *is* holy.

The foundation of all religion is laid in this truth, That *the Lord reigns.* God governs the world by his providence, governs the church by his grace, and both by his Son. We are to believe not only that *the Lord lives*, but that *the Lord reigns.* This is the triumph of the Christian church, and here it was the triumph of the Jewish church, that Jehovah was their King; and hence it is inferred, *Let the people tremble*, that is, 1. Let even the subjects of this kingdom tremble; for the Old-Testament dispensation had much of terror in it. At Mount Sinai Israel, and even Moses himself, did *exceedingly fear and quake;* and then God was *terrible in his holy places.* Even when he appeared in his people's behalf, he did terrible things. But we are not now come to *that mount that burned with fire*, Heb. xii. 18. Now that *the Lord reigns let the earth rejoice.* Then he ruled more by the power of holy fear; now he rules by the power of holy love. 2. Much more let the enemies of this kingdom tremble; for he will either bring them into obedience to his golden sceptre or crush them with his iron rod. *The Lord reigns, though the people be stirred with indignation* at it; though they fret away all their spirits, their rage is all in vain. He will set his King upon his holy hill of Zion in spite of them (ii. 1—6); first, or last, he will make them *tremble*, Rev. xi. 15, &c. *The Lord reigns, let the earth be moved.* Those that submit to him shall be established, and not *moved* (xcvi. 10); but those that oppose him will be moved. Heaven

611

and earth shall be shaken, and all nations; but the kingdom of Christ is what cannot be moved; the *things which cannot be shaken shall remain,* Heb. xii. 27. *In these is continuance,* Isa. lxiv. 5.

God's kingdom, set up in Israel, is here made the subject of the psalmist's praise.

I. Two things the psalmist affirms:—1. God presided in the affairs of religion: *He sitteth between the cherubim* (*v.* 1), as on his throne, to give law by the oracles thence delivered—as on the mercy-seat, to receive petitions. This was the honour of Israel, that they had among them the Shechinah, or special presence of God, attended by the holy angels; the temple was the royal palace, and the Holy of holies was the presence-chamber. *The Lord is great in Zion* (*v.* 2); there he is known and praised (lxxvi. 1, 2); there he is served as great, more than any where else. *He is high* there *above all people;* as that which is high is exposed to view, and looked up to, so in Zion the perfections of the divine nature appear more conspicuous and more illustrious than any where else. Therefore *let those* that dwell in Zion, and worship there, *praise thy great and terrible name,* and give thee the glory due unto it, *for it is holy.* The holiness of God's name makes it truly great to his friends and terrible to his enemies, *v.* 3. This is that which those above adore—*Holy, holy, holy.* 2. He was all in all in their civil government, *v.* 4. As in Jerusalem was the testimony of Israel, whither the tribes went up, so *there were set thrones of judgment,* cxxii. 4, 5. Their government was a theocracy. God raised up David to rule over them (and some think this psalm was penned upon occasion of his quiet and happy settlement in the throne) and he is *the king* whose *strength loves judgment.* He is strong; all his strength he has from God; and *his strength* is not abused for the support of any wrong, as the power of great princes often is, but it *loves judgment.* He does justice with his power, and does it with delight; and herein he was a type of Christ, to whom God would give *the throne of his father David, to do judgment and justice.* He has power to crush, but his *strength loves judgment;* he does not rule with rigour, but with moderation, with wisdom, and with tenderness. The people of Israel had a good king; but they are here taught to look up to God as he by whom their king reigns: *Thou dost establish equity* (that is, God gave them those excellent laws by which they were governed), and *thou executest judgment and righteousness in Jacob;* he not only by his immediate providences often executed and enforced his own laws, but took care for the administration of justice among them by civil magistrates, who reigned by him and by him did decree justice. Their judges judged for God, and their judgment was his, 2 Chron. xix. 6.

II. Putting these two things together, we see what was the happiness of Israel above

any other people, as Moses had described it (Deut. iv. 7, 8), that they had *God so nigh unto them,* sitting between the cherubim, and that they had *statutes and judgments so righteous,* by which equity was established, and God himself ruled in Jacob, from which he infers this command to that happy people (*v.* 5): " *Exalt you the Lord our God, and worship at his footstool;* give him the glory of the good government you are under, as it is now established, both in church and state." Note, 1. The greater the public mercies are which we have a share in the more we are obliged to bear a part in the public homage paid to God: the setting up of the kingdom of Christ, especially, ought to be the matter of our praise. 2. When we draw nigh to God, to worship him, our hearts must be filled with high thoughts of him, and he must be exalted in our souls. 3. The more we abase ourselves, and the more prostrate we are before God, the more we exalt him. We must *worship at his footstool,* at his ark, which was as the footstool to the mercy-seat between the cherubim; or we must cast ourselves down upon the pavement of his courts; and good reason we have to be thus reverent, *for he is holy,* and his holiness should strike an awe upon us, as it does on the angels themselves, Isa. vi. 2, 3.

6 Moses and Aaron among his priests, and Samuel among them that call upon his name; they called upon the LORD, and he answered them. 7 He spake unto them in the cloudy pillar: they kept his testimonies, and the ordinance *that* he gave them. 8 Thou answeredst them, O LORD our God: thou wast a God that forgavest them, though thou tookest vengeance of their inventions. 9 Exalt the LORD our God, and worship at his holy hill; for the LORD our God *is* holy.

The happiness of Israel in God's government is here further made out by some particular instances of his administration, especially with reference to those that were, in their day, the prime leaders and most active useful governors of that people—Moses, Aaron, and Samuel, in the two former of whom the theocracy or divine government began (for they were employed to form Israel into a people) and in the last of whom that form of government, in a great measure, ended; for when the people rejected Samuel, and urged him to resign, they are said to reject God himself, that he should not be so immediately their king as he had been (1 Sam. viii. 7), for now they would have a king, like all the nations. Moses, as well as Aaron, is said to be *among his priests,* for he executed the priest's office till Aaron was settled in it and he consecrated Aaron and his sons;

therefore the Jews call him the *priest of the priests.* Now concerning these three chief rulers observe,

I. The intimate communion they had with God, and the wonderful favour to which he admitted them. None of all the nations of the earth could produce three such men as these, that had such an intercourse with Heaven, and whom God *knew by name,* Exod. xxxiii. 17. Here is, 1. Their gracious observance of God. No kingdom had men that honoured God as these three men of the kingdom of Israel did. They honoured him, (1.) By their prayers. Samuel, though not among his priests, yet was *among those that called on his name;* and for *this* they were all famous, *They called upon the Lord;* they relied not on their own wisdom or virtue, but in every emergency had recourse to God, towards him was their desire, and on him their dependence. (2.) By their obedience: *They kept his testimonies, and the ordinances that he gave them;* they made conscience of their duty, and in every thing made God's word and law their rule, as knowing that unless they did so they could not expect their prayers should be answered, Prov. xxviii. 9. Moses did all according to the pattern shown him; it is often repeated, *According to all that God commanded Moses, so did he.* Aaron and Samuel did likewise. Those were the greatest men and most honourable that were most eminent for keeping God's testimonies and conforming to the rule of his word. 2. God's gracious acceptance of them: *He answered them,* and granted them the things which they called upon him for. They all wonderfully prevailed with God in prayer; miracles were wrought at their special instance and request; nay, he not only condescended to do that for them which they desired, as a prince for a petitioner, but he communed with them as one friend familiarly converses with another (*v.* 7): *He spoke unto them in the cloudy pillar.* He often spoke to Samuel; from his childhood the word of the Lord came to him, and, probably, sometimes he spoke to him by a bright cloud overshadowing him: however, to Moses and Aaron he often spoke out of the famous *cloudy pillar,* Exod. xvi. 10; Num. xii. 5. Israel are now reminded of this, for the confirming of their faith, that though they had not every day such sensible tokens of God's presence as the cloudy pillar was, yet to those that were their first founders, and to him that was their great reformer, God was pleased thus to manifest himself.

II. The good offices they did to Israel. They interceded for the people, and for them also they obtained many an answer of peace. *Moses stood in the gap,* and *Aaron between the living and the dead;* and, when Israel was in distress, Samuel cried unto the Lord for them, 1 Sam. vii. 9. This is here referred to (*v.* 8): " *Thou answeredst them, O Lord our God!* and, at their prayer, *thou wast a God*

that forgavest the people they prayed for; and, *though thou tookest vengeance of their inventions,* yet thou didst not cut them off from being a people, as their sin deserved." "*Thou wast a God that wast propitious for them* (so Dr. Hammond), for their sakes, and sparedst the people at their request, even when thou wast about to *take vengeance of their inventions,* that is, when thy wrath was so highly provoked against them that it was just ready to break in upon them, to their utter overthrow." These were some of the many remarkable instances of God's dominion in Israel, more than in any other nation, for which the people are again called upon to praise God (*v.* 9): " *Exalt the Lord our God,* on account of what he has done for us formerly, as well as of late, *and worship at his holy hill* of Zion, on which he has now set his temple and will shortly *set his King* (ii. 6), the former a type of the latter; there, as the centre of unity, let all God's Israel meet, with their adorations, *for the Lord our God is holy,* and appears so, not only in his holy law, but in his holy gospel."

PSALM C.

It is with good reason that many sing this psalm very frequently in their religious assemblies, for it is very proper both to express and to excite pious and devout affections towards God in our approach to him in holy ordinances; and, if our hearts go along with the words, we shall make melody in it to the Lord. The Jews say it was penned to be sung with their thank-offerings; perhaps it was; but we say that as there is nothing in it peculiar to their economy so its beginning with a call to all lands to praise God plainly extends it to the gospel-church. Here, I. We are called upon to praise God and rejoice in him, ver. 1, 2, 4. II. We are furnished with matter for praise; we must praise him, considering his being and relation to us (ver. 3) and his mercy and truth, ver. 5. These are plain and common things, and therefore the more fit to be the matter of devotion.

A psalm of praise.

MAKE a joyful noise unto the Lord, all ye lands. 2 Serve the Lord with gladness: come before his presence with singing. 3 Know ye that the Lord he *is* God: *it is* he *that* hath made us, and not we ourselves; *we are* his people, and the sheep of his pasture. 4 Enter into his gates with thanksgiving, *and* into his courts with praise: be thankful unto him, *and* bless his name. 5 For the Lord *is* good; his mercy *is* everlasting; and his truth *endureth* to all generations.

Here, I. The exhortations to praise are very importunate. The psalm does indeed answer to the title, *A psalm of praise;* it begins with that call which of late we have several times met with (*v.* 1), *Make a joyful noise unto the Lord, all you lands,* or *all the earth,* all the inhabitants of the earth. When all nations shall be discipled, and the gospel preached to every creature, then this summons will be fully answered to. But, if we take the foregoing psalm to be (as we have opened it) a call to the Jewish church to rejoice in the administration of God's kingdom, which they were under (as the four psalms before it were calculated for the days of the Messiah), this psalm, perhaps, was intended for proselytes, that came over out of all lands to the Jews' religion. However, we have here, 1. A strong invitation to worship God; not that God needs us, or any thing we have or can do, but it is his will that we should *serve the Lord*, should devote ourselves to his service and employ ourselves in it; and that we should not only serve him in all instances of obedience to his law, but that we should *come before his presence* in the ordinances which he has appointed and in which he has promised to manifest himself (*v.* 2), that we should *enter into his gates and into his courts* (*v.* 4), that we should attend upon him among his servants, and keep there where he keeps court. In all acts of religious worship, whether in secret or in our families, we come into God's presence, and serve him; but it is in public worship especially that we *enter into his gates and into his courts.* The people were not permitted to enter into the holy place; there the priests only went in to minister. But let the people be thankful for their place in the courts of God's house, to which they were admitted and where they gave their attendance. 2. Great encouragement given us, in worshipping God, to do it cheerfully (*v.* 2): *Serve the Lord with gladness.* This intimates a prediction that in gospel-times there should be special occasion for joy; and it prescribes this as a rule of worship: Let God be *served with gladness.* By holy joy we do really serve God; it is an honour to him to rejoice in him; and we ought to serve him with holy joy. Gospel-worshippers should be joyful worshippers; if we serve God in uprightness, let us serve him with gladness. We must be willing and forward to it, glad when we are called to *go up to the house of the Lord* (cxxii. 1), looking upon it as the comfort of our lives to have communion with God; and we must be pleasant and cheerful in it, must say, It is good to be here, approaching to God, in every duty, as *to God our exceeding Joy*, xliii. 4. We must *come before his presence with singing*, not only songs of joy, but songs of praise. *Enter into his gates with thanksgiving*, *v.* 4. We must not only comfort ourselves, but glorify God, with our joy, and let him have the praise of that which we have the pleasure of. *Be thankful to him and bless his name;* that is, (1.) We must take it as a favour to be admitted into his service, and give him thanks that we have liberty of access to him, that we have ordinances instituted and opportunity continued of waiting upon God in those ordinances. (2.) We must intermix praise and thanksgiving with all our services. This golden thread must run through every duty (Heb. xiii. 15), for it is the work of angels. *In every thing give thanks*, in every ordinance, as well as in every providence.

II. The matter of praise, and motives to

it, are very important, *v.* 3, 5. Know you what God is in himself and what he is to you. Note, Knowledge is the mother of devotion and of all obedience: blind sacrifices will never please a seeing God. "Know it; consider and apply it, and then you will be more close and constant, more inward and serious, in the worship of him." Let us know then these seven things concerning the Lord Jehovah, with whom we have to do in all the acts of religious worship:—1. *That the Lord he is God*, the only living and true God—that he is a Being infinitely perfect, self-existent, and self-sufficient, and the fountain of all being; he is God, and not a man as we are. He is an eternal Spirit, incomprehensible and independent, the first cause and last end. The heathen worshipped the creature of their own fancy; the workmen made it, therefore it is not God. We worship him that made us and all the world; he is God, and all other pretended deities are vanity and a lie, and such as he has triumphed over. 2. That he is our Creator: *It is he that has made us, and not we ourselves.* I find that I am, but cannot say, *I am that I am*, and therefore must ask, Whence am I? Who made me? *Where is God my Maker?* And it is the Lord Jehovah. He gave us being, he gave us this being; he is both the former of our bodies and the Father of our spirits. We did not, we could not, make ourselves. It is God's prerogative to be his own cause; our being is derived and depending. 3. That therefore he is our rightful owner. The Masorites, by altering one letter in the Hebrew, read it, *He made us, and his we are*, or *to him we belong.* Put both the readings together, and we learn that because God *made us, and not we ourselves*, therefore we are not our own, but his. He has an incontestable right to, and property in, us and all things. His we are, to be actuated by his power, disposed of by his will, and devoted to his honour and glory. 4. That he is our sovereign ruler: *We are his people* or subjects, and he is our prince, our rector or governor, that gives law to us as moral agents, and will call us to an account for what we do. *The Lord is our judge; the Lord is our lawgiver.* We are not at liberty to do what we will, but must always make conscience of doing as we are bidden. 5. That he is our bountiful benefactor. We are not only his sheep, whom he is entitled to, but *the sheep of his pasture*, whom he takes care of; the *flock of his feeding* (so it may be read); therefore the *sheep of his hand;* at his disposal because *the sheep of his pasture*, xcv. 7. He that made us maintains us, and gives us all good things richly to enjoy. 6. That he is a God of infinite mercy and goodness (*v.* 5): *The Lord is good*, and therefore does good; *his mercy is everlasting;* it is a fountain that can never be drawn dry. The saints, who are now the sanctified vessels of mercy, will be, to eternity, the glorified monuments of mercy. 7.

That he is a God of inviolable truth and faithfulness : *His truth endures to all generations,* and no word of his shall fall to the ground as antiquated or revoked. The promise is sure to all the seed, from age to age.

PSALM CI.

David was certainly the penman of this psalm, and it has in it the genuine spirit of the man after God's own heart ; it is a solemn vow which he made to God when he took upon him the charge of a family and of the kingdom. Whether it was penned when he entered upon the government, immediately after the death of Saul (as some think), or when he began to reign over all Israel, and brought up the ark to the city of David (as others think), is not material ; it is an excellent plan or model for the good government of a court, or the keeping up of virtue and piety, and, by that means, good order, in it : but it is applicable to private families ; it is the householder's psalm. It instructs all that are in any sphere of power, whether larger or narrower, to use their power so as to make it a terror to evil-doers, but a praise to those that do well. Here is, I. The general scope of David's vow, ver. 1, 2. II. The particulars of it, that he would detest and discountenance all manner of wickedness (ver. 3—5, 7, 8) and that he would favour and encourage such as were virtuous, ver. 6. Some think this may fitly be accommodated to Christ, the Son of David, who governs his church, the city of the Lord, by these rules, and who loves righteousness and hates wickedness. In singing this psalm families, both governors and governed, should teach, and admonish, and engage themselves and one another to walk by the rule of it, that peace may be upon them and God's presence with them.

A psalm of David.

I WILL sing of mercy and judgment : unto thee, O LORD, will I sing. 2 I will behave myself wisely in a perfect way. O when wilt thou come unto me ? I will walk within my house with a perfect heart. 3 I will set no wicked thing before mine eyes : I hate the work of them that turn aside ; *it* shall not cleave to me. 4 A froward heart shall depart from me : I will not know a wicked *person.* 5 Whoso privily slandereth his neighbour, him will I cut off : him that hath a high look and a proud heart will not I suffer. 6 Mine eyes *shall be* upon the faithful of the land, that they may dwell with me : he that walketh in a perfect way, he shall serve me. 7 He that worketh deceit shall not dwell within my house : he that telleth lies shall not tarry in my sight. 8 I will early destroy all the wicked of the land ; that I may cut off all wicked doers from the city of the LORD.

David here cuts out to himself and others a pattern both of a good magistrate and a good master of a family ; and, if these were careful to discharge the duty of their place, it would contribute very much to a universal reformation. Observe,

I. The chosen subject of the psalm (*v.* 1) : *I will sing of mercy and judgment,* that is,

1. Of God's mercy and judgment, and then it looks back upon the dispensations of Providence concerning David since he was first anointed to be king, during which time he had met with many a rebuke and much hardship on the one hand, and yet, on the other hand, had had many wonderful deliverances wrought for him and favours bestowed upon him ; of these he will sing unto God. Note, (1.) God's providences concerning his people are commonly mixed—*mercy and judgment ;* God has set the one over-against the other, and appointed them April-days, showers and sunshine. It was so with David and his family ; when there was mercy in the return of the ark there was judgment in the death of Uzza. (2.) When God in his providence exercises us with a mixture of mercy and judgment it is our duty to sing, and sing unto him, both of the one and of the other ; we must be suitably affected with both, and make suitable acknowledgments to God for both. The Chaldee-paraphrase of this is observable : *If thou bestowest mercy upon me,* or, *If thou bring any judgment upon me, before thee, O Lord ! will I sing my hymns for all.* Whatever our outward condition is, whether joyful or sorrowful, still we must give glory to God, and sing praises to him ; neither the laughter of a prosperous condition nor the tears of an afflicted condition must put us out of tune for sacred songs. Or,

2. It may be understood of David's mercy and judgment ; he would, in this psalm, promise to be merciful, and just, or wise, for judgment is often put for discretion. To do justly and love mercy is the sum of our duty ; these he would covenant to make conscience of in that place and relation to which God had called him and this in consideration of the various providences of God that had occurred to him. Family-mercies and family-afflictions are both of them calls to family-religion. David put his vow into a song or psalm, that he might the better keep it in his own mind and frequently repeat it, and that it might the better be communicated to others and preserved in his family, for a pattern to his sons and successors.

II. The general resolution David took up to conduct himself carefully and conscientiously in his court, *v.* 2. We have here,

1. A good purpose concerning his conversation—concerning his conversation in general (how he would behave himself in every thing ; he would live by rule, and not at large, not walk at all adventures ; he would, though a king, by a solemn covenant bind himself to his good behaviour), and concerning his conversation in his family particularly, not only how he would walk when he appeared in public, when he sat in the throne, but how he would *walk within his house,* where he was more out of the eye of the world, but where he still saw himself under the eye of God. It is not enough to put on our religion when we go abroad and appear before men ; but we must govern ourselves by it in our families. Those that are in public stations are not thereby excused from care in governing their families ; nay, rather, they are more concerned to set a good example of *ruling their own houses well,* 1 Tim. iii. 4. When David had his hands full of public

affairs, yet he returned to bless his house, 2 Sam. vi. 20. He resolves, (1.) To act conscientiously and with integrity, to *walk in a perfect way*, in the way of God's commandments; that is *a perfect way*, for *the law of the Lord is perfect.* This he will walk in *with a perfect heart*, with all sincerity, not dissembling either with God or men. When we make the word of God our rule, and are ruled by it, the glory of God our end, and aim at it, then we walk *in a perfect way with a perfect heart.* (2.) To act considerately and with discretion: *I will behave myself wisely; I will understand* or *instruct myself* in a perfect way, so some. I will walk circumspectly. Note, We must all resolve to walk by the rules of Christian prudence in the ways of Christian piety. We must never turn aside out of the perfect way, under pretence of *behaving ourselves wisely;* but, while we keep to the good way, we must be *wise as serpents.*

2. A good prayer: *O when wilt thou come unto me?* Note, It is a desirable thing, when a man has a house of his own, to have God come to him and dwell with him in it; and those may expect God's presence that walk with *a perfect heart* in *a perfect way.* If we compare the account which the historian gives of David (1 Sam. xviii. 14), we shall find how exactly it answers his purpose and prayer, and that neither was in vain. David, as he purposed, *behaved himself wisely in all his ways; and,* as he prayed, *the Lord was with him.*

III. His particular resolution to practise no evil himself (v. 3): "*I will set no wicked thing before my eyes;* I will not design nor aim at any thing but what is for the glory of God and the public welfare." He will never have it in his eye to enrich himself by impoverishing his subjects, or enlarge his own prerogative by encroaching on their property. In all our worldly business we must see that what we set our eyes upon be right and good and not any forbidden fruit, and that we never seek that which we cannot have without sin. It is the character of a good man that he shuts his eyes from seeing evil, Isa. xxxiii. 15. "Nay, I *hate the work of those that turn aside* from the paths of equity (Job xxxi. 7), not only I avoid it, but I abhor it; *it shall not cleave to me.* If any blot of injustice should come on my hands, it shall be washed off quickly."

IV. His further resolution not to keep bad servants, nor to employ those about him that were vicious. He will not countenance them, nor show them any favour, lest thereby he should harden them in their wickedness, and encourage others to do like them. He will not converse with them himself, nor admit them into the company of his other servants, lest they should spread the infection of sin in his family. He will not confide in them, nor put them in power under him; for those who hated to be reformed would certainly

616

hinder every thing that is good. When he comes to mention particulars he does not mention drunkards, adulterers, murderers, or blasphemers; such gross sinners as these he was in no danger of admitting into his house, nor did he need to covenant particularly against having fellowship with them; but he mentions those whose sins were less scandalous, but no less dangerous, and in reference to whom he needed to stand upon his guard with caution and to behave himself wisely. He will have nothing to do, 1. With spiteful malicious people, who are ill-natured, and will bear a grudge a great while, and care not what mischief they do to those they have a pique against (v. 4): "*A froward heart* (one that delights to be cross and perverse) *shall depart from me*, as not fit for society, the bond of which is love. *I will not know*," that is, "I will have no acquaintance or conversation, if I can help it, with such *a wicked person;* for a little of the leaven of malice and wickedness will leaven the whole lump." 2. With slanderers, and those who take a pleasure in wounding their neighbour's reputation secretly (v. 5): "*Whoso privily slanders his neighbour*, either raises or spreads false stories, to the prejudice of his good name, *him will I cut off* from my family and court." Many endeavour to raise themselves into the favour of princes by unjust representations of persons and things, which they think will please their prince. *If a ruler hearken to lies, all his servants are wicked,* Prov. xxix. 12. But David will not only not hearken to them, but will prevent the preferment of those that hope thus to curry favour with him: he will punish not only him that falsely accuses another in open court, but him that privily slanders another. I wish David had remembered this vow in the case of Mephibosheth and Ziba. 3. With haughty, conceited, ambitious people; none do more mischief in a family, in a court, in a church, for *only by pride comes contention:* "Therefore him *that has a high look and a proud heart will I not suffer;* I will have no patience with those that are still grasping at all preferments, for it is certain that they do not aim at doing good, but only at aggrandizing themselves and their families." God resists the proud, and so will David. 4. With false deceitful people, that scruple not to tell lies, or commit frauds (v. 7):- "*He that worketh deceit*, though he may insinuate himself into my family, yet, as soon as he is discovered, *shall not dwell within my house.*" Some great men know how to serve their own purposes by such as are skilful to deceive, and they are fit tools for them to work by; but David will make use of no such persons as agents for him: *He that tells lies shall not tarry in my sight*, but shall be expelled the house with indignation. Herein David was *a man after God's own heart*, for a proud look and a lying tongue are things which God hates; and he was also a type of Christ, who will, in the great day, banish from his presence *all that love and make a lie,* Rev. xxii. 15.

V. His resolution to put those in trust under him that were honest and good (*v.* 6): *My eyes shall be upon the faithful in the land.* In choosing his servants and ministers of state he kept to the land of Israel and would not employ foreigners; none shall be preferred but true-born Israelites, and those such as were Israelites indeed, the *faithful in the land;* for even in that land there were those that were unfaithful. These faithful ones his eyes shall be upon, to discover them and find them out; for they were modest, did not crowd into the city to court preferment, but lived retired in the land, in the country, out of the way of it. Those are commonly most fit for places of honour and trust that are least fond of them; and therefore wise princes will spy out such in their recesses and privacies, and take them to dwell with them and act under them. *He that walks in a perfect way,* that makes conscience of what he says and does, *shall serve me.* The kingdom must be searched for honest men to make courtiers of; and, if any man is better than another, he must be preferred. This was a good resolution of David's; but either he did not keep to it or else his judgment was imposed upon when he made Ahithophel his right hand. It should be the care and endeavour of all masters of families, for their own sakes and their children's, to take such servants into their families as they have reason to hope fear God. The Son of David has his eyes upon *the faithful in the land;* his secret is with them, and they *shall dwell with him.* Saul chose servants for their goodliness (1 Sam. viii. 16), but David for their goodness.

VI. His resolution to extend his zeal to the reformation of the city and country, as well as of the court (*v.* 8): " *I will early destroy all the wicked of the land,* all that are discovered and convicted; the law shall have its course against them." He would do his utmost to *destroy all the wicked,* so that there might be none left that were notoriously wicked. He would do it early; he would lose no time and spare no pains; he would be forward and zealous in promoting the reformation of manners and suppression of vice; and those must rise betimes that will do any thing to purpose in that work. That which he aimed at was not only the securing of his own government and the peace of the country, but the honour of God in the purity of his church, *That I may cut off all wicked doers from the city of the Lord.* Not Jerusalem only, but the whole land, was the *city of the Lord;* so is the gospel-church. It is the interest of the *city of the Lord* to be purged from *wicked doers,* who both blemish it and weaken it; and it is therefore the duty of all to do what they can, in their places, towards so good a work, and to be zealously affected in it. The day is coming when the Son of David shall cut off all wicked doers from the new Jeru-

salem, for there shall not enter into it any that do iniquity.

PSALM CII.

Some think that David penned this psalm at the time of Absalom's rebellion; others that Daniel, Nehemiah, or some other prophet, penned it for the use of the church, when it was in captivity in Babylon, because it seems to speak of the ruin of Zion and of a time set for the rebuilding of it, which Daniel understood by books, Dan. ix. 2. Or perhaps the psalmist was himself in great affliction, which he complains of in the beginning of the psalm, but (as in Ps. lxxvii. and elsewhere) he comforts himself under it with the consideration of God's eternity, and the church's prosperity and perpetuity, how much soever it was now distressed and threatened. But it is clear, from the application of ver. 25, 26, to Christ (Heb. i. 10—12), that the psalm has reference to the days of the Messiah, and speaks either of his affliction or of the afflictions of his church for his sake. In the psalm we have, I. A sorrowful complaint which the psalmist makes, either for himself or in the name of the church, of great afflictions, which were very pressing, ver. 1—11. II. Seasonable comfort fetched in against these grievances, 1. From the eternity of God, ver. 12, 24, 27. 2. From a believing prospect of the deliverance which God would, in due time, work for his afflicted church (ver. 13—22) and the continuance of it in the world, ver. 28. In singing this psalm, if we have not occasion to make the same complaints, yet we may take occasion to sympathize with those that have, and then the comfortable part of this psalm will be the more comfortable to us in the singing of it.

A prayer of the afflicted, when he is overwhelmed, and poureth out his complaint before the Lord.

HEAR my prayer, O LORD, and let my cry come unto thee. 2 Hide not thy face from me in the day *when* I am in trouble; incline thine ear unto me: in the day *when* I call answer me speedily. 3 For my days are consumed like smoke, and my bones are burned as a hearth. 4 My heart is smitten, and withered like grass; so that I forget to eat my bread. 5 By reason of the voice of my groaning my bones cleave to my skin. 6 I am like a pelican of the wilderness: I am like an owl of the desert. 7 I watch, and am as a sparrow alone upon the house top. 8 Mine enemies reproach me all the day; *and* they that are mad against me are sworn against me. 9 For I have eaten ashes like bread, and mingled my drink with weeping, 10 Because of thine indignation and thy wrath: for thou hast lifted me up, and cast me down. 11 My days *are* like a shadow that declineth; and I am withered like grass.

The title of this psalm is very observable; it is *a prayer of the afflicted.* It was composed by one that was himself afflicted, afflicted with the church and for it; and on those that are of a public spirit afflictions of that kind lie heavier than any other. It is calculated for an afflicted state, and is intended for the use of others that may be in the like distress; for *whatsoever things were written aforetime were written* designedly *for our use.* The whole word of God is of use to direct us in prayer; but here, as often elsewhere, the Holy Ghost has drawn up our petition for us, has put words into our mouths.

617

Hos. xiv. 2, *Take with you words.* Here is a prayer put into the hands of the afflicted: let them set, not their hands, but their hearts to it, and present it to God. Note, 1. It is often the lot of the best saints in this world to be sorely affected. 2. Even good men may be almost overwhelmed with their afflictions, and may be ready to faint under them. 3. When our state is afflicted, and our spirits are overwhelmed, it is our duty and interest to pray, and by prayer to *pour out our complaints before the Lord,* which intimates the leave God gives us to be free with him and the liberty of speech we have before him, as well as liberty of access to him; it intimates also what an ease it is to an afflicted spirit to unburden itself by a humble representation of its grievances and griefs. Such a representation we have here, in which,

I. The psalmist humbly begs of God to take notice of his affliction, and of his prayer in his affliction, *v.* 1, 2. When we pray in our affliction, 1. It should be our care that God would graciously hear us; for, if our prayers be not pleasing to God, they will be to no purpose to ourselves. Let this therefore be in our eye that our prayer may *come unto God,* even *to his ears* (xviii. 6); and, in order to that, let us *lift up the prayer,* and our souls with it. 2. It may be our hope that God will graciously hear us, because he has appointed us to seek him and has promised we shall not seek him in vain. If we put up a *prayer in faith,* we may in faith say, *Hear my prayer, O Lord!* "Hear me," that is, (1,) "Manifest thyself to me, *hide not thy face from me* in displeasure, *when I am in trouble.* If thou dost not quickly free me, yet let me know that thou favourest me; if I see not the operations of thy hand for me, yet let me see the smiles of thy face upon me." God's hiding his face is trouble enough to a good man even in his prosperity (xxx. 7, *Thou didst hide thy face, and I was troubled*); but if, when we are in trouble, God hides his face, the case is sad indeed. (2.) "Manifest thyself for me; not only hear me, but answer me; grant me the deliverance I am in want of and in pursuit of; answer me speedily, even *in the day when I call.*" When troubles press hard upon us, God gives us leave to be thus pressing in prayer, yet with humility and patience.

II. He makes a lamentable complaint of the low condition to which he was reduced by his afflictions. 1. His body was macerated and emaciated, and he had become a perfect skeleton, nothing but skin and bones. As prosperity and joy are represented by *making fat the bones,* and the *bones flourishing like a herb,* so great trouble and grief are here represented by the contrary: *My bones are burnt as a hearth* (*v.* 3); they *cleave to my skin* (*v.* 5); nay, *my heart is smitten, and withered like grass* (*v.* 4); it touches the vitals, and there is a sensible decay there. *I am withered like grass* (*v.* 11), scorched with the burning heat of my troubles. If we be
618

thus brought low by bodily distempers, let us not think it strange; the body is like grass, weak and of the earth, no wonder then that it withers. 2. He was very melancholy and of a sorrowful spirit. He was so taken up with the thoughts of his troubles that he *forgot to eat his bread* (*v.* 4); he had no appetite to his necessary food nor could he relish it. When God hides his face from a soul the delights of sense will be sapless things. He was always *sighing* and *groaning,* as one pressed above measure (*v.* 5), and this wasted him and exhausted his spirits. He affected solitude, as melancholy people do. His friends deserted him and were shy of him, and he cared as little for their company (*v.* 6, 7): "*I am like a pelican of the wilderness,* or a *bittern* (so some) that make a doleful noise; *I am like an owl,* that affects to lodge in deserted ruined buildings; *I watch, and am as a sparrow upon the house-top.* I live in a garret, and there spend my hours in poring on my troubles and bemoaning myself." Those who do thus, when they are in sorrow, humour themselves indeed; but they prejudice themselves, and know not what they do, nor what advantage they hereby give to the tempter. In affliction we should sit alone to consider our ways (Lam. iii. 28), but not sit alone to indulge an inordinate grief. 3. He was evil-spoken of by his enemies, and all manner of evil was said against him. When his friends went off from him his foes set themselves against him (*v.* 8): *My enemies reproach me all the day,* designing thereby both to create vexation to him (for an ingenuous mind regrets reproach) and to bring an odium upon him before men. When they could not otherwise reach him they shot these arrows at him, even *bitter words.* In this they were unwearied; they did it *all the day;* it was a continual dropping. His enemies were very outrageous: *They* are *mad against me,* and very obstinate and implacable. *They* are *sworn against me;* as the Jews that bound themselves with an oath that they would kill Paul; or, *They have sworn against me* as accusers, to take away my life. 4. He fasted and wept under the tokens of God's displeasure (*v.* 9, 10): "*I have eaten ashes like bread;* instead of eating my bread, I have lain down in dust and ashes, and *I have mingled my drink with weeping;* when I should have refreshed myself with drinking I have only eased myself with weeping." And what is the matter? He tells us (*v.* 10): *Because of thy wrath.* It was not so much the trouble itself that troubled him as the wrath of God which he was under the apprehensions of as the cause of the trouble. This, this was the *wormwood and the gall* in the affliction and the misery: *Thou hast lifted me up and cast me down,* as that which we cast to the ground with a design to dash it to pieces; we lift up first, that we may throw it down with the more violence; or, "Thou hast formerly lifted me up in honour, and joy, and uncommon prosperity; but the remembrance of that aggravates the present grief and makes it the more grievous." We must eye the hand of God both in lifting us up and casting us down, and say, " Blessed be the name of the Lord, who both gives and takes away." 5. He looked upon himself as a dying man : *My days are consumed like smoke* (*v.* 3), which vanishes away quickly. Or, They are consumed *in smoke*, of which nothing remains; they are *like a shadow that declines* (*v.* 11), like the evening-shadow, or a forerunner of approaching night. Now all this, though it seems to speak the psalmist's personal calamities, and therefore is properly a prayer for a particular person afflicted, yet is supposed to be a description of the afflictions of the church of God, with which the psalmist sympathizes, making public grievances his own. The mystical body of Christ is sometimes, like the psalmist's body here, *withered* and *parched*, nay, like *dead and dry bones.* The church sometimes is forced *into the wilderness,* seems lost, and gives up herself for gone, under the tokens of God's displeasure.

12 But thou, O LORD, shalt endure for ever; and thy remembrance unto all generations. 13 Thou shalt arise, *and* have mercy upon Zion : for the time to favour her, yea, the set time, is come. 14 For thy servants take pleasure in her stones, and favour the dust thereof. 15 So the heathen shall fear the name of the LORD, and all the kings of the earth thy glory. 16 When the LORD shall build up Zion, he shall appear in his glory. 17 He will regard the prayer of the destitute, and not despise their prayer. 18 This shall be written for the generation to come: and the people which shall be created shall praise the LORD. 19 For he hath looked down from the height of his sanctuary; from heaven did the LORD behold the earth; 20 To hear the groaning of the prisoner; to loose those that are appointed to death; 21 To declare the name of the LORD in Zion, and his praise in Jerusalem; 22 When the people are gathered together, and the kingdoms, to serve the LORD.

Many exceedingly great and precious comforts are here thought of, and mustered up, to balance the foregoing complaints; for *unto the upright there arises light in the darkness,* so that, though they are cast down, they are not in despair. It is bad with the psalmist himself, bad with the people of God; but he has many considerations to revive himself with.

I. We are dying creatures, and our inter-

ests and comforts are dying, but God is an everliving everlasting God (*v.* 12): " *My days are like a shadow ;* there is no remedy; night is coming upon me; but, *thou, O Lord! shalt endure for ever.* Our life is transient, but thine is permanent; our friends die, but thou our God diest not ; what threatened us cannot touch thee ; our names will be written in the dust and buried in oblivion, but *thy remembrance shall be unto all generations;* to the end of time, nay, to eternity, thou shalt be known and honoured." A good man loves God better than himself, and therefore can balance his own sorrow and death with the pleasing thought of the unchangeable blessedness of the Eternal Mind. God *endures for ever,* his church's faithful patron and protector; and, his honour and perpetual remembrance being very much bound up in her interests, we may be confident that they shall not be neglected.

II. Poor Zion is now in distress, but there will come a time for her relief and succour (*v.* 13) : *Thou shalt arise and have mercy upon Zion.* The hope of deliverance is built upon the goodness of God—"Thou wilt *have mercy upon Zion,* for she has become an object of thy pity ;" and upon the power of God— " Thou shalt arise and have mercy, shalt stir up thyself to do it, shalt do it in contempt of all the opposition made by the church's enemies." *The zeal of the Lord of hosts shall do this.* That which is very encouraging is that there is a time set for the deliverance of the church, which not only will come some time, but will come at the time appointed, the time which Infinite Wisdom has appointed (and therefore it is the best time) and which Eternal Truth has fixed it to, and therefore it is a certain time, and shall not be forgotten nor further adjourned. At the end of seventy years, the time to favour Zion, by delivering her from the daughter of Babylon, was to come, and at length it did come. Zion was now in ruins, that is, the temple that was built in the city of David: the favouring of Zion is the building of the temple up again, as it is explained, *v.* 16. This is expected from the favour of God; that will set all to rights, and nothing but that, and therefore Daniel prays (Dan. ix. 17), *Cause thy face to shine upon thy sanctuary, which is desolate.* The building up of Zion is as great a favour to any people as they can desire. No blessing more desirable to a ruined state than the restoring and re-establishing of their church-privileges. Now this is here wished for and longed for, 1. Because it would be a great rejoicing to Zion's friends (*v.* 14) : *Thy servants take pleasure* even in *the stones* of the temple, though they were thrown down and scattered, and *favour the dust,* the very rubbish and ruins of it. Observe here, When the temple was ruined, yet the stones of it were to be had for a new building, and there were those who encouraged themselves with that, for they had a favour even for the dust of it. Those who truly love the church of God love it when it is in affliction as well as when it is in prosperity; and it is a good ground to hope that God will favour the ruins of Zion when he puts it into the heart of his people to favour them, and to show that they do so by their prayers and by their endeavours; as it is also a good plea with God for mercy for Zion that there are those who are so affectionately concerned for her, and are *waiting for the salvation of the Lord*. 2. Because it would have a good influence upon Zion's neighbours, *v.* 15. It will be a happy means perhaps of their conversion, at least of their conviction; for *so the heathen shall fear the name of the Lord*, shall have high thoughts of him and his people, and even the kings of the earth shall be affected with his glory. They shall have better thoughts of the church of God than they have had, when God by his providence thus puts an honour upon it; they shall be afraid of doing any thing against it when they see God taking its part; nay, they shall say, We will go with you, for we have *seen that God is with you*, Zech. viii. 23. Thus it is said (Est. viii. 17) that *many of the people of the land became Jews, for the fear of the Jews fell upon them*. 3. Because it would redound to the honour of Zion's God (*v.* 16): *When the Lord shall build up Zion.* They take it for granted it will be done, for God himself has undertaken it, and *he shall then appear in his glory;* and for that reason all that have made his glory their highest end desire it and pray for it. Note, The edifying of the church will be the glorifying of God, and therefore we may be assured it will be done in the set time. Those that pray in faith, *Father, glorify thy name*, may receive the same answer to that prayer which was given to Christ himself by a voice from heaven, *I have both glorified it and I will glorify it yet again*, though now for a time it may be eclipsed.

III. The prayers of God's people now seem to be slighted and no notice taken of them, but they will be reviewed and greatly encouraged (*v.* 17): *He will regard the prayer of the destitute.* It was said (*v.* 16) that God will *appear in his glory*, such a glory as kings themselves shall *stand in awe of, v.* 15. When great men *appear in their glory* they are apt to look with disdain upon the poor that apply to them; but the great God will not do so. Observe, 1. The meanness of the petitioners; they are the *destitute*. It is an elegant word that is here used, which signifies the heath in the wilderness, a low shrub, or bush, like the hyssop of the wall. They are supposed to be in a low and broken state, enriched with spiritual blessings, but destitute of temporal good things—the poor, the weak, the desolate, the stripped; thus variously is the word rendered; or it may signify that low and broken spirit which God looks for in all that draw nigh to him and which he will graciously look upon. This

will bring them to their knees. Destitute people should be praying people, 1 Tim. v. 5. 2. The favour of God to them, notwithstanding their meanness: *He will regard their prayer*, and will look at it, will peruse their petition (2 Chron. vi. 40), and he *will not despise their prayer*. More is implied than is expressed: he will value it and be well pleased with it, and will return an answer of peace to it, which is the greatest honour that can be put upon it. But it is thus expressed because others despise their praying, they themselves fear God will despise it, and he was thought to despise it while their affliction was prolonged and, their prayers lay unanswered. When we consider our own meanness and vileness, our darkness and deadness, and the manifold defects in our prayers, we have cause to suspect that our prayers will be received with disdain in heaven; but we are here assured of the contrary, for we have an advocate with the Father, and are under grace, not under the law. This instance of God's favour to his praying people, though they are destitute, will be a lasting encouragement to prayer (*v.* 18): *This shall be written for the generation to come, that none may despair*, though they be destitute, nor think their prayers forgotten because they have not an answer to them immediately. The experiences of others should be our encouragements to seek unto God and trust in him. And, if we have the comfort of the experiences of others, it is fit that we should give God the glory of them: *The people who shall be created shall praise the Lord* for what he has done both for them and for their predecessors. Many that are now unborn shall, by reading the history of the church, be wrought upon to turn proselytes. The people that shall be created anew by divine grace, that are a kind of *first-fruits of his creatures*, shall praise the Lord for his answers to their prayers when they were more destitute.

IV. The prisoners under condemnation unjustly seem as sheep appointed for the slaughter, but care shall be taken for their discharge (*v.* 19, 20): God has *looked down from the height of his sanctuary, from heaven*, where he has prepared his throne, that high place, that holy place; thence did *the Lord behold the earth*, for it is a place of prospect, and nothing on this earth is or can be hidden from his all-seeing eye; he looks down, not to take a view of the kingdoms of the world and the glory of them, but to do acts of grace, *to hear the groaning of the prisoners* (which we desire to be out of the hearing of), and not only to hear them, but to help them, *to loose those that are appointed to death*, then when there is but a step between them and it. Some understand it of the release of the Jews out of their captivity in Babylon. God heard their groaning there as he did when they were in Egypt (Exod. iii. 7, 9) and came down to deliver them. God takes notice not only of the prayers of his afflicted people, which are the language of grace, but even of their groans, which are the language of nature. See the divine pity in hearing the prisoner's groans, and the divine power in loosing the prisoner's bonds, even when they are appointed to death and are pinioned and double-shackled. We have an instance in Peter, Acts xii. 6. Such instances as these of the divine condescension and compassion will help, 1. *To declare the name of the Lord in Zion,* and to make it appear that he answers to his name, which he himself proclaimed, *The Lord God, gracious and merciful;* and this declaration of his name in Zion shall be the matter of his praise in Jerusalem, *v.* 21. If God by his providences declare his name, we must by our acknowledgments of them declare his praise, which ought to be the echo of his name. God will discharge his people that were prisoners and captives in Babylon, *that they may declare his name in Zion,* the place he has chosen to put his name there, *and his praise in Jerusalem,* at their return thither; in the land of their captivity they could not sing the songs of Zion (cxxxvii. 3, 4), and God brought them again to Jerusalem in order that they might sing them there. For this end God gives liberty from bondage (*Bring my soul out of prison, that I may praise thy name,* cxlii. 7), and life from the dead. *Let my soul live, and it shall praise thee,* cxix. 175. 2. They will help to draw in others to the worship of God (*v.* 22): *When the people of God are gathered together* at Jerusalem (as they were after their return out of Babylon) many out of the kingdoms joined with them *to serve the Lord.* This was fulfilled Ezra vi. 21, where we find that not only the children of Israel that had come out of captivity, but many that had *separated themselves from them among the heathen,* did *keep the feast of unleavened bread with joy.* But it may look further, at the conversion of the Gentiles to the faith of Christ in the latter days. Christ has proclaimed *liberty to the captives,* and *the opening of the prison to those that were bound,* that they may declare the name of the Lord in the gospel-church, in which Jews and Gentiles shall unite.

23 He weakened my strength in the way; he shortened my days. 24 I said, O my God, take me not away in the midst of my days: thy years *are* throughout all generations. 25 Of old hast thou laid the foundation of the earth: and the heavens *are* the work of thy hands. 26 They shall perish, but thou shalt endure: yea, all of them shall wax old like a garment; as a vesture shalt thou change them, and they shall be changed: 27 But thou *art* the same, and thy years shall have no end. 28 The children of thy

servants shall continue, and their seed shall be established before thee.

We may here observe,

I. The imminent danger that the Jewish church was in of being quite extirpated and cut off by the captivity in Babylon (*v.* 23): *He weakened my strength in the way.* They were for many ages in the way to the performance of the great promise made to their fathers concerning the Messiah, longing as much for it as ever a traveller did to be at his journey's end. The legal institutions led them in the way; but when the ten tribes were lost in Assyria, and the two almost lost in Babylon, the strength of that nation was weakened, and, in all appearance, its day shortened; for they said, *Our hope is lost; we are cut off for our parts,* Ezek. xxxvii. 11. And then what becomes of the promise that Shiloh should arise out of Judah, the star out of Jacob, and the Messiah out of the family of David? If these fail, the promise fails. This the psalmist speaks of as in his own person, and it is very applicable to two of the common afflictions of this time:—1. To be sickly. Bodily distempers soon *weaken our strength in the way,* make the keepers of the house to tremble and the strong men to bow themselves. 2. To be short-lived. Where the former is felt, this is feared; when in the midst of our days, according to a course of nature, our strength is weakened, what can we expect but that the *number of our months should be cut off in the midst?* and what should we do but provide accordingly? We must own God's hand in it (for in his hand our strength and time are), and must reconcile it to his love, for it has often been the lot of those that have used their strength well to have it weakened, and of those that could very ill be spared to have their days shortened.

II. A prayer for the continuance of it (*v.* 24): "*O my God! take me not away in the midst of my days;* let not this poor church be cut off in the midst of the days assigned it by the promise; let it not be cut off till the Messiah shall come. *Destroy it not, for that blessing is in it,*" Isa. lxv. 8. She is a criminal, but, for the sake of that blessing which is in her, she pleads for a reprieve. This is a prayer for the afflicted, and which, with submission to the will of God, we may in faith put up, that God would not *take us away in the midst of our days,* but that, if it be his will, he would spare us to do him further service and to be made riper for heaven.

III. A plea to enforce this prayer taken from the eternity of the Messiah promised, *v.* 25—27. The apostle quotes these verses (Heb. i. 10—12) and tells us, *He saith this to the Son,* and in that exposition we must acquiesce. It is very comfortable, in reference to all the changes that pass over the church, and all the dangers it is in, that *Jesus Christ is the same yesterday, to-day, and for ever.*

Thy years are throughout all generations, and cannot be shortened. It is likewise comfortable in reference to the decay and death of our own bodies, and the removal of our friends from us, that God is an everliving God, and that therefore, if he be ours, in him we may have everlasting consolation. In this plea observe how, to illustrate the eternity of the Creator, he compares it with the mutability of the creature; for it is God's sole prerogative to be unchangeable. 1. God made the world, and therefore had a being before it from eternity. The Son of God, the eternal Word, made the world. It is expressly said, *All things were made by him, and without him was not any thing made that was made ;* and *therefore the same was in the beginning* from eternity *with God, and was God,* John i. 1—3; Col. i. 16; Eph. iii. 9; Heb. i. 2. Earth and heaven, and the hosts of both, include the universe and its fulness, and these derive their being from God by his Son (*v.* 25): " *Of old hast thou laid the foundation of the earth,* which is founded *on the seas* and *on the floods* and yet *it abides ;* much more shall the church, which is *built upon a rock.* The *heavens are the work of thy hands,* and by thee are all their motions and influences directed;" God is therefore the fountain, not only of all being, but of all power and dominion. See how fit the great Redeemer is to be entrusted with all power, both in heaven and in earth, since he himself, as Creator of both, perfectly knows both and is entitled to both. 2. God will unmake the world again, and therefore shall have a being to eternity (*v.* 26, 27): *They shall perish,* for *thou shalt change them* by the same almighty power that made them, and therefore, no doubt, *thou shalt endure; thou art the same.* God and the world, Christ and the creature, are rivals for the innermost and uppermost place in the soul of man, the immortal soul; now what is here said, one would think, were enough to decide the controversy immediately and to determine us for God and Christ. For, (1.) A portion in the creature is fading and dying : *They shall perish;* they will not last so long as we shall last. The day is coming when *the earth and all the works that are therein shall be burnt up;* and then what will become of those that have laid up their treasure in it? Heaven and earth shall *wax old as a garment,* not by a gradual decay, but, when the set time comes, they shall be laid aside like an old garment that we have no more occasion for : *As a vesture shalt thou change them, and they shall be changed,* not annihilated, but altered, it may be so that they shall not be at all the same, but *new heavens and a new earth.* See God's sovereign dominion over heaven and earth. He can change them as he pleases and when he pleases ; and the constant changes they are subject to, in the revolutions of day and night, summer and winter, are earnests of their last and final change, when *the heavens* and *time* (which is

622

measured by them) *shall be no more.* (2.) A portion in God is perpetual and everlasting : *Thou art the same,* subject to no change; and *thy years have no end, v.* 27. Christ will be the same in the performance that he was in the promise, the same to his church in captivity that he was to his church at liberty. Let not the church fear the weakening of her strength, or the shortening of her days, while Christ himself is both her strength and her life ; he is the same, and has said, *Because I live you shall live also.* Christ came in the fulness of time, and set up his kingdom in spite of the power of the Old-Testament Babylon, and he will keep it up in spite of the power of the New-Testament Babylon.

IV. A comfortable assurance of an answer to this prayer (*v.* 28): *The children of thy servants shall continue;* since Christ is the same, the church shall continue from one generation to another; from the eternity of the head we may infer the perpetuity of the body, though often weak and distempered, and even at death's door. Those that hope to *wear out the saints of the Most High* will be mistaken. Christ's servants shall have children; those children shall have a seed, a succession, of professing people; the church, as well as the world, is under the influence of that blessing, *Be fruitful and multiply.* These *children shall continue,* not in their own persons, by reason of death, but in their seed, which shall be established before God (that is, in his service, and by his grace); the entail of religion shall not be cut off while the world stands, but, as one generation of good people passes away, another shall come, and thus the throne of Christ shall endure.

PSALM CIII.

This psalm calls more for devotion than exposition ; it is a most excellent psalm of praise, and of general use. The psalmist, I. Stirs up himself and his own soul to praise God (ver. 1, 2) for his favour to him in particular (ver. 3—5), to the church in general, and to all good men, to whom he is, and will be, just, and kind, and constant (ver. 6—18), and for his government of the world, ver. 19. II. He desires the assistance of the holy angels, and all the works of God, in praising him, ver. 20—22. In singing this psalm we must in a special manner get our hearts affected with the goodness of God and enlarged in love and thankfulness.

A psalm of David.

BLESS the LORD, O my soul : and all that is within me, *bless* his holy name. 2 Bless the LORD, O my soul, and forget not all his benefits : 3 Who forgiveth all thine iniquities ; who healeth all thy diseases ; 4 Who redeemeth thy life from destruction ; who crowneth thee with lovingkindness and tender mercies ; 5 Who satisfieth thy mouth with good *things ; so that* thy youth is renewed like the eagle's.

David is here communing with his own heart, and he is no fool that thus talks to himself and excites his own soul to that which is good. Observe,

I. How he stirs up himself to the duty of

praise, *v.* 1, 2. 1. It is the Lord that is to be blessed and spoken well of; for he is the fountain of all good, whatever are the channels or cisterns; it is to his name, his holy name, that we are to consecrate our praise, *giving thanks at the remembrance of his holiness.* 2. It is the soul that is to be employed in blessing God, *and all that is within* us. We make nothing of our religious performances if we do not make heart-work of them, if that which is within us, nay, if *all that is within* us, be not engaged in them. The work requires the inward man, the whole man, and all little enough. 3. In order to our return of praises to God, there must be a grateful remembrance of the mercies we have received from him: *Forget not all his benefits.* If we do not give thanks for them, we do forget them; and that is unjust as well as unkind, since in all God's favours there is so much that is memorable. " O my soul! to thy shame be it spoken, thou hast forgotten many of his benefits; but surely thou wilt not forget them all, for thou shouldst not have forgotten any."

II. How he furnishes himself with abundant matter for praise, and that which is very affecting : " Come, my soul, consider what God has done for thee." 1. " He has pardoned thy sins (*v.* 3); he has forgiven, and *does forgive, all thy iniquities.*" This is mentioned first because by the pardon of sin that is taken away which kept good things from us, and we are restored to the favour of God, which bestows good things on us. Think what the provocation was; it was iniquity, and yet pardoned; how many the provocations were, and yet all pardoned. *He has forgiven all our trespasses.* It is a continued act; he is still forgiving, as we are still sinning and repenting. 2. " He has cured thy sickness." The corruption of nature is the sickness of the soul; it is its disorder, and threatens its death. This is cured in sanctification; when sin is mortified, the disease is healed; though complicated, it is all healed. Our crimes were capital, but God saves our lives by pardoning them; our diseases were mortal, but God saves our lives by healing them. These two go together; for, as for God, his work is perfect and not done by halves; if God take away the guilt of sin by pardoning mercy, he will break the power of it by renewing grace. Where Christ is made righteousness to any soul he is made sanctification, 1 Cor. i. 30. 3. " He has rescued thee from danger." A man may be in peril of life, not only by his crimes, or his diseases, but by the power of his enemies; and therefore here also we experience the divine goodness : *Who redeemed thy life from destruction* (*v.* 4), from the destroyer, *from hell* (so the Chaldee), from the second death. *The redemption of the soul is precious ;* we cannot compass it, and therefore are the more indebted to divine grace that has wrought it out, to him who has *obtained eternal redemp-*

tion for us. See Job xxxiii. 24, 28. 4. " He has not only saved thee from death and ruin, but has made thee truly and completely happy, with honour, pleasure, and long life." (1.) " He has given thee true honour and great honour, no less than a crown : *He crowns thee with his lovingkindness and tender mercies ;*" and what greater dignity is a poor soul capable of than to be advanced into the love and favour of God ? *This honour have all his saints.* What is the crown of glory but God's favour ? (2.) " He has given thee true pleasure : *He satisfies thy mouth with good things*" (*v.* 5); it is only the favour and grace of God that can give satisfaction to a soul, can suit its capacities, supply its needs, and answer to its desires. Nothing but divine wisdom can undertake to *fill its treasures* (Prov. viii. 21); other things will surfeit, but not *satiate*, Eccl. vi. 7; Isa. lv. 2. (3.) " He has given thee a prospect and pledge of long life : *Thy youth is renewed like the eagle's.*" The eagle is long-lived, and, as naturalists say, when she is nearly 100 years old, casts all her feathers (as indeed she changes them in a great measure every year at moulting time), and fresh ones come, so that she becomes young again. When God, by the graces and comforts of his Spirit, recovers his people from their decays, and fills them with new life and joy, which is to them an earnest of eternal life and joy, then they may be said to *return to the days of their youth,* Job xxxiii. 25.

6 The Lord executeth righteousness and judgment for all that are oppressed. 7 He made known his ways unto Moses, his acts unto the children of Israel. 8 The Lord *is* merciful and gracious, slow to anger, and plenteous in mercy. 9 He will not always chide : neither will he keep *his anger* for ever. 10 He hath not dealt with us after our sins; nor rewarded us according to our iniquities. 11 For as the heaven is high above the earth, *so* great is his mercy toward them that fear him. 12 As far as the east is from the west, *so* far hath he removed our transgressions from us. 13 Like as a father pitieth *his* children, so the Lord pitieth them that fear him. 14 For he knoweth our frame; he remembereth that we *are* dust. 15 *As for* man, his days *are* as grass : as a flower of the field, so he flourisheth. 16 For the wind passeth over it, and it is gone; and the place thereof shall know it no more. 17 But the mercy of the Lord *is* from everlasting to everlasting upon them that

623

fear him, and his righteousness unto children's children; 18 To such as keep his covenant, and to those that remember his commandments to do them.

Hitherto the psalmist had only looked back upon his own experiences and thence fetched matter for praise; here he looks abroad and takes notice of his favour to others also; for in them we should rejoice and give thanks for them, all the saints being fed at a common table and sharing in the same blessings.

I. Truly God is good to all (*v.* 6): He *executes righteousness and judgment,* not only for his own people, but *for all that are oppressed;* for even in common providence he is the patron of wronged innocency, and, one way or other, will plead the cause of those that are injured against their oppressors. It is his honour to humble the proud and help the helpless.

II. He is in a special manner good to Israel, to every Israelite indeed, that is of a clean and upright heart.

1. He has revealed himself and his grace to us (*v.* 7): *He made known his ways unto Moses,* and by him *his acts to the children of Israel,* not only by his rod to those who then lived, but by his pen to succeeding ages. Note, Divine revelation is one of the first and greatest of divine favours with which the church is blessed; for God restores us to himself by revealing himself to us, and gives us all good by giving us knowledge. He has *made known his acts and his ways* (that is, his nature, and the methods of his dealing with the children of men), that they may know both what to conceive of him and what to expect from him; so Dr. Hammond. Or by his *ways* we may understand his precepts, the way which he requires us to walk in; and by his *acts,* or *designs* (as the word signifies), his promises and purposes as to what he will do with us. Thus fairly does God deal with us.

2. He has never been rigorous and severe with us, but always tender, full of compassion, and ready to forgive.

(1.) It is in his nature to be so (*v.* 8): The *Lord is merciful and gracious;* this was his way which he made known unto Moses at Mount Horeb, when he thus proclaimed his name (Exod. xxxiv. 6,7), in answer to Moses's request (*ch.* xxxiii. 13), *I beseech thee, show me thy way, that I may know thee.* It is my way, says God, to pardon sin. [1.] He is not soon angry, *v.* 8. He is *slow to anger,* not extreme to mark what we do amiss nor ready to take advantage against us. He bears long with those that are very provoking, defers punishing, that he may give space to repent, and does not speedily execute the sentence of his law; and he could not be thus *slow to anger* if he were not *plenteous in mercy,* the very *Father of mercies.* [2.] He is not long angry; for (*v.* 9) *he will not always chide,* though we always offend and deserve chiding. Though he signify his displeasure against us for our sins by the rebukes of Providence, and the reproaches of our own consciences, and thus cause grief, yet he will have compassion, and will not always keep us in pain and terror, no, not for our sins, but, after the spirit of bondage, will give the spirit of adoption. How unlike are those to God who always chide, who take every occasion to chide, and never know when to cease! What would become of us if God should deal so with us? *He will not keep his anger for ever* against his own people, but will gather them with *everlasting mercies,* Isa. liv. 8; lvii. 16.

(2.) We have found him so; we, for our parts, must own that *he has not dealt with us after our sins, v.* 10. The scripture says a great deal of the mercy of God, and we may all set to our seal that it is true, that we have experienced it. If he had not been a God of patience, we should have been in hell long ago; but *he has not rewarded us after our iniquities;* so those will say who know what sin deserves. He has not inflicted the judgments which we have merited, nor deprived us of the comforts which we have forfeited, which should make us think the worse, and not the better, of sin; for *God's patience should lead us to repentance,* Rom. ii. 4.

3. He has pardoned our sins, not only my *iniquity* (*v.* 3), but *our transgressions, v.* 12. Though it is of our own benefit, by the pardoning mercy of God, that we are to take the comfort, yet of the benefit others have by it we must give him the glory. Observe, (1.) The transcendent riches of God's mercy (*v.* 11): *As the heaven is high above the earth* (so high that the earth is but a point to the vast expanse), so God's mercy is above the merits of those that fear him most, so much above and beyond them that there is no proportion at all between them; the greatest performances of man's duty cannot demand the least tokens of God's favour as a debt, and therefore all the seed of Jacob will join with him in owning themselves *less than the least of all God's mercies,* Gen. xxxii. 10. Observe, God's mercy is thus great *towards those that fear him,* not towards those that trifle with him. We must fear the Lord and his goodness. (2.) The fulness of his pardons, an evidence of the riches of his mercy (*v.* 12): *As far as the east is from the west* (which two quarters of the world are of greatest extent, because all known and inhabited, and therefore geographers that way reckon their longitudes) *so far has he removed our transgressions from us,* so that they shall never be laid to our charge, nor rise up in judgment against us. The sins of believers shall be remembered no more, shall not be mentioned unto them; they shall be sought for, and not found. If we thoroughly forsake them, God will thoroughly forgive them.

4. He has pitied our sorrows, *v.* 13, 14. Observe, (1.) Whom he pities—*those that*

fear him, that is, all good people, who in this world may become objects of pity on account of the grievances to which they are not only born, but born again. Or it may be understood of those who have not yet received *the spirit of adoption,* but are yet *trembling at his word;* those he *pities,* Jer. xxxi. 18, 20. (2.) How he pities—*as a father pities his children,* and does them good as there is occasion. God is a Father to those that fear him and owns them for his children, and he is tender of them as a father. The father pities his children that are weak in knowledge and instructs them, pities them when they are froward and bears with them, pities them when they are sick and comforts them (Isa. lxvi. 13), pities them when they have fallen and helps them up again, pities them when they have offended, and, upon their submission, forgives them, pities them when they are wronged and gives them redress; thus *the Lord pities those that fear him.* (3.) Why he pities—*for he knows our frame.* He has reason to know our frame, for he framed us; and, having himself made man of the dust, *he remembers that he is dust,* not only by constitution, but by sentence. *Dust thou art.* He considers the frailty of our bodies and the folly of our souls, how little we can do, and expects accordingly from us, how little we can bear, and lays accordingly upon us, in all which appears the tenderness of his compassion.

5. He has perpetuated his covenant-mercy and thereby provided relief for our frailty, *v.* 15—18. See here, (1.) How short man's life is and of what uncertain continuance. The lives even of great men and good men are so, and neither their greatness nor their goodness can alter the property of them: *As for man, his days are as grass,* which grows out of the earth, rises but a little way above it, and soon withers and returns to it again. See Isa. xl. 6, 7. Man, in his best estate, seems somewhat more than grass; he flourishes and looks gay; yet then he is but *like a flower of the field,* which, though distinguished a little from the grass, will wither with it. The flower of the garden is commonly more choice and valuable, and, though in its own nature withering, will last the longer for its being sheltered by the garden-wall and the gardener's care; but the flower of the field (to which life is here compared) is not only withering in itself, but exposed to the cold blasts, and liable to be cropped and trodden on by the beasts of the field. Man's life is not only wasting of itself, but its period may be anticipated by a thousand accidents. When the flower is in its perfection a blasting wind, unseen, unlooked for, *passes over it, and it is gone;* it hangs the head, drops the leaves, dwindles into the ground again, *and the place thereof,* which was proud of it, now *knows it no more.* Such a thing is man: God considers this, and pities him; let him consider it himself, and be humble, dead to

this world and thoughtful of another. (2.) How long and lasting God's mercy is to his people (*v.* 17, 18): it will continue longer than their lives, and will survive their present state. Observe, [1.] The description of those to whom this mercy belongs. They are such as fear God, such as are truly religious, from principle. *First,* They live a life of faith; for they *keep God's covenant;* having taken hold of it, they keep hold of it, fast hold, and will not let it go. They keep it as a treasure, keep it as their portion, and would not for all the world part with it, for it is their life. *Secondly,* They live a life of obedience; they *remember his commandments to do them,* else they do not *keep his covenant.* Those only shall have the benefit of God's promises that make conscience of his precepts. See who those are that have a good memory, as well as a *good understanding* (cxi. 10), those that *remember God's commandments,* not to talk of them, but *to do them,* and to be ruled by them. [2.] The continuance of the mercy which belongs to such as these; it will last them longer than their lives on earth, and therefore they need not be troubled though their lives be short, since death itself will be no abridgment, no infringement, of their bliss. God's mercy is better than life, for it will out-live it. *First,* To their souls, which are immortal; to them the mercy of the Lord is *from everlasting to everlasting;* from everlasting in the councils of it to everlasting in the consequences of it, in their election before the world was and their glorification when this world shall be no more; for they are predestinated to the *inheritance* (Eph. i. 11) and *look for the mercy of the Lord,* the Lord Jesus, unto eternal life. *Secondly,* To their seed, which shall be kept up to the end of time (cii. 28): *His righteousness,* the truth of his promise, shall be *unto children's children;* provided they tread in the steps of their predecessors' piety, and *keep his covenant,* as they did, then shall mercy be preserved to them, even to *a thousand generations.*

19 The Lord hath prepared his throne in the heavens; and his kingdom ruleth over all. 20 Bless the Lord, ye his angels, that excel in strength, that do his commandments, hearkening unto the voice of his word. 21 Bless ye the Lord, all *ye* his hosts; *ye* ministers of his, that do his pleasure. 22 Bless the Lord, all his works in all places of his dominion: bless the Lord, O my soul.

Here is, I. The doctrine of universal providence laid down, *v.* 19. He has secured the happiness of his peculiar people by promise and covenant, but the order of mankind, and the world in general, he secures by common providence. *The Lord has* a *throne of* his own, a throne of glory, a throne of government. He that made all rules all, and both by a word of power: *He has prepared his throne,* has fixed and established it that it cannot be shaken; he has afore-ordained all the measures of his government and does all according to the counsel of his own will. He *has prepared* it *in the heavens,* above us, and out of sight; for he *holds back the face of his throne, and spreads a cloud upon it* (Job xxvi. 9); yet he can himself *judge through the dark cloud,* Job xxii. 13. Hence *the heavens are said to rule* (Dan. iv. 26), and we are led to consider this by the influence which even the visible heavens have upon this earth, their *dominion,* Job xxxviii. 33; Gen. i. 16. But though God's throne is in heaven, and there he keeps his court, and thither we are to direct to him *(Our Father who art in heaven),* yet *his kingdom rules over all.* He takes cognizance of all the inhabitants, and all the affairs, of this lower world, and disposes all persons and things according to the counsel of his will, to his own glory (Dan. iv. 35): *His kingdom rules over all* kings and all kingdoms, and from it there is no exempt jurisdiction.

II. The duty of universal praise inferred from it: if all are under God's dominion, all must do him homage.

1. Let the holy angels praise him (*v.* 20, 21): *Bless the Lord, you his angels;* and again, *Bless the Lord, all you his hosts, you ministers of his.* David had been stirring up himself and others to praise God, and here, in the close, he calls upon the angels to do it; not as if they needed any excitement of ours to praise God, they do it continually; but thus he expresses his high thoughts of God as worthy of the adorations of the holy angels, thus he quickens himself and others to the duty with this consideration, That it is the work of angels, and comforts himself in reference to his own weakness and defect in the performance of this duty with this consideration, That there is a world of holy angels who dwell in God's house and are still praising him. In short, the blessed angels are glorious attendants upon the blessed God. Observe, (1.) How well qualified they are for the post they are in. They are able; for they *excel in strength;* they are *mighty in strength* (so the word is); they are able to bring great things to pass, and to abide in their work without weariness. And they are as willing as they are able; they are willing to know their work; for they *hearken to the voice of his word;* they stand expecting commission and instructions from their great Lord, and *always behold his face* (Matt. xviii 10), that they may take the first intimation of his mind. They are willing to do their work: They *do his commandments* (*v.* 20); they *do his pleasure* (*v.* 21); they dispute not any divine commands, but readily address themselves to the execution of them. Nor do

they delay, but fly swiftly: They *do his commandments at hearing,* or *as soon as they hear the voice of his word;* so Dr. Hammond. *To obey is better than sacrifice;* for angels obey, but do not sacrifice. (2.) What their service is. They are *his angels,* and *ministers of his*—his, for he made them, and made them for himself—his, for he employs them, though he does not need them—his, for he is their owner and Lord; they belong to him and he has them at his beck. All the creatures are his servants, but not as the angels that attend the presence of his glory. Soldiers, and seamen, and all good subjects, serve the king, but not as the courtiers do, the ministers of state and those of the household. [1.] The angels occasionally serve God in this lower world; they *do his commandments,* go on his errands (Dan. ix. 21), fight his battles (2 Kings vi. 17), and minister for the good of his people, Heb. i. 14. [2.] They *continually praise him* in the upper world; they began betimes to do it (Job xxxviii. 7), and it is still their business, from which they rest not *day nor night,* Rev. iv. 8. It is God's glory that he has such attendants, but more his glory that he neither needs them nor is benefited by them.

2. Let *all his works* praise him (*v.* 22), all *in all places of his dominion;* for, because they are his works, they are under his dominion, and they were made and are ruled that they may be unto him *for a name and a praise. All his works,* that is, all the children of men, in all parts of the world, let them all praise God; yea, and the inferior creatures too, which are God's works also; let them praise him objectively, though they cannot praise him actually, cxlv. 10. Yet all this shall not excuse David from praising God, but rather excite him to do it the more cheerfully, that he may bear a part in this concert; for he concludes, *Bless the Lord, O my soul!* as he began, *v.* 1. Blessing God and giving him glory must be the alpha and the omega of all our services. He began with *Bless the Lord, O my soul!* and, when he had penned and sung this excellent hymn to his honour, he does not say, Now, O my soul! thou hast blessed the Lord, sit down, and rest thee, but, *Bless the Lord, O my soul!* yet more and more. When we have done ever so much in the service of God, yet still we must stir up ourselves to do more. God's praise is a subject that will never be exhausted, and therefore we must never think this work done till we come to heaven, where it will be for ever in the doing.

PSALM CIV.

It is very probable that this psalm was penned by the same hand, and at the same time, as the former; for as that ended this begins, with "Bless the Lord, O my soul!" and concludes with it too. The style indeed is somewhat different, because the matter is so: the scope of the foregoing psalm was to celebrate the goodness of God and his tender mercy and compassion, to which a soft and sweet style was most agreeable; the scope of this is to celebrate his greatness, and majesty, and sovereign dominion, which ought to be done in the most stately lofty strains of poetry. David, in the former psalm, gave God the glory of his covenant-mercy and love to his own people; in this he gives him the glory of his works of creation and providence, his dominion over, and his bounty to, all the creatures. God is there praised as the God of grace, here as the God of nature. And this psalm is wholly bestowed on that subject; not as Ps. xix., which begins with it, but passes from it to the consideration of the divine law; nor as Ps. viii., which speaks of this but prophetically, and with an eye to Christ. This noble poem is thought by very competent judges greatly to excel, not only for piety and devotion (that is past dispute), but for flight of fancy, brightness of ideas, surprising turns, and all the beauties and ornaments of expression, the Greek and Latin poets upon any subject of this nature. Many great things the psalmist here gives God the glory of. I. The splendour of his majesty in the upper world, ver. 1—4. II. The creation of the sea and the dry land, ver. 5—9. III. The provision he makes for the maintenance of all the creatures according to their nature, ver. 10—18 and again ver. 27, 28. IV. The regular course of the sun and moon, ver. 19—24. V. The furniture of the sea, ver. 25, 26. VI. God's sovereign power over all the creatures, ver. 29—32. And, lastly, he concludes with a pleasant and firm resolution to continue praising God (ver. 23—35), with which we should heartily join in singing this psalm.

BLESS the LORD, O my soul. O LORD my God, thou art very great; thou art clothed with honour and majesty. 2 Who coverest *thyself* with light as *with* a garment: who stretchest out the heavens like a curtain: 3 Who layeth the beams of his chambers in the waters: who maketh the clouds his chariot: who walketh upon the wings of the wind: 4 Who maketh his angels spirits; his ministers a flaming fire: 5 *Who* laid the foundations of the earth, *that* it should not be removed for ever. 6 Thou coveredst it with the deep as *with* a garment: the waters stood above the mountains. 7 At thy rebuke they fled; at the voice of thy thunder they hasted away. 8 They go up by the mountains; they go down by the valleys unto the place which thou hast founded for them. 9 Thou hast set a bound that they may not pass over; that they turn not again to cover the earth.

When we are addressing ourselves to any religious service we must *stir up ourselves to take hold on God* in it (Isa. lxiv. 7); so David does here. "Come, my soul, where art thou? What art thou thinking of? Here is work to be done, good work, angels' work; set about it in good earnest; let all the powers and faculties be engaged and employed in it: *Bless the Lord, O my soul!*" In these verses,

I. The psalmist looks up to the divine glory shining in the upper world, of which, though it is one of the things not seen, faith is the evidence. With what reverence and holy awe does he begin his meditation with that acknowledgment: *O Lord my God! thou art very great!* It is the joy of the saints that he who is their God is a great God. The grandeur of the prince is the pride and pleasure of all his good subjects. The majesty of God is here set forth by various instances, alluding to the figure which great princes in their public appearances covet to make. Their equipage, compared with his (even of the eastern kings, who most affected pomp), is

but as the light of a glow-worm compared with that of the sun, when he goes forth in his strength. Princes appear great, 1. In their robes; and what are God's robes? *Thou art clothed with honour and majesty, v.* 1. God is seen in his works, and these proclaim him infinitely wise and good, and all that is great. Thou *coverest thyself with light as with a garment, v.* 2. God *is light* (1 John i. 5), the *Father of lights* (Jam. i. 17); he *dwells in light* (1 Tim. vi. 16); he clothes himself with it. The residence of his glory is in the highest heaven, that light which was created the first day, Gen. i. 3. Of all visible beings light comes nearest to the nature of a spirit, and therefore with that God is pleased to cover himself, that is, to reveal himself under that similitude, as men are seen in the clothes with which they cover themselves; and so only, for his face cannot be seen. 2. In their palaces or pavilions, when they take the field; and what is God's palace and his pavilion? He *stretches out the heavens like a curtain, v.* 2. So he did at first, when he made the firmament, which in the Hebrew has its name from its being expanded, or *stretched out,* Gen. i. 7. He made it to divide the waters as a curtain divides between two apartments. So he does still: he now *stretches out the heavens like a curtain,* keeps them upon the stretch, and they *continue to this day according to his ordinance.* The regions of the air are stretched out about the earth, like a curtain about a bed, to keep it warm, and drawn between us and the upper world, to break its dazzling light; for, though God *covers himself with light,* yet, in compassion to us, *he makes darkness his pavilion. Thick clouds are a covering to him.* The vastness of this pavilion may lead us to consider how great, how very great, he is that *fills heaven and earth.* He has his *chambers,* his *upper rooms* (so the word signifies), *the beams* whereof *he lays in the waters,* the waters that are above the firmament (*v.* 3), as he has *founded the earth upon the seas and floods,* the waters beneath the firmament. Though air and water are fluid bodies, yet, by the divine power, they are kept as tight and as firm in the place assigned them as a chamber is with beams and rafters. How great a God is he whose presence-chamber is thus reared, thus fixed! 3. In their coaches of state, with their stately horses, which add much to the magnificence of their entries; but God *makes the clouds his chariots,* in which he rides strongly, swiftly, and far above out of the reach of opposition, when at any time he will act by uncommon providences in the government of this world. He descended in a cloud, as in a chariot, to Mount Sinai, to give the law, and to Mount Tabor, to proclaim the gospel (Matt. xvii. 5), and he *walks* (a gentle pace indeed, yet stately) *upon the wings of the wind.* See xviii. 10, 11. He commands the winds, directs them as he pleases, and serves his own purposes by them. 4. In their retinue or train of attendants; and here also God is very great, for (v. 4) he *makes his angels spirits.* This is quoted by the apostle (Heb. i. 7) to prove the pre-eminence of Christ above the angels. The angels are here said to be *his angels* and *his ministers*, for they are under his dominion and at his disposal; they are *winds*, and *a flame of fire*, that is, they appeared in wind and fire (so some), or they are as swift as winds, and pure as flames; or he *makes them spirits*, so the apostle quotes it. They are spiritual beings; and, whatever vehicles they may have proper to their nature, it is certain they have not bodies as we have. Being spirits, they are so much the further removed from the incumbrances of the human nature and so much the nearer allied to the glories of the divine nature. And they are bright, and quick, and ascending, as fire, as *a flame of fire*. In Ezekiel's vision they ran and returned *like a flash of lightning*, Ezek. i. 14. Thence they are called *seraphim—burners*. Whatever they are, they are what God made them, what he still makes them; they derive their being from him, having the being he gave them, are held in being by him, and he makes what use he pleases of them.

II. He looks down, and looks about, to the power of God shining in this lower world. He is not so taken up with the glories of his court as to neglect even the remotest of his territories; no, not the sea and dry land.

1. He has founded the earth, *v.* 5. Though he has *hung it upon nothing* (Job xxvi. 2), *ponderibus librata suis—balanced by its own weight*, yet it is as immovable as if it had been laid upon the surest foundations. He has built the earth upon her basis, so that though it has received a dangerous shock by the sin of man, and the malice of hell strikes at it, yet *it shall not be removed for ever*, that is, not till the end of time, when it must give way to the new earth. Dr. Hammond's paraphrase of this is worth noting: " God has fixed so strange a place for the earth, that, being a heavy body, one would think it should fall every minute; and yet, which way soever we would imagine it to stir, it must, contrary to the nature of such a body, fall upwards, and so can have no possible ruin but by tumbling into heaven.''

2. He has set bounds to the sea; for that also is his. (1.) He brought it within bounds in the creation. At first the earth, which, being the more ponderous body, would subside of course, was *covered with the deep* (v. 6): *The waters were above the mountains;* and so it was unfit to be, as it was designed, a habitation for man; and therefore, on the third day, God said, *Let the waters under the heaven be gathered to one place, and let the dry land appear*, Gen. i. 9. This command of God is here called his *rebuke*, as if he gave it because he was displeased that the earth was thus covered with water and not fit for man to dwell on. Power went along with this

628

word, and therefore it is also called here *the voice of* his *thunder*, which is a mighty voice and produces strange effects, *v.* 7. *At thy rebuke*, as if they were made sensible that they were out of their place, *they fled; they hasted away* (they called, and not in vain, to the rocks and mountains to cover them), as it is said on another occasion (lxxvii. 16), *The waters saw thee, O God! the waters saw thee; they were afraid.* Even those fluid bodies received the impression of God's terror. But *was the Lord displeased against the rivers?* No; it was *for the salvation of his people*, Hab. iii. 8, 13. So here; God rebuked the waters for man's sake, to prepare room for him; for *men must not be made as the fishes of the sea* (Hab. i. 14); they must have air to breathe in. Immediately therefore, with all speed, the waters retired, *v.* 8. *They go over hill and dale* (as we say), *go up by the mountains* and *down by the valleys*; they will neither stop at the former nor lodge in the latter, but make the best of their way *to the place which thou hast founded for them*, and there they make their bed. Let the obsequiousness even of the unstable waters teach us obedience to the word and will of God; for shall man alone of all the creatures be obstinate? Let their retiring to and resting in the place assigned them teach us to acquiesce in the disposals of that wise providence which appoints us the bounds of our habitation. (2.) He keeps it within bounds, *v.* 9. The waters are forbidden to pass over the limits set them; they may not, and therefore they do not, *turn again to cover the earth*. Once they did, in Noah's flood, because God bade them, but never since, because he forbids them, having promised not to drown the world again. God himself glories in this instance of his power (Job xxxviii. 8, &c.) and uses it as an argument with us to fear him, Jer. v. 22. This, if duly considered, would keep the world in awe of the Lord and his goodness, That the waters of the sea would soon cover the earth if God did not restrain them.

10 He sendeth the springs into the valleys, *which* run among the hills. 11 They give drink to every beast of the field : the wild asses quench their thirst. 12 By them shall the fowls of the heaven have their habitation, *which* sing among the branches. 13 He watereth the hills from his chambers : the earth is satisfied with the fruit of thy works. 14 He causeth the grass to grow for the cattle, and herb for the service of man : that he may bring forth food out of the earth ; 15 And wine *that* maketh glad the heart of man, *and* oil to make *his* face to shine, and bread *which* strengtheneth man's heart. 16 The trees of the LORD are

full *of sap ;* the cedars of Lebanon, which he hath planted ; 17 Where the birds make their nests : *as for* the stork, the fir trees *are* her house. 18 The high hills *are* a refuge for the wild goats ; *and* the rocks for the conies.

Having given glory to God as the powerful protector of this earth, in saving it from being deluged, here he comes to acknowledge him as its bountiful benefactor, who provides conveniences for all the creatures.

I. He provides fresh water for their drink : *He sends the springs into the valleys, v.* 10. There is water enough indeed in the sea, that is, enough to drown us, but not one drop to refresh us, be we ever so thirsty—it is all so salt ; and therefore God has graciously provided water fit to drink. Naturalists dispute about the origin of fountains ; but, whatever are their second causes, here is their first cause ; it is God that *sends the springs into the* brooks, *which* walk by easy steps between *the hills,* and receive increase from the rain-water that descends from them. These *give drink,* not only to man, and those creatures that are immediately useful to him, but *to every beast of the field* (*v.* 11) ; for where God has given life he provides a livelihood and takes care of all the creatures. Even *the wild asses,* though untameable and therefore of no use to man, are welcome to *quench their thirst;* and we have no reason to grudge it them, for we are better provided for, though *born like the wild ass's colt.* We have reason to thank God for the plenty of fair water with which he has provided the habitable part of his earth, which otherwise would not be habitable. That ought to be reckoned a great mercy the want of which would be a great affliction ; and the more common it is the greater mercy it is. *Usus communis aquarum—water is common for all.*

II. He provides food convenient for them, both for man and beast : *The heavens drop fatness;* they *hear the earth, but God hears them,* Hos. ii. 21. *He waters the hills from his chambers* (*v.* 13), from those chambers spoken of (*v.* 3), *the beams of which he lays in the waters,* those store-chambers, the clouds that distil fruitful showers. The hills that are not watered by the rivers, as Egypt was by the Nile, are watered by the rain from heaven, which is called *the river of ·God* (lxv. 9), as Canaan was, Deut. xi. 11, 12. Thus *the earth is satisfied with the fruit of his works,* either with the rain it drinks in (the earth knows when it has enough ; it is a pity that any man should not) or with the products it brings forth. It is a satisfaction to the earth to bear the fruit of God's works for the benefit of man, for thus it answers the end of its creation. The *food* which God *brings forth out of the earth* (*v.* 14) is the *fruit of his works,* which *the earth is satisfied with.* Observe

how various and how valuable its products are.

1. For the cattle there is grass, and the beasts of prey, that live not on grass, feed on those that do ; for man there is herb, a better sort of grass (and a dinner of herbs and roots is not to be despised) ; nay, he is furnished with *wine, and oil, and bread, v.* 15. We may observe here, concerning our food, that which will help to make us both humble and thankful. (1.) To make us humble let us consider that we have a necessary dependence upon God for all the supports of this life (we live upon alms ; we are at his finding, for our own hands are not sufficient for us),— that our food comes all out of the earth, to remind us whence we ourselves were taken and whither we must return,—and that therefore we must not think to *live by bread alone,* for that will feed the body only, but must look into the word of God for the meat that endures to eternal life. Let us also consider that we are in this respect fellow-commoners with the beasts ; the same earth, the same spot of ground, that brings grass for the cattle, brings corn for man. (2.) To make us thankful let us consider, [1.] That God not only provides for us, but for our servants. The cattle that are of use to man are particularly taken care of ; grass is made to grow in great abundance for them, when *the young lions,* that are not for the service of man, often *lack and suffer hunger.* [2.] That our food is nigh us, and ready to us. Having our habitation on the earth, there we have our storehouse, and depend not on the *merchant-ships that bring food from afar,* Prov. xxxi. 14. [3.] That we have even from the products of the earth, not only for necessity, but for ornament and delight, so good a Master do we serve. *First,* Does nature call for something to support it, and repair its daily decays ? Here is *bread, which strengthens man's heart,* and is therefore called *the staff of life;* let none who have that complain of want. *Secondly,* Does nature go further, and covet something pleasant ? Here is *wine, that makes glad the heart,* refreshes the spirits, and exhilarates them, when it is soberly and moderately used, that we may not only go through our business, but go through it cheerfully. It is a pity that that should be abused to overcharge the heart, and unfit men for their duty, which was given to revive their heart and quicken them in their duty. *Thirdly,* Is nature yet more humoursome, and does it crave something for ornament too ? Here is that also out of the earth—*oil to make the face to shine,* that the countenance may not only be cheerful but beautiful, and we may be the more acceptable to one another.

2. Nay, the divine providence not only furnishes animals with their proper food, but vegetables also with theirs (*v.* 16) : *The trees of the Lord are full of sap,* not only men's trees, which they take care of and have an eye to, in their orchards, and parks, and other

enclosures, but God's trees, which grow in the wildernesses, and are taken care of only by his providence; they *are full of sap* and want no nourishment. Even *the cedars of Lebanon,* an open forest, though they are high and bulky, and require a great deal of sap to feed them, have enough from the earth; they **are** trees *which he has planted,* and which therefore he will protect and provide for. We may apply this to the trees of righteousness, which are the planting of the Lord, planted in his vineyard; these *are full of sap,* for what God plants he will water, and those that *are planted in the house of the Lord shall flourish in the courts of our God,* xcii. 13.

III. He takes care that they shall have suitable habitations to dwell in. To men God has given discretion to build for themselves and for the cattle that are serviceable to them; but there are some creatures which God more immediately provides a settlement for. 1. The birds. Some birds, by instinct, make their nests in the bushes near rivers (v. 12): *By the springs that run among the hills* some of the *fowls of heaven have their habitation, which sing among the branches.* They sing, according to their capacity, to the honour of their Creator and benefactor, and their singing may shame our silence. Our *heavenly Father feeds them* (Matt. vi. 26), and therefore they are easy and cheerful, and take no thought for the morrow. The birds being made to *fly above the earth* (as we find, Gen. i. 20), they *make their nests* on high, in the tops of trees (v. 17); it should seem as if nature had an eye to this in *planting the cedars of Lebanon,* that they might be receptacles for the birds. Those that fly heavenward shall not want resting-places. *The stork* is particularly mentioned; *the fir-trees,* which are very high, *are her house,* her castle. 2. The smaller sort of beasts (v. 18): *The wild goats,* having neither strength nor swiftness to secure themselves, are guided by instinct to *the high hills,* which are a refuge to them; and *the rabbits,* which are also helpless animals, find shelter in *the rocks,* where they can set the beasts of prey at defiance. Does God provide thus for the inferior creatures; and will he not himself be a refuge and dwelling-place to his own people?

19 He appointed the moon for seasons: the sun knoweth his going down. 20 Thou makest darkness, and it is night: wherein all the beasts of the forest do creep *forth.* 21 The young lions roar after their prey, and seek their meat from God. 22 The sun ariseth, they gather themselves together, and lay them down in their dens. 23 Man goeth forth unto his work and to his labour until the evening. 24 O LORD, how manifold are thy works! in wisdom hast thou made

them all: the earth is full of thy riches. 25 *So is* this great and wide sea, wherein *are* things creeping innumerable, both small and great beasts. 26 There go the ships: *there is* that leviathan, *whom* thou hast made to play therein. 27 These wait all upon thee; that thou mayest give *them* their meat in due season. 28 *That* thou givest them they gather: thou openest thine hand, they are filled with good. 29 Thou hidest thy face, they are troubled: thou takest away their breath, they die, and return to their dust. 30 Thou sendest forth thy spirit, they are created: and thou renewest the face of the earth.

We are here taught to praise and magnify God,

I. For the constant revolutions and succession of day and night, and the dominion of sun and moon over them. The heathen were so affected with the light and influence of the sun and moon, and their serviceableness to the earth, that they worshipped them as deities; and therefore the scripture takes all occasions to show that the gods they worshipped are the creatures and servants of the true God (v. 19): *He appointed the moon for seasons,* for the measuring of the months, the directing of the seasons for the business of the husbandman, and the governing of the tides. The full and change, the increase and decrease, of the moon, exactly observe the appointment of the Creator; so does the sun, for he keeps as punctually to the time and place of his going down as if he were an intellectual being and knew what he did. God herein consults the comfort of man. 1. The shadows of the evening befriend the repose of the night (v. 20): *Thou makest darkness and it is night,* which, though black, contributes to the beauty of nature, and is as a foil to the light of the day; and under the protection of the night *all the beasts of the forest creep forth* to feed, which they are afraid to do in the day, God having put the *fear* and *dread of man upon every beast of the earth* (Gen. ix. 2), which contributes as much to man's safety as to his honour. See how nearly allied those are to the disposition of the wild beasts who *wait for the twilight* (Job xxiv. 15) and have fellowship with the unfruitful works of darkness; and compare to this the danger of ignorance and melancholy, which are both as darkness to the soul; when, in either of those ways, *it is night,* then *all the beasts of the forest creep forth.* Satan's temptations then assault us and have advantage against us. Then the *young lions roar after their prey;* and, as naturalists tell us, their roaring terrifies the timorous beasts so that they have not strength nor spirit to escape from them, which otherwise they might do, and so they become an easy prey to them. They are said to *seek their meat from God*, because it is not prepared for them by the care and forecast of man, but more immediately by the providence of God. The roaring of the young lions, like the crying of the young ravens, is interpreted *asking their meat of God*. Does God put this construction upon the language of mere nature, even in venomous creatures? and shall he not much more interpret favourably the language of grace in his own people, though it be weak and broken, *groanings which cannot be uttered?* 2. The light of the morning befriends the business of the day (*v.* 22, 23): *The sun arises* (for, as he *knows his going down*, so, thanks be to God, he knows his rising again), and then the wild beasts betake themselves to their rest; even they have some society among them, for they *gather themselves together* and *lay down in their dens*, which is a great mercy to the children of men, that while they are abroad, as becomes honest travellers, between sun and sun, care is taken that they shall not be set upon by wild beasts, for they are then drawn out of the field, and the sluggard shall have no ground to excuse himself from the business of the day with this, That there is *a lion in the way*. Therefore then *man goes forth to his work and to his labour*. The beasts of prey creep forth with fear; man goes forth with boldness, as one that has dominion. The beasts creep forth to spoil and do mischief; man goes forth to work and do good. There is the work of every day, which is to be done in its day, which man must apply to every morning (for the lights are set up for us to work by, not to play by) and which he must stick to till evening; it will be time enough to rest when the night comes, in which *no man can work*.

II. For the replenishing of the ocean (*v.* 25, 26): As *the earth is full of God's riches*, well stocked with animals, and those well provided for, so that it is seldom that any creature dies merely for want of food, *so is this great and wide sea*, which seems a useless part of the globe, at least not to answer the room it takes up; yet God has appointed it its place and made it serviceable to man both for navigation *(there go the ships,* in which goods are conveyed, to countries vastly distant, speedily and much more cheaply than by land-carriage) and also to be his storehouse for fish. God made not the sea in vain, any more than the earth; he *made it to be inherited*, for *there are things swimming innumerable, both small and great animals*, which serve for man's dainty food. The whale is particularly mentioned in the history of the creation (Gen. i. 21) and is here called the *leviathan*, as Job xli. 1. He is made to *play in the sea;* he has nothing to do, as man has, who *goes forth to his work;* he has nothing to fear, as the beasts have, that lie down in their dens; and therefore he plays with

the waters. It is a pity that any of the children of men, who have nobler powers and were made for nobler purposes, should live as if they were sent into the world, like leviathan into the waters, to play therein, spending all their time in pastime. The leviathan is said to *play in the waters*, because he is so well armed against all assaults that he sets them at defiance and *laughs at the shaking of a spear*, Job xli. 29.

III. For the seasonable and plentiful provision which is made for all the creatures, *v.* 27, 28. 1. God is a bountiful benefactor to them: He *gives them their meat;* he *opens his hand and they are filled with good.* He supports the armies both of heaven and earth. Even the meanest creatures are not below his cognizance. He is open-handed in the gifts of his bounty, and is a great and good housekeeper that provides for so large a family. 2. They are patient expectants from him: They *all wait upon him.* They seek their food, according to the natural instinct God has put into them and in the proper season for it, and affect not any other food, or at any other time, than nature has ordained. They do their part for the obtaining of it: what God gives them *they gather*, and expect not that Providence should put it into their mouths; and what they gather *they* are satisfied with —*they are filled with good*. They desire no more than what God sees fit for them, which may shame our murmurings, and discontent, and dissatisfaction with our lot.

IV. For the absolute power and sovereign dominion which he has over all the creatures, by which every species is still continued, though the individuals of each are daily dying and dropping off. See here, 1. All the creatures perishing (*v.* 29): *Thou hidest thy face*, withdrawest thy supporting power, thy supplying bounty, and *they are troubled* immediately. Every creature has as necessary a dependence upon God's favours as every saint is sensible he has and therefore says with David (Ps. xxx. 7), *Thou didst hide thy face and I was troubled.* God's displeasure against this lower world for the sin of man is the cause of all the vanity and burden which the whole creation groans under. *Thou takest away their breath*, which is in thy hand, and then, and not till then, *they die and return to their dust*, to their first principles. The *spirit of the beast, which goes downward*, is at God's command, as well as *the spirit of a man, which goes upward.* The death of cattle was one of the plagues of Egypt, and is particularly taken notice of in the drowning of the world. 2. All preserved notwithstanding, in a succession (*v.* 30): *Thou sendest forth thy spirit, they are created.* The same spirit (that is, the same divine will and power) by which they were all created at first still preserves the several sorts of creatures in their being, and place, and usefulness; so that, though one generation of them passes away, another comes, and from time to time they are created;

new ones rise up instead of the old ones, and this is a continual creation. Thus the *face of the earth is renewed* from day to day by the light of the sun (which beautifies it anew every morning), from year to year by the products of it, which enrich it anew every spring and put quite another face upon it from what it had all winter. The world is as full of creatures as if none died, for the place of those that die is filled up. This (the Jews say) is to be applied to the resurrection, which every spring is an emblem of, when a new world rises out of the ashes of the old one.

In the midst of this discourse the psalmist breaks out into wonder at the works of God (*v.* 24): *O Lord! how manifold are thy works!* They are numerous, they are various, of many kinds, and many of every kind; and yet *in wisdom hast thou made them all.* When men undertake many works, and of different kinds, commonly some of them are neglected and not done with due care; but God's works, though many and of very different kinds, are all made in wisdom and with the greatest exactness; there is not the least flaw nor defect in them. The works of art, the more closely they are looked upon with the help of microscopes, the more rough they appear; the works of nature through these glasses appear more fine and exact. They are all made in wisdom, for they are all made to answer the end they were designed to serve, the good of the universe, in order to the glory of the universal Monarch.

31 The glory of the LORD shall endure for ever: the LORD shall rejoice in his works. 32 He looketh on the earth, and it trembleth: he toucheth the hills, and they smoke. 33 I will sing unto the LORD as long as I live: I will sing praise to my God while I have my being. 34 My meditation of him shall be sweet: I will be glad in the LORD. 35 Let the sinners be consumed out of the earth, and let the wicked be no more. Bless thou the LORD, O my soul. Praise ye the LORD.

The psalmist concludes this meditation with speaking,

I. Praise to God, which is chiefly intended in the psalm.

1. He is to be praised, (1.) As a great God, and a God of matchless perfection: *The glory of the Lord shall endure for ever, v.* 31. It shall endure to the end of time in his works of creation and providence; it shall endure to eternity in the felicity and adorations of saints and angels. Man's glory is fading; God's glory is everlasting. Creatures change, but with the Creator there is no variableness. (2.) As a gracious God: *The Lord shall rejoice in his works.* He continues that complacency in the products of his own wisdom

and goodness which he had when he *saw every thing that he had made, and behold it was very good,* and *rested the seventh day.* We often do that which, upon the review, we cannot rejoice in, but are displeased at, and wish undone again, blaming our own management. But God always *rejoices in his works,* because they are all done in wisdom. We regret our bounty and beneficence, but God never does; he rejoices in the works of his grace: his *gifts and callings* are *without repentance.* (3.) As a God of almighty power (*v.* 32): *He looks on the earth, and it trembles,* as unable to bear his frowns—trembles, as Sinai did, *at the presence of the Lord. He touches the hills, and they smoke.* The volcanoes, or burning mountains, such as Ætna, are emblems of the power of God's wrath fastening upon proud unhumbled sinners. If an angry look and a touch have such effects, what will the weight of his heavy hand do and the operations of his outstretched arm? *Who knows the power of his anger?* Who then dares set it at defiance? God rejoices in his works because they are all so observant of him; and he will in like manner *take pleasure in those that fear him and that tremble at his word.*

2. The psalmist will himself be much in praising him (*v.* 33): "*I will sing unto the Lord, unto my God,* will praise him as Jehovah, the Creator, and as *my God,* a God in covenant with me, and this not now only, but *as long as I live,* and *while I have my being.*" Because we have our being from God, and depend upon him for the support and continuance of it, as long as we live and have our being we must continue to praise God; and when we have no life, no being, on earth, we hope to have a better life and better being in a better world and there to be doing this work in a better manner and better company.

II. Joy to himself (*v.* 34): *My meditation of him shall be sweet;* it shall be fixed and close; it shall be affecting and influencing; and therefore it shall be sweet. Thoughts of God will *then* be most pleasing, when they are most powerful. Note, Divine meditation is a very sweet duty to all that are sanctified: "*I will be glad in the Lord;* it shall be a pleasure to me to praise him; I will be glad of all opportunities to set forth his glory; and I will *rejoice in the Lord always* and in him only." All my joys shall centre in him, and in them they shall be full.

III. Terror to the wicked (*v.* 35): *Let the sinners be consumed out of the earth; and let the wicked be no more.* 1. Those that oppose the God of power, and fight against him, will certainly be consumed; none can prosper that harden themselves against the Almighty. 2. Those that rebel against the light of such convincing evidence of God's being, and refuse to serve him whom all the creatures serve, will justly be consumed. Those that make that earth to groan under the burden of their impieties which God thus fills with his riches deserve to be consumed out of it, and that it should spue them out. 3. Those that heartily desire to praise God themselves cannot but have a holy indignation at those that blaspheme and dishonour him, and a holy satisfaction in the prospect of their destruction and the honour that God will get to himself upon them. Even this ought to be the matter of their praise: "While *sinners* are *consumed out of the earth*, let *my soul bless the Lord* that I am not cast away with the workers of iniquity, but distinguished from them by the special grace of God. When *the wicked* are *no more* I hope to be praising God world without end; and therefore, *Praise you the Lord;* let all about me join with me in praising God. *Hallelujah;* sing praise to Jehovah." This is the first time that we meet with *Hallelujah;* and it comes in here upon occasion of the destruction of the wicked; and the last time we meet with it is upon a similar occasion. When the New-Testament Babylon is consumed, this is the burden of the song, *Hallelujah*, Rev. xix. 1, 3, 4, 6.

PSALM CV.

Some of the psalms of praise are very short, others very long, to teach us that, in our devotions, we should be more observant how our hearts work than how the time passes and neither over-stretch ourselves by coveting to be long nor over-stint ourselves by coveting to be short, but either the one or the other as we find in our hearts to pray. This is a long psalm; the general scope is the same with most of the psalms, to set forth the glory of God, but the subject-matter is particular. Every time we come to the throne of grace we may, if we please, furnish ourselves out of the word of God (out of the history of the New Testament, as this out of the history of the Old) with new songs, with fresh thoughts—so copious, so various, so inexhaustible is the subject. In the foregoing psalm we are taught to praise God for his wondrous works of common providence with reference to the world in general. In this we are directed to praise him for his special favours to his church. We find the first eleven verses of this psalm in the beginning of that psalm which David delivered to Asaph to be used (as it should seem) in the daily service of the sanctuary when the ark was fixed in the place he had prepared for it, by which it appears both who penned it and when and upon what occasion it was penned, 1 Chron. xvi. 7, &c. David by it designed to instruct his people in the obligations they lay under to adhere faithfully to their holy religion. Here is the preface (ver. 1–7) and the history itself in several articles. I. God's covenant with the patriarchs, ver. 8–11. II. His care of them while they were strangers, ver. 12–15. III. His raising up Joseph to be the shepherd and stone of Israel, ver. 16–22. IV. The increase of Israel in Egypt and their deliverance out of Egypt, ver. 23–38. V. The care he took of them in the wilderness and their settlement in Canaan, ver. 39—45. In singing this we must give to God the glory of his wisdom and power, his goodness and faithfulness, must look upon ourselves as concerned in the affairs of the Old-Testament church, both because to it were committed the oracles of God, which are our treasure, and because out of it Christ arose, and these things happened to it for ensamples.

O GIVE thanks unto the LORD; call upon his name: make known his deeds among the people. 2 Sing unto him, sing psalms unto him: talk ye of all his wondrous works. 3 Glory ye in his holy name: let the heart of them rejoice that seek the LORD. 4 Seek the LORD, and his strength: seek his face evermore. 5 Remember his marvellous works that he hath done; his wonders, and the judgments of his mouth; 6 O ye seed of Abraham his servant, ye children of Jacob his chosen. 7 He *is* the LORD our God: his judgments *are* in all the earth.

Our devotion is here warmly excited; and we are stirred up, that we may stir up ourselves to praise God. Observe,

I. The duties to which we are here called, and they are many, but the tendency of them all is to give unto God the glory due unto his name. 1. We must *give thanks to him*, as one who has always been our bountiful benefactor and requires only that we give him thanks for his favours—poor returns for rich receivings. 2. *Call upon his name*, as one whom you depend upon for further favours. Praying for further mercies is accepted as an acknowledgment of former mercies. *Because he has inclined his ear unto me, therefore will I call upon him.* 3. *Make known his deeds* (v. 1), that others may join with you in praising him. *Talk of all his wondrous works* (v. 2), as we talk of things that we are full of, and much affected with, and desire to fill others with. God's wondrous works ought to be the subject of our familiar discourses with our families and friends, and we should talk of them *as we sit in the house and as we go by the way* (Deut. vi. 7), not merely for entertainment, but for the exciting of devotion and the encouraging of our own and others' faith and hope in God. Even sacred things may be the matter of common talk, provided it be with due reverence. 4. *Sing psalms* to God's honour, as those that rejoice in him, and desire to testify that joy for the encouragement of others and to transmit it to posterity, as memorable things anciently were handed down by songs, when writing was scarce. 5. *Glory in his holy name;* let those that are disposed to glory not boast of their own accomplishments and achievements, but of their acquaintance with God and their relation to him, Jer. ix. 23, 24. *Praise you his holy name,* so some; but it comes all to one, for in glorying in him we give glory to him. 6. *Seek him;* place your happiness in him, and then pursue that happiness in all the ways that he has appointed. *Seek the Lord and his strength,* that is, the *ark of his strength;* seek him in the sanctuary, in the way wherein he has appointed us to seek him. *Seek his strength,* that is, his grace, the strength of his Spirit to work in you that which is good, which we cannot do but by strength derived from him, for which he will be enquired of. *Seek the Lord and be strengthened;* so divers ancient versions read it. Those that would be *strengthened in the inward man* must fetch in strength from God by faith and prayer. Seek *his strength,* and then *seek his face;* for by his strength we hope to prevail with him for his favour, as Jacob did, Hos. xii. 3. " *Seek his face evermore;* seek to have his favour to eternity, and therefore continue seeking it to the end of the time of your probation. Seek it while you live in this world, and you shall have it while you live in the other world, and even there shall be for ever seeking it in an infinite progression, and yet be for ever satisfied in it." 7. *Let the hearts of those rejoice that do seek him* (*v.* 3); for they have chosen well, are well fixed, and well employed, and they may be sure that their labour will not be in vain, for he will not only be found, but he will be found the *rewarder of those that diligently seek him.* If those have reason to rejoice that *seek the Lord,* much more those that have *found him.*

II. Some arguments to quicken us to these duties. 1. " Consider both what he has said and what he has done to engage us for ever to him. You will see yourselves under all possible obligations to give thanks to him, and call upon his name, if you remember the wonders which should make deep and durable impressions upon you,—the wonders of his providence which he has *wrought for you* and those who are gone before you, the *marvellous works that he has done,* which will be had in everlasting remembrance with the thoughtful and with the grateful,—the wonders of his law, which he has written to you, and entrusted you with, *the judgments of his mouth,* as well as the judgments of his hand," *v.* 5. 2. " Consider the relation you stand in to him (*v.* 6): *You are the seed of Abraham his servant ;* you are born in his house, and being thereby entitled to the privilege of his servants, protection and provision, you are also bound to do the duty of servants, to attend your Master, consult his honour, obey his commands, and do what you can to advance his interests. You are *the children of Jacob his chosen,* and are *chosen* and *beloved* for the fathers' sake, and therefore ought to tread in the steps of those whose honours you inherit. You are the children of godly parents ; do not degenerate. You are God's church upon earth, and, if you do not praise him, who should ?" 3. Consider your interest in him : *He is the Lord our God, v.* 7. We depend upon him, are devoted to him, and from him our expectation is. *Should not a people seek unto their God* (Isa. viii. 19) and praise their God ? Dan. v. 4. He is *Jehovah our God.* He that is our God is self-existent and self-sufficient, has an irresistible power and incontestable sovereignty : *His judgments are in all the earth ;* he governs the whole world in wisdom, and gives law to all nations, even to those that know him not. The earth is full of the proofs of his power.

8 He hath remembered his covenant for ever, the word *which* he commanded to a thousand generations. 9 Which *covenant* he made with Abraham, and his oath unto Isaac ; 10 And confirmed the same unto Jacob for a law, *and* to Israel *for* an everlasting covenant : 11 Saying, Unto thee will I give the land of Canaan, the lot of your inheritance : 12 When there were *but* a few men in number : yea, very few, and strangers in it. 13 When

they went from one nation to another, from *one* kingdom to another people ; 14 He suffered no man to do them wrong : yea, he reproved kings for their sakes ; 15 *Saying,* Touch not mine anointed, and do my prophets no harm. 16 Moreover he called for a famine upon the land : he brake the whole staff of bread. 17 He sent a man before them, *even* Joseph, *who* was sold for a servant : 18 Whose feet they hurt with fetters : he was laid in iron ; 19 Until the time that his word came : the word of the LORD tried him. 20 The king sent and loosed him, *even* the ruler of the people, and let him go free. 21 He made him lord of his house, and ruler of all his substance : 22 To bind his princes at his pleasure ; and teach his senators wisdom. 23 Israel also came into Egypt ; and Jacob sojourned in the land of Ham. 24 And he increased his people greatly ; and made them stronger than their enemies.

We are here taught, in praising God, to look a great way back, and to give him the glory of what he did for his church in former ages, especially when it was in the founding and forming, which those in its latter ages enjoy the benefit of and therefore should give thanks for. Doubtless we may fetch as proper matter for praise from the histories of the gospels, and the acts of the apostles, which relate the birth of the Christian church, as the psalmist here does from the histories of Genesis and Exodus, which relate the birth of the Jewish church ; and our histories greatly outshine theirs. Two things are here made the subject of praise :—

I. God's promise to the patriarchs, that great promise that he would give to their seed the land of Canaan for an inheritance, which was a type of the promise of eternal life made in Christ to all believers. In all the marvellous works which God did for Israel *he remembered his covenant* (*v.* 8) and he will remember it *for ever ;* it is *the word which he commanded to a thousand generations.* See here the power of the promise ; it is the word which he commanded and which will take effect. See the perpetuity of the promise ; it is commanded *to a thousand generations,* and the entail of it shall not be cut off. In the parallel place it is expressed as our duty (1 Chron. xvi. 15), *Be you mindful always of his covenant.* God will not forget it and therefore we must not. The promise is here called a *covenant,* because there was something required on man's part as the condition of the promise. Observe, 1. The persons with whom this covenant was made—with Abraham, Isaac, and Jacob, grandfather, father, and son, all eminent believers, Heb. xi. 8, 9. 2. The ratifications of the covenant; it was made sure by all that is sacred. Is that sure which is sworn to? It is his oath to Isaac and to Abraham. See to whom God *swore by himself*, Heb. vi. 13, 14. Is that sure which has passed *into a law?* He *confirmed the same for a law*, a law never to be repealed. Is that sure which is reduced to a mutual contract and stipulation? This is confirmed *for an everlasting covenant*, inviolable. 3. The covenant itself: *Unto thee will I give the land of Canaan, v.* 11. The patriarchs had a right to it, not by providence, but by promise; and their seed should be put in possession of it, not by the common ways of settling nations, but by miracles; God will give it to them himself, as it were with his own hand; it shall be given to them as their lot which God assigns them and measures out to them, as *the lot of their inheritance*, a sure title, by virtue of their birth; it shall come to them by descent, not by purchase, by the favour of God, and not any merit of their own. Heaven is the inheritance we have obtained, Eph. i. 11. And *this is the promise which God has promised us* (as Canaan was the promise he promised them), *even eternal life*, 1 John ii. 25; Tit. i. 2.

II. His providences concerning the patriarchs while they were waiting for the accomplishment of this promise, which represent to us the care God takes of his people in this world, while they are yet on this side the heavenly Canaan; for these things *happened unto them for examples* and encouragements to all the heirs of promise, that live by faith as they did.

1. They were wonderfully protected and sheltered, and (as the Jewish masters express it) *gathered under the wings of the divine Majesty*. This is accounted for, *v.* 12—15. Here we may observe,

(1.) How they were exposed to injuries from men. To the three renowned patriarchs, Abraham, and Isaac, and Jacob, God's promises were very rich; again and again he told them he would be their God; but his performances in this world were so little proportionable that, if he had not *prepared for them a city* in the other world, he would have been *ashamed to be called their God* (see Heb. xi. 16), because he was always generous; and yet even in this world he was not wanting to them, but that he might appear, to do uncommon things for them, he exercised them with uncommon trials. [1.] They were few, very few. Abraham was called alone (Isa. li. 2); he had but two sons, and one of them he cast out; Isaac had but two, and one of them was forced for many years to flee from his country; Jacob had more, but some of them, instead of being a defence to him, exposed him, when (as he himself pleads, Gen.

xxxiv. 30) he was but few in number, and therefore might easily be destroyed by the natives, he and his house. God's chosen are but a little flock, few, very few, and yet upheld. [2.] They were strangers, and therefore were the most likely to be abused and to meet with strange usage, and the less able to help themselves. Their religion made them to be looked upon as strangers (1 Pet. iv. 4) and to be hooted at as *speckled birds*, Jer. xii. 9. Though the whole land was theirs by promise, yet they were so far from producing and pleading their grant that they *confessed themselves strangers in it*, Heb. xi. 13. [3.] They were unsettled (v. 13): *They went from one nation to another*, from one part of that land to another (for it was then in the holding and occupation of divers nations, Gen. xii. 8; xiii. 3, 18); nay, *from one kingdom to another people*, from Canaan to Egypt, from Egypt to the land of the Philistines, which could not but weaken and expose them; yet they were forced to it by famine. Note, Though frequent removals are neither desirable nor commendable, yet sometimes there is a just and necessary occasion for them, and they may be the lot of some of the best men.

(2.) How they were guarded by the special providence of God, the wisdom and power of which were the more magnified by their being so many ways exposed, *v.* 14, 15. They were not able to help themselves and yet, [1.] No men were suffered to wrong them, but even those that hated them, and would gladly have done them a mischief, had their hands tied, and could not do what they would. This may refer to Gen. xxxv. 5, where we find that *the terror of God* (an unaccountable restraint) *was upon the cities that were round about them*, so that, though provoked, *they did not pursue after the sons of Jacob.* [2.] Even crowned heads, that did offer to wrong them, were not only checked and chidden for it, but controlled and baffled· *He reproved kings for their sakes* in dreams and visions, saying, "*Touch not my anointed;* it is at your peril if you do, nay, it shall not be in your power to do it; *do my prophets no harm.*" Pharaoh king of Egypt was plagued (Gen. xii. 17) and Abimelech king of Gerar was sharply rebuked (Gen. xx. 6) for doing wrong to Abraham. Note, *First*, Even kings themselves are liable to God's rebukes if they do wrong. *Secondly*, God's prophets are his anointed, for they have the unction *of the Spirit*, that *oil of gladness*, 1 John ii. 27. *Thirdly*, Those that offer to touch God's prophets, with design to harm them, may expect to hear of it one way or other. God is jealous for his prophets; whoso *touches the apple of his eye. Fourthly*, Even those that *touch the prophets*, nay, that *kill the prophets* (as many did), cannot *do them any harm*, any real harm. *Lastly*, God's anointed prophets are dearer to him than anointed kings themselves. Jeroboam's hand was withered when it was stretched out against a prophet.

2. They were wonderfully provided for and supplied. And here also, (1.) They were reduced to great extremity. Even in Canaan, the land of promise, *he called for a famine, v.* 16. Note, All judgments are at God's call, and no place is exempt from their visitation and jurisdiction when God sends them forth with commission. To try the faith of the patriarchs, God *broke the whole staff of bread,* even in that good land, that they might plainly see God designed them a better country than that was. (2.) God graciously took care for their relief. It was in obedience to his precept, and in dependence upon his promise, that they were now sojourners in Canaan, and therefore he could not in honour suffer any evil to befal them or any good thing to be wanting to them. As he restrained one Pharaoh from doing them wrong, so he raised up another to do them a kindness, by preferring and entrusting Joseph, of whose story we have here an abstract. He was to be the shepherd and stone of Israel and to save that holy *seed alive,* Gen. xlix. 24; l. 20. In order to this, [1.] He was humbled, greatly humbled (*v.* 17, 18): *God sent a man before them, even Joseph.* Many years before the famine began, he was sent before them, to nourish them in the famine; so vast are the foresights and forecasts of Providence, and so long its reaches. But in what character did *he* go to Egypt who was to provide for the reception of the church there? He went not in quality of an ambassador, no, nor so much as a factor or commissary; but *he was sold* thither *for a servant,* a slave for term of life, without any prospect of being ever set at liberty. This was low enough, and, one would think, set him far enough from any probability of being great. And yet he was brought lower; he was made a prisoner (*v.* 18): *His feet they hurt with fetters.* Being unjustly charged with a crime no less heinous than a rape upon his mistress, *the iron entered into his soul,* that is, was very painful to him; and the false accusation which was the cause of his imprisonment did in a special manner grieve him, and went to his heart; yet all this was the way to his preferment. [2.] He was exalted, highly exalted. He continued a prisoner, neither tried nor bailed, *until the time* appointed of God for his release (*v.* 19), when *his word came,* that is, his interpretations of dreams came to pass, and the report thereof came to Pharaoh's ears by the chief butler. And then *the word of the Lord cleared him;* that is, the power God gave him to foretel things to come rolled away the reproach his mistress had loaded him with; for it could not be thought that God would give such a power to so bad a man as he was represented to be. *God's word tried him,* tried his faith and patience, and then it came in power to give command for his release. There is a time

set when God's word will come for the comfort of all that trust in it, Hab. ii. 3. *At the end it shall speak, and not lie.* God gave the word, and then *the king sent and loosed him;* for the king's heart is in the hand of the Lord. Pharaoh, finding him to be a favourite of Heaven, *First,* Discharged him from his imprisonment (*v.* 20): He *let him go free.* God has often, by wonderful turns of providence, pleaded the cause of oppressed innocency. *Secondly,* He advanced him to the highest posts of honour, *v.* 21, 22. He made him lord high chamberlain of his household (*he made him lord of his house);* nay, he put him into the office of lord-treasurer, *the ruler of all his substance.* He made him prime-minister of state, lord-president of his council, to *command his princes at his pleasure* and *teach them wisdom,* and general of his forces. *According to thy word shall all my people be ruled,* Gen. xli. 40, 43, 44. He made him lord chief justice, to judge even his senators and punish those that were disobedient. In all this Joseph was designed to be, 1. A father to the church that then was, to save the house of Israel from perishing by the famine. He was made great, that he might *do good, especially* in *the household of faith.* 2. A figure of Christ, that was to come, who, because he humbled himself and took upon him the form of a servant, was highly exalted, and has all judgment committed to him. Joseph being thus sent before, and put into a capacity of maintaining all his father's house, *Israel also came into Egypt* (*v.* 23), where he and all his were very honourably and comfortably provided for many years. Thus the New-Testament church has a place provided for her even in the wilderness, where *she is nourished for a time, times, and half a time,* Rev. xii. 14. Verily she shall be fed.

3. They were wonderfully multiplied, according to the promise made to Abraham that his seed should be as the sand of the sea for multitude, *v.* 24. In Egypt he *increased his people greatly;* they multiplied like fishes, so that in a little time they became *stronger than their enemies* and formidable to them. Pharaoh took notice of it. Exod. i. 9, *The children of Israel are more and mightier than we.* When God pleases *a little one shall become a thousand;* and God's promises, though they work slowly, work surely.

25 He turned their heart to hate his people, to deal subtilly with his servants. 26 He sent Moses his servant; *and* Aaron whom he had chosen 27 They showed his signs among them, and wonders in the land of Ham. 28 He sent darkness, and made it dark; and they rebelled not against his word. 29 He turned their water

into blood, and slew their fish. 30 Their land brought forth frogs in abundance, in the chambers of their kings. 31 He spake, and there came divers sorts of flies, *and* lice in all their coasts. 32 He gave them hail for rain, *and* flaming fire in their land. 33 He smote their vines also and their fig trees; and brake the trees of their coasts. 34 He spake, and the locusts came, and caterpillars, and that without number, 35 And did eat up all the herbs in their land, and devoured the fruit of their ground. 36 He smote also all the firstborn in their land, the chief of all their strength. 37 He brought them forth also with silver and gold: and *there was* not one feeble *person* among their tribes. 38 Egypt was glad when they departed: for the fear of them fell upon them. 39 He spread a cloud for a covering; and fire to give light in the night. 40 *The people* asked, and he brought quails, and satisfied them with the bread of heaven. 41 He opened the rock, and the waters gushed out; they ran in the dry places *like* a river. 42 For he remembered his holy promise, *and* Abraham his servant. 43 And he brought forth his people with joy, *and* his chosen with gladness: 44 And gave them the lands of the heathen: and they inherited the labour of the people; 45 That they might observe his statutes, and keep his laws. Praise ye the LORD.

After the history of the patriarchs follows here the history of the people of Israel, when they grew into a nation.

I. Their affliction in Egypt (*v.* 25): *He turned* the *heart* of the Egyptians, who had protected them, *to hate* them and *deal subtilely* with them. God's goodness to his people exasperated the Egyptians against them; and, though their old antipathy to the Hebrews (which we read of Gen. xliii. 32; xlvi. 34) was laid asleep for a while, yet now it revived with more violence than ever: formerly they hated them because they despised them, now because they feared them. They *dealt subtilely* with them, set all their politics on work to find out ways and means to weaken them, and waste them, and prevent their growth; they made their burdens heavy and their lives bitter, and slew their male children as soon as they were born. Malice is

crafty to destroy: Satan has the serpent's subtlety, with his venom. It was God that turned the hearts of the Egyptians against them; for every creature is that to us that he makes it to be, a friend or an enemy. Though God is not the author of the sins of men, yet he serves his own purposes by them.

II. Their deliverance out of Egypt, that work of wonder, which, that it might never be forgotten, is put into the preface to the ten commandments. Observe,

1. The instruments employed in that deliverance (*v.* 26): *He sent Moses his servant* on this errand and joined Aaron in commission with him. Moses was designed to be their lawgiver and chief magistrate, Aaron to be their chief priest; and therefore, that they might respect them the more and submit to them the more cheerfully, God made use of them as their deliverers.

2. The means of accomplishing that deliverance; these were the plagues of Egypt. Moses and Aaron observed their orders, in summoning them just as God appointed them, and *they rebelled not against his word* (*v.* 28) as Jonah did, who, when he was sent to denounce God's judgments against Nineveh, went to Tarshish. Moses and Aaron were not moved, either with a foolish fear of Pharaoh's wrath or a foolish pity of Egypt's misery, to relax or retard any of the plagues which God ordered them to inflict on the Egyptians, but stretched forth their hand to inflict them as God appointed. Those that are instructed to execute judgment will find their remissness construed as a rebellion against God's word. The plagues of Egypt are here called God's *signs, and his wonders* (*v.* 27); they were not only proofs of his power, but tokens of his wrath, and to be looked upon with admiration and holy awe. *They showed the words of his signs* (so it is in the original), for every plague had an exposition going along with it; they were not, as the common works of creation and providence, silent signs, but speaking ones, and they spoke aloud. They are all or most of them here specified, though not in the order in which they were inflicted. (1.) The plague of darkness, *v.* 28. This was one of the last, though here mentioned first. God sent *darkness*, and, coming with commission, it came with efficacy; his command *made it dark.* And then *they* (that is, the people of Israel) *rebelled not against God's word*, namely, a command which some think was given them to circumcise all among them that had not been circumcised, in doing which the three days' darkness would be a protection to them. The old translation follows the LXX., and reads it, *They were not obedient to his word*, which may be applied to Pharaoh and the Egyptians, who, notwithstanding the terror of this plague, *would not let the people go;* but there is no ground for it in the Hebrew. (2.) The turning of the river Nilus (which

they idolized) *into blood,* and all their other waters, which *slew their fish* (v. 29), and so they were deprived, not only of their drink, but of the daintiest of their meat, Num. xi. 5. (3.) The frogs, shoals of which their land brought forth, which poured in upon them, not only in such numbers, but with such fury, that they could not keep them out of the *chambers of their kings* and great men, whose hearts had been full of vermin, more nauseous and more noxious—contempt of, and enmity to, both God and his Israel. (4.) Flies of divers sorts swarmed in their air, and lice in their clothes, v. 31; Exod. viii. 17, 24. Note, God can make use of the meanest, and weakest, and most despicable animals, for the punishing and humbling of proud oppressors, to whom the impotency of the instrument cannot but be a great mortification, as well as an undeniable conviction of the divine omnipotence. (5.) Hail-stones shattered their trees, even the strongest timber-trees in *their coasts,* and killed their vines, and their other fruit-trees, v. 32, 33. Instead of rain to cherish their trees, he gave them hail to crush them, and with it thunder and lightning, to such a degree that the *fire ran along upon the ground,* as if it had been a stream of kindled brimstone, Exod. ix. 23. (6.) *Locusts and caterpillars* destroyed *all the* herbs which were made for the service of man and ate the bread out of their mouths, v. 34, 35. See what variety of judgments God has, wherewith to plague proud oppressors, that will not let his people go. God did not bring the same plague twice, but, when there was occasion for another, it was still a new one; for he has many arrows in his quiver. Locusts and caterpillars are God's armies; and, how weak soever they are singly, he can raise such numbers of them as to make them formidable, Joel, i. 4, 6. (7.) Having mentioned all the plagues but those of the murrain and boils, he concludes with that which gave the conquering stroke, and that was the death of *the first-born, v.* 36. In the dead of the night the joys and hopes of their families, *the chief of their strength* and flower of their land, were all struck dead by the destroying angel. They would not release God's first-born, and therefore God seized theirs by way of reprisal, and thereby forced them to dismiss his too, when it was too late to retrieve their own; for *when God judges he will overcome,* and those will certainly sit down losers at last that contend with him.

3. The mercies that accompanied this deliverance. In their bondage, (1.) They had been impoverished, and yet they came out rich and wealthy. God not only brought them forth, but he *brought them forth with silver and gold, v.* 37. God empowered them to ask and collect the contributions of their neighbours (which were indeed but part of payment for the service they had done them) and inclined the Egyptians to furnish them with what they asked. Their wealth was his,

638

and therefore he might, their hearts were in his hand, and therefore he could, give it to the Israelites. (2.) Their lives had been made bitter to them, and their bodies and spirits broken by their bondage; and yet, when God brought them forth, *there was not one feeble person,* none sick, none so much as sickly, *among their tribes.* They went out that very night that the plague swept away all the first-born of Egypt, and yet they went out all in good health, and brought not with them any of the diseases of Egypt. Surely never was the like, that among so many thousands there was not one sick! So false was the representation which the enemies of the Jews, in after-ages, gave of this matter, that they were all sick of a leprosy, or some loathsome disease, and that therefore the Egyptians thrust them out of their land. (3.) They had been trampled upon and insulted over; and yet they were brought out with honour (v. 38): *Egypt was glad when they departed;* for God had so wonderfully owned them, and pleaded their cause, that *the fear of Israel fell upon them,* and they owned themselves baffled and overcome. God can and will make his church *a burdensome stone* to all that *heave at it* and seek to displace it, so that those shall think themselves happy that get out of its way, Zech. xii. 3. *When God judges, he will overcome.* (4.) They had spent their days in sorrow and in sighing, by reason of their bondage; but now he brought them forth *with joy and gladness, v.* 43. When Egypt's cry for grief was loud, their first-born being all slain, Israel's shouts for joy were as loud, both when they looked back upon the land of slavery out of which they were rescued and when they looked forward to the pleasant land to which they were hastening. God now put a new song into their mouth.

4. The special care God took of them in the wilderness. (1.) For their shelter. Besides the canopy of heaven, he provided them another heavenly canopy: He *spread a cloud for a covering* (v. 39), which was to them not only a screen and umbrella, but a cloth of state. A cloud was often God's pavilion (xviii. 11) and now it was Israel's; for they also were his hidden ones. (2.) For their guidance and refreshment in the dark. He appointed a pillar of *fire to give light in the night,* that they might never be at a loss. Note, God graciously provides against all the grievances of his people, and furnishes them with convenient succours for every condition, for day and night, till they come to heaven, where it will be all day to eternity. (3.) He fed them both with necessaries and dainties. Sometimes he furnished their tables with wild fowl (v. 40): *The people asked, and he brought quails;* and, when they were not thus feasted, yet they were abundantly satisfied *with the bread of heaven.* Those are curious and covetous indeed who will not be so satisfied. Man did eat angels' food, and

that constantly and on free-cost. And, as every bit they ate had miracle in it, so had every drop they drank: *He opened the rock, and the waters gushed out,* v. 41. Common providence fetches waters from heaven, and bread out of the earth; but for Israel the divine power brings bread from the clouds and water from the rocks: so far is the God of nature from being tied to the laws and courses of nature. The water did not only gush out once, but it ran *like a river,* plentifully and constantly, and attended their camp in all their removes; hence they are said to have the *rock follow them* (1 Cor. x. 4), and, which increased the miracle, this *river of God* (so it might be truly called) *ran in dry places,* and yet was not drunk in and lost, as one would have expected it to be, by the sands of the desert of Arabia. To this that promise alludes, *I will give rivers in the desert, to give drink to my chosen,* Isa. xliii. 19, 20.

5. Their entrance, at length, into Canaan (v 44): *He gave them the lands of the heathen,* put them in possession of that which they had long been put in hopes of; and what the Canaanites had taken pains for God's Israel had the enjoyment of: *They inherited the labour of the people;* and the wealth of the sinner is laid up for the just. The Egyptians had long inherited their labours, and now they inherited the labours of the Canaanites. Thus sometimes one enemy of the church is made to pay another's scores.

6. The reasons why God did all this for them. (1.) Because he would himself perform the promises of the word, *v.* 42. They were unworthy and unthankful, yet he did those great things in their favour *because he remembered the word of his holiness* (that is, his covenant) *with Abraham his servant,* and he would not suffer one iota or tittle of that to fall to the ground. See Deut. vii. 8. (2.) Because he would have them to perform the precepts of the word, to bind them to which was the greatest kindness he could put upon them. He put them in possession of Canaan, not that they might live in plenty and pleasure, in ease and honour, and might make a figure among the nations, but *that they might observe his statutes and keep his laws,*—that, being formed into a·people, they might be under God's immediate government, and revealed religion might be the basis of their national constitution,—that, having a good land given them, they might out of the profits of it bring sacrifices to God's altar,—and that, God having thus done them good, they might the more cheerfully receive his law, concluding that also designed for their good, and might be sensible of their obligations in gratitude to live in obedience to him. We are *therefore* made, maintained, and redeemed, that we may live in obedience to the will of God; and the hallelujah with which the psalm concludes may be taken both as a thankful acknowledgment of God's favours and as a cheerful concur-

rence with this great intention of them. Has God done so much for us, and yet does he expect so little from us? *Praise you the Lord.*

PSALM CVI.

We must give glory to God by making confession, not only of his goodness but our own badness, which serve as foils to each other. Our badness makes his goodness appear the more illustrious, as his goodness makes our badness the more heinous and scandalous. The foregoing psalm was a history of God's goodness to Israel; this is a history of their rebellions and provocations, and yet it begins and ends with Hallelujah; for even sorrow for sin must not put us out of tune for praising God. Some think it was penned at the time of the captivity in Babylon and the dispersion of the Jewish nation thereupon, because of that prayer in the close, ver. 47. I rather think it was penned by David at the same time with the foregoing psalm, because we find the first verse and the last two verses in that psalm which David delivered to Asaph, at the bringing up of the ark to the place he had prepared for it (1 Chron. xvi. 34—36), "Gather us from among the heathen;" for we may suppose that in Saul's time there was a great dispersion of pious Israelites, when David was forced to wander. In this psalm we have, I. The preface to the narrative, speaking honour to God (ver. 1, 2), comfort to the saints (ver. 3), and the desire of the faithful towards God's favour, ver. 4, 5. II. The narrative itself of the sins of Israel, aggravated by the great things God did for them, an account of which is inter mixed. Their provocations at the Red Sea (ver. 6—12), lusting (ver. 13—15), mutinying (ver. 16—18), worshipping the golden calf (ver. 19—23), murmuring (ver. 24—27), joining themselves to Baal-peor (ver. 28—31), quarrelling with Moses (ver. 32, 33), incorporating themselves with the nations of Canaan, ver. 34—39. To this is added an account how God had rebuked them for their sins, and yet saved them from ruin, ver. 40—46. III. The conclusion of the psalm with prayer and praise, ver. 47, 48. It may be of use to us to sing this psalm, that, being put in mind by it of our sins, the sins of our land, and the sins of our fathers, we may be humbled before God and yet not despair of mercy, which even rebellious Israel often found with God.

PRAISE ye the Lord. O give thanks unto the Lord; for *he is* good: for his mercy *endureth* for ever. 2 Who can utter the mighty acts of the Lord? *who* can show forth all his praise? 3 Blessed *are* they that keep judgment, *and* he that doeth righteousness at all times. 4 Remember me, O Lord, with the favour *that thou bearest unto* thy people: O visit me with thy salvation; 5 That I may see the good of thy chosen, that I may rejoice in the gladness of thy nation, that I may glory with thine inheritance.

We are here taught,

I. To bless God (*v.* 1, 2): *Praise you the Lord,* that is, 1. Give him thanks for his goodness, the manifestation of it to us, and the many instances of it. *He is good* and *his mercy endures for ever;* let us therefore own our obligations to him and make him a return of our best affections and services. 2. Give him the glory of his greatness, his *mighty acts,* proofs of his almighty power, wherein he has done great things, and such as would be opposed. *Who can utter these?* Who is worthy to do it? Who is able to do it? They are so many that they cannot be numbered, so mysterious that they cannot be described; when we have said the most we can of the mighty acts of the Lord, the one half is not told; still there is more to be said; it is a subject that cannot be exhausted. We must *show forth his praise;* we may show forth some of it, but *who can show forth all?* Not the angels themselves. This will not excuse us in not doing what we can, but should quicken us to do all we can.

II. To bless the people of God, to call and account them happy (*v.* 3): *Those that keep judgment are blessed,* for they are fit to be employed in praising God. God's people are those whose principles are sound—*They keep judgment* (they adhere to the rules of wisdom and religion, and their practices are agreeable); they *do righteousness,* are just to God and to all men, and herein they are steady and constant; they do it *at all times,* in all manner of conversation, at every turn, in every instance, and herein persevering to the end.

III. To bless ourselves in the favour of God, to place our happiness in it, and to seek it, accordingly, with all seriousness, as the psalmist here, *v.* 4, 5. 1. He has an eye to the lovingkindness of God, as the fountain of all happiness: " *Remember me, O Lord!* to give me that mercy and grace which I stand in need of, *with the favour which thou bearest to thy people.*" As there are a people in the world who are in a peculiar manner God's people, so there is a peculiar favour which God bears to that people, which all gracious souls desire an interest in; and we need desire no more to make us happy. 2. He has an eye to the salvation of God, the great salvation, that of the soul, as the foundation of happiness: *O visit me with thy salvation.* "Afford me (says Dr. Hammond) that pardon and that grace which I stand in need of, and can hope for from none but thee." Let that salvation be my portion for ever, and the pledges of it my present comfort. 3. He has an eye to the blessedness of the righteous, as that which includes all good (*v.* 5): " *That I may see the good of thy chosen* and be as happy as the saints are; and happier I do not desire to be." God's people are here called his *chosen,* his *nation,* his *inheritance;* for he has set them apart for himself, incorporated them under his own government, is served by them and glorified in them. The chosen people of God have a good which is peculiar to them, which is the matter both of their gladness and of their glorying, which is their pleasure, and their praise. God's people have reason to be a cheerful people, and to boast in their God all the day long; and those who have that gladness, that glory, need not envy any of the children of men their pleasure or pride. The gladness of God's nation, and the glory of his inheritance, are enough to satisfy any man; for they have everlasting joy and glory at the end of them.

6 We have sinned with our fathers, we have committed iniquity, we have done wickedly. 7 Our fathers understood not thy wonders in Egypt; they remembered not the multitude of thy mercies; but provoked *him* at the sea, *even* at the Red sea. 8 Nevertheless

he saved them for his name's sake, that he might make his mighty power to be known. 9 He rebuked the Red sea also, and it was dried up: so he led them through the depths, as through the wilderness. 10 And he saved them from the hand of him that hated *them,* and redeemed them from the hand of the enemy. 11 And the waters covered their enemies: there was not one of them left. 12 Then believed they his words; they sang his praise.

Here begins a penitential confession of sin, which was in a special manner seasonable now that the church was in distress; for thus we must justify God in all that he brings upon us, acknowledging that *therefore* he has done right, because *we have done wickedly;* and the remembrance of former sins, notwithstanding which God did not cast off his people, is an encouragement to us to hope that, though we are justly corrected for our sins, yet we shall not be utterly abandoned.

I. God's afflicted people here own themselves guilty before God (*v.* 6): "*We have sinned with our fathers,* that is, like our fathers, after the similitude of their transgression. We have added to the stock of hereditary guilt, and filled up the measure of our fathers' iniquity, *to augment yet the fierce anger of the Lord,*" Num. xxxii. 14, Matt. xxiii. 32. And see how they lay a load upon themselves, as becomes penitents: "*We have committed iniquity,* that which is in its own nature sinful, and *we have done wickedly;* we have sinned with a high hand presumptuously." Or this is a confession, not only of their imitation of, but their interest in, their fathers' sins: *We have sinned with our fathers,* for we were in their loins and we *bear their iniquity,* Lam. v. 7.

II. They bewail the sins of their fathers when they were first formed into a people, which, since children often smart for, they are concerned to sorrow for, even further than to the third and fourth generation. Even we now ought to take occasion from the history of Israel's rebellions to lament the depravity and perverseness of man's nature and its unaptness to be amended by the most probable means. Observe here,

1. The strange stupidity of Israel in the midst of the favours God bestowed upon them (*v.* 7): *They understood not thy wonders in Egypt.* They saw them, but they did not rightly apprehend the meaning and design of them. *Blessed are those that have not seen, and yet have* understood. They thought the plagues of Egypt were intended for their deliverance, whereas they were intended also for their instruction and conviction, not only to force them out of their

Egyptian slavery, but to cure them of their inclination to Egyptian idolatry, by evidencing the sovereign power and dominion of the God of Israel, above all gods, and his particular concern for them. We lose the benefit of providences for want of understanding them. And, as their understandings were dull, so their memories were treacherous; though one would think such astonishing events should never have been forgotten, yet they remembered them not, at least *they remembered not the multitude of* God's *mercies* in them. *Therefore* God is distrusted because his favours are not remembered.

2. Their perverseness arising from this stupidity: *They provoked him at the sea, even at the Red Sea.* The provocation was, despair of deliverance (because the danger was great) and wishing they had been left in Egypt still, Exod. xiv. 11, 12. Quarrelling with God's providence, and questioning his power, goodness, and faithfulness, are as great provocations to him as any whatsoever. The place aggravated the crime; it was *at the sea, at the Red Sea,* when they had newly come out of Egypt and the wonders God had wrought for them were fresh in their minds; yet they reproach him, as if all that power had no mercy in it, but he had brought them out of Egypt on purpose to *kill them in the wilderness.* They never lay at God's mercy so immediately as in their passage through the Red Sea, yet there they affront it, and provoke his wrath.

3. The great salvation God wrought for them notwithstanding their provocations, *v.* 8—11. (1.) He forced a passage for them through the sea: *He rebuked the Red Sea* for standing in their way and retarding their march, *and it was dried up* immediately; as, in the creation, *at God's rebuke the waters fled,* civ. 7. Nay, he not only prepared them a way, but, by the pillar of cloud and fire, he *led them* into the sea, and, by the conduct of Moses, led them through it as readily as *through the wilderness.* He encouraged them to take those steps, and subdued their fears, when those were their most dangerous and threatening enemies. See Isa. lxiii. 12—14. (2.) He interposed between them and their pursuers, and prevented them from cutting them off, as they designed. The Israelites were all on foot, and the Egyptians had all of them chariots and horses, with which they were likely to overtake them quickly, but God *saved them from the hand of him that hated them,* namely, Pharaoh, who never loved them, but now hated them the more for the plagues he had suffered on their account. *From the hand of* his *enemy,* who was just ready to seize them, *God redeemed them* (*v.* 10), interposing himself, as it were, in the pillar of fire, between the persecuted and the persecutors. (3.) To complete the mercy, and turn the deliverance into a victory, the Red Sea, which was a lane to them, was a grave to the Egyptians (*v.* 11): *The*

waters covered their enemies, so as to slay them, but not so as to conceal their shame; for, the next tide, they were thrown up dead upon the shore, Exod. xiv. 30. *There was not one of them left* alive, to bring tidings of what had become of the rest. And why did God do this for them? Nay, why did he not cover them, as he did their enemies, for their unbelief and murmuring? He tells us (*v.* 8): it was *for his name's sake.* Though they did not deserve this favour, he designed it; and their undeservings should not alter his designs, nor break his measures, nor make him withdraw his promise, or fail in the performance of it. He did this for his own glory, *that he might make his mighty power to be known,* not only in dividing the sea, but in doing it notwithstanding their provocations. Moses prays (Num. xiv. 17, 19), *Let the power of my Lord be great and pardon the iniquity of this people.* The power of the God of grace in pardoning sin and sparing sinners is as much to be admired as the power of the God of nature in dividing the waters.

4. The good impression this made upon them for the present (*v.* 12): *Then believed they his words,* and acknowledged that God was with them of a truth, and had, in mercy to them, brought them out of Egypt, and not with any design to slay them in the wilderness; then *they feared the Lord and his servant Moses,* Exod. xiv. 31. Then *they sang his praise,* in that song of Moses penned on this great occasion, Exod. xv. 1. See in what a gracious and merciful way God sometimes silences the unbelief of his people, and turns their fears into praises; and so it is written, *Those that erred in spirit shall come to understanding,* and *those that murmured shall learn doctrine,* Isa. xxix. 24.

13 They soon forgat his works: they waited not for his counsel: 14 But lusted exceedingly in the wilderness, and tempted God in the desert. 15 And he gave them their request; but sent leanness into their soul. 16 They envied Moses also in the camp, *and* Aaron the saint of the LORD. 17 The earth opened and swallowed up Dathan, and covered the company of Abiram. 18 And a fire was kindled in their company; the flame burned up the wicked. 19 They made a calf in Horeb, and worshipped the molten image. 20 Thus they changed their glory into the similitude of an ox that eateth grass. 21 They forgat God their saviour, which had done great things in Egypt; 22 Wondrous works in the land of Ham, *and* terrible things by the Red sea. 23 Therefore

he said that he would destroy them, had not Moses his chosen stood before him in the breach, to turn away his wrath, lest he should destroy *them.* 24 Yea, they despised the pleasant land, they believed not his word : 25 But murmured in their tents, *and* hearkened not unto the voice of the LORD. 26 Therefore he lifted up his hand against them, to overthrow them in the wilderness : 27 To overthrow their seed also among the nations, and to scatter them in the lands. 28 They joined themselves also unto Baal-peor, and ate the sacrifices of the dead. 29 Thus they provoked *him* to anger with their inventions: and the plague brake in upon them. 30 Then stood up Phinehas, and executed judgment: and *so* the plague was stayed. 31 And that was counted unto him for righteousness unto all generations for evermore. 32 They angered *him* also at the waters of strife, so that it went ill with Moses for their sakes: 33 Because they provoked his spirit, so that he spake unadvisedly with his lips.

This is an abridgment of the history of Israel's provocations in the wilderness, and of the wrath of God against them for those provocations : and this abridgment is abridged by the apostle, with application to us Christians (1 Cor. x. 5, &c.); for these things were *written for our admonition,* that we sin not like them, lest we suffer like them.

I. The cause of their sin was disregard to the works and word of God, *v.* 13. 1. They minded not what he had done for them : *They soon forgot his works,* and lost the impressions they had made upon them. Those that do not improve God's mercies to them, nor endeavour in some measure to render according to the benefit done unto them, do indeed forget them. This people soon forgot them (God took notice of this, Exod. xxxii. 8, *They have turned aside quickly) : They made haste, they forgot his works* (so it is in the margin), which some make to be two separate instances of their sin. *They made haste ;* their expectations anticipated God's promises; they expected to be in Canaan shortly, and because they were not they questioned whether they should ever be there and quarrelled with all the difficulties they met with in their way ; whereas *he that believeth does not make haste,* Isa. xxviii. 16. And, withal, *they forgot his works,* which were the undeniable evidences of his wisdom, power, and goodness, and denied the conclu-

sion as confidently as if they had never seen the premises proved. This is mentioned again (*v.* 21, 22): *They forgot God their Saviour ;* that is, they forgot that he had been their Saviour. Those that forget the works of God forget God himself, who makes himself known by his works. They forgot what was done but a few days before, which we may suppose they could not but talk of, even then, when, because they did not make a good use of it, they are said to forget it : it was what God did for them *in Egypt, in the land of Ham,* and *by the Red Sea,* things which we at this distance cannot, or should not, be unmindful of. They are called *great things* (for, though the great God does nothing mean, yet he does some things that are in a special manner great), *wondrous works,* out of the common road of Providence, therefore observable, therefore memorable, and *terrible things,* awful to them, and dreadful to their enemies, and yet soon forgotten. Even miracles that were seen passed away with them as tales that are told. 2. They minded not what God had said to them nor would they depend upon it : *They waited not for his counsel,* did not attend his word, though they had Moses to be his mouth to them ; they took up resolves about which they did not consult him and made demands without calling upon him. They would be in Canaan directly, and had not patience to tarry God's time. The delay was intolerable, and therefore the difficulties were looked upon as insuperable. This is explained (*v.* 24): *They believed not his word,* his promise that he would make them masters of Canaan ; and (*v.* 25), *They hearkened not to the voice of the Lord,* who gave them counsel which they would not wait for, not only by Moses and Aaron, but by Caleb and Joshua, Num. xiv. 6, 7, &c. Those that will not wait for God's counsel shall justly be given up to their own hearts' lusts, to walk in their own counsels.

II. Many of their sins are here mentioned, together with the tokens of God's displeasure which they fell under for those sins.

1. They would have flesh, and yet would not believe that God could give it to them (*v.* 14): *They lusted a lust* (so the word is) *in the wilderness ;* there, where they had bread enough and to spare, yet nothing would serve them but they must have flesh to eat. They were now purely at God's finding, being supported entirely by miracles, so that this was a reflection upon the wisdom and goodness of their Creator. They were also, in all probability, within a step of Canaan, yet had not patience to stay for dainties till they came thither. They had flocks and herds of their own, but they will not kill them ; God must give them flesh as he gave them bread, or they will never give him credit, or their good word. They did not only wish for flesh, *but* they *lusted exceedingly* after it. A desire, even of lawful

things, when it is inordinate and violent, becomes sinful; and therefore this is called *lusting after evil things* (1 Cor. x. 6), though the quails, as God's gift, were good things, and were so spoken of, Ps. cv. 40. Yet this was not all : *They tempted God in the desert,* where they had had such experience of his goodness and power, and questioned whether he could and would gratify them herein. See lxxviii. 19, 20. Now how did God show his displeasure against them for this. We are told how (*v.* 15): *He gave them their request,* but gave it them in anger, and with a curse, for he *sent leanness into their soul;* he filled them with uneasiness of mind, and terror of conscience, and a self-reproach, occasioned by their bodies being sick with the surfeit, such as sometimes drunkards experience after a great debauch. Or this is put for that great plague with which the Lord smote them, *while the flesh was yet between their teeth,* as we read, Num. xi. 33. It was the consumption of the life. Note, (1.) What is asked in passion is often given in wrath. (2) Many that fare deliciously every day, and whose bodies are healthful and fat, have, at the same time, leanness in their souls, no love to God, no thankfulness, no appetite to the bread of life, and then the soul must needs be lean. Those wretchedly forget themselves that feast their bodies and starve their souls. Then God gives the good things of this life in love, when with them he gives grace to glorify him in the use of them; for then *the soul delights itself in fatness,* Isa. lv. 2.

2. They quarrelled with the government which God had set over them both in church and state (*v.* 16): *They envied Moses* his authority *in the camp,* as generalissimo of the armies of Israel and chief justice in all their courts; they envied *Aaron* his power, as *saint of the Lord,* consecrated to the office of high priest, and Korah would needs put in for the pontificate, while Dathan and Abiram, as princes of the tribe of Reuben, Jacob's eldest son, would claim to be chief magistrates, by the so-much-admired right of primogeniture. Note, Those are preparing ruin for themselves who envy those whom God has put honour upon and usurp the dignities they were never designed for. And justly will contempt be poured upon those who put contempt upon any of the saints of the Lord. How did God show his displeasure for this? We are told how, and it is enough to make us tremble (*v.* 17, 18); we have the story, Num. xvi. 32, 35. (1.) Those that flew in the face of the civil authority were punished by *the earth,* which *opened and swallowed them up,* as not fit to go upon God's ground, because they would not submit to God's government. (2.) Those that would usurp the ecclesiastical authority in things pertaining to God suffered the vengeance of heaven, for *fire came out from the Lord and consumed them,* and the pretending sacrificers were themselves

sacrificed to divine justice. *The flame burnt up the wicked;* for though they vied with *Aaron, the saint of the Lord,* for holiness (Num. xvi. 3, 5), yet God adjudged them wicked, and as such cut them off, as in due time he will destroy the man of sin, that wicked one, notwithstanding his proud pretensions to holiness.

3. They made and worshipped the golden calf, and this in Horeb, where the law was given, and where God had expressly said, *Thou shalt* neither *make any graven image* nor *bow down* to it; they did both: *They made a calf and worshipped* it, *v.* 19.

(1.) Herein they bade defiance to, and put an affront upon, the two great lights which God has made to rule the moral world :—[1.] That of human reason ; for *they changed their glory,* their God, at least the manifestation of him, which always had been in a cloud (either a dark cloud or a bright one), without any manner of visible similitude, *into the similitude of* Apis, one of the Egyptian idols, *an ox that eateth grass,* than which nothing could be more grossly and scandalously absurd, *v.* 20. Idolaters are perfectly besotted, and put the greatest disparagement possible both upon God, in representing him by the image of a beast, and upon themselves, in worshipping it when they have so done. That which is here said to be the changing of their glory is explained by St. Paul (Rom. i. 23) the *changing of the glory of the incorruptible God.* [2.] That of divine revelation, which was afforded to them, not only in the words God spoke to them, but in the works he wrought for them, *wondrous works,* which declared aloud that the Lord Jehovah is the only true and living God and is alone to be worshipped, *v.* 21, 22.

(2.) For this God showed his displeasure by declaring the decree that he would cut them off from being a people, as they had, as far as lay in their power, in effect cut him off from being a God; he spoke *of destroying them* (*v.* 23), and certainly he would have done it if *Moses, his chosen, had not stood before him in the breach* (*v.* 23), if he had not seasonably interposed to deal with God as an advocate about the breach or ruin God was about to devote them to and wonderfully prevailed to turn away his wrath. See here the mercy of God, and how easily his anger is turned away, even from a provoking people. See the power of prayer, and the interest which God's chosen have in heaven. See a type of Christ, God's *chosen,* his *elect,* *in whom his soul delights,* who *stood before him in the breach* to *turn away* his wrath from a provoking world, and ever lives, for this end, making intercession.

4. They gave credit to the report of the evil spies concerning the land of Canaan, in contradiction to the promise of God (*v.* 24): *They despised the pleasant land.* Canaan was a pleasant land, Deut. viii. 7. They undervalued it when they thought it not worth

venturing for, no, not under the guidance of God himself, and therefore were for making a captain and returning to Egypt again. They *believed not God's word* concerning it, but *murmured in their tents*, basely charging God with a design upon them in bringing them thither that they might become a prey to the Canaanites, Num. xiv. 2, 3. And, when they were reminded of God's power and promise, they were so far from hearkening to that voice of the Lord that they attempted to stone those who spoke to them, Num. xiv. 10. The heavenly Canaan is a pleasant land. A promise is left us of entering into it; but there are many that despise it, that neglect and refuse the offer of it, that prefer the wealth and pleasure of this world before it, and grudge the pains and hazards of this life to obtain that. This also was so displeasing to God that *he lifted up his hand against them*, in a way of threatening, *to destroy them in the wilderness;* nay, in a way of swearing, for he swore in his wrath that they should not enter into his rest (xcv. 11; Num. xiv. 28); nay, and he threatened that their children also should be *overthrown and scattered* (v. 26, 27), and the whole nation dispersed and disinherited; but Moses prevailed for mercy for their seed, that they might enter Canaan. Note, Those who despise God's favours, and particularly the pleasant land, forfeit his favours, and will be shut out for ever from the pleasant land.

5. They were guilty of a great sin in the matter of Peor; and this was the sin of the new generation, when they were within a step of Canaan (v. 28): *They joined themselves to Baal-peor*, and so were entangled both in idolatry and in adultery, in corporeal and in spiritual whoredom, Num. xxv. 1—3. Those that did often partake of the altar of the living God now *ate the sacrifices of the dead*, of the idols of Moab (that were dead images, or dead men canonized or deified), or sacrifices to the infernal deities on the behalf of their dead friends. *Thus they provoked God to anger with their inventions* (v. 29), in contempt of him and his institutions, his commands, and his threatenings. The iniquity of Peor was so great that, long after, it is said, *They were not cleansed from it*, Josh. xxii. 17. God testified his displeasure at this, (1.) By sending a plague among them, which in a little time swept away 24,000 of those impudent sinners. (2.) By stirring up Phinehas to use his power as a magistrate for the suppressing of the sin and checking the contagion of it. He stood up in his zeal for the Lord of hosts, and executed judgment upon Zimri and Cozbi, sinners of the first rank, genteel sinners; he put the law in execution upon them, and this was a service so pleasing to God that upon it *the plague was stayed*, v. 30. By this, and some other similar acts of public justice on that occasion (Num. xxv. 4, 5), the guilt ceased to be national, and the general controversy was let

fall. When the proper officers did their duty God left it to them, and did not any longer keep the work in his own hands by the plague. Note, National justice prevents national judgments. But, Phinehas herein signalizing himself, a special mark of honour was put upon him, for what he did was *counted to him for righteousness to all generations* (v. 31), and, in recompence of it, the priesthood was entailed on his family. *He* shall make an atonement by offering up the sacrifices, who had so bravely made an atonement (so some read it, v. 30) by offering up the sinners. Note, It is the honour of saints to be zealous against sin.

6. They continued their murmurings to the very last of their wanderings; for in the fortieth year they *angered God at the waters of strife* (v. 32), which refers to that story, Num. xx. 3—5. And that which aggravated it now was that *it went ill with Moses for their sakes;* for, though he was the meekest of all the men in the earth, yet their clamours at that time were so peevish and provoking that they put him into a passion, and, having now grown very old and off his guard, *he spoke unadvisedly with his lips* (v. 33), and not as became him on that occasion; for he said in a heat, *Hear now, you rebels, must we fetch water out of this rock for you?* This was Moses's infirmity, and is written for our admonition, that we may learn, when we are in the midst of provocation, to keep our mouth as with a bridle (xxxix. 1—3), and to *take heed to our spirits*, that they admit not resentments too much; for, when the spirit is provoked, it is much ado, even for those that have a great deal of wisdom and grace, not to *speak unadvisedly*. But it is charged upon the people as their sin: *They provoked his spirit* with that with which they angered God himself. Note, We must answer not only for our own passions, but for the provocation which by them we give to the passions of others, especially of those who, if not greatly provoked, would be meek and quiet. God shows his displeasure against this sin of theirs by shutting Moses and Aaron out of Canaan for their misconduct upon this occasion, by which, (1.) God discovered his resentment of all such intemperate heats, even in the dearest of his servants. If he deals thus severely with Moses for one unadvised word, what does their sin deserve who have spoken so many presumptuous wicked words? *If this was done in the green tree, what shall be done in the dry?* (2.) God deprived them of the blessing of Moses's guidance and government at a time when they most needed it, so that his death was more a punishment to them than to himself. It is just with God to remove those relations from us that are blessings to us, when we are peevish and provoking to them and grieve their spirits.

34 They did not destroy the nations, concerning whom the LORD

commanded them: 35 But were mingled among the heathen, and learned their works. 36 And they served their idols ⸕ which were a snare unto them. 37 Yea, they sacrificed their sons and their daughters unto devils, 38 And shed innocent blood, *even* the blood of their sons and of their daughters, whom they sacrificed unto the idols of Canaan: and the land was polluted with blood. 39 Thus were they defiled with their own works, and went a whoring with their own inventions. 40 Therefore was the wrath of the Lord kindled against his people, insomuch that he abhorred his own inheritance. 41 And he gave them into the hand of the heathen; and they that hated them ruled over them. 42 Their enemies also oppressed them, and they were brought into subjection under their hand. 43 Many times did he deliver them; but they provoked *him* with their counsel, and were brought low for their iniquity. 44 Nevertheless he regarded their affliction, when he heard their cry: 45 And he remembered for them his covenant, and repented according to the multitude of his mercies. 46 He made them also to be pitied of all those that carried them captives. 47 Save us, O Lord our God, and gather us from among the heathen, to give thanks unto thy holy name, *and* to triumph in thy praise. 48 Blessed *be* the Lord God of Israel from everlasting to everlasting: and let all the people say, Amen. Praise ye the Lord.

Here, I. The narrative concludes with an account of Israel's conduct in Canaan, which was of a piece with that in the wilderness, and God's dealings with them, wherein, as all along, both justice and mercy appeared.

1. They were very provoking to God. The miracles and mercies which settled them in Canaan made no more deep and durable impressions upon them than those which fetched them out of Egypt; for by the time they were just settled in Canaan they corrupted themselves, and forsook God. Observe,

(1.) The steps of their apostasy. [1.] They spared the nations which God had doomed to destruction (*v.* 34); when they had got the good land God had promised them they had no zeal against the wicked inhabitants whom the Lord commanded them to extirpate, pretending pity; but so merciful is God that no

man needs to be in any case more compassionate than he. [2.] When they spared them they promised themselves that, notwithstanding this, they would not join in any dangerous affinity with them. But the way of sin is down-hill; omissions make way for commissions; when they neglect to *destroy the heathen* the next news we hear is, They were *mingled among the heathen*, made leagues with them and contracted an intimacy with them, so that they *learned their works, v.* 35. That which is rotten will sooner corrupt that which is sound than be cured or made sound by it. [3.] When they mingled with them, and learned some of their works that seemed innocent diversions and entertainments, yet they thought they would never join with them in their worship; but by degrees they learned that too (*v.* 36): *They served their idols* in the same manner, and with the same rites, that they served them; and they became *a snare to them.* That sin drew on many more, and brought the judgments of God upon them, which they themselves could not but be sensible of and yet knew not how to recover themselves. [4.] When they joined with them in some of their idolatrous services, which they thought had least harm in them, they little thought that ever they should be guilty of that barbarous and inhuman piece of idolatry the sacrificing of their living children to their dead gods; but they came to that at last (*v.* 37, 38), in which Satan triumphed over his worshippers, and regaled himself in blood and slaughter: *They sacrificed their sons and daughters,* pieces of themselves, to devils, and added murder, the most unnatural murder, to their idolatry; one cannot think of it without horror. They *shed innocent blood,* the most innocent, for it was infant-blood, nay, it was the *blood of their sons and their daughters.* See the power of the spirit that works in the children of disobedience, and see his malice. The beginning of idolatry and superstition, like that of strife, is as the letting forth of water, and there is no villany which those that venture upon it can be sure they shall stop short of, for God justly *gives them up to a reprobate mind,* Rom. i. 28.

(2.) Their sin was, in part, their own punishment; for by it, [1.] They wronged their country: *The land was polluted with blood, v.* 38. That pleasant land, that holy land, was rendered uncomfortable to themselves, and unfit to receive those kind tokens of God's favour and presence in it which were designed to be its honour. [2.] They wronged their consciences (*v.* 39): *They went a whoring with their own inventions,* and so debauched their own minds, and were *defiled with their own works,* and rendered odious in the eyes of the holy God, and perhaps of their own consciences.

2. God brought his judgments upon them; and what else could be expected? For his name is Jealous, and he is a jealous God. (1.) He fell out with them for it, *v.* 40. He

was angry with them : *The wrath of God,* that consuming fire, *was kindled against his people;* for from them he took it as more insulting and ungrateful than from the heathen that never knew him. Nay, he was sick of them: *He abhorred his own inheritance,* which once he had taken pleasure in ; yet the change was not in him, but in them. This is the worst thing in sin, that it makes us loathsome to God ; and the nearer any are to God in profession the more loathsome are they if they rebel against him, like a dunghill at our door. (2.) Their enemies then fell upon them, and, their defence having departed, made an easy prey of them (*v.* 41, 42): *He gave them into the hands of the heathen.* Observe here how the punishment answered to the sin: They *mingled with the heathen and learned their works;* from them they willingly took the infection of sin, and therefore God justly made use of them as the instruments of their correction. Sinners often see themselves ruined by those by whom they have suffered themselves to be debauched. Satan, which is a tempter, will be a tormentor. The heathen hated them. Apostates lose all the love on God's side, and get none on Satan's; and when those that *hated them ruled over them,* and they were brought into subjection under them, no marvel that they oppressed them and ruled them with rigour; and thus God made them know the difference between *his service and the service of the kings of the countries,* 2 Chron xii. 8. (3.) When God granted them some relief, yet they went on in their sins, and their troubles also were continued, *v.* 43. This refers to the days of the Judges, when God often raised up deliverers and wrought deliverances for them, and yet they relapsed to idolatry and *provoked God with their counsel,* their idolatrous inventions, to deliver them up to some other oppressor, so that at last they *were brought* very *low for their iniquity.* Those that by sin disparage themselves, and will not by repentance humble themselves, are justly debased, and humbled, and brought low, by the judgments of God. (4.) At length they cried unto God, and God returned in favour to them, *v.* 44—46. They were chastened for their sins, but not destroyed, cast down, but not cast off. God appeared for them, [1.] As a God of mercy, who looked upon their grievances, *regarded their affliction, beheld when distress was upon them* (so some), who looked over their complaints, for he *heard their cry* with tender compassion (Exod. iii. 7) and overlooked their provocations; for though he had said, and had reason to say it, that he would destroy them, yet he *repented, according to the multitude of his mercies,* and reversed the sentence. Though he is not a *man that he should repent,* so as to change his mind, yet he is a gracious God, who pities us, and changes his way. [2.] As a God of truth, who *remembered for them his covenant,* and made good every word that he had spoken;

656

and therefore, bad as they were, he would not break with them, because he would not break his own promise [3.] As a God of power, who has all hearts in his hand, and turns them which way soever he pleases. *He made them to be pitied even of those that carried them captives,* and hated them, and ruled them with rigour. He not only restrained the remainder of their enemies' wrath, that it should not utterly consume them, but he infused compassion even into their stony hearts, and made them relent, which was more than any art of man could have done with the utmost force of rhetoric. Note, God can change lions into lambs, and, *when a man's ways please the Lord,* will make even *his enemies to pity him* and *be at peace with him.* When God pities men shall. *Tranquillus Deus tranquillat omnia—A God at peace with us makes every thing at peace.*

II. The psalm concludes with prayer and praise. 1. Prayer for the completing of his people's deliverance. Even when the Lord brought back the captivity of his people still there was occasion to pray, *Lord, turn again our captivity* (cxxvi. 1, 4); so here (*v.* 47), *Save us, O Lord our God! and gather us from among the heathen.* We may suppose that many who were forced into foreign countries, in the times of the Judges (as Naomi was, Ruth i. 1), had not returned in the beginning of David's reign, Saul's time being discouraging, and therefore it was seasonable to pray, Lord, gather the dispersed Israelites *from among the heathen, to give thanks to thy holy name,* not only that they may have cause to give thanks and hearts to give thanks, but that they may have opportunity to do it in the courts of the Lord's house, from which they were now banished, and so may *triumph in thy praise,* over those that had in scorn challenged them to *sing the Lord's song in a strange land.* 2. Praise for the beginning and progress of it (*v.* 48): *Blessed be the Lord God of Israel from everlasting to everlasting.* He is a blessed God from eternity, and will be so to eternity, and so let him be praised by all his worshippers. Let the priests say this, and then *let all the people say, Amen, Hallelujah,* in token of their cheerful concurrence in all these prayers, praises, and confessions. According to this rubric, or directory, we find that when this psalm (or at least the closing verses of it) was sung all the people said, *Amen,* and praised the Lord by saying, *Hallelujah.* By these two comprehensive words it is very proper, in religious assemblies, to testify their joining with their ministers in the prayers and praises which, as their mouth, they offer up to God, according to his will, saying *Amen* to the prayers and *Hallelujah* to the praises.

PSALM CVII.

The psalmist, having in the two foregoing psalms celebrated the wisdom, power, and goodness of God, in his dealings with his church in particular, here observes some of the instances of his providential care of the children of men in general, especially in their distresses; for he is not only King of saints, but King of nations, not only the God of Israel, but the God of the whole earth, and a common Father to all mankind. Though this may especially refer to Israelites in their personal capacity, yet there were those who pertained not to the commonwealth of Israel and yet were worshippers of the true God; and even those who worshipped images had some knowledge of a supreme "Numen," to whom, when they were in earnest, they looked above all their false gods. And of these, when they prayed in their distresses, God took a particular care. I. The psalmist specifies some of the most common calamities of human life, and shows how God succours those that labour under them, in answer to their prayers. 1. Banishment and dispersion, ver. 2—9. 2. Captivity and imprisonment, ver. 10 –16. 3. Sickness and distemper of body, ver. 17—22. 4. Danger and distress at sea, ver. 23—32. These are put for all similar perils, in which those that cry unto God have ever found him a very present help. II. He specifies the varieties and vicissitudes of events concerning nations and families, in all which God's hand is to be eyed by his own people, with joyful acknowledgments of his goodness, ver. 33—43. When we are in any of these or the like distresses it will be comfortable to sing this psalm, with application; but, if we be not, others are, and have been, of whose deliverances it becomes us to give God the glory, for we are members one of another.

O GIVE thanks unto the LORD, for *he is* good: for his mercy *endureth* for ever. 2 Let the redeemed of the LORD say *so*, whom he hath redeemed from the hand of the enemy; 3 And gathered them out of the lands, from the east, and from the west, from the north, and from the south. 4 They wandered in the wilderness in a solitary way; they found no city to dwell in. 5 Hungry and thirsty, their soul fainted in them. 6 Then they cried unto the LORD in their trouble, *and* he delivered them out of their distresses. 7 And he led them forth by the right way, that they might go to a city of habitation. 8 Oh that *men* would praise the LORD *for* his goodness, and *for* his wonderful works to the children of men! 9 For he satisfieth the longing soul, and filleth the hungry soul with goodness.

Here is, I. A general call to all to give thanks to God, *v.* 1. Let all that sing this psalm, or pray over it, set themselves herein to *give thanks to the Lord ;* and those that have not any special matter for praise may furnish themselves with matter enough from God's universal goodness. In the fountain *he is good ;* in the streams *his mercy endures for ever* and never fails.

II. A particular demand hereof from *the redeemed of the Lord*, which may well be applied spiritually to those that have an interest in the great Redeemer and are saved by him from sin and hell. They have, of all people, most reason to say that God is good, and his mercy everlasting; these are the *children of God that were scattered abroad,* whom Christ died to *gather together in one,* out of all lands, John xi. 52 ; Matt. xxiv. 31. But it seems here to be meant of a temporal deliverance, wrought for them when in their distress *they cried unto the Lord, v.* 6. *Is any afflicted? Let him pray.* Does any pray? God will certainly hear and help. When troubles be-

come extreme that is man's time to cry; those who but whispered prayer before then cry aloud, and then it is God's time to succour. In the mount he will be seen. 1. They were in an enemy's country, but God wrought out their rescue : He *redeemed them from the hand of the enemy* (v. 2), not by might or power, it may be (Zech. iv. 6), nor by *price or reward* (Isa. xlv. 13), *but by the Spirit of God* working on the spirits of men. 2. They were dispersed as out-casts, but God gathered them out of all the countries whither they were scattered in the cloudy and dark day, that they might again be incorporated, *v.* 3. See Deut. xxx. 4; Ezek. xxxiv. 12. God knows those that are his, and where to find them. 3. They were bewildered, had no road to travel in, no dwelling-place to rest in, *v.* 4. *When they were redeemed* out of the *hand of the enemy, and gathered out of the lands,* they were in danger of perishing in their return home through the dry and barren deserts. *They wandered in the wilderness,* where there was no trodden path, no company, but *a solitary way,* no lodging, no conveniences, no accommodations, no inhabited city where they might have quarters or refreshment. But *God led them forth by the right way* (v. 7), directed them to an inn, nay, directed them to a home, *that they might go to a city of habitation,* which was inhabited, nay, which they themselves should inhabit. This may refer to poor travellers in general, those particularly whose way lay through the wilds of Arabia, where we may suppose they were often at a loss ; and yet many in that distress were wonderfully relieved, so that few perished. Note, We ought to take notice of the good hand of God's providence over us in our journeys, going out and coming in, directing us in our way, and providing for us places both to bait in and rest in. Or (as some think) it has an eye to the wanderings of the children of Israel in the wilderness for forty years ; it is said (Deut. xxxii. 10) *God led them about,* and yet here *he led them by the right way.* God's way, though to us it seems about, will appear at last to have been the right way. It is applicable to our condition in this world; we are here as in a wilderness, have here no *continuing city,* but dwell in tents as strangers and pilgrims. But we are under the guidance of his wise and good providence, and, if we commit ourselves to it, we shall be *led in the right way to the city that has foundations.* 4. They were ready to perish for hunger (v. 5): *Their soul even fainted in them.* They were spent with the fatigues of their journey and ready to drop down for want of refreshment. Those that have constant plenty, and are every day fed to the full, know not what a miserable case it is to be *hungry and thirsty,* and to have no supply. This was sometimes the case of Israel in the wilderness, and perhaps of other poor travellers ; but God's providence finds out ways to *satisfy the longing soul and fill the hungry soul with goodness, v.* 9. Israel's wants were seasonably supplied, and many have been wonderfully relieved when they were ready to perish. The same God that has led us has fed us all our life long unto this day, has fed us with food convenient, has provided food for the soul, *and filled the hungry soul with goodness.* Those that hunger and thirst after righteousness, after God, the living God, and communion with him, shall be abundantly *replenished with the goodness of his house*, both in grace and glory. Now for all this those who receive mercy are called upon to return thanks (*v.* 8): *Oh that men* (it is meant especially of those men whom God has graciously relieved) *would praise the Lord for his goodness* to them in particular, *and for his wonderful works to* others *of the children of men!* Note, (1.) God's works of mercy are wonderful works, works of wonderful power considering the weakness, and of wonderful grace considering the unworthiness, of those he shows mercy to. (2.) It is expected of those who receive mercy from God that they return praise to him. (3.) We must acknowledge God's goodness to the children of men as well as to the children of God, to others as well as to ourselves.

10 Such as sit in darkness and in the shadow of death, *being* bound in affliction and iron; 11 Because they rebelled against the words of God, and contemned the counsel of the most High: 12 Therefore he brought down their heart with labour; they fell down, and *there was* none to help. 13 Then they cried unto the LORD in their trouble, *and* he saved them out of their distresses. 14 He brought them out of darkness and the shadow of death, and brake their bands in sunder. 15 Oh that *men* would praise the LORD *for* his goodness, and *for* his wonderful works to the children of men! 16 For he hath broken the gates of brass, and cut the bars of iron in sunder.

We are to take notice of the goodness of God towards prisoners and captives. Observe, 1. A description of this affliction. Prisoners are said to *sit in darkness* (*v.* 10), in dark dungeons, close prisons, which intimates that they are desolate and disconsolate; they sit *in the shadow of death*, which intimates not only great distress and trouble, but great danger. Prisoners are many times appointed to die; they sit despairing to get out, but resolving to make the best of it. They are *bound in affliction*, and many times *in iron*, as Joseph. Thus sore a calamity is imprisonment, which should make us prize liberty, and be thankful for it. 2. The cause of this affliction, *v.* 11. It is *because they rebelled against the words of God.* Wilful sin is rebellion against the words of God; it is a contradiction to his truths and a violation of his laws. *They contemned the counsel of the Most High*, and thought they neither needed it nor could be the better for it; and those that will not be counselled cannot be helped. Those that despise prophesying, that regard not the admonitions of their own consciences nor the just reproofs of their friends, contemn the counsel of the Most High, and for this they are bound in affliction, both to punish them for and to reclaim them from their rebellions. 3. The design of this affliction, and that is to bring *down their heart* (*v.* 12), to humble them for sin, to make them low in their own eyes, to cast down every high, proud, aspiring thought. Afflicting providences must be improved as humbling providences; and we not only lose the benefit of them, but thwart God's designs and walk contrary to him in them if our hearts be unhumbled and unbroken, as high and hard as ever under them. Is the estate brought down with labour, the honour sunk? Have those that exalted themselves fallen down, and is there none to help them? Let this bring down the spirit to confess sin, to accept the punishment of it, and humbly to sue for mercy and grace. 4. The duty of this afflicted state, and that is to pray (*v.* 13): *Then they cried unto the Lord in their trouble*, though before perhaps they had neglected him. Prisoners have time to pray, who, when they were at liberty, could not find time; they see they have need of God's help, though formerly they thought they could do well enough without him. Sense will make men cry when they are in trouble, but grace will direct them to cry unto the Lord, from whom the affliction comes and who alone can remove it. 5. Their deliverance out of the affliction: *They cried unto the Lord, and he saved them, v.* 13. He *brought them out of darkness into light*, welcome light, and then doubly sweet and pleasant, *brought them out of the shadow of death* to the comforts of life, and their liberty was to them life from the dead, *v.* 14. Were they *fettered? He broke their bands asunder.* Were they imprisoned in strong castles? He broke the *gates of brass* and the *bars of iron* wherewith those gates were made fast; he did not put back, but *cut in sunder.* Note, When God will work deliverance the greatest difficulties that lie in the way shall be made nothing of. Gates of brass and bars of iron, as they cannot keep him out from his people (he was with Joseph in the prison), so they cannot keep them in when the time, the set-time, for their enlargement, comes. 6. The return that is required from those whose bands God has loosed (*v.* 15): *Let them praise the Lord for his goodness*, and take occasion from their own experience of it, and share in it, to bless him for that goodness which the earth is full of, *the world and those that dwell therein.*

17 Fools because of their transgression, and because of their iniquities, are afflicted. 18 Their soul abhorreth all manner of meat; and they draw near unto the gates of death. 19 Then they cry unto the Lord in their trouble, *and* he saveth them out of their distresses. 20 He sent his word, and healed them, and delivered *them* from their destructions. 21 Oh that *men* would praise the Lord *for* his goodness, and *for* his wonderful works to the children of men! 22 And let them sacrifice the sacrifices of thanksgiving, and declare his works with rejoicing.

Bodily sickness is another of the calamities of this life which gives us an opportunity of experiencing the goodness of God in recovering us, and of that the psalmist speaks in these verses, where we may observe,

I. That we, by our sins, bring sickness upon ourselves and then it is our duty to pray, *v.* 17—19. 1. It is the sin of the soul that is the cause of sickness; we bring it upon ourselves both meritoriously and efficiently: *Fools, because of their transgression, are thus afflicted;* they are thus corrected for the sins they have committed and thus cured of their evil inclinations to sin. If we knew no sin, we should know no sickness; but the transgression of our life, and the iniquity of our heart, make it necessary. Sinners are fools; they wrong themselves, and all against their own interest, not only their spiritual, but their secular interest. They prejudice their bodily health by intemperance and endanger their lives by indulging their appetites. This their way is their folly, and they need the rod of correction to drive out the foolishness that is bound up in their hearts. 2. The weakness of the body is the effect of sickness, *v.* 18. When people are sick *their soul abhors all manner of meat;* they not only have no desire to eat nor power to digest it, but they nauseate it, and their stomach is turned against it. And here they may read their sin in their punishment: those that doted most on the meat that perishes, when they come to be sick are sick of it, and the dainties they loved are loathed; what they took too much of now they can take nothing of, which commonly follows upon the overcharging of the heart with surfeiting and drunkenness. And when the appetite is gone the life is as good as gone: *They draw near unto the gates of death;* they are, in their own apprehension and in the apprehension of all about them, at the brink of the grave, as ready to be turned to de-

struction. 3. Then is a proper time for prayer: *Then they cry unto the Lord, v.* 19. Is any sick? Let him pray; let him be prayed for. Prayer is a salve for every sore.

II. That it is by the power and mercy of God that we are recovered from sickness, and then it is our duty to be thankful. Compare with this Job xxxiii. 18, 28. 1. When those that are sick call upon God he returns them an answer of peace. They cry unto him and he *saves them out of their distresses* (*v.* 19); he removes their griefs and prevents their fears. (1.) He does it easily: *He sent his word and healed them, v.* 20. This may be applied to the miraculous cures which Christ wrought when he was upon earth, by a word's speaking; he said, *Be clean, Be whole,* and the work was done. It may also be applied to the spiritual cures which the Spirit of grace works in regeneration; he sends his word, and heals souls, convinces, converts, sanctifies them, and all by the word. In the common instances of recovery from sickness God in his providence does but speak, and it is done. (2.) He does it effectually: *He delivereth them out of their destructions,* that they shall neither be destroyed nor distressed with the fear of being so. Nothing is too hard for that God to do who kills and makes alive again, brings down to the grave and raises up, who *turneth man* almost *to destruction,* and yet saith, *Return.* 2. When those that have been sick are restored they must return to God an answer of praise (*v.* 21, 22): *Let all men praise the Lord for his goodness,* and let those, particularly, to whom God has thus granted a new life, spend it in his service; *let them sacrifice with thanksgiving,* not only bring a thank-offering to the altar, but a thankful heart to God. Thanksgivings are the best thank-offerings, and shall please the Lord better than an ox or bullock. *And let them declare his works with rejoicing,* to his honour and for the encouragement of others. *The living, the living, they shall praise him.*

23 They that go down to the sea in ships, that do business in great waters; 24 These see the works of the Lord, and his wonders in the deep. 25 For he commandeth, and raiseth the stormy wind, which lifteth up the waves thereof. 26 They mount up to the heaven, they go down again to the depths: their soul is melted because of trouble. 27 They reel to and fro, and stagger like a drunken man, and are at their wit's end. 28 Then they cry unto the Lord in their trouble, and he bringeth them out of their distresses. 29 He maketh the storm a calm, so that the waves thereof are still. 30 Then are they glad because

they be quiet; so he bringeth them unto their desired haven. 31 Oh that *men* would praise the LORD *for* his goodness, and *for* his wonderful works to the children of men! 32 Let them exalt him also in the congregation of the people, and praise him in the assembly of the elders.

The psalmist here calls upon those to give glory to God who are delivered from dangers at sea. Though the Israelites dealt not much in merchandise, yet their neighbours the Tyrians and Zidonians did, and for them perhaps this part of the psalm was especially calculated.

I. Much of the power of God appears at all times in the sea, 23, 24. It appears to those *that go down to the sea in ships*, as mariners, merchants, fishermen, or passengers, *that do business in great waters*. And surely none will expose themselves there but those that have business (among all Solomon's pleasant things we do not read of any pleasure-boat he had), but those that go on business, lawful business, may, in faith, put themselves under the divine protection. *These see the works of the Lord, and his wonders*, which are the more surprising, because most are born and bred upon land, and what passes at sea is new to them. The deep itself is a wonder, its vastness, its saltness, its ebbing and flowing. The great variety of living creatures in the sea is wonderful. Let those that go to sea be led, by all the wonders they observe there, to consider and adore the infinite perfections of that God whose the sea is, for he made it and manages it.

II. It especially appears in storms at sea, which are much more terrible than at land. Observe here, 1. How dangerous and dreadful a tempest at sea is. *Then* wonders begin to appear in the deep, when God *commands and raises the* strong *wind*, which *fulfils his word*, cxlviii. 8. He raises the winds, as a prince by his commission raises forces. Satan pretends to be the *prince of the power of the air;* but he is a pretender; the powers of the air are at God's command, not at his. When the wind becomes stormy it *lifts up the waves* of the sea, *v.* 25. Then the ships are kicked like tennis-balls on the tops of the waves; they seem to *mount up to the heavens*, and then they couch again, as if they would *go down to the depths, v.* 26. A stranger, who had never seen it, would not think it possible for a ship to live at sea, as it will in a storm, and ride it out, but would expect that the next wave would bury it and it would never come up again; and yet God, who taught man discretion to make ships that should so strangely keep above water, does by his special providence preserve them, that they answer the end to admiration. When the ships are thus tossed the *soul of* the seaman *melts because of trouble;* and,

650

when the storm is very high, even those that are used to the sea can neither shake off nor dissemble their fears, but *they reel to and fro*, the tossing makes them giddy, *and* they *stagger* and are sick, it may be, *like a drunken man;* the whole ship's crew are in confusion *and* quite *at their wits' end* (*v.* 27), not knowing what to do more for their preservation; all their wisdom is swallowed up, and they are ready to give up themselves for gone, Jonah i. 5, &c. 2. How seasonable it is at such a time to pray. Those that go to sea must expect such perils as are here described, and the best preparation they can make for them is to make sure a liberty of access to God by prayer, for *then they* will *cry unto the Lord, v.* 28. We have a saying, "Let those that would learn to pray go to sea;" I say, Let those that will go to sea learn to pray, and accustom themselves to pray, that they may come with the more boldness to the throne of grace when they are in trouble. Even heathen mariners, in a storm, *cried every man to his god;* but those that have the Lord for their God have a present and powerful help in that and every other time of need, so that when they are at their wits' end they are not at their faith's end. 3. How wonderfully God sometimes appears for those that are in distress at sea, in answer to their prayers: *He brings them out* of the danger; and, (1.) The sea is still: *He makes the storm a calm, v.* 29. The winds fall, and only by their soft and gentle murmurs serve to lull the waves asleep again, so that the surface of the sea becomes smooth and smiling. By this Christ proved himself to be more than a man *that even the winds and the seas obeyed him.* (2.) The seamen are made easy: *They are glad because they are quiet*, quiet from the noise, quiet from the fear of evil. Quietness after a storm is a very desirable thing, and sensibly pleasant. (3.) The voyage becomes prosperous and successful: *So he brings them to their desired haven, v.* 30. Thus he carries his people safely through all the storms and tempests that they meet with in their voyage heaven-ward, and lands them, at length, in the desired harbour. 4. How justly it is expected that all those who have had a safe passage over the sea, and especially who have been delivered from remarkable perils at sea, should acknowledge it with thankfulness, to the glory of God. Let them do it privately in their closets and families. Let them *praise the Lord for his goodness* to themselves and others, *v.* 31. Let them do it publicly (*v.* 32), *in the congregation of the people and in the assembly of the elders;* there let them erect the memorials of their deliverance, to the honour of God, and for the encouragement of others to trust him.

33 He turneth rivers into a wilderness, and the watersprings into dry ground; 34 A fruitful land into barrenness, for the wickedness of them

that dwell therein. 35 He turneth the wilderness into a standing water, and dry ground into watersprings. 36 And there he maketh the hungry to dwell, that they may prepare a city for habitation; 37 And sow the fields, and plant vineyards, which may yield fruits of increase. 38 He blesseth them also, so that they are multiplied greatly; and suffereth not their cattle to decrease, 39 Again, they are minished and brought low through oppression, affliction, and sorrow. 40 He poureth contempt upon princes, and causeth them to wander in the wilderness, *where there is* no way. 41 Yet setteth he the poor on high from affliction, and maketh *him* families like a flock. 42 The righteous shall see *it*, and rejoice: and all iniquity shall stop her mouth. 43 Whoso *is* wise, and will observe these *things*, even they shall understand the lovingkindness of the Lord.

The psalmist, having given God the glory of the providential reliefs granted to persons in distress, here gives him the glory of the revolutions of providence, and the surprising changes it sometimes makes in the affairs of the children of men.

I. He gives some instances of these revolutions.

1. Fruitful countries are made barren and barren countries are made fruitful. Much of the comfort of this life depends upon the soil in which our lot is cast. Now, (1.) The sin of man has often marred the fruitfulness of the soil and made it unserviceable, *v.* 33, 34. Land watered with *rivers* is sometimes *turned into a wilderness,* and that which had been full of water-springs now has not so much as water-streams; it is turned *into dry* and *sandy ground,* that has not consistency and moisture enough to produce any thing valuable. Many *a fruitful land* is turned into saltness, not so much from natural causes as from the just judgment of God, who thus punishes *the wickedness of those that dwell therein;* as was the vale of Sodom became a salt sea. Note, If the land be bad, it is because the inhabitants are so. Justly is the ground made unfruitful to those that bring not forth fruit unto God, but serve Baal with their corn and wine. (2.) The goodness of God has often mended the barrenness of the soil, and turned a *wilderness,* a land of drought, *into water-springs, v.* 35. The land of Canaan, which was once the glory of all lands for fruitfulness, is said to be, at this day, a fruitless, useless, worthless spot of ground, as was foretold, Deut. xxix. 23. This land of ours, which formerly was much of it an uncultivated desert, is now full of all good

things, and *more abundant honour* is *given to that part which lacked.* Let the plantations in America, and the colonies settled there, compared with the desolations of many countries in Asia and Europe, that formerly were famous, expound this.

2. Necessitous families are raised and enriched, while prosperous families are impoverished and go to decay. If we look abroad in the world, (1.) We see many greatly increasing whose beginning was small, and whose ancestors were mean and made no figure, *v.* 36—38. Those that were *hungry* are made *to dwell* in fruitful lands; there they take root, and gain a settlement, and *prepare a city for habitation* for themselves and theirs after them. Providence puts good land under their hands, and they build upon it. Cities took rise from rising families. But as lands will not serve for men without lodgings, and therefore they must *prepare a city of habitation,* so lodgings, though ever so convenient, will not serve without lands, and therefore they must sow *the fields, and plant vineyards (v.* 37), for the king himself is served of the field. And yet the fields, though favoured with water-springs, will not *yield fruits of increase,* unless they be sown, nor will vineyards be had, unless they be planted; man's industry must attend God's blessing, and then God's blessing will crown man's industry. The fruitfulness of the soil should engage, for it does encourage, diligence; and, ordinarily, *the hand of the diligent,* by the blessing of God, *makes rich, v.* 38. *He blesses them also, so that they are,* in a little time, *multiplied greatly, and* he *diminishes not their cattle.* As in the beginning, so still it is, by the blessing of God, that the earth and all the creatures *increase and multiply* (Gen. i. 22), and we depend upon God for the increase of the cattle as well as for the increase of the ground. Cattle would decrease many ways if God should but permit it, and men would soon suffer by it. (2.) We see many that have thus suddenly risen as suddenly sunk and brought to nothing (*v.* 39): *Again they are diminished and brought low* by adverse providences, and end their days as low as they began them; or their families after them lose as fast as they got, and scatter what they heaped together. Note, Worldly wealth is an uncertain thing, and often those that are filled with it, ere they are aware, grow so secure and sensual with it that, ere they are aware, they lose it again. Hence it is called *deceitful riches* and the *mammon of unrighteousness.* God has many ways of making men poor; he can do it by *oppression, affliction, and sorrow,* as he tempted Job and brought him low.

3. Those that were high and great in the world are abased, and those that were mean and despicable are advanced to honour, *v.* 40, 41. We have seen, (1.) Princes dethroned and reduced to straits. *He pours contempt upon* them, even among those that

651

have idolized them. Those that exalt themselves God will abase, and, in order thereunto, will infatuate: He makes *them to wander in the wilderness, where there is no way.* He baffles those counsels by which they thought to support themselves, and their own power and pomp, and drives them headlong, so that they know not what course to steer, nor what measures to take. We met with this before, Job xii. 24, 25. (2.) Those of low degree advanced to the posts of honour (*v.* 41): *Yet setteth he the poor on high,* raiseth *from the dust* to the *throne of glory,* 1 Sam. ii. 8; Ps. cxiii. 7, 8. Those that were afflicted and trampled on are not only delivered, but set on high out of the reach of their troubles, above their enemies, and have dominion over those to whom they had been in subjection. That which adds to their honour, and strengthens them in their elevation, is the multitude of their children: *He maketh him families like a flock* of sheep, so numerous, so useful, so sociable with one another, and so meek and peaceable. He that sent them meat sent them mouths. *Happy is the man that has his quiver filled* with arrows, for he shall boldly *speak with the enemy in the gate,* cxxvii. 5. God is to be acknowledged both in setting up families and in building them up. Let not princes be envied, nor the poor despised, for God has many ways of changing the condition of both.

II. He makes some improvement of these remarks; such surprising turns as these are of use, 1. For the solacing of saints. They observe these dispensations with pleasure (*v.* 42): *The righteous shall see it and rejoice* in the glorifying of God's attributes and the manifesting of his dominion over the children of men. It is a great comfort to a good man to see how God manages the children of men, as the potter does the clay, so as to serve his own purposes by them, to see despised virtue advanced and impious pride brought low to the dust, to see it evinced beyond dispute that *verily there is a God that judges in the earth.* 2. For the silencing of sinners: *All iniquity shall stop her mouth;* it shall be a full conviction of the folly of atheists, and of those that deny the divine providence; and, forasmuch as practical atheism is at the bottom of all sin, it shall in effect *stop the mouth of all iniquity.* When sinners see how their punishment answers to their sin, and how justly God deals with them in taking away from them those gifts of his which they had abused, they shall not have one word to say for themselves; for God will be justified, he will be clear. 3. For the satisfying of all concerning the divine goodness (*v.* 43): *Whoso is wise, and will observe these things,* these various dispensations of divine providence, *even they shall understand the lovingkindness of the Lord.* Here is, (1.) A desirable end proposed, and that is, rightly to *understand the lovingkindness of the Lord.* It is of great use to us, in religion, to be fully assured of

God's goodness, to be experimentally acquainted and duly affected with it, that his *lovingkindness* may be *before our eyes,* xxvi. 3. (2.) A proper means prescribed for attaining this end, and that is a due observance of God's providence. We must lay up these things, mind them, and keep them in mind, Luke ii. 19. (3.) A commendation of the use of this means as an instance of true wisdom: *Whoso is wise,* let him by this both prove his wisdom and improve it. A prudent observance of the providences of God will contribute very much to the accomplishing of a good Christian.

PSALM CVIII.

This psalm begins with praise and concludes with prayer, and faith is at work in both. I. David here gives thanks to God for mercies to himself, ver. 1–5. II. He prays to God for mercies for the land, pleading the promises of God and putting them in suit, ver. 6–13. The former part is taken out of Ps. lvii. 7, &c., the latter out of Ps. lx. 5, &c., and both with very little variation, to teach us that we may in prayer use the same words that we have formerly used, provided it be with new affections. It intimates likewise that it is not only allowable, but sometimes convenient, to gather some verses out of one psalm and some out of another, and to put them together, to be sung to the glory of God. In singing this psalm we must give glory to God and take comfort to ourselves.

A song or psalm of David.

O GOD, my heart is fixed; I will sing and give praise, even with my glory. 2 Awake, psaltery and harp: I *myself* will awake early. 3 I will praise thee, O LORD, among the people: and I will sing praises unto thee among the nations. 4 For thy mercy *is* great above the heavens: and thy truth *reacheth* unto the clouds. 5 Be thou exalted, O God, above the heavens: and thy glory above all the earth.

We may here learn how to praise God from the example of one who was master of the art. 1. We must praise God with fixedness of heart. Our heart must be employed in the duty (else we make nothing of it) and engaged to the duty (*v.* 1): *O God! my heart is fixed,* and then *I will sing and give praise.* Wandering straggling thoughts must be gathered in, and kept close to the business; for they must be told that here is work enough for them all. 2. We must praise God with freeness of expression: I will praise him *with my glory,* that is, with my tongue. Our tongue is our glory, and never more so than when it is employed in praising God. When the *heart is inditing* this *good matter* our *tongue* must be as *the pen of a ready writer,* xlv. 1. David's skill in music was his glory, it made him famous, and this should be consecrated to the praise of God; and therefore it follows, *Awake my psaltery and harp.* Whatever gift we excel in we must praise God with. 3. We must praise God with fervency of affection, and must stir up ourselves to do it, that it may be done in a lively manner and not carelessly (*v.* 2): *Awake, psaltery and harp;* let it not be done with a dull and sleepy tune, but let the airs be all lively. *I myself will awake early* to do it, with all that is within me, and all little enough. Warm devotions honour God. 4. We must praise God publicly, as those that are not ashamed to own our obligations to him and our thankful sense of his favours, but desire that others also may be in like manner affected with the divine goodness (*v.* 3): *I will praise thee among the people* of the Jews; nay, *I will sing to thee among the nations* of the earth. Whatever company we are in we must take all occasions to speak well of God; and we must not be shy of singing psalms, though our neighbours hear us, for it looks like being ashamed of our Master. 5. We must, in our praises, magnify the mercy and truth of God in a special manner (*v.* 4), mercy in promising, truth in performing. The heavens are vast, but the mercy of God is more capacious; the skies are high and bright, but the truth of God is more eminent, more illustrious. We cannot see further than the heavens and clouds; whatever we see of God's mercy and truth there is still more to be seen, more reserved to be seen, in the other world. 6. Since we find ourselves so, defective in glorifying God, we must beg of him to glorify himself, to do all, to dispose all, to his own glory, to get himself honour and make himself a name (*v.* 5): *Be thou exalted, O God! above the heavens*, higher than the angels themselves can exalt thee with their praises, *and let thy glory* be spread over *all the earth. Father, glorify thy own name. Thou hast glorified it; glorify it again.* It is to be our first petition, *Hallowed be thy name.*

6 That thy beloved may be delivered: save *with* thy right hand, and answer me. 7 God hath spoken in his holiness; I will rejoice, I will divide Shechem, and mete out the valley of Succoth. 8 Gilead *is* mine; Manasseh *is* mine; Ephraim also *is* the strength of mine head; Judah *is* my lawgiver; 9 Moab *is* my washpot; over Edom will I cast out my shoe; over Philistia will I triumph. 10 Who will bring me into the strong city? who will lead me into Edom? 11 *Wilt* not *thou*, O God, *who* hast cast us off? and wilt not thou, O God, go forth with our hosts? 12 Give us help from trouble: for vain *is* the help of man. 13 Through God we shall do valiantly: for he *it is that* shall tread down our enemies.

We may here learn how to pray as well as praise. 1. We must be public-spirited in prayer, and bear upon our hearts, at the throne of grace, the concerns of the church of God, *v.* 6. It is God's *beloved*, and therefore must be ours; and therefore we must

pray for its deliverance, and reckon that we are answered if God grant what we ask for his church, though he delay to give us what we ask for ourselves. " *Save* thy church, *and* thou *answerest me;* I have what I would have." *Let the earth be filled with God's glory, and the prayers of David are ended* (lxxii. 19, 20); he desires no more. 2. We must, in prayer, act faith upon the power and promise of God—upon his power *(Save with thy right hand*, which is mighty to save), and upon his promise: *God has spoken in his holiness*, in his holy word, to which he has sworn by his holiness, and therefore *I will rejoice, v.* 7. What he has promised he will perform, for it is the word both of his truth and of his power. An active faith can rejoice in what God has said, though it be not yet done; for with him saying and doing are not two things, whatever they are with us. 3. We must, in prayer, take the comfort of what God has secured to us and settled upon us, though we are not yet put in possession of it. God had promised David to give him, (1.) The hearts of his subjects; and therefore he surveys the several parts of the country as his own already: " *Shechem* and *Succoth, Gilead* and *Manasseh, Ephraim* and *Judah*, are all my own," *v.* 8. With such assurance as this we may speak of the performance of what God has promised to the Son of David; he will, without fail, give him the heathen for his *inheritance and the utmost parts of the earth for his possession*, for so has he *spoken in his holiness;* nay, of all the particular persons that were given him he will *lose none;* he also, as David, shall have the hearts of his subjects, John vi. 37. And, (2.) The *necks of his enemies*. These are promised, and therefore David looks upon *Moab* and *Edom*, and *Philistia*, as his own already (*v.* 9): *Over Philistia will I triumph*, which explains lx. 8, *Philistia, triumph thou because of me*, which some think should be read, *O my soul! triumph thou over Philistia*. Thus the exalted Redeemer is set down at God's right hand, in a full assurance that all his enemies shall in due time *be made his footstool, though all things are not yet put under him*, Heb. ii. 8. 4. We must take encouragement from the beginnings of mercy to pray and hope for the perfecting of it (*v.* 10, 11): " *Who will bring me into the strong cities* that are yet unconquered? Who will make me master of the country of *Edom*, which is yet unsubdued?" The question was probably to be debated in his privy council, or a council of war, what methods they should take to subdue the Edomites and to reduce that country; but he brings it into his prayers, and leaves it in God's hands: *Wilt not thou, O God?* Certainly thou wilt. It is probable that he spoke with the more assurance concerning the conquest of Edom because of the ancient oracle concerning Jacob and Esau, that *the elder should serve the younger*, and the blessing of Jacob, by which he was made Esau's lord,

Gen. xxvii. 37. 5. We must not be discouraged in prayer, nor beaten off from our hold of God, though Providence has in some instances frowned upon us: "Though thou hast *cast us off,* yet thou wilt now *go forth with our hosts, v.* 11. Thou wilt *comfort us again* after the time that thou *hast afflicted us.*" Adverse events are sometimes intended for the trial of the constancy of our faith and prayer, which we ought to persevere in whatever difficulties we meet with, and not to *faint.* 6. We must seek help from God, renouncing all confidence in the creature (*v.* 12): "*Lord, give us help from trouble,* prosper our designs, and defeat the designs of our enemies against us." It is not unseasonable to talk of trouble at the same time that we talk of triumphs, especially when it is to quicken prayer for help from heaven; and it is a good plea, *Vain is the help of man.* "It is really so, and therefore we are undone if thou do not help us; we apprehend it to be so, and therefore depend upon thee for help and have the more reason to expect it." 7. We must depend entirely upon the favour and grace of God, both for strength and success in our work and warfare, *v.* 13. (1.) We must do our part, but we can do nothing of ourselves; it is only *through God that we shall do valiantly.* Blessed Paul will own that even he can *do nothing,* nothing to purpose, *but through Christ strengthening him,* Phil. iv. 13. (2.) When we have acquitted ourselves ever so well, yet we cannot speed by any merit or might of our own; it is God himself that *treads down our enemies,* else we with all our valour cannot do it. Whatever we do, whatever we gain, God must have all the glory.

PSALM CIX.

Whether David penned this psalm when he was persecuted by Saul, or when his son Absalom rebelled against him, or upon occasion of some other trouble that was given him, is uncertain; and whether the particular enemy he prays against was Saul, or Doeg, or Ahithophel, or some other not mentioned in the story, we cannot determine; but it is certain that in penning it he had an eye to Christ, his sufferings and his persecutors, for that imprecation (ver. 8) is applied to Judas, Acts. i. 20. The rest of the prayers here against his enemies were the expressions, not of passion, but of the Spirit of prophecy. I. He lodges a complaint in the court of heaven of the malice and base ingratitude of his enemies and with an appeal to the righteous God, ver. 1—5. II. He prays against his enemies, and devotes them to destruction, ver. 6—20. III. He prays for himself, that God would help and succour him in his low condition, ver. 21—29. IV. He concludes with a joyful expectation that God would appear for him, ver. 30, 31. In singing this psalm we must comfort ourselves with the believing foresight of the certain destruction of all the enemies of Christ and his church, and the certain salvation of all those that trust in God and keep close to him.

To the chief Musician. A psalm of David.

HOLD not thy peace, O God of my praise; 2 For the mouth of the wicked and the mouth of the deceitful are opened against me: they have spoken against me with a lying tongue. 3 They compassed me about also with words of hatred; and fought against me without a cause. 4 For my love they are my adversaries: but I *give myself unto* prayer. 5 And they

have rewarded me evil for good, and hatred for my love.

It is the unspeakable comfort of all good people that, whoever is against them, God is for them, and to him they may apply as to one that is pleased to concern himself for them. Thus David here.

I. He refers himself to God's judgment (*v.* 1): "*Hold not thy peace,* but *let my sentence come forth from thy presence,* xvii. 2. Delay not to give judgment upon the appeal made to thee." God saw what his enemies did against him, but seemed to connive at it, and to keep silence: "Lord," says he, "do not always do so." The title he gives to God is observable: "*O God of my praise!* the God in whom *I glory,* and not in any wisdom or strength of my own, from whom I have every thing that is my praise, or the God whom I have praised, and will praise, and hope to be for ever praising." He had before called God the *God of his mercy* (lix. 10), here he calls him *the God of his praise.* Forasmuch as God is the *God of our mercies* we must make him the *God of our praises;* if all is of him and from him, all must be to him and for him.

II. He complains of his enemies, showing that they were such as it was fit for the righteous God to appear against. 1. They were very spiteful and malicious: They are *wicked;* they delight in doing mischief (*v.* 2); their words are *words of hatred, v.* 3. They had an implacable enmity to a good man because of his goodness. "They open their mouths against me to swallow me up, and *fight against me* to cut me off if they could." 2. They were notorious liars; and lying comprehends two of the seven things which the Lord hates. "They are *deceitful* in their protestations and professions of kindness, while at the same time they speak against me behind my back, *with a lying tongue.*" They were equally false in their flatteries and in their calumnies. 3. They were both politic and restless in their designs: "They *compassed me about* on all sides, so that, which way soever I looked, I could see nothing but what made against me." 4. They were unjust; their accusations of him, and sentence against him, were all groundless: "*They have fought against me without a cause;* I never gave them any provocation." Nay, which was worst of all, 5. They were very ungrateful, and *rewarded him evil for good, v.* 5. Many a kindness he had done them, and was upon all occasions ready to do them, and yet he could not work upon them to abate their malice against him, but, on the contrary, they were the more exasperated because they could not provoke him to give them some occasion against him (*v.* 4): *For my love they are my adversaries.* The more he endeavoured to gratify them the more they hated him. We may wonder that it is possible that any should be so wicked; and yet, since there have been so many instances of it, we should not wonder if any be so wicked against us.

III. He resolves to keep close to his duty and take the comfort of that: *But I give myself unto prayer* (v. 4), *I prayer* (so it is in the original); "I am for prayer, I am a man of prayer, I love prayer, and prize prayer, and practise prayer, and make a business of prayer, and am in my element when I am at prayer." A good man is made up of prayer, *gives himself to prayer*, as the apostles, Acts vi. 4. When David's enemies falsely accused him, and misrepresented him, he applied to God and by prayer committed his cause to him. Though they were his adversaries for his love, yet he continued to pray for them; if others are abusive and injurious to us, yet let not us fail to do our duty to them, nor *sin against the Lord in ceasing to pray for them*, 1 Sam. xii. 23. Though they hated and persecuted him for his religion, yet he kept close to it; they laughed at him for his devotion, but they could not laugh him out of it. "Let them say what they will, *I give myself unto prayer.*" Now herein David was a type of Christ, who was compassed about with *words of hatred* and lying words, whose enemies not only persecuted him without cause, but for his love and his *good works* (John x. 32); and yet he *gave himself to prayer*, to pray for them. *Father, forgive them.*

6 Set thou a wicked man over him : and let Satan stand at his right hand. 7 When he shall be judged, let him be condemned: and let his prayer become sin. 8 Let his days be few ; *and* let another take his office. 9 Let his children be fatherless, and his wife a widow. 10 Let his children be continually vagabonds, and beg: let them seek *their bread* also out of their desolate places. 11 Let the extortioner catch all that he hath; and let the strangers spoil his labour. 12 Let there be none to extend mercy unto him: neither let there be any to favour his fatherless children. 13 Let his posterity be cut off; *and* in the generation following let their name be blotted out. 14 Let the iniquity of his fathers be remembered with the LORD; and let not the sin of his mother be blotted out. 15 Let them be before the LORD continually, that he may cut off the memory of them from the earth. 16 Because that he remembered not to show mercy, but persecuted the poor and needy man, that he might even slay the broken in heart. 17 As

he loved cursing, so let it come unto him : as he delighted not in blessing, so let it be far from him. 18 As he clothed himself with cursing like as with his garment, so let it come into his bowels like water, and like oil into his bones. 19 Let it be unto him as the garment *which* covereth him, and for a girdle wherewith he is girded continually. 20 *Let this be* the reward of mine adversaries from the LORD, and of them that speak evil against my soul.

David here fastens upon some one particular person that was worse than the rest of his enemies, and the ringleader of them, and in a devout and pious manner, not from a principle of malice and revenge, but in a holy zeal for God and against sin and with an eye to the enemies of Christ, particularly Judas who betrayed him, whose sin was greater than Pilate's that condemned him (John xix. 11), he imprecates and predicts his destruction, foresees and pronounces him completely miserable, and such a one as our Saviour calls him, *A son of perdition.* Calvin speaks of it as a detestable piece of sacrilege, common in his time among Franciscan friars and other monks, that if any one had malice against a neighbour he might hire some of them to curse him every day, which he would do in the words of these verses; and particularly he tells of a lady in France who, being at variance with her own and only son, hired a parcel of friars to curse him in these words. Greater impiety can scarcely be imagined than to vent a devilish passion in the language of sacred writ, to kindle strife with coals snatched from God's altar, and to call for fire from heaven with a tongue set on fire of hell.

I. The imprecations here are very terrible —woe, and a thousand woes, to that man against whom God says *Amen* to them; and they are all in full force against the implacable enemies and persecutors of God's church and people, that *will not repent, to give him glory.* It is here foretold concerning this bad man,

1. That he should be cast and sentenced as a criminal, with all the dreadful pomp of a trial, conviction, and condemnation (v. 6, 7): *Set thou a wicked man over him,* to be as cruel and oppressive to him as he has been to others; for God often makes one wicked man a scourge to another, to spoil the spoilers and to deal treacherously with those that have dealt treacherously. *Set the wicked one over him* (so some), that is, Satan, as it follows ; and then it was fulfilled in Judas, whom Satan entered, to hurry him into sin first and then into despair. Set his own wicked heart over him, set his own conscience against him; let that fly in his face.

Let Satan stand on his right hand, and be let loose against him to deceive him, as he did Ahab to his destruction, and then to accuse him and resist him, and then he is certainly cast, having no interest in that advocate who alone can say, *The Lord rebuke thee, Satan* (Zech. iii. 1, 2); when he shall be judged at men's bar let not his usual arts to evade justice do him any service, but let his sin find him out and *let him be condemned;* nor shall he escape before God's tribunal, but be condemned there when the day of inquisition and recompence shall come. *Let his prayer become sin,* as the clamours of a condemned malefactor not only find no acceptance, but are looked upon as an affront to the court. The prayers of the wicked now become sin, because soured with the leaven of hypocrisy and malice; and so they will in the great day, because then it will be too late to cry, *Lord, Lord, open to us.* Let every thing be turned against him and improved to his disadvantage, even his prayers.

2. That, being condemned, he should be executed as a most notorious malefactor. (1.) That he should lose his life, and the number of his months be cut off in the midst, by the sword of justice: *Let his days be few,* or shortened, as a condemned criminal has but a few days to live (*v.* 8); such bloody and *deceitful men shall not live out half their days.* (2.) That consequently all his places should be disposed of to others, and they should enjoy his preferments and employments: *Let another take his office.* This Peter applies to the filling up of Judas's place in the truly sacred college of the apostles, by the choice of Matthias, Acts i. 20. Those that mismanage their trusts will justly have their office taken from them and given to those that will approve themselves faithful. (3.) That his family should be beheaded and beggared, that *his wife* should be made *a widow* and *his children fatherless,* by his untimely death, *v.* 9. Wicked men, by their wicked courses, bring ruin upon their wives and children, whom they ought to take care of and provide for. Yet his children, if, when they lost their father, they had a competency to live upon, might still subsist in comfort; but they shall be *vagabonds and shall beg;* they shall not have a house of their own to live in, nor any certain dwelling-place, nor know where to have a meal's-meat, but shall creep *out of their desolate places* with fear and trembling, like beasts out of their dens, to *seek their bread* (*v.* 10), because they are conscious to themselves that all mankind have reason to hate them for their father's sake. (4.) That his estate should be ruined, as the estates of malefactors are confiscated (*v.* 11): *Let the extortioner,* the officer, seize *all that he has and let the stranger,* who was nothing akin to his estate, *spoil his labour,* either for his crimes or for his debts, Job v. 4, 5. (5.) That his posterity should be miserable. Fatherless children, though they have no-

656

thing of their own, yet sometimes are well provided for by the kindness of those whom God inclines to pity them; but this wicked man having never shown mercy there shall *be none to extend mercy to him,* by *favouring his fatherless children* when he is gone, *v.* 12. The children of wicked parents óften fare the worse for their parents' wickedness in this way that the bowels of men's compassion are shut up from them, which yet ought not to be, for why should children suffer for that which was not their fault, but their infelicity? (6.) That his memory should be infamous, and buried in oblivion and disgrace (*v.* 13): *Let his posterity be cut off; let his end be to destruction* (so Dr. Hammond); *and in the* next *generation let their name be blotted out,* or remembered with contempt and indignation, and (*v.* 15) let an indelible mark of disgrace be left upon it. See here what hurries some to shameful deaths, and brings the families and estates of others to ruin, makes them and theirs despicable and odious, and entails poverty, and shame, and misery, upon their posterity; it is sin, that mischievous destructive thing. The learned Dr. Hammond applies this to the final dispersion and desolation of the Jewish nation for their crucifying Christ; their princes and people were cut off, their country was laid waste, and their posterity were made fugitives and vagabonds.

II. The ground of these imprecations bespeaks them very just, though they sound very severe. 1. To justify the imprecations of vengeance upon the sinner's posterity, the sin of his ancestors is here brought into the account (*v.* 14, 15), *the iniquity of his fathers* and *the sin of his mother.* These God often visits even upon the children's children, and is not unrighteous therein: when wickedness has long run in the blood justly does the curse run along with it. Thus all the innocent blood that had been shed upon the earth, from that of righteous Abel, was required from that persecuting generation, who, by putting Christ to death, *filled up the measure of their fathers,* and left as long a train of vengeance to follow them as the train of guilt was that went before them, which they themselves agreed to by saying, *His blood be upon us and on our children.* 2. To justify the imprecations of vengeance upon the sinner himself, his own sin is here charged upon him, which called aloud for it. (1.) He had loved cruelty, and therefore give him blood to drink (*v.* 16): *He remembered not to show mercy,* remembered not those considerations which should have induced him to show mercy, remembered not the objects of compassion that had been presented to him, but persecuted the poor, whom he should have protected and relieved, and *slew the broken in heart,* whom he should have comforted and healed. Here is a barbarous man indeed, not fit to live. (2.) He had loved cursing, and therefore let the curse come upon his head, *v.* 17—19. Those that were out of the reach of his cruelty he let fly at with his curses, which were impotent and ridiculous; but they shall return upon him. *He delighted not in blessing;* he took no pleasure in wishing well to others, nor in seeing others do well; he would give nobody a good word or a good wish, much less would he do any body a good turn; and *so let all good be far from him. He clothed himself with cursing;* he was proud of it as an ornament that he could frighten all about him with the curses he was liberal of; he confided in it as armour, which would secure him from the insults of those he feared. And let him have enough of it. Was he fond of cursing? *Let God's curse come into his bowels like water* and swell him as with a dropsy, *and* let it soak *like oil into his bones.* The word of the curse *is quick and powerful, and divides between the joints and the marrow;* it works powerfully and effectually; it fastens on the soul; it is a piercing thing, and there is no antidote against it. Let it compass him on every side *as a garment, v.* 19. Let God's cursing him be his shame, as his cursing his neighbour was his pride; let it cleave to him as *a girdle,* and let him never be able to get clear of it. Let it be to him like the waters of jealousy, which caused the *belly to swell* and the *thigh to rot.* This points at the utter ruin of Judas, and the spiritual judgments which fell on the Jews for crucifying Christ. The psalmist concludes his imprecations with a terrible *Amen,* which signifies not only, " I wish it may be so," but "I know it shall be so." *Let this be the reward of my adversaries from the Lord, v.* 20. And this will be the reward of all the adversaries of the Lord Jesus; his enemies that will not have him to reign over them shall be *brought forth and slain before him.* And he will one day recompense tribulation to those that trouble his people.

21 But do thou for me, O GOD the Lord, for thy name's sake: because thy mercy *is* good, deliver thou me. 22 For I *am* poor and needy, and my heart is wounded within me. 23 I am gone like the shadow when it declineth: I am tossed up and down as the locust. 24 My knees are weak through fasting; and my flesh faileth of fatness. 25 I became also a reproach unto them : *when* they looked upon me they shaked their heads. 26 Help me, O LORD my God: O save me according to thy mercy: 27 That they may know that this *is* thy hand; *that* thou, LORD, hast done it. 28 Let them curse, but bless thou: when they arise, let them be ashamed; but let

thy servant rejoice. 29 Let mine adversaries be clothed with shame, and let them cover themselves with their own confusion, as with a mantle. 30 I will greatly praise the LORD with my mouth; yea, I will praise him among the multitude. 31 For he shall stand at the right hand of the poor, to save *him* from those that condemn his soul.

David, having denounced God's wrath against his enemies, here takes God's comforts to himself, but in a very humble manner, and without boasting.

I. He pours out his complaint before God concerning the low condition he was in, which, probably, gave advantage to his enemies to insult over him : " *I am poor and needy,* and therefore a proper object of pity, and one that needs and craves thy help." 1. He was troubled in mind (*v.* 22): *My heart is wounded within me,* not only broken with outward troubles, which sometimes prostrate and sink the spirits, but wounded with a sense of guilt; and *a wounded spirit who can bear?* who can heal? 2. He apprehended himself drawing near to his end: *I am gone like the shadow when it declines,* as good as gone already. Man's life, at best, is like a shadow; sometimes it is like the evening shadow, the presage of night approaching, *like the shadow when it declines.* 3. He was unsettled, *tossed up and down like the locust,* his mind fluctuating and unsteady, still putting him upon new counsels, his outward condition far from any fixation, but still upon the remove, hunted like a partridge on the mountains. 4. His body was wasted, and almost worn away (*v.* 24): *My knees are weak through fasting,* either forced fasting (for want of food when he was persecuted, or for want of appetite when he was sick) or voluntary fasting, when he chastened his soul either for sin or affliction, his own or other's, xxxv. 13 ; lxix. 10. " *My flesh fails of fatness;* that is, it has lost the fatness it had, so that I have become a skeleton, nothing but skin and bones." But it is better to have this leanness in the body, while the soul prospers and is in health, than, like Israel, to have leanness sent into the soul, while the body is feasted. 5. He was ridiculed and reproached by his enemies (*v.* 25); his devotions and his afflictions they made the matter of their laughter, and, upon both those accounts, God's people have been exceedingly filled with the scorning of those that were at ease. In all this David was a type of Christ, who in his humiliation was thus wounded, thus weakened, thus reproached ; he was also a type of the church, which is often *afflicted, tossed with tempests, and not comforted.*

II. He prays for mercy for himself. In general (*v.* 21): " *Do thou for me, O God the Lord!* appear for me, act for me." If God

657

be for us, he will do for us, will do *more abundantly for us than we are able either to ask or think.* He does not prescribe to God what he should do for him, but refers himself to his wisdom : " Lord, do for me what seems good in thy eyes. Do that which thou knowest will be for me, really for me, in the issue for me, though for the present it may seem to make against me." More particularly, he prays (*v.* 26) : " *Help me, O Lord my God! O save me!* Help me under my trouble, save me out of my trouble ; save me from sin, help me to do my duty." He prays (*v.* 28), Though they *curse, bless thou.* Here, (1.) He despises the causeless curses of his enemies : *Let them curse.* He said of Shimei, *So let him curse.* They can but show their malice ; they can do him no more mischief than *the bird by wandering* or *the swallow by flying,* Prov. xxvi. 2. He values the blessing of God as sufficient to counterbalance their curses : *Bless thou,* and then it is no matter though they *curse.* If God bless us, we need not care who curses us ; for *how can they curse those whom God has not cursed,* nay, whom he has blessed ? Num. xxiii. 8. Men's curses are impotent ; God's blessings are omnipotent ; and those whom we unjustly curse may in faith expect and pray for God's blessing, his special blessing. When the Pharisees cast out the poor man for confessing Christ, Christ *found him,* John ix. 35. When men without cause say all the ill they can of us, and wish all the ills they can to us, we may with comfort lift up our heart to God in this petition : *Let them curse, but bless thou.* He prays (*v.* 28), *Let thy servant rejoice.* Those that know how to value God's blessing, let them but be sure of it. and they will be glad of it.

III. He prays that his enemies might *be ashamed* (*v.* 28), *clothed with shame* (*v.* 29), that they might *cover themselves with their own confusion,* that they might be left to themselves, to do that which would expose them and *manifest their folly before all men,* or rather that they might be disappointed in their designs and enterprises against David, and thereby might be *filled with shame,* as the adversaries of the Jews were, Neh. vi. 16. Nay, in this he prays that they might be brought to repentance, which is the chief thing we should beg of God for our enemies. Sinners indeed bring shame upon themselves, but they are true penitents that take shame to themselves and *cover themselves with their own confusion.*

IV. He pleads God's glory, the honour of his name :—*Do for me, for thy name's sake* (*v.* 21), especially the honour of his goodness, by which he has proclaimed his name : " *Deliver me, because thy mercy is good;* it is what thou thyself dost delight in, and it is what I do depend upon. Save me, not according to my merit, for I have none to pretend to, but *according to thy mercy;* let that be the fountain, the reason, the measure, of my salvation."

658

Lastly, He concludes the psalm with joy, the joy of faith, joy in assurance that his present conflicts would end in triumphs. 1. He promises God that he will praise him (*v.* 30) : "*I will greatly praise the Lord,* not only with my heart, but *with my mouth; I will praise him,* not in secret only, but *among the multitude.*" 2. He promises himself that he shall have cause to praise God (*v.* 31): *He shall stand at the right hand of the poor,* nigh to him, a present help ; he shall stand at his right hand as his patron and advocate to plead his cause against his accusers and to bring him off, *to save him from those that condemn his soul* and would execute their sentence if they could. God was David's protector in his sufferings, and was present also with the Lord Jesus in his, *stood at his right hand,* so that he was *not moved* (xvi. 8), saved his soul from those that pretended to be the judges of it, and received it into his own hands. Let all those that *suffer according to the will of God commit the keeping of their souls to him.*

PSALM CX.

This psalm is pure gospel; it is only, and wholly, concerning Christ, the Messiah promised to the fathers and expected by them. It is plain that the Jews of old, even the worst of them, so understood it, however the modern Jews have endeavoured to pervert it and to rob us of it ; for when the Lord Jesus proposed a question to the Pharisees upon the first words of this psalm, where he takes it for granted that David, in spirit, calls Christ his Lord though he was his Son, they chose rather to say nothing, and to own themselves gravelled, than to make it a question whether David does indeed speak of the Messiah or no ; for they freely yield so plain a truth, though they foresee it will turn to their own disgrace, Matt. xxii. 41, &c. Of him therefore, no doubt, the prophet here speaks, of him and of no other man. Christ, as our Redeemer, executes the office of a prophet, of a priest, and of a king, with reference both to his humiliation and his exaltation ; and of each of these we have here an account. I. His prophetical office, ver. 2. II. His priestly office, ver. 4. III. His kingly office, ver. 1, 3, 5, 6. IV. His estates of humiliation and exaltation, ver. 7. In singing this psalm we must act faith upon Christ, submit ourselves entirely to him, to his grace and government, and triumph in him as our prophet, priest, and king, by whom we hope to be ruled, and taught, and saved, for ever, and as the prophet, priest, and king of the whole church, who shall reign till he has put down all opposing rule, principality, and power, and delivered up the kingdom to God the Father.

A psalm of David.

THE Lord said unto my Lord, Sit thou at my right hand, until I make thine enemies thy footstool. 2 The Lord shall send the rod of thy strength out of Zion : rule thou in the midst of thine enemies. 3 Thy people *shall be* willing in the day of thy power, in the beauties of holiness from the womb of the morning : thou hast the dew of thy youth. 4 The Lord hath sworn, and will not repent, Thou *art* a priest for ever after the order of Melchizedek.

Some have called this psalm *David's creed,* almost all the articles of the Christian faith being found in it ; the title calls it *David's psalm,* for in the believing foresight of the Messiah he both praised God and solaced himself, much more may we, in singing it, to whom that is fulfilled, and therefore more clearly revealed, which is here foretold. Glorious things are here spoken of Christ, and such as oblige us to consider how great he is.

I. That he is David's Lord. We must take special notice of this because he himself does. Matt. xxii. 43, *David, in spirit, calls him Lord.* And as the apostle proves the dignity of Melchizedek, and in him of Christ, by this, that so great a man as Abraham was paid him *tithes* (Heb. vii. 4), so we may by this prove the dignity of the Lord Jesus that David, that great man, *called him* his *Lord;* by him that king acknowledges himself to reign, and to him to be acceptable as a servant to his lord. Some think he calls him his *Lord* because he was the Lord that was to descend from him, his son and yet his Lord. Thus his immediate mother calls him her *Saviour* (Luke i. 47); even his parents were his subjects, his saved ones.

II. That he is constituted a sovereign Lord by the counsel and decree of God himself : *The Lord,* Jehovah, *said unto him, Sit* as a king. He *receives of the Father* this honour and glory (2 Pet i. 17), from him who is the fountain of honour and power, and *takes it not to himself.* He is therefore rightful Lord, and his title is incontestable ; for what God has said cannot be gainsaid. He is therefore everlasting Lord ; for what God has said shall not be unsaid. He will certainly take and keep possession of that kingdom which the Father has committed to him, and none can hinder.

III. That he was to be advanced to the highest honour, and entrusted with an absolute sovereign power both in heaven and in earth : *Sit thou at my right hand.* Sitting is a resting posture ; after his services and sufferings, he entered into rest from all his labours. It is a ruling posture ; he sits to give law, to give judgment. It is a remaining posture ; he sits like a king for ever. Sitting at the right hand of God denotes both his dignity and his dominion, the honour put upon him and the trusts reposed in him by the Father. All the favours that come from God to man, and all the service that comes from man to God, pass through his hand.

IV. That all his enemies were in due time to be made his footstool, and not till then ; but then also he must reign in the glory of the Mediator, though the work of the Mediator will be, in a manner, at an end. Note, 1. Even Christ himself has enemies that fight against his kingdom and subjects, his honour and interest, in the world. There are those that will not have him to reign over them, and thereby they join themselves to Satan, who will not have him to reign at all. 2. These enemies will *be made his footstool;* he will subdue them and triumph over them ; he will do it easily, as easily as we put a footstool in its proper place, and such a propriety there will be in it. He will make himself easy by the doing of it, as a man that sits with a footstool under his feet ; he will subdue them in such a way as shall be most for his honour and their perpetual disgrace ; he will *tread down the wicked,* Mal. iv. 3. 3. God the Father has undertaken to do it : *I*

will make them thy footstool, who can do it. 4. It will not be done immediately. All his enemies are now in a chain, but not yet made his footstool. This the apostle observes. Heb. ii. 8, *We see not yet all things put under him.* Christ himself must wait for the completing of his victories and triumphs. 5. He shall wait till it is done ; and all their might and malice shall not give the least disturbance to his government. His sitting at God's right hand is a pledge to him of his setting his feet, at last, on the necks of all his enemies.

V. That he should have a kingdom set up in the world, beginning at Jerusalem (*v.* 2): " *The Lord shall send the rod* or sceptre *of thy strength out of Zion,* by which thy kingdom shall be erected, maintained, and administered." The Messiah, when he sits on the right hand of the Majesty in the heavens, will have a church on earth, and will have an eye to it ; for he is *King upon the holy hill of Zion* (ii. 6), in opposition to Mount Sinai, that frightful mountain, on which the law was given, Heb. xii. 18, 24 ; Gal. iv. 24, 25. The kingdom of Christ took rise from Zion, the city of David, for he was the Son of David, and was to have *the throne of his father David.* By the rod of his strength, or his strong rod, is meant his everlasting gospel, and the power of the Holy Ghost going along with it—the report of the word, and the arm of the Lord accompanying it (Isa. liii. 1, Rom. i. 16),—the gospel coming in word, and in power, and *in the holy Ghost,* 1 Thess. i. 5. By the word and Spirit of God souls were to be reduced first, and brought into obedience to God, and then ruled and governed according to the will of God. This strong rod God sent forth ; he poured out the Spirit, and gave both commissions and qualifications to those that preached the word, and *ministered the Spirit,* Gal. iii. 5. It was sent out of Zion, for there the Spirit was given, and there the preaching of the gospel among all nations must begin, at Jerusalem. See Luke xxiv. 47, 49. *Out of Zion* must *go forth the law* of faith, Isa. ii. 3. Note, The gospel of Christ, being sent of God, is *mighty through God* to do wonders, 2 Cor. x. 4. It is *the rod of Christ's strength.* Some make it to allude not only to the sceptre of a prince, denoting the glory of Christ shining in the gospel, but to a shepherd's crook, his rod and staff, denoting the tender care Christ takes of his church ; for he is both *the great and the good Shepherd.*

VI. That his kingdom, being set up, should be maintained and kept up in the world, in spite of all the oppositions of the power of darkness. 1. Christ shall rule, shall give laws, and govern his subjects by them, shall perfect them, and make them easy and happy, shall do his own will, fulfil his own counsels, and maintain his own interests among men. His kingdom is of God, and it shall stand ; his crown sits firmly on his head, and there it shall flourish. 2. He shall rule *in the midst of his enemies.* He sits in heaven in the midst of his friends; his throne of glory there is surrounded with none but faithful worshippers of him, Rev. v. 11. But he rules on earth in the midst of his enemies, and his throne of government here is surrounded with those that hate him and fight against him. Christ's church is a lily among thorns, and his disciples are sent forth *as sheep in the midst of wolves;* he knows *where they dwell, even where Satan's seat is* (Rev. ii. 13), and this redounds to his honour that he not only keeps his ground, but gains his point, notwithstanding all the malignant policies and powers of hell and earth, which cannot shake the rock on which the church is built. *Great is the truth, and will prevail.*

VII. That he should have a great number of subjects, who should be to him for a name and a praise, *v.* 3.

1. That they should be his own people, and such as he should have an incontestable title to. They are given to him by the Father, who gave them their lives and beings, and to whom their lives and beings were forfeited. *Thine they were and thou gavest them me,* John xvii. 6. They are redeemed by him; he has purchased them to be to himself *a peculiar people,* Tit. ii. 14. They are his by right, antecedent to their consent. He *had much people in Corinth* before they were converted, Acts xviii. 10.

2. That they should be *a willing people,* a people of willingness, alluding to servants that choose their service and are not coerced to it (they love their masters and would not go out free), to soldiers that are volunteers and not pressed men (" Here am I, send me"), to sacrifices that are free-will offerings and not offered of necessity; we *present ourselves living sacrifices.* Note, Christ's people are a willing people. The conversion of a soul consists in its being willing to be Christ's, coming under his yoke and into his interests, with an entire compliancy and satisfaction.

3. That they should be so *in the day of his power, in the day of thy muster* (so some); when thou art enlisting soldiers thou shalt find a multitude of volunteers forward to be enlisted; let but the standard be set up and the *Gentiles* will *seek to it,* Isa. xi. 10; lx. 3. Or when thou art drawing them out to battle they shall be willing to *follow the Lamb whithersoever he goes,* Rev. xiv. 4. *In the day of thy armies* (so some); "when the first preachers of the gospel shall be sent forth, as Christ's armies, to reduce apostate men, and to ruin the kingdom of apostate angels, then all that are *thy people shall be willing;* that will be thy time of setting up thy kingdom." *In the day of thy strength,* so we take it. There is a general power which goes along with the gospel to all, proper to make them willing to be Christ's people, arising from the supreme authority of its great author and the intrinsic excellency of the things themselves contained

in it, besides the undeniable miracles that were wrought for the confirmation of it. And there is also a particular power, the power of the Spirit, going along with the power of the word, to the people of Christ, which is effectual to make them willing. The former leaves sinners without matter of excuse; this leaves saints without matter of boasting. Whoever are willing to be Christ's people, it is the free and mighty grace of God that makes them so.

4. That they should be so *in the beauty of holiness,* that is, (1.) They shall be allured to him by the beauty of holiness; they shall be charmed into a subjection to Christ by the sight given them of his beauty, who is the holy Jesus, and the beauty of the church, which is the holy nation. (2.) They shall be admitted by him into the beauty of holiness, as spiritual priests, to minister in his sanctuary; for *by the blood of Jesus we have boldness to enter into the holiest.* (3.) They shall attend upon him in the beautiful attire or ornaments of grace and sanctification. Note, Holiness is the livery of Christ's family and that which *becomes his house for ever.* Christ's soldiers are all thus clothed; these are the colours they wear. The armies of heaven *follow him in fine linen, clean and white,* Rev. xix. 14.

5. That he should have great numbers of people devoted to him. The multitude of the people is the honour of the prince, and that shall be the honour of this prince *From the womb of the morning thou hast the dew of thy youth,* that is, abundance of young converts, like the drops of dew in a summer's morning. In the early days of the gospel, in the morning of the New Testament, the youth of the church, great numbers flocked to Christ, and there were *multitudes that believed,* a *remnant of Jacob,* that was as a *dew from the Lord,* Mic. v. 7; Isa. lxiv. 4, 8. Or thus ? " *From the womb of the morning* (from their very childhood) *thou hast the dew of thy people's youth,* that is, their hearts and affections when they are young; it is thy youth, because it is dedicated to thee." *The dew of the youth* is a numerous, illustrious, hopeful show of young people flocking to Christ, which would be to the world as dew to the ground, to make it fruitful. Note, The dew of our youth, even in the morning of our days, ought to be consecrated to our Lord Jesus.

6. That he should be not only a king, but a priest, *v.* 4. The same Lord that said, *Sit thou at my right hand, swore, and will not repent, Thou art a priest,* that is, *Be thou a priest;* for by the word of his oath he was consecrated. Note, (1.) Our Lord Jesus Christ is a priest. He was appointed to that office and faithfully executes it; he is *ordained for men in things pertaining to God, to offer gifts and sacrifices for sin* (Heb. v. 1), to make atonement for our sins and to recommend our services to God's acceptance. He is God's minister to us, and our advocate with God,

and so is a Mediator between us and God. (2.) He is *a priest for ever.* He was designed for a priest, in God's eternal counsels; he was a priest to the Old-Testament saints, and will be a priest for all believers to the end of time, Heb. xiii. 8. He is said to be *a priest for ever,* not only because we are never to expect any other dispensation of grace than this by the priesthood of Christ, but because the blessed fruits and consequences of it will remain to eternity. (3.) He is made a priest with an oath, which the apostle urges to prove the pre-eminence of his priesthood above that of Aaron, Heb. vii. 20, 21. *The Lord has sworn,* to show that in the commission there was no implied reserve of a power of revocation; for *he will not repent,* as he did concerning Eli's priesthood, 1 Sam. ii. 30. This was intended for the honour of Christ and the comfort of Christians. The priesthood of Christ is confirmed by the highest ratifications possible, that it might be an unshaken foundation for our faith and hope to build upon. (4.) He is a priest, not of the order of Aaron, but of that of Melchizedek, which, as it was prior, so it was upon many accounts superior, to that of Aaron, and a more lively representation of Christ's priesthood. Melchizedek was *a priest upon his throne,* so is Christ (Zech. vi. 13), king of righteousness and king of peace. Melchizedek had no successor, nor has Christ; his is an unchangeable priesthood. The apostle comments largely upon these words (Heb. vii.) and builds on them his discourse of Christ's priestly office, which he shows was no new notion, but built upon this most sure word of prophecy. For, as the New/Testament explains the Old, so the Old Testament confirms the New, and Jesus Christ is the Alpha and Omega of both.

5 The Lord at thy right hand shall strike through kings in the day of his wrath. 6 He shall judge among the heathen, he shall fill *the places* with the dead bodies; he shall wound the heads over many countries. 7 He shall drink of the brook in the way: therefore shall he lift up the head.

Here we have our great Redeemer

I. Conquering his enemies (*v.* 5, 6) in order to the making of them *his footstool, v.* 1. Our Lord Jesus will certainly bring to nought all the opposition made to his kingdom, and bring to ruin all those who make that opposition and persist in it. He will be too hard for those, whoever they may be, that fight against him, against his subjects and the interest of his kingdom among men, either by persecutions or by perverse disputings. Observe here,

1. The conqueror: *The Lord—Adonai,* the Lord Jesus, he to whom all judgment is committed, he shall make his own part good against his enemies *The Lord at thy right*

hand, *O church!* so some; that is, the Lord that is nigh unto his people, and a very present help to them, that is at their right hand, to strengthen and succour them, shall appear for them against his and their enemies. See cix. 31. *He shall stand at the right hand of the poor,* xvi. 8. Some observe that when Christ is said to do his work at the right hand of his church it intimates that, if we would have Christ to appear for us, we must *bestir ourselves,* 2 Sam. v. 24. Or, rather, *At thy right hand, O God!* referring to *v.* 1, in the dignity and dominion to which he is advanced. Note, Christ's sitting at the right hand of God speaks as much terror to his enemies as happiness to his people.

2. The time fixed for this victory: *In the day of his wrath,* that is, the time appointed for it, when the measure of their iniquities is full and they are ripe for ruin. When the day of his patience has expired, then the day of his wrath comes. Note, (1.) Christ has wrath of his own, as well as grace. It concerns us to *kiss the Son,* for he can be *angry* (ii. 12), and we read of the *wrath of the Lamb,* Rev. vi. 16. (2.) There is a day of wrath set, a year of *recompences for the controversy of Zion, the year of the redeemed.* The time is set for the destruction of particular enemies, and when that time shall come it shall be done, how unlikely soever it may seem; but the great day of his wrath will be at the end of time, Rev. vi. 17.

3. The extent of this victory. (1.) It shall reach very high: He *shall strike through kings.* The greatest of men, that set themselves against Christ, shall be made to fall before him. Though they be *kings of the earth,* and rulers, accustomed to carry their point, they cannot carry it against Christ, they do but make themselves ridiculous by the attempt, ii. 2—5. Be their power among men ever so despotic, Christ will call them to an account; be their strength ever so great, their policies ever so deep, Christ will be too hard for them, and wherein they deal proudly he will be above them. Satan is the prince of this world, Death the king of terrors, and we read of kings that make war with the Lamb; but they shall all be brought down and broken. (2.) It shall reach very far. The trophies of Christ's victories will be set up *among the heathen,* and in many countries, wherever any of his enemies are, not his eye only, but his *hand, shall find them out* (xxi. 8) and his wrath shall follow them. He will *plead with all nations,* Joel iii. 2.

4. The equity of this victory: *He shall judge among them.* It is not a military execution, which is done in fury, but a judicial one. Before he condemns and slays, he will judge; he will make it appear that they have brought this ruin upon themselves, and have themselves rolled the stone which returns upon them, that he may be *justified when he speaks* and *the heavens may declare his righteousness.* See Rev. xix. 1, 2.

5. The effect of this victory; it shall be the complete and utter ruin of all his enemies. He shall strike them through, for he strikes home and gives an incurable wound: He shall *wound the heads*, which seems to refer to the first promise of the Messiah (Gen. iii. 15), that he should *bruise the serpent's head.* He shall *wound the head of his enemies*, Ps. lxviii. 21. Some read it, *He shall wound* him that is *the head over many countries*, either Satan or Antichrist, whom *the Lord shall consume with the breath of his mouth.* He shall make such destruction of his enemies that he shall *fill the places with the dead bodies.* The slain of the Lord shall be many. See Isa. xxxiv. 3, &c.; Ezek. xxxix. 12, 14; Rev. xiv. 20; xix. 17, 18. The filling of *the valleys* (for so some read it) *with dead bodies*, perhaps denotes the *filling of hell* (which is sometimes compared to the valley of *Hinnom*, Isa. xxx. 33; Jer. vii. 32) with *damned souls*, for that will be the portion of those that persist in their enmity to Christ.

II. We have here the Redeemer saving his friends and comforting them (*v.* 7); for their benefit, 1. He shall be humbled: *He shall drink of the brook in the way*, that bitter cup which the Father put into his hand. He shall be so abased and impoverished, and withal so intent upon his work, that he shall drink puddle-water out of the lakes in the highway; so some. The wrath of God, running in the channel of the curse of the law, was *the brook in the way*, in the way of his undertaking, which he must go through, or which ran in the way of our salvation and obstructed it, which lay between us and heaven. Christ drank of this brook when he was made a curse for us, and therefore, when he entered upon his suffering, he *went over the brook Kidron*, John xviii. 1. He drank deeply of this *black brook* (so Kidron signifies), this bloody brook, so drank of the *brook in the way* as to take it out of the way of our redemption and salvation. 2. He shall be exalted: *Therefore shall he lift up the head.* When he died he *bowed the head* (John xix. 30), but he soon lifted up the head by his own power in his resurrection. He lifted up the head as a conqueror, yea, more than a conqueror. This denotes not only his exaltation, but his exultation; not only his elevation, but his triumph in it. Col. ii. 15, *Having spoiled principalities and powers, he made a show of them.* David spoke as a type of him in this (Ps. xxvii. 6), *Now shall my head be lifted up above my enemies.* His exaltation was the reward of his humiliation; because he *humbled himself, therefore God also highly exalted him*, Phil. ii. 9. Because he drank of the brook in the way therefore he lifted up his own head, and so lifted up the heads of all his faithful followers, who, *if they suffer with him, shall also reign with him.*

PSALM CXI.

This and divers of the psalms that follow it seem to have been penned by David for the service of the church in their solemn feasts, and not upon any particular occasion. This is a psalm of praise.

The title of it is "Hallelujah—Praise you the Lord," intimating that we must address ourselves to the use of this psalm with hearts disposed to praise God. It is composed alphabetically, each sentence beginning with a several letter of the Hebrew alphabet, in order exactly, two sentences to each verse, and three a piece to the last two. The psalmist, exhorting to praise God, I. Sets himself for an example, ver. 1. II. Furnishes us with matter for praise from the works of God. 1. The greatness of his works and the glory of them. 2. The righteousness of them. 3. The goodness of them. 4. The power of them. 5. The conformity of them to his word of promise. 6. The perpetuity of them. These observations are intermixed, ver. 2—9. III. He recommends the holy fear of God, and a conscientious obedience to his commands, as the most acceptable way of praising God, ver. 10

PRAISE ye the LORD. I will praise the LORD with *my* whole heart, in the assembly of the upright, and *in* the congregation. 2 The works of the LORD *are* great, sought out of all them that have pleasure therein. 3 His work *is* honourable and glorious: and his righteousness endureth for ever. 4 He hath made his wonderful works to be remembered: the LORD *is* gracious and full of compassion. 5 He hath given meat unto them that fear him: he will ever be mindful of his covenant.

The title of the psalm being *Hallelujah*, the psalmist (as every author ought to have) has an eye to his title, and keeps to his text.

I. He resolves to praise God himself, *v.* 1. What duty we call others to we must oblige and excite ourselves to; nay, whatever others do, whether they will praise God or no, we and our houses must determine to do it, we and our hearts; for such is the psalmist's resolution here: *I will praise the Lord with my whole heart.* My heart, my whole heart, being devoted to his honour, shall be employed in this work; and this *in the assembly*, or secret, *of the upright*, in the cabinet-council, *and in the congregation* of Israelites. Note, We must praise God both in private and in public, in less and greater assemblies, in our own families and in the courts of the Lord's house; but in both it is most comfortable to do it in concert with the upright, who will heartily join in it. Private meetings for devotion should be kept up as well as more public and promiscuous assemblies.

II. He recommends to us the *works of the Lord* as the proper subject of our meditations when we are praising him—the dispensations of his providence towards the world, towards the church, and towards particular persons. 1. God's works are very magnificent, great like himself; there is nothing in them that is mean or trifling: they are the products of infinite wisdom and power, and we must say this upon the first view of them, before we come to enquire more particularly into them, that the *works of the Lord are great, v.* 2. There is something in them surprising, and that strikes an awe upon us. All the *works of the Lord* are spoken of as one (*v.* 3); it is *his work*, such is the beauty and harmony of Providence and so admirably do all its dispensations centre in one design; it was cried to *the wheels, O wheel!* Ezek. x. 13. Take all together, and it is *honourable and glorious,* and such as becomes him. 2. They are entertaining and exercising to the inquisitive—*sought out of all those that have pleasure therein.* Note, (1.) All that truly love God have pleasure in his works, and reckon all well that he does; nor do their thoughts dwell upon any subject with more delight than on the works of God, which the more they are looked into the more they give us of a pleasing surprise. (2.) Those that have pleasure in the works of God will not take up with a superficial transient view of them, but will diligently search into them and observe them. In studying both natural and political history we should have this in our eye, to discover the greatness and glory of God's works. (3.) These works of God, that are humbly and diligently sought into, shall be *sought out;* those that *seek shall find* (so some read it); *they are found of all those that have pleasure in them,* or found in all their parts, designs, purposes, and several concernments (so Dr. Hammond), for the *secret of the Lord is with those that fear him,* xxv. 14. 3. They are all just and holy; *His righteousness endures for ever.* Whatever he does, he never did, nor ever will do, any wrong to any of his creatures; and *therefore* his works *endure for ever* (Eccl. iii. 14) because the righteousness of them endures. 4. They are admirable and memorable, fit to be registered and kept on record. Much that we do is so trifling that it is not fit to be spoken of or told again; the greatest kindness is to forget it. But notice is to be taken of God's works, and an account to be kept of them (*v.* 4). *He has made his wonderful works to be remembered;* he has done that which is worthy to be remembered, which cannot but be remembered, and he has instituted ways and means for the keeping of some of them in remembrance, as the deliverance of Israel out of Egypt by the passover. *He has made himself a memorial by his wonderful works* (so some read it); see Isa. lxiii. 10. By that which God did with his *glorious arm he made himself an everlasting name.* 5. They are very kind. In them the Lord shows that he is *gracious and full of compassion.* As of the works of creation, so of the works of providence, we must say, They are not only all very great, but all very good. Dr. Hammond takes this to be the name which God has made to himself by his wonderful works, the same with that which he proclaimed to Moses, *The Lord God is gracious and merciful,* Exod. xxiv. 6. God's pardoning sin is the most wonderful of all his works and which ought to be remembered to his glory. It is a further instance of his grace and compassion that *he has given meat to those that fear him, v.* 5. He gives them their daily bread, food convenient for them; so he does to others by common providence, but to those that fear him he gives it by covenant and in pursuance of the pro-

mise, for it follows, *He will be ever mindful of his covenant;* so that they can taste covenant-love even in common mercies. Some refer this to the manna with which God fed his people Israel in the wilderness, others to the spoil they got from the Egyptians when they came out with great substance, according to the promise, Gen. xv. 14. When God *broke the heads of leviathan* he gave him to be *meat to his people,* Ps. lxxiv. 14. *He has given* prey *to those that fear him* (so the margin has it), not only fed them, but enriched them, and given their enemies to be a prey to them. 6. They are earnests of what he will do, according to his promise: *He will ever be mindful of his covenant,* for he has ever been so; and, as he never did, so he never will, let one jot or tittle of it fall to the ground. Though God's people have their infirmities, and are often unmindful of his commands, yet he *will ever be mindful of his covenant.*

6 He hath showed his people the power of his works, that he may give them the heritage of the heathen. 7 The works of his hands *are* verity and judgment; all his commandments *are* sure. 8 They stand fast for ever and ever, *and are* done in truth and uprightness. 9 He sent redemption unto his people : he hath commanded his covenant for ever : holy and reverend *is* his name. 10 The fear of the LORD *is* the beginning of wisdom : a good understanding have all they that do *his commandments :* his praise endureth for ever.

We are here taught to give glory to God,

I. For the great things he has done for his people, for his people Israel, of old and of late : *He has shown his people the power of his works* (*v.* 6), in what he has wrought for them; many a time he has given proofs of his omnipotence, and shown them what he can do, and that there is nothing too hard for him to do. Two things are specified to show *the power of his works :*—1. The possession God gave to Israel in the land of Canaan, *that he might give them,* or in giving them, *the heritage of the heathen.* This he did in Joshua's time, when the seven nations were subdued, and in David's time, when the neighbouring nations were many of them brought into subjection to Israel and became tributaries to David. Herein God showed his sovereignty, in disposing of kingdoms as he pleases, and his might, in making good his disposals If God will make the heritage of the heathen to be the heritage of Israel, who can either arraign his counsel or stay his hand ? 2. The many deliverances which he wrought for his people when by their iniquities they had sold themselves into the hand of their enemies (*v.* 9): *He sent redemption unto his people*, not only out of Egypt at first, but often afterwards; and these redemptions were typical of the great redemption which in the fulness of time was to be wrought out by the Lord Jesus, that redemption in Jerusalem which so many waited for.

II. For the stability both of his word and of his works, which assure us of the great things he will do for them. 1. What God has done shall never be undone. He will not undo it himself, and men and devils cannot (*v.* 7): *The works of his hand are verity and judgment* (*v.* 8), that is, they *are done in truth and uprightness;* all he does is consonant to the eternal rules and reasons of equity, all according to the counsel of his wisdom and the purpose of his will, all well done and therefore there is nothing to be altered or amended, but his works are firm and unchangeable. Upon the beginning of his works we may depend for the perfecting of them; work that is done properly will last, will neither go to decay nor sink under the stress that is laid upon it. 2. What God has said shall never be unsaid: *All his commandments are sure*, all straight and therefore all steady. His purposes, the rule of his actions, shall all have their accomplishment: *Has he spoken, and will he not make it good?* No doubt he will; whether he commands light or darkness, it is done as he commands. His precepts, the rule of our actions, are unquestionably just and good, and therefore unchangeable and not to be repealed; his promises and threatenings are all sure, and will be made good; nor shall the unbelief of man make either the one or the other of no effect. They are established, and therefore *they stand fast for ever and ever*, and the scripture cannot be broken. The wise God is never put upon new counsels, nor obliged to take new measures, either in his laws or in his providences. All is said, as all is done, in truth and uprightness, and therefore it is immutable. Men's folly and falsehood make them *unstable in all their ways*, but infinite wisdom and truth for ever exclude retraction and revocation: *He has commanded his covenant for ever.* God's covenant is commanded, for he has made it as one that has an incontestable authority to prescribe both what we must do and what we must expect, and an unquestionable ability to perform both what he has promised in the blessings of the covenant and what he has threatened in the curses of it, cv. 8.

III. For the setting up and establishing of religion among men. Because *holy and reverend is his name, and the fear of* him *is the beginning of wisdom*, therefore *his praise endureth for ever*, that is, he is to be everlastingly praised. 1. Because the discoveries of religion tend so much to his honour. Review what he has made known of himself in his word and in his works, and you will see, and say, that God is great and greatly

to be feared; for his name is holy, his infinite purity and rectitude appear in all that whereby he has made himself known, and because it is holy therefore it is reverend, and to be thought of and mentioned with a holy awe. Note, What is holy is reverend; the angels have an eye to God's holiness when they cover their faces before him, and nothing is more man's honour than his sanctification. It is in his holy places that God appears most terrible, lxviii. 35; Lev. x. 3. 2. Because the dictates of religion tend so much to man's happiness. We have reason to praise God that the matter is so well contrived that our reverence of him and obedience to him are as much our interest as they are our duty. (1.) Our reverence of him is so: *The fear of the Lord is the beginning of wisdom.* It is not only reasonable that we should fear God, because his name is reverend and his nature is holy, but it is advantageous to us. It is wisdom; it will direct us to speak and act as becomes us, in a consistency with ourselves, and for our own benefit. It is the head of wisdom, that is (as we read it), it *is the beginning of wisdom.* Men can never begin to be wise till they begin to fear God; all true wisdom takes its rise from true religion, and has its foundation in it. Or, as some understand it, it is the chief wisdom, and the most excellent, the first in dignity. It is the principal wisdom, and the principle of wisdom, to worship God and give honour to him as our Father and Master. Those manage well who always act under the government of his holy fear. (2.) Our obedience to him is so: *A good understanding have all those that do his commandments.* Where the fear of the Lord rules in the heart there will be a constant conscientious care to keep his commandments, not to talk of them, but to do them; and such have a good understanding, that is, [1.] They are well understood; their obedience is graciously accepted as a plain indication of their mind that they do indeed fear God. Compare Prov. iii. 4, *So shalt thou find favour and good understanding.* God and man will look upon those as meaning well, and approve of them, who make conscience of their duty, though they have their mistakes. What is honestly intended shall be well taken. [2.] They understand well. *First*, It is a sign that they do understand well. The most obedient are accepted as the most intelligent; those understand themselves and their interest best that make God's law their rule and are in every thing ruled by it. A great understanding those have that know God's commandments and can discourse learnedly of them, but a good understanding have those that do them and walk according to them. *Secondly*, It is the way to understand better: *A good understanding are they to all that do them;* the fear of the Lord and the laws of that give men a good understanding, and are able to make them *wise unto salvation.* If any man will do his will, he shall know more and more clearly of the doctrine of Christ, John vii. 17. *Good success have all those that do them* (so the margin), according to what was promised to Joshua if he would observe to do according to the law. Josh. i. 8, *Then thou shalt make thy way prosperous and shalt have good success.* We have reason to praise God, to praise him for ever, for putting man into such a fair way to happiness. Some apply the last words rather to the good man who fears the Lord than to the good God : *His praise endures for ever.* It is *not of men* perhaps, *but* it is *of God* (Rom. ii. 29), and that praise which is of God endures for ever when the praise of men is withered and gone.

PSALM CXII.

This psalm is composed alphabetically, as the former is, and is (like the former) entitled "Hallelujah," though it treats of the happiness of the saints, because it redounds to the glory of God, and whatever we have the pleasure of he must have the praise of. It is a comment upon the last verse of the foregoing psalm, and fully shows how much it is our wisdom to fear God and do his commandments. We have here, I. The character of the righteous, ver. 1. II. The blessedness of the righteous. 1. There is a blessing entailed upon their posterity, ver. 2. 2. There is a blessing conferred upon themselves. (1.) Prosperity outward and inward, ver. 3. (2.) Comfort, ver. 4. (3.) Wisdom, ver. 5. (4.) Stability, ver. 6–8. (5.) Honour, ver. 6, 9. III. The misery of the wicked, ver. 10. So that good and evil are set before us, the blessing and the curse. In singing this psalm we must not only teach and admonish ourselves and one another to answer to the characters here given of the happy, but comfort and encourage ourselves and one another with the privileges and comforts here secured to the holy.

PRAISE ye the LORD. Blessed *is* the man *that* feareth the LORD, *that* delighteth greatly in his commandments. 2 His seed shall be mighty upon earth : the generation of the upright shall be blessed. 3 Wealth and riches *shall be* in his house : and his righteousness endureth for ever. 4 Unto the upright there ariseth light in the darkness: *he is* gracious, and full of compassion, and righteous. 5 A good man showeth favour, and lendeth : he will guide his affairs with discretion.

The psalmist begins with a call to us to praise God, but immediately applies himself to praise the people of God; for whatever glory is acknowledged to be on them it comes from God, and must return to him ; as he is their praise, so they are his. We have reason to praise the Lord that there are a people in the world who fear him and serve him, and that they are a happy people, both which are owing entirely to the grace of God. Now here we have,

I. A description of those who are here pronounced blessed, and to whom these promises are made

1. They are well-principled with pious and devout affections. Those have the privileges of God's subjects, not who cry, Lord, Lord, but who are indeed well affected to his government. (1.) They are such as stand in awe of God and have a constant reverence for his majesty and deference to his will. The happy man is he *that fears the Lord, v.* 1. (2.) They are such as take a pleasure in their

duty. He *that fears the Lord,* as a Father, with the disposition of a child, not of a slave, *delights greatly in his commandments,* is well pleased with them and with the equity and goodness of them ; they are written in his heart ; it is his choice to be under them, and he calls them an easy, a pleasant, yoke ; it is his delight to be searching into and conversing with God's commandments, by reading, hearing, and meditation, Ps. i. 2. He delights not only in God's promises, but in his precepts, and thinks himself happy under God's government as well as in his favour. It is a pleasure to him to be found in the way of his duty, and he is in his element when he is in the service of God. Herein he delights greatly, more than in any of the employments and enjoyments of this world. And what he does in religion is done from principle, because he sees amiableness in religion and advantage by it.

2. They are honest and sincere in their professions and intentions. They are called the *upright* (*v.* 2, 4), who are really as good as they seem to be, and deal faithfully both with God and man. There is no true religion without sincerity ; that is gospel-perfection.

3. They are both just and kind in all their dealings : *He is gracious, full of compassion, and righteous* (*v.* 4), dares not do any wrong to any man, but does to every man all the good he can, and that from a principle of compassion and kindness. It was said of God, in the foregoing psalm (*v.* 4), He *is gracious, and full of compassion ;* and here it is said of the good man that he is so ; for herein we must be *followers of God as dear children;* be merciful as he is. He is *full of compassion, and yet righteous ;* what he does good with is what he came honestly by. God hates robbery for burnt-offerings, and so does he. One instance is given of his beneficence (*v.* 5) : He *shows favour and lends.* Sometimes there is as much charity in lending as in giving, as it obliges the borrower both to industry and honesty. He is *gracious and lends* (xxxvii. 26) ; he does it from a right principle, not as the usurer lends for his own advantage, nor merely out of generosity, but out of pure charity ; he does it in a right manner, not grudgingly, but pleasantly, and with a cheerful countenance.

II. The blessedness that is here entailed upon those that answer to these characters. Happiness, all happiness, to *the man that feareth the Lord.* Whatever men think or say of them, God says that they are blessed ; and his saying so makes them so.

1. The posterity of good men shall fare the better for his goodness (*v.* 2) : *His seed shall be mighty on earth.* Perhaps he himself shall not be so great in the world, nor make such a figure, as his seed after him shall for his sake. Religion has been the raising of many a family, if not so as to advance it high, yet so as to fix it firmly. When good men themselves are happy in heaven their seed perhaps are considerable

665

on earth, and will themselves own that it is by virtue of a blessing descending from them. *The generation of the upright shall be blessed;* if they tread in their steps, they shall be the more blessed for their relation to them, *beloved for the Father's sake* (Rom. xi. 28), for so runs the covenant—*I will be a God to thee, and to thy seed;* while *the seed of evil-doers shall never be renowned.* Let the children of godly parents value themselves upon it, and take heed of doing any thing to forfeit the blessing entailed upon the generation of the upright.

2. They shall prosper in the world, and especially their souls shall prosper, *v.* 3. (1.) They shall be blessed with outward prosperity as far as is good for them: *Wealth and riches shall be in* the upright man's *house,* not in his heart (for he is none of those in whom the love of money reigns), perhaps not so much in his hand (for he only begins to raise the estate), but in his house; his family shall grow rich when he is gone. But, (2.) That which is much better is that they shall be blessed with spiritual blessings, which are the true riches. His *wealth shall be in his house,* for he must leave that to others; but *his righteousness* he himself shall have the comfort of to himself, it *endures for ever.* Grace is better than gold, for it will outlast it. He shall have wealth and riches, and yet shall keep up his religion, and in a prosperous condition shall *still hold fast his integrity,* which many, who kept it in the storm, throw off and let go in the sunshine. *Then* worldly prosperity is a blessing when it does not make men cool in their piety, but they still persevere in that; and when this endures in the family, and goes along with the wealth and riches, and the heirs of the father's estate inherit his virtues too, that is a happy family indeed. However, the good man's *righteousness endures for ever* in the *crown of righteousness which fades not away*

3. They shall have comfort in affliction (*v.* 4): *Unto the upright there arises light in the darkness.* It is here implied that good men may be in affliction; the promise does not exempt them from that. They shall have their share in the common calamities of human life; but, *when they sit in darkness, the Lord shall be a light to them,* Mic. vii. 8. They shall be supported and comforted under their troubles; their spirits shall be lightsome when their outward condition is clouded. *Sat lucis intus*—*There is light enough within.* During the Egyptian darkness the Israelites had *light in their dwellings.* They shall be in due time, and perhaps when they least expect it, delivered out of their troubles; when the night is darkest the day dawns; nay, at *evening-time,* when night was looked for, *it shall be light.*

4. They shall have wisdom for the management of all their concerns, *v.* 5. He that does good with his estate shall, through the providence of God, increase it, not by miracle,

but by his prudence: *He shall guide his affairs with discretion,* and his God *instructs him to discretion* and *teaches him,* Isa. xxviii. 26. It is part of the character of a good man that he will use his discretion in managing his affairs, in getting and saving, that he may have to give. It may be understood of the affairs of his charity: He *shows favour and lends;* but then it is with discretion, that his charity may not be misplaced, that he may give to proper objects what is proper to be given and in due time and proportion. And it is part of the promise to him who thus uses discretion that God will give him more. Those who most use their wisdom see most of their need of it, and *ask it of God,* who has promised to *give it liberally,* Jam. i. 5. *He will guide his words with judgment* (so it is in the original); and there is nothing in which we have more occasion for wisdom than in the government of the tongue; blessed is he to whom God gives that wisdom.

6 Surely he shall not be moved for ever: the righteous shall be in everlasting remembrance. 7 He shall not be afraid of evil tidings: his heart is fixed, trusting in the LORD. 8 His heart *is* established, he shall not be afraid, until he see *his desire* upon his enemies. 9 He hath dispersed, he hath given to the poor; his righteousness endureth for ever; his horn shall be exalted with honour. 10 The wicked shall see *it,* and be grieved; he shall gnash with his teeth, and melt away: the desire of the wicked shall perish.

In these verses we have,

I. The satisfaction of saints, and their stability. It is the happiness of a good man that *he shall not be moved for ever, v.* 6. Satan and his instruments endeavour to move him, but his foundation is firm and he shall never be moved, at least *not moved for ever;* if he be shaken for a time, yet he settles again quickly.

1. A good man will have a settled reputation, and that is a great satisfaction. A good man shall have a good name, a name for good things, with God and good people: *The righteous shall be in everlasting remembrance (v.* 6); in this sense *his righteousness* (the memorial of it) *endures for ever, v.* 9. There are those that do all they can to sully his reputation and to load him with reproach; but his integrity shall be cleared up, and the honour of it shall survive him. Some that have been eminently righteous are *had in a lasting remembrance* on earth; wherever the scripture is read their good deeds are *told for a memorial* of them. And the memory of many a good man that is dead and gone is still blessed; but in heaven their remembrance shall be truly everlasting, and the honour of

their righteousness shall there endure for ever, with the reward of it, in the *crown of glory that fades not away.* Those that are forgotten on earth, and despised, are remembered there, and honoured, and *their righteousness found unto praise, and honour, and glory* (1 Pet. i. 7); then, at furthest, shall the horn of a good man *be exalted with honour,* as that of the unicorn when he is a conqueror. Wicked men, now in their pride, *lift up their horns on high,* but they shall all be *cut off,* lxxv. 5, 10. The godly, in their humility and humiliation, have *defiled their horn in the dust* (Job xvi. 15); but the day is coming when it *shall be exalted with honour.* That which shall especially turn to the honour of good men is their liberality and bounty to the poor: *He has dispersed, he has given to the poor;* he has not suffered his charity to run all in one channel, or directed it to some few objects that he had a particular kindness for, but he has dispersed it, *given a portion to seven and also to eight,* has *sown beside all waters,* and by thus scattering he has increased: and this is *his righteousness, which endures for ever.* Alms are called *righteousness,* not because they will justify us by making atonement for our evil deeds, but because they are good deeds, which we are bound to perform; so that if we are not charitable we are not just; we *withhold good from those to whom it is due.* The honour of this endures for ever, for it shall be taken notice of in the great day. *I was hungry, and you gave me meat.* This is quoted as an inducement and encouragement to charity, 2 Cor. ix. 9.

2. A good man shall have a settled spirit, and that is a much greater satisfaction than the former; for *so shall a man have rejoicing in himself alone, and not in another.* Surely *he shall not be moved,* whatever happens, not moved either from his duty or from his comfort; for *he shall not be afraid; his heart is established, v.* 7, 8. This is a part both of the character and of the comfort of good people. It is their endeavour to keep their minds stayed upon God, and so to keep them calm, and easy, and undisturbed; and God has promised them both cause to do so and grace to do so. Observe, (1.) It is the duty and interest of the people of God not to *be afraid of evil tidings,* not to be afraid of hearing bad news; and, when they do, not to be put into confusion by it and into an amazing expectation of worse and worse, but whatever happens, whatever threatens, to be able to say, with blessed Paul, *None of these things move me,* neither will I *fear, though the earth be removed,* xlvi. 2. (2.) The fixedness of the heart is a sovereign remedy against the disquieting fear of evil tidings. If we keep our thoughts composed, and ourselves masters of them, our wills resigned to the holy will of God, our temper sedate, and our spirits even, under all the unevenness of Providence, we are well fortified against the agitations of

the timorous. (3.) Trusting in the Lord is the best and surest way of fixing and establishing the heart. By faith we must cast anchor in the promise, in the word of God, and so return to him and repose in him as our rest. The heart of man cannot fix any where, to its satisfaction, but in the truth of God, and there it finds firm footing. (4.) Those whose hearts are established by faith will patiently wait till they have gained their point: *He shall not be afraid, till he see his desire upon his enemies,* that is, till he come to heaven, where he shall see Satan, and all his spiritual enemies, trodden under his feet, and, as Israel saw the Egyptians, dead on the sea-shore. *Till he look upon his oppressors* (so Dr. Hammond), till he behold them securely, and look boldly in their faces, as being now no longer under their power. It will complete the satisfaction of the saints, when they shall look back upon their troubles and pressures, and be able to say with St. Paul, when he had recounted the persecutions he endured (2 Tim. iii. 11), *But out of them all the Lord delivered me.*

II. The vexation of sinners, *v.* 10. Two things shall fret them:—1. The felicity of the righteous: *The wicked shall see* the righteous in prosperity and honour and shall *be grieved.* It will vex them to see their innocency cleared and their low estate regarded, and those whom they hated and despised, and whose ruin they sought and hoped to see, the favourites of Heaven, and advanced to have *dominion over them* (xlix. 14); this will make them *gnash with their teeth and pine away.* This is often fulfilled in this world. The happiness of the saints is the envy of the wicked, and that envy is the *rottenness of their bones.* But it will most fully be accomplished in the other world, when it shall make damned sinners *gnash with their teeth,* to see *Abraham afar off, and Lazarus in his bosom,* to see *all the prophets in the kingdom of God and themselves thrust out.* 2. Their own disappointment: *The desire of the wicked shall perish.* Their desire was wholly to the world and the flesh, and they ruled over them; and therefore, when these perish, their joy is gone, and their expectations from them are cut off, to their everlasting confusion; their hope is as a spider's web.

PSALM CXIII.

This psalm begins and ends with "Hallelujah;" for, as many others, it is designed to promote the great and good work of praising God, ver. 1—3. II. We are here furnished with matter for praise, and words are put into our mouths, in singing which we must with holy fear and love give to God the glory of, 1. The elevations of his glory and greatness, ver. 4, 5. 2. The condescensions of his grace and goodness (ver. 6—9), which very much illustrate one another, that we may be duly affected with both.

PRAISE ye the LORD. Praise, O ye servants of the LORD, praise the name of the LORD. 2 Blessed be the name of the LORD from this time forth and for evermore. 3 From the rising of the sun unto the going down of the same the Lord's name *is* to be praised. 4 The Lord *is* high above all nations, *and* his glory above the heavens. 5 Who *is* like unto the Lord our God, who dwelleth on high, 6 Who humbleth *himself* to behold *the things that are* in heaven, and in the earth! 7 He raiseth up the poor out of the dust, *and* lifteth the needy out of the dunghill; 8 That he may set *him* with princes, *even* with the princes of his people. 9 He maketh the barren woman to keep house, *and to be* a joyful mother of children. Praise ye the Lord.

In this psalm,

I. We are exhorted to give glory to God, to give him the glory due to his name.

1. The invitation is very pressing: *Praise you the Lord*, and again and again, *Praise him, praise him ; blessed be his name*, for it is to be praised, *v.* 1—3. This intimates, (1.) That it is a necessary and most excellent duty, greatly pleasing to God, and has a large room in religion. (2) That it is a duty we should much abound in, in which we should be frequently employed and greatly enlarged. (3.) That it is work which we are very backward to, and which we need to be engaged and excited to by precept upon precept and line upon line. (4.) That those who are much in praising God themselves will court others to it, both because they find the weight of the work, and that there is need of all the help they can fetch in (there is employment for all hearts, all hands, and all little enough), and because they find the pleasure of it, which they wish all their friends may share in.

2. The invitation is very extensive. Observe, (1.) From whom God has praise—from his own people ; they are here called upon to praise God, as those that will answer the call : *Praise, O you servants of the Lord !* They have most reason to praise him ; for those that attend him as his servants know him best and receive most of his favours. And it is their business to praise him ; that is the work required of them as his servants : it is easy pleasant work to speak well of their Master, and do him what honour they can ; if they do not, who should ? Some understand it of the Levites ; but, if so, all Christians are a royal priesthood, *to show forth the praises of him that has called them*, 1 Pet. ii. 9. The angels are the servants of the Lord ; they need not be called upon by us to praise God, yet it is a comfort to us that they do praise him, and that they praise him better than we can. (2.) From whom he ought to have praise. [1.] From all ages (*v.* 2)—*from this time forth for evermore*. Let not this work die with us, but let us be doing it in a better world, and let those that come after us be doing it in

668

this. Let not our seed degenerate, but let God be praised through all the generations of time, and not in this only. We must bless the Lord in our day, by saying, with the psalmist, *Blessed be his name now and always*. [2.] From all places—*from the rising of the sun to the going down of the same*, that is, throughout the habitable world. Let all that enjoy the benefit of the sun rising (and those that do so must count upon it that the sun will set) give thanks for that light to the Father of lights. God's *name is to be praised ;* it ought to be praised by all nations ; for in every place, from east to west, there appear the manifest proofs and products of his wisdom, power, and goodness ; and it is to be lamented that so great a part of mankind are ignorant of him, and give that praise to others which is due to him alone. But perhaps there is more in it ; as the former verse gave us a glimpse of the kingdom of glory, intimating that God's name shall be *blessed for ever* (when time shall be no more that praise shall be the work of heaven), so this verse gives us a glimpse of the kingdom of grace in the gospel-dispensation of it. When the church shall no longer be confined to the Jewish nation, but shall spread itself all the world over, when in *every place* spiritual *incense shall be offered to our God* (Mal. i. 11), then from *the rising to the setting of the sun the Lord's name shall be praised* by some in all countries.

II. We are here directed what to give him the glory of.

1. Let us look up with an eye of faith, and see how high his glory is in the upper world, and mention that to his praise, *v.* 4, 5. We are, in our praises, to exalt his name, for he is high, his glory is high. (1.) *High above all nations*, their kings though ever so pompous, their people though ever so numerous. Whether it be true of an earthly king or no that though he is *major singulis—greater than individuals*, he is *minor universis—less than the whole*, we will not dispute ; but we are sure it is not true of the King of kings. Put all the nations together, and he is above them all ; they are before him as the *drop of the bucket and the small dust of the balance*, Isa. xl. 15, 17. Let all nations think and speak highly of God, for he is high above them all. (2.) High *above the heavens ;* the throne of his glory is in the highest heavens, which should raise our hearts in praising him, Lam. iii. 41. *His glory is above the heavens*, that is, above the angels ; he is above what they are, for their brightness is nothing to his,—above what they do, for they are under his command and do his pleasure,—and above what even they can speak him to be. He is exalted above *all blessing and praise*, not only all ours, but all theirs. We must therefore say, with holy admiration, *Who is like unto the Lord our God ?* who of all the princes and potentates of the earth ? who of all the bright and blessed spirits above ? None can equal him, none

dare compare with him. God is to be praised as transcendently, incomparably, and infinitely great; for he *dwells on high*, and from on high sees all, and rules all, and justly attracts all praise to himself.

2. Let us look around with an eye of observation, and see how extensive his goodness is in the lower world, and mention that to his praise. He is a God *who exalts himself to dwell, who humbles himself in heaven, and in earth*. Some think there is a transposition, *He exalts himself to dwell in heaven, he humbles himself to behold on earth;* but the sense is plain enough as we take it, only observe, God is said to *exalt himself* and to *humble himself*, both are his own act and deed; as he is self-existent, so he is both the fountain of his own honour and the spring of his own grace; God's condescending goodness appears,

(1.) In the cognizance he takes of the world below him. His glory is *above the nations* and *above the heavens,* and yet neither is neglected by him. *God is great, yet he despises not any*, Job xxxvi. 5. *He humbles himself to behold* all his creatures, all his subjects, though he is infinitely above them. Considering the infinite perfection, sufficiency, and felicity of the divine nature, it must be acknowledged as an act of wonderful condescension that God is pleased to take into the thoughts of his eternal counsel, and into the hand of his universal Providence, both the armies of heaven and the inhabitants of the earth (Dan. iv. 35); even in this dominion he humbles himself. [1.] It is condescension in him to behold the things in heaven, to support the beings, direct the motions, and accept the praises and services, of the angels themselves; for he needs them not, nor is benefited by them. [2.] Much more is it condescension in him to *behold the things that are in the earth*, to visit the sons of men, and regard them, to order and overrule their affairs, and to take notice of what they say and do, that he may fill the earth with his goodness, and so set us an example of stooping to do good, of taking notice of, and concerning ourselves about, our inferiors. If it be such condescension for God to behold things in heaven and earth, what an amazing condescension was it for the Son of God to come from heaven to earth and take our nature upon him, that he might *seek and save those that were lost!* Herein indeed he humbled himself.

(2.) In the particular favour he sometimes shows to the least and lowest of the inhabitants of this meaner lower world. He not only beholds the great things in the earth, but the meanest, and those things which great men commonly overlook. Nor does he merely behold them, but does wonders for them, and things that are very surprising, out of the common road of providence and chain of causes, which shows that the world is governed, not by a course of nature, for that

would always run in the same channel, but by a God of nature, who delights in doing things we looked not for. [1.] Those that have been long despicable are sometimes, on a sudden, made honourable (*v*. 7, 8): *He raises up the poor out of the dust, that he may set him with princes.* First, Thus God does sometimes magnify himself, and his own wisdom, power, and sovereignty. When he has some great work to do he chooses to employ those in it that were least likely, and least thought of for it by themselves or others, to the highest post of honour: Gideon is fetched from threshing, Saul from seeking the asses, and David from keeping the sheep; the apostles are sent from fishing to be *fishers of men*. The treasure of the gospel is put into earthen vessels, and the weak and foolish ones of the world are pitched upon to be preachers of it, to confound the *wise and mighty* (1 Cor. i. 27, 28), that the excellency of the power may be of God, and all may see that promotion comes from him. Secondly, Thus God does sometimes reward the eminent piety and patience of his people who have long groaned under the burden of poverty and disgrace. When Joseph's virtue was tried and manifested he was raised from the prison-dust and *set with princes*. Those that are wise will observe such returns of Providence, and will understand by them *the loving-kindness of the Lord*. Some have applied this to the work of redemption by Jesus Christ, and not unfitly; for through him poor fallen men are raised out of the dust (one of the Jewish rabbies applies it to the resurrection of the dead), nay, out of the dunghill of sin, and *set among princes*, among angels, those princes of his people. Hannah had sung to this purport, 1 Sam. ii. 6—8. [2.] Those that have been long barren are sometimes, on a sudden, made fruitful, *v*. 9. This may look back to Sarah and Rebecca, Rachel, Hannah, and Samson's mother, or forward to Elizabeth; and many such instances there have been, in which God has looked on the affliction of his handmaids and taken away their reproach. *He makes the barren woman to keep house*, not only builds up the family, but thereby finds the heads of the family something to do. Note, Those that have the comfort of a family must take the care of it; *bearing children* and *guiding the house* are put together, 1 Tim. v. 14. When God *sets the barren in a family* he expects that she should *look well to the ways of her household*, Prov. xxxi. 27. She is said to *be a joyful mother of children*, not only because, even in common cases, the pain is forgotten, *for joy that a man-child is born into the world*, but there is particular joy when a child is born to those that have been long childless (as Luke i. 14) and therefore there ought to be particular thanksgiving. *Praise you the Lord*. Yet, in this case, *rejoice with trembling;* for, though the sorrowful mother be made joyful, the joyful mother may be made sorrowful again, if the children be either removed from her or embittered to her. This, therefore, may be applied to the gospel-church among the Gentiles (the building of which is illustrated by this similitude, Isa. liv. 1, *Sing, O barren! thou that didst not bear,* and Gal. iv. 27), for which we, who, being sinners of the Gentiles, are children of the desolate, have reason to say, *Praise you the Lord.*

PSALM CXIV.

The deliverance of Israel out of Egypt gave birth to their church and nation, which were then founded, then formed; that work of wonder ought therefore to be had in everlasting remembrance. God gloried in it, in the preface to the ten commandments, and Hos. xi. 1, "Out of Egypt have I called my son." In this psalm it is celebrated in lively strains of praise; it was fitly therefore made a part of the great Hallelujah, or song of praise, which the Jews were wont to sing at the close of the passover-supper. It must never be forgotten, I. That they were brought out of slavery, ver. 1. II. That God set up his tabernacle among them, ver. 2. III. That the sea and Jordan were divided before them, ver 3, 5. IV. That the earth shook at the giving of the law, when God came down on Mount Sinai, ver. 4, 6, 7. V. That God gave them water out of the rock, ver. 8. In singing this psalm we must acknowledge God's power and goodness in what he did for Israel, applying it to the much greater work of wonder, our redemption by Christ, and encouraging ourselves and others to trust in God in the greatest straits.

WHEN Israel went out of Egypt, the house of Jacob from a people of strange language; 2 Judah was his sanctuary, *and* Israel his dominion. 3 The sea saw *it*, and fled: Jordan was driven back. 4 The mountains skipped like rams, *and* the little hills like lambs. 5 What *ailed* thee, O thou sea, that thou fleddest? thou Jordan, *that* thou wast driven back? 6 Ye mountains, *that* ye skipped like rams; *and* ye little hills, like lambs? 7 Tremble, thou earth, at the presence of the Lord, at the presence of the God of Jacob; 8 Which turned the rock *into* a standing water, the flint into a fountain of waters.

The psalmist is here remembering *the days of old, the years of the right hand of the Most High,* and the wonders which their fathers told them of (Judg. vi. 13), for time, as it does not wear out the guilt of sin, so it should not wear out the sense of mercy. Let it never be forgotten,

I. That God brought Israel out of the house of bondage with a high hand and a stretched-out arm: *Israel went out of Egypt, v.* 1. They did not steal out clandestinely, nor were they driven out, but fairly went out, marched out with all the marks of honour; they went out from a barbarous people, that had used them barbarously, from *a people of a strange language,* lxxxi. 5. The Israelites, it seems, preserved their own language pure among them, and cared not for learning the language of their oppressors. By this distinction from them they kept up an earnest of their deliverance.

II. That he himself framed their civil and sacred constitution (*v.* 2): *Judah and Israel were his sanctuary, his dominion.* When he

delivered them out of the hand of their oppressors it was *that they might serve him* both *in holiness and in righteousness,* in the duties of religious worship and in obedience to the moral law, in their whole conversation. *Let my people go, that they may serve me.* In order to this, 1. He set up his sanctuary among them, in which he gave them the special tokens of his presence with them and promised to receive their homage and tribute. Happy are the people that have God's sanctuary among them (see Exod. xxv. 8, Ezek. xxxvii. 26), much more those that, like Judah here, are his *sanctuaries,* his living temples, on whom *Holiness to the Lord* is written. 2. He set up his dominion among them, was himself their lawgiver and their judge, and their government was a theocracy: *The Lord was their King.* All the world is God's dominion, but Israel was so in a peculiar manner. What is God's sanctuary must be his dominion. Those only have the privileges of his house that submit to the laws of it; and for this end Christ has redeemed us that he might bring us into God's service and engage us for ever in it.

III. That the Red Sea was divided before them at their coming out of Egypt, both for their rescue and the ruin of their enemies; and the river Jordan, when they entered into Canaan, for their honour, and the confusion and terror of their enemies (*v.* 3): *The sea saw it,* saw there that *Judah was* God's *sanctuary, and Israel his dominion, and* therefore *fled;* for nothing could be more awful. It was this that *drove Jordan back,* and was an invincible dam to his streams; God was at the head of that people, and therefore they must give way to them, must make room for them, they must retire, contrary to their nature, when God speaks the word. To illustrate this the psalmist asks, in a poetical strain (*v.* 5), *What ailed thee, O thou sea! that thou fleddest?* And furnishes the sea with an answer (*v.* 7); it was *at the presence of the Lord.* This is designed to express, 1. The reality of the miracle, that it was not by any power of nature, or from any natural cause, but it was *at the presence of the Lord,* who gave the word. 2. The mercy of the miracle: *What ailed thee?* Was it in a frolic? Was it only to amuse men? No; it was *at the presence of the God of Jacob;* it was in kindness to the Israel of God, *for the salvation* of that chosen people, that God was thus *displeased against the rivers,* and his *wrath was against the sea,* as the prophet speaks, Hab. iii. 8—13; Isa. li. 10; lxiii. 11, &c. 3. The wonder and surprise of the miracle. Who would have thought of such a thing? Shall the course of nature be changed, and its fundamental laws dispensed with, to serve a turn for God's Israel? Well may the *dukes of Edom be amazed* and the *mighty men of Moab tremble,* Exod. xv. 15. 4. The honour hereby put upon Israel, who are taught to triumph over the sea, and Jordan, as unable to stand before them. Note, There is no sea, no Jordan, so deep, so broad, but, when God's time shall come for the redemption of his people, it shall be divided and driven back if it stand in their way. Apply this, (1.) To the planting of the Christian church in the world. What ailed Satan and the powers of darkness, that they trembled and truckled as they did? Mark i. 34. What ailed the heathen oracles, that they were silenced, struck dumb, struck dead? What ailed their idolatries and witchcrafts, that they died away before the gospel, and melted like snow before the sun? What ailed the persecutors and opposers of the gospel, that they gave up their cause, hid their guilty heads, and called to rocks and mountains for shelter? Rev. vi. 15. It was *at the presence of the Lord,* and that power which went along with the gospel. (2.) To the work of grace in the heart. What turns the stream in a regenerate soul? What ails the lusts and corruptions, that they fly back, that the prejudices are removed and the whole man has become new? It is at the presence of God's Spirit that imaginations are *cast down,* 2 Cor. x. 5.

IV. That the earth shook and trembled when God came down on Mount Sinai to give the law (*v.* 4): *The mountains skipped like rams, and* then *the little hills* might well be excused if they skipped *like lambs,* either when they are frightened or when they sport themselves. The same power that fixed the fluid waters and made them stand still shook the stable mountains and made them tremble for all the powers of nature are under the check of the God of nature. Mountains and hills are, before God, but like rams and lambs; even the bulkiest and the most rocky are as manageable by him as *they* are by the shepherd. The trembling of the mountains before the Lord may shame the stupidity and obduracy of the children of men, who are not moved at the discoveries of his glory. The psalmist asks the mountains and hills what ailed them to skip thus; and he answers for them, as for the seas, it was *at the presence of the Lord,* before whom, not only those mountains, but the earth itself, may well tremble (*v.* 7), since it has lain under a curse for man's sin. See Ps. civ. 32; Isa. lxiv. 3, 4. He that made the hills and mountains to skip thus can, when he pleases, dissipate the strength and spirit of the proudest of his enemies and make them tremble.

V. That God supplied them with water out of the rock, which followed them through the dry and sandy deserts. Well may the earth and all its inhabitants tremble before that God who *turned the rock into a standing water* (*v.* 8), and what cannot he do who did that? The same almighty power that turned waters into a rock to be a wall to Israel (Exod. xiv. 22) turned the rock into waters to be a well to Israel: as they were protected, so they were provided for, by miracles, stand-

ing miracles; for such was the standing water, that fountain of waters into which the rock, the flinty rock, was turned, *and that rock was Christ,* 1 Cor. x. 4. For he is a fountain of living waters to his Israel, from whom they receive grace for grace.

PSALM CXV.

Many ancient translations join this psalm to that which goes next before it, the Septuagint particularly, and the vulgar Latin; but it is, in the Hebrew, a distinct psalm. In it we are taught to give glory, I. To God, and not to ourselves, ver. 1. II. To God, and not to idols, ver. 2—8. We must give glory to God, 1. By trusting in him, and in his promise and blessing, ver. 9—15. 2. By blessing him, ver. 16—18. Some think this psalm was penned upon occasion of some great distress and trouble that the church of God was in, when the enemies were insolent and threatening, in which case the church does not so much pour out her complaint to God as place her confidence in God, and triumph in doing so; and with such a holy triumph we ought to sing this psalm.

NOT unto us, O LORD, not unto us, but unto thy name give glory for thy mercy, *and* for thy truth's sake. 2 Wherefore should the heathen say, Where *is* now their God? 3 But our God *is* in the heavens: he hath done whatsoever he hath pleased. 4 Their idols *are* silver and gold, the work of men's hands. 5 They have mouths, but they speak not: eyes have they, but they see not: 6 They have ears, but they hear not: noses have they, but they smell not: 7 They have hands, but they handle not: feet have they, but they walk not: neither speak they through their throat. 8 They that make them are like unto them; *so is* every one that trusteth in them.

Sufficient care is here taken to answer both the pretensions of self and the reproaches of idolaters.

I. Boasting is here for ever excluded, *v.* 1. Let no opinion of our own merits have any room either in our prayers or in our praises, but let both centre in God's glory. 1. Have we received any mercy, gone through any service, or gained any success? We must not assume the glory of it to ourselves, but ascribe it wholly to God. We must not imagine that we do any thing for God by our own strength, or deserve any thing from God by our own righteousness; but all the good we do is done by the power of his grace, and all the good we have is the gift of his mere mercy, and therefore he must have all the praise. Say not, *The power of my hand has gotten me this wealth,* Deut. viii. 17. Say not, *For my righteousness the Lord has done these great and kind things for me,* Deut. ix. 4. No; all our songs must be sung to this humble tune, *Not unto us, O Lord!* and again, *Not unto us, but to thy name,* let all the glory be given; for whatever good is wrought in us, or wrought for us, it is for his mercy and his truth's sake, because he will glorify his mercy and fulfil his promise. All our crowns must be cast at the feet of *him that sits upon the throne*, for that is the proper place for them. 2. Are we in pursuit of any mercy and wrestling with God for it? We must take our encouragement, in prayer, from God only, and have an eye to his glory more than to our own benefit in it. " Lord, do so and so for us, not that we may have the credit and comfort of it, but that thy mercy and truth may have the glory of it." This must be our highest and ultimate end in our prayers, and therefore it is made the first petition in the Lord's prayer, as that which guides all the rest, *Hallowed be thy name;* and, in order to that, *Give us our daily bread,* &c. This also must satisfy us, if our prayers be not answered in the letter of them. Whatever becomes of us, *unto thy name give glory.* See John xii. 27, 28.

II. The reproach of the heathen is here for ever silenced and justly retorted.

1. The psalmist complains of the reproach of the heathen (v. 2): *Wherefore should they say, Where is now their God?* (1) "Why do they say so? Do they not know that our God is every where by his providence, and always nigh to us by his promise and grace?" (2.) " Why does God permit them to say so? Nay, why is Israel brought so low that they have some colour for saying so? Lord, appear for our relief, that thou mayest vindicate thyself, and glorify thy own name."

2. He gives a direct answer to their question, v. 3. " Do they ask where is our God? We can tell where he is." (1.) " In the upper world is the presence of his glory : *Our God is in the heavens,* where the gods of the heathen never were, *in the heavens,* and therefore out of sight ; but, though his majesty be unapproachable, it does not therefore follow that his being is questionable." (2.) " In the lower world are the products of his power : *He has done whatsoever he pleased,* according to the counsel of his will ; he has a sovereign dominion and a universal uncontrollable influence. Do you ask where he is? He is at the beginning and end of every thing, *and not far from any of us.*"

3. He returns their question upon themselves. They asked, Where is the God of Israel? because he is not seen. He does in effect ask, What are the gods of the heathen? because they are seen. (1.) He shows that their gods, though they are not shapeless things, are senseless things. Idolaters, at first, worshipped the sun and moon (Job xxxi. 26), which was bad enough, but not so bad as that which they were now come to (for evil men grow worse and worse), which was the worshipping of images, v. 4. The matter of them was *silver and gold,* dug out of the earth *(man found them poor and dirty in a mine,* Herbert*),* proper things to make money of, but not to make gods of. The make of them was from the artificer · they are creatures of men's vain imaginations and *the works of men's hands,* and therefore

can have no divinity in them. If man is the work of God's hands (as certainly he is, and it was his honour that he was made *in the image of God)* it is absurd to think that that can be God which is the work of men's hands, or that it can be any other than a dishonour to God to make him in the image of man. The argument is irrefragable : *The workmen made it, therefore it is not God,* Hos. viii. 6. These idols are represented here as the most ridiculous things, a mere jest, that would seem to be something, but were really nothing, fitter for a toy-shop than a temple, for children to play with than for men to pray to. The painter, the carver, the statuary, did their part well enough ; they made them with *mouths* and *eyes, ears* and *noses, hands* and *feet,* but they could put no life into them and therefore no sense. They had better have worshipped a dead carcase (for that had life in it once) than a dead image, which neither has life nor can have. *They speak not,* in answer to those that consult them ; the crafty priest must speak for them. In Baal's image there was *no voice, neither any that answered. They see not* the prostrations of their worshippers before them, much less their burdens and wants. *They hear not* their prayers, though ever so loud ; *they smell not* their incense, though ever so strong, ever so sweet ; *they handle not* the gifts presented to them, much less have they any gifts to bestow on their worshippers ; they cannot *stretch forth their hands to the needy. They walk not,* they cannot stir a step for the relief of those that apply to them. Nay, they do not so much as *breathe through their throat;* they have not the least sign or symptom of life, but are as dead, after the priest has pretended to consecrate them and call a deity into them, as they were before. (2.) He thence infers the sottishness of their worshippers (v. 8): *Those that make them* images show their ingenuity, and doubtless are sensible men ; but *those that make them* gods show their stupidity and folly, and *are like unto them,* as senseless blockish things ; *they see not* the invisible things of the true and living God in the works of creation ; *they hear not* the voice of the day and the night, which in every speech and language declare his glory, xix. 2, 3. By worshipping these foolish puppets, they make themselves more and more foolish like them, and set themselves at a greater distance from every thing that is spiritual, sinking themselves deeper into the mire of sense ; and withal they provoke God to *give them up to a reprobate mind, a mind void of judgment,* Rom. i. 28. Those *that trust in them* act very absurdly and very unreasonably, are senseless, helpless, useless, like them ; and they will find it so themselves, to their own confusion. We shall know where our God is, and so shall they, to their cost, when their gods are gone, Jer. x. 3--11 ; Isa. xliv. 9, &c.

9 O Israel, trust thou in the LORD:

he *is* their help and their shield. 10 O house of Aaron, trust in the LORD : he *is* their help and their shield. 11 Ye that fear the LORD, trust in the LORD : he *is* their help and their shield. 12 The LORD hath been mindful of us : he will bless *us;* he will bless the house of Israel ; he will bless the house of Aaron. 13 He will bless them that fear the LORD, *both* small and great. 14 The LORD shall increase you more and more, you and your children. 15 Ye *are* blessed of the LORD which made heaven and earth. 16 The heaven, *even* the heavens, *are* the LORD's : but the earth hath he given to the children of men. 17 The dead praise not the LORD, neither any that go down into silence. 18 But we will bless the LORD from this time forth and for evermore. Praise the LORD.

In these verses,

I. We are earnestly exhorted, all of us, to repose our confidence in God, and not suffer our confidence in him to be shaken by the heathens' insulting over us upon the account of our present distresses. It is folly to trust in dead images, but it is wisdom to trust in the living God, for he is a *help and a shield* to those that do *trust in them,* a help to furnish them with and forward them in that which is good, and a shield to fortify them against and protect them from every thing that is evil. Therefore, 1. Let Israel trust in the Lord ; the body of the people, as to their public interests, and every particular Israelite, as to his own private concerns, let them leave it to God to dispose of all for them, and believe he will dispose of all for the best and will be *their help and shield.* 2. Let the priests, the Lord's ministers, and all the families of the *house of Aaron, trust in the Lord* (v. 10) ; they are most maligned and struck at by the enemies and therefore of them God takes particular care. They ought to be examples to others of a cheerful confidence in God, and a faithful adherence to him in the worst of times. 3. Let the proselytes, who are not of the seed of Israel, but *fear the Lord,* who worship him and make conscience of their duty to him, let them *trust in him,* for he will not fail nor forsake them, *v.* 11. Note, Wherever there is an awful fear of God, there may be a cheerful faith in him : those that reverence his word may rely upon it.

II. We are greatly encouraged to trust in God, and good reason is given us why we should stay ourselves upon him with an entire satisfaction. Consider, 1. What we have experienced (*v.* 12) : *The Lord has been mind-*

ful of us, and never unmindful, has been so constantly, has been so remarkably upon special occasions. He has been mindful of our case, our wants and burdens, mindful of our prayers to him, his promises to us, and the covenant-relation between him and us. All our comforts are derived from God's *thoughts to us-ward;* he *has been mindful of us,* though we have forgotten him. Let *this* engage us to trust in him, that we have found him faithful. 2. What we may expect. From what he has done for us we may infer, He *will bless us;* he that has been our *help and our shield* will be so ; he that has *remembered us in our low estate* will not forget us ; for he is still the same, his power and goodness the same, and his promise inviolable ; so that we have reason to hope that he who has delivered, and does, will yet deliver. Yet this is not all : He *will bless us;* he has promised that he will ; he has pronounced a blessing upon all his people. God's blessing us is not only speaking good to us, but doing well for us ; those whom he blesses are blessed indeed. It is particularly promised that *he will bless the house of Israel,* that is, he will bless the commonwealth, will bless his people in their civil interests. *He will bless the house of Aaron,* that is, the church, the ministry, will bless his people in their religious concerns. The priests were to bless the people ; it was their office (Num. vi. 23) ; but God blessed them, and so blessed their blessings. Nay (*v.* 13), *he will bless those that fear the Lord,* though they be not of the house of Israel or the house of Aaron ; for it was a truth, before Peter perceived it, *That in every nation he that fears God is accepted of him,* and blessed, Acts x. 34, 35. *He will bless them both small and great,* both young and old. God has blessings in store for those that are good betimes and for those that are old disciples, both those that are poor in the world and those that make a figure. The greatest need his blessing, and it shall not be denied to the meanest that fear him. Both the weak in grace and the strong shall be blessed of God, the lambs and the sheep of his flock. It is promised (*v.* 14), *The Lord shall increase you.* Whom God blesses he increases ; that was one of the earliest and most ancient blessings, *Be fruitful and multiply.* God's blessing gives an increase—increase in number, building up the family—increase in wealth, adding to the estate and honour—especially an increase in spiritual blessings, with the increasings of God. He will bless you with the increase of knowledge and wisdom, of grace, holiness, and joy ; those are blessed indeed whom God thus increases, who are made wiser and better, and fitter for God and heaven. It is promised that this shall be, (1.) A constant continual increase : "*He shall increase you more and more;* so that, as long as you live, you shall be still increasing, till you come to perfection, as the shining light," Prov. iv. 18. (2.) An hereditary increase :

" *You and your children;* you in your children." It is a comfort to parents to see their children increasing in wisdom and strength. There is a blessing entailed upon the seed of those that fear God even in their infancy. For (*v.* 15), *You are blessed of the Lord,* you and your children are so ; *all that see them shall acknowledge them, that they are the seed which the Lord has blessed,* Isa. lix. 9. Those that are the blessed of the Lord have encouragement enough to *trust in the Lord,* as *their help and shield,* for it is he that *made heaven and earth;* therefore his blessings are free, for he needs not any thing himself ; and therefore they are rich, for he has all things at command for us if we fear him and trust in him. He that *made heaven and earth* can doubtless make those happy that trust in him, and will do it.

III. We are stirred up to praise God by the psalmist's example, who concludes the psalm with a resolution to persevere in his praises. 1. God is to be praised, *v.* 16. He is greatly to be praised ; for, (1.) His glory is high See how stately his palace is, and the throne he has prepared in the heavens : *The heaven, even the heavens are the Lord's;* he is the rightful owner of all the treasures of light and bliss in the upper and better world, and is in the full possession of them, for he is himself infinitely bright and happy. (2.) His goodness is large, for *the earth he has given to the children of men,* having designed it, when he made it, for their use, to find them with meat, drink, and lodging. Not but that still he is proprietor in chief ; *the earth is the Lord's, and the fulness thereof;* but he has let out that vineyard to these unthankful husbandmen, and from them he expects the rents and services ; for, though he has given them the earth, his eye is upon them, and he will call them to render an account how they use it. Calvin complains that profane wicked people, in his days, perverted this scripture, and made a jest of it, which some in our days do, arguing, in banter, that God, having given the earth to the children of men, will no more look after it, nor after them upon it, but they may do what they will with it, and make the best of it as their portion ; it is as it were thrown like a prey among them, Let him seize it that can. It is a pity that such an instance as this gives of God's bounty to man, and such a proof as arises from it of man's obligation to God, should be thus abused. From the highest heavens, it is certain, God beholds all the children of men ; to them he has given the earth ; but to the children of God heaven is given. 2. The dead are not capable of praising him (*v.* 17), nor *any that go into silence.* The soul indeed lives in a state of separation from the body and is capable of praising God ; and *the souls of the faithful, after they are delivered from the burdens of the flesh,* do praise God, are still praising him ; for they go up to the land of perfect light and constant busi-

674

ness. But the dead body cannot praise God ; death puts an end to our glorifying God in this world of trial and conflict, to all our services in the field ; the grave is a land of darkness and silence, where there is no work or device. This they plead with God for deliverance out of the hand of their enemies, " Lord, if they prevail to cut us off, the idols will carry the day, and there will be none to praise thee, to bear thy name, and to bear a testimony against the worshippers of idols." *The dead praise not the Lord,* so as we do in the business and for the comforts of this life." See Ps. xxx. 9 ; lxxxviii. 10. 3. Therefore it concerns us to praise him (*v.* 18) : " *But we,* we that are alive, *will bless the Lord;* we and those that shall come after us, will do it, *from this time forth and for evermore,* to the end of time ; we and those we shall remove to, *from this time forth* and to eternity. *The dead praise not the Lord,* therefore we will do it the more diligently." (1.) Others are dead, and an end is thereby put to their service, and therefore we will lay out ourselves to do so much the more for God, that we may fill up the gap. *Moses my servant is dead, now therefore, Joshua, arise.* (2.) We ourselves must shortly go to the land of silence ; *but, while we do live, we will bless the Lord,* will improve our time and work that work of him that sent us into the world to praise him before the night comes, and because *the night comes, wherein no man can work. The Lord will bless us* (*v.* 12) ; he will do well for us, and therefore *we will bless* him, we will speak well of him. Poor returns for such receivings ! Nay, we will not only do it ourselves, but will engage others to do it. *Praise the Lord;* praise him with us ; praise him in your places, as we in ours ; praise him when we are gone, that he may be praised *for evermore. Hallelujah.*

PSALM CXVI.

This is a thanksgiving psalm ; it is not certain whether David penned it upon any particular occasion or upon a general review of the many gracious deliverances God had wrought for him, out of six troubles and seven, which deliverances draw from him many very lively expressions of devotion, love, and gratitude ; and with similar pious affections our souls should be lifted up to God in singing it. Observe, I. The great distress and danger that the psalmist was in, which almost drove him to despair, ver. 3, 10, 11. II. The application he made to God in that distress, ver. 4. III. The experience he had of God's goodness to him, in answer to prayer ; God heard him (ver. 1, 2), pitied him (ver. 5, 6), delivered him, ver. 8. IV. His care respecting the acknowledgments he should make of the goodness of God to him, ver. 12. 1. He will love God, ver. 1. 2. He will continue to call upon him, ver. 2, 13, 17. 3. He will rest in him, ver. 7. 4. He will walk before him, ver. 9. 5. He will pay his vows of thanksgiving, in which he will own the tender regard God had to him, and this publicly, ver. 13—15, 17—19. Lastly, He will continue God's faithful servant to his life's end, ver. 16. These are such breathings of a holy soul as bespeak it very happy.

I LOVE the Lord, because he hath heard my voice *and* my supplications. 2 Because he hath inclined his ear unto me, therefore will I call upon *him* as long as I live. 3 The sorrows of death compassed me, and the pains of hell gat hold upon me : I found trouble and sorrow. 4 Then called I upon the name of the Lord ; O Lord,

I beseech thee, deliver my soul. 5 Gracious *is* the LORD, and righteous; yea, our God *is* merciful. 6 The LORD preserveth the simple : I was brought low, and he helped me. 7 Return unto thy rest, O my soul ; for the LORD hath dealt bountifully with thee. 8 For thou hast delivered my soul from death, mine eyes from tears, *and* my feet from falling. 9 I will walk before the LORD in the land of the living.

In this part of the psalm we have,

I. A general account of David's experience, and his pious resolutions (*v.* 1, 2), which are as the contents of the whole psalm, and give an idea of it. 1. He had experienced God's goodness to him in answer to prayer : *He has heard my voice and my supplications.* David, in straits, had humbly and earnestly begged mercy of God, and God had heard him, that is, had graciously accepted his prayer, taken cognizance of his case, and granted him an answer of peace. *He has inclined his ear to me.* This intimates his readiness and willingness to hear prayer; he lays his ear, as it were, to the mouth of prayer, to hear it, though it be but whispered *in groanings that cannot be uttered.* He *hearkens and hears,* Jer. viii. 6. Yet it implies, also, that it is wonderful condescension in God to hear prayer ; it is bowing his ear. Lord, what is man, that God should thus stoop to him !— 2. He resolved, in consideration thereof, to devote himself entirely to God and to his honour. (1.) He will love God the better. He begins the psalm somewhat abruptly with a profession of that which his heart was full of : *I love the Lord* (as xviii. 1); and fitly does he begin with this, in compliance with the first and great commandment and with God's end in all the gifts of his bounty to us. " I love him only, and nothing besides him, but what I love for him." God's love of compassion towards us justly requires our love of complacency in him. (2.) He will love prayer the better : *Therefore I will call upon him.* The experiences we have had of God's goodness to us, in answer to prayer, are great encouragements to us to continue praying ; we have sped well, notwithstanding our unworthiness and our infirmities in prayer, and therefore why may we not ? God answers prayer, to make us love it, and expects this from us, in return for his favour. Why should we glean in any other field when we have been so well treated in this ? Nay, *I will call upon him as long as I live* (Heb., In my days), every day, to the last day. Note, As long as we continue living we must continue praying. This breath we must breathe till we breathe our last, because then we shall take our leave of it, and till then we have continual occasion for it.

II. A more particular narrative of God's gracious dealings with him and the good impressions thereby made upon him.

1. God, in his dealings with him, showed himself a good God, and therefore he bears this testimony to him, and leaves it upon record (*v.* 5): " *Gracious is the Lord, and righteous.* He is righteous, and did me no wrong in afflicting me; he is gracious, and was very kind in supporting and delivering me." Let us all speak of God as we have found ; and have we ever found him otherwise than just and good ? No; *our God is merciful,* merciful to us, and *it is of his mercies that we are not consumed.*

(1.) Let us review David's experiences. [1.] He was in great distress and trouble (*v.* 3): *The sorrows of death compassed me,* that is, such sorrows as were likely to be his death, such as were thought to be the very pangs of death. Perhaps the extremity of bodily pain, or trouble of mind, is called here *the pains of hell,* terror of conscience arising from sense of guilt. Note, The sorrows of death are great sorrows, and the pains of hell great pains. Let us *therefore* give diligence to prepare for the former, that we may escape the latter. These *compassed* him on every side ; they arrested him, *got hold upon him,* so that he could not escape. *Without were fightings, within were fears.* " *I found trouble and sorrow ;* not only they found me, but I found them." Those that are melancholy have a great deal of sorrow of their own finding, a great deal of trouble which they create to themselves, by indulging fancy and passion ; this has sometimes been the infirmity of good men. When God's providence makes our condition bad let us not by our own imprudence make it worse. [2.] In his trouble he had recourse to God by faithful and fervent prayer, *v.* 4. He tells us that he prayed : *Then called I upon the name of the Lord ;* then, when he was brought to the last extremity, then he made use of this, not as the last remedy, but as the old and only remedy, which he had found a salve for every sore. He tells us what his prayer was ; it was short, but to the purpose : " *O Lord! I beseech thee, deliver my soul ;* save me from death, and save me from sin, for that is it that is killing to the soul." Both the humility and the fervency of his prayer are intimated in these words, *O Lord! I beseech thee.* When we come to the throne of grace we must come as beggars for an alms, for necessary food. The following words (*v.* 5), *Gracious is the Lord,* may be taken as part of his prayer, as a plea to enforce his request and encourage his faith and hope : " Lord, *deliver my soul,* for thou art *gracious* and *merciful,* and that only I depend upon for relief." [3.] God, in answer to his prayer, came in with seasonable and effectual relief. He found by experience that God is gracious and merciful, and in his compassion *preserves the simple, v.* 6. Because they are simple (that is, sincere, and upright, and without guile) therefore God preserves them, as he preserved Paul, who had his conversation in the world *not with fleshly wisdom, but in simplicity and godly sincerity.* Though they are simple (that is, weak, and helpless, and unable to shift for themselves, men of no depth, no design) yet God preserves them, because they commit themselves to him and have no confidence in their own sufficiency. Those who by faith put themselves under God's protection shall be safe.

(2.) Let David speak his own experience. [1.] God supported him under his troubles: "*I was brought low,* was plunged into the depth of misery, and then *he helped me,* helped me both to bear the worst and to hope the best, helped me to pray, else desire had failed, helped me to wait, else faith had failed. I was one of the simple ones whom God preserved, the poor man who *cried and the Lord heard him,*" xxxiv. 6. Note, God's people are never brought so low but that everlasting arms are under them, and those cannot sink who are thus sustained. Nay, it is in the time of need, at the dead lift, that God chooses to help, Deut. xxxii. 36. [2.] God saved him out of his troubles (*v.* 8): *Thou hast delivered,* which means either the preventing of the distress he was ready to fall into or the recovering of him from the distress he was already in. God graciously delivered, *First,* His *soul from death.* Note, It is God's great mercy to us that we are alive; and the mercy is the more sensible if we have been at death's door and yet have been spared and raised up, just turned to destruction and yet ordered to return. That a life so often forfeited, and so often exposed, should yet be lengthened out, is a miracle of mercy. The deliverance of the soul from spiritual and eternal death is especially to be acknowledged by all those who are now sanctified and shall be shortly glorified. *Secondly,* His *eyes from tears,* that is, his heart from inordinate grief. It is a great mercy to be kept either from the occasions of sorrow, the evil that causes grief, or, at least, from being swallowed up with overmuch sorrow. When God comforts those that are cast down, looses the mourners' sackcloth and girds them with gladness, then he delivers *their eyes from tears,* which yet will not be perfectly done till we come to that world where God shall *wipe away all tears from our eyes. Thirdly,* His *feet from falling,* from falling into sin and so into misery. It is a great mercy, when our feet are almost gone, to have God *hold us by the right hand* (lxxii. 2, 23), so that though we enter into temptation we are not overcome and overthrown by the temptation. Or, "Thou *hast delivered my feet from falling* into the grave, when I had one foot there already."

2. David, in his returns of gratitude to God, showed himself a good man. God had done all this for him, and therefore,

(1.) He will live a life of delight in God (*v.* 7): *Return unto thy rest, O my soul!* [1.] "Repose thyself and be easy, and do not

agitate thyself with distrustful disquieting fears as thou hast sometimes done. Quiet thyself, and then enjoy thyself. God has dealt kindly with thee, and therefore thou needest not fear that ever he will deal hardly with thee." [2.] "Repose thyself in God. Return to him as thy rest, and seek not for that rest in the creature which is to be had in him only." God is the soul's rest; in him only it can *dwell at ease;* to him therefore it must retire, and rejoice in him. He has *dealt bountifully with us;* he has provided sufficiently for our comfort and refreshment, and encouraged us to come to him for the benefit of it, at all times, upon all occasions; let us therefore be satisfied with that. Return to that rest which Christ gives to the *weary and heavy-laden,* Matt. xi. 28. Return to thy Noah; his name signifies *rest,* as the dove, when she found no rest, returned to the ark. I know no word more proper to close our eyes with at night, when we go to sleep, nor to close them with at death, that long sleep, than this, *Return to thy rest, O my soul!*

(2.) He will live a life of devotedness to God (*v.* 9): *I will walk before the Lord in the land of the living,* that is, in this world, as long as I continue to live in it. Note, [1.] It is our great duty to *walk before the Lord,* to do all we do as becomes us in his presence and under his eye, to approve ourselves to him as a holy God by conformity to him as our sovereign Lord, by subjection to his will, and, as a God all-sufficient, by a cheerful confidence in him. *I am the almighty God; walk before me,* Gen. xvii. 1. *We must walk worthy of the Lord unto all well-pleasing.* [2.] The consideration of this, that we are in the land of the living, should engage and quicken us to do so. We are spared and continued in the land of the living by the power, and patience, and tender mercy of our God, and therefore must make conscience of our duty to him. The *land of the living* is a land of mercy, which we ought to be thankful for; it is a land of opportunity, which we should improve. Canaan is called the *land of the living* (Ezek. xxvi. 20), and those whose lot is cast in such a valley of vision are in a special manner concerned to *set the Lord always before them.* If God has delivered our soul from death, we must walk before him. A new life must be a new life indeed.

10 I believed, therefore have I spoken : I was greatly afflicted : 11 I said in my haste, All men *are* liars. 12 What shall I render unto the LORD *for* all his benefits toward me? 13 I will take the cup of salvation, and call upon the name of the LORD. 14 I will pay my vows unto the LORD now in the presence of all his people. 15 Precious in the sight of the LORD

is the death of his saints. 16 O LORD, truly I *am* thy servant ; I *am* thy servant, *and* the son of thine handmaid: thou hast loosed my bonds. 17 I will offer to thee the sacrifice of thanksgiving, and will call upon the name of the LORD. 18 I will pay my vows unto the LORD now in the presence of all his people, 19 In the courts of the LORD's house, in the midst of thee, O Jerusalem. Praise ye the LORD.

The Septuagint and some other ancient versions make these verses a distinct psalm separate from the former; and some have called it the *Martyr's psalm*, I suppose for the sake of *v.* 15. Three things David here makes confession of:—

I. His faith (*v.* 10): *I believed, therefore have I spoken.* This is quoted by the apostle (2 Cor. iv. 13) with application to himself and his fellow-ministers, who, though they suffered for Christ, were not ashamed to own him. David believed the being, providence, and promise of God, particularly the assurance God had given him by Samuel that he should exchange his crook for a sceptre: a great deal of hardship he went through in the belief of this, and therefore he spoke, spoke to God by prayer (*v.* 4), by praise, *v.* 12. Those that believe in God will address themselves to him. He spoke to himself; because he believed, he said to his soul, *Return to thy rest.* He spoke to others, told his friends what his hope was, and what the ground of it, though it exasperated Saul against him and he was greatly afflicted for it. Note, Those that believe with the heart must confess with the mouth, for the glory of God, the encouragement of others, and to evidence their own sincerity, Rom. x. 10; Acts ix. 19, 20. Those that live in hope of the kingdom of glory must neither be afraid nor ashamed to own their obligation to him that purchased it for them, Matt. x. 22.

II. His fear (*v.* 11): *I was greatly afflicted,* and then *I said in my haste* (somewhat rashly and inconsiderately—in my *amazement* (so some), when I was in a consternation—*in my flight* (so others), when Saul was in pursuit of me), *All men are liars,* all with whom he had to do, Saul and all his courtiers; his friends, who he thought would stand by him, deserted him and disowned him when he fell into disgrace at court. And some think it is especially a reflection on Samuel, who had promised him the kingdom, but deceived him; for, says he, *I shall one day perish by the hand of Saul,* 1 Sam. xxvii. 1. Observe, 1. The faith of the best of saints is not perfect, nor always alike strong and active. David *believed* and *spoke well* (*v.* 10), but now, through unbelief, he spoke amiss. 2. When we are under great and sore afflictions, especially if they continue long, we are apt to grow weary, to despond, and almost to despair of a good issue. Let us not therefore be harsh in censuring others, but carefully watch over ourselves when we are in trouble, xxxix. 1—3. 3. If good men speak amiss, it is in their haste, through the surprise of a temptation, not deliberately and with premeditation, as the wicked man, who *sits in the seat of the scornful* (Ps. i. 1), sits and *speaks against his brother,* l. 19, 20. 4. What we speak amiss, in haste, we must by repentance unsay again (as David, xxxi. 22), and then it shall not be laid to our charge. Some make this to be no rash word of David's. He was greatly afflicted and forced to fly, but he did not trust in man, nor make flesh his arm. No: he said, *"All men are liars;* as *men of low degree are vanity,* so *men of high degree are a lie,* and therefore my confidence was in God only, and in him I cannot be disappointed." In this sense the apostle seems to take it. Rom. iii. 4, *Let God be true and every man a liar* in comparison with God. All men are fickle and inconstant, and subject to change; and therefore let us cease from man and cleave to God.

III. His gratitude, *v.* 12, &c. God had been better to him than his fears, and had graciously delivered him out of his distresses; and, in consideration hereof,

1. He enquires what returns he shall make (*v.* 12): *What shall I render unto the Lord for all his benefits towards me?* Here he speaks, (1.) As one sensible of many mercies received from God—*all his benefits.* This psalm seems to have been penned upon occasion of some one particular benefit (*v.* 6, 7), but in that one he saw many and that one brought many to mind, and therefore now he thinks of all God's benefits towards him. Note, When we speak of God's mercies we should magnify them and speak highly of them. (2.) As one solicitous and studious how to express his gratitude: *What shall I render unto the Lord?* Not as if he thought he could render any thing proportionable, or as a valuable consideration for what he had received; we can no more pretend to give a recompence to God than we can to merit any favour from him; but he desired to render something acceptable, something that God would be pleased with as the acknowledgment of a grateful mind. He asks God, *What shall I render?* Asks the priest, asks his friends, or rather asks himself, and communes with his own heart about it. Note, Having received many benefits from God, we are concerned to enquire, *What shall we render?*

2. He resolves what returns he will make. (1.) He will in the most devout and solemn manner offer up his praises and prayers to God, *v.* 13, 17. [1.] *"I will take the cup of salvation,* that is, I will offer the drink-offerings appointed by the law, in token of my thankfulness to God, and rejoice with my friends in God's goodness to me;"* this is

called *the cup of deliverance* because drunk in memory·of the deliverance. The pious Jews had sometimes a *cup of blessing,* at their private meals, which the master of the family drank first of, with thanksgiving to God, and all at his table drank with him. But some understand it not of the cup that he would present to God, but of the cup that God would put into his hand. *I will receive, First,* The *cup of affliction.* Many good interpreters understand it of that cup, that bitter cup, which is yet sanctified to the saints, so that to them it is a cup of salvation. Phil. i. 19, *This shall turn to my salvation;* it is a means of spiritual health. David's sufferings were typical of Christ's, and we, in ours, have communion with his, and his cup was indeed a cup of salvation. "God, having bestowed so many benefits upon me, whatever cup he shall put into my hands I will readily take it, and not dispute it; welcome his holy will." Herein David spoke the language of the Son of David. John xviii. 11, *The cup that my Father has given me, shall I not* take it and *drink it?* Secondly, The cup of consolation: "I will receive the benefits God bestows upon me as from his hand, and taste his love in them, as that which is *the portion* not only *of my inheritance* in the other world, but *of my cup* in this." [2.] *I will offer to thee the sacrifice of thanksgiving,* the thank-offerings which God required, Lev. vii. 11, 12, &c. Note, Those whose hearts are truly thankful will express their gratitude in thank-offerings. We must first *give our ownselves* to God as *living sacrifices* (Rom. xii. 1, 2 Cor. viii. 5), and then lay out of what we have for his honour in works of piety and charity. *Doing good* and *communicating* are *sacrifices* with which *God is well pleased* (Heb. xiii. 15, 16) and this must accompany our *giving thanks to his name.* If God has been bountiful to us, the least we can do in return is to be bountiful to the poor, Ps. xvi. 2, 3. Why should we offer that to God which costs us nothing? [3.] *I will call upon the name of the Lord.* This he had promised (*v.* 2) and here he repeats it, *v.* 13 and again *v.* 17. If we have received kindness from a man like ourselves, we tell him that we hope we shall never trouble him again; but God is pleased to reckon the prayers of his people an honour to him, and a delight, and no trouble; and therefore, in gratitude for former mercies, we must seek to him for further mercies, and continue to *call upon him.*

(2.) He will always entertain good thoughts of God, as very tender of the lives and comforts of his people (*v.* 15): *Precious in the sight of the Lord is the death of his saints,* so precious that he will not gratify Saul, nor Absalom, nor any of David's enemies, with his death, how earnestly soever they desire it. This truth David had comforted himself with in the depth of his distress and danger; and, the event having confirmed it, he

678

comforts others with it who might be in like manner exposed. God has a people, even in this world, that are his saints, his merciful ones, or men of mercy, that have received mercy from him and show mercy for his sake. The saints of God are mortal and dying; nay, there are those that desire their death, and labour all they can to hasten it, and sometimes prevail to be the death of them; but it is *precious in the sight of the Lord; their life* is so (2 Kings i. 13); their *blood* is so, Ps. lxxii. 14. God often wonderfully prevents the death of his saints when there is but a step between them and it; he takes special care about their death, to order it for the best in all the circumstances of it; and whoever kills them, how light soever they may make of it, they shall be made to pay dearly for it when inquisition is made for the blood of the saints, Matt. xxiii. 35. Though *no man lays it to heart* when *the righteous perish,* God will make it to appear that he lays it to heart. This should make us willing to die, to die for Christ, if we are called to it, that our death shall be registered in heaven; and let that be precious to us which is so to God.

(3.) He will oblige himself to be God's servant all his days. Having asked, *What shall I render?* here he surrenders himself, which was *more than all burnt-offerings and sacrifice* (*v.* 16): *O Lord! truly I am thy servant.* Here is, [1.] The relation in which David professes to stand to God: "*I am thy servant;* I choose to be so; I resolve to be so; I will live and die in thy service." He had called God's people, who are dear to him, *his saints;* but, when he comes to apply it to himself, he does not say, *Truly I am thy saint* (that looked too high a title for himself), but, *I am thy servant.* David was a king, and yet he glories in this, that he was God's servant. It is no disparagement, but an honour, to the greatest kings on earth, to be the servants of the God of heaven. David does not here compliment God, as it is common among men to say, *I am your servant, Sir.* No; "Lord, I am *truly thy servant; thou knowest all things, thou knowest that I am so.*" And he repeats it, as that which he took pleasure in the thoughts of and which he was resolved to abide by: "*I am thy servant, I am thy servant.* Let others serve what master they will, *truly I am* thy servant." [2.] The ground of that relation. Two ways men came to be servants:—*First,* By birth. "Lord, I was born in thy house; I am *the son of thy handmaid,* and therefore thine." It, is a great mercy to be the children of godly parents, as it obliges us to duty and is pleadable with God for mercy. *Secondly,* By redemption. He that procured the release of a captive took him for his servant. "Lord, *thou hast loosed my bonds;* those sorrows of death that compassed me, thou hast discharged me from them, and therefore *I am thy servant,* and entitled to thy protection as well as obliged to thy work." *The very bonds which thou hast loosed shall tie me faster unto thee.* Patrick.

(4.) He will make conscience of paying his vows and making good what he had promised, not only that he would offer the sacrifices of praise, which he had vowed to bring, but perform all his other engagements to God, which he had laid himself under in the day of his affliction (*v.* 14): *I will pay my vows;* and again, (*v.* 18), *now in the presence of all his people.* Note, Vows are debts that must be paid, for it is better not to vow than to vow and not pay. He will pay his vows, [1.] Presently; he will not, like sorry debtors, delay the payment of them, or beg a day; but, "*I will pay them now,*" Eccl. v. 4. [2.] Publicly; he will not huddle up his praises in a corner, but what service he has to do for God he will do it *in the presence of all his people;* not for ostentation, but to show that he was not ashamed of the service of God, and that others might be invited to join with him. He will pay his vows in the courts of the tabernacle, where there was a crowd of Israelites attending, *in the midst of Jerusalem,* that he might bring devotion into more reputation.

PSALM CXVII.

This psalm is short and sweet; I doubt the reason why we sing it so often as we do is for the shortness of it; but, if we rightly understood and considered it, we should sing it oftener for the sweetness of it, especially to us sinners of the Gentiles, on whom it casts a very favourable eye. Here is, I. A solemn call to all nations to praise God, ver. 1. II. Proper matter for that praise suggested, ver. 2. We are soon weary indeed of well-doing if, in singing this psalm, we keep not up those pious and devout affections with which the spiritual sacrifice of praise ought to be kindled and kept burning.

O PRAISE the LORD, all ye nations: praise him, all ye people. 2 For his merciful kindness is great toward us: and the truth of the LORD *endureth* for ever. Praise ye the LORD.

There is a great deal of gospel in this psalm. The apostle has furnished us with a key to it (Rom. xv. 11), where he quotes it as a proof that the gospel was to be preached to, and would be entertained by, the Gentile nations, which yet was so great a stumbling-block to the Jews. Why should that offend them when it is said, and they themselves had often sung it, *Praise the Lord, all you Gentiles, and laud him, all you people.* Some of the Jewish writers confess that this psalm refers to the kingdom of the Messiah; nay, one of them has a fancy that it consists of two verses to signify that in the days of the Messiah God should be glorified by two sorts of people, by the Jews, according to the law of Moses, and by the Gentiles, according to the seven precepts of the sons of Noah, which yet should make one church, as these two verses make one psalm. We have here,

I. The vast extent of the gospel church, *v.* 1. For many ages in Judah only was God known and his name praised. The sons of Levi and the seed of Israel praised him, but the rest of the nations *praised gods of wood*

and stone (Dan. v. 4), while there was no devotion at all paid, at least none openly, that we know of, to the living and true God. But here *all nations* are called to praise the Lord, which could not be applied to the Old-Testament times, both because this call was not then given to any of the Gentile nations, much less to all, in a language they understood, and because, unless the people of the land became Jews and were circumcised, they were not admitted to praise God with them. But the gospel of Christ is ordered to be preached to all nations, and by him the partition-wall is taken down, and those that were *afar off* are *made nigh.* This was the mystery which was hidden in prophecy for many ages, but was at length revealed in the accomplishment, *That the Gentiles should be fellow-heirs,* Eph. iii. 3, 6. Observe here, 1. Who should be admitted into the church—*all nations* and *all people.* The original words are the same that are used for the *heathen that rage* and *the people that imagine* against Christ (ii. 1); those that had been enemies to his kingdom should become his willing subjects. The gospel of the kingdom was to be preached *to all the world, for a witness to all nations,* Matt. xxiv. 14; Mark xvi. 15. All nations shall be called, and to some of all nations the call shall be effectual, and they shall be discipled. 2. How their admission into the church is foretold—by a repeated call to *praise him.* The tidings of the gospel, being sent to all nations, should give them cause to praise God; the institution of gospel-ordinances would give them leave and opportunity to praise God; and the power of gospel-grace would give them hearts to praise him. Those are highly favoured whom God invites by his word and inclines by his Spirit to praise him, and so makes to be to him for a name and a praise, Jer. xiii. 11. See Rev. vii. 9, 10.

II. The unsearchable riches of gospel-grace, which are to be the matter of our praise, *v.* 2. In the gospel, those celebrated attributes of God, his mercy and his truth, shine most brightly in themselves and most comfortably to us; and the apostle, where he quotes this psalm, takes notice of these as the two great things for which the Gentiles should glorify God (Rom. xv. 8, 9), for *the truth of God* and for *his mercy.* We that enjoy the gospel have reason to praise the Lord, 1. For the power of his mercy: *His merciful kindness is great towards us;* it is *strong* (so the word signifies); it is *mighty* for the pardon of *mighty sins* (Amos v. 12) and for the working out of a mighty salvation. 2. For the perpetuity of his truth: *The truth of the Lord endures for ever.* It was mercy, mere mercy, to the Gentiles, that the gospel was sent among them. It was merciful kindness prevailing towards them above their deserts; and in it the *truth of the Lord,* of his promise made unto the fathers, *endures for ever;* for, though the Jews were hardened and expelled, yet the promise took its effect in the believing Gentiles, the spiritual seed of Abraham. God's mercy is the fountain of all our comforts and his truth the foundation of all our hopes, and therefore for both we must praise the Lord.

PSALM CXVIII.

It is probable that David penned this psalm when he had, after many a storm, weathered his point at last, and gained a full possession of the kingdom to which he had been anointed. He then invites and stirs up his friends to join with him, not only in a cheerful acknowledgment of God's goodness and a cheerful dependence upon that goodness for the future, but in a believing expectation of the promised Messiah, of whose kingdom and his exaltation to it his were typical. To him, it is certain, the prophet here bears witness, in the latter part of the psalm. Christ himself applies it to himself (Matt. xxi. 42), and the former part of the psalm may fairly, and without forcing, be accommodated to him and his undertaking. Some think it was first calculated for the solemnity of the bringing of the ark to the city of David, and was afterwards sung at the feast of tabernacles. In it, I. David calls upon all about him to give to God the glory of his goodness, ver. 1—4. II. He encourages himself and others to trust in God, from the experience he had had of God's power and pity in the great and kind things he had done for him, ver. 5—18. III. He gives thanks for his advancement to the throne, as it was a figure of the exaltation of Christ, ver. 19—23. IV. The people, the priests, and the psalmist himself, triumph in the prospect of the Redeemer's kingdom, ver. 24—29. In singing this psalm we must glorify God for his goodness, his goodness to us, and especially his goodness to us in Jesus Christ.

O GIVE thanks unto the LORD; for, *he is* good : because his mercy *endureth* for ever. 2 Let Israel now say, that his mercy *endureth* for ever. 3 Let the house of Aaron now say, that his mercy *endureth* for ever. 4 Let them now that fear the LORD say, that his mercy *endureth* for ever. 5 I called upon the LORD in distress: the LORD answered me, *and set me* in a large place. 6 The LORD *is* on my side ; I will not fear : what can man do unto me ? 7 The LORD taketh my part with them that help me : therefore shall I see *my desire* upon them that hate me. 8 *It is* better to trust in the LORD than to put confidence in man. 9 *It is* better to trust in the LORD than to put confidence in princes. 10 All nations compassed me about : but in the name of the LORD will I destroy them. 11 They compassed me about ; yea, they compassed me about : but in the name of the LORD I will destroy them. 12 They compassed me about like bees ; they are quenched as the fire of thorns : for in the name of the LORD I will destroy them. 13 Thou hast thrust sore at me that I might fall : but the LORD helped me. 14 The LORD *is* my strength and song, and is become my salvation. 15 The voice of rejoicing and salvation *is* in the tabernacles of the righteous : the right hand of the LORD doeth valiantly. 16 The right hand of the LORD *is* exalted : the

right hand of the LORD doeth valiantly. 17 I shall not die, but live, and declare the works of the LORD. 18 The LORD hath chastened me sore : but he hath not given me over unto death.

It appears here, as often elsewhere, that David had his heart full of the goodness of God. He loved to think of it, loved to speak of it, and was very solicitous that God might have the praise of it and others the comfort of it. The more our hearts are impressed with a sense of God's goodness the more they will be enlarged in all manner of obedience. In these verses,

I. He celebrates God's mercy in general, and calls upon others to acknowledge it, from their own experience of it (*v.* 1): *O give thanks unto the Lord, for he is* not only *good* in himself, but good to you, and *his mercy endures for ever*, not only in the everlasting fountain, God himself, but in the never-failing streams of that mercy, which shall run parallel with the longest line of eternity, and in the chosen *vessels of mercy*, who will be everlasting monuments of it. Israel, and the house of Aaron, and all that *fear God*, were called upon to *trust in God* (cxv. 9—11) ; here they are called upon to confess that *his mercy endures for ever*, and so to encourage themselves to trust in him, *v.* 2—4. Priests and people, Jews and proselytes, must all own God's goodness, and all join in the same thankful song ; if they can say no more, let them say this for him, that *his mercy endures for ever*, that they have had experience of it all their days, and confide in it for good things that shall last for ever. The praises and thanksgivings of all that truly *fear the Lord* shall be as pleasing to him as those of the house of Israel or the house of Aaron.

II. He preserves an account of God's gracious dealings with him in particular, which he communicates to others, that they might thence fetch both songs of praise and supports of faith, and both ways God would have the glory. David had, in his time, waded through a great deal of difficulty, which gave him great experience of God's goodness. Let us therefore observe here,

1. The great distress and danger that he had been in, which he reflects upon for the magnifying of God's goodness to him in his present advancement. There are many who, when they are lifted up, care not for hearing or speaking of their former depressions ; but David takes all occasions to remember his own low estate. He was *in distress* (*v.* 5), greatly straitened and at a loss ; there were many that *hated him* (*v.* 7), and this could not but be a great grief to one of an ingenuous spirit, that strove to gain the good affections of all. *All nations compassed me about, v.* 10. All the nations adjacent to Israel set themselves to give disturbance to David, when he had newly come to the throne, Philistines,

Moabites, Syrians, Ammonites, &c. We read of *his enemies round about;* they were confederate against him, and thought to cut off all succours from him. This endeavour of his enemies to surround him is repeated (*v.* 11): *They compassed me about, yea, they compassed me about,* which intimates that they were virulent and violent, and, for a time, prevalent, in their attempts against him, and when put into disorder they rallied again and pushed on their design. *They compassed me about like bees,* so numerous were they, so noisy, so vexatious ; they came flying upon him, came upon him in swarms, set upon him with their malignant stings ; but it was to their own destruction, as the bee, they say, loses her life with her sting, *Animamque in vulnere ponit*—*She lays down her life in the wound. Lord, how are those increased that trouble me !* Two ways David was brought into trouble :—(1.) By the injuries that men did him (*v.* 13) : *Thou* (O enemy!) *hast thrust sore at me,* with many a desperate push, *that I might fall* into sin and into ruin. *Thrusting thou hast thrust at me* (so the word is), so that I was *ready to fall.* Satan is the great enemy that thrusts sorely at us by his temptations, to cast us down from our excellency, that we may fall from our God and from our comfort in him; and, if God had not upheld us by his grace, his thrusts would have been fatal to us. (2.) By the afflictions which God laid upon him (*v.* 18): *The Lord has chastened me sore.* Men thrust at him for his destruction ; God chastened him for his instruction. They thrust at him with the malice of enemies ; God chastened him with the love and tenderness of a Father. Perhaps he refers to the same trouble which God, the author of it, designed for his profit, that by it he *might partake of his holiness* (Heb. xii. 10, 11); howbeit, men, who were the instruments of it, meant not so, *neither did their heart think so, but it was in their heart to cut off and destroy,* Isa. x. 7. What men intend for the greatest mischief God intends for the greatest good, and it is easy to say whose counsel shall stand. God will sanctify the trouble to his people, as it is his chastening, and secure the good he designs ; and he will guard them against the trouble, as it is the enemies' thrusting, and secure them from the evil they design, and then we need not fear.

This account which David gives of his troubles is very applicable to our Lord Jesus. Many there were that *hated him,* hated him without a cause. They *compassed him about;* Jews and Romans surrounded him. *They thrust sorely at him;* the devil did so when he tempted him; his persecutors did so when they reviled him; nay, the Lord himself *chastened him sorely,* bruised him, and put him to grief, that *by his stripes we might be healed.*

2. The favour God vouchsafed to him in his distress. (1.) God heard his prayer (*v.* 5): " *He answered me* with enlargements; he did more for me than I was able to ask ; he en-

larged my heart in prayer and yet gave more largely than I desired." *He answered me, and set me in a large place* (so we read it), where I had room to bestir myself, room to enjoy myself, and room to thrive ; and the large place was the more comfortable because he was brought to it out of distress, iv. 1. (2.) God baffled the designs of his enemies against him : They are *quenched as the fire of thorns* (*v.* 12), which burns furiously for a while, makes a great noise and a great blaze, but is presently out, and cannot do the mischief that it threatened. Such was the fury of David's enemies ; such is *the laughter of the fool,* like the *crackling of thorns under a pot* (Eccl. vii. 6), and such is the anger of the fool, which therefore is not to be feared, any more than his laughter is to be envied, but both to be pitied. They thrust sorely at him, but *the Lord helped him* (*v.* 13), helped him to keep his feet and maintain his ground. Our spiritual enemies would, long before this, have been our ruin if God had not been our helper. (3.) God preserved his life when there was but a step between him and death (*v.* 18): " *He has chastened me,* but he has not *given me over unto death,* for he has not given me over to the will of my enemies." To this St. Paul seems to refer in 2 Cor. vi. 9. *As dying, and behold we live; as chastened, and not killed.* We ought not therefore, when we are chastened sorely, immediately to despair of life, for God sometimes, in appearance, *turns men to destruction,* and yet *says, Return; says unto them, Live.*

This also is applicable to Jesus Christ. God *answered him, and set him in a large place.* He quenched the fire of his enemies' rage, which did but consume themselves ; for *through death he destroyed him that had the power of death.* He helped him through his undertaking; and thus far he did not *give him over unto death* that he did *not leave him in the grave,* nor *suffer him to see corruption. Death had no dominion over him.*

3. The improvement he made of this favour. (1.) It encouraged him to trust in God ; from his own experience he can say, *It is better,* more wise, more comfortable, and more safe, there is more reason for it, and it will speed better, *to trust in the Lord, than to put confidence in man,* yea, though it be *in princes, v.* 8, 9. He that devotes himself to God's guidance and government, with an entire dependence upon God's wisdom, power, and goodness, has a better security to make him easy than if all the kings and potentates of the earth should undertake to protect him. (2.) It enabled him to triumph in that trust. [1.] He triumphs in God, and in his relation to him and interest in him (*v.* 6) : " *The Lord is on my side.* He is a righteous God, and therefore espouses my righteous cause and will plead it." If we are on God's side, he is on ours ; if we be for him and with him, he will be for us and with us (*v.* 7) : " *The Lord takes my part,* and stands up for me, *with*

those that help me. He is to me among my helpers, and so one of them that he is all in all both to them and me, and without him I could not help myself nor could any friend I have in the world help me." Thus (*v.* 14), " *The Lord is my strength and my song;* that is, I make him so (without him I am weak and sad, but on him I stay myself as my strength, both for doing and suffering, and in him I solace myself as my song, by which I both express my joy and ease my grief), and, making him so, I find him so : he strengthens my heart with his graces and gladdens my heart with his comforts." If God be our strength, he must be our song ; if he work all our works in us, he must have all praise and glory from us. God is sometimes the strength of his people when he is not their song; they have spiritual supports when they want spiritual delights. But, if he be both to us, we have abundant reason to triumph in him ; for, if he be our strength and our song, he has become not only our Saviour, but our salvation ; for his being our strength is our protection to the salvation, and his being our song is an earnest and foretaste of the salvation. [2.] He triumphs over his enemies. Now shall his head be lifted up above them ; for, *First,* He is sure they cannot hurt him : " God is for me, and then *I will not fear what man can do against me,*" *v.* 6. He can set them all at defiance, and is not disturbed at any of their attempts. "They can do nothing to me but what God permits them to do ; they can do me no real damage, for they cannot separate between me and God ; they cannot do any thing but what God can make to work for my good. The enemy is a man, a depending creature, whose power is limited, and subordinate to a higher power, and therefore I will not fear him." *Who art thou, that thou shouldst be afraid of a man that shall die ?* Isa. li. 12. The apostle quotes this, with application to all Christians, Heb. xiii. 6. They may boldly say, as boldly as David himself, *The Lord is my helper,* and *I will not fear what man shall do unto me ;* let him do his worst. *Secondly,* He is sure that he shall be too hard for them at last : " *I shall see my desire upon those that hate me* (*v.* 7); I shall see them defeated in their designs against me ; nay, *In the name of the Lord I will destroy them* (*v.* 10 —12); I trust in the name of the Lord that I shall destroy them, and in his name I will go forth against them, depending on his strength, by warrant from him, and with an eye to his glory, not confiding in myself nor taking vengeance for myself." Thus he went forth against Goliath, *in the name of the God of Israel,* 1 Sam. xvii. 45. David says this as a type of Christ, who triumphed over the powers of darkness, destroyed them, and *made a show of them openly.* [3.] He triumphs in an assurance of the continuance of his comfort, his victory, and his life. *First,* Of his comfort (*v.* 15): *The voice of rejoicing and*

salvation is in the tabernacles of the righteous, and in mine particularly, in my family. The dwellings of the righteous in this world are but tabernacles, mean and movable ; here we have no city, *no continuing city.* But these tabernacles are more comfortable to them than the palaces of the wicked are to them ; for in the house where religion rules, 1. There is salvation ; safety from evil, earnests of eternal salvation, which *has come to this house,* Luke xix. 9. 2. Where there is salvation there is cause for rejoicing, for continual joy in God. Holy joy is called *the joy of salvation,* for in that there is abundant matter for joy. 3. Where there is rejoicing there ought to be *the voice* of rejoicing, that is, praise and thanksgiving. Let God be served with joyfulness and gladness of heart, and let the voice of that rejoicing be heard daily in our families, to the glory of God and the encouragement of others. *Secondly,* Of his victory : *The right hand of the Lord does valiantly* (*v.* 15) and *is exalted ;* for (as some read it) *it has exalted me.* The right hand of God's power is engaged for his people, and it acts vigorously for them and therefore victoriously. For what difficulty can stand before the divine valour ? We are weak, and act but cowardly for ourselves ; but God is mighty, and acts valiantly for us, with jealousy and resolution, Isa. lxiii. 5, 6. There is spirit, as well as strength, in all God's operations for his people. And, when God's right hand does valiantly for our salvation, it ought to be exalted in our praises. *Thirdly,* Of his life (*v.* 17): " *I shall not die* by the hands of my enemies that seek my life, *but live and declare the works of the Lord ;* I shall live a monument of God's mercy and power ; his works shall be declared in me, and I will make it the business of my life to praise and magnify God, looking upon that as the end of my preservation." Note, It is not worth while to live for any other purpose than to *declare the works of God,* for his honour and the encouragement of others to serve him and trust in him. Such as these were the triumphs of the Son of David in the assurance he had of the success of his undertaking and that the *good pleasure of the Lord* should *prosper in his hand.*

19 Open to me the gates of righteousness : I will go into them, *and* I will praise the Lord : 20 This gate of the Lord, into which the righteous shall enter. 21 I will praise thee : for thou hast heard me, and art become my salvation. 22 The stone *which* the builders refused is become the head *stone* of the corner. 23 This is the Lord's doing ; it *is* marvellous in our eyes. 24 This *is* the day *which* the Lord hath made ; we will rejoice and be glad in it. 25 Save now, I beseech

thee, O Lord: O Lord, I beseech thee, send now prosperity. 26 Blessed *be* he that cometh in the name of the Lord: we have blessed you out of the house of the Lord. 27 God *is* the Lord, which hath showed us light: bind the sacrifice with cords, *even* unto the horns of the altar. 28 Thou *art* my God, and I will praise thee: *thou art* my God, I will exalt thee. 29 O give thanks unto the Lord; for *he is* good: for his mercy *endureth* for ever.

We have here an illustrious prophecy of the humiliation and exaltation of our Lord Jesus, his sufferings, and the glory that should follow. Peter thus applies it directly to the chief priests and scribes, and none of them could charge him with misapplying it, Acts iv. 11. Now observe here,

I. The preface with which this precious prophecy is introduced, *v.* 19—21. 1. The psalmist desires admission into the sanctuary of God, there to celebrate the glory of him *that cometh in the name of the Lord: Open to me the gates of righteousness.* So the temple-gates are called, because they were shut against the uncircumcised, and forbade the stranger to come nigh, as the sacrifices there offered are called *sacrifices of righteousness.* Those that would enter into communion with God in holy ordinances must become humble suitors to God for admission. And when the gates of righteousness are opened to us we must *go into them*, must enter into the holiest, as far as we have leave, *and praise the Lord.* Our business within God's gates is to praise God; *therefore* we should long till the gates of heaven be opened to us, that we may go into them to dwell in God's house above, where we shall be still praising him. 2. He sees admission granted him (*v.* 20): *This is the gate of the Lord*, the gate of his appointing, *into which the righteous shall enter;* as if he had said, "The gate you knocked at is opened, and you are welcome. *Knock, and it shall be opened unto you."* Some by this gate understand Christ, by whom we are taken into fellowship with God and our praises are accepted; he is *the way;* there is no coming to the Father but by him (John xiv. 6), he is the *door of the sheep* (John x. 9); he is the gate of the temple, by whom, and by whom only, the righteous, and they only, shall enter, and *come into God's righteousness*, as the expression is, lxix. 27. The psalmist triumphs in the discovery that the gate of righteousness, which had been so long shut, and so long knocked at, was now at length opened. 3. He promises to give thanks to God for this favour (*v.* 21): *I will praise thee.* Those that saw Christ's day at so great a distance saw cause to praise God for the prospect; for in him they saw that God had heard them, had heard the prayers

of the Old-Testament saints for the coming of the Messiah, and would be their salvation.

II. The prophecy itself, *v.* 22, 23. This may have some reference to David's preferment; he was the stone which Saul and his courtiers rejected, but was by the wonderful providence of God advanced to be the head-stone of the building. But its principal reference is to Christ; and here we have, 1. His humiliation. He is *the stone which the builders refused;* he is the *stone cut out of the mountain without hands*, Dan. ii. 34. He is a stone, not only for strength, and firmness, and duration, but for life, in the building of the spiritual temple; and yet a *precious stone* (1 Pet. ii. 6), for the foundation of the gospel-church must be *sapphires*, Isa. liv. 11. This stone was *rejected by the builders*, by the rulers and people of the Jews (Acts iv. 8, 10, 11); they refused to own him as the stone, the Messiah promised; they would not build their faith upon him nor join themselves to him; they would make no use of him, but go on in their building without him; they *denied him in the presence of Pilate* (Acts iii. 13) when they said, *We have no king but Cæsar.* They trampled upon this stone, threw it among the rubbish out of the city; nay, they stumbled at it. This was a disgrace to Christ, but it proved the ruin of those that thus made light of him. Rejecters of Christ are rejected of God. 2. His exaltation. He *has become the head-stone of the corner;* he is advanced to the highest degree both of honour and usefulness, to be above all, and all in all. He is the chief corner-stone in the foundation, in whom Jew and Gentile are united, that they may be built up one holy house. He is the chief top-stone in the corner, in whom the building is completed, and who must in all things have the pre-eminence, as the *author and finisher of our faith.* Thus highly has God exalted him, because he humbled himself: and we, in compliance with God's design, must make him the foundation of our hope, the centre of our unity, and the end of our living. *To me to live is Christ.* 3. The hand of God in all this: *This is the Lord's doing;* it is from the Lord; it is with the Lord; it is the product of his counsel; it is contrivance. Both the humiliation and the exaltation of the Lord Jesus were his work, Acts ii. 23; iv. 27, 28. He sent him, sealed him; his hand went with him throughout his whole undertaking, and from first to last he did his Father's will; and this ought to be *marvellous in our eyes.* Christ's name is *Wonderful;* and the redemption he wrought out is the most amazing of all God's works of wonder; it is what the angels *desire to look into*, and will be admiring to eternity; much more ought we to admire it, who owe our all to it. *Without controversy, great is the mystery of godliness.*

III. The joy wherewith it is entertained

and the acclamations which attend this prediction.

1. Let the day be solemnized to the honour of God with great joy (v. 24): *This is the day the Lord has made.* The whole time of the gospel-dispensation, that *accepted time*, that *day of salvation*, is what the Lord has made so; it is a continual feast, which ought to be kept with joy. Or it may very fitly be understood of the Christian sabbath, which we sanctify in remembrance of Christ's resurrection, when the rejected stone began to be exalted; and so, (1.) Here is the doctrine of the Christian sabbath: *It is the day which the Lord has made*, has made remarkable, made holy, has distinguished from other days; he has made it for man: it is therefore called *the Lord's day*, for it bears his image and superscription. (2.) The duty of the sabbath, the work of the day that is to be done in his day: *We will rejoice and be glad in it*, not only in the institution of the day, that there is such a day appointed, but in the occasion of it, Christ's becoming the *head of the corner.* This we ought to rejoice in both as his honour and our advantage. Sabbath days must be rejoicing days, and then they are to us as the days of heaven. See what a good Master we serve, who, having instituted a day for his service, appoints it to be spent in holy joy.

2. Let the exalted Redeemer be met, and attended, with joyful hosannas, v. 25, 26.

(1.) Let him have the acclamations of the people, as is usual at the inauguration of a prince. Let every one of his loyal subjects shout for joy, *Save now, I beseech thee, O Lord!* This is like *Vivat rex—Long live the king,* and expresses a hearty joy for his accession to the crown, an entire satisfaction in his government, and a zealous affection to the interests and honour of it. *Hosanna* signifies, *Save now, I beseech thee.* [1.] "Lord, save me, I beseech thee; let this Saviour be my Saviour, and, in order to that, my ruler; let me be taken under his protection and owned as one of his willing subjects. His enemies are my enemies; Lord, I beseech thee, save me from them. Send me an interest in that prosperity which his kingdom brings with it to all those that entertain it. Let my soul prosper and be in health, in that peace and righteousness which his government brings, lxxii. 3. Let me have victory over those lusts *that war against my soul,* and let divine grace go on in my heart *conquering and to conquer.*" [2.] "Lord, preserve him, I beseech thee, even the Saviour himself, and *send him prosperity* in all his undertakings; give success to his gospel, and let it be *mighty, through God, to the pulling down of strong-holds* and reducing souls to their allegiance to him. Let his name be sanctified, his *kingdom come*, his *will be done.*" Thus *let prayer be made for him continually,* lxxii. 15. On the Lord's day, when we rejoice and are glad in his kingdom, we must

pray for the advancement of it more and more, and its establishment upon the ruins of the devil's kingdom. When Christ made his public entry into Jerusalem he was thus met by his well-wishers (Matt. xxi. 9): *Hosanna to the Son of David;* long live King Jesus; let him reign for ever.

(2.) Let the priests, the Lord's ministers, do their part in this great solemnity, v. 26. [1.] Let them bless the prince with their praises: *Blessed is he that cometh in the name of the Lord.* Jesus Christ is *he that cometh* —ὁ ἐρχόμενος, he that was to come and is yet to come again, Rev. i. 8. He *comes in the name of the Lord*, with a commission from him, to act for him, to do his will and to seek his glory; and therefore we must say, *Blessed be he that cometh;* we must rejoice that he has come; we must speak well of him, admire him, and esteem him highly, as one we are eternally obliged to, call him blessed Jesus, blessed for ever, xlv. 2. We must bid him welcome into our hearts, saying, "Come in, thou blessed of the Lord; come in by thy grace and Spirit, and take possession of me for thy own." We must bless his faithful ministers that come in his name, and receive them for his sake, Isa. lii. 7; John xiii. 20. We must pray for the enlargement and edification of his church, for the ripening of things for his second coming, and then that he who has said, *Surely I come quickly,* would *even so come.* [2.] Let them bless the people with their prayers: *We have blessed you out of the house of the Lord.* Christ's ministers are not only warranted, but appointed to pronounce a blessing, in his name, upon all his loyal subjects that love him and his government in sincerity, Eph. vi. 24. We assure you that in and through Jesus Christ you are blessed; for he came to bless you. "You are *blessed out of the house of the Lord,* that is, *with spiritual blessings in heavenly places* (Eph. i. 3), and therefore have reason to bless him who has thus blessed you."

3. Let sacrifices of thanksgiving be offered to his honour who offered for us the great atoning sacrifice, v. 27. Here is, (1.) The privilege we enjoy by Jesus Christ: *God is the Lord who has shown us light.* God is Jehovah, is known by that name, a God performing what he has promised and perfecting what he has begun, Exod. vi. 3. *He has shown us light,* that is, he has given us the knowledge of himself and his will. He *has shined upon us* (so some); he has favoured us, and lifted up upon us the light of his countenance; he has given us occasion for joy and rejoicing, which is light to the soul, by giving us a prospect of everlasting light in heaven. *The day which the Lord has made* brings light with it, true light. (2.) The duty which this privilege calls for: *Bind the sacrifice with cords,* that, being killed, the blood of it may be sprinkled *upon the horns of the altar*, according to the law; or perhaps it was the custom (though we read not of it

elsewhere) to *bind the sacrifice to the horns of the altar* while things were getting ready for the slaying of it. Or this may have a peculiar significancy here; the sacrifice we are to offer to God, in gratitude for redeeming love, is ourselves, not to be slain upon the altar, but *living sacrifices* (Rom. xii. 1), to be bound to the altar, spiritual sacrifices of prayer and praise, in which our hearts must be fixed and engaged, as the sacrifice was bound *with cords to the horns of the altar* not to start back.

4. The psalmist concludes with his own thankful acknowledgments of divine grace, in which he calls upon others to join with him, *v.* 28, 29. (1.) He will praise God himself, and endeavour to exalt him in his own heart and in the hearts of others, and this because of his covenant-relation to him and interest in him: "*Thou art my God,* on whom I depend, and to whom I am devoted, who ownest me and art owned by me; *and* therefore *I will praise thee.*" (2.) He will have all about him to give thanks to God for these glad tidings of great joy to all people, that there is a Redeemer, even Christ the Lord. In him it is that God *is good* to man and that *his mercy endures for ever;* in him the covenant of grace is made, and in him it is made sure, made good, and made an everlasting covenant. He concludes this psalm as he began it (*v.* 1), for God's glory must be the Alpha and Omega, the beginning and the end, of all our addresses to him. *Hallowed be thy name,* and *thine is the glory.* And this fitly closes a prophecy of Christ. The angels give thanks for man's redemption. *Glory to God in the highest* (Luke ii. 14), for there is *on earth peace,* to which we must echo with our hosannas, as they did, Luke xix. 38. *Peace in heaven* to us through Christ, and therefore *glory in the highest.*

PSALM CXIX.

This is a psalm by itself, like none of the rest; it excels them all, and shines brightest in this constellation. It is much longer than any of them more than twice as long as any of them. It is not making long prayers that Christ censures, but making them for a pretence, which intimates that they are in themselves good and commendable. It seems to me to be a collection of David's pious and devout ejaculations, the short and sudden breathings and elevations of his soul to God, which he wrote down as they occurred, and, towards the latter end of his time, gathered out of his day-book where they lay scattered, added to them many like words, and digested them into this psalm, in which there is seldom any coherence between the verses, but, like Solomon's proverbs, it is a chest of gold rings, not a chain of gold links. And we may not only learn, by the psalmist's example, to accustom ourselves to such pious ejaculations, which are an excellent means of maintaining constant communion with God, and keeping the heart in frame for the more solemn exercises of religion, but we must make use of the psalmist's words, both for the exciting and for the expressing of our devout affections; what some have said of this psalm is true, "He that shall read it considerately, it will either warm him or shame him." The composition of it is singular and very exact. It is divided into twenty-two parts, according to the number of the letters of the Hebrew alphabet, and each part consists of eight verses, all the verses of the first part beginning with Aleph, all the verses of the second with Beth, and so on, without any flaw throughout the whole psalm. Archbishop Tillotson says, It seems to have more of poetical skill and number in it than we at this distance can easily understand. Some have called it the saints' alphabet; and it were to be wished we had it as ready in our memories as the very letters of our alphabet, as ready as our A B C. Perhaps the penman found it of use to himself to observe this method, as it obliged him to seek for thoughts, and search for them, that he might fill up the quota of every part; and the letter he was to begin with might lead him to a word which might suggest a good sentence; and all little enough to raise any thing that is good in the barren soil of our hearts. However, it would be of use to the learners, a help to them both in committing it to memory and in calling it to mind upon occasion;

by the letter the first word would be got, and that would bring in the whole verse; thus young people would the more easily learn it by heart and retain it the better even in old age. If any censure it as childish and trifling, because acrostics are now quite out of fashion, let them know that the royal psalmist despises their censure; he is a teacher of babes, and, if this method may be beneficial to them, he can easily stoop to it; if this be to be vile, he will be yet more vile.

II. The general scope and design of it is to magnify the law, and make it honourable; to set forth the excellency and usefulness of divine revelation, and to recommend it to us, not only for the entertainment, but for the government, of ourselves, by the psalmist's own example, who speaks by experience of the benefit of it, and of the good impressions made upon him by it, for which he praises God, and earnestly prays, from first to last, for the continuance of God's grace with him, to direct and quicken him in the way of his duty. There are ten different words by which divine revelation is called in this psalm, and they are synonymous, each of them expressive of the whole compass of it (both that which tells us what God expects from us and that which tells us what we may expect from him) and of the system of religion which is founded upon it and guided by it. The things contained in the scripture, and drawn from it, are here called, 1. God's law, because they are enacted by him as our Sovereign. 2. His way, because they are the rule both of his providence and of our obedience. 3. His testimonies, because they are solemnly declared to the world and attested beyond contradiction. 4. His commandments, because given with authority, and (as the word signifies) lodged with us as a trust. 5. His precepts, because prescribed to us and not left indifferent. 6. His word, or saying, because it is the declaration of his mind, and Christ, the essential eternal Word, is all in all in it. 7. His judgments, because framed in infinite wisdom, and because by them we must both judge and be judged. 8. His righteousness, because it is all holy, just, and good, and the rule and standard of righteousness. 9. His statutes, because they are fixed and determined, and of perpetual obligation. His truth, or faithfulness, because the principles upon which the divine law is built are eternal truths. And I think there is but one verse (it is ver. 122) in all this long psalm in which there is not one or other of these ten words; only in three or four they are used concerning God's providence or David's practice (as ver 75, 84, 121), and ver. 132 they are called God's name. The great esteem and affection David had for the word of God is the more admirable considering how little he had of it, in comparison with what we have, no more perhaps in writing than the first books of Moses, which were but the dawning of this day, which may shame us who enjoy the full discoveries of divine revelation and yet are so cold towards it. In singing this psalm there is work for all the devout affections of a sanctified soul, so copious, so various, is the matter of it. We here find that in which we must give glory to God both as our ruler and great benefactor, that in which we are to teach and admonish ourselves and one another (so many are the instructions which we here find about a religious life), and that in which we are to comfort and encourage ourselves and one another, so many are the sweet experiences of one that lived such a life. Here is something or other to suit the case of every Christian. Is any afflicted? Is any merry? Each will find that here which is proper for him. And it is so far from being a tedious repetition of the same thing, as may seem to those who look over it cursorily, that, if we duly meditate upon it, we shall find almost every verse has a new thought and something in it very lively. And this, as many other of David's psalms, teaches us to be sententious in our devotions, both alone and when others join with us; for, ordinarily, the affections, especially of weaker Christians, are more likely to be raised and kept by short expressions, the sense of which lies in a little compass, than by long and laboured periods.

1. ALEPH.

BLESSED *are* the undefiled in the way, who walk in the law of the LORD. 2 Blessed *are* they that keep his testimonies, *and that* seek him with the whole heart. 3 They also do no iniquity: they walk in his ways.

The psalmist here shows that godly people are happy people; they are, and shall be, blessed indeed. Felicity is the thing we all pretend to aim at and pursue. He does not say here wherein it consists; it is enough for us to know what we must do and be that we may attain to it, and that we are here told. All men would be happy, but few take the right way; God has here laid before us the right way, which we may be sure will end in happiness, though it be strait and narrow. Blessednesses are to the righteous; all manner of blessedness. Now observe the charac-

ters of the happy people. Those are happy,
1. Who make the will of God the rule of all
their actions, and govern themselves, in their
whole conversation, by that rule : They *walk
in the law of the Lord, v.* 1. God's word is
a law to them, not only in this or that instance, but in the whole course of their conversation ; they walk within the hedges of
that law, which they dare not break through
by doing any thing it forbids ; and they walk
in the paths of that law, which they will not
trifle in, but *press forward* in them *towards
the mark,* taking every step by rule and never
walking at all adventures. This is *walking
in God's ways* (v. 3), the ways which he has
marked out to us and has appointed us to
walk in. It will not serve us to make religion the subject of our discourse, but we
must make it the rule of our walk ; we must
walk *in his ways,* not in the way of the world,
or of our own hearts, Job xxiii. 10, 11;
xxxi. 7. 2. Who are upright and honest in
their religion—*undefiled in the way,* not only
who keep themselves pure from the pollutions of actual sin, *unspotted from the world,*
but who are habitually sincere in their intentions, *in whose spirit there is no guile,* who
are really as good as they seem to be and
row the same way as they look. 3. Who are
true to the trust reposed in them as God's
professing people. It was the honour of the
Jews that *to them were committed the oracles
of God ;* and blessed are those who preserve
pure and entire that sacred deposit, *who keep
his testimonies* as a treasure of inestimable
value, keep them as the apple of their eye,
so keep them as to carry the comfort of them
themselves to another world and leave the
knowledge and profession of them to those
who shall come after them in this world.
Those who would *walk in the law of the Lord*
must *keep his testimonies,* that is, his truths.
Those will not long make conscience of good
practices who do not adhere to good principles. Or *his testimonies* may denote his
covenant ; the ark of the covenant is called
the ark of the testimony. Those do not keep
covenant with God who do not keep the
commandments of God. 4. Who have a
single eye to God as their chief good and
highest end in all they do in religion (v. 2) :
They *seek him with their whole heart.* They
do not seek themselves and their own things,
but God only ; this is that which they aim
at, that God may be glorified in their obedience and that they may be happy in God's
acceptance. He is, and will be, the rewarder,
the reward, of all those who thus *seek him
diligently, seek him with the heart,* for that is
it that God looks at and requires ; and *with
the whole heart,* for if the heart be divided
between him and the world it is faulty. 5.
Who carefully avoid all sin (v. 3) : *They do
no iniquity ;* they do not allow themselves in
any sin ; they do not commit it as those do
who are the servants of sin ; they do not
make a practice of it, do not make a trade of

it. They are conscious to themselves of
much iniquity that clogs them in the ways of
God, but not of that iniquity which draws
them out of those ways. Blessed and holy
are those who thus exercise themselves *to
have always consciences void of offence.*

4 Thou hast commanded *us* to keep
thy precepts diligently. 5 O that my
ways were directed to keep thy statutes ! 6 Then shall I not be ashamed,
when I have respect unto all thy commandments.

We are here taught, 1. To own ourselves
under the highest obligations to walk in God's
law. The tempter would possess men with
an opinion that they are at their liberty whether they will make the word of God their
rule or no, that, though it may be good, yet
it is not so necessary as they are made to believe it is. He taught our first parents to
question the command : *Hath God said, You
shall not eat ?* And therefore we are concerned to be well established in this (v. 4):
Thou hast commanded us to keep thy precepts,
to make religion our rule ; and *to keep* them
diligently, to make religion our business and
to mind it carefully and constantly. We are
bound, and must obey at our peril. 2. To
look up to God for wisdom and grace to do
so (v. 5): *O that my ways were directed* accordingly ! not only that all events concerning us may be so ordered and disposed by
the providence of God as not to be in any
thing a hindrance to us, but a furtherance
rather, in the service of God, but that our
hearts may be so guided and influenced by
the Spirit of God that we may not in any
thing transgress God's commandments—not
only that our eyes may be directed to behold
God's statutes, but our hearts directed to
keep them. See how the desire and prayer
of a good man exactly agree with the will
and command of a good God: " Thou wouldest have me keep thy precepts, and, Lord, I
fain would keep them." *This is the will of
God, even our sanctification ;* and it should be
our will. 3. To encourage ourselves in the
way of our duty with a prospect of the comfort we shall find in it, v. 6. Note, (1.) It is
the undoubted character of every good man
that he has a *respect to all* God's *commandments.* He has a respect to the command,
eyes it as his copy, aims to conform to it, is
sorry wherein he comes short ; and what he
does in religion he does with a conscientious
regard to the command, because it is his duty.
He has *respect to all* the *commandments,* one
as well as another, because they are all backed
with the same authority (Jam. ii. 10, 11) and
all levelled at the same end, the glorifying of
God in our happiness. Those who have a
sincere respect to any command will have a
general respect to every command, to the
commands of both testaments and both tables, to the prohibitions and the precepts, to

those that concern both the inward and the outward man, both the head and the heart, to those that forbid the most pleasant and gainful sins and to those that require the most difficult and hazardous duties (2.) Those who have a sincere *respect to all* God's *commandments shall not be ashamed,* not only they will thereby be kept from doing that which will turn to their shame, but they shall have *confidence towards God* and boldness of access to the throne of his grace, 1 John iii. 21. They shall have credit before men; their honesty will be their honour. And they shall have clearness and courage in their own souls; they shall not be ashamed to retire into themselves, nor to reflect upon themselves, for their hearts shall not condemn them. David speaks this with application to himself. Those that are upright may take the comfort of their uprightness. "As, if I be wicked, woe to me; so, if I be sincere, it is well with me."

7 I will praise thee with uprightness of heart, when I shall have learned thy righteous judgments. 8 I will keep thy statutes: O forsake me not utterly.

Here is, I. David's endeavour to perfect himself in his religion, and to make himself (as we say) master of his business. He hopes to *learn* God's *righteous judgments.* He knew much, but he was still pressing forward and desired to know more, as knowing this, that *he had not yet attained;* but as far as perfection is attainable in this life he reached towards it, and would not take up short of it. As long as we live we must be scholars in Christ's school, and sit at his feet; but we should aim to be head-scholars, and to get into the highest form. God's judgments are all righteous, and therefore it is desirable not only to learn them, but to be learned in them, *mighty in the scriptures.*

II. The use he would make of his divine learning. He coveted to be learned in the laws of God, not that he might make himself a name and interest among men, or fill his own head with entertaining speculations, but, 1. That he might give God the glory of his learning: *I will praise thee when I have learned thy judgments,* intimating that he could not learn unless God taught him, and that divine instructions are special blessings, which we have reason to be thankful for. Though Christ keeps a free-school, and teaches without money and without price, yet he expects his scholars should give him thanks both for his word and for his Spirit; surely it is a mercy worth thanks to be taught so gainful a calling as religion is. Those have learned a good lesson who have learned to praise God, for that is the work of angels, the work of heaven. It is an easy thing to praise God in word and tongue; but those only are well learned in this mystery who have learned to *praise* him *with uprightness of heart,* that is, are inward with him in

praising him, and sincerely aim at his glory in the course of their conversation as well as in the exercises of devotion. God accepts only the praises of the upright. 2. That he might himself come under the government of that learning: *When I shall have learned thy righteous judgments I will keep thy statutes.* We cannot keep them unless we learn them; but we learn them in vain if we do not keep them. Those have well learned God's statutes who have come up to a full resolution, in the strength of his grace, to keep them.

III. His prayer to God not to leave him: " *O forsake me not!* that is, leave me not to myself, withdraw not thy Spirit and grace from me, for then *I shall* not *keep thy statutes.*" Good men see themselves undone if God forsakes them; for then the tempter will be too hard for them. "Though thou seem to forsake me, and threaten to forsake me, and dost, for a time, withdraw from me, yet let not the desertion be total and final; for that is hell. *O forsake me not utterly!* for woe unto me if God departs from me."

2. BETH.

9 Wherewithal shall a young man cleanse his way? by taking heed *thereto* according to thy word.

Here is, 1. A weighty question asked. By what means may the next generation be made better than this? *Wherewithal shall a young man cleanse his way?* Cleansing implies that it is polluted. Besides the original corruption we all brought into the world with us (from which we are not cleansed unto this day), there are many particular sins which young people are subject to, by which they defile their way, *youthful lusts* (2 Tim. ii. 22); these render their way offensive to God and disgraceful to themselves. Young men are concerned to cleanse their way—to get their hearts renewed and their lives reformed, to make clean, and keep clean, from the *corruption that is in the world through lust,* that they may have both a good conscience and a good name. Few young people do themselves enquire by what means they may recover and preserve their purity; and therefore David asks the question for them. 2. A satisfactory answer given to this question. Young men may effectually *cleanse their way by taking heed thereto according to* the *word* of God; and it is the honour of the word of God that it has such power and is of such use both to particular persons and to communities, whose happiness lies much in the virtue of their youth. (1.) Young men must make the word of God their rule, must acquaint themselves with it and resolve to conform themselves to it; that will do more towards the cleansing of young men than the laws of princes or the morals of philosophers. (2.) They must carefully apply that rule and make use of it; they must take heed to their way, must examine it by the word of God as a touchstone and standard, must rectify what is amiss in it by that regulator and steer by that chart and compass. God's word will not do without our watchfulness, and a constant regard both to it and to our way, that we may compare them together. The ruin of young men is either living at large (or by no rule at all) or choosing to themselves false rules: let them ponder the path of their feet, and walk by scripture-rules; so their way shall be clean, and they shall have the comfort and credit of it here and for ever.

10 With my whole heart have I sought thee : O let me not wander from thy commandments.

Here is, 1. David's experience of a good work God had wrought in him, which he takes the comfort of and pleads with God: "*I have sought thee*, sought to thee as my oracle, sought after thee as my happiness, sought thee as my God; for *should not a people seek unto their God?* If I have not yet found thee, the *I have sought thee*, and thou never saidst, Seek in vain, nor wilt say so to me, for *I have sought thee with my heart, with my whole heart*, sought thee only, sought thee diligently." 2. His prayer for the preservation of that work : " Thou that hast inclined me to seek thy precepts, never suffer me to wander from them." The best are sensible of their aptness to wander; and the more we have found of the pleasure there is in keeping God's commandments the more afraid we shall be of wandering from them and the more earnest we shall be in prayer to God for his grace to prevent our wanderings.

11 Thy word have I hid in mine heart, that I might not sin against thee.

Here is, 1. The close application which David made of the word of God to himself: *He hid it in his heart*, laid it up there, that it might be ready to him whenever he had occasion to use it; he laid it up as that which he valued highly, and had a warm regard for, and which he was afraid of losing and being robbed of. God's word is a treasure worth laying up, and there is no laying it up safely but in our hearts; if we have it only in our houses and hands, enemies may take it from us; if only in our heads, our memories may fail us : but if our hearts be delivered into the mould of it, and the impressions of it remain on our souls, it is safe. 2. The good uses he designed to make of it : *That I might not sin against thee.* Good men are afraid of sin, and are in care to prevent it; and the most effectual way to prevent it is to hide God's word in our hearts, that we may answer every temptation, as our Master did, with, *It is written*, may oppose God's precepts to the dominion of sin, his promises to its allurements, and his threatenings to its menaces.

12 Blessed *art* thou, O Lord : teach me thy statutes.

688

Here, 1. David gives glory to God : "*Blessed art thou, O Lord!* Thou art infinitely happy in the enjoyment of thyself and hast no need of me or my services ; yet thou art pleased to reckon thyself honoured by them ; assist me therefore, and then accept me." In all our prayers we should intermix praises. 2. He asks grace from God : *Teach me thy statutes ;* give me to know and do my duty in every thing. Thou art the fountain of all blessedness ; O let me have this drop from that fountain, this blessing from that blessedness : *Teach me thy statutes*, that I may know how to bless thee, who art a blessed God, and that I may be blessed in thee."

13 With my lips have I declared all the judgments of thy mouth. 14 I have rejoiced in the way of thy testimonies, as *much as* in all riches. 15 I will meditate in thy precepts, and have respect unto thy ways. 16 I will delight myself in thy statutes : I will not forget thy word.

Here, I. David looks back with comfort upon the respect he had paid to the word of God. He had the testimony of his conscience for him, 1. That he had edified others with what he had been taught out of the word of God (v. 13): *With my lips have I declared all the judgments of thy mouth.* This he did, not only as a king in making orders, and giving judgment, according to the word of God, nor only as a prophet by his psalms, but in his common discourse. Thus he showed how full he was of the word of God, and what a holy delight he took in his acquaintance with it; for it is *out of the abundance of the heart* that *the mouth speaks.* Thus he did good with his knowledge; he did not hide God's word from others, but hid it for them; and, out of that *good treasure in his heart*, brought *forth good things*, as the householder out of his store *things new and old.* Those whose hearts are fed with the bread of life should with their lips feed many. He had prayed (v. 12) that God would teach him; and here he pleads, " Lord, I have endeavoured to make a good use of the knowledge thou hast given me, therefore increase it;" for *to him that has shall be given.* 2. That he had entertained himself with it: "*Lord, teach me thy statutes;* for I desire no greater pleasure than to know and do them (v. 14): *I have rejoiced in the way of thy commandments*, in a constant even course of obedience to thee ; not only in the speculations and histories of thy word, but in the precepts of it, and in that path of serious godliness which they chalk out to me. *I have rejoiced in* this *as much as in all riches*, as much as ever any worldling rejoiced in the increase of his wealth. In the way of God's commandments I can truly say, *Soul, take thy ease ;*" in true religion there is all riches, the unsearchable riches of Christ.

II. He looks forward with a holy resolution never to cool in his affection to the word of God; what he *does that he will do*, 2 Cor. xi. 12. Those that have found pleasure in the ways of God are likely to proceed and persevere in them. 1. He will dwell much upon them in his thoughts (*v.* 15): *I will meditate in thy precepts.* He not only discoursed of them to others (many do that only to show their knowledge and authority), but he communed with his own heart about them, and took pains to digest in his own thoughts what he had declared, or had to declare, to others. Note, God's words ought to be very much the subject of our thoughts. 2. He will have them always in his eye: *I will have respect unto thy ways*, as the traveller has to his road, which he is in care not to miss and always aims and endeavours to hit. We do not meditate on God's precepts to good purpose unless we have respect to them as our rule and our good thoughts produce good works and good intentions in them. 3. He will take a constant pleasure in communion with God and obedience to him. It is not for a season that he rejoices in this light, but "*I will* still, I will for ever, *delight myself in thy statutes*, not only think of them, but do them with delight," *v.* 16. David took more delight in God's statutes than in the pleasures of his court or the honours of his camp, more than in his sword or in his harp. When the law is written in the heart duty becomes a delight. 4. He will never forget what he has learned of the things of God: "*I will not forget thy word*, not only I will not quite forget it, but I will be mindful of it when I have occasion to use it." Those that meditate in God's word, and delight in it, are in no great danger of forgetting it

3. GIMEL.

17 Deal bountifully with thy servant, *that* I may live, and keep thy word.

We are here taught, 1. That we owe our lives to God's mercy. David prays, *Deal bountifully with* me, *that I may live.* It was God's bounty that gave us life, that gave us this life; and the same bounty that gave it continues it, and gives all the supports and comforts of it; if these be withheld, we die, or, which is equivalent, our lives are embittered and we become weary of them. If God deals in strict justice with us, we die, we perish, we all perish; if these forfeited lives be preserved and prolonged, it is because God deals bountifully with us, according to his mercy, not according to our deserts. The continuance of the most useful life is owing to God's bounty, and on that we must have a continual dependence. 2. That therefore we ought to spend our lives in God's service. Life is *therefore* a choice mercy, because it is an opportunity of obeying God in this world, where there are so few that do glorify him; and this David had in his eye: "Not *that I may live* and grow rich, live and be merry,

but *that I may live and keep thy word*, may observe it myself and transmit it to those that shall come after, which the longer I live the better I shall do."

18 Open thou mine eyes, that I may behold wondrous things out of thy law.

Observe here, 1. That there are *wondrous things* in God's *law*, which we are all concerned, and should covet, to *behold*, not only strange things, which are very surprising and unexpected, but excellent things, which are to be highly esteemed and valued, and things which were long *hidden from the wise and prudent*, but are now *revealed unto babes.* If there were wonders in the law, much more in the gospel, where Christ is all in all, whose name is *Wonderful.* Well may we, who are so nearly interested, desire to behold these wondrous things, when the angels themselves reach *to look into them*, 1 Pet. i. 12. 2. Those that would see the wondrous things of God's law and gospel must beg of him to *open their eyes* and to give them an understanding. We are by nature blind to the things of God, till his grace cause the scales to fall from our eyes; and even those in whose hearts God has said, *Let there be light*, have yet need to be further enlightened, and must still pray to God to open their eyes yet more and more, that those who at first *saw men as trees walking* may come to see all things clearly; and the more God opens our eyes the more wonders we see in the word of God, which we saw not before.

19 I *am* a stranger in the earth: hide not thy commandments from me.

Here we have, 1. The acknowledgment which David makes of his own condition: *I am a stranger in the earth.* We all are so, and all good people confess themselves to be so; for heaven is their home, and the world is but their inn, the land of their pilgrimage. David was a man that knew as much of the world, and was as well known in it, as most men. God built him a house, established his throne; strangers submitted to him, and people that he had not known served him; he had a name like the names of the great men, and yet he calls himself a stranger. We are all strangers on earth and must so account ourselves. 2. The request he makes to God thereupon: *Hide not thy commandments from me.* He means note: "Lord, show thy commandments to me; let me never know the want of the word of God, but, as long as I live, give me to be growing in my acquaintance with it. *I am a stranger*, and therefore stand in need of a guide, a guard, a companion, a comforter; let me have thy commandments always in view, for they will be all this to me, all that a poor stranger can desire. *I am a stranger* here, and must be gone shortly; by thy commandments let me be prepared for my removal hence."

20 My soul breaketh for the longing *that it hath* unto thy judgments at all times.

David had prayed that God would open his eyes (*v.* 18) and open the law (*v.* 19); now here he pleads the earnestness of his desire for knowledge and grace, for it is the fervent prayer that avails much. 1. His desire was importunate: *My soul breaketh for the longing it hath to thy judgments,* or (as some read it) "*It is taken up, and wholly employed, in longing for thy judgments;* the whole stream of its desires runs in this channel. I shall think myself quite broken and undone if I want the word of God, the direction, converse, and comfort of it." 2. It was constant—*at all times.* It was not now and then, in a good humour, that he was so fond of the word of God; but it is the habitual temper of every sanctified soul to hunger after the word of God as its necessary food, which there is no living without.

21 Thou hast rebuked the proud *that are* cursed, which do err from thy commandments.

Here is, 1. The wretched character of wicked people. The temper of their minds is bad. They are *proud;* they magnify themselves above others. And yet that is not all: they magnify themselves against God, and set up their wills in competition with and opposition to the will of God, as if their hearts, and tongues, and all, were their own. There is something of pride at the bottom of every wilful sin, and the tenour of their lives is no better: They *do err from thy commandments,* as Israel, that did *always err in their hearts;* they err in judgment, and embrace principles contrary to thy commandments, and then no wonder that they err in practice, and wilfully turn aside out of the good way. This is the effect of their pride; for they say, *What is the Almighty, that we should serve him?* As Pharaoh, *Who is the Lord?* 2. The wretched case of such. They are certainly cursed, for *God resists the proud;* and those that throw off the commands of the law lay themselves under its curse (Gal. iii. 10), and he that now *beholds them afar off* will shortly say to them, *Go, you cursed.* The proud sinners bless themselves; God curses them; and, though the most direful effects of this curse are reserved for the other world, yet they are often severely rebuked in this world: Providence crosses them, vexes them, and, wherein they dealt proudly, God shows himself above them; and these rebukes are earnests of worse. David took notice of the rebukes proud men were under, and it made him cleave the more closely to the word of God and pray the more earnestly that he might not *err from* God's commandments. Thus saints get good by God's judgments on sinners.

22 Remove from me reproach and contempt; for I have kept thy testimonies.

Here, 1. David prays against the reproach and contempt of men, that they might be *removed,* or (as the word is) *rolled, from off him.* This intimates that they lay upon him, and that neither his greatness nor his goodness could secure him from being libelled and lampooned. Some despised him and endeavoured to make him mean; others reproached him and endeavoured to make him odious. It has often been the lot of those that do well to be ill-spoken of. It intimates that they lay heavily upon him. Hard and foul words indeed break no bones, and yet they are very grievous to a tender and ingenuous spirit; therefore David prays, "Lord, *remove* them from me, that I may not be thereby either driven from my duty or discouraged in it." God has all men's hearts and tongues in his hand, and can silence lying lips, and raise up a good name that is trodden in the dust. To him we may appeal as the assertor of right and avenger of wrong, and may depend on his promise that he will clear up our *righteousness as the light,* xxxvii. 6. Reproach and contempt may humble us and do us good and then it shall be removed. 2. He pleads his constant adherence to the word and way of God: *For I have kept thy testimonies.* He not only pleads his innocency, that he was unjustly censured, but, (1.) That he was jeered for well-doing. He was despised and abused for his strictness and zeal in religion; so that it was for God's name's sake that he suffered reproach, and therefore he could with the more assurance beg of God to appear for him. The reproach of God's people, if it be not removed now, will be turned into the greater honour shortly. (2.) That he was not jeered out of well-doing: "Lord, remove it from me, *for I have kept thy testimonies* notwithstanding." If in a day of trial we still retain our integrity, we may be sure it will end well.

23 Princes also did sit *and* speak against me: *but* thy servant did meditate in thy statutes.

See here, 1. How David was abused even by great men, who should have known better his character and his case, and have been more generous: *Princes did sit,* sit in council, sit in judgment, and *speak against me.* What even princes say is not always right; but it is sad when judgment is thus turned to wormwood, when those that should be the protectors of the innocent are their betrayers. Herein David was a type of Christ, for they were the princes of this world that vilified and *crucified the Lord of glory,* 1 Cor. ii. 8. 2. What method he took to make himself easy under these abuses: he *meditated in God's statutes,* went on in his duty, and did not regard them; as a deaf man, he heard not. When they spoke against him, he found that in the word of God which spoke for him, and spoke comfort to him, and then none of these things moved him. Those that have pleasure in communion with God may easily despise the censures of men, even of princes.

24 Thy testimonies also *are* my delight *and* my counsellors.

Here David explains his meditating in God's statutes (*v.* 23), which was of such use to him when princes sat and spoke against him. 1. Did the affliction make him sad? The word of God comforted him, and was *his delight*, more his delight than any of the pleasures either of court or camp, of city or country. Sometimes it proves that the comforts of the word of God are most pleasant to a gracious soul when other comforts are embittered. 2. Did it perplex him? Was he at a loss what to do when the princes spoke against him? God's statutes were *his counsellors*, and they counselled him to bear it patiently and commit his cause to God. God's *testimonies* will be the best counsellors both to princes and private persons. *They are the men of my counsel;* so the word is. There will be found more safety and satisfaction in consulting them than in the multitude of other counsellors. Observe here, Those that would have God's testimonies to be their delight must take them for their counsellors and be advised by them; and let those that take them for their counsellors in close walking take them for their delight in comfortable walking.

4. DALETH.

25 My soul cleaveth unto the dust: quicken thou me according to thy word.

Here is, I. David's complaint. We should have thought his soul soaring to heaven; but he says himself, *My soul* not only rolls in the dust, but *cleaves to the dust*, which is a complaint either, 1. Of his corruptions, his inclination to the world and the body (both which are dust), and that which follows upon it, a deadness to holy duties. When he would *do good evil was present with him.* God intimated that Adam was not only mortal, but sinful, when he said, *Dust thou art*, Gen. iii. 19. David's complaint here is like St. Paul's of a body of death that he carried about with him. The remainders of in-dwelling corruption are a very grievous burden to a gracious soul. Or, 2. Of his afflictions, either trouble of mind or outward trouble. *Without were fightings, within were fears,* and both together brought him even to the *dust of death* (xxii. 15), and his soul clave inseparably to it.

II. His petition for relief, and his plea to enforce that petition: " *Quicken thou me according to thy word.* By thy providence put life into my affairs, by thy grace put life into my affections; cure me of my spiritual deadness and make me lively in my devotion." Note, When we find ourselves dull we must go to God and beg of him to quicken us; he has an eye to God's word as a means of quickening (for the words which God speaks, *they are spirit and they are life* to those that receive them), and as an encouragement to hope that God would quicken him, having promised grace and comfort to all the saints, and to David in particular. God's word must be our guide and plea in every prayer.

26 I have declared my ways, and thou heardest me: teach me thy statutes. 27 Make me to understand the way of thy precepts: so shall I talk of thy wondrous works.

We have here, 1. The great intimacy and freedom that had been between David and his God. David had opened his case, opened his very heart to God: " *I have declared my ways,* and acknowledged thee in them all, have taken thee along with me in all my designs and enterprises." Thus *Jephthah uttered all his words,* and Hezekiah spread his letters, *before the Lord.* " *I have declared my ways,* my wants, and burdens, and troubles, that I meet with in my way, or my sins, my by-ways (I have made an ingenuous confession of them), and *thou heardest me*, heardest patiently all I had to say, and tookedst cognizance of my case." It is an unspeakable comfort to a gracious soul to think with what tenderness all its complaints are received by a gracious God, 1 John v. 14, 15. 2. David's earnest desire of the continuance of that intimacy, not by visions and voices from heaven, but by the word and Spirit in an ordinary way: *Teach me thy statutes*, that is, *Make me to understand the way of thy precepts.* When he knew God had heard his declaration of his ways he did not say, " Now, Lord, tell me my lot, and let me know what the event will be;" but, " Now, Lord, tell me my duty; let me know what thou wouldst have me to do as the case stands." Note, Those who in all their ways acknowledge God may pray in faith that he will *direct their steps* in the right way. And the surest way of keeping up our communion with God is by learning his statutes and walking intelligently in the *way of his precepts.* See 1 John i. 6, 7. 3. The good use he would make of this for the honour of God and the edification of others: " Let me have a good understanding of *the way of thy precepts;* give me a clear, distinct, and methodical knowledge of divine things; *so shall I talk* with the more assurance, and the more to the purpose, *of thy wondrous works.*" We can talk with a better grace of God's wondrous works, the wonders of providence, and especially the wonders of redeeming love, when we understand the way of God's precepts and walk that way.

28 My soul melteth for heaviness: strengthen thou me according unto thy word. 29 Remove from me the way of lying and grant me thy law graciously.

Here is, 1. David's representation of his own griefs · *My soul melteth for heaviness,* which is to the same purport with *v.* 25, *My soul cleaveth to the dust.* Heaviness in the heart of man makes it to melt, to drop away like a candle that wastes. The penitent soul melts in sorrow for sin, and even the patient soul may melt in the sense of affliction, and it is then its interest to pour out its supplication before God. 2. His request for God's grace. (1.) That God would enable him to bear his affliction well and graciously support him under it: " *Strengthen thou me* with strength in my soul, *according to thy word,* which, as the bread of life, strengthens man's heart to undergo whatever God is pleased to inflict. Strengthen me to do the duties, resist the temptations, and bear up under the burdens, of an afflicted state, that the spirit may not fail. *Strengthen me according to* that *word* (Deut. xxxiii. 25), *As thy days so shall thy strength be.*" (2.) That God would keep him from using any unlawful indirect means for the extricating of himself out of his troubles (*v.* 29): *Remove from me the way of lying.* David was conscious to himself of a proneness to this sin; he had, in a strait, cheated Ahimelech (1 Sam. xxi. 2), and Achish, *v.* 13 and *ch.* xxvii. 10. Great difficulties are great temptations to palliate a lie with the colour of a pious fraud and a necessary self-defence; therefore David prays that God would prevent him from falling into this sin any more, lest he should settle in the way of it. A course of lying, of deceit and dissimulation, is that which every good man dreads and which we are all concerned to beg of God by his grace to keep us from. (3.) That he might always be under the guidance and protection of God's government: *Grant me thy law graciously;* grant me that to keep me from the *way of lying.* David had the law written with his own hand, for the king was obliged to transcribe a copy of it for his own use (Deut. xvii. 18); but he prays that he might have it written in his heart; for then, and then only, we have it indeed, and to good purpose. " Grant it me more and more." Those that know and love the law of God cannot but desire to know it more and love it better. "Grant it me *graciously;*" he begs it as a special token of God's favour. Note, We ought to reckon God's law a grant, a gift, an unspeakable gift, to value it, and pray for it, and to give thanks for it accordingly. The divine code of institutes and precepts is indeed a charter of privileges; and God is truly gracious to those whom he makes gracious by giving them his law.

30 I have chosen the way of truth: thy judgments have I laid *before me.* 31 I have stuck unto thy testimonies: O Lord, put me not to shame. 32 I will run the way of thy commandments, when thou shalt enlarge my heart.

Observe, I. That those who will make any thing to purpose of their religion must first make it their serious and deliberate choice; so David did: *I have chosen the way of truth.* Note, 1. The way of serious godliness is the way of truth; the principles it is founded on are principles of eternal truth, and it is the only true way to happiness. 2. We must choose to walk in this way, not because we know no other way, but because we know no better; nay, we know no other safe and good way. Let us choose that way for our way, which we will walk in, though it be narrow.

II. That those who have chosen the way of truth must have a constant regard to the word of God as the rule of their walking: *Thy judgments have I laid before me,* as he who learns to write lays his copy before him, that he may write according to it, as the workman lays his model and platform before him, that he may do his work exactly. As we must have the word in our heart by an habitual conformity to it, so we must have it in our eye by an actual regard to it upon all occasions, that we may walk accurately and by rule.

III. That those who make religion their choice and rule are likely to adhere to it faithfully: *I have stuck to thy testimonies* with an unchanged affection and an unshaken resolution, stuck to them at all times, through all trials. *I have chosen them,* and therefore *I have stuck* to them." Note, The choosing Christian is likely to be the steady Christian; while those that are Christians by chance tack about if the wind turn.

IV. That those who stick to the word of God may in faith expect and pray for acceptance with God; for David means this when he begs, " *Lord, put me not to shame;* that is, never leave me to do that by which I shall shame myself, and do thou not reject my services, which will put me to the greatest confusion."

V. That the more comfort God gives us the more duty he expects from us, *v.* 32. Here we have, 1. His resolution to go on vigorously in religion: *I will run the way of thy commandments.* Those that are going to heaven should make haste thither and be still pressing forward. It concerns us to redeem time and take pains, and to go on in our business with cheerfulness. We *then* run the way of our duty, when we are ready to it, and pleasant in it, and *lay aside every weight,* Heb. xii. 1. 2. His dependence upon God for grace to do so: " I shall *then* abound in thy work, *when thou shalt enlarge my heart.*" God, by his Spirit, enlarges the hearts of his people when he gives them wisdom (for that is called *largeness of heart,* 1 Kings iv. 29), when he *sheds abroad the love of God* in the heart, and puts gladness there. The joy of our Lord should be wheels to our obedience.

5. HE.

33 Teach me, O Lord, the way of

thy statutes ; and I shall keep it *un-to* the end. 34 Give me understanding, and I shall keep thy law ; yea, I shall observe it with *my* whole heart.

Here, I. David prays earnestly that God himself would be his teacher; he had prophets, and wise men, and priests, about him, and was himself well instructed in the law of God, yet he begs to be taught of God, as knowing that *none teaches like him,* Job xxxvi. 22. Observe here, 1. What he desires to be taught, not the notions or language of God's statutes, but *the way* of them —"the way of applying them to myself and governing myself by them; teach me the way of my duty which thy statutes prescribe, and in every doubtful case let me know what thou wouldst have me to do, let me near the word behind me, saying, *This is the way, walk in it,"* Isa. xxx. 21. 2. How he desires to be taught, in such a way as no man could teach him : *Lord, give me understanding.* As the God of nature, he has given us intellectual powers and faculties; but here we are taught to pray that, as the God of grace, he would give us understanding to use those powers and faculties about the great things which belong to our peace, which, through the corruption of nature, we are averse to : *Give me understanding,* an enlightened understanding ; for it is as good to have no understanding at all as not to have it sanctified. Nor will the spirit of revelation in the word answer the end unless we have the spirit of wisdom in the heart. This is that which we are indebted to Christ for; for the *Son of God has come and has given us understanding,* 1 John v. 20.

II. He promises faithfully that he would be a good scholar. If God would teach him, he was sure he should learn to good purpose : " *I shall keep thy law,* which I shall never do unless I be taught of God, and therefore I earnestly desire that I may be taught." If God, by his Spirit, give us a right and good understanding, we shall be, 1. Constant in our obedience : " *I shall keep it to the end,* to the end of my life, which will be the surest proof of sincerity." It will not avail the traveller to keep the way for a while, if he do not keep it to the end of his journey. 2. Cordial in our obedience : *I shall observe it with my whole heart,* with pleasure and delight, and with vigour and resolution. That way which the whole heart goes the whole man goes; and that should be the way of God's commandments, for the keeping of them is the whole of man.

35 Make me to go in the path of thy commandments; for therein do I delight. 36 Incline my heart unto thy testimonies, and not to covetousness.

He had before prayed to God to enlighten his understanding, that he might know his duty, and not mistake concerning it; here he prays to God to bow his will, and quicken the active powers of his soul, that he might do his duty ; for *it is God that works in us both to will and to do,* as well as to understand, what is good, Phil. ii. 13. Both the good head and the good heart are from the good grace of God, and both are necessary to every good work. Observe here,

I. The grace he prays for. 1. That God would make him able to do his duty : " *Make me to go;* strengthen me for every good work." Since we are not sufficient of ourselves, our dependence must be upon the grace of God, for from him all our sufficiency is. God puts his Spirit within us, and so causes us to *walk in his statutes* (Ezek. xxxvi. 27), and this is that which David here begs. 2. That God would make him willing to do it, and would, by his grace, subdue the aversion he naturally had to it : " *Incline my heart to thy testimonies,* to those things which thy testimonies prescribe ; not only make me willing to do my duty, as that which I must do and therefore am concerned to make the best of, but make me desirous to do my duty as that which is agreeable to the new nature and really advantageous to me." Duty is then done with delight when the heart is inclined to it : it is God's grace that inclines us, and the more backward we find ourselves to it the more earnest we must be for that grace.

II. The sin he prays against, and that is covetousness : " *Incline my heart to keep thy testimonies,* and restrain and mortify the inclination there is in me to *covetousness."* That is a sin which stands opposed to all God's testimonies ; for the love of money is such a sin as is the root of much sin, of all sin. Those therefore that would have the love of God rooted in them must get the love of the world rooted out of them ; for the *friendship of the world is enmity with God.* See in what way God deals with men, not by compulsion, but he draws with the cords of a man, working in them an inclination to that which is good and an aversion to that which is evil.

III. His plea to enforce this prayer : " Lord, bring me to, and keep me in, *the way of thy commandments, for therein do I delight;* and therefore I pray thus earnestly for grace to walk in that way. Thou hast wrought in me this delight in the way of thy commandments; wilt thou not work in me an ability to walk in them, and so crown thy own work?"

37 Turn away mine eyes from beholding vanity ; *and* quicken thou me in thy way.

Here, 1. David prays for restraining grace, that he might be prevented and kept back from that which would hinder him in the way of his duty : *Turn away my eyes from beholding vanity.* The honours, pleasures, and profits of the world are the vanities, the aspect and prospect of which draw multitudes away from the paths of religion and godliness. The eye, when fastened on these, infects the heart with the love of them, and so it is alienated from God and divine things; and therefore, as we ought to *make a covenant with our eyes*, and lay a charge upon them, that they shall not wander after, much less fix upon, that which is dangerous (Job xxxi. 1), so we ought to pray that God by his providence would keep vanity out of our sight and that by his grace he would keep us from being enamoured with the sight of it. 2. He prays for constraining grace, that he might not only be kept from every thing that would obstruct his progress heaven-ward, but might have that grace which was necessary to forward him in that progress: " *Quicken thou me in thy way;* quicken me to redeem time, to improve opportunity, to press forward, and to do every duty with liveliness and fervency of spirit." Beholding vanity deadens us and slackens our pace; a traveller that stands gazing upon every object that presents itself to his view will not rid ground; but, if our eyes be kept from that which would divert us, our hearts will be kept to that which will excite us.

38 Stablish thy word unto thy servant, who *is devoted* to thy fear.

Here is, 1. The character of a good man, which is the work of God's grace in him; he is *God's servant*, subject to his law and employed in his work, that is, *devoted to his fear*, given up to his direction and disposal, and taken up with high thoughts of him and all those acts of devotion which have a tendency to his glory. Those are truly God's servants who, though they have their infirmities and defects, are sincerely *devoted to the fear of God* and have all their affections and motions governed by that fear; they are engaged and addicted to religion. 2. The confidence that a good man has towards God, in dependence upon the word of his grace to him. Those that are God's servants may, in faith and with humble boldness, pray that God would *establish his word to them*, that is, that he would fulfil his promises to them in due time, and in the mean time give them an assurance that they shall be fulfilled. What God has promised we must pray for; we need not be so aspiring as to ask more; we need not be so modest as to ask less.

39 Turn away my reproach which I fear: for thy judgments *are* good.

Here, 1. David prays against *reproach*, as before, *v.* 22. David was conscious to himself that he had done that which might give *occasion to the enemies of the Lord to blaspheme*, which would blemish his own reputation and turn to the dishonour of his family; now he prays that God, who has all men's hearts and tongues in his hands, would be pleased to prevent this, to *deliver him from all his transgressions*, that he *might not be the reproach of the foolish*, which he feared (xxxix. 8); or he means that reproach which his enemies unjustly loaded him with. Let their *lying lips be put to silence*. 2. He

pleads the goodness of God's judgments : " Lord, thou sittest in the throne, and *thy judgments are right* and *good*, just and kind, to those that are wronged, and therefore to thee I appeal from the unjust and unkind censures of men." It is a small thing to be judged of man's judgment, while *he that judges us is the Lord*. Or thus : " Thy word, and ways, and thy holy religion, are very good, but the reproaches cast on me will fall on them; therefore, *Lord, turn them away;* let not religion be wounded through my side."

40 Behold, I have longed after thy precepts: quicken me in thy righteousness.

Here, 1. David professes the ardent affection he had to the word of God: " *I have longed after thy precepts*, not only loved them, and delighted in what I have already attained, but I have earnestly desired to know them more and do them better, and am still pressing forward towards perfection." Tastes of the sweetness of God's precepts will but set us a longing after a more intimate acquaintance with them. He appeals to God concerning this passionate desire after his precepts: " *Behold, I have* thus loved, thus *longed;* thou knowest all things, thou knowest that I am thus affected." 2. He prays for grace to enable him to answer this profession. " Thou hast wrought in me this languishing desire, put life into me, that I may prosecute it; *quicken me in thy righteousness*, in thy righteous ways, according to thy righteous promise." Where God has wrought to will he will work to do, and where he has wrought to desire he will satisfy the desire.

6. VAU.

41 Let thy mercies come also unto me, O LORD, *even* thy salvation, according to thy word. 42 So shall I have wherewith to answer him that reproacheth me : for I trust in thy word.

Here is, 1. David's prayer for the salvation of the Lord. " Lord, thou art my Saviour; I am miserable in myself, and thou only canst make me happy; *let thy salvation come to me*. Hasten temporal salvation to me from my present distresses, and hasten me to the eternal salvation, by giving me the necessary qualifications for it and the comfortable pledges and foretastes of it." 2. David's dependence upon the grace and promise of God for that salvation. These are the two pillars on which our hope is built, and they will not fail us :—(1.) The grace of God: *Let thy mercies come, even thy salvation*. Our salvation must be attributed purely to God's mercy, and not to any merit of our own. Eternal life must be expected as the *mercy of our Lord Jesus Christ*, Jude 21. " Lord, I have by faith thy mercies in view; let me by prayer prevail to have them come to me." (2.) The promise of God: " *Let it* come according to thy word, thy word of promise. *I trust in thy word,* and therefore may expect the performance of the promise." We are not only allowed to trust in God's word, but our trusting in it is the condition of our benefit by it. 3. David's expectation of the good assurance which that grace and promise of God would give him : " *So shall I have wherewith to answer him that reproaches me* for my confidence in God, as if it would deceive me." When God saves those out of their troubles who trusted in him he effectually silences those who would have *shamed that counsel of the poor* (xiv. 6), and their reproaches will be for ever silenced when the salvation of the saints is completed; then it will appear, beyond dispute, that it was not in vain to trust in God.

43 And take not the word of truth utterly out of my mouth ; for I have hoped in thy judgments. 44 So shall I keep thy law continually for ever and ever.

Here is, 1. David's humble petition for the tongue of the learned, that he might know how to *speak a word in season* for the glory of God : *Take not the word of truth utterly out of my mouth.* He means, " Lord, let the word of truth be always in my mouth; let me have the wisdom and courage which are necessary to enable me both to use my knowledge for the instruction of others, and, like the good householder, to bring out of my treasury *things new and old,* and to make profession of my faith whenever I am called to it." We have need to pray to God that we may never be afraid or ashamed to own his truths and ways, nor deny him before men. David found that he was sometimes at a loss, that the *word of truth* was not so ready to him as it should have been, but he prays, " Lord, let it not be taken utterly from me ; let me always have so much of it at hand as will be necessary to the due discharge of my duty." 2. His humble profession of the heart of the upright, without which the tongue of the learned, however it may be serviceable to others, will stand us in no stead. (1.) David professes his confidence in God: "Lord, make me ready and mighty in the scriptures, *for I have hoped in those judgments* of thy mouth, and, if they be not at hand, my support and defence have departed from me." (2.) He professes his resolution to adhere to his duty in the strength of God's grace: " *So shall I keep thy law continually.* If I have thy word not only in my heart, but in my mouth, I shall do all I should do, stand complete in thy whole will." Thus shall the *man of God be perfect, thoroughly furnished for every good work and work,* 2 Tim. iii. 17 ; Col. iii. 16. Observe how he resolves to keep God's law, [1] Continually, without trifling. God must be served in a constant course of obedience every day, and all the day long. [2.] *For ever and ever,* without backsliding. We must

never be *weary of well-doing.* If we serve him to the end of our time on earth, we shall be serving him in heaven to the endless ages of eternity ; so shall we *keep his law for ever and ever.* Or thus : " Lord, let me have the word of truth in *my mouth,* that I may commit that sacred deposit to the rising generation (2 Tim. ii. 2) and by them it may be transmitted to succeeding ages ; so shall thy law be kept *for ever and ever,*" that is, from one generation to another, according to that promise (Isa. lix. 21), *My word in thy mouth shall not depart out of the mouth of thy seed, nor thy seed's seed.*

45 And I will walk at liberty : for I seek thy precepts. 46 I will speak of thy testimonies also before kings, and will not be ashamed. 47 And I will delight myself in thy commandments, which I have loved. 48 My hands also will I lift up unto thy commandments, which I have loved ; and I will meditate in thy statutes.

We may observe in these verses, 1. What David experienced of an affection to the law of God : " *I seek thy precepts, v.* 45. I desire to know and do my duty, and consult thy word accordingly ; I do all I can to *understand what the will of the Lord is* and to discover the intimations of his mind. *I seek thy precepts,* for *I have loved them, v.* 47, 48. I not only give consent to them as good, but take complacency in them as good for me." All that love God love his government and therefore love all his commandments. 2. What he expected from this. Five things he promises himself here in the strength of God's grace :—(1.) That he should be free and easy in his duty : " *I will walk at liberty,* freed from that which is evil, not hampered with the fetters of my own corruptions, and free to that which is good. doing it not by constraint, but willingly." The service of sin is perfect slavery ; the service of God is perfect liberty. Licentiousness is bondage to the greatest of tyrants ; conscientiousness is freedom to the meanest of prisoners, John viii. 32, 36 ; Luke i. 74, 75. (2.) That he should be bold and courageous in his duty : *I will speak of thy testimonies also before kings.* Before David came to the crown kings were sometimes his judges, as Saul, and Achish ; but, if he were called before them to give a reason of the hope that was in him, he would *speak of God's testimonies,* and profess to build his hope upon them and make them his council, his guards, his crown, his all. We must never be afraid to own our religion, though it should expose us to the wrath of kings, but speak of it as that which we will live and die by, like the three children before Nebuchadnezzar, Dan. iii. 16; Acts iv. 20. After David came to the crown kings were sometimes his companions ; they visited him and he returned their visits ; but he did not, in complaisance to them, talk of every thing but religion, for fear of affronting them and making 'his conversation uneasy to them. No ; God's testimonies shall be the principal subject of his discourse with the kings, not only to show that he was not ashamed of his religion, but to instruct them in it and bring them over to it. It is good for kings to hear of God's testimonies, and it will adorn the conversation of princes themselves to speak of them. (3) That he should be cheerful and pleasant in his duty (*v.* 47) : " *I will delight myself in thy commandments,* in conversing with them, in conforming to them. I will never be so well pleased with myself as when I do that which is pleasing to God." The more delight we take in the service of God the nearer we come to the perfection we aim at. (4.) That he should be diligent and vigorous in his duty : *I will lift up my hands to thy commandments,* which denotes not only a vehement desire towards them (cxliii. 6)—" I will lay hold of them as one afraid of missing them, or letting them go ;" but a close application of mind to the observance of them—" I will lay my hands to the command, not only to praise it, but practise it ; nay, I will lift up my hands to it, that is, I will put forth all the strength I have to do it." The hands that hang down, through sloth and discouragement, shall be lifted up, Heb. xii. 12. (5.) That he should be thoughtful and considerate in his duty (*v.* 48): "*I will meditate in thy statutes,* not only entertain myself with thinking of them as matters of speculation, but contrive how I may observe them in the best manner." By *this* it will appear that we truly love God's commandments, if we apply both our minds and our hands to them.

7. ZAIN.

49 Remember the word unto thy servant, upon which thou hast caused me to hope.

Two things David here pleads with God in prayer for that mercy and grace which he hoped for, according to the word, by which his requests were guided :—1. That God had given him the promise on which he hoped : " Lord, I desire no more than that thou wouldst *remember thy word unto thy servant,* and *do as thou hast said;*" see 1 Chron. xvii. 23. " Thou art'wise, and therefore wilt perfect what thou hast purposed, and not change thy counsel. Thou art faithful, and therefore wilt perform what thou hast promised, and not break thy word." Those that make God's promises their portion may with humble boldness make them their plea. " Lord, is not that the word which thou hast spoken ; and wilt thou not make it good ?" Gen. xxxii. 9; Exod. xxxiii. 12. 2. That God, who had given him the promise in the word, had by his grace wrought in him a hope in that promise and enabled him to depend upon it, and had raised his expectations of great things from it. Has God kindled in

us desires towards spiritual blessings more than towards any temporal good things, and will he not be so kind as to satisfy those desires ? Has he filled us with hopes of those blessings, and will he not be so just as to accomplish these hopes ? He that did by his Spirit work faith in us will, according to our faith, work for us, and will not disappoint us.

50 This *is* my comfort in my affliction : for thy word hath quickened me.

Here is David's experience of benefit by the word. 1. As a means of his sanctification : " *Thy word has quickened me.* It made me alive when I was dead in sin ; it has many a time made me lively when I was dead in duty ; it has quickened me to that which is good when I was backward and averse to it, and it has quickened me in that which is good when I was cold and indifferent." 2. Therefore as a means of his consolation when he was in affliction and needed something to support him : " Because thy word has quickened me at other times, it has comforted me then." The word of God has much in it that speaks *comfort in affliction;* but those only may apply it to themselves who have experienced in some measure the quickening power of the word. If through grace it make us holy, there is enough in it to make us easy, in all conditions, under all events.

51 The proud have had me greatly in derision : *yet* have I not declined from thy law.

David here tells us, and it will be of use to us to know it, 1. That he had been jeered for his religion. Though he was a man of honour, a man of great prudence, and had done eminent services to his country, yet, because he was a devout conscientious man, *the proud had him greatly in derision;* they ridiculed him, bantered him, and did all they could to expose him to contempt ; they laughed at him for his praying, and called it *cant,* for his seriousness, and called it *mopishness,* for his strictness, and called it *needless preciseness.* They were the proud that sat in the scorner's seat and valued themselves on so doing. 2. That yet he had not been jeered out of his religion : " They have done all they could to make me quit it for shame, but none of these things move me : *I have not declined from thy law* for all this ; but, *if this be to be vile*" (as he said when Michal had him greatly in derision), " *I will be yet more vile.*" He not only had not quite forsaken the law, but had not so much as declined from it. We must never shrink from any duty, nor let slip an opportunity of doing good, for fear of the reproach of men, or their revilings. The traveller goes on his way though the dogs bark at him. Those can bear but little for Christ that cannot bear a hard word for him.

52 I remembered thy judgments of

old, O LORD; and have comforted myself.

When David was derided for his godliness he not only held fast his integrity, but, 1. He comforted himself. He not only bore reproach, but bore it cheerfully. It did not disturb his peace, nor break in upon the repose of his spirit in God. It was a comfort to him to think that it was for God's sake that he bore reproach, and that his worst enemies could find *no occasion against him, save only in the matter of his God,* Dan. vi. 5. Those that are derided for their adherence to God's law may comfort themselves with this, that *the reproach of Christ* will prove, in the end, *greater riches* to them *than the treasures of Egypt.* 2. That which he comforted himself with was the remembrance of God's *judgments of old,* the providences of God concerning his people formerly, both in mercy to them and in justice against their persecutors. God's judgments of old, in our own early days and in the days of our fathers, are to be remembered by us for our comfort and encouragement in the way of God, for he is still the same.

53 Horror hath taken hold upon me because of the wicked that forsake thy law.

Here is, 1. The character of wicked people; he means those that are openly and grossly wicked : *They forsake thy law.* Every sin is a transgression of the law, but a course and way of wilful and avowed sin is downright forsaking it and throwing it off. 2. The impression which the wickedness of the wicked made upon David ; it frightened him, it put him into an amazement. He trembled to think of the dishonour thereby done to God, the gratification thereby given to Satan, and the mischiefs thereby done to the souls of men. He dreaded the consequences of it both to the sinners themselves (and cried out, *O gather not my soul with sinners ! let my enemy be as the wicked)* and to the interests of God's kingdom among men, which he was afraid would be thereby sunk and ruined. He does not say, " *Horror has taken hold on me* because of their cruel designs against me," but " because of the contempt they put on God and his law." Sin is a monstrous horrible thing in the eyes of all that are sanctified, Jer. v. 30; xxiii. 14; Hos. vi. 10; Jer. ii. 12.

54 Thy statutes have been my songs in the house of my pilgrimage.

Here is, 1. David's state and condition ; he was *in the house of his pilgrimage,* which may be understood either as his peculiar trouble (he was often tossed and hurried, and forced to fly) or as his lot in common with all. This world is the house of our pilgrimage, the house in which we are pilgrims ; it is our tabernacle; it is our inn. We must confess ourselves *strangers and pilgrims upon earth,* who are not at home here, nor must be here long. Even David's palace is but the house of his pilgrimage. 2. His comfort in this state : " *Thy statutes have been my songs,* with which I here entertain myself," as travellers are wont to divert the thoughts of their weariness, and take off something of the tediousness of their journey, by singing a pleasant song now and then. David was the sweet singer of Israel, and here we are told whence he fetched his songs ; they were all borrowed from the word of God. God's statutes were as familiar to him as the songs which a man is accustomed to sing ; and he conversed with them in his pilgrimage-solitudes. They were as pleasant to him as songs, and *put gladness into his heart* more than those have that *chant to the sound of the viol,* Amos vi. 5. *Is any afflicted* then? Let him sing over God's statutes, and try if he cannot so *sing away sorrow,* cxxxviii. 5.

55 I have remembered thy name, O LORD, in the night, and have kept thy law. 56 This I had, because I kept thy precepts.

Here is, 1. The converse David had with the word of God ; he kept it in mind, and upon every occasion he called it to mind. God's name is the discovery he has made of himself to us in and by his word. *This is his memorial unto all generations,* and therefore we should always keep it in memory—remember it *in the night,* upon a waking bed, when we are communing with our own hearts. When others were sleeping David was remembering God's name, and, by repeating that lesson, increasing his acquaintance with it ; in the night of affliction this he called to mind. 2. The conscience he made of conforming to it. The due remembrance of God's name, which is prefixed to his law, will have a great influence upon our observance of the law : *I remembered thy name in the night,* and therefore was careful to *keep thy law* all day. How comfortable will it be in the reflection if our own hearts can witness for us that we have thus remembered God's name, and kept his law! 3. The advantage he got by it (*v.* 56) : *This I had because I kept thy precepts.* Some understand this indefinitely : *This I had* (that is I had that which satisfied me ; I had every thing that is comfortable) *because I kept thy precepts.* Note, All that have made a business of religion will own that it has turned to a good account, and that they have been unspeakable gainers by it. Others refer it to what goes immediately before: " I had the comfort of keeping thy law because I kept it." Note, God's work is its own wages. A heart to obey the will of God is a most valuable reward of obedience ; and the more we do the more we may do, and shall do, in the service of God ; the branch that bears fruit is made *more fruitful,* John xv. 2.

697

8. CHETH.

57 *Thou art* my portion, O LORD: I have said that I would keep thy words.

We may hence gather the character of a godly man. 1. He makes the favour of God his felicity: *Thou art my portion, O Lord!* Others place their happiness in the wealth and honours of this world. Their portion is in this life; they look no further; they desire no more; these are *their good things,* Luke xvi. 25. But all that are sanctified take the Lord for the portion of their inheritance and their cup, and nothing less will satisfy them. David can appeal to God in this matter: "Lord, thou knowest that I have chosen thee for my portion, and depend upon thee to make me happy." 2. He makes the law of God his rule: *I have said that I would keep thy words;* and what I have said by thy grace I will do, and will abide by it to the end." Note, Those that take God for their portion must take him for their prince, and swear allegiance to him; and, having promised to *keep his word,* we must often put ourselves in mind of our promise, xxxix. 1.

58 I intreated thy favour with *my* whole heart : be merciful unto me according to thy word.

David, having in the foregoing verse reflected upon his covenants with God, here reflects upon his prayers to God, and renews his petition. Observe, 1. What he prayed for. Having taken God for his portion, he *entreated his favour,* as one that knew he had forfeited it, was unworthy of it, and yet undone without it, but for ever happy if he could obtain it. We cannot demand God's favour as a debt, but must be humble suppliants for it, that God will not only be reconciled to us, but accept us and smile upon us. He prays, " *Be merciful to me,* in the forgiveness of what I have done amiss, and in giving me grace to do better for the future." 2. How he prayed—*with his whole heart,* as one that knew how to value the blessing he prayed for. The gracious soul is entirely set upon the favour of God, and is therefore importunate for it. *I will not let thee go except thou bless me.* 3. What he pleaded—the promise of God: " *Be merciful to me, according to thy word.* I desire the mercy promised, and depend upon the promise for it." Those that are governed by the precepts of the word and are resolved to keep them (v. 57) may plead the promises of the word and take the comfort of them.

59 I thought on my ways, and turned my feet unto thy testimonies. 60 I made haste, and delayed not to keep thy commandments.

David had said he *would keep God's word* (v 57), and it was well said; now here he tells us how and in what method he pursued

that resolution. 1. He *thought on his ways.* He thought beforehand what he should do, pondering the path of his feet (Prov. iv. 26), that he might walk surely, and not at all adventures. He thought after what he had done, reflected upon his life past, and recollected the paths he had walked in and the steps he had taken. The word signifies a fixed abiding thought. Some make it an allusion to those who work embroidery, who are very exact and careful to cover the least flaw, or to those who cast up their accounts, who reckon with themselves, What do I owe? What am I worth? " *I thought* not on my wealth (as the covetous man, xlix. 11) but *on my ways,* not on what I have, but what I do :" for what we do will follow us into another world when what we have must be left behind. Many are critical enough in their remarks upon other people's ways who never think of their own; but *let every man prove his own work.* 2. He *turned his feet to God's testimonies.* He determined to make the word of God his rule, and to walk by that rule. He turned from the by-paths to which he had turned aside, and returned to God's testimonies. He turned not only his eye to them, but his feet, his affections to the love of God's word and his conversation to the practice of it. The bent and inclinations of his soul were towards God's testimonies and his conversation was governed by them. Penitent reflections must produce pious resolutions. 3. He did this immediately and without demur (v. 60): *I made haste and delayed not.* When we are under convictions of sin we must strike while the iron is hot, and not think to defer the prosecution of them, as Felix did, to *a more convenient season.* When we are called to duty we must lose no time, but set about it *to-day, while it is called to-day.* Now this account which David here gives of himself may refer either to his constant practice every day (he reflected on his ways at night, directed his feet to God's testimonies in the morning, and what his hand found to do that was good he did it without delay), or it may refer to his first acquaintance with God and religion, when he began to throw off the vanity of childhood and youth, and to remember his Creator; that blessed change was, by the grace of God, thus wrought. Note, (1.) Conversion begins in serious consideration, Ezek. xviii. 28; Luke xv. 17. (2.) Consideration must end in a sound conversion. To what purpose have we thought on our ways if we do not turn our feet with all speed to God's testimonies?

61 The bands of the wicked have robbed me : *but* I have not forgotten thy law.

Here is, 1. The malice of David's enemies against him. They were wicked men, who hated him for his godliness. There were bands or troops of them confederate against him. They did him all the mischief they could; they robbed him; having endeavoured to take away his good name (v. 51), they set upon his goods, and spoiled him of them, either by plunder in time of war or by fines and confiscations under colour of law. Saul (it is likely) seized his effects, Absalom his palace, and the Amalekites rifled Ziklag. Worldly wealth is what we may be robbed of. David, though a man of war, could not keep his own. *Thieves break through and steal.* 2. The testimony of David's conscience for him that he had held fast his religion when he was stripped of every thing else, as Job did when the bands of the Chaldeans and Sabeans had robbed him: *But I have not forgotten thy law.* No care nor grief should drive God's word out of our minds, or hinder our comfortable relish of it and converse with it. Nor must we ever think the worse of the ways of God for any trouble we meet with in those ways, nor fear being losers by our religion at last, however we may be losers for it now.

62 At midnight I will rise to give thanks unto thee because of thy righteous judgments.

Though David is, in this psalm, much in prayer, yet he did not neglect the duty of thanksgiving; for those that pray much will have much to give thanks for. See, 1. How much God's hand was eyed in his thanksgivings. He does not say, "*I will give thanks* because of thy favours to me, which I have the comfort of," but, "*Because of thy righteous judgments,*" all the disposals of thy providence in wisdom and equity, which thou hast the glory of." We must give thanks for the asserting of God's honour and the accomplishing of his word in all he does in the government of the world. 2. How much David's heart was set upon his thanksgivings. He would *rise at midnight to give thanks* to God. Great and good thoughts kept him awake, and refreshed him, instead of sleep; and so zealous was he for the honour of God that when others were in their beds he was upon his knees at his devotions. He did not affect to be seen of men in it, but gave thanks in secret, where our heavenly Father sees. He had praised God *in the courts of the Lord's house,* and yet he will do it in his bed-chamber. Public worship will not excuse us from secret worship. When David found his heart affected with God's judgments, he immediately offered up those affections to God, in actual adorations, not deferring, lest they should cool. Yet observe his reverence; he did not lie still and give thanks, but rose out of his bed, perhaps in the cold and in the dark, to do it the more solemnly. And see what a good husband he was of time; when he could not lie and sleep, he would rise and pray.

63 I *am* a companion of all *them* that fear thee, and of them that keep thy precepts.

David had often expressed the great love

he had to God; here he expresses the great love he had to the people of God; and observe, 1. Why he loved them; not so much because they were his best friends, most firm to his interest and most forward to serve him, but because they were such as *feared God* and *kept his precepts,* and so did him honour and helped to support his kingdom among men. Our love to the saints is *then* sincere when we love them for the sake of what we see of God in them and the service they do to him. 2. How he showed his love to them: He was *a companion of them.* He had not only a spiritual communion with them in the same faith and hope, but he joined with them in holy ordinances in the courts of the Lord, where rich and poor, prince and peasant, meet together. He sympathized with them in their joys and sorrows (Heb. x. 33); he conversed familiarly with them, communicated his experiences to them, and consulted theirs. He not only took such to be his companions as did fear God, but he vouchsafed himself to be a companion with all, with any, that did so, wherever he met with them. Though he was a king, he would associate with the poorest of his subjects that feared God, Ps. xv. 4; Jam. ii. 1.

64 The earth, O Lord, is full of thy mercy: teach me thy statutes.

Here, 1. David pleads that God is good to all the creatures according to their necessities and capacities; as the heaven is full of God's glory, so *the earth is full of his mercy,* full of the instances of his pity and bounty. Not only the land·of Canaan, where God is known and worshipped, but the whole earth, in many parts of which he has no homage paid him, is full of his mercy. Not only the children of men upon the earth, but even the inferior creatures, taste of God's goodness. *His tender mercies are over all his works.* 2. He therefore prays that God would be good to him according to his necessity and capacity: "*Teach me thy statutes.* Thou feedest the young ravens that cry, with food proper for them; and wilt thou not feed me with spiritual food, the bread of life, which my soul needs and craves, and cannot subsist without? *The earth is full of thy mercy;* and is not heaven too? Wilt thou not then give me spiritual blessings in heavenly places?" A gracious heart will fetch an argument from any thing to enforce a petition for divine teaching. Surely he that will not let his birds be unfed will not let his children be untaught.

9. TETH.

65 Thou hast dealt well with thy servant, O Lord, according unto thy word. 66 Teach me good judgment and knowledge: for I have believed thy commandments.

Here, 1. David makes a thankful acknowledgment of God's gracious dealings with him all along· *Thou hast dealt well with thy servant.* However God has dealt with us, we must own he has dealt *well* with us, better than we deserve, and all in love and with design to work for our good. In many instances God has done well for us beyond our expectations. He has done well for all his servants; never any of them complained that he had used them hardly. *Thou hast dealt well with* me, not only according to thy mercy, but *according to thy word.* God's favours look best when they are compared with the promise and are seen flowing from that fountain. 2. Upon these experiences he grounds a petition for divine instruction: "*Teach me good judgment and knowledge,* that, by thy grace, I may render again, in some measure, *according to the benefit done unto me.*" Teach me *a good taste* (so the word signifies), a good relish, to discern things that differ, to distinguish between truth and falsehood, good and evil; for *the ear tries words, as the mouth tastes meat.* We should pray to God for a sound mind, that we may have *spiritual senses exercised,* Heb. v. 14. Many have knowledge who have little judgment; those who have both are well fortified against the snares of Satan and well furnished for the service of God and their generation. 3. This petition is backed with a plea: "*For I have believed thy commandments,* received them, and consented to them that they are good, and submitted to their government; therefore, Lord, *teach me.*" Where God has given a good heart a good head too may in faith be prayed for.

67 Before I was afflicted I went astray: but now have I kept thy word.

David here tells us what he had experienced, 1. Of the temptations of a prosperous condition: "*Before I was afflicted,* while I lived in peace and plenty, and knew no sorrow, *I went astray* from God and my duty." Sin is going astray; and we are most apt to wander from God when we are easy and think ourselves at home in the world. Prosperity is the unhappy occasion of much iniquity; it makes people conceited of themselves, indulgent of the flesh, forgetful of God, in love with the world, and deaf to the reproofs of the word. See xxx. 6. It is good for us, when we are afflicted, to remember how and wherein we went astray *before we were afflicted,* that we may answer the end of the affliction. 2. Of the benefit of an afflicted state: "*Now have I kept thy word,* and so have been recovered from my wanderings." God often makes use of afflictions as a means to reduce those to himself who have wandered from him. Sanctified afflictions humble us for sin and show us the vanity of the world; they soften the heart, and open the ear to discipline. The prodigal's distress brought him to himself first and then to his father.

68 Thou *art* good, and doest good; teach me thy statutes

Here, 1. David praises God's goodness and gives him the glory of it: *Thou art good and doest good.* All who have any knowledge of God and dealings with him will own that he does good, and therefore will conclude that he is good. The streams of God's goodness are so numerous, and run so full, so strong, to all the creatures, that we must conclude the fountain that is in himself to be inexhaustible. We cannot conceive how much good our God does every day, much less can we conceive how good he is. Let us acknowledge it with admiration and with holy love and thankfulness. 2. He prays for God's grace, and begs to be under the guidance and influence of it: *Teach me thy statutes.* "Lord, thou doest good to all, art the bountiful benefactor of all the creatures; this is the good I beg thou wilt do to me,—Instruct me in my duty, incline me to it, and enable me to do it. *Thou art good, and doest good;* Lord, *teach me thy statutes,* that I may be good and do good, may have a good heart and live a good life." It is an encouragement to poor sinners to hope that God will *teach them his way* because he is *good and upright,* xxv. 8.

69 The proud have forged a lie against me: *but* I will keep thy precepts with *my* whole heart. 70 Their heart is as fat as grease; *but* I delight in thy law.

David here tells us how he was affected as to the proud and wicked people that were about him. 1: He did not fear their malice, nor was he by it deterred from his duty: *They have forged a lie against me.* Thus they aimed to take away his good name. Nay, all we have in the world, even life itself, may be brought into danger by those who make no conscience of forging a lie. Those that were proud envied David's reputation, because it eclipsed them, and therefore did all they could to blemish him. They took a pride in trampling upon him. They therefore persuaded themselves it was no sin to tell a deliberate lie if it might but expose him to contempt. Their wicked wit forged lies, invented stories which there was not the least colour for, to serve their wicked designs. And what did David do when he was thus belied? He will bear it patiently; he will keep that precept which forbids him to render railing for railing, and will with all his heart sit down silently. He will go on in his duty with constancy and resolution: "Let them say what they will, *I will keep thy precepts,* and not dread their reproach." 2. He did not envy their prosperity, nor was he by it allured from his duty. *Their heart is as fat as grease.* The proud are *at ease* (cxxiii. 4); they are full of the world, and the wealth and pleasures of it; and this makes them, (1.) Senseless, secure, and stupid; they are past feeling: thus the phrase is used, Isa. vi. 10. *Make the heart of this people fat.* They are not sensible of the touch of the word of God or his rod. (2.)

Sensual and voluptuous : " *Their eyes stand out with fatness* (Ps. lxxiii. 7); they roll themselves in the pleasures of sense, and take up with them as their chief good; and much good may it do them. I would not change conditions with them. *I delight in thy law;* I build my security upon the promises of God's word and have pleasure enough in communion with God, infinitely preferable to all their delights." The children of God, who are acquainted with spiritual pleasures, need not envy the children of this world their carnal pleasures.

71 *It is* good for me that I have been afflicted; that I might learn thy statutes.

See here, 1. That it has been the lot of the best saints to be afflicted. The proud and the wicked lived in pomp and pleasure, while David, though he kept close to God and his duty, was still in affliction. *Waters of a full cup are wrung out to* God's people, lxxiii. 10. 2. That it has been the advantage of God's people to be afflicted. David could speak experimentally: *It was good for me;* many a good lesson he had learnt by his afflictions, and many a good duty he had been brought to which otherwise would have been unlearnt and undone. *Therefore* God visited him with affliction, that he might learn God's statutes; and the intention was answered: the afflictions had contributed to the improvement of his knowledge and grace. He that chastened him taught him. *The rod and reproof give wisdom.*

72 The law of thy mouth *is* better unto me than thousands of gold and silver.

This is a reason why David reckoned that when by his afflictions he learned God's statutes, and the profit did so much counterbalance the loss, he was really a gainer by them; for God's *law*, which he got acquaintance with by his affliction, was *better* to him than all the *gold and silver* which he lost by his affliction. 1. David had but a little of the word of God in comparison with what we have, yet see how highly he valued it; how inexcusable then are we, who have both the Old and New Testament complete, and yet account them as a strange thing! Observe, *Therefore* he valued the law, because it is *the law of God's mouth*, the revelation of his will, and ratified by his authority. 2. He had a great deal of gold and silver in comparison with what we have, yet see how little he valued it. His riches increased, and yet he did not set his heart upon them, but upon the word of God. That was better to him, yielded him better pleasures, and better maintenance, and a better inheritance, than all the treasures he was master of. Those that have read, and believe, David's *Psalms* and Solomon's *Ecclesiastes*, cannot but prefer the word of God far before the wealth of this world.

10. JOD.

73 Thy hands have made me and fashioned me : give me understanding, that I may learn thy commandments.

Here, 1. David adores God as the God of nature and the author of his being: *Thy hands have made me and fashioned me*, Job x. 8. Every man is as truly the work of God's hands as the first man was, Ps. cxxxix. 15, 16. " *Thy hands have* not only *made me*, and given me a being, otherwise I should never have been, but *fashioned me*, and given me this being, this noble and excellent being, endued with these powers and faculties ;" and we must own that we are *fearfully and wonderfully made.* 2. He addresses himself to God as the God of grace, and begs he will be the author of his new and better being. God made us to serve him and enjoy him; but by sin we have made ourselves unable for his service and indisposed for the enjoyment of him; and we must have a new and divine nature, otherwise we had the human nature in vain; therefore David prays, " Lord, since thou hast made me by thy power for thy glory, make me anew by thy grace, that I may answer the ends of my creation and live to some purpose : *Give me understanding, that I may learn thy commandments.*" The way in which God recovers and secures his interest in men is by giving them an understanding; for by that door he enters into the soul and gains possession of it.

74 They that fear thee will be glad when they see me; because I have hoped in thy word.

Here is, 1. The confidence of this good man in the hope of God's salvation : " *I have hoped in thy word;* and I have not found it in vain to do so ; it has not failed me, nor have I been disappointed in my expectations from it. It is a hope that *maketh not ashamed;* but is present satisfaction, and fruition at last." 2. The concurrence of other good men with him in the joy of that salvation : " *Those that fear thee will be glad when they see me* relieved by my hope in thy word and delivered according to my hope." The comforts which some of God's children have in God, and the favours they have received from him, should be matter of joy to others of them. Paul often expressed the hope that for God's grace to him thanks would be rendered by many, 2 Cor. i. 11; iv. 15. Or it may be taken more generally; good people are glad to see one another; they are especially pleased with those who are eminent for their hope in God's word.

75 I know, O LORD, that thy judgments *are* right, and *that* thou in faithfulness hast afflicted me.

Still David is in affliction, and being so he owns, 1. That his sin was justly corrected : *I know, O Lord! that thy judgments are right,* are righteousness itself. However God is pleased to afflict us, he does us no wrong, nor can we charge him with any iniquity, but must acknowledge that it is less than we have deserved. We know that God is holy in his nature and wise and just in all the acts of his government, and therefore we cannot but know, in the general, that his *judgments are right,* though, in some particular instances, there may be difficulties which we cannot easily resolve. 2. That God's promise was graciously performed. The former may silence us under our afflictions, and forbid us to repine, but this may satisfy us, and enable us to rejoice; for afflictions are in the covenant, and therefore they are not only not meant for our hurt, but they are really intended for our good: "*In faithfulness thou hast afflicted me,* pursuant to the great design of my salvation." It is easier to own, in general, that God's *judgments are right,* than to own it when it comes to be our own case; but David subscribes to it with application, "Even my afflictions are just and kind."

76 Let, I pray thee, thy merciful kindness be for my comfort, according to thy word unto thy servant. 77 Let thy tender mercies come unto me, that I may live: for thy law *is* my delight.

Here is, 1. An earnest petition to God for his favour. Those that own the justice of God in their afflictions (as David had done, *v.* 75) may, in faith, and with humble boldness, be earnest for the mercy of God, and the tokens and fruits of that mercy, in their affliction. He prays for God's *merciful kindness* (*v* 76), his *tender mercies, v.* 77. He can claim nothing as his due, but all his supports under his affliction must come from mere mercy and compassion to one in misery, one in want. "Let these *come to me,*" that is, " the evidence of them (clear it up to me that thou hast a kindness for me, and mercy in store), and the effects of them; let them work my relief and deliverance." 2. The benefit he promised himself from God's lovingkindness: "Let it *come to me for my comfort* (*v.* 76); that will comfort me when nothing else will; that will comfort me whatever grieves me." Gracious souls fetch all their comfort from a gracious God, as the fountain of all happiness and joy: " Let it *come to me, that I may live,* that is, that I may be revived, and my life may be made sweet to me, for I have no joy of it while I am under God's displeasure. *In his favour is life;* in his frowns are death." A good man cannot live with any satisfaction any longer than he has some tokens of God's favour to him. 3. His pleas for the benefits of God's favour. He pleads, (1.) God's promise: "Let me have thy kindness, *according to thy word unto thy servant,* the kindness which thou hast promised and because thou hast promised it." Our Master

702

has passed his word to all his servants that he will be kind to them, and they may plead it with him. (2.) His own confidence and complacency in that promise: " *Thy law is my delight;* I hope in thy word and rejoice in that hope." Note, Those that delight in the law of God may depend upon the favour of God, for it shall certainly make them happy.

78 Let the proud be ashamed; for they dealt perversely with me without a cause: *but* I will meditate in thy precepts. 79 Let those that fear thee turn unto me, and those that have known thy testimonies.

Here David shows,

I. How little he valued the ill-will of sinners. There were those that dealt perversely with him, that were peevish and ill-conditioned towards him, that sought advantages against him, and misconstrued all he said and did. Even those that deal most fairly may meet with those that deal perversely. But David regarded it not, for, 1. He knew it was *without cause,* and that for his love they were his adversaries. The causeless reproach, like the curse causeless, may be easily slighted; it does not hurt us, and therefore should not move us. 2. He could pray, in faith, that they might *be ashamed* of it; God's dealing favourably with him might make them ashamed to think that they had dealt perversely with him. "*Let* them *be ashamed,*" that is, let them be brought either to repentance or to ruin." 3. He could go on in the way of his duty, and find comfort in that. "However they deal with me, *I will meditate in thy precepts,* and entertain myself with them."

II. How much he valued the good-will of saints, and how desirous he was to stand right in their opinion, and keep up his interest in them and communion with them: *Let those that fear thee turn to me.* He does not mean so much that they might side with him, and take up arms in his cause, as that they might love him, and pray for him, and associate with him. Good men desire the friendship and society of those that are good. Some think it intimates that when David had been guilty of that foul sin in the murder of Uriah, though he was a king, those that feared God grew strange to him and turned from him, for they were ashamed of him; this troubled him, and therefore he prays, Lord, let them *turn to me* again. He desires especially the company of those that were not only honest, but intelligent, *that have known thy testimonies,* have good heads as well as good hearts, and whose conversation will be edifying. It is desirable to have an intimacy with such.

80 Let my heart be sound in thy statutes; that I be not ashamed.

Here is, 1. David's prayer for sincerity, that his heart might be brought to God's *statutes,* and that it might be *sound* in them, not rotten and deceitful, that he might not rest in the form of godliness, but be acquainted with and subject to the power of it,—that he might be hearty and constant in religion, and that his soul might be in health. 2. His dread of the consequences of hypocrisy: *That I be not ashamed.* Shame is the portion of hypocrites, either here, if it be repented of, or hereafter, if it be not: " *Let my heart be sound,* that I fall not into scandalous sin, that I fall not quite off from the ways of God, and so shame myself. *Let my heart be sound,* that I may come *boldly to the throne of grace,* and may lift up my face without spot at the great day."

11. CAPH.

81 My soul fainteth for thy salvation : *but* I hope in thy word. 82 Mine eyes fail for thy word, saying, When wilt thou comfort me ?

Here we have the psalmist,

I. Longing for help from heaven: *My soul faints ; my eyes fail.* He longs *for the salvation of the Lord* and *for his word,* that is, salvation according to the word. He is not thus eager for the creatures of fancy, but for the objects of faith, salvation from the present calamities under which he was groaning and the doubts and fears which he was oppressed with. It may be understood of the coming of the Messiah, and so he speaks in the name of the Old-Testament church ; the souls of the faithful even *fainted to see* that salvation of which the prophets testified. (1 Pet. i. 10); their eyes failed for it. Abraham saw it at a distance, and so did others, but at such a distance that it put their eyes to the stretch and they could not stedfastly see it. David was now under prevailing dejections, and, having been long so, his eyes cried out, " *When wilt thou comfort me ?* Comfort me with *thy salvation,* comfort me with *thy word.*" Observe, 1. The salvation and consolation of God's people are secured to them by the word, which will certainly be fulfilled in its season. 2. The promised salvation and comfort may be, and often are, long deferred, so that they are ready to faint and fall in the expectation of them. 3. Though we think the time long ere the promised salvation and comfort come, yet we must still keep our eye upon that salvation, and resolve to take up with nothing short of it. " Thy salvation, thy word, thy comfort, are what my heart is still upon."

II. Waiting for that help, assured that it will come, and tarrying till it come : *But I hope in thy word ;* and but for hope the heart would break. When the *eyes fail* yet the faith must not ; for *the vision is for an appointed time, and at the end it shall speak and shall not lie.*

83 For I am become like a bottle in the smoke ; *yet* do I not forget thy statutes.

David begs God would make haste to comfort him, 1. Because his affliction was great, and therefore he was an object of God's pity : Lord, make haste to help me, *for I have become like a bottle in the smoke,* a leathern bottle, which, if it hung any while in the smoke, was not only blackened with soot, but dried, and parched, and shrivelled up. David was thus wasted by age, and sickness, and sorrow. See how affliction will mortify the strongest and stoutest of men ! David had been of a ruddy countenance, as fresh as a rose ; but now he is withered, his colour is gone, his cheeks are furrowed. Thus does man's beauty consume under God's rebukes, as a moth fretting a garment. A bottle, when it is thus wrinkled with the smoke, is thrown by, and there is no more use of it. Who will put wine into such old bottles ? Thus was David, in his low estate, looked upon as *a despised broken vessel,* and as *a vessel in which there was no pleasure.* Good men, when they are drooping and melancholy, sometimes think themselves more slighted than really they are. 2. Because, though his affliction was great, yet it had not driven him from his duty, and therefore he was within the reach of God's promise : *Yet do I not forget thy statutes.* Whatever our outward condition is we must not cool in our affection to the word of God, nor let that slip out of our minds ; no care, no grief, must crowd that out. As some *drink and forget the law* (Prov. xxxi. 5), so others weep and forget the law ; but we must in every condition, both prosperous and adverse, have the things of God in remembrance ; and, if we be mindful of God's statutes, we may pray and hope that he will be mindful of our sorrows, though for a time he seems to forget us.

84 How many *are* the days of thy servant? when wilt thou execute judgment on them that persecute me ?

Here, I. David prays against the instruments of his troubles, that God would make haste to execute judgment on those that persecuted him. He prays not for power to avenge himself (he bore no malice to any), but that God would take to himself the vengeance that belonged to him, and *would repay* (Rom. xii. 19), as the God that *sits in the throne judging right.* There is a day coming, and a great and terrible day it will be, when God will execute judgment on all the proud persecutors of his people, *tribulation to those that troubled them ;* Enoch foretold it (Jude 14), whose prophecy perhaps David here had an eye to ; and that day we are to look for and pray for the hastening of. Come, Lord Jesus, come quickly. 2. He pleads the long continuance of his trouble : " *How many are the days of thy servant ? The days of my life are but few*" (so some) ; " therefore let them not all be miserable, and therefore make haste to appear for me against my enemies, *before I go hence and shall be seen no more.*"

Or rather, "*The days of my affliction are many ;* thou seest, Lord, how many they be; when wilt thou return in mercy to me? Sometimes, for the elect's sake, *the days of trouble are shortened.* O let the days of my trouble be shortened; I am *thy servant ;* and therefore, as the eyes of a servant are to the hand of his master, so are mine to thee, until thou have mercy on me." ·

85 The proud have digged pits for me, which *are* not after thy law. 86 All thy commandments *are* faithful: they persecute me wrongfully; help thou me. 87 They had almost consumed me upon earth; but I forsook not thy precepts.

David's state was *herein* a type and figure of the state both of Christ and Christians that he was grievously persecuted; as there are many of his psalms, so there are many of the verses of this psalm, which complain of this, as those here. Here observe,

I. The account he gives of his persecutors and their malice against him. 1. They were *proud,* and in their pride *they persecuted him,* glorying in this, that they could trample upon one who was so much cried up, and hoping to raise themselves on his ruins. 2. They were unjust: *They persecuted him wrongfully ;* so far was he from giving them any provocation that he had studied to oblige them; but *for his love they were his adversaries.* 3. They were spiteful: *They dug pits for him,* which intimates that they were deliberate in their designs against him and that what they did was of malice prepense; it intimates likewise that they were subtle and crafty, and had the serpent's head as well as the serpent's venom, that they were industrious and would refuse no pains to do him a mischief, and treacherous, laying snares in secret for him, as hunters do to take wild beasts, xxxv. 7. Such has been the enmity of the serpent's seed to the seed of the woman. 4. They herein showed their enmity to God himself. The pits they *dug for him* were *not after God's law ;* he means they were very much against his law, which forbids to *devise evil to our neighbour,* and has particularly said, *Touch not my anointed.* The law appointed that, if a man dug a pit which occasioned any mischief, he should answer for the mischief (Exod. xxi. 33, 34), much more when it was dug with a mischievous design. 5. They carried on their designs against him so far that *they had almost consumed him upon earth ;* they went near to ruin him and all his interests. It is possible that those who shall shortly be consummate in heaven may be, for the present, *almost consumed on earth ;* and *it is of the Lord's mercies* (and, considering the malice of their enemies, it is a miracle of mercy) *that they are not quite consumed.* But the bush in

704

which God is, though it burns, shall not be burnt up.

II. His application to God in his persecuted state. 1. He acknowledges the truth and goodness of his religion, though he suffered: "However it be, *all thy commandments are faithful,* and, therefore, whatever I lose for my observance of them, I know I shall not lose by it." True religion, if it be worth any thing, is worth every thing, and therefore worth suffering for. "Men are false; I find them so; men of low degree, men of high degree, are so, there is no trusting them. But *all thy commandments are faithful ;* on them I may rely." 2. He begs that God would stand by him, and succour him: "*They persecute me ; help thou me ;* help me under my troubles, that I may bear them patiently, and as becomes me, and may still hold fast my integrity, and in due time help me out of my troubles." *God help me* is an excellent comprehensive prayer; it is a pity that it should ever be used lightly and as a by-word.

III. His adherence to his duty notwithstanding all the malice of his persecutors (*v.* 87): *But I forsook not thy precepts.* That which they aimed at was to frighten him from the ways of God, but they could not prevail; he would sooner forsake all that was dear to him in this world than forsake the word of God, would sooner lose his life than lose the comfort of doing his duty.

88 Quicken me after thy lovingkindness; so shall I keep the testimony of thy mouth.

Here is, 1. David in care to be found in the way of his duty. His constant desire and design are to *keep the testimony of God's mouth,* to keep to it as his rule and to keep hold of it as his confidence and portion for ever. This we must keep, whatever we lose. 2. David at prayer for divine grace to assist him therein: "*Quicken me after thy lovingkindness* (make me alive and make me lively), *so shall I keep thy testimonies,*" implying that otherwise he should not keep them. We cannot proceed, nor persevere, in the good way, unless God quicken us and put life into us; we are therefore here taught to depend upon the grace of God for strength to do every good work, and to depend upon it as grace, as purely the fruit of God's favour. He had prayed before, *Quicken me in thy righteousness* (*v.* 40); but here, *Quicken me after thy lovingkindness.* The surest token of God's good-will toward us is his good work in us.

12. LAMED.

89 For ever, O LORD, thy word is settled in heaven. 90 Thy faithfulness *is* unto all generations : thou hast established the earth, and it abideth. 91 They continue this day according to thine ordinances : for all *are* thy servants.

Here, 1. The psalmist acknowledges the unchangeableness of the word of God and of all his counsels: "*For ever, O Lord! thy word is settled. Thou art for ever thyself* (so some read it); thou art the same, and with thee there is no variableness, and this is a proof of it. *Thy word,* by which the heavens were made, *is settled* there in the abiding products of it;" or the settling of God's word in heaven is opposed to the changes and revolutions that are here upon earth. *All flesh is grass;* but *the word of the Lord endures for ever.* It *is settled in heaven,* that is, in the secret counsel of God, which is hidden in himself and is far above out of our sight, and is immovable, *as mountains of brass.* And his revealed will is as firm as his secret will; as he will fulfil the thoughts of his heart, so no word of his shall *fall to the ground;* for it follows here, *Thy faithfulness is unto all generations,* that is, the promise is sure to every age of the church and it cannot be antiquated by lapse of time. The promises that look ever so far forward shall be performed in their season. 2. He produces, for proof of it, the constancy of the course of nature: *Thou hast established the earth for ever and it abides;* it is what it was at first made, and where it was at first placed, poised with its own weight, and notwithstanding the convulsions in its own bowels, the agitations of the sea that is interwoven with it, and the violent concussions of the atmosphere that surrounds it, it remains unmoved. "*They*" (the heavens and the earth and all the hosts of both) "*continue to this day according to thy ordinances;* they remain in the posts wherein thou hast set them; they fill up the place assigned them, and answer the purposes for which they were intended." The stability of the ordinances of day and night, of heaven and earth, is produced to prove the perpetuity of God's covenant, Jer. xxxi. 35, 36; xxxiii. 20, 21 It is by virtue of God's promise to Noah (Gen. viii. 22) that *day and night, summer and winter,* observe a steady course. "They have continued to this day, and shall still continue to the end of time, acting according to the ordinances which were at first given them; for all are thy servants; they do thy will, and set forth .thy glory, and in both *are thy servants.*" All the creatures are, in their places, and according to their capacities, serviceable to their Creator, and answer the ends of their creation; and shall man be the only rebel, the only revolter from his allegiance, and the only unprofitable burden of the earth?

92 Unless thy law *had been* my delights, I should then have perished in mine affliction.

Here is, 1. The great distress that David was in. He was in affliction, and ready to *perish in his affliction,* not likely to die, so much as likely to despair; he was ready to give up all for gone, and to look upon himself as cut off from God's sight; he therefore admires the goodness of God to him, that he had not perished, that he kept the possession of his own soul, and was not driven out of his wits by his troubles, but especially that he was enabled to keep close to his God and was not driven off from his religion by them. Though we are not kept from affliction, yet, if we are kept from perishing in our affliction, we have no reason to say, *We have cleansed our hands in vain;* or, *What profit is it that we have served God?* 2. His support in this distress. God's law was his delight, (1.) It had been so formerly, and the remembrance of that was a comfort to him, as it afforded him a good evidence of his integrity. (2.) It was so now in his affliction; it afforded him abundant matter of comfort, and from these fountains of life he drew living waters, when the cisterns of the creature were broken or dried up. His converse with God's law, and his meditations on it, were his delightful entertainment in solitude and sorrow. A Bible is a pleasant companion at any time if we please.

93 I will never forget thy precepts: for with them thou hast quickened me.

Here is, 1. A very good resolution: "*I will never forget thy precepts,* but will always retain a remembrance of and regard to thy word as my rule." It is a resolution for perpetuity, never to be altered. Note, The best evidence of our love to the word of God is never to forget it. We must resolve that we will never, at any time, cast off our religion, and never, upon any occasion, lay aside our religion, but that we will be constant to it and persevere in it. 2. A very good reason for it: "*For by them thou hast quickened me;* not only they are quickening, but," (1.) "They have been so to me; I have found them so." Those speak best of the things of God who speak by experience, who can say that by the word the spiritual life has been begun in them, maintained and strengthened in them, excited and comforted in them. (2.) "Thou hast made them so;" the word of itself, without the grace of God, would not quicken us. Ministers can but prophesy upon the dry bones, they cannot put life into them; but, ordinarily, the grace of God works by the word and makes use of it as a means of quickening, and this is a good reason why we should never forget it, but should highly value what God has put such honour upon, and dearly love what we have found and hope still to find such benefit by. See here what is the best help for bad memories, namely, good affections. If we are quickened by the word, we shall never forget it; nay, that word that does really quicken us to and in our duty is not forgotten; though the expressions be lost, if the impressions remain, it is well

94 I *am* thine, save me; for I have sought thy precepts.

Here, 1. David claims relation to God : " *I am thine*, devoted to thee and owned by thee, thine in covenant." He does not say, *Thou art mine* (as Dr. Manton observes), though that follows of course, because that were a higher challenge ; but, *I am thine*, expressing himself in a more humble and dutiful way of resignation ; nor does he say, *I am thus*, but, *I am thine*, not pleading his own good property or qualification, but God's propriety in him : " *I am thine*, not my own, not the world's." 2. He proves his claim : " *I have sought thy precepts ;* I have carefully enquired concerning my duty and diligently endeavoured to do it." This will be the best evidence that we belong to God ; all that are his, though they have not found perfection, are seeking it. 3. He improves his claim : " *I am thine ; save me ;* save me from sin, save me from ruin." Those that have in sincerity given up themselves to God to be his may be sure that he will protect them and preserve them to his heavenly kingdom, Mal. iii. 18.

95 The wicked have waited for me to destroy me : *but* I will consider thy testimonies.

Here, 1. David complains of the malice of his enemies : *The wicked* (and none but such would be enemies to so good a man) *have waited for me to destroy me*. They were very cruel, and aimed at no less than his destruction; they were very crafty, and sought all opportunities to do him a mischief ; and they were *confident* (they *expected*, so some read it), that they should destroy him ; they thought themselves sure of their prey. 2. He comforts himself in the word of God as his protection : " While they are contriving my destruction, *I consider thy testimonies*, which secure to me my salvation." God's testimonies are *then* likely to be our support, when we consider them, and dwell in our thoughts upon them

96 I have seen an end of all perfection : *but* thy commandment *is* exceeding broad.

Here we have David's testimony from his own experience, 1. Of the vanity of the world and its insufficiency to make us happy : *I have seen an end of all perfection.* Poor perfection which one sees an end of ! Yet such are all those things in this world which pass for perfections. David, in his time, had seen Goliath, the strongest, overcome, Asahel, the swiftest, overtaken, Ahithophel, the wisest, befooled, Absalom, the fairest, deformed ; and, in short, he had *seen an end of perfection*, of *all perfection*. He saw it by faith ; he saw it by observation ; he saw an end of the perfection of the creature both in respect of sufficiency (it was scanty and defective ; there is that to be done for us which the creature cannot do) and in respect of continuance ; it will not last our time, for it will not last to eternity as we must   The glory of

man is but as the flower of the grass. 2. Of the fulness of the word of God, and its sufficiency for our satisfaction : *But thy commandment is broad, exceedingly broad.* The word of God reaches to all cases, to all times. The divine law lays a restraint upon the whole man, is designed to sanctify us wholly. There is a great deal required and forbidden in every commandment. The divine promise (for that also is commanded) extends itself to all our burdens, wants, and grievances, and has that in it which will make a portion and happiness for us when we *have seen an end of all perfection.*

13. MEM.

97 O how love I thy law ! it *is* my meditation all the day.

Here is, 1. David's inexpressible love to the word of God : *O how love I thy law !* He protests his affection to the word of God with a holy vehemency ; he found that love to it in his heart which, considering the corruption of his nature and the temptations of the world, he could not but wonder at, and at that grace which had wrought it in him. He not only loved the promises, but loved the law, and delighted in it after the inner man 2. An unexceptionable evidence of this. What we love we love to think of ; by *this* it appeared that David loved the word of God that it was his *meditation*. He not only read the book of the law, but digested what he read in his thoughts, and was delivered into it as into a mould : it was his meditation not only in the night, when he was silent and solitary, and had nothing else to do, but in the day, when he was full of business and company ; nay, and *all the day ;* some good thoughts were interwoven with his common thoughts, so full was he of the word of God.

98 Thou through thy commandments hast made me wiser than mine enemies : for they *are* ever with me. 99 I have more understanding than all my teachers : for thy testimonies *are* my meditation. 100 I understand more than the ancients, because I keep thy precepts.

We have here an account of David's learning, not that of the Egyptians, but of the Israelites indeed.

I. The good method by which he got it. In his youth he minded business in the country as a shepherd ; from his youth he minded business in the court and camp. Which way then could he get any great stock of learning ? He tells us here how he came by it ; he had it from God as the author : *Thou hast made me wise.* All true wisdom is from God. He had it by the word of God as the means, by *his commandments* and *his testimonies.* These are able to *make us wise to salvation* and *to furnish the man of God for every good work.* 1. These David took for his constant companions : " *They are ever with me*, ever in my mind, ever in my eye." A good man, wherever he goes, carries his Bible along with him, if not in his hands, yet in his head and in his heart. 2. These he took for the delightful subject of his thoughts; they were his *meditation*, not only as matters of speculation for his entertainment, as scholars meditate on their notions, but as matters of concern, for his right management, as men of business think of their business, that they may do it in the best manner. 3. These he took for the commanding rules of all his actions: *I keep thy precepts*, that is, I make conscience of doing my duty in every thing. The best way to improve in knowledge is to abide and abound in all the instances of serious godliness; for, *if any man do his will, he shall know of the doctrine* of Christ, shall know more and more of it, John vii. 17. The love of the truth prepares for the light of it; the *pure in heart shall see God* here.

II. The great eminency he attained to in it. By studying and practising God's commandments, and making them his rule, he learnt to *behave himself wisely in all his ways*, 1 Sam. xviii. 14. 1. He outwitted his enemies; God, by these means, made him wiser to baffle and defeat their designs against him than they were to lay them. Heavenly wisdom will carry the point, at last, against carnal policy. By keeping the commandments we secure God on our side and make him our friend, and therein are certainly wiser than those that make him their enemy. By keeping the commandments we preserve in ourselves that peace and quiet of mind which our enemies would rob us of, and so are wise for ourselves, wiser than they are for themselves, for this world as well as for the other. 2. He outstripped his *teachers*, and had more understanding than all of them. He means either those who would have been his teachers, who blamed his conduct and undertook to prescribe to him (by keeping God's commandments he managed his matters so that it appeared, in the event, he had taken the right measures and they had taken the wrong), or those who should have been his teachers, the priests and Levites, who sat in Moses's chair, and whose lips ought to have kept knowledge, but who neglected the study of the law, and minded their honours and revenues, and the formalities only of their religion; and so David, who conversed much with the scriptures, by that means became more intelligent than they. Or he may mean those who had been his teachers when he was young; he built so well upon the foundation which they had laid that, with the help of his Bible, he became able to teach them, to teach them all. He was not now a babe that needed milk, but had *spiritual senses exercised*, Heb. v. 14. It is no reflection upon our teachers, but rather an honour to them, to improve so as really to excel them, and not to need them. By meditation we preach to ourselves, and so we come to un-

derstand *more than our teachers*, for we come to understand our own hearts, which they cannot. 3. He outdid *the ancients*, either those of his day (he was young, like Elihu, and they were very old, but his keeping God's precepts taught more wisdom than the multitude of their years, Job xxxii. 7, 8) or those of former days; he himself quotes the proverb of the ancients (1 Sam. xxiv. 13), but the word of God gave him to understand things better than he could do by tradition and all the learning that was handed down from preceding ages. In short, the written word is a surer guide to heaven than all the doctors and fathers, the teachers and ancients, of the church; and the sacred writings kept, and kept to, will teach us more wisdom than all their writings.

101 I have refrained my feet from every evil way, that I might keep thy word.

Here is, 1. David's care to avoid the ways of sin: "*I have refrained my feet from the evil ways* they were ready to step aside into. I checked myself and drew back as soon as I was aware that I was entering into temptation." Though it was a broad way, a green way, a pleasant way, and a way that many walked in, yet, being a sinful way, it was an evil way, and he refrained his feet from it, foreseeing the end of that way. And his care was universal; he shunned every evil way. *By the words of thy lips I have kept myself from the paths of the destroyer*, xvii. 4. 2. His care to be found in the way of duty: *That I might keep thy word*, and never transgress it. His abstaining from sin was, (1.) An evidence that he did conscientiously aim to keep God's word and had made that his rule. (2.) It was a means of his keeping God's word in the exercises of religion; for we cannot with any comfort or boldness attend on God in holy duties, so as in them to keep his word, while we are under guilt or in any by-way.

102 I have not departed from thy judgments: for thou hast taught me.

Here is, 1. David's constancy in his religion. He had *not departed from God's judgments;* he had not chosen any other rule than the word of God, nor had he wilfully deviated from that rule. A constant adherence to the ways of God in trying times will be a good evidence of our integrity. 2. The cause of his constancy: "*For thou hast taught me;* that is, they were divine instructions that I learned; I was satisfied that the doctrine was of God, and therefore I stuck to it." Or, rather, "It was divine grace in my heart that enabled me to receive those instructions." All the saints are taught of God, for he it is that gives the understanding; and those, and those only, that are taught of God, will continue to the end in the things that they have learned.

103 How sweet are thy words unto my taste! *yea, sweeter* than honey to my mouth. 104 Through thy precepts I get understanding : therefore I hate every false way.

Here is, 1. The wonderful pleasure and delight which David took in the word of God; it was *sweet to his taste, sweeter than honey.* There is such a thing as a spiritual taste, an inward savour and relish of divine things, such an evidence of them to ourselves, by experience, as we cannot give to others. We have *heard him ourselves,* John iv. 42. To this scripture-taste the word of God is sweet, very sweet, sweeter than any of the gratifications of sense, even those that are most delicious. David speaks as if he wanted words to express the satisfaction he took in the discoveries of the divine will and grace; no pleasure was comparable to it. 2. The unspeakable profit and advantage he gained by the word of God. (1.) It helped him to a good head : "*Through thy precepts I get understanding* to discern between truth and falsehood, good and evil, so as not to mistake either in the conduct of my own life or in advising others." (2.) It helped him to a good heart : "*Therefore,* because I have got understanding of the truth, *I hate every false way,* and am stedfastly resolved not to turn aside into it." Observe here, [1.] The way of sin is a false way; it deceives, and will ruin, all that walk in it; it is the wrong° way, and yet it seems to a man right, Prov. xiv. 12. [2.] It is the character of every good man that he hates the way of sin, and hates it because it is a false way; he not only refrains his feet from it (*v.* 101), but he *hates it,* has an antipathy to it and a dread of it. [3.] Those who hate sin as sin will hate all sin, hate every false way, because every false way leads to destruction. And, [4.] The more understanding we get by the word of God the more rooted will our hatred of sin be (for *to depart from evil, that is understanding,* Job xxviii. 28), and the more ready we are in the scriptures the better furnished we are with answers to temptation.

14. NUN.

105 Thy word *is* a lamp unto my feet, and a light unto my path.

Observe here, 1. The nature of the word of God, and the great intention of giving it to the world; it is a *lamp and a light.* It discovers to us, concerning God and ourselves, that which otherwise we could not have known; it shows us what is amiss, and will be dangerous; it directs us in our work and way, and a dark place indeed the world would be without it. It is a lamp which we may set up by us, and take into our hands for our own particular use, Prov. vi. 23. The commandment is a lamp kept burning with the oil of the Spirit; it is like the lamps in the sanctuary, and the pillar of fire to Israel. 2.

The use we should make of it. It must be not only a *light to our eyes,* to gratify them, and fill our heads with speculations, but a *light to our feet* and *to our path,* to direct us in the right ordering of our conversation, both in the choice of our way in general and in the particular steps we take in that way, that we may not take a false way nor a false step in the right way. We are then truly sensible of God's goodness to us in giving us such a lamp and light when we make it a guide to our feet, our path

106 I have sworn, and I will perform *it,* that I will keep thy righteous judgments.

Here is, 1. The notion David had of religion; it is *keeping God's righteous judgments.* God's commands are his judgments, the dictates of infinite wisdom. They are righteous judgments, consonant to the eternal rules of equity, and it is our duty to keep them carefully. 2. The obligation he here laid upon himself to be religious, binding himself, by his own promise, to that which he was already bound to by the divine precept, and all little enough. "*I have sworn (I have lifted up my hand to the Lord, and I cannot go back)* and therefore must go forward: *I will perform it.*" Note, (1.) It is good for us to bind ourselves with a solemn oath to be religious. We must swear to the Lord as subjects swear allegiance to their sovereign, promising fealty, appealing to God concerning our sincerity in this promise, and owning ourselves liable to the curse if we do not perform it. (2.) We must often call to mind the vows of God that are upon us, and remember that we have sworn. (3.) We must make conscience of performing unto the Lord our oaths (an honest man will be as good as his word); nor have we sworn to our own hurt, but it will be unspeakably to our hurt if we do not perform.

107 I am afflicted very much : quicken me, O LORD, according unto thy word.

Here is, 1. The representation David makes of the sorrowful condition he was in : *I am afflicted very much,* afflicted in spirit; he seems to mean that especially. He laboured under many discouragements; without were fightings, within were fears. This is often the lot of the best saints; therefore think it not strange if sometimes it be ours. 2. The recourse he has to God in this condition; he prays for his grace : "*Quicken me, O Lord!* make me lively, make me cheerful; quicken me by afflictions to greater diligence in my work. *Quicken me,* that is, deliver me out of my afflictions, which will be as life from the dead." He pleads the promise of God, guides his desires by it, and grounds his hopes upon it: *Quicken me according to thy word.* David resolved to perform his promises to God (*v.* 106) and therefore could, with humble boldness, beg of God to make good his word to him.

108 Accept, I beseech thee, the free-will offerings of my mouth, O LORD, and teach me thy judgments.

Two things we are here taught to pray for, in reference to our religious performances :— 1. Acceptance of them. This we must aim at in all we do in religion, that, whether present or absent, we may be accepted of the Lord. What David here earnestly prays for the acceptance of are the *free-will-offerings*, not of his purse, but of his *mouth*, his prayers and praises. *The calves of our lips* (Hos. xiv. 2), *the fruit of our lips* (Heb. i. 15), these are the spiritual offerings which all Christians, as spiritual priests, must offer to God ; and they must be *free-will-offerings*, for we must offer them abundantly and cheerfully, and it is this willing mind that is accepted. The more there is of freeness and willingness in the service of God the more pleasing it is to him. 2. Assistance in them : *Teach me thy judgments.* We cannot offer any thing to God which we have reason to think he will accept of, but what he is pleased to instruct us in the doing of ; and we must be as earnest for the grace of God in us as for the favour of God towards us.

109 My soul *is* continually in my hand : yet do I not forget thy law. **110** The wicked have laid a snare for me : yet I erred not from thy precepts.

Here is, 1. David in danger of losing his life. There is but a step between him and death, for the *wicked have laid a snare* for him ; Saul did so many a time, because he hated him for his piety. Wherever he was he found some design or other laid against him to take away his life, for it was that they aimed at. What they could not effect by open force they hoped to compass by treachery, which made him say, *My soul is continually in my hand.* It was so with him, not only as a *man* (so it is true of us all ; wherever we are we lie exposed to the strokes of death ; what we carry in our hands is easily snatched away from us by violence, or if sandy, as our life is, it easily of itself slips through our fingers), but as a *man of war*, a soldier, who often jeoparded his life in the high places of the field, and especially as *a man after God's own heart*, and, as such, hated and persecuted, and *always delivered to death* (2 Cor. iv. 11), *killed all the day long*. 2. David in no danger of losing his religion, notwithstanding this, thus in jeopardy every hour and yet constant to God and his duty. None of these things move him ; for, (1.) He *does not forget the law*, and therefore he is likely to persevere. In the multitude of his cares for his own safety he finds room in his head and heart for the word of God, and has that in his mind as fresh as ever ; and where

that dwells richly it will be a *well of living water*. (2.) He has not yet erred from God's precepts, and therefore it is to be hoped he will not. He had stood many a shock and kept his ground, and surely that grace which had helped him hitherto would not fail him, but would still prevent his wanderings.

111 Thy testimonies have I taken as a heritage for ever : for they *are* the rejoicing of my heart. **112** I have inclined mine heart to perform thy statutes alway, *even unto* the end.

The psalmist here in a most affectionate manner, like an Israelite indeed, resolves to stick to the word of God and to live and die by it.

I. He resolves to portion himself in it, and there to seek his happiness, nay, there to enjoy it : " *Thy testimonies* (the truths, the promises, of thy word) *have I taken as a heritage for ever, for they are the rejoicing of my heart.*" The present delight he took in them was an evidence that the good things contained in them were in his account the best things, and the treasure which he set his heart upon. 1. He expected an eternal happiness in God's testimonies. The covenant God had made with him was an everlasting covenant, and therefore he took it as a *heritage for ever*. If he could not yet say, " They are my heritage," yet he could say, " I have made choice of them for my heritage ; and will never take up with a portion in this life," xvii. 14, 15. God's testimonies are a heritage to all that have received the Spirit of adoption ; for, *if children, then heirs.* They are a *heritage for ever*, and that no earthly heritage is (1 Pet. i. 4) ; all the saints accept them as such, take up with them, live upon them, and can therefore be content with but little of this world. 2. He enjoyed a present satisfaction in them : *They are the rejoicing of my heart*, because they will be *my heritage for ever*. It requires the heart of a good man to see his portion in the promise of God and not in the possessions of this world.

II. He resolves to govern himself by it and thence to take his measures : *I have inclined my heart to do thy statutes.* Those that would have the blessings of God's testimonies must come under the bonds of his statutes. We must look for comfort only in the way of duty, and that duty must be done, 1. With full consent and complacency : " *I have*, by the grace of God, *inclined my heart to it*, and conquered the aversion I had to it." A good man brings his heart to his work and then it is done well. A gracious disposition to do the will of God is the acceptable principle of all obedience. 2. With constancy and perseverance. He would perform God's statutes always, in all instances, in the duty of every day, in a constant course of holy walking, and this *to the end*, without weariness. This is following the Lord fully.

15. SAMECH.

113 I hate *vain* thoughts : but thy law do I love.

Here we have, 1. David's dread of the risings of sin, and the first beginnings of it : *I hate* vain *thoughts.* He does not mean that he hated them in others, for there he could not discern them, but he hated them in his own heart. Every good man makes conscience of his thoughts, for they are words to God. Vain thoughts, how light soever most make of them, are sinful and hurtful, and therefore we should account them hateful and dreadful, for they not only divert the mind from that which is good, but open the door to all evil, Jer. iv. 14. Though David could not say that he was free from vain thoughts, yet he could say that he hated them ; he did not countenance them, nor give them any entertainment, but did what he could to keep them out, at least to keep them under. *The evil I do I allow not.* 2. David's delight in the rule of duty : *But thy law do I love*, which forbids those vain thoughts, and threatens them. The more we love the law of God the more we shall get the mastery of our vain thoughts, the more hateful they will be to us, as being contrary to the whole law, and the more watchful we shall be against them, lest they draw us from that which we love.

114 Thou *art* my hiding place and my shield : I hope in thy word.

Here is, 1. God's care of David to protect and defend him, which he comforted himself with when his enemies were very malicious against him : *Thou art my hiding-place and my shield.* David, when Saul pursued him, often betook himself to close places for shelter ; in war he guarded himself with his shield. Now God was both these to him, a hiding-place to preserve him from danger and a shield to preserve him in danger, his life from death and his soul from sin. Good people are safe under God's protection. He is their *strength and their shield*, their *help and their shield*, their *sun and their shield*, their *shield and their great reward*, and here their *hiding-place and their shield.* They may by faith retire to him, and repose in him as their hiding-place, where they are kept in secret. They may by faith oppose his power all the might and malice of their enemies, as their shield to quench every fiery dart. 2. David's confidence in God. He is safe, and therefore he is easy, under the divine protection : "*I hope in thy word*, which has acquainted me with thee and assured me of thy kindness to me." Those who depend on God's promise shall have the benefit of his power and be taken under his special protection.

115 Depart from me, ye evildoers: for I will keep the commandments of my God.

Here is, 1. David's firm and fixed resolu-

710

tion to live a holy life : *I will keep the commandments of my God.* Bravely resolved ! like a saint, like a soldier ; for true courage consists in a steady resolution against all sin and for all duty. Those that would keep God's commandments must be often renewing their resolutions to do so : "*I will keep them.* Whatever others do, this I will do; though I be singular, though all about me be evil-doers, and desert me ; whatever I have done hitherto, I will for the future walk closely with God. They are the commandments of God, of my God, and therefore I will keep them. He is God and may command me, my God and will command me nothing but what is for my good." 2. His farewell to bad company, pursuant to this resolution : *Depart from me, you evil-doers.* Though David, as a good magistrate, was a terror to evil-doers, yet there were many such, even about court, intruding near his person ; these he here abdicates, and resolves to have no conversation with them. Note, Those that resolve to keep the commandments of God must have no society with evil-doers ; for bad company is a great hindrance to a holy life. We must not choose wicked people for our companions, nor be intimate with them ; we must not do as they do nor do as they would have us do, Ps. i. 1 ; Eph. v. 11.

116 Uphold me according unto thy word, that I may live : and let me not be ashamed of my hope. **117** Hold thou me up, and I shall be safe : and I will have respect unto thy statutes continually.

Here, 1. David prays for sustaining grace ; for this grace sufficient he besought the Lord twice : *Uphold me;* and again, *Hold thou me up.* He sees himself not only unable to go on in his duty by any strength of his own, but in danger of falling into sin unless he was prevented by divine grace ; and therefore he is thus earnest for that grace to uphold him in his integrity (xli. 12), to keep him from falling and to keep him from tiring, that he might neither turn aside to evil-doing nor be weary of well-doing. We stand no longer than God holds us and go no further than he carries us. 2. He pleads earnestly for this grace. (1.) He pleads the promise of God, his dependence upon the promise, and his expectation from it : " *Uphold me, according to thy word*, which word I hope in ; and, if it be not performed, I shall be made *ashamed of my hope*, and be called a fool for my credulity." But those that hope in God's word may be sure that the word will not fail them, and therefore their hope will not make them ashamed. (2.) He pleads the great need he had of God's grace and the great advantage it would be of to him : *Uphold me, that I may live*, intimating that he could not live without the grace of God; he should fall into sin, into death, into hell, if God did not hold him up; but, supported by his hand, he shall live; his spiritual life shall be maintained and be an earnest of eternal life. *Hold me up, and I shall be safe,* out of danger and out of the fear of danger. Our holy security is grounded on divine supports. (3.) He pleads his resolution, in the strength of this grace, to proceed in his duty: "*Hold me up,* and then *I will have respect unto thy statutes continually* and never turn my eyes or feet aside from them." *I will employ myself* (so some), I *will delight myself* (so others) *in thy statutes.* If God's right hand uphold us, we must, in his strength, go on in our duty both with diligence and pleasure.

118 Thou hast trodden down all them that err from thy statutes: for their deceit *is* falsehood. 119 Thou puttest away all the wicked of the earth *like* dross: therefore I love thy testimonies. 120 My flesh trembleth for fear of thee; and I am afraid of thy judgments.

Here is, I. God's judgment on wicked people, on those that *wander from his statutes,* that take their measures from other rules and will not have God to reign over them. All departure from God's statutes is certainly an error, and will prove a fatal one. These are *the wicked of the earth;* they mind earthly things, lay up their treasures in the earth, live in pleasure on the earth, and are strangers and enemies to heaven and heavenly things. Now see how God deals with them, that you may neither fear them nor envy them. 1. He *treads them all down.* He brings them to ruin, to utter ruin, to shameful ruin; he makes them his footstool. Though they are ever so high, he can bring them low (Amos. ii. 9); he has done it many a time, and he will do it, for he resists the proud and will triumph over those that oppose his kingdom. Proud persecutors trample upon his people, but, sooner or later, he will trample upon them. 2. He *puts them all away like dross.* Wicked people are as dross, which, though it be mingled with the good metal in the ore, and seems to be of the same substance with it, must be separated from it. And in God's account they are worthless things, the scum and refuse of the earth, and no more to be compared with the righteous than dross with fine gold. There is a day coming which will put them away from among the righteous (Matt. xiii. 49), so that they shall have no place *in their congregation* (Ps. i. 5), which will put them away into everlasting fire, the fittest place for the dross. Sometimes, in this world, the wicked are, by the censures of the church, or the sword of the magistrate, or the judgments of God, *put away as dross,* Prov. xxv. 4, 5

II. The reasons of these judgments. God casts them off because they *err from his sta-*

tutes (those that will not submit to the commands of the word shall feel the curses of it) and because *their deceit is falsehood,* that is, because they deceive themselves by setting up false rules, in opposition to God's statutes, which they err from, and because they go about to deceive others with their hypocritical pretences of good and their crafty projects of mischief. *Their cunning is falsehood,* so Dr. Hammond. The utmost of their policy is treachery and perfidiousness; this the God of truth hates and will punish.

III. The improvement David made of these judgments. He took notice of them and received instruction from them. The ruin of the wicked helped to increase, 1. His love to the word of God. "I see what comes of sin; *therefore I love thy testimonies,* which warn me to take heed of those dangerous courses and *keep me from the paths of the destroyer.*" We see the word of God fulfilled in his judgments on sin and sinners, and therefore we should love it. 2. His fear of the wrath of God: *My flesh trembles for fear of thee.* Instead of insulting over those who fell under God's displeasure, he humbled himself. What we read and hear of the judgments of God upon wicked people should make us, (1.) To reverence his terrible majesty, and to stand in awe of him: *Who is able to stand before this holy Lord God?* 1 Sam. vi. 20. (2.) To fear lest we offend him and become obnoxious to his wrath. Good men have need to be restrained from sin by *the terrors of the Lord,* especially when judgment *begins at the house of God* and hypocrites are discovered and *put away as dross.*

16. AIN.

121 I have done judgment and justice: leave me not to mine oppressors. 122 Be surety for thy servant for good: let not the proud oppress me.

David here appeals to God, 1. As his witness that he had not done wrong; he could truly say, "*I have done judgment and justice,* that is, I have made conscience of rendering to all their due, and have not by force or fraud hindered any of their right." Take him as a king, he *executed judgment and justice to all his people,* 2 Sam. viii. 15. Take him in a private capacity, he could appeal to Saul himself that *there was no evil or transgression in his hand,* 1 Sam. xxiv. 11. Note, Honesty is the best policy and will be our rejoicing in the day of evil. 2. As his Judge, that he might not be wronged. Having done justice for others that were oppressed, he begs that God would do him justice and avenge him of his adversaries: "*Be surety for thy servant, for good;* undertake for me against those that would run me down and ruin me." He is sensible that he cannot make his part good himself, and therefore begs that God would appear for him. Christ is our surety with God; and, if he be so, Providence shall be our surety against all the world. Who or what shall harm us if God's power and goodness be engaged for our protection and rescue? He does not prescribe to God what he should do for him; only let it be *for good*, in such way and manner as Infinite Wisdom sees best; "*only let me not be left to my oppressors.*" Though David had *done judgment and justice*, yet he had many enemies; but, having God for his friend, he hoped they should not have their will against him; and in that hope he prayed again, *Let not the proud oppress me.* David, one of the best of men, was oppressed by the proud, whom God beholds afar off; the condition therefore of the persecuted is better than that of the persecutors, and will appear so at last.

123 Mine eyes fail for thy salvation, and for the word of thy righteousness.

David, being oppressed, is here waiting and wishing for the salvation of the Lord, which would make him easy. 1. He cannot but think that it comes slowly: *My eyes fail for thy salvation.* His eyes were towards it and had been long so. He looked for help from heaven (and we deceive ourselves if we look for it any other way), but it did not come so soon as he expected, so that his eyes began to fail, and he was sometimes ready to despair, and to think that, because the salvation did not come when he looked for it, it would never come. It is often the infirmity even of good men to be weary of waiting God's time when *their* time has elapsed. 2. Yet he cannot but hope that it comes surely; for he expects *the word of God's righteousness*, and no other salvation than what is secured by that word, which cannot fall to the ground because it is a word of righteousness. Though our eyes fail, yet God's word does not, and therefore those that build upon it, though now discouraged, shall in due time see his salvation.

124 Deal with thy servant according unto thy mercy, and teach me thy statutes. 125 I *am* thy servant; give me understanding, that I may know thy testimonies.

Here is, 1. David's petition for divine instruction: "*Teach me thy statues;* give me to know all my duty; when I am in doubt, and know not for certain what is my duty, direct me, and make it plain to me; now that I am afflicted, oppressed, and *my eyes* are ready to *fail for thy salvation*, let me know what my duty is in this condition." In difficult times we should desire more to be told what we must do than what we may expect, and should pray more to be led into the knowledge of scripture-precepts than of scripture-prophecies. If God, who gave us his statutes, do not teach us, we shall never learn them. How God teaches is implied in the next petition: *Give me understanding* (a renewed understanding, apt to receive divine light), *that*

I may know thy testimonies. It is God's prerogative to give an understanding, that understanding without which we cannot know God's testimonies. Those who know most of God's testimonies desire to know more, and are still earnest with God to teach them, never thinking they know enough. 2. His pleas to enforce this petition. (1.) He pleads God's goodness to him: *Deal with me according to thy mercy.* The best saints count this their best plea for any blessing, "Let me have it according to thy mercy;" for we deserve no favour from God, nor can we claim any as a debt, but we are most likely to be easy when we cast ourselves upon God's mercy and refer ourselves to it. Particularly, when we come to him for instruction, we must beg it as a mercy, and reckon that in being taught we are well dealt with. (2.) He pleads his relation to God: "*I am thy servant*, and have work to do for thee; therefore *teach me* to do it and to do it well." The servant has reason to expect that, if he be at a loss about his work, his master should teach him, and, if it were in his power, give him an understanding. "Lord," says David, "I desire to serve thee; show me how." If any man resolve to do God's will as his servant, he shall be made to know his testimonies, John vii. 17; Ps. xxv. 14.

126 *It is* time for *thee*, LORD, to work: *for* they have made void thy law.

Here is, 1. A complaint of the daring impiety of the wicked. David, having in himself a holy indignation at it, humbly represents it to God: "Lord, there are those that *have made void thy law*, have set thee and thy government at defiance, and have done what in them lay to cancel and vacate the obligation of thy commands." Those that sin through infirmity transgress the law, but presumptuous sinners do in effect make void the law, saying, *Who is the Lord? What is the Almighty, that we should fear him?* It is possible a godly man may sin against the commandment, but a wicked man would sin away the commandment, would repeal God's laws and enact his own lusts. This is the sinfulness of sin and the malignity of the carnal mind. 2. A desire that God would appear, for the vindication of his own honour: "*It is time for thee, Lord, to work*, to do something for the effectual confutation of atheists and infidels, and the silencing of those that set their mouth against the heavens." God's time to work is when vice has become most daring and the measure of iniquity is full. *Now will I arise, saith the Lord.* Some read it, and the original will bear it, *It is time to work for thee, O Lord!* it is time for every one in his place to appear on the Lord's side—against the threatening growth of profaneness and immorality. We must do what we can for the support of the sinking interests of religion, and, after all, we must beg of God to take the work into his own hands.

127 Therefore I love thy commandments above gold; yea, above fine gold. **128** Therefore I esteem all *thy* precepts *concerning* all *things to be* right; *and* I hate every false way.

David here, as often in this psalm, professes the great love he had to the word and law of God; and, to evidence the sincerity of it, observe, 1. The degree of his love. He loved his Bible better than he loved his money—*above gold, yea, above fine gold.* Gold, fine gold, is what most men set their hearts upon; nothing charms them and dazzles their eyes so much as gold does. It is fine gold, a fine thing in their eyes; they will venture their souls, their God, their all, to get and keep it. But David saw that the word of God answers all purposes better than money does, for it enriches the soul towards God; and therefore he loved it better than gold, for it had done that for him which gold could not do, and would stand him in stead when the wealth of the world would fail him. 2. The ground of his love. He loved all God's commandments because he esteemed them to be right, all reasonable and just, and suited to the end for which they were made. They are all as they should be, and no fault can be found with them; and we must love them because they bear God's image and are the revelations of his will. If we thus *consent to the law that it is good,* we shall delight in it after the inner man. 3. The fruit and evidence of this love: He *hated every false way.* The way of sin being directly contrary to God's precepts, which are right, is a false way, and therefore those that have a love and esteem for God's law hate it and will not be reconciled to it.

17. PE

129 Thy testimonies *are* wonderful: therefore doth my soul keep them.

See here how David was affected towards the word of God. 1. He admired it, as most excellent in itself: *Thy testimonies are wonderful.* The word of God gives us admirable discoveries of God, and Christ, and another world · admirable proofs of divine love and grace. The majesty of the style, the purity of the matter, the harmony of the parts, are all wonderful. Its effects upon the consciences of men, both for conviction and comfort, are wonderful; and it is a sign that we are not acquainted with God's testimonies, or do not understand them, if we do not admire them. 2. He adhered to it as of constant use to him: "*Therefore doth my soul keep them,* as a treasure of inestimable value, which I cannot be without." We do not keep them to any purpose unless our souls keep them. There they must be deposited, as the tables of testimony in the ark

there they must have the innermost and uppermost place. Those that see God's word to be admirable will prize it highly and preserve it carefully, as that which they promise themselves great things from

130 The entrance of thy words giveth light; it giveth understanding unto the simple.

Here is, 1. The great use for which the word of God was intended, to give light, that is, to give understanding, to give us to understand that which will be of use to us in our travels through this world; and it is the outward and ordinary means by which the Spirit of God enlightens the understanding of all that are sanctified. God's testimonies are not only wonderful for the greatness of them, but useful, as a light in a dark place. 2. Its efficacy for this purpose. It admirably answers the end; for, (1.) Even *the entrance of God's word gives light.* If we begin at the beginning, and take it before us, we shall find that the very first verses of the Bible give us surprising and yet satisfying discoveries of the origin of the universe, about which, without that, the world is utterly in the dark. As soon as the word of God enters into us, and has a place in us, it enlightens us; we find we begin to see when we begin to study the word of God. The very first principles of the oracles of God, the plainest truths, the milk appointed for the babes, bring a great light into the soul, much more will the soul be illuminated by the sublime mysteries that are found there. "The exposition or explication of thy word gives light;" then it is most profitable when ministers do their part *in giving the sense,* Neh. viii. 8. Some understand it of the New Testament, which is the opening or unfolding of the Old, which would give light concerning life and immortality. (2.) It would *give understanding* even *to the simple,* to the weakest capacities; for it shows us a way to heaven so plain that the *wayfaring men, though fools, shall not err therein.*

131 I opened my mouth, and panted: for I longed for thy commandments.

Here is, 1. The desire David had towards the word of God: *I longed for thy commandments.* When he was under a forced absence from God's ordinances he longed to be restored to them again; when he enjoyed ordinances he greedily sucked in the word of God, *as new-born babes desire the milk.* When Christ is formed in the soul there are gracious longings, unaccountable to one that is a stranger to the work. 2. The degree of that desire appearing in the expressions of it: *I opened my mouth and panted,* as one overcome with heat, or almost stifled, pants for a mouthful of fresh air. Thus strong, thus earnest, should our desires be towards God

and the remembrance of his name, xlii. 1, 2.
Luke xii. 50.

132 Look thou upon me, and be merciful unto me, as thou usest to do unto those that love thy name.

Here is, 1. David's request for God's favour to himself: " *Look* graciously *upon me;* let me have thy smiles, and the light of thy countenance. Take cognizance of me and my affairs, *and be merciful to me;* let me taste the sweetness of thy mercy and receive the gifts of thy mercy." See how humble his petition is. He asks not for the operations of God's hand, only for the smiles of his face; a good look is enough; and for that he does not plead merit, but implores mercy. 2. His acknowledgment of his favour to all his people: *As thou usest to do unto those that love thy name.* This is either, (1.) A plea for mercy: "Lord, I am one of *those that love thy name,* love thee and thy word, and thou usest to be kind to those that do so; and wilt thou be worse to me than to others of thy people?" Or, (2.) A description of the favour and mercy he desired— "that which thou usest to bestow on those that love thy name, which *thou bearest to thy chosen,*" cvi. 4, 5. He desires no more, no better, than neighbour's fare, and he will take up with no less; common looks and common mercies will not serve, but such as are reserved for those that love him, which are such as *eye has not seen,* 1 Cor. ii. 9. Note, The dealings of God with those that love him are such that a man needs not desire to be any better dealt with, for he will make them truly and eternally happy. And as long as God deals with us no otherwise than as he uses to deal with those that love him we have no reason to complain, 1 Cor. x. 13.

133 Order my steps in thy word: and let not any iniquity have dominion over me.

Here David prays for two great spiritual blessings, and is, in this verse, as earnest for the good work of God in him as, in the verse before, for the good-will of God towards him. He prays, 1. For direction in the paths of duty · " *Order my steps in thy word;* having led me into the right way, let every step I take in that way be under the guidance of thy grace." We ought to walk by rule; all the motions of the soul must not only be kept within the bounds prescribed by the word, so as not to transgress them, but carried out in the paths prescribed by the word, so as not to trifle in them. And therefore we must beg of God that by his good Spirit he would order our steps accordingly. 2. For deliverance from the power of sin: " *Let no iniquity have dominion over me,* so as to gain my consent to it, and that I should be led captive by it." The dominion of sin is to be dreaded and deprecated by every one of us;

714

and, if in sincerity we pray against it, we may receive that promise as an answer to the prayer (Rom. vi. 14), *Sin shall not have dominion over you.*

134 Deliver me from the oppression of man: so will I keep thy precepts.

Here, 1. David prays that he might live a quiet and peaceable life, and might not be harassed and discomposed by those that studied to be vexatious: " *Deliver me from the oppression of man*—man, whom God can control, and whose power is limited. Let them know themselves to be *but men* (ix. 20), and let me be delivered *out of the hands of unreasonable men.*" 2. He promises that then he would live *in all godliness and honesty.* "Let me be delivered out of the hands of my enemies, that I may serve God without fear; *so will I keep thy precepts.*" Not but that he would keep God's precepts, though he should be continued under oppression; "but so shall I keep thy precepts more cheerfully and with more enlargement of heart, my bonds being loosed." *Then* we may expect temporal blessings when we desire them with this in our eye, that we may serve God the better.

135 Make thy face to shine upon thy servant; and teach me thy statutes.

David here, as often elsewhere, writes himself God's servant, a title he gloried in, though he was a king; now here, as became a good servant, 1. He is very ambitious of his Master's favour, accounting that his happiness and chief good. He asks not for corn and wine, for silver and gold, but, " *Make thy face to shine upon thy servant;* let me be accepted of thee, and let me know that I am so. Comfort me with the light of thy countenance in every cloudy and dark day. If the world frown upon me, yet do thou smile." 2. He is very solicitous about his Master's work, accounting that his business and chief concern. This he would be instructed in, that he might do it, and do it well, so as to be accepted in the doing of it: *Teach me thy statutes.* Note, We must pray as earnestly for grace as for comfort. If God hides his face from us, it is because we have been careless in keeping his statutes; and therefore, that we may be qualified for the returns of his favour, we must pray for wisdom to do our duty.

136 Rivers of waters run down mine eyes, because they keep not thy law.

Here we have David in sorrow. 1. It is a great sorrow, to such a degree that he weeps *rivers of tears.* Commonly, where there is a gracious heart, there is a weeping eye, in conformity to Christ, who was a man of sorrows and acquainted with grief. David had prayed for comfort in God's favour (v. 135) now he pleads that he was qualified for that comfort, and had need of it, for he was one of those that mourned in Zion, and those that do so shall be comforted, Isa. lxi. 3. 2. It is godly sorrow. He wept not for his troubles, though they were many, but for the dishonour done to God : *Because they keep not thy law,* either *because my eyes keep not thy law,* so some (the eye is the inlet and outlet of a great deal of sin, and therefore it ought to be a weeping eye), or, rather, *they,* that is, those about me, *v.* 139. Note, The sins of sinners are the sorrows of saints. We must mourn for that which we cannot mend.

18. TZADDI.

137 Righteous *art* thou, O Lord, and upright *are* thy judgments. 138 Thy testimonies *that* thou hast commanded *are* righteous and very faithful.

Here is, 1. The righteousness of God, the infinite rectitude and perfection of his nature. As he is what he is, so he is what he should be, and in every thing acts as becomes him; there is nothing wanting, nothing amiss, in God; his will is the eternal rule of equity, and he is righteous, for he does all according to it. 2. The righteousness of his government. He rules the world by his providence, according to the principles of justice, and never did, nor ever can do, any wrong to any of his creatures : *Upright are thy judgments,* the promises and threatenings and the executions of both. Every word of God is pure, and he will be true to it; he perfectly knows the merits of every cause and will judge accordingly. 3. The righteousness of his commands, which he has given to be the rule of our obedience: " *Thy testimonies that thou hast commanded,* which are backed with thy sovereign authority, and to which thou dost require our obedience, *are* exceedingly *righteous and faithful,* righteousness and faithfulness itself." As he acts like himself, so his law requires that we act like ourselves and like him, that we be just to ourselves and to all we deal with, true to all the engagements we lay ourselves under both to God and man. That which we are commanded to practise is righteous; that which we are commanded to believe is faithful. It is necessary to our faith and obedience that we be convinced of this.

139 My zeal hath consumed me, because mine enemies have forgotten thy words.

Here is, 1. The great contempt which wicked men put upon religion : *My enemies have forgotten thy words.* They have often heard them, but so little did they heed them that they soon forgot them, they willingly forgot them, not only through carelessness let them slip out of their minds, but contrived how to cast them behind their backs. This is at the bottom of all the wickedness of the wicked, and particularly of their malig-

nity and enmity to the people of God ; they have forgotten the words of God, else those would give check to their sinful courses. 2. The great concern which godly men show for religion. David reckoned those his enemies who forgot the words of God because they were enemies to religion, which he had entered into a league with, offensive and defensive. And therefore his *zeal* even *consumed him,* when he observed their impieties. He conceived such an indignation at their wickedness as preyed upon his spirits, even *ate them up* (as Christ's zeal, John ii. 17), swallowed up all inferior considerations, and made him forget himself. *My zeal has pressed or constrained me* (so Dr. Hammond reads it), Acts xviii. 5. Zeal against sin should constrain us to do what we can against it in our places, at least to do so much the more in religion ourselves. The worse others are the better we should be.

140 Thy word *is* very pure : therefore thy servant loveth it.

Here is, 1. David's great affection for the word of God : *Thy servant loves it.* Every good man, being a servant of God, loves the word of God, because it lets him know his Master's will and directs him in his Master's work. Wherever there is grace there is a warm attachment to the word of God. 2. The ground and reason of that affection; he saw it to be *very pure,* and therefore he loved it. Our love to the word of God is *then* an evidence of our love to God when we love it for the sake of its purity, because it bears the image of God's holiness and is designed to make us partakers of his holiness. It commands purity, and, as it is itself refined from all corrupt mixture, so if we receive it in the light and love of it it will refine us from the dross of worldliness and fleshly-mindedness.

141 I *am* small and despised : *yet* do not I forget thy precepts.

Here is, 1. David pious and yet poor. He was a man after God's own heart, one whom the King of kings did delight to honour, and yet *small and despised* in his own account and in the account of many others. Men's real excellency cannot always secure them from contempt; nay, it often exposes them to the scorn of others and always makes them low in their own eyes. *God has chosen the foolish things of the world,* and it has been the common lot of his people to be a despised people. 2. David poor and yet pious, *small and despised* for his strict and serious godliness, yet his conscience can witness for him that he did *not forget God's precepts.* He would not throw off his religion, though it exposed him to contempt, for he knew that was designed to try his constancy. When we are small and despised we have the more need to remember God's precepts, that we may have them to support us under the pressures of a low condition.

142 Thy righteousness *is* an everlasting righteousness, and thy law *is* the truth.

Observe, 1. That God's word *is righteousness,* and it *is an everlasting righteousness.* It is the rule of God's judgment, and it is consonant to his counsels from eternity and will direct his sentence for eternity. The word of God will judge us, it will judge us in righteousness, and by it our everlasting state will be determined. This should possess us with a very great reverence for the word of God that it is righteousness itself, the standard of righteousness, and it is everlasting in its rewards and punishments. 2. That God's word is a law, and that law is truth. See the double obligation we are under to be governed by the word of God. We are reasonable creatures, and as such we must be ruled by truth, acknowledging the force and power of it. If the principles be true, the practices must be agreeable to them, else we do not act rationally. We are creatures, and therefore subjects, and must be ruled by our Creator; and whatever he commands we are bound to obey as a law. See how these obligations are here twisted, these cords of a man. Here is truth brought to the understanding, there to sit chief, and direct the motions of the whole man; but, lest the authority of that should become weak through the flesh, here is a law to bind the will and bring that into subjection. God's truth is a law (John xviii. 37) *and God's law is the truth;* surely we cannot break such words as these asunder.

143 Trouble and anguish have taken hold on me: *yet* thy commandments *are* my delights. 144 The righteousness of thy testimonies *is* everlasting: give me understanding, and I shall live.

These two verses are almost a repetition of the two foregoing verses, but with improvement. 1. David again professes his constant adherence to God and his duty, notwithstanding the many difficulties and discouragements he met with. He had said (*v.* 141), *I am small and despised,* and yet adhere to my duty. Here he finds himself not only mean, but miserable, as far as this world could make him so: *Trouble and anguish have taken hold on me*—trouble without, anguish within; they surprised him, they seized him, they held him. Sorrows are often the lot of saints in this vale of tears; they are *in heaviness through manifold temptations.* There he had said, *Yet do I not forget thy precepts;* here he carries his constancy much higher: *Yet thy commandments are my delights.* All this trouble and anguish did not put his mouth out of taste for the comforts of the word of God, but he could still relish them and find that peace and pleasure in them which all the calamities of this present time could not de-

716

prive him of. There are delights, variety of delights, in the word of God, which the saints have often the sweetest enjoyment of when they are in trouble and anguish, 2 Cor. i. 5. 2. He again acknowledges the everlasting righteousness of God's word as before (*v.* 142): *The righteousness of thy testimonies is everlasting* and cannot be altered; and, when it is admitted in its power into a soul, it is there an abiding principle, *a well of living water,* John iv. 14. We ought to meditate much and often upon the equity and the eternity of the word of God. Here he adds, by way of inference, (1.) His prayer for grace: *Give me understanding.* Those that know much of the word of God should still covet to know more; for there is more to be known. He does not say, "Give me a further revelation," but, *Give me a further understanding;* what is revealed we should desire to understand, and what we know to know better; and we must go to God for a heart to know. (2.) His hope of glory: "Give me this renewed understanding, and then *I shall live,* shall live for ever, shall be eternally happy, and shall be comforted, for the present, in the prospect of it." *This is life eternal, to know God,* John xvii. 3.

19. KOPH.

145 I cried with *my* whole heart; hear me, O LORD: I will keep thy statutes. 146 I cried unto thee; save me, and I shall keep thy testimonies.

Here we have, I. David's good prayers, by which he sought to God for mercy; these he mentions here, not as boasting of them, or trusting to any merit in them, but reflecting upon them with comfort, that he had taken the appointed way to comfort. Observe here, 1. That he was inward with God in prayer; he prayed *with his heart,* and prayer is acceptable no further than the heart goes along with it. Lip-labour, if that be all, is lost labour. 2. He was importunate with God in prayer; he *cried,* as one in earnest, with fervour of affection and a holy vehemence and vigour of desire. He *cried with his whole heart;* all the powers of his soul were not only engaged and employed, but exerted to the utmost, in his prayers. *Then* we are likely to speed when we thus strive and wrestle in prayer. 3. That he directed his prayer to God: *I cried unto thee.* Whither should the child go but to his father when any thing ails him? 4. That the great thing he prayed for was salvation: *Save me.* A short prayer (for we mistake if we think we shall be heard for our much speaking), but a comprehensive prayer: "Not only rescue me from ruin, but make me happy." We need desire no more than God's salvation (l. 23) and the *things that accompany* it, Heb. vi. 9. 5. That he was earnest for an answer; and not only looked up in his prayers, but looked up after them, to see what became of them

(Ps. v. 3): "Lord, *hear me,* and let me know that thou hearest me."

II. David's good purposes, by which he bound himself to duty when he was in the pursuit of mercy. "*I will keep thy statutes;* I am resolved that by thy grace I will;" for, *if we turn away our ear from hearing the law,* we cannot expect an answer of peace to our prayers, Prov. xxviii. 9. This purpose is used as a humble plea (v. 146): "*Save me from my sins, my corruptions, my temptations,* all the hindrances that lie in my way, that I may *keep thy testimonies.*" We must cry for salvation, not that we may have the ease and comfort of it, but that we may have an opportunity of serving God the more cheerfully.

147 I prevented the dawning of the morning, and cried: I hoped in thy word. 148 Mine eyes prevent the *night* watches, that I might meditate in thy word.

David goes on here to relate how he had abounded in the duty of prayer, much to his comfort and advantage: he cried unto God, that is, offered up to him his pious and devout affections with all seriousness. Observe,

I. The handmaids of his devotion. The two great exercises that attended his prayers, and were helpful to them, were, 1. Hope in God's word, which encouraged him to continue instant in prayer, though the answer did not come immediately: "I cried, and hoped that at last I should speed, because *the vision is for an appointed time, and at the end it will speak and not lie. I hoped in thy word,* which I knew would not fail me." 2. Meditation in God's word. The more intimately we converse with the word of God, and the more we dwell upon it in our thoughts, the better able we shall be to speak to God in his own language and the better we shall know what to pray for as we ought. Reading the word will not serve, but we must meditate in it.

II. The hours of his devotion. *He anticipated the dawning of the morning,* nay, and *the night-watches.* See here, 1. That David was an early riser, which perhaps contributed to his eminency. He was none of those that say, *Yet a little sleep.* 2. That he began the day with God. The first thing he did in the morning, before he admitted any business, was to pray, when his mind was most fresh and in the best frame. If our first thoughts in the morning be of God they will help to keep us in his fear all the day long. 3. That his mind was so full of God, and the cares and delights of his religion, that a little sleep served his turn. Even in *the night-watches,* when he awaked from his first sleep, he would rather meditate and pray than turn himself and go to sleep again. He *esteemed the words of God's mouth more than his necessary* repose, which we can as ill spare as our *food,* Job

xxiii. 12. 4. That he would redeem time for religious exercises. He was full of business all day, but that will excuse no man from secret devotion; it is better to take time from sleep, as David did, than not to find time for prayer. And this is our comfort, when we pray in the night, that we can never come unseasonably to the throne of grace; for we may have access to it at all hours. Baal may be asleep, but Israel's God never slumbers, nor are there any hours in which he may not be spoken with.

149 Hear my voice according unto thy lovingkindness: O LORD, quicken me according to thy judgment.

Here, 1. David applies to God for grace and comfort with much solemnity. He begs of God to hear his voice: "Lord, I have something to say to thee; shall I obtain a gracious audience?" Well, what has he to say? What is his petition and what is his request? It is not long, but it has much in a little: "*Lord, quicken me;* stir me up to that which is good, and make me vigorous, and lively, and cheerful in it. Let habits of grace be drawn out into act." 2. He encourages himself to hope that he shall obtain his request; for he depends, (1.) Upon God's lovingkindness: "He is good, therefore he will be good to me, who hope in his mercy. His lovingkindness manifested to me will help to quicken me, and put life into me." (2.) Upon God's *judgment,* that is, his wisdom ("He knows what I need, and what is good for me, and therefore will quicken me"), or his promise, the word which he has spoken, mercy secured by the new covenant: *Quicken me according to* the tenour of that covenant.

150 They draw nigh that follow after mischief: they are far from thy law. 151 Thou *art* near, O LORD; and all thy commandments *are* truth.

Here is, I. The apprehension David was in of danger from his enemies. 1. They were very malicious, and industrious in prosecuting their malicious designs: They *follow after mischief,* any mischief they could do to David or his friends; they would let slip no opportunity nor let fall any pursuit that might be to his hurt. 2. They were very impious, and had no fear of God before their eyes: *They are far from thy law,* setting themselves as far as they can out of the reach of its convictions and commands. The persecutors o God's people are such as make light of God himself; we may therefore be sure that God will take his people's part against them. 3. They followed him closely and he was just ready to fall into their hands: *They draw nigh,* nigher than they were; so that they got ground of him. They were at his heels, just upon his back. God sometimes suffers persecutors to prevail very far against his people, so that, as David said (1 Sam. xx. 3), *There is but a step between them and death*

Perhaps this comes in here as a reason why David was so earnest in prayer, *v.* 149. God brings us into imminent perils, as he did Jacob, that, like him, we may wrestle for a blessing.

II. The assurance David had of protection with God : " *They draw nigh* to destroy me, but *thou art near, O Lord !* to save me, not only mightier than they and therefore able to help me against them, but nearer than they and therefore ready to help." It is the happiness of the saints that, when trouble is near, God is near, and no trouble can separate between them and him. He is never far to seek, but he is within our call, and means are within his call, Deut. iv. 7. *All thy commandments are truth.* The enemies thought to defeat the promises God had made to David, but he was sure it was out of their power ; they were inviolably true, and would be infallibly performed.

152 Concerning thy testimonies, I have known of old that thou hast founded them for ever.

This confirms what he had said in the close of the foregoing verses, *All thy commandments are truth ;* he means the covenant, the word which God has commanded to a thousand generations. This is firm, as true as truth itself. For, 1. God has founded it so ; he has framed it for a perpetuity. Such is the constitution of it, and so well ordered is it in all things, that it cannot but be sure. The promises are *founded for ever,* so that when heaven and earth shall have passed away every iota and tittle of the promise shall stand firm, 2 Cor. i. 20. 2. David had found it so, both by a work of God's grace upon his heart (begetting in him a full persuasion of the truth of God's word and enabling him to rely upon it with a full satisfaction) and by the works of his providence on his behalf, fulfilling the promise beyond what he expected. Thus he *knew of old,* from the days of his youth, ever since he began to look towards God, that the word of God is what one may venture one's all upon. This assurance was confirmed by the observations and experiences of his own life all along, and of others that had gone before him in the ways of God. All that ever dealt with God, and trusted in him will own that they have found him faithful.

20. RESH.

153 Consider mine affliction, and deliver me : for I do not forget thy law. 154 Plead my cause, and deliver me : quicken me according to thy word.

Here, I. David prays for succour in distress. *Is any afflicted ? let him pray ;* let him pray as David does here. 1. He has an eye to God's pity, and prays, " *Consider my affliction ;* take it into thy thoughts, and all the circumstances of it, and sit not by as one unconcerned." God is never unmindful of his

718

people's afflictions, but he will have us to *put him in remembrance* (Isa. xliii. 26), to spread our case before him, and then leave it to his compassionate consideration to do in it as in his wisdom he shall think fit, in his own time and way. 2. He has an eye to God's power and prays, *Deliver me ;* and again, " *Deliver me ;* consider my troubles and bring me out of them." God has promised deliverance (l. 15) and we may pray for it, with submission to his will and with regard to his glory, that we may serve him the better. 3. He has an eye to God's righteousness, and prays, " *Plead my cause ;* be thou my patron and advocate, and take me for thy client." David had a just cause, but his adversaries were many and mighty, and he was in danger of being run down by them ; he therefore begs of God to clear his integrity and silence their false accusations. If God do not plead his people's cause, who will ? He is righteous, and they commit themselves to him, and therefore he will do it, and do it effectually, Isa. li. 22 ; Jer. l. 34. (4.) He has an eye to God's grace, and prays, " *Quicken me.* Lord, I am weak, and unable to bear my troubles ; my spirit is apt to droop and sink. O that thou wouldst revive and comfort me, till the deliverance is wrought !"

II. He pleads his dependence upon the word of God and his obedient regard to its directions : *Quicken* and *deliver me according to thy word* of promise, *for I do not forget thy precepts.* The more closely we cleave to the word of God, both as our rule and as our stay, the more assurance we may have of deliverance in due time.

155 Salvation *is* far from the wicked : for they seek not thy statutes.

Here is, 1. The description of wicked men. They do not only not do God's statutes, but they do not so much as seek them ; they do not acquaint themselves with them, nor so much as desire to know their duty, nor in the least endeavour to do it. Those are wicked indeed who do not think the law of God worth enquiring after, but are altogether regardless of it, being resolved to live at large and to walk in the way of their heart. 2. Their doom : *Salvation is far from* them. They cannot upon any good grounds promise themselves temporal deliverance. *Let not that man think that he shall receive any thing of the Lord.* How can those expect to seek God's favour with success, when they are in adversity, who never sought his statutes when they were in prosperity ? But eternal salvation is certainly far from them. They flatter themselves with a conceit that it is near, and that they are going to heaven ; but they are mistaken : it is far from them. They thrust it from them by thrusting the Saviour from them ; it is so far from them that they cannot reach it, and the longer they persist in sin the further it is : nay, while salvation is far from them, damnation is near; it slumbers not. *Behold, the Judge stands before the door.*

156 Great *are* thy tender mercies, O Lord: quicken me according to thy judgments.

Here, 1. David admires God's grace: *Great are thy tender mercies, O Lord!* The goodness of God's nature, as it is his glory, so it is the joy of all the saints. His mercies are tender, for he is full of compassion; they are many, they are great, a fountain that can never be exhausted. He is rich in mercy to all that call upon him. David had spoken of the misery of the wicked (*v.* 155); but God is good notwithstanding; there were tender mercies sufficient in God to have saved them, if they had not *despised the riches of those mercies.*" Those that are delivered from the sinner's doom are bound for ever to own the greatness of God's mercies which delivered them. 2. He begs for God's grace, reviving quickening grace, *according to his judgments,* that is, according to the tenour of the new covenant (that established rule by which he goes in dispensing that grace) or according to his manner, his custom or usage, with those that love his name, *v.* 132.

157 Many *are* my persecutors and mine enemies; *yet* do I not decline from thy testimonies.

Here is, 1. David surrounded with difficulties and dangers: *Many are my persecutors and my enemies.* When Saul the king was his persecutor and enemy no marvel that many more were so: multitudes will follow the pernicious ways of abused authority. David, being a public person, had many enemies, but withal he had many friends, who loved him and wished him well; let him set the one over-against the other. In this David was a type both of Christ and his church. The enemies, the persecutors, of both, are many, very many. 2. David established in the way of his duty, notwithstanding: "*Yet do I not decline from thy testimonies,* as knowing that while I adhere to them God is for me; and then no matter who is against me." A man who is steady in the way of his duty, though he may have many enemies, needs fear none

158 I beheld the transgressors, and was grieved; because they kept not thy word.

Here is, 1. David's sorrow for the wickedness of the wicked. Though he conversed much at home, yet sometimes he looked abroad, and could not but see the wicked walking on every side. He *beheld the transgressors,* those whose sins were open before all men, and it *grieved* him to see them dishonour God, serve Satan, debauch the world, and ruin their own souls, to see the transgressors so numerous, so daring, so very impudent, and so industrious to draw unstable souls into their snares. All this cannot but be a grief to those who have any regard to the glory of God and the welfare of mankind. 2. The reason of that sorrow. He was grieved, not because they were vexatious to him, but because they were provoking to God: *They kept not thy word.* Those that hate sin truly hate it as sin, as a transgression of the law of God and a violation of his word.

159 Consider how I love thy precepts: quicken me, O Lord, according to thy lovingkindness.

Here is, 1. David's appeal to God concerning his love to his precepts: "Lord, thou knowest all things, thou knowest that I love them; consider it then, and deal with me as thou usest to deal with those that love thy word, which thou hast magnified above all thy name." He does not say, "Consider how I fulfil thy precepts;" he was conscious to himself that in many things he came short; but, "Consider how I love them." Our obedience is pleasing to God, and pleasant to ourselves, only when it comes from a principle of love. 2. His petition thereupon: "*Quicken me,* to do my duty with vigour; revive me, keep me alive, not according to any merit of mine, though I love thy word, *but according to thy lovingkindness;*" to that we owe our lives, nay, that is better than life itself. We need not desire to be quickened any further than God's lovingkindness will quicken us.

160 Thy word *is* true *from* the beginning: and every one of thy righteous judgments *endureth* for ever.

David here comforts himself with the faithfulness of God's word, for the encouragement of himself and others to rely upon it. 1. It has always been found faithful hitherto, and never failed any that ventured upon it: *It is true from the beginning.* Ever since God began to reveal himself to the children of men all he said was true and to be trusted. The church, from its beginning, was built upon this rock. It has not gained its validity by lapse of time, as many governments, whose best plea is prescription and long usage. *Quod initio non valet, tractu temporis convalescit—That which, at first, wanted validity, in the progress of time acquired it.* But the *beginning of God's word was true* (so some read it); his government was laid on a sure foundation. And all, in every age, that have received God's word in faith and love, have found every saying in it *faithful and well worthy of all acceptation.* 2. It will be found faithful to the end, because righteous: "*Every one of thy judgments remains for ever* unalterable and of perpetual obligation, adjusting men's everlasting doom."

21. SCHIN.

161 Princes have persecuted me without a cause: but my heart standeth in awe of thy word.

David here lets us know, 1. How he was discouraged in his duty by the fear of man: *Princes persecuted him.* They looked upon him as a traitor and an enemy to the government, and under that notion sought his life, and bade him *go serve other gods*, 1 Sam. xxvi. 19. It has been the common lot of the best men to be persecuted; and the case is the worse if princes be the persecutors, for they have not only the sword in their hand, and therefore can do the more hurt, but they have the law on their side, and can do it with reputation and a colour of justice. It is sad that the power which magistrates have from God, and should use for him, should ever be employed against him. But *marvel not at the matter*, Eccl. v. 8. It was a comfort to David that when princes persecuted him he could truly say it was without cause, he never gave them any provocation. 2. How he was kept to his duty, notwithstanding, by the fear of God: "They would make me stand in awe of them and their word, and do as they bid me; but *my heart stands in awe of thy word*, and I am resolved to please God, and keep in with him, whoever is displeased and falls out with me." Every gracious soul stands in awe of the word of God, of the authority of its precepts and the terror of its threatenings; and to those that do so nothing appears, in the power and wrath of man, at all formidable. We ought to obey God rather than men, and to make sure of God's favour, though we throw ourselves under the frowns of all the world, Luke xii. 4, 5. The heart that stands in awe of God's word is armed against the temptations that arise from persecution.

162 I rejoice at thy word, as one that findeth great spoil.

Here is, 1. The pleasure David took in the word of God. He rejoiced at it, rejoiced that God had made such a discovery of his mind, that Israel was blessed with that light when other nations sat in darkness, that he was himself let into the understanding of it and had had experience of the power of it. He took a pleasure in reading it, hearing it, and meditating on it, and every thing he met with in it was agreeable to him. He had just now said that his heart stood in awe of his word, and yet here he declares that he rejoiced in it. The more reverence we have for the word of God the more joy we shall find in it. 2. The degree of that pleasure— *as one that finds great spoil.* This supposes a victory over the enemy. It is through much opposition that a soul comes to this, to *rejoice in God's word.* But, besides the pleasure and honour of a conquest, there is great advantage gained by the plunder of the field, which adds much to the joy. By the word of God we become more than conquerors, that is, unspeakable gainers.

163 I hate and abhor lying: *but* thy law do I love.

Love and hatred are the leading affections of the soul; if those be fixed aright, the rest move accordingly. Here we have them fixed aright in David. 1. He had a rooted antipathy to sin; he could not endure to think of it: *I hate and abhor lying*, which may be taken for all sin, inasmuch as by it we deal treacherously and perfidiously with God and put a cheat upon ourselves. Hypocrisy is lying; false doctrine is lying; breach of faith is lying. Lying, in commerce or conversation, is a sin which every good man hates and abhors, hates and doubly hates, because of the seven things which the Lord hates *one* is a *lying tongue* and *another* is a *false witness that speaks lies*, Prov. vi. 16. Every man hates to have a lie told him; but we should more hate telling a lie because by the former we only receive an affront from men, by the latter we give an affront to God. 2. He had a rooted affection to the word of God: *Thy law do I love.* And therefore he abhorred lying, for lying is contrary to the whole law of God; and the reason why he loved the law of God was because of the truth of it. The more we see of the amiable beauty of truth the more we shall see of the detestable deformity of a lie.

164 Seven times a day do I praise thee because of thy righteous judgments.

David, in this psalm, is full of complaints, yet those did neither jostle out his praises nor put him out of tune for them; whatever condition a child of God is in he does not want matter for praise and therefore should not want a heart. See here, 1. How often David praised God—*seven times a day*, that is, very frequently, not only every day, but often every day. Many think that once a week will serve, or once or twice a day, but David would praise God seven times a day at least. Praising God is a duty which we should very much abound in. We must praise God at every meal, praise him upon all occasions, in every thing give thanks. We should praise God seven times a day, for the subject can never be exhausted and our affections should never be tired. See *v.* 62. 2. What he praised God for—*because of thy righteous judgments.* We must praise God for his precepts, which are all just and good, for his promises and threatenings and the performance of both in his providence. We are to praise God even for our afflictions, if through grace we get good by them.

165 Great peace have they which love thy law: and nothing shall offend them.

Here is an account of the happiness of good men, who are governed by a principle of love to the word of God, who make it their rule and are ruled by it. 1. They are easy, and have a holy serenity none enjoy themselves more than they do· *Great peace have* those that love thy law, abundant satisfaction in doing their duty and pleasure in reflecting upon it. *The work of righteousness is peace* (Isa. xxxii. 17), such peace as the world can neither give nor take away. They may be in great troubles without and yet enjoy great peace within, *sat lucis intus—abundance of internal light.* Those that love the world have great vexation, for it does not answer their expectation; those that love God's word have great peace, for it outdoes their expectation, and in it they have sure footing. 2. They are safe, and have a holy security: *Nothing shall offend them*; nothing shall be a scandal, snare, or stumbling-block, to them, to entangle them either in guilt or grief. No event of providence shall be either an invincible temptation or an intolerable affliction to them, but their love to the word of God shall enable them both to hold fast their integrity and to preserve their tranquillity. They will make the best of that which is, and not quarrel with any thing that God does. Nothing shall offend or hurt them, for every thing shall work for good to them, and therefore shall please them, and they shall reconcile themselves to it. Those in whom this holy love reigns will not be apt to perplex themselves with needless scruples, nor to take offence at their brethren, 1 Cor. xiii. 6, 7.

166 Lord, I have hoped for thy salvation, and done thy commandments.

Here is the whole duty of man; for we are taught, 1. To keep our eye upon God's favour as our end : " *Lord, I have hoped for thy salvation,* not only temporal but eternal salvation. I have hoped for that as my happiness and laid up my treasure in it; I have hoped for it as thine, as a happiness of thy preparing, thy promising, and which consists in being with thee. Hope of this has raised me above the world, and borne me up under all my burdens in it." 2. To keep our eye upon God's word as our rule : *I have done thy commandments,* that is, I have made conscience of conforming myself to thy will in every thing. Observe here how God has joined these two together, and let no man put them asunder. We cannot, upon good grounds, hope for God's salvation, unless we set ourselves to do his commandments, Rev. xxii. 14. But those that sincerely endeavour to do his commandments ought to keep up a good hope of the salvation; and that hope will both engage and enlarge the heart in doing the commandments. The more lively the hope is the more lively the obedience will be.

167 My soul hath kept thy testimonies; and I love them exceedingly. 168 I have kept thy precepts and thy testimonies : for all my ways *are* before thee.

David's conscience here witnesses for him, I. That his practices were good. 1. He loved God's testimonies, he loved them exceedingly. Our love to the word of God must be a superlative love (we must love it better than the wealth and pleasure of this world), and it must be a victorious love, such as will subdue and mortify our lusts and extirpate carnal affections. 2. He kept them, his soul kept them. Bodily exercise profits little in religion ; we must make heart-work of it or we make nothing of it. The soul must be sanctified and renewed, and delivered into the mould of the word ; the soul must be employed in glorifying God, for he will be worshipped in the spirit. We must keep both the precepts and the testimonies, the commands of God by our obedience to them and his promises by our reliance on them. II. That he was governed herein by a good principle: " *Therefore* I have kept thy precepts, because by faith I have seen thy eye always upon me ; *all my ways are before thee;* thou knowest every step I take and strictly observest all I say and do. Thou dost see and accept all that I say and do well; thou dost see and art displeased with all I say and do amiss." Note, The consideration of this, that God's eye is upon us at all times, should make us very careful in every thing to keep his commandments, Gen. xvii. 1.

22. TAU.

169 Let my cry come near before thee, O Lord : give me understanding according to thy word. 170 Let my supplication come before thee : deliver me according to thy word.

Here we have, I. A general petition for audience repeated : *Let my cry come near before thee;* and again, *Let my supplication come before thee.* He calls his prayer his *cry,* which denotes the fervency and vehemence of it, and his *supplication,* which denotes the humility of it. We must come to God as beggars come to our doors for an alms. He is concerned that his prayer might come before God, might come near before him, that is, that he might have grace and strength by faith and fervency to lift up his prayers, that no guilt might interpose to shut out his prayers and to separate between him and God, and that God would graciously receive his prayers and take notice of them. His prayer that his supplication might come before God implies a deep sense of his unworthiness, and a holy fear that his prayer should come short or miscarry, as not fit to come before God; nor would any of our prayers have had access to God if Jesus Christ had not approached to him as an advocate for us. II. Two particular requests, which he is thus earnest to present :—1. That God, by his grace, would give him wisdom to conduct himself well under his troubles : *Give me understanding;* he means that wisdom of the prudent which is to understand his way; "Give me to know thee and myself, and my duty to thee." 2. That God, by his providence, would rescue him out of his troubles: *Deliver me*, that is, with the temptation make a way to escape, 1 Cor. x. 13.

III. The same general plea to enforce these requests—*according to thy word*. This directs and limits his desires: "Lord, give me such an understanding as thou hast promised and such a deliverance as thou hast promised; I ask for no other. It also encourages his faith and expectation: "Lord, that which I pray for is what thou hast promised, and wilt not thou be as good as thy word?"

171 My lips shall utter praise, when thou hast taught me thy statutes.

Here is, 1. A great favour which David expects from God, that he will teach him his *statutes*. This he had often prayed for in this psalm, and urged his petition for it with various arguments; and now that he is drawing towards the close of the psalm he speaks of it as taken for granted. Those that are humbly earnest with God for his grace, and resolve with Jacob that they will not let him go unless he bless them with spiritual blessings, may be humbly confident that they shall at length obtain what they are so importunate for. The God of Israel will grant them those things which they request of him. 2. The grateful sense he promises to have of that favour: *My lips shall utter praise when thou hast taught me*. (1.) Then he shall have cause to praise God. Those that are taught of God have a great deal of reason to be thankful, for this is the foundation of all these spiritual blessings, which are the best blessings, and the earnest of eternal blessings. (2.) Then he shall know how to praise God, and have a heart to do it. All that are taught of God are taught this lesson; when God opens the understanding, opens the heart, and so opens the lips, it is that the mouth may show forth his praise. We have learned nothing to purpose if we have not learned to praise God. (3.) *Therefore* he is thus importunate for divine instructions, that he might praise God. Those that pray for God's grace must aim at God's glory, Eph. i. 12.

172 My tongue shall speak of thy word: for all thy commandments *are* righteousness.

Observe here, 1. The good knowledge David had of the word of God; he knew it so well that he was ready to own, with the utmost satisfaction, that all God's commandments are not only righteous, but righteousness itself, the rule and standard of righteousness. 2. The good use he resolved to make of that knowledge: *My tongue shall speak of thy word*, not only utter praise for it to the glory of God, but discourse of it for the instruction and edification of others, as that

722

which he was himself full of (for out of the abundance of the heart the mouth will speak) and as that which he desired others also might be filled with. The more we see of the righteousness of God's commandments the more industrious we should be to bring others acquainted with them, that they may be ruled by them. We should always make the word of God the governor of our discourse, so as never to transgress it by sinful speaking or sinful silence; and we should often make it the subject-matter of our discourse, that it may feed many and *minister grace to the hearers*.

173 Let thine hand help me; for I have chosen thy precepts. 174 I have longed for thy salvation, O LORD; and thy law *is* my delight.

Here, 1. David prays that divine grace would work for him: *Let thy hand help me*. He finds his own hands are not sufficient for him, nor can any creature lend him a helping hand to any purpose; therefore he looks up to God in hopes that the hand that had made him would help him; for, if the Lord do not help us, whence can any creature help us? All our help must be expected from God's hand, from his power and his bounty. 2. He pleads what divine grace had already wrought in him as a pledge of further mercy, being a qualification for it. Three things he pleads:—(1.) That he had made religion his serious and deliberate choice: "*I have chosen thy precepts.* I took them for my rule, not because I knew no other, but because, upon trial, I knew no better." Those are good, and do good indeed, who are good and do good, not by chance, but from choice; and those who have thus chosen God's precepts may depend upon God's helping hand in all their services and under all their sufferings. (2.) That his heart was upon heaven: *I have longed for thy salvation*. David, when he had got to the throne, met with enough in the world to court his stay, and to make him say, "It is good to be here;" but still he was looking further, and longing for something better in another world. There is an eternal salvation which all the saints are longing for, and therefore pray that God's hand would help them forward in their way to it. (3.) That he took pleasure in doing his duty: "*Thy law is my delight.* Not only I delight in it, but it is my delight, the greatest delight I have in this world." Those that are cheerful in their obedience may in faith beg help of God to carry them on in their obedience; and those that expect God's salvation must take delight in his law and their hopes must increase their delight.

175 Let my soul live, and it shall praise thee; and let thy judgments help me.

David's heart is still upon praising God; and therefore, 1. He prays that God would give him time to praise him : *" Let my soul live, and it shall praise thee,* that is, let my life be prolonged, that I may live to thy glory." The reason why a good man desires to live is that he may praise God in the land of the living, and do something to his honour. Not, " Let me live and serve my country, live and provide for my family;" but, " Let me live that, in doing this, I may praise God here in this world of conflict and opposition." When we die we hope to go to a better world to praise him, and that is more agreeable for us, though here there is more need of us. And therefore one would not desire to live any longer than we may do God some service here. *Let my soul live,* that is, let me be sanctified and comforted, for sanctification and comfort are the life of the soul, *and* then *it shall praise thee.* Our souls must be employed in praising God, and we must pray for grace and peace that we may be fitted to praise God. 2. He prays that God would give him strength to praise him : *" Let thy judgments help me;* let all ordinances and all providences" (both are God's judgments) "further me in glorifying God; let them be the matter of my praise and let them help to fit me for that work."

176 I have gone astray like a lost sheep; seek thy servant; for I do not forget thy commandments.

Here is, 1. A penitent confession : *I have gone astray,* or wander up and down, *like a lost sheep.* As unconverted sinners are like lost sheep (Luke xv. 4), so weak unsteady saints are like lost sheep, Matt. xviii. 12, 13. We are apt to wander like the sheep, and very unapt, when we have gone astray, to find the way again. By going astray we lose the comfort of the green pastures and expose ourselves to a thousand mischiefs. 2. A believing petition : *Seek thy servant,* as the good shepherd seeks a wandering sheep to bring it back again, Ezek. xxxiv. 12. "Lord, seek me, as I used to seek my sheep when they went astray;" for David had been himself a tender shepherd. " Lord, own me for one of thine; for, though I am a stray sheep, I have thy mark; concern thyself for me, send after me by the word, and conscience, and providences; bring me back by thy grace." *Seek me,* that is, *find me;* for God never seeks in vain. *Turn me, and I shall be turned.* 3. An obedient plea : " Though I have gone astray, yet I have not wickedly departed, *I do not forget thy commandments.*" Thus he concludes the psalm with a penitent sense of his own sin and a believing dependence on God's grace. With these a devout Christian will conclude his duties, will conclude his life; he will live and die repenting and praying. Observe here, (1.) It is the character of good people that they do not *forget God's commandments,* being well pleased with their convictions and well settled in their resolutions. (2.) Even those who, through grace, are mindful of their duty, cannot but own that they

have in many instances wandered from it (3.) Those that have wandered from their duty, if they continue mindful of it, may with a humble confidence commit themselves to the care of God's grace.

PSALM CXX.

This psalm is the first of those fifteen which are here put together under the title of " songs of degrees." It is well that it is not material what the meaning of that title should be, for nothing is offered towards the explication of it, no, not by the Jewish writers themselves, but what is conjectural. These psalms do not seem to be composed all by the same hand, much less all at the same time. Four of them are expressly ascribed to David, and one is said to be designed for Solomon, and perhaps penned by him; yet cxxvi. and cxxix. seem to be of a much later date. Some of them are calculated for the closet (as cxx. cxxx.), some for the family (as cxxvii. cxxviii.), some for the public assembly (as cxxii. cxxxiv.), and some occasional, as cxxiv. cxxxii. So that, it should seem, they had not this title from the author, but from the publisher. Some conjecture that they are so called from their singular excellency (as the song of songs, so the song of degrees, is a most excellent song, in the highest degree), others from the tune they were set to, or the musical instruments they were sung to, or the raising of the voice in singing them. Some think they were sung on the fifteen steps or stairs, by which they went up from the outward court of the temple to the inner, others at so many stages of the people's journey, when they returned out of captivity. I shall only observe, 1. That they are all short psalms, all but one very short (three of them have but three verses apiece), and that they are placed next to Ps. cxix., which is by much the longest of all. Now as that was one psalm divided into many parts, so these were many psalms, which, being short, were sometimes sung all together, and made, as it were, one psalm, observing only a pause between each; as many steps make one pair of stairs. 2. That, in the composition of them, we frequently meet with the figure they call climax, or an ascent, the preceding word repeated, and then rising to something further, as cxx., " With him that hated peace. I peace." cxxi., " Whence cometh my help; my help cometh." " He that keepeth thee shall not slumber; he that keepeth Israel." cxxii., " Within thy gates, O Jerusalem. Jerusalem is builded." cxxiii., " Until that he have mercy upon us. Have mercy upon us." And the like in most of them, if not all. Perhaps for one of these reasons they are called songs of degrees.

This psalm is supposed to have been penned by David upon occasion of Doeg's accusing him and the priests to Saul, because it is like lii., which was penned on that occasion, and because the psalmist complains of his being driven out of the congregation of the Lord and his being forced among barbarous people. I. He prays to God to deliver him from the mischief designed him by false and malicious tongues, ver. 1, 2. II. He threatens the judgments of God against such, ver. 3, 4. III. He complains of his wicked neighbours that were quarrelsome and vexatious, ver. 5—7. In singing this psalm we may comfort ourselves in reference to the scourge of the tongue, when at any time we fall unjustly under the lash of it, that better than we have smarted from it.

A song of degrees.

IN my distress I cried unto the LORD, and he heard me. 2 Deliver my soul, O LORD, from lying lips, *and* from a deceitful tongue. 3 What shall be given unto thee ? or what shall be done unto thee, thou false tongue ? 4 Sharp arrows of the mighty, with coals of juniper.

Here is, I. Deliverance from a false tongue obtained by prayer. David records his own experience of this.

1. He was brought into distress, into great distress, by *lying lips and a deceitful tongue.* There were those that sought his ruin, and had almost effected it, by lying. (1.) By telling lies to him. They flattered him with professions and protestations of friendship, and promises of kindness and service to him, that they might the more securely and without suspicion carry on their designs against him, and might have an opportunity, by betraying his counsels, to do him a mischief. They smiled in his face and kissed him, even when they were aiming to smite him under the fifth rib. The most dangerous enemies, and those

723

which it is most hard to guard against, are such as carry on their malicious designs under the colour of friendship. The Lord deliver every good man from such lying lips. (2) By telling lies of him. They forged false accusations against him and *laid to his charge things that he knew not.* This has often been the lot not only of the innocent, but of the excellent ones, of the earth, who have been greatly distressed by lying lips, and have not only had their names blackened and made odious by calumnies in conversation, but their lives, and all that is dear to them in this world, endangered by false-witness-bearing in judgment. David was herein a type of Christ, who was distressed by lying lips and deceitful tongues.

2. In this distress he had recourse to God by faithful and fervent prayer : *I cried unto the Lord.* Having no fence against false tongues, he appealed to him who has all men's hearts in his hand, who has power over the consciences of bad men, and can, when he pleases, bridle their tongues. His prayer was, "*Deliver my soul, O Lord! from lying lips,* that my enemies may not by these cursed methods work my ruin." He that had prayed so earnestly to be kept from lying (cxix. 29) and hated it, so heartily in himself (*v.* 163) might with the more confidence pray to be kept from being belied by others, and from the ill consequences of it.

3. He obtained a gracious answer to this prayer. God heard him; so that his enemies, though they carried their designs very far, were baffled at last, and could not prevail to do him the mischief they intended. The God of truth is, and will be, the protector of his people from lying lips, xxxvii. 6.

II. The doom of a false tongue foretold by faith, *v.* 3, 4. As God will preserve his people from this mischievous generation, so he will reckon with their enemies, xii. 3, 7. The threatening is addressed to the sinner himself, for the awakening of his conscience, if he have any left : " Consider *what shall be given unto thee, and what shall be done unto thee,* by the righteous Judge of heaven and earth, *thou false tongue.*" Surely sinners durst not do as they do if they knew, and would be persuaded to think, what will be in the end thereof. Let liars consider what shall be given to them : *Sharp arrows of the Almighty, with coals of juniper,* that is, they will fall and lie for ever under the wrath of God, and will be made miserable by the tokens of his displeasure, which will fly swiftly like arrows, and will strike the sinner ere he is aware and when he sees not who hurts him. This is threatened against liars, lxiv. 7. *God shall shoot at them with an arrow ; suddenly shall they be wounded.* They set God at a distance from them, but from afar his arrows can reach them. They are sharp arrows, and arrows of the mighty, the Almighty; for they will pierce through the strongest armour and strike deep into the hardest heart. The terrors of the

Lord are his arrows (Job vi. 4), and his wrath is compared to burning coals of juniper, which do not flame or crackle, like thorns under a pot, but have a vehement heat, and keep fire very long (some say, a year round) even when they seem to be gone out. This is the portion of the false tongue ; for all that love and make a lie shall have their portion in the lake that burns eternally, Rev. xxii. 15.

5 Woe is me, that I sojourn in Mesech, *that* I dwell in the tents of Kedar ! 6 My soul hath long dwelt with him that hateth peace. 7 I *am for* peace : but when I speak, they *are* for war.

The psalmist here complains of the bad neighbourhood into which he was driven ; and some apply the two foregoing verses to this : " What shall the deceitful tongue give, what shall it do to those that lie open to it ? What shall a man get by living among such malicious deceitful men ? Nothing but *sharp arrows* and *coals of juniper,*" all the mischiefs of a false and spiteful tongue, lvii. 4. *Woe is me,* says David, that I am forced to dwell among such, *that I sojourn in Mesech and Kedar.* Not that David dwelt in the country of Mesech or Kedar ; we never find him so far off from his own native country; but he dwelt among rude and barbarous people, like the inhabitants of Mesech and Kedar : as, when we would describe an ill neighbourhood, we say, We dwell among Turks and heathens. This made him cry out, *Woe is me !* 1. He was forced to live at a distance from the ordinances of God. While he was in banishment, he looked upon himself as a sojourner, never at home but when he was near God's altars ; and he cries out, " *Woe is me* that my sojourning is prolonged, that I cannot get home to my resting-place, but am still kept at a distance !" So some read it. Note, A good man cannot think himself at home while he is banished from God's ordinances and has not them within reach. And it is a great grief to all that love God to be without the means of grace and of communion with God : when they are under a force of that kind they cannot but cry out, as David here, *Woe is me !* 2. He was forced to live among wicked people, who were, upon many accounts, troublesome to him. He *dwelt in the tents of Kedar,* where the shepherds were probably in an ill name for being litigious, like the herdsmen of Abraham and Lot. It is a very grievous burden to a good man to be cast into, and kept in, the company of those whom he hopes to be for ever separated from (like Lot in Sodom ; 2 Pet. ii. 8); to dwell long with such is grievous indeed, for they are thorns, vexing, and scratching, and tearing, and they will show the old enmity that is in the *seed of the serpent* against the *seed of the woman.* Those that David dwelt with were such as not only hated him, but hated peace, and proclaimed war with it, who might write on their weapons of war not *Sic sequimur pacem—Thus we aim at peace,* but *Sic persequimur—Thus we persecute.* Perhaps Saul's court was the Mesech and Kedar in which David dwelt, and Saul was the man he meant that hated peace, whom David studied to oblige and could not, but the more service he did him the more exasperated he was against him. See here, (1.) The character of a very good man in David, who could truly say, though he was a man of war, *I am for peace; for living peaceably with all men and unpeaceably with none. I peace* (so it is in the original); "I love peace and pursue peace; my disposition is to peace and my delight is in it. I pray for peace and strive for peace, will do any thing, submit to any thing, part with any thing, in reason, for peace. *I am for peace,* and have made it to appear that I am so." *The wisdom that is from above is first pure, then peaceable.* (2.) The character of the worst of bad men in David's enemies, who would pick quarrels with those that were most peaceably disposed : "*When I speak they are for war;* and the more forward for war the more they find me inclined to peace." He spoke with all the respect and kindness that could be, proposed methods of accommodation, spoke reason, spoke love; but they would not so much as hear him patiently, but cried out, "'To arms! to arms!'" so fierce and implacable were they, and so bent to mischief. Such were Christ's enemies : for his love they were his adversaries, and for his good words, and good works, they stoned him. If we meet with such enemies, we must not think it strange, nor love peace the less for our seeking it in vain. *Be not overcome of evil,* no, not of such evil as this, *but,* even when thus tried, still try to *overcome evil with good.*

PSALM CXXI.

Some call this the soldier's psalm, and think it was penned in the camp, when David was hazarding his life in the high places of the field, and thus trusted God to cover his head in the day of battle. Others call it the traveller's psalm (for there is nothing in it of military dangers) and think David penned it when he was going abroad, and designed it pro vehiculo— for the carriage, for a good man's convoy and companion in a journey or voyage. But we need not thus appropriate it ; wherever we are, at home or abroad, we are exposed to danger more than we are aware of; and this psalm directs and encourages us to repose ourselves and our confidence in God, and by faith to put ourselves under his protection and commit ourselves to his care, which we must do, with an entire resignation and satisfaction, in singing this psalm. I. David here assures himself of help from God, ver. 1, 2. II. He assures others of it, ver. 3–8.

A song of degrees.

I WILL lift up mine eyes unto the hills, from whence cometh my help. 2 My help *cometh* from the LORD, which made heaven and earth. 3 He will not suffer thy foot to be moved : he that keepeth thee will not slumber. 4 Behold, he that keepeth Israel shall neither slumber nor sleep. 5 The LORD *is* thy keeper : the LORD *is* thy shade upon thy right hand. 6 The sun shall not smite thee by day,

nor the moon by night. 7 The LORD shall preserve thee from all evil : he shall preserve thy soul. 8 The LORD shall preserve thy going out and thy coming in from this time forth, and even for evermore.

This psalm teaches us,

I. To stay ourselves upon God as a God of power and a God all-sufficient for us. David did so and found the benefit of it. 1. We must not rely upon creatures, upon men and means, instruments and second causes, nor make flesh our arm : "*Shall I lift up my eyes to the hills?*"—so some read it. "Does my help come thence?   Shall I depend upon the powers of the earth, upon the strength of the hills, upon princes and great men, who, like hills, fill the earth, and hold up their heads towards heaven?   No; *in vain is salvation hoped for from hills and mountains,* Jer. iii. 23.   I never expect help to come from them ; my confidence is in God only." *We must lift up our eyes above the hills* (so some read it) ; we must look beyond instruments to God, who makes them that to us which they are. 2. We must see all our help laid up in God, in his power and goodness, his providence and grace; and from him we must expect it to come : "*My help comes from the Lord;* the help I desire is what he sends, and from him I expect it in his own way and time. If he do not help, no creature can help; if he do, no creature can hinder, can hurt." 3. We must fetch in help from God, by faith in his promises, and a due regard to all his institutions : "*I will lift up my eyes to the hills*" (probably he meant the hills on which the temple was built, Mount Moriah, and the holy hill of Zion, where the ark of the covenant, the oracle, and the altars were) ; "I will have an eye to the special presence of God in his church, and with his people (his presence by promise) and not only to his common presence." When he was at a distance he would look towards the sanctuary (xxviii. 2 ; xlii. 6); thence *comes* our *help,* from the word and prayer, from the secret of his tabernacle. *My help cometh from the Lord* (so the word is, *v.* 2), *from before the Lord,* or *from the sight and presence of the Lord.* "This (says Dr. Hammond) may refer to Christ incarnate, with whose humanity the Deity being inseparably united, God is always present with him, and, through him, with us, for whom, sitting at God's right hand, he constantly maketh intercession." Christ is called the *angel of his presence,* that saved his people, Isa. lxiii. 9. 4. We must encourage our confidence in God with this that he *made heaven and earth,* and he who did that can do any thing. He made the world out of nothing, himself alone, by a word's speaking, in a little time, and *all very good,* very excellent and beautiful ; and therefore, how great soever our straits and difficulties are, he has power sufficient for our succour and relief. He that made heaven and earth is sovereign Lord of all the hosts of both, and can make use of them as he pleases for the help of his people, and restrain them when he pleases from hurting his people.

II. To comfort ourselves in God when our difficulties and dangers are greatest. It is here promised that if we put our trust in God, and keep in the way of our duty, we shall be safe under his protection, so that no real evil, no mere evil, shall happen to us, nor any affliction but what God sees good for us and will do us good by. 1. God himself has undertaken to be our protector : *The Lord is thy keeper, v.* 5. Whatever charge he gives his angels to keep his people, he has not thereby discharged himself, so that, whether every particular saint has an angel for his guardian or no, we are sure he has God himself for his guardian. It is infinite wisdom that contrives, and infinite power that works, the safety of those that have put themselves under God's protection. Those must needs be well kept that have *the Lord* for their *keeper.* If, by affliction, they be made his prisoners, yet still he is their keeper. 2. The same that is the protector of the church in general is engaged for the preservation of every particular believer, the same wisdom, the same power, the same promises. *He that keepeth Israel (v.* 4) *is thy keeper, v.* 5. The shepherd of the flock is the shepherd of every sheep, and will take care that not one, even of the little ones, shall perish. 3. He is a wakeful watchful keeper : " *He that keepeth Israel,* that keepeth thee, O Israelite! *shall neither slumber nor sleep* ; he never did, nor ever will, for he is never weary ; he not only does not sleep, but he does not so much as slumber ; he has not the least inclination to sleep." 4. He not only protects those whom he is the keeper of, but he refreshes them : He *is their shade.* The comparison has a great deal of gracious condescension in it ; the eternal Being who is infinite substance is what he is in order that he may speak sensible comfort to his people, promises to be their *umbra*—their *shadow,* to keep as close to them as the shadow does to the body, and to shelter them from the scorching heat, as *the shadow of a great rock in a weary land,* Isa. xxxii. 2. Under this shadow they may sit with delight and assurance, Cant. ii. 3. 5. He is always near to his people for their protection and refreshment, and never at a distance ; he *is* their *keeper* and *shade on their right hand ;* so that he is never far to seek. The right hand is the working hand ; let them but turn themselves dexterously to their duty, and they shall find God ready to them, to assist them and give them success, Ps. xvi. 8. 6. He is not only at their right hand, but he will also *keep the feet of his saints,* 1 Sam. ii. 9. He will have an eye upon them in their motions : He *will not suffer thy foot to be moved.* God will provide that his

people shall not be tempted above what they are able, shall not fall into sin, though they may be very near it (lxxiii. 2, 23), shall not fall into trouble, though there be many endeavouring to undermine them by fraud or overthrow them by force. He will keep them from being frightened, as we are when we slip or stumble and are ready to fall. 7. He will protect them from all the malignant influences of the heavenly bodies (*v.* 6) : *The sun shall not smite thee* with his heat *by day nor the moon* with her cold and moisture *by night.* The sun and moon are great blessings to mankind, and yet (such a sad change has sin made in the creation) even the sun and moon, though worshipped by a great part of mankind, are often instruments of hurt and distemper to human bodies ; God by them often smites us ; but his favour shall interpose so that they shall not damage his people. He will keep them *night and day* (Isa. xxvii. 3), as he kept Israel in the wilderness by *a pillar of cloud by day,* which screened them from the heat of the sun, *and of fire by night,* which probably diffused a genial warmth over the whole camp, that they might not be prejudiced by the cold and damp of the night, their father Jacob having complained (Gen. xxxi. 40) that *by day the drought consumed him and the frost by night.* It may be understood figuratively : "Thou shalt not be hurt either by the open assaults of thy enemies, which are as visible as the scorching beams of the sun, or by their secret treacherous attempts, which are like the insensible insinuations of the cold by night." 8. His protection will make them safe in every respect : " *The Lord shall preserve thee from all evil,* the evil of sin and the evil of trouble. He shall prevent the evil thou fearest, and shall sanctify, remove, or lighten, the evil thou feelest. He will keep thee from doing evil (2 Cor. xiii. 7), and so far from suffering evil that whatever affliction happens to thee there shall be no evil in it. Even that which kills shall not hurt." 9. It is the spiritual life, especially, that God will take under his protection : *He shall preserve thy soul.* All souls are his ; and the soul is the man, and therefore he will with a peculiar care preserve them, that they be not defiled by sin and disturbed by affliction. He will keep them by keeping us in the possession of them ; and he will preserve them from perishing eternally. 10. He will keep us in all our ways : " *He shall preserve thy going out and thy coming in.* Thou shalt be under his protection in all thy journeys and voyages, outward-bound or homeward-bound, as he kept Israel in the wilderness, in their removes and rests. He will prosper thee in all thy affairs at home and abroad, in the beginning and in the conclusion of them. He will keep thee in life and death, thy going out and going on while thou livest and thy coming in when thou diest, going out to thy labour in the morning of thy days and coming home to thy rest when the evening of old age calls thee in," civ. 23.

11. He will continue his care over us *from this time forth and even for evermore.* It is a protection for life, never out of date. "He will be thy guide *even unto death,* and will then hide thee in the grave, hide thee in heaven. He will *preserve thee in his heavenly kingdom.*" God will protect his church and his saints always, *even to the end of the world.* The Spirit, who is their preserver and comforter, shall abide with them for ever.

PSALM CXXII.

This psalm seems to have been penned by David for the use of the people of Israel, when they came up to Jerusalem to worship at the three solemn feasts. It was in David's time that Jerusalem was first chosen to be the city where God would record his name. It being a new thing, this, among other means, was used to bring the people to be in love with Jerusalem, as the holy city, though it was but the other day in the hands of the Jebusites. Observe, I. The joy with which they were to go up to Jerusalem, ver. 1, 2. II. The great esteem they were to have of Jerusalem, ver. 3—5. III. The great concern they were to have for Jerusalem, and the prayers they were to put up for its welfare, ver. 6—9. In singing this psalm we must have an eye to the gospel church, which is called the "Jerusalem that is from above."

A song of degrees of David.

I WAS glad when they said unto me, Let us go into the house of the LORD. 2 Our feet shall stand within thy gates, O Jerusalem. 3 Jerusalem is builded as a city that is compact together: 4 Whither the tribes go up, the tribes of the LORD, unto the testimony of Israel, to give thanks unto the name of the LORD. 5 For there are set thrones of judgment, the thrones of the house of David.

Here we have,

I. The pleasure which David and other pious Israelites took in approaching to and attending upon God in public ordinances, v. 1, 2.

1. The invitation to them was very welcome. David was himself glad, and would have every Israelite to say that he *was glad, when* he was called upon to *go up to the house of the Lord.* Note, (1.) It is the will of God that we should worship him in concert, that many should join together to wait upon him in public ordinances. We ought to worship God in our own houses, but that is not enough; we must *go into the house of the Lord,* to pay our homage to him there, and *not forsake the assembling of ourselves together.* (2.) We should not only agree with one another, but excite and stir up one another, to go to worship God in public. *Let us go ;* not, " Do you go and pray for us, and we will stay at home ;" but, *We will go also,* Zech. viii. 21. Not, " Do you go before, and we will follow at our leisure ;" or, " We will go first, and you shall come after us ;" but, " *Let us go* together, for the honour of God and for our mutual edification and encouragement." We ourselves are slow and backward, and others are so too, and therefore we should thus quicken and sharpen one another to that which is good, as iron sharpens iron. (3.) Those that rejoice in God will rejoice in

calls and opportunities to wait upon him. David himself, though he had as little need of a spur to his zeal in religious exercises as any, yet was so far from taking it as an affront that he was glad of it as a kindness when he was called upon to *go up to the house of the Lord* with the meanest of his subjects. We should desire our Christian friends, when they have any good work in hand, to call for us and take us along with them.

2. The prospect of them was very pleasing. They speak it with a holy triumph (*v.* 2): *Our feet shall stand within thy gates, O Jerusalem!* Those that came out of the country, when they found the journey tedious, comforted themselves with this, that they should be in Jerusalem shortly, and that would make amends for all the fatigues of their journey. We shall stand there as servants ; it is desirable to have a place in Jerusalem, though it be *among those that stand by* (Zech. iii. 7), though it be the door-keeper's place, Ps. lxxxiv. 10. We have now got a resting-place for the ark, and where it is there will we be.

II. The praises of Jerusalem, as xlviii. 12.

1. It is the beautiful city, not only for situation, but for building. It is built into *a city,* the houses not scattered, but contiguous, and the streets fair and spacious. It is built uniform, *compact together,* the houses strengthening and supporting one another. Though the city was divided into the higher and lower town, yet the Jebusites being driven out, and it being entirely in the possession of God's people, it is said to be compact together. It was a type of the gospel-church, which is compact together in holy love and Christian communion, so that it is all as one city.

2. It is the holy city, v. 4. It is the place where all Israel meet one another : *Thither the tribes go up,* from all parts of the country, as one man, under the character of *the tribes of the Lord,* in obedience to his command. It is the place appointed for their general rendezvous; and they come together, (1.) To receive instruction from God ; they come to *the testimony of Israel,* to hear what God has to say to them and to consult his oracle. (2.) To ascribe the glory to God, *to give thanks to the name of the Lord,* which we have all reason to do, especially those that have the testimony of Israel among them. If God speak to us by his word, we have reason to answer him by our thanksgivings. See on what errand we go to public worship, *to give thanks.*

3. It is the royal city (v. 5) : *There are set thrones of judgment. Therefore* the people had reason to be in love with Jerusalem, because justice was administered there by a man after God's own heart. The civil interests of the people were as well secured as their ecclesiastical concerns ; and very happy they were in their courts of judicature, which were erected in Jerusalem, as with us in Westminster Hall. Observe, What a goodly sight it was to see *the testimony of Israel* and the

thrones of judgment such near neighbours, and they are good neighbours, which may greatly befriend one another. Let the testimony of Israel direct the thrones of judgment, and the thrones of judgment protect the testimony of Israel.

6 Pray for the peace of Jerusalem: they shall prosper that love thee. 7 Peace be within thy walls, *and* prosperity within thy palaces. 8 For my brethren and companions' sakes, I will now say, Peace *be* within thee. 9 Because of the house of the Lord our God I will seek thy good.

Here, I. David calls upon others to wish well to Jerusalem, *v.* 6, 7. *Pray for the peace of Jerusalem,* for the welfare of it, for all good to it, particularly for the uniting of the inhabitants among themselves and their preservation from the incursions of enemies. This we may truly desire, that' in the peace thereof we may have peace; and this we must earnestly pray for, for it is the gift of God, and for it he will be enquired of. Those that can do nothing else for the peace of Jerusalem can pray for it, which is something more than showing their good-will; it is the appointed way of fetching in mercy. The peace and welfare of the gospel church, particularly in our land, is to be earnestly desired and prayed for by every one of us. Now, 1. We are here encouraged in our prayers for Jerusalem's peace: *Those shall prosper that love thee.* We must pray for Jerusalem, not out of custom, nor for fashion's sake, but out of a principle of love to God's government of man and man's worship of God; and, in seeking the public welfare, we seek our own, for so well does God *love the gates of Zion* that he will love all those that do love them, and therefore they cannot but prosper; at least their souls shall prosper by the ordinances they so dearly love. 2. We are here directed in our prayers for it and words are put into our mouths (*v.* 7): *Peace be within thy walls.* He teaches us to pray, (1.) For all the inhabitants in general, all within the walls, from the least to the greatest. Peace be in thy fortifications; let them never be attacked, or, if they be, let them never be taken, but be an effectual security to the city. (2.) For the princes and rulers especially: Let *prosperity* be *in the palaces* of the great men that sit at the helm and have the direction of public affairs; for, if they prosper, it will be well for the public. The poorer sort are apt to envy the prosperity of the palaces, but they are here taught to pray for it.

II. He resolves that whatever others do he will approve himself a faithful friend to Jerusalem, 1. In his prayers: " *I will now say,* now I see the tribes so cheerfully resorting hither to *the testimony of Israel,* and the matter settled, that Jerusalem must be the place where God will record his name, now I will

say, *Peace be within thee.*" He did not say, " Let others pray for the public peace, the priests and the prophets, whose business it is, and the people, that have nothing else to do, and I will fight for it and rule for it." No ; " I will pray for it too." 2. In his endeavours, with which he will second his prayers: " *I will,* to the utmost of my power, *seek thy good.*" Whatever lies within the sphere of our activity to do for the public good we must do it, else we are not sincere in praying for it. Now it might be said, No thanks to David to be so solicitous for the welfare of Jerusalem; it was his own city, and the interests of his family were lodged in it. This is true; yet he professes that this was not the reason why he was in such care for the welfare of Jerusalem, but it proceeded from the warm regard he had, (1.) To the communion of saints : It is *for my brethren and companions' sakes,* that is, for the sake of all true-hearted Israelites, whom I look upon as my brethren (so he calls them, 1 Chron. xxviii. 2) and who have often been my companions in the worship of God, which has knit my heart to them. (2.) To the ordinances of God : He had *set his affection to the house of his God* (1 Chron. xxix. 3); he took a great pleasure in public worship, and for that reason would pray for the good of Jerusalem. *Then* our concern for the public welfare is right when it is the effect of a sincere love to God's institutions and his faithful worshippers.

PSALM CXXIII.

This psalm was penned at a time when the church of God was brought low and trampled upon; some think it was when the Jews were captives in Babylon, though that was not the only time that they were insulted over by the proud. The psalmist begins as if he spoke for himself only (ver. 1), but presently speaks in the name of the church. Here is, I. Their expectation of mercy from God, ver. 1. 2. II. Their plea for mercy with God, ver. 3, 4. In singing it we must have our eye up to God's favour with a holy concern, and then an eye down to men's reproach with a holy contempt.

A song of degrees.

UNTO thee lift I up mine eyes, O thou that dwellest in the heavens. 2 Behold, as the eyes of servants *look* unto the hand of their masters, *and* as the eyes of a maiden unto the hand of her mistress; so our eyes *wait* upon the Lord our God, until that he have mercy upon us. 3 Have mercy upon us, O Lord, have mercy upon us: for we are exceedingly filled with contempt. 4 Our soul is exceedingly filled with the scorning of those that are at ease, *and* with the contempt of the proud.

We have here,

I. The solemn profession which God's people make of faith and hope in God, *v.* 1, 2. Observe, 1. The title here given to God : *O thou that dwellest in the heavens.* Our Lord Jesus has taught us, in prayer, to have an eye to God as *our Father in heaven;* not that he is confined there, but there especially he manifests his glory, as the King in his court. Heaven is a place of prospect and a place of power; he that dwells there beholds thence all the calamities of his people and thence can send to save them. Sometimes God seems to have forsaken the earth, and the enemies of God's people ask, *Where is now your God?* But then they can say with comfort, *Our God is in the heavens. O thou that sittest in the heavens* (so some), sittest as Judge there; for *the Lord has prepared his throne in the heavens,* and to that throne injured innocency may appeal. 2. The regard here had to God. The psalmist himself *lifted up his eyes* to him. The eyes of a good man are *ever towards the Lord,* xxv. 15. In every prayer we lift up our soul, the eye of our soul, to God, especially in trouble, which was the case here. The *eyes* of the people *waited on the Lord, v.* 2. We find mercy coming towards a people *when the eyes of man, as of all the tribes of Israel, are towards the Lord,* Zech. ix. 1. The eyes of the body are heaven-ward. *Os homini sublime dedit—To man he gave an erect mien,* to teach us which way to direct the eyes of the mind. *Our eyes wait on the Lord,* the eye of desire and prayer, the begging eye, and the eye of dependence, hope, and expectation, the longing eye. Our eyes must wait upon God as *the Lord,* and *our God, until that he have mercy upon us.* We desire mercy from him, we hope he will show us mercy, and we will continue our attendance on him till the mercy come. This is illustrated (*v.* 2) by a similitude : Our eyes are to God *as the eyes of a servant,* and *handmaid, to the hand of their master and mistress.* The eyes of a servant are, (1.) To his master's directing hand, expecting that he will appoint him his work, and cut it out for him, and show him now he must do it. *Lord, what wilt thou have me to do?* (2.) To his supplying hand. Servants look to their master, or their mistress, for their portion of meat in due season, Prov. xxxi. 15. And to God must we look for daily bread, for grace sufficient; from him we must receive it thankfully. (3.) To his assisting hand. If the servant cannot do his work himself, where must he look for help but to his master? And in the strength of the Lord God we must go forth and go on. (4.) To his protecting hand. If the servant meet with opposition in his work, if he be questioned for what he does, if he be wronged and injured, who should bear him out and right him, but his master that set him on work? The people of God, when they are persecuted, may appeal to their Master, *We are thine; save us.* (5.) To his correcting hand. If the servant has provoked his master to beat him, he does not call for help against his master, but looks at the hand that strikes him, till it shall say, "It is enough; I will not contend for ever." The people of God were now under his rebukes; and whither should they turn but to him that *smote*

them? Isa. ix. 13. To whom should they make supplication but to their Judge? They will not do as Hagar did, who ran away from her mistress when she put some hardships upon her (Gen. xvi. 6), but they submit themselves to and humble themselves under God's mighty hand. (6.) To his rewarding hand. The servant expects his wages, his *well-done,* from his master. Hypocrites have their eye to the world's hand; thence *they have their reward* (Matt. vi. 2); but true Christians have their eye to God as their rewarder.

II. The humble address which God's people present to him in their calamitous condition (*v.* 3, 4), wherein, 1. They sue for mercy, not prescribing to God what he shall do for them, nor pleading any merit of their own why he should do it for them, but, *Have mercy upon us, O Lord! have mercy upon us.* We find little mercy with men; their *tender mercies are cruel;* there are *cruel mockings.* But this is our comfort, that *with the Lord there is mercy* and we need desire no more to relieve us, and make us easy, than the mercy of God. Whatever the troubles of the church are, God's mercy is a sovereign remedy. 2. They set forth their grievances : *We are exceedingly filled with contempt.* Reproach is the wound, the burden, they complain of. Observe, (1.) Who were reproached : "We, who have our eyes up to thee." Those who are owned of God are often despised and trampled on by the world. Some translate the words which we render, *those that are at ease,* and *the proud,* so as to signify the persons that are scorned and contemned. "Our soul is troubled to see how those that are at peace, and the excellent ones, are scorned and despised." The saints are a peaceable people and yet are abused (xxxv. 20), the excellent ones of the earth and yet undervalued, Lam. iv. 1, 2. (2.) Who did reproach them. Taking the words as we read them, they were the epicures who lived at ease, carnal sensual people, Job xii. 5. The scoffers are such as walk after their own lusts and serve their own bellies, and the proud such as set God himself at defiance and had a high opinion of themselves; they trampled on God's people, thinking they magnified themselves by vilifying them. (3.) To what degree they were reproached : "*We are filled,* we are surfeited with it. *Our soul is exceedingly filled with it.*" The enemies thought they could never jeer them enough, nor say enough to make them despicable; and they could not but lay it to heart; it was a sword in their bones, Ps. xlii. 10. Note, [1.] Scorning and contempt have been, and are, and are likely to be, the lot of God's people in this world. Ishmael mocked Isaac, which is called *persecuting* him; and so it is now, Gal. iv. 29. [2.] In reference to the scorn and contempt of men it is matter of comfort that there is mercy with God, mercy to our good names when they are barbarously used. *Hear, O our God! for we are despised.*

PSALM CXXIV.

David penned this psalm (we suppose) upon occasion of some great deliverance which God wrought for him and his people from some very threatening danger, which was likely to have involved them all in ruin, whether by foreign invasion, or intestine insurrection, is not certain; whatever it was he seems to have been himself much affected, and very desirous to affect others, with the goodness of God, in making a way for them to escape. To him he is careful to give all the glory, and takes none to himself as conquerors usually do. I. He here magnifies the greatness of the danger they were in, and of the ruin they were at the brink of, ver. 1—5. II. He gives God the glory of their escape, ver. 6, 7, compared with ver. 1, 2. III. He takes encouragement thence to trust in God, ver. 8. In singing this psalm, besides the application of it to any particular deliverance wrought for us and our people, in our days and the days of our fathers, we may have in our thoughts the great work of our redemption by Jesus Christ, by which we were rescued from the powers of darkness.

A song of degrees of David.

IF *it had not been* the LORD who was on our side, now may Israel say; 2 If *it had not been* the LORD who was on our side, when men rose up against us : 3 Then they had swallowed us up quick, when their wrath was kindled against us : 4 Then the waters had overwhelmed us, the stream had gone over our soul : 5 Then the proud waters had gone over our soul.

The people of God, being here called upon to praise God for their deliverance, are to take notice,

I. Of the malice of men, by which they were reduced to the very brink of ruin. Let Israel say that there was but a step between them and death : the more desperate the disease appears to have been the more does the skill of the Physician appear in the cure. Observe, 1. Whence the threatening danger came : *Men rose up against us,* creatures of our own kind, and yet bent upon our ruin. *Homo homini lupus—Man is a wolf to man.* No marvel that the red dragon, the roaring lion, should seek to swallow us up ; but that men should thirst after the blood of men, Absalom after the blood of his own father, that a woman should be drunk with the blood of saints, is what, with St. John, we may wonder at with great admiration. From men we may expect humanity, yet there are those whose *tender mercies are cruel.* But what was the matter with these men? Why *their wrath was kindled against us* (v. 3); something or other they were angry at, and then no less would serve than the destruction of those they had conceived a displeasure against. *Wrath is cruel and anger is outrageous.* Their wrath was kindled as fire ready to consume us. They were proud ; and *the wicked in his pride doth persecute the poor.* They were daring in their attempt; they *rose up against us,* rose in rebellion, with a resolution to *swallow us up* alive. 2. How far it went, and how fatal it would have been if it had gone a little further : "We should have been devoured as a lamb by a lion, not only slain, but *swallowed up,* so that there would have been no relics of us remaining, swallowed

up with so much haste, ere we were aware, that we should have gone down alive to the pit. We should have been deluged as the low grounds by a land-flood or the sands by a high spring-tide." This similitude he dwells upon, with the ascents which bespeak this a song of degrees, or risings, like the rest. *The waters had overwhelmed us.* What of us? Why *the stream had gone over our souls,* our lives, our comforts, all that is dear to us. What waters? Why *the proud waters.* God suffers the enemies of his people sometimes to prevail very far against them, that his own power may appear the more illustrious in their deliverance.

II. Of the goodness of God, by which they were rescued from the very brink of ruin : "*The Lord was on our side;* and, *if he had not been so,* we should have been undone." 1. "God was on our side; he took our part, espoused our cause, and appeared for us. He was our helper, and a very present help, a help on our side, nigh at hand. He was with us, not only for us, but among us, and commander-in-chief of our forces." 2. That God was Jehovah; there the emphasis lies. "If it had not been Jehovah himself, a God of infinite power and perfection, that had undertaken our deliverance, our enemies would have overpowered us." Happy the people, therefore, whose God is Jehovah, a God all-sufficient. Let Israel say this, to his honour, and resolve never to forsake him.

6 Blessed *be* the LORD, who hath not given us *as* a prey to their teeth. 7 Our soul is escaped as a bird out of the snare of the fowlers : the snare is broken, and we are escaped. 8 Our help *is* in the name of the LORD, who made heaven and earth.

Here the psalmist further magnifies the great deliverance God had lately wrought for them.

I. That their hearts might be the more enlarged in thankfulness to him (v. 6): *Blessed be the Lord.* God is the author of all our deliverances, and therefore he must have the glory of them. We rob him of his due if we do not return thanks to him. And we are the more obliged to praise him because we had such a narrow escape. We were delivered, 1. Like a lamb out of the very jaws of a beast of prey: God *has not given us as a prey to their teeth,* intimating that they had no power over God's people but what was given them from above. They could not be a prey to their teeth unless God gave them up, and *therefore* they were rescued, because God would not suffer them to be ruined. 2. Like *a bird,* a little bird (the word signifies a sparrow), *out of the snare of the fowler.* The enemies are very subtle and spiteful ; they lay snares for God's people, to bring them into sin and trouble, and to hold them there. Sometimes they seem to have prevailed so far as to gain their point. God's people are taken in the snare, and are as unable to help themselves out as any weak and silly bird is; and *then* is God's time to appear for their relief, when all other friends fail; then God breaks the snare, and turns the counsel of the enemies into foolishness : *The snare is broken and so we are delivered.* Isaac was saved when he lay ready to be sacrificed. *Jehovah-jireh—in the mount of the Lord it shall be seen.*

II. That their hearts, and the hearts of others, might be the more encouraged to trust in God in the like dangers (v. 8) : *Our help is in the name of the Lord.* David had directed us (cxxi. 2) to depend upon God for help as to our personal concerns—*My help is in the name of the Lord;* here as to the concerns of the public—*Our help is* so. It is a comfort to all that lay the interests of God's Israel near their hearts that Israel's God is the same that made the world, and therefore will have a church in the world, and can secure that church in times of the greatest danger and distress. In him therefore let the church's friends put their confidence, and they shall not be put to confusion.

PSALM CXXV.

This short psalm may be summed up in those words of the prophet (Isa. iii. 10, 11), "Say you to the righteous, It shall be well with him. Woe to the wicked, it shall be ill with him." Thus are life and death, the blessing and the curse, set before us often in the psalms, as well as in the law and the prophets. I. It is certainly well with the people of God : for, 1. They have the promises of a good God that they shall be fixed (ver. 1), and safe (ver. 2), and not always under the hatches, ver. 3. 2. They have the prayers of a good man, which shall be heard for them, ver. 4. II. It is certainly ill with the wicked, and particularly with the apostates, ver. 5. Some of the Jewish rabbies are of opinion that it has reference to the days of the Messiah ; however, we that are members of the gospel-church may certainly, in singing this psalm, take the comfort of these promises, and the more so if we stand in awe of the threatening.

A song of degrees.

THEY that trust in the LORD shall be as mount Zion, *which* cannot be removed, *but* abideth for ever. 2 *As* the mountains *are* round about Jerusalem, so the LORD *is* round about his people from henceforth even for ever. 3 For the rod of the wicked shall not rest upon the lot of the righteous; lest the righteous put forth their hands unto iniquity.

Here are three very precious promises made to the people of God, which, though they are designed to secure the welfare of the church in general, may be applied by particular believers to themselves, as other promises of this nature may. Here is,

I. The character of God's people, to whom these promises belong. Many call themselves God's people who have no part nor lot in this matter. But those shall have the benefit of them and may take the comfort of them, (1.) Who are *righteous* (v. 3), righteous before God, righteous to God, and righteous to all men, for his sake justified and sanctified. (2.) Who *trust in the Lord,* who depend upon his care and devote themselves to his honour. All that deal with God must deal upon trust, and he will give com-

fort to those only that give credit to him, and make it to appear they do so by quitting other confidences, and venturing to the utmost for God. The closer our expectations are confined to God the higher our expectations may be raised from him.

II. The promises themselves.

1. That their hearts shall be established by faith : those minds shall be truly stayed that are stayed on God : *They shall be as Mount Zion.* The church in general is called *Mount Zion* (Heb. xii. 22), and it shall in *this* respect be like *Mount Zion,* it shall be built upon a rock, and its interests shall be so well secured that *the gates of hell shall not prevail against it.* The stability of the church is the satisfaction of all its well-wishers. Particular persons, who trust in God, shall be established (Ps. cxii. 7); their faith shall be their fixation, Isa. vii. 9. *They shall be as Mount Zion,* which is firm as it is a mountain supported by providence, much more as a holy mountain supported by promise. (1.) They *cannot be removed* by the prince of the power of the air, nor by all his subtlety and strength. They cannot be removed from their integrity nor from their confidence in God. (2.) They *abide for ever* in that grace which is the earnest of their everlasting continuance in glory.

2. That, committing themselves to God, they shall be safe, under his protection, from all the insults of their enemies, as Jerusalem had a natural fastness and fortification in the *mountains* that *were round about it, v. 2.* Those mountains not only sheltered it from winds and tempests, and broke the force of them, but made it also very difficult of access for an enemy ; such a defence is God's providence to his people. Observe, (1.) The compass of it : *The Lord is round about his people* on every side. There is no gap in the hedge of protection which he makes round about his people, at which the enemy, who goes about them, seeking to do them a mischief, can find entrance, Job. i. 10. (2.) The continuance of it—*henceforth even for ever.* Mountains may moulder and *come to nought, and rocks be removed out of their place* (Job xiv. 18), but God's covenant with his people cannot be *broken* (Isa. liv. 10) nor his care of them cease. Their being said to stand fast *for ever* (v. 1), and here to have God *round about them for ever,* intimates that the promises of the stability and security of God's people will have their full accomplishment in their everlasting state. In heaven they shall *stand fast for ever,* shall be as *pillars in the temple of our God and go no more out* (Rev. iii. 12), and there God himself, with his glory and favour, will be *round about them for ever.*

3. That their troubles shall last no longer than their strength will serve to bear them up under them, *v. 3.* (1.) It is supposed that the *rod of the wicked* may come, may fall, *upon the lot of the righteous.* The rod of their power may oppress them; the rod of their anger may vex and torment them. It may

fall upon their persons, their estates, their liberties, their families, their names, any thing that falls to their lot, only it cannot reach their souls. (2.) It is promised that, though it may come upon their lot, it shall not rest there; it shall not continue so long as the enemies design, and as the people of God fear, but God will cut the work short in righteousness, so short that even *with the temptation he will make a way for them to escape.* (3.) It is considered as a reason of this promise that if the trouble should continue over-long the righteous themselves would be in temptation to *put forth their hands to iniquity,* to join with wicked people in their wicked practices, to say as they say and do as they do. There is danger lest, being long persecuted for their religion, at length they grow weary of it and willing to give it up, lest, being kept long in expectation of promised mercies, they begin to distrust the promise, and to think of casting God off, upon suspicion of his having cast them off. See lxxiii. 13, 14. Note, God considers the frame of his people, and will proportion their trials to their strength by the care of his providence, as well as their strength to their trials by the power of his grace. *Oppression makes a wise man mad,* especially if it continue long; therefore *for the elect's sake* the days shall be shortened, that, whatever becomes of their lot in this world, they may not lose their lot among the chosen.

4 Do good, O Lord, unto *those that be* good, and to *them that are* upright in their hearts. 5 As for such as turn aside unto their crooked ways, the Lord shall lead them forth with the workers of iniquity: *but* peace *shall be* upon Israel.

Here is, 1. The prayer the psalmist puts up for the happiness of those that are sincere and constant (v. 4): *Do good, O Lord! unto those that are good.* This teaches us to pray for all good people, to *make supplication for all saints;* and we may pray in faith for them, being assured that those who do well shall certainly be well dealt with. Those that are as they should be shall be as they would be, provided they be *upright in heart,* that they be really as good as they seem to be. *With the upright God will show himself upright.* He does not say, Do good, O Lord! to those that are perfect, that are sinless and spotless, but to those that are sincere and honest. God's promises should quicken our prayers. It is comfortable wishing well to those for whom God has engaged to do well. 2. The prospect he has of the ruin of hypocrites and deserters; he does not pray for it *(I have not desired the woeful day, thou knowest),* but he predicts it: *As for those* who, having known the way of righteousness, for fear of the rod of the wicked, basely turn aside out of it *to their wicked ways,* use indirect ways to prevent trouble or extricate themselves out of

732

it, or those who, instead of reforming, grow worse and worse and are more obstinate and daring in their impieties, God shall *send them away, cast them out,* and *lead them forth with the workers of iniquity,* that is, he will appoint them their portion with the worst of sinners. Note, (1.) Sinful ways are *crooked ways;* sin is the perverting of that which is right. (2.) The doom of those who turn aside to those crooked ways out of the right way will be the same with theirs who have all along walked in them, nay, and more grievous, for if any place in hell be hotter than another that shall be the portion of hypocrites and apostates. God shall *lead them forth,* as prisoners are led forth to execution. *Go, you cursed, into everlasting fire;* and *these shall go away;* all their former righteousness shall not be mentioned unto them. The last words, *Peace upon Israel,* may be taken as a prayer: " God preserve his Israel in peace, when his judgments are abroad reckoning with evil-doers. We read them as a promise: *Peace shall be upon Israel;* that is, [1.] When those who have treacherously deserted the ways of God meet with their own destruction those who faithfully adhere to them, though they may have trouble in their way, shall have peace in the end. [2.] The destruction of those who walk in crooked ways will contribute to the peace and safety of the church. When Herod was cut off *the word of God grew,* Acts xii. 23, 24. [3.] The peace and happiness of God's Israel will be the vexation, and will add much to the torment, of those who perish in their wickedness, Luke xiii. 28; Isa. lxv. 13. *My servants shall rejoice, but you shall be ashamed.*

PSALM CXXVI.

It was with reference to some great and surprising deliverance of the people of God out of bondage and distress that this psalm was penned, most likely their return out of Babylon in Ezra's time. Though Babylon be not mentioned here (as it is, Ps. cxxxvii.) yet their captivity there was the most remarkable captivity both in itself and as their return out of it was typical of our redemption by Christ. Probably this psalm was penned by Ezra, or some of the prophets that came up with the first. We read of singers of the children of Asaph, that famous psalmist, who returned then, Ezra ii. 41. It being a song of ascents, in which the same things are twice repeated with advancement (ver. 2, 3, and ver. 4, 5), it is put here among the rest of the psalms that bear that title. I. Those that had returned out of captivity are here called upon to be thankful, ver. 1—3. II. Those that were yet remaining in captivity are here prayed for (ver. 4) and encouraged, ver. 5, 6. It will be easy, in singing this psalm, to apply it either to any particular deliverance wrought for the church or our own land or to the great work of our salvation by Christ

A song of degrees.

WHEN the Lord turned again the captivity of Zion, we were like them that dream. 2 Then was our mouth filled with laughter, and our tongue with singing : then said they among the heathen, The Lord hath done great things for them. 3 The Lord hath done great things for us; *whereof* we are glad.

While the people of Israel were captives in Babylon their harps were hung upon the willow-trees, for then God called to weeping and mourning, then he mourned unto them and they lamented; but now that their captivity is turned they resume their harps; Providence pipes to them, and they dance. Thus must we accommodate ourselves to all the dispensations of Providence and be suitably affected with them. And the harps are never more melodiously tunable than after such a melancholy disuse. The long want of mercies greatly sweetens their return. Here is, 1. The deliverance God had wrought for them: He *turned again the captivity of Zion.* It is possible that Zion may be in captivity for the punishment of her degeneracy, but her captivity shall be turned again when the end is answered and the work designed by it is effected. Cyrus, for reasons of state, proclaimed liberty to God's captives, and yet it was *the Lord's doing,* according to his word many years before. God sent them into captivity, not as dross is put into the fire to be consumed, but as gold to be refined. Observe, The release of Israel is called *the turning again of the captivity of Zion,* the holy hill, where God's tabernacle and dwelling-place were; for the restoring of their sacred interests, and the reviving of the public exercise of their religion, were the most valuable advantages of their return out of captivity. 2. The pleasing surprise that this was to them. They were amazed at it; it came so suddenly that at first they were in confusion, not knowing what to make of it, nor what it was tending to: "We thought ourselves *like men that dream;* we thought it too good news to be true, and began to question whether we were well awake or no, and whether it was not still" (as sometimes it had been to the prophets) "only a representation of it in vision," as St. Peter for a while thought his deliverance was, Acts xii. 9. Sometimes the people of God are thus prevented with the blessings of his goodness before they are aware. *We were like those that are recovered to health* (so Dr. Hammond reads it); "such a comfortable happy change it was to us, as life from the dead or sudden ease from exquisite pain; we thought ourselves in a new world." And the surprise of it put them into such an ecstasy and transport of joy that they could scarcely contain themselves within the bounds of decency in the expressions of it: *Our mouth was filled with laughter and our tongue with singing.* Thus they gave vent to their joy, gave glory to their God, and gave notice to all about them what wonders God had wrought for them. Those that were laughed at now laugh and a *new song is put into their mouths.* It was a laughter of joy in God, not scorn of their enemies. 3. The notice which their neighbours took of it: *They said among the heathen,* Jehovah, the God of Israel, *has done great things* for that people, such as our gods cannot do for us. The heathen had observed their calamity and had triumphed in it, Jer. xxii. 8, 9; Ps. cxxxvii. 7. Now they could not but observe their

deliverance and admire that. It put a reputation upon those that had been scorned and despised, and made them look considerable; besides, it turned greatly to the honour of God, and extorted from those that set up other gods in competition with him an acknowledgment of his wisdom, power, and providence. 4. The acknowledgments which they themselves made of it, *v.* 3. The heathen were but spectators, and spoke of it only as matter of news; they had no part nor lot in the matter; but the people of God spoke of it as sharers in it, (1.) With application: "He has *done great things for us,* things that we are interested in and have advantage by." Thus it is comfortable speaking of the redemption Christ has wrought out as wrought out for us. *Who loved me, and gave himself for me.* (2.) With affection: "*Whereof we are glad.* The heathen are amazed at it, and some of them angry, but we are glad." While Israel went a whoring from their God joy was forbidden them (Hos. ix. 1); but now that the iniquity of Jacob was purged by the captivity, and their sin taken away, now God makes them to rejoice. It is the repenting reforming people that are, and shall be, the rejoicing people. Observe here, [1.] God's appearances for his people are to be looked upon as great things. [2.] God is to be eyed as the author of all the great things done for the church. [3.] It is good to observe how the church's deliverances are for us, that we may rejoice in them.

4 Turn again our captivity, O Lord, as the streams in the south. 5 They that sow in tears shall reap in joy. 6 He that goeth forth and weepeth, bearing precious seed, shall doubtless come again with rejoicing, bringing his sheaves *with him.*

These verses look forward to the mercies that were yet wanted. Those that had come out of captivity were still in distress, even in their own land (Neh. i. 3), and many yet remained in Babylon; and therefore they rejoiced with trembling, and bore upon their hearts the grievances that were yet to be redressed. We have here, 1. A prayer for the perfecting of their deliverance (*v.* 4): "*Turn again our captivity.* Let those that have returned to their own land be eased of the burdens which they are yet groaning under. Let those that remain in Babylon have their hearts stirred up, as ours were, to take the benefit of the liberty granted." The beginnings of mercy are encouragements to us to pray for the completing of it. And while we are here in this world there will still be matter for prayer, even when we are most furnished with matter for praise. And, when we are free and in prosperity ourselves, we must not be unmindful of our brethren that are in trouble and under restraint. The bringing of those that were yet in captivity to join with their brethren that had returned would be as welcome to both sides as streams of water in those countries, which, lying far south, were parched and dry. As cold water to a thirsty soul, so would this good news be from that far country, Prov. xxv. 25. 2. A promise for their encouragement to wait for it, assuring them that, though they had now a sorrowful time, yet it would end well. But the promise is expressed generally, that all the saints may comfort themselves with this confidence, that their seedness of tears will certainly end in a harvest of joy at last, *v.* 5, 6. (1.) Suffering saints have a seedness of tears. They are in tears often; they share in the calamities of human life, and commonly have a greater share in them than others. But they *sow in tears;* they do the duty of an afflicted state and so answer the intentions of the providences they are under. Weeping must not hinder sowing; when we suffer ill we must be doing well. Nay, as the ground is by the rain prepared for the seed, and the husbandman sometimes chooses to sow in the wet, so we must improve times of affliction, as disposing us to repentance, and prayer, and humiliation. Nay, there are tears which are themselves the seed that we must sow, tears of sorrow for sin, our own and others, tears of sympathy with the afflicted church, and tears of tenderness in prayer and under the word. These are precious seed, such as the husbandman sows when corn is dear and he has but little for his family, and therefore weeps to part with it, yet buries it under ground, in expectation of receiving it again with advantage. Thus does a good man sow in tears. (2.) They shall have a harvest of joy. The troubles of the saints will not last always, but, when they have done their work, shall have a happy period. The captives in Babylon were long sowing in tears, but at length were brought forth with joy, and then they reaped the benefit of their patient suffering, and brought their sheaves with them to their own land, in their experiences of the goodness of God to them. Job, and Joseph, and David, and many others, had harvests of joy after a sorrowful seedness. Those that sow in the tears of godly sorrow shall reap in the joy of a sealed pardon and a settled peace. Those that *sow to the spirit,* in this vale of tears, *shall of the spirit reap life everlasting,* and that will be a joyful harvest indeed. *Blessed are those that mourn, for they shall be* for ever *comforted.*

PSALM CXXVII.

This is a family-psalm, as divers before were state-poems and church-poems. It is entitled (as we read it) "for Solomon," dedicated to him by his father. He having a house to build, a city to keep, and seed to raise up to his father, David directs him to look up to God, and to depend upon his providence, without which all his wisdom, care, and industry, would not serve. Some take it to have been penned by Solomon himself, and it may as well be read, "a song of Solomon," who wrote a great many; and they compare it with the Ecclesiastes, the scope of both being the same, to show the vanity of worldly care and how necessary it is that we keep in favour with God. On him we must depend, I. For wealth, ver. 1, 2. II. For heirs to leave it to, ver. 3—5. In singing this psalm we must have our eye up unto God for success in all our undertakings and a blessing upon

all our comforts and enjoyments, because every creature is that to us which he makes it to be and no more.

A song of degrees for Solomon.

EXCEPT the LORD build the house, they labour in vain that build it: except the LORD keep the city, the watchman waketh *but* in vain. 2 *It is* vain for you to rise up early, to sit up late, to eat the bread of sorrows: *for* so he giveth his beloved sleep. 3 Lo, children *are* an heritage of the LORD: *and* the fruit of the womb *is his* reward. 4 As arrows *are* in the hand of a mighty man; so *are* children of the youth. 5 Happy *is* the man that hath his quiver full of them: they shall not be ashamed, but they shall speak with the enemies in the gate.

We are here taught to have a continual regard to the divine Providence in all the concerns of this life. Solomon was cried up for a wise man, and would be apt to lean to his own understanding and forecast, and therefore his father teaches him to look higher, and to take God along with him in his undertakings. He was to be a man of business, and therefore David instructed him how to manage his business under the direction of his religion. Parents, in teaching their children, should suit their exhortations to their condition and occasions. We must have an eye to God,

I. In all the affairs and business of the family, even of the royal family, for kings' houses are no longer safe than while God protects them. We must depend upon God's blessing and not our own contrivance, 1. For the raising of a family: *Except the Lord build the house,* by his providence and blessing, *those labour in vain, that build it.* We may understand it of the material house: except the Lord bless the building it is to no purpose for men to build, any more than for the builders of Babel, who attempted in defiance of heaven, or Hiel, who built Jericho under a curse. If the model and design be laid in pride and vanity, or if the foundations be laid in oppression and injustice (Hab. ii. 11, 12), God certainly does not build there; nay, if God be not acknowledged, we have no reason to expect his blessing, and without his blessing all is nothing. Or, rather, it is to be understood of the making of a family considerable—that was mean; men labour to do this by advantageous matches, offices, employments, purchases; but all in vain, unless God build up the family, and *raise the poor out of the dust.* The best-laid project fails unless God crown it with success. See Mal. i. 4. 2. For the securing of a family or a city (for this is what the psalmist particularly mentions): if the guards of the city cannot secure it without God, much less can the good man of the house save his house from being broken up. *Except the Lord keep the city* from fire, from enemies, *the watchmen,* who *go about the city,* or patrol upon the walls of it, though they neither slumber nor sleep, *wake but in vain,* for a raging fire may break out, the mischief of which the timeliest discoveries may not be able to prevent. The guards may be slain, or the city betrayed and lost, by a thousand accidents, which the most watchful sentinel or most cautious governor could not obviate. 3. For the enriching of a family; this is a work of time and thought, but cannot be effected without the favour of Providence any more than that which is the product of one happy turn: "*It is vain for you to rise up early and sit up late,* and so to deny yourselves your bodily refreshments, in the eager pursuit of the wealth of the world." Usually, those that rise early do not care for sitting up late, nor can those that sit up late easily persuade themselves to rise early; but there are some so hot upon the world that they will do both, will rob their sleep to pay their cares. And they have as little comfort in their meals as in their rest; they *eat the bread of sorrows.* It is part of our sentence that we eat our bread in the sweat of our face; but those go further: *all their days they eat in darkness,* Eccl. v. 17. They are continually full of care, which embitters their comforts, and makes their lives a burden to them. All this is to get money, and all in vain except God prosper them, for *riches are not always to men of understanding,* Eccl. ix. 11. Those that love God, and are beloved of him, have their minds easy and live very comfortably without this ado. Solomon was called *Jedidiah—Beloved of the Lord* (2 Sam. xii. 25); to him the kingdom was promised, and then it was in vain for Absalom to rise up early, to wheedle the people, and for Adonijah to make such a stir, and to say, *I will be king.* Solomon sits still, and, being *beloved of the Lord,* to him he gives sleep and the kingdom too. Note, (1.) Inordinate excessive care about the things of this world is a vain and fruitless thing. We weary ourselves for vanity if we have it, and often weary ourselves in vain for it, Hag. i. 6, 9. (2.) Bodily sleep is God's gift to his beloved. We owe it to his goodness that our sleep is safe (iv. 8), that it is sweet, Jer. xxxi. 25, 26. God gives us sleep as he gives it to his beloved when with it he gives us grace to lie down in his fear (our souls returning to him and reposing in him as our rest), and when we awake to be still with him and to use the refreshment we have by sleep in his service. *He gives his beloved sleep,* that is, quietness and contentment of mind, a comfortable enjoyment of what is present and a comfortable expectation of what is to come. Our care must be to *keep ourselves in the love of God,* and then we may be easy whether we have little or much of this world.

II. In the increase of the family. He shows, 1. That children are *God's gift, v. 3.* If children are withheld it is God that withholds them (Gen. xxx. 2); if they are given, it is God that gives them (Gen. xxxiii. 5); and they are to us what he makes them, comforts or crosses. Solomon multiplied wives, contrary to the law, but we never read of more than one son that he had; for those that desire children as a heritage from the Lord must receive them in the way that he is pleased to give them, by lawful marriage to one wife. Mal. ii. 15, *therefore one, that he might seek a seed of God.* But *they shall commit whoredom and shall not increase. Children are a heritage,* and a *reward,* and are so to be accounted, blessings and not burdens; for he that sends mouths will send meat if we trust in him. Obed-edom had eight sons, for the Lord blessed him because he had entertained the ark, 1 Chron. xxvi. 5. Children are a heritage for the Lord, as well as from him; they are *my children* (says God) *which thou hast borne unto me* (Ezek. xvi. 20); and they are most our honour and comfort when they are accounted to him for a generation. 2. That they are a good gift, and a great support and defence to a family: *As arrows are in the hand of a mighty man,* who knows how to use them for his own safety and advantage, so are children of the youth, that is, children born to their parents when they are young, which are the strongest and most healthful children, and are grown up to serve them by the time they need their service; or, rather, children who are themselves young; they are instruments of much good to their parents and families, which may fortify themselves with them against their enemies. The family that has a large stock of children is like a quiver full of arrows, of different sizes we may suppose, but all of use one time or other; children of different capacities and inclinations may be several ways serviceable to the family. He that has a numerous issue may boldly *speak with his enemy in the gate* in judgment; in battle he needs not fear, having so many good seconds, so zealous, so faithful, and in the vigour of youth, 1 Sam. ii. 4, 5. Observe here, *Children of the youth* are *arrows in the hand,* which, with prudence, may be directed aright to the mark, God's glory and the service of their generation; but afterwards, when they have gone abroad into the world, they are arrows out of the hand; it is too late to bend them then. But these arrows in the hand too often prove arrows in the heart, a constant grief to their godly parents, whose gray hairs they bring with sorrow to the grave.

PSALM CXXVIII.

have the satisfaction of seeing the church of God in a flourishing condition, ver. 5, 6. We must sing this psalm in the firm belief of this truth, That religion and piety are the best friends to outward prosperity, giving God the praise that it is so and that we have found it so, and encouraging ourselves and others with it.

A song of degrees.

BLESSED *is* every one that fear-eth the LORD; that walketh in his ways. 2 For thou shalt eat the labour of thine hands: happy *shalt* thou *be*, and *it shall be* well with thee. 3 Thy wife *shall be* as a fruitful vine by the sides of thine house: thy children like olive plants round about thy table. 4 Behold, that thus shall the man be blessed that feareth the LORD. 5 The LORD shall bless thee out of Zion: and thou shalt see the good of Jerusalem all the days of thy life. 6 Yea, thou shalt see thy child-ren's children, *and* peace upon Israel.

It is here shown that godliness has the promise of the life that now is and of that which is to come.

It is here again and again laid down as an undoubted truth that *those who are truly holy are truly happy.* Those whose blessed state we are here assured of are such as *fear the Lord* and *walk in his ways,* such as have a deep reverence of God upon their spirits and evidence it by a regular and constant conformity to his will. Where the fear of God is a commanding principle in the heart the tenour of the conversation will be accordingly; and in vain do we pretend to be of those that fear God if we do not make conscience both of keeping to his ways and not trifling in them or drawing back. Such are blessed (*v.* 1), and shall be blessed, *v.* 4. God blesses them, and his pronouncing them blessed makes them so. They are blessed now, they shall be blessed still, and for ever. This blessedness, arising from this blessing, is here secured, 1. To all the saints universally: *Blessed is every one that fears the Lord,* whoever he be; in every nation he that fears God and works righteousness is accepted of him, and therefore is blessed whether he be high or low, rich or poor, in the world; if religion rule him, it will protect and enrich him. 2. To such a saint in particular: *Thus shall the man be blessed,* not only the nation, the church in its public capacity, but the particular person in his private interests. 3. We are encouraged to apply it to ourselves (*v.* 2): " *Happy shalt thou be;* thou mayest take the comfort of the promise, and expect the benefit of it, as if it were directed to thee by name, if thou *fear God and walk in his ways. Happy shalt thou be,* that is, It *shall be well with thee;* whatever befals thee, good shall be brought out of it; it shall be well with thee whīle thou livest, better when thou diest, and best of all to eternity." It is as-serted (*v.* 4) with a note commanding atten-

tion: *Behold, thus shall the man be blessed;* behold it by faith in the promise; behold it by observation in the performance of the promise; behold it with assurance that it shall be so, for God is faithful, and with ad-miration that it should be so, for we merit no favour, no blessing, from him.

II. Particular promises are here made to godly people, which they may depend upon, as far as is for God's glory and their good; and that is enough.

1. That, by the blessing of God, they shall get an honest livelihood and live comforta-bly upon it. It is not promised that they shall live at ease, without care or pains, but, *Thou shalt eat the labour of thy hands.* Here is a double promise, (1.) That they shall have something to do (for an idle life is a miserable uncomfortable life) and shall have health, and strength, and capacity of mind to do it, and shall not be forced to be be-holden to others for necessary food, and to live, as the disabled poor do, upon the la-bours of other people. It is as much a mercy as it is a duty *with quietness* to work and *eat our own bread,* 2 Thess. iii. 12. (2.) That they shall succeed in their employments, and they and theirs shall enjoy what they get; others shall not come and eat the bread out of their mouths, nor shall it be taken from them either by oppressive rulers or invading enemies. God will not blast it and blow upon it (as he did, Hag. i. 9), and his bless-ing will make a little go a great way. It is very pleasant to enjoy the fruits of our own industry; as the sleep, so the food, of a la-bouring man is sweet.

2. That they shall have abundance of com-fort in their family-relations. As a wife and children are very much a man's care, so, if by the grace of God they are such as they should be, they are very much a man's de-light, as much as any creature-comfort. (1.) The *wife* shall be *as a vine by the sides of the house,* not only as a spreading vine which serves for an ornament, but as a fruitful vine which is for profit, and with the fruit where-of both God and man are honoured, Judg. ix. 13. The vine is a weak and tender plant, and needs to be supported and cherished, but it is a very valuable plant, and some think (because all the products of it were prohibited to the Nazarites) it was the *tree of knowledge* itself. The wife's place is the husband's house; there her business lies, and that is her castle. *Where is Sarah thy wife? Behold, in the tent;* where should she be else? Her place is *by the sides of the house,* not under-foot to be trampled on, nor yet upon the house-top to domineer (if she be so, she is but *as the grass upon the house-top,* in the next psalm), but on the side of the house, being a rib out of the side of the man. She shall be a loving wife, as the vine, which cleaves to the house-side, an obedient wife, as the vine, which is pliable, and grows as it is directed. She shall be

fruitful as the vine, not only in children, but in the fruits of wisdom, and righteousness, and good management, the *branches* of which *run over the wall* (Gen. xlix. 22; Ps. lxxx. 11), *like a fruitful vine*, not cumbering the ground, nor bringing forth sour grapes, or grapes of Sodom, but good fruit. (2.) The *children* shall be *as olive plants*, likely in time to be olive-trees, and, though *wild by nature*, yet grafted into the good olive, and partaking of its *root and fatness*, Rom. xi. 17. It is pleasant to parents who have a table spread, though but with ordinary fare, to see their children round about it, to have many children, enough to surround it, and those with them, and not scattered, or the parents forced from them. Job makes it one of the first instances of his former prosperity that *his children were about him*, Job xxix. 5. Parents love to have their children at table, to keep up the pleasantness of the table-talk, to have them in health, craving food and not physic, to have them like *olive-plants*, straight and green, sucking in the sap of their good education, and likely in due time to be serviceable.

3. That they shall have those good things which God has promised and which they pray for: *The Lord shall bless thee out of Zion*, where the ark of the covenant was, and where the pious Israelites attended with their devotions. *Blessings out of Zion* are the best blessings, which flow, not from common providence, but from special grace, Ps. xx. 2.

4. That they shall live long, to enjoy the comforts of the rising generations: "Thou shalt *see thy children's children*, as Joseph, Gen. l. 23. Thy family shall be built up and continued, and thou shalt have the pleasure of seeing it." *Children's children*, if they be good children, *are the crown of old men* (Prov. xvii. 6), who are apt to be fond of their grandchildren.

5. That they shall see the welfare of God's church, and the land of their nativity, which every man who fears God is no less concerned for than for the prosperity of his own family. "Thou shalt be blessed in Zion's blessing, and wilt think thyself so. Thou shalt *see the good of Jerusalem* as long as thou shalt live, though thou shouldst live long, and shalt not have thy private comforts allayed and embittered by public troubles." A good man can have little comfort in seeing his children's children, unless withal he see peace upon Israel, and have hopes of transmitting the entail of religion pure and entire to those that shall come after him, for that is the best inheritance.

PSALM CXXIX.

This psalm relates to the public concerns of God's Israel. It is not certain when it was penned, probably when they were in captivity in Babylon, or about the time of their return. I. They look back with thankfulness for the former deliverances God had wrought for them and their fathers out of the many distresses they had been in from time to time, ver. 1—4. II. They look forward with a believing prayer for and prospect of the destruction of all the enemies of Zion, ver. 5—8. In singing this psalm we may apply it both ways to the Gospel-Israel, which, like the Old-Testament Israel, has weathered many a storm and is still threatened by many enemies.

A song of degrees.

MANY a time have they afflicted me from my youth, may Israel now say: 2 Many a time have they afflicted me from my youth: yet they have not prevailed against me. 3 The ploughers ploughed upon my back: they made long their furrows. 4 The LORD *is* righteous: he hath cut asunder the cords of the wicked.

The church of God, in its several ages, is here spoken of, or, rather, here speaks, as one single person, now old and gray-headed, but calling to remembrance the former days, and reflecting upon the times of old. And, upon the review, it is found, 1. That the church has been often greatly distressed by its enemies on earth: *Israel may now say*, "I am the people that has been oppressed more than any people, that has been *as a speckled bird*, pecked at by *all the birds round about*," Jer. xii. 9. It is true, they brought their troubles upon themselves by their sins; it was for them that God punished them; but it was for the peculiarity of their covenant, and the singularities of their religion, that their neighbours hated and persecuted them. "For these *many a time have they afflicted me from my youth*." Note, God's people have always had many enemies, and the state of the church, from its infancy, has frequently been an afflicted state. Israel's youth was in Egypt, or in the times of the Judges; then they were afflicted, and thenceforward more or less. The gospel-church, ever since it had a being, has been at times afflicted; and it bore this yoke most of all in its youth, witness the ten persecutions which the primitive church groaned under. *The ploughers ploughed upon my back, v.* 3. We read (cxxv. 3) of *the rod of the wicked upon the lot of the righteous*, where we rather expected the plough, to mark it out for themselves; here we read of the *plough* of the wicked *upon the back of the righteous*, where we rather expected to find the rod. But the metaphors in these places may be said to be *crossed*; the sense however of both is the same, and is too plain, that the enemies of God's people have all along used them very barbarously. They tore them, as the husbandman tears the ground with his plough-share, to pull them to pieces and get all they could out of them, and so to *wear out the saints of the Most High*, as the ground is worn out that has been long tilled, tilled (as we say) quite out of heart. When God permitted them to plough thus he intended it for his people's good, that, their fallow ground being thus broken up, he might sow the seeds of his grace upon them, and reap a harvest of good fruit from them: howbeit, the enemies meant not so, neither did their hearts think so (Isa. x. 7); *they made long their furrows*, never knew when to have done, aiming at nothing less than the destruction of the church. Many by the *furrows* they made on the backs of God's people understand the stripes they gave them. *The cutters cut upon my back*, so they read it. The saints have often *had trials of cruel scourgings* (probably the captives had) *and cruel mockings* (for we read of the scourge or lash of the tongue, Heb. xi. 36), and so it was fulfilled in Christ, who *gave his back to the smiters*, Isa. l. 6. Or it may refer to the desolations they made of the cities of Israel. *Zion shall, for your sake, be ploughed as a field*, Mic. iii. 12. 2. That the church has been always graciously delivered by her friend in heaven. (1.) The enemies' projects have been defeated. They have afflicted the church, in hopes to ruin it, but they have not gained their point. Many a storm it has weathered; many a shock, and many a brunt, it has borne; and yet it is in being: *They have not prevailed against me.* One would wonder how this ship has lived at sea, when it has been tossed with tempests, and all the waves and billows have gone over it. Christ has built his church upon a rock, and the gates of hell have not prevailed against it, nor ever shall. (2.) The enemies' power has been broken: God *has cut asunder the cords of the wicked*, has cut their gears, their traces, and so spoiled their ploughing, has cut their scourges, and so spoiled their lashing, has cut the bands of union by which they were combined together, has cut the bands of captivity in which they held God's people. God has many ways of disabling wicked men to do the mischief they design against his church and shaming their counsels. These words, *The Lord is righteous*, may refer either to the distresses or to the deliverances of the church. [1.] *The Lord is righteous* in suffering Israel to be afflicted. This the people of God were always ready to own, that, how unjust soever their enemies were, God was *just in all that was brought upon them*, Neh. ix. 33. [2.] *The Lord is righteous* in not suffering Israel to be ruined; for he has promised to preserve to a people to himself, and he will be as good as his word. He is righteous in reckoning with their persecutors, and rendering to them *a recompence*, 2 Thess. i. 6.

5 Let them all be confounded and turned back that hate Zion. 6 Let them be as the grass *upon* the housetops, which withereth afore it groweth up: 7 Wherewith the mower filleth not his hand; nor he that bindeth sheaves his bosom. 8 Neither do they which go by say, The blessing of the LORD *be* upon you: we bless you in the name of the LORD.

The psalmist, having triumphed in the defeat of the many designs that had been laid as deep as hell to ruin the church, here concludes his psalm as Deborah did her song, *So let all thy enemies perish, O Lord!* Judg. v. 31.

I. There are many that hate Zion, that hate Zion's God, his worship, and his worshippers, that have an antipathy to religion and religious people, that seek the ruin of both, and do what they can that God may not have a church in the world.

II. We ought to pray that all their attempts against the church may be frustrated, that in them they may be *confounded* and *turned back* with shame, as those that have not been able to bring to pass their enterprise and expectation: *Let them all be confounded* is as much as, *They shall be* all confounded. The confusion imprecated and predicted is illustrated by a similitude; while God's people shall flourish as the loaded palm-tree, or the green and fruitful olive, their enemies shall *wither as the grass upon the house-top.* As men they are not to be feared, for they shall be made as grass, Isa. li. 12. But as they are enemies to Zion they are so certainly marked for ruin that they may be looked upon with as much contempt as the grass on the house-tops, which is little, and short, and sour, and good for nothing. 1. It perishes quickly: It *withers before it grows up* to any maturity, having no root; and the higher its place is, which perhaps is its pride, the more it is exposed to the scorching heat of the sun, and consequently the sooner does it wither. *It withers before it is plucked up*, so some read it. The enemies of God's church wither of themselves, and stay not till they are rooted out by the judgments of God. 2. It is of no use to any body; nor are *they* any thing but the unprofitable burdens of the earth, nor will their attempts against Zion ever ripen or come to any head, nor, whatever they promise themselves, will they get any more by them than the husbandman does by the grass on his house-top. Their *harvest will be a heap in the day of grief*, Isa. xvii. 11.

III. No wise man will pray God to bless the mowers or reapers, v. 8. Observe, 1. It has been an ancient and laudable custom not only to salute and wish a good day to strangers and travellers, but particularly to pray for the prosperity of harvest-labourers. Thus Boaz prayed for his reapers. Ruth ii. 4, *The Lord be with you.* We must thus acknowledge God's providence, testify our good-will to our neighbours, and commend their industry, and it will be accepted of God as a pious ejaculation if it come from a devout and upright heart. 2. Religious expressions, being sacred things, must never be made use of in light and ludicrous actions. Mowing the grass on the house-top would be a jest, and therefore those that have a reverence for the name of God will not prostitute to it the usual forms of salutation, which savoured of devotion; for holy things must not be jested with. 3. It is a dangerous thing to let the church's enemies have our good wishes in their designs against the church. If we *wish them God speed, we are partakers of their evil deeds,* 2 John 11. When it is said, None will bless them, and show them respect, more is implied, namely, that all wise and good people will cry out shame on them, and beg of God to defeat them; and woe to those that have the prayers of the saints against them. *I cursed his habitation,* Job v. 3.

PSALM CXXX.

This psalm relates not to any temporal concern, either personal or public, but it is wholly taken up with the affairs of the soul. It is reckoned one of the seven penitential psalms, which have sometimes been made use of by penitents, upon their admission into the church; and, in singing it, we are all concerned to apply it to ourselves. The psalmist here expresses, I. His desire towards God, ver. 1, 2. II. His repentance before God, ver 3, 4. III. His attendance upon God, ver. 5, 6. IV. His expectations from God, ver. 7, 8. And, as in water face answers to face, so does the heart of one humble penitent to another.

A song of degrees.

OUT of the depths have I cried unto thee, O LORD. 2 Lord, hear my voice: let thine ears be attentive to the voice of my supplications. 3 If thou, LORD, shouldest mark iniquities, O Lord, who shall stand? 4 But *there is* forgiveness with thee, that thou mayest be feared.

In these verses we are taught,

I. Whatever condition we are in, though ever so deplorable, to continue calling upon God, *v.* 1. The best men may sometimes be in *the depths,* in great trouble and affliction, and utterly at a loss what to do, in the depths of distress and almost in the depths of despair, the spirit low and dark, sinking and drooping, cast down and disquieted. But, in the greatest depths, it is our privilege that we may cry unto God and be heard. A prayer may reach the heights of heaven, though not out of the depths of hell, yet out of the depths of the greatest trouble we can be in in this world, Jeremiah's out of the dungeon, Daniel's out of the den, and Jonah's out of the fish's belly. It is our duty and interest to cry unto God, for that is the likeliest way both to prevent our sinking lower and to recover us out of the *horrible pit and miry clay,* xl. 1, 2.

II. While we continue calling upon God to assure ourselves of an answer of peace from him; for this is that which David in faith prays for (*v.* 2): *Lord, hear my voice,* my complaint and prayer, and *let thy ears be attentive* to the voice both of my afflictions and *of my supplications.*

III. We are taught to humble ourselves before the justice of God as guilty in his sight, and unable to answer him for one of a thousand of our offences (*v.* 3): *If thou, Lord, shouldst mark iniquities, O Lord! who shall stand?* His calling God *Lord* twice, in so few words, *Jah* and *Adonai,* is very emphatic, and intimates a very awful sense of God's glorious majesty and a dread of his wrath. Let us learn here, 1. To acknowledge our iniquities, that we cannot justify ourselves before God, or plead Not guilty. There is that which is remarkable in our iniquities and is liable to be animadverted upon. 2. To own the power and justice of God, which are such that, if he were extreme to mark what we do amiss, there would be no hopes of coming off. His eye can discover enough in the best man to ground a condemnation upon; and, if he proceed against us, we have no way to help ourselves, we cannot stand, but shall certainly be cast. If God deal with us in strict justice, we are undone; if he make remarks upon our iniquities, he will find them to be many and great, greatly aggravated and very provoking; and then, if he should proceed accordingly, he would shut us out from all hope of his favour and shut us up under his wrath; and what could we do to help ourselves? We could not make our escape, nor resist nor bear up under his avenging hand. 3. Let us admire God's patience and forbearance; we should be undone if he were to mark iniquities, and he knows it, and therefore bears with us. *It is of his mercy that we are not consumed* by his wrath.

IV. We are taught to cast ourselves upon the pardoning mercy of God, and to comfort ourselves with that when we see ourselves obnoxious to his justice, *v.* 4. Here is, 1. God's grace discovered, and pleaded with him, by a penitent sinner: *But there is forgiveness with thee.* It is our unspeakable comfort, in all our approaches to God, that there is forgiveness with him, for that is what we need. He has put himself into a capacity to pardon sin; he has declared himself gracious and merciful, and ready to forgive, Exod. xxxiv. 6, 7. He has promised to forgive the sins of those that do repent. Never any that dealt with him found him implacable, but easy to be entreated, and swift to show mercy. With us there is iniquity, and therefore it is well for us that with him there is forgiveness. *There is a propitiation with thee,* so some read it. Jesus Christ is the great propitiation, the ransom which God has found; he is ever with him, as advocate for us, and through him we hope to obtain forgiveness. 2. Our duty designed in that discovery, and inferred from it: " *There is forgiveness with thee,* not that thou mayest be made bold with and presumed upon, but *that thou mayest be feared*—in general, that thou mayest be worshipped and served by the children of men, who, being sinners, could have no dealings with God, if he were not a Master that could pass by a great many faults." But this encourages us to come into his service that we shall not be turned off for every misdemeanour; no, nor for any, if we truly repent. This does in a special manner invite those who have sinned to repent, and return to the fear of God, that he is gracious and merciful, and will receive them upon their repentance, Joel ii. 13; Matt. iii. 2. And, particularly, we are to have a holy awe and reverence of God's pardoning mercy (Hos. iii. 5, *They shall fear the Lord, and his goodness);*

and *then* we may expect the benefit of the forgiveness that is with God when we make it the object of our holy fear.

5 I wait for the LORD, my soul doth wait, and in his word do I hope. 6 My soul *waiteth* for the Lord more than they that watch for the morning: *I say, more than* they that watch for the morning. 7 Let Israel hope in the LORD: for with the LORD *there is* mercy, and with him *is* plenteous redemption. 8 And he shall redeem Israel from all his iniquities.

Here, I. The psalmist engages himself to trust in God and to wait for him, *v.* 5, 6. Observe, 1. His dependence upon God, expressed in a climax, it being a song of degrees, or ascents : "*I wait for the Lord;* from him I expect relief and comfort, believing it will come, longing till it does come, but patiently bearing the delay of it, and resolving to look for it from no other hand. *My soul doth wait;* I wait for him in sincerity, and not in profession only. I am an expectant, and it is *for the Lord* that *my soul waits,* for the gifts of his grace and the operations of his power." 2. The ground of that dependence : *In his word do I hope.* We must hope for that only which he has promised in his word, and not for the creatures of our own fancy and imagination; and we must hope for it because he has promised it, and not from any opinion of our own merit. 3. The degree of that dependence—"*more than those that watch for the morning,* who are, (1.) Well-assured that the morning will come; and so am I that God will return in mercy to me, according to his promise; for God's covenant is more firm than the ordinances of day and night, for they shall come to an end, but that is everlasting." (2.) Very desirous that it would come. Sentinels that keep guard upon the walls, those that watch with sick people, and travellers that are abroad upon their journey, long before day wish to see the dawning of the day; but more earnestly does this good man long for the tokens of God's favour and the visits of his grace, and more readily will he be aware of his first appearances than they are of day. Dr. Hammond reads it thus, *My soul hastens to the Lord, from the guards in the morning, the guards in the morning,* and gives this sense of it, "To thee I daily betake myself, early in the morning, addressing my prayers, and my very soul, before thee, at the time that the priests offer their morning sacrifice."

II. He encourages all the people of God in like manner to depend upon him and trust in him: *Let Israel hope in the Lord* and *wait for him;* not only the body of the people, but every good man, who *surnames himself by the name of Israel,* Isa. xliv. 5. Let all that devote themselves to God cheerfully stay themselves upon him (*v.* 7, 8), for two reasons:—

740

1. Because the light of nature discovers to us that *there is mercy with him,* that the God of Israel is a merciful God and *the Father of mercies. Mercy is with* him; not only inherent in his nature, but it is his delight, it is his darling attribute; it is with him in all his works, in all his counsels. 2. Because the light of the gospel discovers to us that *there is redemption with him,* contrived by him, and to be wrought out *in the fulness of time:* it was in the beginning hidden in God. See here, (1.) The nature of this redemption; it is redemption from sin, from all sin, and therefore can be no other than that eternal redemption which Jesus Christ became the author of; for it is he *that saves his people from their sins* (Matt. i. 21), that *redeems them from all iniquity* (Tit. ii. 14), and *turns away ungodliness from Jacob,* Rom. xi. 26. It is he that redeems us both from the condemning and from the commanding power of sin. (2.) The riches of this redemption; it *is plenteous redemption;* there is an all-sufficient fulness of merit and grace in the Redeemer, enough for all, enough for each; enough for me, says the believer. Redemption from sin includes redemption from all other evils, and therefore is a plenteous redemption. (3.) The persons to whom the benefits of this redemption belong: *He shall redeem Israel,* Israel according to the spirit, all those who are in covenant with God, as Israel was, and who are *Israelites indeed, in whom is no guile.*

PSALM CXXXI.

This psalm is David's profession of humility, humbly made, with thankfulness to God for his grace, and not in vain-glory. It is probable enough that (as most interpreters suggest) David made this protestation in answer to the calumnies of Saul and his courtiers, who represented David as an ambitious aspiring man, who, under pretence of a divine appointment, sought the kingdom, in the pride of his heart. But he appeals to God, that, on the contrary, I. He aimed at nothing high nor great, ver. 1. II. He was very easy in every condition which God allotted him (ver. 2); and therefore, III. He encourages all good people to trust in God as he did, ver. 3. Some have made it an objection against singing David's psalms that there are many who cannot say, "My heart is not haughty," &c. It is true there are; but we may sing it for the same purpose that we read it, to teach and admonish ourselves, and one another, what we ought to be, with repentance that we have come short of being so, and humble prayer to God for his grace to make us so.

A song of degrees of David.

LORD, my heart is not haughty, nor mine eyes lofty: neither do I exercise myself in great matters, or in things too high for me. 2 Surely I have behaved and quieted myself, as a child that is weaned of his mother: my soul *is* even as a weaned child. 3 Let Israel hope in the LORD from henceforth and for ever.

Here are two things which will be comforts to us:—

I. Consciousness of our integrity. This was David's rejoicing, that his heart could witness for him that he had walked humbly with his God, notwithstanding the censures he was under and the temptations he was in.

1. He aimed not at a high condition, nor was he desirous of making a figure in the world, but, if God had so ordered, could

have been well content to spend all his days, as he did the beginning of them, in the sheep-folds. His own brother, in a passion, charged him with pride (1 Sam. xvii. 28), but the charge was groundless and unjust. God, who searches the heart, knew, (1.) That he had no conceited opinion of himself, or his own merits : *Lord, my heart is not haughty.* Humble saints cannot think so well of themselves as others think of them, are not in love with their own shadow, nor do they magnify their own attainments or achievements. The love of God reigning in the heart will subdue all inordinate self-love. (2.) That he had neither a scornful nor an aspiring look : " *My eyes are not lofty*, either to look with envy upon those that are above me or to look with disdain upon those that are below me." Where there is a proud heart there is commonly a proud look (Prov. vi. 17), but the humble publican will not so much as lift up his eyes. (3.) That he did not employ himself in things above his station, *in things too* great or *too high for* him. He did not employ himself in studies too high ; he made God's word his meditation, and did not amuse himself with matters of nice speculation or doubtful disputation, or covet to be wise above what is written. To know God and our duty is learning sufficiently high for us. He did not employ himself in affairs too great; he followed his ewes, and never set up for a politician ; no, nor for a soldier ; for, when his brethren went to the wars, he staid at home to keep the sheep. It is our wisdom, and will be our praise, to keep within our sphere, and not to intrude into things which we have not seen, or meddle with that which does not belong to us. Princes and scholars must not exercise themselves in matters too great, too high, for men : and those in a low station, and of ordinary capacities, must not pretend to that which is out of their reach, and which they were not cut out for. Those will fall under due shame that affect undue honours.

2. He was well reconciled to every condition that God placed him in (*v.* 2): *I have behaved and quieted myself as a child that is weaned of his mother.* As he had not proudly aimed at the kingdom, so, since God had appointed him to it, he had not behaved insolently towards any, nor been restless in his attempts to get the crown before the time set; but, (1.) He had been as humble as a little child about the age of a weanling, as manageable and governable, and as far from aiming at high things ; as entirely at God's disposal as the child at the disposal of the mother or nurse; as far from taking state upon him, though anointed to be king, or valuing himself upon the prospect of his future advancement, as a child in the arms. Our Saviour has taught us humility by this comparison (Matt. xviii. 3); we must *become as little children.* (2.) He had been as indifferent to the wealth and honour of this world as a child is to the breast when it is thoroughly weaned from it. *I have levelled and quieted myself* (so Dr. Hammond reads it) *as a child that is weaned.* This intimates that our hearts are naturally as desirous of worldly things as the babe is of the breast, and in like manner relish them, cry for them, are fond of them, play with them, and cannot live without them. But, by the grace of God, a soul that is sanctified, is weaned from those things. Providence puts wormwood upon the breast, and that helps to wean us. The child is perhaps cross and fretful while it is in the weaning and thinks itself undone when it has lost the breast. But in a day or two it is forgotten ; the fret is over, and it accommodates itself well enough to a new way of feeding, cares no longer for milk, but can bear strong meat. Thus does a gracious soul quiet itself under the loss of that which it loved and disappointment in that which it hoped for, and is easy whatever happens, lives, and lives comfortably, upon God and the covenant-grace, when creatures prove dry breasts. When our condition is not to our mind we must bring our mind to our condition ; and then we are easy to ourselves and all about us; then our souls are *as a weaned child.*

II. Confidence in God; and this David recommends to all the Israel of God, no doubt from his own experience of the benefit of it (*v.* 3): *Let Israel hope in the Lord,* and let them continue to do so *henceforth and for ever.* Though David could himself wait patiently and quietly for the crown designed him yet perhaps Israel, the people whose darling he was, would be ready to attempt something in favour of him before the time; he therefore endeavours to quiet them too, and bids them *hope in the Lord* that they should see a happy change of the face of affairs in due time. *Thus it is good to hope and quietly to wait for the salvation of the Lord.*

PSALM CXXXII.

It is probable that this psalm was penned by Solomon, to be sung at the dedication of the temple which he built according to the charge his father gave him, 1 Chron. xxviii. 2, &c. Having fulfilled his trust, he begs of God to own what he had done. I. He had built this house for the honour and service of God ; and when he brings the ark into it, the token of God's presence, he desires that God himself would come and take possession of it, ver. 8—10. With these words Solomon concluded his prayer, 2 Chron. vi. 41, 42. II. He had built it in pursuance of the orders he had received from his father, and therefore his pleas to enforce these petitions refer to David. 1. He pleads David's piety towards God, ver. 1—7. 2. He pleads God's promise to David, ver. 11—18. The former introduces his petition ; the latter follows it as an answer to it. In singing this psalm we must have a concern for the gospel church as the temple of God, and a dependence upon Christ as David our King, in whom the mercies of God are sure mercies.

A song of degrees.

LORD, remember David, *and* all his afflictions: 2 How he sware unto the LORD, *and* vowed unto the mighty *God* of Jacob: 3 Surely I will not come into the tabernacle of my house, nor go up into my bed; 4 I will not give sleep to mine eyes, *or* slumber to mine eyelids, 5 Until I find out a place for the LORD, a habitation for the mighty *God* of Jacob. 6 Lo, we heard of it at Ephratah : we found it in the fields of the wood. 7 We will go into his tabernacles : we will worship at his footstool. 8 Arise, O LORD, into thy rest ; thou, and the ark of thy strength. 9 Let thy priests be clothed with righteousness ; and let thy saints shout for joy. 10 For thy servant David's sake turn not away the face of thine anointed.

In these verses we have Solomon's address to God for his favour to him and to his government, and his acceptance of his building a house to God's name. Observe,

I. What he pleads—two things :—

1. That what he had done was in pursuance of the pious vow which his father David had made to build a house for God. Solomon was a wise man, yet pleads not any merit of his own : "I am not worthy, for whom thou shouldst do this; but, Lord, *remember David*, with whom thou madest the covenant" (as Moses prayed, Exod. xxxii. 13, *Remember Abraham*, the first trustee of the covenant); "remember *all his afflictions*, all the troubles of his life, which his being anointed was the occasion of," or his care and concern about the ark, and what an uneasiness it was to him that the ark was in curtains, 2 Sam. vii. 2. *Remember all his humility and meekness* (so some read it), all that pious and devout affection with which he had made the following vow. Note, It is not amiss for us to put God in mind of our predecessors in profession, of their afflictions, their services, and their sufferings, of God's covenant with them, the experiences they have had of his goodness, the care they took of, and the many prayers they put up for, those that should come after them. We may apply it to Christ, the Son of David, and to all his afflictions : "Lord, remember the covenant made with him and the satisfaction made by him. *Remember all his offerings* (Ps. xx. 3), that is, all his sufferings." He especially pleads the solemn vow that David had made as soon as ever he was settled in his government, and before he was well settled in a house of his own, that he would build a house for God. Observe, (1.) Whom he bound himself to, *to the Lord, to the mighty God of Jacob.* Vows are to be made to God, who is a party as well as a witness. The Lord is the Mighty One of Jacob, Jacob's God, and a mighty one, whose power is engaged for Jacob's defence and deliverance. Jacob is weak, but the God of Jacob is a mighty one. (2.) What he bound himself to do, to *find out a place for the Lord*, that is, for the ark, the token of his presence. He had observed in the law frequent mention of the *place that God would choose to put his*

name *there*, to which all the tribes should resort. When he came to the crown there was no such place ; Shiloh was deserted, and no other place was pitched upon, for want of which the feasts of the Lord were not kept with due solemnity. "Well," says David, "I will find out such a place for the general rendezvous of all the tribes, a place of *habitation for the Mighty* One *of Jacob*, a place for the ark, where there shall be room both for the priests and people to attend upon it." (3.) How intent he was upon it ; he would not settle in his house, nay, he would not sleep in his bed, till he had brought this matter to some head, *v.* 3, 4. The thing had been long talked of, and nothing done, till at last David, when he went out one morning about public business, made a vow that before night he would come to a resolution in this matter, and would determine the place either where the tent should be pitched for the reception of the ark, at the beginning of his reign, or rather where Solomon should build the temple, which was not fixed till the latter end of his reign, just after the pestilence with which he was punished for numbering the people (1 Chron. xxii. 1, *Then David said, This is the house of the Lord*) ; and perhaps it was upon occasion of that judgment that he made this vow, being apprehensive that one of God's controversies with him was for his dilatoriness in this matter. Note, When needful work is to be done for God it is good for us to task ourselves, and tie ourselves to a time, because we are apt to put off. It is good in the morning to cut out work for the day, binding ourselves that we will do it before we sleep, only with submission to Providence ; for we *know not what a day may bring forth*. Especially in the great work of conversion to God we must be thus solicitous, thus zealous ; we have good reason to resolve that we will not enjoy the comforts of this life till we have laid a foundation for hopes of a better.

2. That it was in pursuance of the expectations of the people of Israel, *v.* 6, 7. (1.) They were inquisitive after the ark ; for they lamented its obscurity, 1 Sam. vii. 2. They *heard of it at Ephratah* (that is, at Shiloh, in the tribe of Ephraim); there they were told it had been, but it was gone. They *found it*, at last, *in the fields of the wood*, that is, in Kirjath-jearim, which signifies *the city of woods*. Thence all Israel fetched it, with great solemnity, in the beginning of David's reign (1 Chron. xiii. 6), so that in building this house for the ark Solomon had gratified all Israel. They needed not to go about to seek the ark any more; they now knew where to find it. (2.) They were resolved to attend it : "Let us but have a convenient place, and *we will go into his tabernacle*, to pay our homage there ; *we will worship at his footstool* as subjects and suppliants, which we neglected to do, for want of such a place, in the days of Saul," 1 Chron. xiii. 3.

II. What he prays for, v. 8—10. 1. That God would vouchsafe, not only to take possession of, but to take up his residence in, this temple which he had built: *Arise, O Lord! into thy rest,* and let this be it, *thou, even the ark of thy strength,* the pledge of thy presence, thy mighty presence. 2. That God would give grace to the ministers of the sanctuary to do their duty: *Let thy priests be clothed with righteousness;* let them appear righteous both in their administrations and in their conversations, and let both be according to the rule. Note, Righteousness is the best ornament of a minister. Holiness towards God, and goodness towards all men, are habits for ministers of the necessity of which there is no dispute. "They are *thy priests,* and will therefore discredit their relation to thee if they *be not clothed with righteousness.*" 3. That the people of God might have the comfort of the due administration of holy ordinances among them: *Let thy saints shout for joy.* They did so when the ark was brought into the city of David (2 Sam. vi. 15); they will do so when the priests are clothed with righteousness. A faithful ministry is the joy of the saints; it is the matter of it; it is a friend and a furtherance to it; we are *helpers of your joy,* 2 Cor. i. 24. 4. That Solomon's own prayer, upon occasion of the dedicating of the temple, might be accepted of God: " *Turn not away the face of thy anointed,* that is, deny me not the things I have asked of thee, send me not away ashamed." He pleads, (1.) That he was the anointed of the Lord, and this he pleads as a type of Christ, the great anointed, who, in his intercession, urges his designation to his office. He is God's anointed, and therefore the Father hears him always. (2.) That he was the son of David: "For his sake do not deny me;" and this is the Christian's plea: "For the sake of Christ" (our David), "*in whom thou art well pleased,* accept me." He is David, whose name signifies *beloved;* and we are made accepted in the beloved. He is God's servant, whom he *upholds,* Isa. xlii. 1. "We have no merit of our own to plead, but for his sake, in whom there is a fulness of merit, let us find favour." When we pray for the prosperity of the church we may pray with great boldness, for Christ's sake, who purchased the church with his own blood. "Let both ministers and people do their duty."

11 The Lord hath sworn *in* truth unto David; he will not turn from it; Of the fruit of thy body will I set upon thy throne. 12 If thy children will keep my covenant and my testimony that I shall teach them, their children shall also sit upon thy throne for evermore. 13 For the Lord hath chosen Zion; he hath desired *it* for his habitation. 14 This *is* my rest for

ever: here will I dwell; for I have desired it. 15 I will abundantly bless her provision : I will satisfy her poor with bread. 16 I will also clothe her priests with salvation : and her saints shall shout aloud for joy. 17 There will I make the horn of David to bud: I have ordained a lamp for mine anointed. 18 His enemies will I clothe with shame: but upon himself shall his crown flourish.

These are precious promises, *confirmed by an oath,* that the heirs of them might have *strong consolation,* Heb. vi. 17, 18. It is all one whether we take them as pleas urged in the prayer or as answers returned to the prayer; believers know how to make use of the promises both ways, with them to speak to God and in them to hear what God the Lord will speak to us. These promises relate to the establishment both in church and state, both to the throne of the house of David and to the testimony of Israel fixed on Mount Zion. The promises concerning Zion's hill are as applicable to the gospel-church as these concerning David's seed are to Christ, and therefore both pleadable by us and very comfortable to us. Here is,

I. The choice God made of David's house and Zion hill. Both were of divine appointment. 1. God chose David's family for the royal family and confirmed his choice by an oath, *v.* 11, 12. David, being a type of Christ, was made king with an oath : *The Lord hath sworn and will not repent,* will not turn from it. Did David swear to the Lord (*v.* 2) that he would find him a house ? The Lord swore to David that he would build him a house; for God will be behind with none of his people in affections or assurances. The promise made to David refers, (1.) To a long succession of kings that should descend from his loins : *Of the fruit of thy body will I set upon thy throne,* which was fulfilled in Solomon ; David himself lived to see it with great satisfaction, 1 Kings i. 48. The crown was also entailed conditionally upon his heirs for ever: *If thy children,* in following ages, *will keep my covenant and my testimony that I shall teach them.* God himself engaged to teach them, and he did his part; they had Moses and the prophets, and all he expects is that they should keep what he taught them, and keep to it, and then *their children shall sit upon thy throne for evermore.* Kings are before God upon their good behaviour, and their commission from him runs *quamdiu se bene gesserint— during good behaviour.* The issue of this was that they did not keep God's covenant, and so the entail was at length cut off, and *the sceptre departed from Judah* by degrees. (2.) To an everlasting successor, a king that should descend from his loins of *the increase of whose government and peace there shall be no end.* St. Peter applies this to Christ, nay, he tells us that David himself so understood it. Acts ii. 30, *He knew that God had sworn with an oath to him that of the fruit of his loins, according to the flesh, he would raise up Christ to sit on his throne ;* and in the fulness of time he did so, and *gave him the throne of his father David,* Luke i. 32. He did fulfil the condition of the promise ; he kept God's covenant and his testimony, did his Father's will, and in all things pleased him ; and therefore to him, and his spiritual seed, the promise shall be made good. He, and the children God has given him, all believers, shall *sit upon the throne for evermore,* Rev. iii. 21.

2. God chose Zion hill for the holy hill, and confirmed his choice by the delight he took in it, *v.* 13, 14. He *chose the Mount Zion which he loved* (lxxviii. 68) ; he chose it for the habitation of his ark, and said of it, *This is my rest for ever,* and not merely my residence for a time, as Shiloh was. Zion was the city of David ; he chose it for the royal city because God chose it for the holy city. God said, *Here will I dwell,* and therefore David said, *Here will I dwell,* for here he adhered to his principle, *It is good for me to be near to God.* Zion must be here looked upon as a type of the gospel-church, which is called *Mount Zion* (Heb. xii. 22), and in it what is here said of Zion has its full accomplishment. Zion was long since ploughed as a field, but the church of Christ *is the house of the living God* (1 Tim. iii. 15), and it is his *rest for ever,* and shall be blessed with his presence always, even to the end of the world. The delight God takes in his church, and the continuance of his presence with his church, are the comfort and joy of all its members.

II. The choice blessings God has in store for David's house and Zion hill. Whom God chooses he will bless.

1. God, having chosen Zion hill, promises to bless that,

(1.) With the blessings of the life that now is ; for godliness has the promise of them, *v.* 15. The earth shall yield her increase ; where religion is set up there shall be provision, and in blessing God will bless it (lxvii. 6) ; he will surely and abundantly bless it. And a little provision, with an abundant blessing upon it, will be more serviceable, as well as more comfortable, than a great deal without that blessing. God's people have a special blessing upon common enjoyments, and that blessing puts a peculiar sweetness into them. Nay, the promise goes further : *I will satisfy her poor with bread.* Zion has her own poor to keep ; and it is promised that God will take care even of them. [1.] By his providence they shall be kept from wanting ; they shall have provision enough. If there be scarcity, the poor are the first that feel it, so that it is a sure sign of plenty if they have sufficient. Zion's poor shall not want, for God has obliged all the sons of Zion to be charitable to the poor, according to their ability, and the church

744

must take care that they be not *neglected,* Acts vi. 1. [2.] By his grace they shall be kept from complaining ; though they have but dry bread, yet they shall be satisfied. Zion's poor have, of all others, reason to be content with a little of this world, because they have better things prepared for them. And this may be understood spiritually of the provision that is made for the soul in the word and ordinances ; God will abundantly bless that for the nourishment of the new man, and satisfy the poor in spirit with the bread of life. What God sanctifies to us we shall and may be satisfied with.

(2.) With the blessings of the life that is to come, things pertaining to godliness (*v.* 16), which is an answer to the prayer, *v.* 9. [1.] It was desired that the priests might be *clothed with righteousness ;* it is here promised that God will *clothe them with salvation,* not only save them, but make them and their administrations instrumental for the salvation of his people ; they shall both *save themselves and those that hear them,* and *add those to the church that shall be saved.* Note, Whom God clothes with righteousness he will clothe with salvation ; we must pray for righteousness and then with it God will give salvation. [2.] It was desired that the saints might *shout for joy ;* it is promised that they *shall shout aloud for joy.* God gives more than we ask, and when he gives salvation he will give an abundant joy.

2. God, having chosen David's family, here promises to bless that also with suitable blessings. (1.) Growing power : *There,* in Zion, *will I make the horn of David to bud, v.* 17. The royal dignity shall increase more and more, and constant additions be made to the lustre of it. Christ is the *horn of salvation* (denoting a plentiful and powerful salvation) which God has raised up, and made to bud, *in the house of his servant David.* David had promised to use his power for God's glory, to cut off the horns of the wicked, and to exalt the horns of the righteous (lxxv. 10) ; in recompence for it God here promises to make his horn to bud, for to those that have power, and use it well, more shall be given. (2.) Lasting honour : *I have ordained a lamp for my anointed.* Thou wilt *light my candle,* xviii. 28. That lamp is likely to burn brightly which God ordains. A lamp is a successor, for, when a lamp is almost out, another may be lighted by it ; it is a succession, for by this means David shall not want a man to stand before God. Christ is the lamp and the light of the world. (3.) Complete victory : " *His enemies,* who have formed designs against him, *will I clothe with shame,* when they shall see their designs baffled." Let the enemies of all good governors expect to be clothed with shame, and especially the enemies of the Lord Jesus and his government, who shall rise, in the great day, *to everlasting shame and contempt.* (4.) Universal prosperity : *Upon himself shall his crown flourish,* that is, his government shall be more and more his honour. This was to have its full accomplish-

ment in Jesus Christ, whose crown of honour and power shall never fade, nor the flowers of it wither. The crowns of earthly princes *endure not to all generations* (Prov. xxvii. 24), but Christ's crown shall endure to all eternity and the crowns reserved for his faithful subjects are such as *fade not away.*

PSALM CXXXIII.

This psalm is a brief encomium on unity and brotherly love, which, if we did not see the miseries of discord among men, we should think needless; but we cannot say too much, it were well if we could say enough, to persuade people to live together in peace. Some conjecture that David penned this psalm upon occasion of the union between the tribes when they all met unanimously to make him king. It is a psalm of general use to all societies, smaller and larger, civil and sacred. Here is, I. The doctrine laid down of the happiness of brotherly love, ver. 1. II. The illustration of that doctrine, in two similitudes, ver. 2, 3. III. The proof of it, in a good reason given for it (ver. 3); and then we are left to make the application, which we ought to do in singing it, provoking ourselves and one another to holy love. The contents of this psalm, in our Bibles, are short, but very proper; it is "the benefit of the communion of saints."

A song of degrees of David.

BEHOLD, how good and how pleasant *it is* for brethren to dwell together in unity! 2 *It is* like the precious ointment upon the head, that ran down upon the beard, *even* Aaron's beard: that went down to the skirts of his garments; 3 As the dew of Hermon, *and as the dew* that descended upon the mountains of Zion: for there the LORD commanded the blessing, *even* life for evermore.

Here see, I. What it is that is commended—*brethren's dwelling together in unity,* not only not quarrelling, and devouring one another, but delighting in each other with mutual endearments, and promoting each other's welfare with mutual services. Sometimes it is chosen, as the best expedient for preserving peace, that brethren should live asunder and at a distance from each other; that indeed may prevent enmity and strife (Gen. xiii. 9), but the goodness and pleasantness are *for brethren to dwell together* and so *to dwell in unity, to dwell even as one* (so some read it), as having one heart, one soul, one interest. David had many sons by many wives; probably he penned this psalm for their instruction, to engage them to love another, and, if they had done this, much of the mischief that arose in his family would have been happily prevented. The tribes of Israel had long had separate interests during the government of the Judges, and it was often of bad consequence; but now that they were united under one common head he would have them sensible how much it was likely to be for their advantage, especially since now the ark was fixed, and with it the place of their rendezvous for public worship and the centre of their unity. Now let them live in love.

II. How commendable it is: *Behold, how good and how pleasant it is!* It is good in itself, agreeable to the will of God, the conformity of earth to heaven. It is good for us, for our honour and comfort. It is pleasant and pleasing to God and all good men; it

brings constant delight to those who do thus live in unity. *Behold, how good!* We cannot conceive or express the goodness and pleasantness of it. Behold it is a rare thing, and therefore admirable. Behold and wonder that there should be so much goodness and pleasantness among men, so much of heaven on this earth! Behold it is an amiable thing, which will attract our hearts. Behold it is an exemplary thing, which, where it is, is to be imitated by us with a holy emulation.

III. How the pleasantness of it is illustrated.

1. It is fragrant as the holy anointing oil, which was strongly perfumed, and diffused its odours, to the great delight of all the by-standers, when it was poured upon the head of Aaron, or his successor the high priest, so plentifully that it ran down the face, even to the collar or binding of the garment, *v.* 2. (1.) This ointment was holy. So must our brotherly love be, with a pure heart, devoted to God. We must love those that are begotten *for his sake that begat,* 1 John v. 1. (2.) This ointment was a composition made up by a divine dispensatory; God appointed the ingredients and the quantities. Thus believers are *taught of God to love one another;* it is a grace of his working in us. (3.) It was very precious, and the like to it was not to be made for any common use. Thus holy love is, in the sight of God, of great price; and that is precious indeed which is so in God's sight. (4.) It was grateful both to Aaron himself and to all about him. So is holy love; it is like *ointment and perfume which rejoice the heart.* Christ's love to mankind was part of that *oil of gladness* with which he was *anointed above his fellows.* (5.) Aaron and his sons were not admitted to minister unto the Lord till they were anointed with this ointment, nor are our services acceptable to God without this holy love; if we have it not we are nothing, 1 Cor. xiii. 1, 2.

2. It is fructifying. It is profitable as well as pleasing; it is *as the dew;* it brings abundance of blessings along with it, as numerous as the drops of dew. It cools the scorching heat of men's passions, as the evening dews cool the air and refresh the earth. It contributes very much to our fruitfulness in every thing that is good; it moistens the heart, and makes it tender and fit to receive the good seed of the word; as, on the contrary, *malice and bitterness* unfit us to receive it, 1 Pet. ii. 1. It is *as the dew of Hermon,* a common hill (for brotherly love is the beauty and benefit of civil societies), *and as the dew that descended upon the mountains of Zion,* a holy hill, for it contributes greatly to the fruitfulness of sacred societies. Both Hermon and Zion will wither without this dew. It is said of the dew that it *tarrieth not for man, nor waiteth for the sons of men,* Mic. v. 7. Nor should our love to our brethren stay for theirs to us (that is publican's love), but should go before it— that is divine love.

IV. The proof of the excellency of brotherly

love. Loving people are blessed people. For, 1. They are blessed of God, and therefore blessed indeed : *There,* where brethren dwell together in unity, *the Lord commands the blessing,* a complicated blessing, including all blessings. It is God's prerogative to command the blessing, man can but beg a blessing. Blessings according to the promise are commanded blessings, for he has commanded *his covenant for ever.* Blessings that take effect are commanded blessings, for *he speaks and it is done.* 2. They are everlastingly blessed. The blessing which God commands on those that dwell in love is *life for ever-more ;* that is the blessing of blessings. Those that dwell in love not only dwell in God, but do already dwell in heaven. As the perfection of love is the blessedness of heaven, so the sincerity of love is the earnest of that blessedness. Those that live in love and peace shall have the God of love and peace with them now, and they shall be with him shortly, with him for ever, in the world of endless love and peace. How good then is it, and how pleasant !

PSALM CXXXIV.

This is the last of the fifteen songs of degrees ; and, if they were at any time sung all together in the temple-service, it is fitly made the conclusion of them, for the design of it is to stir up the ministers to go on with their work in the night, when the solemnities of the day were over. Some make this psalm to be a dialogue. I. In the first two verses, the priests or Levites who sat up all night to keep the watch of the house of the Lord are called upon to spend their time while they were upon the guard, not in idle talk, but in the acts of devotion. II. In the last verse those who were thus called upon to praise God pray for him that gave them the exhortation, either the high priest or the captain of the guard. Or thus : those who did that service did mutually exhort one another and pray for one another. In singing this psalm we must both stir up ourselves to give glory to God and encourage ourselves to hope for mercy and grace from him.

A song of degrees.

BEHOLD, bless ye the LORD, all *ye* servants of the LORD, which by night stand in the house of the LORD. 2 Lift up your hands *in* the sanctuary, and bless the LORD. 3 The LORD that made heaven and earth bless thee out of Zion.

This psalm instructs us concerning a two-fold blessing :—

I. Our blessing God, that is, speaking well of him, which here we are taught to do, *v.* 1, 2. 1. It is a call to the *Levites* to do it. They were *the servants of the Lord* by office, appointed to minister in holy things ; they attended the sanctuary, and kept the charge of the house of the Lord, Num. iii. 6, &c. Some of them did *by night stand in the house of the Lord,* to guard the holy things of the temple, that they might not be profaned, and the rich things of the temple, that they might not be plundered. While the ark was in curtains there was the more need of guards upon it. They attended likewise to see that neither the fire on the altar nor the lamps in the candlestick went out. Probably it was usual for some devout and pious Israelites to sit up with them ; we read of one that *departed not from the temple night or day,* Luke ii. 37. Now these are here called upon to *bless the Lord.*

Thus they must keep themselves awake by keeping themselves employed. Thus they must redeem time for holy exercises ; and how can we spend our time better than in praising God ? It would be an excellent piece of husbandry to fill up the vacancies of time with pious meditations and ejaculations; and surely it is a very modest and reasonable demand to converse with God when we have nothing else to do. Those who stood *in the house of the Lord* must remember where they were, and that holiness and holy work became that house. Let them therefore, bless the Lord *;* let them all do it in concert, or each by himself ; let them *lift up* their *hands* in the doing of it, in token of the lifting up of their hearts. *Let them lift up their hands in holiness* (so Dr. Hammond reads it) or in sanctification, as it is fit when they lift them up *in the sanctuary ;* and let them remember that when they were appointed to wash before they went in to minister they were thereby taught to *lift up holy hands* in prayer and praise. 2. It is a call to us to do it, who, as Christians, are made priests to our God, and Levites, Isa. lxvi. 21. We are the *servants of the Lord ;* we have a place and a name in his house, in his sanctuary ; we stand before him to minister to him. Even by night we are under his eye and have access to him. Let us therefore *bless the Lord,* and again bless him ; think and speak of his glory and goodness. Let us *lift up* our *hands* in prayer, in praise, in vows ; let us do our work with diligence and cheerfulness, and an elevation of mind. This exhortation is ushered in with *Behold !* a note commanding attention. Look about you, Sirs, when you are in God's presence, and conduct yourselves accordingly.

II. God's blessing us, and that is doing well for us, which we are here taught to desire, *v.* 3. Whether it is the watchmen's blessing their captain, or the Levites' blessing the high priest, or whoever was their chief (as many take it, because it is in the singular number, *The Lord bless thee*), or whether the blessing is pronounced by one upon many (" *The Lord bless thee,* each of you in particular, thee and thee ; you that are blessing God, the Lord bless you"), is not material. We may learn, 1. That we need desire no more to make us happy than to be blessed of the Lord, for those whom he blesses are blessed indeed. 2. That blessings out of Zion, spiritual blessings, the blessings of the covenant, and of communion with God, are the best blessings, which we should be most earnest for. 3. It is a great encouragement to us, when we come to God for a blessing, that it is he who *made heaven and earth,* and therefore has all the blessings of both at his disposal, the upper and nether springs. 4. We ought to beg these blessings, not only for ourselves, but for others also ; not only, The Lord bless *me,* but, The Lord bless *thee,* thus testifying our belief of the fulness of divine blessings, that there is enough for others as well as for us, and our good-will also to others. We must pray for those that exhort us. Though *the less is blessed of the greater* (Heb. vii. 7), yet the greater must be prayed for by the less.

PSALM CXXXV.

This is one of the Hallelujah-psalms; that is the title of it, and that is the Amen of it, both its Alpha and its Omega. I. It begins with a call to praise God, particularly a call to the " servants of the Lord " to praise him, as in the foregoing psalm, ver. 1—3. II. It goes on to furnish us with matter for praise. God is to be praised, 1. As the God of Jacob, ver. 4. 2. As the God of gods, ver. 5. 3. As the God of the whole world, ver. 6, 7. 4. As a terrible God to the enemies of Israel, ver. 8—11. 5. As a gracious God to Israel, both in what he had done for them and what he would do, ver. 12—14. 6. As the only living God, all other gods being vanity and a lie, ver. 15—18. III. It concludes with another exhortation to all persons concerned to praise God, ver. 19—21. In singing this psalm our hearts must be filled, as well as our mouths, with the high praises of God.

PRAISE ye the Lord. Praise ye the name of the Lord; praise *him*, O ye servants of the Lord. 2 Ye that stand in the house of the Lord, in the courts of the house of our God, 3 Praise the Lord; for the Lord *is* good : sing praises unto his name; for *it is* pleasant. 4 For the Lord hath chosen Jacob unto himself, *and* Israel for his peculiar treasure.

Here is, 1. The duty we are called to—to *praise the Lord*, to *praise his name : praise him*, and again *praise him*. We must not only thank him for what he has done for us, but praise him for what he is in himself and has done for others ; take all occasions to speak well of God and to give his truths and ways a good word. 2. The persons that are called upon to do this—the *servants of the Lord*, the priests and Levites *that stand in his house*, and all the devout and pious Israelites that stand *in the courts of his house* to worship there, *v.* 2. Those have most reason to praise God who are admitted to the privileges of his house, and those see most reason who there behold his beauty and taste his bounty ; from them it is expected, for to that end they enjoy their places. Who should praise him if they do not ? 3. The reasons why we should praise God. (1.) Because he whom we are to praise *is good*, and goodness is that which every body will speak well of. He is good to all, and we must give him the praise of that. His goodness is his glory, and we must make mention of it to his glory. (2.) Because the work is its own wages: *Sing praises unto his name, for it is pleasant*. It is best done with a cheerful spirit, and we shall have the pleasure of having done our duty. It is a heaven upon earth to be praising God ; and the pleasure of that should quite put our mouths out of taste for the pleasures of sin. (3.) Because of the peculiar privileges of God's people (*v.* 4) : *The Lord hath chosen Jacob to himself*, and therefore Jacob is bound to praise him ; for *therefore* God chose a people to himself that they might be unto him *for a name and a praise* (Jer. xiii. 11), and *therefore*

Jacob has abundant matter for praise, being thus dignified and distinguished. *Israel* is God's *peculiar treasure* above all people (Exod. xix. 5) ; they are his *Segullah*, a people appropriated to him, and that he has a delight in, *precious in his sight and honourable.* For this distinguishing surprising favour, if the seed of Jacob do not praise him, they are the most unworthy ungrateful people under the sun.

5 For I know that the Lord *is* great, and *that* our Lord *is* above all gods. 6 Whatsoever the Lord pleased, *that* did he in heaven, and in earth, in the seas, and all deep places. 7 He causeth the vapours to ascend from the ends of the earth ; he maketh lightnings for the rain ; he bringeth the wind out of his treasuries. 8 Who smote the firstborn of Egypt, both of man and beast. 9 *Who* sent tokens and wonders into the midst of thee, O Egypt, upon Pharaoh, and upon all his servants. 10 Who smote great nations, and slew mighty kings ; 11 Sihon king of the Amorites, and Og king of Bashan, and all the kingdoms of Canaan : 12 And gave their land *for* a heritage, a heritage unto Israel his people. 13 Thy name, O Lord, *endureth* for ever ; *and* thy memorial, O Lord, throughout all generations. 14 For the Lord will judge his people, and he will repent himself concerning his servants.

The psalmist had suggested to us the goodness of God, as the proper matter of our cheerful praises ; here he suggests to us the greatness of God as the proper matter of our awful praises ; and on this he is most copious, because this we are less forward to consider.

I. He asserts the doctrine of God's greatness (*v.* 5) : *The Lord is great*, great indeed, who knows no limits of time or place. He asserts it with assurance, " I know that he is so ; know it not only by observation of the proofs of it, but by belief of the revelation of it. I know it ; I am sure of it ; I know it by my own experience of the divine greatness working on my soul." He asserts it with a holy defiance of all pretenders, though they should join in confederacy against him. He is not only above any god, but above all gods, infinitely above them, between him and them there is no comparison.

II. He proves him to be a great God by the greatness of his power, *v.* 6. 1. He has an absolute power, and may do what he will : *Whatsoever the Lord pleased, that did he*, and none could control him, or say unto him, *What doest thou ?* He does what he pleases, because he pleases, and gives not account of any of his matters. 2. He has an almighty power and can do what he will; if he will work, none shall hinder. 3. This absolute almighty power is of universal extent; he does what he will *in heaven, in earth, in the seas,* and in *all the deep places* that are in the bottom of the sea or the bowels of the earth. The gods of the heathen can do nothing; but our God can do any thing and does do every thing.

III. He gives instances of his great power, 1. In the kingdom of nature, *v.* 7. All the powers of nature prove the greatness of the God of nature, from whom they are derived and on whom they depend. The chain of natural causes was not only framed by him at first, but is still preserved by him. (1.) It is by his power that exhalations are drawn up from the terraqueous globe. The heat of the sun raises them, but it has that power from God, and therefore it is given as an instance of the glory of God that *nothing is hidden from the heat* of the sun, xix. 6. *He causes the vapours to ascend* (not only unhelped, but unseen, by us) from the earth, *from the ends of the earth,* that is, from the seas, by which the earth is surrounded. (2.) It is he who, out of those vapours so raised, forms the rain, so that the earth is no loser by the vapours it sends up, for they are returned with advantage in fruitful showers. (3.) Out of the same vapours (such is his wonderful power) he *makes lightnings for the rain;* by them he opens the bottles of heaven, and shakes the clouds, that they may water the earth. Here are fire and water thoroughly reconciled by divine omnipotence. They come together, and yet the water does not quench the fire, nor the fire lick up the water, as fire from heaven did when God pleased, 1 Kings xviii. 38. (4.) The same exhalations, to serve another purpose, are converted into winds, which blow where they list, from what point of the compass they will, and we are so far from directing them that we cannot tell whence they come nor whither they go, but God *brings them out of his treasuries* with as much exactness and design as a prudent prince orders money to issue out of his exchequer.

2. In the kingdoms of men; and here he mentions the great things God had formerly done for his people Israel, which were proofs of God's greatness as well as of his goodness, and confirmations of the truth of the scriptures of the Old Testament, which began to be written by Moses, the person employed in working those miracles. Observe God's sovereign dominion and irresistible power, (1.) In bringing Israel out of Egypt, humbling Pharaoh by many plagues, and so forcing him to let them go. These plagues are called *tokens* and *wonders,* because they came not in the common course of providence, but there was something miraculous in each of them. They were *sent upon Pharaoh and all his servants,* his subjects; but the Israelites, whom

748

God claimed for his servants, his son, his first-born, his free-born, were exempted from them, and no plague came nigh their dwelling. The death of the first-born both of men and cattle was the heaviest of all the plagues, and that which gained the point. (2.) In destroying the kingdoms of Canaan before them, *v.* 10. Those that were in possession of the land designed for Israel had all possible advantages for keeping possession. The people were numerous, and warlike, and confederate against Israel. They were great nations. Yet, if a great nation has a meek and mean-spirited prince, it lies exposed; but these great nations had *mighty kings,* and yet they were all smitten and slain—*Sihon* and *Og,* and *all the kingdoms of Canaan, v.* 10, 11. No power of hell or earth can prevent the accomplishment of the promise of God when the time, the set time, for it has come. (3.) In settling them in the land of promise. He that gives kingdoms to whomsoever he pleases gave Canaan to be a heritage to Israel his people. It came to them by inheritance, for their ancestors had the promise of it, though not the possession; and it descended as an inheritance to their seed. This was done long before, yet God is now praised for it; and with good reason, for the children were now enjoying the benefit of it.

IV. He triumphs in the perpetuity of God's glory and grace. 1. Of his glory (*v.* 13): *Thy name, O God! endures for ever.* God's manifestations of himself to his people have everlasting fruits and consequences. *What God doeth it shall be for ever,* Eccl. iii. 14. His name endures for ever in the constant and everlasting praises of his people; his memorial endures, has endured hitherto, and shall still endure throughout all generations of the church. This seems to refer to Exod. iii. 15, where, when God had called himself *the God of Abraham, Isaac, and Jacob,* he adds, *This is my name for ever and this is my memorial unto all generations.* God is, and will be, always the same to his church, a gracious, faithful, wonder-working God; and his church is, and will be, the same to him, a thankful praising people; and thus his name *endures for ever.* 2. Of his grace. He will be kind to his people. (1.) He will plead their cause against others that contend with them. *He will judge his people,* that is, he will judge for them, and will not suffer them to be run down. (2.) He will not himself contend for ever with them, but will *repent himself concerning his servants,* and not proceed in his controversy with them; he will be entreated for them, or he will be comforted concerning them; he will return in ways of mercy to them and will delight to do them good. This verse is taken from the song of Moses, Deut. xxxii. 36.

15 The idols of the heathen *are* silver and gold, the work of men's hands. 16 They have mouths, but they

speak not; eyes have they, but they see not; 17 They have ears, but they hear not; neither is there *any* breath in their mouths. 18 They that make them are like unto them: *so is* every one that trusteth in them. 19 Bless the LORD, O house of Israel: bless the LORD, O house of Aaron: 20 Bless the LORD, O house of Levi: ye that fear the LORD, bless the LORD. 21 Blessed be the LORD out of Zion, which dwelleth at Jerusalem. Praise ye the LORD.

The design of these verses is,

I. To arm the people of God against idolatry and all false worships, by showing what sort of gods they were that the heathen worshipped, as we had it before, cxv. 4, &c. 1. They were gods of their own making; being so, they could have no power but what their makers gave them, and then what power could their makers receive from them? The images were the *work of men's hands*, and the deities that were supposed to inform them were as much the creatures of men's fancy and imagination. 2. They had the shape of animals, but could not perform the least act, no, not of the *animal* life. They could neither *see*, nor *hear*, nor *speak*, nor so much as *breathe;* and therefore to make them with *eyes*, and *ears*, and *mouths*, and *nostrils*, was such a jest that one would wonder how reasonable creatures could suffer themselves to be so imposed upon as to expect any good from such mock-deities. 3. Their worshippers were therefore as stupid and senseless as they were, both those that made them to be worshipped and those that trusted in them when they were made, *v.* 18. The worshipping of such gods as were the objects of sense, and senseless, made the worshippers sensual and senseless. Let our worshipping a God that is a Spirit make us spiritual and wise.

II. To stir up the people of God to true devotion in the worship of the true God, *v.* 19—21. The more deplorable the condition of the Gentile nations that worship idols is the more are we bound to thank God that we know better. Therefore, 1. Let us set ourselves about the acts of devotion, and employ ourselves in them: *Bless the Lord*, and again and again, *bless the Lord.* In the parallel place (cxv. 9—11), by way of inference from the impotency of idols, the duty thus pressed upon us is to *trust in the Lord;* here to *bless him;* by putting our trust in God we give glory to him, and those that depend upon God shall not want matter of thanksgiving to him. All persons that knew God are here called to praise him--the *house of Israel* (the nation in general), the *house of Aaron* and the *house of Levi* (the Lord's ministers that attended in his sanctuary), and all others *that feared the Lord*, though they were not of the

house of Israel. 2. Let God have the glory of all: *Blessed be the Lord.* The tribute of praise arises *out of Zion.* All God's works do praise him, but his saints bless him; and they need not go far to pay their tribute, for he *dwells in Jerusalem*, in his church, which they are members of, so that he is always nigh unto them to receive their homage. The condescensions of his grace, in dwelling with men upon the earth, call for our grateful and thankful returns, and our repeated Hallelujahs.

PSALM CXXXVI.

The scope of this psalm is the same with that of the foregoing psalm, but there is something very singular in the composition of it; for the latter half of each verse is the same, repeated throughout the psalm, "for his mercy endureth for ever," and yet no vain repetition. It is allowed that such burdens, or "keepings," as we call them, add very much to the beauty of a song, and help to make it moving and affecting; nor can any verse contain more weighty matter, or more worthy to be thus repeated, than this, that God's mercy endureth for ever; and the repetition of it here twenty-six times intimates, 1. That God's mercies to his people are thus repeated and drawn, as it were, with a continuando from the beginning to the end, with a progress and advance in infinitum. 2. That in every particular favour we ought to take notice of the mercy of God, and to take notice of it as enduring still, the same now that it has been, and enduring for ever, the same always that it is. 3. That the everlasting continuance of the mercy of God is very much his honour and that which he glories in, and very much the saints' comfort and that which they glory in. It is that which therefore our hearts should be full of and greatly affected with, so that the most frequent mention of it, instead of cloying us, should raise us the more, because it will be the subject of our praise to all eternity. This most excellent sentence, that God's mercy endureth for ever, is magnified above all the truths concerning God, not only by the repetition of it here, but by the signal tokens of divine acceptance with which God owned the singing of it, both in Solomon's time (2 Chron. v. 13, when they sang these words, "for his mercy endureth for ever," the house was filled with a cloud) and in Jehoshaphat's time (when they sang these words, God gave them victory, 2 Chron. xx. 21, 22), which should make us love to sing, "His mercies sure do still endure, eternally." We must praise God, I. As great and good in himself, ver. 1—3. II. As the Creator of the world, ver. 5—9. III. As Israel's God and Saviour, ver. 10—22. IV. As our Redeemer, ver. 23, 24. V. As the great benefactor of the whole creation, and God over all, blessed for evermore, ver. 25, 26.

O GIVE thanks unto the LORD; for *he is* good: for his mercy *endureth* for ever. 2 O give thanks unto the God of gods: for his mercy *endureth* for ever. 3 O give thanks to the Lord of lords: for his mercy *endureth* for ever. 4 To him who alone doeth great wonders: for his mercy *endureth* for ever. 5 To him that by wisdom made the heavens: for his mercy *endureth* for ever. 6 To him that stretched out the earth above the waters: for his mercy *endureth* for ever. 7 To him that made great lights: for his mercy *endureth* for ever: 8 The sun to rule by day: for his mercy *endureth* for ever: 9 The moon and stars to rule by night: for his mercy *endureth* for ever.

The duty we are here again and again called to is to *give thanks*, to *offer the sacrifice of praise continually*, not the fruits of our ground or cattle, but *the fruit of our lips, giving thanks to his name*, Heb. xiii. 15. We are never so earnestly called upon to pray and repent as to *give thanks;* for it is the will of God that we should abound most in the most pleasant exercises of religion, in that which is the work of heaven. Now here observe, 1. Whom we must give thanks to—to him that we receive all good from, *to the Lord,* Jehovah, Israel's God (*v.* 1), *the God of gods,* the God whom angels adore, from whom magistrates derive their power, and by whom all pretended deities are and shall be conquered (*v.* 2), *to the Lord of lords,* the Sovereign of all sovereigns, the stay and supporter of all supports; *v.* 3. In all our adorations we must have an eye to God's excellency as transcendent, and to his power and dominion as incontestably and uncontrollably supreme. 2. What we must give thanks for, not as the Pharisee that made all his thanksgivings terminate in his own praise *(God, I thank thee,* that I am so and so), but directing them all to God's glory. (1.) We must give thanks to God for his goodness and mercy (*v.* 1): *Give thanks to the Lord,* not only because he does good, but because he is good (all the streams must be traced up to the fountain), not only because he is merciful to us, but because his mercy endures for ever, and will be drawn out to those that shall come after us. We must give thanks to God, not only for that mercy which is now handed out to us here on earth, but for that which shall endure for ever in the glories and joys of heaven. (2.) We must give God thanks for the instances of his power and wisdom. In general (*v.* 4), he *alone does great wonders.* The contrivance is wonderful, the design being laid by infinite wisdom; the performance is wonderful, being put in execution by infinite power. He alone does marvellous things; none besides can do such things, and he does them without the assistance or advice of any other. More particularly, [1.] He made the heavens, and stretched them out, and in them we not only see his wisdom and power, but we taste his mercy in their benign influences; as long as the heavens endure the mercy of God endures in them, *v.* 5. [2.] He raised the earth out of the waters when he caused the dry land to appear, that it might be fit to be a habitation for man, and therein also his mercy to man still endures (*v.* 6); for *the earth hath he given to the children of men,* and all its products. [3.] Having made both heaven and earth, he settled a correspondence between them, notwithstanding their distance, by making the sun, moon, and stars, which he placed in the firmament of heaven, to shed their light and influences upon this earth, *v.* 7—9. These are called the *great lights* because they appear so to us, for otherwise astronomers tell us that the moon is less than many of the stars, but, being nearer to the earth, it seems much greater. They are said to *rule,* not only because they govern the seasons of the year, but because they are useful to the world, and benefactors are the best rulers, Luke xxii. 25. But the empire is divided, one *rules by day,* the *other by night* (at least, *the stars*), and yet

all are subject to God's direction and disposal. Those rulers, therefore, which the Gentiles idolized, are the world's servants and God's subjects. *Sun, stand thou still, and thou moon.*

10 To him that smote Egypt in their firstborn: for his mercy *endureth* for ever: 11 And brought out Israel from among them: for his mercy *endureth* for ever: 12 With a strong hand, and with a stretched out arm: for his mercy *endureth* for ever: 13 To him which divided the Red sea into parts: for his mercy *endureth* for ever: 14 And made Israel to pass through the midst of it: for his mercy *endureth* for ever: 15 But overthrew Pharaoh and his host in the Red sea: for his mercy *endureth* for ever. 16 To him which led his people through the wilderness: for his mercy *endureth* for ever. 17 To him which smote great kings: for his mercy *endureth* for ever: 18 And slew famous kings: for his mercy *endureth* for ever: 19 Sihon king of the Amorites: for his mercy *endureth* for ever: 20 And Og the king of Bashan: for his mercy *endureth* for ever: 21 And gave their land for a heritage: for his mercy *endureth* for ever: 22 *Even* a heritage unto Israel his servant: for his mercy *endureth* for ever.

The great things God did for Israel, when he first formed them into a people, and set up his kingdom among them, are here mentioned, as often elsewhere in the psalms, as instances both of the power of God and of the particular kindness he had for Israel. See cxxxv. 8, &c. 1. He brought them out of Egypt, *v.* 10—12. That was a mercy which endured long to them, and our redemption by Christ, which was typified by that, does indeed endure for ever, for it is an eternal redemption. Of all the plagues of Egypt, none is mentioned but the death of the first-born, because that was the conquering plague; by that God, who in all the plagues distinguished the Israelites from the Egyptians, brought them at last from among them, not by a wile, but with a strong hand and an arm stretched out to reach far and do great things. These miracles of mercy, as they proved Moses's commission to give law to Israel, so they laid Israel under lasting obligations to obey that law, Exod. xx. 2. 2. He forced them a way through the Red Sea, which obstructed them at their first setting out. By the power he has to control the common course of nature he *divided the sea into two parts,* between which he opened a path, and made Israel to pass between the parts, now that they were to enter into covenant with him; see Jer. xxxiv. 18. He not only divided the sea, but gave his people courage to go through it when it was divided, which was an instance of God's power over men's hearts, as the former of his power over the waters. And, to make it a miracle of justice as well as mercy, the same Red Sea that was a lane to the Israelites was a grave to their pursuers. There he shook off Pharaoh and his host. 3. He conducted them through a vast howling wilderness (*v.* 16); there he led them and fed them. Their camp was victualled and fortified by a constant series of miracles for forty years; though they loitered and wandered there, they were not lost. And in this the mercy of God, and the constancy of that mercy, were the more observable because they often provoked him in the wilderness and grieved him in the desert. 4. He destroyed kings before them, to make room for them (*v.* 17, 18), not deposed and banished them, but smote and slew them, in which appeared his wrath against them, but his mercy, his never-failing mercy, to Israel. And that which magnified it was that they were *great kings* and *famous kings*, yet God subdued them as easily as if they had been the least, and weakest, and meanest, of the children of men. They were wicked kings, and then their grandeur and lustre would not secure them from the justice of God. The more great and famous they were the more did God's mercy to Israel appear in giving such kings for them. Sihon and Og are particularly mentioned, because they were the first two that were conquered on the other side Jordan, *v.* 19, 20. It is good to enter into the detail of God's favours and not to view them in the gross, and in each instance to observe, and own, that God's *mercy endureth for ever.* 5. He put them in possession of a good land, *v.* 21, 22. He whose the earth is, and the fulness thereof, the world and those that dwell therein, took land from one people and gave it to another, as pleased him. The *iniquity of the Amorites was now full*, and therefore it was taken from them. *Israel* was his *servant*, and, though they had been provoking in the wilderness, yet he intended to have some service out of them, for *to them pertained the service of God.* As he said to the Egyptians, *Let my people go*, so to the Canaanites, *Let my people in*, that they may serve me. In this *God's mercy* to them *endureth for ever*, because it was a figure of the heavenly Canaan, the *mercy of our Lord Jesus Christ unto eternal life.*

23 Who remembered us in our low estate: for his mercy *endureth* for ever: 24 And hath redeemed us from our enemies: for his mercy *endureth* for ever. 25 Who giveth food to all flesh: for his mercy *endureth* for ever. 26 O give thanks unto the God of heaven: for his mercy *endureth* for ever.

God's everlasting mercy is here celebrated, 1. In the redemption of his church, *v.* 23, 24. In the many redemptions wrought for the Jewish church out of the hands of their oppressors (when, in the years of their servitude, their estate was very low, God remembered them, and raised them up saviours, the judges, and David, at length, by whom God gave them rest from all their enemies), but especially in the great redemption of the universal church, of which these were types, we have a great deal of reason to say, "*He remembered us*, the children of men, *in our low estate*, in our lost estate, *for his mercy endureth for ever;* he sent his Son to redeem us from sin, and death, and hell, and all our spiritual enemies, *for his mercy endureth for ever;* he was sent to redeem us, and not the angels that sinned, for his mercy endureth for ever." 2. In the provision he makes for all the creatures (*v.* 25): *He gives food to all flesh.* It is an instance of the mercy of God's providence that wherever he has given life he gives food agreeable and sufficient; and he is a good housekeeper that provides for so large a family. 3. In all his glories, and all his gifts (*v.* 26): *Give thanks to the God of heaven.* This denotes him to be a glorious God, and the glory of his mercy is to be taken notice of in our praises. The *riches of his glory* are displayed in the *vessels of his mercy*, Rom. ix. 23. It also denotes him to be the great benefactor, *for every good and perfect gift is from above*, from the Father of lights, the *God of heaven;* and we should trace every stream to the fountain. This and that particular mercy may perhaps endure but a while, but the mercy that is in God *endures for ever;* it is an inexhaustible fountain.

PSALM CXXXVII.

There are divers psalms which are thought to have been penned in the latter days of the Jewish church, when prophecy was near expiring and the canon of the Old Testament ready to be closed up, but none of them appears so plainly to be of a late date as this, which was penned when the people of God were captives in Babylon, and there insulted over by their proud oppressors; probably it was towards the latter end of their captivity; for now they saw the destruction of Babylon hastening on apace (ver. 8), which would be their discharge. It is a mournful psalm, a lamentation; and the Septuagint makes it one of the lamentations of Jeremiah, naming him for the author of it. Here, I. The melancholy captives cannot enjoy themselves, ver. 1, 2. II. They cannot humour their proud oppressors, ver. 3, 4. III. They cannot forget Jerusalem, ver. 5, 6. IV. They cannot forgive Edom and Babylon, ver. 7—9. In singing this psalm we must be much affected with the concernments of the church, especially that part of it that is in affliction, laying the sorrows of God's people near our hearts, comforting ourselves in the prospect of the deliverance of the church and the ruin of its enemies, in due time, but carefully avoiding all personal animosities, and not mixing the leaven of malice with our sacrifices.

BY the rivers of Babylon, there we sat down, yea, we wept, when we remembered Zion. 2 We hanged our harps upon the willows in the midst thereof. 3 For there they that carried us away captive required of us a song; and they that wasted us *required of us* mirth, *saying,* Sing us *one* of the songs of Zion. 4 How shall we sing the LORD's song in a strange land? 5 If I forget thee, O Jerusalem, let my right hand forget *her* cunning. 6 If I do not remember thee, let my tongue cleave to the roof of my mouth; if I prefer not Jerusalem above my chief joy.

We have here the daughter of Zion covered with a cloud, and dwelling with the daughter of Babylon; the people of God in tears, but sowing in tears. Observe,

I. The mournful posture they were in as to their affairs and as to their spirits. 1. They were posted *by the rivers of Babylon,* in a strange land, a great way from their own country, whence they were brought. as prisoners of war. The land of Babylon was now a house of bondage to that people, as Egypt had been in their beginning. Their conquerors quartered them *by the rivers,* with design to employ them there, and keep them to work in their galleys; or perhaps they chose it as the most melancholy place, and therefore most suitable to their sorrowful spirits. If they must build houses there (Jer. xxix. 5), it shall not be in the cities, the places of concourse, but by the rivers, the places of solitude, where they might mingle their tears with the streams. We find some of them by the *river Chebar* (Ezek. i. 3), others by the *river Ulai,* Dan. viii. 2. 2. There they *sat down* to indulge their grief by poring on their miseries. Jeremiah had taught them under this yoke to *sit alone,* and *keep silence,* and *put their mouths in the dust,* Lam. iii. 28, 29. "We sat down, as those that expected to stay, and were content, since it was the will of God that it must be so." 3. Thoughts of Zion drew tears from their eyes; and it was not a sudden passion of weeping, such as we are sometimes put into by a trouble that surprises us, but they were deliberate tears (we *sat down and wept*), tears with consideration—we *wept when we remembered Zion,* the holy hill on which the temple was built. Their affection to God's house swallowed up their concern for their own houses. They remembered Zion's former glory and the satisfaction they had had in Zion's courts, Lam. i. 7. *Jerusalem remembered, in the days of her misery, all her pleasant things which she had in the days of old,* Ps. xlii. 4. They remembered Zion's present desolations, and *favoured the dust thereof,* which was a good sign that the time for God to favour it was not far off, cii. 13, 14. 4. They laid by their instruments of music (v. 2): *We hung our harps upon the willows.* (1.) The harps they used for their own diversion and entertainment. These they laid aside, both because it was their judgment that they ought not to

use them now that God called to weeping and mourning (Isa. xxii. 12), and their spirits were so sad that they had no hearts to use them; they brought their harps with them, designing perhaps to use them for the alleviating of their grief, but it proved so great that it would not admit the experiment. Music makes some people melancholy. *As vinegar upon nitre, so is he that sings songs to a heavy heart.* (2.) The harps they used in God's worship, the Levites' harps. These they did not throw away, hoping they might yet again have occasion to use them, but thy laid them aside because they had no present use for them; God had cut them out other work by *turning their feasting into mourning and their songs into lamentations,* Amos. viii. 10. Every thing is beautiful in its season. They did not hide their harps in the bushes, or the hollows of the rocks; but hung them up in view, that the sight of them might affect them with this deplorable change. Yet perhaps they were faulty in doing this; for praising God is never out of season; it is his will that we should *in every thing give thanks,* Isa. xxiv. 15, 16.

II. The abuses which their enemies put upon them when they were in this melancholy condition, *v.* 3. They had *carried them away captive* from their own land and then *wasted them* in the land of their captivity, took what little they had from them. But this was not enough; to complete their woes they insulted over them: They *required of us mirth and a song.* Now, 1. This was very barbarous and inhuman; even an enemy, in misery, is to be pitied and not trampled upon. It argues a base and sordid spirit to upbraid those that are in distress either with their former joys or with their present griefs, or to challenge those to be merry who, we know, are out of tune for it. This is adding affliction to the afflicted. 2. It was very profane and impious. No songs would serve them but the *songs of Zion,* with which God had been honoured; so that in this demand they reflected upon God himself as Belshazzar, when he drank wine in temple-bowls. Their enemies *mocked at their sabbaths,* Lam. i. 7.

III. The patience wherewith they bore these abuses, *v.* 4. They had laid by their harps, and would not resume them, no, not to ingratiate themselves with those at whose mercy they lay; they would not answer those fools according to their folly. Profane scoffers are not to be humoured, nor pearls cast before swine. David prudently *kept silence even from good* when the *wicked were before him,* who, he knew, would ridicule what he said and make a jest of it, Ps. xxxix. 1, 2. The reason they gave is very mild and pious; *How shall we sing the Lord's song in a strange land?* They do not say, "How shall we sing when we are so much in sorrow?" If that had been all, they might perhaps have put a force upon themselves so far as to oblige their masters with a song; but "It is the

Lord's song; it is a sacred thing; it is peculiar to the temple-service, and therefore we dare not sing it in the land of a stranger, among idolaters." We must not serve common mirth, much less profane mirth, with any thing that is appropriated to God, who is sometimes to be honoured by a religious silence as well as by religious speaking.

IV. The constant affection they retained for Jerusalem, the city of their solemnities, even now that they were in Babylon. Though their enemies banter them for talking so much of Jerusalem, and even doting upon it, their love to it is not in the least abated; it is what they may be jeered for, but will never be jeered out of, *v.* 5, 6. Observe,

1. How these pious captives stood affected to Jerusalem. (1.) Their heads were full of it. It was always in their minds; they remembered it; they did not forget it, though they had been long absent from it; many of them had never seen it, nor knew any thing of it but by report, and by what they had read in the scripture, yet it was graven upon the palms of their hands, and even its ruins were continually before them, which was an evidence of their faith in the promise of its restoration in due time. In their daily prayers they opened their windows towards Jerusalem; and how then could they forget it? (2.) Their hearts were full of it. They *preferred* it *above* their *chief joy,* and therefore they remembered it and could not forget it. What we love we love to think of. Those that rejoice in God do, for his sake, make Jerusalem their joy, and prefer it before that, whatever it is, which is the head of their joy, which is dearest to them in this world. A godly man will prefer a public good before any private satisfaction or gratification whatsoever.

2. How stedfastly they resolved to keep up this affection, which they express by a solemn imprecation of mischief to themselves if they should let it fall : " Let me be for ever disabled either to sing or play on the harp if I so far forget the religion of my country as to make use of my songs and harps for the pleasing of Babylon's sons or the praising of Babylon's gods. *Let my right hand forget her art*" (which the hand of an expert musician never can, unless it be withered), " nay, *let my tongue cleave to the roof of my mouth,* if I have not a good word to say for Jerusalem wherever I am." Though they dare not sing Zion's songs among the Babylonians, yet they cannot forget them, but, as soon as ever the present restraint is taken off, they will sing them as readily as ever, notwithstanding the long disuse.

7 Remember, O LORD, the children of Edom in the day of Jerusalem; who said, Rase *it,* rase *it, even* to the foundation thereof. 8 O daughter of Babylon, who art to be destroyed; happy *shall he be,* that re-wardeth thee as thou hast served us. 9 Happy *shall he be,* that taketh and dasheth thy little ones against the stones.

The pious Jews in Babylon, having afflicted themselves with the thoughts of the ruins of Jerusalem, here please themselves with the prospect of the ruin of her impenitent implacable enemies; but this not from a spirit of revenge, but from a holy zeal for the glory of God and the honour of his kingdom.

I. The Edomites will certainly be reckoned with, and all others that were accessaries to the destruction of Jerusalem, that were aiding and abetting, that *helped forward the affliction* (Zech. i. 15) and triumphed in it, that *said, in the day of Jerusalem,* the day of her judgment, " *Rase it, rase it to the foundations;* down with it, down with it; do not leave one stone upon another." Thus they made the Chaldean army more furious, who were already so enraged that they needed no spur. Thus they put shame upon Israel, who would be looked upon as a people worthy to be cut off when their next neighbours had such an ill-will to them. And all this was a fruit of the old enmity of Esau against Jacob, because he got the birthright and the blessing, and a branch of that more ancient enmity between the seed of the woman and the seed of the serpent: Lord, *remember* them, says the psalmist, which is an appeal to his justice against them. Far be it from us to avenge ourselves, if ever it should be in our power, but we will leave it to him who has said, *Vengeance is mine.* Note, Those that are glad at calamities, especially the calamities of Jerusalem, shall not go unpunished. Those that are confederate with the persecutors of good people, and stir them up, and set them on, and are pleased with what they do, shall certainly be called to an account for it another day, and God will remember it against them.

II. Babylon is the principal, and it will come to her turn too to drink of the cup of tremblings, the very dregs of it (*v.* 8, 9): O *daughter of Babylon!* proud and secure as thou art, we know well, by the scriptures of truth, thou *art to be destroyed,* or (as Dr. Hammond reads it) *who art the destroyer.* The destroyers shall be destroyed, Rev. xiii. 10. And perhaps it is with reference to this that the man of sin, the head of the New-Testament Babylon, is called a *son of perdition,* 2 Thess. ii. 3. The destruction of Babylon being foreseen as a sure destruction (thou *art to be destroyed*), it is spoken of, 1. As a just destruction. She shall be paid in her own coin: "Thou shalt be served *as thou hast served us,* as barbarously used by the destroyers as we have been by thee." See Rev. xviii. 6. Let not those expect to find mercy who, when they had power, did not show mercy. 2. As an utter destruction. The very little ones of Babylon, when it is taken by storm, and all in it are put to the sword, shall be dashed to pieces by the enraged and merciless conqueror. None escape if these little ones perish. Those are the seed of another generation; so that, if they be cut off, the ruin will be not only total, as Jerusalem's was, but final. It is sunk like a millstone into the sea, never to rise. 3. As a destruction which should reflect honour upon the instruments of it. Happy shall those be that do it; for they are fulfilling God's counsels; and therefore he calls Cyrus, who did it, his *servant*, his *shepherd*, his *anointed* (Isa. xliv. 28, xlv. 1), and the soldiers that were employed in it his *sanctified ones*, Isa. xiii. 3. They are making way for the enlargement of God's Israel, and happy are those who are in any way serviceable to that. The fall of the New-Testament Babylon will be the triumph of all the saints, Rev. xix. 1.

PSALM CXXXVIII.

It does not appear, nor is it material to enquire, upon what occasion David penned this psalm; but in it, I. He looks back with thankfulness upon the experiences he had had of God's goodness to him, ver. 1—3. II. He looks forward with comfort, in hopes, 1. That others would go on to praise God like him, ver. 4, 5. 2. That God would go on to do good to him, ver. 6—8. In singing this psalm we must in like manner devote ourselves to God's praise and glory and repose ourselves in his power and goodness.

A psalm of David.

I WILL praise thee with my whole heart: before the gods will I sing praise unto thee. 2 I will worship toward thy holy temple, and praise thy name for thy lovingkindness and for thy truth: for thou hast magnified thy word above all thy name. 3 In the day when I cried thou answeredst me, *and* strengthenedst me *with* strength in my soul. 4 All the kings of the earth shall praise thee, O LORD, when they hear the words of thy mouth. 5 Yea, they shall sing in the ways of the LORD: for great *is* the glory of the LORD.

I. How he would praise God, compare cxi. 1. 1. He will praise him with sincerity and zeal—"*With my heart, with my whole heart*, with that which is within me and with all that is within me, with uprightness of intention and fervency of affection, inward impressions agreeing with outward expressions." 2. With freedom and boldness: *Before the gods will I sing praise unto thee*, before the princes, and judges, and great men, either those of other nations that visited him or those of his own nation that attended on him, even in their presence. He will not only praise God with his heart, which we may do by pious ejaculations in any company, but will sing praise if there be occasion. Note, Praising God is work which the greatest of men need not be ashamed of; it is the work of angels, the work of heaven. *Before the angels* (so some understand it), that is,

754

in religious assemblies, where there is a special presence of angels, 1 Cor. xi. 10. 3. In the way that God had appointed: *I will worship towards thy holy temple*. The priests alone went into the temple; the people, at the nearest, did but worship towards it, and that they might do at a distance. Christ is our temple, and towards him we must look with an eye of faith, as Mediator between us and God, in all our praises of him. Heaven is God's holy temple, and thitherward we must lift up our eyes in all our addresses to God. *Our Father in heaven.*

II. What he would praise God for. 1. For the fountain of his comforts—*for thy lovingkindness and for thy truth*, for thy goodness and for thy promise, mercy hidden in thee and mercy revealed by thee, that God is a gracious God in himself and has engaged to be so to all those that trust in him. *For thou hast magnified thy word* (thy promise, which is truth) *above all thy name.* God has made himself known to us in many ways in creation and providence, but most clearly by his word. The judgments of his mouth are magnified even above those of his hand, and greater things are done by them. The wonders of grace exceed the wonders of nature; and what is discovered of God by revelation is much greater than what is discovered by reason. In what God had done for David his faithfulness to his word appeared more illustriously, and redounded more to his glory, than any other of his attributes. Some good interpreters understand it of Christ, the essential Word, and of his gospel, which are magnified above all the discoveries God had before made of himself to the fathers. He that magnified the law, and made that honourable, magnifies the gospel much more. 2. For the streams flowing from that fountain, in which he himself had tasted that the Lord is gracious, *v.* 3. He had been in affliction, and he remembers, with thankfulness, (1.) The sweet communion he then had with God. He cried, he prayed, and prayed earnestly, and God answered him, gave him to understand that his prayer was accepted and should have a gracious return in due time. The intercourse between God and his saints is carried on by his promises and their prayers. (2.) The sweet communications he then had from God: *Thou strengthenedst me with strength in my soul.* This was the answer to his prayer, for God gives more than good words, xx. 6. Observe, [1.] It was a speedy answer: *In the day when I cried.* Note, Those that trade with heaven by prayer grow rich by quick returns. *While we are yet speaking God hears*, Isa. lxv. 24. [2.] It was a spiritual answer. God gave him strength in his soul, and that is a real and valuable answer to the prayer of faith in the day of affliction. If God give us strength in our souls to bear the burdens, resist the temptations, and do the duties of an afflicted state, if he strengthen us to keep hold of himself by faith, to maintain the peace of our own minds and to wait with patience for the issue, we must own that he has answered us, and we are bound to be thankful.

III. What influence he hoped that his praising God would have upon others, *v.* 4, 5. David was himself a king, and therefore he hoped that kings would be wrought upon by his experiences, and his example, to embrace religion; and, if kings became religious, their kingdoms would be every way better. Now, 1. This may have reference to the kings that were neighbours to David, as Hiram and others. " They shall all praise thee." When they visited David, and, after his death, when they sought the presence of Solomon (as *all the kings of the earth* are expressly said to have done, 2 Chron. ix. 23), they readily joined in the worship of the God of Israel. 2. It may look further, to the calling of the Gentiles and the discipling of all nations by the gospel of Christ, of whom it is said that *all kings shall fall down before him*, Ps. lxxii. 11. Now it is here foretold, (1.) That *the kings of the earth shall hear the words of God*. All that came near David should hear them from him, cxix. 46. In the latter days the preachers of the gospel should be sent into all the world. (2.) That then they shall praise God, as all those have reason to do that hear his word, and receive it in the light and love of it, Acts xiii. 48. (3.) That they shall *sing in the ways of the Lord*, in the ways of his providence and grace towards them; they shall rejoice in God, and give glory to him, however he is pleased to deal with them in the ways of their duty and obedience to him. Note, Those that walk in the ways of the Lord have reason to sing in those ways, to go on in them with a great deal of cheerfulness, for they are ways of pleasantness, and it becomes us to be pleasant in them; and, if we are so, *great is the glory of the Lord*. It is very much for the honour of God that kings should walk in his ways, and that all those who walk in them should sing in them, and so proclaim to all the world that he is a good Master and his work its own wages.

6 Though the LORD *be* high, yet hath he respect unto the lowly: but the proud he knoweth afar off.   7 Though I walk in the midst of trouble, thou wilt revive me: thou shalt stretch forth thine hand against the wrath of mine enemies, and thy right hand shall save me.   8 The LORD will perfect *that which* concerneth me : thy mercy, O LORD, *endureth* for ever : forsake not the works of thine own hands.

David here comforts himself with three things :—

I. The favour God bears to his humble people (*v.* 6) : *Though the Lord be high,* and neither needs any of his creatures nor can be benefited by them, *yet has he respect unto the lowly*, smiles upon them as well pleased with them, overlooks heaven and earth to cast a gracious look upon them (Isa. lvii. 15, lxvi. 1), and, sooner or later, he will put honour upon them, while *he knows the proud afar off*, knows them, but disowns them and rejects them, how proudly soever they pretend to his favour. Dr. Hammond makes this to be the sum of that gospel which the kings of the earth shall hear and welcome—that penitent sinners shall be accepted of God, but the impenitent cast out ; witness the instance of the Pharisee and the publican, Luke xviii.

II. The care God takes of his afflicted oppressed people, *v.* 7. David, though a great and good man, expects to *walk in the midst of trouble*, but encourages himself with hope, 1. That God would comfort him : " When my spirit is ready to sink and fail, *thou* shalt *revive me*, and make me easy and cheerful under my troubles." Divine consolations have enough in them to revive us even when we walk in the midst of troubles and are ready to die away for fear. 2. That he would protect him, and plead his cause : " *Thou shalt stretch forth thy hand*, though not against my enemies to destroy them, yet *against the wrath of my enemies*, to restrain that and set bounds to it." 3. That he would in due time work deliverance for him : *Thy right hand shall save me*. As he has one hand to stretch out against his enemies, so he has another to save his own people. Christ is the right hand of the Lord, that shall save all those who serve him.

III. The assurance we have that whatever good work God has begun in and for his people he will perform it (*v.* 8) : *The Lord will perfect that which concerns me*, 1. That which is most needful for me ; and he knows best what is so. We *are careful and cumbered about many things* that do not concern us, but he knows what are the things that really are of consequence to us (Matt. vi. 32) and he will order them for the best. 2. That which we are most concerned about. Every good man is most concerned about his duty to God and his happiness in God, that the former may be faithfully done and the latter effectually secured ; and if indeed these are the things that our hearts are most upon, and concerning which we are most solicitous, there is a good work begun in us, and he that has begun it will perfect it, we may be confident he will, Phil. i. 6. Observe, (1.) What ground the psalmist builds this confidence upon : *Thy mercy, O Lord! endures for ever*. This he had made very much the matter of his praise (xiii. 6), and therefore he could here with the more assurance make it the matter of his hope. For, if we give God the glory of his mercy, we may take to ourselves the comfort of it. Our hopes that we shall persevere must be founded, not upon our own strength, for that will fail us, but upon the mercy of God, for that will not fail. It is well pleaded, " *Lord, thy mercy endures for ever ;* let me be for ever a monument of it." (2.) What use he makes of this confidence ; it does not supersede, but quicken prayer ; he turns his expectation into a petition : " *Forsake not,* do not let go, *the work of thy own hands.* Lord, I am the work of thy own hands, my soul is so, do not forsake me ; my concerns are so, do not lay by thy care of them." Whatever good there is in us it is the work of God's own hands ; *he works in us both to will and to do ;* it will fail if he forsake it ; but his glory, as Jehovah, a perfecting God, is so much concerned in the progress of it to the end that we may in faith pray, " Lord, do not forsake it." Whom he loves he loves to the end ; and, as for God, his work is perfect.

PSALM CXXXIX.

Some of the Jewish doctors are of opinion that this is the most excellent of all the psalms of David ; and a very pious devout meditation it is upon the doctrine of God's omniscience, which we should therefore have our hearts fixed upon and filled with in singing this psalm. I. This doctrine is here asserted, and fully laid down, ver. 1—6. II. It is confirmed by two arguments :— 1. God is every where present ; therefore he knows all, ver. 7—12. 2. He made us, therefore he knows us, ver. 13—16. III. Some inferences are drawn from this doctrine. 1. It may fill us with pleasing admiration of God, ver. 17, 18. 2. With a holy dread and detestation of sin and sinners, ver. 19—22. 3. With a holy satisfaction in our own integrity, concerning which we may appeal to God, ver. 23, 24. This great and self-evident truth, That God knows our hearts and the hearts of all the children of men, if we did but mix faith with it and seriously consider it and apply it, would have a great influence upon our holiness and upon our comfort.

To the chief musician. A psalm of David.

O LORD, thou hast searched me, and known *me.* 2 Thou knowest my downsitting and mine uprising, thou understandest my thought afar off. 3 Thou compassest my path and my lying down, and art acquainted *with* all my ways. 4 For *there is* not a word in my tongue, *but,* lo, O LORD, thou knowest it altogether. 5 Thou hast beset me behind and before, and laid thine hand upon me. 6 *Such* knowledge *is* too wonderful for me ; it is high, I cannot *attain* unto it.

David here lays down this great doctrine, That the God with whom we have to do has a perfect knowledge of us, and that all the motions and actions both of our inward and of our outward man are naked and open before him.

I. He lays down this doctrine in the way of an address to God ; he says it to him, acknowledging it to him, and giving him the glory of it. Divine truths look fully as well when they are prayed over as when they are preached over, and much better than when they are disputed over. When we speak of God to him himself we shall find ourselves concerned to speak with the utmost degree both of sincerity and reverence, which will be likely to make the impressions the deeper.

II. He lays it down in a way of application

756

to himself, not, " Thou hast known *all*," but, " Thou hast known *me ;* that is it which I am most concerned to believe and which it will be most profitable for me to consider." *Then* we know these things for our good when we know them *for ourselves,* Job v. 27. When we acknowledge, " Lord, all souls are thine," we must add, " My soul is thine ; thou that hatest all sin hatest my sin ; thou that art good to all, good to Israel, art good to me." So here, " *Thou hast searched me, and known me ;* known me as thoroughly as we know that which we have most diligently and exactly searched into." David was a king, and *the hearts of kings are unsearchable* to their subjects (Prov. xxv. 3), but they are not so to their Sovereign.

III. He descends to particulars : " Thou knowest me wherever I am and whatever I am doing, me and all that belongs to me." 1. " *Thou knowest* me and all my motions, *my down-sitting* to rest, *my up-rising* to work, with what temper of mind I compose myself when I sit down and stir up myself when I rise up, what my soul reposes itself in as its stay and support, what it aims at and reaches towards as its felicity and end. Thou knowest me when I come home, how I walk before my house, and when I go abroad, on what errands I go." 2. " Thou knowest all my imaginations. Nothing is more close and quick than thought ; it is always unknown to others ; it is often unobserved by ourselves, and yet *thou understandest my thought afar off.* Though my thoughts be ever so foreign and distant from one another, thou understandest the chain of them, and canst make out their connexion, when so many of them slip my notice that I myself cannot." Or, " *Thou understandest them afar off,* even before I think them, and long after I have thought them and have myself forgotten them." Or, " *Thou understandest them from afar ;* from the height of heaven thou seest into the depths of the heart," xxxiii. 14. 3. " Thou knowest me and all my designs and undertakings ; *thou compassest* every particular *path ; thou siftest* (or *winnowest) my path* " (so some), " so as thoroughly to distinguish between the good and evil of what I do," as by sifting we separate between the corn and the chaff. All our actions are ventilated by the judgment of God, xvii. 3. God takes notice of every step we take, every right step and every by-step. He is *acquainted with all* our *ways,* intimately acquainted with them ; he knows what rule we walk by, what end we walk towards, what company we walk with. 4. " *Thou knowest* me in all my retirements ; thou knowest *my lying down ;* when I am withdrawn from all company, and am reflecting upon what has passed all day and composing myself to rest, thou knowest what I have in my heart and with what thoughts I go to bed." 5. " Thou knowest me, and all I say (*v.* 4) : *There is not a word in my tongue,* not a vain word, nor a good word, *but thou knowest it altogether,* knowest what it meant, from what thought it came, and with what design it was uttered. There is not a word at my tongue's end, ready to be spoken, yet checked and kept in, but thou knowest it." *When there is not a word in my tongue, O Lord! thou knowest all* (so some read it); for thoughts are words to God. 6. "Thou knowest me in every part of me: *Thou hast beset me behind and before,* so that, go which way I will, I am under thy eye and cannot possibly escape it. Thou hast *laid thy hand upon me,* and I cannot run away from thee." Wherever we are we are under the eye and hand of God. Perhaps it is an allusion to the physician's laying his hand upon his patient to feel how his pulse beats or what temper he is in. God knows us as we know not only what we see, but what we feel and have our hands upon. *All his saints are in his hand.*

IV. He speaks of it with admiration (*v.* 6): *It is too wonderful for me; it is high.* 1. "Thou hast such a knowledge of me as I have not of myself, nor can have. I cannot take notice of all my own thoughts, nor make such a judgment of myself as thou makest of me." 2. "It is such a knowledge as I cannot comprehend, much less describe. That thou knowest all things I am sure, but how I cannot tell." We cannot by searching find out how God searches and finds out us; nor do we know how we are known.

7 Whither shall I go from thy spirit? or whither shall I flee from thy presence? 8 If I ascend up into heaven, thou *art* there: if I make my bed in hell, behold, thou *art there.* 9 *If* I take the wings of the morning, *and* dwell in the uttermost parts of the sea; 10 Even there shall thy hand lead me, and thy right hand shall hold me. 11 If I say, Surely the darkness shall cover me; even the night shall be light about me. 12 Yea, the darkness hideth not from thee; but the night shineth as the day: the darkness and the light *are* both alike *to thee.* 13 For thou hast possessed my reins: thou hast covered me in my mother's womb. 14 I will praise thee; for I am fearfully *and* wonderfully made: marvellous *are* thy works; and *that* my soul knoweth right well. 15 My substance was not hid from thee, when I was made in secret, *and* curiously wrought in the lowest parts of the earth. 16 Thine eyes did see my substance, yet being unperfect; and in thy book all *my members* were written, *which* in

continuance were fashioned, when *as yet there was* none of them.

It is of great use to us to know the certainty of the things wherein we have been instructed, that we may not only believe them, but be able to tell why we believe them, and to give a reason of the hope that is in us. David is sure that God perfectly knows him and all his ways,

I. Because he is always under his eye. If God is omnipresent, he must needs be omniscient; but he is omnipresent; this supposes the infinity and immensity of his being, from which follows the ubiquity of his presence; heaven and earth include the whole creation, and the Creator fills both (Jer. xxiii. 24); he not only knows both, and governs both, but he fills both. Every part of the creation is under God's intuition and influence. David here acknowledges this also with application and sees himself thus open before God.

1. No flight can remove us out of God's presence: "*Whither shall I go from thy Spirit, from thy presence,* that is, from thy spiritual presence, from thyself, who art a Spirit?" *God is a Spirit,* and therefore it is folly to think that because we cannot see him he cannot see us: *Whither shall I flee from thy presence?* Not that he desired to go away from God; no, he desired nothing more than to be near him; but he only puts the case, "Suppose I should be so foolish as to think of getting out of thy sight, that I might shake off the awe of thee, suppose I should think of revolting from my obedience to thee, or of disowning a dependence on thee and of shifting for myself, alas! whither can I go?" A heathen could say, *Quocunque te flexeris, ibi Deum videbis occurrentem tibi — Whithersoever thou turnest thyself, thou wilt see God meeting thee.* Seneca. He specifies the most remote and distant places, and counts upon meeting God in them. (1.) In heaven: "*If I ascend* thither, as I hope to do shortly, *thou art there,* and it will be my eternal bliss to be with thee there." Heaven is a vast large place, replenished with an innumerable company, and yet there is no escaping God's eye there, in any corner, or in any crowd. The inhabitants of that world have as necessary a dependence upon God, and lie as open to his strict scrutiny, as the inhabitants of this. (2.) *In hell*—in *Sheol,* which may be understood of the depth of the earth, the very centre of it. Should we dig as deep as we can under ground, and think to hide ourselves there, we should be mistaken; God knows that path which the vulture's eye never saw, and to him the earth is all surface. Or it may be understood of the state of the dead. When we are removed out of the sight of all living, yet not out of the sight of the living God; from his eye we cannot hide ourselves in the grave. Or it may be understood of the place of the damned: *If I make my bed in hell* (an uncomfortable

place to make a bed in, where there is no rest day or night, yet thousands will make their bed for ever in those flames), *behold, thou art there*, in thy power and justice. God's wrath is the fire which will there burn everlastingly, Rev. xiv. 10. (3.) In the remotest corners of this world: "*If I take the wings of the morning*, the rays of the morning-light (called the wings of the sun, Mal. iv. 2), than which nothing more swift, and flee upon them to *the uttermost parts of the sea*, or of the earth (Job xxxviii. 12, 13), should I flee to the most distant and obscure islands (the *ultima Thule*, the *Terra incognita*), I should find thee there; *there shall thy hand lead me*, as far as I go, *and thy right hand shall hold me*, that I can go no further, that I cannot go out of thy reach." God soon arrested Jonah when *he fled to Tarshish from the presence of the Lord*.

2. No veil can hide us from God's eye, no, not that of the thickest darkness, *v.* 11, 12. "*If I say*, Yet *the darkness shall cover me*, when. nothing else will, alas! I find myself deceived; the curtains of the evening will stand me in no more stead than the wings of the morning; *even the night shall be light about me*. That which often favours the escape of a pursued criminal, and the retreat of a beaten army, will do me no kindness in fleeing from thee." When God divided between the light and darkness it was with a reservation of this prerogative, that to himself *the darkness and the light* should still be *both alike*. "*The darkness* darkeneth *not from thee*, for there is no darkness nor shadow of death where the workers of iniquity may hide themselves." No hypocritical mask or disguise, how specious soever, can save any person or action from appearing in a true light before God. Secret haunts of sin are as open before God as the most open and barefaced villanies.

II. Because he is the work of his hands. He that framed the engine knows all the motions of it. God made us, and therefore no doubt he knows us; he saw us when we were in the forming, and can we be hidden from him now that we are formed? This argument he insists upon (*v.* 13—16): "*Thou hast possessed my reins;* thou art Master of my most secret thoughts and intentions, and the innermost recesses of my soul; thou not only knowest, but governest, them, as we do that which we have possession of; and the possession thou hast of my reins is a rightful possession, *for thou coveredst me in my mother's womb*, that is, thou madest me (Job x. 11), thou madest me in secret. The soul is concealed from all about us. *Who knows the things of a man, save the spirit of a man?*" 1 Cor. ii. 11. Hence we read of *the hidden man of the heart*. But it was God himself that thus covered us, and therefore he can, when he pleases, discover us; when he hid us from all the world he did not intend to hide us from himself. Concerning the formation of man, of each of us,

1. The glory of it is here given to God, entirely to him; *for it is he that has made us and not we ourselves*. "*I will praise thee*, the author of my being; my parents were only the instruments of it. It was done, (1.) Under the divine inspection: *My substance*, when hid in the womb, nay, when it was yet but *in fieri—in the forming*, an unshapen embryo, *was not hidden from thee; thy eyes did see my substance*. (2.) By the divine operation. As the eye of God saw us then, so his hand wrought us; we were his work. (3.) According to the divine model: *In thy book all my members were written*. Eternal wisdom formed the plan, and by that almighty power raised the noble structure.

2. Glorious things are here said concerning it. The generation of man is to be considered with the same pious veneration as his creation at first. Consider it, (1.) As a great marvel, a great miracle we might call it, but that it is done in the ordinary course of nature. We are *fearfully and wonderfully made;* we may justly be astonished at the admirable contrivance of these living temples, the composition of every part, and the harmony of all together. (2.) As a great mystery, a mystery of nature: *My soul knows right well* that it is marvellous, but how to describe it for any one else I know not; for *I was made in secret, and curiously wrought* in the womb as *in the lowest parts of the earth*, so privately, and so far out of sight. (3.) As a great mercy, that all our members *in continuance were fashioned*, according as they were written in the book of God's wise counsel, *when as yet there was none of them;* or, as some read it, *and none of them was left out*. If any of our members had been wanting in God's book, they would have been wanting in our bodies, but, through his goodness, we have all our limbs and senses, the want of any of which might have made us burdens to ourselves. See what reason we have then to praise God for our creation, and to conclude that he who saw our substance when it was unfashioned sees it now that it is fashioned.

17 How precious also are thy thoughts unto me, O God! how great is the sum of them! 18 *If* I should count them, they are more in number than the sand: when I awake, I am still with thee. 19 Surely thou wilt slay the wicked, O God: depart from me therefore, ye bloody men. 20 For they speak against thee wickedly, *and* thine enemies take *thy name* in vain. 21 Do not I hate them, O Lord, that hate thee? and am not I grieved with those that rise up against thee? 22 I hate them with perfect hatred: I count them mine enemies. 23 Search me, O

God, and know my heart: try me, and know my thoughts: 24 And see if *there be any* wicked way in me, and lead me in the way everlasting.

Here the psalmist makes application of the doctrine of God's omniscience, divers ways.

I. He acknowledges, with wonder and thankfulness, the care God had taken of him all his days, *v.* 17, 18. God, who knew him, thought of him, and his thoughts towards him were thoughts of love, *thoughts of good, and not of evil,* Jer. xxix. 11. God's omniscience, which might justly have watched over us to do us hurt, has been employed for us, and has watched over us to do us good, Jer. xxxi. 28. God's counsels concerning us and our welfare have been, 1. Precious to admiration : *How precious* are they ! They are deep in themselves, such as cannot possibly be fathomed and comprehended. Providence has had a vast reach in its dispensations concerning us, and has brought things about for our good, quite beyond our contrivance and foresight. They are dear to us ; we must think of them with a great deal of reverence, and yet with pleasure and thankfulness. Our thoughts concerning God must be delightful to us, above any other thoughts. 2. Numerous to admiration : *How great is the sum of them !* We cannot conceive how many God's kind counsels have been concerning us, how many good turns he has done us, and what variety of mercies we have received from him. *If* we would *count them,* the heads of them, much more the particulars of them, *they are more in number than the sand,* and yet every one great and very considerable, xl. 5. We cannot conceive the multitude of God's compassions, which are all new every morning. 3. Constant at all times : " *When I awake,* every morning, *I am still with thee,* under thy eye and care, safe and easy under thy protection." This bespeaks also the continual devout sense David had of the eye of God upon him : *When I awake I am with thee,* in my thoughts ; and it would help to keep us in the 'fear of the Lord all the day long if, when we awake in the morning, our first thoughts were of him and we did then set him before us.

II. He concludes from this doctrine that ruin will certainly be the end of sinners. God knows all the wickedness of the wicked, and therefore he will reckon for it : " *Surely thou wilt slay the wicked, O God!* for all their wickedness is open before thee, however it may be artfully disguised and coloured over, to hide it from the eye of the world. However thou suffer them to prosper for a while, *surely thou wilt slay* them at last." Now observe, 1. The reason why God will punish them, because they daringly affront him and set him at defiance (*v.* 20): *They speak against thee wickedly ;* they *set their mouth against the heavens* (lxxiii. 9),

and shall be called to account for the hard speeches they have *spoken against him,* Jude 15. They are his *enemies,* and declare their enmity by *taking his name in vain,* as we show our contempt of a man if we make a by-word of his name, and never mention him but in a way of jest and banter. Those that profane the sacred forms of swearing or praying by using them in an impertinent irreverent manner take God's name in vain, and thereby show themselves enemies to him. Some make it to be a description of hypocrites : " They speak of thee for mischief ; they talk of God, pretending to piety, but it is with some ill design, for a cloak of maliciousness ; and, being enemies to God, while they pretend friendship, they *take* his *name in vain ;* they swear falsely." 2. The use David makes of this prospect which he has of the ruin of the wicked. (1.) He defies them : " *Depart from me, you bloody men ;* you shall not debauch me, for I will not admit your friendship nor have fellowship with you ; and you cannot destroy me, for, being under God's protection, he shall force you to depart from me." (2.) He detests them (*v.* 21, 22) : " Lord, thou knowest the heart, and canst witness for me ; *do not I hate those that hate thee,* and for that reason, because they hate thee ? I hate them because I love thee, and hate to see such affronts and indignities put upon thy blessed name. *Am not I grieved with those that rise up against thee,* grieved to see their rebellion and to foresee their ruin, which it will certainly end in ?" Note, Sin is hated, and sinners are lamented, by all that fear God. " *I hate them*" (that is, *I hate the work of them that turn aside,*" as he explains himself, ci. 3) " *with a* sincere and *perfect hatred ; I count those* that are enemies to God as enemies to me, and will not have any intimacy with them," lxix. 8.

III. He appeals to God concerning his sincerity, *v.* 23, 24. 1. He desires that as far as he was in the wrong God would discover it to him. Those that are upright can take comfort in God's omniscience as a witness of their uprightness, and can with a humble confidence beg of him to search and try them, to discover them to themselves (for a good man desires to know the worst of himself) and to discover them to others. He that means honestly could wish he had a window in his breast that any man may look into his heart : " Lord, I hope I am not in a wicked way, but *see if there be any wicked way in me,* any corrupt inclination remaining ; let me see it ; and root it out of me, for I do not allow it." 2. He desires that, as far as he was in the right, he might be forwarded in it, which he that knows the heart knows how to do effectually : *Lead me in the way everlasting.* Note, (1.) The way of godliness is an everlasting way ; it is everlastingly true and good, pleasing to God and profitable to us, and will end in everlasting life. *It is the way of antiquity* (so some), *the good old way.* (2.) All the saints desire to be kept and led in this way, that they may not miss it, turn out of it, nor tire in it.

PSALM CXL.

This and the four following psalms are much of a piece, and the scope of them the same with many that we met with in the beginning and middle of the book of Psalms, though with but few of late. They were penned by David (as it should seem) when he was persecuted by Saul; one of them is said to be his "prayer when he was in the cave," and it is probable that all the rest were penned about the same time. In this psalm, I. David complains of the malice of his enemies, and prays to God to preserve him from them, ver. 1—5. II. He encourages himself in God as his God, ver. 6, 7. III. He prays for, and prophesies, the destruction of his persecutors, ver. 8—11. IV. He assures all God's afflicted people that their troubles would in due time end well (ver. 12, 13), with which assurance we must comfort ourselves, and one another, in singing this psalm.

To the chief musician.   A psalm of David.

DELIVER me, O LORD, from the evil man: preserve me from the violent man; 2 Which imagine mischiefs in *their* heart; continually are they gathered together *for* war. 3 They have sharpened their tongues like a serpent; adders' poison *is* under their lips. Selah. 4 Keep me, O LORD, from the hands of the wicked; preserve me from the violent man; who have purposed to overthrow my goings. 5 The proud have hid a snare for me, and cords; they have spread a net by the wayside; they have set gins for me. Selah. 6 I said unto the LORD, Thou *art* my God: hear the voice of my supplications, O LORD. 7 O God the Lord, the strength of my salvation, thou hast covered my head in the day of battle.

In *this,* as in other things, David was a type of Christ, that he suffered before he reigned, was humbled before he was exalted, and that as there were many who loved and valued him, and sought to do him honour, so there were many who hated and envied him, and sought to do him mischief, as appears by these verses, where,

I. He gives a character of his enemies, and paints them out in their own colours, as dangerous men, whom he had reason to be afraid of, but wicked men, whom he had no reason to think the righteous God would countenance. There was one that seems to have been the ring-leader of them, whom he calls *the evil man* and *the man of violences* (v. 1, 4), probably he means Saul. The Chaldee paraphrast (v. 9) names both Doeg and Ahithophel; but between them there was a great distance of time. Violent men are evil men. But there were many besides this one who were confederate against David, who are here represented as the genuine offspring and seed of the serpent. For, 1. They are very subtle, crafty to do mischief; they have imagined it (v. 2), have laid the scheme with all the art and cunning imaginable. They *have purposed* and

plotted *to overthrow* the *goings* of a good man (v. 4), to draw him into sin and trouble, to ruin him by blasting his reputation, crushing his interest, and taking away his life. For this purpose *they have,* like mighty hunters, *hidden a snare,* and *spread a net,* and *set gins* (v. 5), that their designs against him, being kept undiscovered, might be the more likely to take effect, and he might fall into their hands ere he was aware. Great persecutors have often been great politicians, which has indeed made them the more formidable; but *the Lord preserves the simple* without all those arts. 2. They are very spiteful, as full of malice as Satan himself: *They have sharpened their tongues like a serpent,* that infuses his venom with his tongue; and there is so much malignity in all they say that one would think there was nothing *under their lips* but *adders' poison, v.* 3. With their calumnies, and with their counsels, they aimed to destroy David, but secretly, as a man is stung with a serpent, or a snake in the grass. And they endeavoured likewise to infuse their malice into others, and to make them seven times more the children of hell than themselves. A malignant tongue makes men like the old serpent; and poison in the lips is a certain sign of poison in the heart. 3. They are confederate; they are many of them; but they are all *gathered together* against me *for war, v.* 2. Those who can agree in nothing else can agree to persecute a good man. Herod and Pilate will unite in this, and in this they resemble Satan, who is not divided against himself, all the devils agreeing in Beelzebub. 4. They are *proud* (v. 5), conceited of themselves and confident of their success; and herein also they resemble Satan, whose reigning ruining sin was pride. The pride of persecutors, though at present it be the terror, yet may be the encouragement, of the persecuted, for the more haughty they are the faster are they ripening for ruin. *Pride goes before destruction.*

II. He prays to God to keep him from them and from being swallowed up by them: "Lord, *deliver me, preserve me, keep me* (v. 1, 4); let them not prevail to take away my life, my reputation, my interest, my comfort, and to prevent my coming to the throne. *Keep me* from doing as they do, or as they would have me do, or as they promise themselves I shall do." Note, The more malice appears in our enemies against us the more earnest we should be in prayer to God to take us under his protection. In him believers may count upon a security, and may enjoy it and themselves with a holy serenity. Those are safe whom God preserves. If he be for us, who can be against us?

III. He triumphs in God, and thereby, in effect, he triumphs over his persecutors. v. 6, 7. When his enemies sharpened their tongues against him, did he sharpen his against them? No; *adders' poison* was *under their lips,* but grace was poured into his lips, witness what he here said unto the Lord, for to him he looked, to him he directed himself, when he saw himself in so much danger, through the malice of his enemies: and it is well for us that we have a God to go to. He comforted himself, 1. In his interest in God: "*I said, Thou art my God;* and, if my God, then my shield and mighty protector." In troublous dangerous times it is good to claim relation to God, and by faith to keep hold of him. 2. In his access to God. This comforted him, that he was not only taken into covenant with God, but into communion with him, that he had leave to speak to him, and might expect an answer of peace from him, and could say, with a humble confidence, *Hear the voice of my supplications, O Lord!* 3. In the assurance he had of help from God and happiness in him: "*O God the Lord—Jehovah Adonai!* as *Jehovah* thou art self-existent and self-sufficient, an infinitely perfect being; as *Adonai* thou art my stay and support, my ruler and governor, and therefore *the strength of my salvation,* my strong Saviour; nay, not only my Saviour, but my salvation itself, from whom, in whom, my salvation is; not only a strong Saviour, but the very strength of my salvation, on whom the stress of my hope is laid; all in all, to make me happy, and to preserve me to my happiness." 4. In the experience he had had formerly of God's care of him: *Thou hast covered my head in the day of battle.* As he pleaded with Saul, that, for the service of his country, he many a time jeoparded his life in the high places of the field, so he pleads with God that, in those services, he had wonderfully protected him, and provided him a better helmet for the securing of his head than Goliath's was: "Lord, thou hast kept me *in the day of battle* with the Philistines, suffer me not to fall by the treacherous intrigues of false-hearted Israelites." God is as able to preserve his people from secret fraud as from open force; and the experience we have had of his power and care, in dangers of one kind, may encourage us to trust in him and depend upon him in dangers of another nature; for nothing can shorten the Lord's right hand.

8 Grant not, O Lord, the desires of the wicked: further not his wicked device; *lest* they exalt themselves. Selah. 9 *As for* the head of those that compass me about, let the mischief of their own lips cover them. 10 Let burning coals fall upon them: let them be cast into the fire; into deep pits, that they rise not up again. 11 Let not an evil speaker be established in the earth: evil shall hunt the violent man to overthrow *him.* 12 I know that the Lord will maintain the cause of the afflicted, *and* the right of the

poor. 13 Surely the righteous shall give thanks unto thy name: the upright shall dwell in thy presence.

Here is the believing foresight David had, I. Of the shame and confusion of persecutors.
1. Their disappointment. This he prays for (*v.* 8), that their lusts might not be gratified, their lust of ambition, envy, and revenge: "*Grant not, O Lord! the desires of the wicked,* but frustrate them; let them not see the ruin of my interest, which they so earnestly wish to see; but *hear the voice of my supplications.* He prays that their projects might not take effect, but be blasted: "*O further not his wicked device;* let not Providence favour any of his designs, but cross them; suffer *not his wicked device* to proceed, but chain his wheels, and stop him in the career of his pursuits. Thus we are to pray against the enemies of God's people, that they may not succeed in any of their enterprises. Such was David's prayer against Ahithophel, that God would turn his counsels into foolishness. The plea is, *lest they exalt themselves,* value themselves upon their success as if it were an evidence that God favoured them. Proud men, when they prosper, are made prouder, grow more impudent against God and insolent against his people, and therefore, "Lord, do not prosper them."
2. Their destruction. This he prays for (as we read it); but some choose to read it rather as a prophecy, and the original will bear it. If we take it as a prayer, that proceeds from a spirit of prophecy, which comes all to one. He foretels the ruin,
(1.) Of his own enemies: "*As for those that compass me about,* and seek my ruin," [1.] "*The mischief of their own lips* shall *cover* their heads (*v.* 9); the evil they have wished to me shall come upon themselves, their curses shall be blown back into their own faces, and the very designs which they have laid against me shall turn to their own ruin," vii. 15, 16. Let those that make mischief, by slandering, tale-bearing, misrepresenting their neighbours, and spreading ill-natured characters and stories, dread the consequence of it, and think how sad their condition will be when all the mischief they have been accessory to shall be made to return upon themselves. [2.] The judgments of God shall *fall upon them,* compared here to *burning coals,* in allusion to the destruction of Sodom; nay, as in the deluge the waters from above, and those from beneath, met for the drowning of the world, both the windows of heaven were opened and the fountains of the great deep were broken up, so here, to complete the ruin of the enemies of Christ and his kingdom, they shall not only have *burning coals* cast upon them from above (Job xx. 23; xxvii. 22), but they themselves shall *be cast into the fire* beneath; both heaven and hell, the wrath of God the Judge

and the rage of Satan the tormentor, shall concur to make them miserable. And the fire they shall be cast into is not a furnace of fire, out of which perhaps they might escape, but a *deep pit,* out of which they cannot rise. Tophet is said to be *deep and large,* Isa. xxx. 33.

(2.) Of all others that are like them, *v.* 11. [1.] Evil speakers must expect to be shaken, for they shall never *be established in the earth.* What is got by fraud and falsehood, by calumny and unjust accusation, will not prosper, will not last. Wealth gotten by vanity will be diminished. Let not such men as Doeg think to reign long, for his doom will be theirs, ii. 5. A lying tongue is but for a moment, but the *lip of truth shall be established for ever.* [2.] Evil doers must expect to be destroyed : *Evil shall hunt the violent man,* as the blood-hound hunts the murderer to discover him, as the lion hunts his prey to tear it to pieces. Mischievous men will be brought to light, and brought to ruin; the destruction appointed shall run them down and overthrow them. *Evil pursues sinners.*

II. Here is his foresight of the deliverance and comfort of the persecuted, *v.* 12, 13. 1. God will do those justice, in delivering them, who, being wronged, commit themselves to him : "*I know that the Lord will maintain the* just and injured *cause of* his *afflicted* people, and will not suffer might always to prevail against right, though it be but *the right of the poor,* who have but little that they can pretend a right to." God is, and will be, the patron of oppressed innocence, much more of persecuted piety; those that know him cannot but know this. 2. They will do him justice (if I may so speak), in ascribing the glory of their deliverance to him : "*Surely the righteous* (who make conscience of rendering to God his due, as well as to men theirs) *shall give thanks unto thy name* when they find their cause pleaded with jealousy and prosecuted with effect." The closing words, *The upright shall dwell in thy presence,* denote both God's favour to them ("Thou shalt admit them to dwell in thy presence in grace here, in glory hereafter, and it shall be their safety and happiness") and their duty to God : "They shall attend upon thee as servants that keep in the presence of their masters, both to do them honour and to receive their commands." This is true thanksgiving, even thanksliving; and this use we should make of all our deliverances, we should serve God the more closely and cheerfully.

PSALM CXLI.

David was in distress when he penned this psalm, pursued, it is most likely, by Saul, that violent man. Is any distressed? Let him pray; David did so, and had the comfort of it. I. He prays for God's favourable acceptance, ver. 1, 2. II. For his powerful assistance, ver. 3, 4. III. That others might be instrumental of good to his soul, as he hoped to be to the souls of others, ver. 5, 6. IV. That he and his friends being now brought to the last extremity God would graciously appear for their relief and rescue, ver. 7—10. The mercy and grace of God are as necessary to us as they were to him, and therefore we should be humbly earnest for them in singing this psalm.

A psalm of David.

LORD, I cry unto thee : make haste unto me; give ear unto my voice, when I cry unto thee. 2 Let my prayer be set forth before thee *as* incense ; *and* the lifting up of my hands *as* the evening sacrifice. 3 Set a watch, O LORD, before my mouth ; keep the door of my lips. 4 Incline not my heart to *any* evil thing, to practise wicked works with men that work iniquity: and let me not eat of their dainties.

Mercy to accept what we do well, and grace to keep us from doing ill, are the two things which we are here taught by David's example to pray to God for.

I. David loved prayer, and he begs of God that his prayers might be heard and answered, *v.* 1, 2. *David cried unto God.* His crying denotes fervency in prayer; he prayed as one in earnest. His crying to God denotes faith and fixedness in prayer. And what did he desire as the success of his prayer? 1. That God would take cognizance of it : "*Give ear to my voice ;* let me have a gracious audience." Those that cry in prayer may hope to be heard in prayer, not for their loudness, but their liveliness. 2. That he would visit him upon it : *Make haste unto me.* Those that know how to value God's gracious presence will be importunate for it and humbly impatient of delays. He that believes does not make haste, but he that prays may be earnest with God to make haste. 3. That he would be well pleased with him in it, well pleased with his *praying* and the *lifting up of his hands in prayer,* which denotes both the elevation and enlargement of his desire and the out-goings of his hope and expectation, the lifting up of the hand signifying the lifting up of the heart, and being used instead of lifting up the sacrifices which were heaved and waved before the Lord. Prayer is a spiritual sacrifice; it is the offering up of the soul, and its best affections, to God. Now he prays that this may be set forth and directed before God *as the incense* which was daily burnt upon the golden altar, and *as the evening sacrifice,* which he mentions rather than the morning sacrifice, perhaps because this was an evening prayer, or with an eye to Christ, who, in the evening of the world and in the evening of the day, was to offer up himself a sacrifice of atonement, and establish the spiritual sacrifices of acknowledgment, having abolished all the carnal ordinances of the law. Those that pray in faith may expect it will please God better than an ox or bullock. David was now banished from God's court, and could not attend the sacrifice and incense, and therefore begs that his prayer might be instead of them. Note, Prayer is of a sweet-smelling savour to God, as incense, which yet has no savour without fire; nor has prayer without the fire of holy love and fervour.

II. David was in fear of sin, and he begs of God that he might be kept from sin, knowing that his prayers would not be accepted unless he took care to watch against sin. We must be as earnest for God's grace in us as for his favour towards us. 1. He prays that he might not be surprised into any sinful words (*v.* 3): " *Set a watch, O Lord! before my mouth,* and, nature having made my lips to be a door to my words, let grace keep that door, that no word may be suffered to go out which may in any way tend to the dishonour of God or the hurt of others." Good men know the evil of tongue-sins, and how prone they are to them (when enemies are provoking we are in danger of carrying our resentment too far, and of speaking unadvisedly, as Moses did, though the meekest of men), and therefore they are earnest with God to prevent their speaking amiss, as knowing that no watchfulness or resolution of their own is sufficient for the governing of their tongues, much less of their hearts, without the special grace of God. We must *keep our mouths as with a bridle;* but that will not serve: we must pray to God to keep them. Nehemiah prayed to the Lord when he set a watch, and so must we, for without him the watchman waketh but in vain. 2. That he might not be inclined to any sinful practices (*v.* 4): "*Incline not my heart to any evil thing;* whatever inclination there is in me to sin, let it be not only restrained, but mortified, by divine grace." The example of those about us, and the provocations of those against us, are apt to stir up and draw out corrupt inclinations. We are ready to do as others do, and to think that if we have received injuries we may return them; and therefore we have need to pray that we may never be left to ourselves to practise any wicked work, either in confederacy with or in opposition to the *men that work iniquity.* While we live in such an evil world, and carry about with us such evil hearts, we have need to pray that we may neither be drawn in by any allurement nor driven on by any provocation to do any sinful thing. 3. That he might not be ensnared by any sinful pleasures: "*Let me not eat of their dainties.* Let me not join with them in their feasts and sports, lest thereby I be inveigled into their sins." *Better is a dinner of herbs,* out of the way of temptation, than a *stalled ox* in it. Sinners pretend to find dainties in sin. *Stolen waters are sweet;* forbidden fruit is pleasant to the eye. But those that consider how soon the dainties of sin will turn into wormwood and gall, how certainly it will, at last, *bite like a serpent* and *sting like an adder,* will dread those dainties, and pray to God by his providence to take them out of their sight, and by his grace to turn them against them. Good men will pray even against the sweets of sin.

5 Let the righteous smite me; it

shall be a kindness: and let him reprove me; *it shall be* an excellent oil, *which* shall not break my head: for yet my prayer also *shall be* in their calamities. 6 When their judges are overthrown in stony places, they shall hear my words; for they are sweet. 7 Our bones are scattered at the grave's mouth, as when one cutteth and cleaveth *wood* upon the earth. 8 But mine eyes *are* unto thee, O God the Lord: in thee is my trust; leave not my soul destitute. 9 Keep me from the snares *which* they have laid for me, and the gins of the workers of iniquity. 10 Let the wicked fall into their own nets, whilst that I withal escape.

Here, I. David desires to be told of his faults. His enemies reproached him with that which was false, which he could not but complain of; yet, at the same time, he desired his friends would reprove him for that which was really amiss in him, particularly if there was any thing that gave the least colour to those reproaches (*v.* 5): *Let the righteous smite me; it shall be a kindness.* The *righteous God* (so some); " I will welcome the rebukes of his providence, and be so far from quarrelling with them that I will receive them as tokens of love and improve them as means of grace, and will pray for those that are the instruments of my trouble." But it is commonly taken for the reproofs given by righteous men; and it best becomes those that are themselves righteous to reprove the unrighteousness of others, and from them reproof will be best taken. But if the reproof be just, though the reprover be not so, we must make a good use of it and learn obedience by it. We are here taught how to receive the reproofs of the righteous and wise. 1. We must desire to be reproved for whatever is amiss in us, or is done amiss by us: " Lord, put it into the heart of the righteous to smite me and reprove me. If my own heart does not *smite me,* as it ought, let my friend do it; let me never fall under that dreadful judgment of being let alone in sin. 2. We must account it a piece of friendship. We must not only bear it patiently, but take it as a kindness; for *reproofs of instruction are the way of life* (Prov. vi. 23), are means of good to us, to bring us to repentance for the sins we have committed, and to prevent relapses into sin. Though reproofs cut, it is in order to a cure, and therefore they are much more desirable than the kisses of an enemy (Prov. xxvii. 6) or the song of fools, Eccl vii. 5. David blessed God for Abigail's seasonable admonition, 1 Sam. xxv. 32. 3. We must reckon ourselves helped and healed by it: It *shall be as an excellent oil* to a wound, to mollify it and close it up; *it shall not break my head*, as some reckon it to do, who could as well bear to have their heads broken as to be told of their faults; but, says David, "I am not of that mind; it is my sin that has broken my head, that has broken my bones, Ps. li. 8. The reproof is an excellent oil, to cure the bruises sin has given me. It shall not *break my head*, if it may but help to break my heart." 4. We must requite the kindness of those that deal thus faithfully, thus friendly with us, at least by our *prayers for them in their calamities*, and hereby we must show that we take it kindly. Dr. Hammond gives quite another reading of this verse: "*Reproach will bruise me that am righteous, and rebuke me; but that poisonous oil shall not break my head* (shall not destroy me, shall not do me the mischief intended), *for yet my prayer shall be in their mischiefs*, that God would preserve me from them, and my prayer shall not be in vain."

II. David hopes his persecutors will, some time or other, bear to be told of their faults, as he was willing to be told of his (*v.* 6): "*When their judges*" (Saul and his officers who judged and condemned David, and would themselves be sole judges) "*are overthrown in stony places*, among the rocks in the wilderness, then *they shall hear my words, for they are sweet.*" Some think this refers to the relentings that were in Saul's breast when he said, with tears, *Is this thy voice, my son David?* 1 Sam. xxiv. 16; xxvi. 21. Or we may take it more generally: even judges, great as they are, may come to be overthrown. Those that make the greatest figure in this world do not always meet with level smooth ways through it. And those that slighted the word of God before will relish it, and be glad of it, when they are in affliction, for that opens the ear to instruction. When the world is bitter the word is sweet. Oppressed innocency cannot gain a hearing with those that live in pomp and pleasure, but when they come to be overthrown themselves they will have more compassionate thoughts of the afflicted.

III. David complains of the great extremity to which he and his friends were reduced (*v.* 7): *Our bones are scattered at the grave's mouth*, out of which they are thrown up, so long have we been dead, or into which they are ready to be thrown, so near are we to the pit; and they are as little regarded as chips among the hewers of wood, which are thrown in neglected heaps: *As one that cuts and cleaves the earth* (so some read it), alluding to the ploughman who tears the earth in pieces with his plough-share, cxxix. 3. *Can these dry bones live?*

IV. David casts himself upon God, and depends upon him for deliverance: "*But my eyes are unto thee* (*v.* 8); for, when the case is ever so deplorable, thou canst redress all the grievances. From thee I expect relief, bad as things are, and in *thee is my trust.*"

Those that have their eye towards God may have their hopes in him.

V. He prays that God would succour and relieve him as his necessity required. 1. That he would comfort him: "*Leave not my soul desolate and destitute; still let me see where my help is.*" 2. That he would prevent the designs of his enemies against him (*v.* 9): "*Keep me from* being taken in *the snare they have laid for me;* give me to discover it and to evade it." Be the gin placed with ever so much subtlety, God can and will secure his people from being taken in it. 3. That God would, in justice, turn the designs of his enemies upon themselves, and, in mercy, deliver him from being ruined by them (*v.* 10): *Let the wicked fall into their own net*, the net which, intentionally, they procured for me, but which, meritoriously, they prepared for themselves. *Nec lex est justior ulla quàm necis artifices arte perire suâ—No law can be more just than that the architects of destruction should perish by their own contrivances.* All that are bound over to God's justice are held in the cords of their own iniquity. But let me at the same time obtain a discharge. The entangling and ensnaring of the wicked sometimes prove the escape and enlargement of the righteous.

PSALM CXLII.

This psalm is a prayer, the substance of which David offered up to God when he was forced by Saul to take shelter in a cave, and which he afterwards penned in this form. Here is, I. The complaint he makes to God (ver. 1, 2) of the subtlety, strength, and malice, of his enemies (ver. 3, 6), and the coldness and indifference of his friends, ver. 4. II. The comfort he takes in God that he knew his case (ver. 3) and was his refuge, ver. 5. III. His expectation from God that he would hear and deliver him, ver. 6, 7. IV. His expectation from the righteous that they would join with him in praises, ver. 7. Those that are troubled in mind, body, or estate, may, in singing this psalm (if they sing it in some measure with David's spirit), both warrant his complaints and fetch in his comforts.

Maschil of David. A prayer when he was in the cave.

I CRIED unto the LORD with my voice; with my voice unto the LORD did I make my supplication. 2 I poured out my complaint before him; I showed before him my trouble. 3 When my spirit was overwhelmed within me, then thou knewest my path. In the way wherein I walked have they privily laid a snare for me.

Whether it was in the cave of *Adullam*, or that of *Engedi*, that David prayed this prayer, is not material; it is plain that he was in distress. It was a great disgrace to so great a soldier, so great a courtier, to be put to such shifts for his own safety, and a great terror to be so hotly pursued and every moment in expectation of death; yet then he had such a presence of mind as to pray this prayer, and, wherever he was, still he had his religion about him. Prayers and tears were his weapons, and, when he durst not stretch forth his hands against his prince, he lifted them up to his God. There is no cave so deep, so dark, but we may out of it send up our prayers, and our souls in prayer, to God. He calls this prayer *Maschil—a psalm of instruction*, because of the good lessons he had himself learnt in the cave, learnt on his knees, which he desired to teach others. In these verses observe,

I. How David complained to God, *v.* 1, 2. When the danger was over he was not ashamed to own (as great spirits sometimes are) the fright he had been in and the application he had made to God. Let not men of the first rank think it any diminution or disparagement to them, when they are in affliction, to cry to God, and to cry like children to their parents when any thing frightens them. *David poured out his complaint*, which denotes a free and full complaint; he was copious and particular in it. His heart was as full of his grievances as it could hold, but he made himself easy by pouring them out before the Lord; and this he did with great fervency: *He cried unto the Lord with his voice*, with the voice of his mind (so some think), for, being hidden in the cave, he durst not speak with an audible voice, lest that should betray him; but mental prayer is vocal to God, and he hears the groanings which cannot, or dare not, be uttered, Rom. viii. 26. Two things David laid open to God, in this complaint:—1. His distress. He exhibited a remonstrance or memorial of his case: *I showed before him my trouble*, and all the circumstances of it. He did not prescribe to God, nor show him his trouble, as if God did not know it without his showing; but as one that put a confidence in God, desired to keep up communion with him, and was willing to refer himself entirely to him, he unbosomed himself to him, humbly laid the matter before him, and then cheerfully left it with him. We are apt to show our trouble too much to ourselves, aggravating it, and poring upon it, which does us no service, whereas by showing it to God we might cast the care upon him who careth for us, and thereby ease ourselves. Nor should we allow of any complaint to ourselves or others which we cannot with due decency and sincerity of devotion make to God, and stand to before him. 2. His desire. When he made his complaint he *made his supplication* (*v.* 1), not claiming relief as a debt, but humbly begging it as a favour. Complainants must be suppliants, for God will be sought unto.

II. What he complained of: "*In the way wherein I walked*, suspecting no danger, *have they privily laid a snare for me*, to entrap me." Saul gave Michal his daughter to David on purpose that she might be *a snare to him*, 1 Sam. xviii. 21. This he complains of to God, that every thing was done with a design against him. If he had gone out of his way, and met with snares, he might have thanked himself; but when he met with them in the way of his duty he might with humble boldness tell God of them.

III. What comforted him in the midst of these complaints (*v.* 3): "*When my spirit was overwhelmed within me*, and ready to sink under the burden of grief and fear, when I was quite at a loss and ready to despair, *then thou knewest my path*, that is, then it was a pleasure to me to think that thou knewest it. Thou knewest my sincerity, the right path which I have walked in, and that I am not such a one as my persecutors represent me. Thou knewest my condition in all the particulars of it; when my spirit was so overwhelmed that I could not distinctly show it, this comforted me, that thou knewest it, Job xxiii. 10. Thou knewest it, that is, thou didst protect, preserve, and secure it," Ps. xxxi. 7; Deut. ii. 7.

4 I looked on *my* right hand, and beheld, but *there was* no man that would know me: refuge failed me; no man cared for my soul. 5 I cried unto thee, O Lord: I said, Thou *art* my refuge *and* my portion in the land of the living. 6 Attend unto my cry; for I am brought very low: deliver me from my persecutors; for they are stronger than I. 7 Bring my soul out of prison, that I may praise thy name: the righteous shall compass me about; for thou shalt deal bountifully with me.

The psalmist here tells us, for our instruction, 1. How he was disowned and deserted by his friends, *v.* 4. When he was in favour at court he seemed to have a great interest, but when he was made an out-law, and it was dangerous for any one to harbour him (witness Ahimelech's fate), then *no man would know him*, but every body was shy of him. He looked on *his right hand* for an advocate (cix. 31), some friend or other to speak a good word for him; but, since Jonathan's appearing for him had like to have cost him his life, nobody was willing to venture in defence of his innocency, but all were ready to say they knew nothing of the matter. He looked round to see if any would open their doors to him; but *refuge failed him*. None of all his old friends would give him a night's lodging, or direct him to any place of secresy and safety. How many good men have been deceived by such swallow-friends, who are gone when winter comes! David's life was exceedingly precious, and yet, when he was unjustly proscribed, *no man cared for it*, nor would move a hand for the protection of it. Herein he was a type of Christ, who, in his sufferings for us, was forsaken of all men, even of his own disciples, and trod the wine-press alone, for there was *none to help, none to uphold*, Isa. lxiii. 5. 2. How he then found satisfaction in God, *v.* 5. Lovers and friends stood aloof from him, and it was in vain to call to them "But," said he, "*I cried unto thee, O Lord!* who knowest me, and carest for me, when none else will, and wilt not fail me nor forsake me when men do;" for God is constant in his love. David tells us what he said to God in the cave : " *Thou art my refuge and my portion in the land of the living ;* I depend upon thee to be so, *my refuge* to save me from being miserable, *my portion* to make me happy. The cave I am in is but a poor refuge. Lord, *thy name* is the *strong tower* that *I run into.* Thou art *my refuge,* in whom alone I shall think myself safe. The crown I am in hopes of is but a poor portion ; I can never think myself well provided for till I know that *the Lord is the portion of my inheritance and of my cup.*" Those who in sincerity take the Lord for their God shall find him all-sufficient both as a refuge and as a portion, so that, as no evil shall hurt them, so no good shall be wanting to them ; and they may humbly claim their interest : " *Lord, thou art my refuge and my portion;* every thing else is a refuge of lies and a portion of no value. Thou art so *in the land of the living,* that is, while I live and have my being, whether in this world or in a better." There is enough in God to answer all the necessities of this present time. We live in a world of dangers and wants ; but what danger need we fear if God is our refuge, or what wants if he be our portion ? Heaven, which alone deserves to be called *the land of the living,* will be to all believers both a refuge and a portion. 3. How, in this satisfaction, he addressed himself to God (*v.* 6, 7) : " Lord, give a gracious *ear to my cry,* the cry of my affliction, the cry of my supplication, for *I am brought very low,* and, if thou help me not, I shall be quite sunk. Lord, *deliver me from my persecutors,* either tie their hands or turn their hearts, break their power or blast their projects, restrain them or rescue me, *for they are stronger than I,* and it will be thy honour to take part with the weakest. Deliver me from them, or I shall be ruined by them, for I am not yet myself a match for them. Lord, *bring my soul out of prison,* not only bring me safe out of this cave, but bring me out of all my perplexities." We may apply it spiritually : the souls of good men are often straitened by doubts and fears, cramped and fettered through the weakness of faith and the prevalency of corruption ; and it is then their duty and interest to apply themselves to God, and beg of him to set them at liberty and to enlarge their hearts, that they may *run the way of his commandments.* 4. How much he expected his deliverance would redound to the glory of God. (1.) By his own thanksgivings, into which his present complaints would then be turned : " *Bring my soul out of prison,* not that I may enjoy myself and my friends and live at ease, no, nor that I may secure my country, but *that I may praise thy name.*" This we should have an eye to, in all our prayers to God for

deliverance out of trouble, that we may have occasion to praise God and may live to his praise. This is the greatest comfort of temporal mercies that they furnish us with matter, and give us opportunity, for the excellent duty of praise. (2.) By the thanksgivings of many on his behalf (2 Cor. i. 11) : " When I am enlarged *the righteous shall encompass me about ;* for *my cause they shall make thee a crown of praise,* so the Chaldee. They shall flock about me to congratulate me on my deliverance, to hear my experiences, and to receive (Maschil) instructions from me ; they shall encompass me, to join with me in my thanksgivings, *because thou shalt* have dealt *bountifully with me.*" Note, The mercies of others ought to be the matter of our praises to God ; and the praises of others, on our behalf, ought to be both desired and rejoiced in by us.

PSALM CXLIII.

This psalm, as those before, is a prayer of David, and full of complaints of the great distress and danger he was in, probably when Saul persecuted him. He did not only pray in that affliction, but he prayed very much and very often, not the same over again, but new thoughts. In this psalm, I. He complains of his troubles, through the oppression of his enemies (ver. 3) and the weakness of his spirit under it, which was ready to sink notwithstanding the likely course he took to support himself, ver. 4, 5. II. He prays, and prays earnestly (ver. 6), 1. That God would hear him, ver. 1—7. 2. That he would not deal with him according to his sins, ver. 2. 3. That he would not hide his face from him (ver. 7), but manifest his favour to him, ver. 8. 4. That he would guide and direct him in the way of his duty (ver. 8, 10) and quicken him in it, ver. 11. 5. That he would deliver him out of his troubles, ver. 9, 11. 6. That he would in due time reckon with his persecutors, ver. 12. We may more easily accommodate this psalm to ourselves, in the singing of it, because most of the petitions in it are for spiritual blessings (which we all need at all times), mercy and grace.

A psalm of David.

HEAR my prayer, O Lord, give ear to my supplications: in thy faithfulness answer me, *and* in thy righteousness. 2 And enter not into judgment with thy servant : for in thy sight shall no man living be justified. 3 For the enemy hath persecuted my soul ; he hath smitten my life down to the ground ; he hath made me to dwell in darkness, as those that have been long dead. 4 Therefore is my spirit overwhelmed within me ; my heart within me is desolate. 5 I remember the days of old ; I meditate on all thy works ; I muse on the work of thy hands. 6 I stretch forth my hands unto thee : my soul *thirsteth* after thee, as a thirsty land. Selah.

Here, I. David humbly begs to be heard (*v.* 1), not as if he questioned it, but he earnestly desired it, and was in care about it, for, having directed his prayer, he looked up to see how it sped, Hab. ii. 1. He is a suppliant to his God, and he begs that his requests may be granted : *Hear my prayer ; give ear to my supplications.* He is an appellant against his persecutors, and he begs that his case may be brought to hearing and that God will give judgment upon it, in his faithfulness and righteousness, as the Judge of right and wrong. Or, "Answer my petitions in thy faithfulness, according to the promises thou hast made, which thou wilt be just to." We have no righteousness of our own to plead, and therefore must plead God's righteousness, the word of promise which he has freely given us and caused us to hope in.

II. He humbly begs not to be proceeded against in strict justice, *v.* 2. He seems here, if not to correct, yet to explain, his plea (*v.* 1), Deliver me *in thy righteousness ;* "I mean," says he, "the righteous promises of the gospel, not the righteous threatenings of the law; if I be answered according to the righteousness of this broken covenant of innocency, I am quite undone ;" and therefore, 1. His petition is, "*Enter not into judgment with thy servant ;* do not deal with me in strict justice, as I deserve to be dealt with." In this prayer we must own ourselves to be God's servants, bound to obey him, accountable to him, and solicitous to obtain his favour, and we must approve ourselves to him. We must acknowledge that in many instances we have offended him, and have come short of our duty to him, that he might justly enquire into our offences, and proceed against us for them according to law, and that, if he should do so, judgment would certainly go against us ; we have nothing to move in arrest or mitigation of it, but execution would be taken out and awarded and then we should be ruined for ever. But we must encourage ourselves with a hope that there is mercy and forgiveness with God, and be earnest with him for the benefit of that mercy. "*Enter not into judgment with thy servant,* for thou hast already entered into judgment with thy Son, and laid upon him the iniquity of us all. *Enter not into judgment with thy servant,* for thy servant enters into judgment with himself ;" and, if *we will judge ourselves, we shall not be judged.* 2. His plea is, "*In thy sight shall no man living be justified* upon those terms, for no man can plead innocency nor any righteousness of his own, either that he has not sinned or that he does not deserve to die for his sins; nor that he has any satisfaction of his own to offer ;" nay, if God contend with us, *we are not able to answer him for one of a thousand,* Job ix. 3 ; xv. 20. David, before he prays for the removal of his trouble, prays for the pardon of his sin, and depends upon mere mercy for it.

III. He complains of the prevalency of his enemies against him (*v.* 3) : "Saul, that great enemy, *has persecuted my soul,* sought my life, with a restless malice, and has carried the persecution so far that he has already *smitten it down to the ground.* Though I am not yet under ground, I am struck to the ground, and that is next door to it ; he has forced me to *dwell in darkness,* not only in dark caves, but in dark thoughts and apprehensions, in the clouds of melancholy, *as* helpless and hopeless as *those that have been*

long dead. Lord, let me find mercy with thee, for I find no mercy with men. They condemn me ; but, Lord, do not thou condemn me. Am not I an object of thy compassion, fit to be appeared for ; and is not my enemy an object of thy displeasure, fit to be appeared against ?"

IV. He bemoans the oppression of his mind, occasioned by his outward troubles (*v.* 4) : *Therefore is my spirit* overpowered and *overwhelmed within me,* and I am almost plunged in despair ; when without are fightings within are fears, and those fears greater tyrants and oppressors than Saul himself and not so easily out-run. It is sometimes the lot of the best men to have their spirits for a time almost overwhelmed and their hearts desolate, and doubtless it is their infirmity. David was not only a great saint, but a great soldier, and yet even he was sometimes ready to faint in a day of adversity. *Howl, fir-trees, if the cedars be shaken.*

V. He applies himself to the use of proper means for the relief of his troubled spirit. He had no force to muster up against the oppression of the enemy, but, if he can keep possession of nothing else, he will do what he can to keep possession of his own soul and to preserve his inward peace. In order to this, 1. He looks back, and *remembers the days of old* (*v.* 5), God's former appearances for his afflicted people and for him in particular. It has been often a relief to the people of God in their straits to think of the wonders which their fathers told them of, lxxvii. 5, 11. 2. He looks round, and takes notice of the works of God in the visible creation, and the providential government of the world : *I meditate on all thy works.* Many see them, but do not see the footsteps of God's wisdom, power, and goodness in them, and do not receive the benefit they might by them because they do not meditate upon them ; they do not dwell on that copious curious subject, but soon quit it, as if they had exhausted it, when they have scarcely touched upon it. *I muse on,* or (as some read it) *I discourse of, the* operation *of thy hands,* how great, how good, it is ! The more we consider the power of God the less we shall fear the face or force of man, Isa. li. 12, 13. 3. He looks up with earnest desires towards God and his favour (*v.* 6) : *I stretch forth my hands unto thee,* as one begging an alms, and big with expectation to receive something great, standing ready to lay hold on it and bid it welcome. *My soul thirsteth after thee; it is to thee* (so the word is), entire for thee, intent on thee ; it is *as a thirsty land,* which, being parched with excessive heat, gapes for rain ; so do I need, so do I crave, the support and refreshment of divine consolations under my afflictions, and nothing else will relieve me." This is the best course we can take when our spirits are overwhelmed ; and justly do those sink under their load who will not take such a ready way as this to ease themselves.

7 Hear me speedily, O LORD : my spirit faileth : hide not thy face from me, lest I be like unto them that go down into the pit. 8 Cause me to hear thy lovingkindness in the morning ; for in thee do I trust : cause me to know the way wherein I should walk ; for I lift up my soul unto thee. 9 Deliver me, O LORD, from mine enemies ; I flee unto thee to hide me. 10 Teach me to do thy will ; for thou *art* my God : thy spirit *is* good ; lead me into the land of uprightness. 11 Quicken me, O LORD, for thy name's sake : for thy righteousness' sake bring my soul out of trouble. 12 And of thy mercy cut off mine enemies, and destroy all them that afflict my soul : for I *am* thy servant.

David here tells us what he said when he stretched-forth his hands unto God ; he begins not only as one in earnest, but as one in haste : "*Hear me speedily*, and defer no longer, for *my spirit faileth.* I am just ready to faint ; reach the cordial—quickly, quickly, or I am gone." It was not a haste of unbelief, but of vehement desire and holy love. *Make haste, O God ! to help me.* Three things David here prays for :—

I. The manifestations of God's favour towards him, that God would be well pleased with him and let him know that he was so ; this he prefers before any good, iv. 6. 1. He dreads God's frowns : " Lord, *hide not thy face from me ;* Lord, be not angry with me, do not turn from me, as we do from one we are displeased with ; Lord, let me not be left under the apprehensions of thy anger or in doubt concerning thy favour ; if I have thy favour, let it not be hidden from me." Those that have the truth of grace cannot but desire the evidence of it. He pleads the wretchedness of his case if God withdrew from him : " Lord, let me not lie under thy wrath, for then I am *like those that go down to the pit,* that is, down to the grave (I am a dead man, weak, and pale, and ghastly ; thy frowns are worse than death), or down to hell, the bottomless pit." Even those who through grace are delivered from going down to the pit may sometimes, when the terrors of the Almighty set themselves in array against them, look like those who are going to the pit. Disconsolate saints have sometimes cried out of the wrath of God, as if they had been damned sinners, Job vi. 4 ; Ps. lxxxviii. 6. 2. He entreats God's favour (*v.* 8) : *Cause me to hear thy lovingkindness in the morning.* He cannot but think that God has a kindness for him, that he has some kind things to say to him, some good words and comfortable words ; but the present hurry of his affairs, and tu-

mult of his spirits, drowned those pleasing whispers ; and therefore he begs, " Lord, do not only speak kindly to me, but cause me to hear it, to *hear joy and gladness,*" li. 8. God speaks to us by his word and by his providence, and in both we should desire and endeavour to *hear his lovingkindness* (cvii. 43), that we may set that always before us : " *Cause me to hear* it *in the morning,* every morning ; let my waking thoughts be of God's lovingkindness, that the sweet relish of that may abide upon my spirits all the day long." His plea is, " *For in thee do I trust,* and in thee only ; I look not for comfort in any other." God's goodness is commonly wrought *for those who trust in him* (xxxi. 8), who by faith draw it out.

II. The operations of God's grace in him. Those he is as earnest for as for the tokens of God's favour to him, and so should we be. He prays,

1. That he might be enlightened with the knowledge of God's will ; and this is the first work of the Spirit, in order to his other works, for God deals with men as men, as reasonable creatures. Here are three petitions to this effect :—(1.) *Cause me to know the way wherein I should walk.* Sometimes those that are much in care to walk right are in doubt, and in the dark, which is the right way. Let them come boldly to the throne of grace, and beg of God, by his word, and Spirit, and providence, to show them the way, and prevent their missing it. A good man does not ask what is the way in which he must walk, or in which is the most pleasant walking, but what is the right way, the way in which he should walk. He pleads, " *I lift up my soul unto thee,* to be moulded and fashioned according to thy will." He did not only importunately, but impartially, desire to know his duty ; and those that do so shall be taught. (2.) " *Teach me to do thy will,* not only show me what thy will is, but teach me how to do it, how to turn my hand dexterously to my duty." It is the desire and endeavour of all God's faithful servants to know and to do his will, and to stand complete in it. He pleads, " *Thou art my God,* and therefore my oracle, by whom I may expect to be advised—my God, and therefore my ruler, whose will I desire to do." If we do in sincerity take God for our God, we may depend upon him to teach us to do his will, as a master does his servant. (3.) *Lead me into the land of uprightness,* into the communion of saints, that pleasant land of the upright, or into a settled course of holy living, which will lead to heaven, that land of uprightness where holiness will be in perfection, and he that is holy shall be holy still. We should desire to be led, and kept safe, to heaven, not only because it is a land of blessedness, but because it is a land of uprightness ; it is the perfection of grace. We cannot find the way that will bring us to that land unless God show us, nor go in that way unless he take us by the hand and lead us, as

we lead those that are weak, or lame, or timorous, or dim-sighted ; so necessary is the grace of God, not only to put us into the good way, but to keep us and carry us on in it. The plea is, " *Thy Spirit is good,* and able to make me good," good and willing to help those that are at a loss. *Let thy good Spirit lead me,* so some read it. Those that have the Lord for their God have his Spirit for their guide ; and it is both their character and their privilege that they are *led by the Spirit.*

2. He prays that he might be enlivened to do his will (*v.* 11) : " *Quicken me, O Lord !* quicken my graces, that they may be active —quicken my devotions, that they may be lively ; quicken me to my duty, and quicken me in it ; and this *for thy name's sake.*" The best saints often find themselves dull, and dead, and slow, and therefore pray to God to quicken them.

III. The appearance of God's providence for him, 1. That God would, in his own way and time, give him rest from his troubles (*v.* 9) : " *Deliver me, O Lord ! from my enemies,* that they may not have their will against me; *for I flee unto thee to hide me ;* I trust to thee to defend me in my trouble, and therefore to rescue me out of it." Preservations are pledges of salvation, and those shall find God their hiding-place who by faith make him such. He explains himself (*v.* 11): " *For thy righteousness-sake, bring my soul out of trouble,* for thy promise-sake, nay, for thy mercy-sake" (for some by *righteousness* understand *kindness* and *goodness*) ; " do not only deliver me from my outward trouble, but from the trouble of my soul, the trouble that threatens to overwhelm my spirit. Whatever trouble I am in, Lord, let not my heart be troubled," John xiv. 1. 2. That he would reckon with those that were the instruments of his trouble (*v.* 12): " *Of thy mercy* to me *cut off my enemies,* that I may be no longer in fear of them ; *and destroy all those,* whoever they be, how numerous, how powerful, soever, *who afflict my soul,* and create vexation to that ; *for I am thy servant,* and am resolved to continue such, and therefore may expect to be owned and protected in thy service." This prayer is a prophecy of the utter destruction of all the impenitent enemies of Jesus Christ and his kingdom, who will not have him to reign over them, who grieve his Spirit and afflict his soul, by afflicting his people, in whose afflictions he is afflicted.

PSALM CXLIV.

The four preceding psalms seem to have been penned by David before his accession to the crown, when he was persecuted by Saul ; this seems to have been penned afterwards, when he was still in trouble (for there is no condition in this world privileged with an exemption from trouble), the neighbouring nations molesting him and giving him disturbance, especially the Philistines, 2 Sam. v. 17. In this psalm, I. He acknowledges, with triumph and thankfulness, the great goodness of God to him in advancing him to the government, ver. 1—4. II. He prays to God to help him against the enemies who threatened him, ver. 5—8, and again ver. 11. III. He rejoices in the assurance of victory over them, ver. 9, 10. IV. He prays for the prosperity of his own family, and pleases himself with the hopes of it, ver. 12—15. In singing this psalm we may give God the glory of our spiritual privileges and advancements, and fetch in help from him against our spiritual enemies ; we may pray for the pros-perity of our souls, of our families, and of our land ; and, in the opinion of some of the Jewish writers, we may refer the psalm to the Messiah and his kingdom.

A psalm of David.

BLESSED *be* the LORD my strength, which teacheth my hands to war, *and* my fingers to fight: 2 My goodness, and my fortress ; my high tower, and my deliverer; my shield, and *he* in whom I trust; who subdueth my people under me. 3 LORD, what *is* man, that thou takest knowledge of him ! *or* the son of man, that thou makest account of him ! 4 Man is like to vanity : his days *are* as a shadow that passeth away. 5 Bow thy heavens, O LORD, and come down: touch the mountains, and they shall smoke. 6 Cast forth lightning, and scatter them : shoot out thine arrows, and destroy them. 7 Send thine hand from above ; rid me, and deliver me out of great waters, from the hand of strange children ; 8 Whose mouth speaketh vanity, and their right hand *is* a right hand of falsehood.

Here, I. David acknowledges his dependence upon God and his obligations to him, *v.* 1, 2. A prayer for further mercy is fitly begun with a thanksgiving for former mercy; and when we are waiting upon God to bless us we should stir up ourselves to bless him. He gives to God the glory of two things :—

1. What he was to him : *Blessed be the Lord my rock* (*v.* 1), *my goodness, my fortress, v.* 2. He has in the covenant engaged himself to be so, and encouraged us, accordingly, to depend upon him ; all the saints, who by faith have made him theirs, have found him not only to answer but to outdo their expectations. David speaks of it here as the matter of his trust, and that which made him easy, as the matter of his triumph, and that which made him glad, and in which he gloried. See how he multiplies words to express the satisfaction he had in God and his interest in him. (1.) " He is *my strength,* on whom I stay, and from whom I have power both for my work and for my warfare, my rock to build on, to take shelter in." Even when we are weak we may *be strong in the Lord and in the power of his might.* (2.) " *My goodness,* not only good to me, but my chief good, in whose favour I place my felicity, and who is the author of all the goodness that is in me, and *from whom comes every good and perfect gift.*" (3.) " *My fortress,* and *my high tower,* in whom I think myself as safe as ever any prince thought himself in a castle or strong-hold." David had formerly sheltered himself in strongholds at En-gedi (1 Sam. xxiii. 29), which

perhaps were natural fastnesses. He had lately made himself master of the strong-hold of Zion, which was fortified by art, and he *dwelt in the fort* (2 Sam. v. 7, 9), but he depends not on these. "Lord," says he, "thou art *my fortress* and *my high tower.*" The divine attributes and promises are fortifications to a believer, far exceeding those either of nature or art. (4.) *My deliverer,* and, as it is in the original, very emphatically, *my deliverer to me,* "not only a deliverer I have interest in, but who is always nigh unto me and makes all my deliverances turn to my real benefit." (5.) "*My shield,* to guard me against all the malignant darts that my enemies let fly at me, not only *my fortress* at home, but *my shield* abroad in the field of battle." Wherever a believer goes he carries his protection along with him. *Fear not, Abram, I am thy shield.*

2. What he had done for him. He was bred a shepherd, and seems not to have been designed by his parents or himself for any thing more. But, (1.) God had made him a soldier. His hands had been used to the crook and his fingers to the harp, but God *taught his hands to war and his fingers to fight,* because he designed him for Israel's champion; and what God calls men to he either finds them or makes them fit for. Let the men of war give God the glory of all their military skill; the same that teaches the meanest husbandman his art teaches the greatest general his. It is a pity that any whose fingers God has taught to fight should fight against him or his kingdom among men. Those have special reason to acknowledge God with thankfulness who prove to be qualified for services which they themselves never thought of. (2.) God had made him a sovereign prince, had taught him to wield the sceptre as well as the sword, to rule as well as fight, the harder and nobler art of the two: He *subdueth my people under me.* The providence of God is to be acknowledged in making people subject to their prince, and so preserving the order and benefit of societies. There was a special hand of God inclining the people of Israel to be subject to David, pursuant to the promise God had made him; and it was typical of that great act of divine grace, the bringing of souls into subjection to the Lord Jesus and making them willing in the day of his power.

II. He admires God's condescension to man and to himself in particular (*v.* 3, 4): "*Lord, what is man,* what a poor little thing is he, *that thou takest knowledge of him, that thou makest account of him,* that he falls so much under thy cognizance and care, and that thou hast such a tender regard to any of that mean and worthless race as thou hast had to me!" Considering the many disgraces which the human nature lies under, we have reason to admire the honours God has put upon mankind in general (the saints especially, some in a particular manner, as

770

David) and upon the essiah (to whom those words are applied, Heb. ii. 6), who was *highly exalted because he humbled himself to be found in fashion as a man,* and *has authority to execute judgment because he is the Son of man.* A question to this purport David asked (viii. 4), and he illustrated the wonder by the consideration of the great dignity God has placed man in (viii. 5), *Thou hast crowned him with glory and honour.* Here he illustrates it by the consideration of the meanness and mortality of man, notwithstanding the dignity put upon him (*v.* 4): *Man is like to vanity;* so frail is he, so weak, so helpless, compassed about with so many infirmities, and his continuance here so very short and uncertain, that he is as like as may be to vanity itself. Nay, he is vanity, he is so at his best estate. *His days* have little substance in them, considering how many of the thoughts and cares of an immortal soul are employed about a poor dying body; they *are as a shadow,* dark and flitting, transitory and finishing with the sun, and, when that sets, resolving itself into all shadow. They *are as a shadow that passeth away,* and there is no loss of it. David puts himself into the number of those that are thus mean and despicable.

III. He begs of God to strengthen him and give him success against the enemies that invaded him, *v.* 5—8. He does not specify who they were that he was in fear of, but says, *Scatter them, destroy them.* God knew whom he meant, though he did not name them. But afterwards he describes them (*v.* 7, 8): "They are *strange children,* Philistines, aliens, bad neighbours to Israel, heathens, whom we are bound to be strange to and not to make any leagues with, and who therefore carry it strangely towards us." Notwithstanding the advantages with which God had blessed David's arms against them, they were still vexatious and treacherous, and men that one could put no confidence in: "One cannot take their word, for their *mouth speaketh vanity;* nay, if they give their hand upon it, or offer their hand to help you, there is no trusting them; for *their right hand is a right hand of falsehood.*" Against such as these we cannot defend ourselves, but we may depend on the God of truth and justice, who hates falsehood, to defend us from them. 1. David prays that God would appear, that he would do something extraordinary, for the conviction of those who preferred their dung-hill-deities before the God of Israel (*v.* 5): "*Bow thy heavens, O Lord!* and make it evident that they are indeed thine, and that thou art the Lord of them, Isa. lxiv. 1. Let thy providence threaten my enemies, and look black upon them, as the clouds do on the earth when they are thick, and hang very low, big with a storm. Fight against those that fight against us, so that it may visibly appear that thou art for us. *Touch the mountains,* our strong and stately enemies, *and let them smoke.* Show thyself by the ministry of thy angels, as thou didst upon Mount Sinai." 2. That he would appear against his enemies, that he would fight from heaven against them, as sometimes he had done, by lightnings, which are his arrows (his fiery darts, against which the hardest steel is no armour of proof, so penetrating is the force of lightning), that he himself would shoot these arrows, who, we are sure, never misses his mark, but hits where he aims. 3. That he would appear for him, *v.* 7. He begs for their destruction, in order to his own deliverance and the repose of his people: " *Send thy hand*, thy power, *from above*, for that way we look for help; *rid me and deliver me out of these great waters* that are ready to overflow me." God's time to help his people is when they are sinking and all other helps fail.

9 I will sing a new song unto thee, O God: upon a psaltery *and* an instrument of ten strings will I sing praises unto thee. 10 *It is he* that giveth salvation unto kings : who delivereth David his servant from the hurtful sword. 11 Rid me, and deliver me from the hand of strange children, whose mouth speaketh vanity, and their right hand *is* a right hand of falsehood : 12 That our sons *may be* as plants grown up in their youth ; *that* our daughters *may be* as corner stones, polished *after* the similitude of a palace : 13 *That* our garners *may be* full, affording all manner of store : *that* our sheep may bring forth thousands and ten thousands in our streets : 14 *That* our oxen *may be* strong to labour ; *that there be* no breaking in, nor going out ; that *there be* no complaining in our streets. 15 Happy *is that* people, that is in such a case : *yea*, happy *is that* people, whose God *is* the LORD.

The method is the same in this latter part of the psalm as in the former ; David first gives glory to God and then begs mercy from him.

I. He praises God for the experiences he had had of his goodness to him and the encouragements he had to expect further mercy from him, *v.* 9, 10. In the midst of his complaints concerning the power and treachery of his enemies, here is a holy exultation in his God : *I will sing a new song to thee, O God!* a song of praise for new mercies, for those compassions that are new every morning. Fresh favours call for fresh returns of thanks ; nay, we must praise God for the mercies we hope for by his promise as well as those we have received by his providence, 2 Chron. xx. 20, 21. He will join music with his songs of praise, to express and excite his

holy joy in God ; he will praise God *upon a psaltery of ten strings*, in the best manner, thinking all little enough to set forth the praises of God. He tells us what this new song shall be (*v.* 10): *It is he that giveth salvation unto kings.* This intimates, 1. That great kings cannot save themselves without him. Kings have their life-guards, and have armies at command, and all the means of safety that can be devised ; but, after all, it is God that gives them their salvation, and secures them by those means, which he could do, if there were occasion, without them, xxxiii. 16. Kings are the protectors of their people, but it is God that is their protector. How much service do they owe him then with their power who gives them all their salvations ! 2. That good kings, who are his ministers for the good of their subjects, shall be protected and saved by him. He has engaged to give salvation to those kings that are his subjects and rule for him ; witness the great things he had done for *David his servant*, whom he had many a time *delivered from the hurtful sword*, to which Saul's malice, and his own zeal for the service of his country, had often exposed him. This may refer to Christ the Son of David, and then it is a new song indeed, a New-Testament song. God delivered him from the hurtful sword, upheld him as his servant, and brought him off a conqueror over all the powers of darkness, Isa. xlii. 1 ; xlix. 8. To him he gave salvation, not for himself only, but for us, raising him up to be *a horn of salvation.*

II. He prays for the continuance of God's favour.

1. That he might be delivered from the public enemies, *v.* 11. Here he repeats his prayer and plea, *v.* 7, 8. His persecutors were still of the same character, false and perfidious, and who would certainly overreach an honest man and be too hard for him : "Therefore, Lord, do thou *deliver me from* them, for they are a strange sort of people."

2. That he might see the public peace and prosperity : "Lord, let us have victory, that we may have quietness, which we shall never have while our enemies have it in their power to do us mischief." David, as a king, here expresses the earnest desire he had of the welfare of his people, wherein he was a type of Christ, who provides effectually for the good of his chosen. We have here,

(1.) The particular instances of that public prosperity which David desired for his people. [1.] A hopeful progeny (*v.* 12): "*That our sons and our daughters may be* in all respects such as we could wish." He means not those only of his own family, but those of his subjects, that are the seed of the next generation. It adds much to the comfort and happiness of parents in this world to see their children promising and likely to do well. *First*, It is pleasant to see *our sons as plants grown up in their youth*, as olive-plants (cxxviii. 3), the *planting of the Lord* (Isa. lxi. 3),—to see them as plants, not as weeds, not as thorns,—to see them as plants growing great, not withered and blasted,—to see them of a healthful constitution, a quick capacity, a towardly disposition, and especially of a pious inclination, likely to bring forth fruit unto God in their day,—to see them *in their youth*, their growing time, increasing in every thing that is good, growing wiser and better, till they grow strong in spirit. *Secondly*, It is no less desirable to see *our daughters as corner-stones*, or corner-pillars, *polished after the similitude of a palace*, or temple. By daughters families are united and connected, to their mutual strength, as the parts of a building are by the corner-stones; and when they are graceful and beautiful both in body and mind they are then polished after the similitude of a nice and curious structure. When we see our daughters well-established and stayed with wisdom and discretion, as corner-stones are fastened in the building,—when we see them by faith united to Christ,—as the chief corner-stone, adorned with the graces of God's Spirit, which are the polishing of that which is naturally rough, and *become women professing godliness*,—when we see them purified and consecrated to God as living temples, we think ourselves happy in them. [2.] Great plenty. Numerous families increase the care, perhaps more than the comfort, where there is not sufficient for their maintenance; and therefore he prays for a growing estate with a growing family. *First*, That their store-houses might be well-replenished with the fruits and products of the earth: *That our garners may be full*, like those of the good householder, who brings out of them things new and old (those things that are best new he has in that state, those that are best when they are kept he has in that state),—that we may have in them *all manner of stores*, for ourselves and our friends,—that, living plentifully, we may live not luxuriously, for then we abuse our plenty, but cheerfully and usefully,—that, having abundance, we may be thankful to God, generous to our friends, and charitable to the poor; otherwise, what profit is it to have our garners full? Jam. v. 3. *Secondly*, That their flocks might greatly increase: *That our sheep may bring forth thousands, and ten thousands, in our* folds. Much of the wealth of their country consisted in their flocks (Prov. xxvii. 26), and this is the case with ours too, else wool would not be, as it is, a staple commodity. The increase of our cattle is a blessing in which God is to be acknowledged. *Thirdly*, That their beasts designed for service might be fit for it: *That our oxen may be strong to labour* in the plough, *that they may be fat and fleshy* (so some), in good working case. We were none of us made to be idle, and therefore we should pray for bodily health, not that we may be easy and take our pleasures, but that we *may*

772

be strong to labour, that we may do the work of our place and day, else we are worse than the beasts; for when they are strong it is for labour. [3.] An uninterrupted peace. *First*, That there be no war, *no breaking in* of invaders, *no going out* of deserters. " Let not our enemies break in upon us; let us not have occasion to march out against them." War brings with it abundance of mischiefs, whether it be offensive or defensive. *Secondly*, That there be no oppression nor faction—*no complaining in our streets*, that the people may have no cause to complain either of their government or of one another, nor may be so peevish as to complain without cause. It is desirable thus to dwell in quiet habitations.

(2.) His reflection upon this description of the prosperity of the nation, which he so much desired (*v.* 15): *Happy are the people that are in such a case* (but it is seldom so, and never long so), *yea, happy are the people whose God is the Lord.* The relation of a people to God as theirs is here spoken of either, [1.] As that which is the fountain whence all those blessings flow. Happy are the Israelites if they faithfully adhere to the Lord as their God, for they may expect to be *in such a case*. National piety commonly brings national prosperity; for nations as such, in their national capacity, are capable of rewards and punishments only in this life. Or, [2.] As that which is abundantly preferable to all these enjoyments. The psalmist began to say, as most do, *Happy are the people that are in such a case;* those are blessed that prosper in the world. But he immediately corrects himself: *Yea, rather, happy are the people whose God is the Lord,* who have his favour, and love, and grace, according to the tenour of the covenant, though they have not abundance of this world's goods. As all this, and much more, cannot make us happy, unless the Lord be our God, so, if he be, the want of this, the loss of this, nay, the reverse of this, cannot make us miserable.

PSALM CXLV.

The five foregoing psalms were all of a piece, all full of prayers; this, and the five that follow it to the end of the book, are all of a piece too, all full of praises; and though only this is entitled David's psalm, yet we have no reason to think but that they were all his as well as all the foregoing prayers. And it is observable, 1. That after five psalms of prayer follow six psalms of praise; for those that are much in prayer shall not want matter for praise, and those that have sped in prayer must abound in praise. Our thanksgivings for mercy, when we have received it, should even exceed our supplications for it when we were in pursuit of it. David, in the last of his begging psalms, had promised to praise God (cxliv. 9), and here he performs his promise. 2. That the book of Psalms concludes with psalms of praise, all praise, for praise is the conclusion of the whole matter; it is that in which all the psalms centre. And it intimates that God's people, towards the end of their life, should abound much in praise, and the rather because, at the end of their life, they hope to remove to the world of everlasting praise, and the nearer they come to heaven the more they should accustom themselves to the work of heaven. This is one of those psalms which are composed alphabetically (as Ps. xxv. and xxxiv., &c.), that it might be the more easily committed to memory, and kept in mind. The Jewish writers justly extol this psalm as a star of the first magnitude in this bright constellation; and some of them have an extravagant saying concerning it, not much unlike some of the popish superstitions, That whosoever will sing this psalm constantly three times a day shall certainly be happy in the world to come. In this psalm, I. David engages himself and others to praise God, ver. 1, 2, 4—7, 10—12. II. He fastens upon those things that are proper matter for praise, God's greatness (ver. 3), his goodness (ver. 8, 9), the proofs of both in the administration of his kingdom (ver. 13), the kingdom of providence (ver. 14—16), the kingdom of grace (ver. 17—20), and then he concludes with a resolution to continue praising God (ver. 21), with which resolution our hearts must be filled, and in which they must be fixed, in singing this psalm.

David's *psalm* of praise.

I WILL extol thee, my God, O king; and I will bless thy name for ever and ever. 2 Every day will I bless thee; and I will praise thy name for ever and ever. 3 Great *is* the LORD, and greatly to be praised; and his greatness is unsearchable. 4 One generation shall praise thy works to another, and shall declare thy mighty acts. 5 I will speak of the glorious honour of thy majesty, and of thy wondrous works. 6 And *men* shall speak of the might of thy terrible acts: and I will declare thy greatness. 7 They shall abundantly utter the memory of thy great goodness, and shall sing of thy righteousness. 8 The LORD *is* gracious, and full of compassion; slow to anger, and of great mercy. 9 The LORD *is* good to all: and his tender mercies *are* over all his works.

The entitling of this *David's psalm of praise* may intimate not only that he was the penman of it, but that he took a particular pleasure in it and sung it often; it was his companion wherever he went. In this former part of the psalm God's glorious attributes are praised, as, in the latter part of the psalm, his kingdom and the administration of it. Observe,

I. Who shall be employed in giving glory to God.

1. Whatever others do, the psalmist will himself be much in praising God. To this good work he here excites himself, engages himself, and has his heart much enlarged in it. What he does, that he will do, having more and more satisfaction in it. It was his duty; it was his delight. Observe, (1.) How he expresses the work itself: "*I will extol thee, and bless thy name* (*v.* 1); I will speak well of thee, as thou hast made thyself known, and will therein express my own high thoughts of thee and endeavour to raise the like in others." When we speak honourably of God, this is graciously interpreted and accepted as an extolling of him. Again (*v.* 2): *I will bless thee, I will praise thy name;* the repetition intimates the fervency of his affection to this work, the fixedness of his purpose to abound in it, and the frequency of his performances therein. Again (*v.* 5): *I will speak of thy honour*, and (*v.* 6) *I will declare thy greatness.* He would give glory to God, not only in his solemn devotions,

but in his common conversation. If the heart be full of God, out of the abundance of that the mouth will speak with reverence, to his praise, upon all occasions. What subject of discourse can we find more noble, more copious, more pleasant, useful, and unexceptionable, than the glory of God? (2.) How he expresses his resolution to persevere in it. [1.] He will be constant to this work: *Every day will I bless thee.* Praising God must be our daily work. No day must pass, though ever so busy a day, though ever so sorrowful a day, without praising God. We ought to reckon it the most needful of our daily employments, and the most delightful of our daily comforts. God is every day blessing us, doing well for us; there is therefore reason that we should be every day blessing him, speaking well of him. [2.] He will continue in it: *I will bless thee for ever and ever, v.* 1 and again *v.* 2. This intimates, *First,* That he resolved to continue in this work to the end of his life, throughout *his ever* in this world. *Secondly,* That the psalms he penned should be made use of in praising God by the church to the end of time, 2 Chron. xxix. 30. *Thirdly,* That he hoped to be praising God to all eternity in the other world. Those that make praise their constant work on earth shall have it their everlasting bliss in heaven.

2. He doubts not but others also would be forward to this work. (1.) "They shall concur in it now; they shall join with me in it: When *I declare thy greatness men shall speak of* it (*v.* 6); *they shall abundantly utter* it" (*v.* 7), or *pour it out* (as the word is); they shall praise God with a gracious fluency, better than the most curious oratory. David's zeal would provoke many, and it has done so. (2.) "They shall keep it up when I am gone, in an uninterrupted succession (*v.* 4): *One generation shall praise thy works to another.*" The generation that is going off shall tell them to that which is rising up, shall tell what they have seen in their days and what they have heard from their fathers; they *shall* fully and particularly *declare thy mighty acts* (lxxviii. 3); and the generation that is rising up shall follow the example of that which is going off: so that the death of God's worshippers shall be no diminution of his worship, for a new generation shall rise up in their room to carry on that good work, more or less, to the end of time, when it shall be left to that world to do it in in which there is no succession of generations.

II. What we must give to God the glory of.

1. Of his greatness and his great works. We must declare, *Great is the Lord*, his presence infinite, his power irresistible, his brightness insupportable, his majesty awful, his dominion boundless, and his sovereignty incontestable; and therefore there is no dispute, but *great is the Lord, and*, if great, then *greatly to be praised*, with all that is within us, to the utmost of our power, and

with all the circumstances of solemnity imaginable. His greatness indeed cannot be comprehended, for it is unsearchable; who can conceive or express how great God is? But then it is so much the more to be praised. When we cannot, by searching, find the bottom, we must sit down at the brink, and adore the depth, Rom. xi. 33. God is great, for, (1.) His majesty is glorious in the upper world, above the heavens, where he has set his glory; and when we are declaring his greatness we must not fail to *speak of the glorious honour of his majesty*, the splendour of the glory of his majesty (*v.* 5), how brightly he shines in the upper world, so as to dazzle the eyes of the angels themselves, and oblige them to cover their faces, as unable to bear the lustre of it. (2.) His works are wondrous in this lower world. The preservation, maintenance, and government of all the creatures, proclaim the Creator very great. When therefore we declare his greatness we must observe the unquestionable proofs of it, and must *declare his mighty acts* (*v.* 4), *speak of his wondrous works* (*v.* 5), *the might of his terrible acts, v.* 6. We must see God acting and working in all the affairs of this lower world. Various instruments are used, but in all events God is the supreme director; it is he that performs all things. Much of his power is seen in the operations of his providence (they are *mighty acts,* such as cannot be paralleled by the strength of any creature), and much of his justice—they are *terrible acts,* awful to saints, dreadful to sinners. These we should take all occasions to speak of, observing the finger of God, his hand, his arm, in all, that we may marvel.

2. Of his goodness; this is his glory, Exod. xxxiii. 19. It is what he glories in (Exod. xxxiv. 6, 7), and it is what we must give him the glory of: *They shall abundantly utter the memory of thy great goodness, v.* 7. God's goodness is great goodness, the treasures of it can never be exhausted, nay, they can never be lessened, for he ever will be as rich in mercy as he ever was. It is memorable goodness; it is what we ought always to lay before us, always to have in mind and preserve the memorials of, for it is *worthy to be had in everlasting remembrance*; and the remembrance we retain of God's goodness we should utter, we should *abundantly utter,* as those who are full of it, very full of it, and desire that others may be acquainted and affected with it. But, whenever we utter God's great goodness, we must not forget, at the same time, to *sing of his righteousness;* for, as he is gracious in rewarding those that serve him faithfully, so he is righteous in punishing those that rebel against him. Impartial and inflexible justice is as surely in God as inexhaustible goodness; and we must sing of both together, Rom. xi. 22. (1.) There is a fountain of goodness in God's nature (*v.* 8): *The Lord is gracious* to those

that serve him; he is *full of compassion* to those that need him, *slow to anger* to those that have offended him, *and of great mercy* to all that seek him and sue to him. He is ready to give, and ready to forgive, more ready than we are to ask, than we are to repent. (2.) There are streams of goodness in all the dispensations of his providence, *v.* 9. As he is good, so he does good; he *is good to all,* to all his creatures, from the highest angel to the meanest worm, to all but devils and damned sinners, that have shut themselves out from his goodness. *His tender mercies are over all his works.* [1.] All his works, all his creatures, receive the fruits of his merciful care and bounty. It is extended to them all; he hates nothing that he has made. [2.] The works of his mercy out-shine all his other works, and declare him more than any of them. In nothing will the glory of God be for ever so illustrious as in the vessels of mercy ordained to glory. To the divine goodness will the everlasting hallelujahs of all the saints be sung.

10 All thy works shall praise thee, O Lord; and thy saints shall bless thee. 11 They shall speak of the glory of thy kingdom, and talk of thy power; 12 To make known to the sons of men his mighty acts, and the glorious majesty of his kingdom. 13 Thy kingdom *is* an everlasting kingdom, and thy dominion *endureth* throughout all generations. 14 The Lord upholdeth all that fall, and raiseth up all *those that be* bowed down. 15 The eyes of all wait upon thee; and thou givest them their meat in due season. 16 Thou openest thine hand, and satisfiest the desire of every living thing. 17 The Lord *is* righteous in all his ways, and holy in all his works. 18 The Lord *is* nigh unto all them that call upon him, to all that call upon him in truth. 19 He will fulfil the desire of them that fear him: he also will hear their cry, and will save them. 20 The Lord preserveth all them that love him: but all the wicked will he destroy. 21 My mouth shall speak the praise of the Lord: and let all flesh bless his holy name for ever and ever.

The greatness and goodness of him who is *optimus et maximus—the best and greatest* of beings, were celebrated in the former part of the psalm; here, in these verses, we are taught to give him *the glory of his kingdom,* in the administration of which his greatness and goodness shine so clearly, so very brightly. Observe, as before,

I. From whom the tribute of praise is expected (*v.* 10): *All God's works shall praise* him. They all minister to us matter for praise, and so praise him according to their capacity; even those that refuse to give him honour he will get himself honour upon. But his *saints* do *bless* him, not only as they have peculiar blessings from him, which other creatures have not, but as they praise him actively, while his other works praise him only objectively. They bless him, for they collect the rent or tribute of praise from the inferior creatures, and pay it into the treasury above. All God's works do praise him, as the beautiful building praises the builder or the well-drawn picture praises the painter; but the saints bless him as the children of prudent tender parents rise up and call them blessed. Of all God's works, his saints, the workmanship of his grace, the first-fruits of his creatures, have most reason to bless him.

II. For what this praise is to be given: *They shall speak of thy kingdom.* The kingdom of God among men is a thing to be often thought of and often spoken of. As, before, he had magnified God's greatness and goodness in general, so here he magnifies them with application to his kingdom. Consider then,

1. The greatness of his kingdom. It is great indeed, for all the kings and kingdoms of the earth are under his control. To show the greatness of God's kingdom, he observes, (1.) The pomp of it. Would we by faith look within the veil, we should see, and, believing, we should *speak of the glory of his kingdom* (*v.* 11), *the glorious majesty of* it (*v.* 12), for he has prepared his throne in the heavens, and it is high and lifted up, and surrounded with an innumerable company of angels. The courts of Solomon and Ahasuerus were magnificent; but, compared with the glorious majesty of God's kingdom, they were but as glow-worms to the sun. The consideration of this should strike an awe upon us in all our approaches to God. (2.) The power of it: When *they speak of the glory of* God's *kingdom* they must *talk of* his *power*, the extent of it, the efficacy of it—his power, by which he can do any thing and does every thing he pleases (*v.* 11); and, as a proof of it, let them *make known his mighty acts* (*v.* 12), that *the sons of men* may be invited to yield themselves his willing subjects and so put themselves under the protection of such a mighty potentate. (3.) The perpetuity of it, *v.* 13. The thrones of earthly princes totter, and the flowers of their crowns wither, monarchies come to an end; but, Lord, *thy kingdom is an everlasting kingdom.* God will govern the world to the end of time, when the Mediator, who is now entrusted with the administration of his kingdom, shall deliver it up to God, even the Father, that he may be all in

all to eternity. His *dominion endures throughout all generations*, for he himself is eternal, and his counsels are unchangeable and uniform; and Satan, who has set up a kingdom in opposition to him, is conquered and in a chain.

2. The goodness of his kingdom. His royal style and title are, *The Lord God, gracious and merciful;* and his government answers to his title. The goodness of God appears in what he does,

(1.) For all the creatures in general (*v.* 15, 16): He *provides food for all flesh*, and therein appears his everlasting mercy, cxxxvi. 25. All the creatures live upon God, and, as they had their being from him at first, so from him they have all the supports of their being and on him they depend for the continuance of it. [1.] The eye of their expectation attends upon him: *The eyes of all wait on thee.* The inferior creatures indeed have not the knowledge of God, nor are capable of it, and yet they are said to *wait upon God*, because they seek their food according to the instinct which the God of nature has put into them (and *they sow not, neither do they reap*, Matt. vi. 26), and because they take what the God of nature has provided for them, in the time and way that he has appointed, and are content with it. [2.] The hand of his bounty is stretched out to them: *Thou givest them their meat in due season*, the meat proper for them, and in the proper time, when they need it: so that none of the creatures ordinarily perish for want of food, no, not in the winter. *Thou openest thy hand* freely and liberally, *and satisfiest the desire of every living thing*, except some of the unreasonable children of men, that will be satisfied with nothing, but are still complaining, still crying, *Give, give.*

(2.) For the children of men in particular, whom he governs as reasonable creatures.

[1.] He does none of them any wrong, for (*v.* 17) *the Lord is righteous in all his ways*, and not unrighteous in any of them; he is *holy*, and acts like himself, with a perfect rectitude *in all his works.* In all the acts of government he is just, injurious to none, but administering justice to all. *The ways of the Lord are equal*, though ours are unequal. In giving laws, in deciding controversies, in recompensing services, and punishing offences, he is incontestably just, and we are bound to own that he is so.

[2.] He does all of them good, his own people in a special manner.

First, He supports those that are sinking, and it is his honour to help the weak, *v.* 14. He *upholds all that fall*, in that, though they fall, they are not utterly cast down. Many of the children of men are brought very low by sickness and other distresses, and seem ready to drop into the grave, and yet Providence wonderfully upholds them, raises them up, and says, *Return*, xc. 3. If all had died who once seemed dying, the world would have been very thin. Many of the children of God, who have been ready to fall into sin, to fall into despair, have experienced his goodness in preventing their falls, or recovering them speedily by his graces and comforts, so that, though they fell, they were *not utterly cast down*, xxxvii. 24. If those who were *bowed down* by oppression and affliction are *raised up*, it was God that raised them. And, with respect to all those *that are heavy-laden* under the burden of sin, if they come to Christ by faith, he will ease them, he will raise them.

Secondly, He is very ready to hear and answer the prayers of his people, *v.* 18, 19. In this appears the grace of his kingdom, that his subjects have not only liberty of petitioning, but all the encouragement that can be to petition. 1. The grant is very rich, that God will be *nigh to all that call upon him;* he will be always within call of their prayers, and they shall always find themselves within reach of his help. If *a neighbour that is near is better than a brother afar off* (Prov. xxvii. 10), much more a God that is near. Nay, he will not only be *nigh to them,* that they may have the satisfaction of being heard, but *he will fulfil* their *desires;* they shall have what they ask and find what they seek. It was said (*v.* 16) that he *satisfies the desire of every living thing,* much more *will he fulfil the desire of those that fear him:* for he that feeds his birds will not starve his babes. *He will hear their call and will save them;* that is hearing them to purpose, as he heard David (that is, saved him) *from the horn of the unicorn,* xxii. 21. 2. The proviso is very reasonable. He will hear and help us, (1.) If we *fear him,* if we worship and serve him with a holy awe of him; for otherwise how can we expect that he should accept us? (2.) If we *call upon him in truth;* for he desires truth in the inward part. We must be faithful to God, and sincere in our professions of dependence on him, and devotedness to him. In all devotions inward impressions must be answerable to the outward expressions, else they are not performed in truth.

Thirdly, He takes those under his special protection who have a confidence and complacency in him (*v.* 20): *The Lord preserves all those that love him;* they lie exposed in this world, but he, by preserving them in their integrity, will effectually secure them, that no real evil shall befal them.

[3.] If any are destroyed they may thank themselves: *All the wicked he will destroy,* but they have by their wickedness fitted themselves for destruction. This magnifies his goodness in the protection of the righteous, that *with their eyes they shall see the reward of the wicked* (xci. 8); and God will by this means preserve his people, even by destroying the wicked that would do them a mischief.

Lastly, The psalmist concludes, 1. With a resolution to give glory to God himself (*v.* 21): *My mouth shall speak the praise of the Lord.* When we have said what we can, in praising God, still there is more to be said,

and therefore we must not only begin our thanksgivings with this purpose, as he did (*v.* 1), but conclude them with it, as he does here, because we shall presently have occasion to begin again. As the end of one mercy is the beginning of another, so should the end of one thanksgiving be. While I have breath to draw, my mouth shall still speak God's praises. 2. With a call to others to do so too: *Let all flesh,* all mankind, *bless his holy name for ever and ever.* Some of mankind shall be blessing God for ever; it is a pity but that they should be all so engaged.

PSALM CXLVI.

This and all the rest of the psalms that follow begin and end with Hallelujah, a word which puts much of God's praise into a little compass; for in it we praise him by his name Jah, the contraction of Jehovah. In this excellent psalm of praise, I. The psalmist engages himself to praise God, ver. 1, 2. II. He engages others to trust in him, which is one necessary and acceptable way of praising him. 1. He shows why we should not trust in men, ver. 3, 4. 2. Why we should trust in God (ver. 5), because of his power in the kingdom of nature (ver. 6), his dominion in the kingdom of providence (ver. 7), and his grace in the kingdom of the Messiah (ver. 8, 9), that everlasting kingdom (ver. 10), to which many of the Jewish writers refer this psalm, and to which therefore we should have an eye, in the singing of it.

PRAISE ye the LORD. Praise the LORD, O my soul. 2 While I live will I praise the LORD: I will sing praises unto my God while I have any being. 3 Put not your trust in princes, *nor* in the son of man, in whom *there is* no help. 4 His breath goeth forth, he returneth to his earth; in that very day his thoughts perish.

David is supposed to have penned this psalm; and he was himself a prince, a mighty prince; as such, it might be thought, 1. That he should be exempted from the service of praising God, that it was enough for him to see that his priests and people did it, but that he needed not to do it himself in his own person. Michal thought it a disparagement to him to *dance before the ark;* but he was so far from being of this mind that he would himself be first and foremost in the work, *v.* 1, 2. He considered his dignity as so far from excusing him from it that it rather obliged him to lead in it, and he thought it so far from lessening him that it really magnified him; therefore he stirred up himself to it and to make a business of it: *Praise the Lord, O my soul!* and he resolved to abide by it: " I will praise him with my heart, *I will sing praises* to him with my mouth. Herein I will have an eye to him as *the Lord,* infinitely blessed and glorious in himself, and as *my God,* in covenant with me." Praise is most pleasant when, in praising God, we have an eye to him as ours, whom we have an interest in and stand in relation to. " This I will do constantly while I live, every day of my life, and to my life's end; nay, I will do it *while I have any being,* for when I have no being on earth I hope to have a being in heaven, a better being, to be doing it better." That which is the great end of our being ought to be our great employment and delight while we have any being. " In thee must our time and powers be spent." 2. It might be thought that he himself, having been so great a blessing to his country, should be adored, according to the usage of the heathen nations, who deified their heroes, that they should all come and *trust in his shadow* and make him their *stay* and *strong-hold.* "No," says David, "*Put not your trust in princes* (*v.* 3), not in me, not in any other; do not repose your confidence in them; do not raise your expectations from them. Be not too sure of their sincerity; some have thought they knew better how to reign by knowing how to dissemble. Be not too sure of their constancy and fidelity; it is possible they may both change their minds and break their words." But, though we suppose them very wise and as good as David himself, yet we must not be too sure of their ability and continuance, for they are sons of Adam, weak and mortal. There is indeed a Son of man in whom there is help, in whom there is salvation, and who will not fail those that trust in him. But all other sons of men are like the man they are sprung of, who, being in honour, did not abide. (1.) We cannot be sure of their ability. Even the power of kings may be so straitened, cramped, and weakened, that they may not be in a capacity to do that for us which we expect. David himself owned (2 Sam. iii. 39), *I am this day weak, though anointed king.* So that *in the son of man there is* often *no help*, no salvation; he is at a loss, at his wits' end, as *a man astonished*, and then, though *a mighty man*, he *cannot save*, Jer. xiv. 9. (2.) We cannot be sure of their continuance. Suppose he has it in his power to help us while he lives, yet he may be suddenly taken off when we expect most from him (*v.* 4): *His breath goes forth*, so it does every moment, and comes back again, but that is an intimation that it will shortly go for good and all, and then *he returns to his earth.* The earth is his, in respect of his original as a man, the earth out of which he was taken, and to which therefore he must return, according to the sentence, Gen. iii. 19. It is his, if he be a worldly man, in respect of choice, his earth which he has chosen for his portion, and on the things of which he has set his affections. He shall go to his own place. Or, rather, it is his earth because of the property he has in it; and though he has had large possessions on earth a grave is all that will remain to him. *The earth God has given to the children of men*, and great striving there is about it, and, as a mark of their authority, men *call their lands by their own names.* But, after a while, no part of the earth will be their own but that in which the dead body shall make its bed, and that shall be theirs *while the earth remains.* But, when he returns to his earth, *in that very day his thoughts perish;* all the projects and designs he had of kindness to us vanish and are gone, and he cannot take one step further in them all his purposes are cut off and buried with

him, Job xvii. 11. And then what becomes of our expectations from him? Princes are mortal, as well as other men, and therefore we cannot have that assurance of help from them which we may have from that Potentate who hath immortality. *Cease from man, whose breath is in his nostrils* and will not be there long.

5 Happy *is he* that *hath* the God of Jacob for his help, whose hope *is* in the Lord his God: 6 Which made heaven, and earth, the sea, and all that therein *is:* which keepeth truth for ever: 7 Which executeth judgment for the oppressed: which giveth food to the hungry. The Lord looseth the prisoners: 8 The Lord openeth *the eyes of* the blind: the Lord raiseth them that are bowed down: the Lord loveth the righteous: 9 The Lord preserveth the strangers; he relieveth the fatherless and widow: but the way of the wicked he turneth upside down. 10 The Lord shall reign for ever, *even* thy God, O Zion, unto all generations. Praise ye the Lord.

The psalmist, having cautioned us not to trust in princes (because, if we do, we shall be miserably disappointed), here encourages us to put our confidence in God, because, if we do so, we shall be happily secured: *Happy is he that has the God of Jacob for his help*, that has an interest in his attributes and promises, and has them engaged for him, and *whose hope is in the Lord his God.*

I. Let us take a view of the character here given of those whom God will uphold. Those shall have God for their help, 1. Who take him for their God, and serve and worship him accordingly. 2. Who have their hope in him, and live a life of dependence upon him, who have good thoughts of him, and encourage themselves in him, when all other supports fail. Every believer may look upon him as the God of Jacob, of the church in general, and therefore may expect relief from him, in reference to public distresses, and as his God in particular, and therefore may depend upon him in all personal wants and straits. We must hope, (1.) In the providence of God for all the good things we need, which relate to the life that now is. (2.) In the grace of Christ for all the good things which relate to the life that is to come. To this especially the learned Dr. Hammond refers this and the following verses, looking upon the latter part of this psalm to have a most visible remarkable aspect towards the eternal Son of God in his incarnation. He quotes one of the rabbies, who says of *v.* 10 that it belongs to the days of the Messiah. And that it does so he thinks will appear by comparing *v.* 7, 8, with the characters Christ gives of the Messiah (Matt. xi. 5, 6), *The blind receive their sight, the lame walk ;* and the closing words there, *Blessed is he whosoever shall not be offended in me,* he thinks may very well be supposed to refer to *v.* 5. *Happy is the man that hopes in the Lord his God,* and who is not offended in him.

II. Let us take a view of the great encouragements here given us to hope in *the Lord our God.* 1. He is the *Maker of the world,* and therefore has all power in himself, and the command of the powers of all the creatures, which, being derived from him, depend upon him (*v.* 6): *He made heaven and earth, the sea, and all that in them is,* and therefore his arm is not shortened, that it cannot save. It is very applicable to Christ, by whom God made the world, and *without whom was not any thing made that was made.* It is a great support to faith that the Redeemer of the world is the same that was the Creator of it, and therefore has a good-will to it, a perfect knowledge of its case, and power to help it. 2. He is a God of inviolable fidelity. We may venture to take God's word, for he *keepeth truth for ever,* and therefore no word of his shall fall to the ground; it is true *from the beginning,* and therefore true *to the end.* Our Lord Jesus is the Amen, *the faithful witness,* as well as *the beginning,* the author and principle, *of the creation of God,* Rev. iii. 14. The keeping of God's truth for ever is committed to him, for *all the promises* are in him *yea and amen.* 3. He is the patron of injured innocency: *He pleads the cause of the oppressed,* and (as we read it) he *executes judgment* for them. He often does it in his providence, giving redress to those that suffer wrong and clearing up their integrity. He will do it in the judgment of the great day. The Messiah came to rescue the children of men out of the hands of Satan the great oppressor, and, all judgment being committed to him, the executing of judgment upon persecutors is so among the rest, Jude 15. 4. He is a bountiful benefactor to the necessitous: *He gives food to the hungry;* so God does in an ordinary way for the answering of the cravings of nature; so he has done sometimes in an extraordinary way, as when ravens fed Elijah; so Christ did more than once when he fed thousands miraculously with that which was intended but for one meal or two for his own family. This encourages us to hope in him as the nourisher of our souls with the bread of life. 5. He is the author of liberty to those that were bound : *The Lord looseth the prisoners.* He brought Israel out of the house of bondage in Egypt and afterwards in Babylon. The miracles Christ wrought, in making the dumb to speak and the deaf to hear with that one word, *Ephphatha—Be opened,* his cleansing lepers, and so discharging them from their confinement, and his raising the dead out of their graves, may all be included in this one of *loosing the prisoners ;* and we may take encouragement from those to hope in him for that spiritual liberty which he came to proclaim, Isa. lxi. 1, 2. 6. He gives sight to those that have been long deprived of it : *The Lord can open the eyes of the blind,* and has often given to his afflicted people to see that comfort which before they were not aware of ; witness Gen. xxi. 19, and the prophet's servant, 2 Kings vi. 17. But this has special reference to Christ ; for *since the world began was it not heard that any man opened the eyes of one that was born blind* till Christ did it (John ix. 32) and thereby encouraged us to hope in him for spiritual illumination. 7. He sets that straight which was crooked, and makes those easy that were pained and ready to sink : He *raises those that are bowed down,* by comforting and supporting them under their burdens, and, in due time, removing their burdens. This was literally performed by Christ when he made a poor woman straight that had been *bowed together, and could in no wise lift up herself* (Luke xiii. 12); and he still does it by his grace, giving rest to those that were weary and heavily laden, and raising up with his comforts those that were humbled and cast down by convictions. 8. He has a constant kindness for all good people : *The Lord loveth the righteous,* and they may with the more confidence depend upon his power when they are sure of his good-will. Our Lord Jesus showed his love to the righteous *by fulfilling all righteousness.* 9. He has a tender concern for those that stand in special need of his care : *The Lord preserves the strangers.* It ought not to pass without remark that the name of Jehovah is repeated here five times in five lines, to intimate that it is an almighty power (that of Jehovah) that is engaged and exerted for the relief of the oppressed, and that it is as much the glory of God to succour those that are in misery as it is to *ride on the heavens by his name Jah,* lxviii. 4. (1.) Strangers are exposed, and are commonly destitute of friends, but *the Lord preserves them,* that they be not run down and ruined. Many a poor stranger has found the benefit of the divine protection and been kept alive by it. (2.) *Widows and fatherless children,* that have lost the head of the family, who took care of the affairs of it, often fall into the hands of those that make a prey of them, that will not do them justice, nay, that will do them injustice ; but *the Lord relieveth them,* and raiseth up friends for them. See Exod. xxii. 22, 23. Our Lord Jesus came into the world to help the helpless, to receive Gentiles, strangers, into his kingdom, and that with him poor sinners, that are as fatherless, *may find mercy,* Hos. xiv. 3. 10. He will appear for the destruction of all those that oppose his kingdom and oppress the faithful subjects of it : *The way of the wicked he turns upside down,* and therefore let us *hope in him,* and not be *afraid of the fury of the oppressor,* as though he were *ready to destroy.* It is the glory of the Messiah that he will subvert all the counsels of hell and earth that militate against his church, so that, having him for us, we need not fear any thing that can be done against us. 11. His kingdom shall continue through all the revolutions of time, to the utmost ages of eternity, *v.* 10. Let *this* encourage us to trust in God at all times that *the Lord shall reign for ever,* in spite of all the malignity of the powers of darkness, *even thy God, O Zion! unto all generations.* Christ is set King on the holy hill of Zion, and his kingdom shall continue in an endless glory. It cannot be destroyed by an invader; it shall not be left to a successor, either to a succeeding monarch or a succeeding monarchy, but it shall stand for ever. It is matter of unspeakable comfort that *the Lord reigns* as Zion's God, as Zion's king, that the Messiah is head over all things to the church, and will be so while the world stands.

PSALM CXLVII.

This is another psalm of praise. Some think it was penned after the return of the Jews from their captivity ; but it is so much of a piece with Ps. cxlv. that I rather think it was penned by David, and what is said ver. 2, 13, may well enough be applied to the first building and fortifying of Jerusalem in his time, and the gathering in of those that had been out-casts in Saul's time. The Septuagint divides it into two ; and we may divide it into the first and second part, but both of the same import. I. We are called upon to praise God, ver. 1, 7, 12. II. We are furnished with matter for praise, for God is to be glorified, 1. As the God of nature, and so he is very great, ver. 4, 5, 8, 9, 15—18. 2. As the God of grace, comforting his people, ver. 3, 6, 10, 11. 3. As the God of Israel, Jerusalem, and Zion, settling their civil state (ver. 2, 13, 14), and especially settling religion among them, ver. 19, 20. It is easy, in singing this psalm, to apply it to ourselves, both as to personal and national mercies, were it but as easy to do so with suitable affections.

PRAISE ye the LORD: for *it is* good to sing praises unto our God; for *it is* pleasant; *and* praise is comely. 2 The LORD doth build up Jerusalem: he gathereth together the outcasts of Israel. 3 He healeth the broken in heart, and bindeth up their wounds. 4 He telleth the number of the stars; he calleth them all by *their* names. 5 Great *is* our Lord, and of great power: his understanding *is* infinite. 6 The LORD lifteth up the meek: he casteth the wicked down to the ground. 7 Sing unto the LORD with thanksgiving; sing praise upon the harp unto our God: 8 Who covereth the heaven with clouds, who prepareth rain for the earth, who maketh grass to grow upon the mountains. 9 He giveth to the beast his food, *and* to the young ravens which cry. 10 He delighteth not in the strength of the horse: he taketh not pleasure in the legs of a man. 11 The LORD taketh pleasure in them that

fear him, in those that hope in his mercy.

Here, I. The duty of praise is recommended to us. It is not without reason that we are thus called to it again and again: *Praise you the Lord* (*v.* 1), and again (*v.* 7), *Sing unto the Lord with thanksgiving, sing praise upon the harp to our God* (let all our praises be directed to him and centre in him), *for it is good* to do so; it is our duty, and therefore good in itself; it is our interest, and therefore good for us. It is acceptable to our Creator and it answers the end of our creation. The law for it is holy, just, and good; the practice of it will turn to a good account. It is good, for, 1. It is pleasant. Holy joy or delight are required as the principle of it, and that is pleasant to us as men; giving glory to God is the design and business of it, and that is pleasant to us as saints that are devoted to his honour. Praising God is work that is its own wages; it is heaven upon earth; it is what we should be in as in our element. 2. It is comely; it is that which becomes us as reasonable creatures, much more as people in covenant with God. In giving honour to God we really do ourselves a great deal of honour.

II. God is recommended to us as the proper object of our most exalted and enlarged praises, upon several accounts.

1. The care he takes of his chosen people, *v.* 2. Is Jerusalem to be raised out of small beginnings? Is it to be recovered out of its ruins? In both cases, *The Lord builds up Jerusalem.* The gospel-church, the Jerusalem that is from above, is of his building. He framed the model of it in his own counsels; he founded it by the preaching of his gospel; he adds to it daily such as shall be saved, and so increases it. He will build it up unto perfection, build it up as high as heaven. Are any of his people outcasts? Have they made themselves so by their own folly? He gathers them by giving them repentance and bringing them again into the communion of saints. Have they been forced out by war, famine, or persecution? He opens a door for their return; many that were missing, and thought to be lost, are brought back, and those that were scattered in the cloudy and dark day are gathered together again.

2. The comforts he has laid up for true penitents, *v.* 3. They are *broken in heart,* and wounded, humbled, and troubled, for sin, inwardly pained at the remembrance of it, as a man is that is sorely wounded. Their very hearts are not only pricked, but rent, under the sense of the dishonour they have done to God and the injury they have done to themselves by sin. To those whom God heals with the consolations of his Spirit he speaks peace, assures them that their sins are pardoned and that he is reconciled to them, and so makes them easy, pours the balm of Gilead into the bleeding wounds, and then binds

them up, and makes them to rejoice. Those who have had experience of this need not be called upon to praise the Lord ; for when he brought them *out of the horrible pit,* and *set their feet upon a rock,* he *put a new song into their mouths,* xl. 2, 3. And for this let others praise him also.

3. The sovereign dominion he has over the lights of heaven, *v.* 4, 5. The stars are innumerable, many of them being scarcely discernible with the naked eye, and yet he counts them, and knows the exact number of them, for they are all the work of his hands and the instruments of his providence. Their bulk and power are very great ; but *he calleth them all by their names,* which shows his dominion over them and the command he has them at, to make what use of them he pleases. They are his servants, his soldiers ; he musters them, he marshals them ; they come and go at his bidding, and all their motions are under his direction. He mentions this as one instance of many, to show that *great is our Lord and of great power* (he can do what he pleases), and of *his understanding there is no computation,* so that he can contrive every thing for the best. Man's knowledge is soon drained, and you have his utmost length ; hitherto his wisdom can reach and no further. But God's knowledge is a depth that can never be fathomed.

4. The pleasure he takes in humbling the proud and exalting those of low degree (*v.* 6) : *The Lord lifts up the meek,* who abase themselves before him, and whom men trample on ; but *the wicked,* who conduct themselves insolently towards God and scornfully towards all mankind, who lift up themselves in pride and folly, he *casteth down to the ground,* sometimes by very humbling providences in this world, at furthest in the day when their faces shall be *filled with everlasting shame.* God proves himself to be God by *looking on the proud and abasing them,* Job xl. 12.

5. The provision he makes for the inferior creatures. Though he is so great as to command the stars, he is so good as not to forget even the fowls, *v.* 8, 9. Observe in what method he feeds man and beast. (1.) *He covereth the heaven with clouds,* which darken the air and intercept the beams of the sun, and yet in them he *prepareth* that *rain for the earth* which is necessary to its fruitfulness. Clouds look melancholy, and yet without them we could have no rain and consequently no fruit. Thus afflictions, for the present, look black, and dark, and unpleasant, and we are in heaviness because of them, as sometimes when the sky is overcast it makes us dull ; but they are necessary, for from these clouds of affliction come those showers that make the harvest to *yield the peaceable fruits of righteousness* (Heb. xii. 11), which should help to reconcile us to them. Observe the necessary dependence which the earth has upon the heavens, which directs us on earth to depend on God in heaven. All

the rain with which the earth is watered is of God's preparing. (2.) By the rain which distils on the earth he *makes grass to grow upon the mountains,* even the high mountains, which man neither takes care of nor reaps the benefit of. The mountains, which are not watered with the springs and rivers, as the valleys are, are yet watered so that they are not barren. (3.) This grass he *gives to the beast* for *his food,* the beast of the mountains which runs wild, which man makes no provision for. And even the *young ravens,* which, being forsaken by their old ones, *cry,* are heard by him, and ways are found to feed them, so that they are kept from perishing in the nest.

6. The complacency he takes in his people, *v.* 10, 11. In times when great things are doing, and there are great expectations of the success of them, it concerns us to know (since the issue proceeds from the Lord) whom, and what, God will delight to honour and crown with victory. It is not the strength of armies, but the strength of grace, that God is pleased to own. (1.) Not the strength of armies—not in the cavalry, *for he delighteth not in the strength of the horse,* the warhorse, noted for his courage (Job xxxix. 19, &c.)—nor in the infantry, for he *taketh no pleasure in the legs of a man ;* he does not mean the swiftness of them for flight, to quit the field, but the steadiness of them for charging, to stand the ground. If one king, making war with another king, goes to God to pray for success, it will not avail him to plead, " Lord, I have a gallant army, the horse and foot in good order ; it is a pity that they should suffer any disgrace ;" for that is no argument with God, Ps. xx. 7. Jehoshaphat's was much better : *Lord, we have no might,* 2 Chron. xx. 12. But, (2.) God is pleased to own the strength of grace. A serious and suitable regard to God is that which is, in the sight of God, of great price in such a case The Lord accepts and *takes pleasure* in those that *fear him and that hope in his mercy.* Observe, [1.] A holy fear of God and hope in God not only may consist, but must concur. In the same heart, at the same time, there must be both a reverence of his majesty and a complacency in his goodness, both a believing dread of his wrath and a believing expectation of his favour ; not that we must hang in suspense between hope and fear, but we must act under the gracious influences of hope and fear. Our fear must save our hope from swelling into presumption, and our hope must save our fear from sinking into despair ; thus must we take our work before us. [2.] We must *hope in God's mercy,* his general mercy, even when we cannot find a particular promise to stay ourselves upon. A humble confidence in the goodness of God's nature is very pleasing to him, as that which turns to the glory of that attribute in which he most glories. Every man of honour loves to be trusted.

12 Praise the LORD, O Jerusalem ; praise thy God, O Zion. 13 For he hath strengthened the bars of thy gates ; he hath blessed thy children within thee. 14 He maketh peace *in* thy borders, *and* filleth thee with the finest of the wheat. 15 He sendeth forth his commandment *upon* earth : his word runneth very swiftly. 16 He giveth snow like wool : he scattereth the hoarfrost like ashes. 17 He casteth forth his ice like morsels : who can stand before his cold ? 18 He sendeth out his word, and melteth them : he causeth his wind to blow, *and* the waters flow. 19 He showeth his word unto Jacob, his statutes and his judgments unto Israel. 20 He hath not dealt so with any nation : and *as for his* judgments, they have not known them. Praise ye the LORD.

Jerusalem, and Zion, the holy city, the holy hill, are here called upon to *praise God, v.* 12. For where should praise be offered up to God but where his altar is ? Where may we expect that glory should be given to him but in the beauty of holiness ? Let the inhabitants of Jerusalem praise the Lord in their own houses; let the priests and Levites, who attend in Zion, the city of their solemnities, in a special manner praise the Lord. They have more cause to do it than others, and they lie under greater obligations to do it than others; for it is their business, it is their profession. " *Praise thy God, O Zion!* he is thine, and therefore thou art bound to praise him ; his being thine includes all happiness, so that thou canst never want matter for praise." Jerusalem and Zion must praise God,

I. For the prosperity and flourishing state of their civil interests, *v.* 13, 14. 1. For their common safety. They had gates, and kept their gates barred in times of danger; but that would not have been an effectual security to them if God had not *strengthened the bars of their gates* and fortified their fortifications. The most probable means we can devise for our own preservation will not answer the end, unless God give his blessing with them ; we must therefore, in the careful and diligent use of those means, depend upon him for that blessing, and attribute the undisturbed repose of our land more to the wall of fire than to the wall of water round about us, Zech. ii. 5. 2. For the increase of their people. This strengthens the bars of the gates as much as any thing : *He hath blessed thy children within thee,* with that first and great blessing, *Be fruitful, and multiply, and replenish the land.* It is a comfort to parents to see their children blessed of the Lord (Isa. lxi. 9), and a comfort to the generation that

is going off to see the rising generation numerous and hopeful, for which blessing God must be blessed. 3. For the public tranquillity, that they were delivered from the terrors and desolations of war : *He makes peace in thy borders,* by putting an end to the wars that were, and preventing the wars that were threatened and feared. *He makes peace within thy borders,* that is, in all parts of the country, by composing differences among neighbours, that there may be no intestine broils and animosities, and *upon thy borders,* that they may not be attacked by invasions from abroad. If there be trouble any where, it is in the borders, the marches of a country ; the frontier-towns lie most exposed, so that, if there be peace in the borders, there is a universal peace, a mercy we can never be sufficiently thankful for. 4. For great plenty, the common effect of peace : *He filleth thee with the finest of the wheat*—wheat, the most valuable grain, the fat, the finest of that, and a fulness thereof. What would they more ? Canaan abounded with the best wheat (Deut. xxxii. 14) and exported it to the countries abroad, as appears, Ezek. xxvii. 17. The land of Israel was not enriched with precious stones nor spices, but with *the finest of the wheat,* with bread, which strengthens man's heart. This made it the glory of all lands, and for this God was praised in Zion.

II. For the wonderful instances of his power in the weather, particularly the winter-weather. He that protects Zion and Jerusalem is that God of power from whom all the powers of nature are derived and on whom they depend, and who produces all the changes of the seasons, which, if they were not common, would astonish us.

1. In general, whatever alterations there are in this lower world (and it is that world that is subject to continual changes) they are produced by the will, and power, and providence of God (*v.* 15) : *He sendeth forth his commandment upon earth,* as one that has an incontestable authority to give orders, and innumerable attendants ready to carry his orders and put them in execution. As the world was at first made, so it is still upheld and governed, by a word of almighty power. *God speaks and it is done,* for all are his servants. That word takes effect, not only surely, but speedily. *His word runneth very swiftly,* for nothing can oppose or retard it. As the lightning, which passes through the air in an instant, such is the word of God's providence, and such the word of his grace, when it is sent forth with commission, Luke xvii. 24. Angels, who carry his word and fulfil it, *fly swiftly,* Dan. ix. 21.

2. In particular, frosts and thaws are both of them wonderful changes, and in both we must acknowledge the word of his power.

(1.) Frosts are from God. With him are the *treasures of the snow and the hail* (Job xxxviii. 22, 23), and out of these treasures he draws as he pleases. [1.] *He giveth snow like wool.* It is compared to wool for its whiteness (Isa. i. 18), and its softness; it falls silently, and makes no more noise than the fall of a lock of wool; it covers the earth, and keeps it warm like a fleece of wool, and so promotes its fruitfulness. See how God can work by contraries, and bring meat out of the eater, can warm the earth with cold snow. [2.] *He scatters the hoar-frost,* which is dew congealed, as the snow and hail are rain congealed. This looks like ashes scattered upon the grass, and is sometimes pre'udicial to the products of the earth and blasts them as if it were hot ashes, Ps. lxxviii. 47. [3.] *He casts forth his ice like morsels,* which may be understood either of large hail-stones, which are as ice in the air, or of the ice which covers the face of the waters, and when it is broken, though naturally it was as drops of drink, it is as morsels of meat, or crusts of bread. [4.] When we see the frost, and snow, and ice, we feel it in the air: *Who can stand before his cold?* The beasts cannot; they retire into dens (Job xxxvii. 8); they are easily conquered then, 2 Sam. xxiii. 20. Men cannot, but are forced to protect themselves by fires, or furs, or both, and all little enough where and when the cold is in extremity. We see not the causes when we feel the effects; and therefore we must call it *his cold:* it is of his sending, and therefore we must bear it patiently, and be thankful for warm houses, and clothes, and beds, to relieve us against the rigour of the season, and must give him the glory of his wisdom and sovereignty, his power and faithfulness, which appear in the winter-weather, which shall not cease any more than summer, Gen viii. 22. And let us also infer from it, If we cannot stand before the cold of his frosts, how can we stand before the heat of his wrath? (2.) Thaws are from God. When he pleases (v. 18) *he sends out his word and melts them;* the frost, the snow, the ice, are all dissolved quickly, in order to which he *causes the wind,* the *south wind, to blow,* and *the waters,* which were frozen, *flow* again as they did before. We are soon sensible of the change, but we see not the causes of it, but must resolve it into the will of the First Cause. And in it we must take notice not only of the power of God, that he can so suddenly, so insensibly, make such a great and universal alteration in the temper of the air and the face of the earth (what cannot he do that does this every winter, perhaps often every winter?) but also of the goodness of God. Hard weather does not always continue; it would be sad if it should. He does not *contend for ever,* but *renews the face of the earth.* As he remembered Noah, and released him (Gen. viii. 1), so he remembers the earth, and his covenant with the earth, Cant. ii. 11, 12. This thawing word may represent the gospel of Christ, and this thawing wind the Spirit of Christ (for the Spirit is compared to the wind, John iii. 8); both are sent for the melting of frozen

souls. Converting grace, like the thaw, softens the heart that was hard, moistens it, and melts it into tears of repentance; it warms good affections, and makes them to flow, which, before, were chilled and stopped up. The change which the thaw makes is universal and yet gradual; it is very evident, and yet how it is done is unaccountable: such is the change wrought in the conversion of a soul, when God's word and Spirit are sent to melt it and restore it to itself.

III. For his distinguishing favour to Israel, in giving them his word and ordinances, a much more valuable blessing than their peace and plenty (v. 14), as much as the soul is more excellent than the body. Jacob and Israel had God's statutes and judgments among them. They were under his peculiar government; the municipal laws of their nation were of his framing and enacting, and their constitution was a theocracy. They had the benefit of divine revelation; the great things of God's law were written to them. They had a priesthood of divine institution for all things pertaining to God, and prophets for all extraordinary occasions. No people besides went upon sure grounds in their religion. Now this was, 1. A preventing mercy. They did not find out God's statutes and judgments of themselves, but *God showed his word unto Jacob,* and by that word he made known to them his *statutes and judgments.* It is a great mercy to any people to have the word of God among them; for *faith comes by hearing* and reading that word, that faith without which it is impossible to please God. 2. A distinguishing mercy, and upon that account the more obliging: "*He hath not dealt so with every nation,* not with *any* nation; and, *as for his judgments, they have not known them,* nor are likely to know them till the Messiah shall come and take down the partition-wall between Jew and Gentile, that the gospel may be preached to every creature." Other nations had plenty of outward good things; some nations were very rich, others had pompous powerful princes and polite literature, but none were blessed with God's statutes and judgments as Israel were. Let *Israel* therefore *praise the Lord* in the observance of these statutes. *Lord, how is it that thou wilt manifest thyself to us, and not to the world! Even so, Father, because it seemed good in thy eyes.*

PSALM CXLVIII.

This psalm is a most solemn and earnest call to all the creatures, according to their capacity, to praise their Creator, and to show forth his eternal power and Godhead, the invisible things of which are manifested in the things that are seen. Thereby the psalmist designs to express his great affection to the duty of praise; he is highly satisfied that God is praised, is very desirous that he may be more praised, and therefore does all he can to engage all about him in this pleasant work, yea, and all who shall come after him, whose hearts must be very dead and cold if they be not raised and enlarged, in praising God, by the lofty flights of divine poetry which we find in this psalm. I. He calls upon the higher house, the creatures that are placed in the upper world, to praise the Lord, both those that are intellectual beings, and are capable of doing it actively (ver. 1, 2), and those that are not, and are therefore capable of doing it only objectively, ver. 3—6. II. He calls upon the lower house, the creatures of this lower world, both those that can only minister matter of praise (ver. 7—10) and those that, being endued with reason, are capable of offering up this sacrifice (ver. 11—13), especially his own people, who have more cause to do it, and are more concerned to do it, than any other, ver. 14.

PRAISE ye the LORD. Praise ye the LORD from the heavens: praise him in the heights. 2 Praise ye him, all his angels: praise ye him, all his hosts. 3 Praise ye him, sun and moon: praise him, all ye stars of light. 4 Praise him, ye heavens of heavens, and ye waters that *be* above the heavens. 5 Let them praise the name of the LORD: for he commanded, and they were created. 6 He hath also established them for ever and ever: he hath made a decree which shall not pass.

We, in this dark and depressed world, know but little of the world of light and exaltation, and, conversing within narrow confines, can scarcely admit any tolerable conceptions of the vast regions above. But this we know,

I. That there is above us a world of blessed angels by whom God is praised, an innumerable company of them. *Thousand thousands minister unto him, and ten thousand times ten thousand stand before him;* and it is his glory that he has such attendants, but much more his glory that he neither needs them, nor is, nor can be, any way benefited by them. To that bright and happy world the psalmist has an eye here, *v.* 1, 2. In general, to *the heavens,* to *the heights.* The heavens are the heights, and therefore we must lift up our souls above the world unto God in *the heavens,* and on *things above* we must *set our affections.* It is his desire that God may be praised *from the heavens,* that thence a praising frame may be transmitted to this world in which we live, that from the inhabitants of that world we may learn this blessed work. It is his delight to think that God is praised *in the heights,* that while we are so cold, and low, and flat, in praising God, there are those above who are doing it in a better manner, and that while we are so often interrupted in this work they rest not day nor night from it. In particular, he had an eye to God's *angels,* to *his hosts,* and calls upon them to praise God. That God's angels are his hosts is plain enough; as soon as they were made they were enlisted, armed, and disciplined; he employs them in fighting his battles, and they keep ranks, and know their place, and observe the word of command as his hosts. But what is meant by the psalmist's calling upon them, and exciting them to praise God, is not so easy to account for. I will not say, They do not heed it, because we find that *to the principalities and powers is known by the church the manifold wisdom of God* (Eph. iii. 10); but I will say, They do not need it, for they are continually praising God and there is no defi-

ciency at all in their performances; and therefore when, in singing this psalm, we call upon the angels to praise God (as we did, ciii. 20), we mean that we desire God may be praised by the ablest hands and in the best manner,—that we are sure it is fit he should be so,—that we are pleased to think he is so,—that we have a spiritual communion with those that dwell in his house above and are still praising him,—and that we have come by faith, and hope, and holy love, to the *innumerable company of angels,* Heb. xii. 22.

II. That there is above us not only an assembly of blessed spirits, but a system of vast bodies too, and those bright ones, in which God is praised, that is, which may give us occasion (as far as we know any thing of them) to give to God the glory not only of their being, but of their beneficence to mankind. Observe,

1. What these creatures are that thus show us the way in praising God, and, whenever we look up and consider the heavens, furnish us with matter for his praises. (1.) There are the *sun, moon,* and *stars,* which continually, either day or night, present themselves to our view, as looking-glasses, in which we may see a faint shadow (for so I must call it, not a resemblance) of the glory of him that is *the Father of lights, v.* 3. The greater lights, the sun and moon, are not too great, too bright, to praise him; and the praises of the less lights, the stars, shall not be slighted, Idolaters made the sun, moon, and stars, their gods, and praised them, worshipping and serving the creature, because it is seen, more than the Creator, because he is not seen; but we, who worship the true God only, make them our fellow-worshippers, and call upon them to praise him with us, nay, as Levites to attend us, who, as priests, offer this spiritual sacrifice. (2.) There are the *heavens of heavens* above the sun and stars, the seat of the blessed; from the vastness and brightness of these unknown orbs abundance of glory redounds to God, for *the heavens of heavens are the Lord's* (cxv. 16) and yet *they cannot contain him,* 1 Kings viii. 27. The learned Dr. Hammond understands here, by *the heavens of heavens,* the upper regions of the air, or all the regions of it, as Ps. lxviii. 33. We read of the heaven of heavens, whence *God sends forth his voice, and that a mighty voice,* meaning the thunder. (3.) There are *the waters that are above the heavens,* the clouds that hang above in the air, where they are reserved *against the day of battle and war,* Job xxxviii. 23. We have reason to praise God, not only that these waters do not drown the earth, but that they do water it and make it fruitful. The Chaldee paraphrase reads it, *Praise him, you heavens of heavens, and you waters that depend on the word of him who is above the heavens,* for the key of the clouds is one of the keys which God has in his hand, wherewith he

opens and none can shut, he shuts and none can open.

2. Upon what account we are to give God the glory of them: *Let them praise the name of the Lord,* that is, let us praise the name of the Lord for them, and observe what constant and fresh matter for praise may be fetched from them. (1.) Because he made them, gave them their powers and assigned them their places: *He commanded* them (great as they are) out of nothing, *and they were created* at a word's speaking. God created, and therefore may command; for he commanded, and so created; his authority must always be acknowledged and acquiesced in, because he once spoke with such authority. (2.) Because he still upholds and preserves them in their beings and posts, their powers and motions (*v.* 6): *He hath established them for ever and ever,* that is, to the end of time, a short ever, but it is their ever; they shall last as long as there is occasion for them. *He hath made a decree,* the law of creation, *which shall not pass;* it was enacted by the wisdom of God, and therefore needs not be altered, by his sovereignty and inviolable fidelity, and therefore cannot be altered. All the creatures that praised God at first for their creation must praise him still for their continuance. And we have reason to praise him that they are kept within the bounds of a decree; for to that it is owing that the waters above the heavens have not a second time drowned the earth.

7 Praise the LORD from the earth, ye dragons, and all deeps : 8 Fire, and hail ; snow, and vapours ; stormy wind fulfilling his word : 9 Mountains, and all hills ; fruitful trees, and all cedars : 10 Beasts, and all cattle ; creeping things, and flying fowl : 11 Kings of the earth, and all people ; princes, and all judges of the earth : 12 Both young men, and maidens ; old men, and children : 13 Let them praise the name of the LORD: for his name alone is excellent; his glory *is* above the earth and heaven. 14 He also exalteth the horn of his people, the praise of all his saints ; *even* of the children of Israel, a people near unto him. Praise ye the LORD.

Considering that this earth, and the atmosphere that surrounds it, are the very sediment of the universe, it concerns us to enquire after those considerations that may be of use to reconcile us to our place in it ; and I know none more likely than this (next to the visit which the Son of God once made to it), that even in this world, dark and as bad as it is, God is praised : *Praise you the Lord from the earth, v.* 7. As the rays of the sun, which are darted directly from heaven, reflect back (though more weakly) from the earth, so

should the praises of God, with which this cold and infected world should be warmed and perfumed.

I. Even those creatures that are not dignified with the powers of reason are summoned into this concert, because God may be glorified in them, *v.* 7—10. Let the *dragons* or *whales,* that sport themselves in the mighty waters (civ. 26), dance before the Lord, to his glory, who largely proves his own omnipotence by his dominion over the leviathan or whale, Job xli. 1, &c. *All deeps,* and their inhabitants, praise God—the sea, and the animals there—the bowels of the earth, and the animals there. *Out of the depths* God may be praised as well as prayed unto. If we look up into the atmosphere we meet with a great variety of meteors, which, being a kind of new productions (and some of them unaccountable), do in a special manner magnify the power of the great Creator. There are fiery meteors ; lightning is fire, and there are other blazes sometimes kindled which may be so called. There are watery meteors, *hail,* and *snow,* and the *vapours* of which they are gendered. There are airy meteors, *stormy winds :* we know not whence they come nor whither they go, whence their mighty force comes nor how it is spent ; but this we know, that, be they ever so strong, so stormy, they *fulfil God's word,* and do that, and no more than that, which he appoints them ; and by *this* Christ showed himself to have a divine power, that he *commanded even the winds and the seas,* and *they obeyed him.* Those that will not fulfil God's word, but rise up in rebellion against it, show themselves to be more violent and headstrong than even the stormy winds, for they fulfil it. Take a view of the surface of the earth (*v.* 9), and there are presented to our view the exalted grounds, *mountains and all hills,* from the barren tops of some of which, and the fruitful tops of others, we may fetch matter for praise ; there are the exalted plants, some that are exalted by their usefulness, as the *fruitful trees* of various kinds, for the fruits of which God is to be praised, others by their stateliness, as *all cedars,* those *trees of the Lord,* civ. 16. Cedars, the high trees, are not the fruitful trees, yet they had their use even in God's temple. Pass we next to the animal kingdom, and there we find God glorified, even by the *beasts* that run wild, *and all cattle* that are tame and in the service of man, *v.* 10. Nay, even the *creeping things* have not sunk so low, nor do the *flying fowl* soar so high, as not to be called upon to *praise the Lord.* Much of the wisdom, power, and goodness of the Creator appears in the several capacities and instincts of the creatures, in the provision made for them and the use made of them. When we see all so very strange, and all so very good, surely we cannot but acknowledge God with wonder and thankfulness.

II. Much more those creatures that are

dignified with the powers of reason ought to employ them in praising God : *Kings of the earth and all people, v.* 11, 12. 1. God is to be glorified in and for these, as in and for the inferior creatures, for their hearts are in the hand of the Lord and he makes what use he pleases of them. God is to be praised in the order and constitution of kingdoms, the *pars imperans—the part that commands*, and the *pars subdita—the part that is subject : Kings of the earth and all people.* It is by him that kings reign, and people are subject to them; the *princes and judges of the earth* have their wisdom and their commission from him, and we, to whom they are blessings, ought to bless God for them. God is to be praised also in the constitution of families, for he is the founder of them ; and for all the comfort of relations, the comfort that parents and children, brothers and sisters, have in each other, God is to be praised. 2. God is to be glorified by these. Let all manner of persons praise God. (1.) Those of each rank, high and low. The praises of kings, and princes, and judges, are demanded ; those on whom God has put honour must honour him with it, and the power they are entrusted with, and the figure they make in the world, put them in a capacity of bringing more glory to God and doing him more service than others. Yet the praises of the people are expected also, and God will graciously accept of them ; Christ despised not the hosannas of the multitude. (2.) Those of each sex, *young men and maidens*, who are accustomed to make merry together; let them turn their mirth into this channel; let it be sacred, that it may be pure. (3.) Those of each age. *Old men* must still bring forth this fruit in old age, and not think that either the gravity or the infirmity of their age will excuse them from it ; *and children* too must begin betimes to praise God ; even *out of the mouth of babes and sucklings* this good work is perfected. A good reason is given (*v.* 13) why all these should *praise the name of the Lord*, because *his name alone is excellent* and worthy to be praised ; it is a name above every name, no name, no nature, but his, has in it all excellency. *His glory is above* both *the earth and the heaven*, and let all the inhabitants both of earth and heaven praise him and yet acknowledge his name to be exalted *far above all blessing and praise.*

III. Most of all his own people, who are dignified with peculiar privileges, must in a peculiar manner give glory to him, *v.* 14. Observe, 1. The dignity God has put upon *his people, even the children of Israel*, typical of the honour reserved for all true believers, who are God's spiritual Israel. *He exalts their horn*, their brightness, their plenty, their power. The people of Israel were, in many respects, honoured above any other nation, for *to them pertained the adoption, the glory, and the covenants,* Rom. ix. 4. It was their own honour that they were *a people near*

unto God, his *Segulla, his peculiar treasure ;* they were admitted into his courts, when a stranger that came nigh must be put to death. They had him *nigh to them in all that which they called upon him for.* This blessing has now come upon the Gentiles, through Christ, for those that *were afar off are* by *his blood made nigh,* Eph. ii. 13. It is the greatest honour that can be put upon a man to be brought near to God, the nearer the better ; and it will be best of all when nearest of all in the kingdom of glory. 2. The duty God expects from them in consideration of this. Let those whom God honours honour him : *Praise you the Lord.* Let him be *the praise of all his saints*, the object of their praise ; for he is a praise to them. *He is thy praise, and he is thy God,* Deut. x. 21. Some by *the horn of his people* understand David, as a type of Christ, whom God has exalted to be *a prince and a Saviour,* who is indeed the praise of all his saints and will be so for ever; for it is through him that they are *a people near to God.*

PSALM CXLIX.

The foregoing psalm was a hymn of praise to the Creator; this is a hymn of praise to the Redeemer. It is a psalm of triumph in the God of Israel, and over the enemies of Israel. Probably it was penned upon occasion of some victory which Israel was blessed and honoured with. Some conjecture that it was penned when David had taken the strong-hold of Zion, and settled his government there. But it looks further, to the kingdom of the Messiah, who, in the chariot of the everlasting gospel, goes forth conquering and to conquer. To him, and his graces and glories, we must have an eye, in singing this psalm, which proclaims, I. Abundance of joy to all the people of God, ver.1—5. II. Abundance of terror to the proudest of their enemies, ver. 6—9.

P RAISE ye the Lord. Sing unto the Lord a new song, *and* his praise in the congregation of saints. 2 Let Israel rejoice in him that made him: let the children of Zion be joyful in their King. 3 Let them praise his name in the dance : let them sing praises unto him with the timbrel and harp. 4 For the Lord taketh pleasure in his people: he will beautify the meek with salvation. 5 Let the saints be joyful in glory : let them sing aloud upon their beds.

We have here,

I. The calls given to God's Israel to praise. *All his works* were, in the foregoing psalm, excited to *praise him;* but here his saints in a particular manner are required to bless him. Observe then, 1. Who are called upon to praise God. *Israel* in general, the body of the church (*v.* 2), *the children of Zion* particularly, the inhabitants of that holy hill, who are nearer to God than other Israelites ; those that have the word and ordinances of God near to them, that are not required to travel far to them, are justly expected to do more in praising God than others. All true Christians may call themselves *the children of Zion*, for in faith and hope *we have come unto Mount Zion*, Heb. xii. 22. The saints must praise God, saints in profession, saints in power, for this is the intention of their sanctification; they are devoted to the glory of God, and renewed by the grace of God, that *they may be unto him for a name and a praise.* 2. What must be the principle of this praise, and that is holy joy in God : *Let Israel rejoice,* and *the children of Zion be joyful,* and *the saints be joyful in glory.* Our praises of God should flow from a heart filled with delight and triumph in God's attributes, and our relation to him. Much of the power of godliness in the heart consists in making God our chief joy and solacing ourselves in him; and our faith in Christ is described by our rejoicing in him. We then give honour to God when we take pleasure in him. We must *be joyful in glory,* that is, in him as our glory, and in the interest we have in him; and let us look upon it as our glory to be of those that rejoice in God. 3. What must be the expressions of this praise. We must by all proper ways show forth the praises of God : *Sing to the Lord.* We must entertain ourselves, and proclaim his name, by *singing praises to him* (v. 3), *singing aloud* (v. 5), for we should sing psalms with all our heart, as those that are not only not ashamed of it, but are enlarged in it. We must sing a *new song,* newly composed upon every special occasion, sing with new affections, which make the song new, though the words have been used before, and keep them from growing threadbare. Let God be *praised in the dance with timbrel and harp,* according to the usage of the Old-Testament church very early (Exod. xv. 20), where we find God praised with *timbrels and dances.* Those who from this urge the use of music in religious worship must by the same rule introduce dancing, for they went together, as in David's dancing before the ark, and Judg. xxi. 21. But, whereas many scriptures in the New Testament keep up singing as a gospel-ordinance, none provide for the keeping up of music and dancing ; the gospel-canon for psalmody is to *sing with the spirit* and *with the understanding.* 4. What opportunities must be taken for praising God, none must be let slip, but particularly, (1.) We must praise God in public, in the *solemn assembly* (v. 1), *in the congregation of saints.* The more the better ; it is the more like heaven. Thus God's name must be owned before the world ; thus the service must have a solemnity put upon it, and we must mutually excite one another to it. The principle, end, and design of our coming together in religious assemblies is that we may join together in praising God. Other parts of the service must be in order to this. (2.) We must praise him in private. *Let the saints be so transported with their joy in God as to sing aloud upon their beds,* when they awake in the night, full of the praises of God, as David, cxix. 62. When God's Israel are brought to a quiet settlement, let them enjoy that, with thankfulness to God; much more may true be-

786

lievers, that have entered into God's rest, and find repose in Jesus Christ, sing aloud for joy of that. Upon their sick-beds, their death-beds, let them sing the praises of their God.

II. The cause given to God's Israel for praise. Consider, 1. God's doings for them. They have reason to rejoice in God, to devote themselves to his honour and employ themselves in his service ; for it is he that made them. He gave us our being as men, and we have reason to praise him for that, for it is a noble and excellent being. He gave Israel their being as a people, as a church, made them what they were, so very different from other nations. Let that people therefore praise him, for he formed them for himself, on purpose that they might *show forth his praise,* Isa. xliii. 21. Let Israel *rejoice in his Makers* (so it is in the original); for God said, *Let us make man;* and in this, some think, is the mystery of the Trinity. 2. God's dominion over them. This follows upon the former : if he made them, he is their King ; he that gave being no doubt may give law ; and this ought to be the matter of our joy and praise that we are under the conduct and protection of such a wise and powerful King. *Rejoice greatly, O daughter of Zion! for behold thy king comes,* the king Messiah, whom God has *set upon his holy hill of Zion;* let all the children of Zion *be joyful* in him, and go forth to meet him with their hosannas, Zech. ix. 9. 3. God's delight in them. He is a king that rules by love, and therefore to be praised ; for *the Lord takes pleasure in his people,* in their services, in their prosperity, in communion with them, and in the communications of his favour to them. He that is infinitely happy in the enjoyment of himself, and to whose felicity no accession can be made, yet graciously condescends to *take pleasure in his people,* cxlvii. 11. 4. God's designs concerning them. Besides the present complacency he has in them, he has prepared for their future glory : *He will beautify the meek,* the humble, and lowly, and contrite in heart, that tremble at his word and submit to it, that are patient under their afflictions and *show all meekness towards all men.* These men vilify and asperse, but God will justify them, and wipe off their reproach ; nay, he will beautify them ; they shall appear not only clear, but comely, before all the world, with the comeliness that he puts upon them. He will beautify them with salvation, with temporal salvations (when God works remarkable deliverances for his people those that had *been among the pots become as the wings of a dove covered with silver,* lxviii. 13), but especially with eternal salvation. The righteous shall be beautified in that day when they *shine forth as the sun.* In the hopes of this, let them now, in the darkest day, *sing a new song.*

6 *Let* the high *praises* of God *be* in their mouth, and a twoedged sword

in their hand; 7 To execute vengeance upon the heathen, *and* punishments upon the people; 8 To bind their kings with chains, and their nobles with fetters of iron; 9 To execute upon them the judgment written : this honour have all his saints. Praise ye the LORD.

The Israel of God are here represented triumphing over their enemies, which is both the matter of their praise (let them give to God the glory of those triumphs) and the recompence of their praise ; those that are truly thankful to God for their tranquillity shall be blessed with victory. Or it may be taken as a further expression of their praise (*v.* 6): *Let the high praises of God be in their mouth,* and then, in a holy zeal for his honour, let them take a *two-edged sword in their hand,* to fight his battles against the enemies of his kingdom. Now this may be applied, 1. To the many victories which God blessed his people Israel with over the nations of Canaan and other nations that were devoted to destruction. These began in Moses and Joshua, who, when they taught Israel *the high praises of the Lord,* did withal put *a two-edged sword in their hand ;* David did so too, for, as he was the sweet singer of Israel, so he was the captain of their hosts, and taught the children of Judah the use of the bow (2 Sam. i. 18), taught their hands to war, as God had taught his. Thus he and they went on victoriously, fighting the Lord's battles, and avenging Israel's quarrels on those that had oppressed them ; then they *executed vengeance upon the heathen* (the Philistines, Moabites, Ammonites, and others, 2 Sam. viii. 1, &c.) *and punishments upon the people,* for all the wrong they had done to God's people, *v.* 7. Their kings and nobles were taken prisoners (*v.* 8) and on some of them the judgment written was executed, as by Joshua on the kings of Canaan, by Gideon on the princes of Midian, by Samuel on Agag. The honour of this redounded to all the Israel of God ; and to him who put it upon them they return it entirely in their hallelujahs. Jehoshaphat's army had at the same time *the high praises of God in their mouth and a two-edged sword in their hand,* for they went forth to war singing the praises of God, and then their sword did execution, 2 Chron. xx. 23. Some apply it to the time of the Maccabees, when the Jews sometimes gained great advantages against their oppressors. And if it seem strange that the meek should, notwithstanding that character, be thus severe, and upon kings and nobles too, here is one word that justifies them in it ; it is *the judgment written.* They do not do it from any personal malice and revenge, or any bloody politics that they govern themselves by, but by commission from God, according to his direction, and in obedience to his command ;

and Saul lost his kingdom for disobeying a command of this nature. Thus the kings of the earth that shall be employed in the destruction of the New-Testament Babylon will but *execute the judgment written,* Rev. xvii. 16, 17. But, since now no such special commissions can be produced, this will by no means justify the violence either of subjects against their princes or of princes against their subjects, or both against their neighbours, under pretence of religion ; for Christ never intended that his gospel should be propagated by fire and sword or his righteousness wrought by the wrath of man. When the high praises of God are in our mouth with them we should have an olive-branch of peace in our hands. 2. To Christ's victories by the power of his gospel and grace over spiritual enemies, in which all believers are more than conquerors. The word of God is the *two-edged sword* (Heb. iv. 12), the *sword of the Spirit* (Eph. vi. 17), which it is not enough to have in our armoury, we must have it in our hand also, as our Master had, when he said, *It is written.* Now, (1.) With this two-edged sword the first preachers of the gospel obtained a glorious victory over the powers of darkness ; vengeance was executed upon the gods of the heathen, by the conviction and conversion of those that had been long their worshippers, and by the consternation and confusion of those that would not repent (Rev. vi. 15) ; the strongholds of Satan were cast down (2 Cor. x. 4, 5); great men were made to tremble at the word, as Felix ; Satan, the god of this world, was cast out, according to the judgment given against him. *This* is the honour of all Christians, that their holy religion has been so victorious. (2.) With this two-edged sword believers fight against their own corruptions, and, through the grace of God, subdue and mortify them ; the sin that had dominion over them is crucified ; self, that once sat king, is bound with chains and brought into subjection to the yoke of Christ; the tempter is foiled and bruised under their feet. *This honour have all the saints.* (3.) The complete accomplishment of this will be in the judgment of the great day, when *the Lord* shall come *with ten thousands of his saints, to execute judgment upon all,* Jude 14, 15. Vengeance shall then be *executed upon the heathen* (Ps. ix. 17), *and punishments,* everlasting punishments, *upon the people. Kings and nobles,* that cast away the bands and cords of Christ's government (ii. 3), shall not be able to cast away the chains and fetters of his wrath and justice. Then shall be executed *the judgment written,* for *the secrets of men shall be judged according to the gospel. This* honour shall all the saints have, that, as assessors with Christ, they shall *judge the world,* 1 Cor. vi. 2. In the prospect of that let them praise the Lord, and continue Christ's faithful servants and soldiers to the end of their lives.

PSALM CL.

The first and last of the psalms have both the same number of verses, are both short, and very memorable. But the scope of them is very different: the first psalm is an elaborate instruction in our duty, to prepare us for the comforts of our devotion; this is all rapture and transport, and perhaps was penned on purpose to be the conclusion of these sacred songs, to show what is the design of them all, and that is to assist us in praising God. The psalmist had been himself full of the praises of God, and here he would fain fill all the world with them: again and again he calls, "Praise the Lord, praise him, praise him," no less than thirteen times in these six short verses. He shows, I. For what, and upon what account, God is to be praised, ver. 1, 2. II. How, and with what expressions of joy, God is to be praised, ver. 3—5. III. Who must praise the Lord; it is every one's business, ver. 6. In singing this psalm we should endeavour to get our hearts much affected with the perfections of God and the praises with which he is and shall be for ever attended, throughout all ages, world without end.

P RAISE ye the LORD. Praise God in his sanctuary: praise him in the firmament of his power. 2 Praise him for his mighty acts: praise him according to his excellent greatness. 3 Praise him with the sound of the trumpet: praise him with the psaltery and harp. 4 Praise him with the timbrel and dance: praise him with stringed instruments and organs. 5 Praise him upon the loud cymbals: praise him upon the high sounding cymbals. 6 Let every thing that hath breath praise the LORD. Praise ye the LORD.

We are here, with the greatest earnestness imaginable, excited to praise God; if, as some suppose, this psalm was primarily intended for the Levites, to stir them up to do their office in the house of the Lord, as singers and players on instruments, yet we must take it as speaking to us, who are made to our God spiritual priests. And the repeated inculcating of the call thus intimates that it is a great and necessary duty, a duty which we should be much employed and much enlarged in, but which we are naturally backward to and cold in, and therefore need to be brought to, and held to, by precept upon precept, and line upon line. Observe here,

I. Whence this tribute of praise arises, and out of what part of his dominion it especially issues. It comes, 1. From *his sanctuary;* praise him there. Let his priests, let his people, that attend there, attend him with their praises. Where should he be praised, but there where he does, in a special manner, both manifest his glory and communicate his grace? *Praise God* upon the account of *his sanctuary,* and the privileges which we enjoy by having that among us, Ezek. xxxvii. 26. *Praise God in his holy ones* (so some read it); we must take notice of the image of God as it appears on those that are sanctified, and love them for the sake of that image; and when we praise them we must praise God in them. 2. From *the firmament of his power. Praise him* because of his power and glory which appear in the firmament, its vastness, its brightness, and its splendid furniture; and because of the powerful influences it has

788

upon this earth. Let those that have their dwelling *in the firmament of his power,* even the holy angels, lead in this good work. Some, by the *sanctuary,* as well as by *the firmament of his power,* understand the highest heavens, the residence of his glory; that is indeed his sanctuary, his holy temple, and there he is praised continually, in a far better manner than we can praise him. And it is a comfort to us, when we find we do it so poorly, that it is so well done there.

II. Upon what account this tribute of praise is due, upon many accounts, particularly, 1. The works of his power (*v.* 2): *Praise him for his mighty acts;* for *his mightinesses* (so the word is), for all the instances of his might, the power of his providence, the power of his grace, what he has done in the creation, government, and redemption of the world, for the children of men in general, for his own church and children in particular. 2. The glory and majesty of his being: *Praise him according to his excellent greatness, according to the multitude of his magnificence* (so Dr. Hammond reads it); not that our praises can bear any proportion to God's greatness, for it is infinite, but, since he is greater than we can express or conceive, we must raise our conceptions and expressions to the highest degree we can attain to. Be not afraid of saying too much in the praises of God, as we often do in praising even great and good men. *Deus non patitur hyperbolum —We cannot speak hyperbolically of God;* all the danger is of saying too little; and therefore, when we have done our utmost, we must own that though we have praised him in consideration of, yet not in proportion to, *his excellent greatness.*

III. In what manner this tribute must be paid, with all the kinds of musical instruments that were then used in the temple-service, *v.* 3—5. It is well that we are not concerned to enquire what sort of instruments these were; it is enough that they were well known then. Our concern is to know, 1. That hereby is intimated how full the psalmist's heart was of the praises of God and how desirous he was that this good work might go on. 2. That in serving God we should spare no cost nor pains. 3. That the best music in God's ears is devout and pious affections, *non musica chordula, sed cor—not a melodious string, but a melodious heart.* Praise God with a strong faith; praise him with holy love and delight; praise him with an entire confidence in Christ; praise him with a believing triumph over the powers of darkness; praise him with an earnest desire towards him and a full satisfaction in him; praise him by a universal respect to all his commands; praise him by a cheerful submission to all his disposals; praise him by rejoicing in his love and solacing yourselves in his great goodness; praise him by promoting the interests of the kingdom of his grace; praise him by a lively hope and expectation of the kingdom of his glory. 4. That, various instruments being used in praising God, it should yet be done with an exact and perfect harmony; they must not hinder, but help one another. The New-Testament concert, instead of this, is *with one mind and one mouth to glorify God*, Rom. xv. 6.

IV. Who must pay this tribute (*v.* 6): *Let every thing that has breath praise the Lord.* He began with a call to those that had a place in his sanctuary and were employed in the temple-service; but he concludes with a call to all the children of men, in prospect of the time when the Gentiles should be taken into the church, and *in every place*, as acceptably as at Jerusalem, *this incense should be offered*, Mal. i. 11. Some think that in *every thing that has breath* here we must include the inferior creatures (as Gen. vii. 22), all *in whose nostrils was the breath of life*. They praise God according to their capacity. The singing of birds is a sort of praising God. The brutes do in effect say to man, " We would praise God if we could; do you do it for us." John in vision heard a song of praise from *every creature which is in heaven, and on the earth, and under the earth*, Rev. v. 13. Others think that only the children of men are meant; for into them God has in a more peculiar manner *breathed the breath of life*, and they have become *living souls*, Gen. ii. 7. Now that the gospel is ordered to be preached *to every creature*, to every human creature, it is required that every human creature praise the Lord. What have we our breath, our spirit, for, but to spend it in praising God; and how can we spend it better? Prayers are called *our breathings*, Lam. iii. 56. Let every one that breathes towards God in prayer, finding the benefit of that, breathe forth his praises too. Having breath, let the praises of God perfume our breath; let us be in this work as in our element; let it be to us as the air we breathe in, which we could not live without. Having our breath in our nostrils, let us consider that it is still going forth, and will shortly go and not return. Since therefore we must shortly breathe our last, while we have breath let us praise the Lord, and then we shall breathe our last with comfort, and, when death runs us out of breath, we shall remove to a better state to breathe God's praises in a freer better air.

The first three of the five books of psalms (according to the Hebrew division) concluded with *Amen and Amen*, the fourth with *Amen, Hallelujah*, but the last, and in it the whole book, concludes with only *Hallelujah*, because the last six psalms are wholly taken up in praising God and there is not a word of complaint or petition in them. The nearer good Christians come to their end the fuller they should be of the praises of God. Some think that this last psalm is designed to represent to us the work of glorified saints in heaven, who are there continually praising God, and that the musical instruments here said to be used are no more to be understood literally than the gold, and pearls, and precious stones, which are said to adorn the New Jerusalem, Rev. xxi. 18, 19. But, as those intimate that the glories of heaven are the most excellent glories, so these intimate that the praises the saints offer there are the most excellent praises. Prayers will there be swallowed up in everlasting praises; there will be no intermission in praising God, and yet no weariness—hallelujahs for ever repeated, and yet still new songs. Let us often take a pleasure in thinking what glorified saints are doing in heaven, what those are doing whom we have been acquainted with on earth, but who have gone before us thither; and let it not only make us long to be among them, but quicken us to do this part of the will of God on earth as those do it that are in heaven. And let us spend as much of our time as may be in this good work because in it we hope to spend a joyful eternity. *Hallelujah* is the word there (Rev. xix. 1, 3); let us echo to it now, as those that hope to join in it shortly. *Hallelujah, praise you the Lord.*

AN

EXPOSITION,

WITH PRACTICAL OBSERVATIONS,

OF THE

PROVERBS.

We have now before us,

I. A new author, or penman rather, or pen (if you will) made use of by the Holy Ghost for making known the mind of God to us, writing as moved by the *finger of God* (so the Spirit of God is called), and that is Solomon ; through his hand came this book of Scripture and the two that follow it, Ecclesiastes and Canticles, a sermon and a song. Some think he wrote Canticles when he was very young, Proverbs in the midst of his days, and Ecclesiastes when he was old. In the title of his song he only writes himself *Solomon*, perhaps because he wrote it before his accession to the throne, being filled with the Holy Ghost when he was young. In the title of his Proverbs he writes himself *the son of David, king of Israel,* for then he ruled over all Israel. In the title of his Ecclesiastes he writes himself *the son of David, king of Jerusalem,* because then perhaps his influence had grown less upon the distant tribes, and he confined himself very much in Jerusalem. Concerning this author we may observe, 1. That he was a king, and a king's son. The penmen of scripture, hitherto, were most of them men of the first rank in the world, as Moses and Joshua, Samuel and David, and now Solomon; but, after him, the inspired writers were generally poor prophets, men of no figure in the world, because that dispensation was approaching in which God would choose the *weak and foolish things of the world to confound the wise and mighty* and the poor should be employed to evangelize. Solomon was a very rich king, and his dominions were very large, a king of the first magnitude, and yet he addicted himself to the study of divine things, and was a prophet and a prophet's son. It is no disparagement to the greatest princes and potentates in the world to instruct those about them in religion and the laws of it. 2. That he was one whom God endued with extraordinary measures of wisdom and knowledge, in answer to his prayers at his accession to the throne. His prayer was exemplary: *Give me a wise and an understanding heart;* the answer to it was encouraging: he had what he desired and *all other things were added to him.* Now here we find what good use he made of the wisdom God gave him; he not only governed himself and his kingdom with it, but he gave rules of wisdom to others also, and transmitted them to posterity. Thus must we trade with the talents with which we are entrusted, according as they are. 3. That he was one who had his faults, and in his latter end turned aside from those good ways of God which in this book he had directed others in. We have the story of it 1 Kings xi., and a sad story it is, that the penman of such a book as this should apostatize as he did. *Tell it not in Gath.* But let those who are most eminently useful take warning by this not to be proud or secure; and let us all learn not to think the worse of good instructions though we have them from those who do not themselves altogether live up to them.

II. A new way of writing, in which divine wisdom is taught us by Proverbs, or short sentences, which contain their whole design within themselves and are not connected with one another. We have had divine *laws, histories,* and *songs,* and now divine *proverbs;* such various methods has Infinite Wisdom used for our instruction, that, no stone being left unturned to do us good, we may be inexcusable if we perish in our folly. Teaching by proverbs was, 1. An ancient way of teaching. It was the most ancient way among the Greeks; each of the seven wise men of Greece had some one saying that he valued himself upon, and that made him famous. These sentences were inscribed on pillars, and had in great veneration as that which was said to come down from heaven. *A cœlo descendit,* Γνῶθι σεαυτὸν—*Know thyself is a precept which came down from heaven.* 2. It was a plain and easy way of teaching, which cost neither the teachers nor the learners much pains, nor put their understandings nor their memories to the stretch. Long periods, and arguments far-fetched, must be laboured both by him that frames them and by him that would understand them, while a proverb, which carries both its sense and its evidence in a little compass, is quickly apprehended and subscribed to, and is easily retained. Both David's devotions and Solomon's instructions are sentential, which may recommend that way of expression to those who minister about holy things, both in praying and preaching. 3. It was a very profitable way of teaching, and served admirably well to answer the end. The word *Mashal,* here used for a proverb, comes from a word that signifies *to rule* or *have dominion,* because of the commanding power and influence which wise and weighty sayings have upon the children of men; he that teaches by them *dominatur in concionibus—rules his auditory.* It is easy to observe how the world is governed by proverbs. *As saith the proverb of the ancients* (1 Sam. xxiv. 13), or (as we commonly express it) *As the old saying is,* goes very far with most men in forming their notions and fixing their resolves. Much of the wisdom of the ancients has been handed down to posterity by proverbs; and some think we may judge of the temper and character of a nation by the complexion of its vulgar proverbs. Proverbs in conversation are like axioms in philosophy, maxims in law, and postulata in the mathematics, which nobody disputes, but every one endeavours to expound so as to have them on his side. Yet there are many corrupt proverbs, which tend to debauch men's minds and harden them in sin. The devil has his proverbs, and the world and the flesh have their proverbs, which reflect reproach on God and religion (as Ezek. xii. 22; xviii. 2), to guard us against the corrupt influences of which God has his proverbs, which are all wise and good, and tend to make us so. These proverbs of Solomon were not merely a collection of the wise sayings that had been formerly delivered, as some have imagined, but were the dictates of the Spirit of God in Solomon. The very first of them (*ch.* i. 7) agrees with what God said to man in the beginning (Job xxviii. 28, *Behold, the fear of the Lord, that is wisdom*); so that though Solomon was great, and his name may serve as much as any man's to recommend his writings; yet, behold, *a greater than Solomon is here.* It is God, by Solomon, that here speaks to us: I say, to *us;* for these proverbs were *written for our learning,* and, when Solomon speaks to his son, the exhortation is said *to speak to us as unto children,* Heb. xii. 5. And, as we have no book so useful to us in our devotions as David's psalms, so have we none so serviceable to us, for the right ordering of our conversations, as Solomon's proverbs, which, as David says of the commandments, are *exceedingly broad,* containing, in a little compass, a complete body of divine ethics, politics, and economics, exposing every vice, recommending every virtue, and suggesting rules for the government of ourselves in every relation and condition, and every turn of the conversation. The learned bishop Hall has drawn up a system of moral philosophy out of Solomon's Proverbs and Ecclesiastes. The first nine chapters of this book are reckoned as a preface, by way of exhortation to the study and practice of wisdom's rules, and caution against those things that would hinder therein. We have then the first volume of Solomon's proverbs (*ch.* x.—xxiv.); after that a second volume (*ch.* xxv.—xxix.); and then Agur's prophecy (*ch.* xxx.), and Lemuel's, *ch.* xxxi. The scope of all is one and the same, to direct us so to order our conversation aright as that in the end we may see the salvation of the Lord. The best comment on these rules is to be ruled by them.

CHAP. I.

Those who read David's psalms, especially those towards the latter end, would be tempted to think that religion is all rapture and consists in nothing but the ecstasies and transports of devotion; and doubtless there is a time for them, and if there be a heaven upon earth it is in them: but, while we are on earth, we cannot be wholly taken up with them; we have a life to live in the flesh, must have a conversation in the world, and into that we must now be taught to carry our religion, which is a rational thing, and very serviceable to the government of human life, and tends as much to make us discreet as to make us devout, to make the face shine before men, in a prudent, honest, useful conversation, as to make the heart burn towards God in holy and pious affections. In this chapter we have, I. The title of the book, showing the general scope and design of it, ver. 1—6. II. The first principle of it recommended to our serious consideration, ver. 7—9. III. A necessary caution against bad company, ver. 10—19. IV. A faithful and lively representation of wisdom's reasonings with the children of men, and the certain ruin of those who turn a deaf ear to those reasonings, ver. 20—33.

THE proverbs of Solomon the son of David, king of Israel; 2 To know wisdom and instruction; to perceive the words of understanding; 3 To receive the instruction of wisdom, justice, and judgment, and equity; 4 To give subtilty to the simple, to the young man knowledge and discretion. 5 A wise *man* will hear, and will increase learning; and a man of understanding shall attain unto wise counsels: 6 To understand a proverb, and the interpretation: the words of the wise, and their dark sayings.

We have here an introduction to this book, which some think was prefixed by the collector and publisher, as Ezra; but it is rather supposed to have been penned by Solomon himself, who, in the beginning of his book, proposes his end in writing it, that he might keep to his business, and closely pursue that end. We are here told,

I. Who wrote these wise sayings, *v.* 1. They are *the proverbs of Solomon.* 1. His name signifies *peaceable,* and the character both of his spirit and of his reign answered to it; both were peaceable. David, whose life was full of troubles, wrote a book of devotion; for *is any afflicted? let him pray.* Solomon, who lived quietly, wrote a book of instruction; for when the *churches had rest they were edified.* In times of peace we should learn ourselves, and teach others, that which in troublous times both they and we must practise. 2. He was *the son of David;* it was his honour to stand related to that good man, and he reckoned it so with good reason, for he fared the better for it, 1 Kings xi.12. He had been blessed with a good education, and many a good prayer had been put up for him (Ps. lxxii. 1), the effect of both which appeared in his wisdom and usefulness. The

generation of the upright are sometimes thus blessed, that they are made blessings, eminent blessings, in their day. Christ is often called *the Son of David,* and Solomon was a type of him in this, as in other things, that he *opened his mouth in parables* or *proverbs.* 3. He was *king of Israel*—a king, and yet it was no disparagement to him to be an instructor of the ignorant, and a teacher of babes—king of Israel, that people among whom God was known and his name was great; among them he learned wisdom, and to them he communicated it. All the earth sought to Solomon *to hear his wisdom,* which excelled all men's (1 Kings iv. 30; x. 24); it was an honour to Israel that their king was such a dictator, such an oracle. Solomon was famous for apophthegms; every word he said had weight in it, and something that was surprising and edifying. His servants who attended him, and heard his wisdom, had, among them, collected 3000 proverbs of his which they wrote in their day-books; but these were of his own writing, and do not amount to nearly a thousand. In these he was divinely inspired. Some think that out of those other proverbs of his, which were not so inspired, the apocryphal books of *Ecclesiasticus* and the *Wisdom of Solomon* were compiled, in which are many excellent sayings, and of great use; but, take altogether, they are far short of this book. The Roman emperors had each of them his symbol or motto, as many now have with their coat of arms. But Solomon had many weighty sayings, not, as theirs, borrowed from others, but all the product of that extraordinary wisdom which God had endued him with.

II. For what end they were written (*v.* 2—4), not to gain a reputation to the author, or strengthen his interest among his subjects, but for the use and benefit of all that in every age and place will govern themselves by these dictates and study them closely. This book will help us, 1. To form right notions of things, and to possess our minds with clear and distinct ideas of them, that we may *know wisdom and instruction,* that wisdom which is got by instruction, by divine revelation, may know both how to speak and act wisely ourselves and to give instruction to others. 2. To distinguish between truth and falsehood, good and evil—*to perceive the words of understanding,* to apprehend them, to judge of them, to guard against mistakes, and to accommodate what we are taught to our selves and our own use, that we may *discern things that differ* and not be imposed upon, and may *approve things that are excellent* and not lose the benefit of them, as the apostle prays, Phil. i. 10. 3. To order our conversation aright in every thing, *v.* 3. This book will give, that we may *receive, the instruction of wisdom,* that knowledge which will guide our practice in *justice, judgment, and equity* (*v.* 3), which will dispose us to render to all their due, to God the things that are God's, in all the exercises of religion, and to all men what is due to them, according to the obligations which by relation, office, contract, or upon any other account, we lie under to them. Note, Those are truly wise, and none but those, who are universally conscientious ; and the design of the scripture is to teach us that wisdom, *justice* in the duties of the first table, *judgment* in those of the second table, *and equity* (that is sincerity) in both ; so some distinguish them.

III. For whose use they were written, *v.* 4. They are of use to all, but are designed especially, 1. For *the simple, to give subtlety to* them. The instructions here given are plain and easy, and level to the meanest capacity, *the wayfaring men, though fools, shall not err therein ;* and those are likely to receive benefit by them who are sensible of their own ignorance and their need to be taught, and are therefore desirous to receive instruction ;⸱ and those who receive these instructions in their light and power, though they be simple, will hereby be made subtle, graciously crafty to know the sin they should avoid and the duty they should do, and to escape the tempter's wiles. He that is *harmless as the dove* by observing Solomon's rules may become *wise as* the *serpent ;* and he that has been sinfully foolish when he begins to govern himself by the word of God becomes graciously wise. 2. For young people, to give them *knowledge and discretion.* Youth is the learning age, catches at instructions, receives impressions, and retains what is then received ; it is therefore of great consequence that the mind be then seasoned well, nor can it receive a better tincture than from Solomon's proverbs. Youth is rash, and heady, and inconsiderate; *man is born like the wild ass's colt,* and therefore needs to be broken by the restraints and managed by the rules we find here. And, if young people will but take heed to their ways according to Solomon's proverbs, they will soon gain the knowledge and discretion of the ancients. Solomon had an eye to posterity in writing this book, hoping by it to season the minds of the rising generation with the generous principles of wisdom and virtue.

IV. What good use may be made of them, *v.* 5, 6. Those who are young and simple may by them be made wise, and are not excluded from Solomon's school, as they were from Plato's. But is it only for such ? No ; here is not only milk for babes, but strong meat for strong men. This book will not only make the foolish and bad wise and good,

but the wise and good wiser and better ; and though the simple and the young man may perhaps slight those instructions, and not be the better for them, yet the *wise man will hear.* Wisdom will be justified by her own children, though not by the children sitting in the market-place. Note, Even wise men must hear, and not think themselves too wise to learn. *A wise man* is sensible of his own defects *(Plurima ignoro, sed ignorantiam meam non ignoro—I am ignorant of many things, but not of my own ignorance),* and therefore is still pressing forward, that he may *increase* in *learning,* may know more and know it better, more clearly and distinctly, and may know better how to make use of it. As long as we live we should strive to increase in all useful learning. It was a saying of one of the greatest of the rabbin, *Qui non auget scientiam, amittit de ea—If our stock of knowledge be not increasing, it is wasting ;* and those that would increase in learning must study the scriptures ; these *perfect the man of God.* A wise man, by increasing in learning, is not only profitable to himself, but to others also, 1. As a counsellor. *A man of understanding* in these precepts of wisdom, by comparing them with one another and with his own observations, *shall* by degrees *attain unto wise counsels ;* he stands fair for preferment, and will be consulted as an oracle, and entrusted with the management of public affairs; he shall come to *sit at the helm,* so the word signifies. Note, Industry is the way to honour ; and those whom God has blessed with wisdom must study to do good with it, according as their sphere is. It is more dignity indeed to be counsellor to the prince, but it is more charity to be counsellor to the poor, as Job was with his wisdom. Job xxix. 15, *I was eyes to the blind.* 2. As an interpreter (*v.* 6)—*to understand a proverb.* Solomon was himself famous for expounding riddles and resolving hard questions, which was of old the celebrated entertainment of the eastern princes, witness the solutions he gave to the enquiries with which the queen of Sheba thought to puzzle him. Now here he undertakes to furnish his readers with that talent, as far as would be serviceable to the best purposes. "They shall *understand a proverb,* even *the interpretation,* without which the proverb is a nut uncracked ; when they hear a wise saying, though it be figurative, they shall take the sense of it, and know how to make use of it." *The words of the wise* are sometimes *dark sayings.* In St. Paul's epistles there is that which is *hard to be understood ;* but to those who, being well-versed in the scriptures, know how to *compare spiritual things with spiritual,* they will be easy and safe ; so that, if you ask them, Have you *understood all these things ?* they may answer, *Yea, Lord.* Note, It is a credit to religion when men of honesty are men of sense ; all good people therefore should aim to be intelligent, and *run to and fro,* take pains in the use of means, that their *knowledge may be increased.*

7 The fear of the LORD *is* the beginning of knowledge : *but* fools despise wisdom and instruction. 8 My son, hear the instruction of thy father, and forsake not the law of thy mother : 9 For they *shall be* an ornament of grace unto thy head, and chains about thy neck.

Solomon, having undertaken to *teach a young man knowledge and discretion,* here lays down two general rules to be observed in order thereunto, and those are, to fear God and honour his parents, which two fundamental laws of morality Pythagoras begins his golden verses with, but the former of them in a wretchedly corrupted state. *Primum, deos immortales cole, parentesque honora—First worship the immortal gods, and honour your parents.* To make young people such as they should be,

I. Let them have regard to God as their supreme.

1. He lays down this truth, that *the fear of the Lord is the beginning of knowledge* (*v.* 7); it is *the principal part of knowledge* (so the margin); it is the head of knowledge; that is, (1.) Of all things that are to be known this is most evident, that *God is to be feared,* to be reverenced, served, and worshipped; this is so the beginning of knowledge that those know nothing who do not know this. (2.) In order to the attaining of all useful knowledge this is most necessary, that we fear God; we are not qualified to profit by the instructions that are given us unless our minds be possessed with a holy reverence of God, and every thought within us be brought into obedience to him. *If any man will do his will, he shall know of his doctrine,* John vii. 17. (3.) As all our knowledge must take rise from the fear of God, so it must tend to it as its perfection and centre. Those know enough who know how to fear God, who are careful in every thing to please him and fearful of offending him in any thing; this is the Alpha and Omega of knowledge.

2. To confirm this truth, that an eye to God must both direct and quicken all our pursuits of knowledge, he observes, *Fools* (atheists, who have no regard to God) *despise wisdom and instruction;* having no dread at all of God's wrath, nor any desire of his favour, they will not give you thanks for telling them what they may do to escape his wrath and obtain his favour. Those who say to the Almighty, *Depart from us,* who are so far from fearing him that they set him at defiance, can excite no surprise if they desire not the knowledge of his ways, but despise that instruction. Note, Those are fools who do not fear God and value the scriptures; and though they may pretend to be admirers of wit they are really strangers and enemies to wisdom.

II. Let them have regard to their parents as their superiors (*v.* 8, 9) : *My son, hear the instruction of thy father.* He means, not only that he would have his own children to be observant of him, and of what he said to them, nor only that he would have his pupils, and those who came to him to be taught, to look upon him as their father and attend to his precepts with the disposition of children, but that he would have all children to be dutiful and respectful to their parents, and to conform to the virtuous and religious education which they give them, according to the law of the fifth commandment.

1. He takes it for granted that parents will, with all the wisdom they have, instruct their children, and, with all the authority they have, give law to them for their good. They are reasonable creatures, and therefore we must not give them law without instruction; we must draw them with the cords of a man, and when we tell them what they must do we must tell them why. But they are corrupt and wilful, and therefore with the instruction there is need of a law. Abraham will not only catechize, but command, his household. Both the father and the mother must do all they can for the good education of their children, and all little enough.

2. He charges children both to receive and to retain the good lessons and laws their parents give them. (1.) To receive them with readiness : *" Hear the instruction of thy father;* hear it and heed it; hear it and bid it welcome, and be thankful for it, and subscribe to it."* (2.) To retain them with resolution : *" Forsake not their law ;* think not that when thou art grown up, and no longer under tutors and governors, thou mayest live at large; no, *the law of thy mother* was according to the law of thy God, and therefore it must never be forsaken; thou wast trained up in the way in which thou shouldst go, and therefore, when thou art old, thou must not depart from it."* Some observe that whereas the Gentile ethics, and the laws of the Persians and Romans, provided only that children should pay respect to their father, the divine law secures the honour of the mother also.

3. He recommends this as that which is very graceful and will put an honour upon us : *" The instructions and laws of thy parents, carefully observed and lived up to, shall be an ornament of grace unto thy head* (*v.* 9), such an ornament as is, in the sight of God, of great price, and shall make thee look as great as those that wear *gold chains about their necks."* Let divine truths and commands be to us a coronet, or a collar of SS, which are badges of first-rate honours; let us value them, and be ambitious of them, and then they shall be so to us. Those are truly valuable, and shall be valued, who value themselves more by their virtue and piety than by their worldly wealth and dignity.

10 My son, if sinners entice thee, consent thou not. 11 If they say, Come with us, let us lay wait for blood, let us lurk privily for the innocent without cause: 12 Let us swallow them up alive as the grave: and whole, as those that go down into the pit: 13 We shall find all precious substance, we shall fill our houses with spoil: 14 Cast in thy lot among us; let us all have one purse: 15 My son, walk not thou in the way with them; refrain thy foot from their path: 16 For their feet run to evil, and make haste to shed blood. 17 Surely in vain the net is spread in the sight of any bird. 18 And they lay wait for their *own* blood; they lurk privily for their *own* lives. 19 So *are* the ways of every one that is greedy of gain; *which* taketh away the life of the owners thereof.

Here Solomon gives another general rule to young people, in order to their finding out, and keeping in, the paths of wisdom, and that is to take heed of the snare of bad company. David's psalms begin with this caution, and so do Solomon's proverbs; for nothing is more destructive, both to a lively devotion and to a regular conversation (v. 10): "*My son*, whom I love, and have a tender concern for, *if sinners entice thee, consent thou not.*" This is good advice for parents to give their children when they send them abroad into the world; it is the same that St. Peter gave to his new converts, (Acts ii. 40), *Save yourselves from this untoward generation.* Observe, 1. How industrious wicked people are to seduce others into the paths of the destroyer: they will entice. Sinners love company in sin; the angels that fell were tempters almost as soon as they were sinners. They do not threaten or argue, but entice with flattery and fair speech; with a bait they draw the unwary young man to the hook. But they mistake if they think that by bringing others to partake with them in their guilt, and to be bound, as it were, in the bond with them, they shall have the less to pay themselves; for they will have so much the more to answer for. 2. How cautious young people should be that they be not seduced by them: "*Consent thou not;* and then, though they entice thee, they cannot force thee. Do not say as they say, nor do as they do or would have thee to do; have no fellowship with them." To enforce this caution,

I. He represents the fallacious reasonings which sinners use in their enticements, and the arts of wheedling which they have for the beguiling of unstable souls. He speci-

fies highwaymen, who do what they can to draw others into their gang, v. 11—14. See here what they would have the young man to do: "*Come with us* (v. 11); let us have thy company." At first they pretend to ask no more; but the courtship rises higher (v. 14): "*Cast in thy lot among us;* come in partner with us, join thy force to ours, and let us resolve to live and die together: thou shalt fare as we fare; and *let us all have one purse,* that what we get together we may spend merrily together," for that is it they aim it. Two unreasonable insatiable lusts they propose to themselves the gratification of, and therewith entice their prey into the snare:—1. Their cruelty. They thirst after blood, and hate those that are innocent and never gave them any provocation, because by their honesty and industry they shame and condemn them: "*Let us* therefore *lay wait for* their *blood,* and *lurk privily* for them; they are conscious to themselves of no crime and consequently apprehensive of no danger, but travel unarmed; therefore we shall make the more easy prey of them. And, O how sweet it will be to *swallow them up alive!*" v. 12. These bloody men would do this as greedily as the hungry lion devours the lamb. If it be objected, "The remains of the murdered will betray the murderers;" they answer, "No danger of that; we will swallow them whole as those that are buried." Who could imagine that human nature should degenerate so far that it should ever be a pleasure to one man to destroy another! 2. Their covetousness. They hope to get a good booty by it (v. 13): "We shall *find all precious substance* by following this trade. What though we venture our necks by it? we shall *fill our houses with spoil.*" See here, (1.) The idea they have of worldly wealth. They call it *precious substance;* whereas it is neither substance nor precious; it is a shadow; it is vanity, especially that which is got by robbery, Ps. lxii. 10. It is as that which is not, which will give a man no solid satisfaction. It is cheap, it is common, yet, in their account, it is precious, and therefore they will hazard their lives, and perhaps their souls, in pursuit of it. It is the ruining mistake of thousands that they over-value the wealth of this world and look on it as *precious substance.* (2.) The abundance of it which they promise themselves: We shall *fill our houses with it.* Those who trade with sin promise themselves mighty bargains, and that it will turn to a vast account (All this will I give thee, says the tempter); but they only *dream that they eat;* the housefuls dwindle into scarcely a handful, like the grass on the house-tops.

II. He shows the perniciousness of these ways, as a reason why we should dread them (v. 15): "*My son, walk not thou in the way with them;* do not associate with them; get, and keep, as far off from them as thou canst; *refrain thy foot from their path;* do not take example by them, nor do as they do." Such is the corruption of our nature that our foot is very prone to step into the path of sin, so that we must use necessary violence upon ourselves to refrain our foot from it, and check ourselves if at any time we take the least step towards it. Consider, 1. How pernicious their way is in its own nature (*v.* 16): *Their feet run to evil,* to that which is displeasing to God and hurtful to mankind, for they *make haste to shed blood.* Note, The way of sin is down-hill; men not only cannot stop themselves, but, the longer they continue in it, the faster they run, and make haste in it, as if they were afraid they should not do mischief enough and were resolved to lose no time. They said they would proceed leisurely (Let us *lay wait for blood, v.* 11), but thou wilt find they are all in haste, so much has Satan *filled their hearts.* 2. How pernicious the consequences of it will be. They are plainly told that this wicked way will certainly end in their own destruction, and yet they persist in it. Herein, (1.) They are like the silly bird, that sees the net spread to take her, and yet it is in vain; she is decoyed into it by the bait, and will not take the warning which her own eyes gave her, *v.* 17. But we think ourselves *of more value than many sparrows,* and therefore should have more wit, and act with more caution. God has *made us wiser than the fowls of heaven* (Job xxxv. 11), and shall we then be as stupid as they? (2.) They are worse than the birds, and have not the sense which we sometimes perceive them to have; for the fowler knows it is in vain to lay his snare *in the sight of the bird,* and therefore he has arts to conceal it. But the sinner sees ruin at the end of his way; the murderer, the thief, see the jail and the gallows before them, nay, they may see hell before them; their watchmen tell them they shall surely die, but it is to no purpose; they rush into sin, and rush on in it, like the horse into the battle. For really the stone they roll will turn upon themselves, *v.* 18, 19. They lay wait, and lurk privily, for the blood and lives of others, but it will prove, contrary to their intention, to be for *their own blood, their own lives;* they will come, at length, to a shameful end; and, if they escape the sword of the magistrate, yet there is a divine Nemesis that pursues them. *Vengeance suffers* them *not to live.* Their greediness of gain hurries them upon those practices which will not suffer them to live out half their days, but will cut off the number of their months in the midst. They have little reason to be proud of their property in that which *takes away the life of the owners* and then passes to other masters; and what is a man profited, though he gain the world, if he lose his life? For then he can enjoy the world no longer; much less if he lose his soul, and that be drowned in destruction and perdition, as multitudes are by the love of money.

Now, though Solomon specifies only the temptation to rob on the highway, yet he intends hereby to warn us against all other evils which sinners entice men to. Such are the ways of the drunkards and unclean; they are indulging themselves in those pleasures which tend to their ruin both here and for ever; and therefore consent not to them.

20 Wisdom crieth without; she uttereth her voice in the streets: 21 She crieth in the chief place of concourse, in the openings of the gates: in the city she uttereth her words, *saying,* 22 How long, ye simple ones, will ye love simplicity? and the scorners delight in their scorning, and fools hate knowledge? 23 Turn you at my reproof: behold, I will pour out my spirit unto you, I will make known my words unto you. 24 Because I have called, and ye refused; I have stretched out my hand, and no man regarded; 25 But ye have set at nought all my counsel, and would none of my reproof: 26 I also will laugh at your calamity; I will mock when your fear cometh; 27 When your fear cometh as desolation, and your destruction cometh as a whirlwind; when distress and anguish cometh upon you. 28 Then shall they call upon me, but I will not answer; they shall seek me early, but they shall not find me: 29 For that they hated knowledge, and did not choose the fear of the LORD: 30 They would none of my counsel: they despised all my reproof. 31 Therefore shall they eat of the fruit of their own way, and be filled with their own devices. 32 For the turning away of the simple shall slay them, and the prosperity of fools shall destroy them. 33 But whoso hearkeneth unto me shall dwell safely, and shall be quiet from fear of evil.

Solomon, having shown how dangerous it is to hearken to the temptations of Satan, here shows how dangerous it is not to hearken to the calls of God, which we shall for ever rue the neglect of. Observe,

I. By whom God calls to us—by *wisdom.* It is *wisdom* that *crieth without.* The word is plural—*wisdoms,* for, as there is infinite wisdom in God, so there is the *manifold wisdom of God,* Eph. iii. 10. God speaks to the children of men by all the kinds of wisdom, and, as in every will, so in every word, of God there is a counsel. 1. Human understanding is wisdom, the light and law of nature, the powers and faculties of reason, and the office of conscience, Job xxxviii. 36. By these God speaks to the children of men, and reasons with them. *The spirit of a man is the candle of the Lord;* and, wherever men go, they may hear a voice behind them, saying, *This is the way;* and the voice of conscience is the voice of God, and not always a still small voice, but sometimes it cries. 2. Civil government is wisdom; it is God's ordinance; magistrates are his vicegerents. God by David had *said to the fools, Deal not foolishly,* Ps. lxxv. 4. *In the opening of the gates,* and in the *places of concourse,* where courts were kept, the judges, the wisdom of the nation, called to wicked people, in God's name, to repent and reform. 3. Divine revelation is wisdom; all its dictates, all its laws, are wise as wisdom itself. God does, by the written word, by the law of Moses, which sets before us the blessing and the curse, by the priests' lips which keep knowledge, by his servants the prophets, and all the ministers of this word, declare his mind to sinners, and give them warning as plainly as that which is proclaimed in the streets or courts of judicature by the criers. God, in his word, not only opens the case, but argues it with the children of men. *Come, now, and let us reason together,* Isa. i. 18. 4. Christ himself is Wisdom, is Wisdoms, for *in him are hidden all the treasures of wisdom and knowledge,* and he is the centre of all divine revelation, not only the *essential Wisdom,* but the *eternal Word,* by whom God speaks to us and to whom he has *committed all judgment;* he it is therefore who here both pleads with sinners and passes sentence on them. He calls himself *Wisdom,* Luke vii. 35.

II. How he calls to us, and in what manner. 1. Very publicly, that whosoever hath ears to hear may hear, since all are welcome to take the benefit of what is said and all are concerned to heed it. The rules of wisdom are published *without in the streets,* not in the schools only, or in the palaces of princes, but *in the chief places of concourse,* among the common people that pass and repass *in the opening of the gates* and *in the city.* It is comfortable casting the net of the gospel where there is a multitude of fish, in hopes that then some will be enclosed. This was fulfilled in our Lord Jesus, who taught openly in the temple, and in crowds of people, and *in secret said nothing* (John xviii. 20), and charged his ministers to *proclaim* his gospel *on the housetop,* Matt. x. 27. God says (Isa. xlv. 19), *I have not spoken in secret. There is no speech or language where* Wisdom's *voice is not heard.* Truth seeks not corners, nor is virtue ashamed of itself. 2. Very pathetically; she *cries,* and again she *cries,* as one in earnest. *Jesus stood and cried.* She *utters her voice,* she *utters her words* with all possible clearness and affection. God is desirous to be heard and heeded.

796

III. What the call of God and Christ is. 1. He reproves sinners for their folly and their obstinately persisting in it, *v.* 22. Observe, (1.) Who they are that Wisdom here reproves and expostulates with. In general, they are such as are *simple,* and therefore might justly be despised, such as *love simplicity,* and therefore might justly be despaired of; but we must use the means even with those that we have but little hopes of, because we know not what divine grace may do. Three sorts of persons are here called to :— [1.] *Simple ones that love simplicity.* Sin is simplicity, and sinners are simple ones; they do foolishly, very foolishly; and the condition of those is very bad who love simplicity, are fond of their simple notions of good and evil, their simple prejudices against the ways of God, and are in their element when they are doing a simple thing, sporting themselves in their own deceivings and flattering themselves in their wickedness. [2.] *Scorners that delight in scorning*—proud people that take a pleasure in hectoring all about them, jovial people that banter all mankind, and make a jest of every thing that comes in their way. But scoffers at religion are especially meant, the worst of sinners, that scorn to submit to the truths and laws of Christ, and to the reproofs and admonitions of his word, and take a pride in running down every thing that is sacred and serious. [3.] *Fools that hate knowledge.* None but fools hate knowledge. Those only are enemies to religion that do not understand it aright. And those are the worst of fools that hate to be instructed and reformed, and have a rooted antipathy to serious godliness. (2.) How the reproof is expressed : "*How long will you* do so ?" This implies that the God of heaven desires the conversion and reformation of sinners and not their ruin, that he is much displeased with their obstinacy and dilatoriness, that he waits to be gracious, and is willing to reason the case with them.

2. He invites them to repent and become wise, *v.* 23. And here, (1.) The precept is plain : *Turn you at my reproof.* We do not make a right use of the reproofs that are given us for that which is evil if we do not turn from it to that which is good ; for for this end the reproof was given. Turn, that is, return to your right mind, turn to God, turn to your duty, turn and live. (2.) The promises are very encouraging. Those that love simplicity find themselves under a moral impotency to change their own mind and way; they cannot turn by any power of their own. To this God answers, "*Behold, I will pour out my Spirit unto you ;* set yourselves to do what you can, and the grace of God shall set in with you, and work in you both to will and to do that good which, without that grace, you could not do." Help thyself, and God will help thee ; *stretch forth thy* withered *hand,* and Christ will strengthen and heal it. [1.] The author of this grace is the Spirit,

and that is promised : *I will pour out my Spirit unto you,* as oil, as water ; you shall have the Spirit in abundance, *rivers of living water,* John vii. 38. Our heavenly Father *will give the Holy Spirit to those that ask him.* [2.] The means of this grace is the word, which, if we take it aright, will turn us ; it is therefore promised, " *I will make known my words unto you,* not only speak them to you, but make them known, give you to understand them." Note, Special grace is necessary to a sincere conversion. But that grace shall never be denied to any that honestly seek it and submit to it.

3. He reads the doom of those that continue obstinate against all these means and methods of grace. It is large and very terrible, *v.* 24—32. Wisdom, having called sinners to return, pauses awhile, to see what effect the call has, *hearkens and hears ; but they speak not aright* (Jer. viii. 6), and therefore she goes on to tell them what will be in the end hereof.

(1.) The crime is recited and it is highly provoking. See what it is for which judgment will be given against impenitent sinners in the great day, and you will say they deserve it, and the Lord is righteous in it. It is, in short, rejecting Christ and the offers of his grace, and refusing to submit to the terms of his gospel, which would have saved them both from the curse of the *law of God* and from the dominion of the *law of sin.* [1.] Christ called to them, to warn them of their danger ; he *stretched out his hand* to offer them mercy, nay, to help them out of their miserable condition, *stretched out his hand* for them to *take hold of,* but they *refused* and *no man regarded ;* some were careless and never heeded it, nor took notice of what was said to them ; others were wilful, and, though they could not avoid hearing the will of Christ, yet they gave him a flat denial, they refused, *v.* 24. They were in love with their folly, and would not be made wise. They were obstinate to all the methods that were taken to reclaim them. God *stretched out his hand* in mercies bestowed upon them, and, when those would not work upon them, in corrections, but all were in vain; they regarded the operations of his hand no more than the declarations of his mouth. [2.] Christ reproved and counselled them, not only reproved them for what they did amiss, but counselled them to do better (those are *reproofs of instruction* and evidences of love and good-will), but they *set at nought all his counsel* as not worth heeding, and *would none of his reproof,* as if it were below them to be reproved by him and as if they had never done any thing that deserved reproof, *v.* 25. This is repeated (*v.* 30): " They *would none of my counsel,* but rejected it with disdain ; they called reproofs reproaches, and took them as an insult (Jer. vi. 10) ; nay, *they despised all my reproof,* as if it were all a jest, and not worth taking notice of." Note, Those are marked for ruin

that are deaf to reproof and good counsel. [3.] They were exhorted to submit to the government of right reason and religion, but they rebelled against both. *First,* Reason should not rule them, for *they hated knowledge* (*v.* 29), hated the light of divine truth because it discovered to them the evil of their deeds, John iii. 20. They hated to be told that which they could not bear to know. *Secondly,* Religion could not rule them, for they *did not choose the fear of the Lord,* but chose to walk in the way of *their heart and in the sight of their eyes.* They were pressed to *set God always before them,* but they chose rather to cast him and his fear *behind their backs.* Note, Those who do not *choose the fear of the Lord* show that they *have no knowledge.*

(2.) The sentence is pronounced, and it is certainly ruining. Those that will not submit to God's government will certainly perish under his wrath and curse, and the gospel itself will not relieve them. They would not take the benefit of God's mercy when it was offered them, and therefore justly fall as victims to his justice, *ch.* xxix. 1. The threatenings here will have their full accomplishment in the judgment of the great day and the eternal misery of the impenitent, of which yet there are some earnests in present judgments. [1.] Now sinners are in prosperity and secure; they live at ease, and set sorrow at defiance. But, *First,* Their *calamity will come* (*v.* 26); sickness will come, and those diseases which they shall apprehend to be the very arrests and harbingers of death ; other troubles will come, in mind, in estate, which will convince them of their folly in setting God at a distance. *Secondly,* Their calamity will put them into a great fright. Fear seizes them, and they apprehend that bad will be worse. When *public judgments* are abroad the *sinners in Zion are afraid, fearfulness surprises the hypocrites.* Death is the *king of terrors* to them (Job xv. 21, &c.; xviii. 11, &c.) ; this fear will be their continual torment. *Thirdly,* According to their fright will it be to them. Their *fear shall come* (the thing they were afraid of shall befal them) ; it shall *come as desolation,* as a mighty deluge bearing down all before it ; it shall be their *destruction,* their total and final destruction ; and it shall come *as a whirlwind,* which suddenly and forcibly drives away all the chaff. Note, Those that will not admit the fear of God lay themselves open to all other fears, and their fears will not prove causeless. *Fourthly,* Their fright will then be turned into despair : *Distress and anguish shall come upon them,* for, having fallen into the pit they were afraid of, they shall see no way to escape, *v.* 27. Saul cries out (2 Sam. i. 9), *Anguish has come upon me ;* and in hell there is *weeping, and wailing, and gnashing of teeth* for anguish, *tribulation and anguish to the soul* of the sinner, the fruit of the *indignation and wrath of the righteous God,* Rom. ii.

797

8, 9. [2.] Now God pities their folly, but he will then *laugh at their calamity (v.* 26): "I also will laugh at your distress, even as you laughed at my counsel." Those that ridicule religion will thereby but make themselves ridiculous before all the world. The righteous will *laugh at them* (Ps. lii. 6), for God himself will. It intimates that they shall be for ever shut out of God's cōmpassions ; they have so long sinned against mercy that they have now quite sinned it away. *His eye shall not spare, neither will he have pity.* Nay, his justice being glorified in their ruin, he will be pleased with it, though now he would rather they should *turn and live. Ah ! I will ease me of my adversaries.* [3.] Now God is ready to hear their prayers and to meet them with mercy, if they would but seek to him for it ; but then the door will be shut, and they shall cry in vain *(v.* 28) : *" Then shall they call upon me* when it is too late, *Lord, Lord, open to us.* They would then gladly be beholden to that mercy which now they reject and make light of ; but *I will not answer,* because, when I called, they would not answer ;" all the answer then will be, *Depart from me, I know you not.* This has been the case of some even in this life, as of Saul, whom God answered not by *Urim* or *prophets ;* but, ordinarily, while there is life there is room for prayer and hope of speeding, and therefore this must refer to the inexorable justice of the last judgment. Then those that slighted God will *seek him early* (that is, earnestly), but in vain *; they shall not find him,* because they sought him not when he might be found, Isa. lv. 6. The rich man in hell begged, but was denied. [4.] Now they are eager upon their own way, and fond of their own devices ; but then they will have enough of them *(v.* 31), according to the proverb, *Let men drink as they brew ;* they shall *eat the fruit of their own way ;* their wages shall be according to their work, and, as was their choice, *so shall their doom be,* Gal. vi. 7, 8. Note, *First,* There is a natural tendency in sin to destruction, Jam. i. 15. Sinners are certainly miserable if they do but *eat the fruit of their own way. Secondly,* Those that perish must thank themselves, and can lay no blame upon any other. It is *their own device ;* let them make their boast of it. God *chooses their delusions,* Isa. lxvi. 4. [5.] Now they value themselves upon their worldly prosperity ; but then that shall help to aggravate their ruin, *v.* 32. *First,* They are now proud that they can turn away from God and get clear of the restraints of religion; but that very thing shall slay them, the remembrance of it shall cut them to the heart. *Secondly,* They are now proud of their own security and sensuality ; but *the ease of the simple* (so the margin reads it) *shall slay them ;* the more secure they are the more certain and the more dreadful will their destruction be, *and the prosperity of fools shall* help to *destroy them,* by puffing them up with pride, gluing their hearts to the world, fur-

798

nishing them with fuel for their lusts, and hardening their hearts in their evil ways.

4. He concludes with an assurance of safety and happiness to all those that submit to the instructions of wisdom *(v.* 33) : *" Whoso hearkeneth unto me,* and will be ruled by me, he shall," (1.) " Be safe ; he *shall dwell* under the special protection of Heaven, so that nothing shall do him any real hurt." (2.) " He shall be easy, and have no disquieting apprehensions of danger ; he shall not only be safe from evil, but *quiet from the fear of* it." *Though the earth be removed, yet shall not they fear.* Would we be safe from evil, and quiet from the fear of it ? Let religion always rule us and the word of God be our counsellor. That is the way to *dwell safely* in this world, and to *be quiet from the fear of evil* in the other world.

CHAP. II.

Solomon, having foretold the destruction of those who are' obstinate in their impiety, in this chapter applies himself to those who are willing to be taught ; and, I. He shows them that, if they would diligently use the means of knowledge and grace, they should obtain of God the knowledge and grace which they seek, ver. 1—9. II. He shows them of what unspeakable advantage it would be to them. 1. It would preserve them from the snares of evil men (ver. 10—15) and of evil women, ver. 16 —19. 2. It would direct them into, and keep them in, the way of good men, ver. 20—22. So that in this chapter we are taught both how to get wisdom and how to use it when we have it, that we may neither seek it, nor receive it, in vain.

MY son, if thou wilt receive my words, and hide my commandments with thee ; 2 So that thou incline thine ear unto wisdom, *and* apply thine heart to understanding ; 3 Yea, if thou criest after knowledge, *and* liftest up thy voice for understanding ; 4 If thou seekest her as silver, and searchest for her as *for* hid treasures ; 5 Then shalt thou understand the fear of the LORD, and find the knowledge of God. 6 For the LORD giveth wisdom : out of his mouth *cometh* knowledge and understanding. 7 He layeth up sound wisdom for the righteous : *he is* a buckler to them that walk uprightly. 8 He keepeth the paths of judgment, and preserveth the way of his saints. 9 Then shalt thou understand righteousness, and judgment, and equity ; *yea,* every good path.

Job had asked, long before this, *Where shall wisdom be found? Whence cometh wisdom ?* (Job xxviii. 12, 20) and he had given this general answer *(v.* 23), *God knoweth the place* of it ; but Solomon here goes further, and tells us both where we may find it and how we may get it. We are here told,

I. What means we must use that we may obtain wisdom.

1. We must closely attend to the word of God, for that is the word of wisdom, *which is able to make us wise unto salvation, v.* 1, 2.

(1.) We must be convinced that the words of God are the fountain and standard of wisdom and understanding, and that we need not desire to be wiser than they will make us. We must *incline our ear* and *apply our hearts* to them, as to *wisdom* or *understanding* itself. Many wise things may be found in human compositions, but divine revelation, and true religion built upon it, are all wisdom. (2.) We must, accordingly, receive the word of God with all readiness of mind, and bid it welcome, even the commandments as well as the promises, without murmuring or disputing. *Speak, Lord, for thy servant hears.* (3.) We must hide them with us, as we do our treasures, which we are afraid of being robbed of. We must not only receive, but retain, the word of God, and lodge it in our hearts, that it may be always ready to us. (4.) We must incline our ear to them; we must lay hold on all opportunities of hearing the word of God, and listen to it with attention and seriousness, as those that are afraid of letting it slip. (5.) We must apply our hearts to them, else inclining the ear to them will stand us in no stead.

2. We must be much in prayer, *v.* 3. We must *cry after knowledge*, as one that is ready to perish for hunger begs hard for bread. Faint desires will not prevail; we must be importunate, as those that know the worth of knowledge and our own want of it. We must cry, as new-born babes, after *the sincere milk of the word*, 1 Pet. ii. 2. We must *lift our voice for understanding*, lift it up to heaven; thence these good and perfect gifts must be expected, Jam. i. 17; Job. xxxviii. 34. We must *give our voice to understanding* (so the word is), speak for it, vote for it, submit the tongue to the command of wisdom. We must consecrate our voice to it; having applied our heart to it, we must employ our voice in seeking for it. Solomon could write *probatum est—a tried remedy*, upon this method; he prayed for wisdom and so obtained it.

3. We must be willing to take pains (*v.* 4); we must *seek it as silver*, preferring it far before all the wealth of this world, and labouring in search of it as those who dig in the mines, who undergo great toil and run great hazards, with indefatigable industry and invincible constancy and resolution, in pursuit of the ore; or as those who will be rich rise up early, and sit up late, and turn every stone to get money and fill their treasures. Thus diligent must we be in the use of the means of knowledge, following on to know the Lord.

II. What success we may hope for in the use of these means. Our labour shall not be in vain; for, 1. We shall know how to maintain our acquaintance and communion with God: "*Thou shalt understand the fear of the Lord* (*v.* 5), that is, thou shalt know how to worship him aright, shalt be led into the meaning and mystery of every ordinance,

and be enabled to answer the end of its institution." *Thou shalt find the knowledge of God*, which is necessary to our fearing him aright. It concerns us to understand how much it is our interest to know God, and to evidence it by agreeable affections towards him and adorations of him. 2. We shall know how to conduct ourselves aright towards all men (*v.* 9): "*Thou shalt understand*, by the word of God, *righteousness, and judgment, and equity*, shalt learn those principles of justice, and charity, and fair dealing, which shall guide and govern thee in the whole course of thy conversation, shall make thee fit for every relation, every business, and faithful to every trust. It shall give thee not only a right notion of justice, but a disposition to practise it, and to render to all their due; for those that do not do justly do not rightly understand it." This will lead them into *every good path*, for the scripture will *make the man of God perfect*. Note, Those have the best knowledge who know their duty, Ps. cxi. 10.

III. What ground we have to hope for this success in our pursuits of wisdom; we must take our encouragement herein from God only, *v.* 6—8.

1. God has wisdom to bestow, *v.* 6. *The Lord* not only is wise himself, but he *gives wisdom*, and that is more than the wisest men in the world can do, for it is God's prerogative to open the understanding. All the wisdom that is in any creature is his gift, his free gift, and he gives it liberally (Jam. i. 5), has given it to many, and is still giving it; to him therefore let us apply for it.

2. He has blessed the world with a revelation of his will. *Out of his mouth*, by the law and the prophets, by the written word and by his ministers, both which are his mouth to the children of men, *come knowledge and understanding*, such a discovery of truth and good as, if we admit and receive the impressions of it, will make us truly knowing and intelligent. It is both an engagement and encouragement to search after wisdom that we have the scriptures to search, in which we may find it if we seek it diligently.

3. He has particularly provided that good men, who are sincerely disposed to do his will, shall have that *knowledge and* that *understanding* which are necessary for them, John vii. 17. Let them seek wisdom, and they shall find it; let them ask, and it shall be given them, *v.* 7, 8. Observe here, (1.) Who those are that are thus favoured. They are *the righteous*, on whom the image of God is renewed, which consists in righteousness, and those who *walk uprightly*, who are honest in their dealings both with God and man and make conscience of doing their duty as far as they know it. They are *his saints*, devoted to his honour, and set apart for his service. (2.) What it is that is provided for them. [1.] Instruction. The means of wisdom are given to all, but wisdom itself, *sound wisdom*, is laid

up for the righteous, laid up in Christ their head, in whom *are hidden all the treasures of wisdom and knowledge*, and who *is made of God to us wisdom.* The same that is the Spirit of revelation in the word is a Spirit of wisdom in the souls of those that are sanctified, that wisdom of the prudent which is to understand his way; and it is sound wisdom, its foundations firm, its principles solid, and its products of lasting advantage. [2.] Satisfaction. Some read it, He *lays up, substance for the righteous*, not only substantial knowledge, but substantial happiness and comfort, Prov. viii. 21. Riches are things that are not, and those that have them only fancy themselves happy; but what is laid up in the promises and in heaven for the righteous will make them truly, thoroughly, and eternally happy. [3.] Protection. Even those who *walk uprightly* may be brought into danger for the trial of their faith, but God is, and will be, *a buckler to them*, so that nothing that happens to them shall do them any real hurt, or possess them with any terrific apprehensions; they are safe, and they shall think themselves so. *Fear not, Abraham; I am thy shield.* It is their way, the paths of judgment in which they walk, that the Lord knows, and owns, and takes care of. [4.] Grace to persevere to the end. If we depend upon God, and seek to him for wisdom, he will uphold us in our integrity, will enable us to *keep the paths of judgment*, however we may be tempted to turn aside out of them; for he *preserves the way of his saints*, that it be not perverted, and so preserves them in it safe and blameless to his heavenly kingdom. The assurances God has given us of his grace, if duly improved, will excite and quicken our endeavours in doing our duty. *Work out your salvation*, for God *works in you.*

10 When wisdom entereth into thine heart, and knowledge is pleasant unto thy soul; 11 Discretion shall preserve thee, understanding shall keep thee: 12 To deliver thee from the way of the evil *man*, from the man that speaketh froward things; 13 Who leave the paths of uprightness, to walk in the ways of darkness; 14 Who rejoice to do evil, *and* delight in the frowardness of the wicked; 15 Whose ways *are* crooked, and *they* froward in their paths: 16 To deliver thee from the strange woman, *even* from the stranger *which* flattereth with her words; 17 Which forsaketh the guide of her youth, and forgetteth the covenant of her God. 18 For her house inclineth unto death, and her paths unto the dead. 19 None

that go unto her return again, neither take they hold of the paths of life. 20 That thou mayest walk in the way of good *men*, and keep the paths of the righteous. 21 For the upright shall dwell in the land, and the perfect shall remain in it. 22 But the wicked shall be cut off from the earth, and the transgressors shall be rooted out of it.

The scope of these verses is to show, 1. What great advantage true wisdom will be of to us; it will keep us from the paths of sin, which lead to ruin, and will therein do us a greater kindness than if it enriched us with all the wealth of the world. 2. What good use we should make of the wisdom God gives us; we must use it for our own guidance in the paths of virtue, and for the arming of us against temptations of every kind. 3. By what rules we may try ourselves whether we have this wisdom or no. This tree will be known by its fruits; if we be truly wise, it will appear by our care to avoid all evil company and evil practices.

This wisdom will be of use to us,

I. For our preservation from evil, from the evil of sin, and, consequently, from the evil of trouble that attends it.

1. In general (*v.* 10, 11), "When wisdom has entire possession of thee, it will *keep thee.*" And when has it an entire possession of us? (1.) When it has dominion over us. When it not only fills the head with notions, but *enters into the heart* and has a commanding power and influence upon that, — when it is upon the throne there, and gives law to the affections and passions, — when it *enters into the heart* as the leaven into the dough, to diffuse its relish there, and to change it into its own image — then it is likely to do us good. (2.) When we have delight in it, when knowledge becomes *pleasant to the soul:* "When thou beginnest to relish it as the most agreeable entertainment, and art subject to its rules, of choice, and with satisfaction, — when thou callest the practice of virtue, not a slavery and a task, but *liberty* and *pleasure*, and a life of serious godliness the most comfortable life a man can live in this world, — then thou wilt find the benefit of it." Though its restraints should be in some respects unpleasant to the body, yet even those must be pleasant to the soul. When it has come to this, with us, *discretion shall preserve* us and keep us. God keeps *the way of his saints* (*v.* 8), by giving them discretion to keep out of harm's way, to keep themselves that the wicked one touch them not. Note, A principle of grace reigning in the heart will be a powerful preservative both against corruptions within and temptations without, Eccl. ix. 16, 18.

2. More particularly, wisdom will preserve us,

(1.) From men of corrupt principles, atheistical profane men, who make it their business to debauch young men's judgments, and instil into their minds prejudices against religion and arguments for vice: "It will *deliver thee from the way of the evil man* (*v.* 12), and a blessed deliverance it will be, as from the very jaws of death, *from the way* in which he walks, and in which he would persuade thee to walk." The enemy is spoken of as one (*v.* 12), an *evil man*, but afterwards as many (*v.* 13); there is a club, a gang of them, that are in confederacy against religion, and join hand in hand for the support of the devil's kingdom and the interests of it. [1.] They have a spirit of contradiction to that which is good: They *speak froward things;* they say all they can against religion, both to show their own enmity to it and to dissuade others from it. They are advocates for Satan; they plead for Baal, and *pervert the right ways of the Lord.* How peevishly will profane wits argue for sin, and with what frowardness will they carp at the word of God! Wisdom will keep us either from conversing with such men or at least from being ensnared by them. [2.] They are themselves apostates from that which is good, and such are commonly the most malicious and dangerous enemies religion has, witness Julian (*v.* 13): *They leave the paths of uprightness,* which they were trained up in and had set out in, shake off the influences of their education, and break off the thread of their hopeful beginnings, *to walk in the ways of darkness,* in those wicked ways which hate the light, in which men are led blindfold by ignorance and error, and which lead men into utter darkness. The ways of sin are ways of darkness, uncomfortable and unsafe; what fools are those that leave the plain, pleasant, lightsome paths of uprightness, to walk in those ways! Ps. lxxxii. 5; 1 John ii. 11. [3.] They take a pleasure in sin, both in committing it themselves and in seeing others commit it (*v.* 14): They *rejoice* in an opportunity *to do evil,* and in the accomplishment and success of any wicked project. It is sport to fools to do mischief; nor is any sight more grateful to them than to see *the frowardness of the wicked,* to see those that are hopeful drawn into the ways of sin, and then to see them hardened and confirmed in those ways. They are pleased if they can discern that the devil's kingdom gets ground (see Rom. i. 32), such a height of impiety have they arrived at. [4.] They are resolute in sin (*v.* 15): Their *ways are crooked,* a great many windings and turnings to escape the pursuit of their convictions and break the force of them; some sly excuse, some subtle evasion or other, their deceitful hearts furnish them with, for the strengthening of their hands in their wickedness; and in the crooked mazes of that labyrinth they secure themselves from the arrests of God's word and their own consciences; for they are *froward in their paths,* that is, they are resolved to go

on in them, whatever is said against it. Every wise man will shun the company of such as these.

(2.) From women of corrupt practices. The former lead to spiritual wickednesses, the lusts of the unsanctified mind; these lead to *fleshly lusts,* which defile the body, that living temple, but withal *war against the soul.* The adulteress is here called *the strange woman,* because no man that has any wisdom or goodness in him will have any acquaintance with her; she is to be shunned by every Israelite as if she were a heathen, and a stranger to that sacred commonwealth. A strange woman indeed! utterly estranged from all principles of reason, virtue, and honour. It is a great mercy to be delivered from the allurements of the adulteress, considering, [1.] How false she is. Who will have any dealings with those that are made up of treachery? She is a strange woman; for, *First,* She is false to him whom she entices. She speaks fair, tells him how much she admires him above any man, and what a kindness she has for him; but she *flatters with her words;* she has no true affection for him, nor any desire of his welfare, any more than Delilah had of Samson's. All she designs is to pick his pocket and gratify a base lust of her own. *Secondly,* She is false to her husband, and violates the sacred obligation she lies under to him. He was *the guide of her youth;* by marrying him she chose him to be so, and submitted herself to his guidance, with a promise to attend him only, and forsake all others. But she has *forsaken* him, and therefore it cannot be thought that she should be faithful to any one else; and whoever entertains her is partaker with her in her falsehood. *Thirdly,* She is false to God himself: She *forgets the covenant of her God,* the marriage-covenant (*v.* 17), to which God is not only a witness, but a party, for, he having instituted the ordinance, both sides vow to him to be true to each other. It is not her husband only that she sins against, but her God, who *will judge whoremongers and adulterers* because they despise the oath and break the covenant, Ezek. xvii. 18; Mal. ii. 14. [2.] How fatal it will prove to those that fall in league with her, *v.* 18, 19. Let the sufferings of others be our warnings. Take heed of the sin of whoredom; for, *First,* The ruin of those who are guilty of it is certain and unavoidable, if they do not repent. It is a sin that has a direct tendency to the killing of the soul, the extinguishing of all good affections and dispositions in it, and the exposing of it to the wrath and curse of God and the sword of his justice. Those that live in forbidden pleasures are dead while they live. Let discretion preserve every man, not only from the evil woman, but from the evil house, for the *house inclines to death;* it is in the road that leads directly to eternal death; *and her paths unto Rephaim,* to the *giants* (so some read it), the sinners of the old world, who, living in luxury and excess of riot, were cut down out of time, and their foundation was overthrown with a flood. Our Lord Jesus deters us from sinful pleasures with the consideration of everlasting torments which follow them. *Where the worm dies not, nor is the fire quenched.* See Matt. v. 28, 29. *Secondly,* Their repentance and recovery are extremely hazardous : *None,* or next to none, *that go unto her, return again.* It is very rare that any who are caught in this snare of the devil recover themselves, so much is the heart hardened, and the mind blinded, by the deceitfulness of this sin. Having once lost their *hold of the paths of life*, they know not how to take hold of them again, but are perfectly besotted and bewitched with those base lusts. Many learned interpreters think that this caution against the *strange woman*, besides the literal sense, is to be understood figuratively, as a caution, 1. Against idolatry, which is spiritual whoredom. Wisdom will keep thee from all familiarity with the worshippers of images, and all inclination to join with them, which had for many ages been of such pernicious consequence to Israel and proved so to Solomon himself: 2. Against the debauching of the intellectual powers and faculties of the soul by the lusts and appetites of the body. Wisdom will keep thee from being captivated by the carnal mind, and from subjecting the spirit to the dominion of the flesh, that notorious adulteress which *forsakes its guide*, violates the *covenant of our God*, which *inclines to death*, and which, when it has got an undisturbed dominion, makes the case of the soul desperate.

II. This wisdom will be of use to guide and direct us in that which is good (*v.* 20) : *That thou mayest walk in the way of good men.* We must avoid the way of the *evil man*, and the *strange woman*, in order that we may walk in good ways ; we must *cease to do evil*, in order that we may *learn to do well* Note, 1. There is a way which is peculiarly the way of good men, the way in which good men, as such, and as far as they have really been such, have always walked. 2. It will be our wisdom to walk in that way, to ask for the good old way and walk therein, Jer. vi. 16; Heb. vi. 12; xii. 1. And we must not only walk in that way awhile, but we must keep it, keep in it, and never turn aside out of it: *The paths of the righteous* are the paths of life, which all that are wise, having taken hold of, will keep their hold of. "That thou mayest imitate those excellent persons, the patriarchs and prophets (so bishop Patrick paraphrases it), and be preserved in *the paths of those righteous* men who followed after them." We must not only choose our way in general by the good examples of the saints, but must also take directions from them in the choice of our particular paths ; observe the track, and go forth by the footsteps of the flock. Two reasons are here given why we should thus choose :—(1.) Be-

cause men's integrity will be their establishment, *v.* 21. It will be the establishment, [1.] Of their persons: *The upright shall dwell in the land*, peaceably and quietly, as long as they live ; and their uprightness will contribute to it, as it settles their minds, guides their counsels, gains them the good-will of their neighbours, and entitles them to God's special favour. [2.] Of their families: *The perfect*, in their posterity, *shall remain in it* They shall dwell and remain for ever in the heavenly Canaan, of which the earthly one was but a type. (2.) Because men's iniquity will be their destruction, *v.* 22. See what becomes of *the wicked*, who choose the way of *the evil man;* they *shall be cut off*, not only from heaven hereafter and all hopes of that, but *from the earth* now, on which they set their affections, and in which they lay up their treasure. They think to take root in it, but they and their families *shall be rooted out of it*, in judgment to them, but in mercy to the earth. There is a day coming which *shall leave them neither root nor branch*, Mal. iv. 1. Let that wisdom then *enter into our hearts*, and be *pleasant to our souls*, which will keep us out of a way that will end thus.

CHAP. III.

This chapter is one of the most excellent in all this book, both for argument to persuade us to be religious and for directions therein. I. We must be constant to our duty because that is the way to be happy, ver. 1—4. II. We must live a life of dependence upon God because that is the way to be safe, ver. 5. III. We must keep up the fear of God because that is the way to be healthful, ver. 7, 8. IV. We must serve God with our estates because that is the way to be rich, ver. 9, 10. V. We must bear afflictions well because that is the way to get good by them, ver. 11, 12. VI. We must take pains to obtain wisdom because that is the way to gain her, and to gain by her, ver. 13 —20. VII. We must always govern ourselves by the rules of wisdom, of right reason and religion, because that is the way to be always easy, ver. 21—26. VIII. We must do all the good we can, and no hurt, to our neighbours, because according as men are just or unjust, charitable or uncharitable, humble or haughty, accordingly they shall receive of God, ver. 27—35. From all this it appears what a tendency religion has to make men both blessed and blessings.

M Y son, forget not my law; but let thine heart keep my commandments : 2 For length of days, and long life, and peace, shall they add to thee. 3 Let not mercy and truth forsake thee : bind them about thy neck ; write them upon the table of thine heart : 4 So shalt thou find favour and good understanding in the sight of God and man. 5 Trust in the Lord with all thine heart ; and lean not unto thine own understanding. 6 In all thy ways acknowledge him, and he shall direct thy paths.

We are here taught to live a life of communion with God ; and without controversy great is this mystery of godliness, and of great consequence to us, and, as is here shown, will be of unspeakable advantage.

I. We must have a continual regard to God's precepts, *v.* 1, 2.

1. We must, (1.) Fix God's law, and his commandments, as our rule, by which we will in every thing be ruled and to which we

will yield obedience. (2.) We must acquaint ourselves with them; for we cannot be said to forget that which we never knew. (3.) We must remember them so that they may be ready to us whenever we have occasion to use them. (4.) Our wills and affections must be subject to them and must in every thing conform to them. Not only our heads, but our hearts, must *keep God's commandments;* in them, as in the ark of the testimony, both the tables of the law must be deposited.

2. To encourage us to submit ourselves to all the restraints and injunctions of the divine law, we are assured (*v.* 2) that it is the certain way to long life and prosperity. (1.) It is the way to be long-lived. God's commandments *shall add to us length of days;* to a good useful life on earth, they shall add an eternal life in heaven, *length of days for ever and ever,* Ps. xxi. 4. God shall be our life and the length of our days, and that will be indeed long life, with an addition. But, because length of days may possibly become a burden and a trouble, it is promised, (2.) That it shall prove the way to be easy too, so that even the days of old age shall not be evil days, but days in which thou shalt have pleasure: *Peace shall they* be continually *adding to thee.* As grace increases, peace shall increase; and *of the increase of Christ's government and peace,* in the heart as well as in the world, *there shall be no end. Great and growing peace have those that love the law.*

II. We must have a continual regard to God's promises, which go along with his precepts, and are to be received, and retained, with them (*v.* 3): " *Let not mercy and truth forsake thee,* God's mercy in promising, and his truth in performing. Do not forfeit these, but live up to them, and preserve thy interest in them; do not forget these, but live upon them, and take the comfort of them. *Bind them about thy neck,* as the most graceful ornament." It is the greatest honour we are capable of in this world to have an interest in the mercy and truth of God. " *Write them upon the table of thy heart,* as dear to thee, thy portion, and most delightful entertainment; take a pleasure in applying them and thinking them over." Or it may be meant of the mercy and truth which are our duty, piety and sincerity, charity towards men, fidelity towards God. Let these be fixed and commanding principles in thee. To encourage us to do this we are assured (*v.* 4) that this is the way to recommend ourselves both to our Creator and fellow-creatures: *So shalt thou find favour and good understanding.* 1. A good man seeks the favour of God in the first place, is ambitious of the honour of being accepted of the Lord, and he shall find that favour, and with it a good understanding; God will make the best of him, and put a favourable construction upon what he says and does. He shall be owned as one of Wisdom's children, and shall have praise with God, as one having that *good understand-*

ing which is ascribed to all those *that do his commandments.* 2. He wishes to have favour with men also (as Christ had, Luke ii. 52), to be *accepted of the multitude of his brethren* (Esth. x. 3), and that he shall have; they shall understand him aright, and in his dealings with them he shall appear to be prudent, shall act intelligently and with discretion. *He shall have good success* (so some translate it), the common effect of good understanding.

III. We must have a continual regard to God's providence, must own and depend upon it in all our affairs, both by faith and prayer. 1. By faith. We must repose an entire confidence in the wisdom, power, and goodness of God, assuring ourselves of the extent of his providence to all the creatures and all their actions. We must therefore *trust in the Lord with all our hearts* (*v.* 5); we must believe that he is able to do what he will, wise to do what is best, and good, according to his promise, to do what is best for us, if we love him, and serve him. We must, with an entire submission and satisfaction, depend upon him to perform all things for us, and not *lean to our own understanding,* as if we could, by any forecast of our own, without God, help ourselves, and bring our affairs to a good issue. Those who know themselves cannot but find their own understanding to be a broken reed, which, if they lean to, will certainly fail them. In all our conduct we must be diffident of our own judgment, and confident of God's wisdom, power, and goodness, and therefore must follow Providence and not force it. That often proves best which was least our own doing. 2. By prayer (*v.* 6): *In all thy ways acknowledge God.* We must not only in our judgment believe that there is an over-ruling hand of God ordering and disposing of us and all our affairs, but we must solemnly own it, and address ourselves to him accordingly. We must ask his leave, and not design any thing but what we are sure is lawful. We must ask his advice and beg direction from him, not only when the case is difficult (when we know not what to do, no thanks to us that we have our eyes up to him), but in every case, be it ever so plain, We must ask success of him, as those who know *the race is not to the swift.* We must refer ourselves to him as one from whom our judgment proceeds, and patiently, and with a holy indifferency, wait his award. *In all our ways* that prove direct, and fair, and pleasant, in which we gain our point to our satisfaction, we must acknowledge God with thankfulness. *In all our ways* that prove cross and uncomfortable, and that are hedged up with thorns, we must acknowledge God with submission. Our eye must be ever towards God; to him we must, in every thing, make our requests known, as Jephthah *uttered all his words before the Lord in Mizpeh,* Judg. xi. 11. For our encouragement to do this, it is promised, " *He shall direct thy daths,* so that thy way shall be safe and good and the issue happy at last." Note, Those that put themselves under a divine guidance shall always have the benefit of it. God will give them that wisdom which is profitable to direct, so that they shall not turn aside into the by-paths of sin, and then will himself so wisely order the event that it shall be to their mind, or (which is equivalent) for their good. Those that faithfully follow the pillar of cloud and fire shall find that though it may lead them about it leads them the right way and will bring them to Canaan at last.

7 Be not wise in thine own eyes: fear the LORD, and depart from evil. 8 It shall be health to thy navel, and marrow to thy bones. 9 Honour the LORD with thy substance, and with the firstfruits of all thine increase: 10 So shall thy barns be filled with plenty, and thy presses shall burst out with new wine. 11 My son, despise not the chastening of the LORD; neither be weary of his correction: 12 For whom the LORD loveth he correcteth; even as a father the son *in whom* he delighteth.

We have here before us three exhortations, each of them enforced with a good reason:—
I. We must live in a humble and dutiful subjection to God and his government (*v.* 7): "*Fear the Lord,* as your sovereign Lord and Master; be ruled in every thing by your religion and subject to the divine will." This must be, 1. A humble subjection: *Be not wise in thy own eyes.* Note, There is not a greater enemy to the power of religion, and the fear of God in the heart, than conceitedness of our own wisdom. Those that have an opinion of their own sufficiency think it below them, and a disparagement to them, to take their measures from, much more to hamper themselves with, religion's rules. 2. A dutiful subjection: *Fear the Lord, and depart from evil;* take heed of doing any thing to offend him and to forfeit his care. To *fear the Lord,* so as to *depart from evil,* is true *wisdom* and *understanding* (Job xxviii. 28); those that have it are truly wise, but self-denyingly so, and not *wise in their own eyes.* For our encouragement thus to live in the fear of God it is here promised (*v.* 8) that it shall be as serviceable even to the outward man as our necessary food. It will be nourishing: *It shall be health to thy navel.* It will be strengthening: It shall be *marrow to thy bones.* The prudence, temperance, and sobriety, the calmness and composure of mind, and the good government of the appetites and passions, which religion teaches, tend very much not only to the health of the soul, but to a good habit of body, which is very desirable, and without which our other

enjoyments in this world are insipid. Envy is *the rottenness of the bones;* the sorrow of the world dries them; but hope and joy in God are marrow to them.
II. We must make a good use of our estates, and that is the way to increase them, *v.* 9, 10. Here is,
1. A precept which makes it our duty to serve God with our estates: *Honour the Lord with thy substance.* It is the end of our creation and redemption to honour God, to be to him for a name and a praise; we are no other way capable of serving him than in his honour. His honour we must show forth and the honour we have for him. We must honour him, not only *with our bodies and spirits which are his,* but with our estates too, for they also are his: we and all our appurtenances must be devoted to his glory. Worldly wealth is but poor substance, yet, such as it is, we must honour God with it, and then, if ever, it becomes substantial. We must honour God, (1.) *With our increase.* Where riches increase we are tempted to honour ourselves (Deut. viii. 17) and to set our hearts upon the world (Ps. lxii. 10); but the more God gives us the more we should study to honour him. It is meant of the increase of the earth, for we live upon annual products, to keep us in constant dependence on God. (2.) *With all our increase.* As God has prospered us in every thing, we must honour him. Our law will allow a prescription for a *modus decimandi*—a mode of *tithing,* but none *de non decimando*—*for exemption from paying tithes.* (3.) *With the first-fruits of all,* as Abel, Gen. iv. 4. This was the law (Exod. xxiii. 19), and the prophets, Mal. iii. 10. God, who is the first and best, must have the first and best of every thing; his right is prior to all other, and therefore he must be served first. Note, It is our duty to make our worldly estates serviceable to our religion, to use them and the interest we have by them for the promoting of religion, to do good to the poor with what we have and abound in all works of piety and charity, *devising liberal things.*
2. A promise, which makes it our interest to serve God with our estates. It is the way to make a little much, and much more; it is the surest and safest method of thriving: *So shall thy barns be filled with plenty.* He does not say thy bags, but thy barns, not thy wardrobe replenished, but thy presses: "God shall bless thee with an increase of that which is for use, not for show or ornament—for spending and laying out, not for hoarding and laying up." Those that do good with what they have shall have more to do more good with. Note, If we make our worldly estates serviceable to our religion we shall find our religion very serviceable to the prosperity of our worldly affairs. *Godliness has the promise of the life that now is* and most of the comfort of it. We mistake if we think that giving will undo us and make us poor. No, giving for

God's honour will make us rich, Hag. ii. 19. What we gave we have.

III. We must conduct ourselves aright under our afflictions, *v.* 11, 12. This the apostle quotes (Heb. xii. 5), and calls it *an exhortation which speaks unto us as unto children*, with the authority and affection of a father. We are here in a world of troubles. Now observe,

1. What must be our care when we are in affliction. We must neither despise it nor be weary of it. His exhortation, before, was to those that are rich and in prosperity, here to those that are poor and in adversity. (1.) We must not despise an affliction, be it ever so light and short, as if it were not worth taking notice of, or as if it were not sent on an errand and therefore required no answer. We must not be stocks, and stones, and stoics, under our afflictions, insensible of them, hardening ourselves under them, and concluding we can easily get through them without God. (2.) We must not be weary of an affliction, be it ever so heavy and long, not *faint* under it, so the apostle renders it, not be dispirited, dispossessed of our own souls, or driven to despair, or to use any indirect means for our relief and the redress of our grievances. We must not think that the affliction either presses harder or continues longer than is meet, nor conclude that deliverance will never come because it does not come so soon as we expect it.

2. What will be our comfort when we are in affliction. (1.) That it is a divine correction; it is *the chastening of the Lord*, which, as it is a reason why we should submit to it (for it is folly to contend with a God of incontestable sovereignty and irresistible power), so it is a reason why we should be satisfied in it; for we may be sure that a God of unspotted purity does us no wrong and that a God of infinite goodness means us no hurt. It is from God, and therefore must not be despised; for a slight put upon the messenger is an affront to him that sends him. It is from God, and therefore we must not be weary of it, for he knows our frame, both what we need and what we can bear. (2.) That it is a fatherly correction; it comes not from his vindictive justice as a Judge, but his wise affection as a Father. The father corrects *the son whom he* loves, nay, and because he loves him and desires he may be wise and good. He delights in that in his son which is amiable and agreeable, and therefore corrects him for the prevention and cure of that which would be a deformity to him, and an alloy to his delight in him. Thus God hath said, *As many as I love I rebuke and chasten,* Rev. iii. 19. This is a great comfort to God's children, under their afflictions, [1.] That they not only consist with, but flow from, covenant-love. [2.] That they are so far from doing them any real hurt that, by the grace of God working with them, they do a great deal of good, and are happy means of their sanctification.

13 Happy *is* the man *that* findeth wisdom, and the man *that* getteth understanding. 14 For the merchandise of it *is* better than the merchandise of silver, and the gain thereof than fine gold. 15 She *is* more precious than rubies : and all the things thou canst desire are not to be compared unto her. 16 Length of days *is* in her right hand ; *and* in her left hand riches and honour. 17 Her ways *are* ways of pleasantness, and all her paths *are* peace. 18 She *is* a tree of life to them that lay hold upon her : and happy *is every one* that retaineth her. 19 The Lord by wisdom hath founded the earth ; by understanding hath he established the heavens. 20 By his knowledge the depths are broken up, and the clouds drop down the dew.

Solomon had pressed us earnestly to seek diligently for wisdom (*ch.* ii. 1, &c.), and had assured us that we should succeed in our sincere and constant pursuits. But the question is, What shall we get by it when we have found it? Prospect of advantage is the spring and spur of industry ; he therefore shows us how much it will be to our profit, laying this down for an unquestionable truth, *Happy is the man that findeth wisdom*, that true wisdom which consists in the knowledge and love of God, and an entire conformity to all the intentions of his truths, providences, and laws. Now observe,

I. What it is to find wisdom so as to be made happy by it.

1. We must get it. He is the happy man who, having found it, makes it his own, gets both an interest in it and the possession of it, who *draws out understanding* (so the word is), that is, (1.) Who derives it from God. Having it not in himself, he draws it with the bucket of prayer from the fountain of all wisdom, *who gives liberally*. (2.) Who takes pains for it, as he does who draws ore out of the mine. If it do not come easily, we must put the more strength to draw it. (3.) Who improves in it, who, having some understanding, draws it out by growing in knowledge and making five talents ten. (4.) Who does good with it, who draws out from the stock he has, as wine from the vessel, and communicates to others, for their instruction, *things new and old*. That is well got, and to good purpose, that is thus used to good purpose.

2. We must trade for it. We read here of the merchandise of wisdom, which intimates, (1.) That we must make it our business, and not a by-business, as the merchant bestows the main of his thoughts and time upon his merchandise. (2.) That we must venture all in it, as a stock in trade, and be willing to

part with all for it. This is that pearl of great price which, when we have found it, we must willingly sell all for the purchase of, Matt. xiii. 45, 46. *Buy the truth* (Prov. xxiii. 23); he does not say at what rate, because we must buy it at any rate rather than miss it.

3. We must lay hold on it as we lay hold on a good bargain when it is offered to us, which we do the more carefully if there be danger of having it taken out of our hands. We must apprehend with all our might, and put forth our utmost vigour in the pursuit of it, lay hold on all occasions to improve in it, and catch at the least of its dictates.

4. We must retain it. It is not enough to lay hold on wisdom, but we must keep our hold, hold it fast, with a resolution never to let it go, but to persevere in the ways of wisdom to the end. We must *sustain it* (so some read it), must embrace it with all our might, as we do that which we would sustain. We must do all we can to support the declining interests of religion in the places where we live.

II. What the happiness of those is who do find it.

1. It is a transcendent happiness, more than can be found in the wealth of this world, if we had ever so much of it, *v.* 14, 15. It is not only a surer, but a more gainful merchandise to trade for wisdom, for Christ, and grace, and spiritual blessings, than for silver, and gold, and rubies. Suppose a man to have got these in abundance, nay, to have all the things he can desire of this world (and who is it that ever had?), yet, (1.) All this would not purchase heavenly wisdom; no, it would *utterly be contemned;* it *cannot be gotten for gold,* Job xxviii. 15, &c. (2.) All this would not countervail the want of heavenly wisdom nor be the ransom of a soul lost by its own folly. (3.) All this would not make a man half so happy, no, not in this world, as those are who have true wisdom, though they have none of all these things. (4.) Heavenly wisdom will procure that for us, and secure that to us, which silver, and gold, and rubies, will not be the purchase of.

2. It is a true happiness; for it is inclusive of, and equivalent to, all those things which are supposed to make men happy, *v.* 16, 17. Wisdom is here represented as a bright and bountiful queen, reaching forth gifts to her faithful and loving subjects, and offering them to all that will submit to her government. (1.) Is length of days a blessing? Yes, the most valuable; life includes all good, and therefore she offers that *in her right hand.* Religion puts us into the best methods of prolonging life, entitles us to the promises of it, and, though our days on earth should be no more than our neighbour's, yet it will secure to us everlasting life in a better world. (2.) Are riches and honour accounted blessings? They are so, and them she reaches out with *her left hand.* For, as she is ready to embrace those that submit to her with both
806

arms, so she is ready to give out to them with both hands. They shall have the wealth of this world as far as Infinite Wisdom sees good for them; while the true riches, by which men are rich towards God, are secured to them. Nor is there any honour, by birth or preferment, comparable to that which attends religion; it makes the *righteous more excellent than his neighbour,* recommends men to God, commands respect and veneration with all the sober part of mankind, and will in the other world make those that are now buried in obscurity to *shine forth as the sun.* (3.) Is pleasure courted as much as any thing? It is so, and it is certain that true piety has in it the greatest true pleasure. *Her ways are ways of pleasantness;* the ways in which she has directed us to walk are such as we shall find abundance of delight and satisfaction in. All the enjoyments and entertainments of sense are not comparable to the pleasure which gracious souls have in communion with God and doing good. That which is the only right way to bring us to our journey's end we must walk in, fair or foul, pleasant or unpleasant; but the way of religion, as it is the right way, so it is a pleasant way; it is smooth and clean, and strewed with roses: *All her paths are peace.* There is not only peace in the end, but peace in the way; not only in the way of religion in general, but in the particular paths of that way, in all her paths, all the several acts, instances, and duties of it. One does not embitter what the other sweetens, as it is with the allays of this world; but they are all peace, not only sweet, but safe. The saints enter into peace on this side heaven, and enjoy a present sabbatism.

3. It is the happiness of paradise (*v.* 18): *She is a tree of life.* True grace is that to the soul which the tree of life would have been, from which our first parents were shut out for eating of the forbidden tree. It is a seed of immortality, a *well of living waters, springing up to life eternal.* It is an earnest of the New Jerusalem, in the midst of which is *the tree of life,* Rev. xxii. 2; ii. 7. Those that feed and feast on this heavenly wisdom shall not only be cured by it of every fatal malady, but shall find an antidote against age and death; they shall *eat and live for ever.*

4. It is a participation of the happiness of God himself, for wisdom is his everlasting glory and blessedness, *v.* 19, 20. This should make us in love with the wisdom and understanding which God gives, that *the Lord by wisdom founded the earth,* so that it cannot be removed, nor can ever fail of answering all the ends of its creation, to which it is admirably and unexceptionably fitted. *By understanding he has* likewise *established the heavens* and directed all the motions of them in the best manner. The heavenly bodies are vast, yet there is no flaw in them—numerous, yet no disorder in them—the motion rapid, yet no wear or tear; the depths of the sea are broken up, and thence come the waters be-

neath the firmament, and *the clouds drop down the dews*, the waters from above the firmament, and all this by the divine wisdom and knowledge ; therefore *happy is the man that finds wisdom*, for he will thereby be *thoroughly furnished for every good word and work.* Christ is that Wisdom, by whom the worlds were made and still consist ; happy therefore are those to whom he is *made of God wisdom*, for he has wherewithal to make good all the foregoing promises of long life, riches, and honour ; for all the wealth of heaven, earth, and seas, is his.

21 My son, let not them depart from thine eyes : keep sound wisdom and discretion : 22 So shall they be life unto thy soul, and grace to thy neck. 23 Then shalt thou walk in thy way safely, and thy foot shall not stumble. 24 When thou liest down, thou shalt not be afraid : yea, thou shalt lie down, and thy sleep shall be sweet. 25 Be not afraid of sudden fear, neither of the desolation of the wicked, when it cometh. 26 For the LORD shall be thy confidence, and shall keep thy foot from being taken.

Solomon, having pronounced those happy who not only lay hold on wisdom, but retain her, here exhorts us therefore to retain her, assuring us that we ourselves shall have the comfort of doing so.

I. The exhortation is, to have religion's rules always in view and always at heart, *v.* 21. 1. To have them always in view: " *My son, let them not depart from thy eyes ;* let not thy eyes ever depart from them to wander after vanity. Have them always in mind, and do not forget them ; be ever and anon thinking of them, and conversing with them, and never imagine that thou hast looked upon them long enough and that it is time now to lay them by ; but, as long as thou livest, keep up and cultivate thy acquaintance with them." He who learns to write must always have his eye upon his copy, and not let that be out of his sight ; and to the words of wisdom must those, in like manner, have a constant respect, who will walk circumspectly. 2. To have them always at heart ; for it is in that treasury, the hidden man of the heart, that we must *keep sound wisdom and discretion*, keep to the principles of it and keep in the ways of it. It is wealth that is worth keeping.

II. The argument to enforce this exhortation is taken from the unspeakable advantage which wisdom, thus kept, will be of to us. 1. In respect of strength and satisfaction : " It will be *life to thy soul* (*v.* 22) ; it will quicken thee to thy duty when thou beginnest to be slothful and remiss ; it will revive thee under thy troubles when thou beginnest to droop and despond. It will be thy spiritual life, an earnest of life eternal." Life

to the soul is life indeed. 2. In respect of honour and reputation : It shall be *grace to thy neck*, as a chain of gold, or a jewel. *Grace to thy jaws* (so the word is), grateful to thy *taste and relish* (so some) ; it shall infuse *grace into all thou sayest* (so others), shall furnish thee with acceptable words, which shall gain thee credit. 3. In respect of safety and security. This he insists upon in four verses, the scope of which is to show that *the effect of righteousness* (which is the same with *wisdom* here) is *quietness and assurance for ever*, Isa. xxxii. 17. Good people are taken under God's special protection, and therein they may have an entire satisfaction. They are safe and may be easy, (1.) In their motions by day, *v.* 23. If our religion be our companion, it will be our convoy : " *Then shalt thou walk in thy way safely.* The natural life, and all that belongs to it, shall be under the protection of God's providence ; the spiritual life, and all its interests, are under the protection of his grace ; so that thou shalt be kept from falling into sin or trouble." Wisdom will direct us into, and keep us in, the safe way, as far as may be, from temptation, and will enable us to walk in it with a holy security. The way of duty is the way of safety. " We are in danger of falling, but wisdom will keep thee, that *thy foot shall not stumble* at those things which are an offence and overthrow to many, but which thou shalt know how to get over." (2.) In their rest by night, *v.* 24. In our retirements we lie exposed and are most subject to frights. " But keep up communion with God, and keep a good conscience, and then *when thou liest down thou shalt not be afraid* of fire, or thieves, or spectres, or any of the terrors of darkness, knowing that when we, and all our friends, are asleep, yet *he that keeps Israel* and every true-born Israelite *neither slumbers nor sleeps*, and to him thou hast committed thyself and taken shelter under the shadow of his wings. *Thou shalt lie down*, and not need to sit up to keep guard ; having lain down, thou shalt sleep, and not have thy eyes held waking by care and fear ; and *thy sleep shall be sweet* and refreshing to thee, being not disturbed by any alarms from without or from within," Ps. iv. 8 ; cxvi. 7. The way to have a good night is to keep a good conscience ; and the sleep, as of the labouring man, so of the wise and godly man, is sweet. (3.) In their greatest straits and dangers. Integrity and uprightness will preserve us, so that we need *not be afraid of sudden fear, v.* 25. The harms that surprise us, unthought of, giving us no time to arm ourselves by consideration, are most likely to put us into confusion. But let not the wise and good man forget himself, and then he will not give way to any fear that has torment, be the alarm ever so sudden. Let him not fear the *desolation of the wicked, when it comes*, that is, [1.] The desolation which the wicked ones make of religion and the religious ;

though it comes, and seems to be just at the door, yet be not afraid of it; for, though God may make use of the wicked as instruments of his people's correction, yet he will never suffer them to be the authors of their desolation. Or rather, [2.] The desolation which wicked men will be brought into in a moment. It will come, and timorous saints may be apprehensive that they shall be involved in it; but let this be their comfort, that though judgments lay waste generally, at least promiscuously, yet God knows who are his and how to separate between the precious and the vile. Therefore be not afraid of that which appears most formidable, for (v. 26) "*the Lord shall be* not only thy protector to keep thee safe, but *thy confidence* to keep thee secure, so that thy foot *shall not be taken* by thy enemies nor ensnared by thy own fears." God has engaged to keep the feet of his saints.

27 Withhold not good from them to whom it is due, when it is in the power of thine hand to do *it*. 28 Say not unto thy neighbour, Go, and come again, and to morrow I will give; when thou hast it by thee. 29 Devise not evil against thy neighbour, seeing he dwelleth securely by thee. 30 Strive not with a man without cause, if he have done thee no harm. 31 Envy thou not the oppressor, and choose none of his ways. 32 For the froward *is* abomination to the LORD: but his secret *is* with the righteous. 33 The curse of the LORD *is* in the house of the wicked: but he blesseth the habitation of the just. 34 Surely he scorneth the scorners: but he giveth grace unto the lowly. 35 The wise shall inherit glory: but shame shall be the promotion of fools.

True wisdom consists in the due discharge of our duty towards man, as well as towards God, in honesty as well as piety, and therefore we have here divers excellent precepts of wisdom which relate to our neighbour.

I. We must render to all their due, both in justice and charity, and not delay to do it (v. 27, 28): "*Withhold not good from those to whom it is due* (either for want of love to them or through too much love to thy money) *when it is in the power of thy hand to do it*, for, if it be not, it cannot be expected; but it was thy great fault if thou didst, by thy extravagances, disable thyself to do justly and show mercy, and it ought to be the greatest of thy griefs if God had disabled thee, not so much that thou art straitened in thy own comforts and conveniences as that thou hast not wherewithal to give to those to whom it is due." *Withhold* it not; this implies that it is called for and expected, but that the

hand is drawn in and the *bowels of compassion are shut up*. We must not hinder others from doing it, nor be ourselves backward to it. "If thou hast it by thee to-day, hast it in the power of thy hand, say not to thy neighbour, *Go thy way for this time*, and come at a more convenient season, and I will then see what will be done; *to-morrow I will give;* whereas thou art not sure that thou shalt live till to-morrow, or that to-morrow thou shalt *have it by thee*. Be not thus loth to part with thy money upon a good account. Make not excuses to shift off a duty that must be done, nor delight to keep thy neighbour in pain and in suspense, nor to show the authority which the giver has over the beggar; but readily and cheerfully, and from a principle of conscience towards God, give good to *those to whom it is due*," to the *lords and owners of it* (so the word is), to those who upon any account are entitled to it. This requires us, 1. To pay our just debts without fraud, covin, or delay. 2. To give wages to those who have earned them. 3. To provide for our relations, and those that have dependence on us, for to them it is due. 4. To render dues both to church and state, magistrates and ministers. 5. To be ready to all acts of friendship and humanity, and in every thing to be neighbourly; for these are things that are due by the law of doing as we would be done by. 6. To be charitable to the poor and necessitous. If others want the necessary supports of life, and we have wherewithal to supply them, we must look upon it as due to them and not withhold it. Alms are called *righteousness* because they are a debt to the poor, and a debt which we must not defer to pay, *Bis dat, qui cito dat*—He gives twice who gives speedily.

II. We must never design any hurt or harm to any body (v. 29): "*Devise not evil against thy neighbour;* do not contrive how to do him an ill-turn undiscovered, to prejudice him in his body, goods, or good name, and the rather because *he dwells securely by thee*, and, having given thee no provocation, entertains no jealousy or suspicion of thee, and therefore is off his guard." It is against the laws both of honour and friendship to do a man an ill-turn and give him no warning *Cursed be he that smites his neighbour secretly*. It is a most base ungrateful thing, if our neighbours have a good opinion of us, that we will do them no harm, and we thence take advantage to cheat and injure them.

III. We must not be quarrelsome and litigious (v. 30): "Do not *strive with a man without cause;* contend not for that which thou hast no title to; resent not that as a provocation which peradventure was but an oversight. Never trouble thy neighbour with frivolous complaints and accusations, or vexatious law-suits, when either there is no harm done thee or none worth speaking of, or thou mightest right thyself in a friendly way." Law must be the last refuge; for it is not only our duty, but our interest, *as much as in us lies, to live peaceably with all men.* When accounts are balanced, it will be found there is little got by striving.

IV. We must not envy the prosperity of evil-doers, *v.* 31. This caution is the same with that which is so much insisted on, Ps. xxxvii. "*Envy not the oppressor;* though he be rich and great, though he live in ease and pleasure, and make all about him to stand in awe of him, yet do not think him a happy man, nor wish thyself in his condition. *Choose none of his ways;* do not imitate him, nor take the courses he takes to enrich himself. Never think of doing as he does, though thou wert sure to get by it all that he has, for it would be dearly bought." Now, to show what little reason saints have to envy sinners, Solomon here, in the last four verses of the chapter, compares the condition of sinners and saints together (as his father David had done, Ps. xxxvii.), sets the one over against the other, that we may see how happy the saints are, though they be oppressed, and how miserable the wicked are, though they be oppressors. Men are to be judged of as they stand with God, and as he judges of them, not as they stand in the world's books. Those are in the right who are of God's mind; and, if we be of his mind, we shall see, whatever pretence one sinner may have to envy another, that saints are so happy themselves that they have no reason at all to envy any sinner, though his condition be ever so prosperous. For, 1. Sinners are hated of God, but saints are beloved, *v.* 32. The froward sinners, who are continually going from-ward him, whose lives are a perverse contradiction to his will, are *abomination to the Lord.* He that hates nothing that he has made yet abhors those who have thus marred themselves; they are not only abominable in his sight, but an abomination. The righteous therefore have no reason to envy them, for they have his secret with them; they are his favourites; he has that communion with them which is a secret to the world and in which they have a joy that a stranger does not intermeddle with; he communicates to them the secret tokens of his love; his covenant is with them; they know his mind, and the meanings and intentions of his providence, better than others can. *Shall I hide from Abraham the thing that I do?* 2. Sinners are under the curse of God, they and their houses; saints are under his blessing, they and their habitation, *v.* 33. The wicked has a house, a strong and stately dwelling perhaps, but *the curse of the Lord* is upon it, it is *in it,* and, though the affairs of the family may prosper, yet the very blessings are cursed, Mal. ii. 2. There is *leanness in the soul,* when the body is fed to the full, Ps. cvi. 15. The curse may work silently and slowly; but it is as a fretting leprosy; it will consume the *timber thereof and the stones thereof,* Zech. v. 4; Hab. ii. 11. The just have a habitation, a poor cottage (the word

is used for **sheep-cotes**), a very mean dwelling; but God blesses it; he is continually blessing it, from the beginning of the year to the end of it. The curse or blessing of God is upon the house according as the inhabitants are wicked or godly; and it is certain that a blessed family, though poor, has no reason to envy a cursed family, though rich. 3. God puts contempt upon sinners, but shows respect to saints, *v.* 34. (1.) Those who exalt themselves shall certainly be abased: *Surely he scorns the scorners.* Those who scorn to submit to the discipline of religion, scorn to take God's yoke upon them, scorn to be beholden to his grace, who scoff at godliness and godly people, and take a pleasure in bantering and exposing them, God will scorn them, and lay them open to scorn before all the world. He despises their impotent malice, *sits in heaven and laughs at them,* Ps. ii. 4. He retaliates upon them (Ps. xviii. 26); he *resists the proud.* (2.) Those who humble themselves shall be exalted, for *he gives grace to the lowly;* he works that in them which puts honour upon them and for which they are *accepted of God and approved of men.* Those who patiently bear contempt from scornful men shall have respect from God and all good men, and then they have no reason to envy the scorners or to choose their ways. 4. The end of sinners will be everlasting shame, the end of saints endless honour, *v.* 35. (1.) Saints are wise men, and act wisely for themselves; for though their religion now wraps them up in obscurity, and lays them open to reproach, yet they are sure to inherit glory at last, the far more exceeding and eternal weight of glory. They shall have it, and have it by inheritance, the sweetest and surest tenure. God gives them grace (*v.* 34), and therefore they shall inherit glory, for grace is glory, 2 Cor. iii. 18. It is glory begun, the earnest of it, Ps. lxxxiv. 11. (2.) Sinners are fools, for they are not only preparing disgrace for themselves, but at the same time flattering themselves with a prospect of honour, as if they only took the way to be great. Their end will manifest their folly: *Shame shall be their promotion.* And it will be so much the more their punishment as it will come instead of their promotion; it will be all the promotion they must ever expect, that God will be glorified in their everlasting confusion

CHAP. IV.

HEAR, ye children, the instruction of a father, and attend to know understanding. 2 For I give you good doctrine, forsake ye not my law. 3 For I was my father's son, tender and only *beloved* in the sight of my mother. 4 He taught me also, and said unto me, Let thine heart retain my words : keep my commandments, and live. 5 Get wisdom, get understanding : forget *it* not ; neither decline from the words of my mouth. 6 Forsake her not, and she shall preserve thee : love her, and she shall keep thee. 7 Wisdom *is* the principal thing ; *therefore* get wisdom : and with all thy getting get understanding. 8 Exalt her, and she shall promote thee : she shall bring thee to honour, when thou dost embrace her. 9 She shall give to thine head an ornament of grace : a crown of glory shall she deliver to thee. 10 Hear, O my son, and receive my sayings ; and the years of thy life shall be many. 11 I have taught thee in the way of wisdom ; I have led thee in right paths. 12 When thou goest, thy steps shall not be straitened ; and when thou runnest, thou shalt not stumble. 13 Take fast hold of instruction ; let *her* not go : keep her ; for she *is* thy life.

Here we have,

I. The invitation which Solomon gives to his children to come and receive instruction from him (*v.* 1, 2): *Hear, you children, the instruction of a father.* That is, 1. "Let my own children, in the first place, receive and give good heed to those instructions which I set down for the use of others also." Note, Magistrates and ministers, who are entrusted with the direction of larger societies, are concerned to take a more than ordinary care for the good instruction of their own families ; from this duty their public work will by no means excuse them. This charity must begin at home, though it must not end there ; for he that has not his children in subjection with all gravity, and does not take pains in their good education, how shall he do his duty as he ought *to the church of God?* 1 Tim. iii. 4, 5. The children of those that are eminent for wisdom and public usefulness ought to improve in knowledge and grace in proportion to the advantages they derive from their relation to such parents. Yet it may be observed, to save both the credit and the comfort of those parents whose children do not answer the hopes that arose from their education, that Rehoboam, the

son of Solomon, was far from being either one of the wisest or one of the best. We have reason to think that thousands have got more good by Solomon's proverbs than his own son did, to whom they seem to have been dedicated. 2. Let all young people, in the days of their childhood and youth, take pains to get knowledge and grace, for that is their learning age, and then their minds are formed and seasoned. He does not say, *My* children, but *You* children. We read but of one son that Solomon had of his own ; but (would you think it?) he is willing to set up for a schoolmaster, and to teach other people's children ! for at that age there is most hope of success ; the branch is easily bent when it is young and tender. 3. Let all that would receive instruction come with the disposition of children, though they be grown persons. Let all prejudices be laid aside, and the mind be as white paper. Let them be dutiful, tractable, and self-diffident, and take the word as the word of a father, which comes both with authority and with affection. We must see it coming from God as *our Father in heaven*, to whom we pray, from whom we expect blessings, the Father of our spirits, to whom we ought to be in subjection, that we may live. We must look upon our teachers as our fathers, who love us and seek our welfare ; and therefore though the instruction carry in it reproof and correction, for so the word signifies, yet we must bid it welcome. Now, (1.) To recommend it to us, we are told, not only that it is the *instruction of a father*, but that it is *understanding*, and therefore should be welcome to intelligent creatures. Religion has reason on its side, and we are taught it by fair reasoning. It is a law indeed (*v.* 2), but that law is founded upon doctrine, upon unquestionable principles of truth, upon *good doctrine*, which is not only faithful, but worthy of all acceptation. If we admit the doctrine, we cannot but submit to the law. (2.) To rivet it in us, we are directed to receive it as a gift, to attend to it with all diligence, to attend so as to know it, for otherwise we cannot do it, and not to forsake it by disowning the doctrine or disobeying the law.

II. The instructions he gives them. Observe,

1. How he came by these instructions ; he had them from his parents, and teaches his children the same that they taught him, *v.* 3, 4. Observe, (1.) His parents loved him, and therefore taught him : *I was my father's son.* David had many sons, but Solomon was his son *indeed*, as Isaac is called (Gen. xvii. 19) and for the same reason, because on him the covenant was entailed. He was his father's darling, above any of his children. God had a special kindness for Solomon (the prophet called him *Jedidiah*, because the Lord loved him, 2 Sam. xii. 25), and for that reason David had a special kindness for him, for he was a man after God's own heart. If

parents may ever love one child better than another, it must not be till it plainly appears that God does so. He was *tender, and only beloved, in the sight of his mother.* Surely there was a manifest reason for making such a distinction when both the parents made it. Now we see how they showed their love; they catechised him, kept him to his book, and held him to a strict discipline. Though he was a prince, and heir-apparent to the crown, yet they did not let him live at large; nay, therefore they tutored him thus. And perhaps David was the more strict with Solomon in his education because he had seen the ill effects of an undue indulgence in Adonijah, whom he had not *crossed in any thing* (1 Kings i. 6), as also in Absalom. (2.) What his parents taught him he teaches others. Observe, [1.] When Solomon was grown up he not only remembered, but took a pleasure in repeating, the good lessons his parents taught him when he was a child. He did not forget them, so deep were the impressions they made upon him. He was not ashamed of them, such a high value had he for them, nor did he look upon them as the childish things, the mean things, which, when he became a man, a king, he should put away, as a disparagement to him; much less did he repeat them: as some wicked children have done, to ridicule them, and make his companions merry with them, priding himself that he had got clear from grave lessons and restraints. [2.] Though Solomon was a wise man himself, and divinely inspired, yet, when he was to teach wisdom, he did not think it below him to quote his father and to make use of his words. Those that would learn well, and teach well, in religion, must not affect new-found notions and new-coined phrases, so as to look with contempt upon the knowledge and language of their predecessors; if we must keep to the good old way, why should we scorn the good old words? Jer. vi. 16. [3.] Solomon, having been well educated by his parents, thought himself thereby obliged to give his children a good education, the same that his parents had given him; and this is one way in which we must requite our parents for the pains they took with us, even by showing piety at home, 1 Tim. v. 4. They taught us, not only that we might learn ourselves, but that we might teach our children, the good knowledge of God, Ps. lxxviii. 6. And we are false to a trust if we do not; for the sacred deposit of religious doctrine and law was lodged in our hands with a charge to transmit it pure and entire to those that shall *come after us,* 2 Tim. ii. 2. [4.] Solomon enforces his exhortations with the authority of his father David, a man famous in his generation upon all accounts. Be it taken notice of, to the honour of religion, that the wisest and best men in every age have been most zealous, not only for the practice of it themselves, but for the propagating of it to others; and we should therefore *continue in*

the things which we have learned, knowing of whom we have learned them, 2 Tim. iii. 14.

2. What these instructions were, *v.* 4—13.

(1.) By way of precept and exhortation. David, in teaching his son, though he was a child of great capacity and quick apprehension, yet to show that he was in good earnest, and to affect his child the more with what he said, expressed himself with great warmth and importunity, and inculcated the same thing again and again. So children must be taught. Deut. vi. 7, *Thou shalt whet them diligently upon thy children.* David, though he was a man of public business, and had tutors for his son, took all this pains with him himself.

[1.] He recommends to him his Bible and his catechism, as the means, his father's *words* (*v.* 4), the *words of his mouth* (*v.* 5), his *sayings* (*v.* 10), all the good lessons he had taught him; and perhaps he means particularly the book of Psalms, many of which were *Maschils* —*psalms of instruction,* and two of them are expressly said to be *for Solomon.* These, and all his other words, Solomon must have an eye to. *First,* He must *hear and receive them* (*v.* 10), diligently attend to them, and imbibe them, *as the earth drinks in the rain that comes often upon it,* Heb. vi. 7. God thus bespeaks our attention to his word: *Hear, O my son! and receive my sayings. Secondly,* He must *hold fast the form of sound words* which his father gave him (*v.* 4): *Let thy heart retain my words;* and except the word be hid in the heart, lodged in the will and affections, it will not be retained. *Thirdly,* He must govern himself by them: *Keep my commandments,* obey them, and that is the way to increase in the knowledge of them, John vii. 17. *Fourthly,* He must stick to them and abide by them· " *Decline not from the words of my mouth* (*v.* 5), as fearing they will be too great a check upon thee, but *take fast hold of instruction* (*v.* 13), as being resolved to keep thy hold and never let it go. Those that have a good education, though they strive to shake it off, will find it hang about them a great while, and, if it do not, their case is very sad.

[2.] He recommends to him wisdom and understanding as the end to be aimed at in the use of these means; that *wisdom* which is the *principal wisdom,* get that. *Quod caput est sapientiæ eam acquire sapientiam*—*Be sure to mind that branch of wisdom which is the top branch of it,* and that is the *fear of God,* ch. i. 7. Junius and Tremellius. A principle of religion in the heart is the one thing needful; therefore, *First,* Get this *wisdom,* get this *understanding, v.* 5. And again, " *Get wisdom,* and, *with all thy getting, get understanding, v.* 7. Pray for it, take pains for it, give diligence in the use of all appointed means to attain it. *Wait at wisdom's gate,* Prov. viii. 34. Get dominion over thy corruptions, which are thy follies: get possession of wise principles and the habits of wisdom. Get wisdom by experience, get it *above all thy getting;* be more in care and take more pains to get this than to get the wealth of this world; whatever thou forgettest, get this; reckon it a great achievement, and pursue it accordingly." True wisdom is God's gift, and yet we are here commanded to get it, because God gives it to those that labour for it; yet, after all, we must not say, *Our might and the power of our hand have gotten us this wealth. Secondly, Forget her not* (v. 5), *forsake her not* (v. 6), *let her not go* (v. 13), *but keep her.* Those that have got this wisdom must take heed of losing it again by returning to folly: it is indeed a good part, that shall not be *taken from us;* but then we must take heed lest we throw it from us, as those do that forget it first, and let it slip out of their minds, and then forsake it and turn out of its good ways. That good thing which is committed to us we must keep, and not let it drop, through carelessness, nor suffer it to be forced from us, nor suffer ourselves to be wheedled out of it; never let go such a jewel. *Thirdly, Love her* (v. 6), and *embrace her* (v. 8), as worldly men love their wealth and set their hearts upon it. Religion should be very dear to us, dearer than any thing in this world; and, if we cannot reach to be great masters of wisdom, yet let us be true lovers of it; and what grace we have let us embrace it with a sincere affection, as those that admire its beauty. *Fourthly, "Exalt her, v.* 8. Always keep up high thoughts of religion; speak of it with value and veneration, and do all thou canst to bring it into reputation, and maintain the credit of it among men. Concur with God in his purpose, which is to magnify the law and make it honourable, and do what thou canst to serve that purpose." Let *Wisdom's* children not only justify her, but magnify her, and prefer her before that which is dearest to them in this world. In honouring those that fear the Lord, though they are low in the world, and in regarding a *poor wise man,* we exalt wisdom.

(2.) By way of motive and inducement thus to labour for wisdom, and submit to the guidance of it, consider, [1.] It is the main matter, and that which ought to be the chief and continual care of every man in this life (v. 7): *Wisdom is the principal thing:* other things which we are solicitous to get and keep are nothing to it. It is the *whole of man,* Eccl. xii. 13. It is that which recommends us to God, which beautifies the soul, which enables us to answer the end of our creation, to live to some good purpose in the world, and to get to heaven at last; and therefore it is the principal thing. [2.] It has reason and equity on its side (v. 11): "*I have taught thee in the way of wisdom,* and so it will be found to be at last. *I have led thee,* not in the crooked ways of carnal policy, which does wrong under colour of wisdom, but *in right paths,* agreeable to the eternal rules and reasons of good and evil." The rectitude of the divine nature appears in the

rectitude of all the divine laws. Observe, David not only taught his son by good instructions, but led him both by a good example and by applying general instructions to particular cases; so that nothing was wanting on his part to make him wise. [3.] It would be much for his own advantage: "If thou be wise and good, thou shalt be so for thyself." First, "It will be thy life, thy comfort, thy happiness; it is what thou canst not live without:" *Keep my commandments and live, v.* 4. That of our Saviour agrees with this, *If thou wilt enter into life, keep the commandments,* Matt. xix. 17. It is upon pain of death, eternal death, and in prospect of life, eternal life, that we are required to be religious. "Receive wisdom's sayings, *and the years of thy life shall be many* (v. 10), as many in this world as Infinite Wisdom sees fit, and in the other world thou shalt live that life the years of which shall never be numbered. *Keep her* therefore, whatever it cost thee, *for she is thy life, v.* 13. All thy satisfaction will be found in this;" and a soul without true wisdom and grace is really a dead soul. *Secondly,* "It will be thy guard and guide, thy convoy and conductor, through all the dangers and difficulties of thy journey through this wilderness. Love wisdom, and cleave to her, and she shall *preserve thee, she shall keep thee* (v. 6) from sin, the worst of evils, the worst of enemies; she shall keep thee from hurting thyself, and then none else can hurt thee." As we say, "Keep thy shop, and thy shop will keep thee;" so, "Keep thy wisdom, and thy wisdom will keep thee." It will keep us from straits and stumbling-blocks in the management of ourselves and our affairs, v. 12. 1. That our steps be not straitened when we go, that we bring not ourselves into such straits as David was in, 2 Sam. xxiv. 14. Those that make God's word their rule shall walk at liberty, and be at ease in themselves. 2. That our feet do not stumble when we run. If wise and good men be put upon sudden resolves, the certain rule of God's word which they go by will keep them even then from stumbling upon any thing that may be pernicious. Integrity and uprightness will preserve us. *Thirdly,* "It will be thy honour and reputation (v. 8): *Exalt* wisdom (do thou but show thy good-will to her advancement) and though she needs not thy service she will abundantly recompense it, *she shall promote thee, she shall bring thee to honour.*" Solomon was to be a king, but his wisdom and virtue would be more his honour than his crown or purple; it was that for which all his neighbours had him so much in veneration; and no doubt, in his reign and David's, wise and good men stood fairest for preferment. However, religion will, first or last, bring all those *to honour* that cordially *embrace her;* they shall be accepted of God, respected by all wise men, owned in the great day, and shall inherit everlasting glory. This he insists on (v. 9): "*She shall give to thy head an orna-*

ment of grace in this world, shall recommend thee both to God and man, and in the other world *a crown of glory shall she deliver to thee*, a crown that shall never totter, a crown of glory that shall never wither." That is the true honour which attends religion. *Nobilitas sola est atque unica virtus—Virtue is the only nobility!* David having thus recommended wisdom to his son, no marvel that when God bade him ask what he would he prayed, Lord, *give me a wise and an understanding heart.* We should make it appear by our prayers how well we are taught.

14 Enter not into the path of the wicked, and go not in the way of evil men. 15 Avoid it, pass not by it, turn from it, and pass away. 16 For they sleep not, except they have done mischief; and their sleep is taken away, unless they cause *some* to fall. 17 For they eat the bread of wickedness, and drink the wine of violence. 18 But the path of the just *is* as the shining light, that shineth more and more unto the perfect day. 19 The way of the wicked *is* as darkness : they know not at what they stumble.

Some make David's instructions to Solomon, which began *v.* 4, to continue to the end of the chapter ; nay, some continue them to the end of the ninth chapter ; but it is more probable that Solomon begins here again, if not sooner. In these verses, having exhorted us to walk in the paths of wisdom, he cautions us against the path of the wicked. 1. We must take heed of the ways of sin and avoid them, every thing that looks like sin and leads to it. 2. In order to this we must keep out of the ways of sinners, and have no fellowship with them. For fear of falling into wicked courses, we must shun wicked company. Here is,

I. The caution itself, *v.* 14, 15. 1. We must take heed of falling in with sin and sinners : *Enter not into the paths of the wicked.* Our teacher, having like a faithful guide shown us the *right paths* (*v.* 11), here warns us of the by-paths into which we are in danger of being drawn aside. Those that have been well educated, and trained up in the way they should go, let them never turn aside into the way they should not go ; let them not so much as enter into it, no, not to make trial of it, lest it prove a dangerous experiment and difficult to retreat with safety. " Venture not into the company of those that are infected with the plague, no, not though thou think thyself guarded with an antidote." 2. If at any time we are inveigled into an evil way, we must hasten out of it. " If, ere thou wast aware, thou didst enter in at the gate, because it was wide, *go not on in the way of evil men.* As soon as thou art made sensible of thy mis-

take, retire immediately, take not a step more, stay not a minute longer, in the way that certainly leads to destruction." 3. We must dread and detest the ways of sin and sinners, and decline them with the utmost care imaginable. *" The way of evil men* may seem a pleasant way and sociable, and the nearest way to the compassing of some secular end we may have in view ; but it is an evil way, and will end ill, and therefore if thou love thy God and thy soul *avoid it, pass not by it,* that thou mayest not be tempted to enter into it ; and, if thou find thyself near it, *turn from it and pass away,* and get as far off it as thou canst." The manner of expression intimates the imminent danger we are in, the need we have of this caution, and the great importance of it, and that our watchmen are, or should be, in good earnest, in giving us warning. It intimates likewise at what a distance we should keep from sin and sinners ; he does not say, Keep at a due distance, but at a great distance, the further the better ; never think you can get far enough from it. *Escape for thy life : look not behind thee.*

II. The reasons to enforce this caution.

1. " Consider the character of the men whose way thou art warned to shun." They are mischievous men (*v.* 16, 17) ; they not only care not what hurt they do to those that stand in their way, but it is their business to do mischief, and their delight, purely for mischief-sake. They are continually designing and endeavouring to *cause some to fall,* to ruin them body and soul. Wickedness and malice are in their nature, and violence is in all their actions. They are spiteful in the highest degree ; for, (1.) Mischief is rest and sleep to them. As much satisfaction as a covetous man has when he has got money, an ambitious man when he has got preferment, and a good man when he has done good, so much have they when they have said or done that which is injurious and ill-natured ; and they are extremely uneasy if they cannot get their envy and revenge gratified, as Haman, to whom every thing was unpleasant as long as Mordecai was unhanged. It intimates likewise how restless and unwearied they are in their mischievous pursuits ; they will rather be deprived of sleep than of the pleasure of being vexatious. (2.) Mischief is meat and drink to them ; they feed and feast upon it. *They eat the bread of the wickedness (they eat up my people as they eat bread,* Ps. xiv. 4) *and drink the wine of violence* (*v.* 17), *drink iniquity like water,* Job. xv. 16. All they eat and drink is got by rapine and oppression. Do wicked men think the time lost in which they are not doing hurt? Let good men make it as much their business and delight to do good. *Amici, diem perdidi—Friends, I have lost a day.* And let all that are wise, and wish well to themselves, avoid the society of the wicked ; for, [1.] It is very scandalous ; for there is no disposition of mind that is a greater re-

proach to human nature, a greater enemy to human society, a bolder defiance to God and conscience, that has more of the devil's image in it, or is more serviceable to his interests, than a delight to do mischief and to vex, and hurt, and ruin every body. [2.] It is very dangerous. "Shun those that delight to do mischief as thou tenderest thy own safety; for, whatever friendship they may pretend, one time or other they will do thee mischief; thou wilt ruin thyself if thou dost concur with them (*ch.* i. 18) and they will ruin thee if thou dost not."

2. "Consider the character of the way itself which thou art warned to shun, compared with the right way which thou art invited to walk in."

(1.) The way of righteousness is light (*v.* 18): *The path of the just,* which they have chosen, and in which they walk, *is as light; the light shines on their ways* (Job xxii. 28) and makes them both safe and pleasant. Christ is *their way* and he is *the light.* They are guided by the word of God and that is a *light to their feet;* they themselves are *light in the Lord* and they *walk in the light as he is in the light.* [1.] It is a *shining light.* Their way shines to themselves in the joy and comfort of it; it shines before others in the lustre and honour of it; *it shines before men, who see their good works,* Matt. v. 16. They go on in their way with a holy security and serenity of mind, as those that *walk in the light.* It is as the morning-light, which *shines out of obscurity* (Isa. lviii. 8, 10) and puts an end to the *works of darkness.* [2.] It is a growing light; it *shines more and more,* not like the light of a meteor, which soon disappears, or that of a candle, which burns dim and burns down, but like that of the rising sun, which goes forward shining, mounts upward shining. Grace, the guide of this way, is growing; *he that has clean hands shall be stronger and stronger.* That joy which is the pleasure of this way, that honour which is the brightness of it, and all that happiness which is indeed its light, shall be still increasing. [3.] It will arrive, in the end, at *the perfect day.* The light of the dayspring will at length be noon-day light, and it is this that the enlightened soul is pressing towards. The saints will not be perfect till they come to heaven, but there they shall themselves *shine as the sun when he goes forth in his strength,* Matt. xiii. 43. Their graces and joys shall be all consummate. Therefore it is our wisdom to keep close to *the path of the just.*

(2.) The *way of* sin *is as darkness, v.* 19. The works he had cautioned us not to have fellowship with are *works of darkness.* What true pleasure and satisfaction can those have who know no pleasure and satisfaction but what they have in doing mischief? What sure guide have those that cast God's word behind them? *The way of the wicked is dark,* and therefore dangerous; for they stumble,

814

and yet *know not at what they stumble.* They fall into sin, but are not aware which way the temptation came by which they were overthrown, and therefore know not how to avoid it the next time. They fall into trouble, but never enquire wherefore God contends with them; they *consider not that they do evil,* nor what will be in the end of it, Ps. lxxxii. 5; Job xviii. 5, 6. This is the way we are directed to shun.

20 My son, attend to my words; incline thine ear unto my sayings. 21 Let them not depart from thine eyes; keep them in the midst of thine heart. 22 For they *are* life unto those that find them, and health to all their flesh. 23 Keep thy heart with all diligence; for out of it *are* the issues of life. 24 Put away from thee a froward mouth, and perverse lips put far from thee. 25 Let thine eyes look right on, and let thine eyelids look straight before thee. 26 Ponder the path of thy feet, and let all thy ways be established. 27 Turn not to the right hand nor to the left: remove thy foot from evil.

Solomon, having warned us not to do evil, here teaches us how to do well. It is not enough for us to shun the occasions of sin, but we must study the methods of duty.

I. We must have a continual regard to the word of God and endeavour that it may be always ready to us.

1. The sayings of wisdom must be our principles by which we must govern ourselves, our monitors to warn us of duty and danger; and therefore, (1.) We must receive them readily: "*Incline thy ear to them* (*v.* 20); humbly bow to them; diligently listen to them." The attentive hearing of the word of God is a good sign of a work of grace begun in the heart and a good means of carrying it on. It is to be hoped that those are resolved to do their duty who are inclined to know it. (2.) We must retain them carefully (*v.* 21); we must lay them before us as our rule: "*Let them not depart from thy eyes;* view them, review them, and in every thing aim to conform to them." We must lodge them within us, as a commanding principle, the influences of which are diffused throughout the whole man: "*Keep them in the midst of thy heart,* as things dear to thee, and which thou art afraid of losing." Let the word of God be written in the heart, and that which is written there will remain.

2. The reason why we must thus make much of the words of wisdom is because they will be both food and physic to us, like *the tree of life,* Rev. xxii. 2; Ezek. xlvii. 12. Those that seek and find them, find and keep them, shall find in them, (1.) Food: *For they*

are life unto those that find them, v. 22. As the spiritual life was begun by the word as the instrument of it, so by the same word it is still nourished and maintained. We could not live without it; we may by faith live upon it. (2.) Physic. They are *health to all their flesh,* to the whole man, both body and soul; they help to keep both in good plight. They are *health to all flesh,* so the LXX. There is enough to cure all the diseases of this distempered world. They are *a medicine to all their flesh* (so the word is), to all their corruptions, for they are called flesh, to all their grievances, which are as thorns in the flesh. There is in the word of God a proper remedy for all our spiritual maladies.

II. We must keep a watchful eye and a strict hand upon all the motions of our inward man, *v.* 23. Here is, 1. A great duty required by the laws of wisdom, and in order to our getting and preserving wisdom: *Keep thy heart with all diligence.* God, who gave us these souls, gave us a strict charge with them: Man, woman, *keep thy heart; take heed to thy spirit,* Deut. iv. 9. We must maintain a holy jealousy of ourselves, and set a strict guard, accordingly, upon all the avenues of the soul; keep our hearts from doing hurt and getting hurt, from being defiled by sin and disturbed by trouble; keep them as our jewel, as our vineyard; keep a conscience void of offence; keep out bad thoughts; keep up good thoughts; keep the affections upon right objects and in due bounds. *Keep them with all keepings* (so the word is); there are many ways of keeping things—by care, by strength, by calling in help, and we must use them all in keeping our hearts; and all little enough, so deceitful are they, Jer. xvii. 9. Or *above all keepings:* we must keep our hearts with more care and diligence than we keep any thing else. We must keep our eyes (Job xxxi. 1), keep our tongues (Ps. xxxiv. 13), keep our feet (Eccl. v. 1), but, above all, keep our hearts. 2. A good reason given for this care, because *out of it are the issues of life.* Out of a heart well kept will flow living issues, good products, to the glory of God and the edification of others. Or, in general, all the actions of the life flow from the heart, and therefore keeping that is making the tree good and healing the springs. Our lives will be regular or irregular, comfortable or uncomfortable, according as our hearts are kept or neglected.

III. We must set a *watch before the door of our lips,* that we offend not with our tongue (*v.* 24): *Put away from thee a froward mouth and perverse lips.* Our hearts being naturally corrupt, out of them a great deal of corrupt communication is apt to come, and therefore we must conceive a great dread and detestation of all manner of evil words, cursing, swearing, lying, slandering, brawling, filthiness, and foolish talking, all which come

from a *froward mouth and perverse lips,* that will not be governed either by reason or religion, but contradict both, and which are as unsightly and ill-favoured before God as a crooked distorted mouth drawn awry is before men. All manner of tongue sins, we must, by constant watchfulness and stedfast resolution, *put from us,* put *far from us,* abstaining from all words that have an appearance of evil and fearing to learn any such words.

IV. We must make a covenant with our eyes: "Let them *look right on and straight before thee, v.* 25. Let the eye be fixed and not wandering; let it not rove after every thing that presents itself, for then it will be diverted from good and ensnared in evil. Turn it from beholding vanity; let thy eye be single and not divided; let thy intentions be sincere and uniform, and look not asquint at any by-end." We must keep our eye upon our Master, and be careful to approve ourselves to him; keep our eye upon our rule, and conform to that; keep our eye upon our mark, the *prize of the high calling,* and direct all towards that. *Oculum in metam—The eye upon the goal.*

V. We must act considerately in all we do (*v.* 26): *Ponder the path of thy feet, weigh it* (so the word is); "put the word of God in one scale, and what thou hast done, or art about to do, in the other, and see how they agree; be nice and critical in examining whether thy way be good before the Lord and whether it will end well." We must consider our past ways and examine what we have done, and our present ways, what we are doing, whither we are going, and *see that we walk circumspectly.* It concerns us to consider what are the duties and what the difficulties, what are the advantages and what the dangers, of our way, that we may act accordingly. "Do nothing rashly."

VI. We must act with steadiness, caution, and consistency: " *Let all thy ways be established* (*v.* 26) and be not unstable in them, as the double-minded man is; halt not between two, but go on in an even uniform course of obedience; *turn not to the right hand nor to the left,* for there are errors on both hands, and Satan gains his point if he prevails to draw us aside either way. Be very careful to *remove thy foot from evil;* take heed of extremes, for in them there is evil, and *let thy eyes look right on,* that thou mayest keep the golden mean." Those that would approve themselves wise must always be watchful.

CHAP. V.

The scope of this chapter is much the same with that of ch. ii. To write the same things, in other words, ought not to be grievous, for it is safe, Phil. iii. 1. Here is, I. An exhortation to get acquaintance with and submit to the laws of wisdom in general, ver. 2. II. A particular caution against the sin of whoredom, ver. 3—14. III. Remedies prescribed against that sin. 1. Conjugal love, ver. 15—20. 2. A regard to God's omniscience, ver. 21. 3. A dread of the miserable end of wicked people, ver. 22, 23. And all little enough to arm young people against those fleshly lusts which war against the soul.

M Y son, attend unto my wisdom, *and* bow thine ear to my understanding: 2 That thou mayest regard discretion, and *that* thy lips may keep knowledge. 3 For the lips of a strange woman drop *as* a honeycomb, and her mouth *is* smoother than oil: 4 But her end is bitter as wormwood, sharp as a twoedged sword. 5 Her feet go down to death; her steps take hold on hell. 6 Lest thou shouldest ponder the path of life, her ways are moveable, *that* thou canst not know *them*. 7 Hear me now therefore, O ye children, and depart not from the words of my mouth. 8 Remove thy way far from her, and come not nigh the door of her house: 9 Lest thou give thine honour unto others, and thy years unto the cruel: 10 Lest strangers be filled with thy wealth; and thy labours *be* in the house of a stranger; 11 And thou mourn at the last, when thy flesh and thy body are consumed, 12 And say, How have I hated instruction, and my heart despised reproof; 13 And have not obeyed the voice of my teachers, nor inclined mine ear to them that instructed me! 14 I was almost in all evil in the midst of the congregation and assembly.

Here we have,

I. A solemn preface, to introduce the caution which follows, v. 1, 2. Solomon here addresses himself to his son, that is, to all young men, as unto his children, whom he has an affection for and some influence upon. In God's name, he demands attention; for he writes by divine inspiration, and is a prophet, though he begins not with, *Thus saith the Lord.* "*Attend, and bow thy ear;* not only hear what is said, and read what is written, but apply thy mind to it and consider it diligently." To gain attention he urges, 1. The excellency of his discourse: "It is *my wisdom, my understanding;* if I undertake to teach thee wisdom I cannot prescribe any thing to be more properly called so; moral philosophy is my philosophy, and that which is to be learned in my school." 2. The usefulness of it: "Attend to what I say," (1.) "That thou mayest act wisely—*that thou mayest regard discretion.*" Solomon's lectures are not designed to fill our heads with notions, with matters of nice speculation, or doubtful disputation, but to guide us in the government of ourselves, that we may act prudently, so as becomes us and so as will be for our true interest. (2.) "That thou mayest speak wisely—*that thy lips may keep knowledge,* and thou mayest have it ready
816

at thy tongue's end" (as we say), "for the benefit of those with whom thou dost converse." The priest's lips are said to *keep knowledge* (Mal. ii. 7); but those that are ready and mighty in the scriptures may not only in their devotions, but in their discourses, be spiritual priests.

II. The caution itself, and that is to abstain from fleshly lusts, from adultery, fornication, and all uncleanness. Some apply this figuratively, and by the adulterous woman here understand idolatry, or false doctrine, which tends to debauch men's minds and manners, or the sensual appetite, to which it may as fitly as any thing be applied; but the primary scope of it is plainly to warn us against seventh-commandment sins, which youth is so prone to, the temptations to which are so violent, the examples of which are so many, and which, where admitted, are so destructive to all the seeds of virtue in the soul that it is not strange that Solomon's cautions against it are so very pressing and so often repeated. Solomon here, as a faithful watchman, gives fair warning to all, as they regard their lives and comforts, to dread this sin, for it will certainly be their ruin. Two things we are here warned to take heed of:—

1. That we do not listen to the charms of this sin. It is true *the lips of a strange woman drop as a honey-comb (v. 3);* the pleasures of fleshly lust are very tempting (like the wine that *gives its colour in the cup* and *moves itself aright);* its mouth, the kisses of its mouth, the words of its mouth, are *smoother than oil,* that the poisonous pill may go down glibly and there may be no suspicion of harm in it. But consider, (1.) How fatal the consequences will be. What fruit will the sinner have of his honey and oil when the end will be, [1.] The terrors of conscience: It *is bitter as wormwood, v. 4.* What was luscious in the mouth rises in the stomach and turns sour there; it cuts, in the reflection, like *a two-edged sword;* take it which way you will, it wounds. Solomon could speak by experience, Eccl. vii. 26. [2.] The torments of hell. If some that have been guilty of this sin have repented and been saved, yet the direct tendency of the sin is to destruction of body and soul; the *feet* of it *go down to death,* nay, they *take hold on hell,* to pull it to the sinner, as if the damnation slumbered too long, v. 5. Those that are entangled in this sin should be reminded that there is but a step between them and hell, and that they are ready to drop into it. (2.) Consider how false the charms are. The adulteress flatters and speaks fair, her words are honey and oil, but she will deceive those that hearken to her: *Her ways are movable, that thou canst not know them;* she often changes her disguise, and puts on a great variety of false colours, because, if she be rightly known, she is certainly hated. Proteus-like, she puts on many shapes, that she may keep in with those whom she has a design upon. And

what does she aim at with all this art and management? Nothing but to keep them from *pondering the path of life,* for she knows that, if they once come to do that, she shall certainly lose them. Those are *ignorant of Satan's devices* who do not understand that the great thing he drives at in all his temptations is, [1.] To keep them from choosing the path of life, to prevent them from being religious and from going to heaven, that, being himself shut out from happiness, he may keep them out from it. [2.] In order hereunto, to keep them from pondering the path of life, from considering how reasonable it is that they should walk in that path, and how much it will be for their advantage. Be it observed, to the honour of religion, that it certainly gains its point with all those that will but allow themselves the liberty of a serious thought and will weigh things impartially in an even balance, and that the devil has no way of securing men in his interests but by diverting them with continual amusements of one kind or other from the calm and sober consideration of the *things that belong to their peace.* And uncleanness is a sin that does as much as any thing blind the understanding, sear the conscience, and keep people from pondering the path of life. Whoredom *takes away the heart,* Hos. iv. 11.

2. That we do not approach the borders of this sin, *v.* 7, 8.

(1.) This caution is introduced with a solemn preface : " *Hear me now therefore, O you children !* whoever you are that read or hear these lines, take notice of what I say, and mix faith with it, treasure it up, and *depart not from the words of my mouth,* as those will do that hearken to the words of the strange woman. Do not only receive what I say, for the present merely, but cleave to it, and let it be ready to thee, and of force with thee, when thou art most violently assaulted by the temptation."

(2.) The caution itself is very pressing : " *Remove thy way far from her ;* if thy way should happen to lie near her, and thou shouldst have a fair pretence of being led by business within the reach of her charms, yet change thy way, and alter the course of it, rather than expose thyself to danger; *come not nigh the door of her house ;* go on the other side of the street, nay, go through some other street, though it be about." This intimates, [1.] That we ought to have a very great dread and detestation of the sin. We must fear it as we would a place infected with the plague; we must loathe it as the odour of carrion, that we will not come near. Then we are likely to preserve our purity when we conceive a rooted antipathy to all fleshly lusts. [2.] That we ought industriously to avoid every thing that may be an occasion of this sin or a step towards it. Those that would be kept from harm must keep out of harm's way. Such tinder there is in the corrupt nature that it is madness, upon any pre-

tence whatsoever, to come near the sparks. If we thrust ourselves into temptation, we mocked God when we prayed, *Lead us not into temptation.* [3.] That we ought to be jealous over ourselves with a godly jealousy, and not to be so confident of the strength of our own resolutions as to venture upon the brink of sin, with a promise to ourselves that *hitherto we will come and no further.* [4.] That whatever has become a snare to us and an occasion of sin, though it be as a *right eye* and a *right hand,* we must *pluck it out, cut it off, and cast it from us,* must part with that which is dearest to us rather than hazard our own souls; this is our Saviour's command, Matt. v. 28—30.

(3.) The arguments which Solomon here uses to enforce this caution are taken from the same topic with those before, the many mischiefs which attend this sin. [1.] It blasts the reputation. " Thou wilt *give thy honour unto others* (v. 9) ; thou wilt lose it thyself ; thou wilt put into the hand of each of thy neighbours a stone to throw at thee, for they will all, with good reason, cry shame on thee, will despise thee, and trample on thee, as a foolish man." Whoredom is a sin that makes men contemptible and base, and no man of sense or virtue will care to keep company with one that keeps company with harlots. [2.] It wastes the time, gives *the years,* the years of youth, the flower of men's time, *unto the cruel,* " that base lust of thine, which with the utmost cruelty *wars against the soul,* that base harlot which pretends an affection for thee, but really hunts for the precious life." Those years that should be given to the honour of a gracious God are spent in the service of a cruel sin. [3.] It ruins the estate (v. 10): " *Strangers* will be *filled with thy wealth,* which thou art but entrusted with as a steward for thy family ; and the fruit of *thy labours,* which should be provision for thy own house, will be in *the house of a stranger,* that neither has right to it nor will ever thank thee for it." [4.] It is destructive to the health, and shortens men's days : *Thy flesh and thy body* will be *consumed* by it, *v.* 11. The lusts of uncleanness not only *war against the soul,* which the sinner neglects and is in no care about, but they war against the body too, which he is so indulgent of and is in such care to please and pamper, such deceitful, such foolish, such hurtful lusts are they. Those that give themselves to work uncleanness with greediness waste their strength, throw themselves into weakness, and often have their bodies filled with loathsome distempers, by which the number of their months is cut off in the midst and they fall unpitied sacrifices to a cruel lust. [5.] It will fill the mind with horror, if ever conscience be awakened. " Though thou art merry now, *sporting thyself in thy own deceivings,* yet thou wilt certainly *mourn at the last, v.* 11. Thou art all this while making work for repentance, and laying up matter for vexation and torment in the reflection, when the sin is set before thee in its own colours." Sooner or later it will bring sorrow, either when the soul is humbled and brought to repentance or when the *flesh and body are consumed,* either by sickness, when conscience flies in the sinner's face, or by the grave; when the body is rotting there, the soul is racking in the torments of hell, where the worm dies not, and " *Son, remember,*" is the constant peal. Solomon here brings in the convinced sinner reproaching himself, and aggravating his own folly. He will then most bitterly lament it. *First,* That because he hated to be reformed he therefore hated to be informed, and could not endure either to be taught his duty *(How have I hated* not only the discipline of being instructed, but the *instruction* itself, though all true and good!) or to be told of his faults—*My heart despised reproof, v.* 12. He cannot but own that those who had the charge of him, parents, ministers, had done their part; they had been his teachers; they had instructed him, had given him good counsel and fair warning (*v.* 13); but to his own shame and confusion does he speak it, and therein justifies God in all the miseries that were brought upon him, he had not *obeyed their voice,* for indeed he *never inclined his ear to those that instructed him,* never minded what they said nor admitted the impressions of it. Note, Those who have had a good education and do not live up to it will have a great deal to answer for another day; and those who will not now remember what they were taught, to conform themselves to it, will be made to remember it as an aggravation of their sin, and consequently of their ruin. *Secondly,* That by the frequent acts of sin the habits of it were so rooted and confirmed that his heart was fully set in him to commit it (*v.* 14): *I was almost in all evil in the midst of the congregation and assembly.* When he came into the synagogue, or into the courts of the temple, to worship God with other Israelites, his unclean heart was full of wanton thoughts and desires and his eyes of adultery. Reverence of the place and company, and of the work that was doing, could not restrain him, but he was almost as wicked and vile there as any where. No sin will appear more frightful to an awakened conscience than the profanation of holy things; nor will any aggravation of sin render it more exceedingly sinful than the place we are honoured with in the congregation and assembly, and the advantages we enjoy thereby. Zimri and Cozbi avowed their villany *in the sight of Moses and all the congregation* (Num. xxv. 6), and heart-adultery is as open to God, and must needs be most offensive to him, when we draw nigh to him in religious exercises. *I was in all evil* in defiance of the magistrates and judges, and their assemblies; so some understand it. Others refer it to the evil of punishment, not to the evil of sin · " I was

made an example, a spectacle to the world. I was under almost all God's sore judgments *in the midst of the congregation of Israel,* set up for a mark. *I stood up and cried in the congregation,*" Job xxx. 28. Let that be avoided which will be thus rued at last.

15 Drink waters out of thine own cistern, and running waters out of thine own well. 16 Let thy fountains be dispersed abroad, *and* rivers of waters in the streets. 17 Let them be only thine own, and not strangers' with thee. 18 Let thy fountain be blessed: and rejoice with the wife of thy youth. 19 *Let her be as* the loving hind and pleasant roe; let her breasts satisfy thee at all times; and be thou ravished always with her love. 20 And why wilt thou, my son, be ravished with a strange woman, and embrace the bosom of a stranger? 21 For the ways of man *are* before the eyes of the LORD, and he pondereth all his goings. 22 His own iniquities shall take the wicked himself, and he shall be holden with the cords of his sins. 23 He shall die without instruction; and in the greatness of his folly he shall go astray.

Solomon, having shown the great evil that there is in adultery and fornication, and all such lewd and filthy courses, here prescribes remedies against them.

I. Enjoy with satisfaction the comforts of lawful marriage, which was ordained for the prevention of uncleanness, and therefore ought to be made use of in time, lest it should not prove effectual for the cure of that which it might have prevented. Let none complain that God has dealt unkindly with them in forbidding them those pleasures which they have a natural desire of, for he has graciously provided for the regular gratification of them. " Thou mayest not indeed eat of every tree of the garden, but choose thee out one, which thou pleasest, and of that thou mayest freely eat; nature will be content with that, but lust with nothing." God, in thus confining men to one, has been so far from putting any hardship upon them that he has really consulted their true interest; for, as Mr. Herbert observes, " *If God had laid all common, certainly man would have been the encloser.*" —Church-porch. Solomon here enlarges much upon this, not only prescribing it as an antidote, but urging it as an argument against fornication, that the allowed pleasures of marriage (however wicked wits may ridicule them, who are factors for the unclean spirit) far transcend all the false forbidden pleasures of whoredom.

1. Let young men marry, marry and not

burn. Have *a cistern, a well of thy own* (v. 15), even the wife *of thy youth, v.* 18. *Wholly abstain, or wed.*—Herbert. "The world is wide, and there are varieties of accomplishments, among which thou mayest please thyself."

2. Let him that is married take delight in his wife, and let him be very fond of her, not only because she is the wife that he himself has chosen and he ought to be pleased with his own choice, but because she is the wife that God in his providence appointed for him and he ought much more to be pleased with the divine appointment, pleased with her because she is his own. *Let thy fountain be blessed* (v. 18); think thyself very happy in her, look upon her as a blessed wife, let her have thy blessing, pray daily for her, and then *rejoice with her.* Those comforts we are likely to have joy of that are sanctified to us by prayer and the blessing of God. It is not only allowed us, but commanded us, to be pleasant with our relations ; and it particularly becomes yoke-fellows to rejoice together and in each other. Mutual delight is the bond of mutual fidelity. It is not only taken for granted that the *bridegroom rejoices over his bride* (Isa. lxii. 5), but given for law. Eccl. ix. 9, *Live joyfully with the wife whom thou lovest all the days of thy life.* Those take not their comforts where God has appointed who are jovial and merry with their companions abroad, but sour and morose with their families at home.

3. Let him be fond of his wife and love her dearly (v. 19): *Let her be as the loving hind and the pleasant roe*, such as great men sometimes kept tame in their houses and played with. Desire no better diversion from severe study and business than the innocent and pleasant conversation of thy own wife ; let her lie in thy bosom, as the poor man's ewe lamb did in his (2 Sam. xii. 3), and do thou repose thy head in hers, and let that *satisfy thee at all times ;* and seek not for pleasure in any other. *"Err thou always in her love.* If thou wilt suffer thy love to run into an excess, and wilt be dotingly fond of any body, let it be only of thy own wife, where there is least danger of exceeding. This is *drinking waters*, to quench the thirst of thy appetite, *out of thy own cistern*, and *running waters*, which are clear, and sweet, and wholesome, *out of thy own well, v.* 15. 1 Cor. vii. 2, 3.

4. Let him take delight in his children and look upon them with pleasure (v. 16, 17): "Look upon them as streams from thy own pure fountains" (the Jews are said to *come forth out of the waters of Judah*, Isa. xlviii. 1), "so that they are parts of thyself, as the streams are of the fountain. Keep to thy own wife, and thou shalt have," (1.) "A numerous offspring, like *rivers of water*, which run in abundance, and they shall be dispersed abroad, matched into other families, whereas those that *commit whoredom* shall *not increase*,"

Hos. iv. 10. (2.) "A peculiar offspring, which shall be *only thy own*, whereas the children of whoredom, that are fathered upon thee, are, probably, not so, but, for aught thou knowest, are the offspring of strangers, and yet thou must keep them." (3.) "A creditable offspring, which are an honour to thee, and which thou mayest send abroad, and appear with, in the streets, whereas a spurious brood is thy disgrace, and that which thou art ashamed to own." In this matter, virtue has all the pleasure and honour in it ; justly therefore it is called *wisdom.*

5. Let him then scorn the offer of forbidden pleasures when he is *always ravished with the love* of a faithful virtuous wife ; let him consider what an absurdity it will be for him to be *ravished with a strange woman* (v. 20), to be in love with a filthy harlot, and *embrace the bosom of a stranger*, which, if he had any sense of honour or virtue, he would loathe the thoughts of. "Why wilt thou be so sottish, such an enemy to thyself, as to prefer puddle-water, and that poisoned too and stolen, before pure living waters out of thy own well?" Note, If the dictates of reason may be heard, the laws of virtue will be obeyed.

II. "See the eye of God always upon thee and let his fear rule in thy heart," v. 21. Those that live in this sin promise themselves secresy *(the eye of the adulterer waits for the twilight*, Job xxiv. 15) ; but to what purpose, when it cannot be hidden from God ? For, 1. He sees it. *The ways of man*, all his motions, all his actions, are *before the eyes of the Lord,* all the workings of the heart and all the outgoings of the life, that which is done ever so secretly and disguised ever so artfully. God sees it in a true light, and knows it with all its causes, circumstances, and consequences. He does not cast an eye upon men's ways now and then, but they are always actually in his view and under his inspection ; and darest thou sin against God in his sight, and do that wickedness under his eye which thou durst not do in the presence of a man like thyself? 2. He will call the sinner to an account for it ; for he not only sees, but *ponders all his goings*, judges concerning them, as one that will shortly judge the sinner for them. Every action is *weighed*, and shall be *brought into judgment* (Eccl. xii. 14), which is a good reason why we should *ponder the path of our feet* (ch. iv. 26), and so *judge ourselves* that we *may not be judged.*

III. "Foresee the certain ruin of those that go on still in their trespasses." Those that live in this sin promise themselves impunity, but they deceive themselves ; their sin will find them out, v. 22, 23. The apostle gives the sense of these verses in a few words. Heb. xiii. 4, *Whoremongers and adulterers God will judge.* 1. It is a sin which men with great difficulty shake off the power of. When the sinner is old and weak his lusts are strong and active, in *calling to remembrance the days of his youth,* Ezek. xxiii. 19. Thus *his own iniquities* having *seized the wicked himself* by his own consent, and he having voluntarily surrendered himself a captive to them, he is *held in the cords of his own sins,* and such full possession they have gained of him that he cannot extricate himself, but in the *greatness of his folly* (and what greater folly could there be than to yield himself a servant to such cruel task-masters?) he shall *go astray,* and wander endlessly. Uncleanness is a sin from which, when once men have plunged themselves into it, they very hardly and very rarely recover themselves. 2. It is a sin which, if it be not forsaken, men cannot possibly escape the punishment of; it will unavoidably be their ruin. As their own iniquities do arrest them in the reproaches of conscience and present rebukes (Jer. vii. 19), so their own iniquities shall arrest them and bind them over to the judgments of God. There needs no prison, no chains; they shall be *holden in the cords of their own sins,* as the fallen angels, being incurably wicked, are thereby *reserved in chains of darkness.* The sinner, who, having been *often reproved, hardens his neck,* shall *die at length without instruction.* Having had general warnings sufficient given him already, he shall have no particular warnings, but he shall die without seeing his danger beforehand, shall die because he would not receive instruction, but *in the greatness of his folly* would *go astray;* and so shall his doom be, he shall never find the way home again. Those that are so foolish as to choose the way of sin are justly left of God to themselves to go in it till they come to that destruction which it leads to, which is a good reason why we should guard with watchfulness and resolution against the allurements of the sensual appetite.

CHAP. VI.

In this chapter we have, I. A caution against rash suretiship, ver. 1—5. II. A rebuke to slothfulness, ver. 6—11. III. The character and fate of a malicious mischievous man, ver. 12—15. IV. An account of seven things which God hates, ver. 16—19. V. An exhortation to make the word of God familiar to us, ver. 20—23. VI. A repeated warning of the pernicious consequences of the sin of whoredom, ver. 24—35. We are here dissuaded from sin very much by arguments borrowed from our secular interests, for it is not only represented as damning in the other world, but as impoverishing in this.

MY son, if thou be surety for thy friend, *if* thou hast stricken thy hand with a stranger, 2 Thou art snared with the words of thy mouth, thou art taken with the words of thy mouth. 3 Do this now, my son, and deliver thyself, when thou art come into the hand of thy friend; go, humble thyself, and make sure thy friend. 4 Give not sleep to thine eyes, nor slumber to thine eyelids. 5 Deliver thyself as a roe from the hand *of the hunter,* and as a bird from the hand of the fowler.

It is the excellency of the word of God that it

teaches us not only divine wisdom for another world, but human prudence for this world, that we may order our affairs with discretion; and this is one good rule, To avoid suretiship, because by it poverty and ruin are often brought into families, which take away that comfort in relations which he had recommended in the foregoing chapter. 1. We must look upon suretiship as a snare and decline it accordingly, *v.* 1, 2. "It is dangerous enough for a man to be bound for his friend, though it be one whose circumstances he is well acquainted with, and well assured of his sufficiency, but much more to *strike the hands with a stranger,* to become surety for one whom thou dost not know to be either able or honest." Or the stranger here with whom the hand is stricken is the creditor, "the usurer to whom thou art become bound, and yet as to thee he is a stranger, that is, thou owest him nothing, nor hast had any dealings with him. If thou hast rashly entered into such engagements, either wheedled into them or in hopes to have the same kindness done for thee another time, know that *thou art snared with the words of thy mouth;* it was easily done, with a word's speaking; it was but setting thy hand to a paper, a bond is soon sealed and delivered, and a recognizance entered into. But it will not be so easily got clear of; thou art *in a snare* more than thou art aware of." See how little reason we have to make light of tongue-sins; if by a word of our mouth we may become indebted to men, and lie open to their actions, by the words of our mouth we may become obnoxious to God's justice, and even so may be snared. It is false that words are but wind: they are often snares. 2. If we have been drawn into this snare, it will be our wisdom by all means, with all speed, to get out of it, *v.* 3—5. It sleeps for the present; we hear nothing of it. The debt is not demanded; the principal says, "Never fear, we will take care of it." But still the bond is in force, interest is running on, the creditor may come upon thee when he will and perhaps may be hasty and severe, the principal may prove either knavish or insolvent, and then thou must rob thy wife and children, and ruin thy family, to pay that which thou didst neither eat nor drink for. And therefore *deliver thyself;* rest not till either the creditor give up the bond or the principal give thee counter-security; when *thou art come into the hand of thy friend,* and he has advantage against thee, it is no time to threaten or give ill language (that will provoke and make ill worse), but *humble thyself,* beg and pray to be discharged, go down on thy knees to him, and give him all the fair words thou canst; engage thy friends to speak for thee; leave no stone unturned till thou hast agreed with thy adversary and compromised the matter, so that thy bond may not come against thee or thine. This is a care which may well break thy sleep, and let it do so till thou hast got through it. *Give not sleep to thy eyes* till thou hast *delivered thyself.* Strive and struggle to the utmost, and hasten with all speed, *as a roe* or a *bird* delivers herself out of the snare of *the fowler* or hunter. Delays are dangerous, and feeble efforts will not serve." See what care God, in his word, has taken to make men good husbands of their estates, and to teach them prudence in the management of them. *Godliness* has precepts, as well as promises, relating to *the life that now is.*

But how are we to understand this? We are not to think it is unlawful in any case to become surety, or bail, for another; it may be a piece of justice or charity; he that has friends may see cause in this instance to show himself friendly, and it may be no piece of imprudence. Paul became bound for Onesimus, Philem. 19. We may help a young man into business that we know to be honest and diligent, and gain him credit by passing our word for him, and so do him a great kindness without any detriment to ourselves. But, 1. It is every man's wisdom to keep out of debt as much as may be, for it is an incumbrance upon him, entangles him in the world, puts him in danger of doing wrong or suffering wrong. The *borrower is servant to the lender,* and makes himself very much a slave to the world. Christians therefore, who are *bought with a price,* should not thus, without need, make themselves *the servants of men,* 1 Cor. vii. 23. 2. It is great folly to entangle ourselves with necessitous people, and to become bound for their debts, that are ever and anon taking up money, and lading, as we say, out of one hole into another, for it is ten to one but, some time or other, it will come upon us. A man ought never to be bound as surety for more than he is both able and willing to pay, and can afford to pay without wronging his family, in case the principal fail, for he ought to look upon it as his own debt. Ecclesiasticus viii. 13, *Be not surety above thy power, for, if thou be surety, thou must take care to pay it.* 3. It is a necessary piece of after-wit, if we have foolishly entangled ourselves, to get out of the snare as fast as we can, to lose no time, spare no pains, and stick at no submission to make ourselves safe and easy, and get our affairs into a good posture. It is better to humble ourselves for an accommodation than to ruin ourselves by our stiffness and haughtiness. *Make sure thy friend* by getting clear from thy engagements from him; for rash suretiship is as much the bane of friendship as that which is prudent is sometimes the bond of it. Let us take heed lest we any way make ourselves guilty of other men's sins against God (1 Tim. v. 22), for that is worse, and much more dangerous, than being bound for other men's debts; and, if we must be in all this care to get our debts to men forgiven, much more to get our peace made with God. "*Humble thyself* to him; *make sure* of Christ *thy friend,* to intercede for thee; pray earnestly

that thy sins may be pardoned, and thou mayest be delivered from going down to the pit, and it shall not be in vain. *Give not sleep to thy eyes nor slumber to thy eye-lids,* till this be done."

6 Go to the ant, thou sluggard; consider her ways, and be wise: 7 Which having no guide, overseer, or ruler, 8 Provideth her meat in the summer, *and* gathereth her food in the harvest. 9 How long wilt thou sleep, O sluggard? when wilt thou arise out of thy sleep? 10 *Yet* a little sleep, a little slumber, a little folding of the hands to sleep: 11 So shall thy poverty come as one that travelleth, and thy want as an armed man.

Solomon, in these verses, addresses himself to the sluggard who loves his ease, lives in idleness, minds no business, sticks to nothing, brings nothing to pass, and in a particular manner is careless in the business of religion. Slothfulness is as sure a way to poverty, though not so short a way, as rash suretiship. He speaks here to the sluggard,

I. By way of instruction, v. 6—8. He sends him to school, for sluggards must be schooled. He is to take him to school himself, for, if the scholar will take no pains, the master must take the more; the sluggard is not willing to come to school to him (dreaming scholars will never love wakeful teachers) and therefore he has found him out another school, as low as he can desire. Observe,

1. The master he is sent to school to: *Go to the ant, to the bee,* so the LXX. Man is taught more than the beasts of the earth, and made wiser than the fowls of heaven, and yet is so degenerated that he may learn wisdom from the meanest insects and be shamed by them. When we observe the wonderful sagacities of the inferior creatures we must not only give glory to the God of nature, who has made them thus strangely, but receive instruction to ourselves; by spiritualizing common things, we may make the things of God both easy and ready to us, and converse with them daily.

2. The application of mind that is required in order to learn of this master: *Consider her ways.* The sluggard is so because he does not consider; nor shall we ever learn to any purpose, either by the word or the works of God, unless we set ourselves to consider. Particularly, if we would imitate others in that which is good, we must consider their ways, diligently observe what they do, that we may do likewise, Phil. iii. 17.

3. The lesson that is to be learned. In general, learn wisdom, *consider, and be wise;* that is the thing we are to aim at in all our learning, not only to be knowing, but to be wise. In particular, learn to *provide meat in summer;* that is, (1.) We must prepare for

hereafter, and not mind the present time only, not eat up all, and lay up nothing, but in gathering time treasure up for a spending time. Thus provident we must be in our worldly affairs, not with an anxious care, but with a prudent foresight; lay in for winter, for straits and wants that may happen, and for old age; much more in the affairs of our souls. We must provide meat and food, that which is substantial and will stand us in stead, and which we shall most need. In the enjoyment of the means of grace provide for the want of them, in life for death, in time for eternity; in the state of probation and preparation we must provide for the state of retribution. (2.) We must take pains, and labour in our business, yea, though we labour under inconveniences. Even *in summer*, when the weather is hot, the ant is busy in *gathering food* and laying it up, and does not indulge her ease, nor take her pleasure, as the grasshopper, that sings and sports in the summer and then perishes in the winter. The ants help one another; if one have a grain of corn too big for her to carry home, her neighbours will come in to her assistance. (3.) We must improve opportunities, we must gather when it is to be had, as the ant does in summer and harvest, in the proper time. It is our wisdom to improve the season while that favours us, because that may be done then which cannot be done at all, or not so well done, at another time. *Walk while you have the light.*

4. The advantages which we have of learning this lesson above what the ant has, which will aggravate our slothfulness and neglect if we idle away our time. She has *no guides*, *overseers*, and *rulers*, but does it of herself, following the instinct of nature; the more shame for us who do not in like manner follow the dictates of our own reason and conscience, though besides them we have parents, masters, ministers, magistrates, to put us in mind of our duty, to check us for the neglect of it, to quicken us to it, to direct us in it, and to call us to an account about it. The greater helps we have for working out our salvation the more inexcusable shall we be if we neglect it.

II. By way of reproof, *v.* 9—11. In these verses,

1. He expostulates with the sluggard, rebuking him and reasoning with him, calling him to his work, as a master does his servant that has over-slept himself: "*How long wilt thou sleep, O sluggard?* How long wouldst thou sleep if one would let thee alone? *When wilt thou* think it time to *arise?*" Sluggards should be roused with a *How long?* This is applicable, (1.) To those that are slothful in the way of work and duty, in the duties of their particular calling as men or their general calling as Christians. "*How long wilt thou* waste thy time, and *when wilt thou* be a better husband of it? *How long wilt thou* love thy ease, and *when wilt thou* learn to deny thyself, and to take pains? *How*

long *wilt thou* bury thy talents, and *when wilt thou* begin to trade with them? *How long wilt thou* delay, and put off, and trifle away thy opportunities, as one regardless of hereafter; and *when wilt thou* stir up thyself to do what thou hast to do, which, if it be not done, will leave thee for ever undone?" (2.) To those that are secure in the way of sin and danger: "Hast thou not slept enough? Is it not far in the day? Does not thy Master call? Are not the Philistines upon thee? When then wilt thou arise?

2. He exposes the frivolous excuses he makes for himself, and shows how ridiculous he makes himself. When he is roused he stretches himself, and begs, as for alms, for more *sleep*, more *slumber;* he is well in his warm bed, and cannot endure to think of rising, especially of rising to work. But, observe, he promises himself and his master that he will desire but *a little* more *sleep, a little* more *slumber*, and then he will get up and go to his business. But herein he deceives himself; the more a slothful temper is indulged the more it prevails; let him sleep awhile, and slumber awhile, and still he is in the same tune; still he asks for *a little* more *sleep, yet a little* more; he never thinks he has enough, and yet, when he is called, pretends he will come presently. Thus men's great work is left undone by being put off yet a little longer, *de die in diem—from day to day;* and they are cheated of all their time by being cheated of the present moments. A little more sleep proves an everlasting sleep. *Sleep on now, and take your rest.*

3. He gives him fair warning of the fatal consequences of his slothfulness, *v.* 11. (1.) *Poverty and want* will certainly come upon those that are slothful in their business. If men neglect their affairs, they not only will not go forward, but they will go backward. He that leaves his concerns at sixes and sevens will soon see them go to wreck and ruin, and bring his noble to nine-pence. Spiritual poverty comes upon those that are slothful in the service of God; those will want oil, when they should use it, that provide it not in their vessels. (2.) "It will come silently and insensibly, will grow upon thee, and come step by step, *as one that travels*, but will without fail come at last." *It will leave thee as naked as if thou wert stripped by a highwayman;* so bishop Patrick. (3.) "It will come irresistibly, *like an armed man*, whom thou canst not oppose nor make thy part good against."

12 A naughty person, a wicked man, walketh with a froward mouth. 13 He winketh with his eyes, he speaketh with his feet, he teacheth with his fingers; 14 Frowardness *is* in his heart, he deviseth mischief continually: he soweth discord. 15 Therefore shall his calamity come suddenly;

suddenly shall he be broken without remedy. 16 These six *things* doth the Lord hate: yea, seven *are* an abomination unto him: 17 A proud look, a lying tongue, and hands that shed innocent blood, 18 A heart that deviseth wicked imaginations, feet tha be swift in running to mischief, 19 A false witness *that* speaketh lies, and he that soweth discord among brethren.

Solomon here gives us,

I. The characters of one that is mischievous to man and dangerous to be dealt with. If the slothful are to be condemned, that do nothing, much more those that do ill, and contrive to do all the ill they can. It is a *naughty person* that is here spoken of, Heb. *A man of Belial:* I think it should have been so translated, because it is a term often used in scripture, and this is the explication of it. Observe,

1. How a man of Belial is here described. He is *a wicked man,* that makes a trade of doing evil, especially with his tongue, he *walks* and works his designs *with a froward mouth* (v. 12), by lying and perverseness, and a direct opposition to God and man. He says and does every thing, (1.) Very artfully and with design. He has the subtlety of the serpent, and carries on his projects with a great deal of craft and management (v. 13), *with his eyes, with his feet, with his fingers.* He expresses his malice *when he dares not speak out* (so some), or, rather, thus he carries on his plot; those about him, whom he makes use of as the tools of his wickedness, understand the ill meaning of a wink of his eye, a stamp of his feet, the least motion of his fingers. He gives orders for evil-doing, and yet would not be thought to do so, but has ways of concealing what he does, so that he may not be suspected. He is a close man, and upon the reserve; those only shall be let into the secret that would do any thing he would have them to do. He is a cunning man, and upon the trick; he has a language by himself, which an honest man is not acquainted with, nor desires to be. (2.) Very spitefully and with ill design. It is not so much ambition or covetousness that *is in his heart,* as downright *frowardness,* malice, and ill nature. He aims not so much to enrich and advance himself as to do an ill turn to those about him. He is *continually devising* one *mischief* or other, purely for mischief-sake—a man of Belial indeed, of the devil, resembling him not only in subtlety, but in malice.

2. What his doom is (v. 15): *His calamity shall come* and *he shall be broken;* he that devised mischief shall fall into mischief. His ruin shall come, (1.) Without warning. It shall come suddenly: *Suddenly shall he be broken,* to punish him for all the wicked arts

he had to surprise people into his snares. (2.) Without relief. He shall be irreparably broken, and never able to piece again: *He shall be broken without remedy.* What relief can he expect that has disobliged all mankind? *He shall come to his end and none shall help him,* Dan. xi. 45.

II. A catalogue of those things which are in a special manner odious to God, all which are generally to be found in those men of Belial whom he had described in the foregoing verses; and the last of them (which, being the seventh, seems especially to be intended, because he says they are six, yea, seven) is part of his character, that he *sows discord.* God hates sin; he hates every sin; he can never be reconciled to it; he hates nothing but sin. But there are some sins which he does in a special manner hate; and all those here mentioned are such as are injurious to our neighbour. It is an evidence of the good-will God bears to mankind that those sins are in a special manner provoking to him which are prejudicial to the comfort of human life and society. *Therefore* the men of Belial must expect their ruin to *come suddenly,* and *without remedy,* because their practices are such as the Lord hates and *are an abomination to him, v.* 16. Those things which God hates it is no thanks to us to hate in others, but we must hate them in ourselves. 1. Haughtiness, conceitedness of ourselves, and contempt of others—*a proud look.* There are seven things that God hates, and pride is the first, because it is at the bottom of much sin and gives rise to it. God sees the pride in the heart and hates it there; but, when it prevails to that degree that the show of men's countenance witnesses against them that they overvalue themselves and undervalue all about them, this is in a special manner hateful to him, for then pride is proud of itself and sets shame at defiance. 2. Falsehood, and fraud, and dissimulation. Next to a *proud look,* nothing is more an abomination to God than *a lying tongue;* nothing more sacred than truth, nor more necessary to conversation than speaking truth. God and all good men hate and abhor lying. 3. Cruelty and blood-thirstiness. The devil was, from the beginning, a liar and a murderer (John viii. 44), and therefore, as *a lying tongue,* so *hands that shed innocent blood* are hateful to God, because they have in them the devil's image and do him service. 4. Subtlety in the contrivance of sin, wisdom to do evil, *a heart that* designs and a head that *devises wicked imaginations,* that is acquainted with the depths of Satan and knows how to carry on a covetous, envious, revengeful plot, most effectually. The more there is of craft and management in sin the more it is an abomination to God. 5. Vigour and diligence in the prosecution of sin—*feet that are swift in running to mischief,* as if they were afraid of losing time or were impatient of delay in a thing they are so greedy of. The policy and vigilance, the eagerness and industry, of sinners, in their sinful pursuits, may shame us who go about that which is good so awkwardly and so coldly. 6. False-witness bearing, which is one of the greatest mischiefs that the wicked imagination can devise, and against which there is least fence. There cannot be a greater affront to God (to whom in an oath appeal is made) nor a greater injury to our neighbour (all whose interests in this world, even the dearest, lie open to an attack of this kind) than knowingly to give in a false testimony. There are seven things which God hates, and lying involves two of them; he hates it, and doubly hates it. 7. Making mischief between relations and neighbours, and using all wicked means possible, not only to alienate their affections one from another, but to irritate their passions one against another. The God of love and peace hates *him that sows discord among brethren,* for he delights in concord. Those that by tale-bearing and slandering, by carrying ill-natured stories, aggravating every thing that is said and done, and suggesting jealousies and evil surmises, blow the coals of contention, are but preparing for themselves a fire of the same nature.

20 My son, keep thy father's commandment, and forsake not the law of thy mother : 21 Bind them continually upon thine heart, *and* tie them about thy neck. 22 When thou goest, it shall lead thee ; when thou sleepest, it shall keep thee ; and *when* thou awakest, it shall talk with thee. 23 For the commandment *is* a lamp ; and the law *is* light ; and reproofs of instruction *are* the way of life : 24 To keep thee from the evil woman, from the flattery of the tongue of a strange woman. 25 Lust not after her beauty in thine heart; neither let her take thee with her eyelids. 26 For by means of a whorish woman *a man is brought* to a piece of bread : and the adulteress will hunt for the precious life. 27 Can a man take fire in his bosom, and his clothes not be burned ? 28 Can one go upon hot coals, and his feet not be burned ? 29 So he that goeth in to his neighbour's wife ; whosoever toucheth her shall not be innocent. 30 *Men* do not despise a thief, if he steal to satisfy his soul when he is hungry ; 31 But *if* he be found, he shall restore sevenfold; he shall give all the substance of his house. 32 *But* whoso committeth adultery with a woman lacketh understanding : he *that* doeth it destroyeth his own soul. 33 A wound and dishonour shall he get ; and his reproach shall not be wiped away. 34 For jealousy *is* the rage of a man : therefore he will not spare in the day of vengeance. 35 He will not regard any ransom ; neither will he rest content, though thou givest many gifts.

Here is, I. A general exhortation faithfully to adhere to the word of God and to take it for our guide in all our actions.

1. We must look upon the word of God both as a light (*v.* 23) and as a law, *v.* 20, 23. (1.) By its arguments it is a light, which our understandings must subscribe to; it *is a lamp* to our eyes for discovery, and so to our feet for direction. The word of God reveals to us truths of eternal certainty, and is built upon the highest reason. Scripture-light is the sure light. (2.) By its authority it is a law, which our wills must submit to. As never such a light shone out of the schools of the philosophers, so never such a law issued from the throne of any prince, so well framed, and so binding. It is such a law as is a lamp and a light, for it carries with it the evidence of its own goodness.

2. We must receive it as *our father's commandment* and *the law of our mother, v.* 20. It is God's commandment and his law. But, (1.) Our parents directed us to it, put it into our hands, trained us up in the knowledge and observance of it, its original and obligation being most sacred. We believe indeed, not for their saying, for we have tried it ourselves and find it to be of God; but we were beholden to them for recommending it to us, and see all the reason in the world to *continue in the things we have learned, knowing of whom we have learned them.* (2.) The cautions, counsels, and commands which our parents gave us agree with the word of God, and therefore we must hold them fast. Children, when they are grown up, must remember *the law of* a good *mother,* as well as the *commandment* of a good *father,* Ecclesiasticus iii. 2. *The Lord has given the father honour over the children and has confirmed the authority of the mother over the sons.*

3. We must retain the word of God and the good instructions which our parents gave us out of it. (1.) We must never cast them off, never think it a mighty achievement (as some do) to get clear of the restraints of a good education: "*Keep thy father's commandment,* keep it still, and never forsake it." (2.) We must never lay them by, no, not for a time (*v.* 21): *Bind them continually,* not only *upon thy hand* (as Moses had directed, Deut. vi. 8) but *upon thy heart.* Phylacteries upon the hand were of no value at all, any further than they occasioned pious thoughts and affections

in the heart. There the word must be written, there it must be hid, and laid close to the conscience. *Tie them about thy neck,* as an ornament, a bracelet, or gold chain,—*about thy throat* (so the word is); let them be a guard upon that pass; tie them about thy throat, that no forbidden fruit may be suffered to go in nor any evil word suffered to go out through the throat; and thus a great deal of sin would be prevented. Let the word of God be always ready to us, and let us feel the impressions of it, as of that which is bound upon our hearts and about our necks.

4. We must make use of the word of God and of the benefit that is designed us by it. If we bind it continually upon our hearts, (1.) It will be our guide, and we must follow its direction. *" When thou goest, it shall lead thee* (v. 22); it shall lead thee into, and lead thee in, the good and right way, shall lead thee from, and lead thee out of, every sinful dangerous path. It will say unto thee, when thou art ready to turn aside, *This is the way; walk in it.* It will be that to thee that the pillar of cloud and fire was to Israel in the wilderness. Be led by that, let it be thy rule, and then thou shalt be led by the Spirit; he will be thy monitor and support." (2.) It will be our guard, and we must put ourselves under the protection of it: *" When thou sleepest,* and liest exposed to the malignant powers of darkness, *it shall keep thee ;* thou shalt be safe, and shalt think thyself so." If we govern ourselves by the precepts of the word all day, and make conscience of the duty God has commanded to us, we may shelter ourselves under the promises of the word at night, and take the comfort of the deliverances God does and will command for us. (3.) It will be our companion, and we must converse with it: *"When thou awakest* in the night, and knowest not how to pass away thy waking minutes, if thou pleasest, *it shall talk with thee,* and entertain thee with pleasant meditations in the night-watches; *when thou awakest* in the morning, and art contriving the work of the day, *it shall talk with thee* about it, and help thee to contrive for the best," Ps. i. 2. The word of God has something to say to us upon all occasions, if we would but enter into discourse with it, would ask it what it has to say, and give it the hearing. And it would contribute to our close and comfortable walking with God all day if we would begin with him in the morning and let his word be the subject of our first thoughts. *When I awake I am still with thee;* we are so if the word be still with us. (4.) It will be our life; for, as the law *is a lamp* and *a light* for the present, so the *reproofs of instruction are the way of life.* Those reproofs of the word which not only show us our faults, but instruct us how to do better, are the way that leads to life, eternal life. Let not faithful reproofs therefore, which have such a direct tendency to make us happy, ever make us uneasy.

II. Here is a particular caution against the sin of uncleanness.

1. When we consider how much this iniquity abounds, how heinous it is in its own nature, of what pernicious consequence it is, and how certainly destructive to all the seeds of the spiritual life in the soul, we shall not wonder that the cautions against it are so often repeated and so largely inculcated. (1.) One great kindness God designed men, in giving them his law, was to preserve them from this sin, v. 24. " The reproofs of instruction are therefore *the way of life* to thee, because they are designed *to keep thee from the evil woman,* who will be certain death to thee, from being enticed by *the flattery of the tongue of a strange woman,* who pretends to love thee, but intends to ruin thee." Those that will be wrought upon by flattery make themselves a very easy prey to the tempter; and those who would avoid that snare must take well-instructed reproofs as great kindnesses and be thankful to those that will deal faithfully with them, Prov. xxvii. 5, 6. (2.) The greatest kindness we can do ourselves is to keep at a distance from this sin, and to look upon it with the utmost dread and detestation (v. 25): *"Lust not after her beauty,* no, not *in thy heart,* for, if thou dost, thou hast *there* already *committed adultery with her.* Talk not of the charms in her face, neither be thou smitten with her amorous glances; they are all snares and nets; *let her* not *take thee with her eye-lids.* Her looks are arrows and fiery darts; they wound, they kill, in another sense than what lovers mean; they call it a pleasing captivity, but it is a destroying one, it is worse than Egyptian slavery."

2. Divers arguments Solomon here urges to enforce this caution against the sin of whoredom.

(1.) It is a sin that impoverishes men, wastes their estates, and reduces them to beggary (v. 26): *By means of a whorish woman a man is brought to a piece of bread ;* many a man has been so, who has purchased the ruin of his body and soul at the expense of his wealth. The prodigal son spent his living on harlots, so that he brought himself to be fellow-commoner with the swine. And that poverty must needs lie heavily which men bring themselves into by their own folly, Job xxxi. 12.

(2.) It threatens death; it kills men : *The adulteress will hunt for the precious life,* perhaps designedly, as Delilah for Samson's, at least, eventually, the sin strikes at the life. Adultery was punished by the law of Moses as a capital crime. *The adulterer and the adulteress shall surely be put to death.* Every one knew this. Those therefore who, for the gratifying of a base lust, would lay themselves open to the law, could be reckoned no better than self-murderers.

(3.) It brings guilt upon the conscience and debauches that. He that *touches his neighbour's wife,* with an immodest touch,

825

cannot *be innocent, v.* 29. [1.] He is in imminent danger of adultery, as he that *takes fire in his bosom,* or *goes upon hot coals,* is in danger of being *burnt.* The way of this sin is down-hill, and those that venture upon the temptations to it hardly escape the sin itself. The fly fools away her life by playing the wanton with the flames. It is a deep pit, which it is madness to venture upon the brink of. He that keeps company with those of ill fame, that goes in with them, and touches them, cannot long preserve his innocency; he thrusts himself into temptation and so throws himself out of God's protection. [2.] He that commits adultery is in the high road to destruction. The bold presumptuous sinner says, " I may venture upon the sin and yet escape the punishment; I shall have peace though I go on." He might as well say, I will *take fire into my bosom and not burn my clothes,* or I will *go upon hot coals and not burn my feet. He that goes in to his neighbour's wife,* however he holds himself, God will not hold him guiltless. The fire of lust kindles the fire of hell.

(4.) It ruins the reputation and entails perpetual infamy upon that. It is a much more scandalous sin than stealing is, *v.* 30—33. Perhaps it is not so in the account of men, at least not in our day. A thief is sent to the stocks, to the gaol, to Bridewell, to the gallows, while the vile adulterer goes unpunished, nay, with many, unblemished; he dares boast of his villanies, and they are made but a jest of. But, in the account of God and his law, adultery was much the more enormous crime; and, if God is the fountain of honour, his word must be the standard of it. [1.] As for the sin of stealing, if a man were brought to it by extreme necessity, if he stole meat for the *satisfying of his soul when he was hungry,* though that will not excuse him from guilt, yet it is such an extenuation of his crime that *men do not despise* him, do not expose him to ignominy, but pity him. Hunger will break through stone-walls, and blame will be laid upon those that brought him to poverty, or that did not relieve him. Nay, though he have not that to say in his excuse, *if he be found* stealing, and the evidence be ever so plain upon him, yet he shall only make restitution *seven-fold.* The law of Moses appointed that he who stole a sheep should restore four-fold, and an ox five-fold (Exod. xxii. 1); accordingly David adjudged, 2 Sam. xii. 6. But we may suppose in those cases concerning which the law had not made provision the judges afterwards settled the penalties in proportion to the crimes, according to the equity of the law. Now, if he that stole an ox out of a man's field must restore five-fold, it was reasonable that he that stole a man's goods out of his house should *restore seven-fold;* for there was no law to put him to death, as with us, for burglary and robbery on the highway, and of this worst kind of theft Solomon here speaks; the greatest

826

punishment was that a man might be forced to *give all the substance of his house* to satisfy the law and his blood was not attainted. But, [2.] Committing adultery is a more heinous crime; Job calls it so, and *an iniquity to be punished by the judge,* Job xxxi. 11. When Nathan would convict David of the evil of his adultery he did it by a parable concerning the most aggravated theft, which, in David's judgment, deserved to be punished with death (2 Sam. xii. 5), and then showed him that his sin was *more exceedingly sinful* than that. *First,* It is a greater reproach to a man's reason, for he cannot excuse it, as a thief may, by saying that it was to satisfy his hunger, but must own that it was to gratify a brutish lust which would break the hedge of God's law, not for want, but for wantonness. Therefore *whoso commits adultery with a woman lacks understanding,* and deserves to be stigmatized as an arrant fool. *Secondly,* It is more severely punished by the law of God. A thief suffered only a pecuniary mulct, but the adulterer suffered death. The thief *steals to satisfy his soul,* but the adulterer *destroys his own soul,* and falls an unpitied sacrifice to the justice both of God and man. " Sinner, thou hast destroyed thyself." This may be applied to the spiritual and eternal death which is the consequence of sin; *he that does it* wounds his conscience, corrupts his rational power, extinguishes all the sparks of the spiritual life, and exposes himself to the wrath of God for ever, and thus *destroys his own soul. Thirdly,* The infamy of it is indelible, *v.* 33. It will be *a wound* to his good name, a *dishonour* to his family, and, though the guilt of it may be done away by repentance, the *reproach* of it never will, but will stick to his memory when he is gone. David's sin in the matter of Uriah was not only a perpetual blemish upon his own character, but gave occasion to the enemies of the Lord to blaspheme his name too.

(5.) It exposes the adulterer to the rage of the jealous husband, whose honour he puts such an affront upon, *v.* 34, 35. He that touches his neighbour's wife, and is familiar with her, gives him occasion for jealousy, much more he that debauches her, which, if kept ever so secret, might then be *discovered by the waters of jealousy,* Num. v. 12. " When discovered, thou hadst better meet a bear robbed of her whelps than the injured husband, who, in the case of adultery, will be as severe an avenger of his own honour as, in the case of manslaughter, of his brother's blood. If thou art not afraid of the wrath of God, yet be afraid of the *rage of a man.* Such jealousy is; it is *strong as death* and *cruel as the grave.* In the *day of vengeance,* when the adulterer comes to be tried for his life, the prosecutor will not spare any pains or cost in the prosecution, will not relent towards thee, as he would perhaps towards one that had robbed him. He will not accept of any commutation, any composition;

he will not regard any ransom. Though thou offer to bribe him, and *give him many gifts* to pacify him, he *will not rest content* with any thing less than the execution of the law. Thou must be *stoned to death.* If *a man would give all the substance of his house,* it would atone for a theft (*v.* 31), but not for adultery; in that case it would utterly be contemned. *Stand in awe therefore, and sin not ;* expose not thyself to all this misery for a moment's sordid pleasure, which will be bitterness in the end."

CHAP. VII.

The scope of this chapter is, as of several before, to warn young men against the lusts of the flesh. Solomon remembered of what ill consequence it was to his father, perhaps found himself, and perceived his son, addicted to it, or at least had observed how many hopeful young men among his subjects had been ruined by those lusts ; and therefore he thought he could never say enough to dissuade men from them, that " every one may possess his vessel in sanctification and honour, and not in the lusts of uncleanness." In this chapter we have, I. A general exhortation to get our minds principled and governed by the word of God, as a sovereign antidote against this sin, ver. 1—5. II. A particular representation of the great danger which unwary young men are in of being inveigled into this snare, ver. 6—23. III. A serious caution inferred thence, in the close, to take heed of all approaches towards this sin, ver. 24—27. We should all pray, " Lord, lead us not into this temptation."

M Y son, keep my words, and lay up my commandments with thee. 2 Keep my commandments, and live ; and my law as the apple of thine eye. 3 Bind them upon thy fingers, write them upon the table of thine heart. 4 Say unto wisdom, Thou *art* my sister ; and call understanding *thy* kinswoman : 5 That they may keep thee from the strange woman, from the stranger *which* flattereth with her words.

These verses are an introduction to his warning against fleshly lusts, much the same with that, *ch.* vi. 20, &c., and ending (*v.* 5) as that did (*v.* 24), *To keep thee from the strange woman ;* that is it he aims at; only there he had said, *Keep thy father's commandment,* here (which comes all to one), *Keep my commandments,* for he speaks to us as unto sons. He speaks in God's name; for it is God's *commandments* that we are to *keep,* his *words,* his *law.* The word of God must be to us, 1. As that which we are most careful of. We must keep it as our treasure ; we must *lay up God's* commandments with us, lay them up safely, that we may not be robbed of them by the wicked one, *v.* 1. We must keep it as our life : *Keep my commandments and live* (*v.* 2), not only, " Keep them, and you shall live ;" but, " Keep them as you would your life, as those that cannot live without them." It would be death to a good man to be deprived of the word of God, for by it he lives, and not *by bread alone.* 2. As that which we are most tender of : Keep *my law as the apple of thy eye.* A little thing offends the eye, and therefore nature has so well guarded it. We pray, with David, that God would keep us as the apple of his eye (Ps. xvii. 8),

that our lives and comforts may be precious in his sight ; and they shall be so (Zech. ii. 8) if we be in like manner tender of his law and afraid of the least violation of it. Those who reproach strict and circumspect walking, as needless preciseness, consider not that the law is to be kept as the apple of the eye, for indeed it is the *apple of our eye ;* the law is light ; the law in the heart is the eye of the soul. 3. As that which we are proud of and would be ever mindful of (*v.* 3) : " *Bind them upon thy fingers ;* let them be precious to thee ; look upon them as an ornament, as a diamond-ring, as the *signet on thy right hand ;* wear them continually as thy wedding-ring, the badge of thy espousals to God. Look upon the word of God as putting an honour upon thee, as an ensign of thy dignity. *Bind them on thy fingers,* that they may be constant memorandums to thee of thy duty, that thou mayest have them always in view, as that which is *graven upon the palms of thy hands.*" 4. As that which we are fond of and are ever thinking of : *Write them upon the table of thy heart,* as the names of the friends we dearly love, we say, are written in our hearts. *Let the word of God dwell richly in us,* and be written there where it will be always at hand to be read. Where sin was written (Jer. xvii. 1) let the word of God be written. It is the matter of a promise (Heb. viii. 10, *I will write my law in their hearts),* which makes the precept practicable and easy. 5. As that which we are intimately acquainted and conversant with (*v.* 4) : " *Say unto wisdom, Thou art my sister,* whom I dearly love and take delight in ; *and call understanding thy kinswoman,* to whom thou art nearly allied, and for whom thou hast a pure affection ; call her thy friend, whom thou courtest. We must make the word of God familiar to us, consult it, and consult its honour, and take a pleasure in conversing with it. 6. As that which we make use of for our defence and armour, to keep us *from the strange woman,* from sin, that flattering but destroying thing, that adulteress ; particularly from the sin of uncleanness, *v.* 5. Let the word of God confirm our dread of that sin and our resolutions against it ; let it discover to us its fallacies and suggest to us answers to all its flatteries.

6 For at the window of my house I looked through my casement, 7 And beheld among the simple ones, I discerned among the youths, a young man void of understanding, 8 Passing through the street near her corner ; and he went the way to her house, 9 In the twilight, in the evening, in the black and dark night : 10 And, behold, there met him a woman *with* the attire of a harlot, and subtil of heart. 11 (She *is* loud and stubborn ;

her feet abide not in her house: 12 Now *is she* without, now in the streets, and lieth in wait at every corner.) 13 So she caught him, and kissed him, *and* with an impudent face said unto him, 14 *I have* peace offerings with me; this day have I paid my vows. 15 Therefore came I forth to meet thee, diligently to seek thy face, and I have found thee. 16 I have decked my bed with coverings of tapestry, with carved *works*, with fine linen of Egypt. 17 I have perfumed my bed with myrrh, aloes, and cinnamon. 18 Come, let us take our fill of love until the morning: let us solace ourselves with loves. 19 For the good man *is* not at home, he is gone a long journey: 20 He hath taken a bag of money with him, *and* will come home at the day appointed. 21 With her much fair speech she caused him to yield, with the flattering of her lips she forced him. 22 He goeth after her straightway, as an ox goeth to the slaughter, or as a fool to the correction of the stocks; 23 Till a dart strike through his liver; as a bird hasteth to the snare, and knoweth not that it *is* for his life.

Solomon here, to enforce the caution he had given against the sin of whoredom, tells a story of a young man that was ruined to all intents and purposes by the enticements of an adulterous woman. Such a story as this would serve the lewd profane poets of our age to make a play of, and the harlot with them would be a heroine; nothing would be so entertaining to the audience, nor give them so much diversion, as her arts of beguiling the young gentleman and drawing in the country squire; her conquests would be celebrated as the triumphs of wit and love, and the comedy would conclude very pleasantly; and every young man that saw it acted would covet to be so picked up. Thus *fools make a mock at sin.* But Solomon here relates it, and all wise and good men read it, as a very melancholy story. The impudence of the adulterous woman is very justly looked upon, by all that have any sparks of virtue in them, with the highest indignation, and the easiness of the young man with the tenderest compassion; and the story concludes with sad reflections, enough to make all that read and hear it afraid of the snares of fleshly lusts and careful to keep at the utmost distance from them. It is supposed to be a parable, or imagined case, but I doubt it was too true, and, which is

worse, that notwithstanding the warning it gives of the fatal consequences of such wicked courses it is still too often true, and the agents for hell are still playing the same game and with similar success.

Solomon was a magistrate, and, as such, inspected the manners of his subjects, looked often through his casement, that he might see with his own eyes, and made remarks upon those who little thought his eye was upon them, that he might know the better how to make the sword he bore a terror to evil-doers. But here he writes as a minister, a prophet, who is by office a watchman, to give warning of the approach of the enemies, and especially where they lie in ambush, that we may not be ignorant of Satan's devices, but may know where to double our guard. This Solomon does here, where we may observe the account he gives,

I. Of the person tempted, and how he laid himself open to the temptation, and therefore must thank himself if it end in his destruction. 1. He was a *young man, v.* 7. Fleshly lusts are called *youthful lusts* (2 Tim. ii. 22), not to extenuate them as tricks of youth, and therefore excusable, but rather to aggravate them, as robbing God of the first and best of our time, and, by debauching the mind when it is tender, laying a foundation for a bad life ever after, and to intimate that young people ought in a special manner to fortify their resolutions against this sin. 2. He was a young man *void of understanding*, that went abroad into the world, not principled as he ought to have been with wisdom and the fear of God, and so ventured to sea without ballast, without pilot, cord, or compass; he knew not how to depart from evil, which is the best understanding, Job xxviii. 28. Those become an easy prey to Satan who, when they have arrived to the stature of men, have scarcely the understanding of children. 3. He kept bad company. He was a *young man among the youths*, a silly young man *among the simple* ones. If, being conscious of his own weakness, he had associated with those that were older and wiser than himself, there would have been hopes of him. Christ, at twelve years old, conversed with the doctors, to set young people an example of this. But, if those that are simple choose such for their companions as are like themselves, simple they will still be, and hardened in their simplicity. 4. He was sauntering, and had nothing to do, but *passed through the street* as one that knew not how to dispose of himself. One of the sins of filthy Sodom was *abundance of idleness*, Ezek. xvi. 49. He went in a starched stately manner, so (it is said) the word signifies. He appeared to be a nice formal fop, the top of whose accomplishments was to dress well and walk with a good air; fit game for that bird of prey to fly at. 5. He was a night-walker, that hated and scorned the business that is to be done by day-light, from which the evening calls men in to their repose; and, having fellowship with the unfruitful works of darkness, he begins to move *in the twilight in the evening, v.* 9. And he chooses *the black and dark night* as fittest for his purpose, not the moonlight nights, when he might be discovered. 6. He steered his course towards the house of one that he thought would entertain him, and that he might be merry with; he went *near her corner*, the *way to her house* (v. 8), contrary to Solomon's advice (*ch.* v. 8), *Come not nigh the door of her house.* Perhaps he did not know it was the way to an infamous house, but, however, it was a way that he had no business in; and when we have nothing to do the devil will quickly find us something to do. We must take heed, not only of idle days, but of idle evenings, lest they prove inlets to temptation.

II. Of the person tempting, not a common prostitute, for she was a married wife (v. 19), and, for aught that appears, lived in reputation among her neighbours, not suspected of any such wickedness, and yet, in the *twilight of the evening*, when her husband was abroad, abominably impudent. She is here described, 1. By her dress. She had the *attire of a harlot* (v. 10), gaudy and flaunting, to set her off as a beauty; perhaps she was painted as Jezebel, and went with her neck and breasts bare, loose, and *en deshabille.* The purity of the heart will show itself in the modesty of the dress, which *becomes women professing godliness.* 2. By her craft and management. She is *subtle of heart,* mistress of all the arts of wheedling, and knowing how by all her caresses to serve her own base purposes. 3. By her temper and carriage. *She is loud and stubborn,* talkative and self-willed, noisy and troublesome, wilful and headstrong, all tongue, and will have her saying, right or wrong, impatient of check and control, and cannot bear to be counselled, much less reproved, by husband or parents, ministers or friends. She is a *daughter of Belial,* that will endure no yoke. 4. By her place, not her own house; she hates the confinement and employment of that; her *feet abide not there* any longer than needs must. She is all for gadding abroad, changing place and company. *Now is she without* in the country, under pretence of taking the air, now *in the streets* of the city, under pretence of seeing how the market goes. She is here, and there, and every where but where she should be. She *lies in wait at every corner,* to pick up such as she can make a prey of. Virtue is a penance to those to whom home is a prison.

III. Of the temptation itself and the management of it. She met the young spark. Perhaps she knew him; however she knew by his fashions that he was such a one as she wished for; so she *caught him about* the neck and *kissed* him, contrary to all the rules of modesty (v. 13), and waited not for his com-

pliments or courtship, but *with an impudent face* invited him not only to *her house,* but to *her bed.*

1. She courted him to sup with her (v. 14, 15): *I have peace-offerings with me.* Hereby she gives him to understand, (1.) Her prosperity, that she was compassed about with so many blessings that she had occasion to offer peace-offerings, in token of joy and thankfulness; she was before-hand in the world, so that he needed not fear having his pocket picked. (2.) Her profession of piety. She had been to-day at the temple, and was as well respected there as any that worshipped in the courts of the Lord. She had paid her vows, and, as she thought, made all even with God Almighty, and therefore might venture upon a new score of sins. Note, The external performances of religion, if they do not harden men against sin, harden them in it, and embolden carnal hearts to venture upon it, in hopes that when they come to count and discount with God he will be found as much in debt to them for their peace-offerings and their vows as they to him for their sins. But it is sad that a show of piety should become the shelter of iniquity (which really doubles the shame of it, and makes it more exceedingly sinful) and that men should baffle their consciences with those very things that should startle them. The Pharisees made long prayers, that they might the more plausibly carry on their covetous and mischievous designs. (3.) Her present plenty of good provisions. The greatest part of the flesh of the peace-offerings was by the law returned back to the offerers, to feast upon with their friends, which (if they were peace-offerings of thanksgiving) was to be all eaten *the same day* and *none of it left until the morning,* Lev. vii. 15. This law of charity and generosity is abused to be a colour for gluttony and excess: "Come," says she, "come home with me, for I have good cheer enough, and only want good company to help me off with it." It was a pity that the peace-offerings should thus become, in a bad sense, sin-offerings, and that what was designed for the honour of God should become the food and fuel of a base lust. But this is not all. (4.) To strengthen the temptation, [1.] She pretends to have a very great affection for him above any man: "*Therefore,* because I have a good supper upon the table, *I came forth to meet thee,* for no friend in the world shall be so welcome to it as thou shalt, v. 15. Thou art he whom I came on purpose to seek, to *seek diligently,* came myself, and would not send a servant." Surely he cannot deny her his company when she put such a value upon it, and would take all this pains to obtain the favour of it. Sinners take pains to do mischief, and are as the roaring lion himself; they *go about seeking to devour,* and yet pretend they are seeking to oblige. [2.] She would have it thought that Providence itself countenanced her choice of him for her

companion; for how quickly had she found him whom she sought!

2. She courted him to lie with her. They will sit down to eat and drink, and then rise up to play, to play the wanton, and there is, a bed ready for them, where he shall find that which will be in all respects agreeable to him. To please his eye, it is *decked with coverings of tapestry* and *carved works*, exquisitely fine; he never saw the like. To please his touch, the sheets are not of home-spun cloth; they are far-fetched and dear bought; they are of *fine linen of Egypt, v.* 16. To gratify his smell, it is *perfumed* with the sweetest scents, *v.* 17. Come, therefore, and *let us take our fill of love, v.* 18. Of *love*, does she say? Of *lust* she means, brutish lust; but it is a pity that the name of love should be thus abused. True love is from heaven; this is from hell. How can those pretend to solace themselves and love one another who are really ruining themselves and one another?

3. She anticipated the objection which he might make of the danger of it. Is she not another man's wife, and what if her husband should catch them in adultery, in the very act? he will make them pay dearly for their sport, and where will the solace of their love be then? "Never fear," says she, "the *good man is not at home*" (*v.* 19); she does not call him her *husband*, for she *forsakes the guide of her youth* and *forgets the covenant of her God;* but "the *good man* of the house, whom I am weary off." Thus Potiphar's wife, when she spoke of her husband, would not call him so, but *he*, Gen. xxxix. 14. It is therefore with good reason taken notice of, to Sarah's praise, that she spoke respectfully of her husband, calling him *lord.* She pleases herself with this that he is not at home, and therefore she is melancholy if she have not some company, and therefore whatever company she has she may be free with them, for she is from under his eye, and he shall never know. But will he not return quickly? No: "he has *gone a long journey*, and cannot return on a sudden; he *appointed the day* of his return, and he never comes home sooner than he says he will. *He has taken a bag of money with him,* either," (1.) "To trade with, to buy goods with, and he will not return till he has laid it all out. It is a pity that an honest industrious man should be thus abused, and advantage taken of his absence, when it is upon business, for the good of his family. Or, (2.) "To spend and revel with." Whether justly or not, she insinuates that he was a bad husband; so she would represent him, because she was resolved to be a bad wife, and must have that for an excuse; it is often groundlessly suggested, but is never a sufficient excuse. "He follows his pleasures, and wastes his estate abroad" (says she), "and why should not I do the same at home?"

IV. Of the success of the temptation. Promising the young man every thing that was pleasant, and impunity in the enjoyment, she gained her point, *v.* 21. It should seem, the youth, though very simple, had no ill design, else a word, a beck, a wink, would have served, and there would have been no need of all this harangue; but though he did not intend any such thing, nay, had something in his conscience that opposed it, yet *with her much fair speech she caused him to yield.* His corruptions at length triumphed over his convictions, and his resolutions were not strong enough to hold out against such artful attacks as these, but *with the flattery of her lips she forced him;* he could not stop his ear against such a charmer, but surrendered himself her captive. Wisdom's maidens, who plead her cause, and have reason on their side, and true and divine pleasures to invite men to, have a deaf ear turned to them, and with all their rhetoric cannot compel men to come in, but such is the dominion of sin in the hearts of men that its allurements soon prevail by falsehood and flattery. With what pity does Solomon here look upon this foolish young man, when he sees him follow the adulterous woman! (1.) He gives him up for gone; alas! he is undone. He goes to the slaughter (for houses of uncleanness are slaughter-houses to precious souls); a dart will presently *strike through his liver;* going without his breast-plate, he will receive his death's wound, *v.* 23. It is his life, his precious life, that is thus irrecoverably thrown away, he is perfectly lost to all good; his conscience is debauched; a door is opened to all other vices, and this will certainly end in his endless damnation. (2.) That which makes his case the more piteous is that he is not himself aware of his misery and danger; he goes blindfold, nay, he goes laughing to his ruin. The ox thinks he is led to the pasture when he is led to the slaughter; *the fool* (that is, the drunkard, for, of all sinners, drunkards are the greatest fools, they wilfully turn themselves into fools) is led *to the correction of the stocks*, and is not sensible of the shame of it, but goes to it as if he were going to a play. The *bird* that *hastes to the snare* looks only at the bait, and promises herself a good bit from that, and considers not that *it is for her life.* Thus this unthinking unwary young man dreams of nothing but the pleasures he shall have in the embraces of the harlot, while really he is running headlong upon his ruin. Though Solomon does not here tell us that he put the law in execution against this base harlot, yet we have no reason to think but that he did, he was himself so affected with the mischief she did and had such an indignation at it.

24 Hearken unto me now therefore, O ye children, and attend to the words of my mouth. 25 Let not thine heart decline to her ways, go not astray

in her paths. 26 For she hath cast down many wounded : yea, many strong *men* have been slain by her. 27 Her house *is* the way to hell, going down to the chambers of death.

We have here the application of the foregoing story: "*Hearken to me therefore*, and not to such seducers (*v.* 24); give ear to a father, and not to an enemy." 1. "Take good counsel when it is given you. *Let not thy heart decline to her°ways* (*v.* 25); never leave the paths of virtue, though strait and narrow, solitary and up-hill, for the way of the adulteress, though green, and broad, and crowded with company. Do not only keep thy feet from those ways, but let not so much as thy heart incline to them; never harbour a disposition this way, nor think otherwise than with abhorrence of• such wicked practices as these. Let reason, and conscience, and the fear of God ruling in the heart, check the inclinations of the sensual appetite. If thou goest in her paths, in any of the paths that lead to this sin, thou goest astray, thou art out of the right way, the safe way; therefore take heed, *go not astray*, lest thou wander endlessly." 2. "Take fair warning when it is given you." (1.) "Look back, and see what mischief this sin has done. The adulteress has been the ruin not of here and there one, but she has *cast down many wounded.*" Thousands have been undone, now and for ever, by this sin; and those not only the weak and simple youths, such as he was of whom he had now spoken, but *many strong men have been slain by her*, *v.* 26. Herein, perhaps, he has an eye especially to Samson, who was slain by this sin, and perhaps to David too, who by this sin entailed a sword upon his house, though so far the Lord took it away that he himself should not die. These were men not only of great bodily strength, but of eminent wisdom and courage, and yet their fleshly lusts prevailed over them. *Howl, fir-trees, if the cedars be shaken. Let him that thinks he stands take heed lest he fall.* (2.) "Look forward with an eye of faith, and see what will be in the end of it," *v.* 27. Her house, though richly decked and furnished, and called a *house of pleasure*, is the *way to hell*; and her chambers are the stair-case that goes down to the *chambers of death* and everlasting darkness. The cup of fornication must shortly be exchanged for the cup of trembling; and the flames of lust, if not quenched by repentance and mortification, will burn to the lowest hell. Therefore *stand in awe and sin not.*

CHAP. VIII.

The word of God is two-fold, and, in both senses, is wisdom ; for a word without wisdom is of little value, and wisdom without a word is of little use. Now, I. Divine revelation is the word and wisdom of God, and that pure religion and undefiled which is built upon it; and of that Solomon here speaks, recommending it to us as faithful, and well worthy of all acceptation, ver. 1—21. God, by it, instructs, and governs, and blesses, the children of men. II. The Redeemer is the eternal Word and wisdom, the Logos. He is the Wisdom that speaks to the children of men in the former part of the chapter. All divine revelation

passes through his hand, and centres in him ; but of him as the personal Wisdom, the second person in the Godhead, in the judgment of many of the ancients, Solomon here speaks, ver. 22—31. He concludes with a repeated charge to the children of men diligently to attend to the voice of God in his word, 32—36.

DOTH not wisdom cry ? and understanding put forth her voice? 2 She standeth in the top of high places, by the way in the places of the paths. 3 She crieth at the gates, at the entry of the city, at the coming in at the doors. 4 Unto you, O men, I call ; and my voice *is* to the sons of man. 5 O ye simple, understand wisdom : and, ye fools, be ye of an understanding heart. 6 Hear; for I will speak of excellent things ; and the opening of my lips *shall be* right things. 7 For my mouth shall speak truth ; and wickedness *is* an abomination to my lips. 8 All the words of my mouth *are* in righteousness ; *there is* nothing froward or perverse in them. 9 They *are* all plain to him that understandeth, and right to them that find knowledge. 10 Receive my instruction, and not silver ; and knowledge rather than choice gold. 11 For wisdom *is* better than rubies; and all the things that may be desired are not to be compared to it.

The will of God revealed to us for our salvation is here largely represented to us as easy to be known and understood, that none may have an excuse for their ignorance or error, and as worthy to be embraced, that none may have an excuse for their carelessness and unbelief.

I. The things revealed are easy to be known, for they *belong to us and to our children* (Deut. xxix. 29), and we need not soar up to heaven, or dive into the depths, to get the knowledge of them (Deut. xxx. 11), for they are published and proclaimed in some measure by the works of the creation (Ps. xix. 1), more fully by the consciences of men and the eternal reasons and rules of good and evil, but most clearly by Moses and the prophets ; let them hear them. The precepts of wisdom may easily be known ; for, 1. They are proclaimed aloud (*v.* 1): *Does not Wisdom cry?* Yes, she cries aloud, and does not spare (Isa. lviii. 1); she *puts forth her voice*, as one in earnest and desirous to be heard. *Jesus stood and cried*, John vii. 37. The curses and blessings were read with a loud voice by the Levites, Deut. xxvii. 14. And men's own hearts sometimes speak aloud to them ; there are clamours of conscience, as well as whispers. 2. They are proclaimed from on high (*v.* 2): *She stands in the top of high places;* it was from the top of Mount Sinai that the law was given, and Christ expounded it in a sermon upon the mount. Nay, if we slight divine revelation, we *turn away from him that speaks from heaven,* a high place indeed, Heb. xii. 25. The adulterous woman spoke in secret, the oracles of the heathen muttered, but Wisdom speaks openly; truth seeks no corners, but gladly appeals to the light. 3. They are proclaimed *in the places of concourse,* where multitudes are gathered together, the more the better. Jesus spoke *in the synagogues and in the temple, whither the Jews always resorted,* John xviii. 20. Every man that passes by on the road, of what rank or condition soever, may know what is good, and what the Lord requires of him, if it be not his own fault. There is no speech nor language where Wisdom's voice is not heard; her discoveries and directions are given to all promiscuously. *He that has ears to hear, let him hear.* 4. They are proclaimed where they are most needed. They are intended for the guide of our way, and therefore are published *in the places of the paths,* where many ways meet, that travellers may be shown, if they will but ask, which is the right way, just then when they are at a loss; thou shalt then *hear the word behind thee, saying, This is the way,* Isa. xxx. 21. The foolish man *knows not how to go to the city* (Eccl. x. 15), and therefore Wisdom stands ready to direct him, stands *at the gates, at the entry of the city,* ready to tell him where the seer's house is, 1 Sam. ix. 18. Nay, she follows men to their own houses, and cries to them *at the coming in at the doors,* saying, *Peace be to this house; and, if the son of peace be there,* it shall certainly abide upon it. God's ministers are appointed to testify to people both publicly and from house to house. Their own consciences follow them with admonitions wherever they go, which they cannot be out of the hearing of while they carry their own heads and hearts about with them, which are a law unto themselves. 5. They are directed to the children of men. We attend to that discourse in which we hear ourselves named, though otherwise we should have neglected it; therefore Wisdom speaks to us: " *Unto you, O men! I call* (v. 4), not to angels (they need not these instructions), not to devils (they are past them), not to the brute-creatures (they are not capable of them), but *to you, O men!* who are taught more than the beasts of the earth and made wiser than the fowls of heaven. To you is this law given, to you is the word of this invitation, this exhortation sent. *My voice is to the sons of men,* who are concerned to receive instruction, and to whom, one would think, it should be very welcome. It is not, to you, O Jews! only, that Wisdom cries, nor to you, O gentlemen! nor to you, O scholars! but *to you, O men! O sons of men!* even the meanest." 6. They are designed to make them wise (v. 5); they are calculated not only for men that are capable of wisdom, but for sinful men, fallen men, foolish men, that need it, and are undone without it: " *O you simple ones! understand wisdom.*

832

Though you are ever so simple, Wisdom will take you for her scholars, and not only so, but, if you will be ruled by her, will undertake to give you *an understanding heart.*" When sinners leave their sins, and become truly religious, then the *simple understand wisdom.*

II. The things revealed are worthy to be known, well worthy of all acceptation. We are concerned to hear; for, 1. They are of inestimable value. They are *excellent things* (v. 6), *princely things,* so the word is. Though they are level to the capacity of the meanest, yet there is that in them which will be entertainment for the greatest. They are divine and heavenly things, so excellent that, in comparison with them, all other learning is but children's play. Things which relate to an eternal God, an immortal soul, and an everlasting state, must needs be *excellent things.* 2. They are of incontestable equity, and carry along with them the evidence of their own goodness. They are *right things* (v. 6), *all in righteousness* (v. 8), and *nothing froward or perverse in them.* All the dictates and directions of revealed religion are consonant to, and perfective of, the light and law of nature, and there is nothing in them that puts any hardship upon us, that lays us under any undue restraints, unbecoming the dignity and liberty of the human nature, nothing that we have reason to complain of. *All God's precepts concerning all things are right.* 3. They are of unquestionable truth. Wisdom's doctrines, upon which her laws are founded, are such as we may venture our immortal souls upon: *My mouth shall speak truth* (v. 7), the whole truth, and nothing but the truth, for it is a testimony to the world. Every word of God is true; there are not so much as pious frauds in it, nor are we imposed upon in that which is told us for our good. Christ is a faithful witness, the truth itself; *wickedness* (that is, lying) *is an abomination to his lips.* Note, Lying is wickedness, and we should not only refrain from it, but it should be an abomination to us, and as far from what we say as from what God says to us. His word to us is *yea, and amen;* never then let ours be *yea and nay.* 4. They are wonderfully acceptable and agreeable to those who take them aright, who understand themselves aright, who have not their judgments blinded and biassed by the world and the flesh, are not under the power of prejudice, are taught of God, and whose understanding he·has opened, who impartially *seek knowledge,* take pains for it, and have found it in the enquiries they have hitherto made. To them, (1.) They are all *plain,* and not hard to be understood. If the book is sealed, it is to those who are willingly ignorant. *If our gospel is hidden, it is hidden to those who are lost;* but to those who *depart from evil,* which *is understanding,* who have that *good understanding* which those have who *do the commandments,* to them *they are all plain* and there is nothing difficult in them. The way of religion is a highway, and *the way-faring men, though fools, shall not err therein,* Isa. xxxv. 8. Those therefore do a great wrong to the common people who deny them the use of the scripture under pretence that they cannot understand it, whereas it is plain for plain people. (2.) They are all *right,* and not hard to be submitted to. Those who discern things that differ, who know good and evil, readily subscribe to the rectitude of all Wisdom's dictates, and therefore, without murmuring or disputing, govern themselves by them.

III. From all this he infers that the right knowledge of those things, such as transforms us into the image of them, is to be preferred before all the wealth of this world (*v.* 10, 11): *Receive my instruction, and not silver.* Instruction must not only be heard, but received. We must bid it welcome, receive the impressions of it, and submit to the command of it; and this *rather than choice gold,* that is, 1. We must prefer religion before riches, and look upon it that, if we have the knowledge and fear of God in our hearts, we are really more happy and better provided for every condition of life than if we had ever so much silver and gold. *Wisdom is* in itself, and therefore must be in our account, *better than rubies.* It will bring us in a better price, be to us a better portion; show it forth, and it will be a better ornament than jewels and precious stones of the greatest value. Whatever we can sit down and wish for of the wealth of this world would, if we had it, be unworthy to be compared with the advantages that attend serious godliness. 2. We must be dead to the wealth of this world, that we may the more closely and earnestly apply ourselves to the business of religion. We must receive instruction as the main matter, and then be indifferent whether we receive silver or no; nay, we must not receive it as our portion and reward, as the rich man in his life-time *received his good things.*

12 I wisdom dwell with prudence, and find out knowledge of witty inventions. 13 The fear of the LORD *is* to hate evil: pride, and arrogancy, and the evil way, and the froward mouth, do I hate. 14 Counsel *is* mine, and sound wisdom: I *am* understanding; I have strength. 15 By me kings reign, and princes decree justice. 16 By me princes rule, and nobles, *even* all the judges of the earth. 17 I love them that love me; and those that seek me early shall find me. 18 Riches and honour *are* with me; *yea,* durable riches and righteousness. 19 My fruit *is* better than gold, yea, than fine gold; and my revenue than choice silver. 20 I lead

in the way of righteousness, in the midst of the paths of judgment: 21 That I may cause those that love me to inherit substance; and I will fill their treasures.

Wisdom here is Christ, *in whom are hidden all the treasures of wisdom and knowledge;* it is Christ in the word and Christ in the heart, not only Christ revealed to us, but Christ revealed in us. It is the word of God, the whole compass of divine revelation; it is God the Word, in whom all divine revelation centres; it is the soul formed by the word; it is Christ formed in the soul; it is religion in the purity and power of it. Glorious things are here spoken of this excellent person, this excellent thing.

I. Divine wisdom gives men good heads (*v.* 12): *I Wisdom dwell with prudence,* not with carnal policy (the wisdom that is from above is contrary to that, 2 Cor. i. 12), but with true discretion, which serves for the right ordering of the conversation, that wisdom of the prudent which is to *understand his way* and is in all cases *profitable to direct,* the wisdom of the serpent, not only to guard from harm, but to guide in doing good. *Wisdom dwells with prudence;* for prudence is the product of religion and an ornament to religion; and there are more *witty inventions* found out with the help of the scripture, both for the right understanding of God's providences and for the effectual countermining of Satan's devices and the doing of good in our generation, than were ever discovered by the learning of the philosophers or the politics of statesmen. We may apply it to Christ himself; he *dwells with prudence,* for his whole undertaking is the *wisdom of God in a mystery,* and in it God *abounds towards us in all wisdom and prudence.* Christ *found out the knowledge of* that great *invention,* and a costly one it was to him, man's salvation, by his satisfaction, an admirable expedient. We had found out many inventions for our ruin; he found out one for our recovery. The covenant of grace is so well ordered in all things that we must conclude that he who ordered it *dwelt with prudence.*

II. It gives men good hearts, *v.* 13. True religion, consisting in *the fear of the Lord,* which is the wisdom before recommended, teaches men, 1. To hate all sin, as displeasing to God and destructive to the soul: *The fear of the Lord is to hate evil, the evil way,* to hate sin as sin, and therefore to *hate every false way.* Wherever there is an awe of God there is a dread of sin, as an evil, as only evil. 2. Particularly to hate pride and passion, those two common and dangerous sins. Conceitedness of ourselves, *pride and arrogancy,* are sins which Christ hates, and so do all those who have the Spirit of Christ; every one hates them in others, but we must hate them in ourselves. *The froward mouth,* peevishness towards others, God hates, because it is such an enemy to the peace of mankind, and therefore we should hate it. Be it spoken to the honour of religion that, however it is unjustly accused, it is so far from making men conceited and sour that there is nothing more directly contrary to it than pride and passion, nor which it teaches us more to detest.

III. It has a great influence upon public affairs and the well-governing of all societies, *v.* 14. Christ, as God, has strength and wisdom; wisdom and might are his; as Redeemer, he is *the wisdom of God and the power of God.* To all that are his he is made of God both *strength* and *wisdom;* in him they are laid up for us, that we may both know and do our duty. He is the wonderful counsellor and gives that grace which alone is *sound wisdom.* He *is understanding* itself, and *has strength* for all those that strengthen themselves in him. True religion gives men the best counsel in all difficult cases, and helps to make their way plain. Wherever it is, it is *understanding,* it has *strength;* it will be all that to us that we need, both for services and sufferings. Where the word of God dwells richly it makes a man *perfect* and *furnishes him thoroughly for every good word and work.* Kings, princes, and judges, have of all men most need of wisdom and strength, of counsel and courage, for the faithful discharge of the trusts reposed in them, and that they may be blessings to the people over whom they are set. And therefore Wisdom says, *By me kings reign* (*v.* 15, 16), that is, 1. Civil government is a divine institution, and those that are entrusted with the administration of it have their commission from Christ: it is a branch of his kingly office that *by him kings reign;* from him to whom all judgment is committed their power is derived. They reign by him, and therefore ought to reign for him. 2. Whatever qualifications for government any kings or princes have they are indebted to the grace of Christ for them; he gives them the spirit of government, and they have nothing, no skill, no principles of justice, but what he endues them with. *A divine sentence is in the lips of the king;* and kings are to their subjects what he makes them. 3. Religion is very much the strength and support of the civil government; it teaches subjects their duty, and so *by it kings reign* over them the more easily; it teaches kings their duty, and so *by it kings reign* as they ought; they *decree justice,* while they *rule in the fear of God.* Those rule well whom religion rules.

IV. It will make all those happy, truly happy, that receive and embrace it.

1. They shall be happy in the love of Christ; for he it is that says, *I love those that love me, v.* 17. Those that *love the Lord Jesus Christ in sincerity* shall be beloved of him with a peculiar distinguishing love: he will *love them and manifest himself to them.*

2. They shall be happy in the success of their enquiries after him: " *Those that seek*

me early, seek an acquaintance with me and an interest in me, seek me *early,* that is, seek me earnestly, seek me first before any thing else, that begin betimes in the days of their youth to seek me, they shall find what they seek." Christ shall be theirs, and they shall be his. He never said, *Seek in vain.*

3. They shall be happy in the wealth of the world, or in that which is infinitely better. (1.) They shall have as much riches and honour as Infinite Wisdom sees good for them (*v.* 18); they are *with Christ,* that is, he has them to give, and whether he will see fit to give them to us must be referred to him. Religion sometimes helps to make people rich and great in this world, gains them a reputation, and so increases their estates; and the riches which Wisdom gives to her favourites have these two advantages:—[1.] That they are *riches and righteousness,* riches honestly got, not by fraud and oppression, but in regular ways, and riches charitably used, for alms are called *righteousness.* Those that have their wealth from God's blessing on their industry, and that have a heart to do good with it, have *riches and righteousness.* [2.] That therefore they are *durable riches.* Wealth gotten by vanity will soon be diminished, but that which is well got will wear well and will be left to the children's children, and that which is well spent in works of piety and charity is put out to the best interest and so will be durable; for the friends made by *the mammon of unrighteousness when we fail will receive us into everlasting habitations,* Luke xvi. 9. It will be found after many days, for the days of eternity. (2.) They shall have that which is infinitely better, if they have not riches and honour in this world (*v.* 19): "*My fruit is better than gold,* and will turn to a better account, will be of more value in less compass, *and my revenue better than the choicest silver,* will serve a better trade." We may assure ourselves that not only Wisdom's products at last, but her income in the mean time, not only her fruit, but her revenue, is more valuable than the best either of the possessions or of the reversions of this world.

4. They shall be happy in the grace of God now; that shall be their guide in the good way, *v.* 20. This is that fruit of wisdom which is *better than gold, than fine gold,* it *leads us in the way of righteousness,* shows us that way and goes before us in it, the way that God would have us walk in and which will certainly bring us to our desired end. It leads *in the midst of the paths of judgment,* and saves us from deviating on either hand. *In medio virtus—Virtue lies in the midst.* Christ by his Spirit guides believers into all truth, and so *leads them in the way of righteousness,* and they *walk after the Spirit.*

5. They shall be happy in the glory of God hereafter, *v.* 21. *Therefore* Wisdom *leads in the paths of righteousness,* not only that she may keep her friends in the way of duty and

obedience, but that she may *cause them to inherit substance* and may *fill their treasures,* which cannot be done with the things of this world, nor with any thing less than God and heaven. The happiness of those that love God, and devote themselves to his service, is substantial and satisfactory. (1.) It is substantial; it is substance itself. It is a happiness which will subsist of itself, and stand alone, without the accidental supports of outward conveniences. Spiritual and eternal things are the only real and substantial things. Joy in God is substantial joy, solid and well-grounded. The promises are their bonds, Christ is their surety, and both substantial. They *inherit substance;* that is, their inheritance hereafter is-substantial; it is a weight of glory; it is substance, Heb. x. 34. All their happiness they have as heirs; it is grounded upon their sonship. (2.) It is satisfying; it will not only fill their hands, but *fill their treasures,* not only maintain them, but make them rich. The things of this world may fill men's bellies (Ps. xvii. 14), but not their treasures, for they cannot in them secure to themselves *goods for many years;* perhaps they may be deprived of them *this night.* But let the treasures of the soul be ever so capacious there is enough in God, and Christ, and heaven, to fill them. In Wisdom's promises believers have goods laid up, not for days and years, but for eternity; her fruit therefore *is better than gold.*

22 The LORD possessed me in the beginning of his way, before his works of old. 23 I was set up from everlasting, from the beginning, or ever the earth was. 24 When *there were* no depths, I was brought forth; when *there were* no fountains abounding with water. 25 Before the mountains were settled, before the hills was I brought forth: 26 While as yet he had not made the earth, nor the fields, nor the highest part of the dust of the world. 27 When he prepared the heavens, I *was* there: when he set a compass upon the face of the depth: 28 When he established the clouds above: when he strengthened the fountains of the deep: 29 When he gave to the sea his decree, that the waters should not pass his commandment: when he appointed the foundations of the earth: 30 Then I was by him, *as* one brought up *with him:* and I was daily *his* delight, rejoicing always before him; 31 Rejoicing in the habitable part of his earth; and my delights *were* with the sons of men.

That it is an intelligent and divine person that here speaks seems very plain, and that it is not meant of a mere essential property of the divine nature, for Wisdom here has personal properties and actions; and that intelligent divine person can be no other than the Son of God himself, to whom the principal things here spoken of wisdom are attributed in other scriptures, and we must explain scripture by itself. If Solomon himself designed only the praise of wisdom as it is an attribute of God, by which he made the world and governs it, so to recommend to men the study of that wisdom which belongs to them, yet the Spirit of God, who indited what he wrote, carried him, as David often, to such expressions as could agree to no other than the Son of God, and would lead us into the knowledge of great things concerning him. All divine revelation is *the revelation of Jesus Christ, which God gave unto him,* and here we are told who and what he is, as God, designed in the eternal counsels to be the Mediator between God and man. The best exposition of these verses we have in the first four verses of St. John's gospel. *In the beginning was the Word,* &c. Concerning the Son of God observe here,

I. His personality and distinct subsistence, one with the Father and of the same essence, and yet a person of himself, whom *the Lord possessed* (v. 22), *who was set up* (v. 23), *was brought forth* (v. 24, 25), *was by him* (v. 30), for he was *the express image of his person,* Heb. i. 3.

II. His eternity; he was begotten of the Father, for *the Lord possessed* him, as his own Son, his beloved Son, laid him in his bosom; he was *brought forth as the only-begotten of the Father,* and this *before all worlds,* which is most largely insisted upon here. The Word was eternal, and had a being before the world, before the beginning of time; and therefore it must follow that it was from eternity. *The Lord possessed him in the beginning of his way,* of his eternal counsels, for those were *before his works.* This way indeed had no beginning, for God's purposes in himself are eternal like himself, but God speaks to us in our own language. Wisdom explains herself (v. 23): *I was set up from everlasting.* The Son of God was, in the eternal counsels of God, designed and advanced to be the wisdom and power of the Father, light and life, and all in all, both in the creation and in the redemption of the world. That he *was brought forth* as to his being, and *set up* as to the divine counsels concerning his office, before the world was made, is here set forth in a great variety of expressions, much the same with those by which the eternity of God himself is expressed Ps. xc. 2, *Before the mountains were brought forth.* 1. *Before the earth was,* and that was made *in the beginning,* before man was made; therefore the second Adam had a being before the first, for the first Adam was *made of the earth*, the second had a being *before the earth*, and therefore is *not of the earth*, John iii. 31. 2. Before the sea was (*v*. 24), *when there were no depths* in which the waters were gathered together, *no fountains* from which those waters might arise, none of that deep on which the Spirit of God moved for the production of the visible creation, Gen. i. 2. 3. Before the mountains were, the everlasting mountains, *v*. 25. Eliphaz, to convince Job of his inability to judge of the divine counsels, asks him (Job xv. 7), *Wast thou made before the hills?* No, thou wast not. But *before the hills was* the eternal Word *brought forth*. 4. Before the habitable parts of the world, which men cultivate, and reap the profits of (*v*. 26), *the fields* in the valleys and plains, to which the mountains are as a wall, which are *the highest part of the dust of the world;* the *first part of the dust* (so some), the atoms which compose the several parts of the world; *the chief or principal part of the dust*, so it may be read, and understood of man, who was made of the dust of the ground and is dust, but is the principal part of the dust, dust enlivened, dust refined. The eternal Word had a being before man was made, for *in him was the life of men.*

III. His agency in making the world. He not only had a being before the world, but he was present, not as a spectator, but as the architect, when the world was made. God silenced and humbled Job by asking him, "*Where wast thou when I laid the foundations of the earth? Who hath laid the measures thereof?*" (Job xxxviii. 4, &c.) Wast thou that eternal Word and wisdom, who was the prime manager of that great affair? No; thou art of yesterday." But here the Son of God, referring, as it should seem, to the discourse God had with Job, declares himself to have been engaged in that which Job could not pretend to be a witness of and a worker in, the creation of the world. *By him God made the worlds*, Eph. iii. 9; Heb. i. 2; Col. i. 16. 1. When, on the first day of the creation, in the very beginning of time, God said, *Let there be light*, and with a word produced it, this eternal Wisdom was that almighty Word: Then *I was there, when he prepared the heavens*, the fountain of that light, which, whatever it is here, is there substantial. 2. He was no less active when, on the second day, he stretched out the firmament, the vast expanse, and *set* that as *a compass upon the face of the depth* (*v*. 27), surrounded it on all sides with that canopy, that curtain. Or it may refer to the exact order and method with which God framed all the parts of the universe, as the workman marks out his work with his line and compasses. The work in nothing varied from the plan of it formed in the eternal mind. 3. He was also employed in the third day's work, when the *waters above the heavens* were gathered together by *establishing the clouds above*, and those under the heavens by *strengthening the fountains of*

the deep, which send forth those waters (*v*. 28), and by preserving the bounds of the sea, which is the receptacle of those waters, *v*. 29. This speaks much the honour of this eternal Wisdom, for by this instance God proves himself a God greatly to be feared (Jer. v. 22) that *he has placed the sand for the bound of the sea*, that the dry land might continue to appear above water, fit to be a habitation for man; and thus he has *appointed the foundation of the earth*. How able, how fit, is the Son of God to be the Saviour of the world, who was the Creator of it!

IV. The infinite complacency which the Father had in him, and he in the Father (*v*. 30): *I was by him, as one brought up with him.* As by an eternal generation he was brought forth of the Father, so by an eternal counsel he was brought up with him, which intimates, not only the infinite love of the Father to the Son, who is therefore called *the Son of his love* (Col. i. 13), but the mutual consciousness and good understanding that were between them concerning the work of man's redemption, which the Son was to undertake, and about which the *counsel of peace was between them both*, Zech. vi. 13. He was *alumnus patris—the Father's pupil*, as I may say, trained up from eternity for that service which in time, in the fulness of time, he was to go through with, and is therein taken under the special tuition and protection of the Father; he is *my servant whom I uphold*, Isa. xlii. 1. He did what he saw the Father do (John v. 19), pleased his Father, sought his glory, did according to the commandment he received from his Father, and all this *as one brought up with him.* He was *daily his Father's delight (my elect, in whom my soul delighteth*, says God, Isa. xlii. 1), and he also *rejoiced always before him.* This may be understood either, 1. Of the infinite delight which the persons of the blessed Trinity have in each other, wherein consists much of the happiness of the divine nature. Or, 2. Of the pleasure which the Father took in the operations of the Son, when he *made the world;* God saw every thing that the Son made, *and, behold, it was very good*, it pleased him, and therefore his Son was *daily*, day by day, during the six days of the creation, upon that account, *his delight*, Exod. xxxix. 43. And the Son also did himself *rejoice before him* in the beauty and harmony of the whole creation, Ps. civ. 31. Or, 3. Of the satisfaction they had in each other, with reference to the great work of man's redemption. The Father delighted in the Son, as Mediator between him and man, was well-pleased with what he proposed (Matt. iii. 17), and *therefore* loved him because he undertook to *lay down his life for the sheep;* he put a confidence in him that he would go through his work, and not fail nor fly off. The Son also *rejoiced always before him*, delighted to do his will (Ps. xl. 8), adhered closely to his undertaking, as one that was well-satisfied in it, and, when it came to the setting to, expressed as much satisfaction in it as ever, saying, *Lo, I come, to do as in the volume of the book it is written of me.*

V. The gracious concern he had for mankind, *v.* 31. Wisdom *rejoiced*, not so much in the rich products of the earth, or the treasures hid in the bowels of it, as *in the habitable parts of* it, for her *delights were with the sons of men;* not only in the creation of man is it spoken with a particular air of pleasure (Gen. i. 26), *Let us make man,* but in the redemption and salvation of man. The Son of God was *ordained, before the world,* to that great work, 1 Pet. i. 20. A remnant of the sons of men were given him to be brought, through his grace, to his glory, and these were those in whom his delights were. His church was the habitable part of his earth, made habitable for him, *that the Lord God might dwell* even *among those* that had been rebellious; and this he rejoiced in, in the prospect of seeing his seed. Though he foresaw all the difficulties he was to meet with in his work, the services and sufferings he was to go through, yet, because it would issue in the glory of his Father and the salvation of those sons of men that were given him, he looked forward upon it with the greatest satisfaction imaginable, in which we have all the encouragement we can desire to come to him and rely upon him for all the benefits designed us by his glorious undertaking.

32 Now therefore hearken unto me, O ye children: for blessed *are they that* keep my ways. 33 Hear instruction, and be wise, and refuse it not. 34 Blessed *is* the man that heareth me, watching daily at my gates, waiting at the posts of my doors. 35 For whoso findeth me findeth life, and shall obtain favour of the LORD. 36 But he that sinneth against me wrongeth his own soul: all they that hate me lo,·e death.

We have here the application of Wisdom's discourse; the design and tendency of it is to bring us all into an entire subjection to the laws of religion, to make us wise and good, not to fill our heads with speculations, or our tongues with disputes, but to rectify what is amiss in our hearts and lives. In order to this, here is,

I. An exhortation to hear and obey the voice of Wisdom, to attend and comply with the good instructions that the word of God gives us, and in them to discern the voice of Christ, as the sheep know the shepherd's voice.

1. We must be diligent *hearers of the word;* for how can we believe in him of whom we have not heard? *"Hearken unto me, O you children!" v.* 32. " Read the word written, sit under the word preached, bless God for

both, and hear him in both speaking to you." Let children in age hearken, for it is their learning age, and what they hearken to then, it is likely, they will be so seasoned by as to be governed by all their days. Let children in relation hearken to God as their Father, to Wisdom as their mother, to whom they ought to be in subjection and live. Let Wisdom's children justify Wisdom by hearkening to her, and show themselves to be indeed her children. We must hear Wisdom's words, (1.) Submissively, and with a willing heart (*v.* 33): " *Hear instruction, and refuse it not,* either as that which you need not or as that which you like not; it is offered you as a kindness, and it is at your peril if you refuse it." Those that reject the counsel of God reject it against themselves, Luke vii. 30. " Refuse it not now, lest you should not have another offer." (2.) Constantly, and with an attentive ear. We must hear Wisdom so as to *watch daily at her gates,* as beggars to receive an alms, as clients and patients to receive advice, and to wait as servants, with humility, and patience, and ready observance, *at the posts of her doors.* See here what a good house Wisdom keeps, for every day is doleday; what a good school, for every day is lecture-day. While we have God's works before our eyes, and his word in our hand, we may be every day hearing Wisdom, and learning instruction from her. See here what a dutiful and diligent attendance is required of all Christ's disciples; they must *watch at the gates.* [1.] We must lay hold on all opportunities of getting knowledge and grace, and must get into, and keep in, a constant settled course of communion with God. [2.] We must be very humble in our attendance on divine instructions, and be glad of any place, even the meanest, so we may but be within hearing of them, as David, who would gladly be a door-keeper in the house of God. [3.] We must raise our expectations of these instructions, and hearken to them with care, and patience, and perseverance, must watch and wait, as Christ's hearers, that *hanged on him* to hear him, as the word in the original is (Luke xix. 48) and (*ch.* xxi. 38) *came early in the morning to hear him.*

2. We must be conscientious *doers of the work,* for we are *blessed only in our deed.* It is not enough to hearken unto Wisdom's words, but we must *keep her ways* (*v.* 32), do every thing that she prescribes, keep within the hedges of her ways, and not transgress them, keep in the tracks of her ways, proceed and persevere in them. " *Hear instruction and be wise;* let it be a means to make you wise in ordering your conversation." What we know is known in vain if it do not make us wise, *v.* 33.

II. An assurance of happiness to all those that do hearken to Wisdom. They are blessed, *v.* 32 and again *v.* 34. Those are blessed that watch and wait at Wisdom's gates; even their attendance there is their happiness; it is the

best place they can be in. Those are blessed
that wait there, for they shall not be put to
wait long; let them continue to knock awhile
and it shall be opened to them. They are
seeking Wisdom, and they shall find what
they seek. •But will it make them amends if
they do find it? Yes (*v.* 35): *Whoso finds me
finds life,* that is, all happiness, all that good
which he needs or can desire. He finds life
in that grace which is the principle of spiritual life and the pledge of eternal life. He
finds life, for he shall *obtain favour of the
Lord,* and *in his favour is life.* If the king's
favour is towards a wise son, much more the
favour of the King of kings. Christ is Wisdom, and he that finds Christ, that obtains
an interest in him, he *finds life;* for Christ is
life to all believers. *He that has the Son of
God has life,* eternal life, and he *shall obtain
favour of the Lord,* who is well-pleased with
all those that are in Christ; nor can we obtain God's favour, unless we find Christ and
be found in him.

III. The doom passed upon all those that
reject Wisdom and her proposals, *v.* 36. They
are left to ruin themselves, and Wisdom will
not hinder them, because they have set at
nought all her counsel. 1. Their crime is
very great; they *sin against Wisdom,* rebel
against its light and laws, thwart its designs,
and by their folly offend it. They *sin against
Christ;* they act in contempt of his authority,
and in contradiction to all the purposes of his
life and death. This is construed into hating
Wisdom, hating Christ; they are his enemies,
who will not have him to reign over them.
What can appear worse than hating him who
is the centre of all beauty and fountain of all
goodness, love itself? 2. Their punishment
will be very just, for they wilfully bring it
upon themselves. (1.) Those that offend
Christ do the greatest wrong to themselves;
they *wrong their own souls;* they wound their
own consciences, bring a blot and stain upon
their souls, which renders them odious in the
eyes of God, and unfit for communion with
him; they deceive themselves, disturb themselves, destroy themselves. Sin is a wrong
to the soul. (2.) Those that are at variance
with Christ are in love with their own ruin:
Those that hate me love death; they love that
which will be their death, and put that from
them which would be their life. Sinners die
because they will die, which leaves them inexcusable, makes their condemnation the more
intolerable, and will for ever justify God when
he judges. *O Israel! thou hast destroyed
thyself.*

CHAP. IX.

Christ and sin are rivals for the soul of man, and here we are told
how they both make their court to it, to have the innermost and
uppermost place in it. The design of this representation is to
set before us life and death, good and evil; and there needs no
more than a fair stating of the case to determine us which of
those to choose, and surrender our hearts to. They are both
brought in making entertainment for the soul, and inviting it to
accept of the entertainment; concerning both we are told what
the issue will be; and, the matter being thus laid before us, let
us consider, take advice, and speak our minds. And we are
therefore concerned to put a value upon our own souls, because
we see there is such striving for them. I. Christ, under the
name of Wisdom, invites us to accept of his entertainment, and

so to enter into acquaintance and communion with him, ver. 1
—6. And having foretold the different success of his invitation
(ver. 7—9) he shows, in short, what he requires from us (ver.
10) and what he designs for us (ver. 11), and then leaves it to
our choice what we will do, ver. 12. II. Sin, under the character of a foolish woman, courts us to accept of her entertainment,
and (ver. 13—16) pretends it is very charming, ver. 17. But Solomon tells us what the reckoning will be, ver. 18. And now
choose you, this day, whom you will close with.

WISDOM hath builded her house,
she hath hewn out her seven
pillars: 2 She hath killed her beasts;
she hath mingled her wine; she hath
also furnished her table. 3 She hath
sent forth her maidens: she crieth
upon the highest places of the city,
4 Whoso *is* simple, let him turn in
hither: *as for* him that wanteth understanding, she saith to him, 5 Come,
eat of my bread, and drink of the
wine *which* I have mingled. 6 Forsake the foolish, and live; and go in
the way of understanding. 7 He that
reproveth a scorner getteth to himself shame: and he that rebuketh a
wicked *man getteth* himself a blot.
8 Reprove not a scorner, lest he hate
thee: rebuke a wise man, and he will
love thee. 9 Give *instruction* to a
wise *man,* and he will be yet wiser:
teach a just *man,* and he will increase
in learning. 10 The fear of the LORD
is the beginning of wisdom: and the
knowledge of the holy *is* understanding. 11 For by me thy days shall be
multiplied, and the years of thy life
shall be increased. 12 If thou be
wise, thou shalt be wise for thyself:
but *if* thou scornest, thou alone shalt
bear it.

Wisdom is here introduced as a magnificent and munificent queen, very great and
very generous; that Word of God is this Wisdom in which God makes known his good-
will towards men; God the Word is this Wisdom, to whom the Father has committed all
judgment. He who, in the chapter before,
showed his grandeur and glory as the Creator of the world, here shows his grace and
goodness as the Redeemer of it. The word
is plural, *Wisdoms;* for in Christ are hid
treasures of wisdom, and in his undertaking
appears the manifold wisdom of God in a
mystery. Now observe here,

I. The rich provision which Wisdom has
made for the reception of all those that will
be her disciples. This is represented under
the similitude of a sumptuous feast, whence,
it is probable, our Saviour borrowed those
parables in which he compared the *kingdom
of heaven* to a great supper, Matt. xxii. 2;
Luke xiv. 16. And so it was prophesied of,
Isa. xxv. 6. It is such a feast as Ahasuerus

made to *show the riches of his glorious kingdom.* The grace of the gospel is thus set before us in the ordinance of the Lord's supper. To bid her guests welcome, 1. Here is a stately palace provided, *v.* 1. Wisdom, not finding a house capacious enough for all her guests, has built one on purpose, and, both to strengthen it and to beautify it, she has *hewn out her seven pillars,* which make it to be very firm, and look very great. Heaven is the house which Wisdom has built to entertain all her guests that are called to the marriage-supper of the Lamb; that is her Father's house, where there are many mansions, and whither she has gone to prepare places for us. She has hanged the earth upon nothing, therefore in it we have no continuing city; but heaven is a city that has foundations, has pillars. The church is Wisdom's house, to which she invites her guests, supported by the power and promise of God, as by *seven pillars.* Probably, Solomon refers to the temple which he himself had lately built for the service of religion, and to which he would persuade people to resort, both to worship God and to receive the instructions of Wisdom. Some reckon the schools of the prophets to be here intended. 2. Here is a splendid feast got ready (*v.* 2) : *She has killed her beasts; she has mingled her wine;* plenty of meat and drink are provided, and all of the best. *She has killed her sacrifice* (so the word is); it is a sumptuous, but a sacred feast, a feast upon a sacrifice. Christ has offered up himself a sacrifice for us, and it is *his flesh* that is *meat indeed* and *his blood* that is *drink indeed.* The Lord's supper is a feast of reconciliation and joy upon the sacrifice of atonement. The wine is *mingled* with something richer than itself, to give it a more than ordinary spirit and flavour. *She has* completely *furnished her table* with all the satisfactions that a soul can desire—righteousness and grace, peace and joy, the assurances of God's love, the consolations of the Spirit, and all the pledges and earnests of eternal life. Observe, It is all Wisdom's own doing ; *she* has killed the beasts, *she* has mingled the wine, which denotes both the love of Christ, who makes the provision (he does not leave it to others, but takes the doing of it into his own hands), and the excellency of the preparation. That must needs be exactly fitted to answer the end which Wisdom herself has the fitting up of.

II. The gracious invitation she has given, not to some particular friends, but to all in general, to come and take part of these provisions. 1. She employs her servants to carry the invitation round about in the country : *She has sent forth her maidens, v.* 3. The ministers of the gospel are commissioned and commanded to give notice of the preparations which God has made, in the everlasting covenant, for all those that are willing to come up to the terms of it ; and they, with maiden purity, not corrupting themselves or the word

of God, and with an exact observance of their orders, are to call upon all they meet with, even in *the highways and hedges,* to come and feast with Wisdom, for *all things are now ready,* Luke xiv. 23. 2. She herself *cries upon the highest places of the city,* as one earnestly desirous of the welfare of the children of men, and grieved to see them rejecting their own mercies for lying vanities. Our Lord Jesus was himself the publisher of his own gospel ; when he had sent forth his disciples he followed them to confirm what they said ; nay, it *began to be spoken by the Lord,* Heb. ii. 3. He stood, and cried, *Come unto me.* We see who invites ; now let us observe,

(1.) To whom the invitation is given : *Whoso is simple* and *wants understanding, v.* 4. If we were to make an entertainment, of all people we should not care for, much less court, the company of such, but rather of philosophers and learned men, that we might hear their wisdom, and whose table-talk would be improving. " Have I need of madmen ?" But Wisdom invites such, because what she has to give is what they most need, and it is their welfare that she consults, and aims at, in the preparation and invitation. He that is simple is invited, that he may be made wise, and he that *wants a heart* (so the word is) let him come hither, and he shall have one. Her preparations are rather physic than food, designed for the most valuable and desirable cure, that of the mind. Whosoever he be, the invitation is general, and excludes none that do not exclude themselves ; though they be ever so foolish, yet, [1.] They shall be welcome. [2.] They may be helped ; they shall neither be despised nor despaired of. Our Saviour came, *not to call the righteous, but sinners,* not the wise in their own eyes, who say they see (John ix. 41), but the simple, those who are sensible of their simplicity and ashamed of it, and him that is willing to *become a fool, that he may be wise,* 1 Cor. iii. 18.

(2.) What the invitation is. [1.] We are invited to Wisdom's house : *Turn in hither.* I say *we* are, for which of us is there that must not own the character of the invited, that are *simple and want understanding ?* Wisdom's doors stand open to such, and she is desirous to have some conversation with them, one word for their good, nor has she any other design upon them. [2.] We are invited to her table (*v.* 5) : *Come, eat of my bread,* that is, taste of the true pleasures that are to be found in the knowledge and fear of God. By faith acted on the promises of the gospel, applying them to ourselves and taking the comfort of them, we feed, we feast, upon the provisions Christ has made for poor souls. What we eat and drink we make our own, we are nourished and refreshed by it, and so are our souls by the word of God ; it has that in it which is *meat and drink* to those that have understanding.

(3.) What is required of those that may

have the benefit of this invitation, *v.* 6. [1.] They must break off from all bad company : "*Forsake the foolish,* converse not with them, conform not to their ways, have no fellowship with the works of darkness, or with those that deal in such works." The first step towards virtue is to shun vice, and therefore to shun the vicious. *Depart from me, you evil-doers.* [2.] They must awake and arise from the dead ; they must live, not in pleasure (for those that do so are dead while they live), but in the service of God ; for those only that do so live indeed, live to some purpose. " Live not a mere animal-life, as brutes, but now, at length, live the life of men. *Live* and *you shall live ;* live spiritually, and you shall live eternally," Eph. v. 14. [3.] They must choose the paths of Wisdom, and keep to them : "*Go in the way of understanding ;* govern thyself henceforward by the rules of religion and right reason." It is not enough to forsake the foolish, but we must join ourselves with those that walk in wisdom, and walk in the same spirit and steps.

III. The instructions which Wisdom gives to the maidens she sends to invite, to the ministers and others, who in their places are endeavouring to serve her interests and designs. She tells them,

1. What their work must be, not only to tell in general what preparation is made for souls, and to give a general offer of it, but they must address themselves to particular persons, must tell them of their faults, *reprove, rebuke,* v. 7, 8. They must instruct them how to amend—*teach,* v. 9. The word of God is intended, and therefore so is the ministry of that word, *for reproof, for correction, and for instruction in righteousness.*

2. What different sorts of persons they would meet with, and what course they must take with them, and what success they might expect.

(1.) They would meet with some *scorners* and *wicked men* who would mock the messengers of the Lord, and misuse them, would *laugh those to scorn* that invite them to the feast of the Lord, as they did, 2 Chron. xxx. 10, would *treat them spitefully,* Matt. xxii. 6. And, though they are not forbidden to invite those simple ones to Wisdom's house, yet they are advised not to pursue the invitation by reproving and rebuking them. *Reprove not a scorner ; cast not these pearls before swine,* Matt. vii. 6. Thus Christ said of the Pharisees, *Let them alone,* Matt. xv .14. "Do not reprove them." [1.] "In justice to them, for those have forfeited the favour of further means who scorn the means they have had. Those that are thus *filthy, let them be filthy still ;* those that are *joined to idols, let them alone ; lo, we turn to the Gentiles.*" [2.] "In prudence to yourselves ; because, if you reprove them," First, "You lose your labour, and so *get to yourselves shame* for the disappointment." *Secondly,* " You exasperate them ; do it ever so wisely and tenderly, if you do it faithfully, they will hate you, they will load 840

you with reproaches, and say all the ill they can of you, and so you will get a blot ; therefore you had better not meddle with them, for your reproofs will be likely to do more hurt than good."

(2.) They would meet with others, who are wise, and good, and just ; thanks be to God, all are not scorners. We meet with some who are so wise for themselves, so just to themselves, as to be willing and glad to be taught ; and when we meet with such, [1.] If there be occasion, we must reprove them ; for wise men are not so perfectly wise but there is that in them which needs a reproof ; and we must not connive at any man's faults because we have a veneration for his wisdom, nor must a *wise man* think that his wisdom exempts him from reproof when he says or does any thing foolishly ; but the more wisdom a man has the more desirous he should be to have his weaknesses shown him, because a *little folly* is a great blemish to *him that is in reputation for wisdom and honour.* [2.] With our reproofs we must *give* them *instruction,* and must *teach* them, v. 9. [3.] We may expect that our doing so will be taken as a kindness, Ps. cxli. 5. A wise man will reckon those his friends who deal faithfully with him : " Rebuke such a one, and *he will love thee* for thy plain dealing, will thank thee, and desire thee to do him the same good turn another time, if there be occasion." It is as great an instance of wisdom to take a reproof well as to give it well, [4.] Being taken well, it will do good, and answer the intention. A *wise man* will be made wiser by the reproofs and instructions that are given him ; he *will increase in learning,* will grow in knowledge, and so grow in grace. None must think themselves too wise to learn, nor so good that they need not be better and therefore need not be taught. We must still press forward, and follow on to know till we come to the perfect man. *Give to a wise man* (so it is in the original), give him advice, give him reproof, give him comfort, and *he will be yet wiser ; give him occasion* (so the LXX.), occasion to show his wisdom, and he will show it, and the acts of wisdom will strengthen the habits.

IV. The instructions she gives to those that are invited, which her maidens must inculcate upon them.

1. Let them know wherein true wisdom consists, and what will be their entertainment at Wisdom's table, v. 10. (1.) The heart must be principled with *the fear of God ; that is the beginning of wisdom.* A reverence of God's majesty, and a dread of his wrath, are that fear of him which is the beginning, the first step towards true religion, whence all other instances of it take rise. This fear may, at first, have torment ; but love will, by degrees, cast out the torment of it. (2.) The head must be filled with the knowledge of the things of God. *The knowledge of holy things* (the word is plural) *is under-*

standing, the things pertaining to the service of God (those are called *holy things*), that pertain to our own sanctification; reproof is called *that which is holy*, Matt. vii. 6. Or the knowledge which holy men have, which was taught by the holy prophets, of those things which *holy men spoke as they were moved by the holy Ghost*, this *is understanding;* it is the best and most useful understanding, will stand us in most stead and turn to the best account.

2. Let them know what will be the advantages of this wisdom (*v.* 11): "*By me thy days shall be multiplied.* It will contribute to the health of thy body, and so *the years of thy life* on earth *shall be increased*, while men's folly and intemperance shorten their days. It will bring thee to heaven, and there thy days shall be multiplied *in infinitum—to infinity*, and the *years of thy life shall be increased without end.*" There is no true wisdom but in the way of religion and no true life but in the end of that way.

3. Let them know what will be the consequence of their choosing or refusing this fair offer, *v.* 12. Here is, (1.) The happiness of those that embrace it: "*If thou be wise, thou shalt be wise for thyself;* thou wilt be the gainer by it, not Wisdom." A man cannot be profitable to God. It is to our own good that we are thus courted. "Thou wilt not leave the gain to others" (as we do our worldly wealth when we die, which is therefore called *another man's*, Luke xvi. 12), "but thou shalt carry it with thee into another world." Those that are wise for themselves are wise for themselves, for the soul is the man; nor do any consult their own true interest but those that are truly religious. This recommends us to God, and recovers us from that which is our folly and degeneracy; it employs us in that which is most beneficial in this world, and entitles us to that which is much more so in the world to come. (2.) The shame and ruin of those that slight it: "*If thou scornest* Wisdom's proffer, *thou alone shalt bear it.*" [1.] "Thou shalt bear the blame of it." Those that are good must thank God, but those that are wicked may thank themselves; it is not owing to God (he is not the author of sin); Satan can only tempt, he cannot force; and wicked companions are but his instruments; so that all the fault must lie on the sinner himself. [2.] "Thou shalt bear the loss of that which thou scornest; it will be to thy own destruction; thy blood will be upon thy own head, and the consideration of this will aggravate thy condemnation. *Son, remember,* that thou hadst this fair offer made thee, and thou wouldst not accept of it; thou stoodest fair for life, but didst choose death rather."

13 A foolish woman *is* clamorous: *she is* simple, and knoweth nothing. 14 For she sitteth at the door of her house, on a seat in the high places of the city. 15 To call passengers who go right on their ways: 16 Whoso *is* simple, let him turn in hither: and *as for* him that wanteth understanding, she saith to him, 17 Stolen waters are sweet, and bread *eaten* in secret is pleasant. 18 But he knoweth not that the dead *are* there; *and that* her guests *are* in the depths of hell.

We have heard what Christ has to say, to engage our affections to God and godliness, and one would think the whole world should go after him; but here we are told how industrious the tempter is to seduce unwary souls into the paths of sin, and with the most he gains his point, and Wisdom's courtship is not effectual. Now observe,

I. Who is the tempter—*a foolish woman*, Folly herself, in opposition to Wisdom. Carnal sensual pleasure I take to be especially meant by this *foolish woman* (*v.* 13); for that is the great enemy to virtue and inlet to vice; that defiles and debauches the mind, stupifies conscience, and puts out the sparks of conviction, more than any thing else. This tempter is here described to be, 1. Very ignorant: *She is simple and knows nothing*, that is, she has no sufficient solid reason to offer; where she gets dominion in a soul she works out all the knowledge of holy things; they are lost and forgotten. *Whoredom, and wine, and new wine, take away the heart;* they besot men, and make fools of them. (2.) Very importunate. The less she has to offer that is rational the more violent and pressing she is, and carries the day often by dint of impudence. She *is clamorous* and noisy (*v.* 13), continually haunting young people with her enticements. *She sits at the door of her house* (*v.* 14), watching for a prey; not as Abraham at his tent-door, seeking an opportunity to do good. *She sits on a seat (on a throne,* so the word signifies) *in the high places of the city*, as if she had authority to give law, and we were all *debtors to the flesh, to live after the flesh*, and as if she had reputation, and were in honour, and thought worthy of *the high places of the city;* and perhaps she gains upon many more by pretending to be fashionable than by pretending to be agreeable. "Do not all persons of rank and figure in the world" (says she) "give themselves a greater liberty than the strict laws of virtue allow; and why shouldst thou humble thyself so far as to be cramped by them?" Thus the tempter affects to seem both kind and great.

II. Who are the tempted—young people who have been well educated; these she will triumph most in being the ruin of. Observe, 1. What their real character is; they are *passengers that go right on their ways* (*v.* 15), that have been trained up in the paths of religion and virtue and set out very hopefully and well, that seemed determined and designed for good, and are not (as that young man, *ch.* vii. 8) *going the way to her house.* Such as these she has a design upon, and lays snares for, and uses all her arts, all her charms, to pervert them; if they *go right on,* and will not look towards her, she will call after them, so urgent are these temptations. (2) How she represents them. She calls them *simple* and *wanting understanding,* and therefore courts them to her school, that they may be cured of the restraints and formalities of their religion. This is the method of the stage (which is too close an exposition of this paragraph), where the sober young man, that has been virtuously educated, is the fool in the play, and the plot is to make him *seven times more a child of hell* than his profane companions, under colour of polishing and refining him, and setting him up for a wit and a beau. What is justly charged upon sin and impiety (*v.* 4), that it is folly, is here very unjustly retorted upon the ways of virtue; but the day will declare who are the fools.

III. What the temptation is (*v.* 17): *Stolen waters are sweet.* It is to water and bread, whereas Wisdom invites to the beasts she has killed and the wine she has mingled; however, bread and water are acceptable enough to those that are hungry and thirsty; and this is pretended to be more *sweet* and *pleasant* than common, for it is *stolen water and bread eaten in secret,* with a fear of being discovered. The pleasures of prohibited lusts are boasted of as more relishing than those of prescribed love; and dishonest gain is preferred to that which is justly gotten. Now this argues, not only a bold contempt, but an impudent defiance, 1. Of God's law, in that the waters are the sweeter for being stolen and come at by breaking through the hedge of the divine command. *Nitimur in vetitum—We are prone to what is forbidden.* This spirit of contradiction we have from our first parents, who thought the forbidden tree of all others *a tree to be desired.* 2. Of God's curse. The *bread is eaten in secret,* for fear of discovery and punishment, and the sinner takes a pride in having so far baffled his convictions, and triumphed over them, that, notwithstanding that fear, he dares commit the sin, and can make himself believe that, being eaten in secret, it shall never be discovered or reckoned for. Sweetness and pleasantness constitute the bait; but, by the tempter's own showing, even that is so absurd, and has such allays, that it is a wonder how it can have any influence upon men that pretend to reason.

IV. An effectual antidote against the temptation, in a few words, *v.* 18. He that so far wants understanding as to be drawn aside by these enticements is led on, ignorantly, to his own inevitable ruin: *He knows not,* will not believe, does not consider, the tempter will not let him know, *that the dead are there,* that those who live in pleasure are *dead while they live, dead in trespasses and sins.* Terrors attend these pleasures like the terrors of death itself. The giants are there —*Rephaim.* It was this that ruined the sinners of the old world, the giants that were *in the earth in those days. Her guests,* that are treated with these *stolen waters,* are not only in the highway to hell and at the brink of it, but they are already *in the depths of hell,* under the power of sin, led captive by Satan at his will, and ever and anon lashed by the terrors of their own consciences, which are a hell upon earth. The depths of Satan are *the depths of hell.* Remorseless sin is remediless ruin; it is the bottomless pit already. Thus does Solomon show the hook; those that believe him will not meddle with the bait.

CHAP. X.

Hitherto we have been in the porch or preface to the proverbs, here they begin. They are short but weighty sentences; most of them are distichs, two sentences in one verse, illustrating each other; but it is seldom that there is any coherence between the verses, much less any thread of discourse, and therefore in these chapters we need not attempt to reduce the contents to their proper heads, the several sentences will appear best in their own places. The scope of them all is to set before us good and evil, the blessing and the curse. Many of the proverbs in this chapter relate to the good government of the tongue, without which men's religion is vain.

THE proverbs of Solomon. A wise son maketh a glad father: but a foolish son *is* the heaviness of his mother.

Solomon, speaking to us as unto children, observes here how much the comfort of parents, natural, political, and ecclesiastical, depends upon the good behaviour of those under their charge, as a reason, 1. Why parents should be careful to give their children a good education, and to train them up in the ways of religion, which, if it obtain the desired effect, they themselves will have the comfort of it, or, if not, they will have for their support under their heaviness that they have done their duty, have done their endeavour. 2. Why children should conduct themselves wisely and well, and live up to their good education, that they may gladden the hearts of their parents and not sadden them. Observe, (1.) It adds to the comfort of young people that are pious and discreet that thereby they do something towards recompensing their parents for all the care and pains they have taken with them, and occasion pleasure to them in the evil days of old age, when they most need it; and it is the duty of parents to rejoice in their children's wisdom and well-doing, yea, though it arrive at such an eminency as to eclipse them. (2.) It adds to the guilt of those that conduct themselves ill that thereby they grieve those whom they ought to be a joy to, and are a heaviness particularly to their poor mothers who bore them with sorrow, but with greater sorrow see them wicked and vile.

2 Treasures of wickedness profit nothing: but righteousness delivereth from death. 3 The LORD will not

suffer the soul of the righteous to famish: but he casteth away the substance of the wicked.

These two verses speak to the same purport, and the latter may be the reason of the former. 1. That wealth which men get unjustly will do them no good, because God will blast it: *Treasures of wickedness profit nothing, v.* 2. The treasures of wicked people, much more the treasure which they have made themselves masters of by any wicked arts, by oppression or fraud, though it be ever so much, as a treasure, and laid up ever so safely, though it be hidden treasure, yet it *profits nothing ;* when profit and loss come to be balanced the profit gained by the treasures will by no means countervail the loss sustained by the wickedness, Matt. xvi. 26. They do not profit the soul; they will not purchase any true comfort or happiness. They will stand a man in no stead at death, or in the judgment of the great day; and the reason is because God *casts away the substance of the wicked* (v. 3) ; he takes that from them which they have unjustly gotten; he rejects the consideration of it, not regarding the rich more than the poor. We often see that scattered by the justice of God which has been gathered together by the injustice of men. How can the treasures of wickedness profit, when, though it be counted substance, God casts it away and it vanishes as a shadow? 2. That which is honestly got will turn to a good account, for God will bless it. *Righteousness delivers from death,* that is, wealth gained, and kept, and used, in a right manner (righteousness signifies both honesty and charity); it answers the end of wealth, which is to keep us alive and be a defence to us. It will deliver from those judgments which men bring upon themselves by their wickedness. It will profit to such a degree as to deliver, though not from the stroke of death, yet from the sting of it, and consequently from the terror of it. For *the Lord will not suffer the soul of the righteous to famish* (v. 3), and so their *righteousness delivers from death,* purely by the favour of God to them, which is their life and livelihood, and which will keep them alive in famine. The soul of the righteous shall be kept alive by the word of God, and faith in his promise, when *young lions shall lack and suffer hunger.*

4 He becometh poor that dealeth *with* a slack hand: but the hand of the diligent maketh rich.

We are here told, 1. Who those are who, though rich, are in a fair way to *become poor* —those *who deal with a slack hand,* who are careless and remiss in their business, and never mind which end goes foremost, nor ever set their hands vigorously to their work or stick to it; those *who deal with a deceitful hand* (so it may be read); those who think

to enrich themselves by fraud and tricking will, in the end, impoverish themselves, not only by bringing the curse of God on what they have, but by forfeiting their reputation with men ; none will care to deal with those who deal with sleight of hand and are honest only with good looking to. 2. Who those are who, though poor, are in a fair way to become rich—those who are diligent and honest, who are careful about their affairs, and, what their hands find to do, do it with all their might, in a fair and honourable way, those are likely to increase what they have. *The hand of the acute* (so some), of those who are sharp, but not sharpers ; *the hand of the active* (so others); the stirring hand gets a penny. This is true in the affairs of our souls as well as in our worldly affairs; slothfulness and hypocrisy lead to spiritual poverty, but those who are *fervent in spirit, serving the Lord,* are likely to be *rich in faith* and *rich in good works.*

5 He that gathereth in summer *is* a wise son : *but* he that sleepeth in harvest *is* a son that causeth shame.

Here is, 1. The just praise of those who improve their opportunities, who take pains to gather and increase what they have, both for soul and body, who provide for hereafter while provision is to be made, who *gather in summer,* which is gathering time. He who does so *is a wise son,* and it is his honour; he acts wisely for his parents, whom, if there be occasion, he ought to maintain, and he gives reputation to himself, his family, and his education. 2. The just reproach and blame of those who trifle away these opportunities : *He who sleeps,* loves his ease, idles away his time, and neglects his work, especially *who sleeps in harvest,* when he should be laying in for winter, who lets slip the season of furnishing himself with that which he will have occasion for, *is a son that causes shame ;* for he is a foolish son ; he prepares shame for himself when winter comes, and reflects shame upon all his friends. He who gets knowledge and wisdom in the days of his youth *gathers in summer,* and he will have the comfort and credit of his industry; but he who idles away the days of his youth will bear the shame of his indolence when he is old.

6 Blessings *are* upon the head of the just: but violence covereth the mouth of the wicked.

Here is, 1. *The head of the just* crowned with *blessings,* with the blessings both of God and man. Variety of blessings, abundance of blessings, shall descend from above, and visibly abide on the head of good men, real blessings ; they shall not only be spoken well of, but done well to. Blessings shall be on their head as a coronet to adorn and dignify them and as a helmet to protect and secure them. 2. *The mouth of the wicked co* vered with *violence.* Their mouths shall be stopped with shame for the violence which they have done; they shall not have a word to say in excuse for themselves (Job v. 16); their breath shall be stopped with the violence that shall be done to them, when their violent dealings shall return on their heads, shall be returned to their teeth.

7 The memory of the just *is* blessed: but the name of the wicked shall rot.

Both the just and the wicked, when their days are fulfilled, must die. Between their bodies in the grave there is no visible difference; between the souls of the one and the other, in the world of spirits, there is a vast difference, and so there is, or ought to be, between their memories, which survive them.

I. Good men are and ought to be well spoken of when they are gone; it is one of the blessings that *comes upon the head of the just,* even when their head is laid. Blessed men leave behind them blessed memories. 1. It is part of the dignity of the saints, especially those who excel in virtue and are eminently useful, that they are remembered with respect when they are dead. Their good name, their name with good men, for good things, is then in a special manner as *precious ointment,* Eccl. vii. 1. Those that honour God he will thus honour, Ps. cxii. 3, 6, 9. *The elders* by faith *obtained a good report* (Heb. xi. 2), and, being dead, are yet spoken of. 2. It is part of the duty of the survivors: *Let the memory of the just be blessed,* so the Jews read it, and observe it as a precept, not naming an eminently just man that is dead without adding, *Let his memory be blessed.* We must delight in making an honourable mention of good men that are gone, bless God for them, and for his gifts and graces that appeared in them, and especially be followers of them in *that which is good.*

II. Bad men are and shall be forgotten, or spoken of with contempt. When their bodies are putrefying in the grave their *names* also *shall rot.* Either they shall not be preserved at all, but buried in oblivion (no good can be said of them, and therefore the greatest kindness that can be done them will be to say nothing of them), or they shall be loathsome, and mentioned with detestation, and that rule of honour, *De mortuis nil nisi bonum—Say nothing to the disadvantage of the dead,* will not protect them. Where the wickedness has been notorious, and cannot but be mentioned, it ought to be mentioned with abhorrence.

8 The wise in heart will receive commandments: but a prating fool shall fall.

Here is, 1. The honour and happiness of the obedient. They *will receive commandments;* they will take it as a privilege, and really an ease to them, to be under govern-

ment, which saves them the labour of deliberating and choosing for themselves; and they will take it as a favour to be told their duty and admonished concerning it. And this is their wisdom; those are *wise in heart* who are tractable, and those who thus bend, thus stoop, shall stand and be established, shall prosper, being well advised. 2. The shame and ruin of the disobedient, that will not be governed, nor endure any yoke, that will not be taught, nor take any advice. They are fools, for they act against themselves and their own interest; they are commonly *prating fools,* fools of lips, full of talk, but full of nonsense, boasting of themselves, prating spitefully against those that admonish them (3 John 10), and pretending to give counsel and law to others. Of all fools, none more troublesome than the *prating fools,* nor that more expose themselves; but they *shall fall* into sin, into hell, because they received not commandments. Those that are full of tongue seldom look well to their feet, and therefore stumble and fall.

9 He that walketh uprightly walketh surely: but he that perverteth his ways shall be known.

We are here told, and we may depend upon it, 1. That men's integrity will be their security: *He that walks uprightly* towards God and man, that is faithful to both, who designs as he ought and means as he says, *walks surely;* he is safe under a divine protection and easy in a holy security. He goes on his way with a humble boldnesss, being well armed against the temptations of Satan, the troubles of the world, and the reproaches of men. He knows what ground he stands on, what guide he follows, what guard he is surrounded with, and what glory he is going to, and therefore proceeds with assurance and *great peace,* Isa. xxxii. 17; xxxiii. 15, 16. Some understand it as part of the character of an upright man, that he *walks surely,* in opposition to walking at all adventures. He will not dare to do that which he is not fully satisfied in his own conscience concerning the lawfulness of, but will see his way clear in every thing. 2. That men's dishonesty will be their shame: *He that perverts his way,* that turns aside into crooked paths, that dissembles with God and man, looks one way and rows another, though he may for a time disguise himself, and pass current, *shall be known* to be what he is. It is a thousand to one but some time or other he betrays himself; at least, God will discover him in the great day. *He that perverts his ways documento erit—shall be made an example of,* for warning to others; so some.

10 He that winketh with the eye causeth sorrow: but a prating fool shall fall.

Mischief is here said to attend, 1. Politic, designing, self-disguising sinners: *He that*

844

winks with the eye, as if he took no notice of you, when at the same time he is watching an opportunity to do you an ill turn, that makes signs to his accomplices when to come in to assist him in executing his wicked projects, which are all carried on by trick and artifice, *causes sorrow* both to others and to himself. Ingenuity will be no excuse for iniquity, but the sinner must either repent or do worse, either rue it or be ruined by it. 2. Public, silly, self-exposing sinners : A *prating fool,* whose sins go before unto judgment, *shall fall,* as was said before, *v.* 8. But his case is less dangerous of the two, and, though he destroy himself, he does not create so much sorrow to others as *he that winks with his eyes.* The dog that bites is not always the dog that barks.

11 The mouth of a righteous *man is* a well of life: but violence covereth the mouth of the wicked.

See here, 1. How industrious a good man is, by communicating his goodness, to do good with it: *His mouth,* the outlet of his mind, *is a well of life;* it is a constant spring, whence issues good discourse for the edification of others, like streams that water the ground and make it fruitful, and for their consolation, like streams that quench the thirst of the weary traveller. It is like *a well of life,* that is pure and clean, not only not poisoned, but not muddled, with any corrupt communication. 2. How industrious a bad man is, by concealing his badness, to do hurt with it : *The mouth of the wicked covers violence,* disguises the designed mischief with professions of friendship, that it may be carried on the more securely and effectually, as Joab kissed and killed, Judas kissed and betrayed; this is his sin, to which the punishment answers (*v.* 6): *Violence covers the mouth of the wicked;* what he got by violence shall by violence be taken from him, Job v 4, 5.

12 Hatred stirreth up strifes : but love covereth all sins.

Here is, 1. The great mischief-maker, and that is malice. Even where there is no manifest occasion of strife, yet *hatred* seeks occasion and so *stirs it up* and does the devil's work. Those are the most spiteful ill-natured people that can be who take a pleasure in setting their neighbours together by the ears, by tale-bearing, evil surmises, and misrepresentations, blowing up the sparks of contention, which had lain buried, into a flame, at which, with an unaccountable pleasure, they warm their hands. 2. The great peace-maker, and that is *love,* which *covers all sins,* that is, the offences among relations which occasion discord. Love, instead of proclaiming and aggravating the offence, conceals and extenuates it as far as it is capable of being concealed and extenuated. Love will excuse the offence which we give through mistake and unadvisedly; when we are able to say that

there was no ill intended, but it was an oversight, and we love our friend notwithstanding, this covers it. It will also overlook the offence that is given us, and so cover it, and make the best of it: by this means strife is prevented, or, if begun, peace is recovered and restored quickly. The apostle quotes this, 1 Pet. iv. 8. *Love will cover a multitude of sins.*

13 In the lips of him that hath understanding wisdom is found: but a rod *is* for the back of him that is void of understanding.

Observe, 1. Wisdom and grace are the honour of good men: He *that has understanding,* that good understanding which those have that do the commandments, *wisdom is found in his lips,* that is, it is discovered to be there, and consequently that he has within a good treasure of it, and it is derived thence for the benefit of others. It is a man's honour to have wisdom, but much more to be instrumental to make others wise. 2. Folly and sin are the shame of bad men: *A rod is for the back of him that is void of understanding—of* him that wants a heart ; he exposes himself to the lashes of his own conscience, to the scourges of the tongue, to the censures of the magistrate, and to the righteous judgments of God. Those that foolishly and wilfully go on in wicked ways are preparing rods for themselves, the marks of which will be their perpetual disgrace.

14 Wise *men* lay up knowledge : but the mouth of the foolish *is* near destruction.

Observe, 1. It is the wisdom of the wise that they treasure up a stock of useful knowledge, which will be their preservation : *Wisdom is* therefore *found in their lips* (*v.* 13), because it is laid up in their hearts, out of which store, like the good householder, they bring things new and old. Whatever knowledge may be at any time useful to us we must *lay it up,* because we know not but some time or other we may have occasion for it. We must continue laying up as long as we live; and be sure to lay it up safely, that it may not be to seek when we want it. 2. It is the folly of fools that they lay up mischief in their hearts, which is ready to them in all they say, and works terror and destruction both to others and to themselves. They *love devouring words* (Ps. lii. 4), and these come uppermost. Their *mouth is near destruction,* having the *sharp arrows of bitter words* always at hand to throw about.

15 The rich man's wealth *is* his strong city : the destruction of the poor *is* their poverty.

This may be taken two ways:—1. As a reason why we should be diligent in our business, that we may avoid that sinking dispiriting uneasiness which attends poverty, and may enjoy the benefit and comfort which those have that are beforehand in the world. Taking pains is really the way to make ourselves and our families easy. Or, rather 2. As a representation of the common mistakes both of rich and poor, concerning their outward condition. (1.) Rich people think themselves happy because they are rich; but it is their mistake: *The rich man's wealth is*, in his own conceit, *his strong city*, whereas the worst of evils it is too weak and utterly insufficient to protect them from. It will prove that they are not so safe as they imagine; nay, their wealth may perhaps expose them. (2.) Poor people think themselves undone because they are poor; but it is their mistake: *The destruction of the poor is their poverty;* it sinks their spirits, and ruins all their comforts; whereas a man may live very comfortably, though he has but a little to live on, if he be but content, and keep a good conscience, and live by faith.

16 The labour of the righteous *tendeth* to life: the fruit of the wicked to sin.

Solomon here confirms what his father had said (Ps. xxxvii. 16), *A little that a righteous man has is better than the riches of many wicked.* 1. Perhaps a righteous man has no more than what he works hard for; he eats only *the labour of his hands*, but that *labour tends to life;* he aims at nothing but to get an honest livelihood, covets not to be rich and great, but is willing to live and maintain his family. Nor does it tend only to his own life, but he would enable himself to do good to others; he labours *that he may have to give* (Eph. iv. 28); all his business turns to some good account or other. Or it may be meant of his labour in religion; he takes most pains in that which has a tendency to eternal life; he *sows to the Spirit*, that he may *reap life everlasting.* 2. Perhaps a wicked man's wealth is fruit which he did not labour for, but came easily by, but it tends *to sin.* He makes it the food and fuel of his lusts, his pride and luxury; he does hurt with it and not good; he gets hurt by it and is hardened by it in his wicked ways. The things of this world are good or evil, life or death, as they are used, and as those are that have them.

17 He *is in* the way of life that keepeth instruction: but he that refuseth reproof erreth.

See here, 1. That those are in the right that do not only receive instruction, but retain it, that do not let it slip through carelessness, as most do, nor let it go to those that would rob them of it, that *keep instruction* safely, keep it pure and entire, keep it for their own use, that they may govern themselves by it, keep it for the benefit of others, that they may instruct them; those that do so are *in the way of life*, the way that has true comfort in it and eternal life at the end of it. 2. That those are in the wrong that do not only not receive instruction, but wilfully and obstinately refuse it when it is offered them. They will not be taught their duty because it discovers their faults to them; that instruction which carries reproof in it they have a particular aversion to, and certainly they err; it is a sign that they err in judgment, and have false notions of good and evil; it is a cause of their erring in conversation. The traveller that has missed his way, and cannot bear to be told of it and shown the right way, must needs err still, err endlessly; he certainly misses *the way of life.*

18 He that hideth hatred *with* lying lips, and he that uttereth a slander, *is* a fool.

Observe here, Malice is folly and wickedness. 1. It is so when it is concealed by flattery and dissimulation: He *is a fool*, though he may think himself a politician, *that hides hatred with lying lips*, lest, if it break out, he should be ashamed before men and should lose the opportunity of gratifying his malice. *Lying lips* are· bad enough of themselves, but have a peculiar malignity in them when they are made *a cloak of maliciousness.* But he *is a fool* who thinks to hide any thing from God. 2. It is no better when it is vented in spiteful and mischievous language: *He that utters slander is a fool* too, for God will sooner or later bring forth that righteousness as the light which he endeavours to cloud, and will find an expedient to roll the reproach away.

19 In the multitude of words there wanteth not sin: but he that refraineth his lips *is* wise.

We are here admonished concerning the government of the tongue, that necessary duty of a Christian. 1. It is good to say little, because *in the multitude of words there wanteth not sin*, or *sin doth not cease.* Usually, those that speak much speak much amiss, and among many words there cannot but be many idle words, which they must shortly give an account of. Those that love to hear themselves talk do not consider what work they are making for repentance; for that will be wanted, and first or last will be had, where *there wanteth not sin.* 2. It is therefore good to *keep our mouth as with a bridle: He that refrains his lips*, that often checks himself, suppresses what he has thought, and holds in that which would transpire, is a wise man; it is an evidence of his wisdom, and he therein consults his own peace. Little said is soon amended, Amos v. 13; Jam. i. 19.

20 The tongue of the just *is as* choice silver: the heart of the wicked *is* little worth. 21 The lips of the righteous feed many: but fools die for want of wisdom.

We are here taught how to value men, not

by their wealth and preferment in the world, but by their virtue.

I. Good men are good for something. Though they may be poor and low in the world, and may not have power and riches to do good with, yet, as long as they have a mouth to speak, that will make them valuable and useful, and upon that account we must honour those that fear the Lord, because *out of the good treasure of their heart they bring forth good things.* 1. This makes them valuable : *The tongue of the just is as choice silver ;* they are sincere, freed from the dross of guile and evil design. God's words are compared to silver *purified* (Ps. xii. 6), for they may be relied on; and such are the words of just men. They are of weight and worth, and will enrich those that hear them with wisdom, which is better than *choice silver.* 2. It makes them useful : *The lips of the righteous feed many ;* for they are full of the word of God, which is the bread of life, and that sound doctrine wherewith souls are nourished up. Pious discourse is spiritual food to the needy, to the hungry.

II. Bad men are good for nothing. 1. One can get no good by them : *The heart of the wicked is little worth,* and therefore that which comes out of the abundance of his heart cannot be worth much. His principles, his notions, his thoughts, his purposes, and all the things that fill him, and affect him, are worldly and carnal, and therefore of no value. *He that is of the earth speaks of the earth,* and neither understands nor relishes the things of God, John iii. 31 ; 1 Cor. ii. 14. The wicked man pretends that, though he does not talk of religion as the just do, yet he has it within him, and thanks God that his heart is good; but he that searches the heart here says the contrary : *It is nothing worth.* 2. One can do no good to them. While many are fed by *the lips of the righteous, fools die for want of wisdom ;* and fools indeed they are to die for want of that which they might so easily come by. *Fools die for want of a heart* (so the word is) ; they perish for want of consideration and resolution ; they have no heart to do any thing for their own good. While the righteous feed others fools starve themselves.

22 The blessing of the LORD, it maketh rich, and he addeth no sorrow with it.

Worldly wealth is that which most men have their hearts very much upon, but they generally mistake both in the nature of the thing they desire and in the way by which they hope to obtain it ; we are therefore told here, 1. What that wealth is which is indeed desirable, not having abundance only, but having it and *no sorrow with it,* no disquieting care to get and keep it, no vexation of spirit in the enjoyment of it, no tormenting grief for the loss of it, no guilt contracted by the abuse of it—to have it and to have a heart

to take the comfort of it, to do good with it and to serve God with joyfulness and gladness of heart in the use of it. 2. Whence this desirable wealth is to be expected, not by making ourselves drudges to the world (Ps. cxxvii. 2), but by *the blessing of God.* It is this that *makes rich and adds no sorrow ;* what comes from the love of God has the grace of God for its companion, to preserve the soul from those turbulent lusts and passions of which, otherwise, the increase of riches is commonly the incentive. He had said (v. 4), *The hand of the diligent makes rich,* as a means ; but here he ascribes it to *the blessing of the Lord ;* but that blessing is upon *the hand of the diligent.* It is thus in spiritual riches. Diligence in getting them is our duty, but God's blessing and grace must have all the glory of that which is acquired, Deut. viii. 17, 18.

23 *It is* as sport to a fool to do mischief : but a man of understanding hath wisdom.

Here is, 1. Sin exceedingly sinful : *It is as laughter to a fool to do mischief ;* it is as natural to him, and as pleasant, as it is to a man to laugh. *Wickedness is his Isaac* (that is the word here) ; it is his delight, his darling, and that in which he pleases himself. He makes a laughing matter of sin. When he is warned not to sin, from the consideration of the law of God and the revelation of his wrath against sin, he makes a jest of the admonition, and laughs at the shaking of the spear ; when he has sinned, instead of sorrowing for it, he boasts of it, ridicules reproofs, and laughs away the convictions of his own conscience, *ch.* xiv. 9. 2. Wisdom exceedingly wise, for it carries along with it the evidence of its own excellency ; it may be predicated of itself, and this is encomium enough ; you need say no more in praise of *a man of understanding* than this, " He is an *understanding man ;* he *has wisdom ;* he is so wise as not to do mischief, or if he has, through oversight, offended, he is so wise as not to make a jest of it." Or, to pronounce wisdom wise indeed, read it thus : *As it is a sport to a fool to do mischief, so it is to a man of understanding to have wisdom and to show it.* Besides the future recompence, a good man has as much present pleasure in the restraints and exercises of religion as sinners can pretend to in the liberties and enjoyments of sin, and much more, and much better.

24 The fear of the wicked, it shall come upon him : but the desire of the righteous shall be granted. **25** As the whirlwind passeth, so *is* the wicked no *more :* but the righteous *is* an everlasting foundation.

It is here said, and said again, to the righteous, that *it shall be well with them,* and to the wicked, *Woe to them ;* and these are set the one over against the other, for their mutual illustration.

I. It shall be as ill with the wicked as they can fear, and as well with the righteous as they can desire. 1. The wicked, it is true, buoy themselves up sometimes in their wickedness with vain hopes which will deceive them, but at other times they cannot but be haunted with just fears, and those *fears shall come upon them;* the God they provoke will be every whit as terrible as they, when they are under their greatest damps, apprehend him to be. *As is thy fear, so is thy wrath,* Ps. xc. 11. Wicked men fear the punishment of sin, but they have not wisdom to improve their fears by making their escape, and so the thing they feared comes upon them, and their present terrors are earnests of their future torments. 2. The righteous, it is true, sometimes have their fears, but their desire is towards the favour of God and a happiness in him, and that *desire shall be granted.* According to their faith, not according to their fear, it shall be *unto them,* Ps. xxxvii. 4.

II. The prosperity of the wicked shall quickly end, but the happiness of the righteous shall never end, *v.* 25. The wicked make a great noise, hurry themselves and others, like a *whirlwind,* which threatens to bear down all before it; but, like a *whirlwind,* they are presently gone, and they pass irrecoverably; they are *no more;* all about them are quiet and glad when the storm is over, Ps. xxxvii. 10, 36; Job xx. 5. *The righteous,* on the contrary, make no show; they lie hid, like a *foundation,* which is low and out of sight, but they are fixed in their resolution to cleave to God, established in virtue, and they shall be an *everlasting foundation,* immovably good. He that is holy shall be holy still and immovably happy; his hope is built on a rock, and therefore not shocked by the storm, Matt. vii. 24. *The righteous is the pillar of the world* (so some read it); the world stands for their sakes; the holy seed is the substance thereof.

26 As vinegar to the teeth, and as smoke to the eyes, so *is* the sluggard to them that send him.

Observe, 1. Those that are of a slothful disposition, that love their ease and cannot apply their minds to any business, are not fit to be employed, no, not so much as to be sent on an errand, for they will neither deliver a message with any care nor make any haste back. Such therefore are very unmeet to be ministers, Christ's messengers; he will not own the sending forth of sluggards into his harvest. 2. Those that are guilty of so great an oversight as to entrust such with any affair, and put confidence in them, will certainly have vexation with them. A slothful servant is to his master as uneasy and troublesome as *vinegar to the teeth* and *smoke to the eyes;* he provokes his passion, as vinegar sets the teeth on edge, and occasions him grief

848

to see his business neglected and undone, as smoke sets the eyes a weeping.

27 The fear of the LORD prolongeth days : but the years of the wicked shall be shortened. 28 The hope of the righteous *shall be* gladness : but the expectation of the wicked shall perish.

Observe, 1. Religion lengthens men's lives and crowns their hopes. *What man is he that loves life?* Let him *fear God,* and that will secure him from many things that would prejudice his life, and secure to him life enough in this world and eternal life in the other; *the fear of the Lord* will add days more than was expected, will add them endlessly, will prolong them to the days of eternity. *What man is he that would see good days?* Let him be religious, and then his days shall not only be many, but happy, very happy as well as very many, for *the hope of the righteous shall be gladness;* they shall have what they hope for, to their unspeakable satisfaction. It is something future and unseen that they place their happiness in (Rom. viii. 24, 25), not what they have in hand, but what they have in hope, and their hope will shortly be swallowed up in fruition, and it will be their everlasting *gladness. Enter thou into the joy of thy Lord.* 2. Wickedness shortens men's lives, and frustrates their hopes: *The years of the wicked,* that are spent in the pleasures of sin and the drudgery of the world, *shall be shortened.* Cut down the trees that cumber the ground. And whatever comfort or happiness a wicked man promises himself, in this world or the other, he will be frustrated; for *the expectation of the wicked shall perish;* his hope shall be turned into endless despair.

29 The way of the LORD *is* strength to the upright : but destruction *shall be* to the workers of iniquity. 30 The righteous shall never be removed : but the wicked shall not inhabit the earth.

These two verses are to the same purport with those next before, intimating the happiness of the godly and the misery of the wicked; it is necessary that this be inculcated upon us, so loth are we to believe and consider it. 1. Strength and stability are entailed upon integrity: *The way of the Lord* (the providence of God, the way in which he walks towards us) *is strength to the upright,* confirms him in his uprightness. All God's dealings with him, merciful and afflictive, serve to quicken him to his duty and animate him against his discouragements. Or *the way of the Lord* (the way of godliness, in which he appoints us to walk) is *strength to the upright;* the closer we keep to that way, the more our hearts are enlarged to proceed in it, the better fitted we are both for services and sufferings. A good conscience, kept pure from sin, gives a man boldness in a dangerous time, and constant diligence in duty makes a man's work easy in a busy time. The more we do for God the more we may do, Job xvii. 9. That *joy of the Lord* which is to be found only in the *way of the Lord* will be our strength (Neh. viii. 10), and therefore *the righteous shall never be removed.* Those that have an established virtue have an established peace and happiness which nothing can rob them of; they *have an everlasting foundation,* v. 25. 2. Ruin and destruction are the certain consequences of wickedness. *The wicked shall not* only not inherit the earth, though they lay up their treasure in it, but they shall not so much as *inhabit the earth;* God's judgments will root them out. *Destruction,* swift and sure destruction, *shall be to the workers of iniquity,* destruction from the presence of the Lord and the glory of his power. Nay, that way of the Lord which is the strength of the upright is consumption and terror *to the workers of iniquity;* the same gospel which to the one is a *savour of life unto life* to the other is a *savour of death unto death;* the same providence, like the same sun, softens the one and hardens the other, Hos. xiv. 9.

31 The mouth of the just bringeth forth wisdom: but the froward tongue shall be cut out. 32 The lips of the righteous know what is acceptable: but the mouth of the wicked *speaketh* frowardness.

Here, as before, men are judged of, and, accordingly, are justified or condemned, by their words, Matt. xii. 37. 1. It is both the proof and the praise of a man's wisdom and goodness that he speaks wisely and well. A good man, in his discourse, *brings forth wisdom* for the benefit of others. God gives him wisdom as a reward of his righteousness (Eccl. ii. 26), and he, in gratitude for that gift and justice to the giver, does good with it, and with his wise and pious discourses edifies many. He *knows what is acceptable,* what discourse will be pleasing to God (for that is it that he studies more than to oblige the company), and what will be agreeable both to the speaker and to the hearers, what will become him and benefit them, and that he will speak. 2. It is the sin, and will be the ruin, of a wicked man, that he speaks wickedly like himself. *The mouth of the wicked speaks frowardness,* that which is displeasing to God and provoking to those he converses with; and what is the issue of it? Why, *the froward tongue shall be cut out,* as surely as the *flattering one,* Ps. xii. 3.

CHAP. XI.

A FALSE balance *is* abomination to the LORD: but a just weight *is* his delight.

As religion towards God is a branch of universal righteousness (he is not an honest man that is not devout), so righteousness towards men is a branch of true religion, for he is not a godly man that is not honest, nor can he expect that his devotion should be accepted; for, 1. Nothing is more offensive to God than deceit in commerce. *A false balance* is here put for all manner of unjust and fraudulent practices in dealing with any person, which are all an *abomination to the Lord,* and render those abominable to him that allow themselves in the use of such accursed arts of thriving. It is an affront to justice, which God is the patron of, as well as a wrong to our neighbour, whom God is the protector of. Men make light of such frauds, and think there is no sin in that which there is money to be got by, and, while it passes undiscovered, they cannot blame themselves for it; a blot is no blot till it is hit, Hos. xii. 7, 8. But they are not the less an abomination to God, who will be the avenger of those that are defrauded by their brethren. 2. Nothing is more pleasing to God than fair and honest dealing, nor more necessary to make us and our devotions acceptable to him: *A just weight is his delight.* He himself goes by a just weight, and holds the scale of judgment with an even hand, and therefore is pleased with those that are herein followers of him. A balance cheats, under pretence of doing right most exactly, and therefore is the greater abomination to God.

2 *When* pride cometh, then cometh shame: but with the lowly *is* wisdom.

Observe, 1. How he that exalts himself is here abased, and contempt put upon him. *When pride comes then comes shame.* Pride is a sin which men have reason to be themselves ashamed of; it is a shame to a man who springs out of the earth, who lives upon alms, depends upon God, and has forfeited all he has, to be proud. It is a sin which others cry out shame on and look upon with disdain; he that is haughty makes himself contemptible; it is a sin for which God often brings men down, as he did Nebuchadnezzar and Herod, whose ignominy immediately attended their vain-glory; for God *resists the proud,* contradicts them, and counterworks them, in the thing they are proud of, Isa. ii. 11, &c. 2. How he that humbles himself is here exalted, and a high character is given him. As with the proud there is folly, and will be shame, so *with the lowly there is wisdom,* and will be honour, for a man's wisdom gains him respect and makes his face to shine before men; or, if any be so base as to trample upon the humble, God will give them grace, which will be their glory. Considering how safe, and quiet, and easy, those are that are of a humble spirit, what communion they have with God and comfort in themselves, we will say, *With the lowly is wisdom.*

3 The integrity of the upright shall guide them: but the perverseness of transgressors shall destroy them.

It is not only promised that God will guide

the upright, and threatened that he will destroy the transgressors, but, that we may be the more fully assured of both, it is here represented as if the nature of the thing were such on both sides that it would do it itself. 1. The integrity of an honest man will itself be his guide in the way of duty and the way of safety. His principles are fixed, his rule is certain, and therefore his way is plain; his sincerity keeps him steady, and he needs not tack about every time the wind turns, having no other end to drive at than to keep a good conscience. *Integrity and uprightness* will *preserve* men, Ps. xxv. 21. 2. The iniquity of a bad man will itself be his ruin. As the plainness of a good man will be his protection, though he is ever so much exposed, so the perverseness of sinners will be their destruction, though they think themselves ever so well fortified. They shall fall into pits of their own digging, *ch.* v. 22.

4 Riches profit not in the day of wrath : but righteousness delivereth from death.

Note, 1. The *day of death* will be a *day of wrath*. It is a messenger of God's wrath; therefore when Moses had meditated on man's mortality he takes occasion thence to admire *the power of God's anger*, Ps. xc. 11. It is a debt owing, not to nature, but to God's justice. *After death the judgment*, and that is a *day of wrath*, Rev. vi. 17. 2. Riches will stand men in no stead in that day. They will neither put by the stroke nor ease the pain, much less take out the sting; what profit will this world's birth-rights be of then? In the day of public judgments riches often expose men rather than protect them, Ezek. vii. 19. 3. It is righteousness only that will *deliver from* the evil of *death*. A good conscience will make death easy, and take off the terror of it; it is the privilege of the righteous only not to be hurt of the second death, and so not much hurt by the first.

5 The righteousness of the perfect shall direct his way: but the wicked shall fall by his own wickedness. 6 The righteousness of the upright shall deliver them: but transgressors shall be taken in *their own* naughtiness.

These two verses are, in effect, the same, and both to the same purport with *v.* 3. For the truths are here of such certainty and weight that they cannot be too often inculcated. Let us govern ourselves by these principles. I. That the ways of religion are plain and safe, and in them we may enjoy a holy security. A living principle of honesty and grace will be, 1. Our best direction in the right way, in every doubtful case to say to us, *This is the way, walk in it.* He that acts without a guide looks right on and sees his way before him. 2. Our best deliverance from every false way: *The righteousness of*

the upright shall be armour of proof to them, to deliver them from the allurements of the devil and the world, and from their menaces. II. The ways of wickedness are dangerous and destructive : *The wicked shall fall* into misery and ruin *by their own wickedness*, and be *taken in their own naughtiness* as in a snare. *O Israel! thou hast destroyed thyself.* Their sin will be their punishment; that very thing by which they contrived to shelter themselves will make against them.

7 When a wicked man dieth, *his* expectation shall perish : and the hope of unjust *men* perisheth.

Note, 1. Even wicked men, while they live, may keep up a confident expectation of a happiness when they die, or at least a happiness in this world. The hypocrite has his hope, in which he wraps himself as the spider in her web. The worldling expects great matters from his wealth; he calls it *goods laid up for many years*, and hopes to take his ease in it and to be merry; but in death their expectation will be frustrated: the worldling must leave this world which he expected to continue in and the hypocrite will come short of that world which he expected to remove to, Job xxvii. 8. 2. It will be the great aggravation of the misery of wicked people that their hopes will sink into despair just when they expect them to be crowned with fruition. When a godly man dies his expectations are out-done, and all his fears vanish; but when a wicked man dies his expectations are dashed, dashed to pieces; in that very day his thoughts perish with which he had pleased himself, his hopes vanish.

8 The righteous is delivered out of trouble, and the wicked cometh in his stead.

As always in death, so sometimes in life, the righteous are remarkably favoured and the wicked crossed. 1. Good people are helped out of the distresses which they thought themselves lost in, and their feet are set in a large room, Ps. lxvi. 12; xxxiv. 19. God has found out a way to deliver his people even when they have despaired and their enemies have triumphed, as if the wilderness had shut them in. 2. The wicked have fallen into the distresses which they thought themselves far from, nay, which they had been instrumental to bring the righteous into, so that they seem to come in their stead, as a ransom for the just. Mordecai is saved from the gallows, Daniel from the lion's den, and Peter from the prison; and their persecutors *come in their stead*. The Israelites are delivered out of the Red Sea and the Egyptians drowned in it. So precious are the saints in God's eye that he *gives men for them*, Isa. xliii. 3, 4.

9 A hypocrite with *his* mouth destroyeth his neighbour : but through knowledge shall the just be delivered.

Here is, 1. Hypocrisy designing ill. It is not only the murderer with his sword, but the *hypocrite with his mouth,* that *destroys his neighbour,* decoying him into sin, or into mischief, by the specious pretences of kindness and good-will. *Death and life are in the power of the tongue,* but no tongue more fatal than the flattering tongue. 2. Honesty defeating the design and escaping the snare: *Through knowledge* of the devices of Satan *shall the just be delivered* from the snares which the hypocrite has laid for him; seducers shall not deceive the elect. By the knowledge of God, and the scriptures, and their own hearts, shall the just be delivered from those that lie in wait to deceive, and so to destroy, Rom. xvi. 18, 19.

10 When it goeth well with the righteous, the city rejoiceth: and when the wicked perish, *there is* shouting. 11 By the blessing of the upright the city is exalted: but it is overthrown by the mouth of the wicked.

It is here observed,

I. That good men are generally well-beloved by their neighbours, but nobody cares for wicked people. 1. It is true there are some few that are enemies to the righteous, that are prejudiced against God and godliness, and are therefore vexed to see good men in power and prosperity; but all indifferent persons, even those that have no great stock of religion themselves, have a good word for a good man; and therefore *when it goes well with the righteous,* when they are advanced and put into a capacity of doing good according to their desire, it is so much the better for all about them, and *the city rejoices.* For the honour and encouragement of virtue, and as it is the accomplishment of the promise of God, we should be glad to see virtuous men prosper in the world, and brought into reputation. 2. Wicked people may perhaps have here and there a well-wisher among those who are altogether such as themselves, but among the generality of their neighbours they get ill-will; they may be feared, but they are not loved, and therefore *when they perish there is shouting;* every body takes a pleasure in seeing them disgraced and disarmed, removed out of places of trust and power, chased out of the world, and wishes no greater loss may come to the town, the rather because they hope *the righteous may come in their stead,* as they into trouble instead of the righteous, *v.* 8. Let a sense of honour therefore keep us in the paths of virtue, that we may live desired and die lamented, and not be hissed off the stage, Job xxvii. 23; Ps. lii. 6.

II. That there is good reason for this, because those that are good do good, but *(as saith the proverb of the ancients) wickedness proceeds from the wicked.* 1. Good men are public blessings—*Vir bonus est commune bonum.*

By the blessing of the upright, the blessings with which they are blessed, which enlarge their sphere of usefulness,—by the blessings with which they bless their neighbours, their advice, their example, their prayers, and all the instances of their serviceableness to the public interest,—by the blessings with which God blesses others for their sake,—by these *the city is exalted,* and made more comfortable to the inhabitants, and more considerable among its neighbours. 2. Wicked men are public nuisances, not only the burdens, but the plagues of their generation. The city is *overthrown by the mouth of the wicked,* whose evil communications corrupt good manners, are enough to debauch a town, to ruin virtue in it, and bring down the judgments of God upon it.

12 He that is void of wisdom despiseth his neighbour: but a man of understanding holdeth his peace. 13 A talebearer revealeth secrets: but he that is of a faithful spirit concealeth the matter.

I. Silence is here recommended as an instance of true friendship, and a preservative of it, and therefore an evidence, 1. Of wisdom: *A man of understanding,* that has rule over his own spirit, if he be provoked, *holds his peace,* that he may neither give vent to his passion nor kindle the passion of others by any opprobrious language or peevish reflections. 2. Of sincerity: *He that is of a faithful spirit,* that is true, not only to his own promise, but to the interest of his friend, *conceals every matter* which, if divulged, may turn to the prejudice of his neighbour.

II. This prudent friendly concealment is here opposed to two very bad vices of the tongue:—1. Speaking scornfully of a man to his face: *He that is void of wisdom discovers his folly by this;* he *despises his neighbour,* calls him *Raca,* and *Thou fool,* upon the least provocation, and tramples upon him as not worthy to be set with the dogs of his flock. He undervalues himself who thus undervalues one that is made of the same mould. 2. Speaking spitefully of a man behind his back: *A tale-bearer,* that carries all the stories he can pick up, true or false, from house to house, to make mischief and sow discord, *reveals secrets* which he has been entrusted with, and so breaks the laws, and forfeits all the privileges, of friendship and conversation.

14 Where no counsel *is,* the people fall: but in the multitude of counsellors *there is* safety.

Here is, 1. The bad omen of a kingdom's ruin: *Where no counsel is,* no consultation at all, but every thing done rashly, or no prudent consultation for the common good, but only caballing for parties and divided interests. *the people fall,* crumble into factions, fall to pieces, fall together by the ears, and fall an easy prey to their common enemies. Councils of war are necessary to the operations of war; two eyes see more than one; and mutual advice is in order to mutual assistance. 2. The good presage of a kingdom's prosperity: *In the multitude of counsellors,* that see their need one of another, and act in concert and with concern for the public welfare, *there is safety;* for what prudent methods one discerns not another may. In our private affairs we shall often find it to our advantage to advise with many; if they agree in their advice, our way will be the more clear; if they differ, we shall hear what is to be said on all sides, and be the better able to determine.

15 He that is surety for a stranger shall smart *for it :* and he that hateth suretiship is sure.

Here we are taught, 1. In general, that we may not use our estates as we will (he that gave them to us has reserved to himself a power to direct us how we shall use them, for they are not our own; we are but stewards), and further that God in his law consults our interests and teaches us that charity which begins at home, as well as that which must not end there. There is a good husbandry which is good divinity, and a discretion in ordering our affairs which is part of the character of a good man, Ps. cxii. 5. Every man must be just to his family, else he is not true to his stewardship. 2. In particular, that we must not enter rashly into suretiship, (1.) Because there is danger of bringing ourselves into trouble by it, and our families too when we are gone: *He that is surety for a stranger,* for any one that asks him and promises him to be bound for him another time, for one whose person perhaps he knows, and thinks he knows his circumstances, but is mistaken, he *shall smart for it. Contritione conteretur—He shall be certainly and sadly crushed and broken by it,* and perhaps become a bankrupt. Our Lord Jesus was surety for us when we were strangers, nay, enemies, and he smarted for it; *it pleased the Lord to bruise him.* (2.) Because he that resolves against all such suretiship keeps upon sure grounds, which a man may do if he take care not to launch out any further into business than his own credit will carry him, so that he needs not ask others to be bound for him.

16 A gracious woman retaineth honour: and strong *men* retain riches.

Here, 1. It is allowed that *strong men retain riches,* that those who bustle in the world, who are men of spirit and interest, and are able to make their part good against all who stand in their way, are likely to keep what they have and to get more, while those who are weak are preyed upon by all about them. 2. It is taken for granted that *a gracious woman* is as solicitous to preserve her reputation for wisdom and modesty, humility and courtesy, and all those other graces that are the true ornaments of her sex, as strong men are to secure their estates; and those women who

are truly gracious will, in like manner, effectually secure their honour by their prudence and good conduct. *A gracious woman* is as honourable as a valiant man and her honour is as sure.

17 The merciful man doeth good to his own soul: but *he that is* cruel troubleth his own flesh.

It is a common principle, Every one for himself. *Proximus egomet mihi—None so near to me as myself.* Now, if this be rightly understood, it will be a reason for the cherishing of gracious dispositions in ourselves and the crucifying of corrupt ones. We are friends or enemies to ourselves, even in respect of present comfort, according as we are or are not governed by religious principles. 1. A *merciful,* tender, good-humoured *man, does good to his own soul,* makes and keeps himself easy. He has the pleasure of doing his duty, and contributing to the comfort of those that are to him as *his own soul;* for *we are members one of another.* He that waters others with his temporal good things shall find that God will water him with his spiritual blessings, which will do the best *good to his own soul.* See Isa. lviii. 7, &c. *If thou hide not thy eyes from thy own flesh,* but do good to others, as to thyself, if thou do good with thy own soul and *draw that out to the hungry,* thou wilt do good to thy own soul; for the Lord shall *satisfy thy soul* and *make fat thy bones.* Some make it part of the character of a *merciful man,* that he will make much of himself; that disposition which inclines him to be charitable to others will oblige him to allow himself also that which is convenient and to *enjoy the good of all his labour.* We may by the *soul* understand the *inward man,* as the apostle calls it, and then it teaches us that the first and great act of mercy is to provide well for our own souls the necessary supports of the spiritual life. 2 A *cruel,* froward, ill-natured man, *troubles his own flesh,* and so his sin becomes his punishment; he starves and dies for want of what he has, because he has not a heart to use it either for the good of others or for his own. He is vexatious to his nearest relations, that are, and should be, to him as his own flesh, Eph. v. 29. Envy, and malice, and greediness of the world, are the rottenness of the bones and the consumption of the flesh.

18 The wicked worketh a deceitful work: but to him that soweth righteousness *shall be* a sure reward.

Note, 1. Sinners put a most fatal cheat upon themselves: *The wicked works a deceitful work,* builds himself a house upon the sand, which will deceive him when the storm comes, promises himself *that* by his sin which he will never gain; nay, it is cutting his throat when it smiles upon him. *Sin deceived me, and by it slew me.* 2. Saints lay up the best securities for themselves : He *that sows righteousness*, that is good, and makes it his business to do good, with an eye to a future recompence, he shall have *a sure reward;* it is made as sure to him as eternal truth can make it. If the seedness fail not, the harvest shall not, Gal. vi. 8.

19 As righteousness *tendeth* to life : so he that pursueth evil *pursueth it* to his own death.

It is here shown that righteousness, not only by the divine judgment, will end in life, and wickedness in death, but that righteousness, in its own nature, has a direct tendency to life and wickedness to death. 1. True holiness is true happiness; it is a preparative for it, a pledge and earnest of it. *Righteousness* inclines, disposes, and leads, the soul *to life.* 2. In like manner, those that indulge themselves in sin are fitting themselves for destruction. The more violent a man is in sinful pursuits the more eagerly bent he is upon his own destruction; he awakens it when it seemed to slumber and hastens it when it seemed to linger.

20 They that are of a froward heart *are* abomination to the LORD : but *such as are* upright in *their* way are his delight.

It concerns us to know what God hates and what he loves, that we may govern ourselves accordingly, may avoid his displeasure and recommend ourselves to his favour. Now here we are told, 1. That nothing is more offensive to God than hypocrisy and double-dealing, for these are signified by the word which we translate *frowardness*, pretending justice, but intending wrong, walking in crooked ways, to avoid discovery. Those are *of a froward heart* who act in contradiction to that which is good, under a profession of that which is good, and such are, more than any sinners, an *abomination to the Lord*, Isa. lxv. 5. 2. That nothing is more pleasing to God than sincerity and plain-dealing : *Such as are upright in their way*, such as aim and act with integrity, such as have their conversation in the world *in simplicity and godly sincerity, not with fleshly wisdom*, these God delights in, these he even boasts of *(Hast thou considered my servant Job?)* and will have us to admire. *Behold an Israelite indeed!*

21 *Though* hand *join* in hand, the wicked shall not be unpunished : but the seed of the righteous shall be delivered.

Observe, 1. That confederacies in sin shall certainly be broken, and shall not avail to protect the sinners : *Though hand join in hand*, though there are many that concur by their practice to keep wickedness in countenance, and engage to stand by one another in defending it against all the attacks of virtue and justice,—though they are in league for the support and propagation of it,—though wicked children tread in the steps of their wicked parents, and resolve to keep up the trade, in defiance of religion,—yet all this will not protect them from the justice of God ; they shall not be held guiltless ; it will not excuse them to say that they did as the most did and as their company did ; they *shall not be unpunished;* witness the flood that was brought upon a whole world of ungodly men. Their number, and strength, and unanimity in sin will stand them in no stead when the day of vengeance comes. 2. That entails of religion shall certainly be blessed : *The seed of the righteous*, that follow the steps of their righteousness, though they may fall into trouble, shall, in due time, *be delivered.* Though justice may come slowly to punish the wicked, and mercy may come slowly to save the righteous, yet both will come surely. Sometimes *the seed of the righteous*, though they are not themselves righteous, are delivered for the sake of their godly ancestors, as Israel often, and the seed of David.

22 *As* a jewel of gold in a swine's snout, *so is* a fair woman which is without discretion.

By *discretion* here we must understand *religion* and *grace*, a true taste and relish (so the word signifies) of the honours and pleasures that attend an unspotted virtue ; so that *a woman without discretion* is a woman of a loose and dissolute conversation ; and then observe, 1. It is taken for granted here that beauty or comeliness of body is *as a jewel of gold*, a thing very valuable, and, where there is wisdom and grace to guard against the temptations of it, it is a great ornament, *(Gratior est pulchro veniens de corpore virtus—Virtue appears peculiarly graceful when associated with beauty);* but a foolish wanton woman, of a light carriage, is fitly compared to a swine, though she be ever so handsome, wallowing in the mire of filthy lusts, with which the mind and conscience are defiled, and, though washed, returning to them. 2. It is lamented that beauty should be so abused as it is by those that have not modesty with it. It seems ill-bestowed upon them; it is quite misplaced, *as a jewel in a swine's snout*, with which he roots in the dunghill. If beauty be not guarded by virtue, the virtue is exposed by the beauty. It may be applied to all other bodily endowments and accomplishments; it is a pity that those should have them who have not discretion to use them well.

23 The desire of the righteous *is* only good : *but* the expectation of the wicked *is* wrath.

This tells us what *the desire* and *expectation of the righteous* and *of the wicked* are and how they will prove, what they would have and what they shall have. 1. *The righteous* would have *good, only good;* all they desire is that it may go well with all about them; they wish no hurt to any, but happiness to all; as to themselves, their desire is not to gratify any evil lust, but to obtain the favour of a good God and to preserve the peace of a good conscience; and good they shall have, that good which they desire, Ps. xxxvii. 4. 2. *The wicked* would have *wrath;* they desire the woeful day, that God's judgments may gratify their passion and revenge, may remove those that stand in their way, and that they may make an advantage to themselves by fishing in troubled waters; and wrath they shall have, so shall their doom be. They expect and desire mischief to others, but it shall return upon themselves; as they loved cursing, they shall have enough of it.

24 There is that scattereth, and yet increaseth; and *there is* that withholdeth more than is meet, but *it tendeth* to poverty.

Note, 1. It is possible a man may grow rich by prudently spending what he has, may scatter in works of piety, charity, and generosity, and yet may increase; nay, by that means may increase, as the corn is increased by being sown. By cheerfully using what we have our spirits are exhilarated, and so fitted for the business we have to do, by minding which closely what we have is increased; it gains a reputation which contributes to the increase. But it is especially to be ascribed to God; he blesses the giving hand, and so makes it a getting hand, 2 Cor. ix. 10. *Give, and it shall be given you.* 2. It is possible a man may grow poor by meanly sparing what he has, *withholding more than is meet,* not paying just debts, not relieving the poor, not providing what is convenient for the family, not allowing necessary expenses for the preservation of the goods; this *tends to poverty;* it cramps men's ingenuity and industry, weakens their interest, destroys their credit, and forfeits the blessing of God: and, let men be ever so saving of what they have, if God blast it and blow upon it, it comes to nothing. *A fire not blown* shall *consume it,* Hag. i. 6, 9.

25 The liberal soul shall be made fat: and he that watereth shall be watered also himself.

So backward we are to works of charity, and so ready to think that giving undoes us, that we need to have it very much pressed upon us how much it is for our own advantage to do good to others, as before, *v.* 17. 1. We shall have the comfort of it in our own bosoms: *The liberal soul,* the soul of blessing, that prays for the afflicted and provides for them, that scatters blessings with gracious lips and generous hands, that soul *shall be made fat* with true pleasure and enriched with more grace. 2. We shall have the recompence of it both from God and man: *He that waters* others with the streams of his bounty *shall be also watered himself;* God will certainly return it in the dews, in the plentiful showers, of his blessing, which he will *pour out, till there be not room enough to receive it,* Mal. iii. 10. Men that have any sense of gratitude will return it if there be occasion; the *merciful shall find mercy* and the kind be kindly dealt with. 3. We shall be enabled still to do yet more good: *He that waters, even he shall be as rain* (so some read it); he shall be recruited as the clouds are which return after the rain, and shall be further useful and acceptable, as the rain to the new-mown grass. *He that teaches shall learn* (so the Chaldee reads it); he that uses his knowledge in teaching others shall himself be taught of God; to him that has, and uses what he has, more shall be given.

26 He that withholdeth corn, the people shall curse him: but blessing *shall be* upon the head of him that selleth *it.*

See here, 1. What use we are to make of the gifts of God's bounty; we must not hoard them up merely for our own advantage, that we may be enriched by them, but we must bring them forth for the benefit of others, that they may be supported and maintained by them. It is a sin, when corn is dear and scarce, to withhold it, in hopes that it will still grow dearer, so to keep up and advance the market, when it is already so high that the poor suffer by it; and at such a time it is the duty of those that have stocks of corn by them to consider the poor, and to be willing to sell at the market-price, to be content with moderate profit, and not aim to make a gain of God's judgments. It is a noble and extensive piece of charity for those that have stores wherewithal to do it to help to keep the markets low when the price of our commodities grows excessive. 2. What regard we are to have to the voice of the people. We are not to think it an indifferent thing, and not worth heeding, whether we have the ill will and word, or the good will and word, of our neighbours, their prayers or their curses; for here we are taught to dread their curses, and forego our own profit rather than incur them; and to court their blessings, and be at some expense to purchase them. Sometimes, *vox populi est vox Dei—the voice of the people is the voice of God.*

27 He that diligently seeketh good procureth favour: but he that seeketh mischief, it shall come unto him.

Observe, 1. Those that are industrious to do good in the world get themselves beloved both with God and man: *He that rises early to that which is good* (so the word is), that seeks opportunities of serving his friends and relieving the poor, and lays out himself therein, *procures favour.* All about him love him, and speak well of him, and will be ready to do him a kindness; and, which is better than that, better than life, he has God's loving-kindness. 2. Those that are industrious to do mischief are preparing ruin for themselves : *It shall come unto them;* some time or other they will be paid in their own coin. And, observe, *seeking mischief* is here set in opposition to *seeking good;* for those that are not doing good are doing hurt.

28 He that trusteth in his riches shall fall : but the righteous shall flourish as a branch.

Observe, 1. Our riches will fail us when we are in the greatest need : *He that trusts in them,* as if they would secure him the favour of God and be his protection and portion, *shall fall,* as a man who lays his weight on a broken reed, which will not only disappoint him, but run into his hand and pierce him. 2. Our righteousness will stand us in stead when our riches fail us : *The righteous shall* then *flourish as a branch,* the branch of righteousness, like a tree whose leaf shall not wither, Ps. i. 3. Even in death, when riches fail men, the *bones* of the righteous *shall flourish as a herb,* Isa. lxvi. 14. When those that take root in the world wither those that are grafted into Christ and partake of his root and fatness shall be fruitful and flourishing.

29 He that troubleth his own house shall inherit the wind : and the fool *shall be* servant to the wise of heart.

Two extremes in the management of family-affairs are here condemned and the ill consequences of them foretold :—1. Carefulness and carnal policy, on the one hand. There are those that by their extreme earnestness in pursuit of the world, their anxiety about their business and fretfulness about their losses, their strictness with their servants and their niggardliness towards their families, *trouble their own houses* and give continual vexation to all about them ; while others think, by supporting factions and feuds in their families, which are really a trouble to their houses, to serve some turn for themselves, and either to get or to save by it. But they will both be disappointed ; they will *inherit the wind.* All they will get by these arts will not only be empty and worthless as the wind, but noisy and troublesome, vanity and vexation. 2. Carelessness and want of common prudence, on the other. He that is a fool in his business, that either minds it not or goes awkwardly about it, that has no contrivance and consideration, not only loses his reputation and interest, but becomes a *servant to the wise in heart.* He is impoverished, and forced to work for his living ; while those that manage wisely raise themselves, and come to have dominion over him, and others like him. It is rational, and very fit, that *the fool* should *be servant to the wise in heart,* and upon that account, among others, we are bound to submit our wills to

the will of God, and to be subject to him, because we are fools and he is infinitely wise.

30 The fruit of the righteous *is* a tree of life ; and he that winneth souls *is* wise.

This shows what great blessings good men are, especially those that are eminently wise, to the places where they live, and therefore how much to be valued. 1. The righteous are as *trees of life;* the fruits of their piety and charity, their instructions, reproofs, examples, and prayers, their interest in heaven, and their influence upon earth, are like the fruits of that tree, precious and useful, contributing to the support and nourishment of the spiritual life in many ; they are the ornaments of paradise, God's church on earth, for whose sake it stands. 2. The wise are something more ; they are as trees of knowledge, not forbidden, but commanded knowledge. *He that is wise,* by communicating his wisdom, *wins souls,* wins upon them to bring them in love with God and holiness, and so wins them over into the interests of God's kingdom among men. The wise are said to *turn many to righteousness,* and that is the same with winning souls here, Dan. xii. 3. Abraham's proselytes are called *the souls that he had gotten,* Gen. xii. 5. Those that would win souls have need of wisdom to know how to deal with them ; and those that do win souls show that they are wise.

31 Behold, the righteous shall be recompensed in the earth : much more the wicked and the sinner.

This, I think, is the only one of Solomon's proverbs that has that note of attention prefixed to it, *Behold !* which intimates that it contains not only an evident truth, which may be beheld, but an eminent truth, which must be considered. 1. Some understand both parts of a recompence in displeasure : *The righteous,* if they do amiss, shall be punished for their offences in this world ; much more shall wicked people be punished for theirs, which are committed, not through infirmity, but with a high hand. If judgment begin at the house of God, what will become of the ungodly? 1 Pet. iv. 17, 18 ; Luke xxiii. 31. 2. I rather understand it of a recompence of reward to the righteous and punishment to sinners. Let us behold providential retributions. There are some recompences *in the earth,* in this world, and in the things of this world, which prove that *verily there is a God that judges in the earth* (Ps. lviii. 11) ; but they are not universal ; many sins go unpunished in the earth, and services unrewarded, which indicates that there is a judgment to come, and that there will be more exact and full retributions in the future state. Many times *the righteous* are *recompensed* for their righteousness here *in the earth,* though that is not the principal, much less the only reward either intended for them or intended by them; but whatever the word of God has promised them, or the wisdom of God sees good for them, they shall have *in the earth. The wicked* also, *and the sinner*, are sometimes remarkably punished in this life, nations, families, particular persons. And if the righteous, who do not deserve the least reward, yet have part of their recompence here on earth, much more shall the wicked, who deserve the greatest punishment, have part of their punishment on earth, as an earnest of worse to come. Therefore *stand in awe and sin not.* If those have two heavens that merit none, much more shall those have two hells that merit both.

CHAP. XII.

WHOSO loveth instruction loveth knowledge: but he that hateth reproof *is* brutish.

We are here taught to try whether we have grace or no by enquiring how we stand affected to the means of grace. 1. Those that have grace and love it will delight in all the instructions that are given them by way of counsel, admonition, or reproof, by the word or providence of God; they will value a good education, and think it not a hardship, but a happiness, to be under a strict and prudent discipline. Those that love a faithful ministry, that value it, and sit under it with pleasure, make it to appear that they *love knowledge.* 2. Those show themselves not only void of grace, but void of common sense, that take it as an affront to be told of their faults, and an imposition upon their liberty to be put in mind of their duty: *He that hates reproof is* not only foolish, but *brutish,* like the horse and the mule that have no understanding, or the ox that kicks against the goad. Those that desire to live in loose families and societies, where they may be under no check, that stifle the convictions of their own consciences, and count those their enemies that tell them the truth, are the *brutish* here meant.

A good *man* obtaineth favour of the LORD: but a man of wicked devices will he condemn.

Note, 1. We are really as we are with God. Those are happy, truly happy, for ever happy, that *obtain favour of the Lord,* though the world frown upon them, and they find little favour with men; for in God's favour is life, and that is the fountain of all good. On the other hand those are miserable whom *he condemns,* however men may applaud them, and cry them up; whom he condemns he condemns to the second death. 2. We are with God as we are with men, as we have our conversation in this world. Our Father judges of his children very much by their conduct one to another; and therefore *a good man,* that is merciful, and charitable, and does good, *draws out favour from the Lord* by his prayers; but a malicious man, that devises

856

wickedness against his neighbours, *he will condemn,* as unworthy of a place in his kingdom.

3 A man shall not be established by wickedness: but the root of the righteous shall not be moved.

Note, 1. Though men may advance themselves by sinful arts, they cannot by such arts settle and secure themselves; though they may get large estates they cannot get such as will abide: *A man shall not be established by wickedness;* it may set him in high places, but they are slippery places, Ps. lxxiii. 18. That prosperity which is raised by sin is built on the sand, and so it will soon appear. 2. Though good men may have but little of the world, yet that little will last, and what is honestly got will wear well: *The root of the righteous shall not be moved,* though their branches may be shaken. Those that by faith are rooted in Christ are firmly fixed; in him their comfort and happiness are so rooted as never to be rooted up.

4 A virtuous woman *is* a crown to her husband: but she that maketh ashamed *is* as rottenness in his bones.

Note, 1. He that is blessed with a good wife is as happy as if he were upon the throne, for she is no less than *a crown* to him *A virtuous woman,* that is pious and prudent, ingenious and industrious, that is active for the good of her family and looks well to the ways of her household, that makes conscience of her duty in every relation, a woman of spirit, that can bear crosses without disturbance, such a one owns her husband for her head, and therefore she *is a crown* to him, not only a credit and honour to him, as *a crown* is an ornament, but supports and keeps up his authority in his family, as *a crown* is an ensign of power. She is submissive and faithful to him and by her example teaches his children and servants to be so too. 2. He that is plagued with a bad wife is as miserable as if he were upon the dunghill; for she is no better than *rottenness in his bones,* an incurable disease, besides that *she makes him ashamed.* She that is silly and slothful, wasteful and wanton, passionate and ill-tongued, ruins both the credit and comfort of her husband. If he go abroad, his head is hung down, for his wife's faults turn to his reproach. If he retire into himself, his heart is sunk; he is continually uneasy; it it is an affliction that preys much upon the spirits.

5 The thoughts of the righteous *are* right: *but* the counsels of the wicked *are* deceit.

Note, 1. The word of God is a discerner of the thoughts and intents of the heart, and judges them. We mistake if we imagine that thoughts are free. No, they are under the divine cognizance, and therefore under the divine command. 2. We ought to be observers of the thoughts and intents of our own hearts, and to judge of ourselves by them; for they are the first-born of the soul, that have most of its image undisguised. Right thoughts are a righteous man's best evidences, as nothing more certainly proves a man wicked than wicked contrivances and designs. A good man may have in his mind bad suggestions, but he does not indulge them and harbour them till they are ripened into bad projects and resolutions. 3. It is a man's honour to mean honestly, and to have his thoughts right, though a word or action may be misplaced, or mistimed, or at least misinterpreted. But it is a man's shame to lie always at catch, to act with deceit, with trick and design, not only with a long reach, but with an overreach.

6 The words of the wicked *are* to lie in wait for blood: but the mouth of the upright shall deliver them.

In the foregoing verse the *thoughts* of the wicked and righteous were compared; here their *words*, and those are as the abundance of the heart is. 1. Wicked people speak mischief to their neighbours; and wicked indeed those are whose *words* are to *lie in wait for blood;* their tongues are swords to those that stand in their way, to good men whom they hate and persecute. See an instance, Luke xx. 20, 21. 2. Good men speak help to their neighbours: The *mouth of the upright* is ready to be opened in the cause of those that are oppressed (*ch.* xxxi. 8), to plead for them, to witness for them, and so to *deliver them,* particularly those whom the wicked *lie in wait* for. A man may sometimes do a very good work with one good word.

7 The wicked are overthrown, and *are* not: but the house of the righteous shall stand.

We are here taught as before (*v.* 3 and *ch.* x. 25, 30), 1. That the *triumphing of the wicked is short.* They may be exalted for a while, but in a little time they are *overthrown and are not;* their trouble proves their overthrow, and those who made a great show disappear, and their place knows them no more. *Turn the wicked, and they are not;* they stand in such a slippery place that the least touch of trouble brings them down, like the apples of Sodom, which look fair, but touch them and they go to dust. 2. That the prosperity of the righteous has a good bottom and will endure. Death will remove them, but their *house* shall *stand,* their families shall be kept up, and the generation of the upright shall be blessed.

8 A man shall be commended according to his wisdom: but he that is of a perverse heart shall be despised.

We are here told whence to expect a good name. Reputation is what most have a high regard to and stand much upon. Now it is certain, 1. The best reputation is that which attends virtue and serious piety, and the pru-

dent conduct of life: *A man shall be commended* by all that are wise and good, in conformity to the judgment of God himself, which we are sure is *according to truth,* not according to his riches or preferments, but craft and subtlety, but *according to his wisdom,* the honesty of his designs and the prudent choice of means to compass them. 2. The worst reproach is that which follows wickedness and an opposition to that which is good: *He that is of a perverse heart,* that turns aside to crooked ways, and goes on frowardly in them, *shall be despised.* Providence will bring him to poverty and contempt, and all that have a true sense of honour will despise him as unworthy to be dealt with and unfit to be trusted, as a blemish and scandal to mankind.

9 *He that is* despised, and hath a servant, *is* better than he that honoureth himself, and lacketh bread.

Note, 1. It is the folly of some that they covet to make a great figure abroad, take place, and take state, as persons of quality, and yet want necessaries at home, and, if their debts were paid, would not be worth a morsel of bread, nay, perhaps, pinch their bellies to put it on their backs, that they may appear very gay, because fine feathers make fine birds. 2. The condition and character of those is every way better who content themselves in a lower sphere, where they are despised for the plainness of their dress and the meanness of their post, that they may be able to afford themselves, not only necessaries, but conveniences, in their own houses, not only bread, but a servant to attend them and take some of their work off their hands. Those that contrive to live plentifully and comfortably at home are to be preferred before those that affect nothing so much as to appear splendid abroad, though they have not wherewithal to maintain their appearance, whose hearts are unhumbled when their condition is low.

10 A righteous *man* regardeth the life of his beast: but the tender mercies of the wicked *are* cruel.

See here, 1. To how great a degree a good man will be merciful; he has not only a compassion for the human nature under its greatest abasements, but he regards even *the life of his beast,* not only because it is his servant, but because it is God's creature, and in conformity to Providence, which *preserves man and beast.* The beasts that are under our care must be provided for, must have convenient food and rest, must in no case be abused or tyrannised over. Balaam was checked for beating his ass. The law took care for oxen. Those therefore are unrighteous men that are not just to the brute-creatures; those that are furious and barbarous to them evidence, and confirm in themselves, a habit of barbarity, and help to make the creation groan, Rom. viii. 22. 2. To how great a degree a wicked man will be unmerciful; even his *tender mercies* are *cruel;* that natural compassion which is in him, as a man, is lost, and, by the power of corruption, is turned into hard-heartedness; even that which they will have to pass for compassion is really cruel, as Pilate's resolution concerning Christ the innocent, *I will chastise him and let him go.* Their pretended kindnesses are only a cover for purposed cruelties.

11 He that tilleth his land shall be satisfied with bread: but he that followeth vain *persons is* void of understanding.

Note, 1. It is men's wisdom to mind their business and follow an honest calling, for that is the way, by the blessing of God, to get a livelihood: *He that tills his land,* of which he is either the owner or the occupant, that keeps to his work and is willing to take pains, if he do not raise an estate by it (what need is there of that?), yet he *shall be satisfied with bread,* shall have food convenient for himself and his family, enough to bear his charges comfortably through the world. Even the sentence of wrath has this mercy in it, Thou shalt *eat bread,* though it be *in the sweat of thy face.* Cain was denied this, Gen. iv. 12. Be busy, and that is the true way to be easy. Keep thy shop and thy shop will keep thee. *Thou shalt eat the labour of thy hands.* 2. It is men's folly to neglect their business. Those are *void of understanding* that do so, for then they fall in with idle companions and follow them in their evil courses, and so come to want bread, at least bread of their own, and make themselves burdensome to others, eating the bread out of other people's mouths.

12 The wicked desireth the net of evil *men:* but the root of the righteous yieldeth *fruit.*

See here, 1. What is the care and aim of a wicked man; he would do mischief: He *desires the net of evil men.* "Oh that I were but as cunning as such a man, to make a hand of those I deal with, that I had but his art of over-reaching, that I could but take my revenge on one I have spite to as effectually as he can!" He desires the *strong-hold, or fortress,* of evil men (so some read it), to act securely in doing mischief, that it may not turn upon him. 2. What is the care and aim of a good man: His *root yields fruit,* and is his strength and stability, and that is it that he desires, to do good and to be fixed and confirmed in doing good. The wicked desires only a net wherewith to fish for himself; the righteous desires to yield fruit for the benefit of others and God's glory, Rom. xiv. 6.

13 The wicked is snared by the transgression of *his* lips: but the just shall come out of trouble.

858

See here, 1. The wicked entangling themselves in trouble by their folly, when God in justice leaves them to themselves. They are often *snared by the transgression of their lips* and their throats are cut with their own tongues. By *speaking evil of dignities* they expose themselves to public justice; by giving ill language they become obnoxious to private resentments, are sued for defamation, and actions on the case for words are brought against them. Many a man has paid dearly in this world for the transgression of his lips, and has felt the lash on his back for want of a bridle upon his tongue, Ps. lxiv. 8. 2. The righteous extricating themselves out of trouble by their own wisdom, when God in mercy comes in for their succour: *The just shall come out* of such troubles as the wicked throw themselves headlong into. It is intimated that the just may perhaps come into trouble; but, *though they fall, they shall not be utterly cast down,* Ps. xxxiv. 19.

14 A man shall be satisfied with good by the fruit of *his* mouth: and the recompence of a man's hands shall be rendered unto him.

We are here assured, for our quickening to every good word and work, 1. That even good words will turn to a good account (*v.* 14): *A man shall be satisfied with good* (that is, he shall gain present comfort, that inward pleasure which is truly satisfying) *by the fruit of his mouth,* by the good he does with his pious discourse and prudent advice. While we are teaching others we may ourselves learn, and feed on the bread of life we break to others. 2. That good works, much more, will be abundantly rewarded: The *recompence of a man's hands* for all his work and labour of love, all he has done for the glory of God and the good of his generation, *shall be rendered unto him,* and he shall reap as he has sown. Or it may be understood of the general rule of justice; God will *render to every man according to his work,* Rom. ii. 6.

15 The way of a fool *is* right in his own eyes: but he that hearkeneth unto counsel *is* wise.

See here, 1. What it is that keeps a fool from being wise: *His way is right in his own eyes;* he thinks he is in the right in every thing he does, and *therefore* asks no advice, because he does not apprehend he needs it; he is confident he knows the way, and cannot miss it, and therefore never enquires the way. The rule he goes by is to do that which is *right in his own eyes,* to walk in the way of his heart. *Quicquid libet, licet—He makes his will his law.* He is a fool that is governed by his eye, and not by his conscience. 2. What it is that keeps a wise man from being a fool; he is willing to be advised, desires to have counsel given him, and *hearkens to counsel,* being diffident of his own judgment and having a value for the directions of those that are wise and good. He is wise (it is a sign he is so, and he is likely to continue so) whose ear is always open to good advice.

16 A fool's wrath is presently known: but a prudent *man* covereth shame.

Note, 1. Passion is folly: *A fool is known by his anger* (so some read it); not but that a wise man may be angry when there is just cause for it, but then he has his anger under check and direction, is *lord of his anger,* whereas a fool's anger lords it over him. He that, when he is provoked, breaks out into indecent expressions, in words or behaviour, whose passion alters his countenance, makes him outrageous, and leads him to forget himself, *Nabal* certainly is his name and *folly is with him. A fool's indignation is known in the day;* he proclaims it openly, whatever company he is in. Or it is known in the day he is provoked; he cannot defer showing his resentments. Those that are soon angry, that are quickly put into a flame by the least spark, have not that rule which they ought to have over their own spirits. 2. Meekness is wisdom: *A prudent man covers shame.* (1.) He covers the passion that is in his own breast; when his *spirit is stirred,* and his *heart hot within him,* he keeps his mouth as with a bridle, and suppresses his resentments, by smothering and stifling them. Anger is shame, and, though a wise man be not perfectly free from it, yet he is ashamed of it, rebukes it, and suffers not the evil spirit to speak. (2.) He covers the provocation that is given him, the indignity that is done him, winks at it, covers it as much as may be from himself, that he may not carry his resentments of it too far. It is a kindness to ourselves, and contributes to the repose of our own minds, to extenuate and excuse the injuries and affronts that we receive, instead of aggravating them and making the worst of them, as we are apt to do.

17 *He that* speaketh truth showeth forth righteousness : but a false witness deceit.

Here is, 1. A faithful witness commended for an honest man. *He that* makes conscience of *speaking truth,* and representing every thing fairly, to the best of his knowledge, whether in judgment or in common conversation, whether he be upon his oath or no, he *shows forth righteousness;* he makes it to appear that he is governed and actuated by the principles and laws of righteousness, and he promotes justice by doing honour to it and serving the administration of it. 2. A false witness condemned for a cheat; he *shows forth deceit,* not only how little conscience he makes of deceiving those he deals with, but how much pleasure he takes in it, and that he is possessed by a lying spirit,

Jer. ix. 3—5. We are all concerned to possess ourselves with a dread and detestation of the sin of lying (Ps. cxix. 163) and with a reigning principle of honesty.

18 There is that speaketh like the piercings of a sword : but the tongue of the wise *is* health.

The tongue is death or life, poison or medicine, as it is used. 1. There are words that are cutting and killing, that are *like the piercings of a sword.* Opprobrious words grieve the spirits of those to whom they are spoken, and cut them to the heart. Slanders, like a sword, wound the reputation of those of whom they are uttered, and perhaps incurably. Whisperings and evil surmises, like a sword, divide and cut asunder the bonds of love and friendship, and separate those that have been dearest to each other. 2. There are words that are curing and healing: *The tongue of the wise is health,* closing up those wounds which the backbiting tongue had given, making all whole again, restoring peace, and accommodating matters in variance and persuading to reconciliation. Wisdom will find out proper remedies against the mischiefs that are made by detraction and evil-speaking.

19 The lip of truth shall be established for ever : but a lying tongue *is* but for a moment.

Be it observed, to the honour of truth, that sacred thing, 1. That, if truth be spoken, it will hold good, and, whoever may be disobliged by it and angry at it, yet it will keep its ground. Great is the truth and will prevail. What is true will be always true ; we may abide by it, and need not fear being disproved and put to shame. 2. That, if truth be denied, yet in time it will transpire. A *lying tongue,* that puts false colours upon things, *is but for a moment.* The lie will be disproved. The liar, when he comes to be examined, will be found in several stories, and not consistent with himself as he is that speaks truth; and, when he is found in a lie, he cannot gain his point, nor will he afterwards be credited. Truth may be eclipsed, but it will come to light. Those therefore that make a lie their refuge will find it a refuge of lies.

20 Deceit *is* in the heart of them that imagine evil: but to the counsellors of peace *is* joy.

Note, 1. Those that devise mischief contrive, for the accomplishing of it, how to impose upon others ; but it will prove, in the end, that they deceive themselves. Those that *imagine evil,* under colour of friendship, have their hearts full of this and the other advantage and satisfaction which they shall gain by it, but it is all a cheat. Let them imagine it ever so artfully, deceivers will be deceived. 2. Those that consult the good of their neighbours, that study the things which make for peace and give peaceable advice, promote healing attempts and contrive healing methods, and, according as their sphere is, further the public welfare, will have not only the credit, but the comfort of it. They will have joy and success, perhaps beyond their expectation. *Blessed are the peace-makers.*

21 There shall no evil happen to the just : but the wicked shall be filled with mischief.

Note, 1. Piety is a sure protection. If men be sincerely righteous, the righteous God has engaged that no evil shall happen to them. He will, by the power of his grace in them, that principle of justice, keep them from the evil of sin; so that, though they be tempted, yet they shall not be overcome by the temptation, and though they may come into trouble, into many troubles, yet to them those troubles shall have no evil in them, whatever they have to others (Ps. xci. 10), for they shall be overruled to work for their good. 2. Wickedness is as sure a destruction. Those that live in contempt of God and man, that are set on mischief, with mischief they *shall be filled.* They shall be more mischievous, shall be *filled with all unrighteousness,* Rom. i. 29. Or they shall be made miserable with the mischiefs that shall come upon them. Those that delight in mischief shall have enough of it. Some read the whole verse thus, *There shall no evil happen to the just, though the wicked be filled with mischief* and spite against them. They shall be safe under the protection of Heaven, though hell itself break loose upon them.

22 Lying lips *are* abomination to the Lord : but they that deal truly *are* his delight.

We are here taught, 1. To hate lying, and to keep at the utmost distance from it, because it is an abomination to the Lord, and renders those abominable in his sight that allow themselves in it, not only because it is a breach of his law, but because it is destructive to human society. 2. To make conscience of truth, not only in our words, but in all our actions, because those that *deal truly* and sincerely in all their dealings are *his delight,* and he is well pleased with them. We delight to converse with, and make use of, those that are honest and that we may put a confidence in; such therefore let us be, that we may recommend ourselves to the favour both of God and man.

23 A prudent man concealeth knowledge : but the heart of fools proclaimeth foolishness.

Note, 1. He that is wise does not affect to proclaim his wisdom, and it is his honour that he does not. He communicates his

knowledge when it may turn to the edification of others, but he conceals it when the showing of it would only tend to his own commendation. Knowing men, if they be prudent men, will carefully avoid every thing that savours of ostentation, and not take all occasions to show their learning and reading, but only to use it for good purposes, and then let *their own works praise them.* *Ars est celare artem—The perfection of art is to conceal it.* 2. He that is foolish cannot avoid proclaiming his folly, and it is his shame that he cannot: *The heart of fools,* by their foolish words and actions, *proclaims foolishness;* either they do not desire to hide it, so little sense have they of good and evil, honour and dishonour, or they know not how to hide it, so little discretion have they in the management of themselves, Eccl. x. 3.

24 The hand of the diligent shall bear rule : but the slothful shall be under tribute.

Note, 1. Industry is the way to preferment. Solomon advanced Jeroboam because he saw that he was an industrious young man, and minded his business, 1 Kings xi. 28. Men that take pains in study and serviceableness will thereby gain such an interest and reputation as will give them a dominion over all about them, by which means many have risen strangely. He that has been *faithful in a few things* shall be made *ruler over many things.* The elders, that *labour in the word and doctrine,* are *worthy of double honour;* and those that are diligent when they are young will get that which will enable them to rule, and so to rest, when they are old. 2. Knavery is the way to slavery : The slothful and careless, or rather the *deceitful* (for so the word signifies), *shall be under tribute.* Those that, because they will not take pains in an honest calling, live by their shifts and arts of dishonesty, are paltry and beggarly, and will be kept under. Those that are diligent and honest when they are apprentices will come to be masters; but those that are otherwise are the fools who, all their days, must be *servants to the wise in heart.*

25 Heaviness in the heart of man maketh it stoop : but a good word maketh it glad.

Here is, 1. The cause and consequence of melancholy. It is *heaviness in the heart;* it is a load of care, and fear, and sorrow, upon the spirits, depressing them, and disabling them to exert themselves with any vigour in what is to be done or fortitude in what is to be borne; it makes them stoop, prostrates and sinks them. Those that are thus oppressed can neither do the duty nor take the comfort of any relation, condition, or conversation. Those therefore that are inclined to it should watch and pray against it. 2. The cure of it : *A good word* from God, applied by faith, *makes it glad;* such a word is that (says one of the rabbin), *Cast thy burden upon the Lord, and he shall sustain thee;* the good word of God, particularly the gospel, is designed to make the hearts glad that are weary and heavy-laden, Matt. xi. 28. Ministers are to be helpers of this joy.

26 The righteous *is* more excellent than his neighbour: but the way of the wicked seduceth them.

See here, 1. That good men do well for themselves; for they have in themselves an excellent character, and they secure to themselves an excellent portion, and in both they excel other people: *The righteous is more abundant than his neighbour* (so the margin); he is richer, though not in this world's goods, yet in the graces and comforts of the Spirit, which are the true riches. There is a true excellency in religion; it ennobles men, inspires them with generous principles, makes them substantial; it is an excellency which is, in the sight of God, of great price, who is the true Judge of excellency. His neighbour may make a greater figure in the world, may be more applauded, but the righteous man has the intrinsic worth. 2. That wicked men do ill for themselves; they walk in a way which *seduces them.* It seems to them to be not only a pleasant way, but the right way; it is so agreeable to flesh and blood that they therefore flatter themselves with an opinion that it cannot be amiss, but they will not gain the point they aim at, nor enjoy the good they hope for. It is all a cheat; and therefore the righteous is wiser and happier than his neighbour, that yet despise him and trample upon him.

27 The slothful *man* roasteth not that which he took in hunting: but the substance of a diligent man *is* precious.

Here is, 1. That which may make us hate slothfulness and deceit, for the word here, as before, signifies both: *The slothful* deceitful *man* has roast meat, but that which he roasts is not what he himself *took in hunting;* no, it is what others took pains for, and he lives upon the fruit of their labours, like the drones in the hive. Or, if slothful deceitful men have taken any thing by hunting (as sportsmen are seldom men of business), yet they do not roast it when they have taken it; they have no comfort in the enjoyment of it; perhaps God in his providence cuts them short of it. 2. That which may make us in love with industry and honesty, that the *substance of a diligent man,* though it be not great perhaps, *is* yet *precious.* It comes from the blessing of God; he has comfort in it; it does him good, and his family. It is his own daily bread, not bread out of other people's mouths, and therefore he sees God gives it to him in answer to his prayer.

28 In the way of righteousness *is*

life; and *in* the pathway *thereof there is* no death.

The way of religion is here recommended to us, 1. As a straight, plain, easy way; it is *the way of righteousness.* God's commands (the rule we are to walk by) are all holy, just, and good. Religion has right reason and equity on its side; it is a *path-way,* a way which God has cast up for us (Isa. xxxv. 8); it is a highway, the king's highway, the King of kings' highway, a way which is tracked before us by all the saints, the good old way, full of the footsteps of the flock. 2. As a safe, pleasant, comfortable way. (1.) There is not only life at the end, but there is life in the way; all true comfort and satisfaction. The favour of God, which is better than life; the Spirit, who is life. (2.) There is not only life in it, but so as that in it *there is no death,* none of that sorrow of the world which works death and is an allay to our present joy and life. There is no end of that life that is in the way of righteousness. Here there is life, but there is death too. *In the way of righteousness* there *is life, and no death,* life and immortality.

CHAP. XIII.

A WISE son *heareth* his father's instruction: but a scorner heareth not rebuke.

Among the children of the same parents it is no new thing for some to be hopeful and others the contrary; now here we are taught to distinguish. 1. There is great hope of those that have a reverence for their parents, and are willing to be advised and admonished by them. He is *a wise son,* and is in a fair way to be wiser, that *hears his father's instruction,* desires to hear it, regards it, and complies with it, and does not merely give it the hearing. 2. There is little hope of those that will not so much as *hear rebuke* with any patience, but scorn to submit to government and scoff at those that deal faithfully with them. How can those mend a fault who will not be told of it, but count those their enemies who do them that kindness?

2 A man shall eat good by the fruit of *his* mouth: but the soul of the transgressors *shall eat* violence.

Note, 1. If that which comes from within, out of the heart, be good, and from a good treasure, it will return with advantage. Inward comfort and satisfaction will be daily bread; nay, it will be a continual feast to those who delight in that communication which is *to the use of edifying.* 2. Violence done will recoil in the face of him that does it: *The soul of the transgressors* that harbours and plots mischief, and vents it by word and deed, *shall eat violence;* they shall have their belly full of it. *Reward her as she has rewarded thee,* Rev. xviii. 6. Every man shall drink as he brews, eat as he speaks; for by our words we must be justified or condemned,

Matt. xii. 37. As our fruit is, so will our food be, Rom. vi. 21, 22.

3 He that keepeth his mouth keepeth his life : *but* he that openeth wide his lips shall have destruction.

Note, 1. A guard upon the lips is a guard to the soul. He that is cautious, that thinks twice before he speaks once, that, if he have *thought evil, lays his hand upon his mouth* to suppress it, that keeps a strong bridle on his tongue and a strict hand on that bridle, he *keeps his soul* from a great deal both of guilt and grief and saves himself the trouble of many bitter reflections on himself and reflections of others upon him. 2. There is many a one ruined by an ungoverned tongue: *He that opens widely his lips,* to let out *quod in buccam venerit—whatever comes uppermost,* that loves to bawl, and bluster, and make a noise, and affects such a liberty of speech as bids defiance both to God and man, he *shall have destruction.* It will be the destruction of his reputation, his interest, his comfort, and his soul for ever, Jam. iii. 6.

4 The soul of the sluggard desireth, and *hath* nothing : but the soul of the diligent shall be made fat.

Here is, 1. The misery and shame of the slothful. See how foolish and absurd they are; they desire the gains which the diligent get, but they hate the pains which the diligent take; they covet every thing that is to be coveted, but will do nothing that is to be done; and therefore it follows, They have nothing ; for he that will not labour let him hunger, and let him not *eat,* 2 Thess. iii. 10. *The desire of the slothful,* which should be his excitement, is his torment, which should make him busy, makes him always uneasy, and is really a greater toil to him than labour would be. 2. The happiness and honour of the diligent : Their *soul shall be made fat;* they shall have abundance, and shall have the comfortable enjoyment of it, and the more for its being the fruit of their diligence. This is especially true in spiritual affairs. Those that rest in idle wishes know not what the advantages of religion are ; whereas those that take pains in the service of God find both the pleasure and profit of it.

5 A righteous *man* hateth lying : but a wicked *man* is loathsome, and cometh to shame.

Note, 1. Where grace reigns sin is loathsome. It is the undoubted character of every *righteous man* that he *hates lying* (that is, all sin, for every sin is a lie, and particularly all fraud and falsehood in commerce and conversation), not only that he will not tell a lie, but he abhors lying, from a rooted reigning principle of love to truth and justice, and conformity to God. 2. Where sin reigns the *man is loathsome.* If his eyes were opened, and his conscience awakened, he would be so to himself, he would *abhor himself and repent in dust*
862

and ashes; however, he is so to God and all good men ; particularly, he makes himself so by lying, than which there is nothing more detestable. And, though he may think to face it out awhile, yet he will *come to shame* and contempt at last and will blush to show his face, Dan. xii. 2.

6 Righteousness keepeth *him that is* upright in the way: but wickedness overthroweth the sinner.

See here, 1. Saints secured from ruin. Those that are *upright in their way,* that mean honestly in all their actions, adhere conscientiously to the sacred and eternal rules of equity, and deal sincerely both with God and man, their integrity will keep them from the temptations of Satan, which shall not prevail over them, the reproaches and injuries of evil men, which shall not fasten upon them, to do them any real mischief, Ps. xxv. 21.

> Hic murus aheneus esto, nil conscire sibi.
> Be this thy brazen bulwark of defence,
> Still to preserve thy conscious innocence.

2. Sinners secured for ruin. Those that are wicked, even their wickedness will be their overthrow at last, and they are held in the cords of it in the mean time. Are they corrected, destroyed? It is their own wickedness that corrects them, that destroys them; they alone shall bear it.

7 There is that maketh himself rich, yet *hath* nothing: *there is* that maketh himself poor, yet *hath* great riches.

This observation is applicable,

I. To men's worldly estate. The world is a great cheat, not only the things of the world, but the men of the world. *All men are liars.* Here is an instance in two sore evils under the sun :—1. Some that are really poor would be thought to be rich and are thought to be so ; they trade and spend as if they were rich, make a great bustle and a great show as if they had hidden treasures, when perhaps, if all their debts were paid, they are not worth a groat. This is sin, and will be shame ; many a one hereby ruins his family and brings reproach upon his profession of religion. Those that thus live above what they have choose to be subject to their own pride rather than to God's providence, and it will end accordingly. 2. Some that are really rich would be thought to be poor, and are thought to be so, because they sordidly and meanly live below what God has given them, and choose rather to bury it than to use it, Eccl. vi. 1, 2. In this there is an ingratitude to God, injustice to the family and neighbourhood, and uncharitableness to the poor.

II. To their spiritual state. Grace is the riches of the soul ; it is true riches ; but men commonly misrepresent themselves, either designedly or through mistake and ignorance of themselves. 1. There are many presuming hypocrites, that are really poor and empty of grace and yet either think themselves rich, and will not be convinced of their poverty, or pretend themselves rich, and will not own their poverty. 2. There are many timorous trembling Christians, that are spiritually rich, and full of grace, and yet think themselves poor, and will not be persuaded that they are rich, or, at least, will not own it; by their doubts and fears, their complaints and griefs, they *make themselves poor.* The former mistake is destroying at last; this is disquieting in the mean time.

8 The ransom of a man's life *are* his riches: but the poor heareth not rebuke.

We are apt to judge of men's blessedness, at least in this world, by their wealth, and that they are more or less happy accordingly as they have more or less of this world's goods; but Solomon here shows what a gross mistake it is, that we may be reconciled to a poor condition, and may neither covet riches ourselves nor envy those that have abundance. 1. Those that are rich, if by some they are respected for their riches, yet, to balance that, by others they are envied and struck at, and brought in danger of their lives, which therefore they are forced to ransom with their riches. *Slay us not, for we have treasures in the field,* Jer. xli. 8. Under some tyrants, it has been crime enough to be rich; and how little is a man beholden to his wealth when it only serves to redeem that life which otherwise would not have been exposed! 2. Those that are poor, if by some, that should be their friends, they are despised and overlooked, yet, to balance that, they are also despised and overlooked by others that would be their enemies if they had any thing to lose: *The poor hear not rebuke,* are not censured, reproached, accused, nor brought into trouble, as the rich are; for nobody thinks it worth while to take notice of them. When the rich Jews were carried captives to Babylon *the poor of the land were left,* 2 Kings xxv. 12. Welcome nothing, once in seven years. *Cantabit vacuus coram latrone viator—When a traveller is met by a robber he will rejoice at not having much property about him.*

9 The light of the righteous rejoiceth: but the lamp of the wicked shall be put out.

Here is, 1. The comfort of good men flourishing and lasting: *The light of the righteous rejoices,* that is, it increases, and makes them glad. Even their outward prosperity is their joy, and much more those gifts, graces, and comforts, with which their souls are illuminated; these *shine more and more, ch.* iv. 18. The Spirit is their light, and he gives them a fulness of joy, and *rejoices to do them good.* 2. The comfort of bad men withering and dying: *The lamp of the wicked* burns dimly and faint; it looks melancholy, like a taper in an urn, and it will shortly *be put out* in

utter darkness, Isa. l. 11. The light of the righteous is as that of the sun, which may be eclipsed and clouded, but will continue; that of the wicked is as a lamp of their own kindling, which will presently go out and is easily put out.

10 Only by pride cometh contention: but with the well advised *is* wisdom.

Note, 1. Foolish pride is the great makebate. Would you know *whence come wars and fightings?* They come from this root of bitterness. Whatever hand other lusts may have in contention (passion, envy, covetousness), pride has the great hand; it is its pride that it will itself sow discord and needs no help. Pride makes men impatient of contradiction in either their opinions or their desires, impatient of competition and rivalship, impatient of contempt, or any thing that looks like a slight, and impatient of concession, and receding, from a conceit of certain right and truth on their side; and hence arise quarrels among relations and neighbours, quarrels in states and kingdoms, in churches and Christian societies. Men will be revenged, will not forgive, because they are proud. 2. Those that are humble and peaceable are wise and *well advised.* Those that will ask and take advice, that will consult their own consciences, their Bibles, their ministers, their friends, and will do nothing rashly, are wise, as in other things, so in this, that they will humble themselves, will stoop and yield, to preserve quietness and prevent quarrels.

11 Wealth *gotten* by vanity shall be diminished: but he that gathereth by labour shall increase.

This shows that riches wear as they are won and woven. 1. That which is won ill will never wear well, for a curse attends it which will waste it, and the same corrupt dispositions which incline men to the sinful ways of getting will incline them to the like sinful ways of spending: *Wealth gotten by vanity* will be bestowed upon vanity, and then it *will be diminished.* That which is got by such employments as are not lawful, or not becoming Christians, such as only serve to feed pride and luxury, that which is got by gaming or by the stage, may as truly be said to be *gotten by vanity* as that which is got by fraud and lying, and *will be diminished. De male quæsitis vix gaudet tertius hæres—Ill-gotten wealth will scarcely be enjoyed by the third generation.* 2. That which is got by industry and honesty will grow more, instead of growing less; it will be a maintenance; it will be an inheritance; it will be an abundance. *He that labours, working with his hands, shall so increase as that he shall have to give to him that needs* (Eph. iv. 28); and, when it comes to that, it will increase yet more and more.

12 Hope deferred maketh the **heart**

sick: but *when* the desire cometh, *it is* a tree of life.

Note, 1. Nothing is more grievous than the disappointment of a raised expectation, though not in the thing itself by a denial, yet in the time of it by a delay : *Hope deferred makes the heart sick* and languishing, fretful and peevish ; but hope quite dashed kills the heart, and the more high the expectation was raised the more cutting is the frustration of it. It is therefore our wisdom not to promise ourselves any great matters from the creature, nor to feed ourselves with any vain hopes from this world, lest we lay up matter for our own vexation ; and what we do hope for let us prepare to be disappointed in, that, if it should prove so, it may prove the easier ; and let us not be hasty. 2. Nothing is more grateful than to enjoy that, at last, which we have long wished and waited for : *When the desire does come* it puts men into a sort of paradise, a garden of pleasure, for *it is a tree of life.* It will aggravate the eternal misery of the wicked that their hopes will be frustrated ; and it will make the happiness of heaven the more welcome to the saints that it is what they have earnestly longed for as the crown of their hopes.

13 Whoso despiseth the word shall be destroyed : but he that feareth the commandment shall be rewarded.

Here is, 1. The character of one that is marked for ruin : He that *despises the word* of God, and has no regard to it, no veneration for it, nor will be ruled by it, certainly he *shall be destroyed,* for he slights that which is the only means of curing a destructive disease and makes himself obnoxious to that divine wrath which will certainly be his destruction. Those that prefer the rules of carnal policy before divine precepts, and the allurements of the world and the flesh before God's promises and comforts, despise his word, giving the preference to those things that stand in competition with it ; and it is to their own just destruction : they would not take warning. 2. The character of one that is sure to be happy : He *that fears the commandment,* that stands in awe of God, pays a deference to his authority, has a reverence for his word, is afraid of displeasing God and incurring the penalties annexed to the commandment, shall not only escape destruction, but *shall be rewarded* for his godly fear. *In keeping the commandment there is great reward.*

14 The law of the wise *is* a fountain of life, to depart from the snares of death.

By *the law of the wise* and righteous, here, we may understand either the principles and rules by which they govern themselves or (which comes all to one) the instructions which they give to others, which ought to be as a law to all about them ; and if they be so,

1. They will be constant springs of comfort and satisfaction, as *a fountain of life,* sending forth streams of living water ; the closer we keep to those rules the more effectually we secure our own peace. 2. They will be constant preservatives from the temptations of Satan. Those that follow the dictates of this law will keep at a distance from the snares of sin, and so escape *the snares of death* which those run into that forsake *the law of the wise.*

15 Good understanding giveth favour : but the way of transgressors *is* hard.

If we compare not only the end, but the way, we shall find that religion has the advantage ; for, 1. The way of saints is pleasant and agreeable : *Good understanding* gains *favour* with God and man : our Saviour grew in that favour when he *increased in wisdom.* Those that conduct themselves prudently, and order their conversation aright in every thing, that *serve Christ in righteousness, and peace, and joy in the Holy Ghost,* are *accepted of God and approved of men,* Rom. xiv. 17, 18. And how comfortably will that man pass through the world who is well understood and is therefore well accepted ! 2. The way of sinners is rough and uneasy, and, for *this* reason, unpleasant to themselves, because unacceptable to others. It is *hard,* hard upon others, who complain of it, hard to the sinner himself, who can have little enjoyment of himself while he is doing that which is disobliging to all mankind. The service of sin is perfect slavery, and the road to hell is strewed with the thorns and thistles that are the products of the curse. Sinners labour in the very fire.

16 Every prudent *man* dealeth with knowledge : but a fool layeth open *his* folly.

Note, 1. It is wisdom to be cautious. *Every prudent* discreet *man* does all *with knowledge* (considering with himself and consulting with others), acts with deliberation and is upon the reserve, is careful not to meddle with that which he has not some knowledge of, nor to launch out into business which he has not acquainted himself with, will not *deal with* those that he has not some *knowledge* of, whether they may be confided in. He is still dealing in knowledge, that he may increase the stock he has. 2. It is folly to be rash, as the *fool* is, who is forward to talk of things he knows nothing of and undertake that which he is no way fit for, and so *lays open his folly* and makes himself ridiculous. He *began to build and was not able to finish.*

17 A wicked messenger falleth into mischief : but a faithful ambassador *is* health.

Here we have, 1. The ill consequences of betraying a trust. *A wicked messenger,* who, being sent to negociate any business, is false to him that employed him, divulges his counsels, and so defeats his designs, cannot expect to prosper, but will certainly *fall into* some *mischief* or other, will be discovered and punished, since nothing is more hateful to God and man than the treachery of those that have a confidence reposed in them. 2. The happy effects of fidelity : An *ambassador* who *faithfully* discharges his trust, and serves the interests of those who employ him, *is health ;* he is health to those by whom and for whom he is employed, heals differences that are between them, and preserves a good understanding ; he is health to himself, for he secures his own interest. This is applicable to ministers, Christ's messengers and ambassadors ; those that are wicked and false to Christ and the souls of men do mischief and *fall into mischief*, but those that are faithful will find sound words to be healing words to others and themselves.

18 Poverty and shame *shall be to* him that refuseth instruction : but he that regardeth reproof shall be honoured.

Note, 1. He that is so proud that he scorns to be taught will certainly be abased. He that *refuses* the good *instruction* offered him, as if it were a reflection upon his honour and an abridgment of his liberty, *poverty and shame shall be to him :* he will become a beggar and live and die in disgrace ; every one will despise him as foolish, and stubborn, and ungovernable. 2. He that is so humble that he takes it well to be told of his faults shall certainly be exalted : *He that regards a reproof*, whoever gives it to him, and will mend what is amiss when it is shown him, gains respect as wise and candid ; he avoids that which would be a disgrace to him and is in a fair way to make himself considerable.

19 The desire accomplished is sweet to the soul : but *it is* abomination to fools to depart from evil.

This shows the folly of those that refuse instruction, for they might be happy and will not. 1. They might be happy. There are in man strong desires of happiness ; God has provided for the accomplishment of those desires, and that would be *sweet to the soul,* whereas the pleasures of sense are grateful only to the carnal appetite. *The desire of* good men towards the favour of God and spiritual blessings brings that which *is sweet to their souls ;* we know those that can say so by experience, Ps. iv. 6, 7. 2. Yet they will not be happy ; for *it is* an *abomination to* them *to depart from evil*, which is necessary to their being happy. Never let those expect any thing truly sweet to their souls that will not be persuaded to leave their sins, but that roll them under their tongues as a sweet morsel.

20 He that walketh with wise *men* shall be wise : but a companion of fools shall be destroyed.

Note, 1. Those that would be good must keep good company, which is an evidence for them that they would be good (men's character is known by the company they choose) and will be a means of making them good, of showing them the way and of quickening and encouraging them in it. He that would be himself wise must walk with those that are so, must choose such for his intimate acquaintance, and converse with them accordingly ; must ask and receive instruction from them, and keep up pious and profitable talk with them. *Miss not the discourse of the elders, for they also learned of their fathers,* Ecclesiasticus viii. 9. And (Ecclesiasticus vi. 35), *Be willing to hear every godly discourse, and let not the parables of understanding escape thee.* 2. Multitudes are brought to ruin by bad company : *A companion of fools shall be broken* (so some), *shall be known* (so the LXX.), known to be a fool ; *noscitur ex socio—he is known by his company.* He *will be like them* (so some), *will be made wicked* (so others) ; it comes all to one, for all those, and those only, that make themselves wicked, will *be destroyed*, and those that associate with evil-doers are debauched, and so undone, and at last ascribe their death to it.

21 Evil pursueth sinners : but t᾽ the righteous good shall be repayed.

Here see, 1. How unavoidable the destruction of sinners is ; the wrath of God pursues them, and all the terrors of that wrath : *Evil pursues* them closely wherever they go, as the avenger of blood pursued the manslayer, and they have no city of refuge to flee to ; they attempt an escape, but in vain. Whom God pursues he is sure to overtake. They may prosper for a while and grow very secure, but their damnation slumbers not, though they do. 2. How indefeasible the happiness of the saints is ; the God that cannot lie has engaged that *to the righteous good shall be repaid.* They shall be abundantly recompensed for all the good they have done, and all the ill they have suffered, in this world ; so that, though many have been losers for their righteousness, they shall not be losers by it. Though the recompence do not come quickly, it will come in the day of payment, in the world of retribution ; and it will be an abundant recompence.

22 A good *man* leaveth an inheritance to his children's children : and the wealth of the sinner *is* laid up for the just.

See here, 1. How *a good man's* estate lasts : He *leaves an inheritance to his children's children.* It is part of his praise that he is thoughtful for posterity, that he does not lay all out upon himself, but is in care to do well for those that come after him, not by withholding more than is meet, but by a prudent and decent frugality. He trains up his children to this, that they may leave it to their children; and especially he is careful, both by justice and charity, to obtain the blessing of God upon what he has, and to entail that blessing upon his children, without which the greatest industry and frugality will be in vain: *A good man,* by being good and doing good, by honouring the Lord with his substance and spending it in his service, secures it to his posterity; or, if he should not leave them much of this world's goods, his prayers, his instructions, his good example, will be the best entail, and the promises of the covenant will be an inheritance to his *children's children,* Ps. ciii. 17. 2. How it increases by the accession of *the wealth of the sinner* to it, for that *is laid up for the just.* If it be asked, How should good men grow so rich, who are not so eager upon the world as others are and who commonly suffer for their well-doing? It is here answered, God, in his providence, often brings into their hands that which wicked people had laid up for themselves. *The innocent shall divide the silver,* Job xxvii. 16, 17. The Israelites shall spoil the Egyptians (Exod. xii. 36) and *eat the riches of the Gentiles,* Isa. lxi. 6.

23 Much food *is in* the tillage of the poor : but there is *that is* destroyed for want of judgment.

See here, 1. How a small estate may be improved by industry, so that a man, by making the best of every thing, may live comfortably upon it: *Much food is in the tillage of the poor,* the poor farmers, that have but a little, but take pains with that little and husband it well. Many make it an excuse for their idleness that they have but a little to work on, a very little to be doing with; but the less compass the field is of the more let the skill and labour of the owner be employed about it, and it will turn to a very good account. Let him dig, and he needs not beg. 2. How a great estate may be ruined by indiscretion : *There is that* has a great deal, but it *is destroyed* and brought to nothing *for want of judgment,* that is, prudence in the management of it. Men over-build themselves or over-buy themselves, keep greater company, or a better table, or more servants, than they can afford, suffer what they have to go to decay and do not make the most of it; by taking up money themselves, or being bound for others, their estates are sunk, their families reduced, and all *for want of judgment.*

24 He that spareth his rod hateth his son : but he that loveth him chasteneth him betimes.

Note, 1. To the education of children in that which is good there is necessary a due correction of them for what is amiss; every child of ours is a child of Adam, and there-

fore has that foolishness bound up in its heart which calls for rebuke, more or less, the rod and reproof which give wisdom. Observe, It is *his* rod that must be used, the rod of a parent, directed by wisdom and love, and designed for good, not the rod of a servant. 2. It is good to begin betimes with the necessary restraints of children from that which is evil, before vicious habits are confirmed. The branch is easily bent when it is tender. 3. Those really hate their children, though they pretend to be fond of them, that do not keep them under a strict discipline, and by all proper methods, severe ones when gentle ones will not serve, make them sensible of their faults and afraid of offending. They abandon them to their worst enemy, to the most dangerous disease, and therefore hate them. Let this reconcile children to the correction their good parents give them; it is from love, and for their good, Heb. xii. 7—9.

25 The righteous eateth to the satisfying of his soul : but the belly of the wicked shall want.

Note, 1. It is the happiness of the righteous that they shall have enough and that they know when they have enough. They desire not to be surfeited, but, being moderate in their desires, they are soon satisfied. Nature is content with a little and grace with less; enough is as good as a feast. Those that feed on the bread of life, that feast on the promises, meet with abundant satisfaction of soul there, eat, and are filled. 2. It is the misery of the wicked that, through the insatiableness of their own desires, they are always needy; not only their souls shall not be satisfied with the world and the flesh, but even their *belly shall want;* their sensual appetite is always craving. In hell they shall be denied a drop of water.

CHAP. XIV.

EVERY wise woman buildeth her house : but the foolish plucketh it down with her hands.

Note, 1. A good wife is a great blessing to a family. By a fruitful wife a family is multiplied and replenished with children, and so built up. But by a prudent wife, one that is pious, industrious, and considerate, the affairs of the family are made to prosper, debts are paid, portions raised, provision made, the children well educated and maintained, and the family has comfort within doors and credit without; thus is the house built. She looks upon it as her own to take care of, though she knows it is her husband's to bear rule in, Esth. i. 22. 2. Many a family is brought to ruin by ill housewifery, as well as by ill husbandry. A *foolish* woman, that has no fear of God nor regard to her business, that is wilful, and wasteful, and humoursome, that indulges her ease and appetite, and is all for jaunting and feasting, cards and the play-house, though she come to a plentiful estate, and to a family beforehand, she will impoverish and waste it, and will as certainly be the ruin of her house as if she *plucked it down with her hands;* and the husband himself, with all his care, can scarcely prevent it.

2 He that walketh in his uprightness feareth the LORD : but *he that is* perverse in his ways despiseth him.

Here are, 1. Grace and sin in their true colours. Grace reigning is a reverence of God, and gives honour to him who is infinitely great and high, and to whom all honour is due, than which what is more becoming or should be more pleasing to the rational creature? Sin reigning is no less than a contempt of God. In *this*, more than in any thing, sin appears exceedingly sinful, that it despises God, whom angels adore. Those that despise God's precepts, and will not be ruled by them, his promises, and will not accept of them, despise God himself and all his attributes. 2. Grace and sin in their true light. By this we may know a man that has grace, and the fear of God, reigning in him, *he walks in his uprightness,* he makes conscience of his actions, is faithful both to God and man, and every stop he makes, as well as every step he takes, is by rule; here is one that honours God. But, on the contrary, *he that is perverse in his ways,* that wilfully follows his own appetites and passions, that is unjust and dishonest and contradicts his profession in his conversation, however he may pretend to devotion, he is a wicked man, and will be reckoned with as a despiser of God himself.

3 In the mouth of the foolish *is* a rod of pride : but the lips of the wise shall preserve them.

See here, 1. A proud fool exposing himself. Where there is pride in the heart, and no wisdom in the head to suppress it, it commonly shows itself in the words : *In the mouth there is pride,* proud boasting, proud censuring, proud scorning, proud commanding and giving law ; this is the *rod,* or branch, *of pride;* the word is used only here and Isa. xi. 1. It grows from that root of bitterness which is in the heart; it is a rod from that stem. The root must be plucked up, or we cannot conquer this branch. Or it is meant of a smiting beating rod, a *rod of pride* which strikes others. The proud man with his tongue lays about him and deals blows at pleasure, but it will in the end be a rod to himself; the proud man shall come under an ignominious correction by the words of his own mouth, not cut as a soldier, but caned as a servant; and herein he will be beaten with his own rod, Ps. lxiv. 8. 2. A humble wise man saving himself and consulting his own good : *The lips of the wise shall preserve them* from doing that mischief to others which

proud men do with their tongues, and from bringing that mischief on themselves which haughty scorners are often involved in.

4 Where no oxen *are,* the crib *is* clean : but much increase *is* by the strength of the ox.

Note, 1. The neglect of husbandry is the way to poverty : *Where no oxen are,* to till the ground and tread out the corn, *the crib* is empty, *is clean;* there is no straw for the cattle, and consequently no bread for the service of man. Scarcity is represented by *cleanness of teeth,* Amos iv. 6. *Where no oxen are* there is nothing to be done at the ground, and then nothing to be had out of it ; *the crib* indeed *is clean* from dung, which pleases the neat and nice, that cannot endure husbandry because there is so much dirty work in it, and therefore will sell their oxen to keep the crib clean; but then not only the labour, but even the dung of the ox is wanted. This shows the folly of those who addict themselves to the pleasures of the country, but do not mind the business of it, who (as we say) keep more horses than kine, more dogs than swine; their families must needs suffer by it. 2. Those who take pains about their ground are likely to reap the profit of it. Those who keep that about them which is for use and service, not for state and show, more husbandmen than footmen, are likely to thrive. *Much increase is by the strength of the ox;* that is made for our service, and is profitable alive and dead.

5 A faithful witness will not lie : but a false witness will utter lies.

In the administration of justice much depends upon the witnesses, and therefore it is necessary to the common good that witnesses be principled as they ought to be; for, 1. A witness that is conscientious will not dare to give in a testimony that is in the least untrue, nor, for good-will or ill-will, represent a thing otherwise than according to the best of his knowledge, whoever is pleased or displeased, and then judgment runs down like a river. 2. But a witness that will be bribed, and biassed, and browbeaten, *will utter lies* (and not stick nor startle at it), with as much readiness and assurance as if what he said were all true.

6 A scorner seeketh wisdom, and *findeth it* not : but knowledge *is* easy unto him that understandeth.

Note, 1. The reason why some people seek wisdom, and do not find it, is because they do not seek it from a right principle and in a right manner. They are scorners, and it is in scorn that they ask instruction, that they may ridicule what is told them and may cavil at it. Many put questions to Christ, tempting him, and that they might have whereof to accuse him, but they were never the wiser. No marvel if those who seek wisdom, as Simon Magus sought the gifts of the Holy

Ghost, to serve their pride and covetousness, do not find it, for they seek amiss. Herod desired to see a miracle, but he was a scorner, and therefore it was denied him, Luke xxiii. 8. Scorners speed not in prayer. 2. To those who understand aright, who *depart from evil* (for *that is understanding*), the *knowledge* of God and of his will *is easy.* The parables which harden scorners in their scorning, and make divine things more difficult to them, enlighten those who are willing to learn, and make the same things more plain, and intelligible, and familiar to them, Matt. xiii. 11, 15, 16. The same word which to the scornful *is a savour of death unto death* to the humble and serious *is a savour of life unto life.* He *that understands,* so as to *depart from evil* (for *that is understanding*), to quit his prejudices, to lay aside all corrupt dispositions and affections, will easily apprehend instruction and receive the impressions of it.

7 Go from the presence of a foolish man, when thou perceivest not *in him* the lips of knowledge.

See here, 1. How we may discern a fool and discover him, a wicked man, for he is *a foolish man.* If we *perceive not in him the lips of knowledge,* if we find there is no relish or savour of piety in his discourse, that his communication is all corrupt and corrupting, and nothing in it *good and to the use of edifying,* we may conclude the treasure is bad. 2. How we must decline such a one and depart from him: *Go from his presence,* for *thou perceivest* there is no good to be gotten by his company, but danger of getting hurt by it. Sometimes the only way we have of reproving wicked discourse and witnessing against it is by leaving the company and going out of the hearing of it.

8 The wisdom of the prudent *is* to understand his way: but the folly of fools *is* deceit.

See here, 1. The good conduct of a wise and good man; he manages himself well. It is not the wisdom of the learned, which consists only in speculation, that is here recommended, but *the wisdom of the prudent,* which is practical, and is of use to direct our counsels and actions. Christian prudence consists in a right *understanding of our way;* for we are travellers, whose concern it is, not to spy wonders, but to get forward towards their journey's end. It *is to understand our own way,* not to be critics and busybodies in other men's matters, but to look well to ourselves and *ponder the path of our feet,* to understand the directions of our way, that we may observe them, the dangers of our way, that we may avoid them, the difficulties of our way, that we may break through them, and the advantages of our way, that we may improve them—to understand the rules we are to walk by and the ends we are to walk towards, and walk accordingly. 2.

The bad conduct of a bad man; he puts a cheat upon himself. He does not rightly understand his way; he thinks he does, and so misses his way, and goes on in his mistake: *The folly of fools is deceit;* it cheats them into their own ruin. The folly of him that built on the sand was deceit.

9 Fools make a mock at sin: but among the righteous *there is* favour.

See here, 1. How wicked people are hardened in their wickedness: they *make a mock at sin.* They make a laughing matter of the sins of others, making themselves and their companions merry with that for which they should mourn, and they make a light matter of their own sins, both when they are tempted to sin and when they have committed it; they *call evil good and good evil* (Isa. v. 20), turn it off with a jest, rush into sin (Jer. viii. 6) and say they shall have peace though they go on. They care not what mischief they do by their sins, and laugh at those that tell them of it. They are advocates for sin, and are ingenious at framing excuses for it. *Fools make a mock at the sin-offering* (so some); those that make light of sin make light of Christ. Those are fools that make light of sin, for they make light of that which God complains of (Amos ii. 13), which lay heavily upon Christ, and which they themselves will have other thoughts of shortly. 2. How good people are encouraged in their goodness: *Among the righteous there is favour;* if they in any thing offend, they presently repent and obtain the favour of God. They have a goodwill one to another; and among them, in their societies, there is mutual charity and compassion in cases of offences, and no mocking.

10 The heart knoweth his own bitterness; and a stranger doth not intermeddle with his joy.

This agrees with 1 Cor. ii. 11, *What man knows the things of a man,* and the changes of his temper, *save the spirit of a man?* 1. Every man feels most from his own burden, especially that which is a burden upon the spirits, for that is commonly concealed and the sufferer keeps it to himself. We must not censure the griefs of others, for we know not what they feel; their stroke perhaps is heavier than their groaning. 2. Many enjoy a secret pleasure, especially in divine consolations, which others are not aware of, much less are sharers in; and, as the sorrows of a penitent, so the joys of a believer are such as a *stranger does not intermeddle with* and therefore is no competent judge of.

11 The house of the wicked shall be overthrown: but the tabernacle of the upright shall flourish.

Note, 1. Sin is the ruin of great families: *The house of the wicked,* though built ever so strong and high, *shall be overthrown,* shall be brought to poverty and disgrace, and at length be extinct. His hope for heaven, the house on which he leans, shall not stand, but fail in the storm; the deluge that comes will sweep it away. 2. Righteousness is the rise and stability even of mean families: Even *the tabernacle of the upright*, though movable and despicable as a tent, *shall flourish*, in outward prosperity if Infinite Wisdom see good, at all events in graces and comfort, which are true riches and honours.

12 There is a way which seemeth right unto a man, but the end thereof *are* the ways of death.

We have here an account of the way and end of a great many self-deluded souls. 1. Their way is seemingly fair: It *seems right* to themselves; they please themselves with a fancy that they are as they should be, that their opinions and practices are good, and such as will bear them out. The way of ignorance and carelessness, the way of worldliness and earthly-mindedness, the way of sensuality and flesh-pleasing, seem right to those that walk in them, much more the way of hypocrisy in religion, external performances, partial reformations, and blind zeal; this they imagine will bring them to heaven; they flatter themselves in their own eyes that all will be well at last. 2. Their end is really fearful, and the more so for their mistake: It is *the ways of death*, eternal death; their iniquity will certainly be their ruin, and they will perish with a lie in their right hand. Self-deceivers will prove in the end self-destroyers.

13 Even in laughter the heart is sorrowful: and the end of that mirth *is* heaviness.

This shows the vanity of carnal mirth, and proves what Solomon said of laughter, that *it is mad;* for, 1. There is sadness under it. Sometimes when sinners are under convictions, or some great trouble, they dissemble their grief by a forced mirth, and put a good face on it, because they will not seem to yield: they cry not when he binds them. Nay, when men really are merry, yet at the same time there is some alloy or other to their mirth, something that casts a damp upon it, which all their gaiety cannot keep from their heart. Their consciences tell them they have no reason to be merry (Hos. ix. 1); they cannot but see the vanity of it. Spiritual joy is seated in the soul; the joy of the hypocrite is but from the teeth outward. See John xvi. 22; 2 Cor. vi. 10. 2. There is worse after it: *The end of that mirth is heaviness.* It is soon over, like the crackling of thorns under a pot; and, if the conscience be awake, all sinful and profane mirth will be reflected upon with bitterness; if not, the heaviness will be so much the greater when *for all these things God shall bring the* sinner *into judgment.* The sorrows of the saints will end in everlasting joys (Ps. cxxvi. 5),

but the laughter of fools will end in endless weeping and wailing.

14 The backslider in heart shall be filled with his own ways : and a good man *shall be satisfied* from himself.

Note, 1. The misery of sinners will be an eternal surfeit upon their sins: The *backslider in heart*, who for fear of suffering, or in hope of profit or pleasure, forsakes God and his duty, shall be *filled with his own ways;* God will give him enough of them. They would not leave their brutish lusts and passions, and therefore they shall stick by them, to their everlasting terror and torment. *He that is filthy shall be filthy still.* "Son, remember," shall *fill them with their own ways,* and set their sins in order before them. Backsliding begins in the heart; it is the evil heart of unbelief that departs from God; and of all sinners backsliders will have most terror when they reflect on *their own ways,* Luke xi. 26. 2. The happiness of the saints will be an eternal satisfaction in their graces, as tokens of and qualifications for God's peculiar favour: *A good man shall be* abundantly *satisfied from himself,* from what God has wrought in him. He has *rejoicing in himself alone,* Gal. vi. 4. As sinners never think they have sin enough till it brings them to hell, so saints never think they have grace enough till it brings them to heaven.

15 The simple believeth every word: but the prudent *man* looketh well to his going.

Note, 1. It is folly to be credulous, to heed every flying report, to give ear to every man's story, though ever so improbable, to take things upon trust from common fame, to depend upon every man's profession of friendship and give credit to every one that will promise payment; those are *simple* who thus *believe every word,* forgetting that all men, in some sense, are liars in comparison with God, all whose words we are to believe with an implicit faith, for he cannot lie. 2. It is wisdom to be cautious: *The prudent man* will try before he trusts, will weigh both the credibility of the witness and the probability of the testimony, and then give judgment as the thing appears or suspend his judgment till it appears. *Prove all things,* and *believe not every spirit.*

16 A wise *man* feareth, and departeth from evil: but the fool rageth, and is confident.

Note, 1. Holy fear is an excellent guard upon every holy thing, and against every thing that is unholy. It is wisdom to depart *from evil,* from the evil of sin, and thereby from all other evil; and therefore it is wisdom to fear, that is, to be jealous over ourselves with a godly jealousy, to keep up a dread of God's wrath, to be afraid of coming near the borders of sin or dallying with the beginnings of it. A wise man, for fear of harm, keeps out of harm's way, and starts back in a fright when he finds himself entering into temptation. 2. Presumption is folly. He who, when he is warned of his danger, *rages and is confident*, furiously pushes on, cannot bear to be checked, bids defiance to the wrath and curse of God, and, fearless of danger, persists in his rebellion, makes bold with the occasions of sin, and plays upon the precipice, he is a fool, for he acts against his reason and his interest, and his ruin will quickly be the proof of his folly.

17 *He that is* soon angry dealeth foolishly: and a man of wicked devices is hated.

Note, 1. Passionate men are justly laughed at. Men who are peevish and touchy, and are *soon angry* upon every the least provocation, *deal foolishly;* they say and do that which is ridiculous, and so expose themselves to contempt; they themselves cannot but be ashamed of it when the heat is over. The consideration of this should engage those especially who are in reputation for wisdom and honour with the utmost care to bridle their passion. 2. Malicious men are justly dreaded and detested, for they are much more dangerous and mischievous to all societies : *A man of wicked devices,* who stifles his resentments till he has an opportunity of being revenged, and is secretly plotting how to wrong his neighbour and to do him an ill turn, as Cain to kill Abel, such a man as this is hated by all mankind. The character of an angry man is pitiable; through the surprise of a temptation he disturbs and disgraces himself, but it is soon over, and he is sorry for it. But that of a spiteful revengeful man is odious; there is no fence against him nor cure for him.

18 The simple inherit folly : but the prudent are crowned with knowledge.

Note, 1. Sin is the shame of sinners : *The simple,* who love simplicity, get nothing by it; they *inherit folly.* They have it *by inheritance,* so some. This corruption of nature is derived from our first parents, and all the calamities that attend it we have by kind; it was the inheritance they transmitted to their degenerate race, an hereditary disease. They are as fond of it as a man of his inheritance, hold it as fast, and are as loth to part with it. What they value themselves upon is really foolish ; and what will be the issue of their simplicity but folly? They will for ever rue their own foolish choice. 2. Wisdom is the honour of the wise : *The prudent crown* themselves *with knowledge,* they look upon it as their brightest ornament, and there is nothing they are so ambitious of; they bind it to their heads as a crown, which they will by no means part with; they press towards the top and perfection of knowledge, which will crown their beginnings and pro-

870

gress. They shall have the praise of it; wise heads shall be respected as if they were crowned heads. They *crown knowledge* (so some read it); they are a credit to their profession. Wisdom is not only justified, but glorified, of all her children.

19 The evil bow before the good; and the wicked at the gates of the righteous.

That is, 1. The wicked are oftentimes impoverished and brought low, so that they are forced to beg, their wickedness having reduced them to straits; while good men, by the blessing of God, are enriched, and enabled to give, and do give, even to the evil; for where God grants life we must not deny a livelihood. 2. Sometimes God extorts, even from bad men, an acknowledgment of the excellency of God's people. The evil ought always to *bow before the good,* and sometimes they are made to do it and *to know that God has loved them,* Rev. iii. 9. They desire their favour (Esth. vii. 7), their prayers, 2 Kings iii. 12. 3. There is a day coming when the upright shall have the dominion (Ps. xlix. 14), when the foolish virgins shall come begging to the wise for oil, and shall knock in vain at that gate of the Lord at which the righteous entered.

20 The poor is hated even of his own neighbour : but the rich *hath* many friends.

This shows, not what should be, but what is the common way of the world—to be shy of the poor and fond of the rich. 1. Few will give countenance to those whom the world frowns upon, though otherwise worthy of respect : *The poor,* who should be pitied, and encouraged, and relieved, *is hated,* looked strange upon, and kept at a distance, even *by his own neighbour,* who, before he fell into disgrace, was intimate with him and pretended to have a kindness for him. Most are swallow-friends, that are gone in winter. It is good having God our friend, for he will not desert us when we are poor. 2. Every one will make court to those whom the world smiles upon, though otherwise unworthy : *The rich have many friends,* friends to their riches, in hope to get something out of them. There is little friendship in the world but what is governed by self-interest, which is no true friendship at all, nor what a wise man will either value himself on or put any confidence in. Those that make the world their God idolize those that have most of its good things, and seek their favour as if indeed they were Heaven's favourites.

21 He that despiseth his neighbour sinneth : but he that hath mercy on the poor, happy *is* he.

See here how men's character and condition are measured and judged of by their conduct towards their poor neighbours. 1. Those that look upon them with contempt have here assigned them a bad character, and their condition will be accordingly: *He that despises his neighbour* because he is low in the world, because he is of a mean extraction, rustic education, and makes but a mean figure, that thinks it below him to take notice of him, converse with him, or concern himself about him, and sets him with the dogs of his flock, *is a sinner*, is guilty of a sin, is in the way to worse, and shall be dealt with as a sinner; unhappy is he. 2. Those that look upon them with compassion are here said to be in a good condition, according to their character: *He that has mercy on the poor*, is ready to do all the good offices he can to him, and thereby puts an honour upon him, *happy is he;* he does that which is pleasing to God, which he himself will afterwards reflect upon with great satisfaction, for which the loins of the poor will bless him, and which will be abundantly recompensed in the resurrection of the just.

22 Do they not err that devise evil? but mercy and truth *shall be* to them that devise good.

See here, 1. How miserably mistaken those are that not only do evil, but devise it: *Do they not err?* Yes, certainly they do; every one knows it. They think that by sinning with craft and contrivance, and carrying on their intrigues with more plot and artifice than others, they shall make a better hand of their sins than others do, and come off better. But they are mistaken. God's justice cannot be out-witted. Those that devise evil against their neighbours greatly err, for it will certainly turn upon themselves and end in their own ruin, a fatal error! 2. How wisely those consult their own interest that not only do good but devise it: *Mercy and truth* shall be to them, not a reward of debt (they will own that they merit nothing), but a reward of mercy, mere mercy, mercy according to the promise, mercy and truth, to which God is pleased to make himself a debtor. Those that are so liberal as to devise liberal things, that seek opportunities of doing good, and contrive how to make their charity most extensive and most acceptable to those that need it, *by liberal things they shall stand*, Isa. xxxii. 8.

23 In all labour there is profit: but the talk of the lips *tendeth* only to penury.

Note, 1. Working, without talking, will make men rich: *In all labour* of the head, or of the hand, *there is profit;* it will turn to some good account or other. Industrious people are generally thriving people, and where there is something done there is something to be had. *The stirring hand gets a penny.* It is good therefore to keep in business, and to keep in action, and what our hand finds to do to do it with all our might. 2. Talking, without working, will make men poor Those that love to boast of their business and make a noise about it, and that waste their time in tittle-tattle, in telling and hearing new things, like the Athenians, and, under pretence of improving themselves by conversation, neglect the work of their place and day, they waste what they have, and the course they take *tends to penury*, and will end in it. It is true in the affairs of our souls; those that take pains in the service of God, that strive earnestly in prayer, will find profit in it. But if men's religion runs all out in talk and noise, and their praying is only the labour of the lips, they will be spiritually poor, and come to nothing.

24 The crown of the wise *is* their riches: *but* the foolishness of fools *is* folly.

Observe, 1. If men be wise and good, riches make them so much the more honourable and useful: *The crown of the wise is their riches*; their riches make them to be so much the more respected, and give them the more authority and influence upon others. Those that have wealth, and wisdom to use it, will have a great opportunity of honouring God and doing good in the world. *Wisdom is good* without *an inheritance*, but better *with* it. 2. If men be wicked and corrupt, their wealth will but the more expose them: *The foolishness of fools*, put them in what condition you will, *is folly*, and will show itself and shame them; if they have riches, they do mischief with them and are the more hardened in their foolish practices.

25 A true witness delivereth souls: but a deceitful *witness* speaketh lies.

See here, 1. How much praise is due to a faithful witness: He *delivers the souls* of the innocent, who are falsely accused, and their good names, which are as dear to them as their lives. A man of integrity will venture the displeasure of the greatest, to bring truth to light and rescue those who are injured by falsehood. A faithful minister, who truly witnesses for God against sin, is thereby instrumental to deliver souls from eternal death. 2. How little regard is to be had to a false witness. He forges *lies*, and yet pours them out with the greatest assurance imaginable for the destruction of the innocent. It is therefore the interest of a nation by all means possible to detect and punish false-witness-bearing, yea, and lying in common conversation; for truth is the cement of society.

26 In the fear of the LORD *is* strong confidence: and his children shall have a place of refuge. 27 The fear of the LORD *is* a fountain of life, to depart from the snares of death.

In these two verses we are invited and encouraged to live in the fear of God by the advantages which attend a religious life. The *fear of the Lord* is here put for all gracious principles, producing gracious practices 1.

Where this reigns it produces a holy security and serenity of mind. There is in it a *strong confidence;* it enables a man still to hold fast both his purity and his peace, whatever happens, and gives him boldness before God and the world. *I know that I shall be justified—None of these things move me;* such is the language of this confidence. 2. It entails a blessing upon posterity. The children of those that by faith make God their confidence shall be encouraged by the promise that God will be a God to believers and to their seed to flee to him as their refuge, and they shall find shelter in him. The children of religious parents often do the better for their parents' instructions and example and fare the better for their faith and prayers. " *Our fathers trusted in thee,* therefore we will." 3. It is an over-flowing ever-flowing spring of comfort and joy; it is *a fountain of life,* yielding constant pleasure and satisfaction to the soul, joys that are pure and fresh, are life to the soul, and quench its thirst, and can never be drawn dry; it is a *well of living water,* that is springing up to, and is the earnest of, eternal life. 4. It is a sovereign antidote against sin and temptation. Those that have a true relish of the pleasures of serious godliness will not be allured by the baits of sin to swallow its hook; they know where to obtain better things than any it can pretend to offer, and therefore it is easy to them *to depart from the snares of death* and to keep their foot from being taken in them.

28 In the multitude of people *is* the king's honour: but in the want of people *is* the destruction of the prince.

Here are two maxims in politics, which carry their own evidence with them:—1. That it is much for the honour of a king to have a populous kingdom; it is a sign that he rules well, since strangers are hereby invited to come and settle under his protection and his own subjects live comfortably; it is a sign that he and his kingdom are under the blessing of God, the effect of which is being fruitful and multiplying. It is his strength, and makes him considerable and formidable; happy is the king, the father of his country, who has his *quiver full of arrows;* he *shall not be ashamed, but shall speak with his enemy in the gate,* Ps. cxxvii. 4, 5. It is therefore the wisdom of princes, by a mild and gentle government, by encouraging trade and husbandry, and by making all easy under them, to promote the increase of their people. And let all that wish well to the kingdom of Christ, and to his honour, do what they can in their places that many may be added to his church. 2. That when the people are lessened the prince is weakened: *In the want of people is the leanness of the prince* (so some read it); trade lies dead, the ground lies untilled, the army wants to be recruited, the navy to be manned, and all because there are not hands sufficient. See how much the ho-

nour and safety of kings depend upon their people, which is a reason why they should rule by love, and not with rigour. Princes are corrected by those judgments which abate the number of the people, as we find, 2 Sam. xxiv. 13.

29 *He that is* slow to wrath *is* of great understanding: but *he that is* hasty of spirit exalteth folly.

Note, 1. Meekness is wisdom. *He* rightly understands himself, and his duty and interest, the infirmities of human nature, and the constitution of human society, who *is slow to anger,* and knows how to excuse the faults of others as well as his own, how to adjourn his resentments, and moderate them, so as by no provocation to be put out of the possession of his own soul. A mild patient man is really to be accounted an intelligent man, one that learns of Christ, who is Wisdom itself. 2. Unbridled passion is folly proclaimed: *He that is hasty of spirit,* whose heart is tinder to every spark of provocation, that is all fire and tow, as we say, he thinks hereby to magnify himself and make those about stand in awe of him, whereas really he *exalts his own folly;* he makes it known, as that which is lifted up is visible to all, and he submits himself to it as to the government of one that is exalted.

30 A sound heart *is* the life of the flesh: but envy the rottenness of the bones.

The foregoing verse showed how much our reputation, this how much our health, depends on the good government of our passions and the preserving of the temper of the mind. 1. A healing spirit, made up of love and meekness, a hearty, friendly, cheerful disposition, is *the life of the flesh;* it contributes to a good constitution of body; people grow fat with good humour. 2. A fretful, envious, discontented spirit, is its own punishment; it consumes the flesh, preys upon the animal spirits, makes the countenance pale, and is the *rottenness of the bones.* Those that see the prosperity of others and are grieved, let them *gnash with their teeth and melt away,* Ps. cxii 10.

Rumpatur, quisquis rumpitur invidia.
Whoever bursts for envy, let him burst.

31 He that oppresseth the poor reproacheth his Maker: but he that honoureth him hath mercy on the poor.

God is here pleased to interest himself more than one would imagine in the treatment given to the poor. 1. He reckons himself affronted in the injuries that are done them. Whosoever he be that wrongs a poor man, taking advantage against him because he is poor and cannot help himself, let him know that he puts an affront upon his Maker. God made him, and gave him his being, the same that is the author of our being; we have all one Father, one Maker; see how Job considered this, Job xxxi. 15. God made him poor, and appointed him his lot, so that, if we deal hardly with any because they are poor, we reflect upon God as dealing hardly with them in laying them low, that they might be trampled upon. 2. He reckons himself honoured in the kindnesses that are done them; he takes them as done to himself, and will show himself accordingly pleased with them. *I was hungry, and you gave me meat.* Those therefore that have any true honour for God will show it by compassion to the poor, whom he has undertaken in a special manner to protect and patronise.

32 The wicked is driven away in his wickedness: but the righteous hath hope in his death.

Here is, 1. The desperate condition of a wicked man when he goes out of the world: He *is driven away in his wickedness.* He cleaves so closely to the world that he cannot find in his heart to leave it, but is driven away out of it; his soul is required, is forced from him. And sin cleaves so closely to him that it is inseparable; it goes with him into another world; he *is driven away in his wickedness,* dies in his sins, under the guilt and power of them, unjustified, unsanctified. His wickedness is the storm in which he is hurried away, as chaff before the wind, chased out of the world. 2. The comfortable condition of a godly man when he finishes his course: He *has hope in his death* of a happiness on the other side death, of better things in another world than ever he had in this. *The righteous* then have the grace of hope in them; though they have pain, and some dread of death, yet they have hope. They have before them the good hoped for, even the blessed hope which God, who cannot lie, has promised.

33 Wisdom resteth in the heart of him that hath understanding: but *that which is* in the midst of fools is made known.

Observe, 1. Modesty is the badge of wisdom. He that is truly wise hides his treasure, so as not to boast of it (Matt. xiii. 44), though he does not hide his talent, so as not to trade with it. His *wisdom rests in his heart;* he digests what he knows, and has it ready to him, but does not unseasonably talk of it and make a noise with it. The heart is the seat of the affections, and there wisdom must rest in the practical love of it, and not swim in the head. 2. Openness and ostentation are a mark of folly. If fools have a little smattering of knowledge, they take all occasions, though very foreign, to produce it, and bring it in by head and shoulders. Or the folly that *is in the midst of fools is made known* by their forwardness to talk. Many a foolish man takes more pains to show his

folly than a wise man thinks it worth his while to take to show his wisdom.

34 Righteousness exalteth a nation: but sin *is* a reproach to any people.

Note, 1. Justice, reigning in a nation, puts an honour upon it. A righteous administration of the government, impartial equity between man and man, public countenance given to religion, the general practice and profession of virtue, the protecting and preserving of virtuous men, charity and compassion to strangers *(alms* are sometimes called *righteousness),* these *exalt a nation;* they uphold the throne, elevate the people's minds, and qualify a nation for the favour of God, which will make them high, as a *holy nation,* Deut. xxvi. 19. 2. Vice, reigning in a nation, puts disgrace upon it: *Sin is a reproach to any* city or kingdom, and renders them despicable among their neighbours. The people of Israel were often instances of both parts of this observation; they were great when they were good, but when they forsook God all about them insulted them and trampled on them. It is therefore the interest and duty of princes to use their power for the suppression of vice and support of virtue.

35 The king's favour *is* toward a wise servant: but his wrath is *against* him that causeth shame.

This shows that in a well-ordered court and government smiles and favours are dispensed among those that are employed in public trusts according to their merits; Solomon lets them know he will go by that rule, 1. That those who behave themselves wisely shall be respected and preferred, whatever enemies they may have that seek to undermine them. No man's services shall be neglected to please a party or a favourite. 2. That those who are selfish and false, who betray their country, oppress the poor, and sow discord, and thus *cause shame,* shall be displaced and banished the court. whatever friends they may make to speak for them.

CHAP. XV.

A SOFT answer turneth away wrath: but grievous words stir up anger.

Solomon, as conservator of the public peace, here tells us, 1. How the peace may be kept, that we may know how in our places to keep it; it is by soft words. If wrath be risen like a threatening cloud, pregnant with storms and thunder, *a soft answer* will disperse it and turn it away. When men are provoked, speak gently to them, and give them good words, and they will be pacified, as the Ephraimites were by Gideon's mildness (Judg. viii. 1—3); whereas, upon a like occasion, by Jephthah's roughness, they were exasperated, and the consequences were bad, Judg. xii. 1—3. Reason will be better spoken, and a righteous cause better pleaded, with meekness than with passion; hard arguments do best with soft words. 2. How the peace will be broken, that we, for our parts, may do nothing towards the breaking of it. Nothing stirs up anger, and sows discord, like *grievous words,* calling foul names, as *Raca,* and *Thou fool,* upbraiding men with their infirmities and infelicities, their extraction or education, or any thing that lessens them and makes them mean; scornful spiteful reflections, by which men affect to show their wit and malice, stir up the anger of others, which does but increase and inflame their own anger. Rather than lose a jest some will lose a friend and make an enemy.

2 The tongue of the wise useth knowledge aright : but the mouth of fools poureth out foolishness.

Note, 1. A good heart by the tongue becomes very useful. He that has knowledge is not only to enjoy it, for his own entertainment, but to use it, to use it aright, for the edification of others ; and it is *the tongue* that must make use of it in pious profitable discourse, in giving suitable and seasonable instructions, counsels, and comforts, with all possible expressions of humility and love, and then *knowledge is used aright ;* and to him that has, and thus uses what he has, more shall be given. 2 A wicked heart by the tongue becomes very hurtful; for *the mouth of fools belches out foolishness,* which is very offensive; and the corrupt communication which proceeds from an evil treasure within (the filthiness, and foolish talking, and jesting) corrupts the good manners of some and debauches them, and grieves the good hearts of others and disturbs them.

3 The eyes of the LORD *are* in every place, beholding the evil and the good.

The great truths of divinity are of great use to enforce the precepts of morality, and none more than this—That the eye of God is always upon the children of men. 1. An eye to discern all, not only from which nothing can be concealed, but by which every thing is actually inspected, and nothing overlooked or looked slightly upon : *The eyes of the Lord are in every place ;* for he not only sees all from on high (Ps. xxxiii. 13), but he is every where present. Angels are *full of eyes* (Rev. iv. 8), but God is all eye. It denotes not only his omniscience, that he sees all, but his universal providence, that he upholds and governs all. Secret sins, services, and sorrows, are under his eye. 2. An eye to distinguish both persons and actions. He *beholds the evil and the good,* is displeased with the evil and approves of the good, and will judge men according to the sight of his eyes, Ps. i. 6; xi. 4. The wicked shall not go unpunished, nor the righteous unrewarded, for God has his eye upon both and knows

their true character; this speaks as much comfort to saints as terror to sinners.

4 A wholesome tongue *is* a tree of life : but perverseness therein *is* a breach in the spirit.

Note, 1. A good tongue is healing, healing to wounded consciences by comforting them, to sin-sick souls by convincing them, to peace and love when it is broken by accommodating differences, compromising matters in variance, and reconciling parties at variance ; this is the healing of the tongue, which *is a tree of life,* the leaves of which have a sanative virtue, Rev. xxii. 2. He that knows how to discourse will make the place he lives in a paradise. 2. An evil tongue is wounding *(perverseness,* passion, falsehood, and filthiness *there, are a breach in the spirit) ;* it wounds the conscience of the evil speaker, and occasions either guilt or grief to the hearers, and both are to be reckoned *breaches in the spirit.* Hard words indeed break no bones, but many a heart has been broken by them.

5 A fool despiseth his father's instruction : but he that regardeth reproof is prudent.

Hence, 1. Let superiors be admonished to give instruction and reproof to those that are under their charge, as they will answer it in the day of account. They must not only instruct with the light of knowledge, but reprove with the heat of zeal ; and both these must be done with the authority and affection of a father, and must be continued, though the desired effect be not immediately perceived. If the instruction be despised, give reproof, and rebuke sharply. It is indeed against the grain with good-humoured men to find fault, and make those about them uneasy ; but better so than to suffer them to go on undisturbed in the way to ruin. 2. Let inferiors be admonished, not only to submit to instruction and reproof (even hardships must be submitted to), but to value them as favours and not despise them, to make use of them for their direction, and always to have a regard to them ; this will be an evidence that they are wise and a means of making them so ; whereas he that slights his good education is a fool and is likely to live and die one.

6 In the house of the righteous *is* much treasure : but in the revenues of the wicked is trouble.

Note, 1. Where righteousness is riches are, and the comforts of them : *In the house of the righteous is much treasure.* Religion teaches men to be diligent, temperate, and just, and by these means, ordinarily, the estate is increased. But that is not all : God *blesses the habitation of the just,* and that blessing makes rich without trouble. Or, if there be not much of this world's goods, yet where there is grace there is true treasure ; and those who have but little, if they have a heart to be therewith content, and to enjoy the comfort of that little, it is enough; it is all riches. The righteous perhaps are not themselves enriched, but there is treasure in their house, a blessing in store, which their children after them may reap the benefit of. A wicked worldly man is only for having his belly filled with those treasures, his own sensual appetite gratified (Ps. xvii. 14); but a righteous man's first care is for his soul and then for his seed, to have treasure in his heart and then in his house, which his relations and those about him may have the benefit of. 2. Where wickedness is, though there may be riches, yet there is vexation of spirit with them: *In the revenues of the wicked,* the great incomes they have, *there is trouble;* for there is guilt and a curse; there is pride and passion, and envy and contention; and those are troublesome lusts, which rob them of the joy of their revenues and make them troublesome to their neighbours.

7 The lips of the wise disperse knowledge : but the heart of the foolish *doeth* not so.

This is to the same purport with *v.* 2, and shows what a blessing a wise man is and what a burden a fool is to those about him. Only here observe further, 1. That we then use knowledge aright when we disperse it, not confine it to a few of our intimates, and grudge it to others who would make as good use of it, but *give a portion* of this spiritual alms *to seven and also to eight,* not only be communicative, but diffusive, of this good, with humility and prudence. We must take pains to spread and propagate useful knowledge, must teach some that they may teach others, and so it is dispersed. 2. That it is not only a fault to *pour out foolishness,* but it is a shame not to *disperse knowledge,* at least not to drop some wise word or other: *The heart of the foolish does not so ;* it has nothing to disperse that is good, or, if it had, has neither skill nor will to do good with it and therefore is little worth.

8 The sacrifice of the wicked *is* an abomination to the LORD : but the prayer of the upright *is* his delight.

Note, 1. God so hates wicked people, whose hearts are malicious and their lives mischievous, that even their *sacrifices are an abomination to* him. God has sacrifices brought him even by wicked men, to stop the mouth of conscience and to keep up their reputation in the world, as malefactors come to a sanctuary, not because it is a holy place, but because it shelters them from justice; but their sacrifices, though ever so costly, are not accepted of God, because not offered in sincerity nor from a good principle; they dissemble with God, and in their conversations give the lie to their devotions, and for that reason they are *an abomination* to him, because they are

made a cloak for sin, *ch.* vii. 14. See Isa. i. 11. 2. God has such a love for upright good people that, though they are not at the expense of a sacrifice (he himself has provided that), their *prayer is a delight* to him. Praying graces are his own gift, and the work of his own Spirit in them, with which he is well pleased. He not only answers their prayers, but delights in their addresses to him, and in doing them good.

9 The way of the wicked *is* an abomination unto the LORD : but he loveth him that followeth after righteousness.

This is a reason of what was said in the foregoing verse. 1. *The sacrifices of the wicked are an abomination to God,* not for want of some nice points of ceremony, but because *their way,* the whole course and tenour of their conversation, is wicked, and consequently an abomination to him. Sacrifices for sin were not accepted of those that resolved to go on in sin, and were to the highest degree abominable if intended to obtain a connivance at sin and a permission to go on in it. 2. Therefore *the prayer of the upright is his delight,* because he is a friend of God, and *he loves him who,* though he have not yet attained, is *following after righteousness,* aiming at it and pressing towards it, as St. Paul, Phil. iii. 13.

10 Correction *is* grievous unto him that forsaketh the way: *and* he that hateth reproof shall die.

This shows that those who cannot bear to be corrected must expect to be destroyed. 1. It is common for those who have known the way of righteousness, but have forsaken it, to reckon it a great affront to be reproved and admonished. They are very uneasy at reproof; they cannot, they will not, bear it; nay, because they hate to be reformed, they hate to be reproved, and hate those who deal faithfully and kindly with them. Of all sinners, reproofs are worst resented by apostates. 2. It is certain that those who will not be reproved will be ruined : *He that hates reproof,* and hardens his heart against it, is joined to his idols; let him alone. He *shall die,* and perish for ever, in his sins, since he would not be parted from his sins. 2 Chron. xxv. 16, *I know that God has determined to destroy thee,* because thou couldst not bear to be reproved; see also *ch.* xxix. 1.

11 Hell and destruction *are* before the LORD : how much more then the hearts of the children of men ?

This confirms what was said (*v.* 3) concerning God's omnipresence, in order to his judging of evil and good. 1. God knows all things, even those things that are hidden from the eyes of all living : *Hell and destruction are before the Lord,* not only the centre of the earth, and its subterraneous caverns, but the grave, and all the dead bodies which are there buried out of our sight; they are all *before the Lord*, all under his eye, so that none of them can be lost or be to seek when they are to be raised again. He knows where every man lies buried, even Moses, even those that are buried in the greatest obscurity; nor needs he any monument with a *Hic jacet—Here he lies*, to direct him. The place of the damned in particular, and all their torments, which are inexpressible, the state of separate souls in general, and all their circumstances, are under God's eye. The word here used for *destruction* is *Abaddon*, which is one of the devil's names, Rev. ix. 11. That destroyer, though he deceives us, cannot evade or elude the divine cognizance. God examines him whence he comes (Job i. 7), and sees through all his disguises though he is sly, and subtle, and swift, Job xxvi. 6. 2. He knows particularly *the hearts of the children of men*. If he sees through the depths and wiles of Satan himself, *much more* can he search men's hearts, though they be deceitful, since they learned all their fraudulent arts of Satan. *God is greater than our hearts*, and knows them better than we know them ourselves, and therefore is an infallible Judge of every man's character, Heb. iv. 13.

12 A scorner loveth not one that reproveth him : neither will he go unto the wise.

A scorner is one that not only makes a jest of God and religion, but bids defiance to the methods employed for his conviction and reformation, and, as an evidence of that, 1. He cannot endure the checks of his own conscience, nor will he suffer it to deal plainly with him : *He loves not to reprove him* (so some read it); he cannot endure to retire into his own heart and commune seriously with that, will not admit of any free thought or fair reasoning with himself, nor let his own heart smite him, if he can help it. That man's case is sad who is afraid of being acquainted and of arguing with himself. 2. He cannot endure the advice and admonitions of his friends : *He will not go unto the wise*, lest they should give him wise counsel. We ought not only to bid the wise welcome when they come to us, but to go to them, as beggars to the rich man's door for an alms ; but this the scorner will not do, for fear of being told of his faults and prevailed upon to reform.

13 A merry heart maketh a cheerful countenance : but by sorrow of the heart the spirit is broken.

Here, 1. Harmless mirth is recommended to us, as that which contributes to the health of the body, making men lively and fit for business, and to the acceptableness of the conversation, making the face to shine and rendering us pleasant one to another. A cheerful spirit, under the government of wisdom and grace, is a great ornament to reli-

876

gion, puts a further lustre upon the beauty of holiness, and makes men the more capable of doing good. 2. Hurtful melancholy is what we are cautioned against, as a great enemy to us, both in our devotion and in our conversation : *By sorrow of the heart*, when it has got dominion and plays the tyrant, as it will be apt to do if it be indulged awhile, *the spirit is broken* and sunk, and becomes unfit for the service of God. *The sorrow of the world works death.* Let us therefore *weep as though we wept not*, in justice to ourselves, as well as in conformity to God and his providence.

14 The heart of him that hath understanding seeketh knowledge : but the mouth of fools feedeth on foolishness.

Here are two things to be wondered at :— 1. A wise man not satisfied with his wisdom, but still seeking the increase of it ; the more he has the more he would have : *The heart of him that has understanding*, rejoices so in the knowledge it has attained to that it is still coveting more, and in the use of the means of knowledge is still labouring for more, *growing in grace, and in the knowledge of Christ. Si dixisti, Sufficit, periisti—If you say, I have enough, you are undone.* 2. A fool well satisfied with his folly and not seeking the cure of it. While a good man hungers after the solid satisfactions of grace, a carnal mind feasts on the gratifications of appetite and fancy. Vain mirth and sensual pleasures are its delight, and with these it can rest contented, flattering itself in these foolish ways.

15 All the days of the afflicted *are* evil : but he that is of a merry heart *hath* a continual feast.

See here what a great difference there is between the condition and temper of some and others of the children of men. 1. Some are much in affliction, and of a sorrowful spirit, and all their days are evil days, like those of old age, and days of which they say they *have no pleasure in them*. They *eat in darkness* (Eccl. v. 17) and never *eat with pleasure*, Job. xxi. 25. How many are the afflictions of the afflicted in this world! Such are not to be censured or despised, but pitied and prayed for, succoured and comforted. It might have been our own lot, or may be yet, merry as we are at present. 2. Others enjoy great prosperity and are of a cheerful spirit ; and they have not only good days, but have *a continual feast ;* and if in the abundance of all things they serve God with gladness of heart, and it is oil to the wheels of their obedience (all this, and heaven too), then they serve a good Master. But let not such feast without fear ; a sudden change may come ; therefore *rejoice with trembling.*

16 Better *is* little with the fear of the LORD than great treasure and

trouble therewith. **17** Better *is* a dinner of herbs where love is, than a stalled ox and hatred therewith.

Solomon had said in the foregoing verse that he who has not a large estate, or a great income, but a cheerful spirit, has *a continual feast ;* Christian contentment, and joy in God, make the life easy and pleasant ; now here he tells us what is necessary to that cheerfulness of spirit which will furnish a man with *a continual feast,* though he has but little in the world—holiness and love.

I. Holiness. A *little,* if we manage it and enjoy it in *the fear of the Lord,* if we keep a good conscience and go on in the way of duty, and serve God faithfully with the little we have, will be more comfortable, and turn to a better account, *than great treasure and trouble therewith.* Observe here, 1. It is often the lot of those that fear God to have but a little of this world. *The poor receive the gospel,* and poor they still are, Jam. ii. 5. 2. Those that have *great treasure* have often great *trouble therewith ;* it is so far from making them easy that it increases their care and hurry. *The abundance of the rich will not suffer them to sleep.* 3. If great treasure bring trouble with it, it it for want of the fear of God. If those tha have great estates would do their duty with them, and then trust God with them, their treasure would not have so much trouble attending it. 4. It is therefore far better, and more desirable, to have but a little of the world and to have it with a good conscience, to keep up communion with God, and enjoy him in it, and live by faith, than to have the greatest plenty and live without God in the world.

II. Love. Next to the fear of God, peace with all men is necessary to the comfort of this life. 1. If *brethren dwell together in unity,* if they are friendly, and hearty, and pleasant, both in their daily meals and in more solemn entertainments, that will make *a dinner of herbs* a feast sufficient ; though the fare be coarse, and the estate so small that they can afford no better, yet love will sweeten it and they may be as merry over it as if they had all dainties. 2. If there be mutual enmity and strife, though there be a whole ox for dinner, a fat ox, there can be no comfort in it ; the leaven of malice, of hating and being hated, is enough to sour it all. Some refer it to him that makes the entertainment ; better have a slender dinner and be heartily welcome than a table richly spread with a grudging evil eye.

Cum torvo vultu mihi cœnula nulla placeoit,
Cum placido vultu cœnula ulla placet.

The most sumptuous entertainment, presented with a sullen brow, would offend me ; while the plainest repast, presented kindly, would delight me.

18 A wrathful man stirreth up strife : but *he that is* slow to anger appeaseth strife.

Here is, 1. Passion the great make-bate.

Thence *come wars and fightings.* Anger strikes the fire which sets cities and churches into a flame : *A wrathful man,* with his peevish passionate reflections, *stirs up strife,* and sets people together by the ears ; he gives occasion to others to quarrel, and takes the occasion that others give, though ever so trifling. When men carry their resentments too far, one quarrel still produces another. 2. Meekness the great peace-maker : *He that is slow to anger* not only *prevents* strife, that it be not kindled, but *appeases* it if it be already kindled, brings water to the flame, unites those again that have fallen out, and by gentle methods brings them to mutual concessions for peace-sake.

19 The way of the slothful *man is* as a hedge of thorns : but the way of the righteous *is* made plain.

See here, 1. Whence those difficulties arise which men pretend to meet with in the way of their duty, and to be insuperable ; they arise not from any thing in the nature of the duty, but from the slothfulness of those that have really no mind to it. Those that have no heart to their work pretend that their way is hedged up with thorns, and they cannot do their work at all (as if God were a hard Master, reaping where he had not sown), at least that their way is strewed with thorns, that they cannot do their work without a great deal of hardship and danger ; and therefore they go about it with as much reluctance as if they were to go barefoot through a thorny hedge. 2. How these imaginary difficulties may be conquered. An honest desire and endeavour to do our duty will, by the grace of God, make it easy, and we shall find it strewed with roses : *The way of the righteous is made plain ;* it is easy to be trodden and not rough, easy to be found, and not intricate.

20 A wise son maketh a glad father : but a foolish man despiseth his mother.

Observe here, 1. To the praise of good children, that they are the joy of their parents, who ought to have joy of them, having taken so much care and pains about them. And it adds much to the satisfaction of those that are good if they have reason to think that they have been a comfort to their parents in their declining years, when evil days come 2. To the shame of wicked children, that by their wickedness they put contempt upon their parents, slight their authority, and make an ill requital for their kindness : *A foolish son despises his mother,* that had most sorrow with him and perhaps had too much indulged him, which makes his sin in despising her the more sinful and her sorrow the more sorrowful.

21 Folly *is* joy to *him that is* destitute of wisdom : but a man of understanding walketh uprightly.

Note, 1. It is the character of a wicked man that he takes pleasure in sin; he has an appetite to the bait, and swallows it greedily, and has no dread of the hook, nor feels from it when he has swallowed it : *Folly is joy to him;* the folly of others is so, and his own much more. He sins, not only without regret, but with delight, not only repents not of it, but makes his boast of it. This is a certain sign of one that is graceless. 2. It is the character of a wise and good man that he makes conscience of his duty. A fool lives at large, walks at all adventures, by no rule, acts with no sincerity or steadiness; *but a man of understanding*, the eyes of whose understanding are enlightened by the Spirit (and those that have not a good understanding have no understanding), *walks uprightly*, lives a sober, orderly, regular life, and studies in every thing to conform himself to the will of God; and this is a constant pleasure and *joy to him*. But what foolishness remains in him, or proceeds from him at any time, is a grief to him, and he is ashamed of it. By these characters we may try ourselves.

22 Without counsel purposes are disappointed : but in the multitude of counsellors they are established.

See here, 1. Of what ill consequence it is to be precipitate and rash, and to act without advice : Men's *purposes are disappointed*, their measures broken, and they come short of their point, gain not their end, because they would not ask counsel about the way. If men will not take time and pains to deliberate with themselves, or are so confident of their own judgment that they scorn to consult with others, they are not likely to bring any thing considerable to pass; circumstances defeat them which, with a little consultation, might have been foreseen and obviated. It is a good rule, both in public and domestic affairs, to do nothing rashly and of one's own head. *Plus vident oculi quam oculus—Many eyes see more than one.* That often proves best which was least our own doing. 2. How much it will be for our advantage to ask the advice of our friends : *In the multitude of counsellors* (provided they be discreet and honest, and will not give counsel with a spirit of contradiction) *purposes are established.* Solomon's son made no good use of this proverb when he acquiesced not in the counsel of the old men, but because he would have a *multitude of counsellors*, regarding number more than weight, advised with the young men.

23 A man hath joy by the answer of his mouth : and a word *spoken* in due season, how good *is it!*

Note, 1. We speak wisely when we speak seasonably : *The answer of the mouth* will be our credit and joy when it is pertinent and

to the purpose, and is *spoken in due season*, when it is needed and will be regarded, and, as we say, hits the joint. Many a good word comes short of doing the good it might have done, for want of being well-timed. Nor is any thing more the beauty of discourse than to have a proper answer ready off-hand, just when there is occasion for it, and it comes in well. 2. If we speak wisely and well, it will redound to our own comfort and to the advantage of others : *A man has joy by the answer of his mouth;* he may take a pleasure, but may by no means take a pride, in having spoken so acceptably and well that the hearers admire him and say, " How *good is it,* and how much good does it do !"

24 The way of life *is* above to the wise, that he may depart from hell beneath.

The way of wisdom and holiness is here recommended to us, 1. As very safe and comfortable : It is *the way of life*, the way that leads to eternal life, in which we shall find the joy and satisfaction which will be the life of the soul, and at the end of which we shall find the perfection of blessedness. Be wise and live. It is the way to escape that misery which we cannot but see ourselves exposed to, and in danger of. It is to *depart from hell beneath*, from the snares of hell, the temptations of Satan, and all his wiles, from the pains of hell, that everlasting destruction which our sins have deserved. 2. As very sublime and honourable : It *is above.* A good man sets his *affections on things above*, and deals in those things. His *conversation is in heaven;* his way leads directly thither; there his treasure is, *above*, out of the reach of enemies, above the changes of this lower world. A good man is truly noble and great; his desires and designs are high, and he lives above the common rate of other men. It is above the capacity and out of the sight of foolish men.

25 The Lord will destroy the house of the proud : but he will establish the border of the widow.

Note, 1. Those that are elevated God delights to abase, and commonly does it in the course of his providence : *The proud*, that magnify themselves, bid defiance to the God above them and trample on all about them, are such as God resists and *will destroy*, not them only, but *their houses*, which they are proud of and are confident of the continuance and perpetuity of. Pride is the ruin of multitudes. 2. Those that are dejected God delights to support, and often does it remarkably : *He will establish the border of the* poor *widow*, which proud injurious men break in upon, and which the poor widow is not herself able to defend and make good. It is the honour of God to protect the weak and appear for those that are oppressed.

26 The thoughts of the wicked *are*

an abomination to the LORD : but *the words* of the pure *are* pleasant words.

The former part of this verse speaks of thoughts, the latter of words, but they come all to one; for thoughts are words to God, and words are judged of by the thoughts from which they proceed, so that, 1. *The thoughts* and words *of the wicked*, which are, like themselves, wicked, which aim at mischief, and have some ill tendency or other, *are an abomination to the Lord;* he is displeased at them and will reckon for them. The thoughts of wicked men, for the most part, are such as God hates, and are an offence to him, who not only knows the heart and all that passes and repasses there, but requires the innermost and uppermost place in it. 2. The thoughts and *words of the pure*, being pure like themselves, clean, honest, and sincere, *are pleasant words* and pleasant thoughts, well-pleasing to the holy God, who delights in purity. It may be understood both of their devotions to God *(the words of their mouth and the meditations of their heart*, in prayer and praise, are *acceptable to God*, Ps. xix. 14; lxix. 13) and of their discourses with men, tending to edification. Both are pleasant when they come from a pure, a purified, heart.

27 He that is greedy of gain troubleth his own house; but he that hateth gifts shall live.

Note, 1. Those that are covetous entail trouble upon their families: *He that is greedy of gain*, and therefore makes himself a slave to the world, rises up early, sits up late, and eats the bread of carefulness, in pursuit of it —he that hurries, and puts himself and all about him upon the stretch, in business, frets and vexes at every loss and disappointment, and quarrels with every body that stands in the way of his profit—he *troubles his own house*, is a burden and vexation to his children and servants. He that, in his greediness of gain, takes bribes, and uses unlawful ways of getting money, leaves a curse with what he gets to those that come after him, which sooner or later will bring trouble into the house, Hab. ii. 9, 10. 2. Those that are generous as well as righteous entail a blessing upon their families: *He that hates gifts*, that shakes his hands from holding the bribes that are thrust into his hand to pervert justice and abhors all sinful indirect ways of getting money —that hates to be paltry and mercenary, and is willing, if there be occasion, to do good gratis—he shall live; he shall have the comfort of life, shall live in prosperity and reputation; his name and family shall live and continue.

28 The heart of the righteous studieth to answer : but the mouth of the wicked poureth out evil things.

Here is, 1. A good man proved to be a wise man by this, that he governs his tongue

well; he that does so *the same is a perfect man*, Jam. iii. 2. It is part of the character of a righteous man that being convinced of the account he must give of his words, and of the good and bad influence of them upon others, he makes conscience of speaking truly (it is his *heart* that *answers*, that is, he speaks as he thinks, and dares not do otherwise, he *speaks the truth in his heart*, Ps. xv. 2), and of speaking pertinently and profitably, and therefore he *studies to answer*, that his speech may be with grace, Neh. ii. 4; v. 7. 2. A wicked man is proved to be a fool by this, that he never heeds what he says, but his *mouth pours out evil things*, to the dishonour of God and religion, his own reproach, and the hurt of others. Doubtless that is an evil heart which thus overflows with evil.

29 The LORD *is* far from the wicked: but he heareth the prayer of the righteous.

Note, 1. God sets himself at a distance from those that set him at defiance: *The wicked say to the Almighty, Depart from us*, and he is, accordingly, *far from* them; he does not manifest himself to them, has no communion with them, will not hear them, will not help them, no, not in the time of their need. They shall be for ever banished from his presence and he will behold them afar off. *Depart from me, you cursed.* 2. He will draw nigh to those in a way of mercy who draw nigh to him in a way of duty: *He hears the prayer of the righteous*, accepts it, is well pleased with it, and will grant an answer of peace to it. It is *the prayer of a righteous man* that *avails much*, Jam. v. 16. *He is nigh to them*, a present help, *in all that they call upon him for.*

30 The light of the eyes rejoiceth the heart : *and* a good report maketh the bones fat.

Two things are here pronounced pleasant: —1. It is pleasant to have a good prospect, to see the light of the sun (Eccl. xi. 7) and by it to see the wonderful works of God, with which this lower world is beautified and enriched. Those that want the mercy know how to value it; how would *the light of the eyes rejoice their hearts!* The consideration of this should make us thankful for our eyesight. 2. It is more pleasant to have *a good name*, a name for good things with God and good people; this *is as precious ointment*, Eccl. vii. 1. *It makes the bones fat;* it gives a secret pleasure, and that which is strengthening. It is also very comfortable to hear (as some understand it) *a good report* concerning others; a good man has no greater joy than to hear that his friends walk in the truth.

31 The ear that heareth the reproof of life abideth among the wise.

Note, 1. It is the character of a wise man that he is very willing to be reproved, and therefore chooses to converse with those that, both by their words and example, will show him what is amiss in him : *The ear that* can take *the reproof* will love the reprover. Faithful friendly reproofs are here called *the reproofs of life,* not only because they are to be given in a lively manner, and with a prudent zeal (and we must reprove by our lives as well as by our doctrine), but because, where they are well-taken, they are means of spiritual life, and lead to eternal life, and (as some think) to distinguish them from rebukes and reproaches for well-doing, which are rather reproofs of death, which we must not regard nor be influenced by. 2. Those that are so wise as to bear reproof well will hereby be *made wiser (ch.* ix. 9), and come at length to be numbered among the wise men of the age, and will have both ability and authority to reprove and instruct others. Those that learn well, and obey well, are likely in time to teach well and rule well.

32 He that refuseth instruction despiseth his own soul : but he that heareth reproof getteth understanding.

See here, 1. The folly of those that will not be taught, that *refuse instruction,* that will not heed it, but turn their backs upon it, or will not hear it, but turn their hearts against it. They *refuse correction* (margin); they will not *take it,* no, not from God himself, but kick against the pricks. Those that do so *despise their own souls;* they show that they have a low and mean opinion of them, and are in little care and concern about them, considered as rational and immortal, instruction being designed to cultivate reason and prepare for the immortal state. The fundamental error of sinners is undervaluing their own souls; therefore they neglect to provide for them, abuse them, expose them, prefer the body before the soul, and wrong the soul to please the body. 2. The wisdom of those that are willing, not only to be taught, but to be reproved : *He that hears reproof,* and amends the faults he is reproved for, *gets understanding,* by which his soul is secured from bad ways and directed in good ways, and thereby he both evidences the value he has for his own soul and puts true honour upon it.

33 The fear of the LORD *is* the instruction of wisdom ; and before honour is humility.

See here how much it is our interest, as well as duty, 1. To submit to our God, and keep up a reverence for him : *The fear of the Lord,* as it is *the beginning of wisdom,* so it is *the instruction* and correction *of wisdom;* the principles of religion, closely adhered to, will improve our knowledge, rectify our mistakes, and be the best and surest guide of our way. An awe of God upon our spirits will put us upon the wisest counsels and chastise us

880

when we say or do unwisely. 2. To stoop to our brethren, and keep up a respect for them. Where there is humility there is a happy presage of honour and preparative for it. Those that humble themselves shall be exalted here and hereafter.

CHAP. XVI.

THE preparations of the heart in man, and the answer of the tongue, *is* from the LORD.

As we read this, it teaches us a great truth, that we are not sufficient of ourselves to *think or speak any thing of ourselves* that is wise and good, but that all *our sufficiency is of God,* who is with the heart and with the mouth, and *works in us both to will and to do,* Phil. ii. 13 ; Ps. x. 17. But most read it otherwise : *The preparation of the heart is in man* (he may contrive-and design this and the other) but *the answer of the tongue,* not only the delivering of what he designed to speak, but the issue and success of what he designed to do, *is of the Lord.* That is, in short, 1. *Man purposes.* He has a freedom of thought and **a** freedom of will permitted him ; let him form his projects, and lay his schemes, as he thinks best : but, after all, 2. *God disposes.* Man cannot go on with his business without the assistance and blessing of God, who *made man's mouth* and teaches us what we shall say. Nay, God easily can, and often does, cross men's purposes, and break their measures. It was a curse that was prepared in Balaam's heart, but the answer of the tongue was a blessing.

2 All the ways of a man *are* clean in his own eyes; but the LORD weigheth the spirits.

Note, 1. We are all apt to be partial in judging of ourselves : *All the ways of a man,* all his designs, all his doings, *are clean in his own eyes,* and he sees nothing amiss in them, nothing for which to condemn himself, or which should make his projects prove otherwise than well ; and therefore he is confident of success, and that the answer of the tongue shall be according to the expectations of the heart ; but there is a great deal of pollution cleaving to our ways, which we are not aware of, or do not think so ill of as we ought. 2. The judgment of God concerning us, we are sure, is according to truth : He *weighs the spirits* in a just and unerring balance, knows what is in us, and passes a judgment upon us accordingly, writing *Tekel* upon that which passed our scale with approbation— *weighed in the balance and found wanting ;* and by his judgment we must stand or fall. He not only sees men's ways but tries their spirits, and we are as our spirits are.

3 Commit thy works unto the LORD, and thy thoughts shall be established.

Note, 1. It is a very desirable thing to have *our thoughts established,* and not tossed, and put into a hurry, by disquieting cares and fears,—to go on in an even steady course of honesty and piety, not disturbed, or put out of frame, by any event or change,—to be satisfied that all shall work for good and issue well at last, and therefore to be always easy and sedate. 2. The only way to have our *thoughts established* is to *commit our works to the Lord.* The great concerns of our souls must be committed to the grace of God, with a dependence upon and submission to the conduct of that grace (2 Tim. i. 12); all our outward concerns must be committed to the providence of God, and to the sovereign, wise, and gracious disposal of that providence. *Roll thy works upon the Lord* (so the word is); roll the burden of thy care from thyself upon God. Lay the matter before him by prayer. *Make known thy works unto the Lord* (so some read it), not only the works of thy hand, but the workings of thy heart; and then leave it with him, by faith and dependence upon him, submission and resignation to him. *The will of the Lord be done.* We may then be easy when we resolve that whatever pleases God shall please us.

4 The LORD hath made all *things* for himself: yea, even the wicked for the day of evil.

Note, 1. That God is the first cause. He is the former of all things and all persons, the fountain of being; he gave every creature the being it has and appointed it its place. Even the wicked are his creatures, though they are rebels; he gave them those powers with which they fight against him, which aggravates their wickedness, that they will not let him that made them rule them, and therefore, though he made them, he will not save them. 2. That God is the last end. All is of him and from him, and therefore all is to him and for him. He made all according to his will and for his praise; he designed to serve his own purposes by all his creatures, and he will not fail of his designs; all are his servants. The wicked he is not glorified by, but he will be glorified upon. He makes no man wicked, but he made those who he foresaw would be wicked: yet he made them (Gen. vi. 6), because he knew how to *get himself honour upon them.* See Rom. ix. 22. Or (as some understand it) he made the wicked to be employed by him as the instruments of his wrath in the day of evil, when he brings judgments on the world. He makes some use even of wicked men, as of other things, to be his sword, his hand (Ps. xvii. 13, 14), *flagellum Dei*—*the scourge of God.* The king of Babylon is called his *servant.*

5 Every one *that is* proud in heart *is* an abomination to the LORD: *though* hand *join* in hand, he shall not be unpunished.

Note, 1. The pride of sinners sets God against them. He that, being high in estate is proud

in heart, whose spirit is elevated with his condition, so that he becomes insolent in his conduct towards God and man, let him know that though he admires himself, and others caress him, yet he is *an abomination to the Lord.* The great God despises him; the holy God detests him. 2. The power of sinners cannot secure them against God, though they strengthen themselves with both hands. Though they may strengthen one another with their confederacies and combinations, joining forces against God, they shall not escape his righteous judgment. *Woe unto him that strives with his Maker, ch.* xi. 21; Isa. xlv. 9.

6 By mercy and truth iniquity is purged: and by the fear of the LORD men depart from evil.

See here, 1. How the guilt of sin is taken away from us—by the *mercy and truth* of God, mercy in promising, truth in performing, the mercy and truth which kiss each other in Jesus Christ the Mediator—by the covenant of grace, in which mercy and truth shine so brightly—by our mercy and truth, as the condition of the pardon and a necessary qualification for it—by these, and not by the legal sacrifices, Mic. vi. 7, 8. 2. How the power of sin is broken in us. By the principles of *mercy and truth* commanding in us the corrupt inclinations are purged out (so we may take the former part); however, *by the fear of the Lord*, and the influence of that fear, *men depart from evil;* those will not dare to sin against God who keep up in their minds a holy dread and reverence of him.

7 When a man's ways please the LORD, he maketh even his enemies to be at peace with him.

Note, 1. God can turn foes into friends when he pleases. He that has all hearts in his hand has access to men's spirits and power over them, working insensibly, but irresistibly upon them, can make *a man's enemies to be at peace with him*, can change their minds, or force them into a feigned submission. He can slay all enemies, and bring those together that were at the greatest distance from each other. 2. He will do it for us when we please him. If we make it our care to be reconciled to God, and to keep ourselves in his love, he will incline those that have been envious towards us, and vexatious to us, to entertain a good opinion of us and to become our friends. God made Esau to be at peace with Jacob, Abimelech with Isaac, and David's enemies to court his favour and desire a league with Israel. The image of God appearing upon the righteous, and his particular loving kindness to them, are enough to recommend them to the respect of all, even of those that have been most prejudiced against them.

8 Better *is* a little with righteous-

ness than great revenues without right.

Here, 1. It is supposed that an honest good man may have but a little of the wealth of this world (all the righteous are not rich),— that a man may have but little, and yet may be nonest (though poverty is a temptation to dishonesty, *ch.* xxx. 9, yet not an invincible one),—and that a man may grow rich, for a while, by fraud and oppression, may have *great revenues*, and those got and kept *without right*, may have no good title to them nor make any good use of them. 2. It is maintained that a small estate, honestly come by, which a man is content with, enjoys comfortably, serves God with cheerfully, and puts to a right use, is much better and more valuable than a great estate ill-got, and then ill-kept or ill-spent. It carries with it more inward satisfaction, a better reputation with all that are wise and good; it will last longer, and will turn to a better account in the great day, when men will be judged, not according to what they had, but what they did.

9 A man's heart deviseth his way: but the LORD directeth his steps.

Man is here represented to us, 1. As a reasonable creature, that has the faculty of contriving for himself: *His heart devises his way*, designs an end, and projects ways and means leading to that end, which the inferior creatures, who are governed by sense and natural instinct, cannot do. The more shame for him if he do not devise the way how to please God and provide for his everlasting state. 2. But as a depending creature, that is subject to the direction and dominion of his Maker. If men *devise their way*, so as to make God's glory their end and his will their rule, they may expect that he will *direct their steps* by his Spirit and grace, so that they shall not miss their way nor come short of their end. But let men devise their worldly affairs ever so politicly, and with ever so great a probability of success, yet God has the ordering of the event, and sometimes *directs their steps* to that which they least intended. The design of this is to teach us to say, *If the Lord will, we shall live and do this or that* (Jam. iv. 14, 15), and to have our eye to God, not only in the great turns of our lives, but in every step we take. *Lord, direct my way*, 1 Thess. iii. 11.

10 A divine sentence *is* in the lips of the king: his mouth transgresseth not in judgment.

We wish this were always true as a proposition, and we ought to make it our prayer for kings, and all in authority, that a *divine sentence* may be in their lips, both in giving orders, that they may do that in wisdom, and in giving sentence, that they may do that in equity, both which are included in *judgment*, and that in neither *their mouth may transgress*, 1 Tim. ii. 1. But it is often otherwise;

882

and therefore, 1. It may be read as a precept to the kings and judges of the earth to be wise and instructed. Let them be just, and rule in the fear of God; let them act with such wisdom and conscience that there may appear a holy divination in all they say or do, and that they are guided by principles supernatural: let not their mouths transgress in judgment, for the judgment is God's. 2. It may be taken as a promise to all good kings, that if they sincerely aim at God's glory, and seek direction from him, he will qualify them with wisdom and grace above others, in proportion to the eminency of their station and the trusts lodged in their hands. When Saul himself was made king God gave him another spirit. 3. It was true concerning Solomon who wrote this; he had extraordinary wisdom, pursuant to the promise God made him, See 1 Kings iii. 28.

11 A just weight and balance *are* the LORD's: all the weights of the bag *are* his work.

Note, 1. The administration of public justice by the magistrate is an ordinance of God; in it the scales are held, and ought to be held by a steady and impartial hand; and we ought to submit to it, for the Lord's sake, and to see his authority in that of the magistrate, Rom. xiii. 1; 1 Pet. ii. 13. 2. The observance of justice in commerce between man and man is likewise a divine appointment. He taught men discretion to make scales and weights for the adjusting of right exactly between buyer and seller, that neither may be wronged; and all other useful inventions for the preserving of right are from him. He has also appointed by his law that they be just. It is therefore a great affront to him, and to his government, to falsify, and so to do wrong under colour and pretence of doing right, which is *wickedness in the place of judgment.*

12 *It is* an abomination to kings to commit wickedness: for the throne is established by righteousness.

Here is, 1. The character of a good king, which Solomon intended not for his own praise, but for instruction to his successors, his neighbours, and the viceroys under him. A good king not only does justice, but it is *an abomination* to him to do otherwise. He hates the thought of doing wrong and perverting justice; he not only abhors the wickedness done by others, but abhors to do any himself, though, having power, he might easily and safely do it. 2. The comfort of a good king: His *throne is established by righteousness*. He that makes conscience of using his power aright shall find that to be the best security of his government, both as it will oblige people, make them easy, and keep them in the interest of it, and as it will obtain the blessing of God, which will be a firm basis to the throne and a strong guard about it.

13 Righteous lips *are* the delight

of kings; and they love him that speaketh right.

Here is a further character of good kings, that they *love* and *delight* in those that *speak right*. 1. They hate parasites and those that flatter them, and are very willing that all about them should deal faithfully with them and tell them that which is true, whether it be pleasing or displeasing, both concerning persons and things, that every thing should be set in a true light and nothing disguised, *ch.* xxix. 12. 2. They not only do righteousness themselves, but take care to employ those under them that do righteousness too, which is of great consequence to the people, who must be subject not only to the king as supreme, but to the governors sent by him, 1 Pet. ii. 14. A good king will therefore put those in power who are conscientious, and will say that which is righteous and discreet, and know how to speak aright and to the purpose.

14 The wrath of a king *is as* messengers of death: but a wise man will pacify it. 15 In the light of the king's countenance *is* life; and his favour *is* as a cloud of the latter rain.

These two verses show the power of kings, which is every where great, but was especially so in those eastern countries, where they were absolute and arbitrary. Whom they would they slew and whom they would they kept alive. Their will was a law. We have reason to bless God for the happy constitution of the government we live under, which maintains the prerogative of the prince without any injury to the liberty of the subject. But here it is intimated, 1. How formidable *the wrath of a king is:* It is *as messengers of death;* the wrath of Ahasuerus was so to Haman. An angry word from an incensed prince has been to many a *messenger of death,* and has struck so great a terror upon some as if a sentence of death had been pronounced upon them. He must be a very *wise man* that knows how to *pacify* the wrath of a king with a word fitly spoken, as Jonathan once pacified his father's rage against David, 1 Sam. xix. 6. A prudent subject may sometimes suggest that to an angry prince which will cool his resentments. 2. How valuable and desirable the king's favour is to those that have incurred his displeasure; it is life from the dead if the king be reconciled to them. To others it is *as a cloud of the latter rain,* very refreshing to the ground. Solomon put his subjects in mind of this, that they might not do any thing to incur his wrath, but be careful to recommend themselves to his favour. We ought by it to be put in mind how much we are concerned to escape the wrath and obtain the favour of the King of kings. His frowns are worse than death, and his favour is better than life; and therefore those are fools who to escape the wrath, and obtain the favour, of an earthly prince, will throw themselves out of God's favour, and make themselves obnoxious to his wrath.

16 How much better *is it* to get wisdom than gold? and to get understanding rather to be chosen than silver?

Solomon here not only asserts that it is better to get wisdom than gold (*ch.* iii. 14, viii. 19), but he speaks it with assurance, that it is much better, better beyond expression—with admiration *(How much better!)* as one amazed at the disproportion—with an appeal to men's consciences ("Judge in yourselves how much better it is")—and with an addition to the same purport, that understanding is *rather to be chosen than silver* and all the treasures of kings and their favourites. Note, 1. Heavenly wisdom is better than worldly wealth, and to be preferred before it. Grace is more valuable than gold. Grace is the gift of God's peculiar favour; gold only of common providence. Grace is for ourselves; gold for others. Grace is for the soul and eternity; gold only for the body and time. Grace will stand us in stead in a dying hour, when gold will do us no good. 2. The getting of this heavenly wisdom is better than the getting of worldly wealth. Many take care and pains to get wealth, and yet come short of it; but grace was never denied to any that sincerely sought it. There is vanity and vexation of spirit in getting wealth, but joy and satisfaction of spirit in getting wisdom. *Great peace have those that love it.*

17 The highway of the upright *is* to depart from evil: he that keepeth his way preserveth his soul.

Note, 1. It is *the way of the upright* to avoid sin, and every thing that looks like it and leads towards it; and this is a highway marked out by authority, tracked by many that have gone before us, and in which we meet with many that keep company with us; it is easy to find and safe to be travelled in, like a highway, Isa. xxxv. 8. *To depart from evil is understanding.* 2. It is the care of the upright to preserve their own souls, that they be not polluted with sin, and that by the troubles of the world they may not be put out of the possession of them, especially that they may not perish for ever, Matt. xvi. 26. And it is therefore their care to keep their way, and not turn aside out of it, on either hand, but to press towards perfection. Those that adhere to their duty secure their felicity. Keep thy way and God will keep thee.

18 Pride *goeth* before destruction, and a haughty spirit before a fall.

Note, 1. Pride will have a fall. Those that are of a *haughty spirit,* that think of themselves above what is meet, and look with contempt upon others, that with their pride affront God and disquiet others, will be brought down, either by repentance or by ruin. It is the honour of God to humble the proud, Job xl. 11, 12. It is the act of justice that those who have lifted up themselves should be laid low. Pharaoh, Sennacherib, Nebuchadnezzar, were instances of this. Men cannot punish pride, but either admire it or fear it, and therefore God will take the punishing of it into his own hands. Let him alone to deal with proud men. 2. Proud men are frequently most proud, and insolent, and haughty, just before their destruction, so that it is a certain presage that they are upon the brink of it. When proud men set God's judgments at defiance, and think themselves at the greatest distance from them, it is a sign that they are at the door; witness the case of Benhadad and Herod. *While the word was in the king's mouth,* Dan. iv. 31. Therefore let us not fear the pride of others, but greatly fear pride in ourselves.

19 Better *it is to be* of a humble spirit with the lowly, than to divide the spoil with the proud.

This is a paradox which the children of this world cannot understand and will not subscribe to, that it is better to be poor and humble than to be rich and proud. 1. Those that *divide the spoil* are commonly proud; they value themselves and despise others, and their mind rises with their condition; those therefore that are *rich in this world* have need to be charged that they *be not high-minded,* 1 Tim. vi. 17. Those that are proud and will put forth themselves, that thrust, and shove, and scramble, for preferment, are the men that commonly *divide the spoil* and share it among them; they have the world at will and the ball at their foot. 2. It is upon all accounts better to take our lot with those whose condition is low, and their minds brought to it, than to covet and aim to make a figure and a bustle in the world. Humility, though it should expose us to contempt in the world, yet while it recommends us to the favour of God, qualifies us for his gracious visits, prepares us for his glory, secures us from many temptations, and preserves the quiet and repose of our own souls, is much better than that high-spiritedness which, though it carry away the honour and wealth of the world, makes God a man's enemy and the devil his master.

20 He that handleth a matter wisely shall find good: and whoso trusteth in the LORD, happy *is* he.

Note, 1. Prudence gains men respect and success: *He that handles a matter wisely* (that is master of his trade and makes it to appear he understands what he undertakes, that is considerate in his affairs, and, when he speaks or writes on any subject, does it pertinently) shall *find good,* shall come into good repute, and perhaps may make a good hand of it. 2. But it is piety only that will secure men's true happiness: Those that

handle a matter wisely, if they are proud and lean to their own understanding, though they may find some good, yet they will have no great satisfaction in it; but he that *trusts in the Lord,* and not in his own wisdom, *happy is he,* and shall speed better at last. Some read the former part of the verse so as to expound it of piety, which is indeed true wisdom: *He that attends to the word* (the word of God, ch. xiii. 13) shall *find good* in it and good by it. And whoso *trusts in the Lord,* in his word which he attends to, is happy.

21 The wise in heart shall be called prudent: and the sweetness of the lips increaseth learning.

Note, 1. Those that have solid wisdom will have the credit of it; it will gain them reputation, and they *shall be called prudent* grave men, and a deference will be paid to their judgment. *Do that which is wise and good and thou shalt have praise of the same.* 2. Those that with their wisdom have a happy elocution, that deliver their sentiments easily and with a good grace, are communicative of their wisdom and have words at will, and good language as well as good sense, *increase learning;* they diffuse and propagate knowledge to others, and do good with it, and by that means increase their own stock. They add doctrine, improve sciences, and do service to the commonwealth of learning. *To him that has,* and uses what he has, *more shall be given.*

22 Understanding *is* a wellspring of life unto him that hath it: but the instruction of fools *is* folly.

Note, 1. There is always some good to be gotten by a wise and good man. His *understanding is a well-spring of life to him,* which always flows and can never be drawn dry; he has something to say upon all occasions that is instructive, and of use to those that will make use of it, things new and old to bring out of his treasure; at least, his understanding is a *spring of life* to himself, yielding him abundant satisfaction; within his own thoughts he entertains and edifies himself, if not others. 2. There is nothing that is good to be gotten by a fool. Even his instruction, his set and solemn discourses, are but folly, like himself, and tending to make others like him. When he does his best it is but folly, in comparison even with the common talk of a wise man, who speaks better at table than a fool in Moses's seat.

23 The heart of the wise teacheth his mouth, and addeth learning to his lips.

Solomon had commended eloquence, or *the sweetness of the lips* (v. 21), and seemed to prefer it before wisdom; but here he corrects himself, as it were, and shows that unless there be a good treasure within to support the eloquence it is worth little. Wisdom in *the heart* is the main matter. 1. It is this that directs us in speaking, that *teaches the mouth* what to speak, and when, and how, so that what is spoken may be proper, and pertinent, and seasonable; otherwise, though the language be ever so fine, it had better be unsaid. 2. It is this that gives weight to what we speak and *adds learning* to it, strength of reason and force of argument, without which, let a thing be ever so well worded, it will be rejected, when it comes to be considered, as trifling. Quaint expressions please the ear, and humour the fancy, but it is learning in the lips that must convince the judgment, and sway that, to which wisdom in the heart is necessary.

24 Pleasant words *are as* a honey-comb, sweet to the soul, and health to the bones.

The *pleasant words* here commended must be those which *the heart of the wise teaches, and adds learning to* (v. 23), words of seasonable advice, instruction, and comfort, words taken from God's word, for that is it which Solomon had learned from his father to account *sweeter than honey and the honey-comb,* Ps. xix. 10. These words, to those that know how to relish them, 1. Are pleasant. They are like the *honey-comb, sweet to the soul,* which tastes in them that *the Lord is gracious;* nothing more grateful and agreeable to the new man than the word of God, and those words which are borrowed from it, Ps. cxix. 103. 2. They are wholesome. Many things are pleasant that are not profitable, but these *pleasant words are health to the bones,* to the inward man, as well as *sweet to the soul.* They make *the bones,* which sin has broken and put out of joint, *to rejoice.* The bones are the strength of the body; and the good word of God is a means of spiritual strength, curing the diseases that weaken us.

25 There is a way that seemeth right unto a man, but the end thereof *are* the ways of death.

This we had before (*ch.* xiv. 12), but here it is repeated, as that which is very necessary to be thought of, 1. By way of caution to us all to take heed of deceiving ourselves in the great concerns of our souls by resting in that which *seems right* and is not really so, and, for the preventing of a self-delusion, to be impartial in self-examination and keep up a jealousy over ourselves. 2. By way of terror to those whose way is not right, is not as it should be, however it may seem to themselves or others; the end of it will certainly be death; to that it has a direct and certain tendency.

26 He that laboureth laboureth for himself; for his mouth craveth it of him.

This is designed to engage us to diligence, and quicken us, *what our hand finds to do, to do it with all our might,* both in our worldly

business and in the work of religion; for in the original it is, *The soul that labours labours for itself.* It is heart-work which is here intended, the labour of the soul, which is here recommended to us, 1. As that which will be absolutely needful. Our mouth is continually craving it of us; the necessities both of soul and body are pressing, and require constant relief, so that we must either work or starve. Both call for daily bread, and therefore there must be daily labour; for in the sweat of our face we must eat, 2 Thess. iii. 10. 2. As that which will be unspeakably gainful. We know on whose errand we go: *He that labours* shall reap the fruit of his labour; it shall be *for himself;* he shall rejoice in his own work and *eat the labour of his hands.* If we make religion our business, God will make it our blessedness.

27 An ungodly man diggeth up evil: and in his lips *there is* as a burning fire. 28 A froward man soweth strife: and a whisperer separateth chief friends.

There are those that are not only vicious themselves, but spiteful and mischievous to others, and they are the worst of men; two sorts of such are here described:—1. Such as envy a man the honour of his good name, and do all they can to blast that by calumnies and misrepresentations: They *dig up evil;* they take a great deal of pains to find out something or other on which to ground a slander, or which may give some colour to it. If none appear above ground, rather than want it they will dig for it, by diving into what is secret, or looking a great way back, or by evil suspicions and surmises, and forced innuendoes. In the lips of a slanderer and backbiter *there is as a fire,* not only to brand his neighbour's reputation, to smoke and sully it, but *as a burning fire* to consume it. And how great a matter does a little of this fire kindle, and how hardly is it extinguished! James iii. 5, 6. 2. Such as envy a man the comfort of his friendship, and do all they can to break that, by suggesting that on both sides which will set those at variance that are most nearly related and have been long intimate, or at least cool and alienate their affections one from another: *A froward man,* that cannot find in his heart to love any body but himself, is vexed to see others live in love, and therefore makes it his business to *sow strife,* by giving men base characters one of another, telling lies, and carrying ill-natured stories between *chief friends,* so as to *separate* them one from another, and make them angry at or at least suspicious of one another. Those are bad men, and bad women too, that do such ill offices; they are doing the devil's work, and his will their wages be.

29 A violent man enticeth his neighbour, and leadeth him into the

way *that is* not good. 30 He shutteth his eyes to devise froward things : moving his lips he bringeth evil to pass.

Here is another sort of evil men described to us, that we may neither do like them nor have any thing to do with them. 1. Such as (like Satan) do all the mischief they can by force and violence, as roaring lions, and not only by fraud and insinuation, as subtle serpents : They are *violent men*, that do all by rapine and oppression, that *shut their eyes*, meditating with the closest intention and application of mind *to devise froward things*, to contrive how they may do the greatest mischief to their neighbour, to do it effectually and yet securely to themselves ; and then *moving their lips*, giving the word of command to their agents, they *bring the evil to pass*, and accomplish the wicked device, *biting his lips* (so some read it) for vexation. When *the wicked plots against the just* he *gnasheth upon him with his teeth*. 2. Such as (like Satan still) do all they can to *entice* and draw in others to join with them in doing mischief, *leading them in a way that is not good*, that is not honest, nor honourable, nor safe, but offensive to God, and which will be in the end pernicious to the sinner. Thus he aims to ruin some in this world by bringing them into trouble, and others in the other world by bringing them into sin.

31 The hoary head *is* a crown of glory, *if* it be found in the way of righteousness.

Note, 1. It ought to be the great care of old people to *be found in the way of righteousness*, the way of religion and serious godliness. Both God and man will look for them in that way ; it will be expected that those that are old should be good, that the multitude of their years should teach them the best wisdom ; let them therefore be found in that way. Death will come ; the Judge is coming ; *the Lord is at hand*. That they may *be found of him in peace*, let them *be found in the way of righteousness* (2 Pet. iii. 14), *found so doing*, Matt. xxiv. 46. Let old people be old disciples ; let them persevere to the end *in the way of righteousness*, which they long since set out in, that they may then be found in it. 2. If old people *be found in the way of righteousness*, their age will be their honour. Old age, as such, is honourable, and commands respect *(Thou shalt rise up before the hoary head*, Lev. xix. 32) ; but, if it be found in the way of wickedness, its honour is forfeited, its crown profaned and laid in the dust, Isa. lxv. 20. Old people therefore, if they would preserve their honour, must still hold fast their integrity, and then their gray hairs are indeed *a crown* to them ; they are *worthy of double honour*. Grace is the glory of old age.

32 *He that is* slow to anger *is* better than the mighty ; and he that ruleth his spirit than he that taketh a city.

This recommends the grace of meekness to us, which will well become us all, particularly *the hoary head*, v. 31. Observe, 1. The nature of it. It is to be *slow to anger*, not easily put into a passion, nor apt to resent provocation, taking time to consider before we suffer our passion to break out, that it may not transgress due bounds, so slow in our motions towards anger that we may be quickly stopped and pacified. It is to have the rule of our own spirits, our appetites and affections, and all our inclinations, but particularly our passions, our anger, keeping that under direction and check, and the strict government of religion and right reason. We must be lords *of our anger*, as God is, Nah. i. 3. *Æolus sis, affectuum tuorum—Rule your passions, as Æolus rules the winds*. 2. The honour of it. He that gets and keeps the mastery of his passions *is better than the mighty*, better *than he that* by a long siege *takes a city* or by a long war subdues a country. Behold, a greater than Alexander or Cæsar is here. The conquest of ourselves, and our own unruly passions, requires more true wisdom, and a more steady, constant, and regular management, than the obtaining of a victory over the forces of an enemy. A rational conquest is more honourable to a rational creature than a brutal one. It is a victory that does nobody any harm ; no lives or treasures are sacrificed to it, but only some base lusts. It is harder, and therefore more glorious, to quash an insurrection at home than to resist an invasion from abroad ; nay, such are the gains of meekness that by it *we are more than conquerors*.

33 The lot is cast into the lap ; but the whole disposing thereof is of the LORD.

Note, 1. The divine Providence orders and directs those things which to us are perfectly casual and fortuitous. Nothing comes to pass by chance, nor is an event determined by a blind fortune, but every thing by the will and counsel of God. What man has neither eye nor hand in God is intimately concerned in. 2. When solemn appeals are made to Providence by the casting of lots, for the deciding of that matter of moment which could not otherwise be at all, or not so well, decided, God must be eyed in it, by prayer, that it may be disposed aright *(Give a perfect lot,* 1 Sam. xiv. 41 ; Acts i. 24), and by acquiescing in it when it is disposed, being satisfied that the hand of God is in it and that hand directed by infinite wisdom. All the disposals of Providence concerning our affairs we must look upon to be the directing of our lot, the determining of what we referred to God, and must be reconciled to them accordingly.

CHAP. XVII.

BETTER *is* a dry morsel, and quietness therewith, than a house full of sacrifices *with* strife.

These words recommend family-love and peace, as conducing very much to the comfort of human life. 1. Those that live in unity and quietness, not only free from jealousies and animosities, but vying in mutual endearments, and that study to make themselves easy and obliging to one another, live very comfortably, though they are low in the world, work hard and fare hard, though they have but each of them *a morsel,* and that *a dry morsel.* There may be peace and quietness where there are not three meals a day, provided there be a joint satisfaction in God's providence and a mutual satisfaction in each other's prudence. Holy love may be found in a cottage. 2. Those that live in contention, that are always jarring and brawling, and reflecting upon one another, though they have plenty of dainties, *a house full of sacrifices,* live uncomfortably; they cannot expect the blessing of God upon them and what they have, nor can they have any true relish of their enjoyments, much less any peace in their own consciences. Love will sweeten a *dry morsel,* but strife will sour and embitter a *house full of sacrifices.* A little of the leaven of malice will leaven all the enjoyments.

2 A wise servant shall have rule over a son that causeth shame, and shall have part of the inheritance among the brethren.

Note 1. True merit does not go by dignity. All agree that the son in the family is more worthy than the servant (John viii. 35), and yet sometimes it so happens that the servant is wise, and a blessing and credit to the family, when the son is a fool, and a burden and shame to the family. Eliezer of Damascus, though Abram could not bear to think that he should be his heir, was a stay to the family, when he obtained a wife for Isaac; whereas Ishmael, a son, was a shame to it, when he mocked Isaac. 2. True dignity will go by merit. If a servant be wise, and manage things well, he shall be further trusted, and not only *have rule* with, but *rule over a son that causes shame;* 'for God and nature have designed that *the fool shall be servant to the wise in heart.* Nay, a prudent servant may perhaps come to have such an interest in his master as to be taken in for a child's share of the estate and to *have part of the inheritance among the brethren.*

3 The fining pot *is* for silver, and the furnace for gold: but the LORD trieth the hearts.

Note, 1. The hearts of the children of men are subject, not only to God's view, but to his judgment: As *the fining-pot is for silver,* both to prove it and to improve is so the

Lord tries the hearts; he searches whether they are standard or no, and those that are he refines and makes purer, Jer. xvii. 10. God tries the heart by affliction (Ps. lxvi. 10, 11), and often chooses his people in that furnace (Isa. xlviii. 10) and makes them choice. 2. It is God only that *tries the hearts.* Men may try their *silver* and *gold* with *the fining-pot and the furnace,* but they have no such way of trying one another's hearts; God only does that, who is both the searcher and the sovereign of the heart.

4 A wicked doer giveth heed to false lips; *and* a liar giveth ear to a naughty tongue.

Note, 1. Those that design to do ill support themselves by falsehood and lying: *A wicked doer gives* ear, with a great deal of pleasure, *to false lips,* that will justify him in the ill he does, to those that aim to make public disturbances, catch greedily at libels, and false stories, that defame the government and the administration. 2. Those that take the liberty to tell lies take a pleasure in hearing them told: *A liar gives* heed to a malicious backbiting tongue, that he may have something to graft his lies upon, and with which to give them some colour of truth and so to support them. Sinners will strengthen one another's hands; and those show that they are bad themselves who court the acquaintance and need the assistance of those that are bad.

5 Whoso mocketh the poor reproacheth his Maker: *and* he that is glad at calamities shall not be unpunished.

See here, 1. What a great sin those are guilty of who trample upon the poor, who ridicule their wants and the meanness of their appearance, upbraid them with their poverty, and take advantage from their weakness to be abusive and injurious to them. They *reproach their Maker,* put a great contempt and affront upon him, who allotted the poor to the condition they are in, owns them, and takes care of them, and can, when he pleases, reduce us to that condition. Let those that thus reproach their Maker know that they shall be called to an account for it, Matt. xxv. 40, 41; Prov. xiv. 31. 2. What great danger those are in of falling into trouble themselves who are pleased to see and hear of the troubles of others: *He that is glad at calamities,* that he may be built up upon the ruins of others, and regales himself with the judgments of God when they are abroad, let him know that he *shall not go unpunished;* the cup shall be put into his hand, Ezek. xxv. 6, 7.

6 Children's children *are* the crown of old men; and the glory of children *are* their fathers.

They are so, that is, they should be so, and, if they conduct themselves worthily, they are so. 1. It is an honour to parents when they are old to leave children, and *children's child-ren*, growing up, that tread in the steps of their virtues, and are likely to maintain and advance the reputation of their families. It is an honour to a man to live so long as to see his children's children (Ps. cxxviii. 6; Gen. l. 23), to see his house built up in them, and to see them likely to serve their genera-tion according to the will of God. This crowns and completes their comfort in this world. 2. It is an honour to children to have wise and godly parents, and to have them continued to them even after they have them-selves grown up and settled in the world. Those are unnatural children who reckon their aged parents a burden to them, and think they live too long; whereas, if the children be wise and good, it is as much their honour as can be that thereby they are com-forts to their parents in the unpleasant days of their old age.

7 Excellent speech becometh not a fool: much less do lying lips a prince.

Two things are here represented as very absurd: 1. That men of no repute should be dictators. What can be more unbecoming than for fools, who are known to have little sense and discretion, to pretend to that which is above them and which they were never cut out for? A fool, in Solomon's proverbs, sig-nifies a wicked man, whom *excellent speech* does not become, because his conversation gives the lie to his excellent speech. What have those to do to declare God's statutes who *hate instruction?* Ps. l. 16. Christ would not suffer the unclean spirits to say that they knew him to be the Son of God. See Acts xvi. 17, 18. 2. That men of great repute should be deceivers. If it is unbecoming a despicable man to presume to speak as a philosopher or politician, and nobody heeds him, being prejudiced against his character, much more unbecoming is it for a prince, for a man of honour, to take advantage from his character and the confidence that is put in him to lie, and dissemble, and make no con-science of breaking his word. Lying ill be-comes any man, but worst a prince, so cor-rupt is the modern policy, which insinuates that princes ought not to make themselves slaves to their words further than is for their interest, and *Qui nescit dissimulare nescit regnare—He who knows not how to dissemble knows not how to reign.*

8 A gift *is as* a precious stone in the eyes of him that hath it: whitherso-ever it turneth, it prospereth.

The design of this observation is to show, 1. That those who have money in their hand think they can do any thing with it. Rich men value a little money as if it were a *pre-cious stone*, and value themselves on it as if it gave them not only ornament, but power, and every one were bound to be at their beck, even justice itself. Whithersoever they turn this sparkling diamond they expect it should

dazzle the eyes of all, and make them do just what they would have them do in hopes of it. The deepest bag will carry the cause. Fee high, and you may have what you will. 2. That those who have money in their eye, and set their hearts upon it, will do any thing for it: *A bribe is as a precious stone in the eyes of him that takes it;* it has a great influ-ence upon him, and he will be sure to go the way that it leads him, hither and thither, though contrary to justice and not consistent with himself.

9 He that covereth a transgression seeketh love; but he that repeateth a matter separateth *very* friends.

Note, 1. The way to preserve peace among relations and neighbours is to make the best of every thing, not to tell others what has been said or done against them when it is not at all necessary to their safety, nor to take no-tice of what has been said or done against ourselves, but to excuse both, and put the best construction upon them. " It was an oversight; therefore overlook it. It was done through forgetfulness; therefore forget it. It perhaps made nothing of you; do you make nothing of it." 2. The ripping up of faults is the ripping out of love, and nothing tends more to the separating of friends, and setting them at variance, than the *repeating of matters* that have been in variance; for they commonly lose nothing in the repetition, but the things themselves are aggravated and the passions about them revived and exaspe-rated. The best method of peace is by an amnesty or act of oblivion.

10 A reproof entereth more into a wise man than a hundred stripes into a fool.

Note, 1. A word is enough to the wise. A gentle reproof will enter not only into the head, but into the heart of a wise man, so as to have a strong influence upon him; for, if but a hint be given to conscience, let it alone to carry it on and prosecute it. 2. Stripes are not enough for a fool, to make him sen-sible of his errors, that he may repent of them, and be more cautious for the future. He that is sottish and wilful is very rarely bene-fited by severity. David is softened with, *Thou art the man;* but Pharaoh remains hard under all the plagues of Egypt.

11 An evil *man* seeketh only rebel-lion: therefore a cruel messenger shall be sent against him.

Here is the sin and punishment of an evil man. 1. His sin. He is an evil man indeed that seeks all occasions to rebel against God, and the government God has set over him, and to contradict and quarrel with those about him. *Quærit jurgia—He picks quar-rels;* so some. There are some that are ac-tuated by a spirit of opposition, that will con-tradict for contradiction-sake, that will go on frowardly in their wicked ways in spite of all restraint and check. *A rebellious man seeks mischief* (so some read it), watches all opportunities to disturb the public peace. 2. His punishment. Because he will not be reclaimed by mild and gentle methods, *a cruel messenger shall be sent against him,* some dreadful judgment or other, as a messenger from God. Angels, God's messengers, shall be employed as ministers of his justice against him, Ps. lxxviii. 49. Satan, the angel of death, shall be let loose upon him, and the *messengers* of Satan. His prince shall send a sergeant to arrest him, an executioner to cut him off. He that *kicks against the pricks* is *waited for of the sword.*

12 Let a bear robbed of her whelps meet a man, rather than a fool in his folly.

Note, 1. A passionate man is a brutish man. However at other times he may have some wisdom, take him in his passion ungoverned, and he is a *fool in his folly ;* those are fools in whose bosom anger rests and in whose countenance anger rages. He has put off man, and is become like a bear, a raging bear, *a bear robbed of her whelps ;* he is as fond of the gratifications of his lusts and passions as a bear of her whelps (which, though ugly, are her own), as eager in the pursuit of them as she is in quest of her whelps when they are missing, and as full of indignation if crossed in the pursuit. 2. He is a dangerous man, falls foul of every one that stands in his way, though innocent, though his friend, as a bear robbed of her whelps sets upon the first man she meets as the robber. *Ira furor brevis est—Anger is temporary madness.* One may more easily stop, escape, or guard against an enraged bear, than an outrageous angry man. Let us therefore watch over our own passions (lest they get head and do mischief) and so consult our own honour; and let us avoid the company of furious men, and get out of their way when they are in their fury, and so consult our own safety. *Currenti cede furori—Give place unto wrath.*

13 Whoso rewardeth evil for good, evil shall not depart from his house.

A malicious mischievous man is here represented, 1. As ungrateful to his friends. He oftentimes is so absurd and insensible of kindnesses done him that he renders *evil for good.* David met with those that were his adversaries for his love, Ps. cix. 4. To render evil for evil is brutish, but to render evil for good is devilish. He is an ill-natured man who, because he is resolved not to return a kindness, will revenge it. 2. As therein unkind to his family, for he entails a curse upon it. This is a crime so heinous that it shall be punished, not only in his person, but in his posterity, for whom he thus treasures up wrath. *The sword shall not depart from* David's *house* because he rewarded

Uriah with evil for his good services. The Jews stoned Christ for his good works; therefore is his blood upon them and upon their children.

14 The beginning of strife *is as* when one letteth out water : therefore leave off contention. before it be meddled with.

Here is, 1. The danger that there is in *the beginning of strife.* One hot word, one peevish reflection, one angry demand, one spiteful contradiction, begets another, and that a third, and so on, till it proves like the cutting of a dam ; when the water has got a little passage it does itself widen the breach, bears down all before it, and there is then no stopping it, no reducing it. 2. A good caution inferred thence, to take heed of the first spark of contention and to put it out as soon as ever it appears. Dread the breaking of the ice, for, if once broken, it will break further ; *therefore leave it off,* not only when you see the worst of it, for then it may be too late, but when you see the first of it. *Obsta principiis—Resist its earliest display.* Leave it off even *before it be meddled with ;* leave it off, if it were possible, before you begin.

15 He that justifieth the wicked, and he that condemneth the just, even they both *are* abomination to the LORD.

This shows what an offence it is to God, 1. When those that are entrusted with the administration of public justice, judges, juries, witnesses, prosecutors, counsel, do either acquit the guilty or condemn those that are not guilty, or in the least contribute to either; this defeats the end of government, which is to protect the good and punish the bad, Rom. xiii. 3, 4. It is equally provoking to God to *justify the wicked,* though it be in pity and *in favorem vitæ—to safe life,* as to *condemn the just.* 2. When any private persons plead for sin and sinners, palliate and excuse wickedness, or argue against virtue and piety, and so *pervert the right ways of the Lord* and confound the eternal distinctions between good and evil.

16 Wherefore *is there* a price in the hand of a fool to get wisdom, seeing *he hath* no heart *to it ?*

Two things are here spoken of with astonishment :—1. God's great goodness to foolish man, in putting *a price into his hand to get wisdom,* to get knowledge and grace to fit him for both worlds. We have rational souls, the means of grace, the strivings of the Spirit, access to God by prayer ; we have time and opportunity. He that has a good estate (so some understand it) has advantages thereby of getting wisdom by purchasing instruction. Good parents, relations, ministers, friends, are helps to get wisdom. It is *a price,* therefore of value, a talent. It is *a price in the hand,* in possession ; *the word is nigh thee.* It is a price for getting ; it is for our own advantage ; it is for getting wisdom, the very thing which, being fools, we have most need of. We have reason to wonder that God should so consider our necessity, and should entrust us with such advantages, though he foresaw we should not make a right improvement of them. 2. Man's great wickedness, his neglect of God's favour and his own interest, which is very absurd and unaccountable : *He has no heart to it,* not to the wisdom that is to be got, nor to the price in the use of which it may be got. *He has no heart,* no skill, nor will, nor courage, to improve his advantages. He has set his heart upon other things, so that he has no heart to his duty or the great concerns of his soul. Wherefore should a price be thrown away and lost upon one so undeserving of it ?

17 A friend loveth at all times, and a brother is born for adversity.

This intimates the strength of those bonds by which we are bound to each other and which we ought to be sensible of. 1. Friends must be constant to each other *at all times.* That is not true friendship which is not constant ; it will be so if it be sincere, and actuated by a good principle. Those that are fanciful or selfish in their friendship will love no longer than their humour is pleased and their interest served, and therefore their affections turn with the wind and change with the weather. Swallow-friends, that fly to you in summer, but are gone in winter ; such friends there is no loss of. But if the friendship be prudent, generous, and cordial, if I love my friend because he is wise, and virtuous, and good, as long as he continues so, though he fall into poverty and disgrace, still I shall love him. Christ is a friend that loves at all times (John xiii. 1) and we must so love him, Rom. viii. 35. 2. Relations must in a special manner be careful and tender of one another in affliction : *A brother is born* to succour a brother or sister in distress, to whom he is joined so closely by nature that he may the more sensibly feel from their burdens, and be the more strongly inclined and engaged, as it were by instinct, to help them. We must often consider what we were *born for,* not only as men, but as in such a station and relation. *Who knows but we came* into such a family *for such a time as this ?* We do not answer the end of our relations if we do not do the duty of them. Some take it thus : *A friend that loves at all times is born* (that is, becomes) *a brother in adversity,* and is so to be valued.

18 A man void of understanding striketh hands, *and* becometh surety in the presence of his friend.

Though Solomon had commended friendship in adversity (*v.* 17), yet let not any, under pretence of being generous to their friends, be unjust to their families and wrong them ;

one part of our duty must be made to consist with another. Note, 1. It is a piece of wisdom to keep out of debt as much as may be, especially to dread suretiship. There may be a just occasion for a man to pass his word for his friend in his absence, till he come to engage himself ; but to be *surety in the presence of his friend,* when he is upon the spot, supposes that his own word will not be taken, he being deemed insolvent or dishonest, and then who can with safety pass his word for him? 2. Those that are *void of understanding* are commonly taken in this snare, to the prejudice of their families, and therefore ought not to be trusted too far with their own affairs, but to be under direction.

19 He loveth transgression that loveth strife : *and* he that exalteth his gate seeketh destruction.

Note, 1. Those that are quarrelsome involve themselves in a great deal of guilt : *He that loves strife,* that in his worldly business loves to go to law, in religion loves controversies, and in common conversation loves to thwart and fall out, that is never well but when he is in the fire, *he loves transgression ;* for a great deal of sin attends that sin, and the way of it is down-hill. He pretends to stand up for truth, and for his honour and right, but really he loves sin, which God hates. 2. Those that are ambitious and aspiring expose themselves to a great deal of trouble, such as often ends in their ruin : *He that exalts his gate,* builds a stately house, at least a fine frontispiece, that he may overtop and outshine his neighbours, seeks his own destruction and takes a deal of pains to ruin himself ; he makes his gate so large that his house and estate go out at it.

20 He that hath a froward heart findeth no good : and he that hath a perverse tongue falleth into mischief.

Note, 1. Framing ill designs will be of no advantage to us ; there is nothing got by them : *He that has a froward heart,* that sows discord and is full of resentment, cannot promise himself to get by it sufficient to counterbalance the loss of his repose and reputation, nor can he take any rational satisfaction in it ; he *finds no good.* 2. Giving ill language will be a great disadvantage to us : *He that has a perverse tongue,* spiteful and abusive, scurrilous or backbiting, *falls into* one *mischief* or other, loses his friends, provokes his enemies, and pulls trouble upon his own head. Many a one has paid dearly for an unbridled tongue.

21 He that begetteth a fool *doeth it* to his sorrow : and the father of a fool hath no joy

This expresses that very emphatically which many wise and good men feel very sensibly, what a grievous vexatious thing it is to have a foolish wicked child. See here,

1. How uncertain all our creature-comforts are, so that we are often not only disappointed in them, but that proves the greatest cross in which we promised ourselves most satisfaction. There was *joy when a man-child was born into the world,* and yet, if he prove vicious, his own father will wish he had never been born. The name of Absalom signifies his *father's peace,* but he was his greatest trouble. It should moderate the desire of having children, and the delight of their parents in them, that they may prove a grief to them; yet it should silence the murmurings of the afflicted father in that case that if his son be a fool he is a fool of his own begetting, and therefore he must make the best of him, and take it up as his cross, the rather because Adam begets a son in his own likeness. 2. How unwise we are in suffering one affliction (and that of an untoward child as likely as any other) to drown the sense of a thousand mercies: *The father of a fool* lays that so much to heart that he *has no joy* of any thing else. For this he may thank himself; there are joys sufficient to counterbalance even that sorrow.

22 A merry heart doeth good *like* a medicine: but a broken spirit drieth the bones.

Note, 1. It is healthful to be cheerful. The Lord is for the body, and has provided for it, not only meat, but medicine, and has here told us that the best medicine is *a merry heart,* not a heart addicted to vain, carnal, sensual mirth; Solomon himself said of that mirth, It is not medicine, but madness; it is not food, but poison; *what doth it?* But he means a heart rejoicing in God, and serving him with gladness, and then taking the comfort of outward enjoyments and particularly that of pleasant conversation. It is a great mercy that God gives us leave to be cheerful and cause to be cheerful, especially if by his grace he gives us hearts to be cheerful. This *does good to a medicine* (so some read it); it will make physic more efficient. Or *it does good as a medicine* to the body, making it easy and fit for business. But, if mirth be a medicine (understand it of diversion and recreation), it must be used sparingly, only when there is occasion, not turned into food, and it must be used medicinally, *sub regimine—as a prescribed regimen,* and by rule. 2. The sorrows of the mind often contribute very much to the sickliness of the body: *A broken spirit,* sunk by the burden of afflictions, and especially a conscience wounded with the sense of guilt and fear of wrath, *dries the bones,* wastes the radical moisture, exhausts the very marrow, and makes the body a mere skeleton. We should therefore watch and pray against all melancholy dispositions, for they lead us into trouble as well as into temptation.

23 A wicked *man* taketh a gift out of the bosom to pervert the ways of judgment.

See here, 1. What an evil thing bribery is: He is *a wicked man* that will *take a gift* to engage him to give a false testimony, verdict, or judgment; when he does it he is ashamed of it, for he takes it, with all the secresy imaginable, *out of the bosom* where he knows it is laid ready for him; it is industriously concealed, and so slily that, if he could, he would hide it from his own conscience. *A gift is taken out of the bosom of a wicked man* (so some read it); for he is a bad man that gives bribes, as well as he that takes them. 2. What a powerful thing it is. It is of such force that it *perverts the ways of judgment.* The course of justice is not only obstructed, but turned into injustice; and the greatest wrongs are done under colour of doing right.

24 Wisdom *is* before him that hath understanding; but the eyes of a fool *are* in the ends of the earth.

Note, 1. He is to be reckoned an intelligent man that not only has wisdom, but has it ready when he has occasion for it. He lays his *wisdom before him,* as his card and compass which he steers by, has his eye always upon it, as he that writes has on his copy; and then he has it *before him;* it is not to seek, but still at hand. 2. He that has a giddy head, a roving rambling fancy, will never be fit for any solid business. He is a fool, and good for nothing, whose *eyes are in the ends of the earth,* here, and there and every where, any where but where they should be, who cannot fix his thoughts to one subject nor pursue any one purpose with any thing of steadiness. When his mind should be applied to his study and business it is filled with a thousand things foreign and impertinent.

25 A foolish son *is* a grief to his father, and bitterness to her that bare him.

Observe, 1. Wicked children are an affliction to both their parents. They are an occasion of *anger* to the father (so the word signifies), because they contemn his authority, but of sorrow and *bitterness* to the mother, because they abuse her tenderness. The parents, being joint-sufferers, should therefore bring mutual comfort to bear them up under it, and strive to make it as easy as they can, the mother to mollify the father's anger, the father to alleviate the mother's grief. 2. That Solomon often repeats this remark, probably because it was his own case; however, it is a common case.

26 Also to punish the just *is* not good, *nor* to strike princes for equity.

In differences that happen between magistrates and subjects, and such differences often arise, 1. Let magistrates see to it that they never *punish the just,* that they be in no case a *terror to good works,* for that is to abuse their power and betray that great trust which is reposed in them. It is *not good,* that is, it is a very evil thing, and will end ill, whatever end they may aim at in it. When princes become tyrants and persecutors their thrones will be neither easy nor firm. 2. Let subjects see to it that they do not find fault with the government for doing its duty, for it is a wicked thing *to strike princes for equity,* by defaming their administration or by any secret attempts against them to strike at them, as the ten tribes that revolted reflected upon Solomon for imposing necessary taxes. Some read it, *Nor to strike the ingenuous for equity.* Magistrates must take heed that none suffer under them for well doing; nor must parents *provoke their children to wrath* by unjust rebukes.

27 He that hath knowledge spareth his words : *and* a man of understanding is of an excellent spirit. 28 Even a fool, when he holdeth his peace, is counted wise : *and* he that shutteth his lips *is esteemed* a man of understanding.

Two ways a man may show himself to be a wise man :—1. By the good temper, the sweetness and the sedateness, of his mind : *A man of understanding is of an excellent spirit,* a *precious spirit* (so the word is); he is one that looks well to his spirit, that it be as it should be, and so keeps it in an even frame, easy to himself and pleasant to others. A gracious spirit is a precious spirit, and renders a man amiable and *more excellent than his neighbour.* He is of a *cool spirit* (so some read it), not heated with passion, nor put into any tumult or disorder by the *impetus* of any corrupt affection, but even and stayed. A cool head with a warm heart is an admirable composition. 2. By the good government of his tongue. (1.) A wise man will be *of few words,* as being afraid of speaking amiss : *He that has knowledge,* and aims to do good with it, is careful, when he does speak to speak to the purpose, and says little in order that he may take time to deliberate. He *spares his words,* because they are better spared than ill-spent. (2.) This is generally taken for such a sure indication of wisdom that a fool may gain the reputation of being a wise man if he have but wit enough to hold his tongue, to hear, and see, and say little. If a fool hold his peace, men of candour will think him wise, because nothing appears to the contrary, and because it will be thought that he is making observations on what others say, and gaining experience, and is consulting with himself what he shall say, that he may speak pertinently. See how easy it is to gain men's good opinion and to impose upon them. But when a *fool holds his peace* God knows his heart, and the folly that is bound up there; thoughts are words to him, and there-

fore he cannot be deceived in his judgment of men.

CHAP. XVIII.

THROUGH desire a man, having separated himself, seeketh *and* intermeddleth with all wisdom.

The original here is difficult, and differently understood. 1. Some take it as a rebuke to an affected singularity. When men take a pride in *separating themselves* from the sentiments and society of others, in contradicting all that has been said before them and advancing new notions of their own, which, though ever so absurd, they are wedded to, it is to gratify a desire or lust of vain-glory, and they are seekers and meddlers with that which does not belong to them. He *seeks according to his desire, and intermeddles with every business,* pretends to pass a judgment upon every man's matter. He is morose and supercilious. Those generally are so that are opinionative and conceited, and they thus make themselves ridiculous, and are vexatious to others. 2. Our translation seems to take it as an excitement to diligence in the pursuit of wisdom. If we would get knowledge or grace, we must desire it, as that which we need and which will be of great advantage to us, 1 Cor. xii. 31. We must *separate ourselves* from all those things which would divert us from or retard us in the pursuit, retire out of the noise of this world's vanities, and then *seek and intermeddle with all* the means and instructions of *wisdom,* be willing to take pains and try all the methods of improving ourselves, be acquainted with a variety of opinions, that we may prove all things and hold fast that which is good.

2 A fool hath no delight in understanding, but that his heart may discover itself.

A fool may pretend to understanding, and to seek and intermeddle with the means of it, but, 1. He has no true delight in it ; it is only to please his friends or save his credit ; he does not love his book, nor his business, nor his Bible, nor his prayers ; he would rather be playing the fool with his sports. Those who take no pleasure in learning or religion will make nothing to purpose of either. No progress is made in them if they are a task and a drudgery. 2. He has no good design in it, only *that his heart may discover itself,* that he may have something to make a show with, something wherewith to varnish his folly, that that may pass off the better, because he loves to hear himself talk.

3 When the wicked cometh, *then* cometh also contempt, and with ignominy reproach.

This may include a double sense:—1. That wicked people are scornful people, and put *contempt* upon others. *When the wicked comes* into any company, comes into the schools of wisdom or into the assemblies for religious worship, *then comes contempt* of God, of his people and ministers, and of every thing that is said and done. You can expect no other from those that are profane than that they will be scoffers ; they will be an *ignominy* and *reproach ;* they will flout and jeer every thing that is serious and grave. But let not wise and good men regard it, for the proverb of the ancients says, such *wickedness proceeds from the wicked.* 2. That wicked people are shameful people, and bring *contempt* upon themselves, for God has said that those *who despise him shall be lightly esteemed.* As soon as ever sin entered shame followed it, and sinners make themselves despicable. Nor do they only draw contempt upon themselves, but they bring *ignominy* and *reproach* upon their families, their friends, their ministers, and all that are in any way related to them. Those therefore who would secure their honour must retain their virtue.

4 The words of a man's mouth *are as* deep waters, *and* the wellspring of wisdom *as* a flowing brook.

The similitudes here seem to be elegantly transposed. 1. The *well-spring of wisdom* is *as deep waters.* An intelligent knowing man has in him a good treasure of useful things, which furnishes him with something to say upon all occasions that is pertinent and profitable. This is as *deep waters,* which make no noise, but never run dry. 2. The words of such *a man's mouth are as a flowing brook.* What he sees cause to speak flows naturally from him and with a great deal of ease, and freedom, and natural fluency ; it is clean and fresh, it is cleansing and refreshing ; from his *deep waters* there flows what there is occasion for, to water those about him, as the brooks do the low grounds.

5 *It is* not good to accept the person of the wicked, to overthrow the righteous in judgment.

This justly condemns those who, being employed in the administration of justice, pervert judgment, 1. By conniving at men's crimes, and protecting and countenancing them in oppression and violence, because of their dignity, or wealth, or some personal kindness they have for them. Whatever excuses men may make for it, certainly *it is not good* thus to *accept the person of the wicked ;* it is an offence to God, an affront to justice, a wrong to mankind, and a real service done to the kingdom of sin and Satan. The merits of the cause must be regarded, not the person. 2. By giving a cause against justice and equity, because the person is poor and low in the world, or not of the same party or persuasion, or a stranger of another country. This is *overthrowing the righteous in judgment,* who ought to be supported, and whom God will make to stand.

6 A fool's lips enter into contention, and his mouth calleth for strokes.

7 A fool's mouth *is* his destruction, and his lips *are* the snare of his soul.

Solomon has often shown what mischief bad men do to others with their ungoverned tongues ; here he shows what mischief they do to themselves. 1. They embroil themselves in quarrels : *A fool's lips,* without any cause or call, *enter into contention,* by advancing foolish notions which others find themselves obliged to oppose, and so a quarrel is begun, or by giving provoking language, which will be resented, and satisfaction demanded, or by setting men at defiance, and bidding them *do if they dare.* Proud, and passionate men, and drunkards, are fools, whose lips *enter into contention.* A wise man may, against his will, be drawn into a quarrel, but he is a fool that of choice enters into it when he might avoid it, and he will repent it when it is too late. 2. They expose themselves to correction : The *fool's mouth* does, in effect, *call for strokes ;* he has said that which deserves to be punished with strokes, and is still saying that which needs to be checked, and restrained with strokes, as Ananias unjustly commanded that Paul should be *smitten on the mouth.* 3. They involve themselves in ruin : A *fool's mouth,* which has been, or would have been, the destruction of others, proves at length *his own destruction,* perhaps from men. Shimei's mouth was his own destruction, and Adonijah's, who spoke against his own head. And when a fool, by his foolish speaking, has run himself into a premunire, and thinks to bring himself off by justifying or excusing what he has said, his defence proves his offence, and his lips are still the snare of his soul, entangling him yet more and more. However, when men by their evil words shall be condemned at God's bar their mouths will be their destruction, and it will be such an aggravation of their ruin as will not admit one drop of water, one drop of comfort, to *cool their tongue,* which is their snare and will be their tormentor.

8 The words of a talebearer *are* as wounds, and they go down into the innermost parts of the belly.

Tale-bearers are those who secretly carry stories from house to house, which perhaps have some truth in them, but are secrets not fit to be told, or are basely misrepresented, and false colours put upon them, and are all told with design to blast men's reputation, to break their friendship, to make mischief between relations and neighbours, and set them at variance. Now the words of such are here said to be, 1. *Like as when men are wounded* (so the margin reads it) ; they pretend to be very much affected with the miscarriages of such and such, and to be in pain for them, and pretend that it is with the greatest grief and reluctance imaginable that they speak of them. They look as if they themselves were wounded by it, whereas really they *rejoice in iniquity,* are fond of the story, and tell it with pride and pleasure. Thus their words seem; but they *go down as poison into the innermost parts of the belly,* the pill being thus gilded, thus sugared. 2. *As wounds* (so the text reads it), as deep wounds, deadly wounds, *wounds in the innermost parts of the belly ;* the *venter medius vel infimus—the middle or lower belly,* the *thorax* or the *abdomen,* in either of which wounds are mortal. The words of the tale-bearer wound him of whom they are spoken, his credit and interest, and him to whom they are spoken, his love and charity. They occasion sin to him, which is a wound to the conscience. Perhaps he seems to slight them, but they wound insensibly, by alienating his affections from one he ought to love.

9 He also that is slothful in his work is brother to him that is a great waster.

Note, 1. Prodigality is very bad husbandry. Those are not only justly branded as fools among men, but will give an uncomfortable account to God of the talents they are entrusted with, who are wasters of their estates, who live above what they have, spend and give more than they can afford, and so, in effect, throw away what they have, and suffer it to run to waste. 2. Idleness is no better. He that is remiss in his work, whose *hands hang down* (so the word signifies), that stands, as we say, with his thumbs in his mouth, that neglects his business, does it not at all, or as if he did it not, he is own brother to him that is a prodigal, that is, he is as much a fool and in as sure and ready a way to poverty ; one scatters what he has, the other lets it run through his fingers. The observation is too true in the affairs of religion ; he that is trifling and careless in praying and hearing is brother to him that does not pray or hear at all ; and omissions of duty and in duty are as fatal to the soul as commissions of sin.

10 The name of the Lord *is* a strong tower : the righteous runneth into it, and is safe.

Here is, 1. God's sufficiency for the saints: His *name is a strong tower* for them, in which they may take rest when they are weary and take sanctuary when they are pursued, where they may be lifted up above their enemies and fortified against them. There is enough in God, and in the discoveries which he has made of himself to us, to make us easy at all times. The wealth laid up in this tower is enough to enrich them, to be a continual feast and a continuing treasure to them. The strength of this tower is enough to protect them ; *the name of the Lord* is all that whereby he has made himself known as God, and our God, not only his titles and attributes, but his covenant and all the promises of it ;

these make up a tower, a strong tower, impenetrable, impregnable, for all God's people. 2. The saints' security in God. It is a strong tower to those who know how to make use of it as such. *The righteous,* by faith and prayer, devotion towards God and dependence on him, *run into it,* as their city of refuge. Having made sure their interest in God's name, they take the comfort and benefit of it ; they go out of themselves, retire from the world, live above, dwell in God and God in them, and so they are safe, they think themselves so, and they shall find themselves so.

11 The rich man's wealth *is* his strong city, and as a high wall in his own conceit.

Having described the firm and faithful defence of the righteous man (*v.* 10), Solomon here shows what is the false and deceitful defence of the rich man, that has his portion and treasure in the things of this world, and sets his heart upon them. His wealth is as much his confidence, and he expects as much from it, as a godly man from his God. See, 1. How he supports himself. He makes his *wealth his city,* where he dwells, where he rules, with a great deal of self-complacency, as if he had a whole city under his command. It *is his strong city,* in which he intrenches himself, and then sets danger at defiance, as if nothing could hurt him. *His scales are his pride ;* his wealth is his wall in which he encloses himself, and he thinks it a *high wall,* which cannot be scaled or got over, Job xxxi. 24 ; Rev. xviii. 7. 2. How herein he cheats himself. It is a *strong city,* and a *high wall,* but it is so only *in his own conceit ;* it will not prove to be really so, but like the house built on the sand, which will fail the builder when he most needs it.

12 Before destruction the heart of man is haughty, and before honour *is* humility.

Note, 1. Pride is the presage of ruin, and ruin will at last be the punishment of pride ; for *before destruction* men are commonly so infatuated by the just judgment of God that they are more haughty than ever, that their ruin may be the sorer and the more surprising. Or, if that do not always hold, yet after the heart has been lifted up with pride, a fall comes, *ch.* xvi. 18. 2. Humility is the presage of honour and prepares men for it, and honour shall at length be the reward of humility, as he had said before, *ch.* xv. 33. That has need to be often said which men are so loth to believe.

13 He that answereth a matter before he heareth *it,* it *is* folly and shame unto him.

See here how men often expose themselves by that very thing by which they hope to gain applause. 1. Some take a pride in being quick. They *answer a matter before they hear it,* hear it out, nay, as soon as they but hear of it. They think it is their honour to take up a cause suddenly; and, when they have heard one side, they think the matter so plain that they need not trouble themselves to hear the other; they are already apprized of it, and masters of all the merits of the cause. Whereas, though a ready wit is an agreeable thing to play with, it is solid judgment and sound wisdom that do business. 2. Those that take a pride in being quick commonly fall under the just reproach of being impertinent. It is folly for a man to go about to speak to a thing which he does not understand, or to pass sentence upon a matter which he is not truly and fully informed of, and has not patience to make a strict enquiry into; and, if it be folly, it is and will be shame.

14 The spirit of a man will sustain his infirmity; but a wounded spirit who can bear?

Note, 1. Outward grievances are tolerable as long as the mind enjoys itself and is at ease. Many infirmities, many calamities, we are liable to in this world, in body, name, and estate, which a man may bear, and bear up under, if he have but good conduct and courage, and be able to act with reason and resolution, especially if he have a good conscience, and the testimony of that be for him; and, if the *spirit of a man* will *sustain the infirmity*, much more will the spirit of a Christian, or rather the Spirit of God witnessing and working with our spirits in a day of trouble. 2. The grievances of the spirit are of all others most heavy, and hardly to be borne; these make sore the shoulders which should sustain the other infirmities. If the spirit be wounded by the disturbance of the reason, dejection under the trouble, whatever it is, and despair of relief, if the spirit be wounded by the amazing apprehensions of God's wrath for sin, and the fearful expectations of judgment and fiery indignation, *who can bear* this? Wounded spirits cannot help themselves, nor do others know how to help them. It is therefore wisdom to keep conscience void of offence.

15 The heart of the prudent getteth knowledge; and the ear of the wise seeketh knowledge.

Note, 1. Those that are prudent will seek knowledge, and apply their ear and heart to the pursuit of it, their ear to attend to the means of knowledge and their heart to mix faith with what they hear and make a good improvement of it. Those that are prudent do not think they have prudence enough, but still see they have need of more; and the more prudent a man is the more inquisitive will he be after knowledge, the knowledge of God and his duty, and the way to heaven, for that is the best knowledge. 2. Those that prudently seek knowledge shall certainly get knowledge, for God never said to such, *Seek*

in vain, but, *Seek and you shall find.* If the ear seeks it, the heart gets it, and keeps it, and is enriched by it. We must get knowledge, not only into our heads, but into our hearts, get the savour and relish of it, apply what we know to ourselves and experience the power and influence of it.

16 A man's gift maketh room for him, and bringeth him before great men.

Of what great force gifts (that is, bribes) are he had intimated before, *ch.* xvii. 8, 23. Here he shows the power of gifts, that is, presents made even by inferiors to those that are above them and have much more than they have. A good present will go far, 1. Towards a man's liberty: *A man's gift*, if he be in prison, may procure his enlargement; there are courtiers, who, if they use their interest even for oppressed innocency, expect to receive a gratuity for it. Or, if a mean man know not how to get access to a great man, he may do it by a fee to his servants or a present to himself; those will make room for him. 2. Towards his preferment. It will bring him to sit among *great men*, in honour and power. See how corrupt the world is when men's gifts will do that for them which their merits will not do, though ever so great; nay, will gain that for them which they are unworthy of and unfit for; and no wonder that those take bribes in their offices who gave bribes for them. *Vendére jura potest, emerat ille prius—He that bought law can sell it.*

17 *He that is* first in his own cause *seemeth* just; but his neighbour cometh and searcheth him.

This shows that one tale is good till another is told. 1. He that speaks first will be sure to tell a straight story, and relate that only which makes for him, and put the best colour he can upon it, so that his cause shall appear good, whether it really be so or no. 2. The plaintiff having done his evidence, it is fit that the defendant should be heard, should have leave to confront the witnesses and cross-examine them, and show the falsehood and fallacy of what has been alleged, which perhaps may make the matter appear quite otherwise than it did. We must therefore remember that we have two ears, to hear both sides before we give judgment.

18 The lot causeth contentions to cease, and parteth between the mighty.

Note, 1. Contentions commonly happen among the mighty, that are jealous for their honour and right and stand upon the punctilios of both, that are confident of their being able to make their part good and therefore will hardly condescend to the necessary terms of an accommodation; whereas those that are poor are forced to be peaceable, and sit down losers. 2. Even the contentions of the mighty may be ended by lot if they cannot otherwise be compromised, and sometimes better so than by arguments which are endless, or concessions which they are loth to stoop to, whereas it is no disparagement to a man to acquiesce in the determination of the lot when once it is referred to that. To prevent quarrels Canaan was divided by lot; and, if lusory lots had not profaned this way of appeal to Providence, perhaps it might be very well used now for the deciding of many controversies, both to the honour of God and the satisfaction of the parties, provided it were done with prayer and due solemnity, this and some other scriptures seeming to direct to it, especially Acts i. 26. If the law be a lottery (as some have called it), it were as well that a lottery were the law.

19 A brother offended *is harder to be won* than a strong city : and *their* contentions *are* like the bars of a castle.

Note, 1. Great care must be taken to prevent quarrels among relations, and those that are under special obligation to each other, not only because they are most unnatural and unbecoming, but because between such things are commonly taken most unkindly, and resentments are apt to be carried too far. Wisdom and grace would indeed make it most easy to us to forgive our relations and friends if they offend us, but corruption makes it most difficult to forgive them ; let us therefore take heed of disobliging a brother, or one that has been as a brother ; ingratitude is very provoking. 2. Great pains must be taken to compromise matters in variance between relations, with all speed, because it is a work of so much difficulty, and consequently the more honourable if it be done. Esau was a *brother offended*, and seemed *harder to be won than a strong city*, yet by a work of God upon his heart, in answer to Jacob's prayer, he was won.

20 A man's belly shall be satisfied with the fruit of his mouth ; *and* with the increase of his lips shall he be filled.

Note, 1. Our comfort depends very much upon the testimony of our own consciences, for us or against us. The *belly* is here put for the conscience, as *ch.* xx. 27. Now it is of great consequence to us whether that be satisfied, and what that is filled with, for, accordingly, will our satisfaction be and our inward peace. 2. The testimony of our consciences will be for us, or against us, according as we have or have not governed our tongues well. According as *the fruit of the mouth* is good or bad, unto iniquity or unto righteousness, so the character of the man is, and consequently the testimony of his conscience concerning him. " We ought to take as great care about the words we speak as we do about the fruit of our trees or the increase of the earth, which we are to eat ; for, according as they are wholesome or unwhole-

some, so will the pleasure or the pain be wherewith we shall be filled." So bishop Patrick.

21 Death and life *are* in the power of the tongue : and they that love it shall eat the fruit thereof.

Note, 1. A man may do a great deal of good, or a great deal of hurt, both to others and to himself, according to the use he makes of his tongue. Many a one has been his own death by a foul tongue, or the death of others by a false tongue ; and, on the contrary, many a one has saved his own life, or procured the comfort of it, by a prudent gentle tongue, and saved the lives of others by a seasonable testimony or intercession for them. And, if by our words we must be justified or condemned, *death and life are*, no doubt, *in the power of the tongue.* Tongues were Æsop's best meat, and his worst. 2. Men's words will be judged of by the affections with which they speak ; he that not only speaks aright (which a bad man may do to save his credit or please his company), but loves to speak so, speaks well of choice, and with delight, to him it will be life; and he that not only speaks amiss (which a good man may do through inadvertency), but loves to speak so (Ps. lii. 4), to him it will be death. As men *love it* they shall *eat the fruit of it.*

22 *Whoso* findeth a wife findeth a good *thing*, and obtaineth favour of the LORD.

Note, 1. A good wife is a great blessing to a man. He that *finds a wife* (that is, a wife indeed ; a bad wife does not deserve to be called by a name of so much honour), that finds a help meet for him (that is a wife in the original acceptation of the word), that sought such a one with care and prayer and has found what he sought, he has found a *good thing,* a jewel of great value, a rare jewel ; he has found that which will not only contribute more than any thing to his comfort in this life, but will forward him in the way to heaven. 2. God is to be acknowledged in it with thankfulness ; it is a token of his favour, and a happy pledge of further favours ; it is a sign that God delights in a man to do him good and has mercy in store for him ; for this, therefore, God must be sought unto.

23 The poor useth entreaties ; but the rich answereth roughly.

Note, 1. Poverty, though many inconveniences to the body attend it, has often a good effect upon the spirit, for it makes men humble and submissive, and mortifies their pride. It teaches them to *use entreaties.* When necessity forces men to beg it tells them they must not prescribe or demand, but take what is given them and be thankful. At the throne of God's grace we are all poor, and must use entreaties, not answer, but make application, must sue *sub formâ pauperis—as a pauper.* 2. A prosperous condition, though it has many advantages, has often this mischief attending it, that it makes men proud, haughty, and imperious : *The rich answers the entreaties of the poor roughly,* as Nabal answered David's messengers with railing. It is a very foolish humour of some rich men, especially those who have risen from little, that they think their riches will warrant them to give hard words, and, even where they do not design any rough dealing, that it becomes them to answer roughly, whereas gentlemen ought to be gentle, Jam. iii. 17.

24 A man *that hath* friends must show himself friendly : and there is a friend *that* sticketh closer than a brother.

Solomon here recommends friendship to us, and shows, 1. What we must do that we may contract and cultivate friendship ; we must *show ourselves friendly.* Would we have friends and keep them, we must not only not affront them, or quarrel with them, but we must love them, and make it appear that we do so by all expressions that are endearing, by being free with them, pleasing to them, visiting them and bidding them welcome, and especially by doing all the good offices we can and serving them in every thing that lies in our power ; that is *showing ourselves friendly.*

Si vis amari, ama—
If you wish to gain affection, bestow it. Sen.

Ut ameris, amabilis esto—
The way to be beloved is to be lovely. Ovid.

2. That it is worth while to do so, for we may promise ourselves a great deal of comfort in a true friend. A *brother* indeed *is born for adversity,* as he had said, *ch.* xvii. 17. In our troubles we expect comfort and relief from our relations, but sometimes *there is a friend,* that is nothing akin to us, the bonds of whose esteem and love prove stronger than those of nature, and therefore he *sticks closer than a brother,* and, when it comes to the trial, will do more for us than a brother will. Christ is a friend to all believers that *sticks closer than a brother ;* to him therefore let them show themselves friendly.

CHAP. XIX.

BETTER *is* the poor that walketh in his integrity, than *he that is* perverse in his lips, and is a fool.

Here see, 1. What will be the credit and comfort of a poor man, and make him more excellent than his neighbour, though his poverty may expose him to contempt and may dispirit him. Let him be honest and *walk in integrity,* let him keep a good conscience and make it appear that he does so, let him always speak and act with sincerity when he is under the greatest temptations to dissemble and break his word, and then let him value himself upon that, for all wise and good men will value him. He is better, has a better character, is in a better condition, is better be-

loved, and lives to better purpose, than many a one that looks great and makes a figure. 2. What will be the shame of a rich man, notwithstanding all his pomp. If he have a shallow head and an evil tongue, if he is *perverse in his lips and is a fool,* if he is a wicked man and gets what he has by fraud and oppression, he *is a fool,* and an honest poor man is to be preferred far before him.

2 Also, *that* the soul *be* without knowledge, *it is* not good ; and he that hasteth with *his* feet sinneth.

Two things are here declared to be of bad consequence :—1. Ignorance : *To be without the knowledge of the soul is not good,* so some read it. Know we not our own selves, our own hearts? *A soul without knowledge is not good ;* it is a great privilege that we have souls, but, if these souls have not knowledge, what the better are we ? If man *has not understanding, he is as the beasts,* Ps. xlix. 20. An ignorant soul cannot be a good soul. That the soul be without knowledge is not safe, nor pleasant ; what good can the soul do, or what is it good for, if it be without knowledge ? 2. Rashness. *He that hastes with his feet* (that does things inconsiderately and with precipitation, and will not take time to ponder the path of his feet) *sins ;* he cannot but often miss the mark and take many a false step, which those prevent that consider their ways. As good not know as not consider.

3 The foolishness of man perverteth his way : and his heart fretteth against the LORD.

We have here two instances of men's folly :—1. That they bring themselves into straits and troubles, and run themselves a-ground, and embarrass themselves : *The foolishness of man perverts his way.* Men meet with crosses and disappointments in their affairs, and things do not succeed as they expected and wished, and it is owing to themselves and their own folly ; it is their own iniquity that corrects them. 2. That when they have done so they lay the blame upon God, and their hearts fret against him, as if he had done them wrong, whereas really they wrong themselves. In fretting, we are enemies to our own peace, and become self-tormentors ; in *fretting against the Lord* we affront him, his justice, goodness, and sovereignty ; and it is very absurd to take occasion from the trouble which we pull upon our own heads by our wilfulness, or neglect, to quarrel with him, when we ought to blame ourselves, for it is our own doing. See Isa. l. 1.

4 Wealth maketh many friends ; but the poor is separated from his neighbour.

Here, 1. We may see how strong men's love of money is, that they will love any man, how undeserving soever he be otherwise, if he has but a deal of money and is free with it, so that they may hope to be the better for it. Wealth enables a man to send many presents, make many entertainments, and do many good offices, and so gains him many friends, who pretend to love him, for they flatter him and make their court to him, but really love what he has, or rather love themselves, hoping to get by him. 2. We may see how weak men's love of one another is. He who, while he prospered, was beloved and respected, if he fall into poverty is *separated from his neighbour*, is not owned nor looked upon, not visited nor regarded, is bidden to keep his distance and told he is troublesome. Even one that has been his neighbour and acquaintance will turn his face from him and pass by on the other side. Because men's consciences tell them they ought to relieve and succour such, they are willing to have this excuse, that they did not see them.

5 A false witness shall not be unpunished, and *he that* speaketh lies shall not escape.

Here we have, 1. The sins threatened—bearing *false witness* in judgment and *speaking lies* in common conversation. Men could not arrive at such a pitch of impiety as to bear false witness (where to the guilt of a lie is added that of perjury and injury) if they had not advanced to it by allowing themselves to speak untruths in jest and banter, or under pretence of doing good. Thus men *teach their tongues to speak lies*, Jer. ix. 5. Those that will take a liberty to tell lies in discourse are in a fair way to be guilty of the greater wickedness of false-witness-bearing, whenever they are tempted to it, though they seemed to detest it. Those that can swallow a false word debauch their consciences, so that a false oath will not choke them. 2. The threatening itself: They *shall not go unpunished;* they *shall not escape.* This intimates that that which emboldens them in the sin is the hope of impunity, it being a sin which commonly escapes punishment from men, though the law is strict, Deut. xix. 18, 19. But it *shall not escape* the righteous judgment of God, who is jealous, and will not suffer his name to be profaned; we know where all liars will have their everlasting portion.

6 Many will entreat the favour of the prince : and every man *is* a friend to him that giveth gifts. 7 All the brethren of the poor do hate him : how much more do his friends go far from him ? he pursueth *them with* words, *yet* they *are* wanting *to him.*

These two verses are a comment upon *v.* 4, and show, 1. How those that are rich and great are courted and caressed, and have suitors and servants in abundance. The

prince that has power in his hand, and preferments at his disposal, has his gate and his ante-chamber thronged with petitioners, that are ready to adore him for what they can get. *Many will entreat his favour*, and think themselves happy in it. Even great men are humble suppliants to the prince. How earnest then should we be for the favour of God, which is far beyond that of any earthly prince. But, it should seem, liberality will go further than majesty itself to gain respect, for there are many that court the prince, but *every man is a friend to him that gives gifts;* not only those that have received, or do expect, gifts from him, will, as friends, be ready to serve him, but others also will, as friends, give him their good word. Prodigals, who are foolishly free of what they have, will have many hangers-on who will cry them up as long as it lasts, but will leave them when it is done. Those that are prudently generous make an interest by it which may stand them in good stead; those that are accounted benefactors exercise an authority which may give them an opportunity of doing good, Luke xxii. 25. 2. How those that are poor and low are slighted and despised. It should not be so; we must honour all men, even under their greatest abasements. Men may, if they please, court the prince, and the princely, but they may not trample upon the poor and look at them with disdain. Yet so it often is : *All the brethren of the poor do hate him;* even his own relations are shy of him, because he is needy and craving, and expects something from them, and because they look upon him as a blemish to their family; and then no marvel if others of his friends, that were nothing akin to him, *go far from him*, to get out of his way. *He pursues them with words*, hoping to prevail with them by his importunity to be kind to him, but all in vain; they have nothing for him. *They pursue him with words* (so some understand it), to excuse themselves from giving him any thing; they tell him that he is idle and impertinent, that he has brought himself into poverty, and therefore ought not to be relieved; as Nabal said to David's messengers: *" There are many servants now a days that run away from their masters;* and how do I know but that David may be one of them ?"* Let poor people therefore make God their friend, pursue him with their prayers, and he will not be wanting to them.

8 He that getteth wisdom loveth his own soul : he that keepeth understanding shall find good.

Those are here encouraged, 1. That take pains to *get wisdom*, to get knowledge, and grace, and acquaintance with God; those that do so show that they *love their own souls*, and will be found to have done themselves the greatest kindness imaginable. No man ever *hated his own flesh*, but loves that, yet many are wanting in love to their own souls, for only those love their souls, and consequently love themselves, aright, that *get wisdom,* true wisdom. 2. That take care to keep it when they have got it; it is health, and wealth, and honour, and all, to the soul, and therefore he that *keeps understanding,* as he shows that he *loves his own soul,* so he shall certainly *find good,* all good. He that retains the good lessons he has learnt, and orders his conversation according to them, shall find the benefit and comfort of it in his own soul and shall be happy here and for ever.

9 A false witness shall not be unpunished, and *he that* speaketh lies shall perish.

Here is, 1. A repetition of what was said before (*v.* 5), for we have need to be again and again warned of the danger of the sin of lying and false-witness-bearing, since nothing is of more fatal consequence. 2. An addition to it in one word; there it was said, *He that speaks lies shall not escape,* and intimated that he shall be punished. Here it is said, His punishment shall be such as will be his destruction: he *shall perish;* the lies he forged against others will be his own ruin. It is a damning destroying sin.

10 Delight is not seemly for a fool; much less for a servant to have rule over princes.

Note, 1. Pleasure and liberty ill become a fool: *Delight is not seemly for* such a one. A man that has not wisdom and grace has no right nor title to true joy, and therefore it is unseemly. It ill becomes those that do not delight in God to delight in any thing else. They know not how to use any thing, nor how to manage themselves, and therefore they do but expose themselves. It becomes ungracious fools to be afflicted, and mourn, and weep, not to laugh and be merry; rebukes are more proper for them than delights. Delight is seemly for a man of business, to refresh him when he is fatigued, but not *for a fool,* that lives an idle life and abuses his recreations. *The prosperity of fools* discovers their folly and *destroys them.* 2. Power and honour ill become a man of a servile spirit. Nothing is more unseemly than *for a servant to have rule over princes;* it is absurd in itself, and very preposterous, for none are so insolent and intolerable as a beggar on horseback, *a servant when he reigns, ch.* xxx. 22. It is very unseemly for one that is a servant to sin and his lusts to rule over and oppress those that are God's freemen and made kings and priests to him.

11 The discretion of a man deferreth his anger; and *it is* his glory to pass over a transgression.

A wise man will observe these two rules about his anger: 1. Not to be over-hasty in his resentments: *Discretion* teaches us to *defer our anger,* to defer the admission of it till we have thoroughly considered all the merits of the provocation, seen them in a true light and weighed them in a just balance; and then to defer the prosecution of it till there be no danger of running into any indecencies. Plato said to his servant, " I would beat thee, but that I am angry." Give it time, and it will cool. 2. Not to be over-critical in his resentments. Whereas it is commonly looked upon as a piece of ingenuity to apprehend an affront quickly, it is here made a man's *glory to pass over a transgression,* to appear as if he did not see it (Ps. xxxviii. 13), or, if he sees fit to take notice of it, yet to forgive it and meditate no revenge.

12 The king's wrath *is* as the roaring of a lion; but his favour *is* as dew upon the grass.

This is to the same purport with what we had *ch.* xvi. 14, 15, and the design of it is, 1. To make kings wise and considerate in dispensing their frowns and smiles. They are not like those of common persons; their frowns are very terrible and their smiles very comfortable, and therefore it concerns them to be very careful that they never frighten a good man from doing well with their frowns, nor ever give countenance to a wicked man in doing ill with their smiles, for then they abuse their influence, Rom. xiii. 3. 2. To make subjects faithful and dutiful to their princes. Let them be restrained from all disloyalty by the consideration of the dreadful consequence of having the government against them; and let them be encouraged in all good services to the public by the hopes of the favour of their prince. Christ is a King whose wrath against his enemies will be *as the roaring of a lion* (Rev. x. 3) and his favour to his own people as the refreshing dew, Ps. lxxii. 6.

13 A foolish son *is* the calamity of his father: and the contentions of a wife *are* a continual dropping.

It is an instance of the vanity of the world that we are liable to the greatest grief in those things wherein we promise ourselves the greatest comfort. It is as it proves. What greater temporal comfort can a man have than a good wife and good children? Yet, 1. *A foolish son is* a great affliction, and may make a man wish a thousand times he had been written childless. A son that will apply himself to no study or business, that will take no advice, that lives a lewd, loose, rakish life, and spends what he has extravagantly, games it away and wastes it in the excess of riot, or that is proud, foppish, and conceited, such a one is the grief *of his father,* because he is the disgrace, and is likely to be the ruin, of his family. He hates all his labour, when he sees to whom he must leave the fruit of it. 2. A cross peevish wife is as great an affliction: Her *contentions are continual;* every day, and every hour in the day, she finds some occasion to make herself and those about her uneasy. Those that are accustomed to chide never want something or other to chide at; but it is *a continual dropping*, that is, a continual vexation, as it is to have a house so much out of repair that it rains in and a man cannot lie dry in it. That man has an uncomfortable life, and has need of a great deal of wisdom and grace to enable him to bear his affliction and do his duty, who has a sot for his son and a scold for his wife.

14 House and riches *are* the inheritance of fathers : and a prudent wife *is* from the Lord.

Note, 1. A discreet and virtuous wife is a choice gift of God's providence to a man—a wife that is *prudent*, in opposition to one that is contentious, *v.* 13. For, though a wife that is continually finding fault may think it is her wit and wisdom to be so, it is really her folly ; *a prudent wife* is meek and quiet, and makes the best of every thing. If a man has such a wife, let him not ascribe it to the wisdom of his own choice or his own management (for the wisest have been deceived both in and by a woman), but let him ascribe it to the goodness of God, who made him a help meet for him, and perhaps by some hits and turns of providence that seemed casual brought her to him. Every creature is what he makes it. Happy marriages, we are sure, are made in heaven ; Abraham's servant prayed in the belief of this, Gen. xxiv. 12. 2. It is a more valuable gift than *house and riches*, contributes more to the comfort and credit of a man's life and the welfare of his family, is a greater token of God's favour, and about which the divine providence is in a more especial manner conversant. A good estate may be *the inheritance of fathers*, which, by the common direction of Providence, comes in course to a man ; but no man has a good wife by descent or entail. Parents that are worldly, in disposing of their children, look no further than to match them to *house and riches*, but, if withal it be to *a prudent wife*, let God have the glory.

15 Slothfulness casteth into a deep sleep ; and an idle soul shall suffer hunger.

See here the evil of a sluggish slothful disposition. 1. It stupifies men, and makes them senseless, and mindless of their own affairs, as if they were *cast into a deep sleep*, dreaming much, but doing nothing. Slothful people doze away their time, bury their talents, live a useless life, and are the unprofitable burdens of the earth ; for any service they do when they are awake they might as well be always asleep. Even their souls are idle and lulled asleep, their rational powers chilled and frozen. 2. It impoverishes men and brings them to want. Those that will not labour cannot expect to eat, but must *suffer hunger: An idle soul*, one that is idle in the affairs of his soul, that takes no care or

900

pains to work out his salvation, shall perish for want of that which is necessary to the life and happiness of the soul.

16 He that keepeth the commandment keepeth his own soul; *but* he that despiseth his ways shall die.

Here is, 1. The happiness of those that walk circumspectly. Those that make conscience of *keeping the commandment* in every thing, that live by rule, as becomes servants and patients, *keep their own souls;* they secure their present peace and future bliss, and provide every way well for themselves. If we keep God's word, God's word will keep us from every thing really hurtful. 2. The misery of those that live at large and never mind what they do : Those *that despise their ways shall die*, shall perish eternally ; they are in the high road to ruin. With respect to those that are careless about the end of their ways, and never consider whither they are going, and about the rule of their ways, that will walk in the way of their hearts and after the course of the world (Eccl. xi. 9), that never consider what they have done nor what they are concerned to do, but *walk at all adventures* (Lev. xxvi. 21), right or wrong, it is all one to them—what can come of this but the greatest mischief?

17 He that hath pity upon the poor lendeth unto the Lord ; and that which he hath given will he pay him again.

Here is, I. The duty of charity described. It includes two things:—1. Compassion, which is the inward principle of charity in the heart; it is to *have pity on the poor*. Those that have not a penny for the poor, yet may have pity for them, a charitable concern and sympathy ; and, if a man *give all his goods to feed the poor* and have not this charity in his heart, *it is nothing*, 1 Cor. xiii. 3. We must *draw out our souls to the hungry*, Isa. lviii. 10. 2. Bounty and liberality. We must not only pity the poor, but give, according to their necessity and our ability, Jam. ii. 15, 16. *That which he has given.* Margin, *His deed.* It is charity to do for the poor, as well as to give ; and thus, if they have their limbs and senses, they may be charitable to one another.

II. The encouragement of charity. 1. A very kind construction shall be put upon it. What is given to the poor, or done for them, God will place it to account as lent to him, *lent upon interest* (so the word signifies); he takes it kindly, as if it were done to himself, and he would have us to take the comfort of it and to be as well pleased as ever any usurer was when he had let out a sum of money into good hands. 2. A very rich recompence shall be made for it : *He will pay him again*, in temporal, spiritual, and eternal blessings. Almsgiving is the surest and safest way of thriving.

18 Chasten thy son while there is hope, and let not thy soul spare for his crying.

Parents are here cautioned against a foolish indulgence of their children that are untoward and viciously inclined, and that discover such an ill temper of mind as is not likely to be cured but by severity. 1. Do not say that it is all in good time to correct them; no, as soon as ever there appears a corrupt disposition in them check it immediately, before it gets head, and takes root, and is hardened into a habit: *Chasten thy son while there is hope*, for perhaps, if he be let alone awhile, he will be past hope, and a much greater chastening will not do that which now a less would effect. It is easiest plucking up weeds as soon as they spring up, and the bullock that is designed for the yoke should be betimes accustomed to it. 2. Do not say that it is a pity to correct them, and that, because they cry and beg to be forgiven, you cannot find in your heart to do it. If the point can be gained without correction, well and good; but if you find, as it often proves, that your forgiving them once, upon a dissembled repentance and promise of amendment, does but embolden them to offend again, especially if it be a thing that is in itself sinful (as lying, swearing, ribaldry, stealing, or the like), in such a case put on resolution, *and let not thy soul spare for his crying.* It is better that he should cry under thy rod than under the sword of the magistrate, or, which is more fearful, that of divine vengeance.

19 A man of great wrath shall suffer punishment: for if thou deliver *him*, yet thou must do it again.

1. As we read this, it intimates, in short, that angry men never want woe. Those that are of strong, or rather headstrong, passions, commonly bring themselves and their families into trouble by vexatious suits and quarrels and the provocations they give; they are still smarting, in one instance or other, for their ungoverned heats; and, if their friends deliver them out of one trouble, they will quickly involve themselves in another, and they *must do it again,* all which troubles to themselves and others would be prevented if they would mortify their passions and get the rule of their own spirits. 2. It may as well be read, *He that is of great wrath* (meaning the child that is to be corrected and is impatient of rebuke, cries and makes a noise, even that wrath of his against the rod of correction) *deserves to be punished; for, if thou deliver him* for the sake of that, thou wilt be forced to punish him so much the more the next time. A stomachful high-spirited child must be subdued betimes, or it will be the worse for it.

20 Hear counsel, and receive instruction, that thou mayest be wise in thy latter end.

Note, 1. It is well with those that are *wise in their latter end,* wise for their latter end, for their future state, wise for another world, that are found wise when their latter end comes, wise virgins, wise builders, wise stewards, that are wise at length, and *understand the things that belong to their peace, before they be hidden from their eyes.* A carnal worldling *at his end shall be a fool* (Jer. xvii. 11), but godliness will prove wisdom at last. 2. Those that would *be wise in their latter end* must *hear counsel* and *receive instruction,* in their beginnings must be willing to be taught and ruled, willing to be advised and reproved, when they are young. Those that would be stored in winter must gather in summer.

21 *There are* many devices in a man's heart; nevertheless the counsel of the LORD, that shall stand.

Here we have, 1. Men projecting. They keep their designs to themselves, but they cannot hide them from God; he knows the *many devices that are in men's hearts,*—devices against his counsels (as those, Ps. ii. 1—3, Micah iv. 11),—devices without his counsel (no regard had to his providence, as those Jam. iv. 13, this and the other they will do, and not take God along with them),—devices unlike God's counsels; men are wavering in their devices, and often absurd and unjust, but God's counsels are wise and holy, steady and uniform. 2. God overruling. Various men have various designs, according as their inclination or interest leads them, but *the counsel of the Lord, that shall stand,* whatever becomes of the devices of men. His counsel often breaks men's measures and baffles their devices; but their devices cannot in the least alter his counsel, nor disturb the proceedings of it, nor put him upon new counsels, Isa. xiv. 24; xlvi. 11. What a check does this give to politic designing men, who think they can outwit all mankind, that there is a God in heaven that laughs at them! Ps. ii. 4. What comfort does this speak to all God's people, that all God's purposes, which we are sure are right and good, shall be accomplished in due time!

22 The desire of a man *is* his kindness: and a poor man *is* better than a liar.

Note, 1. The honour of doing good is what we may laudably be ambitious of. It cannot but be *the desire of a man,* if he have any spark of virtue in him, to be kind; one would not covet an estate for any thing so much as thereby to be put into a capacity of relieving the poor and obliging our friends. 2. It is far better to have a heart to do good and want ability for it than have ability for it and want a heart to it: *The desire of a man* to be kind, and charitable, and generous, *is his kindness,* and shall be so construed; both God and man will accept his good-will, *according to what he has,* and will not expect more. *A poor man,* who wishes you well, but can promise you nothing, because he has nothing to be kind with, *is better than a liar,* than a rich man who makes you believe he will do mighty things, but, when it comes to the setting to, will do nothing. The character of the men of low degree, that they *are vanity,* from whom nothing is expected, is better than that of men of high degree, that they *are a lie,* they deceive those whose expectations they raised.

23 The fear of the Lord *tendeth* to life : and *he that hath it* shall abide satisfied ; he shall not be visited with evil.

See what those get by it that live in the fear of God, and always make conscience of their duty to him. 1. Safety : They *shall not be visited with evil;* they may be visited with sickness or other afflictions, but there shall be no evil in them, nothing to hurt them, because nothing to separate them *from the love of God,* or to hurt the soul. 2. Satisfaction : They *shall abide satisfied;* they shall have those comforts which are satisfying, and shall have a constant contentment and complacency in them. It is a satisfaction which will abide, whereas all the satisfactions of sense are transient and soon gone. *Satur pernoctabit, non cubabit incœnatus—He shall not go supperless to bed;* he shall have that which will make him easy and be an entertainment to him in his silent and solitary hours, Ps. xvi. 6, 7. 3. True and complete happiness. Serious godliness has a direct tendency *to life,* to all good, to eternal life ; it is the sure and ready way to it ; there is something in the nature of it fitting men for heaven and so leading them to it.

24 A slothful *man* hideth his hand in *his* bosom, and will not so much as bring it to his mouth again.

A sluggard is here exposed as a fool, for, 1. All his care is to save himself from labour and cold. See his posture : He *hides his hand in his bosom,* pretends he is lame and cannot work ; his hands are cold, and he must warm them in his bosom ; and, when they are warm there, he must keep them so. He hugs himself in his own ease and is resolved against labour and hardship. Let those work that love it ; for his part he thinks there is no such fine life as sitting still and doing nothing. 2. He will not be at the pains to feed himself, an elegant hyperbole ; as we say, A man is so lazy that he would not shake fire off him, so here, He cannot find in his heart to take his hand out of his bosom, no, not to put meat into his own mouth. If the law be so that those that will not labour must not eat, he will rather starve than stir. Thus his sin is his punishment, and therefore is egregious folly.

25 Smite a scorner, and the simple will beware : and reprove one that

hath understanding, *and* he will understand knowledge.

Note, 1. The punishment of scorners will be a means of good to others. When men are so hardened in wickedness that they will not themselves be wrought upon by the severe methods that are used to reclaim and reform them, yet such methods must be used for the sake of others, that *they may hear and fear,* Deut. xix. 20. If the *scorner* will not be recovered from his sin, the disease being inveterate, yet *the simple will beware* of venturing upon the sin which exposes men thus. If it cure not the infected, it may prevent the spreading of the infection. 2. The reproof of wise men will be a means of good to themselves. They need not be smitten ; a word to the wise is enough. Do but *reprove one that has understanding and he will* so far understand himself and his own interest that he will *understand knowledge* by it, and not miss it again through ignorance and inadvertency when once he has been told of it ; so kindly does he take reproof and so wisely improve it.

26 He that wasteth *his* father, *and* chaseth away *his* mother, *is* a son that causeth shame, and bringeth reproach.

Here is, 1. The sin of a prodigal son. Besides the wrong he does to himself, he is injurious to his good parents, and basely ungrateful to those that were the instruments of his being and have taken so much care and pains about him, which is a great aggravation of his sin and renders it exceedingly sinful in the eyes of God and man : *He wastes his father,* wastes his estate which he should have to support him in his old age, wastes his spirits, and breaks his heart, and brings his gray head *with sorrow to the grave.* He *chases away his mother,* alienates her affections from him, which cannot be done without a great deal of regret and uneasiness to her ; he makes her weary of the house, with his rudeness and insolence, and glad to retire for a little quietness ; and, when he has spent all, he turns her out of doors. 2. The shame of a prodigal son. It is a shame to himself that he should be so brutish and unnatural. He makes himself odious to all mankind. It is a shame to his parents and family, who are reflected upon, though, perhaps, without just cause, for teaching him no better, or being in some way wanting to him.

27 Cease, my son, to hear the instruction *that causeth* to err from the words of knowledge.

This is a good caution to those who have had a good education to take heed of hearkening to those who, under pretence of instructing them, draw them off from those good principles under the influence of which they were trained up. Observe, 1. There is that which seems designed for the instruction, but really tends to the destruction of young men. The factors for vice will undertake to teach them free thoughts and a fashionable conversation, how to palliate the sins they have a mind to and stop the mouth of their own consciences, how to get clear of the restraints of their education and to set up for wits and beaux. This is *the instruction* which *causes to err from the* forms of sound words, which should be held fast in faith and love. 2. It is the wisdom of young men to turn a deaf ear to such instructions, as the adder does to the charms that are designed to ensnare her. "Dread hearing such talk as tends to instil loose principles into the mind; and, if thou art linked in with such, break off from them; thou hast heard enough, or too much, and therefore hear no more of the evil communication which corrupts good manners."

28 An ungodly witness scorneth judgment: and the mouth of the wicked devoureth iniquity.

Here is a description of the worst of sinners, whose *hearts are fully set in them to do evil.* 1. They set that at defiance which would deter and detain them from sin: *An ungodly witness* is one that bears false witness against his neighbour, and will forswear himself to do another a mischief, in which there is not only great injustice, but great impiety; this is one of the worst of men. Or *an ungodly witness* is one that profanely and atheistically witnesses against religion and godliness, whose instructions seduce *from the words of knowledge* (v. 27); such a one *scorns judgment,* laughs at the terrors of the Lord, mocks at that fear, Job xv. 26. Tell him of law and equity, that the scriptures and an oath are sacred things, and not to be jésted with, that there will come a reckoning day; he laughs at it all, and scorns to heed it. 2. They are greedy, and glad of that which gives them an opportunity to sin: *The mouth of the wicked eagerly devours iniquity, drinks it in like water,* Job xv. 16.

29 Judgments are prepared for scorners, and stripes for the back of fools.

Note, 1. Scorners are fools. Those that ridicule things sacred and serious do but make themselves ridiculous. *Their folly shall be manifest unto all men.* 2. Those that scorn judgments cannot escape them, *v.* 28. The unbelief of man shall not make God's threatenings of no effect; those that *devour iniquity* swallow the hook with the bait. The civil magistrate has *judgments prepared for scorners,* for otherwise he would *bear the sword in vain;* but if he be remiss, and connive at sin, yet God's judgments slumber not; they are prepared, Matt. xxv. 41.

CHAP. XX.

WINE *is* a mocker, strong drink *is* raging: and whosoever is deceived thereby is not wise.

Here is, 1. The mischief of drunkenness: *Wine is a mocker; strong drink is raging.* It is so to the sinner himself; it mocks him, makes a fool of him, promises him that satisfaction which it can never give him. It smiles upon him at first, but *at the last it bites.* In reflection upon it, it rages in his conscience. It is raging in the body, puts the humours into a ferment. *When the wine is in the wit is out,* and then the man, according as his natural temper is, either mocks like a fool or rages like a madman. Drunkenness, which pretends to be a sociable thing, renders men unfit for society, for it makes them abusive with their tongues and outrageous in their passions, *ch.* xxiii. 29. 2. The folly of drunkards is easily inferred thence. He that *is deceived thereby,* that suffers himself to be drawn into this sin when he is so plainly warned of the consequences of it, *is not wise :* he shows that he has no right sense or consideration of things; and not only so, but he renders himself incapable of getting wisdom; for it is a sin that infatuates and besots men, and takes away their heart. A drunkard is a fool, and a fool he is likely to be.

2 The fear of a king *is* as the roaring of a lion : *whoso* provoketh him to anger sinneth *against* his own soul.

See here, 1. How formidable kings are, and what a terror they strike upon those they are angry with, Their *fear,* with which (especially when they are absolute and their will is a law) they keep their subjects in awe, *is as the roaring of a lion,* which is very dreadful to the creatures he preys upon, and makes them tremble so that they cannot escape from him. Those princes that rule by wisdom and love rule like God himself, and bear his image; but those that rule merely by terror, and with a high hand, do but rule like a lion in the forest, with a brutal power. *Oderint, dum metuant*—*Let them hate, provided they fear.* 2. How unwise therefore those are that quarrel with them, that are angry at them, and so *provoke them to anger.* They *sin against their own lives.* Much more do those do so that provoke the King of kings to anger. *Nemo me impune lacesset*—*No one shall provoke me with impunity.*

3 *It is* an honour for a man to cease from strife : but every fool will be meddling.

This is designed to rectify men's mistakes concerning strife. 1. Men think it is their wisdom to engage in quarrels; whereas it is the greatest folly that can be. He thinks himself a wise man that is quick in resenting affronts, that stands upon every nicety of honour and right, and will not abate an ace of either, that prescribes, and imposes, and gives law, to every body; but he that thus meddles is a fool, and creates a great deal of needless vexation to himself. 2. Men think, when they are engaged in quarrels, that it would be a shame to them to go back and let fall the weapon ; whereas really *it is an honour for a man to cease from strife,* an honour to withdraw an action, to drop a controversy, to forgive an injury, and to be friends with those that we have fallen out with. It is the honour of a man, a wise man, a man of spirit, to show the command he has of himself by *ceasing from strife,* yielding, and stooping, and receding from his just demands, for peace-sake, as Abraham, the better man, Gen. xiii. 8.

4 The sluggard will not plough by reason of the cold ; *therefore* shall he beg in harvest, and *have* nothing.

See here the evil of slothfulness and the love of ease. 1. It keeps men from the most necessary business, from ploughing and sowing when the season is : *The sluggard* has ground to occupy, and has ability for it ; he can plough, but he *will not ;* some excuse or other he has to shift it off, but the true reason is that it is *cold* weather. Though ploughing time is not in the depth of winter, it is in the borders of winter, when he thinks it too cold for him to be abroad. Those are scandalously sluggish who, in the way of their business, cannot find in their hearts to undergo so little toil as that of ploughing and so little hardship as that of a cold blast. Thus careless are many in the affairs of their souls ; a trifling difficulty will frighten them from the most important duty ; but good soldiers must endure hardness. 2. Thereby it deprives them of the most necessary supports : Those that *will not plough* in seed-time cannot expect to reap in harvest ; and therefore they must beg their bread with astonishment when the diligent are bringing home their sheaves with joy. He that will not submit to the labour of ploughing must submit to the shame of begging. They *shall beg in harvest, and* yet *have nothing ;* no, not then when there is greatest plenty. Though it may be charity to relieve sluggards, yet a man may, in justice, not relieve them ; they deserve to be left to starve. Those that would not provide oil in their vessels begged when the bridegroom came, and were denied.

5 Counsel in the heart of man *is like* deep water ; but a man of understanding will draw it out.

A man's wisdom is here said to be of use to him for the pumping of other people, and diving into them, 1. To get the knowledge of them. Though men's counsels and designs are ever so carefully concealed by them, so that they are as *deep water* which one cannot fathom, yet there are those who by sly insinuations, and questions that seem foreign, will get out of them both what they have done and what they intend to do. Those therefore who would keep counsel must not only put on resolution, but stand upon their guard. 2. To get knowledge by them. Some are

904

very able and fit to give counsel, have an excellent faculty of cleaving a hair, hitting the joint of a difficulty, and advising pertinently, but they are modest, and reserved, and not communicative ; they have a great deal in them, but it is loth to come out. In such a case *a man of understanding will draw it out,* as wine out of a vessel. We lose the benefit we might have by the conversation of wise men for want of the art of being inquisitive.

6 Most men will proclaim every one his own goodness : but a faithful man who can find ?

Note, 1. It is easy to find those that will pretend to be kind and liberal. Many a man will call himself a man of mercy, will boast what good he has done and what good he designs to do, or, at least, what an affection he has to well-doing. Most men will talk a great deal of their charity, generosity, hospitality, and piety, will sound a trumpet to themselves, as the Pharisees, and what little goodness they have will proclaim it and make a mighty matter of it. 2. But it is hard to find those that really are kind and liberal, that have done and will do more than either they speak of or care to hear spoken of, that will be true friends in a strait ; such a one as one may trust to is like a black swan.

7 The just *man* walketh in his integrity : his children *are* blessed after him.

It is here observed to the honour of a good man, 1. That he does well for himself. He has a certain rule, which with an even steady hand he governs himself by : He *walks in his integrity ;* he keeps a good conscience, and he has the comfort of it, for *it is his rejoicing.* He is not liable to those uneasinesses, either in contriving what he shall do or reflecting on what he has done, which those are liable to that walk in deceit. 2. That he does well for his family : *His children are blessed after him,* and fare the better for his sake. God has mercy in store for the seed of the faithful.

8 A king that sitteth in the throne of judgment scattereth away all evil with his eyes.

Here is, 1. The character of a good governor : He is *a king* that deserves to be called so who *sits in the throne,* not as a throne of honour, to take his ease, and take state upon him, and oblige men to keep their distance, but as a *throne of judgment,* that he may do justice, give redress to the injured and punish the injurious, who makes his business his delight and loves no pleasure comparably to it, who does not devolve the whole care and trouble upon others, but takes cognizance of affairs himself and sees with his own eyes as much as may be, 1 Kings x. 9. 2. The happy effect of a good government. The presence of the prince goes far towards the putting of wickedness out of countenance; if he inspect his affairs himself, those that are employed under him will be kept in awe and restrained from doing wrong. If great men be good men, and will use their power as they may and ought, what good may they do and what evil may they prevent!

9 Who can say, I have made my heart clean, I am pure from my sin?

This question is not only a challenge to any man in the world to prove himself sinless, whatever he pretends, but a lamentation of the corruption of mankind, even that which remains in the best. Alas! *Who can say,* "I am sinless?" Observe, 1. Who the persons are that are excluded from these pretensions—all, one as well as another. Here, in this imperfect state, no person whatsoever can pretend to be without sin. Adam could say so in innocency, and saints can say so in heaven, but none in this life. Those that think themselves as good as they should be cannot, nay, and those that are really good will not, dare not, say this. 2. What the pretension is that is excluded. We cannot say, We *have made our hearts clean.* Though we can say, through grace, "We are cleaner than we have been," yet we cannot say, "We are clean and pure from all remainders of sin." Or, though we are clean from the gross acts of sin, yet we cannot say, "Our hearts are clean." Or, though we are washed and cleansed, yet we cannot say, "We ourselves made our own hearts clean;" it was the work of the Spirit. Or, though we are pure from the sins of many others, yet we cannot say, "We are *pure from our sin, the sin that easily besets us,* the *body of death* which Paul complained of," Rom. vii. 24.

10 Divers weights, *and* divers measures, both of them *are* alike abomination to the LORD.

See here, 1. The various arts of deceiving that men have, all which evils the *love of money* is the root of. In paying and receiving money, which was then commonly done by the scale, they had *divers weights,* an under-weight for what they paid and an over-weight for what they received; in delivering out and taking in goods they had *divers measures,* a scanty measure to sell by and a large measure to buy by. This was doing wrong with plot and contrivance, and under colour of doing right. Under these is included all manner of fraud and deceit in commerce and trade. 2. The displeasure of God against them. Whether they be about the money or the goods, in the buyer or in the seller, they are all *alike an abomination to the Lord.* He will not prosper the trade that is thus driven, nor bless what is thus got. He hates those that thus break the common faith by which justice is maintained, and will be *the avenger of all such.*

11 Even a child is known by his do-

ings, whether his work *be* pure, and whether *it be* right.

The tree is known by its fruits, a man *by his doings,* even a young tree by its first fruits, *a child by his* childish things, *whether his work be clean* only, appearing good (the word is used *ch.* xvi. 2), or *whether it be right,* that is, really good. This intimates, 1. That children will discover themselves. One may soon see what their temper is, and which way their inclination leads them, according as their constitution is. Children have not learned the art of dissembling and concealing their bent as grown people have. 2. That parents should observe their children, that they may discover their disposition and genius, and both manage and dispose of them accordingly, drive the nail that will go and draw out that which goes amiss. *Wisdom is* herein *profitable to direct.*

12 The hearing ear, and the seeing eye, the LORD hath made even both of them.

Note, 1. God is the God of nature, and all the powers and faculties of nature are derived from him and depend upon him, and therefore are to be employed for him. It was he that *formed the eye* and *planted the ear* (Ps. xciv. 9), and the structure of both is admirable; and it is he that preserves to us the use of both; to his providence we owe it that our eyes are *seeing eyes* and our ears *hearing ears.* Hearing and seeing are the learning senses, and we must particularly own God's goodness in them. 2. God is the God of grace. It is he that gives the ear that hears God's voice, the eye that sees his beauty, for it is he that opens the understanding.

13 Love not sleep, lest thou come to poverty; open thine eyes, *and* thou shalt be satisfied with bread.

Note, 1. Those that indulge themselves in their ease may expect to want necessaries, which should have been gotten by honest labour. "Therefore, though thou must sleep (nature requires it), yet *love not sleep,* as those do that hate business. Love not sleep for its own sake, but only as it fits for further work. Love not much sleep, but rather grudge the time that is spent in it, and wish thou couldst live without it, that thou mightest always be employed in some good exercise." We must allow it to our bodies as men allow it to their servants, because they cannot help it and otherwise they shall have no good of them. Those that love sleep are likely to *come to poverty,* not only because they lose the time they spend in excess of sleep, but because they contract a listless careless disposition, and are still half asleep, never well awake. 2. Those that stir up themselves to their business may expect to have conveniences: "*Open thy eyes,* awake and shake off sleep, see how far in the day it is, how thy work wants thee, and how busy others are about thee! And, when thou art awake, look up, look to thy advantages, and do not let slip thy opportunities; apply thy mind closely to thy business and be in care about it. It is the easy condition of a great advantage : *Open thy eyes and thou shalt be satisfied with bread;* if thou dost not grow rich, yet thou shalt have enough, and that is as good as a feast."

14 *It is* naught, *it is* naught, saith the buyer: but when he is gone his way, then he boasteth.

See here, 1. What arts men use to get a good bargain and to buy cheap. They not only cheapen carelessly, as if they had no need, no mind for the commodity, when perhaps they cannot go without it (there may be prudence in that), but they vilify and run down that which yet they know to be of value; they cry, "*It is naught, it is naught;* it has this and the other fault, or perhaps may have; it is not good of the sort; and it is too dear; we can have better and cheaper elsewhere, or have bought better and cheaper." This is the common way of dealing; and after all, it may be, they know the contrary of what they affirm; but the buyer, who may think he has no other way of being even with the seller, does as extravagantly commend his goods and justify the price he sets on them, and so there is a fault on both sides; whereas the bargain would be made every jot as well if both buyer and seller would be modest and speak as they think. 2. What pride and pleasure men take in a good bargain when they have got it, though therein they contradict themselves, and own they dissembled when they were driving the bargain. When the buyer has beaten down the seller, who was content to lower his price rather than lose a customer (as many poor tradesmen are forced to do—small profit is better than none), then he goes his way, and boasts what excellent goods he has got at his own price, and takes it as an affront and a reflection upon his judgment if any body disparages his bargain. Perhaps he knew the worth of the goods better than the seller himself did and knows how to get a great deal by them. See how apt men are to be pleased with their gettings and proud of their tricks; whereas a fraud and a lie are what a man ought to be ashamed of, though he have gained ever so much by them.

15 There is gold, and a multitude of rubies: but the lips of knowledge *are* a precious jewel.

The *lips of knowledge* (a good understanding to guide the lips and a good elocution to diffuse the knowledge) are to be preferred far before gold, and pearl, and rubies; for, 1. They are more rare in themselves, more scarce and hard to be got. *There is gold* in many a man's pocket that has no grace in

his heart. In Solomon's time there was plenty of gold (1 Kings x. 21) and *abundance of rubies;* every body wore them; they were to be bought in every town. But wisdom is a rare thing, a precious jewel; few have it so as to do good with it, nor is it to be purchased of the merchants. 2. They are more enriching to us and more adorning. They make us rich towards God, rich in good works, 1 Tim. ii. 9, 10. Most people are fond of gold, and a ruby or two will not serve, they must have a multitude of them, a cabinet of jewels; but he that has the lips of knowledge despises these, because he knows and possesses better things.

16 Take his garment that is surety *for* a stranger: and take a pledge of him for a strange woman.

Two sorts of persons are here spoken of that are ruining their own estates, and will be beggars shortly, and therefore are not to be trusted without good security:—1. Those that will be bound for any body that will ask them, that entangle themselves in rash suretiship to oblige their idle companions; they will break at last, nay, they cannot hold out long; these waste by wholesale. 2. Those that are in league with abandoned women, that treat them, and court them, and keep company with them. They will be beggars in a little time; never give them credit without a good pledge. Strange women have strange ways of impoverishing men to enrich themselves.

17 Bread of deceit *is* sweet to a man; but afterwards his mouth shall be filled with gravel.

Note, 1. Sin may possibly be pleasant in the commission: *Bread of deceit,* wealth gotten by fraud, by lying and oppression, may be *sweet to a man,* and the more sweet for its being ill-gotten, such pleasure does the carnal mind take in the success of its wicked projects. All the pleasures and profits of sin are *bread of deceit.* They are stolen, for they are forbidden fruit; and they will deceive men, for they are not what they promise. For a time, however, they are *rolled under the tongue as a sweet morsel,* and the sinner blesses himself in them. But, 2. It will be bitter in the reflection. Afterwards the sinner's *mouth shall be filled with gravel.* When his conscience is awakened, when he sees himself cheated, and becomes apprehensive of the wrath of God against him for his sin, how painful and uneasy then is the thought of it! The pleasures of sin are but for a season, and are succeeded with sorrows. Some nations have punished malefactors by mingling gravel with their bread.

18 *Every* purpose is established by counsel: and with good advice make war.

Note, 1. It is good in every thing to act with deliberation, and to consult with ourselves at least, and, in matters of moment, with our friends too, before we determine, but especially to ask counsel of God, and beg direction from him, and observe the guidance of his eye. This is the way to have both our minds and our purposes established, and to succeed well in our affairs; whereas what is done hastily and with precipitation is repented of at leisure. Take time, and you will have done the sooner. *Deliberandum est diu, quod statuendum est semel—A final decision should be preceded by mature deliberation.* 2. It is especially our wisdom to be cautious in making war. Consider, and take advice, whether the war should be begun or no, whether it be just, whether it be prudent, whether we be a match for the enemy, and able to carry it on when it is too late to retreat (Luke xiv. 31); and, when it is begun, consider how and by what arts it may be prosecuted, for management is as necessary as courage. Going to law is a kind of going to war, and therefore must be done with good advice, Prov. xxv. 8. The rule among the Romans was *nec sequi bellum, nec fugere—neither to urge war nor yet to shun it.*

19 He that goeth about *as* a talebearer revealeth secrets: therefore meddle not with him that flattereth with his lips.

Two sorts of people are dangerous to be conversed with:—1. Tale-bearers, though they are commonly flatterers, and by fair speeches insinuate themselves into men's acquaintance. Those are unprincipled people that go about carrying stories, that make mischief among neighbours and relations, that sow in the minds of people jealousies of their governors, of their ministers, and of one another, that reveal secrets which they are entrusted with or which by unfair means they come to the knowledge of, or, under pretence of guessing at men's thoughts and intentions, tell that of them which is really false. "Be not familiar with such; do not give them the hearing when they tell their tales and reveal secrets, for you may be sure that they will betray your secrets too and tell tales of you." 2. Flatterers, for they are commonly tale-bearers. If a man fawn upon you, compliment and commend you, suspect him to have some design upon you, and stand upon your guard; he would pick that out of you which will serve him to make a story of to somebody else to your prejudice; therefore *meddle not with him that flatters with his lips.* Those too dearly love, and too dearly buy, their own praise, that will put confidence in a man and trust him with a secret or business because he flatters them.

20 Whoso curseth his father or his mother, his lamp shall be put out in obscure darkness.

Here is, 1. An undutiful child become very wicked by degrees. He began with despis-

ing his father and mother, slighting their instructions, disobeying their commands, and raging at their rebukes, but at length he arrives at such a pitch of impudence and impiety as to curse them, to give them scurrilous and opprobrious language, and to wish mischief to those who were the instruments of his being and have taken so much care and pains about him, and this in defiance of God and his law, which has made this a capital crime (Exod. xxi. 17, Matt. xv. 4), and in violation of all the bonds of duty, natural affection, and gratitude. 2. An undutiful child become very miserable at last: *His lamp shall be put out in obscure darkness;* all his honour shall be laid in the dust, and he shall for ever lose his reputation. Let him never expect any peace or comfort in his own mind, no, nor to prosper in this world. His days shall be shortened, and the lamp of his life extinguished, according to the reverse of the promise in the fifth commandment. His family shall be cut off and his posterity be a curse to him. And it will be his eternal ruin; the lamp of his happiness shall *be put out in the blackness of darkness* (so the word is), even that which is *for ever,* Jude 13, Matt. xxii. 13.

21 An inheritance *may be* gotten hastily at the beginning; but the end thereof shall not be blessed.

Note, 1. It is possible that an estate may be suddenly raised. There are those who will be rich, by right or wrong, who make no conscience of what they say or do if they can but get money by it, who, when it is in their power, will cheat their own father, and who sordidly spare and hoard up what they get, grudging themselves and their families food convenient and thinking all lost but what they buy land with or put out to interest. By such ways as these a man may grow rich, may grow very rich, in a little time, at his first setting out. 2. An estate that is suddenly raised is often as suddenly ruined. It was raised hastily, but, not being raised honestly, it proves *soon ripe and soon rotten: The end thereof shall not be blessed* of God, and, if he do not bless it, it can neither be comfortable nor of any continuance; so that he who got it at the end will be a fool. He had better have taken time and built firmly.

22 Say not thou, I will recompense evil; *but* wait on the LORD, and he shall save thee.

Those that live in this world must expect to have injuries done them, affronts given them, and trouble wrongfully created them, for we dwell among briers. Now here we are told what to do when we have wrong done us. 1. We must not avenge ourselves, no, nor so much as think of revenge, or design it: " *Say not thou,* no, not in thy heart, *I will recompense evil* for evil. Do not please thyself with the thought that some time or other thou shalt have an opportunity of being quits with him. Do not wish revenge, or hope for it, much less resolve upon it, no, not when the injury is fresh and the resentment of it most deep. Never say that thou wilt do a thing which thou canst not in faith pray to God to assist thee in, and *that* thou canst not do in meditating revenge." 2. We must refer ourselves to God, and leave it to him to plead our cause, to maintain our right, and reckon with those that do us wrong in such a way and manner as he thinks fit and in his own due time: "*Wait on the Lord,* attend his pleasure, acquiesce in his will, and he does not say that he will punish him that has injured thee (instead of desiring that thou must forgive him and pray for him), but *he will save thee,* and that is enough. He will protect thee, so that thy passing by one injury shall not (as is commonly feared) expose thee to another; nay, he will recompense good to thee, to balance thy trouble and encourage thy patience," as David hoped, when Shimei cursed him, 2 Sam. xvi. 12.

23 Divers weights *are* an abomination unto the LORD; and a false balance *is* not good.

This is to the same purport with what was said *v.* 10. 1. It is here repeated, because it is a sin that God doubly hates (as lying, which is of the same nature with this sin, is mentioned twice among the seven things that God hates, *ch.* vi. 17, 19), and because it was probably a sin very much practised at that time in Israel, and therefore made light of as if there were no harm in it, under pretence that, being commonly used, there was no trading without it. 2. It is here added, *A false balance is not good,* to intimate that it is not only abominable to God, but unprofitable to the sinner himself; there is really no good to be got by it, no, not a good bargain, for a bargain made by fraud will prove a losing bargain in the end.

24 Man's goings *are* of the LORD; how can a man then understand his own way?

We are here taught that in all our affairs, 1. We have a necessary and constant dependence upon God. All our natural actions depend upon his providence, all our spiritual actions upon his grace. The best man is no better than God makes him; and every creature is that to us which it is the will of God that it should be. Our enterprises succeed, not as we desire and design, but as God directs and disposes. The goings even of a strong man (so the word signifies) *are of the Lord,* for his strength is weakness without God, nor is the battle always to the strong. 2. We have no foresight of future events, and therefore know not how to forecast for them: *How can a man understand his own way?* How can he tell what will befal him, since God's counsels concerning him are secret, and therefore how can he of himself

contrive what to do without divine direction? We so little understand our own way that we know not what is good for ourselves, and therefore we must make a virtue of necessity, and commit our way unto the Lord, in whose hand it is, follow the guidance and submit to the disposal of Providence.

25 *It is* a snare to the man *who* devoureth *that which is* holy, and after vows to make enquiry.

Two things, by which God is greatly affronted, men are here said to be ensnared by, and entangled not only in guilt, but in trouble and ruin at length:—1. Sacrilege, men's alienating holy things and converting them to their own use, which is here called *devouring* them. What is devoted in any way to the service and honour of God, for the support of religion and divine worship or the relief of the poor, ought to be conscientiously preserved to the purposes designed; and those that directly or indirectly embezzle it, or defeat the purpose for which it was given, will have a great deal to answer for. *Will a man rob God in tithes and offerings?* Mal. iii. 8. Those that hurry over religious offices (their praying and preaching) and huddle them up in haste, as being impatient to get done, may be said to *devour that which is holy.* 2. Covenant-breaking. *It is a snare to a man, after* he has made *vows* to God, *to enquire* how he may evade them or get them dispensed with, and to contrive excuses for the violating of them, If the matter of them was doubtful, and the expressions were ambiguous, that was his fault; he should have made them with more caution and consideration, for it will involve his conscience (if it be tender) in great perplexities, if he be to enquire concerning them afterwards (Eccl. v. 6); for, when we have opened our mouth to the Lord, it is too late to think of going back, Acts v. 4.

26 A wise king scattereth the wicked, and bringeth the wheel over them.

See here, 1. What is the business of magistrates. They are to be a terror to evil-doers. They must *scatter the wicked,* who are linked in confederacies to assist and embolden one another in doing mischief; and there is no doing this but by *bringing the wheel over them,* that is, putting the laws in execution against them, crushing their power and quashing their projects. Severity must sometimes be used to rid the country of those that are openly vicious and mischievous, debauched and debauching. 2. What is the qualification of magistrates, which is necessary in order to this. They have need to be both pious and prudent, for it is the wise king, who is both religious and discreet, that is likely to effect the suppression of vice and reformation of manners.

27 The spirit of man *is* the candle of the LORD, searching all the inward parts of the belly.

We have here the dignity of the soul, the great soul of man, that light which lighteth every man. 1. It is a divine light; it is the *candle of the Lord*, a candle of his lighting, for it is *the inspiration of the Almighty* that *gives us understanding.* He *forms the spirit of man within him.* It is after the image of God that man is created in knowledge. Conscience, that noble faculty, is God's deputy in the soul; it is a candle not only lighted by him, but lighted for him. The Father of spirits is therefore called the *Father of lights.* 2. It is a discovering light. By the help of reason we come to know men, to judge of their characters, and dive into their designs; by the help of conscience we come to know ourselves. The spirit of a man has a self-consciousness (1 Cor. ii. 11); it searches into the dispositions and affections of the soul, praises what is good, condemns what is otherwise, and judges of the thoughts and intents of the heart. This is the office, this the power, of conscience, which we are therefore concerned to get rightly informed and to keep void of offence.

28 Mercy and truth preserve the king: and his throne is upholden by mercy.

Here we have, 1. The virtues of a good king. Those are *mercy and truth*, especially mercy, for that is mentioned twice here. He must be strictly faithful to his word, must be sincere, and abhor all dissimulation, must religiously discharge all the trusts reposed in him, must support and countenance truth. He must likewise rule with clemency, and by all acts of compassion gain the affections of his people. *Mercy and truth* are the glories of God's throne, and kings are called *gods.* 2. The advantages he gains thereby. These virtues will preserve his person and support his government, will make him easy and safe, beloved by his own people and feared by his enemies, if it be possible that he should have any.

29 The glory of young men *is* their strength: and the beauty of old men *is* the gray head.

This shows that both young and old have their advantages, and therefore must each of them be, according to their capacities, serviceable to the public, and neither of them despise nor envy the other. 1. Let not old people despise the young, for they are strong and fit for action, able to go through business, and break through difficulties, which the aged and weak cannot grapple with. The *glory of young men is their strength,* provided they use it well (in the service of God and their country, not of their lusts), and that they be not proud of it nor trust to it. 2. Let not young people despise the old, for they are grave, and fit for counsel, and, though they have not the strength that young men have, yet they have more wisdom and

experience. *Juniores ad labores, seniores ad honores—Labour is for the young, honour for the aged.* God has put honour upon the old man; for his *gray head* is his beauty. See Dan. vii. 9.

30 The blueness of a wound cleanseth away evil: so *do* stripes the inward parts of the belly.

Note, 1. Many need severe rebukes. Some children are so obstinate that their parents can do no good with them without sharp correction; some criminals must feel the rigour of the law and public justice; gentle methods will not work upon them; they must be beaten black and blue. And the wise God sees that his own children sometimes need very sharp afflictions. 2. Severe rebukes sometimes do a great deal of good, as corrosives contribute to the cure of a wound, eating out the proud flesh. The rod drives out even that foolishness which was bound up in the heart, and cleanses away the evil there. 3. Frequently those that most need severe rebukes can worst bear them. Such is the corruption of nature that men are as loth to be rebuked sharply for their sins as to be beaten till their bones ache. *Correction is grievous to him that forsakes the way,* and yet it is good for him, Heb. xii. 11.

CHAP. XXI.

THE king's heart *is* in the hand of the Lord, *as* the rivers of water: he turneth it whithersoever he will.

Note, 1. Even the *hearts* of men are in God's hand, and not only their *goings,* as he had said, *ch.* xx. 24. God can change men's minds, can, by a powerful insensible operation upon their spirits, turn them from that which they seemed most intent upon, and incline them to that which they seemed most averse to, as the husbandman, by canals and gutters, turns the water through his grounds as he pleases, which does not alter the nature of the water, nor put any force upon it, any more than God's providence does upon the native freedom of man's will, but directs the course of it to serve his own purpose. 2. Even kings' hearts are so, notwithstanding their powers and prerogatives, as much as the hearts of common persons. The *hearts of kings are unsearchable* to us, much more unmanageable by us; as they have their *arcana imperii—state secrets,* so they have the prerogatives of their crown; but the great God has them not only under his eye, but in his hand. Kings are what he makes them. Those that are most absolute are under God's government; he *puts things into their hearts,* Rev. xvii. 17; Ezra vii. 27.

2 Every way of a man *is* right in his own eyes: but the Lord pondereth the hearts.

Note, 1. We are all apt to be partial in judging of ourselves and our own actions, and to think too favourably of our own character, as if there were nothing amiss in it: *Every way of a man,* even his by-way, *is right in his own eyes.* The proud heart is very ingenious in putting a fair face upon a foul matter, and in making that appear right to itself which is far from being so, to stop the mouth of conscience. 2. We are sure that the judgment of God concerning us is according to truth. Whatever our judgment is concerning ourselves, *the Lord ponders the heart.* God looks at the heart, and judges of men according to that, of their actions according to their principles and intentions; and his judgment of that is as exact as ours is of that which we ponder most, and more so; he weighs it in an unerring balance, *ch.* xvi. 2.

3 To do justice and judgment *is* more acceptable to the LORD than sacrifice.

Here, 1. It is implied that many deceive themselves with a conceit that, if they offer sacrifice, that will excuse them from doing justice, and will procure them a dispensation for their unrighteousness; and this makes their way *seem right, v.* 2. *We have fasted,* Isa. lviii. 3. *I have peace-offerings with me,* Prov. vii. 14. 2. It is plainly declared that living a good life (doing justly and loving mercy) is more pleasing to God than the most pompous and expensive instances of devotion. Sacrifices were of divine institution, and were acceptable to God if they were offered in faith and with repentance, otherwise not, Is. i. 11, &c. But even then moral duties were preferred before them (1 Sam. xv. 22), which intimates that their excellency was not innate nor the obligation to them perpetual, Mic. vi. 6—8. Much of religion lies in doing judgment and justice from a principle of duty to God, contempt of the world, and love to our neighbour; and this is more pleasing to God than all burnt-offerings and sacrifices, Mark xii. 33.

4 A high look, and a proud heart, *and* the ploughing of the wicked, *is* sin.

This may be taken as showing us, 1. The marks of a wicked man. He that has a *high look and a proud heart,* that carries himself insolently and scornfully towards both God and man, and that is always ploughing and plotting, designing and devising some mischief or other, is indeed a wicked man. *The light of the wicked is sin.* Sin is *the pride, the ambition, the glory and joy,* and *the business of wicked men.* 2. The miseries of a wicked man. His raised expectations, his high designs, and most elaborate contrivances and projects, are sin to him; he contracts guilt in them and so prepares trouble for himself. The very business of all wicked men, as well as their pleasure, is nothing but sin; so Bishop Patrick. They do all to serve their lusts, and have no regard to the glory of God in it, and therefore *their ploughing is*

910

sin, and no marvel when their sacrificing is so, *ch.* xv. 8.

5 The thoughts of the diligent *tend* only to plenteousness; but of every one *that is* hasty only to want.

Here is, 1. The way to be rich. If we would live plentifully and comfortably in the world, we must be diligent in our business, and not shrink from the toil and trouble of it, but prosecute it closely, improving all advantages and opportunities for it, and doing what we do with all our might; yet we must not be hasty in it, nor hurry ourselves and others with it, but keep doing fair and softly, which, we say, goes far in a day. With diligence there must be contrivance. The *thoughts of the diligent* are as necessary as the hand of the diligent. Forecast is as good as work. Seest thou a man thus prudent and diligent? He will have enough to live on. 2. The way to be poor. Those that are hasty, that are rash and inconsiderate in their affairs, and will not take time to think, that are greedy of gain, by right or wrong, and make haste to be rich by unjust practices or unwise projects, are in the ready road to poverty. Their thoughts and contrivances, by which they hope to raise themselves, will ruin them.

6 The getting of treasures by a lying tongue *is* a vanity tossed to and fro of them that seek death.

This shows the folly of those that hope to enrich themselves by dishonest practices, by oppressing and over-reaching those with whom they deal, by false-witness-bearing, or by fraudulent contracts, of those that make no scruple of lying when there is any thing to be got by it. They may perhaps heap up treasures by these means, that which they make their treasure; but, 1. They will not meet with the satisfaction they expect. It is a *vanity tossed to and fro;* it will be disappointment and vexation of spirit to them; they will not have the comfort of it, nor can they put any confidence in it, but will be perpetually uneasy. It will be *tossed to and fro* by their own consciences, and by the censures of men; let them expect to be in a constant hurry. 2. They will meet with the destruction they do not expect. While they are seeking wealth by such unlawful practices they are really seeking death; they lay themselves open to the envy and ill-will of men by the treasures they get, and to the wrath and curse of God by the lying tongue wherewith they get them, which he will make to fall upon themselves and sink them to hell.

7 The robbery of the wicked shall destroy them; because they refuse to do judgment.

See here, 1. The nature of injustice. Getting money by lying (*v.* 6) is no better than downright robbery. Cheating is stealing; you might as well pick a man's pocket as impose upon him by a lie in making a bargain, which he had no fence against but by not believing you; and it will be no excuse from the guilt of robbery to say that he might choose whether he would believe you, for that is a debt we should owe to all men. 2. The cause of injustice. Men *refuse to do judgment;* they will not render to all their due, but withhold it, and omissions make way for commissions; they come at length to robbery itself. Those that refuse to do justice will choose to do wrong. 3. The effect of injustice; it will return upon the sinner's own head. The robbery of the wicked will *terrify them* (so some); their consciences will be filled with horror and amazement, will cut them, will *saw them asunder* (so others); it will *destroy them* here and for ever, therefore he had said (*v.* 6), *They seek death.*

8 The way of man *is* froward and strange: but *as for* the pure, his work *is* right.

This shows that as men are so is their way. 1. Evil men have evil ways. If the man be *froward*, his way also is *strange;* and this is the way of most men, such is the general corruption of mankind. *They have all gone aside* (Ps. xiv. 2, 3); all flesh have perverted their way. But the froward man, the man of deceit, that acts by craft and trick in all he does, his way is strange, contrary to all the rules of honour and honesty. It is strange, for you know not where to find him nor when you have him; it is strange, for it is alienated from all good and estranges men from God and his favour. It is what he beholds afar off, and so do all honest men. 2. Men that are pure are proved to be such by their work, for it *is right,* it is just and regular; and they are accepted of God and approved of men. The way of mankind in their apostasy is froward and strange; but as for the pure, those that by the grace of God are recovered out of that state, of which there is here and there one, *their work is right,* as Noah's was in the old world, Gen. vii. 1.

9 *It is* better to dwell in a corner of the housetop, than with a brawling woman in a wide house.

See here, 1. What a great affliction it is to a man to have a brawling scolding woman for his wife, who upon every occasion, and often upon no occasion, breaks out into a passion, and chides either him or those about her, is fretful to herself and furious to her children and servants, and, in both, vexatious to her husband. If a man has a wide house, spacious and pompous, this will embitter the comfort of it to him—*a house of society* (so the word is), in which a man may be sociable, and entertain his friends; this will make both him and his house unsociable, and unfit for the enjoyments of true friendship. It makes a man ashamed of his choice and his management, and disturbs his company. 2 What many a man is forced to do

under such an affliction. He cannot keep up his authority. He finds it to no purpose to contradict the most unreasonable passion, for it is unruly and rages so much the more; and his wisdom and grace will not suffer him to render railing for railing, nor his conjugal affection to use any severity, and therefore he finds it his best way to retire *into a corner of the house-top,* and sit alone there, out of the hearing of her clamour; and if he employ himself well there, as he may do, it is the wisest course he can take. Better do so than quit the house, and go into bad company, for diversion, as many, who, like Adam, make their wife's sin the excuse of their own.

10 The soul of the wicked desireth evil: his neighbour findeth no favour in his eyes.

See here the character of a very wicked man. 1. The strong inclination he has to do mischief. His very *soul desires evil,* desires that evil may be done and that he may have the pleasure, not only of seeing it, but of having a hand in it. The root of wickedness lies in the soul; the desire that men have to do evil, that is the lust which conceives and brings forth sin. 2. The strong aversion he has to do good: *His neighbour,* his friend, his nearest relation, *finds no favour in his eyes,* cannot gain from him the least kindness, though he be in the greatest need of it. And, when he is in the pursuit of the evil his heart is so much upon, he will spare no man that stands in his way; his next neighbour shall be used no better than a stranger, than an enemy.

11 When the scorner is punished, the simple is made wise: and when the wise is instructed, he receiveth knowledge.

This we had before (*ch.* xix. 25), and it shows that there are two ways by which the simple may be made wise:—1. By the punishments that are inflicted on those that are incorrigibly wicked. Let the law be executed upon a scorner, and even he that is simple will be awakened and alarmed by it, and will discern, more than he did, the evil of sin, and will take warning by it and take heed. 2. By the instructions that are given to those that are wise and willing to be taught: *When the wise is instructed* by the preaching of the word *he* (not only the wise himself, but the simple that stands by) *receives knowledge.* It is no injustice at all to take a good lesson to ourselves which was designed for another.

12 The righteous *man* wisely considereth the house of the wicked: *but* God overthroweth the wicked for *their* wickedness.

1. As we read this verse, it shows the reason why good men, when they come to understand things aright, will not envy the prosperity of evil-doers. When they see *the*

house of the wicked, how full it is perhaps of all the good things of this life, they are tempted to envy; but when they *wisely consider* it, when they look upon it with an eye of faith, when they see *God overthrowing the wicked for their wickedness,* that there is a curse upon their habitation which will certainly be the ruin of it ere long, they see more reason to despise them, or pity them, than to fear or envy them. 2. Some give another sense of it: *The righteous man* (the judge or magistrate, that is entrusted with the execution of justice, and the preservation of public peace) *examines the house of the wicked,* searches it for arms or for stolen goods, makes a diligent enquiry concerning his family and the characters of those about him, that he may by his power *overthrow the wicked for their wickedness* and prevent their doing any further mischief, that he may fire the nests where the birds of prey are harboured or the unclean birds.

13 Whoso stoppeth his ears at the cry of the poor, he also shall cry himself, but shall not be heard.

Here we have the description and doom of an uncharitable man. 1. His description: He *stops his ears at the cry of the poor,* at the cry of their wants and miseries (he resolves to take no cognizance of them), at the cry of their requests and supplications—he resolves he will not so much as give them the hearing, turns them away from his door, and forbids them to come near him, or, if he cannot avoid hearing them, he will not heed them, nor be moved by their complaints, nor be prevailed with by their importunities; he *shuts up the bowels of his compassion,* and that is equivalent to the stopping of his ears, Acts vii. 57. 2. His doom. He shall himself be reduced to straits, which will make him *cry,* and then *he shall not be heard.* Men will not hear him, but reward him as he has rewarded others. God will not hear him; for he that *showed no mercy shall have judgment without mercy* (Jam. ii. 13), and he that on earth denied a crumb of bread in hell was denied a drop of water. God will be deaf to the prayers of those who are deaf to the cries of the poor, which, if they be not heard by us, will be heard against us, Exod. xxii. 23.

14 A gift in secret pacifieth anger: and a reward in the bosom strong wrath.

Here is, 1. The power that is commonly found to be in gifts. Nothing is more violent than *anger.* O the force of *strong wrath!* And yet a handsome present, prudently managed, will turn away some men's wrath when it seemed implacable, and disarm the keenest and most passionate resentments. Covetousness is commonly a master-sin and has, the command of other lusts. *Pecuniæ obediunt omnia—Money commands all things.* Thus Jacob pacified Esau and Abigail David.

2. The policy that is commonly used in giving and receiving bribes. It must be *a gift in secret and a reward in the bosom,* for he that takes it would not be thought to covet it, nor known to receive it, nor would he willingly be beholden to him whom he has been offended with; but, if it be done privately, all is well. No man should be too open in giving any gift, nor boast of the presents he sends; but, if it be a bribe to pervert justice, that is so scandalous that those who are fond of it are ashamed of it.

15 *It is* joy to the just to do judgment: but destruction *shall be* to the workers of iniquity.

Note, 1. It is a pleasure and satisfaction to good men both to see justice administered by the government they live under, right taking place and iniquity suppressed, and also to practise it themselves, according as their sphere is. They not only do justice, but do it with pleasure, not only for fear of shame, but for love of virtue. 2. It is a terror to wicked men to see the laws put in execution against vice and profaneness. It is destruction to them; as it is also a vexation to them to be forced, either for the support of their credit or for fear of punishment, *to do judgment* themselves. Or, if we take it as we read it, the meaning is, There is true pleasure in the practice of religion, but certain destruction at the end of all vicious courses.

16 The man that wandereth out of the way of understanding shall remain in the congregation of the dead.

Here is, 1. The sinner upon his ramble: He *wanders out of the way of understanding,* and when once he has left that good way he wanders endlessly. The way of religion is *the way of understanding;* those that are not truly pious are not truly intelligent; those *that wander out of this way* break the hedge which God has set, and follow the conduct of the world and the flesh; and they go astray like lost sheep. 2. The sinner at his rest, or rather his ruin: He *shall remain (quiescet—he shall rest,* but not *in pace—in peace) in the congregation of the giants,* the sinners of the old world, that were swept away by the deluge; to that destruction the damnation of sinners is compared, as sometimes to the destruction of Sodom, when they are said to have their portion in fire and brimstone. Or *in the congregation of the damned,* that are under the power of the second death. There is a vast congregation of damned sinners, bound in bundles for the fire, and in that those shall remain, remain for ever, who are shut out from the congregation of the righteous. He that forsakes the way to heaven, if he return not to it, will certainly sink into the depths of hell.

17 He that loveth pleasure *shall be* a poor man: he that loveth wine and oil shall not be rich.

Here is an argument against a voluptuous luxurious life, taken from the ruin it brings upon men's temporal interests. Here is, 1. The description of an epicure: *He loves pleasure.* God allows us to use the delights of sense soberly and temperately, *wine to make glad the heart* and put vigour into the spirits, and *oil to make the face to shine* and beautify the countenance; but he that loves these, that sets his heart upon them, covets them earnestly, is solicitous to have all the delights of sense wound up to the height of pleasure-ableness, is impatient of every thing that crosses him in his pleasures, relishes these as the best pleasures, and has his mouth by them put out of taste for spiritual delights, he is an epicure, 2 Tim. iii. 4. 2. The punishment of an epicure in this world: *He shall be a poor man:* for the lusts of sensuality are not maintained but at a great expense, and there are instances of those who want necessaries, and live upon alms, who once could not live without dainties and varieties. Many a beau becomes a beggar.

18 The wicked *shall be* a ransom for the righteous, and the transgressor for the upright.

This intimates, 1. What should be done by the justice of men: *The wicked,* that are the troublers of a land, ought to be punished, for the preventing and turning away of those national judgments which otherwise will be inflicted and in which even the righteous are many times involved. Thus when Achan was stoned he was *a ransom for the* camp of *righteous* Israel; and the seven sons of Saul, when they were hanged, were *a ransom for the* kingdom of *righteous* David. 2. What is often done by the providence of God: *The righteous is delivered out of trouble, and the wicked comes in his stead,* and so seems as if he were a *ransom for him,* ch. xi. 8. God will rather leave many wicked people to be cut off than abandon his own people. *I will give men for thee,* Isa. xliii. 3, 4.

19 *It is* better to dwell in the wilderness, than with a contentious and an angry woman.

Note, 1. Unbridled passions embitter and spoil the comfort of all relations. A peevish angry wife makes her husband's life uneasy, to whom she should be a comfort and a meet help. Those cannot dwell in peace and happiness that cannot dwell in peace and love. Even those that are one flesh, if they be not withal one spirit, have no joy of their union. 2. It is better to have no company than bad company. The wife of thy covenant is thy companion, and yet, if she be peevish and provoking, *it is better to dwell in* a solitary *wilderness,* exposed to wind and weather, than in company with her. A man may better enjoy God and himself in a wilderness than among quarrelsome relations and neighbours. See *v.* 9.

20 *There is* treasure to be desired and oil in the dwelling of the wise; but a foolish man spendeth it up.

Note, 1. Those that are wise will increase what they have and live plentifully; their wisdom will teach them to proportion their expenses to their income and to lay up for hereafter; so that *there is a treasure* of things *to be desired,* and as much as needs be desired, a good stock of all things convenient, laid up in season, and particularly of *oil,* one of the staple commodities of Canaan, Deut. viii. 8. This is *in the habitation,* or cottage, *of the wise;* and it is better to have an old-fashioned house, and have it well furnished, than a fine modern one, with sorry housekeeping. God blesses the endeavours of the wise and then their houses are replenished. 2. Those that are foolish will mispend what they have upon their lusts, and so bring the stock they had to nothing. Those manage wretchedly that are in haste to spend what they have, but not in care which way to get more. Foolish children spend what their wise parents had laid up. *One sinner destroys much good,* as the prodigal son.

21 He that followeth after righteousness and mercy findeth life, righteousness, and honour.

See here, 1. What it is to make religion our business; it is to *follow after righteousness and mercy,* not to content ourselves with easy performances, but to do our duty with the utmost care and pains, as those that are pressing forward and in fear of coming short. We must both do justly and love mercy, and must proceed and persevere therein; and, though we cannot attain to perfection, yet it will be a comfort to us if we aim at it and follow after it. 2. What will be the advantage of doing so: Those that do *follow after righteousness* shall *find righteousness;* God will give them grace to do good, and they shall have the pleasure and comfort of doing it; those that make conscience of being just to others shall be justly dealt with by others and others shall be kind to them. The Jews *followed after righteousness,* and did not find it, because they sought amiss, Rom. ix. 31 Otherwise, *Seek and you shall find,* and with it shall find both *life and honour,* everlasting life and honour, the *crown of righteousness.*

22 A wise *man* scaleth the city of the mighty, and casteth down the strength of the confidence thereof.

Note, 1. Those that have power are apt to promise themselves great things from their power. *The city of the mighty* thinks itself impregnable, and therefore its strength is *the confidence thereof,* what it boasts of and trusts in, bidding defiance to danger. 2. Those that have wisdom, though they are so modest as not to promise much, often perform great things, even against those that are so confident of their strength, by their wisdom.

Good conduct will go far even against great force; and a stratagem, well managed, may effectually *scale the city of the mighty and cast down the strength* it had such a confidence in. *A wise man* will gain upon the affections of people and conquer them by strength of reason, which is a more noble conquest than that obtained by strength of arms. Those that understand their interest will willingly submit themselves to a wise and good man, and the strongest walls shall not hold out against him.

23 Whoso keepeth his mouth and his tongue keepeth his soul from troubles.

Note, 1. It is our great concern to keep our souls from straits, from being entangled in snares and perplexities, and disquieted with troubles, that we may preserve the possession and enjoyment of ourselves and that our souls may be in frame for the service of God. 2. Those that would keep their souls must keep a watch before the door of their lips, must *keep the mouth* by temperance, that no forbidden fruit go into it, no stolen waters, that nothing be eaten or drunk to excess; they must *keep the tongue* also, that no forbidden word go out of the door of the lips, no corrupt communication. By a constant watchfulness over our words we shall prevent abundance of mischiefs which an ungoverned tongue runs men into. Keep thy heart, and that will keep thy tongue from sin; keep thy tongue, and that will keep thy heart from trouble.

24 Proud *and* haughty scorner *is* his name, who dealeth in proud wrath.

See here the mischief of pride and haughtiness. 1. It exposes men to sin; it makes them passionate, and kindles in them the fire of *proud wrath.* They are continually dealing in it, as if it were their trade to be angry, and they had nothing so much to do as to barter passions and exchange bitter words. Most of the wrath that inflames the spirits and societies of men is *proud wrath.* Men cannot bear the least slight, nor in any thing to be crossed or contradicted, but they are out of humour, nay, in a heat, immediately. It likewise makes them scornful when they are angry, very abusive with their tongues, insolent towards those above them and imperious towards all about them. *Only by pride* comes all this. 2. It exposes men to shame. They get a bad name by it, and every one calls them *proud and haughty scorners,* and therefore nobody cares for having any thing to do with them. If men would but consult their reputation a little and the credit of their profession, which suffers with it, they would not indulge their pride and passion as they do.

25 The desire of the slothful killeth him; for his hands refuse to labour.

26 He coveteth greedily all the day

914

long: but the righteous giveth and spareth not.

Here we have, 1. The miseries of the slothful, whose *hands refuse to labour* in an honest calling, by which they might get an honest livelihood. They are as fit for labour as other men, and business offers itself, to which they might lay their hands and apply their minds, but they will not; herein they fondly think they do well for themselves, see *ch.* xxvi. 16. *Soul, take thy ease.* But really they are enemies to themselves; for, besides that their slothfulness starves them, depriving them of their necessary supports, their desires at the same time stab them. Though their hands refuse to labour, their hearts cease not to covet riches, and pleasures, and honours, which yet cannot be obtained without labour. Their desires are impetuous and insatiable; they *covet greedily all the day long,* and cry, *Give, give;* they expect every body should do for them, though they will do nothing for themselves, much less for any body else. Now these *desires kill them;* they are a perpetual vexation to them, fret them to death, and perhaps put them upon such dangerous courses for the satisfying of their craving lusts as hasten them to an untimely end. Many that must have money with which to make provision for the flesh, and would not be at the pains to get it honestly, have turned highwaymen, and that has killed them. Those that are slothful in the affairs of their souls, and yet have desires towards that which would be the happiness of their souls, those *desires kill them,* will aggravate their condemnation and be witnesses against them that they were convinced of the worth of spiritual blessings, but refused to be at the pains that were necessary to the obtaining of them. 2. The honours of the honest and diligent. The righteous and industrious have their desires satisfied, and enjoy not only that satisfaction, but the further satisfaction of doing good to others. The slothful are always craving and gaping to receive, *but the righteous* are always full and contriving to give; and *it is more blessed to give than to receive.* They *give and spare not,* give liberally and upbraid not; they *give a portion to seven and also to eight,* and do not spare for fear of wanting.

27 The sacrifice of the wicked *is* abomination: how much more, *when* he bringeth it with a wicked mind?

Sacrifices were of divine institution; and when they were offered in faith, and with repentance and reformation, God was greatly honoured by them and well-pleased in them. But they were often not only unacceptable, but an *abomination,* to God, and he declared so, which was an indication both that they were not required for their own sakes and that there were better things, and more effectual, in reserve, when sacrifice and offering should be done away. They were an *abomination,* 1. When they were brought by wicked men, who did not, according to the true intent and meaning of sacrificing, repent of their sins, mortify their lusts, and amend their lives. Cain brought his offering. Even wicked men may be found in the external performances of religious worship. Many can freely give God their beasts, their lips, their knees, who would not give him their hearts; the Pharisees gave alms. But when the person is an *abomination,* as every wicked man is to God, the performance cannot but be so; *even when he brings it diligently;* so some read the latter part of the verse. Though their offerings are continually before God (Ps. l. 8), yet they are an abomination to him. 2. *Much more when* they were brought with *wicked minds,* when their sacrifices were made, not only consistent with, but serviceable to, their wickedness, as Absalom's vow, Jezebel's fast, and the Pharisees' long prayers. When men make a show of devotion, that they may the more easily and effectually compass some covetous or malicious design, when holiness is pretended, but some wickedness intended, then especially the performance is an abomination, Isa. lxvi. 5.

28 A false witness shall perish: but the man that heareth speaketh constantly.

Here is, 1. The doom of *a false witness.* He who, for favour to one side or malice to the other, gives in a false evidence, or makes an affidavit of that which he knows to be false, or at least does not know to be true, if it be discovered, his reputation will be ruined. A man may tell ⁊ lie perhaps in his haste; but he that gives in a false testimony does it with deliberation and solemnity, and it cannot but be a presumptuous sin, and a forfeiture of man's credit. But, though it should not be discovered, he himself shall be ruined; the vengeance he imprecated upon himself, when he took the false oath, will come upon him. 2. The praise of him that is conscientious: He *who hears* (that is, obeys) the command of God, which is to *speak every man truth with his neighbour,* he who testifies nothing but what he has heard and knows to be true, *speaks constantly* (that is, consistently with himself); he is always in the same story; he speaks *in finem—to the end;* people will give credit to him and hear him out; he speaks unto victory; he carries the cause, which the *false witness* shall lose; he shall speak to eternity. What is true is true eternally. *The lip of truth is established for ever.*

29 A wicked man hardeneth his face: but *as for* the upright, he directeth his way.

Here is, 1. The presumption and impudence of a wicked man: He *hardens his face* —brazens it, that he may not blush—steels it, that he may not tremble when he commits the greatest crimes; he bids defiance to the terrors of the law and the checks of his own conscience, the reproofs of the word and the rebukes of Providence; he will have his way and nothing shall hinder him, Isa. lvii. 17. 2. The caution and circumspection of a good man: *As for the upright,* he does not say, What *would* I do? What have I a mind to? and that I will have; but, What *should* I do? What does God require of me? What is duty? What is prudence? What is for edification? And so he does not force his way, but *direct his way* by a safe and certain rule.

30 *There is* no wisdom nor understanding nor counsel against the LORD. 31 The horse *is* prepared against the day of battle: but safety *is* of the LORD.

The designing busy part of mankind are here directed, in all their counsels and undertakings, to have their eye to God, and to believe, 1. That there can be no success against God, and therefore they must never act in opposition to him, in contempt of his commands, or in contradiction to his counsels. Though they think they have *wisdom,* and *understanding,* and *counsel,* the best politics and politicians, on their side, yet, if it be *against the Lord,* it cannot prosper long; it shall not prevail at last. He that sits in heaven laughs at men's projects against him and his anointed, and will carry his point in spite of them, Ps. ii. 1—6. Those that fight against God are preparing shame and ruin for themselves; whoever *make war with the Lamb,* he will certainly *overcome them,* Rev. xvii. 14. 2. That there can be no success without God, and therefore they must never act but in dependence on him. Be the cause ever so good, and the patrons of it ever so strong, and wise, and faithful, and the means of carrying it on, and gaining the point, ever so probable, still they must acknowledge God and take him along with them. Means indeed are to be used; *the horse* must be *prepared against the day of battle,* and the foot too; they must be armed and disciplined. In Solomon's time even Israel's kings used horses in war, though they were forbidden to multiply them. *But,* after all, *safety* and salvation *are of the Lord;* he can save without armies, but armies cannot save without him; and therefore he must be sought to and trusted in for success, and when success is obtained he must have all the glory. When we are preparing for *the day of battle* our great concern must be to make God our friend and secure his favour.

CHAP. XXII.

A GOOD name *is* rather to be chosen than great riches, *and* loving favour rather than silver and gold.

Here are two things which are more valuable and which we should covet more than great riches:—1. To be well spoken of: *A name* (that is, *a good name,* a name for good things with God and good people) *is rather to be chosen than great riches ;* that is, we should be more careful to do that by which we may get and keep a good name than that by which we may raise and increase a great estate. Great riches bring great cares with them, expose men to danger, and add no real value to a man. A fool and a knave may have *great riches,* but *a good name* makes a man easy and safe, supposes a man wise and honest, redounds to the glory of God, and gives a man a greater opportunity of doing good. By great riches we may relieve the bodily wants of others, but by a good name we may recommend religion to them. 2. To be well beloved, to have an interest in the esteem and affections of all about us; this is better *than silver and gold.* Christ had neither silver nor gold, but he *grew in favour with God and man,* Luke ii. 52. This should teach us to look with a holy contempt upon the wealth of this world, not to set our hearts upon that, but with all possible care to *think of those things that are lovely and of good report,* Phil. iv. 8.

2 The rich and poor meet together : the LORD *is* the maker of them all.

Note, 1. Among the children of men divine Providence has so ordered it that some are *rich* and others *poor,* and these are intermixed in societies : *The Lord is the Maker of both,* both the author of their being and the disposer of their lot. The greatest man in the world must acknowledge God to be his Maker, and is under the same obligations to be subject to him that the meanest is ; and the poorest has the honour to be the work of God's hands as much as the greatest. *Have they not all one Father ?* Mal. ii. 10 ; Job xxxi. 15. God makes some rich, that they may be charitable to the poor, and others poor, that they may be serviceable to the rich; and they have need one of another, 1 Cor. xii. 21. He makes some poor, to exercise their patience, and contentment, and dependence upon God, and others rich, to exercise their thankfulness and beneficence. Even *the poor* we *have always with* us ; they shall never cease out of the land, nor the rich neither. 2. Notwithstanding the distance that is in many respects between *rich and poor,* yet in most things they *meet together,* especially before *the Lord,* who *is the Maker of them all,* and *regards not the rich more than the poor,* Job xxxiv. 19. *Rich and poor meet together* at the bar of God's justice, all guilty before God, concluded under sin, and shapen in iniquity, the rich as much as the poor; and they meet at the throne of God's grace ; the poor are as welcome there as the rich. There is the same Christ, the same scripture, the same Spirit, the same covenant of promises, for them both. There is the same heaven for poor saints that there is for rich : Lazarus is in the bosom of Abraham. And there is the same hell for rich sinners that there is for poor. All stand upon the same

level before God, as they do also in the grave. *The small and great are there.*

3 A prudent *man* foreseeth the evil, and hideth himself : but the simple pass on, and are punished.

See here, 1. The benefit of wisdom and consideration : *A prudent man,* by the help of his prudence, will *foresee an evil,* before it comes, *and hide himself;* he will be aware when he is entering into a temptation and will put on his armour and stand on his guard. When the clouds are gathering for a storm he takes the warning, and flies to the name of the Lord as his strong tower. Noah foresaw the deluge, Joseph the years of famine, and provided accordingly. 2. The mischief of rashness and inconsideration. *The simple,* who believe every word that flatters them, will believe none that warns them, and so they *pass on and are punished.* They venture upon sin, though they are told what will be in the end thereof; they throw themselves into trouble, notwithstanding the fair warning given them, and they repent their presumption when it is too late. See an instance of both these, Exod. ix. 20, 21. Nothing is so fatal to precious souls as this, they will not take warning.

4 By humility *and* the fear of the LORD *are* riches, and honour, and life.

See here, 1. Wherein religion does very much consist—in *humility and the fear of the Lord;* that is, walking humbly with God. We must so reverence God's majesty and authority as to submit with all humility to the commands of his word and the disposals of his providence. We must have such low thoughts of ourselves as to behave humbly towards God and man. Where the fear of God is there will be humility. 2. What is to be gotten by it—*riches, and honour,* and comfort, *and* long *life,* in this world, as far as God sees good, at least spiritual *riches and honour* in the favour of God, and the promises and privileges of the covenant of grace, *and* eternal *life* at last.

5 Thorns *and* snares *are* in the way of the froward : he that doth keep his soul shall be far from them.

Note, 1. The way of sin is vexatious and dangerous : *In the way of the froward,* that crooked way, which is contrary to the will and word of God, *thorns and snares are* found, thorns of grief for past sins and snares entangling them in further sin. He that makes no conscience of what he says and does will find himself hampered by that imaginary liberty, and tormented by his pleasures. Froward people, who are soon angry, expose themselves to trouble at every step. Every thing will fret and vex him that will fret and vex at every thing. 2. The way of duty is safe and easy : *He that keeps his soul,* that watches carefully over his own heart and ways, is *far from* those *thorns and snares,* for his way is both plain and pleasant

6 Train up a child in the way he should go : and when he is old, he will not depart from it.

Here is, 1. A great duty enjoined, particularly to those that are the parents and instructors of children, in order to the propagating of wisdom, that it may not die with them : *Train up children* in that age of vanity, to keep them from the sins and snares of it, in that learning age, to prepare them for what they are designed for. *Catechise* them ; initiate them ; keep them under discipline. *Train* them as soldiers, who are taught to handle their arms, keep rank, and observe the word of command. *Train* them up, not in the way they would go (the bias of their corrupt hearts would draw them aside), but *in the way they should go,* the way in which, if you love them, you would have them go. *Train up a child according as he is capable* (so some take it), with a gentle hand, as nurses feed children, little and often, Deut. vi. 7. 2. A good reason for it, taken from the great advantage of this care and pains with children: When they *grow up,* when they *grow old,* it is to be hoped, they *will not depart from it.* Good impressions made upon them then will abide upon them all their days. Ordinarily the vessel retains the savour with which it was first seasoned. Many indeed have departed from the good way in which they were trained up ; Solomon himself did so. But early training may be a means of their recovering themselves, as it is supposed Solomon did. At least the parents will have the comfort of having done their duty and used the means

7 The rich ruleth over the poor, and the borrower *is* servant to the lender,

He had said (*v.* 2), *Rich and poor meet together ;* but here he finds, here he shows, that, as to the things of this life, there is a great difference ; for, 1. Those that have little will be in subjection to those that have much, because they have dependence upon them, they have received, and expect to receive, support from them : *The rich rule over the poor,* and too often more than becomes them, with pride and rigour, unlike to God, who, though he be great, yet despises not any. It is part of the affliction of the poor that they must expect to be trampled upon, and part of their duty to be serviceable, as far as they can, to those that are kind to them, and study to be grateful. 2. Those that are but going behindhand find themselves to lie much at the mercy of those that are before hand : *The borrower is servant to the lender,* is obliged to him, and must sometimes beg, *Have patience with me.* Therefore it is part of Israel's promised happiness that they should lend and not borrow, Deut. xxviii. 12. And it should be our endeavour to keep as much as may be out of debt. Some sell their liberty to gratify their luxury

8 He that soweth iniquity shall reap vanity : and the rod of his anger shall fail.

Note, 1. Ill-gotten gains will not prosper : *He that sows iniquity,* that does an unjust thing in hopes to get by it, *shall reap vanity ;* what he gets will never do him any good nor give him any satisfaction. He will meet with nothing but disappointment. Those that create trouble to others do but prepare trouble for themselves. Men shall reap as they sow. 2. Abused power will not last. If the rod of authority turn into a *rod of anger,* if men rule by passion instead of prudence, and, instead of the public welfare, aim at nothing so much as the gratifying of their own resentments, it *shall fail* and be broken, and their power shall not bear them out in their exorbitances, Isa. x. 24, 25.

9 He that hath a bountiful eye shall be blessed ; for he giveth of his bread to the poor.

Here is, 1. The description of a charitable man ; he has a *bountiful eye,* opposed to the evil eye (*ch.* xxiii. 6) and the same with the *single eye* (Matt. vi. 22),—an eye that seeks out objects of charity, besides those that offer themselves,—an eye that, upon the sight of one in want and misery, affects the heart with compassion,—an eye that with the alms gives a pleasant look, which makes the alms doubly acceptable. He has also a liberal hand : *He gives of his bread to* those that need—*his bread,* the bread appointed for his own eating. He will rather abridge himself than see the poor perish for want ; yet he does not give all *his bread,* but *of his bread ;* the poor shall have their share with his own family. 2. The blessedness of such a man. The loins of the poor will bless him, all about him will speak well of him, and God himself will bless him, in answer to many a good prayer put up for him, and he *shall be blessed*

10 Cast out the scorner, and contention shall go out ; yea, strife and reproach shall cease.

See here, 1. What *the scorner* does. It is implied that he sows discord and makes mischief wherever he comes. Much of the *strife and contention* which disturb the peace of all societies is owing to *the evil interpreter* (as some read it), that construes every thing into the worst, to those that despise and deride every one that comes in their way and take a pride in bantering and abusing all mankind. 2. What is to be done with the scorner that will not be reclaimed : *Cast* him *out* of your society, as Ishmael, when he mocked Isaac, was thrust out of Abraham's family. Those that would secure the peace must exclude the scorner

11 He that loveth pureness of heart, *for* the grace of his lips the king *shall be* his friend.

Here is, 1. The qualification of an accomplished, a complete gentleman, that is fit to be employed in public business. He must be an honest man, a man *that loves pureness of heart* and hates all impurity, not only pure from all fleshly lusts, but from all deceit and dissimulation, from all selfishness and sinister designs, that takes care to approve himself a man of sincerity, is just and fair from principle, and delights in nothing more than in keeping his own conscience clean and void of offence. He must also be able to speak with a good grace, not to daub and flatter, but to deliver his sentiments decently and ingeniously, in language as clean and smooth as his spirit. 2. The preferment such a man stands fair for: *The king*, if he be wise and good, and understand his own and his people's interest, *will be his friend*, will make him of his cabinet-council, as there was one in David's court, and another in Solomon's, that was called the *king's friend;* or, in any business that he has, the king will befriend him. Some understand it of the King of kings. A man *in whose spirit there is no guile*, and whose speech is always with grace, God will be his friend, Messiah, the Prince, will be his friend. *This honour have all the saints.*

12 The eyes of the LORD preserve knowledge, and he overthroweth the words of the transgressor.

Here is, 1. The special care God takes to *preserve knowledge*, that is, to keep up religion in the world by keeping up among men the knowledge of himself and of good and evil, notwithstanding the corruption of mankind, and the artifices of Satan to blind men's minds and keep them in ignorance. It is a wonderful instance of the power and goodness of *the eyes of the Lord*, that is, his watchful providence. He preserves *men of knowledge*, wise and good men (2 Chron. xvi. 9), particularly faithful witnesses, who speak what they know; God protects such, and prospers their counsels. He does by his grace *preserve knowledge* in such, secures his own work and interest in them. See Prov. ii. 7, 8. 2. The just vengeance God takes on those that speak and act against knowledge, against their own knowledge and against the interests of knowledge and religion in the world: *He overthrows the words of the transgressor*, and *preserves knowledge* in spite of him. He defeats all the counsels and designs of false and treacherous men, and turns them to their own confusion.

13 The slothful *man* saith, *There is* a lion without, I shall be slain in the streets.

Note, 1. Those that have no love for their business will never want excuses to shake it off. Multitudes are ruined, both for soul and body, by their slothfulness, and yet still they have something or other to say for themselves, so ingenious are men in putting a

cheat upon their own souls. And who, I pray, will be the gainer at last, when the pretences will be all rejected as vain and frivolous? 2. Many frighten themselves from real duties by imaginary difficulties: *The slothful man* has work to do *without* in the fields, but he fancies *there is a lion* there; nay, he pretends he dares not go along the streets for fear somebody or other should meet him and kill him. He does not himself think so; he only says so to those that call him up. He talks of *a lion without*, but considers not his real danger from the devil, that *roaring lion*, which is in bed with him, and from his own slothfulness, which kills him.

14 The mouth of strange women *is* a deep pit: he that is abhorred of the LORD shall fall therein.

This is designed to warn all young men against the lusts of uncleanness. As they regard the welfare of their souls, let them take heed of *strange women*, lewd women, whom they ought to be *strange* to, of *the mouth of strange women*, of the kisses of their lips (ch. vii. 13), of the words of their lips, their charms and enticements. Dread them; have nothing to do with them; for, 1. Those who abandon themselves to that sin give proof that they are abandoned of God: it *is a deep pit*, which those *fall* into that are *abhorred of the Lord*, who leaves them to themselves to enter into that temptation, and takes off the bridle of his restraining grace, to punish them for other sins. Value not thyself upon thy being in favour with such women, when it proclaims thee under the wrath of God. 2. It is seldom that they recover themselves, for it *is a deep pit;* it will be hard getting out of it, it so besots the mind and debauches the conscience, by pleasing the flesh.

15 Foolishness *is* bound in the heart of a child; *but* the rod of correction shall drive it far from him.

We have here two very sad considerations: —1. That corruption is woven into our nature. Sin is *foolishness;* it is contrary both to our right reason and to our true interest. It *is in the heart;* there is an inward inclination to sin, to speak and act foolishly. It *is in the heart of children;* they bring it into the world with them; it is what they were shapen and conceived in. It is not only *found* there, but it is *bound* there; it is annexed to the heart (so some); vicious dispositions cleave closely to the soul, are bound to it as the cion to the stock into which it is grafted, which quite alters the property. There is a knot tied between the soul and sin, a true lover's knot; they two become one flesh. It is true of ourselves, it is true of our children, whom we have begotten in our own likeness. *O God! thou knowest* this *foolishness*. 2. That correction is necessary to the cure of it. It will not be got out by fair means and gentle methods; there must be strictness and severity, and that which will cause grief. Children need to be corrected, and kept under discipline, by their parents; and we all need to be corrected by our heavenly Father (Heb. xii. 6, 7), and under the correction we must stroke down folly and kiss the rod.

16 He that oppresseth the poor to increase his *riches, and* he that giveth to the rich, *shall* surely *come* to want.

This shows what evil courses rich men sometimes take, by which, in the end, they will impoverish themselves and provoke God, notwithstanding their abundance, to bring them to want; they *oppress the poor and give to the rich.* 1. They will not in charity relieve the poor, but withhold from them, that by saving that which is really the best, but which they think the most needless part of their expenses, they may *increase their riches;* but they will make presents *to the rich,* and give them great entertainments, either in pride and vain-glory, that they may look great, or in policy, that they may receive it again with advantage. Such *shall surely come to want.* Many have been beggared by a foolish generosity, but never any by a prudent charity. Christ bids us invite the poor, Luke xiv. 12, 13. 2. They not only will not relieve *the poor,* but they *oppress* them, rob the spital, extort from their poor tenants and neighbours, invade the rights of those who have not wherewithal to defend themselves, and then *give* bribes *to the rich,* to protect and countenance them in it. But it is all in vain; they *shall come to want.* Those that rob God, and so make him their enemy, cannot secure themselves by *giving to the rich,* to make them their friends.

17 Bow down thine ear, and hear the words of the wise, and apply thine heart unto my knowledge. 18 For *it is* a pleasant thing if thou keep them within thee; they shall withal be fitted in thy lips. 19 That thy trust may be in the LORD, I have made known to thee this day, even to thee. 20 Have not I written to thee excellent things in counsels and knowledge, 21 That I might make thee know the certainty of the words of truth; that thou mightest answer the words of truth to them that send unto thee?

Solomon here changes his style and manner of speaking. Hitherto, for the most part, since the beginning of *ch.* x., he had laid down doctrinal truths, and but now and then dropped a word of exhortation, leaving us to make the application as we went along; but here, to the end of *ch.* xxiv., he directs his speech to his son, his pupil, his reader, his hearer, speaking as to a particular person. Hitherto, for the most part, his sense was comprised in one verse, but here usually it is

drawn out further. See how Wisdom tries variety of methods with us, lest we should be cloyed with any one. To awaken attention and to assist our application the method of direct address is here adopted. Ministers must not think it enough to preach before their hearers, but must preach to them, nor enough to preach to them all in general, but should address themselves to particular persons, as here: Do *thou* do so and so. Here is,

I. An earnest exhortation to get wisdom and grace, by attending to *the words of the wise* men, both written and preached, the words of the prophets and priests, and particularly to that *knowledge* which Solomon in this book gives men of good and evil, sin and duty, rewards and punishments. To these *words,* to this *knowledge,* the ear must be *bowed down* in humility and serious attention and the *heart applied* by faith, and love, and close consideration. The ear will not serve without the heart.

II. Arguments to enforce this exhortation. Consider,

1. The worth and weight of the things themselves which Solomon in this book gives us the *knowledge* of. They are not trivial things, for amusement and diversion, not jocular proverbs, to be repeated in sport and in order to pass away time. No; they are *excellent things,* which concern the glory of God, the holiness and happiness of our souls, the welfare of mankind and all communities; they are *princely things* (so the word is), fit for kings to speak and senates to hear; they are things that concern *counsels and knowledge,* that is, wise counsels, relating to the most important concerns; things which will not only make us knowing ourselves, but enable us to advise others.

2. The clearness of the discovery of these things and the directing of them to us in particular. "They are *made known,* publicly known, that all may read,—plainly known, that he that runs may read,—*made known this day* more fully than ever before, in this day of light and knowledge,—*made known in this thy day.* But it is only a little while that this light is with thee; perhaps the things that are *this day made known to thee,* if thou improve not the day of thy visitation, may, before to-morrow, be *hidden from thy eyes.* They are *written,* for the greater certainty, and that they may be received and the more safely transmitted pure and entire to posterity. But that which the emphasis is here most laid upon is that they are *made known to thee, even to thee,* and *written to thee,* as if it were a letter directed to thee by name. It is suited to thee and to thy case; thou mayest in this glass see thy own face; it is intended for thee, to be a rule to thee, and by it thou must be judged." We cannot say of these things, "They are good things, but they are nothing to us;" no, they are of the greatest concern imaginable to us.

3. The agreeableness of these things to us, in respect both of comfort and credit. (1.) If we hide them in our hearts, they will be very pleasing and yield us an abundant satisfaction (*v.* 18): "*It is a pleasant thing*, and will be thy constant entertainment, *if thou keep them within thee ;* if thou digest them, and be actuated and governed by them, and delivered into them as into a mould." The form of godliness, when that is rested in, is but a force put upon a man, and he does but do penance in that white clothing ; those only that submit to the power of godliness, and make heart-work of it, find the pleasure of it, *ch.* ii. 10. (2.) If we make use of them in our discourse, they will be very becoming, and gain us a good reputation. *They shall be fitted in thy lips.* " Speak of these things, and thou speakest like thyself, and as is fit for thee to speak considering thy character; thou wilt also have pleasure in speaking of these things as well as in thinking of them."

4. The advantage designed us by them. The *excellent things* which God has *written to* us are not like the commands which the master gives his servant, which are all intended for the benefit of the master, but like those which the master gives his scholar, which are all intended for the benefit of the scholar. These things must be kept by us, for they are written to us, (1.) That we may have a confidence in him and communion with him · *That thy trust may be in the Lord, v.* 19. We cannot trust in God except in the way of duty ; we are *therefore* taught our duty, that we may have reason to trust in God. Nay, this is itself one great duty we are to learn, and a duty that is the foundation of all practical religion, to live a life of delight in God and dependence on him. (2.) That we may have a satisfaction in our own judgment : " *That I might make thee know the certainty of the words of truth ;* that thou mayest know what is truth, mayest plainly distinguish between it and falsehood, and mayest know upon what grounds thou receivest and believest the truths of God." Note, [1.] It is a desirable thing to know, not only *the words of truth*, but *the certainty of* them, that our faith may be intelligent and rational, and may grow up to a full assurance. [2.] The way to *know the certainty of the words of truth* is to make conscience of our duty ; for, *if any man do his will, he shall know* for certain that the doctrine is of God, John vii. 17. (3.) That we may be useful and serviceable to others for their instruction : " *That thou mayest give a good account of the words of truth to those that send to thee* to consult thee as an oracle," or (as the margin reads it) " *to those that send thee*, that employ thee as an agent or ambassador in any business." Knowledge is given us to do good with, that others may light their candle at our lamp, and that we may in our place serve our generation according to the will of God ; and those who make conscience of keeping God's commandments

930

will be best able to *give a reason of the hope that is in* them.

22 Rob not the poor, because he *is* poor : neither oppress the afflicted in the gate : 23 For the Lord will plead their cause, and spoil the soul of those that spoiled them.

After this solemn preface, one would have expected something new and surprising; but no; here is a plain and common, but very needful caution against the barbarous and inhuman practice of oppressing poor people. Observe,

I. The sin itself, and that is *robbing the poor* and making them poorer, taking from those that have but little to lose and so leaving them nothing. It is bad to rob any man, but most absurd to rob the poor, whom we should relieve,—to squeeze those with our power whom we should water with our bounty,—*to oppress the afflicted*, and so to add affliction to them,—to give judgment against them, and so to patronise those that do rob them, which is as bad as if we robbed them ourselves. Rich men will not suffer themselves to be wronged; poor men cannot help themselves, and therefore we ought to be the more careful not to wrong them.

II. The aggravations of the sin. 1. If their inability, by reason of their poverty, to right themselves, embolden us to rob them, it is so much the worse; this is *robbing the poor because he° is poor ;* this is not only a base and cowardly thing, to take advantage against a man because he is helpless, but it is unnatural, and proves men worse than beasts. 2. Or, if it be done under colour of law and justice, that is oppressing *the afflicted in the gate*, where they ought to be protected from wrong and to have justice done them against those that oppress them.

III. The danger that attends this sin. He that robs and oppresses the poor does it at his peril; for, 1. The oppressed will find God their powerful patron. He *will plead their cause*, and not suffer them to be run down and trampled upon. If men will not appear for them, God will. 2. The oppressors will find him a just avenger. He will make reprisals upon them, will *spoil the souls of those that spoil them ;* he will repay them in spiritual judgments, in curses to their souls. He that robs the poor will be found in the end a murderer of himself.

24 Make no friendship with an angry man; and with a furious man thou shalt not go : 25 Lest thou learn his ways, and get a snare to thy soul.

Here is, 1. A good caution against being intimate with a passionate man. It is the law of friendship that we accommodate ourselves to our friends and be ready to serve them, and therefore we ought to be wise and wary in the choice of a friend, that we come not under that sacred tie to any one whom it would be our folly to accommodate ourselves to. Though we must be civil to all, yet we must be careful whom we lay in our bosoms and contract a familiarity with. And, among others, a man who is easily provoked, touchy, and apt to resent affronts, who, when he is in a passion, cares not what he says or does, but grows outrageous, such a one is not fit to be made a friend or companion, for he will be ever and anon angry with us and that will be our trouble, and he will expect that we should, like him, be angry with others, and that will be our sin. 2. Good cause given for this caution : *Lest thou learn his way.* Those we go with we are apt to grow like. Our corrupt hearts have so much tinder in them that it is dangerous conversing with those that throw about the sparks of their passion. We shall thereby *get a snare to our souls,* for a disposition to anger is a great snare to any man, and an occasion of much sin. He does not say, " Lest thou have ill language given thee or get a broken head," but, which is much worse, " Lest thou imitate him, to humour him, and so contract an ill habit."

26 Be not thou *one* of them that strike hands, *or* of them that are sureties for debts. 27 If thou hast nothing to pay, why should he take away thy bed from under thee ?

We have here, as often before, a caution against suretiship, as a thing both imprudent and unjust. 1. We must not associate ourselves, nor contract an intimacy, with men of broken fortunes, and reputations, who need and will urge their friends to be bound for them, that they may cheat their neighbours to feed their lusts, and by keeping up a little longer may do the more damage at last to those that give them credit. Have nothing to do with such ; be not thou among them. 2. We must not cheat people of their money, by *striking hands* ourselves, or *becoming surety for others,* when we *have not to pay.* If a man by the divine providence is disabled to pay his debts, he ought to be pitied and helped ; but he that takes up money or goods himself, or is bound for another, when he knows that he has not wherewithal to pay, or that what he has is so settled that the creditors cannot come at it, does in effect pick his neighbour's pocket, and though, in all cases, compassion is to be used, yet he may thank himself if the law have its course and his *bed* be *taken from under him,* which might not be taken for a pledge to secure a debt, Exod. xxii. 26, 27. For, if a man appeared to be so poor that he had nothing else to give for security, he ought to be relieved, and it was honestly done to own it ; but, for the recovery of a debt, it seems it might be taken by the *summum jus—the strict operation of law.* 3. We must not ruin our own estates and families. Every man ought to be just to himself and to his wife and children ;

those are not so who live above what they have, who by the mismanagement of their own affairs, or by encumbering themselves with the debts of others, waste what they have and bring themselves to poverty. We may *take joyfully the spoiling of our goods* if it be for the testimony of a good conscience ; but, if it be for our own rashness and folly, we cannot but take it heavily.

28 Remove not the ancient landmark which thy fathers have set.

1. We are here taught not to invade another man's right, though we can find ways of doing it ever so secretly and plausibly, clandestinely and by fraud, without any open force. Let not property in general be entrenched upon, by robbing men of their liberties and privileges, or of any just ways of maintaining them. Let not the property of particular persons be encroached upon. The land-marks, or meer-stones, are standing witnesses to every man's right ; let not those be removed quite away, for thence come wars, and fightings, and endless disputes ; let them not be removed so as to take from thy neighbour's lot to thy own, for that is downright robbing him and entailing the fraud upon posterity. 2. We may infer hence that a deference is to be paid, in all civil matters, to usages that have prevailed time out of mind and the settled constitutions of government, in which it becomes us to acquiesce, lest an attempt to change it, under pretence of changing it for the better, prove of dangerous consequence.

29 Seest thou a man diligent in his business ? he shall stand before kings ; he shall not stand before mean *men.*

Here is, 1. A plain intimation what a hard thing it is to find a truly ingenious industrious man : "*Seest thou a man diligent in his business?* Thou wilt not see many such, so epidemical are dulness and slothfulness." He is here commended who lays out himself to get business, though it be but in a very low and narrow sphere, and is not easy when he is out of business, who loves business, is quick and active in it, and goes through it, not only with constancy and resolution, but with dexterity and expedition, a man of despatch, who knows how to bring a deal of business into a little compass. 2. A moral prognostication of the preferment of such a man ; though now he *stands before mean men,* is employed by them and attends upon them, yet he will rise, and is likely enough to *stand before kings,* as an ambassador to foreign kings or prime-minister of state to his own. *Seest thou a man diligent* in the business of religion ? He is likely to excel in virtue, and shall stand before the King of kings.

CHAP. XXIII.

WHEN thou sittest to eat with a ruler, consider diligently what *is* before thee : 2 And put a knife to thy throat, if thou *be* a man given to appetite. 3 Be not desirous of his dainties : for they *are* deceitful meat.

The sin we are here warned against is luxury and sensuality, and the indulgence of the appetite in eating and drinking, a sin that most easily besets us. 1. We are here told when we enter into temptation, and are in most danger of falling into this sin: "*When thou sittest to eat with a ruler* thou hast great plenty before thee, varieties and dainties, such a table spread as thou hast seldom seen; thou art ready to think, as Haman did, of nothing but the honour hereby done thee (Esth. v. 12), and the opportunity thou hast of pleasing thy palate, and forgettest that there is a snare laid for thee." Perhaps the temptation may be stronger, and more dangerous, to one that is not used to such entertainments, than to one that always sits down to a good table. 2. We are here directed to double our guard at such a time. We must, (1.) Apprehend ourselves to be in danger: "*Consider diligently what is before thee,* what meat and drink are before thee, that thou mayest choose that which is safest for thee and which thou art least likely to eat and drink of to excess. Consider what company is before thee, the ruler himself, who, if he be wise and good, will take it as an affront for any of his guests to disorder themselves at his table." And, if when we sit to eat with a ruler, much more when we sit to eat with the ruler of rulers at the Lord's table, must we *consider diligently what is before us,* that we may not in any respect *eat and drink unworthily,* unbecomingly, lest that table become a snare. (2.) We must alarm ourselves into temperance and moderation: "*Put a knife to thy throat,* that is, restrain thyself, as it were with a sword hanging over thy head, from all excess. Let these words, *Take heed lest at any time your hearts be overcharged with surfeiting and drunkenness, and so that day come upon you unawares*—or those, *For all these things, God shall bring thee into judgment*—or those, *Drunkards shall not inherit the kingdom of God,* be a knife to the throat.*" The Latins call luxury *gula—the throat.* "Take up arms against that sin. Rather be so abstemious that thy craving appetite will begin to think thy throat cut than indulge thyself in voluptuousness.*" We must never *feed ourselves without fear* (Jude 12), but we must in a special manner fear when temptation is before us. (3.) We must reason ourselves into a holy contempt of the gratifications of sense : "*If thou be a man given to appetite,* thou must, by a present resolution, and an application of the terrors of the Lord, restrain thyself. When thou art in danger of falling into any excess *put a knife to thy throat;* that may serve for once. But that is not enough: lay the axe to the root; mortify that appetite which has such a power over thee: *Be not desirous of dain-*

ties." Note, We ought to observe what is our own iniquity, and, if we find ourselves addicted to flesh-pleasing, we must not only stand upon our guard against temptations from without, but subdue the corruption within. Nature is desirous of food, and we are taught to pray for it, but it is lust that is desirous of dainties, and we cannot in faith pray for them, for frequently they are not food convenient for mind, body, or estate They are deceitful meat, and therefore David, instead of praying for them, prays against them, Ps. cxli. 4. They are pleasant to the palate, but perhaps rise in the stomach, turn sour there, upbraid a man, and make him sick. They do not yield men the satisfaction they promised themselves from them; for those that are given to appetite, when they have that which is very dainty, are not pleased; they are soon weary of it; they must have something else more dainty. The more a luxurious appetite is humoured and indulged the more humoursome and troublesome it grows, and the more hard to please; dainties will surfeit, but never satisfy. But especially they are upon *this* account deceitful meat, that, while they please the body, they prejudice the soul, they overcharge the heart, and unfit it for the service of God, nay, they take away the heart, and alienate the mind from spiritual delights, and spoil its relish of them. Why then should we covet that which will certainly cheat us ?

4 Labour not to be rich : cease from thine own wisdom. 5 Wilt thou set thine eyes upon that which is not? for *riches* certainly make themselves wings; they fly away as an eagle toward heaven.

As some are given to appetite (*v.* 2) so others to covetousness, and those Solomon here takes to task. Men cheat themselves as much by setting their hearts on money (though it seems most substantial) as by setting them on dainties. Observe,

I. How he dissuades the covetous man from toiling and tormenting himself (*v.* 4) "Do not *aim to be rich,* to raise an estate, and to make what thou hast in abundance more than it is." We must endeavour to live comfortably, and provide for our children and families, according as our rank and condition are, but we must not seek great things Be not of those that will be rich, that desire it as their chief good and design it as their highest end, 1 Tim. vi. 9. Covetous men think it is their wisdom, imagining that if they be rich to such a degree they shall be completely happy. *Cease from that wisdom,* for it is a mistake; *a man's life consists not in the abundance of the things which he possesses,* Luke xii. 15. 1. Those that aim at great things fill their hands with business more than they can grasp, so that their life is both a perfect drudgery and a perpetual hurry; but be not thou such a fool; *labour not to be rich.* What thou hast, or doest, be master of it, and not a slave to it as those that *rise up early, sit up late,* and *eat the bread of carefulness,* and all to be rich. Moderate labour, *that we may have to give,* is our wisdom and duty, Eph. iv. 28. Immoderate labour, that we may have to hoard, is our sin and folly. 2. They fill their heads with projects more than they understand, so that their life is a constant toss of care and fear; but do not thou thus vex thyself: *Cease from thy own wisdom;* go on quietly in the way of thy business, not contriving new ways and setting thy wits to work to find out new inventions. Acquiesce in God's wisdom, and cease from thy own, *ch.* iii. 5, 6.

II. How he dissuades the covetous man from cheating and deceiving himself by an inordinate love and pursuit of that which is vanity and vexation of spirit; for,

1. It is not substantial and satisfying: *"Wilt thou* be such a fool as to *set thy eyes,* to cause thy eyes to fly with eagerness and violence, *upon that which is not?"* Note, (1.) The things of this world are things that are not. They have a real existence in nature and are the real gifts of Providence, but in the kingdom of grace they are things that are not; they are not a happiness and portion for a soul, are not what they promise to be nor what we expect them to be; they are a show, a shadow, a sham upon the soul that trusts to them. They are not, for in a little while they will not be, they will not be ours; they perish in the using; the fashion of them passes away. (2.) It is therefore folly for us to set our eyes upon them, to admire them as the best things, to appropriate them to ourselves as our good things, and to aim at them as our mark at which all our actions are levelled, to fly upon them as the eagle upon her prey. "Wilt thou do a thing so absurd in itself? What thou, a reasonable creature, wilt thou dote upon shadows? The eyes are put for rational and intellectual powers; wilt thou throw those away upon such undeserving objects? To set the hands and feet upon the world is well enough, but not the eyes, the eyes of the mind; those were made to contemplate better things. Wilt thou, my son, that professest religion, put such an affront upon God (towards whom thy eyes should ever be) and such an abuse upon thy soul?"

2. It is not durable and abiding. Riches are very uncertain things; certainly they are so: *They make themselves wings, and fly away.* The more we cause our eyes to fly upon them the more likely they are to fly away from us. (1.) Riches will leave us. Those that hold them ever so fast cannot hold them long; either they must be taken from us or we must be taken from them. The goods are said to flow away as a stream (Job xx. 28), here to flee away as a bird. (2.) Perhaps they may leave us suddenly, when we have taken a great deal of pains for them and be-

gin to take a great deal of pride and pleasure in them. The covetous man sits hatching upon his wealth, and brooding over it, till it is fledged, as the young ones under the hen, and then it is gone. Or, as if a man should be fond of a flight of wild-fowl that light in his field, and call them his own because they are upon his ground, whereas, if he offer to come near them, they take wing immediately and are gone to another man's field. (3.) The wings they fly away upon are of their own making. They have in themselves the principles of their own corruption, their own moth and rust. They are wasting in their own nature, and like a handful of dust, which, if it be grasped, slips through the fingers. Snow will last awhile, and look pretty, if it be left to lie on the ground where it fell, but, if gathered up and laid in the bosom, it is dissolved and gone immediately (4.) They go irresistibly and irrecoverably, as *an eagle towards heaven,* that flies strongly (there is no stopping her), and flies out of sight and out of call (there is no bringing her back); thus do riches leave men, and leave them in grief and vexation if they set their hearts upon them.

6 Eat thou not the bread of *him that hath* an evil eye, neither desire thou his dainty meats: 7 For as he thinketh in his heart, so *is* he: Eat and drink, saith he to thee; but his heart *is* not with thee. 8 The morsel *which* thou hast eaten shalt thou vomit up, and lose thy sweet words.

Those that are voluptuous and given to appetite (*v.* 2) are glad to be where there is good cheer stirring, and those that are covetous and saving, that they may spare at home, will be glad to get a dinner at another man's table; and therefore both are here advised not to be forward to accept of every man's invitation, but especially not to thrust themselves in uninvited. Observe, 1. There are those that pretend to bid their friends welcome that are not hearty and sincere in it. They have a fair tongue, and know what they should say: *Eat and drink,* saith he, because it is expected that the master of the feast should so compliment his guests; but they have *an evil eye,* and grudge their guests every bit they eat, especially if they eat freely. They would seem to be liberal in making the entertainment, and would have the credit of it, but they have so great a love to their money, and so little to their friends, that they cannot have the comfort of it, nor any enjoyment of themselves or their friends. The miser's feast is his penance. If a man be so very selfish, and sordid, and mean that he cannot find in his heart to bid his friends welcome to what he has, he ought not to add to that the guilt of dissimulation by inviting them, but let him own himself to be what he is, that *the vile person may not be called liberal nor the churl bountiful,* Isa. xxxii. 5. 2. One can have no comfort in accepting the entertainments that are given grudgingly: "*Eat not thou the bread* of such a man; let him keep it to himself. Do not sponge upon those that are bountiful, nor make thyself burdensome to any; but especially scorn to be beholden to those that are paltry and not sincere. Better have a dinner of herbs, and true welcome, than *dainty meats* without it. Therefore," (1.) "Judge of the man as his mind is. Thou thinkest to pay thy respect to him as a friend, so thou takest him to be, because he compliments thee, but *as he thinks in his heart so is he,* not as he speaks with his tongue." We are that really, both to God and man, which we are inwardly; and neither religion nor friendship is worth any thing further than as it is sincere. (2.) "Judge of the meat as the digestion is and as it agrees with thee. He bids thee eat freely, but, first or last, he will discover his sordid covetous humour, and *as he thinks in his heart* so he will look, and give thee to understand that thou art not welcome, and then *the morsel thou hast eaten thou shalt vomit up;* the very thought of that will make thee even to vomit the meat thou hast eaten, and eat the words thou hast spoken in returning his compliments and giving him thanks for his civilities. Thou shalt *lose thy sweet words,* which he has given thee and thou hast given him."

9 Speak not in the ears of a fool: for he will despise the wisdom of thy words.

We are here directed not to *cast pearls before swine* (Matt. vii. 6) and not to expose things sacred to the contempt and ridicule of profane scoffers. It is our duty to take all fit occasions to speak of divine things; but, 1. There are some that will make a jest of every thing, though it be ever so prudently and pertinently spoken, that will not only despise a wise man's words, but despise even the wisdom of them, that in them which is most improvable for their own edification; they will particularly reproach that, as if it had an ill design upon them, which they must guard against. 2. Those that do so forfeit the benefit of good advice and instruction, and a wise man is not only allowed, but advised, not to *speak in the ears* of such fools; let them be foolish still, and let not precious breath be thrown away upon them. If what a wise man says in his wisdom will not be heard, let him hold his peace, and try whether the wisdom of that will be regarded.

10 Remove not the old landmark: and enter not into the fields of the fatherless: 11 For their redeemer *is* mighty; he shall plead their cause with thee

Note, 1. The fatherless are taken under God's special protection; with him they not

only find mercy shown to them (Hos. xiv. 3) but justice done for them. He is *their Redeemer,* their *Goël,* their near kinsman, that will take their part and stand up for them with jealousy, as taking himself affronted in the injuries done to them. As their Redeemer *he will plead their cause* against those that do them any injury, and, one way or other, will not only defend their right, and recover it for them, but avenge the wrongs done to them. And he *is mighty,* almighty; his omnipotence is engaged and employed for their protection, and their proudest and most powerful oppressors will not only find themselves an unequal match for this, but will find that it is at their peril to contend with it. 2. Every man therefore must be careful not to injure them in any thing, or to invade their rights, either by a clandestine removal of the old land-marks or by a forcible entry into their fields. Being fatherless, they have none to redress their wrongs, and, being in their childhood, they do not so much as apprehend the wrong that is done them. Sense of honour, and much more the fear of God, would restrain men from offering any injury to children, especially fatherless children.

12 Apply thine heart unto instruction, and thine ears to the words of knowledge. 13 Withhold not correction from the child: for *if* thou beatest him with the rod, he shall not die. 14 Thou shalt beat him with the rod, and shalt deliver his soul from hell. 15 My son, if thine heart be wise, my heart shall rejoice, even mine. 16 Yea, my reins shall rejoice, when thy lips speak right things.

Here is, 1. A parent instructing his child. He is here brought in persuading him to give his mind to his book, and especially to the scriptures and his catechism, to attend *to the words of knowledge,* by which he might come to know his duty, and danger, and interest, and not to think it enough to give them the hearing, but to apply his heart to them, to delight in them, and bow his will to the authority of them. The heart is *then* applied to the instruction when the instruction is applied to the heart. 2. A parent correcting his child. A tender parent can scarcely find in his heart to do this; it goes much against the grain. But he finds it is necessary; it is his duty, and therefore he dares not *withhold correction* when there is occasion for it *(spare the rod and spoil the child);* he *beats him with the rod,* gives him a gentle correction, the *stripes of the sons of men,* not such as we give to beasts. *Beat him with the rod and he shall not die.* The rod will not kill him; nay, it will prevent his killing himself by those vicious courses which the rod will be necessary to restrain him from. For the present *it is not joyous, but grievous,* both to the parent and to the child; but when it is given with wisdom, designed for good, accompanied with prayer, and blessed of God, it may prove a happy means of preventing his utter destruction and *delivering his soul from hell.* Our great care must be about our children's souls; we must not see them in danger of hell without using all possible means, with the utmost care and concern, to snatch them as brands out of everlasting burnings. Let the body smart, so that the spirit be *saved in the day of the Lord Jesus.* 3. A parent encouraging his child, telling him, (1.) What was all he expected, nothing but what would be for his own good, that *his heart be wise* and that his *lips speak right things,* that he be under the government of good principles, and that by those principles he particularly maintain a good government of his tongue. It is to be hoped that those will do *right things* when they grow up who learn to *speak right things* when they are young, and dare not speak any bad words. (2.) What a comfort it would be to him if herein he answered his expectation: " *If thy heart be wise, my heart shall rejoice,* shall rejoice in thee, *even mine,* who have taken so much care and pains about thee, my heart, that has many a time ached for thee, for which thou shouldst study thus to make a grateful requital." Note, The wisdom of children will be the joy of their parents and teachers, who have no greater joy than to see them *walk in the truth,* 3 John 4. "Children, if you be wise and good, devout and conscientious, God will be pleased with you, and that will be our joy: we shall think our labour in instructing you well bestowed; it will be a comfortable answer for the many prayers we have put up for you; we shall be eased of a great deal of care, shall not need to be so strict and severe in watching over you, and shall consequently be the easier both to you and to ourselves. We shall rejoice in hope that you will be a credit and comfort to us, if we should live to be old, that you will bear up the name of Christ in your generation, that you will live comfortably in this world and happily in another."

17 Let not thine heart envy sinners: but *be thou* in the fear of the LORD all the day long. 18 For surely there is an end; and thine expectation shall not be cut off.

Here is, 1. A necessary caution against entertaining any favourable thoughts of prospering profaneness: "*Let not thy heart envy sinners;* do not grudge them either the liberty they take to sin or the success they have in sin; it will cost them dearly and they are to be pitied rather than envied. Their prosperity is their portion (Ps. xvii. 14), nay, it is their poison," Prov. i. 32. We must not harbour in our hearts any secret discontent at the providence of God, though it seem to smile upon them, nor wish ourselves in

their condition. ' *Let not thy heart imitate sinners*" (so some read it); do not as they do; walk not in the way with them; use not the methods they take to enrich themselves, though they thrive by them. 2. An excellent direction to maintain high thoughts of God in our minds at all times: *Be thou in the fear of the Lord* every day and *all the day long.* We must be in the fear of the Lord as in our employment, exercising ourselves in holy adorings of God, in subjection to his precepts, submission to his providences, and a constant care to please him; we must be in it as in our element, taking a pleasure in contemplating God's glory and complying with his will. We must be *devoted to his fear* (Ps. cxix. 38); and governed by it as our commanding principle in all we say and do. All the days of our life we must constantly keep up an awe of God upon our spirits, must pay a deference to his authority, and have a dread of his wrath. We must be always so in his fear as never to be out of it. 3. A good reason for both of these (*v.* 18): *Surely there is an end,* an end and expectation, as Jer. xxix. 11. *There will be an end of the prosperity of the wicked,* therefore *do not envy them* (Ps. lxxiii. 17); there will be an end of thy afflictions, therefore be not weary of them, an end of thy services, thy work and warfare will be accomplished, *perfect love will shortly cast out fear,* and *thy expectation* of the reward not only will be *not cut off,* or disappointed, but it will be infinitely outdone. The consideration of the end will help to reconcile us to all the difficulties and discouragements of the way.

19 Hear thou, my son, and be wise, and guide thine heart in the way. 20 Be not among winebibbers; among riotous eaters of flesh: 21 For the drunkard and the glutton shall come to poverty: and drowsiness shall clothe *a man* with rags. 22 Hearken unto thy father that begat thee, and despise not thy mother when she is old. 23 Buy the truth, and sell *it* not; *also* wisdom, and instruction, and understanding. 24 The father of the righteous shall greatly rejoice: and he that begetteth a wise *child* shall have joy of him. 25 Thy father and thy mother shall be glad, and she that bare thee shall rejoice. 26 My son, give me thine heart, and let thine eyes observe my ways. 27 For a whore *is* a deep ditch; and a strange woman *is* a narrow pit. 28 She also lieth in wait as *for* a prey, and increaseth the transgressors among men.

Here is good advice for parents to give to their children; words are put into their mouths, that they may *train them up in the way they should go.* Here we have,

I. An earnest call to young people to attend to the advice of their godly parents, not only to this that is here given, but to all other profitable instructions : " *Hear, my son, and be wise, v.* 19. This will be an evidence that thou art wise and a means to make thee wiser." Wisdom, as *faith, comes by hearing.* And again (*v.* 22): " *Hearken unto thy father who begot thee,* and who therefore has an authority over thee and an affection for thee, and, thou mayest be sure, can have no other design than thy own good." We ought to *give reverence to the fathers of our flesh,* who begot us, and were the instruments of our being; much more ought we to obey and be in subjection to the *Father of our spirits,* who made us and is the author of our being. And since *the mother* also, from a sense of duty to God and from love to her child, gives him good instructions, let him not *despise her,* nor her advice, *when she is old.* When the mother was grown old we may suppose the children to be grown up; but let them not think themselves past being taught, even by her, but rather respect her the more for the multitude of her years and the wisdom which they teach. Scornful and insolent young men will make a jest, it may be, of the good advice of an aged mother, and think themselves not concerned to heed what an old woman says; but such will have a great deal to answer for another day, not only as having set at nought good counsel, but as having slighted and grieved a good mother, *ch.* xxx. 17.

II. An argument to enforce this call, taken from the great comfort which this will be to their parents, *v.* 24, 25. Note, 1. It is the duty of children to study how they may gladden the hearts of their good parents, and do it yet more and more, so that they may *greatly rejoice* in them, even when the *evil days come and the years of which they say they have no pleasure in them* but this, to see their children do well, as *Barzillai* to see *Chimham* preferred. 2. Children will be a joy to their parents if they be *righteous and wise.* Righteousness is true wisdom ; those who do good do well for themselves. Those are completely such as they should be who are not only *wise* (that is, knowing and learned), but *righteous* (that is, honest and good), and not only *righteous* (that is, conscientious and well-meaning), but *wise* (that is, prudent and discreet) in the management of themselves. If such the children be, especially all the children, the father and mother will be glad, and think nothing too much that they have done, or do, for them ; they will please themselves in them, and give God thanks for them ; particularly she that bore them with pain, and nursed them with pains, will rejoice in them, and reckon herself well requited, and the sorrow more than forgotten, because a wise and good man is the product of it, who is a blessing to the world he was born into.

III. Some general precepts of wisdom and virtue.

1. *Guide thy heart in the way, v.* 19. It is the heart that must be taken care of and directed aright; the motions and affections of the soul must be towards right objects and under a steady guidance. If the heart be guided in the way, the steps will be guided and the conversation well ordered.

2. *Buy the truth and sell it not, v.* 23. Truth is that by which the heart must be guided and governed, for without truth there is no goodness ; no regular practices without right principles. It is by the power of truth, known and believed, that we must be kept back from sin and constrained to duty. The understanding must be well-informed with wisdom and instruction, and therefore, (1.) We must buy it, that is, be willing to part with any thing for it. He does not say at what rate we must buy it, because we cannot buy it too dear, but must have it at any rate ; whatever it costs us, we shall not repent the bargain. When we are at expense for the means of knowledge, and resolved not to starve so good a cause, then we *buy the truth* Riches should be employed for the getting of knowledge, rather than knowledge for the getting of riches. When we are at pains in searching after truth, that we may come to the knowledge of it and may distinguish between it and error, then we buy it. *Dii laboribus omnia vendunt—Heaven concedes every thing to the laborious.* When we choose rather to suffer loss in our temporal interest than to deny or neglect the truth then we buy it; and it is a pearl of such great price that we must be willing to part with all to purchase it, must make shipwreck of estate, trade, preferment, rather than of faith and a good conscience. (2.) We must not sell it. Do not part with it for pleasures, honours, riches, any thing in this world. Do not neglect the study of it, nor throw off the profession of it, nor revolt from under the dominion of it, for the getting or saving of any secular interest whatsoever. *Hold fast the form of sound words,* and never let it go upon any terms

3. *Give me thy heart, v.* 26. God, in this exhortation, speaks to us as unto children : " Son, Daughter, *Give me thy heart.*" The heart is that which the great God requires and calls for from every one of us ; whatever we give, if we do not give him our hearts, it will not be accepted. We must set our love upon him. Our thoughts must converse much with him, and on him, as our highest end. *The intents of our hearts* must be fastened. We must make it our own act and deed to devote ourselves to the Lord, and we must be free and cheerful in it. We must not think to divide the heart between God and the world ; he will have all or none. *Thou shalt love the Lord thy God with all thy heart.* To this call we must readily answer, " *My father, take my heart,* such as it is, and

make it such as it should be ; take possession of it, and set up thy throne in it."

4. *Let thy eyes observe my ways ;* have an eye to the rule of God's word, the conduct of his providence, and the good examples of his people. Our eyes must observe these, as he that writes observes his copy, that we may keep in the right paths and may proceed and persevere in them.

IV. Some particular cautions against those sins which are, of all sins, the most destructive to the seeds of wisdom and grace in the soul, which impoverish and ruin it. 1. Gluttony and drunkenness, v. 20, 21. The world is full of examples of this sin and temptations to it, which all young people are concerned to stand upon their guard against and keep at a distance from. *Be not a wine-bibber ;* we are allowed to drink *a little wine* (1 Tim. v. 23), but not much, not to make a trade of it, never to drink to excess. *Be not a riotous eater of flesh,* as the Israelites were, who lusted exceedingly after it, saying, *Who will give us flesh to eat ?* Whereas Paul, though he is free to eat flesh, yet resolves that *he will eat no flesh while the world stands rather than make his brother to offend ;* so indifferent is he to it, 1 Cor. viii. 13. *Be not an* excessive *eater of flesh.* Intemperance must be avoided in meat as well as drink. *Be not a* luxurious *eater of flesh,* not pleased with any thing but what is very nice and delicate, savoury dishes, and forced meat. Some take not only a pleasure, but a pride, in being curious about their diet, and, as they call it, eating well ; as if that were the ornament of a gentleman, which is really the shame of a Christian, making a God of the belly. *" Be not a wine-bibber,* and *be not a riotous eater ;* and therefore, *be not among wine-bibbers* nor *among riotous eaters ;* do not give them countenance, lest thou learn their ways and insensibly fall into those sins, or at least lose the dread and detestation of them. They covet to have thee among them ; for those that are debauched themselves are very desirous to debauch others ; therefore do not gratify them, lest thou endanger thyself."* He fetches an argument against this sin from the expensiveness of it and its tendency to impoverish men : and if men will not be deterred from it by the ruin it brings on their secular interests, which lie nearest their hearts, no marvel that they are not frightened from it by what they are told out of the word of God of the mischief it does them in their spiritual and eternal concerns. *The drunkard and the glutton* hate to be reformed, though they are told they *shall come to poverty,* nay, though they are told they shall come to hell. Drunkenness is the cause of *drowsiness ;* it stupifies men, and makes them inattentive to business, and then all goes to wreck and ruin : thus men that have lived creditably come to be *clothed with rags.* 2. Whoredom. This is another sin which *takes away the heart* that should be given to God, Hos. iv. 11. He

shows the danger which attends that sin, *v.* 27, 28, (1.) It is a sin from which few recover themselves when once they are entangled in it. It is like *a deep ditch* and *a narrow pit,* which it is almost impossible to get out of ; and therefore it is wisdom to keep far enough from the brink of it. Take heed of making any approaches towards this sin, because it is so hard to make a retreat from it, conscience, which should head the retreat, being debauched by it, and divine grace forfeited. (2.) It is a sin which bewitches men to their ruin : *The adulteress lies in wait as a robber,* pretending friendship, but designing the greatest mischief, to rob them of all they have that is valuable, to strip them both of their armour and of their ornaments. Even those who, being virtuously educated, endeavour to shun the adulteress, she will *lie in wait* for, that she may assault them when they are off their guard and she has them at an advantage. Let none therefore be at any time secure. (3.) It is a sin that contributes more than any other to the spreading of vice and immorality in a kingdom : It *increases the transgressors among men.* One adulteress may be the ruin of many a precious soul and may help to debauch a whole town. It increases the treacherous or perfidious ones ; it not only occasions husbands to be false to their wives and servants to their masters, but many that have professed religion to throw off their profession and break their covenants with God. Houses of uncleanness are therefore such pest-houses as ought to be suppressed by those whose office it is to take care of the public welfare.

29 Who hath woe ? who hath sorrow ? who hath contentions ? who hath babbling ? who hath wounds without cause ? who hath redness of eyes ? 30 They that tarry long at the wine ; they that go to seek mixed wine. 31 Look not thou upon the wine when it is red, when it giveth his colour in the cup, *when it* moveth itself aright. 32 At the last it biteth like a serpent, and stingeth like an adder. 33 Thine eyes shall behold strange women, and thine heart shall utter perverse things. 34 Yea, thou shalt be as he that lieth down in the midst of the sea, or as he that lieth upon the top of a mast. 35 They have stricken me, *shalt thou say, and* I was not sick ; they have beaten me, *and* I felt *it* not : when shall I awake ? I will seek it yet again.

Solomon here gives fair warning against the sin of drunkenness, to confirm what he had said, v. 20.

I. He cautions all people to keep out of

the way of temptations to this sin (v 31): *Look not thou upon the wine when it is red.* Red wine was in Canaan looked upon as the best wine , it is therefore called *the blood of the grape.* Critics judge of wine, among other indications, by the colour o*ͬ* it; some wine, they say, looks charmingly, looks so well that it even says, "Come and drink me;" *it moves itself aright,* goes down very smoothly, or perhaps the roughness of it is grateful. It is said of generous strong-bodied wine that it even *causes the lips of those that are asleep to speak,* Cant. vii. 9. But *look not thou upon it.* 1. "Be not ruled by sense, but by reason and religion. Covet not that which pleases the eye, in hopes that it will please the taste; but let thy serious thoughts correct the errors of thy senses and convince thee that that which seems delightful is really hurtful, and resolve against it accordingly. Let not the heart walk after the eye, for it is a deceitful guide." 2. "Be not too bold with the charms of this or any other sin; *look not,* lest thou lust, lest thou take the forbidden fruit." Note, Those that would be kept from any sin must keep themselves from all the occasions and beginnings of it, and be afraid of coming within the reach of its allurements, lest they be overcome by them.

II. He shows the many pernicious consequences of the sin of drunkenness, for the enforcement of this caution. Take heed of the bait, for fear of the hook: *At the last it bites, v.* 32. All sin will be bitterness in the end, and this sin particularly. *It bites like a serpent,* when the drunkard is made sick by his surfeit, thrown by it into a dropsy or some fatal disease, beggared and ruined in his estate, especially when his conscience is awakened and he cannot reflect upon it without horror and indignation at himself, but worst of all, at last, when the cup of drunkenness shall be turned into a cup of trembling, the cup of the Lord's wrath, the dregs of which he must be for ever drinking, and shall not have a drop of water to cool his inflamed tongue. To take off the force of the temptation that there is in the pleasure of the sin, foresee the punishment of it, and what it will at last end in if repentance prevent not. In *its latter end it bites* (so the word is); think therefore what will be *in the end thereof.* But the inspired writer chooses to specify those pernicious consequences of this sin which are present and sensible.

1. It embroils men in quarrels, makes them quarrel with others, and say and do that which gives others occasion to quarrel with them, *v.* 29. He asks, *Who hath woe? Who hath sorrow?* Who has not, in this world? Many have woe and sorrow, and cannot help it; but drunkards wilfully create woe and sorrow to themselves. Those that have *contentions* have *woe and sorrow ;* and drunkards are the fools whose *lips enter into contention.* When the wine is in the wit is out and the passions are

928

up; and thence come drunken scuffles, and drunken frays, and drunken disputes over the cups; many a vexatious ruining law-suit has begun thus. There is *babbling,* quarrels in word and the exchanging of scurrilous language; yet it rests not there: you shall have *wounds without cause,* for causes are things which drunkards are in no capacity to judge of, and therefore they deal blows about without the least consideration why or wherefore, and must expect to be in like manner treated themselves. The wounds which men receive in defence of their country and its just rights are their honour; but *wounds without cause,* received in the service of their lusts, are marks of their infamy. Nay, drunkards wound themselves in a tender part, for they have *redness of eyes,* symptoms of an inward inflammation; their sight is weakened by it, and their looks are deformed. This comes, (1.) Of drinking long, *tarrying long at the wine,* and spending that time in drunken company which should be spent in useful business, or in sleep, which should fit for business, *v.* 30. O the precious hours which thousands throw away thus, every one of which will be brought into the account at the great day ! (2.) Of drinking that which is strong and intoxicating. *They go* up and down *to seek wine* that will please them ; their great enquiry is, "Where is the best liquor?" *They seek mixed wine,* which is most palatable, but most heady, so willingly do they sacrifice their reason to please their palate !

2. It makes men impure and insolent, *v.* 33. (1.) The *eyes* grow unruly and *behold strange women* to lust after them, and so let in adultery into the heart. *Est Venus in vinis* —Wine is oil to the fire of lust. *Thy eyes shall behold strange things* (so some read it); when men are drunk the house turns round with them, and every thing looks strange to them, so that then they cannot trust their own eyes. (2.) The tongue also grows unruly and talks extravagantly; by it the *heart utters perverse things,* things contrary to reason, religion, and common civility, which they would be ashamed to speak if they were sober. What ridiculous incoherent nonsense men will talk when they are drunk who at another time will speak admirably well and to the purpose !

3. It stupifies and besots men, *v.* 34. When men are drunk they know not where they are nor what they say and do. (1.) Their heads are giddy, and when they lie down to sleep they are as if they were tossed by the rolling waves *of the sea,* or *upon the top of a mast ;* hence they complain that their heads swim; their sleep is commonly unquiet and not refreshing, and their dreams are tumultuous. (2.) Their judgments are clouded, and they have no more steadiness and consistency than he that sleeps *upon the top of a mast :* they *drink and forget the law* (ch. xxxi. 5): *they err through wine* (Isa. xxviii. 7), and think as extravagantly as they talk. (3.)

They are heedless and fearless of danger, and senseless of the rebukes they are under either from God or man. They are in imminent danger of death, of damnation, lie as much exposed as if they slept *upon the top of a mast,* and yet are secure and sleep on. They fear no peril when the terrors of the Lord are laid before them ; nay, they feel no pain when the judgments of God are actually upon them; they cry not when he binds them. Set a drunkard in the stocks, and he is not sensible of the punishment. *" They have stricken me, and I was not sick ; I felt it not :* it made no impression at all upon me." Drunkenness turns men into stocks and stones; they are scarcely to be reckoned animals; they are dead while they live.

4. Worst of all, the heart is hardened in the sin, and the sinner, notwithstanding all these present mischiefs that attend it, obstinately persists in it, and hates to be reformed : *When shall I awake ?* Much ado he has to shake off the chains of his drunken sleep ; he can hardly get clear of the fumes of the wine, though he strives with them, that (being thirsty in the morning) he may return to it again. So perfectly lost is he to all sense of virtue and honour, and so wretchedly is his conscience seared, that he is not ashamed to say, *I will seek it yet again. There is no hope ; no, they have loved* drunkards, and *after them they will go,* Jer. ii. 25. This is *adding drunkenness to thirst,* and *following strong drink ;* those that do so may read their doom Deut. xxix. 19, 20, their *woe* Isa. v. 11, and, if this be the end of the sin, with good reason were we directed to stop at the beginning of it : *Look not upon the wine when it is red.*

CHAP. XXIV.

BE not thou envious against evil men, neither desire to be with them. 2 For their heart studieth destruction, and their lips talk of mischief.

Here, 1. The caution given is much the same with that which we had before (*ch.* xxiii. 17), not to envy sinners, not to think them happy, nor to wish ourselves in their condition, though they prosper ever so much in this world, and are ever so merry and ever so secure. " Let not such a thought ever come into thy mind, O that I could shake off the restraints of religion and conscience, and take as great a liberty to indulge the sensual appetite, as I see such and such do ! No ; *desire not to be with them,* to do as they do and fare as they fare, and to *cast in thy lot among* them." 2. Here is another reason given for this caution : " *Be not envious against* them, not only because their end will be bad, but because their way is so, *v.* 2. Do not think with them, *for their heart studies destruction* to others, but it will prove destruction to themselves. Do not speak like them, for *their lips talk of their mischief.* All they say

has an ill tendency, to dishonour God, reproach religion, or wrong their neighbour ; but it will be mischief to themselves at last. It is therefore thy wisdom to have nothing to do with them. Nor hast thou any reason to look upon them with envy, but with pity rather, or a just indignation at their wicked practices."

3 Through wisdom is a house builded; and by understanding it is established : 4 And by knowledge shall the chambers be filled with all precious and pleasant riches. 5 A wise man *is* strong ; yea, a man of knowledge increaseth strength. 6 For by wise counsel thou shalt make thy war : and in multitude of counsellors *there is* safety.

We are tempted to envy those that grow rich, and raise their estates and families, by such unjust courses as our consciences will by no means suffer us to use. But, to set aside that temptation, Solomon here shows that a man, with prudent management, may raise his estate and family by lawful and honest means, with a good conscience, and a good name, and the blessing of God upon his industry ; and, if the other be raised a little sooner, yet these will last a great deal longer. 1. That which is here recommended to us as having the best influence upon our outward prosperity is *wisdom,* and *understanding,* and *knowledge ;* that is, both piety towards God (for that is true wisdom) and prudence in the management of our outward affairs. We must govern ourselves in every thing by the rules of religion and then of discretion. Some that are truly pious do not thrive in the world, for want of prudence ; and some that are prudent enough, yet do not prosper, because they lean to their own understanding and do not acknowledge God in their ways ; therefore both must go together to complete a wise man. 2. That which is here set before us as the advantage of true wisdom is that it will make men's outward affairs prosperous and successful. (1.) It will *build a house and establish it, v.* 3. Men may by unrighteous practices build their houses, but they cannot establish them, for the foundation is rotten (Hab. ii. 9, 10); whereas what is honestly got will wear like steel and be an inheritance to children's children. (2.) It will enrich a house and furnish it, *v.* 4. Those that manage their affairs with wisdom and equity, that are diligent in the use of lawful means for increasing what they have, that spare from luxury and spend in charity, are in a fair way to have their shops, their warehouses, their *chambers, filled with all precious and pleasant riches—precious* because got by honest labour, and *the substance of a diligent man is precious—pleasant* because enjoyed with holy cheerfulness. Some think this is to be understood chiefly of spiritual riches. *By knowledge the chambers of the soul are filled with the graces and comforts of the Spirit, those precious and pleasant riches ;* for the Spirit, by enlightening the understanding, performs all his other operations on the soul. (3.) It will fortify a house and turn it into a castle : *Wisdom is better than weapons of war,* offensive or defensive. *A wise man is in strength,* is in a strong-hold, *yea, a man of knowledge strengthens might,* that is, increases it, *v.* 5. As we grow in knowledge we grow in all grace, 2 Pet. iii. 18. Those that *increase in wisdom* are *strengthened with all might,* Col. i. 9, 11. A wise man will compass that by his wisdom which a strong man cannot effect by force of arms. The spirit is strengthened both for the spiritual work and the spiritual warfare by true wisdom. (4.) It will govern a house and a kingdom too, and the affairs of both, *v.* 6. Wisdom will erect a college, or council of state. Wisdom will be of use, [1.] For the managing of the public quarrels, so as not to engage in them but for an honest cause and with some probability of success, and, when they are engaged in, to manage them well, and so as to make either an advantageous peace or an honourable retreat : *By wise counsel thou shalt make war,* which is a thing that may prove of ill consequence if not done by wise counsel. [2.] For the securing of the public peace : *In the multitude of counsellors there is safety,* for one may foresee the danger, and discern the advantages, which another cannot. In our spiritual conflicts we need wisdom, for our enemy is subtle.

7 Wisdom *is* too high for a fool : he openeth not his mouth in the gate. 8 He that deviseth to do evil shall be called a mischievous person. 9 The thought of foolishness *is* sin : and the scorner *is* an abomination to men.

Here is the description, 1. Of a weak man : *Wisdom is too high* for him ; he thinks it so, and therefore, despairing to attain it, he will take no pains in the pursuit of it, but sit down content without it. And really it is so; he has not capacity for it, and therefore the advantages he has for getting it are all in vain to him. It is no easy thing to get wisdom ; those that have natural parts good enough, yet if they be foolish, that is, if they be slothful and will not take pains, if they be playful and trifling, and given to their pleasures, if they be viciously inclined and keep bad company, it *is too high* for them ; they are not likely to reach it. And, for want of it, they are unfit for the service of their country : They *open not their mouth in the gate ;* they are not admitted into the council or magistracy, or, if they are, they are dumb statues, and stand for cyphers; they say nothing, because they have nothing

930

to say, and they know that if they should offer any thing it would not be heeded, nay, it would be hissed at. Let young men take pains to get wisdom, that they may be qualified for public business, and do it with reputation. 2. Of a wicked man, who is not only despised as a fool is, but detested. Two sorts of wicked men are so :—(1.) Such as are secretly malicious. Though they speak courteously and conduct themselves plausibly, they *devise to do evil,* are contriving to do an ill turn to those they bear a grudge to, or have an envious eye at. He that does so *shall be called a mischievous person,* or *a master of mischief,* which perhaps was then a common name of reproach ; he shall be branded as an *inventor of evil things* (Rom. i. 30), or, if any mischief be done, he shall be suspected as the author of it, or at least accessory to it. This *devising evil* is the *thought of foolishness, v.* 9. It is made light of, and turned off with a jest, as only a foolish thing, but really it *is sin,* it is exceedingly sinful ; you cannot call it by a worse name than to call it *sin.* It is bad to do evil, but it is worse to devise it ; for that has in it the subtlety and poison of the old serpent. But it may be taken more generally. We contract guilt, not only by the act of foolishness, but by the thought of it, though it go no further ; the first risings of sin in the heart are sin, offensive to God, and must be repented of or we are undone. Not only malicious, unclean, proud thoughts, but even foolish thoughts, are sinful thoughts. If *vain thoughts lodge in the heart,* they defile it (Jer. iv. 14), which is a reason why we should *keep our hearts with all diligence,* and harbour no thoughts there which cannot give a good account of themselves, Gen. vi. 5. (2.) Such as are openly abusive : *The scorner,* who gives ill-language to every body, takes a pleasure in affronting people and reflecting upon them, *is an abomination to men ;* none that have any sense of honour and virtue will care to keep company with him. *The seat of the scornful* is the *pestilential chair* (as the LXX. call it, Ps. i. 1), which no wise man will come near, for fear of taking the infection. Those that strive to make others odious do but make themselves so.

10 *If* thou faint in the day of adversity, thy strength *is* small.

Note, 1. In *the day of adversity* we are apt to *faint,* to droop and be discouraged, to desist from our work, and to despair of relief. Our spirits sink, and then our hands hang down and our knees grow feeble, and we become unfit for any thing. And often those that are most cheerful when they are well droop most, and are most dejected, when any thing ails them. 2. This is an evidence that our *strength is small,* and is a means of weakening it more. " It is a sign that thou art not a man of any resolution, any firmness of thought, any consideration, any faith (for that is the strength of a soul), if thou canst not bear up under an afflictive change of thy condition." Some are so feeble that they can bear nothing; if a trouble does but *touch* them (Job iv. 5), nay, if it does but threaten them, they faint immediately and are ready to give up all for gone; and by this means they render themselves unfit to grapple with their trouble and unable to help themselves. *Be of good courage* therefore, *and God shall strengthen thy heart.*

11 If thou forbear to deliver *them that are* drawn unto death, and *those that are* ready to be slain; 12 If thou sayest, Behold, we knew it not; doth not he that pondereth the heart consider *it?* and he that keepeth thy soul, doth *not* he know *it?* and shall *not* he render to *every* man according to his works?

Here is, 1. A great duty required of us, and that is to appear for the relief of oppressed innocency. If we see the lives or livelihoods of any in danger of being taken away unjustly, we ought to bestir ourselves all we can to save them, by disproving the false accusations on which they are condemned and seeking out proofs of their innocency. Though the persons be not such as we are under any particular obligation to, we must help them, out of a general zeal for justice. If any be set upon by force and violence, and it be in our power to rescue them, we ought to do it. Nay, if we see any through ignorance exposing themselves to danger, or fallen in distress, as travellers upon the road, ships at sea, or any the like, it is our duty, though it be with peril to ourselves, to hasten with help to them and not *forbear to deliver them,* not to be slack, or remiss, or indifferent, in such a case. 2. An answer to the excuse that is commonly made for the omission of this duty. Thou wilt say, " *Behold, we knew it not;* we were not aware of the imminency of the danger the person was in; we could not be sure that he was innocent, nor did we know how to prove his innocence, nor which way to do any thing in favour of him, else we would have helped him." Now, (1.) It is easy to make such an excuse as this, sufficient to avoid the censures of men, for perhaps they cannot disprove us when we say, *We knew it not,* or, *We forgot;* and the temptation to tell a lie for the excusing of a fault is very strong when we know that it is impossible to be disproved, the truth lying wholly in our own breast, as when we say, *We thought so and so, and really designed it,* which no one is conscious of but ourselves. (2.) It is not so easy with such excuses to evade the judgment of God; and to the discovery of that we lie open and by the determination of that we must abide. Now, [1.] God *ponders the heart and keeps the soul;* he keeps an eye upon it, observes all the mo-

tions of it; its most secret thoughts and intents are all naked and open before him. It is his prerogative to do so, and that in which he glories. Jer. xvii. 10, *I the Lord search the heart.* He *keeps the soul,* holds it in life. This is a good reason why we should be tender of the lives of others, and do all we can to preserve them, because our lives have been precious in the sight of God and he has graciously kept them. [2.] He knows and considers whether the excuse we make be true or no, whether it was because we did not know it or whether the true reason was not because we did not love our neighbour as we ought, but were selfish, and regardless both of God and man. Let this serve to silence all our frivolous pleas, by which we think to stop the mouth of conscience when it charges us with the omission of plain duty: *Does not he that ponders the heart consider it?* [3.] He will judge us accordingly. As his knowledge cannot be imposed upon, so his justice cannot be biassed, but he will *render to every man according to his works,* not only the commission of evil works, but the omission of good works.

13 My son, eat thou honey, because *it is* good; and the honeycomb, *which is* sweet to thy taste: 14 So *shall* the knowledge of wisdom *be* unto thy soul: when thou hast found *it,* then there shall be a reward, and thy expectation shall not be cut off.

We are here quickened to the study of wisdom by the consideration both of the pleasure and the profit of it. 1. It will be very pleasant. We *eat honey because it is sweet to the taste,* and upon that account we call it *good,* especially that which runs first from the *honey-comb.* Canaan was said to flow with milk and honey, and honey was the common food of the country (Luke xxiv. 41, 42), even for children, Isa. vii. 15. Thus should we feed upon wisdom, and relish the good instructions of it. Those that have tasted honey need no further proof that it is sweet, nor can they by any argument be convinced of the contrary; so those that have experienced the power of truth and godliness are abundantly satisfied of the pleasure of both; they have tasted the sweetness of them, and all the atheists in the world with their sophistry, and the profane with their banter, cannot alter their sentiments. 2. It will be very profitable. Honey may be *sweet to the taste* and yet not wholesome, but wisdom has a future recompence attending it, as well as a present sweetness in it. "Thou art permitted to *eat honey,* and the agreeableness of it to thy taste invites thee to it; but thou hast much more reason to relish and digest the precepts *of wisdom,* for, *when thou hast found* that, *there shall be a reward;* thou shalt be paid for thy pleasure, while the servants of sin pay dearly for their pains. Wisdom does indeed set thee to work, but *there shall be a reward ;* it does indeed raise great expectations in thee, but as thy labour, so thy hope, shall not be in vain ; *thy expectation shall not be cut off (ch.* xxiii. 18), nay, it shall be infinitely outdone."

15 Lay not wait, O wicked *man,* against the dwelling of the righteous ; spoil not his resting place : 16 For a just *man* falleth seven times, and riseth up again : but the wicked shall fall into mischief.

This is spoken, not so much by way of counsel to wicked men (they will not receive instruction, *ch.* xxiii. 9), but rather in defiance of them, for the encouragement of good people that are threatened by them. See here, 1. The designs of the wicked against the righteous, and the success they promise themselves in those designs. The plot is laid deeply : They *lay wait against the dwelling of the righteous,* thinking to charge some iniquity upon it, or compass some design against it ; they lie in wait at the door, to catch him when he stirs out, as David's persecutors, Ps. lix. *title.* The hope is raised high ; they doubt not but to *spoil his dwelling-place* because he is weak and cannot support it, because his condition is low and distressed, and he is almost down already. All this is a fruit of the old enmity in the seed of the serpent against the seed of the woman. *The blood-thirsty hate the upright.* 2. The folly and frustration of these designs. (1.) The righteous man, whose ruin was expected, recovers himself. He *falls seven times* into trouble, but, by the blessing of God upon his wisdom and integrity, he *rises again,* sees through his troubles and sees better times after them. The *just man falls,* sometimes *falls seven times* perhaps, into sin, sins of infirmity, through the surprise of temptation ; but he *rises again* by repentance, finds mercy with God, and regains his peace. (2.) The *wicked* man, who expected to see his ruin and to help it forward, is undone. He *falls into mischief ;* his sins and his troubles are his utter destruction.

17 Rejoice not when thine enemy falleth, and let not thine heart be glad when he stumbleth : 18 Lest the LORD see *it,* and it displease him, and he turn away his wrath from him.

Here, 1. The pleasure we are apt to take in the troubles of an enemy is forbidden us. If any have done us an ill turn, or if we bear them ill-will only because they stand in our light or in our way, when any damage comes to them (suppose they fall), or any danger (suppose they stumble), our corrupt hearts are too apt to conceive a secret delight and satisfaction in it—*Aha ! so would we have it ; they are entangled ; the wilderness has shut them in*—or, as Tyrus said concerning Jerusalem (Ezek. xxvi. 2), *I shall be replenished, now she is laid waste.* "Men hope in the ruin of their enemies or rivals to wreak their revenge or to find their account ; but be not thou so inhuman ; *rejoice not when* the worst *enemy* thou hast *falls.*" There may be a holy joy in the destruction of God's enemies, as it tends to the glory of God and the welfare of the church (Ps. lviii. 10) ; but in the ruin of our enemies, as such, we must by no means rejoice ; on the contrary, we must weep even with them when they weep (as David, Ps. xxxv. 13, 14), and that in sincerity, not so much as letting our hearts be secretly glad at their calamities. 2. The provocation which that pleasure gives to God is assigned as the reason of that prohibition : *The Lord will see it,* though it be hidden in the heart only, *and it* will *displease him,* as it will displease a prudent father to see one child triumph in the correction of another, which he ought to tremble at, and take warning by, not knowing how soon it may be his own case, he having so often deserved it. Solomon adds an argument *ad hominem—addressed to the individual :* "Thou canst not do a greater kindness to *thy enemy,* when he has fallen, than to rejoice in it ; for then, to cross thee and vex thee, God will *turn his wrath from him ;* for, as *the wrath of man works not the righteousness of God,* so the righteousness of God was never intended to gratify the wrath of man, and humour his foolish passions ; rather than seem to do that he will adjourn the execution of his wrath : nay, it is implied that when he *turns his wrath from him* he will turn it against thee and the cup of trembling shall be put into thy hand."

19 Fret not thyself because of evil *men,* neither be thou envious at the wicked ; 20 For there shall be no reward to the evil *man ;* the candle of the wicked shall be put out.

Here, 1. He repeats the caution he had before given against envying the pleasures and successes of wicked men in their wicked ways. This he quotes from his father David, Ps. xxxvii. 1. We must not in any case *fret* ourselves, or make ourselves uneasy, whatever God does in his providence ; how disagreeable soever it is to our sentiments, interests, and expectations, we must acquiesce in it. Even that which grieves us must not *fret* us ; nor must our eye be evil against any because God is good. Are we more wise or just than he ? If wicked people prosper, we must not therefore incline to do as they do. 2. He gives a reason for this caution, taken from the end of that way which wicked men walk in. Envy not their prosperity ; for, (1.) There is no true happiness in it : *There shall be no reward to the evil man ;* his prosperity only serves for his present subsistence ; these are all the good things he must ever expect ; there is none intended him in the world of retribution. *He has his reward,* Matt. vi. 2.

He shall have none. Those are not to be envied that have their portion in this life and must out-live it, Ps. xvii. 14. (2.) There is no continuance in it; their *candle* shines brightly, but it shall presently *be put out*, and a final period put to all their comforts, Job xxi. 17; Ps. xxxvii. 1, 2.

21 My son, fear thou the LORD and the king : *and* meddle not with them that are given to change : 22 For their calamity shall rise suddenly ; and who knoweth the ruin of them both ?

Note, 1. Religion and loyalty must go together. As men, it is our duty to honour our Creator, to worship and reverence him, and to be always in his fear ; as members of a community, incorporated for mutual benefit, it is our duty to be faithful and dutiful to the government God has set over us, Rom. xiii. 1, 2. Those that are truly religious will be loyal, in conscience towards God ; the godly in the land will be the *quiet in the land ;* and those are not truly loyal, or will be so no longer than is for their interest, that are not religious. How should he be true to his prince that is false to his God? And, if they come in competition, it is an adjudged case, we must *obey God rather than men.* 2. Innovations in both are to be dreaded. Have nothing to do, he does not say, with those that *change,* for there may be cause to change for the better, but *those that are given to change,* that affect change for change-sake, out of a peevish discontent with that which is and a fondness for novelty, or a desire to fish in troubled waters: *Meddle not with those that are given to change* either in religion or in the civil government ; *come not into their secret ;* join not with them in their cabals, nor enter into the mystery of their iniquity. 3. Those that are of restless, factious, turbulent spirits, commonly pull mischief upon their own heads ere they are aware: *Their calamity shall rise suddenly.* Though they carry on their designs with the utmost secresy, they will be discovered, and brought to condign punishment, when they little think of it. *Who knows* the time and manner of *the ruin* which both God and the king will bring on their contemners, *both* on them and those that meddle with them?

23 These *things* also *belong* to the wise. *It is* not good to have respect of persons in judgment. 24 He that saith unto the wicked, Thou *art* righteous ; him shall the people curse, nations shall abhor him : 25 But to them that rebuke *him* shall be delight, and a good blessing shall come upon them. 26 *Every man* shall kiss *his* lips that giveth a right answer.

Here are lessons for *wise* men, that is, judges and princes. As subjects must do their duty, and be obedient to magistrates, so magistrates must do their duty in administering justice to their subjects, both in pleas of the crown and causes between party and party. These are lessons for them. 1. They must always weigh the merits of a cause, and not be swayed by any regard, one way or other, to the parties concerned : *It is not good* in itself, nor can it ever do well, *to have respect of persons in judgment ;* the consequences of it cannot but be the perverting of justice and doing wrong under colour of law and equity. A good judge will know the truth, not know faces, so as to countenance a friend and help him out in a bad cause, or so much as omit any thing that can be said or done in favour of a righteous cause, when it is the cause of an enemy. 2. They must never connive at or encourage wicked people in their wicked practices. Magistrates in their places, and ministers in theirs, are to deal faithfully with the wicked man, though he be a great man or a particular friend, to convict him of his wickedness, to show him what will be in the end thereof, to discover him to others, that they may avoid him. But if those whose office it is thus to show people their transgressions palliate them and connive at them, if they excuse the wicked man, much more if they prefer him and associate with him (which is, in effect, to say, Thou art righteous), they shall justly be looked upon as enemies to the public peace and welfare, which they ought to advance, and *the people shall curse them* and cry out shame on them; and even those of other *nations shall abhor them,* as base betrayers of their trust. 3. They must discountenance and give check to all fraud, violence, injustice, and immorality; and, though thereby they may disoblige a particular person, yet they will recommend themselves to the favour of God and man. Let magistrates and ministers, and private persons too that are capable of doing it, *rebuke* the wicked, that they may bring them to repentance or put them to shame, and they shall have the comfort of it in their own bosoms: *To them shall be delight,* when their consciences witness for them that they have been witnesses for God; *and a good blessing shall come upon them,* the blessing of God and good men; they shall be deemed religion's patrons and their country's patriots. See *ch.* xxviii. 23. 4. They must always give judgment according to equity (*v.* 26); they must *give a right answer,* that is, give their opinion and pass sentence according to law and the true merits of the cause; and *every one shall kiss his lips that* does so, that is, shall love and honour him, and be subject to his orders, for there is a kiss of allegiance as well as of affection. He that in common conversation likewise speaks pertinently and with sincerity recommends himself to his company and is beloved and respected by all.

27 Prepare thy work without, and

make it fit for thyself in the field ; and afterwards build thine house.

This is a rule of prudence in the management of household affairs ; for all good men should be good husbands, and manage with discretion, which would prevent a great deal of sin, and trouble, and disgrace to their profession. 1. We must prefer necessaries before conveniences, and not lay that out for show which should be expended for the support of the family. We must be content with a mean cottage for a habitation, rather than want, or go in debt for, food convenient. 2. We must not think of building till we can afford it : " First apply thyself to *thy work without in the field ;* let thy ground be put into good order ; look after thy husbandry, for it is that by which thou must get ; and, when thou hast got well by that, then, and not till then, thou mayest think of rebuilding and beautifying *thy house,* for that is it upon which, and in which, thou wilt have occasion to spend." Many have ruined their estates and families by laying out money on that which brings nothing in, beginning *to build* when they were *not able to finish.* Some understand it as advice to young men not to marry (for by that the house is built) till they have set up in the world, and got wherewith to maintain a wife and children comfortably. 3. When we have any great design on foot it is wisdom to take it before us, and make the necessary preparations, before we fall to work, that, when it is begun, it may not stand still for want of materials. Solomon observed this rule himself in building the house of God ; all was made ready *before it was brought to the ground,* 1 Kings vi. 7.

28 Be not a witness against thy neighbour without cause ; and deceive *not* with thy lips. 29 Say not, I will do so to him as he hath done to me : I will render to the man according to his work.

We are here forbidden to be in any thing injurious to our neighbour, particularly in and by the forms of law, either, 1. As *a witness :* " Never bear a testimony against any man *without cause,* unless what thou sayest thou knowest to be punctually true and thou hast a clear call to testify it. Never bear a false testimony against any one ;" for it follows, " *Deceive not with thy lips ;* deceive not the judge and jury, deceive not those whom thou conversest with, into an ill opinion of thy neighbour. When thou speakest of thy neighbour do not only speak that which is true, but take heed lest, in the manner of thy speaking, thou insinuate any thing that is otherwise and so shouldst deceive by innuendos or hyperboles." Or, 2. As a plaintiff or prosecutor. If there be occasion to bring an action or information against thy neighbour, let it not be from a spirit of revenge. " *Say not,* I am resolved I will be even with

934

him : *I will do so to him as he has done to me.*" Even a righteous cause becomes unrighteous when it is thus prosecuted with malice. *Say not, I will render to the man according to his work,* and make him pay dearly for it ; for it is God's prerogative to do so, and we must leave it to him, and not step into his throne, or take his work out of his hands. If we will needs be our own carvers, and judges in our own cause, we forfeit the benefit of an appeal to God's tribunal ; therefore we must not avenge ourselves, because he has said, *Vengeance is mine.*

30 I went by the field of the slothful, and by the vineyard of the man void of understanding ; 31 And, lo, it was all grown over with thorns, *and* nettles had covered the face thereof, and the stone wall thereof was broken down. 32 Then I saw, *and* considered *it* well : I looked upon *it, and* received instruction. 33 *Yet* a little sleep, a little slumber, a little folding of the hands to sleep : 34 So shall thy poverty come *as* one that travelleth ; and thy want as an armed man.

Here is, 1. The view which Solomon took of *the field and vineyard of the slothful* man. He did not go on purpose to see it, but, as he passed by, observing the fruitfulness of the ground, as it is very proper for travellers to do, and his subjects' management of their land, as it is very proper for magistrates to do, he cast his eye upon a *field* and a *vineyard* unlike all the rest ; for, though the soil was good, yet there was nothing growing in them but *thorns and nettles,* not here and there one, but they were all overrun with weeds ; and, if there had been any fruit, it would have been eaten up by the beasts, for there was no fence : *The stone-wall was broken down* See the effects of that curse upon the ground (Gen. iii. 18), " *Thorns and thistles shall it bring forth unto thee,* and nothing else unless thou take pains with it." See what a blessing to the world the husbandman's calling is, and what a wilderness this earth, even Canaan itself, would be without it. *The king himself is served of the field,* but he would be ill served if God did not teach the husbandman discretion and diligence to clear the ground, plant it, sow it, and fence it. See what a great difference there is between some and others in the management even of their worldly affairs, and how little some consult their reputation, not caring though they proclaim their slothfulness, in the manifest effects of it, to all that pass by, shamed by their neighbour's diligence. 2. The reflections which he made upon it. He paused a little *and considered it, looked* again *upon it, and received instruction.* He did not break out into any passionate censures of the owner, did not call him any ill names, but he endeavoured himself to get good by the observation and to be quickened by it to diligence. Note, Those that are to give instruction to others must receive instruction themselves, and instruction may be received, not only from what we read and hear, but from what we see, not only from what we see of the works of God, but from what we see of the manners of men, not only from men's good manners, but from their evil manners. Plutarch relates a saying of Cato Major, "That wise men profit more by fools than fools by wise men; for wise men will avoid the faults of fools, but fools will not imitate the virtues of wise men." Solomon reckoned that he *received instruction* by this sight, though it did not suggest to him any new notion or lesson, but only put him in mind of an observation he himself had formerly made, both of the ridiculous folly of the sluggard (who, when he has needful work to do, lies dozing in bed and cries, *Yet a little sleep, a little slumber,* and still it will be a little more, till he has slept his eyes out, and, instead of being fitted by sleep for business, as wise men are, he is dulled, and stupified, and made good for nothing) and of the certain misery that attends him: his *poverty comes as one that travels ;* it is constantly coming nearer and nearer to him, and will be upon him speedily, and want seizes him as irresistibly *as an armed man,* a highwayman that will strip him of all he has. Now this is applicable, not only to our worldly business, to show what a scandalous thing slothfulness in that is, and how injurious to the family, but to the affairs of our souls. Note, (1.) Our souls are our fields and vineyards, which we are every one of us to take care of, to dress, and to keep. They are capable of being improved with good husbandry; that may be got out of them which will be fruit abounding to our account. We are charged with them, to occupy them till our Lord come; and a great deal of care and pains it is requisite that we should take about them. (2.) These fields and vineyards are often in a very bad state, not only no fruit brought forth, but all overgrown with *thorns* and *nettles* (scratching, stinging, inordinate lusts and passions, pride, covetousness, sensuality, malice, those are the thorns and nettles, the wild grapes, which the unsanctified heart produces), no guard kept against the enemy, but the *stone-wall broken down,* and all lies in common, all exposed. (3.) Where it is thus it is owing to the sinner's own slothfulness and folly. He is a sluggard, loves sleep, hates labour; and he is void of understanding, understands neither his business nor his interest; he is perfectly besotted. (4.) The issue of it will certainly be the ruin of the soul and all its welfare. It is everlasting want that thus comes upon it as an armed man. We know the place assigned to the wicked and slothful servant.

CHAP. XXV.

THESE *are* also proverbs of Solomon, which the men of Hezekiah king of Judah copied out.

This verse is the title of this latter collection of Solomon's proverbs, for he *sought out and set in order many proverbs,* that by them he might be still *teaching the people knowledge,* Eccl. xii. 9. Observe, 1. The proverbs were Solomon's, who was divinely inspired to deliver, for the use of the church, these wise and weighty sentences; we have had many, but still there are more. Yet herein Christ is greater than Solomon, for if we had all upon record that Christ said, and did, that was instructive, *the world could not contain the books that would be written,* John xxi. 25. 2. The publishers were Hezekiah's servants, who, it is likely, herein acted as his servants, being appointed by him to do this good service to the church, among other good offices that he did *in the law and in the commandments,* 2 Chron. xxxi. 21. Whether he employed the prophets in this work, as Isaiah, Hosea, or Micah, who lived in his time, or some that were trained up in the schools of the prophets, or some of the priests and Levites, to whom we find him giving a charge concerning divine things (2 Chron. xxix. 4), or (as the Jews think) his *princes* and ministers of state, who were more properly called his *servants,* is not certain; if the work was done by Eliakim, and Joah, and Shebna, it was no diminution to their character. They copied out these proverbs from the records of Solomon's reign, and published them as an appendix to the former edition of this book. It may be a piece of very good service to the church to publish other men's works that have lain hidden in obscurity, perhaps a great while. Some think they culled these out of the 3000 proverbs which Solomon spoke (1 Kings iv. 32), leaving out those that were physical, and that pertained to natural philosophy, and preserving such only as were divine and moral; and in this collection some observe that special regard was had to those observations which concern kings and their administration.

2 *It is* the glory of God to conceal a thing : but the honour of kings *is* to search out a matter. 3 The heaven for height, and the earth for depth, and the heart of kings *is* unsearchable.

Here is, 1. An instance given of the honour of God: *It is his glory to conceal a matter.* He needs not search into any thing, for he perfectly knows every thing by a clear and certain view, and nothing can be hidden from him; and yet his own *way is in the sea* and his *path in the great waters.* There is an unfathomable depth in his counsels, Rom. xi. 33. It is but a little portion that is heard of him. *Clouds and darkness are round about him.* We see what he does, but we know not the reasons. Some refer it to the sins of men; it is his glory to pardon sin, which is covering it, not remembering it, not mentioning it; his forbearance, which he exercises towards sinners, is likewise his honour, in which he seems to keep silence and take no notice of the matter. 2. A double instance of the honour of kings:—(1.) It is God's glory that he needs not *search into a matter*, because he knows it without search; but it is the honour of kings, with a close application of mind, and by all the methods of enquiry, to search out the matters that are brought before them, to take pains in examining offenders, that they may discover their designs and bring to light the hidden works of darkness, not to give judgment hastily or till they have weighed things, nor to leave it wholly to others to examine things, but to see with their own eyes. (2.) It is God's glory that he cannot himself be found out by searching, and some of that honour is devolved upon kings, wise kings, that *search out matters;* their *hearts* are *unsearchable,* like the *height of heaven* or the *depth of the earth,* which we may guess at, but cannot measure. Princes have their *arcana imperii* —state secrets, designs which are kept private, and reasons of state, which private persons are not competent judges of, and therefore ought not to pry into. Wise princes, when they *search into a matter,* have reaches which one would not think of, as Solomon, when he called for a sword to divide the living child with, designing thereby to discover the true mother.

4 Take away the dross from the silver, and there shall come forth a vessel for the finer. 5 Take away the wicked *from* before the king, and his throne shall be established in righteousness.

This shows that the vigorous endeavour of a prince to suppress vice, and reform the manners of his people, is the most effectual way to support his government. Observe, 1. What the duty of magistrates is: To *take away the wicked,* to use their power for the terror of evil works and evil workers, not only to banish those that are vicious and profane from their presence, and forbid them the court, but so to frighten them and restrain them that they may not spread the infection of their wickedness among their subjects. This is called *taking away the dross from the silver,* which is done by the force of fire. Wicked people are the dross of a nation, the scum of the country, and, as such, to be taken away. If men will not take them away, God will, Ps. cxix. 119. If the *wicked be taken away from before the king,* if he abandon them and show his detestation of their wicked courses, it will go far towards the disabling of them to do mischief. The reformation of the court will promote the re-

formation of the kingdom, Ps. ci. 3, 8. 2. What the advantage will be of their doing this duty. (1.) It will be the bettering of the subjects; they shall be made like silver refined, fit to be made *vessels of honour.* (2.) It will be the settling of the prince. *His throne shall be established in* this *righteousness,* for God will bless his government, the people will be pliable to it, and so it will become durable.

6 Put not forth thyself in the presence of the king, and stand not in the place of great *men :* 7 For better *it is* that it be said unto thee, Come up hither; than that thou shouldest be put lower in the presence of the prince whom thine eyes have seen.

Here we see, 1. That religion is so far from destroying good manners that it teaches us to behave ourselves lowly and reverently towards our superiors, to keep our distance, and give place to those to whom it belongs · *" Put not forth thyself* rudely and carelessly *in the king's presence,* or in the presence of great men; do not *compare with them"* (so some understand it); "do not vie with them in apparel, furniture, gardens, house-keeping, or retinue, for that is an affront to them and will waste thy own estate." 2. That religion teaches us humility and self-denial, which is a better lesson than that of good manners: " Deny thyself the place thou art entitled to; covet not to make a fair show, nor aim at preferment, nor thrust thyself into the company of those that are above thee; be content in a low sphere if that is it which God has allotted to thee." The reason he gives is because this is really the way to advancement, as our Saviour shows in a parable that seems to be borrowed from this, Luke xiv. 9. Not that we must *therefore* pretend modesty and humility, and make a stratagem of it, for the courting of honour, but *therefore* we must really be modest and humble, because God will put honour on such and so will men too. It is better, more for a man's satisfaction and reputation, to be advanced above his pretensions and expectations, than to be thrust down below them, *in the presence of the prince,* whom it was a great piece of honour to be admitted to the sight of and a great piece of presumption to look upon without leave.

8 Go not forth hastily to strive, lest *thou know not* what to do in the end thereof, when thy neighbour hath put thee to shame. 9 Debate thy cause with thy neighbour *himself;* and discover not a secret to another: 10 Lest he that heareth *it* put thee to shame, and thine infamy turn not away.

I. Here is good counsel given about going to law:—1. " Be not hasty in bringing an action, before thou hast thyself considered it, and consulted with thy friends about it: *Go not forth hastily to strive;* do not send for a writ in a passion, or upon the first appearance of right on thy side, but weigh the matter deliberately, because we are apt to be partial in our own cause; consider the certainty of the expenses and the uncertainty of the success, how much care and vexation it will be the occasion of, and, after all, the cause may go against thee; surely then thou shouldst not *go forth hastily to strive.*" 2. " Bring not an action before thou hast tried to end the matter amicably (*v.* 9): *Debate thy cause with thy neighbour* privately, and perhaps you will understand one another better and see that there is no occasion to go to law." In public quarrels the war that must at length end might better have been prevented by a treaty of peace, and a great deal of blood and treasure spared. It is so in private quarrels: " Sue not thy neighbour as a *heathen man and a publican* until thou hast told him his fault between thee and him alone, and he has refused to refer the matter, or to come to an accommodation. Perhaps the matter in variance is a secret, not fit to be divulged to any, much less to be brought upon the stage before the country; and therefore end it privately, that it may not be discovered." *Reveal not the secret of another,* so some read it. " Do not, in revenge, to disgrace thy adversary, disclose that which should be kept private and which does not at all belong to the cause."

II. Two reasons he gives why we should be thus cautious in going to law:—1. " Because otherwise the cause will be in danger of going against thee, and thou wilt *not know what to do* when the defendant has justified himself in what thou didst charge upon him, and made it out that thy complaint was frivolous and vexatious and that thou hadst no just cause of action, and so *put thee to shame,* non-suit thee, and force thee to pay costs, all which might have been prevented by a little consideration." 2. " Because it will turn very much to thy reproach if thou fall under the character of being litigious. Not only the defendant himself (*v.* 8), but he that hears the cause tried will *put thee to shame,* will expose thee as a man of no principle, and *thy infamy will not turn away;* thou wilt never retrieve thy reputation."

11 A word fitly spoken *is like* apples of gold in pictures of silver. 12 *As* an earring of gold, and an ornament of fine gold, *so is* a wise reprover upon an obedient ear.

Solomon here shows how much it becomes a man, 1. To speak pertinently: *A word upon the wheels,* that runs well, is well-circumstanced, in proper time and place—instruction, advice, or comfort, given seasonably, and in apt expressions, adapted to the case of the person spoken to and agreeing with

the character of the person speaking—*is like golden* balls resembling *apples,* or like true apples of a golden colour (golden rennets), or perhaps gilded, as sometimes we have gilded laurels, and those embossed *in pictures of silver,* or rather brought to table in a silver network basket, or in a silver box of that which we call *philligree*-work, through which the golden apples might be seen. Doubtless it was some ornament of the table, then well known. As that was very pleasing to the eye, so is *a word fitly spoken* to the ear. 2. Especially to give a reproof with discretion, and so as to make it acceptable. If it be well given, by *a wise reprover,* and well taken, by an *obedient ear,* it is an *earring of gold* and an *ornament of fine gold,* very graceful and well becoming both the reprover and the reproved; both will have their praise, the reprover for giving it so prudently and the reproved for taking it so patiently and making a good use of it. Others will commend them both, and they will have satisfaction in each other; he who gave the reproof is pleased that it had the desired effect, and he to whom it was given has reason to be thankful for it as a kindness. *That is well given,* we say, *that is well taken;* yet it does not always prove that that is well taken which is well given. It were to be wished that a *wise reprover* should always meet with an *obedient ear,* but often it is not so.

13 As the cold of snow in the time of harvest, *so is* a faithful messenger to them that send him: for he refresheth the soul of his masters.

See here, 1. What ought to be the care of a servant, the meanest that is sent on an errand and entrusted with any business, much more the greatest, the agent and ambassador of a prince; he ought to be *faithful to him that sends him,* and to see to it that he do not, by mistake or with design, falsify his trust, and that he be in nothing that lies in his power wanting to his master's interest. Those that act as factors, by commission, ought to act as carefully as for themselves. 2. How much this will be the satisfaction of the master; it will *refresh his soul* as much as ever the *cold of snow* (which in hot countries they preserve by art all the year round) refreshed the labourers in the harvest, that *bore the burden and heat of the day.* The more important the affair was, and the more fear of its miscarrying, the more acceptable is the messenger, if he have managed it successfully and well. A faithful minister, Christ's messenger, should be thus acceptable to us (Job xxxiii. 23); however, he will be a *sweet savour to God,* 2 Cor. ii. 15.

14 Whoso boasteth himself of a false gift *is like* clouds and wind without rain.

He may be said to boast of a false gift, 1. Who pretends to have received or given that which he never had, which he never gave, makes a noise of his great accomplishments and his good services, but it is all false; he is not what he pretends to be. Or, 2. Who promises what he will give and what he will do, but performs nothing, who raises people's expectations of the mighty things he will do for his country, for his friends, what noble legacies he will leave, but either he has not wherewithal to do what he says or he never designs it. Such a one is like the morning-cloud, that passes away, and disappoints those who looked for rain from it to water the parched ground (Jude 12), *clouds without water*.

15 By long forbearing is a prince persuaded, and a soft tongue breaketh the bone.

Two things are here recommended to us, in dealing with others, as likely means to gain our point:—1. Patience, to bear a present heat without being put into a heat by it, and to wait for a fit opportunity to offer our reasons and to give persons time to consider them. By this means even a *prince* may be *persuaded* to do a thing which he seemed very averse to, much more a common person. That which is justice and reason now will be so another time, and therefore we need not urge them with violence now, but wait for a more convenient season. 2. Mildness, to speak without passion or provocation : *A soft tongue breaks the bone;* it mollifies the roughest spirits and overcomes those that are most morose, like lightning, which, they say, has sometimes broken the bone, and yet not pierced the flesh. Gideon with a soft tongue pacified the Ephraimites and Abigail turned away David's wrath. *Hard words*, we say, *break no bones*, and therefore we should bear them patiently ; but, it seems, *soft words* do, and therefore we should, on all occasions, give them prudently.

16 Hast thou found honey ? eat so much as is sufficient for thee, lest thou be filled therewith, and vomit it.

Here, 1. We are allowed a sober and moderate use of the delights of sense: " *Hast thou found honey ?* It is not forbidden fruit to thee, as it was to Jonathan ; thou mayest eat of it with thanksgiving to God, who, having created things grateful to our senses, has given us leave to make use of them. *Eat as much as is sufficient*, and no more. *Enough is as good as a feast*. 2. We are cautioned to take heed of excess. We must use all pleasures as we do honey, with a check upon our appetite, lest we take more than does us good and make ourselves sick with it. We are most in danger of surfeiting upon that which is most sweet, and therefore those that fare sumptuously every day have need to watch over themselves, *lest their hearts be at any time overcharged*. The pleasures of sense lose their sweetness by the excessive use of

them and become nauseous, as honey, which turns sour in the stomach ; it is therefore our interest, as well as our duty, to use them with sobriety.

17 Withdraw thy foot from thy neighbour's house ; lest he be weary of thee, and *so* hate thee.

Here he mentions another pleasure which we must not take too much of, that of visiting our friends, the former for fear of surfeiting ourselves, this for fear of surfeiting our neighbour. 1. It is a piece of civility to visit our neighbours sometimes, to show our respect to them and concern for them, and to cultivate and improve mutual acquaintance and love, and that we may have both the satisfaction and advantage of their conversation. 2. It is wisdom, as well as good manners, not to be troublesome to our friends in our visiting them, not to visit too often, nor stay too long, nor contrive to come at meal-time, nor make ourselves busy in the affairs of their families ; hereby we make ourselves cheap, mean, and burdensome. Thy neighbour, who is thus plagued and haunted with thy visits, will be *weary of thee and hate thee*, and *that* will be the destruction of friendship which should have been the improvement of it. *Post tres sæpe dies piscis vilescit et hospes—After the third day fish and company become distasteful.* Familiarity breeds contempt. *Nulli te facias nimis sodalem—Be not too intimate with any.* He that sponges upon his friend loses him. How much better a friend then is God than any other friend ; for we need not withdraw our foot from his house, the throne of his grace (*ch.* viii. 34); the oftener we come to him the better and the more welcome.

18 A man that beareth false witness against his neighbour *is* a maul, and a sword, and a sharp arrow.

Here, 1. The sin condemned is *bearing false witness against our neighbour*, either in judgment or in common conversation, contrary to the law of the ninth commandment. 2. That which it is here condemned for is the mischievousness of it ; it is in its power to ruin not only men's reputation, but their lives, estates, families, all that is dear to them. A false testimony is every thing that is dangerous ; it *is a maul* (or *club* to knock a man's brains out with), a flail, which there is no fence against ; it is *a sword* to wound near at hand and a *sharp arrow* to wound at a distance ; we have therefore need to pray, *Deliver my soul, O Lord ! from lying lips*, Ps. cxx. 2.

19 Confidence in an unfaithful man in time of trouble *is like* a broken tooth, and a foot out of joint.

1. The *confidence of an unfaithful man* (so some read it) will be *like a broken tooth ;* his policy, his power, his interest, all that which he trusted in to support him in his wicked-

ness, will fail him in time of trouble, Ps. lii. 7. 2. *Confidence in an unfaithful man* (so we read it), in a man whom we thought trusty and therefore depended on, but who proves otherwise; it proves not only unserviceable, but painful and vexatious, like a *broken tooth, or a foot out of joint,* which, when we put any stress upon it, not only fails us, but makes us feel from it, especially *in time of trouble,* when we most expect help from it; it is like a broken reed, Isa. xxxvi. 6. Confidence in a faithful God, in time of trouble, will not prove thus; on him we may rest and in him dwell at ease.

20 *As* he that taketh away a garment in cold weather, *and as* vinegar upon nitre, so *is* he that singeth songs to a heavy heart.

1. The absurdity here censured is *singing songs to a heavy heart.* Those that are in great sorrow are to be comforted by sympathizing with them, condoling with them, and concurring in their lamentation. If we take that method, the *moving of our lips may assuage their grief* (Job xvi. 5); but we take a wrong course with them if we think to relieve them by being merry with them, and endeavouring to make them merry; for it adds to their grief to see their friends so little concerned for them; it puts them upon ripping up the causes of their grief, and aggravating them, and makes them harden themselves in sorrow against the assaults of mirth. 2. The absurdities this is compared to are, *taking away a garment* from a man in *cold weather,* which makes him colder, and pouring *vinegar upon nitre,* which, like water upon lime, puts it into a ferment; so improper, so incongruous, is it to sing pleasant songs to one that is of a sorrowful spirit. Some read it in a contrary sense: *As he that puts on a garment in cold weather* warms the body, or as *vinegar upon nitre* dissolves it, so he that *sings songs* of comfort to a person in sorrow refreshes him and dispels his grief.

21 If thine enemy be hungry, give him bread to eat; and if he be thirsty, give him water to drink: 22 For thou shalt heap coals of fire upon his head, and the LORD shall reward thee.

By this it appears that, however the scribes and Pharisees had corrupted the law, not only the commandment of loving our brethren, but even that of loving our enemies, was not only a new, but also an old commandment, an Old-Testament commandment, though our Saviour has given it to us with the new enforcement of his own great example in loving us when we were enemies. Observe, 1. How we must express our love to our enemies by the real offices of kindness, even those that are expensive to ourselves and most acceptable to them: "If they be *hungry* and *thirsty,* instead of pleasing thyself with their distress and contriving how to cut off supplies from

them, relieve them, as Elisha did the Syrians that came to apprehend him," 2 King vi. 22. 2. What encouragement we have to do so. (1.) It will be a likely means to win upon them, and bring them over to be reconciled to us; we shall mollify them as the refiner melts the metal in the crucible, not only by putting it over the fire, but by heaping coals of fire upon it. The way to turn an enemy into a friend is, to act towards him in a friendly manner. If it do not gain him, it will aggravate his sin and punishment, and heap the burning coals of God's wrath upon his head, as rejoicing in his calamity may be an occasion of God's turning his wrath from him, *ch.* xxiv. 17. (2.) However, we shall be no losers by our self-denial: "Whether he relent towards thee or no, *the Lord shall reward thee;* he shall forgive thee who thus showest thyself to be of a forgiving spirit. He shall provide for thee when thou art in distress (though thou hast been evil and ungrateful), as thou dost for thy enemy; at least it shall be recompensed in the resurrection of the just, when kindnesses done to our enemies shall be remembered as well as those shown to God's friends."

23 The north wind driveth away rain: so *doth* an angry countenance a backbiting tongue.

Here see, 1. How we must discourage sin and witness against it, and particularly the sin of slandering and backbiting; we must frown upon it, and, by giving it an angry countenance, endeavour to put it out of countenance. Slanders would not be so readily spoken as they are if they were not readily heard; but good manners would silence the slanderer if he saw that his tales displeased the company. We should show ourselves uneasy if we heard a dear friend, whom we value, evil-spoken of; the same dislike we should show of evil-speaking in general. If we cannot otherwise reprove, we may do it by our looks. 2. The good effect which this might probably have; who knows but it may silence and drive away a *backbiting tongue?* Sin, if it be countenanced, becomes daring, but, if it receive any check, it is so conscious of its own shame that it becomes cowardly, and this sin in particular, for many abuse those they speak of only in hopes to curry favour with those they speak to.

24 *It is* better to dwell in the corner of the housetop, than with a brawling woman and in a wide house.

This is the same with what he had said, *ch.* xxi. 9. Observe, 1. How those are to be pitied that are unequally yoked, especially with such as are brawling and contentious, whether husband or wife; for it is equally true of both. It is better to be alone than to be joined to one who, instead of being a meet-help, is a great hindrance to the comfort of life. 2. How those may sometimes be envied that live in solitude; as they want the comfort of society, so they are free from the vexation of it. And as there are cases which give occasion to say, "Blessed is the womb that has not borne," so there are which give occasion to say, "Blessed is the man who was never married, but who lies like a servant in *a corner of the house-top.*"

25 *As* cold waters to a thirsty soul, so *is* good news from a far country.

See here, 1. How natural it is to us to desire to hear good news from our friends, and concerning our affairs at a distance. It is sometimes with impatience that we expect to hear from abroad; our souls thirst after it. But we should check the inordinateness of that desire; if it be bad news, it will come too soon, if good, it will be welcome at any time. 2. How acceptable such good news will be when it does come, as refreshing as cold water to one that is thirsty. Solomon himself had much trading abroad, as well as correspondence by his ambassadors with foreign courts; and how pleasant it was to hear of the good success of his negociations abroad he well knew by experience. Heaven is a country afar off; how refreshing is it to hear good news thence, both in the everlasting gospel, which signifies glad tidings, and in the witness of the Spirit with our spirits that we are God's children.

26 A righteous man falling down before the wicked *is as* a troubled fountain, and a corrupt spring.

It is here represented as a very lamentable thing, and a public grievance, and of ill consequence to many, like the *troubling* of a *fountain* and the *corrupting* of a *spring*, for the righteous to *fall down before the wicked*, that is, 1. For the righteous to fall into sin in the sight of the wicked—for them to do any thing unbecoming their profession, which is *told in Gath*, and *published in the streets of Ashkelon*, and in which the *daughters of the Philistines rejoice.* For those that have been *in reputation for wisdom and honour* to fall from their excellency, this *troubles the fountains* by grieving some, and *corrupts the springs* by infecting others and emboldening them to do likewise. 2. For the righteous to be oppressed, and run down, and trampled upon, by the violence or subtlety of evil men, to be displaced and thrust into obscurity, this is the troubling of the fountains of justice and corrupting the very springs of government, *ch.* xxviii. 12, 28; xxix. 2. 3. For the righteous to be cowardly, to truckle to the wicked, to be afraid of opposing his wickedness and basely to yield to him, this is a reflection upon religion, a discouragement to good men, and strengthens the hands of sinners in their sins, and so is like a *troubled fountain* and a *corrupt spring.*

27 *It is* not good to eat much honey:

940

so *for men* to search their own glory *is not* glory.

I. Two things we must be graciously dead to:—1. To the pleasures of sense, for *it is not good to eat much honey;* though it pleases the taste, and, if eaten with moderation, is very wholesome, yet, if eaten to excess, it becomes nauseous, creates bile, and is the occasion of many diseases. It is true of all the delights of the children of men that they will surfeit, but never satisfy, and they are dangerous to those that allow themselves the liberal use of them. 2. To the praise of men. We must not be greedy of that any more than of pleasure, because, *for men to search their own glory,* to court applause and covet to make themselves popular, is not their glory, but their shame; every one will laugh at them for it; and the glory which is so courted *is not glory* when it is got, for it is really no true honour to a man.

II. Some give another sense of this verse: *To eat much honey is not good,* but to search into glorious and excellent things is a great commendation, it is true glory; we cannot therein offend by excess. Others thus: "As honey, though pleasant to the taste, if used immoderately, oppresses the stomach, so an over-curious search into things sublime and glorious, though pleasant to us, if we pry too far, will overwhelm our capacities with a greater glory and lustre than they can bear." Or thus: "You may be surfeited with eating too much honey, but the last of glory, of their glory, the glory of the blessed, is glory; it will be ever fresh, and never pall the appetite.

28 He that *hath* no rule over his own spirit *is like* a city *that is* broken down, *and* without walls.

Here is, 1. The good character of a wise and virtuous man implied. He is one that has *rule over his own spirit;* he maintains the government of himself, and of his own appetites and passions, and does not suffer them to rebel against reason and conscience. He has the rule of his own thoughts, his desires, his inclinations, his resentments, and keeps them all in good order. 2. The bad case of a vicious man, who has not this rule over his own spirit, who, when temptations to excess in eating or drinking are before him, has no government of himself, when he is provoked breaks out into exorbitant passions, such a one is *like a city that is broken down and without walls.* All that is good goes out, and forsakes him; all that is evil breaks in upon him. He lies exposed to all the temptations of Satan and becomes an easy prey to that enemy; he is also liable to many troubles and vexations; it is likewise as much a reproach to him as it is to a city to have its walls ruined, Neh. i. 3.

CHAP. XXVI.

AS snow in summer, and as rain in harvest, so honour is not seemly for a fool.

Note, 1. It is too common a thing for honour to be given to fools, who are utterly unworthy of it and unfit for it. Bad men, who have neither wit nor grace, are sometimes preferred by princes, and applauded and cried up by the people. *Folly is set in great dignity*, as Solomon observed, Eccl. x. 6. 2. It is very absurd and unbecoming when it is so. It is as incongruous *as snow in summer*, and as great a disorder in the commonwealth as that is in the course of nature and in the seasons of the year; nay, it is as injurious *as rain in harvest*, which hinders the labourers and spoils the fruits of the earth when they are ready to be gathered. When bad men are in power they commonly abuse their power, in discouraging virtue, and giving countenance to wickedness, for want of wisdom to discern it and grace to detest it.

2 As the bird by wandering, as the swallow by flying, so the curse causeless shall not come.

Here is, 1. The folly of passion. It makes men scatter *causeless curses*, wishing ill to others upon presumption that they are bad and have done ill, when either they mistake the person or misunderstand the fact, or they call evil good and good evil. Give honour to a fool, and he thunders out his anathemas against all that he is disgusted with, right or wrong. Great men, when wicked, think they have a privilege to keep those about them in awe, by cursing them, and swearing at them, which yet is an expression of the most impotent malice and shows their weakness as much as their wickedness. 2. The safety of innocency. He that is cursed without cause, whether by furious imprecations or solemn anathemas, the curse shall do him no more harm than the bird that flies over his head, than Goliath's curses did to David, 1 Sam. xvii. 43. It will fly away like the sparrow or the wild dove, which go nobody knows where, till they return to their proper place, as the curse will at length return upon the head of him that uttered it.

3 A whip for the horse, a bridle for the ass, and a rod for the fool's back.

Here, 1. Wicked men are compared to *the horse* and *the ass*, so brutish are they, so unreasonable, so unruly, and not to be governed but by force or fear, so low has sin sunk men, so much below themselves. Man indeed is *born like the wild ass's colt*, but as some by the grace of God are changed, and become rational, so others by custom in sin are hardened, and become more and more sottish, *as the horse and the mule*, Ps. xxxii. 9. 2. Direction is given to use them accordingly. Princes, instead of giving *honour to a fool* (*v.* 1), must put disgrace upon him—instead of putting power into his hand, must exercise power over him. A *horse* unbroken needs *a whip* for correction, and an *ass a bridle* for direction and to check him when he would turn out of the way; so a vicious man, who

will not be under the guidance and restraint of religion and reason, ought to be whipped and bridled, to be rebuked severely, and made to smart for what he has done amiss, and to be restrained from offending any more.

4 Answer not a fool according to his folly, lest thou also be like unto him. 5 Answer a fool according to his folly, lest he be wise in his own conceit.

See here the noble security of the scripture-style, which seems to contradict itself, but really does not. Wise men have need to be directed how to deal with fools; and they have never more need of wisdom than in dealing with such, to know when to keep silence and when to speak, for there may be a time for both. 1. In some cases a wise man will not set his wit to that of a fool so far as to *answer him according to his folly*. "If he boast of himself, do not answer him by boasting of thyself. If he rail and talk passionately, do not thou rail and talk passionately too. If he tell one great lie, do not thou tell another to match it. If he calumniate thy friends, do not thou calumniate his. If he banter, do not answer him in his own language, *lest thou be like him*, even thou, who knowest better things, who hast more sense, and hast been better taught." 2. Yet, in other cases, a wise man will use his wisdom for the conviction of a fool, when, by taking notice of what he says, there may be hopes of doing good, or at least preventing further mischief, either to himself or others. "If thou have reason to think that thy silence will be deemed an evidence of the weakness of thy cause, or of thy own weakness, in such a case *answer him*, and let it be an answer *ad hominem—to the man*, beat him at his own weapons, and that will be an answer *ad rem—to the point*, or as good as one. If he offer any thing that looks like an argument, answer that, and suit thy answer to his case. If he think, because thou dost not answer him, that what he says is unanswerable, then *give* him an answer, *lest he be wise in his own conceit* and boast of a victory." For (Luke vii. 35) Wisdom's children must justify her.

6 He that sendeth a message by the hand of a fool cutteth off the feet, *and* drinketh damage. 7 The legs of the lame are not equal: so *is* a parable in the mouth of fools. 8 As he that bindeth a stone in a sling, so *is* he that giveth honour to a fool. 9 *As* a thorn goeth up into the hand of a drunkard, so *is* a parable in the mouth of fools.

To recommend wisdom to us, and to quicken us to the diligent use of all the means for the getting of wisdom, Solomon here shows that fools are fit for nothing; they are either sottish men, who will never think and design at all, or vicious men, who will never think and design well. 1. They are not fit to be entrusted with any business, not fit to go on an errand (*v.* 6): *He that* does but *send a message by the hand of a fool,* of a careless heedless person, one who is so full of his jests and so given to his pleasures that he cannot apply his mind to any thing that is serious, will find his message misunderstood, the one half of it forgotten, the rest awkwardly delivered, and so many blunders made about it that he might as well have *cut off his legs,* that is, never have sent him. Nay, he will *drink damage;* it will be very much to his prejudice to have employed such a one, who, instead of bringing him a good account of his affairs, will abuse him and put a trick upon him; for, in Solomon's language, a knave and a fool are of the same signification. It will turn much to a man's disgrace to make use of the service of a fool, for people will be apt to judge of the master by his messenger. 2. They are not fit to have any honour put upon them. He had said (*v.* 1), *Honour is not seemly for a fool;* here he shows that it is lost and thrown away upon him, as if a man should throw a precious stone, or a stone fit to be used in weighing, into a heap of common stones, where it would be buried and of no use; it is as absurd as if a man should *dress up a stone in purple* (so others); nay, it is dangerous, it is like *a stone bound in a sling,* with which a man will be likely to do hurt. To *give honour to a fool* is to put a sword in a madman's hand, with which we know not what mischief he may do, even to those that put it into his hand. 3. They are not fit to deliver wise sayings, nor should they undertake to handle any matter of weight, though they should be instructed concerning it, and be able to say something to it. Wise sayings, as a foolish man delivers them and applies them (in such a manner that one may know he does not rightly understand them), lose their excellency and usefulness: *A parable in the mouth of fools* ceases to be a parable, and becomes a jest. If a man who lives a wicked life, yet speaks religiously and takes God's covenant into his mouth, (1.) He does but shame himself and his profession: As *the legs of the lame are not equal,* by reason of which their going is unseemly, so unseemly is it for a fool to pretend to speak apophthegms, and give advice, and for a man to talk devoutly whose conversation is a constant contradiction to his talk and gives him the lie. His good words raise him up, but then his bad life takes him down, and so his *legs are not equal.* "A wise saying," (says bishop Patrick) "doth as ill become a fool as dancing doth a cripple; for, as his lameness never so much appears as when he would seem nimble, so the other's folly is never so ridiculous as when he would seem wise." As therefore it is best for a lame man to keep his seat, so it is best for a silly

942

man, or a bad man, to hold his tongue. (2.) He does but do mischief with it to himself and others, as a drunkard does with a thorn, or any other sharp thing which he takes in his hand, with which he tears himself and those about him, because he knows not how to manage it. Those that talk well and do not live well, their good words will aggravate their own condemnation and others will be hardened by their inconsistency with themselves. Some give this sense of it: The sharpest saying, by which a sinner, one would think, should be pricked to the heart, makes no more impression upon a fool, no, though it come out of his own mouth, than the scratch of a thorn does upon the hand of a man when he is drunk, who then feels it not nor complains of it, *ch.* xxiii. 35.

10 The great *God* that formed all *things* both rewardeth the fool, and rewardeth transgressors.

Our translation gives this verse a different reading in the text and in the margin; and accordingly it expresses either, 1. The equity of a good God. The *Master,* or *Lord* (so *Rab* signifies), or, as we read it, *The great God that formed all things* at first, and still governs them in infinite wisdom, renders to every man according to his work. He *rewards the fool,* who sinned through ignorance, *who knew not his Lord's will, with few stripes;* and he *rewards the transgressor,* who sinned presumptuously and with a high hand, who *knew his Lord's will and would not do it, with many stripes.* Some understand it of the goodness of God's common providence even to fools and transgressors, on whom he *causes his sun to shine* and *his rain to fall.* Or, 2. The iniquity of a bad prince (so the margin reads it): *A great man grieves all, and he hires the fool; he hires also the transgressors.* When a wicked man gets power in his hand, by himself, and by the fools and knaves whom he employs under him, whom he hires and chooses to make use of, he grieves all who are under him and is vexatious to them. We should therefore *pray for kings and all in authority,* that, under them, our lives may be quiet and peaceable.

11 As a dog returneth to his vomit, so a fool returneth to his folly.

See here, 1. What an abominable thing sin is, and how hateful sometimes it is made to appear, even to the sinner himself. When his conscience is convinced, or he feels smart from his sin, he is sick of it, and vomits it up; he seems then to detest it and to be willing to part with it. It is in itself, and, first or last, will be to the sinner, more loathsome than the vomit of a dog, Ps. xxxvi. 2. 2. How apt sinners are to relapse into it notwithstanding. As the dog, after he has gained ease by vomiting that which burdened his stomach, yet goes and licks it up again, so sinners, who have been convinced only and not converted, return to sin again, forgetting how sick it made them. The apostle (2 Pet. ii. 22) applies this proverb to those that *have known the way of righteousness* but are *turned from it; but* God will *spue them out of his mouth*, Rev. iii. 16.

12 Seest thou a man wise in his own conceit? *there is* more hope of a fool than of him.

Here is, 1. A spiritual disease supposed, and that is self-conceit: *Seest thou a man?* Yes, we see many a one, *wise in his own conceit*, who has some little sense, but is proud of it, thinks it much more than it is, more than any of his neighbours have, and enough, so that he needs no more, has such a conceit of his own abilities as makes him opinionative, dogmatical, and censorious; and all the use he makes of his knowledge is that it puffs him up. Or, if by a wise man we understand a religious man, it describes the character of those who, making some show of religion, conclude their spiritual state to be good when really it is very bad, like Laodicea, Rev. iii. 17. 2. The danger of this disease. It is in a manner desperate: *There is more hope of a fool*, that knows and owns himself to be such, *than of* such a one. Solomon was not only a wise man himself, but a teacher of wisdom; and this observation he made upon his pupils, that he found his work most difficult and least successful with those that had a good opinion of themselves and were not sensible that they needed instruction. Therefore he that *seems* to himself *to be wise* must *become a fool, that he may be wise*, 1 Cor. iii. 18. There is more hope of a publican than of a proud Pharisee, Matt. xxi. 32. Many are hindered from being truly wise and religious by a false and groundless conceit that they are so, John ix. 40, 41.

13 The slothful *man* saith, *There is* a lion in the way; a lion *is* in the streets.

When a man talks foolishly we say, He talks idly; for none betray their folly more than those who are idle and go about to excuse themselves in their idleness. As men's folly makes them slothful, so their slothfulness makes them foolish. Observe, 1. What *the slothful man* really dreads. He dreads *the way, the streets*, the place where work is to be done and a journey to be gone; he hates business, hates every thing that requires care and labour. 2. What he dreams of, and pretends to dread—*a lion in the way*. When he is pressed to be diligent, either in his worldly affairs or in the business of religion, this is his excuse (and a sorry excuse it is, as bad as none), *There is a lion in the way*, some insuperable difficulty or danger which he cannot pretend to grapple with. Lions frequent woods and deserts; and, in the day-time, when man has business to do, they are in their dens, Ps. civ. 22, 23. But the sluggard

fancies, or rather pretends to fancy, *a lion in the streets*, whereas the lion is only in his own fancy, nor is he so fierce as he is painted. Note, It is a foolish thing to frighten ourselves from real duties by fancied difficulties, Eccl. xi. 4.

14 *As* the door turneth upon his hinges, so *doth* the slothful upon his bed.

Having seen the slothful man in fear of his work, here we find him in love with his ease; he lies in his bed on one side till he is weary of that, and then turns to the other, but still in his bed, when it is far in the day and work is to be done, as the door is moved, but not removed; and so his business is neglected and his opportunities are let slip. See the sluggard's character. 1. He is one that does not care to get out of his bed, but seems to be hung upon it, *as the door upon the hinges*. Bodily ease, too much consulted, is the sad occasion of many a spiritual disease. Those that love sleep will prove in the end to have loved death. 2. He does not care to get forward with his business; in that he stirs to and fro a little, but to no purpose; he is where he was. Slothful professors turn, in profession, like *the door upon the hinges*. The world and the flesh are the two hinges on which they are hung, and though they move in a course of external services, have got into a road of duties, and tread around in them like the horse in the mill, yet they get no good, they get no ground, they are never the nearer heaven—sinners unchanged, saints unimproved.

15 The slothful hideth his hand in *his* bosom; it grieveth him to bring it again to his mouth.

The sluggard has now, with much ado, got out of his bed, but he might as well have lain there still for any thing he is likely to bring to pass in his work, so awkwardly does he go about it. Observe, 1. The pretence he makes for his slothfulness: He *hides his hand in his bosom* for fear of cold; next to his warm bed is his warm bosom. Or he pretends that he is lame, as some do that make a trade of begging; something ails his hand; he would have it thought that it is blistered with yesterday's hard work. Or it intimates, in general, his aversion to business; he has tried, and his hands are not used to labour, and therefore he hugs himself in his own ease and cares for nobody. Note, It is common for those that will not do their duty to pretend they cannot. *I cannot dig*, Luke xvi. 3. 2. The prejudice he sustains by his slothfulness. He himself is the loser by it, for he starves himself: *It grieves him to bring his hand to his mouth*, that is, he cannot find in his heart to feed himself, but dreads, as if it were a mighty toil, to lift his hand to his head. It is an elegant hyperbole, aggravating his sin, that he cannot endure to take the least pains, no, not for the greatest profit, and showing how his sin is his punishment. Those that are slothful in the business of religion will not be at the pains to feed their own souls with the word of God, the bread of life, nor to fetch in promised blessings by prayer, though they might have them for the fetching.

16 The sluggard *is* wiser in his own conceit than seven men that can render a reason.

Observe, 1. The high opinion which the sluggard has of himself, notwithstanding the gross absurdity and folly of his slothfulness: He thinks himself *wiser than seven men*, than seven wise men, for they are such as *can render a reason*. It is the wisdom of a man to be able to *render a reason*, of a good man to be able to give *a reason of the hope that is in him*, 1 Pet. iii. 15. What we do we should be able to *render a reason* for, though perhaps we may not have wit enough to show the fallacy of every objection against it. He that takes pains in religion can render a good reason for it; he knows that he is working for a good Master and that *his labour shall not be in vain.* But *the sluggard* thinks himself *wiser than seven* such; for let seven such persuade him to be diligent, with all the reasons they can render for it, it is to no purpose; his own determination, he thinks, answer enough to them and all their reasons. 2. The reference that this has to his slothfulness. It is *the sluggard*, above all men, that is thus self-conceited; for, (1.) His good opinion of himself is the cause of his slothfulness; he will not take pains to get wisdom because he thinks he is wise enough already. A conceit of the sufficiency of our attainments is a great enemy to our improvement. (2.) His slothfulness is the cause of his good opinion of himself. If he would but take pains to examine himself, and compare himself with the laws of wisdom, he would have other thoughts of himself. Indulged slothfulness is at the bottom of prevailing self-conceitedness. Nay, (3.) So wretchedly besotted is he that he takes his slothfulness to be his wisdom; he thinks it is his wisdom to make much of himself, and take all the ease he can get, and do no more in religion than he needs must, to avoid suffering, to sit still and see what other people do, that he may have the pleasure of finding fault with them. Of such sluggards, who are proud of that which is their shame, there is little hope, *v.* 12.

17 He that passeth by, *and* meddleth with strife *belonging* not to him, *is like* one that taketh a dog by the ears.

1. That which is here condemned is *meddling with strife that belongs not to us.* If we must not be hasty to strive in our own cause (*ch.* xxv. 8), much less in other people's, especially theirs that we are no way related to or concerned in, but light on accidentally as we pass by. If we can be instrumental to make peace between those that are at variance we must do it, though we should thereby get the ill-will of both sides, at least while they are in their heat; but to make ourselves busy in other men's matters, and parties in other men's quarrels, is not only to court our own trouble, but to thrust ourselves into temptation. *Who made* me *a judge?* Let them end it, as they began it, between themselves. 2. We are cautioned against it because of the danger it exposes us to; it is like taking a snarling cur *by the ears*, that will snap at you and bite you; you had better have let him alone, for you cannot get clear of him when you would, and must thank yourselves if you come off with a wound and dishonour. He that has got *a dog by the ears*, if he lets him go he flies at him, if he keeps his hold, he has his hands full, and can do nothing else. Let every one *with quietness work and mind his own business*, and not with unquietness quarrel and meddle with other people's business.

18 As a mad *man* who casteth firebrands, arrows, and death, 19 So *is* the man *that* deceiveth his neighbour, and saith, Am not I in sport?

See here, 1. How mischievous those are that make no scruple of *deceiving their neighbours:* they are as *madmen that cast firebrands, arrows, and death,* so much hurt may they do by their deceits. They value themselves upon it as politic cunning men, but really they are *as madmen.* There is not a greater madness in the world than a wilful sin. It is not only the passionate furious man, but the malicious deceitful man, that is *a madman;* he does in effect *cast fire-brands, arrows, and death;* he does more mischief than he can imagine. Fraud and falsehood burn like fire-brands, kill, even at a distance, like arrows. 2. See how frivolous the excuse is which men commonly make for the mischief they do, that they did it in jest; with this they think to turn it off when they are reproved for it, *Am not I in sport?* But it will prove dangerous playing with fire and jesting with edge-tools. Not that those are to be commended who are captious, and can take no jest (those that themselves are *wise must suffer fools*, 2 Cor. xi. 19, 20), but those are certainly to be condemned who are any way abusive to their neighbours, impose upon their credulity, cheat them in their bargains with them, tell lies to them or tell lies of them, give them ill language, or sully their reputation, and then think to excuse it by saying that they did but jest. *Am not I in sport?* He that sins in jest must repent in earnest, or his sin will be his ruin. Truth is too valuable a thing to be sold for a jest, and so is the reputation of our neighbour. By lying and slandering in jest men learn themselves, and teach others, to lie and slander in earnest; and a false report, raised in mirth, may be spread in malice; besides, if a man may tell a lie to make himself merry, why not to make himself rich, and so *truth quite perishes,* and men *teach their tongues to tell lies,* Jer. ix. 5. If men would consider that a lie comes from the devil, and brings to hell-fire, surely that would spoil the sport of it; it is *casting arrows and death* to themselves.

20 Where no wood is, *there* the fire goeth out: so where *there is* no tale-bearer, the strife ceaseth. 21 *As* coals *are* to burning coals, and wood to fire; so *is* a contentious man to kindle strife. 22 The words of a talebearer *are* as wounds, and they go down into the innermost parts of the belly.

Contention is as a fire; it heats the spirit, burns up all that is good, and puts families and societies into a flame. Now here we are told how that fire is commonly kindled and kept burning, that we may avoid the occasions of strife and so prevent the mischievous consequences of it. If then we would keep the peace, 1. We must not give ear to *tale-bearers,* for they feed the fire of contention with fuel; nay, they spread it with combustible matter; the tales they carry are fire-balls. Those who by insinuating base characters, revealing secrets, and misrepresenting words and actions, do what they can to make relations, friends, and neighbours, jealous one of another, to alienate them one from another, and sow discord among them, are to be banished out of families and all societies, and then strife will as surely cease as the fire will go out when it has no fuel; the contenders will better understand one another and come to a better temper; old stories will soon be forgotten when there are no new ones told to keep up the remembrance of them, and both sides will see how they have been imposed upon by a common enemy. Whisperers and backbiters are incendiaries not to be suffered. To illustrate this, he repeats (*v.* 22) what he had said before (*ch.* xviii. 8), that *the words of a tale-bearer are as wounds,* deep and dangerous wounds, wounds in the vitals. They wound the reputation of him who is belied, and perhaps the wound proves incurable, and even the plaster of a recantation (which yet can seldom be obtained) may not prove wide enough for it. They wound the love and charity which he to whom they are spoken ought to have for his neighbour and give a fatal stab to friendship and Christian fellowship. We must therefore not only not be tale-bearers ourselves at any time, nor ever do any ill offices, but we should not give the least countenance to those that are. 2. We must not associate with peevish passionate people, that are exceptious, and apt to put the worst constructions upon everything, that pick quarrels upon the least occasion, and are quick, and high, and hot, in resenting affronts. These are *contentious men,* that *kindle strife, v.* 21. The less we have to do

with such the better, for it will be very difficult to avoid quarrelling with those that are quarrelsome.

23 Burning lips and a wicked heart *are like* a potsherd covered with silver dross.

This may be meant either, 1. Of *a wicked heart* showing itself in *burning lips,* furious, passionate, outrageous words, burning in malice, and persecuting those to whom, or of whom, they are spoken; ill words and ill-will agree as well together as *a potsherd* and the *dross of silver,* which, now that the pot is broken and the dross separated from the silver, are fit to be thrown together to the dunghill. 2. Or of *a wicked heart* disguising itself with *burning lips,* burning with the professions of love and friendship, and even persecuting a man with flatteries; this is *like a potsherd covered with* the scum or *dross of silver,* with which one that is weak may be imposed upon, as if it were of some value, but a wise man is soon aware of the cheat. This sense agrees with the following verses.

24 He that hateth dissembleth with his lips, and layeth up deceit within him; 25 When he speaketh fair, believe him not: for *there are* seven abominations in his heart. 26 *Whose* hatred is covered by deceit, his wickedness shall be showed before the *whole* congregation.

There is cause to complain, not only of the want of sincerity in men's profession of friendship, and that they do not love so well as they pretend nor will serve their friends so much as they promise, but, which is much worse, of wicked designs in the profession of friendship, and the making of it subservient to the most malicious intentions. This is here spoken of as a common thing (*v.* 24): *He that hates* his neighbour, and is contriving to do him a mischief, yet *dissembles with his lips,* professes to have a respect for him and to be ready to serve him, talks kindly with him, as Cain with Abel, asks, *Art thou in health, my brother?* as Joab to Amasa, that his malice may not be suspected and guarded against, and so he may have the fairer opportunity to execute the purposes of it, this man *lays up deceit within him,* that is, he keeps in his mind the mischief he intends to do his neighbour till he catches him at an advantage. This is malice which has no less of the subtlety than it has of the venom of the old serpent in it. Now, as to this matter, we are here cautioned, 1. Not to be so foolish as to suffer ourselves to be imposed upon by the pretensions of friendship. Remember to distrust when a man *speaks fair;* be not too forward to *believe him* unless you know him well, for it is possible there may be *seven abominations in his heart,* a great many projects of mischief against you, which he is labouring so industriously to conceal with his fair speech. Satan is an enemy that hates us, and yet in his temptations speaks fair, as he did to Eve, but it is madness to give credit to him, *for there are seven abominations in his heart; seven other spirits* does one unclean spirit bring *more wicked than himself.* 2. Not to be so wicked as to impose upon any with a profession of friendship; for, though the fraud may be carried on plausibly awhile, it will be brought to light, *v.* 26. He *whose hatred is covered by deceit* will one time or other be discovered, and *his wickedness shown,* to his shame and confusion, *before the whole congregation;* and nothing will do more to make a man odious to all companies. Love (says one) is the best armour, but the worst cloak, and will serve dissemblers as the disguise which Ahab put on and perished in.

27 Whoso diggeth a pit shall fall therein : and he that rolleth a stone, it will return upon him.

See here, 1. What pains men take to do mischief to others. As they put a force upon themselves by concealing their design with a profession of friendship, so they put themselves to a great deal of labour to bring it about; it is *digging a pit,* it is *rolling a stone,* hard work, and yet men will not stick at it to gratify their passion and revenge. 2. What preparation they hereby make of mischief to themselves. Their violent dealing will return upon their own heads; they shall themselves *fall into the pit they digged,* and the stone they rolled *will return upon them,* Ps. vii. 15, 16; ix. 15, 16. The righteous God will take the wise, not only *in their own craftiness,* but in their own cruelty. It is the plotter's doom. Haman is hanged on a gallows of his own preparing.

———nec lex est justior ulla
Quam necis artifices arte perire sua—

Nor is there any law more just than that the contrivers of destruction should perish by their own arts.

28 A lying tongue hateth *those that are* afflicted by it; and a flattering mouth worketh ruin.

There are two sorts of lies equally detestable :—1. A slandering lie, which avowedly hates those it is spoken of : *A lying tongue hates those that are afflicted by it;* it afflicts them by calumnies and reproaches because it hates them, and can thus smite them secretly where they are without defence; and it hates them because it has afflicted them and made them its enemies. The mischief of this is open and obvious; it afflicts, it hates, and owns it, and every body sees it. 2. A flattering lie, which secretly works the ruin of those it is spoken to. In the former the mischief is plain, and men guard against it as well as they can, but in this it is little suspected, and men betray themselves by being credulous of their own praises and the compliments that are passed upon them. A wise man therefore will be more afraid of a flat-

946

terer that kisses and kills than of a slanderer that proclaims war.

CHAP. XXVII.

BOAST not thyself of to morrow; for thou knowest not what a day may bring forth.

Here is, 1. A good caution against presuming upon time to come : *Boast not thyself,* no, not *of to-morrow,* much less of many days or years to come. This does not forbid preparing for to-morrow, but presuming upon to-morrow. We must not promise ourselves the continuance of our lives and comforts till to-morrow, but speak of it with submission to the will of God and as those who with good reason are kept at uncertainty about it. We must not *take thought for the morrow* (Matt. vi. 34), but we must cast our care concerning it upon God. See James iv. 13—15. We must not put off the great work of conversion, that one thing needful, till to-morrow, as if we were sure of it, *but to-day, while it is called to-day,* hear God's voice. 2. A good consideration, upon which this caution is grounded : *We know not what a day may bring forth,* what event may be in the teeming womb of time; it is a secret till it is born, Eccl. xi. 5. A little time may produce considerable changes, and such as we little think of. We *know not what* the present *day may bring forth;* the evening must commend it. *Nescis quid serus vesper vehat—Thou knowest not what the close of evening may bring with it.* God has wisely kept us in the dark concerning future events, and reserved to himself the knowledge of them, as a flower of the crown, that he may train us up in a dependence upon himself and a continued readiness for every event, Acts i. 7.

2 Let another man praise thee, and not thine own mouth ; a stranger, and not thine own lips.

Note, 1. We must do that which is commendable, for which even strangers may praise us. Our *light* must *shine before men,* and we must do good works that may be seen, though we must not do them on purpose that they may be seen. Let our own works be such as will praise us, even *in the gates,* Phil. iv. 8. 2. When we have done it we must not commend ourselves, for that is an evidence of pride, folly, and self-love, and a great lessening to a man's reputation. Every one will be forward to run him down that cries himself up. There may be a just occasion for us to vindicate ourselves, but it does not become us to applaud ourselves. *Proprio laus sordet in ore—Self-praise defiles the mouth.*

3 A stone *is* heavy, and the sand weighty; but a fool's wrath *is* heavier than them both. 4 Wrath *is* cruel, and anger *is* outrageous; but who *is* able to stand before envy?

These two verses show the intolerable mischief, 1. Of ungoverned passion. The wrath of a fool, who when he is provoked cares not what he says and does, is more grievous than a great stone or a load of sand. It lies heavily upon himself. Those who have no command of their passions do themselves even sink under the load of them. The wrath of a fool lies heavily upon those he is enraged at, to whom, in his fury, he will be in danger of doing some mischief. It is therefore our wisdom not to give provocation to a fool, but, if he be in a passion, to get out of his way. 2. Of rooted malice, which is as much worse than the former as coals of juniper are worse than a fire of thorns. *Wrath* (it is true) *is cruel,* and does many a barbarous thing, *and anger is outrageous;* but a secret enmity at the person of another, an envy at his prosperity, and a desire of revenge for some injury or affront, are much more mischievous. One may avoid a sudden heat, as David escaped Saul's javelin, but when it grows, as Saul's did, to a settled envy, there is no *standing before it ;* it will pursue ; it will overtake. He that grieves at the good of another will be still contriving to do him hurt, and will keep his anger for ever.

5 Open rebuke *is* better than secret love. 6 Faithful *are* the wounds of a friend ; but the kisses of an enemy *are* deceitful.

Note, 1. It is good for us to be reproved, and told of our faults, by our friends. If true love in the heart has but zeal and courage enough to show itself in dealing plainly with our friends, and reproving them for what they say and do amiss, this is really *better,* not only than secret hatred (as Lev. xix. 17), but *than secret love,* that love to our neighbours which does not show itself in this good fruit, which compliments them in their sins, to the prejudice of their souls. *Faithful are the reproofs of a friend,* though, for the present they are painful as *wounds.* It is a sign that our friends are faithful indeed if, in love to our souls, they will not suffer sin upon us, nor let us alone in it. The physician's care is to cure the patient's disease, not to please his palate. 2. It is dangerous to be caressed and flattered by *an enemy,* whose *kisses are deceitful.* We can take no pleasure in them because we can put no confidence in them (Joab's kiss and Judas's were deceitful), and therefore we have need to stand upon our guard, that we be not deluded by them ; they are to be deprecated. Some read it : *The Lord deliver us from an enemy's kisses, from lying lips, and from a deceitful tongue.*

7 The full soul loatheth a honey-comb ; but to the hungry soul every bitter thing is sweet.

Solomon here, as often in this book, shows that the poor have in some respects the advantage of the rich ; for, 1. They have a better relish of their enjoyments than the rich have. Hunger is the best sauce. Coarse fare, with a good appetite to it has a sensible pleasantness in it, which those are strangers to whose hearts are *overcharged with surfeiting.* Those that fare sumptuously every day nauseate even delicate food, as the Israelites did the quails ; whereas those that have no more than their necessary food, though it be such as *the full soul* would call *bitter,* to them it *is sweet ;* they eat it with pleasure, digest it, and are refreshed by it. 2. They are more thankful for their enjoyments : *The hungry* will bless God for bread and water, while those that are *full* think the greatest dainties and varieties scarcely worth giving thanks for. The virgin Mary seems to refer to this when she says (Luke i. 53), *The hungry,* who know how to value God's blessings, *are filled with good things,* but *the rich,* who despise them, are justly *sent empty away.*

8 As a bird that wandereth from her nest, so *is* a man that wandereth from his place.

Note, 1. There are many that do not know when they are well off, but are uneasy with their present condition, and given to change. God, in his providence, has appointed them a place fit for them and has made it comfortable to them ; but they affect unsettledness ; they love to wander ; they are glad of a pretence to go abroad, and do not care for staying long at a place ; they needlessly absent themselves from their own work and care, and meddle with that which belongs not to them. 2. Those that thus desert the post assigned to them are like *a bird that wanders from her nest.* It is an instance of their folly ; they are like a silly bird ; they are always wavering, like the wandering bird that hops from bough to bough and rests nowhere. It is unsafe ; the bird that wanders is exposed ; a man's place is his castle ; he that quits it makes himself an easy prey to the fowler. When the bird wanders from her nest the eggs and young ones there are neglected. Those that love to be abroad leave their work at home undone. *Let every man therefore, in the calling wherein he is called, therein abide,* therein abide *with God.*

9 Ointment and perfume rejoice the heart : so *doth* the sweetness of a man's friend by hearty counsel. 10 Thine own friend, and thy father's friend, forsake not ; neither go into thy brother's house in the day of thy calamity : *for* better *is* a neighbour *that is* near than a brother far off.

Here is, 1. A charge given to be faithful and constant to our friends, our old friends, to keep up an intimacy with them, and to be ready to do them all the good offices that lie in our power. It is good to have a friend, a bosom-friend, whom we can be free with, and with whom we may communicate counsels.

It is not necessary that this friend should be a relation, or any way akin to us, though it is happiest when, among those who are so, we find one fit to make a friend of. Peter and Andrew were brethren, so were James and John; yet Solomon frequently distinguishes between a friend and a brother. But it is advisable to choose a friend among our neighbours who live near us, that acquaintance may be kept up and kindnesses the more frequently interchanged. It is good also to have a special respect to those who have been friends to our family: " *Thy own friend*, especially if he have been *thy father's friend, forsake not ;* fail not both to serve him and to use him, as there is occasion. He is a tried friend; he knows thy affairs; he has a particular concern for thee; therefore be advised by him." It is a duty we owe to our parents, when they are gone, to love their friends and consult with them. Solomon's son undid himself by forsaking the counsel of his father's friends. 2. A good reason given why we should thus value true friendship and be choice of it. (1.) Because of the pleasure of it. There is a great deal of *sweetness* in conversing and consulting with a cordial friend. It is like *ointment and perfume*, which are very grateful to the smell, and exhilarate the spirits. It *rejoices the heart ;* the burden of care is made lighter by unbosoming ourselves to our friend, and it is a great satisfaction to us to have his sentiments concerning our affairs. *The sweetness of* friendship lies not in hearty mirth, and hearty laughter, but in *hearty counsel*, faithful advice, sincerely given and without flattery, *by counsel of the soul* (so the word is), counsel which reaches the case, and comes to the heart, counsel about soul-concerns, Ps. lxvi. 16. We should reckon that the most pleasant conversation which is about spiritual things, and promotes the prosperity of the soul. (2.) Because of the profit and advantage of it, especially in a *day of calamity*. We are here advised not to go into a *brother's house*, not to expect relief from a kinsman merely for kindred-sake, for the obligation of that commonly goes little further than calling cousin and fails when it comes to the trial of a real kindness, but rather to apply ourselves to our neighbours, who are at hand, and will be ready to help us at an exigence. It is wisdom to oblige them by being neighbourly, and we shall have the benefit of it in distress, by finding them so to us, *ch.* xviii. 24.

11 My son, be wise, and make my heart glad, that I may answer him that reproacheth me.

Children are here exhorted to be wise and good, 1. That they may be a comfort to their parents and may *make their hearts glad*, even when *the evil days come*, and so recompense them for their care, *ch.* xxiii. 15. 2. That they may be a credit to them: " *That I may answer him that reproaches me* with having

been over-strict and severe in bringing up my children, and having taken a wrong method with them in restraining them from the liberties which other young people take. *My son, be wise*, and then it will appear, in the effect, that I went the wisest way to work with my children." Those that have been blessed with a religious education should in every thing conduct themselves so as to be a credit to their education and to silence those who say, *A young saint, an old devil ;* and to prove the contrary, *A young saint, an old angel.*

12 A prudent *man* foreseeth the evil, *and* hideth himself; *but* the simple pass on, *and* are punished.

This we had before, *ch.* xxii. 3. Note, 1. Evil may be foreseen. Where there is temptation, it is easy to foresee that if we thrust ourselves into it there will be sin, and as easy to foresee that if we venture upon the evil of sin there will follow the evil of punishment; and, commonly, God warns before he wounds, having *set watchmen over us*, Jer. vi. 17. 2. It will be well or ill with us according as we do or do not improve the foresight we have of evil before us : The *prudent man, foreseeing the evil*, forecasts accordingly, *and hides himself, but the simple* is either so dull that he does not foresee it or so wilful and slothful that he will take no care to avoid it, and so he *passes on securely and is punished*. We do well for ourselves when we provide for hereafter.

13 Take his garment that is surety for a stranger, and take a pledge of him for a strange woman.

This also we had before, *ch.* xx. 16. 1. It shows who those are that are hastening to poverty, those that have so little consideration as to be bound for every body that will ask them and those that are given to women. Such as these will take up money as far as ever their credit will go, but they will certainly cheat their creditors at last, nay, they are cheating them all along. An honest man may be made a beggar, but he is not honest that makes himself one. 2. It advises us to be so discreet in ordering our affairs as not to lend money to those who are manifestly wasting their estates, unless they give very good security for it. Foolish lending is injustice to our families. He does not say, " Get another to be bound with him," for he that makes himself a common voucher will have those to be his security who are as insolvent as himself; therefore *take his garment.*

14 He that blesseth his friend with a loud voice, rising early in the morning, it shall be counted a curse to him.

Note, 1. It is a great folly to be extravagant in praising even the best of our friends and benefactors. It is our duty to give every one his due praise, to applaud those who excel in knowledge, virtue, and usefulness, and to acknowledge the kindnesses we have received with thankfulness ; but to do this *with a loud voice, rising early in the morning,* to be always harping on this string, in all companies, even to our friend's face, or so as that he may be sure to hear it, to do it studiously, as we do that which we rise early to, to magnify the merits of our friend above measure and with hyperboles, is fulsome, and nauseous, and savours of hypocrisy and design. Praising men for what they have done is only to get more out of them; and every body concludes the parasite hopes to be well paid for his panegyric or epistle dedicatory. We must not give that praise to our friend which is due to God only, as some think is intimated in *rising early* to do it; for in the morning God is to be praised. We must not *make too much haste to praise men* (so some understand it), not cry up men too soon for their abilities and performances, but let them first be proved ; lest they be lifted up with pride, and laid to sleep in idleness. 2. It is a greater folly to be fond of being ourselves extravagantly praised. A wise man rather counts it *a curse,* and a reflection upon him, not only designed to pick his pocket, but which may really turn to his prejudice. Modest praises (as a great man observes) invite such as are present to add to the commendation, but immodest immoderate praises tempt them to detract rather, and to censure one that they hear over-commended. And, besides, over-praising a man makes him the object of envy ; every man puts in for a share of reputation, and therefore reckons himself injured if another monopolize it or have more given him than his share. And the greatest danger of all is that it is a temptation to pride ; men are apt to think of themselves above what is meet when others speak of them above what is meet. See how careful blessed Paul was not to be over-valued, 2 Cor. xii. 6.

15 A continual dropping in a very rainy day and a contentious woman are alike. 16 Whosoever hideth her hideth the wind, and the ointment of his right hand, *which* bewrayeth *itself.*

Here, as before, Solomon laments the case of him that has a peevish passionate wife, that is continually chiding, and making herself and all about her uneasy. 1. It is a grievance that there is no avoiding, for it is like *a continual dropping in a very rainy day.* The contentions of a neighbour may be like a sharp shower, troublesome for the time, yet, while it lasts, one may take shelter; but *the contentions of a wife* are like a constant soaking rain, for which there is no remedy but patience. See *ch.* xix. 13. 2. It is a grievance that there is no concealing. A wise man would hide it if he could, for the sake both of his own and his wife's reputation, but he cannot, any more than he can conceal the noise of the wind when it blows or the smell of a strong perfume. Those that are froward and brawling will proclaim their own shame, even when their friends, in kindness to them, would cover it.

17 Iron sharpeneth iron ; so a man sharpeneth the countenance of his friend.

This intimates both the pleasure and the advantage of conversation. One man is nobody; nor will poring upon a book in a corner accomplish a man as the reading and studying of men will. Wise and profitable discourse sharpens men's wits; and those that have ever so much knowledge may by conference have something added to them. It sharpens men's looks, and, by cheering the spirits, puts a briskness and liveliness into the countenance, and gives a man such an air as shows he is pleased himself and makes him pleasing to those about him. Good men's graces are sharpened by converse with those that are good, and bad men's lusts and passions are sharpened by converse with those that are bad, as iron is sharpened by its like, especially by the file. Men are filed, made smooth, and bright, and fit for business (who were rough, and dull, and inactive), by conversation. This is designed, 1. To recommend to us this expedient for sharpening ourselves, but with a caution to take heed whom we choose to converse with, because the influence upon us is so great either for the better or for the worse. 2. To direct us what we must have in our eye in conversation, namely to improve both others and ourselves, not to pass away time or banter one another, but to *provoke one another to love and to good works* and so to make one another wiser and better.

18 Whoso keepeth the fig tree shall eat the fruit thereof : so he that waiteth on his master shall be honoured.

This is designed to encourage diligence, faithfulness, and constancy, even in mean employments. Though the calling be laborious and despicable, yet those who keep to it will find there is something to be got by it. 1. Let not a poor gardener, who *keeps the fig-tree,* be discouraged; though it require constant care and attendance to nurse up fig-trees, and, when they have grown to maturity, to keep them in good order, and gather the figs in their season, yet he shall be paid for his pains: He *shall eat the fruit* of it, 1 Cor. ix. 7. 2. Nay, let not a poor servant think himself incapable of thriving and being preferred; for if he be diligent in *waiting on his master,* observant of him and obedient to him, if *he keep his master* (so the word is), if he do all he can for the securing of his person and reputation and take care that his estate be not wasted or damaged, such a one *shall be honoured,* shall not only get a good word, but be preferred and rewarded. God is a Master who has engaged to put an honour on those that serve him faithfully, John xii. 26.

19 As in water face *answereth* to face, so the heart of man to man.

This shows us that there is a way, 1. Of knowing ourselves. As the water is a looking-glass in which we may see our faces by reflection, so there are mirrors by which the *heart of a man* is discovered to *a man*, that is, to himself. Let a man examine his own conscience, his thoughts, affections, and intentions. Let him behold his *natural face in the glass* of the divine law (Jam. i. 23), and he may discern what kind of man he is and what is his true character, which it will be of great use to every man rightly to know. 2. Of knowing one another by ourselves; for, as there is a similitude between the face of a man and the reflection of it in the water, so there is between one man's heart and another's; for God has fashioned men's hearts alike; and in many cases we may judge of others by ourselves, which is one of the foundations on which that rule is built of doing to others as we would be done by, Exod. xxiii. 9. *Nihil est unum uni tam simile, tam par, quam omnes inter nosmet ipsos sumus. Sui nemo ipse tam similis quam omnes sunt omnium*—No one thing *is so like another as man is to man. No person is so like himself as each person is to all besides.* Cic. de Legib. lib. 1. One corrupt heart is like another, and so is one sanctified heart, for the former bears the same image of the earthy, the latter the same image of the heavenly.

20 Hell and destruction are never full; so the eyes of man are never satisfied.

Two things are here said to be insatiable, and they are two things near of kin—death and sin. 1. Death is insatiable. The first death, the second death, both are so. The grave is not clogged with the multitude of dead bodies that are daily thrown into it, but is still an *open sepulchre,* and cries, *Give, give.* Hell also has enlarged itself, and still has room for the damned spirits that are committed to that prison. *Tophet is deep and large,* Isa. xxx. 33. 2. Sin is insatiable: *The eyes of man are never satisfied,* nor the appetites of the carnal mind towards profit or pleasure. The *eye is not satisfied with seeing,* nor is he that *loves silver satisfied with silver.* Men labour for that which surfeits, but satisfies not; nay, it is dissatisfying; such a perpetual uneasiness have men justly been doomed to ever since our first parents were not satisfied with all the trees of Eden, but they must meddle with the forbidden tree. Those whose eyes are ever towards the Lord in him are satisfied, and shall for ever be so.

21 *As* the fining pot for silver, and the furnace for gold; so *is* a man to his praise.

This gives us a touchstone by which we may try ourselves. Silver and gold are tried by putting them into the furnace and fining-pot; so is a man tried by praising him. Let him be extolled and preferred, and then he will show himself what he is. 1. If a man be made, by the applause that is given him, proud, conceited, and scornful,—if he take the glory to himself which he should transmit to God, as Herod did,—if, the more he is praised, the more careless he is of what he says and does,—if he *lie in bed till noon* because *his name is up,* thereby it will appear that he is a vain foolish man, and a man who, though he be praised, has nothing in him truly praise-worthy. 2. If, on the contrary, a man is made by his praise more thankful to God, more respectful to his friends, more watchful against every thing that may blemish his reputation, more diligent to improve himself, and do good to others, that he may answer the expectations of his friends from him, by this it will appear that he is a wise and good man. He has a good temper of mind who knows how to pass by evil report and good report, and is still the same, 2 Cor. vi. 8.

22 Though thou shouldest bray a fool in a mortar among wheat with a pestle, *yet* will not his foolishness depart from him.

Solomon had said (*ch.* xxii. 15), *The foolishness* which *is bound in the heart of a child may be driven out by the rod of correction,* for then the mind is to be moulded, the vicious habits not having taken root; but here he shows that, if it be not done then, it will be next to impossible to do it afterwards; if the disease be inveterate, there is a danger of its being incurable. *Can the Ethiopian change his skin?* Observe, 1. Some are so bad that rough and severe methods must be used with them, after gentle means have been tried in vain; they must be *brayed in a mortar.* God will take this way with them by his judgments; the magistrates must take this way with them by the rigour of the law. Force must be used with those that will not be ruled by reason, and love, and their own interest. 2. Some are so incorrigibly bad that even those rough and severe methods do not answer the end, their *foolishness will not depart from them,* so fully are their *hearts set in them to do evil;* they are often under the rod and yet not humbled, in the furnace and yet not refined, but, like Ahaz, trespass yet more (2 Chron. xxviii. 22); and what remains then but that they should be rejected as reprobate silver?

23 Be thou diligent to know the state of thy flocks, *and* look well to thy herds. 24 For riches *are* not for ever: and doth the crown *endure* to every generation? 25 The hay appeareth, and the tender grass showeth itself, and herbs of the mountains are

gathered. 26 The lambs *are* for the clothing, and the goats *are* the price of the field. 27 And *thou shalt have* goats' milk enough for thy food, for the food of thy household, and *for* the maintenance for thy maidens.

Here is, I. A command given us to be diligent in our callings. It is directed to husbandmen and shepherds, and those that deal in cattle, but it is to be extended to all other lawful callings; whatever our business is, within doors or without, we must apply our minds to it. This command intimates, 1. That we ought to have some business to do in this world and not to live in idleness. 2. We ought rightly and fully to understand our business, and know what we have to do, and not meddle with that which we do not understand. 3. We ought to have an eye to it ourselves, and not turn over all the care of it to others. We should, with our own eyes, inspect the *state of our flocks*; it is the master's eye that makes them fat. 4. We must be discreet and considerate in the management of our business, *know the state* of things, and *look well* to them, that nothing may be lost, no opportunity let slip, but every thing done in proper time and order, and so as to turn to the best advantage. 5. We must be *diligent* and take pains; not only sit down and contrive, but be up and doing: "Set thy heart to thy herds, as one in care; lay thy hands, lay thy bones, to thy business."

II. The reasons to enforce this command. Consider,

1. The uncertainty of worldly wealth (*v.* 24): *Riches are not for ever.* (1.) Other riches are not so durable as these are: "*Look well to thy flocks and herds,* thy estate in the country and the stock upon that, for these are staple commodities, which, in a succession, will be for ever, whereas riches in trade and merchandise will not be so; the *crown* itself may perhaps not be so sure to thy family as thy flocks and herds." (2.) Even these riches will go to decay if they be not well looked after. If a man had *an abbey* (as we say), and were slothful and wasteful, he might make an end of it. Even the crown and the revenues of it, if care be not taken, will suffer damage, nor will it *continue to every generation* without very good management. Though David had the crown entailed on his family, yet he *looked well to his flocks,* 1 Chron. xxvii. 29, 31.

2. The bounty and liberality of nature, or rather of the God of nature, and his providence (*v.* 25): *The hay appears.* In taking care of the *flocks and herds,* (1.) "There needs no great labour, no ploughing or sowing; the food for them is the spontaneous product of the ground; thou hast nothing to do but to turn them into it in the summer, *when the grass shows itself,* and to *gather the herbs of the mountains* for them against winter. God

has done his part; thou art ungrateful to him, and unjustly refusest to serve his providence, if thou dost not do thine." (2.) "There is an opportunity to be observed and improved, a time when *the hay appears;* but, if thou let slip that time, thy flocks and herds will fare the worse for it. As for ourselves, so for our cattle, we ought, with the ant, to provide meat in summer.

3. The profit of good husbandry in a family: "Keep thy sheep, and thy sheep will help to keep thee; thou shalt have food for thy children and servants, *goats' milk enough* (*v.* 27); and *enough is as good as a feast.* Thou shalt have raiment likewise: the *lambs' wool shall be for thy clothing.* Thou shalt have money to pay thy rent; the goats thou shalt have to sell shall be *the price of thy field;*" nay, as some understand it, "*Thou shalt become a purchaser,* and buy land to leave to thy children," *v.* 26. Note, (1.) If we have food and raiment, and wherewithal to give every body his own, we have enough, and ought to be not only content, but thankful. (2.) Masters of families must provide not only for themselves, but for their families, and see that their servants have a fitting maintenance. (3.) Plain food and plain clothing, if they be but competent, are all we should aim at. "Reckon thyself well done to if thou be clothed with home-spun cloth with the fleece of thy own lambs, and fed with goats' milk; let that serve for thy food which serves for the *food of thy household and the maintenance of thy maidens.* Be not desirous of dainties, *far-fetched and dear-bought.*" (4.) This should encourage us to be careful and industrious about our business, that that will bring in a sufficient maintenance for our families; we shall *eat the labour of our hands.*

CHAP. XXVIII.

THE wicked flee when no man pursueth: but the righteous are bold as a lion.

See here, 1. What continual frights those are subject to that go on in wicked ways. Guilt in the conscience makes men a terror to themselves, so that they are ready *to flee when none pursues;* like one that absconds for debt, who thinks every one he meets a bailiff. Though they pretend to be easy, there are secret fears which haunt them wherever they go, so that they fear where no present or imminent danger is, Ps. liii. 5. Those that have made God their enemy, and know it, cannot but see the whole creation at war with them, and therefore can have no true enjoyment of themselves, no confidence, no courage, but a *fearful looking for of judgment.* Sin makes men cowards.

Degeneres animos timor arguit—
Fear argues a degenerate soul. VIRGIL.

Quos diri conscia facti mens habet attonitos—
The consciousness of atrocious crimes astonishes and confounds
JUVENAL

If they flee when none pursues, what will

they do when they shall see God himself pursuing them with his armies? Job xx. 24; xv. 24. See Deut. xxviii. 25; Lev. xxvi. 36. 2. What a holy security and serenity of mind those enjoy who *keep conscience void of offence* and so keep themselves in the love of God : *The righteous are bold as a lion,* as a young lion; in the greatest dangers they have a God of almighty power to trust to. *Therefore will not we fear though the earth be removed.* Whatever difficulties they meet with in the way of their duty, they are not daunted by them. *None of those things move me.*

> Hic murus aheneus esto, nil conscire sibi—
> Be this thy brazen bulwark of defence,
> Still to preserve thy conscious innocence. Hor.

2 For the transgression of a land many *are* the princes thereof : but by a man of understanding *and* knowledge the state *thereof* shall be prolonged.

Note, 1. National sins bring national disorders and the disturbance of the public repose : *For the transgression of a land,* and a general defection from God and religion to idolatry, profaneness, or immorality, *many are the princes thereof,* many at the same time pretending to the sovereignty and contending for it, by which the people are crumbled into parties and factions, biting and devouring one another, or many successively, in a little time, one cutting off another, as 1 Kings xvi. 8, &c., or soon cut off by the hand of God or of a foreign enemy, as 2 Kings xxiv. 5, &c. As the people suffer for the sins of the prince,

> Delirant reges, plectuntur Achivi—
> Kings play the madmen, and their people suffer for it,

so the government sometimes suffers for the sins of the people. 2. Wisdom will prevent or redress these grievances : *By a man,* that is, by a people, *of understanding,* that come again to themselves and their right mind, things are kept in a good order, or, if disturbed, brought back to the old channel again. Or, By a prince of *understanding and knowledge,* a privy-counsellor, or minister of state, that will restrain or suppress *the transgression of the land,* and take the right methods of healing the state thereof, the good estate of it will be prolonged. We cannot imagine what a great deal of service one wise man may do to a nation in a critical juncture.

3 A poor man that oppresseth the poor *is like* a sweeping rain which leaveth no food.

See here, 1. How hard-hearted poor people frequently are to one another, not only not doing such good offices as they might do one to another, but imposing upon and overreaching one another. Those who know by experience the miseries of poverty should be compassionate to those who suffer the like, but they are inexcusably barbarous if they be injurious to them. 2. How imperious and griping those commonly are who, being

indigent and necessitous, get into power. If a prince prefer a poor man, he forgets that ever he was poor, and none shall be so oppressive to the poor as he, nor squeeze them so cruelly. The hungry leech and the dry sponge suck most. *Set a beggar on horseback, and he will ride* without mercy. He *is like a sweeping rain,* which washes away the corn in the ground, and lays and beats out that which has grown, so that it *leaves no food.* Princes therefore ought not to put those into places of trust who are poor, and in debt, and behind-hand in the world, nor any who make it their main business to enrich themselves.

4 They that forsake the law praise the wicked : but such as keep the law contend with them.

Note, 1. Those that *praise the wicked* make it to appear that they do themselves *forsake the law,* and go contrary to it, for that curses and condemns the wicked. Wicked people will speak well of one another, and so strengthen one another's hands in their wicked ways, hoping thereby to silence the clamours of their own consciences and to serve the interests of the devil's kingdom, which is not done by any thing so effectually as by keeping vice in reputation. 2. Those that do indeed make conscience of the law of God themselves will, in their places, vigorously oppose sin, and bear their testimony against it, and do what they can to shame and suppress it. They will reprove the works of darkness, and silence the excuses which are made for those works, and do what they can to bring gross offenders to punishment, that others may hear and fear.

5 Evil men understand not judgment : but they that seek the LORD understand all *things.*

Note, I. As the prevalency of men's lusts is owing to the darkness of their understandings, so the darkness of their understandings is very much owing to the dominion of their lusts : *Men understand not judgment,* discern not between truth and falsehood, right and wrong ; they understand not the law of God as the rule either of their duty or of their doom ; and, 1. *Therefore* it is that they are *evil men ;* their wickedness is the effect of their ignorance and error, Eph. iv. 18. 2. *Therefore* they *understand not judgment,* because they are *evil men ;* their corruptions blind their eyes, and fill them with prejudices, and because they do evil they *hate the light.* It is just with God also to *give them up to strong delusions.*

II. As men's *seeking the Lord* is a good sign that they do understand much, so it is a good means of their understanding more, even of their understanding all things needful for them. Those that set God's glory before them as their end, his favour as their felicity, and his word as their rule, and apply to him upon all occasions by prayer, *they seek the Lord,* and he will give them the spirit of wisdom. If a man *do his will,* he shall *know his doctrine,* John vii. 17. *A good understanding those have,* and a better they shall have, that *do his commandments,* Ps. cxi. 10; 1 Cor. ii. 12, 15.

6 Better *is* the poor that walketh in his uprightness, than *he that is* perverse *in his* ways, though he *be* rich.

Here, 1. It is supposed that a man may *walk in his uprightness* and yet be poor in this world, may be poor in the world, which is a temptation to dishonesty, and yet may resist the temptation and continue to *walk in his uprightness*—also that a man may be *perverse in his ways,* injurious to God and man, and yet be rich, and prosper in the world, for a while, may be rich, and so lie under great obligations and have great opportunities to do good, and yet be *perverse in his ways* and do a great deal of hurt. 2. It is maintained as a paradox to a blind world that an honest, godly, poor man, is better than a wicked, ungodly, rich man, has a better character, is in a better condition, has more comfort in himself, is a greater blessing to the world, and is worthy of much more honour and respect. It is not only certain that his case will be better at death, but it is better in life. When Aristides was by a rich man upbraided with his poverty he answered, *Thy riches do thee more hurt than my poverty does me.*

7 Whoso keepeth the law *is* a wise son : but he that is a companion of riotous *men* shameth his father.

Note, 1. Religion is true wisdom, and it makes men wise in every relation. He that conscientiously *keeps the law* is wise, and he will be particularly *a wise son,* that is, will act discreetly towards his parents, for the law of God teaches him to do so. 2. Bad company is a great hindrance to religion. Those that are *companions of riotous men,* that choose such for their companions and delight in their conversation, will certainly be drawn from *keeping the law of God* and drawn to transgress it, Ps. cxix. 115. 3. Wickedness is not only a reproach to the sinner himself, but to all that are akin to him. He that keeps rakish company, and spends his time and money with them, not only grieves his parents, but shames them; it turns to their disrepute, as if they had not done their duty to him. They are ashamed that a child of theirs should be scandalous and abusive to their neighbours.

8 He that by usury and unjust gain increaseth his substance, he shall gather it for him that will pity the poor.

Note, 1. That which is ill-got, though it may increase much, will not last long. A man may perhaps raise a great estate, in a little time, by usury and extortion, fraud, and oppression of the poor, but it will not con-

tinue; he gathers it for himself, but it shall prove to have been gathered for somebody else that he has no kindness for. His estate shall go to decay, and another man's shall be raised out of the ruins of it. 2. Sometimes God in his providence so orders it that that which one got unjustly another uses charitably; it is strangely turned into the hands of one *that will pity the poor* and do good with it, and so cut off the entail of the curse which he brought upon it who got it by deceit and violence. Thus the same Providence that punishes the cruel, and disables them to do any more hurt, rewards the merciful, and enables them to do so much the more good. *To him that has the ten pounds give the pound* which the wicked servant *hid in the napkin ;* for *to him that has,* and uses it well, more *shall be given,* Luke xix. 24. Thus the poor are repaid, the charitable are encouraged, and God is glorified.

9 He that turneth away his ear from hearing the law, even his prayer *shall be* abomination.

Note, 1. It is by the word and prayer that our communion with God is kept up. God speaks to us by his law, and expects we should hear him and heed him ; *we* speak to him by prayer, to which we wait for an answer of peace. How reverent and serious should we be, whenever we are hearing from and speaking to the Lord of glory ! 2. If God's word be not regarded by us, our prayers shall not only not be accepted of God, but they shall be an abomination to him, not only our sacrifices, which were ceremonial appointments, but even our prayers, which are moral duties, and which, when they are put up by the upright, are so much his delight. See Isa. i. 11, 15. The sinner whose prayers God is thus angry at is one who wilfully and obstinately refuses to obey God's commandments, who will not so much as give them the hearing, but causes his *ear to decline the law,* and refuses when God calls ; God will therefore justly refuse him when he calls. See Prov. i. 24, 28.

10 Whoso causeth the righteous to go astray in an evil way, he shall fall himself into his own pit : but the upright shall have good *things* in possession.

Here is, 1. The doom of seducers, who attempt to draw good people, or those who profess to be such, into sin and mischief, who would take a pride in *causing the righteous to go astray in an evil way,* in drawing them into a snare, that they may insult over them. They shall not gain their point; it is impossible to deceive the elect. But they shall *fall themselves into their own pit ;* and having been not only sinners, but tempters, not only unrighteous, but enemies to the righteous, their condemnation will be so much the greater, Matt. xxiii. 14, 15. 2. The happiness of the sincere. They shall not only be preserved from the evil way which the wicked would decoy them into, but they shall *have good things*, the best things, *in possession*, the graces and comforts of God's Spirit, besides what they have in reversion.

11 The rich man *is* wise in his own conceit; but the poor that hath understanding searcheth him out.

Note, 1. Those that are rich are apt to think themselves wise, because, whatever else they are ignorant of, they know how to get and save; and those that are purse-proud expect that all they say should be regarded as an oracle and a law, and that none should dare to contradict them, but every sheaf bow to theirs; this humour is fed by flatterers, who, because (like Jezebel's prophets) they are fed at their table, cry up their wisdom. 2. Those that are poor often prove themselves wiser than they: A *poor man*, who has taken pains to get wisdom, having no other way (as the rich man has) to get a reputation, *searches him out*, and makes it to appear that he is not such a scholar, nor such a politician, as he is taken to be. See how variously God dispenses his gifts; to some he gives wealth, to others wisdom, and it is easy to say which of these is the better gift, which we should *covet more earnestly.*

12 When righteous *men* do rejoice, *there is* great glory: but when the wicked rise, a man is hidden.

Note, 1. The comfort of the people of God is the honour of the nation in which they live. There is a *great glory* dwelling in the land when *the righteous do rejoice*, when they have their liberty, the free exercise of their religion, and are not persecuted, when the government countenances them and speaks comfortably to them, when they prosper and grow rich, and, much more, when they are preferred and employed and have power put into their hands. 2. The advancement of the wicked is the eclipsing of the beauty of a nation: *When the wicked rise* and get head they make head against all that is sacred, and then *a man is hidden*, a good man is thrust into obscurity, is necessitated to abscond for his own safety; corruptions prevail so generally that, as in Elijah's time, there seem to be no good men left, the *wicked walk* so thickly *on every side.*

13 He that covereth his sins shall not prosper: but whoso confesseth and forsaketh *them* shall have mercy.

Here is, 1. The folly of indulging sin, of palliating and excusing it, denying or extenuating it, diminishing it, dissembling it, or throwing the blame of it upon others: *He that* thus *covers his sins shall not prosper*, let him never expect it. He shall not succeed in his endeavour to cover his sin, for it will be discovered, sooner or later. *There is nothing hid which shall not be revealed.* A *bird*

954

of the air shall carry the voice. Murder will out, and so will other sins. He *shall not prosper*, that is, he shall not obtain the pardon of his sin, nor can he have any true peace of conscience. David owns himself to have been in a constant agitation while he *covered his sins*, Ps. xxxii. 3, 4. While the patient conceals his distemper he cannot expect a cure. 2. The benefit of parting with it, both by a penitent confession and a universal reformation: *He that confesses* his guilt to God, and is careful not to return to sin again, shall *find mercy* with God, and shall have the comfort of it in his own bosom. His conscience shall be eased and his ruin prevented. See 1 John i. 9; Jer. iii. 12, 13. When we set sin before our face (as David, *My sin is ever before me*) God casts it behind his back.

14 Happy *is* the man that feareth alway: but he that hardeneth his heart shall fall into mischief.

Here is, 1. The benefit of a holy caution. It sounds strangely, but it is very true: *Happy is the man that feareth always.* Most people think that those are happy who never fear; but there is a fear which is so far from having torment in it that it has in it the greatest satisfaction. Happy is the man who always keeps up in his mind a holy awe and reverence of God, his glory, goodness, and government, who is always afraid of offending God and incurring his displeasure, who keeps conscience tender and has a dread of the appearance of evil, who is always jealous of himself, distrustful of his own sufficiency, and lives in expectation of troubles and changes, so that, whenever they come, they are no surprise to him. He who keeps up such a fear as this will live a life of faith and watchfulness, and therefore happy is he, blessed and holy. 2. The danger of a sinful presumption: *He that hardens his heart*, that mocks at fear, and sets God and his judgments at defiance, and receives not the impressions of his word or rod, *shall fall into mischief;* his presumption will be his ruin, and whatever sin (which is the greatest mischief) he falls into it is owing to the hardness of his heart.

15 *As* a roaring lion, and a ranging bear; *so is* a wicked ruler over the poor people.

It is written indeed, *Thou shalt not speak evil of the ruler of thy people;* but if he be a wicked ruler, that oppresses the people, especially the poor people, robbing them of the little they have and making a prey of them, whatever we may call him, this scripture calls him *a roaring lion and a ranging bear.* 1. In respect of his character. He is brutish, barbarous, and blood-thirsty; he is rather to be put among the beasts of prey, the wildest and most savage, than to be reckoned of that noble rank of beings whose glory is reason and humanity. 2. In respect of the mischief he does to his subjects. He is dreadful as the *roaring lion,* who makes the forest tremble; he is devouring as a hungry *bear,* and the more necessitous he is the more mischief he does and the more greedy of gain he is.

16 The prince that wanteth understanding *is* also a great oppressor: *but* he that hateth covetousness shall prolong *his* days.

Two things are here intimated to be the causes of the mal-administration of princes: —1. The love of money, that *root of all evil;* for *hating covetousness* here stands opposed to *oppression,* according to Moses's character of good magistrates, *men fearing God and hating covetousness* (Exod. xviii. 21), not only not being covetous, but hating it, and shaking the hands from the holding of bribes. A ruler that is covetous will neither do justly nor love mercy, but the people under him shall be bought and sold. 2. Want of consideration: *He that hates covetousness shall prolong* his government and peace, shall be happy in the affections of his people and the blessing of his God. It is as much the interest as the duty of princes to reign in righteousness. Oppressors therefore and tyrants are the greatest fools in the world; they *want understanding;* they do not consult their own honour, ease, and safety, but sacrifice all to their ambition of an absolute and arbitrary power. They might be much happier in the hearts of their subjects than in their necks or estates.

17 A man that doeth violence to the blood of *any* person shall flee to the pit; let no man stay him.

This agrees with that ancient law, *Whoso sheddeth man's blood, by man shall his blood be shed* (Gen. ix. 6), and proclaims, 1. The doom of the shedder of blood. He that has committed murder, though he flees for his life, shall be continually haunted with terrors, shall himself *flee to the pit,* betray himself, and torment himself, like Cain, who, when he had killed his brother, became a fugitive and a vagabond, and trembled continually. 2. The duty of the avenger of blood, whether the magistrate or the next of kin, or whoever are concerned in making inquisition for blood, let them be close and vigorous in the prosecution, and let it not be bought off. Those that acquit the murderer, or do any thing to help him off, come in sharers in the guilt of blood; nor can the land be purged from blood but by the blood of him that shed it, Num. xxxv. 33.

18 Whoso walketh uprightly shall be saved: but *he that is* perverse *in his* ways shall fall at once.

Note, 1. Those that are honest are always safe. He that acts with sincerity, that speaks as he thinks, has a single eye, in every thing, to the glory of God and the good of his brethren, that would not, for a world, do an unjust thing if he knew it, that in all manner of conversation *walks uprightly,* he *shall be saved* hereafter. We find a glorious company of those *in whose mouth was found no guile,* Rev. xiv. 5. They shall be safe now. Integrity and uprightness will preserve men, will give them a holy security in the worst of times; for it will preserve their comfort, their reputation, and all their interests. They may be injured, but they cannot be hurt. 2. Those that are false and dishonest are never safe: *He that is perverse in his ways,* that thinks to secure himself by fraudulent practices, by dissimulation and treachery, or by an estate ill-got, he *shall fall,* nay, he *shall fall at once,* not gradually, and with warning given, but suddenly, without previous notice, for he is least safe when he is most secure. He *falls at once,* and so has neither time to guard against his ruin nor to provide for it; and, being a surprise upon him, it will be so much the greater terror to him.

19 He that tilleth his land shall have plenty of bread: but he that followeth after vain *persons* shall have poverty enough.

Note, 1. Those that are diligent in their callings take the way to live comfortably: He that *tills his land,* and tends his shop, and minds his business, whatever it is, he *shall have plenty of bread,* of that which is necessary for himself and his family and with which he may be charitable to the poor; he shall *eat the labour of his hands.* 2. Those that are idle, and careless, and company-keepers, though they indulge themselves in living (as they think) easily and pleasantly, they take the way to live miserably. He that has land and values himself upon that, but does not till it, neglects his business, will not take pains, but *follows after vain persons,* drinks with them, joins with them in their frolics and vain sports, and idles away his time with him, he shall have *poverty enough,* shall be *satiated* or *replenished* with poverty (so the word is); he takes those courses which lead so directly to it that he seems to court it, and he shall have his fill of it.

20 A faithful man shall abound with blessings: but he that maketh haste to be rich shall not be innocent.

Here, 1. We are directed in the true way to be happy, and that is to be holy and honest. He that is *faithful* to God and man shall be blessed of the Lord, and he *shall abound with blessings* of the upper and nether springs. Men shall praise him, and pray for him, and be ready to do him any kindness. He shall abound in doing good, and shall himself be a blessing to the place where he lives. Usefulness shall be the reward of faithfulness, and it is a good reward. 2. We are cautioned against a false and deceitful way to happiness, and that is, right or wrong, raising an estate suddenly. Say not, This is the way to *abound with blessings,* for *he that makes haste to be rich,* more haste than good speed, *shall not be innocent;* and, if he be not, he shall not be blessed of God, but rather bring a curse upon what he has; nor, if he be not innocent, can he long be easy to himself; he shall not be accounted innocent by his neighbour's, but shall have their ill will and ill word. He does not say that he *cannot be innocent,* but there is all the probability in the world that he will not prove so: *He that hasteth with his feet sinneth,* stumbleth, falleth. *Sed quæ reverentia legum, quis metus, aut pudor, est unquam properantis avari?—What reverence for law, what fear, what shame, was ever indicated by an avaricious man hasting to be rich?*

21 To have respect of persons *is* not good : for for a piece of bread *that* man will transgress.

Note, 1. It is a fundamental error in the administration of justice, and that which cannot but lead men to abundance of transgression, to consider the parties concerned more than the merits of the cause, so as to favour one because he is a gentleman, a scholar, my countryman, my old acquaintance, has formerly done me a kindness, or may do me one, or is of my party and persuasion, and to bear hard on the other party because he is a stranger, a poor man, has done me an ill turn, is or has been my rival, or is not of my mind, or has voted against me. Judgment is perverted when any consideration of this kind is admitted into the scale, any thing but pure right. 2. Those that are partial will be paltry. Those that have once broken through the bonds of equity, though, at first, it must be some great bribe, some noble present, that would bias them, yet, when they have debauched their consciences, they will, at length, be so sordid that *for a piece of bread* they will give judgment against their consciences; they will rather play at small game than sit out.

22 He that hasteth to be rich *hath* an evil eye, and considereth not that poverty shall come upon him.

Here again Solomon shows the sin and folly of those that will *be rich;* they are resolved that they will be so, *per fas, per nefas—right or wrong;* they will be so with all speed ; they are getting hastily an estate. 1. They have no comfort in it : They *have an evil eye,* that is, they are always grieving at those that have more than they, and always grudging their necessary expenses, because they think the former keep them from seeming rich, the latter from being so, and between both they must needs be perpetually uneasy. 2. They have no assurance of the continuance of it, and yet take no thought to

provide against the loss of it : *Poverty shall come upon* them, and the riches which they made wings for, that they might fly to them, will make themselves wings to fly from them ; but they are secure and improvident, and do *not consider* this, that while they are making *haste to be rich* they are really making haste to be poor, else they would not *trust to uncertain riches.*

23 He that rebuketh a man afterwards shall find more favour than he that flattereth with the tongue.

Note, 1. Flatterers may please those for a time who, upon second thoughts, will detest and despise them. If ever they come to be convinced of the evil of those sinful courses they were flattered in, and to be ashamed of the pride and vanity which were humoured and gratified by those flatteries, they will hate the fawning flatterers as having had an ill design upon them, and the fulsome flatteries as having had an ill effect upon them and become nauseous. 2. Reprovers may displease those at first who yet afterwards, when the passion is over and the bitter physic begins to work well, will love and respect them. He that deals faithfully with his friend, in telling him of his faults, though he may put him into some heat for the present, and perhaps have hard words, instead of thanks, for his pains, yet afterwards he will not only have the comfort in his own bosom of having done his duty, but he also whom he reproved will acknowledge that it was a kindness, will entertain a high opinion of his wisdom and faithfulness, and look upon him as fit to be a friend. He that cries out against his surgeon for hurting him when he is searching his wound will yet pay him well, and thank him too, when he has cured it.

24 Whoso robbeth his father or his mother, and saith, *It is* no transgression ; the same *is* the companion of a destroyer.

As Christ shows the absurdity and wickedness of those children who think it is no duty, in some cases, to maintain their parents (Matt. xv. 5), so Solomon here shows the absurdity and wickedness of those who think it is no sin to rob their parents, either by force or secretly, by wheedling them or threatening them, or by wasting what they have, and (which is no better than robbing them) running into debt and leaving them to pay it. Now, 1. This is commonly made light of by untoward children ; they say, " *It is no transgression,* for it will be our own shortly, our parents can well enough spare it, we have occasion for it, we cannot live as gentlemen upon the allowance our parents give us, it is too strait for us." With such excuses as these they endeavour to shift off the conviction. But, 2. How lightly soever an ungoverned youth makes of it, it is really a very great sin; he that does it *is the companion of a destroyer,* no better than a robber on the highway. What wickedness will he scruple to commit who will rob his own parents?

25 He that is of a proud heart stirreth up strife: but he that putteth his trust in the LORD shall be made fat.

Note, 1. Those make themselves lean, and continually unquiet, that are haughty and quarrelsome, for they are opposed to those that *shall be made fat: He that is of a proud heart,* that is conceited of himself and looks with a contempt upon all about him, that cannot bear either competition or contradiction, he *stirs up strife,* makes mischief, and creates disturbance to himself and every body else. 2. Those make themselves fat, and always easy, that live in a continual dependence upon God and his grace: *He who puts his trust in the Lord,* who, instead of struggling for himself, commits his cause to God, *shall be made fat.* He saves the money which others spend upon their pride and contentiousness; he enjoys himself, and has abundant satisfaction in his God; and thus his soul dwells at ease, and he is most likely to have plenty of outward good things. None live so easily, so pleasantly, as those who live by faith.

26 He that trusteth in his own heart is a fool: but whoso walketh wisely, he shall be delivered.

Here is, 1. The character of a fool: *He trusts to his own heart,* to his own wisdom and counsels, his own strength and sufficiency, his own merit and righteousness, and the good opinion he has of himself; he that does so *is a fool,* for he trusts to that, not only which *is deceitful above all things* (Jer. xvii. 9), but which has often deceived him. This implies that it is the character of a wise man (as before, *v.* 25) to *put his trust in the Lord,* and in his power and promise, and to follow his guidance, Prov. iii. 5, 6. 2. The comfort of a wise man : He that *walks wisely,* that trusts not to his own heart, but is humble and self-diffident, and goes on in the strength of the Lord God, *he shall be delivered;* when the fool, *that trusts in his own heart,* shall be destroyed.

27 He that giveth unto the poor shall not lack: but he that hideth his eyes shall have many a curse.

Here is, 1. A promise to the charitable: *He that gives to the poor* shall himself be never the poorer for so doing; he *shall not lack.* If he have but little, and so be in danger of lacking, let him give out of his little, and that will prevent it from coming to nothing; as the bounty of the widow of Sarepta to Elijah (for whom she made a little cake first) saved what she had, when it was reduced to a handful of meal. If he have much, let him give much out of it, and that will prevent its growing less; he and his

shall not want what is given in pious charity. What we gave we have. 2. A threatening to the uncharitable: *He that hides his eyes,* that he may not see the miseries of the poor nor read their petitions, lest his eye should affect his heart and extort some relief from him, he *shall have many a curse,* both from God and man, and neither causeless, and therefore they shall come. Woeful is the condition of that man who has the word of God and the prayers of the poor against him.

28 When the wicked rise, men hide themselves: but when they perish, the righteous increase.

This is to the same purport with what we had, *v.* 12. 1. When bad men are preferred, that which is good is clouded and run down. When power is put into the hands of *the wicked, men hide themselves;* wise men retire into privacy, and decline public business, not caring to be employed under them; rich men get out of the way, for fear of being squeezed for what they have; and, which is worst of all, good men abscond, despairing to do good and fearing to be persecuted and ill-treated. 2. When bad men are disgraced, degraded, and their power taken from them, then that which is good revives again, then *the righteous increase;* for, *when they perish,* good men will be put in their room, who will, by their example and interest, countenance religion and righteousness. It is well with a land when the number of good people increases in it; and it is therefore the policy of all princes, states, and potentates, to encourage them and to take special care of the good education of youth.

CHAP. XXIX.

HE, that being often reproved hardeneth *his* neck, shall suddenly be destroyed, and that without remedy.

Here, 1. The obstinacy of many wicked people in a wicked way is to be greatly lamented. They are *often reproved* by parents and friends, by magistrates and ministers, by the providence of God and by their own consciences, have had their sins set in order before them and fair warning given them of the consequences of them, but all in vain; they *harden their necks.* Perhaps they fling away, and will not so much as give the reproof a patient hearing; or, if they do, yet they go on in the sins for which they are reproved; they will not bow their necks to the yoke, but are children of Belial; they refuse reproof (*ch.* x. 17), despise it (*ch.* v. 12), hate it, *ch.* xii. 1. 2. The issue of this obstinacy is to be greatly dreaded : Those that go on in sin, in spite of admonition, *shall be destroyed;* those that will not be reformed must expect to be ruined; if the rods answer not the end, expect the axes. They *shall be suddenly destroyed,* in the midst of their security, *and without remedy;* they have sinned against the prevent-

ing remedy, and therefore let them not expect any recovering remedy. Hell is remediless destruction. They *shall be destroyed,
and no healing,* so the word is. If God wounds,
who can heal?

**2 When the righteous are in au-
thority, the people rejoice : but when
the wicked beareth rule, the people
mourn.**

This is what was said before, ch. xxviii.
12, 28. 1. *The people* will have cause to *rejoice* or *mourn* according as their rulers are
righteous or *wicked ;* for, if *the righteous* be in
authority, sin will be punished and restrained,
religion and virtue will be supported and kept
in reputation ; *but,* if *the wicked* get power in
their hands, wickedness will abound, religion
and religious people will be persecuted, and
so the ends of government will be perverted.
2. *The people* will actually *rejoice* or *mourn*
according as their rulers are *righteous* or
wicked. Such a conviction are even the common people under of the excellency of virtue
and religion that they will rejoice when they
see them preferred and countenanced ; and,
on the contrary, let men have ever so much
honour or power, if they be wicked and vicious, and use it ill, they *make themselves contemptible and base before all the people* (as
those priests, Mal. ii. 9) and subjects will
think themselves miserable under such a government.

**3 Whoso loveth wisdom rejoiceth
his father : but he that keepeth company with harlots spendeth *his* substance.**

Both the parts of this verse repeat what
has been often said, but, on comparing them
together, the sense of them will be enlarged
from each other. 1. Be it observed, to the
honour of a virtuous young man, that he *loves
wisdom,* he is *a philosopher* (for that signifies
a lover of wisdom), for religion is the best philosophy ; he avoids bad company, and especially the company of lewd women. Hereby
he *rejoices his* parents, and has the satisfaction of being a comfort to them, and increases
his estate, and is likely to live comfortably.
2. Be it observed, to the reproach of a vicious
young man, that he hates *wisdom ; he keeps
company with* scandalous women, who will be
his ruin, both in soul and body ; he grieves
his parents, and, like the prodigal son, devours their living *with harlots.* Nothing will
beggar men sooner than the lusts of uncleanness ; and the best preservative from those
ruinous lusts is *wisdom.*

**4 The king by judgment establish-
eth the land : but he that receiveth
gifts overthroweth it.**

Here is, 1. The happiness of a people under a good government. The care and business of a prince should be to *establish the
land,* to maintain its fundamental laws, to

settle he minds of his subjects and make
them easy, to secure their liberties and properties from hostilities and for posterity, and
to set in order the things that are wanting ;
this he must do *by judgment,* by wise counsels, and by the steady administration of justice, without respect of persons, which will
have these good effects. 2. The misery of
a people under a bad government : *A man
of oblations* (so it is in the margin) *overthrows the land ;* a man that is either sacri-
legious or superstitious, or that invades the
priest's office, as Saul and Uzziah—or a man
that aims at nothing but getting money, and
will, for a good bribe, connive at the most
guilty, and, in hope of one, persecute the innocent—such governors as these will ruin a
country.

**5 A man that flattereth his neigh-
bour spreadeth a net for his feet.**

Those may be said to *flatter their neighbours* who commend and applaud that good
in them (the good they do or the good they
have) which really either is not or is not such
as they represent it, and who profess that esteem and that affection for them which really
they have not ; these *spread a net for their
feet.* 1. For their neighbours' feet, whom
they *flatter.* They have an ill design in it ;
they would not praise them as they do but
that they hope to make an advantage of them ;
and it is therefore wisdom to suspect those
who flatter us, that they are secretly laying a
snare for us, and to stand on our guard accordingly. Or it has an ill effect on those
who are flattered ; it puffs them up with pride,
and makes them conceited and confident of
themselves, and so proves a net that entangles them in sin. 2. For their own feet ; so
some understand it. He that flatters others,
in expectation that they will return his compliments and flatter him, does but make himself ridiculous and odious even to those he
flatters.

**6 In the transgression of an evil
man *there is* a snare : but the righteous doth sing and rejoice.**

Here is, 1. The peril of a sinful way. There
is not only a punishment at the end of it, but
a snare in it. One sin is a temptation to another, and there are troubles which, as *a
snare,* come suddenly upon evil men in the
midst of their transgressions ; nay, their transgression itself often involves them in vexations ; their sin is their punishment, and they
are *holden in the cords of their own iniquity,*
ch. v. 22. 2. The pleasantness of the way of
holiness. The snare that is *in the transgression of evil men* spoils all their mirth, *but
righteous* men are kept from those snares, or
delivered out of them ; they walk at liberty,
walk in safety, and therefore they *sing and
rejoice.* Those that make God their chief joy
have him for their exceeding joy, and it is
their own fault if they do not *rejoice ever-*

more. If there be any true joy on this side heaven, doubtless those have it whose conversation is in heaven.

7 The righteous considereth the cause of the poor: *but* the wicked regardeth not to know *it.*

It is a pity but that every one who sues *sub formâ pauperis—as a pauper*, should have an honest cause (they are of all others inexcusable if they have not), because the scripture has so well provided that it should have a fair hearing, and that the judge himself should be of counsel, as for the prisoner, so for the pauper. 1. It is here made the character of a *righteous* judge that he *considers the cause of the poor.* It is every man's duty to consider the poor (Ps. xli. 1), but the judgment of the poor is to be considered by those that sit in judgment; they must take as much pains to find out the right in a poor man's cause as in a rich man's. Sense of justice must make both judge and advocate as solicitous and industrious in the poor man's cause as if they hoped for the greatest advantage. 2. It is made the character of a *wicked* man that because it is a poor man's cause, which there is nothing to be got by, he *regards not to know it,* in the true state of it, for he cares not which way it goes, right or wrong. See Job xxix. 16.

8 Scornful men bring a city into a snare: but wise *men* turn away wrath.

See here, 1. Who are the men that are dangerous to the public—*scornful men.* When such are employed in the business of the state they do things with precipitation, because they scorn to deliberate, and will not take time for consideration and consultation; they do things illegal and unjustifiable, because they scorn to be hampered by laws and constitutions; they break their faith, because they scorn to be bound by their word, and provoke the people, because they scorn to please them. Thus they *bring a city into a snare* by their ill conduct, or (as the margin reads it) they *set a city on fire;* they sow discord among the citizens and run them into confusion. Those are *scornful men* that mock at religion, the obligations of conscience, the fears of another world, and every thing that is sacred and serious. Such men are the plagues of their generation; they bring God's judgments upon a land, set men together by the ears, and so bring all to confusion. 2. Who are the men that are the blessings of a land—the *wise men* who by promoting religion, which is true wisdom, *turn away the wrath* of God, and who, by prudent counsels, reconcile contending parties and prevent the mischievous consequences of divisions. Proud and foolish men kindle the fires which wise and good men must extinguish.

9 *If* a wise man contendeth with a foolish man, whether he rage or laugh, *there is* no rest.

A wise man is here advised not to set his wit to a fool's, not to dispute with him, or by contending with him to think either of fastening reason upon him or gaining right from him: *If a wise man contend with a wise man,* he may hope to be understood, and, as far as he has reason and equity on his side, to carry his point, at least to bring the controversy to a head and make it issue amicably; but, if he *contend with a foolish man, there is no rest;* he will see no end of it, nor will he have any satisfaction in it, but must expect to be always uneasy. 1. Whether the foolish man he contends with *rage or laugh,* whether he take angrily or scornfully what is said to him, whether he rail at it or mock at it, one of the two he will do, and so there will be *no rest.* However it is given, it will be ill-taken, and the wisest man must expect to be either scolded or ridiculed if he *contend with a fool.* He that fights with a dunghill, whether he be conqueror or conquered, is sure to be defiled. 2. Whether the wise man himself *rage or laugh,* whether he take the serious or the jocular way of dealing with the fool, whether he be severe or pleasant with him, whether he come with a rod or with *the spirit of meekness* (1 Cor. iv. 21), it is all alike, no good is done. *We have piped unto you, and you have not danced, mourned unto you, and you have not lamented.*

10 The bloodthirsty hate the upright: but the just seek his soul.

Note, 1. Bad men hate their best friends: *The blood-thirsty,* all the seed of the old serpent, who *was a murderer from the beginning,* all that inherit his enmity against the seed of the woman, *hate the upright;* they seek the ruin of good men because they condemn the wicked world and witness against it. Christ told his disciples that they should be *hated of all men.* Bloody men do especially *hate upright* magistrates, who would restrain and reform them, and put the laws in execution against them, and so really do them a kindness. 2. Good men love their worst enemies: *The just,* whom the bloody men hate, *seek their soul,* pray for their conversion, and would gladly do any thing for their salvation. This Christ taught us. *Father, forgive them. The just seek his soul,* that is, the soul of the upright, whom the bloody hate (so it is commonly understood), seek to protect it from violence, and save it from, or avenge it at, the hands of *the blood-thirsty.*

11 A fool uttereth all his mind: but a wise *man* keepeth it in till afterwards.

Note, 1. It is a piece of weakness to be very open: He is *a fool who utters all his mind,*—who tells every thing he knows, and has in his mouth instantly whatever he has in his thoughts, and can keep no counsel,—who, whatever is started in discourse, quickly shoots his bolt,—who, when he is provoked, will say any thing that comes uppermost, whoever is reflected upon by it,—who, when he is to speak of any business, will say all he thinks, and yet never thinks he says enough, whether choice or refuse, corn or chaff, pertinent or impertinent, you shall have it all. 2. It is a piece of wisdom to be upon the reserve: *A wise man* will not *utter all his mind* at once, but will take time for a second thought, or reserve the present thought for a fitter time,· when it will be more pertinent and likely to answer his intention; he will not deliver himself in a continued speech, or starched discourse, but with pauses, that he may hear what is to be objected and answer it. *Non minus interdum oratorium est tacere quam dicere—True oratory requires an occasional pause.* Plin. Ep. vii. 6.

12 If a ruler hearken to lies, all his servants *are* wicked.

Note, 1. It is a great sin in any, especially in rulers, to *hearken to lies;* for thereby they not only give a wrong judgment themselves of persons and things, according to the lies they give credit to, but they encourage others to give wrong informations. Lies will be told to those that will hearken to them; but the receiver, in this case, is as bad as the thief. 2. Those that do so will have *all their servants wicked.* All their servants will appear wicked, for they will have lies told of them; and they will be wicked, for they will tell lies to them. All that have their ear will fill their ear with slanders and false characters and representations; and so if princes, as well as people, will be deceived, they shall be deceived, and, instead of devolving the guilt of their own false judgments upon their servants that misinformed them, they must share in their servants' guilt, and on them will much of the blame lie for encouraging such misinformations and giving countenance and ear to them·

13 The poor and the deceitful man meet together: the LORD lighteneth both their eyes.

This shows how wisely the great God serves the designs of his providence by persons of very different tempers, capacities, and conditions in the world, even, 1. By those that are contrary the one to the other. Some are *poor* and forced to borrow; others are rich, have a great deal of the *mammon of unrighteousness (deceitful riches* they are called), and they are creditors, or *usurers,* as it is in the margin. Some are *poor,* and honest, and laborious; others are rich, slothful, and *deceitful.* They *meet together* in the business of this world, and have dealings with one another, and the *Lord enlightens both their eyes;* he causes his sun to shine upon both and gives them both the comforts of this life. To some of both sorts he gives his grace. He enlightens the eyes of the poor by giving them patience, and of the deceitful by giving them repentance, as Zaccheus. 2. By those that we think could best be spared. *The poor and*

the deceitful we are ready to look upon as blemishes of Providence, but God makes even them to display the beauty of Providence; he has wise ends not only in leaving the poor always with us, but in permitting *the deceived and the deceiver,* for both *are his* (Job xii. 16) and turn to his praise.

14 The king that faithfully judgeth the poor, his throne shall be established for ever.

Here is, 1. The duty of magistrates, and that is, to judge faithfully between man and man, and to determine all causes brought before them, according to truth and equity, particularly to take care of *the poor,* not to countenance them in an unjust cause for the sake of their poverty (Exod. xxiii. 3), but to see that their poverty do not turn to their prejudice if they have a just cause. The rich will look to themselves, but *the poor* and needy the prince must *defend* (Ps. lxxxii. 3) and plead for, Prov. xxxi. 9. 2. The happiness of those magistrates that do their duty. Their *throne* of honour, their tribunal of judgment, *shall be established for ever.* This will secure to them the favour of God and strengthen their interest in the affections of their people, both which will be the establishment of their power, and help to transmit it to posterity and perpetuate it in the family.

15 The rod and reproof give wisdom: but a child left *to himself* bringeth his mother to shame.

Parents, in educating their children, must consider, 1. The benefit of due correction. They must not only tell their children what is good and evil, but they must chide them, and correct them too, if need be, when they either neglect that which is good or do that which is evil. If a *reproof* will serve without *the rod,* it is well, but *the rod* must never be used without a rational and grave *reproof;* and then, though it may be a present uneasiness both to the father and to the child, yet it will *give wisdom. Vexatio dat intellectum—Vexation sharpens the intellect.* The child will take warning, and so will get *wisdom.* 2. The mischief of undue indulgence: *A child* that is not restrained or reproved, but is *left to himself,* as Adonijah was, to follow his own inclinations, may do well if he will, but, if he take to ill courses, nobody will hinder him; it is a thousand to one but he proves a disgrace to his family, and *brings his mother,* who fondled him and humoured him in his licentiousness, *to shame,* to poverty, to reproach, and perhaps will himself be abusive to her and give her ill language.

16 When the wicked are multiplied, transgression increaseth: but the righteous shall see their fall.

Note, 1. The more sinners there are the more sin there is: *When the wicked,* being countenanced by authority, grow numerous, and walk on every side, no marvel if *transgression increases*, as a plague in the country is said to increase when still more and more are infected with it. *Transgression* grows more impudent and bold, more imperious and threatening, when there are many to keep it in countenance. In the old world, when *men began to multiply*, they began to degenerate and corrupt themselves and one another. 2. The more sin there is the nearer is the ruin threatened. Let not *the righteous* have their faith and hope shocked by the increase of sin and sinners. Let them not say that they have *cleansed their hands in vain*, or that *God has forsaken the earth*, but wait with patience; the transgressors shall fall, the measure of their iniquity will be full, and then they shall fall from their dignity and power, and fall into disgrace and destruction, and *the righteous shall* have the satisfaction of *seeing their fall* (Ps. xxxvii. 34), perhaps in this world, certainly in the judgment of the great day, when the fall of God's implacable enemies will be the joy and triumph of glorified saints. See Isa. lxvi. 24; Gen. xix. 28.

17 Correct thy son, and he shall give thee rest; yea, he shall give delight unto thy soul.

Note, 1. It is a very happy thing when children prove the comfort of their parents. Good children are so; they *give them rest*, make them easy, and free from the many cares they have had concerning them; *yea*, they *give delight unto their souls*. It is a pleasure to parents, which none know but those that are blessed with it, to see the happy fruit of the good education they have given their children, and to have a prospect of their well-doing for both worlds; it *gives delight* proportionable to the many thoughts of heart that have been concerning them. 2. In order to this, children must be trained up under a strict discipline, and not suffered to do what they will and to go without rebuke when they do amiss. The foolishness bound up in their hearts must by correction be driven out when they are young, or it will break out, to their own and their parents' shame, when they are grown up.

18 Where *there is* no vision, the people perish: but he that keepeth the law, happy *is* he.

See here, I. The misery of the people that want a settled ministry: *Where there is no vision*, no prophet to expound the law, no priest or Levite to teach the good knowledge of the Lord, no means of grace, the word of the Lord is scarce, there is *no open vision* (1 Sam. iii. 1), where it is so *the people perish;* the word has many significations, any of which will apply here. 1. *The people are made naked*, stripped of their ornaments and so exposed to shame, stripped of their armour and so exposed to danger. How bare

does a place look without Bibles and ministers, and what an easy prey is it to the enemy of souls! 2. *The people rebel*, not only against God, but against their prince; good preaching would make people good subjects, but, for want of it, they are turbulent and factious, and *despise dominions*, because they know no better. 3. *The people are idle*, or *they play*, as the scholars are apt to do when the master is absent; they do nothing to any good purpose, but stand all the day idle, and sporting in the market-place, for want of instruction what to do and how to do it. 4. *They are scattered as sheep having no shepherd*, for want of the masters of assemblies to call them and keep them together, Mark vi. 34. They are scattered from God and their duty by apostasies, from one another by divisions; God is provoked to scatter them by his judgments, 2 Chron. xv. 3, 5. 5. *They perish ;* they are *destroyed for lack of knowledge*, Hos. iv. 6. See what reason we have to be thankful to God for the plenty of *open vision* which we enjoy.

II. The felicity of a people that have not only a settled, but a successful ministry among them, the people that hear and *keep the law*, among whom religion is uppermost; *happy* are such a people and every particular person among them. It is not having the law, but obeying it, and living up to it, that will entitle us to blessedness.

19 A servant will not be corrected by words: for though he understand he will not answer.

Here is the description of an unprofitable, slothful, wicked servant, a slave that serves not from conscience, or love, but purely from fear. Let those that have such servants put on patience to bear the vexation and not disturb themselves at it. See their character. 1. No rational words will work upon them; they *will not be corrected* and reformed, not brought to their business, nor cured of their idleness and laziness, by fair means, no, nor by foul *words ;* even the most gentle master will be forced to use severity with them; no reason will serve their turn, for they are unreasonable. 2. No rational words will be got from them. They are dogged and sullen; and, *though they understand* the questions you ask them, they *will not* give you an *answer ;* though you make it ever so plain to them what you expect from them, they will not promise you to mend what is amiss nor to mind their business. See the folly of those servants whose mouth by their silence calls for strokes; they might *be corrected by words* and save blows, but they *will not*.

20 Seest thou a man *that is* hasty in his words? *there is* more hope of a fool than of him.

Solomon here shows that there is little hope of bringing a man to wisdom that is hasty either, 1. Through rashness and inconsideration : *Seest thou a man that is hasty in his matters,* that is of a light desultory wit, that seems to take a thing quickly, but takes it by the halves, gallops over a book or science, but takes no time to digest it, no time to pause or muse upon a business ? *There is more hope of* making a scholar and a wise man of one that is dull and heavy, and slow in his studies, than of one that has such a mercurial genius and cannot fix. 2. Through pride and conceitedness : *Seest thou a man that is* forward to speak to every matter that is started, and affects to speak first to it, to open it, and speak last to it, to give judgment upon it, as if he were an oracle ? *There is more hope of a* modest *fool,* who is sensible of his folly, than of such a self-conceited one.

21 He that delicately bringeth up his servant from a child shall have him become *his* son at the length.

Note, 1. It is an imprudent thing in a master to be too fond of a servant, to advance him too fast, and admit him to be too familiar with him, to suffer him to be over-nice and curious in his diet, and clothing, and lodging, and so to bring him up delicately, because he is a favourite, and an agreeable servant ; it should be remembered that he is a servant, and, by being thus indulged, will be spoiled for any other place. Servants must endure hardness. 2. It is an ungrateful thing in a servant, but what is very common, to behave insolently because he has been used tenderly. The humble prodigal thinks himself unworthy *to be called a son,* and is content to be a servant ; the pampered slave thinks himself too good to be called *a servant,* and will be *a son at the length,* will take his ease and liberty, will be on a par with his master, and perhaps pretend to the inheritance. Let masters *give their servants that which is equal* and fit for them, and neither more nor less. This is very applicable to the body, which is a servant to the soul ; those that *delicately bring up* the body, that humour it, and are over-tender of it, will find that at length it will forget its place, and *become a son,* a master, a perfect tyrant.

22 An angry man stirreth up strife, and a furious man aboundeth in transgression.

See here the mischief that flows from an angry, passionate, furious disposition. 1. It makes men provoking to one another : *An angry man stirs up strife,* is troublesome and quarrelsome in the family and in the neighbourhood, blows the coals, and even forces those to fall out with him that would live peaceably and quietly by him. 2. It makes men provoking to God : *A furious man,* who is wedded to his humours and passions, cannot but *abound in transgressions.* Undue anger is a sin which is the cause of many sins ; it not only hinders men from calling upon

God's name, but it occasions their swearing, and cursing, and profaning God's name.

23 A man's pride shall bring him low : but honour shall uphold the humble in spirit.

This agrees with what Christ said more than once, 1. That those who *exalt themselves shall be abased.* Those that think to gain respect by lifting up themselves above their rank, by looking high, talking big, appearing fine, and applauding themselves, will on the contrary expose themselves to contempt, lose their reputation, and provoke God by humbling providences to bring them down and lay them *low.* 2. That those who *humble themselves shall be exalted,* and shall be established in their dignity : *Honour shall uphold the humble in spirit ;* their humility is their honour, and that shall make them truly and safely great, and recommend them to the esteem of all that are wise and good.

24 Whoso is partner with a thief hateth his own soul : he heareth cursing, and bewrayeth *it* not.

See here what sin and ruin those involve themselves in who are drawn away by the enticement of sinners. 1. They incur a great deal of guilt : *He* does so that goes *partner with* such as rob and defraud, and *casts in his lot among* them, ch. i. 11, &c. The receiver is as bad as the thief ; and, being drawn in to join with him in the commission of the sin, he cannot escape joining with him in the concealment of it, though it be with the most horrid perjuries and execrations. They *hear cursing* when they are sworn to tell the whole truth, but they will not confess. 2. They hasten to utter ruin : They even *hate their own souls,* for they wilfully do that which will be the inevitable destruction of them. See the absurdities sinners are guilty of ; they love death, than which nothing is more dreadful, and *hate their own souls,* than which nothing is more dear.

25 The fear of man bringeth a snare : but whoso putteth his trust in the LORD shall be safe.

Here, 1. We are cautioned not to dread the power of man, neither the power of a prince nor the power of the multitude ; both are formidable enough, but the slavish fear of either *brings a snare,* that is, exposes men to many insults (some take a pride in terrifying the timorous), or rather exposes men to many temptations. Abraham, for *fear of man,* denied his wife, and Peter his Master, and many a one his God and religion. We must not shrink from duty, nor commit sin, to avoid the wrath of man, nor, though we see it coming upon us, be disquieted with fear, Dan. iii. 16 ; Ps. cxviii. 6. He must himself die (Isa. li. 12) and can but kill our body, Luke xii. 5. 2. We are encouraged to depend upon the power of God, which would keep us from all that *fear of man* which has either torment or temptation in it. *Whoso puts his trust in the Lord,* for protection and supply in the way of duty, *shall be* set on high, above the power of man and above the fear of that power. A holy confidence in God makes a man both great and easy, and enables him to look with a gracious contempt upon the most formidable designs of hell and earth against him. If God be my salvation, *I will trust and not be afraid.*

26 Many seek the ruler's favour; but *every* man's judgment *cometh* from the LORD.

See here, 1. What is the common course men take to advance and enrich themselves, and make themselves great: they *seek the ruler's favour,* and, as if all their judgment proceeded from him, to him they make all their court. Solomon was himself a *ruler,* and knew with what sedulity men made their application to him, some on one errand, others on another, but all for his *favour.* It is the way of the world to make interest with great men, and expect much from the smiles of second causes, which yet are uncertain, and frequently disappoint them. *Many* take a great deal of pains in seeking *the ruler's favour* and yet cannot have it; many have it for a little while, but they cannot keep themselves in it, by some little turn or other they are brought under his displeasure; many have it, and keep it, and yet it does not answer their expectation, they cannot make that hand of it that they promised themselves they should. Haman had *the ruler's favour,* and yet it availed him nothing. 2. What is the wisest course men can take to be happy. Let them look up to God, and seek the favour of the Ruler of rulers; for *every man's judgment proceeds from the Lord.* It is not with us as the ruler pleases; his favour cannot make us happy, his frowns cannot make us miserable. But it is as God pleases; every creature is that to us that God makes it to be, no more and no other. He is the first Cause, on which all second causes depend; if he help not, they cannot, 2 Kings vi. 27; Job xxxiv. 29.

27 An unjust man *is* an abomination to the just: and *he that is* upright in the way *is* abomination to the wicked.

This expresses not only the innate contrariety that there is between virtue and vice, as between light and darkness, fire and water, but the old enmity that has always been between the seed of the woman and the seed of the serpent, Gen. iii. 15. 1. All that are sanctified have a rooted antipathy to wickedness and wicked people. They have a good will to the souls of all (God has, and would have none perish); but they hate the ways and practices of those that are impious towards God and injurious towards men; they cannot hear of them nor speak of them without a holy indignation; they loathe the society of the ungodly and unjust, and dread the thought of giving them any countenance, but do all they can to bring the wickedness of the wicked to an end. Thus *an unjust* man makes himself odious *to the just,* and it is one part of his present shame and punishment that good men cannot endure him. 2. All that are unsanctified have a like rooted antipathy to godliness and godly people: *He that is upright in the way,* that makes conscience of what he says and does, *is an abomination to the wicked,* whose wickedness is restrained perhaps and suppressed, or, at least, shamed and condemned, by the uprightness of the upright. Thus Cain did, who was *of his father the devil.* And this is not only the wickedness of the wicked, that they hate those whom God loves, but their misery too, that they hate those whom they shall shortly see in everlasting bliss and honour, and who shall have *dominion over them in the morning,* Ps. xlix. 14.

CHAP. XXX.

This and the following chapter are an appendix to Solomon's proverbs; but they are both expressly called prophecies in the first verses of both, by which it appears that the penmen of them, whoever they were, were divinely inspired. This chapter was penned by one that bears the name of "Agur Ben Jakeh." What tribe he was of, or when he lived, we are not told; what he wrote, being indited by the Holy Ghost, is here kept upon record. We have here, I. His confession of faith, ver. 1—6. II. His prayer, ver. 7—9. III. A caution against wronging servants, ver. 10. IV. Four wicked generations, ver. 11—14. V. Four things insatiable (ver. 15, 16), to which is added fair warning to undutiful children, ver. 17. VI. Four things unsearchable, ver. 18—20. VII. Four things intolerable, ver. 21—23. VIII. Four things little and wise, ver. 24—28. IX. Four things stately, ver. 29 to the end.

THE words of Agur the son of Jakeh, *even* the prophecy: the man spake unto Ithiel, even unto Ithiel and Ucal, 2 Surely I *am* more brutish than *any* man, and have not the understanding of a man. 3 I neither learned wisdom, nor have the knowledge of the holy. 4 Who hath ascended up into heaven, or descended? who hath gathered the wind in his fists? who hath bound the waters in a garment? who hath established all the ends of the earth? what *is* his name, and what *is* his son's name, if thou canst tell? 5 Every word of God *is* pure: he *is* a shield unto them that put their trust in him. 6 Add thou not unto his words, lest he reprove thee, and thou be found a liar.

Some make *Agur* to be not the name of this author, but his character; he was a *collector* (so it signifies), a gatherer, one that did not compose things himself, but collected the wise sayings and observations of others, made abstracts of the writings of others, which some think is the reason why he says (*v.* 3), " I have not *learned wisdom* myself, but have been a scribe, or amanuensis, to other wise and learned men." Note, We must not bury our talent, though it be but one, but, as we have received the gift, so minister the same, if it be but to collect what others have written. But we rather suppose it to be his name, which, no doubt, was well known then, though not mentioned elsewhere in scripture. *Ithiel and Ucal* are mentioned, either, 1. As the names of his pupils, whom he instructed, or who consulted him as an oracle, having a great opinion of his wisdom and goodness. Probably they wrote from him what he dictated, as Baruch wrote from the mouth of Jeremiah, and by their means it was preserved, and they were ready to attest it to be his, for it was spoken to them; they were two witnesses of it. Or, 2. As the subject of his discourse. *Ithiel* signifies *God with me,* the application of *Immanuel, God with us.* The word calls him *God with us;* faith appropriates this, and calls him " *God with me,* who loved me, and gave himself for me, and into union and communion with whom I am admitted." *Ucal* signifies *the Mighty One,* for it is upon one that is mighty that help is laid for us. Many good interpreters therefore apply this to the Messiah, for to him all the prophecies bear witness, and why not this then? It is what Agur spoke concerning *Ithiel, even* concerning *Ithiel* (that is the name on which the stress is laid) *and Ucal—the mighty God* (Isa. ix. 6) *with us,* Isa. vii. 14.

Three things the prophet here aims at:—

I. To abase himself. Before he makes confession of his faith he makes confession of his folly and the weakness and deficiency of reason, which make it so necessary that we be guided and governed by faith. Before he speaks concerning the Saviour he speaks of himself as needing a Saviour, and as nothing without him; we must go out of ourselves before we go into Jesus Christ. 1. He speaks of himself as wanting a righteousness, and having done foolishly, very foolishly. When he reflects upon himself he owns, *Surely I am more brutish than any man. Every man has become brutish,* Jer. x. 14. But he that knows his own heart knows so much more evil of himself than he does of any other that he cries out, " *Surely* I cannot but think that *I am more brutish than any man;* surely no man has such a corrupt deceitful heart as I have. I have acted as one that has *not the understanding* of Adam, as one that is wretchedly degenerated from the knowledge and righteousness in which man was at first created; nay, I have not the common sense and reason of a man, else I should not have done as I have done." Agur, when he was applied to by others as wiser than most, acknowledged himself more foolish than any. Whatever high opinion others may have of us, it becomes us to have low thoughts of ourselves. 2. He speaks of himself as wanting a revelation to guide him in the ways of truth and wisdom. He owns (*v.* 3) " *I neither learned wisdom* by any power of my own (the depths of it cannot be fathomed by my line and

plummet) *nor know I the knowledge of the holy ones,* the angels, our first parents in innocency, nor of the holy things of God; I can get no insight into them, nor make any judgment of them, further than God is pleased to make them known to me." The natural man, the natural powers, perceive not, nay, they *receive not, the things of the Spirit of God.* Some suppose Agur to be asked, as Apollo's oracle was of old, *Who was the wisest man?* The answer is, *He that is sensible of his own ignorance,* especially in divine things. *Hoc tantum scio, me nihil scire—All that I know is that I know nothing.*

II. To advance Jesus Christ, and the Father in him (*v.* 4): *Who hath ascended up into heaven,* &c. 1. Some understand this of God and of his works, which are both incomparable and unsearchable. He challenges all mankind to give an account of the heavens above, of the winds, the waters, the earth: "Who can pretend to have *ascended up to heaven,* to take a view of the orbs above, and then to have descended, to give us a description of them? Who can pretend to have had the command of the winds, to have grasped them in his hand and managed them, as God does, or to have bound the waves of the sea with a swaddling band, as God has done? Who has *established the ends of the earth,* or can describe the strength of its foundations or the extent of its limits? Tell me what is *the man's name* who can undertake to vie with God or to be of his cabinet-council, or, if he be dead, what is his name to whom he has bequeathed this great secret." 2. Others refer it to Christ, to Ithiel and Ucal, the Son of God, for it is the Son's name, as well as the Father's, that is here enquired after, and a challenge given to any to vie with him. We must now exalt Christ as one revealed; they then magnified him as one concealed, as one they had heard something of but had very dark and defective ideas of. *We have heard the fame of him with our ears,* but cannot describe him (Job xxviii. 22); certainly it is God that has *gathered the wind in his fists* and *bound the waters as in a garment;* but *what is his name?* It is, *I am that I am* (Exod. iii. 14), a name to be adored, not to be understood. What is *his Son's name,* by whom he does all these things? The Old-Testament saints expected the Messiah to be the *Son of the Blessed,* and he is here spoken of as a person distinct from the Father, but his name as yet secret. Note, The great Redeemer, in the glories of his providence and grace, can neither be paralleled nor found out to perfection. (1.) The glories of the kingdom of his grace are unsearchable and unparalleled; for who besides has *ascended into heaven and descended?* Who besides is perfectly acquainted with both worlds, and has himself a free correspondence with both, and is therefore fit to settle a correspondence between them, as Mediator, as Jacob's ladder? He was *in heaven* in the *Father's bosom* (John i. 1, 18);

thence he descended to take our nature upon him; and never was there such condescension. In that nature he again ascended (Eph. iv. 9), to receive the promised glories of his exalted state; and who besides has done this? Rom. x. 6. (2.) The glories of the kingdom of his providence are likewise unsearchable and unparalleled. The same that reconciles heaven and earth was the Creator of both and governs and disposes of all. His government of the three lower elements of *air, water,* and *earth,* is here particularised. [1.] The motions of the air are of his directing. Satan pretends to be *the prince of the power of the air,* but even there Christ has *all power;* he *rebuked the winds* and they obeyed him. [2.] The bounds of the water are of his appointing: He *binds the waters as in a garment; hitherto they shall come, and no further,* Job xxxviii. 9—11. [3.] The foundations of the earth are of his establishing. He founded it at first; he upholds it still. If Christ had not interposed, the foundations of the earth would have sunk under the load of the curse upon the ground, for man's sin. Who and what is the mighty He that does all this? We cannot *find out God,* nor the *Son of God, unto perfection. Oh the depth of that knowledge!*

III. To assure us of the truth of the word of God, and to recommend it to us, *v.* 5, 6. Agur's pupils expect to be instructed by him in the things of God. "Alas!" says he, "I cannot undertake to instruct you; go to the word of God; see what he has there revealed of himself, and of his mind and will; you need know no more than what that will teach you, and that you may rely upon as sure and sufficient. *Every word of God is pure;* there is not the least mixture of falsehood and corruption in it." The words of men are to be heard and read with jealousy and with allowance, but there is not the least ground to suspect any deficiency in the word of God; it is *as silver purified seven times* (Ps. xii. 6), without the least dross or alloy. *Thy word is very pure,* Ps. cxix. 140. 1. It is sure, and therefore we must trust to it and venture our souls upon it. God in his word, God in his promise, is *a shield,* a sure protection, to all those that put themselves under his protection and *put their trust in him.* The word of God, applied by faith, will make us easy in the midst of the greatest dangers, Ps. xlvi. 1, 2. 2. It is sufficient, and therefore we must not add to it (*v.* 6): *Add thou not unto his words,* because they are pure and perfect. This forbids the advancing of any thing, not only in contradiction to the word of God, but in competition with it; though it be under the plausible pretence of explaining it, yet, if it pretend to be of equal authority with it, it is *adding to his words,* which is not only a reproach to them as insufficient, but opens a door to all manner of errors and corruptions; for, that one absurdity being granted, that the word of any man, or company of men, is to be received with the same faith and vene-

ration as the word of God, a thousand follow. We must be content with what God has thought fit to make known to us of his mind, and not covet to be *wise above what is written;* for, (1.) God will resent it as a heinous affront: "*He* will *reprove thee,* will reckon with thee as a traitor against his crown and dignity, and lay thee under the heavy doom of those that add to his words, or diminish from them," Deut. iv. 2; xii. 32. (2.) We shall run ourselves into endless mistakes: "Thou wilt be found a liar, a corrupter of the word of truth, a broacher of heresies, and guilty of the worst of forgeries, counterfeiting the broad seal of heaven, and pretending a divine mission and inspiration, when it is all a cheat. Men may be thus deceived, but *God is not mocked.*"

7 Two *things* have I required of thee; deny me *them* not before I die: 8 Remove far from me vanity and lies: give me neither poverty nor riches; feed me with food convenient for me: 9 Lest I be full, and deny *thee,* and say, Who *is* the LORD? or lest I be poor, and steal, and take the name of my God *in vain.*

After Agur's confession and creed, here follows his litany, where we may observe,

I. The preface to his prayer: *Two things have I required* (that is, *requested)* of thee, O God! Before we go to pray it is good to consider what we need, and what the things are which we have to ask of God.—What does our case require? What do our hearts desire? What would we that God should do for us?—that we may not have to seek for our petition and request when we should be presenting it. He begs, *Deny me not before I die.* In praying, we should think of dying, and pray accordingly. "Lord, give me pardon, and peace, and grace, before I die, *before I go hence and be no more;* for, if I be not renewed and sanctified before I die, the work will not be done after; if I do not prevail in prayer before I die, prayers afterwards will not prevail, no, not Lord, Lord. There is none of this wisdom or working in the grave. *Deny me not* thy grace, for, if thou do, I die, I perish; if thou be silent to me, *I am like those that go down to the pit,* Ps. xxviii. 1. *Deny me not before I die;* as long as I continue in the land of the living, let me continue under the conduct of thy grace and good providence."

II. The prayer itself. The *two things* he requires are grace sufficient and food convenient. 1. Grace sufficient for his soul· *Remove from me vanity and lies;* deliver me from sin, from all corrupt principles, practices, and affections, from error and mistake, which are at the bottom of all sin, from the love of the world and the things of it, which are all *vanity and a lie.*" Some understand it as a prayer for the pardon of sin, for, when

God forgives sin, he removes it, he takes it away. Or, rather, it is a prayer of the same import with that, *Lead us not into temptation.* Nothing is more mischievous to us than sin, and therefore there is nothing which we should more earnestly pray against than that we may *do no evil.* 2. Food convenient for his body. Having prayed for the operations of divine grace, he here begs the favours of the divine Providence, but such as may tend to the good and not to the prejudice of the soul. (1.) He prays that of God's free gift he might receive a competent portion of the good things of this life: *" Feed me with the bread of my allowance,* such bread as thou thinkest fit to allow me." As to all the gifts of the divine Providence, we must refer ourselves to the divine wisdom. Or, *" the bread that is fit for me,* as a man, a master of a family, that which is agreeable to my rank and condition in the world." For *as is the man so is his competency.* Our Saviour seems to refer to this when he teaches us to pray, *Give us this day our daily bread,* as this seems to refer to Jacob's vow, in which he wished for no more than *bread to eat and raiment to put on.* Food convenient for us is what we ought to be content with, though we have not dainties, varieties, and superfluities—what is for necessity, though we have not for delight and ornament; and it is what we may in faith pray for and depend upon God for. (2.) He prays that he may be kept from every condition of life that would be a temptation to him. [1.] He prays against the extremes of abundance and want: *Give me neither poverty nor riches.* He does not hereby prescribe to God, nor pretend to teach him what condition he shall allot to him, nor does he pray against poverty or riches absolutely, as in themselves evil, for either of them, by the grace of God, may be sanctified and be a means of good to us; but, *First,* He hereby intends to express the value which wise and good men have for a middle state of life, and, with submission to the will of God, desires that that might be his state, neither great honour nor great contempt. We must learn how to manage both (as St. Paul, Phil. iv. 12), but rather wish to be always between both. *Optimus pecuniæ modus qui nec in paupertatem cedit nec procul à paupertate discedit*—*The best condition is that which neither implies poverty nor yet recedes far from it.* Seneca. *Secondly,* He hereby intimates a holy jealousy he had of himself, that he could not keep his ground against the temptations either of an afflicted or a prosperous condition. Others may preserve their integrity in either, but he is afraid of both, and therefore grace teaches him to pray against riches as much as nature against poverty; but *the will of the Lord be done.* [2.] He gives a pious reason for his prayer, *v.* 9. He does not say, *" Lest I be rich,* and cumbered with care, and envied by my neighbours, and eaten up with a multitude of servants, or, *lest I be poor*

and trampled on, and forced to work hard and fare hard;" but, *" Lest I be rich* and sin, or *poor* and sin." Sin is that which a good man is afraid of in every condition and under every event; witness Nehemiah (*ch.* vi. 13), *that I should be afraid, and do so, and sin.* *First,* He dreads the temptations of a prosperous condition, and therefore even deprecates that: *Lest I be full and deny thee* (as Jeshurun, who *waxed fat and kicked, and forsook God who made him,* Deut. xxxii. 15), and say, as Pharaoh in his pride, *Who is the Lord, that I should obey his voice?* Prosperity makes people proud and forgetful of God, as if they had no need of him and were therefore under no obligation to him. *What can the Almighty do for them?* Job xxii. 17. And therefore they will do nothing for him. Even good men are afraid of the worst sins, so deceitful do they think their own hearts to be; and they know that the greatest gains of the world will not balance the least guilt. *Secondly,* He dreads the temptations of a poor condition, and for that reason, and no other, deprecates that: *Lest I be poor and steal.* Poverty is a strong temptation to dishonesty, and such as many are overcome by, and they are ready to think it will be their excuse; but it will not bear them out at God's bar any more than at men's to say, "I stole because I was poor;" yet, if a man *steal for the satisfying of his soul when he is hungry,* it is a case of compassion (*ch.* vi. 30) and what even those that have some principles of honesty in them may be drawn to. But observe why Agur dreads this, not because he should endanger himself by it, " Lest I steal, and be hanged for it, whipped or put in the stocks, or sold for a bondman," as among the Jews poor thieves were, who had not wherewithal to make restitution; but lest he should dishonour God by it: *" Lest I should steal, and take the name of my God in vain,* that is, discredit my profession of religion by practices disagreeable to it." Or, " Lest I steal, and, when I am charged with it, forswear myself." He *therefore* dreads one sin, because it would draw on another, for the way of sin is downhill. Observe, He calls God *his* God, and *therefore* he is afraid of doing any thing to offend him because of the relation he stands in to him.

10 Accuse not a servant unto his master, lest he curse thee, and thou be found guilty. 11 *There is* a generation *that* curseth their father, and doth not bless their mother. 12 *There is* a generation *that are* pure in their own eyes, and *yet* is not washed from their filthiness. 13 *There is* a generation, O how lofty are their eyes! and their eyelids are lifted up. 14 *There is* a generation, whose teeth *are* as swords, and their jaw teeth *as*

knives, to devour the poor from off the earth, and the needy from *among* men.

Here is, I. A caution not to abuse other people's servants any more than our own, nor to make mischief between them and their masters, for it is an ill office, invidious, and what will make a man odious, v. 10. Consider, 1. It is an injury to the servant, whose poor condition makes him an object of pity, and therefore it is barbarous to add affliction to him that is afflicted : *Hurt not a servant with thy tongue* (so the margin reads it); for it argues a sordid disposition to smite any body secretly with the scourge of the tongue, especially a servant, who is not a match for us, and whom we should rather protect, if his master be severe with him, than exasperate him more. 2. " It will perhaps be an injury to thyself. If a servant be thus provoked, perhaps he will curse thee, will accuse thee and bring thee into trouble, or give thee an ill word and blemish thy reputation, or appeal to God against thee, and imprecate *his* wrath upon thee, who is the patron and protector of oppressed innocency."

II. An account, upon occasion of this caution, of some wicked generations of men, that are justly abominable to all that are virtuous and good. 1. Such as are abusive to their parents, give them bad language and wish them ill, call them bad names and actually injure them. *There is a generation* of such ; young men of that black character commonly herd together, and irritate one another against their parents. A *generation of vipers* those are who curse their natural parents, or their magistrates, or their ministers, because they cannot endure the yoke; and those are near of kin to them who, though they have not yet arrived at such a pitch of wickedness as to curse their parents, yet do not bless them, cannot give them a good word, and will not pray for them. 2. Such as are conceited of themselves, and, under a show and pretence of sanctity, hide from others, and perhaps from themselves too, abundance of reigning wickedness in secret (v. 12); they are *pure in their own eyes*, as if they were in all respects such as they should be. They have a very good opinion of themselves and their own character, that they are not only righteous, but *rich and increased with goods* (Rev. iii. 17), and yet *are not cleansed from their filthiness*, the filthiness of their hearts, which they pretend to be the best part of them. They are, it may be, swept and garnished, but they are not washed, not sanctified; as the Pharisees that within were *full of all uncleanness*, Matt. xxiii. 25, 26. 3. Such as are haughty and scornful to those about them, v. 13. He speaks of them with amazement at their intolerable pride and insolence : " *Oh how lofty are their eyes !* With what disdain do they look upon their neighbours, as not worthy to be set with the dogs of their flock ! What a

distance do they expect every body should keep ; and, when they look upon themselves, how do they strut and vaunt like the peacock, thinking they make themselves illustrious when really they make themselves ridiculous ! There is a generation of such, on whom he that *resists the proud* will pour contempt. 4. Such as are cruel to the poor and barbarous to all that lie at their mercy (v. 14); their teeth are iron and steel, *swords and knives*, instruments of cruelty, with which they *devour the poor* with the greatest pleasure imaginable, and as greedily as hungry men cut their meat and eat it. God has so ordered it that the *poor we shall always have with us*, that they shall *never cease out of the land ;* but there are those who, because they hate to relieve them, would, if they could, abolish them *from the earth, from among men*, especially God's poor. Some understand it of those who wound and ruin others by slanders and false accusations, and severe censures of their everlasting state; their tongues, and their teeth too (which are likewise organs of speech), are *as swords and knives*, Ps. lvii. 4.

15 The horseleech hath two daughters, *crying*, Give, give. There are three *things that* are never satisfied, *yea*, four *things* say not, *It is* enough : 16 The grave ; and the barren womb; the earth *that* is not filled with water; and the fire *that* saith not, *It is* enough. 17 The eye *that* mocketh at *his* father, and despiseth to obey *his* mother, the ravens of the valley shall pick it out, and the young eagles shall eat it.

He had spoken before of those that devoured the poor (v. 14), and had spoken of them last, as the worst of all the four generations there mentioned ; now here he speaks of their insatiableness in doing this. The temper that puts them upon it is made up of cruelty and covetousness. Now those are *two daughters* of the *horse-leech*, its genuine offspring, that still cry, " *Give, give*, give more blood, give more money ;" for the bloody are still blood-thirsty; being drunk with blood, they add thirst to their drunkenness, and will seek it yet again. Those also that *love silver* shall never *be satisfied with silver*. Thus, while from these two principles they are devouring the poor, they are continually uneasy to themselves, as David's enemies, Ps. lix. 14, 15. Now, for the further illustration of this,

I. He specifies four other things which are insatiable, to which those devourers are compared, which say not, *It is enough*, or *It is wealth*. Those are never rich that are always coveting. Now these four things that are always craving are, 1. The grave, into which multitudes fall, and yet still more will fall, and it swallows them all up, and returns none,

Hell and destruction are never full, ch. xxvii. 20. When it comes to our turn we shall find the grave ready for us, Job xvii. 1. 2. The *barren womb,* which is impatient of its affliction in being barren, and cries, as Rachel did, *Give me children.* 3. The *parched ground* in time of drought (especially in those hot countries), which still soaks in the rain that comes in abundance upon it and in a little time wants more. 4. The *fire,* which, when it has consumed abundance of fuel, yet still devours all the combustible matter that is thrown into it. So insatiable are the corrupt desires of sinners, and so little satisfaction have they even in the gratification of them.

II. He adds a terrible threatening to disobedient children (*v.* 17), for warning to the first of those four wicked generations, that curse their parents (*v.* 11), and shows here,

1. Who they are that belong to that generation, not only those that curse their parents in heat and passion, but, (1.) Those that *mock* at them, though it be but with a scornful eye, looking with disdain upon them because of their bodily infirmities, or looking sour or dogged at them when they instruct or command, impatient at their checks and angry at them. God takes notice with what eye children look upon their parents, and will reckon for the leering look and the casts of the evil eye as well as for the bad language given them. (2.) Those that *despise to obey* them, that think it a thing below them to be dutiful to their parents, especially to the *mother,* they scorn to be controlled by her; and thus she that bore them in sorrow in greater sorrow bears their manners.

2. What their doom will be. Those that dishonour their parents shall be set up as monuments of God's vengeance; they shall be hanged in chains, as it were, for the birds of prey to pick out their eyes, those eyes with which they looked so scornfully on their good parents. The dead bodies of malefactors were not to hang all night, but before night the ravens would have picked out their eyes. If men do not punish undutiful children, God will, and will load those with the greatest infamy that conduct themselves haughtily towards their parents. Many who have come to an ignominious end have owned that the wicked courses that brought them to it began in a contempt of their parents' authority.

18 There be three *things which* are too wonderful for me, yea, four which I know not: 19 The way of an eagle in the air; the way of a serpent upon a rock; the way of a ship in the midst of the sea; and the way of a man with a maid. 20 Such *is* the way of an adulterous woman; she eateth, and wipeth her mouth, and saith, I have done no wickedness. 21 For

three *things* the earth is disquieted, and for four *which* it cannot bear: 22 For a servant when he reigneth; and a fool when he is filled with meat; 23 For an odious *woman* when she is married; and a handmaid that is heir to her mistress.

Here is, I. An account of four things that are unsearchable, *too wonderful* to be fully known. And here,

1. The first three are natural things, and are only designed as comparisons for the illustration of the last. We cannot trace, (1.) *An eagle in the air.* Which way she has flown cannot be discovered either by the footstep or by the scent, as the way of a beast may upon ground; nor can we account for the wonderful swiftness of her flight, how soon she has gone beyond our ken. (2.) *A serpent upon a rock.* The way of a serpent in the sand we may find by the track, but not of a serpent upon the hard rock; nor can we describe how a serpent will, without feet, in a little time creep to the top of a rock. (3.) *A ship in the midst of the sea.* The leviathan indeed *makes a path to shine after him, one would think the deep to be hoary* (Job xli. 32), but a ship leaves no mark behind it, and sometimes it is so tossed upon the waves that one would wonder how it lives at sea and gains its point. The kingdom of nature is full of wonders, marvellous things which the God of nature does, *past finding out.*

2. The fourth is a mystery of iniquity, more unaccountable than any of these; it belongs to the depths of Satan, that deceitfulness and that desperate wickedness of the heart which none can know, Jer. xvii. 9. It is twofold :—(1.) The cursed arts which a vile adulterer has to debauch a maid, and to persuade her to yield to his wicked and abominable lust. This is what a wanton poet wrote a whole book of, long since, *De arte amandi—On the art of love.* By what pretensions and protestations of love, and all its powerful charms, promises of marriage, assurances of secresy and reward, is many an unwary virgin brought to sell her virtue, and honour, and peace, and soul, and all to a base traitor; for so all sinful lust is in the kingdom of love. The more artfully the temptation is managed the more watchful and resolute ought every pure heart to be against it. (2.) The cursed arts which a vile adulteress has to conceal her wickedness, especially from her husband, from whom she treacherously departs; so close are her intrigues with her lewd companions, and so craftily disguised, that it is as impossible to discover her as to track an *eagle in the air.* She eats the forbidden fruit, after the similitude of Adam's transgression, and then *wipes her mouth,* that it may not betray itself, and with a bold and impudent face says, *I have done no wickedness.* [1.] To the world she denies the fact,

and is ready to swear it that she is as chaste and modest as any woman, and never did the wickedness she is suspected of. Those are the works of darkness which are industriously kept from coming to the light. [2.] To her own conscience (if she have any left) she denies the fault, and will not own that that *great wickedness* is any wickedness at all, but an innocent entertainment. See Hos. xii. 7, 8. Thus multitudes ruin their souls by calling evil good and out-facing their convictions with a self-justification.

II. An account of four things that are intolerable, that is, four sorts of persons that are very troublesome to the places where they live and the relations and companies they are in; the earth is *disquieted for them*, and groans under them as a burden it cannot bear, and they are all much alike.—1. *A servant* when he is advanced, and entrusted with power, who is, of all others, most insolent and imperious; witness Tobiah the servant, the Ammonite, Neh. ii. 10. 2. *A fool*, a silly, rude, boisterous, vicious man, who when he has grown rich, and is partaking of the pleasures of the table, will disturb all the company with his extravagant talk and the affronts he will put upon those about him. 3. An ill-natured, cross-grained, *woman*, when she gets a husband, one who, having made herself odious by her pride and sourness, so that one would not have thought any body would ever love her, yet, if at last she be married, that honourable estate makes her more intolerably scornful and spiteful than ever. It is a pity that that which should sweeten the disposition should have a contrary effect. A gracious woman, when she is married, will be yet more obliging. 4. An old maid-servant that has prevailed with her mistress, by humouring her, and, as we say, getting the length of her foot, to leave her what she has, or is as dear to her as if she was to be her heir, such a one likewise will be intolerably proud and malicious, and think all too little that her mistress gives her, and herself wronged if any thing be left from her. Let those therefore whom Providence has advanced to honour from mean beginnings carefully watch against that sin which will most easily beset them, pride and haughtiness, which will in them, of all others, be most insufferable and inexcusable; and let them humble themselves with the remembrance of the rock out of which they were hewn.

24 There be four *things which are* little upon the earth, but they *are* exceeding wise: 25 The ants *are* a people not strong, yet they prepare their meat in the summer; 26 The conies *are but* a feeble folk, yet make they their houses in the rocks; 27 The locusts have no king, yet go they forth all of them by bands; 28 The

spider taketh hold with her hands, and is in kings' palaces.

I. Agur, having specified four things that seem great and yet are really contemptible, here specifies four things that are little and yet are very admirable, great in miniature, in which, as bishop Patrick observes, he teaches us several good lessons; as, 1. Not to admire bodily bulk, or beauty, or strength, nor to value persons or think the better of them for such advantages, but to judge of men by their wisdom and conduct, their industry and application to business, which are characters that deserve respect. 2. To admire the wisdom and power of the Creator in the smallest and most despicable animals, in an ant as much as in an elephant. 3. To blame ourselves who do not act so much for our own true interest as the meanest creatures do for theirs. 4. Not to despise the weak things of the world; there are those that are *little upon the earth*, poor in the world and of small account, and yet *are exceedingly wise*, wise for their souls and another world, and those *are exceedingly wise, wiser than their neighbours.* Margin, *They are wise, made wise* by the special instinct of nature. All that are wise to salvation are made wise by the grace of God.

II. Those he specifies are, 1. The *ants*, minute animals and very weak, and yet they are very industrious in gathering proper food, and have a strange sagacity to do it in the summer, the proper time. This is so great a piece of wisdom that we may learn of them to be wise for futurity, *ch.* vi. 6. When the ravening *lions lack, and suffer hunger*, the laborious ants have plenty, and know no want. 2. The *conies*, or, as some rather understand it, the Arabian mice, field-mice, weak creatures, and very timorous, yet they have so much wisdom as to *make their houses in the rocks*, where they are well guarded, and their feebleness makes them take shelter in those natural fastnesses and fortifications. Sense of our own indigence and weakness should drive us to him that is a *rock higher than we* for shelter and support; there let us make our habitation. 3. The *locusts;* they are little also, and *have no king*, as the bees have, but *they go forth all of them by bands*, like an army in battle-array; and, observing such good order among themselves, it is not any inconvenience to them that they *have no king.* They are called God's *great army* (Joel ii. 25); for, when he pleases, he musters, he marshals them, and wages war by them, as he did upon Egypt. *They go forth all of them gathered together* (so the margin); sense of weakness should engage us to keep together, that we may strengthen the hands of one another. 4. The *spider*, an insect, but as great an instance of industry in our houses as the ants are in the field. Spiders are very ingenious in weaving their webs with a fineness and exactness such as no art can pretend to come near : They *take hold with their hands,* and spin a fine thread out of their own bowels, with a great deal of art ; and they are not only in poor men's cottages, but in *kings' palaces,* notwithstanding all the care that is there taken to destroy them. Providence wonderfully keeps up those kinds of creatures, not only which men provide not for, but which every man's hand is against and seeks the destruction of. Those that will mind their business, and *take hold* of it *with their hands,* shall be *in kings' palaces ;* sooner or later, they will get preferment, and may go on with it, notwithstanding the difficulties and discouragements they meet with. If one well-spun web be swept away, it is but making another.

29 There be three *things* which go well, yea, four are comely in going : 30 A lion *which is* strongest among beasts, and turneth not away for any ; 31 A greyhound ; a he goat also ; and a king, against whom *there is* no rising up. 32 If thou hast done foolishly in lifting up thyself, or if thou hast thought evil, *lay* thine hand upon thy mouth. 33 Surely the churning of milk bringeth forth butter, and the wringing of the nose bringeth forth blood : so the forcing of wrath bringeth forth strife.

Here is, I. An enumeration of four things which are majestic and stately in their going, which look great :—1. *A lion,* the king of beasts, because *strongest among beasts.* Among beasts it is strength that gives the pre-eminence, but it is a pity that it should do so among men, whose *wisdom* is their honour, not their *strength* and *force.* The lion *turns not away,* nor alters his pace, for fear of any pursuers, since he knows he is too hard for them. Herein *the righteous are bold as a lion,* that they *turn not away* from their duty for fear of any difficulty they meet with in it. 2. *A greyhound* that is girt in the loins and fit for running ; or (as the margin reads it) *a horse,* which ought not to be omitted among the creatures that *are comely in going,* for so he is, especially when he is dressed up in his harness or trappings. 3. *A he-goat,* the comeliness of whose going is when he goes first and leads the flock. It is the comeliness of a Christian's going to go first in a good work and to lead others in the right way. 4. *A king,* who, when he appears in his majesty, is looked upon with reverence and awe, and all agree that *there is no rising up against* him ; none can vie with him, none can contend with him, whoever does it, it is at his peril. And, if *there is no rising up* against an earthly prince, *woe to him* then *that strives with his Maker.* It is intended that we should learn courage and fortitude in all virtuous actions

970

from the *lion* and *not to turn away for any* difficulty we meet with ; from the *greyhound* we may learn quickness and despatch, from the *he-goat* the care of our family and those under our charge, and from *a king* to have our children in subjection with all gravity, and from them all to *go well,* and to order the steps of our conversation so as that we may not only be safe, but *comely, in going.*

II. A caution to us to keep our temper at all times and under all provocations, and to take heed of carrying our resentments too far upon any occasion, especially when there is *a king* in the case, *against whom there is no rising up,* when it is a ruler, or one much our superior, that is offended ; nay, the rule is always the same.

1. We must bridle and suppress our own passion, and take shame to ourselves, whenever we are justly charged with a fault, and not insist upon our own innocency : If we have *lifted up ourselves,* either in a proud conceit of ourselves or a peevish opposition to those that are over us, if we have transgressed the laws of our place and station, we have therein *done foolishly.* Those that magnify themselves over others or against others, that are haughty and insolent, do but shame themselves and betray their own weakness. Nay, if we have but *thought evil,* if we are conscious to ourselves that we have harboured an ill design in our minds, or it has been suggested to us, we must *lay our hand upon our mouth,* that is, (1.) We must humble ourselves for what we have done amiss, and even lie in the dust before God, in sorrow for it, as Job did, when he repented of what he had said foolishly *(ch.* xl. 4, *I will lay my hand upon my mouth),* and as the convicted leper, who *put a covering upon his upper lip.* If we have *done foolishly,* we must not stand to it before men, but by silence own our guilt, which will be the best way of appeasing those we have offended. 2. We must keep the evil thought we have conceived in our minds from breaking out in any evil speeches. Do not give the evil thought an *imprimatur—a license ;* allow it not to be published ; but *lay thy hand upon thy mouth ;* use a holy violence with thyself, if need be, and enjoin thyself silence ; as Christ *suffered not the evil spirits to speak.* It is bad to think ill, but it is much worse to speak it, for that implies a consent to the evil thought and a willingness to infect others with it.

2. We must not irritate the passions of others. Some are so very provoking in their words and conduct that they even *force wrath,* they make those about them angry whether they will or no, and put those into a passion who are not only inclined to it, but resolved against it. Now this *forcing of wrath brings forth strife,* and where that *is there is confusion and every evil work.* As the violent agitation of the cream fetches all the good out of the milk, and the hard *wringing of the nose* will extort blood from it, so this *forcing*

of wrath wastes both the body and spirits of a man, and robs him of all the good that is in him. Or, as it is in *the churning of milk and the wringing of the nose, that* is done by force which otherwise would not be done, so the spirit is heated by degrees with strong passions; one angry word begets another, and that a third; one passionate debate makes work for another, and so it goes on till it ends at length in irreconcilable feuds. Let nothing therefore be said or done with violence, but every thing with softness and calmness.

CHAP. XXXI.

This chapter is added to Solomon's proverbs, some think because it is of the same author, supposing king Lemuel to be king Solomon; others only because it is of the same nature, though left in writing by another author, called Lemuel; however it be, it is a prophecy, and therefore given by inspiration and direction of God, which Lemuel was under in the writing of it, and putting it into this form, as his mother was in dictating to him the matter of it. Here is, I. An exhortation to Lemuel, a young prince, to take heed of the duties of the place he was called to, ver. 1—9. II. The description of a virtuous woman, especially in the relation of a wife and the mistress of a family, which Lemuel's mother drew up, not as an encomium of herself, though, no doubt, it was her own true picture, but either as an instruction to her daughters, as the foregoing verses were to her son, or as a direction to her son in the choice of a wife; she must be chaste and modest, diligent and frugal, dutiful to her husband, careful of her family, discreet in her discourse, and in the education of her children, and, above all, conscientious in her duty to God: such a one as this, if he can find her, will make him happy, ver. 10—31.

THE words of king Lemuel, the prophecy that his mother taught him. 2 What, my son? and what, the son of my womb? and what, the son of my vows? 3 Give not thy strength unto women, nor thy ways to that which destroyeth kings. 4 *It is* not for kings, O Lemuel, *it is* not for kings to drink wine; nor for princes strong drink: 5 Lest they drink, and forget the law, and pervert the judgment of any of the afflicted. 6 Give strong drink unto him that is ready to perish, and wine unto those that be of heavy hearts. 7 Let him drink, and forget his poverty, and remember his misery no more. 8 Open thy mouth for the dumb in the cause of all such as are appointed to destruction. 9 Open thy mouth, judge righteously, and plead the cause of the poor and needy.

Most interpreters are of opinion that Lemuel is Solomon; the name signifies one that is *for God*, or *devoted to God;* and so it agrees well enough with that honourable name which, by divine appointment, was given to Solomon (2 Sam. xii. 25), *Jedediah—beloved of the Lord.* Lemuel is supposed to be a pretty, fond, endearing name, by which his mother used to call him; and so much did he value himself upon the interest he had in his mother's affections that he was not ashamed to call himself by it. One would the rather incline to think it is Solomon that

here tells us what *his mother taught him* because he tells us (ch. iv. 4) what his father taught him. But some think (and the conjecture is not improbable) that Lemuel was a prince of some neighbouring country, whose mother was a daughter of Israel, perhaps of the house of David, and taught him these good lessons. Note, 1. It is the duty of mothers, as well as fathers, to teach their children what is good, that they may do it, and what is evil, that they may avoid it; when they are young and tender they are most under the mother's eye, and she has then an opportunity of moulding and fashioning their minds well, which she ought not to let slip. 2. Even kings must be catechised; the greatest of men is less than the least of the ordinances of God. 3. Those that have grown up to maturity should often call to mind, and make mention of, the good instructions they received when they were children, for their own admonition, the edification of others, and the honour of those who were the guides of their youth.

Now, in this mother's (this queen mother's) catechism, observe,

I. Her expostulation with the young prince, by which she lays hold of him, claims an interest in him, and awakens his attention to what she is about to say (v. 2): "*What! my son?* What shall I say to thee?" She speaks as one considering what advice to give him, and choosing out words to reason with him; so full of concern is she for his welfare! Or, *What is it that thou doest?* It seems to be a chiding question. She observed, when he was young, that he was too much inclined to women and wine, and therefore she found it necessary to take him to task and deal roundly with him. "*What! my son?* Is this the course of life thou intendest to lead? Have I taught thee no better than thus? I must reprove thee, and reprove thee sharply, and thou must take it well, for," 1. "Thou art descended from me; thou art *the son of my womb*, and therefore what I say comes from the authority and affection of a parent and cannot be suspected to come from any ill-will. Thou art a piece of myself. I bore thee with sorrow, and I expect no other return for all the pains I have taken with thee, and undergone for thee, than this, Be wise and good, and then I am well paid." 2. "Thou art devoted to my God; thou art *the son of my vows*, the son I prayed to God to give me and promised to give back to God, and did so" (thus Samuel was the son of Hannah's vows); "thou art the son I have often prayed to God to give his grace to (Ps. lxxii. 1), and shall a child of so many prayers miscarry? And shall all my hopes concerning thee be disappointed?" Our children that by baptism are dedicated to God, for whom and in whose name we covenanted with God, may well be called *the children of our vows;* and, as this may be made a good plea with God in our prayers

971

for them, so it may be made a good plea with them in the instructions we give them; we may tell them they are baptized, are *the children of our vows,* and it is at their peril if they break those bonds in sunder which in their infancy they were solemnly brought under.

II. The caution she gives him against those two destroying sins of *uncleanness* and *drunkenness,* which, if he allowed himself in them, would certainly be his ruin. 1. Against uncleanness (*v.* 3): *Give not thy strength unto women,* unto strange women. He must not be soft and effeminate, nor spend that time in a vain conversation with the ladies which should be spent in getting knowledge and despatching business, nor employ that wit (which is the strength of the soul) in courting and complimenting them which he should employ about the affairs of his government. " Especially shun all adultery, fornication, and lasciviousness, which waste the strength of the body, and bring into it dangerous diseases. *Give not thy ways,* thy affections, thy conversation, *to that which destroys kings,* which has destroyed many, which gave such a shock to the kingdom even of David himself, in the matter of Uriah. Let the sufferings of others be thy warnings." It lessens the honour of kings and makes them mean. Are those fit to govern others that are themselves slaves to their own lusts? It makes them unfit for business, and fills their court with the basest and worst of animals. Kings lie exposed to temptations of this kind, having wherewith both to please the humours and to bear the charges of the sin, and therefore they ought to double their guard; and, if they would preserve their people from the unclean spirit, they must themselves be patterns of purity. Meaner people may also apply it to themselves. Let none give their strength *to that which destroys souls.* 2. Against drunkenness, *v.* 4, 5. He must not *drink wine* or *strong drink* to excess; he must never sit to drink, as they used to do *in the day of their king,* when *the princes made him sick with bottles of wine,* Hos. vii. 7. Whatever temptation he might be in from the excellency of the wine, or the charms of the company, he must deny himself, and be strictly sober, considering, (1.) The indecency of drunkenness in a king. However some may call it a fashionable accomplishment and entertainment, *it is not for kings, O Lemuel! it is not for kings, to* allow themselves that liberty; it is a disparagement to their dignity, and profanes their crown, by confusing the head that wears it; that which for the time unmans them does for the time unking them. Shall we say, *They are gods?* No, they are *worse than the beasts that perish.* All Christians are *made to our God kings and priests,* and must apply this to themselves. *It is not for* Christians, *it is not for* Christians, *to drink* to excess; they debase themselves if they do; it ill becomes the heirs of

the kingdom and the spiritual priests, Lev. x. 9. (2.) The ill consequences of it (*v.* 5): *Lest they drink* away their understandings and memories, *drink and forget the law* by which they are to govern; and so, instead of doing good with their power, do hurt with it, *and pervert* or *alter the judgment of all the sons of affliction,* and, when they should right them, wrong them, and add to their affliction. It is a sad complaint which is made of the priests and prophets (Isa. xxviii. 7), that *they have erred through wine, and through strong drink they are out of the way;* and the effect is as bad in kings, who when they are drunk, or intoxicated with the love of wine, cannot but stumble in judgment. Judges must have clear heads, which those cannot have who so often make themselves giddy, and incapacitate themselves to judge of the most common things.

III. The counsel she gives him to do good. 1. He must do good with his wealth. Great men must not think that they have their abundance only that out of it they may *make provision for the flesh, to fulfil the lusts of it,* and may the more freely indulge their own genius; no, but that with it they may relieve such as are in distress, *v.* 6, 7. " Thou hast wine or strong drink at command; instead of doing thyself hurt with it, do others good with it; let those have it that need it." Those that have wherewithal must not only give bread to the hungry and water to the thirsty, but they must *give strong drink to him that is ready to perish* through sickness or pain *and wine to those that* are melancholy and *of heavy heart;* for it was appointed to cheer and revive the spirits, and *make glad the heart* (as it does where there is need of it), not to burden and oppress the spirits, as it does where there is no need of it. We must deny ourselves in the gratifications of sense, that we may have to spare for the relief of the miseries of others, and be glad to see our superfluities and dainties better bestowed upon those whom they will be a real kindness to than upon ourselves whom they will be a real injury to. Let those that are *ready to perish* drink soberly, and it will be a means so to revive their drooping spirits that they will *forget their poverty* for the time *and remember their misery no more,* and so they will be the better able to bear it. The Jews say that upon this was grounded the practice of giving a stupifying drink to condemned prisoners when they were going to execution, as they did to our Saviour. But the scope of the place is to show that wine is a cordial, and therefore to be used for want and not for wantonness, by those only that need cordials, as Timothy, who is advised to *drink a little wine,* only *for his stomach's sake and his often infirmities,* 1 Tim. v. 23. 2. He must do good with his power, his knowledge, and interest, must administer justice with care, courage, and compassion, *v.* 8, 9. (1.) He must himself take cognizance of the causes his subjects have depending in his courts, and inspect what his judges and officers do, that he may support those that do their duty, and lay those aside that neglect it or are partial. (2.) He must, in all matters that come before him, *judge righteously*, and, without fear of the face of man, boldly pass sentence according to equity: *Open thy mouth*, which denotes the liberty of speech that princes and judges ought to use in passing sentence. Some observe that only wise men *open* their mouths, for fools have their mouths always open, are full of words. (3.) He must especially look upon himself as obliged to be the patron of oppressed innocency. The inferior magistrates perhaps had not zeal and tenderness enough to *plead the cause of the poor and needy;* therefore the king himself must interpose, and appear as an advocate, [1.] For those that were unjustly charged with capital crimes, as Naboth was, that were *appointed to destruction,* to gratify the malice either of a particular person or of a party. It is a case which it well befits a king to appear in, for the preserving of innocent blood. [2.] For those that had actions unjustly brought against them, to defraud them of their right, because they were *poor and needy*, and unable to defend it, not having wherewithal to fee counsel; in such a case also kings must be advocates for the poor. Especially, [3.] For those that were *dumb,* and knew not how to speak for themselves, either through weakness or fear, or being over-talked by the prosecutor or over-awed by the court. It is generous to speak for those that cannot speak for themselves, that are absent, or have not words at command, or are timorous. Our law appoints the judge to be of counsel for the prisoner.

10 Who can find a virtuous woman? for her price *is* far above rubies. 11 The heart of her husband doth safely trust in her, so that he shall have no need of spoil. 12 She will do him good and not evil all the days of her life. 13 She seeketh wool, and flax, and worketh willingly with her hands. 14 She is like the merchants' ships; she bringeth her food from afar. 15 She riseth also while it is yet night, and giveth meat to her household, and a portion to her maidens. 16 She considereth a field, and buyeth it: with the fruit of her hands she planteth a vineyard. 17 She girdeth her loins with strength, and strengtheneth her arms. 18 She perceiveth that her merchandise *is* good: her candle goeth not out by night. 19 She layeth her hands to the spindle, and her hands hold the distaff. 20 She stretcheth out her hand to the

poor; yea, she reacheth forth her hands to the needy. 21 She is not afraid of the snow for her household: for all her household *are* clothed with scarlet. 22 She maketh herself coverings of tapestry; her clothing *is* silk and purple. 23 Her husband is known in the gates, when he sitteth among the elders of the land. 24 She maketh fine linen, and selleth *it;* and delivereth girdles unto the merchant. 25 Strength and honour *are* her clothing; and she shall rejoice in time to come. 26 She openeth her mouth with wisdom; and in her tongue *is* the law of kindness. 27 She looketh well to the ways of her household, and eateth not the bread of idleness. 28 Her children arise up, and call her blessed; her husband *also*, and he praiseth her. 29 Many daughters have done virtuously, but thou excellest them all. 30 Favour *is* deceitful, and beauty *is* vain: *but* a woman *that* feareth the LORD, she shall be praised. 31 Give her of the fruit of her hands; and let her own works praise her in the gates.

This description of the *virtuous woman* is designed to show what wives the women should make and what wives the men should choose; it consists of twenty-two verses, each beginning with a letter of the Hebrew alphabet in order, as some of the *Psalms*, which makes some think it was no part of the lesson which Lemuel's mother taught him, but a poem by itself, written by some other hand, and perhaps had been commonly repeated among the pious Jews, for the ease of which it was made alphabetical. We have the abridgment of it in the New Testament (1 Tim. ii. 9, 10, 1 Pet. iii. 1—6), where the duty prescribed to wives agrees with this description of a good wife; and with good reason is so much stress laid upon it, since it contributes as much as any one thing to the keeping up of religion in families, and the entail of it upon posterity, that the mothers be wise and good; and of what consequence it is to the wealth and outward prosperity of a house every one is sensible. He that will thrive must ask his wife leave. Here is,

I. A general enquiry after such a one (*v.* 10), where observe, 1. The person enquired after, and that is *a virtuous woman—a woman of strength* (so the word is), though the weaker vessel, yet made strong by wisdom and grace, and the fear of God: it is the same word that is used in the character of good judges (Exod. xviii. 21), that they are *able men*, men qualified for the business to which they are called, *men of truth, fearing God.* So it follows,

A virtuous woman is a woman of spirit, who has the command of her own spirit and knows how to manage other people's, one that is pious and industrious, and a help meet for a man. In opposition to this strength, we read of the weakness of the heart *of an imperious whorish woman*, Ezek. xvi. 30. *A virtuous woman* is a woman of resolution, who, having espoused good principles, is firm and steady to them, and will not be frightened with winds and clouds from any part of her duty. 2. The difficulty of meeting with such a one : *Who can find* her? This intimates that good women are very scarce, and many that seem to be so do not prove so; he that thought he had found *a virtuous woman* was deceived; *Behold, it was Leah*, and not the Rachel he expected. But he that designs to marry ought to seek diligently for such a one, to have this principally in his eye, in all his enquiries, and to take heed that he be not biassed by beauty or gaiety, wealth or parentage, dressing well or dancing well; for all these may be and yet the woman not be virtuous, and there is many a woman truly virtuous who yet is not recommended by these advantages. 3. The unspeakable worth of such a one, and the value which he that has such a wife ought to put upon her, showing it by his thankfulness to God and his kindness and respect to her, whom he must never think he can do too much for. *Her price is far above rubies*, and all the rich ornaments with which vain women adorn themselves. The more rare such good wives are the more they are to be valued.

II. A particular description of her and of her excellent qualifications.

1. She is very industrious to recommend herself to her husband's esteem and affection. Those that are good really will be good relatively. A good woman, if she be brought into the marriage state, will be a good wife, and make it her business to *please her husband*, 1 Cor. vii. 34. Though she is a woman of spirit herself, yet *her desire is to her husband*, to know his mind, that she may accommodate herself to it, and she is willing that *he should rule over her*. (1.) She conducts herself so that he may repose an entire confidence in her. He trusts in her chastity, which she never gave him the least occasion to suspect or to entertain any jealousy of; she is not morose and reserved, but modest and grave, and has all the marks of virtue in her countenance and behaviour; her husband knows it, and therefore his *heart doth safely trust in her ;* he is easy, and makes her so. He trusts in her conduct, that she will speak in all companies, and act in all affairs, with prudence and discretion, so as not to occasion him either damage or reproach. He trusts in her fidelity to his interests, and that she will never betray his counsels nor have any interest separate from that of his family. When he goes abroad, to attend the concerns of the public, he can confide in her to order all his affairs at home, as well as if he him-

self were there. She is a good wife that is fit to be trusted, and he a good husband that will leave it to such a wife to manage for him. (2.) She contributes so much to his content and satisfaction *that he shall have no need of spoil ;* he needs not be griping and scraping abroad, as those must be whose wives are proud and wasteful at home. She manages his affairs so that he is always before-hand, has such plenty of his own that he is in no temptation to prey upon his neighbours. He thinks himself so happy in her that he envies not those who have most of the wealth of this world; he needs it not, he has enough, having such a wife. Happy the couple that have such a satisfaction as this in each other ! (3.) She makes it her constant business to *do him good*, and is afraid of doing any thing, even through inadvertency, that may turn to his prejudice, *v.* 12. She shows her love to him, not by a foolish fondness, but by prudent endearments, accommodating herself to his temper, and not crossing him, giving him good words, and not bad ones, no, not when he is out of humour, studying to make him easy, to provide what is fit for him both in health and sickness, and attending him with diligence and tenderness when any thing ails him ; nor would she, no, not for the world, wilfully do any thing that might be a damage to his person, family, estate, or reputation. And this is her care *all the days of her life ;* not at first only, or now and then, when she is in a good humour, but perpetually ; and she is not weary of the good offices she does him : *She does him good*, not only all the days of *his* life, but *of her own* too ; if she survive him, still she is doing him good in her care of his children, his estate, and good name, and all the concerns he left behind him. We read of kindness shown, not only *to the living*, but *to the dead*, Ruth ii. 20. (4.) She adds to his reputation in the world (*v.* 23): *Her husband is known in the gates*, known to have a good wife. By his wise counsels, and prudent management of affairs, it appears that he has a discreet companion in his bosom, by conversation with whom he improves himself. By his cheerful countenance and pleasant humour it appears that he has an agreeable wife at home ; for many that have not have their tempers strangely soured by it. Nay, by his appearing clean and neat in his dress, every thing about him decent and handsome, yet not gaudy, one may know he has a good wife at home, that takes care of his clothes.

2. She is one that takes pains in the duty of her place and takes pleasure in it. This part of her character is much enlarged upon here. (1.) She hates to sit still and do nothing : *She eats not the bread of idleness, v.* 27. Though she needs not work for her bread (she has an estate to live upon), yet she will not eat it in idleness, because she knows that we were none of us sent into this world to be idle, that when we have nothing

to do the devil will soon find us something to do, and that it is not fit that those who *will not labour* should *eat.* Some eat and drink because they can find themselves nothing else to do, and needless visits must be received with fashionable entertainments; these are eating the bread of idleness, which she has no relish for, for she neither gives nor receives idle visits nor idle talk. (2.) She is careful to fill up time, that none of that be lost. When day-light is done, she does not then think it time to lay by her work, as those are forced to do whose business lies abroad in the fields (Ps. civ. 23), but her business lying within-doors, and her work worth candle-light, with that she lengthens out the day; and *her candle goes not out by night, v.* 18. It is a mercy to have candle-light to supply the want of day-light, and a duty, having that advantage, to improve it. We say of an elaborate piece, It smells of the lamp. (3.) *She rises* early, *while it is yet night* (*v.* 15), to give her servants their breakfast, that they may be ready to go cheerfully about their work as soon as the day breaks. She is none of those who sit up playing at cards, or dancing, till midnight, till morning, and then lie in bed till noon. No; the *virtuous woman* loves her business better than her ease or her pleasure, is in care to be found in the way of her duty every hour of the day, and has more true satisfaction in having *given meat to her household* betimes in the morning than those can have in the money they have won, much more in what they have lost, who sat up all night at play. Those that have a family to take care of should not love their bed too well in a morning. (4.) She applies herself to the business that is proper for her. It is not in scholar's business, or statesman's business, or husbandman's business, that she employs herself, but in women's business: *She seeks wool and flax,* where she may have the best of each at the best hand, and cheapest; she has a stock of both by her, and every thing that is necessary to the carrying on both of the woollen and the linen manufacture (*v.* 13), and with this she does not only set the poor on work, which is a very good office, but does herself work, *and work willingly, with her hands;* she *works with the counsel or delight of her hands* (so the word is); she goes about it cheerfully and dexterously, lays not only her hand, but her mind to it, and goes on in it without weariness in well-doing. *She lays her own hands to the spindle,* or spinning-wheel, *and her hands hold the distaff* (*v.* 19), and she does not reckon it either an abridgment of her liberty or a disparagement to her dignity, or at all inconsistent with her repose. The spindle and the distaff are here mentioned as her honour, while the ornaments of the daughters of Zion are reckoned up to their reproach, Isa. iii. 18, &c. (5.) She does what she does with all her might, and does not trifle in it (*v.* 17): *She girds her loins with strength and strengthens her arms;* she does not employ herself in sitting work only, or in that which is only the nice performance of the fingers (there are works that are scarcely one remove from doing nothing); but, if there be occasion, she will go through with work that requires all the strength she has, which she will use as one that knows it is the way to have more.

3. She is one that makes what she does to turn to a good account, by her prudent management of it. She does not toil all night and catch nothing; no, she herself *perceives that her merchandise is good* (*v.* 18); she is sensible that *in all* her *labour there is profit,* and that encourages her to go on in it. She perceives that she can make things herself better and cheaper than she can buy them; she finds by observation what branch of her employment brings in the best returns, and to that she applies herself most closely. (1.) She brings in provisions of all things necessary and convenient for her family, *v.* 14. No *merchants' ships,* no, not Solomon's navy, ever made a more advantageous return than her employments do. Do they bring in foreign commodities with the effects they export? So does she with the fruit of her labours. What her own ground does not produce she can furnish herself with, if she have occasion for it, by exchanging her own goods for it; and so *she brings her food from afar.* Not that she values things the more for their being far-fetched, but, if they be ever so far off, if she must have them she knows how to come by them. (2.) She purchases lands, and enlarges the demesne of the family (*v.* 16): *She considers a field, and buys it.* She considers what an advantage it will be to the family and what a good account it will turn to, and therefore she buys it; or, rather, though she have ever so much mind to it she will not buy it till she has first considered it, whether it be worth her money, whether she can afford to take so much money out of her stock as must go to purchase it, whether the title be good, whether the ground will answer the character given of it, and whether she has money at command to pay for it. Many have undone themselves by buying without considering; but those who would make advantageous purchases must consider, and then buy. *She* also *plants a vineyard, but it is with the fruit of her hands;* she does not take up money, or run into debt, to do it, but she does it with what she can spare out of the gains of her own housewifery. Men should not lay out any thing upon superfluities, till, by the blessing of God upon their industry, they have got before-hand, and can afford it; and *then* the fruit of the vineyard is likely to be doubly sweet, when it is the fruit of honest industry. (3.) She furnishes her house well and has good clothing for herself and her family (*v.* 22): *She makes herself coverings of tapestry* to hang her rooms, and

975

she may be allowed to use them when they are of her own making. *Her* own *clothing* is rich and fine : it is *silk and purple,* according to her place and rank. Though she is not so vain as to spend much time in dressing herself, nor makes the putting on of apparel her adorning, nor values herself upon it, yet she has rich clothes and puts them on well. The senator's robes which her husband wears are of her own spinning, and they look better and wear better than any that are bought. She also gets good warm clothing for her children, and her servants' liveries. She needs not fear the cold of the most pinching winter, for she and her family are well provided with clothes, sufficient to keep out cold, which is the end chiefly to be aimed at in clothing : *All her household are clothed in scarlet,* strong cloth and fit for winter, and yet rich and making a good appearance. They are *all, double clothed* (so some read it), have change of raiment, a winter suit and a summer suit. (4.) She trades abroad. She makes more than she and her household have occasion for ; and therefore, when she has sufficiently stocked her family, *she sells fine linen and girdles to the merchants* (v. 24), who carry them to Tyre, the mart of the nations, or some other trading city. Those families are likely to thrive that sell more than they buy ; as it is well with the kingdom when abundance of its 'home manufactures are exported. It is no disgrace to those of the best quality to sell what they can spare, nor to deal in trade and send ventures by sea. (5.) She lays up for hereafter : *She shall rejoice in time to come,* having laid in a good stock for her family, and having good portions for her children. Those that take pains when they are in their prime will have the pleasure and joy of it when they are old, both in reflecting upon it and in reaping the benefit of it.

4. She takes care of her family and all the affairs of it, *gives meat to her household* (v. 15), to every one *his portion of meat in due season,* so that none of her servants have reason to complain of being kept short or faring hard. She gives also *a portion* (an allotment of work, as well as meat) *to her maidens ;* they shall all of them know their business and have their task. *She looks well to the ways of her household* (v. 27) ; she inspects the manners of all her servants, that she may check what is amiss among them, and oblige them all to behave properly and do their duty to God and one another, as well as to her ; as Job, who put away iniquity far from his tabernacle, and David, who would suffer no wicked thing in his house. She does not intermeddle in the concerns of other people's houses ; she thinks it enough for her to look well to her own.

5. She is charitable *to the poor, v.* 20. She is as intent upon giving as she is upon getting ; she often serves the poor with her own hand, and she does it freely, cheerfully, and very liberally, with an out-stretched hand.

Nor does she relieve her poor neighbours only, and those that are nigh at hand, but *she reaches forth her hands to the needy* that are at a distance, seeking opportunities *to do good and to communicate,* which is as good housewifery as any thing she does.

6. She is discreet and obliging in all her discourse, not talkative, censorious, nor peevish, as some are, that know how to take pains ; no, *she opens her mouth with wisdom ;* when she does speak, it is with a great deal of prudence and very much to the purpose ; you may perceive by every word she says how much she governs herself by the rules of wisdom. She not only takes prudent measures herself, but gives prudent advice to others ; and this not as assuming the authority of a dictator, but with the affection of a friend and an obliging air : *In her tongue is the law of kindness ;* all she says is under the government of that law. The law of love and kindness is written in the heart, but it shows itself in the tongue ; if we are *kindly affectioned one to another,* it will appear by affectionate expressions. It is called a *law of kindness,* because it gives law to others, to all she converses with. Her wisdom and kindness together put a commanding power into all she says ; they command respect, they command compliance. How forcible are right words ! *In her tongue is the law of grace,* or *mercy* (so some read it), understanding it of the word and law of God, which she delights to talk of among her children and servants. She is full of pious religious discourse, and manages it prudently, which shows how full her heart is of another world even when her hands are most busy about this world.

7. That which completes and crowns her character is that she *fears the Lord, v.* 30. With all those good qualities she lacks not that *one thing needful ;* she is truly pious, and, in all she does, is guided and governed by principles of conscience and a regard to God ; this is that which is her preferred far before *beauty :* that *is vain and deceitful ;* all that are wise and good account it so, and value neither themselves nor others on it. Beauty recommends none to God, nor is it any certain indication of wisdom and goodness, but it has deceived many a man who has made his choice of a wife by it. There may be an impure deformed soul lodged in a comely and beautiful body ; nay, many have been exposed by their beauty to such temptations as have been the ruin of their virtue, their honour, and their precious souls. It is a fading thing at the best, and therefore *vain* and *deceitful.* A fit of sickness will stain and sully it in a little time ; a thousand accidents may blast this flower in its prime ; old age will certainly wither it and death and the grave consume it. But the fear of God reigning in the heart is the beauty of the soul ; it recommends those that have it to the favour of God, and is, in his sight, of

great price; it will last for ever, and bid defiance to death itself, which consumes the beauty of the body, but consummates the beauty of the soul.

III. The happiness of this virtuous woman. 1. She has the comfort and satisfaction of her virtue in her own mind (*v.* 25): *Strength and honour are her clothing,* in which she wraps herself, that is, enjoys herself, and in which she appears to the world, and so recommends herself. She enjoys a firmness and constancy of mind, has spirit to bear up under the many crosses and disappointments which even the wise and virtuous must expect to meet with in this world; and this is her clothing, for defence as well as decency. She deals honourably with all, and she has the pleasure of doing so, *and shall rejoice in time to come;* she shall reflect upon it with comfort, when she comes to be old, that she was not idle or useless when she was young. In the day of death it will be a pleasure to her to think that she has lived to some good purpose. Nay, *she shall rejoice in an eternity to come;* she shall be recompensed for her goodness with *fulness of joy and pleasures for evermore.*

2. She is a great blessing to her relations, *v.* 28. (1.) *Her children* grow up in her place, *and* they *call her blessed.* They give her their good word, they are themselves a commendation to her, and they are ready to give great commendations of her; they pray for her, and bless God that they had such a good mother. It is a debt which they owe her, a part of that honour which the fifth commandment requires to be paid to father and mother; and it is a double honour that is due to a good father and a good mother. (2.) *Her husband* thinks himself so happy in her that he takes all occasions to speak well of her, as one of the best of women. It is no indecency at all, but a laudable instance of conjugal love, for husbands and wives to give one another their due praises.

3. She gets the good word of all her neighbours, as Ruth did, whom *all the city of her people knew* to be *a virtuous woman,* Ruth iii. 11. Virtue will have its praise, Phil. iv. 8. A woman that fears the Lord, shall have praise *of God* (Rom. ii. 29) and of men too. It is here shown, (1.) That she shall be highly praised (*v.* 29): *Many have done virtuously.* Virtuous women, it seems, are precious jewels, but not such rare jewels as was represented *v.* 10. There have been many,

but such a one as this cannot be paralleled. *Who can find* her equal? *She excels them all.* Note, Those that are good should aim and covet to excel in virtue. *Many daughters,* in their father's house, and in the single state, *have done virtuously, but* a good wife, if she be virtuous, *excels them all,* and does more good in her place than they can do in theirs. Or, as some explain it, A man cannot have his house so well kept by good daughters, as by a good wife. (2.) That she shall be incontestably praised, without contradiction, *v.* 31. Some are praised above what is their due, but those that praise her do but *give her of the fruit of her hands;* they give her that which she has dearly earned and which is justly due to her; she is wronged if she have it not. Note, Those ought to be praised the fruit of whose hands is praise-worthy. The tree is known by its fruits, and therefore, if the fruit be good, the tree must have our good word. If her children be dutiful and respectful to her, and conduct themselves as they ought, they then *give her of the fruit of her hands;* she reaps the benefit of all the care she has taken of them, and thinks herself well paid. Children must thus study to *requite their parents,* and this is *showing piety at home,* 1 Tim. v. 4. But, if men be unjust, the thing will speak itself, *her own works* will *praise her in the gates,* openly before all the people. [1.] She leaves it to her own works to praise her, and does not court the applause of men. Those are none of the truly virtuous women that love to hear themselves commended. [2.] *Her own works* will *praise her;* if her relations and neighbours altogether hold their peace, her good works will proclaim her praise. The widows gave the best encomium of Dorcas when they *showed the coats and garments she had made for the poor,* Acts ix. 39. [3.] The least that can be expected from her neighbours is that they should *let her own works praise her,* and do nothing to hinder them. Those that *do that which is good,* let them *have praise of the same* (Rom. xiii. 3) and let not us enviously say, or do, any thing to the diminishing of it, but be provoked by it to a holy emulation. Let none have an ill report from us, that have *a good report* even *of the truth itself.* Thus is shut up this looking-glass for ladies, which they are desired to open and dress themselves by; and, if they do so, their adorning will be found to praise, and honour, and glory, at the appearing of Jesus Christ.

Twenty chapters of the book of *Proverbs* (beginning with *ch.* x. and ending with *ch.* xxix), consisting mostly of entire sentences in each verse, could not well be reduced to proper heads, and the contents of them gathered; I have therefore here put the contents of all these chapters together, which perhaps may be of some use to those who desire to see at once all that is said of any one head in these chapters. Some of the verses, perhaps, I have not put under the same heads that another would have put them under, but the most of them fall (I hope) naturally enough to the places I have assigned them.

PROVERBS.—CONTENTS.

AN

EXPOSITION,

WITH PRACTICAL OBSERVATIONS,

OF THE BOOK OF

ECCLESIASTES.

WE are still among Solomon's happy men, his happy servants, that *stood continually before him to hear his wisdom;* and they are the choicest of all the dictates of his wisdom, such as were more immediately given by divine inspiration, that are here transmittted to us, not to be heard, as by them, but once, and then liable to be mistaken or forgotten, and by repetition to lose their beauty, but to be read, reviewed, revolved, and had in everlasting remembrance. The account we have of Solomon's apostasy from God, in the latter end of his reign (1 Kings xi. 1), is the tragical part of his story ; we may suppose that he spoke his *Proverbs* in the prime of his time, while he kept his integrity, but delivered his *Ecclesiastes* when he had grown old (for of the burdens and decays of age he speaks feelingly *ch.* xii.), and was, by the grace of God, recovered from his backslidings. There he dictated his observations ; here he wrote his own experiences ; this is what days speak, and wisdom which the multitude of years teaches. The title of the book and the penman we shall meet with in the first verse, and therefore shall here only observe,

I. That it is a sermon, a sermon in print; the text is (*ch.* i. 2), *Vanity of vanities, all is vanity;* that is the doctrine too ; it is proved at large by many arguments and an induction of particulars, and divers objections are answered, and in the close we have the use and application of all, by way of exhortation, to *remember our Creator,* to *fear him,* and to *keep his commandments.* There are indeed many things in this book which are dark and hard to be understood, and some things which men of corrupt minds *wrest to their own destruction,* for want of distinguishing between Solomon's arguments and the objections of atheists and epicures ; but there is enough easy and plain to convince us (if we will admit the conviction) of the vanity of the world, and its utter insufficiency to make us happy, the vileness of sin, and its certain tendency to make us miserable, and of the wisdom of being religious, and the solid comfort and satisfaction that are to be had in doing our duty both to God and man. This should be intended in every sermon, and that is a good sermon by which these points are in any measure gained. II. That it is a penitential sermon, as some of David's psalms are penitential psalms ; it is a recantation-sermon, in which the preacher sadly laments his own folly and mistake, in promising himself satisfaction in the things of this world, and even in the forbidden pleasures of sense, which now he finds more bitter than death. His fall is a proof of the weakness of man's nature : *Let not the wise man glory in his wisdom,* nor say, " I shall never be such a fool as to do so and so," when Solomon himself, the wisest of men, played the fool so egregiously ; nor *let the rich man glory in his riches,* since Solomon's wealth was so great a snare to him, and did him a great deal more hurt than Job's poverty did him. His recovery is a proof of the power of God's grace, in bringing one back to God that had gone so far from him ; it is a proof too of the riches of God's mercy in accepting him notwithstanding the many aggravations of his sin, pursuant to the promise made to David, that *if his children should commit iniquity* they should be corrected, but not abandoned and disinherited, 2 Sam. vii. 14, 15. Let him therefore that *thinks he stands take heed lest he fall ;* and let him that has fallen make haste to get up again, and not despair either of assistance or acceptance therein. III. That it is a practical profitable sermon. Solomon, being brought to repentance, resolves, like his father, to *teach transgressors God's way* (Ps. li. 13) and to give warning to all to take heed of splitting upon those rocks which had been fatal to him ; and these were *fruits meet for repentance.* . The fundamental error of the children of men, and that which is at the bottom of all their departures from God, is the same with that of our first parents, hoping to be *as gods* by entertaining themselves with that which seems *good for food, pleasant to the eyes,* and *desirable to make one wise.* Now the scope of this book is to show that this is a great mistake, that our happiness consists not in being as gods to ourselves, to have what we will and do what we will, but in having him that made us to be a God to us. The moral philosophers disputed much about man's felicity, or chief good. Various opinions they had about it ; but Solomon, in this book, determines the question, and assures us that *to fear God and to keep his commandments is the whole of man.* He tried what satisfaction might be found in the wealth of the world and the pleasures of sense, and at last pronounced *all vanity and vexation ;* yet multitudes will not take his word, but will make the same dangerous experiment, and it proves fatal to them. He, 1. Shows the vanity of those things in which men commonly look for happiness, as human learning and policy, sensual delight, honour and power, riches and great possessions. And then, 2. He prescribes remedies against the vexation of spirit that attends them. Though we cannot cure them of their vanity, we may prevent the trouble they give us, by sitting loose to them, enjoying them comfortably, but laying our expectations low from them, and acquiescing in the will of God concerning us in every event, especially by remembering God in the days of our youth, and continuing in his fear and service all our days, with an eye to the judgment to come.

CHAP. I.

In this chapter we have, I. The inscription, or title of the book, ver. 1. II. The general doctrine of the vanity of the creature laid down (ver. 2) and explained, ver. 3. III. The proof of this doctrine, taken, 1. From the shortness of human life and the multitude of births and burials in this life, ver. 4. 2. From the inconstant nature, and constant revolutions, of all the creatures, and the perpetual flux and reflux they are in, the sun, wind, and water, ver. 5—7. 3. From the abundant toil man has about them and the little satisfaction he has in them, ver. 8. 4. From the return of the same things again, which shows the end of all perfection, and that the stock is exhausted, ver. 9, 10. 5. From the oblivion to which all things are condemned, ver. 11. IV. The first instance of the vanity of men's knowledge, and all the parts of learning, especially natural philosophy and politics. Observe, 1. The trial Solomon made of these, ver. 12, 13, 16, 17. 2. His judgment of them, that all is vanity, ver. 14. For, (1.) There is labour in getting knowledge, ver. 13. (2.) There is little good to be done with it, ver. 15. (3.) There is no satisfaction in it, ver. 18. And, if this is vanity and vexation, all other things in this world, being much inferior to it in dignity and worth, must needs be so too. A great scholar cannot be happy unless he be a true saint.

THE words of the Preacher, the son of David, king of Jerusalem. 2 Vanity of vanities, saith the Preacher, vanity of vanities; all *is* vanity. 3 What profit hath a man of all his labour which he taketh under the sun ?

Here is, I. An account of the penman of this book ; it was Solomon, for no other son of David was king of Jerusalem ; but he conceals his name *Solomon, peaceable,* because by his sin he had brought trouble upon himself and his kingdom, had broken his peace with God and lost the peace of his conscience, and therefore was no more worthy of that name. Call me not *Solomon,* call me *Marah,* for, *behold, for peace I had great bitterness.* But he calls himself,

1. *The preacher,* which intimates his present character. He is *Koheleth,* which comes from a word which signifies *to gather ;* but it is of a feminine termination, by which perhaps Solomon intends to upbraid himself

980

with his effeminacy, which contributed more than any thing to his apostasy ; for it was to please his wives that he set up idols, Neh. xiii. 26. Or the word *soul* must be understood, and so *Koheleth* is,

(1.) A *penitent soul,* or one *gathered,* one that had rambled and gone astray like a lost sheep, but was now reduced, gathered in from his wanderings, gathered home to his duty, and come at length to himself. The spirit that was dissipated after a thousand vanities is now collected and made to centre in God. Divine grace can make great sinners great converts, and renew even those to repentance who, *after they had known the way of righteousness, turned aside from it,* and heal their *backslidings,* though it is a difficult case. It is only the penitent soul that God will accept, the heart that is broken, not the head that is bowed down like a bulrush only for a day, David's repentance, not Ahab's. And it is only the gathered soul that is the penitent soul, that comes back from its by-paths, that no longer *scatters its way to the strangers* (Jer. iii. 13), but is *united to fear God's name. Out of the abundance of the heart the mouth will speak,* and therefore we have here the words of the penitent, and those published. If eminent professors of religion fall into gross sin, they are concerned, for the honour of God and the repairing of the damage they have done to his kingdom, openly to testify their repentance, that the antidote may be administered as extensively as the poison.

(2.) A *preaching soul,* or one *gathering.* Being himself *gathered* to the congregation of saints, out of which he had by his sin thrown himself, and being reconciled to the church, he endeavours to gather others to it that had gone astray like him, and perhaps were led astray by his example. He that has done any thing to seduce his brother ought to do all he can to restore him. Perhaps Solomon called together a congregation of his people, as he had done at the dedication of the temple (1 Kings viii. 2), so now at the re-dedicating of himself. In that assembly he presided as the people's mouth to God in prayer (*v.* 12); in this as God's mouth to them in preaching. God by his Spirit made him a preacher, in token of his being reconciled to him; a commission is a tacit pardon. Christ sufficiently testifies his forgiving Peter by committing his lambs and sheep to his trust. Observe, Penitents should be preachers; those that have taken warning themselves to turn and live should give warning to others not to go on and die. *When thou art converted strengthen thy brethren.* Preachers must be preaching *souls*, for that only is likely to reach to the heart that comes from the heart. Paul served God *with his spirit in the gospel of his Son*, Rom. i. 9.

2. *The son of David.* His taking this title intimates, (1.) That he looked upon it as a great honour to be the son of so good a man, and valued himself very much upon it. (2.) That he also looked upon it as a great aggravation of his sin that he had such a father, who had given him a good education and put up many a good prayer for him; it cuts him to the heart to think that he should be a blemish and disgrace to the name and family of such a one as David. It aggravated the sin of Jehoiakim that he was the son of Josiah, Jer. xxii. 15—17. (3.) That his being the son of David encouraged him to repent and hope for mercy, for David had fallen into sin, by which he should have been warned not to sin, but was not; but David repented, and therein he took example from him and found mercy as he did. Yet this was not all; he was that son of David concerning whom God had said that though he would *chasten his transgression with the rod*, yet he would not *break his covenant* with him, Ps. lxxxix. 34. Christ, the great preacher, was the *Son of David.*

3. *King of Jerusalem.* This he mentions, (1.) As that which was a very great aggravation of his sin. He was a king. God had done much for him, in raising him to the throne, and yet he had so ill requited him; his dignity made the bad example and influence of his sin the more dangerous, and many would follow his pernicious ways; especially as he was king of Jerusalem, the holy city, where God's temple was, and of his own building too, where the priests, the Lord's ministers, were, and his prophets who had taught him better things. (2.) As that which might give some advantage to what he wrote, for *where the word of a king is there is power.* He thought it no disparagement to him, as a king, to be a preacher; but the people would regard him the more as a preacher because he was a king. If men of honour would lay

out themselves to do good, what a great deal of good might they do! Solomon looked as great in the pulpit, preaching the vanity of the world, as in his throne of ivory, judging.

The Chaldee-paraphrase (which, in this book, makes very large additions to the text, or comments upon it, all along) gives this account of Solomon's writing this book, That by the spirit of prophecy he foresaw the revolt of the ten tribes from his son, and, in process of time, the destruction of Jerusalem and the house of the sanctuary, and the captivity of the people, in the foresight of which he said, *Vanity of vanities, all his vanity;* and to that he applies many passages in this book.

II. The general scope and design of the book. What is it that this royal preacher has to say? That which he aims at is, for the making of us truly religious, to take down our esteem of and expectation from the things of this world. In order to this, he shows,

1. That they are *all vanity, v.* 2. This is the proposition he lays down and undertakes to prove: *Vanity of vanities, all is vanity.* It was no new text; his father David had more than once spoken to the same purport. The truth itself here asserted is, that *all is vanity,* all besides God and considered as abstract from him, the *all* of this world, all worldly employments and enjoyments, the *all* that *is in the world* (1 John ii. 16), all that which is agreeable to our senses and to our fancies in this present state, which gains pleasure to ourselves or reputation with others. It is *all vanity,* not only in the abuse of it, when it is perverted by the sin of man, but even in the use of it. Man, considered with reference to these things, is vanity (Ps. xxxix. 5, 6), and, if there were not another life after this, were made in vain (Ps. lxxxix. 47); and those things, considered in reference to man (whatever they are in themselves), are *vanity.* They are impertinent to the soul, foreign, and add nothing to it; they do not answer the end, nor yield any true satisfaction; they are uncertain in their continuance, are fading, and perishing, and passing away, and will certainly deceive and disappoint those that put a confidence in them. Let us not therefore *love vanity* (Ps. iv. 2), nor *lift up our souls* to it (Ps. xxiv. 4), for we shall but weary ourselves for it, Heb. ii. 13. It is expressed here very emphatically; not only, *All is vain,* but in the abstract, *All is vanity;* as if vanity were the *proprium quarto modo*—*property in the fourth mode,* of the things of this world, that which enters into the nature of them. They are not only *vanity,* but *vanity of vanities,* the vainest vanity, vanity in the highest degree, nothing but vanity, such a vanity as is the cause of a great deal of vanity. And this is redoubled, because the thing is certain and past dispute, it is *vanity of vanities.* This intimates that the wise man had his own heart fully convinced of and much affected with this truth, and that he was very desirous that

others should be convinced of it and affected with it, as he was, but that he found the generality of men very loth to believe it and consider it (Job xxxiii. 14); it intimates likewise that we cannot comprehend and express the vanity of this world. But who is it that speaks thus slightly of the world? Is it one that will stand to what he says? Yes, he puts his name to it—*saith the preacher.* Is it one that was a competent judge? Yes, as much as ever any man was. Many speak contemptuously of the world because they are hermits, and know it not, or beggars, and have it not; but Solomon knew it. He had dived into nature's depths (1 Kings iv. 33), and he had it, more of it perhaps than ever any man had, his head filled with its notions and *his belly* with its *hidden treasures* (Ps. xvii. 14), and he passes this judgment on it. But did he speak as one having authority? Yes, not only that of a king, but that of a prophet, a preacher; he spoke in God's name, and was divinely inspired to say it. But did he not say it in his haste, or in a passion, upon occasion of some particular disappointment? No; he said it deliberately, said it and proved it, laid it down as a fundamental principle, on which he grounded the necessity of being religious. And, as some think, one main thing he designed was to show that the everlasting throne and kingdom which God had by Nathan promised to David and his seed must be of another world; for all things in this world are subject to vanity, and therefore have not in them sufficient to answer the extent of that promise. If Solomon find all to be vanity, then the kingdom of the Messiah must come, in which we shall inherit substance.

2. That they are insufficient to make us happy. And for this he appeals to men's consciences: *What profit has a man of all the pains he takes? v.* 3. Observe here, (1.) The business of this world described. It is *labour;* the word signifies both care and toil. It is work that wearies men. There is a constant fatigue in worldly business. It is *labour under the sun;* that is a phrase peculiar to this book, where we meet with it twenty-eight times. There is a world above the sun, a world which needs not the sun, for the glory of God is its light, where there is work without labour and with great profit, the work of angels; but he speaks of the work *under the sun,* the pains of which are great and the gains little. It is *under the sun,* under the influence of the sun, by its light and in its heat; as we have the benefit of the light of the day, so we have likewise the burden and heat of the day (Matt. xx. 12), and therefore *in the sweat of our face we eat bread.* In the dark and cold grave the weary are at rest. (2.) The benefit of that business enquired into: *What profit has a man of all that labour?* Solomon says (Prov. xiv. 23), *In all labour there is profit;* and yet here he denies that there is any profit. As to our present condition in 982

the world, it is true that by labour we get that which we call *profit;* we *eat the labour of our hands;* but as the wealth of the world is commonly called *substance,* and yet it is *that which is not* (Prov. xxiii. 5), so it is called *profit,* but the question is whether it be really so or no. And here he determines that it is not, that it is not a real benefit, that it is not a remaining benefit. In short, the wealth and pleasure of this world, if we had ever so much of them, are not sufficient to make us happy, nor will they be a portion for us. [1.] As to the body, and the life that now is, *What profit has a man of all his labour? A man's life consists not in an abundance,* Luke xii. 15. As goods are increased care about them is increased, and *those are increased that eat of them,* and a little thing will embitter all the comfort of them; and then *what profit has a man* of all his labour? Early up, and never the nearer. [2.] As to the soul, and the life that is to come, we may much more truly say, *What profit has a man of all his labour?* All he gets by it will not supply the wants of the soul, nor satisfy its desires, will not atone for the sin of the soul, nor cure its diseases, nor countervail the loss of it; what profit will they be of to the soul in death, in judgment, or in the everlasting state? The fruit of our labour in heavenly things is *meat that endures to eternal life,* but the fruit of our labour for the world is only *meat that perishes.*

4 *One* generation passeth away, and *another* generation cometh: but the earth abideth for ever. 5 The sun also ariseth, and the sun goeth down, and hasteth to his place where he arose. 6 The wind goeth toward the south, and turneth about unto the north; it whirleth about continually, and the wind returneth again according to his circuits. 7 All the rivers run into the sea; yet the sea *is* not full; unto the place from whence the rivers come, thither they return again. 8 All things *are* full of labour; man cannot utter *it:* the eye is not satisfied with seeing, nor the ear filled with hearing.

To prove the vanity of all things under the sun, and their insufficiency to make us happy, Solomon here shows, 1. That the time of our enjoyment of these things is very short, and only while we *accomplish as a hireling his day.* We continue in the world but for one generation, which is continually passing away to make room for another, and we are passing with it. Our worldly possessions we very lately had from others, and must very shortly leave to others, and therefore to us they are vanity; they can be no more substantial than that life which is the *substratum* of them, and that is but a *vapour, which appears for a little while and then vanishes away.* While the stream of mankind is continually flowing, how little enjoyment has one drop of that stream of the pleasant banks between which it glides! We may give God the glory of that constant succession of generations, in which the world has hitherto had its existence, and will have to the end of time, admiring his patience in continuing that sinful species and his power in continuing that dying species. We may be also quickened to do the work of our generation diligently, and serve it faithfully, because it will be over shortly; and, in concern for mankind in general, we should consult the welfare of succeeding generations; but as to our own happiness, let us not expect it within such narrow limits, but in an eternal rest and consistency. 2. That when we leave this world we leave the earth behind us, that *abides for ever* where it is, and therefore the things of the earth can stand us in no stead in the future state. It is well for mankind in general that the earth endures to the end of time, when it and all the works in it shall be burnt up; but what is that to par-, ticular persons, when they remove to the world of spirits? 3. That the condition of man is, in this respect, worse than that even of the inferior creatures: *The earth abides for ever,* but man abides upon the earth but a little while. The sun sets indeed every night, yet it rises again in the morning, as bright and fresh as ever; the winds, though they shift their point, yet in some point or other still they are; the waters that go to the sea above ground come from it again under ground. *But man lies down and rises not,* Job xiv. 7, 12. 4. That all things in this world are movable and mutable, and subject to a continual toil and agitation, constant in nothing but inconstancy, still going, never resting; it was but once that the sun stood still; when it is risen it is hastening to set, and, when it is set, hastening to rise again (*v.* 5); the winds are ever and anon shifting (*v.* 6), and the waters in a continual circulation (*v.* 7), it would be of as bad consequence for them to stagnate as for the blood in the body to do so. And can we expect rest in a world where all things are thus full of labour (*v.* 8), on a sea that is always ebbing and flowing, and her waves continually working and rolling? 5. That though all things are still in motion, yet they are still where they were; The sun *parts* (as it is in the margin), but it is to the same place; the wind turns till it comes to the same place, and so the waters return to the place whence they came. Thus man, after all the pains he takes to find satisfaction and happiness in the creature, is but where he was, still as far to seek as ever. Man's mind is as restless in its pursuits as the sun, and wind, and rivers, but never satisfied, never contented; the more it has of the world the more it would have; and it would be no sooner filled with the streams of outward prosperity, the brooks of *honey and butter* (Job. xx. 17), than the sea

is with *all the rivers that run into it;* it is still as it was, *a troubled sea that cannot rest.* 6. That *all things continue as they were from the beginning of the creation,* 2 Pet. iii. 4. The earth is where it was; the sun, and winds, and rivers, keep the same course that ever they did; and therefore, if they have never yet been sufficient to make a happiness for man, they are never likely to be so, for they can but yield the same comfort that they have yielded. We must therefore look above the sun for satisfaction, and for a new world. 7. That this world is, at the best, a weary land: *All is vanity,* for all is *full of labour.* The whole creation is made subject to this vanity ever since man was sentenced to *eat bread in the sweat of his brows.* If we survey the whole creation, we shall see all busy; all have enough to do to mind their own business; none will be a portion or happiness for man; all labour to serve him, but none prove a *help-meet* for him. Man cannot express how full of labour all things are, can neither number the laborious nor measure the labours. 8. That our senses are unsatisfied, and the objects of them unsatisfying. He specifies those senses that perform their office with least toil, and are most capable of being pleased: *The eye is not satisfied with seeing,* but is weary of seeing always the same sight, and covets novelty and variety. *The ear* is fond, at first, of a pleasant song or tune, but soon nauseates it, and must have another; both are surfeited, but neither satiated, and what was most grateful becomes ungrateful. Curiosity is still inquisitive, because still unsatisfied, and the more it is humoured the more nice and peevish it grows, crying, *Give, give.*

9 The thing that hath been, it *is that* which shall be; and that which is done *is* that which shall be done: and *there is* no new *thing* under the sun. 10 Is there *any* thing whereof it may be said, See, this *is* new? it hath been already of old time, which was before us. 11 *There is* no remembrance of former *things;* neither shall there be *any* remembrance of *things* that are to come with *those* that shall come after.

Two things we are apt to take a great deal of pleasure and satisfaction in, and value ourselves upon, with reference to our business and enjoyments in the world, as if they helped to save them from vanity. Solomon here shows us our mistake in both.

1. The novelty of the invention,—that it is such as was never known before. How grateful is it to think that none ever made such advances in knowledge, and such discoveries by it, as we, that none ever made such improvements of an estate or trade, and had the art of enjoying the gains of it, as we have. Their contrivances and compo-

sitions are all despised and run down, and we boast of new fashions, new hypotheses, new methods, new expressions, which jostle out the old, and put them down. But this is all a mistake: *The thing that* is, and *shall be, is* the same with *that which has been, and that which shall be done* will be but the same with *that which is done,* for *there is no new thing under the sun, v.* 9. It is repeated (*v.* 10) by way of question, *Is there any thing* of which *it may be said,* with wonder, *See, this is new;* there never was the like? It is an appeal to observing men, and a challenge to those that cry up modern learning above that of the ancients. Let them name any thing which they take to be new, and though perhaps we cannot make it to appear, for want of the records of former times, yet we have reason to conclude *that it has been already of old time, which was before us.* What is there in the kingdom of nature of which we may say, *This is new? The works were finished from the foundation of the world* (Heb. iv. 3); things which appear new to us, as they do to children, are not so in themselves. The heavens were *of old;* the earth abides for ever; the powers of nature and the links of natural causes are still the same that ever they were. In the kingdom of Providence, though the course and method of it have not such known and certain rules as that of nature, nor does it go always in the same track, yet, in the general, it is still the same thing over and over again. Men's hearts, and the corruptions of them, are still the same; their desires, and pursuits, and complaints, are still the same; and what God does in his dealings with men is according to the scripture, according to the manner, so that it is all repetition. What is surprising to us needs not be so, for there has been the like, the like strange advancements and disappointments, the like strange revolutions and sudden turns, sudden turns of affairs; the miseries of human life have always been much the same, and mankind tread a perpetual round, and, as the sun and wind, are but where they were. Now the design of this is, (1.) To show the folly of the children of men in affecting things that are new, in imagining that they have discovered such things, and in pleasing and priding themselves in them. We are apt to nauseate old things, and to grow weary of what we have been long used to, as Israel of the manna, and covet, with the Athenians, still to tell and hear of some new thing, and admire this and the other as new, whereas it is all what has been. Tatianus the Assyrian, showing the Grecians how all the arts which they valued themselves upon owed their original to those nations which they counted barbarous, thus reasons with them: "For shame, do not call those things εὑρήσεις—*inventions,* which are but μίμησεις—*imitations.*" (2.) To take us off from expecting happiness or satisfaction in the creature. Why should we look for it

984

there, where never any yet have found it? What reason have we to think that the world should be any kinder to us than it has been to those that have gone before us, since there is nothing in it that is new, and our predecessors have made as much of it as could be made? *Your fathers did eat manna, and yet they are dead.* See John viii. 8, 9; vi. 49. (3.) To quicken us to secure spiritual and eternal blessings. If we would be entertained with new things, we must acquaint ourselves with the things of God, get a new nature; then *old things pass away, and all things become new,* 2 Cor. v. 17. The gospel puts *a new song into our mouths.* In heaven *all is new* (Rev. xxi. 5), all new at first, wholly unlike the present state of things, a new world indeed (Luke xx. 35), and all new to eternity, always fresh, always flourishing. This consideration should make us willing to die, That in this world there is nothing but the same over and over again, and we can expect nothing from it more or better than we have had.

2. The memorableness of the achievement, that it is such as will be known and talked of hereafter. Many think they have found satisfaction enough in this, that their names shall be perpetuated, that posterity will celebrate the actions they have performed, the honours they have won, and the estates they have raised, that *their houses shall continue for ever* (Ps. xlix. 11); but herein they deceive themselves. How many *former things* and persons were there, which in their day looked very great and made a mighty figure, and yet *there is no remembrance* of them; they are buried in oblivion. Here and there one person or action that was remarkable met with a kind historian, and had the good hap to be recorded, when at the same time there were others, no less remarkable, that were dropped: and therefore we may conclude that *neither shall there be any remembrance of things to come,* but that which we hope to be remembered by will be either lost or slighted.

12 I the Preacher was king over Israel in Jerusalem. 13 And I gave my heart to seek and search out by wisdom concerning all *things* that are done under heaven: this sore travail hath God given to the sons of man to be exercised therewith. 14 I have seen all the works that are done under the sun; and, behold, all *is* vanity and vexation of spirit. 15 *That which is* crooked cannot be made straight: and that which is wanting cannot be numbered. 16 I communed with mine own heart, saying, Lo, I am come to great estate, and have gotten more wisdom than all *they* that have been before me in Jerusalem: yea,

my heart had great experience of wisdom and knowledge. 17 And I gave my heart to know wisdom, and to know madness and folly : I perceived that this also is vexation of spirit. 18 For in much wisdom *is* much grief : and he that increaseth knowledge increaseth sorrow.

Solomon, having asserted in general that *all is vanity,* and having given some general proofs of it, now takes the most effectual method to evince the truth of it, 1. By his own experience ; he tried them all, and found them vanity. 2. By an induction of particulars ; and here he begins with that which bids fairest of all to be the happiness of a reasonable creature, and that is knowledge and learning ; if this be vanity, every thing else must needs be so. Now as to this,

I. Solomon tells us here what trial he had made of it, and that with such advantages that, if true satisfaction could have been found in it, he would have found it. 1. His high station gave him an opportunity of improving himself in all parts of learning, and particularly in politics and the conduct of human affairs, *v.* 12. He that is *the preacher* of this doctrine *was king over Israel,* whom all their neighbours admired as *a wise and understanding people,* Deut. iv. 6. He had his royal seat in *Jerusalem,* which then deserved, better than Athens ever did, to be called *the eye of the world.* The heart of a king is unsearchable ; he has reaches of his own, and *a divine sentence is often in his lips.* It is his honour, it is his business, to search out every matter. Solomon's great wealth and honour put him into a capacity of making his court the centre of learning and the rendezvous of learned men, of furnishing himself with the best of books, and either conversing or corresponding with all the wise and knowing part of mankind then in being, who made application to him to learn of him, by which he could not but improve himself ; for it is in knowledge as it is in trade, all the profit is by barter and exchange ; if we have that to say which will instruct others, they will have that to say which will instruct us. Some observe how slightly Solomon speaks of his dignity and honour. He does not say, *I the preacher am* king, but I *was king,* no matter what I am. He speaks of it as a thing past, because worldly honours are transitory. 2. He applied himself to the improvement of these advantages, and the opportunities he had of getting wisdom, which, though ever so great, will not make a man wise unless he give his mind to it. Solomon *gave his heart to seek and search out* all things to be known *by wisdom,* v. 13. He made it his business to acquaint himself with *all the things that are done under the sun,* that are done by the providence of God or by the art and prudence of man. He set himself to get

all the insight he could into philosophy and mathematics, into husbandry and trade, merchandise and mechanics, into the history of former ages and the present state of other kingdoms, their laws, customs, and policies, into men's different tempers, capacities, and projects, and the methods of managing them ; he set himself not only to seek, but to search, to pry into, that which is most intricate, and which requires the closest application of mind and the most vigorous and constant prosecution. Though he was a prince, he made himself a drudge to learning, was not discouraged by its knots, nor took up short of its depths. And this he did, not merely to gratify his own genius, but to qualify himself for the service of God and his generation, and to make an experiment how far the enlargement of the knowledge would go towards the settlement and repose of the mind. 3. He made a very great progress in his studies, wonderfully improved all the parts of learning, and carried his discoveries much further than any that had been before him. He did not condemn learning, as many do, because they cannot conquer it and will not be at the pains to make themselves masters of it ; no, what he aimed at he compassed ; he *saw all the works that were done under the sun (v.* 14), works of nature in the upper and lower world, all within this vortex (to use the modern gibberish) which has the sun for its centre, works of art, the product of men's wit, in a personal or social capacity. He had as much satisfaction in the success of his searches as ever any man had ; he *communed with his own heart* concerning his attainments in knowledge, with as much pleasure as ever any rich merchant had in taking account of his stock. He could say, " *Lo, I* have magnified and increased *wisdom,* have not only gotten more of it myself, but have done more to propagate it and bring it into reputation, than any, *than all that have been before me in Jerusalem.*" Note, It becomes great men to be studious, and delight themselves most in intellectual pleasures. Where God gives great advantages of getting knowledge he expects improvements accordingly. It is happy with a people when their princes and noblemen study to excel others as much in wisdom and useful knowledge as they do in honour and estate ; and they may do that service to the commonwealth of learning by applying themselves to the studies that are proper for them which meaner persons cannot do. Solomon must be acknowledged a competent judge of this matter, for he had not only got his head full of notions, but his *heart had great experience of wisdom and knowledge,* of the power and benefit of knowledge, as well as the amusement and entertainment of it ; what he knew he had digested, and knew how to make use of. *Wisdom entered into his heart,* and so became *pleasant to his soul,* Prov. ii. 10, 11 ; xxii. 18. 4. He applied his studies especially to that part of learning which is most serviceable to the conduct of human life, and consequently is the most valuable (*v.* 17): "*I gave my heart to know* the rules and dictates of *wisdom,* and how I might obtain it; *and to know madness and folly,* how I might prevent and cure it, to know the snares and insinuations of it, that I might avoid them, and guard against them, and discover its fallacies." So industrious was Solomon to improve himself in knowledge that he gained instruction both by the wisdom of prudent men and by the madness of foolish men, by *the field of the slothful,* as well as of *the diligent.*

II. He tells us what was the result of this trial, to confirm what he had said, that *all is vanity.*

1. He found that his searches after knowledge were very toilsome, and a weariness not only to the flesh, but to the mind (*v.* 13): *This sore travail,* this difficulty that there is in searching after truth and finding it, *God has given to the sons of men to be* afflicted *therewith,* as a punishment for our first parents' coveting forbidden knowledge. As bread for the body, so that for the soul, must be got and eaten *in the sweat of our face,* whereas both would have been had without labour if Adam had not sinned.

2. He found that the more he saw of *the works done under the sun* the more he saw of their vanity; nay, and the sight often occasioned him *vexation of spirit* (*v.* 14): "*I have seen all the works* of a world full of business, have observed what the children of men are doing; *and behold,* whatever men think of their own works, I see *all is vanity and vexation of spirit.*" He had before pronounced all *vanity* (*v.* 2), needless and unprofitable, and that which does us no good; here he adds, It is all *vexation of spirit,* troublesome and prejudicial, and that which does us hurt. It is *feeding upon wind;* so some read it, Hos. xii. 1. (1.) The works themselves which we see done are *vanity and vexation* to those that are employed in them. There is so much care in the contrivance of our worldly business, so much toil in the prosecution of it, and so much trouble in the disappointments we meet with in it, that we may well say, It is *vexation of spirit.* (2.) The sight of them is *vanity and vexation of spirit* to the wise observer of them. The more we see of the world the more we see to make us uneasy, and, with Heraclitus, to look upon all with weeping eyes. Solomon especially perceived that the knowledge of *wisdom and folly* was *vexation of spirit, v.* 17. It vexed him to see many that had wisdom not use it, and many that had folly not strive against it. It vexed him when he knew wisdom to see how far off it stood from the children of men, and, when he saw folly, to see how fast it was bound in their hearts.

3. He found that when he had got some knowledge he could neither gain that satisfaction to himself nor do that good to others with it which he expected, *v.* 15. It would

not avail, (1.) To redress the many grievances of human life: "After all, I find that *that which is crooked* will be crooked still and *cannot be made straight.*" Our knowledge is itself intricate and perplexed; we must go far about and fetch a great compass to come at it. Solomon thought to find out a nearer way to it, but he could not. The paths of learning are as much a labyrinth as ever they were. The minds and manners of men are crooked and perverse. Solomon thought, with his wisdom and power together, thoroughly to reform his kingdom, and make that straight which he found crooked; but he was disappointed. All the philosophy and politics in the world will not restore the corrupt nature of man to its primitive rectitude; we find the insufficiency of them both in others and in ourselves. Learning will not alter men's natural tempers, nor cure them of their sinful distempers; nor will it change the constitution of things in this world; a vale of tears it is and so it will be when all is done. (2.) To make up the many deficiencies in the comfort of human life: *That which is wanting* there *cannot be numbered,* or counted out to us from the treasures of human learning, but what *is wanting* will still be so. All our enjoyments here, when we have done our utmost to bring them to perfection, are still lame and defective, and it cannot be helped; as they are, so they are likely to be. *That which is wanting* in our knowledge is so much that it *cannot be numbered.* The more we know the more we see of our own ignorance. *Who can understand his errors,* his defects?

4. Upon the whole, therefore, he concluded that great scholars do but make themselves great mourners; *for in much wisdom is much grief, v.* 18. There must be a great deal of pains taken to get it, and a great deal of care not to forget it; the more we know the more we see there is to be known, and consequently we perceive with greater clearness that our work is without end, and the more we see of our former mistakes and blunders, which occasions *much grief.* The more we see of men's different sentiments and opinions (and it is that which a great deal of our learning is conversant about) the more at a loss we are, it may be, which is in the right. Those *that increase knowledge* have so much the more quick and sensible perception of the calamities of this world, and for one discovery they make that is pleasing, perhaps, they make ten that are displeasing, and so they *increase sorrow.* Let us not therefore be driven off from the pursuit of any useful knowledge, but put on patience to break through the sorrow of it; but let us despair of finding true happiness in this knowledge, and expect it only in the knowledge of God and the careful discharge of our duty to him. *He that increases* in heavenly wisdom, and in an experimental acquaintance with the principles, powers, and

pleasures of the spiritual and divine life, *increases* joy, such as will shortly be consummated in everlasting joy.

CHAP. II.

Solomon having pronounced all vanity, and particularly knowledge and learning, which he was so far from giving himself joy of that he found the increase of it did but increase his sorrow, in this chapter he goes on to show what reason he has to be tired of this world, and with what little reason most men are fond of it. I. He shows that there is no true happiness and satisfaction to be had in mirth and pleasure, and the delights of sense, ver. 1—11. II. He reconsiders the pretensions of wisdom, and allows it to be excellent and useful, and yet sees it clogged with such diminutions of its worth that it proves insufficient to make a man happy, ver. 12—16. III. He enquires how far the business and wealth of this world will go towards making men happy, and concludes, from his own experience, that, to those who set their hearts upon it, "it is vanity and vexation of spirit," (ver. 17—23), and that, if there be any good in it, it is only to those that sit loose to it, ver. 24—26.

I SAID in mine heart, Go to now, I will prove thee with mirth, therefore enjoy pleasure: and, behold, this also *is* vanity. 2 I said of laughter, *It is* mad: and of mirth, What doeth it? 3 I sought in mine heart to give myself unto wine, yet acquainting mine heart with wisdom; and to lay hold on folly, till I might see what *was* that good for the sons of men, which they should do under the heaven all the days of their life. 4 I made me great works; I builded me houses; I planted me vineyards: 5 I made me gardens and orchards, and I planted trees in them of all *kind of* fruits: 6 I made me pools of water, to water therewith the wood that bringeth forth trees: 7 I got *me* servants and maidens, and had servants born in my house; also I had great possessions of great and small cattle above all that were in Jerusalem before me: 8 I gathered me also silver and gold, and the peculiar treasure of kings and of the provinces: I gat me men singers and women singers, and the delights of the sons of men, *as* musical instruments, and that of all sorts. 9 So I was great, and increased more than all that were before me in Jerusalem: also my wisdom remained with me. 10 And whatsoever mine eyes desired I kept not from them, I withheld not my heart from any joy; for my heart rejoiced in all my labour: and this was my portion of all my labour. 11 Then I looked on all the works that my hands had wrought, and on the labour that I had laboured to do: and, behold, all *was* vanity and vexation of spirit, and *there was* no profit under the sun.

Solomon here, in pursuit of the *summum bonum—the felicity* of man, adjourns out of his study, his library, his elaboratory, his council-chamber, where he had in vain sought for it, into the park and the playhouse, his garden and his summer-house; he exchanges the company of the philosophers and grave senators for that of the wits and gallants, and the beaux-esprits, of his court, to try if he could find true satisfaction and happiness among them. Here he takes a great step downward, from the noble pleasures of the intellect to the brutal ones of sense; yet, if he resolve to make a thorough trial, he must knock at this door, because here a great part of mankind imagine they have found that which he was in quest of.

I. He resolved to try what mirth would do and the pleasures of wit, whether he should be happy if he constantly entertained himself and others with merry stories and jests, banter and drollery; if he should furnish himself with all the pretty ingenious turns and repartees he could invent or pick up, fit to be laughed over, and all the bulls, and blunders, and foolish things, he could hear of, fit to be ridiculed and laughed at, so that he might be always in a merry humour. 1. This experiment made (*v.* 1): "Finding that *in much wisdom is much grief*, and that those who are serious are apt to be melancholy, *I said in my heart*" (to my heart), "*Go to now, I will prove thee with mirth;* I will try if that will give thee satisfaction." Neither the temper of his mind nor his outward condition had any thing in them to keep him from being merry, but both agreed, as did all other advantages, to further it; *therefore* he resolved to take a lease this way, and said, "*Enjoy pleasure*, and take thy fill of it; cast away care, and resolve to be merry." So a man may be, and yet have none of these fine things which he here got to entertain himself with; many that are poor are very merry; beggars in a barn are so to a proverb. Mirth is the entertainment of the fancy, and, though it comes short of the solid delights of the rational powers, yet it is to be preferred before those that are merely carnal and sensual. Some distinguish man from the brutes, not only as *animal rationale—a rational animal,* but as *animal risibile—a laughing animal;* therefore he that said to his soul, *Take thy ease, eat and drink,* added, *And be merry,* for it was in order to that that he would eat and drink. "Try therefore," says Solomon, "to laugh and be fat, to laugh and be happy." 2. The judgment he passed upon this experiment: *Behold, this also is vanity,* like all the rest; it yields no true satisfaction, *v.* 2. *I said of laughter, It is mad,* or, *Thou art mad,* and therefore I will have nothing to do with thee; *and of mirth* (of all sports and recreations, and whatever pretends to be diverting), *What doeth it?* or, *What doest thou?* Innocent mirth, soberly, seasonably, and moderately used, is a good thing, fits for busi-

ness, and helps to soften the toils and cha-
grins of human life; but, when it is excessive
and immoderate, it is foolish and fruitless.
(1.) It does no good: *What doeth it? Cui
bono—Of what use is it?* It will not avail to
quiet a guilty conscience; no, nor to ease a
sorrowful spirit; nothing is more ungrateful
than *singing songs to a heavy heart.* It will
not satisfy the soul, nor ever yield it true
content. It is but a palliative cure to the
grievances of this present time. Great laughter commonly ends in a sigh. (2.) It does a
great deal of hurt: *It is mad,* that is, it makes
men mad, it transports men into many indecencies, which are a reproach to their reason
and religion. They are mad that indulge
themselves in it, for it estranges the heart
from God and divine things, and insensibly
eats out the power of religion. Those that
love to be merry forget to be serious, and,
while they take the timbrel and harp, they
say to the Almighty, Depart from us, Job xxi.
12, 14. We may, as Solomon, *prove* ourselves, *with mirth,* and judge of the state of
our souls by this: How do we stand affected
to it? Can we be merry and wise? Can we
use it as sauce, and not as food? But we
need not try, as Solomon did, whether it will
make a happiness for us, for we may take
his word for it, *It is mad;* and *What does
it?* Laughter and pleasure (says Sir William
Temple) come from very different affections
of the mind; for, as men have no disposition
to laugh at things they are most pleased with,
so they are very little pleased with many
things they laugh at.

II. Finding himself not happy in that which
pleased his fancy, he resolved next to try that
which would please the palate, *v.* 3. Since
the knowledge of the creature would not satisfy, he would see what the liberal use of it
would do: *I sought in my heart to give myself
unto wine,* that is, to good meat and good
drink. Many give themselves to these without consulting their hearts at all, not looking
any further than merely the gratification of
the sensual appetite; but Solomon applied
himself to it rationally, and as a man, critically, and only to make an experiment. Observe, 1. He did not allow himself any liberty
in the use of the delights of sense till he had
tired himself with his severe studies. Till
his *increase* of wisdom proved an *increase* of
sorrow, he never thought of giving himself *to
wine.* When we have spent ourselves in doing good we may then most comfortably refresh ourselves with the gifts of God's bounty.
Then the delights of sense are rightly used
when they are used as we use cordials, only
when we need them; as Timothy drank wine
for his health's sake, 1 Tim. v. 23. *I thought
to draw my flesh with wine* (so the margin
reads it) or *to wine.* Those that have addicted themselves to drinking did at first put
a force upon themselves; they drew their
flesh to it, and with it; but they should remember to what miseries they hereby draw

themselves. 2. He then looked upon it as
folly, and it was with reluctance that he gave
himself to it; as St. Paul, when he commended himself, called it a *weakness,* and desired to be borne with in his *foolishness,* 2 Cor.
xi. 1. He sought *to lay hold on folly,* to see
the utmost that that folly would do towards
making men happy; but he had like to have
carried the jest (as we say) too far. He resolved that the folly should not take hold of
him, not get the mastery of him, but he would
lay hold on it, and keep it at a distance; yet
he found it too hard for him. 3. He took
care at the same time to *acquaint* himself *with
wisdom,* to manage himself wisely in the use
of his pleasures, so that they should not do
him any prejudice nor disfit him to be a competent judge of them. When he *drew his
flesh with wine* he *led his heart with wisdom*
(so the word is), kept up his pursuits after
knowledge, did not make a sot of himself,
nor become a slave to his pleasures, but his
studies and his feasts were foils to each other,
and he tried whether both mixed together
would give him that satisfaction which he
could not find in either separately. This Solomon proposed to himself, but he found it
vanity; for those that think to give themselves
to wine, and yet to acquaint their hearts with
wisdom, will perhaps deceive themselves as
much as those do that think to serve both
God and mammon. *Wine is a mocker;* it is
a great cheat; and it will be impossible for
any man to say that thus far he will give himself to it and no further. 4. That which he
aimed at was not to gratify his appetite, but
to find out man's happiness, and this, because
it pretended to be so, must be tried among
the rest. Observe the description he gives
of man's happiness—it is *that good for the
sons of men which they should do under the
heaven all their days.* (1.) That which we are
to enquire after is not so much the good we
must have (we may leave that to God), but the
good we must do; that ought to be our care.
Good Master, what good thing shall I do?
Our happiness consists not in being idle, but
in doing aright, in being well employed. If
we *do that which is good,* no doubt we shall
have comfort and *praise of the same.* (2.) It
is good to be done *under the heaven,* while we
are here in this world, while it is day, while
our doing time lasts. This is our state of
work and service; it is in the other world
that we must expect the retribution. Thither
our works will follow us. (3.) It is to be
done *all the days of our life.* The good we
are to do we must persevere in the doing of
to the end, while our doing time lasts, *the
number of the days of our life* (so it is in the
margin); the days of our life are numbered
to us by him in whose hand our times are and
they are all to be spent as he directs. But
that any man should give himself to wine, in
hopes to find out in that the best way of living
in this world, was an absurdity which Solomon here, in the reflection, condemns him-

self for. Is it possible that this should be the good that men should do? No; it is plainly very bad.

III. Perceiving quickly that it was folly to give himself to wine, he next tried the most costly entertainments and amusements of princes and great men. He had a vast income; the revenue of his crown was very great, and he laid it out so as might most please his own humour and make him look great.

1. He gave himself much to building, both in the city and in the country; and, having been at such vast expense in the beginning of his reign to build a house for God, he was the more excusable if afterwards he pleased his own fancy in building for himself; he began his work at the right end (Matt. vi. 33), not as the people (Hag. i. 4), that *ceiled their own houses* while God's lay waste, and it prospered accordingly. In building, he had the pleasure of employing the poor and doing good to posterity. We read of Solomon's buildings (1 Kings ix. 15—19), and they were all *great works,* such as became his purse, and spirit, and great dignity. See his mistake; he enquired after the *good* works he should do (v. 3), and, in pursuit of the enquiry, applied himself to *great* works. *Good* works indeed are truly great, but many are reputed great works which are far from being good, wondrous works which are not gracious, Matt. vii. 22.

2. He took to love a garden, which is to some as bewitching as building. He *planted himself vineyards,* which the soil and climate of the land of Canaan favoured; he *made himself* fine *gardens and orchards* (v. 5), and perhaps the art of gardening was no way inferior then to what it is now. He had not only forests of timber-trees, but *trees of all kinds of fruit,* which he himself had planted; and, if any worldly business would yield a man happiness, surely it must be that which Adam was employed in while he was in innocency.

3. He laid out a great deal of money in water-works, ponds, and canals, not for sport and diversion, but for use, *to water the wood that brings forth trees* (v. 6); he not only planted, but watered, and then left it to God to give the increase. *Springs of water* are great *blessings* (Josh. xv. 19); but where nature has provided them art must direct them, to make them serviceable, Prov. xxi. 1.

4. He increased his family. When he proposed to himself to do *great works* he must employ many hands, and therefore procured *servants and maidens,* which were bought with his money, and of those he *had servants born in his house, v.* 7. Thus his retinue was enlarged and his court appeared more magnificent. See Ezra ii. 58.

5. He did not neglect country business, but both entertained and enriched himself with that, and was not diverted from it either by his studies or by his pleasures. He *had large possessions of great and small cattle,*

herds and flocks, as his father had before him (1 Chron. xxvii. 29, 31), not forgetting that his father, in the beginning, was a keeper of sheep. Let those that deal in cattle neither despise their employment nor be weary of it, remembering that Solomon puts his having *possessions of cattle* among his *great works* and his pleasures.

6. He grew very rich, and was not at all impoverished by his building and gardening, as many are, who, for that reason only, repent it, and call it *vanity and vexation.* Solomon scattered and yet increased. He filled his exchequer with *silver and gold,* which yet did not stagnate there, but were made to circulate through his kingdom, so that he made *silver to be in Jerusalem as stones* (1 Kings x. 27); nay, he had the *segullah, the peculiar treasure of kings and of the provinces,* which was, for richness and rarity, more accounted of than *silver and gold.* The neighbouring kings, and the distant provinces of his own empire, sent him the richest presents they had, to obtain his favour and the instructions of his wisdom.

7. He had every thing that was charming and diverting, all sorts of melody and music, vocal and instrumental, *men-singers and women-singers,* the best voices he could pick up, and all the wind and band-instruments that were then in use. His father had a genius for music, but it should seem he employed it more to serve his devotion than the son, who made it more his diversion. These are called *the delights of the sons of men;* for the gratifications of sense are the things that the generality of people set their affections upon and take the greatest complacency in. The delights of the children of God are of quite another nature, pure, spiritual, and heavenly, and the delights of angels.

8. He enjoyed, more than ever any man did, a composition of rational and sensitive pleasures at the same time. He was, in this respect, *great, and increased more than all that were before him,* that he was wise amidst a thousand earthly enjoyments. It was strange, and the like was never met with, (1.) That his pleasures did not debauch his judgment and conscience. In the midst of these entertainments *his wisdom remained with him, v.* 9. In the midst of all these childish delights he preserved his spirit manly, kept the possession of his own soul, and maintained the dominion of reason over the appetites of sense; such a vast stock of wisdom had he that it was not wasted and impaired, as any other man's would have been, by this course of life. But let none be emboldened hereby to lay the reins on the neck of their appetites, presuming that they may do that and yet retain their wisdom, for they have not such a strength of wisdom as Solomon had; nay, and Solomon was deceived; for how did *his wisdom remain with him* when he lost his religion so far as to build altars to strange gods, for the humouring of his strange wives? But

thus far *his wisdom remained with him* that he was master of his pleasures, and not a slave to them, and kept himself capable of making a judgment of them.   He went over into the enemies' country, not as a deserter, but as a *spy, to discover the nakedness of their land.* (2.) Yet his judgment and conscience gave no check to his pleasures, nor hindered him from extracting the very quintessence of the delights of sense, *v.* 10.   It might be objected against his judgment in this matter that if *his wisdom remained with him* he could not take the liberty that was necessary to a full experimental acquaintance with it : " Yea," said he, " I took as great a liberty as any man could take, for *whatsoever my eyes desired I kept not from them,* if it could be compassed by lawful means, though ever so difficult or costly ; and as *I withheld not any joy from my heart* that I had a mind to, so *I withheld not my heart from any joy,* but, with a *non-obstante —with the full exercise* of my wisdom, I had a high gust of my pleasures, relished and enjoyed them as much as ever any Epicure did;" nor was there any thing either in the circumstances of his condition or in the temper of his spirit to sour or embitter them, or give them any alloy.   In short, [1.] He had as much pleasure in his business as ever any man had : *My heart rejoiced in all my labour ;* so that the toil and fatigue of that were no damp to his pleasures.   [2.] He had no less profit by his business.   He met with no disappointment in it to give him any disturbance: *This was my portion of all my labour ;* he had this added to all the rest of his pleasures that in them he did not only see, but eat, the labour of his hands ; and this was all he had, for indeed it was all he could expect, from his labours.   It sweetened his business that he enjoyed the success of it, and it sweetened his enjoyments that they were the product of his business ; so that, upon the whole, he was certainly as happy as the world could make him.

9. We have, at length, the judgment he deliberately gave of all this, *v.* 11.   When the Creator had made his great works he reviewed them, and *behold, all was very good ;* every thing pleased him.   But when Solomon reviewed *all his works that his hands had wrought* with the utmost cost and care, *and the labour that he had laboured to do* in order to make himself easy and happy, nothing answered his expectation ; *behold, all was vanity and vexation of spirit ;* he had no satisfaction in it, no advantage by it ; *there was no profit under the sun,* neither by the employments nor by the enjoyments of this world.

12 And I turned myself to behold wisdom, and madness, and folly: for what *can* the man *do* that cometh after the king ? *even* that which hath been already done.   13 Then I saw that wisdom excelleth folly, as far as light excelleth darkness.   14 The wise man's

eyes *are* in his head ; but the fool walketh in darkness: and I myself perceived also that one event happeneth to them all.   15 Then said I in my heart, As it happeneth to the fool, so it happeneth even to me ; and why was I then more wise ?   Then I said in my heart, that this also *is* vanity. 16 For *there is* no remembrance of the wise more than of the fool for ever ; seeing that which now *is* in the days to come shall all be forgotten. And how dieth the wise *man ?* as the fool.

Solomon having tried what satisfaction was to be had in learning first, and then in the pleasures of sense, and having also put both together, here compares them one with another and passes a judgment upon them.

I. He sets himself to consider both wisdom and folly.   He had considered these before (*ch.* i. 17) ; but lest it should be thought he was then too quick in passing a judgment upon them, he here turns himself again to behold them, to see if, upon a second view and second thoughts, he could gain more satisfaction in the search than he had done upon the first.   He was sick of his pleasures, and, as nauseating them, he turned from them, that he might again apply himself to speculation ; and if, upon this rehearing of the cause, the verdict be still the same, the judgment will surely be decisive ; *for what can the man do that comes after the king ?* especially such a king, who had so much of this world to make the experiment upon and so much wisdom to make it with.   The baffled trial needs not be repeated.   No man can expect to find more satisfaction in the world than Solomon did, nor to gain a greater insight into the principles of morality ; when a man has done what he can still it is *that which has been already done.*   Let us learn, 1. Not to indulge ourselves in a fond conceit that we can mend that which has been well done before us.   Let us *esteem others better than ourselves,* and think how unfit we are to attempt the improvement of the performances of better heads and hands than ours, and rather own how much we are beholden to them, John iv. 37, 38.   2. To acquiesce in Solomon's judgment of the things of this world, and not to think of repeating the trial ; for we can never think of having such advantages as he had to make the experiment nor of being able to make it with equal application of mind and so little danger to ourselves.

II. He gives the preference to wisdom far before folly.   Let none mistake him, as if, when he speaks of the vanity of human literature, he designed only to amuse men with a paradox, or were about to write (as a great wit once did) *Encomium moriæ—A panegyric in praise of folly.* No, he is maintaining sacred truths, and therefore is careful to guard against being misunderstood. I soon *saw* (says he) *that there is an excellency in wisdom more than in folly*, as much as there is in light above darkness. The pleasures of wisdom, though they suffice not to make men happy, yet vastly transcend the pleasures of wine. Wisdom enlightens the soul with surprising discoveries and necessary directions for the right government of itself; but sensuality (for that seems to be especially the folly here meant) clouds and eclipses the mind, and is as darkness to it; it puts out men's eyes, makes them to stumble in the way and wander out of it. Or, though wisdom and knowledge will not make a man happy (St. Paul shows a *more excellent way* than gifts, and that is grace), yet it is much better to have them than to be without them, in respect of our present safety, comfort, and usefulness; for *the wise man's eyes are in his head* (v. 14), where they should be, ready to discover both the dangers that are to be avoided and the advantages that are to be improved; a wise man has not his reason to seek when he should use it, but looks about him and is quick-sighted, knows both where to step and where to stop; whereas *the fool walks in darkness*, and is ever and anon either at a loss, or at a plunge, either bewildered, that he knows not which way to go, or embarrassed, that he cannot go forward. A man that is discreet and considerate has the command of his business, and acts decently and safely, as those that walk in the day; but he that is rash, and ignorant, and sottish, is continually making blunders, running upon one precipice or other; his projects, his bargains, are all foolish, and ruin his affairs. Therefore *get wisdom, get understanding.*

III. Yet he maintains that, in respect of lasting happiness and satisfaction, the wisdom of this world gives a man very little advantage; for, 1. Wise men and fools fare alike. "It is true the wise man has very much the advantage of the fool in respect of foresight and insight, and yet the greatest probabilities do so often come short of success that *I myself perceived,* by my own experience, that *one event happens to them all* (v. 14); those that are most cautious of their health are as soon sick as those that are most careless of it, and the most suspicious are imposed upon." David had observed that *wise men die,* and are involved in the same common calamity with the fool and the brutish person, Ps. xlix. 12. See *ch.* ix. 11. Nay, it has of old been observed that *Fortune favours fools,* and that half-witted men often thrive most, while the greatest projectors forecast worst for themselves. The same sickness, the same sword, devours wise men and fools. Solomon applies this mortifying observation to himself (v. 15), that though he was a wise man, he might not *glory in his wisdom: I said to my heart,* when it began to be proud or secure, *As it happens to the fool,*

so it happens to me, even to me; for thus emphatically it is expressed in the original: "So, *as for me,* it happens to me. Am I rich? So is many a Nabal that fares as sumptuously as I do. Is a foolish man sick, does he get a fall? So do I, *even I;* and neither my wealth nor my wisdom will be my security. *And why was I then more wise?* Why should I take so much pains to get wisdom, when, as to this life, it will stand me in so little stead? *Then I said in my heart that this also is vanity."* Some make this a correction of what was said before, like that (Ps. lxxvii. 10), "*I said, This is my infirmity:* it is my folly to think that wise men and fools are upon a level;" but really they seem to be so, in respect of the event, and therefore it is rather a confirmation of what he had before said, That a man may be a profound philosopher and politician and yet not be a happy man. 2. Wise men and fools are forgotten alike (v. 16): *There is no remembrance of the wise more than of the fool.* It is promised to the righteous that they *shall be had in everlasting remembrance,* and *their memory shall be blessed,* and they shall shortly *shine as the stars;* but there is no such promise made concerning the wisdom of this world, that that shall perpetuate men's names, for those names only are perpetuated that are *written in heaven,* and otherwise the names of this world's wise men are written with those of its fools in the dust. *That which now is in the days to come shall all be forgotten.* What was much talked of in one generation is, in the next, as if it had never been. New persons and new things jostle out the very remembrance of the old, which in a little time are looked upon with contempt and at length quite buried in oblivion. *Where is the wise? Where is the disputer of this world?* 1 Cor. i. 20. And it is upon this account that he asks, *How dies the wise man? As the fool.* Between the death of a godly and a wicked man there is a great difference, but not between the 'death of a wise man and a fool; the fool is buried and forgotten (*ch.* viii. 10), *and no one remembered the poor man that by his wisdom delivered the city* (*ch.* ix. 15); so that to both the grave is a *land of forgetfulness;* and wise and learned men, when they have been awhile there out of sight, grow out of mind, a new generation arises that *knew them not.*

17 Therefore I hated life; because the work that is wrought under the sun *is* grievous unto me: for all *is* vanity and vexation of spirit. 18 Yea, I hated all my labour which I had taken under the sun: because I should leave it unto the man that shall be after me. 19 And who knoweth whether he shall be a wise *man* or a fool? yet shall he have rule over all my labour wherein I have laboured, and

wherein I have showed myself wise under the sun. This *is* also vanity. 20 Therefore I went about to cause my heart to despair of all the labour which I took under the sun. 21 For there is a man whose labour *is* in wisdom, and in knowledge, and in equity; yet to a man that hath not laboured therein shall he leave it *for* his portion. This also *is* vanity and a great evil. 22 For what hath man of all his labour, and of the vexation of his heart, wherein he hath laboured under the sun? 23 For all his days *are* sorrows, and his travail grief; yea, his heart taketh not rest in the night. This is also vanity. 24 *There is* nothing better for a man, *than* that he should eat and drink, and *that* he should make his soul enjoy good in his labour. This also I saw, that it *was* from the hand of God. 25 For who can eat, or who else can hasten *hereunto*, more than I? 26 For *God* giveth to a man that *is* good in his sight wisdom, and knowledge, and joy: but to the sinner he giveth travail, to gather and to heap up, that he may give to *him that is* good before God. This also *is* vanity and vexation of spirit.

Business is a thing that wise men have pleasure in. They are in their element when they are in their business, and complain if they be out of business. They may sometimes be tired with their business, but they are not weary of it, nor willing to leave it off. Here therefore one would expect to have found the good that men should do, but Solomon tried this too; after a contemplative life and a voluptuous life, he betook himself to an active life, and found no more satisfaction in it than in the other; still it is all *vanity and vexation of spirit*, of which he gives an account in these verses, where observe,

I. What the business was which he made trial of; it was business *under the sun* (v. 17—20), about the things of this world, sublunary things, the riches, honours, and pleasures of this present time; it was the business of a king. There is business *above the sun*, perpetual business, which is perpetual blessedness; what we do in conformity to that business (doing *God's will as it is done in heaven)* and in pursuance of that blessedness, will turn to a good account; we shall have no reason to hate that labour, nor to despair of it. But it is *labour under the sun*, labour for the *meat that perishes* (John vi. 27; Isa. lv. 2), that Solomon here speaks of

992

with so little satisfaction. It was the better sort of business, not that of the *hewers of wood and drawers of water* (it is not so strange if men hate all that labour), but it was *in wisdom, and knowledge, and equity, v.* 21. It was rational business, which related to the government of his kingdom and the advancement of its interests. It was labour managed by the dictates of wisdom, of natural and acquired knowledge, and the directions of justice. It was labour at the council-board and in the courts of justice. It was labour wherein he *showed himself wise* (v. 19), which as much excels the labour wherein men only show themselves strong as the endowments of the mind, by which we are allied to angels, do those of the body, which we have in common with the brutes. That which many people have in their eye more than any thing else, in the prosecution of their worldly business, is to *show themselves wise*, to get the reputation of ingenious men and men of sense and application.

II. His falling out with this business. He soon grew weary of it. 1. He *hated all his labour*, because he did not meet with that satisfaction in it which he expected. After he had had his fine houses, and gardens, and water-works, awhile, he began to nauseate them, and look upon them with contempt, as children, who are eager for a toy and fond of it at first, but, when they have played with it awhile, are weary of it, and throw it away, and must have another. This expresses not a gracious hatred of these things, which is our duty, to love them less than God and religion (Luke xiv. 26), nor a sinful hatred of them, which is our folly, to be weary of the place God has assigned us and the work of it, but a natural hatred of them, arising from a surfeit upon them and a sense of disappointment in them. 2. He *caused his heart to despair of all his labour* (v. 20); he took pains to possess himself with a deep sense of the vanity of worldly business, that it would not bring in the advantage and satisfaction he had formerly flattered himself with the hopes of. Our hearts are very loth to quit their expectations of great things from the creature; we must go about, must fetch a compass, in arguing with them, to convince them that there is not that in the things of this world which we are apt to promise ourselves from them. Have we so often bored and sunk into this earth for some rich mine of satisfaction, and found not the least sign or token of it, but been always frustrated in the search, and shall we not at length set our hearts at rest and despair of ever finding it? 3. He came to that, at length, that he *hated life itself* (v. 17), because it is subject to so many toils and troubles, and a constant series of disappointments. God had given Solomon such largeness of heart, and such vast capacities of mind, that he experienced more than other men of the unsatisfying nature of all the things of this life and their insufficiency to make him happy. Life itself, that is so precious to a man, and such a blessing to a good man, may become a burden to a man of business.

III. The reasons of this quarrel with his life and labours. Two things made him weary of them :—

1. That his business was so great a toil to himself: The *work that he had wrought under the sun was grievous unto him, v.* 17. His thoughts and cares about it, and that close and constant application of mind which was requisite to it, were a burden and fatigue to him, especially when he grew old. It is the effect of a curse on that we are to work upon. Our business is said to be *the work and toil of our hands, because of the ground which the Lord had cursed* (Gen. v. 29) and of the weakening of the faculties we are to work with, and of the sentence pronounced on us, that in *the sweat of our face we must eat bread.* Our labour is called *the vexation of our heart (v. 22)*; it is to most a force upon themselves, so natural is it to us to love our ease. A man of business is described to be uneasy both in his *going out* and his *coming in, v.* 23. (1.) He is deprived of his pleasure by day, for *all his days are sorrow,* not only sorrowful, but sorrow itself, nay, many sorrows and various; his travail, or labour, all day, is grief. Men of business ever and anon meet with that which vexes them, and is an occasion of anger or sorrow to them. Those that are apt to fret find that the more dealings they have in the world the oftener they are made to fret. The world is a *vale of tears,* even to those that have much of it. Those that *labour* are said to be *heavy-laden,* and are therefore called to come to Christ for rest, Matt. xi. 28. (2.) He is disturbed in his repose *by night.* When he is overcome with the hurries of the day, and hopes to find relief when he lays his head on his pillow, he is disappointed there; cares *hold his eyes waking,* or, if he sleep, yet his heart wakes, and that *takes no rest in the night.* See what fools those are that make themselves drudges to the world, and do not make God their rest; night and day they cannot but be uneasy. So that, upon the whole matter, it is *all vanity, v.* 17. *This is vanity* in particular *(v.* 19, 23), nay, it is *vanity and a great evil, v.* 21. It is a great affront to God and a great injury to themselves, therefore a *great evil;* it is a vain thing *to rise up early and sit up late* in pursuit of this world's goods, which were never designed to be our chief good.

2. That the gains of his business must all be left to others. Prospect of advantage is the spring of action and the spur of industry; *therefore* men labour, because they hope to get by it; if the hope fail, the labour flags; and *therefore* Solomon quarrelled with all the works, the great works, he had made, because they would not be of any lasting advantage to himself. (1.) He must leave them.

He could not at death take them away with him, nor any share of them, nor should he return any more to them (Job vii. 10), nor would the remembrance of them do him any good, Luke xvi. 25. But I must *leave all to the man that shall be after me,* to the generation that comes up in the room of that which is passing away. As there were many before us, who built the houses that we live in, and into whose purchases and labours we have entered, so there shall be many after us, who shall live in the houses that we build, and enjoy the fruit of our purchases and labours. Never was land lost for want of an heir. To a gracious soul this is no uneasiness at all; why should we grudge others their turn in the enjoyments of this world, and not rather be pleased that, when we are gone, those that come after us shall fare the better for our wisdom and industry? But to a worldly mind, that seeks for its own happiness in the creature, it is a great vexation to think of leaving the beloved pelf behind, at this uncertainty. (2.) He must leave them to those that would never have taken so much pains for them, and will thereby excuse himself from taking any pains. He that raised the estate did it by *labouring in wisdom, and knowledge, and equity ;* but he that enjoys it and spends it (it may be) *has not laboured therein (v.* 21), and, more than that, never will. The bee toils to maintain the drone. Nay, it proves a snare to him : it is left him *for his portion,* which he rests in, and takes up with; and miserable he is in being put off with it for a portion. Whereas, if an estate had not come to him thus easily, who knows but he might have been both industrious and religious? Yet we ought not to perplex ourselves about this, since it may prove otherwise, that what is well got may come to one that will use it well and do good with it. (3.) He knows not whom he must leave it to (for God makes heirs), or at least what *he* will prove to whom he leaves it, whether *a wise man or a fool,* a wise man that will make it more or a fool that will bring it to nothing; *yet he shall have rule over all my labour,* and foolishly undo that which his father wisely did. It is probable that Solomon wrote this very feelingly, being afraid what Rehoboam would prove. St. Jerome, in his commentary on this passage, applies this to the good books which Solomon wrote, in which he had shown himself wise, but he knew not into whose hands they would fall, perhaps into the hands of a fool, who, according to the perverseness of his heart, makes a bad use of what was well written. So that, upon the whole matter, he asks *(v.* 22), *What has man of all his labour ?* What has he to himself and to his own use? What has he that will go with him into another world?

IV. The best use which is therefore to be made of the wealth of this world, and that is to use it cheerfully, to take the comfort of it, and do good with it. With this he concludes the chapter, *v.* 24—26. There is no true happiness to be found in these things. They are *vanity*, and, if happiness be expected from them, the disappointment will be *vexation of spirit*. But he will put us in a way to make the best of them, and to avoid the inconveniencies he had observed. We must neither over-toil ourselves, so as, in pursuit of more, to rob ourselves of the comfort of what we have, nor must we over-hoard for hereafter, nor lose our own enjoyment of what we have to lay it up for those that shall come after us, but serve ourselves out of it first. Observe,

1. What that good is which is here recommended to us ; and which is the utmost pleasure and profit we can expect or extract from the business and profit of this world, and the furthest we can go to rescue it from its *vanity* and the *vexation* that is in it. (1.) We must do our duty with them, and be more in care how to use an estate well, for the ends for which we were entrusted with it, than how to raise or increase an estate. This is intimated *v.* 26, where *those* only are said to have the comfort of this life who are good in *God's sight*, and again, *good before God*, truly good, as Noah, whom *God saw righteous before him.* We must set God always before us, and give diligence in every thing to approve ourselves to him. The Chaldee-paraphrase says, *A man should make his soul to enjoy good by keeping the commandments of God and walking in the ways that are right before him,* and (*v.* 25) by *studying the words of the law, and being in care about the day of the great judgment that is to come.* (2.) We must take the comfort of them. These things will not make a happiness for the soul ; all the good we can have out of them is for the body, and if we make use of them for the comfortable support of that, so that it may be fit to serve the soul and able to keep pace with it in the service of God, then they turn to a good account. *There is* therefore *nothing better for a man,* as to these things, than to allow himself a sober cheerful use of them, according as his rank and condition are, to have meat and drink out of them for himself, his family, his friends, and so delight his senses and make his *soul enjoy good,* all the good that is to be had out of them ; do not lose that, in pursuit of that good which is not to be had out of them. But observe, He would not have us to give up business, and take our ease, that we may *eat and drink;* no, we must *enjoy good in our labour;* we must use these things, not to excuse us from, but to make us diligent and cheerful in, our worldly business. (3.) We must herein *acknowledge God ;* we must see that *it is from the hand of God,* that is, [1.] The *good things* themselves that we enjoy are so, not only the products of his creating power, but the gifts of his providential bounty to us. And *then* they are truly pleasant to us when we take them from the hand of God as a Father, when we eye his wisdom giving

us that which is fittest for us, and acquiesce in it, and taste his love and goodness, relish them, and are thankful for them. [2.] A heart to enjoy them is so ; this is the gift of God's grace. Unless he give us wisdom to make a right use of what he has, in his providence, bestowed upon us, and withal peace of conscience, that we may discern God's favour in the world's smiles, we cannot make our souls enjoy any good in them.

2. Why we should have this in our eye, in the management of ourselves as to this world, and look up to God for it. (1.) Because Solomon himself, with all his possessions, could aim at no more and desire no better (*v.* 25) : *"Who can hasten to this more than I ?"* This is that which I was ambitious of : I wished for no more ; and those that have but little, in comparison with what I have, may attain to this, to be content with what they have and enjoy the good of it." Yet Solomon could not obtain it by his own wisdom, without the special grace of God, and therefore directs us to expect it from the hand of God and pray to him for it. (2.) Because riches are a blessing or a curse to a man according as he has or has not a heart to make good use of them. [1.] God makes them a reward to a good man, if with them he give him *wisdom, and knowledge, and joy,* to enjoy them cheerfully himself and to communicate them charitably to others. To those who are *good in God's sight,* who are of a good spirit, honest and sincere, pay a deference to their God and have a tender concern for all mankind, *God will give wisdom and knowledge in this world, and joy with the righteous in the world to come ;* so the Chaldee. Or he will give that wisdom and knowledge in things natural, moral, political, and divine, which will be a constant joy and pleasure to them. [2.] He makes them a punishment to a bad man if he denies him a heart to take the comfort of them, for they do but tantalize him and tyrannize over him : *To the sinner God gives travail,* by leaving him to himself and his own foolish counsels, to *gather and to heap up* that, which, as to himself, will not only burden him like *thick clay* (Hab. ii. 6), but be *a witness against him and eat his flesh as it were fire* (Jam. v. 3) ; while God designs, by an overruling providence, to give it to him that is *good before him;* for the *wealth of the sinner is laid up for the just,* and *gathered for him that will pity the poor.* Note, *First, Godliness, with contentment, is great gain ;* and *those* only have true joy that are *good in God's sight,* and that have it from him and in him. *Secondly,* Ungodliness is commonly punished with discontent and an insatiable covetousness, which are sins that are their own punishment. *Thirdly,* When God gives abundance to wicked men it is with design to force them to a resignation in favour of his own children, when they are of age and ready for it, as the Canaanites kept possession of the good land till the time appointed for Israel's entering upon it. [3.]

The burden of the song is still the same : *This is also vanity and vexation of spirit.* It is vanity, at the best, even to the good man ; when he has all that the sinner has scraped together it will not make him happy without something else ; but it is *vexation of spirit* to the sinner to see what he had laid up enjoyed by him that is *good in God's sight,* and therefore evil in his. So that, take it which way you will, the conclusion is firm, *All is vanity and vexation of spirit.*

CHAP. III.

Solomon having shown the vanity of studies, pleasures, and business, and made it to appear that happiness is not to be found in the schools of the learned, nor in the gardens of Epicurus, nor upon the exchange, he proceeds, in this chapter, further to prove his doctrine, and the inference he had drawn from it, That therefore we should cheerfully content ourselves with, and make use of, what God has given us, by showing, I. The mutability of all human affairs, ver. 1—10. II. The immutability of the divine counsels concerning them and the unsearchableness of those counsels, ver. 11—15. III. The vanity of worldly honour and power, which are abused for the support of oppression and persecution if men be not governed by the fear of God in the use of them, ver. 16. For a check to proud oppressors, and to show them their vanity, he reminds them, 1. That they will be called to account for it in the other world, ver. 17. 2. That their condition, in reference to this world (for of that he speaks), is no better than that of the brutes, ver. 18—21. And therefore he concludes that it is our wisdom to make use of what power we have for our own comfort, and not to oppress others with it.

TO every *thing there is* a season, and a time to every purpose under the heaven: 2 A time to be born, and a time to die; a time to plant, and a time to pluck up *that which is* planted ; 3 A time to kill, and a time to heal ; a time to break down, and a time to build up ; 4 A time to weep, and a time to laugh ; a time to mourn, and a time to dance ; 5 A time to cast away stones, and a time to gather stones together ; a time to embrace, and a time to refrain from embracing ; 6 A time to get, and a time to lose ; a time to keep, and a time to cast away ; 7 A time to rend, and a time to sew ; a time to keep silence, and a time to speak ; 8 A time to love, and a time to hate ; a time of war, and a time of peace. 9 What profit hath he that worketh in that wherein he laboureth ? 10 I have seen the travail, which God hath given to the sons of men to be exercised in it.

The scope of these verses is to show, 1. That we live in a world of changes, that the several events of time, and conditions of human life, are vastly different from one another, and yet occur promiscuously, and we are continually passing and repassing between them, as in the revolutions of every day and every year. In the *wheel of nature* (Jam. iii. 6) sometimes one spoke is uppermost and by and by the contrary ; there is a constant ebbing and flowing, waxing and waning ; from one extreme to the other does the *fashion of this world change,* ever did, and ever

will. 2. That every change concerning us, with the time and season of it, is unalterably fixed and determined by a supreme power ; and we must take things as they come, for it is not in our power to change what is appointed for us. And this comes in here as a reason why, when we are in prosperity, we should be easy, and yet not secure—not to be secure because we live in a world of changes and therefore have no reason to say, *To-morrow shall be as this day* (the lowest valleys join to the highest mountains), and yet to be easy, and, as he had advised (*ch.* ii. 24), *to enjoy the good of our labour,* in a humble dependence upon God and his providence, neither lifted up with hopes, nor cast down with fears, but with evenness of mind expecting every event. Here we have,

I. A general proposition laid down : *To every thing there is a season, v.* 1. 1. Those things which seem most contrary the one to the other will, in the revolution of affairs, each take their turn and come into play. The day will give place to the night and the night again to the day. Is it summer ? It will be winter. Is it winter ? Stay a while, and it will be summer. Every purpose has its time. The clearest sky will be clouded, *Post gaudia luctus—Joy succeeds sorrow ;* and the most clouded sky will clear up, *Post nubila Phœbus —The sun will burst from behind the cloud.* 2. Those things which to us seem most casual and contingent are, in the counsel and foreknowledge of God, punctually determined, and the very hour of them is fixed, and can neither be anticipated nor adjourned a moment.

II. The proof and illustration of it by the induction of particulars, twenty-eight in number, according to the days of the moon's revolution, which is always increasing or decreasing between its full and change. Some of these changes are purely the act of God, others depend more upon the will of man, but all are determined by the divine counsel. Every thing *under heaven* is thus changeable, but in heaven there is an unchangeable state, and an unchangeable counsel concerning these things. 1. There is *a time to be born and a time to die.* These are determined by the divine counsel ; and, as we were born, so we must die, at the time appointed, Acts xvii. 26. Some observe that here is *a time to be born and a time to die,* but no time to live ; that is so short that it is not worth mentioning ; as soon as we are born we begin to die. But, as there is *a time to be born and a time to die,* so there will be a time to rise again, a set time when those that lie in the grave shall be remembered, Job xiv. 13. 2. *A time* for God *to plant* a nation, as that of Israel in Canaan, *and,* in order to that, *to pluck up* the seven nations *that were planted* there, to make room for them ; and at length there was a time when God spoke concerning Israel too, to *pluck up and to destroy,* when the measure of their iniquity was full, Jer. xviii. 7, 9. There is *a time* for men *to plant,* a time of the year, a time of their lives; but, when *that which was planted* has grown fruitless and useless, it is *time to pluck it up.* 3. *A time to kill,* when the judgments of God are abroad in a land and lay all waste; but, when he returns in ways of mercy, then is *a time to heal* what *he has torn* (Hos. vi. 1, 2), to comfort a people after the time that he has *afflicted them,* Ps. xc. 15. There is a time when it is the wisdom of rulers to use severe methods, but there is a time when it is as much their wisdom to take a more gentle course, and to apply themselves to lenitives, not corrosives. 4. *A time to break down* a family, an estate, a kingdom, when it has ripened itself for destruction; but God will find *a time,* if they return and repent, to rebuild what he has broken down; there is *a time,* a set time, for the Lord *to build up Zion,* Ps. cii. 13, 16. There is *a time* for men *to break up* house, and break off trade, and so *to break down,* which those that are busy in *building up* both must expect and prepare for. 5. *A time* when God's providence calls *to weep and mourn,* and when man's wisdom and grace will comply with the call, and will *weep and mourn,* as in times of common calamity and danger, and then it is very absurd to *laugh, and dance,* and make merry (Isa. xxii. 12, 13; Ezek. xxi. 10); but then, on the other hand, there is a time when God calls to cheerfulness, *a time to laugh and dance,* and then he expects we should *serve him with joyfulness and gladness of heart.* Observe, The time of mourning and weeping is put first, before that of laughter and dancing, for we must first *sow in tears* and then *reap in joy.* 6. *A time to cast away stones,* by breaking down and demolishing fortifications, when God gives peace in the borders, and there is no more occasion for them; but there is *a time to gather stones together,* for the making of strong holds, *v.* 5. A time for old towers to fall, as that in Siloam (Luke xiii. 4), and for the temple itself to be so ruined as that *not one stone should be left upon another;* but also a time for towers and trophies too to be erected, when national affairs prosper. 7. *A time to embrace* a friend when we find him faithful, but *a time to refrain from embracing* when we find he is unfair or unfaithful, and that we have cause to suspect him; it is then our prudence to be shy and keep at a distance. It is commonly applied to conjugal embraces, and explained by 1 Cor. vii. 3—5; Joel ii. 16. 8. *A time to get,* get money, get preferment, get good bargains and a good interest, when opportunity smiles, a time when a wise man will *seek* (so the word is); when he is setting out in the world and has a growing family, when he is in his prime, when he prospers and has a run of business, then it is time for him to be busy and make hay when the sun shines. There is *a time to get* wisdom, and knowledge, and grace, when a man has a price put into his hand; but then let him expect there will come a time to spend, when all he has will be little enough

to serve his turn. Nay, there will come *a time to lose,* when what has been soon got will be soon scattered and cannot be held fast. 9. *A time to keep,* when we have use for what we have got, and can keep it without running the hazard of a good conscience; but there may come *a time to cast away,* when love to God may oblige us to cast away what we have, because we must deny Christ and wrong our consciences if we keep it (Matt. x. 37, 38), and rather to make shipwreck of all than of the faith; nay, when love to ourselves may oblige us to cast it away, when it is for the saving of our lives, as it was when Jonah's mariners heaved their cargo into the sea. 10. *A time to rend* the garments, as upon occasion of some great grief, *and a time to sew* them again, in token that the grief is over. A time to undo what we have done and a time to do again what we have undone. Jerome applies this to the rending of the Jewish church and the sewing and making up of the gospel church thereupon. 11. *A time* when it becomes us, and is our wisdom and duty, *to keep silence,* when it is an *evil time* (Amos v. 13), when our speaking would be the *casting of pearl before swine,* or when we are in danger of speaking amiss (Ps. xxxix. 2); but there is also *a time to speak* for the glory of God and the edification of others, when silence would be the betraying of a righteous cause, and when with the mouth confession is to be made to salvation; and it is a great part of Christian prudence to know when to speak and when to hold our peace. 12. *A time to love,* and to show ourselves friendly, to be free and cheerful, and it is a pleasant time; but there may come *a time to hate,* when we shall see cause to break off all familiarity with some that we have been fond of, and to be upon the reserve, as having found reason for a suspicion, which love is loth to admit. 13. *A time of war,* when God draws the sword for judgment and gives it commission to devour, when men draw the sword for justice and the maintaining of their rights, when there is in the nations a disposition to war; but we may hope for *a time of peace,* when the sword of the Lord shall be sheathed and he shall *make wars to cease* (Ps. xlvi. 9), when the end of the war is obtained, and when there is on all sides a disposition to peace. War shall not last always, nor is there any peace to be called lasting on this side the everlasting peace. Thus in all these changes God has set the one over-against the other, that we may *rejoice as though we rejoiced not and weep as though we wept not.*

III. The inferences drawn from this observation. If our present state be subject to such vicissitude, 1. Then we must not expect our portion in it, for the good things of it are of no certainty, no continuance (*v.* 9): *What profit has he that works?* What can a man promise himself from planting and building, when that which he thinks is brought to perfection may so soon, and will so surely, be plucked up and broken down? All our pains and care will not alter either the mutable nature of the things themselves or the immutable counsel of God concerning them. 2 Then we must look upon ourselves as upon our probation in it. There is indeed no profit *in that wherein we labour ;* the thing itself, when we have it, will do us little good; but, if we make a right use of the disposals of Providence about it, there will be profit in that (*v.* 10): *I have seen the travail which God has given to the sons of men,* not to make up a happiness by it, but *to be exercised in it,* to have various graces exercised by the variety of events, to have their dependence upon God tried by every change, and to be trained up to it, and taught both *how to want and how to abound,* Phil. iv. 12. Note, (1.) There is a great deal of toil and trouble to be seen among the children of men. Labour and sorrow fill the world. (2.) This toil and this trouble are what God has allotted us. He never intended this world for our rest, and therefore never appointed us to take our ease in it. (3.) To many it proves a gift. God gives it to men, as the physician gives a medicine to his patient, to do him good. This travail is given to us to make us weary of the world and desirous of the remaining rest. It is given to us that we may be kept in action, and may always have something to do; for we were none of us sent into the world to be idle. Every change cuts us out some new work, which we should be more solicitous about, than about the event.

11 He hath made every *thing* beautiful in his time : also he hath set the world in their heart, so that no man can find out the work that God maketh from the beginning to the end. 12 I know that *there is* no good in them, but for *a man* to rejoice, and to do good in his life. 13 And also that every man should eat and drink, and enjoy the good of all his labour, it *is* the gift of God. 14 I know that, whatsoever God doeth, it shall be for ever : nothing can be put to it, nor any thing taken from it : and God doeth *it,* that *men* should fear before him. 15 That which hath been is now ; and that which is to be hath already been ; and God requireth that which is past.

We have seen what changes there are in the world, and must not expect to find the world more sure to us than it has been to others. Now here Solomon shows the hand of God in all those changes; it is he that has made every creature to be that to us which it is, and therefore we must have our eye always upon him.

I. We must make the best of *that which is,* and must believe it best for the present, and accommodate ourselves to it : *He has made every thing beautiful in his time* (*v.* 11), and therefore, while its time lasts, we must be reconciled to it : nay, we must please ourselves with the beauty of it. Note, 1. Every thing is as God has made it; it is really as he appointed it to be, not as it appears to us. 2. That which to us seems most unpleasant is yet, in its proper time, altogether becoming. Cold is as becoming in winter as heat in summer; and the night, in its turn, is a black beauty, as the day, in its turn, is a bright one. 3. There is a wonderful harmony in the divine Providence and all its disposals, so that the events of it, when they come to be considered in their relations and tendencies, together with the seasons of them, will appear very beautiful, to the glory of God and the comfort of those that trust in him. Though we see not the complete beauty of Providence, yet we shall see it, and a glorious sight it will be, when the mystery of God shall be finished. Then every thing shall appear to have been done in the most proper time and it will be the wonder of eternity, Deut. xxxii. 4. Ezek. i. 18.

II. We must wait with patience for the full discovery of that which to us seems intricate and perplexed, acknowledging that we *cannot find out the work that God makes from the beginning to the end,* and therefore must judge nothing before the time. We are to believe that God has made all beautiful. Every thing is done well, as in creation, so in providence, and we shall see it when the end comes, but till then we are incompetent judges of it. While the picture is in drawing, and the house in building, we see not the beauty of either; but when the artist has put his last hand to them, and given them their finishing strokes, then all appears very good. We see but the middle of God's works, not from the beginning of them (then we should see how admirably the plan was laid in the divine counsels), nor to the end of them, which crowns the action (then we should see the product to be glorious); but we must wait till the veil be rent, and not arraign God's proceedings nor pretend to pass a judgment on them. *Secret things belong not to us.* Those words, *He has set the world in their hearts,* are differently understood. 1. Some make them to be a reason why we may know more of God's works than we do; so Mr. Pemble: " God has not left himself without witness of his righteous, equal, and beautiful ordering of things, but has set it forth, to be observed in the book of *the world,* and this he has *set in men's hearts,* given man a large desire, and a power, in good measure, to comprehend and understand the history of nature, with the course of human affairs, so that, if men did but give themselves to the exact observation of things, they might in most of them perceive an admirable order and contrivance." 2. Others make them to be a reason why we do not know so much of God's works as we might; so bishop Reynolds: "We have the world so much in our hearts, are so taken up with thoughts and cares of worldly things, and are so exercised in our travail concerning them, that we have neither time nor spirit to eye God's hand in them." The world has not only gained possession of the heart, but has formed prejudices there against the beauty of God's works.

III. We must be pleased with our lot in this world, and cheerfully acquiesce in the will of God concerning us, and accommodate ourselves to it. *There is no* certain, lasting, *good in* these things; what good there is in them we are here told, *v.* 12, 13. We must make a good use of them, 1. For the benefit of others. All the *good* there is *in them* is *to do good* with them, to our families, to our neighbours, to the poor, to the public, to its civil and religious interests. What have we our beings, capacities, and estates for, but to be some way serviceable to our generation? We mistake if we think we were born for ourselves. No; it is our business *to do good;* it is in doing good that there is the truest pleasure, and what is so laid out is best laid up and will turn to the best account. Observe, It is *to do good in this life,* which is short and uncertain; we have but a little time to be doing good in, and therefore had need to redeem time. It is *in this life,* where we are in a state of trial and probation for another life. Every man's life is his opportunity of doing that which will make for him in eternity. 2. For our own comfort. Let us make ourselves easy, *rejoice, and enjoy the good of our labour,* as *it is the gift of God,* and so enjoy God in it, and taste his love, return him thanks, and make him the centre of our joy, *eat and drink* to his glory, and *serve him with joyfulness of heart, in the abundance of all things.* If all things in this world be so uncertain, it is a foolish thing for men sordidly to spare for the present, that they may hoard up all for hereafter; it is better to live cheerfully and usefully upon what we have, and let to-morrow *take thought for the things of itself.* Grace and wisdom to do this *is the gift of God,* and it is a good gift, which crowns the gifts of his providential bounty.

IV. We must be entirely satisfied in all the disposals of the divine Providence, both as to personal and public concerns, and bring our minds to them, because God, in all, performs the thing that is appointed for us, acts according to the counsel of his will; and we are here told, 1. That that counsel cannot be altered, and therefore it is our wisdom to make a virtue of necessity, by submitting to it. It must be as God wills: *I know* (and every one knows it that knows any thing of God) *that whatsoever God does it shall be for ever. v.*14. *He is in one mind, and who can turn*

him? His measures are never broken, nor is he ever put upon new counsels, but what he has purposed shall be effected, and all the world cannot defeat nor disannul it. It behoves us therefore to say, "Let it be as God wills," for, how cross soever it may be to our designs and interests, God's will is his wisdom. 2. That that counsel needs not to be altered, for there is nothing amiss in it, nothing that can be amended. If we could see it altogether at one view, we should see it so perfect that *nothing can be put to it,* for there is no deficiency in it, *nor any thing taken from it,* for there is nothing in it unnecessary, or that can be spared. As the word of God, so the works of God are every one of them perfect in its kind, and it is presumption for us either to add to them or to diminish from them, Deut. iv. 2. It is therefore as much our interest, as our duty, to bring our wills to the will of God.

V. We must study to answer God's end in all his providences, which is in general to make us religious. *God does* all *that men should fear before him,* to convince them that there is a God above them that has a sovereign dominion over them, at whose disposal they are and all their ways, and in whose hands their times are and all events concerning them, and that therefore they ought to have their eyes ever towards him, to worship and adore him, to acknowledge him in all their ways, to be careful in every thing to please him, and afraid of offending him in any thing. God thus changes his disposals, and yet is unchangeable in his counsels, not to perplex us, much less to drive us to despair, but to teach us our duty to him and engage us to do it. That which God designs in the government of the world is the support and advancement of religion among men.

VI. Whatever changes we see or feel in this world, we must acknowledge the inviolable steadiness of God's government. The sun rises and sets, the moon increases and decreases, and yet both are where they were, and their revolutions are in the same method from the beginning according to *the ordinances of heaven;* so it is with the events of Providence (*v.* 15): *That which has been is now.* God has not of late begun to use this method. No; things were always as mutable and uncertain as they are now, and so they will be: *That which is to be has already been;* and therefore we speak inconsiderately when we say, "Surely the world was never so bad as it is now," or, "None ever met with such disappointments as we meet with," or, "The times will never mend;" they may mend with us, and after a time to mourn there may come a time to rejoice, but that will still be liable to the common character, to the common fate. The world, as it has been, is and will be constant in inconstancy; for *God requires that which is past,* that is, repeats what he has formerly done and deals with us no otherwise than as he has used to deal with good men; and *shall the earth be forsaken for us, or the rock removed out of his place?* There has no change befallen us, nor any temptation by it overtaken us, *but such as is common to men.* Let us not be proud and secure in prosperity, for God may recal a past trouble, and order that to seize us and spoil our mirth (Ps. xxx. 7); nor let us despond in adversity, for God may call back the comforts that are past, as he did to Job. We may apply this to our past actions, and our behaviour under the changes that have affected us. God will call us to account for *that which is past;* and therefore, when we enter into a new condition, we should judge ourselves for our sins in our former condition, prosperous or afflicted.

16 And moreover I saw under the sun the place of judgment, *that* wickedness *was* there; and the place of righteousness, *that* iniquity *was* there. 17 I said in mine heart, God shall judge the righteous and the wicked: for *there is* a time there for every purpose and for every work. 18 I said in mine heart concerning the estate of the sons of men, that God might manifest them, and that they might see that they themselves are beasts. 19 For that which befalleth the sons of men befalleth beasts; even one thing befalleth them: as the one dieth, so dieth the other; yea, they have all one breath; so that a man hath no preeminence above a beast: for all *is* vanity. 20 All go unto one place; all are of the dust, and all turn to dust again. 21 Who knoweth the spirit of man that goeth upward, and the spirit of the beast that goeth downward to the earth? 22 Wherefore I perceive that *there is* nothing better, than that a man should rejoice in his own works; for that *is* his portion: for who shall bring him to see what shall be after him?

Solomon is still showing that every thing in this world, without piety and the fear of God, is vanity. Take away religion, and there is nothing valuable among men, nothing for the sake of which a wise man would think it worth while to live in this world. In these verses he shows that power (than which there is nothing men are more ambitious of) and life itself (than which there is nothing men are more fond, more jealous of) are nothing without the fear of God.

I. Here is the vanity of man as mighty, man in his best estate, man upon the throne,

where his authority is submitted to, man upon the judgment-seat, where his wisdom and justice are appealed to, and where, if he be governed by the laws of religion, he is God's vicegerent; nay, he is of those to whom it is said, *You are gods;* but without the fear of God it *is vanity,* for, set that aside, and,

1. The judge will not judge aright, will not use his power well, but will abuse it; instead of doing good with it he will do hurt with it, and then it is not only vanity, but a lie, a cheat to himself and to all about him, *v.* 16. Solomon perceived, by what he had read of former times, what he heard of other countries, and what he had seen in some corrupt judges, even in the land of Israel, notwithstanding all his care to prefer good men, that there was *wickedness in the place of judgment.* It is not so above the sun: far be it from God that he should do iniquity, or pervert justice. But *under the sun* it is often found that that which should be the refuge, proves the prison, of oppressed innocency. *Man being in honour, and not understanding* what he ought to do, *becomes like the beasts that perish,* like the beasts of prey, even the most ravenous, Ps. xlix. 20. Not only from the persons that sat in judgment, but even *in the places* where judgment was, in pretence, administered, and righteousness was expected, *there was iniquity;* men met with the greatest wrongs in those courts to which they fled for justice. This is *vanity and vexation;* for, (1.) It would have been better for the people to have had no judges than to have had such. (2.) It would have been better for the judges to have had no power than to have had it and used it to such ill purposes; and so they will say another day.

2. The judge will himself be judged for not judging aright. When Solomon saw how judgment was perverted among men he looked up to God the Judge, and looked forward to the day of his judgment (*v.* 17): "*I said in my heart* that this unrighteous judgment is not so conclusive as both sides take it to be, for there will be a review of the judgment; *God shall judge* between *the righteous and the wicked,* shall judge for the righteous and plead their cause, though now it is run down, and judge against the wicked and reckon with them for all their *unrighteous decrees* and the *grievousness which they have prescribed,* Isa. x. 1. With an eye of faith we may see, not only the period, but the punishment of the pride and cruelty of oppressors (Ps. xcii. 7), and it is an unspeakable comfort to the oppressed that their cause will be heard over again. Let them therefore wait with patience, for there is another *Judge* that *stands before the door.* And, though the day of affliction may last long, yet *there is a time,* a set time, for the examination of *every purpose, and every work* done under the sun. Men have their day now, but God's day is coming, Ps. xxxvii. 13. With God

there is a time for the re-hearing of causes, redressing of grievances, and reversing of unjust decrees, though as yet we see it not here, Job xxiv. 1.

II. Here is the vanity of man as mortal. He now comes to speak more generally *concerning the estate of the sons of men* in this world, their life and being on earth, and shows that their reason, without religion and the fear of God, advances them but little above the beasts. Now observe,

1. What he aims at in this account of man's estate. (1.) That God may be honoured, may be justified, may be glorified—*that they might clear God* (so the margin reads it), that if men have an uneasy life in this world, full of vanity and vexation, they may thank themselves and lay no blame on God; let them clear him, and not say that he made this world to be man's prison and life to be his penance; no, God made man, in respect both of honour and comfort, *little lower than the angels;* if he be mean and miserable, it is his own fault. Or, *that God* (that is, the word of God) *might manifest them,* and discover them to themselves, and so appear to be *quick and powerful,* and a judge of men's characters; and we may be made sensible how open we lie to God's knowledge and judgment. (2.) That men may be humbled, may be vilified, may be mortified—*that they might see that they themselves are beasts.* It is no easy matter to convince proud men that *they are but men* (Ps. ix. 20), much more to convince bad men *that they are beasts,* that, being destitute of religion, they are as *the beasts that perish,* as *the horse and the mule that have no understanding.* Proud oppressors are as beasts, as *roaring lions and ranging bears.* Nay, every man that minds his body only, and not his soul, makes himself no better than a brute, and must wish, at least, to die like one.

2. The manner in which he verifies this account. That which he undertakes to prove is that a worldly, carnal, earthly-minded *man, has no preëminence above the beast, for all* that which he sets his heart upon, places his confidence, and expects a happiness in, *is vanity, v.* 19. Some make this to be the language of an atheist, who justifies himself in his iniquity (*v.* 16) and evades the argument taken from the judgment to come (*v.* 17) by pleading that there is not another life after this, but that when man dies there is an end of him, and therefore while he lives he may live as he lists; but others rather think Solomon here speaks as he himself thinks, and that it is to be understood in the same sense with that of his father (Ps. xlix. 14), *Like sheep they are laid in the grave,* and that he intends to show the vanity of this world's wealth and honours " by the equal condition in mere outward respects (as bishop Reynolds expounds it) between men and beasts," (1.) The events concerning both seem much alike (*v.* 19); *That which befals the sons of*

1000

men is no other than that which *befals beasts;* a great deal of knowledge of human bodies is gained by the anatomy of the bodies of brutes. When the deluge swept away the old world the beasts perished with mankind. Horses and men are killed in battle with the same weapons of war. (2.) The end of both, to an eye of sense, seems alike too : *They have all one breath,* and breathe in the same air, and it is the general description of both that *in their nostrils is the breath of life* (Gen. vii. 22), and therefore, *as the one dies, so dies the other;* in their expiring there is no visible difference, but death makes much the same change with a beast that it does with a man. [1.] As to their bodies, the change is altogether the same, except the different respects that are paid to them by the survivors. Let a man be *buried with the burial of an ass* (Jer. xxii. 19) and what preëminence then has he *above a beast?* The touch of the dead body of a man, by the law of Moses, contracted a greater ceremonial pollution than the touch of the carcase even of an unclean beast or fowl. And Solomon here observes that *all go unto one place;* the dead bodies of men and beasts putrefy alike; *all are of the dust,* in their original, for we see *all turn to dust again* in their corruption. What little reason then have we to be proud of our bodies, or any bodily accomplishments, when they must not only be reduced to the earth very shortly, but must be so in common with the beasts, and we must mingle our dust with theirs! [2.] As to their spirits there is indeed a vast difference, but not a visible one, *v.* 21. It is certain that *the spirit of* the sons of men at death is ascending; it *goes upwards* to the Father of spirits, who made it, to the world of spirits to which it is allied; it dies not with the body, but *is redeemed from the power of the grave,* Ps. xlix. 15. It *goes upwards* to be judged and determined to an unchangeable state. It is as certain that *the spirit of the beast goes downwards to the earth;* it dies with the body; it perishes and is gone at death. The soul of a beast is, at death, like a candle blown out—there is an end of it; whereas the soul of a man is then like a candle taken out of a dark lantern, which leaves the lantern useless indeed, but does itself shine brighter. This great difference there is between the spirits of men and beasts; and a good reason it is why men should *set their affections on things above,* and lift up their souls to those things, not suffering them, as if they were the souls of brutes, to cleave to this earth. But *who knows* this difference? We cannot see the ascent of the one and the descent of the other with our bodily eyes; and therefore those that live by sense, as all carnal sensualists do, that *walk in the sight of their eyes* and will not admit any other discoveries, by their own rule of judgment have no *preëminence above the beasts. Who knows,* that is, who considers this? Isa. liii. 1. Very few. Were it better considered, the world would be every way better; but most men live as if they were to be here always, or as if when they die there were an end of them; and it is not strange that those live like beasts who think they shall die like beasts, but on such the noble faculties of reason are perfectly lost and thrown away.

3. An inference drawn from it (*v.* 22): *There is nothing better*, as to this world, nothing better to be had out of our wealth and honour, *than that a man should rejoice in his own works*, that is, (1.) Keep a clear conscience, and never admit *iniquity* into *the place of righteousness. Let every man prove his own work*, and approve himself to God in it, *so shall he have rejoicing in himself alone*, Gal. vi. 4. Let him not get nor keep any thing but what he can rejoice in. See 2 Cor. i. 12. (2.) Live a cheerful life. If God have prospered the work of our hands unto us, let us rejoice in it, and take the comfort of it, and not make it a burden to ourselves and leave others the joy of it; *for that is our portion*, not the portion of our souls (miserable are those that have their portion in this life, Ps. xvii. 14, and fools are those that choose it and take up with it, Luke xii. 19), but it is the portion of the body; that only which we enjoy is ours out of this world; it is taking what is to be had and making the best of it, and the reason is because none can give us a sight of *what shall be after us*, either who shall have our estates or what use they will make of them. When we are gone it is likely we shall not see what is after us; there is no correspondence that we know of between the other world and this, Job xiv. 21. Those in the other world will be wholly taken up with that world, so that they will not care for seeing what is done in this; and while we are here we cannot foresee *what shall be after us*, either as to our families or the public. *It is not for us to know the times and seasons* that *shall be after* us, which, as it should be a restraint to our cares about this world, so it should be a reason for our concern about another. Since death is a final farewell to this life, let us look before us to another life.

CHAP. IV.

Solomon, having shown the vanity of this world in the temptation which those in power feel to oppress and trample upon their subjects, here further shows, I. The temptation which the oppressed feel to discontent and impatience, ver. 1—3. II. The temptation which those that love their ease feel to take their ease and neglect business, for fear of being envied, ver. 4—6. III. The folly of hoarding up abundance of worldly wealth, ver. 7, 8. IV. A remedy against that folly, in being made sensible of the benefit of society and mutual assistance, ver. 9—12. V. The mutability even of royal dignity, not only through the folly of the prince himself (ver. 13, 14), but through the fickleness of the people, let the prince be ever so discreet, ver. 15, 16. It is not the prerogative even of kings themselves to be exempted from the vanity and vexation that attend these things; let none else then expect it.

SO I returned, and considered all the oppressions that are done under the sun: and behold the tears of *such as were* oppressed, and they had no comforter; and on the side of their oppressors *there was* power; but they had no comforter. 2 Wherefore I praised the dead which are already dead more than the living which are yet alive. 3 Yea, better *is he* than both they, which hath not yet been, who hath not seen the evil work that is done under the sun.

Solomon had a large soul (1 Kings iv. 29) and it appeared by this, among other things, that he had a very tender concern for the miserable part of mankind and took cognizance of the afflictions of the afflicted. He had taken the oppressors to task (*ch.* iii. 16, 17) and put them in mind of the judgment to come, to be a curb to their insolence; now here he observes the oppressed. This he did, no doubt, as a prince, to do them justice and *avenge them of their adversaries*, for he both *feared God and regarded men ;* but here he does it as a preacher, and shows,

I. The troubles of their condition (*v.* 1); of these he speaks very feelingly and with compassion. It grieved him, 1. To see might prevailing against right, to see so much *oppression done under the sun*, to see servants, and labourers, and poor workmen, oppressed by their masters, who take advantage of their necessity to impose what terms they please upon them, debtors oppressed by cruel creditors and creditors too by fraudulent debtors, tenants oppressed by hard landlords and orphans by treacherous guardians, and, worst of all, subjects oppressed by arbitrary princes and unjust judges. Such *oppressions are done under the sun ;* above the sun righteousness reigns for ever. Wise men will *consider these oppressions*, and contrive to do something for the relief of those that are oppressed. *Blessed is he that considers the poor.* 2. To see how those that were wronged laid to heart the wrongs that were done them. He *beheld the tears of such as were oppressed*, and perhaps could not forbear weeping with them. The world is a place of weepers; look which way we will, we have a melancholy scene presented to us, *the tears of* those that are *oppressed* with one trouble or other. They find it is to no purpose to complain, and therefore mourn in secret (as Job, *ch.* xvi. 20; xxx. 28); but *Blessed are those that mourn.* 3. To see how unable they were to help themselves : *On the side of their oppressors there was power*, when they had done wrong, to stand to it and make good what they had done, so that the poor were borne down with a strong hand and had no way to obtain redress. It is sad to see power misplaced, and that which was given men to enable them to do good perverted to support them in doing wrong. 4. To see how they and their calamities were slighted by all about them. They wept and needed comfort, but there was none to do that friendly office : *They had no comforter ;* their oppressors were powerful and threatening, and therefore *they had no com-*

forter; those that should have comforted them durst not, for fear of displeasing the oppressors and being made their companions for offering to be their comforters. It is sad to see so little humanity among men.

II. The temptations of their condition. Being thus hardly used, they are tempted to hate and despise life, and to envy those that are dead and in their graves, and to wish they had never been born (*v.* 2, 3); and Solomon is ready to agree with them, for it serves to prove that *all is vanity and vexation,* since life itself is often so; and if we disregard it, in comparison with the favour and fruition of God (as St. Paul, Acts xx. 24, Phil. i. 23), it is our praise, but, if (as here) only for the sake of the miseries that attend it, it is our infirmity, and we judge therein after the flesh, as Job and Elijah did. 1. He here thinks those happy who have ended this miserable life, have done their part and quitted the stage; "*I praised the dead that are already dead,* slain outright, or that had a speedy passage through the world, made a short cut over the ocean of life, dead already, before they had well begun to live; I was pleased with their lot, and, had it been in their own choice, should have praised their wisdom for but looking into the world and then retiring, as not liking it. I concluded that it is better with them than with *the living that are yet alive* and that is all, dragging the long and heavy chain of life, and wearing out its tedious minutes." This may be compared not with Job iii. 20, 21, but with Rev. xiv. 13, where, in times of persecution (and such Solomon is here describing), it is not the passion of man, but the Spirit of God, that says, *Blessed are the dead which die in the Lord from henceforth.* Note, The condition of the saints that are dead, and gone to rest with God, is upon many accounts better and more desirable than the condition of living saints that are yet continued in their work and warfare. 2. He thinks those happy who never began this miserable life; nay, they are happiest of all: *He that has not been is happier than both they.* Better never to have been born than be born to *see the evil work that is done under the sun,* to see so much wickedness committed, so much wrong done, and not only to be in no capacity to mend the matter, but to suffer ill for doing well. A good man, how calamitous a condition soever he is in in this world, cannot have cause to wish he had never been born, since he is glorifying the Lord even in the fires, and will be happy at last, for ever happy. Nor ought any to wish so while they are alive, for while there is life there is hope; a man is never undone till he is in hell.

4 Again, I considered all travail, and every right work, that for this a man is envied of his neighbour. This *is* also vanity and vexation of spirit.

5 The fool foldeth his hands together,

and eateth his own flesh. 6 Better *is* a handful *with* quietness, than both the hands full *with* travail and vexation of spirit.

Here Solomon returns to the observation and consideration of the vanity and vexation of spirit that attend the business of this world, which he had spoken of before, *ch.* ii. 11.

I. If a man be acute, and dexterous, and successful in his business, he gets the ill-will of *his neighbours, v.* 4. Though he takes a great deal of pains, and goes through *all travail,* does not get his estate easily, but it costs him a great deal of hard labour, nor does he get it dishonestly, he wrongs no man, defrauds no man, but by *every right work,* by applying himself to his own proper business, and managing it by all the rules of equity and fair-dealing, yet *for this he is envied of his neighbour,* and the more for the reputation he has got by his honesty. This shows, 1. What little conscience most men have, that they will bear a grudge to a neighbour, give him an ill word and do him an ill turn, only because he is more ingenious and industrious than themselves, and has more of the blessing of heaven. Cain envied Abel, Esau Jacob, and Saul David, and all for their right works. This is downright diabolism. 2. What little comfort wise and useful men must expect to have in this world. Let them behave themselves ever so cautiously, they cannot escape being envied; and *who can stand before envy?* Prov. xxvii. 4. Those that excel in virtue will always be an eye-sore to those that exceed in vice, which should not discourage us from any right work, but drive us to expect the praise of it, not from men, but from God, and not to count upon satisfaction and happiness in the creature; for, if *right works* prove *vanity and vexation of spirit,* no works *under the sun* can prove otherwise. But for *every right work* a man shall be accepted of his God, and then he needs not mind though he be *envied of his neighbour,* only it may make him love the world the less.

II. If a man be stupid, and dull, and blundering in his business, he does ill for himself (*v.* 5): *The fool* that goes about his work as if *his hands* were muffled and *folded together,* that does every thing awkwardly, *the sluggard* (for he is a fool) that loves his ease and *folds his hands together* to keep them warm, because they refuse to labour, he *eats his own flesh,* is a cannibal to himself, brings himself into such a poor condition that he has nothing to eat but his own flesh into such a desperate condition that he is ready to eat his own flesh for vexation. He has a dog's life—hunger and ease. Because he sees active men that thrive in the world envied, he runs into the other extreme; and, lest he should be envied for his right works, he does every thing wrong, and does not deserve to be pitied. Note, Idleness is a sin that is its own punishment. The following words (*v.* 6), *Better is a handful with quiet-*

ness than both the hands full with travail and vexation of spirit, may be taken either, 1. As the sluggard's argument for the excuse of himself in his idleness. He *folds his hands together*, and abuses and misapplies a good truth for his justification, as if, because *a little with quietness is better than* abundance with strife, therefore a little with idleness is better than abundance with honest labour : thus *wise in his own conceit* is he, Prov xxvi. 16. But, 2. I rather take it as Solomon's advice to keep the mean between that *travail* which will make *a man envied* and that slothfulness which will make a man *eat his own flesh*. Let us by honest industry lay hold on the handful, that we may not want necessaries, but not grasp at both the hands full, which will but create us vexation of spirit. Moderate pains and moderate gains will do best. A man may have but a handful of the world, and yet may enjoy it and himself with a great deal of *quietness*, with content of mind, peace of conscience, and the love and good-will of his neighbours, while many that have both their hands full, have more than heart could wish, have a great deal of travail and vexation with it. Those that cannot live on a little, it is to be feared, would not live as they should if they had ever so much.

7 Then I returned, and I saw vanity under the sun. 8 There is one *alone*, and *there is* not a second; yea, he hath neither child nor brother: yet *is there* no end of all his labour; neither is his eye satisfied with riches; neither *saith he*, For whom do I labour, and bereave my soul of good ? This *is* also vanity, yea, it *is* a sore travail. 9 Two *are* better than one; because they have a good reward for their labour. 10 For if they fall, the one will lift up his fellow : but woe to him *that is* alone when he falleth; for *he hath* not another to help him up. 11 Again, if two lie together, then they have heat: but how can one be warm *alone?* 12 And if one prevail against him, two shall withstand him ; and a threefold cord is not quickly broken.

Here Solomon fastens upon another instance of the vanity of this world, that frequently the more men have of it the more they would have; and on this they are so intent that they have no enjoyment of what they have. Now Solomon here shows,

I. That selfishness is the cause of this evil (*v.* 7, 8): *There is one alone*, that minds none but himself, cares for nobody, but would, if he could, be placed alone in the midst of the earth ; *there is not a second*, nor does he desire there should be : one mouth he thinks enough in a house, and grudges every thing

that goes beside him. See how this covetous muckworm is here described. 1. He makes himself a mere slave to his business. Though *he has no charge, neither child nor brother*, none to take care of but himself, none to hang upon him, or draw from him, no poor relations, nor dares he marry, for fear of the expense of a family, *yet is there no end of his labour ;* he is at it night and day, early and late, and will scarcely allow necessary rest to himself and those he employs. He does not confine himself within the bounds of his own calling, but is for having a hand in any thing that he can get by. See Ps. cxxvii. 2. 2. He never thinks he has enough : *His eye is not satisfied with riches*. Covetousness is called *the lust of the eye* (1 John ii. 16) because the *beholding of it with his eyes* is all that the worldling seems to covet, Eccl. v. 11. He has enough for his back (as bishop Reynolds observes), for his belly, for his calling, for his family, for his living decently in the world, but he has not enough for his eyes. Though he can but see it, can but count his money, and not find in his heart to use it, yet he is not easy because he has not more to regale his eyes with. 3. He denies himself the comfort of what he has : He *bereaves his soul of good*. If our souls be bereaved of good, it is we ourselves that do bereave them. Others may bereave us of outward good, but cannot rob us of our graces and comforts, our spiritual good things. It is our own fault if we do not enjoy ourselves. Yet many are so set upon the world that, in pursuit of it, they *bereave their souls of good* here and for ever, make shipwreck of faith and of a good conscience, bereave themselves not only of the favour of God and eternal life, but of the pleasures of this world too and this present life. Worldly people, pretending to be wise for themselves, are really enemies to themselves. 4. He has no excuse for doing this : He has neither child nor *brother*, none that he is bound to, on whom he may lay out what he has to his satisfaction while he lives, none that he has a kindness for, for whom he may lay it up to his satisfaction and to whom he may leave it when he dies, none that are poor or dear to him. 5. He has not consideration enough to show himself the folly of this. He never puts this question to himself, " *For whom do I labour* thus? Do I labour, as I should, for the glory of God, and that I may have to give to those that need ? Do I consider that it is but for the body that I am labouring, a dying body; it is for others, and I know not for whom—perhaps for a fool, that will scatter it as fast as I have gathered it—perhaps for a foe, that will be ungrateful to my memory ?" Note, It is wisdom for those that take pains about this world to consider whom they take all this pains for, and whether it be really worth while to bereave themselves of good that they may bestow it on a stranger. If men do not consider this, it *is vanity, and a sore travail ;* they shame and vex themselves to no purpose.

II. That sociableness is the cure of this evil. Men are thus sordid because they are all for themselves. Now Solomon shows here, by divers instances, that *it is not good for man to be alone* (Gen. ii. 18); he designs hereby to recommend to us both marriage and friendship, two things which covetous misers decline, because of the charge of them; but such are the comfort and advantage of them both, if prudently contracted, that they will very well quit cost. Man, in paradise itself, could not be happy without a mate, and therefore is no sooner made than matched. 1. Solomon lays this down for a truth, That *two are better than one,* and more happy jointly than either of them could be separately, more pleased in one another than they could be in themselves only, mutually serviceable to each other's welfare, and by a united strength more likely to do good to others: *They have a good reward of their labour ;* whatever service they do, it is returned to them another way. He that serves himself only has himself only for his paymaster, and commonly proves more unjust and ungrateful to himself than his friend, if he should serve him, would be to him ; witness him that *labours endlessly* and yet *bereaves his soul of good*; he has no *reward of his labour.* But he that is kind to another has *a good reward ;* the pleasure and advantage of holy love will be an abundant recompence for all the *work and labour of love.* Hence Solomon infers the mischief of solitude: *Woe to him that is alone.* He lies exposed to many temptations which good company and friendship would prevent and help him to guard against; he wants that advantage which a man has by the countenance of his friend, as iron has of being sharpened by iron. A monastic life then was surely never intended for a state of perfection, nor should those be reckoned the greatest lovers of God who cannot find in their hearts to love any one else. 2. He proves it by divers instances of the benefit of friendship and good conversation. (1.) Occasional succour in an exigency. It is good for two to travel together, *for if* one happen to *fall,* and perhaps so as not to be able to get up himself, the other will be ready *to help him up* (a friend in need is a friend indeed); whereas if one travel alone, and get a fall, he may be lost for want of a little help. If a man fall *into sin,* his friend will help to *restore him with the spirit of meekness ;* if he fall into trouble, his friend will help to comfort him and assuage his grief. (2.) Mutual warmth. As a fellow-traveller is of use *(amicus pro vehiculo—a friend is a good substitute for a carriage)* so is a bedfellow : *If two lie together, they have heat.* So virtuous and gracious affections are excited by good society, and Christians warm one another by *provoking one another to love and to good works.* (3.) United strength. If an

enemy find a man alone, he is likely to *prevail against him ;* with his own single strength he cannot make his part good, but, if he have a second, he may do well enough : *two shall withstand him.* "You shall help me against my enemy, and I will help you against yours ;" according to the agreement between Joab and Abishai (2 Sam. x. 11), and so both are conquerors ; whereas, acting separately, both would have been conquered ; as was said of the ancient Britons, when the Romans invaded them, *Dum singuli pugnant, universi vincuntur—While they fight in detached parties, they sacrifice the general cause.* In our spiritual warfare we may be helpful to one another as well as in our spiritual work ; next to the comfort of communion with God, is that of the communion of saints. He concludes with this proverb, *A threefold cord is not easily broken,* any more than a bundle of arrows, though each single thread, and each single arrow, is. Two together he compares to *a threefold cord ;* for where two are closely joined in holy love and fellowship, Christ will by his Spirit come to them, and make the third, as he joined himself to the two disciples going to Emmaus, and then there is *a threefold cord* that can never be *broken. They that dwell in love, dwell in God, and God in them.*

13 Better *is* a poor and a wise child than an old and foolish king, who will no more be admonished. 14 For out of prison he cometh to reign; whereas also *he that is* born in his kingdom becometh poor. 15 I considered all the living which walk under the sun, with the second child that shall stand up in his stead. 16 *There is* no end of all the people, *even* of all that have been before them : they also that come after shall not rejoice in him. Surely this also *is* vanity and vexation of spirit.

Solomon was himself a king, and therefore may be allowed to speak more freely than another concerning the vanity of kingly state and dignity, which he shows here to be an uncertain thing; he had before said so (Prov. xxvii. 24, *The crown doth not endure to every generation),* and his son found it so. Nothing is more slippery than the highest post of honour without wisdom and the people's love.

I. A king is not happy unless he have wisdom, *v.* 13, 14. He that is truly *wise,* prudent, and pious, though he be *poor* in the world, and very young, and upon both accounts despised and little taken notice of, *is better,* more truly valuable and worthy of respect, is likely to do better for himself and to be a greater blessing to his generation, *than a king, than an old king,* and therefore venerable both for his gravity and for his dignity, if he be *foolish*, and knows not how to manage public affairs himself nor *will be admonished* and advised by others—*who* knows not to *be admonished*, that is, will not suffer any counsel or admonition to be given him (no one about him dares contradict him) or will not hearken to the counsel and admonition that are given him. It is so far from being any part of the honour of kings that it is the greatest dishonour to them that can be not to be *admonished*. Folly and wilfulness commonly go together, and those that most need admonition can worst bear it; but neither age nor titles will secure men respect if they have not true wisdom and virtue to recommend them; while wisdom and virtue will gain men honour even under the disadvantages of youth and poverty. To prove the *wise child better than the foolish king* he shows what each of them comes to, *v.* 14. 1. *A poor* man by his wisdom comes to be preferred, as Joseph, who, when he was but young, was brought *out of prison* to be *the second* man in the kingdom, to which story Solomon seems here to refer. Providence sometimes *raises the poor out of the dust, to set them among princes,* Ps. cxiii. 7, 8. Wisdom has wrought not only the liberty of men, but their dignity, raised them from the dunghill, from the dungeon, to the throne. 2. *A king* by his folly and wilfulness comes to be impoverished. Though he was *born in his kingdom,* came to it by inheritance, though he has lived to be old in it and has had time to fill his treasures, yet if he take all courses, and *will no more be admonished* as he has been, thinking, because he is old, he is past it, he *becomes poor ;* his treasure is exhausted, and perhaps he is forced to resign his crown and retire into privacy.

II. A king is not likely to continue if he have not a confirmed interest in the affections of the people; this is intimated, but somewhat obscurely, in the last two verses. 1. He that is king must have a successor, a *second,* a *child that shall stand up in his stead,* his own, suppose, or perhaps that *poor and wise child* spoken of, *v.* 13. Kings, when they grow old, must have the mortification of seeing those that are to jostle them out and stand up in their stead. 2. It is common with the people to adore the rising sun : *All the living who walk under the sun* are *with the second child,* are in his interests, are conversant with him, and make their court to him more than to the father, whom they look upon as going off, and despise because his best days are past. Solomon considered this; he saw this to be the disposition of his own people, which appeared immediately after his death, in their complaints of his government and their affectation of a change. 3. People are never long easy and satisfied : *There is no end,* no rest, *of all the people ;* they are continually fond of changes, and know not what they would have. 4. This is no new thing, but it has been the way *of all that*

have been before them ; there have been instances of this in every age : even Samuel and David could not always please. 5. As it has been, so it is likely to be still: *Those that come after* will be of the same spirit, and *shall not* long *rejoice in him* whom at first they seemed extremely fond of. To-day, *Hosanna*—to-morrow, *Crucify.* 6. It cannot but be a great grief to princes to see themselves thus slighted by those they have studied to oblige and have depended upon; there is no faith in man, no stedfastness. *This is vanity and vexation of spirit.*

CHAP. V.

Solomon, in this chapter, discourses, I. Concerning the worship of God, prescribing that as a remedy against all those vanities which he had already observed to be in wisdom, learning, pleasure, honour, power, and business. That we may not be deceived by those things, nor have our spirits vexed with the disappointments we meet with in them, let us make conscience of our duty to God and keep up our communion with him ; but, withal, he gives a necessary caution against the vanities which are too often found in religious exercises, which deprive them of their excellency and render them unable to help against other vanities. If our religion be a vain religion, how great is that vanity ! Let us therefore take heed of vanity, 1. In hearing the word, and offering sacrifice, ver. 1. 2. In prayer, ver. 2, 3. 3. In making vows, ver. 4—6. 4. In pretending to divine dreams, ver. 7. Now, (1.) For a remedy against those vanities, he prescribes the fear of God, ver. 7. (2.) To prevent the offence that might arise from the present sufferings of good people, he directs us to look up to God, ver. 8. II. Concerning the wealth of this world and the vanity and vexation that attend it. The fruits of the earth indeed are necessary to the support of life (ver. 9), but as for silver, and gold, and riches, 1. They are unsatisfying, ver. 10. 2. They are unprofitable, ver. 11. 3. They are disquieting, ver. 12. 4. They often prove hurtful and destroying, ver. 13. 5. They are perishing, ver. 14. 6. They must be left behind when we die, ver. 15, 16. 7. If we have not a heart to make use of them, they occasion a great deal of uneasiness, ver. 17. And therefore he recommends to us the comfortable use of that which God has given us, with an eye to him that is the giver, as the best way both to answer the end of our having it and to obviate the mischiefs that commonly attend great estates, ver. 18—20. So that if we can but learn out of this chapter how to manage the business of religion, and the business of this world (which two take up most of our time), so that both may turn to a good account, and neither our sabbath days nor our week-days may be lost, we shall have reason to say, We have learned two good lessons.

KEEP thy foot when thou goest to the house of God, and be more ready to hear, than to give the sacrifice of fools : for they consider not that they do evil. 2 Be not rash with thy mouth, and let not thine heart be hasty to utter *any* thing before God : for God *is* in heaven, and thou upon earth : therefore let thy words be few. 3 For a dream cometh through the multitude of business ; and a fool's voice *is known* by multitude of words.

Solomon's design, in driving us off from the world, by showing us its vanity, is to drive us to God and to our duty, that we may not walk in the way of the world, but by religious rules, nor depend upon the wealth of the world, but on religious advantages; and therefore,

I. He here sends us to *the house of God,* to the place of public worship, to the temple, which he himself had built at a vast expense. When he reflected with regret on all his other works (*ch.* ii. 4), he did not repent of that, but reflected on it with pleasure, yet mentions it not, lest he should seem to reflect on it with pride; but he here sends those to it that would know more of the vanity of the world and would find that happiness which is in vain sought for in the creature. David, when he was perplexed, *went into the sanctuary of God,* Ps. lxxiii. 17. Let our disappointments in the creature turn our eyes to the Creator ; let us have recourse to the word of God's grace and consult that, to the throne of his grace and solicit that. In the word and prayer there is a balm for every wound.

II. He charges us to behave ourselves well there, that we may not miss of our end in coming thither. Religious exercises are not vain things, but, if we mismanage them, they become vain to us. And therefore,

1. We must address ourselves to them with all possible seriousness and care : "*Keep thy foot,* not keep it back from the house of God (as Prov. xxv. 17), nor go slowly thither, as one unwilling to draw nigh to God, but *look well to thy goings, ponder the path of thy feet,* lest thou take a false step. Address thyself to the worship of God with a solemn pause, and take time to compose thyself for it, not going about it with precipitation, which is called *hasting with the feet,* Prov. xix. 2. Keep thy thoughts from roving and wandering from the work ; keep thy affections from running out towards wrong objects, for in the business of God's house there is work enough for the whole man, and all too little to be employed." Some think it alludes to the charge given to Moses and Joshua to *put off their shoes* (Exod. iii. 5, Josh. v. 15,) in token of subjection and reverence. *Keep thy feet* clean, Exod. xxx. 19.

2. We must take heed that the sacrifice we bring be not *the sacrifice of fools* of wicked men, for they are fools and their *sacrifice is an abomination to the Lord* (Prov. xv. 8), that we bring not *the torn, and the lame, and the sick for sacrifice,* for we are plainly told that it will not be accepted, and therefore it is folly to bring it,—that we rest not in the sign and ceremony, and the outside of the performance, without regarding the sense and meaning of it, for that is the *sacrifice of fools.* Bodily exercise, if that be all, is a jest ; none but fools will think thus to please him who is a Spirit and requires the heart, and they will see their folly when they find what a great deal of pains they have taken to no purpose for want of sincerity. They are *fools,* for they *consider not that they do evil ;* they think they are doing God and themselves good service when really they are putting a great affront upon God and a great cheat upon their own souls by their hypocritical devotions. Men may be doing evil even when they profess to be doing good, and even when they do not know it, when they do not consider it. *They know not but to do evil,* so some read it. Wicked minds cannot choose but sin, even in the acts of devotion. Or, They *consider not that they do evil ;* they act at a venture, right or wrong, pleasing to God or not, it is all one to them.

3. That we may not bring *the sacrifice of fools,* we must come to God's house with hearts disposed to know and do our duty. We must be *ready to hear,* that is, (1.) We must diligently *attend* to the word of God read and preached. "*Be swift to hear* the exposition which the priests give of the sacrifices, declaring the intent and meaning of them, and do not think it enough to gaze upon what they do, for it must be *a reasonable service,* otherwise it is *the sacrifice of fools.*" (2.) We must resolve to comply with the will of God as it is made known to us. *Hearing* is often put for *obeying,* and that is it that is *better than sacrifice,* 1 Sam. xv. 22 ; Isa. i. 15, 16. We come in a right frame to holy duties when we come with this upon our heart, *Speak, Lord, for thy servant hears. Let the word of the Lord come* (said a good man), *and if I had* 600 *necks I would bow them all to the authority of it.*

4. We must be very cautious and considerate in all our approaches and addresses to God (*v.* 2)· *Be not rash with thy mouth,* in making prayers, or protestations, or promises; *let not thy heart be hasty to utter any thing before God.* Note, (1.) When we are in the *house of God,* in solemn assemblies for religious worship, we are in a special manner before God and in his presence, there where he has promised to meet his people, where his eye is upon us and ours ought to be unto him. (2.) We have something to say, something to utter before God, when we *draw nigh to him* in holy duties; he is one *with whom we have to do,* with whom we have business of vast importance. If we come without an errand, we shall go away without any advantage. (3.) What we *utter before God* must come from *the heart,* and therefore we must not be *rash with our mouth,* never let our tongue outrun our thoughts in our devotions; the *words of our mouth* must always be the product of the *meditation of our hearts.* Thoughts are words to God, and words are but wind if they be not copied from the thoughts. Lip-labour, though ever so well laboured, if that be all, is but lost labour in religion, Matt. xv. 8, 9. (4.) It is not enough that what we say comes from the heart, but it must come from a composed heart, and not from a sudden heat or passion. As the mouth must not be rash, so the heart must not be hasty ; we must not only think, but think twice, before we speak, when we a.e to speak either from God in preaching or to God in prayer, and not utter any thing indecent and undigested, 1 Cor. xiv. 15.

5. We must be sparing of our words in the presence of God, that is, we must be reverent and deliberate, not talk to God as boldly and carelessly as we do to one another, not speak what comes uppermost, not repeat things over and over, as we do to one another, that what we say may be understood and remembered and may make impression; no, when we speak to God we must consider,

(1.) That between him and us there is an infinite distance: *God is in heaven, where he reigns in glory over us* and all the children of men, where he is attended with an innumerable company of holy angels and is *far exalted above all our blessing and praise. We are on earth,* the footstool of his throne; we are mean and vile, unlike God, and utterly unworthy to receive any favour from him or to have any communion with him. Therefore we must be very grave, humble, and serious, and be reverent in speaking to him, as we are when we speak to a great man that is much our superior; and, in token of this, *let our words be few,* that they may be *well chosen,* Job ix. 14. This does not condemn all long prayers; were they not good, the Pharisees would not have used them for a pretence; Christ prayed all night; and we are directed to *continue in prayer.* But it condemns careless heartless praying, *vain repetitions* (Matt. vi. 7), repeating *Pater-nosters* by tale. Let us speak to God, and of him, in his own words, words which the scripture teaches; and let our words, words of our own invention, be few, lest, not speaking by rule, we speak amiss. (2.) That the multiplying of words in our devotions will make them *the sacrifices of fools, v.* 3. As confused dreams, frightful and perplexed, and such as disturb the sleep, are an evidence of a hurry of business which fills our head, so many words and hasty ones, used in prayer, are an evidence of folly reigning in the heart, ignorance of and unacquaintedness with both God and ourselves, low thoughts of God, and careless thoughts of our own souls. Even in common conversation *a fool is known by the multitude of words;* those that know least talk most (*ch.* x. 11), particularly in devotion; there, no doubt, *a prating fool shall fall* (Prov. x. 8, 10), shall fall short of acceptance. Those are fools indeed who think they *shall be heard,* in prayer, *for their much speaking.*

4 When thou vowest a vow unto God, defer not to pay it; for *he hath no pleasure in fools:* pay that which thou hast vowed. 5 Better *is it* that thou shouldest not vow, than that thou shouldest vow and not pay. 6 Suffer not thy mouth to cause thy flesh to sin; neither say thou before the angel, that it *was* an error: wherefore should God be angry at thy voice, and destroy the work of thine hands? 7 For in the multitude of dreams and many words *there are* also *divers* vanities: but fear thou God. 8 If thou seest the oppression of the poor, and violent perverting of judgment and justice in a province, marvel not at the matter: for *he that is* higher than the highest regardeth; and *there be* higher than they.

Four things we are exhorted to in these verses:—

I. To be conscientious in paying our vows.

1. A vow is a bond upon the soul (Num. xxx. 2), by which we solemnly oblige ourselves, not only, in general, to do that which we are already bound to do, but, in some particular instances, to do that to do which we were not under any antecedent obligation, whether it respects honouring God or serving the interests of his kingdom among men. When, under the sense of some affliction (Ps. lxvi. 14), or in the pursuit of some mercy (1 Sam. i. 11), thou hast vowed such a vow as this *unto God,* know that *thou hast opened thy mouth unto the Lord and thou canst not go back;* therefore, (1.) Pay it; perform what thou hast promised; bring to God what thou hast dedicated and devoted to him: *Pay that which thou hast vowed;* pay it in full and *keep not back any part of the price;* pay it in kind, do not *alter it or change it,* so the law was, Lev. xxvii. 10. Have we vowed to *give our own selves unto the Lord?* Let us then be as good as our word, act in his service, to his glory, and not sacrilegiously alienate ourselves. (2.) *Defer not to pay it.* If it be in the power of thy hands to pay it to-day, leave it not till to-morrow; do not *beg a day,* nor put it off to a more convenient season. By delay the sense of the obligation slackens and cools, and is in danger of wearing off; we thereby discover a lothness and backwardness to perform our vow; and *qui non est hodie cras minus aptus erit—he who is not inclined to-day will be averse to-morrow.* The longer it is put off the more difficult it will be to bring ourselves to it; death may not only prevent the payment, but fetch thee to judgment, under the guilt of a broken vow, Ps. lxxvi. 11.

2. Two reasons are here given why we should speedily and cheerfully pay our vows:—(1.) Because otherwise we affront God; we play the fool with him, as if we designed to put a trick upon him; and *God has no pleasure in fools.* More is implied than is expressed; the meaning is, He greatly abhors such fools and such foolish dealings. *Has he need of fools?* No; *Be not deceived, God is not mocked,* but will surely and severely reckon with those that play fast and loose with him. (2.) Because otherwise we wrong ourselves, we lose the benefit of the making of the *vow,* nay, we incur the penalty for the breach of it; so that it would have been better a great deal *not to have vowed,* more safe and more to our advantage, than to *vow and not to pay.* Not to have *vowed* would have been but an omission, but to *vow and not pay* incurs the guilt of treachery and perjury; it is *lying to God,* Acts v. 4.

II. To be cautious in making our vows. This is necessary in order to our being conscientious in performing them, *v.* 6. 1. We must take heed that we never vow any thing that is sinful, or that may be an occasion of sin, for such a vow is ill-made and must be broken. *Suffer not thy mouth,* by such a vow, *to cause thy flesh to sin,* as Herod's rash promise caused him to cut off the head of John the Baptist. 2. We must not vow that which, through the frailty of the flesh, we have reason to fear we shall not be able to perform, as those that vow a single life and yet know not how to keep their vow. Hereby, (1.) They shame themselves; for they are forced to *say before the angel, It was an error,* that either they did not mean or did not consider what they said; and, take it which way you will, it is bad enough. "When thou hast made a *vow,* do not seek to evade it, nor find out excuses to get clear of the obligation of it; *say not before the priest,* who is called the *angel* or *messenger of the Lord of hosts,* that, upon second thoughts, thou hast changed thy mind, and desirest to be absolved from the obligation of thy vow; but stick to it, and do not seek a hole to creep out at." Some by *the angel* understand the guardian angel which they suppose to attend every man and to inspect what he does. Others understand it of Christ, *the Angel of the covenant,* who is present with his people in their assemblies, who searches the heart, and cannot be imposed upon; *provoke him not, for God's name is in him,* and he is represented as strict and jealous, Exod. xxiii. 20, 21. (2.) They expose themselves to the wrath of God, for he is *angry at the voice of* those that thus *lie unto him with their mouth and flatter him with their tongue,* and is displeased at their dissimulation, and *destroys the works of their hands,* that is, blasts their enterprises, and defeats those purposes which, when they made these vows, they were seeking to God for the success of. If we treacherously cancel the words of our mouths, and revoke our vows, God will justly overthrow our projects, and walk contrary, and at all adventures, with those that thus walk contrary, and at all adventures with him. It is *a snare to a man, after vows, to make enquiry.*

III. To keep up the fear of God, *v.* 7. Many, of old, pretended to know the mind of God by *dreams,* and were so full of them that they almost made God's people forget his name by their *dreams* (Jer. xxiii. 25, 26); and many now perplex themselves with their frightful or odd dreams, or with other people's dreams, as if they foreboded this or the other disaster. Those that heed dreams shall have a multitude of them to fill their heads with; but in them all *there are divers vanities,* as there are in many words, and the more if we regard them. "They are but like the idle impertinent chat of children and fools, and therefore never heed them; forget them; instead of repeating them lay no stress upon them, draw no disquieting conclusions from them, but *fear thou God;* have an eye to

his sovereign dominion, set him before thee, keep thyself in his love, and be afraid of offending him, and then thou wilt not disturb thyself with foolish dreams." The way not to be dismayed at the signs of heaven, nor afraid *of the idols of the heathen,* is to *fear God as King of nations,* Jer. x. 2, 5, 7.

IV. With that to keep down the fear of man, *v.* 8. "Set God before thee, and then, if *thou seest the oppression of the poor,* thou wilt not *marvel at the matter,* nor find fault with divine Providence, nor think the worse of the institution of magistracy, when thou seest the ends of it thus perverted, nor of religion, when thou seest it will not secure men from suffering wrong. Observe here, 1. A melancholy sight on earth, and such as cannot but trouble every good man that has a sense of justice and a concern for mankind, to see *the oppression of the poor* because they are poor and cannot defend themselves, and the *violent perverting of judgment and justice in a province,* oppression under colour of law and backed with power. The kingdom in general may have a good government, and yet it may so happen that a particular province may be committed to a bad man, by whose mal-administration justice may be perverted; so hard it is for the wisest of kings, in giving preferments, to be sure of their men; they can but redress the grievance when it appears. 2. A comfortable sight in heaven. When things look thus dismal we may satisfy ourselves with this, (1.) That, though oppressors be *high,* God is *above them,* and in that very thing wherein *they deal proudly,* Exod. xviii. 11. God is *higher than the highest* of creatures, than the highest of princes, than the king that is *higher than Agag* (Num. xxiv. 7), than the highest angels, the *thrones and dominions* of the upper world. God is the *Most High over all the earth,* and his *glory is above the heavens;* before him princes are worms, the brightest but glow-worms. (2.) That, though oppressors be secure, God has his eye upon them, takes notice of, and will reckon for, all their violent perverting of judgment; *he regards,* not only sees it but observes it, and keeps it on record, to be called over again; his *eyes are upon their ways.* See Job xxiv. 23. (3.) That there is a world of angels, for there are *higher than they,* who are employed by the divine justice for protecting the injured and punishing the injurious. Sennacherib valued himself highly upon his potent army, but one angel proved too hard for him and all his forces. Some, by those *that are higher than they* understand the great council of the nation, the presidents to whom the *princes of the provinces are accountable* (Dan. vi. 2), the senate that receive complaints against the proconsuls, the courts above to which appeals are made from the inferior courts, which are necessary to the good government of a kingdom. Let it be a check to oppressors that perhaps their superiors on earth may call them to an account; however, God the Supreme in heaven will.

9 Moreover the profit of the earth is for all: the king *himself* is served by the field. 10 He that loveth silver shall not be satisfied with silver; nor he that loveth abundance with increase: this *is* also vanity. 11 When goods increase, they are increased that eat them: and what good *is there* to the owners thereof, saving the beholding *of them* with their eyes? 12 The sleep of a labouring man *is* sweet, whether he eat little or much: but the abundance of the rich will not suffer him to sleep. 13 There is a sore evil *which* I have seen under the sun, *namely*, riches kept for the owners thereof to their hurt. 14 But those riches perish by evil travail: and he begetteth a son, and *there is* nothing in his hand. 15 As he came forth of his mother's womb, naked shall he return to go as he came, and shall take nothing of his labour, which he may carry away in his hand. 16 And this also *is* a sore evil, *that* in all points as he came, so shall he go: and what profit hath he that hath laboured for the wind? 17 All his days also he eateth in darkness, and *he hath* much sorrow and wrath with his sickness.

Solomon had shown the vanity of pleasure, gaiety, and fine works, of honour, power, and royal dignity; and there is many a covetous worldling that will agree with him, and speak as slightly as he does of these things; but money, he thinks, is a substantial thing, and if he can but have enough of that he is happy. This is the mistake which Solomon attacks, and attempts to rectify, in these verses; he shows that there is as much vanity in great riches, and the *lust of the eye* about them, as there is in the *lusts of the flesh* and the *pride of life*, and a man can make himself no more happy by hoarding an estate than by spending it.

I. He grants that the products of the earth, for the support and comfort of human life, are valuable things (*v.* 9): *The profit of the earth is for all.* Man's body, being made of the earth, thence has its maintenance (Job xxviii. 5); and that it has so, and that a *barren land* is not *made his dwelling* (as he has deserved for being rebellious, Ps. lxviii. 6), is an instance of God's great bounty to him. There is *profit to be got out of the earth*, and it is *for all;* all need it; it is appointed for all; there is enough for all. It is not only for all men, but for all the inferior creatures;

the same ground brings *grass for the cattle* that brings *herbs for the service of men.* Israel had *bread from heaven, angels' food*, but (which is a humbling consideration) the earth is our storehouse and the beasts are fellow-commoners with us. *The king himself is served of the field,* and would be ill served, and would be quite starved, without its products. This puts a great honour upon the husbandman's calling, that it is the most necessary of all to the support of man's life. The many have the benefit of it; the mighty cannot live without it; it is *for all;* it is for the *king himself.* Those that have an abundance of the fruits of the earth must remember *they are for all*, and therefore must look upon themselves but as stewards of their abundance, out of which they must give to those that need. Dainty meats and soft clothing are only *for some*, but the *fruit of the earth is for all.* And even those that *suck the abundance of the seas* (Deut. xxxiii. 19) cannot be without the fruit of the earth, while those that have a competency of the *fruit of the earth* may despise the *abundance of the seas.*

II. He maintains that the riches that are more than these, that are for hoarding, not for use, are *vain things*, and will not make a man easy or happy. That which our Saviour has said (Luke xii. 15), *that a man's life consists not in the abundance of the things which he possesses*, is what Solomon here undertakes to prove by various arguments.

1. The more men have the more they would have, *v.* 10. A man may have but a little silver and be satisfied with it, may know when he has enough and covet no more. *Godliness, with contentment, is great gain. I have enough*, says Jacob; *I have all, and abound*, says St. Paul: but, (1.) He that *loves silver*, and sets his heart upon it, will never think he has enough, but *enlarges his desire as hell* (Hab. ii. 5), *lays house to house and field to field* (Isa. v. 8), and, like *the daughters of the horse-leech, still cries, Give, give.* Natural desires are at rest when that which is desired is obtained, but corrupt desires are insatiable. Nature is content with little, grace with less, but lust with nothing. (2.) He that has silver in abundance, and has it increasing ever so fast upon him, yet does not find that it yields any solid satisfaction to his soul. There are bodily desires which silver itself will not satisfy; if a man be hungry, ingots of silver will do no more to satisfy his hunger than clods of clay. Much less will worldly abundance satisfy spiritual desires; he that has ever so much silver covets more, not only of that, but of something else, something of another nature. Those that make themselves drudges to the world are spending their *labour for that which satisfies not* (Isa. lv. 2), which fills the belly, but will never fill the soul, Ezek. vii. 19.

2. The more men have the more occasion they have for it, and the more they have to do with it, so that it is as broad as it is long:

When *goods increase, they are increased that eat them, v.* 11. *The more meat the more mouths.* Does the estate thrive? And does not the family at the same time grow more numerous and the children grow up to need more? The more men have the better house they must keep, the more servants they must employ, the more guests they must entertain, the more they must give to the poor, and the more they will have hanging on them, for where *the carcase is the eagles will be.* What we have more than food and raiment we have *for others;* and then *what good is there to the owners* themselves, but the pleasure of *beholding it with their eyes?* And a poor pleasure it is. An empty speculation is all the difference between the owners and the sharers; the owner sees that as his own which those about him enjoy as much of the real benefit of as he; only he has the satisfaction of doing good to others, which indeed is a satisfaction to one who believes what Christ said, that *it is more blessed to give than to receive;* but to a covetous man, who thinks all lost that goes beside himself, it is a constant vexation to see others eat of his increase.

3. The more men have the more care they have about it, which perplexes them and disturbs their repose, *v.* 12. Refreshing sleep is as much the support and comfort of this life as food is. Now, (1.) Those commonly sleep best that work hard and have but what they work for: *The sleep of the labouring man is sweet,* not only because he has tired himself with his labour, which makes his sleep the more welcome to him and makes him sleep soundly, but because he has little to fill his head with care and so break his sleep. His sleep is sweet, though he eat but little and have but little to eat, for his weariness rocks him asleep; and, though he eat much, yet he can sleep well, for his labour gets him a good digestion. The sleep of the diligent Christian, and his long sleep, is sweet; for, having spent himself and his time in the service of God, he can cheerfully return to God and repose in him as his rest. (2.) Those that have every thing else often fail to secure a good night's sleep. Either their eyes are held waking or their sleeps are unquiet and do not refresh them; and it is their abundance that breaks their sleep and disturbs it, both the abundance of their care (as that rich man's who, when his ground brought forth plentifully, thought within himself, *What shall I do?* Luke xii. 17) and the abundance of what they eat and drink, which overcharges the heart, makes them sick, and so hinders their repose. Ahasuerus, after a banquet of wine, could not sleep; and perhaps consciousness of guilt, both in getting and using what they have, breaks their sleep as much as any thing. But *God gives his beloved sleep.*

4. The more men have the more danger they are in both of doing mischief and of having mischief done them (*v.* 13): *There is an evil, a sore evil,* which Solomon himself

had *seen under the sun,* in this lower world, this theatre of sin and woe—*riches kept for the owners thereof* (who have been industrious to hoard them and keep them safely) *to their hurt;* they would have been better without them. (1.) Their riches *do them hurt,* make them proud, secure, and in love with the world, draw away their hearts from God and duty, and make it very difficult for them to enter into the kingdom of heaven, nay, help to shut them out of it. (2.) They *do hurt with their riches,* which not only put them into a capacity of gratifying their own lusts and living luxuriously, but give them an opportunity of oppressing others and dealing hardly with them. (3.) Often they sustain *hurt by their riches.* They would not be envied, would not be robbed, if they were not rich. It is the fat beast that is led first to the slaughter. A very rich man (as one observes) has sometimes been excepted out of a general pardon, both as to life and estate, merely on account of his vast and overgrown estate; so riches *often take away the life of the owners thereof,* Prov. i. 19.

5. The more men have the more they have to lose, and perhaps they may lose it all, *v.* 14. Those riches that have been laid up with a great deal of pains, and kept with a great deal of care, *perish by evil travail,* by the very pains and care which they take to secure and increase them. Many a one has ruined his estate by being over-solicitous to advance it and make it more, and has lost all by catching at all. Riches are perishing things, and all our care about them cannot make them otherwise; they *make themselves wings and fly away.* He that thought he should have made his son a gentleman leaves him a beggar; he *begets a son,* and brings him up in the prospect of an estate, but, when he dies, leaves it under a charge of debt as much as it is worth, so that *there is nothing in his hand.* This is a common case; estates that made a great show do not prove what they seemed, but cheat the heir.

6. How much soever men have when they die, they must leave it all behind them (*v.* 15, 16): *As he came forth of his mother's womb naked, so shall he return;* only as his friends, when he came naked into the world, in pity to him, helped him with swaddling-clothes, so, when he goes out, they help him with grave-clothes, and that is all. See Job i. 21; Ps. xlix. 17. This is urged as a reason why we should be content with such things as we have, 1 Tim. vi. 7. In respect of the body we must go as we came; the dust shall return to the earth as it was. But sad is our case if the soul return as it came, for we were born in sin, and if we die in sin, unsanctified, we had better never have been born; and that seems to be the case of the worldling here spoken of, for he is said to *return in all points as he came,* as sinful, as miserable, and much more so. This is a *sore evil;* he thinks it so whose heart is glued to the world, that he

shall take nothing of his labour which he may carry away in his hand; his riches will not go with him into another world nor stand him in any stead there. If we labour in religion, the grace and comfort we get by that labour we may carry away in our hearts, and shall be the better for it to eternity; that is meat that endures. But if we labour only for the world, to fill our hands with that, we cannot take that away with us; we are born with our hands griping, but die with them extended, letting go what we held fast. So that, upon the whole matter, he may well ask, *What profit has he that has laboured for the wind?* Note, Those that labour for the world labour for the wind, for that which has more sound than substance, which is uncertain, and always shifting its point, unsatisfying, and often hurtful, which we cannot hold fast, and which, if we take up with it as our portion, will no more feed us than the *wind*, Hos. xii. 1. Men will see that they have *laboured for the wind* when at death they find the profit of their labour is all gone, gone like the wind, they know not whither.

7. Those that have much, if they set their hearts upon it, have not only uncomfortable deaths, but uncomfortable lives too, *v.* 17. This covetous worldling, that is so bent upon raising an estate, *all his days eats in darkness and much sorrow, and it is his sickness and wrath;* he has not only no pleasure of his estate, nor any enjoyment of it himself, for he *eats the bread of sorrow* (Ps. cxxvii. 2), but a great deal of vexation to see others eat of it. His necessary expenses make him sick, make him fret, and he seems as if he were angry that himself and those about him cannot live without meat. As we read the last clause, it intimates how ill this covetous worldling can bear the common and unavoidable calamities of human life. When he is in health he *eats in darkness,* always dull with care and fear about what he has; but, if he be sick, *he has much sorrow and wrath with his sickness;* he is vexed that his sickness takes him off from his business and hinders him in his pursuits of the world, vexed that all his wealth will not give him any ease or relief, but especially terrified with the apprehensions of death (which his diseases are the harbingers of), of leaving this world and the things of it behind him, which he has set his affections upon, and removing to a world he has made no preparation for. He has not any *sorrow after a godly sort*, does not *sorrow to repentance,* but he has *sorrow and wrath,* is angry at the providence of God, angry at his sickness, angry at all about him, fretful and peevish, which doubles his affliction, which a good man lessens and lightens by patience and joy in his sickness.

18 Behold *that* which I have seen: *it is* good and comely *for one* to eat and to drink, and to enjoy the good of all his labour that he taketh under the sun all the days of his life, which God giveth him : for it *is* his portion. 19 Every man also to whom God hath given riches and wealth, and hath given him power to eat thereof, and to take his portion, and to rejoice in his labour; this *is* the gift of God. 20 For he shall not much remember the days of his life; because God answereth *him* in the joy of his heart.

Solomon, from the vanity of riches hoarded up, here infers that the best course we can take is to use well what we have, to serve God with it, to do good with it, and take the comfort of it to ourselves and our families; this he had pressed before, *ch.* ii. 24; iii. 22. Observe, 1. What it is that is here recommended to us, not to indulge the appetites of the flesh, or to take up with present pleasures or profits for our portion, but soberly and moderately to make use of what Providence has allotted for our comfortable passage through this world. We must not starve ourselves through covetousness, because we cannot afford ourselves food convenient, nor through eagerness in our worldly pursuits, nor through excessive care and grief, but *eat and drink* what is fit for us to keep our bodies in good plight for the serving of our souls in God's service. We must not kill ourselves with *labour,* and then leave others *to enjoy the good* of it, but take the comfort of that which our hands have laboured for, and that not now and then, but *all the days of our life which God gives us.* Life is God's gift, and he has appointed us *the number of the days* of our life (Job. xiv. 5); let us therefore spend those days in *serving the Lord our God with joyfulness and gladness of heart.* We must not do the business of our calling as a drudgery, and make ourselves slaves to it, but we must *rejoice in our labour,* not grasp at more business than we can go through without perplexity and disquiet, but take a pleasure in the calling wherein God has put us, and go on in the business of it with cheerfulness. This is to *rejoice in our labour,* whatever it is, as *Zebulun in his going out and Issachar in his tents.* 2. What is urged to recommend it to us. (1.) That *it is good and comely* to do this. It is well, and it looks well. Those that cheerfully use what God has given them thereby honour the giver, answer the intention of the gift, act rationally and generously, do good in the world, and make what they have turn to the best account, and this is both their credit and their comfort; *it is good and comely;* there is duty and decency in it. (2.) That it is all the good we can have out of the things of this world : *It is our portion,* and in doing thus we take our portion, and make the best of bad. This is our part of our worldly possessions. God must have his part, the poor theirs, and our families theirs, but this is ours; it is all that falls to our lot out of them. (3.) That a heart to do thus is such a gift of God's grace as crowns all the gifts of his providence. If God has given a man *riches and wealth,* he completes the favour, and makes that a blessing indeed, if withal he *gives him power to eat thereof,* wisdom and grace to take the good of it and to do good with it. If this *is God's gift,* we must *covet* it *earnestly* as *the best gift* relating to our enjoyments in this world. (4.) That this is the way to make our own lives easy and to relieve ourselves against the many toils and troubles which our lives on earth are incident to (*v.* 20): *He shall not much remember the days of his life,* the days of his sorrow and sore travail, his working days, his weeping days. He shall either forget them or remember them as waters that pass away; he shall not much lay to heart his crosses, nor long retain the bitter relish of them, *because God answers him in the joy of his heart,* balances all the grievances of his labour with the joy of it and recompenses him for it by giving him to *eat the labour of his hands.* If he does not answer all his desires and expectations, in the letter of them, yet he answers them with that which is more than equivalent, *in the joy of his heart.* A cheerful spirit is a great blessing; it makes the yoke of our employments easy and the burden of our afflictions light.

CHAP. VI.

In this chapter, I. The royal preacher goes on further to show the vanity of worldly wealth, when men place their happiness in it and are eager and inordinate in laying it up. Riches, in the hands of a man that is wise and generous, are good for something, but in the hands of a sordid, sneaking, covetous miser, they are good for nothing. 1. He takes an account of the possessions and enjoyments which such a man may have. He has wealth (ver. 2), he has children to inherit it (ver. 3), and lives long, ver. 3, 6. 2. He describes his folly in not taking the comfort of it; he has no power to eat of it, lets strangers devour it, is never filled with good, and at last has no burial, ver. 2, 3. 3. He condemns it as an evil, a common evil, vanity, and a disease, ver. 1, 2. 4. He prefers the condition of a still-born child before the condition of such a one, ver. 3. The still-born child's infelicity is only negative (ver. 4, 5), but that of the covetous worldling is positive; he lives a great while to see himself miserable, ver. 6. 5. He shows the vanity of riches as pertaining only to the body, and giving no satisfaction to the mind (ver. 7, 8), and of those boundless desires with which covetous people vex themselves (ver. 9), which, if they be gratified ever so fully, leave a man but a man still, ver. 10. II. He concludes this discourse of the vanity of the creature with this plain inference from the whole, That it is folly to think of making up a happiness for ourselves in the things of this world, ver. 11, 12. Our satisfaction must be in another life, not in this.

THERE is an evil which I have seen under the sun, and it *is* common among men: 2 A man to whom God hath given riches, wealth, and honour, so that he wanteth nothing for his soul of all that he desireth, yet God giveth him not power to eat thereof, but a stranger eateth it: this *is* vanity, and it *is* an evil disease. 3 If a man beget a hundred *children,* and live many years, so that the days of his years be many, and his soul be not filled with good, and also *that* he have no burial; I say, *that* an untimely birth *is* better than he. 4 For he cometh in with

vanity, and departeth in darkness, and his name shall be covered with darkness. 5 Moreover he hath not seen the sun, nor known *any thing*: this hath more rest than the other. 6 Yea, though he live a thousand years twice *told,* yet hath he seen no good: do not all go to one place?

Solomon had shown, in the close of the foregoing chapter, how good it is to make a comfortable use of the gifts of God's providence; now here he shows the evil of the contrary, having and not using, gathering to lay up for I know not what contingent emergencies to come, not to lay out on the most urgent occasions present. This *is an evil which* Solomon himself saw *under the sun, v.* 1. A great deal of evil there is *under the sun.* There is a world above the sun where there is no evil, yet God *causes his sun to shine upon the evil* as well as upon *the good,* which is an aggravation of the evil. God has lighted up a candle for his servants to work by, but they bury their talent as slothful and unprofitable, and so waste the light and are unworthy of it. Solomon, as a king, inspected the manners of his subjects, and took notice of this evil as a prejudice to the public, who are damaged not only by men's prodigality on the one hand, but by their penuriousness on the other. As it is with the blood in the natural body, so it is with the wealth of the body politic, if, instead of circulating, it stagnates, it will be of ill consequence. Solomon as a preacher observed the evils that were done that he might reprove them and warn people against them. This evil was, in his days, *common,* and yet then there was great plenty of silver and gold, which, one would think, should have made people less fond of riches; the times also were peaceable, nor was there any prospect of trouble, which to some is a temptation to hoard. But no providence will of itself, unless the grace of God work with it, cure the corrupt affection that is in the carnal mind to the world and the things of it; nay, when *riches increase* we are most apt to set our *hearts upon them.* Now concerning this miser observe,

I. The abundant reason he has to serve God with joyfulness and gladness of heart; how well God has done for him.

1. He *has given* him *riches, wealth, and honour, v.* 2. Note, (1.) *Riches* and *wealth* commonly gain people *honour* among men. Though it be but an image, if it be a *golden* image, *all people, nations, and languages,* will *fall down and worship it.* (2.) *Riches, wealth, and honour,* are God's gifts, the gifts of his providence, and not given, as his rain and sunshine, alike to all, but to some, and not to others, as God sees fit. (3.) Yet they are given to many that do not make a good use of them, to many to whom God does not give wisdom and grace to take the comfort of

them and serve God with them. The gifts of common providence are bestowed on many to whom are denied the gifts of special grace, without which the gifts of providence often do more hurt than good.

2. *He wants nothing for his soul of all that he desires.* Providence has been so liberal to him that he has as much as *heart could wish,* and *more,* Ps. lxxiii. 7. He does not desire grace for his soul, the better part; all he desires is enough to gratify the sensual appetite, and that he has; his *belly is filled with these hidden treasures,* Ps. xvii. 14.

3. He is supposed to have a numerous family, to *beget a hundred children,* which are the stay and strength of his house and as a *quiver full of arrows* to him, which are the honour and credit of his house, and in whom he has the prospect of having his name built up and having all the immortality this world can give him. *They are full of children* (Ps. xvii. 14), while many of God's people are written childless and stripped of all.

4. To complete his happiness, he is supposed to *live many years,* or rather many *days,* for our life is to be reckoned rather by days than years : *The days of his years are many,* and so healthful is his constitution, and so slowly does age creep upon him, that they are likely to be many more. Nay, he is supposed to *live a thousand years* (which no man, that we know of, ever did), nay, *a thousand years twice told,* a small part of which time, one would think, were enough to convince men, by their own experience, of the folly both of those that expect to find all good in worldly wealth, and of those that expect to find any good in it but in using it.

II. The little heart he has to use this which God gives him, for the ends and purposes for which it was given him. This is his fault and folly that he *renders not again according to the benefit done unto him,* and *serves not the Lord God* his benefactor, *with joyfulness and gladness of heart, in the abundance of all things.* In the day of prosperity he is not joyful. *Tristis es, et felix?—Art thou happy, yet sad?* See his folly : 1. He cannot find in his heart to take the comfort of what he. has himself. He has meat before him; he has wherewith to maintain himself and his family comfortably, but he has *not power to eat thereof.* His sordid niggardly temper will not suffer him to lay it out, no, not upon himself, no, not upon that which is most necessary for himself. He has not power to reason himself out of this absurdity, to conquer his covetous humour. He is weak indeed, who has not power to use what God gives him, for *God gives him not* that *power,* but withholds it from him, to punish him for his other abuses of his wealth. Because he has not the will to serve God with it, God denies him the power to serve himself with it. 2. He suffers those to prey upon him that he is under no obligation to: *A stranger eateth it.* This is the common fate of misers;

they will not trust their own children perhaps, but retainers and hangers-on, that have the art of wheedling, insinuate themselves into them, and find ways of devouring what they have, or getting it to be left to them by their wills. God orders it so that *a stranger eats it. Strangers devour his strength,* Hos. vii. 9; Prov. v. 10. This may be well called *vanity, and an evil disease.* What we have we have in vain if we do not use it; and that temper of mind which keeps us from using it. Our worst diseases are those that arise from the corruption of our own hearts. 3. He deprives himself of the good that he might have had of his worldly possessions, not only forfeits it, but robs himself of it and throws it from him: *His soul is not filled with good, v.* 3. He is still unsatisfied and uneasy. His hands are filled with riches, his barns filled, and his bags filled, but *his soul is not filled with good,* no, not with that good, for it is still craving more. Nay (*v.* 6), *he has not seen good;* he cannot so much as please his eye, for that is still looking further and looking with envy on those that have more. He has not even the sensible good of an estate. Though he looks not beyond the things that are seen, yet he looks not with any true pleasure even on them. 4. *He has no burial,* none agreeable to his rank, no decent burial, but *the burial of an ass.* Through the sordidness of his temper he will not allow himself a fashionable burial, but forbids it, or the strangers that have eaten him up leave him so poor, at last, that he has not wherewithal, or those to whom he leaves what he has have so little esteem for his memory, and are so greedy of what they are to have from him, that they will not be at the charges of burying him handsomely, which his own children, if he had left it to them, would not have grudged him.

III. The preference which the preacher gives to an untimely birth before him : *An untimely birth,* a child that is carried from the womb to the grave, *is better than he.* Better is the fruit that drops from the tree before it is ripe than that which is left to hang on till it is rotten. Job, in his passion, thinks the condition of *an untimely birth* better than his when he was in adversity (Job iii. 16); but Solomon here pronounces it better than the condition of a worldling in his greatest prosperity, when the world smiles upon him. 1. He grants the condition of *an untimely birth,* upon many accounts, to be very sad (*v.* 4, 5): *He comes in with vanity* (for, as to this world, he that is born and dies immediately was born in vain), and he *departs in darkness;* little or no notice is taken of him; being an abortive, he has no *name,* or, if he had, it would soon be forgotten and buried in oblivion; it would *be covered with darkness,* as the body is with the earth. Nay (*v.* 5), *he has not seen the sun,* but from the darkness of the womb he is hurried immediately to that of the grave, and, which is worse than not being known to any, he has not *known any thing*, and therefore has come short of that which is the greatest pleasure and honour of man. Those that live in wilful ignorance, and know nothing to purpose, are no better than *an untimely birth* that *has not seen the sun nor known any thing.* 2. Yet he prefers it before that of a covetous miser. *This* untimely birth *has more rest than the other*, for *this* has some rest, but *the other* has none; *this* has no trouble and disquiet, but *the other* is in perpetual agitation, and has nothing but trouble, trouble of his own making. The shorter the life is the longer the rest; and the fewer the days, and the less we have to do with this troublesome world, the less trouble we know.

> 'Tis better die a child at four,
> Than live, and die so at fourscore.

The reason he gives why *this has more rest* is because *all go to one place* to rest in, and this is sooner at his rest, *v.* 6. He that *lives a thousand years* goes to the same place with the child that does not live an hour, *ch.* iii. 20. The grave is the place we shall all meet in. Whatever differences there may be in men's condition in this world, they must all die, are all under the same sentence, and, to outward appearance, their deaths are alike. The grave is to one, as well as another, a land of silence, of darkness, of separation from the living, and a sleeping-place. It is the common rendezvous of rich and poor, honourable and mean, learned and unlearned; the short-lived and long-lived meet in the grave, only one rides post thither, the other goes by a slower conveyance; the dust of both mingles, and lies undistinguished.

7 All the labour of man *is* for his mouth, and yet the appetite is not filled. **8** For what hath the wise more than the fool? what hath the poor, that knoweth to walk before the living? **9** Better *is* the sight of the eyes than the wandering of the desire: this *is* also vanity and vexation of spirit. **10** That which hath been is named already, and it is known that it *is* man: neither may he contend with him that is mightier than he.

The preacher here further shows the vanity and folly of heaping up worldly wealth and expecting happiness in it.

I. How much soever we toil about the world, and get out of it, we can have for ourselves no more than a maintenance (*v.* 7): *All the labour of man is for his mouth*, which *craves it of him* (Prov. xvi. 26); it is but *food and raiment;* what is more others have, not we; it is all *for the mouth. Meats* are but *for the belly and the belly for meats;* there is nothing for the head and heart, nothing to nourish or enrich the soul. A little will serve

to sustain us comfortably and a great deal can do no more.

II. Those that have ever so much are still craving; let a man labour ever so much *for his mouth, yet the appetite is not filled.* 1. Natural desires are still returning, still pressing; a man may be feasted to-day and yet hungry to-morrow. 2. Worldly sinful desires are insatiable, *ch.* v. 10. Wealth to a worldling is like drink to one in a dropsy, which does but increase the thirst. Some read the whole verse thus: *Though all a man's labour fall out to his own mind (ori ejus obveniat—so as to correspond with his views,* Juv.), just as himself would have it, *yet his desire is not satisfied*, still he has a mind to something more. 3. The desires of the soul find nothing in the wealth of the world to give them any satisfaction. *The soul is not filled*, so the word is. When God *gave* Israel *their request* he *sent leanness into their souls*, Ps. cvi. 15. He was a fool who, when his barns were full, said, *Soul, take thine ease.*

III. A fool may have as much worldly wealth, and may enjoy as much of the pleasure of it, as a wise man; nay, and perhaps not be so sensible of the vexation of it: *What has the wise more than the fool?* v. 8. Perhaps he has not so good an estate, so good a trade, nor such good preferment as the fool has. Nay, suppose them to be equal in their possessions, what can a wise man, a scholar, a wit, a politician, squeeze out of his estate more than needful supplies? and a half-witted man may do this. A fool can fare as well and relish it, can dress as well, and make as good a figure in any public appearance, as a wise man; so that if there were not pleasures and honour peculiar to the mind, which *the wise man has more than the fool*, as to this world they would be upon a level.

IV. Even a poor man, who has business, and is discreet, diligent, and dexterous, in the management of it, may get as comfortably through this world as he that is loaded with an overgrown estate. Consider *what the poor has* less than the rich, if he but *knows to walk before the living*, knows how to conduct himself decently, and do his duty to all, how to get an honest livelihood by his labour, how to spend his time well and improve his opportunities. *What has* he? Why, he is better beloved and more respected among his neighbours, and has a better interest than many a rich man that is griping and haughty. *What has* he? Why he has as much of the comfort of this life, has *food and raiment*, and is *therewith content*, and so is as truly rich as he that has abundance.

V. The enjoyment of what we have cannot but be acknowledged more rational than a greedy grasping at more (*v.* 9): *Better is the sight of the eyes*, making the best of that which is present, *than the wandering of the desire*, the uneasy walking of the soul after things at a distance, and the affecting of a variety of imaginary satisfactions. He is much happier that is always content, though he has ever so little, than he that is always coveting, though he has ever so much. We cannot say, *Better is the sight of the eyes than the fixing of the desire* upon God, and the resting of the soul in him; it is better to live by faith in things to come than to live by sense, which dwells only upon present things; but *better is the sight of the eyes than the* roving *of the desire* after the world, and the things of it, than,which nothing is more uncertain nor more unsatisfying at the best. *This wandering of the desire is vanity and vexation of spirit.* It *is vanity* at the best; if what is desired, be obtained, it proves not what we promised ourselves from it, but commonly *the wandering desire* is crossed and disappointed, and then it turns to *vexation of spirit.*

VI. Our lot, whatever it is, is that which is appointed us by the counsel of God, which cannot be altered, and it is therefore our wisdom to reconcile ourselves to it and cheerfully to acquiesce in it (*v.* 10): *That which has been,* or (as some read it) *that which is,* and so likewise that which shall be, *is named already;* it is already determined in the divine foreknowledge, and all our care and pains cannot make it otherwise than as it is fixed. *Jacta est alea—The die is cast.* It is therefore folly to quarrel with that which will be as it is, and wisdom to make a virtue of necessity. We shall have what pleases God, and let that please us.

VII. Whatever we attain to in this world, still we are but men, and the greatest possessions and preferments cannot set us above the common accidents of human life: *That which has been,* and is, that busy animal that makes such a stir and such a noise in the world, *is named already.* He that made him gave him his name, *and it is known that it is man;* that is his name by which he must know himself, and it is a humbling name, Gen. v. 2. He *called their name Adam;* and all theirs have the same character, *red earth.* Though a man could make himself master of all the treasures of kings and provinces, yet he is a man still, mean, mutable, and mortal, and may at any time be involved in the calamities that are *common to men.* It is good for rich and great men to know and consider that they are *but men,* Ps. ix. 20. *It is known that* they are but men; let them put what face they will upon it, and, like the king of Tyre, *set their heart as the heart of God,* yet the Egyptians are men, and not gods, and it is known that they are so.

VIII. How far soever our desires wander, and how closely soever our endeavours keep pace with them, we cannot strive with the divine Providence, but must submit to the disposals of it, whether we will or no. If *it is man, he may not contend with him that is mightier than he.* It is presumption to arraign God's proceedings, and to charge him

with folly or iniquity; nor is it to any purpose to complain of him, for *he is in one mind and who can turn him?* Elihu pacifies Job with this incontestable principle, That *God is greater than man* (Job xxxiii. 12) and therefore *man may not contend with him,* nor resist his judgments, when they come with commission. A man cannot with the greatest riches make his part good against the arrests of sickness or death, but must yield to his fate.

11 Seeing there be many things that increase vanity, what *is* man the better? 12 For who knoweth what *is* good for man in *this* life, all the days of his vain life which he spendeth as a shadow? for who can tell a man what shall be after him under the sun?

Here, 1. Solomon lays down his conclusion which he had undertaken to prove, as that which was fully confirmed by the foregoing discourse: *There be many things that increase vanity;* the life of man is vain, at the best, and there are abundance of accidents that concur to make it more so; even that which pretends to increase the wealth and pleasure does but increase the vanity and make it more vexatious. 2. He draws some inferences from it, which serve further to evince the truth of it. (1.) That a man is never the nearer to true happiness for the abundance that he has in this world. *What is man the better* for his wealth and pleasure, his honour and preferment? What remains to man? What residuum has he, what overplus, what real advantage, when he comes to balance his accounts? Nothing that will do him any good or turn to account. (2.) That we do not know what to wish for, because that which we promise ourselves most satisfaction in often proves most vexatious to us: *Who knows what is good for a man in this life,* where every thing is vanity, and any thing, even that which we most covet, may prove a calamity to us? Thoughtful people are in care to do every thing for the best, if they knew it; but as it is an instance of the corruption of our hearts that we are apt to desire that as good for us which is really hurtful, as children that cry for knives to cut their fingers with, so is it an instance of the vanity of this world that what, according to all probable conjectures, seems to be for the best, often proves otherwise; such is our shortsightedness concerning the issues and events of things, and such broken reeds are all our creature-confidences. We know not how to advise others for the best, nor how to act ourselves, because that which we apprehend likely to be for our welfare may become a trap. (3.) That therefore our life upon earth is what we have no reason to take any great complacency in, or to be confident of the continuance of. It is to be reckoned by *days;* it is but a *vain life,* and we spend it *as a shadow,* so little is there in it substantial, so fleeting, so uncertain, so transitory is it, and so little in it to be fond of or to be depended on. If all the comforts of life be vanity, life itself can have no great reality in it to constitute a happiness for us. (4.) That our expectations from this world are as uncertain and deceitful as our enjoyments are. Since every thing is vanity, *Who can tell a man what shall be after him under the sun?* He can no more please himself with the hopes of *what shall be after him,* to his children and family, than with the relish of what is with him, since he can neither foresee himself, nor can any one else foretel to him, *what shall be after him.* Nor shall he have any intelligence sent him of it when he is gone. *His sons come to honour, and he knows it not.* So that, look which way we will, *Vanity of vanity, all is vanity.*

CHAP. VII.

Solomon had given many proofs, and instances of the vanity of this world and the things of it; now, in this chapter, I. He recommends to us some good means proper to be used for the redress of these grievances and the arming of ourselves against the mischief we are in danger of from them, that we may make the best of the bad, as, 1. Care of our reputation, ver. 1. 2. Seriousness, ver. 2—6. 3. Calmness of spirit, ver. 7—10. 4. Prudence in the management of all our affairs, ver. 11, 12. 5. Submission to the will of God in all events, accommodating ourselves to every condition, ver. 13—15. 6. A conscientious avoiding of all dangerous extremes, ver. 16—18. 7. Mildness and tenderness towards those that have been injurious to us, ver. 19—22. In short, the best way to save ourselves from the vexation which the vanity of the world creates us is to keep our temper and to maintain a strict government of our passions. II. He laments his own iniquity, as that which was more vexatious than any of these vanities, that mystery of iniquity, the having of many wives, by which he was drawn away from God and his duty, ver. 23—29.

A GOOD name *is* better than precious ointment; and the day of death than the day of one's birth. 2 *It is* better to go to the house of mourning, than to go to the house of feasting: for that *is* the end of all men; and the living will lay *it* to his heart. 3 Sorrow *is* better than laughter: for by the sadness of the countenance the heart is made better. 4 The heart of the wise *is* in the house of mourning; but the heart of fools *is* in the house of mirth. 5 *It is* better to hear the rebuke of the wise, than for a man to hear the song of fools. 6 For as the crackling of thorns under a pot, so *is* the laughter of the fool: this also *is* vanity.

In these verses Solomon lays down some great truths which seem paradoxes to the unthinking part, that is, the far greatest part, of mankind.

I. That the honour of virtue is really more valuable and desirable than all the wealth and pleasure in this world (*v.* 1): *A good name is before good ointment* (so it may be read); it is preferable to it, and will be rather chosen by all that are wise. *Good ointment* is here put for all the profits of the earth (among the products of which oil was reckoned one of the most valuable), for all the delights of

sense (for *ointment and perfume* which *rejoice the heart, and it is called the oil of gladness*), nay, and for the highest titles of honour with which men are dignified, for kings are anointed. *A good name is* better than all *riches* (Prov. xxii. 1), that is, a name for wisdom and goodness with those that are wise and good—*the memory of the just;* this is a good that will bring a more grateful pleasure to the mind, will give a man a larger opportunity of usefulness, and will go further, and last longer, than the most *precious box of ointment;* for Christ paid Mary for her ointment with a *good name,* a name in the gospels (Matt. xxvi. 13), and we are sure he always pays with advantage.

II. That, all things considered, our going out of the world is a greater kindness to us than our coming into the world was: *The day of death* is preferable to the *birth-day;* though, as to others, there was joy *when a child was born into the world,* and where there is death there is lamentation, yet, as to ourselves, if we have lived so as to merit a *good name, the day of our death,* which will put a period to our cares, and toils, and sorrows, and remove us to rest, and joy, and eternal satisfaction, *is better than the day of our birth,* which ushered us into a world of so much sin and trouble, vanity and vexation. We were born to uncertainty, but a good man does not die at uncertainty. *The day of our birth* clogged our souls with the burden of the flesh, but *the day of our death* will set them at liberty from that burden.

III. That it will do us more good to go to a funeral than to go to a festival (*v.* 2): *It is better to go to the house of mourning,* and there *weep with those that weep, than to go to the house of feasting,* to a wedding, or a wake, there to *rejoice with those that do rejoice.* It will do us more good, and make better impressions upon us. We may lawfully go to both, as there is occasion. Our Saviour both feasted at the wedding of his friend in Cana and wept at the grave of his friend in Bethany; and we may possibly glorify God, and do good, and get good, in the house of feasting; but, considering how apt we are to be vain and frothy, proud and secure, and indulgent of the flesh, *it is better* for us *to go to the house of mourning,* not to see the pomp of the funeral, but to share in the sorrow of it, and to learn good lessons, both from the dead, who is going thence to his long home, and from the mourners, who go about the streets.

1. The uses to be gathered from *the house of mourning* are, (1.) By way of information: *That is the end of all men.* It *is the end of man* as to this world, a final period to his state here; he shall return no more to his house. It *is the end of all men;* all *have sinned* and therefore *death passes upon all.* We must thus be left by our friends, as the mourners are, and thus leave, as the dead do. What is the lot of others will be ours; the

cup is going round, and it will come to our turn to pledge it shortly. (2.) By way of admonition : *The living will lay it to his heart.* Will they ? It were well if they would. Those that are spiritually alive *will lay it to heart,* and, as for all the survivors, one would think they should ; it is their own fault if they do not, for nothing is more easy and natural than by the death of others to be put in mind of our own. Some perhaps *will lay that to heart,* and *consider their latter end,* who would not lay a good sermon to heart.

2. For the further proof of this (*v.* 4) he makes it the character, (1.) Of a wise man that his *heart is in the house of mourning ;* he is much conversant with mournful subjects, and this is both an evidence and a furtherance of his wisdom. *The house of mourning* is the wise man's school, where he has learned many a good lesson, and there, where he is serious, he is in his element. When he *is in the house of mourning* his *heart* is there to improve the spectacles of mortality that are presented to him ; nay, when he is in *the house of feasting,* his *heart is in the house of mourning,* by way of sympathy with those that are in sorrow. (2.) It is the character of a fool that his *heart is in the house of mirth ;* his heart is all upon it to be merry and jovial ; his whole delight is in sport and gaiety, in merry stories, merry songs, and merry company, merry days and merry nights. If he be at any time in *the house of mourning,* he is under a restraint ; his heart at the same time *is in the house of mirth ;* this is his folly, and helps to make him more and more foolish.

IV. That gravity and seriousness better become us, and are better for us, than mirth and jollity, *v.* 3. The common proverb says, " An ounce of mirth is worth a pound of sorrow ;" but the preacher teaches us a contrary lesson : *Sorrow is better than laughter,* more agreeable to our present state, where we are daily sinning and suffering ourselves, more or less, and daily seeing the sins and sufferings of others. While we are in a vale of tears, we should conform to the temper of the climate. It is also more for our advantage ; *for, by the sadness that appears in the countenance, the heart is* often *made better.* Note, 1. That is best for us which is best for our souls, by which *the heart is made better,* though it be unpleasing to sense. 2. Sadness is often a happy means of seriousness, and that affliction which is impairing to the health, estate, and family, may be improving to the mind, and make such impressions upon that as may alter its temper very much for the better, may make it humble and meek, loose from the world, penitent for sin, and careful of duty. *Vexatio dat intellectum*—*Vexation sharpens the intellect. Periissem nisi periissem*—*I should have perished if I had not been made wretched.* It will follow, on the contrary, that by the mirth and frolicsomeness of the countenance the heart is made worse, more vain, carnal, sensual, and secure, more in love with the world and more estranged from God and spiritual things (Job xxi. 12, 14), till it become utterly unconcerned in *the afflictions of Joseph,* as those Amos vi. 5, 6, and *the king and Haman,* Esth. iii. 15.

V. That it is much better for us to have our corruptions mortified by the *rebuke of the wise* than to have them gratified by *the song of fools, v.* 5. Many that would be very well pleased to hear the information of the wise, and much more to have their commendations and consolations, yet do not care for *hearing their rebukes,* that is, care not for being told of their faults, though ever so wisely ; but therein they are no friends to themselves, for *reproofs of instruction are the way of life* (Prov. vi. 23), and, though they be not so pleasant as *the song of fools,* they are more wholesome. *To hear,* not only with patience, but with pleasure, *the rebuke of the wise,* is a sign and means of wisdom ; but to be fond of *the song of fools* is a sign that the mind is vain and is the way to make it more so. And what an absurd thing is it for a man to dote so much upon such a transient pleasure as *the laughter of a fool* is, which may fitly be compared to the burning *of thorns under a pot,* which makes a great noise and a great blaze, for a little while, but is gone presently, scatters its ashes, and contributes scarcely any thing to the production of a boiling heat, for that requires a constant fire! *The laughter of a fool* is noisy and flashy, and is not an instance of true joy. *This is also vanity ;* it deceives men to their destruction, for *the end of that mirth is heaviness.* Our blessed Saviour has read us our doom : *Blessed are you that weep now, for you shall laugh ; woe to you that laugh now, for you shall mourn and weep,* Luke vi. 21, 25.

7 Surely oppression maketh a wise man mad ; and a gift destroyeth the heart. 8 Better *is* the end of a thing than the beginning thereof : *and* the patient in spirit *is* better than the proud in spirit. 9 Be not hasty in thy spirit to be angry : for anger resteth in the bosom of fools. 10 Say not thou, What *is the cause* that the former days were better than these ? for thou dost not enquire wisely concerning this.

Solomon had often complained before of the *oppressions* which he saw *under the sun,* which gave occasion for many melancholy speculations and were a great discouragement to virtue and piety. Now here,

I. He grants the temptation to be strong (*v.* 7) : *Surely* it is often too true that *oppression makes a wise man mad.* If a wise man be much and long oppressed, he is very apt to speak and act unlike himself, to lay the reins on the neck of his passions, and break out into indecent complaints against God and man, or to make use of unlawful dishonourable means of relieving himself. *The righteous,* when the *rod of the wicked rests* long *on their lot,* are in danger of *putting forth their hands to iniquity,* Ps. cxxv. 3. When even wise men have unreasonable hardships put upon them they have much ado to keep their temper and to keep their place. *It destroys the heart of a gift* (so the latter clause may be read); even the generous heart that is ready to give gifts, and a gracious heart that is endowed with many excellent gifts, is destroyed by being oppressed. We should therefore make great allowances to those that are abused and ill-dealt with, and not be severe in our censures of them, though they do not act so discreetly as they should; we know not what we should do if it were our own case.

II. He argues against it. Let us not fret at the power and success of oppressors, nor be envious at them, for, 1. The character of oppressors is very bad, so some understand *v.* 7. If he that had the reputation of *a wise man* becomes an *oppressor,* he becomes a *madman;* his reason has departed from him; he is no better than a roaring lion and a ranging bear, *and the gifts,* the bribes, he takes, the gains he seems to reap by his oppressions, do but *destroy his heart* and quite extinguish the poor remains of sense and virtue in him, and therefore he is rather to be pitied than envied; let him alone, and he will act so foolishly, and drive so furiously, that in a little time he will ruin himself. 2. The issue, at length, will be good: *Better is the end of a thing than the beginning thereof.* By faith see what the end will be, and with patience expect it. When proud men begin to oppress their poor honest neighbours they think their power will bear them out in it; they doubt not but to carry the day, and gain the point. But it will prove better in the end than it seemed at the beginning; their power will be broken, their wealth gotten by oppression will be wasted and gone, they will be humbled and brought down, and reckoned with for their injustice, and oppressed innocency will be both relieved and recompensed. *Better was the end of* Moses's treaty with Pharaoh, that proud oppressor, when Israel was brought forth with triumph, *than the beginning* of it, when the tale of bricks was doubled, and every thing looked discouraging.

III. He arms us against it with some necessary directions. If we would not be driven mad by oppression, but preserve the possession of our own souls,

1. We must be clothed with humility; *for the proud in spirit* are those that cannot bear to be trampled upon, but grow outrageous, and fret themselves, when they are hardly bestead. That will break a proud man's heart, which will not break a humble man's sleep. Mortify pride, therefore, and a lowly spirit will easily be reconciled to a low condition.

2. We must put on patience, *bearing* patience, to submit to the will of God in the affliction, and *waiting* patience, to expect the issue in God's due time. *The patient in spirit* are here opposed to *the proud in spirit,* for where there is humility there will be patience. Those will be thankful for any thing who own they deserve nothing at God's hand, *and the patient* are said to be *better than the proud;* they are more easy to themselves, more acceptable to others, and more likely to see a good issue of their troubles.

3. We must govern our passion with wisdom and grace (*v.* 9): *Be not hasty in thy spirit to be angry;* those that are hasty in their expectations, and cannot brook delays, are apt to be angry if they be not immediately gratified. "Be not angry at proud oppressors, or any that are the instruments of your trouble." (1.) "Be not soon angry, not quick in apprehending an affront and resenting it, nor forward to express your resentments of it." (2.) "Be not long angry;" for though anger may come into the bosom of a wise man, and pass through it as a wayfaring man, it *rests* only *in the bosom of fools;* there it resides, there it remains, there it has the innermost and uppermost place, there it is hugged as that which is dear, and laid in the bosom, and not easily parted with. He therefore that would approve himself so wise as not to *give place to the devil,* must not *let the sun go down upon his wrath,* Eph. iv. 26, 27.

4. We must make the best of that which is (*v.* 10): "Take it not for granted *that the former days were better than these,* nor enquire *what is the cause* that they were so, for therein *thou dost not enquire wisely,* since thou enquirest into the reason of the thing before thou art sure that the thing itself is true; and, besides, thou art so much a stranger to the times past, and such an incompetent judge even of the present times, that thou canst not expect a satisfactory answer to the enquiry, and therefore *thou dost not enquire wisely;* nay, the supposition is a foolish reflection upon the providence of God in the government of the world." Note, (1.) It is folly to complain of the badness of our own times when we have more reason to complain of the badness of our own hearts (if men's hearts were better, the times would mend) and when we have more reason to be thankful that they are not worse, but that even in the worst of times we enjoy many mercies, which help to make them not only tolerable, but comfortable. (2.) It is folly to cry up the goodness of former times, so as to derogate from the mercy of God to us in our own times; as if former ages had not the same things to complain of that we have, or if perhaps, in some respects, they had not, yet as if God had been unjust and unkind to us in casting our lot in an iron age, compared with the golden ages that went before us; this arises from nothing but fretfulness and discontent, and an aptness to pick

quarrels with God himself. We are not to think there is any universal decay in nature, or degeneracy in morals. God has been always good, and men always bad; and if, in some respects, the times are now worse than they have been, perhaps in other respects they are better.

11 Wisdom *is* good with an inheritance: and *by it there is* profit to them that see the sun. 12 For wisdom *is* a defence, *and* money *is* a defence: but the excellency of knowledge *is, that* wisdom giveth life to them that have it. 13 Consider the work of God: for who can make *that* straight, which he hath made crooked? 14 In the day of prosperity be joyful, but in the day of adversity consider: God also hath set the one over against the other, to the end that man should find nothing after him. 15 All *things* have I seen in the days of my vanity: there is a just *man* that perisheth in his righteousness, and there is a wicked *man* that prolongeth *his life* in his wickedness. 16 Be not righteous over much; neither make thyself over wise: why shouldest thou destroy thyself? 17 Be not over much wicked, neither be thou foolish: why shouldest thou die before thy time? 18 *It is* good that thou shouldest take hold of this; yea, also from this withdraw not thine hand: for he that feareth God shall come forth of them all. 19 Wisdom strengtheneth the wise more than ten mighty *men* which are in the city. 20 For *there is* not a just man upon earth, that doeth good, and sinneth not. 21 Also take no heed unto all words that are spoken; lest thou hear thy servant curse thee: 22 For oftentimes also thine own heart knoweth that thou thyself likewise hast cursed others.

Solomon, in these verses, recommends wisdom to us as the best antidote against those distempers of mind which we are liable to, by reason of the vanity and vexation of spirit that there are in the things of this world. Here are some of the praises and the precepts of wisdom.

I. The praises of wisdom. Many things are here said in its commendation, to engage us to get and retain wisdom. 1. Wisdom is necessary to the right managing and improving of our worldly possessions: *Wisdom is good with an inheritance*, that is, an inheritance is good for little without wisdom. Though a man have a great estate, though it come easily to him, by descent from his ancestors, if he have not wisdom to use it for the end for which he has it, he had better have been without it. Wisdom is not only good for the poor, to make them content and easy, but it is good for the rich too, good with riches to keep a man from getting hurt by them, and to enable a man to do good with them. *Wisdom is good* of itself, and makes a man useful; but, if he have a good estate with it, that will put him into a greater capacity of being useful, and with his wealth he may be more serviceable to his generation than he could have been without it; he will also *make friends to himself*, Luke xvi. 9. *Wisdom is as good as an inheritance, yea, better too* (so the margin reads it); it is more our own, more our honour, will make us greater blessings, will remain longer with us, and turn to a better account. 2. It is of great advantage to us throughout the whole course of our passage through this world: *By it there is* real *profit to those that see the sun*, both to those that have it and to their contemporaries. It is pleasant to *see the sun* (ch. xi. 7), but that pleasure is not comparable to the pleasure of wisdom. The light of this world is an advantage to us in doing the business of this world (John xi. 9); but to those that have that advantage, unless withal they have wisdom wherewith to manage their business, that advantage is worth little to them. The clearness of the eye of the understanding is of greater use to us than bodily eye-sight. 3. It contributes much more to our safety, and is a shelter to us from the storms of trouble and its scorching heat; it *is a shadow* (so the word is), *as the shadow of a great rock in a weary land.* *Wisdom is a defence, and money* (that is, as *money) is a defence.* As a rich man makes his wealth, so a wise man makes his wisdom, a *strong city. In the shadow of wisdom* (so the words run) *and in the shadow of money* there is safety. He puts wisdom and money together, to confirm what he had said before, that *wisdom is good with an inheritance.* Wisdom is as a wall, and money may serve as a thorn hedge, which protects the field. 4. It is joy and true happiness to a man. This is *the excellency of knowledge,* divine knowledge, not only above money, but above wisdom too, human wisdom, *the wisdom of this world,* that it *gives life to those that have it. The fear of the Lord, that is wisdom,* and that is life; it prolongs life. Men's wealth exposes their lives, but their wisdom protects them. Nay, whereas wealth will not lengthen out the natural life, true wisdom will give spiritual life, the earnest of eternal life; so much *better is it to get wisdom than gold.* 5. It will put strength into a man, and be his stay and support (v. 19): *Wisdom strengthens the wise,* strengthens their spirits, and makes them bold and resolute, by keeping them always on sure grounds. It strengthens their interest, and gains them friends and reputation. It strengthens them for their services under their sufferings, and against the attacks that are made upon them, *more than ten mighty men*, great commanders, strengthen *the city*. Those that are truly wise and good are taken under God's protection, and are safer there than if ten of the mightiest men in the city, men of the greatest power and interest, should undertake to secure them, and become their patrons.

II. Some of the precepts of wisdom, that wisdom which will be of so much advantage to us.

1. We must have an eye to God and to his hand in every thing that befals us (*v.* 13): *Consider the work of God.* To silence our complaints concerning cross events, let us consider the hand of God in them and not open our mouths against that which is his doing ; let us look upon the disposal of our condition and all the circumstances of it as the *work of God*, and consider it as the product of his eternal counsel, which is fulfilled in every thing that befals us. Consider that every work of God is wise, just, and good, and there is an admirable beauty and harmony in his works, and all will appear at last to have been for the best. Let us therefore give him the glory of all his works concerning us, and study to answer his designs in them. *Consider the work of God* as that which we cannot make any alteration of. *Who can make that straight which he has made crooked ?* Who can change the nature of things from what is settled by the God of nature ? If he speak trouble, who can make peace ? And, if he hedge up the way with thorns, who can get forward ? If desolating judgments go forth with commission, who can put a stop to them ? Since therefore we cannot mend God's work, we ought to make the best of it.

2. We must accommodate ourselves to the various dispensations of Providence that respect us, and do the work and duty of the day in its day, *v.* 14. Observe, (1.) How the appointments and events of Providence are counterchanged. In this world, at the same time, some are in prosperity, others are in adversity ; the same persons at one time are in great prosperity, at another time in great adversity ; nay, one event prosperous, and another grievous, may occur to the same person at the same time. Both come from the hand of God ; *out of his mouth both evil and good proceed* (Isa. xiv. 7), and *he has set the one overagainst the other*, so that there is a very short and easy passage between them, and they are a foil to each other. Day and night, summer and winter, are set *the one overagainst the other*, that in prosperity we may rejoice *as though we rejoiced not*, and in adversity may weep *as though we wept not*, for we may plainly see the one from the other and quickly exchange the one for the other ; and it is *to the end that man may find nothing*

after him, that he may not be at any certainty concerning future events or the continuance of the present scene, but may live in a dependence upon Providence and be ready for whatever happens. Or that man may find nothing in the work of God which he can pretend to amend. (2.) How we must comply with the will of God in events of both kinds. Our religion, in general, must be the same in all conditions, but the particular instances and exercises of it must vary, as our outward condition does, that we may *walk after the Lord*. [1.] In a *day of prosperity* (and it is but a day) we must *be joyful*, be in good, be doing good, and getting good, maintain a holy cheerfulness, *and serve the Lord with gladness of heart in the abundance of all things*. "When the world smiles, *rejoice in God* and praise him, and let *the joy of the Lord be thy strength*." [2.] In a *day of adversity* (and that is but a day too) *consider*. Times of affliction are proper times for consideration, then God calls to *consider* (Hag. i. 5), then, if ever, we are disposed to it, and no good will be gotten by the affliction without it. We cannot answer God's end in afflicting us unless we consider why and wherefore he contends with us. And consideration is necessary also to our comfort and support under our afflictions.

3. We must not be offended at the greatest prosperity of wicked people, nor at the saddest calamities that may befal the godly in this life, *v.* 15. Wisdom will teach us how to construe those dark chapters of Providence so as to reconcile them with the wisdom, holiness, goodness, and faithfulness of God. We must not think it strange ; Solomon tells us there were instances of this kind in his time : *All things have I seen in the days of my vanity; I have taken notice of all that passed, and this has been as surprising and perplexing to me as any thing.*" Observe, Though Solomon was so wise and great a man, yet he calls the days of his life *the days of his vanity*, for the best days on earth are so, in comparison with the days of eternity. Or perhaps he refers to the days of his apostasy from God (those were indeed the days of his vanity) and reflects upon this as one thing that tempted him to infidelity, or at least to indifference in religion, that he saw *just men perishing in their righteousness*, that the greatest piety would not secure men from the greatest afflictions by the hand of God, nay, and sometimes did expose men to the greatest injuries from the hands of wicked and unreasonable men. Naboth perished in his righteousness, and Abel long before. He had also seen wicked men prolonging their lives in their wickedness ; they *live, become old, yea, are mighty in power* (Job xxi. 7), yea, and by their fraud and violence they screen themselves from the sword of justice. "Now, in this, consider the work of God, and let it not be a stumbling-block to thee." The calamities of the righteous are preparing them for their future blessedness, and the wicked, while their

days are prolonged, are but ripening for ruin. There is a judgment to come, which will rectify this seeming irregularity, to the glory of God and the full satisfaction of all his people, and we must wait with patience till then.

4. Wisdom will be of use both for caution to saints in their way, and for a check to sinners in their way. (1.) As to saints, it will engage them to proceed and persevere in their righteousness, and yet will be an admonition to them to take heed of running into extremes : *A just man may perish in his righteousness,* but let him not, by his own imprudence and rash zeal, pull trouble upon his own head, and then reflect upon Providence as dealing hardly with him. " *Be not righteous overmuch, v.* 16. In the acts of righteousness govern thyself by the rules of prudence, and be not transported, no, not by a zeal for God, into any intemperate heats or passions, or any practices unbecoming thy character or dangerous to thy interests." Note, There may be over-doing in well-doing. Self-denial and mortification of the flesh are good ; but if we prejudice our health by them, and unfit ourselves for the service of God, we are *righteous overmuch.* To reprove those that offend is good, but to cast that pearl before swine, who will turn again and rend us, is to be *righteous overmuch.* "*Make not thyself over-wise.* Be not opinionative, and conceited of thy own abilities. Set not up for a dictator, nor pretend to give law to, and give judgment upon, all about thee. Set not up for a critic, to find fault with every thing that is said and done, nor busy thyself in other men's matters, as if thou knewest every thing and couldst do any thing. *Why shouldst thou destroy thyself,* as fools often do by meddling with strife that belongs not to them? Why shouldst thou provoke authority, and run thyself into the briers, by needless contradictions, and by going out of thy sphere to correct what is amiss? *Be wise as serpents;* beware of men." (2.) As to sinners, if it cannot prevail with them to forsake their sins, yet it may restrain them from growing very exorbitant. It is true *there is a wicked man that prolongs his life in his wickedness* (*v.* 15); but let none say that therefore they may safely be as wicked as they will; no, *be not overmuch wicked* (*v.* 17) ; do not run to an excess of riot. Many that will not be wrought upon by the fear of God, and a dread of the torments of hell, to avoid all sin, will yet, if they have ever so little consideration, avoid those sins that ruin their health and estate, and expose them to public justice. And Solomon here makes use of these considerations. " *The magistrate bears not the sword in vain,* has a quick eye and a heavy hand, and is *a terror to evil-doers ;* therefore be afraid of coming within his reach, be not so foolish as to lay thyself open to the law, *why shouldst thou die before thy time ?*" Solomon, in these two cautions, had probably a special

regard to some of his own subjects that were disaffected to his government and were meditating the revolt which they made immediately after his death. Some, it may be, quarrelled with the sins of their governor, and made them their pretence ; to them he says, *Be not righteous overmuch.* Others were weary of the strictness of the government, and the temple-service, and that made them desirous to set up another king ; but he frightens both from their seditious practices with the sword of justice, and others likewise from meddling *with those that were given to change.*

5. Wisdom will direct us in the mean between two extremes, and keep us always in the way of our duty, which we shall find a plain and safe way (*v.* 18): "*It is good that thou shouldst take hold of this,* this wisdom, this care, not to run thyself into snares. *Yea, also from this withdraw not thy hand;* never slacken thy diligence, nor abate thy resolution to maintain a due decorum, and a good government of thyself. Take hold of the bridle by which thy head-strong passions must be held in from hurrying thee into one mischief or other, as *the horse and mule that have no understanding;* and, having taken hold of it, keep thy hold, and withdraw not thy hand from it, for, if thou do, the liberty that they will take will be *as the letting forth of water,* and thou wilt not easily recover thy hold again. Be conscientious, and yet be cautious, and to this exercise thyself. Govern thyself steadily by the principles of religion, and thou shalt find that *he that fears God shall come forth out of all* those straits and difficulties which those run themselves into that cast off that fear." *The fear of the Lord* is that wisdom which will serve as a clue to extricate us out of the most intricate labyrinths. *Honesty is the best policy.* Those that truly fear God have but one end to serve, and therefore act steadily. God has likewise promised to direct those that fear him, and to order their steps not only in the right way, but out of every dangerous way, Ps. xxxvii. 23, 24.

6. Wisdom will teach us how to conduct ourselves in reference to the sins and offences of others, which commonly contribute more than any thing else to the disturbance of our repose, which contract both guilt and grief. (1.) Wisdom teaches us not to expect that those we deal with should be faultless ; we ourselves are not so, none are so, no, not the best. This *wisdom strengthens the wise* as much as any thing, and arms them against the danger that arises from provocation (*v.* 19), so that they are not put into any disorder by it. They consider that those they have dealings and conversation with are not incarnate angels, but sinful sons and daughters of Adam : even the best are so, insomuch that *there is not a just man upon earth, that doeth good and sinneth not, v.* 20. Solomon had this in his prayer (1 Kings viii. 46), in

his proverbs (Prov. xx. 9), and here in his preaching. Note, [1.] It is the character of just men that they *do good;* for the tree is known by its fruits. [2.] The best men, and those that do most good, yet cannot say that they are perfectly free from sin; even those that are sanctified are not sinless. None that live on this side heaven live without sin. *If we say, We have not sinned, we deceive ourselves.* [3.] We sin even in our doing good; there is something defective, nay, something offensive, in our best performances. That which, for the substance of it, is good, and pleasing to God, is not so well done as it should be, and omissions in duty are sins, as well as omissions of duty. [4.] It is only just men upon earth that are subject thus to sin and infirmity; *the spirits of just men,* when they have got clear of the body, are made *perfect* in holiness (Heb. xii. 23), and in heaven they *do good and sin not.*

(2.) Wisdom teaches us not to be quick-sighted, or quickscented, in apprehending and resenting affronts, but to wink at many of the injuries that are done us, and act as if we did not see them (v. 21): " *Take no heed to all words that are spoken; set not thy heart to them.* Vex not thyself at men's peevish reflections upon thee, or suspicions of thee, but be *as a deaf man that hears not,* Ps. xxxviii. 13, 14. Be not solicitous or inquisitive to know what people say of thee; if they speak well of thee, it will feed thy pride, if ill, it will stir up thy passion. See therefore that thou approve thyself to God and thy own conscience, and then heed not what men say of thee. *Hearkeners,* we say, *seldom hear good of themselves;* if thou heed every word that is spoken, perhaps *thou wilt hear thy own servant curse thee* when he thinks thou dost not hear him; thou wilt be told that he does, and perhaps told falsely, if thou have thy ear open to tale-bearers, Prov. xxix. 12. Nay, perhaps it is true, and thou mayest stand behind the curtain and hear it thyself, mayest hear thyself not only blamed and despised, but cursed, the worst evil said of thee and wished to thee, and that by a servant, one of the meanest rank, of the abjects, nay, by thy own servant, who should be an advocate for thee, and protect thy good name as well as thy other interests. Perhaps it is a servant thou hast been kind to, and yet he requites thee thus ill, and this will vex thee; thou hadst better not have heard it. Perhaps it is a servant thou hast wronged and dealt unjustly with, and, though he dares not tell thee so, he tells others so, and tells God so, and then thy own conscience will join with him in the reproach, which will make it much more uneasy." The good names of the greatest lie much at the mercy even of the meanest. And perhaps there is a great deal more evil said of us than we think there is, and by those from whom we little expected it. But we do not consult our own repose, no, nor our credit, though we pretend to be jealous

1022

of it, if we take notice of every word that is spoken diminishingly of us; it is easier to pass by twenty such affronts than to avenge one.

(3.) Wisdom puts us in mind of our own faults (v. 22): " Be not enraged at those that speak ill of thee, or wish ill to thee, *for oftentimes,* in that case, if thou retire into thyself, thy own conscience will tell thee *that thou thyself hast cursed others,* spoken ill of them and wished ill to them, and thou art paid in thy own coin." Note, When any affront or injury is done us it is seasonable to examine our consciences whether we have not done the same, or as bad, to others; and if, upon reflection, we find we have, we must take that occasion to renew our repentance for it, must justify God, and make use of it to qualify our own resentments. If we be truly angry with ourselves, as we ought to be, for backbiting and censuring others, we shall be the less angry with others for backbiting and censuring us. We must show all meekness towards all men, for we ourselves *were sometimes foolish,* Tit. iii. 2, 3; Matt. vii. 1, 2; James iii. 1, 2.

23 All this have I proved by wisdom: I said, I will be wise; but it *was* far from me. 24 That which is far off, and exceeding deep, who can find it out? 25 I applied mine heart to know, and to search, and to seek out wisdom, and the reason *of things,* and to know the wickedness of folly, even of foolishness *and* madness: 26 And I find more bitter than death the woman, whose heart *is* snares and nets, *and* her hands *as* bands: whoso pleaseth God shall escape from her; but the sinner shall be taken by her. 27 Behold, this have I found, saith the preacher, *counting* one by one, to find out the account: 28 Which yet my soul seeketh, but I find not: one man among a thousand have I found; but a woman among all those have I not found. 29 Lo, this only have I found, that God hath made man upright; but they have sought out many inventions.

Solomon had hitherto been proving the vanity of the world and its utter insufficiency to make men happy; now here he comes to show the vileness of sin, and its certain tendency to make men miserable; and this, as the former, he proves from his own experience, and it was a dear-bought experience. He is here, more than any where in all this book, putting on the habit of a penitent. He reviews what he had been discoursing of already, and tells us that what he had said was what he knew and was well assured of, and what he resolved to stand by: *All this have I proved by wisdom, v.* 23. Now here,

I. He owns and laments the deficiencies of his wisdom. He had wisdom enough to see the vanity of the world and to experience that that would not make a portion for a soul. But, when he came to enquire further, he found himself at a loss; his eye was too dim, his line was too short, and, though he discovered this, there were many other things which he could not prove by wisdom.

1. His searches were industrious. God had given him a capacity for knowledge above any; he set up with a great stock of wisdom; he had the largest opportunities of improving himself that ever any man had; and, (1.) He resolved, if it were possible, to gain his point: *I said, I will be wise.* He earnestly desired it as highly valuable; he fully designed it as that which he looked upon to be attainable; he determined not to sit down short of it, Prov. xviii. 1. Many are not wise because they never said they would be so, being indifferent to it; but Solomon set it up for the mark he aimed at. When he made trial of sensual pleasures, he still thought *to acquaint his heart with wisdom* (*ch.* ii. 3), and not to be diverted from the pursuits of that; but perhaps he did not find it so easy a thing as he imagined to keep up his correspondence with wisdom, while he addicted himself so much to his pleasures. However, his will was good; he said, *I will be wise.* And that was not all: (2.) He resolved to spare no pains (*v.* 25): "*I applied my heart;* I and my heart turned every way; I left no stone unturned, no means untried, to compass what I had in view. I set *myself to know, and to search, and to seek out wisdom,* to accomplish myself in all useful learning, philosophy, and divinity." If he had not thus closely applied himself to study, it would have been but a jest for him to say, *I will be wise,* for those that will attain the end must take the right way. Solomon was a man of great quickness, and yet, instead of using that (with many) as an excuse for slothfulness, he pressed it upon himself as an inducement to diligence, and the easier he found it to master a good notion the more intent he would be that he might be master of the more good notions. Those that have the best parts should take the greatest pains, as those that have the largest stock should trade most. He applied himself not only to know what lay on the surface, but to search what lay hidden out of the common view and road; nor did he search a little way, and then give it over because he did not presently find what he searched for, but he *sought it out,* went to the bottom of it; nor did he aim to know things only, but the reasons of things, that he might give an account of them.

2. Yet his success was not answerable or satisfying: "*I said, I will be wise, but it was far from me;* I could not compass it. After all, *This only I know that I know nothing,* and the more I know the more I see there is to

be known, and the more sensible I am of my own ignorance. *That which is far off, and exceedingly deep, who can find it out?*" He means God himself, his counsels and his works; when he searched into these he presently found himself puzzled and run aground. He *could not order his speech by reason of darkness. It is higher than heaven, what can he do?* Job xi. 8. Blessed be God, there is nothing which we have to do which is not plain and easy; *the word is nigh us* (Prov. viii. 9); but there is a great deal which we would wish to know which is *far off, and exceedingly deep,* among the secret things which belong not to us. And probably it is a culpable ignorance and error that Solomon here laments, that his pleasures, and the many amusements of his court, had blinded his eyes and cast a mist before them, so that he could not attain to true wisdom as he designed.

II. He owns and laments the instances of his folly in which he had exceeded, as, in wisdom, he came short. Here is,

1. His enquiry concerning the evil of sin. He *applied his heart to know the wickedness of folly, even of foolishness and madness.* Observe, (1.) The knowledge of sin is a difficult knowledge, and hard to be attained; Solomon took pains for it. Sin has many disguises with which it palliates itself, as being loth to appear sin, and it is very hard to strip it of these and to see it in its true nature and colours. (2.) It is necessary to our repentance for sin that we be acquainted with the evil of it, as it is necessary to the cure of a disease to know its nature, causes, and malignity. St. Paul *therefore* valued the divine law, because it discovered sin to him, Rom. vii. 7. Solomon, who, in the days of his folly, had set his wits on work to invent pleasures and sharpen them, and was ingenious in making provision for the flesh, now that God had opened his eyes is as industrious to find out the aggravations of sin and so to put an edge upon his repentance. Ingenious sinners should be ingenious penitents, and wit and learning, among the other spoils of the *strong man armed,* should be divided by the Lord Jesus. (3.) It well becomes penitents to say the worst they can of sin, for the truth is we can never speak ill enough of it. Solomon here, for his further humiliation, desired to see more, [1.] Of the sinfulness of sin; that is it which he lays the greatest stress upon in this inquiry, to *know the wickedness of folly,* by which perhaps he means his own iniquity, the sin of uncleanness, for that was commonly called *folly in Israel,* Gen. xxxiv. 7; Deut. xxii. 21; Judg. xx. 6; 2 Sam. xiii. 12. When he indulged himself in it, he made a light matter of it; but now he desires to see the *wickedness* of it, its *great wickedness,* so Joseph speaks of it, Gen. xxxix. 9. Or it may be taken there generally for all sin. Many extenuate their sins with this, They were *folly;* but Solomon sees *wicked-*

ness in those follies, an offence to God and a wrong to conscience. *This is wickedness,* Jer. iv. 18; Zech. v. 8. [2.] Of the folly of sin; as there is a wickedness in folly, so there is a folly in wickedness, even foolishness and madness. Wilful sinners are fools and madmen; they act contrary both to right reason and to their true interest.

2. The result of this enquiry.

(1.) He now discovered more than ever of the evil of that great sin which he himself had been guilty of, the *loving of many strange women,* 1 Kings xi. 1. This is that which he here most feelingly laments, and in very pathetic expressions. [1.] He found the remembrance of the sin very grievous. O how heavily did it lie upon his conscience! what an agony was he in upon the thought of it— the wickedness, the foolishness, the madness, that he had been guilty of! *I find it more bitter than death.* As great a terror seized him, in reflection upon it, as if he had been under the arrest of death. Thus do those that have their sins set in order before them by a sound conviction cry out against them; they are bitter as gall, nay, bitter as death, to all true penitents. Uncleanness is a sin that is, in its own nature, more pernicious than death itself. Death may be made honourable and comfortable, but this sin can be no other than shame and pain, Prov. v. 9, 11. [2.] He had found the temptation to the sin very dangerous, and that it was extremely difficult, and next to impossible, for those that ventured into the temptation to escape the sin, and for those that had fallen into the sin to recover themselves by repentance. The heart of the adulterous woman is *snares and nets;* she plays her game to ruin souls with as much art and subtlety as ever any fowler used to take a silly bird. The methods such sinners use are both deceiving and destroying, as snares and nets are. The unwary souls are enticed into them by the bait of pleasure, which they greedily catch at and promise themselves satisfaction in; but they are taken before they are aware, and taken irrecoverably. Her hands are as bands, with which, under colour of fond embraces, she holds those fast that she has seized; they are *held in the cords of their own sin,* Prov. v. 22. Lust gets strength by being gratified and its charms are more prevalent. [3.] He reckoned it a great instance of God's favour to any man if by his grace he has kept him from this sin: *He that pleases God shall escape from her,* shall be preserved either from being tempted to this sin or from being overcome by the temptation. Those that are kept from this sin must acknowledge it is God that keeps them, and not any strength or resolution of their own, must acknowledge it a great mercy; and those that would have grace sufficient for them to arm them against this sin must be careful to please God in every thing, by keeping his ordinances, Lev. xviii. 30. [4.] He reckoned it a

sin that is as sore a punishment of other sins as a man can fall under in this life: *The sinner shall be taken by her.* First, Those that allow themselves in other sins, by which their minds are blinded and their consciences debauched, are the more easily drawn to this *Secondly,* It is just with God to leave them to themselves to fall into it. See Rom. i. 26, 28; Eph. iv. 18, 19. Thus does Solomon, as it were, with horror, bless himself from the sin in which he had plunged himself.

(2.) He now discovered more than ever of the general corruption of man's nature. He traces up that stream to the fountain, as his father had done before him, on a like occasion (Ps. li. 5): *Behold, I was shapen in iniquity.* [1.] He endeavoured to find out the number of his actual transgressions (v. 27): "*Behold, this have I found,* that is, this I hoped to find; I thought I could have understood my errors and have brought in a complete list, at least, of the heads of them; I thought I could have counted them one by one, and have found out the account." He desired to find them out as a penitent, that he might the more particularly acknowledge them; and, generally, the more particular we are in the confession of sin the more comfort we have in the sense of the pardon; he desired it also as a preacher, that he might the more particularly give warning to others. Note, A sound conviction of one sin will put us upon enquiring into the whole confederacy; and the more we see amiss in ourselves the more diligently we should enquire further into our own faults, that what we see not may be discovered to us, Job xxxiv. 32. [2.] He soon found himself at a loss, and perceived that they were innumerable (v. 28): "*Which yet my soul seeks;* I am still counting, and still desirous to find out the account, but I find not, I cannot count them all, nor find out the account of them to perfection. I still make new and amazing discoveries of the desperate wickedness that there is in my own heart," Jer. xvii. 9, 10. *Who can know it? Who can understand his errors? Who can tell how often he offends?* Ps. xix. 12. He finds that if God enters into judgment with him, or he with himself, for all his thoughts, words, and actions, he is *not able to answer for one of a thousand,* Job ix. 3. This he illustrates by comparing the corruption of his own heart and life with the corruption of the world, where he scarcely found one good man among a thousand; nay, among all the thousand wives and concubines which he had, he did not find *one good woman.* "Even so," says he, " when I come to recollect and review my own thoughts, words, and actions, and all the passages of my life past, perhaps among those that were manly I might find one good among a thousand, and that was all; the rest even of those had some corruption or other in them." He found (v. 20) that he had sinned even in doing good. But for those that were effeminate, that passed in the indulgence of his pleasures, they were all naught; in that part of his life there did not appear so much as one of a thousand good. In our hearts and lives there appears little good, at the best, but sometimes none at all. Doubtless this is not intended as a censure of the female sex in general; it is probable that there have been and are more good women than good men (Acts xvii. 4, 12); he merely alludes to his own sad experience. And perhaps there may be this further in it: he does, in his proverbs, warn us against the snares both of the *evil man* and of the *strange woman* (Prov. ii. 12, 16; iv. 14; v. 3); now he had observed the ways of the *evil women* to be more deceitful and dangerous than those of the *evil men*, that it was more difficult to discover their frauds and elude their snares, and therefore he compares sin to an adulteress (Prov. ix, 13), and perceives he can no more find out the deceitfulness of his own heart than he can that of a strange woman, whose ways are movable, that thou canst not know them. [3] He therefore runs up all the streams of actual transgression to the fountain of original corruption. The source of all the folly and madness that are in the world is in man's apostasy from God and his degeneracy from his primitive rectitude (*v.* 29): " *Lo, this only have I found*; when I could not find out the particulars, yet the gross account was manifest enough; it is as clear as the sun that man is corrupted and revolted, and is not as he was made." Observe, *First*, How man was made by the wisdom and goodness of God: *God made man upright; Adam the first man*, so the Chaldee. God made him, and he made him *upright*, such a one as he should be; being made a rational creature, he was, in all respects, such a one as a rational creature should be, *upright*, without any irregularity; one could find no fault in him; he was *upright*, that is, determined to God only, in opposition to the *many inventions* which he afterwards turned aside to. Man, as he came out of God's hands, was (as we may say) a little picture of his Maker, who is *good and upright*. *Secondly*, How he was marred, and in effect unmade, by his own folly and badness: *They have sought out many inventions*—they, our first parents, or the whole race, all in general and every one in particular. *They have sought out great inventions* (so some), inventions to become great as gods (Gen. iii. 5), or *the inventions of the great ones* (so some), of the angels that fell, the *Magnates*, or *many inventions*. Man, instead of resting in what God had found for him, was for seeking to better himself, like the prodigal that left his father's house to seek his fortune. Instead of being for one, he was for many; instead of being for God's institutions, he was for his own inventions. The law of his creation would not hold him, but he would be at his own disposal and follow his own sentiments

and inclinations. *Vain man would be wise*, wiser than his Maker; he is giddy and unsettled in his pursuits, and therefore has *many inventions*. Those that forsake God wander endlessly. Men's actual transgressions are multiplied. Solomon could not find out how many they are (*v.* 28); but he found they were *very many*. Many kinds of sins, and those often repeated. *They are more than the hairs on our heads*, Ps. xl. 12.

CHAP. VIII.

Solomon, in this chapter, comes to recommend wisdom to us as the most powerful antidote against both the temptations and vexations that arise from the vanity of the world. Here is, I. The benefit and praise of wisdom, ver 1. II. Some particular instances of wisdom prescribed to us. 1. We must keep in due subjection to the government God has set over us, ver. 2—5. 2. We must get ready for sudden evils, and especially for sudden death, ver. 6—8. 3. We must arm ourselves against the temptation of an oppressive government and not think it strange, ver. 9, 10. The impunity of oppressors makes them more daring (ver. 11), but is the issue it will be well with the righteous and ill with the wicked (ver. 12, 13), and therefore the present prosperity of the wicked and afflictions of the righteous ought not to be a stumbling-block to us, ver. 14. 4. We must cheerfully use the gifts of God's providence, ver. 15. 5. We must with an entire satisfaction acquiesce in the will of God, and, not pretending to find the bottom, we must humbly and silently adore the depth of his unsearchable counsels, being assured they are all wise, just, and good, ver. 16, 17.

WHO *is* as the wise *man?* and who knoweth the interpretation of a thing? a man's wisdom maketh his face to shine, and the boldness of his face shall be changed. 2 I *counsel thee* to keep the king's commandment, and *that* in regard of the oath of God. 3 Be not hasty to go out of his sight: stand not in an evil thing; for he doeth whatsoever pleaseth him. 4 Where the word of a king *is, there is* power: and who may say unto him, What doest thou? 5 Whoso keepeth the commandment shall feel no evil thing: and a wise man's heart discerneth both time and judgment.

Here is, I. An encomium of *wisdom* (*v.* 1), that is, of true piety, guided in all its exercises by prudence and discretion. The wise man is the good man, that knows God and glorifies him, knows himself and does well for himself; his wisdom is a great happiness to him, for, 1. It advances him above his neighbours, and makes him more excellent than they: *Who is as the wise man?* Note, Heavenly wisdom will make a man an incomparable man. No man without grace, though he be learned, or noble, or rich, is to be compared with a man that has true grace and is therefore accepted of God. 2. It makes him useful among his neighbours and very serviceable to them: *Who but the wise man knows the interpretation of a thing*, that is, understands the times and the events of them, and their critical junctures, so as to direct *what Israel ought to do*, 1 Chron. xii. 32 3. It beautifies a man in the eyes of his friends: *It makes his face to shine*, as Moses's did when he came down from the mount; it puts honour upon a man and a lustre ou his whole conversation, makes him to be regarded and taken notice of, and gains him respect (as Job xxix. 7, &c.); it makes him lovely and amiable, and the darling and blessing of his country. *The strength of his face*, the sourness and severity of his countenance (so some understand the last clause), *shall be changed* by it into that which is sweet and obliging. Even those whose natural temper is rough and morose by *wisdom* are strangely altered; they become mild and gentle, and learn to look pleasant. 4. It emboldens a man against his adversaries, their attempts and their scorn: *The boldness of his face shall be* doubled by wisdom; it will add very much to his courage in maintaining his integrity when he not only has an honest cause to plead, but by his wisdom knows how to manage it and where to find *the interpretation of a thing. He shall not be ashamed, but shall speak with his enemy in the gate.*

II. A particular instance of wisdom pressed upon us, and that is subjection to authority, and a dutiful and peaceable perseverance in our allegiance to the government which Providence has set over us. Observe,

1. How the duty of subjects is here described. (1.) We must be observant of the laws. In all those things wherein the civil power is to interpose, whether legislative or judicial, we ought to submit to its order and constitutions: *I counsel thee ;* it may as well be supplied, *I charge thee*, not only as a prince but as a preacher: he might do both ; "I recommend it to thee as a piece of wisdom ; I say, whatever those say that are given to change, *keep the king's commandment;* wherever the sovereign power is lodged, be subject to it. *Observe the mouth of a king*" (so the phrase is); "say as he says ; do as he bids thee; let his word be a law, or rather let the law be his word." Some understand the following clause as a limitation of this obedience : "*Keep the king's commandment,* yet so as to have a *regard to the oath of God,* that is, so as to keep a good conscience and not to violate thy obligations to God, which are prior and superior to thy obligations to the king. *Render to Cæsar the things that are Cæsar's,* but so as to reserve pure and entire *to God the things that are* his." (2.) We must not be forward to find fault with the public administration, or quarrel with every thing that is not just according to our mind, nor quit our post of service under the government, and throw it up, upon every discontent (*v.* 3) : "*Be not hasty to go out of his sight,* when he is displeased at thee (*ch.* x. 4), or when thou art displeased at him; fly not off in a passion, nor entertain such jealousies of him as will tempt thee to renounce the court or forsake the kingdom." Solomon's subjects, as soon as his head was laid low, went directly contrary to this rule, when, upon the rough answer which Rehoboam gave them, they were *hasty to go out*

of his sight, would not take time for second thoughts nor admit proposals of accommodation, but cried, *To your tents, O Israel !* "There may perhaps be a just cause *to go out of his sight ;* but *be not hasty to* do it; act with great deliberation." (3.) We must not persist in a fault when it is shown us : "*Stand not in an evil thing ;* in any offence thou hast given to thy prince humble thyself, and do not justify thyself, for that will make the offence much more offensive. In any ill design thou hast, upon some discontent, conceived against thy prince, do not proceed in it ; but *if thou hast done foolishly in lifting up thyself, or hast thought evil, lay thy hand upon thy mouth,*" Prov. xxx. 32. Note, Though we may by surprise be drawn into an evil thing, yet we must not stand in it, but recede from it as soon as it appears to us to be evil. (4.) We must prudently accommodate ourselves to our opportunities, both for our own relief, if we think ourselves wronged, and for the redress of public grievances : *A wise man's heart discerns both time and judgment* (*v.* 5) ; it is the wisdom of subjects, in applying themselves to their princes, to enquire and consider both at what season and in what manner they may do it best and most effectually, to pacify his anger, obtain his favour, or obtain the revocation of any grievous measure prescribed. Esther, in dealing with Ahasuerus, took a deal of pains to *discern both time and judgment,* and she sped accordingly. This may be taken as a general rule of wisdom, that every thing should be well timed ; and our enterprises are *then* likely to succeed, when we embrace the exact opportunity for them.

2. What arguments are here used to engage us to be subject to the higher powers; they are much the same with those which St. Paul uses, Rom. xiii. 1, &c. (1.) We *must needs be subject, for conscience-sake,* and that is the most powerful principle of subjection. We must be subject because *of the oath of God,* the oath of allegiance which we have taken to be faithful to the government, *the covenant between the king and the people,* 2 Chron. xxiii. 16. *David made a covenant,* or contract, *with the elders of Israel,* though he was king by divine designation, 1 Chron. xi. 3. "*Keep the king's commandments,* for he has sworn to rule thee in the fear of God, and thou hast sworn, in that fear, to be faithful to him." It is called *the oath of God* because he is a witness to it and will avenge the violation of it. (2.) *For wrath's sake,* because of the sword which the prince bears and the power he is entrusted with, which make him very formidable : *He does whatsoever pleases him ;* he has a great authority and a great ability to support that authority (*v.* 4) : *Where the word of a king is,* giving orders to seize a man, *there is power ;* there are many that will execute his orders, which makes *the wrath of a king,* or supreme government, like *the roaring of a lion* and

like *messengers of death. Who may say unto him, What doest thou?* He that contradicts him does it at his peril. Kings will not bear to have their orders disputed, but expect they should be obeyed. In short, it is dangerous contending with sovereignty, and what many have repented. A subject is an unequal match for a prince. *He* may command me who has legions at command. (3.) For the sake of our own comfort: *Whoso keeps the commandment,* and lives a quiet and peaceable life, *shall feel no evil thing,* to which that of the apostle answers (Rom. xiii. 3), *Wilt thou then not be afraid of the power* of the king? *Do that which is good,* as becomes a dutiful and loyal subject, *and thou shalt* ordinarily *have praise of the same.* He that does no ill shall feel no ill and needs fear none.

6 Because to every purpose there is time and judgment, therefore the misery of man *is* great upon him. 7 For he knoweth not that which shall be: for who can tell him when it shall be? 8 *There is* no man that hath power over the spirit to retain the spirit; neither *hath he* power in the day of death: and *there is* no discharge in *that* war; neither shall wickedness deliver those that are given to it.

Solomon had said (*v.* 5) that *a wise man's heart discerns time and judgment,* that is, a man's wisdom will go a great way, by the blessing of God, in moral prognostications; but here he shows that few have that wisdom, and that even the wisest may yet be surprised by a calamity which they had not any foresight of, and therefore it is our wisdom to expect and prepare for sudden changes. Observe, 1. All the events concerning us, with the exact time of them, are determined and appointed in the counsel and foreknowledge of God, and all in wisdom: *To every purpose there is a time* prefixed, and it is the best time, for it *is time and judgment,* time appointed both in wisdom and righteousness; the appointment is not chargeable with folly or iniquity. 2. We are very much in the dark concerning future events and the time and season of them: Man *knows not that which shall be* himself; and *who can tell him when* or how *it shall be? v.* 7. It cannot either be foreseen by him or foretold him; the stars cannot foretel a man what shall be, nor any of the arts of divination. God has, in wisdom, concealed from us the knowledge of future events, that we may be always ready for changes. 3. It is our great unhappiness and misery that, because we cannot foresee an evil, we know not how to avoid it, or guard against it, and, because we are not aware of the proper successful season of actions, therefore we lose our opportunities and miss our way: *Because to every purpose there is* but one way, one method, one proper opportun-

ity, *therefore the misery of man is great upon him;* because it is so hard to hit that, and it is a thousand to one but he misses it. Most of the miseries men labour under would have been prevented if they could have been foreseen and the happy time discovered to avoid them. Men are miserable because they are not sufficiently sagacious and attentive. 4. Whatever other evils may be avoided, we are all under a fatal necessity of dying, *v.* 8. (1.) When the soul is required it must be resigned, and it is to no purpose to dispute it, either by arms or arguments, by ourselves, or by any friend: *There is no man that has power over* his own *spirit, to retain it,* when it is summoned to return to God who gave it. It cannot fly any where out of the jurisdiction of death, nor find any place where its writs do not run. It cannot abscond so as to escape death's eye, though it is hidden from the eyes of all living. A man has no power to adjourn the day of his death, nor can he by prayers or bribes obtain a reprieve; no bail will be taken, no essoine [excuse], protection, or imparlance [conference], allowed. We have not *power over the spirit* of a friend, *to retain* that; the prince, with all his authority, cannot prolong the life of the most valuable of his subjects, nor the physician with his medicines and methods, nor the soldier with his force, nor the orator with his eloquence, nor the best saint with his intercessions. The stroke of death can by no means be put by when our days are determined and the hour appointed us has come. (2.) Death is an enemy that we must all enter the lists with, sooner or later: *There is no discharge in that war,* no dismission from it, either of the men of business or of the faint-hearted, as there was among the Jews, Deut. xx. 5, 8. While we live we are struggling with death, and we shall never put off the harness till we put off the body, never obtain a discharge till death has obtained the mastery; the youngest is not released as a fresh-water soldier, nor the oldest as *miles emeritus—a soldier whose merits have entitled him to a discharge.* Death is a battle that must be fought, *There is no sending to that war* (so some read it), no substituting another to muster for us, no champion admitted to fight for us; we must ourselves engage, and are concerned to provide accordingly, as for a battle. (3.) Men's wickedness, by which they often evade or outface the justice of the prince, cannot secure them from the arrest of death, nor can the most obstinate sinner harden his heart against those terrors. Though he *strengthen himself* ever so much *in his wickedness* (Ps. lii. 7), death will be too strong for him. The most subtle wickedness cannot outwit death, nor the most impudent wickedness outbrave death. Nay, the wickedness which men give themselves to will be so far from delivering them from death that it will deliver them up to death.

9 All this have I seen, and applied

my heart unto every work that is done under the sun: *there is* a time wherein one man ruleth over another to his own hurt. 10 And so I saw the wicked buried, who had come and gone from the place of the holy, and they were forgotten in the city where they had so done: this *is* also vanity. 11 Because sentence against an evil work is not executed speedily, therefore the heart of the sons of men is fully set in them to do evil. 12 Though a sinner do evil a hundred times, and his *days* be prolonged, yet surely I know that it shall be well with them that fear God, which fear before him: 13 But it shall not be well with the wicked, neither shall he prolong *his* days, *which are* as a shadow; because he feareth not before God.

Solomon, in the beginning of the chapter, had warned us against having any thing to do with seditious subjects; here, in these verses, he encourages us, in reference to the mischief of tyrannical and oppressive rulers, such as he had complained of before, *ch.* iii. 16; iv. 1.

1. He had observed many such rulers, *v.* 9. In the serious views and reviews he had taken of the children of men and their state he had observed that many a time *one man rules over another to his hurt;* that is, (1.) To the hurt of the ruled (many understand it so); whereas they ought to be God's ministers unto their subjects *for their good* (Rom. xiii. 14), to administer justice, and to preserve the public peace and order, they use their power for their hurt, to invade their property, encroach upon their liberty, and patronise the acts of injustice. It is sad with a people when those that should protect their religion and rights aim at the destruction of both. (2.) To the hurt of the rulers (so we render it), *to their own hurt*, to the feeling of their pride and covetousness, the gratifying of their passion and revenge, and so to the filling up of the measure of their sins and the hastening and aggravating of their ruin. *Agens agendo repatitur—What hurt men do to others will return, in the end, to their own hurt.*

2. He had observed them to prosper and flourish in the abuse of their power (*v.* 10): *I saw* those *wicked* rulers *come and go from the place of the holy*, go in state to and return in pomp from the place of judicature (which is called *the place of the Holy One* because *the judgment is the Lord's*, Deut. i. 17, and he *judges among the gods*, Ps. lxxxii. 1, and *is with them in the judgment*, 2 Chron. xix. 6), and they continued all their days in office, were never reckoned with for their mal-ad-

ministration, but died in honour and were buried magnificently; their commissions were *durante vitâ—during life*, and not *quamdiu se bene gesserint—during good behaviour*. *And they were forgotten in the city where they had so done:* their wicked practices were not remembered against them to their reproach and infamy when they were gone. Or, rather, it denotes the vanity of their dignity and power, for that is his remark upon it in the close of the verse: *This is also vanity.* They are proud of their wealth, and power, and honour, because they sit in the *place of the holy;* but all this cannot secure, (1.) Their bodies from being buried in the dust; *I saw* them laid in the grave; and their pomp, though it attended them thither, could *not descend after them*, Ps. xlix. 17. (2.) Nor their names from being buried in oblivion; for *they were forgotten*, as if they had never been.

3. He had observed that their prosperity hardened them in their wickedness, *v.* 11. It is true of all sinners in general, and particularly of wicked rulers, that, *because sentence against their evil works is not executed speedily*, they think it will never be executed, and therefore they set the law at defiance and *their hearts are full in them to do evil;* they venture to do so much the more mischief, fetch a greater compass in their wicked designs, and are secure and fearless in it, and commit iniquity with a high hand. Observe, (1.) Sentence is passed against evil works and evil workers by the righteous Judge of heaven and earth, even against the evil works of princes and great men, as well as of inferior persons. (2.) The execution of this sentence is often delayed a great while, and the sinner goes on, not only unpunished, but prosperous and successful. (3.) Impunity hardens sinners in impiety, and the patience of God is shamefully abused by many who, instead of being led by it to repentance, are confirmed by it in their impenitency. (4.) Sinners herein deceive themselves, for, though the *sentence* be *not executed speedily*, it will be executed the more severely at last. Vengeance comes slowly, but it comes surely, and wrath is in the mean time *treasured up against the day of wrath.*

4. He foresaw such an end of all these things as would be sufficient to keep us from quarrelling with the divine Providence upon account of them. He supposes a wicked ruler to do an unjust thing *a hundred times*, and that yet his punishment is deferred, and God's patience towards him *is prolonged*, much beyond what was expected, and the days of his power are lengthened out, so that he continues to oppress; yet he intimates that we should not be discouraged. (1.) God's people are certainly a happy people, though they be oppressed: "*It shall be well with those that fear God*, I say with all those, and those only, *who fear before him.*" Note, [1.] It is the character of God's people that they *fear God*, have an awe of him upon

their hearts and make conscience of their duty to him, and this because they see his eye always upon them and they know it is their concern to approve themselves to him. When they lie at the mercy of proud oppressors they fear God more than they fear them. They do not quarrel with the providence of God, but submit to it. [2.] It is the happiness of *all that fear God*, that in the worst of times *it shall be well with them;* their happiness in God's favour cannot be prejudiced, nor their communion with God interrupted, by their troubles; they are in a good case, for they are kept in a good frame under their troubles, and in the end they shall have a blessed deliverance from and an abundant recompence for their troubles. And therefore *" surely I know,* I know it by the promise of God, and the experience of all the saints, *that,* however it goes with others, *it shall go well with them.*" All is well that ends well. (2.) Wicked people are certainly a miserable people; though they prosper, and prevail, for a time, the curse is as sure to them as the blessing is to the righteous : *It shall not be well with the wicked,* as others think it is, who judge by outward appearance, and as they themselves expect it will be ; nay, *woe to the wicked ; it shall be ill with them* (Isa. iii. 10, 11); they shall be reckoned with for all the ill they have done ; nothing that befals them shall be really well for them. *Nihil potest ad malos pervenire quod prosit, imo nihil quod non noceat—No event can occur to the wicked which will do them good, rather no event which will not do them harm.* Seneca. Note, [1.] The wicked man's days *are as a shadow,* not only uncertain and declining, as all men's days are, but altogether unprofitable. A good man's days have some substance in them; he lives to a good purpose. A wicked man's days are all *as a shadow,* empty and worthless. [2.] These days *shall not be prolonged* to what he promised himself; he *shall not live out half his days,* Ps. lv. 23. Though they may be *prolonged* (v. 12) beyond what others expected, yet his day shall come to fall. He shall fall short of everlasting life, and then his long life on earth will be worth little. [3.] God's great quarrel with wicked people is for their *not fearing before* him; that is at the bottom of their wickedness, and cuts them off from all happiness.

14 There is a vanity which is done upon the earth; that there be just *men,* unto whom it happeneth according to the work of the wicked ; again, there be wicked *men,* to whom it happeneth according to the work of the righteous : I said that this also *is* vanity. 15 Then I commended mirth, because a man hath no better thing under the sun, than to eat, and to drink, and to be merry: for that shall abide with him of his labour the days of his life, which God giveth him under the sun. 16 When I applied mine heart to know wisdom, and to see the business that is done upon the earth : (for also *there is that* neither day nor night seeth sleep with his eyes :) 17 Then I beheld all the work of God, that a man cannot find out the work that is done under the sun : because though a man labour to seek *it* out, yet he shall not find *it ;* yea farther ; though a wise *man* think to know *it,* yet shall he not be able to find *it.*

Wise and good men have, of old, been perplexed with this difficulty, how the prosperity of the wicked and the troubles of the righteous can be reconciled with the holiness and goodness of the God that governs the world. Concerning this Solomon here gives us his advice.

I. He would not have us to be surprised at it, as though some strange thing happened, for he himself saw it in his days, *v.* 14. 1. He saw *just men to whom it happened according to the work of the wicked,* who, notwithstanding their righteousness, suffered very hard things, and continued long to do so, as if they were to be punished for some great wickedness. 2. He saw *wicked men to whom it happened according to the work of the righteous,* who prospered as remarkably as if they had been rewarded for some good deed, and that from themselves, from God, from men. We see the just troubled and perplexed in their own minds, the wicked easy, fearless, and secure,—the just crossed and afflicted by the divine Providence, the wicked prosperous, successful, and smiled upon,—the just, censured, reproached, and run down, by the higher powers, the wicked applauded and preferred.

II. He would have us to take occasion hence, not to charge God with iniquity, but to charge the world with vanity. No fault is to be found with God ; but, as to the world, This *is vanity upon the earth,* and again, *This is also vanity,* that is, it is a certain evidence that the things of this world are not the best things nor were ever designed to make a portion and happiness for us, for, if they had, God would not have allotted so much of this world's wealth to his worst enemies and so much of its troubles to his best friends ; there must therefore be another life after this the joys and griefs of which must be real and substantial, and able to make men truly happy or truly miserable, for this world does neither.

III. He would have us not to fret and perplex ourselves about it, or make ourselves uneasy, but cheerfully to enjoy what God has given us in the world, to be content with it and make the best of it, though it be much better with others, and such as we think very unworthy (*v.* 15): *Then I commended joy,* a holy security and serenity of mind, arising from a confidence in God, and his power, providence, and promise, *because a man has no better thing under the sun* (though a good man has much better things *above* the sun) *than to eat and drink,* that is, soberly and thankfully to make use of the things of this life according as his rank is, *and to be cheerful,* whatever happens, *for that shall abide with him of his labour.* That is all the fruit he has for himself of the pains that he takes in the business of the world; let him therefore take it, and much good may it do him; and let him not deny himself that, out of a peevish discontent because the world does not go as he would have it. *That shall abide with him* during *the days of his life which God gives him under the sun.* Our present life is a life *under the sun,* but we look for *the life of the world to come,* which will commence and continue when *the sun shall be turned into darkness* and shine no more. This present life must be reckoned by days; this life is given us, and the days of it are allotted to us, by the counsel of God, and therefore while it does last we must accommodate ourselves to the will of God and study to answer the ends of life.

IV. He would not have us undertake to give a reason for that which God does, for *his way is in the sea and his path in the great waters,* past finding out, and therefore we must be contentedly and piously ignorant of the meaning of God's proceedings in the government of the world, *v.* 16, 17. Here he shows, 1. That both he himself and many others had very closely studied the point, and searched far into the reasons of the prosperity of the wicked and the afflictions of the righteous. He, for his part, had *applied his heart to know* this *wisdom, and to see the business that is done,* by the divine Providence, *upon the earth,* to find out if there were any certain scheme, any constant rule or method, by which the affairs of this lower world were administered, any course of government as sure and steady as the course of nature, so that by what is done now we might as certainly foretel what will be done next as by the moon's changing now we can foretel when it will be at the full; this he would fain have found out. Others had likewise set themselves to make this enquiry with so close an application that they could not find time for *sleep, either day or night,* nor find in their hearts to sleep, so full of anxiety were they about these things. Some think Solomon speaks of himself, that he was so eager in prosecuting this great enquiry that he could not sleep for thinking of it. 2. That it was all labour in vain, *v.* 17. When we look upon *all the works of God* and his providence, and compare one part with another, we *cannot find* that there is any such certain method by which *the work that is done under the sun* is directed; we cannot discover

1030

any key by which to decypher the character, nor by consulting precedents can we know the practice of this court, nor what the judgment will be. [1.] *Though a man* be ever so industrious, though he *labour to seek it out.* [2.] Though he be ever so ingenious, *though* he be *a wise man* in other things, and can fathom the counsels of kings themselves and trace them by their footsteps. Nay, [3.] Though he be very confident of success, though he *think to know it, yet he shall not;* he cannot *find it out.* God's ways are above ours, nor is he tied to his own former ways, but *his judgments are a great deep.*

CHAP. IX.

Solomon, in this chapter, for a further proof of the vanity of this world, gives us four observations which he had made upon a survey of the state of the children of men in it:—I. He observed that commonly, as to outward things, good and bad men fare much alike, ver. 1—3. II. That death puts a final period to all our employments and enjoyments in this world (ver. 4—6), whence he infers that it is our wisdom to enjoy the comforts of life and mind the business of life, while it lasts, ver. 7—10. III. That God's providence often crosses the fairest and most hopeful probabilities of men's endeavour, and great calamities often surprise men ere they are aware, ver. 11, 12. IV. That wisdom often makes men very useful, and yet gains them little respect, for that persons of great merit are slighted, ver. 13—18. And what is there then in this world that should make us fond of it?

FOR all this I considered in my heart even to declare all this, that the righteous, and the wise, and their works, *are* in the hand of God: no man knoweth either love or hatred *by* all *that is* before them. 2 All *things* **come** alike to all: *there is* one event to the righteous, and to the wicked; to the good and to the clean, and to the unclean; to him that sacrificeth, and to him that sacrificeth not: as *is* the good, so *is* the sinner; *and* he that sweareth, as *he* that feareth an oath. 3 This *is* an evil among all *things* that are done under the sun, that *there is* one event unto all: yea, also the heart of the sons of men is full of evil, and madness *is* in their heart while they live, and after that *they go* to the dead.

It has been observed concerning those who have pretended to search for the philosophers' stone that, though they could never find what they sought for, yet in the search they have hit upon many other useful discoveries and experiments. Thus Solomon, when, in the close of the foregoing chapter, he *applied his heart to know the work of God,* and took a great deal of pains to search into it, though he despaired of finding it out, yet he found out that which abundantly recompensed him for the search, and gave him some satisfaction, which he here gives us; *for* therefore *he considered all this in his heart,* and weighed it deliberately, that he might *declare* it for the good of others. Note, What we are *to declare* we should first *consider;* think twice before we speak once; and what we have con-

sidered we should then *declare   I believed, therefore have I spoken.*

The great difficulty which Solomon met with in studying the book of providence was the little difference that is made between good men and bad in the distribution of comforts and crosses, and the disposal of events. This has perplexed the minds of many wise and contemplative men. Solomon discourses of it in these verses, and, though he does not undertake to find out this *work of God*, yet he says that which may prevent its being a stumbling-block to us.

I. Before he describes the temptation in its strength he lays down a great and unquestionable truth, which he resolves to adhere to, and which, if firmly believed, will be sufficient to break the force of the temptation. This has been the way of God's people in grappling with this difficulty. Job, before he discourses of this matter, lays down the doctrine of God's omniscience (Job xxiv. 1), Jeremiah the doctrine of his righteousness (Jer. xii. 1), another prophet that of his holiness (Hab. i. 13), the psalmist that of his goodness and peculiar favour to his own people (Ps. lxxiii. 1), and that is it which Solomon here fastens upon and resolves to abide by, that, though good and evil seem to be dispensed promiscuously, yet God has a particular care of and concern for his own people: *The righteous and the wise, and their works, are in the hand of God*, under his special protection and guidance ; all their affairs are managed by him for their good; all their wise and righteous actions *are in his hand*, to be recompensed in the other world, though not in this. They seem as if they were given up *into the hand of their enemies*, but it is not so. Men have *no power against them but what is given them from above.* The events that affect them do not come to pass by chance, but all according to the will and counsel of God, which will turn that to be for them which seemed to be most against them. Let this make us easy, whatever happens, that all God's saints are in his hand, Deut. xxxiii. 3; John x. 29; Ps. xxxi. 15.

II. He lays this down for a rule, that the love and hatred of God are not to be measured and judged of by men's outward condition. If prosperity were a certain sign of God's love, and affliction of his hatred, then it might justly be an offence to us to see the wicked and godly fare alike. But the matter is not so: *No man knows either love or hatred by all that is before him* in this world, by those things that are the objects of sense. These we may know by that which is within us ; if we love God with all our heart, thereby we may know that he loves us, as we may know likewise that we are under his wrath if we be governed by that carnal mind which is enmity to him. These will be known by that which shall be hereafter, by men's everlasting state ; it is certain that men are happy or miserable according as they are under the love or hatred of God, but not ac-

cording as they are under the smiles or frowns of the world ; and therefore if God loves a righteous man (as certainly he does) he is happy, though the world frown upon him ; and if he hates a wicked man (as certainly he does) he is miserable, though the world smile upon him. Then the offence of this promiscuous distribution of events has ceased.

III. Having laid down these principles, he acknowledges that *all things come alike to all;* so it has been formerly, and therefore we are not to think it strange if it be so now, if it be so with us and our families. Some make this, and all that follows to *v.* 13, to be the perverse reasoning of the atheists against the doctrine of God's providence; but I rather take it to be Solomon's concession, which he might the more freely make when he had fixed those truths which are sufficient to guard against any ill use that may be made of what he grants. Observe here (*v.* 2),

1. The great difference that there is between the characters of the righteous and the wicked, which, in several instances, are set the one over-against the other, to show that, though *all things come alike to all*, yet that does not in the least confound the eternal distinction between moral good and evil, but that remains immutable. (1.) The righteous are *clean*, have *clean hands and pure hearts;* the wicked are *unclean*, under the dominion of unclean lusts, *pure* perhaps *in their own eyes*, but not *cleansed from their filthiness.* God will certainly put a difference *between the clean and the unclean, the precious and the vile*, in the other world, though he does not seem to do so in this. (2.) The righteous *sacrifice*, that is, they make conscience of worshipping God according to his will, both with inward and outward worship ; the wicked *sacrifice not*, that is, they live in the neglect of God's worship and grudge to part with any thing for his honour. *What is the Almighty, that they should serve him?* (3.) The righteous are *good*, good in God's sight, they do good in the world; the wicked are *sinners*, violating the laws of God and man, and provoking to both. (4.) The wicked man *swears*, has no veneration for the name of God, but profanes it by swearing rashly and falsely ; but the righteous man *fears an oath*, swears not, but is sworn, and then with great reverence ; he fears to take an oath, because it is a solemn appeal to God as a witness and judge ; he fears, when he has taken an oath, to break it, because God is righteous who takes vengeance.

2. The little difference there is between the conditions of the righteous and the wicked in this world: *There is one event to* both. Is David rich? So is Nabal. Is Joseph favoured by his prince? So is Haman. Is Ahab killed in a battle? So is Josiah. Are the bad figs carried to Babylon? So are the good, Jer. xxiv. 1. There is a vast difference between the original, the design, and the nature, of the same event to the one and to the other ; the effects and issues of it are likewise vastly

different; the same providence to the one is a *savour of life unto life,* to the other *of death unto death,* though, to outward appearance, it is the same.

IV. He owns this to be a very great grievance to those that are wise and good: "*This is an evil,* the greatest perplexity, *among all things that are done under the sun* (v. 3); nothing has given me more disturbance than this, *that there is one event unto all.* It hardens atheists, and strengthens the hands of evil-doers; for therefore it is that *the hearts of the sons of men are full of evil* and *fully set in them to do evil, ch.* viii. 11. When they see that *there is one event to the righteous and the wicked* they wickedly infer thence that it is all one to God whether they are righteous or wicked, and therefore they stick at nothing to gratify their lusts.

V. For the further clearing of this great difficulty, as he began this discourse with the doctrine of the happiness of the righteous (whatever they may suffer, they *and their works are in the hands of God,* and therefore in good hands, they could not be in better), so he concludes with the doctrine of the misery of the wicked; however they may prosper, *madness is in their heart while they live, and after that they go to the dead.* Envy not the prosperity of evil-doers, for, 1. They are now madmen, and all the delights they seem to be blessed with are but like the pleasant dreams and fancies of a distracted man. They are *mad upon their idols* (Jer 1. 38), are mad against God's people, Acts xxvi. 11. When the prodigal repented, it is said, *He came to himself* (Luke xv. 17), which intimates that he had been beside himself before. 2. They will shortly be dead men. They make a mighty noise and bustle *while they live,* but, after awhile, *they go to the dead,* and there is an end of all their pomp and power; they will then be reckoned with for all their madness and outrage in sin. Though, on this side death, the righteous and the wicked seem alike, on the other side death there will be a vast difference between them.

4 For to him that is joined to all the living there is hope: for a living dog is better than a dead lion. 5 For the living know that they shall die: but the dead know not any thing, neither have they any more a reward; for the memory of them is forgotten. 6 Also their love, and their hatred, and their envy, is now perished; neither have they any more a portion for ever in any *thing* that is done under the sun. 7 Go thy way, eat thy bread with joy, and drink thy wine with a merry heart; for God now accepteth thy works. 8 Let thy garments be always white; and let thy head lack

no ointment. 9 Live joyfully with the wife whom thou lovest all the days of the life of thy vanity, which he hath given thee under the sun, all the days of thy vanity: for that *is* thy portion in *this* life, and in thy labour which thou takest under the sun. 10 Whatsoever thy hand findeth to do, do *it* with thy might; for *there is* no work, nor device, nor knowledge, nor wisdom, in the grave, whither thou goest.

Solomon, in a fret, had *praised the dead more than the living* (*ch.* iv. 2); but here, considering the advantages of life to prepare for death and make sure the hope of a better life, he seems to be of another mind.

I. He shows, the advantages which the living have above those that are dead, *v.* 4—6. 1. While there is life *there is hope. Dum spiro, spero—While I breathe, I hope.* It is the privilege of the living that they are *joined to the living,* in relation, commerce, and conversation, and, while they are so, *there is hope.* If a man's condition be, upon any account, bad, *there is hope* it will be amended. If *the heart be full of evil, and madness be in it,* yet while there is life *there is hope* that by the grace of God there may be a blessed change wrought; but after men *go to the dead* (*v.* 3) it is too late then; he that is then filthy will be filthy still, for ever filthy. If men be thrown aside as useless, yet, while they are *joined to the living, there is hope* that they may yet again take root and bear fruit; he that is alive is, or may be, good for something, but he that is dead, as to this world, is not capable of being any further serviceable. Therefore *a living dog is better than a dead lion;* the meanest beggar alive has that comfort of this world and does that service to it which the greatest prince, when he is dead, is utterly incapable of. 2. While there is life there is an opportunity of preparing for death: *The living know* that which the dead have no knowledge of, particularly they *know that they shall die,* and are, or may be, thereby influenced to prepare for that great change which will come certainly, and may come suddenly. Note, *The living* cannot but *know that they shall die,* that they must needs die. They know they are under a sentence of death; they are already taken into custody by its messengers, and feel themselves declining. This is a needful useful knowledge; for what is our business, while we live, but to get ready to die? *The living know they shall die;* it is a thing yet to come, and therefore provision may be made for it. The dead know they are dead, and it is too late; they are on the other side the great gulf fixed. 3. When life is gone all this world is gone with it, as to us. (1.) There is an end of all our acquaintance with this world and the things of it: *The dead know not any thing* of that which, while they lived, they were intimately conversant with. It does not appear that they know any thing of what is done by those they leave behind. Abraham is ignorant of us; they are removed *into darkness*, Job x. 22. (2.) There is an end of all our enjoyments in this world : *They have no more a reward* for their toils about the world, but all they got must be left to others ; they have a reward for their holy actions, but not for their worldly ones. The meats and the belly will be destroyed together, John vi. 27 ; 1 Cor. vi. 13. It is explained *v.* 6. *Neither have they any more a portion for ever,* none of that which they imagined would be *a portion for ever,* of that which *is done* and got *under the sun.* The things of this world will not be a portion for the soul because they will not be a portion for ever ; those that choose them, and have them for *their good things,* have only a *portion in this life,* Ps. xvii. 14. The world can only be an annuity for life, not a *portion for ever.* (3.) There is an end of their name. There are but few whose names survive them long ; the grave is a land of forgetfulness, *for the memory of those* that are laid there *is* soon *forgotten ;* their *place knows them no more,* nor the lands they called by their own names. (4.) There is an end of their affections, their friendships and enmities : *Their love, and their hatred, and their envy have now perished ;* the good things they loved, the evil things they hated, the prosperity of others, which they envied, are now all at an end with them. Death parts those that loved one another, and puts an end to their friendship, and those that hated one another too, and puts an end to their quarrels. *Actio moritur cum personâ*—*The person and his actions die together.* There we shall be never the better for our friends (their love can do us no kindness), nor ever the worse for our enemies— their hatred and envy can do us no damage. *There the wicked cease from troubling.* Those things which now so affect us and fill us, which we are so concerned about and so jealous of, will there be at an end.

II. Hence he infers that it is our wisdom to make the best use of life that we can while it does last, and manage wisely what remains of it.

1. Let us relish the comforts of life while we live, and cheerfully take our share of the enjoyments of it. Solomon, having been himself ensnared by the abuse of sensitive delights, warns others of the danger, not by a total prohibition of them, but by directing to the sober and moderate use of them ; we may use the world, but must not abuse it, take what is to be had out of it, and expect no more. Here we have,

(1.) The particular instances of this cheerfulness prescribed : "Thou art drooping and melancholy, *go thy way,* like a fool as thou art, and get into a better temper of mind." [1.] " Let thy spirit be easy and pleasant ; then let there be *joy* and *a merry heart* within," *a good heart* (so the word is), which distinguishes this from carnal mirth and sensual pleasure, which are the evil of the heart, both a symptom and a cause of much evil there. We must enjoy ourselves, enjoy our friends, enjoy our God, and be careful to keep a good conscience, that nothing may disturb us in these enjoyments. We must serve God with gladness, in the use of what he gives us, and be liberal in communicating it to others, and not suffer ourselves to be oppressed with inordinate care and grief about the world. We must eat our bread as Israelites, *not in our mourning* (Deut. xxvi. 14), as Christians, *with gladness and* liberality *of heart,* Acts ii. 46. See Deut. xxviii. 47. [2.] " Make use of the comforts and enjoyments which God has given thee : *Eat thy bread, drink thy wine,* thine, not another's, not *the bread of deceit,* nor *the wine of violence,* but that which is honestly got, else thou canst not eat it with any comfort nor expect a blessing upon it— *thy bread* and *thy wine,* such as are agreeable to thy place and station, not extravagantly above it nor sordidly below it ; lay out what God has given thee for the ends for which thou art entrusted with it, as being but a steward." [3.] " Evidence thy cheerfulness (*v.* 8) : *Let thy garments be always white.* Observe a proportion in thy expenses ; reduce not thy food in order to gratify thy pride, nor thy clothing in order to gratify thy voluptuousness. Be neat, wear clean linen, and be not slovenly." Or, " *Let thy garments be white* in token of joy and cheerfulness," which were expressed by *white raiment* (Rev. iii. 4) ; "and as a further token of joy, *let thy head lack no ointment* that is fit for it." Our Saviour admitted this piece of pleasure at a feast (Matt. xxvi. 7), and David observes it among the gifts of God's bounty to him. Ps. xxiii. 5, *Thou anointest my head with oil.* Not that we must place our happiness in any of the delights of sense, or set our hearts upon them, but what God has given us we must make as comfortable a use of as we can afford, under the limitations of sobriety and wisdom, and not forgetting the poor. [4.] " Make thyself agreeable to thy relations : *Live joyfully with the wife whom thou lovest.* Do not engross thy delights, making much of thyself only, and not caring what becomes of those about thee, but let them share with thee and make them easy too. Have a wife ; for even in paradise *it was not good for man to be alone* Keep to thy wife, to one, and do not multiply wives" (Solomon had found the mischief of that) ; " keep to her only, and have nothing to do with any other." How can a man live joyfully with one with whom he does not live honestly ? " Love thy wife ; and *the wife whom thou lovest* thou wilt be likely to *live joyfully with.*" When we do the duty of relations we may expect the comfort of them. See Prov. v. 19. " Live with thy wife, and delight in her society. *Live joyfully with her,* and be most cheerful when thou art with her. Take pleasure in thy family, thy vine and thy olive plants."

(2.) The qualifications necessary to this cheerfulness: " Rejoice and have *a merry heart,* if *God now accepts thy works.* If thou art reconciled to God, and recommended to him, then thou hast reason to be cheerful, otherwise not." *Rejoice not, O Israel! for joy, as other people, for thou hast gone a whoring from thy God,* Hos. IX. 1. Our first care must be to make our peace with God, and obtain his favour, to do that which he will accept of, and then, *Go thy way, eat thy bread with joy.* Note, Those whose works God has accepted have reason to be cheerful and ought to be so. " Now that thou eatest the bread of thy sacrifices *with joy,* and partakest of the wine of thy drink-offerings *with a merry heart,* now *God accepts thy works.* Thy religious services, when performed with holy joy, are pleasing to God; he loves to have his servants sing at their work, it proclaims him a good Master.

(3.) The reasons for it. " Live joyfully, for," [1.] " It is all little enough to make thy passage through this world easy and comfortable: *The days of thy life* are the days *of thy vanity ;* there is nothing here but trouble, and disappointment. Thou wilt have time enough for sorrow and grief when thou canst not help it, and therefore *live joyfully* while thou canst, and perplex not thyself with thoughts and cares about to-morrow; *sufficient to the day is the evil thereof.* Let a gracious serenity of mind be a powerful antidote against the vanity of the world." [2.] " It is all thou canst get from this world: *That is thy portion in* the things of *this life.* In God, and another life, thou shalt have a better portion, and a better recompence for thy labours in religion; but for thy pains *which thou takest* about the things *under the sun* this is all thou canst expect, and therefore do not deny this to thyself."

2. Let us apply ourselves to the business of life while life lasts, and so use the enjoyments of it as by them to be fitted for the employments: " Therefore *eat with joy* and *a merry heart,* not that thy soul may take its ease (as Luke xii. 19), but that thy soul may take the more pains and the joy of the Lord may be its strength and oil to its wheels," *v.* 10. *Whatsoever thy hand finds to do do it with thy might.* Observe here, (1.) There is not only something to be had, but something to be done, in this life, and the chief good we are to enquire after is *the good we should do,* Eccl. ii. 3. This is the world of service; that to come is the world of recompence. This is the world of probation and preparation for eternity; we are here upon business, and upon our good behaviour. (2.) Opportunity is to direct and quicken duty. That is to be done which *our hand finds to do,* which occasion calls for; and an active hand will always find something to do that will turn to a good account. What must be done, of necessity, our hand will here find a price in it for the doing of, Prov. xvii. 16.

(3.) What good we have an opportunity of doing we must do while we have the opportunity, and *do it with our might,* with care, vigour, and resolution, whatever difficulties and discouragements we may meet with in it. Harvest-days are busy days; and we must make hay while the sun shines. Serving God and working out our salvation must be done with *all that is within us,* and all little enough. (4.) There is good reason why we should *work the works of him that sent us while it is day, because the night comes, wherein no man can work,* John ix. 4. We must up and be doing now with all possible diligence, because our doing-time will be done shortly and we know not how soon. But this we know that, if the work of life be not done when our time is done, we are undone for ever: " *There is no work* to be done, *nor device* to do it, *no knowledge* for speculation, *nor wisdom* for practice, *in the grave whither thou goest.*" We are all going towards the grave; every day brings us a step nearer to it; when we are *in the grave* it will be too late to mend the errors of life, too late to repent and make our peace with God, too late to lay up any thing in store for eternal life; it must be done now or never. The grave is a land of darkness and silence, and therefore there is no doing any thing for our souls there; it must be done now or never, John xii. 35.

11 I returned, and saw under the sun, that the race *is* not to the swift, nor the battle to the strong, neither yet bread to the wise, nor yet riches to men of understanding, nor yet favour to men of skill; but time and chance happeneth to them all. 12 For man also knoweth not his time: as the fishes that are taken in an evil net, and as the birds that are caught in the snare; so *are* the sons of men snared in an evil time, when it falleth suddenly upon them.

The preacher here, for a further proof of the vanity of the world, and to convince us that *all our works are in the hand of God,* and not in our own hand, shows the uncertainty and contingency of future events, and how often they contradict the prospects we have of them. He had exhorted us (*v.* 10) to do what we have to do *with all our might ;* but here he reminds us that, when we have done all, we must leave the issue with God, and not be confident of the success.

I. We are often disappointed of the good we had great hopes of, *v.* 11. Solomon had himself made the observation, and so has many a one since, that events, both in public and private affairs, do not always agree even with the most rational prospects and probabilities. *Nulli fortuna tam dedita est ut multa tentanti ubique respondeat—Fortune surrenders herself to no one so as to ensure him success, however numerous his undertakings.* Seneca. The issue of affairs is often unaccountably cross to every one's expectation, that the highest may not presume, nor the lowest despair, but all may live in a humble dependence upon God, from whom every man's judgment proceeds.

1. He gives instances of disappointment, even where means and instruments were most encouraging and promised fair. (1.) One would think that the lightest of foot should, in running, win the prize; and yet *the race is not* always *to the swift;* some accident happens to retard them, or they are too secure, and therefore remiss, and let those that are slower get the start of them. (2.) One would think that, in fighting, the most numerous and powerful army should be always victorious, and, in single combat, that the bold and mighty champion should win the laurel; but *the battle is not* always *to the strong;* a host of Philistines was once put to flight by Jonathan and his man; *one of you shall chase a thousand;* the goodness of the cause has often carried the day against the most formidable power. (3.) One would think that men of sense should always be men of substance, and that those who know how to live in the world should not only have a plentiful maintenance, but get great estates; and yet it does not always prove so; even *bread is not* always *to the wise,* much less *riches* always *to men of understanding.* Many ingenious men, and men of business, who were likely to thrive in the world, have strangely gone backward and come to nothing. (4.) One would think that those who understand men, and have the art of management, should always get preferment and obtain the smiles of great men; but many ingenious men have been disappointed, and have spent their days in obscurity, nay, have fallen into disgrace, and perhaps have ruined themselves by those very methods by which they hoped to raise themselves, for *favour is not* always *to men of skill,* but fools are favoured and wise men frowned upon.

2. He resolves all these disappointments into an over-ruling power and providence, the disposals of which to us seem casual, and we call them *chance,* but really they are according to the determinate counsel and foreknowledge of God, here called *time,* in the language of this book, *ch.* iii. 1; Ps. xxxi. 15. *Time and chance happen to them all.* A sovereign Providence breaks men's measures, and blasts their hopes, and teaches them that the way of man is not in himself, but subject to the divine will. We must use means, but not trust to them; if we succeed, we must give God the praise (Ps. xliv. 3); if we be crossed, we must acquiesce in his will and take our lot.

II. We are often surprised with the evils we were in little fear of (*v.* 12): *Man knows not his time,* the time of his calamity, his fall, his death, which, in scripture, is called *our day* and *our hour.* 1. We know not what

troubles are before us, which will take us off our business, and take us out of the world, what *time and chance will happen to us,* nor what *one day,* or a night, *may bring forth.* It is *not for us to know the times,* no, not our own time, when or how we shall die. God has, in wisdom, kept us in the dark, that we may be always ready. 2. Perhaps we may meet with trouble in that very thing wherein we promise ourselves the greatest satisfaction and advantage; as the fishes and the birds are drawn into the snare and net by the bait laid to allure them, which they greedily catch at, so are the sons of men often *snared in an evil time,* when it falls suddenly upon them, before they are aware. And these things too *come alike to all.* Men often find their bane where they sought their bliss, and catch their death where they thought to find a prize. Let us therefore never be secure, but always ready for changes, that, though they may be sudden, they may be no surprise or terror to us.

13 This wisdom have I seen also under the sun, and it *seemed* great unto me: 14 *There was* a little city, and few men within it; and there came a great king against it, and besieged it, and built great bulwarks against it: 15 Now there was found in it a poor wise man, and he by his wisdom delivered the city; yet no man remembered that same poor man. 16 Then said I, Wisdom *is* better than strength: nevertheless the poor man's wisdom *is* despised, and his words are not heard. 17 The words of wise *men are* heard in quiet more than the cry of him that ruleth among fools. 18 Wisdom *is* better than weapons of war: but one sinner destroyeth much good.

Solomon still recommends wisdom to us as necessary to the preserving of our peace and the perfecting of our business, notwithstanding the vanities and crosses which human affairs are subject to. He had said (*v.*11), *Bread is not always to the wise;* yet he would not therefore be thought either to disparage, or to discourage, wisdom, no, he still retains his principle, that *wisdom excels folly as much as light excels darkness* (ch. ii. 13), and we ought to love and embrace it, and be governed by it, for the sake of its own intrinsic worth, and the capacity it gives us of being serviceable to others, though we ourselves should not get wealth and preferment by it. This wisdom, that is, this which he here describes, wisdom which enables a man to serve his country out of pure affection to its interests, when he himself gains no advantage by it, no, not so much as thanks for his pains, or the reputation of it, this is the wisdom which, Solomon says, *seemed great unto him,* *v.* 13. A public spirit, in a private sphere, is wisdom which those who understand things that differ cannot but look upon as very magnificent.

I. Solomon here gives an instance, which probably was a case in fact, in some neighbouring country, of a *poor man* who with his wisdom did great service in a time of public distress and danger (*v.* 14): *There was a little city* (no great prize, whoever was master of it); there were but *few men within it*, to defend it, and men, if men of fortitude, are the best fortifications of a city; here were *few men*, and, because few, feeble, fearful, and ready to give up their city as not tenable. Against this little city a *great king* came with a numerous army, and besieged it, either in pride, or covetousness to possess it, or in revenge for some affront given him, to chastise and destroy it. Thinking it stronger than it was, he *built great bulwarks against it*, from which to batter it, and doubted not but in a little time to make himself master of it. What a great deal of unjust vexation do ambitious princes give to their harmless neighbours! This *great king* needed not fear this *little city*; why then should he frighten it? It would be little profit to him; why then should he put himself to such a great expense to gain it? But as unreasonably and insatiably greedy as little people sometimes are to *lay house to house, and field to field*, great kings often are to lay city to city, and province to province, *that they may be placed alone in the earth*, Isa. v. 8. Did victory and success attend the *strong?* No; there was found in this little city, among the few men that were in it, *one poor wise man*—a wise man, and yet poor, and not preferred to any place of profit or power in the city; places of trust were not given to men according to their merit, and meetness for them, else such a wise man as this would not have been a poor man. Now, 1. Being wise, he served the city, though he was poor. In their distress they found him out (Judg. xi. 7) and begged his advice and assistance; and *he by his wisdom delivered the city*, either by prudent instructions given to the besieged, directing them to some unthought-of stratagem for their own security, or by a prudent treaty with the besiegers, as the woman at Abel, 2 Sam. xx. 16. He did not upbraid them with the contempt they had put upon him, in leaving him out of their council, nor tell them he was poor and had nothing to lose, and therefore cared not what became of the city; but he did his best for it, and was blessed with success. Note, Private interests and personal resentments must always be sacrificed to the public good and forgotten when the common welfare is concerned. 2. Being poor, he was slighted by the city, though he was wise and had been an instrument to save them all from ruin: *No man remembered that same poor man;* his good

services were not taken notice of, no recompence was made him, no marks of honour were put upon him, but he lived in as much poverty and obscurity as he had done before. *Riches were not* to this *man of understanding*, nor *favour to* this *man of skill.* Many who have well-merited of their prince and country have been ill-paid; such an ungrateful world do we live in. It is well that useful men have a God to trust to, who will be their bountiful rewarder; for, among men, great services are often envied and rewarded with evil for good.

II. From this instance he draws some useful inferences, looks upon it and receives instruction. 1. Hence he observes the great usefulness and excellency of wisdom, and what a blessing it makes men to their country: *Wisdom is better than strength, v.* 16. A prudent mind, which is the honour of a man, is to be preferred before a robust body, in which many of the brute creatures excel man. A man may by his wisdom effect that which he could never compass by his strength, and may overcome those by out-witting them who are able to overpower him. Nay, *wisdom is better than weapons of war*, offensive or defensive, *v.* 18. *Wisdom,* that is, religion and piety (for the wise man is here opposed to a sinner), is better than all military endowments or accoutrements, for it will engage God for us, and then we are safe in the greatest perils and successful in the greatest enterprises. *If God be for us, who can be against us* or stand before us? 2. Hence he observes the commanding force and power of wisdom, though it labour under external disadvantages (*v.* 17): *The words of wise men are heard in quiet;* what they speak, being rational and to the purpose, being spoken calmly and with deliberation (though, not being rich and in authority, they dare not speak aloud nor with any great assurance), will be hearkened to and regarded, will gain respect, nay, will gain the point, and sway with men more than the imperious clamour of him that *rules among fools*, who, like fools, chose him to be their ruler, for his noise and blustering, and, like fools, think he must by those methods carry the day with every body else. A few close arguments are worth a great many big words; and those will strike sail to fair reasoning who will answer those that hector and insult *according to their folly*. How forcible are *right words!* What is spoken wisely should be spoken calmly, and then it will be heard in quiet and calmly considered. But passion will lessen the force even of reason, instead of adding any force to it. 3. Hence he observes that wise and good men, notwithstanding this, must often content themselves with the satisfaction of having done good, or at least attempted it, and offered at it, when they cannot do the good they would do nor have the praise they should have. Wisdom capacitates a man to serve his neighbours, and he offers his service; but, alas! if he be poor his wisdom is despised, and *his words are not heard, v.* 16. Many a man is buried alive in poverty and obscurity who, if he had but fit encouragement given him, might be a great blessing to the world; many a pearl is lost in its shell. But there is a day coming when wisdom and goodness shall be in honour, and the *righteous shall shine forth.*

4. From what he had observed of the great good which one wise and virtuous man may do he infers what a great deal of mischief one wicked man may do, and what a great deal of good he may be the hindrance of: *One sinner destroyeth much good.* (1.) As to himself, a sinful condition is a wasteful condition. How many of the good gifts both of nature and Providence does one sinner destroy and make waste of—good sense, good parts, good learning, a good disposition, a good estate, good meat, good drink, and abundance of God's good creatures, all made use of in the service of sin, and so destroyed and lost, and the end of giving them frustrated and perverted! He who destroys his own soul destroys much good. (2.) As to others, what a great deal of mischief may one wicked man do in a town or country! One sinner, who makes it his business to debauch others, may defeat and frustrate the intentions of a great many good laws and a great deal of good preaching, and draw many into his pernicious ways; one sinner may be the ruin of a town, as one Achan troubled the whole camp of Israel. The wise man who delivered the city would have had his due respect and recompence for it but that some one sinner hindered it, and invidiously diminished the service. And many a good project, well laid for the public welfare, has been destroyed by some one subtle adversary to it. The wisdom of some would have healed the nation, but, through the wickedness of a few, it would not be healed. See who are a kingdom's friends and enemies, if one saint does much good, and one sinner destroys much good.

CHAP. X.

This chapter seems to be like Solomon's proverbs, a collection of wise sayings and observations, rather than a part of his sermon ; but the preacher studied to be sententious, and " set in order many proverbs," to be brought in in his preaching. Yet the general scope of all the observations in this chapter is to recommend wisdom to us, and its precepts and rules, as of great use for the right ordering of our conversation and to caution us against folly. I. He recommends wisdom to private persons, who are in an inferior station. 1. It is our wisdom to preserve our reputation, in managing our affairs dexterously, ver. 1—3. 2. To be submissive to our superiors if at any time we have offended them, ver. 4. 3. To live quiet and peaceable lives, and not to meddle with those that are factious and seditious, and are endeavouring to disturb the government and the public repose, the folly and danger of which disloyal and turbulent practices he shows, ver. 8—11. 4. To govern our tongues well, ver. 12—15. 5. To be diligent in our business and provide well for our families, ver. 18, 19. 6. Not to speak ill of our rulers, no, not in secret, ver. 20. II. He recommends wisdom to rulers ; let them not think that, because their subjects must be quiet under them, therefore they may do what they please ; no, but, 1. Let them be careful whom they prefer to places of trust and power, ver. 5 —7. 2. Let them manage themselves discreetly, be generous and not childish, temperate and not luxurious, ver. 16, 17. Happy the nation when princes and people make conscience of their duty according to these rules.

DEAD flies cause the ointment of the apothecary to send forth a stinking savour: *so doth* a little folly

---

him that is in reputation for wisdom *and* honour. 2 A wise man's heart *is* at his right hand ; but a fool's heart at his left. 3 Yea also, when he that is a fool walketh by the way, his wisdom faileth *him,* and he saith to every one *that* he *is* a fool.

In these verses Solomon shows,

I. What great need wise men have to take heed of being guilty of any instance of folly; for *a little folly* is a great blemish to him that *is in reputation for wisdom and honour,* and is as hurtful to his good name as *dead flies* are to a sweet perfume, not only spoiling the sweetness of it, but making it *to send forth a stinking savour.* Note, 1. True wisdom is true honour, and will gain a man a reputation, which is like a box of precious ointment, pleasing and very valuable. 2. The reputation that is got with difficulty, and by a great deal of wisdom, may be easily lost, and by a *little folly,* because envy fastens upon eminency, and makes the worst of the mistakes and miscarriages of those who are cried up for wisdom, and improves them to their disadvantage; so that the folly which in another would not be taken notice of in them is severely censured. Those who make a great profession of religion have need to walk very circumspectly, to *abstain from all appearances of evil,* and approaches towards it, because many eyes are upon them, that watch for their halting; their character is soon sullied, and they have a great deal of reputation to lose.

II. What a deal of advantage a wise man has above a fool in the management of business (*v.* 2): *A wise man's heart is at his right hand,* so that he goes about his business with dexterity, turns his hand readily to it, and goes through it with despatch; his counsel and courage are ready to him, whenever he has occasion for them. But a *fool's heart is at his left hand;* it is always to seek when he has any thing to do that is of importance, and therefore he goes awkwardly about it, like a man that is left-handed; he is soon at a loss and at his wits' end.

III. How apt fools are at every turn to proclaim their own folly, and expose themselves; he that is either witless or graceless, either silly or wicked, if he be ever so little from under the check, and left to himself, if he but *walk by the way,* soon shows what he is; his *wisdom fails him,* and, by some impropriety or other, *he says to every one he meets that he is a fool (v.* 3), that is, he discovers his folly as plainly as if he had told them so. He cannot conceal it, and he is not ashamed of it. Sin is the reproach of sinners wherever they go.

4 If the spirit of the ruler rise up against thee, leave not thy place; for yielding pacifieth great offences. 5

There is an evil *which* I have seen under the sun, as an error *which* proceedeth from the ruler : 6 Folly is set in great dignity, and the rich sit in low place. 7 I have seen servants upon horses, and princes walking as servants upon the earth. 8 He that diggeth a pit shall fall into it ; and whoso breaketh a hedge, a serpent shall bite him. 9 Whoso removeth stones shall be hurt therewith ; *and* he that cleaveth wood shall be endangered thereby. 10 If the iron be blunt, and he do not whet the edge, then must he put to more strength : but wisdom *is* profitable to direct. 11 Surely the serpent will bite without enchantment ; and a babbler is no better.

The scope of these verses is to keep subjects loyal and dutiful to the government. In Solomon's reign the people were very rich, and lived in prosperity, which perhaps made them proud and petulant, and when the taxes were high, though they had enough to pay them with, it is probable that many conducted themselves insolently towards the government and threatened to rebel. To such Solomon here gives some necessary cautions.

I. Let not subjects carry on a quarrel with their prince upon any private personal disgust (*v.* 4): "*If the spirit of the ruler rise up against thee,* if upon some misinformation given him, or some mismanagement of thine, he is displeased at thee, and threaten thee, yet *leave not thy place,* forget not the duty of a subject, revolt not from thy allegiance, do not, in a passion, quit thy post in his service and throw up thy commission, as despairing ever to regain his favour. No, wait awhile, and thou wilt find he is not implacable, but that *yielding pacifies great offences.*" Solomon speaks for himself, and for every wise and good man that is a master, or a magistrate, that he could easily forgive those, upon their submission, whom yet, upon their provocation, he had been very angry with. It is safer and better to yield to an angry prince than to contend with him.

II. Let not subjects commence a quarrel with their prince, though the public administration be not in every thing as they would have it. He grants *there is an evil often seen under the sun,* and it is a king's-evil, an evil which the king only can cure, for *it is an error which proceeds from the ruler* (*v.* 5); it is a mistake which rulers, consulting their personal affections more than the public interests, are too often guilty of, that men are not preferred according to their merit, but *folly is set in great dignity,* men of shattered brains, and broken fortunes, are put in places of power and trust, while the rich men of good sense and good estates, whose interest would oblige

them to be true to the public, and whose abundance would be likely to set them above temptations to bribery and extortion, yet sit in low places, and can get no preferment (*v.* 6), either the ruler knows not how to value them or the terms of preferment are such as they cannot in conscience comply with. It is ill with a people when vicious men are advanced and men of worth are kept under hatches. This is illustrated *v.* 7. "*I have seen servants upon horses,* men not so much of mean extraction and education (if that were all, it were the more excusable, nay, there is many a wise servant who with good reason *has rule over a son that causes shame),* but of sordid, servile, mercenary dispositions. I have seen these riding in pomp and state as princes, while princes, men of noble birth and qualities, fit to rule a kingdom, have been forced to *walk as servants upon the earth,* poor and despised. Thus God, in his providence, punishes a wicked people; but, as far as it is the ruler's act and deed, it is certainly his *error,* and a *great evil,* a grievance to the subject and very provoking; but it is *an error under the sun,* which will certainly be rectified above the sun, and when it shall shine no more, for in heaven it is only wisdom and holiness that are set in great dignity. But, if the prince be guilty of his error, yet let not the subjects *leave their place,* nor rise up against the government, nor form any project for the alteration of it; nor let the prince carry on the humour too far, nor set such servants, such beggars, on horseback, as will ride furiously over the ancient land-marks of the constitution, and threaten the subversion of it.

1. Let neither prince nor people violently attempt any changes, nor make a forcible entry upon a national settlement, for they will both find it of dangerous consequence, which he shows here by four similitudes, the scope of which is to give us a caution not to meddle to our own hurt. Let not princes invade the rights and liberties of their subjects; let not subjects mutiny and rebel against their princes ; for, (1.) *He that digs a pit* for another, it is ten to one but he *falls into it* himself, and his violent dealing returns upon his own head. If princes become tyrants, or subjects become rebels, all histories will tell both what is likely to be their fate and that it is at their utmost peril, and *it were better* for both to be content within their own bounds. (2.) *Whoso breaks a hedge,* an old hedge, that has long been a land-mark, let him expect that a *serpent,* or *adder,* such as harbour in rotten hedges, will *bite him;* some viper or other will fasten upon his hand, Acts xxviii. 3. God, by his ordinance, as by a hedge, has inclosed the prerogatives and powers of princes; their persons are under his special protection; those therefore that form any treasonable designs against their peace, their crown, and dignity, are but twisting halters for themselves. (3.) *Whoso*

removes stones, to pull down a wall, or build-ing, does but pluck them upon himself; he shall be *hurt therewith*, and will wish that he had let them alone. Those that go about to alter a well-modelled well-settled government, under colour of redressing some grievances and correcting some faults in it, will quickly perceive not only that it is easier to find fault than to mend, to demolish that which is good than to build up that which is better, but that they thrust their own fingers into the fire and overwhelm themselves in the ruin they occasion. (4.) *He that cleaves the wood*, es-pecially if, as it follows, he has sorry tools (*v.* 10), *shall be endangered thereby;* the chips, or his own axe-head, will fly in his face. If we meet with knotty pieces of timber, men of perverse and ungovernable spirits, and we think to master them by force and violence, and hew them to pieces, they may not only prove too hard for us, but the attempt may turn to our own damage.

2. Rather let both prince and people act towards each other with prudence, mildness, and good temper: *Wisdom is profitable to direct* the ruler how to manage a people that are inclined to be turbulent, so as neither, on the one hand, by a supine negligence to em-bolden and encourage them, nor, on the other hand, by rigour and severity to exas-perate and provoke them to any seditious practices. It is likewise profitable to direct the subjects how to act towards a prince that is inclined to bear hard upon them, so as not to alienate his affections from them, but to win upon him by humble remonstrances (not insolent demands, such as the people made upon Rehoboam), by patient submissions and peaceable expedients. The same rule is to be observed in all relations, for the pre-serving of the comfort of them. Let wisdom direct to gentle methods and forbear violent ones. (1.) Wisdom will teach us to whet the tool we are to make use of, rather than, by leaving it blunt, oblige ourselves to exert so much the *more strength, v.* 10. We might save ourselves a great deal of labour, and pre-vent a great deal of danger, if we did whet before we cut, that is, consider and preme-ditate what is fit to be said and done in every difficult case, that we may accommodate our-selves to it and may do our work smoothly and easily both to others and to ourselves. Wisdom will direct how to sharpen and put an edge upon both ourselves and those we employ, not to *work deceitfully* (Ps. lii. 2), but to work cleanly and cleverly. The mower loses no time when he is whetting his scythe. (2.) Wisdom will teach us to en-chant the serpent we are to contend with, rather than think to out-hiss it (*v.* 11): *The serpent will bite* if he be not by singing and music charmed and enchanted, against which therefore he *stops his ears* (Ps. lviii. 4, 5); *and a babbler is no better* to all those who enter the lists with him, who therefore must not think by dint of words to out-talk him,

but by prudent management to enchant him. *He that is lord of the tongue* (so the phrase is), a ruler that has liberty of speech and may say what he will, it is as dangerous dealing with him as with a serpent uncharmed; but, if you use the enchantment of a mild and humble submission, you may be safe and out of danger; herein *wisdom*, the meekness of wisdom, *is profitable to direct. By long forbearing is a prince persuaded*, Prov. xxv. 15. Jacob enchanted Esau with a present and Abigail David. To those that may say any thing it is wisdom to say nothing that is provoking.

12 The words of a wise man's mouth *are* gracious; but the lips of a fool will swallow up himself. 13 The be-ginning of the words of his mouth *is* foolishness: and the end of his talk *is* mischievous madness. 14 A fool also is full of words: a man cannot tell what shall be; and what shall be after him, who can tell him? 15 The labour of the foolish wearieth every one of them, because he knoweth not how to go to the city.

Solomon, having shown the benefit of wis-dom, and of what great advantage it is to us in the management of our affairs, here shows the mischief of folly and how it exposes men, which perhaps comes in as a reflection upon those rulers who *set folly in great dignity.*

I. Fools talk a great deal to no purpose, and they show their folly as much by the multitude, impertinence, and mischievousness of their words, as by any thing; whereas *the words of a wise man's mouth are gracious*, are grace, manifest grace in his heart and minis-ter grace to the hearers, are good, and such as become him, and do good to all about him, *the lips of a fool* not only expose him to reproach and make him ridiculous, but *will swallow up himself* and bring him to ruin, by provoking the government to take cognizance of his seditious talk and call him to an ac-count for it. Adonijah foolishly *spoke against his own life*, 1 Kings ii. 23. Many a man has been sunk by having *his own tongue fall upon him*, Ps. lxiv. 8. See what a fool's talk is. 1. It takes rise from his own weakness and wickedness: *The beginning of the words of his mouth is foolishness*, the foolishness bound up in his heart, that is the corrupt spring out of which all these polluted streams flow, the evil treasure out of which evil things are brought. As soon as he begins to speak you may perceive his folly; at the very first he talks idly, and passionately, and like him-self. 2. It rises up to fury, and tends to the hurt and injury of others: *The end of his talk*, the end it comes to, *is madness*. He will presently talk himself into an indecent heat, and break out into the wild extravagances of a distracted man. The end he aims at is mischief; as, at first, he appeared to have little government of himself, so, at last, it appears he has a great deal of malice to his neighbours; that root of bitterness bears gall and wormwood. Note, It is not strange if those that begin foolishly end madly; for an ungoverned tongue, the more liberty is allowed, grows the more violent. 3. It is all the same over and over (*v.* 14): *A fool also is full of words,* a passionate fool especially, that runs on endlessly and never knows when to leave off. He will have the last word, though it be but the same with that which was the first. What is wanting in the weight and strength of his words he endeavours in vain to make up in the number of them; and they must be repeated, because otherwise there is nothing in them to make them regarded. Note, Many who are empty of sense are *full of words;* and the least solid are the most noisy. The following words may be taken either, (1.) As checking him for his vainglorious boasting in the multitude of his words, what he will do and what he will have, not considering that which every body knows that *a man cannot tell what shall be* in his own time, while he lives (Prov. xxvii. 1), much less can one tell *what shall be after him,* when he is dead and gone. Would we duly consider our own ignorance of, and uncertainty about, future events, it would cut off a great many of the idle words we foolishly multiply. Or, (2.) As mocking him for his tautologies. He is *full of words,* for if he do but speak the most trite and common thing, *a man cannot tell what shall be,* because he loves to hear himself talk, he will say it again, *what shall be after him who can tell him?* like Battus in Ovid:

———— Sub illis
Montibus (inquit) erant, et erant sub montibus illis—
Under those mountains were they,
They were under those mountains, I say—

whence vain repetitions are called *Battologies,* Matt. vi. 7.

II. Fools toil a great deal to no purpose (*v.* 15); *The labour of the foolish,* to accomplish their designs, *wearies every one of them.* 1. They weary themselves in that labour which is very foolish and absurd. All their labour is for the world and the body, and the meat that perishes, and in this labour they spend their strength, and exhaust their spirits, and *weary themselves for very vanity,* Hab. ii. 13; Isa. lv. 2. They choose that service which is perfect drudgery rather than that which is perfect liberty. 2. That labour which is necessary, and would be profitable, and might be gone through with ease, wearies them, because they go about it awkwardly and foolishly, and so make their business a toil to them, which, if they applied themselves to it prudently, would be a pleasure to them. Many complain of the labours of religion as grievous, which they would have no reason to complain of if the exercises of Christian piety were always under the direction of

Christian prudence. The foolish tire themselves in endless pursuits, and never bring any thing to pass, *because they know not how to go to the city,* that is, because they have not capacity to apprehend the plainest thing, such as the entrance into a great city is, where one would think it were impossible for a man to miss his road. Men's imprudent management of their business robs them both of the comfort and of the benefit of it. But it is the excellency of the way to the heavenly city that it is a high-way, in which the *wayfaring men, though fools, shall not err* (Isa. xxxv. 8); yet sinful folly makes men miss that way.

16 Woe to thee, O land, when thy king *is* a child, and thy princes eat in the morning! 17 Blessed *art* thou, O land, when thy king *is* the son of nobles, and thy princes eat in due season, for strength, and not for drunkenness! 18 By much slothfulness the building decayeth; and through idleness of the hands the house droppeth through. 19 A feast is made for laughter, and wine maketh merry: but money answereth all *things.* 20 Curse not the king, no not in thy thought; and curse not the rich in thy bedchamber: for a bird of the air shall carry the voice, and that which hath wings shall tell the matter.

Solomon here observes,

I. How much the happiness of a land depends upon the character of its rulers; it is well or ill with the people according as the princes are good or bad. 1. The people cannot be happy when their princes are childish and voluptuous (*v.* 16): *Woe unto thee, O land!* even the land of Canaan itself, though otherwise the glory of all lands, when *thy king is a child,* not so much in age (Solomon himself was young when his kingdom was happy in him) as in understanding; when the prince is weak and foolish as a child, fickle and fond of changes, fretful and humoursome, easily imposed upon, and hardly brought to business, it is ill with the people. The body staggers if the head be giddy. Perhaps Solomon wrote this with a foresight of his son Rehoboam's ill conduct (2 Chron. xiii. 7); he was a child all the days of his life and his family and kingdom fared the worse for it. Nor is it much better with a people when their princes *eat in the morning,* that is, make a god of their belly and make themselves slaves to their appetites. If the king himself be a child, yet if the princes and privy-counsellors are wise and faithful, and apply themselves to business, the land may do the better; but if they addict themselves to their pleasures, and prefer the gratifications of the flesh before the despatch of the public business, which they disfit themselves for by eating and drinking *in a morning*, when judges are epicures, and do not eat to live, but live to eat, what good can a nation expect! 2. The people cannot but be happy when their rulers are generous and active, sober and temperate, and men of business, *v.* 17. The land is then blessed, (1.) When the sovereign is governed by principles of honour, *when the king is the son of nobles*, actuated and animated by a noble spirit, which scorns to do any thing base and unbecoming so high a character, which is solicitous for the public welfare, and prefers that before any private interests. Wisdom, virtue, and the fear of God, beneficence, and a readiness to do good to all mankind, these ennoble the royal blood. 2. When the subordinate magistrates are more in care to discharge their trusts than to gratify their appetites; when they *eat in due season*, that is, when they have despatched their business, and got them an appetite. God gives the creatures *their meat in due season* (Ps. cxlv. 15); let us not take ours unseasonably, lest we lose the comfort of seeing God give it to us. Magistrates should *eat for strength*, that their bodies may be fitted to serve their souls in the service of God and their country, *and not for drunkenness*, to make themselves unfit to do any thing either for God or man, and particularly to *sit in judgment*, for they will *err through wine* (Isa. xxviii. 7), will *drink and forget the law*, Prov. xxxi. 5. It is well with a people when their princes are examples of temperance, when those that have most to spend upon themselves know how to deny themselves.

II. Of what ill consequence slothfulness is both to private and public affairs (*v.* 18): *By much slothfulness and idleness of the hands*, the neglect of business, and the love of ease and pleasure, *the building decays, drops through* first, and by degrees drops down. If it be not kept well covered, and care be not taken to repair the breaches, as any happen, it will rain in, and the timber will rot, and the house will become unfit to dwell in. It is so with the family and the affairs of it; if men cannot find in their hearts to take pains in their callings, to tend their shops and look after their own business, they will soon run in debt and go behind-hand, and, instead of making what they have more for their children, will make it less. It is so with the public; if the king be *a child* and will take no care, if the *princes eat in the morning* and will take no pains, the affairs of the nation suffer loss, and its interests are prejudiced, its honour is sullied, its power is weakened, its borders are encroached upon, the course of justice is obstructed, the treasure is exhausted, and all its foundations are out of course, and all this through the slothfulness and self-seeking of those that should be the *repairers of its breaches and the restorers of paths to dwell in*, Isa. lviii. 12.

III. How industrious generally all are, both princes and people, to get money, because that serves for all purposes, *v.* 19. He seems to prefer money before mirth: *A feast is made for laughter*, not merely for eating, but chiefly for pleasant conversation and the society of friends, not the laughter of the fool, which is madness, but that of wise men, by which they fit themselves for business and severe studies. Spiritual feasts are made for spiritual laughter, holy joy in God. *Wine makes merry, makes glad the* life, *but money is* the measure of all things and *answers all things. Pecuniæ obediunt omnia—Money commands all things.* Though *wine make merry*, it will not be a house for us, nor a bed, nor clothing, nor provisions and portions for children; *but money*, if men have enough of it, will be all these. The feast cannot be made without money, and, though men have wine, they are not so much disposed to be merry unless they have money for the necessary supports of life. Money of itself answers nothing; it will neither feed nor clothe; but, as it is the instrument of commerce, it answers all the occasions of this present life. What is to be had may be had for money. But it answers nothing to the soul; it will not procure the pardon of sin, the favour of God, the peace of conscience; the soul, as it is not redeemed, so it is not maintained, with *corruptible things as silver and gold.* Some refer this to rulers; it is ill with the people when they give up themselves to luxury and riot, feasting and making merry, not only because their business is neglected, but because money must be had to *answer all* these *things*, and, in order to that, the people squeezed by heavy taxes.

IV. How cautious subjects have need to be that they harbour not any disloyal purposes in their minds, nor keep up any factious cabals or consultations against the government, because it is ten to one that they are discovered and brought to light, *v.* 20. "Though rulers should be guilty of some errors, yet be not, upon all occasions, arraigning their administration and running them down, but make the best of them." Here, 1. The command teaches us our duty: "*Curse not the king, no, not in thy thought*, do not wish ill to the government in thy mind." All sin begins there, and therefore the first risings of it must be curbed and suppressed, and particularly of treason and sedition. "*Curse not the rich*, the princes and governors, *in thy bed-chamber*, in a conclave or club of persons disaffected to the government; associate not with such; *come not into their secret;* join not with them in speaking ill of the government or plotting against it." 2. The reason consults our safety. "Though the design be carried on ever so closely, *a bird of the air shall carry the voice* to the king, who has more spies about than thou art aware of, *and that which has wings shall tell the matter*, to thy confusion and ruin." God sees what men do, and hears what they say, in secret;

and, when he pleases, he can bring it to light by strange and unsuspected ways. Wouldst *thou then not be hurt by the powers* that be, nor *be afraid of* them? *Do that which is good, and thou shalt have praise of the same; but, if thou do that which is evil, be afraid,* Rom. xiii. 3, 4.

CHAP. XI.

In this chapter we have, I. A pressing exhortation to works of charity and bounty to the poor, as the best cure of the vanity which our worldly riches are subject to and the only way of making them turn to a substantial good account, ver. 1—6. II. A serious admonition to prepare for death and judgment, and to begin betimes, even in the days of our youth, to do so, ver. 7—10.

CAST thy bread upon the waters: for thou shalt find it after many days. 2 Give a portion to seven, and also to eight; for thou knowest not what evil shall be upon the earth. 3 If the clouds be full of rain, they empty *themselves* upon the earth: and if the tree fall toward the south, or toward the north, in the place where the tree falleth, there it shall be. 4 He that observeth the wind shall not sow; and he that regardeth the clouds shall not reap. 5 As thou knowest not what *is* the way of the spirit, *nor* how the bones *do grow* in the womb of her that is with child: even so thou knowest not the works of God who maketh all. 6 In the morning sow thy seed, and in the evening withhold not thine hand: for thou knowest not whether shall prosper, either this or that, or whether they both *shall be* alike good.

Solomon had often, in this book, pressed it upon rich people to take the comfort of their riches themselves; here he presses it upon them to do good to others with them and to abound in liberality to the poor, which will, another day, abound to their account. Observe,

I. How the duty itself is recommended to us, *v.* 1. 1. *Cast thy bread upon the waters,* thy *bread-corn upon the low places* (so some understand it), alluding to the husbandman, who *goes forth, bearing precious seed,* sparing bread-corn from his family for the seedness, knowing that without that he can have no harvest another year; thus the charitable man takes from his bread-corn for seed-corn, abridges himself to supply the poor, that he may *sow beside all waters* (Isa. xxxii. 20), because as he sows so he must *reap,* Gal. vi. 7. We read of the *harvest of the river,* Isa. xxiii. 3. Waters, in scripture, are put for multitudes (Rev. xvi. 5), and there are multitudes of poor (we do not want objects of charity); waters are put also for mourners: the poor are men of sorrows. Thou must give *bread,* the necessary supports of life, not only give

good words, but *good things,* Isa. lviii. 7. It must be *thy* bread, that which is honestly got; it is no charity, but injury, to give that which is none of our own to give; first *do justly,* and then *love mercy.* "*Thy bread,* which thou didst design for thyself, let the poor have a share with thee, as they had with Job, *ch.* xxxi. 17. Give freely to the poor, though it may seem thrown away and lost, as that which is *cast upon the waters.* Send it a voyage, send it as a venture, as merchants that trade by sea. Trust it *upon the waters;* it shall not sink."

2. "*Give a portion to seven and also to eight,* that is, be free and liberal in works of charity." (1.) "Give much if thou hast much to give, not a pittance, but *a portion,* not a bit or two, but a mess, a meal; give a large dole, not a paltry one; give *good measure* (Luke vi. 38); be generous in giving, as those were when, on festival days, they *sent portions to those for whom nothing was prepared* (Neh. viii. 10), worthy portions." (2.) "Give to many, *to seven, and also to eight;* if thou meet with seven objects of charity, give to them all, and then, if thou meet with an eighth, give to that, and, if with eight more, give to them all too. Excuse not thyself with the good thou hast done from the good thou hast further to do, but hold on, and mend. In hard times, when the number of the poor increases, let thy charity be proportionably enlarged." God is rich in mercy to all, to us, though unworthy; he *gives liberally, and upbraids not* with former gifts, and we must be merciful as our heavenly Father is.

II. The reasons with which it is pressed upon us. Consider,

1. Our reward for well-doing is very certain. "Though thou *cast it upon the waters,* and it seem lost, thou thinkest thou hast given thy good word with it and art likely never to hear of it again, yet *thou shalt find it after many days,* as the husbandman finds his seed again in a plentiful harvest and the merchant his venture in a rich return. It is not lost, but well laid out, and well laid up; it brings in full interest in the present gifts of God's providence, and graces and comforts of his Spirit; and the principal is sure, laid up in heaven, for it is *lent to the Lord.*" Seneca, a heathen, could say, *Nihil magis possidere me credam, quam bene donata—I possess nothing so completely as that which I have given away. Hoc habeo quodcunque dedi; hæ sunt divitiæ certæ in quacunque sortis humanæ levitate—Whatever I have imparted I still possess; these riches remain with me through all the vicissitudes of life.* "Thou shalt find it," perhaps not quickly, *but after many days;* the return may be slow, but it is sure and will be so much the more plentiful." Wheat, the most valuable grain, lies longest in the ground. Long voyages make the best returns.

2. Our opportunity for well-doing is very uncertain: "*Thou knowest not what evil*

may be upon the earth, which may deprive thee of thy estate, and put thee out of a capacity to do good, and therefore, while thou hast wherewithal, be liberal with it, improve the present season, as the husbandman in sowing his ground, before the frost comes." We have reason to expect *evil upon the earth,* for we are born to trouble; what the evil may be we *know not,* but that we may be ready for it, whatever it is, it is our wisdom, in the day of prosperity, to be in good, to be doing good. Many make use of this as an argument against giving to the poor, because they know not what hard times may come when they may want themselves; whereas we should therefore be the rather charitable, that, when *evil days come,* we may have the comfort of having done good while we were able; we would then hope to find mercy both with God and man, and therefore should now show mercy. If by charity we trust God with what we have, we put it into good hands against bad times.

III. How he obviates the objections which might be made against this duty and the excuses of the uncharitable.

1. Some will say that what they have is their own and they have it for their own use, and will ask, Why should we *cast it thus upon the waters?* Why should *I take my bread, and my flesh, and give it to I know not* whom? So Nabal pleaded, 1 Sam. xxv. 11. " Look up, man, and consider how soon thou wouldest be starved in a barren ground, *if the clouds* over thy head should plead thus, that they have their waters for themselves; but thou seest, when they are *full of rain, they empty themselves upon the earth,* to make it fruitful, till they are wearied and spent with watering it, Job xxxvii. 11. Are the heavens thus bountiful to the poor earth, that is so far below them, and wilt thou grudge thy bounty to thy poor brother, who is *bone of thy bone?* Or thus: some will say, Though we give but little to the poor, yet, thank God, we have as charitable a heart as any." Nay, says Solomon, *if the clouds be full of rain, they will empty themselves;* if there be charity in the heart, it will show itself, Jam. ii. 15, 16. He that *draws out his soul to the hungry* will reach forth his hand to them, as he has ability.

2. Some will say that their sphere of usefulness is low and narrow; they cannot do the good that they see others can, who are in more public stations, and therefore they will sit still and do nothing. Nay, says he, *in the place where the tree falls,* or happens to be, *there it shall be,* for the benefit of those to whom it belongs; every man must labour to be a blessing to that place, whatever it is, where the providence of God casts him; wherever we are we may find good work to do if we have but hearts to do it. Or thus: some will say, " Many present themselves as objects of charity who are unworthy, and I do not know whom it is fit to give it to."

" Trouble not thyself about that" (says Solomon); " give as discreetly as thou canst, and then be satisfied that, though the person should prove undeserving of thy charity, yet, if thou give it with an honest heart, thou shalt not lose thy reward; which way soever the charity is directed, *north* or *south,* thine shall be the benefit of it." This is commonly applied to death; *therefore* let us do good, and, as good trees, *bring forth the fruits of righteousness,* because death will shortly come and cut us down, and we shall then be determined to an unchangeable state of happiness or misery according to what was done in the body. As the tree falls at death, so it is likely to lie to all eternity.

3. Some will object the many discouragements they have met with in their charity. They have been reproached for it as proud and pharisaical; they have but little to give, and they shall be despised if they do not give as others do; they know not but their children may come to want it, and they had better lay it up for them; they have taxes to pay and purchases to make; they know not what use will be made of their charity, nor what construction will be put upon it; these, and a hundred such objections, he answers, in one word (v. 4): *He that observes the wind shall not sow,* which signifies doing good; *and he that regards the clouds shall not reap,* which signifies getting good. If we stand thus magnifying every little difficulty and making the worst of it, starting objections and fancying hardship and danger where there is none, we shall never go on, much less go through with our work, nor make any thing of it. If the husbandman should decline, or leave off, sowing for the sake of every flying cloud, and reaping for the sake of every blast of wind, he would make but an ill account of his husbandry at the year's end. The duties of religion are as necessary as sowing and reaping, and will turn as much to our own advantage. The discouragements we meet with in these duties are but as winds and clouds, which will do us no harm, and which those that put on a little courage and resolution will despise and easily break through. Note, Those that will be deterred and driven off by small and seeming difficulties from great and real duties will never bring any thing to pass in religion, for there will always arise some wind, some cloud or other, at least in our imagination, to discourage us. Winds and clouds are in God's hands, are designed to try us, and our Christianity obliges us to endure hardness.

4. Some will say, " We do not see in which way what we expend in charity should ever be made up to us; we do not find ourselves ever the richer; why should we depend upon the general promise of a blessing on the charitable, unless we saw which way to expect the operation of it?" To this he answers, " *Thou knowest not the work of God,* nor is it fit thou shouldst. Thou mayest be sure he

will make good his word of promise, though he does not tell thee how, or which way, and though he works in a way by himself, according to the counsels of his unsearchable wisdom. He will work, and none shall hinder; but then he will work and none shall direct or prescribe to him. The blessing shall work insensibly but irresistibly. God's work shall certainly agree with his word, whether we see it or no." Our ignorance of the work of God he shows, in two instances :—(1.) We *know not what is the way of the Spirit, of the wind* (so some), we *know not whence it comes, or whither it goes,* or when it will turn; yet the seamen lie ready waiting for it, till it turns about in favour of them; so we must do our duty, in expectation of the time appointed for the blessing. Or it may be understood of the human soul; we know that God made us, and gave us these souls, but how they entered into these bodies, are united to them, animate them, and operate upon them, we know not; the soul is a mystery to itself, no marvel then that *the work of God* is so to us. (2.) We know not *how the bones are fashioned in the womb of her that is with child.* We cannot describe the manner either of the formation of the body or of its information with a soul; both, we know, are *the work of God,* and we acquiesce in his work, but cannot, in either, trace the process of the operation. We doubt not of the birth of the child that is conceived, though we know not how it is formed; nor need we doubt of the performance of the promise, though we perceive not how things work towards it. And we may well trust God to provide for us that which is convenient, without our anxious disquieting cares, and therein to recompense us for our charity, since it was without any knowledge or forecast of ours that our bodies were curiously wrought in secret and our souls found the way into them; and so the argument is the same, and urged to the same intent, with that of our Saviour (Matt. vi. 25), *The life,* the living soul that God has given us, *is more than meat; the body,* that God has made us, *is more than raiment;* let him therefore that has done the greater for us be cheerfully depended upon to do the less.

5. Some say, " We have been charitable, have given a great deal to the poor, and never yet saw any return for it; many days are past, and we have not *found it again,*" to which he answers (*v.* 6), " Yet go on, proceed and persevere in well-doing; let slip no opportunity. *In the morning sow thy seed* upon the objects of charity that offer themselves early, *and in the evening do not withhold thy hand,* under pretence that thou art weary; as thou hast opportunity, be doing good, some way or other, all the day long, as the husbandman follows his seedness from morning till night. *In the morning* of youth lay out thyself to do good; give out of the little thou hast to begin the world with; *and in the evening* of old age yield not to the com-

mon temptation old people are in to be penurious; even then *withhold not thy hand,* and think not to excuse thyself from charitable works by purposing to make a charitable will, but do good to the last, *for thou knowest not* which work of charity and piety *shall prosper,* both as to others and as to thyself, *this or that,* but hast reason to hope that *both shall be alike good. Be not weary of well-doing, for in due season,* in God's time and that is the best time, *you shall reap,*" Gal. vi. 9. This is applicable to spiritual charity, our pious endeavours for the good of the souls of others; let us continue them, for, though we have long laboured in vain, we may at length see the success of them. Let ministers, in the days of their seedness, sow both morning and evening; *for who* can tell *which shall prosper?*

7 Truly the light *is* sweet, and a pleasant *thing it is* for the eyes to behold the sun : 8 But if a man live many years, *and* rejoice in them all; yet let him remember the days of darkness; for they shall be many. All that cometh *is* vanity. 9 Rejoice, O young man, in thy youth; and let thy heart cheer thee in the days of thy youth, and walk in the ways of thine heart, and in the sight of thine eyes : but know thou, that for all these *things* God will bring thee into judgment. 10 Therefore remove sorrow from thy heart, and put away evil from thy flesh : for childhood and youth *are* vanity.

Here is an admonition both to old people and to young people, to think of dying, and get ready for it. Having by many excellent precepts taught us how to live well, the preacher comes now, towards the close of his discourse, to teach us how to die well and to put us in mind of our latter end.

I. He applies himself to the aged, writes to them as fathers, to awaken them to think of death, *v.* 7, 8. Here is, 1. A rational concession of the sweetness of life, which old people find by experience : *Truly the light is sweet;* the light of *the sun* is so; it is *a pleasant thing for the eyes to behold* it. Light was the first thing made in the formation of the great world, as the eye is one of the first in the formation of the body, the little world. It is pleasant to see the light; the heathen were so charmed with the pleasure of it that they worshipped the sun. It is pleasant by it to see other things, the many agreeable prospects this world gives us. The light of life is so. Light is put for life, Job iii. 20, 23. It cannot be denied that life is sweet. It is sweet to bad men because they have *their portion in this life;* it is sweet to good men because they have this life as the time of their preparation for a better life; it is sweet to all men; nature says it is so, and there is no disputing against it; nor can death be desired for its own sake, but dreaded, unless as a period to present evils or a passage to future good. Life is sweet, and therefore we have need to double a guard upon ourselves, lest we love it too well. 2. A caution to think of death, even in the midst of life, and of life when it is most sweet and we are most apt to forget death: *If a man live many years, yet let him remember the days of darkness* are coming. Here is, (1.) A summer's day supposed to be enjoyed—that life may continue long, even many years, and that, by the goodness of God, it may be made comfortable and a man may *rejoice in them all.* There are those that *live many years* in this world, escape many dangers, receive many mercies, and therefore are secure that they shall want no good, and that no evil shall befal them, that the pitcher which has come so often from the well safe and sound shall never come home broken. But who are those that *live many years and rejoice in them all?* Alas! none; we have but hours of joy for months of sorrow. However, some rejoice in their years, their many years, more than others; if these two things meet, a prosperous state and a cheerful spirit, these two indeed may do much towards enabling a man to *rejoice in them all,* and yet the most prosperous state has its alloys and the most cheerful spirit has its damps; jovial sinners have their melancholy qualms, and cheerful saints have their gracious sorrows; so that it is but a supposition, not a case in fact, that a man should *live many years and rejoice in them all.* But, (2.) Here is a winter's night proposed to be expected after this summer's day: *Yet let* this hearty old man *remember the days of darkness, for they shall be many.* Note, [1.] There are *days of darkness* coming, the days of our lying in the grave; there the body will lie in the dark; there the eyes see not, the sun shines not. The darkness of death is opposed to the light of life; the grave is a *land of darkness,* Job x. 21. [2.] Those *days of darkness* will *be many;* the days of our lying under ground will be more than the days of our living above ground. They are many, but they are not infinite; many as they are, they will be numbered and finished when *the heavens are no more,* Job xiv. 12. As the longest day will have its night, so the longest night will have its morning. [3.] It is good for us often to remember those *days of darkness,* that we may not be lifted up with pride, nor lulled asleep in carnal security, nor even transported into indecencies by vain mirth. [4.] Notwithstanding the long continuance of life, and the many comforts of it, *yet* we must *remember the days of darkness,* because those will certainly come, and they will come with much the less terror if we have thought of them before.

II. He applies himself to the young, and writes to them as children, to awaken them to think of death (*v.* 9, 10); here we have,

1. An ironical concession to the vanities and pleasures of youth: *Rejoice, O young man! in thy youth.* Some make this to be the counsel which the atheist and the epicure give to the young man, the poisonous suggestions against which Solomon, in the close of the verse, prescribes a powerful antidote. But it is more emphatic if we take it, as it is commonly understood, by way of irony, like that of Elijah to the priests of Baal *(Cry aloud, for he is a god),* or of Micaiah to Ahab *(Go to Ramoth-Gilead, and prosper),* or of Christ to his disciples, *Sleep on now.* "*Rejoice, O young man! in thy youth,* live a merry life, follow thy sports, and take thy pleasures; *let thy heart cheer thee in the days of thy youth,* cheer thee with its fancies and foolish hopes; entertain thyself with thy pleasing dreams; *walk in the ways of thy heart;* do whatever thou hast a mind to do, and stick at nothing that may gratify the sensual appetite. *Quicquid libet, licet—Make thy will thy law. Walk in the ways of thy heart, and* let thy heart walk after *thy eyes,* a rambling heart after a roving eye; what is pleasing in thy own eyes do it, whether it be pleasing in the eyes of God or no." Solomon speaks thus ironically to the young man to intimate, (1.) That this is that which he would do, and which he would fain have leave to do, in which he places his happiness and on which he sets his heart. (2.) That he wishes all about him would give him this counsel, would prophesy to him such smooth things as these, and cannot brook any advice to the contrary, but reckons those his enemies that bid him be sober and serious. (3.) To expose his folly, and the great absurdity of a voluptuous vicious course of life. The very description of it, if men would see things entirely, and judge of them impartially, is enough to show how contrary to reason those act that live such a life. The very opening of the cause is enough to determine it, without any argument. (4.) To show that if men give themselves to such a course of life as this it is just with God to give them up to it, to abandon them to their own hearts' lusts, that they may *walk in their own counsels,* Hos. iv. 7.

2. A powerful check given to these vanities and pleasures: "*Know thou that for all these things God shall bring thee into judgment,* and duly consider that, and then live such a luxurious life if thou canst, if thou darest." This is a κολαστήριον—*a corrective* to the foregoing concession, and plucks in the reins he had laid on the neck of the young man's lust. "*Know then,* for a certainty, that, if thou dost take such a liberty as this, it will be thy everlasting ruin; thou hast to do with a God who will not let it go unpunished." Note, (1.) There is a judgment to come. (2.) We must every one of us be brought into judgment, however we may

now put far from us that evil day. (3.) We shall be reckoned with for all our carnal mirth and sensual pleasures in that day. (4.) It is good for all, but especially for young people, to know and consider this, that they may not, by the indulgence of their youthful lusts, *treasure up unto themselves wrath against that day of wrath*, the wrath of the Lamb.

3. A word of caution and exhortation inferred from all this, *v.* 10. Let young people look to themselves and manage well both their souls and their bodies, their heart and their flesh. (1.) Let them take care that their minds be not lifted up with pride, nor disturbed with anger, or any sinful passion : *Remove sorrow*, or anger, *from thy heart ;* the word signifies any disorder or perturbation of the mind. Young people are apt to be impatient of check and control, to vex and fret at any thing that is humbling and mortifying to them, and their proud hearts rise against every thing that crosses and contradicts them. They are so set upon that which is pleasing to sense that they cannot bear any thing that is displeasing, but it goes with sorrow to their heart. Their pride often disquiets them, and makes them uneasy. " Put that away, and the love of the world, and lay thy expectations low from the creature, and then disappointments will not be occasions of sorrow and anger to thee." Some by sorrow here understand that carnal mirth described *v.* 9, the end of which will be bitterness and sorrow. Let them keep at a distance from every thing which will be sorrow in the reflection. (2.) Let them take care that their bodies be not defiled by intemperance, uncleanness, or any fleshly lusts : " *Put away evil from the flesh*, and let not the members of thy body be instruments of unrighteousness. The evil of sin will be the evil of punishment, and that which thou art fond of, as good for the flesh, because it gratifies the appetites of it, will prove evil, and hurtful to it, and therefore put it far from thee, the further the better."

III. The preacher, to enforce his admonition both to old and young, urges, as an effectual argument, that which is the great argument of his discourse, the vanity of all present things, their uncertainty and insufficiency. 1. He reminds old people of this (*v.* 8): *All that comes is vanity ;* yea, though *a man live many years and rejoice in them all,* All that has come already, and all that is yet to come, how much soever men promise themselves from the concluding scenes, it is all *vanity.* What will be will do no more to make men happy than what has been. *All that come* into the world are *vanity ;* they are altogether so, at their best estate. 2. He reminds young people of this : *Childhood and youth are vanity.* The dispositions and actions of childhood and youth have in them a great deal of impertinence and iniquity, sinful vanity, which young people have need to

watch against and get cured. The pleasures and advantages of childhood and youth have in them no certainty, satisfaction, nor continuance. They are passing away ; these flowers will soon wither, and these blossoms fall ; let them therefore be knit into good fruit, which will continue and abound to a good account.

CHAP. XII.

The wise and penitent preacher is here closing his sermon ; and he closes it, not only like a good orator, but like a good preacher, with that which was likely to make the best impressions and which he wished might be powerful and lasting upon his hearers. Here is, I. An exhortation to young people to begin betimes to be religious and not to put it off to old age (ver. 1), enforced with arguments taken from the calamities of old age (ver. 1—5) and the great change that death will make upon us, ver. 6, 7. II. A repetition of the great truth he had undertaken to prove in this discourse, the vanity of the world, ver. 8. III. A confirmation and recommendation of what he had written in this and his other books, as worthy to be duly weighed and considered, ver. 9—12. IV. The whole matter summed up and concluded, with a charge to all to be truly religious, in consideration of the judgment to come, ver. 13, 14.

REMEMBER now thy Creator in the days of thy youth, while the evil days come not, nor the years draw nigh, when thou shalt say, I have no pleasure in them ; 2 While the sun, or the light, or the moon, or the stars, be not darkened, nor the clouds return after the rain : 3 In the day when the keepers of the house shall tremble, and the strong men shall bow themselves, and the grinders cease because they are few, and those that look out of the windows be darkened, 4 And the doors shall be shut in the streets, when the sound of the grinding is low, and he shall rise up at the voice of the bird, and all the daughters of music shall be brought low ; 5 Also *when* they shall be afraid of *that which is* high, and fears *shall be* in the way, and the almond tree shall flourish, and the grasshopper shall be a burden, and desire shall fail : because man goeth to his long home, and the mourners go about the streets : 6 Or ever the silver cord be loosed, or the golden bowl be broken, or the pitcher be broken at the fountain, or the wheel broken at the cistern. 7 Then shall the dust return to the earth as it was : and the spirit shall return unto God who gave it.

Here is, I. A call to young people to think of God, and mind their duty to him, when they are young : *Remember now thy Creator in the days of thy youth.* This is, 1. The royal preacher's application of his sermon concerning the vanity of the world and every thing in it. " You that are young flatter yourselves with expectations of great things from it, but believe those that have tried; it yields no solid satisfaction to a soul; therefore, that you may not be deceived by this vanity, nor too much disturbed by it, *remember your Creator*, and so guard yourselves against the mischiefs that arise from the vanity of the creature." 2. It is the royal physician's antidote against the particular diseases of youth, the love of mirth, and the indulgence of sensual pleasures, the vanity which childhood and youth are subject to; to prevent and cure this, *remember thy Creator.* Here is, (1.) A certain duty pressed upon us, to *remember* God as our *Creator*, not only to remember that God is our Creator, that he *made us and not we ourselves*, and is therefore our rightful Lord and owner, but we must engage ourselves to him with the considerations which his being our Creator lay us under, and pay him the honour and duty which we owe him as our Creator. *Remember thy Creators;* the word is plural, as it is Job xxxv. 10, *Where is God my Makers?* For God said, *Let us make man*, us, Father, Son, and Holy Ghost. (2.) The proper season for this duty —*in the days of thy youth*, the *days of thy choice* (so some), thy choice days, thy choosing days. "Begin in the beginning of thy days to remember him from whom thou hadst thy being, and go on according to that good beginning. Call him to mind when thou art young, and keep him in mind throughout all the days of thy youth, and never forget him. Guard thus against the temptations of youth, and thus improve the advantages of it."

II. A reason to enforce this command: *While the evil days come not, and the years of which thou shalt say I have no pleasure in them.*

1. Do it quickly, (1.) "Before sickness and death come. Do it while thou livest, for it will be too late to do it when death has removed thee from this state of trial and probation to that of recompence and retribution." The days of sickness and death are *the days of evil*, terrible to nature, *evil days* indeed to those that have forgotten their Creator. These *evil days* will *come* sooner or later; as yet they *come not*, for God is *long-suffering to us-ward*, and gives us *space to repent;* the continuing of life is but the deferring of death, and, while life is continued and death deferred, it concerns us to prepare, and get the property of death altered, that we may die comfortably. (2.) Before old age comes, which, if death prevent not, will come, and they will be *years of which we shall say, We have no pleasure in them*,— when we shall not relish the delights of sense, as Barzillai (2 Sam. xix. 35),—when we shall be loaded with bodily infirmities, old and blind, or old and lame,—when we shall be taken off from our usefulness, and our *strength* shall be *labour and sorrow*,—when we shall either have parted with our relations, and all our old friends, or be afflicted in them and

see them weary of us,—when we shall feel ourselves die by inches. These *years draw nigh*, when *all that comes* will be *vanity*, the remaining months all months of vanity, and there will be *no pleasure* but in the reflection of a good life on earth and the expectation of a better life in heaven.

2. These two arguments he enlarges upon in the following verses, only inverting the order, and shows,

(1.) How many are the calamities of old age, and that if we should live to be old, our days will be such as we shall *have no pleasure in*, which is a good reason why we should return to God, and make our peace with him, *in the days of our youth*, and not put it off till we come to be old; for it will be no thanks to us to leave the pleasures of sin when they have left us, nor to return to God when need forces us. It is the greatest absurdity and ingratitude imaginable to give the cream and flower of our days to the devil, and reserve the bran, and refuse, and dregs of them for God; this is offering *the torn, and the lame, and the sick for sacrifice;* and, besides, old age being thus clogged with infirmities, it is the greatest folly imaginable to put off that needful work till then, which requires the best of our strength, when our faculties are in their prime, and especially to make the work more difficult by a longer continuance in sin, and, laying up treasures of guilt in the conscience, to add to the burdens of age and make them much heavier. If the calamities of age will be such as are here represented, we shall have need of something to support and comfort us then, and nothing will be more effectual to do that than the testimony of our consciences for us that we began betimes to remember our Creator and have not since laid aside the remembrance of him. How can we expect God should help us when we are old, if we will not serve him when we are young? See Ps. lxxi. 17, 18.

[1.] The decays and infirmities of old age are here elegantly described in figurative expressions, which have some difficulty in them to us now, who are not acquainted with the common phrases and metaphors used in Solomon's age and language; but the general scope is plain—to show how uncomfortable, generally, the days of old age are. *First*, Then *the sun* and *the light* of it, *the moon* and *the stars*, and the light which they borrow from it, will *be darkened*. They look dim to old people, in consequence of the decay of their sight; their countenance is clouded, and the beauty and lustre of it are eclipsed; their intellectual powers and faculties, which are as lights in the soul, are weakened; their understanding and memory fail them, and their apprehension is not so quick nor their fancy so lively as it has been; the days of their mirth are over (light is often put for joy and prosperity) and they have not the pleasure either of the converse of the day or the repose of the night, for both *the sun* and the moon are *darkened* to them. *Secondly,* Then *the clouds return after the rain;* as, when the weather is disposed to wet, no sooner has one cloud blown over than another succeeds it, so it is with old people, when they have got free from one pain or ailment, they are seized with another, so that their distempers are *like a continual dropping in a very rainy day.* The end of one trouble is, in this world, but the beginning of another, and deep calls unto deep. Old people are often afflicted with defluxions of rheum, like soaking rain, after which still more clouds return, feeding the humour, so that it is continually grievous, and therein the body, as it were, melts away. *Thirdly,* Then *the keepers of the house tremble.* The head, which is as the watch-tower, shakes, and the arms and hands, which are ready for the preservation of the body, shake too, and grow feeble, upon every sudden approach and attack of danger. That vigour of the animal spirits which used to be exerted for self-defence fails and cannot do its office; old people are easily dispirited and discouraged. *Fourthly,* Then *the strong men shall bow themselves;* the legs and thighs, which used to support the body, and bear its weight, bend, and cannot serve for travelling as they have done, but are soon tired. Old men that have been in their time *strong men* become weak and stoop for *age,* Zech. viii. 4. *God takes no pleasure in the legs of a man* (Ps. cxlvii. 10), for their strength will soon fail; but *in the Lord Jehovah there is everlasting strength;* he has everlasting arms. *Fifthly,* Then the *grinders cease because they are few;* the teeth, with which we grind our meat and prepare it for concoction, cease to do their part, *because they are few.* They are rotted and broken, and perhaps have been drawn because they ached. Some old people have lost all their teeth, and others have but few left; and this infirmity is the more considerable because the meat, not being well chewed, for want of teeth, is not well digested, which has as much an influence as any thing upon the other decays of age. *Sixthly, Those that look out of the windows* are *darkened;* the eyes wax dim, as Isaac's (Gen. xxvii. 1), and Ahijah's, 1 Kings xiv. 4. Moses was a rare instance of one who, when 120 years old, had good eye-sight, but ordinarily the sight decays in old people as soon as any thing, and it is a mercy to them that art helps nature with spectacles. We have need to improve our sight well while we have it, because the light of the eyes may be gone before the light of life. *Seventhly, The doors are shut in the streets.* Old people keep within doors, and care not for going abroad to entertainments. The lips, the doors of the mouth, are shut in eating, because the teeth are gone and *the sound of the grinding* with them is *low,* so that they have not that command of their meat in their mouths which they used to have; they cannot digest their meat, and

therefore little grist is brought to the mill. *Eighthly,* Old people *rise up at the voice of the bird.* They have no sound sleep as young people have, but a little thing disturbs them, even the chirping of a bird; they cannot rest for coughing, and therefore rise up at cock-crowing, as soon as any body is stirring; or they are apt to be jealous, and timorous, and full of care, which breaks their sleep and makes them rise early; or they are apt to be superstitious, and *rise up* as in a fright, *at those voices of birds,* as of ravens, or screech-owls, which soothsayers call ominous. *Ninthly,* With them *all the daughters of music* are *brought low.* They have neither voice nor ear, can neither sing themselves nor take any pleasure, as Solomon had done in the days of his youth, in *singing men, and singing women, and musical instruments,* ch. ii. 8. Old people grow hard of hearing, and unapt to distinguish sounds and voices. *Tenthly,* They are *afraid of that which is high,* afraid to go to the top of any high place, either because, for want of breath, they cannot reach it, or, their heads being giddy or their legs failing them, they dare not venture to it, or they frighten themselves with fancying that *that which is high* will fall upon them. *Fear* is *in the way;* they can neither ride nor walk with their former boldness, but are afraid of every thing that lies in their way, lest it throw them down. *Eleventhly, The almond-tree flourishes.* The old man's hair has grown white, so that his head looks like an almond-tree in the blossom. The almond-tree blossoms before any other tree, and therefore fitly shows what haste old age makes in seizing upon men; it prevents their expectations and comes faster upon them than they thought of. Gray hairs are here and there upon them, and they perceive it not. *Twelfthly, The grasshopper is a burden and desire fails.* Old men can bear nothing; the lightest thing sits heavily upon them, both on their bodies and on their minds, a little thing sinks and breaks them. Perhaps *the grasshopper was* some food that was looked upon to be very light of digestion (John Baptist's meat *was locusts*), but even that lies heavily upon an old man's stomach, and therefore *desire fails,* he has no appetite to his meat, neither shall he *regard the desire of woman,* as that king, Dan. xi. 37. Old men become mindless and listless, and the pleasures of sense are to them tasteless and sapless.

[2.] It is probable that Solomon wrote this when he was himself old, and could speak feelingly of the infirmities of age, which perhaps grew the faster upon him for the indulgence he had given himself in sensual pleasures. Some old people bear up better than others under the decays of age, but, more or less, the days of old age are and will be *evil days* and of little pleasure. Great care therefore should be taken to pay respect and honour to old people, that they may have something to balance these grievances and nothing may be done to add to them. And all this, put together, makes up a good reason why we should *remember our Creator in the days of our youth,* that he may remember us with favour when these *evil days come,* and his comforts may delight our souls when the delights of sense are in a manner worn off.

(2.) He shows how great a change death will make with us, which will be either the prevention or the period of the miseries of old age. Nothing else will keep them off, nor any thing else cure them. "Therefore *remember thy Creator in the days of thy youth,* because death is certainly before thee, perhaps it is very near thee, and it is a serious thing to die, and thou shouldst feel concerned with the utmost care and diligence to prepare for it." [1.] Death will fix us in an unchangeable state: *Man* shall then *go to his long home,* and all these infirmities and decays of age are harbingers of and advances towards that awful remove. At death *man goes* from this world and all the employments and enjoyments of it. He has gone for good and all, as to his present state. He has gone *home,* for here he was a stranger and pilgrim; both soul and body go to the place whence they came, *v.* 7. He has gone to his rest, to the place where he is to fix. He has gone *to his home, to the house of his world* (so some), for this world is not his. He has gone *to his long home,* for the days of his lying in the grave will be many. He has gone *to his house of eternity,* not only to his house whence he shall never return to this world, but to the house where he must be for ever. This should make us willing to die, that, at death, we must *go home;* and why should we not long to go to our Father's house? And this should quicken us to get ready to die, that we must then go to our *long home,* to an *everlasting habitation.* [2.] Death will be an occasion of sorrow to our friends that love us. When *man goes to his long home the mourners go about the streets*— the real mourners, and those, as now with us, distinguished by their habits as they go along the streets,—the mourners for ceremony, that were hired to weep for the dead, both to express and to excite the real mourning. When we die we not only remove to a melancholy house before us, but we leave a melancholy house behind us. Tears are a tribute due to the dead, and this, among other circumstances, makes it a serious thing to die. But in vain do we *go to the house of mourning,* and see *the mourners go about the streets,* if it do not help to make us serious and pious mourners in the closet. [3.] Death will dissolve the frame of nature and take down the earthly house of this tabernacle, which is elegantly described, *v.* 6. Then shall *the silver cord,* by which soul and body were wonderfully fastened together, *be loosed,* that sacred knot untied, and those old friends be forced to part; then shall *the golden bowl,* which held the waters of life for us, *be broken;* then shall *the pitcher* with which we used to fetch up water, for the con-

stant support of life and the repair of its decays, *be broken,* even *at the fountain,* so that it can fetch up no more; and *the wheel* (all those organs that serve for the collecting and distributing of nourishment) shall be *broken,* and disabled to do their office any more. The body shall become like a watch when the spring is broken, the motion of all the wheels is stopped and they all stand still; the machine is taken to pieces; the heart beats no more, nor does the blood circulate. Some apply this to the ornaments and utensils of life; rich people must, at death, leave behind them their clothing and furniture of *silver* and *gold,* and poor people their earthen *pitchers,* and the drawers of water will have their *wheel broken.* [4.] Death will resolve us into our first principles, *v.* 7. Man is a strange sort of creature, a ray of heaven united to a clod of earth; at death these are separated, and each goes to the place whence it came. *First,* The body, that clod of clay, *returns to* its own *earth.* It is made of *the earth;* Adam's body was so, and we are of the same mould; it is a house of clay. At death it is laid in *the earth,* and in a little time will be resolved into earth, not to be distinguished from common earth, according to the sentence (Gen. iii. 19), *Dust thou art and* therefore *to dust thou shalt return.* Let us not therefore indulge the appetites of the body, nor pamper it (it will be worms' meat shortly), nor let *sin reign in our mortal bodies,* for they are mortal, Rom. vi. 12. *Secondly,* The soul, that beam of light, *returns to* that God who, when he *made man of the dust of the ground, breathed into him the breath of life,* to make him *a living soul* (Gen. ii. 7), and forms the spirit of every man within him. When the fire consumes the wood the flame ascends, and the ashes *return to the earth* out of which the wood grew. The soul does not die with the body; it is *redeemed from the power of the grave* (Ps. xlix. 15); it can subsist without it and will in a state of separation from it, as the candle burns, and burns brighter, when it is taken out of the dark lantern. It removes to the world of spirits, to which it is allied. It goes *to God* as a Judge, to give account of itself, and to be lodged either with *the spirits in prison* (1 Pet. iii. 19) or with *the spirits in paradise* (Luke xxiii. 43), according to what was done in the body. This makes death terrible to the wicked, whose souls go to God as an avenger, and comfortable to the godly, whose souls go to God as a Father, into whose hands they cheerfully commit them, through a Mediator, out of whom sinners may justly dread to think of going *to God.*

8 Vanity of vanities, saith the preacher; all *is* vanity. 9 And moreover, because the preacher was wise, he still taught the people knowledge; yea, he gave good heed, and sought out, *and* set in order many

proverbs. 10 The preacher sought to find out acceptable words : and *that which was* written *was* upright, *even* words of truth. 11 The words of the wise *are* as goads, and as nails fastened *by* the masters of assemblies, *which* are given from one shepherd. 12 And further, by these, my son, be admonished : of making many books *there is* no end; and much study *is* a weariness of the flesh.

Solomon is here drawing towards a close, and is loth to part till he has gained his point, and prevailed with his hearers, with his readers, to seek for that satisfaction in God only and in their duty to him which they can never find in the creature.

I. He repeats his text (*v.* 8), 1. As that which he had fully demonstrated the truth of, and so made good his undertaking in this sermon, wherein he had kept closely to his text, and both his reasons and his application were to the purpose. 2. As that which he desired to inculcate both upon others and upon himself, to have it ready, and to make use of it upon all occasions. We see it daily proved; let it therefore be daily improved: *Vanity of vanities, all is vanity.*

II. He recommends what he had written upon this subject by divine direction and inspiration to our serious consideration. The words of this book are faithful, and well worthy our acceptance, for,

1. They are the words of one that was a convert, a penitent, that could speak by dear-bought experience of the vanity of the world and the folly of expecting great things from it. He was *Coheleth,* one gathered in from his wanderings and gathered home to that God from whom he had revolted. *Vanity of vanities, saith the* penitent. All true penitents are convinced of the vanity of the world, for they find it can do nothing to ease them of the burden of sin, which they complain of.

2. They are the words of one that was wise, wiser than any, endued with extraordinary measures of wisdom, famous for it among his neighbours, who all sought unto him *to hear his wisdom,* and therefore a competent judge of this matter, not only wise as a prince, but wise as a preacher—and preachers have need of wisdom to win souls.

3. He was one that made it his business to do good, and to use wisdom aright. *Because* he *was* himself *wise,* but knew he had not his wisdom for himself, any more than he had it from himself, *he still taught the people* that *knowledge* which he had found useful to himself, and hoped might be so to them too. It is the interest of princes to have their people well taught in religion, and no disparagement to them to teach them themselves *the good knowledge of the Lord,* but their duty to encourage those whose office it is to teach

them and to speak comfortably to them, 2 Chron. xxx. 22. Let not the people, the common people, be despised, no, not by the wisest and greatest, as either unworthy or incapable of good knowledge : even those that are well taught have need to be *still taught,* that they may grow in knowledge.

4. He took a great deal of pains and care to do good, designing to *teach the people knowledge.* He did not put them off with any thing that came next to hand, because they were inferior people, and he a very wise man, but, considering the worth of the souls he preached to and the weight of the subject he preached on, he *gave good heed* to what he read and heard from others, that, having stocked himself well, he might *bring out of his treasury things new and old.* He *gave good heed* to what he spoke and wrote himself, and was choice and exact in it; all he did was elaborate. (1.) He chose the most profitable way of preaching, by proverbs or short sentences, which would be more easily apprehended and remembered than long and laboured periods. (2.) He did not content himself with a few parables, or wise sayings, and repeat them again and again, but he furnished himself with *many proverbs,* a great variety of grave discourses, that he might have something to say on every occasion. (3.) He did not only give them such observations as were obvious and trite, but he *sought out* such as were surprising and uncommon; he dug into the mines of knowledge, and did not merely pick up what lay on the surface. (4.) He did not deliver his heads and observations at random, as they came to mind, but methodised them, and *set them in order* that they might appear in more strength and lustre.

5. He put what he had to say in such a dress as he thought would be most pleasing : *He sought to find out acceptable words,* words of delight (*v.* 10); he took care that good matter might not be spoiled by a bad style, and by the ungratefulness and incongruity of the expression. Ministers should study, not for big words, nor for fine words, but *acceptable words,* such as are likely to please men for their good, to edification, 1 Cor. x. 33. Those that would win souls must contrive how to win upon them with *words fitly spoken.*

6. That which he wrote for our instruction is of unquestionable certainty, and what we may rely upon : *That which was written was upright* and sincere, according to the real sentiments of the penman, even *words of truth,* the exact representation of the thing as it is. Those are sure not to miss their way who are guided by these words. What good will *acceptable words* do us if they be not *upright and words of truth?* Most are for smooth things, that flatter them, rather than right things, that direct them (Isa. xxx. 10), but to those that understand themselves, and their own interest, *words of truth* will always be *acceptable words.*

7. That which he and other holy men wrote

will be of great use and advantage to us, especially being inculcated upon us by the exposition of it, *v.* 11. Here observe, (1.) A double benefit accruing to us from divine truths if duly applied and improved ; they are *profitable for doctrine, for reproof, for correction, and instruction in righteousness.* They are of use, [1.] To excite us to our duty. They are as goads to the ox that draws the plough, putting him forward when he is dull and quickening him, to amend his pace. The truths of God *prick men to the heart* (Acts ii. 37) and put them upon bethinking themselves, when they trifle and grow remiss, and exerting themselves with more vigour in their work. While our good affections are so apt as they are to grow flat and cool, we have need of these *goads.* [2.] To engage us to persevere in our duty. They are *as nails* to those that are wavering and inconstant, to fix them to that which is good. They are *as goads* to such as are dull and draw back, and *nails* to such as are desultory and draw aside, means to establish the heart and confirm good resolutions, that we may not sit loose to our duty, nor even be taken off from it, but that what good there is in us may be *as a nail fastened in a sure place,* Ezra ix. 8. (2.) A double way of communicating divine truths, in order to these ~~benefits~~ :—[1.] By the scriptures, as the standing rule, the *words of the wise,* that is, of the prophets, who are called *wise men,* Matt. xxiii. 34. These we have in black and white, and may have recourse to them at any time, and make use of them as *goads and as nails.* By them we may teach ourselves ; let them but come with pungency and power to the soul, let the impressions of them be deep and durable, and they will *make us wise to salvation.* [2.] By the ministry. To make the *words of the wise* more profitable to us, it is appointed that they should be impressed and fastened by the *masters of assemblies.* Solemn assemblies for religious worship are an ancient divine institution, intended for the honour of God and the edification of his church, and are not only serviceable, but necessary, to those ends. There must be masters of these assemblies, who are Christ's ministers, and as such are to preside in them, to be God's mouth to the people and theirs to God. Their business is to fasten the *words of the wise,* and drive them as *nails* to the head, in order to which the word of God is likewise as *a hammer,* Jer. xxiii. 29.

8. That which is written, and thus recommended to us, is of divine origin. Though it comes to us through various hands (many *wise men,* and many *masters of assemblies),* yet it is *given by one* and the same *shepherd,* the great *shepherd of Israel, that leads Joseph like a flock,* Ps. lxxx. 1. God is that one Shepherd, whose good Spirit indited the scriptures, and assists the *masters of the assemblies* in opening and applying the scriptures. These *words of the wise* are the true

sayings of God, on which we may rest our souls. From that one Shepherd all ministers must receive what they deliver, and speak according to the light of the written word.

9. The sacred inspired writings, if we will but make use of them, are sufficient to guide us in the way to true happiness, and we need not, in the pursuit of that, to fatigue ourselves with the search of other writings (*v.* 12): "*And further,* nothing now remains but to tell thee that *of making many books there is no end,*" that is, (1.) Of *writing* many books. " If what I have written, serve not to convince thee of the vanity of the world, and the necessity of being religious, neither wouldst thou be convinced if I should write ever so much." If the end be not attained in the use of those books of scripture which God has blessed us with, neither should we obtain the end, if we had twice as many more ; nay, if we had so many that the whole world could not contain them (John xxi. 25), and much study of them would but confound us, and would rather be *a weariness to the flesh* than any advantage to the soul. We have as much as God saw fit to give us, saw fit for us, and saw us fit for. Much less can it be expected that those who will not by these be admonished should be wrought upon by other writings. Let men write ever so many books for the conduct of human life, write till they have tired themselves with much study, they cannot give better instructions than those we have from the word of God. Or, (2.) Of *buying* many books, making ourselves masters of them, and masters of what is in them, by much study ; still the desire of learning would be unsatisfied. It will give a man indeed the best entertainment and the best accomplishment this world can afford him ; but if we be not by these *admonished* of the vanity of the world, and human learning, among other things, and its insufficiency to make us happy without true piety, alas ! there is no end of it, nor real benefit by it ; it will weary the body, but never give the soul any true satisfaction. The great Mr. Selden subscribed to this when he owned that in all the books he had read he never found that on which he could rest his soul, but in the holy scripture, especially Tit. ii. 11, 12. By these therefore let us be admonished.

13 Let us hear the conclusion of the whole matter : Fear God, and keep his commandments : for this *is* the whole *duty* of man. 14 For God shall bring every work into judgment, with every secret thing, whether *it be* good, or whether *it be* evil.

The great enquiry which Solomon prosecutes in this book is, *What is that good which the sons of men should do ? ch.* ii. 3. What is the true way to true happiness, the certain means to attain our great end ? He had in vain sought it among those things which most men are eager in pursuit of, but here, at length, he has found it, by the help of that discovery which God anciently made to man (Job xxviii. 28), that serious godliness is the only way to true happiness : *Let us hear the conclusion of the whole matter,* the return entered upon the writ of enquiry, the result of this diligent search ; you shall have all I have been driving at in two words. He does not say, *Do you hear it,* but, *Let us hear it ;* for preachers must themselves be hearers of that word which they preach to others, must hear it as from God; those are teachers by the halves who teach others and not themselves, Rom. ii. 21. Every word of God is pure and precious, but some words are worthy of more special remark, as this; the Masorites begin it with a capital letter, as that Deut. vi. 4. Solomon himself puts a *nota bene* before it, demanding attention in these words, *Let us hear the conclusion of the whole matter.* Observe here,

I. The summary of religion. Setting aside all matters of doubtful disputation, to be religious is to *fear God and keep his commandments.* 1. The root of religion is the fear of God reigning in the heart, a reverence of his majesty, a deference to his authority, and a dread of his wrath. *Fear God,* that is, worship God, give him the honour due to his name, in all the instances of true devotion, inward and outward. See Rev. xiv. 7. 2. The rule of religion is the law of God revealed in the scriptures. Our fear towards God must be taught by his commandments (Isa. xxix. 13), and those we must keep and carefully observe. Wherever the fear of God is uppermost in the heart, there will be *a respect to all his commandments* and care to keep them. In vain do we pretend to fear God if we do not make conscience of our duty to him.

II. The vast importance of it : *This is the whole of man ;* it is all his business and all his blessedness ; our whole duty is summed up in this and our whole comfort is bound up in this. It is the concern of every man, and ought to be his chief and continual care ; it is the common concern of all men, of their whole time. It is nothing to a man whether he be rich or poor, high or low, but it is the main matter, it is all in all to a man, to fear God and do as he bids him.

III. A powerful inducement to this, *v.* 14. We shall see of what vast consequence it is to us that we be religious if we consider the account we must every one of us shortly give of himself to God; thence he argued against a voluptuous and vicious life (*ch.* xi. 9), and here for a religious life: *God shall bring every work into judgment.* Note, 1. There is a judgment to come, in which every man's eternal state will be finally determined. 2. God himself will be the Judge, God-man will, not only because he has a right to judge, but because he is perfectly fit for it, infinitely wise and just. 3. *Every work* will then be *brought into judgment,* will be enquired into and called over again. It will be a day to *bring to remembrance every thing done in the body.* 4. The great thing to be then judged of concerning *every work* is whether it be good or evil, conformable to the will of God or a violation of it. 5. Even *secret things,* both good and evil, will be brought to light, and brought to account, in the judgment of the great day (Rom. ii. 16); there is no good work, no bad work, hid, but shall then be made manifest. 6. In consideration of the judgment to come, and the strictness of that judgment, it highly concerns us now to be very strict in our walking with God, that we may *give up our account with joy.*

AN

EXPOSITION,

WITH PRACTICAL OBSERVATIONS,

OF THE

SONG OF SOLOMON.

ALL *scripture,* we are sure, *is given by inspiration of God, and is profitable* for the support and advancement of the interests of his kingdom among men, and it is never the less so for there being found in it some things *dark and hard to be understood, which those that are unlearned and unstable wrest to their own destruction.* In our belief both of the divine extraction and of the spiritual exposition of this book we are confirmed by the ancient, constant, and concurring testimony both of the church of the Jews, to whom were *committed the oracles of God,* and who never made any doubt of the authority of this book, and of the Christian church, which happily succeeds them in that trust and honour. I. It must be confessed, on the one hand, that if he who barely reads this book be asked, as the eunuch was, *Understandest thou what thou readest?* he will have more reason than he had to say, *How can I, except some man shall guide me?* The books of scripture-history and prophecy are very much like one another, but this *Song of Solomon's* is very much unlike the songs of his father David; here is not the name of God in it; it is never quoted in the New Testament; we find not in it any expressions of natural religion or pious devotion, no, nor is it introduced by vision, or any of the marks of immediate revelation. It seems as hard as any part of scripture to be made a *savour of life unto life*, nay, and to those who come to the reading of it with carnal minds and corrupt affections, it is in danger of being made a *savour of death unto death;* it is a flower out of which they extract poison; and therefore the Jewish doctors advised their young people not to read it till they were thirty years old, lest by the abuse of that which is most pure and sacred (*horrendum dictu—horrible to say!*) the flames of lust should be kindled with fire from heaven, which is intended for the altar only. But, II. It must be confessed, on the other hand, that with the help of the many faithful guides we have for the understanding of this book it appears to be a very bright and powerful ray of heavenly light, admirably fitted to excite pious and devout affections in holy souls, to draw out their desires towards God, to increase their delight in him, and improve their acquaintance and communion with him. It is an allegory, the letter of which kills those who rest in that and look no further, but the spirit of which gives life, 2 Cor. iii. 6; John vi. 63. It is a parable, which makes divine things more difficult to those who do not love them, but more plain and pleasant to those who do, Matt. xiii. 14, 16. Experienced Christians here find a counterpart of their experiences, and to them it is intelligible, while *those* neither understand it nor relish it who have no part nor lot in the matter. It is a song, an *Epithalamium*, or nuptial song, wherein, by the expressions of love between a bridegroom and his bride, are set forth and illustrated the mutual affections that pass between God and a distinguished remnant of mankind. It is a pastoral; the bride and bridegroom, for the more lively representation of humility and innocence, are brought in as a shepherd and his shepherdess. Now, 1. This song might easily be taken in a spiritual sense by the Jewish church, for whose use it was first composed, and was so taken, as appears by the Chaldee-Paraphrase and the most ancient Jewish expositors. God betrothed the people of Israel to himself; he entered into covenant with them, and it was a marriage-covenant. He had given abundant proofs of his love to them, and required of them that they should love him with all their heart and soul. Idolatry was often spoken of as spiritual adultery, and doting upon idols, to prevent which this song was penned, representing the complacency which God took in Israel and which Israel ought to take in God, and encouraging them to continue faithful to him, though he might seem sometimes to withdraw and hide himself from them, and to wait for the further manifestation of himself in the promised Messiah. 2. It may more easily be taken in a spiritual sense by the Christian church, because the condescensions and communications of divine love appear more rich and free under the gospel than they did under the law, and the communion between heaven and earth more familiar. God sometimes spoke of himself as the husband of the Jewish church (Isa. lxiv. 5, Hos. ii. 16, 19), and rejoiced in it as his bride, Isa. lxii. 4, 5. But more frequently is Christ represented as the bridegroom of his church (Matt. xxv. 1, Rom. vii. 4, 2 Cor. xi. 2, Eph. v. 32), and the church as the bride, the Lamb's wife, Rev. xix. 7; xxi. 2, 9. Pursuant to this metaphor Christ and the church in general, Christ and particular believers, are here discoursing with abundance of mutual esteem and endearment. The best key to this book is the 45th Psalm, which we find applied to Christ in the New Testament, and therefore this ought to be so too. It requires some pains to find out what may, probably, be the meaning of the Holy Spirit in the several parts of this book; as David's songs are many of them level to the capacity of the meanest, and there are shallows in them in which a lamb may wade, so this of Solomon's will exercise the capacities of the most learned, and there are depths in it in which an elephant may swim. But, when the meaning is found out, it will be of admirable use to excite pious and devout affections in us; and the same truths which are plainly laid down in other scriptures when they are extracted out of this come to the soul with a more pleasing power. When we apply ourselves to the study of this book we must not only, with Moses and Joshua, *put off our shoe from off our foot*, and even forget that we have bodies, because *the place where we stand is holy ground*, but we must, with John, *come up hither*, must spread our wings, take a noble flight, and soar upwards, till by faith and holy love we *enter into the holiest*, for *this is no other than the house of God and this is the gate of heaven.*

CHAP. I.

In this chapter, after the title of the book (ver. 1), we have Christ and his church, Christ and a believer, expressing their esteem for each other. I. The bride, the church, speaks to the bridegroom (ver. 2—4), to the daughters of Jerusalem (ver. 5, 6), and then to the bridegroom, ver. 7. II. Christ, the bridegroom, speaks in answer to the complaints and requests of his spouse, ver. 8—11. III. The church expresses the great value she has for Christ, and the delights she takes in communion with him, ver. 12—14. IV. Christ commends the church's beauty, ver. 15. V The church returns the commendation, ver. 16, 17. Where there is a fire of true love to Christ in the heart this will be of use to blow it up into a flame.

THE song of songs, which *is* Solomon's.

We have here the title of this book, showing, 1. The nature of it; it is a *song*, that it might the better answer the intention, which is to stir up the affections and to heat them, which poetry will be very instrumental to do. The subject is pleasing, and therefore fit to be treated of in a song, in singing which we may *make melody with our hearts unto the Lord*. It is evangelical; and gospel-times should be times of joy, for gospel-grace puts *a new song* into our mouths,

Ps. xcviii. 1. **2.** The dignity of it; it is *the song of songs*, a most excellent song, not only above any human composition, or above all the other songs which Solomon penned, but even above any other of the scripture-songs, as having more of Christ in it. **3.** The penman of it; it is Solomon's. It is not the song of fools, as many of the songs of love are, but the song of the wisest of men; nor can any man give a better proof of his wisdom than to celebrate the love of God to mankind and to excite his own love to God and that of others with it. Solomon's songs were a thousand and five (1 Kings iv. 32); those that were of other subjects are lost, but this of seraphic love remains, and will to the end of time. Solomon, like his father, was addicted to poetry, and, which way soever a man's genius lies, he should endeavour to honour God and edify the church with it. One of Solomon's names was *Jedidiah—beloved of the Lord* (2 Sam. xii. 25); and none so fit to write of the Lord's love as he that had himself so great an interest in it; none of all the apostles wrote so much of love as he that was himself the beloved disciple and lay in Christ's bosom. Solomon, as a king, had great affairs to mind and manage, which took up much of his thoughts and time, yet he found heart and leisure for this and other religious exercises. Men of business ought to be devout men, and not to think that business will excuse them from that which is every man's great business — to keep up communion with God. It is not certain when Solomon penned this sacred song. Some think that he penned it after he recovered himself by the grace of God from his backslidings, as a further proof of his repentance, and as if by doing good to many with this song he would atone for the hurt he had perhaps done with loose, vain, amorous songs, when he *loved many strange wives;* now he turned his wit the right way. It is more probable that he penned it in the beginning of his time, while he kept close to God and kept up his communion with him; and perhaps he put this song, with his father's psalms, into the hands of the chief musician, for the service of the temple, not without a key to it, for the right understanding of it. Some think that it was penned upon occasion of his marriage with Pharaoh's daughter, but that is uncertain; the tower of Lebanon, which is mentioned in this book (*ch.* vii. 4), was not built, as is supposed, till long after that marriage. We may reasonably think that when in the height of his prosperity he *loved the Lord* (1 Kings iii. 3) he thus *served him with joyfulness and gladness of heart in the abundance of all things.* It may be rendered, *The song of songs, which is concerning Solomon,* who as the son and successor of David, on whom the covenant of royalty was entailed, as the founder of the temple, and as one that excelled in wisdom and wealth, was a type of Christ, in whom are *hidden all the treasures of*

wisdom and knowledge, and yet is a greater than Solomon; this is therefore a song concerning him. It is here fitly placed after *Ecclesiastes;* for when by that book we are thoroughly convinced of the vanity of the creature, and its insufficiency to satisfy us and make a happiness for us, we shall be quickened to seek for happiness in the love of Christ, and that true transcendent pleasure which is to be found only in communion with God through him. The voice in the wilderness, that was to prepare Christ's way, cried, *All flesh is grass.*

2 Let him kiss me with the kisses of his mouth: for thy love *is* better than wine. **3** Because of the savour of thy good ointments thy name *is as* ointment poured forth, therefore do the virgins love thee. **4** Draw me, we will run after thee: the king hath brought me into his chambers: we will be glad and rejoice in thee, we will remember thy love more than wine: the upright love thee. **5** I *am* black, but comely, O ye daughters of Jerusalem, as the tents of Kedar, as the curtains of Solomon. **6** Look not upon me, because I *am* black, because the sun hath looked upon me: my mother's children were angry with me; they made me keeper of the vineyards; *but* mine own vineyard have I not kept.

The spouse, in this dramatic poem, is here first introduced addressing herself to the bridegroom and then to the daughters of Jerusalem.

I. To the bridegroom, not giving him any name or title, but beginning abruptly: *Let him kiss me;* like Mary Magdalen to the supposed gardener (John xx. 15), *If thou have borne him hence,* meaning Christ, but not naming him. The heart had been before taken up with the thoughts of him, and to this relative those thoughts were the antecedent, that good matter which the heart was inditing, Ps. xlv. 1. Those that are full of Christ themselves are ready to think that others should be so too. Two things the spouse desires, and pleases herself with the thoughts of:—

1. The bridegroom's friendship (*v.* 2): " *Let him kiss me with the kisses of his mouth,* that is, be reconciled to me, and let me know that he is so; let me have the tokens of his favour." Thus the Old-Testament church desired Christ's manifesting himself in the flesh, to be no longer under the law as a schoolmaster, under a dispensation of bondage and terror, but to receive the communications of divine grace in the gospel, in w ich God is reconciling the world unto himself, binding up and healing what by the law was torn and

smitten; as the mother kisses the child that she has chidden. " Let him no longer send to me, but come himself, no longer speak by angels and prophets, but let me have the word of his own mouth, those *gracious words* (Luke iv. 22), which will be to me as the *kisses of his mouth,* sure tokens of reconciliation, as Esau's kissing Jacob was." All gospel duty is summed up in our kissing the Son (Ps. ii. 12) ; so all gospel-grace is summed up in his kissing us, as the father of the prodigal kissed him when he returned a penitent. It is a kiss of peace. Kisses are opposed to wounds (Prov. xxvii. 6), so are the kisses of grace to the wounds of the law. Thus all true believers earnestly desire the manifestations of Christ's love to their souls; they desire no more to make them happy than the assurance of his favour, the lifting up of the light of his countenance upon them (Ps. iv. 6, 7), and the knowledge of that love of his which surpasses knowledge; this is the one thing they desire, Ps. xxvii. 4. They are ready to welcome the manifestation of Christ's love to their souls by his Spirit, and to return them in the humble professions of love to him and complacency in him, above all. *The fruit of his lips is peace,* Isa. lvii. 19. " Let him give me ten thousand kisses whose very fruition makes me desire him the more, and, whereas all other pleasures sour and wither by using, those of the Spirit become more delightful." So bishop Reynolds. She gives several reasons for this desire. (1.) Because of the great esteem she has for his love : *Thy love is better than wine.* Wine *makes glad the heart,* revives the drooping spirits, and exhilarates them, but gracious souls take more pleasure in loving Christ and being beloved of him, in the fruits and gifts of his love and in the pledges and assurances of it, than any man ever took in the most exquisite delights of sense, and it is more reviving to them than ever the richest cordial was to one ready to faint. Note, [1.] Christ's love is in itself, and in the account of all the saints, more valuable and desirable than the best entertainments this world can give. [2.] Those only may expect the kisses of Christ's mouth, and the comfortable tokens of his favour, who prefer his love before all the delights of the children of men, who would rather forego those delights than forfeit his favour, and take more pleasure in spiritual joys than in any bodily refreshments whatsoever. Observe here the change of the person : *Let him kiss me;* there she speaks of him as absent, or as if she were afraid to speak to him; but, in the next words, she sees him near at hand, and therefore directs her speech to him : " *Thy love, thy loves*" (so the word is), " I so earnestly desire, because I highly esteem it." (2.) Because of the diffusive fragrancy of his love and the fruits of it (v. 3): " *Because of the savour of thy good ointment* (the agreeableness and acceptableness of thy graces and comforts to all that

rightly understand both them and themselves), *thy name is as ointment poured forth,* thou art so, and all that whereby thou hast made thyself known; thy very name is precious to all the saints ; it is an ointment and perfume which rejoice the heart." The unfolding of Christ's name is as the opening of a box of precious ointment, which the room is filled with the odour of. The preaching of his gospel was the *manifesting the savour of his knowledge in every place,* 2 Cor. ii. 14. The Spirit was the *oil of gladness* wherewith Christ was anointed (Heb. i. 9), and all true believers have that *unction* (1 John ii. 27), so that he is precious to them, and they to him and to one another. *A good name* is *as precious ointment,* but Christ's name is more fragrant than any other. Wisdom, like oil, *makes the face to shine;* but the Redeemer outshines, in beauty, all others. The name of Christ is not now like ointment sealed up, as it had been long *(Ask not after my name, for it is secret),* but like *ointment poured forth,* which denotes both the freeness and fulness of the communications of his grace by the gospel. (3.) Because of the general affection that all holy souls have to him : *Therefore do the virgins love thee.* It is Christ's *love shed abroad in our hearts* that draws them out in love to him; all that are pure from the corruptions of sin, that preserve the chastity of their own spirits, and are true to the vows by which they have devoted themselves to God, that not only suffer not their affections to be violated, but cannot bear so much as to be solicited by the world and the flesh, those are the virgins that love Jesus Christ and *follow him whithersoever he goes,* Rev. xiv. 4. And, because Christ is the darling of all the *pure in heart,* let him be ours, and let our desire be towards him and towards the *kisses of his mouth.*

2. The bridegroom's fellowship, v. 4. Observe here,

(1.) Her petition for divine grace : *Draw me.* This implies sense of distance from him, desire of union with him. " Draw me to thyself, draw me nearer, draw me home to thee." She had prayed that he would draw nigh to her (v. 2); in order to that, she prays that he would draw her nigh to him. " *Draw me,* not only with the moral suasion which there is in the fragrancy of the good ointments, not only with the attractives of that name which is as ointment poured forth, but with supernatural grace, with the *cords of a man* and the *bands of love,*" Hos. xi. 4. Christ has told us that none come to him but such as the Father draws, John vi. 44. We are not only weak, and cannot come of ourselves any further than we are helped, but we are naturally backward and averse to come, and therefore must pray for those influences and operations of the Spirit, by the power of which we are of unwilling made willing, Ps. cx. 3. " *Draw me,* else I move not; overpower the world and the flesh that would draw me from thee. We are not driven to Christ, but drawn in such a way as is agreeable to rational creatures.

(2.) Her promise to improve that grace: *Draw me,* and then *we will run after thee.* See how the doctrine of special and effectual grace consists with our duty, and is a powerful engagement and encouragement to it, and yet reserves all the glory of all the good that is in us to God only. Observe, [1.] The flowing forth of the soul after Christ, and its ready compliance with him, are the effect of his grace; we could not run after him if he did not draw us, 2 Cor. iii. 5; Phil. iv. 13. [2.] The grace which God gives us we must diligently improve. When Christ by his Spirit draws us we must with our spirits run after him. As God says, *I will,* and *you shall* (Ezek. xxxvi. 27), so we must say, " *Thou shalt* and *we will;* thou shalt *work in us both to will and to do,* and therefore we will work out our own salvation" (Phil. ii. 12, 13); not only we will walk, but we will run after thee, which denotes eagerness of desire, readiness of affection, vigour of pursuit, and swiftness of motion. *When thou shalt enlarge my heart* then *I will run the way of thy commandments* (Ps. cxix. 32); when *thy right hand upholds me* then *my soul follows hard after thee* (Ps. lxiii. 8); when with lovingkindness to us he draws us (Jer. xxxi. 3) we with lovingkindness to him must run after him, Isa. xl. 31. Observe the difference between the petition and the promise: " Draw me, and then we will run." When Christ pours out his Spirit upon the church in general, which is his bride, all the members of it do thence receive enlivening quickening influences, and are made to run to him with the more cheerfulness, Isa. lv. 5. Or, " Draw me" (says the believing soul) " and then I will not only follow thee myself as fast as I can, but will bring all mine along with me: *We will run after thee,* I and the *virgins that love thee* (v. 3), I and all that I have any interest in or influence upon, *I and my house* (Josh. xxiv. 15), I and the *transgressors whom I will teach thy ways,*" Ps. li. 13. Those that put themselves forth, in compliance with divine grace, shall find that their *zeal will provoke many,* 2 Cor. ix. 2. Those that are lively will be active; when Philip was drawn to Christ he drew Nathanael; and they will be exemplary, and so will win those that would not be won by the word.

(3.) The immediate answer that was given to this prayer: *The King has* drawn me, has *brought me into his chambers.* It is not so much an answer fetched by faith from the word of Christ's grace as an answer fetched by experience from the workings of his grace. If we observe, as we ought, the returns of prayer, we may find that sometimes, *while we are yet speaking,* Christ hears, Isa. lxv. 24. The bridegroom is a king; so much the more wonderful is his condescension in the invitations and entertainments that he gives

us, and so much the greater reason have we to accept of them and to *run after him.* God is the King that has made *the marriage-supper* for his Son (Matt. xxii. 2) and brings in even *the poor and the maimed,* and even the most shy and bashful are *compelled to come in.* Those that are drawn to Christ are brought, not only into his courts, into his palaces (Ps. xlv. 15), but into his presence-chamber, where his secret is with them (Ps. xxv. 14), where he is free with them (John xiv. 21), and where they are safe in his pavilion, Ps. xxvii. 5; Isa. xxvi. 20. Those that *wait at wisdom's gates* shall be *made to come* (so the word is) *into her chambers;* they shall be led into truth and comfort.

(4.) The wonderful complacency which the spouse takes in the honour which the king put upon her. Being *brought into the chamber,* [1.] " We have what we would have. Our desires are crowned with unspeakable delights; all our griefs vanish, and *we will be glad and rejoice.* If a *day in the courts,* much more an hour in the chambers, *is better than a thousand,* than ten thousand, elsewhere." Those that are, through grace, brought into covenant and communion with God, have reason to *go on their way rejoicing,* as the eunuch (Acts viii. 39), and that joy will enlarge our heart and be our strength, Neh. viii. 10. [2.] All our joy shall centre in God: " *We will rejoice,* not in the ointments, or the chambers, but *in thee.* It is God only that is our *exceeding joy,* Ps. xliii. 4. We have no joy but in Christ, and which we are indebted to him for." *Gaudium in Domino —Joy in the Lord,* was the ancient salutation, and *Salus in Domino sempiterna—Eternal salvation in the Lord.* [3.] " We will retain the relish and savour of this kindness of thine and never forget it: *We will remember thy loves more than wine;* not only thy love itself (v. 2), but the very remembrance of it shall be more grateful to us than the strongest cordial to the spirits, or the most palatable liquor to the taste. We will remember to give thanks for thy love, and it shall make more durable impressions upon us than any thing in this world."

(5.) The communion which a gracious soul has with all the saints in this communion with Christ. In the chambers to which we are brought we not only meet with him, but meet with one another (1 John i. 7); for the *upright love thee;* the congregation, the generation, of *the upright love thee.* Whatever others do, all that are Israelites indeed, and faithful to God, will love Jesus Christ. Whatever differences of apprehension and affection there may be among Christians in other things, this they are all agreed in, Jesus Christ is precious to them. *The upright* here are the same with the *virgins,* v. 3. All that *remember his love more than wine* will love him with a superlative love. Nor is any love acceptable to Christ but the love of *the upright,* love in sincerity, Eph. vi. 24.

II. To *the daughters of Jerusalem, v.* 5, 6. The church in general, being in distress, speaks to particular churches to guard them against the danger they were in of being offended at the church's sufferings, 1 Thess. iii. 3. Or the believer speaks to those that were professors at large in the church, but not of it, or to weak Christians, babes in Christ, that labour under much ignorance, infirmity, and mistake, not perfectly instructed, and yet willing to be taught in the things of God. She observed these by-standers look disdainfully upon her because of her blackness, in respect both of sins and sufferings, upon the account of which they thought she had little reason to expect the kisses she wished for (*v.* 2) or to expect that they should join with her in her joys, *v.* 4. She therefore endeavours to remove this offence; she owns she is *black*. Guilt blackens; the heresies, scandals, and offences, that happen in the church, make her *black;* and the best saints have their failings. Sorrow blackens; that seems to be especially meant; the church is often in a low condition, mean, and poor, and in appearance despicable, her beauty sullied and her face foul with weeping; she is in mourning weeds, clothed with sackcloth, as the Nazarites that had become *blacker than a coal,* Lam. iv. 8. Now, to take off this offence,

1. She asserts her own comeliness notwithstanding (*v.* 5): *I am black, but comely,* black *as the tents of Kedar,* in which the shepherds lived, which were very coarse, and never whitened, weatherbeaten and discoloured by long use, but comely *as the curtains of Solomon,* the furniture of whose rooms, no doubt, was sumptuous and rich, in proportion to the stateliness of his houses. The church is sometimes *black* with persecution, *but comely* in patience, constancy, and consolation, and never the less amiable in the eyes of Christ, *black in the account of men, but comely* in God's esteem, *black* in some that are a scandal to her, *but comely* in others that are sincere and are an honour to her. True believers are *black* in themselves, *but comely* in Christ, with the comeliness that he puts upon them, *black* outwardly, for the *world knows them not,* but *all glorious within,* Ps. xlv. 13. St. Paul was *weak,* and yet *strong,* 2 Cor. xii. 10. And so the church is *black* and yet *comely;* believer is a sinner and yet a saint; his own righteousnesses are *as filthy rags,* but he is clothed with the robe of Christ's righteousness. The Chaldee Paraphrase applies it to the people of Israel's blackness when they made the golden calf and their comeliness when they repented of it.

2. She gives an account how she came to be so black. The blackness was not natural, but contracted, and was owing to the hard usage that had been given her: *Look not upon me so scornfully because I am black.* We must take heed with what eye we look upon the church, especially when she is in black. *Thou shouldst not have looked upon*

the day of thy brother, the day of his affliction, Obad. 12. Be not offended; for,

(1.) *I am black* by reason of my sufferings: *The sun has looked upon me.* She was fair and comely; whiteness was her proper colour; but she got this blackness by *the burden and heat of the day,* which she was forced to bear. She was sun-burnt, scorched with tribulation and persecution (Matt. xiii. 6, 21); and the greatest beauties, if exposed to the weather, are soonest tanned. Observe how she mitigates her troubles; she does not say, as Jacob (Gen. xxxi. 40), *In the day the drought consumed me,* but, *The sun has looked upon me;* for it becomes not God's suffering people to make the worst of their sufferings. But what was the matter? [1.] She fell under the displeasure of those of her own house: *My mother's children were angry with me.* She was *in perils by false brethren;* her foes were *those of her own house* (Matt. x. 36), brethren by nature as men, by profession as members of the same sacred corporation, the children of the church her mother, but not of God her Father; they *were angry with* her. The Samaritans, who claimed kindred to the Jews, were vexed at any thing that tended to the prosperity of Jerusalem, Neh. ii. 10. Note, It is no new thing for the people of God to fall under the anger of their own mother's children. *It was thou, a man, my equal,* Ps. lv. 12, 13. This makes the trouble the more irksome and grievous; from such it is taken unkindly, and the anger of such is implacable. *A brother offended is hard to be won.* [2.] They dealt very hardly with her: *They made me the keeper of the vineyards,* that is, *First,* "They seduced me to sin, drew me into false worships, to serve their gods, which was like dressing their vineyards, *keeping the vine of Sodom;* and they would not let me *keep my own vineyard,* serve my own God, and observe those pure worships which he gave me in charge, and which I do and ever will own for mine." These are the grievances which good people complain most of in a time of persecution, that their consciences are forced, and that those who rule them with rigour say *to their souls, Bow down, that we may go over,* Isa. li. 23. Or, *Secondly,* "They brought me into trouble, imposed that upon me which was toilsome, and burdensome, and very disgraceful." Keeping the vineyards was base servile work, and very laborious, Isa. lxi. 5. Her mother's children made her the drudge of the family. *Cursed be their anger, for it was fierce, and their wrath, for it was cruel.* The spouse of Christ has met with a great deal of hard usage.

(2.) "My sufferings are such as I have deserved; for *my own vineyard have I not kept.* How unrighteous soever my brethren are in persecuting me, God is righteous in permitting them to do so. I am justly made a slavish keeper of men's vineyards, because I have been a careless keeper of the vineyards God has entrusted me with." Slothful servants of God are justly made to serve their enemies, *that they may know his service, and the service of the kings of the countries,* 2 Chron. xii. 8; Deut. xxviii. 47, 48; Ezek. xx. 23, 24. "Think not the worse of the ways of God for my sufferings, for I smart for my own folly." Note, When God's people are oppressed and persecuted it becomes them to acknowledge their own sin to be the procuring cause of their troubles, especially their carelessness in keeping their vineyards, so that it has been like *the field of the slothful.*

7 Tell me, O thou whom my soul loveth, where thou feedest, where thou makest *thy flock* to rest at noon: for why should I be as one that turneth aside by the flocks of thy companions? 8 If thou know not, O thou fairest among women, go thy way forth by the footsteps of the flock, and feed thy kids beside the shepherds' tents. 9 I have compared thee, O my love, to a company of horses in Pharaoh's chariots. 10 Thy cheeks are comely with rows *of jewels,* thy neck with chains *of gold.* 11 We will make thee borders of gold with studs of silver.

Here is, I. The humble petition which the spouse presents to her beloved, the shepherdess to the shepherd, the church and every believer to Christ, for a more free and intimate communion with him. She turns from the *daughters of Jerusalem,* to whom she had complained both of her sins and of her troubles, and looks up to heaven for relief and succour against both, v. 7. Here observe, 1. The title she gives to Christ: *O thou whom my soul loveth.* Note, It is the undoubted character of all true believers that their souls love Jesus Christ, which intimates both the sincerity and the strength of their love; they *love him with all their hearts;* and those that do so may come to him boldly and may humbly plead it with him. 2. The opinion she has of him as the good shepherd of the sheep; she doubts not but he *feeds his flock* and *makes them rest at noon.* Jesus Christ graciously provides both repast and repose for his sheep; they are not starved, but well fed, not scattered upon the mountains, but fed together, fed *in green pastures* and in the hot time of the day *led by the still waters* and made to lie down under a cool refreshing shade. Is it with God's people a noon-time of outward troubles, inward conflicts? Christ has rest for them; he *carries them in his arms,* Isa. xl. 11. 3. Her request to him that she might be admitted into his society: *Tell me where thou feedest.* Those that would be told, that would be taught, what they are concerned to know and do, must apply to Jesus Christ, and beg of him to teach them, to tell them. "Tell me where to find thee, where I may

have conversation with thee, *where thou feedest* and tendest thy flock, that there I may have some of thy company." Observe, by the way, We should not, in love to our friends and their company, tempt them or urge them to neglect their business, but desire such an enjoyment of them as will consist with it, and rather, if we can, to join with them in their business and help to forward it. "*Tell me where thou feedest,* and there I will sit with thee, walk with thee, feed my flocks with thine, and not hinder thee nor myself, but bring my work with me." Note, Those whose souls love Jesus Christ earnestly desire to have communion with him, by his word in which he speaks to us and by prayer in which we speak to him, and to share in the privileges of his flock; and we may learn from the care he takes of his church, to provide convenient food and rest for it, how to take care of our own souls, which are our charge. 4. The plea she uses for the enforcing of this request: "*For why should I be as one that turns aside by* (or after) *the flocks of thy companions,* that pretend to be so, but are really thy competitors, and rivals with thee." Note, Turning aside from Christ after other lovers is that which gracious souls dread, and deprecate, more than any thing else. "Thou wouldst not have me to *turn aside,* no, nor to *be as one that turns aside; tell me* then, O tell me, where I may be near thee, and I will never leave thee." (1.) "*Why should I* lie under suspicion, and look as if I belonged to some other and not to thee? *Why should I be* thought *by the flocks of our companions* to be a deserter from thee, and a retainer to some other shepherd?" Good Christians will be afraid of giving any occasion to those about them to question their faith in Christ and their love to him; they would not do any thing that looks like unconcernedness about their souls, or uncharitableness towards their brethren, or that savours of indifference and disaffection to holy ordinances; and we should pray to God to direct us into and keep us in the way of our duty, that we may not so much as *seem to come short,* Heb. iv. 1. (2.) "*Why should I* lie in temptation to *turn aside,* as I do while I am absent from thee?" We should be earnest with God for a settled peace in communion with God through Christ, that we may not be as waifs and strays, ready to be picked up by him that next passes by.

II. The gracious answer which the bridegroom gives to this request, v. 8. See how ready God is to answer prayer, especially prayers for instruction; even while she is yet speaking, he hears. Observe, 1. How affectionately he speaks to her: *O thou fairest among women!* Note, Believing souls are fair, in the eyes of the Lord Jesus, above any other. Christ sees a beauty in holiness, whether we do or no. The spouse had called herself black, but Christ calls her fair. Those that are low in their own eyes are so much the more amiable in the eyes of Jesus Christ.

Blushing at their own deformity (says Mr. Durham) is a chief part of their beauty. 2. How mildly he checks her for her ignorance, in these words, *If thou know not*, intimating that she might have known it if it had not been her own fault. What! dost thou not know where to find me and my flock? Compare Christ's answer to a like address of Philip's (John xiv. 9), *Have I been so long time with you, and yet hast thou not known me, Philip?* But, 3. With what tenderness he acquaints her where she might find him. If men say, *Lo, here is Christ, or, Lo, he is there, believe them not, go not after them*, Matt. xxiv. 23, 26. But, (1.) *Walk in the way of good men* (Prov. ii. 20), follow the track, ask for the good old way, observe *the footsteps of the flock*, and *go forth by* them. It will not serve to sit still and cry, "Lord, show me the way," but we must bestir ourselves to enquire out the way; and we may find it by looking which way *the footsteps of the flock* lead, what has been the practice of godly people all along; let that practice be ours, Heb. vi. 12; 1 Cor. xi. 1. (2.) Sit under the direction of good ministers: "*Feed* thyself *and thy kids beside the tents of the under-shepherds.* Bring thy charge with thee" (it is probable that the custom was to commit the lambs and kids to the custody of the women, the shepherdesses); "they shall all be welcome; *the shepherds* will be no hindrance to thee, as they were to Reuel's daughters (Exod. ii. 17), but helpers rather, and therefore abide by their tents." Note, Those that would have acquaintance and communion with Christ must closely and conscientiously adhere to holy ordinances, must join themselves to his people and attend his ministers. Those that have the charge of families must bring them with them to religious assemblies; let their *kids*, their children, their servants, have the benefit of *the shepherds' tents.*

III. The high encomiums which the bridegroom gives of his spouse. To be *given in marriage*, in the Hebrew dialect, is to be *praised* (Ps. lxxviii. 63, margin), so this spouse is here; her *husband praises* this *virtuous woman* (Prov. xxxi. 28); he praises her, as is usual in poems, by similitudes. 1. He calls her his *love* (v. 9); it is an endearing compellation often used in this book: "My friend, my companion, my familiar." 2. He compares her to a set of strong and stately *horses in Pharaoh's chariots.* Egypt was famous for the best horses. Solomon had his thence; and Pharaoh, no doubt, had the choicest the country afforded for his own chariots. The church had complained of her own weakness, and the danger she was in of being made a prey of by her enemies: "Fear not," says Christ; "*I have made thee like a company of horses;* I have put strength into thee as I have done into *the horse* (Job xxxix. 19), so that thou shalt with a gracious boldness *mock at fear, and not be affrighted,* like *the lion,* Prov. xxviii. 1. *The Lord has made thee as his* goodly horse *in the day of battle,* Zech. x. 3: *I have compared thee to my company of horses* which triumphed over *Pharaoh's chariots,* the holy angels, *horses of fire.*" Hab. iii. 15, *Thou didst walk through the sea with thy horses;* and see Isa. lxiii. 13. We are weak in ourselves, but if Christ make us as horses, strong and bold, we need not fear what all the powers of darkness can do against us. 3. He admires the beauty and ornaments of her countenance (v. 10): *Thy cheeks are comely with rows of jewels,* the attire of the head, curls of hair, or favourites (so some), or knots of ribbons; *thy neck also with chains,* such as persons of the first rank wear, *chains of gold.* The ordinances of Christ are the ornaments of the church. The graces, gifts, and comforts of the Spirit, are the adorning of every believing soul, and beautify it; these render it, *in the sight of God, of great price.* The ornaments of the saints are many, but all orderly disposed in *rows* and *chains*, in which there is a mutual connexion with and dependence upon each other. The beauty is not from any thing in themselves, from the *neck* or from the *cheeks*, but from the ornaments with which they are set off. It was *comeliness which I put upon thee, saith the Lord God;* for we were born not only naked, but polluted, Ezek. xvi. 14.

IV. His gracious purpose to add to her ornaments; for where God has given true grace he will give more grace; *to him that has shall be given.* Is the church courageous in her resistance of sin, as the *horses in Pharaoh's chariots?* Is she *comely* in the exercise of grace, as *with rows of jewels* and *chains of gold?* She shall be yet further beautified (v. 11): *We will make thee borders of gold,* inlaid, or enamelled, *with studs of silver.* Whatever is wanting shall be made up, till the church and every true believer come to be *perfect in beauty;* see Ezek. xvi. 14. This is here undertaken to be done by the concurring power of the three persons in the Godhead: *We will* do it; like that (Gen. i. 26), "*Let us make man;* so let us new-make him, and perfect his beauty." The same that is the author will be the finisher of the good work; and it cannot miscarry.

12 While the king *sitteth* at his table, my spikenard sendeth forth the smell thereof. 13 A bundle of myrrh *is* my wellbeloved unto me; he shall lie all night betwixt my breasts. 14 My beloved *is* unto me *as* a cluster of camphire in the vineyards of En-gedi. 15 Behold, thou *art* fair, my love; behold, thou *art* fair; thou *hast* doves' eyes. 16 Behold, thou *art* fair, my beloved, yea, pleasant: also our bed *is* green. 17 The beams of our house *are* cedar, *and* our rafters of fir.

Here the conference is carried on between Christ and his spouse, and endearments are mutually exchanged.

I. Believers take a great complacency in Christ, and in communion with him. *To you that believe he is precious,* above any thing in this world, 1 Pet. ii. 7. Observe,

1. The humble reverence believers have for Christ as their Sovereign, *v.* 12. He is a *King* in respect both of dignity and dominion; he wears the crown of honour, he bears the sceptre of power, both which are the unspeakable satisfaction of all his people. This King has his royal table spread in the gospel, in which is *made for all nations a feast of fat things,* Isa. xxv. 6. Wisdom has *furnished her table,* Prov. ix. 1. He *sits at this table to see his guests* (Matt. xxii. 11), to see that nothing be wanting that is fit for them; he *sups with them* and *they with him* (Rev. iii. 20); he has fellowship with them and rejoices in them; he *sits at his table* to bid them welcome, and to carve for them, as Christ *broke the five loaves* and gave to his disciples, that they might distribute to the multitude. He sits there to receive petitions, as Ahasuerus admitted Esther's petition at *the banquet of wine.* He has promised to be present with his people in his ordinances always. Then believers do him all the honour they can, and study how to express their esteem of him and gratitude to him, as Mary did when she anointed his head with *the ointment of spikenard* that was *very costly,* one pound of it worth *three hundred pence,* and so fragrant that *the house was filled with the pleasing odour of it* (John xii. 3), which story seems as if it were designed to refer to this passage, for Christ was then *sitting at table.* When good Christians, in any religious duty, especially in the ordinance of the Lord's supper, where the King is pleased, as it were, to *sit* with us *at his* own *table,* have their graces exercised, their hearts broken by repentance, healed by faith, and inflamed with holy love and desire towards Christ, and with joyful expectations of the glory to be revealed, then the *spikenard sends forth the smell thereof.* Christ is pleased to reckon himself honoured by it, and to accept of it as an instance of respect to him, as it was in the wise men of the east, who paid their homage to the new-born King of the Jews by presenting to him *frankincense and myrrh.* The graces of God's Spirit in the hearts of believers are exceedingly precious in themselves and pleasing to Christ, and his presence in ordinances draws them out into act and exercise. If he withdraw, graces wither and languish, as plants in the absence of the sun; if he approach, the face of the soul is renewed, as of the earth in the spring; and then it is time to bestir ourselves, that we may not lose the gleam, not lose the gale; for nothing is done acceptably but what grace does, Heb. xii. 28.

2. The strong affection they have for Christ as their *beloved,* their *well-beloved, v.* 13.

Christ is not only *beloved* by all believing souls, but is their *well-beloved,* their best-beloved, their only beloved; he has that place in their hearts which no rival can be admitted to, the innermost and uppermost place. Observe, (1.) How Christ is accounted of by all believers: He is *a bundle of myrrh* and *a cluster of camphire,* something, we may be sure, nay, every thing, that is pleasant and delightful. The doctrine of his gospel, and the comforts of his Spirit, are very refreshing to them, and they rest in his love; none of all the delights of sense are comparable to the spiritual pleasure they have in meditating on Christ and enjoying him. There is a complicated sweetness in Christ and an abundance of it; there is *a bundle of myrrh* and *a cluster of camphire.* We are not straitened in him in whom there is *all fulness.* The word translated *camphire* is *copher,* the same word that signifies *atonement* or *propitiation.* Christ is *a cluster of* merit and righteousness to all believers; *therefore* he is dear to them because *he is the propitiation for their sins.* Observe what a stress the spouse lays upon the application: He *is unto me,* and again *unto me,* all that is sweet; whatever he is to others, he is so *to me.* He *loved me, and gave himself for me.* He *is my Lord, and my God.* (2.) How he is accepted: *He shall lie all night between my breasts,* near my heart. Christ lays the beloved disciples in his bosom; why then should not they lay their beloved Saviour in their bosoms? Why should not they embrace him with both arms, and hold him fast, with a resolution never to let him go? Christ must *dwell in the heart* (Eph. iii. 17), and, in order to that, the adulteries must be put from *between the breasts* (Hos. ii. 2), no pretender must have his place in the soul. He shall be as *a bundle of myrrh,* or perfume bag, between *my breasts,* always sweet to me; or his effigies in miniature, his love-tokens, shall be hung between *my breasts,* according to the custom of those that are dear to each other. He shall not only be laid there for a while, but shall lie there, shall abide there.

II. Jesus Christ has a great complacency in his church and in every true believer; they are amiable in his eyes (*v.* 15): *Behold, thou art fair, my love;* and again, *Behold, thou art fair.* He says this, not to make her proud (humility is one principal ingredient in spiritual beauty), but, 1. To show that there is a real beauty in holiness, that all who are sanctified are thereby beautified; they are truly fair. 2. That he takes great delight in that good work which his grace has wrought on the souls of believers; so that though they have their infirmities, whatever they think of themselves, and the world thinks of them, he thinks them fair. He calls them friends. The *hidden man of the heart, in that which is not corruptible,* is *in the sight of God of great price,* 1 Pet. iii. 4. 3. To comfort weak believers, who are discouraged by their own blackness; let them be told again and again that they are fair. 4. To engage all who are sanctified to be very thankful for that grace which has made them fair, who by nature were deformed, and changed the Ethiopian's skin. One instance of the beauty of the spouse is here mentioned, that she *has doves' eyes,* as *ch.* iv. 1. Those are fair, in Christ's account, who have, not the piercing eye of the eagle, but the pure and chaste eye of the *dove,* not like the hawk, who, when he soars upwards, still has his eye upon the prey on earth, but a humble modest eye, such an eye as discovers a simplicity and godly sincerity and a dove-like innocency, eyes enlightened and guided by the Holy Spirit, that blessed Dove, weeping eyes. I did *mourn as a dove,* Ezek. vii. 16.

III. The church expresses her value for Christ, and returns esteem for esteem (*v.* 16): *Behold, thou art fair.* See how Christ and believers praise one another. Israel saith of God, *Who is like thee?* Exod. xv. 11. And God saith of Israel, *Who is like thee?* Deut. xxxiii. 29. Lord, saith the church, "Dost thou call me *fair?* No; if we speak of strength, *thou art strong* (Job ix. 19), so, if of beauty, *thou art fair.* I am fair no otherwise than as I have thy image stamped upon me. Thou art the great Original; I am but a faint and imperfect copy, I am but thy *umbra—the shadow of thee,* John i. 16; iii. 34. Thou art fair in thyself and (which is more) *pleasant* to all that are thine. Many are fair enough to look at, and yet the sourness of their temper renders them unpleasant; but *thou art fair, yea, pleasant."* Christ is pleasant, as he is ours, in covenant with us, in relation to us. "Thou art pleasant now, when the *King sits at his table."* Christ is always precious to believers, but in a special manner pleasant when they are admitted into communion with him, when they hear his voice, and see his face, and taste his love. *It is good to be here.* Having expressed her esteem of her husband's person, she next, like a loving spouse, that is transported with joy for having disposed of herself so well, applauds the accommodations he had for her entertainment, his *bed,* his *house,* his *rafters* or *galleries* (*v.* 16), which may fitly be applied to those holy ordinances in which believers have fellowship with Jesus Christ, receive the tokens of his love and return their pious and devout affections to him, increase their acquaintance with him and improve their advantages by him. Now, 1. These she calls *ours,* Christ and believers having a joint-interest in them. As husband and wife are *heirs together* (1 Pet. iii. 7), so believers are *joint-heirs with Christ,* Rom. viii. 17. They are his institutions and their privileges; in them Christ and believers meet. She does not call them *mine,* for a believer will own nothing as his but what Christ shall have an interest in, nor *thine,* for Christ has said, *All that I have is thine,* Luke xv. 31. All is ours

if we are Christ's. Those that can by faith lay claim to Christ may lay claim to all that is his. 2. These are the best of the kind. Does the colour of the bed, and the furniture belonging to it, help to set it off? *Our bed is green,* a colour which, in a pastoral, is preferred before any other, because it is the colour of the fields and groves where the shepherd's business and delight are. It is a refreshing colour, good for the eyes; and it denotes fruitfulness. *I am like a green olive-tree,* Ps. lii. 8. We are *married to* Christ, *that we should bring forth unto God,* Rom. vii. 4. *The beams of our house are cedar* (*v.* 17), which probably refers to the temple Solomon had lately built for communion between God and Israel, which was of *cedar,* a strong sort of wood, sweet, durable, and which will never rot, typifying the firmness and continuance of the church, the gospel-temple. The galleries for walking are *of fir,* or *cypress,* some sort of wood that was pleasing both to the sight and to the smell, intimating the delight which the saints take in walking with Christ and conversing with him. Every thing in the covenant of grace (on which foot all their treaties are carried on) is very firm, very fine, and very fragrant.

CHAP. II.

I AM the rose of Sharon, *and* the lily of the valleys. 2 As the lily among thorns, so *is* my love among the daughters.

See here, I. What Christ is pleased to compare himself to; and he condescends very much in the comparison. He that is the Son of the Highest, the bright and morning star, calls and owns himself *the rose of Sharon, and the lily of the valleys,* to express his presence with his people in this world, the easiness of their access to him, and the beauty and sweetness which they find in him, and to teach them to adorn themselves with him, as shepherds and shepherdesses, when they appeared gay, were decked with roses and lilies, garlands and chaplets of flowers. *The rose,* for beauty and fragrancy, is the chief of flowers, and our Saviour prefers the clothing of *the lily* before that of *Solomon in all his glory.* Christ is *the rose of Sharon,* where probably the best roses grew and in most plenty, *the rose of the field* (so some), denoting that the gospel salvation is a common salvation; it lies open to all; whoever will may come and gather the rose-buds of privileges and comforts that grow in the covenant of grace. He is not a rose locked up in a garden, but all may come and receive benefit by him and comfort in him. He is a *lily* for whiteness, a *lily of the valleys* for sweetness, for those which we call so yield a strong perfume. He is a *lily of the valleys*, or *low places*, in his humiliation, exposed to injury. Humble souls see most beauty in him. Whatever he is to others, to those that are in the *valleys* he is a *lily*. He is the *rose, the lily;* there is none besides. Whatever excellency is in Christ, it is in him singularly and in the highest degree.

II. What he is pleased to compare his church to, v. 2. 1. She is as a *lily;* he himself is *the lily* (v. 1), she is *as the lily*. The beauty of believers consists in their conformity and resemblance to Jesus Christ. They are his love, and so they are as lilies, for those are made like Christ in whose hearts his *love is shed abroad*. 2. *As a lily among thorns, as a lily* compared with *thorns*. The church of Christ as far excels all other societies as a bed of roses excels a bush of thorns. *As a lily* compassed with *thorns*. The wicked, *the daughters* of this world, such as have no love to Christ, are as *thorns*, worthless and useless, good for nothing but to stop a gap; nay, they are noxious and hurtful; they came in with sin and are a fruit of the curse; they choke good seed, and hinder good fruit, and their *end is to be burned*. God's people are *as lilies among them*, scratched and torn, shaded and obscured, by them; they are dear to Christ, and yet exposed to hardships and troubles in the world; they must expect it, for they are planted *among thorns* (Ezek. ii. 6), but they are nevertheless dear to him; he does not overlook nor undervalue any of his lilies for their being *among thorns*. When they are *among thorns* they must still be *as lilies*, must maintain their innocency and purity, and, though they are *among thorns*, must not be turned into *thorns*, must *not render railing for railing*, and, if they thus preserve their character, they shall be still owned as conformable to Christ. Grace in the soul is a *lily among thorns;* corruptions are *thorns in the flesh* (2 Cor. xii. 7), are as Canaanites to God's Israel (Josh. xxiii. 13); but *the lily* that is now *among thorns* shall shortly be transplanted out of this wilderness into that paradise where there is no *pricking brier* nor *grieving thorn*, Ezek. xxviii. 24.

3 As the apple tree among the trees of the wood, so *is* my beloved among the sons. I sat down under his shadow with great delight, and his fruit *was* sweet to my taste. 4 He brought me to the banqueting house, and his banner over me *was* love. 5 Stay me with flagons, comfort me with apples: for I *am* sick of love. 6 His left hand *is* under

my head, and his right hand doth embrace me. 7 I charge you, O ye daughters of Jerusalem, by the roes, and by the hinds of the field, that ye stir not up, nor awake *my* love, till he please.

Here, I. The spouse commends her beloved and prefers him before all others: *As the apple-tree among the trees of the wood*, which perhaps does not grow so high, nor spread so wide, as some other trees, yet is useful and serviceable to man, yielding pleasant and profitable fruit, while the other trees are of little use, no, not the cedars themselves, till they are cut down, *so is my beloved among the sons*, so far does he excel them all,—all *the sons* of God, the angels (that honour was put upon him which was never designed for them, Heb. i. 4),—all *the sons* of men; he is *fairer* than them all, fairer than the choicest of them, Ps. xlv. 2. Name what creature you will, and you will find Christ has the pre-eminence above them all. The world is a barren tree to a soul; Christ is a fruitful one.

II. She remembers the abundant comfort she has had in communion with him: She *sat down* by him *with great delight*, as shepherds sometimes repose themselves, sometimes converse with one another, under a tree. A double advantage she found in sitting down so near the Lord Jesus:—1. A refreshing shade: *I sat down under his shadow*, to be sheltered by him from the scorching heat of the sun, to be cooled, and so to take some rest. Christ is to believers *as the shadow* of a great tree, nay, *of a great rock in a weary land*, Isa. xxxii. 2; xxv. 4. When a poor soul is parched with convictions of sin and the terrors of the law, as David (Ps. xxxii. 4), when fatigued with the troubles of this world, as Elijah when he *sat down under the juniper tree* (1 Kings xix. 4), they find that in Christ, in his name, his graces, his comforts, and his undertaking for poor sinners, which revives them and keeps them from fainting; those that *are weary and heavily laden* may find *rest* in Christ. It is not enough to pass by this *shadow*, but we must *sit down under* it *(here will I dwell, for I have desired it);* and we shall find it not like Jonah's gourd, that soon withered, and left him in a heat, both inward and outward, but like the tree of life, the leaves whereof were not only for shelter, but for the healing of the nations. We must *sit down under this shadow with delight*, must put an entire confidence in the protection of it (as Judges ix. 15), and take an entire complacency in the refreshment of it. But that is not all: 2. Here is pleasing nourishing food. This tree drops its fruits to those that *sit down under its shadow*, and they are welcome to them, and will find them *sweet unto their taste*, whatever they are to others. Believers have tasted that the Lord

Jesus is *gracious* (1 Pet. ii. 3); his *fruits* are all the precious privileges of the new covenant, purchased by his blood and communicated by his Spirit. Promises are sweet to a believer, yea, and precepts too. *I delight in the law of God after the inward man.* Pardons are sweet, and peace of conscience is sweet; assurances of God's love, joys of the Holy Ghost, the hopes of eternal life, and the present earnests and foretastes of it are sweet, all sweet to those that have their spiritual senses exercised. If our mouths be put out of taste for the pleasures of sin, divine consolations will be *sweet to our taste, sweeter than honey and the honeycomb.*

III. She owns herself obliged to Jesus Christ for all the benefit and comfort she had in communion with him (*v.* 4): "*I sat down under* the apple-tree, glad to be there, but he admitted me, nay, he pressed me, to a more intimate communion with him: *Come in, thou blessed of the Lord, why standest thou without?* He brought me to the house of wine, the place where he entertains his special friends, from lower to higher measures and degrees of comfort, from the fruit of *the apple tree* to the more generous fruit of the vine. *To him that* values the divine joys *he has more shall be given.* One of the rabbin by *the banqueting-house* understands *the tabernacle of the congregation, where the interpretation of the law was given;* surely then we may apply it to Christian assemblies, where the gospel is preached and gospel-ordinances are administered, particularly the Lord's supper, that *banquet of wine,* especially to the inside of those ordinances, communion with God in them. Observe, 1. How she was introduced: "*He brought me,* wrought in me an inclination to draw nigh to God, helped me over my discouragements, took me by the hand, guided and led me, and gave me an *access* with boldness to God as a *Father,*" Eph. ii. 18. We should never have come *into the banqueting-house,* never have been acquainted with spiritual pleasures, if Christ had not brought us, by opening for us a new and living way and opening in us a new and living fountain. 2. How she was entertained: *His banner over me was love; he brought me* in with a banner displayed over my head, not as one he triumphed over, but as one he triumphed in, and whom he always caused to triumph with him and in him, 2 Cor. ii. 14. The gospel is compared to a *banner* or *ensign* (Isa. xi. 12), and that which is represented in this banner, written in it in letters of gold, letters of blood, is *love, love;* and this is the entertainment in *the banqueting-house.* Christ is the *captain of our salvation,* and he enlists all his soldiers under the *banner of love;* in that they centre; to that they must continually have an eye, and be animated by it. *The love of Christ* must *constrain* them to fight manfully. When a city was taken the conqueror set up his standard in it. "He has conquered me with his love, overcome

me with kindness, and that is the *banner over me.*" This she speaks of as what she had formerly had experience of, and she remembers it with delight. Eaten bread must not be forgotten, but remembered with thankfulness to that God who has fed us with manna in this wilderness.

IV She professes her strong affection and most passionate love to Jesus Christ (*v.* 5): *I am sick of love,* overcome, overpowered, by it. David explains this when he says (Ps. cxix. 20), *My soul breaks for the longing that it has unto thy judgments,* and (*v.* 81), *My soul faints for thy salvation,* languishing with care to make it sure and fear of coming short of it. The spouse was now absent perhaps from her beloved, waiting for his return, and cannot bear the grief of distance and delay. Oh how much better is it with the soul when it is *sick of love* to Christ than when it is surfeited with the love of this world! She cries out for cordials: "Oh *stay me with flagons,* or *ointments,* or *flowers,* any thing that is reviving; *comfort me with apples,* with the fruits of that *apple-tree,* Christ (*v.* 3), with the merit and mediation of Christ and the sense of his love to my soul." Note, Those that are *sick of love* to Christ shall not want spiritual supports, while they are yet waiting for spiritual comforts.

V. She experiences the power and tenderness of divine grace, relieving her in her present faintings, *v.* 6. Though he seemed to have withdrawn, yet he was even then a very present help, 1. To sustain the love-sick soul, and to keep it from fainting away: "*His left hand is under my head,* to bear it up, nay, as a pillow to lay it easy." David experienced God's hand upholding him then when *his soul was following hard after God* (Ps. lxiii. 8), and Job in a state of desertion yet found that God *put strength* into him, Job xxiii. 6. *All his saints are in his hand,* which tenderly holds their aching heads. 2. To encourage the love-sick soul to continue waiting till he returns: "For, in the mean time, *his right hand embraces me,* and thereby gives me an unquestionable assurance of his love." Believers owe all their strength and comfort to the supporting left hand and embracing right hand of the Lord Jesus.

VI. Finding her beloved thus nigh unto her she is in great care that her communion with him be not interrupted (*v.* 7): *I charge you, O you daughters of Jerusalem.* Jerusalem, the mother of us all, charges all her daughters, the church charges all her members, the believing soul charges all its powers and faculties, the spouse charges herself and all about her, not to *stir up, or awake, her love until he please,* now that he is asleep in her arms, as she was borne up in his, *v.* 6. She gives them this charge *by the roes and the hinds of the field,* that is, by every thing that is amiable in their eyes, and dear to them, *as the loving hind and the pleasant roe.* "My love is to me dearer than those can be to you, and will be disturbed, like them, with a very little noise." Note, 1. Those that experience the sweetness of communion with Christ, and the sensible manifestations of his love, cannot but desire the continuance of these blessed views, these blessed visits. Peter would make tabernacles upon the holy mount, Matt. xvii. 4. 2. Yet Christ will, when he pleases, withdraw those extraordinary communications of himself, for he is a free-agent, and the Spirit, as *the wind, blows where* and when *it listeth*, and in his pleasure it becomes us to acquiesce. But, 3. Our care must be that we do nothing to provoke him to withdraw and to hide his face, that we carefully watch over our own hearts and suppress every thought that may grieve his good Spirit. Let those that have comfort be afraid of sinning it away.

8 The voice of my beloved! behold, he cometh leaping upon the mountains, skipping upon the hills. 9 My beloved is like a roe or a young hart: behold, he standeth behind our wall, he looketh forth at the windows, showing himself through the lattice. 10 My beloved spake, and said unto me, Rise up, my love, my fair one, and come away. 11 For, lo, the winter is past, the rain is over *and* gone; 12 The flowers appear on the earth; the time of the singing *of birds* is come, and the voice of the turtle is heard in our land; 13 The fig tree putteth forth her green figs, and the vines *with* the tender grape give a *good* smell. Arise, my love, my fair one, and come away.

The church is here pleasing herself exceedingly with the thoughts of her further communion with Christ after she has recovered from her fainting fit.

I. She rejoices in his approach, *v.* 8. 1. She hears him speak: "It is *the voice of my beloved*, calling to me to tell me he is coming." Like one of his own sheep, she *knows his voice* before she sees him, and can easily distinguish it from *the voice of a stranger* (John x. 4, 5), and, like a faithful friend of the bridegroom, she *rejoices greatly because of the bridegroom's voice*, John iii. 29. With what an air of triumph and exultation does she cry out, "*It is the voice of my beloved*, it can be the voice of no other, for none besides can speak to the heart and make that burn." 2. She sees him come, sees the goings of our God, our King, Ps. xlviii. 24. *Behold, he comes.* This may very well be applied to the prospect which the Old-Testament saints had of Christ's coming in the flesh. *Abraham saw his day* at a distance, *and was glad.* The nearer the time came the clearer discoveries

were made of it; and those that waited for the consolation of Israel with an eye of faith saw him come, and triumphed in the sight: *Behold, he comes;* for they had heard him say (Ps. xl. 7), *Lo, I come,* to which their faith here affixes its seal: *Behold, he comes* as he has promised. (1.) He comes cheerfully and with great alacrity; he comes leaping and skipping *like a roe* and like *a young hart* (*v.* 9), as one pleased with his own undertaking, and that had his heart upon it and his delights with the sons of men. When he came to be baptized with the baptism of blood, how was he *straitened till it was accomplished!* Luke xii. 50. (2.) He comes slighting and surmounting all the difficulties that lay in his way; he comes *leaping over the mountains, skipping over the hills* (so some read it), making nothing of the discouragements he was to break through; the curse of the law, the death of the cross, must be undergone, all the powers of darkness must be grappled with, but, before the resolutions of his love, these great mountains become plains. Whatever opposition is given at any time to the deliverance of God's church, Christ will break through it, will get over it. (3.) He comes speedily, *like a roe* or *a young hart;* they thought the time long (every day a year), but really he hastened; as now, so then, *surely he comes quickly; he that shall come will come, and will not tarry.* When he comes for the deliverance of his people he *flies upon a cloud,* and never stays beyond his time, which is the best time. We may apply it to particular believers, who find that even when Christ has withdrawn sensible comforts, and seems to forsake, yet it is but for a small moment, and he will soon return with everlasting lovingkindness.

II. She pleases herself with the glimpses she has of him, and the glances she has of his favour: "He *stands behind our wall;* I know he is there, for sometimes *he looks forth at the window,* or *looks in* at it, and displays *himself through the lattice.*" Such was the state of the Old-Testament church while it was in expectation of the coming of the Messiah. The ceremonial law is called a *wall of partition* (Eph. ii. 14), a *veil* (2 Cor. iii. 13); but Christ stood behind that wall. They had him near them; they had him with them, though they could not see him clearly. He that was the substance was not far off from the shadows, Col. ii. 17. They saw him looking through the windows of the ceremonial institutions and smiling through those lattices; in their sacrifices and purifications Christ discovered himself to them, and gave them intimations and earnests of his grace, both to engage and to encourage their longings for his coming. Such is our present state in comparison with what it will be at Christ's second coming. We now *see him through a glass darkly* (the body is a wall between us and him, through the windows of which we now and then get a sight of him), but not *face to face*, as we hope to see him shortly. In the sacraments Christ is near us, but it is *behind the wall* of external signs, through *those lattices* he manifests himself to us; but we shall shortly *see him as he is*. Some understand this of the state of a believer when he is under a cloud; Christ is out of sight and yet not far off. See Job xxxiv. 14, and compare Job xxiii. 8—10. She calls the wall that interposed between her and her beloved *our wall*, because it is sin, and nothing else, that separates between us and God, and that is a wall of our own erecting (Isa. lix. 1); behind that he stands, as *waiting to be gracious*, and ready to be reconciled, upon our repentance. Then *he looks in at the window*, observes the frame of our hearts and the working of our souls; he looks forth at the window, and shows himself in giving them some comfort, that they may continue hoping for his return.

III. She repeats the gracious invitation he had given her to come a walking with him, *v.* 10—13. She remembers what her beloved said to her, for it had made a very pleasing and powerful impression upon her, and the *word that quickens us* we shall *never forget*. She relates it for the encouragement of others, telling them what he had said to her soul and *done for her soul*, Ps. lxvi. 16.

1. He called her his love and his fair one. Whatever she is to others, to him she is acceptable, and in his eyes she is amiable. Those that take Christ for their beloved, he will own as his; never was any love lost that was bestowed upon Christ. Christ, by expressing his love to believers, invites and encourages them to follow him.

2. He called her to *rise and come away, v.* 10, and again *v.* 13. The repetition denotes backwardness in her (we have need to be often called to come away with Jesus Christ; *precept must be upon precept and line upon line)*, but it denotes earnestness in him; so much is his heart set upon the welfare of precious souls that he importunes them most pressingly to that which is for their own good.

3. He gave for a reason the return of the spring, and the pleasantness of the weather.

(1.) The season is elegantly described in a great variety of expressions. [1.] *The winter is past*, the dark, cold, and barren winter. Long winters and hard ones pass away at last; they do not endure always. And the spring would not be so pleasant as it is if it did not succeed the winter, which is a foil to its beauty, Eccl. vii. 14. Neither the face of the heavens nor that of the earth is always the same, but subject to continual vicissitudes, diurnal and annual. *The winter is past*, but has not passed away for ever; it will come again, and we must provide for it in summer, Prov. vi. 6, 8. We must weep in winter, and rejoice in summer, as though we wept and rejoiced not, for both are passing. [2.] *The rain is over and gone*, the winter-rain, the cold stormy rain; it is over now, and *the dew is as*

the dew of herbs. Even the rain that drowned the world was over and gone at last (Gen. viii. 1—3), and God promised to drown the world no more, which was a type and figure of the covenant of grace, Isa. liv. 9. [3.] *The flowers appear on the earth.* All winter they are dead and buried in their roots, and there is no sign of them; but in the spring they revive, and show themselves in a wonderful variety and verdure, and, like the dew that produces them, *tarry not for man*, Mic. v. 7. They appear, but they will soon disappear again, and man is herein like *the flower of the field*, Job xiv. 2. [4.] *The time of the singing of birds has come.* The little birds, which all the winter lie hid in their retirements and scarcely live, when the spring returns forget all the calamities of the winter, and to the best of their capacity chant forth the praises of their Creator. Doubtless he who understands the birds that cry for want (Ps. cxlvii. 9) takes notice of those that *sing for joy*, Ps. civ. 12. The singing of the birds may shame our silence in God's praises, who are better fed (Matt. vi. 26), and better taught (Job xxxv. 11), and are of *more value than many sparrows*. They live without inordinate care (Matt. vi. 26) and therefore they sing, while we murmur. [5.] *The voice of the turtle is heard in our land*, which is one of the season-birds mentioned Jer. viii. 7, that observe the time of their coming and the time of their singing, and so shame us who *know not the judgment of the Lord*, understand not the times, nor do that which is *beautiful in its season*, do not sing in singing time. [6.] *The fig-tree puts forth her green figs*, by which *we know that summer is nigh* (Matt. xxiv. 32), when the green figs will be ripe figs and fit for use; and the *vines with the tender grape give a good smell*. The earth produces not only *flowers* (v. 12), but *fruits;* and the smell of the fruits, which are profitable, is to be preferred far before that of the flowers, which are only for show and pleasure. Serpents, they say, are driven away by the smell of vines; and who is the old serpent, and who the true vine, we know very well.

(2.) Now this description of the returning spring, as a reason for coming away with Christ, is applicable, [1.] To the introducing of the gospel in the room of the Old-Testament dispensation, during which it had been winter time with the church. Christ's gospel warms that which was cold, makes that fruitful which before was dead and barren; when it comes to any place it puts a beauty and glory upon that place (2 Cor. iii. 7, 8) and furnishes occasion for joy. Spring-time is pleasant time, and so is gospel-time. *Aspice venturo lætentur ut omnia seclo—Behold what joy the dawning age inspires!* said Virgil, from the Sibyls, perhaps with more reference to the setting up of the Messiah's kingdom at that time than he himself thought of. See Ps. xcvi. 11. *Arise then*, and improve this spring-time. *Come away* from the world and the flesh, come into *fellowship with Christ*, 1 Cor. i. 9. [2.] To the delivering of the church from the power of persecuting enemies, and the restoring of liberty and peace to it, after a severe winter of suffering and restraint. When the storms of trouble are over and gone, when the *voice of the turtle*, the joyful sound of the gospel of Christ, is again heard, and ordinances are enjoyed with freedom, then *arise and come away* to improve the happy juncture. Walk in the light of the Lord; sing in the ways of the Lord. When the churches had rest, then were they edified, Acts ix. 31. [3.] To the conversion of sinners from a state of nature to a state of grace. That blessed change is like the return of the spring, a universal change and a very comfortable one; it is a new creation; it is being born again. The soul that was hard, and cold, and frozen, and unprofitable, like the earth in winter, becomes fruitful, like the earth in spring, and by degrees, like it, brings its fruits to perfection. This blessed change is owing purely to the approaches and influences of the sun of righteousness, who calls to us from heaven to *arise and come away;* come, gather in summer. [4.] To the consolations of the saints after a state of inward dejection and despondency. A child of God, under doubts and fears, is like the earth in winter, its nights long, its days dark, good affections chilled, nothing done, nothing got, the hand sealed up. But comfort will return; the birds shall sing again, and the flowers appear. Arise therefore, poor drooping soul, and *come away* with thy beloved. *Arise, and shake thyself from the dust*, Isa. lii. 2. *Arise, shine, for thy light has come* (Isa. lx. 1); *walk in that light*, Isa. ii. 5. [5.] To the resurrection of the body at the last day, and the glory to be revealed. The bones that lay in the grave, as the roots of plants in the ground during the winter, shall then *flourish as a herb*, Isa. lxvi. 14; xxvi. 19. That will be an eternal farewell to winter and a joyful entrance upon an everlasting spring.

14 O my dove, *that art* in the clefts of the rock, in the secret *places* of the stairs, let me see thy countenance, let me hear thy voice; for sweet *is* thy voice, and thy countenance *is* comely. 15 Take us the foxes, the little foxes, that spoil the vines: for our vines *have* tender grapes. 16 My beloved *is* mine, and I *am* his: he feedeth among the lilies. 17 Until the day break, and the shadows flee away, turn, my beloved, and be thou like a roe or a young hart upon the mountains of Bether.

Here is, I. The encouraging invitation which Christ gives to the church, and every believing soul, to come into communion with him, *v.* 14.

1. His love is now his *dove;* David had called the church God's *turtle-dove* (Ps. lxxiv. 19), and so she is here called; a dove for beauty, her *wings covered with silver* (Ps. lxviii. 13), for innocence and inoffensiveness; a gracious spirit is a dove-like spirit, harmless, loving quietness and cleanliness, and faithful to Christ, as the turtle to her mate. The Spirit descended *like a dove* on Christ, and so he does on all Christians, making them of a *meek and quiet spirit*. She is Christ's *dove*, for he owns her and delights in her; she can find no rest but in him and his ark, and therefore to him, as her Noah, she returns.

2. This dove is *in the clefts of the rock and in the secret places of the stairs*. This speaks either, (1.) Her praise. Christ is the rock, to whom she flies for shelter and in whom alone she can think herself safe and find herself easy, as a dove in the hole of a rock, when struck at by the birds of prey, Jer. xlviii. 28. Moses was hid in a cleft of the rock, that he might behold something of God's glory, which otherwise he could not have borne the brightness of. She retires *into the secret places of the stairs*, where she may be alone, undisturbed, and may the better commune with her own heart. Good Christians will find time to be private. Christ often withdrew to a mountain *himself alone, to pray*. Or, (2.) Her blame. She crept into the *clefts of the rock*, and the *secret places*, for fear and shame, any where to hide her head, being heartless and discouraged, and shunning even the sight of her beloved. Being conscious to herself of her own unfitness and unworthiness to come into his presence, and speak to him, she drew back, and was *like a silly dove without heart*, Hos. vii. 11.

3. Christ graciously calls her out of her retirements: Come, *let me see thy countenance, let me hear thy voice*. She was *mourning like a dove* (Isa. xxxviii. 14), bemoaning herself like the *doves of the valleys*, where they are near the clefts of the impending rocks, *mourning for her iniquities* (Ezek. vii. 16) and refusing to be comforted. But Christ calls her to *lift up her face without spot*, being purged from an evil conscience (Job xi. 15; xxii. 26), to *come boldly to the throne of grace*, having a great *high priest* there (Heb. iv. 16), to tell what her petition is and what her request: Let me *hear thy voice*, hear what thou hast to say; *what would you that I should do unto you?* Speak freely, speak up, and fear not a slight or repulse.

4. For her encouragement, he tells her the good thoughts he had of her, whatever she thought of herself: *Sweet is thy voice;* thy praying voice, though thou canst but *chatter like a crane or a swallow* (Isa. xxxviii. 14); it is music in God's ears. He has assured us that *the prayer of the upright is his delight;* he smelled a sweet savour from Noah's sacrifice, and the *spiritual sacrifices* are no less *acceptable*, 1 Pet. ii. 5. This does not so much commend our services as God's gracious con-

descension in making the best of them, and the efficacy of the *much incense* which is *offered with the prayers of saints,* Rev. viii. 3. "That countenance of thine, which thou art ashamed of, is comely, though now mournful, much more will it be so when it becomes cheerful." *Then* the voice of prayer is sweet and acceptable to God when the countenance, the conversation in which we show ourselves before men, is holy, and so comely, and agreeable to our profession. Those that are sanctified have the best comeliness.

II. The charge which Christ gives to his servants to oppose and suppress that which is a terror to his church and drives her, like a poor frightened dove, into the clefts of the rock, and which is an obstruction and prejudice to the interests of his kingdom in this world and in the heart (*v.* 15): *Take us the foxes* (take them for us, for it is good service both to Christ and the church), *the little foxes,* that creep in insensibly; for, though they are little, they do great mischief, they *spoil the vines,* which they must by no means be suffered to do at any time, especially now when our vines have *tender grapes* that must be preserved, or the vintage will fail. Believers are as vines, weak but useful plants; their fruits are as *tender grapes* at first, which must have time to come to maturity. This charge to *take the foxes* is, 1. A charge to particular believers to mortify their own corruptions, their sinful appetites and passions, which are as *foxes, little foxes,* that destroy their graces and comforts, quash good motions, crush good beginnings, and prevent their coming to perfection. Seize the *little foxes,* the first risings of sin, the little ones of Babylon (Ps. cxxxvii. 9), those sins that seem little, for they often prove very dangerous. Whatever we find a hindrance to us in that which is good we must put away. 2. A charge to all in their places to oppose and prevent the spreading of all such opinions and practices as tend to corrupt men's judgments, debauch their consciences, perplex their minds, and discourage their inclinations to virtue and piety. Persecutors are foxes (Luke xiii. 32); false prophets are foxes, Ezek. xiii. 4. Those that sow the tares of heresy or schism, and, like Diotrephes, trouble the peace of the church and obstruct the progress of the gospel, they are the *foxes, the little foxes,* which must not be knocked on the head *(Christ came not to destroy men's lives),* but taken, that they may be tamed, or else restrained from doing mischief.

III. The believing profession which the church makes of her relation to Christ, and the satisfaction she takes in her interest in him and communion with him, *v.* 16. He had called her to *rise* and *come away* with him, to let him see her face and hear her voice; now this is her answer to that call, in which, though at present in the dark and at a distance,

1. She comforts herself with the thoughts

of the mutual interest and relation that were between her and her beloved: *My beloved to me* and *I to him,* so the original reads it very emphatically; the conciseness of the language speaks the largeness of her affection: "What he is to me and I to him may better be conceived than expressed." Note, (1.) It is the unspeakable privilege of true believers that Christ is theirs: *My beloved is mine;* this denotes not only propriety (" I have a title to him") but possession and tenure—" I receive from his fulness." Believers are partakers of Christ; they have not only an interest in him, but the enjoyment of him, are taken not only into covenant, but into communion with him. All the benefits of his glorious undertaking, as Mediator, are made over to them. He is that to them which the world neither is nor can be, all that which they need and desire, and which will make a complete happiness for them. All he is is theirs, and all he has, all he has done, and all he is doing; all he has promised in the gospel, all he has prepared in heaven, all is yours. (2.) It is the undoubted character of all true believers that they are Christ's, and then, and then only, he is theirs. They have given their own selves to him (2 Cor. viii. 5); they receive his doctrine and obey his laws; they bear his image and espouse his interest; they belong to Christ. If we be his, his wholly, his only, his for ever, we may take the comfort of his being ours.

2. She comforts herself with the thoughts of the communications of his grace to his people: *He feeds among the lilies.* When she wants the tokens of his favour to her in particular, she rejoices in the assurance of his presence with all believers in general, who are as lilies in his eye. He *feeds* among them, that is, he takes as much pleasure in them and their assemblies as a man does in his table or in his garden, for he *walks in the midst of the golden candlesticks;* he delights to converse with them, and to do them good.

IV. The church's hope and expectation of Christ's coming, and her prayer grounded thereupon. 1. She doubts not but that the *day will break* and the *shadows* will *flee away.* The gospel-day will dawn, and the shadows of the ceremonial law will flee away. This was the comfort of the Old-Testament church, that, after the long night of that dark dispensation, the *day-spring from on high would* at length *visit them,* to *give light to those that sit in darkness.* When the sun rises the shades of the night vanish, so do the shadows of the day when the substance comes. The day of comfort will come after a night of desertion. Or it may refer to the second coming of Christ, and the eternal happiness of the saints; the shadows of our present state will flee away, our darkness and doubts, our griefs and all our grievances, and a glorious day shall dawn, a morning when the *upright shall have dominion,* a day that shall have no night after it. 2. She begs the presence of her beloved, in the mean time, to support and comfort her : " *Turn, my beloved,* turn to me, come and visit me, come and relieve me, *be with me always to the end of the age.* In the day of my extremity, make haste to help me, *make no long tarrying.* Come over even *the mountains of division,* interposing time and days, with some gracious anticipations of that light and love." 3. She begs that he would not only turn to her for the present, but hasten his coming to fetch her to himself. " *Even so, come, Lord Jesus, come quickly.* Though there be mountains in the way, thou canst, *like a roe, or a young hart,* step over them with ease. *O show thyself to me, or take me up to thee.*"

CHAP. III.

In this chapter, I. The church gives an account of a sore trial wherewith she was exercised through the withdrawing of her beloved from her, the pains she was at before she recovered the comfortable sense of his favour again, and the resolution she took, when she did recover it, not to lose it again, as she had done through her own carelessness, ver. 1—5. II. The daughters of Jerusalem admire the excellencies of the church, ver. 6. III. The church admires Jesus Christ under the person of Solomon, his bed, and the life-guards about it (ver. 7, 8), his chariot, ver. 9, 10. She calls upon the daughters of Zion, who were admiring her, to admire him rather, especially as he appeared on his coronation day and the day of his nuptials, ver. 11.

BY night on my bed I sought him whom my soul loveth : I sought him, but I found him not. 2 I will rise now, and go about the city in the streets, and in the broad ways I will seek him whom my soul loveth : I sought him, but I found him not. 3 The watchmen that go about the city found me : *to whom I said,* Saw ye him whom my soul loveth ? 4 *It was* but a little that I passed from them, but I found him whom my soul loveth : I held him, and would not let him go, until I had brought him into my mother's house, and into the chamber of her that conceived me. 5 I charge you, O ye daughters of Jerusalem, by the roes, and by the hinds of the field, that ye stir not up, nor awake *my* love, till he please.

God is not wont to say to the seed of Jacob, *Seek you me in vain;* and yet here we have the spouse for a great while seeking her beloved in vain, but finding him at last, to her unspeakable satisfaction. It was hard to the Old-Testament church to find Christ in the ceremonial law, and the types and figures which then were *of good things to come.* Long was the consolation of Israel looked for before it came. The watchman of that church gave little assistance to those who enquired after him ; but at length Simeon had *him* in his arms *whom his soul loved.* It is applicable to the case of particular believers, who often walk in darkness a great while, but *at even time it shall be light,* and those that seek

1068

Christ to the end shall find him at length. Observe,

I. How the spouse sought him in vain *upon her bed (v.* 1) ; when she was up and looking about her, grace in act and exercise, though her beloved was withdrawn, yet she could see him at a distance *(ch.* ii. 8), but now it was otherwise. She still continued her affection to him, still it was *he whom her soul loved,* that bond of the covenant still continued firm. " *Though he slay me, I will trust in him;* though he leave me, I will love him. When I have him not in my arms, I have him in my heart." But she wanted the communion she used to have with him, as David when he *thirsted for God, for the living God.* She sought him, but, 1. It was *by night on her bed;* it was late and lazy seeking. Her understanding was clouded ; it was by night, in the dark. Her affections were chilled, it was on her bed half asleep. The wise virgins slumbered in the absence of the bridegroom. It was a dark time with the believer ; she saw not her signs, and yet she sought them. Those whose souls love Jesus Christ will continue to seek him even in silence and solitude : their *reins* instruct them to do so, even *in the night season.* 2. She failed in her endeavour. Sometimes he is *found of those that seek him not* (Isa. lxv. 1), but here he is not found of one that sought him, either for the punishment of her corruptions, her slothfulness and security (we miss of comfort because we do not seek it aright), or for the exercise of graces, her faith and patience, to try whether she will continue seeking. The woman of Canaan sought Christ, and found him not at first, that she might find him, at length, so much the more to her honour and comfort.

II. How she sought him in vain abroad, *v.* 2. She had made trial of secret worship, and had gone through the duties of the closet, had remembered him on her bed and meditated on him in the *night-watches* (Ps. lxiii. 6), but she did not meet with comfort. *My sore ran in the night,* and then I *remembered God and was troubled,* Ps. lxxvii. 2, 3. And yet she is not driven off by the disappointment from the use of further means ; she resolves, " *I will rise now;* I will not lie here if I cannot find my beloved here, nor be content if he be withdrawn. *I will rise now* without delay, and seek him immediately, lest he withdraw further from me." Those that would seek Christ so as to find him must lose no time. " *I will rise* out of a warm bed, and go out in a cold dark night, in quest of my beloved." Those that seek Christ must not startle at difficulties. " *I will rise, and go about the city,* the holy city, in the streets, and the broad-ways ;" for she knew he was not to be found in any blind by-ways. We must seek him in the city, in Jerusalem, which was a type of the gospel-church. The likeliest place to find Christ is in the temple (Luke ii. 46), in the streets of the gospel-church, in holy ordinances, where the children of Zion pass and repass at all hours. She had a good purpose when she said, *I will arise now*, but the good performance was all in all. She arose, and *sought him* (those that are in pursuit of Christ, the knowledge of him and communion with him, must turn every stone, seek every where), and yet she *found him not;* she was still unsatisfied, uneasy, as Job, when he looked on all sides, but could not perceive any tokens of the divine favour (Job xxiii. 8, 9), and the Psalmist often, when he complained that God hid his face from him, Ps. lxxxviii. 14. We may be in the way of our duty and yet may miss of comfort, for *the wind bloweth where it listeth.* How heavy is the accent on this repeated complaint: *I sought him, but I found him not!* like that of Mary Magdalen, *They have taken away my Lord, and I know not where they have laid him*, John xx. 13.

III. How she enquired of the watchmen concerning him, *v.* 3. In the night the watchmen *go about the city*, for the preservation of its peace and safety, to guide and assist the honest and quiet, as well as to be a check upon those that are disorderly; these met her in her walks, and she asked them if they could give her any tidings of her beloved. In the streets and broad-ways of Jerusalem she might meet with enough to divert her from her pursuit and to entertain her, though she could not meet her beloved; but she regards none in comparison with him. Gracious souls press through crowds of other delights and contentments in pursuit of Christ, whom they prefer before their chief joy. Mary Magdalen sees angels in the sepulchre, but that will not do unless she see Jesus. *Saw you him whom my soul loveth?* Note, We must evince the sincerity of our love to Christ by our solicitous enquiries after him. *The children of the bride-chamber will mourn when the bridegroom is taken away* (Matt. ix. 15), especially for the sin which provoked him to withdraw; and, if we do so, we shall be in care to recover the sense of his favour and diligent and constant in the use of proper means in order thereunto. We must search the scriptures, be much in prayer, keep close to ordinances, and all with this upon our heart, *Saw you him whom my soul loveth?* Those only who have seen Christ themselves are likely to direct others to a sight of him. When the Greeks came to worship at the feast they applied to Philip, with such an address as this of the spouse to the watchmen, *Sir, we would see Jesus*, John xii. 21.

IV. How she found him at last, *v.* 4. She *passed from* the watchmen as soon as she perceived they could give her no tidings of her beloved; she would not stay with them, because he was not among them, but went on seeking, for (as Ainsworth observes) the society neither of brethren, nor of the church, nor of ministers, can comfort the afflicted

conscience unless Christ himself be apprehended by faith. But soon after she parted from the watchmen she found him whom she sought, and then called him *him whom my soul loveth*, with as much delight as before with desire. Note, Those that continue seeking Christ shall find him at last, and when perhaps they were almost ready to despair of finding him. See Ps. xlii. 7, 8; lxxvii. 9, 10; Isa. liv. 7, 8. Disappointments must not drive us away from gracious pursuits. Hold out, faith and patience; *the vision is for an appointed time*, and, though the watchman can give us no account of it, *at the end* it shall itself *speak and not lie*; and the comfort that comes in after long waiting, in the use of means, will be so much the sweeter at last.

V. How close she kept to him when she had found him. She is now as much in fear of losing him as before she was in care to find him: *I held him*, held him fast, as the women, when they met with Christ after his resurrection, *held him by the feet, and worshipped him*, Matt. xxviii. 9. *"I would not let him go.* Not only, I would never do any thing to provoke him to depart, but I would by faith and prayer prevail with him to stay, and by the exercise of grace preserve inward peace." Those that know how hard comfort is come by, and how dearly it is bought, will be afraid of forfeiting it and playing it away, and will think nothing too much to do to keep it safe. *Non minor est virtus quam quærere parta tueri—As much is implied in securing our acquisitions as in making them.* Those that have laid hold on wisdom must *retain her*, Prov. iii. 18. Those that hold Christ fast in the arms of faith and love shall *not let him go;* he will abide with them.

VI. How desirous she was to make others acquainted with him: *"I brought him to my mother's house*, that all my relations, all who are dear to me, might have the benefit of communion with him." When Zaccheus found Christ, or rather was found of him, *salvation came to his house*, Luke xix. 9. Wherever we find Christ we must take him home with us to our houses, especially to our hearts. The church is our mother, and we should be concerned for her interests, that she may have Christ present with her and be earnest in prayer for his presence with his people and ministers always. Those that enjoy the tokens of Christ's favour to their own souls should desire that the church, and all religious assemblies in their public capacity, might likewise enjoy the tokens of his favour.

VII. What care she was in that no disturbance might be given him (*v.* 5); she repeats the charge she had before given (*ch.* ii. 7) to the *daughters of Jerusalem* not to *stir up or awake her love.* When she *had brought him into her mother's house*, among her sisters, she gives them a strict charge to keep all quiet and in good order, to be very observant of him, careful to please him, and afraid of offending him. The charge given to the church in the wilderness concerning the angel of the covenant, who was among them, explains this. Exod. xxiii. 21, *Beware of him and obey his voice ; provoke him not.* See that none of you stir out of your places, lest you disturb him, but *with quietness work and mind your own business ;* make no noise ; let all *clamour and bitterness be put* far *from you,* for that *grieves the Holy Spirit of God,* Eph. iv. 30, 31. Some make this to be Christ's charge to the *daughters of Jerusalem* not to disturb or disquiet his church, nor trouble the minds of the disciples ; for Christ is very tender of the peace of his church, and all the members of it, even the little ones ; and those that trouble them *shall bear their judgment,* Gal. v. 10.

6 Who *is* this that cometh out of the wilderness like pillars of smoke, perfumed with myrrh and frankincense, with all powders of the merchant ?

These are the words of the *daughters of Jerusalem,* to whom the charge was given, *v.* 5. They had looked shily upon the bride because she was black (*ch.* i. 6); but now they admire her, and speak of her with great respect : *Who is this ?* How beautiful she looks ! Who would have expected such a comely and magnificent person to *come out of the wilderness ?* As, when Christ rode in triumph into Jerusalem, they said, *Who is this ?* And of the accession of strangers to the church she herself says, with wonder (Isa. xlix. 21), *Who has begotten me these ?* 1. This is applicable to the Jewish church, when, after forty years' wandering in the wilderness, they came out of it, to take a glorious possession of the land of promise ; and this may very well be illustrated by what Balaam said of them at that time, when they ascended *out of the wilderness like pillars of smoke,* and he stood admiring them : *From the top of the rocks I see him. How goodly are thy tents, O Jacob !* Num. xxiii. 9 ; xxiv. 5. 2. It is applicable to any public deliverance of the church of God, as particularly of Babylon, the Old-Testament and the New-Testament Babylon ; then the church is *like pillars of smoke,* ascending upwards in devout affections, the incense of praise, from which, as from Noah's sacrifice, God *smells a sweet savour ;* then she is amiable in the eyes of her friends, and her enemies too cannot but have a veneration for her, and *worship at her feet, knowing that God has loved her,* Rev. iii. 9. Sometimes *the fear of the Jews* was upon their neighbours, when they saw that God *was with them of a truth,* Esth. viii. 17. 3. It is applicable to the recovery of a gracious soul out of a state of desertion and despondency. (1.) She ascends *out of the wilderness,* the dry and barren land, where there is *no way,* where there is *no water,* where travellers are still in want and ever at

a loss ; here a poor soul may long be left to wander, but shall come up, at last, under the conduct of the Comforter. (2.) She comes up *like pillars of smoke,* like a cloud of incense ascending from the altar or the smoke of the burnt-offerings. This intimates a fire of pious and devout affections in the soul, whence this smoke arises, and the mounting of the soul heaven-ward in this smoke (as Judges xiii. 20), the heart lifted up to God in the heavens, *as the sparks fly upward.* Christ's return to the soul gives life to its devotion, and its communion with God is most reviving when it ascends out *of a wilderness.* (3.) She is *perfumed with myrrh and frankincense.* She is replenished with the graces of God's Spirit, which are as sweet spices, or as the holy incense, which, being now kindled by his gracious returns, sends forth a very fragrant smell. Her devotions being now peculiarly lively, she is not only acceptable to God, but amiable in the eyes of others also, who are ready to cry out with admiration, *Who is this ?* What a monument of mercy is this ! The graces and comforts with which she is *perfumed* are called the *powders of the merchant,* for they are far-fetched and dear-bought, by our Lord Jesus, that blessed merchant, who took a long voyage, and was at vast expense, no less than that of his own blood, to purchase them for us. They are not the products of our own soil, nor the growth of our own country ; no, they are imported from the heavenly Canaan, the better country.

7 Behold his bed, which *is* Solomon's ; threescore valiant men *are* about it, of the valiant of Israel. 8 They all hold swords, *being* expert in war : every man *hath* his sword upon his thigh because of fear in the night. 9 King Solomon made himself a chariot of the wood of Lebanon. 10 He made the pillars thereof *of* silver, the bottom thereof *of* gold, the covering of it *of* purple, the midst thereof being paved *with* love, for the daughters of Jerusalem. 11 Go forth, O ye daughters of Zion, and behold king Solomon with the crown wherewith his mother crowned him in the day of his espousals, and in the day of the gladness of his heart.

The *daughters of Jerusalem* stood admiring the spouse and commending her, but she overlooks their praises, is not puffed up with them, but transfers all the glory to Christ, and directs them to look off from her to him, recommends him to their esteem, and sets herself to applaud him. Here he is three times called *Solomon,* and we have that name but three times besides in all this song, *ch.* i. 5 ; viii. 11, 12. It is Christ that is here meant, who is greater than Solomon, and of whom Solomon was an illustrious type for his wisdom and wealth, and especially his building the temple.

Three things she admires him for :—

I. The safety of his bed (*v.* 7): *Behold his bed,* even *Solomon's,* very rich and fine ; for such *the curtains of Solomon* were. *His bed, which is above Solomon's,* so some read it. Christ's bed, though he had *not where to lay his head,* is better than Solomon's best bed. The church is his bed, for he has said of it. *This is my rest for ever ; here will I dwell.* The hearts of believers are his bed, for he lies all night between their breasts, Eph. iii. 17. Heaven is his bed, the rest into which he entered when he had done his work. Or it may be meant of the sweet repose and satisfaction which gracious souls enjoy in communion with him ; it is called *his bed,* because, though we are admitted to it, and therefore it is called *our bed* (*ch.* i. 16), yet it is his peace that is our rest, John xiv. 27. *I will give you rest,* Matt. xi. 28. It *is Solomon's bed,* whose name signifies *peace,* because in his days Judah and Israel *dwelt safely under their vines and fig-trees.* That which she admires his bed for is the guard that surrounded it. Those that rest in Christ not only dwell at ease (many do so who yet are in the greatest danger) but they dwell in safety. Their holy serenity is under the protection of a holy security. This bed had *threescore valiant men about it,* as yeomen of the guard, or the band of gentlemen-pensioners; they are *of the valiant of Israel,* and a great many bold and brave men David's reign had produced. The life-guard men are well armed : *They all hold swords,* and know how to hold them ; they are *expert in war,* well skilled in all the arts of it. They are posted about the bed at a convenient distance. They are in a posture of defence, *every man* with *his sword upon his thigh* and his hand upon his sword, ready to draw upon the first alarm, and this *because of fear in the night,* because of the danger feared ; for the lives of princes, even the wisest and best, as they are more precious, so they are more exposed, and require to be more guarded than the lives of common persons. Or, *because of the fear* of it, and the apprehension which the spouse may have of danger, these guards are set for her satisfaction, that she may be *quiet from the fear of evil,* which believers themselves are subject to, especially *in the night,* when they are under a cloud as to their spiritual state, or in any outward trouble more than ordinary. Christ himself was under the special protection of his Father in his whole undertaking. *In the shadow of his hand has he hid me* (Isa. xlix. 2); he had legions of angels at his command. The church is well guarded ; more are with her than against her. Lest any hurt this vineyard, God himself *keeps it night and day* (Isa. xxvii. 2, 3); particular believers, when they repose them-

selves in Christ and with him, though it may be night-time with them, and they may have their *fears in the night,* are yet safe, as safe as Solomon himself in the midst of his guards ; the angels have a charge concerning them, ministers are appointed to *watch for their souls,* and *they* ought to be *valiant* men, *expert in* the spiritual warfare, holding *the sword of the Spirit, which is the word of God,* and having that girt *upon their thigh,* always ready to them for the silencing *of the fears* of God's people *in the night.* All the attributes of God are engaged for the safety of believers ; they are kept as in a strong-hold by his power (1 Pet. i. 5), are safe in *his name* (Prov. xviii. 10), his peace protects those in whom it rules (Phil. iv. 7), and the effect of righteousness in them is *quietness* and *assurance,* Isa. xxxii. 17. Our danger is from *the rulers of the darkness of this world,* but we are safe in the *armour of light.*

II. The splendour of his chariot, *v.* 9, 10. As Christ and believers rest in safety under a sufficient guard, so when they appear publicly, as kings in their coaches of state, they appear in great magnificence. This chariot was of Solomon's own contriving and making, the materials very rich, *silver,* and *gold,* and *cedar,* and *purple.* He made it for himself, and yet made it *for the daughters of Jerusalem,* to oblige them. Some by this *chariot,* or *coach,* or *chaise* (the word is nowhere else used in scripture), understand the human nature of Christ, in which the divine nature rode as in an open chariot. It was a divine workmanship *(A body hast thou prepared me) ;* the structure was very fine, but that which was at the bottom of it was love, pure love to the children of men. Others make it to represent the everlasting gospel, in which, as in an open chariot, Christ shows himself, and as in a chariot of war rides forth triumphantly, *conquering and to conquer. The pillars,* the seven pillars (Prov. ix. 1), are of *silver,* for the words of the Lord are *as silver tried* (Ps. xii. 6), nay, they are better *than thousands of gold and silver.* It is hung with *purple,* a princely colour ; all the adornings of it are dyed in the precious blood of Christ, and that gives them this colour. But that which completes the glory of it is *love ; it is paved with love,* it is lined with love, not love of strangers, as Solomon's was in the days of his defection, but *love* of *the daughters of Jerusalem,* a holy *love.* Silver is better than cedar, gold than silver, but love is better than gold, better than all, and it is put last, for nothing can be better than that. The gospel is all *love.* Mr. Durham applies it to the covenant of redemption, the way of our salvation, as it is contrived in the eternal counsel of God, and manifested to us in the scripture. This is that work of Christ himself wherein the glory of his grace and love to sinners most eminently appears, and which makes him amiable and admirable in the eyes of believers. In this covenant love is con·

veyed to them, and they are carried in it to the perfection of love, and, as it were, ride in triumph. It is admirably framed and contrived, both for the glory of Christ and for the comfort of believers. It is *well ordered in all things, and sure* (2 Sam. xxiii. 5); it has *pillars* that cannot be shaken; it is *made of the wood of Lebanon,* which can never rot; the basis of it is *gold,* the most lasting metal; the blood of the covenant, that rich *purple,* is the cover of this chariot, by which believers are sheltered from the wind and storms of divine wrath, and the troubles of this world; but the midst of it, and that which is all in all in it, is *love,* that *love of Christ which surpasses knowledge* and the dimensions of which are immeasurable.

III. The lustre of his royal person, when he appears in his greatest pomp, *v.* 11. Here observe,

1. The call that is given to the *daughters of Zion* to acquaint themselves with the glories of *king Solomon: Go forth, and behold* him. The multitude of the spectators adds to the beauty of a splendid cavalcade. Christ, in his gospel, manifests himself. Let each of us add to the number of those that give honour to him, by giving themselves the satisfaction of looking upon him. Who should pay respects to Zion's king but Zion's daughters? They have reason to rejoice greatly when he comes, Zech. ix. 9. (1.) *Behold him* then. Look with pleasure upon Christ in his glory. Look upon him with an eye of faith, with a fixed eye. Here is a sight worth seeing; *behold,* and admire him, *behold,* and love him; look upon him, and know him again. (2.) *Go forth and behold* him; go off from the world, as those that see no beauty and excellency in it in comparison with what is to be seen in the Lord Jesus. Go out of yourselves, and let the sight of his transcendent beauty put you out of conceit with yourselves. *Go forth* to the place where he is to be seen, to the street through which he passes, as Zaccheus.

2. The direction that is given them to take special notice of that which they would not see every day, and that was his *crown,* either the crown of gold, adorned with jewels, which he wore on his coronation-day (Solomon's mother, Bathsheba, though she did not procure that for him, yet, by her seasonable interposal, she helped to secure it to him when Adonijah was catching at it), or the garland or crown of flowers and green tied with ribbons which his mother made for him, to adorn the solemnity of his nuptials. Perhaps Solomon's coronation day was his marriage-day, *the day of his espousals,* when the garland his mother crowned him with was added to the crown his people crowned him with. Applying this to Christ, it speaks, (1.) The many honours put upon him, and the power and dominion he is entrusted with: *Go forth,* and see king Jesus, *with the crown wherewith his* Father *crowned him,* when he declared him

1072

his *beloved Son, in whom* he was *well-pleased,* when he *set him as King upon his holy hill of Zion,* when he advanced him to his own right hand, and invested him with a sovereign authority, both *in heaven and in earth,* and *put all things under his feet.* (2.) The dishonour put upon him by his persecutors. Some apply it to the *crown of thorns* with which *his mother,* the Jewish church, *crowned him* on the day of his death, which was *the day of his espousals* to his church, when he *loved it, and gave himself for it* (Eph. v. 25); and it is observable that when he was *brought forth wearing the crown of thorns* Pilate said, and said it to the *daughters of Zion, Behold the man* (3.) It seems especially to mean the honour done him by his church, as his mother, and by all true believers, in whose hearts he is formed, and of whom he has said, *These are my mother, and sister, and brother,* Matt. xii. 50. They give him the glory of his undertaking; to him is glory *in the church,* Eph. iii. 21. When believers accept of him as theirs, and join themselves to him in an everlasting covenant, [1.] It is his coronation-day in their souls. Before conversion they were crowning themselves, but then they begin to crown Christ, and continue to do so from that day forward. They appoint him their head; they bring *every thought into obedience to* him; they set up his throne in their hearts, and cast all their crowns at his feet. [2.] It is *the day of his espousals,* in which he betroths them to him for ever in lovingkindness and in mercies, joins them to himself in faith and love, and gives himself to them in the promises and all he has, to be theirs. *Thou shalt not be for another, so will I also be for thee,* Hos. iii. 3. And to him they are presented as *chaste virgins.* [3.] It is *the day of the gladness of his heart;* he is pleased with the honour that his people do him, pleased with the progress of his interest among them. Does *Satan fall* before them? *In that hour Jesus rejoices in spirit,* Luke x. 18, 21. There is joy in heaven over repenting sinners; the family is glad when the prodigal son returns. *Go forth and behold* Christ's grace towards sinners, as his *crown,* his brightest glory.

CHAP. IV.

In this chapter, I. Jesus Christ, having espoused his church to himself (ch. iii. 11), highly commends her beauty in the several expressions of it, concluding her fair, all fair, ver. 1—5 and again, ver. 7. II. He retires himself, and invites her with him, from the mountains of terror to those of delight, ver. 6, 8. III. He professes his love to her and his delight in her affection to him, ver. 9—14. IV. She ascribes all she had that was valuable in her to him, and depends upon the continued influence of his grace to make her more and more acceptable to him, ver. 15, 16.

BEHOLD, thou *art* fair, my love; behold, thou *art* fair; thou *hast* doves' eyes within thy locks: thy hair *is* as a flock of goats, that appear from mount Gilead. 2 Thy teeth *are* like a flock *of sheep that are even* shorn, which came up from the washing; whereof every one bear twins, and none *is* barren among them. 3 Thy lips *are* like a thread of scarlet, and thy speech *is* comely: thy temples *are* like a piece of a pomegranate within thy locks. 4 Thy neck *is* like the tower of David builded for an armoury, whereon there hang a thousand bucklers, all shields of mighty men. 5 Thy two breasts *are* like two young roes that are twins, which feed among the lilies. 6 Until the day break, and the shadows flee away, I will get me to the mountain of myrrh, and to the hill of frankincense. 7 Thou *art* all fair, my love; *there is* no spot in thee.

Here is, I. A large and particular account of the beauties of the church, and of gracious souls on whom the image of God is renewed, consisting *in the beauty of holiness.* In general, he that is a competent judge of beauty, whose *judgment,* we are sure, *is according to truth,* and what all must subscribe to, he has said, *Behold, thou art fair.* She had commended him, and called all about her to take notice of his glories; and hereby she recommends herself to him, gains his favour, and, in return for her respects, he calls to all about him to take notice of her graces. Those that honour Christ he will honour, 1 Sam. ii. 30.

1. He does not flatter her, nor design hereby either to make her proud of herself or to court her praises of him; but, (1.) It is to encourage her under her present dejections. Whatever others thought of her, she was amiable in his eyes. (2.) It is to teach her what to value herself upon, not any external advantages (which would add nothing to her, and the want of which would deprive her of nothing that was really excellent), but upon the comeliness of grace which he had put upon her. (3.) It is to invite others to think well of her too, and to join themselves to her: "Thou art *my love,* thou lovest me and art beloved of me, and therefore *thou art fair.*" All the beauty of the saints is derived from him, and they shine by reflecting his light; it is *the beauty of the Lord our God* that is *upon us,* Ps. xc. 17. She was espoused to him, and that made her beautiful. *Uxor fulget radiis mariti—The spouse shines in her husband's rays.* It is repeated: *Thou art fair,* and again, *Thou art fair,* denoting not only the certainty of it, but the pleasure he took in speaking of it.

2. As to the representation here made of the beauty of the church, the images are certainly very bright, the shades strong, and the comparisons bold, not proper indeed to represent any external beauty, for they were not designed to do so, but *the beauty of holiness, the new man, the hidden man of the heart, in that which is not corruptible.* Seven par-

ticulars are specified, a number of perfection, for the church is enriched with manifold graces by *the seven spirits* that *are before the throne,* Rev. i. 4; 1 Cor. i. 5, 7.

(1.) Her *eyes.* A good eye contributes much to a beauty: *Thou hast doves' eyes,* clear and chaste, and often cast up towards heaven. It is not the eagle's eye, that can face the sun, but the *dove's eye,* a humble, modest, mournful eye, that is the praise of those whom Christ loves. Ministers are the church's eyes (Isa. lii. 8, *thy watchmen shall see eye to eye);* they must be like *doves' eyes,* harmless and inoffensive (Matt. x. 16), having their *conversation in the world in simplicity and godly sincerity.* Wisdom and knowledge are the eyes of the new man; they must be clear, but not haughty, *not exercised in things too high for us.* When our aims and intentions are sincere and honest, then we have *doves' eyes,* when we look not unto *idols* (Ezek. xviii. 6), but have our *eyes ever towards the Lord,* Ps. xxv. 15. The *doves' eyes are within the locks,* which are as a shade upon them, so that, [1.] They cannot fully see. As long as we are here in this world we *know but in part,* for a hair hangs in our eyes; *we cannot order our speech by reason of darkness;* death will shortly cut those locks, and then we shall see all things clearly. [2.] They cannot be fully seen, but as the stars through the thin clouds. Some make it to intimate the bashfulness of her looks; she suffers not her eyes to wander, but limits them with her locks.

(2.) Her *hair;* it is compared to *a flock of goats,* which looked white, and were, on the top of the mountains, like a fine head of hair; and the sight was the more pleasant to the spectator because the goats have not only gravity from their beards, but they are *comely in going* (Prov. xxx. 29), but it was most pleasant of all to the owner, much of whose riches consisted in his flocks. Christ puts a value upon that in the church, and in believers, which others make no more account of than of their hair. He told his disciples that *the very hairs of their head were all numbered,* as carefully as men number their flocks (Matt. x. 30), and that *not a hair of their head should perish,* Luke xxi. 18. Some by the *hair* here understand the outward conversation of a believer, which ought to be comely, and decent, and agreeable to the holiness of the heart. The apostle opposes good works, such as become the professors of godliness, to *the plaiting of the hair,* 1 Tim. ii. 9, 10. Mary Magdalen's hair was beautiful when she wiped the feet of Christ with it.

(3.) Her *teeth, v.* 2. Ministers are the church's teeth; like nurses, they chew the meat for the babes of Christ. The Chaldee paraphrase applies it to the priests and Levites, who fed upon the sacrifices as the representatives of the people. Faith, by which we feed upon Christ, meditation, by which we ruminate on the word and chew the cud upon what we have heard, in order to the digesting of it, are the teeth of the new man. These are here compared to *a flock of sheep.* Christ called his disciples and ministers a *little flock.* It is the praise of teeth to be *even*, to be white, and kept clean, *like sheep from the washing*, and to be firm and well fixed in the gums, and not like sheep that cast their young; for so the word signifies which we translate *barren*. It is the praise of ministers to be even in mutual love and concord, to be pure and clean from all moral pollutions, and to be fruitful, bringing forth souls to Christ, and nursing his lambs.

(4.) Her *lips;* these are compared to *a thread of scarlet, v.* 3. Red lips are comely, and a sign of health, as the paleness of the lips is a sign of faintness and weakness; her *lips* were of the colour *of scarlet*, but thin *lips, like a thread of scarlet.* The next words explain it: *Thy speech is comely*, always with grace, *good*, and *to the use of edifying*, which adds much to the beauty of a Christian. When we praise God with *our lips, and with the mouth make confession* of him *to salvation*, then they are as *a thread of scarlet.* All our good works and good words must be *washed in the blood of Christ*, dyed like the *scarlet thread*, and then, and not till then, they are acceptable to God. The Chaldee applies it to the chief priest, and his prayers for Israel on the day of atonement.

(5.) Her *temples*, or cheeks, which are here compared to *a piece of a pomegranate*, a fruit which, when cut in two, has rich veins or specks in it, like a blush in the face. Humility and modesty, blushing to lift up our faces before God, blushing at the remembrance of sin and in a sense of our unworthiness of the honour put upon us, will beautify us very much in the eyes of Christ. The blushes of Christ's bride are *within her locks*, which intimates (says Mr. Durham) that she blushes when no other sees, and for that which none sees but God and conscience; also that she seeks not to proclaim her humility, but modestly covers that too; yet the evidences of all these, in a tender walk, appear and are comely.

(6.) Her *neck ;* this is here compared to *the tower of David, v.* 4. This is generally applied to the grace of faith, by which we are united to Christ, as the body is united to the head by the neck; this *is like the tower of David*, furnishing us with weapons of war, especially *bucklers* and *shields*, as the soldiers were supplied with them out of that tower, for *faith* is our *shield* (Eph. vi. 16): those that have it never want a *buckler*, for God will compass them *with his favour as with a shield.* When this *neck is like a tower*, straight, and stately, and strong, a Christian goes on in his way, and works with courage and magnanimity, and does not hang a drooping head, as he does when faith fails. Some make the *shields of* the *mighty men*, that are here said to hang up in *the tower of David*, to be the monuments of the valour of David's worthies.

Their shields were preserved, to keep in remembrance them and their heroic acts, intimating that it is a great encouragement to the saints to hold up their heads, to see what great things the saints in all ages have accomplished and won by faith. In Heb. xi. we have the *shields of* the *mighty men* hung up, the exploits of believers and the trophies of their victories.

(7.) Her *breasts ;* these *are like two young roes that are twins, v.* 5. The church's breasts are both for ornament (Ezek. xvi. 7) and for use; they are the *breasts of her consolation* (Isa. lxvi. 11), as she is said to *suck the breasts of kings*, Isa. lx. 16. Some apply these to the two Testaments; others to the two sacraments, the seals of the covenant of grace; others to ministers, who are to be spiritual nurses to the children of God and to give out to them the *sincere milk of the word, that they may grow thereby*, and, in order to that, are themselves to *feed among the lilies* where Christ feeds (*ch.* ii. 16), that they may be to the babes of the church as full breasts. Or the breasts of a believer are his love to Christ, which he is pleased with, as a tender husband is with the affections of his wife, who is therefore said to be to him *as the loving hind and the pleasant roe*, because *her breasts satisfy him at all times*, Prov. v. 19 This includes also his edifying others and communicating grace to them, which adds much to a Christian's beauty.

II. The bridegroom's resolution hereupon to retire *to the mountain of myrrh* (*v.* 6) and there to make his residence. This *mountain of myrrh* is supposed to signify Mount Moriah, on which the temple was built, where incense was daily burnt to the honour of God. Christ was so pleased with the beauty of his church that he chose this to be his rest for ever; here he will dwell *till the day break and the shadows flee away.* Christ's parting promise to his disciples, as the representatives of the church, answers to this: *Lo, I am with you always, even to the end of the world.* Where the ordinances of God are duly administered there Christ will be, and there we must meet him at the door of the tabernacle of meeting. Some make these to be the words of the spouse, either modestly ashamed of the praises given her, and willing to get out of the hearing of them, or desirous to be constant to the holy hill, not doubting but there to find suitable and sufficient succour and relief in all her straits, and there to cast anchor, and wish for the day, which, at the time appointed, would *break and the shadows flee away.* The holy hill (as some observe) is here called both a *mountain of myrrh*, which is bitter, and a *hill of frankincense*, which is sweet, for there we have occasion both to mourn and rejoice; repentance is a bitter sweet. But in heaven it will be all frankincense, and no myrrh. Prayer is compared to incense, and Christ will meet his praying people and will bless them.

III. His repeated commendation of the beauty of his spouse (*v.* 7): *Thou art all fair, my love.* He had said (*v.* 1), *Thou art fair;* but here he goes further, and, in review of the particulars, as of those of the creation, he pronounces *all very good:* "*Thou art all fair, my love;* thou art all over beautiful, and there is nothing amiss in thee, and thou hast all beauties in thee; thou art *sanctified wholly* in every part; *all things have become new* (2 Cor. v. 17); there is not only a new face and a new name, but a new man, a new nature; *there is no spot in thee,* as far as thou art renewed." The spiritual sacrifices must be without blemish. *There is no spot* but such as is often the spot of God's children, none of the leopard's spots. The church, when Christ shall present it to himself a glorious church, will be altogether *without spot or wrinkle,* Eph. v. 27.

8 Come with me from Lebanon, *my* spouse, with me from Lebanon: look from the top of Amana, from the top of Shenir and Hermon, from the lions' dens, from the mountains of the leopards. 9 Thou hast ravished my heart, my sister, *my* spouse; thou hast ravished my heart with one of thine eyes, with one chain of thy neck. 10 How fair is thy love, my sister, *my* spouse! how much better is thy love than wine! and the smell of thine ointments than all spices! 11 Thy lips, O *my* spouse, drop *as* the honeycomb: honey and milk *are* under thy tongue; and the smell of thy garments *is* like the smell of Lebanon. 12 A garden inclosed *is* my sister, *my* spouse; a spring shut up, a fountain sealed. 13 Thy plants *are* an orchard of pomegranates, with pleasant fruits; camphire, with spikenard, 14 Spikenard and saffron; calamus and cinnamon, with all trees of frankincense; myrrh and aloes, with all the chief spices.

These are still the words of Christ to his church, expressing his great esteem of her and affection to her, the opinion he had of her beauty and excellency, the desire he had of, and the delight he had in, her converse and society. And so ought men to love their wives as Christ loves the church, and takes pleasure in it as if it were spotless and had no fault, when yet it is compassed with infirmity. Now, observe here,

I. The endearing names and titles by which he calls her, to express his love to her, to assure her of it, and to engage and excite her love to him. Twice here he calls her *My spouse* (*v.* 8, 11) and three times *My sister,*

my spouse, *v.* 9, 10, 12. Mention was made (*ch.* iii. 11) of *the day of his espousals,* and, after that, she is called his *spouse,* not before. Note, There is a marriage-covenant between Christ and his church, between Christ and every true believer. Christ calls his church his *spouse,* and his calling her so makes her so. "I have betrothed thee unto me for ever; and, as the bridegroom rejoices over the bride, so shall thy God rejoice over thee." He is not ashamed to own the relation, but, as becomes a kind and tender husband, he speaks affectionately to her, and calls her his *spouse,* which cannot but strongly engage her to be faithful to him. Nay, because no one relation among men is sufficient to set forth Christ's love to his church, and to show that all this must be understood spiritually, he owns her in two relations, which among men are incompatible, *My sister, my spouse.* Abraham's saying of Sarah, *She is my sister,* was interpreted as a denying of her to be his wife; but Christ's church is to him both a *sister* and a *spouse,* as Matt. xii. 50, a *sister and mother.* His calling her *sister* is grounded upon his taking our nature upon him in his incarnation, and his making us partakers of his nature in our sanctification. He clothed himself with a *body* (Heb. ii. 14), and he clothes believers with his *Spirit* (1 Cor. vi. 17), and so they become his *sisters.* They are children of God his Father (2 Cor. vi. 18) and so they become his *sisters;* he that sanctifies, and those that are sanctified, are all of one (Heb. ii. 11); and he owns them, and loves them, as his sisters.

II. The gracious call he gives her to come along with him as a faithful bride, that must forget her own people and her father's house, and leave all to cleave to him. *Ubi tu Caius, ibi ego Caia—Where thou Caius art, I Caia will be. Come with me from Lebanon, v.* 8.

1. It is a precept; so we take it, like that (*ch.* ii. 10, 13), *Rise up, and come away.* All that have by faith come to Christ must come with Christ, in holy obedience to him and compliance with him. Being joined to him, we must walk with him. This is his command to us daily: "*Come with me, my spouse;* come with me to God as a Father; come with me onward, heavenward; come forward with me; come up with me; *come with me from Lebanon, from the top of Amana, from the lions' dens.*" These mountains are to be considered, (1.) As seemingly delightful places. Lebanon is called *that goodly mountain,* Deut. iii. 25. We read of the *glory of Lebanon* (Isa. xxxv. 2) and its goodly smell, Hos. xiv. 6. We read of the pleasant *dew of Hermon* (Ps. cxxxiii. 3) and the *joy of Hermon* (Ps. lxxxix. 12); and we may suppose the other mountains here mentioned to be pleasant ones, and so this is Christ's call to his spouse to come off from the world, all its products, all its pleasures, to sit loose to all the delights of sense. All those must do so that would come with Christ; they must

take their affections off from all present things; yea, though they be placed at the upper end of the world, on *the top of Amana* and *the top of Shenir,* though they enjoy the highest satisfactions the creature can propose to give, yet they must *come away* from them all, and live above the tops of the highest hills on earth, that they may have *their conversation in heaven. Come from* those mountains, to go along with Christ to the holy mountain, the *mountain of myrrh, v.* 6. Even while we have our residence on these mountains, yet we must look from them, look above them. Shall we *lift up our eyes to the hills?* No; *our help comes from the Lord,* Ps. cxxi. 1, 2. We must look beyond them, to *the things that are not seen* (as these high hills are), that *are eternal. From the tops of Shenir and Hermon,* which were on the other side Jordan, as from Pisgah, they could see the land of Canaan; from this world we must look forward to the better country. (2.) They are to be considered as really dangerous. These hills indeed are pleasant enough, but there are in them *lions' dens;* they are *mountains of the leopards,* mountains of prey, though they seem *glorious and excellent,* Ps. lxxvi. 4. Satan, that *roaring lion,* is the *prince of this world;* in the things of it he lies in wait to devour. On the tops of these mountains there are many dangerous temptations to those who take up their residence in them; and therefore *come with me from* them; let us not set our hearts upon the things of this world, and then they can do us no hurt. *Come with me from* the temples of idolaters, and the societies of wicked people (so some understand it); *come out from among them, and be you separate. Come from* under the dominion of your own lusts, which are as *lions* and *leopards,* fierce upon us, and making us fierce.

2. It may be taken as a promise: Thou shalt *come with me from Lebanon, from the lions' dens;* that is, (1.) "Many shall be brought home to me, as living members of the church, from every point, from Lebanon in the north, Amana in the west, Hermon in the east, Shenir in the south, from all parts, to *sit down with Abraham, Isaac, and Jacob,* Matt. viii. 11. See Isa. xlix. 11, 12. Some *from the tops of* these mountains, some of the great men of this world, shall give themselves to Christ. (2.) The church shall be delivered from her persecutors, in due time; though now she *dwells among lions* (Ps. lvii. 4), Christ will take her with himself from among their dens.

III. The great delight Christ takes in his church and in all believers. He delights in them,

1. As in an agreeable bride, *adorned for her husband* (Rev. xxi. 2), who *greatly desires her beauty,* Ps. xlv. 11. No expressions of love can be more passionate than these here, in which Christ manifests his affection to his church; and yet that great proof of his love,

his dying for it, that he might present it to himself a glorious church, goes far beyond them all. A spouse so dearly bought and paid for could not but be dearly loved. Such a price being given for her, a high value must needs be put upon her accordingly; and both together may well set us a wondering at *the height and depth, and length and breadth, of the love of Christ, which surpasses knowledge,* that love in which he *gave himself for us* and gives himself to us. Observe, (1.) How he is affected towards his spouse: *Thou hast ravished my heart;* the word is used only here. *Thou hast hearted me,* or *Thou hast unhearted me.* New words are coined to express the inexpressibleness of Christ's surprising love to his church; and the strength of that love is set forth by that which is a weakness in men, the being so much in love with one object as to be heartless to every thing else. This may refer to that love which Christ had to the chosen remnant, before the worlds were, when *his delights were with the sons of men* (Prov. viii. 31), that first love, which brought him from heaven to earth, to *seek and save* them at such vast expense, yet including the complacency he takes in them when he has brought them to himself. Note, Christ's heart is upon his church; so it has appeared all along. His treasure is in it; it is his *peculiar treasure* (Exod. xix. 5); and therefore there his heart is also. "Never was love like unto the love of Christ, which made him even mindless of himself, when he emptied himself of his glory, and despised all shame and pain, for our sakes. The wound of love towards us, which he had from eternity in himself, made him neglect all the wounds and reproaches of the cross;" so bishop Reynolds. Thus let us love him. (2.) What it is that thus affects him with delight. [1.] The regard she has to him: *Thou hast ravished my heart with one of thy eyes,* those doves' eyes, clear and chaste (which were commended, *v.* 1), with one glance of those eyes. Christ is wonderfully pleased with those that look unto him as their Saviour, and through the eye of faith dart their affections to him, above any rival whatsoever, and whose *eyes are ever towards him;* he is soon aware of the first look of a soul towards him and meets it with his favours. [2.] The ornaments she has from him, that is, the obedience she yields to him, for that is the *chain of her neck,* the graces that enrich her soul, which are connected as links in a chain, the exercise of these graces in a conversation which adorns both herself and the doctrine of Jesus Christ, which she professes to believe (as a gold chain is an ornament to persons of quality), and an entire submission to the commanding power of his law and the constraining power of his love. Having shaken off the *bands of our neck,* by which we were tied to this world (Isa. lii. 2), and *the yoke of our transgressions,* we are bound with the *cords of love,* as *chains of gold,* to

Jesus Christ, and our necks are brought under his sweet and easy yoke, to draw in it. This recommends us to Jesus Christ, for this is that true wisdom which, in his account, is *an ornament of grace unto the head and chains about the neck,* Prov. i. 9. [3.] The affection she has for him: *How fair is thy love!* how beautiful is it! Not only thy love itself, but all the fruits and products of it, its working in the heart, its works in the life. How well does it become a believer thus to love Christ, and what a pleasure does Christ take in it! Nothing recommends us to Christ as this does. *How much better is thy love than wine,* than all the wine that was poured out to the Lord in the drink-offerings! Hence the fruit of the vine is said to *cheer God and man,* Judges ix. 13. She had said of Christ's love, *It is better than wine (ch.* i. 2), and now Christ says so of hers; there is nothing lost by praising Christ, nor will he be behindhand with his friends in kindness. [4.] The ointments, the odours wherewith she is perfumed, the gifts and graces of the Spirit, her good works, which are *an odour of a sweet smell, a sacrifice acceptable, well-pleasing to God,* Phil. iv. 18. *The smell of thy ointment* is better *than all spices,* such as the queen of Sheba presented to Solomon, camel-loads of them (1 Kings x. 2), or, rather, than all the spices that were used in compounding the holy incense which was burned daily on the golden altar. Love and obedience to God are more pleasing to Christ than sacrifice or incense. *The smell of her garments* too, the visible profession she makes of religion, and relation to Christ, before men, and wherein she appears to the world, this is very grateful to Christ, as *the smell of Lebanon.* Christ having put upon his spouse the *white raiment* of his own righteousness (Rev. iii. 18), and *the righteousness of saints* (Rev. xix. 8), and this perfumed with holy joy and comfort, he is well pleased with it. [5.] Her words, both in her devotions to God and her discourses with men (*v.* 11): *Thy lips O my spouse! drop as the honeycomb,* drop that which is very sweet, and drop it freely and plentifully. If what God speaks to us be *sweeter* to us *than the honey and the honeycomb* (Ps. xix. 10), what we say to him in prayer and praise shall also be pleasing to him: *Sweet is thy voice.* And if *out of a good treasure* in the *heart* we *bring forth good things,* if our *speech be always with grace,* if our *lips use knowledge aright,* if they *disperse knowledge,* they then, in Christ's account, even *drop the honeycomb,* out-drop it. *Honey and milk* (the two staple commodities of Canaan) *are under thy tongue;* that is, in thy heart, not only reserved there for thy own use as a sweet morsel for thyself, but ready there for the use of others. In the word of God there is sweet and wholesome nourishment, milk for babes, honey for those that are grown up. Christ is well-pleased with those that are full of his word.

2. As in a pleasant garden. And well may a very great delight be compared to the delight taken in a garden, when the happiness of Adam in innocency was represented by the putting of him into a garden, a garden of pleasure. This comparison is pursued, *v.* 12—14. The church is fitly compared to a *garden,* to a garden which, as was usual, had *a fountain* in it. Where Solomon made himself *gardens* and *orchards,* he made himself *pools of water* (Eccl. ii. 5, 6), not only for curiosity and diversion, in water-works, but for use, to *water the gardens.* Eden was *well watered,* Gen. ii. 10; xiii. 10. Observe, (1.) The peculiarity of this garden: It is *a garden enclosed,* a paradise separated from the common earth. It is appropriated to God; he has *set it apart for himself;* Israel is God's portion, the lot of his inheritance. It is enclosed for secrecy; the saints are God's hidden ones, therefore *the world knows them not;* Christ walks in his garden unseen. It is enclosed for safety; a hedge of protection is made about it, which all the powers of darkness cannot either find or make a gap in. God's vineyard is *fenced* (Isa. v. 2); there is a wall about it, a wall of fire. It has a spring in it, and a fountain, but it is *a spring shut up* and *a fountain sealed,* which sends its streams *abroad* (Prov. v. 16), but is itself carefully locked up, that it may not by any injurious hand be muddied or polluted. The souls of believers are as *gardens enclosed;* grace in them is as *a spring shut up* there in *the hidden man of the heart,* where the water that Christ gives is *a well of living water,* John iv. 14; vii. 38. The Old-Testament church was *a garden enclosed* by the partition wall of the ceremonial law. The Bible was then *a spring shut up* and *a fountain sealed;* it was confined to one nation; but now the wall of separation is removed, the gospel preached to every nation, and *in Jesus Christ there is neither Greek nor Jew.* (2.) The products of this garden. It is as the garden of Eden, where *the Lord God made to grow every tree that is pleasant to the sight and good for food,* Gen. ii. 9. *Thy plants,* or plantations, *are an orchard of pomegranates with pleasant fruits, v.* 13. It is not like the *vineyard of the man void of understanding,* that was *all grown over with thorns and nettles;* but here are *fruits, pleasant fruits, all trees of frankincense,* and *all the chief spices, v.* 14. Here is great plenty of fruits and great variety, nothing wanting which might either beautify or enrich this garden, might make it either delightful or serviceable to its great Lord. Every thing here is the best of the kind. Their *chief spices* were much more valuable, because much more durable, than the choicest of our flowers. Solomon was a great master in botany as well as other parts of natural philosophy; he treated largely of trees (1 Kings iv. 33), and perhaps had reference to some specific qualities of the fruits here specified, which made them very fit for

the purpose for which he alludes to them; but we must be content to observe, in general, that saints in the church, and graces in the saints, are very fitly compared to these *fruits and spices;* for, [1.] They are planted, and do not grow of themselves; *the trees of righteousness* are the *planting of the Lord* (Isa. lxi. 3); grace springs from an incorruptible seed. [2.] They are precious and of high value; hence we read of the *precious sons of Zion* and their *precious faith;* they are *plants of renown.* [3.] They are pleasant, and of a sweet savour to God and man, and, as strong aromatics, diffuse their fragrancy. [4.] They are profitable and of great use. Saints are the blessings of this earth, and their graces are their riches, with which they trade as the merchants of the east with their spices. [5.] They are permanent, and will be preserved to good purpose, when flowers are withered and good for nothing. Grace, ripened into glory, will last for ever.

15 A fountain of gardens, a well of living waters, and streams from Lebanon. 16 Awake, O˙north wind; and come, thou south; blow upon my garden, *that* the spices thereof may flow out. Let my beloved come into his garden, and eat his pleasant fruits.

These seem to be the words of the spouse, the church, in answer to the commendations which Christ, the bridegroom, had given of her as a pleasant fruitful garden. Is she a garden?

I. She owns her dependence upon Christ himself to make this garden fruitful. To him she has an eye (v.ᵉ 15) as the *fountain of gardens,* not only the founder of them, by whom they are planted and to whom they owe their being, but the fountain of them, by which they are watered and to which they owe their continuance and well-being, and without whose constant supplies they would soon become like the dry and barren wilderness. To him she gives all the glory of her fruitfulness, as being nothing without him: O *fountain of gardens!* fountain of all good, of all grace, do not thou fail me. Does a believer say to the church, *All my springs are in thee,* in thee, O Zion? (Ps. lxxxvii. 7), the church transmits the praise to Christ, and says to him, *All my springs are in thee;* thou art *the well of living waters* (Jer. ii. 13), out of which flow the *streams of Lebanon,* the river Jordan, which had its rise at the foot of Mount Lebanon, and the waters of the sanctuary, which issued out *from under the threshold of the house,* Ezek. xlvii. 1. Those that are gardens to Christ must acknowledge him a fountain to them, from whose fulness they receive and to whom it is owing that their souls are as *a watered garden,* Jer. xxxi. 12. *The city of God* on earth is made *glad* with the *river* that flows from this fountain (Ps. xlvi. 4), and the new Jerusalem has its

1078

pure river of water of life proceeding out of the throne of God and of the Lamb, Rev. xxii. 1.

II. She implores the influences of the blessed Spirit to make this garden fragrant (v. 16): *Awake, O north wind! and come, thou south.* This is a prayer, 1. For the church in general, that there may be a plentiful effusion of the Spirit upon it, in order to its flourishing estate. Ministers' gifts are *the spices;* when the Spirit is poured out these flow forth, and then *the wilderness becomes a fruitful field,* Isa. xxxii. 15. This prayer was answered in the pouring out of the Spirit on *the day of pentecost* (Acts ii. 1), ushered in by a *mighty wind;* then the apostles, who were bound up before, flowed forth, and were a *sweet savour to God,* 2 Cor. ii. 15. 2. For particular believers. Note, (1.) Sanctified souls are as gardens, gardens of the Lord, enclosed for him. (2.) Graces in the soul are as spices in these gardens, that in them which is valuable and useful. (3.) It is very desirable that the spices of grace should flow forth both in pious and devout affections and in holy gracious actions, that with them we may honour God, adorn our profession, and do that which will be grateful to good men. (4.) The blessed Spirit, in his operations upon the soul, is as the *north and the south wind,* which *blows where it listeth,* and from several points, John iii. 8. There is the north wind of convictions, and the south wind of comforts; but all, like the wind, brought *out of God's treasuries* and *fulfilling his word.* (5.) The flowing forth of the spices of grace depends upon the gales of the Spirit; he stirs up good affections, and works in us both to will and to do that which is good; it is he that makes manifest the savour of his knowledge by us. (6.) We ought therefore to wait upon the Spirit of grace for his quickening influences, to pray for them, and to lay our souls under them. God has promised to give us his Spirit, but he will for this be enquired of.

III. She invites Christ to the best entertainment the garden affords: " *Let my beloved* then *come into his garden and eat his pleasant fruits;* let him have the honour of all the products of the garden (it is fit he should), and let me have the comfort of his acceptance of them, for that is the best account they can be made to turn to." Observe, 1. She calls it *his* garden; for those that are espoused to Christ call nothing their own, but what they have devoted to him and desire to be used for him. When the spices flow forth then it is fit to be called his garden, and not till then. The fruits of the garden are his pleasant fruits, for he planted them, watered them, and gave the increase. What can we pretend to merit at Christ's hands when we can invite him to nothing but what is his own already? 2. She begs he would visit it, and accept of what it produced. The believer can take little pleasure in his garden, unless Christ, the beloved of his soul, come to him, nor have any joy of the fruits of it, unless they redound some way or other to the glory of Christ, and he will think all he has well bestowed upon him.

CHAP. V.

In this chapter we have, I. Christ's gracious acceptance of the invitation which his church had given him, and the kind visit which he made to her, ver. 1. II. The account which the spouse gives of her own folly, in putting a slight upon her beloved, and the distress she was in by reason of his withdrawings, ver. 2—8. III. The enquiry of the daughters of Jerusalem concerning the amiable perfections of her beloved (ver. 9), and her particular answer to that enquiry, ver. 10—16. " Unto you that believe he is thus precious."

I AM come into my garden, my sister, *my* spouse : I have gathered my myrrh with my spice; I have eaten my honeycomb with my honey; I have drunk my wine with my milk : eat, O friends; drink, yea, drink abundantly, O beloved.

These words are Christ's answer to the church's prayer in the close of the foregoing chapter, *Let my beloved come into his garden;* here he has come, and lets her know it. See how ready God is to hear prayer, how ready Christ is to accept the invitations that his people give him, though we are backward to hear his calls and accept his invitations. He is free in condescending to us, while we are shy of ascending to him. Observe how the return answered the request, and outdid it. 1. She called him *her beloved* (and really he was so), and invited him because she loved him; in return to this, he called her his *sister and spouse,* as several times before, *ch.* iv. Those that make Christ their best beloved shall be owned by him in the nearest and dearest relations. 2. She called the garden *his,* and the pleasant fruits of it *his,* and he acknowledges them to be so: It is *my garden,* it is *my spice.* When God was displeased with Israel he turned them off to Moses (They are *thy people,* Exod. xxxii. 7); and he called the appointed feasts of the Lord *their appointed feasts* (Isa. i. 14); but now that they are in his favour he owns them for his garden. "Though of small account, yet it is mine." Those that in sincerity give up themselves and all they have and can do to Jesus Christ, he will do them the honour to stamp them, and what they have and do for him, with his own mark, and say, *It is mine.* 3. She invited him to *come into his garden,* and he says, *I have come.* Isa. lviii. 9, *Thou shalt cry, and he shall say, Here I am.* When Solomon prayed that God would come and take possession of the house he had built for him, he did come; *his glory filled the house* (2 Chron. vii. 2), and (*v.* 16) he let him know that he had chosen and sanctified this house, that his *name might be there for ever.* Those that throw open the door of their souls to Jesus Christ shall find him ready to come in to them; and in every place where he records his name he will meet his people, and bless them, Exod. xx. 24. 4. She desired him to *eat his pleasant fruits,* to accept of the

sacrifices offered in his temple, which were as the fruits of his garden, and he does so, but finds they are not gathered and ready for eating, therefore he does himself gather them. As the fruits are his, so is the preparation of them; he finds the heart unready for his entertainment, but does himself draw out into exercise those gracious habits which he had planted there. What little good there is in us would be shed and lost if he did not gather it, and preserve it to himself. 5. She only desired him to *eat the fruits* of the garden, but he brought along with him something more, *honey,* and *wine,* and *milk,* which yield substantial nourishment, and which were the products of Canaan, Immanuel's land. Christ delights himself greatly in that which he has both conferred upon his people and wrought in them. Or we may suppose this to have been prepared by the spouse herself, as Esther prepared for the king her husband *a banquet of wine;* it is but plain fare, and what is natural, honey and milk, but, being kindly designed, it is kindly accepted; imperfections are overlooked; the honey-comb is eaten with the honey, and the weakness of the flesh passed by and pardoned, because the *spirit is willing.* When Christ appeared to his disciples after his resurrection he did eat with them a piece of a honey-comb (Luke xxiv. 42, 43), in which this scripture was fulfilled. He did not drink the wine only, which is liquor for men, for great men, but the milk too, which is liquor for children, little children, for he was to be the *holy child Jesus,* that had need of milk. 6. She only invited him to come himself, but he, bringing his own entertainment along with him, brings his friends too, and invites them to share in the provisions. *The more the merrier,* we say; and here, where there was so great a plenty, there was not the worse fare. When our Lord Jesus fed 5000 at once *they did all eat and were filled.* Christ invites all his friends to the *wine and milk* which he himself drinks of (Isa. lv. 1), to the *feast of fat things* and *wines on the lees,* Isa. xxv. 6. The great work of man's redemption, and the riches of the covenant of grace, are a feast to the Lord Jesus and they ought to be so to us. The invitation is very free, and hearty, and loving: *Eat, O friends!* If Christ comes to sup with us, it is we that sup with him, Rev. iii. 20. *Eat, O friends!* Those only that are Christ's friends are welcome to his table; his enemies, *that will not have him to reign over them,* have *no part nor lot in the matter. Drink, yea, drink abundantly.* Christ, in his gospel, has made plentiful provision for poor souls. *He fills the hungry with good things;* there is enough for all, there is enough for each; *we are not straitened in him* or in his grace, let us not therefore be straitened in our own bosoms. *Open thy mouth widely, and Christ will fill it. Be not drunk with wine,* but *be filled with the Spirit,* Eph. v. 18. Those that entertain

Christ must bid his friends welcome with him; Jesus and his disciples were called together to the marriage (John ii. 2), and Christ will have all his friends to rejoice with him in the day of his espousals to his church, and, in token of that, to feast with him. In spiritual and heavenly joys there is no danger of exceeding; there we may *drink abundantly, drink of the river of God's pleasures* (Ps. xxxvi. 8), and be *abundantly satisfied,* Ps. lxv. 4.

2 I sleep, but my heart waketh: *it is* the voice of my beloved that knocketh, *saying,* Open to me, my sister, my love, my dove, my undefiled: for my head is filled with dew, *and* my locks with the drops of the night. 3 I have put off my coat; how shall I put it on? I have washed my feet; how shall I defile them? 4 My beloved put in his hand by the hole *of the door,* and my bowels were moved for him. 5 I rose up to open to my beloved; and my hands dropped *with* myrrh, and my fingers *with* sweet smelling myrrh, upon the handles of the lock. 6 I opened to my beloved; but my beloved had withdrawn himself, *and* was gone: my soul failed when he spake: I sought him, but I could not find him; I called him, but he gave me no answer. 7 The watchmen that went about the city found me, they smote me, they wounded me; the keepers of the walls took away my veil from me. 8 I charge you, O daughters of Jerusalem, if ye find my beloved, that ye tell him, that I *am* sick of love.

In this song of loves and joys we have here a very melancholy scene; the spouse here speaks, not to her beloved (as before, for he has withdrawn), but of him, and it is a sad story she tells of her own folly and ill conduct towards him, notwithstanding his kindness, and of the just rebukes she fell under for it. Perhaps it may refer to Solomon's own apostasy from God, and the sad effects of that apostasy after God had come into his garden, had taken possession of the temple he had built, and he had feasted with God upon the sacrifices (*v.* 1); however, it is applicable to the too common case both of churches and particular believers, who by their carelessness and security provoke Christ to withdraw from them. Observe,

I. The indisposition that the spouse was under, and the listlessness that had seized her (*v.* 2): *I sleep, but my heart wakes.* Here is, 1. Corruption appearing in the actings of it:

1080

I sleep. The wise virgins slumbered. She was *on her bed* (ch. iii. 1), but now she sleeps. Spiritual distempers, if not striven against at first, are apt to grow upon us and to get ground. *She slept,* that is, pious affections cooled, she neglected her duty and grew remiss in it, she indulged herself in her ease, was secure and off her watch. This is sometimes the bad effect of more than ordinary enlargements—a good cause. St. Paul himself was in danger of being puffed up with abundant revelations, and of saying, Soul, *take thy ease,* which made a *thorn in the flesh* necessary for him, to keep him from sleeping. Christ's disciples, when he had come into his garden, the garden of his agony, were heavy with sleep, and could not watch with him. True Christians are not always alike lively and vigorous in religion. 2. Grace remaining, notwithstanding, in the habit of it: "*My heart wakes;* my own conscience reproaches me for it, and ceases not to rouse me out of my sluggishness. *The spirit is willing,* and, *after the inner man, I delight in the law of God,* and *with my mind I serve that.* I am, for the present, overpowered by temptation, but all does not go one way in me. I sleep, but it is not a dead sleep; I strive against it; it is not a sound sleep; I cannot be easy under this indisposition." Note, (1.) We ought to take notice of our own spiritual slumbers and distempers, and to reflect upon it with sorrow and shame that we have fallen asleep when Christ has been nigh us in his garden. (2.) When we are lamenting what is amiss in us, we must not overlook the good that is wrought in us, and preserved alive: "My heart wakes in Christ, who is dear to me as my own heart, and is my life; when I sleep, *he neither slumbers nor sleeps.*"

II. The call that Christ gave to her, when she was under this indisposition: *It is the voice of my beloved;* she knew it to be so, and was soon aware of it, which was a sign that her heart was awake. Like the child Samuel, she heard at the first call, but did not, like him, mistake the person; she knew it to be the voice of Christ. He knocks, to awaken us to come and let him in, knocks by his word and Spirit, knocks by afflictions and by our own consciences; though this is not expressly quoted, yet probably it is referred to (Rev. iii. 20), *Behold, I stand at the door, and knock.* He calls sinners into covenant with him and saints into communion with him. Those whom he loves he will not let alone in their carelessness, but will find some way or other to awaken them, to rebuke and chasten them When we are unmindful of Christ he thinks of us, and provides that our faith fail not. Peter denied Christ, but the Lord turned and looked upon him, and so brought him to himself again. Observe how moving the call is · *Open to me, my sister, my love.* 1. He sues for entrance who may demand it; he knocks who could easily knock the door down. 2 He gives her all the kind and most endearing titles imaginable: *My sister, my love, my dove, my undefiled;* he not only gives her no hard names, nor upbraids her with unkindness in not sitting up for him, but, on the contrary, studies how to express his tender affection to her still. *His loving-kindness he will not utterly take away.* Those that by faith are espoused to Christ he looks upon as his sisters, his loves, his doves, and all that is dear; and, being clothed with his righteousness, they are undefiled. This consideration should induce her to open to him. Christ's love to us should engage ours to him, even in the most self-denying instances. *Open to me.* Can we deny entrance to such a friend, to such a guest? Shall we not converse more with one that is infinitely worthy of our acquaintance, and so affectionately desirous of it, though we only can be gainers by it? 3. He pleads distress, and begs to be admitted *sub formâ pauperis—under the character of a poor traveller* that wants a lodging: "*My head is wet with the dew,* with the cold drops of the night; consider what hardships I have undergone, to merit thee, which surely may merit from thee so small a kindness as this." When Christ was crowned with thorns, which no doubt fetched blood from his blessed head, then was his head *wet with the dew.* "Consider what a grief it is to me to be thus unkindly used, as much as it would be to a tender husband to be kept out of doors by his wife in a rainy stormy night." Do we thus requite him for his love? The slights which careless souls put upon Jesus Christ are to him as a *continual dropping in a very rainy day.*

III. The excuse she made to put off her compliance with this call (*v.* 3): *I have put off my coat; how shall I put it on again?* She is half asleep; she knows the voice of her beloved; she knows his knock, but cannot find in her heart to open to him. She was undressed, and would not be at the pains to dress herself again; she had *washed her feet,* and would not have occasion to wash them again. She could not send another to open the door (it must be our own act and deed to let Christ into our hearts), and yet she was loth to go herself; she did not say, *I will not open,* but, *How shall I?* Note, Frivolous excuses are the language of prevailing slothfulness in religion; Christ calls to us to open to him, but we pretend we have no mind, or we have no strength, or we have no time, and therefore think we may be excused, as the *sluggard* that *will not plough by reason of cold.* And those who ought to *watch for the Lord's coming* with their *loins girt,* if they ungird themselves and put off their coat, will find it difficult to recover their former resolution and to put it on again; it is best therefore to keep tight. Making excuses (Luke xiv. 18) is interpreted making light of Christ (Matt. xxii. 5), and so it is. Those put a great contempt upon Christ that cannot find in their hearts to

bear a cold blast for him, or get out of a warm bed.

IV. The powerful influences of divine grace, by which she was made willing to rise and open to her beloved. When he could not prevail with her by persuasion he *put in his hand by the hole of the door,* to unbolt it, as one weary of waiting, *v.* 4. This intimates a work of the Spirit upon her soul, by which she was of unwilling made willing, Ps. cx. 3. The conversion of Lydia is represented by the *opening of her heart* (Acts xvi. 14) and Christ is said to open his disciples' understandings, Luke xxiv. 45. He that *formed the spirit of man within him* knows all the avenues to it, and which way to enter into it; he can find the *hole of the door* at which to put in his hand for the conquering of prejudices and the introducing of his own doctrine and law. He has the *key of David* (Rev. iii. 7), with which he opens the door of the heart in such a way as is suited to it, as the key is fitted to the wards of the lock, in such a way as not to put a force upon its nature, but only upon its ill nature.

V. Her compliance with these methods of divine grace at last: *My bowels were moved for him.* The will was gained by a good work wrought upon the affections: *My bowels were moved for him,* as those of the two disciples were when Christ made their *hearts to burn within them.* She was moved with compassion to her beloved, because his *head was wet with the dew.* Note, Tenderness of spirit, and a heart of flesh, prepare the soul for the reception of Christ into it; and therefore his love to us is represented in such a way as is most affecting. Did Christ redeem us in his pity? Let us in pity receive him, and, for his sake, those that are his, when at any time they are in distress. This good work, wrought upon her affections, raised her up, and made her ashamed of her dulness and slothfulness (*v.* 5, *I rose up, to open to my beloved*), his grace inclining her to do it and conquering the opposition of unbelief. It was her own act, and yet he wrought it in her. And now her *hands dropped with myrrh upon the handles of the lock.* Either, 1. She found it there when she applied her hand to the lock, to shoot it back; he that *put in his hand by the hole of the door* left it there as an evidence that he had been there. When Christ has wrought powerfully upon a soul he leaves a blessed sweetness in it, which is very delightful to it. With this he oiled the lock, to make it go easy. Note, When we apply ourselves to our duty, in the lively exercises of faith, under the influence of divine grace, we shall find it will go on much more readily and sweetly than we expected. If we will but rise up, to open to Christ, we shall find the difficulty we apprehended in it strangely overcome, and shall say with Daniel, *Now let my Lord speak, for thou hast strengthened me,* Dan. x. 19. Or, 2. She brought it thither. Her *bowels being moved for her beloved,* who had stood so long in the cold and wet, when she came to open to him she prepared to anoint his head, and so to refresh and comfort him, and perhaps to prevent his catching cold; she was in such haste to meet him that she would not stay to make the usual preparation, but dipped her hand in her box of ointment, that she might readily anoint his head at his first coming in. Those that open the doors of their hearts to Christ, those *everlasting doors,* must meet him with the lively exercises of faith and other graces, and with these must anoint him.

VI. Her sad disappointment when she did open to her beloved. And here is the most melancholy part of the story: *I opened to my beloved,* as I intended, but, alas! *my beloved had withdrawn himself, and was gone. My beloved was gone, was gone,* so the word is.

1. She did not open to him at his first knock, and now she came too late, when afterwards she *would have inherited this blessing.* Christ will be sought while he may be found; if we slip our time, we may lose our passage. Note, (1.) Christ justly rebukes our delays with his denials, and suspends the communications of comfort from those that are remiss and drowsy in their duty. (2.) Christ's departures are matter of great grief and lamentation to believers. The royal psalmist never complains of any thing with such sorrowful accents as God's *hiding his face* from him, and *casting him off,* and *forsaking him.* The spouse here is ready to tear her hair, and rend her clothes, and wring her hands, crying, *He is gone, he is gone;* and that which cuts her to the heart is that she may thank herself, she provoked him to withdraw. If Christ departs, it is because he takes something unkindly.

2. Now observe what she does, in this case, and what befel her. (1.) She still calls him her *beloved,* being resolved, how cloudy and dark soever the day be, she will not quit her relation to him and interest in him. It is a weakness, upon every apprehension either of our own failings or of God's withdrawings, to conclude hardly as to our spiritual state. Every desertion is not despair. I will say, *Lord, I believe,* though I must say, *Lord, help my unbelief.* Though he leave me, I love him; he is mine. (2.) She now remembers the words he said to her when he called her, and what impressions they made upon her, reproaching herself for her folly in not complying sooner with her convictions: "*My soul failed when he spoke;* his words melted me when he said, *My head is wet with the dew;* and yet, wretch that I was, I lay still, and made excuses, and did not open to him." The smothering and stifling of our convictions is a thing that will be very bitter in the reflection, when God opens our eyes. Sometimes the word has not its effect immediately upon the heart, but it melts it afterwards, upon second thoughts. *My soul* now *melted because of his words* which he had spoken before. (3.) She did not go to bed again, but went in pursuit of him: *I sought him; I called him.* She

might have saved herself this labour if she would but have bestirred herself when he first called; but we cut ourselves out a great deal of work, and create ourselves a great deal of trouble, by our own slothfulness and carelessness in improving our opportunities. Yet it is her praise that, when her beloved has withdrawn, she continues seeking him; her desires towards him are made more strong, and her enquiries after him more solicitous, by his withdrawings. She calls him by prayer, calls after him, and begs of him to return; and she not only prays but uses means, she seeks him in the ways wherein she used to find him. (4.) Yet still she missed of him: *I could not find him; he gave me no answer.* She had no evidence of his favour, no sensible comforts, but was altogether in the dark, and in doubt concerning his love towards her. Note, There are those who have a true love for Christ, and yet have not immediate answers to their prayers for his smiles; but he gives them an equivalent if he strengthens them with strength in their souls to continue seeking him, Ps. cxxxviii. 3. St. Paul could not prevail for the removing of the *thorn in the flesh,* but was answered with grace sufficient for him. (5.) She was ill-treated by the watchmen: *They found me; they smote me; they wounded me, v. 7.* They took her for a lewd woman (because she went about the streets at that time of night, when they were walking their rounds), and beat her accordingly. Disconsolate saints are taken for sinners, and are censured and reproached as such. Thus Hannah, when she was praying in the *bitterness of her soul,* was wounded and smitten by Eli, one of the prime watchmen, when he said to her, *How long wilt thou be drunken?* so counting her a daughter of Belial, 1 Sam. i. 14, 15. It is no new thing for those that are the loyal loving subjects of Zion's King to be misrepresented by the watchmen of Zion, as enemies or scandals to his kingdom; they could not abuse and persecute them but by putting them into an ill name. Some apply it to those ministers who, though watchmen by office, yet misapply the word to awakened consciences, and through unskilfulness, or contempt of their griefs, add affliction to the afflicted, and *make the hearts of the righteous sad whom God would not have made sad* (Ezek. xiii. 22), discouraging those who ought to be encouraged and talking to the grief of those *whom God has wounded,* Ps. lix. 26. Those watchmen were bad enough that could not, or would not, assist the spouse in her enquiries after her beloved (*ch.* iii. 3); but these were much worse, that hindered her with their severe and uncharitable censures, *smote her* and *wounded her* with their reproaches, and though they were the *keepers of the wall of Jerusalem,* as if they had been the breakers of it, *took away her veil* from her rudely and barbarously, as if it had been only a pretence of modesty, but a cover of the contrary. Those whose outward appearances are all good, and who yet are invidiously condemned and run down as hypocrites, have reason to complain, as the spouse here, of the *taking away of their veil* from them. (6.) When she was disabled by the abuses the watchmen gave her to prosecute her enquiry herself she gave charge to those about her to assist her in the enquiry (v. 8): *I charge you, O you daughters of Jerusalem!* all my friends and acquaintance, *if you find my beloved*, it may be you may meet with him before I shall, *what shall you tell him?* so some read. "Speak a good word for me; tell him that *I am sick of love.*" Observe here, [1.] What her condition was. She loved Jesus Christ to such a degree that his absence made her sick, extremely sick, she could not bear it, and she was in pain for his return as a woman in travail, as Ahab for Naboth's vineyard, which he so passionately coveted. This is a sickness which is a sign of a healthy constitution of soul, and will certainly end well, a sickness that will be not death, but life. It is better to be sick of love to Christ than at ease in love to the world. [2.] What course she took in this condition. She did not sink into despair, and conclude she should die of her disease, but she sent after her beloved; she asked the advice of her neighbours, and begged their prayers for her, that they would intercede with him on her behalf. "Tell him, though I was careless, and foolish, and slothful, and rose not up so soon as I should have done to open to him, yet I love him; he *knows all things*, he *knows that I do*. Represent me to him as sincere, though in many instances coming short of my duty; nay, represent me to him as an object of his pity, that he may have compassion on me and help me." She does not bid them tell him how the watchmen had abused her; how unrighteous soever they were in it, she acknowledges that *the Lord is righteous*, and therefore bears it patiently. "But tell him that I am wounded with love to him." Gracious souls are more sensible of Christ's withdrawings than of any other trouble whatsoever.

> Languet amans, non languet amor—
> The lover languishes, but not his love.

9 What *is* thy beloved more than *another* beloved, O thou fairest among women? what *is* thy beloved more than *another* beloved, that thou dost so charge us? 10 My beloved *is* white and ruddy, the chiefest among ten thousand. 11 His head *is as* the most fine gold, his locks *are* bushy, *and* black as a raven. 12 His eyes *are* as *the eyes* of doves by the rivers of waters, washed with milk, *and* fitly set. 13 His cheeks *are* as a bed of spices, *as* sweet flowers: his lips *like* lilies, dropping sweet smelling myrrh. 14 His hands *are* as gold

rings set with the beryl: his belly *is* as bright ivory overlaid *with* sapphires. 15 His legs *are as* pillars of marble, set upon sockets of fine gold: his countenance *is* as Lebanon, excellent as the cedars. 16 His mouth *is* most sweet: yea, he *is* altogether lovely. This *is* my beloved, and this *is* my friend, O daughters of Jerusalem.

Here is, I. The question which the daughters of Jerusalem put to the spouse concerning her beloved, in answer to the charge she had given them, v. 9. Observe, 1. The respectful title they give to the spouse: *O thou fairest among women!* Our Lord Jesus makes his spouse truly amiable, not only in his eyes, but in the eyes of all the daughters of Jerusalem. The church is the most excellent society in the world, the communion of saints the best communion, and the beauty of the sanctuary a transcendent beauty. The saints are the most excellent people; holiness is the symmetry of the soul; it is its agreement with itself; it recommends itself to all that are competent judges of it. Even those that have little acquaintance with Christ, as those daughters of Jerusalem here, cannot but see an amiable beauty in those that bear his image, which we should love wherever we see it, though in different dresses. 2. Their enquiry concerning her beloved: "*What is thy beloved more than another beloved?* If thou wilt have us to find him for thee, give us his marks, that we may know him when we see him." (1.) Some take it for a scornful question, blaming her for making such ado about him: "Why shouldst thou be so passionate in enquiring after thy beloved, more than others are after theirs? Why shouldst thou be so set upon him, more than others that yet have a kindness for him?" Those that are zealous in religion are men wondered at by such as are indifferent to it. The many careless ones laugh at the few that are solicitous and serious. "What is there in him that is so very charming, more than in another person? If he be gone, thou, who art the *fairest among women*, wilt soon have another with an equal flame." Note, Carnal hearts see nothing excellent or extraordinary in the Lord Jesus, in his person or offices, in his doctrine or in his favours; as if there were no more in the knowledge of Christ, and in communion with him, than in the knowledge of the world and in its conversation. (2.) Others rather take it for a serious question, and suppose that those who put it intended, [1.] To comfort the spouse, who, they knew, would recover new spirits if she did but talk awhile of her beloved; nothing would please her better, nor give a more powerful diversion to her grief, than to be put upon the pleasing task of describing the beauties of her beloved. [2.] To inform themselves; they had heard, in general, that he was excellent and glorious, but they desired to know more particularly. They wondered what moved the spouse to charge them concerning her beloved with so much vehemence and concern, and therefore concluded there must be something more in him than in another beloved, which they are willing to be convinced of. *Then* there begin to be some hopes of people when they begin to enquire concerning Christ and his transcendent perfections. And sometimes the extraordinary zeal of one, in enquiring after Christ, may be a means to provoke many (2 Cor. ix. 2), as the apostle, by the faith of the Gentiles, would stir up the Jews to a holy emulation, Rom. xi. 14. See John iv. 10.

II. The account which the spouse gives of her beloved in answer to this question We should always be ready to instruct and assist those that are enquiring after Christ. Experienced Christians, who are well acquainted with Christ themselves, should do all they can to make others acquainted with him.

1. She assures them, in general, that he is one of incomparable perfections and unparalleled worth (*v.* 10): " Do not you know my beloved ? Can the daughters of Jerusalem be ignorant of him that is Jerusalem's crown and crowned head ? Let me tell you then," (1.) That he has every thing in him that is lovely and amiable : *My beloved is white and ruddy,* the colours that make up a complete beauty. This points not at any extraordinary beauty of his body, when he should be incarnate (it was never said of the child Jesus, as of the child Moses, when he was born, that he was *exceedingly fair* (Acts vii. 20); nay, *he had no form nor comeliness,* Isa. liii. 2); but his divine glory, and the concurrence of every thing in him as Mediator, to make him truly lovely in the eyes of those that are enlightened to discern spiritual things. In him we may behold the *beauty of the Lord ;* he was the *holy child Jesus ;* that was his fairness. If we look upon him as made to us *wisdom, righteousness, sanctification, and redemption,* he appears, in all, very amiable. His love to us renders him lovely. He is *white* in the spotless innocency of his life, *ruddy* in the bloody sufferings he went through at his death,—*white* in his glory, as God (when he was transfigured *his raiment was white as the light), ruddy* in his assuming the nature of man, *Adam—red earth,—white* in his tenderness towards his people, *ruddy* in his terrible appearances against his and their enemies. His complexion is a very happy composition. (2.) That he has that loveliness in him which is not to be found in any other : He is *the chief among ten thousand,* a nonsuch for beauty, *fairer than the children of men,* than any of them, than all of them; there is none like him, nor any to be compared with him; every thing else is to be accounted *loss and dung in comparison of him,* Phil. iii. 8.

1084

He is higher than the kings of the earth (Ps. lxxxix. 27) and has *obtained a more excellent name* than any of the principalities and powers of the upper or lower world, Phil. ii. 9 ; Heb. i. iv. He is a *standard-bearer among ten thousand* (so the word is), the tallest and comeliest of the company. He is himself *lifted up as an ensign* (Isa. xi. 10), to whom we must be gathered and must always have an eye. And there is all the reason in the world why he should have the innermost and uppermost place in our souls who is the *fairest of ten thousands* in himself and the fittest of twenty thousands for us.

2. She gives a particular detail of his accomplishments, conceals not his power or comely proportion. Every thing in Christ is amiable. Ten instances she here gives of his beauty, which we need not be nice in the application of, lest the wringing of them bring forth blood and prove the wresting of them. The design, in general, is to show that he is every way qualified for his undertaking, and has all that in him which may recommend him to our esteem, love, and confidence. Christ's appearance to John (Rev. i. 13, &c.) may be compared with the description which the spouse gives of him here, the scope of both being to represent him transcendently glorious, that is, both great and gracious, made lovely in the eyes of believers and making them happy in himself. (1.) *His head is as the most fine gold. The head of Christ is God* (1 Cor. xi. 3), and it is promised to the saints that *the Almighty shall be their gold* (Job xxii. 25), their defence, their treasure; much more was he so to Christ, *in whom dwells all the fulness of the Godhead bodily,* Col. ii. 9. Christ's head bespeaks his sovereign dominion over all and his vital influence upon his church and all its members. This is as *gold, gold;* the former word in the original signifies shining gold, the latter strong solid gold; Christ's sovereignty is both beautiful and powerful. Nebuchadnezzar's monarchy is compared to a *head of gold* (Dan. ii. 38), because it excelled all the other monarchies, and so does Christ's government. (2.) *His locks are bushy and black,* not *black as the tents of Kedar,* whose blackness was their deformity, to which therefore the church compares herself (*ch.* i. 5), but *black as a raven,* whose blackness is his beauty. Sometimes Christ's hair is represented as *white* (Rev. i. 14), denoting his eternity, that he is *the ancient of days;* but here as *black and bushy,* denoting that he is ever young and that there is in him no decay, nothing that waxes old. Every thing that belongs to Christ is amiable in the eyes of a believer, even his hair is so; it was pity that it should be wet, as it was, *with the dew,* and these *locks with the drops of the night,* while he waited to be gracious, *v.* 2. (3.) *His eyes are as the eyes of doves,* fair and clear, and chaste and kind, *by the rivers of waters,* which doves delight in, and in which,

as in a glass, they see themselves. They are washed, to make them clean, *washed with milk*, to make them white, *and fitly set*, neither starting out nor sunk in. Christ is *of purer eyes than to behold iniquity*, for they are doves' eyes, Hab. i. 13. All believers speak with pleasure of the omniscience of Christ, as the spouse here of *his eyes ;* for, though it be terrible to his enemies as *a flame of fire* (Rev. i. 14), yet it is amiable and comfortable to his friends, as *doves' eyes*, for it is a witness to their integrity. *Thou knowest all things, thou knowest that I love thee.* Blessed and holy are those that walk always as under the eye of Christ. (4.) *His cheeks* (the risings of the face) *are as a bed of spices*, raised in the gardens, which are the beauty and wealth of them, and *as sweet flowers*, or towers of sweetness. There is that in Christ's countenance which is amiable in the eyes of all the saints, in the least glimpse of him, for the cheek is but a part of the face. The half discoveries Christ makes of himself to the soul are reviving and refreshing, fragrant above the richest flowers and perfumes. (5.) *His lips are like lilies*, not white like lilies, but sweet and pleasant. Such are *the words of his lips* to all that are sanctified, *sweeter than honey and the honey-comb ;* such are the *kisses of his lips*, all the communications of his grace; *grace is poured into his lips*, and those that heard him *wondered at the gracious words which proceeded out of his mouth. His lips are as* lilies, *dropping sweet-smelling myrrh.* Never any lilies in nature dropped myrrh, but nothing in nature can fully set forth the beauty and excellency of Christ, and therefore, to do it by comparison, there must be a composition of images. (6.) *His hands are as gold rings set with the beryl*, a noted precious stone, *v*. 14. Great men had their hands adorned with gold rings on their fingers, set with diamonds or other precious stones, but, in her eye, *his hands* themselves were *as gold rings ;* all the instances of his power, the works of his hands, all the performances of his providence and grace, are all rich, and pure, and precious, as gold, *as the precious onyx and the sapphire*, all fitted to the purpose for which they were designed *as gold rings* to the finger, and all beautiful and very becoming, *as rings set with beryl.* His hands, which are stretched forth both to receive his people and to give to them, are thus rich and comely. (7.) *His bowels are as bright ivory*, for so it should be rendered, rather than *his belly*, for it is the same word that was used for *bowels* (*v*. 4) and is often ascribed to God (as Isa. lxiii. 15 ; Jer. xxxi. 20), and so it denotes his tender compassion and affection for his spouse, and the love he has to her even in her desolate and deserted state. This love of his is like *bright ivory*, finely polished, and richly *overlaid with sapphires.* The love itself is strong and firm, and the instances and circumstances of it are bright and sparkling, and add much to

the inestimable value of it. (8.) *His legs are as pillars of marble*, so strong, so stately, and no disgrace, no, not to the *sockets of fine gold upon* which they are *set, v*. 15. This bespeaks his stability and stedfastness ; where he sets his foot he will fix it ; he is able to bear all the weight of the government that is upon his shoulders, and his legs will never fail under him. This sets forth the stateliness and magnificence of *the goings of our God, our King, in his sanctuary* (Ps. lxviii. 24), and the steadiness and evenness of all his dispensations towards his people. *The ways of the Lord are equal ;* they are all *mercy and truth ;* these are the *pillars of marble*, more lasting than the pillars of heaven. (9.) *His countenance* (his port and mien) *is as Lebanon*, that stately hill; his aspect beautiful and charming, like the prospect of that pleasant forest or park, *excellent as the cedars*, which, in height and strength, excel other trees, and are of excellent use. Christ is a goodly person; the more we look upon him the more beauty we shall see in him. (10.) *His mouth is most sweet ;* it is sweetness itself; it is *sweetnesses* (so the word is); it is pure essence, nay, it is the quintessence of all delights, *v*. 16. The words of his mouth are all sweet to a believer, sweet as milk to babes (to whom it is agreeable), as honey to those that are grown up (Ps. cxix. 103), to whom it is delicious. The kisses of his mouth, all the tokens of his love, have a transcendent sweetness in them, and are most delightful to those who have their *spiritual senses exercised. To you that believe he is precious.*

3. She concludes with a full assurance both of faith and hope, and so gets the mastery of her trouble. (1.) Here is a full assurance of faith concerning the complete beauty of the Lord Jesus : " *He is altogether lovely.* Why should I stand to mention particulars, when throughout there is nothing amiss?" She is sensible she does him wrong in the particular descriptions of him, and comes far short of the dignity and merit of the subject, and therefore she breaks off with this general encomium : *He is* truly *lovely*, he is wholly so; there is nothing in him but what is amiable, and nothing amiable but what is in him. *He is all desires ;* he has all in him that one can desire. And therefore all her desire is towards him, and she seeks him thus carefully and cannot rest contented in the want of him. Who can but love him who is so lovely ? (2.) Here is a full assurance of hope concerning her own interest in him : " *This is my beloved, and this is my friend ;* and therefore wonder not that I thus long after him." See with what a holy boldness she claims relation to him, and then with what a holy triumph she proclaims it. It is property that sweetens excellency. To see Christ, and not to see him as ours, would be rather a torture than a happiness; but to see one that is thus lovely, and to see him as ours, is a complete satisfaction. Here is a

true believer, [1.] Giving an entire consent to Christ: "He is mine, *my Lord and my God* (John xx. 28), mine according to the tenour of the gospel-covenant, mine in all relations, bestowed upon me, to be all that to me that my poor soul stands in need of." [2.] Taking an entire complacency in Christ. It is spoken of here with an air of triumph: "This is he whom I have chosen, and to whom I have given up myself. None but Christ, none but Christ. This is he on whom my heart is, for he is my best-beloved; this is he in whom I trust, and from whom I expect all good, for *this is my friend.*" Note, Those that make Christ their beloved shall have him their friend; he has been, is, and will be, a special friend to all believers. He loves those that love him; and those that have him their friend have reason to glory in him, and speak of him with delight. "Let others be governed by the love of the world, and seek their happiness in its friendship and favours, *This is my beloved and this is my friend.* Others may do as they please, but this is my soul's choice, my soul's rest, my life, my joy, my all; this is he whom I desire to live and die with."

CHAP. VI.

In this chapter, I. The daughters of Jerusalem, moved with the description which the church had given of Christ, enquire after him, ver. 1. II. The church directs them where they may meet with him, ver. 2, 3. III. Christ is now found of those that sought him, and very highly applauds the beauty of his spouse, as one extremely smitten with it (ver. 4—7), preferring her before all others (ver. 8, 9), recommending her to the love and esteem of all her neighbours (ver. 10), and, lastly, acknowledging the impressions which her beauty had made upon him and the great delight he took in it, ver. 11—13.

WHITHER is thy beloved gone, O thou fairest among women? whither is thy beloved turned aside? that we may seek him with thee. 2 My beloved is gone down into his garden, to the beds of spices, to feed in the gardens, and to gather lilies. 3 I *am* my beloved's, and my beloved *is* mine: he feedeth among the lilies.

Here is, I. The enquiry which the daughters of Jerusalem made concerning Christ, *v.* 1. They still continue their high thoughts of the church, and call her, as before, the *fairest among women;* for true sanctity is true beauty. And now they raise their thoughts higher concerning Christ: *Whither has thy beloved gone, that we may seek him with thee?* This would be but an indecent, unacceptable, compliment, if the song were not to be understood spiritually; for love is jealous of a rival, would monopolize the beloved, and cares not that others should join in seeking him; but those that truly love Christ are desirous that others should love him too, and be joined to him; nay, the greatest instance of duty and respect that the church's children can show to their mother is to join with her in seeking Christ. The *daughters of Jerusalem,* who had asked (*ch.* v. 9), *What is thy beloved more than another beloved?* wondering that

the spouse should be so passionately in love with him, are now of another mind, and are themselves in love with him; for, 1. The spouse had described him, and shown them his excellencies and perfections; and therefore, though they have not seen him, yet, believing, they love him. Those that undervalue Christ do so because they do not know him; when God, by his word and Spirit, discovers him to the soul, with that ray of light the fire of love to him will be kindled. 2. The spouse had expressed her own love to him, her rest in that love, and had triumphed in it: *This is my beloved;* and that flame in her breast scattered sparks into theirs. As sinful lusts, when they break out, defile many, so the pious zeal of some may *provoke many,* 2 Cor. ix. 2. 3. The spouse had bespoken their help in seeking her beloved (*ch.* v. 8); but now they beg hers, for they perceive that now the cloud she had been under began to scatter, and the sky to clear up, and, while she was describing her beloved to them, she herself retrieved her comfort in him. Drooping Christians would find benefit themselves by talking of Christ, as well as do good to others. Now here, (1.) They enquire concerning him, "*Whither has thy beloved gone?* which way must we steer our course in pursuit of him?" Note, Those that are made acquainted with the excellencies of Christ, and the comfort of an interest in him, cannot but be inquisitive after him and desirous to know where they may meet with him. (2.) They offer their service to the spouse to accompany her in quest of him: *We will seek him with thee.* Those that would find Christ must seek him, seek him early, seek him diligently; and it is best seeking Christ in concert, to join with those that are seeking him. We must seek for communion with Christ in communion with saints. We know *whither our beloved has gone;* he has gone to heaven, *to his Father, and our Father.* He took care to send us notice of it, that we might know how to direct to him, John xx. 17. We must by faith see him there, and by prayer seek him there, with boldness *enter into the holiest,* and herein must join with *the generation of those that seek him* (Ps. xxiv. 6), even with *all that in every place call upon him,* 1 Cor. i. 2. We must pray with and for others.

II. The answer which the spouse gave to this enquiry, *v.* 2, 3. Now she complains not any more, as she had done (*ch.* v. 6), "He is gone, he is gone," that she knew not where to find him, or doubted she had lost him for ever; no,

1. Now she knows very well where he is (*v.* 2): "*My beloved* is not to be found in the streets of the city, and the crowd and noise that are there; there I have in vain looked for him" (as his parents *sought him among their kindred and acquaintance, and found him not*); "but he *has gone down to* his garden, a place of privacy and retire-

ment." The more we withdraw from the hurry of the world the more likely we are to have acquaintance with Christ, who took his disciples into a garden, there to be witnesses of the agonies of his love. Christ's church is a garden enclosed, and separated from the open common of the world; it is *his garden*, which he has planted as he did the garden of Eden, which he takes care of, and delights in. Though he has gone up to the paradise above, yet he comes down to his garden on earth; it lies low, but he condescends to visit it, and wonderful condescension it is. *Will God in very deed dwell with man upon the earth?* Those that would find Christ may expect to meet with him in *his garden* the church, for *there he records his name* (Exod. xx. 24); they must attend upon him in the ordinances which he has instituted, the word, sacraments, and prayer, wherein he will be with us *always, even to the end of the world.* The spouse here refers to what Christ had said (*ch.* v. 1), *I have come into my garden.* It is as if she had said, "What a fool was I to fret and fatigue myself in seeking him where he was not, when he himself had told me where he was!" Words of direction and comfort are often out of the way when we have occasion to use them, till the blessed Spirit brings them to our remembrance, and then we wonder how we overlooked them. Christ has told us that he would *come into his garden ;* thither therefore we must go to seek him. *The beds,* and smaller *gardens,* in this greater, are the particular churches, the *synagogues of God in the land* (Ps. lxxiv. 8); the *spices* and *lilies* are particular believers, the planting of the Lord, and pleasant in his eyes. When Christ comes down to his church it is, (1.) *To feed* among *the gardens,* to feed his flock, which he feeds not, as other shepherds, in the open fields, but in his garden, so well are they provided for, Ps. xxiii. 2. He comes to feed his friends, and entertain them; there you may not only find him, but find his table richly furnished, and a hearty welcome to it. He comes to feed himself, that is, to please himself with the products of his own grace in his people ; *for the Lord takes pleasure in those that fear him.* He has many gardens, many particular churches of different sizes and shapes ; but, while they are his, he feeds in them all, manifests himself among them, and is well pleased with them. (2.) *To gather lilies,* wherewith he is pleased to entertain and adorn himself. He picks the lilies one by one, and gathers them to himself; and there will be a general harvest of them at the great day, when he will send forth his angels, to gather all his lilies, that he may be for ever glorified and admired in them.

2. She is very confident of her own interest in him (*v.* 3): " *I am my beloved's, and my beloved is mine ;* the relation is mutual, and the knot is tied, which cannot be loosed; for *he feeds among the lilies,* and my commu-nion with him is a certain token of my interest in him." She had said this before (*ch.* ii. 16); but, (1.) Here she repeats it as that which she resolved to abide by, and which she took an unspeakable pleasure and satisfaction in; she liked her choice too well to change. Our communion with God is very much maintained and kept up by the frequent renewing of our covenant with him and rejoicing in it. (2.) She had occasion to repeat it, for she had acted unkindly to her beloved, and, for her so doing, he had justly withdrawn himself from her, and therefore there was occasion to take fresh hold of the covenant, which continues firm between Christ and believers, notwithstanding their failings and his frowns, Ps. lxxxix. 30—35. " I have been careless and wanting in my duty, and yet *I am my beloved's ;*" for every transgression in the covenant does not throw us out of covenant. " He has justly hidden his face from me and denied me his comforts, and yet *my beloved is mine ;*" for rebukes and chastenings are not only consistent with, but they flow from covenant-love. (3.) When we have not a full assurance of Christ's love we must live by a faithful adherence to him. " Though I have not the sensible consolation I used to have, yet I will cleave to this, *Christ is mine and I am his.*" (4.) Though she had said the same before, yet now she inverts the order, and asserts his interest in her first: *I am my beloved's,* entirely devoted and dedicated to him; and then her interest in him and in his grace: " *My beloved is mine,* and I am happy, truly happy in him." If our own hearts can but witness for us that we are his, there is no room left to question his being ours; for the covenant never breaks on his side. (5.) It is now her comfort, as it was then, that *he feeds among the lilies,* that he takes delight in his people and converses freely with them, as we do with those with whom we feed; and therefore, though at present he be withdrawn, " I shall meet with him again. *I shall yet praise him who is the health of my countenance, and my God.*"

4 Thou *art* beautiful, O my love, as Tirzah, comely as Jerusalem, terrible as *an army* with banners. 5 Turn away thine eyes from me, for they have overcome me : thy hair *is* as a flock of goats that appear from Gilead. 6 Thy teeth *are* as a flock of sheep which go up from the washing, whereof every one beareth twins, and *there is* not one barren among them. 7 As a piece of a pomegranate *are* thy temples within thy locks. 8 There are threescore queens, and fourscore concubines, and virgins without number. 9 My dove, my undefiled is *but* one ; she *is* the *only* one of her

mother, she *is* the choice *one* of her that bare her. The daughters saw her, and blessed her ; *yea,* the queens and the concubines, and they praised her. 10 Who *is* she *that* looketh forth as the morning, fair as the moon, clear as the sun, *and* terrible as *an army* with banners ?

Now we must suppose Christ graciously returned to his spouse, from whom he had withdrawn himself, returned to converse with her (for he speaks to her and *makes her to hear joy and gladness),* returned to favour her, having forgiven and forgotten all her unkindness, for he speaks very tenderly and respectfully to her.

I. He pronounces her truly amiable (*v.* 4): *Thou art beautiful, O my love! as Tirzah,* a city in the tribe of Manasseh, whose name signifies *pleasant,* or *acceptable,* the situation, no doubt, being very happy and the building fine and uniform. *Thou art comely as Jerusalem,* a city *compact together* (Ps. cxxii. 3), and which Solomon had built and beautified, *the joy of the whole earth;* it was an honour to the world (whether they thought so or no) that there was such a city in it. It was the holy city, and that was the greatest beauty of it ; and fitly is the church compared to it, for it was figured and typified by it. The gospel-church is *the Jerusalem that is above* (Gal. iv. 26), *the heavenly Jerusalem* (Heb. xii. 22) ; in it God has *his sanctuary,* and is, in a special manner, present ; thence he has the tribute of praise issuing ; it is his rest for ever, and therefore it is *comely as Jerusalem,* and, being so, is *terrible as an army with banners.* Church-censures, duly administered, strike an awe upon men's consciences ; the word (the weapons of her warfare) *casts down imaginations* (2 Cor. x. 5), and even an unbeliever is convinced and judged by the solemnity of holy ordinances, 1 Cor. xiv. 24, 25. The saints by faith *overcome the world* (1 John v. 4) ; nay, like Jacob, they have *power with God and prevail,* Gen. xxxii. 28.

II. He owns himself in love with her, *v.* 5. Though, for a small moment, and in a little wrath, he had hid his face from her, yet now he gathers her with very surprising instances of *everlasting lovingkindness,* Isa. liv. 8. *Turn thy eyes towards me* (so some read it), " turn the eyes of faith and love towards me, *for they have lifted me up* ; look unto me, and be comforted." When we are calling to God to turn the eye of his favour towards us he is calling to us to turn the eye of our obedience towards him. We read it as a strange expression of love, " *Turn away thy eyes from me, for* I cannot bear the brightness of them; *they have* quite *overcome me,* and I am prevailed with to overlook all that is past ;" as God said to Moses, when he interceded for Israel, " *Let me alone,* or I must yield," Exod.

xxxii. 10. Christ is pleased to borrow these expressions of a passionate lover only to express the tenderness of a compassionate Redeemer, and the delight he takes in his redeemed and in the workings of his own grace in them.

III. He repeats, almost word for word, part of the description he had given of her beauty (*ch.* iv. 1—3), her *hair,* her *teeth,* her *temples* (*v.* 5—7), not because he could not have described it in other words, and by other similitudes, but to show that he had still the same esteem for her since her unkindness to him, and his withdrawings from her, that he had before. Lest she should think that, though he would not quite cast her off, yet he would think the worse of her while he knew her, he says the same of her now that he had done ; for those°*to whom much is forgiven will love the more,* and, consequently, will be the more beloved, for Christ has said, *I love those that love me.* He is pleased with his people, notwithstanding their weaknesses, when they sincerely repent of them and return to their duty, and commends them as if they had already arrived at perfection.

IV. He prefers her before all competitors, and sees all the beauties and perfections of others meeting and centering in her (*v.* 8, 9): "*There are,* it may be, *threescore queens,* who, like Esther, have by their beauty attained to the royal state and dignity, *and fourscore concubines,* whom kings have preferred before their own queens, as more charming, and these attended by their maids of honour, *virgins without number,* who, when there is a ball at court, appear in great splendour, with beauty that dazzles the eyes of the spectators; but *my dove, my undefiled, is but one,* a holy one." 1. She excels them all. Go through all the world, and view the societies of men that reckon themselves wise and happy, kingdoms, courts, senates, councils, or whatever incorporations you may think valuable, they are none of them to be compared with the church of Christ ; their honours and beauties are nothing to hers. *Who is like unto thee, O Israel!* Deut. xxxiii. 29 ; iv. 6, 7. There are particular persons, as *virgins without number,* who are famed for their accomplishments, the beauties of their address, language, and performances, but the beauty of holiness is beyond all other beauty : " *My dove, my undefiled, is one,* has that one beauty that she is a dove, an undefiled dove, and mine, and that makes her excel the queens and virgins, though they were ever so many." 2. She includes them all. " Other kings have many queens, and concubines, and virgins, with whose conversation they entertain themselves, but *my dove, my undefiled,* is to me instead of all ; in that one I have more than they have in all theirs." Or, " Though there are many particular churches, some of greater dignity, others of less, some of longer, others of shorter, standing, and many particular believers, of different gifts and attainments, some more eminent, others less so, yet they all constitute but one catholic church, are all but parts of that whole, and that is *my dove, my undefiled."* Christ is the centre of the church's unity; all the children of God that are scattered abroad are gathered by him (John xi. 52), and meet in him (Eph. i. 10), and are all his doves.

V. He shows how much she was esteemed, not by him only, but by all that had acquaintance with her and stood in relation to her. It would add to her praise to say, 1. That she was her mother's darling; she had that in her, from a child, which recommended her to the particular affection of her parents. As Solomon himself is said to have been *tender and an only one in the sight of his mother* (Prov. iv. 3), so was she *the only one of her mother,* as dear as if she had been an only one, and, if there were many more, yet she was *the choice one of her that bore her,* more excellent than all the societies of men this world ever produced. All the kingdoms of the world, and the glory of them, are nothing, in Christ's account, compared with the church, which is made up of *the excellent ones of the earth,* the *precious sons of Zion, comparable to fine gold,* and *more excellent than their neighbours.* 2. That she was admired by all her acquaintance, not only *the daughters,* who were her juniors, but even *the queens and the concubines,* who might have reason to be jealous of her as a rival; *they* all *blessed her,* and wished well to her, *praised her,* and spoke well of her. The *daughters of Jerusalem* called her the *fairest among women;* all agreed to give her the pre-eminence for beauty, and every sheaf bowed to hers. Note, (1.) Those that have any correct sense of things cannot but be convinced in their consciences (whatever they say) that godly people are excellent people; many will give them their good word, and more their good-will. (2.) Jesus Christ takes notice what people think and speak of his church, and is well pleased with those that honour such as fear the Lord, and takes it ill of those that despise them, particularly when they are under a cloud, that *offend any of his little ones.*

VI. He produces the encomium that was given of her, and makes it his own (*v.* 10): *Who is she that looks forth as the morning?* This is applicable both to the church in the world and to grace in the heart.

1. They are amiable as the light, the most beautiful of all visible things. Christians are, or should be, the lights of the world. The patriarchal church *looked forth as the morning* when the promise of the Messiah was first made known, and *the day-spring from on high visited* this dark world. The Jewish church was *fair as the moon;* the ceremonial law was an imperfect light; it shone by reflection; it was changing as the moon, did not make day, nor had *the sun of righteousness yet risen.* But the Christian church is *clear as the sun,* exhibits a great *light to those that sat in dark-*

ness. Or we may apply it to the kingdom of grace, the gospel-kingdom. (1.) In its rise, it *looks forth as the morning* after a dark night; it is discovering (Job xxxviii. 12, 13), and very acceptable, *looks forth* pleasantly as a clear morning; but it is small in its beginnings, and scarcely perceptible at first. (2.) It is, at the best, in this world, but *fair as the moon,* which shines with a borrowed light, which has her changes and eclipses, and her spots too, and, when at the full, does but rule by night. But, (3.) When it is perfected in the kingdom of glory then it will be *clear as the sun,* the church *clothed with the sun,* with Christ *the sun of righteousness,* Rev. xii. 1. Those that love God will then be *as the sun when he goes forth in his strength* (Judg. v. 31; Matt. xiii. 43); they shall shine in inexpressible glory, and that which is perfect will then come; there shall be no darkness, no spots, Isa. xxx. 26.

2. The beauty of the church and of believers is not only amiable, but *awful as an army with banners.* The church, in this world, is *as an army,* as the camp of Israel in the wilderness; its state is militant; it is in the midst of enemies, and is engaged in a constant conflict with them. Believers are soldiers in this army. It has its *banners;* the gospel of Christ is an ensign (Isa. xi. 12), the love of Christ, *ch.* ii. 4. It is marshalled, and kept in order and under discipline. It is *terrible* to its enemies, as Israel in the wilderness was, Exod. xv. 14. When Balaam saw Israel encamped according to their tribes, by their standards, with colours displayed, he said, *How goodly are thy tents, O Jacob!* Num. xxiv. 5. When the church preserves her purity she secures her honour and victory; when she is *fair as the moon,* and *clear as the sun,* she is truly great and formidable.

11 I went down into the garden of nuts to see the fruits of the valley, *and* to see whether the vine flourished, *and* the pomegranates budded. 12 Or ever I was aware, my soul made me *like* the chariots of Amminadib. 13 Return, return, O Shulamite; return, return, that we may look upon thee. What will ye see in the Shulamite? As it were the company of two armies.

Christ having now returned to his spouse, and the breach being entirely made up, and the falling out of these lovers being the renewing of love, Christ here gives an account both of the distance and of the reconciliation.

I. That when he had withdrawn from his church as his spouse, and did not comfort her, yet even then he had his eye upon it as his garden, which he took care of (*v.* 11): " *I went down into the garden of nuts,* or nutmegs, *to see the fruits of the valley,* with complacency and concern, to see them as my own." When he was out of sight ne was no further off than the garden, hid among the trees of the garden, in a low and dark valley; but then he was observing *how the vine flourished,* that he might do all that to it which was necessary to promote its flourishing, and might delight himself in it as a man does in a fruitful garden. He went to see whether *the pomegranates budded.* Christ observes the first beginnings of the good work of grace in the soul and the early buddings of devout affections and inclinations there, and is well pleased with them, as we are with the blossoms of the spring.

II. That yet he could not long content himself with this, but suddenly felt a powerful, irresistible, inclination in his own bosom to return to his church, as his spouse, being moved with her lamentations after him, and her languishing desire towards him (*v.* 12): " *Or ever I was aware, my soul made me like the chariots of Ammi-nadib;* I could not any longer keep at a distance; my repentings were kindled together, and I presently resolved to fly back to the arms of my love, my dove." Thus Joseph made himself strange to his brethren, for a while, to chastise them for their former unkindnesses, and make trial of their present temper, till he could no longer refrain himself, but, *or ever he was aware,* burst out into tears, and said, *I am Joseph,* Gen. xlv. 1, 3. And now the spouse perceives, as David did (Ps. xxxi. 22), that though she *said in her haste, I am cut off from before thy eyes,* yet, at the same time, he *heard the voice of her supplications,* and became *like the chariots of Ammi-nadib,* which were noted for their beauty and swiftness. *My soul put me into the chariots of my willing people* (so some read it), "the chariots of their faith, and hope, and love, their desires, and prayers, and expectations, which they sent after me, to fetch me back, as chariots of fire with horses of fire." Note, 1. Christ's people are, and ought to be, a willing people. 2. If they continue seeking Christ and longing after him, even when he seems to withdraw from them, he will graciously return to them in due time, perhaps sooner than they think and with a pleasing surprise. No chariots sent for Christ shall return empty. 3. All Christ's gracious returns to his people take rise from himself. It is not they, it is his own soul, that puts him into the chariots of his people; for he is gracious because he will be gracious, and loves his Israel because he would love them; not for their sakes, be it known to them.

III. That he, having returned to her, kindly courted her return to him, notwithstanding the discouragements she laboured under. Let her not despair of obtaining as much comfort as ever she had before this distance happened, but take the comfort of the return of her beloved, *v.* 13. Here, 1. The church is called the *Shulamite,* referring either to *Solomon,* the bridegroom in type, by whose name she

is called, in token of her relation to him and union with him (thus believers are called *Christians* from *Christ*), or referring to *Salem,* the place of her birth and residence, as the woman of *Shunem* is called the *Shunamite.* Heaven is the Salem whence the saints have their birth, and where they have their citizenship; those that belong to Christ, and are bound for heaven, shall be called *Shulamites.* 2. She is invited to return, and the invitation most earnestly pressed : *Return, return;* and again, " *Return, return;* recover the peace thou hast lost and forfeited ; come back to thy former composedness and cheerfulness of spirit." Note, Good Christians, after they have had their comfort disturbed, are sometimes hard to be pacified, and need to be earnestly persuaded to return again to their rest. As revolting sinners have need to be called to again and again *(Turn you, turn you, why will you die?)* so disquieted saints have need to be called to again and again, *Turn you, turn you,* why will you droop; *Why art thou cast down, O my soul?* 3. Having returned, she is desired to show her face : *That we may look upon thee.* Go no longer with thy face covered like a mourner. Let those that have made their peace with God *lift up their faces without spot* (Job xxii. 26); let them come boldly to his throne of grace. Christ is pleased with the cheerfulness and humble confidence of his people, and would have them look pleasant. "Let us *look upon thee,* not I only, but the holy angels, who rejoice in the consolation of saints as well as in the conversion of sinners; not I only, but all the daughters." Christ and believers are pleased with the beauty of the church. 4. A short account is given of what is to be seen in her. The question is asked, *What will you see in the Shulamite?* And it is answered, *As it were the company of two armies.* (1.) Some think she gives this account of herself; she is shy of appearing, unwilling to be looked upon, having, in her own account, no form nor comeliness. Alas! says she, *What will you see in the Shulamite?* nothing that is worth your looking upon, nothing but *as it were the company of two armies* actually engaged, where nothing is to be seen but blood and slaughter. The watchmen had smitten her, and wounded her, and she carried in her face the marks of those wounds, looked as if she had been fighting. She had said (*ch.* i. 6), *Look not upon me because I am black;* here she says, "Look not upon me because I am bloody." Or it may denote the constant struggle that is between grace and corruption in the souls of believers; they are in them *as two armies* continually skirmishing, which makes her ashamed to show her face. (2.) Others think her beloved gives this account of her. "I will tell you what you shall *see in the Shulamite;* you shall see as noble a sight as that of two armies, or two parts of the same army, drawn out in rank and file; not only *as an army with banners,* but as *two armies*, with a majesty double to what was before spoken; she is as *Mahanaim*, as the two hosts which Jacob saw (Gen. xxxii. 1, 2), a host of saints and a host of angels ministering to them; the church militant, the church triumphant." Behold *two armies;* in both the church appears beautiful.

CHAP. VII.

In this chapter, I. Christ, the royal bridegroom, goes on to describe the beauties of his spouse, the church, in many instances, and to express his love to her and the delight he has in her conversation, ver. 1—9. II. The spouse, the church, expresses her great delight in him, and the desire that she had of communion and fellowship with him, ver. 10—13. Such mutual esteem and endearment are there between Christ and believers. And what is heaven but an everlasting interchanging of loves between the holy God and holy souls!

HOW beautiful are thy feet with shoes, O prince's daughter! the joints of thy thighs *are* like jewels, the work of the hands of a cunning workman. 2 Thy navel *is like* a round goblet, *which* wanteth not liquor: thy belly *is like* a heap of wheat set about with lilies. 3 Thy two breasts *are* like two young roes *that are* twins. 4 Thy neck *is* as a tower of ivory; thine eyes *like* the fishpools in Heshbon, by the gate of Bath-rabbim: thy nose *is* as the tower of Lebanon which looketh toward Damascus. 5 Thine head upon thee *is* like Carmel, and the hair of thine head like purple; the king *is* held in the galleries. 6 How fair and how pleasant art thou, O love, for delights! 7 This thy stature is like to a palm tree, and thy breasts to clusters *of grapes*. 8 I said, I will go up to the palm tree, I will take hold of the boughs thereof: now also thy breasts shall be as clusters of the vine, and the smell of thy nose like apples; 9 And the roof of thy mouth like the best wine for my beloved, that goeth *down* sweetly, causing the lips of those that are asleep to speak.

The title which Jesus Christ here gives to the church is new: *O prince's daughter!* agreeing with Ps. xlv. 13, where she is called *the king's daughter*. She is so in respect of her new birth, born from above, begotten of God, and his workmanship, bearing the image of the King of kings, and guided by his Spirit. She is so by marriage; Christ, by betrothing her to himself, though he found her mean and despicable, has made her a *prince's daughter*. She has a princely disposition, something in her truly noble and generous; she is daughter and heir to the prince of the kings of the earth. *If children, then heirs.* Now here we have,

I. A copious description of the beauty of the spouse, which, some think, is given by the virgins her companions, and that those were they who called upon her to return; it seems rather to be given by Christ himself, and to be designed to express his love to her and delight in her, as before, *ch.* iv. 1, &c., and *ch.* vi. 5, 6. The similitudes are here different from what they were before, to show that the beauty of holiness is such as nothing in nature can reach; you may still say more of it, and yet still come short of it. That commendation of the spouse, *ch.* iv., was immediately upon the espousals (*ch.* iii. 11), this upon her return from a by-path (*ch.* vi. 13); yet this exceeds that, to show the constancy of Christ's love to his people; *he loves them to the end*, since he made them *precious in his sight and honourable*. The spouse had described the beauty of her beloved in ten particulars (*ch.* v. 11, &c.); and now he describes her in as many, for he will not be behindhand with her in respects and endearments. Those that honour Christ he will certainly honour, and make honourable. As the prophet, in describing the corruptions of degenerate Israel, reckons *from the sole of the foot even unto the head* (Isa. i. 6), so here the beauties of the church are reckoned from foot to head, that, as the apostle speaks, when he is comparing the church, as here, to the natural body (1 Cor. xii. 23), *more abundant honour might be bestowed on those parts of the body which we think to be less honourable, and which therefore lacked honour, v. 24.* 1. Her *feet* are here praised; the feet of Christ's ministers are beautiful in the eyes of the church (Isa. lii. 7), and her feet are here said to be beautiful in the eyes of Christ. *How beautiful are thy feet with shoes!* When believers, being made free from the captivity of sin (Acts xii. 8), *stand fast in the liberty with which they are made free*, preserve the tokens of their enfranchisement, have *their feet shod with the preparation of the gospel of peace*, and walk steadily according to the rule of the gospel, then their *feet are beautiful with shoes;* they tread firmly, being well armed against the troubles they meet with in their way. When we rest not in good affections, but they are accompanied with sincere endeavours and resolutions, then our feet are beautified *with shoes*. See Ezek. xvi. 10. 2. *The joints of the thighs are* here said to be *like jewels*, and those curiously wrought by *a cunning workman*. This is explained by Eph. iv. 16 and Col. ii. 19, where the mystical body of Christ is said to be held together by *joints and bands*, as the hips and knees (both which are *the joints of the thighs)* serve the natural body in its strength and motion. The church is *then* comely in Christ's eyes when those joints are kept firm by holy love and unity, and the communion of saints. When believers act in religion from good principles, and are steady and regular in their whole conversation, and turn themselves easily to every duty in its time and place, then *the joints are like jewels*. 3. The *navel* is here compared to a round cup or *goblet*, that *wants not* any of the agreeable *liquor* that one would wish to find in it, such as David's cup that ran over (Ps. xxiii. 5), well shaped, and not as that miserable infant whose navel was not cut, Ezek. xvi. 4. The fear of the Lord is said to be *health to the navel*. See Prov. iii. 8. When the soul wants not that fear then the *navel wants not liquor*. 4. The *belly is like a heap of wheat* in the store-chamber, which perhaps was sometimes, to make show, adorned with flowers. The *wheat* is useful, the *lilies* are beautiful; there is every thing in the church which may be to the members of that body either for use or for ornament. All the body is nourished from the *belly;* it denotes the spiritual prosperity of a believer and the healthful constitution of the soul, all in good plight. 5. The *breasts are like two young roes that are twins, v.* 3. By the breasts of the church's consolations those are nourished who are born from its belly (Isa. xlvi. 3), and by the navel received nourishment in the womb. This comparison we had before, *ch.* iv. 5. 6. The *neck*, which before was compared to *the tower of David* (*ch.* iv. 4), is here compared to *a tower of ivory*, so white, so precious; such is the faith of the saints, by which they are joined to Christ their head. The name of the Lord, improved by faith, is to the saints as a strong and impregnable tower. 7. The *eyes* are compared to *the fish-pools in Heshbon*, or the artificial fish-ponds, *by a gate*, either of Jerusalem or of Heshbon, which is called *Bath-rabbim*, the daughter of a multitude, because a great thoroughfare. The understanding, the intentions of a believer, are clean and clear as these ponds. The eyes, weeping for sin, are as fountains (Jer. ix. 1), and comely with Christ. 8. The *nose* is like *the tower of Lebanon*, the forehead or face set *like a flint* (Isa. l. 7), undaunted as that tower was impregnable. So it denotes the magnanimity and holy bravery of the church, or (as others) a spiritual sagacity to discern things that differ, as animals strangely distinguish by the smell. This tower *looks towards Damascus*, the head city of Syria, denoting the boldness of the church in facing its enemies and not fearing them. 9. The *head like Carmel*, a very high hill near the sea, *v.* 5. The head of a believer is *lifted up above his enemies* (Ps. xxvii. 6), above the storms of the lower region, as the top of Carmel was, pointing heaven-ward. The more we get above this world, and the nearer to heaven, and the more secure and serene we become by that means, the more amiable we are in the eyes of the Lord Jesus. 10. The *hair of the head* is said to be *like purple*. This denotes the universal amiableness of a believer in the eyes of Christ, even to *the hair*, or (as some understand it) the pins with which *the hair* is dressed. Some by *the head and the hair* understand the governors of the church, who, if they be careful to do their duty, add much to her comeliness. *The head*

like crimson (so some read it) *and the hair like purple*, the two colours worn by great men.

II. The complacency which Christ takes in his church thus beautified and adorned. She is lovely indeed if she be so in his eyes; as he puts the comeliness upon her, so it is his love that makes this comeliness truly valuable, for he is an unexceptionable judge. 1. He delighted to look upon his church, and to converse with it, rejoicing in that habitable part of his earth : *The king is held in the galleries*, and cannot leave them. This is explained by Ps. cxxxii. 13, 14, *The Lord has chosen Zion*, saying, *This is my rest for ever; here will I dwell;* and Ps. cxlvii. 11, *The Lord takes pleasure in those that fear him.* And, if Christ has such delight *in the galleries* of communion with his people, much more reason have they to delight in them, and to reckon *a day there better than a thousand*. 2. He was even struck with admiration at the beauty of his church (*v.* 6) : *How fair and how pleasant art thou, O love! How art thou made fair!* (so the word is), "not born so, but made so with the comeliness which I have put upon thee." Holiness is a beauty beyond expression; the Lord Jesus is wonderfully pleased with it; the outward aspect of it is fair; the inward disposition of it is pleasant and highly agreeable, and the complacency he has in it is inexpressible. *O my dearest for delights!* so some read it. 3. He determined to keep up communion with his church. (1.) To *take hold of* her as of *the boughs* of *a palm-tree*. He compares her *stature to a palm-tree* (*v.* 7), so straight, so strong, does she appear, when she is looked upon in her full proportion. The *palm-tree* is observed to flourish most when it is loaded ; so the church, the more it has been afflicted, the more it has multiplied ; and the branches of it are emblems of victory. Christ says, "*I will go up to the palm-tree*, to entertain myself with the shadow of it (*v.* 8) and *I will take hold of its boughs* and observe the beauty of them." What Christ has said he will do, in favour to his people ; we may be sure he will do it, for his kind purposes are never suffered to fall to the ground ; and if he *take hold of the boughs* of his church, take early hold of her branches, when they are young and tender, he will keep his hold and not let them go. (2.) To refresh himself with her fruits. He compares her *breasts* (her pious affections towards him) *to clusters of grapes*, a most pleasant fruit (*v.* 7), and he repeats it (*v.* 8) : They *shall be* (that is, they shall be to me) *as clusters of the vine*, which *make glad the heart*. "Now that I come *up to the palm-tree* thy graces shall be exerted and excited." Christ's presence with his people kindles the holy heavenly fire in their souls, and then their *breasts shall be as clusters of the vine*, a cordial to themselves and acceptable to him. And since God, at first, *breathed into man's nostrils the breath of life*, and breathes the breath of the new life still, the smell *of* their nostrils is *like the smell of apples*, or oranges, which is pleasing and reviving. *The Lord smelt a sweet savour* from Noah's sacrifice, Gen. viii. 21. And, *lastly, the roof of her mouth is like the best wine (v. 9)* ; her spiritual taste and relish, or the words she speaks to God and man, which come not from the teeth outward, but from *the roof of the mouth*, these are pleasing to God. *The prayer of the upright is his delight.* And, when *those that fear the Lord speak one to another* as becomes them, *the Lord hearkens, and hears* with pleasure, Mal. iii. 16. It is like that wine which is, [1.] Very palatable and grateful to the taste. It *goes down sweetly* ; it *goes straightly* (so the margin reads it); it *moves itself aright*, Prov. xxiii. 31. The pleasures of sense seem right to the carnal appetite, and go down smoothly, but they are often wrong, and, compared with the pleasure of communion with God, they are harsh and rough. Nothing *goes down* so *sweetly* with a gracious soul as the wine of God's consolations. [2.] It is a great cordial. The presence of Christ by his Spirit with his people shall be reviving and refreshing to them, as that strong wine which makes *the lips* even *of those that are asleep* (that are ready to faint away in a deliquium), *to speak*. Unconverted sinners are asleep ; saints are often drowsy, and listless, and half asleep ; but the word and Spirit of Christ will put life and vigour into the soul, and *out of the abundance of the heart* that is thus filled *the mouth* will *speak*. When the apostles were filled with the Spirit they spoke *with tongues the wonderful works of God* (Acts ii. 10, 12) ; and those who in opposition to being *drunk with wine, wherein is excess*, are *filled with the Spirit, speak to themselves in psalms and hymns*, Eph. v. 18, 19. When Christ is thus commending the sweetness of his spouse's love, excited by the manifestation of his, she seems to put in that word, *for my beloved*, as in a parenthesis. "Is there any thing in me that is pleasant or valuable? As it is from, so it is for my beloved." Then he delights in our good affections and services, when they are all for him and devoted to his glory.

10 I *am* my beloved's, and his desire *is* toward me. 11 Come, my beloved, let us go forth into the field ; let us lodge in the villages. 12 Let us get up early to the vineyards ; let us see if the vine flourish, *whether* the tender grape appear, *and* the pomegranates bud forth : there will I give thee my loves. 13 The mandrakes give a smell, and at our gates *are* all manner of pleasant *fruits*, new and old, *which* I have laid up for thee, O my beloved.

These are the words of the spouse, the church, the believing soul, in answer to the

kind expressions of Christ's love in the foregoing verses.

I. She here triumphs in her relation to Christ and her interest in him, and in his name will she boast all the day long. With what a transport of joy and holy exultation does she say (*v.* 10), " *I am my beloved's*, not my own, but entirely devoted to him and owned by him." If we can truly say that Christ is our *best beloved*, we may be confident that we are his and he *will save us*, Ps. cxix. 94. The gracious discoveries of Christ's love to us should engage us greatly to rejoice in the hold he has of us, his sovereignty over us and property in us, which is no less a spring of comfort than a bond of duty. Intimacy of communion with Christ should help to clear up our interest in him. Glorying in this, that she is his, to serve him, and reckoning that her honour, she comforts herself with this, that his *desire is towards her*, that is, he is her husband ; it is a periphrasis of the conjugal relation, Gen. iii 16. Christ's desire was strongly towards his chosen remnant, when he came from heaven to earth to seek and save them ; and when, in pursuance of his undertaking, he was even straitened till the baptism of blood he was to pass through for them *was accomplished*, Luke xii. 50. He desired *Zion for a habitation;* this is a comfort to believers that, whosoever slights them, Christ has a desire towards them, such a desire as will again bring him from heaven to earth to receive them to himself; for he longs to have them all with him, John xvii. 24 ; xiv. 3.

II. She humbly and earnestly desires communion with him (*v.* 11, 12): " Come, *my beloved*, let us take a walk together, that I may receive counsel, instruction, and comfort from thee, and may make known my wants and grievances to thee, with freedom, and without interruption." Thus Christ walked with the two disciples that were going to the village called *Emmaus*, and talked with them, till he made their *hearts burn within them*. Observe here, 1. Having received fresh tokens of his love, and full assurances of her interest in him, she presses forward towards further acquaintance with him ; as blessed Paul, who desired yet more and more of *the excellency of the knowledge of Christ Jesus*, Phil. iii. 8. Christ has made it to appear how much his desire is towards us, and we are very ungrateful if ours be not towards him. Note, Communion with Christ is that which all that are sanctified earnestly breathe after ; and the clearer discoveries he makes to them of his love the more earnestly do they desire it. Sensual pleasures pall the carnal appetite, and soon give it a surfeit, but spiritual delights whet the desires, the language of which is, *Nothing more than God*, but still *more and more of him*. Christ had said, *I will go up to the palm-tree.* Come, saith she, *Let us go.* The promises Christ has made us of communion with him are not to supersede, but quicken and encourage, our prayers for that communion. 2. She desires to go forth into the fields and villages to have this communion with him. Those that would converse with Christ must go forth from the world and the amusements of it, must avoid every thing that would divert the mind and be a hindrance to it when it should be wholly taken up with Christ; we must contrive how to *attend upon the Lord without distraction* (1 Cor. vii. 35), for therefore the spouse here covets to get out of the noise of the town. *Let us go forth to him without the camp,* Heb. xiv. 13. Solitude and retirement befriend communion with God; therefore *Isaac went out into the field to meditate* and pray. *Enter into thy closet, and shut thy door.* A believer is never less alone than when alone with Christ, where no eye sees. 3. Having business to go abroad, to look after the grounds, she desires the company of her beloved. Note, Wherever we are, we may keep up our communion with God, if it be not our own fault, for he is always at our right hand, his eye always upon us, and both his word and his ear always nigh us. By going about our worldly affairs with heavenly holy hearts, mixing pious thoughts with common actions, and having our eyes ever towards the Lord, we may take Christ along with us whithersoever we go. Nor should we go any whither where we cannot in faith ask him to go along with us. 4. She is willing to rise betimes, to go along with her beloved: *Let us get up early to the vineyards.* It intimates her care to improve opportunities of conversing with her beloved; when the time appointed has come, we must lose no time, but, as the woman (Mark xvi. 2), *go very early,* though it be to a *sepulchre,* if we be in hopes to meet him there. Those that will go abroad with Christ must begin betimes with him, early in the morning of their days, must begin every day with him, seek him early, seek him diligently. 5. She will be content to take up her lodging in the villages, the huts or cottages which the country people built for their shelter when they attended their business in the fields; there, in these mean and cold dwellings, she will gladly reside, if she may but have her beloved with her. His presence will make them fine and pleasant, and convert them into palaces. A gracious soul can reconcile itself to the poorest accommodations, if it may have communion with God in them. 6. The most pleasant delightful fields, even in the spring-time, when the country is most pleasant, will not satisfy her, unless she have her beloved with her. No delights on earth can make a believer easy, unless he enjoy God in all.

III. She desires to be better acquainted with the state of her own soul and the present posture of its affairs (*v.* 12): *Let us see if the vine flourish.* Our own souls are our vineyards; they are, or should be, planted with vines and pomegranates, choice and useful trees. We are made keepers of these vineyards, and therefore are concerned often to look into them, to examine the state of our own souls, to seek whether the *vine flourishes,* whether our graces be in act and exercise, whether we be fruitful in the fruits of righteousness, and whether our fruit abound. And especially let us enquire whether *the tender grape appear* and whether *the pomegranates bud forth,* what good motions and dispositions there are in us that are yet but young and tender, that they may be protected and cherished with a particular care, and may not be nipped, or blasted, or rubbed off, but cultivated, that they may bring forth fruit unto perfection. In this enquiry into our own spiritual state, it will be good to take Christ along with us, because his presence will make the *vine flourish* and the *tender grape appear,* as the returning sun revives the gardens, and because to him we are concerned to approve ourselves. If he sees the *vine flourish,* and the *tender grape appear* —if we can appeal to him, *Thou knowest all things, thou knowest that I love thee,*—if his Spirit witness with our spirit that our souls prosper, it is enough. And, if we would be acquainted with ourselves, we must beg of him to search and try us, to help us in the search, and discover us to ourselves.

IV. She promises to her beloved the best entertainment she can give him at her country seat; for he will come in to us, and sup with us, Rev. iii. 20. 1. She promises him her best affections; and, whatever else she had for him, it would utterly be contemned if her heart were not entire for him: " *There* therefore *will I give thee my love;* I will repeat the professions of it, honour thee with the tokens of it; and the out-goings of my soul towards thee in adorations and desires shall be quickened and enlarged, and my heart offered up to thee in a holy fire." 2. She promises him her best provision, *v.* 13. "There we shall find pleasant odours, for *the mandrakes give a smell;*" the *love-flowers* or *lovely ones* (so the word signifies), or the *love-fruits;* it was something that was in all respects very grateful, so valuable that Rachel and Leah had like to have fallen out above it, Gen. xxx. 14. "We shall also find that which is good for food, as well as pleasant to the eye, all the rarities that the country affords: *At our gates are all manner of pleasant fruits.*" Note, (1.) The fruits and exercises of grace are pleasant to the Lord Jesus. (2.) These must be carefully laid up for him, devoted to his service and honour, must be always ready to us when we have occasion for them, as that is which is laid up at our gates, that, by our bringing forth much fruit, he may be glorified, John xv. 18. (3.) There is a great variety of these pleasant fruits, with which our souls should be well stocked; we must have all sorts of them, grace for all occasions, *new and old,* as the good householder has in his treasury, not only the products of this year, but remainders of the last, Matt. xiii. 52. We must not only have that ready to us, for the service of Christ, which we have heard, and learned, and experienced lately, but must retain that which we have formerly gathered; nor must we content ourselves only with what we have laid up in store in the days of old, but, as long as we live, must be still adding something new to it, that our stock may increase, and we may be *thoroughly furnished for every good work.* (4.) Those that truly love Christ will think all they have, even their most *pleasant fruits,* and what they have treasured up most carefully, too little to be bestowed upon him, and he is welcome to it all; if it were more and better, it should be at his service. It is all from him, and therefore it is fit it should be all for him.

CHAP. VIII.

The affections between Christ and his spouse are as strong and lively here, in this closing chapter of the song, as ever, and rather more so. I. The spouse continues her importunity for a more intimate communion and fellowship with him, ver. 1–3. II. She charges the daughters of Jerusalem not to interrupt her communion with her beloved (ver. 4); and they, thereupon, admire her dependence on him, ver. 5. III. She begs of her beloved, whom she raises up by her prayers (ver. 5), that he would by his grace confirm that blessed union with him to which she was admitted, ver. 6, 7. IV. She makes intercession for others also, that care might be taken of them (ver. 8, 9), and pleases herself with the thoughts of her own interest in Christ and his affection to her, ver. 10. V. She owns herself his tenant for a vineyard she held of him at Baal-hamon, ver. 11, 12. VI. The song concludes with an interchanging of parting requests. Christ charges his spouse that she should often let him hear from her (ver. 13), and she begs of him that he would hasten his return to her, ver. 14.

O THAT thou *wert* as my brother, that sucked the breasts of my mother! *when* I should find thee without, I would kiss thee; yea, I should not be despised. 2 I would lead thee, *and* bring thee into my mother's house, *who* would instruct me: I would cause thee to drink of spiced wine of the juice of my pomegranate. 3 His left hand *should be* under my head, and his right hand should embrace me. 4 I charge you, O daughters of Jerusalem, that ye stir not up, nor awake *my* love, until he please.

Here, 1. The spouse wishes for a constant intimacy and freedom with the Lord Jesus. She was already betrothed to him, but, the nuptials being not yet solemnized and published (the bride, the Lamb's wife, will not be completely ready till his second coming), she was obliged to be shy and to keep at some distance; she therefore wishes she may be taken for his sister, he having called her so (*ch.* v. 1), and that she might have the same chaste and innocent familiarity with him that a sister has with a brother, an own brother, that *sucked the breasts* of the same *mother* with her, who would therefore be exceedingly tender of her, as Joseph was of his brother Benjamin. Some make this to be the prayer of the Old-Testament saints for the hastening of Christ's incarnation, that the church might be the better acquainted with

him, when, *forasmuch as the children are partakers of flesh and blood,* he should also himself likewise take part of the same, and not be ashamed to call them brethren. It is rather the wish of all believers for a more intimate communion with him, that they might *receive the Spirit of sanctification,* and so Christ might be as their brother, that is, that they might be as his brethren, which *then* they are when by grace they are made partakers of a divine nature, and *he that sanctifies, and those that are sanctified, are both of one,* Heb. ii. 11, &c. It becomes brethren and sisters, the children of the same parents, that have been nursed at the same breast, to be very loving to and tender of one another; such a love the spouse desires might be between her and her beloved, that she might call him brother. 2. She promises herself then the satisfaction of making a more open profession of her relation to him than at present she could make: " *When I should find thee without,* any where, even before company, *I would kiss thee,* as a sister does her own brother, especially her little brother that is now *sucking the breasts of her mother"* (for so some understand it); " I would use all the decent freedom with thee that could be, and *should not be despised* for it, as doing any thing unbecoming the modesty of my sex." The church, since Christ's incarnation, can better own him than she could before, when she would have been laughed at for being so much in love with one that was not yet born. Christ has become as our brother; wherever we find him, therefore, let us be ready to own our relation to him and affection for him, and not fear being despised for it, nor regard that any more than David did when he danced before the ark. *If this be to be vile, I will be yet more vile.* Nay, let us hope that we shall not be despised so much as some imagine. *Of the maid-servants of whom thou hast spoken I shall be had in honour.* Wherever we find the image of Christ, though it be without, among those that do not follow him with us, we must love it, and testify that love, and we *shall not be despised* for it, but catholic charity will gain us respect. 3. She promises to improve the opportunity she should then have for cultivating an acquaintance with him (*v.* 2): " *I would lead thee,* as my brother, by the arm, and hang upon thee; I would show thee all the house of my precious things, would bring *thee into my mother's house,* into the church, into the solemn assemblies (*ch.* iii. 4), into my closet" (for there the saints have most familiar communion with Christ), "and *there thou wouldst instruct me"* (so some read it), as brethren inform their sisters of what they desire to be instructed in. Those that know Christ shall be taught of him; and *therefore* we should desire communion with Christ that we may receive instruction from him. He has come that he might give us an understanding. Or, " My mother would instruct me when I have thee with me." It is the presence of Christ in and with his church that makes the word and ordinances instructive to her children, who shall all be taught of God. 4. She promises him to bid him welcome to the best she had; she would *cause him to drink of her spiced wine and the juice of her pomegranate,* and bid him welcome to it, wishing it better for his sake. The exercise of grace and the performance of duty are spiced wine to the Lord Jesus, very acceptable to him, as expressive of a grateful sense of his favours. Those that are pleased with Christ must study to be pleasing to him; and they will not find him hard to be pleased. He reckons hearty welcome his best entertainment; and, if he have that, he will bring his entertainment along with him. 5. She doubts not but to experience his tender care of her and affection to her (*v.* 3), that she should be supported by his power and kept from fainting in the hardest services and sufferings *(His left hand shall be under my head)* and that she should be comforted with his love—*His right hand should embrace me.* Thus Christ laid his right hand upon John when he was ready to die away, Rev. i. 17. See also Dan. x. 10, 18. It may be read as it is *ch.* ii. 6, *His left hand is under my head* (for the words are the same in the original) and so it expresses an immediate answer to her prayer; she was answered with *strength in her soul,* Ps. cxxxviii. 3. While we are following hard after Christ his *right hand sustains us,* Ps. lxiii. 8. *Underneath are the everlasting arms.* 6. She charges those about her to take heed of doing any thing to interrupt the pleasing communion she now had with her beloved (*v.* 4), as she had done before, when he thus strengthened and comforted her with his presence (*ch.* ii. 7): Let me *charge you, O you daughters of Jerusalem,* and reason with you, *Why should you stir up, and why should you awake, my love, until he will?* The church, our common mother, charges all her children that they never do any thing to provoke Christ to withdraw, which we are very prone to do. Why should you put such an affront upon him? Why should you be such enemies to yourselves? We should thus reason with ourselves when we are tempted to do that which will grieve the Spirit. "What! Am I weary of Christ's presence, that I affront him and provoke him to depart from me? Why should I do that which he will take so unkindly and which I shall certainly repent of?

5 Who *is* this that cometh up from the wilderness, leaning upon her beloved? I raised thee up under the apple tree: there thy mother brought thee forth: there she brought thee forth *that* bare thee. 6 Set me as a seal upon thine heart, as a seal upon thine arm: for love *is* strong as death;

jealousy *is* cruel as the grave: the coals thereof *are* coals of fire, *which hath* a most vehement flame. 7 Many waters cannot quench love, neither can the floods drown it: if a man would give all the substance of his house for love, it would utterly be contemned.

Here, I. The spouse is much admired by those about her. It comes in in a parenthesis, but in it gospel-grace lies as plain, and as much above ground, as any where in this mystical song: *Who is this that comes up from the wilderness, leaning upon her beloved?* Some make these the words of the bridegroom, expressing himself well pleased with her reliance on him and resignation of herself to his guidance. They are rather the words of the daughters of Jerusalem, to whom she spoke (*v.* 4); they see her, and bless her. The angels in heaven, and all her friends on earth, are the joyful spectators of her bliss. The Jewish church came up from the wilderness supported by the divine power and favour, Deut. xxxii. 10, 11. The Christian church raised up from a low and desolate condition by the grace of Christ relied on, Gal. iv. 27. Particular believers are amiable, nay, admirable, and divine grace is to be admired in them, when by the power of that grace they are brought *up from the wilderness, leaning* with a holy confidence and complacency *upon* Jesus Christ *their beloved.* This bespeaks the beauty of a soul, and the wonders of divine grace, 1. In the conversion of sinners. A sinful state is a *wilderness,* remote from communion with God, barren and dry, and in which there is no true comfort; it is a wandering wanting state. Out of this wilderness we are concerned to *come up,* by true repentance, in the strength of the grace of Christ, supported by our beloved and carried in his arms. 2. In the consolation of saints. A soul convinced of sin, and truly humbled for it, is in a *wilderness,* quite at a loss; and there is no coming out of this *wilderness* but *leaning* on Christ as our beloved, by faith, and not *leaning to our own understanding,* nor trusting to any righteousness or strength of our own as sufficient for us, but going forth, and going on, in the strength of the Lord God, and making mention of his righteousness, even his only, who is *the Lord our righteousness.* 3. In the salvation of those that belong to Christ. We must go up from the wilderness of this world having our conversation in heaven; and, at death, we must remove thither, *leaning* upon Christ, must live and die by faith in him. *To me to live is Christ,* and it is he that is gain in death.

II. She addresses herself to her beloved.

1. She puts him in mind of the former experience which she and others had had of comfort and success in applying to him. (1.) For her own part: "*I raised thee up under the apple tree,* that is, I have many a time

wrestled with thee by prayer and have prevailed. When I was alone in the acts of devotion, retired in the orchard, under *the apple-tree*" (which Christ himself was compared to, *ch.* ii. 3), as *Nathanael under the fig-tree* (John i. 48), "meditating and praying, then *I raised thee up,* to help me and comfort me," as the disciples raised him up in the storm, saying, *Master, carest thou not that we perish?* (Mark iv. 38), and the church (Ps. xliv. 23), *Awake, why sleepest thou?* Note, The experience we have had of Christ's readiness to yield to the importunities of our faith and prayer should encourage us to continue instant in our addresses to him, to strive more earnestly, and not to faint. *I sought the Lord, and he heard me,* Ps. xxxiv. 4. (2.) Others also had had like experience of comfort in Christ, as it follows there (Ps. xxxiv. 5), *They looked unto him,* as well as I, *and were lightened.* There *thy mother brought thee forth,* the universal church, or believing souls, in whom Christ was formed, Gal. iv. 15. They were in pain for the comfort of an interest in thee, and *travailed in pain* with *great sorrow* (so the word here signifies); but they *brought thee forth;* the pangs did not continue always; those that had *travailed* in convictions at last *brought forth* in consolations, and the *pain was forgotten* for joy of the Saviour's birth. By this very similitude our Saviour illustrates the joy which his disciples would have in his return to them, after a mournful separation for a time, John xvi. 21, 22. After the bitter pangs of repentance many a one has had the blessed birth of comfort; why then may not I?

2. She begs of him that her union with him might be confirmed, and her communion with him continued and made more intimate (*v.* 6): *Set me as a seal upon thy heart, as a seal upon thy arm.* (1.) "Let me have a place in thy heart, an interest in thy love." This is that which all those desire above any thing that know how much their happiness is bound up in the love of Christ. (2.) "Let me never lose the room I have in thy heart; let thy love to me be ensured, as that deed which is sealed not to be revoked, that cabinet which is sealed up not to be robbed. Let nothing ever prevail either to separate me from thy love, or, by suspending the communications of it, to deprive me of the comfortable sense of it." (3.) "Let me be always near and dear to thee, as the *signet on thy right hand,* not to be parted with (Jer. xxii. 24), *engraven upon the palms of thy hands* (Isa. xlix. 14), be loved with a peculiar love." (4.) "Be thou my high priest; let my name be written on thy breast-plate, nearer thy heart, as the names of all the tribes were engraven like the engravings of a signet in twelve precious stones on the breast-plate of Aaron, and also on two precious *stones* on the *two shoulders* or arms of the ephod," Exod. xxviii. 11, 12, 21. (5.) "Let thy power be engaged for me, as an evidence of thy love to

me; let me be not only a *seal upon thy heart,* but a *seal upon thy arm;* let me be ever borne up in thy arms, and know it to my comfort." Some make these to be the words of Christ to his spouse, commanding her to be ever mindful of him and of his love to her; however, if we desire and expect that Christ should set us as a *seal on his heart,* surely we cannot do less than set him as a seal on ours.

3. To enforce this petition, she pleads the power of love, of her love to him, which constrained her to be thus pressing for the tokens of his love to her.

(1.) Love is a violent vigorous passion. [1.] It is *strong as death.* The pains of a disappointed lover are like the pains of death; nay, the pains of death are slighted, and made nothing of, in pursuit of the beloved object. Christ's love to us was *strong as death,* for it broke through death itself. *He loved us, and gave himself for us.* The love of true believers to Christ is *strong as death,* for it makes them dead to every thing else; it even parts between soul and body, while the soul, upon the wings of devout affections, soars upwards to heaven, and even forgets that it is yet clothed and clogged with flesh. Paul, in a rapture of this love, knew not whether he was in *the body or out of the body.* By it a believer is crucified to the world. [2.] *Jealousy is cruel as the grave,* which swallows up and devours all; those that truly love Christ are jealous of every thing that would draw them from him, and especially jealous of themselves, lest they should do any thing to provoke him to withdraw from them, and, rather than do so, would *pluck out a right eye* and *cut off a right hand,* than which what can be more cruel? Weak and trembling saints, who conceive a jealousy of Christ, doubting of his love to them, find that jealousy to prey upon them like the grave; nothing wastes the spirits more; but it is an evidence of the strength of their love to him. [3.] *The coals thereof,* its lamps, and flames, and beams, are very strong, and burn with incredible fury and irresistible force, as the *coals of fire that have a most vehement flame,* a *flame of the Lord* (so some read it), a powerful piercing flame, as the lightning, Ps. xxix. 7. Holy love is a fire that begets a vehement heat in the soul, and consumes the dross and chaff that are in it, melts it down like wax into a new form, and carries it upwards as the sparks towards God and heaven.

(2.) Love is a valiant victorious passion. Holy love is so; the reigning love of God in the soul is constant and firm, and will not be drawn off from him either by fair means or foul, by *life or death,* Rom. viii. 38. [1.] Death, and all its terrors, will not frighten a believer from loving Christ: *Many waters,* though they will quench fire, *cannot quench this love,* no, nor the *floods drown it, v.* 7.

The noise of these waters will strike no terror upon it; let them do their worst, Christ shall still be the best beloved. The overflowing of these waters will strike no damp upon it, but it will enable a man to rejoice in tribulation. *Though he slay me,* I will love him and *trust in him.* No waters could quench Christ's love to us, nor any floods drown it; he waded through the greatest difficulties, even seas of blood. Love sat king upon the floods ; let nothing then abate our love to him. [2.] Life, and all its comforts, will not entice a believer from loving Christ : *If a man* could hire him with *all the substance of his house,* to take his love off from Christ and set it upon the world and the flesh again, he would reject the proposal with the utmost disdain ; as Christ, when the kingdoms of this world and the glory of them were offered him, to buy him off from his undertaking, said, *Get thee hence, Satan.* It would utterly be contemned. Offer those things to those that know no better. Love will enable us to repel and triumph over temptations from the smiles of the world, as much as from its frowns. Some give this sense of it : *If a man would give all the substance of his house to* Christ, as an equivalent instead of love, to excuse it, *it would be contemned.* He seeks not ours, but us, the heart, not the wealth. *If I give all my goods to feed the poor, and have not love, it is nothing,* 1 Cor. xiii. 1. Thus believers stand affected to Christ : the gifts of his providence cannot satisfy them without the assurances of his love.

8 We have a little sister, and she hath no breasts : what shall we do for our sister in the day when she shall be spoken for ? 9 If she *be* a wall, we will build upon her a palace of silver : and if she *be* a door, we will inclose her with boards of cedar. 10 I *am* a wall, and my breasts like towers : then was I in his eyes as one that found favour. 11 Solomon had a vineyard at Baal-hamon ; he let out the vineyard unto keepers ; every one for the fruit thereof was to bring a thousand *pieces* of silver. 12 My vineyard, which *is* mine, *is* before me : thou, O Solomon, *must have* a thousand, and those that keep the fruit thereof two hundred.

Christ and his spouse having sufficiently confirmed their love to each other, and agreed it to be on both sides *strong as death* and inviolable, they are here, in these verses, like a loving husband and his wife, consulting together about their affairs, and considering what they should do. Yoke-fellows, having laid their hearts together, lay their heads together, to contrive about their relations and about their estates ; and, accordingly, this happy pair are here advising with one another about a sister, and a vineyard.

I. They are here consulting about their sister, their little sister, and the disposing of her.

1. The spouse proposes her case with a compassionate concern (*v.* 8): *We have a little sister and she has no breasts* (she has not grown up to maturity); *what shall we do for* this *little sister* of ours *in the day that she shall be spoken for,* so as that we may do well for her ? (1.) This may be understood as spoken by the Jewish church concerning the Gentile world. God had espoused the church of the Jews to himself, and she was richly endowed, but what shall become of the poor Gentiles, *the barren that has not borne,* and *the desolate?* Isa. liv. 1. Their condition (say the pious Jews) is very deplorable and forlorn ; they are *sisters,* children of the same fathers, God and Adam, but they are *little,* because not dignified with the knowledge of God ; they *have no breasts,* no divine revelation, no scriptures, no ministers, no breasts of consolation drawn out to them, whence they might suck, being *strangers to the covenants of promise,* no breasts of instruction themselves to draw out to their children, to nourish them, 1 Pet. ii. 2. *What shall we do for* them ? We can but pity them, and pray for them. Lord, what wilt thou do for them ? The saints, in Solomon's time, might know, from David's psalms, that God had mercy in store for them, and they begged it might be hastened to them. Now the tables are turned ; the Gentiles are betrothed to Christ, and ought to return the kindness by an equal concern for the bringing in of the Jews again, our eldest sister, that once had breasts, but now has none. If we take it in this sense, the unbelieving posterity of these pious Jews contradicted this prayer of their fathers; for, when the day came that the Gentiles should be *spoken for* and courted to Christ, instead of considering what to do for them they plotted to do all they could against them, which filled up the measure of their iniquity, 1 Thess. ii. 16. Or, (2.) It may be applied to any other that belong to the election of grace, but are yet uncalled. They are remotely related to Christ and his church, and sisters to them both, *other sheep that are not of this fold,* John x. 16; Acts xviii. 10. They *have no breasts,* none yet fashioned (Ezek. xvi. 7), no affection to Christ, no principle of grace. *The day* will come *when* they *shall be spoken for,* when the chosen shall be called, shall be courted for Christ, by the ministers, the friends of the bridegroom. A blessed day it will be, a day of visitation. What shall we do, in that day, to promote the match, to conquer their coyness, and persuade them to consent to Christ and present themselves chaste virgins to him ? Note, Those that through grace are brought to Christ them-

selves should contrive what they may do to help others to him, to carry on the great design of his gospel, which is to espouse souls to Christ and convert sinners to him from whom they have departed.

2. Christ soon determines what to do in this case, and his spouse agrees with him in it (*v.* 9): "*If she be a wall,* if the good work be once begun with the Gentiles, with the souls that are to be called in, if the *little sister, when she shall be spoken for* by the gospel, will but receive the word, and build herself upon Christ the foundation, and frame her doings to turn to the Lord, as the wall is in order to the house, *we will build upon her a palace of silver,* or build her up into such a palace; we will carry on the good work that is begun, till the wall become a palace, the wall of stone a palace of silver," which goes beyond the boast of Augustus Cæsar, that what he found brick he left marble. This *little sister,* when once she is joined to the Lord, shall be made to *grow into a holy temple, a habitation of God through the Spirit,* Eph. ii. 21, 22. *If she be a door,* when this palace comes to be finished, and the doors of this wall set up, which was the last thing done (Neh. vii. 1), then *we will enclose her with boards of cedar;* we will carefully and effectually protect her, that she shall receive no damage. *We will* do it; Father, Son, and Holy Ghost, all concur in contriving, carrying on, and crowning, the blessed work when the time comes. Whatever is wanting shall be set in order, and the work of faith shall be fulfilled with power. Though the beginnings of grace be small, the latter end shall greatly increase. The church is in care concerning those that are yet uncalled. " Let me alone," says Christ; " I will do all that which is necessary to be done for them. Trust me with it."

3. The spouse takes this occasion to acknowledge with thankfulness his kindness to her, *v.* 10. She is very willing to trust him with her *little sister,* for she herself had had great experience of his grace, and, for her part, she owed her all to him: *I am a wall, and my breasts like towers.* This she speaks, not as upbraiding her little sister that had no breasts, but comforting herself concerning her, that he who had made her what she was, who had built her up upon himself and made her to grow up to maturity, could and would do the same kindness for those whose case she bore upon her heart. *Then was I in his eyes as one that found favour.* See, (1.) What she values herself upon, her having found favour in the eyes of Jesus Christ. Those are happy, truly happy, and for ever so, that have the favour of God and are accepted of him. (2.) How she ascribes the good work of God in her to the good-will of God towards her: " He has *made me a wall and my breasts as towers,* and then, in that instance more than in any thing, I experienced his love to me." *Hail, thou that art highly favoured,* for in thee Christ is formed.

(3.) What pleasure God takes in the work of his own hands. When we are made as a *wall,* as a *brazen wall* (Jer. i. 18; xv. 20), that stands firmly against the *blast of the terrible ones* (Isa. xxv. 4), then God takes delight in us to do us good. (4.) With what joy and triumph we ought to speak of God's grace towards us, and with what satisfaction we should look back upon the special times and seasons when *we were in his eyes as those that find favour;* these were days never to be forgotten.

II. They are here consulting about *a vineyard* they had in the country, the church of Christ on earth considered under the notion of *a vineyard* (*v.* 11, 12): *Solomon had a vineyard at Baal-hamon,* had a kingdom in the possession of a multitude, a numerous people. As he was a type of Christ, so his vineyard was a type of the church of Christ. Our Saviour has given us a key to these verses in the parable of the vineyard let out to unthankful husbandmen, Matt. xxi. 33. The bargain was that, every one of the tenants having so much of the vineyard assigned him as would contain 1000 vines, he was to pay the annual rent of 1000 *pieces of silver;* for we read (Isa. vii. 23) that in a fruitful soil there were 1000 *vines at* 1000 *silverlings.* Observe, 1. Christ's church is his vineyard, a pleasant and peculiar place, privileged with many honours; he delights to walk in it, as a man in his vineyard, and is pleased with its fruits. 2. He has entrusted each of us with his vineyard, as *keepers* of it. The privileges of the church are that good thing which he has committed to us, to be kept as a sacred trust. The service of the church is to be our business, according as our capacity is. *Son, go work to-day in my vineyard.* Adam, in innocency, was *to dress the garden, and to keep it.* 3. He expects rent from those that are employed in his vineyard and entrusted with it. *He comes, seeking fruit,* and requires gospel-duty of all those that enjoy gospel-privileges. Every one, of what rank or degree soever, must bring glory and honour to Christ, and do some service to the interest of his kingdom in the world, in consideration of what benefit and advantage they enjoy by their share of the privileges of the vineyard. 4. Though Christ has *let out his vineyard to keepers,* yet still it is his, and he has his eye always upon it for good; for, if he did not watch over it *night and day* (Isa. xxvii. 1, 2), *the watchmen,* to whom he has let it out, would keep it *but in vain,* Ps. cxxvii. 1. Some take these for Christ's words (*v.* 12): *My vineyard, which is mine, is before me;* and they observe how he dwells upon his property in it: It is *my vineyard, which is mine;* so dear is his church to him, it is *his own in the world* (John xiii. 1), and therefore he will always have it under his protection; it is his own, and he will look after it. 5. The church, that enjoys the privileges of the vineyard, must have them always before her. The keeping of the vineyard requires constant care and diligence. They are rather the words of the spouse: *My vineyard, which is mine, is before me.* She had lamented her fault and folly in not keeping her *own vineyard* (*ch.* i. 6), but now she resolves to reform. Our hearts are our vineyards, which we must *keep with all diligence;* and therefore we must have a watchful jealous eye upon them at all times. 6. Our great care must be to pay our rent for what we hold of Christ's vineyard, and to see that we do not go behind-hand, nor disappoint the messengers he sends to *receive the fruits* (Matt. xxi. 34): *Thou, O Solomon! must have* 1000, and shalt have. The main of the profits belong to Christ; to him and his praise all our fruits must be dedicated. 7. If we be careful to give Christ the praise of our church-privileges, we may then take to ourselves the comfort and benefit of them. If the owner of the vineyard have had his due, the keepers of it shall be well paid for their care and pains; they shall have 200, which sum, no doubt, was looked upon as good profit. Those that work for Christ are working for themselves, and shall be unspeakable gainers by it.

13 Thou that dwellest in the gardens, the companions hearken to thy voice: cause me to hear *it.* 14 Make haste, my beloved, and be thou like to a roe or to a young hart upon the mountains of spices.

Christ and his spouse are here parting for a while; she must stay below *in the gardens* on earth, where she has work to do for him; he must remove to *the mountains of spices* in heaven, where he has business to attend for her, as *an advocate with the Father.* Now observe with what mutual endearments they part.

I. He desires to hear often from her. She is ready at her pen; she must be sure to write to him; she knows how to direct (*v.* 13): "*Thou that,* for the present, *dwellest in the gardens,* dressing and keeping them till thou remove from the garden below to the paradise above—*thou,* O believer! whoever thou art, *that dwellest in the gardens* of solemn ordinances, *in the gardens* of church-fellowship and communion, *the companions* are so happy as to hear *thy voice, cause me to hear it* too." Observe, 1. Christ's friends should keep a good correspondence one with another, and, as dear companions, speak often to one another (Mal. iii. 16) and hearken to one another's voice; they should edify, encourage, and respect one another. They are companions in the kingdom and patience of Christ, and therefore, as fellow-travellers, should keep up mutual freedom, and not be shy of, nor strange to, one another. *The communion of saints* is an article of our covenant, as well as an article of our creed, *to exhort one another daily,* and be glad to be exhorted one by another. *Hearken to the voice* of the church, as far as it agrees with the voice of Christ; his companions will do so. 2. In the midst of our communion with one another we must not neglect our

communion with Christ, but let him see our countenance and hear our voice; he here bespeaks it: "*The companions hearken to thy voice;* it is a pleasure to them; *cause me to hear it.* Thou makest thy complaints to them when any thing grieves thee; why dost thou not bring them to me, and let me hear them? Thou art free with them; be as free with me; pour out thy heart to me." Thus Christ, when he left his disciples, ordered them to send to him upon every occasion. *Ask, and you shall receive.* Note, Christ not only accepts and answers, but even courts his people's prayers, not reckoning them a trouble to him, but an honour and a *delight,* Prov. xv. 8. We *cause him to hear* our prayers when we not only pray, but wrestle and strive in prayer. He loves to be pressingly importuned, which is not the manner of men. Some read it, "*Cause me to be heard;* thou hast often an opportunity of speaking to thy companions, and they hearken to what thou sayest; speak of me to them; let my name be heard among them; let me be the subject of thy discourse." "One word of Christ" (as archbishop Usher used to say) "before you part." No subject is more becoming, or should be more pleasing.

II. She desires his speedy return to her (*v.* 14): *Make haste, my beloved,* to come again, and receive me to thyself; *be thou like a roe, or a young hart, upon the mountains of spices;* let no time be lost; it is pleasant dwelling here *in the gardens, but to depart, and be with thee, is far better;* that therefore is what I wish, and wait, and long for. *Even so, come, Lord Jesus, come quickly.* Observe, 1. Though Jesus Christ be now retired, he will return. The heavens, those high *mountains of* sweet *spices,* must *contain him till the times of refreshing shall come;* and those times will come, *when every eye shall see him,* in all the pomp and power of the upper and better world, the mystery of God being finished and the mystical body completed. 2. True believers, as they are looking for, so they are hastening to, the coming of that *day of the Lord,* not that they would have him make more haste than good speed, but that the intermediate counsels may all be fulfilled, and then that the end may come—the sooner the better. Not that they think him *slack concerning his promise, as some men count slackness,* but thus they express the strength of their affections to him and the vastness of their expectations from him when he comes again. 3. Those only that can in sincerity call Christ their *beloved,* their *best beloved,* can, upon good grounds, desire him to hasten his second coming. As for those whose hearts go a whoring after the world, and who set their affections on the things of the earth, they cannot love his appearing, but dread it rather, because then the earth, and all the things of it which they have chosen for their portion, will be burnt up. But those that truly love Christ long for his second coming, because it will be the crown both of his glory and their bliss. 4. The comfort and satisfaction which we sometimes have in communion with God in grace here should make us breathe the more earnestly after the immediate vision and complete fruition of him in the kingdom of glory. The spouse, after an endearing conference with her beloved, finding it must break off, concludes with this affectionate request for the perfecting and perpetuating of this happiness in the future state. The clusters of grapes that meet us in this wilderness should make us long for the full vintage in Canaan. If a day in his courts be so sweet, what then will an eternity within the veil be! If this be heaven, O that I were there! 5. It is good to conclude our devotions wi..h a joyful expectation of the glory to be revealed, and holy humble breathings towards it. We should not part but with the prospect of meeting again. It is good to conclude every sabbath with thoughts of the everlasting sabbath, which shall have no night at the end of it, nor any week-day to come after it. It is good to conclude every sacrament with thoughts of the everlasting feast, when we shall sit down with Christ at his table in his kingdom, to rise no more, and drink of the wine new there, and to break up every religious assembly in hopes of *the general assembly of the church of the first-born,* when time and days shall be no more: Let the blessed Jesus hasten that blessed day. *Why are his chariot-wheels so long a coming? Why tarry the wheels of his chariots?*